International Dictionary of Architects and Architecture - 2

ARCHITECTURE

International Dictionary of Architects and Architecture - 2

ARCHITECTURE

EDITOR
RANDALL J. VAN VYNCKT

EUROPEAN CONSULTANT
DOREEN YARWOOD

PHOTO and GRAPHIC RESEARCHER
SUHAIL BUTT

R
720.9
Interna
v. 2

St J

St James Press

Detroit   London   Washington D.C.

STAFF

Randall J. Van Vynckt, *Editor*
Doreen Yarwood, *European Consultant*
Suhail Butt, *Photo and Graphic Researcher*
Jim Kamp, *Project Editor*
Linda Irvin, *Contributing Editor*
Paul E. Schellinger, *Associate Editor*

Cynthia Baldwin, *Art Director*
Barbara J. Yarrow, *Graphic Services Supervisor*
Kathleen Hourdakis, *Designer*
C. J. Jonik, *Keyliner*

Mary Beth Trimper, *Production Director*
Evi Seoud, *Assistant Production Manager*
Shanna P. Heilveil, *Production Assistant*

Margaret A. Chamberlain, *Permissions Supervisor*
Pamela A. Hayes and Keith Reed, *Permissions Associates*
Arlene Johnson and Barbara Wallace, *Permissions Assistants*

Cover photo: Basilica di S. Andrea, Mantoua, Italy. Courtesy of Archiv Alinari/Art Resource, New York

The paper used in this publication meets the minimum requirements of American National Standard for Informational Sciences—Permanence Paper for Printed Library Materials, ANSI Z39.48-1984. ∞™

Library of Congress Cataloging-in-Publication Data
International dictionary of architects and architecture / editor, Randall J. Van Vynckt;
European consultant, Doreen Yarwood; photo and graphic researcher, Suhail Butt.
p. cm.
Includes bibliographical references and indexes.
Contents: v. 1. Architects — v. 2. Architecture
ISBN 1-55862-089-3 (set: not sold sep.): $250.00. — ISBN 1-55862-087-7
(v. 1). — ISBN 1-55862-088-5 (v. 2).
1. Architects—Biography—Dictionaries. 2. Architecture—Dictionaries.
I. Yarwood, Doreen. II. Butt, Suhail.
NA40.I48 1993
720'.9—dc20   93-13431
                                                                                CIP
A CIP catalogue record of this book is available from the British Library.

Printed in the United States of America.
Published simultaneously in the United Kingdom.

The trademark **ITP** is used under license.

CONTENTS

INTRODUCTION

Scope

The *International Dictionary of Architects and Architecture* features 523 architects and 467 buildings and sites that have figured prominently in Western architectural history. The *Architects* volume covers architects, theorists and engineers, as well as personalities involved in architectural decoration, landscape design and urban planning. Many buildings and sites in the *Architecture* volume were selected to compensate for coverage that simply could not be provided in the *Architects* volume. Arranged geographically, the *Architecture* volume covers a range of periods and styles, from Ancient Greece to examples of postmodernism and deconstruction, and includes Classical sites, cathedrals, buildings, and other works whose architects generally are not known. The geographic ordering of the *Architecture* volume is intended to provide users with a convenient means of accessing related works.

Selection

The selection of subjects was based on original research, published sources, many writers who served as de facto advisers, and Doreen Yarwood, who shared her valuable experience of more than forty years of canvassing European architecture. Despite the size of this dictionary, the space is nonetheless limited in terms of the entire spectrum of architectural history, especially in terms of the depth of information we intended to provide for each topic; we therefore decided to limit our focus to architects and architecture within what has been considered the Western tradition. This dictionary, then, should serve as a valuable complement to original sources, monographs and reference works that deal with the wealth of architecture that has been promulgated within this tradition. Notable within our presentation of this Western realm are many important buildings and architects from areas of Eastern Europe that often have been excluded from English-language reference books, but that have recently become more accessible.

Entry Content

Entries in the *International Dictionary of Architects and Architecture* contain the following information:

- HEADNOTES: Compiled by the editor and his staff from a number of different sources as well as from information supplied by contributors, headnotes provide key information at a glance. The content varies according to volume:

  - *Architects*—Begins with biographical data, including nationality, birth and death locations and dates, educational background, and principal affiliations. Next follows a concise chronology of the architect's major built works.

vii

- ▸ *Architecture*—Features dates of construction, architect(s) if known, and listings of notable additions or alterations.

- BIBLIOGRAPHIC CITATIONS: The dictionary's thousands of bibliographic citations—books and articles ranging from the general to the specific—were selected to aid everyone from the beginning student to the more advanced researcher.

  - ▸ *Architects*—Contains chronological lists of books and/or articles by the architect as well as alphabetical lists (by author or, if unavailable, by title) of books and/or articles about the architect.

  - ▸ *Architecture*—Features books and articles about a specific site or building.

- SIGNED CRITICAL ESSAYS: Some 220 international contributors knowledgeable about their respective subjects wrote the original essays in both volumes. Averaging about 1000 words, the essays discuss the key developments in an architect's life and career or the design, construction and impact of an architectural masterwork. Since the essays reflect each writer's scholarship and orientation, the approach to the subject matter ranges from detailed, matter-of-fact reporting to impressionistic musings. To learn more about any contributor, refer to the "Notes on Contributors" in the back of each volume.

- ILLUSTRATIONS: The *Dictionary* is highlighted by 964 photographs and 169 floor plans. Providing a wealth of information in their own right, these 1,133 illustrations appear in the majority of entries in *Architects* and **all** of the entries in *Architecture*.

Indexes

The Geographic, Building, and Architect indexes in these two volumes were designed to provide significant assistance in pinpointing desired information and in relating various architects to their buildings, and vice-versa.

Special Thanks

During the final months of book preparation, several people made special efforts to help complete *International Dictionary of Architects and Architecture*. Those who helped with final proofing and headnote compilation and coding include assistant editors Joanna Brod, Pamela S. Dear, Jeff Hill, Thomas F. McMahon, Terrie A. Rooney, Aarti D. Stephens, Linda Tidrick, Brandon R. Trenz and Roger M. Valade III along with associate editors Shelly Andrews, Elizabeth A. Des Chenes, Kathleen J. Edgar, Marie Ellavich, David M. Galens, Motoko Huthwaite, Mark F. Mikula, Michelle M. Motowski, Susan R. Reicha, Kenneth R. Shepherd, Deborah A. Stanley, Polly A. Vedder and Thomas Wiloch. In addition, "Notes on Contributors" was compiled by associate editor Mary K. Ruby and all photo captions were prepared by assistant editor Jane M. Kelly.

Geographic List of Architecture

(BOOK ORDER)

Classical Sites and Monuments

Akragas
Aspendos
Athens: Acropolis
Athens: Agora
Athens: Choragic Monument of Lysicrates
Athens: Tower of the Winds
Baalbek
Delphi
Ephesos
Epidauros
Herculaneum
Miletos
Mycenae
Nîmes: Amphitheater
Nîmes: Maison Carrée.
Nîmes: Pont du Gard
Olympia
Ostia Antica
Paestum
Palmyra
Pergamon
Pompeii
Priene
Pula: Amphitheater
Rome: Arch of Constantine
Rome: Arch of Titus
Rome: Baths of Diocletian
Rome: Colosseum
Rome: Forum Romanum
Rome: Pantheon
Rome: Temple of Fortuna Virilis
Rome: Theater of Marcellus
Segesta
Split: Imperial Palace of Diocletian
Syracuse
Tiryns
Tivoli: Hadrian's Villa

Europe

Austria

Salzburg: Schloss Mirabell

Vienna: Belvedere
Vienna: Hofburg
Vienna: Karlskirche
Vienna: Majolica House
Vienna: Piaristenkirche
Vienna: Postal Savings Bank
Vienna: St. Stephen's Cathedral
Vienna: Schloss Schönbrunn
Vienna: Secession Building

Belgium

Antwerp: Grote Markt
Antwerp: Town Hall
Bruges: Town Hall (Stadhuis)
Brussels: Grand' Place
Brussels: Hôtel Tassel
Brussels: Palais Stoclet
Louvain: Town Hall
Tournai Cathedral

Croatia

Porec: Euphrasius Basilica
Trogir: Trogir Cathedral
Zadar Cathedral
Zadar: Church of St. Donato

Czech Republic

Brno: Villa Tugendhat
Kutna Hora: Cathedral of St. Barbara
Prague: Černín Palace
Prague: National Theater
Prague: St. Nicholas
Prague: St. Vitus' Cathedral
Prague: Vladislav Hall
Tabor: Zizka Square

Denmark

Copenhagen: Amalienborg
Copenhagen: Bourse
Copenhagen Cathedral
Copenhagen: Rosenborg Palace

Finland

Helsinki: Railway Station and Administration Building
Helsinki: Senate Square
Helsinki: Telephone Company Building
Paimio: Tuberculosis Sanatorium
Seinäjoki: Civic Center
Tampere Cathedral
Tampere: Kaleva Church

France

Amiens Cathedral
Anet: Château
Beauvais Cathedral
Blois: Château
Bordeaux: Grande Théâtre
Bourges: House of Jacques Coeur
Carcassonne: City Walls and Fortifications
Centula: St. Riquier
Chambord: Château
Chartres Cathedral
Conques: Church of Ste. Foy
Fontainebleau Palace
Laon Cathedral
Le Raincy: Church of Notre Dame
Marseilles: Unité d'Habitation
Metz Cathedral
Nancy: Place Royale (Place Stanislas)
Paris: Arc de Triomphe
Paris: Bibliothèque Nationale
Paris: Centre Georges Pompidou
Paris: La Défense
Paris: Eiffel Tower
Paris: Les Halles Centrales
Paris: Hôtel de Cluny
Paris: Institut du Monde Arabe
Paris: Les Invalides
Paris: Louvre
Paris: Louvre, Pyramide
Paris: Madeleine
Paris: Métro Stations
Paris: Notre-Dame Cathedral
Paris: Opéra
Paris: Panthéon (Ste. Geneviève)
Paris: Place de la Concorde
Paris: Place Vendôme
Paris: Place des Vosges
Paris: Sacré Coeur
Paris: La Sainte-Chapelle
Paris: St. Sulpice
Paris: UNESCO Headquarters
Paris: Val de Grâce
Périgueux: St. Front
Poissy: Villa Savoye
Reims Cathedral
Ronchamp: Notre-Dame-du-Haut
Strasbourg Cathedral
Vaux-le-Vicomte: Château
Versailles: Palace
Versailles: Grand Trianon

Versailles: Petite Trianon
Versailles: Park
Vézelay: La Madeleine

Germany

Aachen: Royal Chapel
Augsburg: Zeughaus
Berlin: AEG Turbine Hall
Berlin: Altes Museum
Berlin: Brandenburg Gate
Berlin: Gross-Siedlung Siemensstadt
Berlin: IBA
Berlin: Neue Wache
Cologne Cathedral
Cologne: Werkbund Exposition, 1914
Dessau: Bauhaus
Hamburg: Chilehaus
Hannover: Altes Rathaus
Karlsruhe: Marktplatz
Kassel: Löwenburg
Lübeck: Marktplatz
Munich: Amalienburg
Munich: Königsbau
Munich: Michaelskirche
Munich: Olympic Games Complex
Munich: Propyläen
Munich: St. John Nepomuk
Ottobeuren: Abbey Church
Potsdam: Nikolaikirche
Potsdam: Palace of Sans Souci
Steinhausen: Pilgrimage Church
Stuttgart: Neue Staatsgalerie
Stuttgart: Schocken Department Store
Stuttgart: Weissenhofsiedlung
Vierzehnheiligen: Pilgrimage Church
Weingarten: Abbey Church
Wurzburg: Residenz

Great Britain

England

Bath: Circus/Crescent/Square
Berkshire: Windsor Castle
Berkshire: St. George's Chapel, Windsor
Bradford-on-Avon: St. Lawrence
Brighton: Royal Pavilion
Bristol: St. Mary Redcliffe
Cambridge: King's College
Canterbury Cathedral
Derbyshire: Kedleston Hall
Durham Cathedral
Exeter Cathedral
Gloucester Cathedral
Leicester: Engineering Faculty Building
Lincoln Cathedral
Liverpool: Anglican Cathedral
Liverpool: Metropolitan Cathedral
Liverpool: St. George's Hall
London: Banqueting House, Whitehouse

Alphabetical List of Architecture

A

Abbey Church: Alcobaça, Portugal
Abbey Church: Ottobeuren, Germany
Abbey Church: Weingarten, Germany
Acropolis: Athens, Classical Sites and Monuments
Admiralty: St. Petersburg, Russia
AEG Turbine Hall: Berlin, Germany
Agora: Athens, Classical Sites and Monuments
Agrigento: See Akragas, Classical Sites and
    Monuments
Akragas (Agrigento): Classical Sites and Monuments
Alhambra: Granada, Spain
Altes Museum: Berlin, Germany
Altes Rathaus: Hannover, Germany
Amalienborg: Copenhagen, Denmark
Amalienburg: Nymphenburg, near Munich,
    Germany
Amphitheater: Nîmes, Classical Sites and
    Monuments
Amphitheater: Pula, Classical Sites and Monuments
Andronikov Monastery: Moscow, Russia
Arc de Triomphe: Paris, France
Arch of Constantine: Rome, Classical Sites and
    Monuments
Arch of Titus: Rome, Classical Sites and
    Monuments
Aspendos: Classical Sites and Monuments
AT&T Building: New York City, New York,
    U.S.A.
Auditorium Building: Chicago, Illinois, U.S.A.

B

Baalbek: Classical Sites and Monuments
Banqueting House, Whitehall: London, England,
    Great Britain
Baths of Diocletian (Thermae Diocletiani): Rome,
    Classical Sites and Monuments
Battersea Power Station: London, England, Great
    Britain
Battery Park City: New York City, New York,
    U.S.A.
Bauhaus: Dessau, Germany
Beauvais Cathedral: Beauvais, France
Belvedere: Vienna, Austria

Best Products Showroom: See Indeterminate Facade
    Showroom, Houston, Texas, U.S.A.
Bibliothèque Nationale: Paris, France
Blenheim Palace: Oxfordshire, England, Great
    Britain
Boots Factory, Beeston: Nottinghamshire, England,
    Great Britain
Boston Public Library: Boston, Massachusetts,
    U.S.A.
Bourse: Copenhagen, Denmark
Bourse: See Exchange, St. Petersburg, Russia
Brandenburg Gate: Berlin, Germany
British Museum: London, England, Great Britain
Brooklyn Bridge: New York City, New York,
    U.S.A.
Burgos Cathedral: Burgos, Spain

C

Ca' d'Oro: Venice, Italy
Caernarvon Castle: Caernarvonshire, Wales, Great
    Britain
Canterbury Cathedral: Canterbury, England, Great
    Britain
Carson Pirie Scott Store: See Schlesinger and Mayer
    Store, Chicago, Illinois, U.S.A.
Casa del Fascio: Como, Italy
Casa Milá: Barcelona, Spain
Castel Nuovo: Naples, Italy
Castle Howard: Yorkshire, England, Great Britain
Castle of the Teutonic Knights: Malbork, Poland
Cathedral: Amiens, France
Cathedral/Mosque of Cordoba: Cordoba, Spain
Cathedral of St. Barbara: Kutna Hora, Czech
    Republic
Cathedral of St. Lawrence: Trogir, Croatia
Cathedral of Santa Maria del Fiore: Florence, Italy
Cathedral of Santa Maria la Nuova: Monreale,
    Sicily
Cathedral of Santiago de Compostela: Santiago de
    Compostela, Spain
Cathedral of Seville: Seville, Spain
Catholic Cathedral: Baltimore, Maryland, U.S.A.
Central Park: New York City, New York, U.S.A.
Central Railway Station: Milan, Italy
Centre Georges Pompidou: Paris, France

International Dictionary of Architects and Architecture - 2

ARCHITECTURE

CLASSICAL
SITES
and
MONUMENTS

AKRAGAS (AGRIGENTO)
Sicily

Sixth century B.C.: Foundation. **Fifth century B.C.:** Temples of Hera Lacinia, Hephaistos, Castor and Pollux constructed. **406 B.C.:** Temple of Herakles burned. **Sixth century A.D.:** Walls erected between columns of Temple of Concord, and temple reroofed.

Publications

COCKERELL, C. R.: *The Temple of Jupiter Olympius at Agrigentum*. London, 1830.

DINSMOOR, WILLIAM BELL: *The Architecture of Ancient Greece*. New York, 1975.

DINSMOOR, WILLIAM BELL: "The Olympieum at Acragas." *Memoirs of the American Academy at Rome* 20 (1950).

DRERUP, H.: "Der Tempel des Zeus Olympios in Akragas." In *Bericht über den VI. internationalen Kongress für Archäologie, Berlin 21-26 August 1939*. Berlin, 1940.

GRIFFO, P.: *Ultimi scavi e ultime scoperte in Agrigento*. Agrigento, 1946.

KLENZE, LEO VON: *Der Tempel des olympischen Jupiter zu Agrigent*. Stuttgart and Tübingen, 1821.

KOLDEWEY, R., and PUCHSTEIN, O.: *Die griechischen Tempel Unteritalien und Sicilien*. Berlin, 1899.

MARCONI, P.: *Agrigento*. Rome, 1933.

PACE, B.: *Arte e civiltà della Sicilia antica*. 3 vols. Milan, 1935-46.

RANDALL-MACIVER, D.: *Greek Cities in Italy and Sicily*. Oxford, 1931.

SERRADIFALCO, DUCA DI: *Le antichità della Sicilia*. 5 vols. Palermo, 1834-42.

Studi e documenti relativi alle antichità agrigentine. Palermo, 1887.

*

The place name "Agrigento" is a deliberate archaism, revived in the 1930s from the Latin *Agrigentum* for the town that was previously called Girgenti, a name that occurs in older accounts of its remains. These remains belong essentially to the Greek colony of Akragas, one of the last of those founded in Sicily in the great age of Greek colonization in the west, which had begun with the east Sicilian cities settled in the last third of the eighth century B.C. The "traditional" date for the foundation of Akragas is 580 B.C., which is probably an approximation. It is certain that the site was known to the Greeks long before they settled there; indeed, Late Bronze Age vases from Greece found there suggest at least a trade connection in the second millennium B.C. Its later occupation may well be linked to an increase in trade along the south coast of Sicily, and across the Mediterranean to Carthage, but, like all the Sicilian Greek cities, the great attraction must have been the availability of land for the settlers, and an existing population that either acquiesced in the Greek takeover of their region or was too weak to resist.

The site occupies two hills, three to four kilometers from the coast, which is a sheltered but extended beach (the present harbor of Porto Empedocle is a modern development), the best landing point for seafarers along the southern coast of Sicily. The northern hill, now occupied by the modern town, formed an acropolis. The southern, more extensive hill bears traces of the grid-plan layout of ancient streets and houses (mostly built

quite late in the city's history), but terminates along its southern edge in an east-west ridge, steep-sided to the south. The ridge was an obvious line for the city wall which runs along the top, and, of course, extended around both hills to include the acropolis, spectacularly crowned by a line of magnificent temples of the fifth century B.C.

The foundation was a joint one, by the earlier Sicilian Greek colony of Gela (to the east of Akragas) and the Aegean island of Rhodes. It is likely that a large number of the original settlers came from Rhodes (the historian Polybius, writing in the second century B.C., thought of Akragas as a Rhodian colony) but although Rhodes is in the East Greek area, and so under the influence of the East Greek Ionic architectural style (the earliest cults of the gods are Rhodian), Akragas built its principal temples in the Doric order. The choice may have resulted from the fact that the Rhodians were in origin Dorians. In any case, the form of the temples is that developed for the Doric order within Sicily itself, so it was clearly a local tradition that prevailed.

There was certainly a temple on the acropolis, dedicated to Athena, probably Athena Lindia, since the Akragantines sent offerings to the "mother" sanctuary of Athena at Lindos in Rhodes. The remains of this temple, visible beneath the Church of Santa Maria dei Greci, into which six of its columns are embedded, suggest that it was constructed in the early part of the fifth century B.C., but it is likely that the cult was established before that, and that there was an earlier building on the site. There are traces of other early-sixth-century temples in Akragas, which must have been provided with religious buildings from the moment of its foundation, but the surviving buildings, for which the site is important, belong to a second phase.

The earliest of these is the most stupendous, the largest temple building in Sicily, and certainly the most unusual. It was dedicated, appropriately, to Olympian Zeus, and may have been inspired to rival the colossal Temple "G" at Selinus, another Greek colony to the west of Akragas. Its date is not absolutely certain. Diodorus, the Sicilian historian writing at the end of the first century B.C. (but certainly relying on earlier sources of information), says that Carthaginian prisoners captured after the Battle of Himera in 480 B.C. were put to work on it. Comparison with other temples is difficult because of its idiosyncratic design, but, like the Selinus temple it rivaled, it was probably begun toward the end of the sixth century. It measures 173 by 361 feet (about 52 by 110 meters), proportions found in other temples of that date. Despite this great size, its design called for facades of six columns only. For these, a lower diameter of more than four meters was required to maintain the proportions appropriate to the Doric order of that date, and this was too large to be quarried in the form of a complete drum, the method of building up columns which was evolving then (the earlier technique, of monolithic shafts, was of course even more impossible). Instead, half columns were built up from smaller blocks; the intervening spaces were walled up (presumably for added strength), enabling the architrave also to be constructed from small blocks without the normal requirement of a free span from column to column. Against the upper parts of these walls gigantic male figures (atlantes) were built in, their arms raised also to support the architrave. Internally, the cella consisted of a series of square piers, linked by a thinner curtain and possibly open at both ends, set in line with the third column from either end of the facade. The resulting division, into three spaces each of approximately 17 meters in width, was too great for the normal Greek techniques of roofing, and in fact the temple was left roofless and unfinished when the Carthaginians captured Akragas in 406 B.C. The temple now lies in ruins; much of the material was taken for the construction of Porto Empedocle, but one of the atlantes has been reconstructed, though it lies prone on the ground.

Temple of Concord, Akragas: Sicily, Italy, 6th century B.C.

The other temples along the southern ridge follow this odd building, but are by comparison perfectly conventional, in the Sicilian Doric manner. They extend to the east (and west) of the Temple of Olympian Zeus. The correct dedications for them, unlike the Zeus temple, are unknown, and they are popularly referred to by later nicknames which are not those of their original "owners." First in chronological sequence, a short distance to the east of Zeus is "Herakles" or "Hercules," hexastyle with 15 flank columns. The column spacing, apparently for the first time in Sicily, was uniform, except for angle contraction to improve the appearance of the facade (but not the ends of the flanks). This temple was burned by the Carthaginians

in 406 B.C. and repaired in Roman times. Further along the southern ridge are two more temples, both hexastyle and with 13 columns on the flanks, proportions normal in the fifth century for Doric temples in mainland as well as western Greece. "Hera Lacinia" at the east end of the ridge dates to the first half of the fifth century, "Concord" to about 430 B.C. Concord is one of the best preserved of all ancient Greek temples, having been converted into a church in the sixth century A.D. with the spaces between its columns walled up, and the whole structure reroofed. Most later accretions were removed in the 18th century. Hera Lacinia is less well preserved: in front of it are the remains of a very wide altar.

By comparison with the near-contemporary temples of Athens, Concord seems stodgy and dull. It suffers, as do all other Sicilian Greek temples, from the unavailability of marble (Pentelic marble not only improved the general appearances of the Athenian temples, but enabled Athenian architecture to lighten the structure, especially the proportions of the columns). Concord has columns whose height is approximately $4\frac{2}{3}$ times their lower diameter, while at Athens the Temple of Hephaistos has columns $5\frac{2}{3}$ times their diameter. Since column diameters roughly determine the proportion of the different elements in the entablatures, Concord also appears heavy in this respect; compared with column height, the entablature is about half the column height, while at Hephaistos the height is only roughly one third of that of the column. At Akragas, also, the cornice is relatively heavy, giving a particularly solid and massive appearance to the pediment. Perhaps to compensate for this heaviness, Concord is raised on a platform of four full steps, a feature found in other Sicilian temples, and contrasting with the lower bases of the Athenian marble temples, where the stricter Doric convention of three steps was adhered to. There is no surviving trace of sculptural decoration, though Sicilian temples frequently used carved decoration on their metopes. The external appearance of the temple at the present day is misleading. The brown color of the limestone predominates, and the individual blocks, particularly the steps, show marked striations, which appear to have been arranged to a pattern of opposing alignments, apparently deliberate, and in marked contrast to the finely smoothed surfaces given to the Athenian marble buildings. In fact, the surfaces were once covered with a fine stucco, traces of which survive, which would have given the stonework the smooth surfaces and crisper lines similar to that of marble.

Other structural aspects of this temple are interesting. It is not a large building, measuring approximately 17 by $39\frac{1}{2}$ meters, slightly larger than Hephaistos at Athens. There were no internal colonnades to support the timbers of the roof, whose ridge was supported on the main cross beams spanning the cella with a length of about eight meters. These beams also held up a flat ceiling, which came immediately above a cornice at the top of the cella wall, which is still preserved. Access to the area above the ceiling was provided by two stone staircases behind the porch wall, one to either side of the door, a feature repeated from other Sicilian temples. These staircases suggest that access to the roof space was needed for more than mere utilitarian or maintenance purposes. There is a large opening through the pedimental upper section of the cella rear wall, with inclined sides and curved top: this opening would be accessible from the attic (via the staircases) and visible from outside, since the roof over the porch and behind the end colonnades is supported not by the usual flat beams and ceiling (which would have hidden the opening) but by a series of purlins along the upper edges of the pediments. All these details are well preserved in Concord. Since they repeat features found in other, less well-preserved Sicilian temples, we may argue that they are consistent with a strong local Sicilian style of building, which presents characteristics of its own distinct from those of mainland Doric.

The other temples "Hephaistos" and "Castor and Pollux" are less well preserved. They too date to the fifth century B.C. Outside the walls is a smaller, nonperipteral temple, of "Asklepios," of uncertain date. Also outside the walls, close to the southern gate near the temple of Olympian Zeus, is a well-preserved monumental tomb, called that of Theron, who ruled Akragas in the early part of the fifth century B.C. However, the structure is clearly Hellenistic, having a main section (over a high-raised podium) embellished with Ionic columns engaged at each corner supporting a Doric architrave. The ultimate inspiration for the tomb was the Mausoleum at Halicarnassus, which also inspired another Hellenistic tomb at Akragas, inside the old city limits, known as the "Oratory of Phalaris."

—R. A. TOMLINSON

ASPENDOS
Roman Asia Minor (Turkey)

Ca. 161-180 A.D.: Roman theater built; **Architect:** Zeno.

Publications

BIEBER, MARGARETE: *The History of the Greek and Roman Theater*. Princeton, New Jersey, 1961.
DINSMOOR, WILLIAM BELL: *The Architecture of Ancient Greece*. New York, 1975.
FREELY, JOHN: *Classical Turkey*. London, 1990.
LANCKORONSKI, K., et al.: *Städte Pamphyliens und Pisidiens*. Prague, Vienna and Leipzig, 1890.
ROBERTSON, D. S.: *Handbook of Greek and Roman Architecture*. Cambridge, 1954.
WARD-PERKINS, J. B.: *Roman Imperial Architecture*. Harmondsworth, England, 1981.

Considered among the great cities of Pamphylia beside Attaleia, Sillyum and Side, Aspendos is best known today for its nearly intact theater, whose reputation has eclipsed that of the site itself. Remains of several vaulted buildings, an aqueduct and curved thoroughfares, all of Roman date, give the ambiance of a city with Roman character, rather than a Romanized one, being relatively free of compromising Hellenistic tradition. In its present state of preservation, the site is stripped of the ostentation resulting from the so-called marble style (contrasting with Perge and Side nearby). In this respect, the parsimony of applied detail in marble allows a more balanced appreciation of well-rehearsed construction techniques with local materials, engineering skills and a flair for transforming topographical impediments into advantage.

In spite of bread riots under Trajan and a questionable reputation as a conniving ally, the city seems to have been free from major devastation. As early as the beginning of the fifth century B.C., it was the only city in the region (except Side) to issue its own silver coinage, bearing testimony to a strong economy that was probably based on the local salt and olive-oil industry. Aspendos was no backwater. Its superb location on an elongated, flat-topped spur overlooks the navigable Eurymedon River, and it commanded water and land routes between east and west Pamphylia (including the main road traversing Asia Minor from Pergamon to Side on the coast). Not surprisingly, abundant remains point to prosperity in the second century A.D., also attested to by a sizable population in the beginning of the Christian era. All major buildings of the Roman city fabric, except the amphitheater, which is rare in Asia Minor and elsewhere, are represented: entertainment buildings (theater, stadium) and functional buildings (bath, gymnasium) on the low-lying periphery to the east, and the governmental-commercial-judicial functions centrally organized with populist expression around the agora high up on the spur. Three city gates, cardinally placed on the north, south and east, formed the entry points for the Roman thoroughfares. The latter curved and twisted,

Theater: Aspendos, ca. 161-180 A.D.

following the lay of the land, showing no effort to enforce the more common straight street pattern of Hellenistic legacy in the east. The verve and pace of the streets are arrested by at least two sculptural edifices, adroitly placed. One of them, an exedra on the southeast corner of the agora, had seats for the public to listen to orators and a row of niches for statues. It overlooked the street leading to the agora from the south gate of the city. On the other end, a ceremonial arch was erected between the east gate and the agora. Both structures were well calculated to anticipate the approach to the city center visually and symbolically. Within the agora itself, a nymphaeum (fountain house), with its screen-like vertical eminence and gushing water, provided both accent and rapport between the covered market, basilica and bouleuterion. Its water (as well as the water for the baths on the plain below) was carried by an impressive aqueduct/viaduct combination, ingeniously furnished with two pressure towers 30 meters high.

The marriage of Roman engineering proficiency and showy aesthetic, however, is consummated in the theater. The overall tectonic unity and economy of construction in the structure, with its visibility from afar, represents the apex of Roman canonical design. Although the *cavea* partially utilizes the hillside, it rests on vaulted arches. Unlike most Roman theaters in Asia Minor, it describes a semicircle which is completely integrated with the stage building in accordance with Vitruvian prescription. Totally cut off from the rest of the world, the audience was encapsulated in a tightly controlled world of the stage and drama. Ingress and egress were also efficiently resolved with a formal but highly practical systematization of the circulation through side entrances (*paradoi*), a horizontal

passage (*diazoma*) which divided the *cavea* equally in the middle, and a series of stairs that fanned out toward the periphery. Alternating curvilinear and triangular pediments crowned the rhythmic projections (*aediculae*) of the stage wall on the inside. They were focused with a wider broken pediment in the center, which was crowned with a Bacchus relief, a concession to histrionic propriety. In a bilingual inscription in Greek and Latin, the two brothers Curtius Crispinus and Curtius Auspicatus proclaimed to posterity their dedication of the theater, built by Zeno, to the gods of the country and to the Imperial House.

—SUNA GÜVEN

ACROPOLIS
Athens, Greece

448-438 B.C.: Parthenon built; **Architects:** Iktinos and Kallikrates. **437-432 B.C.:** Propylaia replaces earlier gateway; **Architect:** Mnesikles. **Ca. 427-424 B.C.:** Temple of Athena Nike built; **Architect:** Iktinos. **Ca. 421-405 B.C.:** Erechtheion built.

Publications
Acropolis

BALANOS, N. M.: *Les monuments de l'Acropole.* 2 vols. Paris, 1938.
BEULÉ, C. E.: *L'acropole d'Athènes.* 2 vols. Paris, 1853-54.

BÖTTICHER, A. G.: *Die Akropolis von Athen.* Berlin, 1888.

BOWRA, C. M.: *Periklean Athens.* London, 1971.

BURNOUF, E. L.: *Le ville et l'acropole d'Athènes.* Paris, 1877.

DINSMOOR, WILLIAM BELL: *The Architecture of Ancient Greece.* New York, 1975.

D'OOGE, M. L.: *The Acropolis of Athens.* New York and London, 1908.

FERGUSON, W. S.: *Hellenistic Athens.* London, 1911.

GARDNER, E. A.: *Ancient Athens.* New York and London, 1902.

HARRISON, J. E., and VERRALL, M. G.: *The Mythology and Monuments of Ancient Athens.* London and New York, 1890.

HEGE, W.: *Akropolis.* Munich, 1956.

HILL, I. T.: *The Ancient City of Athens, Its Topography and Monuments.* Chicago, 1969.

PICARD, C., and BOISSONNAS, F.: *L'acropole d'Athènes, l'enceinte, l'entrée, le bastion d'Athéna Niké, les Propylées.* Paris, 1930.

PICARD, C., and BOISSONNAS, F.: *L'acropole d'Athènes, le plateau supérieur, l'Erechtheion, les annexes sud.* Paris, 1930.

RODENWALDT, G., and HEGE, W.: *The Acropolis.* London, 1930.

SCHEDE, M.: *The Acropolis of Athens.* Berlin, 1924.

STEVENS, G. P.: *The Periclean Entrance Court of the Acropolis of Athens.* Cambridge, Massachusetts, 1936.

STEVENS, G. P.: *The Setting of the Periclean Parthenon.* Cambridge, Massachusetts, 1940.

STUART, J., and REVETT, N.: *The Antiquities of Athens.* 4 vols. London, 1762-1816.

WALTER, O.: *Athen, Akropolis.* Vienna, 1929.

WELLER, C. H.: *Athens and Its Monuments.* New York, 1913.

WYCHERLEY, R. E.: *The Stones of Athens.* Princeton, New Jersey, 1978.

Erechtheion

DELL, J.: *Das Erechtheion in Athen, bauanalytisch untersucht, erklärt und ergänzt.* Brunn, 1934.

DÖRPFELD, W., and SCHLEIF, H.: *Erechtheion.* Berlin, 1942.

INWOOD, HENRY W.: *The Erechtheion at Athens.* London, 1827.

PATON, J. M., and STEVENS, G. P.: *The Erechtheum.* Cambridge, Massachusetts, 1927.

RODENWALDT, G.: "Die Form des Erechtheions." *Neue Jahrbuch für das klassische Altertumsgeschichte* 47 (1921).

WELLER, C. H.: "The Original Plan of the Erechtheum." *American Journal of Archaeology* 25 (1921).

Nike Temple

BLÜMEL, C.: *Der Fries des Tempels der Athena Nike.* Berlin, 1923.

CARPENTER, RHYS: *The Sculpture of the Nike Temple Parapet.* Cambridge, Massachusetts, 1929.

DINSMOOR, W. B.: "The Sculptured Parapet of Athena Nike." *American Journal of Archaeology* 30 (1926).

MARK, I. S.: "Nike and the Cult of Athena Nike on the Athenian Acropolis." Ph.D. Dissertation. New York University, New York, 1979.

MATTINGLY, H. B.: "The Athena Nike Temple Reconsidered." *The American Journal of Archaeology* 86 (1982): 381-385.

MÖBIUS, H.: "Zu Ilissosfries und Nikebalustrade." *Athenische Mitteilungen des Deutschen Archäologischen Instituts* 53 (1928).

ORLANDOS, A. K.: "Zum Tempel der Athena Nike." *Athenische Mitteilungen des Deutschen Archäologischen Instituts* 40 (1915).

Acropolis: Athens, Greece, 5th century B.C.

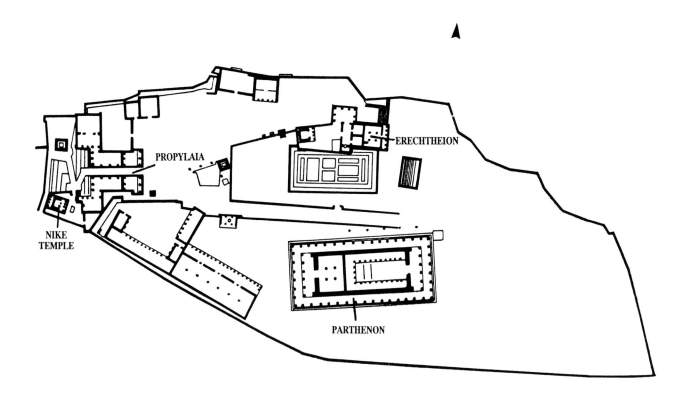

PROPYLAIA

ERECHTHEION

NIKE
TEMPLE

PARTHENON

ORLANDOS, A. K.: ''Nouvelles observations sur la construction du temple d'Athéna Niké.'' *Bulletin de correspondance héllénique* 71-72 (1947-48).

ROSS, L.; SCHAUBERT, E.; and HANSEN, C.: *Der Tempel der Nike Apteros.* Berlin, 1839.

WESENBERG, B.: ''Zur Baugeschichte des Niketemples.'' *Jahrbuch des Deutschen Archäologischen Instituts* 96 (1981) 28:54.

Parthenon

BOARDMAN, J.: *The Parthenon and Its Sculptures.* Austin, Texas, 1990.

CARPENTER, RHYS: *The Architects of the Parthenon.* Harmondsworth, England, 1970.

COLLIGNON, M., and BOISSONNAS, F.: *Le Parthénon, l'histoire, l'architecture et la sculpture.* Paris, 1910-12.

DINSMOOR, W. B.: ''The Construction and Arrangement of the Panathenaic Frieze of the Parthenon.'' *Journal of Hellenic Studies* 68 (1948).

DINSMOOR, W. B.: ''How the Parthenon Was Planned: Modern Theory and Ancient Practice.'' *Architecture* 47-48 (1923).

GOODYEAR, W. H.: *Greek Refinements: Studies in Temperamental Architecture.* New Haven, Connecticut, 1912.

HAMBRIDGE, J.: *The Parthenon and Other Greek Temples: Their Dynamic Symmetry.* New Haven, Connecticut, 1924.

KNELL, H.: ''Iktinos: Baumeister des Parthenon und des Apollontempels von Philaglia-Basse?'' *Jahrbuch des Deutschen Archäologischen Instituts* 83 (1968): 100-117.

MAGNE, L.: *Le Parthénon.* Paris, 1895.

MICHAELIS, A.: *Der Parthenon.* Leipzig, 1870-71.

MURRAY, A. S.: *The Sculptures of the Parthenon.* London, 1903.

PENNETHORNE, J.: *The Geometry and Optics of Ancient Architecture.* London and Edinburgh, 1878.

PRASCHNIKER, C.: *Parthenonstudien.* Augsburg and Vienna, 1928.

STEVENS, G. P.: ''Concerning the Curvature of the Steps of the Parthenon.'' *American Journal of Archaeology* 38 (1934).

VON LÜCKEN, G.: *Die Entwicklung der Parthenonskulpturen.* Augsburg, 1930.

WESENBERG, B.: ''Wer Erbaute den Parthenon?'' *Athenische Mitteilungen des Deutschen Archäologischen Instituts* 97 (1982): 99-125.

WILKINS, WILLIAM: ''On the Sculptures of the Parthenon.'' In ROBERT WALPOLE (ed.): *Travels in Various Countries of the East.* London, 1820.

WOLFER-SULZER, L.: *Das geometrische Prinzip der griechisch-dorischen Tempel.* Winterthur, 1939.

ZILLER, E.: ''Über die ursprüngliche Existenz der Curvaturen des Parthenon.'' *Zeitschrift für Bauwesen* 15 (1865).

Propylaia

BOHN, R.: *Die Propyläen der Akropolis zu Athen.* Berlin and Stuttgart, 1882.

DINSMOOR, W. B.: ''The Gables of the Propylaea.'' *American Journal of Archaeology* 14 (1910).

DÖRPFELD, W.: ''Die Propyläen der Akropolis zu Athen.'' *Athenische Mitteilungen des Deutschen Archäologischen Instituts* 10 (1885).

*

EARLY HISTORY

The Acropolis of Athens, a large outcropping of gray limestone and red schist, rises steeply above its surroundings. Easily defended, it attracted human occupation in both the Neolithic Era

Temple of Nike: Athens, Greece, ca. 427-424 B.C.

(ca. 5000 B.C.) and the Bronze Age (ca. 3000 to 1100 B.C.). In the Late Bronze Age, Mycenaean kings resided in a palace on the north side. The plan of that palace is unknown, although it may be safe to conjecture that a megaron formed part of the structure. In the late 13th century B.C., during a time of upheaval and anticipated invasion, the Mycenaeans turned the Acropolis into a stronghold complete with a Cyclopean circuit wall, a fortified entrance gate on the southwest (oriented north-south), and a postern gate on the north reached by a steep staircase partly hewn from the rock itself. Access to a natural well deep in a cleft in the north face of the rock was also effected at that time. Current research indicates that the Mycenaean gateway remained in place until the early fifth century B.C.

THE ARCHAIC PERIOD

The Acropolis was sacred to the goddess Athena (from whom the Athenians took their name) early on. She shared it with Athenian kings (*Iliad* 2.546-556, *Odyssey* 7.78-81) until the monarchy changed into an aristocracy in the seventh century B.C. From that time forward, until the Middle Ages, the citadel served primarily as her residence. One or more temples dedicated to her must have stood on the Acropolis in the seventh century, but as they were built largely of perishable materials, their remains are scanty. In the sixth century at least two noteworthy stone structures were erected on the Acropolis: the temple of Athena Polias (Protectress of the City), a peripteral Doric limestone temple from about 550 B.C., located on the north side; and a second limestone temple to Athena, known as the Hekatompedon (hundred-footer), which apparently stood on the south side. Both temples faced east, as was usual for Greek temples, and thus were built with their backs toward the gateway.

The Polias temple, the foundations of which can still be seen on the Acropolis just south of the Erechtheion, had multiple cellas, suggesting that it housed several cults. The eastern cella was dedicated to Athena, and in it the ancient olive-wood statue of Athena Polias (which Pausanias relates "fell from heaven") was housed. That half of the temple was destroyed during the Persian sack of Athens in 479 B.C. The western half was then repaired, and the cult statue, which had been evacuated from Athens before the conflict for safekeeping, was placed within. Referred to in fifth-century accounts as "The Opisthodomos," it stood in place until it was demolished in the middle of the fourth century B.C. The Hekatompedon, like the Temple of Athena Polias, was a peripteral Doric temple. Its exact layout is unknown, for it was dismantled in the early fifth century B.C. (ca. 490-488) to make way for a new all-marble temple, known today as the Older (or Marathonian) Parthenon. This new temple was unfinished at the time of the Persian sack of Athens, and was damaged when the invaders set fire to the Acropolis. Some of its marble was reused 30 years later in the Periklean Parthenon, and some of its unfluted column drums were built into the northern portion of the new Acropolis defense wall, along with part of the entablature from the Temple of Athena Polias, "to serve as a reminder for all time of Persian impiety."

THE CLASSICAL PERIOD

The Acropolis was transformed into a citadel of breathtaking beauty during an extensive building campaign begun in 448 B.C., under the auspices of Perikles (who died in 429, two years after the outbreak of the Peloponnesian Wars), and completed in about 405 B.C., just before Sparta dealt Athens its final resounding defeat. During that half century a new gateway and three temples to Athena were built there, all of Pentelic marble: the Parthenon, 448-438 B.C., referred to in contemporary accounts as "the new temple"; the Propylaia, 437-432 B.C., which replaced an earlier fifth-century gateway of disputed form; the temple of Athena Nike (Bringer of Victory), circa 427-424 B.C., set atop an impressive new stone bastion; and the Erechtheion, circa 421-405 B.C., a temple which Athena shared with several local heroes and other gods, and which was referred to in contemporary accounts as "the temple on the Acropolis within which is the archaic statue" (*I.G.* I² 372).

The present-day visitor to the Acropolis often approaches it from a broad modern road along the south side where tour buses stop to let off passengers. From there, walking westward, one gets a tantalizing glimpse of the back (western portion) of the Parthenon above the medieval fortification wall before it disappears from view behind the ruins of the Roman Odeion, built by Herodes Atticus at the base of the southwestern slope. In ancient times, however, visitors approached the Acropolis from the north, following the Sacred Way diagonally across the Agora to where it ascended the lower northwestern edge of the Acropolis. Midway up the slope the path leveled out, bringing the pilgrim around to the western ascent and up through the Propylaia. The Beulé Gate, which today controls entrance to the Acropolis, was built in the third century A.D. and placed axially with respect to the Classical Propylaia. The partly preserved monumental staircase leading up to the Propylaia was added by the Roman Emperor Claudius in about 52 A.D.

THE TEMPLE OF ATHENA NIKE

Perched at the northwestern edge of its lofty bastion, which narrows perceptibly toward the front, the tiny tetrastyle amphiprostyle Temple of Athena Nike greets the visitor to the Acropolis like a winged Victory alighting on, or about to spring forth

Propylaia: Athens, Greece, 437-432 B.C.

from, the prow of a ship. Several "refinements"—such as the upwardly curving *krepidoma,* and the inward inclination of steps, side walls and columns—give the temple a soaring quality, while others—a heavier-than-normal entablature and stocky Ionic columns with squashed bases—keep the temple firmly rooted to the spot. Resembling a *naiskos,* it is a broad, compact, one-room temple, lacking both pronaos and opisthodomos, and like a *naiskos* the eastern end of the cella is left open. There two piers *in-antis* suggest both the wall, which normally closes off the eastern end of a temple cella, and the columns *in-antis* found at the front of a temple pronaos. The Nike temple was reached in antiquity by a staircase built against and into the northern wall of the bastion, and from the southern wing of the Propylaia. From there it appears as an exquisite jewel set against a spectacular and unforgettable backdrop of mountains, sea and sky.

THE PROPYLAIA

The west slope of the Acropolis is crowned by a magnificent Doric gateway, designed and built by Mnesikles, which today is difficult to fully appreciate due to its ruinous state, and because it is partly obscured from below by both the Beulé Gate and a huge Hellenistic pedestal, reused by the Romans for a monument to Agrippa. Adapted to a rising and uneven terrain (partly through terracing and partly through ingenious design), the Propylaia spans the western side of the Acropolis, its splendid central hexastyle portico towering over its low, horizontal wings. The wings project forward, embracing the visitor, and drawing him upward and inward, their tristyle *in-antis* porches giving the illusion of perfect symmetry. The south wing, however, is only a facade, its length sharply curtailed so

that it would not encroach unduly on the tiny precinct of Athena Nike. The asymmetrical placement of the doorway in the north wing suggests that dining couches were installed within for use during sacred meals associated with the precinct of Athena Nike. This wing is often referred to as the Pinakotheke because it contained a series of paintings by famous artists (Pliny *N.H.* 35.101; Pausanias 1.22.6-7).

As the ancient visitor approached the central porch of the Propylaia from the west, he could see from certain vantage points a second pediment behind, and slightly higher than, the first, added by Mnesikles to mark the location of the gate wall itself, and the change in levels between the western and eastern porticoes. The resulting design has a complexity, strength and grandeur worthy of Michelangelo or Borromini. The four-stepped *krepidoma* is split in two by a wide ramp, leaving an extra wide intercolumniation in the center, so that the Panathenaic Procession and its attendant sacrificial beasts could pass easily through the gate. Directly above the ramp Mnesikles used a double cantilever arrangement in the frieze course to relieve extra stress on the architrave. Inside the porch, Ionic columns, which once supported a splendid marble ceiling much admired in antiquity (Pausanias 1.22.4), flank the central passage, and lead to the gate wall, which rests atop a pair of five steps and is pierced by five doorways.

The eastern aspect of the Propylaia must have been as disappointing in antiquity as it is today. The central hexastyle porch projects forward excessively, and rests on a mere two-stepped *krepidoma,* which is often obscured by the Acropolis rock into which it is sunk. Mnesikles' original design called for two large symmetrical rooms flanking the eastern hexastyle portico, which would have transformed this side of the Propylaia into a vision of monumental grandeur all its own. Recent analysis suggests that these rooms were to serve as *hestiatoria* for sacrificial meals during the Panathenaic Festival. Unfortunately, these rooms were never built because it would have necessitated demolishing more of the surviving Mycenaean wall on the southwest and would have interfered with the precinct of Artemis Brauronia.

THE PARTHENON

The Parthenon rises majestically above its surroundings, dominating not only the Acropolis rock but the city of Athens itself by its sheer size and extraordinary beauty. In ancient times it could be seen clearly from miles away, a symbol of the greatness of Athens and of her patron goddess. Built of white Pentelic marble, which has weathered to a golden hue, and framed against a deep blue sky, the Parthenon is hidden from view on the western ascent until one passes through the Propylaia. Set at an angle to the line of sight, the laws of linear perspective reinforcing its three-dimensionality, the Parthenon impresses the viewer with its sculptural solidity. Although larger temples existed in Greece, none commanded such an impressive setting, nor could have evoked in the beholder the same sense of breathless exhilaration.

In planning the Parthenon, architects Iktinos and Kallikrates retained the two-cella arrangement, and the truncated pronaos and opisthodomos (with prostyle columns), of its unfinished predecessor, but dispensed with the long Archaic (6 by 16) proportions of the earlier structure. They shortened and broadened the new temple, making the two cellas unusually wide, the *pteroma* excessively narrow, and giving it a majestic peristyle of 8 by 17 slender, closely packed Doric columns, a combination of elements which gives the temple an extraordinary breadth and dignity. In the eastern cella they devised a new π-shaped arrangement of double-tiered Doric columns, to frame the new colossal cryselephantine statue of Athena being prepared by

Parthenon, from the northwest: Athens, Greece, 448-438 B.C.

Pheidias, while in the smaller western cella, four single-story Ionic columns bore the weight of the ceiling and roof. The use of Ionic elements within Doric structures was characteristic of Archaic and Classical Athens, an Ionian city-state surrounded by Dorian neighbors.

The very slenderness of the peristyle columns (approximately 5.5 diameters high), with their new subtle entasis and taper, is a High Classical refinement of the Doric order. The *echinoi* now form truncated cones, effortlessly transmitting the horizontal load of the entablature down through the vertical shafts of the columns, the load and non-load-bearing members in perfect harmony. Mnesikles copied the proportions and profiles of the Parthenon peristyle columns for the Doric porticoes of the Propylaia, thus preparing the approaching visitor for the sight which lay beyond, and reminding him of it on his way out.

The temple seems organic, growing vigorously from the rock to which it is firmly rooted, an impression achieved through a series of sophisticated "refinements," some of which appeared for the first time on the Parthenon. The upward curvature of the *krepidoma* and entablature, slight inward tilting of the columns and lower entablature, and slight outward tilt of the corona create the impression that the temple is soaring upward in the center but is also weighted down at the corners. The extra-thick corner columns and strong angle contraction on all four sides strengthen the corners visually as they hold the vital mass of the temple in check. Most of these refinements are visible to the naked eye, proving that they were not mere optical corrections.

The Parthenon was also extraordinarily rich in its sculptural adornment, which fell under the supervision of Pheidias. Both pediments held figures carved fully in the round, the east pediment representing the Birth of Athena, the west the Contest of Athena and Poseidon for the land of Attica. All 92 exterior metopes were sculpted with legendary battle scenes: the Gigantomachy (east), the Fall of Troy (north), an Amazonomachy (west) and a Centauromachy (south). And above the exterior cella walls ran an Ionic frieze depicting the Panathenaic Procession, the most important religious festival in Athens, celebrating the Birth of Athena.

THE ERECHTHEION

On the extreme northern section of the Acropolis rock, placed midway between the western and eastern slopes, stands a delicate Ionic temple known today as the Erechtheion. Dwarfed by the Parthenon, the Erechtheion nevertheless holds its own, attracting the visitor by its eccentric layout and splendid Caryatid Porch. One glance at the temple reveals that it cannot be fully grasped from any one angle, but must be explored from every aspect. Not surprisingly the most harmonious (although not the most intriguing) view of the temple is from the southeast, at the spot where the great open-air altar of Athena stood. It was there that the Panathenaic Procession culminated after first visiting the Parthenon.

Given the task of building this temple on terrain which rose dramatically upward along the south and east, and of incorporating into its structure and surroundings a large number of cults and holy spots of great antiquity, the unknown architect organized the temple into a central block facing east-west, with a single entablature and roof spanning its entire length, and added two extraordinary porches to the northern and southern flanks

Erechtheion: Athens, Greece, ca. 421-405 B.C.

at the western edge. The interior of the temple was totally destroyed by Christian and Turkish modifications, but it seems that the central block was divided in two by a cross wall, the floor level of the eastern section being considerably higher than that of the west. The eastern cella, dedicated to Athena Polias and containing her ancient olive-wood statue (transferred there from ''The Opisthodomos''), has a prostyle porch of six elegant Ionic columns. The western section was subdivided into three rooms, with slightly differing floor levels, by short marble walls leaving a single high ceiling above them. The exact arrangement of these compartments is unknown, but it may have echoed those of the old Polias temple. Here the altars of Poseidon-Erechtheus, Hephaistos and Boutes were placed. Below the westernmost of the three compartments, the sacred snake dwelt, and a small cistern held the famous salt sea of Poseidon. The western facade is decorated by four Ionic half columns *in-antis* ''backed by pilasters'' resting on a molded base above a plain ashlar wall, giving the impression of a western portico matching that of the east. The lower wall was (and is) hidden from view by the foundations of the Archaic Polias temple and the walls of the Pandroseion, an open-air precinct that abuts the Erech-theion and was sacred to Pandrosos, daughter of Kekrops, an early king of Athens whose tomb was next to or under the South Porch. On the upper wall the intervals between the engaged columns and antae ''were walled to the height of four courses,'' the open spaces above filled in with wooden grilles, save the southernmost ''intercolumniation,'' which, for cult reasons, was left completely open, perhaps to allow for a close association with the sacred olive tree of Athena which grew in the Pandroseion. These openings served as a clerestory for the western section, letting abundant light and air into this portion

of the temple. (The Romans replaced the grilles with the wall and three windows found there today.)

The small South Porch (commonly referred to as the Porch of the Maidens), built over a holy spot associated with early Athenian Kings, contains a symmetrical arrangement of 4 by 2 stately caryatids, resting on a tall wall base. (The original statues, severely damaged by modern pollution, have been removed to the Acropolis museum; copies stand in their stead). The maidens carry fancy Doric capitals (carved with an egg and dart, and a bead and reel), reminiscent of baskets, on their heads, leading some to identify them as the Arrephoroi, who carried secret sacred things in this way (Pausanias 1.27.3), or the daughters of Kekrops, who kept the snake-child Erichthonios in a basket (Pausanias 1.18.2). The Caryatid Porch served as a minor entrance to the western section by means of a small door in the northeast corner of its base which led to a staircase and doorway in the temple wall. The large and imposing North Porch is best seen from the north side, where the monumentality of its impressive 4 by 2 Ionic portico can be fully appreciated. Raised on a four-stepped *krepidoma,* the North Porch marks the spot where Poseidon hit the rock with his trident in his contest with Athena for the land of Attica. (The marks are visible through a hole built into the *krepidoma.* A corresponding hole in the roof above leaves this section open to the sky). At the back, a monumental doorway, with elaborately carved door jambs, served as the main entrance to the western section. The North Porch projects slightly beyond the western facade (an awkward juncture which has given rise to the suggestion that the original plan for the Erechtheion was quite different from the one finally executed), giving access to the Pandroseion through a small doorway, and from there to the Erechtheion through a doorway cut in the lower western wall. To the east of the North Porch is the open-air precinct of Zeus Hypatos (Most High), a paved courtyard, and a monumental staircase which allowed the ancient visitor to ascend to the level of the East Porch.

From every vantage point the Parthenon and the Erechtheion play off against one another in a neverending symphony of architectural point and counterpoint. The majestic Parthenon contrasts with the jewel-like Erechtheion, with its plethora of exquisitely carved moldings and colorful decorations, which once also included white marble figures in relief attached to the frieze course of blue Eleusinian limestone, and brightly colored beads glued in the interstices of the carved guilloches below the volutes on the Ionic capitals of the North Porch. Of different orders, unequal in size, and completely different in expression, these two temples nevertheless balance each other, and provide for a lively interchange across the Acropolis rock.

OTHER BUILDINGS AND SANCTUARIES

Aside from the major structures and sanctuaries dedicated to Athena, the Acropolis housed many other cults (some of great antiquity), and a number of other buildings. Between the Propylaia and the Parthenon lay the altar of Hygeia, the sanctuary of Artemis Brauronia, and the Chalkotheke (a storage hall). Somewhere on the eastern portion of the rock the sanctuaries of Zeus Polieos and the Pandion were located, and on the north, near a stair which led through the fortification wall down to the sacred caves in the northwest rock, stood the house of the Arrephoroi, the young girls who weaved the *peplos* presented to Athena yearly at the Panathenaic Festival. Numerous statues lined the Acropolis rock, the most impressive of which was the colossal bronze statue of Athena Promachos by Pheidias, cast in about 458 B.C. from the spoils of the Persian Wars. It stood halfway between the Propylaia and the foundations of the Archaic Polias temple, and was so tall that the tip of her spear and the crest of her helmet could be seen from the sea. In the Roman period a small monopteros dedicated to Rome and Augustus was erected just east of the Parthenon.

Along the north slope were the Klepsydra spring, the sanctuary of the Nymphs, caves sacred to Apollo, Pan and Aglauros, and the sanctuary of Aphrodite and Eros. The sanctuary of Asklepios, dedicated in 418 B.C., complete with a small temple

Erechtheion, Caryatid Porch, ca. 421-405 B.C.

and several stoas (rebuilt in stone in the fourth century B.C.), is found on the south slope, next to the sanctuary of Dionysos with the ruins of its fourth-century temple and stone theater. Nearby, Eumenes added a long stoa in the second century B.C., and Herodes Atticus an Odeion in the Roman period.

CONCLUSION

Although in ruins, the Acropolis, with its magnificent marble gateway and splendid marble temples dedicated to Athena, impresses the visitor as forcefully today as it did in ancient times. As testimony to the vision of Perikles in initiating this project and the greatness of all who participated in it, we cannot improve on the words of Plutarch (*Perikles* 13), who remarked that despite the remarkable speed with which the Periklean Acropolis had been built, each structure "possessed a beauty which seemed venerable the moment it was born, and at the same time had a youthful vigour which makes it appear to this day as if it were newly built. A bloom of eternal freshness hovers over these works . . . and preserves them from the touch of time, as if some unfading spirit of youth, some ageless vitality, had been breathed into them." (*Paraphrase of translation by Ian Scott-Kilvert for Penguin Books*).

—PATRICIA A. MARX

AGORA
Athens, Greece

Seventh century B.C.: Construction. **Sixth century B.C.:** Relocated to second site. **Fifth century B.C.:** Temple of Hephaistos constructed. **Second century B.C.:** Stoa of Attalos II. **267 A.D.:** Destruction.

Publications

COULTON, J. J.: *The Architectural Development of the Greek Stoa.* Oxford, 1976.
DINSMOOR, WILLIAM BELL: *The Architecture of Ancient Greece.* New York, 1975.
THOMPSON, H. A.: "The Odeion in the Athenian Agora." *Hesperia* 19 (1950).

*

Research by the Greek Archaeological Society carried out between 1859 and 1912 has established that the first Athenian Agora was set out by Theseus, who dedicated a shrine to Aphrodite Pandemos in a clearing much nearer to the Acropolis in the seventh century B.C. The name *agora* comes from *agorai*, which is the Greek word for assembly, and this first long and narrow space, which extended to the Eleusinion on the lower north slope of the Acropolis, was presumably used in this way. From earliest times, the Agora was the place where the citizens of Athens would gather to pay respect to their ancestors, honor their heroes, hold festivals and athletic contests, as well as musical, dramatic and equestrian competitions.

The Panathenaic Procession, which was eventually to become one of the most visible of all of the religious rituals held in the city, was also initiated by Theseus, in honor of Athena Polias, the patron goddess of the city. This procession took place every year, and in a particularly memorable fashion every fourth year, moving from the Dipylon Gate in the city wall, across the Agora, and up to a statue of the goddess Athena placed at the base of the slope of the Acropolis. Unlike the celebratory parades normally held in cities today, which provide a preorganized spectacle involving specific organizations that march by while others look on, the Panathenaic Procession included everyone in Athens. The procession was an expression of civic unity, which was also symbolized by the statue of Athena herself. A graphic representation of this unity is given by the last scene in the Oresteian Trilogy of Aeschylus, in which the actors, who walk out of the theater, are joined by the audience, who walk together into the city in commemoration of the Panathenaic Procession. According to ancient tradition, a ship, carried in the procession, was taken in a circle around the Eleusinion and then past all of the buildings in the old Agora before coming to rest at the base of the Acropolis. Early in the sixth century B.C., the Agora was moved by Solon, to a level area between the Aeropagus and the Eridanos River where the oldest cemetery in Athens was once located. These facts have been verified by the archaeological research of the American School of Classical Studies, systematically carried out on this site since 1931. The research has uncovered remains from the Mycenaean, sub-Mycenaean and Geometric periods. From its establishment at this second site in 583 B.C. the Agora was to remain a thriving and indispensible part of the city for 850 years, until its final destruction by the Herulians in 267 A.D.

Prior to the invasion of Athens by the Persians in 490 B.C., and the burning of the temples on the Acropolis, the most important buildings in the Agora were the Altar of the Twelve Gods and the Leokorian on the northern side, and the shrine of Theseus and the Enneakrisungs on the south. Strung along a low ridge that runs along almost the entire western edge of the Agora were the Shrine of Zeus Eleutherias, the Temple of Apollo Patrous, the Temple of the Mother of the Gods, the Bouleuterion, and the Prytamikon, which was built on the site later occupied by the Tholos. The basic institutions represented on the Agora were the first manifestations of democracy as we know it, and while they may have begun to emerge in places like Chios as early as 550 B.C., it was really in Athens, following the Cleisthenian reforms of 507 B.C., that democracy as the rule of the *demos*, or people, began to be fully recognized. The Assembly, which consisted of the entire free male adult population of the city, fell far short of the type of extended franchise that is familiar to democratic societies today, but it represented a vast improvement over the despotism that had preceded it, as well as a historical shift in the collective perception of the individual's role in government. The Assembly was advised by the Boule, or elected council of 500, chosen in equal numbers from each of the 10 main tribes in Athens. The Boule, in turn, was guided by the Prytany, which was made up of 50 members, selected in the same way, which met only in a short session amounting to about one month a year. Both of these bodies only had powers of consultation, with final decisions being left to the Assembly itself.

After the Persians were defeated and many of the buildings that had been damaged had been repaired, a campaign to expand the Agora was launched by Kimon, resulting in many of the structures that are most familiar to us today. By 420 B.C., these included the Temple of Hephaistos or the Hephaisteion, which was built on top of the western ridge in axial alignment with a circular orchestra in the center of the Agora that serves as a graphic reminder of the celebratory, as well as the social and commercial, function of the central open space surrounded by these buildings. The Hephaisteion was flanked by the Stoa of Zeus Eleutherios on the northern end of the ridge, which was closest to the entry into the Agora from the Dipylon gate, on the one hand, and a semicircular *bouletari* on the other. Steps

Stoa of Attalos II (restored), Agora: Athens, Greece, 2nd century B.C.

leading up to the temple occupied the space between these two buildings, forming a linear grouping that was effectively terminated by the circular Tholos at the southern end of the ridge. On the south side of the Agora, the ancient precinct of Theseus had by then been joined to the Enneakrdands by a long stoa which created a second linear wall of buildings extending out at a right angle from the ridge.

In the Hellenistic period, the Stoa of Attalos II, which was donated to the city by the king of Pergamon, was built along the entire eastern end of the Agora, and it, along with a long middle stoa built in front of the Thesion on the south, created a space that was then entirely enclosed on three sides. The Stoa of Attalos, which has been completely restored, is two stories high, and in typical Hellenistic fashion superimposes one order upon another. The colonnade on the lower level facing the Agora is Doric, and that on the upper is Ionic, indicating the cosmopolitan character of the period, as well as the role that Athens played as a center of learning at the time. The ridge beam of the roof was also supported by a colonnade running down the middle of the stoa, and the petal-like, quasi-Egyptian

capitals are further proof of the eclecticism of the time. Shops originally lined the entire length of both stories of the stoa on the edge opposite the Agora. Today, these serve as the Agora Museum on the lower level, and as a work space for the American School of Classical Studies above. This long colonnade must have been an impressive sight for those in the Panathenaic Procession, who entered the open space directly opposite from it, and moved in a diagonal path in front of it toward the Acropolis on the southeast. Along with the middle stoa, this colonnade served both to direct and to echo the line of the march—which has been immortalized on the inner frieze of the Parthenon itself—giving it rhythm and an almost theatrical architectural background.

During that period, another important alteration was made to the Agora that greatly changed its appearance. A third stoa, less than half the length of either the middle or Attalion additions, was built in front of the old *bouletari*, effectively closing the visual gate that had previously existed between it and the Stoa of Zeus on the north. What this meant for those in the Agora itself was that they were surrounded by a nearly continuous

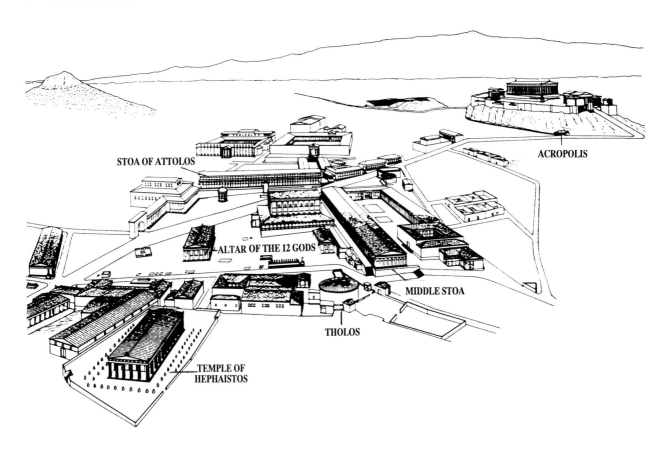

monumental colonnade instead of the clearly distinguishable individual buildings that had served to mark the boundaries of the space in the past. Rather than being the civic representation of the classical ideal of a loosely arranged assembly of buildings that could each be visually appreciated as individual, sculptural elements against the sky, the Agora was transformed into an urban entity, in which each part contributed to the impression of the whole.

While the population of Periclean Athens is estimated to have been about 150,000 free citizens and 100,000 slaves, this had actually declined by the Hellenistic period to about 200,000. While Athens had by then ceased to be the center of an empire, which it had lost at the end of the fifth century after a disastrous war with Sparta, Athens remained the psychological focus of the Greek world, which had then been so dramatically expanded by Alexander the Great. As the self-appointed champion of Greek culture, Alexander sought—through the establishment of new cities in the territory that he conquered, as well as the frequent presentation of athletic contests and theatrical productions—to promote Hellenic ideals, and he himself looked to Athens as their source. Although Alexander claimed that his invasion of Asia Minor was a revenge of the Persian destruction of the Athenian Agora and Acropolis two centries earlier, it is likely that overpopulation and an apalling poverty on the mainland were more direct incentives.

Following his dramatic success, scores of mercenaries followed to fight at his side, and they either died in the east, or stayed and settled there, rather than returning to Greece. Teachers and philosophers followed as well, eager to participate in this Panhellenic renaissance. Aristotle, for example, who had been Alexander's teacher, had a school of philosophy at Assos,

south of Troy on the Aegean coast of Asia Minor, and eventually returned to Athens to teach there, too. The long stoas of the Agora were a perfect background for such teaching, which was usually conducted peripatetically, while students and teacher walked, with the rational repetition of columns acting as an architectural mirror of the increasingly structured nature of philosophy in the Hellenistic period.

As the place where others such as Socrates, Plato, Chrysippos and Demosthenes also taught, and the apostle Paul paused on his travels to argue to all who would listen in favor of Christianity, the Agora remained the intellectual, if not the political, center of the Hellenic world, and a mandatory point of pilgrimage for those who wanted to learn to live within that world. Contemporary guidebooks to the city and its center, such as that written by Pausanias in the second century A.D., give some indication of the Agora's importance as a stop on the tourist circuit at a time when the traditional values that had evolved out of the polis were being questioned, and people looked to Athens as both a symbol as well as the embodiment of past ideals.

In 86 B.C., Athens made a fatal political miscalculation by placing its still considerable prestige behind Mithridates VI of Pantus, who had revolted against Roman rule in Asia and had massacred many colonists there. In retaliation, the Roman dictator Sulla leveled Athens, saying that he was more interested in punishing rebels than in learning architectural history.

While the Panathenaic Procession continued to be held, and still guided the placement of all new buildings in the Agora, in the second century B.C. the spirit had disappeared from both. The sense of balance that had prompted the transfer of the people's assembly to the Pnyx after the Lykourgian building campaign in the fourth century B.C. and that led to the construction of a new Theater and Odeion on the south side of the Acropolis in order to prevent overcrowding in the Periclean age was by that time missing. The Romans built a new temple of Ares in front of the Stoa of Zeus, below the western ridge on which the Hephaisteion is located, that directly intruded into the central space that had always remained open in the past. A second Odeion, which was built perpendicular to the face of the Middle Stoa, also projected to the center of the Agora, reaching nearly to the middle of the original circular orchestra where theatrical performances had once taken place, and which had served as the point around which more respectful growth had taken place in the past. Other statues and fountains compounded this clutter, creating a jumble that effectively destroyed the classical simplicity that had previously characterized the space.

In a sense the change that took place in the architectural feeling of the Agora between the fifth and second century A.D. accurately reflects the difference between the Greek and Roman conceptions of urban space, in which the Hellenistic period represents a transitional, rather than abnormal phase. While the Greek attitude may generally be said to have been one of accretion, in which the space between buildings was palpably an important entity in itself, or an outdoor room, the Roman approach was not nearly as sensitive. Rather than being concerned with the external relationships between buildings, the Romans concentrated instead on internal space, which led to expedient and often awkward combinations of buildings in their cities. This is most easily seen in the comparison of the Panathenaic Way of Athens with the route taken by the Triumphal Procession in Rome. Instead of being linear, and influencing the structural, proportional and directional characteristics of the buildings flanking its path, as in the Athenian example, the Roman procession began with several turns around the Circus Maximus and then proceeded through the crush of buildings in the Forum toward the Capitoline Hill, where each victorious general would surrender his weapons at the Temple of Jupiter as a symbol of his submission to Jupiter's authority. While the Athenian Agora had obviously grown in a carefully planned way prior to Roman rule, urban growth similar to that of the Forum, in which individual buildings were placed next to each other in total disregard for the consequences that this had for exterior civic space, followed the Roman occupation of the Greek city.

While this continuous formal evolution was undoubtedly important in an architectural sense, the real significance of the Agora goes far beyond the compositional arrangement of a series of buildings. As the heart of the most famous Greek polis of all, the Athenian Agora has become the historical symbol of the beginning of democracy itself. While it is well known that in its earliest permutation, this democracy was hardly multilateral, and that citizenship was granted only to a select few, the very idea of allowing different opinions to be voiced and votes to be counted, as an expression of the intrinsic worth of the individual, began here. Following the decline of the strong monarchies of the Bronze Age, semidemocratic governmental forms began to emerge in several places throughout the Greek world, and in the Periclean Age the Athenian Agora had unquestionably become the physical manifestation of the idea that government was best if it was guided by institutions and laws, and not by a single individual. While it is now mostly in ruins, the Agora still remains the most durable representation of that ideal.

—JAMES M. STEELE

CHORAGIC MONUMENT OF LYSICRATES
Athens, Greece

Late fourth century B.C.

Publications

DINSMOOR, WILLIAM BELL: *The Architecture of Ancient Greece*. New York, 1975.
VON LÜTZOW, C.: *Das choragische Denkmal des Lysikrates*. Leipzig, 1868.

*

The Choragic Monument of Lysicrates is a synthesis of formal and iconographic elements drawn from the realms of ancient theater, architecture and pagan ritual. For the purposes of discussion such diverse activities can be conveniently linked, at least etymologically, by the complex antique term *thymele,* a word that survives in various literary and architectural remains. Though its potential meanings are numerous and subject to debate, the term was undoubtedly applied in all three cultural contexts, and therefore may serve as a suitable vehicle for the interpretation of this important Greek monument.

One known usage of *thymele* was to designate the altar and accompanying offering table that stood at the center of the orchestra prior to the development of the permanent theater structure. The orchestra then was simply an open area of circular plan, possibly bordered with a stone curb, inside of which the primitive chorus danced in a cyclic motion. The performance consisted of a dithyramb, or chant, delivered to accompanying flute music in honor of the patron god of the theater, Dionysus.

Choragic Monument of Lysicrates: Athens, Greece, 4th century B.C.

As primarily religious affairs, dramatic events were preceded by sacrifices; victims slain on the *thymele*-altar were carved and dressed on the *thymele*-table.

Increasingly theatrical performances came to be conducted primarily in the format of festival competitions, the premiated chorus being rewarded with a bronze tripod. Moreover, from the dithyramb there eventually developed an exchange of dialogue between the chorus and its leader, who stood upon the *thymele*-table at the center of the dance. Consequently the word was extended to mean not only the two pieces of sacrificial furniture but also the performing space around them—the orchestra—with which they had become dramatically linked. Still later, in the Roman era, *thymele* denoted the by-then-raised proscenium stage and the theater in general.

The same term carries connotations of a more broadly architectural nature. An inscription calls the tholos, or circular building, at Epidauros a *thymele,* and scholars have attempted to draw a connection between the term and structures of round plan generally, especially as these buildings might carry mythological associations of death and resurrection. The Epidauros tholos, for instance, is said to have represented the tomb of Asklepius, the god of healing, while its mysterious subterranean labyrinth could be explained as signifying the mythical underworld. The existence of circular tombs in the Late Bronze Age, and more important, of a common type of round underground Greek tomb called the tumulus, reinforces such a relation between form and content.

Erected for the display of a prize tripod won by the poet Lysicrates for his dithyramb at the Athenian festival of 334 B.C., the choragic monument named after him is composed of a square pedestal and a diminutive circular structure above. To indicate its function as support, the base, or socle, is fashioned in rudimentary tectonic form: its unornamented cubic volume expresses the solidity of a sustaining mass, as does the large-scale ashlar coursing, which is then further emphasized by drafted reveals—an articulation of the individual block rarely found in the typically sheer wall surface of mortarless Attic construction. The considerable proportion of the base relative to the monument height and the overall vertical proportions of the monument itself are similarly unusual, and convey the vertical optimism of victory.

In contrast, the ring of six Corinthian columns and its superstructure comprise one of the most exuberantly decorative compositions in the Greek tradition. Recent studies suggest that it was originally conceived as a monopteros; however, an unforeseen structural instability in what would have been the first executed example of this building type may have required the insertion of intermediate wall slabs for cross-bracing. Only the slightly wider east bay facing the adjoining avenue, called the Street of the Tripods, was apparently left open, as the subtle alteration of the ground-plan geometry would suggest. This opening, neglected in many restorations, may have afforded a glimpse of a small figure of Bacchus, much like the placement of a cult statue in a temple cella. Surrounded by a grove of tree-like Corinthian columns capped by a simulated thatched roof, the divinity would have appeared enshrined in the sort of primitive hut that was his abode before the age of monumental temple architecture.

In addition to an inscription and the exhibited tripod, the representations of the god inside and on the frieze—where the myth of Dionysus and the failed resistance to his power by Tyrrhenian pirates is narrated—identify the monument with him and the theater, of which he is patron. The circular arrangement of the columns thus may be an allusion to the geometry of the ancient *thymele*-orchestra, while their rhythmic intercolumniations could recall the original cyclic chorus of the dithyramb,

as the Corinthian supports appear to dance about the structure.

The round plan of the upper monument, of course, also qualifies it as a tholos, with the potential connotations of the resurrection theme tied to the Epidaurian *thymele*. Again, Dionysus provides the thematic link, for among his legends, he is said to have been dismembered (as was the sacrificial victim on the *thymele*-table) and then reconstructed when stewed in a cauldron not unlike that of a tripod bowl. Moreover, as a vegetation god, he is connected with rituals designed to overcome nature's resistance to new spring growth, symbolized in the monument by the phyllotactic Corinthian columns; the frieze iconography translates the idea of resistance into human terms. Even the tall base may contain funereal implications in light of similar treatments at the tombs of Halicarnassus, Belevi, the Nereid Monument and so forth. Finally, the acanthus-based Corinthian order itself evokes the idea of rebirth described in the Vitruvian myth tracing its origin to the death of a young maiden (IV.I.9-10). This order, whose circular capitals accord well with the round plan, was employed externally for the very first time at the Lysicrates monument.

Such self-conscious unconventionality also informs the urban dimension, for the monument is deliberately sited to stand just forward of the facades of the adjoining choragic monuments designed chiefly as regular oblong temples. Moreover, a slightly oblique vista generated by an adjacent curve in the Street of the Tripods was balanced visually by the monument's cylindrical shape, the whole lending the urban topography an exceptionally scenographic quality.

The emphasis on visual content characterizes the details of the monument as well. The hitherto incompatible combination of frieze and dentils, the use of a *cyma recta* in the bed mold, the elimination of a proper *sima* for Vitruvian wave ornament, and a diminished calathos in the capital signal an increasing divorce of apparent and real structure when judged against the generally rational tectonicity of the previous century.

Two details in the monument are especially significant: the sweeping inverted cavetto forming a continuous sub-base beneath the columns, and the proportion of the dentils. The former recalls the exceptional bases of the Ionic columns inside the Temple of Apollo at Bassae, while the latter reproduces almost exactly those of the caryatid porch in the nearby Erechtheion. Like both these structures, the Choragic Monument of Lysicrates pursues deviation over canon, Dionysian individualism over Apollonian orthodoxy, and thereby stands with them as a counterpart to the intensely typological investigations of ancient Greek architecture.

—DONALD M. RATTNER

TOWER OF THE WINDS
Athens, Greece

40 B.C.: Construction.

Publications

DINSMOOR, WILLIAM BELL: *The Architecture of Ancient Greece*. New York, 1975.

Tower of the Winds: Athens, Greece, 40 B.C.

ROBINSON, H. S.: "The Tower of the Winds and the Roman Market Place." *American Journal of Archaeology* 47 (1943).

*

Constructed to house a water clock in its interior, a weather vane on its roof and a series of sundials on its sides, the Tower of the Winds (or Horologium) is among the most singular designs of classical Greek architecture. Though the atypical nature of a number of its formal features, including octagonal plan with apsidal projection, extreme vertical orientation and height, and emphasis on mural rather than columnar elements, is in part amplified by the loss of probable prototypes, the structure is strikingly original, and represents a successful adaptation of traditional classical vocabulary to the increasingly diverse building types of antiquity.

Indicative of the capacity for inventive arrangement are the two porches sheltering the entry doors. There the conventional temple portico, whose pediment is typically continuous with the gable roof of the building behind it, has been diminished in size and scale to that of an appendage to the main octagonal volume. In addition to providing a pleasing contrast between the deeply cast shadows of the columned porches and the faceted planar walls beyond, the relatively small coverings endow the structure with a human scale not inappropriate for the openly public contents of its interior. Moreover, the reduced span of the lintel supporting the pediment permits an economical distyle arrangement of columns, requiring only two supports across its width.

The individual columns are especially worthy of study, for they were the first instances of a variant type that was to enjoy remarkable longevity in later architecture. While frequently designated as Corinthian by virtue of the ring of acanthus leaves

encircling a campaniform, or bell-shaped capital, they differ from their canonical counterpart in significant ways. In the capital the abacus is square and lacks a fleuron; the upper volutes, helices and acanthus have been eliminated and substituted with narrow lotus petals; and the shaft contains only 20 flutes, has no base and is fewer than seven diameters in height to the astragal. The more tectonic character of the Doric order suggested by these last three characteristics is echoed in the simplified capital, where the decorative elements of the regular Corinthian have been replaced with forms that emphasize rather than conceal the supporting element of the bell, or calathos, whose concave profile clearly expresses the bearing of superincumbent weight. The origins of the campaniform capital and its water lily ornament, the lotus, are generally traced to the architecture of Egypt, and further underscore the degree of inventive eclecticism characteristic of the Horologium. At the same time, the engaged piers responding to the columns at the octagon have capitals of a different profile, thus perpetuating the traditional Greek distinction between orthogonal wall and circular point support.

Both the distyle porch and its order are visually rich compositions yet relatively simple to assemble, and therefore well suited to contexts requiring fiscal economy, relative severity of appearance, or domestic scale, but desirous of architectural status. Not surprisingly, then, each was enthusiastically adopted into the permanent classical repertory, especially for the adornment of 19th-century American and English residential structures (even continuing to be produced today by manufacturers of architectural ornaments). Also of some importance for subsequent developments is the conception of the tall building as a reiteration of the column, to be composed of a base, middle section or shaft, and crowning member or capital; accordingly, figurative ornament, like the personifications of the winds, appears primarily in the upper strata, while the features nearer the rude earth assume the more tectonic geometric forms of sustaining elements.

Inside, the vertically oriented volume is balanced by a series of horizontal stringcourses corresponding to significant divisions on the exterior. Most intriguingly, the interior arrangement strongly resembles First Style mural decoration, an instance of architecture imitating painting imitating architecture; this transmutation of media and material is consistent with the Greek attitude toward form, and is evident outside, where the 24 trapezoidal roof slabs have been carved to look like individually laid tiles. The derivation of the interior from decorative sources also explains the atectonic design of the middle bracketed cornice, whose modillions were thenceforth to be associated with the Corinthian order. The modern misconception of Greek architecture as a purely rational affair is thus disproved.

Equally notable is the conical dome made by shaping the underside of the slabs into a circular plan, the transition to the octagonal perimeter effected by eight diminutive Doric columns standing in turn on a round stringcourse. The key to understanding the significance of the dome may lie in the building's contents, consisting primarily of the public display of a large water-powered anaphoric clock, which not only told time but simulated the diurnal rotation of the celestial bodies. The Horologium itself may be interpreted as representing the cosmos architecturally, for the image of the dome as a heavenly canopy supported by columns occurs not infrequently in ancient art; Varro discusses one such example in the same section mentioning the Horologium (IV.5.9,17). Similarly, the Doric columns could be disguised versions of atlantes, described by Vitruvius (VI.VII.6) as masculine supports based on Atlas, the mythical figure who carried the heavens on his shoulders.

Most compelling for this reading is the conspicuous geometry by which the Horologium was designed. In the ancient world, geometry (literally "earth measurement") was inextricably linked not only to philosophical speculation (Plato, *Timaeus*) and to the calendar and time (Vitr. I.I.16, IX.I-VIII), but to practical and theoretical issues of ideal urban planning (Vitr. I.VI; Plato, *Critias, Laws*). Thus the domains of science and art, geometry and nature, heaven and earth, and time and space are united in a single work of architecture where all the world might be exhibited to the wondering spectator.

—DONALD M. RATTNER

BAALBEK
Bekaa Valley, Lebanon

16 B.C.: Roman colony founded. **60 A.D.:** Front columns of Temple of Jupiter completed. **Second century A.D.:** Porticoes built to enclose north, south, west sides of courtyard; Temple of Bacchus constructed. **Third century A.D.:** Propylaea finished; Temple of Venus constructed.

Publications

COLLART, P., and COUPEL, J.: *L'autel monumental de Baalbek*. Beirut, 1951.
KRENCKER, VON LÜPKE and WINNEFELD: *Baalbek: Ergebnisse der Ausgrabungen*. Berlin and Leipzig, 1923.
WIEGAND, T.: *Baalbek*. 2 vols. Berlin and Leipzig, 1921-23.
WOOD, ROBERT: *The Ruins of Palmyra and Balbec*. London, 1827.

*

Baalbek is an ancient site located in the Bekaa Valley between the Lebanon and Anti-Lebanon mountain ranges. The area was dominated by the Persians from the sixth to the fourth centuries B.C., until the conquest of Alexander the Great. After that Baalbek became part of the Hellenistic Egyptian Empire of the Ptolemies; Baal was identified with their sun god, Helios, and the name of the city was changed to Heliopolis. About the same time, the sacred triad Baal-Aliyan-Anat was associated with the Greek gods Zeus-Hermes-Aphrodite and later the Roman gods Jupiter-Mercury-Venus. Baalbek became part of the Hellenistic empire of the Seleucids under Antiochus in about 200 B.C. It came under Roman control with the conquest of Pompey in 64 B.C. and was founded as the Roman Colonia Julia Augusta Felix Heliopolitana in 16 B.C.

Baalbek appears to have been the center for the development of a distinctive provincial style in the Roman East. There were three sanctuaries at Baalbek of great architectural note during the Roman period: the sanctuaries of Jupiter Heliopolitanus, Bacchus and Venus.

One sanctuary was located on an artificial mound (tell) which had become a raised Altar Court during the late second millennium B.C. At some point, a large staircase with flanking towers was constructed to provide access to the high Altar Court above. During the Hellenistic period, a classical temple was planned

Sanctuary of Jupiter Heliopolitarus: Baalbek, Bekaa Valley, Lebanon

for the religious ceremonies in this sanctuary. To build this temple, the construction of a high podium was begun on the west side of the sanctuary so that a large temple could be placed on axis with the altar. Most of the podium was completed by the time the Romans took over Phoenicia. Shortly after the Roman foundation of a colony at Baalbek, plans were developed to expand this sanctuary as the Sanctuary of Jupiter Heliopolitanus. The result was one of the most extraordinary examples of the design of ensembles in classical architecture.

Characteristic of much Roman design, the plan followed a very strict axis. All of its parts were symmetrical and concluded in a grand climactic fashion. Within this axiality and symmetry, the architects attempted to create a deeply moving religious experience through the design of a sequence of varying spaces and levels. The sanctuary was composed of an imposing propylaea, a hexagonal peristyle court, a large rectangular Altar Court, and a colossal temple, the dominant feature in this group design.

The Temple of Jupiter (48 by 88 meters), which was constructed entirely of hard local limestone, was peripteral in plan, reflecting Hellenistic traditions established in Syria. Its grand scale was surpassed only by a handful of its Greek predecessors. It was placed on a raised podium and reached only from the front by a wide flight of steps, a characteristic of Roman temple design. The temple was planned shortly after the establishment of the Roman colony; the columns on its front were completed by 60 A.D. The original Corinthian capitals are of a type found in Rome during the reign of Augustus. The entablature above the colonnade follows Roman proportions used in the first century A.D. The style of carving developed in western Asia Minor appears in this limestone entablature, presumably as a result of the ever-increasing use of marble imported to this region. The ornament of the moldings is an interesting admixture of Hellenistic and Near Eastern types. The interior design of the now-destroyed cella is uncertain and has been restored based only on traces and comparisons with other temples in the region. It is thought to have been a raised sanctuary reached by a flight of steps at the rear of the cella. There, presumably, stood the famous cult statue of Jupiter (Baal), which was carried about on the shoulders of priests during the function of the oracle.

The Altar Court was widened on its north and south sides by the construction of two large parallel barrel-vaulted galleries.

This gave the space of the courtyard a scale more commensurable with the size of the great temple which overlooked it. In the second century A.D. porticoes enclosed the north, south and west sides of the courtyard. The colonnades were constructed of red granite imported from Aswan and gray granite from the Bosphorus, providing beautiful color and textural accents and contrasts with the local honey-gray limestone. The porticoes were designed with alternating, rectangular and curved exedrae. The rectangular ones were timber-roofed, and the hemicycles received semidomes in stone.

Shortly after the completion of the Temple of Jupiter, the ancient altar which had been the focus of the cult was replaced by an altar-tower (17 meters high). It was designed with two interior staircases with richly carved, coffered ceilings. While it was constructed to fulfill the needs of the local cult, the altar-tower blocked the view of the temple—in decidedly un-Roman fashion—as one entered the courtyard. The altar-tower was a traditional Syrian type.

A hexagonal peristyle forecourt—a design unique to Roman architecture—was constructed at the level of the Altar Court. It differed both in shape and scale from the larger Altar Court, providing visitors with variety and a heightened sense of ceremony as they proceeded through this space to the Altar Court.

The Propylaea was finished during the reigns of Caracalla (211-217 A.D.) and Philip the Arab (244-249 A.D.). It was designed with two imposing towers that flanked a monumental staircase, which led to the great colonnaded facade of the entranceway. The towers probably reflected the much older pre-Roman entrance, which had consisted of a more modest stairway flanked by two towers. The use of flanking towers at entrances was common in the architecture of the ancient Near East. The space between the central columns of the Propylaea was spanned by a monumental arch. The use of an arch not only permitted a wider spacing to provide an unobstructed view of the wide central doorway, but also marked the axis of the sanctuary as it dramatically stressed the entrance. An open courtyard 70 meters in length was constructed in front of the grand staircase of the Propylaea, providing ample space for large gatherings. The scale and importance of the Propylaea are emphasized by this great open space before it.

Within the sanctuary then, there is a distinct sense of sequence

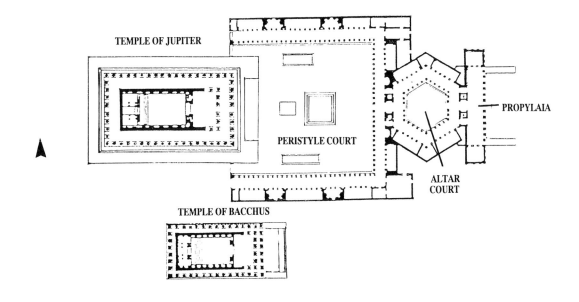

TEMPLE OF JUPITER

PERISTYLE COURT

PROPYLAIA

ALTAR COURT

TEMPLE OF BACCHUS

in spaces and levels. In moving from the open courtyard at ground level one climbs to and through the richly adorned Propylaea, into the more concentrated, centered hexagonal space, and out to the expanse of the Altar Court with the Temple of Jupiter as the climax. This sequence of levels and spaces is a clear example of the Roman ability to instill a sense of wonder and awe.

The Temple of Bacchus (35 by 65 meters) stood within a colonnaded courtyard located immediately to the south of the Jupiter sanctuary. It was constructed about the middle of the second century A.D. of the local honey-gray limestone. It was peripteral in plan, reflecting Hellenistic influence; however, the peristyle rested on a high podium with a flight of steps permitting only a frontal approach, which is characteristic of Roman temples. A study has demonstrated that the design of this temple carefully followed the modular proportions set forth in the work of the Roman architect Vitruvius.

The cella with its raised sanctuary (*adyton*) shows clear Syrian influence. The cella is one of the best-preserved examples of Roman temple interiors extant. A masterpiece of Roman wall design, it demonstrates a rich plastic sense, at once lavish and restrained. It is remarkable for its skilled, controlled alternation of compressed and expanding planes and the interplay of curvilinear and rectilinear elements. On the interior, the side walls were constructed with pilasters (with Corinthian capitals) on a podium. To these pilasters, fluted Corinthian half columns were attached. Two niches for statuary were placed between the pilasters—wide-arched niches below and somewhat narrower, pedimental niches above. Within the cella there is a monumental flight of steps leading up to the *adyton*. At the first landing were placed two large freestanding piers with attached Corinthian columns of the same height as those of the side walls. These piers continued the entablature of the side walls out into the cella space and back to the west wall of the cella. Thus, there is a continuously running entablature visible all around the cella. In doing this, the architect attempted to link the *adyton* with the cella as a whole.

To the southeast, the Temple of Venus (third century A.D.) stood in a courtyard a short distance from the sanctuaries of Bacchus and Jupiter. Like the Temple of Bacchus, it had a peristyle which rested on a podium with a flight of steps on the front. But the resemblance ends there. Unlike the other two temples, it is circular and domed, and in terms of scale strikes one as a little jewel box compared with its neighbors.

The Temple of Venus was constructed on a rectangular platform. In plan, the temple was designed with a circular cella with a rectangular porch on the front. The cylindrical space was domed with stone masonry, unlike the vaults and domes in the Roman West, which were constructed of brick and concrete. Presumably, because of the lateral thrust of the dome, the columns of the peristyle around the cella carried five horizontal arches which were designed so that their crowns were tangential to the dome. Thus, the horizontal arches—along with the columns—would act as buttresses. So, the columns of the peristyle placed around the cella wall did not carry a continuous curving entablature. The resulting effect was remarkable in that the entablature looped inward toward the cella wall between the columns. The podium was made to curve inward between the columns as well, repeating the lines of the entablature above. Therefore, the traditional covered porch around the cella wall was completely eliminated. In addition, the cella wall was designed with curving arched niches on its exterior. This building, then, evinces one of the boldest uses of curve and countercurve in Roman Baroque design. The independent thinking on the part of the architect also can be seen in certain details, such as the use of five-sided Corinthian capitals, which here are unique

to Roman architecture. This temple is said to have been the inspiration for the design of the lantern above the dome of Sant'Ivo della Sapienza in Rome by Francesco Borromini in about 1650.

—CHARLES W. WHITE

DELPHI
Delphi, Greece

Ca. 490 B.C.: Treasury of the Athenians. **Ca. 390 B.C.:** Tholos. **Fourth century B.C.:** Temple of Apollo and Theater.

Publications

AGARD, W.: "The Date of the Metopes of the Athenian Treasury." *American Journal of Archaeology* 27 (1923).

AMANDRY, P.: "Le portique des Athéniens à Delphes." *Bulletin de correspondance héllénique* 70 (1946).

BOURGUET, E.: *Les ruines de Delphes*. Paris, 1914.

BOURGUET, E.: *Delphes*. Paris, 1925.

BOUSQUET, J.: "Le Trésor de Syracuse à Delphes." *Bulletin de correspondance héllénique* 64-65 (1940-41).

COSTE-MESSELIÈRE, P. DE LA: *Au musée de Delphes*. Paris, 1936.

COSTE-MESSELIÈRE, P. DE LA: "Chapiteaux doriques de Delphes." *Bulletin de correspondance héllénique* 66-67 (1942-43).

COSTE-MESSELIÈRE, P. DE LA: *Delphes*. Paris, 1943.

COURBY, F.: "Sur la frise du trésor de 'Cnide' à Delphes." *Revue archéologique* 17 (1911).

COURBY, F.: "La tholos du trésor de Sicyone à Delphes." *Bulletin de correspondance héllénique* 35 (1911).

DAUX, G.: *Pausanias à Delphes*. Paris, 1936.

DAUX, G., and COSTE-MESSELIÈRE, P. DE LA: "La frise du trésor de Siphnos." *Bulletin de correspondance héllénique* 51 (1927).

DINSMOOR, WILLIAM BELL: *The Architecture of Ancient Greece*. New York, 1975.

DINSMOOR, WILLIAM BELL: "The Aeolic Capitals of Delphi." *American Journal of Archaeology* 27 (1923).

DINSMOOR, WILLIAM BELL: "Studies of the Delphian Treasuries." *Bulletin de correspondance héllénique* 36-37 (1912-13).

GRAINDOR, P.: *Delphes et son oracle*. Cairo, 1930.

KENNEDY, C.: *The Treasury of the Siphnians at Delphi*. Northampton, Massachusetts, 1935.

PICARD, C., and COSTE-MESSELIÈRE, P. DE LA: *La sculpture grecque à Delphes*. Paris, 1929.

POMTOW, H.: *Beiträge zur Topographie von Delphi*. Berlin, 1889.

POULSEN, F.: *Delphi*. London, 1920.

*

The rugged character of Delphi's natural terrain on the slopes of Mount Parnassus added wonder and mystery to its presence for the pilgrims who sought its oracle during the thousand years or more in which the Sanctuary of Apollo was in operation. The precipitous cliffs towering above its monuments and the breathtaking view over the Pleistos plain to the sea still inspire a sense of magic, and undoubtedly contributed to Delphi's

Treasury of the Athenians: Delphi, Greece, ca. 490 B.C.

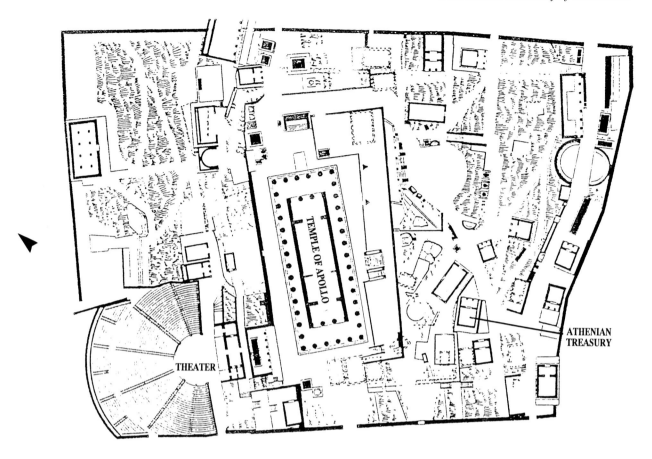

reputation as the most famous oracular shrine in Greece. The irregular surface of the site, as well as the periodic stages of construction, prevented an organized planning of the various structures so that few buildings or monuments were placed with any religious or architectural scheme. Yet the more natural arrangement, clustered along the winding Sacred Way, provides a harmonious setting with the overwhelming backdrop of the cliffs and enhances the religious essence of the site. Located on the crossing of ancient routes from eastern Greece to the Gulf of Corinth and from southwestern Greece to the north, Delphi's geographical position is in accord with the traditional claim that it occupied the center of the earth. This belief was supported by the dedication of numerous votives in the form of an omphalos or navel, while a large stone omphalos stood in Apollo's temple on the site, and the god was depicted seated on it in ancient art.

Although Neolithic and Bronze Age finds have been recovered from the area, the growth of Apollo's cult at Delphi stems from the Greek Dark Ages after the collapse of the Mycenaean civilization. The site was referred to as Pytho by Homer as well as in the somewhat later *Homeric Hymn to Pythian Apollo,* where the traditional details recounting the foundation of the shrine first appeared. The Sanctuary of Apollo consisted of a specific area of sacred ground known as a *temenos,* in which were the primary temple, an altar, several treasuries containing dedications from various city-states, a theater, and votive monuments and statues. Clustered nearby were a stadium and other athletic facilities, lesser shrines for other divinities and structures to accomodate visiting pilgrims. As a major religious center for pan-Hellenic worship, Delphi was the scene for sacred festivities, processionals, dances, poetic recitations, dramatic performances with mythical reenactments and athletic contests. Above all, it was famous for its oracular presentations in which

Apollo addressed his audience through the medium of a priestess known as the Pythia.

The Delphic oracle epitomized the morality of Greek culture personified by Apollo, who represented prudence and moderation. The renowned maxims "Know Thyself" and "Nothing in Excess" affixed to Apollo's temple underscored the essence of his cult at Delphi. Upholding a position of compromise and tolerance did much to foster tremendous support for Delphi from the far reaches of the Greek world. Whereas Olympia represented cultural homogeneity and national unity, Delphi became an international shrine, having an appeal to powers on the edges and Greek civilization. During its periods of greatest prestige, Delphi enjoyed the patronage of the Kings of Egypt, Lydia, Phrygia, Etruria and Pergamon. During the great period of Greek colonizations, from the eighth to sixth centuries B.C., the prestige of the Delphic oracle rose dramatically as it became the supreme consultant for those seeking to found new cities abroad. City-states on the Greek mainland and those ringing the Aegean basin sought the advice of Apollo at Delphi prior to establishing their colonies as far away as the Black Sea coast, North Africa and the far reaches of the western Mediterranean. Much of their gratitude took the form of buildings and shrines, statues and other votives erected in the Delphic sanctuary. Given the large quantities of Corinthian pottery of that period found at Delphi, it seems clear that the Corinthians were bent on influencing Delphic opinion in matters of overseas expansion from the earliest times. It is not surprising, therefore, that Corinth dedicated the earliest treasury on the site.

The establishment of treasuries at Delphi by various city-states served a variety of purposes. The shrine-like buildings were meant to store the ex-votes offered by the city-state responsible for each structure. In isolating the growing quantity of dedications on the site, the responsible parties established a

Tholos: Delphi, Greece, ca. 390 B.C.

viable basis for their own prestige. This was accomplished not only under the appreciative gaze of the Delphic priesthood but in the eyes of the rival city-states as well. In at least some instances the dedicators of a treasury decorated the structure itself with boastful propaganda or elaborate and expensive ornamentation, such as the Siphnian Treasury, which was the earliest completely Ionic building on the Greek mainland. Datable to the years around 530 B.C. on historical grounds, this elaborately decorated edifice was constructed of Parian marble under the supervision of the Cycladic islanders of Siphnos, a city-state made rich from its gold and silver mines. A continuous sculptured frieze, nearly 30 meters in length and depicting four different myths, encircled the building. Two caryatids (reflective

of those on the earlier Cnidian Treasury) attired in Ionic chitons stood on bases between the antae. Highly unusual for the Ionic order and enhancing the building's opulence even further were pedimental sculptures depicting Hercules and Apollo in the Struggle for the Delphic Tripod. Other Ionic and/or Aeolic treasuries at Delphi, such as the Cnidian, Massalian and Clazomenian, were also made of marble but did not display the elaborate combinations of ornamentation found on the Siphnian Treasury.

Obtaining a prime location for one's treasury was also a means of claiming superiority among peers in the sanctuary. The Athenian dedication occupies a conspicuous and certainly prestigious position at the point where the Sacred Way makes its first turn. This treasury, perhaps constructed immediately after the Athenian victory at Marathon in 490 B.C., if not some 15 years before with the foundation of democracy in Athens, touted Athenian pride and self-assured preeminence among the Greek people in general, while claiming distinctive recognition within the international arena of the Delphic sanctuary. Built entirely of island marble, this Doric structure displayed sculptured metopes depicting the heroic exploits of Hercules, champion of the Greeks, and of Theseus, symbol of Athenian democracy, over various mythical adversaries. The choice location at this point along the Sacred Way was perhaps granted to Athens out of deference to Cleisthenes (or his followers) who, at the head of the exiled Alcmæonid family of Athens during the Peisistratid tyranny, embellished the facade of the recently rebuilt limestone Temple of Apollo with marble at his own expense. Nearly a century after the Athenians had proudly dedicated their treasury, the Syracusans gained political clout at the expense of Athens and positioned their treasury directly across the Sacred Way after their devastating defeat of the Athenian expedition during the Peloponnesian War.

Other structures of interest at Delphi include the early-fourth-century B.C. *tholos,* or circular building, in the lower Sanctuary of Athena Pronaia. Its elegant design included 20 slender Doric columns of Pentelic marble on the exterior and Corinthian half columns lining the wall of the interior. Its position in a line of temples and treasuries does not provide clarity as to its function and dedication which remain unknown. The magnificent polygonal retaining wall which supports the terrace on which the Temple of Apollo and its altar rest stretches more than 80 meters across the site. Each limestone block with curving joints is unique in shape, creating an irregular interlocking pattern which is both aesthetically pleasing to the eye and pragmatically suited to resist seismic shocks.

In addition to the oracular cult of Apollo, other deities enjoyed patronage at various times at Delphi. Prior to the advent of the Apollo cult, the earth goddess Gæa was worshiped there in conjunction with her mate Poseidon, he not as a sea god but as one of earthquakes. The Muses were worshiped there during historical times as well as Athena. The Sanctuary of Athena Pronaia, by virtue of its name, lies along the eastern approach road *before* the naos or shrine of Apollo. However, since terracotta female figurines of the Bronze Age were recovered from that site, it seems plausible to consider the cult of Athena there as an historical continuance of the prehistoric earth goddess in the form of a huge snake worshiped in that area. The cult of this earth goddess would have been a survivor of Minoan-Mycenaean religion at the time that it was usurped by the divination cult of Apollo. That a ritual vessel in the form of a lion-headed stone rhyton was retrieved from layers beneath the Temple of Apollo indicates that religious ceremonies were probably performed in the area from very early times. The style of the rhyton recalls that of Minoan vessels and it, along with the terra-cotta female figurines, testifies to the antiquity of religious practice on the site. The Minoan presence also recalls the tradition in the *Homeric Hymn* that Apollo brought Cretan sailors to Delphi and made them his priests. At other sanctuaries of Apollo a man served as the high priest. That a woman filled the role of prophetic medium at Delphi was a concession on the part of the priesthood in acknowledging the antecedent female divinity on the site. Her title, Pythia, also reflects this acknowledgment.

Dionysus as a god of emotional expression and orgiastic celebration was also worshiped at Delphi. During the winter months Apollo was believed to have vacated the site for the northern regions, and Dionysus took up residence at Delphi. During that period dramatic performances were enacted in the Delphic theater, and Dionysiac rituals transpired on the snow-covered slopes of Parnassus. The theater dates from the fourth century B.C., with Hellenistic and Roman remodeling. It is one of the best-preserved theaters in Greece, with seats of white marble from Parnassus; scenes of Hercules' exploits in relief sculpture once decorated the stage facade. That there is no evidence of a theater at Olympia testifies to the lack of artistic and intellectual contests in the Olympic Games, while such events were very much a part of the religious activities in the Sanctuary of Apollo at Delphi. The renowned Pythian Games were held in honor of the divine twins, Apollo and Artemis, and their mother, Leto. They were instituted to commemorate Apollo's triumph over the serpent Python, and originally consisted of musical recitals in honor of the god. Second only to the Olympic Games in importance, the Pythian Games provided an international arena for Greeks to compete, gaining glory not only for the individuals but for their own city-states as well.

Delphi flourished during the Archaic and Classical periods and continued to exercise its power, somewhat lessened, even under the Macedonian Kings who held sway over the Amphityonic League during the years after Philip and Alexander the Great. A second period of exalted reputation was experienced during the third and second centuries B.C. under the Aetolian Confederacy, only to be curtailed under Roman rule after 168 B.C., when the oracle was virtually ignored. In its twilight years the oracle's sphere of influence was sadly diminished to matters of money, marriages and other private concerns. While some Roman leaders such as Augustus and Hadrian embellished the ancient sanctuary, primarily through restoration, others such as Sulla and Nero pillaged its treasures. By the fourth century A.D., when Julian the Apostate (360-363 A.D.) attempted to revive paganism, his envoy to Delphi was told that the prophetic voice lived no more and that the sanctuary was in serious decay. Stripped of its treasures and deserted by its followers, the Sanctuary of Apollo was finally closed in 394 A.D. under the edict of Theodosius the Great forbidding pagan worship.

—KARL KILINSKI II

EPHESOS
Asia Minor

Sixth century B.C.: Artemision of Ephesos constructed; **Architects:** Theodoros, Chersiphron the Cretan, Metagenes. **First century A.D.:** Lower two stories of Roman theater constructed. **118-138 A.D.:** Temple of Hadrian constructed; **Architect:** P. Quintillus. **Third century:** Upper story of Roman stage building constructed.

Publications

DINSMOOR, WILLIAM BELL: *The Architecture of Ancient Greece.* New York, 1975.
Forschungen in Ephesos veröffentlicht vom Österreichischen Archäologischen Institut in Wien. 7 vols. 1906-71.
KEIL, J.: *Führer durch Ephesos.* 5th ed. Vienna, 1964.
MILTNER, F.: *Ephesos: Stadt der Artemis und des Johannes.* Vienna, 1958.

Celsus Library: Ephesos, Asia Minor

The foundation myth of Ephesos credits Androkles, who was one of the sons of King Codrus of Athens, as the first colonist of the city. Archaeologists believe this myth may have an element of truth, considering the repeated Athenian claim to a hereditary connection with Ionia. The colony was most probably established in the 10th century B.C., when other settlements were also established in this area. The original town of Ephesos is thought to have been located to the west of the present ruins, near a port that was called Koressos. During the first half of the seventh century, the Cimmerians took the city, only to be displaced by the Lydians 100 years later under the leadership of the famous King Croesus. Following the death of Alexander the Great, Ephesos and the remainder of Ionia were claimed by Lysimachus, one of Alexander's generals, and the entire city was moved further north. The Selucids succeeded Lysimachus and were followed by the Pergamene kings, who ruled there from 190 B.C. until Pergamon itself was bequeathed to Rome and the city fell within the province of Asia. During the 200 years of the Pax Romana, the city entered its most glorious period, becoming one of the most prosperous cities of the Near East.

Ephesos was dependent on its deep harbor for this prosperity, but this harbor, which penetrated to the edge of the town's agora, has long since silted up, leaving only a barren plain in its place. Lying in a protected cleft between Mt. Pion (Bülbuldag) to the north and Mt. Coressos (Panayirdag) to the south, Ephesos seems stately, self-controlled and secure as it looks out to what was once a frenetic harbor to the west. This same harbor was extremely popular when it was in operation because of its central position along the Aegean coast of Asia Minor. The convenient location also made pilgrimage to the Artemesion, which was

the largest temple in Ionia, very easy. Rather than facing its harbor with a screen-like, column-lined stoa placed at right angles to the water as Miletus did, Ephesos greeted those landing by ship with the sight of an enormous gymnasium. While the position of this particular building may initially seem to have been dictated by a wish to place it as close to the area of highest activity in the city as possible, it also seems to have been selected as a way to show off what was obviously considered to be the most impressive civic monument that Ephesos had to offer. Resting on a platform supported by large vaulted substructions of perpendicular corridors near the harbor, the "great gymnasium" featured huge granite columns and more than 500 feet of central corridor.

Gymnasia, baths and theaters were major status symbols and the most creative architectural achievements of urban Asia Minor. In serving the multiple functions of civic center, clubhouse and school, the gymnasium replaced the palace and the temple as the social focal point of the city. A long stoa running perpendicular to the Ephesian harbor separated this gymnasium from a broad street bordered by the irregular city wall to the south, leading all pedestrian traffic inexorably toward the famous theater that still forms the town's center of gravity.

The ruins of this theater as seen today date from the Roman period, as do most other remains still visible there. It is most famous as the background for the riot against Saint Paul, mentioned in Acts, that took place around 50 A.D., which was led by a craftsman who represented all those involved in making votive statues of the goddess Artemis for sale to the tourists. The riot was clearly caused by the fear that many in the city felt about the spread of Christianity and the economic consequences of it, but in spite of opposition from souvenir sellers

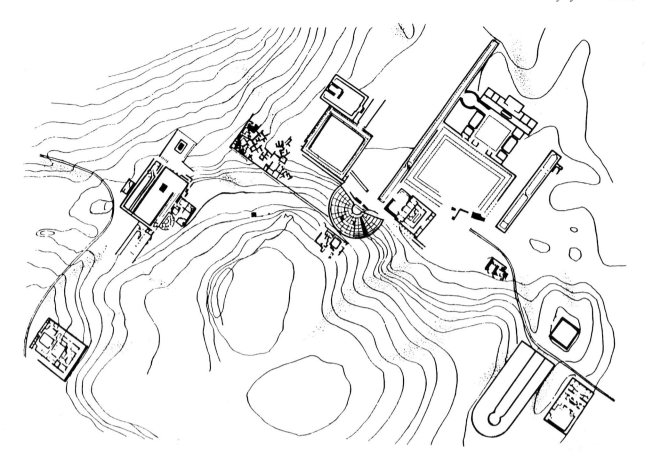

to whom the cult of Artemis was a big business, Paul was later to establish a strong Christian congregation at Ephesos, which went on to become one of the key churches in Asia Minor. One of his most moving letters is one written to that congregation soon after the incident at the theater, which has entered the Bible as the Book of Ephesians and stands as one of the most beautifully written statements of the basic tenets of Christian belief. In it, Paul clearly states that the new religion should not be confined by its Hebraic roots but should be, rather, a religion predestined for the entire world. He concludes with a memorable admonition to the entire congregation of the church of Ephesos that displays an acute consciousness of the impression that good behavior would have upon others judging this new faith, and he carefully outlines correct Christian actions that will serve as a model for others. Paul's travels throughout Anatolia, which make Acts almost read like a Turkish itinerary in places, made it possible for him to ensure almost singlehandedly that Christianity would rise above the numerous mystery cults, such as Mithraism, that had begun to flourish in the later Hellenistic and Roman period, when religions based on self-involvement and discovery began to proliferate.

Within 100 years after the death of Christ, thanks to efforts like Paul's, Christianity spread throughout Asia Minor. Developing as it did within the framework of the Roman legal, magisterial system, the fledgling church established a simple administrative structure and held services that were organized around singing, prayer and spoken commentary, usually performed in an intimate domestic setting. By 250 A.D., with more than 60 percent of Anatolia converted to Christianity, and with a more wealthy and powerful congregation, an intentionally pragmatic liturgy began to evolve, and dogma became more clearly defined. After Paul's death in Rome, the apostle John assumed the role of titular head of all the churches under the auspices

of the church of Ephesus, and upon his death he was buried in Ephesos in accordance with his wishes.

After the Edict of Milan, in which Emperor Constantine formally recognized the Christian church in 313 A.D., a basilica with a wooden roof was built over John's grave; this building was greatly enlarged two centuries later by Emperor Justinian, resulting in the church that can be seen today. Even though its layout deviates considerably from that of other, more straightforward, basilicas in this region—such as that of St. Mary in Ephesos—which were to have such a profound effect on church building throughout the Christian world, it accurately reflects the growing formality of the church liturgy, which had been affected by the elevation of Christianity to a state religion. St. John's was a pilgrimage church, with a main focus of attention on the grave of Saint John, located at the center of the crossing. The apse section of the building was reserved for the use of the clergy only, in order to isolate them from the frenetic comings and goings of the pilgrims, who were increasingly drawn by the reputation of the healing powers of the shrine. Otherwise, the main body of the church, with its three naves, side aisles, forecourt and baptistery, adapted itself reasonably well to a liturgy that had by then evolved into two distinct parts. The first part included both members and prospective members, who shared in prayer, hymns and readings from scripture, while the second part of the service, for members only, consisted of the Mass, from which the catechumens were excused, withdrawing into the forecourt and narthex. A bishop and other members of the clergy presided over both segments of the service from a semicircular seating area. This was a holdover from the magisterial tribunal of the Roman basilica, or law court, and was taken as a model for the early church buildings because of its straightforward form and ability to hold a great number of people easily. In its final form the Church of St. John of Ephesos was quite imposing, with three large domes covering the main nave, and one dome each over the transepts. The use of domes in this particular situation lends support to the theory, held by some, that there is a direct connection between the dome form and the martyrium, or the burial place of a saint.

Roman ruins comprise most of the major Classical sites visible in Asia Minor today, and at Ephesos the well-preserved temple of Hadrian is one of the most impressive of these. It was built by a certain P. Quintillus between 118 and 138 A.D. and faces "Curetes Street," marking the full transfer of power from the gods and goddesses of the Greek world to the worship of the world of mortals, which the Hellenistic age had helped to make possible. There had been cases before the Romans when exceptional mortals had been granted full status of a divinity, as with Heracles and Asclepius, for example, but such instances were rare and not nearly on the scale of the Roman cult of emperors. There were individuals, such as Augustus and Tiberius, who were known to have been less than enthusiastic about this trend, but hesitancy in this matter was soon to become rare. It is only the delicate face of Tyche, the goddess of victory, that acts as a keystone on Hadrian's arched disregard for the classic Greek architrave and that offers a small reminder of the degree of human sensitivity that had been sacrificed to make possible the construction of his temple here.

The Celsus Library in Ephesos is directly across from Hadrian's temple. Originally the monumental tomb of Julius Celsus Polemaeamus, who had been governor of the Roman province of Asia at one time and was buried there in 110 A.D, it was converted to a library by his son Tiberius Aquila, to commemorate the achievements of his father in a more vibrant way. The front facade of the building, which is all that remains, is treated with the stately and dramatic flourish considered worthy of a man of such status, as well as being placed at a strategic location at the junction of two of the most important streets in Ephesos. The library, which is particularly visible at the terminus of "Curetes Street," which gently slopes toward it in the east, had to be accommodated into a long and narrow site between two flanking buildings that have long since disappeared. Its designers, taking all of these factors into consideration, cleverly chose to use the form of the *scaenae frons* normally reserved for the backdrop of a theater stage in Roman times. The symbolic associations of such an architectural decision were surely not lost on the typologically conditioned minds of the citizens of Ephesos, who must have felt that they were thereby invited to penetrate the normally forbidden zone of the theater stage, and enter through its doors into the backstage to meet the "actors"— the thousands of books housed in the library.

Like the *scaenae frons* of a theater, the elevation of the library has its obligatory three doors that lead from the entry portico into the interior. The central door, the Porta Regia, like the doors on either side of it, was set into a deep recess, just as was normally done in backstage design, with a two-tier screen of columns around it. In another reference to theatrical architecture, each columnar projection frames a niche filled with statuary, personifiying the wisdom (*sophis*), knowledge (*episterne*) and destiny (*ennoia*) that the departed was felt to possess. Above the projecting columns there is an alternately arched and gabled entablature that breaks forward to emphasize, frame and shade these niches, and then backward to announce the doorways, thus setting up an interlocking rhythm that takes the eye in and out and up and down the entire facade, creating a feeling of increased scale, movement and harmony. In addition, recent studies there have revealed that minor adjustments in measurements were made between the columns to increase the space between those nearest the edge of the building, in order to make it look wider than its actual 11 meters. The interior of the library

extended back for 17 meters and was, as at Pergamon, dominated by a statue of Athena in its center. Books were protected from humidity by a double wall, and were brought forward by librarians from shelves located within a three-story gallery attached to the interior wall.

—JAMES STEELE

EPIDAUROS
Peloponnese

Ca. 420-375 B.C.: Temple constructed; **Architect:** Theodorus. **Ca. 360-20 B.C.:** Thymele constructed; **Architect:** Polykleitos the Younger. **Ca. 350 B.C.:** Theater constructed; **Architect:** Polykleitos the Younger. **86 B.C.:** Sanctuary looted. **67 B.C.:** Sanctuary looted.

Publications

BURFORD, ALISON: *The Greek Temple Builders at Epidauros.* Toronto, 1969.
DINSMOOR, WILLIAM BELL: *The Architecture of Ancient Greece.* New York, 1975.
MÜLLER-WIENER, M.: *Das Theater von Epidauros.* Stuttgart, 1961.

*

Epidauros, a small Greek city on the Saronic gulf in the northern Peloponnese, is most noted for its inland valley sanctuary of the healing god Asklepius. Pan-Hellenic athletic games, which included poetry and music contests, were celebrated in Epidauros also. The sanctuary, which is entered through a ceremonial propylaeum, consisted of the great temple of Asklepius as well as smaller temples and colonnades. There were also hospitals, hotels, and houses for the physician-priests, as well as a palaestra, gymnasium, Greek and Roman baths, and a theater. Although there is architectural coherence to the sanctuary, there is no specific alignment for the buildings as is found in some sanctuaries. It is the sacred road—which led into the sacred precinct, up a slight grade to the temple, past other monuments, and to the theater—which seems to unify this sanctuary by connecting the buildings necessary for the sacrifices, ritual healing, feasting and dramatic performance.

Apollo, the father of Asklepius, was associated with Epidauros as Apollo Malos or Maleatas long before Asklepius himself, whose earliest connection with this sanctuary was during the Archaic period. It was at Epidauros that Asklepius— because of his association with Apollo Maleatas, whose cult may have dated from the Mycenean period and was revived in the seventh century B.C.—achieved prominence, and by the fourth century Epidauros was celebrated as his birthplace and the sanctuary was developed. The cult—originally Thessalian— seems to have been most active in Epidauros in the fourth and later centuries before it was transferred to Athens, Rome and other locations.

The sanctuary belonged to the city of Epidauros, and the priest and a board of financial officials were in charge. Frequently patients who had been healed presented offerings and votive inscriptions, the number of which attest to the popularity of the cult. The sanctuary was looted by Sulla in 86 B.C. and by pirates in 67 B.C. In 395 A.D. Visigoths overran the sanctuary,

Theater: Epidauros, Peloponnese, 350 B.C.

and in the sixth century A.D. Christ replaced the pagan healing god, as is evident from the construction of a Christian church not far from the propylaeum.

Except for the fourth-century theater, which has been restored and in which ancient Greek tragedy is still performed, little remains of the structures connected with the sanctuary. Architectural fragments as well as sculpture from the sanctuary buildings are on display in the museum at the site (which also contains architectural reconstructions) and in the National Museum in Athens.

The theater, the acoustics of which are excellent, is one of the most renowned of its type and the best preserved of all Greek theaters. By the fourth century B.C. the plan of the Greek theater had become firmly established; the structure at Epidauros, built by Polykleitos the Younger from local limestone about 350 B.C., is typical of this form. Two passageways provided access to the theater. The orchestra (performing area) of beaten earth is circular, approximately 80 feet in diameter, with an altar in the center. The cavea (seating area), which is slightly more than a semicircle in shape and 125 yards across, faces north; it has 55 rows of seats, 34 in the lower section and 21 above. The lower section is separated into 12 wedges by 13 staircases, while the upper section is divided by 23 staircases. The seats of honor, with arm rails and backs, were made of red limestone, and the remaining 14,000 seats were of white limestone. A semicircular depression, nearly seven feet wide and paved, was placed between the circle and front row of seats to collect rainwater. The auditorium was completely separate from the stage building.

The great temple of Asklepius, which is variously dated between 420 and 375 B.C., was one of the major buildings at

Epidauros. A Doric peripteral hexastyle about 80 feet in length, it has a pronaos but no opisthodomos; because of this design, there are only 11 columns along the sides. A paved road and a ramp led to the east end of the temple; to the south was the altar of Asklepius. Although nothing of the temple is preserved except for the foundations and some fragments housed in the museum, an incomplete inscription from the first quarter of the fourth century survives that details specific expenditures during the temple's construction. According to these records, the architect in charge was Theodotus and the temple was completed in four years, eight-and-a-half months; the relatively short period of construction may reflect the availability of funds. Specific sculptors (Hektoridas and Timotheos) are linked with the execution of the pediments (the Amazonomachy on the west and either the destruction of Troy or the battle of the Greeks and Centaurs on the east), the acroteria and other reliefs. Although not mentioned in the building inscription, the lost chryselephantine cult statue of the seated Asklepius—known to us from its representation on coins and from Pausanias' account—was most likely executed in about 375 B.C. by Thrasymedes of Paros.

There are remains of the other temples in the sanctuary: a fourth-century Doric hexastyle temple of Artemis, which had heads of hunting dogs or wild boars as water spouts, and two smaller temples, perhaps dedicated to Themis and Aphrodite, which had Ionic columns lining the cellas on three sides.

A large tholos, or circular building also known as the Thymele, was constructed in the mid-fourth century (ca. 360-320 B.C.) by Polykleitos the Younger. Tholoi, such as those erected within the precincts at Delphi, Olympia and Epidauros and in the marketplace at Athens, represent an important development of Greek fourth-century architecture: these circular structures with two concentric rings of columns—often of different orders—probably served various functions. Whereas the tholos in Athens served as a council chamber, the function of those within the sanctuaries remains unclear.

The tholos at Epidauros is more elaborate than its counterparts at the other sanctuaries; the elegant decoration as well as its prominent position in the sanctuary—close to the temple and to the place where patients slept awaiting divine visitation—attest to its importance. It has been suggested that in contrast to the temple, which honors Asklepius as a god, this structure may honor his death as a man.

The tholos contains the earliest example of metopes filled with rosettes in relief. Lion's head gargoyles were placed at regular intervals at the roof's edge, and the ceiling had marble coffered plaques with floral designs carved in the center. The external peristyle of 26 Doric columns rested on a base slightly more than 66 feet in diameter, and the cella's inner circle of 14 freestanding columns—with notably beautiful capitals— were Corinthian. One surviving Corinthian capital, unfinished and intentionally buried, most likely served as a preliminary model. Two windows on either side of the entrance provided light for the elaborate interior, which had a floor of black and white rhomboidal slabs. The foundation is comprised of six concentric walls (with an outermost diameter of 72 feet). Beneath the floor is an underground labyrinth formed by the three inner foundation walls and connecting doorways. It may have been a sacred well or a maze related to the snake cult of Asklepius. It shows some similarity to the snakepits in the Asklepium and the Erechtheion at Athens. The possible identification of Asklepius with the chthonic deities may explain his association with snakes.

North of the tholos are two Ionic stoas which formed the Abaton or Endkoimeterion in which patients slept while they were expecting divine visitation and dream cures. Doubled in length during the Roman era, the stoa is 232 feet long. Tablets with inscriptions pertaining to miraculous cures have been found there.

There are also the remains of a *katagogion* (a hotel for patients waiting for cures) with four peristyle courts, each surrounded by rooms. The relatively large size of this two-story structure further attests to the popularity of the cult.

Another courtyard building, approximately 247 feet by 228 feet, is variously identified as a gymnasium or banqueting hall. Sixteen Doric columns were on each side of the courtyard, which may have been used for dramatic performances and which was surrounded by a variety of rooms. The projecting porch had six Doric columns.

The remains of such other structures as the stadium, the Roman odeion, the great propylaeum of the gymnasium, and the palaestra are not extensive.

Although the extent of destruction of the buildings associated with the sanctuary of Asklepius is regrettable, evidence suggests the existence of a fourth-century sanctuary that was both opulent and popular.

—ANN THOMAS WILKINS

HERCULANEUM
Italy

120 B.C.: Samnite House. **1st Century A.D.:** House of the Large Portal, House of the Beautiful Courtyard, House of the Deer, Palaestra, and Suburban Baths. **79 A.D.:** Town destroyed by eruption of Mount Vesuvius. **1709:** Town discovered and excavations begun.

Publications

ACCADEMIA ERCOLANESE DI ACHEOLOGIA: *Antichita di Ercolano*. Naples, 1755-1792.

BALZANO, F.: *L'Antica Erclano, ovvero la Torre del Greco tolta all'Obblio*. Naples, 1688.

BRION, M.: *Pompeii and Herculaneum*. Trans. J. Rosenberg. New York, 1960.

COCHIN, CHARLES-NICOLAS, and BELLICARD, JÉRÔME-CHARLES: *Observations sur les antiquités de la ville de d'Herculanum, avec quelques réflexions sur la peinture et la sculpture des ancients*. Paris, 1754.

KRAUS, T. and VON MATT, L.: *Pompeii and Herculaneum*. Trans. E. Wolf. New York, 1973.

MAIURI, A.: *Ercolano: i nuovi scavi (1927-1958)*. Rome, 1958.

MAIURI, A.: *Herculaneum*. Naples, 1964.

An ancient town on the eastern shore of the bay of Naples, Herculaneum was about 10 miles from the more well known inland city of Pompeii, and was destroyed at the same time by the eruption of Vesuvius in 79 A.D. Unlike Pompeii, however, which was asphyxiated by a cloud of volcanic gas and ash, Herculaneum was overwhelmed by a landslide of gravel and mud, mixed with ash and pumice, to a depth of as much as 65 feet. This effluvium not only caused the complete disappearance of the town, but its gradual consolidation into a massy material rendered the remains exceptionally difficult to access, even though digging on the site began as long ago as its rediscovery at the beginning of the 18th century. Yet although the particular facts of destruction of the site made it very hard to clear, the mud slide had preserved various kinds of things, especially objects made of wood, which had been completely destroyed at Pompeii. As later excavations were to reveal, the importance of Herculaneum as a recovered ancient site lay as much as anything else in the degree to which its remains differed from, rather than resembled, those of Pompeii.

In 1709 a well was sunk from the ground level above and struck a part of the theater; tunnels were driven in several directions, and numerous sculptures and decorative elements were removed, but little effort was made to record architectural information. Further attempts to recover more of the ancient town took place between 1738 and 1765, but those too consisted of little more than scavenging over a limited area. More purposeful excavation occurred from 1828 to 1835, when two city blocks were exposed. After a pause, digging was resumed in 1869, but ceased again in 1875 with little more revealed than before. It was not until 1927 that a major excavation campaign was undertaken, as the result of which the site as it is known today has come to light.

What can be seen now are four blocks of buildings, together with the streets separating them, along the edge of the town plan closest to the shore. In addition, the edges of five adjacent blocks have been explored, along with some remains standing outside and below the town walls on the side toward the bay. Almost all of the structures uncovered were dwellings of one sort or another, along with the remains of an arch across what may have been the main street, and evidence of several public buildings. One of the public buildings, on the north side of the modern excavations, may have been the town basilica, although only one edge of the structure has been uncovered so far. On the east side of the site a large court surrounded by porticoes

Herculaneum, Samnite House: Herculaneum, Italy, 120 B.C.

has been mostly revealed, possibly an exercise area or palaestra; its center was occupied by a large cross-shaped pool, an unusual feature in a public space. Finally, two bath buildings have been uncovered, one in the town and one outside. The remains of the theater, to the northwest of the modern excavations, are still buried beneath the surrounding modern town. It has been estimated, by rough analogy, that ancient Herculaneum covered about one third the area of Pompeii, or not more than 55 acres. The present excavated area covers less than 12 acres, or no more than a quarter of the estimated total area of the ancient town.

Herculaneum may have been originally a settlement of local Italic (Oscan) people; despite its name there is no evidence that it was a Greek colony. The first occupation of the site is thought to have occurred no earlier than the end of the sixth century B.C. In any case, Herculaneum was never a large place—its maximum population was perhaps about 5,000—and it was absorbed by the expanding Roman state at the same time as its neighboring cities, Pompeii and Naples. But unlike Pompeii, which was further inland, larger and more dependent on agriculture, Herculaneum was basically a maritime center and a resort town. Even the small excavated area visible today was marked by features much less familiar or even unknown at Pompeii, most of all the predominance of two-story buildings. Pompeii, with a few exceptions, was a single-story town. Herculaneum, by contrast, was apparently two stories almost everywhere, the result no doubt of higher land values near the shore. But while that was important as evidence of the economic forces that were driving the local building industry, it was even more important as evidence of the social forces that were causing the development of new types of residential buildings. For it seems that

the multistory buildings that were to be so prominent in the urban environments of the later Roman world were prefigured in part in towns like Herculaneum.

Among other architectural innovations, Herculaneum provided examples of the house with two-story atrium, such as the Samnite House; the house with upper stories overhanging the sidewalk below, such as the House with Half-timbering; and simple versions of what later became the dominant residential type in ancient cities, the apartment building. The House with the Wooden Partition had a splendid two-story atrium, its inner wall opening onto a columned loggia at the second story, and the wall to the street side marvelously mimicking the inner face in carved and painted plaster. The small rooms at the sides retain painted interiors of high quality, with tiny vignettes of landscapes and classical subjects set against grounds of uniformly forceful color.

The House of Neptune and Amphitrite has preserved unique decorative features. In plan it was little different from its neighbors, with the entrance giving onto a two-story atrium with tablinum beyond. In this house a visual axis extended from the entrance through a window in the back wall of the tablinum, and was terminated by a brilliant polychrome mosaic on the rear wall of a court beyond. Not until the viewer reached the court was it revealed that there was a second visual axis, at right angles to the first, and focused in turn on a niched wall, again decorated with polychrome mosaic. The courts stand as the single finest example of such decoration preserved from antiquity. Between the two mosaic panels lay an open air triclinium, showing that the space, though minute, walled and paved, was understood as a garden. In each of those cases, the pressure created by high land values caused significant transformations

Herculaneum, House of the Mosaic Atrium

in the traditional house form, while preserving its traditional dispositions.

More radical was an example such as the House of the Corinthian Atrium, in which the ground-floor plan was not that of a traditional house, with central atrium and flanking lesser chambers left and right, but something quite novel in domestic architecture up to that time. To begin with, the plan was not symmetrical about a central axis, but had lesser rooms on one side of the central space only. Second, the central space was not an atrium, that is, a room with a hole in the center of its roof, but a courtyard, that is, an unroofed space with a portico on its sides. Third, it was clear from the presence of a stair in the left rear corner that the building was more than one story high. In other words, the House of the Corinthian Atrium was not an atrium house, nor a house at all, but an early version of the apartment building, probably in this case with one apartment per floor, and not more than two stories in height altogether.

There were also numerous smaller houses, the homes of shopkeepers and artisans, which were abbreviated in their architectural effects, and were so compressed in plan as to require vertical extension. Along the western edge of the public court called the palaestra, mentioned above, was a row of shops and offices at ground level, which had small accommodations above them, as a kind of linear apartment building. This too was a novel form, and one not seen at Pompeii.

Equally dramatic were the changes in domestic architecture that appeared in the houses of the wealthiest families, those built above the town walls and facing onto the bay, such as the House of the Mosaic Atrium and the adjoining House of the Deer. In these buildings the spatial dispositions preserved the traditional order of the Italic house vestigially at the entrance,

led then to a peristyle of Hellenistic inspiration, and terminated finally in a row of belvederes, pavilions and dining and sitting rooms oriented outward to the view over the sea, in the manner of a country villa. The great urban palaces of later ages, in Rome and elsewhere, were prefigured in examples such as these.

Beyond the transformations in the space of domestic architecture, fascinating enough, above all Herculaneum's buildings preserve *in situ* many of their original decorative finishes, not more splendid than the remains from Pompeii, but astonishing in their ability to convey the emotive qualities of an intensely coloristic architecture. The houses mentioned above all shared these features, and there is evidence to suggest that the same characteristics were found in the public buildings. The public baths within the town, similar in disposition to the Forum Baths at Pompeii, preserve fine examples of plaster work on the ceilings of the main chambers. Most outstanding for surface decoration among the public buildings were the Suburban Baths, immediately outside the town walls on the side toward the shore. In this building the viewer was provided with unexpected visual and spatial surprises. The entrance was through a corridor, dark and narrow, which led without preamble to a small vestibule, scarcely 15 feet square, whose center was articulated by four columns carrying arches; upon those were four more columns carrying arches, the whole lit from a skylight above its center with an effect almost mysterious. Dramatic effects of lighting such as these were to play a major part in later Roman architecture. The principal interior spaces, almost fully preserved in terms of surface finishes and illumination, are overwhelming to the modern eye in their sensory qualities. They were marked by a density of color—red, green, black—combined with stucco reliefs, white against potent grounds, unmatched for effect in any other ancient examples.

In conclusion, as an ancient site, Herculaneum is spectacular for its preservation in a minute space of so much valuable information on architecture and decoration. It owes its importance not least to the circumstances of its burial, noted above. The relative ease with which Pompeii was uncovered led to the destruction of a vast amount of information about the site, as until the 20th century excavation on ancient sites was little more than treasure-hunting; anything that could not be removed from the site and sold was considered to be of no value. The architectural evidence suffered most of all from this abuse. At Herculaneum, by contrast, the extreme difficulty of getting at the site has rendered most of it intact up to the present day. As a result, within that small compass has been preserved more information on ancient art and architecture than at virtually any other ancient site known today, of whatever size. The splendid remains of architectural decoration, wall paintings, stuccos, plaster and mosaic work, furniture, hardware, bronze and marble statuary all testify to the unusual richness of the built environment and the quality of life in the ancient town, at least for the wealthy.

—BERNARD M. BOYLE

MILETOS
Maiandros River, Asia Minor

---

495 B.C.: Destroyed, reconstruction begins. **170 B.C.:** Council House restored.

Publications

BACON, EDMUND N.: "The Growth of Greek Cities." In *Design of Cities*, 67-81. Rev. ed. Harmondsworth, 1974.

BOYLE, BERNARD: "Hippodamos." In *Macmillan Encyclopedia of Architects*, edited by Adolf Placzek. New York, 1982.

CASTAGNOLI, FERDINANDO: *Orthogonal Town Planning in Antiquity*. Cambridge, Massachusetts, and London, 1971.

DINSMOOR, WILLIAM BELL: *The Architecture of Ancient Greece*. New York, 1975.

EGLI, ERNST: *Geschichte des Städtebaus*. Zürich and Stuttgart, 1962.

GUTKIND, E. A.: *Urban Development in Southern Europe: Italy and Greece*. New York, 1969.

HIORNS, F.: *Town-Building in History*. London, 1956.

KLEINER, G.: *Alt-Milet*. Wiesbaden, 1966.

KLEINER, G.: *Die Ruinen von Milet*. Berlin, 1968.

KOLB, F.: *Die Stadt in Altertum*. Munich, 1984.

KOSTOF, SPIRO.: *A History of Architecture: Settings and Rituals*. New York and Oxford, 1985.

KRIESIS, A.: *Greek Town Building*. Athens, 1965.

LAVEDAN, PIERRE: *Histoire de l'urbanisme: Antiquité*. 2nd ed. Paris, 1966.

LAWRENCE, A. W. N.: *Greek Architecture*. 4th integrated ed. Harmondsworth, England, 1983.

LINTOTT, A.: *Violence, Civil Strife and Revolution in the Classical City*. London and New York, 1982.

MARCHESE, R. T. (ed.): *Aspects of Graeco-Roman Urbanism*. Oxford, 1984.

MARTIENSSEN, R. D.: *The Idea of Space in Greek Architecture*. Johannesburg, 1968.

MARTIN, ROLAND: *Greek Architecture*. History of World Architecture series. New York, 1980.

MCDONALD, WILLIAM A.: *The Political Meeting Places of the Greeks*. Baltimore, 1943.

MUMFORD, LEWIS: *The City in History*. New York, 1961.

NORBERG-SCHULZ, CHRISTIAN: *Meaning in Western Architecture*. Rev. ed. New York, 1980.

OWENS, E. J.: *The City in the Greek and Roman World*. London and New York, 1991.

PELLETIER, A.: *L'urbanisme romain sous l'empire*. Paris, 1982.

RICH, J., and WALLACE-HADRILL, A. (eds.): *City and Country in the Ancient World*. London and New York, 1991.

RYKWERT, JOSEPH: *The Idea of a Town: The Anthropology of Urban Form in Rome, Italy and the Ancient World*. Cambridge, Massachusetts, 1988.

SCULLY, VINCENT: *The Earth, the Temple, and the Gods*. Rev. ed. New York, 1969.

TRITSCH, F.: "Die Stadtbildungen des Altertums und die griechische Polis," *Klio* 22 (1928): 1-83.

VON GERKAN, A.: *Griechische Städteanlagen*. Berlin, 1924.

WARD-PERKINS, JOHN B.: *Cities of Ancient Greece and Italy: Planning in Classical Antiquity*. New York, 1974.

WIEGAND, T., and SCHRADER, H. (eds.): *Milet, Ergebnisse der Ausgrabungen und Untersuchungen seit dem Jahre 1899*. Berlin, 1906-36.

WYCHERLEY, R. E.: "The Agora of Miletus." *Journal of the Royal Institute of British Architects* 45 (1938): 1005-1011.

WYCHERLEY, R. E.: *How the Greeks Built Cities*. 2nd ed. London, 1962.

WYMER, J. E.: *Marktplatz-Anlagen der Griechen und Römer*. Munich, 1920.

*

Situated at the mouth of the Maiandros River on the southwestern shore of Asia Minor, Miletos boasted the largest and most sophisticated of the early rationalized city plans in classical antiquity that were named after Hippodamos. Founded by Cretans, then settled by Mycenaean Achaeans, Miletos enjoyed proud prominence as early as the first millennium B.C., when it became a leading settlement of the Ionian League. In archaic times too, the commercial wealth of the city was the main impetus in founding a plethora of colonies and markets from Egypt to the Black Sea, as many as 90, according to Pliny. As a thriving center of learning, Miletos became a veritable melting pot for ideas from the East and the West. Revolutionary hypotheses concerning the essence of matter, advances in mathematics and geometry, and the forewarning of the eclipse of the sun in 585 B.C. were dispensed to the world by Thales the Milesian. Renowned natural philosophers such as Anaximandros and Anaximenes, and the historian geographer Hecataios also lived and worked in this city.

After Miletos was completely destroyed by Persians in 495 B.C., historical consciousness stemming from a proud past and the operative force of established scientific tradition engendered the reconstruction of the city from scratch according to a new orthogonal idiom. With four harbors, one in the east and three on the western promontory, Miletos once again became the busiest port in Ionia, and flourished into the Roman era with prolific and impressive public building befitting its status as an independent metropolis of the Asia Province. Unable to escape the fate of other silted-up cities, however, the city shrank in size during the Byzantine period. Another spurt of commercial activity signaled the swansong of Miletos in the 15th century

City Gate: Miletos, Asia Minor, ca. 495 B.C.

when the mosque of İlyas Bey, with exquisite marble workmanship, was built. During the Ottoman period, partly due to earthquakes, the city was reduced to the status of a village, which continues today.

Public building in Miletos was in the forefront of architectural development during the Hellenistic and Roman periods, respectively. Evolution of the stoa as a building in its own right in the former and the uncontrollable rise of flamboyant facade architecture in the latter reached their zenith in Miletos. In spite of the name, the ''Hippodamian'' system of streets intersecting one another at right angles was not actually an invention of Hippodamos, since it had already been used at Ephesos and Olbia during the archaic period, and even before further in the east. Because of the need for systematization, several of the Milesian colonies may have served as experimental pilot areas for the plan before its large-scale application in Miletos and Piraeus, which is also thought to have been planned by Hippodamos. What makes the Hippodamian plan at Miletos unique, however, is that it was the first instance of applied social urban theory combining Aristotelian notions of the ideal city state with actual town planning. The eminent master plan associated with

Hippodamos envisaged a city with a population of 10,000 people: the land was divided up into three areas—sacred, public and private—and the population was comprised of three classes—artisans, farmers and warriors. Considering, though, that the population of Miletos had already reached 64,000 in 494 B.C., and that the actual area in grid was nearly 100 hectares, it is clear that the city was laid out on a larger scale than anticipated.

In the new scheme, the importance of the sacred tradition was maintained by making the shrines of Athena and of Apollo Delphinios the starting point for the plan. The classical Athena temple received a new orientation from north to south, while the principal and longest road of the grid commenced at the Athena temple, and joined the sacral avenue that led to the oracular center at Didyma. However, the archaic physical dominance of these religious foci held no longer. Instead, the three agoras, or marketplaces, which had a natural relationship with the four harbors of the town, controlled the most extensive and central area in the public and sacred domain. Government buildings, the Prytaneion and the new Bouleuterion, or Council House, were centrally situated adjacent to the markets, increasing their symbolic importance, while the housing constituting

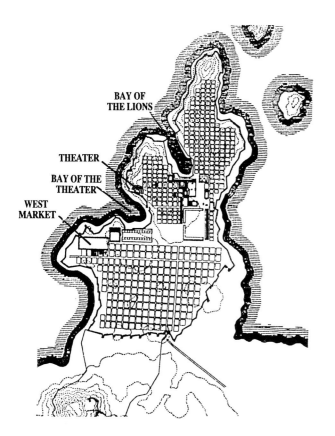

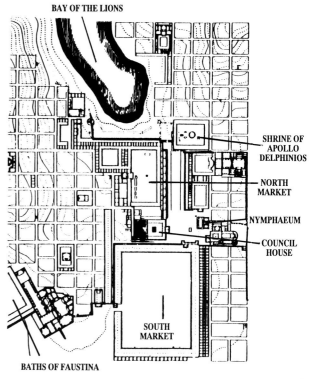

some 400 blocks in the plan was peripherally organized in three clusters beyond.

In the planning of the new town, the piecemeal growth of the so-called North, South and West markets within the framework of the precisely defined public areas and functions reserved for them reveals the stage-by-stage genesis of a remarkably versatile building type: the stoa. A colonnade, with or without a single or a double row of shops, the stoa served to scale outdoor spaces. It could stand on its own or it could be bent into an L or pi shape. In the North Market, the oldest agora of Miletos, three stages of development spanning the fifth, fourth and the first centuries B.C. may be traced culminating in the transformation of the stoa into a formalized enclosure. In contrast to the hermetically sealed North Market, the four-sided articulation of the South Market, the largest of Greek market buildings (33,000 square meters), embodies a more flexible and airy arrangement of stoas: a pair of double-aisled L-shaped stoas, one with a row of shops at the back, face each other, forming a pi, while a lengthy single-aisled stoa with a double row of shops on the eastern side completes the circuit. There is no architectural symbiosis. Although the three stoas conform to the rectilinear grid, the monumentalization of the commercial complex is achieved organically. The elongated West Market is the latest of the market complexes in the late Hellenistic era. Its intrusion into the terraces of the Athena temple points to the declining importance of the sacral function.

During the Roman period, richly articulated showy structures reflected the desire for highly wrought decorative civic imagery. A new building boom was realized first under Trajan (A.D. 53-117), who dedicated to his father the ostentatious Nymphaeum (fountain house) facing the tetrastyle propylon of the Bouleuterion. The three-story marble facade gleaming with columns and statues utilized the devices of stage design, and it acted as an urban screen closing off one end of a ceremonial avenue. The southern vista of the avenue was terminated with the North Gate of the South Market, which matched the visual splendor of the Nymphaeum. The North Gate was a two-story tabernacular structure with three arched passageways and four pavilions surmounted by a broken pediment in the center. Its projecting and retreating forms which were emphasized by twin Corinthian columns, contrasted with the classical austerity of the Bouleuterion, bringing about a pulsating terminus to the ceremonial avenue. The avenue itself (100 meters long and about 28 meters wide), with colonnaded wide pavements on both sides (each nearly six meters wide), connected the religious, commercial and government centers, its formal grandiosity forming a parallel to the pomp and ceremony of Roman rulership. Visitors arriving at the Port of Lions received their first glimpse of the city in the impressive facade of the Harbor Stoa. They went through the Harbor Gate, which had been refurbished with 16 columns in conformity with the Roman taste for grandeur, before they entered the equally overwhelming ceremonial avenue.

Two buildings, the Baths of Faustina and the Theater, deviate from the grid plan, and their well-preserved ruins dominate the site of Miletos today. Commissioned by Faustina, the wife of Marcus Aurelius, the former consists of a large palaestra (62 by 64 meters) in Greek fashion and the bathing complex with an unusually long *apodyterium* (dressing room). Unlike the Baths of Capito and the Bouleuterion, characteristic Roman features of strict axial and symmetrical regularity are not found in this structure, perhaps due to its location outside the grid. The Roman sequence of bathing is well represented: from the *apodyterium* one entered the *frigidarium* (cold room) consisting of three rooms, the central one with a shallow pool. Two apsidal rooms in the southeast constituted the *caldarium* (hot room) heated vertically and from below. Although stripped of its marble now, the bath with its vaulted halls embodies an introverted sensibility—the use of polychromatic marble was reserved for creating slick interiors. No attempt was made to embellish the brick-faced walls of mortared rubble on the outside, revealing the antithetical attitude toward buildings propagating the official image and utilitarian architecture.

Situated on the promontory between the Bay of Lions and the Bay of the Theater, the theater was enlarged in Roman times after four successive restorations of the scene building and the auditorium in the Hellenistic period. As the largest theater in Asia Minor, it could accommodate 15,000 spectators. Since it utilized a natural slope for its *cavea*, it deviated from the grid plan. The orchestra is almost in the form of a semicircle in Roman fashion but the scene building, originally three stories high (140 by 30 meters), does not form a fully integrated architectural unity with the *cavea*. Nevertheless, the spectators were cut off from the outside world by an impressive frontispiece decorated with statues and a frieze with reliefs. Galleries covered with vaulted roofs built of blocks of stone led to the seats and allowed easily controlled access to the three divisions of seats at different levels. Exactly in the center on the lowest row was a box of honor with four extant columns reserved for important officials. Perhaps more than any other building at Miletos, the theater extols the Romanized aggrandizement of the city: from a modest building of entertainment for only 5,300 people, it became a colossal pleasure palace dispensing amusement to local citizens and international visitors alike.

—SUNA GÜVEN

MYCENAE
Greece

16th century B.C.: Grave Circle A, cemetery, Knossos tholos tomb constructed. **15th century B.C.:** Kato Phournos tholos tomb and defense walls constructed. **14th century B.C.:** Panagia tholos tomb constructed. **Ca. 1400 B.C.:** Defense walls constructed. **13th century B.C.:** Defense walls enlarged. **1300-1250 B.C.:** Treasury of Atreus constructed. **1250 B.C.:** Lion Gate constructed.

Publications

BUSCHOR, E., and HAMANN, R.: *Die Skulpturen des Zeustempels zu Olympia*. Marburg, Germany, 1924.

COULTON, J. J.: *Ancient Greek Architects at Work: Problems of Structure and Design*. Ithaca, New York, 1977.

CURTIUS, E., et al.: *Die Ausgrabungen zu Olympia*. 5 vols. Berlin, 1876-81.

CURTIUS, E.; ADLER, F.; et al.: *Olympia: Die Ergebnisse der vom Deutschen Reich veranstalteten Ausgrabungen*. 10 vols. Berlin, 1890-97.

DINSMOOR, WILLIAM BELL: *The Architecture of Ancient Greece*. New York, 1975.

DINSMOOR, WILLIAM BELL: "An Archaeological Earthquake at Olympia." *American Journal of Archaeology* 45 (1941).

DÖRPFELD, W.: *Alt-Olympia, Untersuchungen und Ausgrabungen zur Geschichte des ältesten Heiligtums von Olympia*. 2 vols. Berlin, 1935.

EVANS, A. J.: *The Shaft Graves and Beehive Tombs of Mycenae and Their Interrelation*. London, 1929.

GARDINER, E. N.: *Olympia, Its History and Remains*. Oxford, 1925.

HERMANN, H.-V.: *Olympia*. Munich, 1972.

KARO, G.: *Die Schachtgräber von Mykenai*. 2 vols. Munich, 1930-33.

LALOUX, V., and MONCEAUX, P.: *Restauration d'Olympie*. Paris, 1889.

LAWRENCE, A. W. N.: *Greek Architecture*. Rev. ed. Harmondsworth, England, 1983.

MALLWITZ, A.: *Olympia und seine Bauten*. Munich, 1972.

ROBERTSON, D. S.: "New Light on the Facade of the Treasury of Atreus." *Journal of Hellenic Studies* 61 (1941).

RODENWALDT, G.: *Der Fries des Megarons von Mykenai*. Halle, Germany, 1921.

RODENWALDT, G., and HEGE, W.: *Olympia*. London, 1936.

SCHLEIF, H.: *Die neuen Ausgrabungen in Olympia und ihre bisherigen Ergebnisse für die antike Bauforschung*. Berlin, 1943.

SCHLIEMANN, HEINRICH: *Mycenae: A Narrative of Researches and Discoveries at Mycenae and Tiryns*. New York, 1880.

SCULLY, VINCENT: *The Earth, the Temple, and the Gods: Greek Sacred Architecture*. New York, 1969.

SIMPSON, W.: "Notes upon the Smaller 'Treasuries' at Mycenae." *Journal of the Royal Institute of British Architects* 2 (1894-95).

THIERSCH, F.: "Die Tholos des Atreus zu Mykenae." *Athenische Mitteilungen des Deutschen Archäologischen Instituts* 4 (1879).

WACE, A. J. B.: *Mycenae*. Princeton, New Jersey, 1949.

*

Renowned in antiquity as the homeland of King Agamemnon, who led the Greek warriors to Troy, Mycenae was demonstrably a powerful center of Helladic civilization from which the Mycenaean culture derives its name. In the annals of Mediterranean archaeology Mycenae has come to typify the powerful and militant people whose monumental citadels and elaborately decorated palaces are tangible reminders of a way of life shaped by specific aristocratic codes of conduct which were later paraphrased by Homer in his epic poetry.

Like other major Bronze Age sites in the Aegean area (for example, Athens, Corinth and Knossos), Mycenae was situated approximately five miles from the sea as a caution against piratical raids. The threat of such invasions was vividly portrayed by Homer. Mycenae's strategic location near the head of the Argolic plain provided it with a commanding view of this agriculturally important terrain and its access points, including the coast. Mycenae's position on a low hill nestled between Mount Ayios Ilias on the north and Mount Zara to the south, with the Kokoretsa and Chavos ravines running, respectively, along its northern and southern flanks, provided natural defenses in these areas. The earliest known defense walls, which encircled the palace area on the summit of the hill shortly after 1400 B.C., were greatly enlarged during the 13th century B.C. to create the massive fortification walls seen today, and attest to the growth of the site as an important administrative center. Portions of these walls and its famous Lion Gate had remained visible over the intervening millennia so that Homer may have had contemporary as well as traditional knowledge in calling Mycenae "well-built"; the first-hand impressions of Pausanias caused him to repeat an ancient belief that they were made by the Cyclopes.

One of the most distinctive features of Mycenaean architecture is the megaron, a rectangular design with a fixed hearth

Perseia Spring: Mycenae, Greece

in the main room and a vestibule and/or columned porch attached to one of its short sides, and all on axis with the only entry. This structure could support a second floor, presumably with a gallery above the hearth room, and a lantern of sorts fitted with terra-cotta pipes for channeling smoke out of the building. Reflections of such a second story structure are found in Homer's description of Telemachos' upstairs chambers in the palace of Odysseus on Ithaca. The megaron was utilized in palatial and other domestic structures at Mycenae and has stylistic ties to other examples going back perhaps into the Neolithic Period on the Balkan peninsula, in Anatolia and the Near East.

Mycenaean building techniques included the use of enormous, roughly worked stones as well as ashlar stone blocks, which, following ancient sources, have been termed "Cyclopean." At the primary entrance gates an enormous stone bastion was thrown out from the walls on an attacker's unshielded, right-hand side, forcing him into a confined passage before the gates, where he would be vulnerable to attack from above. This defensive device typifies the Mycenaean anticipation of armed conflict, at least by the 13th century B.C., when these bastions were constructed.

Other important and characteristic Mycenaean architectural

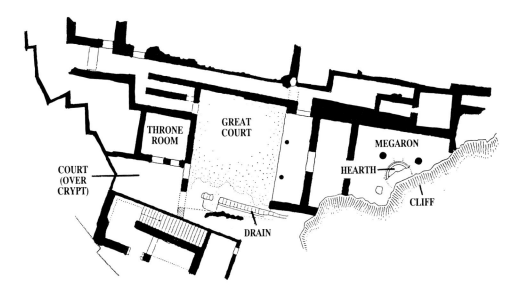

traits include corbelled vaults, which were used to shelter rectangular and circular spaces, ranging in size from relatively narrow passages up to areas nearly 50 feet in diameter. Over prominent doorways, such as those of the so-called Treasury of Atreus and Tomb of Clytemnestra, the megalithic structures were interrupted by a ''relieving triangle,'' which, by means of corbelling, minimized the weight on the lintel block. The open space above the lintel could be filled with lighter material or fitted with a carved block as in the Lion Gate at the main entrance to the citadel.

This impressive, 10-foot-high stone relief with its two heraldic lionesses flanking a single column of Minoan design is awe-inspiring to one approaching it today just as it must have been to those standing before it in antiquity. It is a powerful testament to the Mycenaean predilection for the heroic, and stands as the earliest example of monumental sculpture in Western art. The heads of the creatures are lost and may have been of a different material, but they would have been set at right angles to their bodies, confronting the approach to the gate. Besides its decorative effect befitting the massive fortification walls, one purpose of the lion sculpture could have been to serve as a coat of arms for the ruling monarchy within the walls. Homer likened Agamemnon to a lion in the Trojan campaign, and this may have had a basis beyond the use of poetic language. The Lion Gate at Mycenae has been dated to about 1250 B.C., a date also associated through archaeological excavation with the destruction of Homer's Troy. If Agamemnon was actually King of Mycenae and led a Greek force against Troy, which served as the basis of Homer's account, then he would have been the reigning monarch of Mycenae at about the time the Lion Gate was created. It is important to note, however, that the concept of monumental sculpture in the form of lions decorating a prominent gateway of a Bronze Age citadel is not unique, since the Lion Gate at the Hittite capital of Hattusas, although of different design, predates the example at Mycenae by about a century.

The walls of Mycenae enclosed a portion of the prehistoric cemetery known to archaeologists as Grave Circle A, excavated primarily by Heinrich Schliemann in the 1870s. At the western edge of this cemetery a second cluster of burials was later found and called Grave Circle B. Circle B is older than Circle A but overlaps it in time for about two generations. Both contained

a combination of deep shaft graves with multiple burials of seemingly royal personages, and other, shallower graves. The amount of worked gold in the form of death masks, body ornaments and weapons, and other skillfully wrought precious materials testifies to the wealth and apparent power of the ruling families at Mycenae, a point echoed by Homer, who referred to the city as ''rich in gold.'' Since the majority of the wealth appeared in Circle A, which dates to most of the 16th century B.C., it has been conjectured that the elite of Mycenae served as mercenaries in Egypt in the wars against the Hyksos at the end of the 17th dynasty (ca. 1570 B.C). In Egypt they would have been exposed to local funerary practices of embalming, shaft burials, gold death masks and other forms of ornamentation of the dead, and presumably rewarded for their military assistance with gold and other precious objects which subsequently were used in the burials at Mycenae. That Greek myth claims Danaos of neighboring Argos to be an Egyptian is perhaps a reflection of a distant memory of Mycenae's contact with Egypt during that period.

Following the development of shaft-grave burials and their smaller and shallower cist-grave counterparts at Mycenae, there emerged the rock-cut chamber tombs and the more elaborate and stone-constructed tholos tombs, of which the so-called Treasury of Atreus is the largest and finest example known in the Mycenaean world. The nine tholos tombs at Mycenae demonstrate a clear development in structural refinement from the late 16th century well into the 13th century B.C. Built into the hillsides west of the citadel, these beehive-shaped vaults of corbelled construction are approached by long entranceways called *dromoi*. The latest and largest examples bore elaborately decorated facades, while one of these, the Treasury of Atreus, had interior ornamentation in the form of bronze rosette studs on the main chamber walls and perhaps decorated walls in its unconventional side chamber. The entire structure of a tholos tomb would be concealed underneath the earth as part of the normal terrain when not open for interment. In this way these tombs also reflect Egyptian funerary architecture in combining the concepts prevalent in contemporay Egyptian royal burials of the 18th dynasty as well as those of the Old Kingdom. The monumental stone-built pyramids approached by long causeways west of Memphis and the hidden, pharaonic tombs with long rock-cut corridors in the Valley of the Kings must have attracted the attention of Mycenaeans, whose pottery is found in sizable quantities on 18th-dynasty sites.

It is even possible to consider that the Mycenaeans utilized aspects of Egyptian construction techniques in maneuvering large blocks into position in the superstructures of their monuments. The larger of the two lentil blocks over the entrance to the Treasury of Atreus weighs in excess of 100 tons and rests nearly 18 feet above ground level. To move the cumbersome block into position, the workmen must have used an earthen ramp, which was later removed, in a similar way to the way in which the Egyptians constructed large mud-brick ramps against the great pylons at Karnak, portions of which still exist.

The tholos tombs at Mycenae have long been robbed of their contents, but intact examples elsewhere in the Peloponnesus have yielded beautifully wrought objects of gold and ivory. We must assume that the tholos tombs of Mycenae once concealed such treasures buried with the dead. It is therefore plausible to consider the clearly related yet sizably and structurally different types of contemporary burial chambers at Mycenae to be reflections of class distinctions. The larger and elaborately made shaft graves followed by the impressive tholos tombs would have been the final resting places for members of Mycenae's ruling class. The smaller cist graves supplanted by the rock-cut chamber tombs would have filled the needs of the local nobility. Other shallow burials at Mycenae, known as pit graves, would have been those of the common people. The funerary architecture, therefore, provides an important glimpse at the developed social structure of this prehistoric site.

At the height of its power, the ruling population of Mycenae enjoyed the airy, palatial structures on the summit of the hill. The strong axiality of the megaron with its open forecourt is reflective of Mycenaean formalism and regimentation. The use of gypsum slabs and brightly painted stucco walls, floors and ceilings created an awe-inspiring atmosphere not lost on the visitor to the court. The exact nature of all the rooms within the palace area is not known, since much of the construction in this region has been lost. However, within the walls of Mycenae is clear evidence of drainage systems that undoubtedly improved the quality of life for the inhabitants and may have been influenced by even more sophisticated plumbing in the Minoan palaces on Crete. Within the protection of its walls, Mycenae maintained religious shrines, multistory houses for its nobility, elaborate facilities for court-supported artists, storage areas for food supplies, access to a water source, and a refuge for its people in times of need.

Archival records in the form of Linear B tablets found at the site provide further evidence that Mycenae was a prominent administrative center. The large number of other, important Mycenaean sites in the area of the Argolic plain (including the walled citadel of Tiryns) provides an indication of its agricultural significance and productive capabilities. Given the impressive quality and magnitude of its archaeological remains and the prominence given to Agamemnon and his city in the Homeric tradition, Mycenae must have governed this region as a suzerain. It does not seem probable, however, that Mycenae's political influence extended in any dominating fashion beyond the Argolic plain, as Homer would have us believe. Mycenaean sites across Greece seem to have been banded together in politically unified clusters, anticipating the polis system of historical Greece. The extensive walls fortifying most prominent Mycenaean centers and echoes of internal conflicts, such as those involving Thebes, in the literary tradition of the Greeks, indicate that the Mycenaean civilization consisted of several politically independent yet culturally unified states, over one of which Mycenae surely presided.

—KARL KILINSKI II

AMPHITHEATER
Nîmes, France

First century A.D.

Publications

BESSAC, J. C.; FINCKER, M.; GARMY, P.; and PEY, J.: "Recherches sur les fondations de l'amphithéâtre de Nîmes (Gard, France)." *Revue archéologique de Narbonnaise* 17 (1984): 223-237.

ESPÉRANDIEU, E.: *L'amphithéâtre de Nîmes.* Paris, 1933.

ETIENNE, R.: "La date de l'amphithéâtre de Nîmes." *Melanges d'archéologie et d'histoire offerts à A. Piganiol.* Vol. 2. Paris, 1966.

GOLVIN, JEAN-CLAUDE: *L'amphithéâtre romain: Essai sur la théorisation de sa forme et des ses fonctions.* 1988.

LASSALLE, V., and PEYRON, J.: "L'escalier de service de l'amphithéâtre de Nîmes." *Revue archéologique de Narbonnaise* 5 (1972): 167-173.

LUGLI, G.: "La datazione degli anfiteatri di Arles e di Nîmes in Provenza." *Rivista dell'Istituto Nazionale d'Archaeologia e Storia dell'Arte* New Series 13-14 (1964-65): 145-199.

MAZAURIC: "Les souterrains des arènes de Nîmes." *Mém. Acad. Nîmes* 33 (1910): 1-35.

PEYRE, ROGER RAYMOND: *Nîmes, Arles, Orange, St. Remy.* Paris, 1903.

STURGIS, RUSSELL: *A Dictionary of Architecture and Building.* New York, 1902.

*

Tucked in the southernmost section of the ancient city of Nîmes, eight meters from the Augustan wall, is a magnificent, well-preserved limestone amphitheater dating to about 100 A.D. Hemmed in today by buildings on three sides, and encircled by modern roads, the amphitheater still dominates its surroundings. Its aspect, best appreciated from the south, resembles the Colosseum in Rome, upon which it is based, but its numerous receding and advancing planes gives it a greater sculptural definition and a baroque play of light and shade.

The circular arcades of the amphitheater rise in two stories capped off by a narrow attic punctuated by pairs of brackets for the wooden poles which carried the *velum* (*velarium*). The ground floor is adorned with fat Tuscan pilasters, the second with Tuscan Doric columns resting on pedestals, both carrying Ionic entablatures which break forward above them—a recent innovation in Roman architectural design. Arcades with trabeated decoration occurred frequently in Roman architecture of the first centuries B.C. and A.D., and appeared on a number of theaters and amphitheaters, including the Colosseum. But the strong vertical accent, rising from the ground all the way up through the attic, was new, introduced here—and at the nearby amphitheater at Arles (designed by the same architect)—to counteract an otherwise squat appearance.

The second story is the more ornate of the two. Between its piers, which rest on podia, ran a series of parapets, and projecting from the piers the column pedestals. (Only three of the parapets are in place today, on the southeast side). This multilayered design forms, along with the entablature of the first story, a continuous projecting and receding band around the amphitheater. A similar band, composed of the upper entablature and

Amphitheater: Nîmes, France, 1st century A.D.

attic story, crowns the structure. These strong circular accents reinforce the elliptical shape of the amphitheater, and play off against both the semicircular arcades and the vertical members of the design.

The amphitheater is oriented with its long axis running northeast-southwest. Along this axis two well-marked passageways lead into the arena. The entrances to these passageways—the Gate of Libitina, goddess of death, on the southwest, through which the dead were carried out, and the Triumphal Gate, on the northeast, through which processions entered at the beginning of the games—have slightly larger arches than those of the surrounding arcades. The Triumphal Gate is further distinguished by a two-story aedicula culminating in a fastigium at attic level. Four bull protomes, two to a story, located between arch and lintel, greet those who enter there. The bull protome is found on a number of ancient buildings at Nîmes and at nearby Arles. Its meaning is not certain, but on the amphitheater it may represent courage and valor.

Although the amphitheater gives an overall impression of massive ruggedness, accentuated by the weathering of its once-ashlar masonry, the architect's uses of fine decorative moldings—on the cornices, architraves, voussoirs, podia, pedestals and parapets—adds a delicate linear definition to the relief depth of the facade. This combination of rugged strength and decorative detail is continued on the interior. Just inside the arcade at ground level is an annular passageway of great height, covered by a concrete barrel vault with thick transverse masonry ribs resting on small finely carved entablatures supported on three corbels each. Above this corridor is another, constricted in height, and severely compartmentalized by the use of radial

vaulting. The individual vaults rest on massive monolithic lintels which span the passageway. Although the use of radial barrel vaults in this manner is an old-fashioned feature, found on the theater of Marcellus in Rome (ca. 13-11 B.C.), the construction is more complex here. There are two lintels per pier, instead of the one in the Theater of Marcellus, separated by a narrow transverse vault, and carved on their outer faces by Ionic fasciae. Massive *cyma reverse* moldings soften the transitions from vertical pier to horizontal lintel; these "slip down" in the center of the pier below the transverse vaults, adding a delightful and unexpected mannerist touch. The result is a sophisticated updated design, exploited for its spatial qualities, dramatic accents of light and shade, and decorative potential.

The radial vaults of the second story are lower in height than the arches of the exterior arcade which they abut, and the piers upon which they rest are wider. Together with the parapet they partly enclose the openings of the arcade, adding further relief depth to the facade at that level, and greatly enhancing the chiaroscuro effect.

The layout of the amphitheater, like that of the Colosseum, is eminently functional. The arches of the lower arcade, each of which serves as an entrance, together with annular and radial passageways and numerous staircases, provide for the easy ingress and egress of large crowds. A half-barrel vault behind the attic gives access to the *velum*. The *cavea*, supported on a series of radial barrel vaults (as in the Colosseum), is divided into four horizontal sections to separate the spectators according to class. And a well-designed series of drains keeps the arena from turning into a pond during rainy weather. The amphitheater lacks, however, the complex underground rooms and passage-ways found beneath the arena in the Colosseum. The simple cross-shaped passageway that exists at Nîmes is probably late, and its function has yet to be determined.

The amphitheater at Nîmes, then, while relying heavily on the Colosseum in Rome, goes beyond it in introducing both the complete vertical accent and a stronger sculptural quality to the facade. Together with its "twin" at Arles it belongs to the developing baroque phase of Roman architecture and stands at the forefront of the bold architectural experimentation which characterizes Roman architecture of the second century A.D.

—PATRICIA MARX

MAISON CARRÉE
Nîmes, France

1 B.C.: Dedication of temple. **1824:** Restoration into museum.

Publications

STURGIS, RUSSELL: *A Dictionary of Architecture and Building.* New York, 1902.

A temple dedicated in 1 B.C. during the reign of the Emperor Augustus, it stood at the south end of the forum of the Roman colony of Nemausus (today, Nîmes), in the province of Gallia Narbonensis (today, Gard, France). The name Maison Carrée (literally, square house), is post-antique, and refers obviously to the form rather than the function of the building. The dedication was to Lucius and Gaius Caesar, grandchildren of Augustus, and was notable as one of the earliest recorded dedications to the cult of the imperial house. The building's subsequent fame was owed most of all to the fact that it survived as one of the best-preserved of all ancient Roman temples. It was constructed up to the roof entirely of stone, and stands today almost complete. Only the timber beams of the roof and the ceilings of porch and cella, along with the tiles of the roof, are not original. Over the many centuries since its construction it served as an assembly hall, a house, a stable, a church, a granary, the seat of the prefecture and, finally, after major restoration in 1824, the building was turned into a museum, its present function.

It was not a large temple by ancient standards, nor architecturally distinctive, but its very typicality suggests its importance. To the extent that the official buildings of the Roman state were very often the products of a formulaic approach, the temple of Nîmes was a totally characteristic example of the state architecture of the time. It was hexastyle prostyle, pseudoperipteral, in the Corinthian order, with six columns across the front and 11 on the long sides. The podium was 43 feet wide by 86 feet deep, and the overall height was 50 feet, allowing 10 feet for the podium, 30 feet for the colonnade and 10 feet more to the top of the pediment. The careful articulation of exterior details,

Maison Carrée: Nîmes, France, dedicated in 1 B.C.

the columns, half-columns, and especially the rear corner columns and the entablature, above all, speak of the influence of Augustan classicism on the form of the traditional Italo-Roman temple. In fact, the sculptural details and other elements of the building were based directly on the designs for the just completed Forum Augustum in Rome, although the temple at Nîmes appears to have been carried out by local workers.

As it stands today the original ground level is recorded in the paving of the surrounding space. This is important, as it permits the modern observer to experience the effect of the proportions of the building much as they were felt in antiquity. The great height of the podium, relative to the height of the entire building, still conveys the intended feeling of separation between secular and sacred, a feeling that the great moldings that project from the top and bottom of the podium were designed to enhance. The colonnade above is vertically extended, as is the superstructure, emphasizing the importance of the building; most of all, the cornice and pedimental molding that surmount the rest project outward beyond the plane of the structure below to an astonishing degree. The overall effect is one of total dominance of the foreground space, all the more impressive in that the temple is in its overall dimensions not a large building, and does not stand today in its original setting. In every way, but especially in its spatial qualities, the temple of Nîmes preserves the sense of kinesthetic force which the hellenized temples of the Roman Empire inherited from their ancient Italic origins.

As much as its importance for our knowledge of Roman architecture, the temple was equally or even more important to the later history of architecture, especially in America. It was in the 18th century that the United States came into existence as a democratic republic, its political ideology modeled in part on what was then believed to be true of the ancient states of Greece and Rome. It was no accident that Thomas Jefferson, one of the framers of the Constitution and at the same time a dedicated amateur of architecture, should have sought in antiquity the examples that would instruct his countrymen in art as he and his collaborators sought there the inspiration for the constitution of the new state. Indeed, Jefferson said so himself in letters written from Paris in 1785, when he was a U.S. ambassador to France.

He was consulted on the design for the state capitol to be built at Richmond, Virginia, and sent drawings for the building, which were based in turn on drawings of the temple at Nîmes that had been made specially for Jefferson by C.-L. Clérisseau. Jefferson's design was, in his own words, copied from ''the most precious the most perfect model of ancient architecture remaining on earth.'' The Virginia State Capitol was a good deal larger than the temple at Nîmes, and there were differences of detail, but the resemblances between the ancient building and the modern were undeniable, and intended. Again, in Jefferson's words, ''How is a taste in this beautiful art [that is, architecture] to be formed in our countrymen, unless we avail ourselves of every occasion when public buildings are to be erected, of presenting to them models for their study and imitation?'' The importance of the borrowing from antiquity in this instance can hardly be overestimated, in that the form and content of official architecture in America, up to as late as 1940, were influenced directly by the iconographic choices made originally by Jefferson at Richmond in 1785.

—BERNARD M. BOYLE

PONT DU GARD
Nîmes, France

Ca. 14 A.D.

Publications

STURGIS, RUSSELL: *A Dictionary of Architecture and Building.* New York, 1902.

*

A section of a Roman aqueduct that brought the water of the river Aizon some 25 miles from Uzés to Nîmes (Roman Nemausus), France, the Pont du Gard was built in the late first century B.C. or early first century A.D. The name Pont du Gard (literally, bridge over the Gard), is post-antique. The last remaining section of the original aqueduct, it carried the water across the valley of the river Gard at a height of about 160 feet above the river below. It consisted of three levels of arches on piers; the lowest level had six arches, the level above had 11 arches with the same spans as those below, while the topmost level had 35 arches, four to each lower one. The largest span, in the center of the first and second levels, was about 80 feet; the other arches of those levels spanned about 60 feet, while the arches of the top level have spans of about 14 feet. The piers were 20 feet deep. Above the third level of arches ran the water channel, roofed over with stone slabs, today still mostly preserved. The entire construction was of huge blocks of locally quarried stone, laid without mortar and strengthened with iron cramps. Numbers of the stone blocks were laid so as to project from the faces of the structure, and clearly were used to support timber centering during the construction process. In 1747 the piers of the lowest level were increased in depth to carry a roadway above; restoration of the entire structure took place between 1855 and 1858.

As a monument of its own time the Pont du Gard stood as an outstanding example of the simplicity and directness of expression achieved by so much of the architectural construction of the Roman world. Although by no means the longest stretch of Roman aqueduct preserved today—it is about 900 feet long—it was certainly one of the highest. But it was not size alone that made the Pont du Gard famous. The architecture of the ancient Roman world was transmitted to later ages—in part as a result of the kind of record surviving from antiquity—largely as what would be called today architectural engineering, that is, works remarkable as much for their structural skill or daring as for their more purely architectural qualities. Even today, everywhere in the former Roman world, there can be seen remains of temples, tombs, baths, basilicas, honorific arches and various other kinds of buildings, many preserved in fragmentary form, and almost all of them lacking their original and often elaborate decorative finishes. On the other hand, and precisely because the more utilitarian Roman structures such as aqueducts, roads, bridges, walls and gates did not usually have elaborate finishes, or any finishes at all, where they have survived they stand before us much as they did in antiquity, in unvarnished simplicity. It is among the latter group that the Pont du Gard takes its place, an immediately apprehensible embodiment of the architectonic culture of the Roman world.

In the later history of architecture, the early Romanesque buildings of southern France were clearly influenced by local Roman remains, among which the Pont du Gard would have occupied then as now a prominent place. The structurally based

Pont du Gard: Nîmes, France, ca. 14 A.D.

expression of Romanesque architecture, as the name implies, owed much to the architecture of the Roman world before it. Later, the great scale combined with modular regularity so characteristic of the Roman aqueduct as a type found echoes in the architecture of the Florentine Renaissance, for example, the Palazzo Pitti in Florence (first phase, ca. 1460). Later still, in the 18th century, it was those qualities of Roman architecture, among others, that inspired the engravings of G. B. Piranesi, to take only one example. And again, a further echo of that simplified monumentality appeared in the 19th century, for example, the Bibliothèque Ste.-Geneviève, in Paris (1838-50), by Henri Labrouste, followed by its re-echo in the Boston Public Library (1887-98) by McKim, Mead and White.

More important for the history of American and world architecture was the influence of the Roman aqueduct as a type, and especially its most well-known exemplar, the Pont du Gard, on the work of H. H. Richardson (1838-86). From the imitative Romanesque of Trinity Church in Boston (1872-78), to the true Romanism of the Allegheny County Courthouse and Jail in Pittsburgh (1884-88) and the Marshall Field Wholesale Store in Chicago (1885-87), Richardson's personal style moved inexorably from the historical to the universal.

Louis Sullivan and, after him, Frank Lloyd Wright were to benefit from Richardson's recognition that the essentials of architecture lay in simplicity of expression and truthfulness in use of materials, and that Roman architecture provided notable models suitable for emulation even by the architects of the new world, models of a formal abstractness so direct as virtually to detach from them the limitations imposed by historical content. Far from being so utilitarian as to be insignificant, the Pont

du Gard and structures like it were to play essential roles in establishing the definition of what was to become the architecture of the modern age.

—BERNARD M. BOYLE

OLYMPIA
Alpheios River Valley, Greece

Seventh century B.C.: Temple of Hera constructed. **Seventh century B.C.:** Gela treasury constructed. **Sixth century B.C.:** First, second Bouleuterion constructed. **Sixth century B.C.:** Treasuries erected. **Fifth century B.C.:** Temple of Zeus constructed. **Fourth century B.C.:** Metroon constructed. **Fourth century B.C.:** Philippieion tholos constructed. **Fourth century B.C.:** Leonidaion constructed. **Fourth century B.C.:** Stadium constructed. **Second century A.D.:** Nymphaeum fountain house constructed. **394 A.D.:** Destruction of shrines ordered by Emperor Theodosius.

Publications

DINSMOOR, WILLIAM BELL: *The Architecture of Ancient Greece.* New York, 1975.

Palaestra: Olympia, Greece, 4th century B.C.

The most important sanctuary of Zeus in Greece, Olympia was also the location of the renowned Olympic festival which was founded, according to different traditions, by Herakles or by Pelops. Olympia is situated in the river valley of the Alpheios and—in contrast to most Greek sites—is well watered, green and shady. The architecture of the sacred precinct and its environs includes temples, dwellings for officials and priests, and public buildings connected with the games, as well as many fine works of Greek sculpture.

The importance of the games and sanctuary is reflected in the quality and quantity of architecture and sculpture in Olympia. Interest in athletic contests continually increased throughout the sixth century B.C., and ultimately this site—accessible to mainland Greece, Asia Minor and Greek colonies in southern Italy and Sicily—became the center for athletics. Thus people from all over the Greek world frequented this pan-Hellenic sanctuary of Zeus, the supreme Greek divinity. Expenditures for the sanctuary must have been great; conversely, revenues from the games would have been substantial.

One of the major sources of our knowledge of the architecture and sculpture of the sanctuary is the description by Pausanias, who visited the site in the late second century A.D. Comparative studies also provide us with further information about the site. For instance, in the Greek city of Poseidonia (now known as Paestum) in southern Italy, the second temple of Hera was probably constructed shortly after the Olympian temple of Zeus; its similar size and plan and its far better preservation provide us with some idea of the appearance of the temple at Olympia.

Within Olympia the walled sanctuary known as the Altis (meaning "grove" in the local dialect, according to Pausanias) housed the temples of Hera and of Zeus, the Metroon (a temple dedicated to the mother of the gods), the shrine of Pelops, many altars to Zeus and other gods, 11 treasuries, the "Philippieion," a fountain house, and many commemorative statues of victors, gods and heroes. It is likely that the original walls of the sanctuary were low stone parapets and that high walls were not added until the Roman period. The Altis precinct was rectangular, approximately 650 by 520 feet. Its ritual center was the altar of Zeus, the original focus of the cult.

Until the time of the Persian wars in the early fifth century B.C., the major constructions at Olympia were the temple to Zeus and Hera (now known as the Heraion) in the northwest

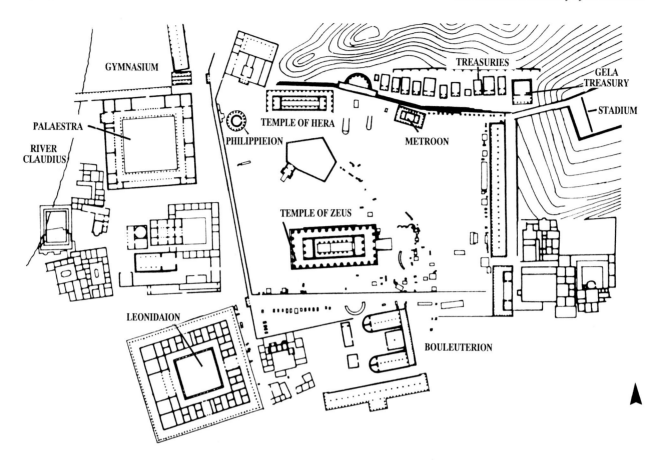

corner of the sacred precinct, the treasuries along the northern boundary, and the council house south of the Altis. The temple of Hera, constructed during the seventh century B.C., was perhaps the first monumental temple built on the Greek mainland; soon overshadowed by the larger and grander temple of Zeus, it is now the best preserved building at Olympia. This temple dedicated to Hera was originally constructed of wood (a fact which suggests a lack of good building stone around Olympia); gradually the wooden columns, at least one of which still existed in Pausanias' time, were replaced with stone. The surviving columns, which represent a variety of styles, provide an index of the gradual change in Doric proportions.

The Heraion, initially dedicated to both Hera and Zeus, was reserved for Hera alone after Zeus' temple was constructed. The temple was a Doric peripteral hexastyle, approximately 61 by 164 feet, with 16 columns on the sides, resulting in relatively long and narrow proportions. In addition, two rows of columns line the cella. The roof of terra-cotta tiles was supported by timber rafters and beams. Since the columns were relatively short (slightly over 17 feet tall) and the roof must have seemed heavy, the temple most likely seemed squat and massive. It seems that the most important decorations were terra-cotta acroterial discs; no evidence of decorated metopes or pedimental sculpture survives. Inside, at the western end of the cella, stood an archaic sculpture of Zeus and Hera; only the pedestal and head of Hera survive. Praxiteles' Hermes was also placed in this temple.

The Bouleuterion, or council house, which was the seat of the Olympic senate, consisted of two apsidal structures which faced east and had porches with three Doric columns *in antis*. The earlier building, the northern one, was erected perhaps in the mid-sixth century, while the second dates to the end of that century. Originally separate, they were later joined by a central room and Ionic colonnade. It has been suggested that since the forms of the two original buildings were similar, the structures were equivalent in function, providing housing for two groups which performed similar duties. Close to the sanctuary but later separated from it by the boundary wall, this building must have been an important ancillary structure.

The treasuries, small temples with a single chamber and distyle portico *in antis* built along the north wall of the sanctuary on a low terrace, were erected by various Greek cities as dedications or commemorations of military victories. They may have been used for the storage of sacrificial vessels and, perhaps, equipment for the games. The majority and the earliest of the treasuries were erected by cities geographically distant from Olympia, such as Sybaris and Metapontum in Italy, and Gela in Sicily. All but three of the treasuries were constructed in the sixth century B.C.; the earliest, belonging to Gela, seems to have been constructed in approximately 600 B.C. The custom of erecting treasuries was common in the sixth century; in the fifth century sculptural dedications became more prevalent.

By the end of the fifth century B.C., numerous nonarchitectural, primarily sculptural, monuments adorned the sanctuary. Some were located inside the buildings while many other marble, bronze, terra-cotta and limestone figures were placed outside. Paeonius' Nike, located in front of the temple of Zeus and dedicated to him possibly at the Peace of Nicias in 421 B.C., is a surviving example.

The first architectural addition to the sanctuary after the Persian Wars, the temple of Zeus, came to dominate the precinct. This temple, one of the largest on the Greek mainland, measured approximately 90 by 210 feet. It was designed by Libon of Elis and built from the spoils of Pisa (a district around Olympia independent of the Eleans) after its destruction by the Eleans. The temple must have been essentially completed by 456 B.C., when an inscribed block was placed in the east gable to support a dedicatory shield given by the Spartans in commemoration of their victory at the battle of Tanagra.

Since the region of Olympia is subject to earthquake damage and the temple site was on alluvial soil rather than directly on rock, unconventional building methods were needed. A Doric peripteral hexastyle with two rows of columns in the cella, the temple of Zeus evidences no innovation in design from that built at Aegina more than 20 years previously, and there is no evidence of optical curvature in the design as used for the Parthenon in Athens. The massive columns (6 by 13), constructed of shell limestone and covered with white stucco, gave the illusion of marble. The pedimental sculptures, gutters, roof tiles and metopes of the inside porches were made of Parian marble.

The theme of Zeus and his children was pervasive throughout the sculptural decoration of the temple. On the east pediment Zeus, larger than the other figures, presides over the chariot race between Oenomaus and Pelops that provided the prototype for the races at the Olympian games. The poses are quiet, since the race is portrayed in its preparation rather than its enactment. The lack of motion of this pediment contrasts with the motion of its western counterpart: the central figure of the west pediment is Apollo, a son of Zeus, who calms the uproar of the battle between the Lapiths and Centaurs—a conflict symbolizing the victory of civilization over barbarians that may well apply to the early-fifth-century struggle between the Greeks and Persians. The external metopes remained undecorated, but inside the main colonnade, above the columns *in antis* of the pronaos and the opisthodomos, were 12 high-relief metopes depicting the canonical version of the labors of Herakles, another son of Zeus. The acroteria consisted of gilded bronze Victories by Paeonius and gilded bronze tripods. Dominating the interior of the temple was one of Phidias' masterpieces—one of the seven wonders of the ancient world—the chryselephantine statue of the seated Zeus, which was most likely completed several years after the building of the temple. We have a detailed description of the sculpture from the writings of Pausanias. Phidias' workshop, also described by Pausanius, was located outside the Altis. Terra-cotta molds and tools used in the construction of the chryselephantine statue of Zeus and a cup inscribed with Phidias' name were found during excavation. The workshop was later converted into a church.

Structures erected in later years include the Metroon, which is a small (67 by 34 feet) peripteral hexastyle temple. This Doric temple of the fourth century B.C. was dedicated to the "Mother of the Gods." The suggestion that during the Roman period the temple was reconsecrated to Augustus' family is substantiated by statues of Claudius and Titus found in its foundations.

A distinctive circular structure, the tholos erected by Philip II of Macedon (and most likely completed by Alexander) to commemorate his victory over Athens and Thebes in Chaironeia in 338 B.C., is located in the northwest corner of the Altis. This tholos, the Philippieion, consisted of two concentric colonnades on a base of three steps (nearly 46 feet in diameter) and a conical roof with marble tiles. The outer colonnade consisted of 18 Ionic columns, and the inner consisted of nine engaged columns with Corinthian capitals. Inside the circular structure, lighted by windows on each side of the doorway, was a group of five chryselephantine statues by Leochares: Philip, his parents, his wife Olympias and their son Alexander. Their carved

bases survive in fragmentary form. Other tholoi were constructed during the fourth century as well: those in the sanctuaries of Delphi, Epidauros and Olympia and the council house in Athens represent an important fourth-century development of Greek architecture.

By the end of the fourth century B.C., the sanctuary was essentially complete. Further development, mostly of the Hellenistic period, took place outside the Altis and includes another stoa, gymnasium, the palaestra, an open court with a Doric peristyle surrounded by rooms. A rather complicated courtyard building, the Leonidaion, was erected by Leonidas in the fourth century B.C., perhaps as a hostel for visitors; later it became the Roman governor's residence. It originally had an open court surrounded by a Doric colonnade. Outside was a continuous Ionic colonnade of 138 columns; most of the bases for these remain *in situ*. In general, the later structures reflect the desire to make the sanctuary more comfortable and convenient for its visitors. Furthermore, these elegantly constructed later additions outside the actual sanctuary emphasized the boundaries of the sacred precinct.

The restored fourth-century stadium is located northeast of the sanctuary and is entered through a vaulted passageway. It probably replaced the stadium constructed before the mid-fifth century, which in turn had replaced the archaic one that had been, in part, within the Altis boundaries. As the games became more professional, the stadium was moved outside the Altis, and the long stoa, the "Echo Colonnade," was built at the sanctuary's eastern boundary.

The Romans continued to alter and add to the sanctuary. For instance, the remains of the official residence of the priests, the Theokoleon, survives from three periods: the original Greek structure (ca. 350 B.C., consisting of eight rooms surrounding a central court), a later addition and a Roman addition. The Prytaneion, used as a formal dining room, dates from the early Greek period and was remodeled several times during the Roman era. Most noteworthy of the Roman additions was the Nymphaeum, a fountain house, erected by Herodes Atticus in the second century A.D. for piped water to replace earlier wells.

An edict of the Emperor Theodosius in 394 A.D. dictating the destruction of pagan shrines ended the role of Olympia as a thriving and active sanctuary.

—ANN THOMAS WILKINS

OSTIA ANTICA
Greece

Second century B.C.: Synagogue, House of Fortuna Annonaria. **Ca. 12 B.C.:** Theater, Forum of the Corporations. **Ca. 30-40 A.D.:** Granary of Hortensius. **Second century A.D.:** House of Diana, House of Lararium. **117-138 A.D.:** Barracks of the Vigiles, Baths of Neptune, House of the Triple Windows, House of the Charioteers. **Ca. 145-150 A.D.:** Horrea Epagathiana of Epaphroditiana. **Ca. 300 A. D.:** House of Cupid and Psyche.

Publications

BECATTI, G.: 'Case Ostiensi del Tardo Impero,' *Bollettino d'Arte* 33 (1948).
CALZA, R.: 'Topografia generale,' *Scavi di Ostia, I*, Rome, 1953.
CALZA, R., and NASH, E.: *Ostia*. Florence, 1959.
MEIGGS, R.: *Roman Ostia*. Oxford, 1960.

House of Diana, Ostia Antica: Greece, 2nd century B.C.

WATTS, CAROL MARTIN, and WATTS, DONALD J.: "Geometrical Ordering of the Garden Houses at Ostia." *Journal of the Society of Architectural Historians* 46 (September 1987): 265-276.

*

The architectural and urban history of Ostia Antica illustrates the development of a Roman city over 900 years, from the fourth century B.C. to the fifth century A.D. Its close political and economic ties to Rome make Ostia an archaeological mirror of the urban planning and architectural changes that transformed that city. While Pompeii gives a more vivid picture of Roman daily life, only Ostia documents the rapid changes in architectural and artistic styles occurring at the very time Pompeii ceased to exist.

Although tradition says that Ancus Marcius, the fourth king of Rome, founded Ostia at the mouth of the Tiber River, the earliest archaeological evidence of the colony dates to circa 349-338 B.C. The small colony was one of several established to guard the coastline and served also as an important naval base during the Punic Wars. The outline of the original colony (*castrum*) with its grid of streets can still be traced, and the tufa blocks of its defensive wall were incorporated into shops and buildings erected as Ostia developed into the port for Rome's growing population during the second century B.C. The colony's *decumanus maximus* became the main east-west street and led to the Via Ostiensis, the road to Rome; the *cardo maximus* went straight from the riverfront to the forum.

Though the growing population of republican Rome made increasingly greater demands on Ostia as a port city, its urban development was first systematically handled by Sulla (ca. 80 B.C.), who built new walls enclosing 160 acres (63.5 hectares), an area some 30 times as large as before. As the center of the city has not been fully excavated, it is difficult to determine whether this larger enclosure was preparation for a future expansion of the city or was accommodating an already-established larger population, though the haphazard street plan of the southeast quarter may reflect a period of unregulated urban growth. The wealthy peristyle and atrium houses built in that period indicate that the southwest quarter toward the sea was the most attractive residential area. The section of the city between the *decumanus maximus* and the river was public property, and its development with the building of warehouses, shipyards, temples and other structures was strictly regulated. Even though by the end of the republic the river harbor had become inadequate due to the silting up of the mouth of the Tiber River and the increasing volume of shipping traffic in ever larger and larger merchant vessels, Emperor Claudius (41-54 A.D.) was the first to construct a coastal harbor, some four kilometers north of Ostia.

More important to the city, however, were the urban developments in the reign of Claudius' successor, Nero (54-68 A.D.), which reflect developments in Rome after the great fire of A.D. 64. When he rebuilt Rome, Nero straightened its archaic crooked streets and lined them with beautiful porticoes. Likewise, Ostian streets had porticoes modeled on those built in Rome. The porticoes lining the northern *cardo maximus* from the river to the forum created a dignified ceremonial entrance to the heart of the city, but the other major axes, the southern *cardo maximus* and the eastern *decumanus maximus,* were also lined with porticoes to impress visitors coming from southern cities along the coast and from Rome.

Nero's new urban design, distinctly different from the older Italic urban architecture seen at Pompeii and Herculaneum, was used at Ostia in the late first and second centuries A.D., when Ostia experienced its greatest growth. The main building material in republican Ostia and Rome had been small, square facing blocks cut from tufa and laid in a diamond-shaped, network pattern (*opus reticulatum*). An alternative method of construction used a framework of sturdy beams and walls made of wattle and daub or rubble (*opus craticum*). To prevent another fiery catastrophe, Nero directed that apartment blocks should instead be built of fireproof materials, such as concrete vaulting and brick-faced concrete.

The need to rebuild Rome quickly also led to the increasing use of brick and the development of the rich clay fields in its vicinity. Ostian buildings dating to the later first century A.D. reflect the growing use of brick at Rome. Though at first the bricks were laid in conjunction with tufa (*opus mixtum*), by the early second century A.D. fine brickwork (*opus testaceum*) became dominant. The Horrea Epagathiana et Epaphroditiana, though primarily a warehouse, was beautifully built of tawny orange brick, with brick engaged columns and contrasting light pink molded brick capitals framing its entrance and supporting a brick pediment and cornice. In other buildings, rose or yellow bricks or squares of dark red tufa were employed for decorative contrast to tawny orange brick facades.

The new urban planning affected housing as well. Republican Ostia contained many houses of the Pompeian, atrium-peristyle type, which could expand only horizontally. The increase in working-class population required the more economical use of space that the multistory apartment block (*insula*) provided. A typical *insula,* such as the House of Diana or the House of the Charioteers, had its ground floors opening off the street, an arrangement common today in Italian cities. Above, in accordance with the legal restrictions on height (50 feet), rose several stories of apartments that provided reasonably spacious living quarters well lit by large windows with panes of mica or steatite. Usually, each apartment had one large room and several small rooms decorated with wall paintings and mosaic floors. Apartments looked out over the street or a courtyard that contained a water cistern for all residents. Apartment dwellers shared a

lavatory on each floor. The most luxurious *insula* was the complex of Hadrianic date called the Garden Houses. These two apartment houses were located in a large garden screened from the surrounding neighborhood to form a separate quarter for the wealthier citizens of Ostia. Each apartment had a long passage with large windows facing the garden; off this passage opened three rooms. At each end of the passage were two principal rooms, also lit by large windows. Each apartment on the upper floors had its own stairway. This floor plan was one of the most common in *insulae.*

The aqueduct that supplied Ostia with drinking water was constructed by Tiberius (14-37 A.D.) or by Caligula (37-41 A.D.). This water was brought to the capacious city cisterns by a lead pipe, 20 inches in diameter, which ran about three feet below the *decumanus maximus* and its pavement of close-fitting volcanic stones. Numerous fountains throughout the city provided inhabitants with water for drinking. In the larger apartment buildings and in the baths and other public buildings were rooms serving as public latrines; only a few houses of late date had private latrines. The public latrines had keyhole-shaped seats cut into long marble benches; under these seats, running water collected the human refuse and poured it into the sewer system lying below the lead water pipe. This sewer system ultimately emptied into the Tiber.

The two most extensive developments of Ostia, during the reign of Hadrian (117-138 A.D.), involved the area north of the *decumanus maximus* to the riverfront. The public property between the forum and the river was given dignity by the brick porticoes leading from the river to the immense new Capitolium built of brick and faced with marble. Its extremely tall podium raised it 10 Roman feet above the legal limit for apartment blocks and made it a monument noticeable from all parts of the city. East of the forum and theater, the Barracks of the Firefighters (*Vigiles*) was enlarged in response to the construction of more and ever-larger warehouses along the riverfront. The grand Baths of Neptune, with their marine mosaics, were obvious imitations of the imperial baths in Rome. The Piazza of the Corporations, part of an Augustan theater complex, became an even greater monument of civic pride when its porticoes were adorned with mosaics advertising some 60 shipping and exporting corporations (*collegia*) established in Ostia; that of the ivory traders from Sabratha in North Africa displays a mosaic elephant. The porticoes frame a large square with a

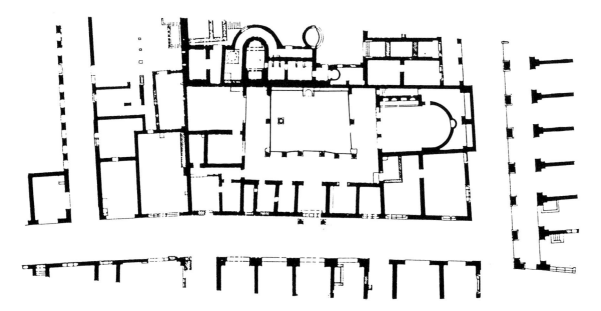

temple (to an unknown deity) in the center. Clearly, this complex—modeled on the portico Pompey built behind his theater in Rome, which contained shady walks and works of art—was an attempt to emulate the capital city.

Along with such municipal showplaces were many shops and warehouses. While earlier ones were single-story, those built after the second century had two or more stories to accommodate an increased demand for storage. Grain warehouses had floors raised so air could circulate to prevent spoilage; wine and oil were stored in huge jars sunk into the warehouse floors. Even such functional buildings were made attractive by brick columns, travertine pediments, bricks and stones of contrasting color, and floor mosaics such as were used in the Horrea Epagathiana. More than 800 shops have been identified, including two bakeries, several fish shops, many small restaurants and bars, and several fulling establishments with vats for dying and cleansing cloth. Such shops were also decorated with paintings of their wares (as at the Thermopolium in the Via di Diana) and floor mosaics (at the Shop of the Fishsellers).

The emperor Trajan (98-117 A.D.) had found it necessary to build a large port with an inner, hexagonal harbor and a canal connecting it to the Tiber upstream from Ostia, thus effectively bypassing Ostia. As more trade and population began to transfer to Portus in the mid to late second century A.D., under the Antonine emperors, urban expansion and building in Ostia began to slacken. Nevertheless, Ostia continued to receive marks of imperial favor, such as the Forum Baths built by Antoninus Pius (138-161 A.D.). These, the most luxurious of the 18 baths of Ostia, were lavishly decorated with marbles of various colors, which were imported from all over the empire. The plan of the Forum Baths is remarkable for the warm and hot rooms that were warmed by solar radiation during winter. The octagonal room, with its four immense windows, had no hot-air flues for subsidiary heat and functioned as a room heated entirely by solar radiation (*heliocaminus*).

By the third century A.D., the decline in population had enabled the rich of Rome to purchase apartment blocks in Ostia to rebuild or to remodel into single-family houses (*domus*). One common house plan was that of rooms around a central peristyle, as in the House of Fortuna Annonaria. Such houses had one principal room, richly decorated. In this house, that room was apse-shaped with a niche holding a statue of Ceres. Along one side was a marble, niched fountain, and the floors and walls of the room were also made of marble. This main room was entered through a triple arcade formed by marble pilasters with travertine capitals. Another common house plan, seen in the House of Cupid and Psyche, seems to have developed out of the layout of rooms in the Garden Houses. Three rooms opened off the side of a long colonnaded passage running the length of the house; at one end of the passage was the main room. All rooms were indirectly lit by light passing through the collonade from the area of the garden and its fountain (*nymphaeum*). As was typical of such houses, the rooms were lavishly adorned with marble walls and floors of marble blocks inlaid in geometric patterns (*opus sectile*) and were heated by hot air passing under the raised floor and rising through wall flues.

Like all port cities, Ostia was home to many religions, especially from the eastern Mediterranean. In addition to the Roman state cult centered on the Capitolium, the temples of several Roman cults have been excavated, such as that of Hercules, whose worship dates to the first century B.C. Fifteen Mithraea have been found, many decorated with mosaic symbols of their rites to the Eastern god Mithras. A shrine to the Egyptian god Serapis was located in the courtyard of one *insula* (Insula of Serapis). A large, open area by the Porta Laurentina became the precinct of the Great Goddess Cybele from Asia Minor;

near her large temple is a smaller shrine to Attis, her consort. Several Christian churches (*basilicae*) have been identified, and in a Christian hall by the Porta Marina a portrait of a bearded, haloed Christ was placed in a handsome wall decorated with slabs of marble inlaid in geometric designs. Outside of the city, along the shore, the Jewish community erected in the first century A.D. the first synagogue in Europe. It remained in use into the fourth century.

In 314 A.D. Constantine deprived Ostia of its rank as a *municipium* and transferred its bishopric to Portus. Nonetheless, Ostia continued as a residential town for the rich until the end of the century, when civic authorities began to neglect maintenance of the river embankments, aqueduct and drainage, and so permitted the spread of malaria and depopulation of the city. Disease and attacks by pirates led to the virtual abandonment of Ostia by the ninth century. During the Middle Ages, Ostia was quarried for building materials and lime, and during the Renaissance for art treasures. Systematic excavation of the site began in the 19th century. The present excavated area is 33 hectares, amounting to about half the city area.

—JUDITH LYNN SEBESTA

PAESTUM (POSEIDONIA)
Greek/Sicily

700-650 B.C.: Settlement established. **Sixth century B.C.:** Basilica temple constructed. **Sixth-Fifth century B.C.:** City designed. **Fifth century B.C.:** Fortifications constructed. **500 B.C.:** Sele River shrine constructed. **500 B.C.:** Temple of Ceres constructed. **450 B.C.:** Temple of Neptune constructed.

Publications

DINSMOOR, WILLIAM BELL: *The Architecture of Ancient Greece.* New York, 1975.
DUMONT, G.-P.-M.: *Les vues, plans, coupes, élévations de trois temples antiques faisant partie de l'ancienne ville de Paestum.* Paris, 1764.
PICKERING, HENRY: *The Ruins of Paestum.* Salem, Massachusetts, 1822.

*

The Greek colonial city of Poseidonia offers one of the finest demonstrations of regularized urban planning in antiquity as well as some of the best and most complete peristyle temples from the Archaic and Early Classical periods. One of a number of colonies founded along the coast of southern Italy, in what is known as Magna Graecia, Poseidonia was established in about 700-650 B.C. by Doric settlers emigrating from the Achaean-dominated city of Sybaris on the Ionian Sea. The site selected for their colony, on the Gulf of Salerno, was especially attractive because it was situated on top of a limestone shelf that offered both stability during seismic tremors and ready building stone. The perimeter of this limestone shelf determined the configuration of Poseidonia.

The wealth of the Greek colony was based upon the rich agricultural resources of the region, and the settlement enjoyed great prosperity throughout the Archaic and Early Classical periods. By the end of the fifth century, however, the indigenous Lucanian peoples rose against the Greek communities of the

Temple of Neptune: Paestum, Greek/Sicily, 450 B.C.

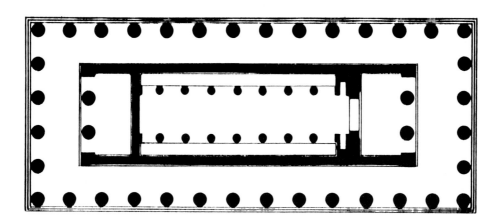

region, and Poseidonia was overrun in about 410 B.C. The Lucanians enjoyed dominance over Poseidonia, which they renamed Paiston, until 332 B.C., when their rule was interrupted by Alexander of Molossia, the king of Epirus and a nephew of Alexander the Great. Alexander's army of federated Italian Greeks defeated the Lucanians at Paiston, but the Lucanians regained the city at the death of Alexander in 326 B.C. Once reestablished, Lucanian rule lasted until 273, when the region came under Roman control. Paiston-Poseidonia received an influx of Latin settlers, assumed the character of a military colony and was once again renamed, this time Paestum.

Much rebuilding took place as Paestum took on the aspect of a Roman town, complete with new prostyle temples, communal baths, amphitheater, and a new forum and civic buildings. By the early years of the first century A.D., however, a general decline in population set in, accelerated by malarial disease. Only a small community remained by the Early Christian era to convert the ancient Athenaion (''Temple of Ceres'') into a church and cluster a little hamlet about that building. Fear of Saracen raiders in the ninth century forced the removal of what remained of Paestum's residents into the mountains, where they founded the town of Capaccio Vecchio.

Paestum itself remained deserted, overgrown and overlooked until its rediscovery in the mid-18th century. The first archaeological surveys were made at that time, and excavations have continued. The site today is a national archaeological monument with a museum building constructed in 1952 in a severely modernist style after earlier designs by Marcello De Vita and Genio Civile, with more recent additions in 1966 by De Felice and in 1970 by De Francisci.

The fifth-century B.C. fortifications surrounding the ancient Poseidonia follow the line of the underlying limestone shelf and may represent a rebuilding of earlier defenses of the sixth century. The circuit of walls measures 4,750 meters and is well preserved along its entire length, thus providing an unusually complete picture of Greek fortification techniques, although considerably amended by both Lucanians and Romans. The walls range in average thickness from five to seven meters and were surrounded by a deep moat. The remains of 32 towers may be counted along the cincture, either square or round, with one pentagonal example. Four main gates flanked by towers, and in two cases with internal vestibules, were situated according to the cardinal points, and a number of postern gates were placed at strategic positions. Bridges over the moat at the north and

west entrances are well preserved; the bastion salient wall of the west (sea) gate is of particular interest, as is the arched Lucanian entryway of the east gate.

Poseidonia-Paestum presents an extraordinary opportunity to study the layout of an ancient city. It figures prominently in the history of the orthogonal system in city planning that developed simultaneously throughout the Mediterranean world by Greeks, Etruscans and Carthaginians. In general, these deliberate urbanscapes featured widely spaced and parallel avenues intersected at right angles by more numerous and closely spaced side streets. The resulting grid divided up the community into a series of long residential blocks, often (as at Poseidonia) with a 1:9 ratio. Specially designated areas, generally centrally located, were reserved for religious and civic purposes.

Such a situation is found in ancient Poseidonia, one of the most intact examples of this sort of disciplined urban planning. At Poseidonia, there were three broad east-west thoroughfares, the central one running between two of the principal gates to the city. More than 30 north-south streets crossed these avenues, the central one of which ran between the two other gates and paralleled the eastern border of the central religious and civic precinct, serving as sort of a ''Sacred Way.'' Thus a suggestion of the later Latin system of the *cardo* and *decumanus* appears to have been present.

Stretching right through Poseidonia from the northern to the southern wall was a broad strip of public land devoted to temples, a marketplace (agora) and communal buildings and monuments. Lacking the elevation of an acropolis, Poseidonia's center was divided into two sacred zones (*temenoi*) surrounded by precinct walls and separated by the agora.

Despite the fact that Greek Poseidonia underwent a significant Roman occupation, the grid plan (quite discernible in aerial photos) can be dated to the late sixth or early fifth century B.C. Whether or not this orderly design represents a revision of an older city plan or simply is evidence of a continued population growth and the necessity of a more orderly development of the urban spaces is unclear. That the present grid may be a reorganization of an older one is suggested by the line of the principal north-south street, which makes a dog-leg detour at one point to reach the northern gate in the fifth-century city wall, and by the fact that the earlier temples along its route are displaced some two degrees out of alignment with the streets.

Aside from its orthogonal plan, Poseidonia's most significant architectural statement lies in the three great Doric temples

Temple of Ceres: Paestum, Greek/Sicily, 500 B.C.

ranged along the public strip, two in the southern sanctuary, popularly known as the "Basilica" and the "Temple of Neptune," and one, in the northern precinct, called the "Temple of Ceres." They are among the best preserved in the Greek world. The earliest of these, the "Basilica," was probably dedicated to Hera. Erected hard by the southern wall, this temple dates to the mid-sixth century and measures nine by 18 columns or 24.5 by 54.3 meters. Unfortunately, this temple has lost its pediments and much of the original entablature. The archaic Doric columns of the peristyle have pronounced entasis, and their anthemion-decorated capitals are of the Achaean variety. Curiously, another line of seven columns ran down the middle of the cella interior. Two smaller temples with frontal columns were located to the north and south of the Basilica and probably served as shrines or chapels; both would seem to date from the early fifth century.

The best-preserved and largest of Poseidonia's temples is the Temple of Neptune, also, it would seem, dedicated to the goddess Hera. Datable to about 450 B.C., this temple measures 24.3 by 59.9 meters with six columns, 8.8 meters tall, across the front and 14 along the sides. That many of the celebrated optical and mathematical refinements of the Parthenon were not unique to that building is made clear in the design of the Temple of Neptune, where horizontal curvature, corner inclination and adjusted alignments of the members also are present. The beauty of this building rested solely upon its architectural niceties, for the metopes of the frieze were left unsculpted and the pediments were bare. The interior cella, set between a vestibule and treasury, both *in antis,* was divided into three aisles by rows of superimposed columns. Adjacent to the northeastern corner of the Temple of Neptune stood another small "chapel," probably

constructed in the late fifth or early fourth century. Associated with both the Basilica and the Temple of Neptune were a number of outdoor altars, votive deposits, smaller temple buildings, purification pools and ceremonial platforms.

Separating the southern sanctuary, dedicated to Hera, from the northern precinct, dedicated to Athena, was an area primarily devoted to civic and commercial functions. This space, organized on an east-west axis, was rebuilt as a forum by the Romans and contains the foundations of buildings which once served them as a curia, baths, nearby gymnasium and amphitheater, and other structures (some of Greek or Lucanian origin), many built with salvaged materials from the earlier Greek agora. Of note is the Italic prostyle temple, which probably served as the *Capitolium* of the new Roman city of Paestum.

The northern sanctuary centered on the so-called Temple of Ceres, now known to have actually been an Athenaion dedicated, circa 500 B.C., to the goddess Athena. This, too, was a Doric temple but utilized Ionic columns in the pronaos to the cella. The peristyle of six by 13 columns (32.9 by 14.5 meters) supported an architrave and frieze with sculpted metopes. The remains of an older and much smaller temple have been found near the southern side of the Temple of Ceres. Also part of this northern *temenos* was a curious subterranean, tomb-like, rectangular shrine. This building, filled with votive deposits of the late sixth century B.C., may have functioned as an honorific burial for Poseidonia's founder or as a chapel dedicated to underworld deities. It is architecturally significant for the "chinese roof" technique used in its gables.

Leading out of the northern gate was a road stretching past a necropolis—which contained a number of gable-roofed tombs constructed of stone slabs (several covered with frescoed scenes)

Columns of the agora with the Turkish Castle in the background: Palmyra, Roman/Syria, 1st century

of the mid-fifth century and later Lucanian period—to an extensive sanctuary at the mouth of the Sele River dedicated to the worship of Hera Argive. Although the establishment of this shrine may antedate the construction of Poseidonia, its principal temple (only foundations survive) was constructed in about 500 B.C.

—CHARLES R. MACK

PALMYRA
Roman/Syria

First century A.D.: Sanctuary of Bel porticoes constructed. **Second century A.D.:** Agora constructed. **Second century A.D.:** Sanctuary of Bel single-aisle portico constructed. **Second century A.D.:** Colonnade streets constructed.

Publications

CALLEDGE, M. A. R.: *The Art of Palmyra*. Boulder, CO. 1976.
WIEGAND, T. (ed.): *Palmyra: Ergebnisse der Expeditionen von 1902 und 1917*. 2 vols. Berlin, 1932.
WOOD, ROBERT: *The Ruins of Palmyra and Balbec*. London, 1827.

Palmyra (biblical Tadmor) was situated at an oasis on the border of a barren steppe and a stony, inhospitable desert midway between the Euphrates to the east and the ports of the Mediterranean to the west. It was a caravan city that lay on the eastern fringe of the Roman world and the western border of the Parthian Empire. From the first century B.C. it grew from a settlement to a city of wealth and importance during Roman times. By carefully policing its trade routes, Palmyra became a key center for the exchange of merchandise in the Roman East. Goods from the Orient were exchanged for those of the West; the city grew rich by levying tariffs on all of it.

During the anarchy within the Roman Empire in the third century A.D., Palmyra gained control of the territories involved with the caravan trade and, for a brief time, established a caravan empire (under Odenath and his queen, Zenobia). Its control stretched from Egypt in the south to southern Anatolia in the north. Roman authority was reestablished by Aurelian and Diocletian. Shortly after that, the city went into a slow, steady decline as the caravan trade found alternate routes.

Typical of most Roman cities in the eastern empire, the main streets of Palmyra were monumentalized by covered porticoes leading from the city gates on the south and southwest to the main thoroughfare of the city; thus they appear to prolong and connect the city with the caravan routes beyond. In addition to being simply passages, they impart a sense of architectural place and moment. Characteristic of the Roman East, many or most of the shafts of the columns had consoles that carried honorary statues of Palmyrene citizens, which added to the sumptuous effect and heightened the sense of occasion as one was led to the various religious, civic and commercial centers.

The principal thoroughfare divides the city from the northwest to the southeast. This central avenue, paved in stone, extended across much of the city. It was 1,100 meters long and 11 meters wide. Porticoes on each side of this central avenue were six meters deep. These porticoes provided convenient shaded passage and easy access to shops and trading stations.

A shift in the axis of the street in two places divides the avenue into three segments, usually referred to as West Colonnade Street, Middle Colonnade Street and East Colonnade Street. At one point the shift in axis is cleverly concealed by an imposing triple archway designed as a *trapezium.* This enables the facades of the archway to be at right angles to both axes of the street. The other change in the direction of the central avenue occurs at an intersection with another thoroughfare. At this intersection, the avenue and the colonnades curve out to form an oval-shaped space in the middle of which the city planners placed a tetrapylon, which effectively masked this change in axis. These were impressive urban landmarks, which punctuated the grand progress through the city. They delimit the middle section of the avenue to the east and west. Between the tetrapylon and the triple archway, the columnar screen of the north portico of Middle Colonnade Street is broken in two places by the projecting columns of an impressive nymphaeum and the columns of the projecting porch of the Baths of Diocletian. These provided climactic accents not only in that they interrupted the alignment of the columns of the portico, but also because of their greater height and difference in ornamentation, color and texture.

The major civic monuments were located to the south of Middle Colonnade Street—the theater, the senate building, the agora and the tariff court. The design of the theater was typical for Roman theaters throughout the Mediterranean. The *scaenae frons* received typical Roman baroque treatment whereby projecting spur walls and *ressauts* with columns were alternated with niches and *aediculae.* The agora was a square peristyle court built in the second century A.D. Here too, the shafts of the columns carried consoles carrying statues of dignitaries. Those on the north columns were city officials; on the south, caravan leaders; on the east (facing the senate), senators; and on the west, military commanders. Contiguous with and connected to the agora on the east was a large courtyard for levying tariffs.

From the monumental triple archway, East Colonnade Street leads to the Sanctuary of Bel, the principal monument in this part of the city. The *temenos* is a large quadrangular enclosure which was entered through an impressive propylaeum. Originally, only the temple (dedicated in 32 A.D.) and altars stood within the enclosure. By the end of the first century A.D., double-aisle porticoes were constructed on the north, south and east sides of this courtyard. In the second century A.D., a much taller single-aisle portico was added on its western side, and an impressive entranceway (propylaeum) was added on the west as well. The propylaeum was designed with a monumental flight of steps (35 meters wide) which led up to an octastyle porch richly adorned with sculpted relief. The entrance proper was of typical Roman design with a very large central doorway with two flanking smaller doorways.

The Temple of Bel, which stands within the enclosure, is a remarkable synthesis of Hellenistic, Roman and Near Eastern architecture. While the architecture is expressed in the classical idiom, the ideas reflect very different religious functions. Typically Hellenistic, it was originally a rectangular peristyle on a raised platform which was stepped on all sides. While it has typical triangular pediments on either short end, the temple did not have a pitched roof. Instead, there was a flat terrace reached by staircases from the cella. Above the classical cornice, a

Columns of the Temple of Bel: Palmyra, Roman/Syria, 1st century

parapet of "Assyrian" (crowstep) merlons has been conjecturally restored. If they did exist here, they would stem, along with the flat-terraced roof, from traditional Near Eastern architecture. The rich acanthus foliations of the Corinthian capitals of the peristyle were of bronze and were attached to the stone bells which were roughly worked to receive them.

In contrast to classical temples, the approach is not to one of the short ends. In this case, a portal was framed in between two columns on one of the long sides of the *peristasis.* This entrance and a projecting flight of steps in front were placed off axis. This framed portal was aligned with the doorway of the cella. The cella is a type with a long history in the ancient Near East. Typically, it is a long rectangular chamber with an entrance on one of the long sides with the focus at one of the short ends. This design of a bent-axis approach to the focus is found here in the Temple of Bel. In this case, however, there is a raised sanctuary (*adyton*) at either short end. The *adyton* on the northern end was a raised recess flanked by *aediculae* on either side. The recess held the images of Bel, Iarhibal and Aglibal—the sacred triad. To the south, the raised chamber reached by a flight of steps is thought to have housed a statue of Bel, which was carried in procession during sacred festivals.

The terrain rises as one moves from the tetrapylon to the west end of the central avenue. The street becomes gradually stepped and the colonnades become shorter to provide for a continuous entablature. The street is terminated by a gate in the form of a columnar screen, which provides a view of a mausoleum at a higher level just beyond. This tomb probably was incorporated into the city by the construction of a later city wall. It is one of the three tomb types to be found at Palmyra. It is in the form of a prostyle classical temple with a pedimental porch and a chamber behind. In this so-called "Funerary Temple" there was a two-story baldachino in the center of the room, below which a sarcophagus of the tomb founder was placed. The side walls carried pilasters between which vertical rows of *loculi* were built. These were closed off by stone slabs carved in relief with portraits of the deceased.

All of the other tombs at Palmyra are extramural and are located to the west and southwest of the city. The tower-tomb, another type common to Palmyra, originated in Asia and spread throughout the Roman Empire. At Palmyra, some rose to a height of five stories and held up to 400 skeletons. At each landing of their staircases were *loculi* closed by slabs with sculpted portraits of the deceased.

The third type of tomb was the hypogeum, usually in the shape of an inverted T-shaped hall in whose walls were carved *cubicula*. The walls of these *cubicula* were, in turn, carved with *loculi*. This subterranean rock-cut type was reached by a large flight of stairs from above. The tombs were lavishly decorated with relief and received extensive fresco decorations, which have proved invaluable for the study of art in the Roman East.

—CHARLES W. WHITE

PERGAMON
Asia Minor

Second century B.C.: Theater constructed. **Second century B.C.:** Great Altar of Zeus constructed. **Second century B.C.:** Main gate constructed. **Second century B.C.:** Stoa of Athena constructed.

Publications

Altertümer von Pergamon. 11 vols. Berlin, 1912-68.
BOEHRINGER, E.: *Pergamon, in Neue deutsche Ausgrabungen im Mittelmeergebiet und im Vorderen Orient*. Berlin, 1959.
DEUBNER, O.: *Das Asklepieion von Pergamon*. Berlin, 1938.
DINSMOOR, WILLIAM BELL: *The Architecture of Ancient Greece*. New York, 1975.
HANSEN, E. V.: *The Attalids of Pergamon*. Ithaca, 1971.
ZIEGENAUS, O.: "Die Ausgrabungen zu Pergamon in Asklepieion." *Archäologischer Anzeiger* (1970).

*

Pergamon was one of the first capital cities in the modern sense of the word, that is, a large conglomerate serving simultaneously as the political, administrative, economic and cultural center of a relatively extensive state. In earlier times, the small city-states of classical Greece were nearly co-extensive with the areas of their jurisdiction, while large cities of the empire, from Memphis to Susa, were more like overgrown temple-palaces. Although from the third century B.C. onward, Alexandria was undoubtedly Ptolemaic Egypt's capital, it was so far from the center, so different and separate from the rest of the country, that it was called "Alexandria on the edge of Egypt" (*Alexandria ad Aegyptum*). Located in northwestern Asia Minor, Pergamon was in the very heart of the Greek Hellenistic kingdoms. These facts notwithstanding, Pergamon was even more important for its development, under the Attalid kings, of an original model of urban planning.

Most likely occupied since the beginning of the first millennium B.C., the site is in no way exceptional: there is an acropolis,

Great Altar: Pergamon, Asia Minor, 2nd century B.C.

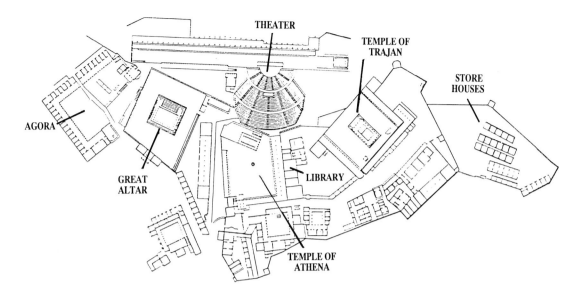

large enough to serve as a place of refuge, dominating a vast plain well supplied with water, which could support a large population, and would allow the expansion of the city beyond the fortifications. The coast and port are too distant (about 30 kilometers) to have played an important part in the development of the urban conglomerate.

Pergamon's real and symbolic dominance over the plain was marked very early on by the foundation of a sanctuary, situated a little over a kilometer from the city and near a spring alleged to have healing powers. In the fourth century B.C. it was consecrated to the healer god Asklepios. A "sacred way" lined with monuments connects this Asklepieion to the city. Part of it was lined with colonnaded porticoes, as was common in Asia Minor, and another part was covered with a vault supported by regularly spaced pillars. This "covered way" (*via tecta*), which was an exclusively pedestrian walkway, was laid out in the second century A.D. parallel to the paved road open to chariots. Constructed in order to shelter pilgrims on their way to the sanctuary, it alone testifies to a sophisticated lifestyle.

The architecture of the Asklepieion at the height of its development under the reign of the emperor Hadrian represents an odd combination of religious, thermal and cultural elements, somewhat like a mixture of Lourdes and Vichy. In the center of a large courtyard (120 by 90 meters), the original sacred spring was surrounded by an ensemble of small religious buildings and shelters for pilgrims. It could also be reached by a vaulted underground passage (*cryptoporticus*), 70 meters long, whose entrance was located in the southwest corner of the courtyard, opposite a partly subterranean rotunda. The rotunda had a central cupola flanked by six apses. No inscription specifies its function, and archaeologists remain uncertain about the purpose of this building. Earlier it was thought to be of a religious nature and was called "temple of Telesphore" after a healing spirit associated with Asklepios. It is now thought (and this is the opinion of present director of excavations, W. Radt) that it was a "therapy building" serving purely medical purposes. The six apses constitute six "treatment units" reserved for cure-takers. Certainly the building's structure is not obviously that of a temple. However, one may wonder if the distinction is meaningful in a situation where every cure is to be credited to divine benevolence, and where medical practice cannot be efficacious unless it is religious practice at the same time.

The influence of Roman architecture, already perceptible

in this elaborate rotunda, was even more pronounced in the neighboring building, a temple consecrated to Zeus Asklepios the Savior. It is, in fact, a scale model of the Roman Pantheon. Its construction was financed by a Roman citizen, as was a library nearby. In the library another function of the Asklepieion—as a cultural center—becomes apparent. Neither the library, nor, above all, a covered theater (*odeion*) with 3,500 seats, located in the northeast corner of the courtyard, could have been reserved exclusively for the use of patients. Concerts, lectures and a variety of performances would have turned the "season" into a veritable festival. The works of the Roman rhetor Aelius Aristidus, a vignette writer of the second century A.D., recreate the atmosphere, both sacred and secular, medical and cultural, which parallels the simultaneously multiform and unified architecture.

The acropolis proper was surrounded by a circular boulevard. The city developed inside the enclosure, which was gradually enlarged as the city expanded from the third century B.C. to the third century A.D. During the Byzantine era, from the fourth to 12th century A.D., the enclosure contracted again little by little. The construction of houses and public monuments on the steep slope of the acropolis follows neither geometrical logic, nor abstract theory. Colonial models of urban planning, developed by Hippodamos of Miletus and in slightly different manner by Plato in his *Laws*, imposed an orthogonal grid (Hippodamos) or circular plan (Plato) on the terrain, regardless of its configuration and at the risk of ignoring problems of viability—as was the case with Priene, where all north-south streets were stairways of necessity. Planning at Pergamon, in contrast, obeys only the logic of a monumental aesthetics. Separated by a winding road, the successive terraces spread out following the contour of the slopes in such a manner as to highlight the monuments erected to the glory of gods and kings. Pergamon's architects exploited both the horizontal and vertical aspects of the terrain.

The northern sector of the acropolis is exemplary in this regard. The *koilon* of the theater, built on a very steep slope of the hillside, is highlighted at the level of the orchestra by a long and narrow platform (250 meters long by 23 meters wide) punctuated at one end by a temple built against the cliff. Above the upper curve of the *koilon*, cult buildings follow one another on a series of terraces laid out in tiers from the summit down to form a concentric arc. Looking south and down, one sees first the Temple of Trajan, which was recently restored by the German Archaeological Institute under the direction of architect

Klaus Nohlen. Completed some time around 125 A.D., it stands in the middle of a courtyard surrounded by porticoes. The northern portico, behind the temple, was a story taller and thus served as a backdrop. The terrace development required significant support: the exterior terrace wall is 23 meters high. The temple of Athena, also set in a courtyard, was situated below the Trajaneum and next to the library, the most important in the ancient world (with the exception of Alexandria) and containing 200,000 volumes. Further down was a terrace housing the ''Great Altar'' consecrated to Zeus; further south and in a final position, closing the semicircle and joining in horizontal layout the extremity of the lower terrace of the theater, was a market lined with porticoes. A little to the side of this extraordinary ensemble, arsenals and, more importantly, royal residences occupied the remaining area of the upper terrace in a more modest manner.

The general impression is of something both disparate and unified. Disparity becomes apparent when one refers to details of style and chronology: almost four centuries separate the completion of the Athena sanctuary from the construction of the temple of Trajan. However, the ideological unity is indisputable. The emperor-god, master of the universe, dominates the city as he dominates the world. Although coming to an end in 133 B.C., the dynasty of the Attalids, who made Pergamon into a capital and finally succeeded in integrating it with the *Pax romana*, keeps its presence alive in the memories of its victories over the Celts, who had invaded and ravaged Asia Minor in the third and second centuries B.C. Athena was in fact venerated as Nikephoros, the bearer of victory, and the temple terrace was covered with the ex-votos celebrating the defeat of the barbarians.

The allegorical glorification of the dynasty also comes across in the Great Altar, probably completed around 150 B.C. The Great Altar is in all respects an exceptional monument. In the first place, it constitutes an independent entity: its size and position prevent an association with the Athena temple: a difference of 25 meters in height separates the two. The Great Altar is also exceptional for its monumentality: the whole, measuring 36 meters in length, 34 meters in width and 10 meters in height, consists of a large portico in the shape of a letter *pi*, erected on a six-meter-high base, that surrounds the platform on top of which the sacrificial altar itself is positioned. The monument is above all famous for the lavish wealth of its sculpture: a frieze, measuring 120 meters in total length and 2.3 meters in height, ran around the entire length of the exterior. Excavated between 1871 and 1886 by the engineer-archaeologist Karl Humann and housed today in the Pergamon Museum in Berlin, it celebrates the victory of the gods of Olympus over the chthonic Giants in a baroque style that evokes the successors of Michelangelo. This founding story of Greek mythology (one encounters it as early as the beginning of the seventh century B.C. in the works of the poet Hesiod) serves as an allegorical representation of the victory of the kings of Pergamon over the Celts. A second frieze, which is both shorter and smaller and in a more reserved style, portrays the myth of Telephus, the city's founding hero. The iconographic program thus associates the gods, the city and its rulers. It is expressed through a unique architectural program, which impressed the Ancients powerfully enough to reckon the Altar of Pergamon among the World Wonders.

This area of the Pergamon acropolis thus fuses the images and symbols of earthly power with those of the divine power

Theater: Pergamon, Asia Minor, 2nd century B.C.

legitimizing it, effecting the fusion with a density of architectural and iconographic expression unparalleled in the Greek world except by Athenian Acropolis of Athens. Given this effect, there was no need for any ostentatious palace to assert the actual power of the Attalid dynasts: it was sufficient to evoke the gods who were their guarantors. Contenting themselves with rich but not extravagant residences, the rulers of Pergamon escaped accusations of excess, the *hybris* typical of tyrants and liable to provoke the wrath of gods. In this way they implicitly associated themselves with the ideological tradition of the classical city-states, whose heirs they claimed to be.

Among numerous other sanctuaries of Pergamon, the one consecrated to the Egyptian divinities Serapis, Isis and Harpocrates, situated in the lower city, deserves mention for the originality of its architecture. Erected in the second century A.D., it is an enormous complex (270 meters by 100 meters) with a huge courtyard in front of a building of worship consisting of three bodies measuring 70 by 100 meters and 20 meters in height. Its walls, whose preservation is due to the fact that the temple was converted to a Christian church in the fifth century A.D., are constructed of baked brick clad with polychrome marble facing at the time of completion. This technique was quite unusual in Asia Minor, and has given rise to speculation that masons familiar with these materials were expressly invited from Rome. The spacious courtyard was laid out over the bed of the river Selinus, the main river in Pergamon, which had been canalized by making it pass through two vaulted tunnels. It is possible that this artistic achievement did not serve only a hydraulic purpose: the course of the Selinus may well have had a symbolic meaning similar to that of the Nile, inseparable companion of the Egyptian gods.

Besides sanctuaries and the theaters affiliated with them, the most typical buildings of a Hellenistic city are those places reserved for the athletic exercises of children and adults: gymnasiums, palaestras and stadiums. Athletic training and competitions are an essential component of Greek culture (*paideia*). In barbaric countries, sports provided a means of confirming a Greek identity. In Pergamon the largest gymnasiums in the Hellenistic world were constructed, and their number continued to increase throughout the Roman era: there were seven of them in the times of the emperor Hadrian. Their organization followed the model of a hierarchical society divided into different age groups. Consequently, the largest gymnasium in Pergamon had a three-fold structure, spread out over three terraces: the top one was reserved for men of military age (*neoi*), the middle one for those receiving their first military training (*ephebi*), and the lowest one for children (*paides*). Each of these separate structures consisted of training tracks, either covered or open, and halls serving various purposes opening onto huge courtyards with porticoes. Construction of the terraces required significant underground work and supports. For this reason, an underground gallery 212 meters long, seven meters wide and four meters high ran under the top of the terrace. The complex was supplemented in Roman times by the thermal baths.

All of this, in addition to the residential buildings, required a significant supply of water. To make matters worse, there was no natural water source inside the enclosure. Almost every house had a cistern, with an average volume of 60 cubic meters, for private use. Regulations provided for periodical inspections, checking for watertightness, and prescribed penalties in case of pollution. However, every city worthy of the name owed itself the construction of aqueducts to supply fountains and public buildings. The works executed by the Attalids and their successors are altogether remarkable. One aqueduct 42 kilometers long carries water to the city from the mountain, from an altitude of 1930 meters. The aqueduct first uses the force of

gravity, then it carries water under pressure in pipes 25 centimeters in external diameter and six to eight centimeters thick, ensuring a flow of 45 liters a second. A water tower with a device preventing overflow was constructed at the top of the acropolis, which ensured regular distribution across the entire city, for a population estimated at 40,000 in the second century B.C. The population increased considerably in the Roman era, reaching about 160,000 in the second century A.D. The number of aqueducts increased proportionally. One of them was 85 kilometers long and crossed a valley by means of a bridge, 500 meters long and 40 meters high. The total flow of water has been calculated to be as high as 26,000 cubic meters a day, to which the volume of the private cisterns is to be added.

Such a water supply seems sufficient to ensure a reasonable quality of life for the inhabitants of Pergamon. However, the residential areas have been less extensively researched than the public monuments (less so, for instance, than in Delos or Priene), so that generalizations cannot be made. Nevertheless, the general impression remains that Pergamon's city plan, whose apparent freedom cannot hide its deliberate character, could and should have been quite efficient. In identifying their own cause with that of Greek civilization, as did many other Hellenistic kings, the Attalids of Pergamon managed to translate their ideology into the development of a powerful and prosperous metropolis, whose proud claim was to be a new Athens in the Orient.

—CHRISTIAN LE ROY
Translated from the French by Alla Melamed

POMPEII
Pompeii, Italy

4th century B.C.: House of the Surgeon built. **3rd century B.C.:** House of the Sallust built. **150 B.C.:** House of the Pansa built. **c. 150-120 B.C.:** Forum built. **120 B.C.:** Stabian Baths built. **2nd century B.C.:** House of the Menander, House of the Vetti, House of the Silver Wedding, and House of the Faun built. **c. 80 B.C.:** Amphitheater built. **c. 80-75 B.C.:** Odeum built. **1st century B.C.:** Caldarium, Forum Baths, House of the Labyrinth, House of Venus built. **1st century A.D.:** Large Theater, Eumachia Building built. **62-79 A.D.:** Villa of Julia Felix, House of Marcus Loreius Tiburtinus built. **63-79 A.D.:** Central Baths built. **79 A.D.:** Town destroyed by volcanic eruption.

Publications

BRION, M.: *Pompeii and Herculaneum.* New York, 1960.
CURTIUS, L.: *Die Wandmalerei Pompeiis.* Leipzig, 1929.
DYER, T. H.: *Pompeii: The History, Buildings and Antiquities.* London, 1891.
JASHEMSKI, WILHELMINA M. F.: *The Gardens of Pompeii, Herculaneum and the Villas Destroyed by Vesuvius.* New York, 1979.
KRAUS, T., and VON MATT, L.: *Pompeii and Herculaneum.* New York, 1973.

Pompeii, Italy

MAIURI, A.: *Pompeii*. Naples, 1964.

MAIURI, A.: *La Villa dei Misteri*. Rome, 1947.

MAU, AUGUST: *Pompeii: Its Life and Art*. London, 1904.

MAZOIS, F.: *Les ruines de Pompeii*. 4 vols. Paris, 1812-38.

PLOMMER, H.: *Vitruvius and Later Roman Building Manuals*. Cambridge, 1973.

RICHARDSON, L.: *Pompeii: An Architectural History*. Baltimore and London, 1988.

SPINAZZOLA, V.: *Pompei alla luce degli scavi di Via dell'Abbondanza*. Rome, 1953.

WARD-PERKINS, J. B., and CLARIDGE, A.: *Pompeii A.D. 79*. New York, 1978.

*

Pompeii is famous for its preservation, as a showcase of Roman architecture almost miraculously preserved by a blanket of volcanic ash. As such, it justly deserves attention, but is the town more than an archaeological freak? Is it more than a place

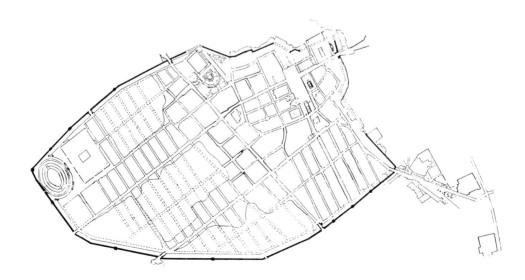

where, thanks to the vagaries of preservation, Roman life comes vividly alive for multitudes of tourists? The answer is assuredly yes. Even if Vesuvius had not erupted in 79 A.D.—entombing the Roman towns of Pompeii, Herculaneum and Stabiae—Pompeii would still be remembered as a flourishing commercial center, a thriving port and a leading city in one of the richest areas, artistically and culturally, of the Roman empire. It is this element that makes Pompeii important historically, archaeologically and architecturally. Pompeii is not just another buried city; it is a fine example of a mid-sized Roman town (with a population around 20,000) with the amenities, town planning, and private and public architecture that such a city embodies.

The excavations of the site have revealed a city that developed over eight centuries from a small town, built along Greek lines with separate acropolis and habitation area, to a fully realized Roman city with new, orthogonally planned sections, a monumentalized forum area and extensive public buildings (commercial, civic and religious). The city's development and growth through succeeding stages provides vital evidence for town planning and typifies the increasing tendency toward rational planning and monumentality in the Hellenistic and Roman periods. In addition, some of Pompeii's public buildings are either the best-preserved examples or the earliest buildings of their type. The basilica, because of its preservation (although partially restored), provides a vivid impression of a longitudinally aligned early Roman basilica. The amphitheater, built in the southeastern (newer) part of town around 80 B.C., is the earliest known Roman amphitheater; it is clearly an experimental building (with exterior ramps and little awareness of the problems of crowd control) but provides evidence for the experimentation that eventually led to larger, more sophisticated structures such as the Flavian amphitheater in Rome.

Pompeii, because of its location in an area in close proximity to the great cultural centers of Magna Graecia, and because of its commercial connections as an important port, provides early evidence for types of buildings not found in Rome until a later date, or not preserved in Rome at all. The former would include the two theaters at Pompeii, the larger of which is Hellenistic in date, Greek in plan, and earlier than any of the theaters in Rome. The smaller theater, an odeum or covered music hall, is one of the finest examples of its type. The exquisite and idiosyncratic Temple of Isis shows the increasing importance of syncretic cults in the first century A.D., as well as the mutability of Roman temple forms when adapted to the needs of new religions. Three public bath complexes, richly stuccoed and decorated, are smaller and more intimate than the great imperial bath complexes encountered in Rome.

But not all the architecture is within the walls. As in any Roman city, cemeteries of the wealthy stretched in every direction outside the city gates. While the houses of the living at Pompeii are turned inward, paying little attention to the impression that they make at street level, the tombs that line the arterial highways outside the town are entirely concerned with the image of the owner and are often far more eclectic than the architecture within the walls.

The private architecture of Pompeii is perhaps its greatest claim to fame. Row upon row of the Roman town house, the *domus,* line the streets. Beautifully adapted to the climate, urban setting and social needs of the Roman upper classes, the Roman *domus* was the characteristic dwelling of a mid-size Roman city such as Pompeii, a city where the population density was low enough to preclude the need for extensive high-density structures such as the Roman *insula,* well known from Ostia and Rome.

The largest houses take up an entire block and can cover as much as 30,000 square feet. The House of the Faun, the best

example of one of these large mansions, has two atria and two peristyles, lavishly encrusted with Hellenistic figural mosaics, including the elaborate Alexander mosaic, made up of more than a million pieces. Other houses, such as the House of the Menander, are no less patrician but were the result of gradual growth rather than of careful planning. This house is made up of several houses, bought at different times and eventually joined together through remodeling. In this way, through the buying and selling of property and the reshuffling of interior spaces over several centuries, Pompeii seems almost organic, an urban organism whose various parts were growing and shifting in response to varied social and economic factors.

The houses of Pompeii are our best evidence for Roman patronage in the private sphere. Paintings in the four Campanian styles that span the last three centuries of the city's history, decorative sculpture and landscaping combine to provide an impression of a city where matters of taste and patronage were as important in the private sphere as in the public. Even the styles of painting there are architectural in the way that they shape and articulate space to enhance the effects of the architecture. Recent research on Pompeian gardens, thanks to the pioneering work of Wilhelmina Jashemski, has revealed the importance of landscaping, hydraulic effects and garden imagery in Roman domestic planning, both urban and suburban.

This evidence for Roman domestic architecture is supplemented by the excavation of nearby Herculaneum, smaller and more of a resort town than a thriving commercial center like Pompeii. There, mansions such as the House of the Stags and the House of the Mosaic Atrium reveal the adaptability of the *domus* plan, how its basic components of atrium, peristyle and subsidiary rooms could be adapted to fit almost any situation. In these two houses the axis of the house was bent, and the peristyle areas were overscaled to create bigger garden areas and outdoor living spaces with better views of the seashore. This type of planning was clearly intended to maximize the fair-weather spaces, a type of house plan appropriate to a resort town.

Excavation of the countryside around Pompeii and Herculaneum has provided valuable evidence for Roman villa planning. The Villa of the Mysteries, just outside the northwestern gate of Pompeii, is a classic *villa suburbana* of the platform type, placed high on an arcaded podium and arranged to maximize the spectacular views of sea and town. Even more spectacular is the recently excavated Villa of the Empress Poppaea at Torre Annunziata (ancient Oplontis, about seven kilometers north of Pompeii), with its sprawling colonnaded wings, extensive landscaping, large swimming pool, and lavish sculptural and pictorial decoration, planned to take advantage of views of countryside and sea.

Both public and private sectors come alive at Pompeii. It is the range of architecture, the evidence of town planning and urban life, not just the exceptional quality of preservation, that make Pompeii valuable and unique.

—P. GREGORY WARDEN

PRIENE
Asia Minor

Third century B.C.: Agora constructed. **Third century B.C.:** Ecclesiasterion constructed. **Third century B.C.:** Auditorium constructed. **Second century B.C.:** Stoa added to agora. **Second century B.C.:** Altar constructed; **Architect:** Hermogenes.

Mansion House: Prienne, Asia Minor, ca. 3rd century B.C.

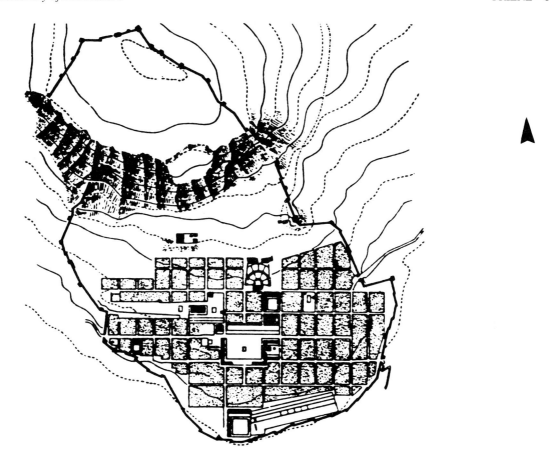

Publications

DINSMOOR, WILLIAM BELL: *The Architecture of Ancient Greece*. New York, 1975.

LAWRENCE, A. W.: *Greek Architecture*. Pelican History of Art, Harmondsworth, 1974.

SCHEDE, M.: *Die Ruinen von Priene*. 2nd ed. Berlin, 1964.

WIEGAND, T., and SCHRADER, H. (eds.): *Priene, Ergebnisse der Ausgrabung in den Jahren 1895-98*. Berlin, 1904.

*

The city of Priene is carved into a steep precipice called Samsun Dag near the village of Gullubache, in Turkey, and the flat plain far below, which was called Naulochos, was once one of the busiest harbors in Asia Minor. Because of Priene's relatively inaccessible location, much of its formidable circuit wall and many of its public buildings have remained basically intact, still presenting a vivid image of the city as it must have been when it was built in the Hellenistic period.

Priene is a masterpiece of Hippodamian planning in which a rectilinear system was imposed on a difficult site to create open public spaces that are effectively separated from the private residential areas that surround them. As such, it is also very instructive of the ways in which a regular grid can become a liberating rather than a restrictive device in urban planning.

In the private realm, the courtyard houses that have survived in the western part of the city are also in a good state of preservation, and easily rival those in other Greek cities, such as Ephesus and Delos, in their ability to recall the everyday life of the people who once lived there. Priene provides a clear

example of what urbanist Jaqueline Trywhitt once called the "human scale intermediary" in civic spaces, in which there was a logical graduation of open zones from the public agora to the private residential courtyard in the city that never visually or psychologically disturbed its inhabitants. Both the variety of scale and high degree of finish in these houses show how far contemporary expectations of what is acceptable in domestic surroundings have deteriorated.

Because of the restrictions of its hillside site, the city faced entirely south, with its main streets, which were typically four and a half meters wide, running east and west, and secondary streets of three and a half meters laid out at a right angle to them, stepping down the hillside from north to south. Principal structures, such as the theater, the stoa of the Temple of Athena, the sacred stoa and the stadium, all face south, both to capitalize on the winter sun and on distant views to the harbor below. Housing blocks typically measure 47.2 by 35.4 meters, with four houses being allocated to a block. Larger religious and governmental buildings were also planned on a modular basis so that they occupied an entire block, or if they were larger, took up two or three. This type of regulated Hippodamian plan, which was also used in cities such as Miletus and Piraeus in the middle of the fifth century B.C., not only marks a determined movement away from the traditional pattern of urban growth by accretion that had characterized the Greek polis in the past, but also indicates the urgency of the policy of colonization that was used to consolidate territory during the Hellenistic period.

Priene received its water supply from the mountains behind the city through an aqueduct that penetrated the circuit wall at a point northeast of the city. After first being collected in three reservoirs, the water was distributed throughout the city by a system of fired clay pipes that still exist. There were also several nymphaeon, or water fountains, located throughout Priene. One of these was located at the southeast corner of the theatre, and the other two were near the eastern end of the sacred stoa and the southern side of the Temple of Athena, respectively, with smaller fountains evenly distributed throughout the residential areas. The agora, midway up the slope, was located on a main transverse street which eventually terminated at the main western gateway in the circuit wall. The Temple of Athena was the oldest building in the agora, and at a height of nearly 100 meters above sea level, was undoubtedly visible from a great distance. The temple is believed to have been built by Pytheos, who was also responsible for the design and construction of the Mausoleum at Halicarnassos, which was one of the "seven wonders" of the ancient world. The Temple of Athena, which was later chosen by Vitruvius as a model of Ionic architecture, demonstrates the same creative combination of empirically derived elements as the mausoleum, as well as a similar disregard of conventional rules. Of the peripteral type, the temple has six columns on its short side and eleven on its longer edge, with a stylobate that measures 37.2 by 19.6 meters. Executed in local Mycale marble, the ornamental sections of the building are now known to have been polychrome in red, yellow and blue, which must have added immeasurably to the temple's visual impact, especially from a distance. Other novel features of the temple, which were also mentioned by Vitruvius, are low, three-step crepidoma column bases that incorporate both Ephesian and Anatolian forms, as well as using a greater ratio of diameter to height of one to ten. The pronaos is especially large in comparison to earlier classical examples, showing a greater tendency toward an emphasis on the interior that was beginning to develop in the Hellenistic period. This significant change in the perception of the space inside the temple, as a positive rather than a negative element, is surprisingly traceable to the Parthenon itself, which is the paragon of an externally focused, classical architecture, but was also one of the first to have an expanded cella, which encouraged worshippers to enter into the temple and not just appreciate it at a distance.

The mathematical precision of the Hippodamian schemes that Priene represents and the ideas of Hellenistic scholars such as Thales and Parmenides of Miletus were a major breakthrough in architectural thinking because they helped to establish an objective relationship between human perception and design, and separated subject and object in a way that could then be analyzed through rational discourse. This then made it possible for others, such as Vitruvius, to dissect the Temple of Athena as a basis for a theory of design that could then be reduced to a mathematical methodology.

In the process, architecture began to be much less of a subjective extension of social values. While the violations of the Classical canon, which was based on essentially anthropomorphic, mythic and emotional elements, make the theories according to which Priene was organized seem apocryphal to fundamentalists, their logic has a clarity all of its own. Even to those who consider the Parthenon to be a model of beauty, the emphasis on space in the agora and Temple of Athena at Priene, and in Hellenistic architecture in general, make both seem more comprehensible and human to us today. The realization that this change in perception began on the Athenian Acropolis makes this transition easier to accept, extending the comprehension of the space-positive tradition back to the Classical model as well, which gives it more than an abstract, iconographic meaning.

The introduction of the stoa at Priene, a concept first thought to have been developed in Asia Minor, extended this idea of space to the exterior groupings as well. While classical Greek

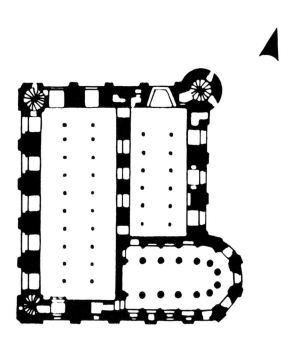

Temple of Athena

plans, from those of sanctuary compounds to cities in general, consistently show an awareness of the invisible forces that adjacent buildings have upon each other, as well as upon people who were moving past them, the stoa added another dimension entirely. By interlocking near and distant space through the right-angled frame of its trabeation, the stoa provided an architectural medium that achieved a link between the man-made and the natural.

Arched openings, which were usually relegated to rather mundane uses, have been found in Priene, showing that, contrary to popular belief, the Greeks did know how to build arches and domes prior to the introduction of those forms in Roman architecture. An arcuated opening, however, especially when placed in conjunction with others, calls attention to its own rhythm and construction, and this natural link, which the Greeks preferred, is lost.

As can be seen with the Temple of Athena, this structure lost much of its individual, sculptural character in the Hellenistic city, becoming only one of the many institutions linked together in a more unified fabric. Such identification was critical in an age in which the city did not have the time to evolve slowly, as in the past, but instead was seen as an educational and political vehicle with which to claim alien territory. While religion had managed to remain more or less aloof from politics in the Classical age, the temple, Bouleuterion, gymnasium, theater and all of the other institutions that can be found in Priene were seen by Alexander the Great and his successors as the requisite evidence of a superior Greek culture in a distant land.

The majority of these institutions are found in the agora, which was built in the third century B.C. and covers two entire blocks within the city module. Stoas line the edge of three of its sides, with the main, transverse street forming the fourth. These colonnades were unusual in that they were built in the Doric order, but typical in the combination of commercial and social uses. Due to the southerly slope, there was a second, basement level below the downhill side of the agora, which was used as a storage area for the shops above. Like most market areas in Greek cities, this agora was also used as a place for festivals, public assemblies and celebrations, serving a number of civic functions. An altar to the god Hermes dominated the center of the square, as did two stone stages, which were the seating platforms used by high-ranking officials during the celebrations. The remains of wooden posts found in these platforms indicate that an awning once covered them to provide shade. There were also many memorial statues placed around the agora, as there also were in Athens and elsewhere, which would have given it a lively, and somewhat cluttered, appearance. Pedestals are all that remain of these memorials, making it difficult to imagine the vibrancy that this space must have had in antiquity. The food market itself was not in the agora, but was located to the west of it, in order to avoid additional congestion.

During the second half of the second century B.C., many new buildings were added to the agora, including the sacred stoa, which finally closed the agora's fourth, northern edge, on the other side of the main street. It is 116 meters long and, according to an inscription found on a fragment of its architrave, was donated to the city by King Ariarathes VI in 130 B.C. Six steps, running along its entire length, gave access to it, and also provided seating for the processions along the main street itself. This stoa, like the other three around the agora, had a roof supported by wooden trusses and covered in red clay tiles.

The Bouleuterion and the adjacent Prytaneion are also well preserved today, and together they occupy an entire city block behind the sacred stoa. The Bouleuterion is almost square, with an altar in the middle. Unlike the Ecclesiasterion, or people's assembly, which was made up of everyone in Priene who was eligible to vote, the Bouleuterion served an advisory capacity and held about 650 people. The Ecclesiasterion met in the theater north of the agora, which has also survived, and is known to have accommodated 5,000. Special seats, or prohedria, were reserved for dignitaries, and had specially carved backrests that are still intact. An altar in the center, dedicated to Dionysus, recalls the origins of this and every other Greek theater as the place for seeing the rituals related to this deity, which eventually evolved into more formal structure. The presence of altars in all public buildings at Priene is a reminder of the important part that the religious act of sacrifice had in public life at that time, similar to the opening of a governmental function with a convocation today. The existence of small details like those at Priene tend to bring it alive in a way that is very unusual for cities of that period, and make it a particularly important example of the urban attitudes of the age.

—JAMES M. STEELE

AMPHITHEATER
Pula, Yugoslavia

41 A.D.: Construction begun.

Publications

SMITH, GARY E.: *A Guide to the Roman Amphitheaters.* Los Angeles, 1984.
"Studietur til Pola." *Arkitekten* 63, No. 9 (3 May 1961): 157-165.

*

Pula, an Adriatic city located in what was Yugoslavia, had been occupied continuously for 3,000 years by numerous peoples, including the Romans. As a colony of Rome under Augustus (ruled 27 B.C.-14 A.D.) the city was rebuilt. The new city followed the Roman tradition of a grid plan. During that construction campaign, numerous public facilities and social spaces were built; among them was the amphitheater. Construction was begun in 41 A.D. on the western hillside overlooking the sea, immediately outside of the city proper. Between the amphitheater and the Adriatic was the Via Flavia, which led to Trieste.

The architect of the amphitheater is unknown, but the design shares principles with other extant examples. Of these amphitheaters, Pula's is the sixth-largest, yet it is considered by many to be the best preserved. As such, it has been studied and recorded throughout history by numerous scholars, including Andrea Palladio, Sebastiano Serlio and Giovanni Battista Piranesi.

The Pula Amphitheater was constructed of locally quarried stone. The rusticated ashlar masonry was finely cut and laid. It was designed following the contours of the natural terrain of the hillside. As a result, in plan the amphitheater is an imperfect ellipse with the major axis oriented north-south.

In elevation, the amphitheater is three stories high, with the western facade rising the full height, while the eastern facade is lost in the hillside. Each of the lower two stories is defined by 72 arched openings, which spring from Doric pilasters. The third story is delineated by 64 openings, which are rectilinear in form. These horizontal divisions correspond to the three seating sections designated for segregation of the social strata of spectators.

The perimeter of the Pula Amphitheater was defined by four towers. Access into the facility was provided by 15 entrances, eight from the sea facade (west), five from the hill facade (east) and one at each end (north and south). The southernmost was nearest the city, and thus functioned as the main entrance. To identify it as such, the southern entrance was the most monumental.

The interior of the amphitheater was divided into three major components: the arena, the galleries and concentric rows of seating (*muri circulares*). The focal point was the arena, which was the location of gladiator, maritime and animal battles. For land battles, it was covered with sand, while aqueducts located below provided water from the Adriatic when flooding it for maritime battles.

Below the arena were the galleries, which accommodated space for the storage of props, weaponry, background sets and animals being kept for battle. In addition, housing and training facilities for the gladiators were located in this area.

The first level above the arena was the podium, a platform protected from the dangers of battle by an iron fence. It was reserved for the magistrate, jurors and honored guests. Above this rose the 30 rows of seating, which accommodated up to 23,000 spectators. The seating in the western portion of the amphitheater rested on a masonry bearing wall structure, while the lowest story at the eastern side rested on the hillside, and its upper stories on a masonry bearing wall. The three strata of seating were the *maenianum primum,* the *maenianum secundum* and the *porticus,* or loggia. The *porticus* accommodated women

Amphitheater: Pula, Yugoslavia, 41 A.D.

in the bottom rows, and plebeians at the top. The lower two seating areas provided stone benches for the spectators, while the *porticus* contained wooden seats.

Circulation was provided by transverse steps, which divided the entire seating area into sections (*cunei*). Additional egress was provided within the infrastructure of the amphitheater wall. Within this cavity were rest areas, storage space and areas for refreshment.

Following the outlawing of the games in 404 A.D., the Pula Amphitheater was converted into a prison by the barbarians during the fifth century. It eventually fell into disrepair and was looted by local residents for building material. This triggered the passage of legislation in 1260 forbidding the amphitheater's further destruction, and imposing fines. Subsequently, the structure was once again used as a public space, first as the venue of annual fairs and, later, following the infilling of the arena floor with concrete, as an outdoor performance space.

The Pula Amphitheater is significant as a major national landmark dominating the skyline from the Adriatic Sea. It is a reminder of the period of the Roman Empire's domination of the Illyrian and Dalmation coast. As an example of Roman architecture, the Pula Amphitheater is one of the best preserved of that period, even though not the grandest.

—ANDREA URBAS

ARCH OF CONSTANTINE
Rome, Italy

313-315 A.D.

Publications

GIULIANO, A.: *Arco di Costantino*. Milan, 1955.

Arch of Constantine: Rome, Italy, 313-315 A.D.

The last and largest of all triumphal arches preserved in Rome was built by the Senate in 313-315 A.D. on a handsome site near the Colosseum to commemorate Constantine's victory over his rival as emperor, Maxentius, at the Battle of the Milvian Bridge (312). Its lavish sculptural program is partly contemporary and partly removed from a series of earlier public monuments, which, taken together, constitute a unique repertory of Roman official sculptural art from Trajan to Constantine. The arch of Constantine is a curious essay in historical revivalism, a nostalgic attempt to recover the glories of pagan Rome by the emperor who proclaimed the toleration of Christianity with the Edict of Milan (313). It stands at the border between the pagan and Christian Roman Empire; henceforth, triumphal arches were erected in the interiors of churches, not along the Via Sacra leading to the temple of Jupiter on the Capitolium.

The structure is of traditional, characteristically Roman triumphal-arch form. The three-arched shape is clearly modeled in all major features after the great triple Arch of Septimius Severus at the west end of the Roman Forum (203 A.D.). The Arch of Constantine surpasses its third-century Severan model in its open, more dignified setting and proportions, and in the triple

articulation of the attic story to correspond with the pattern of the archways beneath. The structure itself is wide in proportion to its height, giving it a rather solid, earthbound appearance in comparison to the soaring majesty of the Severan monument. The lower story is carefully proportioned so that the two lateral arches reach exactly to the line from which the central arch springs: the result is a triadic stepped arcade. The motion of the semicircular arches is picked up by the circular medallions above the frieze. The vertical effect of the four detached columns is echoed in the pilasters of the facade and continued in the upper story by the plain piers and the pedestals with statues of captive barbarians. The effect of the overall design is, however, impaired by the restless motion of sculptures that overload the two lateral parts of the facade.

The older sculptures were all lifted bodily from monuments erected by the "good" emperors with whom Constantine (or the conservative and pagan Senate) wished to associate: Trajan, Hadrian and Marcus Aurelius, whose heads were recarved into portraits of Constantine and his generals. Their new function and new meaning arise simply from the architect's act of choice. In this way the idea behind the work of art acquired greater importance than the work itself, and all the hard-won technical knowledge for creating spatial depth and other naturalistic illusions cultivated in Classical Greece, the Hellenistic kingdoms and the Roman Empire came to seem irrelevant to the main purpose of art. The Constantinian artisans seem to have been less interested in realistic presentation than in a kind of symbolic expression of historical truths and, shortly afterward, of Christian ideals.

The crisp naturalism of the reused sculptures contrasts strangely with the superficially more primitive style of the long narrative friezes. In one panel, for instance, two Hadrianic roundels representing a boar hunt and a sacrifice to Apollo are inset above the frieze of Constantine delivering a public oration. The roundels are elegantly suave examples of the Hellenized art favored by Emperor Hadrian, delicately cut, naturalistic, vivacious and graceful. By contrast, the Constantinian relief is startling. Uniformly squat figures with oversize heads, stiffly posed in rows, are aligned on either side of the emperor as he addresses the people from the rostrum in the Roman Forum. There is no foreshortening, no indication of movement: space is flattened, scale is ignored, and the buildings have been reduced to toys in the background.

The increasing austerity of architectural exteriors and the greater reliance upon colored marble, stucco and mosaic for interiors during the third century precluded the need for relief-carving in the grand manner. The genre had become all but extinct in Rome; no official relief sculpture had been produced there for some 80 years. Constantine depended on a lively contemporary school of Roman sarcophagus carvers for the narrative panels, with whose work, both in scale and style, they are quite similar. The Constantinian reliefs, therefore, may belong to an ancient popular Italic style, sometimes termed plebeian. This style was patronized by the middle classes and had coexisted with that favored by the more highly educated and consequently more strongly Hellenized patricians. Although the Constantinian reliefs have distressed such critics as the late Bernard Berenson, there can be no serious doubt that they represent the creative mainstream of one of the most vigorous currents in early-fourth-century art.

—PETER J. HOLLIDAY

ARCH OF TITUS
Rome, Italy

82 A.D.

Publications

"Arc de Titus: détail de l'ordre." *Moniteur des architectes* 9 (1875): 170-171.
FROTHINGHAM, A. L.: "A Lost Section of the Frieze of the Arch of Titus?" *American Journal of Archaeology* 18 (1914): 479-483.
MAGI, FILIPPO: "L'iscrizione perduta dell'Arco di Tito, una ipotesi." *Mitteilungen des Deutschen Archäologischen Institut* 82, 1 (1975): 99-116.

*

The most frequently used vehicle for visual propaganda in ancient Rome was the triumphal arch. Half architecture and half sculpture, this Roman invention has surprisingly obscure origins. Monumental entrances to cities, sacred sites and palaces had been embellished with sculpture by the Hittites, Assyrians, Babylonians, Egyptians and Mycenaeans; the Etruscans also built monumental gateways to their cities. But the Roman triumphal arch was essentially different. Although it could serve as a monumental entrance to a forum or a city, it was not necessarily the entrance to anything. It was freestanding and purely ornamental, its only function to carry and display visual propaganda. During the republic temporary arches had been built by commanders to celebrate their triumphal return to Rome at the head of armies bearing the spoils of war; by the end of the empire some 64 arches adorned the capital, and others were scattered throughout the empire. The permanent arch erected in the Roman Forum to commemorate Augustus' victory over the Parthians in 19 B.C. (primarily reconstructed from coin types) seems to have set the pattern for subsequent monuments: a rectangular block with a round-headed opening framed by pilasters and entablature with a large panel for an inscription above, crowned by a group of the emperor in a triumphal chariot.

The Arch of Titus in Rome is one of the finest surviving examples of this monument type. It is prominently placed at the summit where the Via Sacra connects the eastern edge of the Roman Forum with the Colosseum. Probably begun by Titus to commemorate his capture of Jerusalem in 70 A.D., it was finished after his death 11 years later by his brother Domitian. It is built of honey-colored marble from Mount Pentelicus in Greece about a concrete core (*opus caementicium*), and is remarkable both for the simple dignity of its architectural lines and for its sculptured ornament. A single arch between square piers is crowned with an attic story, undoubtedly once supporting a traditional bronze group: the four-horse chariot (*quadriga*) driven by Titus in triumph. The applied decorative (or "screen") architecture is formed of paired columns upholding an entablature with a sculptured frieze. The architects also introduced several innovations here. For example, the Arch of Titus is one of the earliest public monuments to use the Composite order. First mentioned by Vitruvius, this even richer fifth order was an invention of Augustan architects but only came into common use during the Flavian period; it is distinguished from the Corinthian in that the volutes have been enlarged to the scale of those of the Ionic. In addition, the entablature is no longer continuous, but is broken so that it projects over the lateral columns, recedes close to the massive piers, and projects again over the central columns and the connecting arch. Thus, screen architecture had become molded with the same fluidity as the underlying architecture of concrete, permitting freedom of shape and the movement of light and dark. (The unfluted columns and entablature at either side of the arch, which do not share in the chiaroscuro effects so important to Flavian masters, are 19th-century restorations.)

The dedicatory inscription in the attic was originally gilded. Its finely cut letters read: "The Roman Senate and People to the Deified Titus, Vespasian Augustus, son of Deified Vespasian." The Romans placed enormous importance on such colossal inscriptions, and were the first to appreciate their artistic possibilities. The lettering is clear and simple; the form of every letter and the equally important spacing conform to the laws of architectural sculpture, and thereby enhance the authority and dignity of the entire monument. Its boldness, clarity and compactness, its total rejection of any kind of decorative flourish, perfectly reflect the dignified restraint (*gravitas*) and disciplined authority (*auctoritas*) held in esteem by the Romans. Such lettering was one of the greatest Roman inventions, and it was certainly one of their most influential and lasting contributions to the visual arts.

Arch of Titus: Rome, Italy, 82 A.D.

The inscriptions indicate that triumphal arches were conceived as historical statements; sculptural programs complement their message. Titus had died (81 A.D.) before the work was completed, and in the center of the vault his apotheosis is shown, borne up to heaven on the back of an eagle. Although winged figures of Victory, descended from those of Greece, hover in the spandrels, the Roman preoccupation with actuality asserts itself in the other reliefs. The figured frieze in the entablature depicts the triumph which Titus shared with his father, Vespasian, in 71 A.D. to celebrate the suppression of the Jewish revolt. Reliefs on either side of the passageway, the *Triumph of Titus* and the *Spoils from the Temple,* represent the treasures looted from the Temple in Jerusalem (the Menorah, the Table of the Shew bread, the great silver trumpets that called the people to Rosh Hashanah), which were paraded past this spot at the foot of the Palatine. These two reliefs were, if anything, more revolutionary than the architecture carrying them. The stateliness of earlier Augustan carving style was swept away and replaced with a new dynamism. The relief space is deeper, and the figures move freely as though passing on a stage before the viewer. As in the varying levels in depth of the supporting architecture, light and shade have been utilized to enrich the drama.

The Arch of Titus is the first metropolitan Roman building since the republic known to have been built of imported marble. In the Middle Ages it was incorporated into a fortress held by the Frangipane family. Giuseppe Valadier restored it to its familiar form in 1821; his use of travertine to distinguish new from original masonry is an early and entirely successful example of scientific restoration.

—PETER J. HOLLIDAY

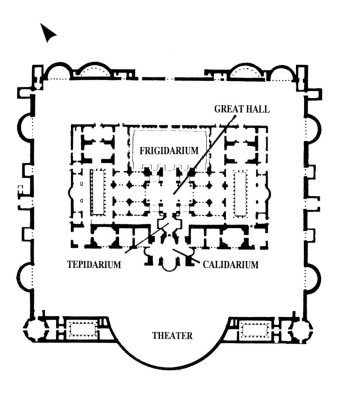

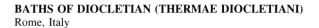

BATHS OF DIOCLETIAN (THERMAE DIOCLETIANI)
Rome, Italy

302 A.D.: Initial construction. **16th century:** Converted to Church of Santa Maria degli Angeli; **Architect:** Michelangelo (1475-1564).

Publications

ACKERMAN, J.: *The Architecture of Michelangelo.* rev. ed. Harmondsworth and Baltimore, 1970.
DE TOLNAY, C.: *Michelangelo.* Princeton, New Jersey, 1975.
VON GEYMÜLLER, HEINRICH: *Documents inédits sur les Thermes d'Agrippa, le Panthéon et les Thermes de Dioclétian.* Lausanne and Rome, 1883.
YEGUL, FIKRET: *Baths and Bathing in Classical Antiquity.* Cambridge, Massachusetts, 1991.

*

The *Thermae Diocletiani* were the largest public baths in the ancient world, designed to hold 3,000 people at a time. They were begun in 298 by Maximian, and completed and dedicated by Diocletian between 1 May 305, and 25 July 306. Inscriptions placed above the four principal gates described and praised the great works of Diocletian and his colleague (*CIL* VI, 1130), and reminded the Romans, who used the baths for communal cultivation of the body and the mind, of the emperor's beneficence.

The baths were built on the high ground in the northeast part of the city of Rome to service the less prosperous citizens in the districts surrounding the Quirinal, Viminal and Esquiline Hills. Two temples and many other private and public buildings were demolished in order to construct the baths, which covered an area of about 136,000 square meters and contained nearly 3,000 marble basins.

The enormous scale of the project provided the architect and builders with an exceptional opportunity to extend their technical mastery to create a symbol of imperial majesty and power. The plan is similar to that of the Baths of Caracalla and of the early-second-century Baths of Trajan designed by Apollodorus of Damascus. Like the earlier baths, a huge central block (250 by 180 meters) contained the large bathing halls. It rose from a vast, level concrete platform honeycombed with cavities for heating and hydraulic installations, and was surrounded by gardens and an enclosing *peribolos* wall with symmetrically placed exedrae, niches and small rooms to provide ample space for relaxation after the baths.

In addition to the main bathing rooms, there were dressing rooms, sweat rooms, latrines, lounges, nymphaea, gymnasia, exercise grounds, halls for strolling and conversation, tanning rooms, ball courts, libraries, and auditoria for lectures and concerts. The complex was designed to heighten the bather's physical sensations and aesthetic awareness. Open-air spaces were often surrounded by sculpture and colonnades in the Greek Palaestra style. Many of the rooms were curved and polygonal with domed and vaulted ceilings. Light sources, such as oculi, raking light shafts and clerestory windows, illuminated the colored marble wall facings of *opus sectile,* mosaic-covered vaults and pavements, stuccoed ceilings and fresco paintings that embellished the interior surfaces.

The whole complex was organized around the axially aligned

Baths of Diocletian (Thermae Diocletiani): Rome, Italy, 302 A.D.

central bathing halls. Its perfect bilateral symmetry made the most economical and efficient use of space and facilitated a progressive current of movement on each side of the central axis, which was a double peripheral sequence of spaces converging on the principal bathing halls. Bathers were conducted from identical lobbies and *apodyteria* at either side, successively through identical pairs of palaestrae and steam rooms, and then, reversing their direction, down the center through the *caldarium, tepidarium, frigidarium* and *natatio*.

The *caldarium* (hot room) at the head of the central axis was oriented southwest to obtain the greatest warmth from the sun for afternoon baths. It was rectangular with a large southwest-facing apse and three semicircular projecting apses that formed lofty groin-vaulted bays. The northeast-facing apse opened directly onto the *tepidarium* (warm room), a domed octagonal hall with two large rectangular exedrae containing baths at either side.

The *tepidarium* opened onto the huge central hall of the baths, sometimes identified as the *frigidarium* (cold room) but more generally accepted as the Great Hall (approximately 91 meters long, 27 meters broad and 22 meters high). Eight enormous monolithic reddish-pink granite columns, each about 15 meters high, and an elaborate system of piers, arches and buttresses supported three large quadripartite vaults. The three bays thus formed were lit by large clerestory windows that were distinctively divided by two vertical mullions into three lights (also known as Diocletian or thermal windows). The ends of the hall opened onto a series of interconnected vaulted rooms of lesser height. These rooms served both as buttresses and as the cross-axis of the baths; they led out to the palaestrae and ended in two semicircular exedrae.

The exterior northeast wall of the great central hall faced the *natatio* (open-air swimming pool), which may have served as the *frigidarium*. The massive wall (believed to have been 100 meters long and 32 meters high) served as a sumptuous *skene*-like backdrop to the massive swimming pool. It was punctuated by three large rectangular *aediculae* that alternated with two semicircular columnar recesses arranged in three tiers; it was adorned with massive projecting piers, attenuated *aediculae*, decorative columns and many windows. The pool itself, the culmination of the bath experience and the termination of the main axis of the baths, covered approximately 3,000 square meters.

Beyond the pool lay meadows and gardens bounded by the *peribolos*. The most striking feature of the outer circuit was the great semicircular exedra that echoed the southwest apse of the *caldarium*. There patrons could sit on the stairs and watch athletic exercises performed by the bathers. By order of the emperor, the libraries of the Biblioteca Ulpia were removed from the Forum of Trajan and installed in the two rectangular rooms flanking the great exedra. At either side were domed circular halls probably used as auditoria. One of the largest domed octagonal halls (23 meters in diameter and 27 meters high), possibly a nymphaeum (fountain room), was located nearby at the west corner of the central block.

The Baths of Diocletian were the most ambitious built in Rome, the culmination of a series of imperial bathing establishments offered to urbanized Romans as ubiquitous public amenities. Although the geometric rigidity of its massive symmetrical forms symbolically expressed the totalitarian order of the tetrarchy's rule, it also made possible a splendid, well-organized setting for leisure that was accessible to nearly everyone. The baths continued in use until 537 and were abandoned when the Acqua Marcia, which supplied its water, was destroyed during the Ostrogothic siege.

—SUSAN SILBERBERG-PEIRCE

COLOSSEUM
Rome, Italy

72-80 A.D.

Publications

PARKER, JOHN H.: *The Colosseum at Rome*. Oxford, 1876.

*

As a type of open amphitheater, the Flavian Amphitheater, or Colosseum, in every way epitomized the enduring characteristics of Roman imperial architecture. It was public, urban, functional, massive in scale, simple in design and built with the most advanced techniques of concrete, brick and stone construction. The Colosseum was not the first of its kind—earlier examples were found in Pompeii and Verona, in Italy, and in Arles and Nîmes, in France—but it was the largest. To produce the best and biggest in Roman design, the anonymous architect capitalized upon the structural and decorative possibilities of arches and vaults. It was characteristic of the period that all types of Roman buildings and techniques reached their peak in the imperial architecture of the capital.

Politics and propaganda inspired the origin and purpose of the Colosseum. Vespasian chose the lake site of Nero's former palace for the new amphitheater as a way of substituting for the ill-famed Golden House, in the conspicuous center of Rome, a symbol of imperial goodwill. The public events that took place in the Colosseum were primarily propagandistic events, often cruel and bloody fights sponsored by the emperor to the delight of the thrill-seeking Roman audiences that could number between 45,000 and 50,000.

The amphitheater type was a Roman invention that resulted from the joining of two Greek theaters to produce an oval plan surrounded by continuous bench-like seats, arranged along a rising elevation. The seats encircled the arena, the focus of the interior, in three stories. While the Greeks built their theaters on natural sloping terrain, the Romans used massive subterranean foundations and a skeletal structure of barrel vaults resting on huge piers and running radially like spokes from the inside to the outer wall. In elevation, the rows and rows of seats, in turn, rested upon these vaults and piers.

In the Roman Colosseum, form and function united to an extent never before seen. A wide, barrel-vaulted corridor ran around the entire periphery and was entered from the street through any one of the 80 wide, round arches of the exterior wall. Other concentric corridors ran around the building parallel to the peripheral corridor. The openness of the vaulted corridors and their placement gave easy access to all parts of the building, perhaps one of the most ingenious aspects of the design, imitating a somewhat similar system in the earlier Theater of Marcellus. The upper stories were reached by steep stairways now worn from centuries of use. The crowds circulated in and out, up and down, and around on every level.

The arena itself covered a network of subterranean chambers in which gladiators, animals and other performers prepared for the lavish spectacles and gruesome battles. A series of cages, ramps, and raising and lowering devices ensured the quick, timely appearance of the animals on the central stage. All structural and functional aspects of the building were thus hidden either under the arena or under the seats in such a way as to produce an interior that contained nothing but space. This combination of hidden structural massiveness and open interior space, roofed or unroofed, was the hallmark of the Roman

Colosseum: Rome, Italy, 72-80 A.D.

Colosseum

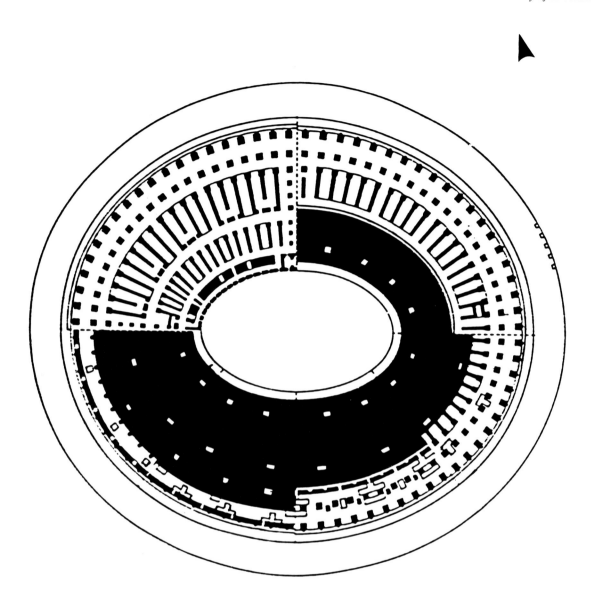

contribution to the history of architecture, and one that has never been duplicated or surpassed. The nearest of kin to the Colosseum, the modern urban stadium, in comparison, gives more the impression of an outdoor area than that of an interior because of its expansive proportions of width to height. These differ from the steeper and narrower proportions of the Colosseum.

Damaged from earthquakes in antiquity and plundered throughout the ages, the Colosseum now stands as a dark and dirty ruin. But besides its sheer massiveness, something of the impressiveness of the original structure is still visible in the articulation of the exterior wall. The exterior is pierced by round, Roman arches on three stories, corresponding to the three-story elevation of the interior. The arches are supported on piers decorated with half columns, which, in turn, support continuous horizontal cornices that form bands around the entire circumference, separating the three stories. By incorporating the round arch flanked by columns supporting an entablature (a combination known as the "Roman arch order") as a fundamental element in his design, the architect formed an early bridge between the monumental and commemorative triumphal arch and the employment of the triumphal arch as an architectural motif. (The commemorative arch, a type invented by the Romans, was nonfunctional, non-space-enclosing and, thus, nonarchitectural.)

The fourth, upper level of the Colosseum, probably later than the rest in date, contains the only true "wall" of the exterior, and it is pierced by rectangular openings framed by flat pilasters. The entire exterior resembles the stage facades of Roman theaters, which were often three stories, with column upon column. In a sense the theater was turned inside out in designing this giant. The combination of rectilinear and curvilinear shapes, vertical and horizontal lines, thick, flat piers and dark, open arches animates the building. The placement of statues in the arched spaces would have turned the hollows into rounded niche-like forms and added a human, or imperfect, touch to the severe and perfect rhythm of the outer wall.

Following the classical, Vitruvian canon, the capitals change from Doric to Ionic to Corinthian from one level to the next, drawing upon the visual properties of the orders as heavy or light and as elements expressive of the structural weight of the building. The upper loads were lightened inside by the use of wooden, rather than stone seats, and by the thin and flatter wall of the fourth exterior level. The combination of diverse building materials—concrete foundations, concrete and brick walls, travertine piers held with iron clamps, tufa walls and marble sheathing—and the lightening of the load in the upper parts of the building were two common characteristics of the period.

Inside, the emperor sat on a special podium, the lower classes sat separately from the upper classes, and women separately from men. A study of these divisions informs us of the wider implications of a building designed for social use. The lower, stone seats were sheathed in white marble, the upper seats were made of wood, and awnings stretched from the upper balconies to shade the spectators. It is primarily from the perspective of how the building functioned that every detail of structure and decoration must be seen.

The fame and symbolism of the Colosseum were great enough in the Middle Ages to cause the Venerable Bede to write, in the eighth century, "As long as the Colosseum stands, Rome shall stand; when the Colosseum falls, Rome shall fall; when Rome falls, the world shall fall." Several key elements, such as the upper wall, decorated with pilasters, inspired the Renaissance architect Leon Battista Alberti in the design of the Palazzo Rucellai in Florence; the multistory open/void and arch/pier combination was used by Donato Bramante in the cloister of Santa Maria della Pace in Rome; and the embracing oval of the enclosure reappeared in Giovanni Lorenzo Bernini's colonnades designed for the Piazza di San Pietro in Rome—all quotations of classical Roman motifs present in the architecture of the Colosseum.

—PAULA D. LEVETO-JABR

FORUM ROMANUM
Rome, Italy

---

497 B.C.: Temple of Saturn, Rostrum, Arch of Septimus Severus, and Miliarium Aureum built (rebuilt 42 B.C.; restored ca. third century A.D.). **484 B.C.:** Temple of the Castor and Pollux and Temple of Caesar constructed. **55-44 B.C.:** Basilica Julia begun. **64 A.D.:** House of the Vestals built. **81 A.D.:** Temple of Vespasian built. **141 A.D.:** Temple of Antonius and Faustina constructed. **191 A.D.:** Temple of Vesta and Regia built. **284 A.D.:** Curia and Basilica Aemilia rebuilt. **Early 4th century A.D.:** Temple of Romulus constructed. **306-312 A.D.:** Basilica of Maxentius and Arch of Titus built. **367 A.D.:** Portico of the Dei Consenti constructed. **608 A.D.:** Phoca's Column and Temple of Concord built.

Publications

GRANT, M.: *The Roman Forum*. London, 1970.
PARKER, JOHN H.: *The Forum Romanum*. Oxford, 1876.
ZANKER, P.: *Forum Romanum: Die Neugestaltung durch Augustus*. Tübingen, 1972.

The *forum romanum*, the long trapezoidal space in the center of Rome, was during the five centuries of the Republican era the principal public space of the city, where the main business of the community was conducted. The *forum romanum* or *forum*

veterum, as it was later called, rendered in English as the Roman Forum, was the oldest such public space in the Roman world, and lent its name, its meaning and its function to innumerable successors. It occupied the bottom of a small valley bounded on the north by the Capitoline Hill, on the east by the Quirinal and Esquiline Hills, on the west by the Palatine Hill, and on the south by the slope of the Velia. Its long axis ran roughly from northwest to southeast, following the lay of the land, with its wider end to the north. As a valley between hill slopes it was for many centuries permanently swampy, yet was from earliest times the nexus of roads leading in from the cardinal directions, thus making it the natural site for a public space.

The history of the Roman Forum reflected the history of Rome itself, and may be divided into similar periods: the prehistoric and regal era (before 500 B.C.), the early republican age (from ca. 500 to ca. 150 B.C.), the later republic (from ca. 150 to ca. 29 B.C.), the imperial age (from ca. 29 B.C. to ca. 320 A.D.), and late antiquity and after. In each period the Forum was the scene of climactic events in city and state history. Later memorials to those events ultimately became so numerous as almost to displace the Forum's original functions. Yet though compressed by huge buildings and filled with monuments, the Forum maintained its position as the historic center of the Roman state. Even when it later fell into disrepair and ultimately decay, the Forum continued to mirror the fortunes of the surrounding city; by the 18th century its only use was as a cow pasture. Not until recently, and principally after 1870, did excavation begin to reveal the ancient monuments; and it was no accident that in the very years that saw the resurgence of a newly unified Italy, aspiring again to a great position among nations, and seeking inspiration in the memorials of its former glory, the Roman Forum should be resurrected to assume once again a role at the center of the Mediterranean world.

The earliest remains from the prehistoric era identified in the Forum were of burials, principally at the southern end of the area. They dated from the ninth through the early sixth centuries B.C., and appeared to have been contemporary with the settlement on the adjacent Palatine Hill. The presence of burials suggests strongly that there was little or no building in the area of the Forum during that period. Yet the myth-history of Rome, as it came down to later ages, contained references to civic buildings of which fragmentary remains seemed to survive into the historic era. Among these were the Comitium (site of public meetings), the Regia (house of the chief priest) and the Temple of Vesta. Tradition if not firm evidence asserts that these remains dated in their origins from the sixth century B.C., as did the Lapis Niger (Black Stone), which marked a religious site that was associated with Romulus, the mythical founder of the city. However, the principal survival from the prehistoric era was of neither religious nor political significance but was something more mundane, namely the Cloaca Maxima (Great Drain), which was constructed near the end of the sixth century B.C. It ran from east of the Forum proper below the northern end of the space, and continued to the west to debouch into the Tiber. Its effect was to relieve the area of continual flooding, and it was from that time forward that the Forum began to assume the built form which has come down to the present.

According to tradition, among the first buildings to be founded in the Forum were the Temple of Saturn (497 B.C.) and the Temple of Castor and Pollux (484 B.C.), placed at the northwest and southwest corners of the space, respectively. Along with these were the sites for the Comitium, the Curia (for the Senate) and the Rostra (a platform for orators), all grouped at the northeast corner. Rows of shops were built on the east and west, defining the space on those sides, while the Temple of Vesta, the Regia and the House of the Vestals

Forum romanum: Rome, Italy, 1st century B.C.-4th century A.D.

combined to mark the southern boundary. The definition of the space established in that early period by the structures along its edges persisted almost unchanged throughout the rest of its long history. In addition, the locations of the streets that connected it to the surrounding city were fixed at about the same time. To the east ran the Argiletum; to the south lay the Sacra Via (Sacred Way), while to the west were the Vicus Tuscus and the Vicus Iugarius; and from the northwest corner a steep street (Clivus Capitolinus) climbed the slope of the Capitoline Hill to the front of the Temple of Jupiter. Another street, the Clivus Argentarius, was opened to the north at a later date. The presence of buildings and streets together show that the city had begun its extension from the Palatine Hill, the foundation site, to the slopes of the adjacent hills, and that the Forum was already at the center rather than the edge of the growing urban complex.

During succeeding centuries the Forum expanded its role in the life of the city, providing room for religious, political, judicial, commercial and even recreational activities. It also began its role as the site of historical memorials. In 366 B.C. the Temple of Concord, commemorating the end of civil struggles, was founded at the north end; and in 388 B.C. the nearby Rostra was decorated with the prows of ships captured in a great naval battle. The first honorific columns were erected in subsequent decades. Further changes in the physical appearance of the Forum occurred in the early second century B.C., when architectural influence from the eastern Mediterranean began to be felt. The first great halls for judicial and commercial affairs, basilicas, were built at that time. First was the Porcia (185 B.C.), followed by the Aemilia (179 B.C.) and the Sempronia (170 B.C.). The basilicas were built on land formerly occupied by

other buildings, and their erection marked the beginning of the long history of building and rebuilding to which the Forum was subjected over the following centuries.

It was in the later republican period that the Forum began to assume its role not only as the center of Rome, but as the center of the Mediterranean world. Older buildings were periodically restored, and new buildings were added, such as the Basilica Opimia (121 B.C.) and the Tabularium (78 B.C.), both at the north end. But in those cases, as in later ones, the literal function of the building began to be overlaid by the symbolic. The struggles for power over the Roman state that culminated in the career and death of Julius Caesar (died 44 B.C.), saw great changes in the Forum. Caesar's plans began with the rebuilding of the Basilica Aemilia in 54 B.C. That was followed by the removal of the Comitium to another location in Rome, the rebuilding of the Curia, the repaving of the central space, and most important, the destruction of the shops on the west side and their replacement by a huge new basilica, the Julia. All of these were not just physical but intentionally political acts, intended to display the beneficence of the first citizen of the state.

Equally important in the transformation of the Forum's role at that time was the building of a second forum, the Forum of Caesar, to the north of the original. Other public spaces had appeared in the city by that time, such as the Forum Boarium and the Forum Holitorium, both near the river bank, but those were for commercial functions. The Forum of Caesar provided space for the moneyers who had previously occupied the Basilica Aemilia and its shops, but its principal function was political as revealed by the erection at its north end of a temple to Venus Genetrix, the mythical ancestress of the Julian clan, and therefore of Julius Caesar

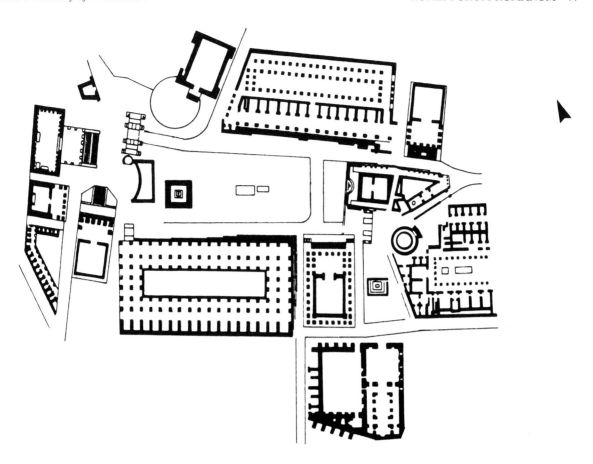

himself. That overtly political act, well understood by contemporaries, was reflected in the original Forum, whose own functions became less practical and more political from that time forward. Although he did not live to see the completion of most of his projects, Caesar's program of public building was continued and expanded by his successors, and effectively marked the end of one age in the history of the Forum and the beginning of the next—the imperial age.

Following the death of Caesar, his successor, Augustus, not only completed Caesar's plans, but continued the work of transforming both the physical appearance and the political function of the ancient public space. One of Augustus' first official acts was to commence the building of a temple to the Deified Julius at the south end of the Forum, in front of the Regia, and the last building to be erected within the space of the Forum proper. Adjacent to the west side of the new temple, an arch dedicated to Augustus himself was added. Many of the older buildings around the Forum underwent major restoration during that time and after, giving them the appearance that survived throughout antiquity. In addition, and equally important, Augustus—like Caesar before him—built a new forum, the Forum of Augustus, to the east of the Forum of Caesar. No commercial or even judicial functions were housed there, but rather a temple to Mars, and memorials of ancient heroes and members of the family of Augustus. The dynastic and symbolic content, even more than the political attributes, of the Forum of Augustus marked a major change in the history of public building in Rome. From that time onward the buildings and memorials that were erected in and around the Forum likewise were usually sacred, commemorative or honorific, which is to say, essentially of symbolic purpose.

Tiberius, the successor of Augustus, provided for the building of a commemorative arch near the Temple of Saturn. Caligula built a series of structures in an attempt to connect the Palatine to the Capitoline across the northwest corner of the Forum, but those structures did not long survive his downfall. In 71 A.D. Vespasian began another commemorative public space, the Temple of Peace, to the east of the Forum. His son Domitian built the Temple of the Deified Vespasian at the north end of the Forum, in front of the Tabularium, and also built a new forum, the Forum Transitorium, between the Forum of Augustus and the Temple of Peace, over the space formerly occupied by the Argiletum. Finally, Domitian's successor, Trajan, built yet another new forum, the Forum of Trajan, north of the Forum of Augustus. By the time of Trajan's death in 117 A.D., there was a huge assemblage of public spaces and buildings in the center of the city, of which the original Forum formed only a small part. By the middle of the second century A.D. it was so closed in by buildings and so crowded with various objects that it could no longer house many of its original functions. The Temple of Antoninus and Faustina was added to the southeast corner at that time. An honorific arch was erected to Septimius Severus in 203 A.D., in front of the Curia; four columns were erected nearby in 303 A.D. to commemorate the Tetrarchy; apart from a number of smaller memorials, those were the last intrusions into the space of the Forum. Yet it continued to hold its place as the historic center of the Roman state.

Many changes to the buildings of the Forum occurred during the Middle Ages. The ancient temples and basilicas were for the most part allowed to fall into decay, when their materials were not carried off for use elsewhere. Christian churches were built in and on the remains, and the collapse of abandoned buildings contributed to the raising of the ground well above the level of the ancient pavement. Virtually all of the smaller buildings and monuments disappeared from sight. The Forum nonetheless continued to function as a sacred place, its old meaning adapted to new purposes. Where formerly it had witnessed processions that entered from the south and terminated at the Temple of Jupiter on the Capitoline, commemorating the sacred history of the pagan city, it became part of the pilgrim route from the Church of San Giovanni in Laterano to St. Peter's, and commemorated the founding of Christianity, the ruin of the old world testifying to the triumph of the new. In addition, the Forum's surviving structures, even when damaged, provided an endless source of information to architects, such as Alberti, Bramante, Palladio and others. At the point of its greatest decay, in the 18th century, the Forum still inspired artists, poets and historians; the names of Giovanni Battista Piranesi and Edward Gibbon come to mind, to name only two.

The latest period in the history of the Forum began at the end of the 18th century, which saw the beginning of serious excavation. At first intermittent, the pace of activity increased gradually as medieval and later incrustations were removed, and more evidence about the ancient condition was revealed. After 1870 excavation became almost continuous, under the sponsorship of the newly created national government, for which the work had national significance. The most extensive demolition and clearing took place under the regime of Mussolini, whose own agenda was attached to the project, so that once more the Forum became a focus of political attention, albeit passively. The recovery of the ancient site was seen as a national goal, valuable in itself, and today most of the area of the original Forum, as it stood at the end of the imperial age, can be seen. Undoubtedly, the information uncovered by modern archaeological activity has been of inestimable historical value; it could be said on the other hand that what had to be destroyed to display that information was itself of historical value, although how great can no longer be determined. Once again the Forum played a role in an historic controversy, this time a peculiarly modern one.

—BERNARD M. BOYLE

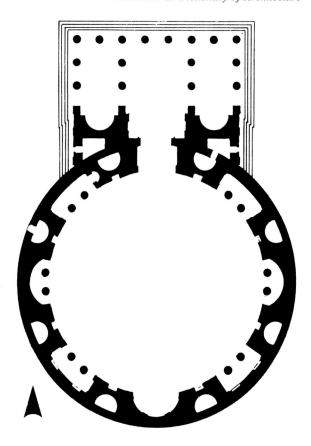

PANTHEON
Rome, Italy

120-124 A.D.

Publications

ARMELLINI, M.: *Le chiese di Roma del secolo IV al XIX*. 3rd ed., 2 vols., Rome, 1942.

BARTOCCETTI, V.: *Santa Maria ad Martyres (Pantheon)*. Rome, 1959.

BELTRAMI, L.: *Il Pantheon rivendicato ad Adriano*. Milan, 1929.

BLOMÉ, B.: "Piazza della Rotunda al Pantheon." *Opuscula romana* 4 (1962): 1-28.

BOATWRIGHT, MARY T.: *Hadrian and the City of Rome*. Princeton, New Jersey, 1989.

BORDINI, S.: "Bernini e il Pantheon." *Quaderni dell'Istituto di Storia dell'Architettura* 79-84 (1967): 53-84.

BUDDENSIEG, T.: "Criticism and Praise of the Pantheon in the Middle Ages and the Renaissance." In BOLGAR, R. R.

(ed.): *Classical Influences of European Culture*. Cambridge, 1971.

CARRETONI, G., et al.: *La pianta marmorea di Roma antica*. 2 vols. Rome, 1960.

CERASOLI, F.: "I restauri del Pantheon dal secolo XV al XVIII." *Bulletino della commissione archeologica communale di Roma* 37 (1909): 280-289.

CHIPIES, C.: "Model of the Pantheon." *American Architect* 33 (1891): 137-138.

COLINI, A. M., and GISMONDI, I.: "Contributi allo studio del Pantheon." *Bulletino della commissione archeologica communale di Roma* 54 (1926): 67-92.

COLONNA, G. B.: "Il Pantheon." *Capitolium* 14 (1934): 240-249.

D'OSSAT, G. DE ANGELIS: "La forma e la costruzione delle cupole nell'architettura romana." *Atti del III convegno nazionale di storia dell'architettura* (1938).

DE FINE LICHT, K.: *The Rotunda in Rome: A Study of Hadrian's Pantheon*. Copenhagen, 1966.

EROLI, G. M.: *Raccolta generale delle inscrizioni pagane e cristiane esistite ed esistente nel Pantheon di Roma*. Narni, 1895.

GIOVANNONI, G.: "Building and Engineering." In BAILEY, C. (ed.): *The Legacy of Ancient Rome*. Oxford, 1951.

GIOVANNONI, G.: "Pantheon." *Architettura et arti decorative* 8 (1928-29): 526-528.

HIRT, L.: *Osservazioni istorico-architettoniche sopra il Pantheon*. Rome, 1791.

KÄHLER, H.: "Das Pantheon in Rom." in STEINGRÄBER, E. (ed.): *Meilensteine europäischer Kunst*. Munich, 1965.

LANCIANI, R.: "Prima relazione sugli scavi per lo isolamento del Pantheon." *Notizie degli scavi di antichità* (1881): 255-294.

Pantheon: Rome, Italy, 120-124 A.D.

LANCIANI, R.: "Seconda relazione sugli scavi per lo isolamento del Pantheon." *Notizie degli scavi di antichità* (1882): 340-359.

LEHMANN, K.: "The Dome of Heaven." *Art Bulletin* 27 (1945): 1-27.

MacDONALD, WILLIAM L.: *The Pantheon: Design, Meaning, and Progeny.* Cambridge, Massachusetts, 1976.

MANETTI, U.: *Il Pantheon di Agrippa e le tombe dei reali d'Italia.* Rome, 1928.

MEEKS, C. L. V.: "Pantheon Paradigm." *Journal of the Society of Architectural Historians* 19 (1960).

MOMMSEN, T., and MEYER, P. M. (eds.): *Codex Theodosianus.* Translated into English by C. Pharr, Princeton, New Jersey, 1952.

MONTANI, C.: "Il Pantheon e i suoi recenti restauri." *Capitolium* 8 (1932): 417-426.

MOORE, F. G.: "The Gilt-Bronze Tiles of the Pantheon." *American Journal of Archaeology* 3 (1899): 40-43.

RIVOIRA, G. T.: "Di Adriano architetto e dei monumenti adrianei." *Rendiconti dell'Accademia nazionale dei Lincei* 18 (1909): 172-177.

RODOCANACHI, E.: "Le Panthéon." *La Revue de l'art ancien et moderne* 34 (1913): 279-286, 365-376.

SANGUINETTI, F.: "Nota sul consolidamento della trabeazione del pronao del Pantheon." *Palladio* 6 (1956): 78-79.

TOMEI, P.: "Le vicende del rivistimento della cupola del Pantheon." *Bollettino d'arte* 32 (1938): 31-39.

VIGHI, R.: *The Pantheon.* Rome, 1957.

VON GERKAN: "Das Pantheon in Rom." *Gnomon* 5 (1929): 273-277.

VON GEYMÜLLER, HEINRICH: *Documents inédits sur les Thermes d'Agrippa, le Panthéon et les Thermes de Dioclétian.* Lausanne and Rome, 1883.

*

The Roman temple dedicated to the pantheon of gods established a classic type in the history of architecture by uniting, for the first time, a domed rotunda with a Greek temple front used as a facade for the porch. The use of Greek columns and pediment was common in Roman architecture, where former structural elements of the post-and-lintel system of construction were adopted purely as facades or decorative members. The combination, in the Pantheon, of the most significant element of the Greek past with the most developed Roman building design, the centralized plan covered by a dome, represented not only a high point in the synthesis of the two traditions but also an astounding engineering achievement.

In plan the circular hall and the rectangular porch and facade of the Pantheon merged quite happily in favor of a frontal orientation of the building, which was the orientation preferred by Roman architects. But in elevation, the joining of the two parts was realized with such difficulty that historians were once tempted to date the porch facade to an earlier period. The precedence of the porch over the rotunda was suggested by an inscription that ran across the entablature stating that it was built by Marcus Agrippus, which would have dated it to the time of Emperor Augustus. Also, an examination of the masonry showed that, at the joining of the curved wall of the rotunda and the straight wall of the porch, a broken joint existed. Despite these incongruities, however, the fact that all parts of the Pantheon belonged to a single building campaign has now generally

Pantheon

Pantheon

been accepted, and the entire structure is dated to the reign of
Hadrian. The inscription apparently commemorated an earlier
building on the same site.

Still, the tentativeness of the novel design was, and is, undeniable. Between the rotunda and the porch stands a transitional
structure, an intermediary rectangular block, often simply considered part of the porch, which is what it appears to be from
the inside. But on the outside, the transitional block rises to the
height of the rotunda wall and spans the entire width of the
porch. Viewed from the front, the effect is twofold: the straight,
tall walls of the transitional block loom higher on either side
of the pediment, presenting a somewhat awkward arrangement
and concealing the dome. From the original street level, some
1.4 meters beneath the modern pavement, and with the original
high podium on which the Pantheon stood, the concealment of
the dome was even more complete. (The high podium and
the unusually tall pediment of the Pantheon recall, perhaps,
Etruscan, rather than Greek, models.)

Another exterior effect is that of the stacking or superposition
of triangular, rectangular and circular volumes in the form of
the pediment, block and rotunda, something that cannot be
gleaned from the plan. This stacking of separate geometric
spaces became a characteristic aesthetic of Romanesque architecture in the later medieval period; the Pantheon sets a Roman
precedent.

One of the strangest elements of the exterior is an engaged
pediment on the transitional block. The cornices of this pediment
line up with the middle of the three cornices that run around
the exterior rotunda wall. And, in correspondence with the taller
height of the transitional block, the engaged pediment reaches
higher than the actual pediment of the porch. If visible from

street level, the engaged pediment would envelope the real
pediment visually and bring the facade and transitional block
closer together, making them appear to be one. However, this
ingenious device was lost from view.

The massiveness of the actual material structure of the Pantheon and the complexity of the structural supports are also
concealed by the simplicity of the plan. The rotunda walls
consist of eight wide piers that alternate with as many niches.
In turn, the niches are alternately rectangular and semicircular
in plan. At the entrance, in place of a niche, the entire thickness
of the wall is pierced to open into the porch. The semicircular
niche opposite the entrance is deeper than the rest, establishing
a definite north-south axis, in keeping with the frontal orientation of the building, and in contrast to the centrality imposed
by the dome. The frontality is consistent also with the original
setting, where the rotunda once stood at one end of an open
rectangular, colonnaded court.

The Pantheon was built with a variety of materials, primarily
used as aggregate in the concrete mix, employed strategically
to strengthen or lighten the weight-bearing load. The aggregate
changed from travertine to tufa to brick and pumice. Foundations were sunk to a depth of approximately 4.5 meters and
were seven meters thick. The rotunda walls, structurally independent of the porch and transitional block, were also an enormous six or so meters thick. For the most part, the concrete
was brick-faced.

The building's sheer mass is phenomenal, especially in light
of the ability of the architect to conceal it, and in light of the
sense of extraordinary spaciousness one feels upon entering the
interior. Herein lies the notoriety of the design, in which so
vast a space is enclosed and so large a dome is sustained without

any inner supports. By incorporating within the rotunda walls a series of semidomes, chambers, brick relieving arches (appearing as brick arches in the exterior masonry) and brick vaults that run perpendicular to the wall for its entire thickness from the inside out, the need for an interior support system, such as walls, piers, or columns, was eliminated. Instead, the weight of the concrete dome, which thins at the top, was distributed down and onto the eight great piers through this complicated series of vaults on top of vaults embedded, and sometimes opened (to facilitate drying), in the thickness of the concrete walls.

The appeal of vaults and domes for Roman builders stemmed exactly from their ability to span great spaces. In the Pantheon the space-spanning qualities and the calculated equilibrium of mass to void, and dome to wall, were realized to a degree never before and never again seen, not even in domes of equal dimensions, such as Filippo Brunelleschi's dome in Florence Cathedral, where the interior forms and proportions were different.

To enter the Pantheon today is still one of the most profound of architectural experiences. The compatibility and tension of spatial openness and mural enclosure are riveting. A diagram of the elevation shows how two imaginary circles, each the diameter of the plan (approximately 43.2 meters), intersect in the interior to form the shape of a sphere. Even the floor has a convex curve, suggesting a spherical contour. The sense of perfection, infiniteness and completeness that one feels in the interior comes largely from the spatial experience of the sphere. Because the center of the sphere is at a height equal to the second interior cornice, the human presence is dwarfed. The idea of a pantheon of gods was thus crystallized in absolute form. The building's "cosmic" nature undoubtedly contributed to its universal appeal.

The schematic and structural phenomena of the Pantheon are impressive and bewildering, insofar as they are completely mysterious. One stands inside in awe and tends not to focus on the interior decoration with its muted marble revetment, aediculae and columns. The interior surfaces are flat and smooth. The tall columns, placed inside the niches, convert the open recesses into screens that stretch from pier to pier. The aediculae, once containing statues, that stand in front of the piers are the only truly three-dimensional decorative elements.

Projecting cornices divide the wall into two levels and separate the dome from the rotunda at a level much lower than on the exterior. Thus, the dome appears to be steeper inside than it does outside, where it looks flat due to the thickness of masonry amassed in steps against its lower circumference. The design of the five rows of coffers, inside the dome, which has lost its original decor, exaggerates the perspective. Rays of sun creep around the rotunda in continual movement, entering through the single light source, the 8.3-meter-wide oculus, in the center of the dome. The play of permanence and motion is another of the Pantheon's spatial conquests.

All of the components of the Pantheon had been used before in Roman building (for example, in the octagonal room in Nero's Golden House), but not on this scale. Whatever made the Romans reach for the limits of technical prowess also produced experiments in the manipulation of space and material that were as great as humankind has ever dared. The confidence of the master planner proved to be well-founded, for the Pantheon still stands intact, in almost perfect form. Its impact reverberated for centuries, inspiring buildings as diverse as Andrea Palladio's 16th century Villa Rotonda in Vicenza, Italy, and Thomas Jefferson's early-19th-century library rotunda at the University of Virginia, in the United States.

—PAULA D. LEVETO-JABR

TEMPLE OF FORTUNA VIRILIS
Rome, Italy

Ca. Second century B.C.: Extant temple constructed. **First century B.C.:** Renovations made.

Publications

FIECHTER, ERNST R.: "Der ionische Tempel am Ponte Rotto in Rom." *Mitteilungen des Kaiserlichen Deutschen Archäologischen Institut* 21 (1906): 220-279.
LYNGBY, HELGE: *Die Tempel Fortuna und der Mater Matuta am Forum Boarium in Rom.* Reprint. Vaduz, Liechtenstein, 1965.
MARCHETTI-LONGHI, G.: "Il tempio ionico di Ponte Rotto, tempio di Fortuna o di Fortune?" *Mitteilungen des Deutschen Archäologischen Institut* 40 (1925): 319-350.
MUÑOZ, ANTONIO: *Il restauro del tempio della Fortuna Virile.* Rome, 1925.

*

The complex political history of the Roman Republic profoundly affected the subsequent development of Roman architecture. With Rome's inexorable advance southward within Italy during the third century B.C. (punctuated by the defeat of Tarentum in 272 and the annexation of Sicily in 241), the conquerors confronted directly Greek monuments and Greek traditions of craftsmanship. The second-century B.C. conquest of the Greek mainland (highlighted by Flaminius' victory over Philip V of Macedonia in 194 and the sack of Corinth in 146) brought into Rome refugee craftsmen and architects, as well as the celebrated flood of gold, silver, paintings and statues. While puritanical traditionalists such as Cato exercised a restraining influence on public opinion, there were also enthusiastic philhellenes, men to whom the richer, more sophisticated cultural traditions of Greece opened up a new world of possibilities.

Aesthetic appreciation, the art market, and even anti-Greek reactions all met on the common ground that art was a typically Greek creation. Architects also maintained the superiority of the Greeks; the traditional Greek orders, for example, remained at the core of Roman monumental building down to late antiquity. Yet with rare exceptions late republican architects avoided slavish copying after Greek models. Italian building traditions readily assimilated and modified new architectural forms, but in matters of building practices and materials were resistant to the wholesale takeover by Greece found in Roman painting and sculpture. The new Romano-Hellenistic architecture was

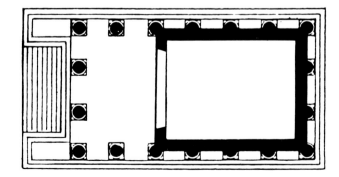

Temple of Fortuna Virilis: Rome, Italy, ca. 2nd-1st century B.C.

a complex phenomenon. Traditional plans were maintained, especially for sacred architecture; nevertheless, new life was given to such traditionally Italic building types as the forward-facing, podium-based temple, now reinterpreted in terms of the outward forms and proportions of the Greek orders.

The rectangular temple in Rome's Forum Boarium (cattle market) near the Tiber provides an excellent example of this architectural synthesis. It is generally known as the Temple of Fortuna Virilis (Manly Fortune), but was probably dedicated to Portunus, the god of harbors. While recent excavations (1947) have revealed ancient remains indicating a foundation in the late fourth century B.C., the extant temple is a remarkably well-preserved monument of the late second century B.C., showing evidence of some rebuilding in the first century B.C. but no later major modifications. Elements of Italic (Etruscan) derivation are immediately visible in the plan: the high podium, the flight of steps at the front leading to the cella, and the deep portico. The construction is purely Roman. The walls of the cella are tufa, a solidified volcanic dust or mud. The podium is concrete, faced with travertine slabs; travertine is also used for the six

freestanding columns of the porch (four in front of the prodomus and one on each side of it) and the four engaged corner columns of the cella. Remains show that the use of these disparate materials was disguised by covering them in stucco scored and finished to imitate dressed stone.

Equally obvious is the attempt to Hellenize the building. Unlike earlier Etruscan building types, the porch takes up less than half the area of the temple and has only four by two columns. The elegantly slender proportions are derived from Greek sources, as are the Ionic style of the columns, although their capitals lack the organic fluidity of Greek models. A compromise between two distinct traditions is apparent in the way in which Roman builders carried the peristyle around the side and back walls of the temple in engaged columns rather than in the freestanding forms generally preferred by Greek architects. In fact, the Temple of Fortuna Virilis is possibly the earliest pseudoperipteral temple and may have influenced the monumental Maison Carrée at Nîmes (1-10 A.D.).

The use of *opus caementicium* (Roman concrete) foreshadowed what was to become a revolutionary building material.

Italian workers readily used it in place of more costly and cumbersome stone; later it would interest Roman architects for its possible use in the creation of new architectural forms. The growing Roman tendency to treat the Greek orders as elements of a decorative facade which might or might not express the constructional logic of underlying structure is also notable. A contemporary Greek would have found the result crude and provincial, but this was because it expressed characteristically Roman needs in terms of specifically local building traditions. The reinterpretation of those traditions in terms of philhellenic taste ensured the enduring Italic contribution to the formal vocabulary of later Roman architecture.

—PETER J. HOLLIDAY

THEATER OF MARCELLUS
Rome, Italy

Ca. 13-11 B.C.: Dedicated. **Middle Ages:** Converted into fortress. **16th century A.D.:** Converted into palace.

Publications

CALZA-BINI, ALBERTO: "Il teatro di Marcello." *Bollettino del Centro di Studi per la Storia dell'Architettura* 7 (1953): 1-44.

FIDENZONI, PAOLO: "La liberazione del teatro di Marcello e lo soprimento di una casetta medioevale." *Capitolium* 2 (1927): 594-600.
FIDENZONI, PAOLO: *Il teatro di Marcello.* Rome, 1970.
ORIGO, BENEDETTA (compiler): *Theatrum marcelli.* Rome, 1973.

*

According to historical tradition, the Theater of Marcellus was the second permanent theater to be built in Rome, the first having been the Theater of Pompey (55-52 B.C.). The Theater of Marcellus may have been projected by Julius Caesar, although this is not at all sure; in any case it was not finished and dedicated before 13-11 B.C., during the reign of Emperor Augustus.

In plan the theater formed a semicircle nearly 400 feet in diameter, enclosing seating for as many as 11,000 spectators, the seats arranged in three tiers, each tier in turn rising at a steeper pitch than the one below. The ends of the semicircle were continued at either side of the stage, incorporating and enclosing both the side entrances and subordinate chambers of the stage block, itself also walled in at the rear.

The outer facade, originally nearly 90 feet high, is preserved today only in its two lower stories, although later additions have maintained the roof line at something close to its original position. Forty-six stone piers carried arches and vaults of stone; in this case travertine was used for the entire exterior facing, the first time in Rome for that application. Behind the facade the stairs, inner ramps and vaults, and the two lower sections of seating were all of concrete. The uppermost tier of seating

Theater of Marcellus: Rome, Italy, ca. 13-11 B.C.

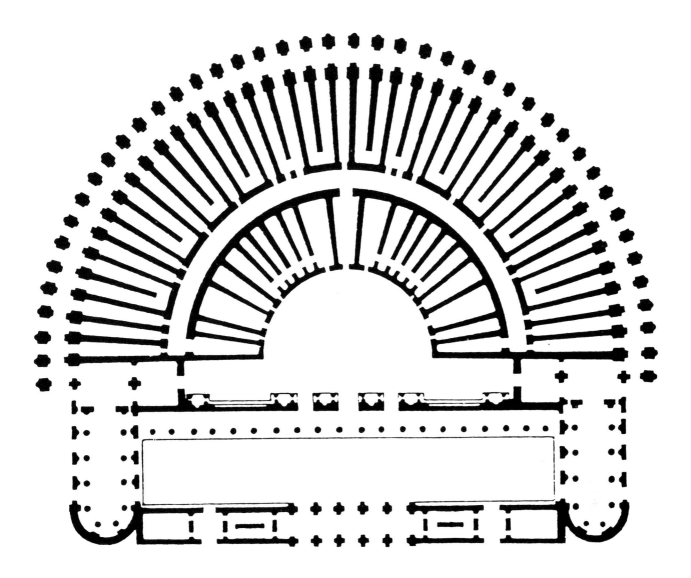

was probably timber. The external arcades were decorated with attached half columns and entablatures, in imitation of post-and-beam construction; the lower rank of half columns was in an elongated version of the Tuscan Doric order, and the upper rank was Ionic, standing on pedestals. The question as to whether or not the uppermost (now lost) story of the exterior had attached half columns or pilasters in the Corinthian order answers itself. All later buildings employing the same expressive mode—such as the Colosseum—used a third order if needed, so it does not matter whether the upper story of the Theater of Marcellus was decorated or plain, for the language had been established below.

In its design as a theater, it represented the final acceptance in Rome of the theater as a separate building type, housing a distinct function. Rome had been until then conservative if not retardataire in its attitude toward the theater as a type. While its stage wall (*scaenae frons*) was apparently not modeled richly in the Hellenistic manner, something that had already appeared by that time elsewhere in Italy, e.g., at Pompeii, most of the other peculiarly Roman elements of theater design were present.

First, the building stood on a completely flat site near the Tiber, and thus was carried entirely on a huge substructure built

mainly of concrete, supplanting the earlier practice of building theaters against hillsides or carving them out of temple platforms. Second, it was totally closed to the outside, with its facade extending above and beyond the entrances at the sides of the stage, and connecting with the high rear wall of the stage house to form a single architectural unit. Third, the ancient connection between theater and sacred site was abandoned, a connection that had been preserved at all the late republican theater sites outside Rome, and in Rome itself as late as at the Theater of Pompey, noted above, where a temple of Venus stood at the crown of the seating area, deliberately referring to Italic tradition. All three features—flat site, total enclosure, secular function—together combined to separate the Roman theater as a building type from its Hellenistic antecedents; the Theater of Marcellus was in effect to become the model that defined the theater for the remainder of the Roman world. What was important about the great building was its typically Roman combination of conservatism with innovation; its use of the classical orders in a decorative and symbolic manner was a continuation of a practice well established during the late republic, while its vaulted concrete interior looked forward to the novel forms of the architecture of the empire. On one hand, historically, the theater was divorced from its site-bound origins by its structural means, and on the other hand, iconographically, it was separated from its traditional connotations by the omission of any sacred reference.

Yet more, the Theater of Marcellus was to contribute, in itself or through its almost innumerable successors, to the definition of the theater in Western architecture from the 15th century to the present. After antiquity, its preservation was owed to its being converted for use as a fortress in the Middle Ages, and as a palace in the 16th century. Modern restoration has revealed what can be seen today. It has always been viewed as a perfect model of ancient theater form; it was represented in plan and part elevation in Sebastiano Serlio's treatise, Book III, whence its influence radiated to Andrea Palladio and his successors. The theater, both as a building and as a function, has been understood since Roman times as providing essentially an internal, secular experience. It was for those qualities above all that the Theater of Marcellus was understood by later ages.

—BERNARD M. BOYLE

SEGESTA
Greek/Sicily

Sixth century B.C.: Sanctuary constructed. **Fifth century B.C.:** Temple constructed. **First century B.C.:** Theater constructed. **1000 A.D.:** Destroyed.

Temple: Segesta, Greek/Sicily, 5th century B.C.

Publications

DINSMOOR, WILLIAM BELL: *The Architecture of Ancient Greece.* New York, 1975.
HITTORFF, JACQUES-IGNACE, and ZANTH, L.: *Architecture antique de la Sicile: Recueil des monuments de Ségeste et de Sélinonte.* Paris, 1870.
KOLDEWEY, R., and PUCHSTEIN, O.: *Die griechischen Tempel in Unteritalien und Sicilien.* Berlin, 1899.
MARCONI, P.: "Segesta, esplorazioni della scena del teatro." *Notizie degli Scavi della Reale Accademia Nazionale dei Lincei* 54 (1929).
SCULLY, VINCENT: *The Earth, the Temple, and the Gods: Greek Sacred Architecture.* New York, 1969.
SERRADIFALCO, DUCA DI: *Le antichità della Sicilia.* 5 vols. Palermo, 1834-42.

*

Located six miles from the sea, on Monte Varvaro in northwestern Sicily, Segesta (Greek *Egesta*) was the capital city of the Elymi. According to Thucydides, the Elymians were a cross between local peoples and Trojan and Phocian refugees. Their two main towns were Eryx, which housed a sanctuary to Astarte-Aphrodite, and Segesta, famed in antiquity for medicinal sulphurous springs. Despite its remote location, Segesta was also the site of a massive fifth-century-B.C. classical Greek temple and a fine Late Hellenistic stone theater.

Although not a Greek city, Segesta was already considerably Hellenized by the sixth century B.C., when the Elymians built a sanctuary surrounded by a large *temenos* enclosure wall at the foot of their settlement and citadel on the Acropolis hill. Broken fragments of columns, triglyphs and other architectural elements comprise the remains of at least three Doric buildings within the sanctuary. By the fifth century B.C., the Elymians wrote their language in Greek characters, used a Greek legend on their coinage, entered into an alliance with Athens against their powerful rival and neighbor Selinus, and undertook the construction of one of the most impressive classical Greek temples in western Sicily.

The unfinished Doric temple stands isolated on the hill opposite the Acropolis. Seen from the higher ground of the theater to the southeast, its eastern front echoes the pyramidal mountain rising behind it. At its west end lies a vast and deep ravine that was perhaps ritually associated with the cult of an earth goddess, such as Demeter or Artemis. According to Cicero, a sacred bronze statue of Diana-Artemis was worshipped as the "god of Segesta." Its extremely fine workmanship was so prized that it was captured by Pyrrhus, returned by Scipio Africanus, and stolen once again by Verres.

The temple was probably begun during the alliance with Athens after 426 B.C. and was left unfinished either because of the war with Selinus in 416 B.C. or the Carthaginian invasion of 409 B.C. Segesta's close relationship with Athens suggests that an Athenian architect was commissioned to design and build the monumental temple in the contemporary classical Greek style. Classical refinements are evident in the curvature of the stereobate, stylobate and top of the abaci, and in the double-angle contraction of the intercolumniations. The scale of the hexastyle temple, measuring 76 by 190 feet on the stylobate and its peristyle of 36 columns standing 31 feet high, is larger than the massive Temple of Concord at Agrigento.

The temple is well preserved with pediments and metope-triglyph friezes intact, but the roof and cella apparently were never completed. This suggests that the peristyle was completed before the cella. In its unfinished state, bosses are left on the blocks of the steps, columns are unfluted, joints are undressed,

Theater: Segesta, Greek/Sicily, 1st century B.C.

the local shell conglomerate remains unstuccoed, and there are no sockets for the roof or ceiling beams. The cornice soffit at each corner, however, received a floral pattern carved in relief, giving an idea of how carefully the peristyle was to have been decorated.

Some speculate that the temple was deliberately left unroofed as an open-air sanctuary, the site of a nature cult. But the architectural vocabulary, mathematical proportions and subtle refinements of the extant portion of the temple are analogous to the Sicilian temples at Agrigento, Syracuse and Himera, which were originally roofed and had inner buildings. One assumes that modifications, such as eliminating the pediments, would have been made if the temple were to be left unroofed. It is more plausible that political and economic circumstances curtailed the building activity, leaving at Segesta a magnificent, unfinished shell.During the fourth century B.C., Segesta endured violent domination and destruction by Carthage and various despots. In the first Punic War of the third century B.C., Segesta surrendered to the Romans, who, on the grounds of their common descent from Troy, treated it generously as a *civitas libera et immunis*. The town was rebuilt and prospered. It had its own trading port at Castellammare, and a theater was built. The stone theater is nestled in the hillside below the Acropolis. Unusual in that it faces north, it is oriented with a spectacular view over the hills and sea, and it is situated so that the actors cast their shadows behind them. It was designed for local plays, with modifications for the convenience of the actors and the audience. As at Syracuse, the orchestra was provided with an underground passage and steps, which enabled the actors to surprise the spectators by suddenly popping up from the underworld.

Because there was no natural amphitheater in the north-facing hill, the builders had to dig into the hillside to construct a high wall to support the *cavea* of about 20 courses of seats, an Italic idea superimposed onto a Greek design. The *skene* building was two stories and elaborately decorated with engaged and freestanding pilasters and columns on both levels, Ionic above and Doric below. The architectural decoration thus served as the permanent scenic background to the raised stage, a characteristic feature of Roman theaters that may indicate a modification of circa 100 B.C.

Projecting obliquely from the *skene* and framing the horseshoe-shaped stage were two-story *parascenia* with open galleries to give the audience seated at the sides of the auditorium a full view of the play. The front faces were decorated on the ground floor with engaged statues of Pan, who was probably associated with an early cult center in the natural cave under the theater. The cave was approached by a doorway from the west part of the *cavea,* a skillful fusion of structure and natural setting.

Segesta was still a significant community in the early first century A.D. (Tacitus, *Annals* 4.43), but declined shortly thereafter when it fell out of Roman favor. It was destroyed by the Saracens in about 1000 A.D.

—SUSAN SILBERBERG-PEIRCE

IMPERIAL PALACE OF DIOCLETIAN

Split, Yugoslavia

3rd-4th centuries A.D.

Publications

ADAM, ROBERT: *Ruins of the Palace of the Emperor Diocletian at Spalatro in Dalmatia.* London, 1764.
MARASOVIĆ, J. and T.: *Diocletian's Palace.* Zagreb, 1970.
NIEMANN, GEORGE: *Der Palast Diokletians in Spalato.* Vienna, 1910.

*

The retirement palace of the Late Roman emperor Diocletian comprises the nucleus of the modern city of Split. A keystone in architectural history, the palace has been continuously inhabited since the Late Roman Empire. Diocletian resided there from the time of his abdication in 305 A.D. until his death in 313. A city developed from within the palace during the early Middle Ages and continued to grow, providing a wealth of architectural remains from all periods in its long history.

Diocletian chose to build his palace at the exact center of the Bay of Aspalathos on the Eastern Adriatic coast in Dalmatia. The landscape afforded protection from winds and high seas

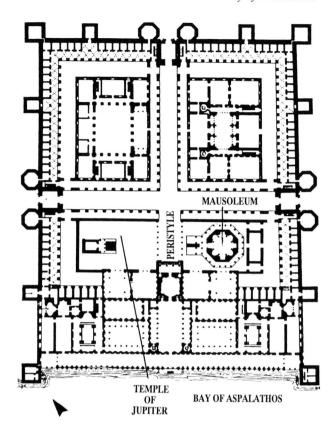

MAUSOLEUM

PERISTYLE

TEMPLE
OF
JUPITER   BAY OF ASPALATHOS

in the winter and offered the advantage of ameliorating breezes in the summer. The island of Brač lies across the bay; the quarry there provided the limestone out of which almost the entire palace was built. Even the architectural ornamentation was carved out of Brač limestone. Undoubtedly, Diocletian, a native of Dalmatia, chose the site primarily so that he could spend his retirement years at his birthplace. It is also likely that, having implemented the new tetrarchic policy of governing, under which the empire was not only divided between East and West and then subdivided but was also co-ruled, Diocletian felt compelled to remain vigilant with regard to political events following his abdication. Geographically, Split held a strategic position, the point at which the Western and Eastern empires met.

Reliable literary sources are silent as to Diocletian's enigmatic personality. But both personality and policy are reflected in the enigmatic home he built for himself. We do know that Diocletian was of a peasant, agrarian background with simple tastes. According to one biographer, Diocletian praised the cabbages grown by his own hands. He was also highly organized and disciplined. An active, accomplished soldier and military leader, Diocletian was a prolific builder of fortifications.

Despite the well-preserved state of the Palace at Split, uncertainties abound, the most pressing being the typology and iconography not only of individual structures but of the palace as a whole. The Scottish architect Robert Adam conducted the first exploration of the palace in 1757. His Vitruvian bias led to romanticized descriptions and drawings of the palace, but they do afford insight into Adam's aesthetic ideal. Scientific explorations conducted by the Austrians and French at the turn of this century contributed factual information and a more accurate plan. Subsequent studies have searched for models in an attempt to explain the anomalies in the palace, only to find that the usual categories are hard to apply. The Palace at Split defies usual methods of analysis.

Imperial Palace of Diocletian: Split, Yugoslavia, 3rd-4th centuries

In many respects the ground plan appears derivative of the Roman *castra* (military camp): both are characterized by a fortification surrounding a systematized plan based on two principal axes intersecting at the center. The palace is enclosed by a circuit of walls with protruding towers and gates at the center of each wall. A row of arched openings articulates each wall at the second level. Neither the walls nor the towers are defensible. The south facade, which rises out of the sea, has towers at the corners only, leaving it vulnerable. The three land gates have two unusual features: the towers that flank them are polygonal as opposed to the more customary rectangular or curved shape, and they have interior courtyards. Interior courtyards in forts were customary during the Augustan period but not later. Those at Split may be deliberately old-fashioned, but more likely served a nonmilitary purpose, perhaps as reception areas. The gates of the Diocletianic camp at Luxor had similar courtyards, but the plan of that camp was more ceremonial than military. The forms within the circuit system at Split do not seem dictated by military tactical necessity. And the presence of civil forms complicates the assessment. Fortifications seem inconsistent with its function as a palace, far from the frontiers, where Diocletian could retire to grow cabbages. More likely, the circuit system reflects the tastes of the soldier-emperor and symbolizes the might of the Roman Empire.

The two principal intersecting axial streets have survived. This feature commonly exists in Roman *castra* and in towns. The *decumanus* connects the east and west gates and bisects the palace. Most of the southern block contains private, residential spaces. Too little of the northern sectors has been excavated to allow precise reconstruction, but presumably they contained shops, workshops, servants' quarters and gardens. The *cardo*

extends from the North Gate, the principal entrance, to the Peristyle, just south of the main intersection.

The North Gate opened onto the main artery connecting the palace with the thriving city of Salona. The ornamentation of the North Gate was both lavish and propagandistic. Five pedestals supporting statues of Diocletian, his self-claimed divine father, Jupiter, and the other three tetrarchs crowned the gate. The gate was meant to convey the authority of the tetrarchy and overwhelm an approaching visitor with a sense of awe and dignity.

All interior spaces are aligned with the *cardo* and *decumanus,* but the palace as a whole is centered in the complex of three buildings just south of the principal intersection. The strongly centralized and tightly systematized plan is testimony to the highly disciplined character of the soldier-emperor and to his goal of centralizing the empire. The four quadrants of the palace symbolically suggest the tetrarchic form of government he boldly implemented.

The Peristyle, its form, function and iconography have been the most debated part of the palace. A clearer understanding of its meaning, as well as that of the two structures that communicate with it to the east and west, will shed considerable light on the meaning of the palace as a whole. The Peristyle, an open-air basilica type form, presents the image of a "classical temple turned inside-out." The space, 27 meters long and 13.5 meters wide, is defined on the east and west sides by closely spaced columns supporting small arches. The south end terminates in a porch. Four massive columns support an arcuated lintel, straight on the sides and arched over the central intercolumniation. Crowning the whole is a pediment on which George Niemann (1910) found a sculpture pedestal with evidence of a

Imperial Palace of Diocletian, octogonal mausoleum

The formal details peculiar to the Peristyle, along with the key role it plays in the centralization of the palace, have suggested to Ejnar Dyggve and Richard Krautheimer a more ceremonial and symbolic interpretation of the Peristyle. Side arcades with a central arch notable in Early Christian churches resemble the Peristyle. Both in form and decoration, the Peristyle and the Porch, especially with the triumphal association of the latter, afforded a framework suitable for imperial ceremony. The panegyrics written in the late third and early fourth centuries testify to processions and elaborate ceremony on the occasion of an emperor's arrival and appearance. The Peristyle, in concert with the North Gate and the *cardo,* provided the requisite setting for such an occasion. But the extent to which the nonreigning emperor would be celebrated, in his retirement home in particular, complicates this interpretation.

An alternative ritual connection is suggested by comparisons with plans of military camps. The shrine for the imperial cult customarily stood at or near the intersection of the *cardo* and *decumanus.* In the Diocletianic camp at Luxor, the shrine had a strong longitudinal approach framed by columns; in Castra Dionysiados the approach was an open processional way; in the Diocletianic camp at Palmyra the shrine was approached by a colonnaded street. The combination of military and ceremonial components is striking. Given the considerable time Diocletian spent in the East and in Egypt, and his predilection for military building, the Peristyle may derive from these forms and functions. The Peristyle at Split, however, accommodated a living figurehead, which may account for the modifications prevalent there.

The presence of a tomb and a temple within the palace, and the intimate formal relationship between them and the Peristyle are without known precedents. Both the literary sources and the early explorations of the palace offer garbled records as to the identification of the two buildings, but recent research has confirmed the building in the eastern *temenos* as the Mausoleum of Diocletian and that in the western *temenos* as the Temple of Jupiter. The plan of the mausoleum, now the Cathedral of Split, derives from a Late Antique tomb type. The porch, the high podium and the circular cella with niches, alternately curved and rectangular, that characterize the mausoleum appear in seven tombs built between 225 and 350 A.D.: the Temple of Portunus in Porto, the tomb of Gallienus on the Via Appia, the tetrarchic examples of the Tor di Schiavi, the Mausoleum of Maxentius and in Salonika the Mausoleum of Galerius; fourth-century examples of the type are the Mausolea of Helen and of Costanza. The Split architects modified the plan with an octagonal exterior wall and podium. While the plan is Western, the construction reflects Eastern methods, most notably in the absence of concrete: even the dome is constructed of bricks laid in fanlike sections. The elevation departs from the Western type as well: an emphasis on verticality raised the podium and cella wall to a height that rises significantly above the ambulatory roof. Lavish decoration dominates the interior, resulting in a shaftlike space. Massive columns carrying heavy continuous entablatures articulate the wall between the niches. Above that is a second order whose height is about half as high as the lower order. A wide frieze with clipeate figures of Diocletian and his wife Prisca, along with funerary imagery, lies behind the capitals of the upper order. The tooling and the style of the ornamentation both there and on the Temple of Jupiter evince the presence of Eastern master craftsmen who worked cooperatively with local masons.

The proximity of the mausoleum to the residential block is unusual but significant, as it anticipated later Christian practice. Its axial and symmetrical relationship to the Temple of Jupiter is equally unusual. Diocletian's anticipation of his apotheosis

bronze triumphal chariot. The Peristyle, open on the north, communicates directly with the intersection of the principal streets.

N. Duval maintains that the Peristyle served as a connective thoroughfare, a continuation of the *cardo,* joining the northern half of the palace and the southern residential block. But several features distinguish the Peristyle and set it apart from the colonnaded street: 1) Recent (1959-60) excavations revealed three steps leading down to the paved floor around the east, west, and north sides. On the south side, two banks of steps led up to the porch and to the residence behind it; under the central arch of the porch was a low stone *transennae,* suggesting a tribunal; below this a vaulted flight of steps led to the basement level. 2) The length of the colonnades of the Peristyle are dictated by the *temenoi* or courtyards that contain Diocletian's Mausoleum to the east and the Temple of Jupiter to the west. 3) The colonnades of the *cardo* and *decumanus* have straight entablatures whereas those of the Peristyle are more closely spaced and are arcuated. 4) The column shafts in the Peristyle and Porch are red Egyptian granite and were appropriated by Diocletian from an Egyptian temple. This marks an early example of the use of *spolia.*

The feasibility of this sunken formalized space serving as a thoroughfare to the residential block is doubtful. Pedestrian traffic through these spaces today is congested. Visually, the Peristyle colonnades harmonize with the Porch as one unit while concurrently creating a link with the *temenoi.* The Peristyle from this perspective marks the culmination of the principal thoroughfare: visually and conceptually it links the three most important areas of the palace. It also serves as "a prelude to the residential block" while the Porch doubles as an impressive facade to the imperial apartments.

Imperial Palace of Diocletian, drawing of palace

and his belief in his eternal divine authority may explain the arrangement.

The presence of a monumental temple on the grounds of a residence is peculiar. Temple-like decorative pavilions such as the Temple of Aphrodite in Hadrian's Villa at Tivoli appear more frequently than actual temples. The Temple of Jupiter is a classic example of a Roman temple with the exception of one element: the cella has a stone barrel-vaulted roof. The vault is coffered and departs from contemporary vaulting in Rome. The closest parallels lie in Western triumphal arches. A Late Imperial funerary building in the west necropolis at Side bears a close formal resemblance to the temple, but the contexts and functions of the two buildings differ. The date of the building is under debate, and may postdate Diocletian's Palace.

The density of carved ornamentation on the Temple of Jupiter exceeds that on any other structure in the palace. Lush vine scrolls animated with birds, exotic creatures and vintaging erotes express prosperity and fertility. Images associated with victory and triumph and with the Roman pantheon embellish the gables, the consoles on the door lintel and the coffers of the vault. Triumphal iconography, in concert with images of Jupiter and Hercules, proclaims eternal victory for the tetrarchic ideology. Diocletian "equated divine filiation with dynastic succession": he considered himself the son of Jupiter and his co-ruler Maximianus the son of Hercules. The prosperity and regeneration of the empire under the tetrarchy was, Diocletian claimed, divinely empowered.

The western *temenos* also contains two small round buildings symmetrically situated in front of the Temple of Jupiter. This configuration is unprecedented in Roman architecture. The two buildings are too small to be temples. The fragments of carved decoration are similar in motif and style to much of the carving on the Temple of Jupiter but more modest in treatment. The decoration and placement of the buildings indicate that they were subsidiary cult structures, shrines or *tropaea:* deliberately linked to the temple but subordinated to it.

The Palace at Split is a highly systematized pastiche of typological categories. We must consider not only "what the spaces were used for but what they were meant to communicate." The experimental nature of the palace must be analyzed in terms of the unique status of the client: a nonreigning, living emperor who professed to found a divinely ordained dynasty. This unprecedented circumstance fostered not only new forms but new functions for those already established: a testimony to the inventiveness of the palace architects.

—JOANNE MANNELL

SYRACUSE
Greek

733 B.C.: Founded. **Sixth century B.C.:** Apollo and Olympian Zeus temples constructed. **Fourth century B.C.:** Theater constructed. **Fourth century B.C.:** Euryalos fort constructed. **Third century B.C.:** Altar constructed.

Greek Theater: Syracuse, Greece, 4th century B.C.

Publications

DINSMOOR, WILLIAM BELL: *The Architecture of Ancient Greece*. New York, 1975.
KOLDEWEY, R., and PUCHSTEIN, O.: *Die griechische Tempel in Unteritalien und Sizilien*. Berlin, 1899.

*

The political and economic development of mainland Greece in the eighth century B.C. saw a massive increase in overseas contacts, dominated by a few (and particularly progressive) states. This in turn led to an enhanced awareness of opportunities for settlement, either to relieve the pressure of rapidly increasing populations, or, perhaps more cogently in some instances, to facilitate a takeover of landed property in Greece itself by dominant communities. Sicily, which earlier had been visited by traders, was suited for such settlement, being fertile, and with an existing population that seems to have been small, ill-organized and unable to resist the newcomers. The Greeks settled on that part of the island which faced toward the east, and a string of colonies was founded there at dates that can be calculated on the basis of information given by the fifth-century-B.C. historian Thucydides to be from 734 B.C. onward.

Syracuse, founded by Corinth in 733 B.C., was the second colony to be established, and it became the most important of the Greek cities of Sicily. It was already a native Sicilian settlement, and had probably served as a point of contact for Greek traders. The advantages of the location were considerable. The nucleus of the settlement was an island, Ortygia, separated from the mainland only by the narrowest of straits (which is now merely a canal). Syracuse was thus easily defendable, and was famous also for its water supply, the spring of Arethusa (which still survives). South of the island an extensive beach sweeps around to another headland, forming the superb, sheltered Grand Harbor. There is extensive agricultural land behind the city, and easy communication with the rest of the island. From the outset Syracuse was a flourishing community, and this condition obviously was matched by its architecture.

There are two relatively early temples, one on Ortygia dedicated to Apollo, the other outside the city to the south by the Grand Harbor, and dedicated to Olympian Zeus. Both belong to the sixth century B.C., though the exact dating is uncertain. The Temple of Apollo has an inscription on its east stylobate, apparently recording the names of its architects (or the dedicator and the architect, the reading being unclear). The letterforms, compared with those used in other inscriptions, have been dated to late in the sixth century, but this seems far too late for the architectural details, which are so undeveloped that the temple appears to be one of the earliest in Sicily. Quite clearly it is very tentative in its handling of stone for the columns and the entablature, suggesting that it was built in an experimental manner in the period of transition between the time when Greek temples (like that of Zeus at Olympia) had wooden columns and wooden entablatures, and the developed stone forms which were becoming general in mainland Greece by the middle of the sixth century. It is particularly significant to compare the Syracuse temple with the second Temple of Apollo, dated to 540 B.C., at Corinth, Syracuse's mother city, with which the colony continued to have a close relationship. Apollo Syracuse seems much older. The problem is to decide whether or not any allowance has to be made for a provincial time lag, and any such estimate is bound to be subjective. Apollo at Syracuse (like the Temple of Zeus, which is very similar in detail, but even more badly preserved) had monolithic shafts for the columns, whose height is barely four times their lower diameter, the most ponderously thick of all Greek temple columns, and suggesting that the architect had no faith in the strength and bearing capacity of the limestone. In addition to that, the columns were placed very close together to reduce the free span of the stone entablature they had to support. There was differential spacing between the columns of the facade and those of the flank. On the facade, the gap between the columns was about the same distance as the diameter of the shafts, but on the flanks it was narrower, the columns there being so close that there would not have been room for the normal pair of metopes to each pair of columns, and the suggestion has been made (the frieze does not in fact survive) that there could have been only one, perhaps rectangular, metope rather than the normal two square ones. On the facade the rhythm was more normal (despite the weight of a pediment over the entablature, assuming the temple had one). Perhaps this was done to preserve an accepted and normal rhythm there, while the architect played for safety on the flanks. He also tried to reduce the weight on the columns by hollowing out the back of the architrave, so that it is L-shaped in section. The plan of this temple is also abnormal compared with the temples of the mainland, though echoed in other Sicilian temples of the sixth century. The cella is long and relatively narrow. Arrangement of the cross walls is not certain, but given the proportions, almost certainly the cella ended with a small inner room (an "adytum") found in other Sicilian temples of the sixth century, which suggests an origin outside the Doric area of the Greek mainland. Another certain peculiarity is the duplication of the facade colonnade at an interval of two flank columnar spacings. This temple cannot have originated out of nothing: probably the lost antecedents for it should be looked for at Syracuse itself, such as the first Temple of Athena, now almost entirely lost.

Much better preserved is the later Temple of Athena, on the island of Ortygia, built as a thank-offering after the victory over the Carthaginians at Himera in 480 B.C., and perhaps paid for out of reparations claimed from the Carthaginians on their defeat. The temple itself is now embedded in the structure of the cathedral. The spaces between the side colonnades have been walled up to form the sides of the cathedral, the original facade has been removed and replaced by a splendid Baroque front, the cella walls of the temple pierced to form the openings between nave and aisles. But from within, as well as from

the sides, the massive limestone Doric columns are visible, including those of the front porch; somehow their position within the structure and embellishments of the cathedral gives a truer impression of their original grandeur than is found in other temples which survive as freestanding ruins, however complete, such as the temples at Agrigento. As a temple, Athena at Syracuse had a facade of six Doric columns and 14 along the flanks. The proportions of the columns, their height being equal to about 4½ times the base diameter, are still much heavier than those of contemporary marble Doric of the mainland, though much closer to those of its limestone near contemporary, Zeus at Olympia. An important feature of the temple is the narrowing of the intercolumnar spacing for the first two pairs of columns on the flank as well as the facades, the first instance of the double contraction designed to counteract the problem caused by the rule that Doric entablatures have to end with a triglyph.

Classical Syracuse was not confined to the island of Ortygia. Political events in the fifth century, in particular, led to the incorporation of the Greek populations from other communities into an enlarged state, and thus its area had to extend over the adjacent mainland. In this area are the remains of the Greek theater, one of the largest known, and dating in its final form essentially to the fourth century B.C., when Syracuse underwent a revival after a period of decline, though a theater must have existed there before. Close to it was the spectacular altar built by Hieron II in the second half of the third century B.C., of the long, narrow form, decorated with a system of triglyphs and metopes, which probably originated at Corinth. This, however, was far more grandiose than the older triglyph altars of the mainland, measuring no less than 198 meters in length.

Most important, though, and especially for the history of military architecture, was the outer defensive system of Syracuse on the hill of Epipolai west of the city, the great fort of Euryalos. The strategical importance of this hill was first recognized during the ill-fated Athenian siege of Syracuse in 415-412 B.C., when seizure of the fort by the Syracusans prevented the Athenians from cutting them off completely. With the development by Dionysus I early in the next century of Syracuse as the dominant Greek city in the west, the walls were extended to run up to the hill itself, and thereafter there was always a major military installation on the summit.

The summit was approached by the strong city wall, which reached it in a section of zigzags. There a powerful tower helped to protect a reentrant angle, at the back of which was a double gateway. The walls of the reentrant, flanking the approach, offered immediate protection, but the whole position was dominated by the fort itself, on the hill just above. There the hill is quite steep, the naturally easier approach to it being along the ridge to the west. So it was there that the most massive fortification was constructed, the final stages (probably not brought to completion) being added by the great Hellenistic scientist and engineer Archimedes, who was a native of Syracuse. The ridge itself was cut through by a deep ditch, which could not be crossed except by a bridge. This led to an open area in front of the fortifications. Next came a broad intermediate ditch, to protect the outwork immediately behind it. Both ditch and outwork were like a broad arrowhead in plan. Behind the outwork was yet another ditch, sheer-sided and topped by an inner wall. Access to it was blocked at the northern end; at the southern end a bridge connected the inner wall with the outwork fortification. Behind this was another, shorter open area, and then the most impressive part of the whole system, a massive tower-like structure, not square as a normal tower, but wide, extending across the whole width of the ridge. This was the "battery"; it is the key to the whole of the complex system, for it was designed to hold the great torsion catapults, the heavy artillery of the ancient world. These had been developed even further by Archimedes at the time of the Roman siege, which despite all these precautions finally reduced the city to submission in 212 B.C. It was the development of catapults in the Hellenistic Age which had led to the system that combined a battery with an elaborate sequence of ditches and outworks intended to prevent an enemy from bringing his siege engines too close to the walls. The fall of Syracuse marks an important stage in the growth of Roman supremacy over the Hellenistic world, and the great fort on Euryalos, even in its ruined state, is a testimony to the science and engineering skills of the Greeks who sought to avert this.

—R. A. TOMLINSON

TIRYNS
Greek Argos

14th-13th century B.C.: Citadel constructed. **13th century B.C.:** Megaron constructed.

Publications

DINSMOOR, WILLIAM BELL: *The Architecture of Ancient Greece*. New York, 1975.
SCHLIEMANN, HEINRICH: *Mycenae: A Narrative of Researches and Discoveries at Mycenae and Tiryns*. New York, 1880.

The citadel of Tiryns is one of the most important and well-preserved centers of occupation in Greece dating to the Late Bronze Age, the second half of the second millenium B.C. It is situated in the plain of Argos, on a low rocky hill, and in the Bronze Age must have been adjacent to the sea, though the present coastline has receded from it. It is a few kilometers distant from the sheltered harbor of Nauplion (which is itself the site of an ancient town), but the long sweep of open beach, reasonably protected from bad weather, provides the conditions which were favored for ancient warships, since these were designed to be drawn up stern first onto land, rather than docked alongside a quay in the modern manner. It is reasonable, therefore, to suggest that Tiryns' obvious importance is due in part at least to the exploitation of this maritime potential. In this respect it differs from the principal fortified Late Bronze city of the plain of Argos, Mycenae, which is situated away from the sea. Given that both sites flourished in the essentially prehistoric Late Bronze Age (though there are some "Linear B" documents from Tiryns as well as Mycenae) it is difficult to assess the relationship between them. Later, when both had decayed considerably, they were separate, independent villages. In the *Iliad,* Tiryns is part of the kingdom of Diomedes, while Mycenae, of course, belongs to the great king Agamemnon. This may reflect the fact that Tiryns, even in the Bronze Age, formed a separate state, but the question is a vexed one (it is debated whether or not the *Iliad* description is based on Bronze Age or later circumstances). Even so, Tiryns had everything architecturally necessary to form the center of an independent state.

The citadel is a natural place for settlement, and was already inhabited in the Neolithic Period. In the Early Bronze Age a substantial but enigmatic circular building 27.9 meters in

Citadel walls: Tiryns, Greek Argos, 13th century B.C.

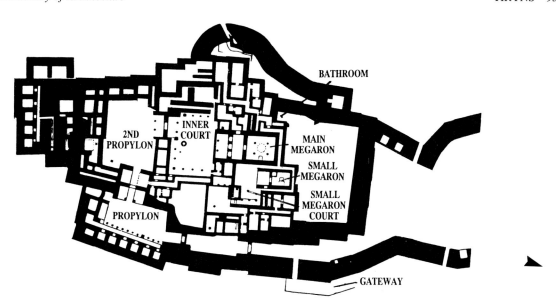

diameter, consisting of concentric walls of unbaked and baked brick, was constructed on the highest point. Its subsequent demolition in the Late Bronze Age makes it impossible to decide what its function was: it bore virtually no resemblance to any other known structure in Greece at that time, and had no demonstrable relationship with buildings in other areas with which the inhabitants of Tiryns at that date may reasonably be supposed to have had contact. Suggestions that it supported a palace or somehow served as a gigantic, domed granary are incapable of proof.

The existing fortifications were developed in the Late Bronze Age. The site itself had been reoccupied, after a destruction toward the end of the Early Bronze Age, and habitation was then continuous. Whether there were any fortifications in the succeeding Middle Bronze Age is uncertain because these earlier phases were completely overridden by later massive development, which makes investigation difficult. The earliest surviving traces of the developed *enceinte* probably belong to the period defined by the stylistic character of pottery, associated in the surviving stratigraphy, as Late Helladic III A2, roughly the equivalent of the second half of the 14th century. These walls surrounded the upper part of the citadel, a restricted area not more than 100 by 50 meters. The monumental masonry of enormous blocks of stone, each weighing several tons, with very little trimming, is fitted together with the help of smaller stones and clay as infill. (This is the style known to later Greeks as "Cyclopean," the supposed work of the legendary giants, the Cyclopes.) The walls themselves can be up to six meters thick. This monumental scale of building appears in mainland Greece without any local antecedents. Again, it is difficult to interpret this, on the basis of later legend only, and in the absence of a true historical record, but it does seem to have been introduced from outside. It is not found in contemporary or earlier Crete, and the real influence, whether direct (perhaps the result of migration or even conquest) or indirect, seems to be the Hittite strongholds of central Asia Minor, places like Hattusas (Boghaz Keui).

This wall was constructed along the top of the citadel rock. The approach was by way of a gradual slope beneath and outside the wall on the east side. At the top of this, almost at the southeast corner, was the entrance, now concealed beneath the later structure, but presumably a defendable gate; there were towers to either side. Subsequently, this initial fortification was added to, a prime reason being to strengthen the system still further, rather than to make any significant increase to the area

contained within the walls, though in fact some increase did result. One of these extensions created a restricted forecourt in front of the original entrance. There, new walls appear to have attained an even more massive thickness, but this was achieved by making them hollow, with a system of internal galleries within the apparent thickness of the wall, roofed over on the corbel principle with the wall continuing above them. These galleries are now easily accessible, and the polish imparted to some of the blocks within the galleries by shoulders of countless generations rubbing against them suggests this dates back to antiquity. The form of these galleries, a passage with a succession of spaces opening off to one side (the east), recalls the storage rooms and passages of Minoan architecture, so the usual interpretation of the galleries at Tiryns is that they were for storage; however, they are in a strangely vulnerable position, outside the main wall and closely within the reach of an attacking enemy. The resemblance to Cretan storage systems may be fortuitous, therefore, and the real reason for them may have been simply to economize in the material required for the thickness of the wall, the gallery in its original form being inaccessible. There is a similar extension, with a similar gallery, at the south end, also outside the main line of the wall.

There was at the same time a strengthening of the entrance and approach. The new wall outside the main gate was extended even further to the north, creating an additional fitting platform, with a gauntlet passageway which had to be traversed by an enemy before reaching the actual entrance to the citadel. In its turn, the passage was blocked by two massive gates, wooden and now, of course, long since disappeared, but with the holes in the side of the gateways where a bar could be inserted to bolt them. On the opposite, west side, a smaller gateway was created, protected by a massive tower surmounting a deep pit; presumably there was some form of drawbridge over the pit. This western entrance was further protected, eventually, by another massive, curving wall which enclosed the staircase that led up to the tower. The purpose of this secondary entrance is no longer clear, but it would seem to have effected communication with a settlement outside the citadel, on the seaward side and presumably connected with the existence of a Tirynthian fleet.

Finally, toward the end of the 13th century B.C. another area of settlement, on the lower part of the hill to the north of the citadel, was enclosed, about 150 meters in length. The area included within this section of fortification, which has not yet been investigated completely, appears to have been given over to a completely haphazard layout of relatively insubstantial structures, presumably private houses, though a totally unpretentious shrine building exists among them. The upper citadel, on the other hand, was devoted to a much more substantial series of structures, not all of them of the same date, much more solid in form and regular in plan, which clearly constitute a palace; this building would have served both as a residence for the man who ruled Tiryns and as an administrative center (in all senses) for him, as well as a place where the material economic resources of the community could be stored, safe from its enemies. The steady increase in the strength and extent of these fortifications reflects the splendor attached to the ruler, but also the increasingly unstable conditions which affected the community, and which ultimately, late in the 13th or early in the 12th century B.C., led to its destruction.

The palace grew in stages, as new and more splendid buildings were added to it. The final form is quite complex, but it clearly did not result from a single, systematic plan. Nevertheless, it is the final form of the palace which is most interesting architecturally, and it is best appreciated for what it became, rather than for the stages of its development.

The palace complex begins with the entrance in the southeast corner of the original citadel. By the final stages this had been demilitarized, replaced by the outer gates along the approach ramp. The final gateway was decorative rather than military, H-shaped in plan with a thin cross-wall for the single doorway, and pairs of columns between the side walls in front and behind. This is the basic plan for the propylon structures of classical Greek sanctuaries a millennium later, and it is tempting to see at Tiryns the prototype for them. But the short life of the Tiryns gateway in this form, and the long gap between its destruction and the emergence of classical forms, makes direct influence unlikely. There may be indirect continuity, perhaps through buildings outside Greece, but a spontaneous reinvention based on essentially similar architectural concepts is the most likely explanation.

The propylon led to an outer courtyard, flanked by utilitarian structures. On the north side of the court was a second propylon, similar in arrangement to the first. This led into the inner court; the gateways, perhaps, though not defensive, did serve the purpose of segregation, restricting entrance to the heart of the royal residence. The southern, eastern and western sides of the inner court were embellished by porticoes, lines of wooden posts, which again anticipated the colonnaded courtyards of classical Greek architecture. The main palace buildings lie beyond—that is, to the north of—this court. Little more than the ground plans and lower sections of the walls are preserved. There are several distinctive features here. The main building of the palace was a great hall, generally termed by modern scholars a "megaron," using the Greek word for the principal hall of the kings described in the Homeric poems. This comprised a near-square room, 9.8 meters wide by 11.8 meters deep, containing at its center a large, circular embellished hearth. Such hearths occurred elsewhere in Bronze Age Greece, not just in the palaces, and is presumed to have had some religious or ritual significance. Round it were placed four wooden columns, which could certainly help support the roof, and may imply some architectural feature above the ceiling and over the hearth itself. The floor of this room was plastered and painted in a system of decorated squares. To one side, a position is marked out for the king's throne, long since vanished but presumably not dissimilar to that in the throne room at Knossos.

This room was entered (by a single door) from a shallow anteroom, the same width as the hall itself. The side walls were extended forward to form a porch, again similar in width, with

two wooden posts for the facade. This set of rooms, like the similar arrangement at Mycenae, anticipated the porch and cella plan of the classical Greek temple, but as with the propylon a direct connection over the intervening centuries is unlikely: both buildings echo a basic house type (though one which was not as common in the Late Bronze Age as is generally assumed). The anteroom was separated from the porch by a "pier-door partition," an arrangement of two piers with folding doors between them, and the side walls. This is a direct borrowing from the architecture of Minoan Crete, though used in a non-Minoan structure (the Cretans used it as part of the "Minoan hall" system, between an enclosed room, anteroom and light well, rather than the open porch of the megaron). Other rooms in the palace at Tiryns included, to the east of the main megaron, an older, smaller and simpler megaron, containing hall and porch only. There was another courtyard by this, but descriptions of it as the "women's megaron" are purely fanciful. Around this were other rooms, whose purpose is uncertain. More significant is the separation of these into "suites" by means of long, narrow corridors, another concept borrowed undoubtedly from the architecture of Minoan Crete. There are also traces of staircases, which prove the former existence of upper stories, again as in Crete. Finally, a room on the west side has a floor formed from a single slab of limestone, calculated to weigh 20 tons, with marks at its edge to receive paneling: it was, undoubtedly, a bathroom.

Thus the architecture of the palace was an amalgamation of Cretan and mainland forms. The Cretan elements give the impression of being superimposed on an essentially non-Cretan type of building, and result assuredly from the capture of that island and its subsequent domination by mainlanders. The result is something of an exotic mixture, its influence on later architecture doubtful. What is less certain is the appearance of these buildings when they were complete. The painted plaster decoration of the floors also extended to the walls, certainly of the principal rooms, and there are fragments of an ornamental dado, half circles forming three decorated upright bands which may (at several removes and with much modification) be the source of the triglyph and metope friezes incorporated into the entablatures of the classical Doric order. The columns are of uncertain form: they may echo those of Minoan Crete, and, again at a remove, anticipate the classical Doric. Roof forms are problematic; the megaron plan, when used for the classical temple, invariable has a tiled, ridged roof, but this seems unlikely in the Tiryns forerunner, for which a flat roof (or even complete upper stories) is more likely. Thus it is difficult, and of dubious value, to try to trace the influence of Tiryns on later buildings. That it, along with other contemporary palaces, formed part of the first truly monumental buildings of the European mainland is clear.

—R. A. TOMLINSON

HADRIAN'S VILLA
Tivoli, Italy

118-138. A.D.: Development of Villa. **Ca. 130 A.D.:** The Canopus.

Publications

AURIGEMMA, S.: *Villa Adriana*. Rome, 1961.
CLARK, ELEANOR: *Hadrian's Villa*. New York, 1974.

Hadrian's Villa, The Canopus: Tivoli, Italy, ca. 130 A.D.

ISOZAKI, ARATA: *Villa Adriana*. Vol. 3 in the *Architectural Pilgrimage to World Architecture* series. Tokyo, 1981.

KÄHLER, H.: *Hadrian und seine Villa bei Tivoli*. Berlin, 1950.

MACDONALD, WILLIAM L., and BOYLE, BERNARD M.: "The Small Baths at Hadrian's Villa." *Journal of the Society of Architectural Historians* 39 (March 1980): 5-27.

*

The landscape villa of the Roman Emperor Hadrian sprawls over a slightly hilly area in the Roman *campagna* just south of Tivoli. The remains of the luxury villa spread over an area of half a square mile. Satisfying the Roman passion for gardens and idyllic settings as well as a propensity for urban living, the villa comprises a plethora of garden peristyles, fountains, reflecting pools, grottoes, libraries, audience halls, reception areas, summer and winter dining rooms, a banquet hall, bath complexes, a music hall, theaters, temples, belvederes, and even a completely self-sufficient island retreat accessed by a drawbridge.

Hadrian resided there as emperor from 117 A.D. until his death in 138. But the original nucleus of the villa, the so-called "palace" in the northern sector, is pre-Hadrianic, and has been assigned to the Late Republic on the basis of construction methods and materials. Reconstructions of the republican villa bear a close relationship to Pompeian atrium houses. Three republican phases are evidenced: that during the reign of Sulla with *opus incertum*; of one during the reign of Caesar with *quasi-reticulatum*; and of one during the reign of Augustus with *reticulatum*.

Hadrian assumed possession of the Tiburtine land and the preexisting villa as early as 100 A.D. through inheritance or his marriage to Sabina. Having lived in and become enamored of the "ancient" villa, Hadrian devoted himself to developing and amplifying the villa when he became emperor.

Ancient literary sources testify to Hadrian's personal involvement with the design of his own additions to the villa. The multifarious forms of the Hadrianic structures mirror the emperor's intellectual versatility as well as his vision for bold and revolutionary design. Born to an aristocratic family in Spain, Hadrian was intensely Roman in sentiment. He was, however, known as "Graeculus" for his love of things Greek. His early education, as well as his later intellectual pursuits, focused on Greek and Latin literature and on the arts: he was a writer, an artist and an architect, according to his ancient biographers. A true diplomat, he spent the major part of his reign traveling to Greece, Egypt and the Eastern Roman provinces to carry out his political aims of establishing peace and consolidating the vast empire through conciliatory acts. He also enjoyed travel for its own sake: it satisfied his passion for exotica and his compelling desire to expand his intellectual horizons.

Three major building phases of the villa coincide with his principal voyages. Modern scholars concur with ancient literary sources that individual structures in the villa were intended to record those places from his travels which most impressed him, namely, Athens, Thessaly and Egypt. The extent to which individual buildings were meant to replicate specific sites or foreign monuments remains speculative. Spartianus in *Vita Hadriani* cites specifically the Lyceum, the Accademia, the Pritaneum and the Stoa Poikile in Athens; the Valley of Tempe in

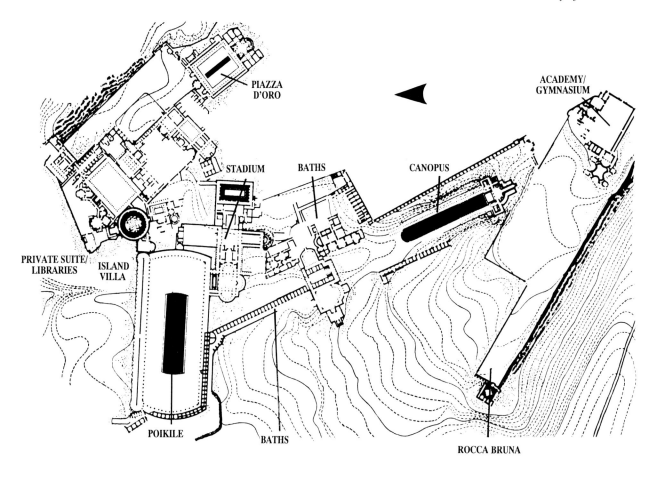

Thessaly; and the Canopus in Egypt. The Canopus is the only complex in the villa that can be identified undoubtedly. This infamous lake-canal joined Alexandria to the city of Canopus and was the site of the mysterious drowning of Antinous, Hadrian's young and intimate companion. The excavations of the Canopus at Hadrian's Villa in the 1950s confirmed the ground plan of the semidomed hemicycle at the north end of the pool, which had previously been associated with the Temple of Serapis in the vicinity of the Egyptian Canopus. The excavator revealed its function as a triclinium *cum* nymphaeum. Cascades of water surrounded the guests not only to refresh them but to enhance the enchantment and the illusion of dining in the exotic canal. The precise iconography of the Canopus complex has attracted the attention of scholars since the late 19th century and underlines the difficulties involved with the interpretation of the villa as a whole. Most identify the hemicycle as a Serapeum, a place for ritualistic meals or cult practices associated with the god Serapis or the god Osiris: a direct tribute to Antinous' death and his apotheosis in the Canopus.

The identification and interpretation of the other structures are less clear. The Poikile, for example, bears no formal relationship to the Athenian Stoa Poikile, a picture gallery, and it lacks any traces of paintings or mosaics. Unlike its alleged Athenian counterpart, the Tiburtine Poikile, especially in light of its direct communication with the large banquet hall at the northeast corner, was more likely one of the many porticoed promenades or belvederes. The Tiburtine Accademia was probably a gymnasium. The so-called Latin and Greek Libraries were convincingly identified by Heinz Kähler as summer triclinia and derivative of Emperor Nero's summer triclinium in his Domus Aurea. The "Casino with three semi-circular esedrae" west of the

stadium was a summer banquet hall, embellished with a reflecting pool and a fountain at one end—a luxurious triclinium of a more official demeanor than the two to the north. Hadrian's plan for the banquet hall was strongly influenced by the Coenatio Jovis, the great triclinium in Domitian's Palace on the Palatine Hill in Rome. Hadrian's formative years were spent in Rome under the dominant tastes of Nero and the Flavians. While emperor, Hadrian entertained officials in the Palatine Palace during the winter months. His installation of hypocausts in the floors of the Coenatio Jovis expressly for these occasions attests to his familiarity with the ground plan of the building. The "stadium" has been identified as a garden stadium, the first grand imperial garden complex. The complex known as the Piazza d'Oro accommodated official guests in a magnificent manner by providing a vestibule, a colonnaded courtyard with a reflecting pool, and a triclinium with a nymphaeum to provide a luxuriant backdrop. The living quarters and offices of the emperor as well as guest apartments were relegated to the original nucleus of the villa, north of the Piazza d'Oro. Romans customarily did not deem very important the rooms of daily life and consequently they are difficult to identify, which is the case here. The purpose for building three bath complexes in the villa remains uncertain. That to the north has a sizable heliocaminus; those on axis with the Canopus, the "Small" and "Large" Baths, have been identified as women's and men's or winter and summer baths.

The dates of Hadrian's trips examined in concert with numerous brick stamps *in situ* aided in the reconstruction of the Hadrianic building program in Tivoli. From this study it became apparent that on the whole Hadrian's villa was completed by his return from his last voyage in 134 A.D., the remaining period devoted to ornamentation of the villa. Brick stamps require conservative interpretation, since many would have remained stockpiled. Consequently, discussion continues about the absolute chronology of some structures. With one exception, Hadrian spent roughly three years in Tivoli between each voyage. This afforded ample time to draw up designs, review them with contractors, acquire necessary construction materials, and to ensure the building program was under way. Three building phases have been assigned: 118-125 A.D. (in absentia 121-125), 125-128 (in absentia for the summer of 128), and 129-138 (in absentia 129-133). During the first building phase the North Palace was refurbished and the buildings in the immediate vicinity were added: the "Ospidale", the Greek and Latin Libraries (or triclinia), the Maritime Theater (Island Casino), the Baths with Heliocaminus, the Garden Stadium, the Banquet Hall, and probably the Poikile. During the second phase, the Piazza d'Oro was added, the Small Baths, and probably the Large Baths, the Vestibule, the Praetorium, the "Piccolo Palazzo," and the surrounding structures which overlook the Valley of Risicoli, such as the Accademia, the Odeon and the Roccabruna. The Canopus has been assigned by some to the second phase, exclusively on the basis of the brick stamps, the latest of which dates 127 A.D., and by others to the third phase, which coincides with Hadrian's fateful voyage down the Nile. The Large Baths may also have been completed in the third building phase.

The Roman West and East are both represented. The villa signaled the inception of a change in which Western Roman forms and aesthetic principles would yield to Eastern ones, producing art and architecture of a broad, ecumenical character. In the extravagant display of colored marbles imported from the East, used in sectile floors, wall revetments, columns and sculpture, and in the intricacy of the carved ornament, a dependence on Eastern craftsmanship is apparent. Apollodorus of Damascus, the architect/engineer employed by Hadrian's predecessor Trajan, was certainly accompanied to Rome by his own Eastern entourage. They stayed to work on subsequent imperial projects, perhaps the Pantheon and parts of Hadrian's Villa.

But the masonry and method of construction of the villa represent the finest of the Western tradition. A high-quality yellow-brown tufa could be quarried in the vicinity and was used for the reticulate facing of the walls and sometimes for blocks. Hadrianic *opus reticulatum* is readily distinguished by its precise regularity, which yielded a uniform, decorative honeycomb pattern. The core of the walls is concrete with medium-size *caementa*, also of the yellow-brown tufa. The bricks and tiles had to be imported from factories in Rome. Therefore they were used sparingly, in reinforcing bands at regular intervals in the *opus reticulatum* facing and occasionally as quoins along with tufa blocks. Tiles were used for pavement and bipedales for facing arches. The exception to this was the Roccabruna, where alternate rows of blocks and bricks were used. This was the first important building in which this type of masonry was employed. But it was the absolute technical confidence in Roman concrete that inspired bold experimentation and revolutionized Roman architecture. Both in the design and construction of Hadrian's Villa, the monolithic quality of Roman concrete was exploited.

One might view the villa as Hadrian's "laboratory" for architectural design. The experimental nature of the architectural forms may account for the redundancy in function of many of the rooms and complexes in the villa. The overall plan and style of the villa reflect the restlessness and versatility of its imperial resident-designer. There is no one, principal axis to the villa, but rather a "jackstraw orientation." There are, however, four groups of buildings, each with its own orientation. Individual axes can be traced along well-defined stretches, and they intersect both perpendicularly and obliquely. This aspect of the villa is common in urban environments. The villa as a whole is loosely hinged at the Island Casino, Hadrian's personal island retreat.

The common denominator in this jigsaw of multiplex forms is curvilinearity both in plan and in elevation. Even the peristyles, which on the whole are rectangular, have curved elements to them. Concavities, convexities and vaulted ceilings, often pierced with numerous openings, create the illusion of the extension of space. Vaulted interiors rose to a variety of heights, echoing the undulation of the terrain itself. Interior spaces were manipulated to rise and fall, to expand and contract, to change shapes and orientation, and to dictate the exterior forms. The theme of curve and countercurve, fully realized in the Island Casino, was further elaborated in the second phase of building, notably in the pavilion of the Piazza d'Oro and the Accademia. Both are characterized by complex, curvilinear cruciform plans of alternating convex and concave colonnaded segments which offered enchanting vistas into counterpoised rooms and courtyards.

The Small Baths are distinguished above all by their protean quality. Both in elevation and plan the multiformed spaces merge into one another, at once abruptly and imperceptibly. The spaces were enclosed under groined, segmental, domical, barrel, quadrant, and quarterspherical vaults, some fenestrated, others pierced with oculi. William MacDonald attests to a remarkable sympathy between the plan of the Small Baths and that of the villa as a whole. The Small Baths present a compacted microcosm of the villa: similar principles of design apply to both. An eccentrically placed focus within a context of multiple, disparate axes is common to both. The baths have spatial groupings that reflect similarly balanced complexes in the villa. Many of the myriad of forms in the baths are akin to those in the Island Casino, the Piazza d'Oro, the Serapeum of the Canopus and the Baths with Heliocaminus. The apparently jumbled nature of the villa, and the baths, is actually characterized by a tightly organized, "flawless economy of design," "a species of minimal building, crowded and immediate while spatially ventilated and brilliantly lit."

The significance and legacy of the villa lies in this early attempt to express interior spaces by exterior forms. The exuberant departure from traditional Vitruvian principles found ready disciples in the Italian masters of the 16th and 17th centuries. Pirro Ligorio, Andrea Palladio, Francesco Borromini and Giovanni Battista Piranesi seized the opportunity to examine against the precepts of Renaissance buildings this example of what was becoming recognized as the less classical character of Roman architecture. The villa has no immediate or obvious progeny in ancient architecture, as the revolution in architecture waned with the death of Hadrian. But the pulsating ovals and ellipses, as well as the bold juxtapositions of disparately shaped spaces in Hadrian's Villa, were vigorously revived by Ligorio, Borromini and Piranesi.

Hadrian's Villa documents a unique circumstance in the history of architecture. It provides us with a portrait of an imperial architect with unlimited resources: in the villa at Tivoli Hadrian boasts of his Romanitas in his expertise in organization, of his Philhellenism in his devotion to aesthetics, and of his Spanish heritage in his love for the grandiose and splendid.

—JOANNE C. MANNELL

EUROPE

AUSTRIA

SCHLOSS MIRABELL
Salzburg, Austria

1606: Built as a country house by Wolf Deitrich von Reitenau, prince-archbishop of Salzburg (1587-1612), and called Altenau. **1689-90:** Gardens designed; **Architect:** Johann Bernhard Fischer von Erlach (1646-1723). **1721-27:** House remodeled; great staircase in west wing, chapel, court facades, Marmorsaal; **Architect:** Johann Lukas von Hildebrandt (1668-1745). **1818:** House destroyed in a fire, but staircase and Marmorsaal by Hildebrandt survive.

Publications

AURENHAMMER, HANS: *J.B. Fischer von Erlach.* London, 1973.

BUCHOWIECKI, WALTER: *Der Barockbau der ehemaligen Hofbibliothek in Wien, ein Werk J.B. Fischer von Erlach.* Vienna, 1957.

FISCHER VON ERLACH, JOHANN BERNHARD: *Entwurf einer historischen Architectur.* Reprint of 1725 edition and 1730 English translation by Thomas Lediard. Farnsborough, England, 1964.

GRIMSCHITZ, BRUNO.: *Johann Lukas von Hildebrandt.* Vienna, 1959.

GRIMSCHITZ, BRUNO: *Wiener Barockpaläste.* Vienna, 1944.

HASELBERGER-BLAHA, HERTA: "Die Triumphtore Bernhard Fischers von Erlachs." *Wiener Jahrbuch für Kunstgeschichte* 17 (1955): 63-85.

ILG, ALBERT: *Die Fischer von Erlach.* Vienna, 1895.

KUNOTH, GEORG: *Die historische Architektur Fischers von Erlach.* Dusseldorf, 1956.

LANCHESTER, H. V.: *Fischer von Erlach.* London, 1924.

MORPER, JOHANN JOSEPH: "Schriftum zum Fischer von Erlach." *Das Münster* 10, 1-2 (1957): 49-51.

PASSMORE, EDWARD: "Fischer von Erlach, Architect to a Monarchy." *Journal of the Royal Institute of British Architects* 58 (1951): 452-475.

SEDLMAYR, HANS: *Fischer von Erlach der Ältere.* Munich, 1925.

SEDLMAYR, HANS: *Johann Bernhard Fischer von Erlach.* Vienna, 1976.

*

Schloss Mirabell began its life in 1606 as a country house called Altenau, which Wolf Dietrich von Reitenau, prince-archbishop of Salzburg from 1587 to 1612, built for his mistress, Salome Alt. This worldly prelate, who began the transformation of Salzburg into an Italianate Baroque city north of the Alps, was to die in 1617 in the fortress of Hohensalzburg as a prisoner. He lost his position because he was drawn into a bitter conflict with the dukes of Bavaria over the lucrative trade in salt (from which Salzburg gets its name): pressure was brought to bear on him by the powerful dukes, and the archbishop was condemned by the ecclesiastical authorities in Rome, not least, one suspects, because of his connection with an exotic Jewess. The unfortunate Wolf Dietrich was replaced by a descendant of the Medicis, Marcus Sitticus, Count Hohenems, prince-archbishop from 1612 to 1619, who gave Altenau the name Schloss Mirabell.

The house was completely remodeled in the Baroque style by Johann Lukas von Hildebrandt in 1721-27, but was badly damaged in a serious fire in 1818, and subsequently went through various indignities. However, Hildebrandt's great staircase (*Erste Stiege*) in the west wing survives, although the stonework is still discolored from the heat of the fire. On the elaborate balustrade are charming *putti* of 1726 by George Raphael Donner (1673-1741), who also carved the figure of Paris on the landing, and the stuccowork is quite fine. The *putti* alternate with elaborate lanterns, and the balustrade itself is composed of bits of broken scrolled pediments, convex and concave curved sections, scrolls and froths, and melting pieces of cartouche, all put together with absolute conviction, sureness of touch and apparent ease. The Marmorsaal also partially survives.

Schloss Mirabell's chief importance today lies in the fact that, like the Kinsky Palace in Vienna, it is the very type of the princely palace, and one of the earliest of such Baroque palaces in Austria, with its grand staircase and formal rooms. But it is also of great significance because of its relationship to its gardens, and in turn in relation to how those gardens are laid out. Not only is the geometry of the garden itself of great interest, connected as it is to the architectonic qualities of the three-story Schloss, but the way in which the axes set up by that geometry terminate in the great *Festung* of the archbishops shows how the Baroque garden could exploit distant views, incorporating them into the scheme of things for additional effects. Those distant vistas, so obvious in many of the French and English gardens of the Baroque age in which the countryside becomes part of the garden, are here used in a town garden, making use of existing buildings. With its terraces, aviary, espaliered and clipped trees and hedges, and many statues, the Mirabell garden is an excellent example of an early-18th-century Baroque landscaped area, laid out to incorporate the vista over the city, with the fortress of Hohensalzburg as the eyecatcher terminating the view.

The sculptures themselves are of outstanding interest. The Pegasus Fountain (1660-61) in the gardens is by Kaspar Graz, and originally was situated in the old chapter-house horse pond, but the chief interest of the sculptures lies in the series of Baroque grotesques. Here we find a curious type of comicality in stone, capturing that odd love of the misshapen and the ugly that was such a feature of court life in the late-17th and early 18th centuries. Many statues feature dwarfs, and there is a Terrible Turk trying unsuccessfully to break a tree that has already been partially cut, a reference perhaps to the all-too-recent Turkish invasion of the Holy Roman Empire, which had itself been partly sundered by the religious strife of the Thirty Years' War. Dwarfs were often found in European courts, and it should be remembered that François Cuvilliés, the genius of Bavarian Rococo who built the Amalienburg in Munich, began his career as the court dwarf to the exiled elector of Bavaria.

There are many lively statues of deities of antiquity, including Flora, Athene and Ceres, and a Paris and a Helen, the former (determined and merry) holding the latter (coy, but ready to surrender). Even the figures of classical subjects have more than a touch of the burlesque about them. The Flora by Ottavio Mostro (ca. 1690) has, in the words of Nikolaus Pevsner, a "merry coarseness" about it, and the "drapery, brimful of flowers, clumsily cuts through the torso." These extraordinary figures combine traditions of sculpture in the German lands with certain new foreign influences, notably those from Italy.

Schloss Mirabell: Salzburg, Austria, 1606

Schloss Mirabell

The gardens also contain superbly inventive carved vases on tall pedestals, and from the terrace-belvedere is a fine view of the rose gardens, the bastions and, of course, the *Festung* of Hohensalzburg.

Johann Bernhard Fischer von Erlach was able to exploit his undoubted abilities as a town planner as well as an architect in Salzburg as nowhere else. In that incomparably lovely city nearly all his architectural and planning projects were realized, and his is the architectural presence that looms largest by the banks of the Salzach. Fischer took up his duties there very soon after Prince-Archbishop Johann Ernst Graf Thun (1687-1709) was appointed to office. In 1689-90 the park of the prince-archbishop's summer residence, as it then was, Schloss Mirabell, was redesigned and laid out according to Fischer's plans. Unfortunately, all that remains of that work are the original entrance (two pairs of symmetrically placed statues of gladiators whose bodies partly form a gateway) and the extraordinarily vigorous carved vases on the pedestals, the designs for which Fischer was to illustrate later in his *Entwurff einer historischen Architektur* in Section V, published first in Vienna in 1721, then in Leipzig in 1725, and subsequently with an English text in 1730. These vases are as interesting as later designs by Giovanni Battista Piranesi.

In spite of all the vicissitudes that Mirabell and its gardens have gone through since Wolf Dietrich first gave the house to Salome Alt, and since two of Austria's greatest architects rebuilt the Schloss and laid out the gardens, Mirabell still offers a town garden with sculptures and ornaments of the most interesting kind, while the great *Treppenhaus* is one of the happiest compositions in a country renowned for its splendid and princely staircases.

—JAMES STEVENS CURL

BELVEDERE
Vienna, Austria

1700-23. Architect: Johann Lukas von Hildebrandt (1668-1745). **1700:** Gardens designed. **1714-16:** Lower Belvedere built. **After 1716:** Upper Belvedere designed. **1723:** Building for palace and gardens completed. **1717:** Additional gardens designed; **Designer:** Dominique Girard. **18th-19th centuries:** Various alterations to Upper and Lower Belvedere interiors, and to Upper Belvedere exterior.

Publications

AURENHAMMER, HANS: ''Ikonographie und Ikonologie des Wiener Belvederegartens.'' *Wiener Jahrbuch für Kunstgeschichte* 17 (1955): 86-108.
AURENHAMMER, HANS: *J. B. Fischer von Erlach.* London, 1973.
GRIMSCHITZ, BRUNO: *Das Belvedere in Wien.* Vienna, 1946.
ILG, ALBERT: *Die Fischer von Erlach.* Vienna, 1895.
KNOPP, NORBERT: *Das Garten-Belvedere.* Munich and Berlin, 1966.
SEDLMAYR, HANS: *Johann Bernhard Fischer von Erlach.* Vienna and Munich, 1956.

*

Johann Lukas von Hildebrandt's masterpiece, the Belvedere Palace and Gardens in Vienna, was designed, laid out and built between 1700 and 1723 for Prince Eugen of Savoy, the commander of the imperial armies which vanquished the Turks at the end of the 17th century; so, like Blenheim Palace in Oxfordshire and the Quinta de Fronteira in Portugal, the Belvedere is really a tribute to a great general and to the renewed fortunes of the country he served. Prince Eugen's victories raised him to the pinnacle of society in the Holy Roman Empire so that his status was almost as grand as that of the Kaiser himself.

Hildebrandt accompanied Prince Eugen during his military campaigns of the 1690s as the prince's chief military engineer. Like J. B. Neumann, Hildebrandt was an expert on fortifications and on military engineering before he found fame as an architect. Hildebrandt took over the responsibility for the design of Prince Eugen's town palace in the Himmelpfortgasse in Vienna, which had been begun by J. B. Fischer von Erlach in 1696, and by 1699 he was well established in the prince's favor, as well as becoming a dangerous rival to the older architect, although the work of the two men was quite different.

The Belvedere, being on the edge of the old city of Vienna (and now surrounded by later developments), is compact, and contains what is probably the finest town garden in all Europe; it is framed by the Lower Belvedere at the bottom end, with walls on either of the long sides, and with the Upper Belvedere at the top or higher level of the gardens. Work began on the Lower Belvedere, a palace and stables that look like an enlarged garden pavilion; Prince Eugen had his summer quarters and orangery with private garden there. The very much bigger, grander and showier Upper Belvedere, which is sited at the top of a series of dramatic terraces, was essentially a palace for entertainment rather than a house to be lived in. It later became the official residence of the heir to the throne of Austria, and

Belvedere, Upper: Vienna, Austria, after 1716

Belvedere, Lower: 1714-16

its last imperial and royal resident was the Archduke Franz Ferdinand and his consort, whose murders in 1914 sparked the catastrophe of 1914-18.

The Upper Belvedere is approached through entrance gates with sumptuous Baroque ironwork and stone gate piers crowned with cartouches supported by lions. These gates give access to a *cour d'honneur* in which is a large pool, suggesting perhaps a canal in a French Baroque garden. Then there is the Upper Belvedere itself.

The garden front faces a series of descending terraces, then the garden slopes downward toward the Lower Belvedere. These gardens were designed by Hildebrandt in basic outline, but completed in detail to designs by Dominique Girard, the French landscape gardener at the Bavarian court, and they exhibit elements of both French and Italian styles. The sloping ground contains platforms for the fountains, and changes of level incorporate cascades. Wide flights of steps on either side lead down from the terraces, with ramps in the centers of each flight to enable sedan chairs to proceed smoothly from one level to the other. The gardens also contained a screened kitchen garden and a circular menagerie, a smaller version of that at Versailles. Planting, in the form of hedges and neatly clipped trees, was arranged in highly geometrical and ordered forms to enhance the architectonic effects and unite the lower and upper palaces in one grand design. Garden statuary includes rearing horses and some delicious Rococo smiling sphinxes, and from the upper terraces is a marvelous view over the city, with the spire of St. Stephen's Cathedral in the center backed by the blue hills of the Vienna Woods.

The Belvedere marks the culmination of Hildebrandt's achievements as a palace architect. He had arrived at his plans

for the gardens by 1700, and produced a project for the Lower Belvedere, which was erected between 1714 and 1716. It seems that the designs for the Upper Belvedere were consolidated quite late, probably after 1716. The significance of the Belvedere ensemble lies not only in its superb Baroque architecture, but in the transformation of the Baroque garden from a design with infinitely expanding perspectives into what is a finite space, although the views over the city (asymmetrical though they are) play no small part in the breathtaking beauty of the place. Echoes of French Baroque gardens in *parterres* and *bosquets* are found, but the changes of level and the formal geometry of the layouts owe even more to Italo-French traditions.

The Upper Belvedere, built 1721-23, dominates the entire scheme, rather as a medieval fortress dominates, so Hildebrant merged in the scheme the tradition of the Austrian Schloss, Franco-Italian taste and Baroque notions of space. Such a relationship of palace to garden was developed by Hildebrandt for the Schönborns at Göllersdorf, for there he placed the garden between the palace buildings and a big orangery in 1710-13; so Göllersdorf was the prototype for the Belvedere, yet both schemes were apparently being developed simultaneously, at least on the drawing board.

French influences are apparent at the entrance to the Lower Belvedere, for the gate is approached through a semi-elliptical space, and the building is set out on an irregular site, fanning out, as it were, from the narrow entrance. The plan itself is of the *cour d'honneur* type, so that a regular garden front is created parallel to the facade of the Upper Belvedere at the top of the garden. Main rooms are contained within a central block which includes a two-story salon in the center of the symmetrical garden front that is joined to the long, low wings on either side by means of cunningly arranged volumes. The roofs of the central pavilion and flanking rooms have pitched hipped roofs (that over the salon is a pyramid), and orders of pilasters embellish the seven-window-wide centerpiece with its three-window-wide, two-story salon. On either side of the centerpiece stretch the long, low, single-story wings with their tall windows with cruciform frames and Mansard roofs with small dormers, while an entablature under the eaves binds the whole composition together.

The Upper Belvedere has a complex and inventive silhouette evolved from the pavilions of which the palace is composed. This silhouette can best be enjoyed from the Lower Belvedere. There is thus a strong French Renaissance influence, although in France buildings with elaborate pavilion roofs were out of fashion by the 1720s. There is even a suggestion of the exoticism of chinoiserie about the roof, especially that over the central pavilion. Three influences are clear from the exterior of the Upper Belvedere: that of Francesco Borromini; that of 17th-century northern European interpretations of classicism, especially in the double-curved pediments and the architectural detail (but then Prince Eugen had spent some time in the Austrian Netherlands, which explains a lot); and that of the French château (obvious in the pavilion roofs and the corner towers).

As the site slopes quite dramatically toward the city, the entrance *cour d'honneur* of the upper palace is half a story higher than the first garden terrace, so from the entrance hall a tremendous stair ascends, while a single flight of steps leads down to the darker Sala Terrena, or garden room, with its low, crushing vaults, and muscular Atlantes agonizingly carrying the complex ceiling. The staircase, with its struggling *termini* figures supporting the vaults, and its leaping, straining *putti* carrying the festive lanterns on the pedestals of the balustrades, was the first in the German lands to exploit fully the dramatic possibilities of space and enclosure offered by the changing levels.

The entrance front thus reads as though it has a *piano-nobile* floor over a basement, and the three-arched entrance with *oeil-de-boeuf* windows over has slipped down below the *piano nobile* and is approached by a ramp. On either side of the entrance rise the attic stories of the five-window-wide pavilions, and set back in the center is the high, Oriental-looking roof. Then, on either side of the tall pavilions are four-window-wide wings with balustrades over the entablatures, and these wings terminate in the octagonal corner pavilions with their green domed roofs. Because of the slope, what appears as a basement on the entrance front becomes a ground floor on the garden elevation.

So the Sala Terrena and stair are held within the three-window-wide centerpiece, and the main salon is also in the center, approached by a flight half a story up from the entrance. In the Sala Terrena, salon, and stair, the articulation and modeling are as rich and as deep as anything ever produced in the Baroque era.

Hildebrandt's importance lies in his mastery of synthesis, and in the way in which he freely interpreted the classical language of architecture. Like Michelangelo, Borromini, Pietro da Cortona and Edwin Lutyens, his complete mastery of that language enabled him to invent his own style, for as with these other architectural innovators, his style is unmistakable, inventive and original.

The Residenz in Würzburg and the great Belvedere complex in Vienna are two of the finest achievements of Late Baroque secular architecture. The Treppenhaus and Sala Terrena, with the stupendous Marmorsaal, can be recognized as triumphs of interior design, where changes of level, interpenetration of volumes and vigorous sculptural effects in the detail all combine in a whole of real quality.

While there are Gallic influences mentioned above, the Upper Belvedere has little evidence of any French restraint in its classical architectural treatment, and while there are Italian notes, they are transmogrified in this Viennese synthesis of forms and decoration. The Belvedere has much that is dynamically alive in it: the massive atlantes, bowed with the stupefying weight of the massive vaults of the Sala Terrena, are almost painfully real, but everywhere one looks in the series of stunning interiors the sheer inventive genius of the architect is apparent in the terms, coupled pilasters and plastic treatment of the surfaces. An enchanted world of magical invention is joined with a severe geometrical logic that cannot be faulted, and there is always that sense of exotic Orientalism prompted, perhaps, by the actual threat of the Turkish invasion (which Hildebrandt's patron had so decisively removed), to give added spice to the extraordinary ensemble.

At the Belvedere, Hildebrandt fused the various elements of his architecture in an harmonious whole, yet expressed them as individual parts: it was this facility, together with his mastery of interpenetration of volume, that makes him so important in the history of architecture. His freedom with architectural expression, too, puts him into the league of the great innovators.
—JAMES STEVENS CURL

HOFBURG
Vienna, Austria

1716: Design begun; **Architect:** Johann Bernhard Fischer von Erlach. **1719:** Construction of the Imperial Stables begun. **1723-37:** Hofburg library constructed; **Architects:** Johann Bernhard Fischer von Erlach and Joseph Emanuel Fischer von Erlach. **1729-35:** Riding School built; **Architects:** Joseph Emanuel Fischer von Erlach and Johann Bernhard Fischer von Erlach. **1850-54:** Stables altered.

Publications

AURENHAMMER, HANS: *J. B. Fischer von Erlach.* London, 1973.
BUCHOWIEKI, WALTER: *Der Barockbau der ehemaligen Hofbibliothek in Wien, ein Werk Johann Bernhard Fischer von Erlach.* Vienna, 1957.
HEMPEL, EBERHARD: *Baroque Art and Architecture in Central Europe.* Harmondsworth, England, 1965.
ILG, ALBERT: *Die Fischer von Erlach.* Vienna, 1895.
KÜHNEL, H.: *Die Hofburg zu Wien.* Graz and Cologne, 1964.
SEDLMAYR, HANS: *Österreichische Barockarchitektur, 1690-1740.* Vienna, 1930.
SEDLMAYR, HANS: *Johann Bernhard Fischer von Erlach.* Vienna and Munich, 1956.
ZACHARIAS, T.: *Joseph Emanuel Fischer von Erlach.* Vienna and Munich, 1960.

*

Near the end of his career, Johann Bernhard Fischer von Erlach was commissioned by the Holy Roman Emperor Charles VI to design two great imperial projects: these were the Karlskirche

Hofburg, library interior: Vienna, Austria, 1723-37

and the rebuilding of the Hofburg, or Imperial Palace, in Vienna. In 1716 the architect began work on the new building to house the imperial library, and also produced plans for an Academy of Sciences, but of the latter very little is known. It seems clear that Fischer von Erlach's conception of the palace was very grand indeed, and in 1719 construction of the Hofstall-Gebäude, or Imperial Stables, commenced; this gigantic project was part of a scheme for the Hofburg conceived on the most imperial scale imaginable. The buildings are situated on the southwestern side of the Maria-Theresien Platz. The design included a semi-circular court and pool of water, and the obvious precedents were the Domus Aurea and the Thermae of Diocletian, imperial Roman buildings which connected Fischer von Erlach's interest in antiquity with a deliberate attempt to suggest Charles VI as a modern Roman emperor and successor to Augustus himself. Another influence was Donato Bramante's design for the Belve-dere courtyard of the Vatican, which the Austrian must have known when he lived in Rome. The stables have a main facade of great length, with the central and lateral pavilions projecting from the front and given emphasis at roof level with accents on the pediments and belvedere-like towers. Regrettably, the Hofstall-Gebäude complex was somewhat drastically altered in 1850-54, and the buildings are used today to house the Vienna International Fair.

Fischer von Erlach conceived the Hofstall-Gebäude as part of a gigantic scheme related to his ideas for extending the Hofburg, and there can be little doubt that some sort of grand project must have existed in the second decade of the 18th century. The Hofstall-Gebäude buildings were designed to be a magnificent termination of one of the views from the palace across the open space outside the fortifications.

By 1722 financing was available for the construction of the Hofburg library, and the building was erected in 1723-37 to Fischer von Erlach's designs under the supervision of his son, Joseph Emanuel. This Hofbibliothek—one of the finest creations to be found in Austrian Baroque architecture—consists of a long, barrel-vaulted hall in the center of which is an elliptical space with its long axis at right angles to the axis of the rectangular space, which is itself subdivided along its length by arrangements of columns carrying entablatures. Around the walls are elaborate bookcases, and an elegant gallery carried on consoles and columns is extended all around the spaces. The Palladian idea of a columnar screen is also found in the gallery of the Palazzo Colonna in Rome (1665), while other precedents are Francesco Borromini's Biblioteca Alessandrina and the library in the Oratory of St. Philip Neri, both in Rome. The imperial theme was further enhanced by the clear influence of the design of the library of the Escorial on Fischer von Erlach, for the Spanish precedent was one of the first with open bookcases, and there are other aspects of the arrangement that are echoed in Vienna. Indeed, in the Hofbibliothek is the French pavilion system of design (with Mansard roofs), a battered rusticated base with horizontal banding (again a French motif), Palladian elements, High Baroque treatment, and a complicated iconography invented partly by Conrad Adolph von Albrecht and partly by Carl Gustaf Heraeus. Here is a temple for books, knowledge, theory and ideas combined with a Temple of Fame. One barrel-vaulted wing was dedicated to Peace and the other to War. The imperial emblems, the Pillars of Hercules, support the vaults of the wings as well as serving as Palladian columnar screens to create an illusion of great length. In the center of the elliptical hall, top-lit by means of *oeil-de-boeuf* windows, is a statue of the emperor, and around the space, in front of the coupled columns which support the gallery, are statues of earlier Haps-burgs, so the space becomes a type of Pantheon, an ancestral hall. The frescoes above (by Daniel Gran) glorify the emperor

as war-lord and peace-lord, and celebrate the achievements of the House of Hapsburg. There are allusions to the Wars with the Turks, to the War of the Spanish Succession, and to the role of the emperor as patron of art and science. Charles VI is himself described as a Hercules of the Muses.

The Hofbibliothek is approached by a stair in the wing next to the Augustinerkirche, and the anteroom on the main long axis was embellished with antique remains. This anteroom was later made into the staircase, by Nikolaus Paccassi, but the upper part of the staircase is still decorated with Roman mile-stones, votive altars, and funerary monuments set into the walls, reflecting the imperial interest in archaeology as well as making a connection with antiquity. There is also the very important fact of Fischer von Erlach's own love of historical themes, which may have played no small part in the creation of the original room.

Other parts of the Hofburg owe their design to the Fischer von Erlachs, father and son. The Winterreitschule (Riding School) of 1729-35 was erected under the direction of Joseph Emanuel, but appears to have been partly Johann Bernhard's design: it is a vast rectangular space with a clear span 18 meters wide, with a gallery carried on 46 columns. It is one of the most impressive interior spaces of the Baroque period. Adjacent to the Riding School is the Michaelertrakt range of buildings commenced by J. E. Fischer von Erlach, but only completed to his designs beginning in 1888; it is not known how much this work owes to original ideas of J. B. Fischer von Erlach. That range, in turn, is joined to the Reichskanzlei-Trakt (on the northeastern side of the square known as "In der Burg") designed by the elder Fischer von Erlach, but completed by his son in 1728; it was the seat of the Imperial Council in the 18th century, and contains some of the former imperial apartments.

Although the Hofburg was not remodeled completely to Fischer von Erlach's intentions, what remains is very impressive. The Hofbibliothek, for example, is one of the noblest buildings of the period, and stands comparison with many other more famous works of architecture. It is among the richest of all 18th-century library interiors, and, in its mix of themes, is unsurpassed in the brilliance of its final form.

—JAMES STEVENS CURL

KARLSKIRCHE
Vienna, Austria

1716-37. Architect: Johann Bernhard Fischer von Erlach (1656-1723).

Publications

AURENHAMMER, HANS: *J. B. Fischer von Erlach*. London, 1973.

CURL, JAMES STEVENS: *The Art and Architecture of Freemasonry*. London, 1991.

DREGER, M.: "Zur Baugeschichte der Wiener Karlskirche." *Wiener Jahrbuch für Kunstgeschichte* (1934): 101ff.

FERGUSSON, FRANCES D.: "St. Charles' Church, Vienna: The Iconography of Its Architecture." *Journal of the Society of Architectural Historians* 29, 4 (1970): 318-326.

Karlskirche: Vienna, Austria, 1716-37

POPELKA, L.: ''Studien zur Wiener Karlskirche.'' *Alte und neue Kunst* 4 (1955): 75ff.

SEDLMAYR, HANS: *Johann Bernhard Fischer von Erlach.* Vienna and Munich, 1956.

SEDLMAYR, HANS: ''Die Schauseite der Karlskirche in Wien.'' In *Kunstgeschichtliche Studien für Hans Kauffmann.* Berlin, 1956.

ZACHARIAS, T.: *Joseph Emanuel Fischer von Erlach.* Vienna and Munich, 1960.

The Holy Roman emperor Charles VI (ruled 1711-40) vowed in 1713 to build a great church if Vienna were delivered from a dreadful visitation of the Plague. The building was to be dedicated to the emperor's patron saint, Saint Charles Borromeo (1538-84), and was also to be a memorial to the last Hapsburg king of Spain (ruled 1704-14), and to the dream of uniting the crown of the empire with that of Spain, as Charles V (emperor 1519-56) had done. Designs were prepared by Johann Bernhard Fischer von Erlach in 1715, and building began the following year on a mound by the River Wien outside the walled city. The main facade of the new church was intended to be viewed from the imperial palace, the Hofburg.

The Karlskirche draws elements from several sources which Fischer von Erlach harmonized in one mighty composition. An obvious allusion is to the Temple of Solomon in Jerusalem: two massive spiral columns stand on each side of the great prostyle hexastyle Corinthian portico, and look like Trajanic columns, but they carry on their spirals reliefs (by Johann Christian

Mader) representing scenes from Saint Charles Borromeo's life and the miracles he performed after his death. These columns were also the emperor's own emblems, inherited from Charles V, who had adopted the Pillars of Hercules to suggest the *plus ultra,* or more beyond, of his great empire across the Atlantic; the ''Pillars'' therefore carry the crown of Spain flanked by the eagles of the Holy Roman Empire. The deeds of Saint Charles also allude to the *constantio et fortitudo* of Emperor Charles VI. The philosopher Gottfried Wilhelm Leibniz had proposed that ancestors and namesakes of the emperor should also be celebrated, with their acts represented on the shafts of the columns, but this idea was not realized. Now the Constantinian Basilica of St. Peter in Rome had twisted spiral columns set up over the tomb of the apostle, columns that were supposed to have been brought from the Temple in Jerusalem when it was destroyed in A.D. 70. Many representations of the Temple in common currency during Fischer von Erlach's lifetime show a domed, Pantheon-like building with twisted ''Solomonic'' or barley-sugar columns in the portico, with two freestanding columns standing before the portico and its steps (as in the drawings by Martin van Heemskerck). Giovanni Lorenzo Bernini also alluded to the earlier spiral columns in his baldachino in St. Peter's, for the twisted columns that stood over the tomb of the Apostle Peter were part of a monument with a prestige un-matched anywhere else in Western Christendom. Fischer von Erlach thus created a mnemonic of the Temple, of the tomb of the Apostle Peter, and a monument to a modern Solomon, the emperor Charles VI. The architect also suggested the Roman Pantheon and antiquity in the great temple front of the portico and in the ''Trajanic'' forms of the columns (which are also, of course, Jachin and Boaz). The Temple allusion is reinforced by the statues of Church and Synagogue placed on each side of the steps leading to the portico, and the reference to Roman antiquity is further emphasized by the resemblance of the pedimented portico to that of the Temple of Concordia that stood in the *Forum romanum.* Within the tympanum is a sculpture depicting Vienna's deliverance from the Plague as a result of the intervention of Saint Charles, while at the apex of the pediment is a statue of the saint as intercessor for mankind; Saint Charles therefore embodies one of the three theological virtues, namely Charity. The other two, Faith and Hope, stand on top of the towers. Statues which are allegories of the virtues of the saint stand on the attic above the pediment. Giovanni Stanetti carved both the tympanum and the statue of Saint Charles.

The Solomonic-Trajanic columns are attached to an extraordinarily wide front that terminates in two Baroque towers, and the general form of the facade suggests the precedents of Borromini's Santa Agnese in Agone in the Piazza Navona in Rome and Fischer von Erlach's earlier Dreifaltigkeitskirche in Salzburg. The wide front, with its terminating tower pavilions and passages, is strange in the extreme, until it is realized that the porch of the Jerusalem Temple was wider by 30 cubits than the house proper behind it, and resembled a transept. Such a wide porch is shown in Claude Perrault's illustration of the Temple in the *Code of Maimonides,* translated into Latin by Compiègne de Veil, and published in Paris in 1678.

Behind this amazing front is a stupendous elliptical space crowned by a dome on a high drum with a lantern. The longer axis of the ellipse is that leading to the high altar, and on the shorter axis on each side of the ellipse are barrel-vaulted rectangular chapels, rather like transepts. On the diagonal axes are four elliptical chapels with galleries above. Fischer originally planned a long sanctuary with a monks' choir behind the columns of the presbytery, an arrangement derived from Andrea Palladio's Venetian churches, but this was not built. The high altar is set beneath a smaller dome, and has a magnificent sunburst around the triangular sign of Yahweh. More immediately influential were Louis Le Vau's Collège des Quatre Nations in Paris of the 1660s, François Mansart's Église des Minimes and the Dôme des Invalides, also in Paris, Christopher Wren's design for St. Paul's Cathedral in London, and, of course, Hagia Sophia in Constantinople and St. Peter's in Rome.

Internally, the Karlskirche is very richly decorated, the prevailing coloring being red, brown, white and gold. Much of this decoration was supervised by Joseph Emanuel, Fischer von Erlach's son (born in 1693), who completed the building, but the overall program of internal works was designed by Conrad Adolph von Albrecht, and was finished in 1738. Fischer von Erlach originally intended a coffered dome to emulate the Pantheon, but instead the ceiling acquired a dramatic fresco showing Saint Charles being received into Heaven, with Mary as intercessor, and adoring the Holy Trinity with angels. The artist was Johann Michael Rottmayr. Illusory architectural perspectives were by Gaetano Fanti.

The Karlskirche is a stunning synthesis of powerful forms, brilliantly joined together in a work of tremendous presence. In this stupendous masterpiece, Fischer von Erlach suggested Vienna as a new Rome (with the emperor as a modern Solomon and a second Augustus), and created a monument to the Hapsburg dynasty. He fused antique, Baroque, Borrominiesque, biblical, iconographical programs, imperial and Talmudic themes all in the one great building. As Hans Aurenhammer has said, in its "spiritual conception it has no predecessor, and in the uniqueness" of its realization "it has no successor."

—JAMES STEVENS CURL

MAJOLICA HOUSE (NO. 40, LINKE WIENZEILE)
Vienna, Austria

Ca. 1898. **Architect:** Otto Wagner (1841-1918).

Publications

HOFMANN, WERNER, and KULTERMANN, UDO: *Modern Architecture in Color.* New York, 1970.

*

In the 1890s Otto Wagner designed and built a number of apartment houses in Vienna. The most famous is Number 40 on the Linke Wienzeile, better known as the Majolica House. The building derives its name from the facade, covered in large glazed earthenware tiles, correctly classified as majolica. The design on the tiles is a pattern of flowers, leaves and vines in green, pinks and blues. The overall impression is as if the vines were growing up the facade of the building.

Undoubtedly the Majolica House is one of the best examples of Secession architecture in Vienna and reveals Wagner's sympathy with the stylistic principles of the Vienna Secession. The young artists who formed the movement sought to break free from over-insistence on historical forms, and sought inspiration in patterns and designs based on nature. Since Wagner held a chair of architecture at the conservative Vienna Academy of Fine Arts, against which the Secession group rebelled, the Majolica House shocked his more conservative colleagues. It was highly criticized because of its modernity, and Wagner lost a number of important commissions of which he might otherwise have been assured. The following year Wagner further identified himself with the goals of the Secession group by formally joining them.

Wagner's treatment of the facade is typical of the Secession style in that the surface nature of the decoration is emphasized by the flatness of the designs. As revolutionary as Wagner was in his facade decoration, he did not break totally with the past, either at the Majolica House or in his other important projects. There is always present a strong, lingering classicism in his work. First, the building itself is a traditional apartment building in terms of structure, derived from the Renaissance palazzo type. Further, the facade is divided into clearly demarcated zones, announcing varied uses of interior space behind the facade. The ground-floor shops or restaurants are marked by the large glass windows and further set off by the iron railing and balcony just above, marking the beginning of the apartments. The roof line is announced by a strong, classicized cornice, projecting from the facade. The strong horizontal zoning of the facade and the regular geometry of the rectangular windows contrast powerfully with the free and expressive flow of the vines, leaves and flowers that decorate the structure. It is interesting that this major statement of Secession-style architecture is just several streets further along the Linke Wienzeile from the Secession Building, built by Josef Olbrich in 1897 as an architectural statement of the group's principles and values.

One cannot discuss the Majolica House without also considering the adjoining apartment building, Number 38, which was designed and built by Wagner at the same time, forming a single unit with the Majolica House. In terms of structure, its facade off the Linke Wienzeile is almost identical to that of the Majolica House, including similar classical divisions of space into visibly separate zones, as well as the use of balcony and cornice. However, Number 38 is a corner building and continues onto

Majolica House (No. 40, Linke Wienzeile): Vienna, Austria, ca. 1898

the side street. There Wagner reveals his particular genius in treating corners, as evidenced in other of his apartment buildings. The convex corner becomes concave below the roof line, creating a kind of loggia—a very successful visual transition from the Linke Wienzeile to the side street. While there are structural similarities, Number 38 serves as a visual foil for the Majolica House, since it is in white stucco and decorated in a more restrained, almost elegant pattern of gold that covers only the two uppermost stories. The more restrained, dignified decoration only serves to highlight the playful spirit and the exuberance of the adjacent Majolica House. Both buildings have been termed urban paintings, and not inappropriately since they recall and reveal an affinity with the then "new" flat paintings of Gustav Klimt, another key figure of the Vienna Secession.

—FRANCIS J. GREENE

PIARISTENKIRCHE (CHURCH OF MARIA TREU)
Vienna, Austria

1698-99: Original designs, and foundation chapel; **Architect:** Johann Lukas von Hildebrandt (1668-1745). **1716-53:** Church erected; **Architect:** Hildebrandt, and continued with revisions probably by Kilian Ignaz Dientzenhofer (1689-1751). **1750:** Additions and changes to upper sections of towers. **1752-53:** Ceiling fresco; **Artist:** Franz Anton Maulbertsch (1724-96). **1858-60:** Final additions and completion of towers.

Publications

GRIMSCHITZ, B.: *Johann Lukas von Hildebrandt.* Vienna, 1959.
WAGNER-RIEGER, RENATE: "Die Piaristenkirche in Wien."
    Wiener Jahrbuch für Kunstgeschichte (1955).

*

Dominating the Jodok-Fink-Platz west of the neo-Gothic Rathaus in Vienna is the twin-towered facade of the great Church of Maria Treu, known as the Piaristenkirche because it is the monastic church of the Piarist Order (*Patres Scholarum Piarum*). The Piarists were found in 1617, and were mostly active in Italy, Spain and Austria. The Church of Maria Treu is also a parish church.

The facade is not in its original state, the upper sections of the towers and other details having been added or changed in 1750, and again more than a century later, and the entire composition has a slenderness, height and elegance unusual in Viennese churches, most of which tend to be powerful architecturally rather than delicate. Basically, the facade has two superimposed orders in a variation on a familiar Italian theme: the lowest order, on pedestals, has a massive entablature and a segmental pediment in the center; the upper order sits on another plinth over the segmental pediment, and carries a triangular pediment. On each side of the frontispiece are towers two stages high over the main entablature and the upper plinth, crowned with triangular pediments on all four sides, over which are

elaborate pyramidal spires capped with metal crosses. The sequence of tall pedestals and base-plinth, main order with high entablature, plinth over entablature, order, plinth, order, and triangular pediments makes the towers exceptionally tall and slender. The towers are linked to the central frontispiece of two superimposed orders by vestigial sweeping scrolls, relating the design to its Roman precedents. However, these towers were not completed until 1858-60, which may help explain their elongated appearance, for many Viennese towers tend to be much more squat and tough, as on the Peterskirche, which was by the same architect. The central portion of the facade between the towers is curved on plan, bowing outward in a convex form.

Johann Lukas von Hildebrandt designed the Piaristenkirche, and the later works of the middle of the 18th century were carried out probably under the direction of Kilian Ignaz Dientzenhofer (1689-1751), who trained as an architect under the direction of Lukas von Hildenbrandt. The Piaristenkirche of Maria Treu was erected between 1716 and 1753, although plans seem to have been drawn up as early as 1698, and the Chapel of Sorrows that exists today was in fact the foundation chapel, built in 1699.

Hildebrandt was born in Italy, and spent the years 1695-96 in Piedmont. In 1699 he started building the Church of St. Lawrence in Gabel, near Prague in northern Bohemia, in which the plan is derived from Guarino Guarini's Church of San Lorenzo in Turin, a connection reinforced by the dedication. The Gabel church has a large, central, basically square space, but with aediculated niches for altars in each corner, and convex forms bowing into the square on each side. Over the space is a circular cupola, so the space actually reads more like a circle in fact. On each side of the central space, on the long axis which is that of the church, is an elliptical space, and off one of the ellipses is an apsidal sanctuary. The other ellipse projects outward between the two three-stage and powerful towers, so that the entrance front is bowed outward. Vestigial passages run along either side of the church on the axes of the towers parallel to the central and main axis. The ellipses have their short axes coincident to the main axis.

The most significant difference between Gabel and Turin is that the former has an elliptical narthex, and the exterior is treated as a whole envelope embracing the towers, a technique Hildebrandt used at the Belvedere to great effect. The spaces in Gabel are juxtaposed rather than interpenetrating, and convexes in one space are answered by concaves in the adjacent space, so there is a sense of statement and response in the forms used.

There are many similarities in treatment to the architecture of the church at Gabel found in the Piaristenkirche. The central space again has altars set in arched aedicules at the corners of the space, and the walls in which the aedicules are formed are convex, bowing out into the space under the cupola (which is lit by means of *oeil-de-boeuf* windows). The plan of the central space is therefore basically an octagon, with the sides of the figure bowing inward. To the north and south are "transeptal" side chapels, and there is an eastern apsidal choir and sanctuary. There are eight chapels in all, including the early foundation chapel. To the west is the entrance with the organ gallery over it set between the twin towers of the noble facade.

While the main influence on the plan and spatial arrangement is Piedmontese, the shade of Francesco Borromini is never far away. Yet the interior of the Piaristenkirche, by far the brightest and most charming of all Baroque church interiors in Vienna, is partly Rococo, and this must be due to Dientzenhofer's—rather than Hildebrandt's—influence. Most of the architecture, orders, arches and so on are white, with no gilding, which enhances the effect of the colored and gilded altars: one can "read" the structure quite clearly. Coloring, in fact, is delicate and subtle, dominated by those pinks and cool greens, with the

Piaristenkirche, fresco: Vienna, Austria, 1752-53

discreet gilding that is found in central-European Rococo at its most refined, while the great fresco on the ceiling by Franz Anton Maulbertsch (1724-96) of 1752-53 covers the space with enchanting color. The theme of the fresco is Marian, with the Triumph of the Cross and the Assumption, but the design has an intensity and a drama quite unlike the work of, say, Johann Baptist Zimmermann, who charms, delights, and never overwhelms with passion. The Maulbertsch fresco in the Piaristenkirche was the first major work of this somewhat mysterious master. Maulbertsch also painted the Christ with the woman of Samaria, and Christ in the house of Martha and Mary, both of which have an almost domestic sense of intimacy compared with the high drama of the ceiling. His picture of Christ on the Cross in the Chapel of the Cross dates from 1772.

Although the Piaristenkirche is not unadultered Hildebrandt, it is important as a synthesis of certain Piedmontese, Roman and Austrian themes, and, ultimately, has an Austrian stamp rather than an Italian flavor. It is, admittedly, less powerful and brilliant in its architectonic qualities than the Dominican church at Gabel (which ought to be better known), but it is nevertheless a work of architecture by a master that deserves close study.

—JAMES STEVENS CURL

Piaristenkirche: 1698-1860

POSTAL SAVINGS BANK
Vienna, Austria

1904-06. Architect: Otto Wagner (1841-1918). **1910-12:** Rear portion added.

Publications

FRAMPTON, KENNETH, and FUTAGAWA, YUKIO: *Modern Architecture: 1851-1919*. New York, 1983.

HOFMANN, WERNER, and KULTERMANN, UDO: *Modern Architecture in Color*. New York, 1970.

''Post Office Savings Bank.'' *Global Architecture* 47.

WAGNER, OTTO: *Einige Skizzen: Projekte und ausgeführte Bauwerke*. 4 vols. Vienna, 1892-1922.

*

Otto Wagner won an open competition in 1903 for the Vienna Postal Savings Bank, to be built on a site facing a small public

Postal Savings Bank, interior hall: Vienna, Austria, 1904-06

square which opened onto the Ringstrasse. The limited site, bounded by four intersecting streets, necessitated a trapezoidal ground plan.

Typical classical organization marks the facade of the Postal Savings Bank: its base is articulated as a separate zone by the use of stone facing larger in size than that covering the rest of the facade above; the roof line is set off by a horizontal attic surmounted by a cornice with balustrade above it; the principal entrance is framed, on each side, by a slight projection forward of the facade itself, and the building's corners are articulated in the same manner. Wagner had been trained in a traditional historicist approach to architecture and held a chair at the Vienna Academy of Fine Arts. Though he was, in many ways, a revolutionary architect for his time, participating in the Vienna Secession, there always remained in his work traces of a deep-rooted classicism, as evident in the articulation of this facade.

Nonetheless, there is much in the Postal Savings Bank that is very modern. The stone slabs covering the facade are all attached with clearly visible metal bolts. The use of metal is continued in the framework and supports of the entrance canopy

in glass, in a balcony above the entrance, and in the use of aluminum for the two female figures at the roof line, one representing Business and the other Thrift. As is often the case in Wagner's buildings, there are strong contrasts of old and new, such as the mixing in this case of granite, iron, aluminum and glass. Thin metal columns support the glass entrance canopy and contrast with the massive stone pilasters, directly behind. This playing-off of elements both large and small, slender and massive, traditional and innovative is a hallmark of Wagner's best work. Further, since the building is situated on a narrow site which limits the range of vision upon approaching it, one actually feels the flatness of the facade, squeezed into this limited urban landscape, as it were.

The entrance vestibule is a vast and welcoming space with a simple, broad staircase. A niche at the left holds the bust of Emperor Franz Josef, and the walls are clad with marble panels, fastened with clearly visible aluminum bolts—again the juxtaposition of traditional and modern materials and technique. The staircase leads to the central interior space where Wagner adapted a traditional architectural form, the basilica, for use as a new building type—a banking hall. The curved glass ceiling, set in a metal frame, is supported by two rows of slender concrete pillars, encased halfway up by aluminum. Further above, where the eye might expect capitals, electric lights emerge from the piers. The floor of the central nave is of heavy glazed glass tiles, and along the left and right side walls are the banking windows. All four side walls are clad in marble, fastened visibly by aluminum bolts. Every element of the design was coordinated by Wagner in the tradition of the *Gesamtkunstwerk* even to include the heating radiators, made of aluminum and positioned around the hall at regular intervals, almost looking like sentinels or guards standing at attention.

Wagner developed an analogy between modern architecture and French *plein air* painting. For Wagner, modern technology in architecture, such as the use of iron and aluminum, was a form of architectural realism, permitting, for example, well-lighted and spacious interiors. For Wagner this had the equivalent impact of viewing a French *plein air* painting, as opposed to the experience of a viewer looking at an historical painting filled with traditional mythological figures. Thus, light plays a major role in all of Wagner's buildings. In his banking hall, light floods through the glass roof. If the visual impact can be likened to that of French *plein air* painting, the historicist approach remains evident nonetheless in the basilican floor plan which all this light reveals.

The Postal Savings Bank is a summation of Wagner's architectural theory, as expressed in his *Moderne Architektur,* published in 1896 for his students at the Vienna Academy of Fine Arts. There Wagner developed his idea of the *Nutzstil,* or functional style, according to which necessity of structure dictates and informs the use of ornament. The Postal Savings Bank is a perfect example of this theory put into practice.

—FRANCIS J. GREENE

ST. STEPHEN'S CATHEDRAL
Vienna, Austria

1137: Original structure begun. **1230s:** Structure torn down; new one begun on its foundations. **1263:** Church consecrated. **1340:** Choir alteration completed. **1430:** Tower added to southern facade. **Late 14th century:** Nave reconstructed. **Late 15th century:** Net vault completed. **1511:** Tower added to north side. **1578:** Steeple completed. **Late 19th/early 20th centuries:** Westwork reconstructed.

Publications

OETTINGER, K.: *Anton Pilgram und die Bildhauer von St. Stephan.* Vienna, 1951.
ZYKAN, J.: *Die Stephankirche in Wien.* Vienna, 1962.

*

The Cathedral of St. Stephen was originally a parish church, though an unusually large one, and it was situated outside Vienna. Political vicissitudes soon promoted the church to a cathedral, and urban expansion gave it a central position in the city. In spite of magnificent reconstructions and enlargements, its humbler origins still show through in its present-day appearance. As Karl Oettinger remarked, the cathedral has the look of a gigantic village church, with its twin facade towers, its steep, patterned roof and its single high tower on the southern facade.

The first, Early Romanesque, structure was begun in 1137 on a site that had once held a Roman settlement. The remains of the Roman walls and gravestones may have been used in the westwork. Built on a cruciform plan, the church had a three-aisle, rib-vaulted nave. The westwork had a central portal and corner towers as was customary at the time. It is not clear whether the original building had shallow side apses besides the strongly projecting central apse, or whether these made their first appearance only in the Late Romanesque reconstruction. The only Early Romanesque survival is the so-called "schwarze Kammer" in the southern facade tower (now Confession Chapel).

In the 1230s the original building was almost completely torn down, and a new one begun on the old foundations, on essentially the same plan. The second church, which was consecrated in 1263, was the last great work of the Late Romanesque in the German-speaking area, and was chiefly notable for its ornamental masonry. The principal changes from its predecessor consisted of a more elaborate westwork and a change in the vaulting system. The simple groin vault was replaced by a complex net vault (completed after 1446 by Hanns Buchsbaum). The corner towers of the western facade, known as the "Heidentürme," were enlarged, and a gallery was built in the interior. The asymmetry of the detail of the towers is typical of the Late Romanesque style. Reconstructed in the late 19th and early 20th centuries, the westwork is the only salient Romanesque feature of the present building. The sculpture in the scattered niches, however, dates from the Gothic period, as does the large rose window. In its plainness, the western facade contrasts sharply with the highly elaborate Gothic exterior of the rest of the building.

Subsequent work has not substantially affected the basic plan, but has nevertheless transformed the cathedral into an undeniably beautiful example of the German Gothic style. Probably due to the influence of the recently constructed Cistercian Abbey Church at Heiligenkreuz and Regensburg Cathedral—both hall churches—an alteration of the choir was undertaken in 1304 (finished in 1340). The result, surviving today, is one of the chief examples of Early Gothic hall choirs in Austria. Although the space is not particularly high, the simple arcades and pillars create a strong vertical impression. In the second half of the 14th century, the Romanesque nave underwent a similar metamorphosis. The side aisles were both widened and heightened to conform to the dimensions of the central nave. Corner chapels were added to the facade on the outsides of the "Heidentürme," to accommodate the greater width of the nave behind.

The effect of the hall church type is the creation of an unusual impression of spaciousness in the interior and a reduced emphasis on the sanctuary, since the gaze is no longer drawn exclusively along the longitudinal axis. On the exterior, the hall church is immediately recognizable for its unbroken wall plane, from ground level up to the roofline. At St. Stephen's, this feature was put to good use, in that the southern wall was in effect made into the principal facade. The enormous windows of the nave are surmounted by ornamental gables with intricate tracery and a forest of pinnacles and turrets. The gables, each one different from the next, also serve to enliven the high roof. The buttresses are almost invisible under their wealth of tracery, pinnacles and figure sculpture.

In 1365 the southern facade was further enriched by the addition of the high tower, built over the greater part of the south transept. By 1395 the first two stories had been completed, but it took another 35 years for the tower to reach its full height of 137 meters. The lower stages of the tower are square, but

St. Stephen's Cathedral: Vienna, Austria, 1137

St. Stephen's Cathedral

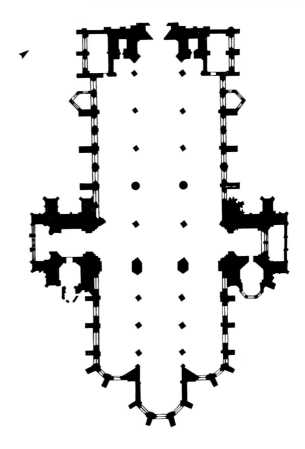

higher up it is transformed into an octagon. A ring of pinnacles obscures the transition to the steeple. The sculptural ornament, consisting of gables, turrets, pinnacles and gargoyles, hides the changes in shape. The gradual stepping back of the mass is almost invisible, as is the slant of the upper parts of the buttresses. The resulting slenderness of the silhouette also relieves the massive expanse of the roof. A tower of identical height, the so-called "Adlerturm," was planned for the northern side of the building, also to be built over the transept. Hanns Buchsbaum developed the design in the mid-15th century, and it was completed to about half its projected height between 1467 and 1511. Then, however, the work stopped. Between 1556 and 1578 Kaspar and Hans Saphoy constructed that tower's steeple, which remains slightly below the top of the roof. The whole of the cathedral benefits by this outcome, since a second high tower would have detracted from the clarity of the church's silhouette.

The interior sculpture in the choir, dating mostly from the early 14th century, is not very remarkable: the figures are heavy and weakly defined. The sculpture in the nave, however, is of extraordinary richness and variety: the gallery over the entrance is richly ornamented in tracery, the piers are carved in complex patterns, and there are many notable pieces among the sculptures along the walls. The most notable interior sculpture, however, is the work of Anton Pilgram, who did the organ pedestal (1513) and the pulpit in the nave (1514-15). Both works are famous for the sculptor's remarkable self-portraits, which function like signatures, but the tracery architecture and the vigorous figure sculpting are of great beauty throughout. The pulpit is attached to a pillar midway down the nave. A richly ornamented spiral staircase leads up to the platform, ringed by high-relief panels containing the figures of the church fathers. Each figure leans "out" of his panel as if out of a window, eyeing the congregation with an expression of rather critical attentiveness. At the

bottom of the pulpit is Anton Pilgram himself, in the act of opening a window, his upper body projecting slightly outward. His expressive, lined face shows him somewhat older, and considerably more worn, than in the self-portrait on the organ pedestal.

The magnificent Gothic alterations and additions to St. Stephen's basic Romanesque structure completely dominate its appearance. They transformed a fairly modest, if large, church into a late medieval monument whose silhouette towers over the modern city, providing a point of reference to visitors and pressing its stamp on the urban plan.

—MARIJKE RIJSBERMAN

SCHLOSS SCHÖNBRUNN
Vienna, Austria

1683: Original structure destroyed. **1692:** New structure designed; **Architect:** Johann Bernhard Fischer (von Erlach). **1696:** Construction. **1705:** Grounds designed; **Architects:** Jean Trehet, Adrian von Steckhoven, and F. H. von Hohenberg. **1711:** Castle completed. **Nineteenth century:** Interior altered.

Publications

HUBALA, E.: "Schleissheim und Schönbrunn." *Kunstchronik* 10 (1957): 341ff.
RASCHAUER, O.: *Schönbrunn.* Vienna, 1960.

Schloss Schönbrunn, with main park: Vienna, Austria, 1696

Before he was ennobled in 1696, Johann Bernhard Fischer (as he was) designed a project in 1692 for a new Schloss Schönbrunn at the request of Emperor Leopold I (1657-1705) to replace that destroyed by the Turks in 1683. This was unquestionably the architect's most ambitious design, and was for a complex of gigantic size: it was later (in 1721) published by Fischer von Erlach in his *Entwurff Einer Historischen Architektur,* and was shown on its intended site, crowning the hill of Schönbrunn. In the event, the finances of the court were insufficient to enable the scheme to be realized, and so Fischer was obliged to design a smaller hunting lodge to be sited in the valley below the hill. Work began on this more modest palace in 1696.

Fischer's original design for Schloss Schönbrunn was clearly intended as the residence of the Holy Roman emperor, with views over Vienna and even as far as the Hungarian border, for the emperor was also ruler of Hungary. This great palace was to be grander than Versailles, and indeed was to outdo all other palaces that had ever been built. The main entrance to the palace was to be in the valley, and was to be flanked by two spiral columns like those of Trajan in Rome; these columns were to support globes on which imperial eagles would perch. This entrance gave access to a huge tilt-yard on each side of which were fountains glorifying the emperor as Hercules and Apollo, while the victory of the Roman Empire over all other ancient empires was also celebrated. Overlooking the tilt-yard was to be the emperor's throne set under a canopy standing on a raised platform.

Beyond the throne and tilt-yard was a massive rock-work fountain, with formal parterres on each side, and vast systems of ramps and arcades leading up to the great platform on which the palace was to be constructed. The park in which the palace was to stand was to stretch as far as the horizon, and was to be bounded on the west by the Wienerwald. It was a stupendous conception.

The great precedent for this stunning scheme was the Temple of Fortuna at Praeneste near Rome, which also had terraces, fountains and cascades; the idea of the Trajanic columns, however, may have come not only from the emblem of Charles V (the Pillars of Hercules), but from Jean Marot's design for the Schloss at Mannheim, from the idea of the emperor as a latter-day Solomon (the twisted "barley-sugar" or "Solomonic" columns associated with the Temple in Jerusalem and with the Tomb of the Apostle Peter in Rome), and from a desire to associate the emperor with Roman antiquity. However, the design for Schönbrunn had three courts of honor on the same axis but on different levels, rising up one behind the other, and so Louis Le Vau's plan of 1668 for Versailles was invoked, while the projection of the central part of the palace into the park derives from the 1678-89 rebuilding of Versailles by Jules Hardouin-Mansart. The central concave feature of the entrance front may be derived from Giovanni Lorenzo Bernini's design for the east front of the Louvre, but the association of the Sun King with Apollo was to be further eclipsed by means of a chariot containing a statue of the emperor as Apollo set above a main facade with obvious quotations from Carlo Maderno's design for the front of the Basilica of St. Peter in Rome. Thus the

Schloss Schönbrunn, Millionenzimmer

Apollonian, God-like, Roman and sacred aspects of the imperial person and position were underscored. Andrea Palladio and Giacomo Barozzi da Vignola are also alluded to in the corner pavilions, which recall the Villa Capra (La Rotonda) at Vicenza and the Villa Lante at Bagnaia in Italy. There are also quotations from Versailles itself.

This Schönbrunn project—the most imperial of Fischer von Erlach's designs—demonstrated his knowledge of the history of architecture, while showing he was up-to-date in being able to draw on elements from the works of Bernini, Le Vau and Mansart, clearly mixed with allusions to Classical antiquity, the Bible, and the world of emblems and iconography. Schönbrunn was intended to be a monument to the power and prestige of the Holy Roman Empire.

The smaller Schönbrunn on the lower site was not complete in 1711 when the emperor Joseph I died. Yet even in the reduced version, Versailles was obviously the model. The palace is approached through a gate flanked by obelisks, and a great *cour d'honneur* is surrounded by low outbuildings. Two fountains, one by Johann G. Hagenauer and the other by Franz Anton Zauner, grace the court. The palace itself has a plain base with two stories above linked by means of a giant order standing on the basement story. On both the court and park sides is a *perron* leading to the *piano-nobile* level. There was to have been a triumphal gate-like construction on the roof, treated as an attic above the main cornice, and this was to shelter an equestrian statue of Joseph I; in the event, however, the palace acquired a central attic story and pitched roofs after 1737, although the

open loggia-*cum*-triumphal gate on the roof as projected by Fischer von Erlach is echoed by Ferdinand Hetzendorf von Hohenberg's *Gloriette* of 1775, which stands as a belvedere on the hill overlooking the formal French gardens of the park side.

The grounds are among the finest examples of Baroque gardens in the French style, with their fountains, great hedges, water and statuary. They were laid out first to designs by Jean Trehet in 1705, and were later altered to designs by Adrian von Steckhoven and F. H. von Hohenberg.

Schönbrunn's interior was radically altered by Nikolaus Paccassi during the reign of Empress Maria Theresa, and there were further changes in the early 19th century. However, many of the rooms are charming examples of the Rococo style, including the enchanting Chinese Cabinets (with lacquer and porcelain panels), the Millionenzimmer (with gilded Chinese rosewood paneling and paintings on parchment) and the Galleries (with ceiling paintings done by Gregor Guglielmi in 1761).

The exterior of Schönbrunn as it is today owes much to Fischer von Erlach, and its restrained elevations have a pleasing unity enhanced by the scheme of Maria-Theresa-yellow walls, cream pilasters and moldings, and green window frames and shutters. In the built palace, which is still very large (far bigger than a "hunting lodge"), it is possible to envisage something of Fischer von Erlach's great proposal for an imperial palace to outshine all imperial palaces in terms of size, splendor, setting, iconography and historical references.

—JAMES STEVENS CURL

Secession Building: Vienna, Austria, 1897-98

SECESSION BUILDING
Vienna, Austria

1897-98. Architect: Joseph Maria Olbrich (1867-1908).

Publications

CLARK, R. J., et. al.: *J. M. Olbrich: Das Werk des Architekten*. Darmstadt, Vienna and Berlin, 1967.

FRAMPTON, KENNETH, and FUTAGAWA, YUKIO: *Modern Architecture: 1851-1919*. New York, 1983.

HAIKO, P. and KRIMMEL, B.: *Josef Maria Olbrich Architecture*. New York, 1988.

HOFMANN, WERNER, and KULTERMANN, UDO: *Modern Architecture in Color*. New York, 1970.

OLBRICH, JOSEPH MARIA: *Architektur/ mit Textbeiträgen von Peter Haiko und Bernd Krimmel und einem Werkkatalog von Renate Ulmer. Vollständiger Nachdruck der drei Originalbände von 1901-1904*. Tübingen, Germany, 1988.

OLBRICH, JOSEPH MARIA: *Architektur von Professor Joseph Maria Olbrich*. 3 vols. Berlin, 1903-07.

*

Joseph Maria Olbrich's Secession Building has long been recognized as one of the seminal works of the early Modern Movement. Historians from Nikolaus Pevsner to Kenneth Framptom—citing the building's chaste white walls, blocky massing

and innovative interior design—have repeatedly described it as one of the earliest attempts to break free of late-19th-century historic revival architecture and create a new, "modern" aesthetic.

Yet for all its modernist redolence the Secession is a transitional work. While its spare exterior and open interior plan seem to anticipate the International Style of the 1920s, the building is still in many ways a product of the cultural and intellectual world of late-19th-century Vienna. Its brooding formal entrance and large gilded dome evoke clearer associations with the architecture of historicists like Friedrich von Schmidt and Karl von Hasenauer than the cool abstractions of Adolf Loos' mature designs. And the building's cultic, ritualistic guise suggests its deep roots in the turn-of-the century interest in mysticism and primitivism.

The Secession Building was erected to serve as an exhibition hall and offices for a group of artists and architects led by the painter Gustav Klimt that had broken away from Vienna's conservative artists' union. The Secessionists, as the rebels were called, sought to revitalize the artistic and cultural life of the city, and the new exhibition building was conceived as a symbol of their movement. The choice to design the building fell on Olbrich, at the time Otto Wagner's chief assistant and an early member of the Secession. It was Olbrich's first independent commission, and he lavished an extraordinary degree of attention on its creation, once remarking that it constituted his "dream house."

Olbrich produced a series of different designs over the course of the 10 months he worked on the project. His early sketches show a building with a small cupola and large freestanding columns, each carrying a draped urn. In later versions he substituted rectangular fluted pylons for the columns. Eventually he abandoned the columns altogether and focused on the cupola, which in the final version rests on four short stacks. In some of Olbrich's early sketches, the front facade is shown with murals—apparently based on an early conceptual sketch of the building by Klimt—but Olbrich left them out in the final drawings, opting instead for white stucco walls with incised and gilded decorations, similar to those at Wagner's nearby apartment house at Wienzeile 38.

What all of Olbrich's designs share, however, is a concern with creating a building that would not only fulfill the functional requirements of a gallery, but also express the Secessionists' beliefs and aims. Appropriately, much of the building's iconography reflects the Secessionists' mission of cultural regeneration. The principal theme is the *Ver Sacrum* (Sacred Spring), the Roman ritual of the consecration of youth in times of national danger. Dominating the composition is an open, gilded wrought-iron dome composed of laurel leaves, creating associations with the myth of Apollo. A Medusa frieze above the door (sculpted by Othmar Schimkowitz) symbolizes the fertile force of the unconscious, while a series of Minerva owls (designed by Koloman Moser) guard the fortunes of the arts inside. Olbrich also reinforced the theme of the Sacred Spring with delicate stucco, graffito-like tree motifs (also designed by Moser) incised on the corners of the building.

But beyond these symbolic representations of artistic renewal, the Secession Building was a reaction to the formal language of late-19th-century Viennese historicism. Rejecting the historic revival styles—neo-Gothic, neo-Renaissance and neo-Baroque—which had dominated Viennese architecture since mid-century, Olbrich sought to cloak the structure in a contemporary drape. As the inscription over its main entry proclaims—"Der Zeit ihre Kunst, der Kunst ihre Freiheit" ("To the age its art, to art its freedom")—the Secession was a manifesto for a new artistic consciousness, one which would respond to the needs and values of a modern industrial society.

Olbrich, however, in contrast to many of his contemporaries, did not abandon history altogether. Instead, he sought to establish a new dialogue between the past and the present, to reconcile the dictates of modern building with the historical tradition. Unlike the historicists, who viewed history as a set of usable quotes, Olbrich attempted to learn the lessons of the past without mimicking past forms. His acknowledged model for the Secession was an early Doric temple at Segesta which he had seen during his travels in Sicily in the early 1890s, but it has been abstracted and transformed so that the original is no longer recognizable.

Olbrich's recourse to "primitive" preclassical forms for a building that celebrated the new reveals one of the principal aims of the Secession movement: to rediscover art's timeless roots. But it was also intended as a repudiation of the historicists' formal language, with its heavy debt to classicism.

Olbrich's attack on historicism is also revealed in other ways: in the building's radically austere surfaces, cubic massing, and its simple block-and-stucco construction. Olbrich also kept the furnishings deliberately simple in order to set them off from the standard interiors of the day.

The most striking contrast with contemporary Viennese architecture, however, is provided by the building's ornamental vocabulary. Olbrich blended the sinuous lines and vegetal forms of French and Belgian art nouveau with geometric motifs that later became characteristic of Austrian Jugendstil. To this he added more traditional motifs, classical laurel wreaths, for example, to create a strikingly original decorative style

This unusual mixture of forms and styles caused a sensation in architectural circles and among the general public. In an essay on Olbrich written shortly after the building's completion, critic Hermann Bahr recorded how the Viennese were both fascinated and repelled by the radically new architecture of the building, describing how passersby stared at it in amazement and found it difficult to walk away without a second look. Local wits dubbed it the "Golden Cabbage" (a reference to the building's gilded dome) or "Mahdi's tomb."

The Secession's interior was as unconventional as its exterior. In contrast to the standard exhibition buildings of the 19th century (which were typically modeled after Italian Renaissance palaces and consisted of a series of partitioned galleries), the building is arranged around a central, glass-roofed courtyard with smaller galleries on three of the four sides. Six thin steel columns support the roof over the main gallery area, creating a large, virtually uninterrupted space. The design allowed for the use of movable panels which could be rearranged to accommodate the needs of different exhibitions. The resulting spaces could be lit from the glass skylight above, or the galleries partitioned off and lit from the side windows or by artificial light.

These functional features appealed to later modernist historians, but Olbrich was guided less by the dictates of rational planning than by the desire to articulate his own subjective impulses. In a statement published at the time of the building's construction, he revealed that his central idea was "to erect a temple of art which would offer the art lover a quiet, elegant place of refuge." The blank white walls, he wrote, expressed "a pure dignity that overcame and shook me as I stood alone before the unfinished temple of Segesta. I wanted only to hear the echo of my own sentiments and see my own warm feelings congeal into cold walls."

Olbrich's description of his moment of creative inspiration suggests how far he—and, indeed, the other early modernists—was from the functionalist aesthetic of the late 1920s. Yet, for all its obscure symbolism, its ponderous formality and its obvious historical debts, the Secession is still the work of a recognizably modernist sensibility. In its complex fusion of historical and modern forms, it represents a first bold step toward a profoundly new concept of architecture.

—CHRISTOPHER LONG

BELGIUM

GROTE MARKT
Antwerp, Belgium

Late 16th century

Publications

DUVERGER, J. (ed.): *Kunstgeschiedenis der Nederlanden.* Utrecht, 1956.

HITCHCOCK, HENRY-RUSSELL: *Netherlandish Scrolled Gables of the Sixteenth and Early Seventeenth Centuries.* New York, 1978.

LEURS, STAN: *Kunstgeschiedenis der Bouwkunst in Vlaanderen.* Antwerp, 1946.

Oude gildehuizen en ambrachtshuizen. Vol. 5 in *Antwerpen die Scone* series. Antwerp, 1972.

THYS, A.: "La Maison Grande Place, 17." *Recueil des Bulletins de la Propriété publiée par le journal L'Escaut* (Antwerp, 1883).

*

While the Grote Markt (or great market) has been the principal public space of Antwerp since the Middle Ages, its civic function has gradually displaced its commercial one. In the mid-16th century the early 15th-century town hall on the southwestern corner of the square was replaced by a much grander, polychromatic structure in the new Renaissance taste, occupying the entire western side of the market's perimeter. The new

Grote Markt: Antwerp, Belgium, late 16th century

town hall served as a splendid backdrop for the increasingly impressive pageants held in the square. Most of the medieval wooden guildhouses and other buildings on the other two sides of this roughly triangular space were replaced by stone facades, from the 16th century onward, in part to lower the chances of conflagration, in part to reflect the growing wealth of the city of Antwerp and its merchants and tradesmen during the city's "Golden Age." In this respect, the development of the Grote Markt of Antwerp typified that of the principal squares of the Hanseatic cities, and indeed of most European cities in general.

Despite appearances, little remains today (besides the town hall) of the 16th-century marketplace. Even the shape and size of the square were drastically modified in the 17th and later centuries by the demolition of large blocks of houses on the southern side. An enormous allegorical fountain, symbolizing the independence of Antwerp as a free-trading city, has animated the center of the market since 1887. As Antwerp remained a dynamic urban area throughout the 18th and 19th centuries, demolitions and remodelings of earlier buildings continued to occur, with new facades conforming to contemporary tastes and building requirements. If the Grote Markt today has the character of a Flemish Renaissance square, it is due entirely to 19th-century efforts to preserve the town hall and the few houses that still retained much of their authentic fabric, and to a major campaign of "restoring" the interstitial facades to a (realistic or imaginary) late medieval or Renaissance appearance.

The inventory of the monuments of central Antwerp carried out by the Rijksdienst voor Monumenten- en Landschapszorg of the Belgian Ministry for Netherlandish Culture, published in 1976, found only six of the 60 house facades on the Grote Markt to be "fairly authentic." This group included two 18th-century Rococo facades (numbers 21 and 24), three 16th-century facades (at numbers 5, 7, and 38, all "restored"), and one from the 17th century (number 40, with considerable modifications to the ground floor). But to dismiss the rest of the houses on the grounds of some putative "inauthenticity" would be very wrong, for all of them are in fact authentic cultural creations of their period and reveal much about the societies that produced them.

The preservation and restoration of the Antwerp town hall, carried out in several campaigns over the course of the whole 19th century, testify to the concern which the citizens of Antwerp shared with their contemporaries throughout the Western world for the protection of ancient monuments.

A number of the facades on the Grote Markt (numbers 4, 26, 52 to 58, 60) still display the simple, classicizing lines and light-colored stucco finish promoted by the stringent Napoleonic and post-Napoleonic building codes of the city of Antwerp. The one at number 26 (1877) is a particularly delightful composition, recalling the scrolled gables of 16th-century Flemish houses without imitating such a house.

The rest of the neo-Gothic or neo-Renaissance facades resulted from a building campaign begun in 1895 and still under way. This campaign was originally given financial impetus by a bequest to the city of Antwerp by a citizen interested in the project. It met with the approval of the city's political and cultural elite, on the one hand because the improvement of the city's physical appearance through municipal construction was already on the agenda, on the other hand because the promotion of Flemish achievements in art was seen as an important component of the popular educational programs advocated by such men as Max Rooses. These programs were intended to raise the ethnic consciousness of a people whose culture had been largely submerged by the Francophone bourgeoisie of Belgium. Inspired, no doubt, by the slightly earlier restorations of the Grand'place in Brussels and the Vrijdagmarkt in Ghent, as well

as by the very successful "Oud Antwerpen" exhibit at the 1894 Antwerp World's Fair (a reconstruction of the medieval Grote Markt and adjacent streets), the restoration of the 16th- and 17th-century Grote Markt of Antwerp has its closest parallel in the early-20th-century construction of the city's Leysstraat. The latter, carried out in a style strongly evocative of the 16th and 17th centuries, comprised a monumental entranceway into the city from the main railway station; the former comprised its monumental, and glorious, heart. Both bore witness to Antwerp's rich history and economic dynamism.

—ALFRED WILLIS

TOWN HALL
Antwerp, Belgium

1561-64. Architects: Cornelis Floris de Vriendt (1504-75), Hans Hendrik van Paesschen (ca. 1515-82), and others. **1576:** Burned by Spanish, then rebuilt according to original design. **19th century:** Restoration; **Architects:** Pierre Bourla, Joseph Schadde and Pieter Dens.

Publications

GELDER, HENDRIK E., and DUVERGER, J. (eds.): *Kunstgeschiedenis der Nederlanden*. 3d. ed. Utrecht, 1954.
GERSON, HORST and TER KUILE, E. H.: *Art and Architecture in Belgium: 1600-1800*. Harmondsworth, England, 1960.
HEDICKE, ROBERT: *Cornelis Floris und die Florisdekoration*. Berlin, 1913.
HITCHCOCK, HENRY-RUSSELL: *Netherlandish Scrolled Gables of the Sixteenth and Early Seventeenth Centuries*. New York, 1978.
HITCHCOCK, HENRY-RUSSELL: *German Renaissance Architecture*. Princeton, New Jersey, 1981.
ROGGEN, D. and WITHOF, J.: "Cornelis Floris." *Gentsche Bijdragen tot de Kunstgeschiedenis* 8 (1942): 79-171.
VERMEULEN, F. A. J.: *Handboek tot de geschiedenis van de Nederlandsche Bouwkunst*. Vol. 2, The Hague, 1931.

*

The history of the Antwerp Town Hall is practically the history of three buildings on the same site. When originally built from 1561 to 1564 to replace an early 15th-century structure that had grown much too small, it was the first great public monument of the Renaissance in northern Europe. Burned by the Spanish in the Fury of 1576 and left with only its outer walls standing, the town hall was subsequently rebuilt to the original designs. This second fabric, after having suffered considerable deteriorations both inside and out over the course of the next two centuries, was subsequently restored in the 19th century.

The original design is usually ascribed to Cornelis Floris de Vriendt, but it was actually the result of a collaborative effort involving several artists appointed to the task by the Antwerp aldermen. Floris was indeed in charge of the first construction. In plan, the building provided a large number of spacious halls grouped around an open court, in the late medieval tradition. Its three stories above a basement supported a high hipped roof with broad eaves. The resulting medieval mass of the town hall was then dressed in Italian Renaissance clothing of remarkable

Town Hall: Antwerp, Belgium, 1561-64; subsequently rebuilt

correctness: the basement arcaded and rusticated, the first two stories with superimposed orders of pilasters on plinths, the top story a balustraded loggia. Set upon this mass was a high scroll-gabled facade in the center of its east front. This slightly projecting facade, with its thoroughly modern profile and its superimposed orders of engaged columns and niches filled with allegorical sculpture, dominated the marketplace before it and affirmed the primarily civic function that that space would have during the following centuries.

The design of the Antwerp Town Hall, and particularly the design of its projecting pavilion, set the tone not only for later 16th- and 17th-century guildhouse facades in Antwerp, but also for northern Renaissance civic architecture in many other cities (including Cologne, Emden and Flushing).

The 19th-century restoration of the town hall's exterior, carried out under the successive directions of Pierre Bourla, Joseph Schadde and Pieter Dens, was apparently quite faithful to what had been built at the end of the 1500s. Comparison with early illustrations attests favorably to this fact. But the simultaneous transformation of the interior was total. In place of the town

hall's original courtyard, Dens inserted a skylighted, monumental double staircase. The new stairhall is one of the most striking interior spaces of its time (early 1880s), combining in a serious setting the aesthetic qualities of neo-Baroque spatial planning with those achieved in glazed commercial passages such as J-P. Cluysenaar's Galeries St. Hubert in Brussels (1846-47).

The wall surfaces of this stairhall, like those of all the principal apartments around it, were covered with decorations—painted and carved—evoking the Golden Age of Antwerp. Some of these decorations were authentic Flemish Renaissance artifacts (for example, the 16th-century chimneypiece from the Hôtel de Moelnere installed in the burgomaster's office in 1824), but most were creations of the revivalist imagination. The earliest complete Flemish Renaissance revival interior in the building is the so-called Leyszaal, a large reception room in the center of the east front. It included paintings of scenes from local history by Hendrik Leys (1859-69) inserted in an architectural decor by Schadde. Schadde had earlier been the architect of Leys' own house in Antwerp. Leys' own dining-room murals (1858-60) were transferred to the town hall and installed in a setting designed by Jean-Jacques Winders (the "Kleine Leyszaal," 1896-99). In the intervening decades the rest of the main-floor rooms in the Antwerp Town Hall were decorated by other leading artists and craftsmen.

Thus, if the exterior of the town hall was properly "restored" to something like its original state, the interior was, on the other hand, completely converted into a scenographic re-creation of the 16th-century. Together, this theatrical interior and its authentic shell explicitly affirmed the political and cultural identity of Antwerp as a Flemish city at a time when Belgium was ruled by a Francophone bourgeoisie that characteristically downgraded all aspects of Flemish culture that it could not easily coopt. The Antwerp Town Hall became simultaneously the expression of Flemish Renaissance and Flemish Renaissance Revival cultures in their ascendancies.

—ALFRED WILLIS

TOWN HALL (STADHUIS)
Bruges, Belgium

1377-1387: Exterior construction. **1402:** Interior vaulted. **Mid 15th century:** Wing added to back of building. **Early 16th century:** Interior remodeled.

Publications

LOUIS, A.: "La petite sculpture à l'hôtel de ville de Bruges: clés de voûte et quadrilobes." *Revue belge d'archéologie et d'histoire de l'art* 9, No. 3 (1939): 201-207.

*

The Town Hall (Stadhuis) of Bruges is the oldest Gothic town hall in Belgium and one of the most beautiful civic buildings in the Low Countries. This meeting place for municipal officials stands on the "Burg" of Bruges, a plaza formed by the most venerable religious and political structures in the city, including the Basilica of the Holy Blood and the now-destroyed Cathedral of St. Donatien. The town hall combines elements from religious and secular architecture of the late Middle Ages into a distinctive and harmonious composition.

The structure was begun in 1377, and the exterior seems to have been completed 10 years later. The interior was vaulted in 1402, and the building was in use by 1420. An additional wing was added to the back of the building in the mid-15th century, and the interior was remodeled in the early 16th century. The building is a two-story rectangle whose long side faces the plaza, but the horizontality of the basic shape is countered by numerous vertical elements in the design. Three octagonal turrets, one at either corner and one in the center, bisect the facade, each half of which is pierced by a door and three tall lancet windows. These are placed in slightly recessed setbacks which, except for the windows over the doors, are continuous across the upper and lower stories, and which establish important vertical accents; a row of reliefs bearing escutcheons of the 24 towns under Bruges' control marks the divisions between stories. Such continuous window setbacks became a Bruges tradition, and were included in local structures until the 17th century.

The most influential aspect of the facade, however, is the series of 48 spired niches affixed to the wall, which once held

statues. These niches are arranged in three ranks of pairs between each window, although a slight asymmetry at the west end required three niches. The niches continue in the lowest level of the turrets, linking them to the rest of the facade. Although adapted from Gothic cathedral portals, most of the niches on the Stadhuis housed images of the political overlords of the city, the counts and countesses of Flanders. Executed by local artists throughout four centuries (including Jan van Eyck), these statues were destroyed in the French Revolution. From a small balcony near the west doorway the counts of Flanders confirmed the privileges of the city.

This treatment of the facade was emulated in town halls built in the 15th and 16th centuries throughout the Netherlands, most vividly in Brussels and Louvain, whose facades are lavishly adorned with rows of sculpted figures in spired niches. At Bruges, however, more of the plane surface of the wall is visible, and the ornament is more restrained. The resulting balance between the architectural and the sculptural elements is enhanced by the linear details of the bar tracery in the windows, the ogival moldings over doors and windows, and by the decoratively crenellated parapet at the base of the steeply pitched roof. The roofline is relieved by small gabled windows and lacy molding along the crest. The facade has the delicacy of a goldsmith's work, and the building has been compared to a reliquary. It is in some ways a civic counterpart to Saint Louis' architectural reliquary in Paris, the Sainte-Chapelle.

Like the Sainte-Chapelle, the Stadhuis encloses two main stories. The ground level is a vaulted hall supported by heavy pillars, where petitioners waited to be heard by the town council. This body met in the upper story in the room now called the Gothic Hall. The most remarkable feature of this rectangular hall is its wooden vault, comprised of two rows of quadripartite ribbed vaults, each row six bays long. Sculpted corbels project from the walls to meet the ribs, but there are no supports for the vaults in the center of the room. Instead, the central ribs drop to the level of the corbels and are suspended from the crown to create an unusual pendant vault. The bosses in the keystones of each vault and the corbels are richly carved with foliage and religious and secular themes. The carving is the work of a local sculptor, Jan van Valenciennes, whose name figures prominently in the building's accounts and who is sometimes identified as the architect. The accounts, however, are missing for the first years of the project, so the architect's name is not documented.

The romantic rediscovery of Bruges in the mid-19th century resulted in a thorough remodeling of the Stadhuis. The Gothic Hall was painted with murals depicting important moments in Bruges' history, the facade was completely reconstructed, and the niches repopulated with modern statues.

—ANN ROBERTS

GRAND' PLACE
Brussels, Belgium

12th century. 15th century: Brussels Town Hall. **16th century:** Broodhuis (or Maison du Roi). **1691-1752:** Guild Houses—Archers, 1691; Shipmasters, Carpenters, Printers, 1696; Mercers, 1699; Butchers, 1720; Brewers, 1752. **1873-74:** Broodhuis demolished and reconstructed; **Architect:** P. V. Jamaer. **1881-90:** Grand' Place reconstruction campaign.

Town Hall: Bruges, Belgium, 1377-1387

Publications

SCHAYES, A. G. B.: *Histoire de l'architecture en Belgique*. 1853.
SCHOY, AUGUSTE: *Histoire de l'influence italienne sur l'architecture dans les Pays-Bas*. Brussels, 1876.

*

The Grand' Place (Grote Markt, or Great Market) of Brussels is one of the great public spaces of the world, boasting an important example of Gothic civil architecture and forming a splendid example of both northern Baroque urban design and 19th-century civic art.

Situated literally in the center of historic Brussels, the Grand' Place has been the principal locus of its economic and civic life since the 12th century. The Brussels Town Hall, one of the principal monuments of the Brabantine Gothic style, dominates its southwest side. The front portion of this building was built in two phases, in the early and in the mid-15th century, respectively. Its lofty tower, which dates from the second building campaign, commands not only the Grand' Place but indeed the whole city—as was typical of Flemish towered town halls of the period (Bruges and Ypres providing significant parallels).

Opposite the town hall stands the Broodhuis, or Maison du Roi, an administrative building of the early 16th century, remodeled often and profoundly until both its character and structural integrity were compromised by the mid-19th century. The Broodhuis was finally demolished and reconstructed (1873-74) by the architect P. V. Jamaer in such a way as to evoke its original Late Gothic appearance. These two buildings stand as massive Gothic poles, anchoring the animated plasticity of the Baroque cityscape between them. This cityscape consists of five discrete rows of guildhouse facades, all but one built between about 1696 and 1704, or restored to their original appearance toward the end of the 19th century.

The 1695 bombardment of Brussels by the French during the Nine Years' War reduced the medieval guildhouses, with their wooden facades, like most of the other buildings on the Grand' Place, to little more than ashes. The rapid reconstruction of these guildhouses—on a larger scale, in permanent materials, and with rich decorations—attests not only to the pride of the Brussels bourgeoisie but also to the wealth the city still enjoyed in the aftermath of a costly siege.

All of the new facades were entirely of stone and designed in the most modern, classicizing fashion by the leading local architects of the age. Most of these facades were enriched not only by a surfeit of architectural ornament (characteristic of southern Netherlandish taste) but sumptuous allegorical and other sculpture as well. As regards their design, they virtually exhaust the variety of the early 17th-century Italianate manners practiced in Flanders and Brabant. Some, like "Den Coninck van Spaigniën," were strongly rectilinear, severely classicizing compositions. Others, like "Den Horen," with a superstructure designed to look like the stern of a ship, displayed the polychromatic, sculptural and fanciful qualities associated with the full-fledged Baroque. A third group, including "De Roos," developed the 16th-century Flemish tradition of scroll-gabled composition. Finally, the row of six houses known collectively as the "Hertogen van Brabant" was designed as a single palatial facade, practically on a Roman scale with two superimposed orders of colossal pilasters and a central segmental pediment.

The French Revolution occasioned considerable damage to

Grand' Place: Brussels, Belgium, 1691-1752

Grand' Place: Brussels, Belgium

the facades of the Grand' Place, and especially to their sculptural decoration, much of which was, or was interpretable as, royalist. Not only their condition, but also their prestige, declined almost inexorably over the next three-quarters of a century. The city of Brussels occasionally (1830, 1847) took steps to prevent further decline, and in 1851 began to appropriate sums for modest restoration work. On the other hand, the city did permit in 1853 the demolition of the house called "De Sterre" in order to widen the street entering the Grand' Place just south of the town hall. A-G-B. Schayes, the great 19th-century chronicler of historic architecture in Belgium, hardly mentioned the Grand' Place in his *Histoire de l'architecture en Belgique* (1853). Even their greatest early admirer—the Belgian architect and architectural historian of the time, Auguste Schoy—wrote of the guildhouses that "frankly, none of the facades is a model of classical style, elegance, or good taste" (*Histoire de l'influence italienne sur l'architecture dans les Pays-Bas.* Brussels: F. Hayez, 1876, p. 409).

Schoy's reluctance to characterize the guildhouses of the Grand' Place as the key monuments in his history of Renaissance architecture in the southern Netherlands, as later scholarship has declared them to be, was due in part to the extremely poor condition in which he found many of their facades. He noted that the houses situated at what are now numbers 21-22, 23, 35, 26-37, 38 and 39 (all on the northeast side of the square, on either side of the Broodhuis) had by the 1870s completely lost any "special architectural character." Interest in these facades was renewed, however, by the enormous popularity enjoyed in the later 1870s and 1880s throughout Belgium, but especially Brussels, by Flemish Renaissance Revival architecture.

The Grand' Place presently appears in the form given it by the major restoration campaign begun in 1881 and largely completed by 1899. Charles Buls, then burgomaster of Brussels, personally promoted that campaign and also made it a part of his political program. Buls, along with Camillo Sitte, was one of the pioneers of "city aesthetics" and thus helped to lay the foundations for modern urban design. Brussels was his laboratory. According to Buls, the improvement of city aesthetics depended, among other things, on the preservation of historic monuments and the rigorous control of the artistic quality of new constructions. He advocated historic preservation and restoration not only as means for achieving picturesque streetscapes, but also for assuring the continued vitality of the city's ethnic (Flemish-speaking) population and thereby sustaining the specific quality of its urban life.

Among the neglected Flemish monuments of Brussels, none was so prominent as the guildhouses neighboring the town hall on the city's main public square. As burgomaster, Buls was in a position to arrange for large municipal subsidies to defray the expenses of those building proprietors willing to cooperate with him and Jamaer (or other architects) in carrying out the restoration project. Most of the restorations were completed under these conditions, in several phases (1883-85, 1888-89 and 1890). Expropriation of uncooperative landlords allowed the city to proceed with the restoration of the remaining guildhouse facades in an expeditious manner. The last facade was restored in 1923.

The one completely modern house on the Grand' Place is the one at number 8. This house, built in 1896-97 to plans by Adolphe Samyn, replaced the house called "De Sterre," demolished almost fifty years earlier. Its design is remarkable in that the entire ground floor was treated as an open, arcaded loggia. Thus the street, above part of which it is built, retained its full width, while the gap in the streetscape of the southern corner of the Grand' Place was closed up. Samyn designed the Flemish Baroque Revival superstructure of this house as something of a pastiche—albeit a successful one—of motifs found on nearby facades.

The restored Grand' Place of Brussels won the approval of many early exponents of modern urban design, including Sitte. As Buls predicted, it did become a point of civic pride for the citizens of Brussels. Restored not only to the period of its greatest magnificence, but adapted in subtle ways to the needs of the modern city, the Grand' Place now not only enjoys the esteem of architectural historians, but has become, along with the center of Bruges (restored to its late medieval appearance at about the same time as the Grand' Place of Brussels, and for much the same reasons), one of the greatest tourist attractions of northern Europe.

—ALFRED WILLIS

HÔTEL TASSEL
Brussels, Belgium

1892-93. Architect: Victor Horta (1861-1947).

Publications

BORSI, FRANCO, and PORTOGHESI, PAOLO: *Horta*. New York, 1991.
HOFMANN, WERNER, and KULTERMANN, UDO: *Modern Architecture in Color*. New York, 1970.

Hôtel Tassel, staircase: Brussels, Belgium, 1892-93

HOPPENBROUWERS, A.; VANDENBREDEN, J.; and BRUGGE-
    MAN, J.: *Victor Horta architectonographie*. Brussels, 1975.
MADSEN, S. TSCHUDI: *Sources of Art Nouveau*. New York,
    1956.

The Hôtel Tassel is the most thoroughly and consistently real-ized work of art nouveau architecture. Each characteristic fea-ture of art nouveau is used to reinforce another. In this building more thoroughly than any other, the identifying marks of art nouveau organically interpenetrate and reinforce one another to make what can properly be called a "statement." The result can be likened to the light blend of whipped rich ingredients which characterized much of the turn-of-the-century cuisine: a consistently subjective, crafty, organic, ornamental, mannered, fresh, multilayered, theatrical, symbolic and perhaps even eso-teric dessert which remains hard to digest.

This house is a subjective portrait—the architect's personal vision of the life and character of the specific client-user, the master of the house (Professor Tassel). The utter subjectivity of this vision can be illustrated by the opinion of the renovator that he would have to have found another bachelor-engineer-professor with a live-in grandmother to inhabit the house in order not to *have to* make physical alterations to the interior space partitions.

The building is a monument to the paradoxical desire of art nouveau to adapt modern materials to craftsmanship. This desire is presented as an element of the "portrait" of Professor Tassel. The clearest examples are the stained-glass windows and the structural-ornamental ironwork.

The complex and interwoven organic ornamentation is itself emblematic of the client; it is precisely the most obdurately "modern" materials that were chosen to undergo the paradoxi-cal metamorphosis to organic form. The objective hard mass of stone, iron and glass has been turned into an architectural essay in the subjective and the personal.

Both "new" and "young," this commission was a new beginning both for architect Victor Horta and Professor Tassel. It was a youthful exercise in a new style—its ornamentation emphasizing swelling, budding and growing youthful new plants.

The Hôtel Tassel unites arts and crafts. It represents architec-ture as sculpture and as personal ornament; it represents the use of excruciatingly complex craftsmanship toward a legitimate artistic goal; it considers interior arrangements and furnishings and their craftsmanship to be within the control of the architect.

"Layering" is its fundamental mode of representation. It is three houses in one, going inward and upward from the street entrance: the facade (public), the stairwell/winter garden (semi-private), the back house (private). The ornamentation is achieved by the layering of one material over another. Interior vistas unfold in "layers" without the use of perspective by relying on the progressive unfolding of screened views as one is forced to move both vertically and horizontally through the house.

The house is as self-consciously mannered and artificial as it is theatrical. The facade, as well as the interiors and their ornamentation, is neo-Mannerist in style, characterized by spa-tial incongruity and an elongation and elaboration of elements. The entire conception of the building is based on artifice—artist as artificer, subject as artificer—the subject of the building is the art of the artifice. Artifice: how to present a bourgeois respectable exterior while holding as secret a jungle-fetid, fin-de-siècle decadent gay-nineties interior. Literally, the house was designed for magic-lantern shows; more figuratively, it is an adaptation of contemporary theater architecture—specifically, the Paris Opéra—to domestic architecture; finally, it is a stage set for a mannered, artificial, theatrical life-style—embraced as an ideal.

The building is symbolic, allusionistic and capable of an esoteric interpretation. Perhaps this dimension of the Hôtel Tas-sel is best understood in reference to its presentation of the relationship between the "natural" and the "artificial." In terms of its organic, plant imagery, the artificial—the sinuous ironwork for example—symbolizes that which it is not: part of the natural world of plants. The most characteristic part of the language of the building, its "organic" ornamentation, is thus a symbol, an allusion which is signified by the absence of that which is being signified—nature represented in the city by "organic" architecture. In reference to this, one must note the centrality, vertically and horizontally, of the "Winter Garden," the hot-house, and its stagy connection to the salon/dining room in which the works of nature are literally incorporated by men. Further, the minuscule garden, of which an elevated "view" as from a ship or train is offered from the same dining salon is actually inaccessible to the inhabitants. The esotericism em-bedded in this view places artifice above fact, symbol above that which is symbolized, the mannered above the ordinary. In this way it is closely allied with the neo-Platonism with which much of high art nouveau is associated.

The line of the building is the "whip." While the open-whip lines are most easily seen in the tracery, the iron ornamentation, or the mosaics, in a more recondite and esoteric way they are clearly represented in the plans and the sections of the building. The use of the central stairwell and the arrangement of staggered half stories creates a line from entrance to attic which is traced by a growing new fern shoot that has been cracked as a whip.

—JOSEPH B. JUHASZ

PALAIS STOCLET
Brussels, Belgium

1905-11. Architect: Josef Hoffmann (1870-1956).

Publications

FRAMPTON, KENNETH, and FUTAGAWA, YUKIO: *Modern Architecture: 1851-1919*. New York, 1983.

HOFMANN, WERNER, and KULTERMANN, UDO: *Modern Architecture in Color*. New York, 1970.

"Josef Hoffmann—Palais Stoclet (1905)." *Architectural Design* 1-2 (1980).

KURRENT, FRIEDRICH, and STRUBL, ALICE: *Das Palais Stoclet in Brussel von Josef Hoffmann mit dem berühmten Fries von Gustav Klimt*. Salzburg, Austria, 1991.

MEYER, CHRISTIAN (ed.): *Josef Hoffman: Architect and Designer, 1870-1956*. Vienna and New York, 1981.

SEKLER, EDUARD F.: *Josef Hoffmann: The Architectural Work*. Princeton, New Jersey, 1985.

SEKLER, EDUARD F.: "The Stoclet House by Josef Hoffmann." In DOUGLAS FRASER (ed.): *Essays in the History of Architecture Presented to Rudolf Wittkower*. London, 1967: 228-244.

When the name Josef Hoffmann comes to mind, one visualizes an early-20th-century architect-designer with a fondness for cubical and rectilinear rational forms, grid patterns, black and white contrasts, and ascetic reserve. One remembers too that this same brilliant young Austrian designer founded the vital and influential atelier known as the Wiener Werkstätte (Viennese Workshop).

Yet, Hoffmann may have caused the most stir with a project outside his homeland, the Palais Stoclet, now considered his most important work. An urban villa, it was built for Belgian industrialist Joseph Stoclet in Brussels between 1905 and about 1911. It is an enigma in architectural history, confounding popular impressions of Hoffmann and of early-20th-century modernism in general. Although it may be considered Hoffmann's signature piece, the structure and gardens contain features somewhat at odds with his general theoretical program. For an architect known for largely ornament-free buildings, spartan simplicity, rigorous accountability and thoughtful unity, the Palais Stoclet is a work with many surprises.

Consider that instead of a reserved, cost-sensitive approach, the Palais Stoclet involved the combined talents of many Wiener Werkstätte members and took from six to ten years to complete. Such notable artists as Kolo Moser, Michael Powolny, Georg Minne, Franz Metzner and Gustav Klimt made contributions, as did others outside the workshop, such as Fernand Knophf.

Hoffmann's buildings were distinctive for their exteriors of cubic clarity, clean surfaces and understated linear accents. The Palais Stoclet continued those tendencies, but the way that they were utilized needs clarification. For example, the massing of this urban-villa complex is rectilinear and rectangular, and (in

Palais Stoclet: Brussels, Belgium, 1905-11

Hoffmann's hands) that usually resulted in monumentality, classical meter, axial dynamics and elegant sobriety. Yet the massing and proportional relationships at the Palais Stoclet result in an almost anticlassical effect, at least in terms of mannered classicism. Giuliano Gresleri noted this in his 1981 study of Hoffmann, observing that "the *piano nobile* of the building has a monumental hall around which Hoffmann placed rooms of unusual dimensions: a bedroom 9×50×5.70 meters, a bathroom 6×6 meters, the dining-room 15×7 meters and the music room 15×7 meters." Along with a covered vehicular entrance, a stair tower and the suspended *paisserelle* over the courtyard, a picturesque roofline and silhouette were the outcome.

Furthermore, the exterior detailing of articulated bronze banding, though acting as uniting seams where the white planar walls meet the roof, has "a tectonically neutral effect," according to historian Kenneth Frampton, "because the resulting lines or bands occur equally along horizontal and vertical junctures." In other words, a strong linear element is present, but it is not coordinated with directions of force in a vertical scheme. Of course, it could be that another, different type of force is operative in the design, one in which there is subtle denial of structure and mass. It is reasonable to suppose that the entire structure was intentionally treated not as architecture but as an architectural object, a precious building—a protected and privileged environment.

The question of design sources for the Palais Stoclet has perplexed experts for decades. This building was initially planned for a site on the Hohe Warte in Vienna, an address relevant to the Palais Stoclet since Hoffmann had designed several distinctive villas in the same area in the years leading up to 1905, including the Villa Henneberg (1902-03) and the Villa Spitzer (1902-03).

Along with those villas and selected smaller commissions, Hoffmann designed the Sanatorium at Purkersdorf near Vienna, which is viewed as essential to the architectural language in the Palais Stoclet. In fact, the Purkersdorf Sanatorium may be seen in hindsight as also having a large number of elements to control. Yet more important, it was a collaboration of design talents among the Wiener Werkstätte staff in which the integration of architectural framework, ornamentation and furnishings was one of the chief goals. The key buildings immediately preceding the Palais Stoclet projected tendencies of exhibition pieces. The Palais Stoclet was conceived as such from the beginning, something undeniable when experiencing its resplendent interior.

If the Palais Stoclet exterior provided design surprises, its interior was not disappointing in that regard either, and has been just as perplexing. The exterior, once again, consists of an asymmetrical massing of white cubic solids representing a mannered synthesis of European and Mediterranean traditions. A statue of Athena stands over this exterior domain as if becalming the building and grounds.

The interior, by contrast, draws the visitor into exotic, ambiguous spaces, highly patterned and polished. For example, one finds marble walls and floors of various colors and veining, onyx and malachite inlays, marquetry, site-specific loomed carpets, suede-covered chairs, and the intoxicating spectacle of gold-and-glass mosaic work in Gustav Klimt's dining-room mural. Experiencing all this could be compared to watching the figure-ground dissolve in an Edouard Vuillard painting of about the same time.

Just as astonishing, Hoffmann allowed structural elements such as walls, cornices, niches, altar-like devices, partitions, boxed or squared columns and typanums to become the architecture itself instead of being merely subordinate parts. To achieve that, he isolated some elements while enlarging or reducing others. Whatever their scale or surface treatment, however, the elements remained architectural objects that were complicated or accented by objects of art.

The designing and building of the Palais Stoclet was, then, an experiment with the ideal of luxury that successfully steered clear of the dangers of gross heaviness or gaudiness. Its range of compositional devices is complex and, in terms of logic, a bit contradictory. The Palais Stoclet is both European and Oriental, both rational and expressive, both disciplined and inventive, and quite possibly anticipates both European functionalism of the International Style, as well as post-modern eclecticism of the late 20th century.

—TOM DEWEY II

TOWN HALL
Louvain, Belgium

1439-69. Architects: Sulpice van Vorst, Jan Kelderman II and Mathieu de Layens.

Publications

BATTARD, M.: *Beffrois, halles, hôtels de ville dans le nord de la France et la Belgique*. Arras, France, 1948.
STURGIS, RUSSELL: *A Dictionary of Architecture and Building*. London, 1902.

*

The Town Hall of Louvain was built between 1439 and 1469, during the heyday of the Brabantine Gothic style. It is situated across from the Collegiate Church of St. Pierre, which also dates to the 15th century. The building has the appearance of an architectural frame for the abundance of sculptures and turrets with which it is ornamented.

The surviving Town Hall was built as a replacement of an older structure, which occupied almost exactly the same site. Since it had to house the city's administrative services, the older building was not demolished immediately. However, nothing remains of it except for the cellars, which are now open to the public. To enlarge the surface between the Town Hall and the church, the facade of the new Town Hall was set back from the location of the older facade by some 12 meters.

The Town Hall was built during two campaigns, one lasting from 1439 to 1445, the other from 1448 to 1469. The architect Sulpice van Vorst, who was responsible for the design, began construction with the rear wing, which was to house the administrative offices and the council chambers. Van Vorst died only a few months after he began construction, however. He was succeeded by Jan Keldermans II, an architect from Mechlin. The rear wing was finished under Keldermans' supervision, but he also died, in 1445, before he was able to begin construction of the projected front wing. Certain elements between the rear and front wings had been built by then, however. After an interruption of several years, construction was resumed under the direction of Mattieu de Layens, an experienced architect who had already designed the Churches of St. Pierre and St. Jacques in Louvain, St. Sulpice in Diest, St. Léonard in Léau and St. Waudru in Mons, among others.

Construction of the front wing was finally begun in 1448, after the older building was demolished. De Layens' design

Town Hall: Louvain, Belgium, 1439-69

was not much different from that of van Vorst. Those original designs, inspired by the Brussels Town Hall, had called for a belfry on the right-hand corner of the facade. When construction was already under way, it turned out that the site was too unstable to support a belfry, and the design had to be changed. Few alterations to the initial design were possible, since construction was already well advanced. To compensate for the absence of the bell tower, de Layens built a second monumental gable in its place, which balances the one on the other corner. Each gable was finished with three small towers. The iconographic program called for Old Testament scenes on the left-hand gable and the principal facade, while the right-hand gable, where the belfry was to have been, was adorned with New Testament scenes. Another modification was also necessary, since the main entry was to have been located in the belfry. De Layens replaced one of the windows on the ground floor with a doorway, and constructed a high platform in front of it.

The general design is thus to be credited to van Vorst, while the alterations necessitated by the suppression of the bell tower were designed by de Layens.

Other alterations have taken place over the course of the centuries. The rear wing was altered in the 17th century, and in the 18th century the old council chambers were transformed into salons and the platform was replaced. In the course of the 19th century, several restorations were done in the romantic spirit. The sculpture of the principal facade has been profoundly modified, and the iconographic program was expanded. Recent statues bear the traits of famous figures—kings, artists, writers. In the 20th century a section of the left rear wing was demolished to make room for a new wing. In the wake of the two world wars, the building required both restoration and reinforcement.

—MONIQUE AND ROGER VAN SCHOUTE
Translated from the French by Marijke Rijsberman

Tournai Cathedral, west facade

TOURNAI CATHEDRAL
Tournai, Belgium

1066-1340: Nave constructed during Romanesque period, followed by five towers (mid-12th century) and choir (from 1243). **15th century:** Chapel of St. Piat added.

Publications

HÉLIOT, P.: "Les parties romanes de la cathédrale de Tournai. Problèmes de date et de filiation." *Revue belge d'archéologie et d'histoire de l'art,* XXV, 1966, pp. 3-76.
ROLLAND, P.: "La cathédrale de Tournai et les courants architecturaux." *Revue belge d'archéologie et d'histoire de l'art,* VII, 1937, p. 229.
ROLLAND, P.: "Chronologie de la cathédrale de Tournai." *Revue belge d'archéologie et d'histoire de l'art,* IV, 1934, pp. 103, 225.
WARICHEZ, J.: *La cathédrale de Tournai.* Brussels, 1935.

*

Tournai, the original seat of the Merovingian dynasty, was made into a bishopric by the end of the fifth century. Several buildings preceded the extant cathedral, the eastern end of which was constructed first, early in the 12th century. The earliest section of the cathedral is the Romanesque nave, which was followed

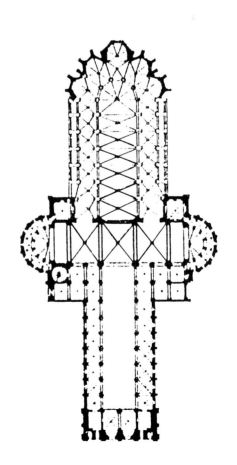

Tournai Cathedral, nave: Tournai, Belgium, 1066-1340

by the transept with its five bell towers, also in the Romanesque style. A Romanesque choir completed the design, but that was later replaced by the choir in the Gothic style, which has been preserved.

The central nave has nine bays, and is 48 meters long, 9 meters wide. It is divided into four levels. The ground-floor arcades are supported by pillars, which are enlarged by four half columns and colonnettes. The arcades are separated from the tribune galleries above by a wide stringcourse, which is repeated between the other levels. The arcades, the tribune galleries and the windows of the fourth level have the same spacing, while the third level has two short bays for every bay on the lower levels. Pilasters support the vault, which was constructed in 1777 to replace the original flat ceiling. The lateral naves still have groin vaults at the first level.

The Romanesque transept contrasts with the nave in several respects, creating a transition to the Gothic choir. The transept was constructed between 1145 and 1170. It is 67 meters long and 10 meters wide, and is separated from the nave by a large arcade of broken arches. A lantern tower was erected over the central bay. The arms of the transept extend in both directions from the central bay by an almost square bay, followed by a rectangular bay, and end in a semicircular apse, with windows on three of the four levels. Four towers flank the short sides of the rectangular bays. The elevation of the transept bays is the same as that of the nave at the two lower levels, but each bay at the level of the triforium has three openings, separated by colonnettes and surmounted by a horizontal lintel. The elevation of the apses has four levels but a different rhythm. The first level, which is pierced by windows, has high columns defining seven narrow bays. The bays of the second level, which is also pierced with windows, are separated by short columns. A triforium without windows is pierced by two arches per bay, and it is surmounted by the high windows of the fourth level, which are set between the ribs of the vault. Sexpartite vaults were planned, but were never carried out except in the square bays of the transept.

The Gothic choir was constructed between 1243 and 1255. It is related to the choir at Beauvais in the vertical emphasis of its design and its rapid rhythm. Its dimensions (61 meters by 12 meters by 36 meters at the crowns of the vaults) and its elevation in three levels contrast with the other two parts of the cathedral. The columns supporting the broken arches of the seven bays of the choir had to be reinforced in the 14th century, but those of the apses have retained their original gracefulness. All three levels are pierced with windows: through the side aisles and chapels at the first level, through the triforium at the second level, and by high windows at the upper level.

On the exterior, the cathedral is distinguished by its five towers and the facade of the Gothic choir, which is entirely pierced with windows and supported by large flying buttresses. The western facade, pierced with a rose window in the 14th century, has undergone restorations and alterations which have significantly modified its appearance.

The exterior elevation of the nave presents the same calm rhythm as the interior, but the decoration of the wall between the bays becomes more complex toward the top. The facade, which is flat at the first level, is pierced with arches supported by colonnettes at the level of the tribune galleries, while an open gallery supported by colonnettes is placed at the level of the high windows. This exterior triforium passage was to become a characteristic element of Scaldian architecture.

The exterior of the apses of the transept presents the same superposition of windows as the nave, but the preponderance of solids over voids is ordered in the opposite direction, as a result of the lesser scope of the upper sections of the structures.

The four upper levels of the towers are pierced with two or three bays. The two eastern towers (the northern one of which is called St. Jean, the southern one St. Marie) are entirely in the Romanesque style. The ones on the side of the nave (the northern one of which is called Brunin, the southern one Treille) were finished later, and have Gothic bays in the upper level. The lantern tower illuminates the transept through three of its sides only, since the fourth side has in effect been opened by the arch of the choir.

The sculpture of the cathedral is extremely rich, and is unique in Belgium. The number of sculptural elements on both the exterior and interior has been set at 1,500. The three sculptural ensembles of the portals are either hardly legible or have altogether disappeared. The western facade must have been ornamented with sculptural portals, pieces of which were discovered during 19th-century restorations. Today, its porch shelters three sculptural orders. The lower level dates to the 14th century, and is inspired by the Old Testament. The second level dates to the 16th century, and evokes the history of Tournai. The large statues of saints and apostles in the upper level are 17th-century replacements of older statues.

Human figures adorn the arch moldings and piers of the two portals on the north (Porte Mantille) and the south sides (Porte du Capitole). The Porte Mantille contains the remains of a Psychomachia and a scene of uncertain subject, representing either Judith and Holofernes, the battles of the Merovingian kings, or an episode from the history of David. The Porte du Capitole has a representation of the Last Judgment.

The sculptural elements in the interior are more easily legible, particularly on capitals and column bases. Decorated capitals are found in the nave, the side aisles, the tribune galleries, the triforium and the high windows. Besides simple cubical capitals, there are great numbers of capitols with human figures, with floral motifs in the Corinthian manner and with animal motifs, both realistic and fantastic. The animal figures are mostly placed on the front or back of the capitals, but their muzzles are sometimes visible around the corners. The interpretation of scenes with human figures is often uncertain. A certain evolution appears in the sculpture, and technique varies also, underlining the importance of the Scaldian school.

—MONIQUE AND ROGER VAN SCHOUTE
Translated from the French by Marijke Rijsberman

CROATIA

EUPHRASIUS BASILICA
Porec, Croatia

Also known as Cathedral of Euphrasius. **3rd century:** Maurian Oratorium constructed. **Ca. 313:** Oratorium remodeled. **5th century:** Baptistery constructed, Oratorium demolished and rebuilt. **535:** Basilica demolished and new cathedral built using prior walls. **6th century:** Baptistery remodeled, consignatorium, memorial chapel, and mausoleum built, mosaics completed. **1277:** Bell tower added. **1440s:** Earthquake damage to south wall, rebuilt and Gothic vaulted ceiling added. **1452:** Choir stall added. **15th century:** Sacristy added. **18th century:** Western chapel added. **19th century:** Eastern chapel added. **20th century:** Middle chapel added.

Publications

MILBURN, ROBERT: *Early Christian Art and Architecture.* Berkeley and Los Angeles, 1988.

MOLAJOLI, BRUNO: *La basilica eufrasiana di Parenzo.* Padua, 1943.

PRELOG, MILAN: *Porec, grad i spomenici.* Belgrade, 1957.

SONJE, A.: *Predeufrazijanske bazilike u Porecu.* Porec, 1971.

TERRY, ANN RAYBIN: "The Architecture and Architectural Sculpture of the Sixth-Century Eufrasius Cathedral Complex at Porec." Ph.D. dissertation. University of Illinois, Champaign-Urbana, Illinois, 1984.

*

The city of Porec, located on the northern coast of the Adriatic, was settled in pre-Roman times and was originally called "Histra." Porec came under Roman domination in 178 B.C. and became a colony in 35 B.C.. Porec met with a series of conquerings, a common occurrence along the Yugoslav coastal areas, and the cultural influences of the Goths, Byzantines and Venetians remain. It was further razed a number of times and required a succession of rebuilding campaigns. Thus, the city remains a rich mixture of cultural artifacts of many periods and architectural styles.

The Euphrasius Basilica stands as one part of an historic church complex dating from the third century to the 16th century. This complex is located to the north of the city of Porec, and south of the city's medieval fortifications. The complex was founded in the third century with the construction of the Maurian Oratorium, a house church, or *ecclesia domestica,* dedicated to martyr Maurus. The building was remodeled in the fourth century (ca. 313) as a simple rectangular double house form, with one portion dedicated to the veneration of relics and the other used as a church. The east side of that structure ran parallel to an ancient street. Although the oratorium no longer stands, an excavated epitaph to the martyr records the chronology of construction.

During the fifth century an octagonal, central-plan baptistery was constructed; it was remodeled during the sixth century. To its west, a bell tower, square in plan and adorned with mosaics, was added in 1277. To the northwest, a consignatorium was constructed during the sixth century. This square, centrally planned structure was built with an apse to its north. During the Middle Ages, it was converted into the Bishop's Palace. To its east and west are ambulatory wings, each terminating in an apse, and a narthex is located to the south.

In the fifth century, in honor of Maurus, the oratorium was demolished and the new structure was doubled in size. This church had been a rectilinear basilica in form, without apses, and had contained ornate mosaics.

In 535 the bishop of Porec, Euphrasius, in an attempt to reinforce architecturally the importance of Christianity and, simultaneously, his own status, demolished the fifth-century basilica to make way for a grander structure. The new cathedral was again constructed as a two-aisle basilica, and employed the walls of the fifth-century church.

The cathedral is the grandest and most significant component of the church complex. It is connected to the baptistery via a square-plan atrium to its west. It was constructed as a three-part basilica with a nave and two side aisles, with three apses. The date 535 would signify that this basilica at Porec was one of the earliest of its type in the region. Stylistically, it is an early Byzantine structure.

In plan, the Euphrasius Basilica is divided into three parts by 18 columns, carrying arches, which were, remarkably, transported in their completed form from Constantinople. The underside of each arch in the arcade is covered with relief work. Flanking the northern side aisle is the sacristy, which was added in the 15th century. To the east, originally constructed as a separate, freestanding structure, is the memorial chapel and mausoleum dedicated to Euphrasius. Dating also to the sixth century, the chapel consists of an oval narthex leading to a trefoil chapel. Flanking the south aisle are three lateral chapels, all relatively recent additions. The oldest of these is the westernmost, which dates to the 18th century; the eastern chapel was installed in the 19th century, and the chapel located in the middle was completed during the 20th century.

During the 1440s an earthquake damaged the south wall of the nave, which required rebuilding. The resulting structure was altered significantly. The south aisle was provided with a Gothic vaulted ceiling, and Gothic pointed windows were installed. In 1452, following the newly adopted style, a choir stall was also added.

The Cathedral of Euphrasius introduced a new robustness to church design. Previously, sacred structures in the region were simple and subdued, with very little ornamentation. In contrast, Euphrasius was monumental in scale and included many adorned wall surfaces. The most significant works of art within its walls are the mosaics. Dating from the sixth century, these works employ a naturalism in their depiction of the human form. The finest examples are located in the central apse, behind the main altar and the ciborium and in the portals.

The exterior of the cathedral is difficult to discern in its totality. The masonry bearing wall—as is the majority of the building fabric of this city—is constructed of coursed rubble. The nave projects above the aisles and is covered with a front-gabled, red clay-tile roof, while red clay-tile shed roofs define the side aisles. Three arched openings provide access to the narthex, and in their hierarchy of size reinforce the three divisions of the basilical plan. Natural lighting is provided to the nave by arched windows, with quarrels at the gallery level in

Ephrasius Basilica: Porec, Croatia, 535

the gable, and centered above each arch separating the nave and aisles. This level is ornamentally articulated with mosaic and relief work between the windows.

The Euphrasius Basilica derives its primary significance both from the importance of the artistic works present on its walls and from its early application of the three-part (three-apsidial) basilical form. It is significant further as a demonstration of the movement and interpretation of popular styles of eastern and western Europe into the eastern regions of the Adriatic.

—ANDREA URBAS

CATHEDRAL OF ST. LAWRENCE
Trogir, Croatia

14th century: Tower on southwest corner. **15th century:** Chapels on north side; ribbed vaults completed. **1430-40:** Gabled end of nave. **1446:** Chapel dedicated to St. Jerome added. **1467:** Baptistery; **Architect:** Andrija Alesi. **1468:** Chapel of Blessed Ivan (John) completed; **Architects:** Niccolo of Florence and Andrija Alesi. **17th century:** Marble altar completed. **1605:** Final story completed.

Publications

BOOZ, P.: *Der Baumeister Der Gotik*, München-Berlin, 1956.

EITELBERGER VON EDELBERG, R.: *Die mittelalterlichen Kunstdenkmale Dalmatiens*. Wien, 1884.

GIBSON, S. and WARD-PERKINS, B.: "The Incised Architectural Drawings of Trogir Cathedral." *The Antiquaries Journal* 57 (1977), 289 ff.

IVEKOVIC, C. M.: *Trogir-Trau*. Wien (1927).

*

The Cathedral of St. Lawrence (Sv. Lovro) represents a succession of building campaigns, and as such is a compilation of architectural styles including Romanesque, Gothic and Renaissance elements. The construction of the cathedral is attributed to the Trogiran bishop Teguan, who became its patron following the destruction of an earlier church on the same site. The cathedral faces the main city square, which has functioned as the community's primary social focal point throughout Trogir's various historical epochs, including its period as an Illyrian settlement, a Greco-Roman city and a Venetian territory.

The cathedral was planned as a basilica with nave and side aisles, each terminating in an apse at the east end of the structure. At the west end is an entry vestibule that provides access to the bell tower and baptistery. Side chapels, constructed during the 15th century, define the north side of the structure.

St. Lawrence dominates the skyline of the island city of Trogir. The main, or west, facade faces the city square, with stone masonry components corresponding to the cathedral's three periods of architectural expression. Half columns define the facade of the first story, dividing it into five bays. In the center is a large Romanesque arched opening leading into the entry vestibule. In addition, two smaller arched windows in the northernmost bay define an interior stair. To the north is located the baptistery, which was constructed in 1467, and designed by Andrija Alesi in the Renaissance style.

Rising to the south of the main facade is the bell tower. Although originally two towers were planned to spring from the entry vestibule for the west facade, only one was built on the southwest corner during the 14th century. It was designed in the Gothic style, and is defined by half columns dividing the facade into two bays, each with a single pointed, arched window with tracery. The three columns each carry one blind pointed arch. This construction is attributed to the master builders Matej and Stjepan. The third story of the bell tower, while maintaining the same major division of bays, clearly belongs to the Late Gothic period. In spirit it belongs to the Late Gothic designs typical of those in Venice during the middle of the 15th century. The architect of this story is unknown; however, it is believed that the masons who executed it were trained in Venice, as was common at the time. The final story was completed in 1605 in the Mannerist style by master builder Trifun Bokanic. It maintains the same bay divisions as the stories below. Each of the bays contains two arched openings, and a pyramidal roof rises above them. This is defined at its juncture by sculptures attributed to the Italian Alessandro Vittoria.

Above the center of the entry vestibule of the western facade rises the gabled end of the nave, which was completed between 1430 and 1440. The focal point of this facade is the central rose window. The south facade can also be viewed from the public square. To the west is a large arched entryway leading into the vestibule, above which rises the bell tower. The balance of this facade was completed in the Romanesque style. It is delineated by pilasters dividing the massive plane into five bays, each with fenestration. In the center is an arched entry leading into one southern aisle of the cathedral, directly opposite the Chapel of Blessed Ivan. The remaining bays contain narrow, arched windows located in the upper third of the wall plane. The second story of the nave repeats this bay pattern with centered narrow, arched windows.

The interior, like the exterior, reflects the stylistic differences associated with each construction campaign. The first space encountered is the entry vestibule. The primary entry portal into the cathedral is centered on the eastern wall of this space and is one of the major artistic works within the building; it is attributed to the master carver Radovan. The doorway is surrounded by a series of arches which spring from pilasters. A gable surmounts this entry, while decorative carved forms depicting both Christian and pagan icons adorn the surface areas. This ornamentation represents a merging of Byzantine, Romanesque and Gothic design.

The main interior space appears heavy, due to large expanses of wall plane with only a few narrow openings. The nave is separated from the aisles by arches springing from piers. It was raised and modernized in the Gothic style during the 15th century, with the introduction of ribbed vaults. Centered on the main axis of the nave is the main altar, adorned with an elaborate ciborium. To the north is a stone masonry pulpit, behind which are elaborately carved Gothic choir benches. Secondary altars are located in the remaining two apses.

The westernmost chapel is dedicated to Saint Jerome, the patron saint of Trogir's coastal region, Dalmatia. Completed in

Cathedral of St. Lawrence: Trogir, Croatia, 14th century onward

1446, this chapel was built in the Gothic style with ribbed vaults by Marco Gruatto and Nikola Racic.

In 1468 the Chapel of Blessed Ivan (John), to house the sarcophagus of the Trogiran bishop, was completed by ''Niccolo of Florence'' and Andrija Alesi. This chapel is rectangular in plan, and has a coffered, barrel-vaulted ceiling. The chapel is architecturally the most significant, designed in the Renaissance style, with ornamentation and statuary depicting, once again, both Christian and pagan icons. The focal point is a marble altar, completed in the 17th century by Zuane Bicogeni, that holds the sarcophagus.

Finally, the sacristy was completed toward the end of the 15th century in the Gothic style. Various reliquaries from the same period are located there.

The Cathedral of St. Lawrence is significant as an example of a Yugoslav interpretation of a transitional Romanesque-Gothic building. It maintains a curious blending of the styles associated with its various building campaigns as well as a synthesis of the cultures of the east and west, and both Christian and pagan beliefs.

—ANDREA URBAS

Zadar Cathedral: Zadar, Croatia, 9th century

ZADAR CATHEDRAL
Zadar, Croatia

Ninth century: Construction begun. **Twelfth century:** Three-part crypt built. **1324:** Initial construction completed. **Fourteenth century:** Gothic sacristy added. **Fifteenth century:** Gothic choir stall added, bell tower begun. **1892:** Bell tower completed; **Architect:** T. G. Jackson (1835-1924).

Publications

JACKSON, THOMAS GRAHAM: *Recollections*. London, 1950.

LONGFELLOW, WILLIAM P. P. (ed.): *A Cyclopædia of Works of Architecture in Italy, Greece, and the Levant*. New York, 1895.

In the ninth century, the bishop of Zadar, an Adriatic city on the northern coast of Yugoslavia, sought to construct a new cathedral, and one of such design as to demonstrate the importance of the city's former function as a papal seat. Thus the Cathedral of St. Stosije (later, St. Anastasia) was constructed and expanded upon from the ninth century to 1324 to fulfill that concept.

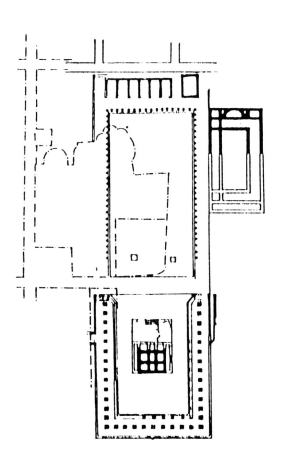

The site selected for the construction of the cathedral already had a history as a building location. St. Stosije was constructed atop the rectilinear walls of an earlier church, which had itself been built upon the foundation walls of an ancient cistern. This earlier church maintained the foundations of the cistern, but part of the eastern wall was demolished in order to straighten the walls, and semicircular apses were added. The earlier church was demolished in the ninth century to accommodate the new cathedral. Once again, the new structure was built to fit the remains of its predecessor.

The Cathedral of St. Stosije faces a public square. The exterior of the cathedral is divided into four levels by blind arcades. The main facade, which is in a gable end, is marked by three ornately carved Romanesque portals that define the nave and side aisles. Statuary is located on each side of the portal. Two tall, narrow blind arches, rising to the height of the nave portal, separate that portal from the aisle portals. Further articulation of the main facade is achieved by three levels of blind arcades atop double engaged columns, adorning the upper levels. Each level is separated by a belt course. Two rose windows, one Romanesque and the other Gothic, are centered below the gable.

The side facades maintain a similar pattern of blind arcades, dividing the structure into three segments. The lower two components are divided by a belt course of a height different from those on the main facade. The top level is the clerestory, again defined by an arcade.

The cathedral is constructed of smooth-faced, coursed ashlar masonry bearing walls. The roof is front-gabled over the nave, and shed over the aisles. It is clad in red clay tiles.

To the rear of the Cathedral of St. Stosije is a bell tower. Originally begun in the 15th century, the bell tower was completed in 1892 by T. G. Jackson. It is a five-story structure, square in plan, with a conical roof. The lowest two stories were built during the 15th century, and are easily distinguishable from their 19th-century counterparts. Each level of the bell tower is defined by two arched openings on each facade, while the earliest construction alternated actual voids with blind arches. Engaged half columns surround each opening, so that single half columns are on the outside edge of the arches, and double half columns are in between the two. Belt courses separate the stories. The lower stories are of rougher construction, with clearly visible courses. The third story attempts to link the old and new. The same arched openings are employed, but a stone balustrade adorns their lower portions. Above the arches are decorative relief panels. Above, defining the story limit, is a blind arcade. The upper two stories are similar; however, each opening is subdivided by a colonette in a tracery surround. Atop the fifth story is a balustrade.

In plan, the cathedral is a basilica with nave and two side aisles, each terminating in an apse. A Gothic sacristy was added in the 14th century, and a seminary was built adjacent to the cathedral in the 18th century. Features of note in the interior include an outstanding marble sarcophagus, ninth-century marble seats, a 13th-century Romanesque fresco and a ninth-century high altar, located in the central apse; the 14th-century sacristy; and a Gothic carved wooden choir stall installed in the 15th century. Below the main altar is a three-part crypt from the 12th century.

The Cathedral of St. Stosije is significant as an outstanding example of Croatian Romanesque design.

—ANDREA URBAS

CHURCH OF ST. DONATO
Zadar, Croatia

Eighth or Ninth century.

Publications

LONGFELLOW, WILLIAM P. P. (ed.): *A Cyclopædia of Works of Architecture in Italy, Greece, and the Levant.* New York, 1895.

*

Zadar was originally an Illyrian settlement, and later was appropriated as a colony of the Roman Empire. As such, it became a major Roman stronghold on the eastern coast of the Adriatic. In the seventh century Slavs conquered the city and established Zadar as a major Byzantine cultural center in the region of Dalmatia. Byzantine influence remained strong until the ninth century, when the territory was continuously in upheaval, coveted by both Italy and Yugoslavia. Thus, the architectural heritage of Zadar maintains a strong blending of the styles of both the East and West.

The Church of St. Donato (originally, the Church of the Holy Trinity) was commissioned at the close of the eighth century or in the early ninth century, on the site of the city's Roman forum, by Donato, the bishop of Zadar. It was to be modeled on the Church of San Vitale in Ravenna (ca. 547). In plan, St. Donato is a central-type church, with three apses reflecting the ground plan of the Carolingian octagonal chapel at Aachen (Aix-le-Chapelle). The diameter measures 21 meters. Six piers and two salvaged columns from various sites separate the structure into two major circular parts, which are the nave and aisles. Eight arches rest on the piers and columns, forming an arcade.

The most significant components of the first level, including the piers, are constructed of smooth-faced, coursed ashlar masonry resting on a coursed ashlar floor, atop a stone foundation.

St. Donato Church: Zadar, Croatia, late 8th or early 9th century

The upper areas of the walls and gallery are of coursed random rubble. These components exhibit a crudeness in design and construction which indicates native craftsmanship.

A narthex and ambulatory wing flank the church to the west. Wide stairs curve from the ambulatory and lead to a gallery above. A barrel-vaulted wooden ceiling covers the aisles, while a conical roof rises above the nave. The flooring material is ashlar masonry. The plan of the gallery mirrors that of the story below: piers rest atop piers, with salvaged columns on the columns, thus echoing the lower arcade.

A domed ceiling rises above the gallery. It is circumscribed by a partial clerestory pierced with narrow arched windows. Ornamentation includes niches located inside of the exterior walls, and parts of salvaged columns, wreaths and pagan altars in the apses. Iron balconies decorate the gallery arcade and separate the gallery level from the main church space below.

The exterior of the Church of St. Donato clearly reads as a two-story structure, with a partial clerestory, and measures 27 meters in height. The central space rises the entire building height, encircled with a smaller massing of the aisle, which extends two stories. The central area consists of coursed random-rubble masonry walls, which appear massive and heavy, with very few openings. Piers with blind colossal arches reinforce the division of the structure into the central nave and the ring of the aisles and nave. This heaviness and the strong sense of verticality are reinforced by the sparseness of openings in the masonry surface. The west facade, containing the narthex, is clearly divided into two stories, while stairs extend to the north.

The fenestration varies in form, size and location. Although some rectilinear openings exist, most windows are horseshoe-shaped. Each window is protected by an iron grate. The four-part segmented conical roof maintains only a single small opening in each bay to function as a source of natural lighting for the clerestory. The roof is clad with clay tiles, laid in segmented parts, and is adorned with a finial.

The apses provide for a symmetrical placement of window openings at each story. The two smaller apses, composed of three bays each, have single windows centered in each bay's colossal blind arch. The main apse also has a window centered in each bay, with four, rather than three, bays located there. The remaining windows are positioned asymmetrically throughout the facade. Carved cruciform shapes adorn windows in the gallery area of the apses.

Although the Church of St. Donato lacks the sophistication of San Vitale, it is significant as an example of the building type interpreted along the eastern coast of the Adriatic. The craftsmanship is rough, and the ornamentation employed was salvaged from Roman spoils during the city's colonial period. As such, the church at Zadar embodies the merging of styles with local culture and traditions, and stands as the premier monumental example of medieval Croatian architecture.

—ANDREA URBAS

CZECH REPUBLIC

VILLA TUGENDHAT
Brno, Czech Republic

1929-30. Architect: Ludwig Mies van der Rohe (1886-1969).
1969: Restoration; **Architects:** Kamil Fuchs, Kutejova, Janececk.

Publications

BIER, JUSTUS: "Kann man im Haus Tugendhat wohnen?" *Form* 6 (15 October 1931): 392-394.
CADBURY-BROWN, H. T.: "Ludwig Mies van der Rohe." *Architectural Association Journal* (special issue, July-August 1959).
FRAMPTON, KENNETH, and FUTAGAWA, YUKIO: *Modern Architecture: 1920-1945*. New York, 1983.
HILBERSEIMER, LUDWIG: "Die Bewohner des Hauses Tugendhat äussern sich." *Form* 7 (15 November 1931): 437-439.
JOHNSON, PHILIP: *Mies van der Rohe*. New York, 1947.
SCHULZE, FRANZ: *Mies van der Rohe: A Critical Biography*. Chicago and London, 1985.
SPAETH, DAVID: *Mies van der Rohe*. New York and London, 1985.
TEGETHOFF, WOLF: *Mies van der Rohe: The Villas and Country Houses*. Cambridge, Massachusetts, 1985.
YORKE, F. R. S.: *The Modern House*. London, 1934.

*

The architectural climate was ripe for the design of a modern house in Brno, Czechoslovakia in the 1920s. The democratic principles of the new republic, founded in 1918 on the ruins of the Austro-Hungarian Empire, provided an ideological platform for liberal intellectuals. In 1923 the Brno division of the Devetsil *avant-garde* group, headed by Karel Teige in Prague, was founded. This society of artists, writers, musicians and architects published a journal and organized lectures. Devetsil members and the Brno Club of Architects invited a number of representatives of the international *avant-garde* to give lectures, among them Theo van Doesburg, Laszlo Moholy-Nagy, J. J. P. Oud, Walter Gropius, Le Corbusier, Amadée Ozenfant and Adolf Loos. The visits of Loos, a native of Brno, were particularly influential on Brno architects.

The second half of the 1920s was marked by a building boom in Brno. A series of lectures called "For a New Architect," the journal *Bytova Kultura* and the activity of the Devetsil group, as well as the works of Brno architects Bohuslav Fuchs, Jindrich Krumpošt and Arnost Wiesner, prepared the grounds for functionalism, which originated in about 1925. The new style rejected the cliches of historicism in architecture. Devoid of any ornament or decoration, expressing functions and their relationship in a building, functionalism was an attempt to reflect the ideals of the new republic and of the 20th century: liberty, equality, justice and fraternity. A series of architectural competitions, the 1924 start of construction of the Brno Exhibition grounds, and the expected future political, economic and cultural significance of the city offered many opportunities for architects. A version of the German Weissenhofsiedlung, a project called "New House 1928," was built under the auspices of the Czechoslovak Werkbund. Nine functionalists were invited to participate; among them were Bohuslav Fuchs, Arnost Wiesner and Jiri Kroha.

Fritz and Grete Tugendhat, clients of Ludwig Mies van der Rohe, were from an old Brno family engaged in the textile business. The founder of the Brno branch of the Tugendhats was Fritz's grandfather Hermann Tugendhat, who opened his textile store in Brno in 1864.

Fritz Tugendhat, born in 1895 in Brno, and Grete Weiss, née Low-Beer, born in 1903 in Brno, were married in July 1928 in Berlin-Wilmersdorf (this was her second marriage). Grete Tugendhat received from her father, Alfred Low-Beer, a textile manufacturer, a wedding gift of a plot of land on the slopes of Cernapole Hill (Schwarzfeldgasse) of an area of almost 2,000

Villa Tugendhat: Brno, Czech Republic, 1929-30

Villa Tugendhat

square meters. Even before their marriage, Fritz and Grete met Ludwig Mies van der Rohe in Berlin, in 1927, and asked him to design a family house for them. They knew Mies' work and were impressed by the celebrated Weissenhofsiedlung.

Mies went to Brno in September 1928 to inspect the site. He discovered a south-facing, steeply sloping lot with commanding views of the Spielberg castle and the old city beneath. He returned to his office in Berlin, where he started designing the villa while continuing work on the Barcelona Pavilion, which opened 26 May 1929.

In December 1928 the architect submitted his design to the clients. Construction began in June 1929 and the building company of Maurice and Arthur Eisler completed it in December 1930, when the Tugendhats moved in. The Tugendhats used the villa until 1938, when they escaped the approaching Nazi occupation of Czechoslovakia and settled in Venezuela. Their two sons, Ernest and Herbert, were born in Brno, in 1930 and 1933, respectively. The two daughters, Ruth, born in 1942, and Marie, born in 1946, both in Venezuela, did not get a chance to live in their parents' house in Brno. The German Nazis occupied the house beginning in March 1939, with official confiscation by the Gestapo occurring in October 1939. One famous inhabitant of the villa during the war was Albert Messerschmidt, a German aircraft manufacturer.

In 1945 the house was plundered and the garden devastated by both the retreating Germans and the advancing Soviet troops. After the end of World War II the badly damaged house was provisionally adapted as a private ballet school. Then it was used by the Pediatric Teaching Hospital of Brno for rehabilitation and physical therapy. In 1950 the property was nationalized and the house came under state ownership. It is not known whether the Tugendhat family, living at that time in Venezuela, claimed ownership of the house.

A number of pleas were made by architects, private individuals and institutions to save the decaying structure from destruction by various unsuitable adaptations. Finally, in 1963 the villa was granted the status of a national cultural monument. The question of restoration of the villa to its original appearance, however, had been repeatedly tabled at the meetings of the National Council of the City of Brno. It was not until 1969 that a motion of "putting an end to the improper use of the villa" and a complete restoration of the structure and its grounds was approved by the council. Undoubtedly, the retrospective exhibition of Mies' work held in Brno in January 1969 and the lecture given at that occasion by Grete Tugendhat had helped the decision on the restoration.

The plans for restoration and supervision of the reconstruction were done by architects Kamil Fuchs (son of the Brno functionalist architect Bohuslav Fuchs) with Kutejova and Janecek of the Brno offices of the State Institute for Reconstruction of Historical Towns and Buildings. Grete Tugendhat and the architect Dirk Lohan, grandson of and a longtime associate of the late Mies van der Rohe in Chicago, were consulted on aspects of the restoration plans.

An exhibition on the reconstruction of the Villa Tugendhat was held in Brno in 1986. Examination of the restoration documents and the original drawings and sketches by Mies, and especially a visit and "sensing out" of the ambience of the house, reveal the design intentions of the architect.

The connection between the Tugendhat house and the Barcelona Pavilion seems obvious. Not only were they conceived at the same time, with cross-shaped chrome-plated columns used in both, but they were a continuation of the De Stijl-inspired project of Mies' Brick Country House from 1922.

Both the Barcelona Pavilion and the Villa Tugendhat were designed to evoke a feeling of endless space. The floor and roof—the horizontal white planes connected by the subtle and mirroring columns—provided a continuum of space separated from the exterior by floor-to-ceiling glass windows and doors. The freestanding partitions organized a flow of spaces and circulation. The furniture was strategically placed in a composition in which the relationship of one piece of furniture to another, of one group to another, and of the groups to the partitions was carefully calculated. The givens the architect faced for the Tugendhat house were the program and the steep sloping site. Accordingly, from the street, the house looks like a sober, single-story work, while a view from the garden reveals a three-story structure with a terrace on the third floor and a monumental stair leading to the middle floor, which is expressed by a large horizontal expanse of glass. This middle floor, containing the Great Room (235 square meters) of the house, perceived as a single interior space, serves a variety of functions, however: reception and entry area, study/office and library, dining space defined by the semicircular partition of Macassar ebony, and a sitting area defined by the polished onyx partition. The cruciform columns with highly reflective chrome-plated covers, on a grid of 5 by 4.6 meters, assist in the creation of a clear geometric order continuously revealing new, surprising views. To the east of the great space is the winter garden, to the west are the kitchen, pantry, servants' rooms and storage, and the north street end is built into the hill. The south side of the great space offers views of the garden and the castle and the city. The Great Room has its own forced-air heating system. Two huge (15 feet of sheer glass) floor-to-ceiling windows can be lowered electrically into the ground. Another temperature control and comfort device included by Mies was the retractable canvas awnings to control the penetration of solar heat into the Great Room.

The top floor, visible from the street, is divided into a larger residential wing to the east and a service wing to the west. The service wing contains a garage and a former chauffeur's residence. Today, that is the residence of a housekeeper. The residential wing, divided into two blocks of bedrooms parallel to the street, was used for the two bedrooms for the boys and a guest room, and the other block for the individual bedrooms of the parents.

Entry to the house is located in a void between the residential wings. A travertine forecourt leads one to a curved milk-glass wall and a recessed entryway leading to a vestibule. From there a round staircase goes downward to the Great Room of the house. The travertine forecourt continues at the entrance floor through the void between the residential wing and the service wing. It connects to the terrace in the front of the bedrooms on the garden side and is opened to the southern view.

The house has been restored with great care. The travertine paving shows clean joints, the white linoleum lies flat, and the chrome of the columns is crisp and shining. What is missing, however, is the original furniture designed by Mies especially for the house. According to the records, there were 49 pieces of furniture in the house when occupied by the Tugendhats. The house seems to be incomplete without them. There were not only the Barcelona chairs and the MR chairs designed for the Barcelona Pavilion, but also the "Tugendhat pieces," such as the Tugendhat chairs, the Brno chairs, the "X" coffee table and other furniture. The colors and materials of the furniture played an important role too: the emerald-green leather, the ruby-red velvet, the white vellum on stools and chairs, the raw silk curtain. Perhaps these pieces will find their way to the house, whose sole function will be to serve as a museum. Mies van der Rohe, the Tugendhats, the legacy of the Brno functionalists and the city of Brno all deserve such distinction.

—PETER LIZON

Cathedral of St. Barbara: Kutna Hora, Czech Republic, late 14th century

CATHEDRAL OF ST. BARBARA
Kutna Hora, Czech Republic

Late 14th century: Construction began. **Ca. 1388:** Choir construction; **Architect:** Peter Parler. **1499:** Main body of church constructed; **Architect:** Matej Rejsek.

Publications

BIALOSTOCKI, J.: *The Art of the Renaissance in Eastern Europe: Hungary, Bohemia and Poland.* Ithaca, NY, 1976.
FEHR, G.: *Benedikt Ried (Rejt).* Munich, 1941.
SAMANKOVA, E.: *Architectura Ceske Renesance.* Prague, 1961.
WIRTH, Z.: *Kutna Hora: Mesto a jeho umeni.* Prague, 1912.

The spectacular Cathedral of St. Barbara, occupying the highest hill in the city of Kutna Hora, is built in a French Flamboyant Gothic style, but informed by native Czech traditions. In the 14th century, ties between Bohemia and France were strong, resulting in the importation of northern French Gothic to the region.

Construction of the cathedral was undertaken in the late 14th century by the owners of the local silver mines, who were trying to establish their city as the foremost cultural and economic center of Bohemia, in competition with Prague, where St. Vitus' Cathedral was then under construction. The church was dedicated to Saint Barbara, because she was the patron saint of miners and of the city of Kutna Hora.

Peter Parler of Gmund designed the choir in about 1388. Two exterior stone spiral staircases, believed to be Parler's work as well, flank the joining of the choir and the rest of the nave. The Bohemian architect Matej Rejsek, whose buildings in Prague had made him one of the leading Gothic architects, began construction of the main body of the church in 1499. The Cathedral of St. Barbara was his greatest achievement.

Rejsek developed a five-nave plan, calling for polygonal towers with steep pointed roofs to be placed at the corners of the cathedral. Rejsek's design left vast areas of the wall space available for stained glass. The five-nave Cistercian basilica actually constructed follows Rejsek's plan closely, even though it was not completed by him, but by a number of architects taking over the task in succession. The cathedral has an eight-chapel apse, an ambulatory and transept naves. The central nave, which is a third again as large as the flanking aisles, rises to the full height of the interior. The aisles on each side support large triforium galleries with vaults similar to that of the central nave. A double set of flying buttresses supports these walls. The exterior aisles, of equal width and height, are set under the buttresses. One of the most striking features of the cathedral is the high-pitched tripartite roof over the nave and aisles. Three hexagonal spires impart variety to the profile of the roof. The highest central one of these towers and the one on the back (or

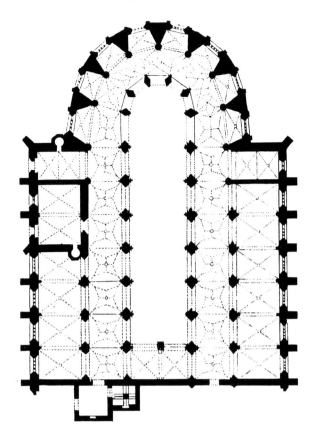

east) side have arcuated galleries about midway up the spire, making for an even more complex silhouette.

As is characteristic of the Flamboyant Gothic style, areas of complex detail are balanced with passages of simplicity, and areas of asymmetrical decoration form a counterpoint to the overall symmetry of the design. The tracery of the stained-glass windows, and the hundreds of pinnacles over each pointed arch and flying buttress, end in flamelike asymmetrical stone decorations. Each element of the building reinforces the verticality of the design. The Gothic portals, completed in about 1400, have stained-glass tympana with a pattern of rotating flames in the tracery. The delicate swirling stone tracery, pointing heavenward, creates an overall effect as of lace in stone. Only the Late French Gothic Reims Cathedral and Church of St. Maclou in Rouen can rival the Cathedral of St. Barbara in Kutna Hora as examples of Flamboyant Late Gothic architecture.

—ROBIN PTACEK

ČERNÍN PALACE
Prague, Czech Republic

1666: Design commissioned; **Architect:** Giovanni Lorenzo Bernini; **Builder:** Francesco Caratti. **1669:** Construction begun. **1673:** Main building exterior completed. **Ca. 1677:** Construction of outer buildings and interior decoration; **Decorators:**

Vaclav Reiner and Ignaz Platzer. **1692:** Exterior completed. **1696:** Decorations for salon commissioned but never completed; **Decorator:** Domenico Egidio Rossi. **1718-22:** Interior altered; **Architect:** Franz Maximilian Kanka. **1722:** Interior decoration completed. **1744-46:** Orangerie completed; **Architect:** Anselmo Lurago. **1747-50:** Portals and porte cochere added; **Architect:** Anselmo Lurago. **1828-34:** Palace restored; **Architect:** Pavel Janák.

Publications

Arte italiana in Cecoslovacchia, Boemia e Moravia. Prague, 1950.
JANAK, P.: "Cerninsky palac v Praze a jeho predkove." *Umeni* 15 (1943-44).
KUPICEK, A.: *Prazske palace*, Prague, 1946.
LORENC, V.: *Cerninsky palac v Praze.* Prague, 1980.
MORPER, J. J.: *Das Czernin Palast in Prag.* Prague, 1940.
POCHE, E.: *Prazske palace.* Prague, 1936.
TRISKA, K.: *Cerninsky palac v Praze.* Prague, 1940.
WIRTH, Z.: "Cerninsky palac v Praze." *Umeni* 9 (1936): 257ff.

Černín Palace, the largest and most imposing of the aristocratic palaces of Prague, and a spectacular specimen of Early Baroque Mannerist architecture, marked the culmination of a long history of Italian influence on Czech architecture.

The palace was, in a manner of speaking, built out of the devastations of the Thirty Years' War, which pitted Catholics against Protestants. Most of the Czech nobility had been on the Protestant side. When the Catholic party, backed by the power of the Hapsburgs, emerged victorious, the "rebels" were massacred. Their lands were divided up among the few Catholic noblemen, along with the properties belonging to the Protestant churches and middle class. In the wake of the war, the victorious nobility began to outdo each other in building sumptuous palaces, to symbolize their newly acquired power and wealth. In 1666, Count Humprecht Jan Černín, who was among the victors and had benefited greatly from the outcome of the war, purchased a large property on the west side of Loretto Square in Prague. Reputedly wishing to outshine even the Vienna Hofburg, Černín commissioned Giovanni Lorenzo Bernini to develop a design for the palace to be constructed there. Francesco Caratti of Bissone, Italy, was retained to execute Bernini's design.

An intensive construction campaign was begun in 1669, resulting in the completion of the main building's exterior by 1673. Construction of the outer buildings and the interior decoration, however, had only just been started when Caratti died in 1677. The exterior was completed by 1692, while work on the interior decoration continued until 1722.

The facade of Černín Palace is 150 meters long, and it is articulated by 30 gigantic half columns surrounding 29 bays. Palaces built before the war—such as the Waldstein palaces at Jičín and Žagań (1626-27)—and the new palace for Prince Lobkowicz at Roudnice (1652-97) had employed colossal pilasters. The substitution of half columns for pilasters allowed for a more forceful articulation of the facade. The half columns hark back to Michelangelo's masterful designs for the Campidoglio in Rome. Beginning at the first floor and resting on massive piers, they are surmounted with capitals in the shape of grotesque heads set between Ionic volutes. Each of the 29 bays has four tiers of casement windows. Alternating rounded and triangular pediments surmount the windows of the third

Černín Palace: Prague, Czech Republic, 1669-1722

tier. The entablature is pierced by the mezzanine windows, as in the Clementinum of Charles University at Prague (1654-58, built by Carlo Lurago). A block between the capitals and entablature cornice further heightens the facade. Nine small demilune dormers extend above the roof at the cornice. The ground floor is finished in large, diamond-shaped rustication.

The massive facade with its robust detail forms exaggerated perspectives when viewed from the side, as was originally intended. The Mannerist vertical thrust terminates abruptly at the cornice and low hipped roof. The facade is very sculptural in form, but does not actually possess a great deal of statuary. The palace has been criticized as "splendid monotony" and a "tasteless mass of stone." When the sunlight plays across the muscular detail, however, the diamond rustication, balcony brackets and demicolumns stand out with Palladian clarity.

Only the portals and the porte cochere relieve the massive severe facade, and these were later additions, built between 1747 and 1750 according to plans by Anselmo Lurago and models by Ignaz Platzer. They contrasted strongly with the strict Palladian forms of the original facade. The simple rounded Roman arches of the porte cochere rise to above 20 feet. A balcony with an ornamental stone balustrade is located above the porte cochere and the portals.

The garden facade is more delicate, but also less cohesive. The lower rustication alternates with sculpture niches and Palladian portals. The half columns rise little more than a story, and support the large rounded arches below the cornice. Perhaps more appropriate to the more secluded and domestic rear area of the palace, this facade nevertheless possesses none of the strength of the public facade on the front.

The interior is dominated by the large salon, located in the center front of the shallow building. Seven bays wide and two and a half stories high, the grand salon was never finished, although brilliant sketches for illusionistic grand architectural vistas were commissioned from Domenico Egidio Rossi in 1696. The interior arrangement contains various rooms at the front, with a corridor running the length of the building behind these rooms, instead of the French enfilade arrangement that was becoming popular at the time.

The original interior decoration was done for the most part by the painter Vaclav Reiner and the sculptor Ignaz Platzer. Franz Maximilian Kanka rearranged much of the interior between 1718 and 1722, according to the prevailing French taste. Reiner's *Fall of the Titans,* with its deep, illusionistic space, was preserved, however. After the French looted the palace in the mid-18th century, the interior was repaired and remodeled by Anselmo Lurago.

Lurago also completed the symmetrical Orangerie in the garden (1744-46). Its Rococo design relieves the extreme severity of the formal gardens. The narrow garden front on the north side has two arcades similar to those of the Villa Medici in Rome. Long, opulent stables in the back support picture galleries above.

In 1851 the Černín family sold the palace to the state, as the building had become a financial burden. A few years later, the Austrian government hired Achille Wolf to turn the palace into a barracks. Both the facade and the interior underwent changes in the reconstruction. With the advent of the independent republic in 1918, Černín Palace became the Ministry of Foreign Affairs. The noted modernist architect Pavel Janák restored the palace between 1928 and 1934, so saving it from complete ruin.

—ROBIN PTACEK

NATIONAL THEATER
Prague, Czech Republic

1881: Construction of original theater, which burned to the ground three months after completion; **Architect:** Josef Zitek. **1881-83:** Reconstruction; **Architect:** Josef Schulz. **1976-83:** Reconstruction and addition; **Chief architect:** Karel Prager; **Architects for historical reconstruction:** Zdenek Vavra and Frantisek Flasar; **Urban planning:** Pavel Kupka and Ivo Loos.

Publications

LIZON, PETER: ''Crystalline Cube Added to Prague's National Theatre.'' *Architecture* (September 1988): 96-97.

*

Prague, Czechoslovakia, commemorated the centennial of its celebrated National Theater in 1983. It took forty years of design and seven years of construction to complete the renovation and expansion of the Theater. Those years were filled with debate over how best to modernize the aging facility. Even as construction ended, the issue of the relationship between the old and the new remained a topic of debate in Prague and throughout the nation.

The original National Theater, designed by Josef Zitek and located prominently on the Vltava River, was completed in 1881. The Theater symbolized the rise and culmination of the Czech National Revival of the 19th century. A national collection made the dream of the nation possible. Tragedy struck just three months later, however, when the theater burned to the ground. A second collection gathered enough funds in forty-seven days to rebuild the Theater. Josef Schulz, Zitek's associate, finished the reconstruction in 1883. The Czech people attach great sentimental value to their National Theater, and have been very emotional about changes to it or its surroundings.

Shortly after World War II, it was clear that both the exterior and the interior of the National Theater needed reconstruction and expansion. After much debate, including two national design competitions and numerous preliminary studies on the subject of expansion, the design team led by Bohuslav Fuchs was granted the contract. However, participating committees' reservations stalled the design development of the project. The design team grew frustrated, and after the death of Fuchs in 1972, the team resigned. In the meantime, the necessity of the reconstruction of the historical building overshadowed the expansion.

Eventually, however, the complex effort of reconstruction and expansion was coordinated, and the old building was connected to the new buildings via an underground network that would allow actors, stage workers, equipment and air to circulate. The architect of reconstruction of the old building was Zdenek Vavra and he was assisted by Frantisek Flasar. The historical building consisted of three parts: the theater of Zitek, the Temporary Theater—which was actually in use before the construction of the first National Theater in 1881—and the Schulz House. In the reconstruction project, these three parts were united to extend the original stage, the stage

National Theater, addition: Prague, Czech Republic, 1976-83

services, the mechanical equipment and the dressing rooms. The capacity of the enlarged theater reached 986 seats.

The expansion's urban design concept was formulated by Pavel Kupka and Ivo Loos. The complex consists of four buildings: the large six-level structure beneath the Theater Plaza, which houses the energy center for all the buildings, storage space, workshops, and parking for 219 cars; the seven-story restaurant building, which has two restaurants, a cafe, a snack bar, and kitchen services; the rehearsals building, which contains a two-story ballet/opera rehearsal hall, a drama rehearsal hall, offices and conference rooms; and the New Scene Building, which is home to a small theater for drama, small opera and ballet as well as other actor and spectator services. The New Scene's flexible stage serves as a proscenium theater of 405 seats or an arena theater of 563 seats. The orchestra pit accommodates 25 musicians. The foyer features a circular monumental stair and conveniently connects to the restaurant building.

The most exposed and controversial part of the expansion project was the building of the New Scene of the National Theater. Set beside the older building, it faces an important street, the Avenue of the Nation (Narodni Trida). Approached from either the direction of Wenceslas Square or the May Day Bridge over the Vltava (Moldau) River, the New Scene confronts its historical neighbor. In general massing, the New Scene and the surrounding buildings of the expansion complex are sympathetic to the older National Theater: they share similar proportions and features such as cornice height, tapered tops, vertical articulation, horizontal layering and ground floors addressing the pedestrian. In addition, the light brown shades of the New Scene exterior relate to the hues of the historical theater. Nevertheless, the core of the controversy remains the design's taking on the shape of a glass crystal, which contrasts with the neo-Renaissance character of the National Theater. Karel Prager, the chief architect of the theater expansion project, explains that, "the vertical and horizontal tapering of the walls is optically reducing the closed compact mass. The outside envelope, made out of hollow glass blocks, mirrors, shimmers and reflects the light and the surrounding objects, thus helping to 'dematerialize' the building mass to become a pendant of the historical building."

The glass-elements enclosure of the New Scene Building serves to provide both acoustic and thermal insulation. Especially crucial is the acoustic muffling of the street noise from ninety-five decibels to thirty-five decibels, achieved by several layers of hollow glass blocks that comprise the perimeter wall. Every one of the 4,306 glass elements installed on the facade was individually blown and exposed to gamma rays which colored the glass to light brown shades to match the sandstone facade of the historical building.

Always at the forefront of architectural innovation, Prager has worked on large-scale redevelopment projects throughout Prague: housing estates in the district of Tesnov and Smichov, a 2,220-bed university hospital, and development of the main railroad station's air rights in the city center. He seeks complex economic solutions that maintain the flexibilities of mixed-use development and offer a variety of architectural expressions. Prager's design for the building of the Czechoslovak Assembly is the best example of his work. A bold spaceframe structure, hovering above an existing building as if defying gravity, the Assembly building is the embodiment of the architect's interest in the exploration of new technologies in architecture.

—PETER LIZON

ST. NICHOLAS
Prague, Czech Republic

1703-11: Construction of nave; **Architect:** Christoph Dientzenhofer (1655-1722). **1737-52:** Dome and chancel built; **Architect:** Kilian Ignaz Dientzenhofer. **1755:** Belfry tower completed. **1755:** Interior decoration completed.

Publications

BLAZICEK, O.: "Poznamky k utaru Davniho oltare u sv. Mikulase v Praze III." *PA* 33 (1948): 85 ff.

BLAZICEK, O.: *Socharstvi Baroku v. Cechah Plasticka 17. a 18. veku*. Prague, 1958.

DVORAKOVA, V.: "Krackerova nastropin malba v kostele sv. Mikulase a problemy jeji resturanu." *ZPP* 14 (1956): 182 ff.

FRANZ, H. G.: *Bauten und Baumeister der Barockzeit in Bohmen*. Leipzig, 1962.

FRANZ, H. G.: *Die Kirchenbauten des Christoph Dientzenhofer*. Brno. 1941.

FRANZ, H. G.: *Studien zur Barockarchitektur in Böhmen und Mähren*. Vienna, 1943.

HEGEMANN, H. W.: *Die Deutsche Barockbaukunst Böhmens*. Munich, 1943.

HEMPEL, E.: *Baroque Art and Architecture in Central Europe*. Penguin, London, 1965.

HLAVSA, V. and VANCURA, J.: *Mala Strana—Mensi Mesto prazske*. Prague, 1983.

KORECKY, M.: "Tvorba Kiliana Ignace Dientzenhofera." *ZPP* 11 and 12 (1952): 45 ff.

MADL, K. B.: "Dientzenhoferovsky motiv." *PA* 32 (1920-21): 201 ff.

MADL, K. B.: "Fresky a sv. Mikulase na Male Strane v Praze." *PA* 17 (1896-97): 17 ff.

NEUMANN, J.: *Cesky Barok*. Prague, 1969.

NOVAK, A.: *Praha Barokni*. Prague, 1947.

PAVLIK, M. and SIMA, J.: "Prispevek k otazce zaklemiti kostelu sv. Mikulase v Praze III." *Umeni* 17 (1965): 76 ff.

STEFAN, O.: *Prazske kostely*. Prague, 1936.

STEFAN, O.: "K otazce klenby kostela sv. Mikulase v Praze III." *Umeni* (1954): 259 ff.

VILIMKOVA, M.: *Stavitele palacu a chramu: Krystof a Kilian Ignac Dientzenhoferove*. Prague, 1986.

VOLAVKA, V. and FUNKE, J.: *Prazske kostely*. Prague, 1946.

YOUNG, M.: *The Flowering of Czech Baroque Art and Architecture*. New York, 1991.

*

The great Church of St. Nicholas in the old Town section of Prague provides a Baroque foil to the imposing Cathedral of St. Vitus, whose Gothic profile dominates the skyline on the peak of the Hradcany, Prague's royal mountain. St. Nicholas' Church represents the Italo-German Baroque filtered through Bohemian sensibilities. Designed by Christoph Dientzenhofer, a follower of Abraham Leuthner, the inspiration came largely from Guarino Guarini. A perfection of the Baroque style, the church also is a landmark of the city of Prague.

The structure occupies the site of an earlier Gothic church dedicated to Saint Nicholas dating from 1283. Although the foundation stone was laid on September 6, 1673, the building of Orsi de Orsini's plans progressed slowly. In March of 1674

St. Nicholas: Prague, Czech Republic, 1703-11

new designs by Francesco Caratti were substituted but construction stopped. A new, innovative structure of interlocking curves was begun in 1703 by Christoph Dientzenhofer, but not completed until 1775 due to several interruptions. Construction was halted in 1750, for example, until a commission of experts could reassure the public that the unprecedented design would not collapse. The shelling of Prague by the Prussians in 1757 resulted in great exterior damage to the unfinished church. Building resumed three years later, only after repairs to the damaged extant sections could be effected.

Dientzenhofer's conception for St. Nicholas' Church refined the ideas of Guarini. The Guarini design for the Church of the Virgin of Alt-Otting was accepted in 1679, and although the church was never built, it greatly influenced the work of Christoph and Johann Dientzenhofer, the most prominent members of one of Prague's leading architectural families. In that same year Dientzenhofer began completion of the Dominican Church of St. Mary Magdalene in Prague, whose construction had been interrupted by the death of its chief architect, Caratti, two years earlier. Dientzenhofer favored the more elaborate forms of the Italo-German Baroque to the more classicizing French and English versions. Guarini's designs were published in 1686 in his *Architectura civile,* which was studied all over Europe.

Between 1703 and 1711, Christoph Dientzenhofer constructed the nave of St. Nicholas for the Jesuits to adjoin their monastery begun in 1665. The building took the Bohemian hall church with internal buttresses as its basic form. The plan is a series of three ovals divided by piers. The walls undulate with movement as concave niches and convex walls alternate in a flowing rhythm. The corner piers display colossal convex pilasters set at an angle with the edges facing the nave. The bases of the pilasters provide pedestals for massive statues. The entablature breaks into individual regular pieces above the capitals in order to allow the upward thrust to the vaults to continue unimpeded. The reddish gray of the veined marble and the gold of the details predominate, avoiding the saccharine color schemes of many German Baroque churches. Light floods the church from upper-story windows. The whole ensemble radiates a cohesive perfection of continuous curves and underlying visual movement.

Christoph's son, Kilian Ignaz Dientzenhofer, became the architect of the church following his father's death in 1722. Between 1737 and 1752 the son built the dome and the chancel. The massive robust ovoid dome provides an appropriate foil to the thin, delicate, concave forms of the spire. The top of the dome measures 75 meters from the ground. The dome rises on a particularly high drum, which some have criticized, but the height allows it to be seen in mass with the tower and, indeed, from much of Prague. Hence the high drum is a visual correction rather than a theoretical mistake. The belfry tower was completed by Anselmo Luragho in 1755 after designs by Kilian Dientzenhofer that Luragho slightly altered.

The exterior of the church was created by an as-yet-unknown Bohemian architect. Continuous curves dominate the facade, giving the entire exterior a flowing, rhythmic play of convex and concave forms. The diagonal position of the pilasters, the convex and concave pediments, and the detached columns form a very plastic surface. The strict symmetry of the facades contrasts beautifully with the marked asymmetry of the belfry and dome.

The interior decoration of the church was not completed until 1775, despite a large number of artists working on it. Tomas Schwartz built the famous organ in 1745-46. Richard and Peter Prachner, as well as Antonin Braun, created much of the sculpture. Ignaz Platzer carved the four immense sculptures beneath the dome and the larger-than-life statue of Saint Nicholas on the high altar. The illusionistic dome frescoes were painted by Frantisek Xaver Balko. Other frescoes were by Jan Hager, Jan Lukacs, Josef Redelmayer, Karel Skreta, Ludvik Kohl, Ignac Raab and Francesco Solimen, but the majority of the frescoes were Jan Lukas Kracker's. His *trompe l'oeil* frescoes on the ceilings visually dissolve the architecture into the illusion of the heavens opening up to the faithful. These frescoes are among the largest in Europe, covering more than 1,500 square meters. They were not painted directly on the vaults, but on shallow oval interpenetrating domes that provide a smooth, albeit curved, surface. The frescoes and sculpture form a dynamic interior space of great harmony and majesty. The major theme of the interior decoration is the glorification of Saint Nicholas, the patron saint of merchants, which was quite appropriate, since the prosperous merchants of Baroque Prague paid for the church.

—ROBIN PTACEK

ST. VITUS' CATHEDRAL
Prague, Czech Republic

1344-67: Construction; **Architects:** Matthias of Arras, Peter Parler of Gmund. **1490-93:** Royal Oratory constructed; **Architect:** Benedikt Rejt. **1556-61:** Gallery constructed. **1873-1929:** Naves of cathedral and tower constructed; **Architects:** Josef Mocker, Kamil Hilbert.

Publications

BIALOSTOCKI, J.: *The Art of the Renaissance in Eastern Europe: Hungary, Bohemia and Poland.* Ithaca, New York, 1976.

BOCK, H.: "Der Beginn spätgotischer Architektur in Prag (Peter Parler) und die Beziehungen zu England." *Wallraf Richartz Jahrbuch* 23 (1961): 191-210.

BRÄUTIGAM, G.: "Gmünd-Prag-Nürnberg. Die Nürnberger Frauenkirche und der Prager Parlerstil vor 1360." *Jahrbuch der Berliner Museen* 3 (1961): 58-75.

FEHR, G.: *Benedikt Ried (Rejt).* Munich, 1941.

FREJKOVA, O.: *Ceska renesance na prazskem hrade.* Prague, 1941.

HAUSHERR, REINER: "Zu Auftrag, Programm und Büstenzyklus des Prager Domchores." *Zeitschrift für Kunstgeschichte* 34 (1971): 21-46.

HILBERT, K.: "Hudebni kruchta v chramu sv. Vita na Hrade prazskem." *Casopis Spolecnosti Pratel Starozitnosti* 17 (1909): 1-17.

KLETZL, O.: *Peter Parler, der Dombaumeister zu Prag.* Leipzig, 1940.

KOTRBA, V.: "Der Dom zu St. Veit in Prag." In SEIBT, F. (ed.): *Bohemia Sacra: Das Christentum in Böhmen, 973-1973.* Düsseldorf, 1974, 511-578.

MENCLOVA, D.: *Ceske hrady.* Prague, 1972.

NEUWIRTH, JOSEF: *Die Wochenrechnungen und der Betrieb des Prager Dombaues in den Jahren 1372-1378.* Prague, 1890.

PODLAHA, A. and SITTLER, E.: *Chramovy Poklad u sv. Vita v Praze.* Prague, 1903.

SAMANKOVA, E.: *Architectura Ceske Renesance.* Prague, 1961.

St. Vitus' Cathedral: Prague, Czech Republic, 1344-67

The Cathedral of St. Vitus is the largest and most significant ecclesiastical structure in Czechoslovakia. Built on the top of the Hradcany, the highest of the seven hills of Prague, the cathedral dominates the skyline of the city. The building is extremely rich in art treasures, and reflects the evolution of Czech architecture, as it was built during a period of six centuries.

In the late 10th century, the Christian king Vaclav I (Saint Wenceslaus) razed an ancient temple occupying the site, and replaced it with a rotunda church (926-929). The rotunda later served as his tomb. That building was replaced by a basilica (1060-90), which in turn was demolished in the mid-14th century by the emperor Charles IV to make room for a sumptuous Gothic cathedral. Matthias of Arras, then the premier architect of Europe, who had just finished the Papal Palace in Avignon, France, was commissioned in 1344 to design and build the structure.

Matthias designed the nave and apse, the choir and the St. Vaclav Chapel, where the king's remains were reinterred. Most of Matthias' work survives unchanged, though very little had

been carried to completion by the time of his death in 1352. The apse, located at the eastern end of the nave, has an ambulatory and five radiating chapels. The nave itself rises to a height of 118 feet. Colonettes clustered in piers rise the entire height of the wall, past the massive pointed arches of the first level, flowing into the ribbed vaults. The height of the colonettes endows the interior space with a soaring verticality. Columns with trefoils rise above the carved interlace of the balcony rail. The main aisle is flanked by two lateral aisles supporting triforium galleries of a later date and a steeply pitched roof. The abundance of stained-glass windows further emphasizes the height and lightness of the structure.

The rib-vaulted St. Vaclav Chapel was built on the foundations of the 10th-century rotunda. Its height and the delicacy and richness of the decoration reflect the Late Gothic ecclesiastical style, also employed in the Ste.-Chapelle in Paris, for example. The chapel was unfinished when Matthias died. Peter Parler of Gmund, who succeeded Matthias as chief architect, completed the chapel in 1376. It was elaborately decorated with frescoes encrusted with thousands of precious

St. Vitus' Cathedral

Parler's system of double buttresses combined innovative engineering with a highly artistic design. The buttresses were decorated with a profusion of gargoyles and other sculptural ornamentation, so that the solid forms tend to dissolve into patterns of light and shadow. The buttresses of the chapels radiating from the apse were furnished with complicated tracery similar to that of the chapels themselves. The elaborate detail of the tracery, which serves no structural function, increases the illusion of height. The oblique flying buttresses and the forest of pinnacles are among the most beautiful features of the church.

Peter Parler also designed the elaborate entrance to the right of the main tower, known as the Golden Door. Three tall, narrow, pointed arches open onto an enclosed porch. Mosaics dating from 1371 fill the wall above the arches. Charles IV and his queen, Elizabeth of Pomerania, are depicted kneeling on each side of the middle arch. Above them the saints and the faithful gather on the Last Judgment Day. Overhead, the archangels blow their horns, just beneath a large mandorla containing the radiant figure of Christ, surrounded by hosts of angels. The other mosaics above the flanking arches depict scenes from the lives of the saints. A parapet and a massive stained-glass window are located above the mosaics. Spiral staircases surrounded by a series of pointed arches winding up to the base of the roof frame this window on each side. The colored roof tiles were laid in a complex pattern of diamond shapes.

The Hussite Wars of the 1460s brought an end to construction, leaving Parler's tower and the nave only half finished. Construction was resumed in 1490, when Benedikt Rejt (also known as Benedikt Ried) built the Royal Oratory, also known as the Vladislav Oratorium, in one of the side chapels. The most salient

and semiprecious stones. Portraits of Charles IV and members of his court were intermingled with saints and biblical figures, all depicted with iconic stylization against embossed gilt plaster backgrounds. High-relief gilt borders, many with precious and semiprecious stones, were used to separate scenes and individuals. Stylized floral patterns resembling medieval tapestry designs covered the vaults between the gilded ribs. Floors were inlaid with marble of many colors. The elaborate metalwork doors and chandeliers were also decorated with jewels. Parler himself carved the tufa statue of Saint Vaclav in 1373 for the St. Vaclav Chapel. An excellent example of the international style of Gothic, the statue conveys little knowledge of musculature, but rather emphasizes courtly grace and a profusion of linear pattern. The small head and features are integrated with the S-curve of the body to convey a refined elegance. The laced tunic displays a floral motif over the intricate pattern of the chain-mail shirt.

Parler also completed five bays of Matthias' nave, installed the triforium galleries, and added the central transepts. The decorative ribbing of the nave vaults displays a highly sculptural quality. Parler's workshop also carved the triforium sculpture, column capitals and other sculptural ornamentation. Each capital has a detailed representation in high relief of a different biblical scene. The Adam and Eve Capital of 1355, for instance, depicts all the essential features of the story—Adam, Eve, the serpent and a bountiful apple orchard. The most important change introduced by Parler consisted in his substitution of Matthias' strict symmetry with an elaborate asymmetry, most notably in the monumental main tower, which he placed near the crossing on the right side of the structure, facing the city.

St. Vitus' Cathedral

feature in the Royal Oratory was the enclosure serving to screen royal visitors from the gaze of the people. Rejt installed a horizontal balustrade projecting into the center of the space like a bay, using the complex pointed vault for support. A medieval sculpture of the Madonna and Christ child was placed in an elaborate Gothic niche above the balustrade. Two smaller niches also containing sculpture are separated from the central niche by ogee-arched windows. A thicket of perpendicular pinnacles surmounts the enclosure. The vault was fitted out with decorative stone ribbing with a *trompe l'oeil* effect of natural wood woven into patterns, framing the coats-of-arms and other sculptural detail covering the vaults and balustrade in profusion. The work was finished in 1493.

A more intensive construction campaign was undertaken in 1509. The tower was finished with an open ambit and five copper cupolas. During the Baroque era, the top of the tower was remodeled to a more complex arrangement of ambits and cupolas. Today, the vertical symmetry of the apse, the old and new sections of the nave, with its absolutely symmetrical western facade, provide a perfect foil to the bulbous shapes of the top of the main tower, which, though not as high as Parler had wanted it to be, is still the highest part of the structure.

Construction was again brought to a halt in 1541, this time by a disastrous fire. When building resumed under the patronage of Leopold I, the Turkish War interrupted completion. Between 1556 and 1561, Boniface Wohlmuth created a classical Renaissance gallery for the organ, which also served to close off the still-unfinished nave. Pilasters with compound capitals separate three rounded arches at the bottom level to support the gallery. Classical brackets replaced keystones over the arches. A curved horizontal balustrade, appropriately decorated with reliefs of musical instruments, projects out before the middle arch. Three more arches at the second level, similar to the ones at ground level, are supported by half columns with Ionic capitals. A blank entablature at the top is surmounted by a cornice with a single row of dentiles.

King Charles VI made another attempt to finish St. Vitus' Cathedral in 1729, but funds ran out, preventing completion once again. The political agenda of the Hapsburg empire included a suppression of Czech culture and a Germanization of the Austro-Hungarian Empire. As a consequence, completion of St. Vitus' Cathedral, a symbol of Czech nationalism and ethnicity, received the lowest of priorities. Construction recommenced in the second half of the 19th century during a resurgence of Czech nationalism. The cathedral was finally finished in 1929, financed by public subscription.

Josef Mocker added the two neo-Gothic spires of the west facade and the openwork spire of the crossing. Mocker also proposed a neo-Gothic renovation for the main tower, but his proposal resulted in public outcry, and the Renaissance addition to Parler's Gothic base was preserved. Kamil Hilbert completed the nave and some of the side chapels. When the cathedral was finally finished in 1929, Hilbert salvaged the organ gallery, and moved it to the transept opposite the Golden Door and main tower, where it serves as a historical link between the old and new sections of the nave.

The late-19th- and early-20th-century additions to the cathedral present a rather romantic version of the Late Gothic, much like the similar neo-Gothic completion of Cologne Cathedral. However, unlike Cologne Cathedral, the Cathedral of St. Vitus benefits from the variety of the earlier construction. The strict symmetry of the early eastern end, the later western section of the nave, and newest western facade provide the perfect counterpoint to Parler's imaginative Gothic asymmetry and the distinctly central European style of the top of the main tower.

The decorations of the western facade include 14 figures of

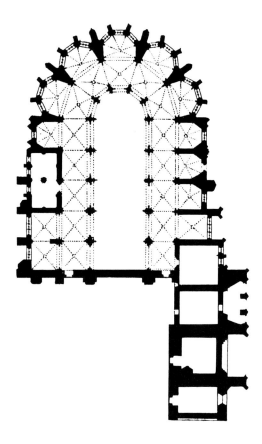

saints and several of the builders of the cathedral, from Matthias of Arras to Mocker and Hilbert. They were done by Vojtech Sucharda. Frantisek Kysela designed the great Rose Window of the west facade in 1929 in a fairly traditional neo-Gothic style. The three sets of bronze portal doors, by Otakar Spaniel, were completed in 1929 to designs by V. H. Brunner. The center set depicts the history of the cathedral, while the flanking sets depict the legends of Saint Vaclav and Saint Adalbert.

The cathedral contains a vast array of art from the 10th to 20th centuries, as well as the Veraicon of Veronica. (A gift to Emperor Charles IV from the pope, this handkerchief is said to preserve the image of Christ's face miraculously imprinted on the material when Veronica wiped his brow on the march to Calvary.) The cathedral's 21 chapels contains the tombs of Czech royalty and archbishops, besides those of Matthias of Arras and Peter Parler. The tombs, by the most prestigious sculptors and metalworkers of their time, are elaborate constructions of sculptural figures surrounded by iron and gold railings with complex interlace patterns. The stained glass in the choir dates from the 14th century. The other stained glass in the cathedral ranges in date from the 15th century through the 20th century. A window of 1931 by the artist Alphonse Mucha represents Saints Cyril and Methodius, who brought Christianity to Bohemia and Moravia. Mucha's lush art nouveau style presents the narrative in rich colors and languid sinuous lines. The St. Vaclav Chapel still contains the tomb and relics of Vaclav, as well as his chain-mail shirt and helmet. The Czech crown jewels, including the crown of Saint Vaclav, the Jagellon crown, and the scepter and orb of Charles IV, are displayed in the Regalia Chamber of the cathedral.

—ROBIN PTACEK

Vladislav Hall: Prague, Czech Republic, 1487-1502

VLADISLAV HALL
Prague, Czech Republic

1487-1502: Construction; **Architect:** Benedikt Rejt.

Publications

FEHR, G.: *Benedikt Ried*. Munich, 1961.
SAMÁNKOVÁ, E.: *Architektura ceski Renesance*. Prague, 1961.

*

Part of the beautiful, rambling Hradčany Castle in Prague, Vladislav Hall far surpasses the other sections of the complex in historical and architectural significance. The hall takes its name from King Vladislav Jagellon II of the Moravian Empire, who introduced Italian Renaissance architecture into Hungary, and subsequently Bohemia, by importing Italian architects for his ambitious building projects in Budapest in the mid-15th century. Vladislav Hall is one of the few remaining portions of the castle-palace complex in the Bohemian Renaissance style. It was an innovative prototype, which influenced both secular and religious architecture in central Europe for generations.

For hundreds of years, the hall was the largest enclosed secular space in Europe. It was used for assemblies and coronations, and was the seat of the Old Diet. It was also used as a riding hall for royalty in inclement weather, and even jousting tournaments took place there. Historical documents indicate that hundreds of riders in ornate heraldic equipage paraded about the hall on special occasions. Vladislav Hall was also the scene of the "defenestration," which set off the Thirty Years' War. On that occasion, Catholic Hapsburg ministers, refusing to yield to the demands of Bohemian Protestants, were thrown from the windows of Vladislav Hall into the moat 40 feet below. Today, the Czech National Assembly still elects the president in Vladislav Hall.

Hradčany Castle was created by a succession of architects over a period of 800 years. The royal architect Benedikt Rejt (also known as Benedikt Ried) built Vladislav Hall between 1487 and 1502, on the north side of the castle, on top of the upper portion of Charles IV's palace. Too original an architect to copy the newly introduced style of the Italian Renaissance slavishly, Rejt fused the new vocabulary of the Italian Renaissance with the decorative Bohemian Late Gothic style. An organically decorative form of the Late Gothic had flourished in Bohemia, which was rivaled only by France as a creative center of Late Gothic art and architecture. The fusion of this strong native tradition with the new forms of the classicizing Italian Renaissance resulted in the Bohemian Renaissance style, which foreshadowed Mannerism.

The hall rests on a series of massive pointed arches. These features were probably dictated by the forms of Charles IV's palace below. A series of five large interlocking vaults creates a tremendous column-free interior space almost 40 feet high, more than 50 feet wide, and 186 feet long. The decorated cavetto ribs of the vaults' bays are interlaced in elegant variations on King Vladislav's monogram. Springing from the low horizontal stone benches that ring the hall, the ribs rise to form knots in the center of the ceiling. Bronze chandeliers are suspended from the knots. The ribs visually organize the large space into a dynamic continuity, both uniting and enlivening it. The ribs are truncated in several places in a surprising manner. They look like dangling ribbon, creating a Mannerist effect.

Several doors pierce the north interior wall of the hall. The lintels are supported by half columns with decorative fluting twists around them. A set of pilasters and lintels provides another frame around the half-column door frame, creating a deep space before each door. The pilasters twist 90 degrees from base to capital, creating a dynamism that matches the fluting on the half columns and the overhead ribs. The Bohemian stonemasons obviously misread the Italian drawings of Corinthian capitals, transforming the fern-like acanthus forms into delightfully charming central European roses. A simple massive entablature supports a lunette of thick, curving stone molding.

On the exterior of the structure, Flamboyant Gothic buttresses with lacelike flat faux-niches topped with ogee arches end in flame-like pinnacles. These provide a strong contrast with the otherwise classical exterior of the south side. Fluted Corinthian pilasters frame the pairs of windows on the north side, while half columns frame the south-side windows. Both pilasters and half columns bear large, simple entablatures. Acanthus brackets support the windows on both sides of the hall. The windows, which have the date of 1493 carved into them, are a sgraffito illusion of regular alternating rusticated blocks of stone, and evoke the calm, clear harmony typical of the Renaissance.

The Equestrian Staircase forms one of the earliest parts of the hall, dating from before 1500. The staircase, which is angled at about 30 degrees, has deep broad steps, constructed especially to allow horses to enter the vast hall. Unlike the massively thick wooden floor of the hall itself, the stairs are made of stone. They lead down to a square corridor, which opens to the hall. The corridor is positioned at right angles to the stairs, in such a way that the two spaces together form an L shape. There are two vaults over the stairs and two over the corridor, which both have the truncated decorative braided ribbing also used in the hall. Two fluted semiclassical columns flank the open portal surmounted by an elaborate ogee-shaped deep molding, again combining Gothic and Renaissance forms.

In 1753, during Maria Theresa's renovations and extensions of the Hradčany, twisted coffers, cartouches and quatrefoils were painted in the spaces between the ribs on the ceiling and walls. This attempt to create the illusion of boiserie in the majestic hall resulted simply in an oddly eclectic clutter. The misguided alteration was undone after World War I, restoring Vladislav Hall to its original dynamic appearance.

The elaborate interlace decorative ribbing of Vladislav Hall appeared in a number of later secular and religious structures of central Europe, most notably the organ loft (1513) in St. Stephen's Cathedral in Vienna. The decorative ribbing in the Church of St. Mary Magdalene in Chvalsiny and the Church of the Virgin Mary at Rozmberk on the Vlatava are other examples of Rejt's influence on Bohemian architecture. The Church of St. Nicholas in Loun (ca. 1518), also built by Rejt, displays truncated decorative cavetto rib vaulting quite similar to that of Vladislav Hall. The ribs at Loun, however, are more elaborate and three-dimensional. The church in Pirna (1540-46) and the church in Most exhibit an even more extreme development, where the ribbing has become sculptural, taking on forms, such as spirals, crossovers and pendants, entirely unrelated to the underlying vaults.

Like the Ca'd'Oro in Venice and the Henry VIII Chapel in England, Vladislav Hall reflects the intersection of different historical styles, periods and cultures. In the case of Vladislav Hall, that intersection foreshadowed the Mannerist compromise of combining the High Renaissance with Late Gothic.

—ROBIN PTACEK

ZIZKA SQUARE
Tabor, Czech Republic

1521: Town Hall constructed. **1556-90:** Church constructed.

Publications

CIKHART, R.: *Popis Taborska*. Tabor, 1947.
DVORAKA, J.H.: "Rozmbersky Iatran pod Pribenicemi." *ZPP* 1947, v. VII, p. 121.
HEJNA, A.: *Tabor*. Odeon, Prague, 1964.
HEROUT, J.: "Tabor." *ZPP* 1950, v. X, pp. 4ff.
JANKOVEC, O.: *Tabori narodni kulturni pamatka, 1969-1973*. Tabor, 1973.
KOLAR, M.: *Kralovske mesto Tabor*. Tabor, 1924.
KROUPA, F.: *Tabor*. 1926.
MACEK, J.: *Tabor v husitskem revolucnim hnuti*. Prague, 1955.
MENCLOVA, D.: "Husitske opevneni Tabora." *ZPP* 1953, v. XIII, pp. 6 & 161ff.
THIR, K.: *Hradiste Hory Tabor jako pevnost v minulosti*. Tabor, 1895.
THIR, K.: *Stare domy a rodiny taborske*. Tabor, 1920.
VOJITISEK, V.: *Na Tabore v letech, 1432-50*. Prague, 1934.
WAGNER, V.: *Tabor, Umelecke pamatky*. Prague, 1924.

*

Zizka Square in Tabor, which lies some 90 kilometers south of Prague, holds a place of great importance in the national and architectural history of the Czechs. Tabor was built on the ashes of an ancient town by followers of Magister Jan Hus. The Taborites adopted a form of communalism based on the sharing of possessions and work, and rejected the authority of Rome in matters of religious governance. The town's motto—"In Tabor nothing belongs to me or you, for everyone has an equal share in everything"—clearly expressed its radical politics. Subsequently, Tabor became the center of the Hussite revolution—the first Protestant challenge to the ascendancy of Roman Catholicism—and the stronghold of the Hussite populist armies. The Old Town of Tabor, centering on the market square, was built on a height above the Luznice River. It had a formidable system of defensive walls, which, however, no longer exists. The narrow, crooked alleys winding away from the square were designed to facilitate defense against an enemy who had managed to breach the walls. Tabor certainly needed its defenses. The town withstood five crusades dispatched by the Holy Roman emperor and the pope, before finally succumbing to the combined forces of Rome and the Hapsburgs. Although a Hussite defeat at the Battle of Lipan in 1434 brought an end to Tabor's socioreligious experiment, it was not until 1621 that the town was finally taken by the Hapsburgs.

The central square is now known as Zizka Square, after Jan Zizka of Trocnov, the one-eyed Hussite hero and leader of the Hussite armies. A statute of Zizka and the original stone communion table in Zizka Square still commemorate the heroic resistance of the Hussites, and Tabor in particular. A vast labyrinth of tunnels and cellars, serving as a hiding place and way of escape from the enemy, was constructed underneath the square. In times of peace, the underground warren provided work space for Tabor's brewers and dyers. The system extends to the subterranean structure of Tabor's Town Hall.

The Town Hall was built in 1521 in the so-called Vladislav style, a combination of Bohemian Gothic and Italian Renaissance architecture, first implemented in the Vladislav Hall at the Hradčany Castle in Prague. The Town Hall is located on

Zizka Square: Tabor, Czech Republic, 15th-16th century

the western side of the square, on a gently sloping site. The three-story structure is symmetrical, except for the side tower, and is surmounted by three end gables fronting the square. Two sets of casement windows flank the main portal on the ground floor. Quatrefoils and other Flamboyant Gothic tracery above the portal form a link with a horizontal band of ogee arches between the ground floor and the main story, which is marked by a balcony. Two more sets of casement windows, vertically aligned with the windows below, flank the large doorway at the center of the balcony. All the openings on the main floor have transoms in the form of small pointed arches. The next story has three large pointed-arch windows. A cornice of elaborate Gothic stone tracery forms the transition to the roof and

gables. The three gabled sections, separated by buttresses, give the design a grid-like appearance. The steep stepped profiles of the gable ends each contain seven tall, narrow, ogee-arched openings. The verticality of these openings and the exterior buttresses balances the horizontality of the windows and cornice.

The eight-story side tower has a clock and a tall, steep hipped roof. By way of a cornice, the tower has a blind gallery of ogee arches, with tall, slender turrets capped by cylindrical roofs at the corners. The turrets emphasize the verticality of the tower, and give the structure a distinctly Bohemian silhouette.

The cross vaulting of the Council Chamber of the Town Hall displays the decorative stone ribbing typical of the Vladislav style. The ribbing springs from the central columns and runs along the edges of the vaults. The Council Chamber now contains the Tabor Escutcheon (1515-16), created by Wendel Roskopf for the exterior of the building. The tall, rectangular stone relief depicts the Bohemian rampant lion before a double-headed eagle on the ramparts of a fortress gate. The gate is most likely a representation of one of Tabor's actual gates. The border of the relief contains the sculpted figures of Jan Hus, Jan Zizka and other important Hussite figures.

The church, which is the tallest structure in Tabor and also faces the square, was built between 1440 and 1512. Construction was begun by Master Stanek to his own designs. Different sections of the church are in different styles, however, among which is the Vladislav style. The building has a steeply pitched tile roof and gable ends masked by arches and cartouches. The ends of the dormer windows on the side away from the square are also finished in this manner. The oldest part of the interior, the apse, is covered with fine diamond-arched vaults. The external buttresses and the verticality of the apse and nave clearly reveal the medieval origins of the building.

The dormers on the side facing the square have a Renaissance treatment with arched niches, pilasters, scrolls and rounded-arch pediments. The nave has less-pointed arches and the decorative rib vaulting of the Vladislav style. The tops of the nave windows end in pointed arches. The tower shows the influence of Renaissance architecture with its quoins and rounded windows. In 1677 a bulbous copper tripartite segmented dome was added to finish the tower as well as a small Baroque cupola on the nave roof.

The fine homes and shops lining the square date mostly from the 16th century, although a few 15th-century buildings survived the destruction of the Thirty Years' War. The older structures have regular casement windows, rather large by medieval standards, capped with a medieval treatment. Many of the buildings are four or five stories high. The steeply pitched roofs present one gable to the street, often masked by ornamentation in the Vladislav style. In the houses dating to the 15th and early 16th century, the ornamentation consists mostly of medieval tracery motifs, often using the Taborite symbol of the chalice. The chalice and inverted-chalice motif, as it can be found on the Ctiboruv and Skochuv houses, for instance, is abstract enough to resemble patterns of interlace lines. Taborite houses dating to the 1560s employ a simpler arch-on-arch motif. Some of the oldest houses even have miniature false flying buttresses on the gables. By the late 16th century, the gables began to reflect Venetian and Lombard influences in the elaborate gable-end designs, combining classicizing pilasters, pediments, scrolls and small windows. Many of the houses were finished with extensive sgraffito adornment. A few town houses of a much later date even exhibit Baroque and neoclassical facades.

The significance of Tabor lies in the preservation not only of the fine church and Town Hall, but especially of its many domestic and commercial buildings dating to the 15th and 16th centuries. The entire Old Town has been declared a national cultural landmark. Restoration and preservation began in 1870 and continue to this day.

—ROBIN PTACEK

DENMARK

AMALIENBORG
Copenhagen, Denmark

Dates: Planned in 1754; **Architect:** Nikolaj Eigtved (1701-54). Not completed until after his death. Facades broken into four separate structures by M. Tuscher; colonnade by C. F. Harsdorff (1735-99).

Publications

ELLING, CHRISTIAN: *Amalienborg Interiors: Christian VII's Palace, 1750-1800*. Copenhagen, 1945.
MØLLER, VIGGO STEN (ed.): *Amalienborg*. Copenhagen, 1932.

Copenhagen is notable for the extent to which the most important features of the original medieval town are discernible in the city today. There is, however, one major part of the modern city in which this is not true, and in the development of this area came an event which shaped a major landmark in another great Nordic city.

The area in question is the Amalienborg, an octagonal plaza containing four palaces and forming the central element in the part of Copenhagen known as Frederiksstad (Frederik's Town). This lies along the harbor on the northeast side of the city. The palaces are now the residences of Denmark's royal family, but this was not the purpose for which they were built.

By the middle of the 17th century Copenhagen Castle, rebuilt and enlarged more than once since a fire in 1375, was becoming less fashionable and more uncomfortable by the year. In 1659

Amalienborg: Copenhagen, Denmark, 1754

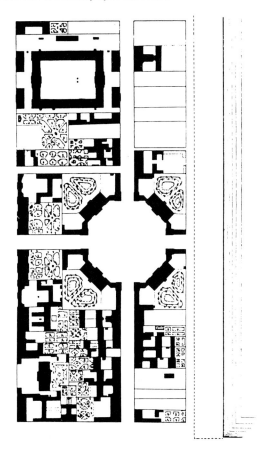

a new palace with gardens was begun for Queen Sophie Amalie, consort of King Frederik III, on the tract of land that still bears her name. She had the enjoyment of this pleasurable retreat until her death in 1685. Shortly thereafter, in 1689, a tragic fire in the palace theater destroyed the entire establishment.

In spite of this disaster the desirability of such a palace was not lost upon the Danish court. Ulrica Eleanora, sister of the new King Christian V, had been married to King Charles XI of Sweden. Her royal architect, Nicodemus Tessin the Younger, was called to Copenhagen to design another palace for the Sophie Amalienborg site. This project was abandoned, but Tessin kept his plan and used it in designing a new Royal Palace in Stockholm when the old Tre Kronor Castle burned in 1697. The palace in Stockholm is, of course, larger and grander than the proposed Danish one would have been, but it preserves in essence the plan for the second Sophie Amalienborg.

It was for one of Denmark's most vigorous patrons of the arts, King Frederik V, to bring about the building of the Amalienborg group that we see today. The House of Oldenburg, Denmark's royal dynasty, marked 300 years of rule in 1749. To celebrate, Frederik V had Frederiksstad laid out, with the plaza as the centerpiece. The four stately palaces and adjoining wings were not, however, planned as royal residences, as they have been used since 1794. The king's idea was that the entire district should be built up by private individuals, and four wealthy noblemen agreed to build the Amalienborg group. Nicholas Eigtved, who was to become the first director of the Royal Danish Academy of Fine Arts, founded by Frederik V in 1754, gave unity to the plaza by using the same design for all four facades. The basement and ground-level stories are finished with shallow pilasters and rustication. Above, the main and attic stories are framed with Ionic pilasters, the whole crowned with a balustrade. Each palace is 11 bays long, the three central bays being wider and projecting slightly, with two pairs of

coupled columns forming the central bay. Above this rises a pediment carved with heraldic motifs and other ornaments. The portals at the ground level of this projection have been closed and replaced by windows, access now being through the wings.

The palaces are not identical in the interiors. The basic scheme of the main level is the central vestibule on the plaza side and behind it a salon overlooking the palace garden. Variations occur in the placement of stairs and disposition of the smaller rooms. The palace built by the king's friend Count Adam Gottlob Moltke is the least changed of the four. Its superb Great Hall is one of the richest expressions of the French Rococo in Denmark. Carved and gilded panels cover the walls from floor to ceiling, with allegorical paintings by François Boucher. The ceiling is adorned with gilded stuccowork as well. Changes in the other palaces brought later fashions, such as the neoclassical, to Amalienborg interiors, making them important repositories of courtly taste.

Symbolism at the Amalienborg is not restricted to the pediment carvings. An equestrian statue of Frederik V by the French sculptor Jacques-François-Joseph Saly was placed in the center of the plaza, looking along Amaliegade, the central cross-axis of Frederiksstad. A great church was begun at the end of the street, and the statue's glance would thereby link church and state. Nicodemus Tessin had planned such an arrangement of palaces and church for Stockholm. If his plan had indeed provided inspiration for Frederiksstad, then even though the Swedish architect's first proposal for this site was rejected, his ideas came back to shape the area as built. While the Amalienborg is a fine contribution of Rococo to the cityscape of Copenhagen, it also has considerable historical significance and some unique links with that other 18th-century Scandinavian royal city, Stockholm.

—MARIAN C. DONNELLY

BOURSE
Copenhagen, Denmark

1619-30: Construction; **Commissioned:** Christian IV (1577-1648).

Publications

SKOVGAARD, JOAKIM: *A King's Architecture: Christian IV and his Buildings.* 1973.

*

By the middle of the 16th century, while Copenhagen Castle itself was still isolated from the city by a moat, the castle island, Slottsholmen, future site of the Bourse, had been enlarged. Christian III built an arsenal across from the southeast side of the castle. Then in 1598 Christian IV built a new arsenal and two storage buildings extending yet farther into the harbor, forming a square basin to serve the ships of the royal navy. A broad parade ground and shipyard for small boats occupied the enlarged island on the northeast, separated from the rest of the growing city by Holmens Canal.

With provision made for the fleet, Christian IV undertook to strengthen Denmark's role in world trade. A decisive move was to send the merchant Ove Giedde to Ceylon in 1618, where he founded the trading post of Tranquebar. On his return in 1622

Bourse: Copenhagen, Denmark, 1619-30

Giedde found the construction of the Bourse well under way beside the canal. The Bourse was one of the most exotic buildings commissioned by the king, and with it the whole administrative complex of Slottsholmen was essentially complete.

Some mystery remains as to who the identity of architect of this remarkable building. The first contract, written 4 May 1619, was with the Netherlandish stonemason Laurens van Steenwinckel, but this was only for some carvings. On his death shortly thereafter, his brother Hans assumed the work. He was then architect general and master builder to the king, but by then the basic design had already been established, and his responsibilities were again for designs for gables and entrances. Attempts to ascribe the building to Inigo Jones, who visited Denmark in 1603-04, have not been very successful. Perhaps, although there is no documentation, the most likely possibility is that the Bourse was designed by Hans van Steenwinckel, probably in consultation with the king, deriving inspiration from the Bourse in Antwerp of 1531. The latter was built in four long wings around a courtyard, with galleries at the ground level and gabled dormers in the attic story. The familiar medieval merchants' hall or guildhall was usually a short rectangle in plan, set in a central marketplace. The Copenhagen Bourse, on the other hand, was to be quayside, serving the merchant ships directly, and for this a long, narrow building like a wing of the Antwerp Bourse was a better solution.

Like so many other buildings remaining from that period, the Bourse was not entirely finished in the first campaign, nor is it now fully in its original condition. The changes are instructive. In order to provide access from ships on both sides, another canal was dug on the south side of the site. This was evidently regarded as the less prestigious side, for it was not

until 1880 that the elaborate gables of the north side were repeated there. Now the south canal has been filled in, and it is actually easier to examine the details of the building from that side.

Built of red brick with sandstone trim, the Bourse is one of the most festive buildings in Copenhagen. On the ground floor it is divided into two rows of 20 small chambers, each for a merchant. A plan in Laurids de Thurah's *Den danske Vitruvius* of 1746-49 shows that the second level originally had a long central room with a series of booths down the middle. These have since been removed. Above the second-story windows there are nine two-story dormers over alternate chambers on the ground level. The central dormer is wider, extending over three openings on the first and second levels, breaking the potential monotony of the long building. The surface of the entire building is lavishly adorned with pilasters, panels, scrolls and cartouches.

The ceremonial entrances at the east and west ends led to the second level, which seems to have offered the more luxurious goods. The east entrance has been changed to give access to the ground level, and its decorative portal is somewhat simpler than that on the west toward the castle. Both entrances are designed as triumphal arches, with double projecting Tuscan columns flanking arched openings and single columns flanking panels above.

The central spire of the Bourse has excited much comment and speculation. Above an open octagonal turret, four dragons crouch heads down, with their tails intertwining to form a spiral rising more than 30 feet. By the 1770s it had fallen into disrepair. Fortunately, a proposal to replace it with a cupola was turned down. There are a number of theories as to the source of inspiration for this extraordinary feature. The Bourse in Antwerp had a more conventional but similar tower, which may have been the prototype, the dragons coming from then-popular Chinese fireworks designs. A number of symbolic references have also been suggested. Whatever the truth of the puzzles about the Bourse, it stands as a monument to the ambitions and taste of Christian IV, its dragon spire proudly taking its place among the towers of Copenhagen.

—MARIAN C. DONNELLY

COPENHAGEN CATHEDRAL (Vor Frue Kirke)
Copenhagen, Denmark

Dates: 1811-29; **Architect:** C. F. Hansen (1756-1845).

Publications

HERMANSEN, VICTOR; ROUSSELL, AAGE; and STEENBERG, JAN: *Danmarks Kirker. København*. Copenhagen, 1945-58.
SMIDT, CLAUS M.: *Vor Frue Kirke*. Copenhagen, 1980.
WOHLERT, VILHELM: "C. F. Hansen's Domkirke." *Architectura* 2 (1980): 49-54.

*

Four or five churches have stood on the site of Vor Frue Kirke (the Church of Our Lady), which in 1536 was designated the preeminent church in newly Reformed Denmark. In history's first bombardment of a civilian population, the English attacked Copenhagen in 1807, and Vor Frue Kirke, whose high Baroque spire had served as a target, once again went up in flames. The spire collapsed into the church, and the tower's bells crashed through the vaults. The entire inventory was destroyed and part of the vaulting, but in the great Gothic choir, which had also survived a serious fire in 1728, the walls and pillars still stood to the height of the roof. The archdeacon's son, later the famous Professor H. N. Clausen, thought that "a complete restoration would scarcely have cost any more than the demolition alone." The chief inspector of buildings, C. F. Hansen, who was called in to discuss the church's rebuilding shortly after the fire, was of a completely different opinion. Hansen, who had singlehandedly formulated for Denmark the principles of neoclassical architecture in the country's greatest monuments, displayed little interest in or veneration for earlier construction. He accordingly expressed his preference for "decorating Vor Frue Kirke in a new taste, instead of restoring it to its earlier condition." The opinion of the country's most important architect carried weight, and in 1811 Frederik VI decreed that Hansen should build the church in the fashion that he considered "most noble and suitable," a choice of words that incidentally reveals the king's own classical orientation.

Over the next 18 years the remaining masonry was removed and a new church built in a form that represents the culmination of Hansen's artistic development: it was his last great project.

Hansen could not rely on antique models for a church for a Reformed congregation, nor on more recent French and Italian prototypes. A Protestant church is not built around a liturgy, but around a sermon; it requires an auditorium where the congregation can be seated during the service, good acoustics and a

pulpit. Hansen's ecclesiastical ideal, on the other hand, was the antique temple—the only one he had so far managed to build took the form of J. Blacker's country house in Blankenese, Holstein (1794-95)—and at Vor Frue Kirke he sought to satisfy both the congregation's understanding of a Reformed house of God, and his own conception of a modern temple in "pure Greek style."

Vor Frue Kirke's plan is that of a traditional basilica with tower, nave and choir. To a great extent it was built on the lines of the former church's external walls, but those of the side aisles, which had been lower than the nave, were now brought up to a powerful, classical cornice, and the old ambulatory was replaced by a semicircular choir crowned by a smooth, copper-roofed halfdome. A smooth band runs around the choir and sides of the building at the height of the doortops; the side walls were ashlar-plastered below it, and smooth-plastered above. Hansen would have preferred to forget the tower, required "only because custom demands that our temples should have towers," he wrote in his description of the building. He did, however, bow to custom and prepared two proposals for the tower, one topped by a cupola and the other with a flat pyramidal roof. Both could find prototypes in the *pharos*, the antique lighthouse that was the only tower type Hansen could accept; moreover, the lighthouse's function as a guide to men in the dark offered symbolic neatness. Hansen himself preferred the lower, roofed-tower proposal; this was the one chosen, after the addition of a gilded cross to its top. With its Serlian windows, gallery and rectangular openings to the bell room, the tower has the character of an Italian campanile.

The tower rises above the church's entrance facade. The old tower's foundations had projected, but Hansen built his into the body of the church, so the tower emerges only at cornice level. The completely unbroken wall surface thus created he used as a backdrop for the building's outstanding external feature, the powerful portico. Like a temple front, the portal with its six Doric columns supports a pediment. The "purity" of the Greek form was reflected in Hansen's choice of fluted columns, the only appearance of this element in his oeuvre.

Equally unknown in Hansen's other buildings is the sense of direction created by the very slight projection of the side walls beside the tower; there is nothing corresponding near the choir, and the arrangement represents a break with the symmetry to which the architect elsewhere adhered so tightly. The resulting movement toward the entrance front contradicts the classical principles that Hansen, with characteristic self-confidence, here chose to relax.

Inside, the nave was made significantly wider than before; and its Gothic groin vaults were replaced by a powerful wooden barrel vault. Through an impressive, cassetted ceiling falls overhead light (as in Hansen's favorite classical building, the Pantheon in Rome), which gives the interior an even illumination: a dead light, according to the critics. In the ambulatory around the choir, where the Gothic choir chapels had been, Hansen envisaged the great men of the nation buried, in a direct continuation of the Pantheon tradition. The idea was rejected; public opinion opposed burial in churches. Hansen expended great care in the design of the interior and himself designed the church's inventory, the cylindrical pulpit, the pews and the candelabras.

Another great Danish neoclassicist, the sculptor Bertel Thorvaldsen (1768-1844), then living in Rome, was commissioned to decorate the church. His Apostle statues were to have stood in niches in the nave piers, but upon their arrival in Copenhagen they turned out to be too tall. The niches were filled in and the figures now stand free, in front of the piers, a solution doubtless highly satisfactory to Thorvaldsen, but which subtly altered the

Copenhagen Cathedral (Vor Frue Kirke): Copenhagen, Denmark, 1811-29

Copenhagen Cathedral (Vor Frue Kirke)

space: less sacral, more museum-like. The nave culminates in the statue of Christ in the apse, originally intended for the Christiansborg Palace Chapel: it has become one of the sculptor's best-loved works. While the placement of the Apostles must have felt like an artistic compromise to Hansen, he was surely delighted by Thorvaldsen's reliefs *John the Baptist Preaching in the Wilderness,* which fills the pediment of the portico, and, above the entrance door itself, *The Entry into Jerusalem.*

In its powerful, naked weight Vor Frue Kirke stands as neoclassicism's most original interpretation of Nordic Protestantism's serious, reflective character. Like Hansen's other buildings it was criticized after his death. Later generations' interest in the ornamental possibilities of various historical styles made it a favorite critical target; the most violent affront was Christian Hansen's insensitive repainting of the interior in brilliant colors, in 1860. (Only in 1977 was the church taken back to its original gray color scale.) But Vor Frue Kirke was also the building that finally put C. F. Hansen back in the dominant position that he deserves in the history of Danish architecture. In 1909 the brewer Carl Jacobson, director of the New Carlsberg Breweries and one of the country's greatest art patrons, offered to pay for the re-erection of the nearly-100-meter-high Baroque spire, which had been destroyed in 1807. This proposal aroused strong opposition in an architectural circle that stated that the spire would "compromise C. F. Hansen's classical masterpiece." Once again neoclassicism's grand old man became the subject of younger architects' interest; but now they put him in the vanguard as a pioneer of functionalism, who had contributed to a new understanding of the beauty of pure form.

—WIVAN MUNK-JØRGENSEN
Translated from the Danish by Christine Stevenson

ROSENBORG PALACE
Copenhagen, Denmark

Ca. 1610: Southeast half of palace constructed. **1613-1614:** Palace completed. **1624:** Third level added. **Architect:** Christian IV (1577-1648).

Publications

SKOVGAARD, J. A.: *A King's Architecture: Christian IV and His Buildings.* London, 1973.
WANSCHER, VILHELM: *Christian IV's bygninger.* Copenhagen, 1947.
WANSCHER, VILHELM: *Rosenborgs historie 1606-1634.* Copenhagen, 1930.

*

In order to understand the role of Rosenborg Palace as its royal patron, King Christian IV, envisioned it, the nature of Copenhagen Castle in 1606 must be recalled. Built on the castle island, Slottsholmen, on the southeast harbor side of the medieval town in 1167, it was attacked, burned and rebuilt several times until Christian IV came to the throne in 1588. He found the castle an irregular structure around a central court, grown deeper over the years by additions of upper stories, gables and turrets, and the whole still isolated by the surrounding canal. By then the castle must have been fairly miserable as a residence, and the pleasure-loving king was already having the great palace of Frederiksborg in the hunting forest at Hillerød built with the splendor so characteristic of his architectural interests. But that was 22 miles from Copenhagen and could be reached only after a day's journey. Therefore, in 1606 he purchased about 30 acres of land outside the north wall of the city in order to provide a pleasant country house to which he could even walk.

Ironically, by the time Christian IV had made the last of the additions to the original simple structure, he had already had the city enlarged by extending the defenses out around the new palace northeast to the stronghold of Kastellet on the Sound. A painting in the Rosenborg Palace collections, however, shows him on horseback in conference, probably with the engineer of the defenses, and with the palace in the background, still in a gentle landscape setting. Although the city has grown up around it, the original plot of land is still Kongens Have, the King's Garden, and Rosenborg Palace is still protected by the tranquility of the beautiful park in which it rises.

As it is, Rosenborg sits on its own little islet, surrounded by a moat and ramparts with four bastions. Built of red brick with sandstone trim, its richly ornamented towers and gables give it a festive appearance. The original designer of the palace has not been identified with certainty. The master mason Bertel Lange has been proposed, as has the participation of the king. As illustrated on a print of 1611, the palace began as a two-story building which became the southeast half after the addition of 1613-14. That this larger structure was planned all along is suggested by the central placement within the ramparts. Had the smaller first structure been centrally located, an awkward asymmetry would have resulted with the enlargement.

The sandstone quoins, stringcourses and window surrounds are set off against the red brick of the main building and its towers. In addition, the north and south gables are decorated with the then-fashionable panels, scrolls and applied pendants of the Netherlandish Renaissance.

The palace ceased to be used as a royal residence early in

Rosenborg Palace: Copenhagen, Denmark, ca. 1610

the 19th century, but it was by then filled with the luxurious appurtenances and various treasures brought to it by Danish kings from Christian IV to Christian VII. Several overseers saw to it until in 1833 a commission was appointed for the Chronological Collections of the Danish Kings. Consequently, visitors can now explore the palace and see how it was furnished over the years, and also see some of the major works of art pertaining to the history of the Danish monarchs. To be sure, the visitor is bound to be impressed by the awkwardness of access between stories, several times rebuilt, and hardly ever convenient for those serving royal occasions.

The ground level is the least altered of the three. There are the rooms occupied by Christian IV and his morganatic wife Kirsten Munk. The Winter Room at the northwest end is dominated by a massive fireplace, with carved scroll brackets on each side and a heavy pediment with strapwork and panels and the king's monogram above. The paneled walls are covered with small Netherlandish paintings. The adjoining King's Bed-

room has an even more elaborate fireplace. On the other side of a smaller chamber behind the central west tower is the so-called Marble Room, originally the bedroom of Kirsten Munk redecorated in the time of Frederik III. The last in the series of rooms on the ground floor is the large daily room of Kirsten Munk, now housing the Danish Regalia: the crown of Christian IV, the queen's crown, the coronation cup, the sword of state and other royal jewels.

The interior of the second level has been much changed, and the rooms now house collections pertaining to the later Danish kings. The third level, added in 1624, is entirely occupied by the Banqueting Hall for royal entertainment. Again richly ornamented, it has at one end the coronation throne of narwhal ivory and the three great silver lions by Ferdinand Küblich.

The King's Park still provides an oasis in the city, but Christian IV's little garden retreat has grown to an opulent demonstration of the tastes and treasures of the monarchy of Denmark.

—MARIAN C. DONNELLY

FINLAND

RAILWAY STATION and ADMINISTRATIVE BUILDING
Helsinki, Finland

1904-14. Architect: Eliel Saarinen (1873-1950).

Publications

FRAMPTON, KENNETH, and FUTAGAWA, YUKIO: *Modern Architecture: 1851-1919*. New York, 1983.

HAUSEN, M.; KIRMO, M.; AMBERG, A.; and VALTO, T. (eds.): *Eliel Saarinen: Projects 1896-1923*. Cambridge, Massachusetts, 1990.

HAUSEN, MARIKA: "The Helsinki Railway Station in Eliel Saarinen's First Versions, 1904." *Taidehistoriallisia Tukimuksia Konsthistoriska Studier* 3 (1977): 57-114.

HOFMANN, WERNER, and KULTERMANN, UDO: *Modern Architecture in Color*. New York, 1970.

MUTO, AKIRA, and SANO, KEIBUN: "Railway Station, Helsinki." *Space Design* (November 1982).

*

The Helsinki Railway Station stands as a remarkable example of architecture's communicative role. To the contemporary traveler, its monumental form symbolizes an independent Finland, a nation no older than the station itself; to its original client and architect, however, the symbolism of the station and its preceding designs was more complex. It not only represented the end of National Romanticism as the dominant architectural language in Finland but also announced the beginning of a new era in which the expression of function was an objective of symbolic form.

By the late 1890s Helsinki's original railway station, a neo-classical building with Tudor arches, was outdated both functionally and stylistically. In December 1903 the Board of Public Buildings announced an open competition to design a new station and administration building. As was typical for competitions in Finland at that time, the architects were given a rigid plan to which their elevations and sections had to comply. This program dictated the site, the U-shaped "terminus" plan, the internal room arrangement and even the exterior materials. As a result, the submissions were judged mainly in terms of facade composition, which must therefore form the basis of our own observations. Eliel Saarinen worked on two of the 21 entries that were received for the competition: one was with his partners Armas Lindgren and Herman Gesellius, the other on his own. It was his independent entry called "Winged Wheel on a Globe" that won first place.

Most of the entries, including Saarinen's design, reflected the style which has come to be known as National Romanticism, an architectural language which Saarinen and his partners were in part responsible for creating with buildings such as the Finnish pavilion for the Paris Exposition of 1900 (1898-1900) and the Finnish National Museum (1902-12). Although the 1800s had been a period of great national awakening, the century closed with Finland's relative autonomy as a Russian grand duchy under attack by the czar's new policy of Russification. The architects responded through work in which national motifs—elements gathered from medieval castles, stone churches and traditional log structures—were used to define national identity and symbolize cultural independence. Finnish granite and soapstone became the building materials of choice, and native flora and fauna became the favored themes of ornamentation. The neo-Romanesque granite architecture of Henry Hobson Richardson was an important model, regarded as an alternative to the earlier continental architectural movements, especially German, with their inherent plaster ornamentation. The railway station gave form to these ideas through a picturesque massing of rectangular medieval-inspired forms including numerous towers and the use of squared-rubble granite, a building technique imported from Scotland. Two winged wheels on globes and eight stone bears adorned the entrance hall.

The only notable exception to this National Romantic style in the competition was the entry by the architect and critic Sigurd Frosterus. A student of Henry van de Velde, Frosterus looked to German and Austrian sources rather than British and American. His entry was a prime example of the developing rationalist school of architecture. Frosterus and another architect-critic, Gustaf Strengell, became adamant critics of Saarinen's entry in particular and National Romanticism in general. In a pamphlet titled *Arkitektur*, published shortly after the competition closed in April 1904, Frosterus argued: "A building is no longer merely a picturesque silhouette. . . . In regard to form, we have much more to learn from the construction of machines, bicycles, automobiles, warships, railway bridges, etc., than from historical styles." But this debate represented more than a shift in architectural styles and an adoption of the belief that form should express function. The political situation was tense in both Russia and Finland, culminating in the general strikes of 1905. With the Russian czar losing power, Finland turned to Germany for support, a political alliance that was reflected in the new artistic sources of the architects.

Saarinen responded to this criticism and changing social context, by developing alternative designs for the station. He studied railroad stations in Germany, England and Scotland, and in December 1904 presented a revised design to the railway administration. Although these revisions were made under the auspices of the partnership of Gesellius, Lindgren and Saarinen, Lindgren's involvement was marginal at best (he left the firm in 1905) and Gesellius' participation seems to have been limited to minor revisions in the plan (Gesellius and Saarinen's partnership ended in 1907). Saarinen signed the drawings for the facades and the sections and is credited with the station's general design. The plans and elevations for the administration building were approved immediately, and construction was completed in 1909. The design of the station proper, however, was modified two more times before construction began in 1912, only to be suspended during World War I when the building served as a Russian military hospital. The station opened for traffic in 1919 after Finland's declaration of independence in 1918 following the Russian Revolution.

In the final building, Saarinen simplified the exterior forms to boldly reflect the interior spaces dominated by a barrel-vaulted central hall and two slightly lower cross-vaulted halls (originally waiting rooms) perpendicular to the entrance hall. The halls are constructed of reinforced concrete—used for the first time in a major public building in Finland—and finished on the exterior with smooth red granite and faceted mansard

Railway Station: Helsinki, Finland, 1904-14

roofs. The main entrance, dominated by a semicircular window, is flanked by four monumental male torchbearers, each holding an illuminable globe. Saarinen's artistic sources relate to the work of German and Austrian architects, including the commercial buildings of Alfred Messel and Herman Billing, Josef Maria Olbrich's Ernst Ludwig House in Darmstadt and Josef Hoffmann's Palais Stoclet in Brussels. As Finland fought for political independence within an international context and not just cultural autonomy within the context of Russia, it was necessary to replace the symbolism of National Romanticism with an architectural language that reflected international styles. Eliel Saarinen's railway station gave visual form to these cultural and political needs, masterfully integrating them with the expressive goals of modernism.

—GREGORY WITTKOPP

Publications

NEUMANN, M.: "Klassizismus in Finnland. Zu den Arbeiten Carl Ludwig Engels." *Zentralblatt der Bauverwaltung*, 62, 1942.
PÖYKKÖ, KALEVI: "Helsinki's Neo-Classical Center." *Apollo* 115, 243 (May 1982): 354-360.
SUOLAHTI, EINO E.: *Helsinki: A City in a Classic Style*. Helsinki, 1973.
WICKBERT, NILS E.: *Carl Ludwig Engel*. Exhibition catalog. Berlin, 1970.
WICKBERG, NILS E.: *Senaatintori*. Helsinki, 1981.

*

SENATE SQUARE
Helsinki, Finland

1819: Construction begun. **Architects:** Johan Albert Ehrenström and Carl Ludwig Engel. **1822:** Main wing of Senate Building built. **1827-32:** University construction. **1828:** Construction of three wings of Senate Building begun. **1833:** City Hall construction. **1833-44:** University Library construction. **1894:** Monument to Czar Alexander II constructed.

The Senate Square in Helsinki is the result of the most monumental and cohesive urban design in Scandinavia. The need for it arose from a combination of disaster and political upheaval, and the realization came through the efforts of two strong creative personalities.

In 1550 Gustavus Vasa had founded Helsinki, which he envisaged as a commercial center for the Gulf of Finland on the eastern edge of the modern city. By 1640 it was clear that the harbor there was inadequate, and the town was moved to its present, better position. There with three major harbors and the

Senate, Senate Square: Helsinki, Finland, 1822

protection of the great fortress of Suomenlinna, begun in 1748, Helsinki had grown modestly to a town of about 4,000 inhabitants by 1808. Finland was then still under the Swedish crown. The long years of struggle between Sweden and Russia, however, led to Russian occupation in 1808 and the final cession of Finland, including the Åland Islands, to Russia in 1809. During the occupation Helsinki had been devastated by fire in 1808 and was seeking plans for reconstruction.

Into this picture came a diplomat and engineer: Johan Albert Ehrenström, a native of Helsinki who had been for 27 years in Sweden and for political reasons had returned to Finland. Through a powerful friend at the court of Czar Alexander I, he was appointed chairman of the committee to reconstruct Helsinki. Perhaps inspired partly by Gustav Adolf's Plaza in Stockholm, Ehrenström developed a plan for Helsinki that included the great plaza now known as the Senate Square.

Helsinki is a city with rocky hills rising from the harbors, and in order to achieve a grandiose plan, many sites had to be leveled and some remaining older buildings cleared away. The elements of Ehrenström's plan still dominate the city: a great square rising to the north of the South Harbor, a broad esplanade running westward from the South Harbor, with then two major boulevards going off diagonally to the northwest and southwest. These are now Mannerheimintie and Bulevardi.

Ehrenström planned the north square, at first called the Great Square, to keep the old Town Hall in the northeast corner, a proposed building to be erected in the northwest corner, and a new Lutheran church to rise on the northern height above them.

To accomplish this would require the removal of the old Main Guard Building and Ulrika Eleanora Church, a wooden structure dating from the previous century.

Ehrenström, however, for all his great vision for the new capital city, was not an architect. As it happened, the German-born and trained architect Carl Ludwig Engel had worked briefly in Turku in 1814, and before going on to work in St. Petersburg had come to Ehrenström's attention. The upshot was that in 1816 Engel was appointed architect to the reconstruction committee. By the time of his death in 1840 he put in place the four major buildings, then not yet entirely finished, that define the Senate Square today: the Senate Building, the Lutheran Church, the University and the University Library.

Proposals for all these buildings went through several stages, Czar Alexander I and Czar Nicholas I after him taking much interest and making numerous suggestions.

Engel's initial proposal for the square included remodeling the Town Hall and building the Post Building and Main Guard Building as Ehrenström had planned. The first two projects were in hand by 1819. The designs for the Senate Building were approved in 1818 and the main wing, facing the square, built by 1822. It is a long four-story building, the first main level rusticated with arched window openings. The central portion has a projecting portico with six Corinthian columns rising through the two upper levels. At each end there is a shallow pavilion motif of four Corinthian pilasters. A grand staircase, of which Engel was very proud, leads from the ground to the second level, where the original grandiose Throne Room is behind the

University, Senate Square: 1827-32

portico, overlooking the square. The other three wings around the central courtyard were begun by 1828.

In the meantime, drawings were in preparation for the church, which became the Lutheran Cathedral of Helsinki in 1959. Dedicated to Saint Nicholas, it is cruciform in plan, covered by a dome and half domes, with a central tower rising above the dome and a six-column Corinthian portico fronting each arm of the cross. The traditional axis of eastern altar and western main entrance was maintained. Engel designed a great cross with icon-like paintings for the main altar, but this was never carried out. There are galleries in the north, south and west wings, but although Engel used the Corinthian order on the interior, it is somewhat severe. The rising ground set the church high above the level of the square, making it a backdrop, with the colonnaded Main Guard Building serving as a base. This was demolished in 1839, giving way to the broad monumental staircase there now.

Another disaster, this time in Turku, changed the nature of the whole idea of the square, by then becoming known as the Senate Square. A fire in 1827 prompted the removal of the University in Turku to Helsinki, where the west side of the square could provide a site. There Engel began another four-story building with central portico and end pavilions echoing the Senate Building opposite. He avoided making the buildings identical, using the Ionic rather than the Corinthian order for the University and changing the window openings. The Assembly Hall on the west side of the University was damaged in World War II and has been altered in the reconstruction.

At first it had been thought to put the university library in the new building, but the space to be provided proved inadequate. Engel's last project for the Senate Square was the University Library, begun in 1833, the interior completed in 1844. Built beside the university and directly opposite the church, the building is shorter, with a colonnade of eight applied Corinthian columns as the central element, pilasters on either side, an attic story rather than a central pediment, and a central low dome. The interior consists of three great colonnaded halls, arranged in an H-plan.

Engel envisaged an urban landscape with plantings in the courtyards and to the north of these four monumental buildings, which then loomed up over the two-story wooden buildings that comprised most of the town. The Senate Square is still impressive, although the turrets and pavilions added to the church shortly after Engel's death interrupt the total unity as he left it. A further obstruction is the monument to Czar Alexander II, built in the center of the square in 1894. The original row of aristocratic stone houses on the south side of the square remains. Several proposals for rebuilding that side have been made, including ones by such prominent Finnish architects as Armas Lindgren and Alvar Aalto. Fortunately, none of these have materialized. The city offices have been moved to the present Town Hall, also a building by Engel, facing the market square beside the South Harbor.

The modern buildings of Helsinki prevent the Senate Square from dominating the city as it once did. Yet, surrounded by automobiles and buses instead of horse-drawn carriages, the

City Hall, Senate Square: 1833

Senate Square in Helsinki remains the grandest urban space in Scandinavia.

—MARIAN C. DONNELLY

TELEPHONE COMPANY BUILDING
Helsinki, Finland

1903-05: Construction. **Architect:** Lars Sonck.

Publications

KIVINEN, P., KORVENMAA, P., and SALOKORPI, A.: *Lars Sonck.* Museum of Finnish Architecture Monograph. Helsinki, 1981.
SPENCE, R.: "Lars Sonck." *Architectural Review* 1020 (Feb. 1982), 40-49.

*

Lars Sonck's Helsinki Telephone Company Building is, along with his Tampere Cathedral, one of the major masterpieces of the Finnish National Romantic Movement, Finland's equivalent to European Jugendstil and art nouveau. It accommodated offices, flats and a telephone exchange. The exchange was one of

the first to be built in Finland and, on receiving the commission in 1901, Sonck traveled abroad to examine similar developments in other parts of Europe. However, the novelty of the building type and its modern technological nature did not lead him to attempt any expression of the new technological age. Indeed, the archaic character of the forms and the rough texture of the stonework are remarkably close to his Cathedral in Tampere. Sonck's buildings of that period serve to highlight the differences between the architects of the National Romantic Movement and rationalists like Peter Behrens in Germany, who began to express the functional nature of a building in its external form, looked for a built equivalent to the new machine age and generally based their forms on ordered classical, rather than picturesque medieval precedent.

In Sonck's building, there was little attempt to make the external composition a logical expression of internal arrangements. The forms are unashamedly independent of the plan. The tower, for example, indicates no significant functional element in planning terms. On the middle floors, the different window shapes and sizes in the right-hand bay—the upper one incorporated into a facade projection—are purely compositional devices to balance the tower visually. This obscures the fact that they light the same open-plan offices as the adjacent rows of windows. Indeed, the smaller windows on the third floor have since been enlarged to admit more light. The one element that seeks to express something about the building's purpose—the decorative carved frieze on the semicircular bay window—reads more readily as archaic Celtic ornament than as the imagery of modern communications technology.

The first design for the building of 1903 is clearly indebted

University Library, Senate Square: 1833-44

to the Helsinki Polytechnic Students Union (1901-03) by Karl Lindahl and Walter Thomé. Thomé had worked in Sonck's office, probably on Tampere Cathedral, so there was almost certainly a mutual exchange of ideas in what was in any case a very close-knit Helsinki architectural community. The circular tower in this design was to stand out from the building, bridging the footpath, a bold move reflecting Sonck's enthusiasm for the kind of urban design landmarks popularized by Camillo Sitte. The final tower, as constructed, still projects somewhat beyond the rest of the building and sits almost on the crown of the hill, providing a very fine climax to the steep cobbled street. Indeed, the power of the forms are only fully appreciated on approaching the building at an acute angle, up the street. The nature of the building as a focal point is dramatized by the giant scale of its individual elements, relative to adjacent structures. This recalls some of Henry Hobson Richardson's work in the United States and even the tricks of scale used by Frank Furness in his Philadelphia buildings.

The Telephone Company Building emphasizes, above all, Sonck's mastery of form and the handling of materials. His use of contrasting smooth and rugged textures is even more striking there than in his cathedral at Tampere. The entrance surround, in the form of an abstracted medieval churchyard gateway, is constructed of smooth, pale gray ashlar and sits proud of the facade, strongly contrasting with the darker, rock-faced pink and gray granite wall behind. It is treated almost as an element of collage, an impression reinforced by the way the form slices through the sill and stringcourse above and invades the territory of the recessed window on the second floor. Similarly, the mullions and sturdy columns between windows on the middle

floors are also of finely dressed stone set off against the surrounding rock-faced granite, and the decorative, sharply-cut incised carving is carefully restricted for maximum intensity of contrast. The texture of the stonework is layered through the height of the building, as in Herman Gesellius, Armas Lindgren and Eliel Saarinen's Pohjola Insurance Company Building (1899-1901), but to greater effect. There is a base of finely dressed stone surmounted by a first floor of coursed rock-faced blocks. Above the massive combined sill and stringcourse with Sonck's characteristic rounded profile, the coursing changes to rock-faced squared rubble, then the whole is capped off by a frieze of pale gray ashlar echoing the stringcourse and entry surround below. As in Tampere Cathedral, Sonck reinterpreted Richardson's powerful stone buildings in the United States in Finnish terms, substituting primitive Gothic arches for Richardson's neo-Romanesque forms. But Sonck stripped away much of the decorative detail characteristic of the late 19th century, and what remains is far less literal in its historic reference, and based rather on abstractions of nature or communications technology.

Sonck's Telephone Company Building principally explores external form rather than internal volume. However, the tunnel-vaulted entry vestibule and the staircase, with its metal balustrade and newel-post lamp standards, are fine examples of Finnish National Romanticism in interior design. The building expresses through its powerful and original forms, probably better than any other Finnish building of the period, Finland's defiant, individualistic, emotive nationalism in the face of Russian oppression.

—RORY SPENCE

Telephone Company Building: Helsinki, Finland, 1903-05

TUBERCULOSIS SANATORIUM
Paimio, Finland

1929-33. Architect: Alvar Aalto (1898-1976).

Publications

AALTO, ALVAR: "Sanatorium i Pemar." *Arkitekten* 36 (1933): 79-91.

BUNNING, W. R.: "Paimio Sanatorium, an Analysis." *Architecture* 29 (1940): 20-25.

FLEIG, KARL (ed.): *Alvar Aalto*. London, 1975.

FRAMPTON, KENNETH, and FUTAGAWA, YUKIO: *Modern Architecture: 1920-1945*. New York, 1983.

HOFMANN, WERNER, and KULTERMANN, UDO: *Modern Architecture in Color*. New York, 1970.

NEUENSCHWANDER, C., and NEUENSCHWANDER, E.: *Alvar Aalto and Finnish Architecture*. London and New York, 1954.

PEARSON, DAVID: *Alvar Aalto and the International Style*. New York, 1978.

QUANTRILL, MALCOLM: *Alvar Aalto: A Critical Study*. London, 1983.

"Un Sanatorium pour touberculeux en Finlande." *Architecture française* 62 (1946).

Tuberculosis Sanatorium: Paimio, Finland, 1929-33

SCHILDT, GORAN (ed.): *Alvar Aalto.* Cambridge, Massachusetts, and London, 1978.
SHAND, P. MORTON: "Tuberculosis Sanatorium, Paimio, Finland." *Architectural Review* (September 1933): 85-90.

*

The Tuberculosis Sanatorium in Paimio, Finland, won in competition by Alvar Aalto in 1929 and completed in 1933, synthesized two potent modernist concerns. First, the design embraces modernism's utopian social commitment and deep confidence in rational design processes. Second, the building expresses, explicitly, the elemental organizational tactics of functionalist architecture and concomitant machine imagery. Metaphorically, if Le Corbusier's Villa Savoye was a "machine for living in," Aalto's Paimio Sanatorium was a machine for regaining health.

During the 1920s and 1930s, modern architects proclaimed the emergence of a spirited and vital new era: a healthier and more orderly age, brought forth by applying the lessons of rational technique to the disorder, chaos and squalor of the existing environment. Rooted in a strong sense of social commitment and reliance upon the effectiveness of serial production and industrial process as a design strategy, modern architects sought a better world. Paimio was both a symbol of the social role of the new architecture and a potent visual paradigm of the new world that modern architecture intended to bring into being. Sun. Light. Fresh air. The physical presence of these natural elements informed the basis of building design, and engendered the qualities of good health associated with modernist social commitment. Moreover, as a polemic, sun, light and fresh air were potent images of a new, healthier world. No other building type was as convincing a symbol of modern architecture as was a sanatorium. The actual medical treatment for tuberculosis—lots of sun, light and fresh air—provided a strong image base for the design and coincided with the health metaphor central to modernist polemics. With the completion of the Paimio Sanatorium, Aalto not only assumed a prominent place among the modern architects of the day, but indicated his understanding of modernism's social and compositional tenets.

Conceptually the Paimio Sanatorium, on first appearance, is a straightforward modernist composition: an articulated, but linked, set of relatively discrete functional elements, expressed in both plan and volumetrics. The primary functional elements include the patients' wing comprised of an elongated suite of rooms with open-air terraces, and the communal dining and assembly areas. These two pieces are linked by a seven-story volume, the entry and control area, housing the vertical circulation. A circulation passage connects to the service area—with its expressed water tank, smokestack and staircase—which in turn is joined to the garage. We have then, the rational and orderly composition of human activity rendered in a highly visible set of forms. Aalto employed the typical material vocabulary associated with achieving the machine aesthetic: concrete, stucco, steel and glass. Each volume incorporates differing glazing patterns and modes of expression of these materials to reinforce the elemental nature of the organization. The housing units for both the doctors and staff are separated from the main building, being located in the surrounding forest.

Despite its mechanistic appearance, Paimio went beyond the conventions of modernist elemental composition. Volumetrically, and in plan, its discrete elements are not unified geometrically or orthogonally, as in Walter Gropius' more regularized Bauhaus building (1926), but forms a more haptic pattern: a chain of architectural pieces in the landscape. Eschewing the modernist tendency to place buildings as isolated elements upon the landscape, Paimio appears as a dialogue between the internal world of space and activity and the exterior concerns of context and form. For instance, the patient wing and communal areas splay away from each other to form a cour d'honneur, allowing the entry court, with its undulating canopy, to gain more prominence. Though the white, rational image stands in contrast to the deep-green forest, the sanatorium is actually a sun trap. The patient wing, facing southeast, provides each patient with morning sunlight. The open-air terraces at the east end of the wing have been rotated further south to catch the sun. The dining and lounge area is oriented, with equal care, to receive the sun at different times during the day.

Paimio is not without precedent, for Aalto was traveling throughout Europe, meeting with avant-garde architects and artists, during the period of its design. Influences from the Dutch architect Johannes Duiker and his Zonnestraal Sanatorium (1926-28), the French architects André Lurçat and Le Corbusier, and Russian constructivism are evident in the work. Yet it was Aalto's ability to meld these into an independent synthesis that is extraordinary. Moreover, Aalto's entry for the earlier Kinkomaa Sanatorium competition (1927) used elemental organization, while his later competition entries for the Kälviä Sanatorium (1929) and the Zagreb Central Hospital (1931) demonstrated further refinement of ideas seen in Paimio. The Paimio Sanatorium stands as witness to Aalto's mastery of modernist design canons and social programs, and its functionalist expression placed his name with Gropius' and Le Corbusier's in the international scene of the day.

The detail level of development in Paimio is extraordinary. Attention was paid to windows, panel heating elements, washbasins and light fixtures. The suite of furnishings developed for Paimio—chairs and tables incorporating continuously curved, bent wood frames and backs, and made of a laminated, molded birch—represents the culmination of a series of furniture studies and wood experiments that began in 1927. In the Paimio furniture Aalto combined serial production with Finnish laminated-plywood technology. The free-form quality of these pieces informed his buildings immediately following the sanatorium, and signaled Aalto's movement away from functionalist tenets toward the more personal style that emerged in the late 1930s.

—WILLIAM C. MILLER

CIVIC CENTER
Seinäjoki, Finland

1959-66. Architect: Alvar Aalto (1898-1976).

Publications

FLEIG, KARL (ed.): *Alvar Aalto.* London, 1975.
SCHILDT, GÖRAN: *Alvar Aalto: The Mature Years.* New York, 1991.

*

In 1960, the year the parish of Seinäjoki achieved status as a township, Alvar Aalto's "Cross of the Plains" Church stood isolated in the landscape. In 1987, with the opening of the municipal theater, the Seinäjoki Civic Center stood complete,

Civic Center: Seimäjoki, Finland, 1959-66

surrounded by the town. Church and parish hall, town hall and government office building, library and theater form a complex embracing two courtyards; it is a complex that took more than 30 years to complete, and exemplifies the best in Aalto's later works. The church, won in competition in 1952, was completed in 1960, while the competition for the overall Civic Center plan was held in 1959. Between 1960 and 1966, the town hall, library and parish center were designed and constructed, yet the theater, designed 20 years earlier, was only recently completed, in 1987.

The Seinäjoki Civic Center illustrates classic Aaltoesque organizational strategies. He began by forming a place in the environment, a civilizing space, often a small plaza or courtyard, within the continuum of the larger landscape. In the Civic Center there are two such spaces, each with a distinctive quality: the terraced, grass court formed by the church and parish hall, and the paved square created by the town hall, theater and library. Once this place was defined, Aalto positioned uniquely configured forms and spaces within the composition. These elements were crafted from the ceremonial or honorific activities of the program. Church sanctuary, bell tower, town council chamber, library reading area and theater auditorium announce themselves volumetrically, receiving expression through exaggerated shaping and profiling, often sinuous and nonrectilinear in form. On the flat Ostrobothnian plain, these forms, which give architectural expression to our human institutions, gather in the surrounding landscape. Binding the courtyard or square and the uniquely formed space together was a neutral, common building order that housed the ordinary, utilitarian functions of the program. Low, horizontal building masses functioned as a datum, weaving together the specialized elements of the composition.

The "Cross of the Plains" Church is the Episcopal See of central and northern Finland, and assumes a cathedral-like stature when compared with Aalto's other churches. The 1952 design was based upon the unbuilt 1950 competition entry for the church and parish center in Lahti. Though the Lahti church was intended as a red brick building, many aspects of the two designs—plan, sectional properties, structural columns—are quite similar. The Seinäjoki church and parish hall plan is in the form of an L (the "head-and-tail" scheme typical of numerous Aalto buildings) enclosing a grassy, terraced square used for open-air worship and celebrations. Crenelated white walls, with slit clerestory windows, surround the sanctuary and appear

to hold in the bulging, black copper roof. The sanctuary, or head of the "head-and-tail" plan, is a specially shaped space in both plan and section. The church has a splayed plan, typical of Aalto church designs, responding to acoustic and processional concerns. The Y-shaped columns hold up the undulating ceiling canopy, giving the space its cathedral-like presence. The low, horizontal parish hall provides the common building order that completes the square, and absorbs the dominating church and bell tower (which assumes landmark status in the open plain).

Clad in blue tile, the Seinäjoki Town Hall stands in contrast to the other white buildings in the complex, yet it repeats the "head-and-tail" organization seen in the church complex. Again, the tail embraces a grass terrace, which is, in turn, adjacent to the second square of the complex: the paved plaza formed by town hall, library and theater. Rising above a columned loggia is the town council chamber, or the head in the composition. It is an undulating form that appears to erupt from the normative geometry of the building. The stair-stepped grass terrace leads from the plaza to the council chamber foyer, and reintroduces nature into this intended urban space. The skylit council chamber is a modest space, yet appropriate for democratic action. The long, two-story mass of the building houses various city agencies, as does the linear governmental office building that terminates the western end of the civic center ensemble.

The Seinäjoki Library, with its low, horizontal mass and fan-plan reading room, is the paradigmatic Aalto library. The honorific reading room, with its sunken reading well, modulated ceiling, expressive roof, clerestory lighting and undulating exterior wall, stands in contrast to the orthogonal order of the utilitarian support areas. Bringing the two seemingly disparate forms together is the control point or checkout counter. The libraries at Viipuri (1933-35), Rovaniemi (1965-68), the Technical Institute in Otaniemi (1964-69) and Mount Angel Benedictine College in Oregon (1965-70), and in the Wolfsburg (Germany) Cultural Center (1958-63) all exhibit the same organizational and volumetric sensibility. Aalto had no hesitation in reusing an organizational *parti*, in the same way he did not hesitate in reusing any element or detail. The planar mass of the support spaces forms an edge of the public plaza, while the undulating wall of the reading room acknowledges a more naturally landscaped area. Like all Aalto libraries, the sense of the reading room spaces is internal, with little focused contact to the outside.

Finished in 1987 by architect Elissa Mäkiniemi Aalto, Aalto's second wife, the Seinäjoki Theater completes the complex. Though its form and shape are in keeping with the original plan, the detail quality suffers in a manner similar to many of the works completed after Aalto's death. These later buildings lack the freshness and tension so often associated with his mature works. The Lahti Church and Jyväskylä Theater, like the Seinäjoki Theater, appear as tepid, stylized realizations of former themes and details.

The Seinäjoki Civic Center is Aalto's most complete and largest single complex. There is among the buildings a positive tension created by their placement, their forms, the colors and their spatial formation that bespeaks the genius of Alvar Aalto. It is as if the buildings and their elements are participating in a dialogue, gesturing and inflecting to each other. But as strong and positive as that dialogue is, it does not quite compensate for the weakness in the qualitative development of the two plazas so essential to the scheme.

—WILLIAM C. MILLER

TAMPERE CATHEDRAL
Tampere, Finland

1899-1907: Construction; **Architect:** Lars Sonck.

Publications

KIVINEN, PAULA: *Tampereen tuomiokirkko.* Porvoo, Finland, and Helsinki, 1986.

Lars Sonck's Tampere Cathedral (formerly St. John's Church), is one of the principal masterpieces of the Finnish National Romantic Movement, Finland's equivalent of European Jugendstil and art nouveau. The commission was won in competition (1899-1900), the usual way of selecting designs for public buildings in Finland at the time.

The overall conception of the building is based on European Gothic Revival prototypes, particularly attempts to adapt the medieval tradition to contemporary Protestant liturgy, which gradually led to more centralized plans that were conducive to communal worship and had already been much used in 18th-century Finnish churches. The almost square plan of the cathedral is close to that of St. James' Congregational Church, Newcastle-upon-Tyne, England (1883), with pews carefully arranged so that everyone could see the preacher. This church had been illustrated in K. E. O. Fritsch's *Der Kirchenbau des Protestantismus von der Reformation bis zur Gegenwart* (1893), a book almost certainly known by Sonck, who was familiar with current German ideas. The spatial arrangement of St. James', however, is still directional, whereas Sonck's spatial conception seems to derive from Johannes Otzen's Gothic Revival work in Germany, which he had already drawn upon in his design for St. Michael's Church, Turku (1894-95). Otzen ingeniously used the star vault of the medieval cathedral crossing in some of his churches, to create a more-centralized spatial form. Sonck adopted this idea at Tampere Cathedral, using a low springing point, which gives the interior a cavernous quality recalling the primitive cross

vaults of medieval Finnish churches. He emphasized the centralized feeling by enclosing the space with the U-shaped balcony fronts supported on very low sweeping arches.

Externally, the cathedral is clad in rock-faced, squared granite rubble. This technique was first used in Finland by Herman Gesellius, Armas Lindgren and Eliel Saarinen on their Pohjola Insurance Company Building, Helsinki (1899-1901) which drew on the architecture of Henry Hobson Richardson, already very influential in Sweden. Finland, however, more than Sweden, specifically took up the rugged primitivism of some of Richardson's buildings. Finnish architects reveled in Richardson's rock-faced stonework, which was very appropriate for the abundant hard Finnish granite. Furthermore, its masculine character seemed to express the celebrated Finnish fortitude (*sisu*) and, even more specifically, their courageous resistance against Russian political oppression, a major issue at that time in Finland, which was still a grand duchy of Russia. Sonck took this Richardsonian primitivism even further than Gesellius, Lindgren, and Saarinen and used undressed boulders for the perimeter walls and gateway to the cathedral, recalling Richardson's Ames Gate Lodge (1880-81), but undoubtedly also inspired by the crude stone walls surrounding many of the Finnish medieval churchyards, later to be an inspiration for Alvar Aalto at the Villa Mairea (1937-39). Although the cathedral remained in the Gothic Revival tradition, Sonck removed most of the conventional medieval details in favour of a new primitivism, which can also be seen in other work of the period, such as the churches of W. R. Lethaby, E. S. Prior and Randall Wells in England. The elegant medieval window tracery became simple grids of mullions and transoms. The subtle form of the Gothic arch became more angular, with a low springing point, again recalling unsophisticated Finnish medieval forms, and some balcony windows even developed a flat top. The main spire, with its little spirelets at each corner, was adapted more directly from the similar but squatter spire on Sonck's local church in Finström, on Åland Island, while earlier designs exhibited the characteristic gable decoration found in many Finnish medieval churches.

Internally, the decorative detail, characteristically for the period, also ignored literal historical precedent in favor of contemporary symbolic images or designs based directly on nature. The interior was the result of the collaborative effort of several artists, creating a *Gesamtkunstwerk* that reflects the influence of the English Arts and Crafts ideal. Hugo Simberg's highly original symbolist frescoes and stained glass, the iconography of which is remarkably unconventional, are particularly impressive.

The siting of the cathedral was seen by Sonck as an integral part of the urban pattern. It was carefully arranged according to the principles that Sonck had learned from Camillo Sitte, whose *City Planning According to Artistic Principles* (1889) was introduced to him by his friend Bertel Jung in 1897. The tower and sacristy were aligned with two streets to close the vistas on approaching the building, while the west front is seen at an angle from a third street which is at 45 degrees to the gridiron plan of the neighborhood. Smaller buildings were planned by Sonck around the church to form a varied enclosure of public space, but sadly were never carried out, as was the case with his earlier church of St. Michael, Turku.

As in Sonck's other masterpiece of National Romanticism, the Helsinki Telephone Company Building, the exterior of Tampere Cathedral is highly idiosyncratic and intuitive. At the time, it was claimed that the composition of the new Finnish architecture should develop from the inside out, but this is only partially the case at Tampere. Sonck apparently went out of his way to model the exterior independently from the principal internal volume. One would never guess from the external form

Tampere Cathedral (formerly St. John's Church): Tampere, Finland, 1899-1907

that the church has a basically square plan with a largely central-ized spatial arrangement. The windows and roofs to the north and south balconies bear little relationship to the internal arrangement or to one another, and there is no clear indication, on the exterior, of the star-vaulted central space. The forms were manipulated to achieve picturesque compositional ends, largely independent of internal spatial design. But the building demonstrates Sonck's sure sense of compositional balance, his sensitive feeling for the contrast of plain walls with restricted areas of decoration and his skillful, seductive juxtaposition of rough and smooth-textured surfaces. Inside and out, Sonck successfully fused a range of overseas influences onto ideas drawn from the indigenous Finnish medieval tradition, to create a brooding, cavernous building of great primitive power.

—RORY SPENCE

Kaleva Church

KALEVA CHURCH
Tampere, Finland

1966: Construction completed; **Architects:** Reima Pietilä and Raili Paatelainen.

Publications

BROCHMANN, ODD: "Kaleva Kirken i Tammerfors." *Arkitektur* 12, 2 (April 1968): 94-100.
"Church at Tampere, Finland." *Progressive Architecture* (December 1961).
"Dipoli and Kaleva Church." *Domus* (December 1964).

*

Public endowment of the Lutheran-Evangelical Church in Finland, through tax revenues from the earnings of church members, greatly helped church building in that country in the period since 1950. This practice led to a number of competitions for parish churches, some of which were won by Alvar Aalto. If Aalto was the architect with the most commissions, many of which are proof of his ingenuity, his energies were mostly directed, after completion of the churches in Imatra (1958) and Seinäjoki (1960), to the residential and civic buildings that became his chosen genre in the 1960s. It is against this background of a church architecture fully adapted to Aalto's free plan forms that we view the emergence of a new talent in church design in Finland at that time: the architect couple Reima Pietilä and Raili Paatelainen.

Their entry with the cryptic pseudonym "Slacken the Rumpstrap Meridian" won first prize in the 1959 architectural competition for a church for Finland's second largest city, Tampere. The environs of the site sloped downhill, with a grassy area to front and rear, and six-to-ten-story apartment blocks on each side. Town planners had reserved the crown of the hill for the new edifice. The competition brief mentioned the ambitious aim of attracting a flock of 30,000 souls. The church was finished in 1966.

One nears the church after crossing under a railroad bridge, reaching a point where the building reveals itself. The visitor is immediately struck by the majesty of the vista. Rising into the clear blue sky of a winter's day, the uneven roofline of the church forms a riveting image. Interest is aroused by the concave

external walls, the squat, cruciform belfry, the vertical ribbon windows set in the spaces between the wall elements. Imperceptibly, one is beckoned by the enveloping reach of the entrance wall. Inside, the soaring perimeter wall sections achieve a striking effect. Indirect light from narrow vertical windows bathes the convex walls, softening their bulk. The *Broken Reed* sculpture in polished pine is outlined eyecatchingly against the clear window behind the altar. It is a carefully proportioned abstract study used by Pietilä to rouse the primitive religious instinct of Finns and Lapps. The unadorned crucifix also of pine stands near the symbolic sculpture as an echo of the newer Christian message. In keeping with Lutheran tradition, no ornamentation is to be found in the church other than the features mentioned above.

Left of the altar stands the concrete pulpit with its acoustic panel of the same material; to the right is the raked choir dais, above which the wood-encased organ pipes are set. The beautifully profiled seats are of pine. They are separated by a wide aisle, whose length is stretched by a barely perceptible incline toward the altar. The floor is faced with a sand-colored burnt tile. The prestressed roof members are faced with rock-wool-filled steel channel sections. Single-casement, double-glazed windows open inward for cleaning. The church nave seats 1,050 people; the choir holds 80. A mortuary chapel, sacristy, parish meeting rooms, choir practice room, lobby with coatracks, reception areas and kitchen are situated on the same level. On the lower level is a crypt chapel, a kindergarten, a caretaker's apartment, plant rooms and workshops.

The architects conceived the form of Kaleva Church by working on models before any drawing was done. They aimed to convey the exalted spirit of medieval cathedrals. One early scheme had the building 10 meters taller than it was afterward built. When the right model was agreed upon, drawings were

Kaleva Church: Tampere, Finland, 1966

made of the "plan-wall" shapes at a scale of 1:10, with individual window and cladding details. The shapes were used to fix the dimensions of the load-bearing structure and were related to fixed points on site. Working drawings were then produced by mechanical reduction of the 1:10 "plan-wall" drawings.

The architects had intended the external wall surfaces to be clad with slipformed, large-format concrete panels and the internal walls finished in acoustic brick, but changes were forced on them. Pietilä thought that brick facades produced incorrect jointing proportions, and weakened the sculptural form of the whole (recounted to Malcolm Quantrill in *Reima Pietilä, Architecture Context and Modernism*).

The preoccupation with form that was central to the development of the design is a direct consequence of the architects' earlier investigation of the influence of form on design exemplified in the Brussels Pavilion (1958). Pietilä acknowledged a debt in that instance to the theories of Aulis Blomstedt, but in the Kaleva Church the confines of his teacher's strictly modular solutions have yielded to a sculpted handling of forms rather than their simple mathematical juxtaposition. Instead of an arid theory for which the building is an apology, there is a vibrant solution that celebrates the spirit behind the theory. Here is a voice exulting in a spatial harmony for which there is no strict precedent in Finnish church architecture.

—DESMOND O'ROURKE

FRANCE

CATHEDRAL
Amiens, France

1220-88: Church rebuilt after fire of 1218; **Architects:** Robert de Luzarches, Thomas de Cormont, Renaud de Cormont, completed by William Macon. **1237-47:** Nave vaults completed. **1258:** Woodwork in abbis destroyed by fire. **1269:** Sanctuary completed. **1288:** Details of the church completed; **Architects:** Geoffrey Evard and Bernard Evard. **14th century:** Entrance towers, balustrades of the sanctuary and nave completed. **Ca. 1400:** Rose windows installed. **1508:** Sculptures added; **Sculptors:** Arnold Boulin, Master carver of Amiens, Alexander Huet, Antoine Avernier. **1527:** Central tower destroyed by fire. **1529:** New steeple begun; **Carpenters:** Louis Gordon, Simon Paneau.

Publications

BARNES, CARL F., JR.: ''Cross-Media Design Motifs in XIIIth-Century France: Architectural Motifs in the Psalter and Hours of Yolande de Soissons and in the Cathedral of Notre-Dame at Amiens.'' *Gesta* 17, 2 (1978): 37-40.

DURAND, G.: *Monographie de l'église Notre Dame, cathédrale d'Amiens.* 3 vols. Amiens/Paris, 1901-03.

ERLANDE-BRANDENBURG, A.: ''La façade de la cathédrale d'Amiens.'' *Bulletin Monumental* 135 (1977): 253-293, esp. 262.

FOUCART-BORVILLE: ''Les projects de Charles de Wailly par la Gloire de la cathèdrale d'Amiens et de Victor Louis pour le maître-antel de la cathédrale de Noyen.'' *Bulletin de la société de l'histoire de l'art français* (1974): 131-144.

GOULD, K.: ''Illumination and Sculpture in Thirteenth-Century Amiens: The Invention of the Body of S. Firmin in the Psalter and Hours of Yolande de Soissons.'' *Art Bulletin* 59 (1977): 161-166.

JANTZEN, HANS: *High Gothic: The Classic Cathedrals of Chartres, Reims and Amiens.* Princeton, New Jersey, 1984.

*

In few buildings is the initial response to their achievement determined quite so much by the direction of approach and entry as is the case with Amiens Cathedral. From the south the impression is of height, reinforced by the cramped surroundings and the flèche, soaring as high as Salisbury Cathedral's spire. To enter via the south transept door is to move through an exquisite simplicity, dominated by the late-13th-century Golden Virgin, into direct confrontation with the most successful expression of the High Gothic period in the Île-de-France. It seems a continuation of the heavenly unity at which the portal has hinted. The whole emphasis is on apparently effortless verticals, and there is an immediate sense of balanced satisfaction. But it is more revealing to enter through the crowded west front, with all its clutter of images and the disorder imposed on it by later additions, to sense the sharp contrast between exterior and interior, to experience the tensions between visions of heaven, patterns of a divinely ordered universe, and the disorderly vitality of medieval daily life which High Gothic only tenuously held together.

To move eastward in this building is very appropriate—it is one of the few cathedrals built that way, largely because of local problems with demolishing extant buildings on the chosen site. As one does so, one receives a clear impression of the pride of the men who paid for it, the wealthy Amiens burghers wishing to rival Paris and Chartres, who wanted an edifice big enough to hold their town's entire population on great days. They brought in a Paris master, Robert de Luzarches, and gave him enough backing to allow the building's completion in 40 years. Amiens Cathedral rivals Salisbury, also begun in 1220, in that respect. However, it also demonstrates how far French style had evolved in comparison to that which the English were by then adopting.

The west front is an impressive failure. Robert's base, an exciting but crowded mix of workaday scenes, the zodiac, and serried ranks of angels, saints and apostles, is dominated by the three great statues which crown the portals named after them: St. Firmin, the local patron; the Virgin Mary; and, in the center, clashing with the awesome portrayal of the Last Judgement which surrounds it, one of the finest portrayals of a benevolent Christ the Middle Ages produced. But the ensemble is too heavy for the lightness of the structure it hides, and peters out just over halfway up the facade. Wedged above it, and spoiled by it, is an exquisite Flamboyant rose window whose tracery can really be tasted only from inside. Above all rise the squashed and ill-balanced towers added some two centuries later.

To pass under these towers is to enter a superb evocation of the structure of heaven. It is the lightest of the big Gothic churches of the Paris region, apparently dispensing with the heavy walls of Chartres or Reims. The strong buttressing is concealed in the stepped walls that provide the outer arcade chapels of the nave aisles. These stepped walls allow a control of the verticals in matching bays, whose formal unity hides the piecemeal nature of some of their details. Further on, beyond the transepts, that unevenness gives way to a complete standardization of masonry pieces, which represents the final emergence of controlled masonic patternmaking in the medieval building process. Henceforth, the blocks could be prefabricated from a single standard model, reducing costs.

Shorn by subsequent warfare of most of its medieval glass, Amiens gives the student a much more readily available sense of its structure than is usually the case. All three levels of each nave bay are balanced, and the stringcourse of the main arcade comes almost halfway up to the vault line. That course is remarkable in itself because its flowing line of leaves encircling the church represents almost the only naturalistic treatment of foliage in the building before the Flamboyant additions; the column capitals are much more solidly formal. The arcade arches are tightly defined without being squashed, and this is repeated in the choir until they give way to the much sharper points of the hemicycle. Because of the lightness of the overall structure, there is little sense of the compression found in the apses of Amiens' neighbors. In most of the triforium Robert inserted double ''window'' arcades with three ''lights''—those in the nave open only onto the darkness of the galleries. In the transepts, choir and hemicycle, however, they break amazingly with both the expectations the eye has so far built up and with Chartres, Paris and the others—the tracery opens onto a glazed exterior. Altar and choir are flooded with light, so that the iconography of the apse as pointing to heaven is reinforced—it offered a model for Tours and an entry point for Rayonnant

Amiens Cathedral, west facade: Amiens, France, 1220-88

Amiens Cathedral, transept

The buttresses continue around the apse, leaping across the double semicircle of ambulatory and radiating chapels. The chevet is much less fussy than the west end—the structure is left to speak for itself. Unlike the main facade with its statement of Aquinas' *Summa* in stone, the mystery is now contained within; the way to heaven from there was on the high altar. Inside, the ambulatory allowed for processions past the six radiating chapels provided for the daily masses. It leads to a central gem, the narrowly extended eastern Lady Chapel. This may be the model for the Sainte-Chapelle in Paris, but it is only partly developed. It is too hemmed in by its neighbors in the chevet for the free flow of light in the rest of the cathedral to carry on there.

The core of the building, the high altar, was overwhelmed by a Baroque sunburst, as in so many cases after Giovanni Lorenzo Bernini encased St. Peter's Chair in Rome. The sunburst is made all the louder as it contrasts with a fine iron screen between the narrow pillars of the apse. This is at odds with the Gothic lightness of its casing, which in turn contrasts even more sharply with the mass of ornate woodwork placed in the choir when the stalls were rebuilt early in the 16th century. The 3,650 carved figures vie for attention; they are exquisite representations of heavenly scenes made up from vignettes of Picardian life. On the outside they are matched by the polychrome stone carvings of the saintly virtues of Firmin and John the Baptist. It would have been a major achievement for any Amiens clergyman to focus on his duties without being distracted by the details of his surroundings. The superabundance of detail clashes remarkably with the simple quadripartite stone vault which soars over the whole cathedral, crossing and hemicycle excepted. At 43 meters it was the highest then built. In more senses than one, the burghers of Amiens could look down on those of Paris and Chartres. The contrast between vault and stalls, both in themselves delicate, replays the tension in the

elsewhere. The "scrubbed" look of the church now (there are a few scattered hints of the initial wall paintings) allows an interplay between light and lightness that Robert de Luzarches must have seen differently. Yet in the clerestory he allowed fully for the brightness of transmitted rather than reflected light. The nave windows are fourlight, those of the choir sixpart, as if the masons in charge had found confidence in the earlier works and made even greater innovations. On the exterior this break, which is quite gentle, is marked systematically by the provision of pointed gables rising above the roof balustrade of the eastern arm, each containing a blank trefoil in its spandrel.

The soaring lightness is nowhere more apparent than in the corner pillars of the crossing—they are so restrained that it requires an effort to notice them. The lack of a central tower, common in these northern French cathedrals, accounts for the lightness of the pillars, and also facilitates the flow of the arcades around the transept corners with little of the disruption that is the English norm. It is closer to the Romanesque right angle than to the breaks of insular Gothic. The lightness is reinforced by the end glazing of the transepts, where the triforium windows are carried up by light bar tracery into vibrant rose windows dating to around 1400. Both from the outside and inside, these are much happier ventures than the one on the west front. On the inside, that one peeps over the organ placed several hundred years later in its favorite French position. By contrast, the transept rose windows flow out of their base structures: the radiant-wheel geometry has moved away from the heavy spokes we find in Chartres and become spaces for light to stream through. They give no clue to their essential place in the structure, which is actually sustained by an increased external sophistication in flying buttresses. The buttresses proclaim their debt to earlier models, but hide their heavier parts, which are concealed in the roof spaces.

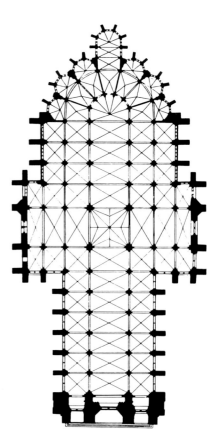

carvings on the west front. To enter the cathedral was to have a vision of the city of heaven, but its structure made the point that the "New Jerusalem" was likely to be spelled "Amiens."

—JOHN LOWERSON

CHÂTEAU
Anet, France

1547-52. Architect: Philibert de l'Orme (ca. 1512-70). **1678-1712:** West wing remodeled, including addition of suspended stone stairway. **1789:** Destroyed during the French Revolution, but monumental entrance gate (at the École des Beaux-Arts, Paris) and the chapel survived.

Publications

BARDON, FRANÇOISE: *Diane de Poiters et le mythe de Diane.* Paris, 1963.

BLUNT, ANTHONY: *Philibert de l'Orme.* London, 1958.

CHASTEL, ANDRÉ: "Escalier du château d'Anet." *Bulletin de la société des antiquaires de France* (1956): 73-74.

GRASHOFF, EHLER W.: "Die Schlosskapelle von Anet und die deutsche Barockarchitektur." *Zeitschrift des deutschen Vereins für Kunstwissenschaft,* 7, 2-3 (1940): 123-130.

HÉLIOT, PIERRE: "Documents inédits sur le château d'Anet." *Mémoires de la société nationale des antiquaires de France,* Series 9, 2 (1951): 257-269.

HOFFMAN, VOLKER: "Philibert de l'Orme und das Schloss Anet." *Architectura,* 2 (1973): 131-152.

MAYER, MARCEL: *Le château d'Anet.* Paris, 1953.

PFNOR, RODOLPHE: *Monographie du château d'Anet, construit par Philibert de l'Orme.* Paris, 1867.

PORCHER, JEAN: "Les premières constructions de Philibert de l'Orme au Château d'Anet." *Bulletin de la société de l'histoire de l'art français* (1939): 6-17.

*

In constructing the Château d'Anet, Philibert de l'Orme demonstrated an extraordinary range of talents: the incorporation of a preexisting structure into a new plan; a technical virtuosity in stone and wood; the melding of French and Italian elements; a masterful handling of geometric forms; the collage of rich materials polychromy and sculpture; and a vigorous iconographic program developed throughout the château and its garden. The result was a building which precisely expressed the desires of the patron, Diane de Poitiers.

On the death of the Grand Sénéchal of Normandy Louis de Brézé in 1531, his wife Diane de Poitiers inherited his late-15th-century château at Anet. About 15 years later she rebuilt the château, located west of Paris in lower Normandy, as a pious memorial to him as well as a token of her affection for the monarch Henri II. The first architect, whose identity remains unknown, began construction on a new *corps de logis.* He seems to have been incompetent, and in 1547, Henri offered

Château: Anet, France, 1547-52

the services of his architect, Philibert de l'Orme. De l'Orme completed the *corps de logis* the following year, and most of the rest of the château by 1552.

The plan of Anet, published in the second volume of Jacques Androuet de Cerceau's *Les plus excellents bastiments de France* (1579), departed from de l'Orme's first château at Saint-Maur (1541-44). Though both shared the basic layout of a rectangular court formed by a U-shaped *corps de logis* with wings and closed by a lower entrance block, Anet comprised a total of three courts: a central *cour d'honneur* with subsidiary courts on each side. The triple-court solution masked the old Château des Brézé from the new *cour d'honneur* by placing the former in a less conspicuous court to the east. To unify the ensemble, de l'Orme invented a long, moated wall extending the entire width of the château. Fortifications by Antonio da Sangallo the Younger or Baldassare Peruzzi may have influenced the trapezium bastions. In the center de l'Orme placed a pyramidal entrance gate flanked by terraces. The rear of the *corps de logis* overlooked a large garden surrounded on three sides by a loggia.

De l'Orme buttressed the weak foundation of the *corps de logis* with a cryptoporticus, open on the north side to the garden. The interpenetrating spaces of this foundation passage have been compared with those of the gallery at Raphael's Villa Madama in Rome, but cast at Anet in the complex stonework of the French master mason's workshop. De l'Orme also demonstrated his knowledge of stonecutting in the vaults of the entrance gate, the startling dome of the chapel, and the squinch added in 1552 on the garden facade of the *corps de logis* to support a new cabinet for the king's apartment. For the roofs of some of the dependencies (including perhaps a bathhouse at the lower end of the garden), he implemented his framing method which substituted overlapping short pieces of wood pegged together for long timbers.

An innovative staircase of twin curving flights began at a terrace above the cryptoporticus and led down to a landing. From there, two short flights headed either to the garden or to the cryptoporticus. De l'Orme had developed this kind of stair for Saint-Maur and employed it again at Fontainebleau. At one end of the cryptoporticus de l'Orme restated Donato Bramante's convex-concave stairs at the Vatican Belvedere in miniature (he placed two others on each side of the entrance gate).

De l'Orme prominently displayed traditional French elements such as bartizans, high-pitched roofs, red brick walls trimmed in stone, and twin chapel towers. For the main entry to the court facade of the *corps de logis,* he constructed a tower or *avant corps,* a common element of French châteaux by that time. The architect used paired columns, perhaps in response to those Pierre Lescot and Jean Goujon were then using at the Louvre, begun in 1546. De l'Orme's innovation, however, was to stack the Doric, Ionic and Corinthian orders in imitation of the Colosseum. Funereal symbolism was an integral part of the iconography of Anet. Sarcophagi inspired chimneys, fountains and other ornament. The black and white marble pavement of the chapel recalled the colors of Diane's widow's weeds, which she always wore. About 1540, Diane commissioned a wall tomb for her husband in the Cathedral of Rouen and inscribed it with a dedication recalling the piety of Queen Artemisia, who built the famous mausoleum for her husband Mausolus at Halicarnassus. The *avant corps* included its own pious dedication to the patron's late husband. De l'Orme may have deliberately imitated the Brézé tomb in his design for the *avant corps;* aside from the dedications, both have paired columns, an effigy of Louis de Brézé, and heraldic crests.

If the *avant corps* was erected as a memorial to Diane's late husband, the entrance wing was a monument to her present relationship with the king. For the entrance gate de l'Orme used a triumphal-arch motif with three openings and articulated with a Doric order. A knowledge of Michelangelo's work for the Medici at San Lorenzo in Florence seems apparent in the tapering pilasters or the detailing of the sarcophagus-like chimneys. The barrel-vaulted passage recalls Sangallo's Palazzo Farnese. As in the *avant corps,* de l'Orme applied a subtle polychromy of black and pink marble ornament against tan Vernon stone, with the additional accent here of bronze ornament. In the tympanum above the center portal, he placed a bronze lunette cast in 1543 by Benevenuto Cellini for the Château de Fontainebleau at the request of François I. The plaque depicted the nymph linked with that château and a stag representing the king. It was never installed in its intended location, the Porte Dorée. Set within its new frame at Anet, it tells a story which differs from the original program. Everywhere—from the exterior balustrades and the brick and stone pavement surrounding the garden, to the interior woodwork, grisaille windows and magnificent tapestries—appear the entwined monograms of Diane de Poitiers and Henri II and the devices they had adopted from the goddess Diana: the crescent moon, bow and quiver. Ovid recounts how the goddess Diana transformed Acteon into a stag for trespassing in her forest sanctuary while she took her bath. Groves of trees on either side of the gate recreate the forest scene and drain spouts in the form of urns on the gate itself deliver the water for Diana's bath. According to Ovid, Acteon was subsequently ripped apart by Diana's dogs. De l'Orme erected a remarkable automaton on top of the entrance gate showing a stag held at bay by hounds. The stag rang the hours with its hoof while the dogs barked and astronomical instruments traced the movement of the heavenly bodies to which Diane and Henri II were compared. The conclusion to Ovid's tale is altered in the lunette and a fountain in the west court; both depict the stag safely under Diana's protection. At Anet the king Henri II submitted to Diane de Poitiers.

The chapel is de l'Orme's most celebrated creation. It extended into the side court from the east wing of the château, which housed a gallery. Following the pattern of royal chapels, the chapel had a tribune above the entrance from which Diane de Poitiers could observe the Mass. The inventive centralized plan, perhaps inspired by a portion of the Baths of Diocletian, combines two concentric circles, a square and Greek cross. The elevation may quote either Antonio da Sangallo the Younger's Medici Chapel at Montecassino or the Pellegrini Chapel at Verona by Michele Sanmicheli. Pilasters with ingenious laurel capitals articulate the interior. The spiral ribs and lozenge coffers of the stone vault follow those in the apsidal vault of the Temple of Venus and Rome. The marble pavement, composed of curving black bands against a white background, reflects the three-dimensional ribs of the dome. It gives the extraordinary impression of a spiraling vortex of infinitely expanding space below and above.

The impact of Anet extended beyond the borders of France. A version of the *avant corps* appears on the facade of Hatfield House (1611) in England. It is intriguing to believe Andrea Palladio had seen a sketch or engraving of the chapel at Anet before designing the chapel at Maser (1579-80). In France, Salomon de Brosse adapted the *avant corps* for the facade of Saint-Gervais (1616) in Paris. François Mansart understood the implications of the *avant corps* best when inventing the taut elevations of Blois (1635-38) and Maisons (1642-46). His centralized plan for Ste. Marie de la Visitation (1632-33) in Paris has its roots in de l'Orme's chapel at Anet.

Two modifications have contributed to the importance of Anet. One is the addition of the remarkable suspended stone stairway built by Claude Desgots when the west wing was remodeled between 1678 and 1712. The second was the destruction of much of the château after the French Revolution. Alexandre Lenoir moved the *avant corps* and the Fountain of Diana to his Musée des Monuments Français in 1802. When the museum was rebuilt as the École des Beaux-Arts by Félix-Jacques Duban between 1832 and 1840, the *avant corps* remained as a monument to one of the definitive creations of the French Renaissance.

—MAURICE S. LUKER III

BEAUVAIS CATHEDRAL
Beauvais, France

1225: Cathedral rebuilt after fire destroyed original. **1250:** Triforium begun. **1272:** Vaults completed. **1284:** Vaults, southwest corner, collapsed. **1284-1334:** Vaults and buttresses, southwest corner, rebuilt. **1337:** Choir rebuilt. **1497:** Work on transepts resumed. **1537:** North transept completed. **1548:** South transept and south front completed; **Architects:** Martin Chambiges (1497-1532), Pierre Chambiges (1532-48). **1573:** Spire fell, and replaced by wooden belfry.

Publications

BORNET, A.: *Les enfants du choeur de la cathédrale de Beauvais aux XIV, XV et XVI siècles.* 1930.

BRANNER, ROBERT: "Le maître de la cathédrale de Beauvais." *Art de France* 2 (1962): 78-92.
DESJARDINS, G.: *Histoire de la cathédrale de Beauvais.* 1865.
LEBLOND, V.: *La cathédrale de Beauvais.* 1926.
McGEE, J. DAVID: "The 'Early Vaults' of Saint-Etienne at Beauvais." *Journal of the Society of Architectural Historians* 45 (March 1986): 20-31.
MURRAY, STEPHEN: *Beauvais Cathedral: Architecture of Transcendence.* Princeton, New Jersey, 1989.
MURRAY, STEPHEN: "The Choir of Saint-Etiènne at Beauvais." *Journal of the Society of Architectural Historians* 36 (1977): 121-139.
WOLFE, M., and MARKS, R.: "The Collapse of the Vaults of Beauvais Cathedral in 1284." *Speculum* (July 1976).

*

One of the distinguishing marks of the French Gothic was the quest for height. When the builders of Salisbury Cathedral were contenting themselves with a vault 78 feet high, the vaults of Bourges and Reims were reaching 123 and 124 feet. In 1220 Amiens added another 14 feet, making a total of 138 feet and ten inches. Finally, in 1225, the builders of Beauvais attained the almost unbelievable altitude of 157 feet and six inches.

The great vaults of Beauvais stood until 1284, when the southwest corner collapsed. It was not until 1337 that the choir was rebuilt, and only in the 16th century were the transepts added. They were made to carry a spire as tall as that of Salisbury, but springing from a building already a hundred feet higher. In 1573 the spire fell, and the builders contented themselves with the truncated edifice we see today.

Beauvais Cathedral: Beauvais, France, 1225-1573

The choir remains one of the most astonishing achievements of the 13th century. On all sides the architecture is strongly vertical. The clustered columns shoot straight into the air for 130 feet before they splay out into the slender ribs of the sexpartite vault. The narrow arches of the great arcade are so tall that the facades of the aisles behind them are three stories high, with their own arcade, their own triforium and their own clerestory. Above them the theme is taken up again. The slender colonettes that subdivide the arcading of the triforium rise without interruption to become the center mullions between the slim lancets of the clerestory, continuing up until they lose themselves in the fretted tracery of the topmost arch. The vertical shafts always pass in front of the horizontal divisions, so that their lines are unbroken and the eye is guided upward and ever further upward with the mounting crescendo of a musical sequence. ''In the movement, unanimous and lofty, of all these stones toward the heavens,'' wrote the comte de Montalembert, ''is there not a sort of renouncing of subjection to the material and a flight of the liberated soul toward its maker?''

The design of the choir is based upon that of Amiens, with some apparent borrowings from Bourges and Le Mans—particularly in the three-story facades of the side aisles and ambulatory. Originally there were only three bays to the choir and the vaults were quadripartite, but in 1284 a portion of those vaults collapsed. The technical reasons for this collapse have been set forth in detail by Stephen Murray, who locates the point of weakness at the angle between the south transept and the choir.

We may infer something of what were considered to be the weaknesses at the time from the reinforcements that the architect of the reconstruction has provided.

First and most obviously, he inserted intermediary columns into the great arcade, dividing each of the arches into two. This created an alternation known as *pile forte-pile faible,* a

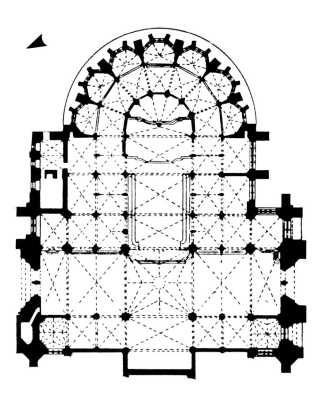

Beauvais Cathedral, nave looking towards east

disposition that almost dictates the use of sexpartite vaulting, which looks archaic in a mid-13th-century cathedral.

The plan reveals also that towers were intended over the two eastern bays of the transepts. The massive piers, which are not repeated on the western side of the transepts, are proof enough, but further evidence can be found on the flying buttress projecting eastward from the south transept. It carries a fluting on its southern face that has no relationship to the surrounding architecture, but would have been part of the decoration of the tower.

In 1497, under Bishop Villiers de l'Isle Adam, it was decided to construct transepts. Martin Chambiges, who did similar work at Senlis and Sens, was put in charge. Work began on the north front, where the presence of ermines, daisies, capital F's and salamanders bear witness to donations from Anne de Bretagne, Marguerite d'Angoulême and François I. On 28 October 1548 the completion of the south front was marked by the setting up of the figure of St. Peter over the gable. Martin Chambiges had died in 1532, but the work was carried on by his son Pierre, and the original design was respected and completed in every detail. These tall facades, with their stone facets almost obscured by the brittle incrustations of their finely chiseled ornament and their niches filled, according to the contemporary Hermant, ''with an infinite number of beautiful figures,'' formed a worthy appendage to the 13th-century choir—a triumph of the late Flamboyant Gothic.

The huge windows offered the greatest possible opportunity to the glaziers at exactly the right time, for during the early 16th century Beauvais became the center of a flourishing school of stained glass associated with the names of Engrand and Nicolas le Prince.

Two years before the completion of the transepts, in March 1546, the decision was made to crown the new building with a spire, and such a spire as the world had never seen. Its height from ground level was 461 feet. By the end of November 1566, the cross was positioned on top of the spire. By the end of the following summer the work was complete.

On 30 April 1573, Ascension Day, the Catholic population of Beauvais were all assembled in the cathedral ready to carry the relics in a procession through the town. As the last person passed out of the south doors, the spire fell. A contemporary witness named Louvet recorded that the fall of this "great mountain of stone caused the whole town to tremble." The cathedral itself disappeared in a cloud of dust that rose into the sky and hung like a pall over the stricken city.

The damage was in due course repaired, but the authorities were by then thoroughly discouraged. It was decided to replace the spire by a simple wooden belfry "fort petit."

—IAN DUNLOP

CHÂTEAU
Blois, France

1498-1638. 1498-1504: East wing built (incorporated 13th-century Salle des États); **Architects:** Colin Biart and Jacques Sourdeau. **1515-24:** François I wing built; **Architect:** Jacques Sourdeau. **1635-38:** Gaston d'Orléans wing built; **Architect:** François Mansart (1598-1666).

Publications

GANAY, E. DE: *Châteaux de France.* Paris, 1949.
GANAY, E. DE: *Châteaux et manoirs de France.* 11 vols. Paris, 1934-38.
GÉBELIN, F.: *Les châteaux de la Renaissance.* Paris, 1927.
LE SUEUR, F. and P.: *Le Château de Blois.* Paris, 1914.

*

If Blois is not the most beautiful château of the Loire, it can at least claim to be the most interesting: it is almost a history of architecture in stone. In the northeast corner the great Salle des États, in the typical form of a double nave divided by an arcade, dates from the 13th century; across the courtyard to the south are the remains of Charles d'Orléans' buildings with the Chapelle St. Calais; adjoining this and forming the eastern facade is Louis XII's wing, which contains the main entrance; on the north side of the courtyard are the elegant Renaissance facades of François I with their great external staircase; finally the western range, rebuilt by François Mansart for Gaston d'Orléans, the brother of Louis XIII, offers a superb example of French early-17th-century architecture.

Charles d'Orléans, prince and poet, grandson of Charles V and father of Louis XII, transformed the feudal fortress into a *maison de plaisance*. Various accounts, dating between 1446

Château, François I Wing: Blois, France, 1515-24

Château, facade des loges: 16th century

and 1457, provide glimpses of the construction. The appearance of the main block, destroyed by Mansart, is known only from the drawings of Jacques Androuet du Cerceau. They show an entirely domestic style of brick with stone dressings. Most of the ground floor was recessed behind an arcade or cloister.

Starting in 1498, Louis XII made his additions in a style that was similar but more ornate. The two balconied windows that overlook the forecourt, deeply recessed behind a lace-like canopy of stone, are disposed without regard for symmetry; otherwise the ornament is concentrated on the central feature, the entrance archway. Above this the statue of the king on horseback is housed in Gothic glory—but among the cusps and pinnacles can already be detected a rather clumsy attempt at Italian arabesque.

Apart from this there is a general atmosphere of quiet good taste built upon the balance between plain surfaces and fine carved enrichment. But the subject matter of the carvings is sometimes obscene. "Some of the figures which support the windows," wrote the 18th-century traveler Wraxall, "are of a nature so very indecent that it excites our surprise how a prince so virtuous as Louis XII could ever have permitted them to be placed in the most conspicuous part of a royal palace." The names of Colin Biart—who had worked at Amboise and Le Verger—and of Jacques Sourdeau—who was to do further work at Blois—are connected with this phase of the building.

Louis XII and his consort Anne de Bretagne occupied the first floor of the wing which they built. They had no son, but their son-in-law the duc d'Angoulême succeeded to the throne on 1 January 1515, with the title of François I. A part of the

dowry that came to him through Claude de France was the Château de Blois.

In June of the same year he set about rebuilding the north range of the courtyard, thus abolishing nearly all that remained of the original fortress. Jacques Sourdeau, by then qualified by the title "maître-maçon de l'oeuvre du chastel de Blois," seems to have been in charge.

The construction was clearly piecemeal and shows no evidence of any overall design. Both Le Sueur and Gebelin insist that this was the work of French craftsmen applying a Renaissance decor of features that had already appeared at Gaillon. At first the medieval outer wall, with its three towers overlooking the town, was retained but slightly embellished by the application of cornices and pilasters to the windows. The western half of the block was built first, the eastern half next and the great staircase added afterward. Finally, a further row of apartments was obtained by advancing the outer wall some seven meters toward the north, thus creating the "facade des loges," which seems to owe something to Bramante. The old curtain wall and its three towers then became an immensely thick partition within the double building. It was there, on 23 December 1588, that the duc de Guise was murdered in the Cabinet Vieux du Roi.

There was, strictly speaking, nothing new about the architectural ordonnance of the François Ier wing. It had appeared already at Gaillon in Normandy, begun in 1501 by Cardinal Georges d'Amboise; it had appeared nearer the Loire region at Champigny-sur-Veude, begun in 1507 by Louis de Bourbon-Montpensier, and wantonly destroyed by Richelieu. There is no reason to seek the hand of an Italian at Blois.

The great staircase, also reflecting earlier ones at Chateaudun, Chaumont and Gaillon, is a mixture of Gothic and Renaissance, of boldness of form and delicacy of ornament—as Balzac described it: "built by giants and decorated by midgets."

The *pierres d'attente* at the east end of François I's wing show that he intended further construction, but on 20 July 1524 Queen Claude died, and work was discontinued.

A century later, in 1635, Gaston d'Orléans commissioned François Mansart to design an entirely new château which, if it had been completed, would have ousted all the previous buildings. The design was dynamic; it would have looked rather like the palais de Luxembourg, lifted out of the flat parterres of its Parisian garden and set on the rocky outcrop of this once feudal foundation. It comprised a new entrance front, surmounted by a dome that gave it an almost ecclesiastical air; two long wings adorned with niches and coupled columns replacing the buildings of Charles d'Orléans and François I; and at the end of this classical perspective, the main block, behind a balustrade. This block was the only part to be built.

The doorway in the center of this facade opens onto the first floor of the great staircase, which, turning left, reaches a landing that marks the center of the obverse facade. The west front, having more space for its development, could be longer than that of the courtyard. Mansart cleverly disguised the difference of axis and the difference of floor level by his use of the staircase.

Gaston d'Orléans died in 1660 without having finished the rebuilding. From that time onward Blois was more or less abandoned. In 1788 Louis XVI decreed its demolition. Curiously enough it was the Revolution that saved the building. It was one of the first in France to be restored under the Commission des Monuments Historiques, by the architect Félix Duban.

—IAN DUNLOP

GRANDE THÉÂTRE
Bordeaux, France

1773-80: Construction; **Architect:** Victor Louis (1731-1800).

Publications

LOUIS, VICTOR: *La Salle de Spectacle de Bordeaux*. Paris, 1782.

MARIONNEAU, CHARLES: *Victor Louis, architecte du Théâtre de Bordeaux*. Bordeaux, 1881.

PRUDENT, HENRI, and GAUDET, PAUL: *Les Salles des Spectacles construites par Victor Louis à Bordeaux, au Palais Royal et à la place Louvois*. Paris, 1903.

RABREAU, DANIEL: "Le grand théâtre de Victor Louis: Des vérités, des impressions." In *Victor Louis et le théâtre:*

Grande Théâtre: Bordeaux, France, 1773-80

Scénographie, mise-en-scène et architecture théâtrale aux XVIIIe et XIXe siècles. Paris, 1982.

TIDWORTH, S.: *Theatres: An Illustrated History.* London, 1973.

*

The Grande Théâtre of Bordeaux, completed in 1780 and considered the first great modern theater, was the hallmark of theater design for more than a century. It was only the second freestanding theater built in France and is the masterpiece of architect Victor Louis.

The theater is an example of the neoclassical design movement that came about in reaction against the rather elaborate Rococo style in the late 18th century. It also is evidence of the increasingly important role played by the public theater in French social life.

Neoclassical architecture, influenced by ancient Rome, emphasizes simplicity and continuity of design, along with archaeological accuracy of detail. Key characteristics include cubic shapes, absence of pavilion roofs (or visible roofs at all), and porticoes with a straight entablature instead of a pediment. Architects who were early influences on the movement were Ange-Jacques Gabriel (1698-1782) and Jacques-Germain Soufflot (1713-80); Victor Louis belonged to the second generation of neoclassicists.

Built on an island site, the theater displays many of these key characteristics. It is a giant rectangle, 325 feet long and half as wide, built of stone. Without pediment, it is fronted by 12 huge Corinthian columns supporting an entablature. It is surrounded by arcades with piers decorated by pilasters.

Inside, Louis' design for the staircase and common areas gives theatergoers a spectacle before they enter the auditorium. His attention to these areas was new in theater design. The monumental staircase ascends to a landing and splits into two flights, rising to galleries with access to the upper portion of the auditorium and the small, oval concert hall above the auditorium. The staircase and the foyer area gave the fashionable citizens of Bordeaux a place to see and be seen; this was important because theater attendance was just at that time becoming available to all who could afford it, rather than being limited to scholarly societies. When Charles Garnier designed his Paris Opéra, built nearly 100 years later, he freely admitted that he copied his staircase hall design from the Grande Théâtre. The design also influenced the staircase of the Fitzwilliam Museum in Cambridge, designed by George Basevi, C. R. Cockerell and E. M. Barry.

The horseshoe-shaped auditorium actually occupies a rather small portion of the building. It has 10 giant columns, four of which support the shallow dome of the ceiling, and there are balconies and three tiers of box seats. On stage, the width of the proscenium is 39 feet. Louis developed the ancillary rooms of the theater far beyond those of France's first freestanding theater, designed by Soufflot at Lyons in the 1750s.

Paris, and later England, followed Bordeaux in theater improvements. Two years after the Bordeaux theater's opening, the Comédie Française (later Odéon) opened in Paris. Its architects, M.-J. Peyre and Charles de Wailly, designed a somewhat different seating arrangement than Louis had for the Bordeaux theater and added columns on each side of the proscenium, but their theater also used many of the same concepts, including the staircase and foyer design. Their theater and Louis' set the standard for theater design for more than 100 years. The Grande Théâtre, however, was considered the most beautiful and the best example of theater architecture.

—TRUDY RING

HOUSE OF JACQUES COEUR
Bourges, France

1443-53: Construction. **1682-1858:** Several alterations during this period, when it was the city hall for Bourges.

Publications

CALLÈDE, B.: "Etude des peintures murales dans la chapelle de l'Hôtel Jacques Coeur à Bourges." *Studies in Conservation* 20, No. 4 (1975): 195-200.

FAVIÈRE, JEAN: *Le palais de Jacques Coeur.* Bourges, 1972.

"French Medieval." *Country Life* 25 (17 and 24 April 1909): 558-567; 594-602.

GAUCHERY, PAUL: *Le palais Jacques-Coeur.* Bourges, 1949.

MERINDOL, C. DE: "L'emblématique des demoures et chapelles de Jacques Coeur." *Histoire médiévale* New series 11 (1985): 153-178.

MOLLAT, MICHEL: *Jacques Coeur, ou, L'esprit d'entreprise au XVe siècle.* Aubier, France, 1988.

VANSITTART, S. N.: "The Hôtels Jacques Coeur, Lallemand, Cujas and the Palace of Duke Jean in Bourges." *Architectural Review* 8 (July-December 1900): 55-64.

VITRY, PAUL: *Hôtels et maisons de la renaissance française.* 3 vols. Paris, 1910.

*

The House of Jacques Coeur in Bourges is the most important urban residence of the mid-15th century surviving in France, and one of the most sumptuous and complete surviving in all of Europe. It was built between 1443 and 1453 for a remarkable man. Jacques Coeur was a new type of entrepreneur in France, a self-made man of business who is reputed to have been the richest man in France. He had a house in Montpellier, the principal seat of his business, and others scattered through France, but his house in Bourges, the city of his birth, reflects the noble status he was granted by Charles VII in 1440, for his services as a diplomat and master of the royal mint. It was princely in pretension, and many of its features set standards for the finest chateaux and town houses of the later 15th century.

The house is roughly rectangular and built around a courtyard. Entrance is gained from the main street facade to the east; the main apartments are built into the remains of Gallo-Roman walls along the west side. These walls include the bases of two round towers, which were incorporated as features of the house, one topped by a hexagonal, crenellated stage, the other by a conical roof. The house is two stories (with cellars below), except at the northwest corner, where there are three stories. The walls are of finely worked ashlar, and liberally decorated with carvings. The chapel, located over the double street entrance (for pedestrian and carriage traffic), is stone-vaulted. It has large, four-light Flamboyant tracery windows in the east and west walls, but otherwise, cross windows are used throughout. Ground-floor rooms have beam ceilings (mostly 2.8 meters high). First-floor rooms (4.9 meters high) are mostly covered by tall king-post roofs, encased in all but the service rooms by wooden planking (those in the galleries in the form of ogee-profiled barrel vaults); this is a seemingly unique feature in central French architecture, and may have contributed to the popularity of paneled ceilings in the 16th century. Six main stair turrets and two other sets provide access to the upper floors. The variety of their decoration and the freedom with which they—and other functional elements—affect the massing create a picturesque effect, which is heightened by the steeply

House of Jacques Coeur: Bourges, France, 1442-53

pitched hips, gables and cones of the roofs and the tall chimneys. There was originally a garden along the Gallo-Roman wall, to the west of the house.

The courtyard has galleries on three sides, open below, enclosed above. The main apartments on the west side are entered through the base of an openwork stair turret, centrally located, adjacent to the banqueting hall (14.6 by 9.9 meters), which was lavishly provided with a minstrels' gallery and a monumental castellated fireplace (over 6 feet long), with statues of Adam and Eve flanking the Tree of Knowledge above. South of the hall is a suite of private rooms, and to the north there are service rooms, including a bath-house (with changing room) which was connected by stairs to the upper rooms. The kitchen in the northwest corner is two stories high, has a small courtyard with a well, and is connected to the street by a service corridor behind the north gallery. Another corridor past the bath-house connects the kitchen with a servery at the end of the great hall. South of the southern gallery is another small courtyard with a well and a porter's lodge.

The first-floor plan is almost identical to that of the ground floor. Above the banqueting hall is another hall, the other rooms comprising private chambers and offices. There is a surprising diversity of rooms; they are larger in number and generally smaller than rooms in most houses of the period. This would seem to indicate a fractionalization of the household, and a more functional specialization of interior spaces. Private access was provided to most rooms.

The decoration of the house is sumptuous. There are blind tracery panels below windows, foliate friezes and openwork parapets on cornices, relief carvings in tympana and panels over doorways, elaborately carved fireplaces in most rooms (the upper hall has two), carved bosses on the vaults in the chapel and lower tower rooms, and the entrance has an interesting ensemble of carvings. Over the entrance portals on the street facade is a large niche, which until the Revolution housed an equestrian statue of Charles VII, a feature which can be found in later residences, such as the Château at Blois. Flanking this niche are two relief panels carved as fictive windows, with half-length stone figures peering over the sills into the street, a charming conceit later copied in the Hôtel de Ville in Bourges. The ground-floor windows on each side of the entrance pavilion were originally much smaller, and for the most part, the ground floor of the street facade was plain, with a stringcourse and cross windows flanked by obliquely set pinnacles above. One of the most famous carvings in the house is a relief scene of Tristan and Isolde in an upper tower room known as the "Chambre des Angelots." The most prominent sculpture, such as this, the facade and chapel carvings, is of very high quality, while a team of less capable masons produced the other sculpture.

The house was lavishly provided with stained glass. Most of this has disappeared, but from descriptions, we know it included images of the Twelve Peers of France and the Nine Heroes and Heroines in the great hall and the 12 months in the Chambre d'Hiver. Coats of arms were plentiful: not only those of Jacques Coeur himself and his wife, Macée de Léodepart, but those of his associates and of the ancient families of Berry. Jacques Coeur's presence was also richly recorded in the stonework, which included not only his arms, but his devices: a heart (*coeur*, in French) and a scallop shell (symbol of St. James, for Jacques). Also to be found was his motto: *A vaillans coeurs rien impossible.*

Much of the wall painting is gone, but we know that some of the interior sculpture was polychrome, and the Chambre des Galées formerly had wall paintings of galleys and ships, as well as reliefs of nautical scenes from romances. The 20 angels painted on the vault cells of the chapel, between gilded ribs, are remarkable not only for the fact that they have survived so well, but for their obviously high quality. These paintings have clear Flemish connections and are stylistically related to the stained glass in Jacques Coeur's chapel in Bourges Cathedral. This is an interesting connection, because the tracery pattern of this four-light window is virtually identical to those in the chapel of Coeur's house, featuring a fleur-de-lys between two hearts; and the same team of masons and painters was probably responsible for both projects.

City Walls: Carcassonne, France, 4th-13th centuries

The chapel is, not surprisingly, the most elaborately treated room in the house, and it also reflects the pretensions Jacques Coeur had for his house, in that it seems strongly related to royal tradition. In locating the chapel on the upper floor of an entrance pavilion, Jacques Coeur was emulating such prestigious aristocratic residences as Coucy and Mehun-sur-Yèvre. And flanking the eastern bay of the chapel, on each side of the altar, are two small oratories built into the walls and lit by small windows. Similar oratories were particularly associated with Ste. Chapelles, not only that built by Saint Louis in Paris, but the later ones in Riom and Bourges. There are also six richly carved niches set in the chapel walls, on corbels carved with Old Testament figures (the niches themselves are now empty). The chapel also had a painted wooden altarpiece with closing wings.

After his arrest in 1451 and banishment in 1453, the house stayed in the Coeur family until the 16th century, when it passed through a succession of owners, including Louis XIV's minister Jean Baptiste Colbert, before becoming the city hall of Bourges between 1682 and 1858. Many alterations were made during that period. After passing to the state, the house was restored by Antoine-Nicolas Bailly, and further work was undertaken in 1920. It is now open to the public.

—JIM BUGSLAG

CITY WALLS AND FORTIFICATIONS
Carcassonne, France

Fourth century-sixth century: Original inner wall built. **13th century:** Additional major fortifications built. **1855-79:** Restored; **Architect:** Eugène-Emmanuel Viollet-le-Duc (1814-79).

Publications

GOUT, PAUL: *Viollet-le-Duc: sa vie, son oeuvre, sa doctrine.* Paris, 1914.
VIOLLET-LE-DUC: *Dictionnaire raisonne de l'Architecture francais.* Paris, 1854-1868.

*

Carcassonne occupies an eminence above the River Aude in southwestern France, providing a natural stronghold in a highly strategic position on an important transportation route between the Mediterranean and Aquitaine. "Carcaso" was inhabited prior to the Romans, who had made it into an outpost by the first century A.D. By 333 it had been fortified. After the breakdown of the empire, it was occupied by the Visigoths and, after the Battle of Vouillé in 506, functioned as a strong point along their border with the Franks. The earliest walls on the site formed a kidney-shaped fortified *castrum* about 525 meters long on its north-south axis and 250 meters wide. These used to be regarded as primarily Visigothic, but opinion has shifted decisively in favor of a Roman origin and a mainly fourth-century date. Much of these walls still survives, built into the 13th-century fortifications. By the 11th century, Carcassonne had come into the hands of the Vicomtes de Trencavel, who built a palace adjoining the western wall between 1130 and 1150.

This region was a center of the Albigensian heresy, against

which the French crown mounted a "crusade" in the early 13th century, initiating the stormiest period in Carcassonne's history. Simon de Montfort took the city by siege in 1209. By 1224 it had been returned to the Trencavels, but the citizens surrendered it to Louis VIII in 1226 rather than undergo another siege. From that time onward, it remained in the hands of the French crown, although local magnates mounted a serious siege in 1240. Carcassonne, along with other fortifications, was in fact used by the French crown as part of their policy to secure the traditionally independent-minded south of France with a strong military presence, and to that end *senechals* were installed there and major building works initiated.

Three major campaigns of building under the French crown through the 13th century turned Carcassonne into essentially what we see today. The first, between 1226 and the siege of 1240, extended the line of the Roman walls at their south end, creating a spur-shaped terminus better adapted to its natural defensive position. An outer wall was also built at that time, making Carcassonne one of the best examples of a concentric fortification in western Europe. As well, the Trencavel palace was fortified, with a rectangular towered wall and ditch, which was a model of northern French military engineering. The campaign after 1240 was far less extensive, being limited mostly to repairing siege damage. Then in the 1280s substantial transformations completed the present arrangements.

These works turned Carcassonne into one of the great walled cities of Europe, along with the fortified port city that Louis IX had built at Aigues-Mortes. It was so imposing that it was never attacked again, not even in 1355 when Edward the Black Prince pillaged the lower town. Over the succeeding centuries, an increasingly ramshackle Carcassonne was maintained as a fortification, and under the ancien régime it became an arsenal and garrison. But in the early 19th century, it was decommissioned, and the walls and towers began to be dismantled for their stone. The walls narrowly escaped complete demolition in 1850, and in 1852 Eugène Viollet-le-Duc began his famous restoration works, which were to occupy him until his death in 1879. Although restoration continued after that time and, indeed, continues today, it is to Viollet-le-Duc that we owe the present impression of the walls and citadel.

The Gallo-Roman walls rested on large foundation blocks and consisted of small, ashlar blocks interrupted at intervals by leveling courses of brick. Their height varied from 4.5 meters to 8 meters, and their width was about half their height. The perimeter measured about 1,070 meters and was punctuated by 30 towers and four gates. The towers were horseshoe-shaped, rounded toward the exterior and rectangular toward the interior. The tops of the walls were crenellated, and the upper chambers of each tower were lit by three small, round-headed windows.

Besides changing the line of the southwest corner of the walls, the 1226 campaign of building made other radical changes to the Roman walls. The new perimeter measured 1,286 meters and added several towers, which were further increased by the fortification of the palace. The outer wall that was built at that time measured 1,500 meters with 17 towers; the lesser number of towers resulted from improvements in projectile weaponry and a change in conception from a passive to an active defensive strategy. The lists between these two sets of walls were leveled, necessitating the underpinning of the Roman walls by, in places, substantial 13th-century masonry of medium-sized ashlar. The walls and towers were also heightened, so that the Roman masonry was untidily sandwiched between 13th-century masonry, resulting in a very irregular arrangement. Apart from two square towers, most of the new towers were round, reflecting contemporary practice, but some of the horseshoe-shaped Roman towers were rebuilt, and others were built anew on this

plan. All the new towers, however, were rib-vaulted in their bottom two or three stories, with wooden floors above; all were provided with multiple arrow-loops and putlog holes for wooden hoardings at the tops of the towers; the bottoms of the walls had glacis to guard against sapping; and watchtowers and bartizans abounded. Also at that time, the Quartier St. Michel, which abutted the eastern walls, was demolished to clear the walls for defense, and the unprotected lower town laid out on a grid system to replace it.

The fortification of the comtal palace was designed as much to provide protection from the town as to form a last line of defense. It was designed by royal engineers and fits firmly into northern military developments. Formerly, it was thought to have dated from the 12th-century Trencavel period, but even as a 13th-century construction it is significantly innovative. The regularity of plan relates to northern fortresses of Philip Augustus's reign like the Louvre and Dourdan. Flanking and commanding fire from the walls is excellent, and ground-level arrow-loops take advantage of the new effectiveness of cross-bows. The twin-towered entrance, with a guardroom above and a covered passage protected by murder holes and a portcullis, appeared in its complete form only at Angers (ca. 1228-38) and Boulogne-sur-Mer (1231).

The third campaign, under Philip III and Philip IV, replaced substantial parts of the patched-together inner wall. The masonry of this campaign is readily identifiable by its regular, rusticated face. Besides the total replacement of walls, the Porte Narbonnaise, the principal gateway into the city, was rebuilt, and the line of wall immediately north of it was redefined with the construction of the Tour du Trésau. Both of the latter make use of horseshoe-shaped plans, the towers of the Porte Narbonnaise also having spurs on the outer faces. Several barbicans were also built on the line of the outer wall, and another guarded the city entrance to the castle.

By the mid-19th century much of this was in jeopardy. Although Viollet-le-Duc's restoration has been strongly criticized, especially for his use of slate instead of tiles for the pepperpot roofs of the towers, he both stabilized the structure and brought it to international prominence. It survives today as one of the best-preserved Roman fortifications in existence and one of the preeminent examples of a medieval fortified city.

—JIM BUGSLAG

ST. RIQUIER
Centula, France

Seventh century A.D.: Benedictine abbey founded. **Eighth century A.D.:** Abbey rebuilt and expanded into Carolingian Abbey Church of St. Riquier; **Architect:** Angilbert. **Eleventh century A.D.:** Outer crypt added. **Architect:** Abbot Gervin I. **Eleventh century A.D.:** Church rebuilt after west tower collapsed. **Architect:** Abbot Gervin II. **1475:** Rebuildings destroyed by fire and construction of Flamboyant church begun. **1507:** New stalls added. **1554:** Nave and choir vaults destroyed by fire. **Seventeenth century:** Church repair and claustral buildings rebuilt. **Architect:** Abbot Charles d'Aligre.

Publications

ACHTER, J.: "Zur Rekonstruction der karolingischen Kloster-kirche Centula." *Zeitschrift für Kunstgeschichte* XIX (1956): 133.

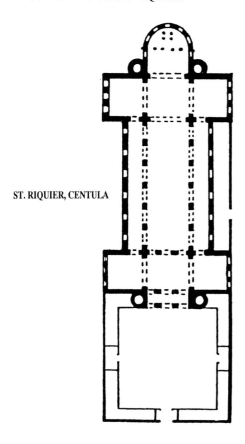

ST. RIQUIER, CENTULA

BERNARD, H.: "Un site prestigieux du monde carolingien: St. Riquier, Peut-on connaitre la grande basillique d'Anilbert?" *Cahiers archeologique de Picardie* 5 (1978): 241-50.

DURAND, G.: *L'église de St. Riquier, La Picardie historique et monumentale.* IV. Amiens and Paris, 1907-11.

EFFMANN, W.: *Centula St. Riquier.* Münster, 1912.

HEITZ, C.: *L'architecture religieuse carolingienne. Les formes et leurs fonctions.* Paris, 1980, pp. 54-63.

HUBERT, J.: "St. Riquier et le monachisme bénédictine en Gaule a l'epoche carolingienne." *Settimana di Studio del Centro Italiano di Studi sull'Atti Medioevo* IV (1957): 293-309.

PARSONS, D.: "The Pre-Romanesque Church of St. Riquier: The Documentary Evidence." *Journal of the British Archaeological Association* 130 (1977): 21-51.

*

The Carolingian Abbey Church of St. Riquier (Ricarius), or Centula, was one of the major churches of its time, and its innovative form was influential for centuries. Although long demolished, it is known through documents and a late-11th-century view of the church and precinct, preserved in three 17th-century copies, and also through H. Bernard's recent excavations.

The body of Saint Ricarius (died 645) was taken to Centula soon after his death, and a Benedictine abbey was founded at his tomb. Charlemagne put one of his favorites, Angilbert, in charge of it as abbot in about 790. With royal help, Angilbert rebuilt the abbey from its foundations on a scale which made it one of the largest monasteries in northern Europe until the 12th century. The buildings, which were finished in 799, included three churches. The main abbey church was dedicated to Saint Ricarius, but had a westwork dedicated to the Savior. Two smaller churches to the south, one dedicated to Saint Mary

and the Apostles, the other to Saint Benedict, were connected to the main church by covered passageways, forming a large, triangular precinct. Although this arrangement was unique and undoubtedly inspired by Trinitarian symbolism, there was also a rectangular cloister attached to the south side of the nave, like those at Lorsch (784-804) and on the paradigmatic St. Gall plan (ca. 820).

Angilbert's abbey church consisted of an apse, aisleless transepts (as wide as the present transepts but two bays further east) with a crossing tower, containing the bells, and staircase turrets in the eastern angles, an aisled, wooden-roofed nave with clerestory, probably of six bays, and a large westwork. The proportions of the westwork and tower (different from those of the eastern transept) can be seen in the present west facade, which is built on the Carolingian foundations. It had a porch, a "crypt" on the ground floor and an upper chapel dedicated to the Holy Savior, which was open toward the nave, and was flanked by transepts. It was reached by staircase turrets at the western angles of the tower, which rose over the western "crossing." Both eastern and western towers had three-staged tops (*tristegum*), again in remembrance of the Trinity.

Much of the liturgical arrangement and use can be reconstructed, although many details must remain hypothetical. The main altar in the apse was dedicated to Saint Ricarius, and before it were the tombs of Saint Ricarius and his two companions, Saint Caidoc and Saint Frigor. The altar of Saint Peter may have been in the crossing, and altars to Saint John and Saint Martin were probably in the transepts. Dominating the nave was the altar of the Holy Cross, with the altar of Saint Denis further west. Altars to Saint Stephen and Saint Quentin were in the north aisle, those to Saint Lawrence and Saint Maurice in the south aisle (or perhaps in the respective transepts). There were also four liturgical stations, each identified by painted stucco reliefs, perhaps like fragments surviving from Disentis in Switzerland, which also made use of gold mosaic decoration. That showing the Passion was over the crossing arch at the east end of the nave, and the Nativity perhaps in the porch over the entrance to the westwork; the other two, the Resurrection and Ascension, are harder to locate, but may have been at the eastern ends of the nave aisles. The abbey's main reliquary was located in the "crypt" of the westwork, as was a font, while 13 minor reliquaries were placed on a beam (*trabes*) carried on six marble columns surrounding the tomb of Saint Savior in the western gallery, that of the Passion in the eastern nave and that of Saint Ricarius in the sanctuary.

Reconstructions based too closely on the 17th-century engravings must be treated with skepticism, but we do know that Charlemagne sent to Rome for columns, capitals, bases and cornices, and provided craftsmen for work in stone, marble, wood, glass and stucco. There were ciboria over the altar of Saint Ricarius in the apse and the altar of Saint Savior in the westwork tribune. Angilbert also paved the area around the Saint Ricarius altar sumptuously in red and green porphyry, fragments of which survive.

The liturgy involved many processions, not only within the church but around it. Three chapels to the archangels Michael, Gabriel and Raphael are impossible to locate; the usual speculation has them occupying the three gatehouses of an atrium. There were also daily processions to the two outlying churches south of the main abbey church, which were connected by two-story, covered passageways, the longest of which, on the west side, was about 1,000 feet long. A stream ran east-west through the precinct, cutting off the southern tip of the triangle and running a water mill. While we must still speculate that the Church of St. Benedict was a small aisleless nave with lower projecting chancel, the Church of St. Mary and the Apostles has been excavated. It was a centralized structure with a hexagonal chamber, probably containing the altar to Saint Mary, covered by a ciborium, surrounded by a dodecahedral outer wall, suggesting the presence of 12 altars to the apostles in the ambulatory. There was a triple tower above, and a short annex projected to the west, flanked by pentises containing staircases; it must have somewhat resembled the rotunda of St. Michael, Fulda (ca. 820).

The monumentality of this ensemble, with its three towers and its liturgical complexity, was one of the great architectural accomplishments of the Carolingian renaissance. St. Riquier not only set standards for later Carolingian buildings, but defined many elements of church structure for the rest of the Middle Ages. Thus, St. Riquier was probably instrumental in defining the ''double-ended'' church so widespread until the Ottonian era. The idea of a semi-independent western church dedicated to the Savior undoubtedly refers to the church of the Holy Sepulcher in Jerusalem. The westwork, however, was a wholly Carolingian invention, and few are known prior to St. Riquier. Certainly, it seems to have influenced that at Corvey (873-85), as well as those formerly at Corbie and Fécamp. The use of imagery at St. Riquier also appears to have been influential: thus, the Nativity relief at the west portal, which developed into a significant focus for relief imagery; thus, also, the Passion relief at the east end of the nave, where ''rood'' imagery later appeared.

The main early addition to Angilbert's church was the outer crypt built east of the apse by Abbot Gervin I (1045-71). This was a rectangular, ground-level building, with a central space flanked by apsed chambers with long passages to the west, connecting them to the transepts. The central chamber has not been excavated, but is known to have been supported by four piers, perhaps, like those of St. Pierre, Lille, dividing it into nine square bays, with an apse at the end of each ''aisle''; this would also resemble the arrangement at St. Philibert de Grandlieu.

After the collapse of the west tower, the church was rebuilt on its old foundations by Abbot Gervin II (1071-97). A further series of rebuildings was destroyed in a disastrous fire in 1475, after which the church was razed to its foundations and the present Flamboyant church begun at the east end. New stalls were ordered in 1507, and the nave and elaborately decorated west front were finished under Abbot Thibaut de Bayencourt (1511-36). Another fire in 1554 caused the nave and choir vaults to collapse.

The ambulatory chapels were walled off for services, and the church remained in a ruinous state for more than a century. Abbot Charles d'Aligre (1645-95) brought the Maurist reform to St. Riquier, repaired the church and rebuilt all the claustral buildings.

—JIM BUGSLAG

CHÂTEAU
Chambord, France

Dates: 1519-47; **Architect:** Domenico da Cortona [Boccadoro].

Publications

GASSEUX, P.: *Chambord.* Zürich (1962).
LESUEUR, L.: ''Les dernières étapes de la construction de Chambord.'' *Bulletin Monumental* 109 (1951): 7.

It was in September 1519, four years after his accession, that François I determined upon the building of ''a beautiful and sumptuous edifice'' at Chambord, and he commissioned François de Pontbriant as superintendant of buildings. The names of Jacques Sourdeau (already employed at Blois) as ''*maître maçon a conduire la maçonnérie*'' and Pierre Nepveu (known as Trinqueau) appear among the letters patent.

The site chosen was that of an old medieval château, miles from anywhere on low-lying marshy ground by the banks of the River Cosson. A model, of which André Félibien has left drawings, and which corresponds with the actual dimensions of the main block, was almost certainly the work of Domenico da Cortona, who was paid in 1553 for his works ''during the past fifteen years at Chambord and other places.''

The model was distinctly Italianate. The symmetry and exact proportions of the ground plan were something new to France. The basic plan of the main block is there, but without the spiral staircase. Its facades are monotonous: every story is treated as an arcade, and every bay has its window. The model gives no indication of what, if anything, was above the cornice. It leaves off where Chambord really begins.

Someone, presumably François, had the elaborate inspiration of the terrace with its high pavilion roofs, its elaborate dormers, its countless cupolas and chimney stacks that create the impression of an overcrowded chessboard, which is the essential character of Chambord. The slender walls of Cortona's model would have been quite inadequate to support his enormous superstructure. The actual masonry is so massive that the rooms seem to have been excavated, like the troglodyte dwellings of Montlouis, out of the solid stone.

It is impossible to imagine the present roofscape without the central cupola in which the whole composition soars to its zenith. The central cupola presupposes the central staircase. Cortona's model shows a staircase with straight flights, as at Chenonçeau. The change from that to the central spiral staircase cannot be separated from the design of the roofscape in its present form.

There are fairly strong reasons for seeing the hand of Leonardo da Vinci in the design of the spiral staircase. He went to France at the king's invitation in May 1517; and died two years later—just before the building began at Chambord. Thus, Leonardo was in France, exactly when the plans would have been under discussion. It would be difficult to believe that François I never mentioned his most important project to his most distinguished guest.

The mere existence of a double spiral staircase at Chambord would not even necessarily imply the intervention of an Italian, for such a staircase existed at the Bernardin Monastery in Paris. But Leonardo had designed plans for villas in which the house was divided into four blocks separated by four vestibules in the form of a cross, sometimes with a chapel in the center. He also designed a number of interlocking staircases. In 1581 Andrea Palladio, writing in his First Book, chapter 28, stated: ''Another remarkable sort of staircase is the one which King François had made at Chambord. It consists of four flights. . . .'' The staircase at Chambord consists of two flights. Palladio must have seen a design for a four-flight staircase and had reason to believe that it belonged to Chambord. Everything points to Leonardo, but the matter cannot be regarded as proven.

The finished plan of the main block or donjon is an exact square. At each corner stands a large tower, 18 meters in diameter, of which three quarters of the circumference projects. The whole is divided into four separated blocks of apartments by cruciform vestibules which link the central windows of each facade. At the center of the crossing is the freestanding spiral staircase with its two interlocking ramps.

Château: Chambord, France, 1519-47

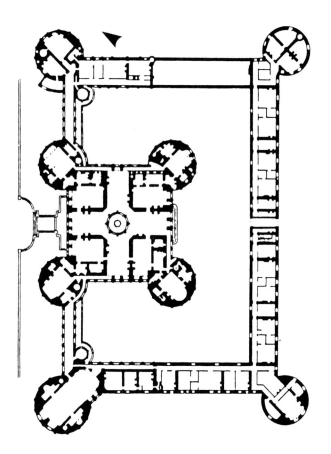

Another feature of the plan of Chambord, which was to become widespread in French architecture, is the grouping of the rooms into an "*appartement*"—one large room (the bedroom), two small rooms and a closet. Anthony Blunt traced the origin of this grouping to Giuliano da Sangallo's villa for Lorenzo de' Medici at Poggio a Caiano.

The north front of the donjon is joined by galleries to two corner towers, that at the northeast angle containing the King's Apartment and that at the northwest the chapel, thus forming a united front of 155 meters in length. It is at first sight symmetrical, but a close inspection reveals a number of what must have been deliberate departures from symmetry. On the south facade this is even more evident and more obviously deliberate. Aesthetically this is important: an absolute symmetry in this sort of building would be boring.

Jacques Androuet du Cerceau, whose architectural drawing often included projects which were as yet unrealized, showed Chambord with two more corner towers as tall as the others, marking the extremities of the south range of the outer court. The buildings of this outer court were restricted to the ground floor so as to give light to the windows of the donjon and so as not to obscure the view of it from the outside. This disposition had first appeared in the Loire Valley at Le Plessis Bourre.

The donjon was largely finished by the death of François I in 1547. The chapel wing and that which answers it on the east of the forecourt were completed by his successor, Henri II. More than a century later, Louis XIV made regular visits to Chambord to hunt in the forest, and further adaptations were made. In the 18th century the château was lived in by Stanislas Leczinski, father-in-law to Louis XV, and the marechal de Saxe. By 1820 it was in a sorry state of disrepair. In 1821, however, the comte de Calonne got up a subscription to purchase Chambord and present it to the posthumous heir to the duc de Berry, *"l'enfant du miracle"* the duc de Bordeaux, who took the title of comte de Chambord. He saw the château for only a few days in July 1871, when he was offered the throne of France but refused it because France refused the white flag of the Bourbons.

—IAN DUNLOP

CHARTRES CATHEDRAL
Chartres, France

1120: Church rebuilt after fire destroyed church built in 858. **1134-40:** North and south tower built, and sculpture of royal portal installed. **1150:** Towers completed, front facade brought forward even with towers, glass over lancet installed. **1165:** South spire completed. **1194:** Church damaged in fire, choir and nave rebuilt. **1197:** North porch begun. **1206:** South porch installed. **1215:** North porch completed, west rose installed. **1220-40:** High vaults and transept roses added. **1260:** Church consecrated. **1316:** Chapter House and Chapel of St. Piat added, **1415:** Vendôme Chapel built. **1506:** North spire destroyed by lightning and rebuilt. **1514:** Screen between choir and side aisles begun; **Architect:** Jean de Beauce. **1757:** Jube ripped down and present stalls added. **1836:** Roof burnt.

Publications

ADAMS, H.: *Mont-Saint-Michel and Chartres: A Study of Thirteenth Century Unity.* Princeton, New Jersey, 1981.

BARNES, C. F.: "The Cathedral of Chartres and the architect of Soissons." *Journal of the Society of Architectural Historians* XXII (1963): 63-74.

BAUCH, KURT: "Chartres und Strassburg." *Oberrheinische Kunst* 4 (1929): 30.

BONY, J.: "The Resistance to Chartres." *Journal of the British Archaeological Association* 3rd series, vols. 20-21 (1957-58).

BRANNER, ROBERT (ed.): *Chartres Cathedral.* New York, 1969.

BULTEAU, A.: *Monographie de la cathédrale de Chartres.* 3 vols. 2nd ed. Chartres, 1887-92.

BUNJES, H.: "Der gotische Lettner der Kathedrale von Chartres." *Wallraf-Richartz Jahrbuch* 12/13 (1943).

DURAND, P. and LASSUS, J. B. A.: *Monographie de la cathédrale de Chartres.* Paris, 1867.

GRODECKI, LOUIS: "The Transept Portals of Chartres Cathedral." *Art Bulletin* (1951).

GRODECKI, LOUIS: "Chronologie de la cathédrale de Chartres." *Bulletin Monumental* CXVI (1958): 91-119.

HENDERSON, G.: *Chartres.* Harmondsworth and Baltimore, 1968.

HOUVET, E.: *La cathédrale de Chartres.* 7 vols. Chartres 1919-1921.

ISOZAKI, ARATA: *Architectural Pilgrimage to World Architecture.* Series, with photographs by Kishin Shinoyama. Vol. 6, *Chartres Cathedral.* Tokyo, 1983.

JAMES, JOHN: *Chartres, The Masons Who Built a Legend.* 1982.

JANTZEN, HANS: *High Gothic: The Classic Cathedrals of Chartres, Reims and Amiens.* Princeton, New Jersey, 1984.

KATZENELLENBOGEN, ADOLF: *The Sculptural Programs of Chartres Cathedral.* Baltimore, 1959.

KIDSON, P.: *Sculpture at Chartres.* London, 1958.

LASSUS, JEAN BAPTISTE ANTOINE: *Monographie de la Cathedrale de Chartres.* Paris, 1842-67.

MALE, EMILE: *Notre-Dame de Chartres.* 1948.

MALE, EMILE: *Chartres.* 1983.

MEULEN, J. V. D.: *Chartres Cathedral: Sources and Literary Interpretation, A Critical Biography.* Boston, 1989.

SCHLAG, GOTTFRIED: "Die Skulpturen des Querhauses der Kathedrale von Chartres." *Wallraf-Richartz Jahrbuch* (1943).

TEICHMANN, FRANK: *Chartres: Schule und Kathedrale.* Stuttgart, 1991.

VAN DER MEULEN, J.: "Histoire de la construction de la cathédrale Notre-Dame de Chartres après 1194." *Bulletin de la Société Archéologique d'Eure-et-Loir* 18 (1965): 5-126.

VON SIMSON, OTTO: *The Gothic Cathedral: Origins of Gothic Architecture and the Medieval Concept of Order.* Princeton, New Jersey, 1987.

*

On 11 July 1144 the new choir of the Abbey of St. Denis built by Abbot Suger near Paris was consecrated. The event could almost be regarded as the launching of the Gothic style in France. Present at the ceremony was Geoffroy de Leves, bishop of Chartres. He had already as his cathedral the imposing Romanesque edifice of Bishop Fulbert, and his first plan may have been to provide that church with a narthex in the new style, providing a new west front. Originally this front was set back between the two west towers, but in 1150 the central facade was brought forward to be flush with the towers as it is today.

Chartres was at that time the center of a flourishing school of theology, and the decoration of the three porches, known collectively as the "Portail Royal," is a statement of theology. The theme chosen was the ultimate unity of all knowledge. To understand Chartres Cathedral we must recapture some of the intellectual excitement which pervaded the era, and above all the idea that all knowledge—spiritual, philosophical and scientific—could be held together in one mighty synthesis with Theology, the "Queen of Sciences," as the keystone of the arch. Chartres was also the chief center for devotion to the Virgin and possessed the chemise allegedly worn by her at the Annunciation.

It is therefore no surprise to find the Seven Liberal Arts represented in the southern archway, dedicated to the Virgin. Music hammers out a chime upon a peal of bells, while Grammar presides grimly with book and birch over two cowering pupils; Aristotle bends over a little writing table, as Euclid traces a geometrical figure; Priscian, Pythagoras, Ptolemy and Cicero complete the scene.

On the northern archway, dedicated to the Ascension, are the manual labors—the ceaseless, seasonal struggle with Nature, combining with the signs of the Zodiac. If the scholar could gaze with satisfaction upon the symbolism of the "Portail de la Vierge," no less could the agricultural laborer see his routine chores ennobled by their inclusion in the "Portail de l'Ascension."

Between these three portals are the famous statue columns. Those of the central bay have a preeminence entirely their own. There is no canopy overhead to break the upward movement; their feet rest upon the slightest of supports; their elongated figures and closely pinioned arms accentuate their architectural allegiance. They are as much columns as statues. In the late 19th century vestiges of paint and gold leaf could still be discerned on these figures. The Portail Royal was brightly colored and richly gilded.

In 1194 a fire destroyed most of Bishop Fulbert's cathedral,

Chartres Cathedral: Chartres, France, begun 1120

Chartres Cathedral, view from choir towards nave

with the exception of the new west front. It was decided to rebuild, but using the foundations of the old church, with which the west front was in alignment. The re-use of the old foundations imposed an important feature upon the new cathedral. Since Fulbert's church had only a wooden ceiling, it could afford to have a span of 16½ meters to the nave. This was at that time the broadest area ever to be vaulted in stone, and it needed a proportionately greater height, which broke all records at 37 meters.

The importance of the architecture of Chartres is that it set the fashion which most of the great cathedrals were to follow. It was at Chartres that the decisive formula was reached: transepts were retained, tribunes abolished and quadripartite vaulting used throughout. A double ambulatory with radiating chapels encircles the choir, but two single aisles accompany the nave.

Nearly everything that was done at Chartres had been done before, though sometimes in a tentative or experimental manner. At Chartres for the first time the new style stepped confidently into its own. The builder seemed to be fully aware of the resources and potentialities at his disposal, and used them to obtain a maximum area of glass. When walls had been a structural necessity, the medieval builder had sought to obtain the rich effect which he desired by mural painting. With the elimination of the wall, it became possible to replace the flatness of pigment with the lovely luminosity of glass.

There was only one element in the Gothic style that was still to be evolved, and that was tracery. The so-called "plate tracery," still in use when Chartres was built, provided the formula of a roundel superimposed above a pair of lancets. In the nave these roundels are so large that they could not be inscribed within a pointed arch. They required a round arch for the wall rib which had to be raised on stilts to attain the same

height as the pointed arches of the nave vault. This in turn twisted the inward facet of the vault into the shape of a plowshare.

The windows were all gifts to the cathedral. Many of them came from the richer clergy—and some were very rich indeed. Forty-four were given by the royal and noble families of France, 42 by the trades guilds of Chartres. These guilds mostly appended their signatures in the form of little scenes of their typical activities at the foot of the windows, where they were most easily seen. Thus, a lady is seen trying on a dress in the drapers' window, and in another a cobbler is depicted threading laces into a newly made shoe. The connection between the trade of the guild and the subject of the window is sometimes farfetched. The stonemasons chose the stoning of Saint Stephen. There was no overriding scheme; each guild chose as it wished. There are five windows dedicated to Saint Nicholas and four to Saint Martin, not to mention the 20 dedicated to the Virgin Mary.

In the great rose windows of the transepts, however, there is a coherent iconography. This is doubtless due in part to the fact that each ensemble was the gift of a single donor. That in the north transept was given by Blanche of Castille, mother of Saint Louis, that in the south transept by Pierre de Dreux, a grandson of Louis VI who had married Alix de Thouars, through whom he became duc de Bretagne. In the north transept the figure of Solomon is almost a portrait of Saint Louis in his coronation robes. The Gothic in France was very much a royal style, and most of the greatest cathedrals following Chartres were built on Capetian territory.

In the south-transept window the risen Christ occupies the center roundel, encircled by the worshipping chorus described in the Book of Revelation. In the lancets below is a deeply theological statement expressed by the mounting of the four

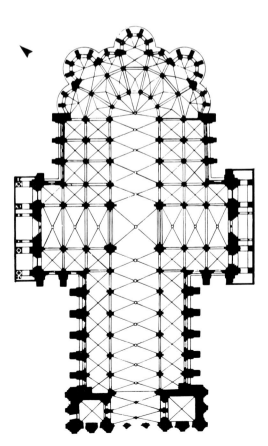

Evangelists upon the shoulders of four of the Prophets. It illustrates what Bernard of Chartres said of the ancient philosophers: "If we could see further than they could, it is not because of the strength of our own vision, it is because we are raised up by them. . . . We are dwarfs mounted on the shoulders of giants."

The north and south facades to the transepts should be seen in close connection with their stained glass, for the sculptured porches reflect the same themes as the windows. On the north is the Portail de la Vierge begun in 1197. The statue columns already show a new conception of the sculptor's art. Essentially the move was toward a greater realism, with the figures no longer motionless and mummified as on the Portail Royal; the postures are more varied and the folds of the drapery more natural, for the underlying anatomy has been considered.

The south porch, like the south rose, was the gift of Pierre de Dreux. The theme of the sculptures is the Last Judgment, with the martyrs of the church in the left-hand bay and the confessors in the right. On the whole these figures seem to lack the vital spark and to be rather wooden, but the scene of the condemned souls being swept to their damnation by a crew of angels is a work of genius and not without humor, for among the condemned can be seen a king, a bishop and a monk.

The facades of the transepts are flanked by towers which do not rise higher than the tops of the rose windows. On the south side there is a further tower over the last bay of the side aisle before the ambulatory. The symmetry of the plan demands that there was to have been an answering tower on the north side. Had these six towers all been completed and crowned with spires, Chartres would have had an exciting, many-towered skyline such as was achieved only at Laon. In fact only the two west towers were completed, and of these only the south one remains as it was built. Otto von Simson has shown in his study *The Gothic Cathedral* that this tower was constructed according to a complex system of harmonic proportions. It is a model of strength and simplicity, and nothing could be more admirable than the way in which the architect has used the ring of tall, attenuated gables to mask the transition from the square to the octagon and from the octagon to the spire.

The north tower was struck by lightning in 1506 and rebuilt to the design of Jean Texier, often known as Jean de Beauce. It was an openwork complexity which defies description, and as a tour-de-force must elicit our astonishment if not our admiration. We can see in the two towers the first and last phases of the Gothic style.

In 1514 Jean de Beauce was commissioned to construct the elaborate screen which separates the choir from its side aisles. It was still unfinished at his death in 1529. A master of the Flamboyant Gothic, he was young enough in his old age to convert to Renaissance ornament. The bishop, Everard de la Marck, had to be specially ordered by the king to contribute to the cost of this addition.

In 1836 the roof of Chartres Cathedral was destroyed by fire. The lead was replaced by a copper covering, which was intended to be temporary, but which is still in place.

—IAN DUNLOP

CHURCH OF STE. FOY
Conques, France

Built on site of chapel of Dadon, a Carolingian hermit. **Ca. eighth century:** Monastary constructed and dedicated to St. Sauveur. **Tenth century:** Golden reliquary constructed. **Ca.**

1800: Destruction of conventual buildings. **19th century:** Addition of west front towers. Present church is the third one to stand on the site.

Publications

SAUERLÄNDER, W.: "Das 7. Colloquium der Société Française d'Archéologie: Ste-Foy in Conques." *Kunstchronik* XXVI (1973): 225.

*

Among Romanesque monuments, the Church of Ste. Foy [St. Faith] at Conques, situated in the Auvergne region of south-central France, remains as one of the most complete medieval buildings available to modern times. The history of the church recounts the story of many medieval monasteries. Its development, from an initial hermitage to the present pilgrimage church, is not unlike that of many churches of a similar period, and its decline during the Wars of Religion and the French Revolution repeats a familiar cycle in French architectural history. What makes Ste. Foy distinctive is the relatively complete survival of the original fabric, treasury, and portal sculpture, all in a setting that has changed very little through the passage of nearly 800 years. (The destruction of the conventual buildings after the Revolution and addition of ungainly west front towers in the 19th century are the major modifications made since construction.) Conques is a small town, comprising perhaps 500 people, about the same number who lived there in the Middle Ages. To visit Ste. Foy, then, is an opportunity to see a major religious monument as it appeared to the people who built it.

In terms of architectural type, Ste. Foy is one of the five great churches of the pilgrimage roads, the smallest in a series which began with St. Martin at Tours and included St. Martial at Limoges, St. Sernin at Toulouse and St. James at Compostela. All showed their dual function as monastic churches and major pilgrim shrines by providing accommodation both for the daily cycle of monastic services and a continual stream of visitors. Divine offices could be celebrated under the lofty vaults of the nave and choir while pilgrims circulated through the aisles and ambulatory, which form a continuous circuit around the central volume. Altars in chapels opening from the transept aisles and ambulatory permitted private devotions and the veneration of relics, while on festival days the generous space of nave, transepts, aisles and galleries could welcome thousands for services. Masonry construction throughout created a fireproof building and at the same time established conditions for resonant acoustics to enhance liturgical chant. Braced by quadrant vaults over the galleries, the banded barrel vaults of nave, transepts and choir were among the highest of the period, but the demands of structure precluded direct clerestory lighting. At the church of Ste. Foy, daylight from the octagonal lantern at the crossing illuminates the area of the main altar and contrasts dramatically with the dimmer nave and transepts. The local stone used for nave and transept construction imparts a warm yellow tone to the interior.

Ste. Foy's plan is a somewhat truncated version of the pilgrimage-road type because of its steep hillside site. The church sits on an artificial terrace, surrounded on the north and east by a retaining wall and bordered on the south by the cloister (now largely destroyed), which steps down a whole story from the level of the church. To the west, the limiting condition was a natural spring, still flowing today, which probably recommended the site to Dadon, the Carolingian hermit whose chapel became the foundation of the subsequent monastery dedicated to St. Sauveur. Conques became a pilgrim stop in part because

Church of Ste. Foy: Conques, France, ca. 8th century

of this abundant source of good water; the town's name refers to the conch shells carried by pilgrims.

The appeal of the site was increased in the ninth century when the relics of Ste. Foy, a 12-year-old girl martyred by the Romans, were brought to Conques from the monastery at Agen. (Legend says they were stolen by Ariviscus, a monk from Conques, after much plotting, but they may have been simply transferred for safekeeping in the face of Viking raids in about 864.) The fame of these relics brought prosperity to the abbey and insured that Conques was included as the pilgrim routes to Compostela were established, although the monastery never affiliated with Cluny, as did many other stations on the Way of St. James. A golden reliquary fashioned in the 10th century in the form of a seated majesty and other precious items in the church's treasury indicate how contributions from the faithful had already enriched the abbey. The present church, the third on the site, was built specifically to house the glorious shrine of Ste. Foy.

Much of the history of the church is encapsulated in the west front tympanum sculpture depicting the Last Judgment. While adhering to established iconographic conventions derived from the Book of Revelation, its sculptors produced a lively composition, rich in detail specific to Conques. In the saintly procession awaiting judgment, one may identify the monastery's founder Dadon; the abbot Odolric, who began construction of the present church; the emperor Charlemagne, whose legendary generosity to the abbey is also remembered with the reliquary, called the A of Charlemagne, preserved in the treasury; and the monk-thief Ariviscus. An image of the saint herself, blessed by the hand of the Holy Spirit, is set beside the empty cells of prisoners unjustly detained, whose freedom was obtained after appeal to Ste. Foy.

Among the damned in hell, one finds that the punishment fits the crime, a concept central to Dante's *Inferno,* but here set forth some two centuries earlier. The crimes depicted include the seven deadly sins as well as lesser transgressions against the abbey: a hunter who poached on the abbey's lands, for example, is roasted on a spit like that used to cook his illegally obtained game, while a miser is choked by the weight of coins in the purse slung around his neck. In comparison with other sculptures of the same general period and subject matter, the tympanum at Conques has been termed popular because its highly ordered composition and clarity make it readily comprehensible by a lay audience. The sculpture unambiguously illustrates in human terms the eternal rewards and punishments promised in church teachings, providing pilgrim and cleric alike with a compelling visual reminder of the importance of avoiding sin.

—MARIAN SCOTT MOFFETT

FONTAINEBLEAU PALACE
France

1528-40: Palace built; **Architect:** Gilles Le Breton. **1533-40:** Galerie Francois I. **1568:** Alterations; **Architect:** Francesco Primaticcio (1504-70) and others. Interior decoration by Primaticcio, Il Rosso and others.

Palace: Fontainebleau, France, 1528-40

Publications

BOTTINEAU, YVES: *L'art d'Ange-Jacques Gabriel à Fontaine-bleau 1735-1774.* Paris, 1962.

BRAY, A.: *Le château de Fontainebleau.* Paris, 1956.

BRAY, A.: *Les plus excellents bâtiments de France: Le château de Fontainebleau.* Paris, 1955.

CHAMPOLLION-FIGEAC, J.-J.: *Le palais de Fontainebleau.* Paris, 1866.

CHASTEL, ANDRÉ: "L'escalier de la Cour Ovale a Fontaine-bleau." *Essays in the History of Architecture presented to Rudolf Wittkower.* London, 1967.

DIMIER, L.: *Le Primatice.* Paris, 1928.

"La Galerie François I au château de Fontainebleau." *Revue de l'art* 16-17 (1972).

GANAY, E. DE: *Châteaux et manoirs de France.* 11 vols. Paris, 1934-38.

GÉBELIN, F.: *Les châteaux de la Renaissance.* Paris, 1927.

GOURNAY, ISABELLE: "Architecture at the Fontainebleau School of Fine Arts." *Journal of the Society of Architectural Historians* 45 (September 1986): 270-285.

GUILBERT, ABBÉ: *Description historique des château, bourg et forest de Fontainebleau.* Paris, 1731.

GUILLAUME, JEAN: "Orion: Fontainebleau poitevin." *Monuments historiques* 101 (1979): 77.

HERBET, F.: "Les travaux de Philibert Delorme à Fontaine-bleau." *Annales de la Société Historique et Archéologique de Gâtinais* 12 (1894): 153-163.

HERBET, F.: *Le château de Fontainebleau.* Paris, 1937.

JAMES, C. F.: "L'hôtel du Cardinal de Ferrare à Fontainebleau d'après un document inédit." *Actes du Colloque international sur l'art de Fontainebleau (1972)* Paris, (1975).

JOHNSON, W. McALLISTER: "Les débuts de Primatice à Fon-tainebleau." *Revue de l'art* 6 (1969): 9.

L'Ecole de Fontainebleau. Exhibition catalog. Fontainebleau, 1972.

PANOFSKY, ERWIN: "The Iconography of the Galerie François I at Fontainebleau." *Gazette des beaux-arts* (1958): 11.

SAMOYAULT, J. P.: "Le Nôtre et le Jardin de la Reine de Fontainebleau." *Bulletin de la Société de l'Histoire de l'Art Français* (1973): 87.

TERRASSE, C.: *Le château de Fontainebleau.* Paris, 1946.

VACQUIER, J. et al: *Les anciens châteaux de France.* 14 vols. Paris, n.d.

WOODBRIDGE, K.: *Princely Gardens: The Origins and Development of the French Formal Style.* New York, 1986.

*

In the second quarter of the 16th century, the Palace of Fontainebleau near Paris became a center of artistic and architectural innovation, and a showcase of Italian art. The most important contribution to the history of art and architecture, however, was a new manner of interior decoration, created by the Italian masters of the so-called School of Fontainebleau.

In 1528 François I decided to expand the medieval castle of Fontainebleau, until then a small hunting lodge, and make it into one of the centers of court life. Unfortunately, the expansion was not planned as a full-scale reconstruction. Piecemeal additions and alterations, which continued through the centuries,

Palace, Galerie Francois I: 1533-40

led to a rather haphazard total effect. Nevertheless, single elements of the complex played a significant role in the development of French architecture.

Master mason Gilles le Breton was responsible for the first phase of additions and alterations, probably supplying designs as well as overseeing execution. His work at Fontainebleau constitutes a significant break with the Gothic style, and moved French architecture into the Renaissance. Though certainly not with a great deal of rigor or correctness, Gilles applied classical principles of articulation to traditional French building types and used decoration very sparingly. The result was a typically French style with classical affinities and a classical simplicity. His most notable work at Fontainebleau is the Porte Dorée (1528-40), a mixture of old and new forms. The design fundamentally adheres to the type of the medieval fortified gate with two towers, but translates it into a Renaissance idiom. The roof is asymmetrical and the strips of windows point to the Gothic love of the vertical. The simplicity of the design and the articulation of the facade, however, are clearly in emulation of classical principles. The superposed loggias in the central bay are flanked by pilasters two stories high, which makes this one of the earliest examples of the colossal order. Interestingly, the pediments of the lower windows in the vertical strips form the bases of the windows above, which in Italy would have been accounted a Mannerist device. More by accident than design, it would seem, Gilles propelled French architecture straight into Mannerism with such features.

Another addition by Gilles le Breton was the elaborate external staircase in the Cour de l'Ovale (destroyed). This monumental staircase, of two opposed lower flights which were united into a single central flight led over an arch, played an important role in stimulating the tradition of monumental staircases in France. Two other early examples were built at Fontainebleau: a horseshoe-shaped staircase by Philibert de l'Orme in the Cour du Cheval Blanc (destroyed), and a staircase by Jean du Cerceau which replaced de l'Orme's work and still stands.

Soon after work was begun, François I started calling Italian artists to Fontainebleau, primarily to decorate the palace interiors. The most significant early arrival was Giovanni Battista Rosso, also known as Rosso Fiorentino, a painter and stuccoworker. Rosso, hailing from Florence, had been active in Rome and had been exposed there to recent Mannerist developments in painting and sculpture, which were to prove influential in his work at Fontainebleau. Francesco Primaticcio, also a painter and stuccoworker, arrived from Mantua in 1532, two years after Rosso. Primaticcio had been a student of Giulio Romano's and had worked with him on the interiors of the Palazzo del Tè. His documented contribution to the Sala degli Stucchi prefigures important elements of his later style. Together, Rosso and Primaticcio were responsible for the interiors at Fontainebleau in the 1530s, creating an altogether new style bearing witness to the work of Giulio Romano, Raphael and Michelangelo. Their work first introduced Mannerism to France, and exploited the full range of the rich vocabulary of Italian Mannerist art, with its mythological figures, swags, garlands, sphinxes, masks, animal heads and so on. Ingenuity and complexity, justified only by the virtuosity with which they were pursued, dominated the decorative schemes. The Fontainebleau interiors were influential not only in interior decoration, but also dominated French painting and sculpture for decades. Many of the better-known sculptors of the next generation, such as

Palace, Minstrel Gallery: 1528-40

Pierre Bontemps and Germain Pilon, were connected to Fontainebleau, and worked in the manner set by Rosso and Primaticcio. Primaticcio in particular had a strong influence on French painting. The group of artists led by Rosso and Primaticcio became known as the School of Fontainebleau.

Rosso and Primaticcio were important not only for importing Mannerism to France, however, but also for the new way in which they combined painting and stucco. Integrating the different media into a unified total decor, they framed their painted panels with elaborate full-relief stuccowork, which seems to stand free from the wall. From the early period before 1540, only the Galerie François I by Rosso and the fireplace from the Chambre de la Reine by Primaticcio survive. The evidence being so scant, it is impossible to tell which of the two artists is to be credited with the new decorative manner, although claims have been put forward for both.

Rosso's splendid Galerie François I (1533-40), which was restored in the 1960s and 1970s, originally had windows along both sides (the restored space has windows only on the side of the Cour du Cheval Blanc). The spaces between the window openings are divided more or less in half horizontally. The bottom half is covered with carved paneling, while the top half carries Rosso's paintings and stucco, showing the particular influence of the art of Raphael. Rosso's stucco figures, seeming to start away from the wall, combine sensuousness with a certain abruptness and vigor, endowing the space with a sense of drama. Mythological scenes and figures are integrated with the symbols of the royal house, most notably the Valois salamander, which recurs above each painted panel. It seems that Rosso was the first to use the characteristic strapwork, imitating rolled and cut

leather in stucco, which serves as a kind of background to the stucco figures. The use of such strapwork spread not only to the rest of France but also to northern Europe.

Primaticcio's early work was a continuance of his training with Giulio Romano, although the full-relief stucco creates a richer effect than any of the younger artist's work at Mantua. In fact, the first interior at Fontainebleau he worked on, the Chambre du Roi (destroyed), was based on a drawing by Giulio Romano. The fireplace from the Chambre de la Reine recalls specific motifs from the interiors of the Palazzo del Tè. Primaticcio's principal works at Fontainebleau are the Chambre de la Duchesse d'Etampes (1541-45) and the Galerie d'Ulysse (ca. 1550), both of which have been restored. Primaticcio's style is principally to be distinguished from Rosso's in its greater ease and elegance, from which the drama of Rosso's work is missing. Primaticcio also used the characteristic strapwork, but rounded and softened the edges so that at times it seems closer to a shell motif.

Primaticcio developed a highly influential style of figure drawing and sculpting, which has been traced to the influence of the Italian painter and etcher Parmigianino. The elongated tapering limbs, long, thin necks, small heads and exaggerated classical features of Primaticcio's figures became one of the most easily recognizable characteristics of French painting of the later 16th century. In Primaticcio's later work, as in the Galerie d'Ulysse, the influence of Michelangelo became more pronounced, particularly in scenes of violent action. A marked illusionism is also to be noted. Although Primaticcio's repeated trips to Italy may have brought him in contact with the recent developments in illusionism, it is more likely that the change was due to the presence of the painter Nicolò dell'Abbate, a more recent arrival from Italy. Nicolò, who was active at Fontainebleau in the 1540s and 1550s and may be considered the third Fontainebleau master, had been trained in an illusionist style.

The year 1540, when Rosso died, brought a number of new artistic stimuli to Fontainebleau, which made the palace into a link with Italy and its most recent artistic developments. Primaticcio returned from a trip to Rome, bringing back molds of ancient and recent sculpture, the casts of which were thenceforward displayed at the palace. Primaticcio also brought the important classical architect Giacomo Barozzi da Vignola with him. Sebastiano Serlio was then also at Fontainebleau, and although he built little there or elsewhere in France, his ideas and particularly his books had a significant influence on architectural developments. Benvenuto Cellini also spent a brief time at Fontainebleau in 1540, leaving a lasting legacy on French sculpture.

In 1559 Primaticcio was made principal architect of the court, upon the rather arbitrary dismissal of Philibert de l'Orme. Among Primaticcio's architectural works at Fontainebleau are the charming grotto in the Jardins des Pins, which shows the influence once again of Giulio Romano. On the other hand, the influence of Vignola is apparent in the classicism of the Aile de la Belle Cheminée. The dual staircase across the entire front of the building is a beautiful feature, but does not compensate for the dry correctness of the building's details.

In the mid-1560s, Fontainebleau ceased to be a center of artistic innovation, becoming more of an academy for the study of Mannerist art. The Second School of Fontainebleau, consisting of French artists, had little influence. Although some of the most prominent French architects contributed to the continuing reconstructions at Fontainebleau, the palace was never again a fulcrum of change. For a few decades Fontainebleau was the port of entry for Renaissance and Mannerist art and architecture to France, and in that capacity had a lasting influence on the course of French art history.

—MARIJKE RIJSBERMAN

LAON CATHEDRAL
Laon, France

1112: Previous cathedral burned. 1160: Rebuilding begun on choir, three bays, an apse, east bays of new transepts. 1180s: Ambulatory torn down, square eastern end bebun, crossing, 11-bay nave, remainder of transepts begun. 1190s: East and west rose windows installed, vaulting and crossing lantern added. 1215: West front completed. Ca. 1225: Work on towers abandoned with only southwest spire completed. Late 13th-early 14th century: Side chapels, cloister, three-bay chapter house added, southern picture window added. 1572-75: Side chapels divided from aisles by stone screens. 1681: Pulpit carved. 1793: Southwest spire destroyed. 1845: Massive restoration.

Publications

ADENAUER, H.: *Die Kathedrale von Laon*. Dusseldorf, 1934.

Only Lincoln Cathedral in England can compare with Laon Cathedral in its superb siting, crowning a steep-sided hill 300 feet above the surrounding Aisne plain and easily visible 25 miles away. Unlike Lincoln, however, Laon Cathedral is almost wholly the product of a single determined program, with relatively little stylistic development along the way. No other cathedral in France approaches so closely the ideal of a seven-tower silhouette, which was really achieved only at Tournai (now in Belgium). If Laon fell short of the ideal through lack of funds or structural problems, at least the completed work has an unmatched combination of power and grace; even in the 13th century Villard de Honnecourt could write that he had never seen towers like those of Laon.

A previous cathedral burned in civil riots in 1112; its successor can only have been a patching-up of the remains, for construction started entirely afresh in 1160 with a new choir of three bays and an apse, and the east bays of new transepts. After a pause, it recommenced in about 1180 with the crossing and 11-bay nave, the remainder of the transepts (including the bases of towers against the two outer corners of each), and then the west front with its own two towers, which was finished by about 1215.

For reasons possibly connected with the bay design and awkward shapes of vaulting, the semicircular east end was quickly taken down and replaced by seven more bays and a square end—a plan type much more typical of England than of France, and a precedent for the similar change made at Lincoln. No satisfactory explanation of the great length of the quire (the longest in France) is known, but the care to ensure a match with earlier work contrasts strikingly with the sort of enthusiasm that elsewhere might have led to "improvements" and a lack of harmony or balance in the finished result.

The four-story internal bay design is unusual but by no means unique. It had been used at Noyon and Senlis. The tribunes, or galleries over the aisles, are extraordinarily spacious, as wide and nearly as high as the aisles themselves, and yet serve little practical purpose except as parts of a homogeneous structure. To the interior they show generous twin openings and daringly slender shafts with Corinthian-type capitals, beneath single blind arches. Across the transept ends these tribunes broaden still further to form bridges on pairs of arches, linking the twin towers, and they terminate in apses projecting from the easternmost towers. Inside, the northern of these vaulted spaces is like a generously sized church in itself; the small southern one was a treasury connected by a stair to the sacristy below. Seen from outside, with their emphasis on windows and buttresses, the lofty apses are a foretaste of medieval designs in which the wall hardly exists. Their two upper stories light the tribunes, and the lower the ground-floor chapels.

Above the tribunes is a low triforium passage, expressed by triplet arches, again on Corinthian-type shafts. It is skillfully linked to the tower stairs and to four separate stairs in the piers of the crossing (probably it was the weakness caused by these that resulted in the completion of the central tower being abandoned). Finally, the clerestory: single large pointed windows with shafted jambs once flooded the whole interior with incandescent light.

Each pair of main bays is spanned by a typically French sexpartite vault, producing a slower rhythm that contrasts with the lively, transparent verticality of the nave walls—walls so pierced and hollowed as to be little more than screens through which space flows in true Gothic manner, punctuated but seldom interrupted. Clustered shafts descend from the vault right down to the main column caps—in fives between the main bays and in threes intermediately. Mostly the columns themselves are circular, and have Corinthianesque capitals in various shapes

Laon Cathedral, west facade: Laon, France, 1215

Laon Cathedral, nave and choir

to suit the upper shafts, but the east part of the nave differs; there big clustered piers alternate with round ones—rather in the older Romanesque manner but also anticipating the many-shafted columns of later Gothic. Nor had the round arches of Romanesque been entirely discarded in this early flowering of Gothic; they appear quite innocently here and there in the triforium and tribune. The thrusts of the high vaults are countered by those of the tribunes and aisles and by a complex system of stepped buttresses beyond the aisles.

Between these buttresses numerous side chapels were inserted in the latter part of the 13th century and the beginning of the 14th, and by about 1500 as many as 50 chaplains were attached to the cathedral. A much bigger chapel like a small separate church adjoins the south nave aisle near its west end. Though called the Chapel of Fonts, it is unlikely to have been meant as a baptistry; rather it would have been used by the canons for celebrating Mass at times when the main building was too cold.

Two vaulted square compartments, the present-day sacristy and treasury, occupy the angles between the transepts and choir aisles. The adjoining parts of these aisles (the three bays built first) have an unusual "domed" form of vaulting—evidently an experiment and not repeated.

The west front of Laon is one of the great masterpieces of the Gothic style, an adventurous composition so complex yet unified, so typical of its time and yet displaying such originality that it defies description in mere words. Perhaps it can be considered in three planes: three gabled portals thrusting boldly forward into the tiny town square, wall and windows above (expressing the nave and aisles), and finally twin towers leaping like natural growths from the corners. Or it can be looked at as three vertical units expressing the aisle-nave-aisle behind, each symmetrical in itself, and each a perfect composition in its own right. Its general form was to be widely imitated—for example at Chartres, Strasbourg and Reims—but was itself derived from such forerunners as St. Denis and Noyon. None of these, however, matches the sense of movement and poise achieved at Laon.

The central sculpture of the portals, its subject matter based on the "Universal Mirror" of Vincent of Beauvais and on sermons of Honorius d'Autun, is of outstanding importance, in spite of renewals that followed severe damage during the Revolution. Some of the 19th-century work was copied from Chartres, which had in its time been itself much influenced by Laon. Each of the three openings has four outer rings with figure carving of marvelous delicacy, fourfold jambs with more figures in two tiers, and an upper and a lower tympanum. The central entrance has a center post with a renewed figure of the Virgin Mary, to whom both this and the northern portal are dedicated. In its two outer rings the latter displays a range of Old Testament subjects unique in its variety and quality, in the third ring a series of Virtues overcoming Vices, and in the innermost a group of angels witnessing the Adoration scene that adorns the upper tympanum. The southern portal, with the Last Judgment as its theme, is noticeably earlier in character,

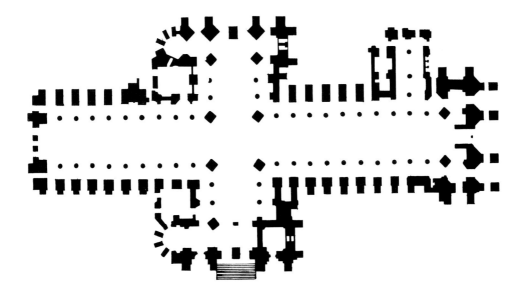

and is therefore believed to have been actually carved at the time of the rebuilding of the choir a generation earlier.

Tucked in behind the big square pinnacles that separate and stabilize the barrel vaults of the portals is a row of eight small windows. Above, with deep arches echoing those of the portals, are the great circular west window with its lace-like tracery, and big lancets flanking it. Though hard to appreciate from ground level, the lancet arches continue the iconography of the doorways below, with representations of the Liberal Arts (north side) and the Creation (south side). Above these again, crowning the main screen wall, runs an open arcade—stepped in the middle to cross the rose window and topped there by a balustraded footbridge connecting the stairs and the triforium passages.

The towers begin prosaically enough with square belfries and pairs of louvered windows on each face. Then the transformation to octagons starts. The corner buttresses become square turrets diagonal to the original square, with three deftly poised open arches, and then octagons themselves—no more than cage-like screens of stone transparent to the sky. Each little octagon was meant to carry an eight-sided spirelet, and each principal one a tall spire. A bizarre touch is added by the unmistakable figures of 16 oxen peering down on passers-by, two from each "cage" at the top of each turret. They commemorate the yoked beasts who toiled up the hill with building stone, and one ox in particular who, according to legend, joined his fellows when most needed and mysteriously disappeared when the work was done.

Only the southwest spire was actually completed, and that was destroyed in 1793. Only one of the towers at each end of the transepts was completed; with slight variations they are similar in design and date to the west ones. What should have been the grandest tower of all, over the crossing, was to have had a steeple doubling the height of the ridge on which the cathedral stands, but it was finished merely as a pyramid-capped lantern with an eight-ribbed vault soaring to 130 feet above the church floor.

Laon's medieval glass suffered badly during the Revolution, and only five windows out of 200 remain in anything like their original state—four in the quire, and the north transept rose. Much of the internal carving has fared better. The earliest capitals, in the east parts of the transept, depict acanthus (as on the traditional Corinthian pattern) and other formalized leaves, along with scrolls and figures of men and animals. Further west the sculpture becomes more naturalistic, portraying local wildflowers such as buttercup and watercress.

In 1572-75 nearly all the side chapels were divided from the aisles by stone screens—unusual but not inelegant compositions of the Doric and Ionic orders profusely ornamented with cartouches and caryatids, birds, heraldry and arabesques, and originally colored and gilded. The pulpit was carved in 1681 for the Charterhouse of Val St. Pierre.

The cloister and rectangular three-bay chapter house, standing south of the nave, are of the same period as the rebuilt choir, dating to the late 13th century. Both are vaulted, but the former has been spoiled by division into dwellings and stables.

—ANTHONY NEW

NOTRE DAME DU RAINCY
Le Raincy, France

1922-24. Architect: Auguste Perret (1874-1954).

Church of Notre Dame: Le Raincy, France, 1922-24

Publications

"Auguste Perret and Brothers." *Architects' Journal* (December 1926).

BADOVICI, JEAN: "Auguste et Gustave Perret." *Architecture vivante* (Summer 1925): 17-28.

COLLINS, PETER: *Concrete: The Vision of a New Architecture. A Study of Auguste Perret and His Predecessors.* London, 1959.

FRAMPTON, KENNETH, and FUTAGAWA, YUKIO: *Modern Architecture: 1920-1945.* New York, 1983.

JAMOT, P.: *Auguste and Gustave Perret et l'architecture du béton armé.* Paris and Brussels, 1927.

"Notre Dame of Le Raincy." *Space Design* (September 1980).

*

Auguste Perret's first religious monument, Notre Dame du Raincy, stands with solemn simplicity on an infill site. Perret applied for the first time his philosophies about reinforced concrete with amazing purity, stripping the elements of the structure to their bare essence: a columnar structural system sits within a nonbearing enclosing envelope.

From the exterior the building appears quiet and grave, with materials that until then were known only to industrial architecture. A continuous wall of precast perforated panels, with small, repetitive motifs filled with glass, wraps around the building, reinforcing a sense of stability, and maintaining a sense of scale and detail. It is this wall of repetitive perforations that allows the vertical surfaces to disappear from the interior, in a multicolored lace of light. The vaulted ceiling seems to soar over the

Church of Notre Dame

slender columns, embracing the worshippers. The uniformity of the shallow central vault is broken by the wrinkles generated by the transverse vaults on either side. This creates a subtle sense of movement that makes the ceiling appear weightless. The roughness of the finished concrete, although due to financial restraints, promotes an earthly character that, by contrast, reinforces the ethereal quality of the space.

This building epitomizes Perret's philosophy of design. Reinforced concrete, the material of the modern age, is explored there in many different ways, and is manipulated to achieve a space that fulfills traditional sensibilities. Structure becomes the essence of the space. The different architectural elements—columns, vaults, walls—are arranged with great precision and are beautifully proportioned. The syntactic relationship of the different elements transcends the realm of construction.

The church in plan is very traditional, a rectangular basilica plan with a central nave, aisles and a shallow apse on the eastern end. Twenty-eight tall and thin columns support two vaulting systems in the ceiling. A longitudinal vault along the center nave is supported by a series of short transverse vaults over the aisles. Rows of four columns march in procession, reinforcing the internal spatial organization. The columns are not there for purely functional purposes, but instead reinforce the rhythm and grandeur that, juxtaposed to the continuity of the exterior envelope, maintain a sense of scale on the inside.

Among the refinements of this simple rectangular space, the gentle slope of the ground floor is notable. While the chancel remains horizontal, by means of a plinth, the floor slopes down toward the altar. Besides the functional advantage of this move, which permits the creation of sacristies and vestries under the

chancel, it dramatizes the procession and modifies our spatial understanding as we enter or leave the space.

Perret's attention to detail is present in the articulation of the exterior wall. The repetitive precast concrete panels are arranged around pictorial pieces at the center of each lateral bay. This creates a transition of scale necessary because of the lack of structural expression on the outside. The panels filled with colored glass are arranged in a chromatic progression from yellow at the entrance to deep purple at the apse. This arrangement is reminiscent of Gothic magnificence in its manipulation of light and spatial transparency.

The church, like most of Perret's architecture, does not rely on structural gymnastics to express the qualities of reinforced concrete. Perret instead searched for structural efficiency within a conservative spatial formulation. With the use of reinforced concrete he was able to achieve an integrated system of vaulting that traditionally would have been understood as two separate elements, the vault and the roof. The longitudinal and transverse shallow vaults of the ceiling were stiffened by fins on the upper side that supported large precast tiles. Combined, these tiles formed the single segmental vault of the roof. The thinness that, by these means, Perret was able to achieve in the interior vaults is heightened not only by the sense of movement of their juxtaposing directions but also by perforations along the center of the interior vaults.

Perret's logic and intuitive ingenuity, which allowed him to solve problems of planning as in the Rue Franklin apartment building, and problems of structure as at the Théâtre des Champs-Elysées, rendered him as the one architect capable of designing a significant monument under tight conditions. With limited economic means, Perret had to design a large church, 185 feet by 63 feet, as a memorial to those killed in the Battle of Ourcq. Perret's thoughts of architecture are so embedded in this work that it is arguable whether his solution would have been different had there been a reasonable budget for this enterprise. Perret once again succeeded in finding a worthy solution under very difficult circumstances.

Perret achieved in this church a new aesthetic identity that reinforced his rational concerns of expressing the essential qualities of the work through a technical system representative of the time. He pursued this through a restrained acknowledgment of classical spatial concerns in a quest for permanent and timeless values in architecture.

—ANNABEL DELGADO

UNITÉ D'HABITATION
Marseilles, France

1946-52. Architect: Le Corbusier (1887-1965).

Publications

HOFMANN, WERNER, and KULTERMANN, UDO: *Modern Architecture in Color.* New York, 1970.
LE CORBUSIER: *L'Unité d'Habitation de Marseille.* Paris, 1950, published as *The Marseilles Block,* London, 1950.
WINTER, JOHN: *Modern Buildings.* London, 1969.

*

Le Corbusier had devoted much of his sojourn in the Pyrenees during World War II to writing and to sporadic approaches to the French Vichy government with a view to realizing self-build housing programs. However, after liberation in 1945, he set about rebuilding a war-torn France with missionary zeal. Finally, it seemed that his *Ville Radieuse* idea could become reality after its two decades of gestation.

In 1922, Le Corbusier's *Ville Contemporaine* was exhibited at the Salon d'Automne, Paris, followed by the *Voisin* plan for Paris at L'Exposition des Arts Décoratifs, Paris, 1925. Projects followed for Nemours (1934) and Zlín (1935), with postwar city plans for Saint-Gaudens, La Rochelle-Pallice and Saint-Dié, all of which developed the *unité* concept of an autonomous community of high density within a lush parkland setting.

Even though the Marseilles Unité was to emerge as *the* seminal building from Le Corbusier's postwar oeuvre, as realized, it was only part of a much more ambitious project to include four such slab blocks. Even in its reduced form, however, the Marseilles Unité was beset by difficulties throughout its extended design and construction period, but they were overcome largely by the unswerving commitment to the project of Claudius-Petit, the minister of reconstruction. The project was also hindered by a notoriously unstable government in postwar France in addition to a disrupted building industry with attendant material shortages.

L'Unité d'Habitation was commissioned in 1946 and early projects for it were in steel, a radical development of the machine aesthetic. The basis was a steel support structure with factory-made apartment units slotted into the frame. At once this seemed a logical development of Le Corbusier's *machine à habiter* mass-produced at city scale. However, acute steel shortages in postwar France provided a catalyst for the new architectural language which emerged, *béton brut:* in the event, the role of L'Unité d'Habitation as form giver was to prove as influential as any utopian views it expressed concerning the nature of collective living or urbanism.

The *unité* not only demonstrated a logical development of Le Corbusier's previous mass housing projects, but like all his truly seminal works, it represented a synthesis of profound experiences to date. The Marseilles apartments with double-height living space evoked his visit to the monastery at Ema in 1907, where its relationship with nature and the notion of a collective monastic community had such a lasting influence. *La Ville Radieuse,* published in 1933, had presented another model for communal living, the Cunard ocean liner embracing, like the *unité,* a range of facilities supporting the everyday needs of its inhabitants, the voyagers. Furthermore, the size of the Marseilles Unité community was no accident: Charles Fourier had suggested in the mid-19th century an ideal community for his *phalanstère* of 1,800 inhabitants.

The formal language of the *unité* similarly represented a synthesis: the pilotis, albeit in monumental guise, reinterpreted *Les cinq points* of two decades previously, and the careful disposition of plastic forms at roof level not only suggested an "acropolis" but reflected Le Corbusier's deep understanding of Mediterranean vernacular forms. However, even more potent was the realization in built form of his prewar painterly investigations. Le Corbusier had always utilized the canvas as a laboratory for formal development.

The key to the *unité* was its sectional organization embracing a generous internal corridor, *la rue intérieure.* This gave access to a series of interlocking apartments varying in size through some 23 types, from the equivalent of a *pension* bedroom for a single itinerant to generous dwellings for large families.

The apartments were physically isolated in the interests of sound attenuation and were, for their time, technically advanced in terms of their integration of services. A typically Corbusian double-height living space with bed balcony was shaded from the strong Mediterranean sunlight by a *brise-soleil,* a device which like *béton brut* was to be absorbed as part of a new mainstream architectural language. The apartments were of narrow frontage with a deep plan. Critics have consistently condemned such a configuration, but unlike many subsequent interpretations of the *unité* idea, the Marseilles prototype, because of its ingenious section, afforded a dual aspect for each dwelling. Furthermore, a deep plan which effectively prevented the penetration of strong Mediterranean sunlight, allied to the *brise-soleil,* averted the potential problems of excessive solar heat gain. While provisions for leisure and physical culture certainly supported the "collective" ethos, the shopping street halfway up the building was an overprovision for a modest community of fewer than 2,000 inhabitants, and shop units remained empty long after completion in 1952.

As a new brutal architectural language, the *unité* was as seductive as the smooth mechanistic vocabulary of Villa Savoye had been two decades previously. Le Corbusier promoted *béton brut* as a *natural* material while the balconies and *brise-soleil* demonstrated a wholly new expression for the facade of a multistory building that was quite remote from the smooth, glazed curtain wall of *Cité de Refuge.* The duplex section showed not only the alternate expression of double-height living room and single-story bedroom to modulate the facade but endowed an appropriate scale to the building. The deep reveals

Unité d'Habitation: Marseilles, France, 1946-52

to the balconies generated rich shadow patterns while oblique views exposed the primary-colored reveals. Furthermore, the whole building was fashioned according to *Le Modulor,* Le Corbusier's successor to *Traces Régulateurs,* and both based upon the golden section.

The *unité* model was repeated at Nantes, Briey, Berlin and Firminy, but it was the English who were to absorb with unique commitment the Brutalist architectural language. A massive program of public housing in postwar Britain allied with a stable socialist government allowed architects to realize their Corbusian aspirations. The outcome was often a sad parody of the Marseilles prototype, but to blame Le Corbusier for such crass misinterpretation of the *unité* idea is a grotesque caricature; for the *second* time in his career, his atelier had produced both a seminal building and a new architectural language of unmatched authority.

—A. PETER FAWCETT

METZ CATHEDRAL
Metz, France

1215-ca. 1240: Nave begun, aisle vaults, four monocylindrical piers, eastern portal, stair tower, some exterior walls completed. **1250:** Designs altered, nave elevated, apsidal westwork made into an independent church. **1302-16:** Westwork reintegrated into the cathedral, three bays added to the south end of nave. **Ca. 1330:** Stained-glass window at the west end of nave added; **Glazier:** Hermann von Munster. **Late 15th-early 16th centuries:** Carolingian transepts and choir demolished and rebuilt. **1769:** Classical portico added to west end; **Architect:** François Blondel. **1898-1903:** Blondel's portal replaced; **Architect:** Paul Tornow.

Publications

AUBERT, MARCEL (ed.): *La cathédrale de Metz.* Paris, 1931.
BOINET, AMÈDÉE: "La cathédrale de Metz." *Congrés archéologique de France, LXXXIIIe session tenue a Metz, Strasbourg et Colmar en 1920* (Paris, 1922).
BURNAND, MARIE CLAIRE: *Lorraine gothique.* Paris, 1990.
PELT, JEAN BAPTISTE: *Etudes sur la cathédrale de Metz.* 3 vols. Metz, 1930-37.
WAGNER, PIERRE EDOUARD, and JOLIN, JEAN LOUIS: *La cathédrale de Metz.* Metz, 1988.

*

The cathedral of Metz is one of the largest Gothic churches in Europe. Its great scale, huge clerestory windows and unusually slender structure make it one of the most important French buildings of the 13th century. Despite this, until recently it attracted limited scholarly attention outside local antiquarian circles, due in part to its limited sculptural programs and to the historical vicissitudes of the Lorraine since the Franco-Prussian War of 1870.

The first Gothic campaign began around 1215 under the reign

Metz Cathedral: Metz, France, begun 1215

Metz Cathedral, nave toward east

of Bishop Conrad von Scharfeneck. Building on the foundations of an important late-Carolingian cathedral unconventionally oriented north-south due to terrain slope, construction proceeded slowly until the 1240s, when important changes were made to the first design. The early plan was Germanic, with twin towers flanking an apsidal westwork, reflecting the influence of the archbishopric of Trier and its cathedral. However, the execution, as at the contemporary Liebfrauenkirche in Trier, was carried out by a French workshop. The Metz builders came from Reims, and brought with them the innovative ideas of the circle of the architect Jean d'Orbais, as is evident from the elevation with

Champenois passages on the side aisles, Remois bar tracery windows, cantonnated piers with continuous capitals, and a classic balance of verticals and horizontals. The building was very spacious, with an exceptionally broad nave and widely spaced piers. In that first 30-odd-year campaign, the nave was constructed up to the level of the aisle vaults. The westwork, dedicated to Notre Dame, had four monocylindrical piers, an eastern portal, a stair tower and some exterior walls completed.

Around 1250, under Bishop Jacques de Lorraine, two major design changes were made. The first, keeping up with contemporary visionary projects at the cathedrals of Amiens, Beauvais and Cologne, was to raise dramatically the elevation of the nave and to change the articulation of shafts to conform with the absolute vertical binding of triforium and clerestory established around 1230 at St. Denis. The typical 3: 1: 3 ratio of nave arcade, triforium and clerestory elevations of High Gothic churches was elongated to an unconventional 3: 1.8: 3.8. Thus the clerestory became one-fourth taller than the nave arcade, and the triforium almost twice as tall as a conventional one. The only unhappy element in this new interior elevation was the broad and dark drapery frieze placed between the triforium and clerestory. Its carvings may have been leftovers from the first campaign, originally intended for a lower setting, as at the portals of Reims cathedral.

At the same time that the height was raised, the depth of the upper structural members was reduced. The outer pier buttresses are the lightest of any major French Gothic cathedral, as is the ratio of supporting stone volume to void. The tracery of the high windows was redesigned toward the end of the century using more complex, richer patterns characteristic of the later Rayonnant. The combination of vertical swelling, structural attenuation and elaborate upper tracery is particularly striking from the exterior, where the enormous windows and thin structural frame suggest a vastly enlarged reliquary chapel, a monumental version of La Sainte-Chapelle in Paris. This vision is reflected in the local name of the cathedral, *la lanterne de Dieu*.

The second design change under Bishop Jacques de Lorraine was the transformation of the apsidal westwork into an independent church, Notre-Dame-la-Ronde, oriented at right angles to the nave of the cathedral. Notre-Dame received a new, highly luminous chevet, added at the east end of the transverse axis between the four piers of the old westwork, and a west portal opening onto the Place St. Etiènne.

Sometime later, probably under Bishop Reginald de Bar

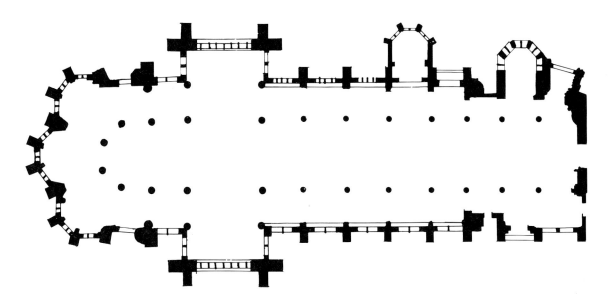

(1302-16), the decision was made to reintegrate Notre-Dame-la-Ronde into the space of the cathedral. Three bays were added at the geographic south end (ecclesiastical west) of the nave, matching loosely the five earlier bays. The new structure was heavier and much more conservative than that of 13th-century bays, but had as an innovation a three-story stained-glass window at the end of the nave, the largest window of the Gothic period, executed about 1330 by the glazier Hermann von Munster. This was a splendid development of the vision of the second designer, wrapping the upper glazed stories of the nave around a luminous western end. Although the sources for such an end window are found in Reims, first at St. Nicaise and later at the cathedral, it also recalls the contemporary English Decorated Gothic choir at Gloucester, but again at a much larger scale. Unfortunately, this window was partly mutilated by a classical portal added to the cathedral in 1769 by François Blondel. This portal was in turn replaced in 1898-1903 by a Gothic Revival one by the *dombaumeister* Paul Tornow. Despite the spatial unification, Notre-Dame-la-Ronde and the cathedral remained physically separated by a wall which was demolished only in 1380, and remained ecclesiastically separate until the 18th century.

After completion of the nave, construction was interrupted for more than one century. The Carolingian transepts and choir were demolished in the late 15th and early 16th centuries and replaced by splendid Late Gothic vessels. Metz and Amiens were the only two of the giant northern Gothic cathedrals, which also include Beauvais, Cologne, Palma de Majorca and Narbonne, completed in the Middle Ages.

Despite a complex and fragmented design history, clearly a collective sustained effort from many masters and administrators who intervened in its construction, the cathedral of Metz attained an extraordinary spatial unit and integrity. Its complex archaeological collage enriches rather than confuses its magnificent central focus. The final building synthesizes visionary scale and rich detail, structural daring and solid competence, and stretches the Sugerian conception of *lux nova* to its most quantitatively extreme medieval statement. Even though Metz Cathedral makes few radical breaks with its sources, it exemplifies through its scale, refinements and innovations some of the most advanced structural and aesthetic aspirations of the Rayonnant Gothic of the second half of the 13th century.

—SERGIO L. SANABRIA

PLACE ROYALE (PLACE STANISLAS)
Nancy, France

1750-57. Architect: Emmanuel Héré de Corny (1705-63).

Publications

HÉRÉ DE CORNY, EMANUELE: *Plans et élévations de la place royale de Nancy et des autres edifices a l'environment bâtis par les ordres du Roy du Pologne duc de Lorraine.* Paris, 1753.

Place Royal (Place Stanislas): Nancy, France, 1750-57

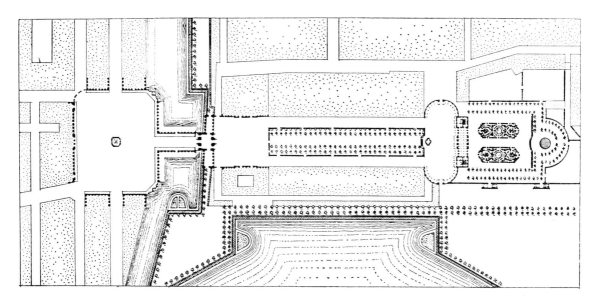

JACQUOT, T.: "Emmanuel Héré premier architecte de Stanislas et ses collaborateurs." *Le pays lorrain* (1952).

MAROT, PIERRE: "La genèse de la Place Royale de Nancy." *Annales de l'est* (1954).

MAROT, PIERRE: *Emmanuel Héré.* Nancy, 1954.

MAROT, PIERRE: *La place royale de Nancy: Image de la réunion de la Lorraine à la France, du monument du Bien-Aimé à la statue du Bienfaisant.* Paris, 1966.

PFISTER, C.: *Emmanuel Héré et la place Stanislas.* Nancy, 1906.

*

The layout of the Place Royale in Nancy is one of the great achievements of urban planning of the Rococo. Stanislas Leszczynski, father-in-law of Louis XV and duke of Lorraine, commissioned Emmanuel Héré to do the design in 1751. By 1755 Héré had completed the design for the modern, innovative, architectonically brilliant and politically consequential monumental axis of Nancy.

The layout consists of a principal square, which is in fact almost square (the former Place Royale), and a long promenade (the Place de la Carrière), which ends in the so-called "Hémicycle." In contradistinction to the design of traditional squares, which are ringed round by high buildings, the Place Royale was opened up to all the principal streets, and thus became the main focus of the city center. The immediate urban planning goal was to connect the Old Town and the New Town, which Héré sought to realize not only by designing diverse open spaces, but also by building a triumphal arch, and by incorporating a fountain by Guibal and the rich railings by Jean Lamour (1698-1771).

Rigorous symmetry is conspicuously absent in the tense sequence of spaces. The differences in height and articulation of the surrounding buildings contribute to the asymmetrical effect. The former Place Royale is surrounded by the Hôtel de Ville (Town Hall), four palaces of equal height and one-story buildings on the side opening up to the Place de la Carrière. The Place de la Carrière (originally the Place Tunier of the Old Town) itself is lined with simple residential buildings, and ends in a grand manner in the Hémicycle. The latter is marked by a curved peristyle and the sumptuous Hôtel de l'Intendence, which stands in an axial relationship to the Hôtel de Ville. The Hémicycle is nevertheless much more intimate than the Place Royale, mostly because of its narrow passages to the Old Town

on the western side and to the Pépinière Gardens on the eastern side.

The originality of the triple design is not diminished by the fact that the Lorraine architect Héré used Parisian models, and consulted Germain Boffrand's *Livre d'Architecture,* which appeared after 1745. Even the classicizing triumphal arch between the Place Royale and the Place de la Carrière was built after the example of Boffrand's Place du Carrousel in Paris. The close relationship with the French Rococo also brought in its wake the attempt to apply the aesthetic "*standards des embellissement,*" a fundamental architectural concept of the mid-18th century, urging urban beautification.

The adoption of French architectural styles was also politically motivated: Nancy had been occupied by French troops in 1702, and the union of Lorraine and France was also to receive an official architectural expression. It was not Leszczynski, the patron of the work, but his son-in-law, Louis XV, who was commemorated in a monumental fashion in the center of the principal square. This unambiguous presence at the heart of Nancy made clear who the ruler of Lorraine really was. Even the splendid railings by Lamour glorify French royalty in the use of the symbols of the sun, lily and rooster.

In its avoidance of any form of monotony, in its successful urban planning, and in its iconologic expressiveness, the public space of Nancy became an important influence on the Place de la Concorde in Paris and the Place Royale in Brussels.

—RICHARD HÜTTEL
Translated from the German by Marijke Rijsberman

ARC DE TRIOMPHE
Paris, France

1806-36. Architect: Jean François Thérèse Chalgrin.

Publications

GAEHTGENS, THOMAS W.: *Napoleons Arc de Triomphe.* Göttingen, Germany, 1974.

GAEHTGENS, THOMAS W.: "Four Newly Discovered Designs

Arc de Triomphe: Paris, France, 1806-36

for the Arc de Triomphe by Jean-François Chalgrin." *Print Review* 5 (1976): 58-68.

HIRSCHFELD, GUSTAVE: *Arcs de triomphe et colonnes triomphales de Paris*. Paris, 1938.

Commissioned in 1806 by Napoléon to celebrate the victories of his Grande Armée over the Austrians at the Battle of Austerlitz, on 2 December 1805, the Arc de Triomphe is a testament to Napoléon's manipulation of Roman imperial imagery to glorify his own reign. During its 30-year construction, the arch became a symbol of the aspirations of succeeding political regimes in their efforts to reshape national identity according to their own vision.

Napoléon originally intended to construct the arch on rue St. Antoine, at the Bastille, in eastern Paris. The site had remained deserted since the storming of the infamous fortress in 1789 but nevertheless remained engrained in the collective memory. Furthermore, Napoleon's victorious soldiers traditionally passed by the Bastille on their return from central European campaigns.

At the same time, Napoléon commissioned Percier and Fontaine to build a second arch (1806-08) to celebrate the emperor's victory at Marengo. It would also double as a triumphal entryway to the Palace of the Tuileries at the Place du Carrousel.

The arch, modeled after the Arch of Septimius Severus in Rome, provides an idea, at a much reduced scale, of Jean-François-Thérèse Chalgrin's original intentions for the Arch of Triumph. The Arc du Carrousel is adorned with eight Corinthian columns in the round surmounted by statues revetted by the various uniforms of the Grande Armée. Six bas-reliefs depicting the glories of the empire decorate the facades, while a bronze quadriga crowns the attic, although it was originally destined to display the bronze horses looted from San Marco Cathedral in Venice. Napoléon thus envisioned a series of permanent triumphal arches stretching from one end of the city to the other, remodeling the cityscape on an antique model, and further uniting Napoléon's reign with that of his illustrious Roman predecessors.

At the urging of Napoléon's minister of the interior, Jean-Baptiste Champagny, the cramped urban site of the Bastille was abandoned for a semicountry setting on the Chaillot Hill, at the height of the Champs-Elysées. Champagny persuasively argued the advantages of this commanding and open site, which was complemented by an orderly arrangement of radiating avenues converging on the future arch. There, in splendid isolation and towering over the capital, the gigantic arch would be visible from key points in Paris, with the Place de la Concorde and the Louvre directly on its axis. Champagny correctly foresaw that the heights would eventually become an integral part of the Parisian landscape, although in 1806 there was only pastureland with the ''radiating avenues'' actually tree-lined dirt roads traced in the preceding century.

Chalgrin and Jean-Arnaud Raymond were chosen to design the arch. Chalgrin was nearing the end of a successful architectural career, with his masterpiece being the neoclassical church of St.-Philippe du Roule (1768-75). Preliminary designs called for an arch modeled after Roman examples, with one arch in its principal facade, as in the Arch of Titus, as well as with a smaller transverse arch on the lateral facade. Chalgrin favored a rather strict interpretation of the Roman type, complete with freestanding columns, statues and bas-relief panels, much like his contemporaries' designs for the Arc de Triomphe du Carrousel. Napoléon, however, judged columns unnecessary on his monumental arch, since these would not be clearly visible from afar. In the end, a simpler, columnless design was approved, and construction begun in August 1806.

Although based on Roman prototypes, the 50-meter-high arch dwarfed all examples from antiquity. Its megalomania, in the manner of Etiènne-Louis Boullée, can be compared with other contemporary Napoléonic projects such as the Church of the Madeleine, whose construction resumed in 1806, and the designs for a Palace for the Emperor's Son, the Roi de Rome. Napoléon advocated such grand monuments, stating that ''men are great only through the monuments they leave behind.'' Beauty was intimately linked to monumentality, and simplicity and directness were valued over allegorical detail and complexity. Stylistically, the arch broke with the French tradition of arches as represented in the Porte Saint Denis (1672) and Porte Saint Martin (1674), built during the reign of Louis XIV. Those arches, with their narrow proportions and rich ornamentation, are more decorative than Napoléon's arch. It is the latter's sheer size, coupled with its relative sobriety and antique proportions, that makes it so memorable and impressive.

Construction of the Arc de Triomphe progressed slowly, and by the time Napoléon married Marie-Louise in April 1810, the arch was only five meters high. Napoléon had the whole arch quickly finished to scale, in wood and linen, in time for the imperial procession. It was on that festive occasion that the arch's power to stir the imagination could at last be fully appreciated, and its judicious location was immediately approbated.

Temporary bas-reliefs were installed on the mock arch depicting Napoléon as a man of peace, an interpretation that would not outlast his reign. The following year, in 1811, Chalgrin died and Goust, one of his associates and former students, continued work on the project. Napoléon's defeat at Waterloo and the Allies' entry into Paris in 1815 brought work on the arch to a halt. If Napoléon had usurped Roman imagery to legitimize his reign by associating it with the glories of the Roman Empire, his successors likewise endowed it with their own political imagery. Although barely rising above ground, the arch had already assumed mythic status as a cogent symbol of national identity.

In 1823, under the Restauration, Louis XVIII resumed construction on the arch, retaining Goust as chief architect. He rededicated the arch to his victorious armies in Spain. Aware of Goust's ties to the former imperial regime, and to its chief architect Chalgrin, the king assigned Jean-Nicholas Huyot to collaborate with Goust on the arch. Huyot, intent on lessening the arch's aggressive imagery recalling Napoléonic grandeur, broke up Goust's plain facades by adding engaged Corinthian columns, thereby diluting the arch's austere grandeur and introducing instead a more decorative reading of the arch. Disagreements between the two architects forced Goust to resign his commission in 1830, the same year that brought the downfall of King Charles X during the July Revolution. The conservative yet pragmatic Louis Philippe succeeded Charles and pursued construction of the arch, which took on a new mission: to commemorate the armies of both the 1789 Revolution and the empire. Abel Blouet, who had restored the Baths of Caracalla in Rome, succeeded Huyot in 1832, and remained faithful to Chalgrin's final design, eliminating Huyot's plans for adding engaged columns. The only change Blouet introduced was the addition of a somewhat heavy attic decorated with shields, on which are engraved the principal battles fought by the republic and the empire. Thirty years after its inception, the arch was finally inaugurated on 29 July, although its decorative sculpture was not yet in place.

The subsequent addition of sculptural decoration offers the most important ensemble of French sculpture dating to the early 19th century. The four colossal high-reliefs on the principal facades (1833-36) illustrate the Triumph of 1810, Peace, Resistance, and the Depart des Volontaires de 1792, also known as La Marseillaise. That last sculpture, by Francois Rude, remains the most powerful and moving of the group. Above these high-reliefs and the lateral arches, six bas-reliefs represent the funeral of the revolutionary general Marceau in 1796; the Battle of Aboukir, celebrating Napoléon's victory over the Turks in 1799; the Battle of Jemmapes, glorifying the revolutionary army's victory over the Austrians in 1792; the Crossing on the Pont d'Arcole, Napoléon's victory over the Austrians in 1796; the capture of Alexandria by Napoléon; and finally, the Battle of Austerlitz. The great frieze of the entablature illustrates the departure and return of the Grande Armée. On the vaults are inscribed the names of 660 generals who participated in the military campaigns of the republic and the empire. Thus the sculpture program as approved by Louis Philippe depicts the battles fought between 1792 and 1814, symbolizing the struggles of the young republic and the empire against the ancien régime and despotic European monarchies. The king chose to illustrate the most glorious events of an era which still claimed the allegiance of a bourgeoisie which was becoming increasingly dissatisfied with the current social and political climate. The king's pragmatic approach to artistic programs at a time of political sensitivity can also be seen in his choice of a 2,000-year-old obelisk, free of political controversy, as the centerpiece for the Place de la Concorde.

It was Napoléon's nephew, Napoléon III, who was to give the arch its definitive setting by embellishing the surrounding roundabout, which by the mid-19th century was becoming increasingly urban. It was in Napoléon III's interest to capitalize on his uncle's memory to legitimize his own coup d'état in 1852. The prefect of Paris, Baron George-Eugène Haussmann, who was to transform the capital's urban fabric, added eight new avenues to the preexisting four, thereby creating 12 radiating avenues converging on the Arc de Triomphe. Furthermore, he had Jean-Charles Alphand landscape the small gardens fronting the symmetrical and harmonious facades of the *hôtel particulier* facing the arch.

It is ironic that the arch's original function, to celebrate the return of victorious armies, was not fulfilled until 14 July 1919, when Allied troops marched through it to celebrate the defeat of the Germans in World War I. The arch, however, had already been witness to great moments in French history, from the return of Napoléon's ashes in 1840 to Victor Hugo's state funeral in 1885. The inhumation of an unknown soldier from World War I in January 1921 assured the Arc de Triomphe's unassailable position as France's most patriotic and hallowed monument, embodying the aspirations of the entire nation, and becoming an obligatory site for visiting dignitaries and tourists, as well as for official celebrations and popular demonstrations.

—MARC VINCENT

BIBLIOTHÈQUE NATIONALE
Paris, France

1854: Commission awarded; **Architect:** Henri Labrouste (1801-75). **1854-75:** Construction.

Publications

FRAMPTON, KENNETH, and FUTAGAWA, YUKIO: *Modern Architecture: 1851-1919.* New York, 1983.

*

The Bibliothèque Nationale expresses Henri Labrouste's architectural genius. The building embodies his desire for architectural expression that represents the present without regard for issues of style. Struggling to fulfill his vision early in his career as a revolutionary student at the École des Beaux-Arts, Labrouste finally realized his dream in his two major buildings: the Bibliothèque Sainte-Geneviève and the Bibliothèque Nationale.

Several proposals had been made for the Bibliothèque Nationale that were inspired by Etiènne-Louis Boullée's scheme for the Bibliothèque Imperiale for the same site in 1785, but it wasn't until Labrouste's appointment in 1854 that substantial work began. The site consisted of existing 17th- and 18th-century structures that Labrouste was to restore and adapt. Labrouste's design consists of a sequence of three spaces inset within an existing fabric: an existing entry court, the reading room and the book stacks. Labrouste's interpretation of learning as a process of progressive discoveries is expressed in an architectural sequence of rooms which ultimately leads to the books. The sequence duplicates his earlier project, the Bibliothèque Sainte-Geneviève. Labrouste uses the progression to express his positive view of historical evolution.

On the Bibliothèque Sainte-Geneviève, Labrouste began the progression in the simple austerity of the exterior. The simple arcaded facade of the library recalls early Renaissance buildings. However, through a detailed study of the articulation of its parts, this work reveals a modern transparency that expresses, in both literal and syntactic levels, the interior organization and its contents. A simple entrance leads to a vestibule resembling a hypostile hall that focuses on a dramatically lit stairwell. The vestibule is enhanced with busts of literary figures and pictorial landscapes that make the user aware of a historical past. The solid masonry columns are adorned by very light arched metal trusses creating an unbalanced confrontation of both materials. The focus of the stairwell celebrates the introduction of printing in Paris by featuring a monument to Ulrich Gering. The stairwell leads to the reading room, which occupies the second floor. A central row of thin cast-iron columns creates the main support for the two barrel vaults in the space. An harmonious balance between iron and masonry is achieved in this room. Light, books and technology are combined to represent the essence of learning.

The Bibliothèque Nationale establishes a similar sequence. Filled with books and pictorial landscapes, the enclosure resembles the Bibliothèque Sainte-Geneviève. In the horizontal progression, the reading room occupies the center between an exterior court and the library stacks. The construction of the reading room created an ethereal feel. Its grandeur is reminiscent of Renaissance spaces. The reading room is composed of sixteen cast-iron columns contained within a surrounding masonry shell. The thirty-two feet high by one foot wide columns are crowned with semicircular girders which generate nine domes made of porcelain panels and skylights that enhance the delicacy of the space. The plan generated by the columns in the central space is non-directional. A vertical thrust, however, is emphasized by the light coming from the top of the domes. The masonry shell mediates between the two rooms but follows the rhythm of the iron structure. It recognizes the presence of the book stacks by an apsidal inflection on an otherwise square plan and by a large four-story window that reveals its contents.

The balance and clarity between the constituent parts of the structure express Labrouste's interest in the tectonics of the building. The iron structure is self-supporting. The transition from the columns to the girders, to the domes, to the porcelain panels, and finally to the skylight is smooth. It expands the dialogue between supporting and enclosing elements. The room resembles a garden or an outdoor reading place.

Labrouste's most revolutionary statement in this library dwells in the stack room. Through a large opening, Labrouste revealed this machine-like room, that had an aesthetic vocabulary only previously used in ship construction. Except for the bookcases, the construction is of iron. Five stories high with an open central space throughout its length, the stacks house over 900,000 volumes. The roof is glass and the floor plates are made of cast iron grillwork, allowing the light to filter through the stacks all the way to the lower floors. Small metal bridges cross the central space, connecting both sides of the stack room. The lightness of the horizontal planes accentuates the vertical solidity of the stacks as the essential supports of this room. Labrouste accomplished a true indication of a new aesthetic sensibility in this space. As Kenneth Frampton points out, the potential of this new aesthetic would not be realized until the constructivist work of the 20th century. It is in the stack room that the progression of spaces terminates. The notions of knowledge and progress embodied in this cage of light are indispensable for the understanding of our time.

Labrouste's search for meaningful expression was achieved through a rational understanding of the nature of construction,

Bibliothèque Nationale: Paris, France, 1854-75

its context and its embodiment in the physiognomy of the building. In the Bibliotèque Nationale, Labrouste broke new ground and ventured into a new understanding of the role of architecture. This was a catalytic event that rapidly evolved in the unravelling of the Modern Movement.

—ANNABEL DELGADO

CENTRE GEORGES POMPIDOU
Paris, France

1977: Completed; **Architects:** Renzo Piano and Richard Rogers, with Ove Arup as consultant.

Publications

BAUDRILLARD, J.: *L'effet Beaubourg: Implosion et dissuasion.* Paris, 1977.
"Centre du plateau Beaubourg: concours d'idées." *Techniques et architecture* (special issue, February 1972).
"Centre Pompidou." *Architectural Design* 2 (1977).
MARINELLI, G.: *Il Centro Beaubourg a Parigi: "Macchina" e segno architettonico.* Bari, Italy, 1978.
MASSIMO, DINO: *Renzo Piano: Progetti e architettura 1964-1983.* Milan, 1983.
"Piano and Rogers—Beaubourg." *Domus* (October 1971).

"Piano and Rogers: Centre Beaubourg." *Architectural Design* (July 1972).
"Piano and Rogers." *Architects' Journal* (21 April 1972).
"Piano and Rogers." *Architectural Design* 5 (1975).
"Piano and Rogers: Architectural Method." *Architecture and Urbanism* (June 1976).
Renzo Piano: Buildings and Projects 1971-1989. New York, 1989.
ROGERS, RICHARD, PIANO, RENZO, et al.: *The Building of Beaubourg.* London, 1979.

*

The Centre Pompidou in Paris, designed by Richard Rogers and Renzo Piano, is the result of a 1971 architectural competition for a new center for modern art. It is often called the "Beaubourg," in reference to its neighborhood, and is reputed to be the most visited building in Europe.

In the 1960s architects on the fringe and students were playing with ideas of infinitely variable megastructures—buildings that could change and adapt within a given frame. The Archigram Group explored this theme with numerous beautiful drawings. Cedric Price designed a fun-palace that changed, adapted and glittered. It was all somehow unreal and far removed from the practical world of building. With the Centre Pompidou the dream became a reality, and great credit must go to the French government and to the architects for taking architecture a great leap forward. Rarely has a single building tried to do so much.

The requirement was for a cultural center with four main areas—a museum of modern art, a library, a center for industrial design and facilities for musical research, together with the

Centre Georges Pompidou: Paris, France, 1977

usual backup services such as restaurants, offices and car park. The site on the Rue de Renard is on the northern edge of the historic core of Paris, immediately to the east of Les Halles, the old market area being redeveloped at the time of the competition. The winning design from the 681 entries was to be chosen by an international architectural jury: Jean Prouvé, eminence gris of French metal construction, was jury president, and Philip Johnson and Oscar Niemeyer were among the assessors, so hope ran high among progressive architects that an inventive design would be chosen. They were not to be disappointed.

Richard Rogers and Renzo Piano were the winners: an Englishman and an Italian. They were young, had built little and were completely outside the architectural establishment; in fact, they barely had an architectural practice. In disbelief they went to Paris to be feted as never before, and then set down to the serious business of developing the design, setting up a Paris office and forming the organization to see the building through to completion. The structural engineers, Ove Arup and Partners, played a full part in this, and being a large and successful firm, gave the designers credibility in the early stages.

The design places the building on the east half of the site, leaving the west half open as a public space. Closure of local roads gives the space to the pedestrian. Many modern developments have provided open space, often labeled "plaza," in which the architects hope that life will flourish, but which ends up empty and litter-strewn. The place at the Centre Pompidou is full of life and entertainment, perhaps the only really successful and lively urban space created in Europe since the war. The influence of the building and the millions of culture-hungry tourists it attracts has transformed the area: art shops and cafés abound and spill out on to the streets, buildings around the Pompidou have been spruced up, and Le Marais, the area to the east of the building, is undergoing almost total refurbishment. As a catalyst for urban renewal, the Pompidou is an unparalleled success.

The architects' intention was to make a totally flexible building, with great, open floors that could be replanned and changed in mood according to tastes and requirements. Six great, open-plan floors, each 166 meters by 48 meters by 7 meters high, have no internal columns or service runs; structure and circulation are kept outside these spaces on their long sides, and service connections can be made almost anywhere in floor and ceiling. As a demonstration of the idea of flexible space it is beautiful, but much of the feel of the building is, by this arrangement, handed over by the architects to the curators. The curators have not always risen to the occasion with quite the panache and conviction of Piano and Rogers, so the gallery interiors are often disappointing. However, the designers did not feel the same need to make rooftop restaurants and circulation spaces so flexible, so these have been designed with more permanence. Circulation is concentrated along the west facade, where people are contained in suspended transparent plastic tubes; vertical circulation, by escalator ascending as a diagonal across the east elevation, gives the visitor one of architecture's great experiences as Paris drops away beneath.

The structure is of steel, and is clearly expressed inside and out. Trusses span the enclosed part of the building in one simple span, but there is a six-meter zone on each side of the occupied part of the building. This is for mechanical services on the east side and for circulation of people on the west side. To accommodate these six-meter zones, heavy cast-steel cantilever elements called gerberettes were used. Being cast, they have a different geometry from the fabricated members, and this gives the building its richness.

Conventional buildings have circulation and services in the center, and hence the external skin is logically simple. Here it is the internal spaces that are simple, and the services and circulation are on the outside. Moreover, the services and circulation are not enclosed within a skin of their own, but each air duct and escalator has its own mini-enclosure, and it is these that give such a memorable and complex image to the building. It has been said that each floor has its mechanical services on one side and access for people on the other: to the east, along the Rue du Renard, the pipes run vertically and are painted jolly colors. Jokers may say that it looks like an oil rig, but in fact the large air ducts give a vertical rhythm to the facade and break it up in a way that enables it to sit happily among the older neighbors. The west facade, facing the public square, has less color, but more transparency as the floors are fully glazed and the circulation routes glisten like big glass caterpillars. Though the architect may accept, indeed enjoy, the individual and changeable elements on these two long facades, the formal ideas of architecture are in no way demoted. The outside limits of the six-meter white zones for service and for movement are defined by the outer framework to the steel structure, which, since the main loads are carried on the columns passing through the gerberettes, can be thin and tenuous, with the diagonals giving order and implying some minimum degree of containment.

To the south of the Centre Pompidou is the music research center known as IRCAM. This underground structure is covered with water at ground level, with a Tinguely water sculpture that adds to the fun and activity around the Centre Pompidou.

Seven million visitors a year place a toll on any building, and the structure has not been without its problems. As a machine-made product it must be clean and pristine to be seen at its best. It has not always been clean and pristine, but it remains an unrivaled image of the way we see ourselves in the late 20th century. The building is the greatest work in the collection, and must have surpassed the wildest dreams of the promoters of the competition in 1971.

—JOHN WINTER

LA DÉFENSE
Paris, France

1958-89. 1958: Palais des Expositions (CNIT, Centre National des Industries et Techniques); **Architects:** Bernard Zehrfuss, Robert Camelot and Jean de Mailly. **1966:** Nobel Tower; **Architects:** Jean de Mailly and Jacques Depusse, with Jean Prouvé, engineer. **1974:** Completion of Fiat Tower; **Architects:** Roger Saubot and François Jullien, with Skidmore, Owings and Merrill as consultant. **1983-89:** La Grande Arche; **Architect:** Johan Otto von Spreckelsen. **1985:** Elf Tower; **Architects:** Roger Saubot and François Jullien. **1985-87:** IBM and Sofitel Buildings; **Architect:** Gino Valle. **1989:** Hotel/congress center built in interior of CNIT building.

Publications

AMSONEIT, WOLFGANG: *Contemporary European Architects.* Cologne, 1991.

*

La Défense is the name of Paris' important business district developed in the west of the city since 1958 by the government

La Défense: Paris, France, 1958-89

agency EPAD (Établissement public pour L'aménagement de la Région de La Défense). It is the location for the huge, futuristic Grande Arch de La Défense, one of the "Grands Projets" sponsored by President François Mitterrand to celebrate the bicentenary in 1989 of the French Revolution.

The district is often cited as one of most ambitious and consistent applications of the modernist principles of town planning evolved by Le Corbusier in the 1920s, and codified in the Charter of Athens (1933). These became a series of ideals to which many planners and architects aspired, and became influential in the postwar period: strict zoning of activities; high, widely spaced blocks; the suppression of the traditional street; and the separation of pedestrians and cars.

Le Corbusier lived and worked in Paris from 1916 until his death in 1965, and his urban thinking was conditioned by that city. In 1925 he notoriously proposed the demolition of most of historic Paris in order to build a "Functional City." Le Corbusier's utopianism and aesthetic preferences for society entailed a certain authoritarianism, as was confirmed by the last plate of his book *Urbanisme* (*The City of Tomorrow,* 1925) depicting Louis XIV supervising the building of Les Invalides.

The history of the French capital has been of strong central [state] authority—monarchical and republican—and of urban planning on the grand scale, culminating in the fusion of the formal precepts of the Baroque with modernization under the prefecture of Georges-Eugène Haussmann between 1853 and 1869. In the 20th century, at La Défense, this tradition met with technocratic *dirigiste* economic planning, which was at its height in the 1960s.

La Défense is also inseparable from the architectural-conceptual problem of how to end the great "historical axis," something deeply rooted in the French psyche—its admiration of

rationality and the relation between politics and architecture in the capital. The axis is essentially a procession of national monuments and originated with André Le Nôtre's extension of the perspective of the Tuileries gardens of the Louvre and the creation of what would become *la Voie Triomphale*. At its very end, on the other side of the Seine across the Pont Neuilly (1772), a *rond-point* the same diameter as the "*Étoile*" (where the Arc de Triomphe now stands) took its name from a statute which was erected in 1883 to commemorate the defense of Paris in the Franco-Prussian War of 1870—*La défense.*

In 1931 there was a competition for the planning of the route from "the Étoile to the Rond-Point La Défense," for which Le Corbusier produced a prototype modernist scheme that continued the axis as an urban freeway. By the early 1960s, however, the idea of a notionally indefinite continuation of the axis linked with the actual continuation of the arterial road had been rejected. Instead, the center of La Défense became a huge elevated platform—in accordance with "utopian" modernist principles—of about 45 hectares, which the road circumscribes like an island.

However, apart from the early parabolic roof of CNIT and the Gallic whimsy of the Tours Shadock, the platform has developed into a random landscape of commercial office towers. It does not have the symmetry and consistency of Le Corbusier's vision, or indeed of many other modernist schemes that have been realized, or, for that matter, parts of historical Paris. The amount of residential space was gradually decreased to create a *Centre d'affaires* that would lead Paris' claim to be a world commercial center. After the so-called "first generation" towers, for example, the Tour Nobel, those of the "second generation" were bigger and more monolithic, for example, the Tour Fiat, which is in the rather blank commercial style derived

La Défense

However, the modern technology has if anything dulled the reaction to scale alone; what remains is a gesture that resolves the conundrum of the axis: it "ends" the perspective without "closing" it. A slight turning of the arch with respect to the axis was necessary because of underground transport links, but fortuitously it mirrors the Louvre's Cour Carrée's orientation at the other end of the axis. As with many of the hugely expensive monuments of Mitterrand's presidency, the arch's practical purpose was not firmly based (or financed), and since 1986 the arch has been just another speculative office building. This rather undercuts the architect's idealistic program contained in his description of the project:

Idea
An open cube
A Window on the World
As a temporary Grand Finale to the avenue
With a view to the future.
It is a modern "Arc de Triomphe"
Celebrating the triumph of mankind,
It is a symbol of hope for the future
That all people can meet freely.
Here under "The Triumphal Arch of Man" people will
come from all over the world to learn about other
people, to learn what people have learned,
To learn about their languages, their customs, religions,
arts and cultures,
But first of all to meet people!

—TIMOTHY CLARKE

from Ludwig Mies van der Rohe. There was considerable criticism of the high-rise environment that was being created, which later "third-generation" buildings have, to some extent, attempted to answer with some of the devices of late modern commercial architecture. The Immeuble Élysée La Défense, for example, has returned to the principle of a courtyard building—with an atrium.

La Défense is, in fact, a paradigm of the debate about modernism. Is it strictly necessary to build high to achieve high densities? Are pedestrian platforms preferable to traditional streets? Now that the old *rond-point* has been built over, the statue of the defense now sits rather incongruously in the middle of the "slab." But judged as a commercial center, La Défense must be accounted a planning success (not least for its excellent transport—it is linked by RER, metro, rail and road) and, ironically, perhaps only because it has succeeded in the goal of relieving development pressure on central Paris, which has therefore been preserved.

Although the *Centre d'affaires* was built at the end of the historical axis, there was still controversy as to whether the axis was—conceptually—"open" or "closed." The question was resolved in 1982 when President François Mitterrand launched a competition for a ministry of public works and international "Carrefour of Communication." Otto Von Sprekelsen's winning entry confirms Mitterrand's fondness for geometric abstraction and minimalism in architecture (also seen in I. M. Pei's glass pyramid for the Louvre at the other end of the axis). But the Great Arch is minimalism on a massive and rhetorical scale—it encloses an "open cube" of 105 meters, which is on the axis and the same width as the Champs Élysée; the "Roof Garden" covers one hectare. There is an allusion to the form of the Arc de Triomphe, but the megastructure is perhaps closer to the Eiffel Tower as an expression of technical prowess.

EIFFEL TOWER
Paris, France

1886: Design selected; **Designers/Engineers:** Gustave Eiffel (1832-1923), Maurice Koechlin, Emile Nougier. **1887-89:** Construction.

Publications

BILLINGTON, DAVID P.: *The Tower and the Bridge: The New Art of Structural Engineering.* Princeton, New Jersey, 1983.
BRAIBANT, CHARLES: *Histoire de la Tour Eiffel.* Paris, 1964.
EIFFEL, GUSTAVE: *La Tour Eiffel en 1900.* Paris, 1902.
"The Eiffel Tower: A Victory for Progressive Design." *Architectural Record* 86 (October 1939): 69-72.
HARRISS, JOSEPH: *The Tallest Tower: Eiffel and the Belle Epoque.* Boston, 1975.
HOFMANN, WERNER, and KULTERMANN, UDO: *Modern Architecture in Color.* New York, 1970.
KEIM, J. A.: *La Tour Eiffel.* Paris, 1950.
Revue technique de l'Exposition universelle de 1889. Vol. 1: *L'architecture*; Vol. 2: *La construction.* Paris, 1889-93.

*

The world's tallest structure when it was completed in 1889, the Eiffel Tower still claims a significant portion of the Paris skyline. Gustave Eiffel designed the 300 meter tower as the gateway to the French Exhibition of 1889. The exhibition, located with its major axis perpendicular to the Seine River, between the École Militaire and the Champs-de-Mars facing the

Eiffel Tower: Paris, France, 1887-89

Trocadéro, displayed new technologies, industrial development and the arts, and highlighted the world significance of France and her ideals. In addition, the exhibition commemorated the 100th anniversary of the storming of the Bastille, the beginning of the French Revolution.

Picked out of over 100 entries in the official competition in 1886, Gustave Eiffel's design reflected two decades of his work building a unique type of arched wrought-iron railroad bridge throughout Europe, South America and Indochina. He developed the ability to create structures over 100 meters long that were supported by light, graceful pylons. Under the architectural preparation of Maurice Koechlin and the guidance of structural calculations by Emile Nougier, workers began construction on the Eiffel Tower on 26 January 1887.

Eiffel applied his engineering and architectural genius to the problem of giving the tower a sturdy yet lightweight frame. He considered both the dead and live vertical loads of the tower. The tower was designed so that the structure applied a foundation load no greater than that of a person sitting in a chair per square unit of measure. Yet, a primary consideration in the development of the structural stability was the resistance of wind loading. Eiffel resolved this potential problem by providing diagonal framing within the structure, and by incorporating a system of windbreaks. Paying particular attention to the lacy and open design, he left generous spaces between each component to minimize wind resistance. Eiffel's firm, Levallois-Perret, fabricated all the wrought-iron components of the structure, holding every piece to exacting standards. Rivets and bolts connected the pieces to form the frame. The mathematical precision of the tower's components and the lightness of its lacy design made the tower a sophisticated product much ahead of its time.

Aesthetic decisions of a nonstructural nature played a subordinate role in the design of the tower. The arches springing from the foundation levels to join the four pylons appear to provide lateral stability to the frame; however, their purpose was primarily to offer an entrance and to accent the axis through the tower to the exhibition. Some regard these arches as an engineering compromise to quiet the objections to the tower and its prominent placement in the city.

Some aestheticians of the French Republic objected to the project's nontraditional scheme. Critics called it the Tower of Babel, which "even commercial America would not have," and said that it would become "without a doubt the dishonor of Paris." For years after the exhibition, many wished to raze the tower. A proposal to recycle the tower's iron for military purposes surfaced during the German occupation in the 1940s. Nevertheless, the Eiffel Tower still stands, working much as it did during the Exhibition of 1889, as a vantage point for the observation of the city. Three observation levels can be accessed by cable elevators which follow the pylon legs' profile. The pinnacle, where Eiffel once had his private laboratory, now houses a restaurant.

—GORDON ECHOLS

LES HALLES CENTRALES
Paris, France

1845: Commission awarded; **Architects:** Victor Baltard (1805-74), Félix Callet (1791-1854). **1851:** Cornerstone laid. **1853:**

Construction halted and new design chosen. **1854-57:** Construction. **1886:** Three pavilions added. **1936:** Two pavilions added. **1973:** Destroyed.

Publications

BALTARD, VICTOR, and CALLET, FÉLIX: *Monographie des halles centrales de Paris construites sous le règne de Napoléon III.* Paris, 1863.

CHEMETOV, P. (ed.): *Familièrement inconnues . . . Architectures, Paris 1848-1914.* Paris, 1972.

DECONCHY, M. F.: *Victor Baltard, sa vie, ses oeuvres.* Paris, 1875.

FRAMPTON, KENNETH, and FUTAGAWA, YUKIO: *Modern Architecture: 1851-1919.* New York, 1983.

GIEDION, SIGFRIED: *Space, Time and Architecture.* Cambridge, Massachusetts, 1954.

HAUSSMANN, GEORGES-EUGÈNE: *Mémoires de Baron Haussmann.* 3 vols. Paris, 1890-93.

HAUTECOEUR, LOUIS: *Histoire de l'architecture classique en France.* Vol. 7, Paris, 1957.

PINKNEY, D. H.: *Napoleon III and the Rebuilding of Paris.* Princeton, New Jersey, 1972.

STEINER, F. H.: *French Iron Architecture.* Ann Arbor, Michigan, 1984.

VAN ZANTEN, DAVID: "Victor Baltard." In *The Second Empire: Art in France under Napoleon III.* Exhibition catalog. Philadelphia, 1978.

*

Because Louis Napoleon sought to glorify the Bonapartes in every aspect of Parisian life, it was not surprising that the city's stomach should be of great concern to him. The project of the Central Markets, or Les Halles Centrales, attracted almost as much of his attention as the completion of the Louvre and the other grand projects associated with the renewal of Paris.

King Philip Augustus established markets in the location, on the right bank, just outside the medieval city walls in the 12th century. By the 18th century the area, enclosed by then within the city, had become a conglomeration of many merchants offering grain, vegetables, meats, fish and other commodities. Having grown over the years, the assemblage of structures possessed neither plan nor order. Basic sanitation was wanting.

On 14 February 1811, Napoleon I issued a decree that stated, "There will be constructed a great hall which will occupy all the terrain of the present Hall (markets), from the Market of the Innocents to the Grain Market (Halle au Blé)." The decree even stipulated that the markets be completed by 1814. The municipal authorities acquired the land and cleared some of it, but never began construction because of the empire's collapse. The restored monarchy did not pursue the matter.

The municipal administration under the bourgeois monarchy of Louis Philippe consented to study the project in 1842. It appointed a commission to visit markets in other European countries, but made progress slowly. Debate ensued as to where the markets should best be placed. Some suggested that the original location, virtually in the center of Paris, would result in intolerable urban congestion. Perhaps relocating the markets on the city's outskirts or distributing their functions among a group of dispersed, smaller markets might prove more efficient. By 1845, the municipality decided to hold to the original site and selected the architects Victor Baltard and Félix Callet as the designers.

Almost immediately Hector Horeau proposed a grander project to be placed upon the northern bank of the Seine in order

Les Halles Centrales: Paris, France, 1854-66

to connect the markets directly with barge traffic. He envisioned three subterranean rail lines connected to principal depots, underground streets and parking facilities for wagons. Technologically, his buildings remained conservative; the structures were to be of traditional masonry with little use of iron.

The Revolution of 1848 altered the political situation, but the new president and later emperor, Louis Napoleon, expressed determination to press ahead with what was originally his uncle's project, laying the cornerstone on 15 September 1851. At the urging of Monsieur Berger, prefect of the Seine, he accepted the scheme of Baltard and Callet. Soon, however, the stone pile received the derogatory title of *"le Fort de la Halle"* from disgruntled Parisians. Its thick walls and small windows permitted little light and air. Louis Napoleon therefore ordered construction halted in June 1853 and a new competition held.

The most prominent architects submitted 42 projects. Horeau proposed a possibly unbuildable span of 300 feet for three great market halls facing directly on the river. Eugène Flachat's five pavilions were to be entirely of iron framing. Cast-iron columns would support rigid wrought-iron trusses having the then-immense span of 80 meters (264 feet), twice that used by Flachat in his Gare Saint-Lazare. This railroad station had particularly impressed the emperor, who wanted his markets covered by a similar iron *parapluie*.

Under the urging of the new prefect of the Seine, Baron Georges Eugène Haussmann, the emperor reappointed the prefect's old school chum, Baltard, as architect. The academically trained Baltard (Prix de Rome, 1833) resisted the untraditional material iron, but under Haussmann's urging (*"du fer, du fer, rien que du fer!"*), he developed sketches made by his two patrons. The architect's only concession to his academic training

would be the superb classical, yet functional, overall plan of the grouping.

In conjunction with Callet and a contractor who had had considerable experience in iron construction, Baltard created a scheme of 10 separate pavilions connected by covered streets. Working from a six-meter module, the architects made the larger pavilions 54 meters (172.2 feet) square, and the smaller, 54 meters by 42 meters (138 feet). A vast cellar lay beneath the complex. Cast-iron columns, placed every six meters and corresponding to the supports above, carried quadripartite vaults composed of iron ribs with brick webs and concrete extrados.

Above, Baltard and Callet constructed a strong but delicate framework. Cast-iron exterior supports, resting on a stone plinth course, took the form of columns cast as pilasters; every corner pilaster held two columns. Each was made hollow to carry off rainwater. A brick curtain wall, 11 centimeters (a little over four inches) thick, rose to a height of 2.5 meters (8.25 feet). There adjustable glass windows set in wooden frames rested upon a stone stringcourse. Trellis wall plates and cast-iron arches connected the exterior columns, giving rigidity to the frame. Trellis rafters and interior cast-iron columns supported the shed roofs, clerestories and lanterns to the height of 25 meters (82.5 feet) above the floor.

Construction began in May 1854 and was completed during 1857. It soon became evident that 10 pavilions were inadequate, and Baltard (Callet had died in 1855) proposed six more pavilions to the west of the existing group. Only three were completed by 1886; two more were added in 1936.

Les Halles functioned primarily as a wholesale market. It therefore experienced its greatest period of activity between midnight and about six in the morning, when restaurateurs,

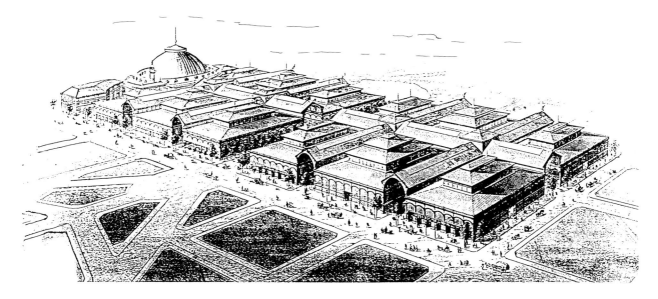

grocers, butchers and fishmongers came to purchase merchandise for the day's trade. They joined a population of porters (*les forts*), wholesalers and prostitutes all rubbing shoulders with elegantly dressed ladies and their escorts, just finishing a night on the town, to savor the famous *soupe à l'oignon* in the neighboring bistros.

During the discussion about the form of the markets, some suggested that modern ventilation devices might serve well in an enclosed building. In the end, however, Parisians chose the French tradition of an open market such as had existed from medieval times. Using iron, Baltard took the genre and translated it into pure poetry. After the morning's activities, the structures retreated into a quietude and grandeur suggestive of a Piranesi print. Destroyed in 1973 and replaced by an underground shopping mall, recollection of them produces an exquisite sorrow.

—THEODORE TURAK

HÔTEL DE CLUNY
Paris, France

1485-98: Built for abbots of the Benedictine Monastery at Cluny. Now a museum for the Middle Ages.

Publications

NORMAND, CHARLES: *L'hôtel de Cluny*. Paris, 1888.
PILLEMENT, G.: *Les hôtels de Paris*. 2 vols. Paris, 1941-45.
VACQUIER, J., and JARRY, P.: *Les vieux hôtels de Paris*. 22 portfolios. Paris, 1910-34.

The Hôtel de Cluny was the Paris residence of the abbots of the great Burgundian monastery of Cluny. The property on which it exists was bought in about 1330 from the bishop of Bayeux. Bordering the rue de la Harpe (now boulevard St. Michel) and the rue des Maturins, it was close to the newly founded Collège de Cluny in the university district. The principal feature of the property was the remains of substantial Roman

baths, onto which a residence was built. Nothing is known of this first residence as it was completely rebuilt between 1485 and 1498, initially on the order of Abbot Jean III de Bourbon, but mostly by Abbot Jacques d'Amboise (1485-1510). This large Flamboyant town house is one of the few buildings of its period remaining in Paris and ranks in importance only behind the House of Jacques Coeur in Bourges among the few secular urban residences of the 15th century surviving in France. Since the mid-19th century, it has housed the Musée de Cluny, with its substantial collection of medieval antiquities.

The thermal baths of Lutetia (the Roman name for Paris), onto which the hôtel was built, date from the beginning of the third century, circa 215. Their large dimensions and the solidity of their construction suggest that they were a public institution. Built in *opus mixtum*, with alternating layers of brick and stone coursing, they comprised a tepidarium abutting a frigidarium, both with alternating segmental and rectangular niches on the interior walls, a caldarium and a piscina, although the exact extent of the complex can no longer be determined. The row of four barrel vaults covering the frigidarium have partially survived and are carried on consoles carved in the shape of ship prows, which has led some to connect the establishment with the Roman corporation of boatmen. This is the only Roman vaulted hall surviving in France. The baths were destroyed in about 285 during the barbarian invasions, and probably suffered further damage at the hands of the Normans in the ninth century. In 1215 the ruins were alienated by Philip Augustus and became royal property.

The residence of Jacques d'Amboise was built into these ruins. The main block of apartments faces the rue des Maturins, separated from the street by a courtyard, formed by a crenellated wall along the street front. From this main block, subsidiary wings project at right angles toward the street at either end, that on the west being longer because of the irregular alignment of the street. Opposite this west wing on the garden side projects the chapel. This is the earliest surviving residence in Paris designed with opposing courtyard and garden. The main entrance into the courtyard was located in a polygonal staircase turret projecting from the center of the main block. The east wing, in which the present entrance to the museum is located, was probably the service block. The west wing features a built-in porch at ground level, with an elaborate arcade of pointed arches, each having a crocketed ogee superarch carved in relief on the wall above it and flanked by tall, slender pinnacles. Apart

Hôtel de Cluny: Paris, France, 1485-98

from this, rectangular cross-windows open on the facade both at ground level and on the first story; between them, the rather plain wall is articulated only by two string courses, and another breaks over the tops of the upper windows. The top of the wall is decorated by an openwork parapet of Flamboyant *mouchettes*. The roofs above are punctuated by tall dormer windows, most gabled, with openwork tracery flanking the gable. The doors of the south wing feature depressed ogee heads; the others are square-headed. The arms and devices of Jacques d'Amboise are plentifully in evidence, notably on the dormer gables.

The interior has been much altered. Apart from the monumental fireplace, a few door passages and four small circular staircases, the only interior space which retains its original character is the chapel. This rectangular chamber features a tall, elegant central column supporting a rather heavy lierne vault, essentially English in character, but similar, as well, to that of the Cathedral of Chalon-sur-Saône. The cells are filled with openwork Flamboyant tracery. On the wall of each bay are pairs of niches, once sheltering statues, with elaborate canopies and foliate bases. While the chapel is basically rectangular, the apse is formed of a projecting, semicircular oriel supported below on a slender column. The oriel contains the only traceried lights in the building.

Besides serving as a residence for the abbots of Cluny, the hôtel was rented out to illustrious and highborn guests, such as Mary Tudor (1515), James V of Scotland (1536) and Cardinal Mazarin (1634). The hôtel belonged to the abbots of Cluny until the Revolution, when it became the property of the state. In 1819 Louis XVIII ordered the demolition of houses bordering the rue de la Harpe, and the ruins of the baths were bought by the city of Paris. They were restored at that time by Albert Lenoir, the son of Alexandre Lenoir. In 1833 the antiquary Alexandre de Sommerard let six rooms on the first floor of the hôtel and installed his collection; the "museum" he established there became one of the most fashionable in Paris. At his death in 1842 the state bought his whole collection and the hôtel, to which the city ceded the Gallo-Roman ruins. The Musée des Thermes et de l'Hôtel de Cluny opened on 16 March 1844. All the buildings were extensively restored in the late 19th century, and further restoration of the hôtel has recently been undertaken.

Although precocious hints of the Italian Renaissance can be found here and there, notably, for instance, on the dormers of the north range, the late-15th-century hôtel was built mostly in a mainstream Flamboyant style. However, the fact that it was tied into the spectacular Roman ruins calls for comment. One might rather have expected the site to have been razed before a town house was erected. Although classical features were not synthesized there into contemporary architectural practice in a "rebirth" of Roman splendor, the ruins were obviously recognized for what they are and valued for their antique associations. By making the Roman ruins an integral part of their hôtel and a feature of its garden, the abbots of Cluny manifested in a unique way the humanist interests of the early Renaissance.

—JIM BUGSLAG

INSTITUT DU MONDE ARABE
Paris, France

1987. Architect: Jean Nouvel.

Publications

LESNIKOWSKI, WOJCIECH G.: *The New French Architecture.* New York, 1990.
NOUVEL, J.: *Institut du Monde Arabe.* Princeton, New Jersey, 1989.

As the result of a competition sponsored by France and 19 Arab countries in 1981, Jean Nouvel—together with Pierre Soria, Gilbert Lezènes and the Architecture Studio—received the commission to build the Institut du Monde Arabe in Paris. The building was intended as a place to expose and explain Arab culture and civilization to the French public. Essentially, the building attempts to express the relationship between Western and Arab cultures, between modernity and tradition, between openness toward the city and architectural interiorization. As a cultural center with facilities similar to the decade-older Centre Pompidou, the Institut du Monde Arabe has a multimedia documentation center, public library, museum, exhibition space and conference rooms.

Although the site selected for the institute, on the southern bank of the Seine, had been barren until then, it was extremely significant in terms of its urban context. Located at the intersection of the Boulevard St. Germain, the Quai St. Bernard and the axis formed by the Pont de Sully on one end and the Place de la Bastille on the other, the site is in visual contact with the historic city center of Paris, the Île de la Cité with Notre-Dame Cathedral, and the neighboring Île St. Louis. In addition, the building complex is confronted with the contradictory urban structures of the old, small-scale buildings and the new, gigantic buildings of the University of Jussieu, dating from the 1960s. Until the Institut du Monde Arabe was built, these had stood next to each other without any kind of architectural transition. Jean Nouvel's glass structure adapts to its environment rather than imposing its architecture on the surrounding space. Its transparency enables an ongoing dialogue between inside and outside. In the closeness in height and the parallel orientation of the facades, the Institut du Monde Arabe stands in a continuous relationship with the university buildings, and simultaneously provides them with a new significance in their urban context.

The concentration of the buildings in the northern part of the available land allows space for a square in front of the buildings, across which one reaches the entrance of the building. Two structurally differentiated blocks—the curved northern wing turned to the river and the smooth cube toward the south—are separated by a canyon-like opening only 3.5 meters wide, which leads to a courtyard on the eastern side. A smooth, windowless facade closes off the complex on the eastern side, without establishing a relationship to the neighboring university buildings. On the exterior, as in the interior, the use of color was avoided wherever possible. The silver-gray tones of glass and aluminum dominate the building.

The curved facade of the northern wing, which contains a museum of Arab and Islamic art and temporary exhibition halls, follows the quay lined with ancient trees. The facade ends at the far corner in a sharp angle. In the rest of the building the square is the basic design element, but here the glass facade is horizontally articulated, a composition underlined by horizontal metal bands. By means of a photographic technique the silhouettes of the surrounding houses, the dome of St. Paul's and the choir of Notre-Dame Cathedral are applied to the surface of the glass. As a result of the transparency of the building, a relationship with the old city comes into being. The opening between the wings, whose axis points directly to the choir of Notre-Dame, leads to the square courtyard and also functions

Institut du Monde Arabe: Paris, France, 1987

as an entrance for special guests. The walls of the courtyard on all sides consist of uniform square marble slabs set in slender aluminum frames, which bathe the interior in a softened daylight. Nouvel attempted to express the emphasis on the interiors typical of Arab architecture, through the closed nature of the opening between the wings and the courtyard.

The southern wing consists of a regular square with smooth facades on all sides. On the narrow eastern side of this wing, the symbolic ''book tower'' is located. Visible from the outside through the glazed facade, the tower is a white concrete spiral clad in marble, which rises the entire height of the three-level wing. Most of the institute's books are housed in the stacks placed along the rising ramp of the tower.

On the smooth southern facade, Nouvel installed an aluminum screen between two panes of glass. It uses traditional decorative elements of Arab architecture—square, circle, polygon and star—and may be seen as a translation of the traditional wooden latticework into a contemporary form. In an adjustment to the Paris climate, the screen facade is built up out of 27,000 mobile aluminum diaphragms, which together form a square. The diaphragms open and close, steered by photoelectric cells, according to the intensity of the sunlight. The ''variable geometry'' of this facade allows for control over sunlight admitted into the building, and simultaneously makes use of the charming play of light and shadow in the interior. The mechanism of the screen is deliberately exposed, in an effort not to veil the fundamentally technological approach of the building.

Behind the screen, the height of the floors in the interior is extremely low by measurement with the human form (in many places the floors are barely higher than two meters). In the basement of the southern wing, a massive, dark hall lined with

columns leads to an auditorium that seats 350 and alludes to Egyptian architecture. The hall stands in stark contrast with the light and airy upper floors.

The selective use of daylight, which plays a great role in Arab architecture, is fundamental to the design of the entire building. This fundamental concept manifests itself not only in the tensions between light and dark spaces, and in the shadow play of the south facade, but also in the transparency of the building, which creates an aesthetic and symbolic dialogue between inside and outside, and between the Arab world and the city in which the Institut du Monde Arabe is integrated.

—ANTJE SENARCLENS DE GRANCY
Translated from the German by Marijke Rijsberman

LES INVALIDES
Paris, France

1671-77: Construction; **Architect:** Libéral Bruant (1635-97). **1678-1708:** Dome constructed; **Architect:** Jules Hardouin-Mansart (1646-1708).

Publications

JESTAZ, B.: ''Jules Hardouin-Mansart et l'église des Invalides.'' *Gazette des beaux-arts* 11 (1965): 59ff.

Hotel, Les Invalides: Paris, France, 1671-77

REUTERSWÄRD, PATRIK: *The Two Churches of the Hôtel des Invalides: A History of Their Design.* Stockholm, 1965.

*

In constructing a military hospital for his soldiers, Louis XIV left a monument that epitomizes French Baroque architecture. Although Cardinal Mazarin had founded the Hôpital de la Salpêtrière in 1654 for the care of the poor and the aged, war veterans had no such facility at their disposal, and were usually cared for in monasteries. To rectify that situation, the Institution des Invalides was founded by royal decree in 1670, and Libéral Bruant was given the contract to construct the hospital in March of the following year.

As *architecte du roi,* Bruant had been involved, along with Louis Le Vau and Pierre Le Muet, with the design and construction of the Hôpital de la Salpêtrière. Born in about 1635, Bruant was well connected to the court, his father having had several official positions such as *maître général des bâtiments* and *maître général des oeuvres de charpenterie du roi.* As was customary, Bruant inherited his father's posts, becoming *architecte du roi* in 1663 and later being elected to the Académie Royale.

Bruant's singular contribution to the Hôpital de la Salpêtrière was its chapel (1657-77). Its centralized, Greek-cross plan was composed of four rectangular wings of identical size radiating from the altar, which was placed in the octagonal crossing and surmounted by an octagonal dome. The division of the chapel into four distinct wings, separated from one another by smaller octagonal chapels, had the function of segregating up to 4,000 participants during Mass. Bruant's chapel was highly unusual

for its date because of its severe sobriety, which emphasized the plan's bold geometry. To modern eyes, the chapel's abstract and pure geometric volumes give credit to Bruant's architectural vision. Bruant, however, was never able to broaden his oeuvre beyond hospital architecture. After the Salpêtrière, the Hôtel des Invalides was his last major commission. Bruant's functional and austere architecture was never able to compete with the grandeur and monumentality of the work of Versailles' main architect, Jules Hardouin-Mansart, who, ironically, was to crown his brilliant architectural career with the construction of the domed Church of the Invalides, overshadowing Bruant's own contribution to the complex.

The king chose to build the Institut des Invalides in the plain of Grenelle, inaugurating royal patronage in the capital's western sector—a tradition that would continue under Louis XV with the construction of Place Louis XV (later Place de la Concorde) and the École Militaire in the 1760s. The hospital was finished in 1677 and soon attended to some 6,000 soldiers.

The monumental four-story facade, some 195 meters in length, follows the traditional French canon: a central *bâtiment* framed by two slightly projecting pavilions. Uncharacteristic for that period, and reminiscent of the chapel of the Salpêtrière, are the simplicity and austerity of the facade. Its most pronounced and original attribute is a semi-circular entrance portal whose arch dramatically breaks both the horizontal cornice and the steep roof. Two pairs of Ionic pilasters support this curved entablature, which is richly decorated by a frieze of trophies. In the center, above three gigantic windows, is an equestrian bas-relief of Louis XIV in Roman dress, added in 1735 by Guillaume Coustou. Two seated statues of Mars and Minerva frame the magnificent entry.

Dome, Les Invalides: 1678-1708

dome, which would mark the apogee of Baroque architecture in France.

François Mansart, Jules Hardouin's great uncle, had previously designed a round funerary royal chapel in 1665 at the Cathedral of St. Denis, the traditional burying place for French royalty. It is believed that Hardouin-Mansart's domed church at the Invalides likewise would have served as a funerary chapel for Louis XIV and his family, once again relating the Invalides to the Escorial. Those plans, however, were never realized, but Hardouin-Mansart kept his innovative design, which reversed traditional church planning: the 70-meter-long nave was utilized by the soldiers, while the church itself was relegated to the area underneath the dome, usually reserved for the sacrarium. The main approach to the church was switched from the *entrée d'honneur* on the central court to the dome facade on the opposite side. Such an arrangement took into consideration the requirement of having a distinct royal entrance, separate from the main entrance. Hardouin-Mansart continued the hospital's austere and severe architecture for the Soldier's Church, which was in character for its use by the military.

The dome church completely overshadows the nave and is generally recognized as the finest of its type in France. It remains the most important French example of a centrally planned church, and is undoubtedly the most audacious religious edifice built under Louis XIV. Although derived from François Mansart's plans for the Bourbon Chapel at St. Denis, itself ultimately based on Michelangelo's design for St. Peter's in Rome, the church dramatically broke away from traditional French domed religious architecture, as realized in the Church of the Sorbonne by Jacques Lemercier (1635) and François Mansart's Val de Grâce (1645). Unlike its tempered and restrained predecessors, the Invalides partakes of the exuberance and bravura of Italian

The windows and doors of the first floor are linked by a continuous stringcourse and by the regular placement of their keystones, transmogrified into grotesque masks. A strongly projecting stringcourse divides the third from the fourth floor, while the steeply pitched roof is enlivened by pronounced chimneystacks and by dormer windows in the form of trophies and armor. Bruant successfully punctuated the potentially monotonous facade with subtle architectural and sculptural devices. Its elaborate arched entrance and the pedimental sculpture on the framing pavilions relieve the horizontality inherent in such a long facade, while the regular placements of keystones, dormer windows and chimneystacks enliven its surface.

The hospital's austere architecture and interior courtyards resemble Juan de Herrera's Escorial monastery and palace near Madrid (1563-82). Both are ordered by a grid plan highlighted by a central court surrounded by two-story galleries and by a chapel on the central axis. The Invalides' large, somewhat monastic central court is highlighted on the south side by a pedimented portico framed by pairs of superimposed columns—the whole marking the main entrance (*entrée d'honneur*) to the Église des Soldats, or Soldier's Church.

Because of the dramatic differences in style between the simple and austere Soldier's Church and the splendor and richness of the dome, it was generally thought that Bruant erected the former, also known as St.-Louis-des-Invalides, and that Jules Hardouin-Mansart added the great dome whose contract dates from November 1676. It is now believed, however, that Hardouin-Mansart was the author of both structures. In 1676, Minister François Michel Louvois dismissed Bruant and replaced him with Hardouin-Mansart, who, between 1678 and 1708, erected both the Soldier's Church and the dome. Hardouin-Mansart retained Bruant's plan for a long nave, but appended it to a new centrally planned church whose chief emblem is a monumental

Church of St. Louis, toward dome, Les Invalides: 1670-76

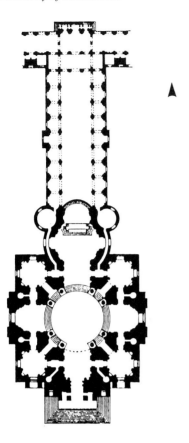

on the church's main axis, as opposed to broad surfaces, Hardouin-Mansart gave great emphasis to vertical movement, which in fact pervades the surface of the entire church, from the columns of the portico, through the piers of the drum, along the consoles and the heavy ribs of the dome, to the lantern, and finally to the three-sided flèche symbolizing the Trinity. Gilded trophies fill in the area of the dome between the ribs, providing Paris with its most decorative and ornate Baroque dome.

Erected at the conclusion of successful military campaigns, the Hôpital des Invalides was also a potent symbol of the military's success and prestige under Louis XIV. The Invalides' stately and noble architecture, coupled with its landmark dome, could only serve to bolster the Crown's recruiting efforts. The Invalides can be seen as combining the functions of a religious edifice, a hospital and a military barracks, each with its own appropriate architectural character. Ironically, it was the juxtaposition of functions and architectural styles, coupled with the reversal of traditional religious iconography, that led to a certain confusion regarding the Invalides' role for succeeding generations. This ambiguity facilitated the church's transformation into a mausoleum in 1841, not for King Louis XIV, but for Napoléon, whose remains were placed under the dome in an open crypt designed by Ludovico Visconti. This fulfilled the emperor's wishes to be "buried along the Seine among the French people which [he] so loved." The return of Napoléon's ashes and their burial underneath the great dome, an epic event in French history, injected new meaning into an institution whose fortunes had declined since the French Revolution. Now forever associated with Napoléon's final resting place, the Church of the Invalides ironically fulfills its original function as a mausoleum, while the hospital, in addition to housing the Musée de l'Armée, still cares for war veterans.

　　　　　　　　　　　　　　　　　　　　　　　—MARC VINCENT

examples, long anathema to the French classical tradition. Indeed, Hardouin-Mansart had originally envisioned a hemicyclical colonnade similar to that of Giovanni Lorenzo Bernini in front of St. Peter's in Rome, but budgetary constraints forced the abandonment of this grandiose project.

The church's exterior facade contains elements never before seen in France. Its lower, rectangular base introduces movement and dynamism more typical of Italian examples. The facade builds up toward the center through a series of projections culminating in the pedimented frontispiece composed of superimposed Doric and Corinthian orders.

The interior is as lively and dynamic as the exterior. Dominating the central space is a set of tall Corinthian columns supporting a deeply projecting entablature of unparalleled richness. Between these columns are the low, narrow openings leading to the circular side chapels. A heavenly glory on the dome is lit by windows concealed in the upper part of the drum. A high altar, a variation of Bernini's Baldacchino in St. Peter's, completes this most Baroque of interiors, characterized by an ingenious combination of shifting volumes, mass and light.

The dome, loosely based on St. Peter's, is perhaps the most singular and original design of the whole ensemble. Hardouin-Mansart abandoned the traditional formula of regularly placed windows separated from each other by buttressing piers. Instead, he introduced a 1-2-1 rhythm of windows between piers, and furthermore placed a pier, and not a bay, on the main axis of the church. These piers are composed of two half columns and form the center of each two-window bay between the buttresses. This unexpected placing of a solid instead of void on the church's principal axis is again repeated in the square lantern atop the dome, which is situated diagonally, with an angle on the main axis. Through the positioning of both piers and angles

LOUVRE
Paris, France

1190: Construction of original fortress begins under Philippe-Auguste. **1360:** Development under Charles V; **Architect:** Raymond du Temple. **1365:** Grand Escalier built. **1546:** Transformation into palace under François I begins; **Architect:** Pierre Lescot (ca. 1510-78), with sculptor Jean Goujon (ca. 1505-ca. 1568). **1594:** Development under Henri IV begins. **1624-54:** Cour Carrée expanded under Louis XIII; **Architect:** Jacques Lemercier (1585-1654). **1660:** Development under Louis XIV; **Architect:** Louis Le Vau (1612-70). **After 1661:** Galerie des Rois, destroyed by fire, rebuilt; **Architect:** Charles Le Brun. **1664:** Colbert becomes Superintendent of Buildings, consults with Bernini. **1667:** Petit Conseil des Bâtiments with Le Vau, Le Brun, and Claude Perrault.

Publications

AULANIER, CHRISTIANE: "Le Palais du Louvre au XVIᵉ siècle." *Bulletin de la Société de l'Histoire de l'Art Français* (1951): 85-100.

BATIFFOL, LOUIS: "Les premières constructions de Pierre Lescot au Louvre d'après de nouveaux documents." *Gazette des beaux-arts* Series 6, 4 (1930): 276-303.

BATIFFOL, LOUIS: "Les travaux du Louvre sous Henry IV." *Gazette des beaux-arts* (1927).

Louvre: Paris, France, 1546ff

BERGER, ROBERT W.: "Charles Le Brun and the Louvre Colonnade." *Art Bulletin* (December 1970).

BIASINI, EMILE, et al.: *Le grand Louvre: metamorphose d'un musée 1981-1993*. Paris, 1989.

BLUNT, ANTHONY: "Two Unpublished Drawings by Lemercier for the Pavillon de l'Horloge." *Burlington Magazine* 102 (1960): 447-448.

CLARAC, CHARLES OTHON FRÉDÉRIC, J. B., COMTE DE: *Description historique et graphique du Louvre et des Tuileries*. Paris, 1853.

CHRIST, YVAN: *Le Louvre et les Tuileries*. Paris, 1949.

CIPRUT, EDOUARD J., and COLLARD, LOUIS: *Nouveaux documents sur le Louvre*. Paris, 1963.

DIMIER: "Fragments de l'ancien hôtel d'O dans la décoration de la Salle des Cariatides au Louvre." *Bulletin de la Société de l'Histoire de l'Art Français* (1924): 20.

DUNLOP, IAN: *Royal Palaces of France*. London, 1985.

ELANDE-BRANDENBURG, A.: "Les Fouilles du Louvre et les projets de Le Vau." *La vie urbaine* (1964): 241.

ESMONIN, E.: "Le Bernin et la construction du Louvre." *Bulletin de la Société de l'Histoire de l'Art Français*. (1911): 31.

HAUTECOEUR, LOUIS: *Histoire du Louvre*. Paris, 1942.

HAUTECOEUR, LOUIS: *Le Louvre et les Tuileries de Louis XIV*. Paris, 1927. English ed.: London, 1964.

HAUTECOEUR, LOUIS: "Le Louvre de Pierre Lescot." *Gazette des beaux-arts* Series 5, 15 (1927): 199-218.

JOSEPHSON, R.: "Les Maquettes du Bernin pour le Louvre." *Gazette des beaux-arts* 1 (1928): 77.

LOWRY, BATES: "Château du Louvre." *Renaissance News* 6 (1953): 10-11.

NOEHLES, K.: "Die Louvre-Projekte von Pietro da Cortona und Carlo Rainaldi." *Zeitschrift für Kunstgeschichte* 24 (1961): 40.

PORTOGHESI, PAOLO: "Gli architetti italiani per il Louvre." In *Saggi di storia dell'architettura*. Rome, 1961.

SAUVEL, TONY: "Les auteurs de la colonnade du Louvre." *Bulletin monumental* (1966).

SAUVEL, TONY: "La date et l'auteur du 'dessein' du Louvre." *Bulletin de la Société Nationale des Antiquaires de France* (1966): 139-149.

WHITELEY, MARY, and BRAHAM, ALLAN: "Louis Le Vau's Projects for the Louvre and the Colonnade." *Gazette des beaux-arts* (1964).

*

Successive French monarchs spent nearly five hundred years building and rebuilding the Louvre, now one of the greatest museums on earth. The Louvre began as a small fort which formed part of the general scheme for the refortification of Paris under Philippe-Auguste, who made it an outwork of his defensive system, guarding the approach to the city from downstream. Charles V diminished the military significance of the Louvre by building an outer line of fortification beyond it and by converting it into a royal residence. Subsequent monarchs allowed the expansion of Paris to envelop the Louvre and the process of in-filling came right up to its walls, making later expansion difficult. François I took the decisive step of pulling down the keep, the famous Tour du Louvre, in order to build a purely palatial structure. But his Louvre was no larger than that of Charles V. By proportioning his facades to so small a building he created a problem for those who were later to enlarge it. The next difficulty arose from the decision of Catherine de Medici to build the palace of the Tuileries outside the line of fortification but near enough to the Louvre for her and her son Henri III to associate the two.

These difficulties, however, might have been overcome had there been any persistent determination to do so, but the monarchs of France showed a recurrent reluctance to live in Paris. Vincennes and Saint-Germain were in many ways more attractive to them. As a result, the many projects for transforming the Louvre from fortress to palace were pursued halfheartedly. Therefore, although the Louvre was for centuries regarded as the seat of the French monarchy—rather like St. James' in England—it was often uninhabited for considerable lengths of time.

Philippe-Auguste began construction on the original fortress in 1190. The building stood four-square with a tower at each corner. At the center of the south and east facades were twin towers guarding narrow entrances. A single tower marked the center of the other two facades, providing covering fire to the whole wall. Inside the courtyard, and placed eccentrically in the northeast corner, was the Grosse Tour—a huge cylinder of stone some 18 1/2 meters in diameter, surrounded by its own moat.

In 1360 Charles V began work on the next phase in the development of the Louvre. He used the architect Raymond du Temple to execute his ideas, which mostly concerned making

the fortress more habitable. New windows were inserted, new lodgings were created on the north and east sides of the courtyard, and new staircases in the corners of the quadrangle facilitated communication. In 1365 a much more important Grand Escalier was built onto the north range. It was in the form of a spiral in an open cage of masonry, somewhat like François I's staircase at Blois. By 1370 the château depicted in the *Très Riches Heures du duc de Berry* was complete. Pol de Limbourg shows the south and east facades, each of which centered on a gatehouse with twin towers between which rose a tall pavilion roof. The corner towers gave birth, above the battlements, to smaller towers capped by poivrières with delicately swept profiles. Towers, turrets and pavilions were crested with gilded weather vanes and banners painted with the royal fleurs-de-lys. Tall white chimney stacks climbed up the towers or sprouted from roofs, contributing to the already exciting skyline of the great conical roof of the Grosse Tour, which towered 31 meters above the level of the court.

François I pulled down the Grosse Tour and the southwest range of buildings and entrusted to Pierre Lescot the task of transforming the fortress into a palace. Lescot was trained as a painter and an architect. His approach to the design of the facade was essentially decorative. It is significant that he worked in close collaboration with the greatest French sculptor of his time, Jean Goujon. Together they produced a style classical in the use of the orders, but distinctly un-Italian in the richness of its decoration—a style that is fully Renaissance and unmistakably French. Henri II completed what François I had begun.

Lescot's block contained a staircase at the north end and two

Louvre, east front

Louvre

superimposed Grandes Salles. The staircase was in the Italian manner, consisting of two straight ramps beneath a barrel vault on which Goujon did some of his most distinctive carving. "The roof over these stairs," wrote Thomas Coryat, "is exceedingly beautiful, being vaulted with very sumptuous frettings or chamferings, wherein the forms of clusters of grapes and many other things are most excellently contrived." The lower of the two Grandes Salles, known as the Salle des Cariatides, still gives some idea of its original appearance. The caryatids take the place of pillars in what is really only an elaborate and purely ornamental porch. Facing the caryatids at the opposite end of the hall was a remarkable and original feature known as the "Tribunal." It was a kind of triumphal arch upheld by groups of pillars of almost Grecian simplicity which formed the canopy to the king's throne.

Adjoining this wing, Lescot built a corner pavilion which housed the king's apartments and thus took the name of "Pavillon du Roi." The external architecture was much plainer than that of the courtyard, but if the outward facades were austere, the rooms behind them were of a richness new even to France. Walls and ceilings were clothed with the most ornate wooden panelling. Coryat recalls the Presence Chamber (more usually the Salle Henri II) as being "adorned with a wondrous sumptuous roof, which, though it be made but of timber work, yet it is exceedingly richly gilt and with that exquisite art, that a stranger upon the first view thereof would imagine it were beaten gold."

Years of war hindered construction until Henri IV made his entry into Paris on 22 March 1594. He and his great minister Sully had the gigantic task of rebuilding a France in ruins. They were builders also in the literal sense of the word. Before the end of 1594 Henri announced his intention of completing the Louvre. The first step was to lay the foundations for the very long gallery linking the Louvre with the Tuileries. This followed the old line of the city wall. By 1607 the work was well advanced. On May 3 Henri IV wrote to Cardinal de Joyeuse: "in Paris you will find my great gallery which goes to the Tuileries finished." At one extremity of this gallery was the Pavillon de Flore which formed the southern extremity of the Tuileries. At the other end was the *petite galerie* which formed the junction between the *grande galerie* and the Louvre. This was later rebuilt by Louis XIV as the Galerie d'Apollon.

Louis XIII made the next most significant extensions of the Louvre with the architect Lemercier. Lemercier decided to quadruple the area of the courtyard, known as the Cour Carrée, by adding a large central pavilion and a repetition of Lescot's building to complete the symmetry of the west range. This set the scale for all future developments.

In October 1660 Louis XIV resolved to complete the building of the Louvre and the Tuileries, which were to be "joined together according to the ancient and magnificent design which has been made by the Kings who preceded him." He ordered the demolition of the remaining parts of the medieval Louvre and the continuation of the great courtyard, the Cour Carrée. The new architect, Le Vau, completed the south front, following the procedure of Lemercier, by building an ornate central pavilion and repeating Lescot's facade beyond it, terminating in a repetition of the Pavillon du Roi. In all, the facade had twenty-nine windows. But before the work had progressed very far, on 16 February 1661, the Galerie des Rois was destroyed by

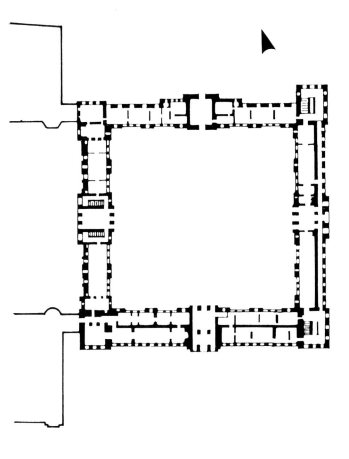

the designs of Louis Le Vau . . . François d'Orbay, his pupil, made no mean contribution to the perfection of this beautiful work."

In 1678 Louis XIV decided on the final enlargement of Versailles. Work continued on the Louvre until 1680, but the annual sums spent decreased steadily. The history of the Louvre as a royal palace had come to an end and that of the Louvre as an art museum had begun.

—IAN DUNLOP

LOUVRE, PYRAMIDE
Paris, France

1983-89: Grand Louvre Phase I and Cour Napoléon and Richelieu Wing Connections Project; **Architect:** I. M. Pei (born 1917).

Publications

ALLAIN-DUPRÉ, E.: "Pyramide du Louvre: Les structures de l'invisible." *Architecture d'aujourd'hui* No. 253 (October 1987): 62-69.

BIASINI, EMILE, et al.: *Le grand Louvre: metamorphose d'un musée 1981-1993.* Paris, 1989.

ELLIS, C.: "Pei in Paris: The Pyramid in Place." *Architecture* 78 (January 1989): 42-47.

FLEURY, MICHEL, et al.: "Le Grand Louvre." *Monuments historique de la France* 136 (December 1984-January 1985): 9-32.

FOUCART, BRUNO: "The Victory of the Pyramid." *Apollo* New series 129 (May 1989): 304-306.

FOUCART, BRUNO; LOSTE, SÉBASTIEN; and SCHNAPPER, ANTOINE: *Paris mystifié: la grande illusion du Grand Louvre.* Paris, 1985.

HECK, SANDY: "Pei's Paris Pyramid." *Journal of the Royal Institute of British Architects* 92 (August 1985): 42-49.

KIMBALL, R.: "The Riddle of the Pyramid." *Architectural Record* 177 (January 1989): 58-61.

KORNBICHLER, THOMAS: "Zwei ehrgeizige Pariser Museumsprojekte." *Kunstwerk* 37 (February 1984): 54-57.

KUHN, JONATHAN: "The Picasso Museum, Christo's Pont Neuf Project, and Pei's Pyramid: Reflections on Artistic Ego and the Artistic Life of Paris." *Arts Magazine* 61 (December 1986): 90-93.

LIPSTADT, HÉLÈNE: "A Paris for the 21st Century?" *Art in America* 72 (November 1984): 104-113.

LORIERS, M. C.: "Perspectives: The Pyramid Prevails." *Progressive Architecture* 70 (June 1989): 37-38.

POISSON, GEORGES: "Avant la pyramide." *Gazette des beaux-arts* 103 (May-June 1984).

TRASKO, MARY: "Unveiling the Pyramid." *Art in America* 76 (May 1988): 31-37.

*

The Grand Louvre Phase I and Cour Napoléon and Richelieu Wing Connections Project (1983-89) made the Louvre Museum not only the world's most famous art institution but also its largest. Architect I. M. Pei effectively manipulated bold geometric forms and state-of-the-art technology to create one of the

fire. The rebuilding of that gallery, now known as the Galerie d'Apollon, was completed by Charles Le Brun, the "Premier Peintre du Roi." The stucco work was executed by Marsy, Girardon and Regnaudin. Already some of the great names connected with the creation of Versailles were found in the annals of the Louvre. Already the great theme of Apollo had been attached to the mythology of Louis XIV.

It was Colbert's great ambition to see the king housed in splendor in the center of his great metropolis. He saw the Louvre, as he told Bernini, as "the principle residence of the kings in the greatest city in the world." In 1664 Colbert became Superintendent of Buildings. He turned to Bernini for a design of a palace worthy of such a position and "worthy, if that were possible, of the greatness and magnificence of the Prince who is to inhabit it." There were two options. One was to accept the architecture and the scale imposed by Lescot and Lemercier and to find the best design for the east front. The other was to pull it down and start again. Bernini, however, arrogant, temperamental, and radically incapable of appreciating anything French, was interested in theatrical effects. His design was a flourish of architecture in a purely Italian style. Bernini made no concession to the difference of climate, let alone the difference of architectural tradition, and considered such matters as how the king was to be lodged and how the servants could be accommodated as being beneath his notice.

Surprisingly the design was accepted, but as soon as Bernini left France it was abandoned. In April 1667 Colbert formed the Petit Conseil des Bâtiments to settle the question of the east front. The Conseil consisted of Le Vau, Le Brun and Claude Perrault. The authorship of the east front, with its dominating colonnade, has usually been attributed to Perrault. Henri Sauval stated that the facade was built "under the oversight and from

Louvre, Pyramide: 1989

most impressive entrances in the history of architecture. By adding a modernist facet to a multiplicity of divergent architectural styles and implementing a rational, spatial organizational plan, Pei has successfully ''brought the Louvre into the twentieth century.''

Despite its prominence, the Louvre was in dire need of remodeling and reorganization. In the absence of any main entrance or centralized plan, visitors, the majority being tourists, frequently became confused and fatigued trying to navigate their way through the museum. These factors prompted French President François Mitterand to fund a major renovation of this national monument. Contrary to French custom, Mitterand eliminated an architectural competition by personally choosing I. M. Pei, a Chinese-born American architect, for the historic project. Pei, experienced in museum architecture, had recently completed his critically acclaimed addition to the National Gallery of Art in Washington, D.C. (1968-78). In the National Gallery project, Pei demonstrated his ability to unify, physically and conceptually, the existing neoclassical structure by John Russell Pope with his own modern design.

In the Grand Louvre project Pei set out to achieve a variety of objectives: he wanted to revitalize interest in the Louvre in order to increase French attendance, renew the urban area immediately surrounding the museum and, most important, provide the facilities necessary for an institution of its caliber. Pei, the only non-French architect ever to work on the Louvre, sought to achieve a ''French solution'' to meet his projected goals. Influenced by the 17th-century French landscape architect André Le Nôtre, Pei devised an image with ''symbolic dignity and architectural excitement''—a large pyramidal glass entrance.

The pyramid is a technological tour-de-force. In order to achieve maximum transparency, Pei chose to use a large number of small structural elements. The result is a web-like frame of handcrafted cablework supporting almost 800 separate glass panes. This technical mastery allows the 71-foot-high structure to remain practically invisible, thereby not infringing upon the architectural integrity of the existing museum. Pei also grappled with complex urban-design considerations in the placement of the pyramid. The pyramid, which was positioned in the Cour Napoléon to correspond with the arms of the Louvre, is slightly off axis with the Voie Triomphale. Pei had a cast of the equestrian statue of Louis XIV by Giovanni Lorenzo Bernini installed west of the pyramid to align with the triumphal way.

Below the Cour Napoléon lies the subterranean addition that contains more than 650,000 square feet of space. This vast new underground area, scheduled for completion in 1993, contains the Hall Napoléon. From this extensive horizontal space, made of Burgundian limestone to correspond with the existing facades and precast concrete, visitors can orient themselves and proceed via escalator directly to the different wings of the museum. Pei also provided for the inclusion of adequate support facilities and public amenities which the museum had sorely lacked.

The history of France is so intimately connected with the history of the Louvre that it was certainly expected that any renovations to this national symbol would be subject to intense skepticism. Initially, the criticism of Pei's plan became so heated that it was questionable if the work would be completed. The right-wing newspaper *Le Figaro,* reflecting public sentiment, labeled the plan ''incoherent and self-deluded.'' In the spring of 1985, in order to allay public fears, Pei had a full-scale cable model of the pyramid erected in order to illustrate that the pyramid, roughly two-thirds the height of the adjacent structures, would not dominate but enhance the existing museum. Since the completion of the project, public and critical opinions have entirely reversed their formerly pessimistic tone. Museum attendance has risen to record highs, and Pei's pyramid is fast on its way to becoming a new, albeit controversial, national treasure.

—LISA VIGNUOLO

MADELEINE
Paris, France

1763: Foundation stone laid. **1842:** Church consecrated. **Architects:** Pierre Contant d'Ivry, Guillame Martin Couture, Pierra

Vignon, Jean-Jacques-Marie Huvé. Originally commissioned by Napoleon to honor the Grande Armée. Since transformed into a church honoring Mary Magdalene.

Publications

BIVER, M. L.: *Le Paris de Napoléon*. Paris, 1963.
GALLET, MICHEL: "Un modèle pour la Madeleine d'aprés le projet de Contant d'Ivry." *Bulletin Carnavalet* 18, 1 (1965).
HAUTECOEUR, LOUIS: *Histoire de l'architecture classique en France*. Vol. 5. Paris, 1953.
HITTORFF, JACQUES IGNACE: "Eglise de la Madeleine." *Journal des artistes* Nos. 20, 21, 22 (1834).
GRUEL, LÉON: *La Madeleine*. Paris, 1910.
KREIGER, ANTOINE: *La Madeleine*. Paris, 1937.
VAUTIER, G.: "Pierre Vignon et l'église de la Madeleine." *Bulletin de la Société d'Histoire de l'Art Français* (1910): 380-422.

Madeleine: Paris, France, 1806-28

Almost a century had passed since its original conception when the Church of the Madeleine was consecrated. Situated in an area of Paris which was annexed only in 1722, the church was constructed following a suggestion made by Louis XV based on an idea of Madame de Pompadour. The chosen site badly needed a building to counterbalance the Palais Bourbon (now the National Assembly), located exactly opposite on the other side of the Seine, and, more important, the interposed magnificent Place Louis XV (Place de la Concorde). The two buildings today provide symmetrical termini to an impressive architectural axis—so much so that when Paris recently decided to repair the facade of the Madeleine, instead of exposing the scaffolding to those on the opposing bank of the Seine, it constructed a life-size image of the facade on canvas to mask the engineering work.

The king expressed interest in 1753, the foundation stone was laid in 1763, and the church was consecrated in 1842. During that time the original design was modified and changed by a succession of architects, including Pierre Contant d'Ivry, Guillaume Martin Couture, Pierre Vignon and Jean-Jacques-Marie Huvé. Napoléon decreed that the incomplete edifice should become a temple to the glory of the French armies, a sort of elaborate war memorial. He commissioned Vignon as architect. Vignon's modification of the plans to recreate a Greco-Roman temple, in accordance with Napoléon's wishes, would probably have been brought to fruition had not the disastrous Russian expedition of 1812 preempted the funding. The concept of a temple was consonant with the pervasive interests of early-19th-century France that called for a revival of the splendors of military Rome and for the praise of ancient virtues. But the decision to revert to the original intention of a church was made.

The classical mold had, however, been cast, and today the Madeleine rises like some displaced Roman temple upon a 4-meter base with all the austerity and simple beauty of an artifact from the past. One could believe that someone had transported the Maison Carrée from Nîmes in the south of France, but although the buildings are similar in architecture, the Madeleine is vastly different in size. Its majestic facade consists of two rows of fluted Corinthian columns supporting a pediment of the Last Judgment (submitted for competition in 1829, it was sculpted by Philippe-Henri Lemaire in 1833); a row of 18 more columns on each side of the sanctuary leads to the rear facade supported by a single row of columns. The rear facade was never completed—the pediment remains without a sculpture, and the bronze door, which, with its depiction of the commandments of the church, should have formed a diptych with that of God's commandments on the main door (by Henri de Triqueti), has not been added.

The interior, at first, intensifies the impression of stepping back in time; through a pronaos-like vestibule one passes beneath the massive organ (by Cavaillé-Coll) into a somber space. It is a space of great volume, for it measures 79.9 meters in length, 21.4 meters in width and 30 meters in height, and can hold 2,000 to 3,000 people. The single nave leading to the hemicycle of the choir is divided into three large bays supported by Corinthian columns and further divided into seven intervening bays along the sides, each decorated with fluted Ionic columns. In the middle of each of these bays—beneath an entablature and galleries—is a chapel, the entrance to which is announced by a projection topped by a triangular pediment.

The marble steps of the altar lead up to an impressive *Rapture of St. Madeleine* by the Italian Carlo Marochetti, and one's eyes move up first to the mosaic à la Puvis de Chavannes of Christ and his disciples bringing Christianity to the Gauls (1888-93)

by Joseph Lameire, then to a strange mural (1835-37) by Jules-Claude Ziégler purporting to honor the history of Christianity. It introduces a mixture of styles, the neo-Byzantine and the Greek, which disturbs the harmony of the whole, for the style of the mosaic and the mural are fixed in much more recent time than that of their surroundings. It is a concession that one has doubtless to make as Christianity tries to come to terms with the architecture conceived basically to serve a different faith.

In the absence of windows, the only natural light filters down from the height of the flattened cupolas that crown the nave and choir. The gentle suffusion of the outside world enhances the impressive awe of the temple become church, with its strategically placed sculptures, its variety of marble and glint of gold leaf. It remains a curious memorial to the continuing prestige of ancient classical art perpetuated by governments anxious to create their own monuments for posterity and at the same time to benefit from the glories of a past age.

—K. C. CAMERON

MÉTRO STATIONS
Paris, France

1900-13: Construction; **Architect:** Hector Guimard (1867-1942).

Publications

FRAMPTON, KENNETH, and FUTAGAWA, YUKIO: *Modern Architecture: 1851-1919*. New York, 1983.

*

Hector Guimard's art nouveau fantasy, the Castel Béranger (1894-98), was just completed when he was asked to perform what would become his most recognized work, the Paris Métro stations. Throughout the years 1900-13, these stations would place the burgeoning art nouveau style on nearly every street corner in Paris, exposing the controversial movement to the general public.

The design of the entrance stations for the new underground rail system had been the topic of much discussion among Parisians. How would these gateways to the modern transportation system adjust to the historicism practiced in Paris by the École des Beaux-Arts throughout the 19th century? Should the stations be, as Charles Garnier (the most prominent architect of Second Empire Parisian architecture) had believed, nonindustrial with "stone and marble, bronze and sculpture, and triumphal columns"?

This debate, which had continued for nearly ten years, was settled by a competition begun in 1896. Not surprisingly, first prize was awarded to Durray, an academic architect who impressed the judges with glass pavilions based on classical sources. The unexpected granting of the commission to Guimard, who had not officially entered the competition, was largely due to the efforts of the president of the Métropolitan Council of Administration, who preferred the arabesque line associated with art nouveau.

Guimard had recently returned from England and Belgium (in 1894 and 1895 respectively) and was experimenting with the new style. While in Brussels he met Victor Horta and was overwhelmed by the Belgian's Hôtel Tassel (1893), one of the

Métro Stations: Paris, France, 1900-1913

very first art nouveau structures on the Continent. Upon his return Guimard began to break away from the historicism he had acquired as a student at the École des Beaux-Arts, and adopted the asymmetry and natural motifs associated with Horta.

Guimard's Métro designs, later known as the "Style Guimard" or the "Style Métro," reflected a newfound love for nature, asymmetry and individuality, all of these part of the art nouveau movement which he had experienced in England and Belgium. Also incorporated into the designs for the Métro stations were many of the practical concerns that would become important to the modern architect, particularly economy and mass production.

From nearly the beginning the underground system was designed in its entirety, to avoid a prolonged period of construction. Therefore, Guimard was immediately aware of the unique concerns involved with the different stations. He designed three basic types of prefabricated structures that could be adapted creatively to fit individual spaces. To achieve this versatility he based his entrances on standardized units of cast-iron materials which could be interchanged according to the station's space and aesthetic requirements, thereby allowing the artist's creativity, as well as the integrity of each site to be maintained without the time and expense involved in creating more than one hundred different designs. Guimard realized further innovation and economy of materials by incorporating the ornamentation into the building materials; thus ornament is not applied but is part of the building's structure.

"Type one" clearly demonstrates this new structural ornament. It is simply a railing and open steps. The railing, reflecting the interpretation of nature so important to the art nouveau

movement, "grows" from the cement base and contains shields molded into a natural ornamental design that sprouts an "M" at the bottom. At the entrance two "stem-like" forms create an arch that holds a pair of lamps, lighting an enameled sign that announces "Métropolitain."

The second "type," represented today by the Porte Dauphine station at the entrance to the Bois de Boulogne, reinforces the art nouveau concept of individuality and craft expressed through unique materials. Embossed with a graphic design, reconstituted-lava panels form side walls, which support plates of glass and iron. In some examples these walls are covered with a glass roof with iron veins. The roof is supported only by a central girder and the front archway, thereby giving the illusion that the entire entrance is covered with the wings of an insect (known today as a "dragonfly" roof).

"Type three" was a complete enclosed pavilion with a waiting room and which, like the other types, amorphously sprouted from the ground, giving the impression not of an industrial complex but of a natural form complete with plant-like stems and translucent materials.

Guimard's remarkable stations were met with mixed reactions—from harsh criticism to admiration. In 1904 his plans for the station in the vicinity of Garnier's Opéra were rejected in favor of a design by an academic, Cassien-Bernard, whose composition promised not to clash with the more historical style of Garnier. There were those, however, who recognized the important step taken by Guimard.

Today Guimard's Métro stations are considered one of the finest examples of the art nouveau style, representing the combined importance accorded nature, industry and handicraft at the turn of the century. Apart from the significance attached to bringing art nouveau to the general public and thus legitimizing the movement, perhaps Guimard's most essential contribution was the combining of prefabricated industrial material with creative individual design for unique situations. He united the perplexing opposition between individual creative ability, inherent in the Arts and Crafts movement of William Morris, and the industrial concerns of a growing bourgeois society.

Guimard's harmonious adaptation of these two poles, however, was not to endure. Already in 1911 the Fagus Factory, by Walter Gropius and Adolf Meyer, had displayed a more austere machine aesthetic, which would become vastly more popular and practical than the intricate designs by Guimard. And although an Arts and Crafts sentiment would continue even through Gropius' Bauhaus, the natural, harmonious and unique forms of Guimard would be replaced by a more functional and geometric austerity.

—TIMOTHY W. HILES

NOTRE-DAME CATHEDRAL
Paris, France

1163: Building begun, arcade piers of the choir with gallery and clerestory, apse. 1182: Choir completed and consecrated, nave and primitive transept begun. 1196: Nave except roofing completed. 1200-50: West front, west towers, gallery of kings built. 1220: Clerestory windows enlarged into the triforium. Ca. 1225: Western rose completed. 1230: Reconstruction of nave and flying buttresses begun. 1240: South tower completed. 1245: North tower completed. 1246-85: South transept built. 1258-early 14th century: North transept built. Late 13th-early 14th century: Side chapels added. 1771: Central portal removed. Early 1790s: Jamb sculpture and western rose window removed. 1795: Window restored and jamb sculpture returned. 1845: Alterations.

Publications

AUBERT, M.: *Notre Dame*. Paris, 1928.
GUILHERMY, FERDINAND: *Monographie de Notre Dame de Paris et de la nouvelle sacristie de MM. Lassus et Viollet-le-Duc*. Paris, 1856.
HUGO, VICTOR: *Notre Dame de Paris*. Edited by Jacques Seebacher and Yves Gohin. Paris, 1975.
PERCIER, C., and FONTAINE: *Recueil de decorations executees dans l'eglise Notre Dame et au Champs-de-Mars*. Paris, 1807.
TEMKO, ALLAN: *Notre-Dame of Paris: The Biography of a Cathedral*. New York, 1990.
VIOLLET-LE-DUC: *Peintures murales des chapelles de Notre Dame*. Paris, 1870.
VLOBERG, M.: *Notre Dame de Paris et le voeu de Louis XIV*. Paris, 1926.

Notre-Dame de Paris was begun by Bishop Maurice de Sully, a peasant who held his post for 36 years. The foundation stone was laid in 1163, possibly by Pope Alexander III.

That the building was conceived as a whole is beyond doubt. The existence of a single, comprehensive master plan can be inferred from the fact that the carvings for the west front were begun at the same time as the first building of the choir. This was, in fact, the normal practice. In the Porte Sainte-Anne the capitals and bases of the colonettes which uphold the canopy over the Virgin and her mother and identical with those in the tribunes of the choir.

Basically, the plan of Maurice de Sully's cathedral is extremely simple: a choir of two double bays—for the vaulting is sexpartite—and a nave of four, ending in a deep narthex beneath the towers of the west front; the whole is surrounded by double aisles except at the crossing, where two shallow transepts interrupt the sequence without projecting beyond the outer wall. The choir ends in an apse, and the aisles curl around into a double ambulatory with no radiating chapels.

A section of the choir would at once reveal the system. The inner aisle is built of two stories—the upper being the tribune, a solid, vaulted corridor running right around the building immediately above the great arcade. This gives abutment to the spring of the vaulting arch and itself receives abutment from the outer aisle. In terms of the interior architecture, this produces the four-story facade. The great arcade is surmounted by the tribune, and above the tribune is a space beneath the clerestory. This space is the upright side of a right-angled triangle, of which the tribune roof is the hypotenuse. At Noyon and Laon this space is occupied by the triforium. At Notre-Dame there was no triforium properly speaking, but this space was occupied by a row of roundels which opened into the roof tent over the tribune. In about 1220 it was decided to suppress those roundels and extend the clerestory window downward. This increased the area available to the glaziers, but it reduced the facade to three stories and made it top-heavy.

There was clearly a break in the construction between the building of the choir, which was completed and consecrated in 1182, and the subsequent construction of the nave. Between those two campaigns a new and important technical device had been added to the repertoire of the Gothic architect—the flying buttress, which made its first known appearance in the Church of St. Remi in Reims. It was the architect of the nave of Notre-Dame who was apparently the first to incorporate flying buttresses into an original design. We can see from the one remaining double flying buttress on the north side of the choir what these looked like. The rest were replaced in the 14th century by the single, slender arches which now span the whole distance in a single, graceful flight.

Another interesting feature of Notre-Dame is that the main arcade presents a regular procession of cylindrical columns of equal girth which retains no trace of the alternation *pile forte-pile faible* that is the logical expression at ground-floor level of sexpartite vaulting. This alternation occurs in the columns which divide the two aisles.

The modifications made in the course of construction in no way obscured the master plan, which, as noted, included a fully thought-out scheme for the west front. This part of the cathedral was to suffer the most from the vandalism of the 18th century, both before and during the Revolution.

Begun in 1200 and completed only 50 years later, the west front has retained an astonishing unity of style, which argues an original master plan faithfully followed by later generations. The west front of Notre-Dame stands historically between that of Laon and that of Amiens, and differs from both in its simplicity and repose. The facade without the towers is an approximate square with a side of some 42 meters. The diagonals intersect at the base of the rose windows—that is to say, at the feet of the figure of the Virgin which occupies the place of honor on the facade.

The plan of the three west porches followed the tradition of placing the Last Judgment in the middle flanked by a Portail

Notre-Dame Cathedral, west front: Paris, France, 1200-50

Notre-Dame Cathedral, apse from northeast: Begun 1163

Notre-Dame Cathedral

de la Vierge to the north and a Portail Sainte-Anne to the south. In 1489 the Armenian Bishop Martyr of Arzenjan described the figure of Christ in the Judgment Porch as ''placed upon a throne of gold and all adorned with ornaments of gold leaf.'' The west front of Notre-Dame had some of the brilliance of an illuminated manuscript.

The iconography of the cathedral was clearly executed by artists working to the precise brief of a theologian. A new feature was the Galérie des Rois, which forms a complete horizontal break in the facade between the portals and the clerestory windows. There has been much learned argument as to whether these were the kings of France or of Israel. The matter was settled in April 1977 when some mutilated fragments were discovered in the course of excavations. The last figure was that of the Virgin Mary; the Galérie des Rois was a Tree of Jesse.

Above the Galérie des Rois is the great rose window, perhaps the most satisfactory ever to be built, for it combines a maximum of strength with a minimum of masonry. The proportion of stonework to open space is 1:146. This is the highest ratio of stone to glass ever achieved, and the system of interlocking support is so good that the masonry has not suffered any deterioration throughout the centuries. Only a few stones, eroded by the weather, were replaced by Eugène-Emmanuele Viollet-le-Duc in the 19th century.

During the late 13th and early 14th centuries there was a proliferation of little chapels, many of them contrived between the piers of the buttresses, which deprived the cathedral of its original lateral facades. This filling out to the level of the buttress piers left the facades of the transepts slightly in retreat. In the middle of the 13th century new transept facades were begun by Jean de Chelles and completed after his death by Pierre de Montreuil. In those fronts the Gothic reached its highest point.

Almost the whole wall space was given over to stained glass, most of which has, happily, survived.

—IAN DUNLOP

OPÉRA
Paris, France

1861-75. Architect: Charles Garnier. **1962-64:** New ceiling panels painted; **Artist:** Marc Chagall.

Publications

GARNIER, CHARLES: *Le nouvel Opéra de Paris.* 4 vols., Paris, 1878-81.
LAVEZZARI, E.: ''Le nouvel Opéra.'' *Revue générale de l'architecture* 32 (1875): 30-33.
STEINHAUSER, MONIKA: *Die Architektur der Pariser Oper.* Munich, 1969.
TIDWORTH, S.: *Theatres: An Illustrated History.* London, 1973.

*

Symbol of the reign of Napoléon III, Charles Garnier's Opéra immediately became the prestige monument of Baron Georges-Eugène Haussmann's Paris, which was being transformed with new boulevards, parks and monumental buildings. The Opéra was planned to be the focus of an important new *carrefour* of banks, businesses and department stores—a cosmopolitan

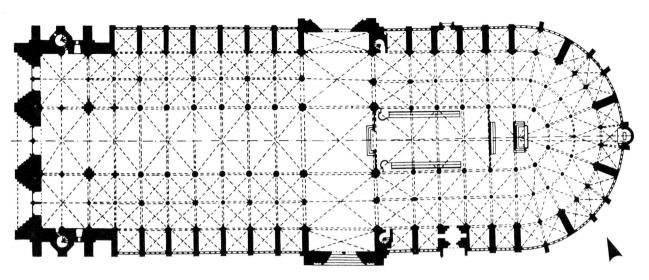

Notre-Dame Cathedral

meeting place lined with uniformly ornate and stately facades. The Place de l'Opéra remains to this day one of the most animated and elegant neighborhoods in the capital, while the Opéra has forever been fixed in the public imagination as a place of intrigue, horror and beauty through Gaston Leroux's *Phantom of the Opera,* written in 1910.

To replace the dilapidated opera house built in 1820 on rue Le Peletier, which had been the site of an assassination attempt against the emperor, a competition was held in 1860 for the construction of an opera house in a new neighborhood, free of the urban congestion and squalor that had characterized rue Le Peletier. Out of the 171 submissions, only five were retained, including those of Léon Ginain and Charles Garnier, two young students from the atelier of Louis-Hippolyte Lebas (1782-1867), whose most famous work was the neoclassical church of Notre-Dame-de-Lorette in Paris (1823-26). Garnier's design was ultimately selected over the objections of Empress Eugénie, who, favoring Eugène Viollet-le-Duc's entry, exclaimed, ''What is this? It is not a style. It is neither Louis XIV, nor Louis XV, nor Louis XVI,'' to which Garnier replied, ''It is Napoléon III

Opéra: Paris, France, 1861-75

and you complain.''

Most French theater design, such as Gabriel Davioud's Théâtre du Châtelet (1864), followed the Palladian box formula,
with a single roof covering both the auditorium and the stage.
What distinguished Garnier's entry, however, was that the theater's interior organization was clearly articulated in the massing
of the exterior: the double colonnade on the facade corresponds
to the grand foyer inside, the dome to the auditorium, and the
proscenium to the main bearing wall, signaled by the sculptural
group atop the Opéra, Eugène-Louis Lequesne's *Fames,* and
Aimé Millet's *Apollo.* Garnier's design was informed by the
ideas of other contestants, such as Ginain's proposal for rotundas, which Garnier placed laterally as in Viollet-le-Duc's design,
so as to provide a rich contrast in massing when viewed from
the side avenues leading to the Opéra. These rotundas fulfilled
practical considerations as well, providing a waiting area for
carriages on one side and representing the emperor's private
loge on the other. The Opéra's richly articulated and legible
massing, together with its impressive silhouette, accentuated by
sculptural groups, gave it monumentality and presence among
the rectilinear facades of the surrounding buildings. Furthermore, Garnier skillfully utilized architectural furnishings, such
as balustrades, grilles and pylons, to ease the transition between
the human scale of the cityscape and the monumentalism of
the opera house.

The first stone was laid in 1862, after the marshy subsoil had
been pumped for 10 months, an operation that inaugurated the
first nighttime construction ever seen in Paris. The Opéra soon
fell victim, however, to budgetary constraints and to the emper-
or's new social politics, which were designed to defend him
against charges of financial misappropriations, and which favored the construction of hospitals and schools over that of the
''temple of pleasure'' that was the Opéra. The main facade was
finally completed in 1867 in time for the Universal Exposition
that year. The Franco-Prussian War of 1870, coupled with the
fall of the empire and the anarchy of the commune that followed,
almost saw the demolition of the incomplete opera house, by
then seen as a symbol of a corrupt and despotic rule. A fire at
the old Opéra on rue Le Peletier, however, made completion
of Garnier's opera house an urgent matter, and it was finally
inaugurated with great pomp on 5 January 1875. Appropriating
the Opéra as its own creation, the Third Republic praised it as
a symbol of regained national pride and vitality, while the
building's sumptuousness was a testament to national economic
and artistic prosperity.

Garnier commented at length on his theater in two publications, *Le Théâtre* (1871) and *Le Nouvel Opéra* (folio, 1878-81).
The Opéra's purpose, Garnier wrote, was to realize the most
primitive desires of society—to hear, see and be seen. Thus the
spectacle was not limited to the stage, but included the spectators
who engaged in a ritual-like procession commencing with their
arrival, continuing to their arrival at their seats, their promenade
during intermission, and concluding with their departure.

The grand facade is characteristically French in conception,
consisting of a central corps with two slightly projecting end
pavilions with arched pediments breaking the horizontality of
the cornice. Above the ground floor is the monumental *piano
nobile,* corresponding to the Grand Foyer in the interior, and
composed of an open loggia with a double colonnade, which
echoes that of the Louvre in its pairing of columns and gigantic
scale. But the Opéra's polychromy and the insertion of smaller
columns within the colonnade make the latter lighter and more
decorative than the 17th-century Louvre. Above the loggia is
an attic, criticized by Viollet-le-Duc for its heaviness, but justified by Garnier in order to respond to the exceptional height
and bulk of the neighboring buildings on the surrounding Place

Opéra, Grand Escalier

de l'Opéra being constructed by Haussmann.

The facade's ornate decoration, reminiscent of Hector Lefuel's Louvre additions of mid-century, was a rebuttal to the
rationalist school's emphasis on functionalism. Although Garnier employed steel for the frame of the opera house, he encased
it in richly ornamented masonry and sculpture. He believed that
steel was a useful agent in construction, but not an end in itself.
Garnier was emphatic about the role of the architect as a creator
and as a manipulator of volume and mass into a coherent and
pleasing whole, something that steel would not allow him to
do. This unity of conception was one of the Opéra's principal
successes. Indeed, its superb profile, with the low dome rising
gracefully from within the mass, convinced Haussmann not to
plant any trees on the new Avenue de L'Opéra, so as not to
obstruct the Opéra's majestic silhouette.

In the interior, the vestibule is highlighted by monumental
sculptures that recall those of the facade, as well as the long
galleries of antique sculpture on the ground floor of the Louvre.
The great marble staircase, leading to the *piano nobile,* the
loges and the Grand Foyer, was inspired by Victor Louis' theater
in Bordeaux (1773-80), and is the Opéra's most original and
grandiose space. Garnier himself stated that the Opéra *was* the
staircase. Surrounded by a three-story arcade and gallery, by
giant pairs of Ionic columns and by round projecting balconies,
the stairs were designed to be the center of attention. On the
staircase's intermediary landing, which leads to the amphitheater, are great bronze doors surmounted by a massive broken
pediment supported by caryatids in polychrome marble, all
reminiscent of Michelangelo's Medici tombs and Ludovico Visconti's tomb and crypt for Napoléon (1841-53). The grand staircase embodies Garnier's genius at injecting emotional character
into classical formulas through a combination of sculptural virtuosity, polychromy, and brilliant control of mass and volume.

Although the accent of the architectural *parti* focuses on the staircase, and not, as might be expected, on the auditorium, the staircase was, surprisingly, left out of the exterior volumetric composition, which announces only the foyer, the auditorium and the stage. The source of the staircase's success, however, is precisely in the fact that its immense volume is not perceived from an exterior reading of the building. One is left ignorant as to the depth of the building between the loggia and the auditorium. The distortion between interior and exterior contradicts the apparent rational disposition of facade. Garnier was a master of such a tour-de-force, typical of a Beaux-Arts education.

The auditorium, even though it was the largest yet built, seems squeezed between the vestibule, the Grand Foyer, the staircase, the stage, the lateral rotundas and the Grand Foyer. The latter, modeled after the Hall of Mirrors at Versailles, rivals the auditorium in splendor and decorative éclat. Its dark and warm tonalities, free of polychromy and dramatic contrasts, lead the eye to the stage with minimal distractions. The cupola, open with grillework, filtered in natural light and doubled as an exhaust for gas-burning chandeliers. The dome's copper shell depicted Jules-Eugène Lenepveu's *Hours of the Day and Night*. In 1962 André Malraux, minister of culture, commissioned Marc Chagall to paint a new ceiling on a shell of plastic panels to be suspended a few centimeters below the original ceiling. Inaugurated in 1964, Chagall's ceiling remains the only heterogeneous element ever introduced into Garnier's creation.

Remaining faithful to the Beaux-Arts emphasis on hierarchy and character, Garnier simplified the decoration of the Opéra's rear facade, which had to be in harmony with the surrounding buildings consisting of offices and department stores. Furthermore, at the rear were located the less formal spaces of the Opéra, including administrative offices and rehearsal areas.

For all its splendor and richness, the new opera house was not spared harsh criticisms, which included the complaint that the main concert hall was sacrificed in favor of the opulent stairs, that the design was akin to superficial competition designs only meant to dazzle the eye, and that the polychromy and gilding were anathema to the gray-limestone tradition of Paris. Garnier, betraying his preference for the vivid Mediterranean color and pattern that had captivated him as a youth, explained that the marble, draperies and chandeliers had to equal the beauty and effervescence of any diva on stage, and that the Opéra was first and foremost a place of enjoyment and pleasure and that all the senses had to contribute to those feelings. Again, Garnier underscored his emphasis on the emotional content inherent in architecture but which too often had been sublimated in favor of rational and functional exigencies.

Forgotten in the contemporary criticism is the fact that the opera house's hallmark was its clear, rational and eminently successful plan, funneling people of all classes to their respective seats. The plan, besides being the linchpin of the exterior massing, introduced a social revolution in theater etiquette by encouraging women to amble to the Grand Foyer to socialize and mingle in the crowd. Theretofore, women had remained in their boxes, where they received visitors as if in their own private salons.

The integrity of the Opéra's volume and mass as governing agents is never challenged by the rich sculptural and mural decoration. This subservience is partly achieved through the repetition of decorative motifs, typical of an age fascinated with scientific classification and categorization. Thus, mythological symbols and deities, zodiac signs, flora and fauna are repeated throughout the mosaic, sculpture and painting decoration. Only Jean-Baptiste Carpeaux's notorious *Dance* (1869) achieved fame as an independent work of art.

The Opéra's success is due to Garnier's bold yet rational articulation of the building's principal volumes, decorating these with a symphony of familiar motifs which satisfied his society's desire for novelty and familiarity. The building influenced theater design all over Europe until the eve of World War I and provided an invaluable working atelier for countless apprentices, many of whom would become the leaders of the next generation of architects, such as Jean-Louis Pascal, Julien Gadet and Emile Bénard.

—MARC VINCENT

PANTHÉON (STE. GENEVIÈVE)
Paris, France

1756-90. Architect: Jacques Germain Soufflot (1713-80). Two square bell towers flanking the apse were destroyed during the Revolution. **1806:** Dome strengthened by Jean Baptiste Rondelet.

Publications

BRAHAM, ALLAN: "The Drawings for Soufflot's Sainte-Geneviève." *Burlington Magazine* 113 (October 1971): 582-590.
CHEVALLIER, PIERRE, and RABREAU, DANIEL: *Le Panthéon.* Paris, 1977.
MONVAL, JEAN: *Soufflot: sa vie, son oeuvre, son ésthétique.* Paris, 1918.
MONVAL, JEAN: *Le Panthéon.* Paris, 1928.
PETZET, MICHEL: *Soufflots Sainte-Geneviève und der französische Kirchenbau des 18. Jahrhunderts.* Berlin, 1961.
VIEL, C. F.: *Des erreurs publiées sur la construction des piliers du dôme du Panthéon français.* Paris, 1806.

*

The Panthéon, built in Paris from 1756 to 1790, is the preeminent masterpiece of early neoclassicism in France. Commissioned by Louis XV and built by Jacques-Germain Soufflot as the Church of Ste. Geneviève, patron saint of Paris, the building was altered significantly and rededicated in 1791 by the revolutionary government to honor the great men of France. The Panthéon is the result of Soufflot's mission to design a church combining the pure, classical style of newly discovered ancient Greek temples and the apparently lightweight structural system of Gothic cathedrals. It also reflects Soufflot's commitment to the functionalist theories of his friend and contemporary Abbé Marc-Antoine Laugier.

Soufflot devoted the second half of his career and, in effect, his health and life to the design and construction of the Church of Ste. Geneviève, from 1756 to the year of his death in 1780. His ambitious goal of combining the purity of the Greek style with the functionalism of Gothic vaulting led to a series of changes in his original plan, and to severe criticism and later alteration of the support system of the dome. Also, his final design and decoration departed from some actual practices of the earlier Greek and Gothic styles he was pursuing. The Greek order he employed was Corinthian, which was used infrequently in Greek architecture but was very popular in imperial Rome; his Gothic vaulting was hidden in the walls and ceilings, like the vaults of St. Paul's Cathedral in London, whose dome also influenced Soufflot's design of the dome for Ste. Geneviève.

Panthéon (Ste. Geneviève): Paris, France, 1756-90

Soufflot's acquaintance with ancient architecture began on his first trip to Rome from about 1731 to 1738. During that period of the Late Baroque style in Rome, his interest in classicism was stimulated by the new classical facades of San Giovanni in Laterano and Santa Maria Maggiore, which were under way at the time of his visit, as well as the ancient Roman monuments. Later, in the company of Abel François Poisson, the marquis de Vandières (created marquis de Marigny in 1755 and marquis de Menars in 1764), Soufflot made a second trip to Italy that further reinforced his classical inclinations. Leaving France in late 1749, Soufflot traveled with Vandières to Italy, visiting Rome and other cities, including Paestum, the site of well-preserved Archaic and Early Classical Greek temples. Soufflot's

study of those temples, which was reinforced by his acceptance of his friend Laugier's theories expressing the purity and superiority of freestanding columns bearing straight entablatures, led to his use of freestanding columns in the portico and the interior of the Church of Ste. Geneviève.

The important friendship Soufflot formed with the future Marigny, who in 1754 became the director of buildings (*surintendant des bâtiments*), was instrumental in the acquisition of the important commission for the Church of Ste. Geneviève. After recovering from a serious illness in 1744, Louis XV had vowed to rebuild the old, deteriorating Abbey Church of Ste. Geneviève. Following a delay of 10 years, the king gave thanks in 1754 and ordered the new church. He was persuaded by

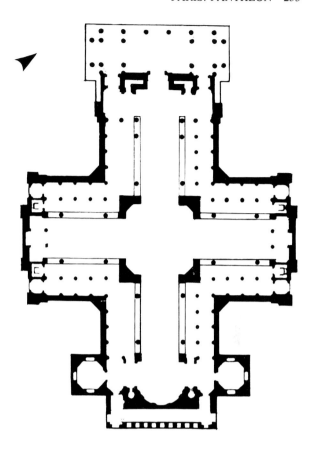

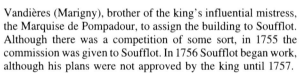

Panthéon (Ste. Geneviève)

Vandières (Marigny), brother of the king's influential mistress, the Marquise de Pompadour, to assign the building to Soufflot. Although there was a competition of some sort, in 1755 the commission was given to Soufflot. In 1756 Soufflot began work, although his plans were not approved by the king until 1757.

Soufflot's original plan, in engravings dated 1757, was a Greek cross with a shallow dome supported by freestanding columns over each of the arms of the cross. The large dome over the crossing was to be supported by triangular piers formed of engaged columns and crowned by a statue of the saint. In his second plan of 1758, he made alterations, including the extension of the nave and the apse arm of the cross, which he lengthened even more in a later stage. In this second version, a statue of the saint was to stand under the crossing next to stairs leading to her tomb in the crypt, which he added to the plan in this stage. The crypt was built 1758-63 and ornamented only by the plain Tuscan Doric order.

Construction of the church proper began in 1764, when Louis XV laid the cornerstone in front of a full-scale, painted model of the facade of the building, and continued to 1770 before Soufflot made additional changes. At that point, he altered the external entablature by replacing rectangular relief panels in the frieze with garland bands and by adding capitals to the corner piers. Then, as Soufflot reached the stage of the dome construction, Pierre Patte, an architectural theorist and critic of contemporary architecture, began a campaign of criticism of the dome. In 1769 Patte predicted future problems for the dome's support system and published these assessments in 1770. In response, engineers, mathematicians and technicians vigorously defended Soufflot's design. After changing the dome design many times from 1770 to 1777, in 1778 Soufflot began work on the final version of the dome based on those designs of the preceding decade. His dome of three shells resembles that of

St. Paul's Cathedral in London, although he used masonry for all three sections in contrast to the masonry, brick and lead-covered wood of Christopher Wren's dome. An inner cone between two hemispherical inner and outer domes continues the comparison; Soufflot's colonnade on the outer dome also was inspired also by Wren's dome.

When Soufflot died in 1780, the church was incomplete; the dome was finished in 1790 according to his plans by his disciple Maximilien Brébion, who was assisted by another follower, Jean Baptiste Rondelet, and Soufflot's nephew François Soufflot Le Romain. Then, shortly afterward, historical events swept away Soufflot's masterful Church of Ste. Geneviève. In 1791 Antoine-Chrysostome Quatremère de Quincy, a nonarchitect appointed commissioner for the works, transformed the church into a secular monument by eliminating all Christian ornament and substituting symbols of the freedom, equality and brotherhood representing the new patriotism of France. Those efforts led to the new pedimental sculpture of French heroes put in place by David d'Angers in the early 19th century. More destructive were the alterations of the structure itself. Quatremère de Quincy decreed that Soufflot's eastern towers erected in 1769 be dismantled. At the same time, the side windows were enclosed so that light could enter the building from the clerestory to simulate what the revolutionaries perceived to be an ancient method of skylighting, although, according to William Dinsmoor, scholar of Greek architecture, Greek temples probably did not have skylights.

One structural change in the building was essential, however. The cracks in the piers supporting the dome worsened, and although some defenders of Soufflot's dome blamed the cracks on poor masonry, there were clearly some design problems. A commission established in 1796 to investigate the cracks yielded no immediate results, but in 1806 Rondelet was charged with further strengthening the piers.

The building became a church again briefly under Napoleon I and the restored Bourbon monarchs, who followed him. Louis Philippe, the "citizen king," resecularized it again later in the century. The sealed, tomb-like exterior and the cold, plain interior of the Panthéon today evoke the chill and solemnity of the Reign of Terror, and serve as fitting symbols of the revolutionary fervor that stripped away all trappings of the life of the *ancièn régime,* although the memory of the titular saint lives in the stripped interior in a fresco series done in 1898 by Pierre Puvis de Chavannes that represents events from the life of Sainte Geneviève.

The Panthéon, although flawed by an overly ambitious original concept, by numerous changes in plans throughout the construction period, and by alterations in external appearance as well as name and function, is significant as a building of the modern age because of its eclectic mixture of styles, its bow to new archaeological discoveries, and Jacques-Germain Soufflot's goal to construct a light, functional Gothic structural system within the frame of a classical Greek temple.

—JOYCE M. DAVIS

PLACE DE LA CONCORDE
Paris, France

1756-73. Architect: Ange-Jacques Gabriel (1698-1782); **1836:** Fountains and Egyptian obelisk replaced royal statue.

Publications

GRANET, SOLANGE: "Images de Paris: La Place de la Concorde." *Revue géographique et industrielle de France* New series, 26 (1963).

LAVEDAN, PIERRE: *Le deuxieme centenaire de la Place de la Concorde.* Paris, 1956.

The Place de la Concorde is at the center of Paris's most impressive crossroads: the east-west axis from the Louvre to the Arc de Triomphe and its north-south counterpart from the Church of the Madeleine to the Palais Bourbon. This urban square is distinguished by its lack of architectural definition, consisting only of a pair of monumental palaces on its northern side. Its eastern and western edges are delineated by the Tuileries and Elysées gardens, respectively, while its southern side is limited by the Seine River. The square is a masterful alliance of urbanity and controlled nature, characterized by ordered vistas opened to the whole city, and has become the site of popular gatherings—even executions during the French Revolution.

To celebrate the Peace of Aix-la-Chapelle in 1748, cities all over France erected equestrian statues of Louis XV, often accompanied by surrounding royal squares. The square serving specifically as a setting for a royal statue had its origins early in the preceding century, when squares such as the Place Dauphine were laid out under Henry IV. That tradition was continued under Louis XIV with the construction of monumental and harmonious squares such as the Place des Victoires in 1685. These squares both beautified the city and underscored royal

power and largesse, but their architectural uniformity and restricted access isolated them visually and physically from the rest of the urban fabric. The Place de la Concorde was one of the last of the type built in the capital, but it was markedly different from its predecessors. It was constructed at a time of renewed interest in great architectural enterprises, contemporary with the building of the École Militaire and the Church of Ste. Geneviève. After 50 years of budgetary constraints, limiting construction to mostly private or small-scale projects, Louis XV sought to leave his mark on the capital, as every preceding monarch had done.

Some 90 projects were presented in the competition held in 1748 for the construction of the new royal square. Most entries situated the square at the heart of the capital and surrounded it with monumental buildings composed of arcaded galleries and superimposed orders. The king, however, not wanting to interfere with commercial activity or destroy a large part of the city's dense urban fabric, proposed a deserted track of land, already belonging to the Crown, at the very western edge of the Tuileries Gardens. If no one had envisioned such an inhospitable area practically outside the city limits, the king was merely continuing the capital's westward expansion inaugurated by Louis XIV with the Hôtel des Invalides (1670), and complemented by Louis XV himself with the École Militaire (1750) and the new royal square. In 1753 the king asked 19 architects to submit designs for the new site on the condition that the views to the Elysées and Tuileries Gardens, as well as to the Palais Bourbon, be preserved. The king charged his *premier architecte,* Ange-Jacques Gabriel, to execute the design, taking into consideration the best features from the competition proposals.

Gabriel at first conceived the square as closed to the north by a large monumental palace. But the idea of a perspective from the north to the royal statue convinced him to build two matching palaces flanking a new street, the rue Royale, which would form the main north-south axis to the center of the square. Thus the Place's disposition was not determined by preexisting urban fabric but by the necessity of preserving views to its center from the periphery. Toward that end, the square's perimeter was kept free of buildings and was broadly defined by the flanking royal gardens and the Seine. Gabriel delineated the square simply by surrounding it with wide landscaped ditches or moats, bordered by balustrades and crossed by bridges. At the angles, eight sentry boxes were to serve as socles for marble statues representing the great cities of France. The square was not, as it is today, the center of converging traffic arteries; the Pont de la Concorde, built in 1786, on axis with the rue Royale, was not planned by Gabriel. Instead, he envisioned the Place as a large landscaped promenade, isolated from the rest of the city by balustrades and moats, but visually linked to it by its openness and broad vistas, forming an element of junction between the Tuileries and the Louvre to the east and the Elysées esplanade to the west. In 1756 the king approved Gabriel's final revisions, and construction began.

The square's chefs d'oeuvre and main architectural elements are the twin palaces on the north side, flanking the rue Royale. East of the square was the royal Garde Meuble, which, after its dissolution during the French Revolution, became the Ministry of the Marine, a function it still serves today. The building to the west was privately developed and is now the home of the Hôtel Crillon and the Automobile Club de France. For these palaces, Gabriel adopted and refined Claude Perrault's Louvre colonnade, thereby affirming the distinctive French classical tradition championed by the influential critic and teacher Jacques-François Blondel, who, through his *Cours d'Architecture,* called for a return to the great 17th-century architecture

Place de la Concorde: Paris, France, 1756-73

of Perrault and François Mansart. Gabriel, however, reversed the Louvre colonnade formula by substituting a straight entablature for Perrault's central pediment, and conversely by adding pediments to the framing pavilions at each end. Furthermore, he lightened the colonnade by reducing it to a row of single columns, bringing it closer to the antique tradition than the Louvre prototype. The palaces are also characterized by their relative sobriety if compared with the prevailing Rococo taste for florid ornamentation. This was due to the palaces' public function and siting, coupled with the great distance from which they were meant to be seen. Thus, decoration was kept to a minimum, and was mostly restricted to architectonic elements, such as the rusticated arcaded basement of Anglo-Palladian derivation, the deeply channeled consoles supporting the end pavilion balconies, and the trophies atop the roof balustrade.

Gabriel also planned two smaller hotels slightly recessed from the alignment of the palaces and separated from them by a street on each side. With their harmonious architectural details, these buildings were to serve as transitions from the surrounding urban environment to the royal *bâtiments*. Only the hôtel to the east, constructed in 1767 by Jean François-Thérèse Chalgrin, was faithful to Gabriel's design.

The Place de la Concorde is a monument to Gabriel's genius of synthesizing the various elements of classical French architecture while still allowing his personal interpretation to shine through. By calling to mind the Louvre colonnade, the square perpetuates the dignity of Louis XIV architecture, a link which was much sought after during the reign of Louis XV, which was generally perceived by contemporaries as lacking in the glory and grandeur that had characterized the preceding reign.

Yet Gabriel's adoption of matching colonnades was an ingenious solution to harmonizing twin buildings into a broad, unified ensemble while respecting their individual identity. The square is also a testament to Gabriel's sensitivity to refinement and *convenance* coupled with *noble simplicité* which emphasized architectonic ornament over superfluous application of decorative details. The palaces, then, can be interpreted as betraying vestiges of the Rococo aesthetic while at the same time foreshadowing the more severe and serious application of the antique that was to characterize the neoclassical period of the following decades.

Edmé Bouchardon's bronze equestrian statue of Louis XV, for which the square would provide a suitable setting, was inaugurated in 1763, while the square itself was finally completed 10 years later. The ensemble, however, survived intact just another 20 years. In 1793 revolutionary mobs toppled the royal statue and erected an allegorical statue of Liberty in its place, while renaming the square Place de la Révolution. That same year, nine months apart, King Louis XVI and Queen Marie-Antoinette were guillotined in the square, inaugurating its infamous use as a site for important executions during the Reign of Terror. In October 1795, under the Directoire, the square was renamed Place de la Concorde, and for the next 40 years, each subsequent political regime tried to remodel the square according to its image. In 1800, for the square's center, Napoléon proposed to build a gigantic bronze column, modeled after the Column of Trajan in Rome, to memorialize his victorious Grande Armée. The imperial column was eventually erected a decade later in the Place Vendôme. Also during Napoléon's reign, construction resumed on the Church of the Madeleine

(1806), fulfilling Gabriel's wishes for a northern terminus on the rue Royale.

Although a competition in 1829 had produced a variety of plans, most of them farfetched, for the square's embellishment, the July Revolution in 1830 halted all such efforts. It was only after the ascent of Louis Philippe to the throne, that same year, that serious efforts were undertaken to beautify the square. In 1833 Jacques-Ignace Hittorff was asked to remodel the Place de la Concorde to reflect its by-then central position in the capital. Hittorff was careful to respect Gabriel's design, adding only candelabras, rostral columns inspired by the maritime theme of the Seine and the Ministry of Marine, and two fountains on the north-south axis, whose iconography consisted of French maritime and river themes.

Between the foundations, at the square's center, Hittorff placed an obelisk from Luxor, a gift from the viceroy of Egypt, Mohammed Ali. Louis Philippe's pragmatic approach toward artistic programs is reflected in his choice of a 2,000-year-old, exotic, geometrically abstract monument which was sure not to enflame political passions. Furthermore, the obelisk placed Paris on par with the Eternal City, Rome, which likewise was embellished with obelisks in the center of its squares, most notably at St. Peter's. In addition, eight statues representing important French cities were placed on top of Gabriel's sentry boxes, with the cities in their approximate geographic relationship to one another, thereby fulfilling a major element of Gabriel's design. Hittorff had transformed the square into a symbol of national unity, inserting a map of France through allegorical statues of its greatest cities and through fountains decorated with French maritime themes. So convincing was Hittorff's program that between the Franco-Prussian War and World War

I, the statue of Strasbourg was shrouded in black and flowers were constantly placed at its feet to mourn the loss of Alsace to Germany.

The only further major modification of the Place de la Concorde occurred under Napoléon III, when the surrounding moats were filled in to facilitate traffic movement. In the process, however, the garden effect so integral to Gabriel's vision was forever lost. The square, witness to pivotal events in French history, retains a fundamental place in the French psyche as a symbol of national aspirations, far surpassing its original function as a frame for a royal statue.

—MARC VINCENT

PLACE VENDÔME
Paris, France

1698-1720: Construction; **Architect:** Jules Hardouin-Mansart (1646-1708); **1810:** Column added.

Publications

BOISLISLE: "La Place des Victoires et la Place Vendôme." *Mémoires de la Société de l'Histoire de Paris* 15 (1888): 1.
CAIN, G.: *La Place Vendôme.* Paris, 1906.

Place Vendôme: Paris, France, 1698-1720

The Place Vendôme defined the elegance and grandeur of the era of Louis XIV. Its classical facades, subtle geometric spatial arrangement and perspectival vista across the length of the enclosure made the square one of the most harmonious and influential projects of city planning in Paris. The square originated as an intellectual, diplomatic and financial center dedicated to the glory of Louis XIV, but it was altered in both style and function during the period of planning and construction, and was completed instead as a residential district for the very wealthy.

In 1685 royal architect Jules Hardouin-Mansart and the chief royal minister, the Marquis de Louvois, persuaded Louis XIV to create a grand Parisian square to be named the Place Louis-le-Grand. After some discussion concerning the location of such a royal square, including one possibility of modifying the earlier Place Dauphine with a statue of Louis XIV facing that of Henry IV, the king's agents purchased the Hôtel Vendôme, in which Hardouin-Mansart and a group of financiers already had a financial interest. To add to the real estate, which was inadequate for the proposed square, the king confiscated the Capucine convent in return for the construction of a new convent in another district of the city.

Louvois envisioned the square as an intellectual site consisting of the royal library, the royal academies, some embassies as well as a mint, and an equestrian statue of Louis XIV at its core. Hardouin-Mansart's design for the square in this original format was a rectangle closed on three sides. On the fourth, a triumphal arch faced the new Church of the Capucines. Progress on these plans moved slowly, however, and in 1696, six years after the death of Louvois, who was instrumental in establishing the square, none of the original separate properties required to complete the square had been sold. After considering abandoning the royal square altogether, in 1698 Louis XIV announced that the square would be built but in an altered form. In the same year, the king abolished the plan for a royal library; at the same time, Hardouin-Mansart began to develop a new octagonal design for the square that would now contain larger spaces behind the individual facades. The king also decided to sell more lots, but the expense of establishing the square remained extremely high. Thus, in August 1699, the king ceded the entire property to the city of Paris in exchange for the costs of the facades that were to be built according to Hardouin-Mansart's new plan and a barracks for the second company of Musketeers. To fulfill this financial obligation, the city sold lots to wealthy individuals, who built town houses behind the facades. Hardouin-Mansart stayed with the project, presenting his new and final plans for the facades in mid-1699 and the roofs in September 1700. Of the individual town houses dated 1702-20, however, he designed only his own and that of a son-in-law.

Hardouin-Mansart's final arrangement of attached facades around the square is a long octagon, in essence a rectangle with its corners chamfered by the pedimented facades of individual houses. There in the square, the royal architect demonstrated the grand Baroque style, in which he integrated classical forms with traditional French features, such as alternating oriel and round arched windows set in high-pitched Mansard roofs. A high arcaded and rusticated base on the ground level or *rez-de-chaussée* is reminiscent of that on the classical garden side of the Château at Versailles. The two upper stories of the facades are unified by a giant Corinthian order of engaged columns on the pedimented houses at the corners and in the middle of the two long sides, while the simpler houses flanking them are adorned by pilasters in the same giant Corinthian order. Satyr heads decorating the keystones of the arcaded ground-floor windows further reinforce the atmosphere of classical antiquity.

Precedents for geometric city spaces surrounded by classical buildings of uniform facades oriented toward central equestrian statues include the Campidoglio in Rome, designed by Michelangelo and known from engravings by Étienne Dupérac, and the Place Royale (Place des Vosges), built in Paris earlier in the 17th century for Henry IV. Although both squares had equestrian statues at their centers, the residential Place Royale in Paris was the more likely source for the residential character of the Place Vendôme in its final state. The focal point of Hardouin-Mansart's square, designating the site as an important civic space while also paying tribute to the glory of a victorious leader, was François Girardon's statue of Louis XIV, which owed a debt to the equestrian statue of Louis XIII in the Place Royale but was derived ultimately from the statue of Marcus Aurelius on the Campidoglio.

The perspectival vista is yet another aspect of the French classical Baroque style apparent in the design of the Place Vendôme. There, in the middle of the city, a geometric formation of uniform classical houses enclosing an open space duplicates the effect of formal garden arrangements of both town houses and country châteaux. A long vista extends from one end of the square to the opposite end along the main axis, which encompasses the equestrian statue at its center. The sides of the square are closed by the continuous uniform facades, which, like geometric tree formations in formal gardens, prevent the eye from being diverted from the straight course determined by the limits of linear perspective. This central axis, like those of formal gardens, leads the eye to a vista consisting of streets and houses instead of trees and pools.

In the Place Vendôme, Hardouin-Mansart, who borrowed extensively from numerous sources, followed earlier traditions of building uniform squares around the central motif of an equestrian statue, and established a new grandeur by employing a giant classical order and an unusual configuration of space. This vision of a royal square influenced later squares throughout the 18th century.

The Place Vendôme, however, like the rest of the architectural patrimony of Louis XIV, was transformed by revolution. Girardon's statue was demolished in 1792 and replaced in 1810 by a victory column based, like the image of Louis XIV it replaced, on a Roman imperial model, the victory column commemorating Trajan's military campaigns. Napoleon's column bearing a similar spiral relief of his military campaigns of 1805-07 was not inviolate, either, and was replaced a number of times, including the last occasion after it was torn down during the Paris Commune of 1871. The tall monolith known now as the Vendôme Column creates a discordant note in the otherwise unchanged and harmonious square, because it towers high above the rooftops of Hardouin-Mansart's classical facades. And its grandiose Roman scale has altered the human proportions of the square determined by the earlier statue of the king. Despite this distortion of scale, however, the square retains its classical Baroque elegance.

—JOYCE M. DAVIS

PLACE DES VOSGES (PLACE ROYALE)
Paris, France

1605-12. Architect: Probably Louis de Métezeau.

Place des Vosges: Paris, France, 1605-12

Publications

BABELON, J. P.: "L'Urbanisme d'Henri IV et de Sully à Paris." In *L'Urbanisme de Paris et l'Europe 1600-1800. Essays in Honor of P. Francastel.* Paris, 1969.

BALLON, HILARY: *The Paris of Henri IV: Architecture and Urbanism.* Cambridge, Massachusetts, 1991.

The Place Royale (later renamed the Place des Vosges), built 1605-12 in the Marais district of Paris, was the first planned residential square in the French capital and a major component of Henry IV's vision for a comprehensive new design for a city that was still crowded and cluttered in medieval fashion upon his accession to the throne in 1589. This square of uniform, symmetrically arranged town houses for the bourgeois and lesser nobles introduced a new classicism in France in the early 17th century and, at the same time, established a distinctive standard for later city planning projects in Paris and elsewhere.

After Henry II met his untimely death in 1559 on the jousting field in the courtyard of the Maison Royale des Tournelles, his widow, Catherine de' Medici, abandoned the old palace. She then ordered its demolition in 1563 and proposed the Place de Valois, a square consisting of uniform houses, to be constructed on the site; but the project failed to materialize because of the Wars of Religion that followed. Her son Francis III, who succeeded his brother Charles IX after a year, later demolished the palace, although large parts of it were still standing when Henry IV came to the throne.

Catherine de' Medici's idea of a planned square later resurfaced in the Place Royale, the residential square of symmetrical facades constructed of brick and stone for Henry IV. The square included his own house, the King's Pavilion, on the south side, opposite the Queen's Pavilion on the north. Initially, he planned a manufacturing center that included a silk factory, which was built but failed and was replaced by the Queen's Pavilion; however, he altered the concept and, in 1603, announced his intention to build one of the grandest and most beautiful squares in Europe. He described it as an open space for the inhabitants of Paris, who were crowded in their sparse quarters, to stroll about freely. In 1605 the idea of a residential center apparently entered his plans as he began the sale of the 34 individual properties to grand lords, officers, financiers and parliamentarians. In July of the same year, he announced his plan for a residential square of uniform houses in a letter stipulating that the houses be constructed of brick and stone and conform to specific dimensions and stylistic appearance.

Louis de Métezeau, who became the royal architect shortly after Henry IV's triumphal entry into Paris and served until his own death in 1615, probably provided the general plan of the square, although engravings by the royal topographer Claude de Chastillon, who also bought one of the individual properties, have led to speculation that he designed the houses according to a general design of the square produced by Métezeau.

In Henry's time, as now, the primary entrance to the square was through the King's Pavilion, which was constructed in 1605-07 by the entrepreneur Jonas Robelin. Both the royal pavilions rise higher than the individual town houses and dominate the square. Entry to each of the town houses is through a *rez-de-chaussée* or ground floor, and each house is linked to its neighbor by a continuous arcade of vaulted stone, whose dimensions were determined also by the stipulations of the letter of patent.

These town houses reflect a new classical simplicity that developed in the architecture of Henry IV's reign and, yet, still consist of typical features of French medieval architecture, such as dormer windows and high-pitched roofs. Each house consists of four bays and has a separate and independent roof. Two upper registers of windows designate the residential floors above the *rez-de-chaussée;* the high-pitched roof studded with dormer windows completes the facade of this new French classical house, which assimilates classical forms of the Italian Renaissance and traditional features of French architecture. The standards of size and materials imposed upon the individual residents by the king assured that the square would be simple and harmonious, although some residents covered their facades with less expensive stucco and painted the surface with simulated brick patterns.

The progressive and far-sighted Henry IV was assassinated in 1610 before the square was finished. Therefore, upon completion, it was inaugurated by his son Louis XIII, who was glorified later in an equestrian statue by Pierre Biard erected in 1639 and still *in situ* at the center of the square.

The Place Royale became a popular residential quarter and housed such illustrious persons as Cardinal Richelieu and Victor Hugo. Some changes occurred in the square, though, with time. A number of the houses were converted to shops and restaurants, and many interiors were stripped of their original furnishings. Other alterations include the planting in 1783 of trees, which are now an integral feature of what has become a small public park, although these trees were not popular at the time of the planting. By the middle of the 20th century, the square was in a state of ill repair, but a law passed in 1962 requires regular maintenance of the Parisian monuments. Modern restoration of the square, which was renamed the Place des Vosges in 1800 in honor of the first French province to pay taxes to the new empire of Napoleon I, has resulted in a revitalization of the square. Now children play in the modern park on the site of the old jousting tournaments, which continued in popularity in the early 17th century under Louis XIII, although they were banned officially by his minister, Cardinal Richelieu. And the well-ordered, open city space planned by a king for the free access of his people and initially also for business is still both commercial and residential in character.

—JOYCE M. DAVIS

SACRÉ COEUR
Paris, France

1875-1919. Architect: Paul Abadie (1812-84).

Publications

"Church of the Sacred Heart." *Architectural Record* 1 (October-December 1891): 201.

Entre archéologie et modernité: Paul Abadie, architecte (1812-1884). Exhibition catalog. Angoulême, France, 1984.

FRAMPTON, KENNETH, and FUTAGAWA, YUKIO: *Modern Architecture: 1851-1919.* New York, 1983.

GUADET, JULIEN: "L'église du Sacré-Coeur." *Revue de l'art* 7 (1900): 103-120.

LOUVET, A.: "La basilique du Sacré-Coeur." *Architecture* 47 (Paris, 15 March 1934): 89-96.

LOYER, F.: "Rehabilitation d'un mal aimé à l'immense succès: le Sacré-Coeur d'Abadie." *Architecture d'aujourd'hui* No. 259 (October 1988): 36-38.

Sacré Coeur: Paris, France, 1875-1919

ROULINE, HENRY: ''The Church of the Sacred Heart at Montmartre.'' *Architectural Record* 3 (July-September 1893): 1-28.

ROUX, F.: ''Eglise du Sacré-Coeur à Montmartre, fondations.'' *Architecture* 1 (Paris, 1888): 269-270.

*

The Sacré Coeur (Sacred Heart Basilica) looms high over the Parisian skyline. With the Eiffel Tower (which alone vies with it in altitude), it has become an international symbol of the capital of France. Born out of a vow made by Alexandre Legentil and Hubert Rohault de Fleury following the military defeat of France in the Franco-Prussian War in 1870, the church was built as a result of the efforts of Cardinal Guibert, who, in 1872, espoused the cause. The *''butte de Montmartre,''* long associated with Roman temples and, later, Saint Denis and Sainte Geneviève, provided, in theory, an ideal site. To finance the construction, an appeal was made on a national scale and the design put open to competition.

Paul Abadie, the architect responsible for the restoration of the cathedrals of Angoulême and Périgueux, won the contest: his design was a triumph for the neo-Romanesque over the neo-Gothic favored by many. Work advanced slowly, as the site proved less attractive for architecture than for panoramas. To assure a solid foundation, it was necessary to sink 83 pillars to a depth of 33 meters, and it was only in 1875 that the foundation stone was laid. Although the building was finished on the eve of World War I, the consecration of the basilica was delayed until 1919; in the intervening period it has survived bomb damage (1944), demonstrations (1971) and a bomb explosion (1974). It has become associated with France's will to survive, and since 1885 lay members of the congregation have maintained a perpetual vigil, even at times of great danger.

Although the basilica is espied from a distance, its full impact becomes truly apparent from the Place Willette at the bottom of the approach gardens. Conceived in 1880 by the engineer Jean-Charles Alphand (1817-91), the gardens were realized by the architect Jean-Camille Formigé (1845-1927). They have been constructed, with difficulty because of the unstable nature of the soil, up the slope with imaginative terraces. From the lower level, the design adopted by Abadie looks unusual and irregular. The cupolas are ovoid in shape and appear to be elongated heavenward.

The stone, from Souppes to the south of Paris, has retained its whiteness (except on the north sides). With time, it has acquired a certain patina but remains somewhat incongruous. This is a building which reminds one of a late-19th-century and early-twentieth-century interest in mosaics, in Romanesque shapes and revitalized forms. The bell tower, which rises to a height of 94 meters behind the basilica and was designed by Lucien Magne, the architect from 1905 to 1910, is a lasting memorial to the popularity of art nouveau.

Above the three-bay peristyle are two equestrian statues, to the left Saint Louis, to the right Joan of Arc. Hippolyte Lefèbvre, their creator, has given them that dignity and stylization which befits heroes of fortitude and resistance. The bronze doors and the tympana reproduce themes associated with the doctrine of the Sacred Heart, as do the stained-glass windows in the narthex with their production of Saints Gertrude, Jean-Eudes and Marguerite-Marie, all associated with the formulation of the cult. There also is a window to Father de Foucauld, a pilgrim to Montmartre; all bear witness to the close link within this church between ecclesiastical politics and spiritual concerns. While the Sacré Coeur was being built, there raged in France bitter discussion between the opposing clerical and anticlerical forces, causing the clerics to become even more entrenched in their conservative depiction of Catholic virtues and responsibilities.

On entering the edifice one is struck by the austerity and perhaps overpowering severity of the architecture. The nave is in the form of a Greek cross, and the stained glass shuts out the harsh light of day. The cupola rises to a height of 83 meters, and then behind it unfurls the mosaic of the choir, executed by Olivier Merson; with an area of 475 square meters, it is one of the biggest mosaics in the world and shows an immense figure of Christ with a ''heart of gold.'' The 11 Romanesque arches upon which the mosaic rests seem to be stretching upward toward the welcoming Christ.

In the apsidal chapels there is more mosaic and a proliferation of neo-Byzantine decoration; the Lady Chapel, which recalls the Immaculate Heart of Mary, has a certain reflective beauty, which is enhanced by the three series of stained-glass windows, and the cupola with its mosaic depicting the Assumption, supported by Romanesque columns.

The crypt is sober and functional, built not only for the intimacy of prayer but for processions which pass under the unseeing eyes of giant statues of saints. Although Abadie's creation is profoundly Romanesque/Byzantine in its conception—use of lanterns, chapel design, columns and mosaics—it fails to recreate the magic of San Vitale in Ravenna, for example. It is a construction which lacks warmth, perhaps because of its size but also perhaps most of all because of its technical ''cleverness.'' It may reproduce the Byzantine design, it may reproduce the Byzantine motif, but it fails to capture and convey the Byzantine presence.

—K. C. CAMERON

LA SAINTE-CHAPELLE
Paris, France

1239-45: Lower and upper chapels built; **Architects:** Pierre de Montreuil and Eudes de Montreuil, Jean Deschamps. **1485:** Western rose replaced. **1838-67:** Chapel restored; **Architects:** Jean Baptiste Antoine Lassus, Eugène Emanuel Viollet-le-Duc.

Publications

GRODECKI, LOUIS: *La Sainte-Chapelle.* Paris, 1975.

GUILHERMY, FERDINAND: *La Sainte-Chapelle de Paris, après les restaurations commencées par M. Duban.* Paris, 1857.

HACKER-SUCK, I.: ''La Sainte-Chapelle et les chapelles palatines du Moyen-Age en France.'' *Cahiers archéologique* 12 (1962): 217-257.

STEIN, HENRI: *Le Palais de Justice et la Sainte-Chapelle de Paris.* Paris, 1912.

*

Few buildings represent quite so clearly the tensions between the development of a logical Gothic order and the mystical elements at the heart of medieval Christianity as does the Sainte-Chapelle. Furthermore, this is done in a remarkably small compass. The skeleton that has survived the desecrations of the French Revolution and the controversial restorations of the mid-19th century is now a framework only for tourists. But its form is inseparable from its original purpose, the adoration of Christ's Passion and the sanctification of the Capetian monarchy.

La Sainte-Chapelle: Paris, France, 1239-45

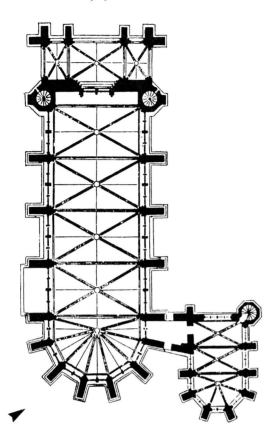

The five years of its initial building, to house the Crown of Thorns, fragment of the True Cross and instruments of Christ's Crucifixion collected by Saint Louis, have tended to mask the amount of detailed work done subsequently; it is perhaps a mistake to see it as quite the epitome of Gothic unity that is usually claimed. The later heavy western porch does detract from the simple linear proportions, but it is so difficult to envisage its original setting, despite the idealization in the Duc de Berry's *Book of Hours,* that the usual deploring of its present neoclassical surrounds is misplaced— if anything, they highlight the elegance of the frame.

Sainte-Chapelle is an oversize reliquary, the exploration in fixed limestone and glass of a familiar portable form. Standing away from Notre-Dame it does not, as is often claimed, mark a departure from the central role played by cathedrals in French architectural development; it grew tangentially from that experience. The most obvious inspiration is the Lady Chapel at Amiens, approaching completion at about the same time. But Sainte-Chapelle takes that source, recasts it, elevates it and proclaims freedom in structure and the use of light that the setting of the Amiens model inhibits. The detachment from a larger ecclesiastical setting was important in the iconography of a monarchy seeking to extend its national authority, although it may not have been as great as the 19th-century redecoration with fleur-de-lis and other royal symbols sought to suggest. They were more a symbol of the tensions within France over the revival of monarchism. At the time of construction it was the privatization of major religious relics that mattered.

The use of two levels, base chapel and main vessel, was not new, since most great churches were built over crypts. Pierre de Montreuil, retained by Louis as the master mason, broke with that tradition by creating a basement which was not subterranean.

Because of that the external proportions belie the nature of the interior; they give a sense of freedom in height which the structure could not have borne had it been undivided, allowing a mini-Beauvais without the structural difficulties. The solid base and limited overall height allow for support by comparatively thin stepped buttresses, avoiding the need for, and the cost of, providing fliers. Only in the arcades which join the main body with the apse is the sense of freedom hindered; they are too squashed. The eye is pulled upward to the flèche, the fifth on a roof much damaged in each century by fire. It stands where a crossing would be in a larger building—here there is none, just the memory.

Entry through the bulging porch masks an adequate view of the flamboyant western rose, which is not in itself an intrusion. The ground chapel, provided for the palace staff and the lesser clergy, must always have been dark, because its hall structure is not exploited by full window space. The golden lining on the arches and the springers gives some sense of mystery and relief. The need to support the much grander upper story demands 40 columns, elegant in themselves but overwhelming in the space available. From there, the narrow spiral stairs which give access upward do not prepare the visitor for what is about to be encountered.

The main chapel is a skeleton for glass, the emphasis being on transmitted rather than reflected light. The effect is overwhelming because the relatively open space rattles with the overcrowded colors of the 15 windows (four for each side of the nave, five for the apse, and the western rose) and the polychrome and gilding that cover the remaining wall and ceiling space and the statuary. It is difficult to realize at first that the whole bears sustained and interrelated themes. The windows take up 15.9 meters of the available vertical 18 meters; they contain 1,134 small vignettes, largely from the Old Testament and the life of Christ, with a few royal interlopers. They rest on a plinth of walls over head height, separated from the glass by a stringcourse of gilded stone leaves. Set into them are arcades to provide seating for royals and other notables, over whose heads angels swing censers.

There is a small "oratory" of uncertain date set at the southeast corner. But the dominant feature at this level is the series of statues of the apostles set in niches from which the springers rise, reconstructed or copied by the 19th-century restorers from the mutilated remains of the originals. They are lively, and articulate the vibrancy of the whole structure. Unfortunately, the later paintings beneath the rose are not of equivalent quality, and they detract from the graceful foliage above them.

The whole effect is to point upward and eastward to the place of honor, not for the monarch, but for the relics once displayed on a baldachino tabernacle over the simple slab of the high altar. The sense of mystery must have been enhanced by the screen which once divided the tiny apsidal choir from the nave. Now its lack leaves open the structure of the whole building but gives to the point of adoration an emphasis which its emptiness of relics is ill equipped to bear. So the attention is drawn back to the details, which are overwhelming. There are too many shifts of focus for the original aim of proclaiming a mystery to work. The details also detract from the building as a skeletal form. But it was never designed to be that, because the contents were far more precious than the container. What remains is exciting, but in the sense that it reflects a conflict between technical skills and decorative mania. It was not that which made the Sainte-Chapelle such an important model for emulation elsewhere in medieval, not least in the now-destroyed Chapel of St. Stephen in England's Westminster. But what was done at the restoration fitted in with the creation of a medieval fantasy as an alternative to an industrializing culture.

—J. R. LOWERSON

ST. SULPICE
Paris, France

1646-70: Choir and transept built; **Architects:** Various, including Louis Le Vau (1612-70); **1719-49:** Nave and facade built; **Architects:** Nave by Gilles-Marie Oppenord and facade by Giovanni Niccolò Servandoni (1695-1766); **1730-32:** Lady Chapel built. **1776-1778:** North tower completed; **Architect:** Jean François-Thérèse Chalgrin.

Publications

LEMESLE, GASTON: *L'Église Saint-Sulpice*. Paris, 1930.

*

The parish church of St. Sulpice in the St. Germain district of Paris, constructed over a long and protracted period from 1646 to about 1780 by numerous architects, is an architectural landmark because its facade by Giovanni Niccolò Servandoni is one of the earliest masterpieces of the neoclassical style.

In the early 17th century, the St. Germain parish determined that its church, which dated from the 13th and 14th centuries, was too small for the rapidly growing area. A neighborhood architect, Gamard, submitted a plan, which was apparently for the enlargement of the existing church; however, the new priest, Olier, decided to rebuild the structure entirely. Gamard thus in 1645 submitted a plan for a new building, which was begun in 1646. Then work ceased at some point because of the death of Gamard and the lack of funds to continue. In 1655 Louis Le Vau was called upon to take up the construction. At that point he modified Gamard's plan but did little else because of extensive commitments elsewhere, and turned the project over to Daniel Gittard, who worked there from 1660, when his drawings were approved, to 1675, when the funds were exhausted again. Under Gittard, the new choir, the radiating chapels and the apsidal Chapel of the Virgin were completed by the time of the archbishop's consecration in December 1673. In the two years left to him, Gittard also began the north transept and the piers of the crossing. Then, nearly a half century later, construction resumed under the priest Languet de Gergy, who in 1719 named Gilles-Marie Oppenord as director of works and, in 1721, was granted a lottery by the regent, the duke of Orleans, to pay for the new work. Before being relieved of the position in 1732, Oppenord, following Gittard's plan, completed the nave, the aisles and the south portal, and began a central tower that was later dismantled. He was succeeded by Servandoni, who had already produced drawings for the decoration of the Chapel of the Virgin in 1729. In 1732 Servandoni also won the competition for the facade announced the year before. In 1733 he began the facade, which was altered many times, by Servandoni himself and by successive architects before completion in about 1780.

The plan of St. Sulpice is the basilican format in the Gothic style popular for French parish churches in the 17th century. The similarity of St. Sulpice to Gothic prototypes is visible in the streamlined nave flanked by single aisles and balanced by a chevet nearly equal in length. Radiating chapels between the buttresses, the apsidal Chapel of the Virgin, and shallow transepts like those of Nôtre Dame on the Île de la Cité further reinforce the comparison with Gothic sources. Inside, classical details blend with Gothic forms. Simple piers adorned by single Ionic pilasters support a straight entablature, above which piers on the second register support tall, domical stone vaults that resemble those of Gothic ribbed construction; a masonry dome covers the crossing.

The fame of the church rests, however, on the severely classical facade by Servandoni; but this came into being only after the submissions of plans by several architects and a number of alterations to Servandoni's design. In 1725 Bullet de Chamblain produced a classical Baroque design similar to facades by the late royal architect Jules Hardouin-Mansart; in 1726 J.A. Meissonier, a decorator of Rococo theatrical constructions, presented a design that borrowed heavily from the undulating Baroque style. Then, in 1731 a competition for the facade was announced. Oppenord entered a project with towers and curving lines reminiscent of the Italian Baroque style, while Servandoni, a French-Italian architect better known as a scene decorator, produced a classical Baroque design that relied on some of the same sources as that by Bullet de Chamblain.

Servandoni's winning design also reveals a close relationship with scenographic architecture. In it, a central projecting frontispiece of two stories employing superimposed Doric and Ionic columns was crowned by a pediment. This frontispiece consisted of a tetrastyle entrance porch on the ground level and an enclosed library behind triple arched windows above. Balancing the frontispiece were lateral towers, which continued the superimposed orders with Corinthian columns in the upper register. The engaged columns of the towers were doubled at the corners, in a way that recalled the towers of the classical facade of St. Paul's Cathedral in London.

Servandoni began revising the original design as early as 1733 to accommodate wide steps that had to be included in the building, because the street facing it was too narrow. In this second version, which he engraved in 1642, a larger pediment extended over the doubled inner columns of the porch. Also, the upper wall was pushed back to form a porch on the second level. The resulting large two-story porch then resembled the narthex of an Early Christian basilica. Servandoni went to England in 1749 but submitted a third and final version of the facade in an engraving dated 1752. In it, he omitted the pediment at the request of the building committee. While Servandoni was in England, Oudot de Maclaurin was put in charge of the building and later became director of works after Servandoni died in 1766.

Because the facade was still unfinished at the time of Servandoni's death, the Académie Royale d'Architecture, at the request of Louis XV, examined the plans and sought advice concerning completion of the facade. After Maclaurin and the theorist Pierre Patte presented ideas, the academy accepted Patte's advice and, in 1768, required Maclaurin to construct a small recessed Corinthian pediment as the third level. This was, however, struck by lightning and demolished in 1770. Finally, from 1776 to 1778, Jean-François-Thérèse Chalgrin fluted the columns and built the heavy north tower.

By the time of Chalgrin's alterations, Servandoni's facade was no longer the classical Baroque church of his original design. Instead, the style of the facade at its completion in the late 18th century was neoclassical. Its severity was emphasized by a straight entablature that had broken forward in both portico and towers in the original plan. It was the elimination of a pedimented central focus, which Servandoni had included repeatedly in his early designs, that altered the impact of the facade and stripped the facade of the inherent Baroque unity and vertical direction of the competition design. The classical components, which were distinct but unified in the first plan, now stand as separate and isolated elements. Servandoni's final scheme of 1752 reflects his awareness of Palladian classicism, which was at its peak of popularity in England during the time of his visit there from 1749 to 1754. The similarity of his third facade design to Andrea Palladio's Palazzo Chiericati in Vicenza is striking, but a grand residential square Servandoni

St. Sulpice: Paris, France, 1646-ca. 1780.

St. Sulpice

planned for the front of the church like the open piazza facing the Chiericati was not completed.

The credit accorded Servandoni for his neoclassical masterpiece must be weighed in the context of the many alterations of his original plan; however, it is clear that, in his changes of the facade, he was exploring classicism in a new context and was in the forefront of a stylistic transformation of French architecture. By the time of its completion, the facade of St. Sulpice that originated as a unified classical Baroque design became one of the exemplars of the neoclassical mainstream of late-18th-century French architecture.

—JOYCE M. DAVIS

UNESCO HEADQUARTERS
Paris, France

1958. Architects: Marcel Breuer (1902-81) and Bernard Zehrfuss (b. 1911), with Pier Luigi Nervi (1891-1979), engineer.

Publications

"Ausführungsprojekt des Unescogebäudes, Paris." *Bauen und Wohnen* 7 (August 1953): 196-200.

JONES, CRANSTON (ed.): *Marcel Breuer: Buildings and Projects, 1921-1961.* New York, 1962.

NERVI, PIER LUIGI: "Le strutture dell'Unesco." *Casabella* (April 1959).

ROGERS, ERNESTO NATHAN: "Il dramma del Palazzo dell'UNESCO." *Casabella* No. 226 (April 1959): 2-25.

SHAPIRO, BARBARA E.: "Tout ça est foutaise, foutaise et demi! Le Corbusier and UNESCO." *Revue d'art canadienne* 16, No. 2 (1989): 171-179.

"La siege de l'UNESCO à Paris." *Architecture d'aujourd'hui* 3 (September 1957): 48-61.

SMITH, G. E. KIDDER: *The New Architecture of Europe.* Cleveland and New York, 1961.

*

The UNESCO Headquarters complex was designed and reviewed by one of the most sophisticated and accomplished teams of architects and artists of the time. The design concepts for the complex were developed over an extended period, during which the designers examined several sites and the very restrictive criteria regulating the visual and physical conditions of location, height, vistas and sense of place in the city of Paris. The product is a highly successful urban complex appropriately located and composed to fit into the rigorous design sensitivities of the city.

The complex is located immediately across a major axis, leading to the River Seine and the Eiffel Tower, from the 18th-century École Militaire. The Y-shaped, eight-story Secretariat, the dominant of the three major buildings in the complex, faces the circle Place de Fontenoy immediately across from the École Militaire. The second of three buildings composing the mass is the trapezoidal Conference Building connected to the Secretariat by the Salle des Pas Perdus, a lobby and information center. The third building is the five-floor Delegates Building.

The three buildings, only one of them having a rectangular volumetric form, are carefully composed to create an architectural order of heterogeneous forms, each maintaining its own

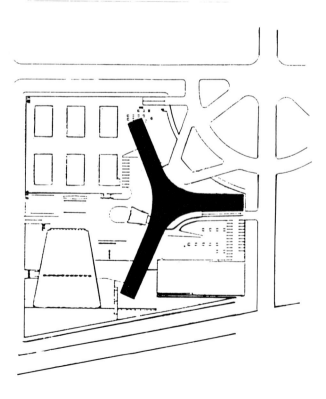

UNESCO Headquarters: Paris, France, 1958

identity and simultaneously creating an arrangement of organized open spaces between the composite building masses.

The open plazas are scaled to the urban community and to the comfort of the human being. The open spaces are animated in their spatial shapes and relations, and objects of art by a group of the leading artists of the 1950s are included within the volumetric composition. An integration of the arts, the architecture and the exterior open spaces has been carefully orchestrated: Henry Moore's monumental-scale reclining stone sculpture placed in the larger courtyard as a counterpoint to the highly polished glass facade of the Secretariat as the backdrop; Joan Miró's ceramic mural on a freestanding wall placed in front of the Salle des Pas Perdus and facing the Moore sculpture in the large courtyard that is, the focus of the space; the relief by Hans Arp at the first-floor level of the Secretariat; the Picasso mural in the Conference Center lobby; the Japanese garden in the small outdoor space between the Secretariat and the Delegates Building. Marcel Breuer described it as "art and architecture

complementing each other, rather than parts of the same."

In consideration of the synthesizing of the sciences, humanities and cultural emphasis of UNESCO, a primary consideration of the design team was to express these characteristics in the visual interpretation of the total architecture beyond just functionalism. The product is the synthesis of architecture, art and technology. The sculptural composition of the three major forms, creating the open spaces between, and the detail of the plastic configurations of the monolithic concrete shapes in the columns, the fire stairs, the folded plates, the concrete shell form at the pedestrian entrance from the large courtyard, all contribute to the sculptural form derived from the technology of contemporary concepts in concrete structure. The detailing of the monolithic concrete structure of the seven floors and roof for the Secretariat offer a statement in engineering technology of plastic structure form.

The outstanding statement of engineering technology is expressed in the boldness of the folded plate roof and the end walls of the Conference Building. Breuer had designed earlier buildings using such structural concepts; however, in the UNESCO Headquarters the opportunity to work with engineer Pier Luigi Nervi opened additional exploration of anesthetics in plastic sculptural structural technology as an art form. The monumental scale of the complex, the contemporary expression of the architecture, and the finite detail of each element unite the UNESCO Headquarters and conform with the historic cityscape of scale and detail of Paris. The subtle and simultaneously complex forms and elements, the simple yet elegant details, and the carefully finished materials are prime factors in the success of the building group within the city environment.

The sun-protection devices attached to the exterior walls of the Secretariat, which use technology to control heat gain and minimize sun glare, represent a traditional expression that Breuer developed in the design development of glass-facade buildings. The consideration for introducing sun, shade and shadow is significant to the articulation of form and space in architecture—another of Breuer's thoughts well illustrated in the buildings' grouping.

—GORDON ECHOLS

VAL DE GRÂCE
Paris, France

1645-65. Architects: François Mansart (1598-1666) in 1645-46, followed by Jacques Lemercier (1585-1654) in 1646-54, and others.

Publications

BEAULIEU, M.: ''G. Le Duc, M. Anguier et le maître-autel du Val-de-Grâce.'' *Bulletin de la Société de l'Histoire de l'Art Français* (1945-46): 150.
MIGNOT, C.: ''L'Eglise du Val-de-Grâce.'' *Bulletin de la Société de l'Histoire de l'Art Français* (1975).

*

Although its aging dome rises up against the Parisian skyline, dominating the military quarters which surround it, and it is one of the landmarks on the Left Bank, the Church of the Val de Grâce is not well situated to be appreciated. Since 1793 its fortune has been linked to that of the army, as a miliary hospital. The main body of the church backs on to the grounds of a spacious hospital green and is not easily visible for the general public. The imposing facade faces the rue Saint Jacques, and in spite of the hemicycle in front of the church, there is scarcely enough space to absorb the magnificence of its line.

It was in 1621 that Anne of Austria, wife of Louis XIII and mother of Louis XIV, patroness of the nuns of the ''Val de Grâce de Notre Dame de la Crèche,'' founded the Benedictine convent in the rue Saint Jacque—the church is the only one of the 14 which were founded during Louis XIII's reign along that thoroughfare to have survived. As a haven of peace it found great favor with the queen, and when after years of unfilled

hopes she eventually gave birth to a son in 1638, the future Louis XIV, she vowed to build a church there as a sign of her gratitude toward God. The foundation stone was laid by the infant king himself in 1645, when he was but six years old.

The church, constructed mainly between 1645 and 1665, yet consecrated only in 1710, is the masterpiece of a succession of royal architects and artists whose very names suffice to evoke the spirit of 17th-century France: François Mansart, responsible for the Gaston d'Orléans wing of the Château de Blois; Jacques Lemercier, architect of the Sorbonne; Pierre Le Muet, and Gabriel Le Duc. Decorating the interior were Pierre Mignard, an artist immortalized for his portrait of Louis XIV and for his work at Versailles, and the sculptors Philippe Buyster and the Anguier brothers, François and Michel.

Lemercier modified Mansart's original plans, and in this edifice we detect a little bit of Rome in Paris insofar as its conception was influenced by the Church of Il Gesù and St. Peter's. It is a church, however, which unites the aspirations and the beliefs of an age. In the power of its lines and its neoclassical symmetry it shows the spirit of René Descartes, a spirit of mathematical precision and reason. The space in front of the church is an essential part of the harmony of the whole: like St. Peter's Square in Rome, it cannot be separated from the main building. Sixteen steps lead up to the magnificent portico of four Corinthian columns. As Boinet points out, the lower elevation is wider than that of the upper, and the perspective is made harmonious by the use of consoles. Behind the portico rises the immense dome on its base of 16 pilasters; on top of each pilaster is an erect guardian angel, bearing a flame ornament, a motif repeated at the base of the dome's ribs.

The plan of Il Gesù also is mirrored within that of the Val-de-Grâce's nave, with its three-color marble floor, three large bays and wrought-iron screen to the altar with its cupola, which is supported by massive pillars; at the base of these pillars, however, are not round chapels as in Rome, but ones of oval form. The cruciform pillars, with fluted Corinthian pilasters, support splendiferous capitals sculpted by Buyster. Along the nave, each of the arches is topped with two recumbent Virtues based upon Cesare Ripa's *Iconologia* and are, according to Emile Mâle, the finest representations of Ripa to be seen in France.

If the facade of the construction stresses the orders, which lead from earth to heaven and symbolically point to the church's being a microcosmic representation of the world order, in its interior there is the awareness of the role inherent in the Counter-Reformation to affect the senses and to transport the mind of the beholder from terrestrial to celestial matters. The fluted pilasters, the confusion of the classical with the theatrical, the dais with its six cable columns (by Gabriel Le Duc) over the altar all take our eyes upward toward the cupola with its splendid ''Home of the Blessed'' (*le séjour des bienheureux*), which Mignard painted in 1663. All the decoration lends itself to the theme of the Holy Family and the Child Jesus, yet includes a representation of Anne of Austria led by Saint Louis, laying down her crown as a sign of her humility and offering a model of the church to God. Molière was so moved by this fresco that he was prompted to write *La Gloire du Val de Grâce*. To the right of the altar, the chapel contains original designs of the 17th century, recently restored.

Behind the main altar is the Chapel of the Blessed Sacrament. Square in shape, it is surmounted by a cupola which reposes on four pillars, echoing those of the nave. The pendentives bear four sculptures by Michel Anguier showing four of the best known of the Church fathers: Saints Ambrose, Jerome, Gregory and Augustine. For some, this chapel is an anomaly which interferes with the harmony of the whole; for others, its presence

Val de Grâce: Paris, France, 1645-65

Val de Grâce

is justified by the use for which it was intended—that is, to provide Communion for the nuns and a place for the Blessed Sacrament to be adored.

Thus it stands, the church of the former Abbey of the Val de Grâce (which, like the Basilica of St. Denis, was once the repository for the hearts of royalty), witness to an era that is now gone. As one looks at its facade and remembers that the statues of Saint Benedict and Saint Scholastica which flank the main door are but copies of statues that were mutilated during the Revolution, and that the crowning pediment has seen the arms of France and Navarre replaced by a clock which itself has now been replaced, it seems that these features are symbolic of the difficulty with which the church exists, besieged within its present surroundings.

—K. C. CAMERON

ST. FRONT
Périgueux, France

500-36: First church built. **1047:** New church consecrated. **Ca. 1120:** New domed church begun. **1173.** Domed church probably completed. **1347:** Alterations. **1583:** Repair of Huguenot damage. **1852:** Paul Abadie begins "restorations."

Publications

AUBERT, M.: "Eglise Saint-Front." *Congres archeologique* 90 (1928): 45-65.
ROUX, J.: *La basilique Saint-Front de Prigueux.* Prigueux, 1919.

*

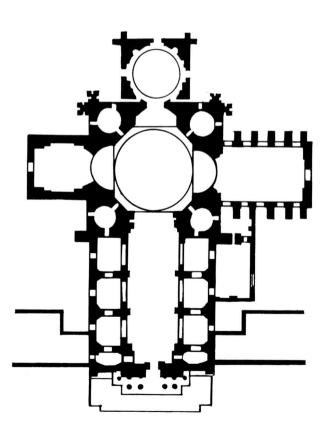

Among the many regional schools of Romanesque architecture, the domed churches of Périgord form one of the most distinctive groups, and St. Front in Périgueux, one of the largest churches in southwestern France, is the most spectacular example. Yet far from being characteristic, it displays many unusual and unique features. Whereas most of these churches have an aisleless plan, with a row of domes over the central vessel (cf. St. Étienne-de-la-Cité in Périgueux and Cahors Cathedral), St. Front has five domes in a Greek-cross plan. Moreover, this centralized structure was added as an eastern appendage to an earlier church, with the choir and crypt under its westernmost dome, thus, in effect, reversing its orientation. Its stylistic features and chronology pose many interesting problems, which unfortunately may always remain unanswered, due to the much-criticized "restoration" by Paul Abadie, who went on to build the Sacré Coeur in Paris. He unnecessarily razed and rebuilt the domes and piers, respecting neither style nor constructional methods, replacing sculpture and making additions of his own. While the centralized domed interior of St. Front is still impressive, Abadie rebuilt the life out of it, and it now gives an impression of dryness and falsity.

A first church was built on the site by Bishop Chronopius II (500-36) to house the relics of Saint Front, the apostle of Périgord and legendary disciple of Saint Peter. These relics formed the goal of a substantial regional pilgrimage, augmented by its position on one of the main pilgrimage routes to Santiago de Compostela in Spain, making the fortunes of the church. Bishop Froterius (976-91) began a new church, consecrated in

St. Front: Périgueux, France, begun ca. 1120

St. Front

1047, which was heavily damaged by fire in 1120. Substantial remains of this church were retained west of the main, domed church which was then built. The earliest surviving structures, however, perhaps from as early as the eighth to ninth centuries, are two small, barrel-vaulted buildings (*confessio*), once at least semi-independent, which flanked Froterius' (and probably Chronopius') choir and now adjoin the westernmost dome bay. The six bays of Froterius' aisled nave were preceded by a porch and followed by an east end with a small crypt, containing the relics of Saint Front. The central vessel of the nave was wooden-roofed, but the aisles carried transverse barrel vaults, some of which survive. The east end, on the site of the westernmost dome, has not been excavated, and its form is unknown. A tower was built over the eastern two nave bays after 1120, with the western bays left open as a small atrium to the domed church, although four large piers were begun at the corners of the atrium, unquestionably to support a dome which was never built. The two east bays under the tower appear initially to have been domed (as they are now), a significantly early use of the feature in this region. In 1077 Guinamundus, a monk of La Chaise-Dieu who was also a goldsmith and enameler, built an aedicular shrine over the crypt, which was retained in the domed church. This was apparently "antique" in character and liberally decorated with figure sculpture, precious stones and enamels, some fragments of which survive.

The new domed church may well have been begun before the 1120 fire, but most of it was built thereafter. A translation of the tombs of nine early bishops in 1173 probably indicates its completion. The five great domes, 45 meters in diameter, were built in a Greek cross on massive square piers, which were, however, hollowed out by cross passages. All of these features were undoubtedly copied from the newly built church of San Marco in Venice (1063-94); they remained virtually

unique in France. Contrary to former opinion, these domes are nowhere near the earliest in the region. The piers supported pointed arches (rebuilt by Abadie as round), which carried pendentives from which the domes sprang. The pendentives had a sinuous profile peculiar to this region. Piers and pendentives were built of ashlar, but the domes were of plastered rubble (again changed by Abadie). A circulation gallery runs around the church below the stepped, triple clerestory windows. Apsidioles project from the eastern sides of the north and south arms, and there was a monumental stairway on the eastern facade. The high altar and crypt of the old church retained their positions, under the west dome. Because of the crypt, the floor level of this bay was more than a meter higher than in the rest of the church; access between them was by stairs in the passages of the two western central piers.

The western bell tower, nearly 60 meters (or 200 feet) high, is an unusual feature among Périgord domed churches and takes an equally unusual form. It is similar in structure to the towers of Notre-Dame-la-Grande, Poitiers, and Notre-Dame, Saintes, but with more "antique" features. Above the lower story, two setback rectangular stages are surmounted by a round turret. The two rectangular stages both feature two rows of windows. The upper three rows are round-headed, but the bottom ones are trabeated, with pediments in relief over them. Each of these stages is also articulated by giant orders, attached pilasters below, attached shafts above, with acanthus capitals. The strongly antique character is maintained in the crowning turret with a drum of closely set columns carrying an entablature and an imbricated conoidal roof. The four piers in the atrium were finished as pylons, two flanking the entrance to the atrium, two the church facade. The facade featured a double portal surmounted by a blind arcade on fluted pilasters. It also had scattered relief sculpture, some of it apparently reused, but most of it, as with the foliage capitals inside the church, was replaced by Abadie.

There were many subsequent changes. In 1347 the eastern entrance was suppressed and a projecting Gothic chapel built, dedicated to Saint Anthony. The Huguenots occupied Périgueux between 1575 and 1581; they pillaged the church, scattered Saint Front's relics and destroyed his shrine. When the damage was repaired in 1583, the high altar was moved to its present position under the east dome and the crypt abandoned. The floor level of the west arm was then lowered to make it level with the rest of the church. Until that time, St. Front had been a collegiate church, but in 1669 it replaced St. Étienne as the cathedral.

In 1841 St. Front was classified as a *monument historique,* and in 1852 Abadie began his "restoration." Besides the damage already catalogued, he demolished the 14th-century eastern chapel and did one in his version of Romanesque, rebuilt the northern apsidiole (which had been transformed in the 16th century) on the model of the southern one, and added a porch to the northern arm and several picturesque lanterns to the roofline, removing the 16th-century roof above the domes (only the central dome was previously lanterned). His depredations were continued by Louis-Clément Bruyere (1883-87), after which Emile Boeswillwald exercised a more moderate hand until 1913, restoring the tower, atrium and cloister. This, however, was not before the west facade had been "massacred" and 460 square meters of claustral buildings destroyed, including the kitchen, refectory and prison, much of which dated from the 11th and 12th centuries. Ironically, although the 12th-century domes had been basically sound in the mid-19th century, Abadie's replacements are now showing signs of weakness, a situation which undoubtedly will pose considerable future "conservation" problems.

—JIM BUGSLAG

Villa Savoye: Poissy, France, 1929-31

VILLA SAVOYE
Poissy, France

1929-31. Architect: Le Corbusier (1887-1965).

Publications

BENTON, TIM: *Les villas de Le Corbusier et Pierre Jeanneret 1920-1930.* Paris, 1984.
BLAKE, PETER: *Le Corbusier: Architecture and Form.* Baltimore, 1964.
FRAMPTON, KENNETH, and FUTAGAWA, YUKIO: *Modern Architecture: 1920-1945.* New York, 1983.
FUTAGAWA, YUKIO (ed.): *Le Corbusier: Villa Savoye.* Tokyo, 1973.
FUTAGAWA, YUKIO and MEIER, RICHARD: *Global Architecture 13: Villa Savoye, Poissy.* Tokyo, 1972.
LE CORBUSIER: *The Complete Architectural Work.* 8 vols. London, 1966-70.
MEIER, RICHARD: "Villa Savoye, Poissy." *Global Architecture* 13 (1972).

*

When completed in 1931, the Villa Savoye represented a synthesis of Le Corbusier's attitudes and experiences to that date. He was 44 years old, and his most influential building of the prewar years in turn established a new architectural language of astonishing maturity.

The last and most "pure" of a series of houses commissioned during the 1920s, it was, unlike its predecessors, for bourgeois clients, M. and Mme. Savoye, who nevertheless had oblique affiliations with some members of the Parisian artistic community. The brief was for a weekend home, a stylish retreat poised in a rustic landscape one hour's drive downriver from Paris. For once Le Corbusier had a free hand, his clients being without strong preconceptions concerning form or style. Accordingly, Villa Savoye encapsulated with enormous clarity *Les cinq points,* reinforced-concrete technology and the *promenade,* but also powerful references to classicism. Colin Rowe has alluded to the fundamental similarity between Villa Savoye and Andrea Palladio's Villa Rotunda: the pilotis elevate the living floor to *piano nobile* status, the four identical Savoye elevations address the Poissy landscape as its classical model relates to an arcadian setting, and the geometry of Rotunda's plan and the structural grid of Savoye's reinforced-concrete columns is similar.

However, Villa Savoye demonstrated how the new architecture could not only embrace classical order, but could also espouse a burgeoning reinforced-concrete technology. One of *the* icons of modern architecture, *Maison Domino,* had appeared as a model for mass housing as early as 1914, and a development of its structural system incorporating reinforced-concrete columns and cantilevered floor slabs was employed at Villa Savoye. This in turn facilitated an exposition of *Les cinq points.* Pilotis elevated the building above the landscape so that Euclidean architectural forms were set in dramatic juxtaposition with nature. This also enabled the ground floor to be given over to service functions. Bedrooms for maids and chauffeur (devoid of hot-water services, incidentally) were relegated to the northern sector of the ground-floor plan, allowing a southwestern location for the entrance hall, where the dog-leg stair (for servants) and the formal *promenade* via the celebrated ramp assume sculptural significance. The route toward and through the building expressed with great authority Le Corbusier's notion of the *promenade.* The curved curtain wall to the ground floor reflected the turning circle of an automobile allowing passengers to alight under the *porte-cochère* provided by the first-floor reinforced-concrete slab. The route then engaged the ramp, which arrived at an identical location on plan at first-floor, finally to provide an external route via the first-floor terrace to terminate at the roof-level solarium. The central role of the ramp in the three-dimensional organization of the plan is made clear; it determines a dynamic link vertically and horizontally between internal and external spaces and terminates at roof level, providing a controlled view over the surrounding landscape, reinforcing the views already provided from identical positions *on plan* at ground and first-floor levels.

Le Corbusier also took the concepts of *fenêtre longue* and free facade to their logical conclusion. At Villa Savoye, the strip window embraced not only habitable rooms and circulation

Villa Savoye

demonstration of his architectural development to that date, the final expression of *machine à habiter,* an *objet-type* capable of infinite repetition. Indeed, Le Corbusier proposed such a development at Le Vingtième, Buenos Aires, an eponymous assembly of 20 such Savoye house types, suggesting an ideal suburban form.

The role of Villa Savoye in shaping 20th-century architectural history has been at variance with the apparent insignificance of its architectural program, a weekend dwelling for occasional use by its wealthy Parisian owners. Nevertheless, in microcosm it suggested a new architecture with utopian vision, and subsequent generations of architects were eager to sustain this model long after Le Corbusier's own development had eschewed Purism and the machine aesthetic.

—A. PETER FAWCETT

spaces but also, devoid of glazing, was employed for the first-floor sun terrace. This was in turn expressed as a living room without a roof so that the distinction between inside and outside was minimal. The ambiguity was reinforced by the ramp which alternately engaged with "inside" and "outside" space. Finally, the solarium or roof garden reached its definitive form—an enclosure of freestanding curved walls, "forms brought together in light" evoking not only grain silos from *Vers une Architecture* but also Le Corbusier's painterly explorations in purist art from the early 1920s.

In its detailing, Villa Savoye also demonstrated Le Corbusier's obsession with contemporary technological imagery; the balustrade to ramp and staircase had distinct nautical overtones, while the smooth, crisp detailing of the facade suggested a machine aesthetic. This highlights the paradoxical nature of Savoye, for such detailing was entirely dependent on traditional plastering skills. While the aesthetic hinted at *machine à habiter,* a factory-made *objet-type,* the reality was a crude constructional device of breeze wall with stuccoed finish. Another paradox was more fundamental; since *Maison Domino,* Le Corbusier's published projects had focused on idealized mass housing forms, in marked contrast to his built oeuvre of lavish houses for a wealthy bourgeoisie. Villa Savoye heightened this apparent paradox.

As a formal language, Villa Savoye was authoritative, accessible and entirely seductive. It at once suggested a building's relationship with its site for universal application. The formal contrast of smooth white planar facades poised over delicate pilotis with an eruption of plastic forms at roof level constituted a compelling and lasting visual image.

Villa Savoye represents the zenith of Le Corbusier's achievement during that heroic period, and remains as the most lucid

REIMS CATHEDRAL
Reims, France

401: Original cathedral built. **852-1152:** Second cathedral built on same site. **1210:** Church destroyed in fire. **1211:** Rebuilding begun. **1241:** Choir completed, stained glass installed. **1255:** Western end of nave, doors begun. **Mid-15th century:** Towers completed. **1481:** Fire damage, roof rebuilt. **17th and 18th centuries:** Interior alterations. **19th century:** Wooden steeple added. **Early 20th century:** Vault, roof, beams, statues, damaged in World War I, and restored. **1974:** Stained-glass window, center chapel installed; **Artist:** Marc Chagall.

Publications

BRANNER, R.: "The North Transept and the First West Façades of Reims Cathedral." *Zeitschrift für Kunstgeschichte 24* (1961): 231ff.

BRANNER, R.: "Villard de Honnecourt, Reims and the origin of Gothic architectural drawing." *Gazette des Beaux-Arts* 61 (1963): 129-146.

"Chronologie de la cathédrale." *Bulletin Monumental* 125 (1967): 382f.

DENEUX, H.: "Signes lapidaires et épures du XIIIe siècle à la cathédrale de Reims." *Bulletin Monumental* 84 (1925): 123ff.

HAMANN-MacLEAN, R.: "Zur Baugeschichte der Kathedrale von Reims." *Gedenkschrift Ernst Gall* (1965): 195-234.

HINKLE, W. M.: "Kunze's Theory of an Earlier Project for the West Portals of the Cathedral of Reims." *Journal of the Society of Architectural Historians* 34 (1975): 208ff.

JANTZEN, HANS: *High Gothic: The Classic Cathedrals of Chartres, Reims and Amiens.* Princeton, New Jersey, 1984.

KURMANN, P.: *La façade de la cathédrale de Reims.* Lausanne, 1987.

LAMY, E.: "Études à Notre-Dame de Reims." *Travaux de l'Académie nationale de Reims* 84 (1887/88): 388f.

PANOFSKY, ERWIN: "Über die Reihenfolge der vier Meister von Reims." *Jahrbuch für Kunstwissenschaft* (1927).

Reims Cathedral, west facade: Reims, France, 401

Reims Cathedral

his mitered head in his hand is among the cathedral's sculptures. A second cathedral consecrated by Archbishop Hincmar in 852 was extended to cover almost the present area in 1152. The bulk of the edifice, however, was constructed between two fires. The first, on 6 May 1210, destroyed the old church, and building was begun on the new one in 1211; there followed a century of concentrated building, and then 150 years of more sporadic efforts, progress coming virtually to a halt after a fire of 1481 that necessitated a new roof. A 16th-century project to build an immense spire was not realized. In the 17th and 18th centuries the internal disposition of the church was modified by changing the place of the altars, remains of the choir stalls, the rood screen and some of the stained glass.

The Revolution more or less spared Reims Cathedral, but the general attention paid to ecclesiastical buildings in the 19th century led to its being given a new wooden steeple above the apse. World War I damage was greater: the beams in the roof were burned, statues shattered and the vault damaged. The roof was repaired, but the stairs either were not replaced or were replaced with poor materials.

Work on the cathedral was, therefore, most intense in the 13th century. Reims was by then a rich and flourishing town. Already under the Carolingians it had been one of 22 archbishoprics with 11 dependent dioceses. Champagne had become by that time a nodal point, the scene of international fairs and a manufacturer of linen. The influx of foreigners allowed the Champenois to familiarize themselves with new ideas and new styles. Thus a concatenation of circumstances allowed Jean d'Orbais and subsequently Jean de Loup, Gaucher de Reims and Bernard de Soissons to create a Gothic splendor worthy of their archbishop and worthy of the role the town played in the world.

REINHARD, H.: *La cathédrale de Reims*. Paris, 1963.
SALET, F.: *Le premier colloque international de la Société française d'archéologie*. Reimes, 1er-2 juin 1965.
SCHÜSSLER, I.: "Die Reimser Visitatio-Maria als erste Trumeau-Madonna." *Marburger Jahrbuch für Kunstwissenschaft* 18 (1969): 132ff.

*

Cathedrals have an administrative purpose: they constitute the mother church of a diocese or an archdiocese. Their size and their magnificence, however, depend upon historical factors, many of which are political and economic. The Cathedral of Reims rises in majesty above a town rich in history and in importance. It is a church which means much to the French, for it is connected with the baptism of Clovis by Saint Remy in 496, and with the coronation of the kings of France—33 in all, from Louis I (778-840) in 816 to Charles X (1757-1836) in 1825, including the coronation of Charles VII in 1429 in the presence of Joan of Arc. Reims Cathedral is a symbol then, for all, of faith and fortitude, symbols which have been underlined in the 20th century by the way in which the cathedral, victim of mortar bombs in World Ward I, remained standing amid the rubble and the widespread bloodshed throughout the surrounding district. In 1962 it was no coincidence that General Charles de Gaulle chose Reims to celebrate with German Chancellor Konrad Adenauer an act of Franco-German reconciliation.

There have been a series of religious buildings on the site since the beginning of the fifth century. Saint Nicaise consecrated the first cathedral in 401. He was decapitated as a martyr in 487, and his statue showing him in episcopal robes holding

Reims Cathedral, nave west

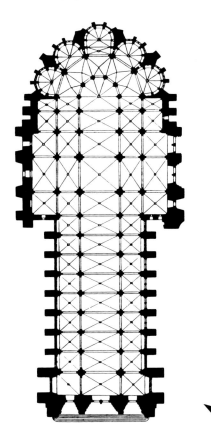

The medieval cathedral is representative of a corporate mentality, of a society united in its aims, of a society which felt part of the wide world of Christendom for which the individual was but a component of a much greater whole. As Maurice Eschapasse wrote in *La Cathédrale de Reims,* the medieval cathedral "unites the past, the present and the end of the world, the moral and the physical worlds, the reigns on earth and the heavenly powers/hierarchies. . . . God is a constructor represented [in the world] . . . the master craftsman is his imitator."

Although it is the fate of many illustrious buildings of the past to be hemmed in by modern constructions, Reims is fortunate in that it is reasonably free; it is possible to approach the cathedral along a wide avenue from a distance. Its highly decorated west front looms large topped by two rectangular towers, which were completed only in the 15th century. Up to 1914 it was calculated that there were 2,302 sculptures—2061 were on the outside and 241 on the inside. The multiplicity of the statues becomes apparent as one draws closer to the facade: Christ the Savior, the Virgin, Saints and martyrs, bishops of Reims and kings they have crowned. Worn by weather and time, a world of petrified personages opens up. In the central portico the Virgin is glorified; to the right are scenes of the Apocalypse and the Last Judgment, to the left the saints and martyrs who followed Christ: examples of passion and death including a statue of an angel with a smiling face, which has become one of the tourist attractions. These three themes are repeated on the sculptures of the north facade.

Passing beneath the terrifying scenes of the Day of Judgment, one enters a colossal space—the removal of much of the stained glass makes the interior much lighter and in some ways much more impressive as architecture than, say, Notre-Dame in Paris;

Reims is also slightly bigger than Notre-Dame, covering a surface of more than 6,000 square meters. The characteristic three-story elevation of Gothic cathedrals is visible: arches, triforium and windows. The genius of the architects there is to be seen in the way in which there is a normal transition from the more widely spaced arches of the central nave, flanked by side aisles, to the more closely spaced columns of the choir.

From the nave one glimpses the splendors of the central window, reresenting Christ on the cross, and of the west rose, representing the death of the Virgin—a kaleidoscope of details and precision, and yet impossible to really decipher from such a distance. Stained glass in these cathedrals has to be viewed from ground level as a sort of glimpse of the beyond, a sort of music for the eye. Similarly, the splendors of the rose in the south transept (the Resurrection) or those of the rose in the west transept (the Creation) are testimony to mysteries of which we can distinguish merely the outlines but of which the true sense is not readily apparent. Not so, however, the more modern glass designed by J. Simon and placed in 1954 in the south transept: three windows sing the praises of Champagne and its viticulturists. From there one begins the deambulatory around the apse of five chapels, each behind a single arch. The center chapel reveals the source of blue and green perceived from the nave, a set of windows designed in 1974 by Marc Chagall that show the hand of the modern master and his interpretation of scenes from the Bible. The design links a rejected Saul, David, a resplendent Good Samaritan, the baptism of Christ, Saint Louis and the coronation of Charles VII. The neighboring Chapel of St. Joseph has 20 paving stones depicting the life of Joseph as depicted in Genesis—the naïve figures were created by pouring lead into the carved stone. Other chapels bear the traces of unfortunate 19th-century restoration, walls patterned in fading fleurs-de-lis, a sad reminder of bad taste.

As the sun filters through the stained and unstained glass, casting a motley of shadows upon the pillars that reach up to gigantic vaults, symbolizing the close union between man and God, the greatness that was once Reims', if not now complete, can still be imagined in part.

—K. C. CAMERON

NOTRE-DAME-DU-HAUT
Ronchamp, Haute Saône, France

1950-55: Construction; **Architect:** Le Corbusier (1887-1965).

Publications

"Chappelle Notre-Dame-du-Haut, Ronchamp." *Global Architecture* 7 (1971).
HENZ, ANTON: *Ronchamp: Le Corbusiers erster Kirchenbau.* Recklinghausen, West Germany, 1956.
LE CORBUSIER: *Textes et dessins pour Ronchamp.* Paris, 1965.
LE CORBUSIER: *The Chapel at Ronchamp.* London, 1957.
PAULY, DANIÈLE: *Ronchamp, lecture d'une architecture.* Paris, 1980.
PAULY, DANIELE: "The Chapel of Ronchamp as an Example of Le Corbusier's Creative Process." In H. ALLEN BROOKS (ed.): *The Le Corbusier Archive.* Vol. 20. New York and Paris, 1983.
PETIT, JEAN (ed.): *Chapelle Notre-Dame-du-Haut à Ronchamp.* Paris, 1957.

Notre-Dame-du-Haut: Ronchamp, Haute Saône, France, 1950-55

ROHNA, KARL ANTON: *Besuch in Ronchamp.* Nuremberg, Germany, 1958.

STIRLING, JAMES: "Ronchamp: Corbusier's Chapel and the Crisis of Rationalism." *Architecture and Urbanism* 105, 6 (1979): 3-10.

TZONIS, ALEXANDER (ed.): "Drawings from the Le Corbusier Archive: Villas, Public Buildings, Ronchamp." *Architectural Design* (1986).

WALDEN, RUSSELL (ed.): *The Open Hand: Essays on Le Corbusier.* Cambridge, Massachusetts, 1977.

WALDEN, RUSSELL: *Bon Anniversaire Le Corbusier 1887-1987, The Joy of Ronchamp.* Auckland, New Zealand, 1987.

WALDEN, RUSSELL: "Le Corbusier, Ideals and Realities." Dissertation. University of Birmingham, England, 1978.

*

Great architecture is rare in history. The mark of real distinction in form, volume, space, color and acoustics is that exceptional quality which moves and uplifts the human spirit. Such is the destiny of Notre-Dame-du–Haut. It is an experience of silence, peace and inner sweetness. Ronchamp is never easy to understand or explain because ultimately Le Corbusier's later work defies rational explanation. At best, we can only experience Ronchamp and be grateful that this miracle of the imagination was built at all, for great works of architecture which speak of the human spirit are an uncommon excellence in any age. Ronchamp is Le Corbusier's jewel. It is a very real part of his inner journey as a spiritual person.

Notre-Dame-du-Haut is situated on the southern foothills of the Vosges, 33 kilometers from Belfort. Its completion in June 1955 was certainly a creative shock to the village of Ronchamp, to the clergy, and to a whole generation that followed World War II. Revulsion from militarism, from hatred and oppression, from the tyranny of the right angle is marked high and heroically on this ancient building site of Bourlémont. Yet this plastic work is in deep harmony with nature and the four horizons. We need to remember that architects of genius can never be understood as predictable creatures. Ronchamp is Le Corbusier's most enigmatic building, where he liberated himself irrevocably from the logic of straight lines. Like a true composer, he was also indifferent to worldly applause. As he exclaimed:

> "This pilgrim's chapel is no baroque pennon
> May Ronchamp bear witness to
> five years of work isolated on a hill.
> I have never in my life explained a work,
> The work may be liked or disliked,
> understood or not,
> What difference does that make to me."

This chapel can be seen from a long way off, like a white lighthouse, set in the middle of a huge landscape of earth and sky. It too sees a long way: to the south, the last outposts of the Vosges, to the west, the plain of the River Soane, to the north a valley and a village, to the east d'Alsace. This landscape, these four horizons were the deciding factors. They are nature's

Notre-Dame-du-Haut

hosts—they are always present. It is to them that the chapel speaks.

Ronchamp is contact with a place. A situation in a place. A word spoken to this place. Ronchamp is freedom. It is totally unrestricted. There is no functional program other than the Mass—one of the oldest rites in Christendom. Ronchamp is a place of pilgrimage, a source of consolation to the lonely. But Ronchamp speaks of inner joy. As Le Corbusier understood it: ''Inside alone with yourself, outside 10,000 pilgrims in front of the altar.''

Le Corbusier's disciplined plan cherished this compelling dream. He used the east wall as a cyclorama against which the public and more private altars were set, incorporating a swiveling Virgin in the reredos wall. This was a stroke of genius. Not only did it give due honor to the Virgin—Notre-Dame-du-Haut—but this detail shows us how Le Corbusier approached the notion of the spiritual. To deny this link between the interior and exterior would have been a direct contradiction of his approach to the spiritual. On this point it is vital to realize that Le Corbusier's spirituality came not through the Catholic Mass but direct from nature.

To celebrate pilgrimage Mass outdoors before nature was in great sympathy with Le Corbusier's approach to the spiritual. He was supremely receptive to the world of nature, and before nature he was himself. Nature in fact reveals Le Corbusier in all his Rousseauist glory. At Ronchamp nature becomes the loudspeaker for Le Corbusier's architecture. The manner in which the concrete shell roof, thick walls and vertical towers define this chamber of silence is pure poetry. Such a controlled space is alive in light. Light is the key, and this space carries a rich variety of meanings woven into its cave-like synthesis.

It is this experience which produces amazing and varying responses in pilgrims.

Without a doubt, this chapel is Le Corbusier's most available and popular building. It captured the imagination of a whole architectural generation, and historians have been writing about it ever since. It has entered the popular mythology of stamps and posters, and finds a place on the front cover of many books which deal with 20th-century civilization.

Why, one might ask? Simply because in an era of deep spiritual poverty, the architectural language of Ronchamp is incredibly rich. At Ronchamp Le Corbusier gave living form to dead matter—his curving forms are alive in spirit. At Ronchamp Le Corbusier sought to express the ineffable, and the inner voice of the artist. For this very reason, Ronchamp was, and still is, a masterpiece. But it is a poetic masterpiece that has to be creatively experienced. It is also a help to the understanding if the visitor has personally experienced the Mediterranean, for it was there that the seal was set on Le Corbusier's sensibility.

To answer the question whether or not Le Corbusier's vision as an architect changed fundamentally between his purist and mature periods, the answer must be categorically no, but it must be realized that until he built the Chapel of Ronchamp, his nature mysticism was not fully visible to the world. It was this deep experience in nature which provided the visual force behind all his work. Le Corbusier's work was never dull. At Ronchamp Le Corbusier created architecture that was not only original to the postwar period in which he worked, but also within his own oeuvre. Above the village of Ronchamp he followed his own path; he was master of his own fate. At the end of the day, for those who seek to climb the hill of Bourlémont,

Ronchamp is a unique moment in a unique landscape, created by a spiritual person who moved his generation in a heroic way.

—RUSSELL WALDEN

STRASBOURG CATHEDRAL
Strasbourg, France

1015: Original church built. **1176-90:** Chancel, apse, crossing and transepts reconstructed after damage in fire. **1230s:** South transept built. **1260s-70s:** Nave rebuilt. **1277:** West front begun; **Architects:** Master Rudolf (designs from 1265), Master Erwin of Steinbach (designs from 1277). **1296:** Work on west front halted due to fire. **1349:** St. Catherine's Chapel added. **1360s:** Belfry built between two towers. **1399:** Plans for extension of north and south towers designed; **Architect:** Ulrich von Ensingen. **1439:** North steeple completed; **Architect:** Johann Hültz. **1515:** St. Lawrence's Chapel added. **1759:** Gothic 'bishop's bonnet' destroyed by fire. **1793:** Sculptures damaged and restored. **1860-78:** Central octagon built; **Architect:** Gustave Klotz. **1944:** Octagon damaged in air raid; being restored.

Publications

BAUCH, KURT: "Chartres und Strassburg." *Oberrheinische Kunst*, 4 (1929).

BEYE, V., HAEUSSER, J.R., LUDMANN, J.D., and RECHT, R.: *La cathédrale de Strasbourg.* Strasbourg, 1974.

GRANDIDIER, ABBÉ PHILIPPE ANDRÉ: *Essais Historiques et Topographiques sur l'Eglise Cathédrale de Strasbourg.* Strasbourg, 1782.

KUNZE, H.: "Der Stand unseres Wissens um die Baugeschichte des Strassburger Münsters." In *Elsass-Lothringen Jahrbuch* XVIII (1939): 63-115.

PARISET, F.: *Etude sur l'Atelier de la Cathédrale de Strasbourg, entre 1681 et 1789.* Paris, 1929.

RECHT, ROLAND: *La cathédrale de Strasbourg.* Stuttgart, 1971.

REINHARDT, H.: *La cathédrale de Strasbourg.* Paris, 1972.

WILL, R.: *La cathédrale de Strasbourg.* Strasbourg, 1957.

*

Strasbourg as a town has hovered between French and German cultures, to its equal profit and peril. Its cathedral perfectly reflects that balancing act. It is the *beau idéal* of the urban Gothic cathedral, romantically, almost savagely different from the buildings that encircle and even abut it. It eschews the icy perfection of the masterpieces of French "great church" architecture in favor of a sheer, tumultuous west end and lofty single steeple which bespeak the vigor and culture of one of the leading German-speaking city-states of the Holy Roman Empire.

The cathedrals of other former city-states like Florence or Cologne are in many respects apter points of comparison with Strasbourg than those of Reims or Paris. For, like many other of Europe's cathedrals, Strasbourg once functioned not just as a center of worship and pilgrimage but as an emblem of the renewed civic life of the late Middle Ages. Before the 1260s the town's secular as well as religious authority was squarely in clerical hands; legal proceedings took place before and perhaps

within the south portal, while from the 15th century the magistracy swore the annual oath of loyalty to Strasbourg's constitution in front of the cathedral's great west door. In later times, the cathedral was to become a symbol of conflicting national prides.

The first prelate we hear of in connection with its construction was a Hapsburg, Prince-Bishop Wernher. In an ambitious rebuilding of the church—then already long fixed in the heart of the ancient Roman town of Argentoratum—from 1015 onward, Wernher set the dimensions of the cathedral we have today. The crypt beneath the chancel may or may not date from that period. The chancel, apse, crossing and transepts, reconstructed gradually after a fire of 1176, are in essence refinements of Wernher's scheme translated into the idiom of the earliest Rhenish Gothic, heavy in mass, modest in height by later standards and distinctly of the Empire.

The architectural shock waves sent out from the Île-de-France were first felt in the south transept, of the 1230s. At first they affected the sculpture more than the architecture. For the lithe, attenuated effigies of the arresting Last Judgement Pillar in the center of the transept and those of Church and Synagogue flanking the south portal (the originals of all of these are now in the Musée de l'Oeuvre Notre-Dame), we must predicate a sculptor-mason of consummate ability trained at Chartres, and probably a team of French-speaking masons working with him. With these figures, the ideal beauty of French religious art reached the Rhine. French also, by then in the full architectural sense, was the Strasbourg nave, rebuilt with dispatch in the 1260s and 1270s. If it is less admired than the naves of other great French Gothic churches of the period, that is because it lacks the height and the long chancel which it demands. The crossing and east end had been rebuilt only a century before, and therefore could hardly be reconstructed so soon—or, for that matter, extended, because of cloister buildings abutting behind. Nevertheless, in precision of structure and luminous elegance, the Strasbourg nave attained the highest level of Rayonnant refinement. The stained glass, too, is of exceptional completeness and loveliness.

Thus far, Strasbourg represented anonymous architecture on a high but by no means original level, procured and paid for by clerics. After the 1270s that changed, and Strasbourg for two centuries moved to the forefront of Gothic achievement. The means by which that was managed was the Frauenwerk or Oeuvre Notre-Dame, a highly efficient fund-raising and building organization controlled by the municipality. The Oeuvre's employees included a chief architect, after 1300 always German-speaking and usually of high international standing, and up to 150 building craftsmen and others. Strasbourg's special reputation is attested by the fact that in 1459 its mason's lodge was voted the foremost in the Holy Roman Empire and by its surviving archive, which includes the world's richest cache of Gothic architectural drawings.

The change of control and mood can be read in the cathedral's west front, one of the supreme achievements of Gothic architecture. It was built over more than a century and embodies several changes of plan. But the basic idea is clear. In front of a *facade harmonique* of classic French type, reflecting the proportions and window openings of the nave and aisles, the Strasbourg architects hung a "wall-veil," or fretted screen of stone, to mask and enrich the zone between the four great buttresses and the west wall proper. Made from the easily worked pink Vosges sandstone, it is a creation of great daring and delicacy. An elaborate sculptural program (mostly renewed after revolutionary vandalism in 1793) occupies focal points of the portals and buttresses. The main architectural function of the veil is to draw the eye upward by insistent finials and tracery panels. The

Strasbourg Cathedral: Strasbourg, France, 1015

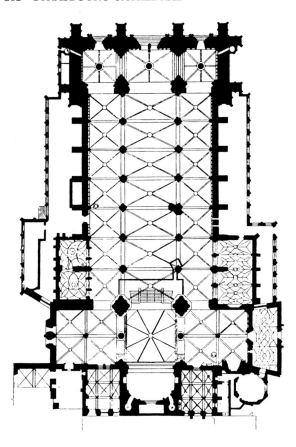

author of this exceptional design is uncertain. Since the 17th century, tradition has given the leading role in the cathedral's design to Erwin of Steinback (died 1318), certainly the master mason at the time the sumptuous rose window was built. But there are difficulties to the hypothesis that Erwin originated the wall-veil.

At first the idea was to complete the front in an orthodox manner, with equal north and south towers and steeples above the level of the rose window. Then in the 1360s it was decided to fill the gap between the towers with a massive belfry, thus creating a huge rectangular *Westwerk* in the German Romanesque tradition, perhaps to be capped with a single monolithic central steeple of the kind later built at Ulm or Freiburg-im-Breisgau. But Ulrich von Ensingen, appointed architect in 1399 and an expert on tall structures, reverted to the idea of north and south towers, starting then a whole stage higher. The north steeple, completed by Johann Hültz in 1439 to a revised version of Ulrich's design rises to 142 meters, a height not matched in Europe till the 1840s. The south tower and steeple were never to be built, though a hut on the high platform, probably there in one form or another since the 1480s, almost suggests they may yet be.

The rugged, pierced and bristling outline of the single Strasbourg spire, combined with the verticality of the west front, gives the exterior of Strasbourg an exuberance and a lush intricacy that foreshadow the independent path followed by central European Gothic. The front, together with the beautiful St. Catherine's Chapel off the south aisle where stained glass and fenestration unite to give the same sense of dramatic upward movement, was directly influential upon Cologne, Ulm and the Parlers' work in Prague. The point which this "Germanic" path reached before Reformation and Renaissance together

caused the collapse of the Gothic vision is represented at Strasbourg by Hans Hammer's ornate pulpit of 1480, erected for the humanist reformer Geiler von Kayserberg, and by the tracery of the St. Lawrence portal on the north side, (1494-1503) by Jakob von Landshut, where bough-like arches and crockets entwine, break free and are cut off in an "organic" manner prophetic of Louis Sullivan's ornament.

Although Strasbourg became Lutheran in the 1520s and the cathedral was adapted for Protestant worship, it is noteworthy that no major acts of vandalism took place then. Only when Louis XIV conquered the city for France in 1681 and restored Catholicism did the sculptured chancel screen disappear, in response to Counter-Reformation requirements. Much of the external sculpture was torn down by French atheists in 1793, but adequately replaced thereafter. Since then, the city has changed countries five times. For symbolic reasons, French and German regimes alike have cherished its fabric. It is appropriate that the most visible change to the cathedral's architecture, Gustave Klotz's scholarly central octagon of about 1860-78 (replacing a Gothic "bishop's bonnet" destroyed by fire in 1759), should have been begun under French rule and finished under the Germans. Klotz's octagon is now being fully restored, after impairment by American bombs in 1944.

Strasbourg has, however, played a lively and fascinating role in what may be called the history of Gothic propaganda. This was inaugurated by Goethe, who in a wrongheaded but memorable early essay written from a largely literary standpoint, *Von Deutscher Baukunst* (1772), hazarded that the whole structure was due to a single Germanic, medieval genius, the mastermason Erwin. The subtleties and allusive brilliance of Goethe's essay were obscured over the following hundred years. During that time romantic German nationalists elaborated a fictitious "Erwin legend," to justify their political claims to Strasbourg

Strasbourg Cathedral, nave south flank

Strasbourg Cathedral

and their cultural claims to priority or preeminence in Gothic architecture. Thereafter the ownership, history and meaning of the great church were bound up with political contention. The final such episode occurred in 1941 when General Leclerc's Free French swore at Koufra, an oasis in Libya, ''never to lay down arms until our colors, our beautiful colors, are flying on Strasbourg Cathedral.'' The Oath of Koufra having been redeemed in 1945, the cathedral is now among the foremost symbols of a united Europe.

—ANDREW SAINT

VAUX-LE-VICOMTE CHÂTEAU
Mélun, France

1657-61. Architect: Louis Le Vau (1612-70).

Publications

ADAMS, WILLIAM HOWARD: *The French Garden 1500-1800.* New York, 1979.

CORDEY, J.: ''Le grand salon ovale de Vaux-le-Vicomte et sa décoration.'' *Revue de l'Art Français* 46 (1924): 233.

PFNOR, RODOLPHE: *Le Chateau de Vaux-le-Vicomte.*

*

A visit to Vaux-le-Vicomte is a strange experience, an authentic trip into the past. It is rare to be able to absorb the atmosphere of a setting where dimensions, proportions and decor are in harmony, surrounded by gardens which after a period of abandon in the 19th century have assumed the form and aspect they had in the 17th.

Vaux-le-Vicomte has its place in history and in legend. It is associated with the splendors of Louis XIV's court, and with the implied moral that ambition has its pitfalls. Nicholas Fouquet (1615-80) purchased the *demesne* in 1641 when he was only 26. Intelligent and ambitious, some would say subject to the ''*folie des grandeurs,*'' he gained royal favor and in 1653 was appointed by the influential statesman Jules Mazarin as Louis XIV's *surintendant des finances.* Fouquet was a successful state minister in righting the nation's finances, and like all good entrepreneurs he was able to ensure his own share in the national company's wealth. His success, however, provoked jealousies, and in 1661 he fell into disgrace, was tried and found guilty of misappropriation of funds and condemned to imprisonment in Pignerol in the Alps, where he died in 1680. It has often been said that the reason for his downfall was a reception he held for Louis XIV at Vaux-le-Vicomte in August 1661: the king is reported to have been incensed with jealousy at the way in which one of his subjects could receive him, and to have decided that he would surpass all of them by developing his own château at Versailles. Although this interpretation of history may be apocryphal, it is certain that Vaux-le-Vicomte did foreshadow Versailles, and that Fouquet's fall from favor was due above all to the machinations of the king's envious chief minister, Jean Baptiste Colbert.

The construction of the château was relatively rapid, and brought together the minds and skills of three of the most outstanding creative spirits to have marked the architecture of 17th-century France: Louis Le Vau was responsible for the buildings, Charles Le Brun for the decoration and André Le Nôtre for the gardens; in fact, Vaux-le-Vicomte was Le Nôtre's first major undertaking. Begun in 1656, the château was inhabitable in 1659—just three years in which to create a masterpiece of symmetry, harmony and taste.

Le Vau did not know Italy firsthand, but like so many others he was under its influence either through what he had heard or what he had seen. The edifice and gardens bear lasting testimony to the French genius which succeeded in importing neoclassical forms and ideas from south of the Alps and giving them a certain ''*je ne sais quoi*'' which is distinctive and embellishing. The heaviness of the Italian building has been replaced with a lightness and a sense of life.

Central to the design is the use of space and of water. The forest was cut away to provide a progression from the profusion of nature in the world, via the symmetry of nature under the control of man, to man triumphant in stone and artistry. The earlier intention of building the house in brick was abandoned in favor of stone, although brick was maintained for the outer buildings. The result is that there is a transition from the ''rustic,'' albeit dignified, dependencies to the majestic stone of the central edifice. The moat of the medieval castle was retained to become a source of ornamentation, its waters reflecting the pilastered main building.

The facade, with its mixture of straight and curve bays, rises up from the bailey, and the pilasters and columns of the entrance

Château Vaux-le-Vicomte: Mélun, France, 1657-61

Château Vaux-le-Vicomte

Château Vaux-le-Vicomte, oval salon

take one's eyes up to the pediment and thence to the high, steep roof so typical of the French château. Vaux-le-Vicomte is not large if compared with Versailles, but it is imposing. Through the square entrance hall one enters the great oval salon, which although never finished has a grandeur of its own—16 bays flanked by 16 pilasters lead up to a cornice topped by square windows and impressive caryatids representing the 12 signs of

the Zodiac and the four seasons, and then a second cornice which borders the cupola.

Normally in 17th-century buildings the main reception rooms were on the first floor, necessitating an ornate and impressive staircase; Le Vau placed them on the ground floor at Vaux-le-Vicomte, which explains the "discreet" first staircases within and the elaborate steps without.

There is much to attract the lover of 17th- and 18-century decoration, and the various guest bedrooms show the reflections of changing taste. Fouquet's hasty departure meant that decoration of much of the upper story was not completed. Notable, however, is the ceiling of the Grande Chambre Carrée, the only one to show Louis XIII beams decorated with gold leaf, which mirrors the gold of the cornice and the classical frieze. Gold leaf is a characteristic of much of the interior decoration, whether it be in the Salon d'Hercule, with its Italian-style ceiling; the Salon of the Muses, in which Le Brun excelled himself; or in the grandiloquent Chambre du Roi, which set the algorithms of the Louis XIV style for Versailles, and hence for the whole of Europe. Around a painted ceiling of Time and Truth by Le Brun descend ornate stuccowork of *putti,* figures and goldwork. All the rooms on the ground floor overlooking the park reveal the innovation of linking doors so that from the Cabinet des Jeux to the Anciens Cabinets due Roi there is the possibility of an uninterrupted view of magnificence through the seven "state rooms."

A walk through the gardens makes one aware of Le Nôtre's genius—his attempt to rationalize nature, to introduce in the form of a grotto an artificial view of the world. The art of the topiary is present all around, and statuary allows the intellectual to combine the pleasure of watching with intellectual pursuits, for the garden was to represent an introduction to the divine and to wisdom. The symmetrical designs divide up space and lead the eye to the natural disposition of the forest—the view from the house is now reached by a gigantic statue of the Farnese Hercules which overlooks the cascades, the waterways, the canal, the rolling lawns.

Since the 17th century through the Fouquet, the Villars, the Choiseul-Praslin, the Sommier and more recently the de Vogüé, Vaux-le-Vicomte has resisted, somewhat anachronistically, the great worldly pressures which have brought destruction and ruin to many similar buildings. It may be symbolic that this

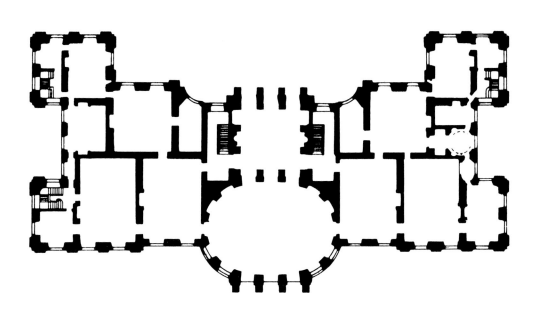

Château de Versailles, west facade: Versailles, France, 17th century

should be the case for a château that was to be the prototype for ''royal living'' not only in France but throughout the whole world.

—K. C. CAMERON

VERSAILLES: PALACE
Versailles, France

17th century. 1661-87: Gardens; **Architect:** André Le Nôtre (1613-1700). **1668:** Construction begun on Grand Appartement and Appartement de la Reine. **1670:** Trianon de Porcelaine; **Architect:** Louis Le Vau (1612-70). **1678-89:** Two great wings added and Hall of Mirrors; **Architect:** Jules Hardouin-Mansart (1646-1708). **1684:** Grande Galerie completed; **Architect:** Charles Le Brun (1619-90). **1687:** Trianon de Porcelaine razed and Trianon de Marbre constructed in its place; **Architects:** Jules Hardouin-Mansart and Robert de Cotte. **1710:** Chapel; **Architects:** Jules Hardouin-Mansart and Robert de Cotte. **1727ff:** Petite Cabinets du Roi; **Architect:** Ange-Jacques Gabriel. **1748ff:** Opera House; **Architect:** Ange-Jacques Gabriel. **1755:** Cabinet du Conseil. **1774:** Library.

Publications

BERGER, ROBERT: *Versailles, The Chateau of Louis XIV.* 1984.

BLUNT, ANTHONY: *Art and Architecture in France: 1500-1700.* 2nd ed. Harmondsworth, England, 1973.

BRIÈRE, G.: *Le château de Versailles.* 2 vols. Paris, ca. 1910.

Charles Le Brun 1619-1690. Catalogue of the exhibtion held at Versailles (1963).

FÉLIBIEN, ANDRÉ, SIEUR DES AVAUX ET DE JAVERCY: *Description du Château de Versailles, de ses Peintures et d'Autres Ouvrages, Fait pour le roy.* Paris, 1696.

GANAY, E. DE: *Châteaux de France.* Paris, 1949.

GANAY, E. DE: *Châteaux et manoirs de France.* 11 vols. Paris, 1934-38.

GÉBELIN, F.: *Les châteaux de la Renaissance.* Paris, 1927.

HAUTECOEUR, LOUIS: Pp. 527-688 in *Le règne de Louis XIV.* Vol. 2 in *Histoire de l'architecture classique en France.* Paris, 1948.

JESTAZ, B.: ''Le Trianon de Marbre ou Louis XIV architecte.'' *Gazette des Beaux-Arts* 11, 259 (1969).

KIMBALL, F.: ''Mansart and Lebrun in the Genesis of the Grande Galerie de Versailles.'' *Art Bulletin* 22 (1940).

KIMBALL, F.: ''The Genesis of the Château Neuf at Versailles, 1668-71.'' *Art Bulletin* 31 (1949): 355.

MARIE, ALFRED: ''Trianon de Porcelaine et Grand Trianon.'' *Bulletin de la Société de l'Histoire de l'Art Français* 88 (1945-46).

MARIE, ALFRED: *Versailles au temps de Louis XIV. Mansart et de Cotte.* Paris, 1976.

MARIE, ALFRED and JEANNE: *Mansart à Versailles.* 2 vols. Paris, 1972.

Château de Versailles

NOLHAC, P. DE: *Versailles et la Cour de France.* 10 portfolios. Paris, 1925-30.

NOLHAC, P. DE: *Versailles.* Paris, 1901.

NOLHAC, P. DE: *Histoire du château de Versailles: Versailles au XVIIIe siècle.* Paris, 1918.

PÜHRINGEN-ZWANOWITZ, LEONORE: "Ein Entwurf Bernins für Versailles." *Wiener Jahrbuch für Kunstgeschichte,* 29 (1976): 101.

RACINAIS, HENRY: *Un Versailles inconnu: Les petits appartements des rois Louis XV et Louis XVI au château de Versailles.* Paris, 1950.

VERLET, P.: *Versailles.* Paris, 1961.

WALTON, GUY: *Louis XIV's Versailles.* 1986.

*

"When you arrive at Versailles," wrote Voltaire, "from the courtyard side you see a wretched, top-heavy building, with a facade seven windows long, surrounded with everything which the imagination could conceive in the way of bad taste. When you see it from the garden side, you see an immense palace whose defects are more than compensated by its beauties." Thus Voltaire identified the essential duality of Versailles. No one seeing for the first time a picture of the entrance courts alongside one of the garden front could ever infer that they were two views of the same building.

Voltaire's "immense palace" was a work of art not achieved at a single sitting. As it stands today it represents a revision by Jules Hardouin-Mansart of an earlier building by Louis Le Vau, who had twice enlarged and reshaped a small hunting lodge built by Louis XIII.

More than any other royal house of France, Versailles was the expression of a theory of monarch of which Louis XIV himself was the truest impersonation. In March 1661, Cardinal Mazarin died. It was the moment of Louis' true coming of age. "Only then," he wrote in his memoirs, "did it seem to me that I was king: born to be king." It was his good fortune to be served on all sides by men of the first quality, which made his reign truly the Grand Siècle. Versailles was the architectural expression of the Grand Siècle.

The first work of Le Vau was to make the little hunting lodge into a *maison de plaisance* of brick and stone, to which Louis could invite a few favored guests for a few delectable days of brilliant entertainment. The second phase was the enclosing of this *maison de plaisance* on three sides by a great stone palace known as the "Enveloppe," providing behind its classical facades two magnificent suites of state rooms: the Grand Appartement to the north and the Appartement de la Reine to the south. This was put into execution in 1668.

Ten years later the Peace of Nijmegen marked the zenith of Louis' military success. It was no longer tolerable that he should not have a palace proportioned to his greatness. Jules Hardouin-Mansart was commissioned to make Versailles a building that would lodge both the court and government in appropriate splendor. Two great wings, thrown out to north and south, left the stately block of the "Enveloppe" a mere projection on the garden front. The finished building had 2,143 windows, 1,252 fireplaces and 67 staircases; the length of the garden front was 670 meters.

The layout of the gardens was as important to Louis as the design of the palace. André Le Nôtre gave a new symmetry and a new shape to the land itself making use of the natural declivity of the site to form a series of terraces; hollowing out a vast amphitheater for the Parterre de Latone; clothing the slopes with woods and hedges within which were contrived an astonishing variety of "bosquets." The whole layout was an attempt to impose upon the landscape a form conceived by the human intellect—a form in which every part was related to the whole in a manner that could be easily grasped and readily understood.

It is significant that the names of the bosquets were largely drawn from the vocabulary of the interior of a house—names such as the *Galerie* des Antiques, the *Salle* des Festins, the *Cabinet* or even the *Appartement* de Verdure. The gardens were in fact conceived as an outdoor extension to the palace and often used as such. As if to heighten the impression of being outdoor rooms, the statues were set against a united wall of foliage in the form of a *charmille* or hornbeam hedge. In 1685 an order of nearly 3 million hornbeam plants was sent to Versailles from the nearby Fôret de Lyons.

There were some 1,400 fountains comprised within the layout. For their "ordinary" display they required 12,960 cubic meters of water for every 12 hours. For the full glory of the *grands eaux* the fountains consumed 9,458 cubic meters every two and a half hours. A vast network of canals, siphons and reservoirs, including a gigantic pump at Marly which raised the waters of the Seine, was established to fulfil this need. "Le Sieur Denis," it was reported in the *Mercure Galant,* "conducts them by means of the most admirable pumps and aqueducts, and Monsieur (Francois) de Francine makes them do things which are beyond our imagining."

The palace and its gardens together were to be the visible symbol of Louis' own conception of the role and status of the French monarchy. He chose the sun as his emblem, and this was to provide the iconography for the layout—"this vast poem of mythology," wrote Mauricheau-Beaupré, "in honor of Apollo, which dominates the whole conception of the gardens."

The gardens were the greatest achievement of André Le Nôtre, but the greatest name in the creation of Versailles was that of Charles Le Brun, for it was he who integrated the work of all the painters and sculptors into one harmonious whole.

Le Vau's facades consisted of a rusticated ground floor with round-arched windows, a first floor proportioned to an Ionic order, and an attic story surmounted by a balustrade crowned with urns and trophies. The windows of the first floor came right down to the base of the pilasters and were surmounted each by a bas-relief.

When Mansart made his alterations, he gave these facades a "facelift." Each first-floor window was raised by the superimposition of a round arch in place of the bas-relief, and the apparent base of the window raised by screening its lower part behind a balustrade.

The interior decoration was in a style that had been developed at Vaux-le-Vicomte by Le Vau and Le Brun, but its appearance in France was probably the Appartement d'Eté in the Louvre begun in 1655 by Le Vau and Giovanni Francesco Romanelli. It is essentially a combination of stucco and gilding and painting. The triumvirate of Le Brun, Le Vau and Le Nôtre who created Vaux-le-Vicomte was also to create Versailles.

Above all, Versailles should be seen as an example of artistic collaboration. An immense team of artists, trained at Jean-Baptiste Colbert's new Académies and orchestrated by Le Brun, produced an ensemble in which it is often difficult to tell the hand of one artist from the hand of another.

The most famous of the interiors, the Grande Galerie or Galerie des Glaces, was completed in November 1684. "This sort of royal beauty," exclaimed Mme. de Sévigné, "is unique in the world." In place of any classical order, Le Brun created

Château de Versailles, Galerie des Glaces

an *ordre français* incorporating the sun, the fleurs de lis and two cocks.

There were important architectural appendages to Versailles—the Ménagerie (now destroyed), at the south extremity of the Canal, and Trianon answering it to the north. Trianon was conceived as a place where Louis could retreat from the formalities of the court. The first building there, designed by Le Vau in 1670, was known as the Trianon de Porcelaine on account of its exterior decoration in Delft tiles. Closely connected with Louis' mistress Mme. de Montespan, it was pulled down in 1787 and replaced by the present building, known as the Trianon de Marbre. In the designing of this, Mansart was assisted by his son-in-law Robert de Cotte. They were jointly responsible also for creation of the last important part of Versailles, the Chapel, finished in 1710.

The court at Versailles had had to be content with a rather makeshift chapel until that date. An early design by Mansart, which fairly closely resembles that at Les Invalides, was replaced in about 1687 with one which made a very different approach in which the medieval and French tradition were represented, although translated into a classical idiom. "The clear, white light of the Age of Reason," wrote Guy Walton, "replaces the more mysterious ambiance created by the rich reds and blues of Gothic stained glass."

The chapel of Charlemagne at Aix and the Sainte-Chapelle in the Palais de la Cité, built by Saint Louis, were the obvious models—and both Charlemagne and Saint Louis are represented in the painted ceiling. The medieval formula of arcade, tribunes and clerestory was reintroduced, but with the accent on the tribunes, which were level with the Grand Appartement. The royal tribune at the west end placed the king in the same relationship to the congregation as at the coronation in Reims Cathedral. The 12 piers of the nave support the 12 columns of the tribunes, which curl into a graceful ambulatory around the altar.

The chapel is built of a beautiful white stone, known as *banc royal*, decorated with low relief carvings that give a brocade-like texture to the stone. Gilding is concentrated on the altar, from which it leads the eye upward, by way of the organ case, to the Baroque splendors of the painted ceiling.

The work of Antoine Coypel, this is one of the finest examples of Baroque illusionist painting extant in France. The artist seems to have been inspired by Baciccio's ceiling for Il Gesù church in Rome, which depends, according to Anthony Blunt, "on the most melodramatic forms of *trompe l'oeil*." The heavens seems to have opened, and Father, Son and Holy Ghost are revealed to the world.

The chapel was Louis XIV's last important work at Versailles. At his death in 1715 the "grand design" was almost completed. All that he left to his successor was the realization of the opera house at the extremity of the Aisle du Nord.

The Versailles of Louis XIV was the architectural expression of his own conception of monarchy. It was the vast theater of a continuous pageant of royalty. When in the mid-18th century François Blondel pronounced his verdict on Versailles, he made a criticism that would not have been made in the 17th century: he complained of the lack of "essential commodities." He was also severe in his strictures on the style, calling the Cour de Marbre "semi-Gothic" and asserting how contrary to propriety it was "to place a visible roof over the residence of a crowned head." Versailles was condemned as uncomfortable and out of date.

It is probable that Louis XV, had he been able to afford it, would have remedied both these defects. His first work, however, was a continuation of the grand style. The Salon d'Hercule, the link between the vestibule to the chapel and the Grand Appartement, not only continued the style of Louis XIV but, in the eyes of some, surpassed it. It was the design of Robert de Cotte, but it depended largely for its effect on the ceiling painted by Antoine le Moyne between 1733 and 1736. Voltaire said of it: "There is hardly in Europe a painting more vast than the ceiling of le Moyne and I do not know of any more beautiful."

In the person of Louis XIV the natures of private individual and of king were hardly to be distinguished, so completely was the man identified with his role. With Louis XV the distinction was so marked as to amount almost to dual personality. "To separate Louis de Bourbon from the King of France," wrote Mme. Campan, "was what this monarch found most piquant in his royal existence."

The emphasis on his life as a private individual was soon reflected in the alterations he made to Versailles. He began at the top. High up under the roof he started, as early as 1727, to construct a network of little *cabinets*, decorated with delicately carved panels, painted in soft colors and finished with *vernis Martin*, which gave them the gloss and freshness of porcelain.

These rooms were known as the "Petits Cabinets du Roi" to distinguish them from the Petits Appartements that were at first-floor level on the north side of the Cour de Marbre. The first of these is a private bedroom in which the king slept after having observed the ceremony of the *coucher* in Louis XIV's bedroom; next comes the Cabinet de la Pendule, so named after the famous clock made by Dauthiau after the design of Passement; last is the Cabinet Intérieur du Roi, which was Louis XV's study and contains his desk started by Oeben and completed by Riesner. These rooms offer a perfect example of the style to which Louis XV gave his name.

It was largely the creation of Ange-Jacques Gabriel, who became Premier Architecte in 1742, and the wood carvers Jacques Verberckt and Antoine Rousseau, who between them covered acres of wall space with their exquisite paneling.

It was a style adaptable both to the intimate and to the grand. Of the grand there are two fine examples: the Chambre de la Reine and the Cabinet du Conseil. The former was redecorated by order of Louis XV in 1729, the year of the birth of the dauphin. This was begun by Robert de Cotte, who thus had a share in the creation of the new style, and finished by Gabriel. The use of tall, narrow panels in place of pilasters is one of the successes of the style.

The Cabinet du Conseil was not only decorated but created in 1755. Louis XIV had a Salle du Conseil on the ground floor and used the Salon de l'Oeil de Boeuf when that proved too small. This was really the central piece of the king's apartment. The decorations by Rousseau form a significant contrast with those of Le Brun in the Grande Galérie. In place of the deified warriors and airborne civil servants of the latter are cockleshells and anchors, shields, military and peacetime functions of the council. In the medallions Rousseau depicts boys—the chubby cherubs of a François Boucher painting—playing with scales, dogs, and mirrors, which represent Justice, Loyalty and Sincerity, the qualities demanded of a minister.

But by far the most important work at Versailles during the reign of Louis XV was the completion of the Opera House at the extremity of the north wing.

As early as 1748 Gabriel had brought out his preliminary designs, comprising the elegant new facade, whose simple rectilinear proportions and stately attached portico were reflected in the reservoirs. The custom had been, when any large-scale entertainment such as a royal marriage was given, to rig up a ballroom for temporary use in the *manège* of the Grande Ecurie. But in 1767 the marriages of the dauphin's four children were looming on the horizon, and the prospect of them was disquieting the royal exchequer. To improvise four temporary but costly decorations and to have nothing to show for it at the end would have been extremely wasteful. It was decided to proceed with the "theater of the Reservoirs."

It was not, however, an extravagantly conceived design. In the interests of acoustics most of the structure of the auditorium was of wood painted to resemble marble. This marbling was achieved in a warm salmon pink against a background of dull gray-green known as *vert-de-mer*, both of an infinitely subtle variety of tones and enriched with gilding. Contrasting with this is the cold, bright cobalt of the silk hangings and the more somber blue of the patterned velvet upholstery.

The auditorium, in the shape of a truncated ellipse, is encircled by a colonnade, which breaks into a graceful apse over the royal box. Each bay of the colonnade is backed by a mirror, and each mirror reflects and thus completes a half chandelier that hangs against its surface. A total of 3,000 candles was required for the lighting of the whole theater. The duc de Croÿ noted how beautifully they illuminated the huge ceiling painted by Du Rameau.

The theater was also a potential *salle de bal*. A floor could be laid down over the pit, thus joining the auditorium with the stage, the scene set to reflect the amphitheater, and the whole opera house turned into one enormous ballroom or banqueting hall. It was first used for the festivities following the wedding of Marie-Antoinette and the dauphin.

In June 1774, within a month of his accession, Louis XVI gave orders for the construction of a library in what had been the bedroom of Mme. Adelaîde, next to her charming Salon de Musique. These rooms formed a continuation of the Petits Appartements du Roi. The new library was designed by Gabriel and executed by Antoine Rousseau. It was the last work either of them was to do at Versailles. It bears impressive testimony to their versatility that two of the greatest exponents of the style

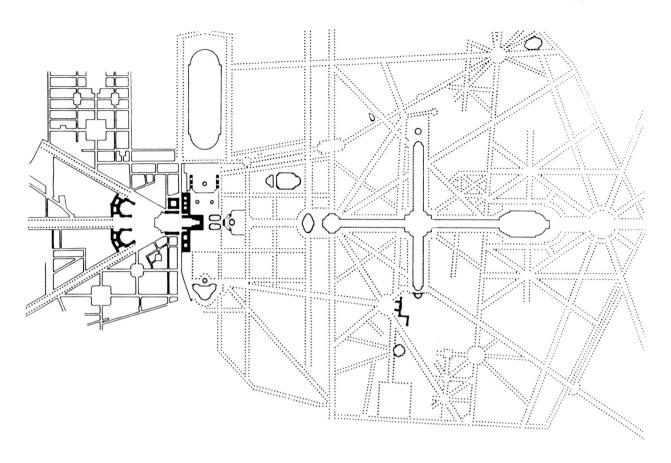

of Louis XV should have created the first and finest example of the style of Louis XVI.

Louis was a great reader, and it was the beautiful bindings of the books themselves which formed the chief decoration of the room. The lines are simple and rectilinear, in keeping with the tall glazed bookcases; the ornament is restrained and subtle. The rounded corners of the room are relieved with gilded drops representing the wide diversity of subject matter of the books—a globe, a telescope, a Roman sword, a shepherd's hat, the masks of Comedy and Tragedy all joined together by a network of flowers and ribbons. Of all the rooms at Versailles this has the most "lived-in" look.

The last important changes to Versailles before the Revolution were in the Cabinets de la Reine, situated behind the state bedroom. They had been created for Marie-Leczinska and were completely remodeled for Marie-Antoinette from the designs of her own architect, Richard Mique. The decorations were executed by the two sons of Antoine Rousseau, Jean-Antoine, the sculptor, and Jean-Siméon, the painter.

The most important of these rooms is the Méridienne, where the queen had her midday rest. It is provided with an alcove and daybed. The delicate patterns carved on the panels have all the precision of the bronze appliqués on the glasses and mirrors; they incorporate peacocks and flowers, hearts pierced with arrows and dolphins—the latter, of course, referring to the fact that since 22 October 1781 France had an heir to the throne.

Two years later the largest of these rooms, the Cabinet Intérieur, was redecorated and became known as the Cabinet Dore. The decor is in a style which would pass for Empire if its date were not fully attested in the accounts. Marie-Antoinette

was still busy redecorating her apartments when the Revolution came.

—IAN DUNLOP

VERSAILLES: GRAND TRIANON
Versailles, France

1687-88: Construction; **Architect:** Robert de Cotte.

Publications

DANIS, R.: *La Première Maison Royale de Trianon*, 1927.
DE NOLHAC, P.: *Trianon*, 1927.
DUNLOP, I.: *Royal Palaces of France*, 1985.
JESTAZ, B.: "Le Trianon de Marbre ou Louis XIV architecte." *Gazette des Beaux-Arts* 11, 259 (1969).
MARIE, ALFRED: "Trianon de Porcelaine et Grand Trianon." *Bulletin de la Société de l'Histoire de l'Art Français* 88 (1945-46).
SCHNAPPER, A.: *Peintures commandées par Louis XIV pour le Grand Trianon*. The Hague, 1967.

Grand Trianon (artist's rendering): Versailles, France, 1687-88

Grand Trianon

Trianon was first conceived as a garden, and a garden in which Louis XIV could walk in *parterre des fleurs* even in winter. "Visit Trianon often," wrote Jean-Baptiste Colbert to his agent Petit. "See that Le Bouteux (the head gardener) has flowers for the King for the whole winter and that he has enough workers." In order to maintain these constant transformation scenes, Le Bouteux had nearly two million flower pots.

It was not a place endowed by nature. There are frequent mentions in the accounts of transporting "good earth" to provide the gardens with topsoil, and an immense quantity of manure was also supplied.

The architectural focus of this garden was little more than a pavilion with a Doric order and with a high and highly decorated roof which seemed to be tiled in blue and white porcelain, from which the pavilion derived its name—the "Trianon de Porcelaine."

The construction of this pavilion between the spring and autumn of 1670 was when Madame de Montespan was at the peak of her favor. Ten years later she was replaced in the king's affection by Madame de Maintenon. However, it was not until July 1687 that Louis decided to demolish the Trianon de Porcelaine and to replace it with something much larger. Perhaps no structure at Versailles illustrates more clearly Louis' method of building. It was the way of an amateur, a succession of trials and errors, of building, pulling down and rebuilding, which may have produced in the end the desired effect, but was certainly the most expensive procedure possible.

The original intention had been to retain the main block of the Trianon de Porcelaine as the center of the new facades, which were given mansard roofs to match. In September 1687, Louis decided to pull it all down. The center of the facade was

to be taken up by an open peristyle and the roofs abolished. "His Majesty," wrote the marquis de Louvois to François Mansart, "did not wish the continuation of work on the roofs, which he found too heavy and to give Trianon the appearance of a big house." The roofs were to be flat and concealed behind a balustrade. The chimneys were to rise only 12 inches above the roof, "His Majesty preferring the risk that they might smoke to their being visible from outside." Mansart was unwell at the time and taking the waters at Vichy, so Robert de Cotte, his son-in-law and future successor, took over the design.

The ground plan is a most unusual one, and can only be explained by its relationship to the gardens of the first Trianon. The controlling factor was a garden room called the Cabinet des Parfums. This was situated at the northwest corner of the parterre which formed a square west of the château. Running from the Cabinet des Parfums for the whole length of the parterre was a trellis pergola. In the finished design for Trianon the pergola was replaced by the Galérie and the Cabinet des Parfums by the Salon des Jardins at its extremity.

The forecourt, with the king's apartment to the north and that of the dauphin to the south, occupied the former site of the Trianon de Porcelaine. More lodgings were needed, so a further block was appended at right angles to the Galérie, which was known from its sylvan setting as "Trianon-sous-Bois." One could easily believe Trianon-sous-Bois, with its two stories, its smaller windows and its beautifully carved masks and consoles, to be a later addition, but it was not. Trianon was conceived and built as a whole.

By the end of 1788 the new building was finished and furnished. Perhaps the fairest description of it came from the duc de Croÿ: "It is the most charming piece of architecture in the world,'' he stated, but he added this qualification: "The view from the entrance to the court is admirable, but the rest does not answer to it.'' There is a certain monotony about the facades seen from the parterre, but the historical imagination must make one alteration which would mitigate the severity of the skyline. One must replace upon the balustrade that regiment of urns and statues which provided animation to the silhouette.

The decoration of marble pilasters and marble plaques between the windows, carried out in the red marble of Languedoc, gave to the building the name of "Trianon de Marbre,'' by which it was usually known.

Indoors, Trianon contains a suite of interiors which still afford, in their carved friezes, paneling and overdoors, an important souvenir of the Grand Siècle, although most of the decor was modified by Napoléon and Louis-Philippe, both of whom made much use of Trianon. The furniture, especially, is almost entirely Empire. Only in the pictures does the decor of the Grand Siècle survive, and this is particularly true of the Galérie. A set of 24 views of the bosquets of Versailles, mostly by Jean Cotelle (1642-1708), is still in place. They should be compared with the comte de Saint-Simon's description of Versailles as it was—"the most sad and barren of places, with no view, no water and no woods.'' Cotelle's paintings show the incredible transformation brought about by Louis XIV. But the last and loveliest of the views comes not from a painting, but from the windows of the Salon des Jardins on the site of the former Cabinet des Parfums—over the parterre and across the Canal to the site of the Ménagerie.

Invitation to Trianon was one of the most coveted privileges which could be conferred upon a courtier. Saint-Simon revealed how the niceties of etiquette were used to his own discomfiture. When a lady was invited to Marly, her husband accompanied her without need of personal application, but this was not the case with an invitation to Trianon. By consistently inviting the duchesse de Saint-Simon to Trianon and by equally consistently refusing her applications for Marly, Louis was able to convey in no uncertain terms his displeasure with the duke.

—IAN DUNLOP

VERSAILLES: PETIT TRIANON
Versailles, France

1764ff. Architect: Ange-Jacques Gabriel. **1774ff:** Gardens added. **1778:** Theater designed; **Architect:** Richard Mique. **1787:** Boudoir added.

Publications

ARNOTT, JAMES A. and WILSON, JOHN: *The Petit Trianon Versailles*. New York, 1929.
DE NOLHAC, P.: *Trianon*, 1927.
DESJARDINS, GUSTAVE: *Le Petit Trianon*. Versailles, 1885.
DUNLOP, I.: *Royal Palaces of France*, 1985.
GROMORT, GEORGES: *Le Hameau de Trianon*. Paris, 1928.
RACINAIS, HENRY: *Un Versailles inconnu: Les petits appartements des rois Louis XV et Louis XVI au château de Versailles*. Paris, 1950.
REY, LÉON: *Le Petit Trianon et le Hameau de Marie-Antoinette*. Paris, 1936.

In 1749 the duc de Croÿ observed that Louis XV and Madame de Pompadour were collecting pigeons and poultry. The fowl were to be housed to the northeast of the Jardin du Roi at Trianon. By November the duke could report that the "New Menagerie'' was almost finished. It was little more than a farmyard the architectural focus of which was a pavilion, designed by Ange-Jacques Gabriel, in the shape of an Irish cross; it became known as the Pavillon Français.

"The King was very fond of plans and buildings,'' wrote Croÿ. "He took me into his pretty pavilion in the gardens of Trianon and observed that that was the style in which I ought to build . . . he worked on his drawing for a long time with M. Gabriel.''

A passing fancy for poultry was succeeded by a more serious interest in botany, which necessitated a considerable extension of the gardens toward the east. It was not long before the idea occurred to Madame de Pompadour of building there something more habitable than the Pavillon Français. The building was to become known as the Petit Trianon.

The earliest designs are dated 1761 and show a building smaller than the one which we see today. The main facades were of only three windows, with an attached portico and coupled columns framing the central window or door. It was not built. The Seven Years' War still had two years to run, but on 10 February 1763 the Treaty of Paris put an end to the war. A fortnight later the duc de Praslin, minister of foreign affairs, was ordered to pay from his budget for most of the cost of the new house and chapel. By July of the following year 120 masons and 75 stonecarvers were at work on the site.

The important carvings were done by Honoré Guibert (ca. 1720-91). He worked mostly in the "Greek'' style, and his partnership with Gabriel was probably fruitful for both of them. Together they produced a building which, by the simplicity of its conception, the purity of its line and the delicacy of its ornament is the first and finest example of the Classical Revival in France, a style usually labeled "Louis XVI.'' The treatment was entirely new, and it is difficult to believe that the Petit Trianon was planned by the same architect who had designed the Pavillon Français.

Simplicity is the keynote of the Petit Trianon, but simplicity is nearly always deceptive. It cannot be achieved without a perfect command of technique. In designing his facades, Gabriel appreciated nicely the variety of texture possible in the fine honey-colored stone. A rusticated lower story, fluted pilasters and a delicately chiseled entablature set off the contrasting smoothness of the undecorated wall surfaces. A subtle use has been made of a drop in the ground level to obtain two facades of two stories and two of three stories. The north and west fronts have their basements masked by a perron, whereby the reception rooms can be approached directly from the gardens. The more imposing height of the entrance front is balanced by the low buildings of the forecourt. The original orientation being toward the Pavillon Français, the west front was accorded the richest treatment. The east front, which used to overlook the botanical gardens, is the plainest.

The interior reflects in its decoration the original purpose of the building, and is derived from the vegetable kingdom. The beautiful lilies in their circular wreaths which adorn the panels of the Salon de Musique, the swagged drops over the mirrors and bunches of roses in the Cabinet du Roi are carved with an accuracy and precision which had to pass the scrutiny of a botanist king. In the festoons of fruit which appropriately ornament the panels and fireplace of the dining room. The strawberry is given a prominent place. The cultivation of this fruit was of particular interest to Louis.

A contemporary plan of the top floor shows 18 bedrooms,

Petit Trianon: Versailles, France, 1764ff.

half of which were little more than cupboards for servants to sleep in. Servants were obviously a necessity, but they were to be excluded from the dining room. Louis had already installed at Choisy-le-Roi a *table volante* which descended through the dining room floor to the kitchens to be reloaded with the next course. Such a table was designed for Trianon by the sieur Loriot and exhibited in the Louvre in May 1766. The baronne d'Oberkirch described the *table volante* at Choisy in June 1782. It had not been used since the new reign and was all rusty.

One of the first acts of Louis XVI on succeeding to the throne was to offer the Petit Trianon to Marie-Antoinette. Her mother wrote enthusiastically: "The generosity of the King over Trianon, which I am told is the most adorable of houses, gives me great pleasure." But her second thoughts were more penetrating: "May this charming first gift of the King not be the occasion of incurring too great an expense, let alone of dissipations."

There was little scope in the actual building for expensive additions, for it was already perfect. The little boudoir behind the queen's bedroom, made in 1787, is the only alteration which she made. It was in the gardens that she was to realize her mother's worst fears.

On 2 July 1774, the Austrian ambassador Mercy reported to the empress that her daughter was wholly occupied with a *jardin à l'anglaise*. A visit to the comte de Caraman, whose garden in Paris was considered one of the most successful in the new fashion, provided Marie-Antoinette with the adviser for which she was looking; Caraman was duly appointed "*Directeur des Jardins de la Reine*."

Two years later the duc de Croÿ, visiting Trianon for the first time since Louis XV's reign, wrote: "I thought I must be mad or dreaming. Never have two hectares of land so completely changed their form nor cost so much money."

The ground to the northeast had been cast into a miniature range of hills, and a lake had been dug, fed by a cascade which gushed from the mouth of a mysterious grotto. Next to the grotto stood the Belvedere designed by the architect Richard Mique, who, in January 1775, had succeeded Gabriel as *controleur general des batiments de la Reine*.

East of the lake, through green meadows and loosely planted groves, wandered a river, at once forming a little backwater toward the château, then dividing its stream to leave an island planted with lilac and laburnam from which rose the 12 stately columns of Mique's Temple de l'Amour, carrying their stone cupola over Edmé Bouchardon's statue *Cupid Making a Bow from Hercules' Club*. There was a rich variety of trees, many of them recently acclimatized at Trianon. Only the trickle of water and the song of the nightingales could be heard. "One could fancy oneself," wrote Prince de Ligne, "three hundred miles from Court." The truth of that statement is the measure of Marie-Antoinette's success.

In 1778 Mique was invited to design a special theater for Trianon. The queen's instructions were that the stage should correspond exactly with those of Fontainebleau and Choisy-le-Roi, so that scenery made for one could be used at the others. Mique produced a design that is almost a miniature of the Opéra at Versailles.

Between 1783 and 1785 the gardens were extended northward by the laying out, after designs by Mique, of the Hameau. Around the borders of a small lake were disposed a dozen rustic houses such as might have formed a tiny village—or the background of a painting by Jean-Baptiste Greuze: a farm with a monumental gateway, several thatched cottages and a mill

Park: Versailles, France, 1630s

worked by a rivulet fed from the lake. The whole scene was an idealized *tableau vivant* of rural life. Cows grazed upon the meadows, chickens strutted in the farmyard; women brought their washing to the *lavanderie* and gathered the fruit in autumn; peasants cultivated the land and dug their gardens, the miller ground his corn, and fishermen plied their nets on the lake, which was well stocked with carp and pike.

Marie-Antoinette lived there more than at Versailles. Her life was innocent and idyllic, but it was not the life of a queen. Calumnies spread about her extravagance. It was there that she earned the fatal title of "Madame Deficit."

—IAN DUNLOP

VERSAILLES: PARK
Versailles, France

1630s: Original gardens; **Architects:** Jacques de Menours and Jacques du Boyceau. **1661-87:** Gardens enlarged, including the creation of the Petite Park and the Grand Park; **Architect:** André Le Nôtre (1613-1700).

Publications

BARBET, L. A.: *Les Grandes Eaux de Versailles*. Paris, 1907.
FOX, HELEN M.: *André Le Nôtre, Garden Architect to Kings*. New York, 1962.
HAZLEHURST, F. HAMILTON: *Gardens of Illusion: The Genius of Andre Le Nostre*. Nashville, Tennessee, 1980.
NOLHAC, P. DE: *Les Jardins de Versailles*. Paris, 1906.
WOODBRIDGE, K.: *Princely Gardens: The Origins and Development of the French Formal Style*. New York, 1986.

*

André Le Nôtre designed the gardens of the park at Versailles to enhance the architecture of the château and to create a majestic outdoor stage for the enactment of the daily, ongoing glorification of the Sun King, Louis XIV. Like Louis Le Vau, who built an enclosure (*enveloppe*) around the hunting lodge of Louis XIII, Le Nôtre made additions to an existing garden. Although a geometric design was in place when he entered the service of Louis XIV in late 1661, Le Nôtre began plans for an enlargement of the garden and initiated a program to honor the young king, who would soon identify himself with the sun god Apollo.

Two dominant features of Le Nôtre's additions to the park were perspectival vistas and water decorations. Both reveal his interest in Italian art and its influence on his gardens. His early study of optics and perspective led to his illusionistic vistas across the broad axes of his earlier masterwork at Vaux-le-Vicomte, and his practice of creating dramatic, illusionistic views continued at Versailles. And, in the midst of these settings, Le Nôtre introduced aquatic elements. His fountains, which contained statuary depicting themes of varying iconography, created dramatic effects for strollers in the park, just as the fountains in the gardens of ancient and Renaissance Italy had done. The sources of water at Versailles were limited; and the transmission of it into the park was a continuous problem for the architects and engineers, who built four reservoirs on the north side of the château in 1666-67. When these supplies proved inadequate for the increasing number of fountains added to the park, the designers sought new sources; but, because the demand for water at Versailles was all-consuming, the practice developed of playing the fountains only when the king was passing by, and turning them off at other times.

Le Nôtre inherited the garden scheme begun by Jacques de Menours and Jacques du Boyceau for Louis XIII in the 1630s, when the château was under reconstruction. To the established format of a dominant east-west axis with an intricate network of cross axes and radial paths, he added a complex series of garden decorations on each side of the main axis and to the north and south of the château. And, throughout the park, he created theatrical settings of gardens (*parterres*), fountains (*fontaines*) and groves (*bosquets*). Many of these half-hidden groves and fountains were decorated like rooms of the château itself and served as outdoor salons for royal functions.

The gardens developed under Le Nôtre comprise an inner core known as the Petite Park and an outer range called the Grand Park. The immediate area surrounding the château and extending outward to the Basin of Apollo (*Bassin d'Apollon*) on the west, to the Basin of the Dragon (*Bassin du Dragon*) on the north, and to the Orangery (*Orangerie*) on the south comprises the Petite Park. Beyond this inner park, the Grand Park encompasses the Grand Canal on the west and extends southward to include a large are below the Orangery and northward to include the village of Trianon.

Le Nôtre's first efforts appear in engravings made to illustrate events of the first of a series of major fêtes held at Versailles in 1664. By that time, he had established the basic lines of his primary axis. Directly in front of the château, he added a long *parterre* and continued the main axis through a circular pool and a long walkway (*allée*), which spread out at the next pool into two radial pathways like the orthogonals of linear perspective in what has become identified with Le Nôtre's plans and known as the goose-foot (*patte d'oie*) pattern.

Shortly after the fête of 1664, additional new features continued to appear in engravings. In this phase of the garden work at Versailles, the central axis continued to evolve into its final form as Le Nôtre moved earth to raise the level of the garden directly in front of the château and thus create a new *parterre* (*Nouveau Parterre* and *Jardin Bas*) below. To reach the new lower level, he created a grand Baroque staircase in two parts. A single grand staircase leads down to a double horseshoe ramp (*Fer à Cheval*).

Another significant project from the period following the fête of 1664 is the Grotto of Thetis (*Grotte de Téthys*), constructed on the northeastern side of the château in 1665-66, which introduced the Apollo theme at Versailles. Inside the single-story, triple-arched building decorated with relief scenes from the story of Apollo and Thetis, a statue group by François Girardon represents the sun god resting in the palace of Thetis after his long day of transporting the sun across the heavens. And so Louis XIV would rest at Versailles after his pressing duties as king in Paris. The grotto setting, like many of Le Nôtre's other features, was employed in Italian gardens of the Renaissance and antiquity, and clearly expresses the strong Italian influence on the decoration at Versailles during Le Nôtre's tenure. Although the theme of Apollo became the pervasive motif of the château and the park, the grotto itself was demolished later to make way for the north wing of the expanding château.

For the next fête in 1668, Le Nôtre came even closer to his final general form. He widened the walkway of the main axis and planted its green carpet (*Tapis Vert*). In its new proportions, the walkway became the Royal Walkway (*Allée Royale*). He also began the Grand Canal (1668-71), which was just beyond

the outer edge of the Petite Park and continued the dominant east-west axis outward to the outer reaches of the Grand Park. Visible also in illustrations of 1668 is the development of the north garden (*Parterre du Nord*), which had been doubled in width in the previous phase and was beginning to be developed. Also belonging to this phase was a new flower garden (*Parterre à Fleurs*) on the south *parterre* (*Parterre du Midi*).

Some of Le Nôtre's most distinctive pools and fountains date from the period of the next fête in 1674. In the Basin of Latona (*Bassin de Latone*), on the lower terrace below the horseshoe ramp, and in the Basin of Apollo (*Bassin d'Apollon*), on the main axis beyond the Royal Walkway, statuary figures enact the legends of Apollo. In the Basin of Latona, the goddess is surrounded by her subjects who have refused to pay her enough respect and, as a result, have been transformed into frogs by her lover Zeus. In his own pool beyond the Royal Walkway, changed from the Basin of Swans (*Bassin des Cygnes*) to continue the theme of Apollo throughout the park, Apollo, in the form of Tuby's gilded lead statue, drives his sun chariot across the heavens. Other aquatic decorations from that period were created on the north *parterre*, which is devoted to water projects. One of these is the Water Walkway (*Allée d'Eau*), or passage between the two halves of the north *parterre* leading to the new Basin of the Dragon (*Bassin du Dragon*), which forms the outer boundary of the Petite Park on the north.

A second brilliant aquatic series from that time consists of secluded groves on the northern side of the garden. There, in a row from east to west, the water theme is employed in varying geometric plans in the diamond-shaped Water Theater (*Théâtre d'Eau*), the circular Water Mountain (*Montagne d'Eau*), and the quatrefoil Room of Banquets or Feasts (*Salle du Festins* or *Conseil*). These water fountains, which have been transformed into less interesting groves, once produced elaborate hydraulic spectacles. The Marais grove, adjacent to and south of the Water Theater, is one of the most unusual features of the park. There, an artificial tree set in the middle of a rectangular pool is a fountain shooting off sprays of water. The idea for it was developed by Louise de Vallière, mistress of the king; the charm of this grove, which was destroyed in a later phase, was matched only by its peculiarity.

Located at the intersections of two secondary east-west and two secondary north-south walkways, about halfway between the château and the Pool of Latona, are four geometric fountains with sculptural groups representing the Four Seasons. Although some of the accompanying sculptural figures are missing, the primary sculptural groups, *in situ* at the centers of their pools, still have the power to delight park visitors.

The last major additions to the garden of the Petite Park were in place by 1680, when Jules Hardouin-Mansart completed his revision of the garden side of the château by enclosing the balcony of Le Vau's envelope to create the Hall of Mirrors (*Galerie des Glaces*). At that time, Le Nôtre seemed to be trying to match the grandeur and monumental scale of Hardouin-Mansart's building with groves and fountains of architectural character. Among these were the complex Gallery of Water or Room of Antiques (*Galerie d'Eau* or *Salle des Antiques*), the Ballroom Grove or Rockeries (*Salle de Bal* or *Salle des Rocailles*), and the Colonnade south of the main axis. North of the main axis are the Enceladus (*Encelade*) and the Grove of Fame (*Bosquet de la Renommée*). The Arch of Triumph (*Arc de Triomphe*) and the Three Fountains (*Trois Fontaines*) on the north *parterre* belong to this group also.

The Grove of Fame, which was Le Nôtre's last significant grove decoration at Versailles, and the Colonnade, which was designed by Hardouin-Mansart, are the most architectural of all the garden components. In the Grove of Fame, begun in

1676 to honor Louis XIV's military victories, Le Nôtre built two outer classical balustrades around the central pool containing a statuary fountain of Fame. This entire enclosure was then flanked by two domed, classical pavilions with pedimented facades by Hardouin-Mansart. This little grove, which resembles a park in miniature, in which the pavilions arc châteaux, did not survive. After the figure of Fame was replaced by Girardon's statue group of Apollo, moved from the demolished Grotto of Thetis, it became the Grove of Domes (*Bosquet des Domes*). And later the pavilions themselves were destroyed.

Hardouin-Mansart's Colonnade, directly opposite the Grove of Fame/Domes on the south side of the Royal Walkway, is still intact. The elegant, circular arcade of alternating blue and pink marble Corinthian columns continues the strong architectural trend in late-17th-century garden decoration. This could be a result of the favor Hardouin-Mansart was able to achieve with the new superintendant of buildings (*surintendent des bâtiments*) the Marquis de Louvois, who succeeded Le Nôtre's champion, Jean-Baptiste Colbert. There is reason to believe that Louvois led Le Nôtre to a premature retirement, as the trend toward more architectural motifs in the gardens suggests. Another trend apparent in the decorative reliefs of children on the spandrels of the arches of the Colonnade is the lighter theme employed by Hardouin-Mansart in some of his late-17th-century work and a new interest of the king in less somber themes.

Hardouin-Mansart's architectural contributions to the gardens of Versailles culminate in the Orangery, whose grand scale and simplicity make it the perfect backdrop for the orange trees and flowers on the lower level of the south *parterre*. Le Vau's original Orangery was replaced circa 1679-80 by Hardouin-Mansart, but the authorship of it has led to controversy. Contemporary attributions of its design to Le Nôtre and the modern rejection of these claims by Hardouin-Mansart's biographers cannot be settled in the absence of additional documents. It is true that Hardouin-Mansart often borrowed ideas or motifs from colleagues and contemporaries, but he also was able to assimilate a wide array of sources into his own personal architectural expression. Therefore, since the Orangery is a grandiose building, whose scale far exceeds the scope of any of the quasi-architectural groves designed by Le Nôtre, there is plausible reason to accept the building in its spartan simplicity as a grand project of Hardouin-Mansart, based possibly on an idea expressed earlier by Le Nôtre.

The recurring theme of water reappeared in the completion of the Basin of Neptune (*Bassin du Neptune*), which terminates the park on the north *parterre*, and the Swiss Lake (*Lac des Suisses*), which encloses the south side of the park. They frame and balance the internal order of the park as harmoniously as do the landscape elements flanking the central scenes of the heroic landscapes of Annibale Carracci and Nicolas Poussin. Le Nôtre also realized his final form for the decoration directly in front of the château. After substituting pools (*miroirs d'eau*) for a large embroidered plot (*Parterre de Broderie*), during that period he simplified the forms so that the large, clear pools would symbolically link the gardens on the exterior of the château with the glass mirrors (*miroirs des glaces*) of the Hall of Mirrors on the interior.

In 1668 Louis XIV had acquired the neighboring village of Trianon for additions to the royal property at Versailles; in 1670 Le Vau built for the king a royal retreat named the Porcelain Trianon (*Trianon de Porcelaine*) after the numerous Oriental tiles applied to the surface of the house. Although Le Nôtre employed a formal and structural landscape there similar to that of the main château, he introduced more flowers into this landscape. There, in the gardens of the Porcelain Trianon, Le Nôtre planted a wide variety of flowers to be enjoyed for their bouquet as well as their color and design qualities. And later in 1687, when Hardouin-Mansart rebuilt the house as the Grand Trianon in pink and yellow marble, Le Nôtre maintained the garden in its general form.

The Grand Trianon is located at the junction of the Grand Canal and the northern orthogonal of the goose-foot radial path. Because the position of the house is off-center, Le Nôtre compromised his usually strict geometric formula by planting two tree plots of unequal size that could not be distinguished from a distance, and thus achieved a simulation of balance and symmetry. Arrival at the Grand Trianon by boat brought visitors to a grand horseshoe staircase leading from the landing up to the Orangery on the garden side of the house.

Le Nôtre planned the garden, whose general configuration was as formal and ordered as that of the main château; but he also paid careful attention to planning special vistas and landscape features to be seen from every window. Hardouin-Mansart's unusual addition of an L-shaped extension on the western side of an otherwise symmetrical plan stimulated Le Nôtre to create additional garden vistas to be seen from this portion, which included a short northern extension for the royal children. This part was named the Trianon-in-the-Woods (*Trianon-sous-Bois*) because of its extension into the wooded area. One of the garden features still intact is the garden visible from the king's apartments in the northern wing, called a "particular garden" ("*jardin particulier*") by Le Nôtre but known now as the King's Garden. A second is the Garden of Springs (*Les Sources*). Although it is now only a plain lawn, it seems to be an early anticipation there at Versailles of the natural style of landscape that became popular in the 18th century.

In Louis XIV's last years, he accepted a number of changes in the garden design of the Petite Park of the main château. Thus, after Le Nôtre died, many of his groves were altered or totally transformed. Then an increasingly popular interest in nature and the unstructured settings based on the new English landscape style, "*le jardin anglais*," as well as the new reverence for nature expressed in the works of Jean Jacques Rousseau and already anticipated in the Garden of Springs at the Grand Trianon, created a demand for the new style at the expense of many of Le Nôtre's artificial constructions of nature. Many of his creations were destroyed or altered to make way for such natural settings as the new Grove of Apollo (*Bosquet d'Apollon*), designed by the painter Hubert Robert in 1778 to replace the Marais grove inspired by Vallière. Other groves from the period of the 1670s also yielded to new styles.

Further changes during the succeeding reign of Louis XV included the addition of a garden of exotic plants in the Trianon village area of the park and the construction of the French Pavilion and the Petit Trianon as additional royal retreats during the king's sojourns into his fancy garden, which included such delicacies as fig trees, coffee shrubs, and pineapples.

The exotic plant garden was displaced, however, in the reign of Louis XVI, by a *jardin anglais* designed by Richard Mique and Hubert Robert for Marie Antoinette in the new natural style that began sweeping away 17th century order and formalism as the winds of revolution would soon sweep away the royal and aristocratic hierarchies of the ancièn régime. Mique and Robert left some trees intact, but otherwise created a new landscape that included an artificial lake and ponds and streams, and set some small classical structures into their midst. One of these is the Temple of Love (*Temple d'Amour*), a round, domed pavilion with Corinthian columns, designed by Mique in 1778. Also by Mique is the Belvedere, a small, octagonal pavilion designed in 1781. These structures and the natural spaces they occupy lead out to the artificial village (*Le Hameau*) that Mique built for Marie Antoinette at the outer reaches of the north side of the park. There, in the hamlet of rustic buildings based on houses of Norman villages, the queen and her maids of honor attempted to live the new natural lifestyle in the simple white dresses she introduced to the French court, whose dress and manners were as structured as Le Nôtre's 17th-century landscapes. Set in the rustic, quasi-rural landscape were the queen's house and the secondary buildings of the village. In this new natural setting, Marie Antoinette's hegemony ended; but so did the formal landscape style associated with Le Nôtre, which had been transformed continually since the early 18th century onward by the writings of Rousseau and the changing political climate in which England became the dominant world power and, as a result, the arbiter of tastes in landscape design.

—JOYCE M. DAVIS

LA MADELEINE
Vézelay, France

After 1096: New church begun. **1132:** Church consecrated. **1161-65:** New chapter house built. **Ca. 1880-1210 or ca. 1860-80:** Choir and transepts rebuilt. **19th century:** Restoration by Eugène Emmanuel Viollet-le-Duc (1814-79).

Publications

CONANT, K.J.: "Deux traditions dans la chronologie du Roman bourguignon." *Annales de Bourgogne* 44 (1972): 94-103.
SALET, F.: *La Madeleine de Vézelay.* Melun, 1948.

*

The Abbey Church of La Madeleine commands a hilltop in western Burgundy near the Yonne River. A dramatic climb up the steep road winding through the tow climaxes in an exhilarating combination of topography and architecture. A monastery was established on this site shortly after 873. From the early 11th century, the legend grew that the body of Mary Magdalene rested in the church. A pilgrimage began to develop, and in 1050 the church was rededicated principally to her. Pilgrims also began to rendezvous there for the pilgrimage to Santiago de Compostela in Spain, and Vézelay became the head of one of the main pilgrimage roads in western Europe.

Although a new church was begun shortly after 1096, the present Romanesque nave was probably built only after a disastrous fire in 1120. Immediately after the nave was finished, a narthex was added; a consecration in 1132 is sometimes taken to indicate the completion of the narthex, but Francis Salet puts the completion of the nave circa 1140-50 and that of the narthex circa 1160. A new chapter house was built in 1161-65. Finally, the choir and transepts were rebuilt in Early Gothic style. This is usually taken to have been begun about 1180-85 and finished about 1205-10, although recently a substantially earlier date of circa 1160-80 has also been proposed.

A rival claim to the relics of Mary Magdalene from Provence effectively ended the pilgrimage to Vézelay in the later 13th century, and its fortunes remained modest thereafter. In 1537 the abbey was secularized, and in 1569 the Huguenots dispersed relics and defaced the outer facade sculpture. In 1790 the college of canons was suppressed, and La Madeleine became a parish church. After a fire consumed the spire of the southwest tower in 1819, attention was called to the poor condition of the church, and from 1840 until 1859 Eugène Emmanuel Viollet-le-Duc

was put in charge of a restoration which, although less archaeologically scrupulous than is now allowable, was a model for its time.

The 10-bay Romanesque nave features a two-story elevation. The cruciform piers have attached shafts on each face, carrying slightly horseshoed arcade arches to the sides, transverse arches across the aisles and vault responds toward the nave. A stringcourse above the arcade is all that relieves the wall surface below the modest clerestory windows. Both nave and aisles are covered with groin vaults. In all this, Vézelay exemplifies a well-established Burgundian tradition (cf. Anzy-le-Duc).

The transverse arches across the nave feature a distinctive alternation of light- and dark-colored voussoirs. Tournus, Lombardy and Muslim Spain have all been claimed as the source of this feature. Lombardy or Tournus seems more likely, as the unusual vault support system at Vézelay can also be found in both places. Initially, and until flying buttresses were added, metal tie-rods ran across the nave between the tops of the responds. The flyers possibly date from the end of the 12th century, although they may have been added much later under Abbot Erard de Rochefort (1601-30); their complete rebuilding by Viollet-le-Duc makes the question unresolvable.

The facade features three sculpted portals which, together with the carved capitals in the nave, form one of the masterpieces of Burgundian Romanesque sculpture. All three feature carved tympana, depicting the Pentecost in the center, the Appearance of the Resurrected Christ to the Apostles on the north and the Adoration of the Magi on the south. The central portal also has a statue of John the Baptist on the *trumeau* and small apostle figures at the tops of the jambs, anticipating the standard Gothic arrangement.

The three-bay narthex added west of the nave, enclosing the facade sculpture, is as wide as the nave and of two stories. The U-shaped tribune story rests on groin vaults over the aisles and eastern central bay. It is open toward the nave and contained an altar dedicated to Saint Michael. Most of the tribune is also groin vaulted, but the central and southeast bays both received quadripartite rib vaults. Towers were planned, but only the south one was built. The narthex facade also featured three portals, and the central one had a carved Last Judgment tympanum, which was defaced by the Huguenots and replaced by Viollet-le-Duc. The upper part of the facade was reworked in about 1230, with five stepped lancets, a wall passage and statuary recalling that of Auxerre Cathedral in style.

The new chapter house, of six bays, with two freestanding columns, was covered with rib vaults, although round arches are used throughout. Relief medallions were set into each vault cell. Viollet-le-Duc rebuilt the vaults and built a largely fanciful adjoining cloister walk to buttress them.

The first master of the Gothic choir was soon replaced by a second master who was less familiar with the Gothic idiom. The choir was laid out with two straight bays and a hemicycle, flanked by aisles and ambulatory, with two rectangular chapels opening off the aisles and five radiating apsidal chapels. The second straight bay is subdivided, with a single colonnette on the south, a pair of colonnettes on the north. The crossing and aisleless, two-bay transepts were also rebuilt. The pointed choir arcades are supported by elegantly slender monolithic columns, very slightly tapered. Above the arcades, the triforium is open to the space under the aisle and ambulatory roofs; in the hemicycle there are twin pointed openings under a round relieving arch, in the straight bays two such units. Large clerestory lancets fill almost all the upper wall surface. It seems likely that the first master foresaw sexpartite vaults over the straight choir bays, but only the westernmost bay received one. Then comes a quadripartite vault over a half bay, and finally eight radiating

La Madeleine, west facade: Vézelay, France, ca. 1104-32

La Madeleine, south flank

La Madeleine

ribs converge on the chord of the hemicycle. The many irregularities of layout in the new east end probably reflect reuse of earlier foundations and accommodation of existing structures. The flying buttresses of the choir pose something of a problem. While the extension of the clerestory windows below the vault springings might suggest their presence from the outset, the elaborate vaulting of the area over the aisles and ambulatory may just as well have been considered adequate support and the flyers added later.

The design of the choir reflects a wide knowledge of Gothic buildings. There are similarities of plan and elevation with Sens Cathedral, St. Germain-des-Prés and also St. Denis. In fact, the upper parts of the elevation probably reflect those of Abbé Suger's choir at St. Denis, making Vézelay, along with Avila Cathedral, one of its closest copies (one can only speculate on the presence of Sugerian stained glass here, but the much-discussed effects of illumination at Vézelay would be much changed by it.) The arcade columns and triple *en delit* shafts of the vault responds are of a highly polished bluish stone, which contrasts with the light oolitic limestone of the walls. This use of contrasting materials must reflect input from such northern French churches as Arras Cathedral. The arrangement of the radiating chapels, which are separated from one another only by a dado wall and are open above, recalls that of St. Etienne, Caen.

The old crypt, in which the relics of Mary Magdalene were kept, was also expanded to encompass the area covered by the crossing and central choir vessel. The area above it is slightly raised, and openings in the resulting bench on the outer side of the arcades provide modest lighting. Two rows of columns create three aisles, seven bays long, all covered by groin vaults. The present crypt stairs in the transepts, by Viollet-le-Duc, replace stairs probably descending from the western choir aisle bays.

The choir campaign also included the revaulting of the four eastern nave bays, and towers over the eastern nave aisle bays were planned, although only the southern one was built and crowned with an octagonal stone spire (now gone). The Gothic rib vaults were somewhat higher than the Romanesque groin vaults, and the ''impurity'' of the nave was more than Viollet-le-Duc could stand. He rebuilt the Gothic bays in Romanesque, his only really irresponsible act there.

—JIM BUGSLAG

GERMANY

ROYAL CHAPEL
Aachen, Germany

Also called the Palatine Chapel (part of Charlemagne's palace complex); the location is variously known as Aix-la-Chapelle. **792-805:** Construction. **Architect:** Odo of Metz. **983:** Underwent restoration. **13th century:** Survived fire that destroyed rest of palace. **1353-1413:** Choir built. **1881:** Underwent restoration.

Publications

BANDMANN, G.: "Die Vorbilder der Aachener Pfalzkapelle." in BRAUNFELS, W. (ed.): *Karl der Grosse.* Düsseldorf, 1965-67: vol. 3: 424.

BEENKEN, H.: "Die Aachener Pfalzkapelle." in *Aachen zum Jahr 1951* (Rheinischer Verein für Denkmalpflege und Heimatschutz) 67.

BRAUNFELS, W. (ed.): *Karl der Grosse.* 4 vols. Düsseldorf, 1965-67.

KLEINBAUER, E.: "Charlemagne's Palace Chapel at Aachen and Its Copies." *Gesta* (International Center of Romanesque Art) 4 (1965): 2-11.

KREUSCH, F.: *Aachen. Über Pfalzkapelle und Atrium zur Zeit Karls des Grossen.* Aachen, 1958.

SCHNITZLER, H.: *Der Dom zu Aachen.* Düsseldorf, 1950.

VERBEEK, A.: "Die architektonische Nachfolge der Aachener Pfalzkapelle." in BRAUNFELS, W. (ed.): *Karl der Grosse.* Düsseldorf, 1965-67: vol. 4: 113.

*

Charlemagne's Royal Chapel, and now tomb, stood at the south end of a long colonnade that connected the chapel to the royal audience hall and other buildings of the palace at Aachen. It remains an important relic because the rest of the palace was destroyed by fire in the 13th century and so few other Carolingian buildings survive. The chapel, built by Odo of Metz, is today incorporated into the cathedral of Aachen. The dome has been rebuilt and decorated with a mosaic imitating the iconography of the original mosaic, showing Christ adored by the Twenty-Four Elders of the Apocalypse.

Originally, the approach to the chapel was from a large atrium at the west end. From the exterior an octagonal cloister vault rose above the central core of the chapel, and the ambulatory vaults and roof formed a lower, outer ring. The entrance was unlike any seen before: a separate tall, narrow and very deep structure of three stories that reached higher than the ambulatory roof and was flanked by twin cylindrical stair towers as high as the central dome. The monumental development of the entrance corresponded to its function as the imperial box, for the emperor's throne and balcony stood in the gallery on the second interior level; there the emperor could address the people and look out onto the chapel below and across the gallery to the chapel dedicated to Christ. A chapel for relics was located on the third story of the entrance block. The entrance to the Royal

Chapel stood at the beginning of the development of the "Westwerk" in Carolingian architecture and was, therefore, an original and prototypical creation.

In plan, the chapel was designed with a central, octagonal inner core, defined by eight huge, angular piers, surrounded by an ambulatory with a 16-sided outer wall. At the east end a rectangular apse projected to the exterior; the present choir is 14th century. The main altar, which was dedicated to Mary—reflecting the dual dedication of the church to Mary and Christ—was located in the ambulatory on the ground floor between the two eastern piers and the projecting apse.

The two projecting structures at east and west (entrance and apse) imparted a longitudinal axis to the centralized plan. The Royal Chapel was one among several round medieval chapels dedicated to Mary, all imitating, perhaps, the seventh-century transformation and the Marian rededication of the Pantheon, which came to be known as Santa Maria Rotonda. In this regard, it is perhaps noteworthy that the Pantheon rotunda was also preceded by a tall, rectangular, three-story entrance block.

The novelty of the plan of the Aachen chapel was seen primarily in the regularization of all of its spaces into separate, clearly defined entities. The ambulatory, for example, was not conceived as a continuous ring—as it had been earlier, say, in Santa Costanza in Rome or in San Vitale in Ravenna—but as a juxtaposition of individual geometric units of space, each covered with its own groin vault, alternately rectangular and triangular, just as the "bays" were in plan. Horn and Born have shown that the entire palace complex was laid out in a square-grid modular system, which can be demonstrated in the plan of the chapel as well as in its elevation. The squaring off of the design, in fact, is one of the major differences between the Royal Chapel at Aachen and San Vitale, to which it has often been compared as copy to model.

The construction in stone represented a departure from the tradition of wood building in northern Europe and revived ancient Roman building practices, in particular, the return to stone vaulting. In the interior elevation heavy stone piers supported wide round arches on the ground floor, opening onto the ambulatory, and, in the second story, even taller arches spanned the piers and opened onto the gallery. The second-story arches were divided in two by a double order of columns, the lower two columns supporting a straight arcade with three openings that were divided from the upper two columns by a straight cornice. The upper columns rose to the intrados of the main arch. The round columns, with their Corinthian capitals, were brought from ancient buildings in Italy. Above, in the drum, eight round-arched windows formed a clerestory.

In comparison with the interior of San Vitale, the Royal Chapel is heavy and ponderous, dictating a reinstatement of wall mass and flat, rather than billowing, surfaces. The regularization and squaring off of spaces was evident in the interior elevation, too. The horizontals of the projecting cornices that separated the two stories balanced the rows of verticals. The overall emphasis, nevertheless, was toward greater overall verticality. The proportions of height to width breathed a new medieval aesthetic, not Early Christian or Byzantine, each having emphasized lateral developments of space.

The ambulatory bays on both stories contained round-arched windows. The gallery bays were separated by a diaphragm arch and vaulted with radial barrel vaults like those used in the Roman Colosseum. Their function was to help support the

Royal Chapel: Aachen, Germany, 792-805

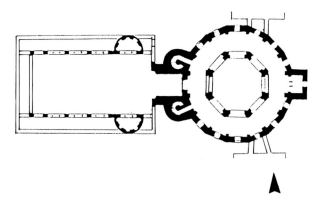

dome. So, not only was stone construction revived, but with it were revived the engineering accomplishments of the Romans and their many diverse structural solutions.

The decorative elements were low-key, consisting of bronze doors with lion-head handles, bronze balustrades in the gallery, and marble sheathing on the walls.

The Royal Chapel at Aachen inspired numerous buildings in the medieval period. The chapel at Nijmegen in the Netherlands and the Chapel of Our Lady at Ottmarsheim in Alsace were both later copies.

—PAULA D. LEVETO-JABR

ZEUGHAUS
Augsburg, Germany

1602-07: Construction; **Architects:** Elias Holl (1573-1646) and Josef Heintz the Elder (1564-1609).

Publications

ALBRECHT, INGEBORG: "Elias Holl, Stil und Werk des 'Maurmaisters' und der Augsburger Malerarchitekten Heinz und Kager." *Münchner Jahrbuch der bildenden Kunst* 12 (1937): 101-136.

BAUM, JULIUS: *Die Bauwerke des Elias Holl*. Strasbourg, 1908.

BUSHART, BRUNO (ed.): *Augsburger Barock*. Exhibition catalog. Augsburg, 1968.

HITCHCOCK, HENRY-RUSSELL: *German Renaissance Architecture*. Princeton, New Jersey, 1981.

LIEB, NORBERT: *Rettet das Augsburger Zeughaus*. Augsburg, 1967.

RAUCH, M.: *Zwei Jahrtausende Farb und Stein: Augsburger Baugeschichte im Wandel der Zeit*. Augsburg, 1973.

ROECK, BERND: *Elias Holl: Architekt einer europäischen Stadt*. Regensburg, 1985.

STANGE, ALFRED: *Die deutsche Baukunst der Renaissance*. Munich, 1926.

VON BEZOLD, G.: *Die Baukunst der Renaissance in Deutschland*. Leipzig, 1908.

ZIMMER, JÜRGEN: *Joseph Heintz der Ältere als Maler*. Heidelberg, 1967.

*

The Augsburg Zeughaus (Armory) was built between 1602 and 1607 to a design by the German Renaissance architect Elias Holl. The building has art-historical significance particularly for its principal facade. It is the first facade in secular architecture shaped by a diverse sculptural design that exemplifies both Renaissance decorative effects and the dynamic pictorial forms of the Italian Baroque.

A granary ("*Kornhaus*"), dating from 1505 and situated southwest of St. Moritz Church, was transformed into the Augsburg Zeughaus in 1584/85. The Augsburg city architect, Jacob Eschay (died 1606), undertook an expansion of that building in 1598. After a great open space was created by the demolition of a building behind the church, the city council decided to build an extension of the Zeughaus on the site. In 1602 the project was entrusted to the new city architect, Elias Holl. He was charged with the demolition of the imperfect building elements constructed by his predecessor Eschay and with the construction of a new wing in their stead.

The older building on the western part of the site was to be connected to a new north wing by means of a square tower set in the inner angle of the courtyard thus created. Holl, faithful to the commission, designed a six-story building consisting of two wings situated at a right angle to each other: a new main building on an east-west axis with the principal facade on the short eastern side, and the older wing on a north-south axis. This right-angle composition was quite common in 16th-century Germany. The most important building of this nature is the Jesuit College of St. Michael at Munich, which was built two decades earlier. The Augsburg Zeughaus is one of the clearest designs built according to this scheme, however. Because of the location of the two-wing structure, across from the Fugger House, a rectangular public space was created—a significant intervention in the urban plan of the western Old Town area.

In the inner angle of the two six-story wings a square tower with a staircase was erected. Both wings have large columned and vaulted halls at ground level, with spacious attics. In the north-south wing (the former *Kornhaus*), a hall with two rows of 10 freestanding pillars is divided into three by six bays. The groin vault rests on two rows of two round columns with Tuscan capitals. Two rows of nine columns support the groin vaults between the wall arches, which are anchored to the side walls by means of corbels.

The hall in the Hainhofer House (1578), built by Hans Holl, Elias' father, served as the model for the design of the hall in the new east-west wing. The hall charms with its artful appearance and size (65 by 200 meters). Such vaulted halls, a practical design considering the function of the space, are to be found in many German armories of the time. The Cologne Zeughaus (1594), which has a two-aisle hall of 13 bays and a groin vault, and the Wolfsbüttel Zeughaus (1613), which has a three-aisle hall of 12 bays over 22 pillars, may serve as examples.

The eastern facade of the new east-west wing was designed as the principal facade. Three designs for this facade were done in collaboration with the painter and architect Josef Heintz the Elder (1564-1609), whose influence is clearly visible. The magnificent facade has a three-story elevation and a two-story gable. It is divided into three axes. The central one, narrower

Zeughaus: Augsburg, Germany, 1602-07

than the two side axes, rises into the gable. Steep volutes are set over the side axes, and form a transition to the gable, which is crowned with a pinecone. The individual stories, each with its own order, are separated by stringcourses. The ground floor is rusticated like a base, and the central axis there contains the portal framed by rusticated columns. Over the portal is a monumental bronze of the archangel Michael, flanked by *putti* with trophies. The bronze was designed by Hans Reichel, a pupil of Giovanni da Bologna, and cast by Wolfgang Neidhardt.

The courtyard created by the two wings was originally enclosed with a high wall designed in the style of the principal facade.

Elements in the articulation of the facade—particularly the vertical front, the emphasized central axis, and the projecting verticals—already had gone beyond the Late Renaissance. Nevertheless, the individual building forms and their application in the overall design were still clearly determined by the Renaissance. What took this building beyond, into the era of the Early Baroque, was the expressive nature of the sculptural ornamentation, the emphasized stringcourses and gable volutes, the shape of the windows, the dissolution of horizontals and the ornamental gables, which break up the surface.

With this grand collaboration of architecture and sculpture in the monumental facade, the Augsburg Zeughaus belongs to the most important achievements of early-17th-century German architecture.

—PETRA LESER
Translated from the German by Marijke Rijsberman

AEG TURBINE HALL
Berlin, Germany

1908-10. Architects: Peter Behrens and Karl Bernhard.

Publications

ANDERSON, STANFORD: "Modern Architecture and Industry: Peter Behrens and the AEG Factories." *Oppositions* 23 (1981): 53-83.

BEHRENS, PETER: "The Turbine Hall of the AEG (1910)." *Documents* (Milton Keynes, England) (1975): 56-57.

BEHRENS, PETER: "Über Aesthetik in der Industrie." *AEG-Zeitung* (June 1909).

BERNHARDT, KARL: "The New Turbine Hall for AEG (1910)." *Documents* (Milton Keynes, England) (1975): 54-56.

BUDDENSIEG, TILMANN, and ROGGE, HENNING: *Industriekultur. Peter Behrens and the AEG, 1907-1914*. Cambridge, Massachusetts, 1984.

FRAMPTON, KENNETH, and FUTAGAWA, YUKIO: *Modern Architecture: 1851-1919*. New York, 1983.

GROPIUS, WALTER: *Internationale Architekur*. 1925.

"Industriearchitekur—Exhibition on Peter Behrens and the AEG." *Architecture d'aujourd'hui* (April 1980).

"Peter Behrens and the AEG." *Bauwelt* (16 March 1979).

"Peter Behrens and the AEG Architecture." *Lotus* (September 1976).

Since its completion, the AEG Turbine Hall has been a virtual symbol of the beginnings of modern, functional architecture. The building was included in Walter Gropius' book *Internationale Architekur* (1925), and since then has appeared in nearly every publication about the development of architecture before World War I. It is probably the absence of the historicizing formal idiom that had been customary until then, and the visible incorporation of construction elements in the architectural concept that have given this design its privileged place.

When Peter Behrens accepted a position as consultant to the Allgemeine Elektricitäts-Gesellschaft (AEG) in 1907, he had already distanced himself from the Jugenstil movement, and adopted the formal language of abstract classicism. His new position not only enabled him to design more buildings, but also provided him with a new challenge as an architect. Industrial buildings had not yet come to be considered as expressly architectural assignments. Moreover, industry was widely and more and more strongly perceived as the enemy of individual artistic accomplishment. It was no coincidence, then, that Behrens cofounded the Deutscher Werkbund in the same year he joined AEG. The Werkbund sought to raise the quality of German industrial production, through the involvement of artists in industrial design.

The commission for the Turbine Hall in 1908 was Behrens' first assignment for a large building for AEG. The key space was a hall for the building of steam engines, with a projected length of 200 meters and a width of 35 meters. The structure actually built was somewhat smaller (123 by 40 meters), and consisted of a main hall whose support system comprised 22 iron columns, which are set 9.22 meters apart. The distance between the columns was determined by the width of the railroad tracks entering the hall. Next to the main hall there is also a smaller hall. The construction materials are iron, concrete and glass.

The Turbine Hall distinguished itself in two respects from the usual forms of industrial architecture. The support system proper, with the 22 gigantic iron columns, was incorporated into the long side facade as an element of its articulation. The columns create a clear rhythm in the facade, which is underscored by their contrast to the glass surfaces in between. An image of machine-like precision is created, which is expressive of the precision of industrial production. The principal short facade is dominated by a massive concrete gable, carried by two corner pylons. These corner supports, however, do not in actuality have a supporting function, but were chosen for reasons of design only. The participating engineer, Karl Bernhard, did not agree with this design. It was his opinion that the thin shell of reinforced concrete in front of the iron construction could lead to the mistaken impression that the building was a massive concrete construction. Behrens, however, wished to accentuate the principal facade so as to achieve a classical, temple-like appearance.

The incorporation of the construction into the architectonic composition and the striving after a new image of the factory as a building type were the most important innovations of the design. In the architectural design of the Turbine Hall, Behrens sought to reconcile the growing contrast between art and industrial production. The relation of the design to the humanistic architectural tradition, in combination with the forms of industrial production, was to give the factory a humanistic and worthy face, and to integrate it architecturally into the urban context. The Turbine Hall thus became an example to the later generation of functionalist architects, not so much for the specific forms of the design as for the successful integration of construction technique and artistic considerations.

—OTAKAR MÁČEL
Translated from the German by Marijke Rijsberman

AEG Turbine Hall: Berlin, Germany, 1908-10

ALTES MUSEUM (MUSEUM AM LUSTGARTEN)
Berlin, Germany

1824-28: Constructed. **Architect:** Karl Friedrich Schinkel (1781-1841).

Publications

JOHNSON, PHILIP: "Schinkel and Mies." *Writings*. New York, 1979: 164-181.

KAUFFMANN, HANS: "Zweckbau und Monument: Zu Friedrich Schinkels Museum am Berliner Lustgarten." in HESS, GERHARD (ed.): *Eine Freundesgabe der Wissenschaft für Ernst Hellmut Vits*. Frankfurt am Main, 1963.

MEYER, GERHARD R., et al.: *Das Alte Museum, 1823-1966*. Festschrift. Berlin, 1966.

MÜTHER, HANS: "Schinkels Museum in Berlin." *Berliner Heimat: Zeitschrift für die Geschichte Berlins*, 2 (1959): 72-82.

PEVSNER, N.: "Karl Friedrich Schinkel." in *Studies in Art, Architecture and Design*. New York, 1968: 186.

PLAGEMANN, VOLKER: *Das deutsche Kunstmuseum 1790-1870*. Munich, 1967.

POSENER, JULIUS: "Schinkel's Eclecticism and 'the Architectural.'" *Architectural Digest* 53 (November-December 1983): 11-12.

Precis des Leçons d'Architecture. Paris, 1801-1805. Vol. 2, 3rd Part: 56-57, and Plate 11.

RAVE, PAUL ORTWIN, and KUHN, G. (eds.): *Karl Friedrich Schinkel: Lebenswerk*. Berlin, 1929-1962.

SCHINKEL, KARL FRIEDRICH: Descriptive commentary, in *Collection of Architectural Designs*. Chicago, 1981.

SPIERO, SABINE: "Schinkels Altes Museum in Berlin: Seine Baugeschichte von den Anfängen bis zur Eröffnung." *Jahrbuch der preussischen Kunstsammlungen*, 55 (1934): 41-86.

UNGERS, L. and MATHIAS, O.: "The Humanist City." *Architectural Design* 52 (November-December 1982): 11-12.

*

When in 1823 Kaiser Friedrich Wilhelm III charged Karl Friedrich Schinkel with the design of a new structure to house the antiquities and art collections amassed by the Prussian crown, Schinkel was already serving the *Oberbaudeputation* (public works administration), which he would eventually head, and had constructed such important buildings as the severely Doric Neue Wache (1816-18) and the monumental Schauspielhaus (1818-21). Schinkel's work was greatly influenced by the Paris of Claude-Nicolas Ledoux and Etiènne-Louis Boullée as instilled in him by his brilliant mentor Friedrich Gilly, and as Schinkel himself experienced during his visit to the French capital in 1805. For Nikolaus Pevsner, the Museum am Lustgarten is ". . . Schinkel's most successful building," while Henry-Russell Hitchcock referred to it as one of the two masterworks of its time.

The building is diagrammatically a collection of simple geometric volumes: a cube housing a hemispherical dome is inserted into a rectangular main solid. The whole is approached on axis, climbing the stairs and continuing through *in antis* colonnade. The middle third of the wall behind it is carved away to reveal a pyramidal element. This two-story central void is visible as

Altes Museum: Berlin, Germany, 1824-28

one approaches the museum, and with the protruding attic of the cube indicates the existence of a centralizing space without revealing its geometry. One then proceeds under the entry element and through the central space, gaining access to the linear galleries which bound two symmetrical inner courtyards. The very regular side and rear facades are accentuated by corner pilasters which, though on the same plane as the wall surface, are articulated by deep recesses. Schinkel was most precise about his intentions: "It is obvious that we had to be very economical to create a building on a site which needed so much preparation prior to construction.... But in spite of the economic constraints, we still wanted to create a building ... which was appropriate for the most beautiful site in the city...," and "... my emphasis was on simplicity for the inside as well as the outside.... Its proximity to both the Royal Palace and the Zeughaus required a very monumental building...."

According to Pevsner, in the museum "Schinkel is entirely uncompromising and gives his building an absolutely straight, smooth, sheer front, with one giant order running right through from the square angle pier on the left to that on the right ... the whole being crowned by the heavy architrave and corner, and the centre slightly raised, again with a roof appearing to be completely flat." Two 19th-century sculptures, Kiss' *Amazon* and Wolff's *Lion-killer,* flank the central stairs of the stylobate. Behind the Ionic columns, the walls of the pronaos were painted with marbleized red square panels along their lower half, and murals designed by Schinkel "... bearing some relation to the purpose of the building" depicted mythological themes on the walls above and on the second-floor vestibule. They were executed under the supervision of Peter Cornelius after the completion of the structure. Upon entry into the rotunda space, one was confronted by a hall displaying "statues of philosophers and poets, thus epitomizing the humanist idea that wisdom, intellect and imagination are the most revered attributes of mankind, and thereby documenting that the human mind is the center of the universe" (Liselotte and O. M. Ungers, "The Humanist City").

The Museum am Lustgarten might remind one of J. N. L. Durand's project in his *Precis des Leçons d'Architecture* with which Schinkel must have been familiar, although Julius Posener does not place much significance in this. What is apparent is that the Durand plan is transformed. Yet the elements assembled by Schinkel present more than the *taxis schemata* of Durand's idealization. They embody nothing less than a journey through the monuments of architecture, by reconfiguring the trabeated *stoa poikile,* the rudimentary form of an archaic Egyptian stepped pyramid, and the hemispherical cella of the Roman Pantheon. Schinkel substituted the usual *acroteria* crowning the entablature of the stoa-colonnade with Hohenzollern eagles; the pyramid through which one enters, formed by the two stairs leading to the mezzanine, also represents a corbeled vault (a nascent arcuated form); the central rotunda rephrases the proportions, coffering, oculus and niches of its Roman antecedent. The didactic role of the museum, a new institution in the 19th century, is integral to the architectural program. In this paradigmatic masterpiece one is to experience architectural time in anticipation of the works housed within. As Pevsner observed, Schinkel was at his best there, compressing and obscuring outside and inside: "The staircase to the upper story, it will be noticed, leads up from the centre ... it is not enclosed by walls, but on both sides open to the colonnade, resulting in an extraordinary interpenetration of space."

The Museum am Lustgarten continued the volumetric clarity of Ledoux's Barrières de la Villette and was a precursor to the architecture of our century. In Schinkel we find an antecedent

for our modernist predilection for precise clarity and structure; his museum is unquestionably connected to such early modernist works as Adolf Loos' Goldman and Salatsch Building (1910-11), Walter Gropius and Adolf Meyer's Fagus Factory (1911), and Peter Behrens' AEG Turbine Factory (1908-09), an affiliation which, as Philip Johnson has noted, continued to later moderns such as Ludwig Mies van der Rohe. The museum's axiality, relation to the ground, regularity of its facades and horizontal disposition of volume are characteristics found in Mies' work at the Illinois Institute of Technology campus, for instance, Crown Hall (1950-56).

Restored in time for the bicentennial of Schinkel's birthday in 1981, the shell and entry sequence of Museum am Lustgarten survive. The rotunda again houses its statuary program, but only the monochromatic lower panels of the pronaos were restored, while the galleries have been thoroughly modernized. The collections housed within are no longer in concert with the didactic nature of the building, and its place in the urban fabric has been lost. In one respect, however, the restoration has improved the original, for the rear facade, which had been detailed in drafted stucco, is now instead sheathed in sandstone. Even so, Schinkel's Museum am Lustgarten remains one of the most significant landmarks of neoclassicist architecture.

—GERARDO BROWN-MANRIQUE

BRANDENBURG GATE
Berlin, Germany

1789-94. **Architect:** Carl Gotthard Langhans (1733-1808).

Publications

BAUCH, KURT: *Das Brandenburger Tor.* Cologne, 1966.
HINRICHS, WALTHER: *Carl Gotthard Langhans: Ein schlesischer Baumeister, 1733-1808.* Strasbourg, 1909.

*

The accession of Friedrich Wilhelm II as king of Prussia in 1787 marked an upsurge of national sentiment and a growing confidence in the development of a specifically German culture that could stand on its own. The king had ambitions to make his capital, Berlin, a great cultural center in which German artists would be preeminent. He cast about him for talent, and in 1788 called to work for him Friedrich Wilhelm Freiherr von Erdmannsdorff (1736-1800) from Dessau in Saxony, Carl Gotthard Langhans (1733-1808) from Breslau in Silesia, David Gilly (1748-1808) from Stettin on the Baltic coast, and the sculptor Johann Gottfried Schadow (1764-1850) (who was a disciple of Antonio Canova and a friend of Gilly's son Friedrich) from Berlin itself.

The Prussian capital thus acquired a first-class academy for the teaching of architecture: there, the main sources for Prussian neoclassicism were identified as springing from Italy (notably the Greek Doric temples at Paestum) and France, and especially Le Camus de Mézières' *Le Génie de l'Architecture, ou l'Analogie de cet Art avec nos Sensations,* published in Paris in 1780.

The first great artifact of Franco-Prussian neoclassicism was the monumental gateway at the western end of the Unter den Linden in Berlin known as the Brandenburg Gate. It was erected in 1789-94 to designs by Langhans, who, in 1788, had been

Brandenburg Gate: Berlin, Germany, 1789-94

appointed *Oberhofbaurat.* The king himself proposed to Langhans that he should use the Athenian Propylaeum as his model.

Now where did the image come from? It is true that the volume of Stuart and Revett's *Antiquities of Athens* containing the illustration of the Propylaeum appeared in 1789, and the work was known and admired in Germany, but it would be a close-run thing if that were truly the source. More likely as a model was J.-D. Le Roy's *Ruines des plus beaux Monuments de la Grèce,* which had been published in Paris in 1758: Langhans never went to Greece, although he had visited Italy in 1768-69, but his sources were probably French.

However, although there are certain affinities with the Athenian original, the Brandenburg Gate does not adopt the Greek Doric order, but a version of Doric that derives from Roman exemplars. The composition is entirely symmetrical (unlike the Athenian Propylaeum), and the central gateway is hexastyle, with three triglyphs over the intercolumniation in the center and two over the rest. The triglyphs are set over the centerlines of columns at the corners, which is a Roman, not Greek Doric, arrangement, and in the small pedimented pavilions on either side of the gate itself there are columns all around, rather than blank walls at the sides terminating in antae. Instead of a pediment over the great gate, Langhans placed an attic platform over the entablature, with a series of steps suggesting the monumental character of a Hellenistic mausoleum and the outline of a pediment: this series of steps on either side of the central attic platform leads the eye to the crowning quadriga by Schadow, who also designed the reliefs of the metopes based on the battles between the Lapiths and the Centaurs. The die of the attic platform carrying the quadriga is enriched with a relief in a panel by Christian Bernhard Rode.

Thus, although the Brandenburg Gate was widely admired, and thought to be a visible expression of the ideals of J. J. Winckelmann and his enthusiasm for Greek art, the axial arrangement on the Unter den Linden and the quadriga make this great building as akin to the Roman triumphal arch as to the Athenian Propylaeum.

Thomas Hope (1769-1831) saw the gate when he visited Berlin in 1794 during a business trip in relation to Flaxman: he described it as ''a superb town gate . . . imitated from the Propylaea,'' and when in 1804 Hope argued that the style for the new Downing College in Cambridge (1807-20) should be Greek, he also suggested that the Brandenburg Gate should be the model for the entrance to the college. William Wilkins (1778-1839), the architect of Downing, actually produced a design for a Propylaeum in 1806, but this was never realized. However, Thomas Harrison (1744-1829) built a Propylaeum at Chester Castle in 1811-13 which has a resemblance to Langhans' masterpiece.

The Brandenburg Gate was the first of several Doric gateways to be erected in Germany, and was an important prototype not only for the building type itself, but as a starting point for a style that was to be associated with a German national identity. Friedrich Weinbrenner's Ettlinger Tor at Karlsruhe (1803) is more ''primitive,'' and is unfluted Greek Doric, while Adolf von Vagedes' Ratinger Tor at Düsseldorf (1810) has two pure Greek Doric pavilions. The greatest gateway to be influenced by the type of the Brandenburg Gate is the Propyläen in the Königsplatz in Munich (1846-60) by Leo von Klenze, the first version of which (1817) has a massing very similar to Langhans' Brandenburg Gate, but the detail is pure Greek.

Langhans' gate has a long history as a symbol, first of national aspirations, then of resistance to Napoleon, then of victory after the wars of liberation and of hope in the future. So significant was the gate as an image of Prussian nationalism that Napoleon removed the quadriga to Paris in 1807, where it remained for the duration of the war. From the 1870s to 1945 it was a significant setting for many military parades associated with the might of Germany, and was the backdrop to the parade of the returning German army after the catastrophe of 1918. After 1945 it became a powerful object marking the divided city of Berlin, and in more recent times it has once more become a potent symbol, this time of unification and of the removal of barriers. In its two centuries of existence it has been many things, but it has always been a great work of architecture, in spite of its patchy "restoration" after war damage. It deserves better of the future.

—JAMES STEVENS CURL

GROSS-SIEDLUNG SIEMENSSTADT
Berlin, Germany

1929-32: Construction; **Architects:** Otto Bartning, Fred Forbat, Walter Gropius (1883-1969), Hugo Häring (1882-1958), and Hans Scharoun (1893-1972).

Publications

BAUER, CATHERINE: *Modern Housing.* Boston, 1934.
GROPIUS, WALTER: *The Scope of Total Architecture.* New York, 1970.
"Gross-Siedlung Siemensstadt." *Housing and Building* 3 (1931): 1-2.
KLEIHUES, JOSEF-PAUL: "Stations in the Architectural History of Berlin in the 20th Century." and "International Building Exhibition Berlin 1987." *Architecture and Urbanism* (special edition, May 1987).
LANE, BARBARA MILLER: *Architects and Politics in Germany 1918-1945.* Cambridge, Massachusetts, 1968.
MUELLER-WULKCOW, W.: *Wohnbauten und Siedlungen.* Koenigstein, 1928.
NERDINGER, WINFRIED: *Walter Gropius.* Berlin, 1985.
"Siemens-Stadt Industrial Suburb." *Architects' Journal* 74 (7 October 1931).
TAFURI, MANFREDO: "Para una crítica de la ideología arquitectónica." *Contraspazio* 1 (1969).
UNGERS, LISELOTTE: *Die Suche nach einer neuen Wohnform: Siedlungen der zwanziger Jahre damals und heute.* Stuttgart, 1983.

*

The Gross-Siedlung Siemensstadt, planned and built from 1929 to 1932 by the building cooperative for the workers at the Siemens industries, is one of the most significant housing complexes to result from reforms undertaken in Germany following late 19th-century unification. Furthermore, it manifests a normative or revolutionary approach to housing conceived by Walter Gropius and other members of the architectural avant-garde of the period between the two world wars. While it is not the purest example of functional-rationalist planning—as Gropius' Dammerstock in Karlsruhe (1928) or Ludwig Hilberseimer's 1930 proposal for Berlin-Friedrichstadt, for instance—Siemensstadt is the most important of the housing estates that respond to concerns of the "Neue Zeitgeist" within the context of an existing urban fabric with all its idiosyncrasies. Henry-Russell Hitchcock called Siemensstadt a "classic" example of the housing block, and for Barbara Miller Lane, "the refined designs they produced (at Siemensstadt) summarized the architectural achievement of the decade."

A law enacted in Prussia in 1868 legalized and regulated cooperative building societies. In 1918 the authorities passed a new housing law, decreeing "the right of every citizen to a sound dwelling within his means," establishing a state fund to finance housing built by the cooperative societies (*gemeinnützige Baugessellschaften*), and requiring that local and regional authorities (WFG: *Wohnungsfürsorgegesellschaften*) regulate and supervise its construction. Following the formation of the Weimar Republic after the 1918 revolution, the new constitution incorporated this legislation. After 1924, a 15 percent tax on rents (*Hauszinssteuer*) was levied to fund the loan program for the construction of new housing. By 1931, some 146,000 dwelling units were built in Berlin under this program, including such other famous housing estates as Bruno Taut and Martin Wagner's Gross-Siedlung Britz (the *Hufeisensiedlung* or "horseshoe estate" also called Taut-Siedlung) and Waldsiedlung (forest estate) Zehlendorf or Onkel-Toms-Hütte (named after the adjacent subway station), both constructed wholly or partly by the largest of the cooperative building societies, the GEHAG. The program accounted for about 75 percent of all housing built in Berlin during the 1920s.

The cooperative building society of the Siemens concern was established in 1914 and built a first housing complex. In 1929 the city government allocated funds for an "additional building program" to finance two large housing estates through funds collected with the *Hauszinssteuer*. One was Weiße Stadt in Berlin-Reinickendorf, designed by Otto Salvisberg and others, and the second Siemensstadt in Berlin-Charlottenburg-Nord.

Planning of the Gross-Siedlung Siemensstadt began early that year when the building society, Gemeinnützige Baugesellschaft Berlin-Heerstrasse, was commissioned to construct the second phase of the estate. The construction company had contracted Paul Mebes and Paul Emmerich, responsible for other housing estates in the city, to prepare a master plan. Martin Wagner, the city architect (*Stadtbaurat*), who performed an excellent role as coordinator of all housing efforts, then recommended Hans Scharoun, Walter Gropius, Hugo Häring, Fred Forbat and Otto Bartning as architects. During their first meeting, the architects chose Scharoun's proposal for the final site plan. The layout included a long building along the principal east-west street as shield to the elevated railway, parallel rows facing east-west to the north, and "a funnel-shaped form would be developed along the existing roads" (Nerdinger). Construction began in July 1929, and was completed in 1932. The program for the four- and five-story structures included a total of 1678 dwelling units—1,425 with two to two-and-a-half rooms, 124 with one to one-and-a-half, and 111 larger (three and three-and-a-half rooms) units, as well as 11 convenience stores (some in one-story structures), five offices, a central laundry and an elementary school.

It was Mebes and Emmerich who originally laid out the complex, and Scharoun who coordinated the site layout, but it was the theories espoused by Gropius which determined its form. Until then, new housing estates were influenced by the

Gross-Siedlung Siemensstadt: Berlin, Germany, 1929-32

Gross-Siedlung Siemensstadt

garden cities movement and were organized either in curvilinear or irregular blocks. In the urban areas, the approach was to enclose large courtyards in superblocks, as one finds in H. P. Berlage's planning for Amsterdam-Zuid or in the Viennese superblocks such as the Karl-Marx-Hof. These were the models for the Hufeisensiedlung and Waldsiedlung. In contrast to these were the proposals by Gropius and others which called for a radical departure from the traditional nature of the urban block. Gropius promoted a rational objectivity for the design of housing which he would later formalize: "The problem of the minimum dwelling is that of establishing the elementary minimum of space, air, light and heat required by man . . . i.e., a minimum *modus vivendi* in place of a *modus non moriendi*" (Gropius, *Scope,* p. 98). In Gropius' mind, this meant *Zeilenbau,* parallel rows of housing slabs which permit equal orientation for all units, preferably to the east and west, to take advantage of sunlight and ventilation. He explored their application according to various combinations of separation between blocks and height of the buildings to argue their viability. By orienting the structures in this manner, the bedrooms and bathrooms of the units would receive morning sun, and the living spaces sun in the afternoon. While one can correctly fault the logic of this proposition, such a diagrammatic approach became widely accepted, as one finds in housing projects around the world.

At Siemensstadt, the housing generally corresponds with the *Zeilenbau* ideal, particularly the slabs by Häring, Forbat and two of those by Gropius. On the other hand, Bartning's long, curving slab along Goebelstrasse and the connecting piece by Gropius across the street, while they do respond to standard functional-rationalist requirements, do so in a less rigid manner. Bartning's is a series of entries with stairs giving access to two

dwellings per floor, and so it does have its living rooms facing north to the street side with the bedrooms receiving southern exposure, while Gropius managed to retain the rigid functionalist diagram by using open corridors for access to the units and facing all the principal spaces to the south. The buildings by Scharoun to the south of the elevated railroad line are more idiosyncratic, as they funnel one into the complex along Jungfernheide Weg. Their orientation, while generally east-west, allows for a greater diversity of orientation and views.

Most of the buildings have point access and two flats per floor with typical layouts, which—in keeping with the modest nature of social housing—are rather minimal. Only one of the buildings by Gropius varies from this. The two segments facing Jungfernheide Weg contain units of two-and-a-half and three-and-a-half rooms. These units separate each function into specific rooms, with the living room at the end of the entry hall. Because of the location of these two buildings, their plans are disparate, so that the living and sleeping spaces could be oriented according to the functionalist principles: the block east of Jungfernheide Weg has the stairwell and entry on the same side as the living room and kitchen, with the bedrooms and bathroom facing the interior garden; the companion block has the stairwell on the same side of two of the bedrooms and the bathroom. The third structure by Gropius, along Goebelstrasse, is the one with flats accessible from an open hall. These are smaller two-room units, each of 43 square meters (463 square feet) each. Their entrance leads one between the service spaces—bathroom and kitchen—into the main living area, from which one enters the bedroom. The balcony is accessible from the living room. The larger units by Fred Forbat are 51.4 square meters (553 square feet). The architect used two unit sizes per floor to permit some differentiation. Scharoun similarly designed interlocking unit plans for the three-room units, resulting in more interesting building plans, since this allows for the alternate location of the stairwells. His two-room units follow a more conventional layout. In all cases, each apartment has a private balcony. The commercial spaces are located at the corners, where the geometric shift enhances their visibility, further reinforced originally by the signs which formed part of their minimal decorations.

Although one initially gets the impression that the complex is one of a "white architecture," this is not the case. The architecture at Siemensstadt did and does use some color, particularly with Häring and Forbat's use of masonry in their blocks. Even Gropius used masonry for decorative purposes in his blocks, which led Adolf Behne to write critically at the time of their completion that "Gropius' attempt in Siemensstadt to make the pillars separating the windows and adjoining apartments disappear by encasing them in back stone (on) an otherwise snow-white wall . . . [seems] to be a forced solution which, unfortunately does not enlarge the living space" (quoted in Nerdinger). These facades are well articulated, some by the rhythmic alternation of solids and voids, others by use of projecting balconies or overhangs. In the blocks by Gropius, facades are articulated by "the protruding or receding staircases, balconies, and glass loggias" (Nerdinger).

Some of the buildings have elicited accurately descriptive pseudonyms. Scharoun's are "*Panzerkreuzer*" (armored cruisers) with gondola balconies, while Bartning's is a "*Langer Jammer*" (long lamentation). Moreover, the housing estate illustrates a tendency counter to the norms of modernism. As Manfredo Tafuri observes "It is incredible that contemporary history hasn't recognized in Berlin's famous Siemensstadt, planned by Scharoun, the historical knot in which one finds one of the largest breaks to the soul of the 'Modern Movement.' " Tafuri further argues this in discussing the characteristics of the specific segments: "Counter to Gropius and Bartning, who remain faithful to the concept of the Siedlung as a chain assemblage . . . [and to] the 'destruction of the aura' traditionally associated with the architectural 'piece,' the 'objects' by Scharoun and Häring tend, on the contrary, to recuperate an 'aura. . . .' '' That observation is similar to one made by Josef-Paul Kleihues: ''The architecture, particularly in the parts designed by Scharoun, Gropius and Häring, reflected a differentiated interpretation of the New Objectivity; the temperament and theoretical demands of these three protagonists of the New Building movement can be distinguished in a wealth of nuances.''

While ignoring the segments of the complex which did not fit her analysis of Siemensstadt's *Zeilenbau* layout, the critic Catherine Bauer wrote in 1934, ''The open space 'flows' around the buildings, and yet the whole is urbane and orderly. . . . There is nothing 'pretty' or 'picturesque' about it, but it can be very handsome—in a way which has seldom been achieved since those two words became terms of architectural approbation.'' The Gross-Siedlung Siemensstadt certainly is a handsome complex. The diversities in building details make palatable the repetitive nature of the *Zeilenbau* layout; with time, the greenery has softened its edges.

—GERARDO BROWN-MANRIQUE

IBA
Berlin, Germany

1984-87.

Publications

''Architecture in Progress; Internationale Bauausstellung Berlin 1984.'' (Issue) *Architectural Design* 53, 1/2 (January/February 1983).

BAUAUSSTELLUNG BERLIN GMBH: *South Friedrichstadt as a Place to Live and Work: International Restricted Competition Kochstrasse/Friedrichstrasse.* Berlin, 1980.

''Berlin as a Model—IBA 1984.'' *Architectural Review* 176, 1051 (special issue, September 1984).

BROWN-MANRIQUE, GERADO: ''The White House.'' *Progressive Architecture* 63, 10 (October 1982): 90-93.

CLELLAND, D.: ''West Berlin 1984; The Milestone & the Millstone.'' *Architectural Review* 176, 1051 (September, 1984) pp. 19-24.

CROSSET, P.-A.: ''Hans Kollhoff a Arthur Ovaska; Abitazioni popolar a Berlino.'' *Casabella* 50, 522 (March 1986): 4-12.

DAL CO, FRANCESCO: ''Where Things Start: The Wissenschaftszentrum in Berlin by Stirling and Wolford.'' *Lotus International* 58, 2 (1988): 30-35.

DE MICHELIS, M.: ''The Myth of the Phoenix; The Case of the IBA 1984, Berlin.'' *Lotus International* 33, 4 (1981): 4-19.

DIETSCH, DEBORAH K.: ''Americans in Berlin.'' *Architectural Record* 177, 8 (July 1989): 82-94.

DOUBILET, S.: ''IBA '84: Exhibition/Collection.'' *Progressive Architecture* 63, 10 (October 1982): 204.

FRAMPTON, K. and BERKE, D.: *Rob Krier: Urban Projects 1968-1982* (IAUS Catalogue 5). New York, 1982.

FRIEBEL, K. (ed.): *Experiment Wohnen—Konzenta Ritterstrasse.* Berlin, 1981.

INTERNATIONAL BAUAUSSTELLUNG BERLIN: *Step by Step: Careful Urban Renewal in Kreuzberg, Berlin—Internationale Bauausstellung Berlin 1987* (Exhibition catalog). Berlin, 1987.

INTERNATIONAL BAUAUSSTELLUNG BERLIN '84 '87: *Projektübersicht: Stadterneuerung und Stadtneubau: Stand Oktober '82.* Berlin, 1982.

''International Building Exhibition Berlin 1987.'' *Architecture † Urbanism* (special issue, May 1987).

KLEIHUES, JOSEF-PAUL, and KLOTZ, HEINRICH (eds.): *Internationale Bauausstellung Berlin 1987: Beispiele einer neuen Architektur.* Stuttgart, 1986. English edition, *International Building Exhibition Berlin 1987: Examples of a New Architecture.* New York, 1987.

KREIS, W.; SCHAAD, U. and SCHAAD, P.: ''Double-faced Building; Residence on Lindenstrasse in Berlin.'' *Lotus International* 48/49, 4/1 (1985-86): 74-82.

KRIER, R. et al.: ''Ritterstrasse Housing.'' *Lotus International* 41, 1 (1984): 30-41.

KRIER, R.: ''City Divided into Building Plots; Dwelling on the Ritterstrasse, Berlin, South Friedrichstadt (1977)-1980.'' *Lotus International* 28, 3 (1980): 74-82.

KRIER, R.: ''South Friedrichstadt; Scheme for an Ideal Project for the Friedrichstadt Zone.'' *Lotus International* 28, 3 (1980): 66-73.

LAMPUGNANI, V. M.: ''How to Put a Contradiction into Effect.'' *Architectural Review* 176, 1051 (September 1984): 25-27.

SENATOR FÜR BAU UND WOHNUNGSWESSEN (ed.): *Leitfaden: Projekte Daten Geschichte: Berichtsjahr 1984.* Berlin, 1984.

Stadt: Monatshefte für Wohnungs-und Städtebau 8 (August 1982): 16-83, 99-100.

STIRLING, JAMES: ''Opening Speech.'' *Lotus International* 58, 2 (1988): 36-37.

*

The Internationale Bauausstellung Berlin (or IBA, the International Building Exhibition) of 1984-87, with the theme of ''Wohnen in der Innenstadt'' (the inner city as a place to live), represents a significant and cohesive use of a building exhibition as a vehicle for positively affecting urban development. While in the tradition of the ''new-spirit'' building exhibitions and model housing estates of the period between the world wars, the very deliberate process initiated by the organizers of the IBA marks a significant departure from those examples by not constructing idealized efforts, as in the earlier housing exhibitions. By addressing concrete issues of housing and urban design, the IBA provides viable alternatives to the predictable process of demolition and new construction devoid of any historical relationships.

In 1979 the Berlin House of Deputies passed an act creating the organizing entity Bauausstellung Berlin GmbH. This action was influenced by activities in the architectural community of Berlin, including symposia organized by the IDZ Berlin (International Design Center), investigations by the IDZ and Cornell University's Berlin Summer Academy on the urban villa and the urban garden, and especially the series ''Models for a City'' appearing between January and August 1977 in the *Berliner Morgenpost.* The newspaper essays, by its editor, Wolf Jobst Siedler, with architect Josef-Paul Kleihues (the eventual codirector of the planning organization), were ideologically

IBA Exhibition: Berlin, Germany, 1984-87

counter to the orthodoxy of functionalist modernism of postwar planning and housing construction. Modernism assumes a *tabula rasa* for all new construction (and no reconstruction). The bases for the new direction are the theoretical propositions of Aldo Rossi, Oswald Mathias Ungers and others of the postwar generation who called for an architecture based on a *genius loci*.

In its role as organizer of the exhibition, the Bauausstellung Berlin GmbH acted as recommending body to city building authorities, identifying sites, selecting architects, then negotiating with the client-developers in order to construct the various projects. The existing minimum space standards, federal subsidy formulas for public and publicly-assisted housing, and conventional financing of market-rate housing constrained the breadth of its program. The IBA was originally scheduled to take place in 1984. Political changes in the city administration, difficulties with developers and other delays forced its rescheduling for 1987, coinciding with the 750th anniversary of the founding of the city.

By considering the whole city as the exhibition site, the IBA was to reweave the urban fabric, to combine new construction under the direction of Kleihues with "careful" renovation and reconstruction directed by Hardt-Waltherr Hämer, and to incorporate community and other facilities within its scope. In short, the IBA was to present "exemplary architecture in the ruined and divided city which is both human and of high artistic quality and provides an alternative to the recognized deficits of modern urban development" (*Step by Step*). For the IBA, "new construction" meant "critical reconstruction" by reevaluating the historical structure of the city vis-à-vis the Modern Movement, and by integrating new projects while addressing new formal concerns and technological needs in housing.

The new construction projects are concentrated in four areas of Berlin: Tegel, Prager Platz, southern area of the Tiergarten, and Südfriedrichstadt. The IBA focused its renovation projects in the Luisenstadt and SO 36 areas of Kreuzberg, restructuring those areas across the former frontier. Their designers were selected through competitions—either closed (invited) or open, and regional, national or international in scope to guarantee a diversity in approaches. The IBA normally awarded the overall design to the first-prize winner, with the other place winners also developing segments of the project. So while the cast of characters was a veritable constellation of nascent and established designers in the contemporary architectural firmament (about 200 designers in all), theirs was a vision guided by one spirit. At the same time, and consistent with West Berlin's role from occupation until 1989 (vis-à-vis the rest of the historic city), there were underlying political motives for the overall program: "It is no coincidence that the most important IBA areas lie directly on the inner-city border, along the Wall" (*Step by Step*).

The Tegel area of Berlin is quite remote from what was the social and economic center of the western half of the divided city. There the task was to redesign the harbor basin with a mixture of housing and community facilities, while also addressing the needs for water decontamination. Moore-Ruble-Yudell (MRY) designed the principal project based on a city landscape. In contrast to the nonwinning "small town on the water" proposal by Leon Krier with its "recollections of ancient cities," Charles Moore and team created a complex which, like a pearl necklace, bends and adjusts to its site. It "achieves the small-scale cohesiveness of a village, offering lessons that are as relevant to market-rate condominiums as public housing" (Dietsch, p. 84). The site plan reflects a decidedly American perspective: housing separated from community facilities. The buildings vary from MRY's serpentine castle complex, to row housing by the Berlin firms of Poly-Steinebach-Weber (PSW)

and Bangert-Jansen-Scholz-Schultes (BJSS), and urban villas by MRY, PSW, Antoine Grumbach, Paolo Portoghesi, Robert Stern, Stanley Tigerman and John Hejduk. The blocks by MRY and the villas by Tigerman and Stern use historicist-picturesque palettes, while those by Hejduk, Grumbach, PSW and BJSS are abstract representations. The success of the harbor project is due to its site and the manner in which the architects handled the water's edge. Other projects in Tegel include a phosphorous elimination plant by Gustav Peichl and additional housing. In Prager Platz, the smallest of the IBA sites, the interventions are more subtle. The master plan, by Gottfried Böhm, follows recommendations made earlier by Rob Krier and Carlo Aymonino as part of the *Morgenpost* articles. The buildings by Böhm, Krier and Aymonino recreate the historic form of the plaza, yet each structure responds in its own unique manner.

It is in the southern Tiergarten and in Südfriedrichstadt that one finds the greatest concentration of IBA projects, where the IBA's vision for reweaving the urban fabric permits analysis. The southern edge of the Tiergarten was once a diplomatic quarter. Now Hans Scharoun's Philharmonie, music museum and city library, as well as Ludwig Mies van der Rohe's New National Gallery and Walter Gropius/TAC's Bauhaus Archives are located there. The IBA projects north of the Landwehrkanal include Hans Hollein's "Kulturforum," which integrates the institutions already mentioned, James Stirling's Wissenschaftszentrum and the Rauchstrasse urban villas adjacent to the former Norwegian embassy. Rob Krier, as winner of the competition, designed the Rauchstrasse master plan and three of the houses. Others are by Brenner Tonon, Aldo Rossi, Nielebock and Partner, Giorgio Grassi, Hermann and Valentiny, and Hans Hollein. The plan uses Rossi's building to balance the former embassy on the western edge, and Krier's connected villas, forming a gateway through its conch-like element, on the eastern side.

The success of the complex is due to the development of the villas as detached multifamily housing, with a central common space shared by the units. Overall the new villas are in keeping with the memory of the site, yet there are some strange bedfellows, for instance Hollein's villa and the adjacent one by Hermann and Valentiny. Nearby is Stirling's piecemeal complex, which, according to Francesco Dal Co, "goes beyond all reasonable expectations and stands as one of the most cryptic of all the British architects' realizations" (*Lotus International*). A larger number of IBA projects are found to the south of the canal. These include Ungers' U-shaped block, which shelters three introverted little tower houses and faces Lützowplatz; Vittorio Gregotti's crisp gateway building on Lützowstrasse with its mews of row houses; the block facing Ungers' Lützowplatz project; the five passive-solar housing towers; and a number of infill blocks along Pohlstrasse and Kurfürstenstrasse.

In the Südfriedrichstadt area, the IBA coordinated its many projects, thus providing a new structure to this once heavily damaged neighborhood. The influence of Rob Krier's dream plan of 1977 is evident particularly in the blocks bound by Oranienstrasse and Lindenstrasse, from Eric Mendelsohn's 1929 building for the Metal Workers Union north to the former Wall. So too are Ungers' proposals of the same year, especially along Friedrichstrasse west to the site of the former Anhalter Bahnhof. The diversity of projects on these sites is impressive. The list of architects with buildings includes Rob Krier, Mathias Ungers, Aldo Rossi, Martorell-Bohigas-Mackay, Rem Koolhaas, Peter Eisenman, John Hejduk, Arata Isozaki and Herman Hertzberger.

Typical of the IBA solutions are the Schinkelplatz complex (the initial IBA effort) and the housing near the Berlin Museum. These two present alternative methods for completing similar blocks. While in Schinkelplatz Rob Krier defined the central square and organized perimeter blocks to reflect the hierarchical differences between bordering streets, Hans Kollhoff (with Arthur Ovaska) divided the site adjacent to the Berlin Museum into segments with their own character. Krier achieved unity at Schinkelplatz by restricting the facade materials and cornice line levels; the segments complement each other, and the inner courtyards work well. Near the Berlin Museum, there is some coordination between components. Kollhoff completed the Victoria Block with perimeter slabs, and defined the site adjacent to the museum with buildings like two bookends holding urban villas in between. Kollhoff's well-conceived and detailed slab is of note, with its variation of a fixed theme according to the location of the segment, including the center one reminiscent of Otto Salvisberg's Weissestadt bridge-building. Less impressive is Isozaki's flamboyant freestanding palazzetto in the Victoria Block's inner court.

The many projects built by the IBA are among the most important international designs of the 1980s. Though some segments of the new constructions still reflect an approach reminiscent of the housing exhibitions of the period between the wars, where the projects were isolated objects of desire, there are truly outstanding parts. Such are the series of projects along Lindenstrasse in Südfriedrichstadt, where the vision of the IBA was for urban blocks, or the urban villas on Rauchstrasse. One can except the projects in the Südfriedrichstadt area to become the models for new development in the rest of Friedrichstadt, while the urban villas provide viable alternatives to this form of development. In the renovations' area, the IBA and its "twelve principles of 'cautious urban renewal' " present a formal structure for a more humane approach for dealing with housing, one which relies on the participation of all involved parties, and on the preservation of the existing structures. These tasks of the IBA are now being carried out by its successor, S.T.E.R.N. GmbH. In the international arena, the program of the IBA provides a model approach for dealing with large-scale renovation. While it may be impossible to replicate the ambitious competition program carried out by the IBA's organizers, the Internationale Bauausstellung's model for inserting new development critically sympathetic to the nature of the historic city ought to be followed, and indeed one sees its influence on Barcelona's preparations for the 1992 Olympic Games, for instance.

Though the program has not been immune to vocal and certainly appropriate criticism, the very broad and coordinated effort of the IBA did reach heroic proportions in trying to redirect the future of the city that was West Berlin. In approaching housing in this manner, housing as theme and building type is an appropriate one for exhibition. One sees its impact in the results: these housing efforts do affect and coordinate the future development of the city. The results in some ways reflect Berlin's split personality, between what had been and what might become: armed with maps which showed the city in two fragmentary moments of its history, the architects for the various IBA interventions proceeded with similar visions to reinvent the city of the past. This is not said disparagingly, as these are for the most part applaudable results.

But in hindsight, there is another reality by which to judge the Internationale Bauausstellung. After a dozen years of planning, construction and completion, what had been proposals placed against the backdrop of a concrete ribbon separating the western half from the rest of historic Berlin now indicate either literally how to bring together fragments of a city developed away from each other and in spite of their history, or how to reinforce the differentiation between its two parts. With reunion, the IBA program will affect the efforts of reconstructing a once-again new Berlin.

—GERARDO BROWN-MANRIQUE

NEUE WACHE
Berlin, Germany

1816-18. Architect: Karl Friedrich Schinkel (1781-1841). **1822:** Statues of Generals Scharnhorst and Bülow added to each side of the Guardhouse; **Artist:** Christian Rauch. **1930-31:** Interior remodeled; **Architect:** Heinrich Tessenow (1876-1950). **1933-45:** Extensive damage in World War II.

Publications

DRONKE, WOLFGANG: "Die Neue Wache in Berlin." Dissertation. Technische Hochschule, Berlin-Charlottenburg, 1931. (Excerpt published in *Zeitschrift für Bauwesen* 81 (1931): 44-52.)

FORSSMAN, ERIK: *Karl Friedrich Schinkel: Bauwerke und Baugedanken.* Munich, 1981.

LEMMER, KLAUS J. (ed.): *Karl Friedrich Schinkel: Berlin, Bauten und Entwürfe.* Berlin, 1973.

RAVE, PAUL ORTWIN, and KUHN, MARGARETE (eds.): *Karl Friedrich Schinkel: Lebenswerk.* 14 vols. Berlin, 1939-68.

WATKIN, DAVID, and MELLINGHOFF, TILMAN: *German Architecture and the Classical Ideal 1740-1840.* London and Cambridge, Massachusetts, 1987.

*

Few buildings can be as memorable yet so simple as the Hauptor Königswache (High or Royal Guardhouse), also known as the Neue Wache (New Guardhouse) on the Unter den Linden in Berlin. It was designed in 1816 and erected in 1817-18 to designs by the great Karl Friedrich Schinkel (1781-1841): it is a significant structure that signals the start of a new phase of Prussian neoclassicism at the hands of a master. Schinkel sought an architectural expression worthy of the highest ideals of the intelligentsia in a country that had been victorious in the wars of liberation against the French, yet had had to face economic depression and austerity because of the war effort. It must be remembered that Berlin itself had been occupied for some time by French troops, and that the Prussian royal family had had to retire to Königsberg during that occupation. The nation had been humiliated, had endured privations, yet had emerged with a new sense of national pride and dignity out of suffering.

Schinkel's plan for the new guardhouse incorporated four massive corner pylons or towers, and the roughly square shape of the plan held between those pylons was subdivided asymmetrically, with an internal rectangular courtyard placed off-center, in spite of the rigidly symmetrical appearance of the exterior. Accommodation included a sentry room, an officers' room, a detention room and utility rooms. A staircase at the rear of the building gave access to the upper floor. As with all Schinkel's buildings, the Neue Wache is most sensitively sited, anchored to the avenue and to its enormous neighbors by means of trees and sculpture. In spite of its size (it is quite a small building), its stands up well to the Baroque Zeughaus beside it: in fact the Neue Wache has a personality that belies its dimensions, and its architect gave it a presence of enormous power, enhanced by the blank walls of its pylons and by the simplified Doric of its portico. The pylons help to form a frame for the portico, and give it an enhanced scale necessary to enable the building to relate to its huge neighbors without being dwarfed.

An earlier version of the front elevation (the plan was the

Neue Wache: Berlin, Germany, 1816-18

same) had a simpler portico of six plain square columns without capitals, giving it an Egyptian air worthy of Queen Hatshepsut's mortuary temple itself. Above each column was the head of a warrior in a *clypeus,* or ornamental circular shield, to suggest the ends of stone beams at right angles to the front leading into the interior. Over the frieze was a low plain pediment, and on top of the corner towers or pylons were oversized trophies, giving the building a primitivist appearance worthy of the best of neoclassical designs of the period. The whole effect was to be stark, simple, and suggestive of the purpose of the building. This was *architecture parlante.*

Schinkel saw his design as loosely fashioned after a Roman *castrum,* which is why he included the corner towers and the inner courtyard. The idea of the *castrum,* of course, would suggest the military, the camp, the guard. The courtyard was also intended to conceal the utility and service rooms from the area around the building, and served to receive water from the roof and to conduct it directly to the covered canal underneath. The external simplicity of the guardhouse was enhanced by the fact of the roofs being hidden and discharging into the court.

However, as built, the guardhouse acquired a prostyle hexa-style Greek Doric portico on three steps, and the trophies on top of the pylon-towers were omitted. Greek Doric was selected because Heinrich Gentz (1766-1811), architect and theoretician, had suggested in his *Elementarbuch* (1803) that this order was apposite for military buildings: its strength, dignity and severity were easily read and understood, and so the order helped to identify the building and its purpose. This identification of Doric with strength, of course, is a Masonic idea, and it is not surprising it is so overtly suggested in a state where the ruling house was long associated with Freemasonry.

Schinkel's Doric order for the portico (erected of Saxon sandstone) is unusual and original, for this architect of genius was no mere copyist. Triglyphs and metopes are omitted, but over the centerlines of columns and antae are winged goddesses of victory carrying wreaths, garlands and palm fronds. Beneath the taenia is a continuous line of guttae, while at the top of the frieze is a continuous Greek key pattern. In the pediment the tympanum has relief sculpture of fine quality representing a battle: the goddess of victory is deciding for the hero fighting on the right-hand side, while on the left are the last effort, the call to arms, flight, pillage, and the anguish of a family awaiting its fate. On the extreme right are mourners and a fallen hero.

The Neue Wache was cunningly sited diagonally across the Unter den Linden from the Kronprinzenpalais (where the king preferred to live rather than in the enormous Schloss), and almost opposite Georg Wenzeslaus von Knobelsdorff's Opera House, while on either side of the guardhouse were placed, in 1822, statues of Generals Scharnhorst and Bülow by Christian Rauch. The subtle relationships of Kronprinzenpalais, Opera House, Zeughaus, statues and trees can only really be appreciated by close study of the plan of the whole area, for the entire ensemble is a brilliant piece of urban design.

In 1930-31 Heinrich Tessenow (1876-1950) remodeled the interior of the Neue Wache as a memorial to Germany's war dead, a task he handled with extraordinary sensitivity and refinement of touch. A further metamorphosis occurred after the catastrophe of 1933-45 when the little building, having been badly damaged, became a shrine to the victims of "Fascism," and goose-stepping guards could still be seen there in 1989. Of Schinkel's interiors, of course, nothing remains.

—JAMES STEVENS CURL

COLOGNE CATHEDRAL
Cologne, Germany

1248: Construction begun. **1388:** Nave completed. **1824-80:** Completed according to original plans; **Supervising Architects:** F. A. Ahlert (1755-1833); Ernst Zwirner (1802-61); R. Voigtel (1829-1902).

Publications

BORGER, H. (ed.): *Der Kölner Dom im Jahrhundert seiner Vollendung.* 3 vols. Cologne, 1980.

CLEMEN, P.: *Der Dom zu Köln.* Düsseldorf, 1937.

PINDER, WILHELM: *Deutsche Dome des Mittelalters.* Königstein im Taunus (1955).

VOGTS, H. (ed.): *Der Kölner Dom: Festschrift zur Siebenhundertjahrfeier 1248-1948 des Zentral-Dombau-Vereins.* Cologne, 1948.

WOLFF, A.: *Der Kölner Dom.* Cologne, 1989.

*

Cologne Cathedral—housing the relics of the three Holy Kings that ensured its role as an imperial cathedral—was planned to

Cologne Cathedral, from southeast: Cologne, Germany, 1248

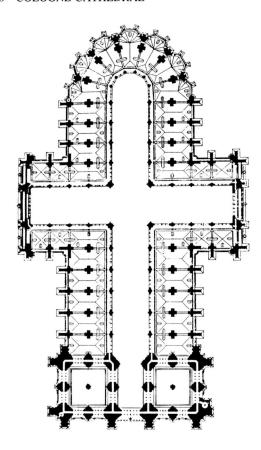

become the largest Gothic cathedral, thereby surpassing anything that had been achieved up to that time in French architecture. These pretensions account for its long construction period, which reached from the mid-13th to the mid-16th century, to be completed, finally only from 1842 to 1880.

Initiator of the project was Archbishop Conrad of Hochstaden (1238-61), who—as archchancellor of the Holy Roman Empire—exercised an important influence on contemporary politics. In particular, the end of the Staufen dynasty gave him the opportunity to have in 1247 and 1257, respectively, William of Holland and Richard of Cornwall elected as German emperors. The cathedral project, begun just before these events, was to demonstrate the importance of an elective system under the supervision of the church. This complex relationship between church, state and, finally, city became the leitmotif of the cathedral throughout its entire history of construction.

Replacing the pre-Romanesque cathedral in the northeastern corner of the Roman city of Cologne, the new ambulatory choir with radiating chapels and double aisles was begun in 1248. By 1265, its ground floor was completed and vaulted, and the inner choir closed by a temporary roof on the triforium level. The upper parts, begun after that and completed in about 1300 (consecrated in 1322), show an architectural style distinguished by its almost complete dissolution of the wall surface into tracery. In such refinements as the opening of the triforium, the design is clearly based on the Parisian court style of Louis IX, the saint, especially his Sainte-Chapelle. A possible importation of Parisian stonemasons would have been only part of a wider cultural exchange, most significant of which was the appointment of Albertus Magnus from the University of Paris to Cologne in the same year, 1248, when the cathedral project in Cologne was begun. Parisian in style, too, and related to the Sainte-Chapelle, are the statues of a *"sacra conversazione"*

between Christ, the Holy Virgin and the twelve apostles at the pillars of the choir. The stained-glass windows of the clerestory pronounce the royal aspect with a sequence of pairs of kings, centering on the adoration of the Three Kings in the axial window.

The building process of the choir was interrupted by class conflicts between archbishop and bourgeoisie, which manifested themselves in several uprisings, culminating in the Battle of Worringen in 1288 that put an end to ecclesiastical rule over Cologne. As an immediate reaction to that, the ambitious project of a double-towered western facade was begun, instead of the transepts and nave which normally would have followed. Of this facade only the massive south tower was built over four bays of the double aisles and completed up to the roof level of the nave, according to a plan that has survived. Developed out of a pattern of vertical buttresses and horizontal stringcourses, a rich architectural system was derived from the main motif of the choir clerestory: the quadripartite tracery window with integrated triforium, and crowned by a traceried gable. During the 15th century the double aisles of the nave were built, but only seven bays of the northern side were vaulted, still faithfully continuing the classical style of the mid-13th century.

As the first major Gothic building in Germany, Cologne Cathedral was to become the most important model for the reception of Gothic architecture outside France. Although entire copies, reduced in scale, remained rare (Utrecht, Altenberg), partial copying became important. The temporary state of the ground floor of the choir influenced the invention of the hall ambulatory choir (Verden, Nuremberg), the double aisles influenced the hall church type (Minden), the clerestory influenced the chapel-like choir (Aachen), and even the uncompleted towers found their followers (Freiburg). In the second half of the 14th century, the choir of Prague Cathedral in the imperial residence of Charles IV, built by Peter Parler from Cologne, transmitted the court style of a century earlier into a new Late Gothic system.

In 1560 the Reformation put an untimely end to the construction of Cologne Cathedral, making the idle crane on the stump of the tower a landmark of the city. The Counter-Reformation saw the revival of the Gothic style in the nearby Jesuits' Church (1618-89) and renewed interest in the completion of the cathedral, the plans of which were published in 1654 by the Jesuit historian H. Crombach. Aside from the introduction of stuccoed wooden vaults to the incomplete nave between 1748 and 1751, little of consequence was done in the 18th century. The cathedral reached the nadir of its fortunes when it was seized after the occupation by the French revolutionary army in 1794, secularized and converted into a warehouse.

Meanwhile, the cathedral was already exerting a fascination over German Romantics who were attracted by its scale and Gothic forms, but above all by the pathos of its ruined state. A fortuitous coincidence changed the cathedral's fate. After the defeat of Napoleon in 1815, the antiquarian Sulpiz Boisserée recovered and published the late-13th-century elevation drawing of the towers, showing them as they would be if completed. Boisserée's friend, Joseph von Görres, one of the promoters of the idea of the cathedral's completion, wanted it to become a symbol of a nationally united and democratic new Germany.

Responsibility for the cathedral, however, passed with the end of the Napoleonic Wars into different hands. The restoration of the Prussian monarchy, which annexed the Catholic Rhineland, created the preconditions for a restoration of the medieval building. From 1825 onward the choir was stabilized. Karl Friedrich Schinkel (1781-1841), head of the Prussian building office, began to plan the cathedral's completion; then politics once again made it the subject of attention, when political and

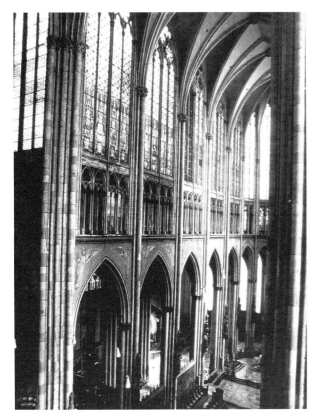

Cologne Cathedral, choir interior

as a structural element. The total of nine portals in the transepts and western facade gave the opportunity to create the most extensive sculptural program of the entire Gothic Revival.

Throughout the decades of construction the cathedral was the most influential model for the German Gothic Revival. Just as its building lodge had served as a school for Gothic architecture in the Middle Ages, so did Germany's most important neo-Gothic architects train in the revived lodge, including Vincenz Statz (Cologne) and Friedrich Schmidt (Vienna). Finally, after four decades of construction, the dedication of the cathedral was celebrated in September 1880, its completion coinciding with a German unity different from what Görres had predicted at the beginning of the century: the Prussian opposition in the Catholic Rhineland being suppressed and its spiritual leader, the archbishop, once again imprisoned.

The completion of the cathedral was not the end of its extended building history, as the worsening of environmental conditions necessitated larger repairs and the exchange of original substance since 1926. While the medieval city of Cologne was nearly completely destroyed in several air-raids between 1941 and 1945, the cathedral suffered severe damage. Nine of its vaults were brought to collapse, and one of the major buttresses of the western facade was destroyed; the degree of the destruction is still shown by a replacement in brick. The subsequent reconstruction copied faithfully the missing medieval parts, but worked more freely with the 19th-century sections, suppressing historicist details. Only since 1968, when the architecture of historicism began to be re-evaluated, has the same method of restoration been applied to all periods of the long construction history of the cathedral.

—HANS J. BÖKER AND MICHAEL J. LEWIS

religious conflict divided the province in the late 1830s. At the climax, the archbishop was arrested by the Prussians. Then, in 1840, as a conciliatory gesture to his Rhenish subjects, and at the same time to create a symbol for the now-conservative national movement headed by Prussia, King Friedrich Wilhelm IV offered to assist in the completion of the cathedral. Construction began in 1842, interrupted by the suppressed 1848 revolution, and was funded in part by Prussia but controlled more directly by the Rhineland, where a vigorous and active network of *Dombauvereine,* or cathedral building societies, raised money, publicized the building campaign and advised on architectural matters.

The two principal figures behind the completion of the cathedral were the architect Ernst Zwirner (1802-61) and the Rhenish jurist and architectural theorist August Reichensperger (1808-95). The latter, in particular, helped establish the *Dombauvereine*'s building policy, pleading for strict fidelity to the original design where possible, but otherwise arguing for bold and creative extrapolation from medieval precedent. Reichensperger was frequently defeated in his call for medieval orthodoxy, losing the battles to build the roof trusses in wood rather than iron, against the more progressive engineers and their idea of a ''future Gothic,'' and to prevent the demolition of parts of the sacristy (mistakenly thought to be a much later addition). Those defeats notwithstanding, Reichensperger and the *Dombauvereine* acted as conscience to the most scrupulous standards of medieval scholarship, expressing the more conservative attitude of the post-1848 restoration.

Among the finest architectural achievements of Zwirner's design are the two transept facades, for which there was little medieval evidence. Instead these facades took as their point of departure the basic arch-and-gable motif of the western facade, enlarging and isolating it in characteristic 19th-century fashion

WERKBUND EXHIBITION, 1914
Cologne, Germany

1914: Glass Pavilion constructed; **Architect:** Bruno Taut (1880-1938). **1914:** Model Factory constructed; **Architects:** Walter Gropius (1883-1969), Adolf Meyer (1881-1929). **1914:** Model Theatre; **Architect:** Henry van de Velde (1863-1957).

Publications

BURCKHARDT, LUCIUS (ed.): *The Werkbund: History and Ideology.* Woodbury, New York, 1977.

CAMPBELL, JOAN: *The German Werkbund—The Politics of Reform in the Applied Arts.* Princeton, New Jersey, 1978.

CUSTOZA, S.; VOGLIAZZO, M.; and POSENER, J.: *Muthesius.* Milan, 1981.

ECKSTEIN, H. (ed.): *50 Jahre Deutscher Werkbund.* Frankfurt and Berlin, 1958.

FRAMPTON, KENNETH, and FUTAGAWA, YUKIO: *Modern Architecture: 1851-1919.* New York, 1983.

MUTHESIUS, H.; NAUMANN, F.; et al.: *Der Werkbund-Gedanke in den germanischen Ländern.* Jena (1914).

NAUMANN, F.: ''Werkbund und Handel.'' *Jahrbuch des Deutschen Werkbundes* (1913).

POSENER, JULIUS (ed.): *Anfänge des Funktionalismus. Von Arts and Crafts zum Deutschen Werkbund.* Berlin, 1964.

RICHARDSON, MARGARET: *The Craft Architects.* London and New York, 1983.

Werkbund Exhibition: Cologne, Germany, 1914

TAUT, BRUNO: *Glashaus: Werkbundausstellung Köln.* Cologne (1914).

∗

Throughout history, exhibitions have been used to introduce new developments to the general public. After the middle of the 19th century, during the period of the industrial revolution, industry and its emerging developments became the center of such exhibitions. Exhibition buildings took on the role of cathedrals of earlier centuries. They changed their form and content with the ongoing development of industrial production and inventions. Such exhibitions and their buildings became a platform to celebrate the comparison of products of different countries, with the purpose of increasing trade and overall industrial standards.

Important exhibitions, such as the one in London (1851), featuring the Crystal Palace, and the exhibition in Paris (1889) with its Eiffel Tower, were important events which announced a change in the meaning and understanding of the complete confidence in an ever-increasing industrial production. From then on, industrial exhibitions seemed to pay less intention to their outward appearances. They were directed toward and focused on the incorporation and adjustment of the machine into the life of contemporary society. That development resulted in 1907 in the founding of the German Werkbund. The founding members included industrial leaders, architects, artists, craftsmen and their spokesmen, whose goal was higher standards in the development and design of manufactured goods through collaboration between their respective groups. The Werkbund sought to educate the general public through exhibitions in which practical, physical examples introduced new developments.

The 1914 Werkbund Exhibition in Cologne, even though interrupted by the outbreak of World War I, was one of the highlights of that attempt, featuring several unique building structures. The exhibition reflected the work of entirely different generations of architects, both of which shared the desire to overcome the architecture of the 19th century and its negative implications. The Werkbund brought together all creative sources in Germany. The older generation of architects such as Theodor Fischer (1862-1938), who together with Freiherr von Schmidt designed the main building, and Henry van de Velde

(1863-1957), who built the Werkbund Theater with its tripartite stage, clearly played a more important role than the second, revolutionary generation of architects such as Bruno Taut (1880-1938). Besides the theater by van de Velde and the exhibition hall by Peter Behrens (1868-1940), the Austrian Pavilion with its temple-like facade designed by Josef Hoffmann (1870-1956) represented the transition between an architecture of the past and the still-undefined potential of the coming decades. The Austrian Pavilion was the only structure at the Werkbund Exhibition erected by a foreign nation, and was understood to be the contribution of and to the friendly Austrian Werkbund members. This pavilion, also known as the "Österreichische Haus," was based on a simple rectangular footprint and developed as a clearly defined volume with its facades loosened up through a dense row of simple, grilled columns. The building also contained the special section of the Bohemian Werkbund, articles of the different areas of the Arts and Crafts movement in Austria.

Hoffmann's, Behrens' and van de Velde's buildings were still built and defined in the ponderous fashion of the 19th century. That approach toward built form in general and toward structure and materials in particular was very different from the approach of the younger generation of architects, who tried to make buildings transparent and to overcome their all-too-apparent heaviness. Architects such as Walter Gropius (1883-1969) and Taut used glass, steel and reinforced concrete, and recalled through their use of these materials associations with the glass pavilions of earlier exhibitions.

Bruno Taut understood his (1880-1938) pavilion for the German glass industry as a space enclosed by glass prisms, glass ceiling, glass paving and glass tiles. He exploited in this building the translucent and prismatic attributes of glass and glass products. The pavilion, which was designed by Taut in the spirit of expressionism and developed in close conjunction with the fantastic poet Paul Scheerbart (1863-1915), appeared like a crystal. Scheerbart, who was a friend of Taut, wrote in 1914 in his pamphlet *Glas Architektur* that glass architecture which turned the dark dwellings of men into cathedrals of light would have the same enlightening influence on mankind itself.

The building which clearly caused the most excitement and was understood as the symbol of the emerging decade of the new spirit, was the model factory designed by Walter Gropius. Gropius showed a medium-sized manufacturing plant, which consisted of an administration building with adjacent open

Werkbund Exhibition

garages/halls, executed as a steel-frame construction, and a manufacturing hall which was separated by a large court from the administration building. The overall building complex was symmetrically organized along a central axis. The only special element in this very strong axial arrangement was an attached pavilion, which was commissioned by the Deutz Corporation to exhibit its gas engines. This pavilion, located at the rear end of the factory hall, featured a high octagon with wide areas of glass between slender columns, placed on a closed, one-story cubical base. The position of the pavilion was similar to the placement of a campanile with regard to its relationship to the main axis. The factory area was designed as engine hall as well as exhibition hall for engines, with a wide, three-part central nave, pitched roof and curved skylights. The overall form of this factory hall demonstrated the success of the close collaboration between architect and engineer.

But the most important architectural feature of the model factory was the two-story office building, with its glass-walled offices and the extended glass curtain around the semicircular staircases that were placed symmetrically on both ends of the building. These two glassed-in spiral staircases, which were located at the ends of the windowless, brick-like wall on the entrance side, led to the roof terrace. The roof terrace contained a covered restaurant and was placed between two taller structures that housed dance floors.

In his earlier design for the Fagus Factory at Alfeld-an-der-Leine (1911, with Adolf Meyer), Gropius had already developed the idea of dematerializing the corners of a building. The notion of the transparency of glass in Gropius' exhibition design stood in opposition to Taut's use of glass in the pavilion for the German Glass Industry. Taut used glass and glass products to enclose space and to direct attention toward the interior of the pavilion. Gropius' notion of glass and its use established an ambiguous reading between exterior and interior space. The simultaneous reading of these phenomena placed the featured staircases in the position of suspended movement. This appearance was reinforced by the juxtaposition of the continuous, solid front wall of yellow limestone and the transparency of the glass curtain.

The use of glass windows in the offices was received by the critics and the general public in several different ways, ranging from the building being compared to a prison—whose occupants would be under constant surveillance—to its being understood

as the most advanced development and integration of new materials. Gropius' model factory, with its simple formal approach and its accentuation of lightness and transparency, introduced a new stage of contemporary architecture which had not been experienced in Europe in such a reduced and defined manner.

The Exhibition of the German Werkbund in Cologne not only was the collaboration of industrial leaders, architects, artists and craftsmen in an awakening Germany, but also was the stage on which the emerging new architecture and its supporters and advocates collided with established architects and their philosophies, which were framed by the closing of the 19th century. The obvious disagreement of the individual parties was passionately discussed in July 1914, on the anniversary of the Werkbund in Cologne. Thousands of the conference's participants witnessed this clash, which nearly developed into a religious war. The antagonists were, on the one hand, Hermann Muthesius (1861-1927), and on the other hand, Henry van de Velde, August Endell (1871-1925), Bruno Taut and others. The main subject of this clash was Muthesius' ideas of art and creation. He called for the standardization of architecture and of all other disciplines associated with the Werkbund. In van de Velde's perception, this approach toward an overall definition of aesthetics did not recognize the artist and his or her spontaneous approach toward creation.

The outbreak of World War I brought the Werkbund Exhibition of Cologne to an abrupt end but did not eliminate the broiling discussion; the war resulted in only a temporary suspension of the new direction in architecture.

—UWE DROST

BAUHAUS
Dessau, Germany

1926. Architects: Walter Gropius (1883-1969) and Adolf Meyer (1881-1929).

Bauhaus: Dessau, Germany, 1926

Publications

ADAMS, G.: ''Memories of a Bauhaus Student.'' *Architectural Review* (September 1968).

ARGAN, GIULIO CARLO: *Walter Gropius e la Bauhaus*. Milan, 1951.

''Bauhaus, Dessau.'' *Architecture and Urbanism* (October 1982).

BAYER, HERBERT; GROPIUS, WALTER; and GROPIUS, ISE: *Bauhaus 1919-1928*. New York, 1938.

COHEN, A.: *Herbert Bayer*. Cambridge, Massachusetts, 1984.

''Dessau: The Glass-Walled Bauhaus.'' *Architects' Journal* 73 (17 June 1931).

FRAMPTON, KENNETH, and FUTAGAWA, YUKIO: *Modern Architecture: 1920-1945*. New York, 1983.

GIEDION, SIGFRIED: *Walter Gropius: Work and Teamwork*. New York, 1954.

GROPIUS, WALTER: *Bauhausbauten Dessau*. Bauhaus Book 12. Munich and Dessau, 1928.

GROPIUS, WALTER: *The New Architecture and the Bauhaus*. London, 1935.

HESSE, FRITZ: *Erinnerungen an Dessau*. 2 vols. Hannover, 1964.

HOFMANN, WERNER, and KULTERMANN, UDO: *Modern Architecture in Color*. New York, 1970.

JAEGER, FALK: ''The Bauhaus Building in Dessau.'' *Deutsche Kunst und Denkmalpflege* 2 (1981).

LANG, L.: *Das Bauhaus 1919-1933. Idee und Wirklichkeit*. Berlin, 1965.

NEUMANN, E.: *Bauhaus and Bauhaus People*. New York, 1970.

ROWLAND, A.: *The Bauhaus Sourcebook*. Florence, Kentucky, 1990.

SCHLEMMER, O.; MOHOLY-NAGY, L.; and MOLNAR, F.: *The Theater of the Bauhaus*. Middletown, Connecticut, 1961.

''Walter Gropius and the Bauhaus.'' *Architektur der DDR* (special issue, April 1983).

WINGLER, HANS: *The Bauhaus: Weimar, Dessau, Berlin and Chicago*. Cambridge, Massachusetts, 1969.

*

Although a department of architecture was not established at the Bauhaus until 1927, it was always the intention of its founder, Walter Gropius (1883-1969), that the curriculum of the school focus on building. As he stated in the Bauhaus manifesto of 1919, *''The ultimate aim of all creative activity is building!* . . . The world of pattern-designer and applied artist, consisting only of drawing and painting, must at last and again become a world in which things are *built.''* (Gropius's emphasis)

The school's early, precarious financial condition in Weimar and the less-than-sympathetic attitude of the populace and local authorities there relative to the school's overall intentions worked against the three-dimensional realization, the ''building,'' of the prototypes designed for industrial production, including architecture. However, the move to Dessau greatly improved opportunities at the Bauhaus. Under the farsighted

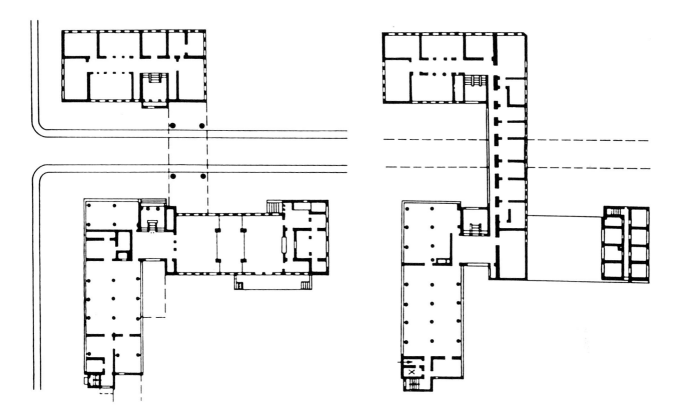

leadership of Fritz Hesse (1881-1973), mayor of Dessau, the city legislature (Landtag) appropriated slightly over one million marks for the construction of new facilities to house the school (902,500 marks for the structure and 126,500 marks for the furnishings and equipment).

Clearly, the design of the new facilities would serve as a means whereby the Bauhaus might realize some of the goals Gropius outlined in the manifesto. The faculty rightly assumed they might play an important role in this process. However, while an architecture "group" had been established in Weimar at the insistence of Marcel Breuer (1902-81), Farkas Molnár (1897-1945) and Georg Muche (1895-1987), it enjoyed no official status. As a result, the design of the school and related facilities was carried out by Gropius as a private commission. Since it was based on the school's programmatic requirements and its "spiritual life," Gropius would claim the Bauhaus had "designed itself." This conceit aside, for the Dessau Bauhaus Gropius was obliged to provide the necessary space for workshops, smaller work rooms, administrative offices, housing for scholarship students, a cafeteria, an auditorium/lecture hall and facilities for the related technical school. According to his own account of the commission, Gropius' overriding concerns were: achieving maximum daylighting through proper solar orientation, ease of internal movement through functional planning, architectonic clarity through the articulation of various programmatic elements, and spatial flexibility for possible future changes in function.

The plan consists of two L-shaped elements intersecting/overlapping one another in a pinwheel-like manner. The resulting asymmetry of the composition, according to Gropius, expressed the "modern spirit" of the building. However, one could not comprehend the whole, according to Gropius, without walking around the structure, "in order to understand the three-dimensional character of its form and the function of its parts." Here fenestration is most revealing: ribbon windows, set outside the plane of the reinforced concrete skeleton structure, indicate smaller spaces of a repetitive nature, while floor-to-ceiling "factory" glazing indicates the studio-workshop spaces. Other window types articulate and differentiate student housing, stairways and service spaces. The unglazed portions of the exterior curtain wall are brick masonry covered with painted stucco.

For the new facilities in Dessau, responsibility for interior finishes and furniture design and production was assigned to the various Bauhaus workshops. For example, interior decoration for the entire building was executed by the wall-painting workshop; the metal workshop was responsible for all lighting fixtures as well as the tubular steel furniture for the auditorium, cafeteria and studios, produced from designs by Marcel Breuer; the printing workshop was responsible for all lettering (exterior and interior graphics). These interior finishes and furniture, coupled with the building's programmatic concerns and its architectonic expression, place the Dessau Bauhaus well within the canon of modern architecture.

Gropius also designed three double houses for the studio masters (Paul Klee and Wassily Kandinsky, Georg Muche and Oskar Schlemmer, Laszlo Moholy-Nagy and Lyonel Feininger) and a larger, freestanding residence for himself. The former, almost identical in plan and elevation, all look different because of their relationship to one another and to the site; the latter, to illustrate the work and the philosophy of the school, was larger, more spacious and "fabulously furnished," according to one account. Like the Bauhaus, interiors and furniture, some designed by the masters for their own residences, were produced in the school's workshops, a fact frequently overlooked in contemporary accounts of the buildings. The houses, located a few hundred yards from the school, were screened from the road by an existing stand of trees and surrounded by lawns rather than separate gardens. Each is within the architectural vocabulary of the Modern Movement: flat roofs and floors of reinforced concrete with cantilevers for balconies and overhangs; exterior surfaces of stucco-covered masonry without ornament; and expanses of glass, carefully proportioned and asymmetrically placed on the elevations, the result of function as much as aesthetic choice.

Considering the times, the place and the speed with which the commission was designed and brought to completion, the ensemble is remarkably good. However, in retrospect we can see that the Bauhaus buildings explored no new structural possibilities, that no new understanding of space resulted. Rather, the Bauhaus buildings are to be appreciated and understood because of the forces from which they derive their existence: Ludwig Mies van der Rohe's (1886-1969) project for a concrete Office Building (1922) and Le Corbusier's (1887-1965) Maison Dom-ino (commencing in 1914). The Bauhaus buildings are living manifestations of the possibilities suggested by the Modern Movement, a rational architecture whose form derives from an articulate expression of function, whose structure derives from the materials and means at hand, whose aesthetic derives from the expression of surface rather than the application of ornament. It would not be too bold to state that the Bauhaus buildings in Dessau are also a clear expression of the artistic and aesthetic aims of the school as well as its pedagogy.

With the rise of National Socialism in Germany, continuation of the Bauhaus was problematic at the very least. The Bauhaus (and modernism in general) represented everything the Nazis rejected and sought to eliminate from German culture. From the moment they gained control of the Dessau city council in 1932, the National Socialists moved to close the school and destroy the building, destruction of which would mean, according to an account in the *Anhalter Tageszeitung,* "the disappearance from German soil of one of the most prominent places of Jewish-Marxist art manifestations." Fortunately for posterity, demolition would have been too costly; however, the workshop wing was badly damaged during World War II. In the immediate postwar period, this wing was bricked up and the building used as a school, although not as a school of design. Restoration was begun in 1976. Further restoration was completed in 1984, and that year the Bauhaus reopened as a school of design and architecture.

Gropius correctly understood that the importance of the Bauhaus was as an idea, an approach to education, rather than as a place or a specific building. Writing to Fritz Hesse in 1953, he commented: "In retrospect one can hardly believe that in spite of difficulties the Bauhaus had made such an impression. When you live in Germany, you can hardly imagine how world-famous the Bauhaus has become, especially in the United States and England. In both countries the curriculum of the schools of art and architecture have followed the teachings of the Bauhaus...."

What Gropius could not see then is that the buildings he designed for the school have transcended their obvious aesthetic limitations and have taken on an historical importance as symbols of artistic freedom. The Bauhaus idea has entered the collected unconscious. We are less and less aware of the origins of this approach to problem solving: it is accepted as pure datum. It falls to these buildings to remind us to look beyond surface and symbol for the generation of thought, the animating idea. The same is also true of the curriculum as developed under

Gropius and his successors, Hannes Meyer (1889-1954) and Mies, and the Bauhaus masters. Education at the Bauhaus began with a student setting aside preconception and examining a problem and the materials for its resolution with an open mind, an unjaundiced eye. As Gropius was fond of telling the students: "We begin at zero." Experience and a rational approach to problem solving gave students the necessary tools to go beyond "zero" and propose new solutions for old problems, and innovative solutions for newly defined problems.

—DAVID SPAETH

CHILEHAUS
Hamburg, Germany

1923: Construction; **Architect:** Fritz Höger (1877-1949).

Publications

"Chile House, Hamburg." *Architectural Review* 58 (November 1925): 192-194.
"Das Chilehaus." In ALFRED KAMPHAUSEN: *Der Baumeister Fritz Höger.* Neumünster, 1972.
FRAMPTON, KENNETH, and FUTAGAWA, YUKIO: *Modern Architecture: 1920-1945.* New York, 1983.
HIPP, H., and MEYER-VEDEN, H.: *Hamburger Kontorhäuser.* Berlin, 1988.

*

The Chilehaus in Hamburg is traditionally included in histories of modern architecture as one of six or eight leading examples of German expressionism, forged in the angst of defeat in the Great War and fraught with catharsis and spiritual regeneration. As a highly crafted brick building it stands opposed to the spirit of industrial classicism associated before the war with the Deutscher Werkbund, Peter Behrens and the AEG—all held somewhat in disrepute after the war as components of a "military-industrial complex" responsible for German humiliation and defeat. It seems like a kindred spirit to Behrens' I. G. Farben Headquarters at Hoechst, to Hans Poelzig's Grosses Schauspielhaus in Berlin, and except for the prospective material, to Eric Mendelsohn's Einstein Observatory in Potsdam.

A closer examination of the cultural and geographical context of the Chilehaus, while not disqualifying the expressionist interpretation, nevertheless establishes it within a broader historical perspective. The Chilehaus may be described as the best-known monument of a Hamburg school, part of a belt of historical brick-building cultures extending along the North Sea from Amsterdam to Copenhagen. In all three of these centers, the 19th-century eclectic tradition gave way at the turn of the century to a species of national romanticism rendered in brick. In the Netherlands, this episode is exemplified by H. P. Berlage's Amsterdam Exchange, in Denmark by Martin Nyrop's Copenhagen City Hall, and in Hamburg by the work of Fritz Schumacher, city architect from 1908 to 1920. Schumacher's prewar work in Hamburg in this faintly eclectic national romantic brick-building idiom includes the Johanneum, the Institute of Tropical

Chilehaus: Hamburg, Germany, 1923

Medicine and the Museum of Hamburg History. Schumacher also designed the Finanzbehörde of 1918, which pioneered the Hamburg *Kontorhaus* or commercial block—the antecedent of Höger's Chilehaus. A nine-story building occupying the full perimeter of its site, but stepped back above the seventh floor to reduce the apparent mass above a consistent cornice height, the *Kontorhaus* paradigm of the Finanzbehörde established one of several alternative models to the American skyscraper, which would bemuse modern European architects after the war.

Fritz Höger's Chilehaus conforms superficially to the *Kontorhaus* model of Schumacher's Finanzbehörde. It completely occupies two city blocks, bridging over the intervening street and rising unbroken from the street line to a seventh-story cornice, whence it steps back in a sequence of receding roof terraces. But Höger totally transformed the prosaic form and details of Schumacher's model. The profile of the Chilehaus undulates to a prow-shaped salient corner, which, while filling out the irregular site, also suggests the imagery of maritime commerce—appropriate to the accommodation of the shipping companies expected to occupy the building.

Beyond the gestalt of the Chilehaus, which might be interpreted as expressing its spiritual purpose to the same degree as Mendelsohn's Einstein Observatory, Höger transformed the brickwork of the Hamburg building into a tour-de-force of expressionist detailing. The surfaces of purple clinker brick—commonly used in 1920s Germany—fairly vibrate in three-dimensional patterns of pushed and pulled coursing. At the ground level, where commercial shop space opens to the street, carved stonework is employed. Aside from a few whimsical figures, the stone carving recalls the stalactite forms with which Hans Poelzig had become familiar in Turkey, and which he had employed at the Grosses Schauspielhaus in 1919. It seems likely, therefore, that Höger was consciously influenced by previous expressionist architecture, not only in postwar Germany but earlier in the neutral Netherlands. Although not copied from any single specific source, the combination of architectonic sculpture with manipulative brick detail strongly suggests the influence of the Amsterdam school of Dutch expressionism. The most proximate Dutch model for the Chilehaus is the Scheepvaarthuis in Amsterdam (1912-16). Like the later Chilehaus, the Scheepvaarthuis was also intended for commercial shipping companies, and in its angular site, approximated the profile of a ship's prow. Höger's Chilehaus thus should be interpreted as the cross-fertilization of a specific Hamburg tradition with an expressionist milieu in Holland and Germany in the early 1920s.

The Chilehaus was not, however, an isolated monument, but part of a colony of similar *Kontorhäuser* erected in the 1920s in the Messberg Quarter of Hamburg Altstadt. These included Höger's own adjacent Sprinkenhof (with Oscar Gerson), Hans and Oscar Gerson's Messberghof, Harman Distel's Montanhof, and many more. All were detailed in manipulative brickwork and carved stone sculpture, less pervasively than the Chilehaus but representing the same prolongation of German expressionism beyond the time of troubles which followed the war—a lingering Hamburg school. Collectively, the Chilehaus and its neighbors comprise a high-density urban commercial quarter reflecting an alternative model to the traditional 19th-century European city and to the American vision of proliferating skyscrapers. As the supreme exemplar of the Hamburg school, Fritz Höger's Chilehaus unites a conservative brick-building tradition with the imperative for novelty superficially equated to modern architecture, if pejoratively described by purists as "modernistic." It survives as the supreme example in Hamburg of the modern decorative style that was European expressionism.

—JAY C. HENRY

ALTES RATHAUS
Hannover, Germany

Ca. 1230: Original structure constructed. **Second half of 14th century:** Main construction begun. **1409-12:** Addition of east wing. **1453-55:** Beer and wine cellars moved to market wing and facade altered by master stone masons Cord and Ludecke Haverkoper. **1453-1503:** Dormers constructed. **1566:** Apothecary wing constructed. **1839:** Prison wing constructed. **Architect:** A. Andreae. **1845-50:** West wing constructed. **Architect:** A. Andreae. **1877-82:** Medieval wings restored. **Architect:** C. W. Hase. **1878:** Entrance gate constructed. **Architect:** C. W. Hase. **1943:** Damaged in World War II. **1954-61:** Reconstruction of the building exterior.

Publications

AHRENS, H.: *Das alte Rathaus zu Hannover: Seine Geschichte, Renovirung und Ausschmückung*. Hannover, 1886.

BÖKER, HANS JOSEF: *Die mittelalterliche Backsteinarchitektur Norddeutschlands*. Darmstadt, 1988.

DEHIO, GEORG: *Handbuch der deutschen Kunstdenkmäler: Bremen, Niedersachsen*. Rev. ed. Munich, 1977.

DENKMALTOPOGRAPHIE BUNDESREPUBLIK DEUTSCHLAND: *Baudenkmale in Niedersachsen 10.1: Stadt Hannover, Teil 1*. Braunschweig and Wiesbaden, 1983.

HAMMER-SCHENK, HAROLD, and KOKKELINK, GÜNTHER: *Laves und Hannover*. Hannover, 1989.

HOELTJE, GEORG: *Hannover*. Berlin, 1931.

JUGLER, AUGUST: *Aus den alten Tagen des hannoverschen Rathauses*. Hannover, 1879.

JÜRGENS, O.: "Aus der Geschichte des alten Rathauses." *Hannoversche Geschichtsblätter* 9 (1906): 116-125.

KOKKELINK, GÜNTHER: "Die Neugotik Conrad Wilhelm Hases." *Hannoversche Geschichtsblätter* New series 22 (1968): 15-16, 46-52, 99, 165, 197.

MASUCH, HORST: "Das alte Rathaus in Hannover—die Leistung der Maurermeister Curd und Ludeke Haverkoper in den Jahren 1453 bis 1455." *Hannoversche Geschichtsblätter* New series 35 (1981): 135-157.

MICHLER, JÜRGEN: "Zum Typus der Giebel am Altstädter Rathaus zu Hannover." *Hannoversche Geschichtsblätter* New series 21 (1967): 1-36.

MITHOFF, H. W. H.: *Archiv für Niedersächsische Kunstgeschichte, 1. Abteilung: Mittelalterliche Kunstwerke in Hannover*. Hannover, 1849.

MITHOFF, H. W. H.: "Die Wappen im Gurtgesimse des alten Rathauses zu Hannover." *Zeitschrift des historischen Vereins für Niedersachsen* (1852): 410-413.

MITHOFF, H. W. H.: "Ergebnisse aus mittelalterlichen Lohnregistern der Stadt Hannover." *Zeitschrift des historischen Vereins für Niedersachsen* (1870): 140-163.

MITHOFF, H. W. H.: *Kunstdenkmale und Alterthümer im Hannoverschen Bd. 1 Fürstenthum Calenberg*. Hannover, 1871.

MITHOFF, H. W. H.: "Ausgabe-Register vom Rathausbau am Markte zu Hannover aus den Jahren 1453, 1454 und 1455." *Zeitschrift des historischen Vereins für Niedersachsen* (1879): 257-281.

"Nachrichten vom alten Rathause." *Hannoversche Geschichtsblätter* New series 35 (1981):

NÖLDEKE, ARNOLD (ed.): *Kunstdenkmälerinventare Niedersachsens: Die Kunstdenkmale der Stadt Hannover, Teil 1*. Hannover, 1932.

Altes Rathaus: Hannover, Germany, ca. 14th century

PLATH, HELMUT: ''Der Marktplatz Hannovers vom 12. bis zum 15. Jahrhundert.'' *Hannoversche Geschichtsblätter* New series 8 (1954): 74-127.

TACK, P.: ''Der Tonfries am alten Rathaus.'' *Hannoversche Geschichtsblätter* 23 (1920): 43-59.

UNGER, THEODOR: *Hannover—Führer durch die Stadt und ihre Bauten.* Hannover, 1882.

*

The Altes Rathaus in Hannover is one of the most important town halls of the northern German *Backsteingotik* (brick Gothic) style. Appearing on the exterior as an exclusively brick construction, the building is the southernmost example of the monumental architecture of northern Germany, which used brick in the Middle Ages. In the cellars and ground floor of the eastern section of the wing which faces the market square, some walls of the preceding structure have been preserved. That earlier structure, erected in about 1230, was built out of rubble. The rise of brick construction in the second half of the 14th century

is immediately visible in the facing and elevation of the market wing.

The Altes Rathaus forms a unified ensemble with the Gothic Marktkirche and the Marktplatz, which lies between these two buildings. The urban layout pairing a parish church with a town hall in this way is typical of cities in northern Germany and the region along the Baltic, such as Lübeck, Goslar, Hannoversch-Münden and Stralsund, while a comparably strong emphasis on the city center by means of a concentration of all public buildings remained foreign to southern cities.

Hannover's medieval town hall accommodated all civic functions: it had room for shops on the ground floor, and a dance hall for the citizens and the council chambers on the upper floors. However, the Hannover Rathaus cannot compete in size with such large complexes as the town halls of Lübeck, Lüneburg or Toruń (now in Poland). These cities began building annexes to house the different municipal services in the Middle Ages, while this tendency asserted itself at Hannover only in the early 15th century, with the addition of the east wing (1409-12) to house the registry. Beer and wine cellars were created in the vaulted cellars of the registry wing, as was traditional in

International Dictionary of Architecture

northern German town halls. The beer and wine cellars were moved to the market wing between 1453 and 1455, where they still are today.

The market and registry wings were at first clearly distinguished as separate buildings by dissimilar roofs and gables. Comparable to the town halls of Goslar, Tangermünde and Braunschweig, an L-shaped building consisting of two structures was thus developed at Hannover. The facade of the Hannover Rathaus was articulated in a manner typical of medieval civic architecture. The floors of the market and registry wings are superposed without vertical connectors, each articulated in a distinct manner. The gables and dormers set over the eaves do not have any connection to the window openings on the floor below, either. This kind of facade articulation was emphasized with an elaborate terra-cotta frieze with coats of arms, and statues of saints and princes. The frieze not only separates the first and second floors but underlines the layered character of the facade. It was first installed at the Hannover Rathaus in the registry wing, and later continued across the facade of the market wing when that was altered (1453-55). The frieze indicates that both wings belong to the same complex. To indicate the unity of the entire complex, a modified form of the frieze was also installed in all later additions to the town hall. Comparable to the separation of the floors by the terra-cotta frieze, the roof and the gables and dormers, which introduce a powerful plastic accent into the ensemble, were separated from the flat area of the facade by a frieze made out of diamond-shaped brick. The contrast between the friezes, like that between the vertically articulated gables and the horizontal, layered facade, is typical of the civic architecture of the northern German brick Gothic style.

The opulent stepped gables of the market wing, whose vertical composition is underlined by pinnacles, were constructed between 1453 and 1455 by the master masons Cord and Ludecke Haverkoper. These gables are a peculiarly Hannoverian creation, only indirectly related to architectural trends in the eastern parts of the German-speaking world. The unusual creative ability of the master masons is particularly evident in the subtle repetition of forms, their virtuosity in working with the peculiarities of brick construction, and in the way the gable steps are diminished in height while the height of the pinnacles is kept constant. These characteristics create an extraordinarily dynamic effect.

The medieval wings of the town hall, with their projecting eaves, face the Marktplatz and the street. To fit the monumental building into the rhythm of the gables of the surrounding medieval structures, the dormers, which articulate the sweep of the roofs, were constructed (1453-1503). The possibility of giving the roof a vertical rhythm by means of windows recalls similar solutions in Braunschweig, Zeitz and Goslar.

The important 19th-century additions to the Altes Rathaus began in 1839, with the erection of a prison wing in the southern side of the courtyard, by A. Andreae. Andreae clearly distanced himself from his classicistic training under Friedrich Weinbrenner in the use of exposed masonry walls and of the Late Medieval motifs, such as the continuation of the terra-cotta frieze separating floors and the installation of blind arches, which cut across the separation between floors. The prison wing was the first step in a well-planned expansion of the old town hall. Between 1845 and 1850, Andreae tore down the so-called "apothecary wing" (1566), building in its stead the west wing, commonly called the "Doge's Palace" because it was built after the model of Venetian Romanesque palaces. The cube-like west wing, with its stone first floor, which is pierced with an arcade, and its upper floors of exposed masonry, is a prominent example of the Hannoverian *Rundbogenstil,* which was prevalent in

northern Germany until after 1860. This style combined historical Italian and English Gothic influences with the architectural language of Friedrich von Gärtner, who was active in Munich, and of Heinrich Hübsch, who was active in Karlsruhe.

Originally, the "Doge's Palace" had one unfinished side (toward the market wing), since further construction was foreseen. It was not until 1878, however, that C. W. Hase created the entrance gate connecting it to the market wing. This gate does not fit with the gables that frame it, whether with regard to coloration, massing or style.

The medieval wings of the town hall were restored by Hase between 1877 and 1882, in the neo-Gothic style of Hannover, which he had developed around 1860, and which had an influence throughout northern Germany and Scandinavia. The restoration of the Altes Rathaus is to be considered one of the Hase's most important works. He used architectural details from the Hannover Rathaus in his later work, with the result that the Hannover style was widely disseminated.

In the design of a new neo-Gothic south wing, built when a new street was created, Hase took up motifs and elements of articulation from the medieval structures, even to the extent of using bricks of the same size. He connected the new building to the buildings along the newly laid out street by adding an extra story.

After extensive damage caused by bombardments in 1943, partial restorations were carried out between 1954 and 1961. The building has been reconstructed to its prewar state only on the exterior. The present-day significance of the Altes Rathaus lies not only in the superior quality of the medieval fabric in the *Backsteingotik* style, but also in its 19th-century neo-Gothic additions. The latter exhibit an exemplary respect for and understanding of the original medieval architecture. Particularly in Hase's work, the Hannover Rathaus became one of the central buildings of the architecture of the Hannover school.

—BERND ADAM
Translated from the German by Marijke Rijsberman

MARKTPLATZ
Karlsruhe, Germany

1797: Construction. **1804, 1811-25:** Rathaus constructed on west side of Marktplatz. **1806-1816:** Evangelische Stadtkirche constructed on east side of Marktplatz. **Architect:** Johann Jakob Friedrich Weinbrenner.

Publications

BERGDOLL, BARRY: "Friedrich Weinbrenner and Neoclassical Karlsruhe: a vision tempered by reality." In *Friedrich Weinbrenner: 1766-1826.* Exhibition catalog. London, 1982.

BROWNLEE, DAVID: *Friedrich Weinbrenner, Architect of Karlsruhe, A Catalogue of the Drawings in the Architectural Archives of the University of Pennsylvania.* Philadelphia, 1986.

Friedrich Weinbrenner 1766-1826. Exhibition catalog. Karlsruhe, Germany, 1977.

GUTKIND, E. A.: "Urban Development in Central Europe" In *International History of City Development.* New York, 1964, 300.

Marktplatz: Karlsruhe, Germany, 1797

VALDENAIRE, ARTHUR: *Friedrich Weinbrenner: Sein Leben und seine Bauten.* Karlsruhe, 1919.

WATKINS, DAVID: *German Architecture and the Classical Ideal.* Cambridge, Massachusetts, 1987.

*

Constructed when the city of Karlsruhe was expanded beyond its original borders, the Marktplatz by Johann Jakob Friedrich Weinbrenner epitomizes the transition in urban planning from the Baroque period to classicism.

Karlsruhe was laid out in 1715 by Friedrich von Batzendorf for Margrave Karl Wilhelm of Baden-Durlach. Its plan reflects the 18th-century concept of the absolutist state and is clearly, according to E. A. Gutkind, "a veritable pattern-book of ideas and prototypes ranging from the radial pattern of Palma Nova . . . the diagonal streets of the Piazza del Popolo, to the gardens of Versailles." In this schema the seat of power, that is, the palace, becomes the literal center of the town and the mediator between city and garden between culture and nature. The principal north-south axis, Schloss Strasse (today's Karl-Friedrich-Strasse), extended south past the parade grounds to its intersection with the main east-west axis, Lange Strasse (now Kaiser Strasse), where the axis ended at the Evangelische Kirche (Lutheran church).

Weinbrenner's early-19th-century expansion of the city altered this relationship, transforming Karlsruhe into what Henry-Russell Hitchcock described as "somewhat less monumental, but more coherently exemplary" romantic classical city (*Architecture: Nineteenth and Twentieth Centuries,* Baltimore, 1958). Appointed *Bauinspektor* in 1797 (he became *Oberbaudirektor*

in 1809), Weinbrenner prepared the comprehensive plan that extended existing streets, introduced new ones and established the standards to be followed in building the blocks. His decision to maintain equal-height facades throughout the streets of Karlsruhe had as much to do with the practicality of construction as with a desire to maintain the height of the palace tower in relation to the other structures. In general, only the palace tower, the bell towers and the spires of the various churches and of the municipal building protrude above the roof line.

As part of the expansion of the city, Weinbrenner projected a three-story arcade for Kaiser Strasse, thereby unifying the existing buildings with a covered promenade, and expanded the *via triumphalis* of Karl-Friedrich-Strasse to the south by first widening the site of the Evangelische Kirche to form the Marktplatz. This central square, which contrasts with the forecourt of the palace, is really two contiguous spaces. The first space has a centralizing pyramidal monument (1823)—which David Watkins describes as the "heir of the abstract monuments of genius of the visionary classicism of late-eighteenth century France"—located where the old church had stood. It is there that the founder of Karlsruhe, Karl Wilhelm, lies buried. Weinbrenner also projected two U-shaped market shelters around its perimeter, and noted: "A fine and most appropriate model for our market place is provided by the markets of antiquity. Pausanias described the market and other public places of Athens in his first book, and has thereby left us a most favourable picture of the ancient Greeks' agora." The second, larger portion of the new square is flanked by the new Evangelische Stadtkirche (1806-16) on the east side and the Rathaus (1804, 1811-25) on the west. The two have pedimented fronts, each is flanked by secondary functions, and their axiality is reinforced by rear towers which balance and complement each other. In all cases, the exteriors are in red sandstone.

The definition of the new space stems from the normative height of the building facades, which are pedimented in their central bays to demarcate the entries of the Rathaus, with its Ionic-order *in antis* central section, and the Evangelische Kirche, with its giant Corinthian order, which is carried into the interior space. The extended axis of the street continues past the Rondellplatz until it is crossed by a new east-west axis, the Kriegs Strasse, terminating in the Ettlinger Tor. From the Rondellplatz, two streets extend as diagonals to the northeast and northwest. Along the diagonal that leads to the northwest, Weinbrenner built the Catholic St. Stephanskirche. The resulting axis is a series of discrete spaces, from the pie-shaped forecourt to the palace, through the double rectangular space of Marktplatz, the circular Rondellplatz, and terminating in a second widening at Ettlinger Tor with Weinbrenner's propylaeum celebrating this point of entry into the city. At its center, each space is punctuated by a monument, and from palace to gate, all these elements reinforce the singular principal axis and the centrality of the palace. From Weinbrenner's perspective, it was important that these introduce asymmetrical yet complementary relationships.

The outcome no longer contains the curvilinear forms of the Baroque, but rather illustrates a rational, logical regimentation in which "the notion of formal and social unity remained Weinbrenner's goal" (Barry Bergdoll, in *Friedrich Weinbrenner: 1766-1826*). For Henry-Russell Hitchcock, "... [the] Karlsruhe Marktplatz stands as one of the happiest ensembles of the early nineteenth century. . . . The ideal of a public square, not walled in in the Baroque way but defined by discrete blocks, balanced but not identical, and focused by the eye-catching diagonals of the central pyramid, a geometrical shape as pure as the cube or sphere yet also an established formal symbol and a subtle memory of the Egyptian past, was fully realized."

In 1979 Rob Krier proposed the building of new versions of the market stalls in Weinbrenner's 1797 proposal, and reintroduction of a constant arcade along Kaiser Strasse. His proposal seeks to recreate the tightly controlled spatial definition of the original while accommodating today's needs. As of yet there is no such reconstruction, though vehicular traffic has been removed from the square except for streetcars, making the space easier to understand. But without these market stalls, the experience remains incomplete.

—GERARDO BROWN-MANRIQUE

LÖWENBURG
Kassel, Germany

1795: Construction begun; **Architect:** Heinrich Christoph Jussow. **World War II:** Damaged in fighting. **1950s:** Partial reconstruction.

Publications

BANGERT, ALBRECHT: "Architektur von Heinrich Christoph Jussow in Kassel um 1800." Dissertation. Ludwigs-Maximilians-Universität. Munich, 1969.
KLEIN, JÜRGEN: "Heinrich Christoph Jussow, Erbauer der 'Löwenburg' zu Kassel und die englische Neogotik." *Architectura* 5 (1975): 138-169.
PAETOW, KARL: *Klassizimus und Romantik auf Wilhelmshohe.* Kassel, Germany, 1929.
VOGEL, H.: *Heinrich C. Jussow, Baumeister in Kassel und Wilhelmshohe.* Exhibition catalog. 1958-59.

Two prominent factors relate to the origins of Löwenburg. First, it was built as an equivalent to the French Bastille, representing the absolute authority of Landgrave Wilhelm IX, who would not tolerate the sort of behavior which had resulted in the French Revolution of 1789. Through this architectural device, Wilhelm intended to return to former times when oaths of fealty established structured control. It was to be both his living quarters and place of burial.

Second, it was built in response to a deficiency in the gardens at Wilhelmshöhe, as determined by C. C. L. Hirschfeld, author of the influential *Théorie de l'art des jardins* (1779-85). Hirschfeld commented on Wilhelmshöhe's lack of historical presence and attributed this failing to the absence of a Gothic castle, just as he had previously suggested that the terraces at Wilhelmshöhe be replaced by a large lawn. Thus, Löwenburg can also be seen as a very large garden building, designed to add quality to an estate, to induce a certain mood, in this case a nostalgia for medieval times. Ideas of the sublime are found in this Gothic Revival architecture and its setting.

Wilhelm IX was strongly nationalistic, and the architects that he chose were usually from Hesse. Heinrich Christoph Jussow, a native of Kassel, was a highly regarded architect who had received his classical training at the Paris school of Charles de Wailly. Löwenburg must be seen as the product of Jussow's fertile imagination, no doubt induced by reading novels such as Horace Walpole's *Castle of Otranto: A Gothic Story*, which was contained in the landgrave's library.

An early drawing possibly by Jussow shows that the original intent was to place the great tower as the main element in the landscape. This would have been similar to England's romantic towers, with their small viewing salons at the top, which Jussow would have observed during his visit from 1784 to 1787.

Today, Löwenburg Castle sits toward the top of the park at Wilhelmshöhe (called Weissenstein prior to 1798), its partially ruined, overgrown state giving the impression that it has been there since medieval times. Its designer well understood that the principal goal of Gothic architecture was to be asymmetrical, not only in interior planning but also externally: the castle has bold, irregular contours and deep, mysterious shadows. The skillful massing and sense of drama with which Jussow endowed the building result in bold forms with no delicacy or fragility. Löwenburg truly has the look of a castle that had been built up over a number of years and then fallen into ruin. That look of dereliction was accentuated during its rebuilding after World War II; the main tower overlooking the gardens and palace below has deliberately been left in a partially ruined state.

As in medieval times, the *bergfrid* or keep is the most important part of the settlement. This tower which dominates both landscape and castle originally contained the knights' room, library and dining room. Untrue to the function of a keep, its windows were not compatible with a defensive structure. On each side of the main tower, arranged in seemingly haphazard manner, are small rooms to the north for the ladies and to the south for the knights. A large, roomy courtyard lies between the *bergfrid* and the opposite side with its armor room and medieval chapel. A knight in full armor reposes on a medieval tomb, portraying Wilhelm IX (who was later entombed in the chapel). Certain details, such as the predella of the church altar, are Renaissance, some stained glass is medieval, and various

Löwenburg Castle: Kassel, Germany, 1795

pieces of furniture were designed by Jussow (as were the medieval knight and tomb described above).

Towers of differing sizes are picturesquely and sometimes strategically ranged around the perimeter of the settlement, which is surrounded on its mountain side by a low wall and a moat with drawbridge. There are two gatehouses, only one of which functions as such today.

While Löwenburg often has been compared with Robert Adam's Culzean Castle in Scotland, Adam's work lacks Löwenburg's ragged outline, its sublime deep gloom and shadows, and its ruined aspect; the main tower at Culzean also does not dominate to the same extent. In comparison with Jussow's building, the Culzean project is compact and almost classical-looking.

No discourse on Löwenburg would be complete without some mention of the gardens at Wilhelmshöhe. Jussow was a highly imaginative artist who placed great emphasis on reconciling building with landscape; the fantastic valley below, the great trees above, the sweeping vista—each variety of scene added to the sublime quality which is realized by Löwenburg. Not only was nature to be enjoyed in this garden—there was also grandeur expressed in the magnificence of broad lawn fronting the neoclassical palace and contrasted with the surrounding forest and the awesome aqueduct. This combination of simple nature and of grandeur is indicative of the changes in taste which had come about through the influence of the English and the writings of contemporary garden theorists, including Hirschfeld; the gardens gradually became more English.

In contrast to the French classicism that reigned at the palace of Landgrave Wilhelm IX and in the buildings of his towns, Löwenburg can be seen as an attempt to imitate the English return to a Gothic style that was felt to be more indigenous than an imitation of Greco-Roman culture. As in its gardens, the Gothic forms used at Löwenburg were based on ideas garnered from English sources as well as on nearby monuments. Jussow's painterly approach resulted in an impressive picture: a castle sitting high on the mountainside overlooking palace and town. The association of Gothic ruins with sentimental dramas is less important in this German edifice than is the association of a powerful lord having a benign, albeit unyielding, control over his people.

—TERESA S. WATTS

MARKTPLATZ
Lübeck, Germany

1250-1330: Marienkirche and Rathaus constructed. **Early 14th century:** Briefkapelle constructed. **1440s:** Lady Chapel added to Marienkirche. **1570s:** Addition to Rathaus constructed. **1939-45:** Severe damage during World War II.

Publications

BELOW, GEORG VON: *Das ältere deutsche Städtewesen und Bürgertum*. Bielefeld and Leipzig, 1898.
FEHLING, EMIL F.: *Lübeckische Ratslinie von den Anfängen der Stadt bis auf die Gegenwart*. Lübeck, 1925.

Rathaus, Marktplaz: Lübeck, Germany, 1251-1330

HOLM, ADOLF: *Lübeck die freie und Hanse-Stadt.* Bielefeld and Leipzig, 1900.

KALLSEN, OTTO: *Gründung und Entwicklung der deutschen Städte im Mittelalter.* Halle a.S., 1891.

LE MANG, IRMGARD: *Die Entwicklung des Backsteinbaues im Mittelalter in Nordostdeutschland.* Strasbourg, 1931.

Lübeck. Vol. 2 in *Die Chroniken der niedersächsischen Städte* series (5 vols.). Leipzig, 1884-1914.

Lübisches Mittelalter. Festgabe zum 800 jährigen Bestehen Lübecks seit der Neugründung unter Heinrich dem Löwen, 1159-1959. Lübeck, 1959.

RÖRIG, FRITZ: *Hansische Beiträge zur deutschen Wirtschaftsgeschichte.* Breslau, 1928.

*

The Hanseatic city of Lübeck, like Venice, is celebrated for its silhouette, its relationship to water and for its remarkably rich architectural legacy. The comparison with Venice can also be made through trade, for both cities were great mercantile centers; in addition, Lübeck's most famous commodity, *Marzipan,* or St. Mark's Bread, recalls the patron saint of the city of the Doges.

Lübeck's Seven Spires dominate the skyline, and the city presents an unforgettable salute to the traveler who approaches the Queen of the Hanse from across the broad expanse of the Wakenitz River. If the long-distance panorama is the first aspect of Lübeck's individual character that strikes an immediate claim on the sensibilities, the second aspect to delight must be the close-knit relationships of spaces and buildings within the *Altstadt,* the core of which is dominated by the enormous bulk of the *Marienkirche,* identified by its twin towers with helm-roof spires. This is one of the largest brick Gothic churches in the world, and was deliberately made as grand as possible to express the mercantile pride of the burghers of Lübeck: the proximity of the *Rathaus* was symbolic of the close link between the city government, the mercantile guilds and the town church. In contrast, the cathedral was sited at the southern tip of the island on which Lübeck stands, almost painfully removed from the center of the life of the *Altstadt.* The commercial power of Lübeck commenced when in 1226 Kaiser Friedrich II granted the status of Free Imperial City, which it retained until 1937, when the Hanseatic port was incorporated into the Prussian province of Schleswig-Holstein.

Nowhere by the Baltic can the qualities of Gothic architecture constructed of brick be appreciated more than in the vicinity of the *Marienkirche* and the *Rathaus,* for these two great buildings complement each other, and form a marvelous ensemble that is an exemplar of what the Germans call *Backsteingotik.* Brick is suitable for large areas of flat wall surface, with perhaps fairly regular and simple modeling, but it is not, like stone, ideal for elaborate carving and decoration. Yet within the confines of the materials, the composition is exceedingly rich, with red and black-glazed bricks contributing to the fabric, and used with vigor, imagination and verve.

The *Marienkirche* dates from the middle of the 13th century, and, like many other German Gothic churches, was to have been of the "hall" type, that is with nave and aisles of similar height. However, during the building the arrangement was changed to a church of the French type, that is with lean-to lower aisles, clerestory, twin western towers and apsidal east end with radiating chapels. It was completed around 1330, although the Lady Chapel was not added until the 1440s. The *Briefkapelle* of the early 14th century has star vaulting that springs from two tall, slender, granite monolithic shafts, and is an example of the elegance that German architects achieved as

Marienkirche, Marktplaz, 1251-1330

Gothic developed as a style. Spatially, the nave is stunning, with its vast volume, thrilling vistas and the geometrical relationships of the various parts contributing to the harmony of the whole. The interior elevation is really divided equally in two vertically, so that the nave arcade is the same height as the clerestory, the lean-to roofs cutting off the lower parts of where the windows should be.

It was one of the many tragedies of World War II that St. Mary's and the *Rathaus* should have been so badly damaged, and it is profoundly moving to reflect on the qualities of the buildings today. Blackened and chipped funerary monuments line the walls of the great church, and much of the elaboration and crafted fixtures have gone, yet the scale and nobility of the architecture somehow survive. At the base of one of the towers is a chapel containing an eloquent memorial to man's madness: the great bells, broken and twisted, lie where they fell the day the Queen of the Hanse was ravaged by bombs.

The *Rathaus,* also built from 1250 onward, stands on the north and eastern sides of the *Marktplatz,* and has massive high protective brick screen walls of dark glazed brick, pierced with huge openings, and with niches, blind arcades and tough architectural detailing, all in brick. They are strengthened and divided into bays by means of buttresses capped with spirelets and cones. The effect is like the illustrations from a fairy tale, and the marvelous ensemble calls to mind a vision of a Northern Venice, reflecting the bright clear light from the gleaming glazed brickwork. The strong reds and blacks, with the green of the copper spires and cones, have a quality of aesthetic excellence admirably suited to the extraordinary clarity of the Baltic light, and are as memorable as the yellows, pinks and greens of the city on the Adriatic.

In front of the northern screen wall is a Renaissance addition to the *Rathaus,* with arcades and gables, erected in the 1570s, of stone. The contrast in scale is extraordinary, and there is nothing half-hearted about these amazing buildings, which are among the finest Gothic structures in northern Europe.

—JAMES STEVENS CURL

AMALIENBURG
Nymphenburg, near Munich, Germany

1734-39. Architect: Jean-François-Vincent-Joseph Cuvilliés the Elder (1695-1768).

Publications

BRAUNFELS, WOLFGANG: *François de Cuvilliés*. Würzburg, Germany, 1938.

HAGER, LUISA: *Nymphenburg: Schloss, Park und Burgen*. Munich, 1955.

MELLENTHIN, HORST: *François Cuvilliés Amalienburg: Ihr Bezug zur französischen Architekturtheorie*. Munich, 1989.

THON, CHRISTINA: *Johann Baptist Zimmermann als Stukkator*. Munich, 1977.

WOLF, FRIEDRICH: *François de Cuvilliés: Der Architekt und Dekorschöpfer*. Munich, 1967.

Once Jean-François-Vincent-Joseph Cuvilliés had demonstrated his prowess as a designer of exquisite Rococo and chinoiserie rooms and details at Brühl for Clemens August, elector-archbishop of Cologne, and carried out the *Reiche Zimmer* at the Residenz in Munich from 1730, his status as an architect was assured. His career had been strange, but blessed with good fortune, for he had entered the service of the exiled Max II Emmanuel, elector of Bavaria from 1679 to 1726, as the court dwarf. When the elector returned to Munich with his entourage in 1715, Cuvilliés worked as a military engineer, and, although he was appointed an ensign in the Life Guards, he could not take part in campaigns of parades because of the figure he would not cut. Aware of Cuvilliés' talents and intelligence, however, the elector sent his dwarf to Paris to study architecture under François Blondel (1683-1756), and Cuvilliés remained in the French capital for four years. On his return he was appointed as one of the court architects in Munich, and his work at Brühl was part of his duties, for Clemens August was a member of the Bavarian electoral house. The elector-archbishop raised Cuvilliés to the rank of "gentleman" in 1730.

Karl Albrecht, elector of Bavaria from 1726 to 1745, commissioned his architect to design the Amalienburg on the grounds of Schloss Nymphenburg outside Munich; the elector was prompted, perhaps, by Cuvilliés' charming hunting lodge at Brühl known as Schloss Falkenlust. The Amalienburg was named after the electress Amalia (or Amélie, as she is known in the Frenchified version). This *maison de plaisance* stands very near the Schloss at Nymphenburg, but is set in woodland so that one comes upon it suddenly. These woods were planted specially for the rearing of pheasants, and nearby was a conservatory in which flowers were forced for the gardens.

Amalienburg, Mirror Room: Nymphenburg, near Munich, Germany, 1734-39

Amalienburg

At the Amalienburg, one of the greatest masterpieces (if not *the* masterpiece) of the Rococo style, the elements of the garden palace or *Lustschloss* are reduced to their essence. Most accounts of the Amalienburg discuss only its interior decoration and basic form, but it is more complicated than that, for the treatment of the landscape (although it is difficult to appreciate today) is significant. The building is basically a long rectangle with a circular salon with domed roof in the center, which is expressed on the front not as a bow, but as two concave curves (in each of which is a window) built out from the straight wings and terminating in a convex entrance facade, the triangular pediment of which is set on a convex plan. The pediment has an open base, and is carried on four Ionic pilasters between which hang garlands and swags with flora and fauna: in the center, between the paired Ionic pilasters, is a large rusticated niche containing the entrance doors, above which is a relief of Diana the Huntress. Before the entrance facade is a small *cour d'honneur,* and to the rear is a *Ressaut* related to the shape of the building.

On each side of the central projection are wings three windows wide. All of these windows are simple rectangular casements with cruciform arrangements of the frames, subdivided by means of glazing bars. Over each window is a Rococo cartouche (in the invention of which Cuvilliés was a master), and over each cartouche is a segmental cornice. Between each window is a raised, flat panel, above which is a recessed roundel containing a bust. Scills are supported on two consoles each. Above the crowning cornice is a parapet, which partially conceals the roof, and over the domed roof of the central salon is the *tir aux faisans* balcony, from which pheasants could be shot.

The segmental eyebrows to the window openings give the

Amalienburg a refined French air, but the Rococo interiors have an exuberance and an inventive gaiety that are entirely German. In this jewel of a building, chinoiserie plays a considerable role in the decorations, of which more anon.

Unquestionably, the central salon is an interior of breathtaking beauty. Doors, windows and mirrors are set under curved frames, surrounded and surmounted by what can only be described as a riot of Rococo decorations with *putti,* garlands, swags, horns of plenty, nets, flora, fauna, cascades, musical instruments, palm leaves, celebrations of the hunt, cartouches and a wondrous display of an apparently inexhaustible invention. The moldings and reliefs are overlaid with silver foil, and the basic color is *à fond blanc,* which is a sort of bluish white, with other shades of blue as well, giving the room with its many mirrors and central chandelier a cool, crystal, even icy appearance, like some magical cave with precious stones and frost glistening everywhere.

Cuvilliés designed the interiors at the Amalienburg, but the silvered stuccowork was executed by Johann Baptist Zimmermann (1680-1758), with carvings by Joachim Dietrich (died 1753) and Egidius Verhelst the Elder (1686-1749). The coloring of the salon is related to white and blue of the Bavarian national colors, and the decorations make the structure dissolve in the play of reflection, light, coloring and ornament.

On each side of the salon are the other rooms, no less exquisite and enchanting, though perhaps less spectacular than the salon. The electress' bedroom is a charming and warm lemon-yellow, with silvered Rococo ornament of the most elegant design (again by Cuvilliés and carried out by Zimmermann). Adjacent is the *Retirade* with the electoral privy, or *Chaise Percée* (as it is known, literally "pierced chair"): this room is decorated in the

Chinese taste. On the other side of the Salon is the *Jagdzimmer,* or hunting room, which is straw-colored, making it extraordinarily light and warm, again with embellished ornament.

At the rear are the hall and gun room: the latter is referred to as the *Hundekammer* or *Hundekabinett,* and contains dog kennels, gun cupboards and a stove of blue and white. The decorations are blue on a white ground, and are again chinoiseries. On the other side of the hall (which is little more than a vestibule) is the kitchen, the walls of which are covered with blue-and-white Delft tiles with panels in full color showing flower vases surrounded by small birds. The ceiling (again of blue and white) is in the Chinese taste. Pascalin Moretti was responsible for these charming chinoiseries.

Throughout, the decorations allude to the hunting of game and fish, as well as to the charms of country life, the whole handled with a dexterity that is all the more impressive for the asymmetry of the cartouches, frames and disposition of elements (although the building itself is virtually symmetrical). The Amalienburg was not only a hunting lodge: it was used for country fêtes like those of the Trianon Farm at Versailles. In the *Lustschloss* the make-believe of simplicity could be acted out in the most exquisite of artificial surroundings.

—JAMES STEVENS CURL

KÖNIGSBAU
Munich, Germany

1826-35. Remodeling of facades of earlier palace; **Architect:** Leo von Klenze (1784-1864).

Publications

HEDERER, OSWALD: *Leo von Klenze—Persönlichkeit und Werk.* Munich, 1981.

KIENER, HANS: *Leon von Klenze.* Unpublished Ph.D. dissertation. University of Munich, 1922.

LIEB, NORBERT and HUFNAGEL, F. (eds.): *Leo von Klenze: Gemalde und Zeichnungen.* Munich, 1979.

WATKIN, D. and MELLINGHOFF, T.: *German Architecture and the Classical Ideal.* Cambridge, Massachusetts, 1987.

When Crown Prince Ludwig of Bavaria ascended the throne of that country as king in 1825, he had in mind the embellishment of his capital city, Munich, with many impressive works of architecture that would allude to antiquity, to the Early Christian period, and to the Renaissance.

One of his first schemes as king was to modernize the large and rambling royal palace, the Residenz, which had grown in stages but which presented little architectural cohesion or grandeur to the world. The king was historically minded and does not seem to have had the intention of demolishing the mix of medieval, Renaissance and Baroque buildings he had inherited: the idea was to construct a series of outer buildings and facades that would be suitably impressive as architecture, and to provide within the complex sufficient state and private apartments to suggest the dignity and modernity of the monarchy.

Leo von Klenze was the architect chosen to design these additions, and between 1826 and 1836 he provided drawings

for and supervised the erection of the Königsbau on the south side of the palace, with its main facade to the Max-Joseph Platz. This southern elevation of the Königsbau is based firmly on Florentine precedents. In general shape, treatment of fenestration and rustication, the obvious source is the Palazzo Pitti, but on the top two stories Klenze added a system of pilasters clearly derived from that of L. B. Alberti's Palazzo Rucellai. Karl von Fischer (1782-1820), who was Königlicher *Oberbaurat* from 1809, and who was to be supplanted by Klenze, had made drawings of the Palazzo Pitti in 1812, and these may have prompted the style eventually chosen for the building of the Königsbau. Another possible source is A.-H.-V. Grandjean de Moligny and A.-P.-Ste.-M. Famin's *Architecture Toscane,* published in Paris in 1815.

The internal arrangement of the rooms behind the regular symmetrical facade was asymmetrical and informal, although individual apartments were decorated with great richness. Interiors had Renaissance, Empire and Antique themes, cunningly mixed. Frescoes illustrated aspects of Greek and German poetry and legend, while artists included Schnorr von Carolsfeld, Hess, Hiltensperger, Kaulbach, Lindenschmitt, Foltz and Schwanthaler. Klenze himself was responsible for furniture and fittings.

The significance of the Königsbau lies in several factors. It, with the Central Post Office (refaced in quattrocento style with quotations from Filippo Brunelleschie's Ospedaledegli Innocenti in Florence in 1836 by Klenze) on the south side of the Max-Joseph Platz, and the grave antique portico of the National Theater to the east, creates a square that is a monument to romantic classicism. The Platz is an eclectic collection of styles, perhaps based on the ideas of J. N. L. Durand, who had influenced Klenze in Paris in 1803. Furthermore, the Königsbau is part of the 19th-century neo-Renaissance movement which saw such a revival of interest in Italian architecture, so it can be seen, with the Leuchtenberg Palais and other important Munich buildings, as just as significant in German terms as Charles Barry's Reform Club was in English. The Königsbau, with Klenze's Pinakothek (begun 1826) are among the two earliest examples of monumental revived High Renaissance design in architecture.

But there was more to it all than that. Klenze believed that in the round-arched styles the essence of Greek architecture could be found. This may seem peculiar, as Greek architecture is columnar and trabeated, but Klenze noted that Greek architecture, alone of all architecture, was characterized by both propriety and beauty. He saw that the essentials of Greek architecture could be found in two phases: the first was when all the apertures and intervals were capped by horizontal elements; and the second was when the arch was used to do the capping. In other words, he saw the Roman merging of the orders with arcuated forms as the second phase of an essentially Greek language of architecture, and that the great buildings of the Italian Renaissance were similarly rooted in Greek precedent. Greek architecture was the architecture of the world, and could be adopted in any period, clime or place.

The Königsbau, therefore, is a synthesis, yet one rooted in antiquity. It is, with the Allerheiligenhofkirche and Pinakothek, among the most important early-19th-century buildings incorporating semicircular arches, and heralds a fashion for the *Rundbogenstil* that was to reach its apogee in South Kensington and in the United States very much later.

Thus the adoption of an Italian Renaissance style by a German architect of genius is far more than a northerner's love affair with the south, and more than the beginnings of the architectural styles we refer to as ''Italianate.'' Klenze's work must be seen as a development of neoclassicism into realms we hardly think

Königsbau: Munich, Germany, 1826-35

of as neoclassical at all, and as an expression of some of the ideas promoted by Durand in lectures and in his *Précis des Lecons d'Architecture données à l'École Polytechnique*, published in Paris in 1802-05. Furthermore, like other architects of the 19th century who used round-arched styles in their designs, Klenze detected in Early Christian, Romanesque and Renaissance architecture powerful survivals from antiquity itself, and not only Roman antiquity, but specifically Greek ideals of beauty, proportion and architectonic themes. Klenze had a vision of Greece as the source for all European architecture: to him, *Ein Griechischer Traum* meant more than archaeology and recording. It was a dream of clarifying the very spring of original architecture in order to enable new forms and images to evolve.

—JAMES STEVENS CURL

MICHAELSKIRCHE
Munich, Germany

1583-97: Church designed and built; **Architects:** Wolfgang Miller and Friedrich Sustris (ca. 1540-99), with some interior contributions by P. Valeriani. **1590:** Choir; **Designer:** Wendel Dietrich; *Fall of the Angels*, High Altar; **Designer:** Christoph Schwarz. **1592:** Facade statue of Saint Michael; **Artist:** Hubert Gerhard; interior stucco apostles, saints and angels in niches

of the choir and nave also by Gerhard. **Late 18th-early 19th century:** Monument to Eugène de Beauharnais; **Designer:** Bertel Thorvaldsen. **1939-45:** Damaged in World War II. **After 1945:** Restorations.

Publications

BRAUN, J.: *Die Kirchenbau der deutschen Jesuiten*. 2 vols. Freiburg-i.B., 1908-10.

HAUTTMANN, M.: *Geschichte der kirchlichen Baukunst in Bayern, Schwaben und Franken*. Munich, 1923.

HITCHCOCK, HENRY-RUSSELL: *German Renaissance Architecture*. Princeton, New Jersey, 1981.

STANGE, ALFRED: *Die deutsche Baukunst der Renaissance*. Munich, 1926.

VON BEZOLD, G.: *Die Baukunst der Renaissance in Deutschland*. Leipzig, 1908.

*

The Michaelskirche in Munich was begun in 1583 by command of Herzog Wilhelm V of Bavaria for the Society of Jesus, and was completed in 1597. It was only some thirty years younger than the parent church of the Jesuits, Il Gesù in Rome, and it is a spectacular artistic expression of the Counter-Reformation north of the Alps. This great church is curiously placed in art-historical terms, because it is both the highest achievement of German Renaissance church architecture and the prototype of much that was to come later in German Baroque ecclesiastical work. The west front, with its flattish, almost secular facade, looks rather like the oversized house of a burgher, with its three

Michaelskirche: Munich, Germany, 1583-97

Michaelskirche

pilastered stories and tall gable with scrolls. The architects appear to have been Wolfgang Miller and Friedrich Sustris. The latter was the son of Lambert Sustris of Augsburg, although the family came originally from Flanders. Sustris was probably a pupil of Giorgio Vasari (1511-74). He settled in Munich in 1580, and became *Surintendant*, or designer and adviser, on all artistic enterprises of the Bavarian court. He directed the building of the Grotto Court of the Residenz from 1581 to 1586. The foundation stone of the Michaelskirche was laid in 1583.

The facade of the church is very un-Roman, and is more like a bucolic remembrance of Il Gesù mixed with northern European gabled domestic architecture and German Renaissance municipal buildings than the more *echt*-Italian model. Miller had been trained in Italy, and Sustris (who was mostly responsible for the transepts and choir) had had not only a solid grounding in the rudiments of architecture in Augsburg, but in the Mannerism of the school of Vasari.

This great German Renaissance church is a variation on the Gesù theme, and marks an epoch in the history of Roman Catholic church building in the South German lands. It was founded as a Jesuit church, became a court church from 1773 to 1918 (which explains the use of the crypt as a burial vault for the House of Wittelsbach—there lie Kings Ludwig II and Otto I, and many other princes), and was returned to the Jesuits in 1921 after the hiatus of the Communist Revolution.

The facade, with the Town Hall in Augsburg, must be regarded as one of the great glories of the period. Between the two doorways framed by aedicules with scrolled broken pediments is a niche containing a bronze statue of Saint Michael done by the Netherlander Hubert Gerhard (ca. 1540-1620) in 1592. The facade also has rows of statues of members of the Wittelsbach House, to demonstrate the alliance of the Church Militant with that house. Yet it is almost ungainly, this tremendous pileup

of crudely modeled pilasters, round-headed windows, niches, roundels, obelisks and *ancones*. There are parallels with Flemish architecture, Elizabethan work, and the strange facades of Augsburg, Lindau-am-Bodensee and Antwerp, yet the Italian theme comes through, even though the two entrances are oddly uncomfortable in their relation to the interior.

Inside, the space is vast and impressive, and owes something to Sebastiano Serlio's illustrations of the Basilica of Constantine as well as to the seminal prototype of Il Gesù. It seems that a Jesuit architect, P. Valeriani, was also involved at some stage in the genesis of the interior. The nave is very wide, and there is a hugh barrel vault over: it is three bays long, with wide pilastered piers defining the shallow side chapels, over which are vaults, and over these again there are galleries with another range of great vaults above them, lit by clerestory windows. The transepts do not project beyond the walls of the "aisles," and read almost as large chapels, breaking the rhythm of the nave as it approaches the triumphal arch of the choir. And it is in this extraordinary and magnificent nave that we find the stunning prototype of the *Wandpfeilerkirche*, or wall-pier church, so typical of the Vorarlberg and of southern Germany for the next century and a half.

The choir is raised above the floor of the nave, and is approached by a flight of steps. It is narrower than the nave, and is entered through the majestic great arch. The Chancel is apsidal, and the barrel vault over it conforms to the shape, producing an almost Gothic effect over the two stories of arcuated walls. Choir stalls were designed with detail that is purely classical, with *guilloches*, shell work and swags, and was completed around 1590.

Stucco angels in the nave and apostles in the choir were by Gerhard, who also made the bronze crucifix with Mary Magdalene in the liturgical south transept. Gerhard's agitated, monumental stucco apostles, saints and angels in the niches of

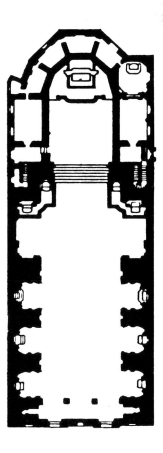

the choir and nave are not easy images with which to come to terms, and exemplify a spiritual struggle, a war in Heaven.

In the north transept is the wonderful and dramatic neoclassical marble monument to Eugène de Beauharnais (1781-1824), duke of Leuchtenberg, made by Pietro Tenerani from designs of Bertel Thorvaldsen (1770-1844). Choir stalls were by Wendel Dietrich (ca. 1535-1621/23), and the Fall of the Angels (1590) on the high altar was by Christoph Schwarz (ca. 1545-92), although the stupendous reredos of three superimposed orders with a lively, almost Baroque attic was by Dietrich.

The outside wall of the "aisle" became a neutral surface, but classical articulation is more than obvious in the continuous architrave between the piers over the chapel vaults. The interior as a whole was very integrated and homogenous, inexpressibly grand and nobly architectonic for its period. Students of the development of Baroque and Rococo in the German lands should start with the Michaelskirche, for there the precedents can be found for much that occurred later. Although the church suffered during World War II, it has been restored. Comparisons with prewar photographs suffice to demonstrate what has been lost, but nevertheless there is still much to be learned from that mighty building.

—JAMES STEVENS CURL

OLYMPIC PARK
Munich, Germany

1972: Construction. **Architects:** Günther Behnisch, Frei Otto, and Jürgen Joedicke.

Publications

BEHNISCH and PARTNER: *Bauten und Entwurfe*. Stuttgart, 1975.

DREW, PHILIP: *Frei Otto: Form und Konstruktion*. Stuttgart, 1976.

KLOTZ, HEINRICH: *Architektur in der Bundesrepublik—Gesprache mit Gunter Behnisch, Wolfgang Doring, Helmut Hentrich, Hans Kammerer, Frei Otto, Oswald Mathias Ungers*. Frankfurt, 1977.

*

The symbol of the 1972 Olympic Games in Munich is an exuberant roof structure of steel cables and acrylic slung over the three main stadiums of the Olympic facilities. This airy construction, though supported by 12 giant pylons and stabilized by anchors and huge cables, seems to float over the grounds, growing into a giant which hovers over the individual facilities.

This great roof embodies more than space or shelter for any sport activities. It encompasses elements of science and art, of humanistic and technocratic beliefs as well as of philosophy and trust. The stadium and its roof construction were designed and proposed by Günther Behnisch and Partners, a relatively young Stuttgart firm which had won the 1967 international competition for the games facilities. Behnisch's emphasis was to be on light, and on lightness. This intention celebrates the victory of the intellectual over technocratic materiality.

The proposed and finally accepted solution features two systems: first, the numerous facilities at ground level, suppressed into the terrain and illustrating the notion of a prehistoric amphitheater; and second, the prestressed grid of cables and acrylic panels, slung over the grounds. The intention was to design an "architectural landscape" in which the individual facilities would become a part of the overall strategy. The landscape was left untouched, so at any point the contours are distinguished and present. The sports facilities are part of this landscape, whereas the roof structure is apart from it. The gigantic roof structure is understood as the integrating element which is lifted off the ground. It covers the Olympic stadium, which seats 80,000, the sports arena, which seats 12,000, and the swimming stadium seating 9,000.

Half a year after the competition jury, the Olympic building authority gave the go-ahead for Behnisch's scheme and for development of the required technology to build the ambitious structure. Frei Otto, who was the head of the Institute for Lightweight Structures at the University of Stuttgart, was named as an expert in such construction: he had previously designed a similar structure for the German pavilion at Montreal's Expo '67. In addition to Otto, the engineering firm of Leonhardt and Andrä, known for their thin bridge structure of prestressed concrete, was hired as structural consultant. The shapes and forms of the final structural configuration at Munich were Frei Otto's. His method of defining the necessary details for the proposed structure proved to be a slow process. While he worked up models and calculations at his institute in Stuttgart, other experts who had never been concerned with or aware of Otto's previous work were required to conduct the necessary counter checks, and were consulted by him on how to build the roof.

The required tests and computer calculations were made by the Institute for Statics and Dynamics of Aviation and Aerospace Design and the Institute for Geodetic Science at Stuttgart University. Fritz Leonhardt and Wolfgang Andrä, who were responsible for the statics, had to struggle with thousands of unknown factors, and it appeared doubtful that the roof would ever be built. Throughout the imperative and incessant adjustments in determining the final forms, many ultimately unneeded calculations were done, which along with the construction of unnecessary foundations increased the overall costs. The problems of the foundation increased when the Bavarian building authorities refused to adjust the existing building codes to include the proposed prestressed foundations, which were cheaper and much more elegant than the imposed deadweight foundations. Finally, three types of foundation were used: slot-and-wedge foundations, which function like tent pegs; deadweight foundations for counterbalancing the tensile forces with their own weight; and great anchor foundations, which operate against a mass of earth to secure stability.

The solutions for the roof covering were as complex as the discussions about the foundations. Otto imagined a lightweight concrete covered with plastics. Other proposed plywood covered with felt and metal foil, placed on a steel cable mesh of 75-centimeter squares. Finally, the intervention of broadcast companies, which insisted on translucent panels, forced the architects and organizers to choose transparent acrylic glass panels, which were to be tinted to give spectators some protection from the sun. These panels, 2.9 meters square, are connected to the intersections of the steel mesh by steel screws and washers, and are separated by neoprene spacers to allow for the individual movement of the different materials. Under the steel cable mesh of the sports and swimming stadium roofs, suspended PVC-coated polyester fabric provides insulation.

Whatever doubts Günther Behnisch and Frei Otto's proposal and structure may have raised with regard to effort, money and the transformation of a temporary architectural idea into a permanent structure, the Olympic complex in Munich has come

Olympic Games Complex: Munich, Germany, 1972

to be recognized as one of the greatest technical and aesthetic achievements in late-20th-century architecture. Besides the technical success of the roof, the stadiums' general success as a vital and integral part of the overall concept of the Munich Olympics seems to be the measure which affected large parts of society.

—UWE DROST

PROPYLÄEN
Munich, Germany

1817: First design created; **Architect:** Leo von Klenze (1784-1864). **1846:** Construction begun with revisions to design of gateway, omission of pavilions, addition of two pylons with centerpiece between, porticoes and columns; **Architect:** Leo von Klenze. **1860:** Building completed.

Publications

BOTTGER, P.: *Die alte Pinakothek in Munchen*. Munich, 1972.
HEDERER, OSWALD: *Leon von Klenze—Personlichkeit und Werk*. Munich, 1981.
KIENER, HANS: *Leon von Klenze*. Unpublished Ph.D. dissertation. University of Munich, 1922.
LIEB, NORBERT and HUFNAGEL, F. (eds.): *Leo von Klenze: Gemalde und Zeichnungen*. Munich, 1979.
WATKIN, D. and MELLINGHOFF, T.: *German Architecture and the Classical Ideal*. Cambridge, Massachusetts, 1987.

*

In the collections of the Bavarian State Museums hangs a remarkable and arresting picture by Leo von Klenze (1784-1864), who was no mean painter. It shows a fascinating reconstruction of Athens, *Ein Griechischer Traum*, and it shows a view of the Acropolis in the distance with, in the foreground on the left, a great polychrome pylon-like tower, the window openings of which have square mullions similar to those used by Karl Friedrich Schinkel at the Berlin Schauspielhaus [and ultimately based on a mixture of the Choragic Monument of Thrasyilus, which James Stuart and Nicholas Revett had illustrated in their *Antiquities of Athens*, and on the square columns of Egyptian temples depicted in Dominique Vivant Denon's *Voyage dans la Basse et la Haute Égypte pendant les Campagnes du Général Bonaparte* (Paris, 1802) and in the Commission des Monuments d'Égypte's *Description de l'Égypte, ou Recueil des Observations et des Recherches qui ont été faites en Égypte pendant l'Expédition de l'Armée Francaise...* (Paris, 1809-28)]. The top of the tower has square piers at the corners, and although between these piers there are male figures based on those of the Temple of Zeus at Agrigentum (which Klenze had drawn on site in 1823-24), this pylon-like tower is similar to the pylons that are such an important part of the composition of Klenze's Propyläen in Munich of 1846-60, one of the most beautiful, most serene, and most startling of all the great monuments of neoclassicism.

The Propyläen, as the name suggests, is a gateway in the Greek taste, and it is a gateway of monumental size. It is situated on the west side of the Königsplatz, and marks the entrance to the city and to the neoclassical square from the direction of the Royal Palace of Nymphenburg. Klenze had prepared a design for the Propyläen as early as 1817, shortly after he had been appointed *Hofbaumeister* by Crown Prince Ludwig of Bavaria (1786-1868) and had started work on the Glyptothek to house the prince's collection of antique sculptures. The first scheme for the gateway consisted of a hexastyle Greek Doric pedimented portico flanked by two lower pavilions, and was clearly modeled on ideas taken from the Athenian Propylaeum and from Carl Gotthard Langhans's celebrated Brandenburg Gate at the end of the Unter den Linden in Berlin. This scheme remained a design on paper only, even after Ludwig ascended the throne of Bavaria as king in 1825.

Eventually, King Ludwig decided to make the Greek War of Independence and the election of his second son (Prince Otto von Wittelsbach) as king of Greece the reasons to justify his commission of a suitable Grecian gateway from his architect. After 1817 Klenze must have long regarded the Propyläen as a dead duck, for the king spent many years dithering about where to put the gate once he got around to having final drawings prepared. At one time the site was to be on the main axis at the northern end of the Ludwigstrasse, but eventually the Siegestor, in the form of a Roman triumphal arch, was built there to designs by Friedrich von Gärtner.

The king finally determined to commemorate Bavaria's connections with Greece by placing an important public monument on the western side of the unfinished Königsplatz: Klenze reworked his ideas accordingly, and the 1817 proposals underwent a change. The revised scheme showed a tougher gateway that was much more monumental, massive, and altogether weightier and more festive. The two small pavilions were scrapped and replaced by two massive Greco-Egyptian pylons with Schauspielhaus square mullions held between the corner piers at high level: between the pylons Klenze placed a lower centerpiece against which were set two hexastyle Greek Doric pedimented porticoes. Inside, the carriageway in the center between the two porticoes was flanked by rows of Ionic columns. This superb piece of urban monumental architecture was built of Untersberger marble, and the pediments and friezes were carved by Ludwig Schwanthaler to represent scenes from the War of Independence and from the reign of King Otto I of Greece (all suitably Grecianised in the antique style by a sculptor who worked closely with Klenze on many commissions).

The Propyläen was completed in 1860, only two years before King Otto lost his throne. The building of the gateway began in the year that "Lola Montez" [née Marie Gilbert (1818-61) of County Limerick] arrived in Munich as an adventuress. Only two years later, in 1848, the scandal of King Ludwig's liaison with the Irishwoman was so great that he was obliged to abdicate.

The new monarch, King Maximilian II, did not share his father's architectural tastes, and so the fruitful collaboration between Leo von Klenze and the ruling house of Bavaria came

Propyläen: Munich, Germany, 1846

to an end. However, the Propyläen was financed throughout the course of its building from the private funds of Ludwig, who would only see the completion of the monument some eight years before his death. The ex-king outlived his architect by just four years.

The Propyläen is a memorial to the collaboration of two extraordinary men: the architect, and the prince who became king. It is also a reminder of the connections between Bavaria and Greece, of the Greek War of Independence and the way in which that war captured the imagination of Europe, and it is an eloquent testimony of the attempt by the king of Bavaria to turn his capital city into a German Athens in modern times, leavened with aspects of the Italian Renaissance. Greek and early Italian Renaissance architecture were ideals, connected in the minds of the king and his architect, and realized in one of Europe's most cultivated and beautiful cities.

—JAMES STEVENS CURL

ST. JOHN NEPOMUK
Munich, Germany

1731-50. Architects: Cosmas Damian Asam (1686-1739) and Egid Quirin Asam (1692-1750). **1860**: Restoration. **1941-42**: Restoration after damage in World War II.

Publications

BAUER, RICHARD, et al.: *St. Johann Nepomuk im Licht der Quellen.* Munich, 1977.

BAUER, RICHARD, and DISCHINGER, GABRIELE: *Die Asamkirchen in München.* Munich, 1981.

HITCHCOCK, HENRY-RUSSELL: *Rococo Architecture in Southern Germany.* London, 1968.

The church of St. John Nepomuk in the Sendlingerstrasse, Munich, was designed and built in 1731-50 by the brothers Egid Quirin and Cosmas Damian Asam at their own expense. It adjoins a house once owned by Egid Quirin, who, as he neared the age of 40, considered the possibility of leaving a monument that would encapsulate the best he and his brother could do, as well as being a private votive offering. He determined on a church as the most appropriate form of memorial, and that church is dedicated to Saint John Nepomuk, a saint not familiar to Anglo-Saxons. Saint John was martyred in 1393: after suffering torture at the hands of Wenceslas IV, the depraved Holy Roman emperor and king of Bohemia, he was taken to Charles Bridge over the Moldau and cast in with his hands tied behind his back. He was killed largely because, as confessor to the queen, he refused to reveal the secrets of the confessional to the dissolute monarch. It is said that on the night of the martyrdom lights appeared over the waters, and toward morning the body floated ashore, the lights twinkling on the water above it. Saint

John is represented with surplice and purple stole, his finger to his lips (to indicate his silence), and wearing a doctor's four-horned biretta. Seven stars surround his head, and he is often shown with water and bridges. Saint John is therefore associated with steadfastness, silence and rock-like devotion; he is also a saint opposed to capricious tyranny.

The building in the Sendlingerstrasse is very small, and is part of a terrace, placed between Egid Quirin's own house on one side and the priests' house (also designed, built and paid for by the Asams). Unfortunately, the balance of the arrangement has been spoiled by the addition of a further story to the priests' house and by other alterations. The facade of the church was therefore intended as the centerpiece of a composition which no longer reads satisfactorily.

Taking the cue from Roman precedents, the front of the "Asamkirche" (as it is known) seems to sway forward, held between two giant pilasters, the capitals of which seem to melt and flow down the shafts. Both the pilasters and the convex front rise from symbolic blocks of rock, so the church is built on "foundations" that have biblical overtones but also allude to the Prague legend of Saint John Nepomuk and his church "on the rocks." Indeed, the facade, springing from the rocks, can be interpreted as a symbol of the bridge associated with the martyrdom of the Saint, for the arches of bridges spring from abutments that require solid, rock-like foundations.

An open-bed pediment carried on a smaller order of Ionic columns marks the porch and supports a sculptural group that rises up before the "west" window. This window has a distorted open-bed pediment that dissolves at its curved top into a burst of glory set beneath a circular window in the tympanum of the incredibly bent and flowing crowning pediment capping the whole composition, and sits above the fragments of concave entablature held on the giant order of pilasters. There was a belfry above, but that is gone.

This is an incredibly complex facade, much more free than even Francesco Borromini could have achieved: it is classicism that has become Baroque, but which seems to have lost any hard lines at all, becoming entirely plastic, molded and freely modeled as though it has melted in the sun or in the heat of its own vitality.

If the exterior amazes, the interior overwhelms, for it is truly sensational, violent and dramatic in the most powerful way. First, the visitor passes from the street to a vestibule that is elliptical on plan, and then into the body of the church proper. The space is tall and narrow, with a gallery that seems to sway and move all around, carried on the fingers of gesticulating angelic terms. There is an altar at gallery level as well as at ground-floor level. Four Solomonic or twisted columns of amazing virtuosity in their detail stand on the pedestals of the gallery, and carry the fragmentary entablatures from which four cherubim spring in joy toward the bursts of gilded rods around the third person of the Trinity, represented in the form of the dove. The gilded glory is actually supported on the tips of the cherubim wings. This dove hovers over the *Gnadenstuhl,* on throne of grace, where God the Father supports the crucified Son flanked by lithe angels. This altar aedicule is completely fused with the architecture of the church, and gives the interior the air of a *Wallfahrtskirche* (pilgrimage church), despite its tiny dimensions. Garlands draped from the capitals of the Solomonic columns double as perches for jubilant *putti.*

The interior of this masterpiece of Bavarian Baroque is theatrical and, like theaters, exploits perspective, color and light to the full. Everything appears to sway back and forth, drop and rise, leap and froth, while the color scheme is powerful in its intensity of deep reds, rose, grays, browns, dark greens and much gold. Light floods from the liturgical west and from

St. John Nepomuk: Munich, Germany, 1731-50

St. John Nepomuk

mysterious sources on high, concealed and magical. The Trinity appears against the light source, intensifying the emotional charge of this extraordinary building.

Above, the frescoed vault, with Cosmas Damian's painting extending the full length from the front wall to the "east" end of the sanctuary, has an almost riotous sense of occasion, and features the presentation of Saint John Nepomuk in Heaven, with scenes from the life of the saint.

Unfortunately, the church was damaged during World War II, and the interior, in any case, underwent "restoration" in 1860 and again in 1941-42. Something of the quality of *Laetitia* is missing, and some of the painting seems to be stylistically unconvincing, and muddily dark. Even worse, the statue of Saint John Nepomuk, the guardian of bridges, the seven-starred, the saint with lips sealed, that once stood until 1824 on the gallery at the "east" end, has not been replaced. This statue was by Egid Quirin, and was silhouetted, like the operatic statue of Saint George at Weltenburg Abbey, against the light from behind.

Yet even with these erosions of detail, destruction of important features and muddying of intent, the Asamkirche remains one of the great buildings of South German Baroque architecture. Its brooding intensity, its theatrical effects and its extraordinary scale make it one of the world's most remarkable buildings.

—JAMES STEVENS CURL

ABBEY CHURCH
Ottobeuren, Germany

1711: Construction process begun. **Architect:** Johann Michael Fischer (1692-1766). **1727:** Excavations for foundations begun. **1737:** Foundation stone laid. **1756:** Church ceiling fresco painting begun; **Artists:** Jakob Zeiller and Franz Anton Zeiller. Church choir stalls; **Designer:** F. X. Feichtmayr. Frescoes in state rooms; **Artists:** E. Zobel and Christopher Voght.

Publications

BLUNT, ANTHONY (ed.): *Kunst und Kultur des Barock und Rokoko: Architektur und Dekoration.* Freiburg, 1979.

LIEB, NORBERT: *Barockkirchen zwischen Donau und Alpen.* Munich, 1983.

LIEB, NORBERT: *Johann Michael Fischer: Baumeister und Raumschöpfer im späten Barock Süddeutschlands.* Regensburg, 1982.

SACHSE, HANS-JOACHIM: *Barocke Dachwerke, Decken und Gewölbe: Zur Baugeschichte und Baukonstruktion in Süddeutschland.* Berlin, 1975.

SCHELL, HUGO: *Ottobeuren: Kloster und Kirche.* Munich, 1979.

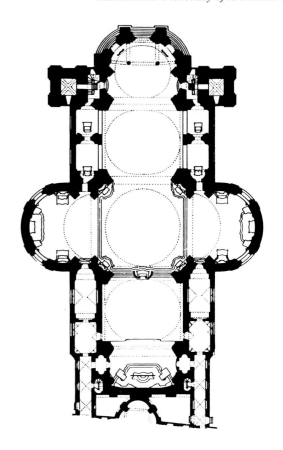

Abbey Church

The Benedictine Abbey of Ottobeuren, once a self-governing entity, lies a little higher than the town of Ottobeuren itself. The Convent Church rises at the northern end of the north-south axis of the convent complex. With its Baroque splendor and its size, the church lends its environment a certain grandeur. The building went through a lengthy planning stage, which continued after construction had already been begun (1711). The construction process was complete in 1731.

Beginning as early as 1712, Peter Vogts developed designs for a new church. Those early designs, based on a cross-shaped plan of a basilican character, show a marked influence by the Kollegienkirche in Salzburg (1715-22) by Johann Bernhard Fischer von Erlach. The connection is particularly clear in the planned high dome with a drum, which emphasizes the crossing. Vogts' early plans seem to have determined the design in a fundamental way, in spite of numerous later designs submitted by a series of different architects. The length of the church and the form of the crossing as planned by Vogts were never changed. In 1727 excavations for the foundations of the church were begun.

Between 1729 and 1731 Kaspar Radmiller and Andrea Maini submitted designs, both with strongly centralized plans. Dominikus Zimmermann's design, submitted in 1732, was somewhat similar to his Pilgrimage Church at Steinhausen (1727-33). Josef Schmuzer submitted a series of designs elaborating on the possibility of a centralized rectangular plan, which gives the space a dynamic center by means of an octagonal crossing. His designs follow the Abbey Church of Weingarten in the disposition of the pilasters.

From all the designs submitted, the abbot of the Ottobeuren convent, Rupert II Ness (1710-40), finally chose a proposal by

Abbey Church: Ottobeuren, Germany, 1711

Simpert Kraemer. In his design, the arms of the cross, all with semicircular ends, recall both the Abbey Church at Weingarten and the Kollegienkirche at Salzburg. In 1737 the foundation stone was laid. In 1740 Abbot Rupert II Ness died. Under his successor, Anselm Erb (1740-67), Kraemer's design was redone by Joseph Effner, then court architect at Munich, in the style of French classicism. In 1748 Johann Michael Fischer, who had finished the Abbey Church at Zwiefalten several years before, was charged with supervision of the construction. One year later Kraemer withdrew from the project.

Fischer changed little in the plan, which takes the shape of a Latin cross, each arm ending in a semicircular structure. Nave and transept are equally wide. Fischer's own contribution, however, is evident in the articulation of the facades and interior elevations. Both are similar to his work at Zwiefalten. The well-balanced exterior gives a clear impression of the interrelations of the different structural elements. The transept is equal in width and height to the central nave, which has low lateral aisles. A roof in the shape of a pyramid is set over the crossing. On the flat southern side, the church is connected to the rest of the convent buildings, while on the northern side a high, convex facade with a gable and two side towers was constructed. A framed stucco relief representing Saint Michael as victor over Lucifer (1761-62, by Johann Michael Feichtmayr) is set in the gable. Two soaring square towers with powerful pilasters and a rhythmic division into levels reinforce the vertical impetus of the facade. The facade composition clearly evinces the influence of Weingarten. For both these churches, the Kollegienkirche at Salzburg had served as a model. The high first level at Ottobeuren and the pilasters are executed in rusticated stone. Windows and portals have wide surrounds.

In the interior, the grand spatial composition expresses the unity of architectural and decorative elements. The bay includes the entry space. The central nave is set between the towers, and starts with a preliminary bay, followed by a square space providing seating for the congregation. This space is framed by interconnected pairs of chapels and a continuous entablature over the chapel entrances. It is crowned with a saucer dome. The equivalent of this space on the other side of the crossing is taken up by the monks' choir, which is flanked by sacristies. The crossing itself is crowned with a suspended dome. Like the beginning of the nave, the arms of the transept have barrel vaults. At the corners of the crossing, the rhythm of the space is underlined by a differentiated order and grouping of colossal pilasters and columns clad in marble. The entablature is generally treated as the architectural completion of the arcades. In the arms of the transept it follows curves and semicircular ends, while it is strongly molded at the corners of the crossing.

The decoration, work on which was begun in 1756, is unusually rich. The plastic and pictorial decoration was mostly done by the stuccoworker and altar specialist Johann Michael Feichtmayr, the sculptor Joseph Christian, and the two painters Johann Jakob Zeiller and Franz Anton Zeiller (frescoes). These artists had already collaborated with Fischer at Zwiefalten. Ornamentation, polychromy and sculpture form a unity with the architecture, and strongly contribute to the grand appearance of this monumental Late Baroque abbey church.

The Abbey Church of Ottobeuren has an important place in the history of the development of the southern German Baroque. As one of the last great religious structures, it stands at the end of an architectural series, of which the abbey churches of Weingarten and Zwiefalten and the Pilgrimage churches at Wies and Vierzehnheiligen also are a part.

—PETRA LESER
Translated from the German by Marijke Rijsberman

NIKOLAIKIRCHE
Potsdam, Germany

1829: Original designs; **Architect:** Karl Friedrich Schinkel (1781-1841). **1830:** Designs modified and construction begun; **Architect:** Karl Friedrich Schinkel; corner bell tower, ceiling construction; **Architect and Construction Supervisor:** Ludwig Persius (1803-45); Cast zinc ceiling panels; **Designer:** Geiss of Berlin. **1843-49:** Drum and dome added. **After 1849:** Building completed; **Architect:** A. Stüler; Apse decorations; **Decorator:** Bernhard Wilhelm Rosendahl; Pulpit decorations; **Decorator:** Kiss (1836-37). **1945:** Church damaged in World War II. **1955:** Cupola reconstruction begun. **1969-72:** Restoration of corner towers and semicircular windows. **1975:** Interior reconstruction.

Publications

Architektur der DDR. 30, 2, (1981).

PEVSNER, N.: "Karl Friedrich Schinkel." In *Studies in Art, Architecture and Design*. New York, 1968.

POSENER, J.: "Schinkel's Eclecticism and 'the Architectural'." *Architectural Digest* 53: (November-December 1983): 11-12.

Precis des Leçons d'Architecture.... Paris, 1801-05, Vol. II, 3rd Part, 56-57, and Plate 11.

RAVE, PAUL ORTWIN: *Karl Friedrich Schinkel Lebenswerk: Berlin. Erster Teil, Bauten für die Kunst, Kirchen, Denkmalpflege*. Berlin, 1941.

RAVE, PAUL ORTWIN, and KUHN, MARGARETE (eds.): *Karl Friedrich Schinkel: Lebenswerk*. 14 vols., Berlin, 1939-68.

SCHINKEL, KARL FRIEDRICH: *Collection of Architectural Designs* (originally published in German in 1866). Princeton, New Jersey, 1989.

UNGERS, L. and MATHIAS, O.: "The Humanist City." In *Architectural Design* 52 (November-December, 1982): 11-12.

*

Karl Friedrich Schinkel prepared his first designs for a new Nikolaikirche in Potsdam in 1829 to replace the earlier church that had been destroyed by fire in 1795. Schinkel proposed a *Zentralbau* with cupola, but in 1830 was obliged to present a modified design without cupola as the royal house was going through one of its periodic fits of economy. Provision for bells was to be in the corners of the massive body of the church, with openings in the attic story: there were to be no overt bell towers. The building itself would have a pitched roof with a pediment at each end. The foundation stone was laid in 1830, but building works proceeded slowly because of the many alterations, arguments and spasmodic funding.

The Nikolaikirche is square on plan, and the overall effect is one of massive grandeur. A prostyle hexastyle Corinthian portico with pediment (in the tympanum of which is a carved relief of the Resurrection) stands on a podium that is gained by a flight of 10 steps. Two antae project from the front wall, partially protecting the entrance from the elements. On the elevation opposite that of the portico is a semicircular apse. All around the church are carried the moldings of the podium, of the column bases and of the entablature, except that the latter terminates in the corner towers. The sides of the building are pierced by five

Nikolaikirche: Potsdam, Germany, 1829

openings with carved architraves and cornices, and the whole church is faced with ashlar.

Above the entablature is a variety of attic story, the same height as the lower story above the topmost molding of the podium: on the front this attic contains a large horizontal inscription with angels in relief set within a rectangular frame. On either side of this frame were to be two two-light openings for the belfry framed by truncated Ionic pilasters. The side elevations of the attic are pierced by huge semicircular windows subdivided by means of wrought-iron glazing bars and pilasters with decorative winged angels, while on either side, immediately below the attic cornice, were to be two three-light openings framed by truncated Ionic pilasters for the belfry, an Ionic variation on the square-mullion

theme of the Schauspielhaus in Berlin. These Ionic-pilastered openings were omitted when the corner towers were substituted for the internal belfry idea.

That part of the apse above the main entablature is subdivided by Ionic pilasters and crowned by a cornice with superimposed antefixae: the attic of the apse is lower than the attic story of the main block of the church.

Above the body of the building rises a drum with a peristyle of Corinthian columns all around, above which is an attic drum with Ionic pilasters over which rises the dome and lantern. The prototype is Jacques-Germain Soufflot's Panthéon cupola in Paris.

Originally, Schinkel planned four massive square constructions in each corner of the square plan to contain stairs, vestibules, ancillary accommodation and, at high level, the bells. The towers (which effectively they were) had no exterior expression except for the belfry-stage openings mentioned earlier. In the final version, the royal building inspector, Ludwig Persius, who supervised the construction of the Nikolaikirche, was obliged to place bell towers at each corner and express them: the belfry stages of these towers have semicircular-headed arches, and are crowned with cornices over which are set plain drums surmounted by fluted cones. Apart from helping to stabilize the structure, these towers seem to have been partly a response to the king's demands for the elimination of the cupola and the erection of two smaller towers with steeples. As completed, the towers stop both the main and attic entablatures.

The clarity of the geometry, though somewhat confused by the four corner towers, is spectacularly expressed inside this great building. The drum of the cupola sits over a square space that is contained by four massive coffered arches of brick, probably the most important example of its date in all Germany. These huge arches are really barrel vaults, the spandrels between which are vaulted to become pendentives supporting a circular gallery, over which rises the drum of the cupola. For the construction of the spandrels the architects used large tiles, taking their cues from Roman building construction.

Within the rectangular spaces under the barrel vaults around three sides of the central square space are galleries carried on a subsidiary Corinthian order. The fourth rectangular space merges with the apse to become the chancel.

Persius was probably responsible for the innovative ceiling construction, which was made of zinc panels set in a lattice, by Geiss of Berlin. Cast zinc was also used for the large, richly ornamented parts of the main cornice, for the sculptures along the railings of the choir lofts and for sculptures above the capitals.

The Nikolaikirche got its drum and dome at last between 1843 and 1849, and the building was completed after Persius' death in 1845 by A. Stüler. The apse was decorated by Bernhard Wilhelm Rosendahl, and the pulpit by Kiss (1836-37).

In 1945 the church was very badly damaged. Work began on the reconstruction of the cupola in 1955, using steel construction clad in copper. The corner towers and semicircular windows were restored between 1969 and 1972, and the interior was reconstructed from 1975, but many details are not quite as designed. Probably the greatest change that has occurred is to the setting of this masterpiece by one of the greatest architects the world has known. The Nikolaikirche was designed to sit in a spacious square, the Alten Markt. War damage and subsequent building of the most banal designs conceivable have wrecked the surroundings, and the juxtaposition of nonarchitecture and Schinkel's great church is painful in the extreme.

The Nikolaikirche is perhaps the most perfect neoclassical church ever built: it is a realization of those concerns with stereometrically pure forms that were a feature of the designs of Etiènne-Louis Boullée and Claude-Nicolas Ledoux. An antique portico set against a blank wall, a simple mass with geometrically pure figures cut into it, an apse placed against a blank surface, and a drum set on a square are all examples of a type of architectural massing that fascinated designers of the second half of the 18th and the first half of the 19th century. In the Nikolaikirche is a resolution of supreme quality, and architecture of the highest order. It is to be hoped that the setting of this incomparably fine building will be radically improved in years to come.

—JAMES STEVENS CURL

PALACE OF SANS SOUCI
Potsdam, Germany

1745-46: Designs for the Marmorsaal, original designs and proportions of all rooms; **Architect:** Georg Wenzeslaus von Knobelsdorff (1699-1753); **Garden Sculptors:** Christian Friedrich Glüme, Lambert-Sigisbert Adam, Jean-Baptiste Pigalle; Garden satyrs; **Carver:** Balthasar Permoser. **After 1746:** Supervision of building taken over; **Architect:** Johann Baumann the Elder; Most interior decorations; **Designers:** Johann Michael Hoppenhaupt and Johann August Nahl. **1750:** Extensions and garden structures for Park of Sans Souci; **Architect:** Georg Wenzeslaus von Knobelsdorff. **1763-64:** Marble terrace wall of the Dutch Garden; **Architect:** Jean-Laurent Legeay. **1786:** Interior decoration for the workroom with bedroom adjoining; **Designer:** Friedrich Wilhelm von Erdmannsdorff (1736-1800). **1841-42:** Extensions; **Architect:** Ludwig Persius and continued by Freidrich August Stüler after Persius' death.

Publications

EGGELING, TILO: *Studien zum friderizianischen Rokoko: Georg Wenceslaus von Knobelsdorff als Entwerfer von Innendekorationen.* Berlin, 1980.
GIERSBERG, HANS JOACHIM: "Studien zur Architektur des 18. Jahrhunderts in Berlin und Potsdam." Ph.D. dissertation. Humboldt Universität, Berlin, 1975.
HEMPEL, EBERHARD: *Baroque Art and Architecture in Central Europe.* Harmondsworth, England, 1965.
KADATZ, HANS-JOACHIM: *Georg Wenzeslaus von Knobelsdorff: Baumeister Friedrichs II.* Leipzig, 1983.
KÜHN, MARGARETE: *Georg Wenzeslaus von Knobelsdorff.* Berlin, 1953.
KURTH, WILLY: *Sanssouci: Ein Beitrag zur Kunst des deutschen Rokoko.* Berlin, 1970.
NOVAK, KARL: *Sans Souci.* Leipzig, n.d.
STREICHHAN, ANNALIESE: *Knobelsdorff und das friderizianische Rokoko.* Burg bei Magdeburg, Germany, 1932.

*

King Frederick II of Prussia (1712-86), better known to us, perhaps, as Frederick the Great, was not only a statesman, philosopher and soldier, but a great patron of the arts, and especially of architecture. In addition, he was a passionate Francophile, and therefore as keen on the courtly Rococo style as on a developing neoclassicism. In fact, much of the architecture built under Frederick's aegis took its themes from France, from Saxony (especially Dresden) and from England. In the latter case, echoes of Castle Howard occur at the Neues Palais at Potsdam, while English Palladianism, and especially Colen Campbell's Wanstead, was the precedent for the Berlin Opera House in the Unter den Linden.

The king was fortunate in having Georg Wenzeslaus von Knobelsdorff (1699-1753), Prussian aristocrat, soldier, painter and architect, as his friend. Knobelsdorff had studied architecture at the Academy in Berlin after he left the army in 1729 on grounds of ill health, and his friendship with Frederick developed when the latter was still crown prince of Prussia.

There were early commissions, then Frederick sent Knobelsdorff on a study tour of Italy in 1736-37; when the latter returned, he became a resident at the prince's court, carrying out various commissions for his patron. When Frederick became king in 1740, Knobelsdorff was appointed *Oberintendant* of the royal

Palace of Sans Souci: Potsdam, Germany, 1745-46

palaces and gardens, and the new king sent him on a second tour to improve his architectural education: this time Knobelsdorff visited Saxony and France. Dresden had made a great impression on the young prince, and he desired his architect to absorb some of the wealth of architectural excellence to be found in the Saxon capital.

Various important commissions, including the prestigious neo-Palladian Opera House mentioned above, followed. Knobelsdorff was also appointed director-in-chief of all buildings in the royal provinces, and a member of the powerful Prussian Council of Ministers.

In 1744 work commenced on the Stadtschloss in Potsdam, which had rich Rococo interiors, and in 1745 the king provided a sketch for a new palace to be called Sans Souci, which Knobelsdorff developed into a full set of design drawings.

The desire to build a retreat called ''Without Care'' was prompted by the king's recent successes in war, the split with his queen (Frederick was homosexual and seems to have found the company of women tedious and wearing), and his wish to organize his time and his life to suit himself. The king was a voracious reader, an accomplished musician and a great lover of animals, especially his horses and dogs.

Knobelsdorff worked closely with Frederick to perfect the designs of Sans Souci, perhaps one of the most enchanting small palaces ever built. It stands on a terrace above a series of terraces set against the slope of the steeply falling ground.

The front of each terrace has glazed opening doors to enable Mediterranean flowers and fruit to be cultivated in the relatively unkind climate of the countryside around Berlin. The total effect, with the curved, glazed terrace fronts leading down to the large pool with its fountain at the bottom of the slope, is like a gigantic and magnificent cascade. It is an entirely memorable and delightful ensemble.

There is a problem, however. From the lowest level, near the pool and fountain, the long, low palace is partially obscured, as it is set back on the upmost terrace: the garden front of the palace with the terraces beneath, therefore, can be seen unobscured only from a distance, while the front of the palace is revealed in detail only when viewed from the topmost terrace (at the east end of which the king's favorite dogs are buried). Knobelsdorff had realized that this would be the case, and he therefore proposed placing the palace on a raised, stepped platform so that the garden front would be more visible from the bottom of the terraces and as one ascended those terraces. Frederick, however, insisted that he should have direct access through the French windows to the top terrace without having to descend any steps on a platform. The two men seem to have had heated arguments about this, and the impasse led to an estrangement: Knobelsdorff ceased to act for the king after 1746. One can see the problem quite clearly: when the palace is viewed from the topmost terrace, its proportions are faultless and its detail agreeable, but, from the descending terraces, the lower part of the facade is obscured, which creates an unhappy architectural effect.

So what exactly is Sans Souci? It is far more than a *Lustschloss*, or a pavilion in a park. It is actually a palace, but it is relatively small and intimate, set on one floor. It consists of a long, single-story building with wings each six windows wide set on either side of an elliptical domed centerpiece (which has a green copper roof and elaborate circular dormer windows set in Baroque stone frames). This long garden front has widely spaced, paired terminal satyrs of the most lively sort carrying the entablature, over which is a balustrade with urns set on the pedestals. The sources for these satyr terms are obviously the vigorous carvings by Balthasar Permoser (1651-1732) on the Zwinger Palace at Dresden, which both Frederick and Knobelsdorff had seen. On the frieze of the central rotunda at Potsdam are the words ''SANS SOUCI.''

This exquisite little palace is approached from a *cour d'honneur* enclosed on one side by the entrance front and by two curved colonnades of paired columns carrying an entablature. These colonnades are of great lightness and elegance, and are quite specifically French in inspiration. The east front of the Louvre and Ribart de Chamoust's ''French'' order feature paired columns. From this court is a view toward the Ruinenberg, an eminence on which are sham ruins built as eye-catchers, a theme derived from English prototypes.

Clipped hedges, pergolas and trelliswork help to define the spaces in the immediate vicinity of the palace, while garden decorations included statuary by Christian Friedrich Glüme, Lambert-Sigisbert Adam and Jean-Baptiste Pigalle. The dominant garden features, however, are the ''cascade'' of glass-fronted terraces, the pool with its fountain, the Ruinenberg and the contrived vistas of the park, which must be one of the loveliest in the world (although in the late 1980s it was not very well kept, as was generally the case in the German Democratic Republic).

The palace is entered through a small vestibule, behind which is the greatest room in the building, the central Marmorsaal, with its coupled Corinthian columns (again a French device): this elliptical room is more neoclassical than Rococo (though there are Rococo touches in the floor inlay and in the *putti* and

other figures that are perched on the cornice), and is inspired by classical antiquity in the form of the Pantheon in Rome.

Knobelsdorff appears to have been responsible only for the design of the Marmorsaal, although he created the proportions of the other rooms. His involvement with Sans Souci seems to have ended before the interior decorators really got down to work. Most of the rooms are decorated in the most wonderful mature light Rococo manner to designs by Johann Michael Hoppenhaupt and Johann August Nahl. In fact, the Sans Souci Rococo is about the finest to be found anywhere, and is the dominant theme of the library, the concert salon and the dining room. The music room has a ceiling decorated with gilded Rococo relief featuring nets and a spider's web, while the delicate paintings of pastoral scenes in asymmetrical Rococo gilt frames are by Antoine Pesne (1683-1757). One of the most delightful rooms is that associated with Voltaire, who stayed there: it was decorated by Hoppenhaupt, and has a distinctly chinoiserie-Rococo flavor enhanced by the colored flora and fauna.

One other room, apart from the Marmorsaal, was decorated in the neoclassical style: this is the workroom with the bedroom off it in which the king died, and it is the creation of Friedrich Wilhelm von Erdmannsdorff (1736-1800), dating from 1786. The main feature of Erdmannsdorff's charming scheme is the screen of fluted seagliola Ionic columns *in antis* set on pedestals which subdivides the working and sleeping quarters of the apartment. Erdmannsdorff was to be one of a number of distinguished architects called to Berlin in 1788 by King Frederick William II, who reigned from 1787 to 1797.

Sans Souci combines elements of Anglo-Palladianism, French coupled columns and neoclassical features, German and French Rococo, and the classical manner of Erdmannsdorff, which he used in Wörlitz and in other projects for Prince Franz of Anhalt-Dessau. The whole is exquisitely put together, and throughout, the scale is perfect. Sans Souci is unparalleled among palace architecture of the period, although the smaller Amalienburg at Schloss Nymphenburg near Munich has certain affinities of composition and decor, while Schloss Benrath near Düsseldorf (1755-57) is more like the Potsdam palace, but sits on a high podium.

The palace is important not only as a very fine example of Knobelsdorff's work in which neoclassical and Rococo elements are combined, but as one element in an extraordinary range of buildings of the highest quality in the park at Potsdam. There, the essence of the *Aufklärung* is given architectural expression. There can be no more delightful secular building on earth, and no palace as agreeable: it is a fitting monument to Frederick the Great.

—JAMES STEVENS CURL

PILGRIMAGE CHURCH (WALLFAHRTSKIRCHE STEINHAUSEN)
Steinhausen, Germany

1727: Church commissioned by Abbot of Schussenried; **Architect:** Dominikus Zimmermann (1685-1766). **1728-35:** Construction of building. Ceiling frescoes and stuccowork; **Artist:** Johann Baptist Zimmermann (1680-1758). **1749-50:** Completion of altars.

Pilgrimage Church: Steinhausen, Germany, 1728-35

Publications

FEULNER, ADOLF: *Bayerisches Rokoko*. Munich, 1923.

HAGER, LUISA: *Nymphenburg*. Munich, 1955.

HITCHCOCK, HENRY-RUSSELL: *German Rococo: The Zimmerman Brothers*. Baltimore, 1968.

KASPER, ALFONS and STRACHE, WOLF: *Steinhausen, ein Juwel unter den Dorfkirchen*. Stuttgart, 1957.

LAMB, CARL: *Die Wies*. Munich, 1948.

LAMPL, SIXTUS: *Johann Baptist Zimmermanns Schlierseer Anfänge*. Schliersee, Germany, 1979.

RUPPRECHT, BERNHARD: *Die Bayerische Rokokokirche*. Kallmünz, Germany, 1959.

SCHNELL, HUGO: *Die Wies*. First published Munich, 1934, revised edition, 1981.

THON, CHRISTINA: *Johann Baptist Zimmermann als Stukkator*. Munich, 1977.

*

Wallfahrtskirche Steinhausen, near Biberach in Württemberg, was commissioned by the Premonstratensian abbot of Schussenried in 1727 as a pilgrimage church of Our Lady of Sorrows. The architect, Dominikus Zimmermann, was first a stucco artist, but later developed his skills as an architect.

The building, which cost much more than was originally intended (resulting in the early retirement of the abbot and a refusal of Zimmermann's request to spend his last days in the abbey), is set in very beautiful, open, partly wooded countryside, and rises high above the pitched roofs of the village. A three-stage tower capped with a small bulbous onion rises somewhat uncomfortably from the steeply pitched and complex roof behind an elaborate shaped gable that features convex and concave sweeping copes. The church has four such gables, giving an oddly north-European Early Renaissance note to the composition, while the upper curve of the gables is echoed in the cornices of the belfry stage of the tower, giving it a slightly surprised appearance. It cannot be said that the single tower works particularly well in architectural terms, any more so than it does at Die Wies, Zimmermann's other famous church: the twin towers found in many south-German Baroque and Rococo churches are infinitely more satisfactory as compositions. The squared and gabled sides and intersecting roofs at Steinhausen give an impression of a crossing and transepts, which is odd, because there are no transepts. The plan is in fact an ellipse with the longer axis that of the church itself: two rectangular elements at either end of the long axis contain the elliptical chancel and the staircases, vestibule and tower. Ten massive piers surround the central ellipse, creating a species of elliptical aisle all around. The aisle walls are pierced by two stories of charmingly shaped windows that widen out at the top in typical Zimmermann fashion (the upper windows are tripartite), and the walls of the two bays in the center of the long axis are thickened so that they are squared outside and give the impression of being transepts. The plan can be explained by the fact that Steinhausen is a pilgrimage church: the number of seats in the center of the ellipse is small, but there was adequate space for pilgrims to process around the aisles.

Internally, the church is wonderfully delicate and light, with much white and gold. It was one of the first full manifestations of the Rococo style, and marked the break with earlier Baroque concerns with mystical indirect lighting in favor of direct, bright

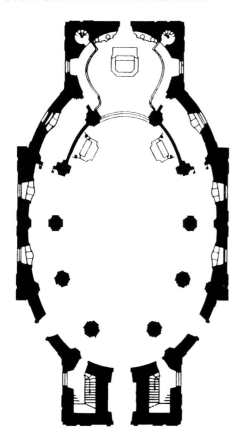

light enhanced by a color scheme that is predominantly white, giving a porcelain-like enchantment to the whole design. The eye is drawn to the elaborate aedicule of the high altar, emphasized by the two side altars set obliquely between the piers on either side of the "chancel arch." The main object of devotion, the *Gnadenbild,* is a *Pietà:* the painting shows a bare Cross, the body having been taken down, and in front of the painting the dead Christ is shown resting on Our Lady's knee. Above, the upper painting framed in the attic story of the reredos depicts the risen Christ. The elliptical chancel contains allusions to the Trinity, for the ceiling fresco (by Johann Baptist Zimmermann [1680-1758]) shows God the Father and the Holy Ghost in the glory of Heaven waiting for the son who is sacrificed on the altar below. Thus the altar itself shows Our Lady with her dead son, in the deepest depths of her sorrow.

Unquestionably, the most successful and arresting part of this masterpiece of South German Rococo is the ceiling of the central ellipse. It is an excellent example of that attempt to create rooflessness by means of illusion, perspective and coloring, for the visitor seems to be looking through the roof into a marvelous sky. Above the arches over the elaborate entablatures of the piers (the capitals of which seem to melt and flow as though made of marine forms trailing in water) is stuccowork that suggests the most delicate of porcelain balconies, worthy of Meissen itself. Over this "balcony" are figures, gardens, landscapes, but the whole of the center of the ellipse is a vision of Heaven and of a glorious riot of angels, *putti* and writhing, gesticulating, joyous saints: this is, of course, Our Lady as queen of Heaven, the gateway to the New Testament after the loss of Paradise. But the pilgrim, versed in Marian imagery, would recognize much more. On axis, for example, on the ceiling fresco, directly above the arch leading to the chancel and the *Pietà,* is a fountain in a magically beautiful garden. This represents the *Hortus Conclusus,* and the *Fons Signatus,*

both Marian attributes derived from the Song of Songs. The pilgrim, therefore, looks upwards to a vision of Heaven where Mary reigns as *Regina Angelorum* and *Regina Sanctorum Omnium:* here are other images such as the potted plant, crowns and roses which represent the *Vas Spirituale,* the *Vas Insigne Devotionis,* the *Rosa Mystica* and the *Stella Matutina.* It is difficult to say where reality ends and illusion begins, for does not the symbol represent what it is? Certainly such a church with its iconography cannot be understood without some knowledge of Marian symbolism. The Litany of the Blessed Virgin, sung at Benediction, is largely a recital of attributes illustrated in Baroque and rococo churches, and Steinhausen is full of such imagery and allusion. This great fresco is by J. B. Zimmermann.

Wallfahrtskirche Steinhausen (completed in 1735) is perhaps the happiest composition, and internally the most satisfactorily unified of all Rococo church interiors. Gloom is banished, and the clear light of a joyous Heaven speaks volumes about the meaning and significance of the sorrows of Our Lady to the fortunate pilgrims who have had the happiness to enjoy this wonderful church.

—JAMES STEVENS CURL

NEUE STAATSGALERIE
Stuttgart, Germany

1977-84: Constructed; **Architect:** James Stirling (1926-).

Publications

KLEIHUES, JOSEF PAUL (ed.): *Dortmunder Architekturhefte 15: Museumbauten—Entwurfe und Projekte seit 1945.* Exhibition catalog. Dortmund, West Germany, 1979.

*

If one were to list the significant museum buildings that were built during the second half of the 20th century, James Stirling and Michael Wilford's Neue Staatsgalerie in Stuttgart should no doubt appear near the top of the roster. The building was the result of a limited competition for an addition to the original Staatsgalerie, a 19th-century neoclassical building. Located along the edge of the once-elegant Schloss garden, the Neue Staatsgalerie fronts the Konrad-Adenauer-Strasse. The Stirling building manipulates its hillside site through a series of terraces and ramps to provide a public cross-site access between the State Theater buildings (located along the Schloss gardens) and the Urban Platz (the address of the city's music academy).

Stirling drew his inspiration for the building from both modern and traditional precedents. The accomplished English architect made specific reference to Karl Friedrich Schinkel's Altes Museum in Berlin (1823-30) through a plan configuration that employs ranges of gallery rooms and a distinct central rotund space in a similar manner to the 19th-century German museum. The architect embraced a planning strategy that uses the characteristics of discrete room-like spaces, otherwise known as the "traditional plan." But, Stirling's building is not solely an assertion of post modern historicist aesthetics, for he synthesized aspects of the "traditional plan" with lessons that he learned from the bard of 20th-century architecture, Le Corbusier. The Staatsgalerie contains a sufficient quantity of space that was planned according to the tenets of the "free plan" to merit

Neue Staatsgalerie: Stuttgart, Germany, 1977-84

examination of an alternative precedent to the Altes Museum. The lower levels of the building house spaces that are composed to suggest lateral continuity in a more free-flowing manner that is characteristic of the "free plan." In these areas, the architect eschewed the discrete room-like division of space in favor of a continuous field of columns punctuated by specific programmatic items and elements of circulation. This portion of the building bears comparison to the Palace of the Assembly by Le Corbusier, in Chandigarh, India. The strategy of combining discrete room-like spatial divisions while simultaneously making provisions for open, free-flowing spaces enhances the flexibility of the museum building.

While part of the agenda of the architect was clearly directed toward addressing the programmatic complexities of a museum, it is equally apparent that the architect used precedent to establish a narrative for the building. Stirling was acutely aware of the city's past, and he used the building to construct a promenade that places the visitor in confrontation with history. It may be argued that there exist two Stuttgarts. There is, of course, the notion of a traditional Stuttgart—a city that once served as home to the rulers of the land of Württemberg. That Stuttgart, the city of the Schloss and its magnificent gardens, the home of a dignified albeit military-dominated culture, and birthplace of Friedrich Schiller, had come to an abrupt conclusion during the later stages of World War II with the massive Allied bombings. An examination of photographs made after the German capitulation illustrates almost complete devastation of the once-elegant city. Estimates concerning the destruction of the city approach 60 percent. Within this context we might also consider a second urban scenario—that of the postwar city—modern Stuttgart. This city retained little of the charm of the traditional

city, and wherever possible the memories of the firestorms and aerial bombardment were expertly eradicated. The war provided an opportunity for rebuilding the city according to modernist ideals. Probably the three best examples of postwar urbanistic strategies can be illustrated by the destruction of the formal axis of the Schloss gardens (for the National Horticultural Show of 1961), the construction of the object-fixated Parliament Building adjacent to the Schloss, and the intervention of an urban autobahn along the line of the Neckar-Strasse (renamed Konrad-Adenauer-Strasse). These projects, along with numerous other infill and rebuilding schemes, made a conscious effort to distance themselves from the traditional city.

Stirling's solution to the dilemma of prewar and postwar Stuttgart was to allow aspects of both cities to exist simultaneously upon the site. He accomplished this partially through the employment of both "abstract" and "representational" elements that allow interpretation as icons of modernity and tradition, respectively. In the Neue Staatsgalerie, we find Stirling making use of "abstract" elements in the form of a series of canopies that mark the entrances to the museum, boldly-colored handrails, and piano-curved curtain walls. These elements clearly belong to the modernist "mind-set" of the architect, while the stone "chassis" of the building—the primary "representational" element, is indicative of his fascination for tradition. The architect exploited the confrontation between contrasting stylistic elements to achieve his ends. He achieved a conceptual framework by allowing his building to benefit from both the traditional spatial strategies of the Altes Museum and the modern paradigm of the Palace of the Assembly. The confrontation between tradition and modernity could have ended there, but he extended the argument to engage memories of the city. He achieved this task by subscribing to urban and architectural ideals that can be seen both as modern and traditional—producing a building that is at once a ruin and a reconstruction.

The Neue Staatsgalerie alludes to both traditional and modern paradigms of the city. The building performs both the tasks of forming space by participating as a fragment of a traditional fabric and making object—standing out against the urban backdrop. The architect was conscious of both traditional construction techniques in his allusions to solid masonry walls and true to modern methods through an exposure of the *trompe l'oeil* effects of those surfaces that become apparent upon close inspection. Ultimately, the architect has created a narrative that involves the building and the viewer in an examination of the memories of the two cities of Stuttgart. He has done so without rejecting the richness and validity of our western architectural traditions and, equally, without dismissing the critique provided by the architecture of the first half of the 20th century. The building addresses the monumental and atemporal qualities necessarily associated with civic architecture. It suggests a civic

architecture that encourages and provokes memories and associations with both ideals and realities. Stirling presents the civic building as a theater of memory, an embodiment of the ideals and aspirations, and too a reminder of the failures, within the public realm.

—BRIAN KELLY

SCHOCKEN DEPARTMENT STORE
Stuttgart, Germany

1926-28: Constructed; **Architect:** Erich Mendelsohn (1887-1953).

Schocken Department Store: Stuttgart, Germany, 1926-27

Publications

DÜSSEL, KARL KONRAD: "Drei Kaufhäuser Schocken in Nürnberg, Stuttgart und Chemnitz von Erich Mendelsohn." *Moderne Bauformen* (November 1930): 461-484.

VON ECKARDT, WOLF: *Eric Mendelsohn.* New York and London, 1960.

WHITTICK, ARNOLD: *Eric Mendelsohn.* London, 1940.

ZEVI, BRUNO: *Erich Mendelsohn: opera completa. Architettore e imagini architettoniche.* Milan, 1970.

*

Erich Mendelsohn, in his sketches, dreamed great dreams and fantasized about monumental, sweeping structures: powerhouses and industrial plants, concert halls and railway stations, the icons of the 20th century. The commissions which actually came to his flourishing practice were of another kind altogether, representing the uncompromising, real-world demands of commerce. In a series of notable buildings, from 1924 to 1930, Mendelsohn applied his considerable design talents to the problem of the department store. In these buildings, he managed to transmute the mundane prose of the business world, if not quite into the soaring palaces of his early fantasies, then at least into an architecture which, while eminently practical, was nevertheless always suffused with his innate poetic vision. The Schocken Department Store at Stuttgart represents the mature midpoint in this development.

This analysis follows Mendelsohn's own design procedure, and begins with the external form. Mendelsohn defined the main elements in his exploratory diagrammatic sketches, and never departed from them in principle, in all subsequent developments of the design. The composition is envisaged as a complex and dynamic interaction of basically simple forms, located on a corner site. The main element is shown as a long, rectilinear prism, whose surface is banded with a repetitive pattern of closely spaced horizontal lines. This block is poised above an unclearly defined base, from which it is separated by the slash of a projecting canopy carrying the name "Schocken" in giant, almost story-height letters. At the corner, the facade pivots around in a semicircular bay, which first projects forward, then sweeps around to carry the banded facade for some distance along the down-sloping side street, before stepping back to link with a lower wing. At the opposite end, projecting above roof level, there is another similarly designed round-ended bay, placed in opposition to the curved corner element, and on an axis at right angles to it.

In reality, the building is basically true to, but somehow less than, the initial concept. In the process of translating aspiration into reality, the dream is inevitably diminished. The building is shorter, squatter, than the sketches would indicate. The close horizontal rhythm translates into broad bands of generously sized windows, whose deep reveals set up an opposed and insistent vertical beat. The wall surfaces between the continuous window heads at one floor and the continuous windowsills of the floor above, are patterned with applied horizontal stripes; the dynamic concept is reduced to a set of lines merely imposed upon the surface, and even these disappear in those night-time views so favored by Mendelsohn. The prismatic form, which had been so ingeniously dissolved in the sketches, is thus revealed in all its substantial reality. Consequently, it sits heavily upon the continuously glazed shopfront to the store, which constitutes its base.

The main facade to the store is competent, if not altogether convincing. Its horizontality is achieved by somewhat contrived means, not integral as in the Herpich Store which preceded it, nor as striking as Mendelsohn's superb store for Schocken at Chemnitz, which followed. However, it is the manipulation of plastic form, rather than mere surface articulation, that is Mendelsohn's forte. The vigorous three-dimensional composition of the Schocken Store, with its contrapuntally balanced geometric forms, curvilinear and prismatic, and its bold supergraphics, is architecturally most effective. Finally, what transforms this good architecture into high drama in the inspired handling of the corner bay. This glass-enclosed staircase tower, ringed by close-spaced horizontal bands, simultaneously expresses both the verticality of the tower, and—for the very first time in an executed building—the dynamic curves and sweeping horizontals which are the very essence of Mendelsohn's vision, dating from his earliest imaginary sketches.

A comparison with Louis Sullivan's Schlesinger and Mayer Store in Chicago, of a previous generation, is irresistible. True, Mendelsohn's rectilinear facade may take us no further than Sullivan's, but the dominant corner treatment of the Schocken Store is architecturally far more successful than the hesitant hinge upon which the Chicago building turns. Moreover, both rounded corners deal essentially with the same pair of linked problems: for the upper floors, how to turn the corner gracefully; and, at street level, how to design a commercially desirable corner entrance to the store, when it penetrates the building at such a visually sensitive point. Sullivan's circular entrance pavilion is a bravura display, but leaves the entrance in an exposed and vulnerable position; Mendelsohn uses the vigorous curve of the shopfront seductively to lead prospective customers into the protected entrance to the store. Once inside, they are confronted with evidence of other facets of Mendelsohn's ineffable skill as an architect: his functional planning of space, his mastery of interior design, his passionate care for detail, and his total control of the entire ensemble, from the design of furniture and fittings, to the lighting and graphics. "The scope of total architecture" was a phrase coined by Walter Gropius; it could most aptly be used to describe the Schocken Store.

—GILBERT HERBERT

WEISSENHOFSIEDLUNG
Stuttgart, Germany

1927: Construction; **Architects:** Ludwig Mies van der Rohe (1886-1969), Richard Döcker (1894-1968).

Publications

BEHRENS, PETER: *Terrassen am Hause.* Stuttgart, 1927.

CADBURY-BROWN, H. T.: "Ludwig Mies van der Rohe." *Architectural Association Journal* (July-August 1959).

"Die Ausstellung 'Die Wohnung' in Stuttgart." *Stavba* (1927): 35-64.

"Die Wohnungsausstellung Stuttgart 1927." *Werk* 9 (1927).

"Exposition du 'Werkbund' a Stuttgart." *Cahiers d'art* 7/8 (1927).

FRAMPTON, KENNETH, AND FUTAGAWA, YUKIO: *Modern Architecture: 1920-1945.* New York, 1983.

JOEDICKE, JÜRGEN, and PLATH, CHRISTIAN: *Die Weissenhofsiedlung.* Stuttgart, 1968.

KIRSCH, KARIN: *The Weissenhofsiedlung: Experimental Housing Built for the Deutscher Werkbund, Stuttgart 1927.* New York, 1987.

Weissenhofsiedlung: Stuttgart, Germany, 1927

LINDER, PAUL: "La exposición 'Werkbund Ausstellung' en Stuttgart." *Arquitectura* 103 (1927).

MIES VAN DER ROHE, LUDWIG: "Werkbundaustellung: Die Wohnung Stuttgart." *Form* (September 1927).

MUELLER-WULCKOW, W.: *Wohnbauten und Siedlungen.* Koenigstein, 1928.

POMMER, RICHARD, and OTTO, CHRISTIAN F.: *Weissenhof 1927 and the Modern Movement in Architecture.* Chicago, 1991.

RASCH, HEINZ, and RASCH, BODO: *Wie Bauen? Bau- und Einrichtung der Werkbundsiedlung am Weissenhof in Stuttgart 1927.* Stuttgart, 1927.

RASCH, BODO: "Wie die Weissenhofsiedlung entstand." *Deutsche Bauzeitung* (November 1977): 28-35.

UNGERS, LISELOTTE: *Die Suche nach einer neuen Wohnform: Siedlungen der zwanziger Jahre damals und heuete.* Stuttgart, Germany. 1983.

Weissenhofsiedlung. Deutscher Werkbund Exhibition catalog. Stuttgart, 1927.

*

For the Modern Movement in architecture, it became an article of faith that better design could improve the quality of life enjoyed by the many, in addition to that already enjoyed by the few. This position was institutionalized and promoted by the German Werkbund, whose membership believed that good design was not an abstraction; to them the benefits of good design could be demonstrated in terms of economy and efficiency, as well as healthfulness. In a series of exhibitions organized during the years following the end of World War I, the Werkbund sought to convince the general public of the value better design offered. However, much of what the public was shown consisted of abstractions, projects and prototypes, rather than the real thing. As a result, among some Werkbund members there was great impetus to translate those ideas about design into three-dimensional reality.

To accomplish that goal, in 1927 Ludwig Mies van der Rohe, then first vice-president of the Werkbund, was invited to organize a group of architects to design a series of housing types that would exemplify the "new living space." Titled "Die Wohnung," this exhibition would be the first major attempt by the Werkbund at reforming German aesthetic thought since the group's initial exposition at Cologne, in 1914. There was, perhaps, a more pressing issue: the need for affordable low-and middle-income housing. Mies and the other architects invited to participate were willing to explore new approaches to solving this most pressing problem.

Because of wartime experience, terms such as "standardization," "rationalization" and "functionalism" found their way into the ordinary vocabularies of architects and designers, and theirs became an overwhelming enthusiasm for forms derived from, or apparently derived from, clear structure and clearly definable function. This idea of an architecture, developed from something other than the study of history or historical prototypes, did not spring full-grown from the Werkbund collective mind. Rather, it had its roots in the 19th-century English Arts and Crafts movement. While that movement eschewed the machine and celebrated the craft of the individual, it also valued pure, unadorned form. It was the quality of pure form that appealed to the modernists, among them Le Corbusier, who summarized their position: "Working by calculation, engineers employ geometrical forms satisfying our eyes by their geometry and our understanding of their mathematics; their work is on the direct line of good art." For modernists, then, in addition to discrediting the old order, the experiences of the "Great War" served to expose designers and architects to the potential that industrialization and serial production offered. As a result, the "idea" of technology became the touchstone of the Modern Movement.

It was in that spirit and with the goal of providing economical alternatives to the problem of housing large numbers of people that a site, overlooking the city of Stuttgart—the Weissenhof—was selected and the project undertaken. Stipulated in the building program was the condition that at the close of the exhibition the structures would be sold or rented. During construction, the city of Stuttgart would simply act as a corporate entity, overseeing construction and guaranteeing initial financing. In retrospect, these conditions seem simple enough, but they ignored the personalities of the individuals involved and the politics of the times.

Initially, neither the modernists' force of numbers nor their talent was enough to convince the officials in Stuttgart of modernism's validity. In contrast to the conservative solution to the subdivision of land and the arrangement of houses advocated by the city's engineers, Mies proposed a more comprehensive and inclusive site plan, one in which a range of housing types and buildings would be linked with low walls, terraces and broad stairs. Conceptually, Mies' proposal was more akin to an Italian hill town of the Middle Ages than to what we have come to associate with large-scale housing developments. With an integrative approach to housing and site development, Mies was attempting to articulate a positive link between modern architecture and the architecture and urban design of the past. The engineers deemed many of the walls, terraces and stairs too expensive and somehow inappropriate for such modest housing. It is to Mies' lasting credit that the final site plan incorporated as many of these architectonic amenities as it did.

There was the problem of bringing in out-of-town talent to design the buildings. Architects in Stuttgart felt that they were capable of providing the necessary talent to plan and design the buildings constructed at the Weissenhof. Mies did not; he felt that for the project to be successful, the best architects and designers, regardless of nationality, should be invited to participate. Further, Mies insisted that the architects be encouraged to explore the possibilities posed by modern architecture and the "free plan." To do this, the fewest restraints should be imposed. Was it not the case that the Werkbund wished to encourage innovation in design at all levels? In any case, the friction already existing among various groups in the Werkbund (and Germany itself) manifested itself in Stuttgart almost at once. It was not only friction between conservatives and liberals, although that played a part; it was the friction between those who saw themselves advancing the cause of modern architecture and those who would be left behind if they did not embrace it, of accepting Germany's (and Europe's) changed conditions or returning to the past. Many times Mies was obliged to seek peace while advancing the cause of modern architecture in what was a hostile environment. From his point of view, there was no other way to give the public an opportunity to see and experience the possibilities modern architecture offered than to make sure that this idea about space, the free plan, was kept as uncompromised as possible.

Curiously, to assure the democracy of ideas, Mies had to be an absolutist. His absolutism extended to the participating architects. The list reads like a European "Who's Who of Modern Architecture": Peter Behrens, Victor Bourgeois, Le Corbusier, Richard Docker, Joseph Frank, Walter Gropius, Ludwig Hilberseimer, Pierre Jeanneret (Le Corbusier's brother), J. J. P. Oud, Hans Poelzig, Adolf Rading, Hans Scharoun, Adolph G. Schneck, Mart Stam, Bruno and Max Taut, and, of course, Mies. Their work ran the gamut of modern architecture, suggesting, in part, that the Modern Movement was not confined to one country or limited to a few architects working in isolation.

Because they were essentially designing prototypes, the architects of the Weissenhofsiedlung could not take advantage of the economy of scale, that is, mass production. As a result, the housing types constructed were more expensive than they would have been had traditional methods of construction and traditional approaches to making space been used. The weather was not much help either, with prolonged rains resulting in costly delays. Without approval, products and materials were substituted for those specified by the architects. In addition, coordination between the architects, the on-site supervisors and the city's engineers was mismanaged at every step.

The exhibition opened despite these problems. The buildings, almost uniformly painted white, were compatible with one another, and the landscaping suggested the homogenous environment and contact with nature that Mies hoped to achieve. The various housing types, testing the validity of the new approach to defining space and articulating function, worked well; but what also became clear was that the attempt to reduce the overall cost of housing by reducing habitable space had not resulted in the hoped-for economies, and the appeal of rational, industrialized housing was more to architects and designers than to the general public. However, as the mayor of Stuttgart was careful to point out at the opening of the Weissenhofsiedlung, "The exhibition departs markedly from outworn tradition. The idea behind it has sprung from the urgent needs of the present day." While the problem of affordable housing was an important one, the mayor's remarks were not enough to ensure general acceptance, and because it was difficult for the public to see beyond the uniform surfaces to the possibilities the free plan offered, the Weissenhofsiedlung did not receive the objective attention the exhibition of prototypes deserved.

In his remarks at the opening of the Weissenhof, Mies commented: "The issues of rationalization and standardization are no more than means to an end; they must never become an end in themselves. The problem of the New Home is ultimately a problem of the mind, and the struggle for the New Home is only one element in the great struggle for new forms of living." As perceptive as Mies' remarks remain, they were insufficient to overcome a general reaction that there was something not quite right with the architecture, with the open spaces and the lack of surface decoration. Very quickly there appeared a postcard of the exhibition depicting it as an Arab village, and the airbrushed palm trees, camels and burnoosed Arabs were meant to be understood as a caustic commentary on the architecture as not German, not of the nation's blood and soil. Concept and content were ignored, and during the Third Reich, it was an easy step to add pitched roofs to some of the buildings and further to discredit modern architecture by destroying others.

With the exception of a few pitched roofs, changes in exterior color, and the addition of garages for automobiles, the present appearance of the Weissenhofsiedlung approaches that of 1927. It remains a prophetic vision as to how space might inform architecture and the landscape; it places a premium on collective rather than individual action; and though its buildings are modern in look and spirit, as an ensemble they speak to an earlier time when people lived in communities and shared a common vision. It may well be that the ultimate value of the Weissenhofsiedlung is as a paradigmatic vision of the future rather than as a preserved piece of the past.

—DAVID SPAETH

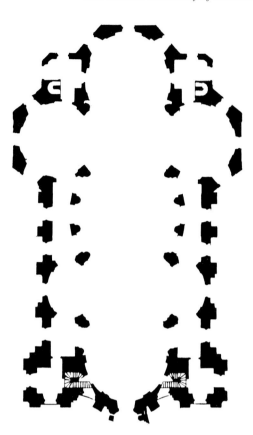

PILGRIMAGE CHURCH
Vierzehnheiligen, Germany

1738: Original designs created; **Architect:** Gottfried Heinrich Krohne (1703-56). **1743:** Construction begun. **1744:** Construction halted and new design created; **Architects:**Johann Balthasar Neumann, Johann Jakob Michael Küchel (1703-69). **1753:** Neumann dies and Küchel takes over as head architect. **1756:** Construction again halted. **1761:** Work resumed. **1763:** Vaulting completed; **Architect:** Johann Jakob Michael Küchel; Stucco decoration begun; **Stuccoists:** Franz Xaver and Johann Michael Feichtmayr and Johann Georg Üblhör; Frescoes begun; **Artist:** Giuseppe Appiani. **1764:** Gnadenaltar; **Architect:** Jakob Michael Küchel. **1772:** Church consecrated.

Publications

ECKSTEIN, H.: *Vierzehnheiligen*. Berlin, 1939.
TEUFEL, R.: *Vierzehnheiligen*. Lichtenfels, 1957.

Pilgrimage Church

The Pilgrimage Church of the Assumption of Mary at Vierzehnheiligen stands on the slopes of the once-beautiful (it has been marred by excessive development in recent years) Main Valley in Franconia, on what was the Frankenthal farm (belonging to the Cistercian Abbey of Langheim) where the shepherd Hermann had visions of the Auxiliary Fourteen Saints, or *Nothelfer,* during 1445-46. In 1735 the abbot of Langheim applied to the bishop of Bamberg (who was also prince-bishop of Würzburg), Friedrich Carl von Schönborn, for permission to demolish the chapel dedicated to the *Nothelfer* and to replace it with a fine new church; Johann Jakob Michael Küchel (1703-69), architect in the employment of the diocesan authorities at Bamberg, titular architect of the Abbey of Langheim, and Johann Balthasar Neumann's assistant at Bamberg, had selected a site which would have its axis aligned with that of Johann Dientzenhofer's Abbey of Banz on the opposite slopes of the valley. In 1738, however, Gottfried Heinrich Krohne (1703-56), court architect of Saxe-Weimar, produced a design on a centralized plan; then Johann Balthasar Neumann, who was working at Würzburg for Schönborn, prepared another design in 1742 that incorporated a drumless dome carried on coupled columns which formed a continuation of the columnar system of the nave, so that the structure would be more or less independently expressed within the envelope of the walls.

In 1743 construction began, and the foundations for the liturgical east end of the church were laid by the master mason, Thomas Niestler, who was working with plans for a long-naved church by Krohne. However, by the end of the year the abbot had informed his bishop that he was unhappy with Krohne's scheme, and Neumann was invited to prepare a new design. The problem then was that Krohne's building had been placed too far up the hill to allow the votive altar (*Gnadenaltar*) to be

Pilgrimage Church: Vierzehnheiligen, Germany, 1743

placed under a crossing, so Neumann and Küchel had to work out a compromise plan in which the *Gnadenaltar* would be set in a large space in the center of the nave, to the liturgical west of the crossing.

From the outside, the church as realized looks like a fairly conventional cruciform basilican arrangement, with canted transepts and chancel, a four-bay clerestoried nave, and a tall, handsome west front flanked by two elegant towers capped by elaborate onion spires, with a centerpiece that bows outward, and is enriched with an engaged order on pedestals above the plainer lower section of the facade. Yet there are sufficient oddities in the design to indicate that the building is unusual inside. To begin with, there are two rows of windows piercing

the walls of the lower part of the church, suggesting a balcony arrangement within. Above the first cornice, which weaves its way continuously around the front, the transepts and the chancel, is the row of windows set in a clerestory that is set back from the walls of the aisles, but flush with the naked transept, chancel and west-front walls. Above this row of windows, the main facade has yet another row of windows alternating with niches, and there are further openings in the belfry stages of the twin towers. The exterior is entirely faced with stone, which glows with a golden hue in the evening light.

Inside, however, the expected basilican arrangement does not apply. Behind the bowed front is an oval space over part of which is the organ gallery. On axis is a large elliptical space to the east, in the center of which is the marvelous *Gnadenaltar,* looking like a cross between a Meissen porcelain grotto and a delicious sedan chair; it was designed by Küchel, and was made in 1764. On each side of the junction between the oval and the large ellipse are two smaller elliptical spaces partially set into the outside walls (indeed, the treatment of the interior generally is one where the curved volumes press into and mold the walls), in which are altars. There is indeed a balcony set behind the giant order of engaged columns that carries the swaying entablature which unifies the geometries of the interior, and this balcony accounts for the two rows of windows which, however, look odd from the inside where there are no balconies (as in the transepts). On each side of the main elliptical space (which enters the crossing space at the liturgical east end) are vestigial spaces that resemble aisles, yet are really little more than passages. The transepts are circular on plan, and the chancel is elliptical, so the junctions between these figures create interesting geometries in the vaulting, where they are more clearly read; the transepts and chancel appear at first glance to be horseshoe-shaped, but the geometries of the ground plan are deliberately confused in the ceiling, to get over the problem of suppressing the crossing. At the "east" end of the presbytery is the fine high altar, which emphasizes the longitudinal axis, but the position and presence of the *Gnadenaltar* in the main ellipse of the nave create two foci: thus the Latin-cross plan merges with Baroque ellipses in an astonishing mix that makes Vierzehnheiligen a virtuoso performance as architecture.

In spite of the sheer delight of the Rococo interior, all white, pink sgagliola, delicate grays, greens, blues and golds, the crossing is odd, for the focus of the *Gnadenaltar* is not under the crossing as one would expect, so the ceiling, where the cupola ought to be, breaks down into the intersection of the four figures of two ellipses and two circles. This problem is highlighted outside, for Küchel placed a roof over the church which is simply cruciform, and has no hint of what lies beneath it. The swaying ogees of the ceiling, although enriched with Rococo stucco of the finest quality, create something of the flowing, syncopated character of late Continental Gothic, but lighter, infinitely more elegant, and joyfully delightful.

Neumann usually gets the credit for this remarkable building, yet Küchel was the man on the spot from 1744. Two years later the Bishop died, and Küchel took charge of all architectural projects in the diocese under the new prince-bishop, Joseph Anton Philipp Freiherr von Frankenstein, who did not combine his position with that of prince-bishop of Würzburg. The abbot died in 1751, Neumann in 1753, and for part of the Seven Years' War from 1756, work on Vierzehnheiligen stopped while Küchel served the empire as a military engineer. He was back on site in 1761, and by 1763 the vaulting was completed, in which year the Feichtmayrs and Johann Georg Üblhör were hired to carry out the stucco decorations. But Üblhör died in 1763, and Franz Xaver Feichtmayr died in 1764, so most of the work was carried out by Johann Michael Feichtmayr, although Küchel designed the altars, Üblhör prepared schemes for the stucco patterns, and Giuseppe Appiani painted the frescoes. Küchel himself died in 1769, before Feichtmayr and Appiani completed their works, and the church was finally consecrated in 1772.

At Vierzehnheiligen the Baroque legacy of Giovanni Lorenzo Bernini, Francesco Borromini and Guarino Guarini, in which ellipses and circles play so important a part, is tempered by the elaborate counterpoint of types of vaulting developed by the Dientzenhofers, notably the churches in Bohemia, but the delicacy of the Rococo decorations lightens the effects, and creates in Vierzehnheiligen an architectural tour-de-force of memorable loveliness.

—JAMES STEVENS CURL

ABBEY CHURCH
Weingarten, Germany

1684-1714: Plans developed; **Architects:** Caspar Moosbrugger (1656-1723), Heinrich Baader, J. J. Herkommer, Andreas Schreck, Christian Thumb, Franz II Beer, and Donato Guiseppe Frisoni. **1714:** Building begun. **1716:** Vaulting of the nave; **Architect:** Beer. **1718:** Designs for the cupola over the crossing; **Architect:** Frisoni; stuccowork; **Stuccoist:** Franz Xaver Schmutzer, with work in side altars by Diego Francesco Carlone; frescoes; **Artist:** Cosmas Damian Asam. **1719:** Designs for the interior, upper facade, towers, altars; **Architect:** Frisoni. **1720:** Choir stalls added; **Architects:** Joseph Anton Feuchtmayer, J. Koch. **1722:** Construction completed. **1737-50:** Organ installed; **Designer:** Josef Gabler. **1762-65:** Pulpit; **Architect:** Fidel Sporer.

Publications

BIRCHER, L.: *Einsiedeln und sein Architekt Bruder Caspar Moosbrugger.* Augsburg, Germany, 1924.

*

The huge Benedictine Abbey Church of Weingarten is situated due north of Lindau on the Bodensee, about halfway between that lovely town and the Premonstratensian Abbey of Schussenried. Weingarten Pilgrimage Church and Abbey stand high on a commanding site above the little town and the great valley of the Schussen in Swabia.

There are problems about precise attribution at Weingarten, which is the grandest of all the churches in southern Germany

Abbey Church

Abbey Church: Weingarten, Germany, 1714

in size: it is representative of a superb ending of one architectural development, that where the Italian influence was preeminent. Stylistically, Weingarten has Baroque themes from Rome, Salzburg and Fulda, and echoes of Einsiedeln near Zurich.

Plans for Weingarten were drawn up by Caspar Moosbrugger (1656-1723), the Benedictine lay brother-cum-architect of Einsiedeln, and most distinguished of the gifted figures of what we now call the Vorarlberg school comprising the families Moosbrugger, Beer and Thumb. Moosbrugger had entered Einsiedeln in 1682 and remained there as a lay brother for the rest of his life. He seems first to have become involved in discussions about Weingarten in 1684, although building work did not begin until 1714. The erection of huge abbeys was a feature of the Baroque Age in central Europe between 1700 and 1760, and Weingarten, in a scheme published in 1723, shows the huge church in the center of a complex of monastic buildings consisting of two vast courts on either side of the church with stretched, elegantly curved smaller outbuildings on all four sides beyond the central five-story buildings and the church. While this vast palatial pile was never completed, other projects, no less grandiose, including Einsiedeln and Melk, were finished.

Weingarten Abbey Church consists of a three-bay nave, shallow apsidal transepts, a two-bay choir with apsidal sanctuary, and a twin-towered west front which bows outward. It is a long church, with a cupola over the crossing, and is of the wall-pier type—with wide nave and massive piers joined to the outside walls—and with a gallery set well back from the faces of the piers so that the rhythm is not interrupted down the full length of the church. However, the piers are designed to look as though they are partially detached from the wall by means of the arches with which they are pierced, so that vestigial aisles are created.

The 18th-century church was built under the aegis of Abbot Sebastian Hyller, who had been a professor at and later rector of the University of Salzburg, and who arrived at Weingarten in 1697, remaining there until his death in 1730. With this in mind, the entrance facade's affinities with the Universitätskirche in Salzburg (1694-1707) by J. B. Fischer von Erlach must owe something to that great church, and so Einsiedeln (1719-35) must also derive partly from the Salzburg church and partly from Weingarten. The apsidal transepts and choir at Weingarten also recall Salzburg Cathedral (1614-28) by Santino Solari of Como, Italy.

The Como connection was maintained at Weingarten too, for the architect in charge in 1717 was Donato Giuseppe Frisoni, who hailed from Laino between Lakes Como and Lugano. By 1717 Frisoni was *Landesbaudirektor* for Württemberg, but although he worked at Weingarten he was not responsible for the original design, and only remained as architect from 1717 to 1719. Before then various architects had been involved: Enrico Zuccalli in 1679 from Munich, Moosbrugger in 1684 from Einsiedeln, and Heinrich Baader in 1687. Once Hyller became abbot, J. J. Herkommer was involved from 1711 to 1713, then the Weingarten monk Andreas Schreck in 1715, then Franz II Beer and Christian Thumb in 1716, and later C. D. Lucchese. The real begetter of the plan does seem to have been Moosbrugger, but there must have been changes as the work proceeded under the executant architects. Beer, for example, seems to have supervised the vaulting of the nave, and then Frisoni provided drawings for the cupola over the crossing in 1718, for the interior, in 1719 for the facade and towers, and later that year for the altars.

From 1718 Franz Xaver Schmutzer, one of the leading Wessobrunn stuccoers, was at work on the fine decorative plasterwork, but it is, if anything, too delicate and refined for such a vast interior, and tends to get lost. The frescoes (again from 1718)

are by Cosmas Damian Asam, and feature the Church triumphant with saints and angels adoring the Trinity in the dome; Saint Benedict in ecstasy with princes, angels and saints over the nave; and the coming of the Holy Ghost over the choir. The latter fresco has many very heavy architectural effects in perspective, which are the least successful parts of this series of paintings.

Especially fine are the choir stalls of 1720 by Josef Anton Feuchtmayer and J. Koch, and the organ of 1737-50 (one of the best in Germany) is by Josef Gabler. Much later, from the 1760s, is the Rococo pulpit by Fidel Sporer: it has two angels, one carrying the pulpit and the other drawing aside the curtain, and it is embellished with the attributes of the Evangelists.

Like the Theatinerkirche in Munich (with which Zuccalli was involved) and Salzburg Cathedral, the Italian Baroque influence is very strong in Weingarten. Apart from the form of the church, which has many Italianate aspects, and the involvement of at least two Italian architects, the side altars have stucco work by Diego Francesco Carlone. The interior has a tough, architectonic appearance quite unlike most of the meltingly tender Baroque and rococo churches of southern Germany.

Weingarten was originally founded by the Guelphs in the 10th century, and the church contains their mausoleum: the monument in the transept is by Leo von Klenze and was erected at the expense of King Georg V of Hannover in the 1850s.

The most precious relic held in the church, and the one that attracted the pilgrims, was the vial of the holy blood of Our Savior. The great church is a worthy reliquary, and is one of the masterpieces of German Baroque architecture.

—JAMES STEVENS CURL

RESIDENZ
Würzburg, Germany

1722: Initial construction begun; **Architects:** Johann Balthasar Neumann (1687-1753) and Maximilian von Welsch, in consultation with Robert de Cotte and Germain Boffrand (1667-1754). **1729:** Construction continues; **Architect:** Johann Lucas von Hildebrandt (1688-1745). **1732:** Construction of church in southwest wing begun; **Architect:** Hildebrandt. **1735:** Construction of main block begun. **1750-53:** Imperial Hall and stairwell ceilings painted; **Artist:** Giovanni Battista Tiepolo. **1755:** Construction completed.

Publications

BACHMANN, E.: *Residenz Würzburg*. Munich, 1970.
FREEDEN, MAX HERMAN VON: *Residenz Würzburg*. Munich, 1952.
SEDLMAIER, RICHARD, and PFISTER, RUDOLF: *Die Fürstbischöfliche Residenz zu Würzburg*. Munich, 1923.

*

In 1683, the Würzburg Cathedral chapter decided to transfer the residence of the prince-bishop from Marienberg Castle to the city. Antonio Petrini built the first city residence, a simple three-wing structure, between 1701 and 1704. It was called the Rennweger Schlößchen, and was situated on the north side of the Residenzplatz in the Rosenbachischer Hof. A part of that early structure was retained in the later building.

Residenz: Würzburg, Germany, 1722

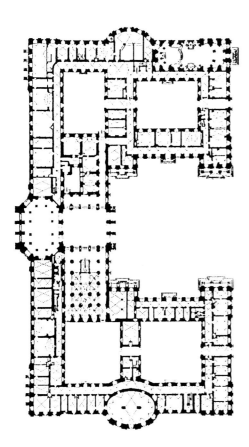

When Johann Philipp Franz von Schönborn became prince-bishop of Würzburg, in 1719, he decided to expand the city residence. Thus began a long and complex history of planning and construction, which resulted in one of the grandest Baroque palaces of the German-speaking world. The disposition and dimensions of the residence were determined by its site, on the eastern bastion of the city's fortifications. The *cour d'honneur* faces west, toward the city, and is flanked by the two symmetrical facades of the side blocks. The side blocks also contain inner courtyards. Both the horseshoe-shaped *cour d'honneur* and the highly developed garden facade, which faces east, are in the traditional style of country residences, while the rest of the building is typical of city palaces. In general terms, the palace at Versailles served as a model for the complex.

The emphasis on the corners of the building, by means of four corner pavilions, is wholly un-French, however. Rather than functioning as connections between separate structures, the pavilions are an integral part of the side blocks. They are set off from these only in the articulation of the facades and the construction of the roofs. The division into floors also turns away from French examples, with the presence of a lower mezzanine. The design of the pavilions, then, points to the kind of architecture that gives a preference to the compact articulation of masses over more cumulative designs.

Balthasar Neumann was responsible for the design of the two corner pavilions on the side facing the city. In each of these, pilasters provide a vertical accent in the arrangement of two full floors and two mezzanines. The floors are separated by an entablature, interrupted by the lower mezzanine windows. The fasciated lower level serves as a kind of pedestal. Each pavilion is crowned by a triangular gable, a balustrade and a mansard roof. The two facades flanking the *cour d'honneur* are

Residenz

closed in by the pavilions, while their central axes are marked by the carriage entrances to the inner courtyards. The facades of the main block, opening onto the *cour d'honneur,* and the garden facade are very different in their articulation. Originally, the *cour d'honneur* was closed off by great wrought-iron gates, interrupted in several places by stone pillars. The gates were removed in 1821.

Some of the most important architects of the age contributed to the design. Schönborn's uncle involved the architect Maximilian von Welsch in the design, while Schönborn's younger brother brought in Johann Lucas von Hildebrandt. Robert de Cotte and Germain Boffrand from France were consulted. The coordination of the design process and the supervision of construction rested with Balthasar Neumann throughout, although he initially had the assistance of Johann Dientzenhofer, who died in 1726.

In the first overall design by Neumann, dating to 1720, the main block was already to be two rooms deep across its entire length, and was to have an entrance hall and stairwells on the side of the courtyard and a main hall on the side of the garden. This design also included pavilion-like projections on the corners and bays on the central axes. Small changes due to the intervention of von Welsch, an international competition opened in 1720, and controversies over particulars do not seem to have

changed the design in any substantial way. On 22 May 1729 the foundation stone of the oval in the northern side block was laid, even before the planning stage had fully come to an end. Schönborn moved to the Rosenbachischer Hof in the immediate vicinity of the construction site, so as to have steady control over construction. In 1723 Neumann presented his designs to the Parisian architects de Cotte and Boffrand for corrections. The double stairwells in the main block were abandoned, and the chapel was moved to a different location as a result of their advice. At Schönborn's death in 1724 only the pavilion on the northwest corner was finished.

Under his successor Franz von Hutten (1724-29), very little construction was carried out. When Friedrich Carl von Schönborn became prince-bishop in 1729, work was resumed on a larger scale, and the architect Hildebrandt was involved in the design process. In 1730 designs for further construction were submitted. It seems that the disposition of the rooms in the main block was changed as a result of Hildebrandt's interventions. A two-level scheme with a *sala terrena* on the garden side was substituted for the originally planned entrance hall with flanking stairwells. The new layout had been developed by Louis Le Vau at Vaux-le-Vicomte (1655-61), but Schloß Pommersfelden seems to have been a more direct influence on the Würzburg Residenz. The height of the different rooms is the same as at Pommersfelden, although the Würzburg Palace is distinguished from the latter by the flanking stairwell. In 1732 construction of the church in the southwest wing was begun, according to a design by Neumann. In 1733 the western part of the southern block, and in 1737 the entire southern block, was roofed over. In 1735 construction of the main block was begun, and the shell was finished in 1739. Between 1739 and 1741 the pavilion in the middle of the garden facade was built. In 1744 construction came to an end with the completion of the northern oval, and the vaulting of the *sala terrena,* the stairwell, the White Hall and the Imperial Hall.

Under the next prince-bishop, Philip von Greifenclau (1749-51), the state rooms in the main block were decorated. In 1750 the greatest fresco painter of the age, Giovanni Battista Tiepolo was called to Würzburg to paint the ceiling frescoes in the Imperial Hall (1750-52) and the stairwell (1752-53). Also employed were the Italian Antonio Bossi, the virtuoso sculptor and carver Johann Wolfgang van der Auvera from Mechlin, and Georg Adam Guthmann from Munich. These artists ornamented the incomparable sequence consisting of the entrance hall, stairwell, White Hall and Imperial Hall, creating a unified artistic result. Upon Greifenclau's death in 1755, construction of the Residenz finally came to an end. In 1753 Balthasar Neumann had died. (The Residenz burned to the ground on 16 March 1945, but in 1950 its reconstruction was undertaken.)

In the Würzburg Residenz the great developments in Western architecture of the time coverage. French palace architecture, the imperial Baroque of Vienna, and northern Italian monumental secular and religious architecture came together in a *Gesamtkunstwerk* of astounding universality, created by the foremost artists of the first half of the 18th century.

—GUNTHER BINDING
Translated from the German by Marijke Rijsberman

GREAT BRITAIN

England

CIRCUS/CRESCENT/SQUARE
Bath, England

1725: Plans drawn for construction; **Architect:** John Wood, Sr., (1704-1754). **1728-35:** Queen Square built; **Architect:** John Wood, Sr. **1754-?:** Circus built; **Architects:** John Wood, Sr. and John Wood, Jr. (1728-1781) **1767-75:** Royal Crescent built; **Architect:** John Wood, Sr., and John Wood, Jr.

Publications

BATH CITY COUNCIL: *Bath, The Georgian City.* Bath, 1954.

BROWNELL, CHARLES E.: *John Wood the Elder and John Wood the Younger: Architects of Bath.* Ph.D. Dissertation. Columbia University, New York, 1976.

CHAMBERLAINE, V. C.: *The City of Bath.* Bristol, 1951.

CUNLIFFE, B. W.: *The City of Bath.* New Haven, Connecticut, 1987.

GIBSON, N.: *Bath and Its Surroundings.* Bradford-on-Avon, 1975.

GREEN, MOWBRAY A.: *The Eighteenth Century Architecture of Bath.* Bath, 1904.

HADDON, J.: *Bath.* London, 1973.

HEAPER, R. G.: *The Soul of Bath; An Architectural Study.* London, 1939.

HONES, GARRY (ed.): *Bath, Museum or City?* Bath, 1978.

HUSSEY, CHRISTOPHER: "9, The Circus, Bath." *Country Life* 102 (1947): 978ff.

ISON, WALTER: *The Georgian Buildings of Bath.* London, 1948.

LITTLE, BRYAN: *Bath Portrait; The Story of Bath, Its Life and Its Buildings.* Bristol, 1961.

LITTLE, BRYAN: *The Building of Bath, 1747-1947: An Architectural and Social Study.* London, 1948.

LOUNDES, W.: *The Royal Crescent in Bath.* London, 1981.

NEALE, R. S.: *Bath 1680 to 1850: A Social History.* London, 1981.

PEACH, R. E. M.: *Historic Houses in Bath and Their Associations.* London, 1883.

PEACH, R. E. M.: *Street-lore of Bath; A Record of Changes in the Highways and Byways of the City.* London, 1893.

ROBERTSON, C. J.: *Bath: An Architectural Guide.* London, 1975.

SUMMERSON, JOHN: "John Wood and the English Town-Planning Tradition." In *Heavenly Mansions and Other Essays on Architecture.* London, 1949.

WOOD, JOHN, THE ELDER: *An Essay Towards a Description of Bath, and of the British Works in Its Neighbourhood.* 2 vols. 1742-43. Reprint: Bath, 1969.

WITHERS, MARGARET: "1 Royal Crescent." *Architect and Building News* 6, 7 (1970): 74-77.

YERBURY, F. R.: *Eighteenth Century Bath.* New York, 1930.

In the early 18th century, John Wood the Elder planned a sequence of a square, a circus and a crescent for the perimeter of the ancient city of Bath. These alterations in the city plan were in part stimulated by the fact that Bath became an extremely fashionable resort in the 18th century, as a result of Queen Anne's visits to Bath. Bath's popularity created a great demand for lodgings, requiring considerable building in the center of the city.

Queen Square, named for Queen Caroline, wife of George II, was the first to be constructed (1728-35). It is situated on a gently sloping site at the bottom of Lansdown. Its leveling was planned, but had to be abandoned for reasons of expense. The formal planning of a Georgian square was thus impossible, and each of the four sides is different. Two of them at first evinced considerable architectural talent, and the northern side is Wood's Palladian masterpiece. The middle of the square was at first laid out as a formal garden and was surrounded by a balustrade. The pointed obelisk, 43 feet high, was put up in honor of Frederick, Prince of Wales. The square is unhappily cluttered by a "motley of odd planting" today.

The northern side is made up of Wood's splendid Palladian terrace, which seems to have been inspired by the Palladian block along one side of Grosvenor Square in London. The houses have Corinthian three-quarter columns and pilasters, and a plain pediment never filled with roundels or coats of arms, as are some other pediments. The pediment was adorned with baroque urns. The windows of the second story and those of the attic stage are smaller than those lower down. The ground floor is rusticated, and its doorways are not given any architectural emphasis. As a consequence, the northern side looks like a unified palace, even though it consists of several separate houses.

The southern side is no real match to the fine composition opposite it. The middle section, now occupied by the Francis Hotel, has three elements, with a simple central pediment. There are 12 windows on each side, and a simple pediment rises at each end of the block. Two of the houses, toward the western end, have baroque doorways. The four houses at the eastern end were bombed in 1942. They have since been rebuilt, and connected to the middle section of the range.

The eastern side of the square, above Wood Street and running up as far as New King Street, contains five houses which are "stepped up" to allow for the slope. Two of them have rich baroque decorations above "open" pediments. Above New King Street an ornate house, with bold rustication blocks which vary its pillars, overlooks the square from the corner. It was once occupied by John Wood the Younger. The appearance of the southern and eastern sides of the square has been much spoiled by the downward enlargement, through the platbands, of many first-floor windows.

The western side of Queen Square was at first lined with three large town houses. The middle one of these was set back from the other two, and had a garden in front of it. This house had a dignified centerpiece, with a pediment set above four Ionic half columns of pilasters. It was pulled down, and the site was filled with an Ionic Greek Revival block by John Pinch

Queen's Square: Bath, England, 1728-35

the Younger in 1831. The side houses were originally split into three residences. One of the two side houses has good interior stuccowork, perhaps by the Italian brothers Franchini.

The Circus is the middle element of Wood's great sequence, and it is also laid out on the lower slopes of Lansdown. Although Wood was prevented from leveling the site for Queen Square, he did level the area for the Circus, at great expense. The Circus was approached by three streets, so that the houses, 30 in all, were arranged in three segments. None of these segments had a central feature such as a pediment. The central space of the Circus was originally open, with nothing but a basin of water, and none of the grass and trees which are there now. The design and the details were the work of Wood the Elder, but construction was supervised, after his death, by John Wood the Younger. The foundation stone was laid in February of 1754, but the breaking of ground, particularly for the major work of leveling, may well have taken place in 1753.

The architectural effect of the Circus lies in its three-tiered combination of the three main classical orders—Roman Doric on the bottom story, Ionic in the middle story, and Corinthian at the top. This combination of the three orders had previously been used in the Colosseum in Rome, in some Italian Renaissance facades, and also in the Elizabethan mansion of Longleat in Wiltshire. The combination is notably bold and effective in the Circus, which has 648 paired three-quarter columns, and whose segments rise to a height of 42 feet above pavement level. The parapets have oval openings to give light to the attics, and they are surmounted by acorns, which refer to the food of Prince Bladud's legendary swine. Usually in Georgian buildings, the height of the individual stories diminishes closer to the top, but this diminution does not occur in the Circus.

The detailed decoration of the Circus is found in the Roman Doric ground-floor story. Roman Doric architraves are shallower than those in Greek Doric, but the alternation of triglyphs and metopes does give scope for varied decoration. In genuine Greek Doric, as in the Parthenon in Athens, this would take the form of figure sculpture. For the Circus, however, Wood the Elder used the "emblemes" of the 17th-century writer George Wither. Most of the 525 metopes are derived from Wither's engravings of animals, but there are also metopes with human faces. The arms of the Freemasons and of the Carpenters' Company are also represented. The designs seem certain to have been chosen by Wood the Elder, but the carving may have been supervised by his son. The Circus is certainly an architectural and decorative tour-de-force. Its interiors vary, and one house has Gothic touches in its decoration. The backs of the houses are not ornamented, although they are better in the southward-facing segment.

The Crescent is the culmination of the great sequence. It was planned by John Wood the Elder, but finished by his son. The Royal Crescent was the first crescent to be built in Bath. Wood the Elder emphasized the point that a terrace of this shape made it possible to put more houses onto a rectangular plot of land, thus increasing the value of the investment. The original setting of the Crescent was rural, with fields running down toward the river.

The Crescent is executed in the son's neoclassical style, rather than the father's Palladianism, and it is often accounted the younger John Wood's masterpiece. It is most impressive by the simplicity of its sweep. It is more than 1,000 feet long, and contains 30 houses. The individual houses vary in size, being three or four windows wide. The variation is emphasized by

Royal Crescent: Bath, England, 1767-75

Circus: Bath, England, 1754-?

the party walls, which project up through the roof. Above a simple ground-floor story, its next two stories are faced with Ionic three-quarter columns; there is no additional emphasis, for example, with a pediment at the central point. The back elevation, as with most Georgian terraces in Bath, is unimpressive.

As the houses were built as lodging houses, and not as the permanent homes of aristocratic owners, internal features, such as ceilings, doorcases and fireplaces, vary much in quality. They are all in the classical taste, however. Number one is the headquarters of the Bath Preservation Trust, and has largely been fitted out as a Georgian museum.

—BRYAN LITTLE

WINDSOR CASTLE
Berkshire, England

Ca. 1066-87: Fortress. **1167-72:** Building and masonry works; **Architects:** Godwin the Mason I (fl.1167-1172) and Ailnoth the Engineer (fl. 1157-1190). **1240:** Apartments constructed. **1357-61:** Royal lodgings rebuilt. **Architect:** William of Wykeham. **1473:** St. George's chapel designed; **Architect:** Henry Janyns (fl. 1453-1483), mason. **1503-6:** Work resumed on St. George's chapel. **1506-11:** Choir to chapel vaulted; **Architect:** William Vertue (d. 1527). **1513-16:** Great Gatehouse with polygonal towers rebuilt. **1582-4:** Long gallery constructed.

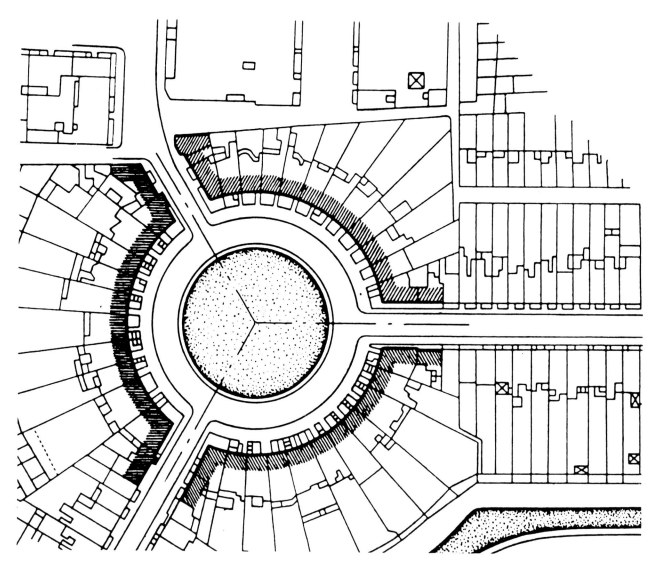

Circus: Bath

1675-84: Lodgings rebuilt; **Architect:** Hugh May (1621-1684). **1795:** Music and dining rooms created. **1800:** Lodgings transformed into Gothic Palace; **Architect:** James Wyatt (1746-1813). **1824:** Repairs; **Architect:** Jeffry Wyatville (1766-1840). **1866:** State stair reconstructed; **Architect:** Anthony Salvin. **1866-72:** Ceremonial staircase constructed, Horseshoe Cloister rebuilt; **Architect:** George Gilbert Scott. **1863-73:** Garter chapter house transformed into memorial chapel; **Architect:** Triqueti.

Publications

AINSWORTH, W. H.: *Windsor Castle*. London, 1844.
BLUNT, ANTHONY: "The Drawings of Carlo Fontana in the Royal Library at Windsor Castle." *Barocco europeo, barocco italiano, barocco salentino.* Lecce, Italy, 1969.
BRAHAM, ALLAN and HAGER, HELLMUT: *Carlo Fontana: The Drawings at Windsor Castle*. London, 1977.
DIXON, WILLIAM H.: *Royal Windsor*. 4 vols. London, 1875.
FLEMING, JOHN: "Cardinal Albani's Drawings at Windsor: Their Purchase by James Adam for George III." *The Connoisseur* 142 (1958): 164-169.
HOPE, W. H. ST. J.: *Windsor Castle*. 2 vols. London, 1913.

*

Built on the first natural strong point in the Thames Valley above London, Windsor Castle, the largest in the British Isles, was founded by William the Conqueror. Its upper and lower baileys stood on either side of its artificial motte. Henry I established a "king's house" above the cliff on the north side of the upper bailey or ward, of which the stone walls and square towers, as well as the shell keep on the motte, were probably built by his grandson, Henry II (1154-89). The stone defenses of the motte and lower ward were completed with rounded towers under Henry III (1216-72), who spent much time at Windsor. The construction under Henry III made Windsor, according to a contemporary chronicler, the finest castle in Europe. A new range of opulent royal apartments including a chapel was constructed from 1240 in the northeast of the lower bailey

Windsor Castle: Berkshire, England, ca. 1066-87

under "Master Henry," doubtless the master mason responsible for rebuilding Westminster Abbey from 1245.

Edward III transformed the castle into a fortified palace. In the lower ward, he founded a college of priests in connection with his newly established Order of the Garter (1348), using the site of Henry III's new lodgings, much damaged by fire in 1295-96, and restoring his chapel. Then in the upper ward the old royal lodgings were nobly rebuilt in stone (William of Wykeham being in charge, 1357-61). Hall and chapel formed a continuous range on the south side of the lodgings, formed around courts—the basis of the state apartments ever since. This plan "closely resembled those later adopted for [Wykeham's] Winchester and New Colleges," according to McKisack. In all, these works cost some £51,000 between 1350 and 1377, and adversely affected building in the rest of the country. Thus, in 1361, masons were requisitioned from 17 counties; stone was purchased from quarries as far afield as Lincolnshire and Yorkshire.

The greatest work for the next three centuries was Edward IV's new chapel, St. George's, for the Order of the Garter (from 1473). Master mason Henry Janyns was presumably responsible for the design, which had square-ended transepts only as deep as the aisles; a central tower was never built. Though the choir had been roofed and the aisles fan-vaulted, little more than the foundations of the nave had been laid by 1485; Henry VII (1485-1509) concentrated on rebuilding Henry III's chapel in 1494-98, intending it then as his burial place. Only a courtier's substantial legacy enabled work on St. George's Chapel to be resumed in 1503-06, when the nave was extended by one bay to the same length as the choir, and additional emphasis given to the now-central transepts: Nikolaus Pevsner saw in the "balance between

E. and W. with the transept in the middle" a sign of "the readiness of England to receive the Italian Renaissance." It is the transepts that principally distinguish St. George's from the other Plantagenet royal chapels. The complex vaulting is flattened, "divided clearly into coving and ceiling," as Pevsner noted. William Vertue vaulted the choir to correspond with the nave, but in a somewhat richer manner, at the expense of the Garter knights in 1506-11.

Henry VII added a new tower to the west of the Lodgings in 1498-1501, lighted by oriels of novel form, the several lights being set at an angle one to another, sometimes flanked by convex lobes; copied at Henry VII's Chapel, Westminster, these set a fashion. Henry VIII rebuilt the Great Gatehouse with polygonal towers in 1513-16. The Tudor sovereigns continued to reside in the Edwardian Lodgings, and under Elizabeth (1558-1603), who was an annual visitor, a great terrace was constructed on the precipitous north side of her apartments. In 1582-84 the essential Elizabethan long gallery was constructed at one end of this terrace, extending west from Henry VII's Tower.

Although the early Stuarts somewhat neglected Windsor, Charles II made amends after his Restoration. Conveniently near London, but too far to be overawed by its citizenry, and defensible, Windsor was also the burial place of Charles' martyred father and seat of his cherished Order of the Garter. He extended the grounds, devising the "Long Walk" to the south. The rebuilding of the Lodgings was carried through in 1675-84, under Hugh May at a cost of some £128,000. May reconstructed most of the north front and the end towers of the east front in a severe character, Norman rather than Plantagenet; it was a style that John Vanbrugh was a few years later to distinguish as "the Castle air." Only a great gilded star enriched the outer face of the new building. May refenestrated throughout, creating tall, round-headed windows in Portland stone surrounds (two survive in Henry III's Tower). Within the palace May created two ranges of state apartments, the king's on the north side, and the queen's on the inner, south and west sides of the Lodgings, each approached by its own grand staircase. The apartments, partly top-lighted and much varied in shape and size, were richly decorated by Grinling Gibbons' carvings, Antonio Verrio's ceiling paintings and C. G. Cousin's gilding, to achieve a frank glorification of the Anglican monarchy. The magnificent Baroque redecoration of the royal chapel and reconstruction of St. George's Hall as a superb setting for Garter ceremonies followed in 1678-84. May's work created the precedent for Christopher Wren's at Whitehall, Hampton Court and Greenwich.

Little beyond maintenance was done to the castle during the 18th century. George III lived much at Windsor, but at first outside the castle at the Queen's Lodge, a building lacking in architectural pretension. In 1795, however, a music room and a dining room were created in the east front, the first stage of a gradual shift of the royal private apartments from the north front, where they had been since the 12th century. From 1800 James Wyatt was employed to transform the Lodgings into a Gothic palace at a cost probably exceeding £150,000, a significant step in popularizing the Gothic Revival. Both the King's and Queen's Stairs were demolished, a new straight flight leading unconventionally directly to the King's Drawing Room, instead of to the Guard Room. An internal corridor improved communications, the monotony of the north front was relieved by new towers, and the windows were redone in a Gothic Revival style. Several of the rooms were enlarged, and new ceiling paintings provided by Matthew Cotes Wyatt, youngest son of architect James Wyatt, who had begun remodeling at Windsor in 1800. From 1782, the king spent freely on embellishing St. George's Chapel, installing a new east window, and in the 1800s converting Henry III's old chapel into a chapter house for the Order of the Garter. This, like the palace works, remained uncompleted at James Wyatt's death in 1813.

His nephew, Jeffry Wyatt, was appointed by George IV in 1824 to improve the castle, thereupon changing his name to Wyatville. He found an ancient structure crumbling into decay, but so soundly did he build that major repairs have not been needed since. Working to a specification drawn up by Sir Charles Long (later Lord Farnborough), the king's artistic adviser, he created a new towered entrance to the inner ward from the south, as a climax to the Long Walk, and reconstructed that into the state apartments, building a new staircase to the Queen's Guard Chamber (thus restoring the conventional approach) in place of his uncle's. He built a grand corridor around the south and east sides of the inner ward, heightened to furnish servants' rooms, and improved communications to the state apartments. He destroyed the old royal chapel and St. George's Hall to form one state room 155 feet long, and created a new dining room, the Waterloo Chamber (hung with Lawrence's portraits of the sovereigns of the powers allied against Napoléon), and a reception room embellished with Louis XV *boiseries*. In the east front he formed a magnificent new suite of private apartments, using material from the lately demolished Carlton House (where George IV had in his younger days given free rein to his enthusiasm for French taste). Their character is similar to contemporaneous neo-Rococo work by James Wyatt's son Benjamin at Belvoir Castle, and York and Apsley Houses, London. In accord with romantic taste, Wyatville enriched the towers with battlements and machicolations (new to Windsor) and raised the Round Tower or keep by some 30 feet, so creating a silhouette

that (despite coarseness of detail) satisfied contemporary concepts of a great castle of the Middle Ages. All this cost about a million pounds. Wyatville and Long thus achieved an appropriate seat for the British monarchy.

Least successful was Wyatville's state entrance: the vestibule was too dark. The state stair was therefore reconstructed by Anthony Salvin in 1866. But the principal Victorian work was in the lower ward, where George Gilbert Scott constructed a ceremonial staircase to the west front of St. George's Chapel and rebuilt the domestic Horseshoe Cloister immediately west of it (1866-72); the unfinished Garter chapter house was transformed by Triqueti in 1863-73 into a memorial chapel for the Prince Consort. Today, however, it is dominated by Gilbert's huge art nouveau tomb of the duke of Clarence, largely of the 1890s, the finest example of the style in the British Isles.

—M. H. PORT

ST. GEORGE'S CHAPEL, WINDSOR
Berkshire, England

1475-1509: Construction. **1478-85:** Choir stalls. **Ca. 1503:** Nave and its vaults; **Architect:** William Vertue. **1506-11:** Choir vaults and lady chapel vaults; **Architect:** William Vertue. **1528:** Crossing vaults; **Architect:** Henry Redman.

Publications

BOND, SHELAGH M.: "A Craftsman of Skill and Invention." *Country Life* 132 (13 September 1962): 607-609.
CAVE, C.: "The Roof Bosses in St. George's Chapel, Windsor." *Archaeologia* 95 (1953): 107-121.
DIXON, WILLIAM H.: *Windsor Castle.* 4 vols. London, 1875.
HARRINGTON, JOHN: *St. George's Chapel, Windsor.* London, 1872.
HOPE, WILLIAM HENRY ST. JOHN: *Windsor Castle.* 2 vols. London, 1913.
WEBB, GEOFFREY: *Architecture in Britain: The Middle Ages.* Baltimore, 1956.
WILLEMENT, THOMAS: *An Account of the Restorations of the Collegiate Chapel of St. George, Windsor.* London, 1844.

*

Begun in 1475 by Edward IV and completed in 1509 by Henry VIII, St. George's Chapel is noted for its expression of fan-vaulted Perpendicular-style architecture. Edward III gave an earlier church on the same site to the College of St. George in 1348 along with the Knights of the Garter. The dean and canons of Windsor, rather than the Crown, own the property, and the chapel remains the home of the Knights of the Garter. Over the centuries, the chapel has been the burial place of several sovereigns and many members of the royal family.

Uniformity and clarity characterize the exterior of the chapel. In keeping with the typical English version of the Gothic, the building is comparatively low. A balustrade with pinnacles completes the top of the walls. The windows of the side aisles and the nave repeat the same size and design. Pier and flying buttresses mark the identical bays of the interior. At the entrance, two slim octagonal towers with reverse curve caps frame the width of the nave. Further out on the facade, octagonal chantry chapels press against the side-aisle walls. The transepts are

St. George's Chapel, Windsor: Berkshire, England, 1475-1509

short, two-story, octagonal projections used as chantry and Curial chapels. Their fenestration matches that of the remainder of the exterior wall. At the end of the choir wall there is another small octagonal projection, a chapel. In this instance it is not matched on the other side of the building, where the cloister is located. This chapel is the same height as the choir wall, but the fenestration differs in that there are three rows of smaller windows. A lady chapel, one story high, completes the longitudinal axis.

The simple rectangular plan is hardly interrupted by its short transepts. They mark the transition between the nave with side aisles and choir, each eight bays long. Because the chapel functioned not as a parish church but as the home of a prayer community and gathering place for the Garter, it had no need for large congregational spaces. Instead, the choir is proportionally larger to accommodate the many choir stalls (1478-85) for the members of the Garter. The banner, helm and crest of each living member of the Garter are positioned over the individual's choir stall. The plan terminates in a lady chapel (now the Albert Memorial Chapel) behind the high altar. The door between it and the choir was the original entrance to Henry III's chapel built on the site in 1240.

In keeping with late medieval English construction, the interior has a flattened, four-centered Tudor vault. This low vault gives the interior its human scale. William Vertue is credited as the master mason who designed and constructed the nave and its vaults (ca. 1503) as well as those of the choir and the lady chapel (1506-11). The crossing vaults date somewhat later and are by Henry Redman (1528). The vaults are elaborated as fans that spread from the tops of thin arcade piers. They form

conoids, which terminate before covering the center of the ceiling. There the decoration is a complex linear pattern of liernes stretching down the center. At the central spandrel of each bay, a pendant drops from the center of the ceiling to mark the procession down the ceiling. The remaining spaces are further enriched by filling spaces with quatrefoils as contrast.

Following the Perpendicular emphasis on linearity in general and upward movement specifically, each bay of the nave and choir has shallow but strongly marked verticals spaced evenly across it, matching the divisions between clerestory windows. The piers dividing the bays are slim and almost unadorned, which allows them to sweep upward unimpeded. Three rows of the same size window are piled on top of each other in the clerestory, a feature that is imitated by those in the side aisle. The vertical motion is countered to some extent by horizontal moldings, which produce the effect of blank paneling. Foliate bands are applied to some of the major horizontals and, like the stringcourse of angels above the nave arcade, do not project so much that they disturb the linear emphasis.

On the end wall of the choir, a single large window fills the entire space between the walls and from the top of the reredos to the vaults. Again the space is defined by tracery that indicates linear divisions with emphasis on the vertical. The large amount of window space throughout the chapel permits the space to be well lighted and is typical of the architectural era. The reredos behind the altar commemorates Prince Albert and is a 19th-century replacement for the original polychrome alabaster screen of 1368-71.

—ANN STEWART BALAKIER

St. Lawrence: Bradford-on-Avon, England, ca. 10th century

ST. LAWRENCE
Bradford-on-Avon, England

10th-11th century: Possible origins.

Publications

PARKINS, T.: *The Abbey Churches of Bath and Malmesbury and the Church of Saint Laurence, Bradford-on-Avon.* London, 1901.

*

Rescued in the mid-19th century from secular use and a clutter of surrounding buildings, this small Late Saxon church illustrates very well the tensions between accessibility and mystery in its originally intended use. It is too small for much else than the priestly celebration of the Mass—indeed, in its original configuration it provided for three altars with a chancel and two lateral chapels combined with porches—yet even its limited space has an openness many later structures lost.

The origins of this church are obscure; for a long time it was given a possible dating to 704, but more recent work has hinted at a 10th- or even 11th-century date. The control over scale is too tight, the craftsmanship in dressed ashlar too polished to justify the earlier attribution. Yet its placing in the canon is still not complete—is it a culmination of Saxon styling or the major impetus for the development of Romanesque on a smaller scale? If the latter, it shows a remarkable lack of the tortuous Byzantine-Celtic ornamentation associated with the Hereford school not many miles further north. It is emphatically a product of the cultural and religious dominance of Late Saxon Wessex.

The building's exterior still acknowledges the wooden structures that dominated English churchbuilding before the mid-11th century. The three tiers of the nave and the two of the chancel both offer a first level with external pilaster strips, and their shared second levels flow with an elegant blank arcading culminating in rounded arches; above them rise the steep gables and slated roofs, which give a far greater impression of height than is really there. There is none of the clumsiness associated with Earl's Barton Church, although it is possible that the Victorian restoration, including an apparently total rebuilding of the arcaded west wall, may have provided rather more polish than was originally intended.

The simple plan, basically two-cell, comprises a small nave and smaller chancel, the latter square rather than apsidal, which might well be anticipated. The nave was buttressed by the two *portici* chapels mentioned above, of which only the northern survives, but there is no hint of the cruciform in the final layout. It is in the geometric interplay of height, length and width that St. Lawrence's triumphs. Both nave and chancel are as high as they are long, and almost twice as high as they are wide. For such a small building, less than 40 feet long, it soars, and all that is borne by the simple layers of carved stone; there is no vaulting. The abutting chapels had the additional virtue of acting as buttresses, as the remains of the southern one still do with some incongruity, otherwise the structure rests on its own solidity and the masons' skills.

Lighting is minimal, and the arched windows may be of a later period. St. Lawrence was designed to contain the Eucharistic mysteries, lit by the candles flickering over walls presumably plastered and frescoed, but now standing bare. In that the church is remarkably similar to many of the tiny Byzantine chapels of the eastern Mediterranean. Access to the main altar was through an arch some 3 feet 6 inches wide, with square capitals and some stripwork. The arches between the nave and the porch chapels were simpler. Possibly, access to the whole structure could originally be gained only from the north. The lateral openings are not central to the northern and southern walls of the separate cells, presumably to allow for the impact of the altars on the space available for movement. It was liturgical use of a fairly simple form that determined this building's layout. It is impossible to tell from surviving manuscript evidence whether this *ecclesiola* (''little church'') was designed for congregational use of any significance. Yet the quality of its construction hints at it as an expression of some major form of contemporary patronage.

This becomes more than clear when the upper reaches of the eastern nave wall are examined. All that remains now of its major initial decoration are two ''reclining'' angels, carved in a vibrant bas-relief. They must once have surrounded a great rood, the crucifix associated in the early Middle Ages with the entrances to the great mysteries of the Mass. The iconoclasm of the Reformation swept away what must have been one of the great examples of pre-Norman sculpture, almost too large for its setting. We are fortunate that its container, the church itself, has survived to continue to challenge simple assumptions about stylistic dominance and derivations.

—JOHN LOWERSON

ROYAL PAVILION
Brighton, England

1786: Farmhouse leased. **1787:** Farmhouse transformed into villa; **Architect:** Henry Holland (1745-1806). **1815-1818:** Domes added, wings added, interior transformed; **Architect:** John Nash (1752-1835).

Publications

COLVIN, HOWARD (ed.): Vol. 6 in *The History of the King's Works*. London, 1973.
DAVIS, TERENCE: *John Nash, the Prince Regent's Architect*. Newton Abbot, England, 1973.
DAVIS, TERENCE: *The Architecture of John Nash*. London, 1960.
MUSGRAVE, CLIFFORD: *Royal Pavilion: An Episode in the Romantic*. London, 1959.
NASH, JOHN: *Views of the Royal Pavilion*. London, 1991.
ROBERTS, HENRY D.: *A History of the Royal Pavilion, Brighton*. London, 1939.
STROUD, DOROTHY: *Henry Holland: His Life and Architecture*. London, 1966.

*

Early-19th-century claims that the Royal Pavilion was the pup of St. Paul's Cathedral, London, may be discounted, but they reveal the degree of controversy that has always surrounded this building. Its only European equivalents are the fantasy castles built for the deranged Ludwig of Bavaria, but its originator, the prince regent, later George IV, was sane. Over some forty years he had created for him one of the great pleasure palaces of Europe. Its eventual derivatives are really local, minor features within Regency Brighton itself; its architectural importance lies in its uniqueness.

The Pavilion's core was simple: a substantial but small farmhouse first leased in 1786. The following year Henry Holland transformed it into a Palladian villa of balanced proportions—two lateral wings, north and south, flanked a rotunda surmounted by a subdued dome. This symmetry dominated all the subsequent work; whatever its decorative fantasies, the Pavilion remains a model of formal order. What made it so different from its rural counterparts was the lack of a park—it is essentially an urban palace. When ''Regency Brighton'' was extended to cope with the influx of fashionable visitors lured to the royal court, it was this simple classicism that remained the dominant model of building rather than the transformations the prince ordered.

The result of these transformations is an apparent conflict in styles: the exterior is Indian in derivation, the interior an essay in chinoiserie. The whole appears as more than vaguely Oriental, but it is the Orientalism of an English gentleman casting more than half an eye at the French influences of the Napoleonic empire. In fact, it seems to have been toned down somewhat by gentle modifications in the early 1820s.

The first venture in the direction of India was in one of the subsidiary buildings that make up the Pavilion ensemble, the stables and indoor riding school, which survive as the Corn Exchange and Dome Concert Hall on the northwest of the site; these were the work of Holland's successor, William Porden, and their main legacy has been their extraordinary acoustics.

After 1815 John Nash transformed the Pavilion. He gave the Palladian rotunda a fully fledged onion dome and added further north and south wings topped with the sawn-off pinnacles of larger domes. Squeezed between them are smaller domes and sundry minarets, as well as the barely decorated chimneys that any English country house, however Oriental its roots, must have. They are ringed with perforated balustrades which ride, in the center and at the edges, over verandas masked with webbed spandrels matching the onion shapes imposed on the

Royal Pavilion: Brighton, England, 1786

rounded earlier windows. Much of the work is stucco over brick or flint, and it has never stood up well to the realities of being a pleasure palace beside one of the world's stormiest seas.

The exterior appears sparse when compared with Nash's interior. There Chinese replaces Indian, except in some parts of the king's own apartments and in the kitchens, where function is interspersed with some of Nash's finest experimental work; iron pillars with capitals cast as palm trees support the roof. Cast iron was exploited skillfully elsewhere, principally in the "bamboo" moldings of the principal staircase, which are repeated in the specially made matching furniture. Most of the rooms and the linking passages retain the Palladian order, not least in the relatively sparsely decorated first-floor bedrooms for lesser royals. It was in the decoration that Nash effected his transformations, and this becomes explosively evident in the two state rooms that he added as the great wings. On the south, the banqueting room almost cowers beneath its own splendor and beneath the 30-foot-high gasolier (weighing a ton) hanging from the claws of a giant silvered dragon under a domed roof, largely taken up with the simulated foliage of a giant tree. When attention came away from that, it roved along the painted walls, paneled with "Chinese" scenes and enveloped with writhing dragons.

This was balanced on the south by a music room whose painted serpents swirl around rather more subdued Eastern landscapes beneath another domed roof given an illusory height by diminishing ranks of gilded cockleshell carvings. Similar beasts are wrapped about much of the rest of the building, including the transformed rotunda, made into a delicate salon as a bridge between the two extravagances. The effect of much of the window and wall decoration is to give the sense of a luxurious

tent, a pavilion in the original sense. Without expensive and repeated maintenance, the quality of the building would have ensured its being folded up decades ago.

—JOHN LOWERSON

ST. MARY REDCLIFFE
Bristol, England

Early 1200s: Rectangular porch constructed. **Ca. 1325:** North porch constructed. **Ca. 1340-1400:** Rebuilding. **1445:** Tower collapsed. **1870s:** Tower restored.

Publications

BETTEY, J. H.: "The Medieval Churches of Bristol." *Ancient Monuments Society Transactions* 34 (1990): 1-27.

BONY, JEAN: *The English Decorated Style: Gothic Architecture Transformed, 1250-1350.* Ithaca, New York, 1979.

BRITTON, JOHN: *An Historical and Architectural Essay Relating to Redcliffe Church, Bristol.* London, 1813.

GOMME, ANDOR; JENNER, MICHAEL; and LITTLE, BRYAN: *Bristol, an Architectural History.* London, 1979.

PRYCE, GEORGE: *Memorials of the Canynges Family and Their Times.* Bristol, 1854.

"St. Mary Redcliffe, Bristol." *Architect* 60 (1898): 265-267, 282-284.

St. Mary Redcliffe: Bristol, England, 13th century

The Parish Church of St. Mary Redcliffe at Bristol derives its name from the exposed face of the low red sandstone ridge south of the River Avon, where the church is located. Queen Elizabeth I, who visited Bristol in 1574, referred to this church as "the fairest, goodliest, and most famous parish church" in England, clearly distinguishing between this building and the run of parish churches. In fact, with its cruciform plan, and a length of about 250 feet, St. Mary Redcliffe has some of the characteristics of a small cathedral or large collegiate church. Distinctive points which elevate it above the standards of the average parish church in England are its complete stone vault, its flying buttresses to support the weight of that vault, its transepts with double aisles and double transom windows. St. Mary Redcliffe is also rare among medieval English parish churches in having an eastern Lady Chapel, which was elongated in the 15th century.

Originally a dependent chapel in the large parish of Bedminster, which at one time included most of southern Bristol, St. Mary's became a separate parish church only in the 19th century. The west end of the building holds important traces of the original 12th-century church. Survivals of about 1190 include the inner north porch, a pair of shallow buttresses in the west wall of the nave, traces of a vaulted nave, and a finely carved corbel. The tower at the northwestern corner with firm foundations on the rocky ridge is in the main of the 13th century, while the spire that surmounts it was put up in the 14th century. It resembled the famous spire, of the same date, at Salisbury Cathedral. Much of it collapsed in a gale in 1445. It long survived in a truncated state, but was restored to its full height in the 1870s.

A gradual reconstruction of the older church was begun about 1340, and continued, after the Black Death of the 1340s, for most of the rest of the 14th century. The work was finished about 1400, but repairs were needed after the collapse of the spire. The building work was financed by prosperous merchants living in the parish. Members of the Canynges family were prominent among them, and the tomb of William Canynges and his wife Joan is to be found in the south transept. Another effigy shows Canynges in the costume of the priesthood, which the death of his wife enabled him to enter.

The hexagonal outer north porch, built in the 14th century, is one of the most splendid porches anywhere in England. It is much finer, for instance than the hexagonal porch of the great parish church of Ludlow in Shropshire. It is particularly noteworthy for the complex vaulting and the excellent carving of the decorative detail, as in the beautiful foliate carving on each side of the entrance doorway.

St. Mary Redcliffe is unusual, among Bristol's churches, in having a fairly good collection of monumental brasses and medieval stained glass.

—BRYAN LITTLE

KING'S COLLEGE
Cambridge University, Cambridge, England

1440s: College founded. **1441:** Work begun on three-story court. **1446:** Work begun on chapel; **Architect:** Reginald of Ely. **1461:** Work continued; **Architect:** John Wolrich (1443-1476). **1515:** Great fan vault completed; **Architect:** John Wastell (1485-?1515). **Early 1500s:** Main windows designed; **Designer:** Dirck Vellert. **1526:** Work continued; **Designer:** Galyon Hone. **1713:** Accommodation blocks commissioned.

Architects: Christopher Wren (1632-1723) and Nicholas Hawksmoor (ca. 1661-1736). **1723:** Western blocks commissioned; **Architect:** James Gibbs (1682-1754). **1822-24:** Perpendicular Gothic constructed; **Architect:** William Wilkins (1778-1839). **1960s:** Development of alley, King's Lane; **Architect:** Fello Atkinson, of James Cubitt and Partners.

Publications

VALE, E.: *Cambridge and Its Colleges*. London, 1959.
WILLIS, ROBERT, and CLARK, JOHN WILLIS: *The Architectural History of the University of Cambridge, and of the Colleges of Cambridge and Eton*. 4 vols. Cambridge, 1886.

*

King's College was founded by King Henry VI in the 1440s. The king and his advisers worked out an elaborate scheme for a large chapel nearly 300 feet long, a hall, domestic buildings, and a cemetery dominated by a tall, pinnacled tower. In 1441 a start was made on a more modest scheme situated to the north of the chapel built later. The site, in what had once been the commercial and trading center of Cambridge, was gradually acquired. The Parish Church of St. John Zachary (the Baptist) was demolished, and many houses and streets were destroyed to make room for the college. The original structure was a court surrounded by three-story buildings, containing a hall and a chapel. The lower stages of its fine gateway survive.

The great stone chapel, of 12 bays, was begun in 1446, to an initial design by Reginald of Ely. Like the unfinished chapel at Eton, King's College Chapel was the culmination of the large college chapels of Winchester and New College at Oxford. It was originally to have been comparatively simple, with a great rib vault of a type still to be seen in the vaulting of some of the side chapels. The royal founder had decided against any excessive elaboration of detail, wanting the chapel "clean and substantial, setting apart superfluity of . . . curious works of entail and busy moulding." The chapel's construction was much impeded by the political collapse of Henry VI, leading to the Wars of the Roses. Some work continued until 1461, but only a little was done under Edward IV, who was the first Yorkist king. Construction was continued in the reigns of Henry VII and Henry VIII.

John Wolrich, the next master mason after Reginald Ely, was followed by John Wastell, under whom the great fan vault with its bold cross arches was finished (ca. 1515). The dominating corner pinnacles were also completed by Wastell.

The two great decorative features of the chapel were inserted in the first half of Henry VIII's reign. The stained or painted glass windows make up a splendid collection, mainly in the large side windows and in the east window. There is also foreign glass of much note in the side chapels, which includes four 15th-century figures from the demolished Church of St. John Zachary. The west window contains glass of 1879.

The designs for the main windows may have been prepared by the designer Dirck Vellert of Antwerp (died in 1544). His work for King's must have been done much earlier in the 16th century, however. The first four windows on the northern side were made by the king's glazier, Barnard Flower (died in 1517). The work was continued, after 1526, by Galyon Hone, of

King's College: Cambridge University, Cambridge, England, 1440s

German, Dutch or Flemish extraction, and other English or foreign glaziers. The great nine-light east window shows scenes from the Passion, while others have scenes from the life of the Blessed Virgin Mary or from the Acts of the Apostles. The rest of the five-light transomed windows use an unusual typological scheme, with scenes from the Old Testament set above parallels from the New Testament, and with dignified figures of messengers, or angels, in the middle light of each window. Thus the torments of Job were set above the scourging of Christ, the crowning of Solomon above the crowning of Christ with the crown of thorns. The ascent of Elijah into Heaven has the Ascension of Christ below it, and the reception of the Law by Moses corresponds to the descent of the Holy Spirit on the disciples. A small-scale equivalent of this unusual arrangement was to be found in some 17th-century windows, unfortunately damaged by a bomb blast, in the choir aisles of Bristol Cathedral.

The other great feature, best seen from the antechapel, is the superb wooden screen, of French or Italian Renaissance workmanship, with a wealth of delicate decoration. There are representations of the royal arms, and the conjoined initials of H and A, which indicate a date between 1533 and 1536, when Anne Boleyn was Henry VIII's queen. Behind the screen, the stalls in the choir have canopies and heraldic panels dating to the 17th century. One of these panels has one of the few representations of the arms of the University of Oxford to be found in Cambridge.

No more building work was done at King's till the early 18th century. Then, in 1713, Provost Adams had a conference in London with Christopher Wren and Nicholas Hawksmoor, and commissioned Hawksmoor to design residential blocks (of which models survive) for the east and west sides of the court. Nothing came of that project before Adams' death, but in 1723 the idea of two residential blocks was revived by Snape. He also planned a fine porticoed hall, flanked by a new provost's lodge, and a buttery and kitchen to be situated on the court's southern side. James Gibbs was chosen as the architect, but only the western of his proposed blocks (the Fellows' or Gibbs Building) was actually constructed. This fine block, of Portland stone, has a central passageway leading through to the Backs and the river. It has a lunette window with a pediment above it, and a finely rusticated ground floor.

No more building was done at King's in the 18th century, and the college continued to use the hall in the Old Court. The remaining buildings now seen on the main site of the college were put up along and behind the southern side of the court. The first of these, in the Perpendicular Gothic of the 1820s, was by William Wilkins, the center of his block being filled by a spacious hall whose oriel window is in the middle of the hall's northern side. Wilkins also designed the entrance lodge and the traceried screen which divides the court from King's Parade.

Later buildings of the 19th century were the Chetwynd Court by George Gilbert Scott, and Webb's Court by Aston Webb. Two ranges, down toward the river, of the three-sided court were planned by G. F. Bodley but only recently finished. Later buildings, and alterations of existing buildings, such as the Provost's Lodge, were done by G. L. Kennedy and Nightingale. Work of the 1960s, in conjunction with St. Catherine's College, is the development of the sites on either side of the unappealing alley of King's Lane. The architect of this work was Fello Atkinson, of James Cubitt and Partners.

A controversial move in recent years has been the installation, at the east end of the chapel, of Peter Paul Rubens' *Adoration of the Magi*. This involved the removal of the reredos, put up early in this century by Dettmar Blow and Fernand Billery to replace the Georgian Gothic reredos by James Essex.

—BRYAN LITTLE

CANTERBURY CATHEDRAL
Canterbury, England

1070: Norman church begun after destruction of Saxon cathedral on the same site; **Architect:** Archbishop Lanfranc. **1093-1130:** Renovations, east end; Architect. **1174:** Central part of church destroyed by fire. **1175-79:** Reconstruction begun, rebuilding of east transepts completed, designs created and building begun for Trinity Chapel, and crypt; **Architect:** William of Sens. **1179-84:** Reconstruction completed, Trinity Chapel, crypt completed; **Architect:** William the Englishman. **Ca. 1391-1405:** New nave, nave transepts built; **Architect:** Henry Yevele. **Late 12th, early 13th century:** Stained glass **Ca. 1405-93:** Additional chapels added. **1418:** South porch built. **1424-34:** Southwest tower built; **Architect:** Thomas Mapleton. **1493-1498:** Bell Harry - Perpendicular tower built; **Architect:** John Wastell. **1831:** Northwest tower replaced with a copy of southwest tower. **1872:** Roof of Trinity Chapel restored.

Publications

CAVINESS, M. H.: *The Early Stained Glass of Canterbury Cathedral: Circa 1175-1220.* Princeton, New Jersey, 1978.
DRAPER, PETER: "William of Sens and the Original Design of the Choir Termination of Canterbury Cathedral." *Journal of the Society of Architectural Historians* 42 (October 1983): 238-248.
G. S.: Chronological History of Canterbury Cathedral.
HARVEY, JOHN H.: *Henry Yevele, c. 1320 to 1400. The Life of an English Architect.* London, 1944.
STUBBS, WILLIAM (ed.): *The Historical Works of Gervase of Canterbury.* London, 1879.
WARREN, S. A.: *Canterbury Cathedral.* London, 1923.
WILLIS, R.: *The Architectural History of Canterbury Cathedral.* London, 1845.
WOODRUFF, C. E., and DANKS, W.: *Memorials of the Cathedral and Priory of Christ in Canterbury.* London, 1912.

*

The see of Canterbury goes back to the arrival of Saint Augustine with his missionary monks from Rome in 597. Nothing remains of the succession of Anglo-Saxon cathedrals, but it is known that the last of these was a building of considerable size, with an apse at each end and flanking towers. It was destroyed by fire in 1067, and a new cathedral was soon started by Archbishop Lanfranc, modeled on the abbey of St. Stephen's at Caen, where Lanfranc had been abbot. The new cathedral at Canterbury, one of whose western towers lasted till the 1830s, was comparatively small. In the 12th century it was strikingly elongated by what amounted to a new church, which had an eastern pair of transepts and was set above a splendid crypt. The new choir was known as "Conrad's glorious choir," after the prior of the cathedral monastery who completed it. It was richly decorated with wall paintings and other furnishings.

The most dramatic event in the history of Canterbury Cathedral was the murder, in 1170, of Archbishop Thomas Becket, who was canonized in 1173. In 1174 the interior of the new choir limb was gutted by fire, and the catastrophe was reckoned to be an act of divine vengeance for the murder of Becket. Becket's shrine became one of England's most important places of pilgrimage.

The monks of the priory were anxious to preserve the crypt and the outer walls of the choir limb, including two arcaded towers. William of Sens, who came from Sens in France, where

Canterbury Cathedral, southwest facade: Canterbury, England, 1070

Canterbury Cathedral, choir

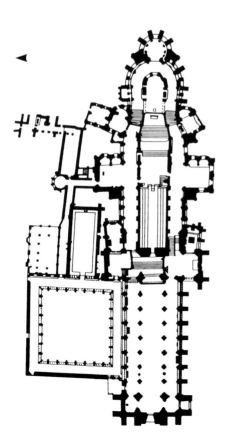

he had participated in the design of the new cathedral, was the designer of the new interior. The reconstructed limb is important as England's first example of "structural" Gothic as this was understood in northern France. The interior has pointed and molded arches, a simple ribbed vault, unobtrusive corbels, and foliate capitals reminiscent of Corinthian work. There is a striking color contrast in the interior resulting from the use of Caen stone and shafts of dark Purbeck marble. The choir limb has fairly thin walls, contrasting with the greater thickness of the walls of the Norman or Romanesque choir limb built earlier in the 12th century.

The reconstructed choir limb is in some ways similar to Sens Cathedral. The paired columns in the eastern part resemble similar columns at Sens, for instance. However, Sens Cathedral was a freestanding building, whereas the new choir at Canterbury was constrained by the deliberate retention of the outer walls and side towers of the earlier choir. The new choir at Canterbury may have had some influence on the apsidal St. Hugh's Choir at Lincoln (1192-1200). The eastern limb of Wells Cathedral, with its squared eastern end, on the other hand, exemplified the English Gothic tradition.

William of Sens had a serious accident in 1178, and he was followed by William the Englishman, who completed the new eastern limb, including the Trinity Chapel and the "Corona," a circular chapel at the extreme eastern end of the cathedral. The construction of the Trinity Chapel was undertaken to accommodate Saint Thomas' tomb, which was moved up from the crypt in 1220 to the eastern part of the building, where the pilgrimage shrine also came to be situated. The eastern bays of the Trinity Chapel are in the Early English Gothic of that period. Below the chapel and the Corona, there is a fine Gothic extension of the crypt. A detached belfry, or clocherium, of

Canterbury Cathedral

uncertain date, was situated to the south of the choir limb. This belfry was damaged by an earthquake in 1382, and was wholly destroyed by 1540.

Canterbury Cathedral has little architectural work of the Decorated style, which prevailed in the 14th century. Only the fine continuous arcade set up above the choir stalls, and two windows in St. Anselm's Chapel are good examples of Decorated work. A chapel in the crypt was fitted up, early in the Perpendicular period, as a chantry for the Black Prince, who died in 1376 and whose splendid tomb, with its gilt bronze effigy, was set in the Trinity Chapel. Across the chapel are the small chantry, and the tomb of Henry IV and Joan of Navarre, his second wife, who long survived the king and died in 1437. Both of these tombs were set as near as possible to the shrine of Saint Thomas. Other important tombs in the cathedral are of cardinals and archbishops, including the tomb of Henry Chichele, which has a vested effigy above a cadaver.

The monastic buildings were constructed to the north of the church. Some of them were executed in the Norman Romanesque, but the rectangular chapter house is of the 15th century, as are the beautifully vaulted cloisters. In the actual

cathedral, the Early Perpendicular nave is comparatively short, its length being determined by the earlier fabric of Lanfranc's nave. The very tall aisle windows allow for a comparatively low triforium and clerestory. The architect was probably Thomas of Hoo.

The southwest tower is of the 15th century, but the culminating feature of the cathedral is the greater central tower, known as the Angel, or the Bell Harry tower, which was finished in 1498. The master mason was John Wastell. The upper stages of the tower are of red brick, faced with stone. The ceiling of the lantern tower has beautiful fan vaulting. To allow for the extra weight which the tower imposed on the central crossing, a set of attractively traceried girder arches was inserted over some of the crossing's main arches and across the aisles. The tower still contains the wooden treadle wheel used to hoist materials to the upper stages.

In 1831 construction of a new northwestern tower, to replace Lanfranc's tower which stood till that year, was begun to the designs of George Austin.

Canterbury Cathedral has important medieval glass of the 12th, 13th and 15th centuries. Its fittings include a beautiful marble font of 1639, Baroque return stalls of 1662, and a brass eagle lectern of 1663 by the London brassfounder William Burroughes.

The first production of T.S. Eliot's *Murder in the Cathedral* was appropriately staged in the cathedral during the Friends Festival of 1935.

—BRYAN LITTLE

KEDLESTON HALL
Derbyshire, England

1758: Building designed; **Architect:** Matthew Brettingham.
1759: Design revised; **Architect:** James Paine (ca. 1716-89).
1760: Design again revised; **Architect:** Robert Adam (1728-92).

Publications

ADAM, ROBERT, and ADAM, JAMES: *The Works in Architecture of Robert and James Adam, Esquires.* 3 vols. 1773-1822.

BOLTON, ARTHUR: *The Architecture of Robert and James Adam.* 2 vols. London, 1922.

HARDY, JOHN, and HAYWARD, HELENA: "Kedleston Hall, Derbyshire." *Country Life* 163, 2 (1978): 262-266.

PAINE, JAMES: *Plans, Elevations and Sections of Noblemen's and Gentlemen's Houses Executed in the Counties of Derby, Durham, Middlesex, Northumberland, Nottingham and York.* 2 vols. London, 1767-83.

Kedleston Hall, south facade

Kedleston Hall, north facade: Derbyshire, England, 1757

Kedleston Hall is one of the pivotal monuments in the evolution of the mid-18th-century country house in England. A building with a complicated design history in which a number of different architects were involved, it illuminates in its successive phases both the central themes in the development of the form of the Anglo-Palladian great house and the nature of the relationship between this and the early stages of English neoclassicism.

Begun very shortly after Sir Nathaniel Curzon, later the first Lord Scarsdale, succeeded to the property in November 1758, it represents the next stage in the development of the great house after Lord Burlington's and William Kent's Holkham Hall, Norfolk, designed more than 20 years earlier. Kedleston's basic form—ultimately derived from Andrea Palladio's project for Leonardo Mocenigo—follows that of Holkham, being intended to consist of a rectangular main block with four subsidiary wings linked to it by quadrant corridors; also taken from Holkham was the idea, based on Palladio's interpretation of the so-called "Egyptian hall," of treating the entrance hall as a great, columned basilica.

The main difference between the two buildings is that whereas at Holkham the main block is of the traditional elongated shape, that at Kedleston is almost square; the significance of this arrangement is that it reflects the influence, even in a house of this very large size, of the other and more innovatory element in Anglo-Palladian country-house design, the compact, centrally planned Palladian villa. In addition, for the subsidiary wings, the specific formula of the villa was adopted, with its characteristic rhythm of a three-bay pedimented centerpiece and single flanking bays. However, the entrance front of the main block, with a five-bay portico and triple flank bays, is a composition in the established great-house manner looking back to such designs as Colen Campbell's Wanstead House (ca. 1714-20).

All of the features enumerated so far were probably due to Lord Scarsdale's first architect, Matthew Brettingham, and the affinities with Holkham Hall are readily explained by the fact that he had been the clerk of works at Holkham. In 1759, however, Brettingham's services were dispensed with, and a revised version of the design was produced by James Paine.

Paine was one of the leading exponents of the villa form as a model for the country house, and he proposed to emphasize further the villa-like qualities of the building, in two respects: first, by introducing a big top-lit central staircase—a feature that was a hallmark of the mature villa-based house—and second, by retaining in his design for the garden front the villa's characteristic single flank bays, managing this in spite of the size of the block by filling the space with big Venetian windows.

A further element in his proposal was the great Pantheon-like circular salon beyond the hall and staircase in the center of the garden front where, half-projecting from the body of the building, domed and colonnaded, it would have had the appearance of an antique peripteral temple. Ironically—since the salon was not executed—this striking composition of a bowed centerpiece flanked by Venetian windows was to be one of Paine's most influential designs, much imitated in the later 18th century.

The final version of the scheme was by Robert Adam, who in 1759 had been engaged to design garden buildings and interior decoration but in the following year was given responsibility for all the design work at Kedleston. He in turn eliminated Paine's villa references, moving the staircase to a less conspicuous position away from the central axis between the hall and salon, and reverting to triple flank bays in his new design for the garden front; however, these changes were in no sense negative.

The relationship which Adam thereby established between the hall and the salon, with the one leading directly into the

Kedleston Hall, rotunda

other, was that which existed between the "atrium" and "vestibulum" in Roman palace and villa planning; so were the Palladian resonances replaced by antique ones. A further consequence of moving the staircase was that the salon no longer projected forward, and Adam also replaced Paine's temple-like garden-front centerpiece with a feature based on the idea of a Roman triumphal arch.

The resulting elevation is frequently cited as an example of the quality of picturesque "movement" that Adam advocated, but that was equally evident in Paine's proposal; the nature of Adam's contribution is perhaps more truly expressed in his interior finishing of the house. Subtly endowing each room in the sequence with a distinct but complementary character, and at the same time underlining the antique references of the building as a whole, it was the type of scheme on which was founded Adam's justified reputation for having "distinguished himself by the superiority of his taste in the nicer and more delicate parts of decoration."

—PETER LEACH

DURHAM CATHEDRAL
Durham, England

1093: Present cathedral begun. **1099:** Choir and crossing completed. **1104:** Single-aisle transepts completed. **1133:** Nave and west towers completed. **1170-75:** Galilee Chapel built. **Ca. 1150-ca. 1226:** Twin west towers built. **Ca. 1260:** Central tower built. **13th century:** Choir vault rebuilt, east chapel, Chapel of

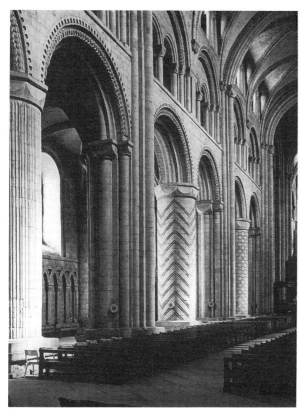

Durham Cathedral, nave

Nine Altars, built to replace apse; **Architect:** Master Richard of Farnham; top stages of twin west towers added. **1429:** Central tower struck by lightning. **1470:** Central tower rebuilt. **15th century:** Flat timber ceiling removed and vaulted ceiling constructed, west end columns strengthened. **Ca. 1490:** Tower extended. **17th century:** Interior damaged. **19th century:** Restoration, interior woodwork. **Architects:** James Wyatt and others. **1801:** Battlements and pinnacles, twin west towers.

Publications

CROOK, J. MORDAUNT and PORT, MICHAEL: Vol. 6 in *The History of the King's Works*. London, 1972.

DALE, ANTHONY: *James Wyatt*. Rev. ed. Oxford, 1936, 1956.

DALE, ANTHONY: "James Wyatt and His Sons." *Architect and Building News* 193 (1948): 294-296.

EASTLAKE, CHARLES: *A History of the Gothic Revival*. Edited by J. Mordaunt Crook. England, 1872, 1970.

ELMES, JAMES: "History of Architecture in Great Britain." *Civil Engineer and Architect's Journal* 10 (1847): 166-170, 209-210, 234-238, 268-271, 300-302, 337-341, 378-383.

FERGUSSON, FRANCES: "James Wyatt and John Penn, Architect and Patron at Stoke Park. Buckinghamshire." *Architectural History* 20 (1977): 45-55.

FERGUSSON, FRANCES: "The Neo-classical Architecture of James Wyatt." Unpublished Ph.D. dissertation, Harvard University, Cambridge, Massachusetts, 1973.

FREW, JOHN M.: "Richard Gough, James Wyatt, and Late 18th-century Preservation." *Journal of the Society of Architectural Historians* 38 (1979): 366-374.

HUNT, THOMAS FREDERICK: "James Wyatt." *Architettura Campestre*. London, 1827, pp. 13-17.

"James Wyatt." *Universal Magazine* 20 (1813): 342-343.

LINSTRUM, D.: *A Catalogue of the Drawings Collection of the R.I.B.A.: the Wyatt Family*. Farnborough, 1973.

ROBINSON, J.M.: *The Wyatts an Architectural Dynasty*. New York, 1979.

"Short Memoirs of the Life of James Wyatt, Esq." *Gentleman's Magazine* 83 (1813): 296-297.

TURNOR, REGINALD: *James Wyatt, 1746-1813*. London, 1950.

*

Late Romanesque architecture in England, or Norman as it is generally known, ranges from simple round-arched village churches at one end of the scale to the magnificence of such cathedrals as Ely and Winchester. None, however, can match the awe-inspiring grandeur of Durham Cathedral, a building perfectly fitted for its superb site.

Its history is in many respects unique. In 995 a monastery and bishopric were set up on this rocky peninsula protected on three sides by the winding River Wear, by monks fleeing from Danish raids on their island priory of Lindisfarne. With them they carried the venerated remains of their founder, Saint Cuthbert, whose seventh-century gold pectoral cross and even his wooden coffin are still preserved; the bones of the famed Venerable Bede were also taken to Durham before the Normans came.

Alongside the might of the cathedral stands the castle with its great octagonal keep on a mound. From the 11th century until the 16th, the bishops of Durham wielded civil and even military power as well as ecclesiastical (an arrangement not unknown in Germany but unique in Britain), and until the establishment of the university in the 1830s this was their palace and personal fortress.

The present cathedral was begun in 1093, which is later than most of the other great Norman churches of England. The choir and crossing were completed in only six years, the single-aisle transepts by 1104, and the nave with its aisles and west towers by 1133. Architecturally all these parts can be considered together, though there are significant differences in detail, particularly in the use of zigzag ornament, which began to appear only at the beginning of the 12th century. The scale and majesty of the interior are overwhelming. Great solemn cylindrical piers, many of them with quite elementary helical and other incised patterns, alternate with even bigger composite ones, so that the rhythm can be interpreted as either single bays or double, a visually satisfying arrangement that occurs in many other great churches of the period and in earlier instances. Hildesheim in Germany (ca. 1000), for example, often involved threes rather than twos.

Up to that time a building of such size would have had a flat ceiling. At Durham, however, quadripartite vaults of stone were ventured on, also arranged in pairs of bays, and each pair separated from the next by big arches that span between the clustered piers. In the nave, which was the last to be vaulted, these big arches are pointed, not semicircular; in England that was a new idea, though it was too early for them to be thought of as Gothic. The tall galleries, which take up the full width of the aisles, have twin round-headed openings internally, contained within a single arch. On the outside of the choir they have two small windows above each main aisle window, while in the nave there is one larger one. The clerestory, expressed externally as a single opening, is triple-arched inside and pushed upward—perhaps a little uncomfortably—into the vaulting.

The choir vault seems to have given trouble from the beginning and was rebuilt in the 13th century, at the time when the east chapels were added in place of the apse. The Norman vault

Durham Cathedral: Durham, England, 1093

may well have been the earliest rib vault in Europe. That was another of the innovations which were ultimately to lead to the Gothic style. The method of construction was simpler than groin vaulting in that the framework of ribs could be erected first on relatively slender timber centering and the spaces filled in afterward with thinner stones. So the building had become lighter in terms of material, and lighter visually as well. Maybe these methods were tried in the choir, not too successfully, and then perfected in the nave; in architectural history it is the successes which have survived for our study and admiration.

One of Durham's best-loved possessions is the 12th-century bronze knocker on the north door, a great cat's or lion's head with eyes that once shone with colored enamels. A replica has replaced the original, which is in the museum.

The central tower stands on four arches of impressive strength and had at first a flat timber ceiling; that was taken out in the 15th century and a lierne vault constructed at a much higher level, the tower itself being extended upward and eventually finished in more or less its present state about 1490. Its rather squat top stage is perhaps the weakest feature in the building's outline when seen from a distance, but it did once have a spire. So did the twin west towers, which are still basically Norman excepting their 13th-century top stages, and battlements and pinnacles of 1801.

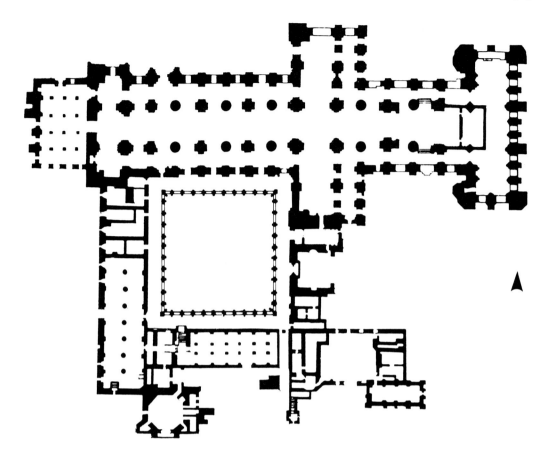

The next great work at Durham was the Galilee Chapel, Norman again in style, but with a lightness and elegance unparalleled at that date (ca. 1170-75)—a contrast indeed to the solemnity of the main building. Attempts had previously been made to build an eastern chapel beyond the choir, but they ran into constructional difficulties and the project was switched to the west end, where the new wall reached almost to the brink of the cliff. In that position its length had to be less than its breadth, so it has five aisles. The four arcades of round arches are profusely ornamented with zigzag and have a grace and poise not normally associated with the Romanesque. Originally their columns were even lighter; in the 15th century they were subtly strengthened by the addition of further shafts—an interesting reversal of the tendency of later Gothic builders to make their supports ever slenderer.

In the middle of the 13th century another attempt at adding an eastern chapel was made, and this was successful. It became known as the Chapel of Nine Altars and is a kind of eastern transept which literally contains nine separate chapels ranged along its far wall. The only other example of such an arrangement is at the ruined Fountains Abbey 50 miles or so to the south. By that time the Early English style was in full flower, and the designer's ambition to build as loftily as possible was helped by being able to lower the floor to a level very much below the rest of the building. Each altar has its own giant lancet window, and the north end has a marvelous Geometric traceried opening with a second, internal set of mullions. The principal attractions of the chapels are the alternating shafts of limestone and dark local "marble" and the vault patterns they support—the outer ones quadripartite, the next an ingenious kind of sexpartite with the central rib missing the boss, and in the center a four-pointed star with a central ring bearing superb carvings of the Evangelists.

At the time of the Civil War the cathedral suffered badly, its worst ordeal being in 1650 when Oliver Cromwell's troops, having taken great numbers of Scots prisoners at the battle of Dunbar, imprisoned 4,000 of them in the building. There they made fires of the medieval woodwork to keep themselves warm. After the restoration of the monarchy and the bishopric, completely new furniture and fittings were made. These are among the most important instances of Gothic Survival, as opposed to Revival, and include pinnacled choir stalls, a great bishop's throne built above a 14th-century bishop's tomb, a much more modest choir pulpit, a towering font cover and various pieces of screenwork—all in somber oak enlivened here and there with gold.

As for memorials and carved stonework, war and decay have left Durham with less of note than most great cathedrals. The chief is the splendid pinnacled late-14th-century Neville screen behind the high altar, dividing the choir from the space where Saint Cuthbert's lavish shrine once stood.

The cloister, the central part of the monastery, was built or rebuilt contemporaneously with the nave, but its present arches and timber ceilings are from the 15th century. The apse-ended chapter house, however, is still largely Norman and has a ribbed vault and zigzag ornament like the cathedral itself. The finest of the monastic buildings is the great dormitory (ca. 1400), nearly 200 feet long and still with its sturdy timber roof; it is now a museum and houses an incredible collection of artifacts from 698 A.D. onward, all closely related to the history of the cathedral and its diocese. The monks' kitchen, too, is a remarkable survival. It dates from 1366-70 and in plan is a square with fireplaces across the corners. The resulting octagon has a star-shaped vault that encloses a smaller octagon on which the vent stands; the resemblance to Moorish vaulting at Cordoba has been commented on but may be no more significant than two minds deriving the same answer from similar data.

—ANTHONY NEW

EXETER CATHEDRAL
Exeter, England

1112-1206: Original cathedral built; twin towers, lower parts of outer walls of the aisles remain. **Mid-late 13th century:** Miserere seats, choir. **1270-1370:** Rebuilding of cathedral, beginning from east end. **1312-18:** Bishop's throne. **Ca. 1320:** Pulpitum. **1389:** Glass, choir window. **15th century:** Battlements and turrets added to twin towers. **1942:** St. James Chapel destroyed; subsequently rebuilt.

Publications

PEVSNER, NIKOLAUS and METCALF, P.: *The Cathedrals of England.* Vol.1 Midland, Eastern & Northern England. Vol.2 Southern England. 1985.

*

Exeter Cathedral represents the epitome of the English Decorated style, though, like almost every other comparable church, it contains elements of different dates and design. In common with the collegiate church of Ottery St. Mary not far away, it has twin towers in the positions of transepts instead of at the west end. So the internal lines and rhythms of the arches and vaults are hardly interrupted from end to end. So too the distant silhouette is satisfyingly solid—no soaring steeples and gables as at Lincoln on its much higher hill, but instead a comfortable four-square massing that dominates the old city without dwarfing it.

The towers are the principal survivals from the Norman building, though the upper part of the north one was rebuilt in the 15th century with unobtrusively similar outline and detail. They once had low spires. Norman too are the lower parts of the outer walls of the aisles, at least as far up as the window sills, and as far east as two bays beyond the towers. Past that point the previous east end was apsidal; the present one continues the scheme of the nave, with a squared-off end followed by a rectangular Lady Chapel and flanked by various smaller rectangular chapels.

The internal piers too stand for the most part in the same places as the Norman ones. The plan is similar, the appearance utterly different—thanks to a rebuilding program continuous from about 1270 to 1370. The east end came first: the Lady Chapel and then the Choir. Differences in detail along the way from east to west are evident to the practiced eye—subtle changes in the manner of carving foliage, and a slight increase in the complexity of window tracery—but fundamentally the same design was used through three generations of building. It seems that no triforium was intended at first, and this accounts for the comparative lowness of the vaulting—13 feet lower than Salibury's, which was already complete when building at Exeter

Exeter Cathedral, west facade: Exeter, England, 1112-1206

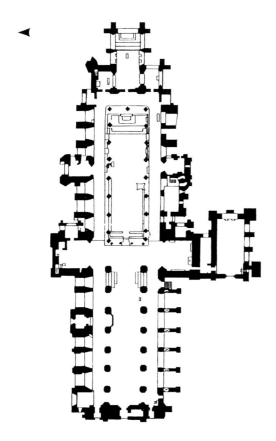

Exeter Cathedral

began. So the interior is not impressively lofty, but is broad and spreading like a palm avenue, and overwhelmingly exuberant at first encounter.

The piers, set diagonally on plan, have each no fewer than 16 shafts, and this proliferation of moldings continues around the main arches and into the upper parts. The triforium is a straightforward run of four small arches to each bay, supporting beneath the clerestory a gallery whose pierced balustrade helps to disguise the relative lack of height. The aisle windows and the equally big ones of the clerestory have five lights, with wonderfully varied tracery based on circles, multifoils and "spherical" triangles. The vaulting is about as complex as is possible for a tierceron system, that is, one with all the ribs radiating from the supporting wall shafts and none of the liernes or intermediate links that were to become customary by the end of the 14th century. It is the longest unbroken length of Gothic vaulting in existence—though in fact there is a subtle punctuation opposite the towers, the inner walls of which were daringly opened so as to create a full cross arm or transept at that point—and it is emphasized by the pulpitum with its towering organ which breaks the vista to just the right degree, concealing the choir and yet revealing it, and suggesting in a way approached by few other cathedrals the mystery and glory of what lies beyond.

A marvel of the vaulting is the abundance of carved stone bosses and corbels, many of naturalistic foliage and nearly all labors of love—for without present-day lights and lenses their detail could hardly be seen once they had been placed in position. Much has been colored and gilded in recent years; though that is how they were intended to be seen, modern eyes accustomed to monochrome stonework may think them needlessly overelaborate if not jarring.

The choir ends with a nine-light Perpendicular window (replacing a Decorated one) as wide and as high as it could be,

and resting on a pair of low arches. Its glass was put in in 1389. The Lady Chapel also has late Geometric tracery patterns, but its slightly earlier character is evident in the stiff-leaf carving, which had not yet fully given way to more realistic forms.

The west gable has another nine-light window, a pure Decorated design based again on circles and spherical triangles, trefoils and quatrefoils. Outside, the base of the window is masked by a stone screen displaying row upon row of standing figures in niches, wrapped around the west front rather like the earlier one at Lincoln. Here, however, there was not the need to bind together a succession of elements of differing dates and styles; this is more like an open-air reredos, a stone procession of saints and kings to impress pilgrims and instill feelings of devotion before they entered the building. Within the wall thickness is the tiny chantry chapel of Bishop Grandisson, who died in 1369 when the cathedral was virtually complete. The head of the statue of Saint Peter, high in the apex above the west window, is said to be the bishop's portrait. All this too was colored when new; the ravages of weather on the paint and the soft red sandstone have reduced it to a mere shadow of its pristine glory.

Inside, a favorite feature is the minstrels' gallery on the north side of the nave, carved with angels bearing a variety of musical instruments. Architecturally more valuable are the galleries corbeled out from the western sides of the transepts, on half vaults or covings like stone versions of the elaborate wooden chancel screens that embellish many local churches.

Other fittings include the stone choir screen, or pulpitum (ca. 1320), with incredibly delicate ogee arches and upper gallery; the choir stalls, mostly 19th-century renewals but with amusingly carved miserere seats said to be the earliest in England (mid- to late 13th century); and the lofty, canopied and pinnacled bishop's throne (1312-18), one of the finest pieces of woodwork of its age.

Exeter Cathedral

The monuments too include many of the first rank, particularly those to bishops of the 13th and 14th centuries and to later Devon worthies with famous names like Gilbert, Speke and Courtenay.

The cloister has all but disappeared, but the chapter house retains its Norman rectangular plan; its lower part is 13th century and its upper 15th including a timber roof with details suggestive of stone vaulting.

—ANTHONY NEW

GLOUCESTER CATHEDRAL
Gloucester, England

1058: Benedictine church built. **1089:** Early Norman rebuilding. **1242:** Early English rib vault added to nave. **1222:** Crossing tower and spire additions begun. **1224-28:** Extension of the axial chapel to form a Lady Chapel. **Ca. 1318:** Decorated rebuilding of south nave aisle. **1320s:** Decorated rebuilding of eastern chapels. **Ca. 1331:** Remodeling, south transept. **1337-1350s:** Remodeling, choir. **1370s:** Remodeling, north transept. **1382-1412:** Fan vaulting, eastern cloister walks. **1421-37:** Two west bays of nave rebuilt. **1450s:** Crossing tower rebuilt. **Ca. 1498:** Perpendicular Lady Chapel completed. **19th century:** Restoration.

Publications

BONY, JEAN: "Gloucester et l'origine des voûtes d'hémicycle gothiques." *Bulletin monumental* 98 (1939).
HARVEY, JOHN: "The Origin of the Perpendicular Style." In E. M. JOPE (ed.): *Studies in Building History.* 1961.
MORRIS, R. K.: "Ballflower Work in Gloucester and Its Vicinity." *British Archeological Association Transactions [Medieval Art and Architecture at Gloucester and Tewkesbury]* 7 (1985).
THURLBY, MALCOLM: "The Elevations of the Romanesque Abbey Churches of St. Mary at Tewkesbury and St. Peter at Gloucester." *British Archeological Association Transactions [Medieval Art and Architecture at Gloucester and Tewkesbury]* 7 (1985).
WILSON, CHRISTOPHER: "Abbot Serlo's Church at Gloucester (1089-1100): Its Place in Romanesque Architecture." *British Archeological Association Transactions [Medieval Art and Architecture at Gloucester and Tewkesbury]* 7 (1985).
WILSON, CHRISTOPHER: *The Gothic Cathedral.* 1990.

Gloucester Cathedral was raised to episcopal status only in 1541. Previous to the Dissolution of the Monasteries it was the church of the wealthy Abbey of St. Peter, founded in about 681. The Benedictine rule had been introduced there in 1022 and a new church built circa 1058, but the earliest remaining fabric belongs to the complete early Norman rebuilding begun by Abbot Serlo in 1089. This was part of the "second wave" of major post-Conquest churches to be built in England and is also one of the best preserved English churches of the late 11th century. The most important alteration to the church was the mid-14th-century renovation of the transepts and east end, producing one of the very earliest manifestations of the Perpendicular style, which set the standard for English architecture for the following 150 years.

Abbot Serlo's church, which was consecrated, although undoubtedly still unfinished, in 1100, featured an east end of three bays terminating in an apse and ambulatory with three radiating chapels (cf. Tewkesbury), a crypt beneath it of the same plan, an aisleless transept with eastern chapels and a crossing tower, an eight-bay nave and a two-towered facade. One of the remarkable aspects of the design was a difference of elevation between the eastern and western parts of the church. In the east end, there was a liturgically functioning gallery of about the same height as the main arcade. The eastern aisles are all groin-vaulted, as is the crypt; the gallery has quadrant vaults and the crypt chapels all have inserted but early rib vaults. Later rebuilding has obscured the original structure above this, but the east end was undoubtedly vaulted and so, perhaps, was the transept; a barrel vault with no clerestory and a groin vault have both been suggested, with a rib-vaulted apse, similar to the crypt chapel vaults. With a barrel vault, the elevation would probably have been two stories, but with groin vaults, it could very well have been of three, or perhaps even four stories, like the Tewkesbury transept.

The nave, on the other hand, was built without galleries. Instead, it has a triforium (cf. Mont-St.-Michel) with chevroned twin openings above a heightened arcade. The arcade piers, like those of the choir, are plain drum piers, but whereas they are relatively stocky in the choir, their tall proportions in the nave create a monumental impression. The subsequently tall nave aisles were rib-vaulted. Above the triforium was a clerestory of chevroned triple openings, with a wall passage, but this has been partially obliterated by the Early English rib vault that was built circa 1242. It was probably covered originally

Gloucester Cathedral: Gloucester, England, 1058

by a wooden ceiling, although a rib vault has also been suggested. This nave elevation, with its redefined three-story elevation and verticality, was an important step on the road to the Gothic wall formulation.

In its use of vaults, Gloucester represents a crucial moment in Anglo-Norman architectural development about which precious little is known, due to lack of survivals. It is now considered that vaulted choirs must have been fairly common in Normandy and England in the late 11th century, and groin vaults were in general the most widely used type of vault. It seems, as well, that rib vaults, which would play such a large role in defining early Gothic architecture, developed out of this predominant use of groin vaults. Serlo's church had vaults over every space

except perhaps for the nave; in the east end they were mostly groin vaults, although the radiating crypt chapels and probably the high apse took advantage of the technical adaptability of ribs, and rib vaults were subsequently used exclusively in the nave. Gloucester thus represents a stage in the use of vaults which led directly to the complete vaulting in rib vaults at Durham Cathedral a decade later. It can be traced back to such Norman progenitors as St. Nicolas (and probably St. Etiènne) in Caen.

To the Norman elements of Gloucester Cathedral were added other continental influences and an idiosyncratic approach to design. These factors produced a recognizable West Country school, which also included nearby Tewkesbury and Pershore

Gloucester Cathedral, north nave elevation: 14th century

abbey churches. The source of certain features, like its three-sided polygonal apse and the plan of the ambulatory, is difficult to pinpoint. Others, most notably the use of tall drum piers, point to Burgundy and churches such as Tournus, and in fact there were churchmen from that area in the West Country.

Besides the nave vault, other Early English additions were made to the church, including a crossing tower and spire (begun in 1222) and an extension of the axial chapel to form a Lady Chapel (1224-28); both the latter have been subsequently rebuilt. Work continued in the early 14th century with the Decorated rebuilding of the south nave aisle (ca. 1318), rich in ball-flower, and several of the eastern chapels in the 1320s.

The burial of King Edward II at Gloucester after his murder

in 1327 provided the impetus for a thorough remodeling of the eastern parts of the church. The south transept was begun first (ca. 1331), followed by the choir, begun in about 1337 and finished probably in the early 1350s; the north transept followed in the early 1370s to a comparable design. The work consisted mainly of cutting back the face of the Norman fabric and sheathing it in a thin skin of tracery panels, in the process of which the choir especially became visually divorced from the aisles and galleries. The idea of defining architectural volumes in terms of tracery extending over a variety of surfaces—window tracery, freestanding tracery in front of gallery and aisle openings, blind tracery against the wall surface—came from the Rayonnant architecture of France, as in such buildings as St.

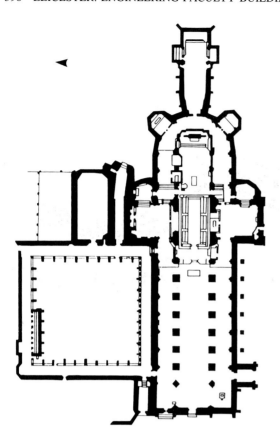

initially been a London-centered style. Another important feature that appears at Gloucester is its magnificent fan vaulting, which was first used in the eastern cloister walks, probably dating between 1382 and 1412; this is the earliest surviving example of the technique. A more mature stage of Perpendicular can be seen at Gloucester in the two west bays of the nave, rebuilt without towers between 1421 and 1437; in the crossing tower, rebuilt in the 1450s; and in the Lady Chapel, which was finished circa 1498. The church underwent only a moderate amount of 19th-century restoration.

—JAMES BUGSLAG

ENGINEERING FACULTY BUILDING (at Leicester University)
Leicester, England

1959-63: Building designed and constructed; **Architects:** James Stirling and James Gowan.

Publications

ARNELL, PETER, and BICKFORD, TED (eds.): *James Stirling: Buildings and Projects 1950-1980*. New York, 1984,.
FRAMPTON, KENNETH: "Leicester University Engineering Laboratory." *Architectural Design* 2 (1964): 61.
HOFMANN, WERNER, and KULTERMANN, UDO: *Modern Architecture in Color*. New York, 1970.
KORN, ARTHUR: "The Work of Stirling and Gowan." *Architecture and Building News* (January 1959).
"James Stirling: Buildings and Projects 1950-1967." *Kentiku Architecture* (January 1968).
James Stirling: Buildings and Projects 1950-74. London, New York, Stuttgart, Milan and Tokyo, 1975.

*

The Engineering Faculty Building of Leicester University by James Gowan and James Stirling was the first building in Britain after modernism. In architecture, this building from 1959-63 is the great symbol of that sense of revulsion and liberation which permeated English art and letters in those years, the years of "pop" and "angry young men." It mirrors with astonishing accuracy the place of All Saints, Margaret Street, the London church that William Butterfield had designed 110 years earlier.

John Summerson, resurrecting Butterfield in his classic 1945 essay subtitled "The Glory of Ugliness," began: "People of taste screw up their faces at the architecture of William Butterfield. . . ."

Certainly Stirling and Gowan at Leicester elicited a parallel response. Nikolaus Pevsner used the building to epitomize the enemy of good (that is, modernist) taste in his talk "The Anti-Pioneers" on BBC radio at the end of 1966. Pevsner's fury led him so to screw up his face that he talked of the building as incorporating "lecture theatres jutting out. These are of exposed concrete; the rest is faced with blue engineering bricks. . . ."

But there is neither blue brick nor raw concrete; on the contrary, the Engineering Faculty Building appears to be quite different from Stirling and Gowan's earlier essays in the "Brutalist" vocabulary. As Stirling commented, "It is clear that when Professor Pevsner approaches a building which he thinks he should not like, he closes his eyes." The lecture theaters

Urbain in Troyes and St. Thibault. But the idea has been transformed at Gloucester into a thoroughly English product.

Many of the features that make the work at Gloucester Perpendicular—including the repetitive use of rectangular panels with arched heads on walls and in windows, the insistence of thin vertical members running virtually the entire height of the interior elevation and, perhaps most fundamentally, tracery patterns featuring mullions running vertically into the arched heads of windows or panels—germinated in London. St. Stephen's Chapel in Westminster Palace supplied many of these ideas, and its second architect, Thomas of Canterbury (died in 1336) has been suggested as the architect of the Gloucester south transept. Another royal master mason, William Ramsey, who was responsible for the chapter house of Old St. Paul's Cathedral in London, has also been strongly linked with Gloucester.

The clerestories and vaults in the transepts and choir were built anew, that in the transepts at the level of the previous vault, that in the choir somewhat higher (about 92 ft). These are highly complex net vaults, i.e., barrel vaults with lateral penetrations overlaid with a dense pattern of ribs, tiercerons and liernes. Unlike other elements there, the vaults appear to be based solidly on a tradition in the west of England, including the choir vaults of Wells Cathedral and Tewkesbury, and there are links, as well, with Bristol Cathedral. The east window of the choir, the largest in the world at the time, forms a complete wall of glass, which is actually wider than the choir itself, as the eastern bay of the choir had to be canted outward slightly to make use of old foundations. It retains much of its medieval glass, and its banked rows of canopied figures across 14 lights create an effect similar to a monumental carved altar screen.

By the time the Gloucester choir was finished, the Perpendicular style was beginning to appear throughout England, and the Gloucester amalgam had some reciprocal effect on what had

Engineering Faculty Building: Leicester, England, 1963

certainly jut out, but they (as elsewhere) are covered with brick-red tiles—red tiles and bricks which remind one, again, of Butterfield's garish, clashing brick church—as well as the more obvious po-face: it is literally for a "red-brick university," as that generation of newer British universities was known.

The extreme of literalness can generate an extravagant rhetoric. At Leicester, Stirling and Gowan straightfacedly demonstrate a direct fit to their program. It is a cheap building, in two clear parts. First, there is a collection of fixed, nonexpanding elements, each clearly articulated at the front (including the requirement for a large water tank 100 feet above the ground for use in the hydraulic labs far below). Second, behind and almost filling the building's tight footprint is a general shed of continually re-equipped and adjusted workshops—heavy machinery on the ground, and higher, overhanging the road to allow vertical access for machinery, the lighter aerodynamic and electrical workshops. Over these sheds, industrial roof lighting aims north—which happens to be 45 degrees to the plan geometry. In front, from the main entrance at first floor, two differently sized lecture theaters rise. Above the smaller theater are stacked four identical laboratories, and above the larger theater rises a tiny, six-story tower of offices served by the only elevator the building could afford. The vertical circulation spaces between the two towers diminish toward the top as the traffic, logically, decreases.

All so logical! Which says nothing about the scintillating crystal waterfall between the towers, about the faceted cylindrical glass escape stair, about why the aerodynamics laboratory is rhetorically *three* floors above the service road—nothing about overall appearance, the forms in subtly dynamic equilibrium ("If you removed the top floor the building would overturn," Stirling remarked later), this Hoover on the hearth rug, this exercise in "bloodyminded élan and sheer zing" (to quote Reyner Banham) which made its neighbors look effete.

Banham recalled how, when at the *Architectural Review,* on getting the first images of Leicester he instantly felt, for almost the only time in his journalistic career, that he had on his hands something extraordinary and important. Today the Engineering Faculty Building's novelty remains refreshing, though we would be less inclined to follow critics of 30 years ago in stressing sadomasochistic qualities or in praising its ugliness. (Moreover, recent recladding of the glazing makes it less easy to see its sharpness in any way.)

This building stands up as a masterpiece of the primitive, in the sense of denying precedent and bluntly facing off smooth, intellectual modernism. Its expressionism "is often exaggerated—in its coarse but honest originality," to quote a contemporary on Butterfield's All Saints. Rough but suave, painful but beautiful, it takes modernist conceits of the 1920s (like entering up a great ramp under the belly of a lecture theater), but forms them in a hard-edged English industrial language that makes even the work of Le Corbusier seem soft.

And it is a tiny building, its three-dimensional organization tight as a clenched fist—just as is the masterly planning of All Saints. It is not necessary to argue how much of the building is Gowan's, but it is certainly not Stirling's alone, as overseas critics too often presume. One might fruitfully look at Stirling's buildings of 1975-85 alongside Alexander Thomson's of 1855-65: great, quixotic and strong. But Leicester is quite different; the unprecedented little masterpiece yet also swansong of a youthful design team which thereafter fragmented, it stands alone twinned with Butterfield's youthful and never-repeated All Saints. Each, bursting out of its chosen, unconventional camouflage (one "gothic," the other "industrial"), amazes with an intense power.

—JOHN McKEAN

LINCOLN CATHEDRAL
Lincoln, England

1092: Norman church consecrated, core of west front, part of the first bay of the nave remain. **Mid-12th century:** First three levels of towers flanking west front, three west doorways built. **1185:** Remains of Norman church damaged in earthquake. **1185-1250:** Restorations and expansion, choir, east transepts, nave, west trancepts, Galilee porch, upper part of west facade; **Architect:** Saint Hugh of Lincoln (except upper part of west facade). **1258-80:** Angel Choir built. **Late 13th century:** Cloisters built. **1307-11:** Geometric Decorated central tower built. **Ca. 1420:** Late Decorated west towers built. **1425-1550:** Perpendicular chantry chapels, doorway across north choir aisle built. **1436-39:** Perpendicular west windows of nave constructed.

Publications

COCKERELL, CHARLES ROBERT: "Ancient Sculptures in Lincoln Cathedral." *Proceedings of the Archaeological Institute* (1850).

FRANKL, P.: "The 'Crazy' Vaults of Lincoln Cathedral." *Art Bulletin* (1953): 95-107.

LAMBERT, E.: "L'eglise du monastere dominicain de Batalha et l'architecture cistercienne." *Melanges d'etudes portugaises, offerts a G. Le Gentil* (1949): 243-56.

PEVSNER, NIKOLAUS and METCALF, P.: *The Cathedrals of England.* Two volumes. 1985.

As a commanding landmark in its city and county, Lincoln Cathedral is second to none. Contrary to any first impression of being a single unified composition, it underwent many changes of design in the centuries since its construction. The homogeneity and coherence of the various phases come partly from the use of stone quarried from the very hill on which the building stands, but more from the instinctive respect of each generation of builders for its predecessors, coupled with the natural limitations of the available materials, whether for spanning openings, or for carving, or for throwing off the weather.

The price the Cathedral pays for its superb site is its exposure to the elements. All three towers once had tall spires, but the central one was blown down and the others have also been removed. The pre-Conquest "minster" or major church at Lincoln was subject to the cathedral of the enormous diocese of Dorchester more than 100 miles away on the Thames. The transfer of the bishop from Dorchester to Lincoln followed the Normans' general policy of moving sees into fortified towns.

The earliest surviving and visible work is of the late 11th century, consisting of five arches forming the core of the west front (the middle one was subsequently heightened). Of the middle of the 12th century are the towers flanking the west front (excluding their tall top stages) and the three rich, round-headed west doorways. Friezes over the side doorways portray Biblical events such as the death of Lazarus and Noah's Ark, and were inspired, it is thought, by similar sculpture at Modena in Italy. Among the supreme examples of Romanesque figure carving in England, they pose the usual conservation problems of artifacts exposed to weather and pollution.

In 1185, during the reign of the saintly Bishop Hugh, an earth tremor did serious damage and precipitated the start of a rebuilding of everything east of the west towers. The western part of the new choir is still called St. Hugh's. With it were

Lincoln Cathedral, west front from southwest: Lincoln, England, 12th century

Lincoln Cathedral

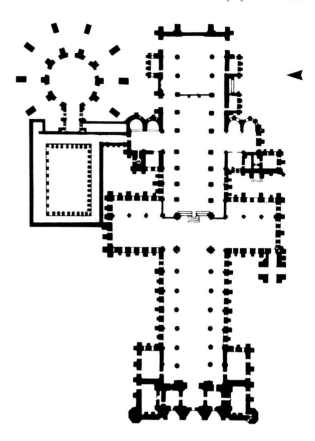

built its aisles, the great crossing arches, the innermost bay of each main transept, and the whole of the additional transept further east—all in a fully developed Early English style, rich with dog-tooth ornament and dark Purbeck marble shafts, features both typical of that period. The type of wall arcading along the aisles, a fascinating design with two separate arcades superimposed, the one out of step with the other, occurs elsewhere in only two other churches. Odder than that, however, is the vault, which is like no other. Its pattern is regular, yet not symmetrical, and has been likened to a series of scissors set diagonally. It is also considered to be the earliest vault to have tierceron ribs.

Next in date came the nave and aisles, only a little later than St. Hugh's Choir and very like it. The variety of treatment of the main piers and capitals is astonishing when the unity of the whole is considered; the Norman west bay, however, enclosed by the towers, remained little changed. The gallery arcade has two richly molded triple arches to each bay, and tracery of the early "plate," not "bar", type. The vaults again have tierceron ribs and are thus quite complex for their period. The aisle wall arcades repeat the "syncopated" rhythm of the choir, on the outside all this Gothic work was tied in to the Norman by a great arcaded screen, which extends right around both towers and masks their lower parts but skillfully leaves the five west arches and doorways almost unaltered. The outer ends of the main transepts are of that period too; the north one contains the great circular "Dean's Eye" window, with original glass, and the south has the sumptuously carved Galilee Porch, with seven splendid stone doorways stacked against one another. Above, in the transept gable, is the "Bishop's Eye," a 14th-century insertion with a wealth of medieval glass fragments. The chapter house, also of the second quarter of the 13th century, is 10-sided. Not only is it the earliest in England of the polygonal

type with central pillar and spreading vault, but its enormous flying buttresses make it also the most spectacular. Parliament met in it on several occasions.

The last major work was the east part of the choir, now known as the Angel Choir from the spandrel carvings of the arcades. Its purpose was to provide space for the pilgrims crowding to the shrine of St. Hugh, and it replaced a marvelous chevet that had stood for little more than 50 years. The Angel Choir is Geometric Decorated at its most lavish. In the triforium, bar tracery takes the place of plate tracery, and the clerestory has complex four-light windows, in two layers with a passage between. The vault is actually simpler than that of the nave, but the main supporting shafts end in big knobby foliage corbels, in one of which is the well-known "Lincoln Imp" carving. The tracery of the eight-light east window, with its delicate quatrefoils and sexfoils, has been called "one of the loveliest of human works," while on the south side of the Angel Choir stands the great Judgment Porch, flanked by two 15th-century chantry chapels, with a wealth of magnificent carving. Perhaps most miraculous of all in its craftsmanship is the doorway built across the north choir aisle at that time. It stands proudly on its own, as if waiting for a wall to be built over it, and its delicate openwork carving is almost beyond belief.

The comparatively small cloister (Lincoln was not a monastic cathedral) was mostly rebuilt just after the Angel Choir, about 1300, and a few years later the magnificent central tower was raised to its present height. The pinnacled stalls in St. Hugh's Choir are of the 14th century, and so is the stone screen dividing them from the crossing. The twin west towers were heightened in about 1400, with soaring belfry windows; octagonal corner turrets, built off the Norman work, strengthen them, both visually and structurally.

In complete contrast is the Honywood Library, built by Christopher Wren on a Tuscan colonnade in place of the north cloister walk. The adjoining medieval library contains one of the four original copies of Magna Carta. The cathedral has a wealth of medieval and later monuments, and a great black font of Tournai marble made for the Norman building.

—ANTHONY NEW

LIVERPOOL ANGLICAN CATHEDRAL
Liverpool, England

1904: Construction begins. **Architects:** Giles Gilbert Scott and G. F. Bodley. **1910:** Lady Chapel constructed. **1924:** Choir, aisles, eastern transept and chapter house constructed. **1951:** Tower constructed. **1964:** Second bay of the nave constructed. **1980:** Cathedral completed.

Publications

REILLY, C. H.: *Representative British Architects of Today*. London, 1931.
WHITE, NORVAL: *The Architecture Book*. New York, 1976.

*

Liverpool Anglican Cathedral is an immense building; its simple and bold exterior is dominated by the huge central tower and its massive but subtle proportions are enhanced by its commanding site, on a ridge of rock high above the city of Liverpool. Giles Gilbert Scott used a vigorous and highly personal version of Gothic to create a building of great power and monumentality, one which was the result of gradual development and many changes of design rather than the inspired creation of a young prodigy.

The Diocese of Liverpool was created in 1880, but it was not until autumn 1901 that a competition, attracting 103 entries from the leading architects of the day, was held. The assessors, G. F. Bodley and Richard Norman Shaw, invited a shortlist of

Anglican Cathedral: Liverpool, England, 1904

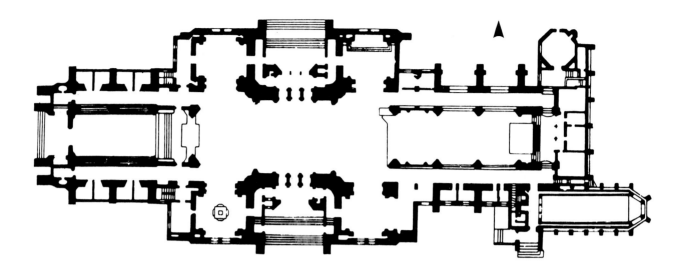

five to submit final designs in April 1903. They were looking for "the best idea and the finest conception . . . the practical and feasible aspect of the designs . . . for that power combined with beauty that makes a great building," which they found to some extent in Scott's entry. As he was only 22 with no experience of construction and administration, he was appointed joint architect with Bodley (the greatest living exponent of the Gothic) as "consultant."

The 1903 design, with twin towers on a single transept, a squat western tower, and a mass of projections and buttresses, was substantially modified to a more monumental and refined conception by the time the foundation stone was laid in July 1904. The only remnants of the first design are the Lady Chapel (dedicated 1910) and the (ritual) east end. The former is lower than the choir, partly because of the rock on which it is founded, and partly so as not to obscure the exterior view of the east. The exterior is a reflection of George Gilbert Scott's (Giles' grandfather's) chapel at Exeter College, Oxford, but the highly decorated interior with its elaborately carved gallery separating the low arcade and lofty clerestory is almost certainly Bodley's.

The Scott-Bodley partnership was a strained one, and Scott was on the point of resignation when in 1907 Bodley died. This allowed Scott to rethink the building, and his third and most radical design followed in 1909-10. The three towers and single transept were given up in favor of the huge central tower, flanked by twin transepts; the nave was reduced to three bays from six. The transepts of the north and south sides act as huge buttresses to the central tower and are linked by a low, wide, semicircular arch that acts as a porch and provides a foil to the mass of masonry above. The most striking feature is the tower: the lower part is rectangular, the upper part octagonal, with the transition masked by octagonal turrets at the four corners. It is there that Scott's approach "as a modeller rather than a draughtsman" is most obvious, and it is no surprise that he contended that "the building must be visualised in the solid" before elevations could be drawn.

Some of the peculiarities of the interior are the result of design changes: the vaulting of the central space (where it meets the narrower choir) springs from columns designed for a different purpose. The nave bridge, an extremely original feature, which breaks the vista from west to east, imparts a sense of mystery and increases the apparent size of the building. Beyond the bridge the interior rises to a great height, "a vast hall quarried out of a solid mass of stone," as Scott described

it. The sensation of height is produced by the unusual interior elevation: a tall arcade and a low triforium (no clerestory); by the darkness of the spaces above; and by the colonettes that rise uninterrupted to the springing of the vault.

The cathedral was constructed in stages so that funding could be raised for each section, which could then be used on completion. The choir, aisles, eastern transept and chapter house were consecrated in 1924 and the central space, great porches and western transept were begun the following year. The tower was complete by 1951, when the first bay of the nave was begun. In that year, power tools were introduced to cut the stone, though all surfaces were still roughed out by hand. Scott died in 1960, before work was finished. By 1964 the second bay of the nave was under construction, and in 1966 F. G. Thomas and R. A. Pinckney, both of whom had worked in Scott's office, were appointed to complete the building.

The final drawings for the west end were produced in September 1977, and the cathedral was completed in 1980. Despite the long time span, the building shows a remarkable unity of design. Rather than being, as Scott once remarked, "the last flare-up of the Gothic Revival," it is almost classical in its form and symmetry—a building out of its time and the final manifestation of the great age of cathedral building, but a building remarkable for its mass and power.

—MOIRA RUDOLF

METROPOLITAN ROMAN CATHOLIC CATHEDRAL
Liverpool, England

1960-67. Architect: Frederick Gibberd (1908-84).

Publications

GIBBERD, FREDERICK: *Metropolitan Cathedral of Christ the King*. London, 1968.

Metropolitan Cathedral: Liverpool, England, 1960-67

Two major commissions, both the result of open architectural competitions, dominated the development of ecclesiastical architecture in postwar Britain. One was Basil Spence's Anglican Cathedral at Coventry, a brilliant but conservative design that did little to reflect progressive liturgical developments; the other was Frederick Gibberd's Roman Catholic Cathedral of Christ the King, Liverpool, by contrast radical in its central planning and uncompromising structural expression. Where Spence's church was a marriage of traditional English liturgical values with an architectural language derived from the Festival of Britain, Gibberd's church was at once progressive and truly international in flavor. Where Spence's church responded to a bomb-damaged medieval precursor, Gibberd's Liverpool Cathedral completed a building operation begun according to Edwin Lutyen's design for the Brownlow Hill site of 1928. That operation was halted by the outbreak of war in 1939, when only the crypt and podium of the Lutyens church were completed.

Gibberd's competition entry responded not only to the existing podium of Lutyens' firmly classical design, but also to a radical brief. The demand for a cathedral ". . . built to enshrine the alter of sacrifice . . ." was answered by a central altar which in turn generated a centroidal plan and ultimately a conical building form, which, along with Giles Gilbert Scott's Anglican Cathedral, dominates the skyline of Liverpool. The high altar sits on a circular dais and is itself located at the center of the crossing in Lutyens' design, the only concession Gibberd made to his illustrious predecessor. However, it is an important one, for it provides a linkage between two wholly dissimilar designs separated by three decades.

In one sense, the building is entirely consistent in that its planning, structure and architectural language derive from a need to engage a congregation of 2,000 in elaborate Roman Catholic ritual, especially the celebration of High Mass. Given the organization of the plan, no communicant is more than 25 meters away from that celebration.

Subsidiary chapels of varying plan forms engage with the periphery of the worship space in radial fashion, fitting between the massive splayed concrete columns of the main structure. While externally these chapels offer formal contrast and relief from the cone and drum of the worship space, internally they

pinnacles and finials, as ample evidence of Gibberd's eclectic tendencies.

The gestation of the Metropolitan Cathedral took no less than 114 years, and in the light of this, the relatively short time devoted to design and particularly to erection may appear surprising. Most certainly it accounts for some of the crude detailing, particularly the way in which mosaic-clad columns crash through the paved podium and reemerge through crudely fashioned openings in the concrete masonry of the podium wall. Similarly ill-conceived junctions occur between these splayed columns and the ring beam supporting the lantern. Serious building failures during the building's short life further identify less-than-well-considered detailing. This is in stark contrast to the "crafted" nature of Scott's Anglican Cathedral half a mile away and, to some extent, Spence's efforts at Coventry, which will forever invite comparison.

At the urban scale, Gibberd's design is most successful and as a counterpoint to Scott's Late Gothic Revival pile, it makes a surprising and dramatic intervention upon Liverpool's skyline. Because of its siting (although Lutyens must take some credit for this), the Metropolitan Cathedral has a presence which dominates many views within the city and has indeed become an image representative of the city itself.

Liverpool remains as Gibberd's finest contribution to postwar British architecture, and despite a decidedly mixed reception from critics (a fate shared with Spence's Coventry), the directness of its design will surely stand the test of time. With three decades' hindsight, it emerges as an important example of its period, thankfully devoid of the meretricious trappings so characteristic of its contemporaries.

—A. PETER FAWCETT

are less successful in their lack of scale occasioned by the use of sprayed concrete finishes, which deny the intensity of detail found with more traditional solutions.

Not only in its planning does Liverpool represent a radical departure from precedent in English greater church building in the 20th century. Gibberd's uncompromising attitude toward structural integrity and expression puts Liverpool in a completely different category from the compromises that denied any such authority to Spence's efforts at Coventry, and puts the Metropolitan Cathedral firmly within the English Brutalist tradition of the 1960s.

There are, however, inconsistencies. The huge splayed columns that form the cone crash arbitrarily through the podium, some reemerging through the podium walls to reveal their springing at ground level, producing a most unfortunate ambiguity. Like Coventry, Gibberd's work harbors artworks, particularly the stained-glass lantern by John Piper and Patrick Reytiens, but arguably they are much better integrated with the structure and fabric of the building than at Coventry. However, this quest for integration can go awry; William Mitchell's incised design of crosses and crowns to the Breueresque entrance canopy reduces Christian iconography to a banal level, and the Gothicized finials and tracery of the "crown" surmounting the lantern seem curiously at odds with the generally powerful integrity of the building.

While Spence's Coventry Cathedral is essentially eclectic, responding to a long English tradition, Gibberd's design at first sight seems to follow another tradition entirely, devoid of picturesque motifs. However, detractors cite references for the crown of thorns (Oscar Niemeyer's Brasília Cathedral), the concrete tracery of the lantern (Auguste Perret), the entrance canopy and bell tower (Marcel Breuer), Mitchell's incised intaglio (Frank Lloyd Wright), and the already noted Gothicized

ST. GEORGE'S HALL
Liverpool, England

1840-56. **Architect:** Harvey Lonsdale Elmes (1814-47). Construction completed by Robert Rawlinson. Interiors completed by C. R. Cockerell (1788-1863).

Publications

HUGHES, O.: "Neo-Classical Ideas and Practice: St. George's Hall, Liverpool." *Architectural Association Quarterly* 5, 2 (1973): 37-44.

KILPIN, J. T.: "The Late Mr. Elmes and St. George's Hall." *Transactions of the Historic Society of Lancashire and Cheshire* New series 9 (1869).

TANNER, J. A.: "A Contemporary Account of St. George's Hall." *Architectural Review* 41 (1917): 122-125.

*

Among the earliest of the 19th-century English town halls, St. George's Hall is a superb expression of the sense of civic pride that impelled the construction of numerous town halls through England. The architect Harvey Lonsdale Elmes won the town hall competition in 1839, and another the following year for a new courthouse. Shortly thereafter, the town fathers decided to combine both projects into one structure. St. George's Hall was Elmes's first major commission, won at the age of 25, and it is the building for which he is most remembered.

St. George's Hall: Liverpool, England, 1840-54

Facing the challenge of constructing a combined town hall and courthouse, into which a concert hall was also to be incorporated, Elmes set out, in 1840, for a grand tour of the Continent. Karl Friedrich Schinkel's first edition of the *Sammlung Architechtonische Entwürfe* had just appeared that year, and Elmes was drawn to Germany by reports of Schinkel's buildings in Berlin—a logical choice for Elmes' attention, since he was firmly committed to the neoclassical tradition. Schinkel's influence can be seen at St. George's Hall, yet Elmes never lapsed into slavish copying in the use of any source of inspiration, be it Schinkel or any other; he created, rather, new and inventive forms in the romantic classical tradition.

Consisting of a pediment (once filled with sculpture), full classical entablature, and a double row of fluted Corinthian columns, the south portico is not the major entrance it appears to be. The impression of this south facade with its portico is neo-Greek, but as one moves to the long east side and principal entrance on Lime Street, the visitor is immediately struck by

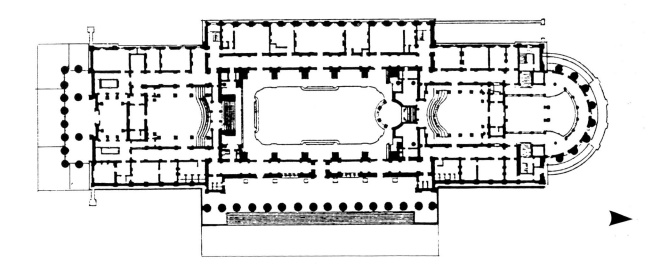

the facade's Roman monumentality. This principal entrance is articulated by a portico of fluted Corinthian columns, approached by a flight of 20 steps. Recalling the Greek stoa colonnade, this portico corresponds to and announces the great interior hall, for concerts and public meetings, directly behind it. The wings on each side of the portico and central hall house the crown and civil courts. Clearly this east portico is inspired by Schinkel's entrance facade to his Altes Museum in Berlin (1830). The attic that rises above St. George's Hall conceals a vast Roman vault and announces the central space of the great hall below. Similarly, the Altes Museum attic conceals a vast dome, crowning a central Pantheon-like exhibition hall.

Elmes's monumental structure was not intended to be viewed at one glance. Its massiveness invites and forces the visitor to walk around it, observing and experiencing, in the process, how the building changes dramatically from side to side in close relationship to the shifting site it occupies. Elmes anticipated, in this way, the later-developing Victorian taste in architecture for irregularity and fragmentation in massing, although that later preference was expressed with a very different vocabulary.

The north end of St. George's Hall is an apse, recalling the Roman basilica, a fitting association for this town hall-courthouse. Unlike Roman prototypes, however, this apse is treated with engaged, fluted Corinthian columns, suggestive of the Greek tholos temple or round Roman temple, such as that of Vesta. As a unifying element, an entablature continues unbroken around the apse, which itself articulates a small concert hall.

The west facade consists of 26 bays of windows at four different levels, separated by freestanding piers crowned with Corinthian columns. This central, projecting expanse of windows articulates the great hall behind it, while the more solid wall surfaces on each side relate to the two courtrooms behind them. By comparison with the other facades, this west side is strikingly modern and sleek.

It is this facade which suggests multiple affinities with Schinkel's Schauspielhaus in Berlin (1818-26). Like Schinkel, Elmes reduced his classical vocabulary to a trabeated grid, expressive of structure, thus relieving the facade's potential massiveness. At the Schauspielhaus, Schinkel had to incorporate a concert hall, at the king's request, and opted for a tripartite plan with central theater—announced by the attic—flanked by concert hall on one side and storage areas on the other. Similarly, Elmes placed his great civic hall at the center, also articulated by an attic, with the two courtrooms on each side, and his concert hall in the apse.

As for the interior, Elmes's concern was for the creation of a major imperial Roman vista of 300 feet—a continuous visual experience from the south end of the crown court through the great central hall and on through the civil court at the north end. Doors separating the great hall from the adjoining courts could be thrown back to provide this visually sublime experience, so sought after by other architects such as John Soane in his Bank of England. Elmes's source of inspiration for his barrel vault was Guillaume-Abel Blouet's *Restauration des Thermes d'Antonin Caracalla à Rome* (1828), and most specifically the sketches of the tepidarium, upon which Elmes freely improvised in his usually creative way. Despite its vastness, the great hall is warm and inviting due to the architect's skillful use of polychromy, particularly through his choice of the finest marbles and granite. Abhorring all sham, Elmes insisted on honesty in materials throughout.

When Elmes died unexpectedly in 1847 at the age of 33, Charles Cockerell was hired to complete the work, most of it interior decoration. His major contribution was the completion of the small concert hall in the north apse. The decorative effect is lavish and opulent with many classical details, including a ring of caryatids beneath the balcony. Truth in materials is not the norm here, as the walls were painted to look like wood, the pilasters are papier-mâché, and the caryatids appear to be of lithodipra, a contemporary synthetic material.

When the concert hall was opened in 1856, St. George's Hall was considered completed at last, although some sculpture was to be added to the exterior years later. It was the last of the important English Romantic Classical civic structures, very possibly the greatest of all the 19th-century English town halls, and the building upon which Harvey Lonsdale Elmes's excellent reputation rests.

—FRANCIS J. GREENE

BANQUETING HOUSE, WHITEHALL
London, England

1619-22: Construction; **Architect:** Inigo Jones. **1698:** Damaged by fire.

Publications

GOTCH, J. A.: *Inigo Jones*. London, 1928.
HARRIS, JOHN: "A Prospect of Whitehall by Inigo Jones." *Burlington Magazine* 109 (1967): 89-90.
LEES-MILNE, J.: *The Age of Inigo Jones*. 1953.
PALME, P.: *Triumph of Peace: A Study of the Whitehall Banqueting House*. Stockholm, 1956.
WARE, I.: *The Designs of Inigo Jones*. London, 1756.
WHINNEY, MARGARET: "John Webb's Drawings for Whitehall Palace." *Walpole Society* 33 (1942-43): 45-107.
WITTKOWER, RUDOLF: "Inigo Jones, Architect and Man of Letters." *RIBA Journal* 3rd series. LX (January 1953).

*

Inigo Jones' Banqueting House, built as a setting for masques and other formal entertainments at the early Stuart court of James I, introduced to England the classical architectural style Jones had learned from the Italian Renaissance architecture of Andrea Palladio.

Jones' simple classical structure of brick and stone, which towered above the complex old Tudor Palace of Whitehall, to which it was added, succeeded earlier structures on the same site. These included an obscure structure of 1572 and a wooden building erected in 1581 to receive the duke of Alençon, a suitor of Elizabeth I. Its immediate predecessor was a masonry banqueting hall built in 1606 by Simon Basil, surveyor of the King's Works. James I did not like Basil's building because of stone posts that obstructed his view of the masques, and the possibility that assassins could lurk in the shadows of these posts. When it burned on 12 January 1619, Jones, who had become surveyor of the King's Works after the death of Basil in 1615, designed the present banqueting hall.

For inspiration, Jones consulted Palladio's publications and discovered two probable sources. His exterior is close to a

Banqueting House, Whitehall: London, England, 1619-22

Venetian palace Palladio described in *I Quattro Libri dell' Architettura* (Book 2) but did not build. The interior Jones based on Vitruvius' description of a Roman basilica as Palladio had interpreted it. And, like the Renaissance architect, inspired by ancient architecture but not a slavish follower of it, Jones used these prototypes freely and created a building that, while indebted to the Italian architect, has its own character. In prints made before 1698—when nearly all of the rest of the palace burned—the Banqueting House's simple classical form contrasts with the clustered medieval elements of the old Whitehall Palace and stands high above the rest of the building. With the Banqueting House, Jones initiated a new architectural age in England based on the application of the classical language of Palladio and Vitruvius, although the new style attracted few followers in the 17th century and reached its apex only in the 18th century, in the Palladian movement begun by Lord Burlington and his circle.

Following Palladio's palace description, which included a pedimented facade, Jones, in an early drawing, featured a central pediment but abandoned it as he progressed, because a pediment implies a grand entrance to a building. Because Jones' entrance was at the north end, he omitted the pediment and designed a slight projection of the three central bays to provide a focal point for the facade.

The main or western facade comprises a rusticated podium base characteristic of Palladian palace design, and an upper region divided into two levels decorated by superimposed Ionic and Composite orders. An open balustrade crowning the roofline balances the podium base and reinforces the classicism of the facade.

Jones emphasized separate elements of the facade by using two different types of stone for the revetment and a third for the decorative features. He faced the basement level with rusticated Oxfordshire stone and adorned it with seven square windows surmounted by rusticated voussoirs. For the main story, he used rusticated Northamptonshire stone; he organized its lower register, which rests on a plinth, into divisions separated by four central engaged columns and lateral pilasters doubled at the ends. To frame the square windows, Jones used aedicular frames made up of slender pilasters and alternating segmental and triangular pediments. His upper register bears the same rhythm of doubled end pilasters and single inner pilasters leading to the projecting engaged columns of the central bays. A continuous frieze of swags and decorative heads and the open balustrade above complete the western elevation.

The internal division comprises a vaulted basement and the great hall above. In the banqueting hall, Jones avoided the structural errors made by Basil in the building of 1606. For the large ceremonial room, he used the format of a rectangular basilican hall with triple aisles but, in a free usage of the classical prototype, created a completely open space by omitting the obstructing posts. He suggested the traditional division of nave and aisles by using engaged columns embedded in the lateral walls instead of the freestanding columns characteristic of ancient basilican interiors. In further reference to the basilican formula, he included a cantilevered gallery on three sides of the hall and large clerestory windows between the Corinthian pilasters. This combination of Corinthian pilasters of the clerestory and the engaged Ionic columns below echo the application of superimposed orders on the facade. Jones also included a frieze of swags and decorative heads like that on the exterior. The hall is a double cube measuring 55 feet in both height and width, and 110 feet in length. Jones revived this spatial prototype popular in the Renaissance for its beauty and harmony.

The only permanent ornamentation of the simple and elegant banqueting hall is a series of nine paintings on canvas by Peter Paul Rubens set into gilded ceiling compartments. These paintings were planned—probably for the ceiling—by Jones in consultation with James I, but it was James' son and successor, Charles I, who commissioned the paintings, which were not installed until 1635. Rubens' brilliantly colored Baroque paintings, which glorify the reign of James I, contrast with the simplicity of the room and emphasize its elegant beauty.

Some internal changes made in the banqueting hall after the fire of 1698, including the immediate fitting of it for the royal chapel and the later additions of items required for use as a museum, altered the effect of Jones' basilican hall. These additions are gone now, and the interior is restored to its original format. External changes were less obvious but longer lasting. When John Soane repaired the deteriorating stonework of the upper level of the facade with Portland stone after William Chambers earlier had refaced the basement level with the same material, he further altered the subtle tricolored original revetment. Despite these few changes, the Banqueting House remains one of the finest classical buildings in England.

—JOYCE M. DAVIS

BATTERSEA POWER STATION
London, England

1934: Construction begun; **Architects:** J. Theo Halliday and Giles Gilbert Scott (1880-1960). **1955:** Construction completed. **1975:** Battersea 'A' closed. **1983:** Battersea 'B' closed.

Publications

REILLY, C. H.: *Representative British Architects of Today*. London, 1931.
WHITE, NORVAL: *The Architecture Book*. New York, 1976.

*

For a generation, the smoking chimneys of Battersea were the image of a power station and an evocative London landmark. The design is strongly associated with Giles Gilbert Scott (1880-1960).

The simple, powerful "upturned stool" silhouette which emphasizes the scale and expanse of the building was not an aesthetic choice. At the start there were doubts about how clean the station would be. (Opposition came from the residents of affluent Chelsea and Kensington rather than poorer Battersea itself; it was also questioned—reasonably—why electricity could not be generated outside the city.) Battersea was therefore planned in two halves—the second to go ahead if the cleaning ("scrubbing") of the exhaust gases proved satisfactory. The plan was symmetrical: two power stations back-to-back with tall boiler houses in parallel flanked by the lower turbine halls. The problem of smoke cleaning led to each station having one flue and two chimneys—one at each corner.

After the form and massing had been determined by these technical considerations, the architect J. Theo Halliday was called in to provide architectural packaging. He proposed the exterior brick skin for the steel frame and stressing the "towers" at the corners. It was Halliday who was also responsible for the extraordinarily elaborate interiors—the turbine halls were designed as temples of modern technology complete with giant, stylized pillars.

Scott's contribution was the detailing of the exterior. He was one of the leading British architects of the interwar years and the grandson of George Gilbert Scott (designer of the Albert Memorial, St. Pancras Station and the Foreign Office, all in London). He was trained in the Victorian Gothic tradition but had developed a Moderne style that owed much to the American deco. He occupied a middle position in the conflicts in the 1920s and 1930s between "modernists" and "traditionalists"; rather than being concerned with functional expression, he saw his role as "humanizing" the products of the industrial age.

At Battersea he was particularly careful in the choice of a light-colored brick and tinted mortar to avoid creating a somber mass. Scott also spent much time carefully modeling the bases of the chimneys. They are reinforced-concrete monoliths, and their "fluting" is entirely decorative. However, the suggestion of double "capitals" resulted from a report advocating an increase in the total height to 337 feet.

Scott had won, at the age of 22, the commission for the huge Liverpool Anglican Cathedral. There are obvious connections in the way, at Battersea, that Scott modeled the elevations without trying to minimize their soaring height—it is perhaps not surprising that Battersea was repeatedly characterized in a revealing mixed metaphor as a "cathedral of power." It was Battersea Power Station rather than the few designs of the Modern Movement that had been built in Britain at that time that caught the imagination and realized the contemporary idea of "modernity" between the wars. Battersea is in the same vein as much of the romantic industrial design of the period, such as the streamlined steam locomotives; there is also perhaps a slight science fiction overtone. The style has been called "Jazz modern"; but as the citric Nikolaus Pevsner, one of the most important exponents of modern design, pointed out, "Whatever criticisms have been levelled against it, it remains one of the first examples in England of a frankly contemporary industrial architecture."

Battersea became an architectural paradigm. Hitherto power stations had not emerged as recognizable architectural types because electricity supply had been provided by a large number of companies through small local generating plants. But in 1926 an act of Parliament set up the Central Electricity Board to coordinate electricity production across the country and to concentrate generation in a limited number of power stations. Battersea was one of the first results of the act, and there followed other stations given a similar architectural treatment until technology, particularly that of the nuclear program, came to dominate over design.

Scott went on to design the oil-fired station Bankside further down the river, opposite Christopher Wren's St. Paul's Cathedral; with its tall brick chimneys, Bankside is really more "cathedral"-like than Battersea. Battersea itself was not completed until 1955, and was in full production only until 1975, when Battersea "A" was closed; Battersea "B" was closed in 1983. Alternative uses were proposed for the structure, and development as a theme park began; however, that has been halted due to a financial crisis. The boilers having been removed, the structure is without a roof, and its future is uncertain.

—TIMOTHY CLARKE

Battersea Power Station: London, England, 1955

BRITISH MUSEUM
London, England

1823: Construction begun; **Architect:** Robert Smirke (1760-1867). **1828:** East wing completed. **1831:** West wing completed. **1842:** Walls completed. **1851:** Ephesus Room completed. **1853:** Forecourt and lodges completed; **Architect:** Sydney Smirke. **1856:** Assyrian Salon completed. **1868:** Northern extension of Elgin Room completed. **1854-56:** Central Reading Room completed; designed by Sydney Smirke. **1907:** Work begun on north side gallery.

Publications

CROOK, J. MORDAUNT: "The Career of Sir Robert Smirke." Oxford doctoral thesis. 1961.
CROOK, J. MORDAUNT: *The British Museum.* London, 1972.
PAPWORTH, WYATT, ed.: *The Dictionary of Architects.* 8 volumes. 1852-92.
WHITE, NORVAL: *The Architecture Book.* New York, 1976.

*

The British Museum, on Great Russell Street in London, is the most important of the great museums of England, is still the largest building in the classical style in England, and is one of the most interesting in the history of museums. It is, as Nikolaus Pevsner put it, "characteristically English in that it was the one great national collection which had no regal or princely origin."

The idea of such a national museum was first spoken of in 1753 when Sir Hans Sloane, a physician, left his library, manuscripts and a collection of objects to the nation. A lottery was organized to raise money, and Montague House was purchased with the proceeds; it was adapted to provide the necessary space, and the museum opened on 15 January 1759. More was added to the collection, including the manuscripts of Sir Robert Cotton and Edward and Robert Harley, and George II gave the royal library of books collected by the sovereigns of England since the time of the Tudors. In 1782 the collection of Greek art of Sir William Hamilton was purchased; after Admiral Nelson's victory in Egypt, and under terms of the Treaty of Alexandria, the Rosetta Stone and many other Egyptian antiquities were taken to London. In 1816 the Elgin Marbles were purchased, and in 1820, upon his accession, King George IV presented the library of his father to the museum.

It was obvious after so many acquisitions that a new building was needed. The noted neoclassicist Robert Smirke was quickly chosen as architect, and he began the work in 1823. The building was designed in the Greek style, as were so many of the public offices and museums of that time; Smirke was firm in his admiration of that manner, it being, as he put it "the noblest" of all possible styles, "simple, grand, magnificent without ostentation."

The plan, which went through several changes after its first unveiling, set a series of wings around a central court; in the first design, Smirke wanted visitors to pass through the courtyard, under a second portico, and to enter at the north wing, past a flight of steps and another portico. But financial and practical problems made this impossible, and the court was, for the moment, left unused. The entrance front was also changed,

British Museum: London, England, 1823

getting more architectural attention as the emphasis on the quadrangle was reduced; Smirke introduced there a stringcourse along the front, sculpture in the pediment and separate sculptured friezes at the center and at the wings, all of which served to soften the general effect. The result is powerful, if perhaps overwhelming: a screen of columns, based essentially, if with careful variation, on those at the Ionic temple of Athena Polias at Priene in Asia Minor, gathered to the center with a pediment that is rooted in the traditions of English Palladianism, the wings being marked only with a simple entablature. The model for all this was perhaps the Parliament House, Dublin, which had been begun in 1728 by Edward Lovett Pearce; there is a sense that all Smirke did was expand the idea Pearce had of an articulated colonnade, and then change the order from Roman to Greek. But the scale and, it must be said, the effect, are quite different.

Building began in 1823; by 1828 the east wing was finished, and in the following year the collection of royal books from Kensington Palace was moved to their new home in what is now the King's Library. Work then started on the west wing to house the Elgin Marbles, and this was completed by 1831. But financial problems were always delaying progress, and it was for this reason that in 1840, a crucial date in the history of the museum, Sir Robert Peel persuaded the Treasury to sanction a higher level of state support. At that moment, plans for the entrance front were put in hand, the construction there finally going to the firm of Samuel Baker of Rochester which was the contractor for most of Smirke's work in London. By 1842 the walls had reached roof level; however, in 1845 ill health forced Smirke to retire from practice, leaving his brother Sydney Smirke to carry on with all the unfinished parts of the museum—

the forecourt and lodges (1849-53), the Ephesus Room (1850-51), the Assyrian Salon (1856) and the northern extension of the Elgin Room (1868).

It was Sydney Smirke who designed the great central Reading Room (1854-56), a dome of glass and iron that may have been based on the model of J. B. Bunning's Coal Exchange in London, which had been finished in 1849. The Reading Room was much larger, though, some 141 feet in diameter (St. Peter's, Rome, being 138 feet across). This was a remarkable idea, though models for such circular plans for libraries went back, in England, to the Radcliffe Camera at Oxford (1737-49); more recently the scholar Benjamin Delessert had proposed such a scheme, based on Jeremy Bentham's idea of the panopticon, for the Royal Library in Paris. Very striking also were the iron stacks and iron floors, set at each level around this central space, an idea suggested by Anthony Panizzi, an Italian political refugee and scholar who had been appointed keeper of printed books in 1837. There had been much dispute about filling this interior court; the trustees and the Treasury recognized the space for the library such a design would provide, however, and it was for this reason, among others, that a proposal of Charles Barry to glaze over the area and make it a gallery was considered unsuitable. We do not know what Robert Smirke thought of it, though, curiously, the form of this new room made the final plan of the museum more similar than ever to that of the Dublin Parliament House.

The building of the British Museum took almost 30 years, and when it was done, the style in which it was designed was completely out of fashion, Regency being much more to the taste of the new generation of Victorian critics of the 1840s. Much, both fair and unfair, was said about the functioning of the building,

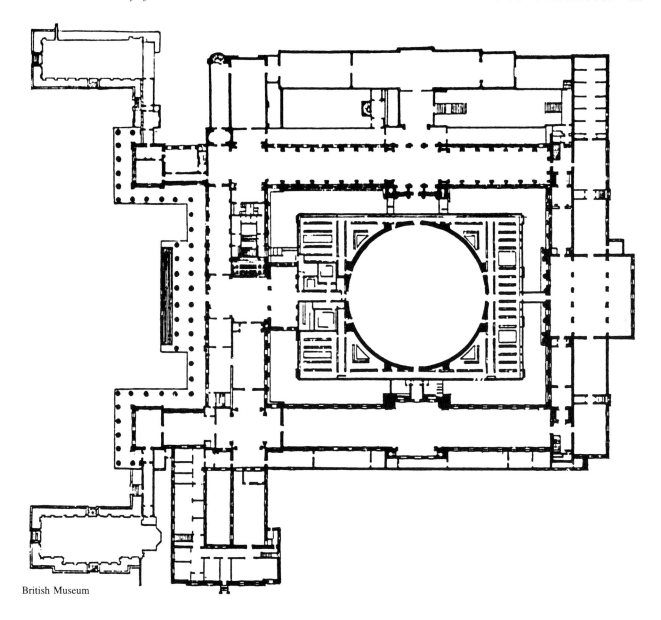

British Museum

and about the way Smirke had been appointed to his position by the Tory government of Peel. And of course there was the style, which one critic called "formalised deformity, shrivelled precision, and starved accuracy." Yet this is a remarkable structure, featuring several new techniques and materials: concrete was used in the foundations, with cast iron in the ceilings and roofs of every room and in the gallery of the King's Library, and the size required brickwork of extraordinary strength and thickness and ceiling beams longer than any used previously in civil architecture. Assisting Sydney Smirke with the structural challenges of the library was John Rastrick, one of the leading railway engineers of the period.

Space had, of course, always been a problem. In the early 1880s, the natural history collections were moved to Alfred Waterhouse's Natural History Museum in South Kensington, and in 1907 work was begun on the large gallery on the north side; in 1939 a new gallery for the Elgin Marbles was given to the nation by Lord Duveen, though, because of the war, this new part was not completed until 1962. In 1970 the Ethnographical Department was moved to Burlington Gardens and is now the Museum of Mankind. And in 1973 an administrative decision was made to separate the museum and the library, for which a completely new home is being built in North London.

—DAVID CAST

CHISWICK HOUSE
Middlesex, London, England

1717: Grounds remodeled. **1725-30:** Villa constructed; **Architect:** Earl of Burlington (1694-1753). **1788:** Wings added; **Architect:** James Wyatt (1746-1813).

Publications

CHARLTON, JOHN: *A History and Description of Chiswick House and Gardens*. London, 1962.

Chiswick House: Middlesex, England, 1725-30

HARRIS, JOHN: ''Chiswick House: A Saga of Possession.''
  Apollo 133 (January 1991): 20-25.
KIMBALL, FISKE: ''Burlington Architectus.'' *Royal Institute of
  British Architects Journal* (1927): 34-35.
WITTKOWER, RUDOLF: ''Lord Burlington and William Kent.''
  Archaeological Journal 102 (1945).
WITTKOWER, RUDOLF: *Palladio and English Palladianism.*
  London, 1974.

*

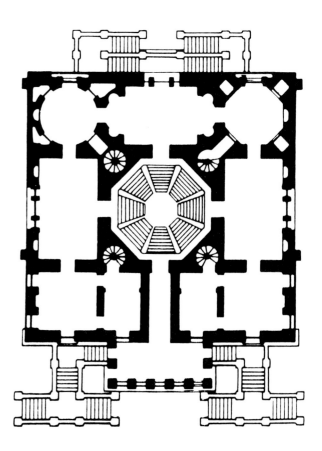

Chiswick House or Villa is usually described as a whimsical
garden building built by Lord Burlington, an adherent to the
precepts of Andrea Palladio. It was, however, the crowning
glory to this small estate.

At his coming of age, Burlington began making alterations
to the layout of his estate at Chiswick. Numerous small garden
buildings were designed to fit into the small, flat area of land.
Burlington's first attempt at architecture, the so-called Bagnio,
was tripartite and included a Doric entablature, triumphal arches,
flat receding wings and a lantern typical of either James Gibbs
or Colen Campbell. Other buildings followed, including an
ancient domed Ionic temple and Inigo Jones' Covent Garden
church portico. Work on what was then termed the Old House,
a Jacobean structure, was restricted to the facade, made more
classical by bringing the central front closer to the level of the
sides and by adding Palladian motifs such as the Diocletian
window. In 1725 the west wing was destroyed by fire. By that
time, Campbell's Mereworth Castle, a copy of Andrea Palladio's
Villa Rotunda, had been built.

New Chiswick House, built shortly thereafter, is evidence of

Burlington's scholarly adherence to Palladian doctrine, particularly in the matter of proportion; Vicentine measurements were used which, when translated into English feet, resulted in a smaller house than Palladio had intended but one with the same proportions. The basic square shape was retained, but the circle was changed into an octagon. Although the sequence of rooms was altered, such an alteration would not have been alien to Palladio; a smooth flow and sense of organization to the rooms demonstrate an understanding and interpretation of Palladio's ideas, rather than the blind copying of his motifs. While Palladio's villa has four facades of equal importance, New Chiswick House has one, consistent with the Palladian preference for dominance of a major part and subordinance of others. Short walls to each side of the facade continue the line of the ground floor for both front and rear facades. The portico rests on a rusticated basement and is linked to the grounds by a complicated series of stairs, more like those used by Palladio at his Villa Malcontenta than at the Rotunda.

Diocletian windows raise the dome and allow light into the central hallway. As Rudolf Wittkower has pointed out, the use of drum and dome can be traced to Vincenzo Scamozzi, a faithful follower of Palladio's. Burlington's Chiswick drum may be even more closer to Palladio's intent than the latter's design for Villa Rotunda (which possibly was not completed as intended).

The garden facade, simpler than the impressive front portico, shares the same rectangular form. Three shallow arched windows, called Venetian or Palladian, break up the mass of the wall. Its staircase is simpler, comparable with Campbell's south front of Houghton. Later, in keeping with some of Palladio's buildings that have lower wings to the side, an addition (now called the Link Building) was built to maintain communication between the old and new houses. Plain and cubic, this link shares its style only in a low wall with Palladian globes extended between the two.

In contrast, interior decoration is abundant and richly decorated, probably due to William Kent (a Burlington protégé) and Lady Burlington. Individual chimneypieces can be traced to various individuals, including Inigo Jones. Recent studies of furniture inventory indicate that Burlington and his wife would have lived very comfortably in their new home, particularly after it was linked to the Old House. A gallery, offices, separate state bedrooms, drawing room and garden room were all appropriately furnished for living. Burlington retired from politics in 1733, and life away from London would have been relatively simple. Paintings were moved from Burlington House to Chiswick, indicating that more time was spent at the latter.

The New House was meant to be seen and appreciated as part of the garden architecture. But although Burlington had included other styles of buildings in his gardens, here he was also proudly displaying a building designed in the spirit of his mentor. Controlled vistas produce a small cosmos of varying styles and moods. An illusion of magnitude is achieved through effective plantings and meandering paths. The balanced geometric avenues, in a *patte d'oie* configuration with the allées terminating in garden buildings, have often been attributed to Charles Bridgeman but were possibly designed by Burlington himself. The winding paths were later introduced by Kent, whose rustic cascade was another of many elements he contributed to the garden.

Acquisition of additional land permitted expansion, and the straight canal was turned into a meandering stream. A classical exedra hedge with statues of Roman worthies was placed in direct line with the garden facade. In front of an Inigo Jones-styled structure, a screen of trees was provided which was later opened up to allow extended vistas. This device has been compared with Palladio's use of screens at the Church of San

Giorgio Maggiore in Venice; perhaps Burlington was trying to achieve with trees what Palladio had executed with columns.

In a commentary on Rigaud's drawings of Chiswick, Jacques Carré observed: "As for the elegant figures sauntering in the foreground of the drawings, if they add little to our knowledge of Chiswick, they appropriately remind us that in the 18th century, aristocratic gardens were not meant to be solitary, but were often visited by the owner's friends and acquaintances."

—TERESA S. WATTS

CHRIST CHURCH, SPITALFIELDS
London, England

1714: Foundations laid; **Architect:** Nicholas Hawksmoor (ca. 1661-1736). **1729:** Completed. **1822-23:** Spire stripped of ornaments. **1851:** Interior altered. **1866:** Side galleries removed.

Publications

GIROUARD, M.; CRUICKSHANK, D.; and SAMUEL, R.: *The Saving of Spitalfields*. London, 1989.
RUFFINIÈRE DU PREY, P.: "Hawksmoor's 'Basilica after the Primitive Christians': Architecture and Theology." *Journal of the Society of Architectural Historians* 48 (1989): 38-52.

*

Christ Church, Spitalfields, a church by Nicholas Hawksmoor in London, originally in the parish of St. Dunstan's, was one of the new churches built under an act of Parliament of 1711 that provided for some 50 new churches and parishes throughout London. The church itself, like so much of Hawksmoor's work, has undergone both minor and major changes: the spire was stripped of its ornaments in 1822-23, and the interior was altered in 1851 and 1866 when the side galleries were taken out, the windows were opened and some of the church furniture was moved. Miraculously, the building escaped the bombing in World War II. The church has been closed now for many years, appearing only in films and commercials where a grand, dramatic interior space is needed. The surrounding area, which also survived the war, has been the site of a spectacular attempt to preserve what remains from the destruction of developers and the prettiness of gentrification.

The site of Christ Church, open on the south and east sides,

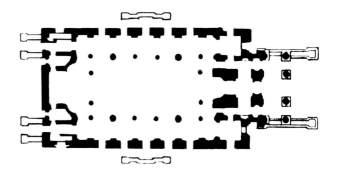

Christ Church, Spitalfields: London, England, 1714

was bought in October 1713, and the foundations were laid in July of the following year, as work began on Hawksmoor's two other Stepney churches, St. Anne's, Limehouse, and St. George's-in-the-East. The first plan, known from surviving drawings, was for a building with a clear west-east axis, an aisled interior of seven bays, a narrow chancel in the seventh bay, and a short, stubby tower at the west end, capped by a small octagonal belfry; it was to that plan, though alterations were made almost immediately, that the foundations were begun.

The final plan as built is a complication of those first suggestions. Hawksmoor introduced a screen of eastern columns to balance those already in place at the west end, and in the middle of the nave, at the third, fourth and fifth bays, he established a central rectangle, with piers at the corners, that suggested a north-south axis, within the firm east-west axis of the plan. The chancel was made deeper, and galleries were set at the sides. The plan was at once that of a basilica with a nave and side aisles, and also, from the opposing axis, a centralized scheme, expanded to the east and with a new, larger entrance at the west. Later, Hawksmoor also added side entrances that emphasized even further this transverse axis; the transversal emphasis would have been completed by the modified articulation of the roof elements and the placing of the pulpit and the reading desk within this rectangle.

The exterior elevation of the church is richly articulated with a series of monumental windows, whose severe and heavy forms recall Roman architecture or, perhaps, the Renaissance walls of Leon Battista Alberti's church at Rimini. The small portholes above those windows, however, seem to be based on 12th-century English churches, such as those at Ely and Norwich. The spire today is plainer than in its original form since the dormer windows that were on each face were removed in the 19th century, as were the crockets at each corner and the large stone finial; in this state the spire may more closely resemble a simple Gothic design than Hawksmoor had intended. But the essential form of this spire remains—a remarkably flat front, with concave cuts on the sides that make the front seem at once subtle and substantial. Below the spire is a base that flows down to the portico with a complex of forms that allude to Venetian windows, to triumphal arches reminiscent of Alberti's work, and perhaps even to Hawksmoor's own earlier work at St. Alfege's, Greenwich. Patterns move up and down this front, from the recessed buttresses of the lower part of the spire to the arch in the center of the belfry, to the huge columns of the portico. The whole design seems remarkable even now; the iconography of its forms matches the kinds of historical allusions to the basilican plan of the early Church, to the models of the Renaissance and to the traditions of church building in England that clearly interested Hawksmoor throughout his life.

The result—by one account, remarkable, but according to Nikolaus Pevsner, original indeed but ugly—may exemplify the originality and difficulty of the style that encouraged the simplifications of the 19th century. Like Hawksmoor's other Stepney churches, Christ Church has suffered from neglect as the economic strength of the area in which it stands has declined. In the early years, Spitalfields was a center of the Huguenot textile trade and, as the size of the houses around the church show, a prosperous and successful one. But there were also many smaller houses and tenements for the textile workers, and when, at the end of the 18th century, the textile trade itself declined, Spitalfields became a neglected, impoverished area. By the mid-19th century, however, with the arrival of Jewish immigrants, the economy of Spitalfields revived, then slipped again, only to be revived in recent years by Bengali immigrants who have continued the small-scale textile tradition. It is in this context that the battles for the preservation of Spitalfields have been fought, and the restoration of Christ Church has become the symbol of a renewal that has been organized to respect the historical and social history of the whole area.

—DAVID CAST

CRYSTAL PALACE
London, England

1850-51: Constructed; **Architect:** Joseph Paxton (1801-1865). **1852-54:** Dismantled and re-erected, Sydenham. **1936:** Destroyed by fire.

Publications

''The Architectural Significance of 1851, the Road Between— The Crystal Palace and the South Bank.'' *Builder* 180 (22 June 1951).

BEAVER, PATRICK: *The Crystal Palace, 1851-1936: A Portrait of Victorian Enterprise.* London, 1970.

BERLYN, P., and FOWLER, C., JR.: *The Crystal Palace, Its Architectural History and Constructive Marvels.* London, 1851.

BRIGGS, ASA: *Iron Bridge to Crystal Palace.* London, 1979.

CAMERON, R.: ''Crystal Palace.'' *Oeil* 62 (February 1960): 60-65.

CHADWICK, G. F.: *The Works of Sir Joseph Paxton.* London, 1961.

COWPER, CHARLES, and DOWNES, CHARLES: *The Building Erected in Hyde Park for the Great Exhibition of Industry of All Nations, 1851.* London, 1852.

The Crystal Palace and Its Contents; Being an Illustrated Cyclopaedia of the Great Exhibition of the Industry of All Nations, 1851. London, 1852.

FAY, C. R.: *Palace of Industry, 1851: A Study of the Great Exhibition and Its Fruits.* Cambridge, 1951.

FENTON, E.: ''Palace Made of Windows.'' *Metropolitan Museum of Art Bulletin* 10 (December 1951): 113-122.

FRAMPTON, KENNETH, and FUTAGAWA, YUKIO: *Modern Architecture: 1851-1919.* New York, 1983.

GIBBS-SMITH, C. H.: ''The Great Exhibition of 1851.'' *Architectural Association Journal* 65 (April 1950): 178-188.

HITCHCOCK, HENRY-RUSSELL: *The Crystal Palace: The Structure, Its Antecedents and Its Immediate Progeny.* Exhibition catalog. Northhampton, Massachusetts, 1951.

HOBHOUSE, C.: *1851 and the Crystal Palace.* New York, 1937.

JORDAN, R. J.: ''Architectural Significance of 1851; with Discussion.'' *Journal of the Royal Institute of British Architects* 58 (June 1951): 340-348.

KING, D. I.: ''The Great Exhibition, 1851, Design and Construction of Paxton's Crystal Palace.'' *Builder* 180 (2 February 1951): 163-165.

The Palace of Industry: A Brief History of Its Origin and Progress; with a Descriptive Account of the Most Interesting Portions of the Machinery Employed in Its Construction. London, 1851.

PEVSNER, NIKOLAUS: *High Victorian Design: A Study of the Exhibits of 1851.* London, 1951.

RICHARDS, J. M.: ''Obituary: The Crystal Palace of London.'' *Architectural Review* 81 (January 1937): 1.

Crystal Palace: London, England, 1851

TIMBS, J.: *The Year-Book of Facts in the Great Exhibition of 1851: Its Origin and Progress; Constructive Details of the Building.* London, 1851.

WYATT, MATTHEW DIGBY: "On the Construction of the Building for the Exhibition of the Works of Industry of All Nations in 1851." *Minutes of the Proceedings of the Institution of Civil Engineers* 10 (1850-51): 127-191.

*

Clearly there were some things miraculous, even mystical, about the Crystal Palace.

First, a crystal building itself: that magical, unworldly place deep in the subconscious—pictured in the West from the castle in the Renaissance tale *Ariosto Furioso,* via Paul Scheerbart or Bruno Taut's "Crystal Chain," to the filmed lair of Superman. Douglas Jarrold, journalist with the humor magazine *Punch,* called it "crystal palace" while it was under construction; the name resonated and stuck.

Second, its unprecedented enclosed space: was it indoors or out? It had elm trees and sparrows, yet was (more or less) rainproof—an artificial climate of incomprehensible, ineffable dimension.

Third, its immense size linked with the speed of its appearance: a litany of celerity and magnitude, repeated in awe by everyone from thronging spectators at the building site to Charles Dickens.

Finally, the systems which produced it: utterly radical, common-sense, addressing every eventuality; linear, logical systems worked on an immense scale; through utterly novel constructional procedures, the whole building grew from the optimum size of a glass pane.

So actually the Victorians got it right. The two qualities which contemporaries of the Crystal Palace stressed above all else remain central today. A paradoxical pair: on the one hand, its practical arithmetic and down-to-earth common sense; on the other, its dissolving spatial identity and immaterial insubstantiality. In more senses than one, here is a building part nononsense industrial accomplishment and part fairy tale.

Early in 1850, a royal commission met to organize an exhibition of British industry, which it planned to open 18 months later. In March it announced a design competition for the temporary building, but in June abandoned all 245 entries received and prepared its own lumpish project—a long, dark structure to be built with 17 million bricks, relieved with a 200-foot-wide metal dome. The commissioners panicked: not only would the structure be ugly, but it would not be even halfway built in time.

Joseph Paxton met one of the organizers, by chance, 10 days before tender documents were to go out; it was agreed that tendering could be on a new design, and Paxton promised one within 10 days. It was done, the commission's hand forced by its publication on 6 July 1850, and both design and priced tender were accepted three weeks later. The first columns were raised in September, and the largest space ever enclosed by man was watertight in January 1851. Fitted out, painted (to a scheme by Owen Jones) and filled, it was opened on 1 May 1851.

It is worth questioning the nature of this achievement in two ways: first, to ask what processes produced this thing; second, what was the effect on the senses of the project thus realized?

In its production, the Crystal Palace bypassed conventional

building and architectural practice, traditional constructional and contractual processes, clearly understood roles, and—perhaps most—it bypassed prejudices and attitudes as to the nature of architecture.

Paxton, gardener turned entrepreneur, left it a couple of days, then quickly sketched the elevation and section of a proposal (on the blotter at a meeting), closely based on a greenhouse he had recently completed, but greatly extended. Then, back with his office staff at the country estate hc managed, he produced a complete set of scale drawings in seven days.

Although largely made of timber and glass, with which Paxton was adept, the main structure at this new scale had to be iron, and here the experience of contracting engineers Fox Henderson and Company of Smethwick was essential. Charles Fox (1810-74) described his task simply as "to mature and realise" Paxton's idea, but this crucial role, linking detail design development and construction control, was unique in its day and, as Fox rightly argued, was the essential element in the building's completion on time.

The tendering was very risky: there were enormous quantities at stake, and the price of a single element to be repeated so many times—a glass pane, girder or column—had to be calculated very precisely. Fox Henderson's tender was the lowest; it and the design were accepted. The structure was built within budget and on time.

Through August 1850, Fox's team "planned and drew, calculating strength and stress and cost and time" (as they said). From that seven-week, 18-hour-per-day spurt came production drawings of every element, component and connection, from girders to rivet holes. As soon as Fox passed a drawing, Henderson set up production of the part. First in Paxton's office and then in Fox Henderson's, the whole enterprise was thought through with radical common sense.

The design process was additive and rooted in reality. For example: the largest glass plate possible was 49 inches by 30 inches; Paxton's experience with garden buildings had taught him the required slope for condensation to run off the underside of the ridge-and-furrow roof into gutters. With ridge bar and two gutters, two panes fitted neatly into an 8-foot bay, this built up into a 24-foot structural grid of cast-iron columns. These are structurally effective around the edge, so hollow columns of minimum section were used (with diagonal bay bracing for rigidity), and rainwater drained down their center.

Paxton and Fox worked out the assembly sequences in detail following an identical logic. Paxton invented a shaping saw into which rough beams were passed and from which profiled gutters, ridge and sash bars appeared. Fox devised a roofed trolley (of which 72 were built) to run in the parallel gutters, carrying glaziers working in all weathers. Eighty glaziers could set 62,000 square feet of glazing in a week. So much for process.

But what *was* this magical place? Certainly the clear, linear connection between realistic detail and ephemeral totality gives a clue. It need not detain us that John Ruskin denied its being architecture, except that part of his argument was that it lacked *difficulty:* "a greenhouse, plus some very ordinary algebra," as he put it. That line was perhaps more interestingly developed by Fyodor Dostoevsky, who recognized a new power in it: "all ready-made and computed with mathematical exactitude" so that "every possible question will vanish, simply because every possible answer will be provided."

In a sense, the Crystal Palace epitomizes the project of modernity. Karl Marx had talked of all that is solid melting into air; the Crystal Palace acted that out. As Lothar Bucher (who knew Marx) said in 1851, "All materiality is blended into the atmosphere." There is a dissolution of corporeality, a disembodiment. "As in a crystal," said Richard Lucae in 1869, "there

is no longer any true interior or exterior. If we imagine that air can be poured like a liquid, then it has, here, achieved a solid form, after the removal of the mould into which it was poured. We find ourselves within a cut-out segment of atmosphere."

Bucher's 1851 description is exemplary: "We see a fine network of symmetrical lines that do not, however, provide any clues whereby one could estimate its distance from the eye or the actual size of the mesh. The side walls stand too far apart to be taken in at a glance, and instead of meeting a facing wall, the eye moves upwards over an endless perspective, or one whose ends appear diffuse and blue. We do not know whether this enclosure hovers a hundred or a thousand feet above us, or whether the ceiling is flat or formed by a number of small parallel ceilings; this is due to the total absence of shadows, which normally aid the eye in comprehending the impressions received by the optical nerve."

This "artificially created environment, . . . no longer a space" (Lucae), clearly retains images of a conservatory—the domesticated tropical dream whose associations stretch back to the Garden of Eden: an enclosed universe, "a world in miniature" (as was said), where all those who entered are enclosed as brothers "under one roof," and all are part of the spectacle, all visible to the panopticon eye, "in the total absence of shadow." The social parallel is clear enough. As the clamor of the Chartists died away, in the only corner of Europe not to boil over into revolt in 1848, Queen Victoria and her ruling class were offered a particularly powerful, harmonious metaphor. Indeed, the queen wept with joy (as she wrote in her diary on 1 May 1851).

Dostoevsky, almost uniquely, but with striking prescience, criticized the Crystal Palace as a modernization of trouble-free but deadening routines. Here also is a hint of its progeny in generations to come of glazed shopping malls for the commodity fetishism of glazed eyes.

As a footnote, we see that on the close of the exhibition, the Crystal Palace was dismantled and Paxton, unfettered by economics of either time or cost, puffed the form up until the glass surface doubled in area, and erected this new building (the one Dostoevsky and so many others actually saw) bombastic on Sydenham Hill. We need not see the Crystal Palace from the view of modernist architecture, encapsulated in Le Corbusier's description of its "triumphant harmony," and with its view of the engineer as the 19th century's noble savage, as the authentic designer of true and honest forms. The nature of Paxton, Fox and Henderson's achievement was quite different—although equally beyond their own declared, earth-bound, intentions.

—JOHN McKEAN

HAMPSTEAD GARDEN SUBURB
London, England

1907: First cottages built; **Architects:** Barry Parker (1867-1941) and Raymond Unwin (1863-1940). **1908-10:** St. Jude's Church designed; **Architect:** Sir Edwin Lutyens (1869-1944).

Hampstead Garden Suburb, the orchard: London, England, 1907

Publications

BAILLIE SCOTT, M.H.; UNWIN, RAYMOND, et al.: *Town Planning and Modern Architecture in the Hampstead Garden
Suburb.* London, 1909.

CREESE, W.: *The Search for Environment. The Garden City:
Before and After.* London, 1966.

DAY, M. G.: "The Contribution of Sir Raymond Unwin (1863-
1940) and R. Barry Parker (1867-1947) to the development
of site planning theory and practice, c. 1890-1918." in SUT-
CLIFFE, A. (ed.): *British Town Planning: The formative
years.* Leicester, 1981.

UNWIN, RAYMOND: *Town Planning and Modern Architecture
at the Hampstead Garden Suburb.* London, 1909.

VON BERLEPSCH-VALENDAS, H. E.: "Hampstead-Eine Studie
über Stadtebau in England." *Kunst und Kunsthandwerk* 12
(1909):241-284.

*

The Hampstead Garden Suburb was the creation of Henrietta Barnett (later Dame Henrietta), wife of Canon Samuel Barnett. After their marriage in 1873, she joined him in his ministry at St. Jude's, Whitechapel, in the East End of London, becoming passionately concerned with the social conditions there and especially with the squalor in which children grew up. The Barnetts also owned a house on the heights of Hampstead Heath, which they used as a retreat for themselves and for others in need. In 1896 Mrs. Barnett learned that the Northern Line Underground was to be extended to Golders Green, then little more than a crossroads in Middlesex to the northwest of London;

this would give access to some 323 acres of farmland owned by Eton College since the Reformation, but now likely to be developed speculatively. Mrs. Barnett determined that 80 acres should be added to the Heath, and that the rest must become a new, ideal garden suburb. Against all the odds—the conventions of the time, her own sex, the amount of money to be raised, the social hazards and the architectural problems in planning—she succeeded indomitably in realizing her ideal more or less completely.

Her scheme, though revolutionary in concept and astonishing in scale, had excellent antecedents. With the exception of Regent's Park, 18th- and 19th-century London had developed on the model of the straight street and the square surrounded by houses. By the second half of Victoria's reign, constant repetition and the sheer weight of overcrowding had undermined the original spruce urban elegance of the metropolis. It was against this sort of city that William Morris reacted, seeking a fresher inspiration in England's medieval, vernacular architecture; Norman Shaw gave expression to these suggestions in the houses he designed from 1875 onward at Bedford Park. Lords Cadbury and Lever had used similar ideas in the estates they planned and built for their factory workers at Bourneville and Port Sunlight, and then, in 1898, Ebenezer Howard published *Garden Cities of Tomorrow.* Five years later work was begun on a garden city at Letchworth in Hertfordshire; the two young architects responsible for its realization were Barry Parker and Raymond Unwin, partners and brothers-in-law. Mrs. Barnett chanced to read a pamphlet by Unwin, and knew that he was the man she needed to build her vision; he produced his first, preliminary scheme in 1905, and the Garden Suburb Trust was formed. Unwin and Parker set up their office at Wyldes, a farmhouse at the southern tip of the estate, and gathered about them an impressive team of young, socially minded architects. This included such men as Charles Wade, Arthur Penty, Alfred Mottram and Samuel Pointon Taylor. The group was reinforced by other architects providing independent designs; they included Michael Bunney, Geoffrey Lucas, Courtney Crickmer, T.M. Wilson, Matthew Dawson, Baillie Scott, Guy Dawber, Arnold Mitchell, Morley Horder and Herbert Welch.

In the planning of this suburb, there were a number of distinct principles. First, all classes were to live together, a proportion of ground rents being kept uneconomically low in order to assist the less well-off, and there were to be proper places for the very old, the very young, the crippled, the mentally distressed and any others who needed help—no one was to be left out. Houses were to stand on average eight to the acre, each with its own garden, and those gardens were to be separated only by hedges and never by walls or high fences. Roads were to be at least 40 feet wide, and lined with trees, preferably flowering. Woods and open spaces were to be for the enjoyment of all; noise was to be avoided as much as possible.

The original 243 acres made a long, thin, awkwardly shaped strip of land, somewhat more than a mile on its main axis running northeast by southwest, and about three-quarters of a mile wide at its broadest point. The main line of communication was the Finchley Road, close to the western boundary, leading away from London to join the Great North Road. The ground undulated, rising to a central ridge, on which Mrs. Barnett determined that churches and a school should stand. Along the edge of the Heath Extension, which she had won as open space, a Great Wall, with garden summerhouses which resembled watch towers, was built on the side facing London as if to declare that here, in the Hampstead Garden Suburb, was a new beginning. The first sod was cut on 2 May 1907 and the first houses, 140 and 142 Hampstead Way, were begun. Two old byways gave access to the estate—Temple Fortune Lane running roughly parallel to, and eventually meeting, the Finchley Road, and Hoop Lane from the west, which was extended eastward to become Meadway and give an approach to the heart of the suburb.

An analysis of the houses on the eastern side of Temple Fortune Lane and along Hampstead Way northward from Meadway defines the ideals which Mrs. Barnett and Unwin, with his acute social consciousness, were trying to achieve. In these roads and in the northern part of the suburb—Asmuns Place and Hill, Erskine Hill, Hogarth Hill, and Willifield Green and Way—the inspiration was the cottages and yeomen's houses of 16th- and 17th-century Essex and Hertfordshire. They were not standard pattern houses, built in straight rows; each one was different, so sited as to take the best advantage of the ground, and to present an agreeable aspect to its neighbors while enjoying the same benefit. Wherever possible the houses were grouped around a green—special legislation had been needed to make this possible. The building materials—bricks dove-gray or soft red, hipped ridge-tiles for the roofs, tile-hanging on or oak-timbering in the walls—were selected with great care for quality and for kindliness of color. The streets of the suburb are full of architectural felicities. Worth particular attention are the six skillfully sited towered houses at the junction of Hogarth Hill and Addison Way; the cottages by G.L. Sutcliffe in Denman Drive North and South; Lucas Square; 40 Hampstead Way at

Hampstead Garden Suburb

the intersection with Willifield Way, which is by Lawrence Dale; the whole of Hill Close; Nos. 12-30 Temple Fortune Lane; and the curving sweep of Meadway Gate by two otherwise unknown architects, Edwin and James Palser.

The Hampstead Garden Suburb Trust confided the planning of the center of the suburb to Edwin Lutyens. Central Square, which commands the highest ground, is a much grander design than the aforementioned housing, and was conceived on a different scale. On the south and north sides of the square stand St. Jude's Church and the Free Church; the eastern side is filled by the Institute, the western left open (eventually Dame Henrietta's memorial would stand there). St. Jude's draws its inspiration from the tithe barns of medieval England, with a great tiled roof which sweeps down almost to the lintels of the doors, and a tower, and spire—the latter perhaps over-sharp and not altogether happy—which answers the spire of Harrow Church, five miles away across the valley of the Brent River. The interior of the church is an enigma; the tunnel vault of the main nave is mysteriously lit from the domes over the central spaces, but the aisles have open, timber roofs. The rectangular interior of the Free Church, lit from a single central dome, is a straightforward, no-nonsense space, but is welcoming, whether empty or filled with a congregation. Emphasizing the church's nondenominationality is Henrietta Barnett's choice of words cut on the foundation stone: "God is greater than the creeds." The Institute, which serves both as the Henrietta Barnett School for Girls and as an adult education center, is modeled on a French *hôtel de ville* and is neither very satisfactory to look at nor encouraging to study in.

The monumental treatment of the center of the suburb meant that grander houses were needed around it. The Early Georgian manor house replaced the cottage as a model. These are to be seen at their best in North Square, in the upper part of Erskine Hill, and in Heathgate, the southern end of which is left open to look out beyond the Great Wall to the protected fields of the Heath Extension.

Some of the most interesting houses lie along, or just off, this extension. The two courtyards, reminiscent of academic life, in Corringham Road, the variety of houses in Heath Close and, above all, the arcaded cloister of Waterlow Court designed by Baillie Scott and opened in 1909 to provide two-room flats of exceptional internal ingenuity and generosity for single working women—an extraordinary innovation for its time—are all enjoyable areas worthy of notice.

One thing the Hampstead Garden Suburb lacks is an active and lively shopping center. Public houses were excluded, being Dame Henrietta's anathema. The churches and Institute were intended to provide the pivot, but a very cold, still center it is. Without a church service, or unless the children are hurrying in or out of school, the heart, with its flowerbeds planned by Lutyens, is dead. The well-proportioned shopping street at Golders Green, beyond the southern tip of the suburb, is now a wilderness of costly boutiques and double parking; the marketplace to the northeast of Falloden Way, added after World War I when the suburb was more than doubled in size and lost a good deal of its first impetus, is now on the line of a trucking route; the true center, where neighbors meet, lies at Temple Fortune, beyond the northern extremity. The entrance to the suburb is marked with two superb ranges of shops, sheltered by arcades at ground level with balconied flats above; designed by Arthur J. Penty and Charles Paget Wade, they draw their inspiration from the walled towns of medieval Germany, such as Nuremberg and Rothenburg.

The motor car has not been kind to the suburb. When the first houses were built, the automobile was a rich man's fancy; the bulk of the residents would not have thought of owning

one and no provision was made, though in Corringway, where cottages were built for the suburb staff, a small garage was established to provide service and vehicle accommodation for the few who might desire and be able to afford such a luxury. After World War I, when the suburb was extended eastward, houses were built with garages, though mercifully, at least in Northway, Middleway and Southway, they retained the proper local individuality of style.

The Hampstead Garden Suburb is nearly a century old, and the intensity of Henrietta Barnett's original dream could hardly be expected to endure. Yet vigilance, self-restraint and the designation of the suburb as a conservation area have protected its fabric from wanton change. The population is now predominantly middle-class and, on the whole, prosperous. Most of the low-rental workmen's cottages have been sold off by the trust. At least part of the original spirit is still there. Neighbors know and greet each other and, when help is needed, it is rare for it not to be forthcoming. The importance of the Hampstead Garden Suburb lies in something more than the plan, or the bricks and mortar; its architecture was intended to express a social ideal as much as an artistic idea, and as such, the suburb has had a widespread influence in Europe and America.

—ANN LOREILLE SAUNDERS

HOUSES OF PARLIAMENT
London, England

1837-43: Initial construction; **Architect:** Charles Barry (1795-1860). **1844-52:** Woodcarvings, furnishings, and other decorations designed by A. W. N. Pugin (1812-52). **1858:** Clock Tower completed; **Architect:** Charles Barry. **1860-70:** Construction completed; **Architect:** Edward Middleton Barry (1830-80). **1958-61:** Victoria Tower reconstructed.

Publications

BARRY, ALFRED: *The Life and Works of Sir Charles Barry.* London, 1867.
BASSIN, JOAN: *Architectural Competitions in 19th Century England.* 1975.
PORT, M. H.: "The New Houses of Parliament." *The History of the King's Works.* Vol. 6. London, 1973.
PORT, M. H. (ed.): *The Houses of Parliament.* New Haven, Connecticut, and London, 1976.
RYDE, H. T.: *Illustrations of the New Palace of Westminster.* London, 1849.
THOMPSON, PETER: *Designs for the Proposed New Houses of Parliament.* London, 1836.

*

The Houses of Parliament are not only the largest single British building of the 19th century; they are significant for three principal reasons: the process by which their design was arrived at; the employment of state-of-the-art techniques in both construction and services; and for their didactic and symbolic role. Stylistically they made comparatively little impact, because their Perpendicular Gothic had become unpopular before their facades emerged.

Houses of Parliament: London, England, 1837-43

Whereas the old Palace of Westminster had been a confused medley of buildings, the Houses of Parliament were purpose-built. Congestion during the Great Reform Bill debates (1831) had provoked demands for a new House of Commons. The rejection of the Franco-American model of speaking from a tribune necessitated a room of moderate size for hearing any member speaking from his place. A bicameral legislature indicated a symmetrical plan, Commons balancing Lords. Although there were fewer peers than commons, the sovereign presided over state ceremonial in the peers' chamber, which was necessarily large and magnificent. A royal entry and robing room were also requisite. Parliament's work required such services as a printing office and means for the distribution of papers and accommodation for innumerable committees. Because members left the chambers to vote, adjacent voting lobbies were necessary. A reformed Parliament needed space for press and public. The traditional "Lobby" was essential for MPs to meet their constituents. Furthermore, legislators were accustomed to ancillary services such as a library and an eating room, and they looked to have all the conveniences of a gentleman's club in their new building.

After the fire that destroyed the chambers on 16 October 1834, a decision to entrust a modest rebuilding to Robert Smirke, a former official architect, united reformers and architectural connoisseurs: their campaign, waged largely through the press, persuaded the government to arrange an open competition, which became the basis for the subsequent great Victorian architectural competitions. A committee of both Houses prepared specifications including an insistence on the Gothic or Elizabethan styles. National pride demanded a national style, and Gothic was commonly believed to be an English invention; some with greater knowledge held that Gothic had achieved its finest flowering in the peculiarly English Perpendicular. And reformers sought to restore the supposed constitutional purity of the Gothic age. "Elizabethan" was architecturally a vaguer concept, but recalled some of England's most glorious days.

Charles Barry responded to the complex brief with a "Perpendicular" design that was at once an expression in stone of

Houses of Parliament

Britain's history, a picturesque composition of the first order satisfying to the prevailing aesthetic taste, and brilliantly planned to accommodate efficiently all the legislature's requirements. The two chambers were protected from the street by a range of offices and flanked toward the river by committee rooms and libraries distant from street noises. A magnificent square tower at one end marked the sovereign's entrance, whence a grand stair mounted to the House of Lords. A smaller tower at the Commons' end assisted in giving elevation, the more necessary because of the low, riverside location. The huge medieval Westminster Hall (which Barry dreamed of cloaking), forced certain compromises in the planning and made the river front the principal facade, but the whole composition grouped picturesquely from those points from which the existing street pattern permitted it to be viewed.

Having won the competition (judged by noted connoisseurs) with exquisite drawings executed by Augustus Welby Pugin, Barry had still to secure the commission. It was not clear who the client was: the government felt obliged to allow Parliament to vet the designs and set additional requirements (e.g., a smoking room), the more so as funds were voted annually by the unreliable Commons. Parliamentary interference continued through the building period. Between 1837 and 1843, Barry went his own way. He was initially permitted to revise his original designs to meet criticisms: he enlarged the building, extending it southward and building out further into the river. Drawings for estimating the cost simplified the ornamental stonework that had been a striking feature of the competition drawings. Parliament approved the revised plans on an estimate of some £707,000, exclusive of embankment, land purchase,

ventilation, fittings and furnishings. Barry optimistically declared that the work could be completed in six years. It was to cost about four times as much and to take four times as long.

Parliament's continued use of the site hindered building. The revised plan required a considerable reclamation from the river, which occupied the period up to 1840: the coffer dam and embankment demanded considerable engineering skill; though Barry called in engineers, he modified their proposals. Then a concrete raft, in some places to a depth of 12 feet, was laid progressively over the whole site, which contained quicksands and springs.

A lump-sum contract for the superstructure of the river front was won by Grissell and Peto, a highly integrated firm in the forefront of innovation in building techniques. They were continued in successive contracts until 1851, when John Jay took over at lower prices. Both Grissell and Peto and Jay were major railway contractors with large businesses. Grissell and Peto's strict discipline over their workforce led to a lengthy masons' strike in 1842. Barry's own office was itself fertile in innovatory techniques: steam engines on rails were employed to move stone and were particularly valuable in the construction of the two great lateral towers, built without external scaffolding by means of ingenious internal climbing platforms. The southern tower, marking the royal entrance, called the Victoria Tower, was the highest square tower in the world. It embraced "several essential ingredients of the skyscraper," according to Henry-Russell Hitchcock. But although the building was largely of iron-framed construction, load-bearing and space-enclosing functions were not wholly separated, the great girders resting ultimately on the external walls of the Norman Porch.

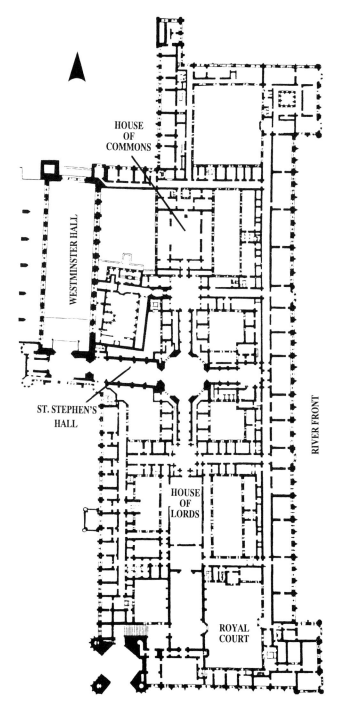

HOUSE
OF
COMMONS

WESTMINSTER HALL

ST. STEPHEN'S
HALL

RIVER FRONT

HOUSE
OF
LORDS

ROYAL
COURT

Required to make his new palace fireproof, Barry employed iron girders rather than wooden framing—a technique already used in industrial buildings, as well as by Smirke (British Museum) and John Nash (Buckingham Palace). Barry roofed the Houses with specially manufactured heavy iron plates. The walls were constructed of a brick core with stone facing on the exterior and in some of the ceremonial parts of the interior. Great care was taken to select a durable stone, a commission being appointed to examine the building stone of the kingdom. But geological science was in its infancy, and these efforts were negated by careless quarrying and bad mason's work, so that the stone early proved susceptible to weathering. Numerous unavailing experiments were made in weatherproofing the stone.

Another application of science was in ventilation. The old House of Commons was notorious for its stench, and members demanded fresher air. A Scotch lecturer in chemistry, David Boswell Reid, applied techniques devised for coal mines to the ventilation of buildings, and had some success in the temporary Commons chamber. He was therefore appointed by the government, without consulting Barry, to install a complete ventilation and heating system. The division of responsibility resulted in major delays. Reid's scheme required the construction of flues to and from every room: fresh air obtained from one or the other tower at the extremities of the building, according to wind direction, would be heated (or cooled if necessary) before transmission to the rooms, whence ducts in the ceilings and roofs would take vitiated air to a central chimney. Barry had to provide a central tower to perform this function, which Peter Collins has described as "the first occasion when mechanical services had a real influence on architectural design." After prolonged disagreement between the two men, parliamentary committees decided on a dual provision of heating systems, open fires as well as hot air. Reid was eventually displaced, though various modifications of his system were used for ventilating the chambers. The problem was exacerbated by the decision to light the palace with gas, which burned at a high temperature.

Using the palace to teach the nation's history involved an elaborate iconographical program of decoration. Barry as a professional was excluded from the royal commission which under the presidency of the art-loving Prince Albert, German husband of Queen Victoria, determined the paintings, sculpture and stained glass. Inspired by the Nazarenes' revival of true fresco painting in Rome and Munich, Prince Albert urged the use of their technique, which proved a failure. More conventional history paintings have illustrated several generations of children's books.

Under heavy pressure from the lords to complete their chamber, Barry turned again to Pugin, who as superintendent of woodcarving from 1844 until his death in 1852 designed fittings and furnishings in great number. Barry, however, exercised close control, dictating, for example, the shape of the throne in the Lords' chamber. To speed up the work, carving machines were used to rough out the woodwork. Pugin also designed tiles, wallpapers, metalwork and stained glass. He appears also to have been engaged in discussions about the completion of external features, and the final form of the upper part of the Clock Tower resembles his design for that at Scarisbrick Hall, Lancashire (1839). The total extent of his collaboration with Barry was fiercely disputed between their sons in 1867, but the evidence shows Barry always in command of the design process, while employing a wide range of expertise. (The argument has continued, from a reluctance to accept the concept of a design team at work at that time.) It was Edward Barry who completed the palace in the decade after his father's death.

—M. H. PORT

ST. STEPHEN'S CHAPEL, HOUSES OF PARLIAMENT
London, England

1292-1320: Construction begins on lower chapel. **1350:** Upper chapel completed. **1360s:** Interior completed. **1526-29:** St. Stephen's Cloister constructed. **1801:** Enlarged; **Architect:** James Wyatt (1746-1813). **1834:** Rebuilt after fire.

Publications

DALE, ANTHONY: *James Wyatt*. Oxford, 1956.
ROBINSON, J. M.: *The Wyatts*. Oxford, 1979.
STURGIS, RUSSELL: *A Dictionary of Architecture and Buildings*. New York, 1902.
WHITE, NORVAL: *The Architecture Book*. New York, 1976.

*

St. Stephen's Chapel, Westminster, founded, according to tradition, by Saint Stephen himself, is part of the great complex of the Palace of Westminster, and one of the few partly preserved sections to have survived the famous fire there of 16 October 1834.

The structure was built in two levels, as were several other such royal chapels, especially that of the French kings at La Sainte-Chapelle in Paris where, as at St. Stephen's, the upper part was reserved for the royal family itself, the crypt or lower chapel being used by all other members of the court. It was the upper part of St. Stephen's Chapel that was completely destroyed in the fire, and to judge what it looked like we have to turn to 17th- and early-19th-century illustrations, most importantly the elevations and sections by John Carter published for the Society of Antiquaries by John Topham in 1801. From these it appears to have been a tall, two-story building with high turrets at the four corners, and long stained-glass windows along its length.

Work was begun on the lower chapel, known also as St. Mary's Undercroft, about 1292 (there had been a fire on the site in 1263), though construction was soon stopped and begun again only in 1320, the upper chapel not being completed until about 1350. The visible details—most notably the vaulting bosses, which are rather crude for so important a building—seem certainly datable to the early 14th century and form part of one of the earliest lierne vaults in England (a lierne being a tertiary rib, one that does not move from either the main springings or from the central bosses). The other details on these ribs and the tracery in the windows cannot be trusted as examples of what was originally there, since these parts were all restored very thoroughly in the early 19th century.

After the 1834 fire, the chapel was replaced by what is now called St. Stephen's Hall, lying to the west of the central lobby of the Palace of Westminster; work and decorations continued there until the early years of this century. Also not far from the chapel is St. Stephen's Cloister (1526-29), of two stories and with a similarly two-story oratory that projects with its polygonal apse into a small, turfed court. This too was rebuilt after the fire, and then again after World War II (the east and south sides needing to be almost completely redone).

St. Stephen's Chapel, Houses of Parliament: London, England, 1292-1320

The Chapel of St. Stephen had an interesting later history. Like all the other religious properties in England, it was taken over in 1547 under the Chantries Act, and by 1550 it had become the meeting place of the Commons. Having no aisles, it was perfectly suited for use as a debating chamber. The Speaker's chair was set where the altar had been (perhaps explaining the habit still of genuflecting before the Speaker); the Members sat in the choir stalls on the north and south walls, and the Mace was set where once the lectern had been. The secular transformation was complete, and for many years it remained the seat of the Commons of England.

—DAVID CAST

WESTMINSTER HALL, HOUSES OF PARLIAMENT
London, England

1097-99: Lower part of Hall built; **Architect:** William Rufus. **1394-1402:** Hall rebuilt; **Architect:** Hugh Herland (ca. 1330-ca. 1411). **1820:** North facade restored. **1834:** Survives fire. **1913:** Steel added to support roof.

Publications

COURTENAY, LYNN T.: "The Westminster Hall Roof and Its 14th-Century Sources." *Journal of the Society of Architectural Historians* 43 (December 1984): 295-309.
COURTENAY, LYNN T, and MARK, ROBERT: "The Westminster Hall Roof: A Historiographic and Structural Study." *Journal of the Society of Architectural Historians* 46 (December 1987): 374-393.

*

Westminster Hall is the oldest surviving part of the Palace of Westminster, the central residence of the Norman kings of England; it is the largest Norman hall in England, and perhaps the largest of its date in Europe. The Palace of Westminster was never a defensible fortress, and there is no evidence of anything there like a keep, the tower of a castle. Building began there in the 11th century, and additions and rebuildings to the whole palace continued through the 13th and 14th centuries. But once Henry VIII replaced Westminster as the seat of the monarchy with Whitehall, the complex became the home of a number of public institutions; Westminster Hall is now part of the whole area of the Houses of Parliament, having survived the great fire there of 1834, together with St. Stephen's Chapel.

The lower part of Westminster Hall, which already had the length of the present hall, some 240 feet, was built by William Rufus in 1097-99, next to the Church of St. Peter, where henceforth all kings were crowned. So far as we know, the walls were plain, and above them were 12 round-headed windows; the hall doubtlessly had two or three aisles, supported perhaps by wooden piers, rather than stone masonry. The whole was slightly bowed, with the two side walls, bay by bay, being slightly off alignment. In 1835 nine sculpted capitals from that first palace were found built into the later medieval masonry fabric; they are now on show at the Jewel Tower.

That early structure lasted a couple of centuries, but in 1394-1402 the hall was rebuilt by Richard II, who had the walls heightened and remodeled, though much of the Norman building still can be seen in the lowest parts of the fabric. The mason

of this new work was Henry Yevele, who had worked also at Westminster Abbey; the carpenter was Hugh Herland, and it is he who earned what Nikolaus Pevsner has called the glory of having transformed this hall—with its mighty hammer-beam roof standing without any inner supports—into one of the most impressive structures in Europe. This was a form to be copied throughout England in the years that followed, and especially in East Anglia. The roof itself weighs some 600 tons—hence the large outer buttresses on the west side; yet only in 1913 was it found necessary to add steelwork to the building to support the roof.

The roof is made of massive timbers—the hammer-posts—the wood for which came from Hampshire and Hertfordshire. Prefabricated at Farnham in Surrey and then carried to Ham for transport up the river, the hammer-posts are about 21 feet long, 39 inches by 25 inches in section. Arched braces intersect this hammer-beam construction, and together with collar arches provide extra support for the structure. Tracery fills in the spandrels throughout the hall, and angels with shields are carved against the hammer-beams. The arched braces and brackets of the hammer-beams rest on stone corbels, which are part of a frieze below the windows on the west and east walls.

The east and west windows seen today are of a later date, though those at the north and south ends are contemporary with the hammer-beam roof. Indeed, the north end still resembles the west end of Westminster Abbey, though the south end was moved back by Charles Barry in the early 19th century to allow space for the dais at the top of the grand staircase. These two windows have nine lights, in a familiar Perpendicular pattern—two center-headed lights and three sidelights on each side, all gathered under a subordinate two-centerhead. Against the end wall of the dais there is now a painting by Benjamin West, *Moses Receiving the Tables of the Law,* done originally in 1784 for King George III's Chapel at Windsor; there also are figures of six kings, dating to the 14th century.

Outside, the north front of Westminster Hall has, on each side of the large window, two square towers that rise only part of the full height of the hall. The facade is decorated with paneling and niches, in which there was originally a set of statues; five of them, damaged, are now inside the hall in the sills of the windows on the east wall. The whole facade was restored in 1820. The floor of the present hall, it should be noted, was originally lower. No other work by Herland is known, yet at Westminster Hall he was able to build a structure without parallel anywhere in England or Europe.

—DAVID CAST

LAW COURTS
London, England

1865: Act authorizing building. **1868:** Competition for Law Courts design. **1868-1922:** Construction completed; **Architect:** George Edmund Street (1824-1881).

Publications

BROWNLEE, DAVID: *The Law Courts, The Architecture of George Edmund Street.* 1984.
BROWNLEE, DAVID B.: *George Edmund Street and the Royal Courts of Justice.* Dissertation. Harvard University, Cambridge, Massachusetts, 1980.

Westminster Hall, Houses of Parliament: London, England, 1097-99

BROWNLEE, DAVID B.: "'To agree would be to commit an act of artistic suicide . . .': The Revision of the Design for the Law Courts." *Journal of the Society of Architectural Historians* 42 (May 1983): 168-188.

KINNARD, JOSEPH: "G. E. Street, the Law Courts and the 'Seventies." In PETER FERRIDAY (ed.): *Victorian Architecture*. London, 1963.

PORT, M. H.: "The New Law Courts Competition: 1866-67." *Architectural History* 11 (1968): 75-93.

SCOTT, GEORGE GILBERT: *Design for the New Law Courts*. London.

STREET, GEORGE EDMUND: *Explanation and Illustrations of His Designs for the Proposed New Courts of Justice*. London, 1867.

SUMMERSON, JOHN: "A Victorian Competition: The Royal Courts of Justice." In JOHN SUMMERSON: *Victorian Architecture: Four Studies in Evaluation*. New York, 1970.

SUMMERSON, JOHN: "The Law Courts Competition of 1866-1877." *Journal of the Royal Institute of British Architects* 77, 1 (1970): 11-18.

WATERHOUSE, ALFRED: *Courts of Justice Competition: General Description of Design*. London, 1867.

Law Courts (or Royal Courts of Justice): London, England, 1868

The Law Courts in the Strand mark the high tide of the Gothic Revival in England. Like most government buildings of the day, they were conceived in controversy. The need for new law courts had been acknowledged for more than 20 years before effective action to build them was taken: because they were to be the seat of civil, not criminal, cases, between private individuals, there was strong resistance to spending public money; and the system agreed upon for financing the building was complex and controversial. Further difficulty arose because the administration of justice was being reformed. The first architectural brief was to concentrate all the superior courts of civil law and equity on one site. That was abandoned because of the cost, and the building eventually went ahead without taking into account the concurrent changes in the legal system. Even when an architect had been commissioned, arguments about the best site delayed progress; then an economically minded minister attempted to cut the heart out of the design.

Building on a site immediately north of the Strand was authorized under an act of 1865: arrangements were to be made by a royal commission dominated by lawyers. The principle of architectural competition for public buildings was adhered to, but because of the controversial results of the government offices open competition of 1856-57, a limited competition of 11 leading architects was held. Somewhat surprisingly, all 11 submitted Gothic designs, whether from their commitment to the style, as with George Gilbert Scott and George Edmund

Street, or from a feeling that Gothic was appropriate to the ancient majesty of the law, or simply a belief that Gothic was the favored style. William Burges' Early French entry was widely admired for its beauty. The judges failed to make a clear decision, commending E. M. Barry's plan and Street's elevation. Exactly what it was in Street's highly eclectic design that attracted the judges is difficult to say: it was a medley of his habitual Early French Gothic (in general massing, window spacing, tourelles and steep roofs), Italian Gothic (in the ventilation towers), English Decorated tracery, and classicizing regularity and uniformity—seen in the general composition of the fronts, a feature probably borrowed from Charles Barry's Houses of Parliament, like the dominant vertical accent of the asymmetrical record tower. Eventually Street was appointed, but the government cut down the scope of his (and the royal commission's) proposals. After he had prepared plans for a new site above the Thames Embankment, Parliament reverted to the Strand site.

Street's problem there was that the Strand was a narrow and exceedingly busy road—indeed, the whole site was hemmed in by narrow, busy streets, except on the west. A grand axial composition in the Beaux-Arts manner of Joseph Poelaert's contemporaneous Palais de Justice in Brussels was clearly not appropriate. Street therefore composed a front of overlapping symmetrical units which could be read successively as one passed down the Strand and provided a picturesque entity viewed in enfilade the length of the street. For John Summerson, it "represents the pathetic collapse of an overstrained imagination."

The distinct routes of communication for the several classes of user—judges, lawyers, witnesses—made a point of intercommunication useful, and lawyers needed somewhere to talk to their clients; this Street provided in his great hall (a traditional feature of principal law courts from Westminster Hall onward), originally designed as an east-west feature surrounded by courtrooms ringed in turn by administrative offices. The limitations of the site and of expense imposed under a restrictive regime at the Treasury and Office of Works caused a recasting of the plan, so that the hall ran north-south, still flanked by courtrooms, but with the offices removed to the east. Street was determined to make the hall his masterpiece: the largest vaulted hall in the country, 238 feet by 48 feet, and 80 feet to the crown of the vault. When the works minister proposed to strike it out to keep down cost, Street appealed successfully to the Cabinet, though the form of the clock tower at the east end of the facade remained undetermined. In its eventual form, it shows the influence of Burges, but it is closely integrated with the rest of the front. (David Brownlee has suggested the contemporary design of Leyswood by R. Norman Shaw, a former pupil of Street's, influenced the front.)

The final design of the Strand front is undoubtedly more responsive to English influences than Street's earlier work. Thus the setting of the entrance to the central hall between two towers recalls, without imitating, the entrance front of Westminster Hall, original seat of the superior courts, while the use of Purbeck shafting within the hall recalls the adjacent Westminster Abbey. The west front, which could be viewed as a whole, was more formally composed. The east or offices front, away from main streets, is of red brick with bands of white stone and a second tower, again Burges-like. Throughout, the varied fenestration asserts the claim that Gothic is the most functional of styles.

Although it can be argued that this highly eclectic design, with its original 1860s muscularity toned down by Queen Anne influences, was very much of the hour, it was nevertheless bitterly attacked in both the professional press and the newspapers, the *Builder* leading the one, *the Times* the other. "Meanness," "feebleness," "ugliness" and "broken outline" were the principal charges; what was needed, the critics declared, was "noble form, exalted dignity." Others came to Street's support, and the *Architect* perciplently identified the attacks as essentially antimedieval: the brief reign of secular Gothic was drawing to its close. Ironically, the *Architect* and the *Building News* (which had also supported Street) were leading advocates of the increasing classicism of the 1870s. The Strand Law Courts were the last great government building in England to be built in Gothic.

—M. H. PORT

LLOYD'S OF LONDON
London, England

1978-86. Construction; **Architect:** Richard Rogers (born 1933).

Publications

DAVIES, COLIN: *High Tech Architecture*. New York, 1988.
"Lloyd's Logic." *Building* (February 1980).
SUDJIC, DEYAN: *Norman Foster, Richard Rogers, James Stirling, New Directions in British Architecture*. 1987.

*

Completed in 1986 to the designs of Richard Rogers, the new building for Lloyd's of London placed one of the city's oldest and most conservative organizations into its most imaginative and adventurous building.

Lloyd's of London, which dates back to the coffee-house trading of the 17th century, is recognized as the center of world insurance. Lloyd's is not a single entity, has no shareholders and takes no corporate liability for the risks insured. It is more like a marketplace in which syndicates of underwriters operate, agreeing on terms and risks with their customers. As a market it requires a great space in which to work; known affectionately as the "Room," this space has been continually rebuilt to a larger and larger size. The growth has been such that the 1928 room was replaced in 1958, with the new room being extended in 1975; soon even that became too small, and a new building was needed. The size of the new room was, inevitably, difficult to insert into the close grain of the city of London, and that problem dominated the planning of the Richard Rogers building.

The site, adjacent to Lloyd's old building, is a typical city of London block bounded by narrow, winding streets of medieval origin. On one side of the site stand the Commercial Union and P&O Towers, a very fine 1960s development of glass towers with central cores and a plaza. On the opposite side is Leadenhall Market, glass-covered streets of delightful Victoriana. Elsewhere the surrounding buildings are low-rise and follow the street line.

Three hundred years earlier, Christopher Wren had inserted Renaissance churches, and surrounded them with minor rooms to fill the leftover spaces and bring them out to the building line within the irregular street pattern. Richard Rogers played the same game. The great "Room" is almost the largest rectangle that could be placed on the site, and Rogers kept it free and open. The odd shapes all around it accept six service towers,

Lloyd's of London: London, England, 1978-88

placed wherever there is space available and bringing the building out to the old, irregular street line. The building also responds to its site in terms of height, with 12 stories on the north side opposite the Commercial Union and P&O Towers, stepping down in stages to six stories at the south, where it fronts 19th-century buildings. The building is, therefore, sensitive to its surroundings. Few would deny, however, that it is a dramatic and surprising insertion into the city, a clear demonstration of the design approach known as "high-tech" and a new landmark for the millions of tourists who crowd London each year.

Circular reinforced concrete columns stand on an 18-by-10.8-meter grid. The three central bays are open to form an atrium, which extends the full height of the building and is topped with a glazed roof—barrel vaulted like the Crystal Palace. This atrium is surrounded by floors that are open to it as galleries at the lower levels; these galleries, which are for underwriters and form natural extensions to the "Room," are connected by escalators in the atrium. At the upper levels the areas around the atrium are offices and other spaces requiring subdivision. Outside the big rectangle the six service cones contain elevators, lavatories, kitchens and plant.

The client's experience of the rapid and costly obsolescence of Lloyd's previous buildings, together with an architectural practice that believes in the importance of change, meant that great thought was given to how the building would perform over time. By placing plant, kitchens and lavatories in stainless-steel boxes on the external service towers, and by mounting permanent cranes on top of these elements, the notion of change is celebrated, for not only did this concept allow the most elaborate and precise parts of the building to be made off-site and hoisted into position late in the building program, it also enables these relatively short-life elements to be changed without disturbing those working in the more permanent spaces within.

The architect's wish to make each element of the building a discrete entity has resulted in a building of staggering complexity. The contrast with the modern architecture of 20 years previously, as exemplified in the Commercial Union Tower opposite, could not be more complete. At Lloyd's every flight of every staircase, every duct and pipe, every piece of structure, every lavatory module is seen as a separate element, usually with its own roof and floor, and often with its own supporting structure. In the hands of lesser architects the result would be chaos, but here all holds together, and the visitor is intrigued and fascinated, marveling at the technical skill of designers and builders. Use of monochrome—gray concrete, stainless steel, aluminum, faceted glass—gives the building a somber look, but the great drama of the elevators, glass wall climbers hung on the outside, brings the outside of the building to life, while inside the change in scene from street level to rooftop is one of the major architectural experiences London has to offer.

—JOHN WINTER

MANSION HOUSE
London, England

1738: Construction begun; **Architect:** George Dance the Elder (1695-1768). **1744:** Pediment carved; **Mason:** Robert Taylor (1714-88). **1752:** Construction completed; **Architect:** George

Dance the Elder. **1842:** Attic building on roof removed. **1931:** Interior refurbished.

Publications

PERKS, SYDNEY: *The History of the Mansion House*. Cambridge, 1922.

English gentlemen on the grand tour in the 17th and 18th centuries took home with them not only Roman relics but an enthusiasm for the style of Andrea Palladio's villas. Palladio molded classical architecture as seen through the eyes of Vitruvius and himself. When George Dance the Elder, clerk of the works to the City of London, was asked in 1737 to submit plans for a public residence for the lord mayor of the city (the restricted competition held in 1735 to find a suitable architect had failed), he, like many of his immediate contemporaries, established yet another filter between the classical style and his own interpretation of it by receiving it through Palladio. But it was a Palladio who had to be adapted to the cramped area of the Stocks Market, a site which backed on to a church and was surrounded by a growing nexus of thoroughfares. Dance was a man associated with public buildings, being responsible for the Fleet Market, the Corn Market and the Surgeon's Hall, all of which have been demolished. The fate of the public building is such that it is often subject to considerable structural changes and uses as needs evolve. The Mansion House is no exception, and there have been a number of transformations since it was constructed. An attic building on the roof was removed in 1842; the interior was refurbished in 1931, and again after World War II.

Externally, the proportions of this striking building are not easily appreciable from the now-crowded streets. It seems to be a little bit of Italy in Britain, in a style that—although it eventually gained favor among municipal authorities—was still a relative novelty in 1738-52, the years of Mansion House's major construction. The ground-floor base is in the rustic mode and shelters the services of the household. The rectangular building (225 feet by 103 feet) is faced on three sides with Portland stone; the fourth side, which is separated by a mere alley from a church, remains in exposed brick. The public reception rooms are on the first floor, with private apartments on the second. There is an impressive ceremonial entrance beneath a portico, supported by six Corinthian columns beneath a pediment sculpted by Robert Taylor and showing a personification of London (turret on her head), over-powering Envy beneath the gaze of Plenty and Old Father Thames. Unfortunately, as in the case of the portico of the National Gallery, also in London, the proportions of the portico allow for only a narrow staircase on each side of the columns. The lord mayor's normal entrance is in Walbrook Street, in the middle of the rustic podium, a befittingly more modest affair, with a Doric columned porch. Through this door is access to the entrance hall converted in 1845 from an area reserved for stables and beyond, a vast modernized kitchen and other offices.

The plan of the reception rooms on the first floor originally resembled that of a Palladian villa, with a small open courtyard in the middle, but with a hall added at the south end across the

Mansion House: London, England, 1739

whole width of the structure. The open courtyard was soon covered over to be the salon. In fact, the functional nature of the building has used space to its greatest advantage. There are high elaborate ceilings decorated by George Fewkes and Humphrey Willmott, doors with elaborate pediments, and chimneypieces sculpted out of stone with ornate classical wooden mantels; the definition of the ceiling decoration and the pillars is highlighted with gold leaf. This pattern is to be found in the adjacent rooms: the Venetian Parlor with its fluted Ionic columns and pilasters; the Hall, with its ceiling modeled on that of Inigo Jones in the Central Hall of Queen Anne's house in Greenwich; the Long Parlour, with its five large windows and pedimented architraves; the State Drawing Room, with its *grisaille* paintings; the Salon, which was once the open courtyard space. There are two rooms that are linked with the special nature of this town representative's office. The first is the Justice Room, in which the lord mayor presides with other magistrates to administer justice in certain cases; the other room is the Banqueting Hall, known as the Egyptian Room (Egyptian because the windows rise above the cornice and an upper row of

columns creates a clerestory effect). This room has a barrel-vaulted ceiling supported by 16 massive Corinthian columns; at each end is a 19th century (Alexander Gibbs, 1868) stained-glass window with two images. The Egyptian Hall has a gallery, which was removed and then restored. The gallery, whose roof was added when the attic building above was removed, thus bears traces of the building's checkered history.

The Mansion House is thus a building modeled on an ancient architectural precedent—the Greek temple with Italian overtones—on a site which has been the center of London since Roman times. As a building it has been the subject of criticism even from the beginning. Now, like so many of London's central constructions, it appears somewhat anachronistic and dwarfed by the proximity of other edifices. The chimneystacks visible from ground level do not, however, enhance it and yet it was, during the recent decade, the center of a conservation debate as people resisted the development plans for the surrounding area which threatened to spoil the unharmonious harmony of the status quo.

—K. C. CAMERON

NATIONAL GALLERY COMPETITION
London, England

1837: Constructed; **Architect:** William Wilkins (1778-1839).
1981: Hampton site commission awarded; **Architect:** Robert Venturi (b. 1925).

Publications

GOLDBERGER, PAUL and FUTAGAWA, YUKIO: *Global Architecture 39: Venturi and Rauch.* Tokyo, 1976.
LISCOMBRE, R. WINDSOR: *William Wilkins 1778-1839.* London, 1980.
MARTIN, GREGORY: "Wilkins and the National Gallery." *Burlington Magazine* 113 (1971): 318-329.
VENTURI, ROBERT: *Complexity and Contradiction in Architecture.* New York, 1966.
VON MOOS, S.: *Venturi, Rauch & Scott Brown: Buildings and Projects.* New York, 1987.
"William Wilkins." *RIBA Journal* (24 December 1932).

Robert Venturi's first building in Britain, the Sainsbury Wing of the National Gallery in London, which opened in July 1991, represents the final chapter in an architectural saga that has lasted well over a century and a half. Most notably, that period has been punctuated by architectural competitions, some of which have been abortive, others of which have realized building stock of varying quality. The National Gallery has also spawned architectural commissions, equally of varying success. Such events have been spiced with intrigue and disappointment (particularly on the part of architect participants), but also with a repeated demonstration of parsimony on the part of the British Government.

Britain's first National Gallery was opened in 1824, at 100 Pall Mall, London, an early manifestation of the infinite versatility of the Georgian terraced house; but it was not until 1837 that William Wilkins' competition-winning design was realized. Following criticism of the finished result, a further competition was instituted in 1866. Not unexpectedly, much debate centered around the question of style; Charles Barry's successful entry was firmly classical (and incidentally recommended the demolition of Wilkins' scheme after a mere three decades), which

National Gallery Competition: London, England, 1837

contrasted with the premiated Gothic designs for the Law Courts and Natural History Museum competitions. In the event, Wilkins' now-famous elevation on Trafalgar Square was retained, and Barry had to be content with eight new galleries at the rear of the Wilkins design. Five further galleries followed in 1911, a product of the Office of Works.

Ironically, it was to be wartime destruction during London's Blitz which set the scene for ensuing events. The bombing of Hampton's furniture store, adjacent to the National Gallery site, freed land for expansion, but the Government did not acquire the site until 1958. Such was the media interest focused upon the Hampton site and the prospect of extending the National Gallery that the London *Sunday Times* promoted a competition in 1959. The winning design by Barrie Dewhurst clearly showed the transatlantic influence of Louis Kahn and Paul Rudolph, incorporating bold cantilevers and repetitive precast concrete cladding panels.

However, pressure to extend the gallery space produced a faceless International Modern effort in 1970 from the office of Ministry of Public Buildings and Works. Inevitably this stopgap was to prove short-lived, and gallery trustees, desperate for further space, urged the then secretary of state for the environment to announce an architectural competition for the still-vacant Hampton site, in December 1981.

The competition, entered by Britain's most celebrated architects, was unusual in that the brief embodied a commercial element, reflecting the then-current values of a burgeoning Thatcherite Britain; if the nation wished to house its art collection, then commerce could underwrite it. The entries, in their range of architectural expression, also demonstrated the essentially pluralist state of late-20th-century British architecture. At one extreme, Richard Rogers' scheme promoted an uncompromising but hugely authoritative high-tech architecture in the manner of his highly acclaimed Beaubourg Center in Paris, while lesser entries embraced the whole fashionable gamut of postmodernism and classical revivalism. The outcome of that first phase of the competition was a shortlist of seven architects who were asked to develop their designs.

From that process Ahrends, Burton and Koralek emerged as the winners. Popular reaction to the winning design was almost universally hostile, a response attributed in part to a modernist architectural language apparently out of sympathy with popular taste. But this populist view was given enormous weight by the intervention of Prince Charles, heir to the British throne. At a dinner celebrating the sesquicentenary of the Royal Institute of British Architects, Prince Charles likened the winning design to a "carbuncle," with disastrous consequences for its architects. The royal intervention threw the already protracted competition process into turmoil, and the trustees, abandoning the competition, renewed their search for a suitable architect. Six architects were shortlisted for the next stage. James Stirling's design demonstrated characteristically masterful planning and contextual concerns in an overtly postmodern envelope, while Piers Gough's effort was typically self-conscious, showing little apparent regard for its venerable neighbor Wilkins.

Venturi, Rauch and Scott Brown were adjudged the winners. However, the brief had fortuitously changed for the better; a philanthropic intervention had removed the always contentious commercial element from the brief, and the Hampton site could be given over entirely to gallery space.

The Venturi firm's design has emerged as a curiously eclectic amalgam, most notably in its controversial elevational treatment, where the Wilkins' classical elevation is diluted gradually from rich classical detail to a Portland stone facade stripped of any ornamentation whatever at its furthermost point. The gallery spaces themselves, the most successful element of the building,

and a generally acclaimed setting for the world's foremost collection of Florentine art, owe much to John Soane's Dulwich Art Gallery. Direct allusions to the work of Filippo Brunelleschi in the willfully truncated *pietra serena* columns co-exist with a robust and distinctly Pironesian entrance hall. The major staircase, redolent of Giovanni Lorenzo Bernini's Scala Regia at the Vatican, links the entrance hall at street level to gallery level via a mezzanine accommodating a restaurant and computerized information room.

Critics have seized upon the building's apparent contradictions, forgetting that such "complexity and contradiction" are the cornerstone of Venturi's theoretical stance. To some, the attempt at reconciliation with Wilkins' original is banal, while the Soanesque lanterns purport to offer daylighting which, in the event, for good conservational reasons, never reaches the priceless exhibits. It is as if Venturi's acknowledged passion for architectural history has allowed him to pillage that huge architectural resource, where disparate historical predilections are applied willfully and even literally, rather than in the interpretive manner of, say, James Stirling.

Nevertheless, the building and, more particularly, the byzantine process by which it was procured have raised the public awareness of architecture in Britain. However, only time will tell whether the Sainsbury Wing of the National Gallery represents an appropriate architectural language for a late-20th-century national monument.

—A. PETER FAWCETT

NATURAL HISTORY MUSEUM
London, England

1864: Commission awarded; **Architect:** Captain Francis Fowke (d.1865). **1868:** Design redeveloped; **Architect:** Alfred Waterhouse (1830-1905). **1873-81:** Constructed; **Architect:** Alfred Waterhouse.

Publications

GIROUARD, MARK: *Alfred Waterhouse and the Natural History Museum*. New Haven, Connecticut, and London, 1981.

*

In 1858 it was proposed to build a new building to house the British Museum's zoological, botanical, geological and mineral collections. This desire reflects the era's extraordinary interest in the study of the natural world. The new museum, as envisioned by Professor Richard Owen, superintendent of the existing museum's natural history departments, was to be revolutionary in its size and the amount of display opened to the public. Owen proposed some 10 acres of top-lighted public display galleries, and, by appealing to national pride and the interests of the middle classes, he was successful in selling the idea over the objections of scholars who wanted most of the collection kept private for the exclusive use of scientific researchers.

In 1864 the site of the 1862 exhibition building was acquired and a competition for a new Natural History and Patent Museum was held. The competition winner was Captain Francis Fowke, who submitted a design in a round-arched High Renaissance style featuring extensive use of terra-cotta. However, Fowke died in 1865 before the design had been affirmed. He was replaced with Alfred Waterhouse, who was appointed by the first commissioner of works, ostensibly to develop Fowke's design.

The program was revised when the government changed in 1866; it was decided to build only the Natural History Museum. By 1868, Waterhouse had developed his own design in the Romanesque style. Romanesque allowed the integration of naturalistic ornament illustrative of the building's function better than did Fowke's classical style and was more acceptable to Waterhouse, who preferred the Gothic style for most of his buildings.

Waterhouse's 1868 scheme featured a central mass inspired by Donate Bramante's design for St. Peter's Basilica; four subsidiary domes at the corners of a square led up to a great central dome located above the stairway hall. This ecclesiological design suggested that the building was a secular cathedral—an appropriate concept inasmuch as the material world was considered to reveal the wisdom and purposes of God.

The 1868 design with its great central dome was not approved. There was talk of moving the site, and the design was considered too expensive. Waterhouse reworked it, eliminating the dome and substituting brick for much of the terra-cotta in the interior, and plaster for the wood ceilings. The ecclesiological reference was changed from Bramante's great Renaissance design to a Romanesque cathedral portal, narthex and nave. The revision was accepted, and work began in 1873. However, another change in government occurred in 1876 that benefited Waterhouse and the museum. The new government was willing to restore much of what had been eliminated before. The dome was not restored, but the great towers that mark the entrance were, as was most of the terra-cotta. The building was opened to the public in April 1881.

The building is frankly symmetrical in plan and form; there is no artificial, forced asymmetry to create a picturesque silhouette. Its symmetrical facade, imposing central entrance, central hall and grand staircase are all elements that were expected of important public buildings. The towers, the end pavilions with their steep Germanic roofs and the wealth of naturalistic decoration in terra-cotta give the building visual interest. Figures on the facade picture living and extinct plants and animals, and the study of zoology, geology and paleontology. The entire surface is terra-cotta constructional polychromy—part buff, part blue-gray. Most interior wall surfaces are covered in the same terra-cotta used on the exterior.

The plan is axially symmetrical; the central foyer leads, under a bridge, to the great hall, 170 feet by 97 feet by 72 feet high, culminating in a monumental stair. The top-lighted hall is treated like a great cathedral nave whose side chapels are used to display samples from the museum's collections. Beyond the great hall, or "index museum," and past the great stair, is the Hall of British Natural History. That part of the museum to the right of the central axis is devoted to geology, that to the left to zoology. Two stories of long galleries run east and west from the foyer to the terminal spaces in the great pavilions at each end of the front facade; these galleries contain the general collections expected to be most popular with visitors. From these long galleries, corridors lead to alternating wide and narrow top-lighted lateral galleries intended to house specialized collections. Originally the wide galleries were for display and the narrow ones for study; however, this program was never enacted in practice as even basement spaces are used for display.

The interior is framed in steel, clearly expressed in the roofs of the great hall and the galleries. A clever fusion of masonry, decoration and iron is evident everywhere. Waterhouse was not ashamed of his ironwork and was not embarrassed to expose

Natural History Museum: London, England, 1873-81

it. His work invariably features an innovative use of industrial methods to achieve decorative richness. In this case Waterhouse combined a direct, axial Beaux-Arts plan, an unfashionable Romanesque style and new industrial materials in a work that is completely, conspicuously modern.

Mark Girouard, in his splendid book on the building published by the British Museum in 1981, said: "(Waterhouse) made arriving, entering and exploring the museum as exciting as possible. Visitors pass through splendid wrought-iron gates up a broad flight of steps to a huge cathedral portal, framed by towers, decorated with carved beasts and twisted columns, and recessed like a cave into the cliff of the front. Through this they come into a hall in scale with the entrance . . . a rectangular cathedral nave, with a triforium above and arcades below, opening into a series of side chapels. . . .

"What turns the great hall from an impressive space into an extraordinary one is the staircase which has been inserted into the cathedral nave. This starts handsomely but conventionally enough at the end of the hall, in the form of a single broad flight that breaks into two at the landing and climbs up to the triforium galleries on the first (second) floor. The exciting bit is the next stage up to the second (third) floor galleries. To get to these one walks along one or other of the galleries to a bridge that spans the hall by means of a single arch towards the end nearest the entrance. Flights of steps climb up either side of this. From the top of the bridge a final flight leaps across the gap between the bridge and the end of the hall. The effect is sensational from every point of view. . . . The combination of complex and dramatic spaces with constantly moving crowds is extraordinarily exhilarating."

—C. MURRAY SMART, JR.

NEW SCOTLAND YARD
London, England

1887: Commission awarded; **Architect:** Richard Norman Shaw (1831-1912). **1888-90:** Construction completed. **1901-03:** Extension foundations built. **1905-07:** Extension superstructure built.

Publications

SAINT, ANDREW: *Richard Norman Shaw*. London, 1976.
STAMP, G. and AMERY, C.: *Victorian Buildings of London, 1837-1887: An Illustrated Guide*. London, 1980.

New Scotland Yard: London, England, 1888-90

New Scotland Yard was built as the central police station for the London Metropolitan Police. The building is transitional between R. Norman Shaw's Queen Anne style and the formal classicism of his late work; it demonstrates his move away from the free Renaissance of Queen Anne toward a more Baroque style. It also represents Shaw's adaptation of what had been a domestic style to a large public building, with remarkable success.

Shaw's appointment as architect is a testimonial to the reputation he had achieved. No open competition for an architect was conducted. The Tory Home Secretary, Henry Matthews, on his own authority consulted Shaw in 1886, and by 1887 Shaw had the commission. The Police Surveyor, J. Dixon Butler, had earlier developed a courtyard scheme for the building which Shaw wisely accepted, thereby diminishing political conflict. Shaw modified Butler's double-loaded corridors to wide, single-loaded ones adjacent to the interior court, thereby allowing the introduction of borrowed light into offices through transoms. This change reduced the size of the court slightly and caused Shaw to heighten the building.

Butler had proposed to construct the building exclusively of granite and Portland stone from government-owned quarries. The granite was to be quarried by convicts and provided free of charge. Shaw kept the granite and used it for the base of the building, but he added red brick to Portland stone for the upper structure. Shaw wanted a ''warm'' material (red brick) to offset the coldness of the granite, stone, and slate roofing. He used $2\frac{1}{8}$" bricks, five courses to the foot; the unbroken passages of thin brickwork give a smart, sharp appearance to the masonry wall. Portland stone was used for the window surrounds, cornices and the bands introduced into the brick.

The building occupies a splendid site on the Thames Embankment. It rises, foursquare, like a Scottish baronial castle; yet its detailing is of an eclectic, rather heavy, academic, later-17th-century, universal sort. Nevertheless, it has great presence because of its form and proportions. The building's details are borrowed from Christopher Wren's Baroque vocabulary. Its corner pendentive turrets suggest ''fortress,'' and in fact the building was designed to be riot-proof. Its two-and-one-half-story-tall granite base carries a superstructure of red brick and Portland stone in alternating horizontal bands. The character of the superstructure is much like the rear of Street's Royal Courts of Justice; even though constructional polychromy was no longer in vogue, Shaw was willing to use it to achieve the desired visual effect of mass diminishing in weight as it rises. The brick and stone superstructure is two full stories in height, plus a third story expressed fully in the gables but only as large dormers on the sides. Two additional attic stories are expressed, German-style, in small dormers on the steeply sloping roof surfaces. The windows in the striated upper portion seem to be in bands because of their connection by Portland stone stripes.

The entry facade is composed of three units. The outer units are gabled; the gables are decorated with broken-pedimented aedicules that rise to break the silhouette against the sky. The inner unit is three bays wide and is given special emphasis through the use of roundheaded windows and dormers, yet it does not contain the entrance. The entrance is in the right gabled unit; consequently, the facade is asymmetrical. The portal is framed by a rusticated arch located within a rusticated aedicular frame topped by a broken segmental pediment. The Baroque details give the facade a vigorous quality similar to that of Nicholas Hawksmoor's buildings.

The fenestration is not as brazenly picturesque and asymmetrical as is Shaw's norm; the windows are regularly placed, some have segmental pediments, others are square-headed or arched. Nevertheless, the play of roof heights, gables, dormers, chimneystacks and obelisks against the sky gives the building a bold silhouette. Shaw liked to suggest that the obelisks were representative of the spikes on policemen's helmets.

Shaw's inspiration for New Scotland Yard seems to be a mixture of Dutch, Danish and English design features. At least one source of inspiration was not historical, however; the Baroque porches were influenced by those on the Institute of Chartered Accountants designed by John Belcher in 1888. What is clear is that this design was strongly influenced by John

Ruskin; the pendentive turrets, the hollow square form, the constructional polychromy and the effect of diminished weight toward the top are all consistent with Ruskin's teaching.

The design of New Scotland Yard was sharply criticized by neo-Gothic purists and many in Parliament, but was widely praised by the architectural press. The attack in Parliament was led by Sir William Harcourt, a former Liberal Party Home Secretary. A long list of distinguished architects and artists came to Shaw's defense. It is interesting that architectural style was such a hot political issue; however, Tory governments were generally concerned about the quality of public buildings and supported architects and architecture in the Gothic Revival mode. Shaw responded to the criticism as follows: "My aim has been to have less of what I should call 'style,' and more of what I should call character. Style gives what we have already got many examples of, viz. dull copies of Italian palaces, medi-aeval buildings, etc., and they are generally found to be unsuited to their purpose, ill lit, and from an artistic point of view dead and so failures. . . . I dwell on New Scotland Yard being a genuine building, in which we have no sham or shew fronts, all is of the same quality and in the court it is the same. In order to secure this, a quality which I consider essential to good building, I have reduced the ornamental features to a minimum, relying on the bulk and outline to give the desired character. Had I sacrificed what I believe to be a sound principle I might have put more ornament on the shew fronts, and so possibly have made it more attractive to a certain class of mind. But after all the whole matter is a question of taste, on which I fear people never can and never will agree, certainly not for some time." (Victorian Buildings of London, p. 152).

The building as originally designed was a simple geometric mass that was complete in itself just as a cube or sphere is complete. It defied addition, yet in 1905-07 it was extended to the south. Earlier, in 1900-02, a new police station to the south-west had been constructed. These additions diminished the impact of the original foursquare mass that had dominated the Embankment even though they were designed by Shaw and were in the style of the original building.

Unfortunately, New Scotland Yard is no longer the home of the Metropolitan Police; the police have moved to an undistinguished modern tower in Victoria Street.

—C. MURRAY SMART, JR.

PADDINGTON STATION
London, England

1850-54: Construction; **Architect:** Isambard Kingdom Brunel (1806-1859).

Publications

BETJEMAN, JOHN: *London's Historic Railway Stations.* London, 1972.
BIDDLE, G.: *Victorian Stations: Railway Stations in England and Wales 1830-1913.* Newton Abbot, England, 1973.
BRUNEL, ISAMBARD K.: *The Life of Isambard Kingdom Brunel, Civil Engineer.* London, 1870.
FRAMPTON, KENNETH, and FUTAGAWA, YUKIO: *Modern Architecture: 1851-1919.* New York, 1983.
HITCHCOCK, HENRY-RUSSELL: "Brunel and Paddington." *Architectural Review* 109 (1951): 240-246.
MEEKS, CARROLL L. V.: *The Railroad Station: An Architectural History.* New Haven, Connecticut, 1956.
PUGSLEY, ALFRED (ed.): *The Works of Isambard Kingdom Brunel: An Engineering Appreciation.* New York, 1980.
ROLT, L. T. C.: *Isambard Kingdom Brunel.* London, 1957.

*

Paddington Station is one of the great railway stations built by Isambard Kingdom Brunel, who was perhaps the leading engineer of the early Victorian period in England. Brunel had been appointed chief engineer for the Great Western Railway in 1833, and that position called for him to build many miles of track—with a wider gauge than usual to permit higher speeds—and numerous tunnels and bridges. At first, however, the company had no London terminus, and it was to a temporary building near Bishop's Bridge that Queen Victoria came by train to London in 1842, having traveled with Brunel from Slough to give royal approval to this new form of transport. In 1850 work began on the present station, located on Praed Street, on the boundary line north of the busiest part of London, which the railways were not allowed to cross. Brunel was helped with the decorative details by Owen Jones and with the architecture by Matthew Digby Wyatt, with whom he had worked earlier on preparations for the Great Exhibition of 1851.

The station itself, which has survived almost intact, was built with three parallel sheds (a fourth was added in the 20th century), four platforms and 10 tracks, with the offices arranged around the departure platform; the arrival platform could be reached by bridges built at each end of the station. The three great glass arches spanned some 240 feet, and the platforms were 700 feet long. Halfway down that length were the so-called "transepts" of the station, an area running across the line of the platforms that was necessary for the traversing frames used for the locomotives in place of the more usual turntables; the only other instance of such "transepts" was also in London, at Liverpool Street Station.

The pattern of intersecting bracings at Paddington was very intricate, and was executed by Fox, Henderson and Company. The firm had worked on the Crystal Palace with Joseph Paxton, and used in the station the same ridge-and-furrow glazing that Paxton made for that project. The decorative details added by Wyatt and Owen were comparatively restrained: the cast-iron columns were octagonal, and at the platforms there were graceful wrought-iron end screens and an iron balcony at the office where Brunel worked. The architectural decorations are, according to Nikolaus Pevsner, both a vague "French Dixhui-tième" on the ground floor and a still vaguer Venetian above that, but the two styles seem to work with the composition as a whole.

To the south of the station, which was completed in 1854, was the Great Western Hotel (1850-52). Designed by Philip Hardwick (1792-1870), who later designed similar hotels at Victoria Station and Euston, the hotel was originally separate, but was later connected to the station. At the time it was built, this was the largest and most sumptuous hotel in England. It

Paddington Station: London, England, 1850-54

was also one of the earliest buildings in England to incorporate elements of French Renaissance and Baroque architecture, perhaps most specifically from the recent additions to the Louvre by Hector Martin Lefuel; most notable were the hotel's curved and mansard roofs, and the multitude of dormers, balconies and ornate brackets, all set within massive corner towers and centered by a pediment by the sculptor John Thomas that illustrated a characteristically Victorian series of figures of Peace, Plenty, Industry and Science.

The mix of structures and styles in this arrangement was perhaps typically Victorian, and the striking manner of the hotel seems to make the more sober forms of the station lurk ignominiously, as Carroll Meeks put it, in its shadow. It is not clear that so grand a structure made true economic sense in the necessarily seedy environs of a train station. But before that became apparent, the idea there of the great hotel was copied by James Knowles at the Grosvenor at Victoria Station (1860-61), and by E. M. Barry at Charing Cross (1864) and Cannon Street Stations (1862-66). Paddington Station is the subject of William Frith's famous painting *The Railway Station* (1861),

which is in the collection of the Royal Holloway College, Egham, Surrey.

—DAVID CAST

REFORM CLUB
London, England

1838-41: Construction; **Architect:** Charles Barry (1795-1860).

Publications

BARRY, ALFRED: *The Life and Works of Sir Charles Barry*. London, 1867.

Reform Club: London, England, 1838-41

FERRIDAY, P. (ed.): *Victorian Architecture*. 1963.
HITCHCOCK, HENRY-RUSSELL: *Early Victorian Architecture in Britain*. 2 volumes. New York, 1972.
WYATT, DIGBY: *The Architectural Career of Sir Charles Barry*. 1859.

*

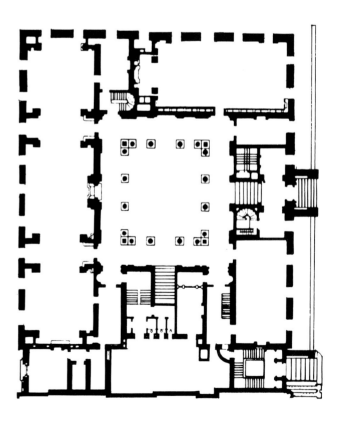

The Reform Club was initiated by a group of British parliamentary Radicals in early 1835 as a place of meeting for the Reformers of the country when they came to London. The more conservatively inclined and aristocratic Whigs, who had seen little need for such a club, were obliged to fall in with the plan, or let the Radicals loose. The club was therefore established as the great rendezvous of all shades of the Reform party, which then dominated the House of Commons. They acquired a three-year lease of a house in Pall Mall a little to the west of the three leading clubs established there in the 1820s: the United Services, the Athenaeum and the Travellers'. The ground landlords' plan to redevelop the immediate area led to a decision to erect a new clubhouse on an enlarged site, to "surpass all others in size and magnificence," combining "the various attractions of other institutions of the class," as the building committee insisted.

They had a magnificent site, with a frontage of 142 feet (twice that of the Travellers') in what was fast becoming the finest street in London, so in May 1837 the club members decided to call on seven leading English architects for designs; in the end four competed—C. R. Cockerell, Edward Blore, Sydney Smirke and Charles Barry. The scale and standard of accommodation exceeded anything previously known: in addition to the usual rooms for meeting friends, eating, writing and reading, there were to be two billiard rooms, a smoking room, baths, dressing- and bed-rooms (an innovation in West End clubs), as well as provision for all the club servants. Barry won. He had success- fully competed for the adjoining Travellers' Clubhouse in 1828, when he introduced the Italian High Renaissance style to Lon- don, and the recent Houses of Parliament competition showed he possessed planning skills of a high order.

His design was a natural evolution from the Travellers', via the Manchester Athenaeum (1836). Appearing more severe than the Travellers' chiefly because of the greater proportion of solid to void in the facade, the Reform aimed at sublimity, a feature of 1840s' design. In comparison with the Travellers', the Reform indicated the future course of Victorian style: stone (a "truth- ful" material) rather than stucco; a form not only more massive, but in higher relief: a more pronounced ornamental stringcourse articulating the first floor, and a deeper *cornicione* which runs around all four sides, not merely on the front. Barry's son, and biographer, commented that the "Farnese Palace was doubtless in his mind during the conception of this design," but pointed out that the resemblances were superficial. There are major differences: the Roman building is without Barry's high base- ment, but has a third story equivalent to its second, whereas Barry's designs have a low top (bedroom) floor. The Reform also has a much less significant doorway, for Barry disliked the break in the unity of the facade that an important entrance involved (as he found in his Manchester Athenaeum).

In plan, the Reform, like the Travellers', followed the Italian manner of being developed around a *cortile*, whereas the earlier clubs in Waterloo Place had the staircase as their central feature. Barry disliked the waste of space resulting from grand staircases: in the Reform he contrived one of considerable splendor that is nevertheless tucked away at one side. Invited by the club's building committee to consider "alterations in the internal ar- rangements," Barry revised his plan so that it was less like the Travellers'. The most striking change was the evolution of the courtyard into a two-story, top-lighted salon, open on both floors to corridors that give access to all the rooms, so creating a sense of great spaciousness. It was treated with considerable richness of decoration, marble and scagliola being extensively employed, and the plasterwork painted or gilded. This salon was the feature of the club that attracted most attention. Barry himself repeated it at Highclere Castle, Bridgewater House and Halifax Town Hall, and it became a popular plan for country houses and commercial palaces alike. All this cost a great deal of money: £78,650, or more than twice the original estimate.

In his Reform Club house, Charles Barry "created a prototype for the great political club-house, often emulated but never equalled" (*Survey of London*). Doubtless its continued survival is in part at least due to the care that the architect took with all aspects of the work: e.g., the kitchens were planned in cooperation with the famous chef Alexis Soyer. It was not only clubhouses that were built in imitation of the Reform (if increasingly in higher relief). The great mansions of Kensington Palace Gardens (from 1844) and others both south and north of Hyde Park represent one line of progeny, the impressive assurance company and banking palaces of the city another. Few buildings have been so intensively imitated.

—M. H. PORT

REGENT'S PARK
London, England

1811: Plan accepted; **Architect:** John Nash (1752-1835). **1812:** Park Crescent constructed. **1818-19:** St. John's Lodge con- structed; **Architect:** John Raffield. **1819:** Holme constructed; **Architect:** Decimus Burton (1800-1881). **1822:** York Terrace constructed; **Architect:** John Nash. **1822-23:** Cornwall and Clarence Terraces, Sussex Place designed; **Architect:** Decimus Burton. **1822-23:** Hanover Terrace constructed; **Architect:** J. M. Aitkens. **1823:** Carlton House Terraces. **1826:** Cumberland Terrace designed; **Designer:** James Thompson. **1826-28:** St. Katherine's Royal Hospital constructed; **Architect:** Ambrose Poynter (1796-1886). **1827:** Kent Terrace constructed; **Archi- tect:** John Nash. **1905-08:** Picadilly Hotel built; **Architect:** Richard Norman Shaw (1831-1912). **Ca. 1920s-30s:** Quadrant rebuilt; **Architect:** Sir Reginald Blomfield.

Publications

DAVIS, TERENCE: *The Architecture of John Nash*. 1960.
HOBHOUSE, HERMIONE: *A History of Regent Street*. London, 1971.
HONOUR, HUGH: "The Regent's Park Colosseum." *Country Life* 113 (1953): 22-24.
OLSEN, DONALD J.: *Town Planning in London*. New Haven, Connecticut, 1982.
"St. Dunstan's Lodge, Regent's Park." *Architect and Building News* 145, Supplement (1936).
SUMMERSON, JOHN: *The Life and Work of John Nash, Archi- tect*. Cambridge, Massachusetts, 1980.
TAYLOR, G. C.: "Holme House, Regent's Park." *Country Life* 86 (1939): 444-448.
TAYLOR, G. C.: "A House in Regent's Park." *Country Life* 87 (1940): 416-418.

*

Regent's Park is an area in the northwest of London, in the borough of St. Marylebone, developed by the architect John Nash in the early years of the 19th century, and named for his patron and friend, the Prince of Wales, later George IV. The history of the project is very complex, London perhaps not taking kindly to any large-scale development. But what Nash was able to produce was a nearly ideal rural landscape near the city and one that has survived, more or less intact, to the present day; the houses have been restored and modernized and, as the prices for them tell, are among the most desirable accommoda- tions in London.

The development was laid out in Marylebone Park, the royal hunting ground of Henry VIII, which is roughly circular in shape. This land had passed, after the Restoration of 1660, through the hands of several favored noblemen and business- men, among whose descendants the holding was split into two leaseholds, one reverting to the Crown in 1803, the other being extended to 1811. But in 1786 a commission had been set up to deal with all the Crown properties, and it was recommended that the estates should be retained by the Crown; a new post of surveyor general of the land revenues was instituted to over- see these properties. John Fordyce was appointed to that position in 1793, and it was under his guidance that Marylebone Park was developed as a comprehensive unit of housing. Reports

Regent's Park, Carlton House Terraces: London, England, 1823

followed, one in 1809 suggesting that the only way to increase the value of the land was to cut a thoroughfare—later Regent's Street—from the park to Charing Cross, giving access to the Law Courts and the Houses of Parliament. It was then that Nash became involved. In 1806 he had been appointed to the Office of Woods and Forests, a government post of little importance. But in 1810 he and Thomas Leverton, an architect attached to the Office of Land Revenues, were asked to submit proposals within six months for the development of the park for consideration by the Treasury.

Leverton's plan was very simple, a crisscross of roads to extend over the whole area, in the manner of the earlier, neighboring estates. Nash had different ideas, and he noted in his proposal that wealthy landowners preferred to live near an open space; that observation was eagerly supported by the prime minister, Spencer Percival, who had seen the gradual encroachment of building in other parts of London. That first plan of 1811 by Nash, which was accepted, was later modified, but it shows, as can be seen even in the later plans, how much Nash owed to the designs done for Bath by John Wood in the mid-18th century. Yet Nash's plan had too many buildings, and he was prompted by Percival to produce a design with a slighter density. Nash heartily endorsed that suggestion and developed a plan with ''a variety of beautiful forms,'' as he put it, ''comprehended in one magnificent whole.''

The villas, of which there were to be some 40 or 50, were dotted everywhere in wooded groves; in the center was to be a vast circus; a serpentine lake and a canal were set amidst the grounds, the canal allowing produce to be delivered; to the side was a series of vast terraces, and it is those sections that have

survived best. The earliest terrace was Park Crescent, done in 1812. Beyond that is the great York Terrace (1822), planned by Nash as one long terrace, but divided by York Gate, through which can be entered the Inner Circle; beyond that stand two of the original villas, the Holme, designed by Decimus Burton, and St. John's Lodge, by John Raffield. On the outer circle are the two blocks, Cornwall and Clarence Terraces, designed in 1823 by Decimus Burton, and then Sussex Place; beyond them is Hanover Terrace (1822-23), built by J. M. Aitkens, and then Kent Terrace (1827), the only block in the whole scheme that does not face the park. To the north side was the Regent's Canal, now filled in; this ran past the site of the Gardens of the Zoological Society of London, purchased in 1824, to the Park Villages, east of Albany Street, which were planned by Nash in the 1820s as a reminiscence of Blaise Hamlet in Gloucestershire, which he had designed a few years earlier. The buildings there were by Nash's chief assistant, James Pennethorne, to whom he assigned his practice in 1834. Beyond these lies St. Katherine's Hospital (1826-28), designed by Ambrose Poynter in the Gothic style.

On this eastern side, in Nash's original plan, a pleasure palace or *guingette* was to be built; on the site opposite where it was to stand is Cumberland Terrace, Nash's most palatial gesture, begun in 1826 to the designs of James Thompson. For all the failure of details that critics have identified there, the effect of the great Ionic blocks at Cumberland Terrace is magnificent. As in so much else of Nash's work, all was designed for effect, and the houses of Cumberland Terrace do not look like houses. Critics also did not like the use of stucco in so many of the buildings in Regent's Park; for all the criticism, though, the

Regent's Park, Cumberland Terrace: 1826

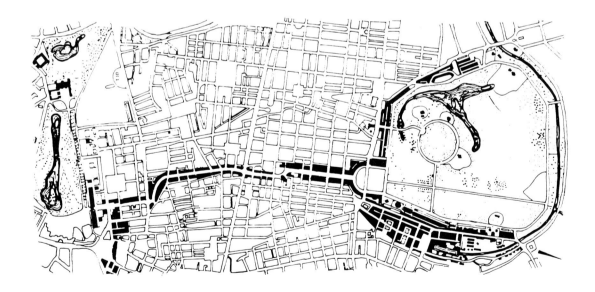

German Prince Pükler-Muskau noted in 1826 that the whole was, as he put it, "worthy of one of the capitals of the world."

Beyond the Park lies Regent Street, another of Nash's remarkable architectural ideas. Regent Street winds down to Piccadilly, with the changes of line being marked, at the upper end, by the Church of All Souls, Langham Place, and toward Piccadilly, by the curving front of the Quadrant. Only a stretch of this part of Nash's plan has survived, in Suffolk Street just east of Lower Regent Street. The destruction began there in 1900 under the hand of Richard Norman Shaw with his building of the Piccadilly Hotel. The rest was the work of Reginald Blomfield in the 1920s and 1930s and his rebuilding of the Quadrant. These disruptions of Nash's plan have been strongly criticized, but despite the destruction, the pattern can still be seen that inspired Pückler-Muskau to speak of the "peculiar beauty of the new street ... though broad, it does not run in straight lines, but makes occasional curves which break its uniformity."

—DAVID CAST

ROYAL FESTIVAL HALL
London, England

1951. Architect: London County Council Architects' Department (under Leslie Martin). **1963-64:** Extension built; **Architect:** Hubert Bennett.

Publications

MARTIN, LESLIE: "Design of the Royal Festival Hall." *Journal of the Royal Institute of British Architects* (April 1952).

McKEAN, JOHN: "The Royal Festival Hall: Master of Building." *Architects' Journal* 11 (October 1991).

McKEAN, JOHN: *The Royal Festival Hall.* London, 1992.

RICHARDS, J. M.: "The Royal Festival Hall." *Architectural Review* (special issue, June 1951).

WILLIAMS-ELLIS, CLOUGH, et al.: *The Royal Festival Hall.* London, 1951.

*

The outstanding British building of the postwar period, the Royal Festival Hall is Britain's greatest monument to modernism. It has had immensely heavy use—40 million visitors in 40 years. It was partially built at immense speed in 1951. Neglected amidst an eyesore of rubble when a new far right government stamped out the Festival of Britain amidst which the building stood, and withheld finance for its completion, it was then disfigured by the construction of an extension in 1964. It has been much knocked about physically, and used as a political football in the 1980s kicked between socialist local government (who built it for the people of London) and reactionary central government (who commandeered it while abolishing London's city government).

And yet, while its character has grown with its scars and weatherbeating, the Festival Hall's initial strength of character, integrity and charm has withstood all vicissitudes. It remains immensely popular among the general public, among a notoriously fashion-swayed and critical design profession, and among its professional users. Such a claim can be made of few public buildings from the mid-20th century, and of very few built amidst such postwar privation and within such tight constraints. That is modernism at its best.

The festival to celebrate the centenary of that which produced the Crystal Palace gave London County Council (LCC) the opportunity to build a much-needed new concert hall after World War II. The building was authorized in autumn 1948, and had to be open on 3 June 1951.

The LCC architect Robert Matthew immediately appointed Leslie Martin to run the project; Martin brought in Peter Moro, who made up the design team with the cream of his wartime students. In a context completely lacking in prestige building of any sort, this young team worked with frantic excitement against an ineluctable deadline on a unique project for Britain.

Martin very quickly produced a strong *parti*: the foyer landscape and associated restaurants would occupy the site, forested with slender trees to support the auditorium centrally over it, within a volume of surrounding galleries and stairs. It was to

Royal Festival Hall, river facade: London, England, 1951

Royal Festival Hall, lounge

be an "egg in a box"—the egg made of two separated concrete skins for acoustic privacy, the box an envelope of space within a light, largely glazed screen. Moro's team aimed first to clarify Martin's central concept as they filled out the detailed design, and second to achieve richness by exploiting the decorative potential of each essential element.

The mid-century, when this hall was germinating, was the moment when scientific method took a grip on architectural practice. Research, analysis, organization and disinterested skill rather than architectural sensibility, it was argued, would produce the almost inevitable result.

The designers of the Royal Festival Hall had a far stronger and richer view of their role than that. Martin, "the father of British Rationalism" (according to Reyner Banham), argued "that science can produce the facts but that art must show us the way in which they can be used." That was almost exactly the formulation of Berthold Lubetkin, Britain's one great prewar immigrant modernist, with whom Moro had worked and to whom he remained close. The Royal Festival Hall has been called the finest tribute to Lubetkin's modernist art; it is much more successfully modernist than the neighboring Royal National Theatre by Denys Lasdun—whom the critic William J. R. Curtis oddly has noted as being the only true successor of Lubetkin.

The key to the Festival Hall's remarkable fast-track completion on time was learned from wartime logistic programming and control procedures—the contract process could not have been achieved before the war even if the building form could have been designed then.

The key to the building's intrinsic strength is the unusual and dynamic unity between the formal central idea (the *parti pris* in Beaux-Arts terms) and the detailed working out at all scales: it is not (like much fine Beaux-Arts work) just a good idea decorated. There is integration between Martin's intellectual skeleton and its fleshing out by an equally rigorous exploitation of actual possibilities. The building has an immediate charm, it attracts foot, hand and eye as one promenades throughout; it pleases the ear as one attends to music.

The acoustic design, based on science, was a test-bed for leading-edge ideas of that moment. But the result was too sharp and dry (an initial reverberation time of 1.5 seconds was later lengthened to about 1.8 seconds with electronic-assisted resonance). Today we see that the rectangular "shoebox" shape was right, that the long section was reasonable, but that the seating capacity, at more than 3,000, was far too high. This demand forced the cross-section to be much too wide, and almost eliminated that acoustic intimacy which depends on side reflections.

The fault was born in that parcel of postwar democratic sensibilities which also produced the Royal Festival Hall's greatness. The times demanded equally good acoustics for every seat in the hall (Festival Hall approaches this better than any hall before and many since). Populist sentiment was imaged in the performance of a Mozart symphony by a small band of 35 virtuosi heard with sparkling clarity by 3,000 (a unique Royal Festival Hall achievement), for if the capacity were less than 2,000 it would seem too exclusive. The whole form of entrance, foyers and refreshment areas is unintimidating, effectively shaping the welcoming hall for a new democratic citizenry.

—JOHN McKEAN

ROYAL HOSPITAL, GREENWICH
London, England

1694: Design proposed. **1698-1707:** Hospital constructed; **Architect:** Christopher Wren (1632-1723). **1704:** Hall dome completed. **1707-12:** Painted hall completed. **1735:** Chapel dome completed; **Architects:**Nicholas Hawksmoor (ca. 1661-1736) and John Vanbrugh (1664-1726).

Publications

CHETTLE, G. H.: *The Queen's House, Greenwich.* London, 1937.
FÜRST, VIKTOR: *The Architecture of Sir Christopher Wren.* London, 1956.
KEITH, W. G.: "The Queen's House, Greenwich." *Journal of the Royal Institute of British Architects* 3rd series, 44 (1937).
LAWRENCE, LESLEY: 'Greece and Rome at Greenwich." *Architectural Review* 109 (1951): 17-24.
LAWRENCE, LESLEY: "The Architects of the Chapel at Greenwich Hospital." *Art Bulletin* 29 (1947): 260-267.
WREN SOCIETY: *Wren Society Papers.* Vol. 6 of 20. London, 1923-43.

*

Although its purpose was to house wounded and infirm navy veterans, the Royal Hospital at Greenwich is Christopher Wren's only executed design expressing his conception of a royal palace, since nothing ever came of his grand plans for Whitehall, Winchester and Hampton Court. Palatial standards for the hospital were established from the beginning by the patronage of the Crown. In 1692 Greenwich Palace, begun in 1662 according to the design of John Webb and only partially completed, was used temporarily to house the wounded from the battle of La Hogue. As a result, William and Mary decided to grant this royal site for a new naval hospital. Although equivalent to Wren's army hospital at Chelsea, it was to outdo it architecturally, Queen Mary having a "fixt Intention for Magnificence," according to Nicholas Hawksmoor's 1728 pamphlet. This desire was appropriate, given the history of the place as well as the proximity of the Queen's House, built from 1616 to 1635 by Inigo Jones. This building, however, proved to be Wren's greatest challenge as he pursued a standard of magnificence borrowed from contemporary French architecture, resulting in a final design that is the flawed, but brilliant, compromise typical of much of his work.

In accordance with the circumstances of its founding, Wren modeled his first design for the hospital, done before October 1694, on the most magnificent palace of his time—Louis XIV's château at Versailles. Wren matched the existing King Charles' block on the opposite side, creating a courtyard opening toward the river, and added successively narrower courtyards to form a receding sequence of three, as at Versailles. The last, however, was formed by curved colonnades that joined to the portico of a central domed vestibule and screened the massive blocks of the hall and chapel on either side of it. Wren had used this dynamic sequence of courtyards centered on a domed vestibule earlier in his design for Winchester Palace. Louis Le Vau's College of the Four Nations, begun in 1662, a riverfront building

Royal Hospital, Greenwich: London, England, 1698-1707

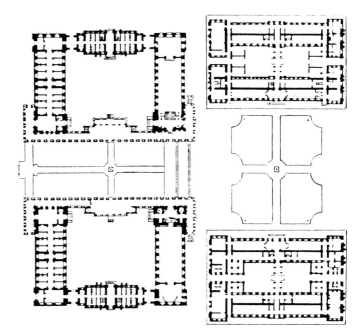

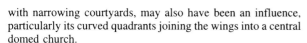

with narrowing courtyards, may also have been an influence, particularly its curved quadrants joining the wings into a central domed church.

The first design, the orientation of the courtyards and the use of curved colonnades as screens, indicates that from the beginning Wren considered the hospital in terms of how it would be viewed from the river, the quickest mode of transportation to Greenwich being by boat. For Wren the issue of "perspective" was of great importance because, in his opinion, beauty was an optical phenomenon. The architect, he wrote in his "Tracts on Architecture," must understand "the principal Views" of the building in terms of angle and distance and design it accordingly. In this first design, however, he blocked out an existing visual element that was given primary importance by Queen Mary and as a result became the major impediment to her requirement for magnificence—the Queen's House. Out of a fondness for the Jones building, Mary called for the preservation of the vista from the Queen's House to the river Thames, represented by a strip of land 115 feet wide running down the center of the site, which in fact remained in the Crown's possession. In terms of the view from the river, this meant that the Queen's House, instead of a new central domed structure, would become the focus of the approach. As such, however, it was a disappointment, for although its north facade was visible and directly faced the river, it was located at such a great distance and at so low an elevation, at the bottom of the park, that it was an extremely weak visual element, overthrowing the magnificent composition Wren had in mind.

In designing the new hospital, Wren was faced with resolving two conflicting architectural values—emulating Louis XIV's château at Versailles, the touchstone of architectural magnificence at that time, and respecting the Queen's House, universally venerated as one of the earliest examples of classical architecture in England. In the next designs he attempted to retain the essence of his initial conception while preserving the Queen's House vista. First he "side-stepped" the vista land, as Kerry Downes describes it, creating two equal, axially organized courtyards to the east which turned their backs toward the Queen's House. Next he tried another approach, attempting to make Jones' building the focus of the entire complex. Seven low-scale blocks, containing dormitories and a chapel or hall, were arranged on either side of the vista land and linked by colonnades to the Queen's House to form an extremely long, narrow courtyard. Neither design incorporated Webb's Greenwich Palace, but, according to Hawksmoor, Queen Mary would not allow its demolition.

In the end Wren incorporated this structure and accepted the reality of visual weakness of the Queen's House, radically reformulating his ideal conception from Versailles. His design from 1698 was based in part on the first scheme with two successive, narrowing courtyards, the largest one formed by duplicating Webb's block. The narrow inner courtyard was derived from the seven-block scheme, but was less than half its length since the site was finally restricted to the land north of what was later to become Romney Road. Continuous colonnades linked only three ranges on each side, built later as three-sided courtyards. At the end of this avenue-like space, at a great distance, was the diminutive Queen's House, standing within a great void created by the introduction of two huge domed vestibules on either side, leading to the hall and chapel.

The idea of punctuating the narrowing and receding courtyards with paired domed structures was used by Wren at Winchester Palace, where he placed chapels crowned by cupolas in the same location. In that case, however, the composition was still resolved by a central domed structure. While the acceptance of a spatial void without an architectural climax down the main axis at Greenwich Hospital may have been simply the result of the unique circumstance of the Queen's House, it may also relate to the use of an infinite vista in the planning of French gardens and Italian cities during that period. In the latter can also be found the use of paired architectural features on either side of the axis, for example, in Carlo Rainaldi's twin domed churches facing the Piazza del Popolo from 1662. Never before, however, had duality rather than centrality within an axial composition been used more boldly than in Wren's building. The magnificence and movement of the ensemble were achieved not—as he had initially proposed—by a gradual crescendo of the wings climaxing in a central dome, but by a series of dramatic contrasts between the two sides and the center. The two huge, soaring vestibules, their various, deeply shadowed shapes crowned by dynamic, diagonally buttressed domes, framed the great void of the sky and beneath it the low, horizontal space of the simple colonnaded avenue, receding and ending in the small, flat facade of the Queen's House. By unexpectedly emphasizing the deficiencies of the Queen's House as a central focus, Wren made it into the monument of the entire ensemble.

With the exception of the overall configuration, the architecture of the main courtyards, and the vigorously simple geometry and decoration of the vestibules and hall, Wren was not involved with the design of the rest of the hospital. His assistant, Nicholas Hawksmoor, played the largest role in completing the courtyards and rear facades of the buildings, followed by a succession of architects over the course of the next 100 years who continued to build according to Wren's final plan. From around 1711, however, Hawksmoor envisioned how other structures might be added to the complex in order to move back in the direction of Wren's first conception. In a series of sketches, he presented elaborate proposals that added a chapel, in some schemes domed and centrally planned, along the main axis in front of the Queen's House. It was to be joined to Wren's building by various complex structures and spaces, one of the most striking being a huge oval forecourt. This attempt to create a grandiose rival to Versailles as well as to St. Peter's in Rome, symbols of the power of absolutism on one hand and Catholicism on the other, was destined to fail in the constitutional, Protestant state of England. Though it may be flawed by continental standards, Wren's hospital at Greenwich is an eloquent expression of the traditional values and cosmopolitan aspirations of that period.

—LYDIA M. SOO

ST. JAMES the LESS, WESTMINSTER
London, England

1858-61: Constructed; **Architect:** George Edmund Street (1824-1881).

Publications

JACKSON, NEIL: "The Un-Englishness of G. E. Street's Church of St. James-the-Less." *Architectural History* 23 (1980): 86-94.

SUMMERSON, JOHN: "Two London Churches." In *Victorian Architecture: Four Studies in Evaluation.* New York, 1970.

Like the much later masterpiece of Ninian Comper, the church of St. Mary at Wellingborough, St. James the Less owes its origin and its architectural excellence to the munificence and aesthetic perception of a family of three sisters who wanted to enrich a "low dirty neighbourhood" (to quote from a contemporary description) with a building embodying, outside and in, the best design and craftsmanship to be had in the country.

Whereas Comper's was the final flowering of the Gothic Revival (St. Mary's was not substantially complete till the 1930s), George Edmund Street's was in many ways a pioneer of that phase of church design, a result of his travels in Spain and France, Germany and Italy, where architects were finding new inspiration and recording details in their sketchbooks with the object of ensuring that their buildings were no mere *pastiche* of real medieval English ones but were far more cosmopolitan in both forms and materials than people had been accustomed to.

St. James the Less is mostly of red brick, inside and out, with black bricks freely used for ornamental bands and in alternating groups in the arches where both colors are molded into arrowhead and other shapes, producing rich effects by simple repetition. For copings, windows and external carvings Street chose a north of England sandstone, but where he wanted special emphasis he did not hesitate to use Scottish granite or even Sicilian marble.

The church is the centerpiece of a carefully ordered group that includes a school and a parish hall, and which was completed after Street's death by his son. Now set within a council estate of the 1960s (itself acclaimed as a pioneer work of its kind), it has only in recent times become sufficiently visible as a whole: the "lily among weeds," as it was described a century earlier, has been revealed. The tower, totally unbuttressed, is virtually detached from the church, linked to it only by a porch designed like one bay of a cloister. In its top stages it blossoms into a great slated spire with four triangular spirelets. In principle this is like Wren's Baroque church towers, which reached upward from plain bases to above the city rooftops, but here the form is decidedly Teutonic, especially in conjunction with the boldly corbelled-out eaves and the splendid twin belfry windows with slate-hung louvres. Over these windows Street introduced strange spandrels of glazed colored tiles, with solid granite spheres as extra accents, for all the world like cannonballs transfixed 80 feet above the ground. (A critic wrote, "the nobs . . . appear ready to fall off, and we really wish they would do so." But Street built to last, and they are still firm.)

The church itself is not large. It did not try to emulate the soaring height of William Butterfield's polychrome tour-de-force All Saints' Margaret Street, two miles away and 12 years older. The plan breaks little with tradition: broad nave and aisles with clerestory, chancel arch, chancel and aisles, and small sacristy. The chancel is short and apse-ended, and its aisles are really double transepts. In addition to the latters' twin gables on each side of the church, there is a third one in the nave clerestory, evidently contrived to light the *Majestas* over the chancel arch. The window tracery, mostly modeled on 13th-century Geometric types, is seen at its best in the boldly buttressed apse.

Facing the apse and the north side of the church are two sets of railings of superb craftsmanship—taut fronds and twirling foliage topped by serried flowery finials, all in iron. A series of delicate carved stone roundels of Old Testament subjects, set in the aisle wall, faces the north railing and adds a special quality to this enclosed space.

The interior, criticized in its day for "a rather crude look," has mellowed to too great an extent, clouding one's judgment

St. James the Less, Westminster: London, England, 1858-61

of the conflicts of materials and colors that were at first complained of. These were particularly thought to detract from the subtler tints of George Frederick Watts' mosaic *Majestas* (which incidentally seems always to have been described as a fresco painting). There are wall facings in tiles of four contrasting plain colors set diagonally, floors with similarly arresting patterns, arcade columns of polished red granite, a boarded nave ceiling with arabesques and golden appliqué stars and medallion portraits based on a Tree of Jesse painted "in vivid color," aisle ceilings busily patterned with stencilwork on their rafters and plaster, and a series of saints in the aisle windows originally by Clayton and Bell but much renewed after war damage. These

outer windows sit happily in marbled wall arcades whose rhythm capriciously ignores the main bay spacing.

Apart from the polychrome tiles and brick, many internal surfaces are encrusted with texts, patterns and figures incised in stone and filled in with black cement. This unusual treatment (called *niello,* though the term really applies to similar work on metal) occurs around the chancel arch and throughout the lower part of the vaulted apse where a series of New Testament women on the north faces Old Testament ones on the south. Further luster is provided by inlays of tiles and Irish marbles and circular marble projections like giant boiled sweets. The apse windows, again by Clayton and Bell, also portray "type and antitype'' themes (i.e., Old and New Testament) in pairs, below and above.

—ANTHONY NEW

ST. JOHN'S, BETHNAL GREEN
London, England

1826-28: Constructed; **Architect:** Sir John Soane (1753-1837). **1870:** Interior remodeled after fire. **1888:** Chancel extended.

Publications

STROUD, DOROTHY: *Sir John Soane, Architect*. London, 1982.

By 1820, Bethnal Green was one of London's poorest and most populous parishes, yet had only one modest church. The Church of England was unable to respond to the growth of cities in late-18th-century England because the building of new churches generally required parliamentary approval. After the Napoleonic Wars, however, the government, under strong pressure from churchmen, found money for church extension, partly as security against revolution. A Church Building Commission was set up in 1818 with a million-pound parliamentary grant, intended to stimulate public subscriptions. The areas in which new churches were most needed, however, were often too poor to raise funds, and were sometimes controlled by interests hostile to the Church of England. Thus the Radical Bethnal Green vestry declared that it could neither support a new church nor provide a site.

As one of the three Crown architects, John Soane had been consulted by the government about designs for the new churches before the legislation was introduced. He prepared two designs that he estimated at not less than £30,000, a sum far too large for the available resources. But the commissioners in any case decided to leave it to the parishes to choose designs for themselves. The lack of local support in Bethnal Green, however,

St. John, Bethnal Green: London, England, 1826-28

obliged the commissioners to act. Some six years after their original decision to build in that parish, they purchased a well-chosen site for £880 and appointed Soane to design the church.

Soane had two other London commissioners' churches to his credit, Holy Trinity St. Marylebone (a wealthy parish) and St. Peter Walworth in a growing southern suburb. St. John's bears a family resemblance to these, but was the cheapest of the three, the contract being taken at £15,999, which was, nevertheless, above the average for commissioners' churches of that period. This was partly accounted for by groined basement vaults and lead roofs. In securing the superior quality of workmanship that Soane constantly sought, he had the assistance of an able, experienced contractor, Robert Streather, who completed the carcass in 11 months.

The design of the west end, visible the length of the Bethnal Green Road, shows how a great architect could achieve an effective composition under the pressure of financial stringency. Soane took the somewhat awkward neoclassical church formula of a temple end with columned portico and steeple riding the pediment, and transcended it in an ultimate exercise in Soanic reductionism. In place of a portico (already at Walworth reduced to a recessed screen of four columns) are doubled pilasters on either side the central door, separated by narrow, full-height recesses containing the flanking doors; windows fill the outer compartments of the flat front; instead of a pediment, there is merely a blocking course, but the vertical line of the pilasters is continued into an attic over the center; above, a square tower with corner piers is surmounted by a pepper-pot bell-turret (a tower like those of the two earlier churches having fallen victim to cost-cutting, though Soane himself offered £100 toward the cost). This neatly triangulated composition recalls in its basic elements John Vanbrugh's Kitchen Court Gate and Tower at

St. Martin-in-the-Fields, with Trafalgar Square: London, England, 1722-26

Blenheim, though it is more immediately a reworking of Soane's Dulwich College Art Gallery Mausoleum (and early scheme for an entrance)—itself designed at a period when, according to John Summerson, Soane was strongly influenced by Vanbrugh. The original east end, replaced by a chancel in 1888, also had a Vanbrughian character.

The Portland stone pilasters offer a bold contrast to the yellow stock-brick walling. Within, a high vestibule, the full width of the church, is articulated by narrow arches demarcating the line of nave and aisles, forming an impressive, characteristically Soanic feature, with a hint of the sublime. Internally the church contains galleries supported on Doric columns and very shallow transverse segmental arches; originally, segmental arches formed an arcade above the gallery fronts, suggesting Gothic principles, though in classical form, an idea that fascinated Soane; these with the roof and windows were altered in the 1870s.

—M. H. PORT

ST. MARTIN-IN-THE-FIELDS
London, England

1722-26. **Architect:** James Gibbs (1682-1754).

Publications

ESDAILE, K. A.: *St. Martin-in-the-Fields, New and Old.* London, 1944.
LITTLE, BRYAN: *The Life and Work of James Gibbs.* London, 1955.
McMASTER, J.: *St. Martin-in-the-Fields.* London, 1916.
WHIFFEN, MARCUS: "The Progeny of St. Martin-in-the-Fields." *Architectural Review* 100 (July 1946).

*

The Parish Church of St. Martin-in-the-Fields took its name from its site in the fields which lay between the City of London and Westminster. It was originally a medieval building. The medieval tower was rebuilt, and a cupola installed, in the course of the 17th century. Christopher Wren, who was a parishioner at the time, designed a combined parish library and school for the church in 1685.

By the end of the 17th century the church was much decayed, and in 1708 it was described as "low and ordinary." In the early months of 1720 an Act of Parliament was passed for the rebuilding of the church at the charge of the inhabitants of the parish, many of whom were wealthy and included George I as a church warden. (The organ which the king gave to the new church is now at Wotton under Edge in Gloucestershire.) Commissioners were appointed to carry out the work.

James Gibbs submitted several schemes for the reconstruction to the commissioners, which included a steeple comparable to steeples by Wren in the City of London. Gibbs was finally chosen as the architect, over John James, and work began in 1722. Gibbs had submitted two designs for a circular church, which were rejected for reasons of expense. He also put in six alternative designs for the steeple, four of them calling for a

St. Martin-in-the-Fields

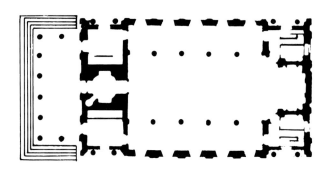

short spire like the one actually built. One of Gibbs' designs included a four-column Ionic portico, but the portico actually approved used the Corinthian order and had six columns.

The new church was finished and consecrated in October 1726. The date and the royal arms are on the pediment and on the architrave. The words "Jacobo Gibbs Architecto" are also on the architrave, in small lettering. The body of the church and the steeple were not finished with the urns of the accepted design, possibly to curtail the expenses of the reconstruction.

St. Martin's, originally hemmed in by other buildings, was greatly enhanced by the creation of John Nash's Trafalgar Square to the southwest in the 19th century. The combination of a western tower with a "Wrennish" steeple and a six-column Corinthian portico has been criticized. The steeple seems to sit heavily on the sloping roof, but in fact its lower structure rests securely on the ground. The steeple itself is a splendid composition, recalling some of Wren's more elaborate steeples. It starts with a square stage with Ionic pilasters. The next stage, which contains the clock, is more fanciful, and has urns at the corners. An octagonal lantern with Corinthian half columns is set above it. The steeple ends with a graceful short spire.

Unlike the broadly similar All Saints' Church at Derby, which Gibbs rebuilt in 1723^25, the interior of St. Martin's has galleries. Its columns are Corinthian, while those at Derby are Roman Doric. The nave has an elliptical rather than a semicircular ceiling, for acoustical reasons. The aisles have saucer domes. The interior stuccowork was by Giuseppe Artari and Giovanni Bagutti. The font of 1689 was retained from the earlier church. The 12 bells were recast by Rudhall of Gloucester. Gibbs' fine bust by Michael Rysbrack is now in the Victoria and Albert Museum.

The sanctuary, to comply with the liturgical requirements of 18th-century Anglicanism, was always to have been short, and

St. Martin's, as a new church on a completely cleared site, formed a pattern for completely new churches in its own time. It also set a pattern for many new churches in England, for example at Gainsborough, St. Paul's at Birmingham, and Christ Church at Bristol, and also St. George's in Dublin. St. John's in Waterloo Road, a Greek Revival church south of the Thames, is also much in debt to the design of St. Martin's.

The influence of St. Martin's is also very apparent in colonial and early Federal America. Gibbs' *Book of Architecture,* an architectural pattern book containing designs of entire buildings and of decorative elements, soon reached America. John Ariss of Virginia visited England in Gibbs' lifetime, and returned to Virginia with copies of Gibbs' books, helping to spread his influence. Several churches on the Eastern Seaboard are clearly influenced by the design of St. Martin-in-the-Fields. Among these are St. Michael's Church in Charleston, South Carolina; Christ Church in Philadelphia, Pennsylvania; Christ Church in Cambridge, Massachusetts; and Center Church in New Haven, Connecticut.

—BRYAN LITTLE

ST. MARY-LE-BOW
London, England

1671-80. Architect: Christopher Wren (1632-1723).

Publications

DOWNES, KERRY: *Christopher Wren.* London, 1971.
DOWNES, KERRY: *The Architecture of Wren.* London, 1982.
ELMES, J.: *Memoirs of Christopher Wren.* London, 1823.
FÜRST, VIKTOR: *The Architecture of Sir Christopher Wren.* London, 1956.
WEBB, GEOFFREY: *Wren.* 1937.
WHINNEY, MARGARET: *Wren.* 1971.

*

In rebuilding London after the Great Fire of 1666, Christopher Wren was faced with the challenge of inventing a new form of church architecture, responding to the liturgical needs of the Anglican church as well as the new classical standards of beauty of the Restoration period. Although the Reformation had taken place well over a century before, very few new churches had

St. Mary-le-Bow: London, England, 1671-80

been constructed, the Gothic parish churches being just adequate enough for the Protestant congregational form of service. For the approximately 50 new city churches, however, Wren sought to correct their manifest deficiencies and, at the same time, to deal with restricted and irregular sites, addressing two separate issues: planning of the interior space and the design of the tower. For both he created several type solutions which, using ancient models, were in the classical style. In terms of its planning St. Mary-le-Bow can be considered a characteristic example; in terms of its tower and spire it can be considered a masterpiece.

Most of the larger city churches, including St. Mary-le-Bow, were given the traditional medieval form of the three-aisle basilica with adjoining tower. The Gothic church, however, with its long, narrow and dark nave, wide side aisles opening to chapels, and altar standing in a remote chancel, was altered to allow clear sight and hearing and thereby full participation of the worshippers in the service of the prayer book. The members of the congregation sat in a broad, brightly lit nave and in galleries over narrow side aisles, their views unobstructed by the widely spaced columns. At the end of the nave stood the altar, which shared its place of prominence with the pulpit and reading desk, these three elements representing the important parts of the liturgy, the Communion service, the sermon and the scripture readings.

Many of these elements and arrangements were developed in two earlier Protestant churches that Wren knew: the French Protestant "Temple" at Charenton near Paris (1623) by Salomon de Brosse and St. Paul's Covent Garden (1630-31) by Inigo Jones. Both were simple rectilinear volumes, based on a nave with side aisles, expressed on the exterior as classical Roman temples. Moreover, both were based on the classical model of Vitruvius' Basilica at Fano, a secular Roman prototype with early Christian connections. Specifically, its plan proportions of 1:2 and use of galleries above the aisles, as described in Vitruvius' treatise, were adopted in the later buildings. Wren probably had this model in mind when he designed five bay aisles with galleries above, as at Fano, in his basilican churches. The one exception, however, was St. Mary-le-Bow, which, according to *Parentalia,* was based on the *Templum Pacis,* that is, the Basilica of Maxentius, which was illustrated by both Sebastiano Serlio and Andrea Palladio. Wren used the same arrangement of a wide three-bay nave with narrow side aisles, but added galleries above. Transverse barrel vaults rise over the aisles in accordance with his model, but instead of groin vaults, an elliptical barrel vault, pierced by clerestory windows, covers the nave. As in the *Templum,* there are Corinthian columns, in this case engaged to the piers of the arcade, that support impost blocks at a level lower than the keystones of the aisle arches.

Despite these similarities, the model is difficult to recognize due to Wren's characteristic use of historical precedent only as a point of departure, altering it beyond recognition to suit the site and functional needs. Reflecting the particular nature of the religion, for the gathering together of the congregation, focusing its attention not on a single point, but on the altar, pulpit and reading desk, at St. Mary-le-Bow Wren gave the longitudinal orientation of the basilican plan greater centrality. A transverse axis was created by a slight widening of the middle intercolumniation in the nave arcade, not noticeable in plan, but quite evident spatially due to the juxtaposition of the elliptical arch of the central intercolumniation with the flanking semicircular arches. The ellipse, a dynamic form with both a longitudinal and centralized character which Wren used on occasion, is repeated in the nave vault and in the oval windows, creating an overall unity. While Wren continued to work with

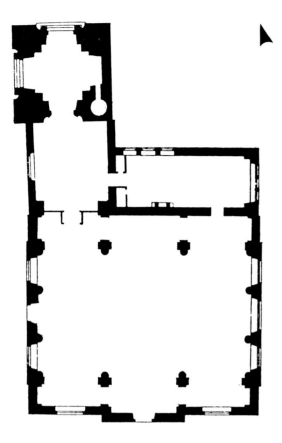

the basilican plan, producing several magnificent examples in St. James, Piccadilly, and St. Clement Danes, the tendency toward centrality that distorted the plan of St. Mary-le-Bow led him to develop other spatial solutions, the most logical being that of the domed church, such as St. Stephen, Walbrook.

Each of the city churches had to be provided with a tower, to serve as a belfry and very often as an entry vestibule, and, most important, to create for the particular church a visual symbol above the cramped city. After completing the church at St. Mary-le-Bow, Wren turned his attention to this problem and created his prototypical solution for a classical tower. Since the beginning of the Renaissance, architects had been frustrated by the absence of classical examples and scant ancient descriptions of monuments such as the Tower of the Winds in Athens and the Tower of Babylon. Leon Battista Alberti had been the first to suggest the idea of a tower as a series of square and round temples, alternating and diminishing as they reached the top. This concept had been tested by Wren in his Warrant Design for St. Paul's in 1675, where he crowned the dome with an awkward pagoda-like spire of octagonal stages.

At St. Mary-le-Bow, Wren vastly improved on this solution by combining Alberti's classical idea with the overall form of the traditional Gothic tower, square in plan, with corner pinnacles and a tapering spire. The main body of the tower is divided into lower, middle and upper stages by stringcourses, the upper stage expressed as a square temple with paired pilasters at the corners and a single arched opening on each side. Above rises the steeple, formed by separate classical elements, gradually decreasing in size: a round tempietto, a square one, and finally an obelisk. As a result, the spire as a whole has a Gothic profile, a quality reinforced by Wren's revival of the Gothic "bows" of the original 15th century tower—the four flying buttresses that supported a short spire, forming a "corona"—as a decorative motif. Instead of pinnacles at the corners of the square

tower, there are sets of four bows, scrolls or volutes leaning on one another, echoing the original "corona," which lead the eye up to the round tempietto. This structure is crowned by a ring of bows that rise to support the smaller square tempietto, which in turn bears up pairs of bows leaning on each face of the base of the obelisk. Visually the columns and volutes form continuous lines and allow a smooth visual transition from one stage to the next, all converging along the edges of the obelisk to unite at its apex.

Wren translated each part of the Gothic tower at St. Mary-le-Bow into an element of ancient architecture, so that as a total composition it achieved the harmonious forms and proportions of the classic, as well as the soaring lightness of Gothic. The potency of his first monumental tower solution was confirmed in the highly original derivatives found among his later churches' steeples. The plan and tower types represented by St. Mary-le-Bow, however, are among several other unique solutions created by Wren for a church architecture, which reflected more directly than ever before the substance and spirit of Anglican worship.

—LYDIA M. SOO

ST. MARY WOOLNOTH
London, England

1716-27: Constructed; **Architect:** Nicholas Hawksmoor (1661-1736) **1875:** Interior altered; **Architect:** William Butterfield (1814-1900). **1897-ca. 1905:** Train station constructed underneath church.

Publications

BILL, E. G. W. (compiler): *The Queen Anne Churches: A Catalogue of the Papers in Lambeth Palace Library of the Commission for Building Fifty New Churches in London and Westminster, 1711-1759.* London, 1979.

COLVIN, H. M. (editor): *The History of the King's Works, 1660-1782.* London, 1976.

DOWNES, KERRY: *Hawksmoor.* London, 1959.

GOODHART-RENDEL, H. S.: *Nicholas Hawksmoor.* London, 1924.

In the city of London St. Mary Woolnoth is a rarity—a classical church not by Christopher Wren. Though its predecessor was within the area ravaged by the Great Fire of 1666, it was able to be patched up, and had lasted in an increasingly precarious state up to the time of Nicholas Hawksmoor's rebuilding (1716-27). William Butterfield altered the interior in 1875, sweeping away galleries and box pews and moving the pulpit to a less commanding position. Thirty years later the church narrowly escaped demolition when the site was wanted for Bank underground railway station. Fortunately, it proved possible to underpin it with a massive steel framework, so the only losses were the greater part of the crypt and a small area of the forecourt. The "tube" entrances, tucked in at the sides, are at the time of writing being changed again to allow the arrival of another railway tunnel from the Docklands area.

Instead of a traditional square-on-plan western tower (which, seen end-on from the complex intersection of roads outside the Royal Exchange and Mansion House, might have asserted itself

St. Mary Woolnoth: London, England, 1716-27

at the expense of the church behind), Hawksmoor created a wide rectangular structure which is both a tower and a screen facade, making its ground stage a narthex. This has a commanding central doorway and subsidiary entrances at both ends, but the end ones were lost in the railway alterations. Hawksmoor never saw the building in its present setting, for it was shrouded with houses to the east and south.

The lower part of the screen, heavily rusticated, has sometimes been criticized for a rather too-forbidding, fortress-like appearance at variance with the welcoming effect expected of a church. Halfway up it divides into two separate twin turrets, so subtly that no one has ever really decided if the church has one tower or two. The transitional story, the actual belfry, is tall and temple-like with Corinthian columns all around.

Behind the tower (or towers) the church itself is slightly less symmetrical and much less conventional than it first seems. Originally the north front to Lombard Street was more important than the south. In it are three roundheaded recesses in heavily rusticated surrounds, each with its own cornice set on flanking Ionic columns. They are pure architectural embellishment, for windows there would be superfluous and would let in street noise. Above them continues the same boldly modillioned main cornice that girdles the tower, capped by a balustrade, which is nearly out of sight from the narrow street. At pavement level there is a line of flat-arched openings into the former crypt. Unfortunately, it is the south front of which passers-by have been more aware since King William Street was driven through toward London Bridge early in the 19th century, and there (because in his time it was hidden) Hawksmoor had economized with much plainer windows—themselves now largely concealed by shops and by comparatively modern vestries and other ancillary rooms.

After the powerful exterior, a bastion of calm above the scurrying traffic, the inside comes as a surprise to anyone neither prepared for its height nor fully aware of Hawksmoor's ingenuity with spaces and volumes. The plan, the smallest and least complex of his six London churches, is to all intents and purposes a square within a bigger square (leaving small squares at the four corners), the inner one being raised high above the outer by means of a clerestory of giant semicircular windows. Below these windows, broken only by a (modern) royal coat-of-arms on the east side, is a rich entablature supported at each corner by no less than three Corinthian columns. Their bases, now exposed, were originally hidden by high box pews.

As well as the tall pews, the interior needs to be imagined with a gallery on three sides, running between the columns at a comfortable height above the main floor. The doors to it still exist in the rear corners, reached from stone stairs that also led downward to the crypt. When Butterfield removed it (except for a short length around the organ above the entrance lobby) he salvaged the dark front panels with their tapered pilasters and had them refixed to the inner face of the outer walls, where they now hang rather forlornly. High over the outer aisle or ambulatory is a heavily modeled plaster ceiling; higher still above the inner square is a contrasting flat ceiling, now painted an arresting sky-blue with encrusted stars.

St. Mary Woolnoth's woodwork is not in the class of the work of Grinling Gibbons, Jonathan Maine or the other incredibly skilled carvers who had enriched Wren's churches a generation earlier. Nevertheless, the bulging canopied pulpit and the reredos with its barley-sugar columns, texts and pelmet-like canopy are splendid objects. The latter stands in a bay which projects beyond the outer square, ever so slightly so as not to spoil the two-way symmetry.

—ANTHONY NEW

ST. PANCRAS CHURCH
London, England

1819-22. Architects: William Inwood (ca. 1771-1843) and Henry William Inwood (1794-1843).

Publications

STURGIS, RUSSELL: *A Dictionary of Architecture and Building.* London, 1902.
SUMMERSON, JOHN: *Victorian Architecture: Four Studies in Evaluation.* New York, 1970.
WHITE, NORVAL: *The Architecture Book.* New York, 1976.

St. Pancras is the most important of the churches constructed in the first wave of church extension in 19th-century England, "*the* parish church *par excellence* of Regency England," according to John Summerson.

The parish of St. Pancras, on the outskirts of London, measuring about four miles north to south by one mile east to west, had grown from a thinly inhabited farming district in the 1770s to a populous town by 1811, with more than 46,000 inhabitants largely concentrated in its southern quarter. It had an old church holding about 150 persons, and a chapel of similar size toward its northern end. Many of the inhabitants were Roman Catholic, and large numbers were poor.

When a new church was proposed in 1812, there was strong opposition, and it was not until 1816 that the church authorities obtained an act of parliament for building a new church and a chapel at a cost of up to £40,000, financed by an annual rate of four pence in the pound on the parish. A site was purchased early in 1818, and a competition for designs launched in January. A month later, 30 designs had been received, and the prizes were awarded to William Inwood and his son, Henry William Inwood (£100); Francis O. Bedford (£50); and Thomas Rickman (£25). Bedford and Rickman were subsequently both to build a number of "Commissioners" churches under the million-pound government grant of 1818, but at St. Pancras it was a local practice that triumphed, giving rise to accusations of favoritism in the competition judging.

The Greek style was at the height of its popularity for town churches at that time, and St. Pancras gave a fashionable gloss to the Anglican model that had been devised by Christopher Wren and perfected by James Gibbs: a temple body with columned portico, the essential steeple that was the hallmark of the Established Church riding somewhat uncomfortably athwart the pedimental roof. But the designs that won the competition were not precisely those executed. With the commission secure, the younger Inwood went to Athens "for the express purpose of making drawings from the Erechtheum and the Temple of the Winds to complete the design" (*The Portfolio,* 1823), not returning until after the construction of the foundations. The contract of 29 April 1819, with Isaac Thomas Seabrook, builder, was for £42,253, but he was ultimately paid £59,556 for the building work, and an additional £6,249 was laid out for terracotta. Including the site (£6,695), Lee has calculated the total cost from surviving accounts at £86,181; from this may be deducted £3,580 recovered in taxes paid, but interest on borrowings resulted in additional charges, so that the final expenditure was about £90,000.

This was far and away the most expensive church of the early 19th century in Great Britain, but it stands as one of the finest works of the Greek Revival. H. W. Inwood brought back

St. Pancras Church: London, England, 1819-22

St. Pancras Church, caryatid porch

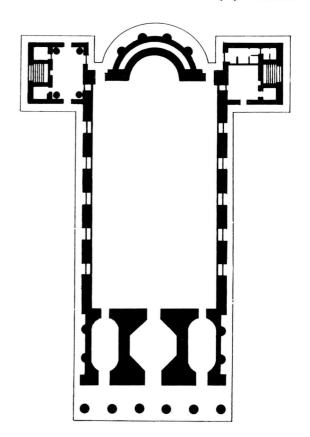

casts from Athens of the ornament of the Erechtheion, which ensured the accurate reproduction of detail, as in the bases and capitals of the scagliola columns of the apse, from the Temple of Minerva Polias. His greatest success was in his adaptation of the Athenian Tower of the Winds for a steeple; he copied Gibbs' device at St. Martin-in-the-Fields of pairs of columns recessed in the first bay of the side elevations to convey that the tower does not "ride" on the pitched roof: an attic story, behind the pediment of the portico, stresses the solidity of the structure from which rises the unusually massive tower. Inwood displayed there a sure sense of proportion and scale, and created a massing of forms that is outstandingly successful, as compared, for example, with Francis Bedford's work at Waterloo Church.

An addition to the competition design was the northeast and southeast features imitated from the southern "caryatid" tribune of the Erechtheion; they extend beyond the end wall of the main building (perhaps modeled on the temple's northern tribune). The caryatids were copied in terra-cotta by Charles Rossi (formerly a sculptor for the Coade factory) from the specimen among the Elgin Marbles, placed in the British Museum in 1816. The twin buildings serve as vestries, as well as providing external entrance to burial vaults: hence the modification of the caryatids to hold reversed torches. Rossi was also responsible for the terra-cotta of the Ionic portico and west doors, likewise imitated from the Erechtheion. The two ranges of windows in the side walls express the galleried interior; the upper windows, like the doors, taper upward.

Internally, the church is a great hall 117 feet by 60 feet; with an apsidal east end for the altar, and a flat ceiling and galleries supported on columns said to be copied from the Elgin Marbles, the church was well suited to the contemporary forms of worship dominated by prayer and preaching. Construction was by traditional techniques: walls of brickwork with timber bond, and timber framing for the roof.

"The queen of early 19-century churches" (Summerson), St. Pancras shows how effectively an architect of limited capacity working within a traditional form could, given adequate funds, reinterpret it in the light of his on-the-spot study of ancient Greek temples.

—M. H. PORT

ST. PANCRAS STATION AND HOTEL
London, England

1863-67: Train shed constructed; **Architect:** W. H. Barlow (1812-1902). **1865-71:** Hotel and station block constructed; **Architect:** Sir George Gilbert Scott (1811-1878).

Publications

BETJEMAN, JOHN: *London's Historic Railway Stations*. London, 1972.
BIDDLE, G.: *Victorian Stations: Railway Stations in England and Wales 1830-1913*. Newton Abbot, England, 1973.
HOFMANN, WERNER, and KULTERMANN, UDO: *Modern Architecture in Color*. New York, 1970.
MEEKS, CARROLL L. V.: *The Railroad Station: An Architectural History*. New Haven, Connecticut, 1956.

St. Pancras Station and Hotel: London, England, 1865-71

St. Pancras Station, train shed interior: 1863-67

To properly evaluate the architectural achievement at St. Pancras Station, we must understand the nature of the design problem set by the railway station, in general terms. By the second half of the 19th century, when St. Pancras was conceived and built, major railway terminals had become complex, multifunctional buildings, whose design presented a unique combination of problems and challenges, in terms of professional procedure, structure, planning and symbolic expression.

Both architects and engineers were professionally involved in the design of the railway station. The degree of architectural unity achieved in the final building depended to a large extent upon the integration of their separate skills, through active cooperation, or at least mutual understanding. Railway engineers laid out the increasingly intricate system of tracks and platforms, which it was then the structural engineer's responsibility to enclose within a vast, well-lit and ventilated train shed, roofed over with broad fireproof spans with a minimum of obstructive intermediate supports: in St. Pancras, by means of an unprecedented single-span arched structure. Upon the architectural design of the complex depended its convenience in daily use, and the appearance it presented to the street.

The functional layout of the plan determined its efficiency. This necessitated the organization of complex circulation paths: to ease the contrary flows of large numbers of incoming and departing passengers and accompanying friends, to give access to administrative and technical staff, and to facilitate the handling of baggage and freight. In St. Pancras this involved not only masses of pedestrians, but horse-drawn cabs and heavy carts, all converging without conflict or accident upon the access points to the trains. Add to this the ancilliary supervisory and administrative offices, the ticket offices, waiting rooms and

public service areas, and technical and maintenance facilities, and a problem emerges of unprecedented planning complexity. But that was not all: it had become standard custom in many major London stations, including St. Pancras (but not neighboring King's Cross, which partly explains the simplicity of its facade), to incorporate, as an integral part of the station complex, a large hotel and restaurant facility, itself a considerable design challenge.

Finally, there was the question of architectural expression, that is the appropriate public face which the railway station was to present toward the city. St. Pancras was set within a cluster of terminal stations around London's heart, competition was intense, and the station was seen as the physical expression of the importance of each railway company. This was the particular area of responsibility of the architect, and it was one of almost intractable difficulty, for he was confronted by a paradox, an inbuilt conflict between progress and conservatism. The duality, nowhere more poignantly in evidence than in St. Pancras, was the need to express both the spirit of progress inherent in the advanced technology of the railways, and the stability and dependability of sound, conservative management. Each symbolic message had its own appropriate architectural language. The problem was their reconciliation and synthesis.

In all of these aspects, the design of St. Pancras Station is remarkably successful. The soaring arches of the single-span iron-and-glass roof, designed by Barlow and Ordish, is a structural achievement of the highest order: the first major station without intermediate supports. Less dramatic, but not less impressive, is the fact that the entire station area, with its tremendous load of trains, tracks and people, is a structural platform carried on columns, a floor above street level. The handling of the complex circulation patterns is exemplary, not only in the separation of entrance and exit, with a bypass road leading to the ticket offices, but in the incorporation of a boldly curved vehicular ramp leading up to the raised station level. Interceding between the train shed and the street is George Gilbert Scott's Midland Hotel, with its rich neo-Gothic detailing, and the romantic silhouette of its towers and spires. The metaphor was that of the cathedral, and the architectural language, so familiar to the Victorian public, was evocative of the most venerable of institutions. The entrance portico to the hotel, at street level, is suitably impressive, yet remains within the measure of human scale. Higher up the ramp, the arched entrance to the station proper, boldly piercing the hotel facade, is much grander, appropriately scaled to vehicular traffic, and a prelude to the vast train shed itself, a symphony of structure, steam and slanting rays of light. The facade of the hotel responds to the curved sweep of the ramp, implying in its dynamism the turbulent movement within, a 19th-century prevision of the futurism of Antonio Sant'Elia. The inner facade of the hotel faces toward the station, but is separated visually and acoustically by the glazed screen of the great arch, across an articulating low roof-lit link.

There is the danger of a schizoid scheme here: eclectic and reminiscent without, all forward-looking and modern within. Yet, as has already been suggested, the first element of synthesis exists in the dynamism of the street facade, where if historicism is dominant, then modernism is emergent. This is subtly reinforced by the sympathetic resonance between Scott's Gothicism and the repetitive pointed arches of Barlow's train shed. Finally, the perimeter walls, which embrace the entire shed at platform level and constitute the immediate environment of its users, insert the architecture of the main facade—its materials, textures, colors and details—into the very fabric of the station, a reassuring assertion of human scale and enduring values where it is most needed, to mute the station's "shock of the new."

—GILBERT HERBERT

ST. PAUL'S CATHEDRAL
London, England

1666: Old St. Paul's destroyed by fire. **1672-73:** Foundations for new church dug. **1675-1710:** Construction; **Architect:** Sir Christopher Wren (1632-1723).

Publications

LANG, J.: *Rebuilding of St. Paul's.* Oxford, 1956.
LYNTON, N.: "A Wren Drawing for St. Paul's." *Burlington Magazine* (February 1955).
POLEY, ARTHUR F. E.: *St. Paul's Cathedral, London: Measured, Drawn and Described.* 2nd ed. London, 1932.
SUMMERSON, JOHN: "The Mind of Wren." In *Heavenly Mansions and Other Essays on Architecture.* London, 1949.
SUMMERSON, JOHN: "The Penultimate Design for St. Paul's." *Burlington Magazine* 103 (1961): 83-89.
WREN SOCIETY: Vols. 13-16 with building accounts of St. Paul's.

The design of St. Paul's Cathedral occupied Christopher Wren from the start of his architectural career, when he became involved with the repairs of the medieval fabric in 1661, until a few years before his retirement, when the new building was completed in 1710. As a result of the long-term, personal attention he gave to this important commission, the process of its design is an illuminating demonstration of his search for a valid architectural language for Restoration England, where tradition was affirmed by the reestablishment of the Stuart monarchy and the Anglican Church, but at the same time challenged by the revolution taking place in the realm of science.

In 1666 Wren produced his first scheme for St. Paul's, known as the Pre-Fire Design, involving repairs and alterations to the medieval Latin-cross church. At that time the building was a wreck from the abuse of weather, time and the Cromwellian soldiers who had used it as a stable. Wren's proposal included the recasing of the interior of the Romanesque nave and transepts in "a good Roman Manner," as he stated in his report, in the same way that Inigo Jones had treated the exterior walls during the 1630s, when he had also added the monumental Corinthian portico. The 13th-century Gothic choir was to remain, but the "heap of deformities"—the Romanesque crossing with its leaning tower caused by a subsiding pier and makeshift bracing arches which obscured the interior space—was to be replaced completely by "a spacious Dome or rotunda with a Cupolo or Hemispherical Roof." In this design, four massive piers occupying the first bays of the nave, transepts and choir supported large arches that carried the high drum of the dome, a two-shell structure with a slightly pointed inner masonry dome and an even taller outer timber one, the whole crowned by an openwork pineapple- or pinecone-shaped metal spire. The inspiration for Wren's idea was the domed church of the Sorbonne by Jacques LeMercier, built from 1635, a building that had deeply impressed him during a recent visit to Paris. Although Wren's design came to nothing after the Great Fire destroyed the old cathedral, the two ideas it contained never left his mind—the classical, domed crossing found in the latest monuments in France and Italy, representing the modernity and greatness of those countries, and the medieval nave of Old St. Paul's, representing English religious and architectural traditions.

Wren's first design for the new building, the First Model, finished in 1670, was an awkward reformulation of these elements. It consisted of two connected structures in the classical style, a long barrel-vaulted nave where the side aisles were transformed into external loggias, and a domed space with three porticoes that served as the vestibule to the nave. The unusual character of this scheme was recognized and criticized by some as being too unlike "the old Gothic Form of Cathedral Churches" and by others as "not stately enough," according to the *Parentalia.* As a result, "in order to find what might satisfy the World, the Surveyor drew several Sketches merely for Discourse-sake. . . ."

The Greek Cross Design of 1672 and the Great Model, designed in 1673 and built in 1673-74, were classical, achieving the stateliness that was lacking earlier. Both were based on the same centrally planned, domed concept, with the four equal arms linked by concave quadrants and articulated by Corinthian pilasters resting on a massive base and supporting an entablature and attic. In the Great Model, however, the aisle spaces were domed rather than cross-vaulted, and a large, freestanding portico and domed vestibule were added to the body of the church. Both schemes had virtually the same dome over the crossing—a double-shell structure with a melon-shaped outer dome on a colonnaded drum, the two joined by buttresses with reentrant curves. Wren derived his designs from St. Peter's in Rome,

St. Paul's Cathedral: London, England, 1675-1710

St. Paul's Cathedral, nave view east

especially the centrally planned schemes of Bramante, Michelangelo and Antonio da Sangallo the Younger, the latter including a domed vestibule that was echoed in the Great Model. These sources for the planning and image of St. Paul's were clearly recognizable to the public, but the connotations were mixed. On one hand the Greek Cross Design and the Great Model meant popery—the domed, centralized classical composition being derived from the monument of the Catholic Church—but on the other hand they meant the New Science based on reason rather than faith, the abstract geometry and the biaxial symmetry expressing not liturgical needs, but universal, natural laws.

Neither image was acceptable to the Anglican clergy, who immediately criticized the Great Model as being "not enough of a Cathedral-fashion." In response Wren produced a scheme in 1675 in the "cathedral form," the Warrant Design. This was a Latin-cross scheme modeled on Old St. Paul's as it had been before the Fire, a classicized Gothic building. On the exterior Wren replicated Jones' "quasi-Tuscan" ornament—plain arched windows separated by Romanesque buttresses treated as broad flat pilasters, which he crowned with pinnacles in the form of stepped pyramids. On the west he created a close version of Jones' giant Corinthian portico standing before a two-story facade where the high nave, with pediment and three arched windows, was joined to the low side aisles by scrolls.

Wren continued the theme begun by Jones in other features of the Warrant Design by using ancient models to classicize the traditional massing and proportions of a Gothic cathedral. The section of the high nave and low side aisles, covered with cross-vaults, was based on the Basilica of Maxentius. At the crossing Wren provided the traditional tower and spire, but placed them on a domed space—an idea he could not abandon—modeled after the Pantheon. Moreover, the tower was treated

as a drum articulated by paired columns and crowned by a two-shell dome, taller on the exterior, as in the Pre-Fire Design. The spire was given a series of stepped stages, giving it a pagoda-like form. By using ancient models, reducing the masses into geometrical and horizontal parts, and applying classical ornament, Wren was able to add classical geometry and proportion to a Gothic conception. Despite the complete absence of Gothic ornament, enough of the Gothic quality remained for the design to be accepted as an English and a Protestant cathedral, and given a warrant in May 1675. Two months later, however, the final "Definitive" design was established, a combination of the Warrant Design and the Great Model in the classical style, although changes continued until the completion of the building.

The sequence of schemes for St. Paul's demonstrates Wren's empirical, almost arbitrary approach to design. His understanding of the origins and particular characteristics of classical and Gothic styles led him to consider them products of custom rather than nature. Therefore he could find nothing authoritative in precedent and did not hesitate to produce classical and Gothic schemes as society might demand them, and to modify and combine Gothic and classical elements without regard to their traditional function or meaning. Yet at the same time he believed in the eternal validity of the classical orders, due to their origin in nature and necessity, and thought the true cause of beauty to be a geometrical appearance, a phenomenon which, like all things in nature, could only be understood based on the perception of the senses. In every design, therefore, he used classical ornament and infused the forms, though they might be Gothic in composition, with geometry.

The consequences of Wren's empirical understanding of architecture are best demonstrated in the final design of St. Paul's. Because the dome of the Great Model was placed over the crossing of the Warrant Design, the crossing piers had to be

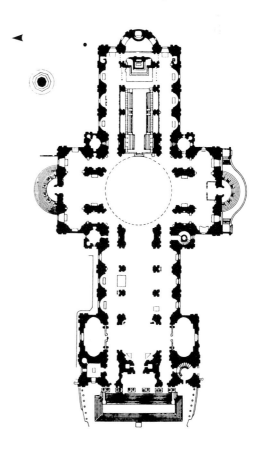

thickened and spaced unequally around the center, the diagonal segmental arches having a lesser span. By inscribing a larger arch above each of them, however, a visual equality was created with the adjacent openings. Greater centralization around the crossing was achieved by using an equal number of bays to the choir and nave, and by creating a wider, visually separate entry complex composed of a large vestibule with side chapels and fronted by a two-story portico with coupled columns, pediment and flanking towers. To create a more massive base for the great dome, a screen wall was placed above the exterior walls, which concealed the high nave and lower side aisles and the flying buttresses that supported the nave vaults. Whereas on the exterior the building appeared to be a simple two-story block articulated by coupled pilasters, on the interior the nave was formed by a tall arcade, with imposts of smaller pilasters, articulated by a giant order of Corinthian pilasters that rose to support saucer-domes—all features first proposed in the Great Model and Pre-Fire Design. The great dome, which appears as a single hemispherical form, was completed as a three-shell structure, a brilliant solution comprised of a structural brick cone hidden within the inner masonry shell and the outer lead-encased timber shell, both nonstructural and hemispherical in appearance and each with their own decorative systems.

Throughout the final design of St. Paul's there is a disunity between the exterior and interior form and decoration, as well as between visual image and actual structure. This was not due to lack of skill as an architect, but rather to Wren's background as a natural philosopher and mathematician, leading him to understand architecture as a phenomenon where, as in nature, the outward appearance often hid the underlying real order. Unlike natural phenomena, however, architecture was a product of society, molded by custom, but needing a standard of good taste—for Wren, a classical standard. As the result of a compromise between native medieval tradition and continental classicism, reconciled by creating a disunity between appearances and reality, the final design of St. Paul's is a clear reflection of social values and scientific philosophy in late-17th-century England.

—LYDIA M. SOO

ST. STEPHEN WALBROOK
London, England

1672-79: Constructed; **Architect:** Sir Christopher Wren (1632-1723). **1686:** Tower completed. **1709-12:** Spire completed. **1830-34:** Interior repaired, restored. **1941:** Dome mostly destroyed. **1951-2:** Dome reconstructed. **1951-54:** Interior repaired, restored.

Publications

DOWNES, KERRY: *Christopher Wren.* London, 1971.
DOWNES, KERRY: *The Architecture of Wren.* London, 1982.
ELMES, J.: *Memoirs of Christopher Wren.* London, 1823.
FÜRST, VIKTOR: *The Architecture of Sir Christopher Wren.* London, 1956.
SUMMERSON, JOHN: *Sir Christopher Wren.* 1953.
WEBB, GEOFFREY: *Wren.* 1937.
WHINNEY, MARGARET: *Wren.* 1971.

St. Stephen Walbrook represents the fulfillment of a design conception that had been on Christopher Wren's mind since his visit to Paris in 1665-66—the domed church. Initially sketched in his pre-Fire design for St. Paul's Cathedral, and then a recurrent theme in his schemes for the new cathedral after the Great Fire of 1666, it was only at St. Stephen that the idea found its most perfect and sophisticated manifestation. In contrast to the cathedral and the other city churches, the design of the former limited by its huge masonry-domed structure, and of the latter by their restricted sites and budgets, St. Stephen was a small building with a wooden roof located on an open site, designed with the full support of a wealthy parish. As a result of these factors, Wren was able to use his skills as a mathematician to their fullest. With "great care and extraordinary pains," according to the churchwardens, he achieved in the spatial design of St. Stephen a clarity and complexity of geometry, as well as a unity of form and need, that he sought, but was not always able to achieve, in all of his churches.

In contrast to the powerful mass of the tower that gives St. Stephen its dominating exterior expression, there is a simple rectilinear volume of space within, containing 16 thin columns that rise to support ceilings, vaults and a dome. In their geometrical arrangement, however, these elements are manipulated subtly to produce varying spatial effects that reflect church liturgy. The grid of columns within the rectangle forms a longitudinal organization of five aisles, the basilican plan found in many of Wren's other city churches, with the wider central aisle creating an appropriate focus on the altar. Since the congregation also turned its attention toward the pulpit and reading desk during the service, the axis of the nave is counterbalanced by a transept equal in width formed within the grid to result in a Latin-cross organization. Originally, this configuration was made even clearer by box-like pews that rose to the height of the column pedestals. Overhead there are barrel vaults over each arm of the cross, reflecting the biaxiality of the plan, although the nave and chancel vaults are cut by clerestory windows to form groin vaults that reemphasize the longitudinal axis.

Equally dominant and functionally logical is the centralized spatial organization, the result of a crossing designed as a regular geometrical volume almost as wide as the entire church. In plan it is simultaneously a three-by-three-bay square, an octagon with eight equal sides and, in conjunction with the adjacent spaces, a Greek cross. Volumetrically the form of a square is further defined at its corners by the entablatures resting on the surrounding columns and flat ceilings above the corner bays. But at the same time, the fact that the space is also octagonal in plan is made clear by the eight equal arches that rest on the entablatures—four opening directly into the nave, chancel and transept vaults, resulting in the concurrent rendering of a Greek cross, and the four in between springing diagonally over the square corners defined by the entablatures to reaffirm the octagon. Finally, the eight arches form pendentives that generate another geometry—the circle of the shallow coffered dome, crowned by a lantern.

The multiple readings of the spatial geometry at St. Stephen, long recognized by historians and critics, are made possible through the treatment of structural elements as thin members so they can all be perceived simultaneously within the open space. The Corinthian columns support a grid of entablatures, creating a horizontal lattice surrounding the edges of the central space that supports the flat ceilings in the corners of the church, the barrel vaults over the nave, altar and transepts, and the eight arches of the crossing. Because they spring from one projecting entablature angle to the next, and are illuminated from behind by large clerestory windows, the arches appear to be thin, rib-like members with light-filled voids in between, suspended over

St. Stephen Walbrook, Bell Tower: London, England, 1686

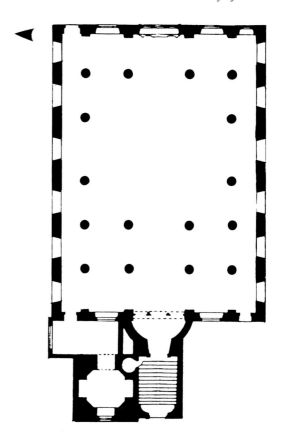

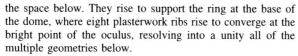
St. Stephen Walbrook: 1672-79

the space below. They rise to support the ring at the base of the dome, where eight plasterwork ribs rise to converge at the bright point of the oculus, resolving into a unity all of the multiple geometries below.

As the result of the wood structure and, more, the particular way in which that structure is articulated, the interior of St. Stephen has a very lightweight as well as light-filled quality. Wren not only combined the Greek trabeated system of columns and entablatures with the Roman arcuated system of vaults, but went further to define their constituent parts, creating a linearity of structure and luminosity of space associated with Gothic architecture. This underlining of the various geometries of the space makes it possible to have the simultaneous readings which give the church its richness and dynamism.

The immediate impact of St. Stephen can be found in Wren's designs for St. Paul's, but beyond his own practice, its influence seems to have been felt only much later outside of England. Wren's son in *Parentalia* (1750) stated that the church, "so little known among us, is famous all over Europe." Legend has it that not until his 1714-15 visit to Rome, after greatly admiring an engraving of what he presumed was a local monument, did Lord Burlington learn, with much astonishment and some shame, of St. Stephen. While designing the Church of Ste. Geneviève (Panthéon) from 1755, the French architect Jacques-Germain Soufflot studied Wren's St. Paul's and, it is very likely, St. Stephen, creating in his own interior a similar unity of classical and Gothic. In the final analysis, however, St. Stephen represents a rare instance, not often repeated, when circumstances and the ingenuity of a mathematician-turned-architect came together to produce a unique and unified expression of a multiplicity of functional requirements, structural forms and spatial geometries.

—LYDIA M. SOO

SIR JOHN SOANE'S MUSEUM
London, England

1808-09: Extension annexed to the rear of Lincoln's Inn Fields; **Architect:** Sir John Soane (1753-1837). **1812:** Rebuilding of Lincoln's Inn Fields into museum; **Architect:** Sir John Soane. **1813-1814:** Front of museum constructed; **Architect:** Sir John Soane. **1824:** Back of museum constructed; **Architect:** Sir John Soane.

Publications

FEINBERG, SUSAN G.: "The Genesis of Sir John Soane's Museum Idea." *Journal of the Society of Architectural Historians* 43 (October 1984): 225-237.

*

The Soane Museum is one of those exceptional creations of the human mind that can be read at many levels, depending on the age, culture and susceptibilities of the visitor. It is at one and the same time a home, an office, a collection for practical use, a gallery of fine art and antiques, a treasure trove of petty curiosities, a medley of nooks and corners to explore, a piece of old-world London in aspic, an essay in picturesque romanticism, a study in lighting effects and techniques, a cabinet of Masonic secrets, a meditation upon death, a manifesto of advanced Regency taste in interior decoration, and the living embodiment of the most original personality in the history of British architecture. For those in search of a single meaning, a hint offered by Sir John Soane himself in the original museum guidebook is the best clue: "One of the objects I had in view was

Sir John Soane's Museum, breakfast room: London, England, 1812

Sir John Soane's Museum, monument yard

to shew . . . the union and close connection between Painting, Sculpture and Architecture—Music and Poetry.'' The added words seem to imply that what lay in the back of Soane's mind was not just the unity of the arts but their combined emotional power.

Unified, in the architectural sense, is the one thing that the Soane Museum is not. It grew by gradual stages. When Soane first came to Lincoln's Inn Fields in 1792, he was an up-and-coming architect of nearly forty, with a young family and a comfortable but limited inheritance recently acquired through his wife. His experience was growing, he had begun to amass public appointments, and he was just building the first master-piece of his very personal neoclassical style, the Bank Stock Office at the Bank of England. So what Soane built on the enclosed and far-from-rectangular site was an orthodox London town house for his family, with room for an architectural office for himself, his assistants and pupils behind. This was No. 12 Lincoln's Inn Fields, to the left of the present museum entrance.

In due course Soane's practice and office expanded. Since he took his responsibilities as an architectural educator seri-ously, the next stage was to extend the office element at the back, so that he and his staff could have ready access to the books, pictures, casts and other objects which he began to amass, partly for his own pleasure, partly as matter for study. In this way the Soane establishment crept behind No. 13, until in 1812-13 he was able to acquire that house, persuade his neighbors to move into No. 12, rebuild No. 13 and transfer his wife and himself in there. Two years later Mrs. Soane died. From then onward the ensemble was in a more or less constant state of alteration, embellishment or intensification, the element of pri-vate museum and fantasy more and more overlaying that of

home and office. Soane effectively retired in 1832. In the next year he obtained a private Act of Parliament which established a trust to maintain the building and its collections to all intents and purposes unaltered after his death (which occurred in 1837) and to guarantee regular free access. These conditions have been respected since, with minor waivers and variations.

The result is paradoxical—a deeply premeditated memorial to one of the great neoclassicists of Europe, yet one which exhibits not a jot of the symmetry, clarity and grandeur which we expect from neoclassicism. The closest parallel, Antonio Canova's cramped and busy house at Possagno in Italy, is lucidity itself in comparison, and lies close to a vast church which sufficiently represents such principles. In the additive, T-shaped rabbit warren of the Soane Museum it is hard to maintain a sense of direction, let alone axiality. Its intensity, confusion and eclecticism belong to the powerful and always personal romantic tradition in English architecture, the tradition of Strawberry Hill, Blaise Hamlet and Cardiff Castle, rather than to the strain of neoclassicism proper. That is not to say that the museum is a Gothic building in the strict stylistic sense. It comprises Gothic fragments, inside and out, but Soane was never able to take Gothic quite seriously, and in the museum's most Gothic corner, the basement Monk's Parlour or ''Parloir of Padre Giovanni,'' there is an evident attempt at what we now call ''grave humor.'' In terms of style, the building's great feature is its succession of small top-lit or one-side-lit interiors. These gave Soane repeated chances to experiment with the fusion of pared-down styles, structural principles and lighting techniques that had obsessed him since the 1790s. In this respect, the museum foreshadows the work of such ''rationalizing'' Victorian eclectics as William Butterfield and Philip Webb as well as the more indulgent strain of romanticism in Victorian architecture.

The front of the museum at No. 13 Lincoln's Inn Fields is a puzzling enough introduction. It is a stone projection of uneven height, jutting some three feet in front of the line of the terrace. It is designed in Soane's most personal style, incised with nervous, linear patterns, topped with Coade-stone figures and acroteria, and ornamented with four large and arbitrary-seeming Gothic capitals taken from Westminster Hall. As built in 1813-14, it was meant to be the left-hand end of an open-windowed composition destined to stretch eastward and cover the whole of Nos. 13-15 Lincoln's Inn Fields. The openings were filled in with windows in 1824, when Soane also added an extra story behind the level of the frontispiece.

Inside, the front rooms retain a semblance of domesticity, especially on the ground floor. There, the library and dining room offer rare surviving evidence of interior decorative taste in London town houses of the 1820s, the decade of John Nash's Regent's Park terraces and George Basevi's Belgrave Square. The tones are somber but colorful, with polished mahogany and ''Pompeian'' hues predominant. The carpets are rich, and their effect was formerly supplemented by plentiful stained glass, much of it lost after bomb damage in 1941. Soane being Soane, the spatial aesthetic and the detailing are far from typical. Hanging arches, recesses and mirrors are used to confuse the edges of the rooms and increase the sense of extent, while the minimal, linear detailing conveys a certain stringency, set off by the sheer profusion of paintings, sculptures, vases and curios.

The breakfast parlor, behind the staircase, functions as a transitional area between the reception rooms at the front and the office-cum-museum behind. For so small a space, it is one of profound complexity. To supplement the single window facing the monument court to the east, Soane covered the room with a low saucer dome, and brought in extra light not only from the opening at the top but also from half-hidden compartments behind the dome. Little round mirrors are set into the pendentives, the crown of the dome and even the undersurfaces of the arches that support it. In this way Soane contrived both to create an original and "architectural" interior and to bathe his art objects in a flattering mixture of top light and side light. Behind this, the museum proper offers many brilliant examples of the manipulation *in parvo* of space and light, always geared to the function of the room. In the great dome, open from a high toplight down to the "sepulchral chamber" in the basement, Soane assembled the best of his classical fragments in a crowded but simply detailed setting that allows them to display their qualities of relief. In the picture room at the northeastern extremity, an addition of 1824, his inventive genius offered not only appropriate natural lighting for the two Hogarth series, *A Rake's Progress* and *The Election* (the jewels of his picture collection), but also an elaborate system for storing extra paintings on sets of concealed screens which never fail to astonish the visitor.

It is mistaken, however, to interpret the Soane Museum just in a functional or aesthetic manner. It also embodies darker currents of a moral or quasireligious nature. Soane never recovered from the death of his wife in 1815, and the testimonies on display of his affection and grief for her are many. Evidently the perfection of the museum represented for Soane a form of therapy for her loss. It contains copious tokens of the architect's morbidity: a stairwell in the shape of a coffin, many funerary objects and designs ancient and modern, and above all the famous Belzoni Sarcophagus of the Egyptian pharaoh Seti I in the sepulchral chamber. This was excavated in 1817, offered to the British Museum but declined, purchased by Soane for the princely sum of £2,000 in 1824, and installed by him with great pomp as the centerpiece of his collections. Seti I was identified at the time with the hero of *Séthos*, a romantic novel by the Abbé Terrusson which seeks to explain the secrets of ancient Egyptian culture and was greatly prized by Freemasons. Soane was not a Christian, but at some stage he became a keen Freemason. Through Masonic investigation and symbolism, it seems that he hoped to arrive at a deeper understanding of life, culture and death. There can be little doubt that the Belzoni Sarcophagus, along with certain other details of the museum, not least its dramatic contrasts of light and darkness, is meant to have secret, Masonic significance. Here is one layer of meaning which this inexhaustible treasure house has yet to yield up completely.

—ANDREW SAINT

SOMERSET HOUSE
London, England

1776-80: Strand block and central court completed; **Architect:** William Chambers (1723-1796). **1835:** Eastern riverfront extension completed; **Architect:** Robert Smirke (1780-1867). **1856:** Western extension completed.

Publications

PEVSNER, NIKOLAUS: "Old Somerset House." *Architectural Review* (September 1954).

During the 18th century Old Somerset House, the dower house of queen's consort, although used occasionally for visiting royalty or state receptions, had been allowed to decay. Troops were quartered there. In 1771 the newly founded Royal Academy was granted some of the rooms. Finally, in 1774 Lord North, first lord of the Treasury, advised of its poor state, proposed that the palace should be demolished and the site used for building new public offices. North was interested in administrative reform, and the offices responsible for the various taxes were scattered about London in rented houses. The Navy Board, too, was in old and inadequate premises. It was therefore a sensible and economical measure to bring together these various branches of administration in one central situation. There is no obvious precedent for a single "palace of administration" (unless it be the Uffizi in Florence), and the credit for the idea must probably go to North. However, in the debate on the act of Parliament for transferring the palace from the queen, Edmund Burke "pressed for Splendour," and a government surveyor, William Robinson, was accordingly instructed to design "an ornament to the Metropolis." His sudden death gave to the royal architect William Chambers the largest public commission of the century, "an object of national splendour," ultimately costing more than £460,000 and taking 25 years to complete.

Building in Portland stone, Chambers laid out a great quadrangle (courtyard is about 310 by 200 feet) that has been compared to a London square. Skilled in domestic design, Chambers had no experience of the monumental. Externally, the principal facades were the river front high above the unembanked Thames, and the much-narrower Strand front. For the latter, devoted to the Royal Academy and other learned societies, Chambers paid tribute to the river front of the old palace attributed to the admired Inigo Jones: an arcaded ground floor supporting a giant Corinthian order. The keystone masks represent English rivers, symbolizing the country's maritime connections. Chambers also used his knowledge of Paris to effect in the central section, where the attic with statuary and the triple-arched vaulted entry were cribbed from Jacques-Denis Antoine's contemporary Hôtel des Monnaies. The Doric loggia may have been further influenced by that of the Palazzo Farnese in Rome. Chambers' work at Somerset House is scholarly and fastidious, as befits an academy for the Muses, with details from Michelangelo, Palladio and other Italian masters. Within the courtyard are statuary groups symbolizing the offices whose entrances they mark.

The river front is plainer. Its position—40 feet above the water—and length of 550 feet invited treatment in the sublime manner (a tribute to Burke?). A granite embankment raised the building sufficiently to permit a merely gentle slope up to the Strand; water gates on either side of a great central arch, decorated with giant swags, struck a Piranesian note. (The Victorian embankment of the Thames has robbed this of its effect.) The building above, however, was handled with more restraint: the central block, articulated by a central recessed portico, crowned by an insignificant dome, and with pilastered wings of slight protrusion, was linked by Palladian bridges to outer ranges of offices and residences. (John Nash was to handle the same pattern with more panache in his Cumberland Terrace, Regent's Park.) The eastern range remained unbuilt until the site was acquired by King's College, and Robert Smirke completed it in 1835. The long, horizontal lines of the river front were emphasized by the continuous stringcourse and the balustrade interrupted only by the pediments of the two bridges.

Although criticized for its cost when it was being built, Chambers' Somerset House came in the 19th century to be regarded as the beau ideal of government offices, restrained in decoration, being constantly recommended as a pattern for the great blocks

Somerset House: London, England, 1776-80

being erected in Whitehall. James Pennethorne copied the same style in 1857 for new offices for the Inland Revenue immediately to the west—so stretching the river front somewhat uncomfortably to a length of 800 feet. When George Gilbert Scott was criticized for the "expensive style" he had adopted for the Foreign Office (1863-68), he pointed out that "Somerset House is a highly palatial building . . . extremely magnificent." But whatever the style or degree of magnificence, the concept of a concentration of government offices that North introduced at Somerset House was one that the Victorians embraced with fervor.

—M. H. PORT

TOWER OF LONDON
London, England

Ca. 1066: White Tower built. **1250:** Turret constructed; **Mason:** Henry de Reyns (*fl.* 1243-ca. 1253). **1282:** Tower vaulted; **Mason:** Simon Pabenham (*fl.* 1282-1334). **1324-25:** Outer curtain wall rebuilt; **Mason:** Walter of Canterbury (*fl.* 1319-1327). **1335-1337:** Recrenellation and cresting of the wall; **Mason:** William de Ramsey (*fl.* 1323-1349). **1389:** Wharf built; **Masons:** John Westcote (*fl.* 1386-1397), Thomas Crumb (*fl.* 1372-1396), Henry Yeveley (*fl.* 1353-1400). **1532:** St. Thomas's Tower (the Traitors' Gate) re-edified; **Carpenter:** James Nedeham (*fl.* 1514-1544). **1532:** Offices built; **Carpenter:** Thomas

Sheres (*fl.* 1532-1545). **1845:** Waterloo Barracks constructed; **Architect:** Anthony Salvin (1799-1881).

Publications

AINSWORTH, W. H.: *The Tower of London*. London, 1840.
BAYLEY, JOHN: *The History and Antiquities of the Tower of London*. 2 vols. London, 1821.
DIXON, WILLIAM H.: *Her Majesty's Tower*. 4 vols. London, 1869.

*

The ancient citadel of London, one of the major castles of Britain, stands by the Thames within the southeast corner of the Roman city wall. Its nucleus is the keep called the White Tower, which was begun under William I shortly after the Norman Conquest. The fortified ward around this keep was developed by stages until by the 14th century the castle had overlapped the Roman wall line on the east and assumed its present "concentric" layout, with inner and outer curtain walls punctuated by numerous defensive towers—named nowadays after their historical associations or their former uses.

As well as being a fortress, the Tower (the term commonly used in London for the whole castle, not just the keep) was a Royal Palace until the 17th century. Up to the early 19th century the Royal Mint and the Royal Menagerie were housed between the inner and outer curtains; some inner buildings were used as a prison, others as a public-records office, and others again as the country's principal military storehouse. These changes

Tower of London, from southeast: London, England, ca. 1066

Tower of London, Chapel of St. John

of use have gradually eroded the defensive nature of the buildings and reduced their value to the military historian. Their outer show of strength is undeniable but is really little more than a symbol.

The White Tower (originally whitewashed) is comparable in Britain only with the less complete one at Colchester in size and design. It has four floors, each divided into three main compartments. For security the entrance is one story above ground and was always reached by an outside stair. The floor above contains a banqueting hall, the "Sword Room" and the lower part of the Chapel of St. John. Square turrets mark three corners, but the fourth, over the chapel apse, is circular; their curved roofs are 14th-century embellishments. All but one of the windows have been enlarged and altered to a classical character (possibly by Christopher Wren), which hardly enhances the building's air of impregnability.

The chapel, within the keep and yet a complete aisled church in its own right, is early Norman work at its most severe, with groin-vaulted aisles and tunnel-vaulted nave and gallery. The aisles and the gallery both curve around the apse as ambulatories. The arches are unmolded, and the piers are low and cylindrical at floor level, but along the gallery no more than squared-off masonry. Most of the capitals are square, of an elementary double scallop type. Architecturally this is by far the most important part of the Tower.

The main water gate to the river is St. Thomas's Tower, popularly known as Traitors' Gate; it leads directly to Garden Tower in the inner curtain (usually called Bloody Tower through association with the murder of Edward V and his brother).

Following the outer curtain clockwise, the southwest or Byward Tower is connected by a causeway (originally by a drawbridge) to Middle Tower on the city bank of the now dry moat.

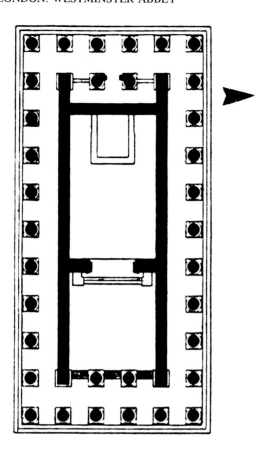

taste, which had earlier acquiesced with the monumental Gothic of the Houses of Parliament, it tried rather too hard to harmonize with the Tower but has long come to be accepted as its permanent companion.

—ANTHONY NEW

WESTMINSTER ABBEY
London, England

Mid-11th century: Original eighth-century church rebuilt. **1245:** Rebuilding begun under Henry III; **Masons:** Henry of Reynes (until ca. 1253), John of Gloucester (until ca. 1261), Robert of Beverley (until ca. 1269), Chapter House built. **1255:** New crossing consisting of transepts, presbytery to the east, one nave bay to the west completed, lower parts of western towers built. **1260s:** Four nave bays rebuilt. **1272:** Tomb, Henry III. **1290:** Tomb, Eleanor of Castile. **Mid-13th century:** Cloister's east and north walk built. **1375:** Rebuilding of remaining nave bays resumed; **Mason:** Henry Yevele. **Mid-14th century:** Cloister completed, flying buttresses added to the Chapter House. **1400:** Tomb built for Richard II. **1422:** Tomb built for Henry V. **1503-07:** Original Lady's Chapel rebuilt and called Henry VII's Chapel. **1509:** Tomb built for Henry VII. **1587:** Tomb built for Mary, Queen of Scots. **1603:** Tomb built for Elizabeth I. **1735-40:** Western towers completed; **Architect:** Nicholas Hawksmoor. **19th century:** Chapter House restored; **Architect:** George Gilbert Scott.

Publications

BRANNER, R.: "Westminster Abbey and the French Court Style." *Journal of the Society of Archeological Historians* XXIII (1964): 3-18.

COTTINGHAM, L. N.: *Plans . . . of the Magnificent Chapel of King Henry the Seventh, at Westminster Abbey Church.* 2 vols. London, 1822-29.

HARVEY, J. H.: *Henry Yevele, c.1320 to 1400. The Life of an English Architect.* London, 1944.

SCOTT, GEORGE GILBERT: *Gleanings from Westminster Abbey.* 2nd ed. rev. Oxford, 1863.

*

Traces of Roman occupation have been found in the vicinity of Westminster Abbey, but stories of a Christian church built in 184 A.D. and made into a temple of Apollo during Diocletian's persecution are probably a product of some medieval monk's fertile imagination. More likely is a seventh-century foundation date, the site being then an island in the Thames marshes called Thorney. The abbey's real history begins with its refoundation under the Benedictine order by Saint Dunstan in about 959 and its rebuilding under Edward the Confessor in the mid-11th century. The church figures in the Bayeux Tapestry, as William the Conqueror was crowned in the abbey in 1066. Architecturally, nothing earlier than the late 11th century survives above ground (there is walling of that date in, for example, the monastic dorter undercroft), but the oldest work of significance was that begun in 1245 on the church itself, which over a period of two and a half centuries was gradually rebuilt.

The high quality of design and workmanship at Westminster stems from royal patronage. But King Henry III was more

---

At the northwest angle is Legge's Mount, a tower rebuilt under Henry VIII, and at the northeast Brass, Mount Battery, a much bigger bastion of the same period. Cradle Tower, one of three other small ones on the riverfront, was a secondary water gate.

The inner curtain consists of a more impressive series of defenses. Just west of Bloody Tower is Queen's (or King's) House, built against the thick wall but showing in contrast on the safe inner side a confidently insubstantial 16th-century timber-framed face. At the southwest angle is Bell Tower, which has some original 12th-century walling mingled with later wooden framing. Beauchamp Tower to its north is of Edward I's period (ca. 1300) and contains numerous graffiti left by prisoners. From there on, the inner wall is slightly earlier (Henry III, mid-12th century), but its towers have been much altered and rebuilt. The principal one on the river side, close to Bloody Tower, is the circular Wakefield Tower of 1221, where the Crown Jewels used to be kept.

Within the northwest angle of the inner wall is the Chapel of St. Peter ad Vincula, an unpretentious Late Gothic building mostly rebuilt in 1512 after a fire. It looks out onto Tower Green, which is bounded on two other sides by purely domestic buildings within the inner curtain, with haphazard gables and chimneys, and overlooked on the fourth by the White Tower.

The remaining buildings within the Tower are of no great architectural importance but contribute handsomely to a hodge-podge that is not unattractive when seen from within the walls but gray and forbidding from without. The biggest is Anthony Salvin's bulky castellated Waterloo Barracks against the north side, a three-story block of 1845 with its own make-believe show of towers and turrets.

The nearby Tower Bridge with its mechanically operated bascules dates only from 1886-94. In accordance with current

Westminster Abbey: London, England, mid-11th century

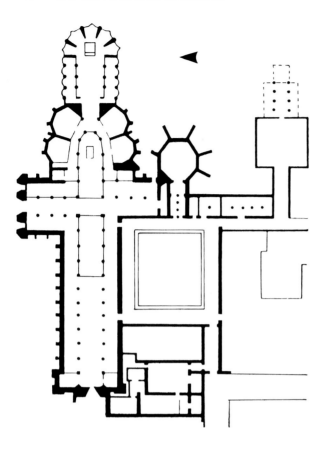

French than English, and his first master designer-mason is believed to have been brought from Reims. That is why the building shows so many French characteristics and indeed many that are derived directly from Reims Cathedral: a very tall clerestory and high vaults, bar-traceried windows of Geometric pattern, big round main columns with four attached shafts, richly molded arches with iron tie-rods, and a radiating chevet of small chapels. Nevertheless, the vaults themselves (the highest medieval ones in Britain) are finished English-fashion with stone ribs at the ridge, and their infilling stones are not parallel to the ridge as they would be in France. Also, the triforium galleries, with double pairs of two-light openings, are more ample than French, and there is lavish use of Purbeck marble, brought a hundred miles or so from Dorset, which is typical of that period in English Gothic design. Materials—and workmen—for the sanctuary pavement came from even further afield; this is so-called Cosmati work, done in 1268 by Roman masons, using Italian porphyry slabs and jasper with marble and glass mosaic in patterns of arches and squares.

The new crossing, consisting of the transepts, presbytery to the east and one nave bay to the west, was complete by 1255; the intended central tower was never built and to this day is represented by a low pyramidal cap. Four more nave bays were rebuilt in the 1260s. For more than a century the remainder of the 12th-century nave bays still stood, and the work of rebuilding, when resumed in 1375, is of special interest in architectural history in that little or no attempt was made—as it would have been almost anywhere else—to incorporate more advanced details of design. The original having been in its day in many respects avant-garde in character, it would have been logical to adopt the Perpendicular style, by then coming into vogue. The work went on in that way until at least 1504, and the later

parts can be distinguished from the original only by the merest subtleties of moldings and minutiae of decoration.

The great eastern chapel, known as Henry VII's, was not part of the original concept; it is as though the designer felt suddenly released from any more need for slavish copying of 13th-century work, and found himself free to indulge in the most daring interpretation of the forms and methods of the ultimate stage of Gothic, beyond which—in retrospect—no further development seems possible—and all still at royal expense. Inside, the contrast of the blacks and white and grays of the architecture with the brilliant colors and metals of heraldic banners, glass and memorials is today as breathtaking as it ever was, though the original window glass is gone. Over it all hangs a vault of paneled stone of the most daring complexity. Above the side aisles it is a true fan vault, that ingenious culmination of medieval English stone roof design which looks like a succession of cantilevered concave cones just touching along the center, yet which in reality spans from wall to wall like any other vault. But here the main roof is an amazing tour-de-force which seems to show off what a fan vault would be like with its intermediate supports removed. The pendants taking the place of columns are actually wedges forming a part of great cusped arches, which are the real bridges from wall to wall. The rest is an intricate system of stone panels, no more than about $3\frac{1}{2}$ inches thick, leaping at all angles from one "bridge" to the next and each one a miracle of the mason's craft. And that is not all; the east end, being polygonal in plan, has its own star-shaped variant on the vault system, different from the remainder yet perfectly in harmony with it.

Outside, the chapel is also faced with paneled stonework, a typically English grid embracing walls and windows, flying buttresses and great polygonal piers that counter their thrusts. What Christopher Wren had called "nice embroidered work" was, alas, refaced in the 18th century with considerable loss of character.

Westminster Abbey's western towers are not, as many people think, wholly medieval, but were completed in 1735-40 by Nicholas Hawksmoor. The lower parts, however, were built with the western parts of the nave, the Geometric motifs of the nave being disciplined to fit into a Perpendicular-style network. Hawksmoor's work is remarkably pure Perpendicular too, though he could not repress the introduction of little scrolly Baroque pediments near the clock faces.

The cloister is unusual in the way it overlaps the south transept, so that part of the east walk is actually within the transept structure. That and the north walk are mid-13th-century and match the Geometric style of the adjoining parts of the nave. The remainder is about a century later, but in contrast with the nave, the designer moved forward to the use of tierceron vaults and Perpendicular tracery.

Off the cloister is the splendid high-roofed chapter house, reached by a vaulted vestibule and stair. It was remarkable in being not only the monastic meeting house but also that of Parliament's House of Commons until 1547. Later it became a public record office, full of galleries and stairs. The 19th-century architect George Gilbert Scott restored it and reopened to view the great four-light Geometric windows which in style and date again match the church. The patterned tiled floor is a remarkable survival, and there are 14th-century wall paintings within a round-headed wall arcade of unique design. The spectacular flying buttresses were 14th-century additions to the 13th-century structure.

Apart from the cloister and chapter house, extensive remains of other monastic rooms and passages still exist, ranging in date from the 11th to the 16th centuries, and intermingled with the buildings of Westminster School. One is the Chapel of the

Westminster Abbey, nave view east

Pyx, which was the king's treasure chamber. The existence of so much that is ancient is due to the fact that Westminster's unique status as the royal coronation and burial church continued after the Reformation; it has its own dean and chapter as though it were a cathedral. But it is one of the anomalies of architectural history that a building so un-English in much of its character has come to be regarded as quintessentially English.

In a description of this kind the monuments present numerous difficulties. To begin with, at Westminster more than in almost any other building, they obscure and confuse the architecture and even in many instances actually mutilate it. Their sheer number defeats a hundredfold any attempt at comprehensive listing; whole books could be, and indeed have been written about them. And, last but not least, many of aesthetic merit are comparative nonentities—and vice-versa.

Central within the main east space of the presbytery is Edward the Confessor's tomb, mid-13th-century, with more Cosmati work. Other royal tombs, all of the richest design and craftsmanship and usually with contemporary effigies, include those of Henry III (1272), Eleanor of Castile (1290), Richard II (1400), Henry V (1422), Henry VII (1509), Mary, Queen of Scots (1587), and Elizabeth I (1603).

In the popular mind, however, it is the clusters of memorials to artists in different fields that are the most celebrated. Many of these are in the south transept, where the so-called Poets' Corner includes the names of many not even buried in the abbey. Statesmen occupy much of the north transept but are extensively commemorated in all parts; the floor slabs in the nave honoring Sir Winston Churchill and the Unknown Warrior of World War I are objects of pilgrimage for many.

Though hardly part of the building, the Stone of Scone is one of its most treasured possessions. It was built into the

coronation chair in 1300-01 following its capture from the Scots, but tales of its previous history and travels are as much a mixture of fact and legend as the early history of Westminster Abbey itself.

—ANTHONY NEW

LONDON ZOO (PENGUIN POOL and GORILLA HOUSE)
London, England

1930s: Construction; **Architect:** Berthold Lubetkin. **1932:** Gorilla House constructed. **1934:** Penguin Pool constructed.

Publications

FRAMPTON, KENNETH, and FUTAGAWA, YUKIO: *Modern Architecture: 1920-1945.* New York, 1983.
WHITE, NORVAL: *The Architecture Book.* New York, 1976.

*

Between the wars Britain remained somewhat isolated from an avant-garde international modernism, which was largely a continental phenomenon. Consequently, response to such progressive movements in architecture was initially cautious, although postwar Britain was to reveal a vastly different picture of enormous commitment to the new architecture serving a new welfare state. With such a background, it is hardly surprising that Britain's most celebrated buildings of the period in the modernist idiom were for animals rather than human beings. However, their existence owes much to enlightened patronage; after 1932 Sir Peter Chalmers Mitchell and his successor, Julian Huxley, as secretaries of the Zoological Society were central to a spate of zoo-building commissions at London, Whipsnade and Dudley which collectively represented a major part of Berthold Lubetkin and Tecton's output during the 1930s.

Lubetkin's first English building was the Gorilla House for London Zoo, commissioned in 1932. The brief was clear; two Congolese gorillas required a habitat with strict control of climate so that jungle conditions could be simulated. Typically, the design followed a program of research into the future inhabitants' habits, a process that was to precede and underpin all of Lubetkin's subsequent work.

The solution was radical, to say the least, particularly when viewed alongside typical zoo buildings of the period. Even by the 1930s, suburban or rural "free range" zoos such as Whipsnade attempted to show animals in environments which reflected their natural habitats as closely as possible, but their pursuit of "naturalism" was rejected by Lubetkin. The whole of this emerging "zoo industry" was seen as part of a burgeoning leisure movement to which Lubetkin responded in the most imaginative fashion. Tecton's zoo buildings in their formal geometry and play of sculptural forms harnessing the latest in reinforced concrete technology were in stark contrast to the "naturalist" norm, but nevertheless were more successful at responding to the needs of the users, both animals and humans.

Following a thorough survey of the climatic and physiological needs of gorillas, Lubetkin's design solution was a radical marriage of Euclidian form and technical virtuosity. The drum-like building was designed to be open in summer when the animals

Penguin Pool, London Zoo: London, England, 1932

could be viewed from outside, but in winter a huge semicylindrical shield slid into position to keep out the severe British climate. A pedestrian bridge on the diameter (also protected from the weather) allowed visitors effectively to share the same space as the gorillas but be separated from them by transparent screens.

The already-well-developed formal language of the gorilla house assumed the status of abstract art at the Penguin Pool (1934) reflecting Lubetkin's formative years in Moscow during the flowering of constructivism. The solution, formalist with its elliptical plan, is at once theatrical, for the whole is reminiscent of a Soviet stage set of 10 years previously, but also in its brilliant exploitation of the interlocking reinforced concrete ramps evokes much of the spirit of constructivist sculpture, particularly the work of Naum Gabo. The ramps, which themselves were to become a symbol of progressive architecture in prewar Britain, were a technical tour-de-force. The young Ove Arup was the engineer responsible for the structural design.

Predictably, the design followed a full program of research into penguins' needs and habits; the ramps, curved poolside promenade and cuboid concrete forms were an eloquent essay in abstract form, a stage set where penguins could strut to the delight of viewers, who were controlled by carefully located openings in the enclosing elliptical reinforced concrete walls. These openings, to develop the theatrical analogy, suggested proscenia framing the activities of the penguins within.

The building embraced delights other than visual; an elliptical plan and hard concrete surfaces provided an excellent acoustic reflector where the curved walls focused the sound of shrieking penguins to most interesting effect. Horizontal canopies, also in reinforced concrete, and supported on slender steel columns,

were arranged to provide shade from the midsummer sun but had a formal role in the composition also, by "balancing" the vertical, curved planar backdrop at the opposite side of the elliptical plan. The whole complex assembly of curved planes, ramps and roofs—and indeed the pool which they in turn framed—were arranged to be looked down upon so that visitors had the equivalent of a gallery view.

Despite the analysis which preceded the design, the pool has prompted criticism from zoological quarters in that it lacks a deep pool facility, thus denying penguins their perceived need for deep water swimming. However, such criticism is leveled with the wisdom of half a century's hindsight and does nothing to diminish the Penguin Pool's central role in the development of modernism in Britain.

In its synthesis of radical ideas in art, architecture and technology, the Penguin Pool rightly became a symbol for progressive architecture in Britain; after World War II architects returned home to practice in peacetime their newfound egalitarian ideals, which a new Labour administration and its welfare state were quick to harness. Theirs was to be a new architecture for "every man," embracing a social dimension denied to Lubetkin in his zoo buildings. Nevertheless, the clear architectural language and the logical design methods which preceded it served as a model for a postwar generation of British architects.

The final recognition of the Penguin Pool's place in British architectural history came in 1987 when, already listed as a building of national historic importance, it was carefully restored to its original pristine form.

—A. PETER FAWCETT

HAMPTON COURT PALACE
Middlesex, England

Early 16th century: Construction of Base Court; construction of Chapel begun. **Late 17th century:** Construction of Fountain Court; **Architect:** Christopher Wren.

Publications

FÜRST, VIKTOR: *The Architecture of Sir Christopher Wren*. London, 1956.

LAW, E.: *History of Hampton Court Palace*. 3 vols. London, 1885-91.

WREN SOCIETY: *Wren Society Papers*. Vol. 4 of 20. London, 1923-43.

*

Hampton Court is one of the greatest of English great houses, no less in its size than in the quality of its architecture and decoration. It falls into two main periods, that of Cardinal Wolsey and Henry VIII (1514-36) and that of Christopher Wren under William and Mary (1689 onward). On a flat site alongside the Thames, to which it is set diagonally, it is surrounded by very extensive landscaped grounds, themselves of some art-historical importance. It consists essentially of three more or less square courts in a line, the first or west (Base Court) being Wolsey's, the east (Fountain Court) Wren's and the middle (Clock Court) a mixture of Wolsey, Henry VIII, Wren and William Kent. Kent became involved in 1732. (It is typical of the changes over two centuries that the earlier emphasis is on the owners' names, the later on the architects'.) Extending along the north side of all three courts is a more haphazard series of service ranges, principally of the Wolsey period.

Wolsey, son of a butcher, achieved riches and power in both politics and the Church to a degree difficult now to comprehend, but surrendered it all to the king only 15 years after commencing his building project with the purchase of the manor of Hampton, and died accused of high treason. By then his private palace was already bigger than François I's great house of Chambord in France. Its most impressive survival is the eight-turreted Great Gatehouse modeled on such British antecedents as the powerful castles of Bodiam and Harlech, and calculated to express a similar sense of defiance—mollified, it is true, by the more domestic color and texture of red brick. Now effectively of three stories, it was originally two floors higher, but even in its present form it mirrors perfectly the personality of its supremely ambitious owner. The moat bridge and the brick wings flanking the gatehouse are due to Henry VIII, but the long utilitarian two-story terraces closing the north side of Outer Green Court were built as soldiers' barracks late in the 17th century.

The Base Court, almost surrounded by modest brick ranges, was for guests and retainers of the cardinal's household. Another gatehouse, in its present form even finer than the Great Gatehouse, leads out on the opposite side. Named after Henry's queen Anne Boleyn, it was nevertheless Wolsey's work too. On the west side it has an oriel window, on the east the famous astronomical clock which gives its name to Clock Court. Made in 1540, this shows, for example, the phases of the moon and the times of high water at London Bridge—in those days matters of great practical importance. At each corner of this gatehouse is an octagonal turret, and on its roof an 18th-century octagonal cupola.

The innumerable tall molded and clustered brick chimneys are a special feature of Hampton Court; all, however, are modern copies. Another feature of great importance is the group of six

Hampton Court Palace, fountain court: Middlesex, England, early 16th century

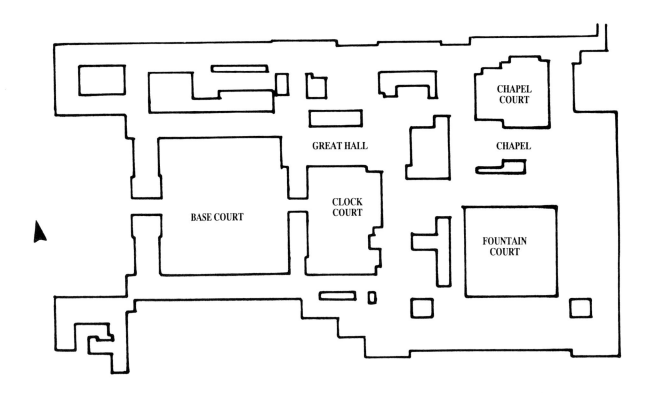

big terra-cotta medallions of Roman emperors made in 1521 by the Italian Giovanni da Maiano. Originally designed for the palace of Whitehall, they are the earliest examples of Italian Renaissance work in England apart from Henry VII's tomb in Westminster Abbey. Two are on each of the main court gateways.

The north side of Clock Court is dominated by the Great Hall (completed by the king), a Perpendicular brick structure high enough to impose itself visually on Base Court, too. It is reached by a broad staircase from Anne Boleyn's Gatehouse. Inside, the outline of its traceried and transomed seven-light end window is echoed in the arches of its splendid hammer-beam roof, and the shapes of the two smaller openings in the gable have their counterparts in wooden traceries high above the tie-beams. Transverse arches link the ends of the projecting hammer-beams on their ornately carved brackets. This is the essentially English type of roof first seen at Westminster Hall a century and a half earlier and thereafter often used for large spans. Like the Forth Bridge and similar much later iron structures, it relies on the cantilevered strength of large supporting brackets. In the side walls five bays have four-light windows with transoms, and the sixth an immensely tall oriel with no fewer than five transoms, lighting the dais. Contemporary Brussels tapestries line the walls beneath the windows. The beer cellars beneath, also with windows to Clock Court, were built by Wolsey; they are 100 feet long.

The Chapel too was begun by Wolsey and completed by Henry. It stands within the denser mass of Tudor buildings toward the northeast corner of the palace, on the same axis as the Great Hall, though that is hardly evident. Like those of some Oxford colleges it has a big antechapel set transversely across the west end. The gallery above that contains the Royal Pew, which is an early 18th-century improvement. So too are

the magnificent wooden reredos with Corinthian columns and segmental pediment carved by Grinling Gibbons, the communion table, the seating and the organ case. Most splendid of all, if a little overwhelming with its giant umbrella-like fans and big carved pendants, is the roof, a superb interpretation in timber of the kind of stone vault at Oxford Cathedral (another Wolsey association) or Henry VII's Chapel at Westminster, but in reality an elaboration of the hammer-beam type.

The south side of Clock Court is closed by a theatrical colonnade of paired Ionic columns by Wren, masking the so-called Wolsey Rooms beyond. Had King William's and Wren's plans all come to fruition those would have been demolished. The rooms' interest lies more in their intimate association with Wolsey than in any architectural merit. However, the upper room called Wolsey's Cabinet has an exquisite Early Renaissance painted ceiling of blue and gold, and an authentic Tudor atmosphere is preserved by old and restored oak paneling.

Against one end of the Great Hall is the Great Watching Chamber. There guards kept watch at the approach to Henry VIII's state rooms, which were demolished during the Wren period but in their time were the most important part of the palace. The chamber has a flat ceiling ornamented with a network of wooden ribs and pendants; beneath are the wine cellars. Communication between the Great Hall and the kitchens was by a servery called the Horn Room. There and in the Watching Chamber more Brussels wall tapestries preserve a 16th-century atmosphere. The Tudor buildings along the north side of the palace are essentially domestic and unassuming, and too many and complex to discuss in detail. From east to west they are ranged around a series of courts of assorted sizes: Chapel Court, Round Kitchen Court, Great Hall Court, Fish Court, Master Carpenter's Court and Lord Chamberlain's Court—associated in that order with worship, food and drink, upkeep, and the

Hampton Court Palace

staff and guests. Serving them all from the north side is Tennis Court Lane. The Tennis Court and some of the other outlying features will be described later.

Wren's principal work is in and around Fountain Court, an apparent square of 11 bays by 12 not on the axis of the Tudor towers and courts, but entered on that axis at one corner. Moreover, it is not itself centered on the external axis, for a yet stronger one had been created to the east by Charles II's landscape gardeners. That was to form the starting line for the vast symmetrical layout of avenues, walks and water created by pupils of André Le Nôtre (of Versailles fame), and is respected by the pedimented central feature of Wren's east elevation. These variations of axis, dictated by the earlier buildings Wren found himself obliged to keep (but which eventually he would have liked to sweep away) are so skillfully managed that they seem, as one walks through from court to court, to be a natural part of the comfortable informality. As in many of his city of London churches, Wren's mathematical genius excelled in adapting and disguising such site awkwardnesses. In any case Hampton Court was never to come near to matching the formal grandeur of the Louvre or Versailles. The splendid figure carving in the east pediment, by the Dane Caius Gabriel Cibber, represents the "Triumph of Hercules over Envy."

All the principal rooms are on the first floor. The king's side was the south, the queen's the north and east, with a linking gallery along the west. To the northeast a small suite allocated to the Prince of Wales (heir to the throne) adjoins the earlier buildings, while at the southwest there is a connection to Wolsey's remaining rooms. In both cases the newer work stands forward of the old, but apart from that it dominates with its white stone and brilliant red brick, contrasting with the mellow

purples and dark reds behind. On the west side there are only two stories; otherwise there are four floors in all, expressed (from the top downward) by square windows, circular ones, tall pedimented ones to the court (and even taller to the gardens), and at ground level windows to the gardens and roundheaded arches inward to the court. There is a certain monotony in all this, and it is not helped by the overweight balustrade. The east front is 23 bays long, and only the seven central ones are strongly emphasized, with Corinthian columns and pilasters and a three-bay pediment; the south front has 25 bays with even less of a central accent, though there each four end bays are brought a few feet forward. Levels are not always what they seem. The floor of the *piano nobile* is below the heads of the Fountain Court arches, thanks to Wren's ingenuity in lowering the cloister vaults behind, while many of the rooms are high enough to extend upward from that story into the next. Moreover, by using painted dummies in place of some of the windows he may be thought to have overstepped the bounds of architectural truthfulness. Though noticeable only by the servants who used them, the top rooms extend back less than half the depth of the range, leaving long, narrow lightwells between.

The interior was badly damaged by fire in the 1980s, but is being restored. Particularly fine are the spacious main staircases, each three-sided with open wells and exquisite wrought-iron balustrades by the French master Jean Tijou. The painted wall and ceiling of the King's Stair by Antonio Verrio depict a gigantic confusion of mythology, religion and martial symbolism. The Queen's Stair is rather less frantic in its decoration; its ceiling is made to look like a dome. The walls of the King's Guard Room, 60 feet long, are patterned with over 3,000 ancient muskets, pistols, swords, helmets and other arms and armour.

The other state rooms—presence chambers, audience chambers, bedrooms, closets, galleries, drawing and dining rooms—contain splendid paneling, tapestries and more Verrio paintings of indifferent quality. Much of the wood carving is again by that supreme master always associated with Wren, Grinling Gibbons. Here and there, however—in the former Music Room for example—the internal design is not by Wren but by his successor, William Kent.

The most remarkable of these principal rooms is the 117-foot-long Great Council Chamber, also called the Cartoon Gallery because it was designed to contain seven large cartoons painted by Raphael and his pupils for tapestries in the Vatican and bought by Charles I. These are now in the Victoria and Albert Museum, but have been replaced with another set of 17th-century tapestries copied from them.

George III refused to live in the palace, and after a period of comparative disuse all but the major rooms were divided into a large number of "grace and favor" apartments by Queen Victoria, their allocation being usually a reward for service to royalty.

Two parks adjoin the palace, both laid out in or just before Wren's time: Home Park to the south and Bushy Park to the east. The latter is outside the scope of this essay. Home Park has a mile-long straight canal. It and two other long, tree-lined avenues converge toward the east front but stop at a big semicircle around the Great Fountain.

Close to the north end of this semicircular water, and lightly connected to the northeast corner of the palace, is the covered Tennis Court, built by Henry VIII for playing "real" or "royal" tennis. With its natural lighting improved by big late-17th century windows, it is as practical as a modern building, without any aesthetic pretensions. Farther away to the north is the famous Maze of high clipped evergreen hedges, first planted in the late 17th century; also there is one surviving Tudor pavilion tower of the former Tilt Yard or tournament ground, along with the Wilderness House, which was the home of the famous landscape gardener Capability Brown, who, while there, did not attempt to alter the layout of the grounds.

On the south are the more intimate gardens: the big Privy Garden stretching toward the river from the king's rooms, the Old Tudor Garden with the Pond or Sunk Garden in the middle, and the tiny recreated Knot Garden. As well as an orangery within the Wren building (beneath the king's rooms), there is a second one built slightly later by him during the time of Queen Anne, a long, unassuming brick structure with very big sash windows—also a vinery with a vine now over 100 feet long planted in 1769. At a little distance from the palace, beyond the Pond Garden, is a little Banqueting House, also by Wren but of battlemented brick out of respect for the Tudor buildings facing it.

There remain to be described a number of important gateways and screens; first the Lion Gates which lead out from near the Maze into Bushy Park and set the axis of its main avenue. Two big square piers with pairs of Doric columns support crouching lions. The delicate iron gates between are probably by Jean Tijou. Close by, at the end of the long Broad Walk which runs along the east front, is the Flower Pot Gate—more attractive than its name implies, for its piers carry graceful leaden figures of boys with baskets of flowers, the work of the Dutch artist John Nost (or Van Ost). At the far end of the Privy Garden is the long curved and angled Tijou screen, which has been called the "most spectacular individual piece of craftsmanship at Hampton Court." Originally made to separate the Fountain Garden from the park beyond, it is thought to have been actually made by a local smith, Huntingdon Shaw.

—ANTHONY NEW

STRAWBERRY HILL, TWICKENHAM
Middlesex, England

1748-54: Eastern part of house constructed; **Architect:** William Robinson (ca. 1720-1775). **1751-61:** Hall, staircase, Holbein Chamber screen, chimney-pieces designed; **Architect:** Richard Bentley (1708-1782). **1754:** Great Parlour and Library constructed; **Architect:** John Chute (1701-1776). **1761-63:** Gallery and round tower constructed; **Architect:** Horace Walpole (1717-1797). **1777:** Beauclerk Tower constructed; **Architect:** James Essex (1722-1784). **1777-97:** Further additions; **Architect:** Horace Walpole. **1790:** Offices constructed; **Architect:** James Wyatt (1747-1813).

Publications

LEWIS, W. S.: *Metropolitan Museum Studies*. New York, 1934-36.

McCARTHY, M.: *The Origins of the Gothic Revival*. New Haven, Connecticut, 1987.

McKINNEY, DAVID D.: "The Castle of My Ancestors: Horace Walpole and Strawberry Hill." *British Journal for Eighteenth-Century Studies* 13, 2 (1990): 199-214.

TOYNBEE, P. (ed.): *Strawberry Hill Accounts . . . from 1747 to 1795*. Oxford, 1927.

*

Despite its small size and its papier-mâché fabric, Strawberry Hill is one of the most significant essays in the Gothic Revival style erected in 18th-century England. Before the property was purchased by Horace Walpole, the house existed as a small cottage known to the residents of Twickenham as Chopp'd Straw Hall. Walpole changed its name to Strawberry Hill and transformed it into a "Gothic castle" during the 50 years between 1747 and 1797.

Walpole was attracted to the house because of its site, and his first improvements to the property involved the development of the garden into a scenic landscape. Statements within his correspondence indicate that he initially chose the Gothic style for the house because the irregular outline created by the use of crenellation and spires would provide a picturesque backdrop for his garden. Despite this interest in the asymmetrical qualities of Gothic, Walpole maintained a basic symmetry on the two garden facades during the first phase of improvements to the house (1750-53), which was not broken until the construction of the gallery and the round tower (1761-63). the facade resulting from the addition of the gallery and tower influenced the design of houses during the picturesque movement of the early 19th century.

In remodeling and expanding Strawberry Hill, Walpole applied the basic tenets of landscape garden design to the improvements within the building. He combined the associative values of the Gothic style with the nationalistic message contained in contemporary gardens like Stowe to establish Strawberry Hill as a Gothic castle that celebrated his family history. Like the routes within 18th-century landscape gardens, path and place were very important to Walpole's plan for Strawberry Hill. The rooms were organized by themes as illustrated by the Holbein chamber, the state bedchamber and Bleauclerc closet. They were placed along a circuit which ran from the outside gate through the house. This circuit provided the visitor with a series of vignettes or prospects that illustrated the links between Walpole's ancestors and English history. The visitor entered the

Strawberry Hill, Twickenham: Middlesex, England, 1748-54

house under the coat of arms indicating Walpole's family lineage. Once inside, one approached the stair through Gothic arches placed to frame the room and to create a perspective view of the hall. Ascending the stair, one passed symbols representative of Walpole heraldic regalia and arrived at the Armoury, which housed the supposed relics of the most illustrious ancestor in the Walpole retinue, Sir Terry Robsart. Relics of notable persons from English history were also displayed throughout Strawberry Hill. These worked in tangent with the Gothic decoration of the house to provide the patina of age that made Walpole's depiction of the past within Strawberry Hill seem plausible.

To enhance the emotional effect of this progression from the exterior to interior and from the present into the past, the house employed light and color in an imaginative way for interior design in the 18th century. The use of stained glass in the windows to color the light, along with the stone and bronze colors in the wallpaper in the stairhall, helped to recreate the ambience of a medieval cathedral. Walpole referred to his attempt to capture this atmosphere as "imprinting the gloomth" of cathedrals upon his house.

Assisting Walpole in the creation of Strawberry Hill were John Chute and Richard Bentley. Together they formed the Committee on Taste. Within the committee, Walpole and Chute served as the archaeologists selecting medieval models for the ornamentation of the house from books on English antiquities. Bentley digested these precedents into designs for the house. The work of the committee continued into the 1760s and expanded to include commissions for Walpole's friends and relations.

During the design for the gallery, Walpole became increasingly dissatisfied with Bentley, and Bentley departed from the committee before the completion of the room. He was replaced briefly by Thomas Pitt, but differences in political alliances made his association with Walpole short-lived. After Pitt, Walpole employed architects on an ad hoc basis.

The design of the gallery also signaled an important change in design for Strawberry Hill. During Bentley's tenure, the Gothic precedents were treated freely in their depiction within the house. After Bentley, Walpole became more concerned with a literal reproduction of the tombs, ceilings and other precedents that he selected for representation within the house. This change resulted in part from a series of "Gothic treks" that Walpole made across England during the 1750s in search of models for his house. As a result of Walpole's first-hand examination of medieval relics, his knowledge of antiquities matured, and he became more concerned with the accurate representation of these items within the design of Strawberry Hill. His knowledge of English art and artifacts was further advanced by his purchase of the manuscripts of the antiquarian George Vertue, which he supplemented and published as *Anecdotes of Painting in England*. This work is important to the Gothic Revival because it contains Walpole's only formal statement on Gothic architecture.

While the essential fabric of Strawberry Hill was completed by 1777, Walpole continued to tinker with the house until his death in 1797. The most significant addition during that period was the construction of the offices by James Wyatt in 1790. During the last years, Walpole intensified the documentation of the house, hiring Edward Edwards and John Carter to provide

Strawberry Hill, Twickenham, gallery interior: 1761-63

pictorial records of the house. He also produced two editions of a *catalogue raisonné* of the house, titled *A Description of Strawberry Hill,* to ensure that the house's place in the Gothic Revival would survive him.

—DAVID D. MCKINNEY

SYON HOUSE, ISLEWORTH
Middlesex, England

1547: House constructed; **Architect:** Edward Seymour. **1762-69:** Interior remodeled; **Architect:** Robert Adam (1728-1792). **1773:** Entrance-screen erected; **Designer:** Robert Adam.

Publications

ADAM, ROBERT and ADAM, JAMES: *The Works in Architecture.* 3 vols. London, 1773-1822.
BOLTON, ARTHUR: *The Architecture of Robert & James Adam.* 2 vol. set. 1922.
ORESKO, ROBERT: *The Works in Architecture of Robert and James Adam.* 1975.
ROWAN, ALISTAIR: *Designs for Castles and Country Villas by Robert & James Adam.* 1985.

*

Robert Adam's redecoration of the interiors of Syon House for Sir Hugh Smithson, duke of Northumberland after 1766,

constitutes one of the grandest conceptions of the neoclassical style in England. Adam's renovation plan reflected the knowledge of ancient art and architecture acquired during his grand tour that extended beyond Italy to Yugoslavia, where, in five weeks with Charles-Louis Clérisseau, he drew and measured the Palace of Diocletian at Split for a publication that appeared in 1764.

At Syon House, built in 1547 by Edward Seymour, Protector Somerset, incorporating parts of a 15th-century Bridgettine monastery, Adam left in place the external shell of the old Tudor house and designed a vast rotunda like that of the Roman Pantheon for the plain central court. In his plan, the combination of geometrical shapes of the round dome, half domes and barrel vaults resembled the juxtaposition of domed and vaulted spaces of Roman *thermae*. Adam completed only the parade rooms on three sides of the court, and, although a temporary dome was erected for a celebration in 1768, the permanent rotunda was not built.

The entry or great hall is nearly a double-cube room. Adam transformed it to resemble the interior of a Roman basilica. A coffered apse at the northern end of the room balances, on the opposite end, a barrel-vaulted, rectangular passage raised above the hall by paired staircases and separated visually by a favorite device of screening columns. The main door and that to the inner court across the short axis Adam framed with projecting triumphal arches, another of his favorite architectural motifs. He surrounded the windows with smaller triumphal arches, whose console supports are reminiscent in their bold style of architectural forms used by Michelangelo, whom Adam admired. In the clerestory, Adam again applied triumphal arches supported by equally bold consoles around the upper windows. And, in his characteristic coordination of floor and ceiling decorations, the large double-x pattern of meander motifs highlighting the black and white marble floor corresponds to a similar design of the ceiling comprising a variety of classical motifs plastered by Joseph Rose.

The antique character of the great hall culminates in its sculptural decoration, including a bronze copy of the Dying Gaul and a plaster cast of the Apollo Belvedere, a statue popular in the 18th century. From this room, which transports the visitor to the ancient past, a set of stairs leads upward, behind the screening columns, across the uneven floors Adam was not permitted to alter, to the anteroom, the brightest at Syon.

The anteroom is yet another evocation of the grandeur of Roman art and architecture admired by Adam, but its brilliant color and lavish materials contrast strongly with the cool, monochromatic great hall. This richness of color results from the materials used, such as Rose's gilded turquoise panels, a brightly colored, floral patterned scagliola floor that conforms with Rose's elegant gilded ceiling, and a series of 12 green columns that both provide color and permitted Adam to simulate a square space in a rectangular room by placing them close to the wall on three sides of the room and at a distance from the wall on the fourth. Of the 12 columns, some are ancient marble shafts dredged from the Tiber River and transported from Rome to Syon House in 1765 by Adam's brother James. The rest are scagliola facsimiles. Adding to the heroic Roman character of the room is a group of gilded statues perched on top of the green columns.

In the dining room, the first he completed at Syon, as in the great hall, Adam used the basilican formula. There, he used gilded white columns to screen apses at either end of the room. And, in this room where he was concerned that the odor of foods could be absorbed by fabrics, Adam kept the decoration simple. His formal gilded white ceiling reflects the similar decoration of the half domes of the apses and the gilded white

Syon House, Isleworth: Middlesex, England, 1547

Syon House, Isleworth, Conservatory

overmantel. Andrea Casali produced a series of chiaroscuro paintings to blend with the antique statuary lining the niches on both sides of the room.

Beyond the dining room is the red drawing room named for its red Spitalfields silk wall covering. In an exquisite ensemble of art and craft, Thomas Moore produced an elaborate, brightly colored carpet that echoes Giambattista Cipriani's painted designs of medallions of classical figures and motifs in the coved ceiling. Adam's attention to all details of his comprehensive design is evident in his inclusion of features such as the door frames inspired by the early Italian Renaissance and mosaics taken from the Roman Baths of Titus for the side tables of this room.

In the long gallery, the last of Adam's interiors reached at Syon, he used a complex scheme of vivid color, painted motifs, classical architectural details, and coordinated floor and ceiling designs to disguise the excessive length of this traditional medieval English room. With these classical forms, Adam transformed a medieval space into a classical, orderly realm. He divided the length into compartments framed by pilasters and decorated by fireplaces, circular niches, unusual temple designs, and paintings of famous personages, including Charlemagne and Northumberland. At the ends of the long room, he created two elegantly decorated small rooms, square and circular, for private use.

Adam's renovated interiors conclude at the end of the long gallery, although he also designed the entrance gate on the London road. Later decorations of the print room, oak passage and west corridor can hardly compete with Adam's rooms and are anticlimactic because it was Adam's synthesis of antique

and Renaissance ornamentation that determined the exquisite character of the interiors of Syon House.

—JOYCE M. DAVIS

HOLKHAM HALL
Norfolk, England

1734-59. Construction; **Architect:** William Kent (ca. 1685-1748). **1854:** Formal terrace added; **Architect:** W. A. Nesfield (1835-88).

Publications

JOURDAIN, MARGARET: *The Work of William Kent*. London and New York, 1948.
LEES-MILNE, JAMES: *Earls of Creation*. 1962.
WITTKOWER, RUDOLF: "Lord Burlington and William Kent." *Architectural Journal* 102, 1945.

*

Holkham, one of the first great English Palladian houses, was constructed on the flat grazing lands of northern Norfolk over a period of 25 years, from 1734 to 1759. The plan, based on

Holkham Hall: Norfolk, England, 1734-65

Andrea Palladio's original unbuilt proposal for the Villa Mocenigo, consists of five pavilions: a large central pavilion, 114 feet by 62 feet, linked at its four corners to four smaller buildings, each 60 feet by 70 feet. The central pavilion is equivalent to the Palladian residential quarters, and indeed it is, at Holkham, a workable residence by itself. The smaller buildings, which in the Italian model would have housed stables and servant quarters, are here used to provide family accommodation (southwest, often called the library wing), guest accommodation (northwest), kitchens (northeast) and chapel, leaving the central pavilion to play the more traditional English role of state apartments—although in this case meant primarily for entertainment and for the display of the owner's superb collection of paintings and ancient statues, rather than for visits from the court. Thus the hierarchy of forms in the Italian Palladian villa comfortably expresses an altogether different set of functions and values in the English Palladian.

Holkham is considered the masterpiece of architect William Kent, but it is certain that Lord Burlington and the earl of Leicester, owner and builder of the house, made significant contributions to the design—as did the Norwich clerk of the works, Matthew Brettingham the Elder. Holkham's chief importance may be its embodiment of the principles advocated by this "Burlington group," which, inspired by Palladio and Inigo Jones, continued ideas already developed by Colen Campbell, especially at nearby Houghton. Strictly Palladian elements are limited in number, and even those are not confined to Palladio's practice: the temple front, the rusticated basement, proportions based upon Vitruvius, the use of the Venetian window. But Holkham, as did Houghton, expressed the new approach that the Burlington group promoted as an alternative, or reaction, to the flamboyant, short-lived English Baroque. This new spirit was to have a long life in Britain and in the American colonies.

Since its completion, Holkham has undergone remarkably little change aside from the addition of a formal terrace to the south (in 1854, by W. A. Nesfield), a Victorian orangery and agricultural outbuildings to the east, and the unfortunate removal of gilded glazing bars in favor of plate glass in all the windows. The important and innovative park design, also by Kent but made more "natural" in later years by Humphry Repton and Capability Brown, provides a bucolic environment for the house, though never dominating it.

The exterior of Holkham is austere: the building material is dun-colored Norfolk brick, and weathered stone dressings add little color or definition; the *piano nobile* and attic stories are smooth and unadorned. The success of the building rests on the play of light and shade on the various forms and on the rustication of the ground-floor level. The south elevation provides the richest variety: the tripartite center block has corner

Holkham Hall

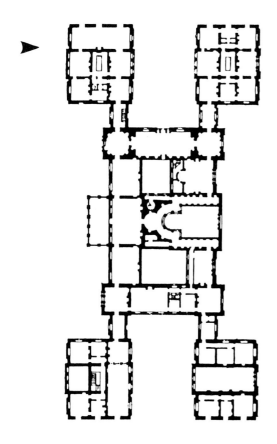

salon there is another Baroque feature—an east/west enfilade which crosses the central block and may be extended into the family and chapel wings to more than 300 feet. In the Baroque, this enfilade would have extended through the state apartments, but here they are a north/south suite of rooms opening into each other and extending along the east side of the center block, returning on the north front to the mezzanine of the great hall.

To the west are a drawing room (on the south) and the principal dining room (on the north), both doubling as passages to a sculpture gallery with tribunes at each end (as at Chiswick, and probably Burlington's idea), the three elements taking the place of the traditional long gallery and extending the full length of the west side of the center block. This compact and practical plan—a development from Colen Campbell—makes it possible for visitors to make a circuit of the public rooms without retracing steps, an innovation which was to find general favor among designers of London town houses.

All of the public rooms are varied in their design, richly decorated and opulently furnished, with much of the furniture being purposely designed by Kent. The salon and drawing room walls are covered with the original Genoese velvet, the gilded ceilings have not required refurbishing in their 200 years; the house retains a sense of freshness which makes it one of the most memorable great houses in Britain.

—KENT C. HURLEY

towers and a pedimented central hexastyle Corinthian temple front on the *piano nobile;* each side pavilion is also tripartite, with a tall central bay encompassing an attic, and lower side bays, all pedimented.

These elements have vertical proportions, but horizontal divisions are provided by an ashlar band extending across the entire 344 feet of the facade above the rustic ground floor; by blind balustrades below the windows; by a stringcourse at sill level; and by cornices at the bases of the pediments. The windows themselves might provide a horizontal accent, but this is avoided by their vertical proportions and varied treatments, and by the pulling forward or pushing back of the various planes of the elements; there are 11 plane surfaces in all. Venetian windows appear in the towers of the central block, with five tall, round-headed windows behind the portico. All of these devices prevent the monotony that can occur on such a long facade. Oddly, there is no external stair from the *piano nobile* to the garden, a serious omission which adds to the sense that the building is isolated from its park.

Holkham is today approached from the north, and the small, inevitably shadowed front door opens directly, in the 18th-century manner, into a great hall that rises the full height of the center block. Eighteen fluted columns of Derbyshire alabaster to the right and left and curving around the apsidal end of the room stand on a windowless ground story faced in the same stone, and support a richly three-dimensional coffered ceiling based on drawings by Inigo Jones. The verticality of the hall is countered by a broad marble staircase that leads upward to the *piano nobile* and the great salon in the center of the south front.

From the door to the salon one can look southward through the portico windows to the distant obelisk erected by Kent in 1730 or back through the window over the main entrance to a monumental column to the north—a Baroque axis. From the

SEATON DELAVAL
Northumberland, England

1721-26: Substantially constructed; **Architect:** Sir John Vanbrugh (1664-1726). **1752:** West wing gutted by fire. **1814-15:** West wing restored; **Architect:** John Dobson (1787-1865). **1822:** Interior of centre block destroyed by fire; later restored under Dobson's direction.

Publications

BEARD, GEOFFREY: *The Work of John Van Brugh.* 1986.
CAMPBELL, COLEN: *Vitruvius Britannicus.* New York, 1967.
DOWNES, KERRY: *English Baroque Architecture.* London, 1966.
DOWNES, KERRY: *Vanbrugh.* London, 1977.
WEBB, G.: *The Complete Works of Sir John Vanbrugh.* vol. IV. London, 1928.

*

A building which expresses the characteristics of its architect more in its ruined state than when originally built must be unique. This is the present situation of Seaton Delaval Hall, designed by John Vanbrugh, substantially erected between 1721 and 1726, and now standing an empty carcass with only the

Seaton Delaval: Northumberland, England, 1721-26

wings in use. Vanbrugh was a Restoration playwright as well as an architect, and overtones of the theater resound in his work.

The sense of theater is apparent when the building suddenly comes into sight from a road which connects a Northumbrian mining village to a nearby coal port. The now-mature landscape forms a curtain of trees which suddenly parts to reveal the house, standing in the grand manner with its dominant central pavilion between the lower supporting elements, linked by arcading to lower wings, which turn forward to enclose the forecourt.

When the great hall is entered directly from the entrance doors at the head of a monumental flight of steps, the theatrical analogy is complete. There is no spatial preparation for the entrance to this room, so there is an immediate visual surprise that the central pavilion is a shell; the intermediate floors and partitions have been removed, giving an uninterrupted view to the underside of the roof with all construction revealed. The design of the original hall, which is itself two stories high, gives a reminder of the grand scale upon which Vanbrugh thought. The upper walls have niches housing statuary and are surmounted by a cornice. As the ceiling of the hall is missing, this architectural essay is cut off at the top of the entablature. The experience is exactly as found in a stage setting, with the space occupied by the original high rooms reproducing the sense of looking up through the set into a fly tower above. The fireplace in this great room seems slightly anachronistic, having overtones of an earlier, almost Jacobean style, especially noticeable in the design of the tapering supports.

In this context Seaton Delaval must be seen as part of the oeuvre. Vanbrugh had a reputation for planning on a magnificent scale, but here there is evidence of a degree of refinement lacking in the gigantism of his earlier work at Blenheim and Castle Howard. True, there is the usual emphasis on a dominant centrality, but on the smaller scale of Seaton Delaval this is quite sophisticated. The stonework to the entrance facade is heavily recessed and framed by linked columns. There is evidence in the remainder of the house that, in this, one of his last major works, he was beginning to appreciate the problem of reconciling his sense of the heroic with necessary domestic arrangements. Externally, Vanbrugh's usual sense of control is present in the design of the facade. There are, of course, those features without which no Vanbrugh house would be complete, such as the crenellated termination to the entablature above the columns, which adds to the Baroque romanticism of the sihouette.

Particularly noticeable is Vanbrugh's handling of the flues, which, taken with the pediments of the pavilion, show a command of composition and massing appropriate to a great designer. He does not allow the eye to wander for long before returning to the central motif, using the play of light across the facade to centralize the view on the entrance block rather than the subordinate elements forming the wings. It is well known that Vanbrugh relied upon others for assistance in the execution of his work. Howard Colvin has recorded that a master mason of York, William Etty, worked at Seaton Delaval from 1719 until 1721. However, this structure, built for Admiral Frances Delaval, unmistakably carries the Vanbrugh stamp.

It is recorded that the house was seriously damaged by fire in 1822 and was later restored under the direction of the Newcastle architect John Dobson, who also added a new wing to complete the composition. It is possible that the correctly detailed classical portico on the facade to the park also dates from that period, although the broken pediment over the doors under the portico is characteristic of Vanbrugh's work.

Seaton Delaval Hall stands gaunt and uncompromising, now a monument rather than a house. In the park, given over to farmland, stands a noble obelisk. Rumor in the village has it that this marks the spot at which the eldest son of the house fell from his horse and was killed. How fortunate for Vanbrugh that this incident occurred on the axis of the central pavilion and just at the range for a suitable vertical element as a response to the hall.

—K. H. MURTA

BOOTS FACTORY, BEESTON
Nottinghamshire, England

1930-32: Wet Goods Factory built; **Architect:** Owen Williams (1890-1969). **1938:** Dry Goods Factory built; **Architect:** Owen Williams.

Publications

COTTAM, DAVID: *Sir Owen Williams, 1890-1969.* London, 1987.

Boots Factory: Beeston, Nottinghamshire, England, 1930-32

FRAMPTON, KENNETH, and FUTAGAWA, YUKIO: *Modern Architecture: 1920-1945*. New York, 1983.

HOFMANN, WERNER, and KULTERMANN, UDO: *Modern Architecture in Color*. New York, 1970.

SHARP, DENNIS: "Utopian Engineering: Sir Owen Williams' 'New Architecture'." *Architecture and Urbanism* 3 (1985): 33-46.

*

The factory buildings designed by Owen Williams for Boots are among the most inventive structures erected in England in the 1930s.

Williams was a practicing engineer involved in the development of reinforced concrete. He made his reputation with the construction of the British Empire Exhibition at Wembley (1921-24) and with some distinguished bridges in Scotland, but usually with the collaboration of an architect. Boots was the first major commission where he was untrammeled by an architect, and he seized the opportunity to the full. In a lecture in 1927 Williams had said that industrial buildings should have "fitness for purpose at minimum cost" and ". . . the factory building is a shell surrounding a process, and I venture to say that many processes are hampered by the imposition of floors." Boots gave him the opportunity to put theory into practice on a grand scale on the company's site at Beeston, near Nottingham.

The Packed Wets Goods Factory (1930-32) is only a third of its intended size, but it was nevertheless the largest British Modern Movement building at the time; it was the coincidence of Williams' functionalist engineering with Modern Movement sensibilities that made the building so important. The original design incorporated the "Drys" building and the "Wets" building as one phased development, but when the time came to build the "Drys" building, it was constructed as a separate structure.

The "Wets" building is a four-story, flat-slab, reinforced-concrete structure with atria and recesses around the perimeter to bring light to the center of the building. The columns are held in from the exterior, with floor slabs cantilevered out to support a cladding of patent glazing. In accordance with Williams' principles, the building is a built version of the production diagram: materials arrive at the south end and enter the ground-floor manufacturing area, which is served by materials stores on the upper floors, delivery being by chutes in the well. On the ground floor the products go to the great packing hall, 600 feet by 76 feet by 70 feet, surrounded by galleries and bridges. From the packing hall the packed goods are taken to store and dispatched at the north end of the building.

Along the west elevation is placed the ancillary accommodation—offices, entrance, canteen and related facilities. At the time, it was usual to treat this accommodation separately, but at Boots it is one with the rest of the building, both structurally and architecturally. Even the entrance is given no special treatment or emphasis, for Williams kept his functionalism pure.

As a young engineer Williams had worked for the British subsidiaries of two American reinforced-concrete firms, the Trussed Concrete Steel Company and the Indented Bar and Concrete Engineering Company, so it is not surprising that Boots conforms to American practice in the use of flat-slab construction with mushroom-type columns, and in the dramatic use of atria with chutes. The entire structure is on a 7-foot 8-inch grid, with a 30-foot 8-inch by 23-foot bay size and a 7-foot 8-inch cantilever around the perimeter and around the atria.

Atria have dramatic roof structures incorporating circular glass blocks. Structurally independent service cores were built after completion of the main structure. Everywhere concrete is exposed as left from the framework.

The original intention was to use black glass for spandrel panels to the exterior in the same way as Williams' Daily Express buildings. However, obscured glass was finally selected for the bottom three feet of all exterior cladding and internal partitions, with heating pipes behind providing some protection. Clear glass was used above. Glass skins were very new in 1932, and because there were problems with overheating in summer, canvas blinds were introduced.

The "Drys" building was constructed in 1938 to make, store and ship dry products such as powders and tablets. Dramatic in its own way, it nevertheless lacks the stunning clarity of its predecessor, and the introduction of large areas of solid wall somehow make it look more "architectural." But Williams retained his directness with regard to the process, with raw materials taken to the tip floor by lifts, and manufacturing proceeding down the building with extensive use of chutes and goods shipped out at ground level. The mushroom columns of the previous building were abandoned in favor of columns that are cruciform on plan and have a head of four tapered arms. Column centers were large for the period, with a 30-foot grid for the multistory section. For the large single-story section of the building, nine-foot-deep Z-section beams at 12-foot centers span over columns at 30-foot and 60-foot centers, with end cantilevers of 30 feet and 48 feet giving an heroic civil engineering scale to the loading bays.

—JOHN WINTER

WOLLATON HALL
Nottinghamshire, England

1580-88: Constructed; **Architect:** Robert Smythson (ca. 1535-1614). **1642:** Damaged in fire. **1680:** Interior remodeling. **19th century:** Remodeled to form a salon, dining room, and library; **Architect:** Jeffrey Wyatville.

Publications

AIRS, MALCOLM: *The Making of the English Country House 1500-1640*. London, 1975.

FRIEDMAN, ALICE T.: *House and Household in Elizabethan England: Wollaton Hall and the Willoughby Family*. Chicago, 1989.

GIROUARD, MARK: "The Smythson Collection of the Royal Institute of British Architects." *Architectural History* 5 (1962): 21-184.

GIROUARD, MARK: *Robert Smythson*. London, 1966.

GIROUARD, MARK: *Robert Smythson and the Architecture of the Elizabethan Era*. London, 1966.

GIROUARD, MARK: *Robert Smythson and the Elizabethan Country House*. 1983.

LEES-MILNE, JAMES: *Tudor Renaissance*. London, 1951.

Wollaton Hall: Nottinghamshire, England, 1580-88

PEVSNER, NIKOLAUS: "Double Profile." *Architectural Review* (March 1950).

SUMMERSON, JOHN: *Architecture in Britain 1530-1830.* 6th ed. Harmondsworth, England, 1977.

*

Sir Francis Willoughby's Wollaton Hall is a premiere example of the elaborate prodigy houses built or remodeled extensively to entertain Elizabeth I and her retinue during her annual royal progresses. Willoughby, who had already entertained the queen in his old house in 1575, built Wollaton in anticipation of a second visit that did not occur, and, in the process of building the extravagant new house, nearly bankrupted himself. Built of Ancaster stone, the house cost Willoughby approximately £8,000 sterling, which he paid with profits from the coal pits on his property. Documentation of builders of Elizabethan houses is rare, but in this case the attribution to Robert Smythson, master mason and architectural genius of the period, is reasonably secure. A grave marker in the Wollaton Church cemetery, where Smythson was buried, indicates that he was the builder of Wollaton Hall.

Smythson's design for Wollaton differs from the H and E plans common in other Elizabethan houses and reveals his knowledge of European architectural books. The plan of Wollaton is a large rectangle disposed around the traditional Elizabethan great hall, and extended outward into four square turrets that rise to three stories. Some probable sources for Smythson

included publications by Sebastiano Serlio and Jacques Androuet du Cerceau. The similarity of Wollaton to French châteaux is evidence of Smythson's dependence on such sources. One drawing, no doubt by Smythson, in the Willoughby collection is almost identical to a plan from du Cerceau's *Petites Habitations*, in its disposition of a centrally placed hall and configuration of two rooms on either side of the hall on the ground floor and stairs on either side leading to the first floor. In du Cerceau's plan and Smythson's drawing, circular turrets common to the French châteaux of the Loire region are linked to the four rooms at the corners of the house, and symmetrical staircases lead to the upper floor. Smythson later modified these plans, however, making corner turrents square rather than round.

Wollaton, located on a high hill overlooking its park, which was enclosed for wild animals in 1492 and enlarged in 1510, is striking because of its breathtaking height, an effect increased by the unusually tall basement above ground and the tall lantern roof enclosing the central great hall and prospect room above it. Notable also are its symmetry, monumental scale and elaborate ornamentation.

Of all English prodigy houses, Wollaton is one of the most eclectic in its decorative details, which exhibit a broad range of medieval and classical motifs. Smythson's sources for medieval features included English Gothic cathedrals and other Elizabethan houses, as well as printed sources such as books by Hans Vredeman de Vries, but the preponderance of classical elements such as the bust portraits of Greek and Roman heroes is attributable probably to Willoughby's interest in the Italian Renaissance. The classical features of Wollaton include superimposed

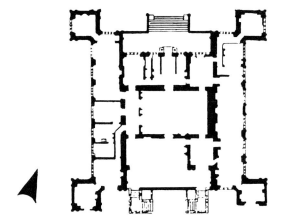

orders of pilasters and niches on the turrets. Also, balustrades on the rooflines of the central block and the prospect room are further examples of classical ornament, which blends with such medieval features as the curving strapwork bases of the small pedimented gables crowning the corner turrets. And, in a typical example of vertical massing on the rooflines of medieval buildings, tall chimneys on the main block coexist with classical obelisks on the rooflines of the turrets.

The most dramatic feature of Wollaton is the prospect room, which—despite its classical balustraded roofline and circular turrets at the corners that are crowned by small cupolas and ornamented by small finials—still evokes the character of a medieval fortification in its dramatic vertical rise high above the countryside and in its large Decorated Gothic windows. Although it is dramatic and beautiful inside and out, particularly in its classical wooden draperies, the functionalism of this room is open to question. At one point, it was a dancing hall, but, since it can be reached only by a frighteningly steep and narrow staircase in one of the circular turrets, the practicality of such activity seems dubious. Other uses for the room included the quartering of servants' guests and the display of rare furniture. The room is no longer used, and its floor and the ceiling below are braced by steel beams.

Like Longleat and Hardwick Hall, two other houses on which Smythson worked, Wollaton is glazed generously. Large banks of mullioned windows on every level of the main body of the house and the square turrets admit as much light as possible in this northern countryside, while the tall lancets of the Gothic windows bring much more light into the higher lantern-like prospect room.

Ornamentation in the central hall includes a screen passage, whose applied decoration is directly related to medieval designs in books by de Vries and to other sources, such as the screens from French church choirs and other English great halls. The dramatic hammer-beam ceiling, though, is a nonfunctioning fake suspended from the ceiling it seems to support.

A fire in 1642 led to later interior remodeling in 1680, when the east and west staircases were painted in the popular style of the Baroque period. Attributed to either Louis Laguerre or Antonio Verrio, these murals contain many stylistic features close to those of Laguerre's documented paintings at Chatsworth. The later remodeling by Jeffrey Wyatville in the 19th century of the small rooms on the ground floor to form a salon, dining room and large library destroyed the original concept of the English medieval house.

After Willoughby's death in 1596, Wollaton devolved upon his heirs and eventually became a natural history museum in 1925 after the death of one of the later heirs. The necessary internal transformation of Wollaton for the display of natural

science exhibits altered forever the original architectural conception of the Elizabethan house. The exterior, however, retains the character of the complex prodigy house built for Willoughby, and Smythson's placement of Wollaton in a picturesque setting was an advanced concept developed more extensively in later centuries.

—JOYCE M. DAVIS

CHRIST CHURCH COLLEGE
Oxford, England

1122: Augustinian canons established. **1100s:** Church rebuilt. **1175:** Canterbury Cathedral choir construction begun. **1200s:** Top of crossing tower added. **Ca. 1160-1200:** Church of St. Frideswide constructed. **1230:** Lady Chapel built. **1330-40:** Latin Chapel added. **1525-29:** Roof of great hall, Cardinal College, constructed; **Architect:** Humphrey Coke (*fl.* 1496-1531). **1640:** Great Staircase completed. **1660-68:** Northern half of Great Quadrangle completed. **1705-14:** Peckwater Quadrangle constructed; **Architect:** Henry Aldrich (1648-1710). **1717-72:** Library building constructed; **Architect:** George Clarke (1661-1736). **1773-83:** Canterbury Quadrangle constructed; **Architect:** James Wyatt (1746-1813). **1862-66:** Gothic Revival Meadow Building constructed; **Architect:** Thomas N. Deane (1828-99).

Publications

CARÖE, W. D.: *Tom Tower.* Oxford, 1923.

*

Christ Church College has a complicated architectural and institutional history. An Anglo-Saxon minster occupied the site, which has uncertain connections with a nunnery founded in the eighth century. Henry I established Augustinian canons there in 1122, forming the Priory of St. Frideswide, and the church, rebuilt in the second half of the 12th century, is one of the highest achievements of the English Romanesque. The priory existed until Cardinal Thomas Wolsey dissolved it in 1525 to make way for his new foundation of Cardinal College. As was his wont, and also his undoing, Wolsey began building on a grand scale, but although it progressed rapidly, the college was left unfinished when he fell from power in 1529.

For what was built, Wolsey had demolished the west part of the priory church and cloister, and intended to demolish the rest eventually, but when Henry VIII refounded the institution as Christ Church College in 1532, he decided to keep what remained of the priory church as the college chapel. Then, in 1546, St. Frideswide's was also made the cathedral of the newly created diocese of Oxford. The new college also absorbed the formerly monastic Canterbury College, where Canterbury Quad now stands. Wolsey's Great Quadrangle was finished in the 17th century, and as was typical of Oxford, the Gothic idiom remained strongly in force, to the point where it is difficult to distinguish between Gothic "survival" and "revival." This resulted in the magnificent fan-vaulted Great Staircase, and even Christopher Wren succumbed to Gothic there, in finishing Tom Tower.

Henry Aldrich, however, introduced an accomplished classicism in his early 18th-century Peckwater Quad, built northwest

Christ Church College: Oxford, England, 1122

of the Great Quad. This was enclosed later in the 18th century by the new library, of a more monumental classicism. Finally, the rebuilding of the smaller Canterbury Quad at the end of the century brought an Adamesque touch, almost at the end of Oxford's cycle of classicism. For Oxford went back to Gothic in the 19th century, as is apparent there in the stately Meadow Building. The college now forms a large, rambling ensemble, to which, however, its two main quads give a semblance of order. It adjoins the 40-odd acres of Christ Church Meadow forming a common anomaly of Oxford's urban development: on one side, the college is in the heart of the city, and on the other, the countryside prevails (the site was just inside the south wall of the medieval city).

The Church of St. Frideswide was begun anew in about 1160 and finished circa 1200. There are no documentary dates, and the unusual nature of this sophisticated building makes stylistic comparison difficult. It featured a rectangular east end of five bays (the aisles are only four bays), three-bay transepts with east and west aisles, a crossing tower, and the nave which was probably of seven bays. The elevation is unusual. The monumental drum piers (with slight "entasis") form a "giant order," with the triforium slung—rather uncomfortably—within their upper half, and then the clerestory above. Although drum piers are not uncommon in English Romanesque, this particular arrangement originated in the choir at Tewkesbury and was also used at Romsey and Jedburgh; Romsey also has another early rectangular east end, a particularly English development. Curiously, the triforium at St. Frideswide, with paired openings, is nonfunctional and does not form a passage. There is, however, a clerestory passage and the usual stepped triple openings (still surviving in transepts and nave). Vault shafts rise from corbels between the bays, and the choir and transepts were originally rib-vaulted, as are all the aisles still. There is a remarkable variety of capitals—Anglo-Norman interlace capitals, volute capitals, waterleaf and crocket capitals.

Two campaigns are distinguishable. Basically, the first comprises the east end and transepts, the second the nave. The influence of Canterbury Cathedral choir, begun in 1175, is apparent in the nave: the drum piers here are alternately round and octagonal, instead of all round, as further east, and there are also pointed arches in the clerestory, rather than the round arches which dominate elsewhere. The top of the crossing tower, with its modest spire, one of the oldest surviving in England, was added in the early 13th century. The chapter house is also Early English, behind its mid-12th-century heavily chevroned facade. The other major work of that period is the Lady Chapel (ca. 1230), built north of the north chancel aisle by knocking an arcade through its outer wall. The same procedure was followed circa 1330-40 when the Latin Chapel was added north of it, probably to house the shrine of Saint Frideswide.

Many of the windows were remodeled in the 14th and 15th centuries, but the main late medieval alteration was the demolition of the 12th-century vaults and the building of magnificent pendant vaults in the choir (ca. 1500), close in design to those in the Divinity School in Oxford and possibly also by William Orchard. The transepts and nave received flat wooden roofs at that time. The church is filled with important monuments and stained glass from many different periods. The western part of the nave, and the western part of the late-15th-century cloisters, were demolished at Wolsey's orders. In the mid-19th century, George Gilbert Scott exercised a heavy hand in his "restorations."

Wolsey's Great Quad, or Tom Quad, was laid out as the largest in Oxford (276.5 by 271 feet). The builders were John Lebons and Henry Redman, both King's master masons. It was meant to have cloisters, like Magdalen College, but only the

wall springers and outer footings were built. The hall, also very large (114.5 by 40 feet) and with a hammer-beam roof by Master Humphrey Cook, is at the east end of the south range, and a chapel was initially planned for the north range, but it was never built. The entrance gateway, in the middle of the west range, was designed like a domestic or monastic gatehouse, with corner turrets, rather than like a college gateway. Only the bottom stages were built in Wolsey's time. Only the southern half of the quad was built then, in fact, and the northern half was finished only in about 1660-68, although to virtually the same design.

The crowning touch was the completion of the entrance gateway, for which Christopher Wren was recruited: "I resolved it ought to be Gothick to agree with the Founder's Worke, Yet I have not continued soe busy as he began." He did so reluctantly, and would rather have used "the better formes of Architecture." Still, the Great Staircase (ca. 1640) in the southeast corner of the quad, giving access to the hall, shows no dissatisfaction with Gothic style and features very elegant fan vaults, supported on a slender central pier, which would not have been out of place 200 years earlier.

These "better formes" were adopted admirably by Henry Aldrich (died 1710), the dean of Christ Church and an academic virtuoso in architectural design, who did much in Oxford. His Peckwater Quad was built 1705-14, forming three sides of a quad, with three stories plus an attic in each range, the ground floor rusticated, the upper two articulated by Ionic pilasters supporting an entablature and balustrade. The middle bays of each range are emphasized by a pediment over the entablature, carried on attached columns rather than pilasters. Triangular and segmental pediments alternate over the first-floor windows. Access to the rooms is by regularly distributed staircases rather than hallways, as in the Great Quad and as was usual in colleges. The design is perfectly regular, although some say a little dry.

The fourth side of the quad is enclosed by the detached library building, which was begun in 1717 but only finished in 1772. The initial designs were also by Aldrich, but they were reworked by that other great Oxford amateur, George Clarke, whose association with Nicholas Hawksmoor is evident in the library's Baroque monumentality and strength. It was built by William Townesend, the prominent Oxford contractor. The seven-day facade features giant Corinthian columns, not set on a rusticated base but rising from the ground, like John Webb's design for the King Charles Building at Greenwich and Wren's for Whitehall Palace, all supporting a heavy cornice and balustrade. Like Peckwater, the upper windows have alternating pediments. The interior has some of the finest 18th-century stuccowork in England, by Thomas Roberts. The ground floor was originally open, but was enclosed in 1769-72 to house the Christ Church Picture Gallery, moved in the 1960s to new premises in Canterbury Quad.

The latter, designed by James Wyatt, was built in 1773-83, adjoining Peckwater and also of three ranges, with the east-end wall of the library forming the fourth side. It is entered by a splendid triumphal arch carried on four attached Doric columns, but the quad itself is quieter. Of later work, the Gothic Revival Meadow Building is noteworthy. Nikolaus Pevsner described that building, designed by Thomas N. Deane of Dublin and built in 1862-66, as "that big, heavy Gothic Chinese wall," but it is more satisfying than that and has a comfortable sense of style that panders neither to archaeological exactitude nor ideological correctness. All the buildings have undergone much restoration.

—JIM BUGSLAG

KEBLE COLLEGE
Oxford, England

1868-82: Construction; **Architect:** William Butterfield (1814-1900).

Publications

The Architect (1870).
PEVSNER, NIKOLAUS, and SHERWOOD, JENNIFER: *Oxfordshire*. London, 1974.
SUMMERSON, JOHN N.: *Heavenly Mansions*. New York, 1963.
THOMPSON, PAUL: *William Butterfield: Victorian Architect*. Cambridge, Massachusetts, 1971.

In the volume on Oxfordshire from the *Buildings of England* series, Nikolaus Pevsner called Keble College "the final triumph of the Oxford Movement." He described it as "earnest and exacting, overwhelmingly what the age called *real*."

The college is composed of two quadrangles and a master's house separate from the other college buildings, all done in William Butterfield's vigorous polychromatic brick Gothic style. The chapel anchors the northeast corner of the composition and is the most interesting architectural piece. Butterfield described his design intention in a letter to the college warden dated 22 January 1873 in which he wrote: "To give the restfulness and strength, and sense of communion that come of quiet order, completeness and proportion, must be our aim" (quoted

in *William Butterfield* by Paul Thompson). Although Butterfield's most direct precedent for the design was the upper Church of St. Francis at Assisi, *The Architect* in 1870 described its style as "Early Decorated, for the purity of which the name of Mr. Butterfield is ample security." To modern viewers the chapel, and the entire college, hardly seems Gothic at all, it is so completely High Victorian in appearance.

The quadrangle ranges are three stories tall with entry and end features of four stories. The chapel, however, is equivalent to an eight-story block. It is extremely tall and vertical in character. Its mass is divided into tall, slender bays by strongly projecting buttresses whose pinnacles project past the roof eave, in the manner of the great single buttress at Butterfield's All Saints, Margaret Street. Here the buttresses establish a rhythm of powerful vertical lines. The chapel has no aisles and the only windows are placed high in the wall, adding to the impression of great height.

The wall panels between the buttresses are composed of a base and four upper stages, all divided by strongly projecting stone moldings. The lower three wall stages are red brick banded with buff stone at regular intervals. The banding increases in width and frequency as it rises, becoming more stone and less brick. The fourth stage begins at the springline of the clerestory arches; it is half brick and half stone in a checkered pattern. Buttresses are banded throughout their height; they function as frames for the checkered panels. Diapering is used on the east and west facades and in the gables. Incised titles filled with sea-green mastic fill the spandrel above the portal in the south entrance recess. Buttress niches and the entrance tympanum are decorated with figural sculpture.

The walls appear to diminish in weight as they rise. Not only

Quad with Chapel, Keble College: Oxford, England, 1868-82

are they opened in the upper stages by the large clerestory windows, but the increased quantity of light-colored stone and the grill-like checkering visually lighten the wall. Butterfield's early preference for smooth surfaces and planar volumes has been replaced with concern for sculptured form, weight and mass.

The interior, as at Assisi, is one great, tall, vaulted, rectangular space. (Keble College Chapel is Butterfield's only completely vaulted work.) The concentration of decorative effort upon the sheer enclosing walls is similar to Assisi, too. Space—great soaring space—is everything. Nothing in the church competes with the space, or even seems to occupy it. All furniture is kept very low, and the choir and sanctuary have only minimal elevation. The altar is simple, and its reredos is very much a part of the wall envelope, not an element in its own right. Side wall bay divisions are marked with tall, slender, full-height shafts that are hardly more than lines; their luxuriantly carved stone capitals receive the slender, linear ribs of the quadripartite vaulting system.

The interior walls are divided into stages much like the exterior walls, except there are only three stages instead of four. The first stage is glazed plum-colored brick with thin stripes of sea-green brick and broader bands of buff stone inlaid with mastic patterns; as on the exterior, a stone arcade of cusped arches on simple round shafts is layered over the brick. The second stage is devoted to a series of glazed-tile mosaic scenes that culminate in the Christ Enthroned in a quatrefoil above the altar. The mosaic scenes are rendered in soft colors—green, pink, pale blue, soft yellow, red and white. The stone veneer of the second stage continues into the third stage as the frames of the clerestory windows. The wall that surrounds the windows is banded, checkered and diapered brick; the predominant color of the brick is vermilion, with the pattern worked in gray and buff.

The ribs of the vaulting are pink and terra-cotta in color. The entire vault surface is painted with formalized jointing patterns in broad bands of buff, sea green and gray. The patterns and colors of the nave continue into the chancel. The tile and stone patterns of the floor in the chancel and the inlaid decoration in the arcade are more elaborate than in the nave, and the central panel is treated as a reredos with a pointed canopy above a great quatrefoil rather than a rectangular panel. Otherwise the decoration is the same.

Color gives the space a special warm glow, an ambience that is enhanced by the great series of Gibbs windows which are predominantly light but glow with bits of scarlet, mauve, yellow and blue-green. Unlike the color in Butterfield's buildings of the previous decade, the color is soft and the color scheme carefully controlled. Butterfield described this work as "largely dependent on, and connected with coloured material." He said, "I should be sorry to see such works published unless that treatment could be done justice to" (Thompson, *William Butterfield*).

Butterfield's color and pattern were already out of style when Keble College was built. Early on, Butterfield's work at the chapel was christened "the holy zebra" style. Even those who had in the past most admired his work found it to be insensitive, startling and restless. Such responses reveal the continuing hold, even in criticism of the Gothic Revival, of classical instincts, of the divinity of whiteness proclaimed by Leon Battista Alberti, Andrea Palladio and the theorists of the Renaissance. Their belief in colorlessness was none the less powerful for being in conflict with most previous architectural tradition, so much so that in the mid-19th century not merely construction polychromy, but even pure red brick was thought a bold gesture.

John Summerson, in his essay on William Butterfield in *Heavenly Mansions,* makes the case that Butterfield is to architecture what Charles Dickens and Emily Brontë were to literature. He says, "In architecture, Butterfield is the great symbol of that sense of revulsion and liberation which permeated English art and letters in those years (1845-65). . . .[Butterfield's way] was to drag the Gothic Revival from its pedestal of scholarship and gentility and recreate it in a builder's yard. . . .Butterfield attacks architecture not as building, but as Gothic-Architecture-as-building."

—C. MURRAY SMART, JR.

QUEEN'S COLLEGE
Oxford, England

1671-72: Williamson Building constructed. **1692-95:** Library constructed; **Mason:** John Townsend. **1709-11:** West range constructed. **1714-18:** Hall and chapel constructed. **1719:** Williamson Building remodeled. **1734:** Screen-wall to High Street constructed; **Architect:** Nicholas Hawksmoor (ca. 1661-1736). **1735-60:** East range constructed. **1841:** Library's cloister enclosed; **Architect:** Charles Robert Cockerell (1788-1863). **1968-70:** Florey Building constructed; **Architect:** James Stirling (b. 1926).

Publications

DOWNES, KERRY: *English Baroque Architecture*. London, 1966.
DOWNES, KERRY: *Hawksmoor*. London, 1959.
HODGKIN, ROBERT H.: *Six Centuries of an Oxford College: A History of the Queen's College, 1340-1940*. Oxford, 1949.
KERSTING, ANTHONY F., and ASHDOWN, JOHN: *The Buildings of Oxford*. New York, 1980.
MAGRATH, JOHN R.: *The Queen's College*. Oxford, 1921.
PEVSNER, NIKOLAUS, and SHERWOOD, JENNIFER: *Oxfordshire*. London, 1974.

*

Although the Queen's College is one of the older colleges in Oxford (founded 1340), it was completely rebuilt in the late 17th and early 18th centuries; it reflects both the initial phase of incursion of the classical idiom into perhaps the most conservative bastion of medieval architectural style in Europe and the full flowering of the short-lived English Baroque, which in a surprising *volte face* Oxford adopted with alacrity.

The first classical building to appear was the Williamson Building (1671-72), immediately north of the old quad on the east side fronting on Queen's Lane. It was extensively remodeled in 1719, though, and little of the original design is now apparent. Although the building still made use of cross-windows, its centrally pedimented long facades and classical detailing were its most significant features. Like all the college's buildings, the authorship of the design is both undocumented and problematic. Christopher Wren's name has been linked with the building, and while this is by no means certain, it is significant. Wren's Sheldonian Theatre (1663-69), in an appropriately bookish classicism, had recently solidified the interruption of Oxford's "*rabies Gothorum,*" which had been initiated in the 1630s with the Canterbury Quad of St. John's College. And Wren's Garden Quad at Trinity College (build in 1668 and

Queen's College, Quad gate detail: Oxford, England, 17th century

Queen's College

1682) is quite comparable to the Williamson Building. Wren soon left Oxford, but he had stirred an enthusiasm for classical architecture among his fellow dons that produced two more amateur architects—Henry Aldrich (died 1710) and George Clarke (died 1736)—who considerably influenced the face of Oxford and more particularly, the nature of the Queen's College.

The new library, a splendid building facing the Williamson Building on the west, was begun in 1692 and finished three years later. The library itself was at first-floor level, with an open cloister passage along the rusticated east side of the ground floor (enclosed by C. R. Cockerell in 1841); the west facade toward the garden was not rusticated, but was of smooth ashlar punctuated by three symmetrically placed doorways and a series of niches with statues of founders and benefactors by Vanderstein. Above the ground floor, both facades are similar, with a row of 11 arched windows focused on a three-bay central sculpted pediment supported on Corinthian pilasters and an entablature. The library was built by John Townesend, the college mason (1688-1712), but again the designer is unknown. As early as 1695 a comparison was made with Wren's Trinity College library, Cambridge (begun 1677), but Wren clearly had no direct part in the design, which was probably in large part due to Henry Aldrich.

In about 1707 Townesend built a north range joining the library and Williamson Building, and its undistinguished design might well have been his own. This, nevertheless, made the north quad a far more imposing ensemble than the old quad, and it was finished in 1719 by the building of the south range and refacing of the Williamson Building to create a homogeneous and complete quadrangle. From about 1708 designs for rebuilding the front quad on an enlarged scale were abroad. In

1708-09 Nicholas Hawksmoor submitted no less than seven different proposals for a completely integrated two-quad layout. As Sir Nathaniel Lloyd observed of Hawksmoor's slightly later designs for All Souls, "He Designs Grandly, for a College," and in fact none of Hawksmoor's grandiose designs were followed exactly, although the screen along the High Street with its gateway is most probably his, and his plans undoubtedly influenced what was begun in 1709. The west range was built first in 1709-11; then the hall and chapel, comprising the north range, in 1714-18; the screen facade along the south in 1734; and finally the east range between 1735 and 1760.

With Radcliffe Square, Queen's is one of the most noticeable manifestations of the encompassing but largely unbuilt pretentions—prominently represented in Hawksmoor's plans—to turn Oxford into a Baroque (or, rather, Roman) city. Prior to this rebuilding the main entrance to Queen's was on Queen's Lane, a row of tenements separating the old quad from the High Street. These tenements were demolished and replaced by the screen facade. This is the most magnificent facade in Oxford and one of the glories of the English Baroque. Flanked by the tall ends of the east and west ranges, with their pediment sculptures and acroterion figures, the center is mostly open above the strongly rusticated arcade that runs the length of the facade. The central gateway is flanked by double columns with vermiculated rustication supporting an entablature and a delicate open cupola above, supported on paired Doric columns with prominent entablatures radiating from the center, which houses a statue of Queen Caroline by Henry Cheere. The inspiration for such a screen enclosing a quad is French, and conscious reference was made there to the Luxembourg Palace in Paris (French, too, are the segmentally pedimented central attics dominating the

Queen's College, Quad gate

building except in Oxford, are all filled with fully colored stained glass, some reused from the earlier chapel, some made specifically for this one.

The college has built since that time, both on this site and on newly acquired land elsewhere in Oxford. Notable among later building is James Stirling's pre-postmodern Florey Building (1968-70) across Magdalen Bridge. The main college buildings, however, are still very much dominated by the albeit heavily refaced Baroque double quad.

—JIM BUGSLAG

RADCLIFFE LIBRARY
Oxford, England

1737-49: Construction; **Architect:** James Gibbs (1682-1754).

Publications

GIBBS, JAMES: *Bibliotheca Radcliviana*. London, 1747.
GILLIAM, S. G.: *The Building Accounts of the Radcliffe Camera*. Oxford, 1958.
LANG, S.: "By Hawksmoor out of Gibbs." *Architectural Review* (April 1949).

*

east and west ranges). Many aspects, particularly of the cupola (but as well of his unbuilt designs), are reminiscent of features in Hawksmoor's later London churches.

Inside the spacious new front quad (140 feet square), the east and west residential ranges were built to the same design, but strikingly, the north range separating the two quads—comprising the hall and chapel, separated by a central passage—was simultaneously built to a different, but coordinated, design. Both, however, make use of a complex play of wall planes. The juxtaposition makes the design of the north range, with its giant attached Tuscan columns and central pediment and cupola, seem even more monumental than it is, and like Hawksmoor's Clarendon Building, its effect belies its size. The mannerist use of detailing also recalls Hawksmoor, but his influence was probably filtered through the significant intervention of Dr. Clarke of All Souls, who also produced designs for the Front Quad. To add to this confusion, the builder William Townesend (died 1739) is known to have modified plans during construction.

The interiors of the hall and particularly the chapel also have Baroque pretensions. The hall has Doric pilasters with entablatures between the windows, a shallow plaster barrel vault, with curved pedimental "facades" on either end wall and a large fireplace centrally placed on the north wall. The chapel, with its apsed east end, has a coved plaster ceiling, and the regular paneling changes to coffering in the apse, surrounding a circular *Ascension* by James Thornhill in *de sotto in sù* perspective, all suggesting, in reserved fashion, a dome. Even though the walls of the east bay are marbled, reserved attention is all the apse—with its plain, decidedly un-Baroque altar table—can stand, and the real focus of the chapel is the wooden carved entrance screen at the west end and the central stalls. The windows, uncharacteristically for a neoclassical

The Radcliffe Library, also called the "Camera," was built in accordance with the will of the eminent physician Dr. John Radcliffe, a graduate and benefactor of University College, Oxford, who died in 1714. Two years before his death, Radcliffe had proposed an enlargement of the Bodleian Library. That proposal finally took shape in the form of a separate building, which only much later became part of the Bodleian proper. Early schemes for the Radcliffe Library, however, involved a circular and a rectangular extension to the Selden end of the Bodleian. There was also a proposal for a rectangular block, with a college library below it, to extend far into the site of Exeter College.

Nicholas Hawksmoor made plans for a circular library attached to the Selden end, and he also developed a plan for a round building on the separate, restricted site bounded by St. Mary's Church, All Souls' College and the Bodleian, which was later actually chosen for the library. Hawksmoor died in 1736 before any design was accepted. James Gibbs developed designs for a rectangular library, but in 1737 he was chosen as the architect of a circular building. Six hundred prints of this design were circulated to possible benefactors. Gibbs made some alterations to the plan as first approved, substituting Headington stone (which had poor wearing quality) for the more durable stone from Burford in the Cotswolds. Instead of pilasters, he opted for three-quarter columns recalling those set around the dome of St. Peter's in Rome.

The foundation stone was laid on 17 May 1737. The building as it was finally constructed had no close relationship to the neighboring structures, and its round plan is unique in England. Its ribbed dome also recalls that of St. Peter's, which was designed by Michelangelo. Gibbs made some changes in the dome in the course of the construction work to diminish the weight. The boldly ribbed dome was to have been of stone, but the stonework already put up was removed, and an alternative

Radcliffe Library: Oxford, England, 1737-49

structure of oak clad with lead was erected instead. A light-weight lantern surmounted the completed dome. The "Camera" was raised over an open piazza, which could be closed off with iron gates, made by Bakewell of Derby, "to preserve that place from being a lurking place for rogues in the night time." The piazza, forming a rusticated base, is now glazed in and used as library space. Gibbs closely and frequently supervised the work.

Inside the library, there is fine stuccowork by Giuseppe Artari, and a prominent statue of Dr. Radcliffe by Michael Rysbrack. The whole interior, with its gallery and bookpresses by a joiner named Phillips, is a good complement to the dignified exterior.

The library was formally opened on 13 May 1749. Gibbs had been made an honorary master of arts at Oxford University the previous day. The opening ceremony was notable for the Jacobite opinions vigorously expressed by Dr. William King, the principal of St. Mary's Hall (now part of Oriel College), who punctuated his address by repetitions of the cry "redeat," to indicate his hope that the "Old Pretender" would come back.

Gibbs' relationship with the Radcliffe trustees was always excellent and much happier than his dealings with the authorities at Cambridge. So it came as no surprise that he left the Radcliffe Library all his books, on architectural and other subjects, and also a large collection of drawings, which are now in the Ashmolean Museum.

—BRYAN LITTLE

BLENHEIM PALACE
Oxfordshire, England

1705-25. Architects: John Vanbrugh (1644-1726) and Nicholas Hawksmoor (ca. 1661-1736). **1764-65:** High Lodge remodeled, Park Farm facade designed; **Architect:** Capability Brown (1716-83).

Publications

BEARD, GEOFFREY: *The Work of Sir John Vanbrugh*. London, 1986.
GREEN, DAVID: *Blenheim Palace*. London, 1951.
MAVOR, WILLIAM: *A New Description of Blenheim*. Oxford, 1810.
VANBRUGH, JOHN: *The Complete Works*. Vol. 4. Edited by Bonany Dobrée and Geoffrey F. Webb. London, 1927-28.

*

Blenheim Palace is the masterwork of John Vanbrugh. In this magnificent edifice, whose monumental size and bold architectural forms epitomize the English Baroque style, Vanbrugh, who desired to create a dramatic, architectural monument and to place the building in a picturesque setting, introduced a trend of romantic historicism that culminated a half century later in the natural English garden style popularized by Lancelot "Capability" Brown.

Accounts vary concerning the selection of the flamboyant Vanbrugh as architect, but his membership in the Whig Kit Cat Club, to which the duke of Marlborough also belonged, was a probable factor. For his assistant, he chose Nicholas Hawksmoor, who probably designed nearly all the interiors. An ensemble cast of artists and craftsmen contributed to the total decoration of the palace.

After the queen approved Vanbrugh's early wooden model, an act of Parliament officially sanctioned the gift of the old royal property of Woodstock Manor as the site of the palace that the Crown would fund. Construction began after the laying of the foundation stone, 18 June 1705, and proceeded at a brisk pace at first. Then, in 1710, when the country, weary of the War of the Spanish Succession, ousted the Whigs, who had conducted it, funding for Blenheim was at risk. The duchess of Marlborough stopped construction that had resumed briefly as a result of Vanbrugh's requests at court. In 1711 Queen Anne dismissed the duke and duchess from their positions and, in the following year, suspended construction of Blenheim again. The Marlboroughs went into exile in Europe in 1712 and returned to England in 1714 after the death of Anne, whose successor,

Blenheim Palace, north main elevation: Oxfordshire, England, 1705-25

Blenheim Palace, south side

George I, restored the duke to all his offices. Marlborough agreed to complete Blenheim with his own funds, but Vanbrugh's concept of a grand military monument on the scale of Roman architecture conflicted with the duchess' preference for a simple and comfortable country home, and led to Vanbrugh's resignation in 1716. After trying to complete the house with master masons, the duchess rehired Hawksmoor, who essentially completed Blenheim by 1725.

Vanbrugh's scheme incorporated a grand design for the house and a majestic setting of gardens. To create a noble setting for the palace, he sited it facing north on a flat terrain overlooking the River Glyme, barely more than a stream at that point; and he planned a monumental bridge over the river leading to his projected great north entrance court. He also proposed to leave the old manor house on the hill above the Glyme, but his decision to build the bridge and retain the manor house as a picturesque curiosity led to unresolved conflicts with the duchess.

The house plan is similar to the French format in which the *corps-de-logis* faces a large court enclosed by corner pavilions,

wings, and a low screening wall containing a grand entrance. Vanbrugh borrowed also from his own design of Castle Howard, although Blenheim is more unified and condensed. Within the main block, he employed a low curving wall decorated by engaged Doric columns to link the central core to massive banded corner pavilions, which he connected by low Doric colonnades to a second pair of pavilions that expand to form large external courts on the eastern and western sides of the main court.

The focus of the north court is a massive Corinthian portico, whose giant order Vanbrugh derived from Michelangelo's apse elevation of St. Peter's Basilica and Capitoline Palace facade in Rome. Above it, a second pediment that is broken, recessed and pierced by large arches joins with the roofline of the rest of the central block to form a lantern-like vertical projection reminiscent of that of Wollaton Hall, which Vanbrugh probably knew. The screening wall that he designed to include a grand arched entrance and to enclose the great north court was not built, and, for various reasons, the eastern approach came into common usage. The best view of the north front, designed to

Blenheim Palace, interior long gallery

impress visitors, is from Vanbrugh's bridge on the axis from the north court to Marlborough's victory monument on the hill above the Glyme. There, in 1731, Robert Pit erected the monument on the site of the old manor house, whose last remains were demolished in 1723.

An unpedimented portico in the form of a Roman triumphal arch crowns the south or garden facade. In his placement of a triumphal arch on a palace facade, Vanbrugh predated by a quarter century Nicola Salvi's similar usage of the triumphal arch on the palace behind the Trevi Fountain in Rome. Surmounting Vanbrugh's portico is not a Roman quadriga but a 30-ton bust of the vanquished Louis XIV, whom Marlborough had captured in his siege of Tournai in 1709. Above the image of the mocked French king, as on the north facade, rises a broken, recessed pediment crowned by classical urns and Vanbrugh's signature cannonball. This central core of the south is linked to the corner pavilions by straight wings, which, like the curving wings on the north, have classical balustrades on their rooflines.

Facing the south front was a military garden set out by the queen's royal gardener, Henry Wise, to resemble army fortifications. Within stone walls marked by eight massive bastions 150 feet in height, the garden consisted of a four-sided arrangement of trees, shrubs and fountains, whose patterns are visible in dry weather, although Capability Brown dismantled the garden in the middle of the 18th century. He replaced it with an English garden.

The eastern and western facades feature curved central bays and present variations of Vanbrugh's Baroque architectural forms. The east facade encloses the private quarters and faces a formal garden that in the early 20th century replaced the original one planted for the first duchess. A new 20th-century formal garden on the western side consists of parterres, water terraces and fountains surrounded by classical sculptures, including a modello reputed to be by Giovanni Lorenzo Bernini.

The north portico leads into the great hall, a vast space divided into two registers of massive arcades flanking a round arch leading to the east-west corridor. Sir James Thornhill's early plan to decorate it as a guardroom with armor lining the arcaded walls did not materialize. His contribution to the room is a

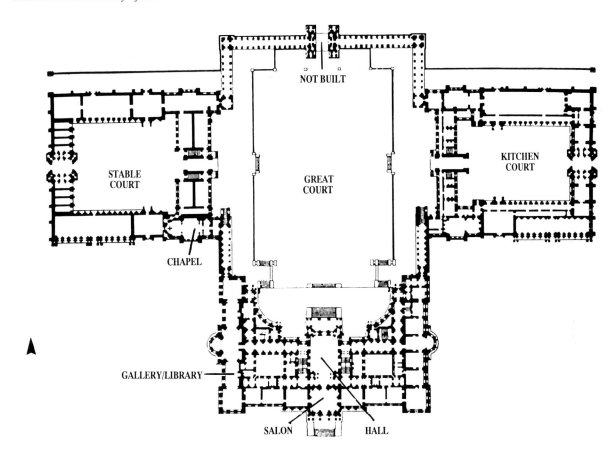

ceiling painting depicting the duke kneeling before Britannia, to whom he offers his Blenheim battle plan. Large clerestory windows provide light for this room, which rises to a height of 67 feet. The sculptor Grinling Gibbons carved the duke's coat-of-arms over the arch leading across the corridor to the salon.

In the salon, Gibbons designed three marble arched door frames and one window, although he carved only the western door that was in place in 1712, when he ceased working at Blenheim. These arches would have harmonized well with Thornhill's design of large niches for the walls of the salon, but the duchess dismissed Thornhill because she found him too expensive. Instead, it was Louis Laguerre's alternative scheme of a monumental, illusionistic tribute to Marlborough that defined the decorative character of the room. Above a simulated dado region, Laguerre painted a colonnaded loggia based on the Ambassadors Staircase painted at Versailles by his former French Academy master, Charles Le Brun. On the ceiling, Laguerre painted the apotheosis of Marlborough, who, in his victory at Blenheim, brought to a premature end the succession of military triumphs of Louis XIV. In one of many ironic twists at Blenheim, the style of Louis XIV's court lives on in this full-scale variant of Le Brun's design, which was demolished in 1752.

In the staterooms, arranged in symmetrical groups of three on either side of the salon, the French style triumphs further in the decoration honoring the defeat of the master of Versailles, whose elaborate interiors provided models for the Blenheim suites.

On the western side of the house, in one of the rooms completed last, Hawksmoor revised Vanbrugh's unfinished original long gallery as a library. In this long room, traditional in English country houses, Hawksmoor counteracted the effect of excessive length by dividing its walls and ceilings into separate compartments. The original plan had called for ceiling paintings by Thornhill, but, at the request of the duchess, Hawksmoor substituted plasterwork by Isaac Mansfield.

The elegant chapel just off the long library has an exquisite plastered ceiling by Mansfield, but a large monument to Marlborough by William Kent dominates the room. Altogether, the entire palace and the assembled structures of the park serve as a monument to the duke, and announce by the grand scale of the ensemble that Marlborough was a giant among military heroes.

—JOYCE M. DAVIS

ROUSHAM PARK
Oxfordshire, England

1720s-41: Landscaping; **Landscaper:** Charles Bridgeman (d. 1738). **1738:** Rousham House interior designed; **Architect:** William Kent (1685-1748).

Publications

WILLIS, PETER: *Charles Bridgeman and the English Landscape Garden*. London, 1977.

Rousham Park, garden: Oxfordshire, England, 1720s-41

WOODBRIDGE, K.: "William Kent's Gardening: the Rousham Letters." *Apollo* (October 1974).

There is a general argument which runs like this: the overwhelming sense that it was "the only possible architecture" that the English felt following their contact with the buildings of the Italian Renaissance, with its rediscovery of precision, of repetition, of the elevated feelings involved in rehandling a sacred formal language and which engendered a flowering of those sensibilities concerning the geometric, the graphic and the theatrical—all this extinguished the old sensibilities that had arisen from the land and from use.

Then one thinks about the city of Bath . . . England's contribution to the architecture of the Renaissance . . . where the sensibilities toward the land, toward use, are overwhelmingly the source of its sense of control . . . the geometric, the graphic, the theatrical inventions of the Renaissance being harnessed to that older notion of ordering which is thereby regenerated beyond our common understanding.

Bath is the consequence of the sensibilities cultivated by the English landscape garden at work in the town. The landscape garden at Rousham in Oxfordshire was there two generations before Lansdown Crescent.

My understanding of what was new in the English landscape garden was the evocation of mood: triggered by condition of enclosure, amount of light, optical distance, time-interval distance, devices to evoke feelings of other places, remembrances of things seen or hoped to be seen, of books read or hoped to be read or just talked about, sound of water, sound of distance, smells. That is, it was dealing with sensibilities which were not only visual.

What was old—from the time before books—was action specific to place . . . the arts of man-occupied land, of man-occupied land-form.

Land and use.

The old sorts of place-rooted understandings maybe, surviving, being revived, in a more bookish form, in an enlightened form, perhaps, after the impact of the Italian Renaissance.

The garden at Rousham, being small, seems to be a distillation of these new and old concerns.

On my first visit, late autumn, a misty day, inclined to rain . . . just barely felt cultivated land beyond the stream . . . was like being enclosed in a dream. I was overwhelmed.

A second visit in sunny weather, over the stream, on the skyline, a military airfield (and barracks?) turned one's focus away from the general landscape onto the enclosed ways of the garden within the confines of the stream.

Its pleasures, different, but undiminished in sun and shade, are of the small walking kind; of interval, surprise, winding around, going up and down, of surprising specimen trees; and the later pleasures of walking scholarship, comparisons, differences.

It is homely, it has peacocks around the house and in the yard and certainly one cannot easily get lost; but it is a homeliness concealing a high art at a new peak, of perfect lock of land and use.

—PETER D. SMITHSON

SALISBURY CATHEDRAL
Salisbury, Wiltshire, England

1220: Building begun; **Supervisor of building:** Elias of Dereham; **Master mason:** Nicholas of Ely. **1258:** Building mostly completed, church consecrated. **Ca. 1260-1284:** Cloisters and Chapter House built. **1265:** West front completed. **1280-1320:** Spire and tower constructed. **Late 13th century:** Vestry and muniment room added. **1856:** Central column, Chapter House, rebuilt.

Publications

PEVSNER, NIKOLAUS, and METCALF, P.: *The Cathedrals of England.* 2 Vols. England, 1985.
RAWLINSON, R.: *The History and Antiquities of the Cathedral Church of Salisbury and the Abbey-Church of Bath.* London, 1719.

*

The outstanding feature of Salisbury Cathedral is its distinctive unity of style. Begun in 1220, it was sufficiently complete to be consecrated in 1258. The west front was finished in 1265 and the last lead placed on the roof in the following year. These dates must have required an almost uninterrupted campaign of building, from which the unity of style derives. The present cathedral was built on an unencumbered site which imposed no restrictions upon the design. The ground plan is a simple cross of Lorraine providing a second pair of transepts to the east of the main transepts. It was an architect's idea, complete in every detail, except that he failed to provide for a vestry and muniment room. These were added before the end of the 13th century and constitute a blemish on the south side.

There was a previous cathedral within the royal castle of Old Sarum. It may have been the difficulties of coexisting with the military that provoked the move, but the arrival of the fully developed Gothic style was tempting bishops everywhere to seek a pretext for reconstruction.

As a Gothic building, however, Salisbury was curiously behind the times. It was the exact contemporary of Amiens, in which the French Gothic reached its point of perfection. Amiens made full use of all the resources of the style—high vaults supported by flying buttresses, windows filled with true tracery, and the almost complete replacement of walls by stained-glass windows. The builders of Salisbury apparently knew nothing of these. Their vaults were half the height of those at Amiens; proper tracery first appeared in the cloisters and chapter house, and the area available to the glazier was relatively limited.

Those who built Salisbury were not trying to do the same thing as the builders of Amiens. The builders of French cathedrals, John Ruskin observed, were essentially concerned with the interior architecture. The exterior was "the wrong side of the stuff in which you find how the threads go that produce the, inside or right side, of the stuff." At Salisbury this seems to have been reversed. The outside seems to be the satisfactory architecture; the inside is comparatively disappointing.

However, the outside depends largely on the effect of the spire. It is difficult to believe that the tower and spire were part of the original intention, because the four piers of the crossing were not strong enough to support it. When the 6.5 tons of

Salisbury Cathedral, from northwest: Wiltshire, England, 1220ff

Salisbury Cathedral, nave toward west

stone were added, the piers began to bend ominously. Flying buttresses were inserted in the clerestory and triforium to take the thrust out onto the arcades of the nave and transepts. The choir, however, was less able to receive this thrust since its arcade was interrupted by the second transepts, the entrances to which had to be in-filled with bracing arches. Finally, the openings to the north and south of the main crossing had also to be strengthened with bracing arches.

From the point of view of the interior, these emergency measures must be regarded as blemishes. From the point of view of the exterior, they may be forgiven as necessary requisites for the sensational elegance of the spire.

The architecture of the interior is as simple as that of the exterior—a three-story facade of arcade, triforium and clerestory with lancet windows. The stone comes from Chilmark, some ten miles west of Salisbury; the marble colonettes are from Purbeck in Dorset. In the 18th century these received a coat of dark brown varnish, which destroyed the original balance, for Purbeck marble, as may still be seen in the Chapter House, is the color of silver lead.

Apart from the bracing arches, the most significant alteration from the original design was the suppression of the choir screen or pulpitum. There have been three screens, the last of which was removed in 1956. The first was probably built at the same time as the Chapter House. It was a two-story structure, which later carried an organ. Part of the lower story, a series of canopied niches, is still to be seen against the west wall of the northeast transept.

The building of the new cathedral, begun under Bishop Richard Poore, was carried out by Elias of Dereham and Nicholas of Ely, but the progress of the work was not recorded. It seems that the west front may have to be credited to another team of workmen and to another master mind, for the architecture of the cathedral proper is extremely simple. The windows are lancets arranged in pairs or in groups of three, four or five. Some of the windows in the upper gables anticipate tracery, using the formula of two lancets surmounted by a roundel inscribed within a containing arch. Almost the only ornament is the very beautiful arcaded parapet that runs right around the cathedral and contributes greatly to the impression of unity.

The west front is an ornate screen, wider than the nave and its aisles, and taller than the lateral facades. The great west window retained the grouped lancets, but the rest of the wall space was divided into five stories filled with niches, many of which were set into blind windows, which repeat the formula of lancets, roundel and retaining arch of the gables. All the niches have plinths, suggesting that they were all intended to receive statues. Only eight of the original figures survive. The rest were put in by Gilbert Scott between 1860 and 1878. Unlike contemporary French cathedrals, Salisbury's west front was not conceived as the main entrance; its doorways are comparatively small. The north porch was clearly meant to be the principal means of access.

On the south side of the nave were built the largest cloisters in England, which gave access from the east gallery to the octagonal Chapter House. The cloisters, completed by 1284, offer in their openings toward the garth the fully developed style of geometrical tracery, which is repeated in the windows of the Chapter House.

The Chapter House is the most beautiful piece of interior architecture in the cathedral. A central column of Purbeck marble, completely rebuilt in 1856, splays out gracefully into the 16 vaulting ribs. Beneath the windows the facets of the wall are arcaded, and above the arcade runs a remarkable sculptured frieze of scenes from the Old Testament. There is evidence that the carvings were originally colored and gilded. Today, the Chapter House is used as a treasury exhibition in which the chief exhibit is one of the four surviving original exemplars of the Magna Carta, sealed by King John in 1215, in a state of almost perfect preservation.

The most probable date for the construction of the tower and spire is between the years 1280 and 1320. The original tower, the height of which is marked by a crenellated parapet, rose only just above the roof ridge.

The tower consists of two stories of the same height. On each story are two pairs of traceried windows, the inward ones glazed, the outward ones blind. The style is much more ornate than that of the cathedral proper. The passage from the square of the tower to the octagon of the spire—always a challenge to the medieval builder—is handled with great skill; the four corners of the tower give birth to lofty pinnacles, studded with ball flowers, which mask the transition.

The other problem facing the builder of the spire was the balance between the need for strength and the need to avoid undue weight. For the first 20 feet the facet walls have a thickness of two feet, but above this it is reduced to eight inches. There are three decorative bands around the spire which are hollowed out of the thickness of the stone, reducing it to between two and three inches of weight-bearing stone. It can only be said that the builders must have gotten the balance exactly right.

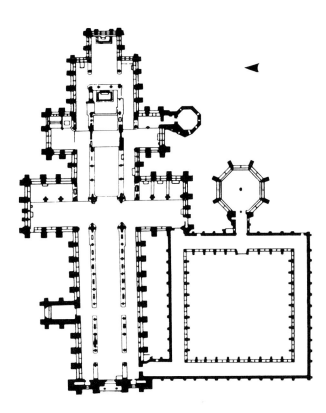

Salisbury Cathedral

The structure is as light as possible, and its strength is manifested by the fact that it is still standing.

Certain reinforcements, however, have been made; the first date from about 1300, when a system of iron braces was inserted into the lower part of the tower to prevent the walls from spreading under the load. This system was noted with approval by Christopher Wren when he made his survey of the building in 1668. The system of internal ties was considerably augmented by Gilbert Scott.

—IAN DUNLOP

IRON BRIDGE
Coalbrookdale, Shropshire, England

1777-79. Architect: Thomas Farnolls Pritchard (1723-77). **Engineer:** Abraham Darby III (1750-91).

Publications

BRACEGIRDLE, BRIAN, and MILES, PATRICIA H.: *The Darbys and the Ironbridge Gorge*. London, 1974.
BRIGGS, ASA: *Iron Bridge to Crystal Palace*. London, 1979.
COSSONS, NEIL, and TRINDER, BARRIE: *The Iron Bridge*. Bradford-on-Avon, 1979.
GLOAG, JOHN, and BRIDGWATER, DEREK: *A History of Cast Iron in Architecture*. London, 1948.
IRONBRIDGE GORGE MUSEUM TRUST: *The Coalbrookdale Ironworks: A Short History*. Telford, England, 1975.

MAGUIRE, R., and MATTHEWS, P.: "The Iron Bridge at Coalbrookdale." *Architectural Association Journal* 70, 4 (1958).

RUDDOCK, TED: *Arch Bridges and Their Builders 1735-1835.* 1979.

*

In a world filled with technological marvels, it may be difficult to understand why people could become excited about a cast-iron bridge, but in the 18th century when the Coalbrookdale Bridge was erected in Shropshire, it rapidly became an international tourist attraction. Widely recognized as the world's first iron bridge, it crosses the River Severn with a single 100-foot arch fabricated from one of the industrial revolution's most important new materials. The Iron Bridge symbolized all that was desirable and progressive about the industrial revolution in an age which regarded smoking factory chimneys and the clamor of foundries as heralds of a better world to come. For those who could not travel to see this marvel of human ingenuity in person, engraved views were widely available.

The Iron Bridge was built to connect the parishes of Madeley and Benthall, replacing passenger ferry service and facilitating local traffic by establishing a road link across the gorge of the River Severn, the major economic thoroughfare for regional commerce. The Severn Gorge had since Elizabethan times been involved in coal mining and other industrial activity, and in the 18th century it became the largest iron-producing county in England. New uses for the material, from rails and railroad-car wheels to engine boilers and farm gates, were developed and used in the district as a direct consequence of industrial production.

Perhaps nowhere else in England could a novel proposal for an iron bridge have been advanced, supported and carried to conclusion with relatively little public criticism being heaped upon the idea. Iron was a logical material to use because the bridge's specific site conditions ruled out traditional masonry or timber construction. The high-masted barges which plied the river required adequate clearance, unstable banks complicated abutment conditions, and sever periodic flooding could be counted upon to wash out foundations of intermediate piers. The design of a single-span, high-arch bridge of iron overcame these difficulties.

The technical accomplishment of the bridge was made possible by the combined talents of several local citizens. The Shrewsbury architect Thomas Farnolls Pritchard (1723-77) is credited with first proposing an iron bridge at Coalbrookdale and being responsible for the bridge's design, although he died before construction actually began. Pritchard's proposal received initial support from John Wilkinson, a leading ironmaster who formed the private subscription company that built the bridge and its associated road connections. After initial organization, however, leadership for the project passed to Abraham Darby III (1750-91), treasurer for the subscribers and contractor for building the bridge. Darby was a third-generation member of an important iron-making family. In 1709 his grandfather had been the first to use coke rather than charcoal in the smelting of iron, pioneering a technique that allowed iron production to use the abundant coal deposits of the English midlands rather than increasingly scarce forest resources, and his father had

Iron Bridge, Coalbrookdale: Shropshire, England, 1777-79

developed the coke-fired blast furnace, which made large-scale production economic. Darby's Coalbrookdale Company was responsible for the innovative casting required for constructing so great an undertaking, and it is no exaggeration to say that his persistence and financial sacrifices on behalf of the bridge project were responsible for its ultimate success.

In design, the bridge represents a synthesis of known forms and techniques. The semicircular arch was well understood from masonry construction, while dovetail joints from wooden construction provided the model for connections between secondary iron members. All the joint designs may well reflect Pritchard's initial training as a joiner. According to modern engineering standards, the iron was not very efficiently used, for the bridge required 378 tons of metal for a 100-foot span. In comparison, the next major iron bridges, both built in 1796, were more sparing in their use of material: Rowland Burdon's bridge over the River Wear at Sunderland spanned 236 feet using 260 tons of iron, and Thomas Telford's bridge over the Severn at Buildwas required 170 tons of iron to span 130 feet. Nevertheless, the pioneering bridge at Coalbrookdale involved considerable technical ingenuity: the castings for the five main arch ribs were done on sand molds at or near the bridge site, each half rib being cast as a single piece. Pig iron was remelted to provide the raw material, and once the castings were completed, the bridge was erected over a three-month period without interruption to river traffic.

Although the design of the Iron Bridge directly influenced that of several later bridges, its lasting importance lies not so much in its design as in its demonstration of iron's structural potential. In a sense, all later developments in metal construction, from framing for high-rise buildings to the graceful lines of steel suspension bridges, may be said to originate with this remarkable bridge over the Severn.

—MARIAN SCOTT MOFFETT

TIGBOURNE COURT, HAMBLEDON
Surrey, England

1899: Constructed; **Architect:** Edwin Lutyens (1869-1944).

Publications

AMERY, COLIN, LUTYENS, M., et al.: *Lutyens: The Work of the English Architect Sir Edwin Lutyens.* London, 1981.

BUTLER, A. S. G.: *The Architecture of Sir Edwin Lutyens.* 3 vols. London, 1950.

O'NEILL, DANIEL: *Edwin Lutyens: Country Houses.* London and New York, 1980.

WEAVER, LAWRENCE: *Houses and Gardens by Edwin Lutyens.* London, 1913.

*

Tigbourne Court belongs to a class of Edwin Lutyens houses that juxtapose the contradictory languages of a medieval vernacular with a more ordered and formal classicism. It is a theme that informed Lutyens' work throughout his career, prompting

Tigbourne Court, Hambledon: Surrey, England, 1899

historians sometimes to misread his life work as having evolved from early vernacular themes to a later interest in neoclassicism, when in fact both architectural languages appear throughout. The commonplace—both forms and materials of the traditional medieval English village house—as well as the historic authority and formal order of classicism touched his work during many periods.

Examples of such contradictions abound. At Marshcourt (Stockbridge, Hampshire, 1901), Lutyens inserted classical interiors within the medieval Tudor forms of a great manor house: pilasters, barrel vaults, marble columns and ceiling plasterwork mix with medieval timbered corridors within a manor house built in dressed Hampshire chalk and accented in brick and flint. At Folly Farm (Sulhamstead, Berkshire), Lutyens arranged extant vernacular farm structures, a 17th-century classic-styled "Dutch wing," and a neovernacular dining room wing in a sequence of additions dating from 1901 to 1912. An extraordinary synthesis of such contradictory elements takes place at Homewood (Knebworth, Hertfordshire, 1901), where (on the garden front) the symbiotic tension of classical forms rising out of the informal farm-vernacular mass informs the architect's most complex, taut and effective smaller-house design.

Tigbourne Court's contradictory design similarly contrasts its front and garden elevations, its materials and form, and its high and low architectural languages. The triple-gabled stone entrance front of Tigbourne Court's main block positions itself historically in Lutyens' work between similar gable threesomes at Munstead Corner (now Munstead Place, Munstead, Surrey, 1891-92), which is both half-timbered and asymmetrical, at Ruckmans (Oakwood, Surrey, 1894), which is clad in tile hanging, and at Homewood, which is clapboarded.

It is, indeed, Lutyens' delight in surface textures and the materiality of building which helps to transform Tigbourne's gabled roadside facade to an extraordinary work of regionalism. The house is principally built of Bargate stone with galletted mortar joints. Its walls are further enriched by courses of diagonally laid roof tiles forming horizontal bands, which strap the building forms and occasionally outline overscaled voussoirs over arched doorways. Thus, a low-style stringcourse begins to shape a voussoir defining a classical doorway. Two more explicitly classical details inform the road facade. Like Elizabethan Hardwick Hall in Derbyshire, a columned loggia accents the main entry at ground level, further elaborated by pairing the columns at Tigbourne. And in a more provincial gesture, the principal windows, classicized by alternating segmental arch and pedimental caps which project as simplified outlines, serve as well to echo similar features on the facade of Lutyens' first completely Georgian building, the Farnham Liberal Club (1894-95) in nearby Farnham, Surrey. Thus, these classical details both universalize and localize the building aesthetic.

But what is most remarkable about Tigbourne is the almost Baroque composition and exaggeration of scale of the concave flanking "pavilions." These present one-story domestic forms to terminate the roadside end of Tigbourne's side wings. With their classical detail, oversized chimneystacks and plasticity of form, these wing/pavilions transcend the strongly native (vernacular) materiality of the building. There Lutyens played what he called the "game" of architecture, speaking a sophisticated language with vernacular expressions but without appearing provincial. The courses of tile accenting the Bargate stone are as colorful as a regional dialect, enriching and localizing the language of architecture.

Moreover, the game involves typical Lutyens surprises. The exaggerated forms, the embracing facade and the site relationship to the road ennobles these outstretched arms that define the half-enclosed courtyard space. The aggrandized pavilions

lead, ironically, merely to the kitchen court at left and to one corner of the garden at right; indeed, the right flank of this second pavilion is merely a garden screen wall.

Lutyens' playful manipulations extended to his floor plans and spatial enrichments inside his houses. At Tigbourne, the axial entry is immediately blocked by an enclosed staircase preventing direct axial access from vestibule to dining room beyond. Such contradictions are found in the architect's most "high classical" house, Heathcote (Ilkley, Yorkshire, 1906) where a fireplace blocks an ordered entry and similarly forces circuitous patterns of circulation.

Tigbourne also gives evidence of Lutyens' delight in providing varied elevations within a single house in order to enrich the experience of walking around the house. The roadside elevation initially presents Tigbourne Court as orderly and balanced, a backdrop for a half-formed entry court. The garden elevations are picturesque and rambling in contrast, much as the axis and spatial sequence leading to the entry courtyard of Berrydown (1897-98, near Ashe, Hampshire) differ from its sweeping, less-formal, gabled garden front. Indeed, the massing of Tigbourne's garden elevations recalls the informal garden forms of Orchards (1897-99) built near (and immediately after) Gertrude Jekyll's Munstead Wood (1896) in Surrey. Such contradictions serve to aggrandize the house as one experiences it; complications of space and requirements for longer lengths of time to circulate make the house seem more extensive.

In these ways, as is the case with so many Lutyens houses, Tigbourne Court is both sophisticated and simple, a reflection of both the architect's respect for local traditions of building, as well as his concern for transforming a house into a work of architecture.

—ROBERT M. CRAIG

MINSTER
York, England

1079: Previous church burned and new cathedral begun. **1154-81:** East end rebuilt and enlarged. **Ca. 1220-40:** South transept added. **1240-53:** North transept added. **1253:** Crossing tower completed. **1280s:** Chapter house built. **1291-ca. 1350:** Nave built. **1342:** Roof completed (destroyed in fire, 1842). **Ca. 1350:** West facade finished. **1360-1405:** Four-bay choir, nonprojecting eastern transepts, four-bay presbytery built. **Ca. 1420:** Crossing tower rebuilt. **1430-50:** South tower added. **Ca. 1470:** North tower added. **19th century:** Fire damage. **1967-72:** Restoration.

Publications

AYLMER, G. E., and CANT, REGINALD (eds.): *A History of York Minster.* Oxford, 1977.

COLDSTREAM, NICOLA: "York Chapter House." *Journal of the British Archeological Association* 35 (1972).

GEE, E. A.: *York Minster: Chapter House and Vestibule.* London, 1980.

HARVEY, JOHN H.: "The Tracing Floor in York Minster." *Friends of York Minster 40th Annual Report* (1968).

HARVEY, JOHN H.: *The Mediaeval Architect.* London, 1972.

PEVSNER, NIKOLAUS, and METCALF, P.: *The Cathedrals of England.* Vol. 1 (Midland, Eastern and Northern England). London, 1985.

WANDER, STEPHEN: "York Chapter House." *Gesta* 17 (1978).

WILSON, CHRISTOPHER: *The Gothic Cathedral.* London, 1990.

Minster Cathedral, west facade: York, England, ca. 1350

There was a bishop in York by 314 and an archbishop by at least 735, but the earliest physical evidence for the metropolitan Church of St. Peter dates from the 11th century. After the minster was burned in 1079, Archbishop Thomas of Bayeux began a new church, probably on a different site, over the remains of the Roman principia. It was a long (362 feet), aisleless church with small transepts, apsidal transept chapels and a long, apsed eastern arm, with a crypt below. The east end was sumptuously rebuilt on an enlarged scale by Archbishop Roger of Pont l'Évêque (1154-81) as an aisled structure of eight bays, with a rectangular east end, small, projecting eastern transepts and a full crypt below, parts of which survive. This elaborate new choir, in a transitional style somewhat less developed than that

of Ripon, served as the basis for a series of rebuildings which eventually transformed the minster into a showcase of various phases of English Gothic architecture, all of the highest quality.

Early English style is represented in the transepts. Rebuilding on a grand scale probably began in about 1220 with the south arm, the north arm being slightly later, and all, including the crossing tower, finished by 1253. Each arm is three bays long with north and south aisles and a three-story elevation of arcades, large triforium or false gallery and clerestory. The aisles are rib-vaulted, although a high vault may have been planned initially. Purbeck marble shafting and stiff-leaf foliage are used lavishly there. Compound piers are used in the arcades, and the triforium is of four lights with nested superarches. All this puts

Minster Cathedral, nave toward west: 1291-ca. 1350

it generally into the Lincoln tradition and more firmly into a northern tradition of Early English building (Whitby, Beverley, Byland, Hexham). Tall lancets are also characteristic of the north, and the lancets called the Five Sisters which grace the north transept end wall (each 5 feet wide and 55 feet tall), epitomize the extent to which lancets could be used to replace stone with glass. In fact, in the north transept facade, remodeled slightly later, lancets are combined with a rose window in the gable and broadened by simple Y-tracery, pointing the way to an acceptance of the French bar-tracery techniques just being introduced at Westminster Abbey.

The freestanding, octagonal chapter house was built northeast of the north transept in the 1280s. The Westminster chapter house had set the standard for octagonal chapter houses in England with its vaults carried on a central pier and its large tracery windows. York continued this tradition. It is as large in plan as Westminster and Salisbury (60 feet), but is taller and does away with the central pier as does the chapter house at Southwell. Even with its flying buttresses, however, it could not carry a stone vault and was given a spectacular wooden imitation vault, which gives evidence of the sophisticated carpentry tradition that eventually created the Ely octagon. The earliest work in the chapter house features Purbeck shafts and mature stiff-leaf foliage. There is evidence, as well, that a central pier was originally foreseen, but a change of design resulted in the present "spatial fluidity." The stiff leaf gives way to naturalistic foliage similar to that at Southwell, and the later parts also provided the opportunity for an unorthodox display of imported Rayonnant features. This can be seen, for instance, in the undulating row of canopies that encircles the chapter house dado above the bench for the canons. This arrangement of projecting, corbeled polygons was developed in France—on the west facade of Strasbourg Cathedral, for instance—to shelter jamb figures on portals, but is used here to far different effect. Rayonnant, too, are the blind gables and pinnacles of the buttresses and the use of "microarchitectural" details; St. Urbain, Troyes, in particular, is recalled in many details, like the tracery patterns in the slightly later L-shaped vestibule to the chapter house. Thus, it is possible to see in the chapter house the demise of Early English style with the appearance of novel French features that would eventually lead to the creation of the Decorated style. This transitional stage can be seen, as well, in the large, five-light windows, in which strictly geometrical tracery patterns were beginning to break down, with a tall central light impaling a pointed trefoil below the more conventional three cusped roundels in the head.

The nave was begun at its east end in 1291, and the west facade was finished ca. 1350. The nave is high for England (99 feet) and wide, as well. The arcades are also high (51 feet) and wide, and Purbeck has been purged from the compound piers. Rayonnant influences intensify in the nave, which is the most purely French-looking of any 13th-century cathedral architecture in England. Vaulting shafts run unbroken from the floor to the vaults (again wooden imitations). The triforium, with its arcade of five gabled arches, is articulated with the clerestory as a single unit, with the triforium mullions running unbroken into the clerestory in classic Rayonnant fashion. The graphic definition of this upper zone is intensified by relegating the clerestory passage to the exterior, bringing the windows flush with the wall plane. In all this, York was part of a diffusion of Rayonnant style that spread in all directions from the Île-de-France: west to Sées, south to Clermont-Ferrand, east to Regensburg and north to Utrecht. The York nave shares many of its elements with such buildings. The designer, although undoubtedly English, must have had a very broad knowledge of recent continental architecture. This treatment of the upper wall plane was revolutionary in England. It prefigured the sheer planes of tracery in the east end of Gloucester choir but was not influential in the same way, although the nave design in general provided a clear precedent for those of Canterbury and Winchester Cathedral naves. Even in the north, the York nave proved only a limited stylistic precedent; the impetus that produced the York nave and chapter house was also at work in London (Eleanor Crosses, St. Stephens' Chapel), where it was developed further into Decorated, and later Perpendicular, which became more or less national styles. Thus, while the York nave and chapter house are important buildings because of the precocious, creative adaptations of their newly imported features, their limited influence makes an evaluation of their place in English architecture difficult.

A definite change of style can be seen in the upper parts of the west facade, the last part of the nave to be built. The lower part of the facade, with its rows of niches extending over buttresses across the breadth of the facade, is in the tradition of the English screen facade, as at Wells, but the effect is decisively transformed by the insertion of a great eight-light window, which dominates the facade. How the facade was originally designed, however, will never be known, as there was a distinct change just below the springing point of the west window arch. At that point, the facade becomes clearly Decorated. The flat gabled arches that define the niches on the

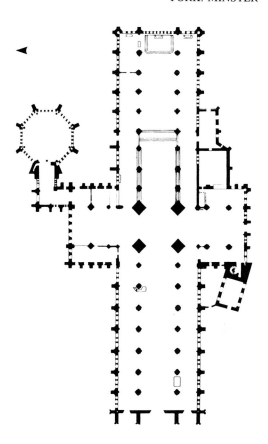

lower wall are replaced with nodding ogees, and the west window itself is a masterpiece of flowing Decorated tracery, in the same northern spirit as Carlisle and Selby. The upper windows opening into the towers are filled with a more standard Decorated pattern of reticulated tracery, here "sub-reticulated" as well.

Within 10 years of the completion of the west facade, the next major rebuilding program was begun at York: the Late Norman east end was replaced by an enlarged structure consisting of a four-bay choir, nonprojecting eastern transepts and a four-bay presbytery. The presbytery, which lay outside of the Norman east end, was built first, from 1361 to about 1370, before the old structure was demolished, and then the presbytery was joined to the transept, between circa 1380 and circa 1400. Although mixed with subdued Decorated elements, such as ogees, in the presbytery, Perpendicular emerges full-blown in the east end, a very early instance of this new style. A concerted effort was made to coordinate the design of this new eastern arm with that of the nave, so that there are equivalences in elevation, pier design and general effect. As the nave had, so to speak, anticipated the Perpendicular style, its design could easily incorporate more up-to-date Perpendicular features. The major difference between presbytery and choir occurs in the clerestory. The presbytery had retained the idea used in the nave of an exterior clerestory passage, and the clerestory and triforium tracery, again linked as in the nave, similarly conform to the wall plane. The interior screening effect culminates, as at Gloucester, in an enormous east window, here of nine lights and slightly larger in area than that at Gloucester, making it the largest Gothic window ever built. In the choir, the clerestory passage has been brought back, as was more usual, into the interior, creating a slightly different surface effect in the screened-off choir. Continuity between presbytery and choir is maintained, despite the presence of the one-bay eastern transept, by means of continuing the main arcades across this bay and placing tracery parapets on top of them, although they are open above this level as far as the vault (again, wooden, like all the York high vaults).

The last major change to the appearance of the cathedral consisted in the addition of three tall Perpendicular towers. The crossing tower was rebuilt beginning in about 1420 and the western towers slightly later, the south one circa 1430-50, the north one circa 1470. At its consecration in 1472, the minster was essentially as it is today. Considerable restoration work has been necessary to replace fire damage and stabilize the structure, most notably a campaign from 1967-72. This last campaign is a masterly piece of engineering which bolstered the foundations and created an undercroft under the crossing area, in which previous stages of construction back to the Roman period can be seen. York Minster has, nevertheless, retained a gratifying amount of its Gothic structure and more of its stained glass than any other church in Britain, making it particularly easy to appreciate the intended effect of its magnificent interior structure.

—JIM BUGSLAG

CASTLE HOWARD
Yorkshire, England

1700-37. **Architects:** John Vanbrugh (1664-1726) and Nicholas Hawksmoor (ca. 1661-1736). **1753-59:** West wing built; **Architect:** Thomas Robinson (ca. 1702-77). **1774-82:** Stables added; **Architect:** John Carr (1723-1807). **1875-88:** Remodeling. **1940:** Some plasterwork destroyed.

Publications

BEARD, GEOFFREY: *The Work of John Vanbrugh*. London, 1986.
SAUSMEREZ SMITH, CHARLES: *The Building of Castle Howard*. Chicago, 1990.
VANBRUGH, JOHN: *The Complete Works*. Vol. 4. Edited by Bonamy Dobrée and Geoffrey F. Webb. London, 1928.

*

Castle Howard, an English Baroque country house in Yorkshire, was built in the early 18th century for the third earl of Carlisle by John Vanbrugh and Nicholas Hawksmoor. It is, as a recent historian put it, a grand and swaggering building, standing in grounds of extraordinary beauty and finish. Like so much other work by Vanbrugh and Hawksmoor, however, Castle Howard and the buildings around it have suffered from the slings of criticism. Thomas Macaulay, in a richly equivocal phrase, called the house ''the most perfect specimen of the most vicious style,'' and Arthur Young in the 1760s spoke of the ornamental buildings on the grounds as being ''in so heavy and clumsy a style as to be perfectly disgusting.'' In 1940 the Great Hall, with its paintings by Gianantonio Pellegrini, the High Salon and the rooms to the east of it were all badly damaged by fire.

Castle Howard, interior hall

But Castle Howard has survived all of that and stands proud, a superb and elegant building, full of the richest architectural detail and wonderfully elaborated spaces. It was used very successfully a few years ago—through the offices of George Howard, then director-general of the British Broadcasting Corporation and a descendant of the third earl of Carlisle—as the setting for the television production of Evelyn Waugh's novel *Brideshead Revisited.*

Castle Howard was built to replace Henderskelfe Castle, which had been the property of the Howard family since 1571. Henderskelfe had been rebuilt in 1683, but it was badly damaged in a fire in 1693; at that point the earl of Carlisle, perhaps for the purpose of advancing in politics, decided to rebuild the house in the new style, calling in the architect William Talman. But Talman was a difficult person to work with, and in 1699, having dismissed Talman over a small detail of payment, the earl turned to Vanbrugh to produce a new plan. The new plans were done by Christmas, and by 1700 construction had begun; the work was completed some 37 years later.

The choice of Vanbrugh was something his political and social enemies made much of, and even now it seems a strange choice for the earl of Carlisle to have made—though the results completely justified his decision. It is known, however, that Hawksmoor was also involved in the work from the very beginning, and indeed it has sometimes been thought that he, rather than Vanbrugh, should be considered the architect of Castle Howard. There is no doubt that Hawksmoor managed the practical side of the building. Yet when in 1721 Hawksmoor spoke of Blenheim Castle, where his responsibilities throughout the years seem to have been the same as at Castle Howard, he talked of tending the building ''like a loving Nurse that almost thinks the Child her own.'' As Nikolaus Pevsner noted, the word ''almost'' is crucial here; and for all Hawksmoor did, it

Castle Howard: Yorkshire, England, 1700-42

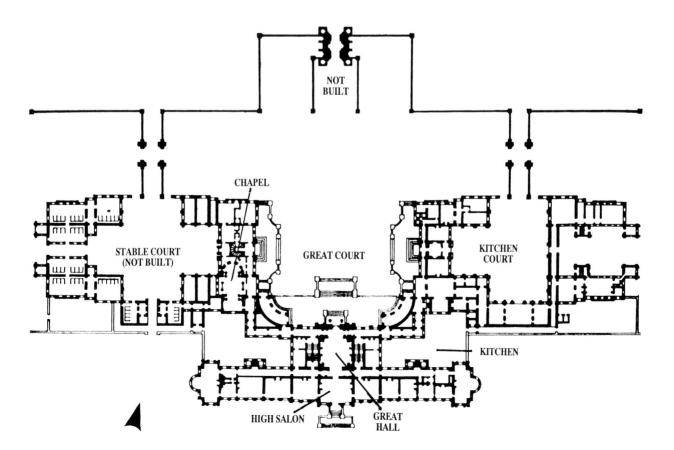

was Vanbrugh, as Charles Saumarez Smith has recently noted, who undertook the first task of designing and watched over the progress of the building, conscientiously and with passion. Help for the gardens, it should be noted, was obtained from George London, who was deputy superintendent of the King's Gardens and owned a nursery in Brompton Park.

Vanbrugh's plan for Castle Howard went through several stages. The first idea, derived perhaps from Talman's suggestion, was for a square central block with two side wings, almost equal in size to this block, that projected forth from arcades extending from the sides of the house. But that was a design for a small house, and in the later schemes, which were essentially those built, the body of the house was extended to a great rectangular plan, some 292 feet long on the clear garden side, with a great hall placed at the center and surmounted by a dome; the wings were brought much closer to the body of the house. According to the first plan, the profile of the house was sharply broken, but the revised profile became that of a great central dome, echoed by the towers and domes of the wings and the corridors, a wildly rhythmic string of masses and voids, roof decorations and stepped blocks.

The house, as built, consists of a nine-bay central block with, on the south side, long, nine-bay wings parallel to the center, and on the north side, ranges set at right angles to the front and connected to it by quadrant wings. The kitchen wing was done by 1701, the house by 1702, the dome by 1706, and the Great Hall by 1712. The gardens were begun in 1703, with the Satyr Gate being completed by 1706, the obelisque by 1714, the wonderful Carrmire Gate by 1725, the Temple of the Four Winds by 1724-26, and the Gothic ruins and towers by 1730; the great Mausoleum by Hawksmoor, though begun in 1731, was not finished until 1742, six years after his death. Further activities included corrections made at the west end by Thomas Robinson, son-in-law of the earl of Carlisle, and it was he who in 1753-59 built the unfinished west wing. Stables were added in 1774-82 by John Carr, and at the center of the south front a great fountain was built in the 19th century by John Thomas. A chapel was added at some point, most of its present decorations coming from a remodeling done in 1875-88.

Castle Howard's interior was filled with decorations painted by Pellegrini and his friend Marco Ricci, and by others, notably the French artist Jean Hervé and a Dutch painter, Jacob Campo Weyerman. Scenes of classical mythology abound, of Phaethon, of Venus and Minerva, of episodes from the Trojan War, and at the west end in the Grand Cabinet at the front, a scene of Diana and Endymion. Filling this out, and surrounding the paintings, was extraordinary plasterwork, some of which in the Great Hall was destroyed in 1940, and colored marble work of the richest and most beautiful kind.

Castle Howard was an expensive project, the whole costing some £78,000, of which the house was £35,000, a large sum of money even for someone as rich as the earl of Carlisle; his income has been calculated recently to have been about £8,000 per annum. These extravagant sums tempt one to view Castle Howard as a house of show. Yet the interiors, for all their decorations, were not grand, and Vanbrugh himself spoke of the expenses of the house as being about £100, no more than was spent "in the Old one." Perhaps the earl of Carlisle had originally nourished political ambitions and had hoped to use the house as the center of a political party. But that was not to be. Money was not free, and after the death of Queen Anne in 1714, he became disillusioned with the factionalism at the court and retired to a somewhat lonely, circumscribed life at Castle Howard. For all its apparent lavishness, Castle Howard ended up as a place where the earl of Carlisle could lead a quiet, domestic old age, or, as Lady Mary Wortley Montague chose to describe it, a nunnery for his three unmarried daughters.

—DAVID CAST

Scotland

CRAIGIEVAR CASTLE
Aberdeenshire, Scotland

1610-26. Architect: William Forbes.

Publications

FENWICK, HUBERT: *Scotland's Historic Buildings*. London, 1974.
HILL, O.: *Scottish Castles of the 16th and 17th Centuries*. London, 1953.
MACGIBBON, DAVID, and ROSS, THOMAS: *Castellated and Domestic Architecture of Scotland*. 5 vols. Edinburgh, 1887-92.
TRANTER, N.: *The Fortified House in Scotland*. 2 vols. Edinburgh, 1962-63.

*

When the National Trust for Scotland took over the running of Craigievar in 1963, on the death of Lord Sempill, the eighth baronet of Craigievar, they described it in their guidebook as "a mountain chateau." It was a description not lightly used, for at almost 1,000 feet elevation, and complete with barmkin and bartizans, Craigievar was in every way the apotheosis of the Scottish Baronial castle. One of the "Castles of Mar," a group of five Aberdeenshire fortalices, Craigievar—or Craigmar, meaning the Rock of Marr—was built as a status symbol for William Forbes, a rich timber merchant and brother to the bishop of Aberdeen, and completed in 1626.

Although neither as fine in its detailing as nearby Crathes, nor, being harled, as good in its stone workmanship as the earlier Amisfield Tower in Dumfries, Craigievar is, nevertheless, a remarkable building. Built apparently for defense—if the remaining evidence of an encompassing barmkin, complete with wall and turrets, is to be believed—Craigievar was a transitional building and thus neither fully a fortress nor wholly a house, but rather a tower infused with the trappings of culture. The plasterwork which adorns the interior was applied, as soon as the building was finished, by, among others, Joseph Fenton, who had recently done work at Glamis Castle; this work is typical of early-17th-century craftsmanship, yet remains strangely at odds, through its use of Renaissance motifs, with the medieval imagery of the exterior. Similarly, the building's defenses were menacing but hardly meaningful, for the cannons which projected from the walls were carved of stone, and the rooftop vantage point was surrounded by Italianate balusters rather than the battlements one would expect. Indeed, as Hubert Fenwick has observed, "Craigievar, with its fake cannon, corbels and turrets, and its rich plasterwork, is a triumph of frivolity and fun in a cold climate inhabited by supposedly unimaginative, miserable men, whose whole beings were governed by the doleful recitation of the psalms and the fight for survival."

In plan Craigievar is typical of Scottish tower houses, although more compact in its lower stories than Castle Fraser, another, and almost contemporary, Castle of Mar, and less frenzied in its upper stories than Claypotts, a late-16th-century building built, like Castle Fraser, on a Z-plan and principally for defense, located to the south at Dundee. Craigievar's heavy

walls contain one main room on each floor, although the spiral stairs, switching and turning within the thickness of the structure, suggest other spaces and relationships which exist beyond and above and below. The plan is L-shaped but, rather surprisingly, the entrance contained within the angle of the L leads not to a winding stair, which it would have done in earlier and more aggressively defensive buildings, but rather to a hall first and then a straight stair. Such an entrance is surely one of procession and not of protection.

Craigievar is beautifully situated and now, largely free from its surrounding barmkin, comes up on the visitor almost unexpectedly, for there are no gardens or drives to herald its approach. Its color, a pale pink, contrasts well with the gray slate roofs and the often leaden sky. But much has changed since William Forbes built it. The 18th century saw the replacement of the leaded lights and wooden shutters with sliding-sash windows common to the Georgian town houses of the lowland cities, and the lower windows have been enlarged and thus robbed of any defensive usefulness. At much the same time many of the rooms were paneled with memel—Scots fir of varied origin—and left unpainted. Yet for all its gentrification over the years, Craigievar remains a late medieval or Early Renaissance building. It could never be mistaken for a piece of Victorian Scottish Baronial Revival, such as William Burn or David Bryce might have built, for theirs were modeled on buildings such as Castle Fraser or even Glamis Castle, where horizontal growth and greater picturesque informality provided precedents more suited to the multiservanted society of that day. Craigievar, remaining tall and upright, was of an earlier time and a more dangerous one.

—NEIL JACKSON

DRUMLANRIG CASTLE
Dumfriesshire, Scotland

1679-90: Castle constructed; **Architects:** William Bruce, Robert Mylne and James Smith.

Publications

CRAWFORD, J.: *Memorials of Alloa*. 1874, p. 91.
MYLNE, R. S.: *The Master Masons to the Crown of Scotland*. 1893.
WOOD, M. and ARMET, H.: *Extracts from the Records of the Burgh of Edinburgh, 1681-9, passim. 1698-1701, passim. 1701-18*.

*

The first sight of Drumlanrig is an unforgettable experience. The drive, having crossed the River Nith, doubles back upon its course and runs straight as an arrow up toward the entrance front, which presents the most dramatic silhouette. Although there is no suggestion of fortification, Drumlanrig has a militant disposition. The towers and cupolas, marshaled on each flank into two well-grouped masses, are united by a classical frontispiece, lower in height, but richer in treatment, centering on a

Craigievar Castle: Aberdeenshire, Scotland, 1610-26

boldly projecting porch which rises to become a clock tower crowned with a ducal coronet.

This facade, which faces north, is a fine piece of architecture. It is built of ashlar in the warm, salmon-pink sandstone of the region. It rises above a terrace which surrounds three sides of the forecourt, from which it is reached by a double *fer-a-cheval* staircase which is possibly modeled on that of the Queen's House by Inigo Jones at Greenwich. The towers are of five stories, the inward blocks of three and the central portion of two. Four large staircase towers on the inward angles of the courtyard project above the balustrade. There are certain touches which only an experienced architect is likely to have thought of. Over the porch the cornice arches into a full semicircle

beneath the clock tower. At the center of the corner towers it does the same, but on a smaller scale. There is something rather French about this: François Mansart used the arching cornice at Blois.

At first sight the north front of Drumlanrig has every appearance of being symmetrical. But it is not. Somewhat astonishingly, the entrance feature, with its ducal coronet, is not central to its facade: it is a few feet right of center. This asymmetry is to be discerned in the ground plan. The eastern range is appreciably wider than the western. The northeast staircase tower therefore projects further into the silhouette than does the northwest one. This strongly suggests an irregularity imposed by the retention of an older building, or at least of its foundations. If this is so,

Drumlanrig Castle: Dumfriesshire, Scotland, 1675-89

the slightly eccentric placing of the central feature of the north front could be seen as a very skilful device on the part of the architect to minimize this apparent lack of symmetry. There was, in fact, a previous design which may have been the cause of this irregularity.

The question of the genesis and authorship of Drumlanrig has been studied by Mark Girouard in *Country Life*. The present building was begun in 1679 by the first duke of Queensberry, but the project seems to date back to 1618 when his grandfather, William, first earl of Queensberry, was thinking of rebuilding the old castle. The only plan known looks unfinished, but it incorporates massive corner towers similar to those built by the first duke. If these corner towers were to have been capped each with four corner turrets, as in the present building (which would not show on a ground plan), this could indeed be the origin of the final design.

The plan of four corner towers capped with smaller cupolas had come to England with the building of the Fountain Court at Theobalds by Lord Burghley in about 1585. It was repeated at Holdenby and later at Audley End. In 1618 Theobalds was still standing. It was the favorite country palace of James I of England and VI of Scotland, and was well known to many Scottish lords. James had visited Drumlanrig in 1617.

When the first duke decided on his rebuilding of Drumlanrig, he annotated the 1618 plan ''to be looked over and advised by Sir Wm Bruise'' (Sir William Bruce) ''as also Mr Mills' (Robert Mylne) draughts both for the house and bridge.'' They were the two most distinguished architects in Scotland. Mylne was the king's master mason, in which post he had succeeded William Wallace, the builder of Heriot's Hospital in Edinburgh, a building that bears a strong resemblance to Drumlanrig. Also involved was James Smith, Mylne's son-in-law, who was certainly

the architect in charge toward the end of the campaign and giving directions to William Lukup, ''Master of Work at Drumlanrig.'' Notably, Smith was also the architect of Dalkeith Palace for the duchess of Buccleuch.

It must be noted that neither Bruce nor Smith ever built or designed anything remotely resembling Drumlanrig. They may have advised on details, but it is unlikely that either of them created the silhouette. Girouard sums up thus: ''It is quite possible that the plans were in fact prepared by William Wallace, the designer of Heriot's Hospital, who was made King's Master Mason in 1617.'' In this case, Heriot's could be a copy of Drumlanrig, rather than vice-versa.

Drumlanrig remained in the possession of the Queensberry family until the death of the fourth duke—''Old Q''—in 1810, when it passed, together with the dukedom, to Henry, third duke of Buccleuch. This nobleman had married, in 1767, Elizabeth, heiress to the duke of Montagu, the owner of Boughton. There thus came into his possession the three ducal estates together with their surnames—Montagu, Douglas, Scott.

The inventory drawn up for the new possessor of Drumlanrig tells a sorry tale of neglect and disrepair, and C. K. Sharpe, writing in 1812, described the gallery as presenting a ''sad scene of desolation.'' The fourth duke of Buccleuch made certain changes in the disposition of the rooms. The original entrance had been ''under piazzas into a small court.'' Across the courtyard was an impressive porch, similar to that in the center of the south facade, leading into what is today the dining room. The arches of the piazza were glazed in anticipation of a visit from Queen Victoria, and this area became the entrance hall. Above this the gallery—''a noble Beautiful room adorned with many portraits''—was divided into bedrooms and the ''carved lym tree work'' of Grinling Gibbons transferred to the drawing room.

The plan of Drumlanrig reproduced in the first volume of Colen Campbell's *Vitruvius Britannicus* (1715) shows the staircase at the west end of what is now the dining room and service room. This staircase was in all probability moved to its present position east of the dining room by the fourth duke of Buccleuch.

As Girouard says, ''There is a bit of everything at Drumlanrig—of French, Dutch and Scottish, of Kinross, Holyrood and Heriot's Hospital.'' I would add the possibility of an English influence through the Fountain Court at Theobalds. But diverse as the influences may be, they are all blended into one harmonious whole at Drumlanrig, creating what is certainly the most dramatic and arguably the finest house in Scotland.

—IAN DUNLOP

PALACE OF HOLYROODHOUSE
Edinburgh, Scotland

1128: Abbey constructed. **13th century:** Abbey lavishly rebuilt. **1501-05:** Shape of present Holyroodhouse set with construction of quadrangle and south range with tower. **1528-32:** North range with tower added. **From 1663:** Full restoration. **Architects:** Begun by John Mylne, Jr. (died in 1667); taken over by his nephew, Robert Mylne (1633-1710), but final plans were by William Bruce (died in 1710). Robert Mylne supervised building from 1671, incorporating early-16th-century tower.

Publications

FENWICK, HUBERT: *Architect Royal: The Life and Works of Sir William Bruce, 1630-1710*. Kineton, England, 1970.

GIFFORD, JOHN, McWILLIAM, COLIN, and WALKER, DAVID: *Edinburgh*. Harmondsworth, 1984.

MYLNE, ROBERT SCOTT: *The Master Masons to the Crown of Scotland and Their Works*. Edinburgh, 1893.

The history of the Palace of Holyroodhouse is as complicated as the history of the Crown of Scotland, with whose fortunes it is inextricably linked. Stylistically it is far from straightforward, Jacobean ceilings being inserted by the Victorians, medieval towers being built during the Enlightenment. Yet when seen with its rugged backdrop of Arthur's Seat and Salisbury Crags, it appears quintessentially Scottish.

The development of the Palace of Holyroodhouse began with the establishment, by David I, King of Scotland, of an abbey about a mile to the east of the castle rock at Edinburgh in 1128. This royal patronage made the abbey important, and its location, so close to a significant stronghold, encouraged its use and growth. Within a hundred years the church was rebuilt on a lavish scale and, a century later, in 1326, Robert I, the Bruce, held parliament there. By that time Holyrood clearly was a major royal residence as well as an abbey, and the royal connection was

Holyroodhouse: Edinburgh, Scotland, from 1663

cemented when David II was interred in the abbey choir in 1370.

Successive monarchs have added to the palace, while invading armies and irate mobs have destroyed it. Thus it has grown fitfully and unharmoniously. The oldest significant works date from James IV's rebuilding of 1501-05, when the shape of the present Holyroodhouse was set: a quadrangle to the west of the abbey cloister garth, and a south range with a tower near the site of William Bruce's later and remaining southwest tower. Following his father's work, James V added a north range to the quadrangle in 1528-32, of which the northwest tower survives, built by the master mason John Ayton. Three years later the west and south sides of the quadrangle were rebuilt, the west elevation being given a symmetrical arrangement of tall, canted-bay and bow windows, the latter framing a central entranceway and suggestive of a barbican. Only the missing southwest tower upset the balance of this now grand facade.

An English invasion in 1544 and destruction by Reformers in 1559 left the palace pillaged and the abbey abandoned. Although it seems likely that the damage to the palace was patched up in 1554-66, no substantial work was done until the royal visits of James VI and I in 1617, and Charles I in 1633, demanded it. But the fall of the Stuarts led to the quartering of Cromwellian troops in the palace in 1650, a resultant fire and the subsequent abandoning of most of the building.

The Restoration of the monarchy in 1660 saw the restoration of the palace's fortunes and, ultimately, its fabric. The king's master mason, John Mylne, carried out a full survey of the buildings in 1663, and the Scottish Privy Council eventually voted £30,000 for the restoration of Holyroodhouse and Stirling Castle. Between 1671 and 1679 William Bruce and Robert Mylne, respectively the king's surveyor-general and (new) master mason, rebuilt the quadrangular buildings, and balanced the old northwest tower with a matching one to the southwest. The west wing was replaced with a long, low, balustraded range with an aedicular central entranceway of coupled Roman Doric columns and a surmounting octagonal cupola, the clock face dated 1680. The courtyard elevations were arcaded and pilastered. With the exception of the battlemented terminal feature, these new buildings were copybook classical. Internally, the ceilings and decorative woodwork and plasterwork in the sequentially arranged rooms were by George Dunterfield, Alexander Eizat, John Houlbert, Jan van Santvoort and others.

Externally little of substance has changed since Bruce recast Holyroodhouse. Internally, however, the logical arrangement of his state and private rooms was never allowed to be fully realized. What was intended to be the Queen's Council Chamber was commandeered as a Roman Catholic chapel for Mary of Modena, and in 1686 her husband, by then James VII and II, ordered the conversion of the Council Chamber into another Roman Catholic chapel; however, the new fittings were destroyed by a Protestant mob in December 1688, the very month the king fled to France.

Holyroodhouse saw little activity following the Act of Union in 1707, except for Prince Charles Edward's brief occupation in 1745. In 1822, however, George IV made his grand visit to Scotland and, for that, the processional route through the Great Apartments was virtually inverted, an arrangement confirmed through Queen Victoria's visit of 1844 and the conversion of Bruce's Guard Hall to Throne Room (and sometime dining room), complete with a new Jacobean ceiling by Robert Matheson.

Little evidence remains of the bustle of outbuildings which had surrounded Holyroodhouse during its varied life as an abbey, monastery, parliament and palace. Today it sits behind heavy wrought-iron screens and gates that are reminiscent of the work of Jean Tijou. The forecourt is naked except for an ornate, octagonal fountain built by Matheson in 1858 and decorated with small, historical figures which are described in *Edinburgh,* by Gifford et al., as having "all the charm and much of the appearance of garden gnomes."

—NEIL JACKSON

EDINBURGH NEW TOWN
Edinburgh, Scotland

1767: Phase I begun; **Architect:** James Craig. **1791:** Charlotte Square begun; **Architect:** Robert Adam. **1802-30:** Phase II. **1800-1830:** Waterloo Place; **Architect:** Archibald Elliot (1761-1823); Moray Estate; **Architect:** James Gillespie Graham; Royal Terrace; **Architect:** William H. Playfair.

Publications

ADAM, R.: *The Works in Architecture of Robert and James Adam, Esquires.* 3 vols. 1773-1822. Reprint. London, 1931.

BOLTON, ARTHUR: *The Architecture of Robert & James Adam.* 2 vol. set. 1922. Reprint 1984.

Dictionary of Architecture, ed. Wyatt Papworth for the Architectural Publication Society, 8 vols. 1852-92.

DUNBAR, JOHN G.: *Architecture of Scotland.* Rev. ed. London, 1978.

GRAHAM, J. M.: "Notice of the Life and Works of W. H. Playfair." *Transactions of the Architectural Institute of Scotland* v, part iv, (1859-61): 13-28.

HAMILTON, THOMAS and BURN, WILLIAM: *Report relative to the proposed approaches from the South and West to the Old Town of Edinburgh.* 1824.

HAMILTON, THOMAS: *A Report relative to Proposed Improvements on the Earthen Mound at Edinburgh.* 1830.

HITCHCOCK, HENRY-RUSSELL: *Early Victorian Architecture in Britain.* 2 vols. New York, 1972.

HUGHES, T. H.: "W. H. Playfair." *Quarterly of the Incorporation of Architects in Scotland* Nos. 17-18 (1926).

LINDSAY, IAN GORDON: *Georgian Edinburgh.* 2nd ed., rev. Edinburgh and London, 1973.

MACAULAY, JAMES: *The Gothic Revival 1745-1845.* Glasgow, 1975.

MACGIBBON, DAVID and ROSS, THOMAS: *The Castellated and Domestic Architecture of Scotland.* Edinburgh, 1887.

MACLACHLAN, JOHN: "Edinburgh Architects" in *Builder* (1882): 667-8.

ORESKO, ROBERT: *The Works in Architecture of Robert and James Adam.* 1975.

YOUNGSON, A. J.: *The Making of Classical Edinburgh, 1750-1840.* Edinburgh, 1966.

*

Edinburgh, the capital of Scotland, was in 1700 a medieval city complete with castle, palace, cathedral and a mass of tall, flatted houses crammed together on a steep-sided defensible ridge. A single, wide High Street linked castle to palace on the crest of the ridge, and a multitude of narrow steeply inclined side streets (known in Scotland as "closes") gave access to the densely populated areas of housing.

After the full union of Scotland and England in 1707 the

Edinburgh New Town: Edinburgh, Scotland, 1760s

economy of Scotland underwent a period of rapid growth, and that led to a large increase in the population of Edinburgh. The scope for natural expansion from the old medieval city was limited, and in the 1750s the town council acquired a flattish area of land to the north, of roughly equal area to that of the "Old Town," as it was from then onward known, with the intention of building a modern city. Several architects were asked to prepare plans, and in 1767 the proposal of the local architect James Craig was selected. Thus the first "New Town" of Edinburgh was initiated.

Craig's plan was very straightforward. It called for a rectangular city consisting of three straight, parallel streets running east to west with the central and principal street, George Street, terminating in a square at either end. The most prominent site in each square, that opposite to the connection with the central street, was reserved for a church. Thus the two churches were to face each other along the principal axis of the new city. The two flanking streets were to have buildings on one side only. The houses on the southerly of these, Princes Street, would look back across an area of marsh (subsequently developed as a city-center park) to the Old Town on its ridge, and that to the north, Queen Street, faced open country, soon to be built up in the expansion of the New Town which occurred in the 19th century.

The area of building between the two squares was subdivided into rectangular blocks by three transverse streets. Further subdivision, but always preserving the rectangular theme, was accomplished by the insertion of narrow minor streets for artisans' houses and a tertiary system of service lanes. The overall plan of this first New Town was therefore a rectangle with two axes of symmetry. It consisted of wide principal streets and squares

laid out in a gridiron pattern. The spaciousness of the layout, which allowed ample fresh air and daylight to penetrate the city, was one of its principal attractions to a population then living in the cramped and unhealthy conditions of the Old Town. The rectilinearity would no doubt also have been attractive to the aesthetic sensibilities of the Neoclassical Age.

Although the town council acquired the land on which the New Town would be built and provided a limited amount of the infrastructure, it was their intention that the project would be funded by private capital. Accordingly, the projected streets and squares were subdivided into building plots and each was feued (leased) to individuals who were required to build their own houses subject to the conditions of the plan. These conditions covered such issues as the building line and the roofline and envisaged a terraced arrangement, but were sufficiently general to allow considerable variations to occur in the appearance of the individual houses. The New Town was to be entirely residential with no commercial property, not even shops. The town council hoped that the feuars would build themselves gracious town palaces and thus create a splendid and magnificent townscape. The reality was to be somewhat different. Many of the feus were in fact taken up by speculative builders, and with a number of exceptions, the houses are of plain, robust appearance. The overall effect, however, which is one of individuality within regularity, is nevertheless magnificent.

Building began at the eastern end of the site in the 1770s. The earliest houses consisted of two stories plus a basement with an outside "area" at basement level enclosed by cast-iron railings, and were versions of the typical terraced town house to be found elsewhere in Britain. They were built entirely of stone rendered with stucco and had dressed quoins and classical doorcases. As building progressed westward in the 1780s the architecture became more refined, with ashlar masonry being used and an attempt being made to give each house a complete classical front; typically, the entrance floors were embellished with chamfered rustication to act as a base for the principal floor, which had become a pilastered *piano nobile*. In a number of cases a unified frontage was placed across three houses, with the central house being given a pedimented temple front.

The glory of the first New Town is Charlotte Square, the westerly of the two squares. There the architect Robert Adam was employed to give the 11 houses which form the entire north side a single unified palace frontage. The houses are of three stories with a basement, but the treatment is typically Georgian. The entrance floor is of chamfered rusticated ashlar forming a base for the two upper floors in plain ashlar, which appear as a *piano nobile* and mezzanine. Three houses form a central block, which is given emphasis by being drawn forward and ornamented with half columns in the Corinthian order. The central house lies behind a temple front. Emphasis is also given to the two end blocks, but there pilasters are used. In both the central and the end blocks the wall plane advances and recedes in typical Adam fashion to create a sense of movement. Individual doorways are underplayed throughout so as not to detract from the unity of the whole block. The overall effect is similar to that sought later in London by John Nash, but, unlike that of Nash, Adam's detailing is controlled and well resolved.

The first New Town of Edinburgh was built almost entirely as planned and was more or less complete by the beginning of the 19th century. The population of the city continued to expand, however, and so the building work did not cease. A "Second New Town" was begun in 1802 on the land north of Craig's New Town, extending from Royal Circus in the west to London Street in the east. This was quickly followed by a "Third," built around Calton Hill to the east of the original New Town, and then a "Fourth" on the Moray Estate to the north and west of the original. The area occupied by the city doubled in the second half of the 18th century with the building of the first New Town, and these new developments caused it to double in area again between 1800 and 1830.

The extensions to the New Town of Edinburgh were planned in the spirit of the picturesque. Instead of the "rational" gridiron plan of symmetrically disposed straight streets and squares of the first New Town, the second wave of building was an affair of crescents, irregular circuses and vistas "closed" by views of prominent buildings. The buildings around Calton Hill, which include Thomas Hamilton's Royal High School, are a particularly fine example of the application of the ideas of the picturesque movement to the creation of a townscape. The underlying topography of Edinburgh was, of course, ideally suited to this romantic approach. It would scarcely have been possible to invent an arrangement of hills and valleys, including an Old Town on a ridge complete with castle and palace, which would have better lent itself to extension and enhancement according to the principles of the picturesque movement.

Although the layouts of the extensions to the New Town were significantly different from that of the original, the character of the architecture was substantially the same. The terraced houses are of ashlar masonry with chamfered rustication on the entrance floors and railinged "areas." The grander streets and crescents have again been given unified frontages ornamented with elements of the classical vocabulary.

Today the First New Town of Edinburgh and its extensions are still in essence a Georgian city. Although commercial pressure has resulted in much rebuilding in the First New Town, which is the business center of present-day Edinburgh, the original layout of streets and squares has been preserved and

a significant number of the original buildings have survived. The 19th-century extensions have fared better; the buildings there have been little altered externally and the majority are still dwelling houses. The essential character of the Georgian city has therefore been preserved, and the New Town of Edinburgh is the largest area of Georgian town planning to be seen anywhere in the United Kingdom. It is one of the architectural treasures of Europe.

—A. J. MACDONALD

GLASGOW SCHOOL OF ART
Glasgow, Scotland

1896: Commission awarded; **Architect:** Charles Rennie Mackintosh (1868-1928). **1896-98:** Eastern section constructed; **Architect:** Charles Rennie Mackintosh. **1906-09:** Western section redesigned; **Architect:** Charles Rennie Mackintosh.

Publications

BILLCLIFFE, ROGER: *Charles Rennie Mackintosh: The Complete Furniture, Furniture Drawings and Interior Designs.* London, 1979.

BLISS, D. P. (ed.): *Charles Rennie Mackintosh and the Glasgow School of Art.* Glasgow, 1961.

BUCHANAN, WILLIAM, et al: *Mackintosh's Masterwork: Charles Rennie Mackintosh and the Glasgow School of Art.* San Francisco, 1989.

COOPER, JACKIE (ed.): *Mackintosh Architecture: The Complete Buildings and Selected Projects.* London, 1978.

EADIE, WILLIAM: *Movements of Modernity: The Case of Glasgow and Art Nouveau.* New York, 1990.

FRAMPTON, KENNETH, and FUTAGAWA, YUKIO: *Modern Architecture: 1851-1919.* New York, 1983.

"Glasgow School of Art." *Global Architecture* 49.

HOFMANN, WERNER, and KULTERMANN, UDO: *Modern Architecture in Color.* New York, 1970.

PEVSNER, NIKOLAUS: "Charles Rennie Mackintosh." In *Studies in Art, Architecture and Design: Victorian and After.* Princeton, New Jersey, 1968.

*

When the foundation stone of the Glasgow School of Art was laid in May 1898, it was already known that the accommodation which the governors required could not be built for the money available. Only half the building—the eastern half up to the main central entrance—was to be erected, the completion necessarily delayed until funds permitted. In the event, this postponement meant that the history of the building's realization stretched from 1896, when conditions for a limited competition were drawn up, until December 1909, when the formal opening took place. For the competition winner, Charles Rennie Mackintosh of the Glasgow practice Honeyman and Keppie, these 14 years lay at the heart of a relatively short career. These were formative years for Mackintosh, and, although the broad concept of the winning design remained unaltered, the form and detail of the building was modified in tune with the evolving ideas of its architect. It is the creative impact of this developing sensibility which imparts a unique and wonderfully disturbing quality to this magnificent building.

Glasgow School of Art: Glasgow, Scotland, 1896-1909

The E-shaped plan extends east-west, placing the main studio accommodation along the northern street edge of the city block site. There is a central entrance leading to the main open staircase; secondary stairs are tucked in behind the returning gable wings at each end. The section of two principal studio floors and an attic steps its basement workshops down a steep slope to the south. All this is unexceptional enough. Yet the staged completion produces remarkable quirks of formal fate: four great glazed studio windows to the west of the central entrance instead of the original three placed to the east; a staircase added at the east into which, "outside inside," the bow windows of the earlier design room project; and, most spectacularly transformed from first elevational intentions, the west wing housing the amazing library. It is these events, and others like them, which release the exhilaration of the unexpected.

Some have argued that it is the specifically functional aspects of the School of Art's design which establish its significance in the history of architecture. Certainly, there is a forthright attitude toward structure in the exposure of brickwork and roof timbers and, in a more sophisticated way, in the neoconstructivist assembling of columns and balcony beams in the library. Moreover, the building's environmental qualities are directly evident in the huge daylighting grids of the studios and, not least, in the ducted system of plenum heating which passes vertically through the central spine wall of the plan.

For others, it is formal inventiveness, not merely in the decorative detail but, more radically, in the creative infraction of conventional compositional schemata, that matters most. The restive tensions of each elevation, as, for example, in the "eccentrically counterbalanced" studio facade and the overlapping symmetries of the west gable, or the abrupt changes in material—ashlar, snecked rubble, roughcast—are fascinating enigmas. Rejecting orthodox resolutions of the whole but retaining recognizable formal tactics, the School of Art admits a beguiling ambiguity.

Neither interpretation alone is adequate. Function and form are always symbiotic; what distinguishes the Glasgow School of Art is the pervasive honesty with which the necessary ambivalence of this relationship is asserted. There is, for instance, a special zest in the interplay of use and ornament. The school is a practical building: it had to serve, and still does, as a workshop for creative activity. No doubt the tight budget curbed excess; in any event, working spaces are generous if austere, finishes raw but robust. This functional response becomes a virtue while no opportunity to exploit any concomitant decorative potential is lost. Stiffening struts to the great grids of the studio windows, ironwork screens at stair landings, timber trusses above the first floor "museum": by "making embellishment intrinsic," all of these show that synthesis of serviceability and formal delight which is a hallmark of Mackintosh's work.

But there is a deeper dialectical aspect to this building, for both the practical needs of the building program and the formal dispositions of solid and void are themselves never entirely divorced from cultural allusion. In the flow of space around the slatted well of the main staircase or in the gridded mullions and transoms of the north facade or on the flat symbol discs of the Renfrew Street railings, Japanese influences are clear. But it is the building's Scottishness that packs the most powerful semantic punch. And this is no mere matter of tower-house memories lingering in the tall cliffs of the east, south and west elevations. In the School of Art, Mackintosh adduced his native architectural tradition—a tradition in which he saw that same unself-conscious integration of function and form—to confront the challenges of *his* time. The result is a contextual masterpiece.

—FRANK ARNEIL WALKER

Wales

CAERNARVON CASTLE
Caernarvonshire, Wales

1283-ca. 1330: Construction; **Architect:** James of St. George.

Publications

COLVIN, HOWARD: *A History of the King's Works*. Vol. 1. London, 1963.
ROYAL COMMISSION ON HISTORICAL MONUMENTS: *Central Caernarvonshire*. Vol. 2. London, 1960.
TAYLOR, A. J.: "Castle-Building in Wales in the Later 13th Century: The Prelude to Construction." In E. M. JOPE (ed.): *Studies in Building History*. 1961.

*

Caernarvon Castle forms part of a massive program of building associated with Edward I's subjugation of north Wales. For this program, which resulted in 10 new castles and much rebuilding and improvement on existing ones, masons, carpenters and diggers were impressed from all over England, and at times as many as 1,500 men were under the direction of the master of the King's Works in Wales, Master James of St. George, who had worked previously in Savoy. Such large, highly organized campaigns of military construction were a new phenomenon of the 13th century, and had been anticipated by that carried out by Master Richard of Lentini for Frederick II in Sicily and by Master Peter of Agincourt for Charles of Anjou in Apulia. They presupposed a highly efficient administration, considerable economic resources and a new scale of strategic importance for castle building.

The first phase of this campaign of castle building, begun in 1277, envisioned only the containment of the Welsh princes in north Wales, but further rebellion in 1282 convinced Edward of the need to conquer this unruly area and to maintain English power permanently by means of further fortifications. Caernarvon, like four of the others, including Conway, combined a castle with a walled town. Modeled on the "bastides" of southern France, these were intended to combine a strongly defended garrison with an imported English population with special civic and trading privileges, in order to create a lasting English presence in the area. All the Welsh castles, as well, had access to the sea, an important military consideration in this mountainous region. Caernarvon, which was designed to be the administrative center of north Wales, was the most important of these sites,

Caernarvon Castle: Caernarvonshire, Wales, 1283-ca. 1330

and the castle there is the most impressive of all the Edwardian castles.

The town and castle occupy a peninsula formed by the rivers Cadnant and Seiont, which with the mill pond that was also built almost isolated the site on the landward side. The strategic importance of the site, which has a harbor and commands both the Menai Strait and the main north-south road along the coast, had long been recognized. The Romans had built nearby Segontium, and in the late 11th century, the earl of Chester, Hugh of Avranches, had built a motte and bailey on the site. Norman occupation, however, was short-lived, and this structure subsequently became a residence of the princes of Gwynedd. When Caernarvon was taken by Edward's forces in June 1283, the Welsh populace was expelled, and work began almost immediately.

Like all the Welsh castles, Caernarvon was designed by Master James of St. George, one of the most capable military architects and engineers in an age renowned for castle building. Generally, his Welsh castles are notable for the innovative combination of three previously unrelated aspects (although anticipated at Caerphilly, begun in 1268): symmetrical plan, concentric walls and a strong gatehouse. Not all of these can be seen at Caernarvon, where the castle was attached to its walled town, occupying an irregular shale outcropping along its southern edge, and where the Norman motte, probably for symbolic reasons, was incorporated into the design, all of which posed special constraints. It is, nevertheless, a masterpiece of military architecture, most closely resembling Conway Castle (also begun in 1283). Caernarvon Castle sprawls in an east-west direction, divided by the substantial King's Gate into an Upper Ward on the east, in which the motte was located (it was cleared away ca. 1870), and a Lower Ward on the west. Its south side was washed by the Seiont, and on the north, it bordered the town, with the town walls adjoining it directly. Only at its east end was it vulnerable to direct landward attack.

It had a dry moat on all landward sides, and its single curtain wall was also provided with a *glacis* on these sides. The curtain is punctuated by eight projecting towers and two twin-towered gateways, the Queen's Gate at the east end and the King's Gate, and the main gate in the middle of the north wall. Most of the towers are provided with turrets, and the largest, the Eagle Tower, has three. All turrets, towers and walls were battlemented, and as well, the curtains contain two mural passages for ease of troop deployment. These passages and the battlements are also provided with arrow loops, and the towers have multiple arrow loops, providing the potential for prodigious firepower from three levels on the walls and more on the towers. Both gateways are similarly designed, but the King's Gate is the more powerful of the two, with a drawbridge leading into a central passage with five doors and six portcullises, covered by "murder holes" above and many interior arrow loops, and then another drawbridge; it remained unfinished on its inner

side, as did the Queen's Gate. There were also three posterns, and a water gate opening from the Eagle Tower remained unfinished. Most of the inner wall faces were lined with buildings, including various offices and a large hall, 100 feet by 40 feet, in the Lower Ward.

The castle was built in three main stages. The first, from 1283 to about 1292, saw the erection of the southern wall, to complete the circuit of the town walls which were also being built. The unfinished state of the castle and town walls was undoubtedly responsible for their being taken by the Welsh during further uprisings in 1294, and work only resumed in 1295. The northwest section of the wall was built next, and a further stoppage from 1301 until 1304 was followed by the completion of the castle, mainly by 1327, although some work probably continued into 1330. The total cost was over £20,000, a staggering sum. Town and castle resisted several sieges by Owen Glyndwr in 1401-04, the last with a castle garrison of only 28 men, a testament to its efficiency and effectiveness.

But Caernarvon Castle owes its magnificence to more than just military considerations. It alone of all the Welsh castles was provided with polygonal, rather than round, towers (cf. Denbigh), and its primarily limestone masonry is decorated with prominent light-brown bands of sandstone (cf. Angers). Together, these features appear to indicate a deliberate imitation of the Theodosian land walls of Constantinople. The symbolic connotations of this connection are rooted in myth of a sort about which Edward I was particularly enthusiastic. There is a tale in the *Mabinogion* about Emperor Constantine's father dreaming in Rome of a maiden in a castle with multicolored towers at the mouth of a river; he found and married her here, and Constantine was born at Caernarvon. It is no coincidence that Edward arranged the birth of his first son, the future Edward II and first Prince of Wales of the royal line, at Caernarvon, and during the building of the town, the body of Constantine's father was reputedly found and solemnly reburied in the new church (similarly, Conway boasted King Arthur's crown). The carved eagles atop the Eagle Tower at Caernarvon probably also recalled this well-known imperial association. These symbolic associations resulted in a castle which not only functioned effectively but also intentionally evoked a romantically chivalric tradition.

The castle's strategic significance virtually disappeared in the 16th century when the borough was opened to Welsh citizens and Wales was more fully integrated into the English state. It became increasingly neglected and was in such a deteriorated condition during the Civil War that it changed hands several times. Thereafter, it languished for some 200 years until efforts were made in the 19th century to restore it, particularly from 1870. In 1908 it became an Ancient Monument, and considerable improvements were made for the investiture of the Prince of Wales in 1911. However much restored, though, an impressive amount of the fabric of the castle and town walls survives.

—JIM BUGSLAG

GREECE

ST. DEMETRIOS
Thessalonica, Greece

Ca. 620s: Construction. Damaged by fires in the seventh century and in 1917. Rebuilt to original plans.

Publications

CORMACK, R. S.: "The Mosaic Decoration of S. Demetrios, Thessaloniki." *Annual of the British School of Athens* 64 (1969): 17ff.

DIEHL, C., LE TOURNEAU, M., and SALADIN, H.: *Les monuments chrétiens de Salonique.* 2 vols. Paris, 1918.

LEMERLE, P.: "Saint-Demetrius de Thessalonique et les problemes du martyrion et du transept." *Bulletin de correspondence hellénique* 77 (1953): 660ff.

SOTIRIOU, G. A., and M.: *St. Demetrius, Salonica.* Athens, 1952.

*

The basilica in Thessalonica consecrated to Saint Demetrios is one of the most important surviving paleochristian monuments in Greece. Its size and its central position in Thessalonica's urban plan, just north of the forum, show that it was conceived as one of the city's major monuments. Its remarkable state of preservation until the fire of 1917, which destroyed a large part of Thessalonica, allows us to give a fairly reliable description of it, even though the later reconstruction does not provide sufficient evidence for definitive conclusions.

St. Demetrios is a basilica constructed for the most part on a northwest/southeast axis, in conformity with the general orientation of the city's streets. It consists of five naves with a projecting transept. On the western side, the naves were preceded by a narthex, according to standard practice, and by a courtyard. The latter, however, does not seem to have taken the form of an atrium with porticoes, possibly because of a lack of available space. The principal nave terminated in the great central apse, which was covered with a timber framework and a pitched roof, and received light from a clerestory. The aisles were covered with sloping roofs at two different levels, allowing for illumination above the tops of the exterior nave roofs.

However, the importance of the monument is due to a number of unusual characteristics which make it exceptional if not unique. Its topographic position is perhaps the foremost of these characteristics, St. Demetrios being constructed on a gentle eastern slope. The builders had to employ the remains of pre-existing structures for the foundations of the eastern part of the church. Those older buildings were *thermae,* later believed to be the place where, before his execution, Saint Demetrios was

St. Demetrios: Thessalonica, Greece, ca. 620s

kept prisoner. (Two annexes in the northwestern part of the church are also vestiges of earlier buildings, perhaps dating from the early fourth century. One of these is believed to be the saint's tomb.) Whether the remains of an earlier church can be found among these surviving portions remains an open question. The eastern basement, continually altered since the first construction, and now known as a crypt, is in fact situated at the level of the street running along the eastern side of the church. It is also accessible from the street. We have no detailed or certain knowledge of the ritual practices for which the space was reserved. It is quite clear, however, that this older section, which lies outside the limits of the apse, was integrated into the master plan of the basilica.

The church's true originality, however, lies in its interior ornamentation. No reliable historical sources give any indication of dates for the decoration, which consequently remain uncertain. The church shows a remarkable alternation between the columns and piers supporting the principal nave. Standing by the piers on the western end, one sees on each side three columns, a pier, four columns, another pier, three columns, and finally the pier marking the eastern end of the sanctuary. This alternation of supports is accompanied by an alternation of the types of marble used for the columns. The columns between the first and second piers, and between the third and fourth piers, are made of light-colored marble. Green marble from Thessaly is used for the columns between the second and third piers (and also for the two columns separating the central nave from the narthex). The capitals of the double colonnade are also characterized by great variety. Next to the traditional composite capitals one finds capitals with animal heads (eagles, rams); multifoil capitals similar to those used in SS. Sergius and Bacchus at Constantinople; and capitals with leaves turned up by the wind. It was traditionally thought that the alternation in the system of supports, the general lack of uniformity, and the re-utilization of material from other buildings were all related to a shortage of materials at the time of a reconstruction. It is known also, from the *Miracula Demetrii* (a valuable historical source for late-sixth- and seventh-century Thessalonica), that the church was damaged by fire in the first quarter of the seventh century.

Nevertheless, the regularity and homogeneity of the plan of St. Demetrios would contradict such a theory. The perfect integration of the piers in the overall design makes it impossible to attribute the peculiarities to a second building stage. It has also been demonstrated that the reutilization of material and diversity in ornamentation, particularly architectural ornamentation, were not a necessary evil or a sign of poverty in paleochristian architecture. Rather, it represents a confirmed aesthetic opposing itself to classical taste. The Arch of Constantine in Rome may well have been the first manifestation of that new aesthetic. It is therefore quite reasonable to suppose that St. Demetrios in Thessalonica, with its lavish ornamentation in *opus sectile* (surviving until 1917) and its mosaics (which may be attributed to the period of its construction, and of which little is preserved), was a part of that trend. Judging from the capitals used, original construction can hardly predate the 620s.

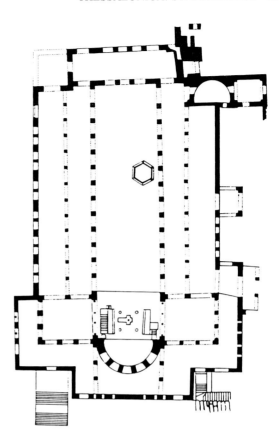

This conclusion is perhaps not definitive, and should not preclude new analysis of the problems associated with this church, particularly the problem of the development of the cult of the saints. It is not impossible that evidence pointing to a somewhat earlier date in the sixth century may still be found.

Whatever the case may be, the church then constructed, in a form similar to that still existing in 1917, was damaged by fire in the first quarter of the seventh century. That fire, undoubtedly limited to the timber framework, led to a restoration immediately afterward, which was commemorated in several surviving mosaics. The reconstruction following the 1917 fire more or less preserved the sixth century building, except for the facing used and the addition of towers to the facade.

There is little indication of the details of the building's later architectural history. In 1481, however, a rich tomb of Venetian workmanship was installed in the northwestern corner of the central nave. The tomb was for Lucas Spandounis, who belonged to a Byzantine family whose numerous members had found refuge in Italy. The church was converted to a mosque at the very end of the 15th century, but it ceased to function as such before the end of the Ottoman era.

—J. -M. SPIESER
Translated from the French by Alla Melamed

HUNGARY

EAST RAILWAY STATION
Budapast, Hungary

1880-82. Construction; **Architects:** Gyula Rochlitz and János Feketeházy. **1960s-1970s:** Construction of underground passages and subway-system connection.

Publications

KUBINSZKY, MIHÁLY: *Régi magyar vasútállomások*. Budapest, 1983.

*

Although the East Railway Station is not the most outstanding monument of Hungarian architecture, it is nevertheless important in view of its historic, urbanistic and economic role.

Buda and Pest were two separate cities until 1872. The two cities, built on opposite banks of the Danube, had long been Hungary's cultural and administrative center. However, the cities turned into a European metropolis only in the last third of the 19th century. Their rapid development was related to two historical events: the formation of the Austro-Hungarian empire in 1867, which gave Hungary equal status within the empire instead of its former subordinate position, and the unification of Pest and Buda into a single city.

The first railway stations in the twin cities were built before the unification. The station in Pest (later rebuilt as West Railway Station) opened in 1846. The station in Buda (which was later called South Railway Station) followed in 1861. The railway stations, which played such a central role in turn-of-the-century life, were built according to sound principles of urban planning. The West Railway Station, built to replace Pest Station, was integral to the layout of the Grand Boulevard. French capital was used to finance the project, and the world-renowned Eiffel Construction Company of Paris participated in the works. The East Railway Station was built further away from the Grand Boulevard, along the main east-west axial road of Pest, which looked like a highway rather than a main city street at the time. The station was built in a neighborhood still awaiting urbanistic reorganization. The numerous pubs frequented by long-distance travelers had given the district a bad reputation. A new main street was designed (today's Rákóczi Street), and the train station, a head station, was set at one end. The construction was accompanied by urban renewal. Great national and local enthusiasm existed for the project, since this station was not being

East Railway Station: Budapest, Hungary, 1880-82

built by foreign companies and engineers but by the Royal Hungarian Railway Company, formed as a consequence of the Austro-Hungarian compromise of 1867. The official name of the station was Budapest Central Railway Station, and it was planned by Hungarian architects.

The East Railway Station was constructed between 1880 and 1882, following 10 years of preparations. The architect, Gyula Rochlitz, was a railway engineer. The designer of the iron-frame hall was János Feketeházy, who had designed several large-scale constructions, including the Franz Joseph Bridge over the Danube in southern Budapest. Urbanistic needs and common European practice dictated the design, which situated the arrival and departure halls in opposite side wings. Large halls, waiting rooms, restaurants, ticket offices, offices of the railway and other agencies such as mail, police and baggage handling found their place in these wings. The monotony of the long wings was broken by three symmetrically arranged pavilion-like masses. The middle one holds a hall decorated with frescoes. The side wings resemble French Renaissance architecture constructed in iron.

The main hall is situated between the side wings and accommodates six tracks. It is 42 meters wide, 179 meters long, and 31.4 meters high. The roof, in the shape of a parabola, is made of welded iron. Glazing on both sides provides light, and ventilation holes in the middle lead away locomotive smoke. The back wall of the hall consists of a glazed curtain wall, which reduces major air movement. Electricity was used for artificial lighting from the first days on.

The principal facade facing the city is reminiscent of a classical triumphal arch. It is situated between the two elevated masses of pavilions, and its opening is covered by a glass wall in an iron frame. The base and stringcourses of the side wings run all the way through the arch-like middle part, so that the glass front is also divided. In the lower level, stone Tuscan columns carrying an attic provide a frame for the extraordinary decorative iron gates. Statues of George Stephenson and James Watt stand on the pillars of the arch, in niches framed by Corinthian half columns. The arch, which holds a large clock, is crowned by a central group of statues allegorically representing Communication.

Modernization in the 1960s and 1970s, which consisted of the construction of underground passages and a connection with the subway system, affected only the park in front of the station. The original architecture of the East Railway Station has remained the same, and the building is now protected as a national monument.

—GYULA ISTVÁNFI
Translated from the Hungarian by Csaba Pleh

ST. STEPHEN'S BASILICA
Budapest, Hugary

1851-68: Construction. **Architect:** József Hild (1789-1867). **1868:** Pillars and drum collapse. **1875-91:** Reconstruction; **Architect:** Miklós Ybl (1814-91). **1891ff.:** Completion of interior; **Architect:** József Kauser (1841-1919)

St. Stephen's Basilica: Budapest, Hungary, 1851-68

Publications

RADOS, JENŐ: *Hild József Életmüve* (with German and French summary). Budapest, 1958.
YBL, ERVIN: *Miklós Ybl*. Budapest, 1956.

*

St. Stephen's Basilica is a remarkable creation in the history of Hungarian architecture, with regard to its architectural qualities, the history of its construction and even with regard to its name. It is the principal church of Budapest, capital of Hungary, which had developed into a metropolis by the time the church was completed. Its construction was begun when historicizing trends held sway in architecture, and it was intended to be the most important neoclassical church in Hungary. By the time it was finished, however, it had turned into a neo-Renaissance building.

At the end of the 18th century, the administrative and cultural center of Hungary consisted of two small cities, Buda and Pest, on opposite sides of the Danube. Pest was situated on the flat left bank, Buda on the hilly right bank. Pest was better situated for purposes of commerce and industry, and had begun to expand toward the north. The new district was called Lipot-Town in 1790, to commemorate the coronation of King Lipot II. The first parochial church on the site of the future cathedral was constructed in 1817, in a temporary manner and without any claims to high architectural standards. It was consecrated to Saint Lipot. During the first half of the 19th century, the district developed into an upper-class area with a carefully planned street system and neoclassical buildings all of similar height.

St. Stephen's Basilica, apse elevation

The striving for uniformity, however, had led to a certain monotony. Thus, the need arose for a larger building to enliven the aesthetic order of the area. At the same time, a strengthening of Hungarian national consciousness gathered momentum and became a political force. From the combination of these two trends the desire to construct a "national sanctuary" in the city of Pest was formed.

József Hild (1789-1867) was the most productive master of the neoclassical period in Hungarian architecture. He designed almost a thousand private and public buildings in the expanding city of Pest. He also designed a series of country churches, two of which have become Hungary's two most important cathedrals, those of Eger and Esztergom. In 1845 he was commissioned to design and build the Pest basilica without competition.

Hild designed a centralized, symmetrical building with a ninefold spatial division focused on the central dome. Only the character of the ground plan was Byzantine, while the domeless chapels in the four corners had low roofs. The name of "basilica" meant no more than cathedral in this case, then, instead of denoting basilican architecture. On the western facade, Hild designed a wide portico crowned with a tympanum carried by eight columns. The eastern side is dominated by a semicircular sanctuary surrounded by a crescent-shaped sacristy. Both facade and mass are similar to the design solutions worked out at Esztergom Cathedral. A hemispheric dome set on a high drum divided by columns looms over the two bulky towers flanking the portico. There is some resemblance to the Italian Renaissance architect Galeazzo Alessi's Church of Santa Maria di Carignano in Genoa.

Construction was to be financed with public donations, which, however, came in rather slowly. The Hungarian Revolution of

1848 also retarded construction. St. Lipot Church, scheduled for dismantling, was destroyed during the fighting in Pest. The foundation stone of the cathedral was finally laid in 1851. The outer walls up to the level of the main cornice and the walls of the drum up to a height of 44 meters were constructed in the next 16 years. However, in January 1868, a year after Hild's death, the pillars and the drum collapsed, following the placement of the cornice under the dome.

Although no human life was lost, the catastrophe compromised the original conception of the building. Some never-to-be-realized advantages of Hild's design had been its balanced elegance, the perfect illumination through the large windows in the walls of the drum and the massing of simple geometric forms. The collapse was due not only to the slimness of the pillars and weak arches but, according to contemporary statements, to a lack of discipline in the construction and to the inferior quality of materials.

Miklós Ybl (1814-91), an experienced, innovative architect and an outstanding figure of late-19th-century historicism, was charged with the reconstruction of the building. His work—170 buildings in Budapest—remarkably enriched the architectural image of the city. Ybl developed several designs during the years construction was interrupted, a period which also saw remarkable changes in the country and the city itself as well as significant developments in architecture. In 1867 Hungary ceased to be subordinate to Austria, gaining equal status in the Austro-Hungarian Empire. The city of Pest, now unified with the city of Buda, obtained the status of national capital in 1873. From 1870 on, all construction was supervised by a professional urban-planning committee (the Committee of Public Works of the Capital), which controlled metropolitan standards. Ybl himself was a member of this committee. Finally, the architectural common sense of the times broke with classical and romantic styles, and architects began choosing historical styles according to a building's function. A preference for Gothic and Renaissance styles became prevalent. Mixtures, with ground plans and facade designs going back to different ages, were not uncommon. Following such guidelines, Budapest became a shining metropolis during the last 30 years of the 19th century and up to World War I.

Ybl thickened the walls of St. Stephen's Basilica and reinforced the pillars. The design of the central dome was similar to that of St. Paul's in London. A double-shell dome was built over a double-wall drum. The outer shell carried a lantern, while the inner shell was spherical to avoid the fluelike impression the lantern might create. Windows in the inner shell let through only secondary light, however, which proved to be the single mistake of Ybl's design. The outer dome, with its dynamic contours, reaches to a height of 100 meters. Ybl removed the eastern towers, and made the western ones more slender by stepping them back. A small dome masks each setback. On the principal facade, the classical portico was replaced by a neo-Renaissance facade of Italian inspiration, related to that of Leon Battista Alberti's Church of San Andrea at Mantua.

The state and city committees and even the artist exercised great care approving the plans. Along with the opinion of home committees, the opinion of two leading Viennese architects was solicited. When Franz Schmidt and Theophilus Hansen approved the designs, construction was restarted in 1875. The work proceeded slowly but continuously under Ybl's direction during the next 16 years. Like his predecessor, however, he never saw his building completed. After his death, the basilica's interior was designed and created by József Kauser (1814-1919), entirely in accordance with Ybl's intentions.

The hidden motivation for construction of the church in Lipot-Town, namely to create a ''national sanctuary,'' became apparent only in 1897, when the church was named after Saint Stephen (970-1038), founding king of Hungary. The goal was truly realized in 1951, when the hand of Saint Stephen was placed in the church.

—GYULA ISTVÁNFI
Translated from the Hungarian by Csaba Pleh

UNIVERSITY CHURCH
Budapest, Hungary

1725-56: Construction. **Architect:** Andreas Mayerhoffer (1690-1771). **1768:** Eastern tower added. **1771:** Western tower added.

Publications

HEKLER, A.: *Ungarische Kunstgeschichte*. Berlin, 1937.
MEYER, SCHUYLER M.: ''Impressions of Budapest.'' *Architectural Record* 26 (December 1909): 428-447.

*

The University Church of Pest is one of the outstanding works of Hungarian Baroque architecture. It is important not only for its artistic merits but also for the pioneering role it played in the development of architectural tradition in Hungary.

In 1686 the allied European Christian troops liberated Pest and Buda after 150 years of Turkish rule. The cities lay in ruins. However, even in Turkish times few notable buildings remained. Contemporary travelers mentioned as worth seeing only the city walls, the mosques, the baths and a bridge over the Danube. For many years following the siege, the city of Pest was no more than a dirty collection of huts in ruins, and its name was cynically associated with the plague (''*pestis*'' in Hungarian).

University Church, Pest: Budapest, Hungary, 1725-56

Several monastic orders were in the forefront of the city's reconstruction, among them the Pauline Order, which had been founded in Hungary. An area with some huts and a small mosque was donated to the order, and this later became the site of University Church.

The construction of the monastery was begun in 1715 and that of the church in 1725. Andreas Mayerhoffer (1690-1771), an architect of Austrian background and training whose work played a decisive role in the development of the Hungarian Baroque, was put in charge of the project. The Baroque style arrived late in Hungary, imported from Italy and Austria already fully formed. The painters, sculptors and craftsmen employed for major building projects such as churches and castles were initially also of Austrian origin, which aided in the dissemination of the new style. Grassalkovich Castle in Gödöllô and Kalocsa Cathedral, Mayerhoffer's other major works, are also examples of mature Baroque architecture.

University Church holds a special place in Mayerhoffer's oeuvre, however. The ground plan of the church is similar to that of Giacomo Barozzi da Vignola's Il Gesù in Rome. The single nave is divided into three bays and is covered by an annular vault. There is an organ loft in the west end, between the two towers of the facade. Three side chapels are ranged along the nave on each side, reinforcing the division into bays. Windows in the niches over the chapels provide ample illumination from both sides. The space is unified by the entablature over the rounded corners and the chapels. There is no transept or dome. The elongated sanctuary, which has a slightly rounded end, is flanked by a sacristy on each side. The internal space of the church is articulated by the five arches that subdivide its tunnel-like length.

The three-story main facade is designed along three axes. A triangular tympanum is set between the two towers on the level of the third story. Two massive stringcourses provide a horizontal counterbalance to the vertical rhythm of the Corinthian pilasters. The towers terminate in bell-shaped cornices and curving roofs. The two-towered church was the first of its kind in the city of Pest. Following the example of University Church, the two-tower facade became a standard feature of city churches, while the majority of village churches continued to be built with one tower. The design of the facade itself was also widely imitated.

The Baroque richness of the interior sculpture and painting,

all in accordance with Pauline thematics, can be credited to Austrian artists. The sculptor Joseph Hebenstreit (1719-83) created the sculptures, stalls and pulpits, and the banister of the organ loft. All are in harmony with the architectural design. The high altar makes a particularly strong impression. Framed by towering architectural and sculptural elements, the altarpiece representing the birth of the Virgin Mary is a sculptural gem. Statues of the saints who dominate the spiritual life of the Pauline Order, Saint Paul and Saint Anthony, are at the sides of the altar. The wooden and gilded pulpit, one of the peak achievements of European Baroque sculptural design, became a model for countless Hungarian naive works.

The most remarkable paintings are the ceiling frescoes, extending over five surfaces and representing scenes from the life of the Virgin Mary. From the organ loft to the sanctuary the scenes are of the Visitation, the Annunciation, the Immaculate Conception, the Presentation in the Temple, and Mary's Assumption. The latter might be the most remarkable of the works. The painter, János Bergl (1718-89), a citizen of Pest, was born to an Austrian family in Bohemia. His harmonious compositions continue skyward in illusionistic designs using the architectural elements.

The main body of the church was finished in 1756, together with the monastery. The towers, however, were completed later: the eastern tower in 1768 and the western one in 1771. In 1786, ten years after its full completion, the complex ceased to be the center of the Pauline province, due to the royal decrees of the emperor Joseph II against religious orders. The church and the monastery were first taken over by a seminary, and in the 19th century the church was annexed to the university, which was then being built on the site. The present name of the church is related to that transfer. The library of the neighboring seminary used to be an important meeting point of the pioneers of Hungarian literature. In 1849 the church also hosted the Hungarian parliament. Even in the mid-19th century the building was a landmark among the mass of one- and two-story buildings of the city. At the end of the 19th century the seminary was rebuilt, and many three-to-five-story buildings rose in the neighborhood. Thus, the church that once dominated the cityscape ended up tightly squeezed into a narrow downtown street. However, it is still a treasure in the jungle of the city.

—GYULA ISTVÁNFI
Translated from the Hungarian by Csaba Pleh

IRELAND

CUSTOM HOUSE
Dublin, Ireland

1781-91. Construction of the Custom House, docks, and stores; **Architect:** James Gandon (1742-1823). **20th century:** Custom House damaged and partially restored.

Publications

CRAIG, MAURICE: *Dublin 1660-1860*. Dublin, 1980.
McPARLAND, EDWARD: *James Gandon: Vitruvius Hibernicus*. New Haven, Connecticut, and London, 1985.

*

The architect James Gandon arrived in Dublin in 1781 to superintend the building of docks, stores and the Custom House, which he had designed in 1780. This very important public building consisted essentially of a large rectangular central block running north-south to which long wings were attached running east-west, so that an H-shaped building was formed. The open ends of the H were partially filled in with two lower blocks, so that two courtyards were formed on each side of the central block. The composition was symmetrically disposed about the central north-south axis.

The site was on the north bank of the River Liffey, and there Gandon applied the principles of composition learned from his master, William Chambers (1723-96). Like Chambers' Somerset House in London, the Dublin Custom House has a long symmetrical facade parallel to the river, and the style is impeccably Roman, with no trace of Grecian modernity or Adamesque delicacy. To ensure that the building would be prominent when seen from the sea, Gandon placed a cupola in the center of the river front which owes much to Christopher Wren's work at Greenwich Hospital, but the fine Corinthian order used in the peristyle of the drum contrasts painfully with the sheer size of the massive Tuscan giant order used for the two-story building itself. Like Greenwich and Somerset House, too, the Custom House was faced in Portland stone.

There are several very original features of Gandon's design. These include the pairs of columns set in a plain wall, the suggestion of two floors by means of a dentiled platband, and a plain entablature which is little more than a deep platband capped by a cornice with massive mutules. This entablature therefore projects slightly over the naked wall below. Gandon also employed subtle means to break up the long facades. The central three bays consist of the prostyle tetrastyle portico with its giant Tuscan order carrying the central pediment: the frieze is enriched with four huge bucrania with swags. On each side of the portico are three wider bays. A setback with a giant order of Tuscan columns marks the center of each group, so that the entablature sails across the top uninterrupted. Over the central nine bays is an attic story, and over the central three is the tall cupola with its high dome. Then, on each side of the central block is a seven-bay wing with a rusticated arcaded ground floor and first-floor windows alternating with aediculated niches, all the windows and niches being pedimented. Over the entablature is a balustrade. The projecting three-bay corner pavilions have giant Tuscan columns on the north and south elevations set within recesses so that the plain entablatures run over them without any projections or breakbacks. The column bases, however, project slightly beyond the face of the wall. Above the entablatures of the pavilions are vigorously carved Royal Arms of Ireland, with the lion and unicorn supporting the Irish Harp.

Most of the carved ornament is by Edward Smyth. The tympanum of the pediment features Britannia and Hibernia embracing, with emblems of Liberty and Peace. The keystones over the arched openings are also by Smyth, and feature the waters of

Custom House: Dublin, Ireland, 1781-91

Ireland: commencing with the keystone over the central door of the river front, they are the Liffey (the only female head of the group), then, moving right, the Boyne, the Barrow, the Blackwater, the Atlantic Ocean, the Bann, the Shannon, the Lee (in the center of the rear elevation), the Lagan, the Suir, the Nore, the Slaney, the Foyle (with 1689 on the headband) and the Erne. The four corners of the globe were represented by four figures over the entablature of the north portico (where there never was a pediment) carved by Thomas Banks (1735-1805), while the Four Continents over the attic on the river front were by Smyth, based on designs by Augustino Carlini (died 1790).

Unfortunately, the Custom House was severely damaged in the Civil War of this century. Ardbraccan stone was used to restore the peristyle of the cupola, and this has darkened, thereby drawing attention to the structure and making the change of scale more obvious. Although the huge statue of Commerce by Smyth still stands sentinel atop her pedestal above the dome, the statues have not been replaced, and neither have the chimneys, so there has been a loss of verticality which has lessened the grandeur of the building, and left it somewhat bare and enfeebled. The splendidly vigorous and oversized urns still stand on the dies of the end-pavilion balustrades, however, but Dublin ought to restore this great building in its entirety.

—JAMES STEVENS CURL

ITALY

SAN NICOLA
Bari, Italy

1087-89: Construction begun. **1098:** Crypt and eastern bays completed. **1196:** Church dedicated.

Publications

BELLI D'ELIA, PINA: *La basilica di S. Nicola a Bari.* Galatina, Italy, 1985.

BERTAUX, EMILE: *L'art dans l'Italie meridionale.* 3 vols. Paris, 1903.

KRAUTHEIMER, RICHARD: "San Nicola in Bari und die apulische Architektur des 12. Jahrhunderts." *Wiener Jahrbuch für Kunstgeschichte* 9 (1934): 5-42.

MILANO, NICOLA: *Le chiese della diocesi di Bari.* Bari, 1982.

SCHETTINI, F.: *La basilica di San Nicola di Bari.* Bari, 1967.

*

The eclectic creativity of southern Italian culture is most artfully expressed in the Church of San Nicola, the fountainhead of Apulian Romanesque architecture. In a city of Italian sailors, Byzantine merchants, Norman soldiers, and pilgrims from both the east and the west, the aesthetic traditions of these varied groups meet in the stones, ornament and spatial arrangements of this church dedicated to Saint Nicholas.

The grand outline of a basilican plan with transept and triple apses reflects the conscious imitation of Early Christian architecture spearheaded by the Benedictine Abbey of Monte Cassino. The church was built on the site of the former governor's palace, and traces of Byzantine masonry are incorporated into San Nicola's foundations. The southwest tower, cleverly integrated into the overall design of the facade, is another remnant of the Byzantine past. The transformation of these elements is so total, however, that the effect can be considered completely Apulian.

The vaulted hall crypt, located under the transept, was the first phase of the Romanesque project. There, 26 columns divide the space into four aisles; similar hall crypts were constructed in many of the churches in the region. Reused Byzantine capitals, as well as expressively carved Romanesque capitals, support the sail vaults of the crypt, while the play of soft light across the colored marbles of the columns contributes to the texture and mystique of the space.

The exterior of San Nicola is also a magnificent blend of influences and effects. The gabled west facade, with its twin towers and soaring verticality, is a dramatic reflection of the recently introduced Norman influence in southern Italy. This facade is divided into three parts by thin pilasters that accentuate the murality of the upper wall. The lower wall is articulated by blind arcades springing from detached columns, and the central portal is accentuated by a plastically rendered, gabled frame reminiscent of the lion portals of Lombardy.

The combination of flat surfaces with applied sculptural decoration is repeated on the east facade. The central window is highlighted by a projecting frame supported by elephant consoles, an innovative variation of the lion portal imitated by other Apulian masons. The rectangular profile of the east facade screens the three semicircular apses of the interior, another distinctly Apulian feature. The shallow, blind arcading on the lower wall is extended around the corners and continues along the faces of the slightly projecting transept arms.

The lateral facades are identical and have a pronounced horizontal emphasis. The three-story elevation corresponds to the arrangement of the interior with an arcade of deep niches, a small gallery and a row of clerestory windows. The enormous arcade is aesthetically distinctive and structurally innovative, with its engaged piers acting as buttresses. A concealed passageway in the west facade, reflecting the Norman technique of "thick wall" construction, leads into the gallery, which is visually akin to the dwarf galleries of Lombardy. The lateral facades are treated sculpturally with recessed planes and a multiplicity of openings. There are also four richly ornamented doorways (two on each side), which further enhance the plastic quality of the walls.

The interior of the basilica is a more simplified arrangement of elements. The church is laid out as a Latin cross with a nave and flanking side aisles. The nave and transept were originally covered by a timber roof with open rafters, while the aisles have groin vaults. The nave arcade has gray granite columns with Byzantine capitals, and above, there is a gallery and a row of small, roundheaded clerestory windows. This three-story elevation was without precedent in Apulia, and San Nicola became the prototype for galleried basilicas in the region. The flow of space in the nave is disrupted by three diaphragm arches,

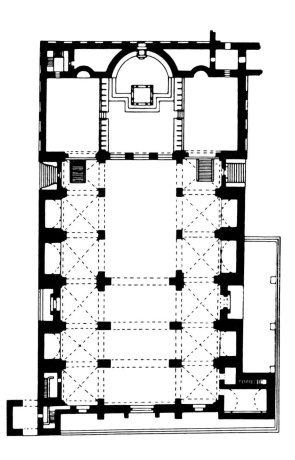

San Nicola: Bari, Italy, 1087-89

which were added centuries later to stabilize the structure after two devastating earthquakes.

An iconostasis with three semicircular arches that separates the transept from the nave imitates the Byzantine practice of screening the sanctuary. The choir is raised on three steps where the Romanesque ciborium and bishop's throne still occupy their original positions. Both are framed by the great vaulted arc of the apse, whose strong vertical emphasis amplifies the simplified grandeur of the interior. Such a skillful combination of elements from so wide a variety of sources was certainly a fitting monument for the relics of Saint Nicholas, one of the most popular and revered saints in both eastern and western Christendom.

—KATHRYN McCLINTOCK

PALAZZO FARNESE
Caprarola (near Rome), Italy

1521-73. Architect: Giacomo Barozzi da Vignola (1507-73).

Publications

PARTRIDGE, LOREN: ''Vignola and the Villa Farnese at Caprarola.'' *Art Bulletin* 52, 1 (1970): 81-87.

Palazzo Farnese: Caprarola, Italy, 1521-73

The Palazzo Farnese, country seat of the powerful Farnese family, is situated in the Cimini Hills overlooking the village of Caprarola, some 50 kilometers northwest of Rome. The palazzo is not only the masterwork of Giacomo Barozzi da Vignola but also is the crowning glory of an urban design that is integral to the palace itself. The ribbon village of Caprarola is laid out along the main street, the Via Nicolai, which continues the central axis of the Palazzo Farnese. Apparently, Vignola had a hand in the shaping of the village, which appears almost as an appendage, doing little more than setting the stage for the grand drama of the commanding palace.

In 1521 Baldassare Peruzzi and Antonio da Sangallo started work on a moated pentagonal castle in accordance with the wishes of Alessandro Farnese (later Pope Paul III). By 1559, when Vignola was taken on to continue the work according to the changed requirements of Farnese, the foundations were laid and most of the basement level may have been completed. The final result, substantially finished at the time of Vignola's death in 1573, is hard to classify, being a combination of castle and villa architecture. The substructure of the building was not significantly changed, and is thus essentially that of a castle with earthworks and bastions at each of the corners of the

Palazzo Farnese, garden

pentagon. The moat was also retained. The superstructure, however, is that of the block-type, centralized villa.

A complex series of ramps and stairways negotiate the transition from the Via Nicolai to the main facade of the palazzo.
Behind this facade, on the *piano nobile,* lies a grand reception
hall with a magnificent spiral staircase to one side and a round
chapel to the other. The spacious and monumental staircase, with
its paired columns and helical vault, rivals the best staircases by
Donato Bramante. Suites of grand *saloni* and their dependencies
are laid out along the remaining four sides of the pentagon in
such a way that the entire building can be circumambulated
through the enfilades. The monumental exterior is marked by
the severe articulation typical of Vignola, being limited to paired
pilasters and recessed oval panels. The windows on the *piano
nobile* have the incongruous rounded tops which are like a
Vignola trademark, while the second-story windows have flat
tops. Rustication is used very sparingly, around entranceways
only.

The grand surprise of the building, however, is the circular
central courtyard which Vignola fitted into the pentagonal
scheme with great ingenuity. Reconciling circular forms with
rectangular and polygonal layouts was something of a specialty
of Vignola's. The most significant earlier example was the Villa
Giulia in Rome, where he fitted a semicircular courtyard into
a rectangular block. The two-story elevation of the courtyard,
at basement and *piano nobile* level, has arcades hiding the five
doorways at each of the sides of the pentagon, giving access
to the suites of rooms behind. The basement level is rusticated,
contributing to the impression of massive solidity seemingly

designed for no other purpose than to function as support for the upper story. The *piano nobile* arcade repeats the articulation of the exterior, with paired pilasters and recessed oval panels in the piers. The spandrels are also recessed. The arcade is topped by a baluster hiding the third floor of the pentagon, which is set back from the lower floors. The upper story has a central corridor lined with small rooms.

Vignola, who was trained as a painter, apparently executed some of the frescoes in the interior, but Federigo Zuccaro was responsible at a somewhat later date for most of the interiors. Though there is great care in the handling of some of the detail, as a whole Zuccaro's interiors are undistinguished except for the fact that they insistently illustrate the lofty station of the Farnese.

The back entrance has a bridge over the moat giving onto a fountain. Halfway down the slope there is another fountain set in a small amphitheater, beyond which the casino and the formal gardens are situated. Apparently laid out by Vignola, the ensemble is of great beauty and somewhat like the Petit Trianon at Versailles in atmosphere.

The Palazzo Farnese in Caprarola had a farflung influence on the architecture of the following centuries. As late as the 19th century, John Soane named the Palazzo Farnese as the inspiration for his State Paper Office in London (1830-34). More immediately, the Palazzo Farnese was a landmark in the development toward the Baroque style.

—MARIJKE RIJSBERMAN

CASA DEL FASCIO
Como, Italy

1932-36. Architect: Giuseppe Terragni (1904-42).

Publications

"The Casa del Fascio at Como, Architect Giuseppe Terragni." *Architect and Building News* (July 1937).

EISENMAN, PETER: "From Object to Relationship: Giuseppe Terragni-"Casa Giuliani Frigerio and Casa del Fascio." *Perspecta* 13/14 (1971): 36-65.

FERRARI, L., and PASTORE, D. (eds.): *Giuseppe Terragni: La Casa del Fascio*. Rome, 1982.

FRAMPTON, KENNETH, and FUTAGAWA, YUKIO: *Modern Architecture: 1920-1945*. New York, 1983.

GHIRARDO, DIANE: "Politics of a Masterpiece: The *Vicenda* of the Decoration of the Facade of the Casa del Fascio, Como 1936-1939." *Art Bulletin* 62 (1980): 466-478.

TERRAGNI, GIUSEPPE: "La Costruzione della Casa del Fascio di Como." *Quadrante* 35 (special issue, 1936).

VERONESI, GIULIA: *Difficoltà politiche dell'architettura in Italia 1920-1940*. Milan, 1953.

Casa del Fascio: Como, Italy, 1932-36

During the past two decades few buildings have been studied, interpreted and analyzed more exhaustively than Giuseppe Terragni's Casa del Fascio in Como. This renewed interest follows a long period of nearly complete neglect, owing largely to the building's disagreeable function as provincial headquarters for the Italian Fascist Party. Today, thanks to the efforts of a group of mostly American scholars, the Casa del Fascio is universally recognized as a major achievement in the history of European modern architecture.

The building was commissioned in 1932, a time of great hope for modernism in Italy. Earlier that year, the rationalists had scored a significant victory by designing an important part of the Tenth Anniversary Exhibition of the Fascist Revolution (to which Terragni contributed one remarkable room). "Traditionalism" was on the defensive, and it seemed as if rationalism was about to become the preferred style of the fascist state. In such a promising climate, Terragni was given a free hand to design a building that epitomized the aspirations of the younger generation of rationalists. Throughout the four years it took to build the Casa del Fascio, Terragni supervised every aspect of construction, including the furniture, lamps and lighting fixtures, while the painter Mario Radice designed the decorations. The result, which ended up costing approximately six times the original estimate, is a credit to Terragni's determination and architectural integrity.

A perfect half cube, clad entirely in the whitest Botticino marble, the Casa del Fascio stands at the edge of the city center, bordering a vast area between the Duomo and Lake Como. This long, rectangular space had been chosen to be the new political center of the city; it was to be surrounded by several other government buildings, which were never built. Without them, the Casa del Fascio appears somewhat isolated against the backdrop of a steeply rising hill. Yet the setting is still spectacular in its relationship to the Duomo, and so it must have appeared to the cheering crowds that assembled in the square to hear the speeches delivered from the Casa's three-tier loggia.

Terragni's design was described by Reyner Banham as "one of the most brilliant formal schemes of the thirties." Its most striking feature was the open trabeated frame, with the fascia-like windows deeply recessed within the frame's protective shade. Here Terragni exploited to great advantage the functional and aesthetic possibilities of the concrete frame, developing an original Italian version of a motif found often in International Style architecture. Contrary to Le Corbusier, whose early buildings usually contained the frame well within the skin of the building, and unlike Ludwig Mies van der Rohe's later work, where the skin and bones tended to occupy the same plane, Terragni conceived the frame as an outermost shell or cage, defining a virtual volume with respect to which all internal articulations appeared to result from a subtractive process, as if material had been removed to reveal a complex inner structure. The dramatic play of light and shade against the glazed surfaces of the recessed wall added to the sense of depth, while the planar expression of each element suggested an intricate layering of surfaces. The result was a highly disciplined composition whose influence can be seen in many other works built in Italy in the late 1930s and 1940s.

But if the Casa del Fascio may thus be seen to express some of the principles of Italian rationalism in their most limpid form, it also conveyed a range of political meanings connected to its function as a "temple of Fascism." As Terragni explained, the guiding theme of the design was "Mussolini's concept of Fascism as a glass house in which everyone can see." This sense of transparency informed the design on many levels, both practical and formal. At the ground floor, a battery of 16 glass doors were designed to open simultaneously through a special electric device; the building could thus be literally thrown open to the square in front, allowing rows of Blackshirts to march in and out without breaking lines. The internal spaces were also designed to facilitate contact between the public and the party officials. Thus the main meeting room (which included Terragni's luxurious glass table and Benita chairs, as well as a magnificent mural by Mario Radice) communicated visually with the entrance atrium through a glass wall. In this way the public was made to witness the meetings of the party. In a house of fascism, Terragni believed, "there must be no barrier, no obstacle between the Fascist leaders and the people."

On a formal level, the design was redolent with political overtones. Just as the square plan alluded to the founding of Rome as a square city (*Roma quadrata*), so the facade evoked the ancient gridded plan of the city of Como, which had survived almost intact over the centuries. The golden proportions of the facade reinforced the link with ancient Rome, immortalizing in marble the rules of *divina proporzione*. Additional historical references included the plan of the Renaissance palazzo, which Terragni adopted but modified by covering the court with a glazed roof, and the medieval city government buildings (*palazzi comunali*), which typically included a loggia and side tower. Such multiple historical allusions reflected Terragni's search for an architecture at once modern and ancient, in which the connections with the past did not entail a direct stylistic reference but were filtered through a contemporary sensibility.

Today, the Casa del Fascio—now known as the Casa del Popolo—is a site of architectural pilgrimages from all over the world. Its enormous popularity seems to derive as much from its modernity as from its rich symbolic content, its consciousness of history and its underlying classicism—that is to say, from its avoidance of some of modernism's most frequently noted shortcomings.

—LIBERO ANDREOTTI

CATHEDRAL OF SANTA MARIA DEL FIORE
Florence, Italy

1296: Initial construction begun; **Architect:** Arnolfo di Cambio. **1334:** Giotto appointed master of the works. **1357:** Scheme enlarged; **Architects:** Andrea Pisano, followed by Francesco Talenti. **1365:** Choir and transepts designed; **Architects:** By commission. **1420-34:** Dome built; **Architect:** Filippo Brunelleschi (1377-1446). **1421:** Three apses complet ed. **1462:** Lantern added; **Architect:** Giuliano da Maiano. **1875-87:** Marble facing added to west facade.

CAMPANILE

1334-59. Architect: Giotto (ca. 1267-1337). Alterations by Andrea Pisano and Francesco Talenti.

BAPTISTERY

Possibly begun in the fifth century as a church, and converted to a baptistery in the mid-11th century; minor adornments added in the 13th century. **1330-36:** Bronze doors added; **Artist:** Andrea Pisano (ca. 1290-1348/49). **1403-52:** Bronze doors added; **Artist:** Lorenzo Ghiberti (1378-1455). **1514:** Iron chain added

Cathedral of Santa Maria del Fiore: Florence, Italy, 1296

Cathedral of Santa Maria del Fiore

at base of dome for more support; **Architect:** Michelangelo (1475-1564).

Publications

BRAUNFELS, WOLFGANG: *Der Dom von Florenz.* Olten, Germany, 1964.

BRAUNFELS, WOLFGANG: "Giottos Campanile." *Das Münster* 1 (1948).

GIOSEFFI, DECIO: *Giotto architetto.* Milan, 1963.

GUASTI, CESARE: *La cupola di S. Maria del Fiore.* Florence, 1857.

GUASTI, CESARE: *Santa Maria del Fiore.* Florence, 1887.

KIESOW, GOTTFRIED: "Zur Baugeschichte des Florentiner Domes." *Mitteilungen des Kunsthistorischen Instituts in Florenz* 10 (1961): 1-22.

KREYTENBERG, GERT: "Der Campanile von Giotto." *Mitteilungen des Kunsthistorischen Instituts in Florenz* 22 (1978): 147-184.

KREYTENBERG, GERT: "Tre cicli di Apostoli dell'antica facciata del duomo fiorentino." *Antichità viva* 16 (1977): 13-39.

KREYTENBERG, GERT: *Der Dom zu Florenz.* Berlin, 1974.

METZ, P.: "Die Florentiner Domfassade des Arnolfo di Cambio." *Jahrbuch der preussischen Kunstsammlungen* (1938).

PAATZ, WALTER and ELISABETH: *Die Kirchen von Florenz.* 6 vols. Frankfurt-am-Main, 1952-55.

PICA, A.: "La cupola di S. Maria del Fiore e la collaborazione Brunellesco-Ghiberti." *Emporium* 97 (1943): 70ff.

POGGI, GIOVANNI: *Il Duomo di Firenze: Documenti sulla decorazione della chiesa e del campanile tratti dall'archivio dell'Opera.* Berlin, 1909.

PRAGER, F. D., and SCAGLIA, G.: *Brunelleschi: Studies of His Technology and Inventions.* Cambridge, Massachusetts, 1970.

SAALMAN, HOWARD: "Santa Maria del Fiore: 1294-1418." *Art Bulletin* 46 (1964): 471-500.

SANPAOLESI, PIERO: "La cupola di Santa Maria del Fiore. Il progetto, la costruzione." *Opere d'arte* 11 (1941).

SWOBODA, K. U.: *Das florentiner Baptisterium.* Berlin and Vienna, 1918.

TOKER, FRANKLIN: "Arnolfo's S. Maria del Fiore: A Working Hypothesis." *Journal of the Society of Architectural Historians* 42 (May 1983): 101-120.

TOKER, FRANKLIN: "Florence Cathedral: The Design Stage." *Art Bulletin* 60 (1978): 214-231.

TRACHTENBERG, MARVIN: "Brunelleschi, Ghiberti, and 'L'occhio' *minore* of Florence Cathedral." *Journal of the Society of Architectural Historians* 42 (October 1983): 249-257.

TRACHTENBERG, MARVIN: *The Campanile of Florence Cathedral: Giotto's Tower.* New York, 1971.

WEINBERGER, M.: "The First Facade of the Cathedral of Florence." *Journal of the Warburg and Courtauld Institutes* 4 (1940-41): 67-79.

The monumental complex of Florence's religious center, consisting of the Cathedral, the Baptistery and the Campanile, with its incredible dimensions and its bright geometric structures covered in polychrome marble, creates an image of wealth and grandeur unequaled in 15th-century Italy. The history of the

Cathedral of Santa Maria del Fiore

complex is connected closely with economic developments of the 14th century. The opening up of markets, and consequently of cities, led to a transformation of traditional secular power structures throughout Italy. A redefinition of ecclesiastical power and influence followed in its wake. The result for urban architecture was more prominent representation of the Church, and indirectly of the citizenry, who intended to assert the shift in power by creating new architectural symbols.

In Florence these historical changes prompted the reconstruction of the Piazza di San Giovanni (now the Piazza del Duomo), which was the location of the ancient Cathedral of Santa Reparata and the Baptistery of San Giovanni. The relationship between these buildings took shape almost accidentally. Although both trace their origins to Late Roman times, one was a temple probably dedicated to Mars, the other a church dedicated to a young imperial martyr. The two buildings, standing at a right angle to each other, are barely 12 meters apart, and exhibit a distinct interdependence and functional complementarity. The octagonal plan of the Baptistery is centered on the ancient baptismal font, which had been used in Early Christian times. Its interior, in the Roman tradition and taste, was of harmonious proportions and had a sequence of round-headed arches that later developed even more in the Romanesque style of the Church of Santi Apostoli and the Church of San Miniato al Monte.

In the late 13th century, the Baptistery was clad in polychrome marble by Arnolfo di Cambio. In the mid-15th century, Filippo Brunelleschi covered the building with a segmented dome with a double shell, surmounted in turn by an octagonal pyramid carrying a graceful lantern. The construction of the dome was seminal in the flowering of Florentine architecture.

In 1296 construction of the new Cathedral, to replace the Cathedral of Santa Reparata, was begun. The new Cathedral was to be the most magnificent and beautiful church human ingenuity and industry could build. Arnolfo di Cambio won the competition with his design, and was appointed architect and supervisor of construction. (His model of the design containing all the details of the immanent construction was later unfortunately lost.) The Cathedral took some 175 years to complete, and the work was interrupted several times by catastrophes such as the flood of 1333, the plague epidemic of 1348, and the failure of the Bardi and Peruzzi banks. Arnolfo was followed by a number of architects, among whom were Giotto, Francesco Talenti and Filippo Brunelleschi.

Arnolfo's design included a gigantic dome, which was prepared for in the foundations and in the form and dimensions of the principal walls. The thickness of the walls at the base of the drum, for instance, was a good four meters. (The allegorical fresco by Andrea Bonaiuto in the Sala Capitolare at Santa Maria Novella contains a fairly accurate portrayal of Arnolfo's initial conception of the cathedral, already depicting the dome and apsidal group.) The dome was not built until the 15th century, however, according to Brunelleschi's design. The design of the double-shelled octagonal dome was as simple as it was stunning. The inner weight-bearing shell was 2.2 meters thick and supported by eight powerful ribs, each a good four meters thick and positioned at the seams of the different segments, and 16 smaller ribs. The external shell was much thinner, and functioned as cover and protection of the dome. The space between the shells was used for the internal connection of the lantern, and to facilitate inspections. The walls of the drum were made out of stone. The inner shell of the dome was made out of brick, laid in a herringbone pattern, to accommodate the octagon and to generate the rotation that made it possible to dispense with scaffolding during construction. The static weight of the lightly arched dome guaranteed sufficient stability.

The white lantern is a splendid finishing touch, as a weight balancing the dome's massiveness and as a pivot of its rotation. The group of smaller apsidal cupolas and the galleries also absorb some of the weight of the dome, relieving it adequately from the earth by exploiting the diagonal reinforcements of the smaller cupolas.

The overall effect of the cathedral complex is of great balance and harmony, with a natural center in the gigantic dome splendidly counterbalanced by the Gothic Campanile (bell-tower) conceived by the painter Giotto, and built in a period of only 25 years. Giotto directed the Campanile's construction from 1334 to 1337, and it is said that he died of heart failure for fear of having made the base too small. Andrea da Pontedera and Andrea Orcagna, who had collaborated with Giotto on the hexagonal decorations of the lower fascia, succeeded him. They decorated the upper fascia with a rhombus motif. The construction was completed by Francesco Talenti in 1359.

The marvelous progression of the marble revetments, which become lighter toward the ample upper window with three lights, makes the tower into a decorative object rather than a functional bell-tower (which Florence never really needed, considering its location in a valley surrounded by hills). The purpose of the Campanile is simply to balance the massive Cathedral dome with a more slender structure. Together the two buildings provide the principal points of reference by which citizens and visitors may orient themselves in the city.

From the beginning, the Cathedral was an object of study, and was frequently described and painted (e.g., the fresco of

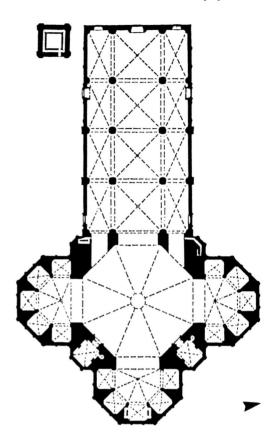

the Madonna della Misericordia at the Bigallo, and the late-14th-century fresco attributed to Giovanni del Biondo at the Cimabue Museum in the cloister of the Church of Santa Croce, besides the abovementioned Bonaiuto fresco). The Cathedral dome was copied on a smaller scale for churches at Semifonte (the Osmannoro) and Pistoia (the Basilica of the Madonna), which used the same ribbing, the same lantern, and the same red segments. It was also copied in miniature for countless ciboria, of which the ciborium over the altar at Santa Maria Novella is a particularly good example.

The dome continues to excite interest, demonstrating its lasting vitality. Architects and engineers are still studying the stupendous simplicity of the dome's construction, which seems impossible without the use of scaffolding. Recently, a Florentine architect has undertaken to build a model of the dome five times smaller than the original, using the same materials, machinery and scaffolding Brunelleschi employed, in order to test his hypotheses concerning Brunelleschi's engineering techniques.

—GIULIANO CHELAZZI
Translated from the Italian by Camille Hurych

Cathedral of Santa Maria del Fiore, detail of the facade

OSPEDALE DEGLI INNOCENTI
Florence, Italy

1421-45. Building constructed; **Architect:** Filippo Brunelleschi (1377-1446).

Ospedale degli Innocenti: Florence, Italy, 1421-45

Publications

ARGAN, GIULIO C.: *Brunelleschi*. Reprint. Milan, 1978.

BATTISTI, E.: *Filippo Brunelleschi*. Milan, Electra, 1976.

BENEVOLO, LEONARDO; CHIEFFI, STEFANO; and MAZZETTI, GIULIO: 'Indagine sul S. Spirito di Brunelleschi.'' *Quaderni dell' Istituto di Storia dell' Architettura, Università di Roma* 15 (1968): 85-90.

BOZZONI, CORRADO and CARBONARA, GIOVANNI: *Filippo Brunelleschi: Saggio di Bibliografia*. 2 vols. Rome, 1977-78.

BRUCKER, GENE: *The Civic World of Early Renaissance Florence*. Princeton, New Jersey, 1977.

BURNS, HOWARD: "Quattrocento Architecture and the Antique: Some Problems." pp. 269-287 in R.R. Bolgar (ed.): *Classical Influences on European Culture, A.D. 500-1500: Proceedings of an International Conference Held at King's College, Cambridge, April, 1969*. Cambridge, England, 1971.

CABLE, CAROLE: *Brunelleschi and His Perspective Panels*. Monticello, Illinois, 1981.

CARLI, E.: *Brunelleschi*. Florence, 1950.

DOUMATO, LAMIA: *Filippo Brunelleschi: 1377-1446*. Monticello, Illinois, 1980.

FABRICZY, CORNELIUS VON: *Filippo Brunelleschi*. Stuttgart, 1892.

FABRICZY, CORNELIUS VON: "Brunelleschiana." *Jahrbuch der königlich preussischen Kunstsammlungen* 28 (1907): 1-84.

FANELLI, GIOVANNI: *Brunelleschi*. Florence, 1977.

FOLMESICS, HANS: *Brunelleschi: Ein Beitrag zur Entwicklungsgeschichte der Frührenaissance-Architektur*. Vienna, 1915.

HEYDENREICH, LUDWIG HEINRICH: "Spätwerke Brunelleschis." *Jahrbuch der preussischen Kunstsammlungen* 52 (1931): 1-28.

HOFFMANN, VOLKER: "Brunelleschis Architektursystem." *Architectura* 1 (1971): 54-71.

HORSTER, MARITA: "Brunelleschi und Alberti in ihrer Stellung zur Römischen Antike." *Mitteilungen des Kunsthistorischen Instituts in Florenz* 17 (1973): 29-64.

HYMAN, ISABELLE: "Brunelleschi, Filippo." Vol. 14, pp. 534-545 in *Dizionario Biografico degli Italiani*. Rome, 1972.

HYMAN, ISABELLE: *Brunelleschi in Perspective*. Englewood Cliffs, New Jersey, 1974.

HYMAN, ISABELLE: *Fifteenth Century Florentine Studies: The Palazzo Medici and a Ledger for the Church of San Lorenzo*. New York, 1977.

KEMP, MARTIN: "Science, Non-science and Nonsense: The Interpretation of Brunelleschi's Perspective." *Art History* 1 2 (1978): 134-161.

KENT, DALE: *The Rise of the Medici: Faction in Florence, 1426-1434*. Oxford, 1978.

KLOTZ, H.: *Filippo Brunelleschi: The Early Works and the Medieval Tradition*. New York, 1990.

LINNENKAMP, R.: "Die Pazzi-Kapelle, S. Croce, Florenz: ein unbekanntes Porportionssystem Brunelleschis." *Deutsche Bauzeitung* LXVI (1961): 277-79.

LUPORINI, EUGENIO: *Brunelleschi: Forma e ragione*. Milan, 1964.

MAINSTONE, ROWLAND: "Brunelleschi's Dome." *Architectural Review* 162 (1977): 156-166.

MANETTI, ANTONIO: *The Life of Brunelleschi*. University Park, Pennsylvania, 1970.

MENDES ATANASIO, M. C., and DALLAI, G.: ''Nuove indagine sullo Spedale degli Innocenti a Firenze.'' *Commentari* 17 (1966): 83-106.

MOLHO, ANTHONY: ''Three Documents Regarding Filippo Brunelleschi.'' *Burlington Magazine* 119 (1977): 851-852.

NYBERG, DOROTHEA F.: ''Brunelleschi's Use of Proportion in the Pazzi Chapel.'' *Marsyas* 7 (1957): 1-7.

PRAGER, F. D. and SCAGLIA, G.: *Brunelleschi: Studies of His Technology and Inventions.* Cambridge, Mass. 1970.

RAGGHIANTI, CARLO L.: *Filippo Brunelleschi: Un uomo, un universo.* Florence, 1977.

SAALMAN, HOWARD: ''Filippo Brunelleschi: Capital Studies.'' *Art Bulletin* XL (1958): 114-115.

SAALMAN, HOWARD: ''Early Renaissance Architectural Theory and Practice in Antonio Filarete's Tratto di Architettura.'' *Art Bulletin* 41 (1959): 89-106.

SANPAOLESI, PIERO: *Brunelleschi.* Milan, 1962.

ZERVAS, DIANE FINIELLO: ''Filippo Brunelleschi's Political Career.'' *Burlington Magazine* 121 (1979): 630-639.

*

The complex of the Ospedale degli Innocenti—an orphanage and foundling hospital—is an assemblage of buildings of different dates, organized around a series of courtyards and gardens. The founding of the hospital, which first opened its doors in 1445, was intimately connected with the flowering of Marianism in Florence. The cult of Mary resulted not only in countless artistic representations of the Virgin and Child, but also stimulated the expansion of charitable institutions for women and children. In the 14th century, for instance, the Ospizio di Orbatello—a hostel for poor women, abandoned by husbands or lovers—was built, under the auspices of the Order of the Holy Annunciation.

In 1294 the Florentine Republic entrusted the care of abandoned children to the silkworkers' guild. At first, the Ospedale di San Gallo, outside the gate of the same name, in the area of what is now the Parterre, and the Ospedale di Santa Maria della Scala were used to house the children. Early in the 14th century, dominance in the regional silk trade passed from Luca to Florence, with the result that the guild grew considerably both in numbers and wealth. In 1421 the Council of the People decided to construct a new building, which was to resemble a palace in its splendor. The silkworkers taxed themselves to finance the construction. Land was bought next to the Church of Santissima Annunziata, away from the historic city center, in an effort to ensure a healthy environment for the foundlings. Filippo Brunelleschi, in his dual capacity as architect and goldsmith, was commissioned to design the complex, a miniature city in itself, and supervise its construction. (He was later succeeded by his pupil Francesco della Lana.) The Carta della Catena and a miniature by Massaio both show the splendid equilibrium of the building's architectural forms, with the fluidly spaced windows on the second floor of the grand hall set against the elegance of the colonnade underneath. The building was positioned at an angle to the Church of Santissima Annunziata, which graced the northeastern part of the piazza.

The current arrangement of the piazza was the result of a

Ospendale degli Innocenti, cloister

slow process of gestation. The Ospedale ended up in an elevated position with respect to the piazza, which is dominated by the colonnade with its chiaroscuro effect. In 1454 a central portico with an arch was added to the facade of the church, by Antonio da Sangallo the Elder, and in 1516 Antonio da Sangallo the Younger and Baccio d'Agnolo amended the oblique angle of the central perspective axis of the Ospedale, to make it correspond to the longitudinal axis of the church. In so doing, they completed the splendid arrangement of the piazza, with the adjacent building faithfully imitating the Ospedale degli Innocent. Giovanni Caccini constructed the lateral arches, three on each side, on the church portico. There is thus considerable continuity in the scenic arrangement of the facades of the three buildings surrounding what is perhaps the most significant piazza of the Florentine Renaissance. The piazza represents the new principles of perspective until then only dreamed of by Piero della Francesca.

The structure of the Ospedale is conceived as a sequence of bodies of various materials, connected to and articulated around the two cloisters, one reserved for boys and one for girls. Spacious outdoor areas and numerous galleries assured outdoor exercise for the children in all seasons and under all weather conditions. The greater cloister seems to recreate, on a reduced scale, the luminous atmosphere of the external piazza. The plan may appear conventional, but the variety in perspective, the galleries and the symbols of childhood make it a place peculiarly suited for children.

On the left side, at the end of the external portico, a double stone staircase is still in existence. It is connected to a square window fitted out with a "wheel" with a wood cylinder which can hold a child. Foundlings were first conveyed into the Ospedale by turning the wheel. The whole contraption was designed to guarantee anonymity to the persons leaving the child, and was used until 1875, when a more dignified system of personal delivery was instituted.

—GIULIANO CHELAZZI
Translated from the Italian by Camille Hurych

PALAZZO PITTI
Florence, Italy

1458-66. Architect: Filippo Brunelleschi (1377-1446); construction supervised by Luca Fancelli. **1558-70:** Construction completed with *cortile* and rear facade. **Architect:** Bartolomeo Ammannati (1511-92). **1620-31:** Extensions, including lateral *cortili*. **Architects:** G. Parigi and A. Parigi. **1794-1839:** Additions.

Publications

SATKOWSKI, LEON: "The Palazzo Pitti: Planning and Use in the Grand-Ducal Era." *Journal of the Society of Architectural Historians* 42 (December 1983): 336-349.

*

The Palazzo Pitti has a curious history, beginning with Filippo Brunelleschi's design for the Palazzo Medici. Commissioned by Cosimo de'Medici the Elder to design the family's principal residence in Florence, Brunelleschi developed a sumptuous, freestanding palace with a square plan, facing the Church of San Lorenzo. Cosimo rejected the design, reputedly fearing that such a splendid work would provoke envy and resentment among the citizens. Whatever his specific motivation, he was in accord with Leon Battista Alberti, who wrote in *De re Aedificatoria,* "The house of the Signore will be gracefully ornate. It will have a pleasing rather than a magnificent appearance." Outraged, Brunelleschi destroyed the design and the model when he learned that his commission had been transferred to Michelozzo Michelozzi, who was to design a less demonstrative palace, more integrated with the urban fabric. Michelozzi's design does seem better suited to its immediate environment. Nonetheless, according to Giorgio Vasari, Cosimo soon regretted his decision.

Not long thereafter, Luca Pitti retained Brunelleschi as the architect for the Palazzo Pitti. Competing with the Medicis, and wishing to build himself a palace that would express his economic and social prestige, Pitti had bought a huge area of land owned by the Boboli family. Homes located on the land were bought from the residing families and immediately demolished, so as to create a sloping site ideal for what was to be the grandest and most magnificent building in Florence. Prompted by Cosimo's disappointing decision, Brunelleschi used his design for the Palazzo Medici as his point of departure, enlarging and elaborating it for his new client. In 1458 work was begun on the central core, which was significantly different from the way it appears today, both in its dimensions and its detail. Judging by axonometric representations of it in the 15th-century *Pianta della Catena* and in Agnolo Bronzino's predella at the Church of Santo Spirito, the core building had rustication on the lower part, windows with round-headed arches on the two upper floors, and a narrow loggia under the steep roof. A strong stringcourse supported by corbels provided a horizontal rhythm.

In 1466 the first block was completed, followed by a long pause in construction due to a crisis in the Pitti finances. In 1549 Luca Pitti's great-grandson, no longer able to manage the family's enormous debts, sold the palace to the Grand Duchess Elenora da Toledo, wife of Cosimo I. She immediately undertook the enlargement of the original block. Bartolommeo Ammannati was put in charge of the architecture, while Niccolo Tribolo was commissioned to arrange the gardens. The appearance of the palace after this second building phase was captured in a lunette by Giusto Utens. Two lateral wings extending back circumscribed a lovely courtyard. Finely worked horizontal strips of rustication created a noble contrast to the large rustic stones of the external facade. Tribolo's garden, including the *teatro della verzura* (theater of verdure) at the end of the courtyard, was laid out on the incline of the hill along the axis of the building, reaching up to the upper basin with its leveled walks.

Before the work was completed, Cosimo himself decided to move into the palace, along with his numerous family. A long corridor that Vasari had designed connected the Palazzo Pitti to the Palazzo Vecchio like an umbilical cord, and assured the grand duke undisturbed movement between the buildings; that in turn enabled him to conduct his political and military affairs from his residence. The symmetrical facade, with the geometrical planning typical of the Renaissance, served to represent the power of the Medici. That representational character made the structure comparable to similar palaces being built all over the city by the Rucellai, Antinori, Pazzi, Strozzi, Guadagni and other families. The Palazzo Pitti was probably very similar to the Palazzo Gondi in its present appearance, which is also characterized by sequences of seven windows, three floors, gradual rustication and a strongly projecting roof.

However, its site predestined the Palazzo Pitti to take on different lines and dimensions. Between 1620 and 1631, the architect Giulio Parigi extended the central block, adding three

Palazzo Pitti: Florence, Italy, 1458-66

windows on each side to each of the three stories. His son, Alfonso, finished the enlargement with another five windows on each side. He lengthened the two lower floors only, to break up the linearity of the building, already accentuated by continuous balustrades at ground level and at the roofline (the latter balustrade being a substitution for the original loggia).

A final building campaign from 1794 to 1839, at the behest of Ferdinand III of Lorena, gave the palace its present appearance. Two lateral projections with colonnaded porticos and terraces, positioned at right angles to the main facade, enclose the piazza. The additions are defined neither by the central axis nor by the longitudinal axis, making it seem as if Cartesian discipline had established an altogether new rule of reason. At the same time, the garden was further extended to the south, and the Palazzina della Meridiana was built by Gaspare Paoletti, parallel to the new gardens.

The entire complex of internal and external spaces, with its symbols of power, works to define the character and position of the prince. But the palace was also the expression of the social and cultural maturity that the Renaissance had fostered. It became the site of cultural representation, a place where the prince could enjoy the pleasures of being a patron of the arts. Many of the rooms were arranged and decorated according to an iconography inspired by ancient mythology, underscoring the openly secular ideology of power. The triumph of the muses was celebrated in the abundance of art—paintings, sculptures, furnishings, cornices with frescoes of mythological subjects—arrayed to demonstrate the passions and sensibility of the art patron. In the rooms dedicated to Venus, Mars, Apollo and other classical gods, works by Raphael, Titian, Murillo, Rubens,

Salvator Rosa and many others create a balanced and harmonious decor.

Naturalistic interests, influenced by the anthropomorphism of the Renaissance, were reinforced by the rationalism of the Cartesian age, which was illustrated best by the gardens. The gardens were not merely appendices to the palace, but actually dominated many of the rooms. The artificial landscape of the gardens was assimilated into the internal decor by means of *trompe l'oeil* painting, reproducing and idealizing the tensions of the squared hedges, and the unshaped trees which nevertheless resemble columns. P. Porcinai wrote about the landscape, "It is a paradise of rationalism, where the philosophical method of Descartes corresponds almost exactly to a method of creating, in green and with a profusion of sculptural elements, an abstract enchanted village around the Palazzo."

In the old plan, the *"teatro della verzura"* became a veritable amphitheater, with the palace courtyard, dominated by the basin, as an unusual backdrop. The southern section was connected to it, and was developed around a wide tree-lined avenue running between the walks of the older gardens and the Fontana dell'Oceana at the far end. A sequence of outdoor spaces, enriched with statues, was thus created, recalling the world of the nymphaeum and the contiguous plans of Hadrian's Villa. The gardens of the Palazzo Pitti became the prototype of *all'italiana* landscape architecture.

In the period 1865-71, when Florence functioned briefly as the Italian capital, the palace was the residence of the ruling House of Savoy. After that time, the Palazzo Pitti and the Boboli Hill were transformed into a giant complex of museums, eight in all—exhibiting paintings, porcelain, costumes, carriages and modern art, among other objects—making it one of the major museum complexes of contemporary Florence.

—GIULIANO CHELAZZI
Translated from the Italian by Camille Hurych

PALAZZO RUCELLAI
Florence, Italy

Ca. 1446-60s: Palazzo rebuilt from houses originally on site; **Architect:** Attributed to Leon Battista Alberti (1404-72) and/or Bernardo Rossellino (1409-64).

Publications

FORSTER, KURT W.: "Discussion: The Palazzo Rucellai and Questions of Typology in the Development of Renaissance Buildings." *Art Bulletin* 58 (1976): 109-113.

KENT, F. W.: "The Rucellai Family and Its Loggia." *Journal of the Warburg and Courtauld Institutes* 35 (1972): 397-401.

MACK, CHARLES R.: *Pienza*. Ithaca, New York, and London, 1987.

MACK, CHARLES R.: "The Rucellai Palace: Some New Proposals." *Art Bulletin* 56 (1974): 517-529.

PREYER, BRENDA: "The Rucellai Loggia." *Mitteilungen des Kunsthistorischen Instituts in Florenz* 21 (1977): 183-198.

PREYER, BRENDA: "The Rucellai Palace." In F. W. KENT, et al.: *Giovanni Rucellai ed il suo Zibaldone, II: A Florentine Patrician and His Palace*. London, 1981.

SAALMAN, HOWARD: "Review of F. W. Kent, A. Perosa, B. Preyer, P. Sanpaolesi and R. Salvini, *Giovanni Rucellai ed il suo Zibaldone, II: A Florentine Patrician and His Palace*." *Journal of the Society of Architectural Historians* 47 (1988): 82-90.

SANPAOLESI, PAOLO: "L'architettura del Palazzo Rucellai." In F. W. KENT, et al.: *Giovanni Rucellai ed il suo Zibaldone, II: A Florentine Patrician and His Palace*. London, 1981.

SANPAOLESI, PAOLO: "Precisazioni sul Palazzo Rucellai." *Palladio* 13 (1963): 61-66.

SCHLOSSER, JULIUS: "Ein Künstlerproblem der Renaissance: L. B. Alberti." In *Akademie der Wissenschaften in Wien: Sitzungsberichte 210*. Vienna, 1929.

*

The Palazzo Rucellai was one of the most important secular buildings to be erected in Florence during the 15th century. Although its internal arrangements contributed little to the development of Renaissance architecture, its elegant facade helped to establish a new standard of harmonious architectural sophistication in keeping with the classically motivated life-style ambitions of the age.

Running along the Via della Vigna Nuova, the facade consists of a three-story grid of seven trabeated bays (and the beginnings of an eighth) separated by tiers of pilasters. Aligned twin-lighted windows are centered in each bay of the two upper stories, while square mezzanine windows appear in each bay of the ground story. Impressively framed doorways are located in the third and sixth bays of the ground floor, that in the third bay leading via a vaulted passageway to a loggia and courtyard; the original function of the opening in the sixth bay is unclear,

and it was perhaps purely decorative. The stonework of the facade is given a channeled rustication against which are set the smooth-faced pilasters and the classical entablatures.

The antiquarian character of the Rucellai facade attracted the admiration of Antonio Filarete, who, in the early 1460s, described it as being designed *al modo antico*. The Roman Colosseum and the Theater of Marcellus have been frequently cited as the inspiration for the articulation of the facade. Even closer prototypes may be found in the now-vanished Septizonium of Septimius Severus and at the Markets of Trajan. Perhaps the best and most appropriate ancient source for the decorative ordering is found in the walls of the ruined villa of Le Mura at Anguilaria. It is also correct to note (as Kurt Forster has) that similar articulation schemes appeared in the fictive architecture painted by Fra Angelico for the Chapel of Pope Nicholas V (1447-50) in the Vatican and in the actual sgraffito enhancements to the facade of certain earlier Florentine palaces such as that of the Gerini.

The patron of the Palazzo Rucellai, Giovanni di Paolo Rucellai, had become one of the wealthiest bankers in Florence, linked by his own marriage to the Strozzi family (although in exile since 1434, still influential) and from 1461, through the betrothal of his son, to the powerful Medici. This latter connection is demonstrated visually on the facade by the use of Medici emblems in the lower frieze (Rucellai devices appear in the upper) and in the spandrels of the windows.

Any evaluation of the stylistic significance of the Rucellai palace must be made in the context of other such Florentine buildings, in particular that of the Medici built by Michelozzo between 1444 and 1455. An accurate appraisal of the importance of the Palazzo Rucellai has been hindered by uncertainties concerning its dates of construction and its architect. Traditionally and, in part based upon some 16th-century notices, it has been dated to the period 1446-51. The discovery and interpretation of the tax statements (*catasti*) of Rucellai, his family and neighbors have revealed a more complex building history, involving several stages of construction. The precise sequence of building events remains difficult to unravel and much debated (Brenda Preyer, Howard Saalman and this writer all have presented varying interpretations based upon essentially the same documentation). According to Rucellai's own testimony (substantiated in the tax records), there originally were eight separate buildings on the property now lying behind the celebrated facade, including his own home at the corner of the Via della Vigna Nuova and the Via dei Palchetti. Beginning in the early 1440s, Rucellai had begun to acquire adjoining properties, probably with a view to enlarging his own quarters in keeping with his growing financial and social importance.

The first phase of this effort (ca. 1446-50) involved the amalgamation of the dwellings along the Via dei Palchetti into a single unit. At that point, the courtyard was constructed either with one, two or three loggias. Shortly thereafter the contiguous house along the Via della Vigna Nuova, owned by Rucellai's mother, was absorbed into the growing complex, and then in about 1460 he added another house next to that. The present internal disposition of the palace continues to reflect the agglutinative character of the building's evolution; the Palazzo Rucellai was not built but rebuilt from houses already on the site, a clear case of adaptive reuse common to other palaces of the period such as that of the Spinelli. The hodgepodge nature of this amalgamation of various structures can still be discerned along the Via dei Palchetti.

It was for the main thoroughfare, the Via della Vigna Nuova, that Rucellai demanded a solidifying front, one in keeping with his aspirations and pretensions. Exactly when this took shape,

Palazzo Rucellai: Florence, Italy, ca. 1446-60s

conceptually and physically, remains uncertain. Paolo Sanpaolesi, seconded by Preyer, has posited a two-phase facade project, the first (ca. 1450) covering the fronts of the houses of Giovanni and his mother and equal to five of the current seven bays and a later expansion. Forster and the present writer have argued for a facade project that awaited the acquisition of the third house along the Via della Vigna Nuova and the inspiration of the engagement of Rucellai's son, which would have occasioned the incorporation of the Medici insignia into the program (Preyer denies the connection of these emblems with the Medici). The latter suggestion, a Rucellai facade of post-1461, calls into question its primacy over the almost identical design used for the Palazzo Piccolomini (1459-62) in the papal city of Pienza. It also raises once again the question of authorship.

Based upon the word of Giorgio Vasari and other mid-to-late-16th-century notations, as well as upon Giovanni Rucellai's known use of the architect at his chapel in the nearby church of San Pancrazio and for the completion of the facade of Santa Maria Novella, the great humanist scholar and artistic theoretician Leon Battista Alberti commonly has been accepted as the architect responsible for the Rucellai palace. Earlier 16th-century writers had, however, linked the name of the sculptor-architect Bernardo Rossellino to the project. Based upon stylistic features, Julius Schlosser questioned Alberti's involvement. The documentary evidence for a later dating for the palace and the possibility of a post-1460 date for the facade caused this writer and Forster to postulate Rossellino's authorship for the facade (almost all scholars credit him with the internal remodeling, citing similarities in sculptural elements and corbel types) and the distinct suggestion that the Palazzo Piccolomini (securely documented to Rossellino) came first. Both Rossellino's authorship and the precedence of the Pienza palace have been denied by Preyer and others. Saalman sees Alberti's mind behind both projects, with Rossellino acting as Alberti's surrogate.

Whatever the case, the facade of the Palazzo Rucellai, due to its prominent position in the Florentine cityscape and "townhouse" features, proved an important influence in reshaping Renaissance attitudes concerning domestic architecture. The appearance of Rucellai's ennobled residence was further embellished through the creation of a little piazza in front of the palace and the construction of family loggia, in a situation reminiscent of Rossellino's designs at Pienza and for the Piccolomini family palace in Siena.

—CHARLES R. MACK

PALAZZO STROZZI
Florence, Italy

1489-1538: Palazzo built; **Architects:** Head architect was Tommaso del Pollaiuolo called Il Cronaca (1457-1508); other contributing architects included Guiliano da Sangallo (ca. 1443-1516) and Benedetto da Maiano (1442-97). **Ca 1492:** *Cortile* designed. **1938:** Extensively restored.

Publications

GOLDWAITE, R. A.: "The Building of the Strozzi Palace: The Construction Industry in Renaissance Florence." Pp. 99-194 in WILLIAM BOWSKY (ed.): *Studies in Medieval and Renaissance History*. Lincoln, Nebraska, 1973.

HEYDENREICH, LUDWIG H., and LOTZ, WOLFGANG: *Architecture in Italy 1400-1600*. Harmondsworth, England, 1974.
PAMPALONI, G.: *Palazzo Strozzi*. Rome, 1963.
PARRONCHI, A.: "Il modello del palazzo Strozzi." *Rinascimento* Series 2, 9 (1969): 95-116.

*

The dominating presence of the Palazzo Strozzi serves to rank it among the most significant of Florence's Renaissance palaces. Unlike the nearby Palazzo Rucellai, which incorporated a number of preexisting structures, but like the Palazzo Medici, which it emulated and sought to surpass in grandeur, the Strozzi family palace was built from the foundations up on land cleared for the purpose.

Work on the palace was begun in 1489 at the instigation of Filippo di Matteo Strozzi, and continued with interruptions until 1538. The Strozzi family, despite its wealth and power as merchant-bankers, was in a politically tenuous position in Florence due to earlier opposition to the Medici. Filippo's palace was intended to solidify the family's position through its impressive size and by the munificence of this contribution to the Florentine cityscape. The Palazzo Strozzi was the largest private residence to have been built in Florence. Original plans called for an enlargement of the piazza to the east (not realized until 1533) and probably for a walled garden area to be attached to the palace, following the example of the Palazzo Medici.

The visual connection with the Palazzo Medici may have intentionally emphasized a reconciliation between these two important families. Three of the facades are public ones (the fourth, left incomplete, parallels a narrow alleyway) and are similar in design, each featuring a centrally placed portal and a row of framed mezzanine windows in the first floor and symmetrically disposed twin-lighted windows in the two upper stories. Bold ashlar rustication enlivens the surfaces of the first and second stories, with a somewhat softer treatment introduced in the third story. Unlike at the earlier Palazzo Medici or the nearby Palazzo Strozzino (begun possibly by Michelozzo and completed by Giuliano da Maiano), the use of pronounced rustication is maintained throughout the elevation. As at the Palazzo Pitti, and in contrast to the Palazzo Medici, the individual stories are equal in height. The lack of pronounced surface gradation, coupled with equal heights of the stories, reduces the illusion of height but contributes to the impression of a weighty mass and sense of unified solidity, thereby adding to the impressive character of the great palatial block. The round arches of the three portals and of the second- and third-story windows are defined by prominent voussoirs. Divisions between the stories are marked by dentilated cornices, and the palace is crowned by a powerfully projecting cornice consisting of dentil, ovolo and modillion moldings resting upon a plain frieze.

The interior is a refinement of the orderly disposition of spaces found at the earlier Palazzo Medici. Symmetry governs the arrangement of rooms about the vast rectangular *cortile*, designed circa 1492. The lower story of the courtyard is traditionally Florentine in appearance, with unfluted Corinthian columns supporting a series of arcades. A departure from the expected occurs in the second story, where Roman-style cross windows and framed oculi are placed within blind arcades springing from Doric pilasters. This level of the *cortile* is clearly the most novel, with features that might be described as proto-High Renaissance. The third story of the courtyard is surrounded by an open loggia of Corinthian columns resting upon an innovative balustrade.

Fortunately, the payment ledgers for the construction of the

Palazzo Strozzi: Florence, Italy, 1489-1538

palace have been preserved, but, while listing the workers involved and their assignments, they do not name the architect in charge. Although authorship of the Strozzi palace is, as a consequence, in dispute, a major role for Simone di Tommaso del Pollaiuolo, called Il Cronaca (1457-1508), is well documented and unchallenged. It was Il Cronaca who designed the great cornice and who probably determined the articulation of the courtyard, but he did not join the project until 1490. Authorities differ in their attribution of the initial designs for the building. In his entry on Il Cronaca in *Lives of the Artists* (1550), Giorgio Vasari credits Benedetto da Maiano with the design for the palace, writing: "Benedetto da Maiano was called in . . . and made a model, standing alone, which was afterwards carried out. . . ." Based upon Vasari's testimony, the authorship of the initial designs traditionally has been assigned to Benedetto, but contemporary scholarship has begun to challenge his role; for example, Richard Goldthwaite has offered convincing arguments in favor of Giuliano da Sangallo, who was given several payments for a wooden model (presumably the one still preserved in the museum of the Palazzo Strozzi) beginning in September 1489. One could argue that Sangallo simply executed

the model according to Benedetto's instructions, but since the latter also was well versed in carpentry, that would seem unlikely. Then, too, many features in the facade of the Strozzi palace are echoed in that of the Palazzo Gondi, begun by Giuliano da Sangallo in about 1490. Two surviving plans of the Piazza degli Strozzi with its surrounding buildings, including the palace (one being a ground plan and the other showing detailed elevations), have been attributed variously to Benedetto da Maiano or Giuliano da Sangallo. Although Benedetto was involved in the project, he received payments only for models of decorative items. Sangallo was given the larger amounts and seemingly played the determining role in the initial stages of construction. Whoever really bore the responsibility, the actual supervision was initially in the hands of a building contractor named Jacopo di Stefano Rosselli.

Early in 1490, Il Cronaca came on the scene, perhaps through the aegis of his father-in-law, Rosselli. It was Il Cronaca who directed the principal states of construction, amending and amplifying the original *modello*, designing the spacious courtyard and the imposing cornice crowning the palace. Already in August of 1490, Il Cronaca was paid for a new model (not extant) which must have altered the original concept appreciably by heightening the elevation, adding rustication to the third story, and providing for the great classicizing cornice which, according to Vasari, was copied "from an antique measured by him at Rome at Spogliacristo."

At the death of Filippo Strozzi, in May 1491, the palace had risen through the first story. Ironwork, including the beautiful lanterns at the corners, were commissioned from Niccolo di Nofri del Sodo, known as Caparra. Work continued under Il Cronaca's oversight and the actual direction of a building foreman named Mariotto di Papi da Balatro. By 1495 the next story had been completed, and the third by 1498. In 1500 work was initiated on the eastern cornice. The building, although still unfinished, was occupied by tenants in 1504. In 1507 work was suspended, but was resumed in 1523. Portions of the northern and western facades remained unfinished when work finally was halted in 1538 with the exile of Filippo's son Lorenzo and the later confiscation of the palace by Duke Cosimo de' Medici. The Strozzi regained possession of the building in 1568.

Extensive restorations were begun in 1938 when the building was ceded to the National Insurance Association. Today the Palazzo Strozzi houses the Studio Italiano di Storia dell'Arte, the Istituto Nazionale di Studi Rinascimento, and the "La Strozzina" museum, and is the frequent site of colloquia and exhibitions.

—CHARLES R. MACK

PALAZZO VECCHIO
Florence, Italy

1299-1315: Palazzo built; **Architect:** Designs attributed to Arnolfo di Cambio (died ca. 1302). **1306:** Main block up to *ballatoio* built. **1308:** Tower built. **1310-15:** Belfry built. **1342-43:** West entrance enlarged and fortified. **1440s:** Extensively renovated, ceilings lowered, mezzanine enlarged, courtyard rebuilt; **Architect:** Michelozzo (1396-1472). **1565:** Courtyard remodeled; **Architect:** Giorgio Vasari (1511-74). **16th century:** Extensive restorations done under Medici dukes.

Publications

LENSI, A.: *Il Palazzo Vecchio di Firenze*. Milan and Rome, 1929.
MOISE, F.: *Palazzo Vecchio*. Florence, 1845.
PAUL, J.: *Der Palazzo Vecchio in Florenz, Ursprung und Bedeutung seiner Form*. Florence, 1969.
TRACHTENBERG, MARVIN: "What Brunelleschi Saw: Monument and Site at the Palazzo Vecchio in Florence." *Journal of the Society of Architectural Historians* 47 (March 1988): 14-44.

*

The Palazzo Vecchio was originally known both as the Palazzo dei Priori and Palazzo della Signoria, or Palace of the Magistrates. Built to accommodate a new political regime, including its many citizen committees, the Palazzo Vecchio also served as the residence of officials elected from the powerful city guilds. During the 1280s and 1290s, just prior to the Palazzo Vecchio's construction, the governance of Florence shifted from the nobility to the guilds of merchants and bankers. This was no smooth political transition, but was marked by constant rebellion, fratricide and violent resistance. By way of solidifying its takeover and imprinting its presence on the face of the city, the victorious mercantile class built its new political center literally to overshadow that of the earlier regime, the relatively new Palazzo del Podestà (built 1250s, known since the 16th century as the Bargello).

The new government's immediate need for expanded and fortified quarters was evident in the speed with which the Palazzo Vecchio was constructed; by 1302 it was sufficiently complete to house the offices of the magistrates, and by 1306 to become their residence. This speed is remarkable by any account, but it is particularly astonishing when compared with the extreme slowness and numerous delays connected to construction at the Cathedral of Florence, begun in 1294.

The fortress-like quality of the original block of the Palazzo Vecchio further attests to the realities of civic strife and the new administration's need for self-preservation within the secured confines of the town hall. The rusticated facade underscores the fact that the palace was built as a defensive fortress for the members of the city council. The tower, too, served a defensive purpose as a watchpost overlooking the city and surrounding valley.

The original block consists of three rusticated horizontal sections, built of local *pietra forte*, separated by thin stringcourses on which rest two rows of mullioned windows with trefoil arches. This main core is topped by a crenelated battlement and covered gallery, the *ballatoio*, carried by arched corbels; between these corbels are frescoed the emblems of the Commune of Florence. The watchtower and belfry rise to the right of center on the south facade; this off-center position was determined by the desire to use an earlier tower on the site as the foundation for the new tower.

As an architectural type, the defensible block with tower was not new with the Palazzo Vecchio; it was, in fact, typical of Italian urban medieval palaces. In a town hall, however, the combination seems to have been first used at the Palazzo Vecchio, and it quickly became the type for 14th-century communal palaces in Tuscany. Its origin may have been the rural *case coloniche*, defensible towered-block structures common to the Tuscan countryside throughout the late medieval period, known from surviving examples as well as early representations (as in *The Castle on the Lakeshore*, one of two small landscapes attributed to Ambrogio Lorenzetti, 1330s, in the Pinacoteca of Siena).

The Palazzo Vecchio is an example of the medieval communal palace type in a transitional phase. Military and civic elements were brought together there as never before. The massive *ballatoio*, planned for protective purposes, is harmoniously proportioned to the facade. The tower juts daringly beyond the main facade, supported in part by corbels under the *ballatoio* only slightly larger than the others. In contrast to these military elements, and as if to assert the dignity, grace and strength of the new Florentine government, the architects incorporated elegant bifora windows into a facade whose rustication is finely graduated. The order and division of facade elements are impressive, and were influential on later quattrocento architecture, particularly that of Michelozzo Michelozzi, whose Palazzo Medici-Riccardi (begun 1444) is an Early Renaissance restatement of architectural principles worked out at the Palazzo Vecchio.

The complex building history of the Palazzo Vecchio has only recently been fully addressed by architectural historians.

Palazzo Vecchio: Florence, Italy, 1299-1315

Begun in 1299, the rusticated main block up to the *ballatoio* was completed by 1306, the *ballatoio* itself was built shortly thereafter, the tower around 1308, and the belfry atop the tower sometime between 1310 and 1315. The significance of these several building campaigns is the apparent concerted attention given the palazzo as a civic monument within an urban setting. Between 1299 and 1315, the design of palazzo and piazza were altered and variations tested. Archaeological evidence suggests that at issue was which facade to make the main entrance, and therefore in which direction the piazza should develop; also considered were the extent of the battlements and the height of

the tower. Work continued at the north and west piazzas into the 1350s as land was gradually reclaimed from private citizens. Together, the palazzo and piazza were considered the city's civic center, and it was as such that this area was joined to the ecclesiastical center by enlarged and regularized streets in the 1380s.

The interior has been greatly modified throughout centuries of constant use by the many governments housed therein. At the center of the original structure was a *cortile*, which most likely supported wooden walkways on the surrounding upper floors; off these walkways were offices for the affairs of state, and dormitories for the priors who were to reside at the palace during their tenure in office. These walkways provided not only ease of communication, but the much-needed fresh air and light into the heart of the palazzo as well as into the rooms surrounding the *cortile*. To the north of the *cortile* on each floor were large assembly rooms, similar in plan to the rooms as they are today.

The one interior space that survives from the original 14th-century structure is the Sala dell'Arme, adjoining the *cortile* on the north side of the ground level. There, six bays of cross vaulting are supported by wall pilasters and two central octagonal piers. The influence of Arnolfo di Cambio (ca. 1245-by 1310), architect of the cathedral, has been detected in the simplicity and planarity of forms in the Sala dell'Arme; Giorgio Vasari' s 16th-century attribution of the palazzo to Arnolfo has often been accepted, but has not been confirmed. It was not uncommon at the time, however, for individuals involved in one civic monument, such as the cathedral, to be similarly involved in other contemporary civic monuments.

The Palazzo Vecchio was modified by nearly every political regime. During the autocratic rule of the duke of Athens in 1342-43, the west entrance was enlarged and fortified; these fortifications were then removed by the citizens upon the duke's expulsion from the city. (The fortifications of the west portal are visible in the fresco depicting the expulsion of the duke of Athens, formerly in the Carceri delle Stinche, now in the Palazzo Vecchio.)

In the 1440s the *Operaio del Palazzo* was formed and given the task of renovation. Michelozzo was appointed superintendent of works; his extensive renovations included the lowering of the ceilings in many rooms, the enlargement of the mezzanine and the rebuilding of the courtyard, which he modeled after his *cortile* at the Palazzo Medici-Riccardi. Architectural echoes of the Medici palace no doubt echoed Medicean influences on that government. The *cortile* was again remodeled in 1565 by Vasari on the occasion of the marriage of Francesco de'Medici and Joan of Austria. The Early (Michelozzo) and Late (Vasari) Renaissance decorations are delineated both architecturally and figuratively. The severity of Michelozzo's architectural details in *pietra serena* against a light stucco is in sharp contrast to Vasari's multicolored *grottesche* and painted histories. Such contrasts are typical throughout the palace's interior, where Late Medieval, Renaissance, Mannerist and even Baroque elements are blended. The interior decoration, although not always harmonious, succeeds in expressing the dynamic use of the structure and the important place it held in the minds of the city's governors.

Other additions to the Palazzo Vecchio included the Salone dei Cinquecento designed by Simone del Pollaiuolo, called Il Cronaca. This large assembly room was built for the Consiglio Maggiore, whose 500 members met there during the brief republican government established by Girolamo Savonarola (1494-98). Even greater modifications were carried out under the Medici dukes. In 1540, Duke Cosimo de Medici and his wife, Eleonora di Toledo, took up residence in the palazzo, which then received the name Palazzo Ducale. In the 1540s, 1550s and 1560s, the palazzo was enlarged to its present size; among the architects involved were Battista del Tasso, Giorgio Vasari and Bernardo Buontalenti. The Palazzo Vecchio was so-named in the 16th century when the Medici dukes moved their private residential quarters to the much larger Palazzo Pitti on the opposite side of the Arno River, and it became the "Old Palace."

Medieval Florence, unlike many other Italian cities, developed distinct geographical urban centers for the city's ecclesiastical and political spheres. These were the areas around the Cathedral of Santa Maria del Fiore (the Duomo) and the Palazzo Vecchio. Begun in the 1290s, these monuments attest to the dramatic growth of the city and to the wealth and pride of its citizens. The magnificent dome of the cathedral and majestic tower of the old town hall were long held to be symbols of the power and organization of one of Europe's wealthiest cities. These buildings form the backdrop against which the remainder of the city's architecture has been viewed for over 500 years, and even today they dominate the city's silhouette. The histories of cathedral and town hall are closely tied to the vicissitudes of Florentine life. The numerous building campaigns at the Palazzo Vecchio are particularly illustrative of the interactions between politics and architecture in a Late Medieval urban setting.

—MARJORIE OCH

PONTE VECCHIO
Florence, Italy

1345: New bridge built on site of original; **Architects:** Attributed to Neri di Fioravante or Taddeo Gaddi. **Ca. 1564:** Loggia built. **After 1593:** Shops on bridge enlarged and extended.

Publications

BORSOOK, E.: *The Companion Guide to Florence.* London, 1966.

*

The medieval Ponte Vecchio, lined with the shops of Florentine goldsmiths and antiquarians, is the oldest bridge in Florence and one of the most picturesque bridges in the world. It was built in 1345, but tradition holds that its foundations incorporated the supports of the ancient Roman bridge built across the Arno River when Florence was founded in about 59 B.C. The earlier bridge was part of the Via Cassia, a major communication and transportation link between the capital in Rome and settlements in the Po Valley and further north; it was probably built of stone piers with a wooden superstructure. After the Roman road crossed the bridge to the north bank of the Arno, it turned slightly at the city gate to became the Cardo Maximus, the north-south axis of Roman Florence that led to the forum and the north gate.

The first historical mention of a bridge on the site of the Ponte Vecchio was in 1117, when a flood destroyed the ancient bridge; it was rebuilt in stone and brick. The bridge had already developed its commercial character by 1206, when a communal agency in charge of renting shops and maintaining the bridge was documented. By the early 13th century, increased trade and traffic made it necessary to erect a second Arno bridge; it was at that time that the older bridge earned its name as the "Ponte Vecchio."

The earliest shops, leased out to tanners and leatherworks, burned on numerous occasions, and the flood of 1333 washed away most of the structure; a temporary wooden bridge was built until a new stone bridge was rebuilt in 1345. The new construction, massive and Tuscan in design, had three bold, low arches; the piers were enlarged, and the shops were built of stone to protect against fire. The heavy arches that support the bridge itself are further strengthened by the pointed buttresses that deflect the force of the Arno waters from the piers. This

Ponte Vecchio, view of bridge: Florence, Italy, 1345

Ponte Vecchio

design is probably by Neri di Fioravante, an architect who also worked on Florence Cathedral, Orsanmichele and the Bargello, but Giorgio Vasari attributed it to the painter Taddeo Gaddi.

The strengthening undertaken in 1345 has proved sufficient, for the Ponte Vecchio has endured six centuries of traffic and several major floods. On the morning of 4 November 1966, it was rumored that the Ponte Vecchio had collapsed from the force of flood waters; while the bridge did survive, most of the goldsmiths' shops were gutted.

By the 16th century the bridge's tenants included shoemakers, flax sellers and other merchants, including butchers, who used the convenient river below to dispose of waste. In 1564-65, in honor of the marriage of Francesco de' Medici and Joanna of Austria, Cosimo I de' Medici commissioned Giorgio Vasari to build a corridor that would pass above the shops to join the new Medici quarters in the Pitti Palace with the offices in the Uffizi and Palazzo Vecchio. It was at that time that the graceful three-arched loggia in the center of the bridge was constructed to support the corridor above.

In 1593 Grand Duke Ferninand I de' Medici banished the butchers and other "low trades" from the bridge, doubled the rents, and ordered that the goldsmiths and jewelers of Florence move to Ponte Vecchio. Under Cosimo III the shops became privately owned, and individual owners began to alter their property by adding windows, balconies, shutters and second stories, and by extending their spaces into the public roadway and out over the river, supporting the new construction on the outside of the bridge on wooden beams that jut out from the structure below. With these developments, the bridge began to develop the picturesque quality that has endured until the present day.

The small piazza in the center of the bridge is one of the unusual features of the Ponte Vecchio, and the bridge's combination of shops, street and piazza make it a microcosm of a typical Italian medieval commune. In 1900 a bust of Benvenuto Cellini, the most famous of Florentine goldsmiths, was erected in the piazza by the goldsmiths of Florence; the sculptor, Raffaelo Romanelli, worked in a style reminiscent of 16th-century goldsmith work.

Other decorations on the bridge include the arms of the Guelphs and of the House of Anjou, while two epigraphs record the flood of 1333 and the reconstruction of the bridge 12 years later. Several bas-reliefs of a tower, in reference to the four original guard-post towers at the ends of the bridge, represent the Capitani di Torre, the medieval group responsible for maintaining the Ponte Vecchio.

As the Germans retreated northward in August 1944, they blew up the Florentine bridges to delay the advancing Allies. Hitler told them to spare the Ponte Vecchio, but in order to block access to the bridge they blew up the old houses and towers at each end. The Nazis left Florence never knowing that Vasari's corridor across the Ponte Vecchio had been used throughout the war by the Italian partisan movement, members of which secretly carried messages and weapons through the city.

—DAVID G. WILKINS and REBECCA WILKINS

SANTA CROCE/PAZZI CHAPEL
Florence, Italy

1295: Construction begun; **Architect:** Attributed to Arnolfo di Cambio (died in 1301). **Ca. 1322:** Sacristy constructed. **Ca. 1371:** Sacristy remodeled. **1385:** Construction essentially completed. **1423:** Cloisters damaged in fire, rebuilding followed. **After 1423:** Loggias of first and second cloister built, Cerchi Chapel built; **Architect:** Michelozzo (1396-1472). **1442-1460s:** Pazzi Chapel built; **Architect:** Filippo Brunelleschi (1377-1446). **1443:** Church consecrated. **1448-52:** Third cloister rebuilt; **Architect:** Bernardo Rossellino; **Decorations:** Workshop of Bernardo Rossellino. **1461:** Outer porch of Pazzi Chapel completed. **1512:** Belltower destroyed in wind storm. **1551:** New belltower designed and construction begun; **Architect:** Giuliano da Sangallo (1443-1516). **1566-84:** Interior alterations and remodeling; **Architect:** Giorgio Vasari (1511-74). **Ca. 1448-52:** Spinelli Cloister (third cloister) completely rebuilt. **17th-19th centuries:** Interior alterations. **1842-63:** Present belltower built; **Architect:** Gaetano Baccini. **1857-63:** Facade completed; **Architect:** Niccola Matas. **19th century:** First and second cloisters destroyed. **Late 19th century:** Extensive restorations. **1925-27:** Extensive restorations. **1966:** Restorations after flood damage.

Publications

BAROLSKY, P.: "Toward an Interpretation of the Pazzi Chapel." *Journal of the Society of Architectural Historians* 32 (1973): 228-231.

BATTISTI, E.: *Filippo Brunelleschi*. Milan, 1976.

BECHERUCCI, L.; BERTI, L.; CHIARELLI, R.; et al.: *Primo Rinascimento in Santa Croce*. Florence, 1968.

BRUES, EVA: "Die Fassade von S. Croce in Florenz, ein Werk des Architekten Matas." *Mitteilungen des Kunsthistorischen Instituts in Florenz* 12 (1965): 151-170.

HALL, MARCIA B.: *Renovation and Counter-Reformation; Vasari and Duke Cosimo in Santa Maria Novella and Santa Croce*. Oxford, 1979.

HALL, MARCIA B.: "The *Tramezzo* in Santa Croce, Florence, Reconstructed." *Art Bulletin* 56 (1974): 325-341.

HECHT, K.: "Masserhältnisse und Masse der Capella Pazzi." *Architectura* 6 (1976): 148-174.

LINNENKAMP, R.: "Die Pazzi-Kapelle, S. Croce, Florenz: ein unbekanntes Proportionssystem Brunelleschis." *Deutsche Bauzeitung* 66 (1961): 277-279.

MOISE, F.: *Santa Croce di Firenze*. Florence, 1845.

NYBERG, D.: "Brunelleschi's Use of Proportion in the Pazzi Chapel." *Marsyas* 7 (1954-57): 1-7.

PAATZ, WALTER and ELISABETH: *Die Kirchen von Florenz*. 6 vols. Frankfurt-am-Main, 1952-55.

POPE-HENNESSY, JOHN: "The Evangelist Roundels in the Pazzi Chapel." *Apollo* 106 (1977): 262-269.

Santa Croce: Florence, Italy, 1295

Santa Croce, west facade

SAALMAN, HOWARD: "Filippo Brunelleschi: Capital Studies." *Art Bulletin* 40 (1958): 114-115.

SAALMAN, HOWARD: "Michelozzo Studies." *Burlington Magazine* 108 (1966): 242-250.

SAALMAN, HOWARD: "Tommaso Spinelli, Michelozzo, Manetti, and Rossellino." *Journal of the Society of Architectural Historians* 25 (1966): 151-160.

SALMI, M.: "Sant'Andrea a Camoggiano e la Cappella de' Pazzi." In ANTJE KOSEGARTEN and PETER TIGLER (eds.): *Festschrift für Ulrich Middeldorf.* Berlin, 1968.

THOMPSON, M.: "A Note on the Pazzi Chapel." *Marsyas* 6 (1950-53): 70-71.

In his biography of the Florentine sculptor and architect Arnolfo di Cambio, Giorgio Vasari wrote that "his next work was the foundation, in 1294, of the church of Santa Croce, where the friars minor are." Already in 1228, the Franciscans had built an oratory (the foundations were revealed following the 1966 flood) on the site of the present church. Beginning in 1285, a number of prominent families began to endow the construction of a new church, and on 3 May 1295, the cornerstone for the new basilica was laid. The traditional attribution to Arnolfo, although unsupported by documents, has gone relatively unchallenged.

Arnolfo's design for Santa Croce befitted the professed simplicity of the Franciscan brotherhood and their desire for a suitably spacious preaching hall. The nave is 115 meters long and 38 meters wide. The plan is that of an Egyptian cross divided into three aisles by 14 octagonal piers from which spring pointed arches. The lower side aisles are cross vaulted, but the nave is covered by a simple open-beam ceiling. That Arnolfo chose not to vault the nave at Santa Croce as he did in the Cathedral of Santa Maria del Fiore is explained by Vasari, who noted that "Arnolfo designed the nave and side aisles . . . on such a scale that he was unable to vault the space under the roof owing to the great distances, so with much judgement he made arches from pillar to pillar, and over these he placed the roof." Each of the seven bays of the nave is nearly twice as wide as it is long, while the flanking aisles are longer than they are wide, repeating a Cistercian formula and giving the church a horizontal emphasis. The walls above the arches in the nave are articulated by pilaster strips that help to preserve the vertical emphasis of the piers and visually divide the elevation of the nave into a sequence of separate units. Lancet windows opening into this clerestory area flood the interior with light. Running above the arcades is a walkway supported by brackets that rises over the higher arches of the crossing. The apse end of the basilica acts as a Gothic triumphal arch, with the towering opening of the main chapel flanked by the lower entrances to the smaller chapels at its side. The Gothic character of the church is best appreciated in the polygonal apse chapel, with its high vaults and tall lancet windows. To either side of the chapel are ranged five smaller chapels, including those of the Bardi and Peruzzi families, with their celebrated fresco cycles by Giotto. It is in this transept area that the original decorative richness of Santa Croce is best preserved, a richness that occasioned the Spiritualist Ubertino da Casale in 1310 to denounce what he viewed as the excessive luxury of the building and to fulminate against the *curiositas picturum* of the many frescoes in the chapels. Along the side walls of the aisles, a number of architecturally significant tombs have been installed, including the 15th-century ones

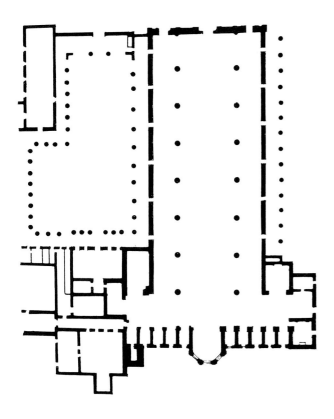

begun in 1551 at the front of the church. Left unfinished, its foundations were removed in 1854 with the construction of the present *campanile* at the end of the south transept; the *campanile* was designed by Gaetano Baccani in 1842 in a compatible neo-Gothic style, and completed in 1863.

Between 1566 and 1584, the character of the interior was extensively altered by Vasari at the instructions of Duke Cosimo. Vasari whitewashed the nave, covering the original frescoed wall, and installed a number of incongruous altar tabernacles framed by classical columns. He also removed the Gothic rood screen and friars' choir from their positions in the nave. Various interior alterations to individual chapels and altars were initiated throughout the 17th and into the 19th centuries. Extensive restorations were carried out at the end of the 19th century, again between 1925 and 1927, and most recently following the damage suffered in the 1966 flood.

Concerning the early history of the adjoining cloister complex, little is known. Such a monastic facility was, no doubt, part of the original Franciscan oratory of 1228. Certainly plans for a new and much enlarged cloister were part of Arnolfo di Cambio's program of the 1290s, and parts of the present structures, including the refectory building, display features consistent with a trecento date and, in fact, have decorations, including frescoes from the 14th-century workshop of Taddeo Gaddi. A devastating fire in 1423 caused grave damage to the monastic buildings and most of what presently exists represents successive stages of rebuilding carried out in the decades that followed.

Within the monastic complex of Santa Croce, at least four major architectural entities must be considered. These are: the first cloister, once divided into smaller and larger cloister yards to form the original first and second cloisters by the Mellini Chapel wing demolished in the 19th century; the second (originally third) or Spinelli Cloister, totally rebuilt in the mid-15th

of Leonardo Bruni by Bernardo Rossellino and of Carlo Marsuppini by Desiderio da Settignano, as well as the Annunciation Tabernacle by Donatello.

Following the death of Arnolfo in 1301, the construction of Santa Croce was placed under the supervision of a series of masters, possibly even including Giotto. Work on the basilica proceeded sufficiently for Mass to be said in 1320. A few years later a spacious sacristy was constructed next to the southeast corner of the south transept (remodeled ca. 1371). Santa Croce was essentially complete by 1385 and finally was consecrated by Pope Eugenius IV in 1443. At mid-century, Santa Croce enjoyed the considerable patronage of Cosimo de' Medici, for whom Michelozzo constructed the Medici Chapel and the handsome corridor connecting it to the south transept arm as well as the L-shaped line of rooms adjoining the Sacristy.

The exterior walls of the nave, never completed with the intended cladding of marble, are distinguished by being divided into a row of gables corresponding to the bays of the interior. Similar lines of gables surround the arms of the transept. Along the sides of the church run elevated arcaded walkways. The round arches of these loggias are supported by octagonal columns. The southern loggia has been attributed to Arnolfo, while that to the north may date to the 15th century but was built in keeping with the earlier design. Plans for the facade of Santa Croce may have been prepared in 1450 and again later in the century, perhaps by Simone del Pollaiuolo (Il Cronaca), but nothing came of them, and the front of the building remained in an unfinished state until the middle of the 19th century. At that time the present three-pointed neo-Gothic facade, with its geometric framing of white Carrara and green Prato marble was carried out (1857-63) following the designs of Niccola Matas. The original bell tower was tumbled in a storm in 1512, and another one designed by Francesco di Giuliano da Sangallo was

Pazzi Chapel, 1442-1460s

Pazzi Chapel

The most famous architectural monument of the Santa Croce cloisters is the Pazzi Chapel. Whether or not this monastic chapter house replaced an earlier and similarly devoted building on its site is debated. The chapel/chapter house was commissioned by Andrea Pazzi in 1429 but not begun until 1442, with the work dragging on through the 1460s. Although Antonio Manetti's biography of Brunelleschi omits mention of this project, the architect's name is connected with the Pazzi Chapel in the *Libro di Antonio Billi* and the *Codice Magliabechiano* and other early records, and his authorship of the original designs has never been questioned. In the interior, Brunelleschi repeated the triumphal arch articulation he had devised at his earlier Sacristy at San Lorenzo, but the result is more harmonious and interrelated. Throughout the cool grandeur of this prime example of the Early Renaissance, Brunelleschi's apparent use of the Euclidian Double Golden Section is obvious, both in plan and elevation. The facade/porch remains unfinished and, despite its obvious correspondence to the totality of the chapel, many authorities prefer to deny Brunelleschi's participation in the design (Michelozzo and B. Rossellino have been suggested as the architects). The trabeated portico with the central archway is a curious feature and, while a connection to such medieval monuments as the cathedrals at Civita Castellana and Pistoia has been suggested, a more likely source can be found in the third-century Roman Tomb of the Calventii on the Via Appia Antica outside of Rome. This is just the sort of antique ruin that Brunelleschi would have studied during his stay in Rome during the early 1430s. If completed as intended, the Pazzi Chapel portico would have included a pediment (this design was repeated in 1470 for the Church of Sant'Andrea at Camoggiano), providing the Pazzi Chapel with an imposing temple front facade.

—CHARLES R. MACK

century; the Pazzi Chapel designed by Filippo Brunelleschi; and the small courtyard situated between the rear of the Pazzi Chapel and the Novitiate Corridor connecting the church with the Medici Chapel.

As part of the postfire reconstruction of Santa Croce's monastic precinct, funded in large part by the Medici, Michelozzo constructed the loggia of the original second cloister, the Cerchi chapel in the rebuilt library wing (situated across the cloister yard from the church) and, perhaps, the loggias in the original first cloister (the construction costs of which were borne by the Spinelli).

The original third cloister, rebuilt about 1448-52 under the patronage of Tommaso Spinelli, has been described by Walter Paatz as the "most delicate and the boldest, the richest and the most cheerful of all cloister yards of the Renaissance." There, two stories of loggias, seven by nine arcades long, surround the ample yard. The treatment of the upper story was conceived with daring novelty. There, convention was abandoned in favor of columns taller than those of the lower arcade, imparting a new feeling of spaciousness to the elevation. Throughout, the architectural details were handled with inventiveness and sculptural precision. The unique design of the capitals and corbels, with their fluted bells and turned-down acanthus-leaf volutes, the finely delineated archivolts, the strigil motif in the entablature, the decorative tondi, the classically graceful doorways, and the subtle use of *sgraffito* decorations all point to the workshop of Bernardo Rossellino. It is to this sculptor and architect that the project should be attributed rather than to Brunelleschi, as has been traditional. Comparisons between the entry portal to the Spinelli Cloister and Rossellino's documented doorway in the Palazzo Pubblico of Siena and between a corbel in the entrance passage of the Palazzo Rucellai and those used at Santa Croce should serve to confirm the role of this architect.

SAN LORENZO—OLD SACRISTY
Florence, Italy

1421-60. Architects: Matteo Dolfini and Filippo Brunelleschi (1377-1446). West facade of main church completed by Antonio Manetti.

Publications

ARGAN, GIULIO C.: *Brunelleschi.* Milan, 1955; 1978.

BATTISTI, EUGENIO: *Filippo Brunelleschi.* Milan, 1976.

BOZZONI, CORRADO and CARBONARA, GIOVANNI: *Filippo Brunelleschi: Saggio di Bibliografia.* 2 vols. Rome, 1977-78.

BRUCKER, GENE: *The Civic World of Early Renaissance Florence.* Princeton, New Jersey, 1977.

BURNS, HOWARD: "San Lorenzo in Florence Before the Building of the New Sacristy: An Early Plan." *Mitteilungen des kunsthistorischen Instituts in Florenz* 23 (1979): 145-154.

CARLI, E.: *Brunelleschi.* Florence, 1950.

FABRICZY, CORNELIUS VON: *Filippo Brunelleschi.* Stuttgart, 1892.

FANELLI, GIOVANNI: *Brunelleschi.* Florence, 1977.

Filippo Brunelleschi: L'uomo e l'artista. Mostra documentaria. Florence, 1977.

GINORI-CONTI, PIERO: *La Basilica di S. Lorenzo di Firenze, e la famiglia Ginori.* Florence, 1940.

GIOVANNI, FANELLO: *Brunelleschi.* 1980.

San Lorenzo, nave towards east: Florence, Italy, 1421-60

HERZNER, VOLKER: "Zur Baugeschichte von San Lorenzo in Florenz." *Zeitschrift für Kunstgeschichte* 37, 2 (1974): 89-115.

HYMAN, ISABELLE: *Fifteenth Century Florentine Studies: The Palazzo Medici and a Ledger for the Church of San Lorenzo.* New York, 1977.

KENT, DALE: *The Rise of the Medici: Faction in Florence, 1426-1434.* Oxford, 1978.

PAATZ, WALTER and ELISABETH: *Die Kirchen von Florenz.* 6 vols. Frankfurt-am-Main, 1952-55.

SAALMAN, HOWARD: "San Lorenzo: The 1434 Chapel Project." *Burlington Magazine* 120 (1978): 361-364.

Any discussion of San Lorenzo in the context of Filippo Brunelleschi's oeuvre must be prefaced by a note of caution, in that the extent of Brunelleschi's involvement in the design of the main body of the church is by no means certain. A start had already been made on the project around 1421 by the then-prior of San Lorenzo, Matteo Dolfini. Brunelleschi had been working on the Old Sacristy for the Medici family, but it was not until the death of Dolfini and the increasing involvement of the Medicis that the earlier work on the main body of the church was abandoned in favor of an alternative design by Brunelleschi. Given the common practice of re-using existing foundations, it is not unlikely that the basic floor plan might owe as much to

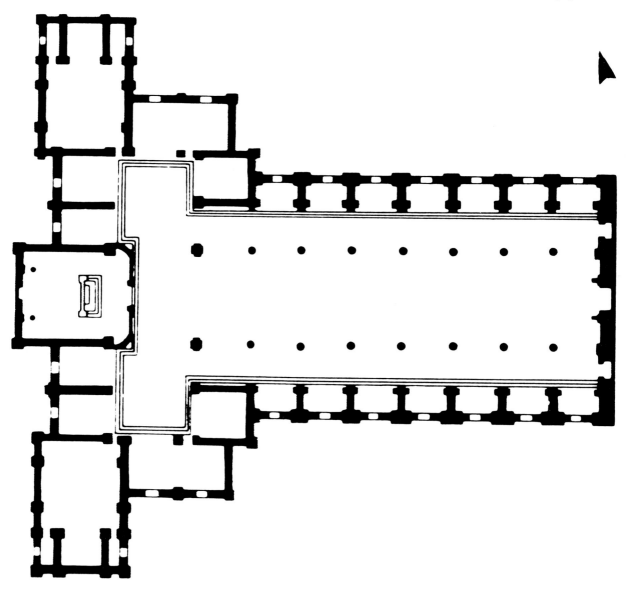

Dolfini as to Brunelleschi. Moreover, although the Old Sacristy was complete by the time of Brunelleschi's death, little of the main body of the church had been built. According to his biographer, Antonio Manetti, much of the subsequent work, especially the cupola, was completed far from Brunelleschi's original intentions, so that "judging it as Filippo's would be to judge it falsely, since his glory is not there."

If Brunelleschi is to be perceived as an architect who sought to develop and refine a specifically Tuscan style of architecture, rather than challenge and counter the accepted tradition, the basilica of San Lorenzo is not uncharacteristic of his work. Although it is known that Brunelleschi was reluctant from the outset to build a church with nave and aisles, San Lorenzo can be read as an attempt to rationalize the traditional basilican form. Along with Santo Spirito, in which Brunelleschi also had a hand, San Lorenzo follows the typical layout of earlier Florentine churches such as Santa Croce. The nave is flanked by two aisles running into a transept lined with chapels. Further chapels were subsequently built off the aisles, and a choir was added, of similar dimensions to the crossing. The chapels, often

inconsistent and haphazard in earlier basilicas, are more uniform and coordinated in San Lorenzo. Proportions throughout have been carefully controlled, with simple mathematical relationships of 1:2 and 1:4. Details are strictly classical, with round rather than octagonal columns, and "correct" Corinthian capitals.

The Old Sacristy lies to the northeast of the transept, opposite the later New Sacristy of Michelangelo. It is the one part of the complex to have been completed within Brunelleschi's lifetime and substantially in accordance with his wishes, although it is known that he was unhappy with the reliefs and doors added by Donatello. The centralized plan of the Old Sacristy contrasts with the axial plan of the basilica, and may offer some clue as to how Brunelleschi might have designed the main body of the church, had he not been constrained into adopting a more traditional plan with nave and aisles. The Old Sacristy is likely to have been built in three phases: the initial "cube," followed by the addition of three small chambers to the west, and finally the encasing of the completed structure within the all-embracing walls of the main church. The structure is crowned with a

San Lorenzo, Old Sacristy: 1421-60

dome of umbrella vaulting. The expressed structural ribs of the vaulting contrast with the classical detailing beneath, which is more ornamental, serving to divide and unify the space according to a complex system of visual relationships. Although the Old Sacristy was probably Brunelleschi's first ecclesiastical building, it displays a number of traits that were to prove hallmarks of his work: the careful control of proportions, a rich interplay of geometrical forms, strict use of classical details, and a sense of overall coordination. These all combine to give the Old Sacristy an air of quiet composure.

San Lorenzo is significant in that it stood at a crucial turning point in humankind's perception of the world. Brunelleschi's own investigations into perspective had signaled a new view of the world, where humankind as spectator assumed the dominant role, and the world was reduced to a perspectival image. The ordered floor plan of San Lorenzo reflects the order of the perspective grid, and the interior of the main body of the church may be read as a perspective view. The detached, rational space that resulted contrasts with the more emotional experience of a Gothic interior.

San Lorenzo also marked a shift in attitudes toward building patronage. The completion of San Lorenzo was secured only by the financial intervention of the Medici family. Sumptuary laws and codes of conduct had previously limited displays of private wealth to the sponsoring of family chapels. The private patronage of an entire church reflects a relaxation of these codes and the growing status of the individual in society. The completion of San Lorenzo was bound up with the construction of the Medici Palace by Michelozzo. Funding for both buildings came from the same account, and the two projects shared the same workmen. It is therefore not unlikely that Michelozzo

might have taken over responsibility for San Lorenzo on the death of Brunelleschi.

—NEIL LEACH

SAN LORENZO—NEW SACRISTY (MEDICI CHAPEL)
Florence, Italy

1517ff. Architect: Michelangelo (1475-1564).

Publications

BRUCKER, GENE: *The Civic World of Early Renaissance Florence*. Princeton, New Jersey, 1977.
ELAM, CAROLINE: "The Site and Early Building History of Michelangelo's New Sacristy." *Mitteilungen des kunsthistorischen Instituts in Florenz* 23 (1979): 155-186.
HERZNER, VOLKER: "Zur Baugeschichte von San Lorenzo in Florenz." *Zeitschrift für Kunstgeschichte* 37, 2 (1974): 89-115.
HYMAN, ISABELLE: *Fifteenth Century Florentine Studies: The Palazzo Medici and a Ledger for the Church of San Lorenzo*. New York, 1977.
KENT, DALE: *The Rise of the Medici: Faction in Florence, 1426-1434*. Oxford, 1978.
MILLON, H. A. and SMYTH, C. H.: *Michelangelo, Architect: The Facade of San Lorenzo and the Drum and Dome of St. Peter's*. Milan, 1988.
VASARI, G.: *Lives of the Artists*. London, 1965.

*

The New Sacristy lies off the transept of San Lorenzo, opposite the earlier Old Sacristy of Brunelleschi. It was commissioned to house the Medici family tombs. According to G. Vasari, Michelangelo sought to model the New Sacristy on the Old Sacristy, but with different decorative features. There are clear similarities between the two structures, most notably in the floor plan, choice of materials and adoption of the fluted Corinthian pilaster order. A number of changes were made, however. The vault was no longer ribbed, but coffered, in the manner of the Pantheon. An attic story was added for extra height, an effect exaggerated by blank windows set in false perspective between the pendentives. But the most striking development took place where Michelangelo set his own free invention against the predominantly Brunelleschian backdrop. A secondary system of pilasters was introduced to frame the niches, tabernacles and doorways around the tombs. The handling of this decoration took its cue from the sculptures. Planes project and recede, forms swell and contract in an organic composition full of movement. By comparison with his nearby Laurentian Library, the sculptural elements are not fully integrated in their architectural setting, and do not form a coherent spatial experience. The tombs and their associated ornaments appear as decorative additions to a larger architectural whole, highlighted by the use of contrasting materials. The tombs and architectural details of the lower section are of finely worked marble, while the rest is finished in the less refined *pietra serena* and in plain stucco.

In the New Sacristy Michelangelo adapted the established language of architecture with considerable license. As Vasari noted, he employed "a style more varied and more original

San Lorenzo, New Sacristy: 1517ff

SAN LORENZO—LAURENTIAN LIBRARY
Florence, Italy

1524-27: Initial construction. **Architect:** Michelangelo (1475-1564). **1533-71:** Construction resumes. **1549-50:** Reading room floor and ceiling completed. **1558-59:** Vestibule stairway completed. **From 1559:** Work continued on library by Giorgio Vasari (1511-74) and Bartolomeo Ammannati (1511-92).

Publications

BRUCKER, GENE: *The Civic World of Early Renaissance Florence*. Princeton, New Jersey, 1977.
WITTKOWER, RUDOLF: "Michelangelo's Biblioteca Laurenzia." In *Idea and Image*. London, 1978.

*

In the design of the Laurentian Library, Michelangelo's *fantasia,* or creative imagination, was uniquely joined with the practical requirements of the commission. The patron, Pope Clement VII (Giulio de' Medici) constantly involved himself in plans for the project, plans which were still evolving even after construction had begun. The Laurentian Library, then, is a synthesis of the ideas of patron and artist, of judicious pragmatism and profound aesthetic inspiration.

The Medici collection of manuscripts, which had been increased by Michelangelo's earlier, benevolent patron, Lorenzo the Magnificent, initially was housed in the Palazzo Medici. In 1524 Michelangelo, who was working in Florence on the Medici Chapel at San Lorenzo (among other commissions), was asked to send preliminary drawings for a new library to Clement VII. It was the pope's desire to place the manuscripts in a library with greater public access. After the site was determined, itself a matter of initial debate between patron and artist, construction of the library, atop the monastic quarters of San Lorenzo, proceeded until the Sack of Rome in 1527. Work resumed in 1533, but a year later Clement VII died and Michelangelo moved permanently to Rome. Amid an abundance of other commissions, including the new St. Peter's and the Campidoglio, Michelangelo continued his designs for the library. The floor and ceiling of the reading room probably were completed by 1549-50; the wondrous stairway of the vestibule was executed by Bartolomeo Ammannati in 1558-59 from a model and instructions sent from Rome.

The Laurentian Library, named to commemorate Lorenzo the Magnificent, was designed with an awareness of Michelozzo's library at San Marco in Florence. Begun 86 years before the Laurentian Library, the San Marco library helped to establish the Renaissance scheme of monastic "public" libraries. After an initial period of exploring diverse approaches to the requirements of the commission, Michelangelo evolved a plan of three distinct yet interrelated units. A vestibule, containing a stairway, would enter on to an elongated reading room. Benches in the reading room, adroitly designed by Michelangelo, would accommodate both the storage and study of the manuscripts. Finally, at the south end of the complex, a rare-book room would complete the library.

It is in the vestibule of the Laurentian Library that Michelangelo's *fantasia* was given unbridled rein. Here, the vocabulary of classical architecture has been imaginatively yet judiciously reconstructed according to a new, and most subjective, invention and aesthetic. The emphatic vertical proportions of the vestibule

than any other master, ancient or modern, has ever been able to achieve." His adaptations were the result not so much of whimsy as of a sculptor's concern for the play of light on form. They must have created quite a stir within a society that lay such store by the accepted truths inherited from antiquity. According to Vasari, Michelangelo proved a great inspiration to others and prompted "the creation of new kinds of fantastic ornamentation." All artists were thereby "under a great and permanent obligation to Michelangelo, seeing that he broke the bonds and chains that had previously confined them to the creation of traditional forms."

The freedom with which Michelangelo handled architectural forms is evidence of a broader underlying shift. Vasari remarked that in designing the New Sacristy, Michelangelo "departed a great deal from the kind of architecture regulated by proportion, order and rule." Michelangelo rejected the static system of proportions derived from Vitruvius, to which his contemporaries had so steadfastly adhered, and moved towards a more dynamic system of formal relationships. Michelangelo represents a move away from the objective approach of the early Renaissance toward a more subjective approach, in which the building becomes an organism and the individual parts are set in a drama of forces and tensions. Such an architecture takes its inspiration not from the calculations of the intellect, but from the feelings and emotions of the body. Michelangelo's building style marks an important step in the development of Renaissance architecture. The New Sacristy was the artist's first significant architectural design and represents an interim stage in his development as an architect. Yet it is the work of a consummate sculptor who had ventured into the field of architecture, though he had not yet fully come to terms with the new discipline.

—NEIL LEACH

San Lorenzo, Laurentian Library: From 1524

are the result of one of the conflicts between architect and patron; Michelangelo's design for skylights was rejected by Clement VII, and so the walls were raised to allow for more conventional windows. Throughout the design, apparent contradictions of form and function abound. Paired columns, recessed behind the plane of the wall, are set above the floor level and "visually" mounted on brackets. The traditional weight-bearing role of columns is denied by the design, yet actually the columns are supporting members of the structure.

Individually, the tabernacles continue this contradiction of Vitruvian standards; the framing pilasters, only partially fluted, taper downward, while their capitals are dramatically reduced in size. Within this evocative environment, center stage is held by an independent and monumental stairway, prophetic of Baroque creations. The stairway, which Michelangelo recalled "as it were in a dream" (letter to Giorgio Vasari, 1555), asserts its own conflict of implied motion. With the vestibule of the Laurentian Library, Michelangelo's approach to architectural design, liberated by invention and imagination, possesses a plasticity and breadth akin to sculpture, if not life, itself.

As one ascends the stairway and enters the door to the reading room, the first impression is of an ordered, yet quickened, pulse of interior space. Drawing from medieval architecture, Michelangelo re-created a bay-like system of articulation. To allow an abundance of light, he reduced the walls to screens with two tiers of windows. The pilasters, which are in accord with the exterior buttresses, are not decorative but structural. They create the rhythmic sequence of the design. This bay-like articulation which determines the wall elevation is reinforced by the patterns of the ceiling and floor. Even the design and placement of Michelangelo's reading benches contribute to this measured articulation of interior space. Unlike the vestibule, where Michelangelo challenged expectations of decoration and structure, here the skeletal supporting system is revealed with clarity and purpose.

Michelangelo's design for the rare-book room, to be built at the south end of the library opposite the vestibule, was not realized. Its approximate triangular plan would have contained a series of concentrically designed and geometrically formulated reading benches. The compact, angular massing of the benches would have contrasted with a vigorous and sculptural undulation of the walls. The rare-book room was to be a resolution of the contrasting designs of the vestibule and reading room.

Giorgio Vasari, in his 1568 edition of *Lives of the Most Eminent Painters, Sculptors, and Architects,* noted how Michelangelo's *fantasia* opened a new artistic license to later architects. In discussing the library at San Lorenzo, Vasari wrote, ''Nor was there ever seen a more resolute grace, both in the whole and in the parts ... nor any staircase more commodious; in which last he made such bizarre breaks in the outlines of the steps, and departed so much from the common use of others, that everyone was amazed.'' Like 16th-century observers, we continue to be ''amazed'' by Michelangelo's prodigious experience of form, function and creative imagination which is the Laurentian Library.

—BERNARD SCHULTZ

SANTA MARIA NOVELLA
Florence, Italy

1246-1350. Architects: Fra Sisto and Fra Ristoro. **1456-70:** Entrance facade. **Architect:** Leon Battista Alberti (1404-72).

Publications

BRAUNFELS, WOLFGANG: *Santa Maria Novella, Florenz, Kirche und Kloster des heiligen Domenicus.* Florence, 1938.
DIACCINI, R.: *La basilica di Santa Maria Novella.* Florence, 1920.

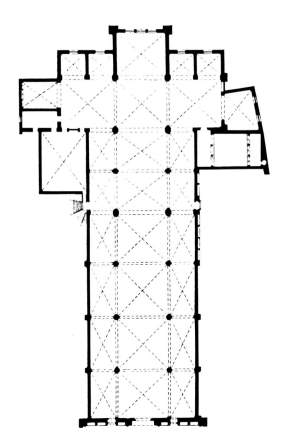

HALL, MARCIA B.: *Renovation and Counter-Reformation; Vasari and Duke Cosimo in Santa Maria Novella and Santa Croce.* Oxford, 1979.
ORLANDI, S.: *Necrologia di Santa Maria Novella.* Florence, 1955.
PAATZ, WALTER and ELISABETH: *Die Kirchen von Florenz.* 6 vols. Frankfurt-am-Main, 1952-55.

*

Santa Maria Novella is best known by contemporary travelers as the name of the train station in the Italian city of Florence. The Gothic structure adjacent to the station that is its namesake is the principal Dominican church in the city. An older church and the lands around it were given to the Dominican order in 1221. The Dominican architects Fra Ristoro da Campi and Fra Sisto began the present church in 1246. The style of this church, whether deliberately intended by the architects or not, was a combination of north and south-central Cistercian traditions. Rather than being a French Cistercian church, Santa Maria Novella clearly established a truly Italian mendicant style.

Santa Maria Novella was the ''airiest'' Gothic church in Italy at the time. This aesthetic in architecture spread, and in fact swept through northern Italy. The origins have been traced to Tuscany, and specifically to Santa Maria Novella.

Although Santa Maria Novella maintains the traditional Christian basilica plan with a central nave flanked by side aisles, it is the earliest example of a vaulted, aisled basilica designed for mendicant needs. These needs, conveyed architecturally, include simplicity and directness. The straight-ended choir, begun in 1279, is flanked by four chapels.

Square or near-square bays are used for the crossing and transepts. There are six contiguous square bays above the nave, while the bays above the side aisles are rectangular in shape. The wide nave, with cool gray-green Tuscan *pietra serena* arches, appears to have a greater height due to its slender supports and narrow side aisles. The height of the side aisles is more than two-thirds that of the nave. This lightness of the interior and elevation of the eye are atypical of the traditional heavy, massive Italian Gothic style.

The Rucellai family commissioned Leon Battista Alberti to design a new facade for the church. The family name is inscribed in large Roman capital letters across the facade, and the family seal, the sail of fortune, is also visible. The six tombs and three doorways in the lower section and large, round windows in the upper portion were incorporated into Alberti's new design. Alberti found his sources for the design from *De architectura* by Vitruvius, his colleague and friend Filippo Brunelleschi, and the Romanesque church of San Miniato al Monte across the Arno River. Alberti's own treatise on architecture, *De re aedificatoria,* states that it is necessary to have harmonic relationships and mathematically proportioned buildings. According to Alberti's treatise, without these components a building cannot be beautiful. At Santa Maria Novella, the height of the facade is equal to its width, so the entire facade can be inscribed in a square. The upper portion can be continued in a square one-fourth that of the entire facade. The lower section of the facade forms a rectangle. The length of the rectangle is twice its height. All of these areas can be related in terms of mathematical proportions. According to Alberti, these numerical ratios indicate harmonic relationships, which are the foundation of beauty. The geometric order evident in Alberti's facade of Santa Maria Novella is indicative of the 15th-century Florentine Renaissance mindset. Alberti was instrumental in the application of mathematics to architecture, as seen on the exterior of this church.

The mural of *The Trinity* at Santa Maria Novella, painted by

Santa Maria Novella: Florence, Italy, 1246-1350

Masaccio in about 1425, exhibits the perspective and geometric proportions advocated in the works and writings of Alberti and Brunelleschi. In 1425 the Signoria, the governing body of Florence, adopted the favorite feast of the Dominicans, Corpus Domini, as an official communal feast. As tribute to this Dominican and public celebration, the subject of the fresco, *The Trinity,* was selected as a new beginning for the relationship of the two groups. The Dominican calendar year begins with the feast of the Trinity.

The Masaccio mural is one of the few works that was not whitewashed under the direction of Giorgio Vasari in the 16th century. The monks' choir and rood screen were demolished and replaced with gabled tabernacles between 1565 and 1571.

The *Chiostro Verde,* or Green Cloister, built between 1330 and 1350 by Fra Giovanni Bracchetti da Campi and Fra Jacopo Talenti, also remains. The Spanish Chapel, or chapter room, was funded by Buonamico di Lapo Guidalotti. Guidalotti was allowed to use it as a family burial chapel.

In addition to the *Chiostro Verde,* there are two other adjacent cloisters, the *Chiostro Grande,* which was built in 1419-20 to house the papal apartments of Pope Martin V, and the *Chiostro dei Morti* (Cloister of the Dead). The refectory was built by Fra Jacopo Talenti, one of the original church architects, in 1353. The murals are by the 16th-century artist Alessandro Allori.

Wealthy Florentine families commissioned contemporary artists to decorate their family chapels from the 14th through 16th

Santa Maria Novella

centuries. The Rucellai, Medici, Bardi, Strozzi, Ricci, Tornabuoni and Cavalcanti families all participated in this patronage. Works by Nino Pisano, Filippino Lippi, Orcagna, Domenico Ghirlandaio, Giuliano da Sangallo, and other prominent Italian artists adorn this elegant church.

—HEIDI J. HORNIK

SAN MINIATO AL MONTE
Florence, Italy

Ca. 1014: Initial restorations of earlier church begun, apse survives. **1018:** Church donated to the Benedictines. **1070:** Major rebuilding campaign begun. **Before 1093:** First story of facade completed. **1207:** Floor mosaics completed. **Ca. 1228-50:** Second story of facade completed. **Early 13th century:** Pediment completed. **1434-59:** Chapel of the Cardinal of Portugal built.

Publications

HARTT, FREDERICK; CORTI, GINO; and KENNEDY, CLARENCE: *The Chapel of the Cardinal of Portugal 1434-1459 at San Miniato at Florence*. Philadelphia, 1964.
PAATZ, WALTER and ELISABETH: *Die Kirchen von Florenz*. 6 vols. Frankfurt-am-Main, 1952-55.

*

San Miniato al Monte has long been considered by visitors to Florence to be a gem perched above the city, visible from the galleries of the Uffizi, and from which the city presents itself in all its glory. Its jewel-like quality is produced by the precious materials of the facade, multicolored stones in geometrical patterns, a decoration more dynamic and fantastic than the better-known Gothic and Renaissance buildings of the city. San Miniato shares this decoration with numerous buildings in Florence,

San Miniato al Monti: Florence, Italy, 11th century

above all the Baptistery, Campanile and Duomo (the facade of which is a 19th-century work in the manner of the earlier period).

For scholars, San Miniato is a magnificent example of the Tuscan Romanesque style, a style whose meaning remains to be fully explored. The Tuscan Romanesque has generally been viewed as a fairly uncomplicated style, perhaps due to the apparent simplicity of buildings such as San Miniato. In plan and ornamentation San Miniato is easily described. The ground plan roughly follows the scheme of an Early Christian basilica, with a rectangular interior divided into nave and single aisles, and a semicircular apse at the east end equal to the width of the nave. The length is divided into three nearly equal segments by two cruciform piers in each of the nave arcades; each of these subdivisions is further divided into a tripartite arcade. The easternmost third of the church is raised 11 feet above the nave, and is accessed by a flight of steps at the end of each aisle. Below this raised choir is a crypt, equal in area to that end of the church.

Many of the columns and capitals throughout the interior are ancient, and were probably mined from local buildings. Some trecento and quattrocento frescoes have survived on the north and south walls, but much of this early decoration has been lost and the bare masonry, as on the exterior, is visible. Several quattrocento works, namely the Chapel of the Crucifix (Michelozzo, 1448, center of nave, directly before one descends into the crypt) and the Chapel of the Cardinal of Portugal (Antonio Manetti, Antonio Rossellino, Luca della Robia, Antonio and Pierro del Pollaiuolo, and Alleso Baldovinetti, begun 1460, north aisle), indicate that San Miniato remained prominent within the Florentine community well into the Renaissance.

The nave clerestory, apse and exterior facade are covered with geometrical marble incrustation, both real and painted, comprised primarily of white, green and black patterns. The choir apse and exterior facade share the common Tuscan Romanesque motif of blind arcading, often executed in multicolored stones (compare with the roughly contemporary Baptistery of Florence, the Collegiata of Empoli, the Badia of Fiesole and the Cathedral Complex of Pisa).

The origins of the church are shrouded in legend. According to tradition, a basilica was founded on this site in the fourth century, and was dedicated to the Florentine deacon Minias, believed to have been martyred in about 250 during the persecutions of the emperor Decius, and subsequently buried on the site. Nothing remains or is known of this Early Christian structure. The earliest surviving records date from the late eighth century, and suggest that by that time both a church and a monastery were located on this hill. By the early 11th century this building, whatever it may have been, was seen by Bishop Hildebrand of Florence to be in need of restoration; the current apse is usually dated to this initial phase of reconstruction begun in 1014.

The nature and extent of the early-11th century building campaign are uncertain, but structural analysis suggests that it was primarily a phase of restoration rather than the beginning of a new building. With Hildebrand's donation of the abbey to the Benedictines in 1018, a period of building activity began and was supported by numerous donations made throughout the 11th and 12th centuries. Indeed, Walter Horn's examination (1943) of the masonry of San Miniato supports what these documents refer to; that is, that repeated efforts were made to

San Miniato al Monti

complete the church, resulting in several campaigns, with the major building carried out after about 1070.

The facade has been examined by several scholars, and its building history is much debated. It is believed that the blind arcading of the lower story was probably the model for the design of the facade in Empoli, known to have been completed by 1093. Through comparisons with similar elements on the Baptistery of Florence (attic, ca. 1090-1128, and lantern, 1150) and securely dated decorative elements in San Miniato (floor mosaic with inscription, 1207), the general consensus is that the second story may be dated between 1128 and 1150, and the pediment to the early 13th century. The pediment is crowned

by an eagle, emblem of the *Arte di Calimala*, the guild responsible for the building from 1288.

The incrustation of exterior and interior is often described as classicizing, a description that is both illuminating and confusing. Nevertheless, the adaptation of a classical vocabulary lies at the heart of the Tuscan Romanesque. This style originated in the late 10th and early 11th centuries during a period of papal and imperial contests of wills. It is entirely likely that the classicizing yet particularly Tuscan elements of this Romanesque style embody something of this debate.

This time period coincides with the reign of Countess Matilda of Canossa (1046-1115), an enlightened pro-papal ruler and great

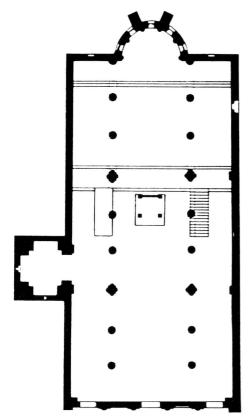

San Miniato al Monti

patron of the arts. The cities under her rule were experiencing expansion and independence, and were unwilling to return to their former status as imperial fiefs. At her death, Matilda left her Tuscan realm under papal protection, perhaps knowing that the military weakness of the papacy at that time assured the cities a continuation of self-rule. If looking to Rome meant freedom from imperial regulations, then stating their Roman alliance on the faces of their cities demonstrated the commitment and determination of the Tuscans.

The contribution of Italy to the architecture of medieval Europe is often overshadowed by scholars' concentration on developments elsewhere on the Continent. This is a curious fact, given the historic, symbolic and material richness of Italy's architecture. Indeed, after the decline of the Roman Empire it was in Italy that ecclesiastical settlements and urban redevelopment first began to flourish, and many of the architectural monuments associated with these social revolutions survive. These circumstances would seem to beg comparisons between ancient and medieval architecture, as well as between medieval and the overtly classicizing monuments of the Renaissance.

Florence is particularly rich for study because of its Roman foundations, wealth of local building materials, and the city's early importance as an ecclesiastical and commercial center of Tuscany. An examination of buildings from that period demonstrates the variety of types constructed to fulfill the growing needs of the expanding Florentine community: communal palaces, commercial offices and church architecture *all' antica*. Suggested, too, is that this architecture has remained largely unstudied because it is as a part of the social fabric, rather than through a purely formal or structural analysis, that it is best understood. The Church of San Miniato al Monte illustrates

both the current state of scholarship and the rich field yet to be mined.

—MARJORIE OCH

UFFIZI
Florence, Italy

1545-59: Palazzo construction ordered, plans designed; **Architect:** Giorgio Vasari (1511-74). **1560:** Construction begun; **1574:** Construction nearly complete; upper loggia glazed and upper-floor rooms converted into gallery; **Architect:** Bernardo Buontalenti (1536-1608).

Publications

BAROCCHI, P.: "Il Vasari." in *Atti dell'Accademia Pontaniana* VI (1958).
BOASE, TSR: *Giorgio Vasari: The Man and The Book*. 1979.
BOTTO, IDA MARIA: *Mostra di disegni di Bernardo Buontalenti (1531-1608)*. Florence, 1968.
FARA, AEMILIO: *Buontalenti: architettura e teatro*. Florence, 1979.
KALLEB, W.: *Vasari-Studien*. 1908.
VASARI, GIORGIO: *Le opere di Giorgio Vasari, con nuove annotazioni e commenti*. 9 vols. Edited by G. Milanesi. Reprint. Florence, 1973. Originally published as *Le vite de più eccelenti architetti*. 1550. Numerous translations and selections from Vasari's *Lives* exist. A standard translation by G. du C. de Vere was published in ten volumes by the Medici Society, London, 1912-1915.
VASARI, GIORGIO: *Vasari on Technique*. 1960.
VENTURI, ADOLFO: "Bernardo Buontalenti." Vol. II, Part 2, pp. 455-546 in *Storia dell'arte italiana*. Milan, 1939.

The history of the Palazzo degli Uffizi began on 3 July 1559, when the grand duke, Cosimo I de'Medici, entrusted to Giorgio Vasari the realization of a major project—to assemble, "for the greater ease of the public," all the offices containing civic administration in one building. This new palace was intended to express the political and administrative unity that the Medici had imposed on diverse governing bodies within their capital city of Florence.

The demolition and reorganization necessary to construct a Via dei Magistrati (the present Piazza degli Uffizi) from the Piazza della Signoria (then Ducale) to the Arno River had been ordered by Cosimo I and begun in 1545. It was, therefore, important that these new governmental offices be housed in a palace of worthy architectural design and style. Vasari received approval from the grand duke for a design for a huge palace composed of two nearly identical wings flanking each side of the newly created street-square and joined at the Arno by an imposing multilevel Serlian loggia. The new structure was designed to incorporate several older structures of some historic value behind a continuous facade. Vasari provided for a unified entity that would be harmonious, balanced and monumental. In doing so he originated a new concept in town planning in which he rejected the practice of emphasizing a single, formal, framed architectural work—such as a freestanding church—and re-

Uffizi: Florence, Italy, 1560-74

placed it with a vision of a total composition, in which particular elements are inserted into an all-encompassing design.

The construction of the Uffizi began 30 June 1560 and proceeded rapidly. It was at a satisfactory stage of completion for some of the festivities marking the marriage of Prince Francesco I to Archduchess Joanna of Austria, which was to be celebrated in its upper salons. At the same time, Vasari also planned and constructed the long corridor that connects the Uffizi to the Palazzo Pitti, carrying it over the superstructure of the Ponte Vecchio; this major extension of the palace was, according to Vasari, completed on schedule in five months. The work on the Uffizi was almost entirely completed at the time of Vasari's death in 1574, the year in which Bernardo Buontalenti glazed the upper loggia and rearranged the rooms on the upper floor to create a gallery for the paintings and sculpture of the ever-growing Medici collection.

The Uffizi represents the major architectural commission in Florence between the completion of the Laurentian Library to the designs of Michelangelo and the enlargement of the Palazzo Pitti to the plans and designs of Bartolomeo Ammannati. As such, it is an architectural composition of major importance of the second generation of *maniera* architects in Florence. It is also a monument of major importance within the development of Mannerist architecture in Italy. It serves as a bridge between the classical works of Donato Bramante and the Baroque compositions of Giovanni Lorenzo Bernini. The Uffizi clearly expresses the confluence of both the severe classicizing elements in Tuscan architecture and the more classical elements of Mannerist architecture. Also, it is a major urban composition linking the town planning of the Renaissance to the grandiose urban compositions of the Baroque.

The Uffizi is a work of architecture commissioned to house the courts and offices of the Thirteen Magistrates. It expresses not only its quotidian functions but also the ideological concepts underlying the state created by Cosimo I de'Medici. Therefore, the Uffizi is a princely forum as well as a public palace, a sacral forecourt as well as a wide public passage, a ceremonial atrium possessed of a presentation festigium as well as a series of utilitarian legal courts. Vasari's design is a stunning solution to the problems presented by the practical need of his client's commission and his ability as a courtier to invest that design with the freight of Cosimo I political's ambitions, social pretensions and dynastic desires. Indeed, the Uffizi is far more than an office building; it is the first example of the architecture of absolute monarchy, the essential link between the villa-palace of the Renaissance, such as the Belvedere in the Vatican, and the state palace of the Baroque, such as Versailles.

Because of its great wealth and political stability, Venice was the great model of impressive civic architecture, and the design of the Uffizi clearly shows parallels with the Piazza di San Marco. Rome provided Vasari's fertile mind with the examples that Michelangelo had created for the popes. The Capitol, for Vasari, was a totally fresh and grand creation, the apogee of civic architecture. Much that was included in the plan for the Uffizi can be traced back to Michelangelo's Roman opus, and much can be traced back to his Florentine opus, especially his work for the Medici at the Church of San Lorenzo. Those works, those early 16th-century manifestations of nascent Florentine Mannerism, are the works on which Vasari depended most heavily, and on which he modeled all his other architectural references. The Laurentian Library at San Lorenzo is the underlying and most obvious source of the design of the Uffizi; it

Uffizi

was not simply copied, but rather became an inspiration. Vasari took forms that Michelangelo had used for the interior of the library and applied them to the exterior of the Uffizi. At the same time, some exterior forms used by Michelangelo at the library appear on the interior of Uffizi's loggia. The "inversion" is typical of both Vasari and Mannerism.

Though Vasari was most obviously dependent on Michelangelo, he was a universal enough artist to make references to the works of other artists, such as Bramante and Baldassare Peruzzi, but these references are always filtered through his Michelangelesque lenses. Through an amalgam of references to Roman and Renaissance princely architecture attached to a basic Michelangelesque framework, Vasari created a series of symbolic references to works created for princes both ancient and modern. Although Vasari was keenly aware of the Florentine-Tuscan tradition in architecture, his architecture goes beyond that tradition's limited scope. His architecture is not static as in the architecture of the Early Renaissance, nor is it the self-absorbed perfection of the High Renaissance. It is an architecture of movement, not the movement of the Baroque leading to a climax, but rather a thwarted, unfulfilled movement unfolding serially and encompassing time as well as space. The movement is within a tight and restricted space, closed at one end and ambiguous at the other, creating tension and confusion as the movement is never resolved.

Vasari chose individual elements from a variety of sources, but he subjected and diminished the individual unit for the sake of the total plan. Vasari was confronted with the need to create new forms to house new institutions. He approached the Uffizi commission by fusing what was already known and accepted

architecturally to a building program, the scope of which was absolutely unprecedented in the annals of Florentine-Tuscan civic architecture. Therefore, his design did not focus on a single monument, but aimed at transforming the entire environment. As the scale of the palaces was unprecedented, Vasari used a modular design which he varied according to the demands of the individual parts of the Uffizi.

Vasari went far beyond the static repose of the Renaissance and far beyond the simple domestic associations of Renaissance architecture. Through him, the palace became charged with expressing not only the status of a specific family, but also, more significantly, the policies of a prince and his state. For Vasari, architecture had become not only an art but an instrument of politics, a method of expressing in the most concrete terms possible the aims of the Medici state. The architecture that Vasari developed for the service of his prince, the architecture of the Uffizi, was derived from many sources: from antiquity, from the Early and High Renaissance, from Rome, Venice and other princely Italian cities, but most especially from Michelangelo, who had "surpassed antiquity." While the forms of the Uffizi are derivative, and while Vasari may be considered a proto-eclectic architect, the Uffizi remains unique in the annals of Italian architecture. Finally, the Uffizi is more than a work of architecture in the service of policies and princes; it is a work that praises the prince who commissioned it. The loggia, the *altana,* the *piano nobile* and the serliana form a perfect *cortile* which serves as the forecourt to his heavenly palace.

At the Uffizi, Vasari created the prototypical urban architecture of power, the model of an architecture charged with expressing the pomp, power, prestige and presence of the prince and his state. As Cosimo I married the old to the new to create his state, so Vasari fused antique with modern architecture to create his monumental masterpiece.

—DONALD FRICELLI

PALAZZO DEL TÈ
Mantua, Italy

1526-34: Palazzo built and decorated; **Architect and artist:** Giulio Romano (1499-1546). **1527-28:** Interiors from Sala di Ovidio to Sala delle Aquile decorated. **1532-34:** Frescoes in Sala dei Giganti painted.

Publications

BELLUZZI, A., and CAPEZZALI, W.: *Il palazzo dei lucidi inganni: Palazzo Tè a Mantova*. Florence, 1976.

FORSTER, K. F., and TUTTLE, R. J.: "The Palazzo del Tè." *Journal of the Society of Architectural Historians* 30 (1971): 267-293.

Giulio Romano. Milan, 1989.

HARTT, FREDERICK: *Giulio Romano*. 2 vols. New Haven, Connecticut, 1958.

ISOZAKI, ARATA: *Palazzo del Tè*. In the *Architectural Pilgrimage to World Architecture* series. Tokyo, 1980.

SHEARMAN, J.: "Osservazioni sulla crónologia e l'evoluzione del Palazzo del Tè." *Bollettino del Centro di Studi di Architettura "Andrea Palladio"* 9 (1967): 438.

"Palazzo del Tè." *Allgemeine Bauzeitung* 49.

VERHEYEN, EGON: *The Palazzo del Tè in Mantua: Images of Love and Politics*. Baltimore, 1977.

VERHEYEN, EGON: "Studien zur Baugeschichte des Palazzo del Tè zu Mantua." *Mitteilungen des Kunsthistorischen Instituts in Florenz* (1972): 63-114.

*

The Palazzo del Tè in Mantua developed from a modest enterprise initially involving a villa and stables into the architectural masterpiece of the Roman painter-architect Giulio Romano. He had been invited to Mantua in 1524 at the invitation of the Marchese Federigo Gonzaga (1500-40).

The observation of the 16th century painter-architect Giorgio Vasari that Giulio had been forced to incorporate older structures into his new layout of spaces for the Palazzo del Tè has been confirmed in independent archival studies by John Shearman (1967), Kurt Forster and Richard Tuttle (1971), and Egon Verheyen (1977). Giulio's initial work at the Gonzaga stud farm, located on the T-shaped island outside the city walls of Mantua, was to renovate a portion of the older stables and villa into a more comfortable but still modest residence. The Tè gradually developed, however, into a low-lying complex of walls, halls and gardens. The core of the older villa was incorporated into the palace's north facade, which Giulio retained in his gradual

Palazzo del Tè: Mantua, Italy, 1526-34

expansion of the inner court and garden, but in the process he changed the main axis of the palace grounds to an east-west orientation.

Giulio's entrance for this facade was neither at the villa's center nor at the center of the building complex as a whole, so that he had to add bays to ensure the structure's symmetry. The walls on the west and south which he included in his designs defined the plan's rectangular shape, but its size and the internal arrangement of rooms remained flexible. In the end, an enormous open courtyard was skirted by a wide perimeter of low walls that gave the palace its horizontal sprawl and made it look grander than its interior spaces would suggest.

On the exterior, Giulio placed attic windows on a stringcourse interrupted by a giant order of Doric pilasters, both of which he made flush with the keystones above the windows. For textural interest, Giulio combined the planar verticality of the pilasters and their busy entablature with the uneven spread of the rusticated window surrounds. Paired pilasters define the endmost bays of the north facade, and three central arches mark its entrance.

At the center of the new west facade, Giulio constructed an enclosed loggia of three bays as a formal ceremonial entrance, but as he gave it only a single portal, it was far less grand on the exterior than the triple arch of the renovated north facade. Its coffered tunnel vault was based on a prototype in the Basilica of Maxentius, but the unfinished marble columns were Giulio's fantasy. In the *cortile* he used half columns, and placed triangular pediments above the keystones of blind tabernacles.

A mosaic of Theodoric's palace in San Apollinare Nuovo in Ravenna provided the model for Giulio's east garden facade with its triple-arched loggia and arcaded wings. He had incorporated the Serliana (often called the Palladian motif) as a royal portal but also as a highly flexible architectural system. Giulio had previously used it in his Villa Lante on the Roman Janiculum. As Federigo's new wife, a Paleologa, was of imperial Byzantine descent, and as Federigo was elevated from marquis to duke in 1530, the year of the Holy Roman emperor's visit to Mantua, the imperial allusions seemed appropriate.

Several major halls, from the Sala di Ovidio to the Sala delle Aquile, had been decorated by 1527-28. These interior mural decorations embedded the windows so that their spacing became a problem on the exterior when Giulio replaced the plaster wall with classical orders. The sprawling window surrounds in each bay allowed Giulio to mask their off-center positions somewhat. His irregular bays, then, were not deliberate attempts at off-center placement so much as asymptotic approaches to symmetry under trying conditions. There is no similar explanation for his decision to allow some of the Doric triglyphs in his garden facades to slip from their entablatures, yet these, too, might have been intended as diversions from those elements over which he had no control. Because the fallen triglyphs occur over windows and cavities, they serve to underscore the classical intervals between solid and void (Giulio used them only on the east and west faces of the garden facades). Among Giulio's interior decorations for the Palazzo del Tè, the Sala dei Cavalli represents a pantheon of champions from the Gonzaga stud farm in painted frescoes framed by personifications of deities in simulated niches. The stallions, placed above the room's wainscoting, are viewed in profile against distant landscapes and between pilasters which the creatures overlap illusionistically. The family's breeds had for decades been noted as winners of horse races throughout the Italian peninsula, and were commemorated in similar decorations in Gonzaga palaces throughout the domain.

The adjacent Sala di Psiche is decorated in warm colors with the grand wedding feast of Cupid and Psyche extending across two contiguous walls. In attendance are deities, nymphs and mythical creatures. Individual scenes of the loves of the gods are framed within the heavy hexagonal and octagonal coffers of the ceiling.

Perhaps the best known of Giulio's fresco decorations are those in the Sala dei Giganti. There a squarish room with a domed ceiling depicts the futile attempt of the arrogant Titans to scale Mount Olympus. The just-vacated throne of Jupiter appears beneath a canopy at the apex of the ceiling as the gods repulse the presumptuous giants, who tumble to earth on all four walls, their caves collapsing about them. The fires of destruction would have been reinforced by light dancing on the walls and ceiling from flames leaping in the room's perforated fireplace. Uneven pavement stones to suggest fallen debris served as an additional sign of Giulio's wit and whimsy in this most entertaining of rooms.

Baldassare Castiglione, whose book *The Courtier* instructed its readers on how court members should serve their prince, had chaperoned Giulio to the Gonzaga household. If Castiglione had ever required evidence of Giulio's suitability for the Mantuan court, his judgment would have been readily confirmed by Giulio's palace and its decoration.

—EDWARD J. OLSZEWSKI

SANT'ANDREA
Mantua, Italy

Ca. 1460-72: Designs for rebuilding of original church created, and construction begun; **Architect:** Leon Battista Alberti (1404-72). **1472-early 1490s:** Nave constructed; west porch built; **Architect:** Luca Fancelli (1430-95). **1530-65:** Walls of transepts, north porch, choir, sacristies built. **1597-1600:** Crypt built. **1697-1702:** Vaulting of transept and choir built; **Architect:** Giulio Torre. **1732-85:** New dome designed and constructed; **Architect:** Filippo Juvarra (1678-1736).

Publications

BORSI, FRANCO: *Leon Battista Alberti*. New York, 1977.
BRANDI, CESARE: "La cupola dello Juvarra a S. Andrea a Mantova e un precedente." *Arte in Europa, Scritti di storia dell'arte in onore di Edoardo Arslan*. Milan, 1966.
BROWN, CHARLOTTE: "Luca Fancelli in Mantua." *Mitteilungen des Kunsthistorischen Instituts in Florenz* 16 (1973): 153ff.
CHAMBERS, DAVID SANDERSON: "Sant'Andrea at Mantua and Gonzaga Patronage: 1460-1472." *Journal of the Warburg and Courtauld Institutes* 40 (1977): 99-127.
GRUGNOLA, G.: *La chiesa di Sant'Andrea in Mantova*. Turin, 1900.
HUBALA, ERICH: "L. B. Albertis Langhaus von Sant'Andrea in Mantua." In *Festschrift für Kurt Behrendt*. Berlin, 1961: 83-120
INTRA, G. B.: *La basilica di Sant'Andre in Mantova*. Milan, 1882.
JOHNSON, EUGENE J.: *S. Andrea in Mantua: The Building History*. London and University Park, Pennsylvania, 1975.
KRAUTHEIMER, RICHARD: "Albertis Templum Etruscum." *Münchner Jahrbuch der bildenden Kunst* 4 (1961): 65-72.
MARIANI, ERCOLANI, et al.: *Il Sant'Andrea di Mantova e Leon Battista Alberti*. Mantua, 1974.

Sant'Andrea: Mantua, Italy, ca. 1460-72

Sant'Andrea

ORIOLI, P.: *Arte ed iscrizioni nella basilica di Leon Battista Alberti fiorentino a Sant'Andrea in Mantova*. Mantua, 1892.

PELATI, P.: *La basilica di Sant'Andrea*. Mantua, 1952.

PERINA, C.: *La basilica di Sant'Andrea in Mantova*. Mantua, 1965.

RITSCHER, ERNST: "Die Kirche S. Andrea in Mantua." *Zeitschrift für Bauwesen* 49 (1899): 1-20, 181-200.

Il Sant'Andrea di Mantova e Leon Battista Alberti: Atti del Convegno di studi nel quinto centenario della basilica di Sant'Andrea. Mantua, 1975.

WITTKOWER, RUDOLF: *Architectural Principles in the Age of Humanism*. London, 1949.

*

The Church of Sant'Andrea in Mantua represents what is probably the culmination of the architectural career of the Renaissance humanist-artist Leon Battista Alberti as well as one of the highpoints of the 18th-century architect Filippo Juvarra. The history of Sant'Andrea is long, involving several major stages of rebuilding and renovation. The original church dated to the 11th century, with later medieval additions including the surviving Late Gothic bell tower flanking the present entry porch. Shortly after 1400, the rulers of Mantua decided to institute public veneration in the church of two vases said to contain the blood of the Crucifixion. So popular did this become with pilgrims that plans to enlarge or rebuild the church were initiated in 1460.

From the beginning, the church's patron, Lodovico Gonzaga, enlisted the architectural advice of Florentines, at first that rather enigmatic carpenter-turned-architect Antonio di Ciaccheri Manetti. The first evidence connecting the name of Alberti with the project came in a letter he sent to Gonzaga offering his services in preparing a plan "more suitable to your intentions . . . more capacious, more enduring, more worthy, and more felicitous." Above all, Alberti assured his potential patron that it would "cost much less" than Manetti's proposal. Alberti had well-established connections with the Gonzaga, having designed the Church of San Sebastiano in Mantua and also having been engaged by them to complete the tribune of Santissima Annunziata in Florence, which was under their patronage. Alberti's offer was accepted, and work began on his "Etruscan type of temple" in 1472. Alberti's design called for a Latin-cross plan with a broad nave covered with a masonry barrel vault. The nave was not to be paralleled with conventional side aisles but instead was flanked, on either side, by three spacious, barrel-vaulted chapels set between large piers. Each of these piers contains a smaller domed chapel. Thus the relationship between the larger nave and its flanking smaller chapels is replicated by these chapels having their own dependent spaces.

For the crossing, Alberti probably intended a hemispherical dome of the type he also may have planned for his earlier architectural endeavors at San Francesco in Rimini and at San Sebastiano. Although the plan in Sant'Andrea is liturgically conventional in its longitudinal direction, the emphasis really is upon the crossing and, therefore, upon the central focus ascribed by Alberti to the "Etruscan temple type." Alberti's intention for the choir area is uncertain.

Although Alberti prepared detailed plans for Sant'Andrea, the cornerstone of the new church was not laid until two months after his death in 1472. Direction of the program was assumed by Alberti's architectural executor, Luca Fancelli, and continued until the early 1490s. During this first campaign the nave was

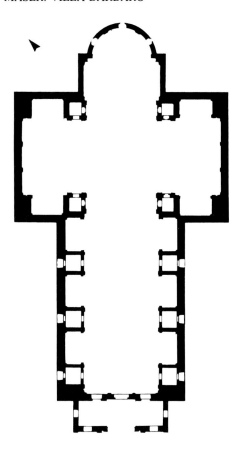

Maria presso San Satiro (ca. 1480) but also the great proto-Baroque church of Il Gesù in Rome.

The interior hall with its major and minor rhythm of chapel openings is visually and temporally anticipated by Alberti's magnificent porch. This prologue to the interior space is in keeping with Alberti's strictures concerning congruity as discussed in his *Ten Books on Architecture*. Here, at the west entrance, the cramping mass of the medieval bell tower dictated the dimensions which, perforce, had to be made smaller than the actual height and width of the church. For his porch entry, Alberti combined the triumphal-arch motif he had used 20 years previously at San Francesco in Rimini with the Mantuan temple front of San Sebastiano of a decade earlier. In Alberti's design (itself, perhaps, inspired by Brunelleschi's intentions for the porch of the Pazzi Chapel or adapted from the Arch of Augustus at Rimini), a giant order of smooth Corinthian pilasters rises the height of the porch facade to support the pediment (the temple front); behind this layer is a minor order of fluted pilasters supporting an entablature and attic story penetrated by the great arched entryway (the triumphal arch). The curious *ombrellone* (or hood) above the porch shielding the Gothic rose window of the nave was part of Alberti's program and intended to control the light entering the nave. His aim was to achieve a monumental diffusion of light, infusing the interior with a sense of macrocosmic mystery, a celestial atmosphere also found in the Roman Pantheon. Sant'Andrea, despite its incomplete state and complicated evolution, represents Alberti's most perfect attempt at reconstructing the grand solemnity of his admired antiquity.

—CHARLES R. MACK

constructed and the west (main) porch built. Work was resumed between 1530 to about 1565 (walls of transepts, north porch, choir, sacristies) and again, briefly, from 1597 to 1600 (crypt), and from 1697 to 1702 under the Bolognese architect Giulio Torre (vaulting of transept and choir). Finally, a new dome was designed in 1732 by Juvarra, following the model of Christopher Wren's domes for Greenwich Hospital, and constructed between 1733 and 1785. Finally, around 1780, a renewal of the internal decoration was carried out under Paolo Pozzo of Verona; exactly how closely this restoration may have reflected Alberti's (or Fancelli's) original intentions or what had been previously executed is unclear. The complex and oft-interrupted building history of Sant'Andrea presents many problems involving intention and execution. As is the case with all such buildings, Sant' Andrea's history was not frozen at the pristine (and Albertian) moment of conception. Reconstructing Alberti's concept involves understanding just how faithful Fancelli might have been to his master's program, how much local tastes and pressures might have interposed, and recognition of the changes rendered during the later phases of construction; Juvarra's great Late Baroque dome was but the most obvious of these.

Without making a specific quotation from an antique monument, the interior of Sant'Andrea definitely conjures up a feeling for classical space, reminiscent of the concourse hall of a great imperial bath or the interior of the Basilica Nova in Rome. The emphatic break from the traditional aisled church, preserved even in the new Renaissance architecture of Filippo Brunelleschi, stands as one of Alberti's most radical contributions. It does recall, however, the Abbey Church of Fiesole north of Florence, which was rebuilt beginning in 1461, perhaps following the plan of Alberti. The treatment anticipated not only Francesco di Giorgio's church of Santa Maria delle Grazie al Calcinaio at Cortona (1485-1509) and Donato Bramante's Santa

VILLA BARBARO
Maser, Italy

Ca. 1549: Designs for villa begun; **Architect:** Andrea Palladio (1508-80). **Ca. 1557:** Construction completed. **1560-61:** Frescoes painted; **Artist:** Paolo Veronese (1528-88).

Publications

ACKERMAN, JAMES S.: *Palladio's Villas*. Locust Valley, New York, 1967.

BASSO, UMBERTO: *La villa e il tempietto dei Barbaro a Maser di Andrea Palladio*. Montebelluna, Italy, 1976.

BURGER, FRITZ: *Die Villen des Andrea Palladio*. Leipzig, 1909.

COCKE, R.: "Veronese and Daniele Barbaro: The Decoration of Villa Maser." *Journal of the Warburg and Courtauld Institutes* (1972): 226-246.

HEINEMANN, W.: *Die Villenbauten des Andrea Palladio*. Berlin, 1909.

IVANOFF, N.: "La tematica degli affreschi di Maser." *Arte Veneta* (1970): 210-213.

MAZZARIOL, G.: *Palladio a Maser*. Venice, 1965.

OBERHUBER, K.: "H. Cock, Battista Pittoni und Paolo Veronese in Villa Maser." In *Munuscula Discipulorum. Festschrift für Hans Kauffmann zum 70. Geburtstag*. Berlin, 1968.

OBERHUBER, K.: "Gli affreschi di Paolo Veronese nella Villa Barbaro." *Bollettino del Centro Internazionale di Studi di Architettura "Andrea Palladio"* (1968): 188-202.

PALLADIO, ANDREA: *I quattro libri d'architettura*. Venice, 1570. English translation: *The Four Books of Architecture*. New York, 1965.

Villa Barbaro: Maser, Italy, ca. 1549

PUPPI, LIONELLO: *Andrea Palladio: The Complete Works.* New
    York, 1986.
SCULLY, VINCENT J., JR.: *The Villas of Palladio.* 1986.
ZORZI, GIAN GIORGIO: *Palladian Villas.* Venice, 1958.

*

Andrea Palladio designed many villas for Venetian patrons who
had large agricultural holdings in the Veneto region of Italy.
The Villa Barbaro in Maser belongs to a group of villas which
were expressly designed as working farms with agricultural
dependencies incorporated into the wings of the main dwelling
block. The taller, pedimented residential quarters are flanked
by long arcades which hide the *barchesse,* or farm structures.
Each wing is then terminated by a taller pavilion holding a
dovecote, so that the entire complex is brought together in a
single monumental form reflecting the noble and humanistic
status of the owner. The basic form of the Villa Barbaro is very
similar to Palladio's Villa Emo in Fanzolo, built just a few
years later. However, the different aesthetic conception and use
of antique imagery in the two structures underscore the impact
of the remarkable patrons, Marc Antonio and Daniele Barbaro.

The Barbaros' wealth and political connections, together with
their humanistic education and knowledge of architecture, distinguishes them as patrons of architecture. They were later
influential in securing Palladio's commission for the Church of
Il Redentore in Venice, and built a smaller version of one of
Palladio's unused variant plans for Il Redentore adjacent to the
villa in Maser which is now used by the local parish. Daniele
Barbaro was especially knowledgeable about architecture, as
he published in 1556 an annotated translation of the architectural
treatise written by the ancient Roman architect Vitruvius. In
fact, Palladio produced the drawings for Barbaro's translation,
and it was during the years of their collaboration when the villa
was designed: the earliest drawings for the villa date from 1549,
and the villa was substantially complete at least by 1557.

Palladio's architecture is often distinguished by the formal
abstraction he gave to column capitals, window architraves and
the proportion of building masses. However, the Villa Barbaro
in Maser is one of Palladio's most ornate commissions for a
suburban villa. The ornate character of this commission is probably due to Daniele Barbaro's collaboration on the design. The

pediment with a broken entablature is unique in Palladio's design (and may have been part of a later alteration, as Palladio's
woodcut of the villa in his treatise shows an unbroken pediment),
as are the curved buttresses which connect the taller dovecotes
to the arcades below. Most of Palladio's suburban commissions
have smooth stucco walls with window openings sharply cut
into the wall surfaces without any intervening molding or articulation. However, at Maser the stucco surface is scored in imitation of ashlar masonry, and the window and door openings are
provided with stone moldings, elements usually reserved for
his urban commissions. Perhaps the most telling influence of
the Barbaros is the inclusion of a nymphaeum, or fountain, at
the rear of the villa. This feature was included in many ancient
Roman villas, and was described in the letters of Pliny the
Younger. Undoubtedly, Barbaro's research on his translation
of Vitruvius would have made him aware of it.

The site of the Villa Barbaro is one of the best of all of
Palladio's villas. Terraced into the hillside, the *piano nobile* of
the villa overlooks the plain to the south and opens to the
fountain and pool behind. Kitchens, stables and storage rooms
originally occupied the ground level built into the hillside, leaving the Barbaros to enjoy the expansive views to the south
while retaining direct access to the delightful courtyard of the
nymphaeum nestled into the hillside. Palladio's genius for combining form and function is evident here, for he carefully explained in his treatise how water from the fountain of the nymphaeum fed the fishpond, which in turn was conducted to the
kitchens, then to the gardens, and then to irrigate the fields.

Because of the difference in height between the ground level
and *piano nobile,* stairs leading directly to the main rooms of
the villa from the front would have been uncomfortably large.
Instead, Palladio provided stairs leading from the flanking arcades into the cruciform hall of the central pavilion. This left
the facade to present a full-height temple front to the valley,
while giving the Barbaros immediate access to the *barchesse*
to supervise their considerable agricultural investment.

Although the cruciform hall is somewhat restricted in size,
Paolo Veronese's frescoes, painted in 1560-61, create a false
architectural framework, behind which illusionistic frescoes
allow the space to expand beyond the confining walls. The
restricted size may result from the reuse of preexisting foundations and walls, for there are fireplaces built into the walls at
the current attic level, and the walls are not built of brick as in

all of Palladio's other residences, but are built of cobbles set in mortar with periodic leveling courses of brick. Palladio's ability to incorporate substantial amounts of preexisting building fabric into his design while achieving a harmonious unity of design amply demonstrates his design skills.

Although the Barbaros' influence is clearly read in the design, their ideas are additions to the monumental villa complex which typifies Palladio's villas. The skillful handling of the sloping site, preexisting structure and functional requirements of the farming operations also typify Palladio's oeuvre. The nymphaeum is an exceptional space whose cooler temperatures and soothing water sounds give relief to oppressive summer heat. These elements, together with Veronese's frescoes, make the Villa Barbaro in Maser one of the most inviting and splendid of all the villas of the Italian Veneto.

—ELWIN C. ROBISON

MILAN CATHEDRAL
Milan, Italy

1387: Building begun; **Architect:** Simone da Orsenigo. **1391:** Foundations completed, walls in construction; **Architects:** Nicolas de Bonaventure and Johann von Freiburg. **1399:** Piers completed. **1500:** Inside of dome and octagonal dome outside completed. **1762:** Concave buttresses and spire built; **Architect:** Francesco Croce. **1806-13:** Facade constructed; **Architect:** Carlo Amati.

Publications

ACKERMAN, JAMES S.: "*Ars sine scientia nihil est*, Gothic Theory of Architecture at the Cathedral of Milan." *Art Bulletin* (June 1949).
BESCAPÉ, G., and MEZZANOTTE, P.: *Il Duomo di Milano*. Milan, 1965.
BOITO, CAMILLO: *Il Duomo di Milano*. Milan, 1889.
CASSI RAMELLI, A.: *Luca Beltrami e il Duomo di Milano*. Milan, 1965.
CATTANEO, ENRICO: *San Carlo Borromeo e il Duomo di Milano*. Milan, 1978.
GAETANO, C. (ed.): *Annali della fabbrica del Duomo di Milano dall'origine fino al presente*. Milan, 1877.
ROCCO, GIOVANNI: *Pellegrino Pellegrini architetto di S. Carlo e le sue opere nel Duomo di Milano*. Milan, 1939.
SIEBENHÜNER, H.: *Deutsche Künstler am Mailänder Dom*. Munich, 1944.
WITTKOWER, RUDOLF: *Gothic vs. Classical, Architectural Projects in 17th Century Italy*. 1974.

*

Milan Cathedral is one of the most interesting medieval monuments in Italy, complicated in its history and vast in scale; its length of 500 feet and its greatest height of 350 feet are surpassed only by the dimensions of St. Peter's in Rome. The details on the exterior, most notably the facade itself, are later in date, from the 16th and 17th centuries; the spire is from the 18th century, and the seemingly innumerable, crocketed pinnacles and gables that spring from every available surface are almost entirely of the 18th and 19th centuries. Yet despite these various

Milan Cathedral: Milan, Italy, 1387

Milan Cathedral

to solve certain of the problems in mensuration and surveying that had arisen. In addition, Heinrich Parler II of Gmund, who may have worked on Cathedrals in Cologne, Prague and Ulm, was summoned to Milan in 1391; his suggestions did not fit the tastes of the existing experts, however, so in May 1392 a desperate gathering of the various parties took place, with the proceedings conducted in the manner of a scholastic dispute. Parler was overruled in all his proposals.

By 1399 the piers had been completed, and the problem of vaulting had to be faced. Again a foreign expert was brought in, Jean Mignot of Paris, and he decided the whole structure was in danger of collapse. His list comprised 54 objections, 25 of which were replied to, the rest being considered insubstantial or simply too time-consuming to consider. This is a remarkable history, the records of which are largely preserved. Scholars have taken notice of what Mignot said about such matters as geometry, mathematical ratios and the symbolism of numbers, all of which were necessary because, as he put it in a remarkable phrase, art without science, or practice without theory, is nothing. Mignot too was dismissed, perhaps because he was too attracted to theory for the Italians, who defended more-practical responses. Whatever Mignot said, the building is still standing. Despite various other changes, the plan remained necessarily similar to what was first laid out: double arcades on both sides of the nave, a transept of three bays and an enormous ambulatory, filled, as is so much else, with a vast expanse of glass. Everything in Milan Cathedral is vast, and on the inside, where there is less detailing than on the exterior, this vastness is especially apparent, because the sculptured figures in the capitals carry a sense of the smallness of the human scale up into the space overhead. The piers are seemingly innumerable, and the rippling contours encourage a sense of all-around movement, which is confirmed by the diagonal views that are opened up at every part of the nave. Yet the width of this nave ensures a

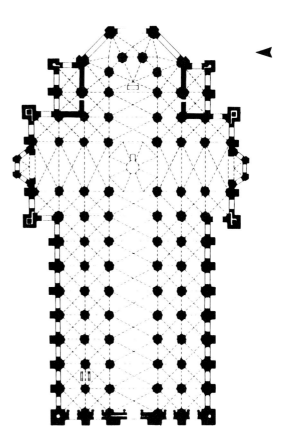

periods of building the effect of the cathedral is perhaps very much like that envisaged by its first builders.

The founding of the cathedral in 1386 was an action symbolizing the emergence of Lombardy from the artistic eclipse that had begun at the end of the Romanesque period; the political activity of the preceding years was brought to an end by Gian Galeazzo Visconti, who annexed to the Lombard domain large areas of the territory of the Venetians and even parts of Tuscany. The revival of such monumental architecture, which included the Certosa of Pavia and the cathedrals of Monza and Como, was a symptom both of the increased wealth and security that came from this political consolidation and the particular interests of Gian Galeazzo himself.

But there was little tradition for building on such a scale, as earlier buildings in Lombardy were stylistically between the Romanesque cathedrals of the area and the newer French Cistercian architecture that had been introduced into Italy in the 13th century; there was very little that included the developments in Gothic architecture, namely flying buttresses, large areas of fenestration and exterior sculpture. In 1387 Simone da Orsenigo was appointed *capomaestro,* and work began on Milan Cathedral. But by 1389 it was recognized that the intended size of the building was beyond the scope of local experts, and Nicolas de Bonaventure was called in from Paris; he was dismissed only a year later, however. Other Italians were appointed, but a year later another foreigner was brought in, the German mason Johann von Freiburg. He too was soon fired, but by then most of the foundations had been laid and the walls and piers were rising.

A conference was called for August 1391 to determine, as the record of the *fabbrica* puts it, "the length of the pilasters, the height of the church, of the windows, doors and accessories." A mathematician, Gabriele Sornaloco, was brought in from Pienza

full flow to the altar; behind that, once the transept is passed, the expanse of glass in the ambulatory opens up, framing all that is in front of it.

Some 3,000 statues are embedded within the fabric of the cathedral, about 2,000 of these on the exterior. Models of the tower to be set over the crossing were made by various architects, perhaps including Donato Bramante, and certainly Leonardo da Vinci; the inside of the dome and the octagonal dome outside were completed by 1500, but it was not until 1762 that a plan for the concave buttresses and the spire by Francesco Croce, architect to the cathedral, were approved and then built. A statue of the Virgin was placed over the spire in 1774.

A similar length of time was spent on the facade. Planning for the facade was not begun seriously until about 1540, when Vincenzo Seregni submitted a plan; he was subsequently appointed architect to the cathedral, but little was accomplished. In 1564 Cardinal Carlo Borromeo, newly appointed archbishop of Milan, replaced Seregni with the artist Pellegrino Tibaldi, who subsequently supervised a considerable program of building. That work did not include the facade, the matter of which by then had become a test of the relationship between the Gothic style of most of the building and the newer schemes of Renaissance proportion and details. Pellegrino's plan was in the modern, or Roman style, and for the moment that was accepted; by 1600 and then by 1735—as surviving engravings show—considerable progress was made. But when in 1745 Luigi Vanvitelli submitted a design, it contained a number of Gothic details, including, at the lowest range, a High Gothic central niche. Disputes followed, and in the next few years a range of other projects were put forward by Bernardo Vittone, Giulio Galliori, Leopoldo Pollak, Luigi Cagnola and Felice Soave, the end coming when Napoléon Bonaparte gave orders that the cathedral should be completed. Most of the work was then carried out by the cathedral architect, Carlo Amati, between 1806 and 1813.

That was not the end of the story, however, for many people objected to the cathedral's mixture of Gothic and classical elements. In 1883 an open competition was arranged for a clearly Gothic facade to be built, with architects entering from countries as far away as England and Russia. The only result of this obviously impractical competition was the addition of yet more decoration on the outside. The last stop was with Mussolini, who approved in 1938 the construction of a Gothic *campanile* next to the cathedral, to be finished in 1942. This tower would have been some 540 feet high, the tallest such structure in the world, but the war, of course, put an end to any such project.

—DAVID CAST

CENTRAL RAILWAY STATION
Milan, Italy

1912: Designs for station completed; **Architect:** Ulisse Stacchini. 1925: Construction begun.

Publications

LE CORBUSIER: *Almanach d'architecture moderne*. Turin, Italy, 1975.

SETA, CESARE DE': *La Cultura Architettonica in Italia tra le due Guerre*. Bari, Italy, 1972.
ZEVI, BRUNO: *Storia dell'Architettura Moderna*. Turin, Italy, 1973.

Premiated over 44 other entries in a national competition held in 1912, Ulisse Stacchini's design for Milan's new passenger railroad station went into construction only in 1925 because World War I and the postwar recession had crippled Italy's building industry. After Mussolini assumed power in 1922, state patronage and Stacchini's redesign incorporated the project into the government's attempts to deal with the chronic poverty and unemployment, the constant crises in industry and agriculture that afflicted the country throughout that and the following decade.

Diane Ghirardo's *Building New Communities: New Deal America and Fascist Italy* (1989) clarifies the precise political context into which the station fit. Like Mussolini's ambitious program for new towns, the station joined "the political economics of labor and the symbolic politics of architecture." Because many of its programs would be long in coming to fruition, the assertively populist and nationalistic government needed other means to demonstrate quickly its efficacy in dealing with severe economic and social dislocations. Since the regime had broken in a number of fundamental ways with previous governments, it had to link itself tangibly to still-viable Italian traditions in order to provide the populace with a sense of continuity. Due to their brief tenure and their position as only the strongest among several competing political parties, the Fascists had to strengthen their still-fragile legitimacy, to effect in the public mind an exclusive identification between the Fascist organization and the state itself.

For all these reasons the train station recommended itself. Construction promised to employ thousands, pump money into one of the two most important regional economies in Italy's industrial heartland, and begin the reconstruction of the nation's historic urban centers, thus attracting the speculators who were to play a major role in the Fascist version of monopoly capitalism. An immense train station fronting on Milan's large Piazza Andrea Doria could be as immediate and rhetorically powerful as charismatic leadership itself. For if the regime could complete such an enterprise, then the appearance of success might cling to a government whose other less visible programs were subject to longer-term development, or to postponement or failure. Monumental architecture's sovereignty in space could invest the station with the government's putatative stability, its capacity to act, its resurrection of Italy's historic prestige.

In these respects, Stacchini's evident knowledge of the three passenger railroad terminals built in New York City and Washington, D.C., during the first decade of the century was telling. Like them, the Milan facility reworked the architecture of imperial Roman baths, in several ways an apt prototype for railroad terminals in an age dominated by Beaux-Arts classicism. In plan, the crossed axes of Roman baths allowed a compact, counterpointed arrangement of otherwise space-consuming functions. The integration of a cross-axial plan with a structural system in which lateral vaults buttressed a much higher central hall not only flooded the interiors with natural light but created a unique spatial and ceremonial amplitude, one that did as much to forestall a sense of overcrowding among the tens of thousands of daily users as did a floor area that, apart from the vaulted expanse overhead, easily accommodated densely peopled activities. This spatial grandeur also fulfilled the railroad station's imperative to serve as the city's formal gateway.

Central Railway Station: Milan, Italy, 1925

The most noteworthy aspect of the three American stations—Pennsylvania and Grand Central stations in New York, and Union Station in Washington, D.C.—had been their planning, and that of the Milanese facility was comparably fluent. This involved more than the titanic barrel vault over the ticket concourse that provided the station's spatial climax, as did similar vaulting in the American stations. Indeed, Stacchini created a sequence of vaulted spaces that had no parallel in American or European railroad station architecture, one intended to enhance with a formidable architectural and political rhetoric the traveler's passage from street level to the station's elevated tracks and platforms. At the head of the piazza was a vast segmentally vaulted vehicular concourse measuring 24 by 185 meters on a transverse axis. Parallel to it ran the full tunnel vault of the more compact but taller ticket concourse. Beyond it and accessible by four flights of stairs was the waiting concourse at track level, a segmentally vaulted space longer and more impressive than that of the vehicular concourse.

Finally, over the platforms and tracks themselves Stacchini threw five contiguous ferrovitreous vaults. Placed on or parallel with the entrance or principal axis, these shed vaults were foils in alignment and materials to the preceding transverse spaces. The shed's trussed, three-pin arches derived from those used in the *Gallerie des Machines* at the 1889 Paris Exposition, and their mutually buttressed structure owed a debt to the twin vaults used in two 19th-century London train sheds (King's Cross Station and Paddington Station). Still, the Milan arches' comparable spans, larger number, heavier proportions, more refined articulation and a more majesterial structural efficiency further embodied the station's last parallel with Roman baths, whose vaulted splendor proferred a ready-made rhetorical magniloquence perfectly suited to the Fascist regime.

That is, the panoply of vaults, crossed axes, coffered soffits, thermal windows and embellishments such as Moderne Dioscuri validated Mussolini's self-proclaimed *imperium* by linking it to the country's most redoubtable period of glory. Despite the station's predictable mural and sculpted allegories, Stacchini, like many architects trained in a Beaux-Arts system, ably employed architectural detail to mediate between human and colossal scales, between function and the demagogic rhetoric inherent in multiplying the number and dimensions of imposing spaces beyond those of ancient and modern precedents. His massing of the piazza facade, and of the two exceptionally long office elevations perpendicular to it, demonstrated a command of the triadic and five-part groupings, of advanced and recessed walls and pavilions that were two of the principal compositional resources in the Beaux-Arts repertoire. Amplifying the station's political speech, the architect worked into many wall surfaces much of the three-dimensional heft of the French Empire style. These features gave the station an architectural probity that set it apart from the regimental repetition in work by Paul Ludwig Troost and Albert Speer for Hitler, from the bombastic *architecture parlante* in Konstantin Melnikov's post-1930 projects for the Stalinist regime, from the dreary blankness resulting from Marcello Piacentini's attempts to mediate between traditional and modern architecture in works for Mussolini from 1932 onward.

Nevertheless, the station embodied some of the deformations of classical architecture evident in many totalitarian and fascist projects, built and unbuilt. Stacchini froze all curvilinear ornament within sharp-edged rectangular frames and profiles. He eschewed the freestanding and engaged columns whose multiplication gave the Empire style much of its sculptural élan. In the few places where he actually used them, as in the paired colossal orders on the triumphal-arch portico, Stacchini vitiated their three-dimensional power by locking them onto the piers behind with rusticated blocks of stone. These and other features confounded the station's careful massing by giving its exteriors a frigid and brutal appearance, an oddly sophisticated bluntness.

There were more flagrant contraventions of the classical canon. Loading a clerestory on top of the attic for the triumphal-arch loggia made this elevation ponderous. Trabeating the openings in the loggia defied the thousand-year association between the triumphal motif and arches. The unusually flat four-centered vaults used for the vehicular and waiting concourses denied the gravity and nobility that are inherent in Roman vaulting. Despite inserting ferrovitreous skylights into the station's major vaults, and uniting these spaces with the platform area through a consistent scale, the design did not fully resolve a typical 19th-century disjunction between a glass and metal shed facility and a masonry head building. However adroitly the design mediated between human and colossal dimensions, it stretched classicism's essentially anthropomorphic proportions to a Ramesside scale. These deformations gave the station a stillborn character consonant with the Fascists' overreaching rhetoric and aims.

—EDWARD W. WOLNER

GALLERIA VITTORIO EMANUELE II
Milan, Italy

1865-77. Architect: Giuseppe Mengoni (1829-77).

Publications

BANDMANN, G.: "Die Galleria Vittorio Emanuele II zu Mailand." *Zeitschrift für Kunstgeschichte* 29 (1966).
GEIST, JOHANN FRIEDRICH: *Arcades: The History of a Building Type.* Cambridge, Massachusetts, and London, 1983.
HOFMANN, WERNER, and KULTERMANN, UDO: *Modern Architecture in Color.* New York, 1970.
RICCI, G.: *La vita e le opere dell'architetto Giuseppe Mengoni.* Milan, 1930.

The 19th-century shopping arcade depended on a politically ascendant middle class, an economic system that throughout the century increasingly if imperfectly resembled a free market, and an industrial revolution whose techniques for the production of iron and glass and whose reorganization of the trade in luxury goods resulted in the development of arcaded galleries of shops. That is, the advent of mass production forced makers of luxury goods to distribute them more efficiently, promote them more effectively and turn them over more quickly.

The arcade fulfilled these and other economic imperatives by offering a range of goods that approached the department store's variety. However, it did so within a public space over which a ferrovitreous vault maintained the character of a city street, and day and night allowed promenading, window shopping and the display of goods undisturbed by adverse weather. The arcade's aggregated shops, complementary commercial uses, central location and internal organization generated the density, heterogeneity and constant flow of visitors that permitted the luxury-goods trade to survive and prosper within the expanded scale and intensified competition of 19th-century capitalism.

The paradigmatic realization of these conditions was Giuseppe Mengoni's Galleria Vittorio Emanuele II in Milan, the arcade that according to Johann Geist's *Arcades,* on which the first third of this entry is based, initiated the monumental phase in the development of this building type. More centrally located than most arcades and department stores, the Galleria on one of its crossed axes connected public squares on which La Scala, Milan's town hall and the cathedral fronted, while on the other axis it linked two of the city's principal streets. In addition to the unusually high number of four separate entrances, the Galleria's internal organization further enhanced its central position within the city through an unprecedented six stories of logically organized uses. Lining the ground floor were restaurants, cafés, a comic opera, a comic theater, and shops whose narrow frontages maximized their number and diversity. The mezzanine carried a second level of shops, the third floor's larger spaces accommodated club rooms, offices and studios, and apartments occupied the upper three stories. Additional unique attractions—a glazed dome crossing and an imposing scale unlike anything else in the city—again reinforced the arcade's centrality, as did its architecture, which is discussed below in relation to its political symbolism.

The Galleria's design, unique attractions, systematic division of levels, diversity and density of consumer and nonconsumer activities, and its linkage of the adjacent civic, cultural, financial and religious sectors of the city transformed visitors into active participants, multiplied unintended or adventitious purchases, and generated the shifting, overlapping flows of people on which the financial health of the arcade depended. In these ways, the Galleria rationalized the selling of luxury goods as thoroughly as machines had transformed artisanal and handcrafted manufacturing into mass production. In other settings, fetishlike attraction of luxury goods seduced consumers by promising to transform them, however momentarily; the Galleria amplified the fetishistic power of commodities and comestibles by proferring to its visitors—with all the completeness of a theatrical, ordered and tasteful city in miniature—their own best versions of themselves as sophisticated urbanites.

The final aspect of the Galleria's centrality involved the political events that by 1859 had resulted in the liberation of northern Italy from Austrian rule. The Galleria's principal architectural features celebrated a new nationhood under the rule of the Piedmontese monarch for whom the Galleria was named. Triumphal arches appeared at the entrances from the cathedral and opera squares, the former a triple arch whose central opening revealed the dimensions of the arcade beyond. In the Galleria's

Galleria Vittorio Emanuele II: Milan, Italy, 1865-77

scale and majesterial glass and iron vault, Mengoni recalled and exploited two salient aspects of imperial Roman baths: their embodiment of Italy's most redoubtable period of national glory, and their provision of an overhead spatial expanse whose grandeur obviated any sense of claustrophobia among the participants in the densely peopled activities below, and conferred on them a ceremonial character and a sense of city life at its most urbane and vivid. So did the arcade elevations, which were free adaptations of Andrea Palladio's Vicentine palace fronts, an appropriately scenographic, street-front architecture: superimposed colossal and single-story orders, and alternating

caryatids and atlantes marked off the unaccented rhythm of facades whose shallow relief responded to the softened light and shadows admitted through the vaulted glass filter above.

Perhaps by intention, the Galleria's Latin-cross plan mirrored the same figure in the coat of arms for the Piedmontese House of Savoy, the royal insignia set in mosaics in the Galleria floor directly below the crossing dome. Mengoni calculated its diameter to equal that of St. Peter's, to identify the Galleria as a secular cathedral honoring the political unification, the cultural progress and the distinct forms of consumption patronized by the newly emergent middle class. Its iconographic program included 24 statues of prominent Italian artists, scientists and political figures ringing the perimeter of the octagonal crossing and flanking each of the four entrances. Over two of the entrances were allegorical frescoes depicting Science, Art, Industry and Agriculture, the four bases of a bourgeois urban order. Lunette frescoes under the dome depicted the continents of Asia, Africa, America and an enthroned Europe, an allegory of the international, imperialistic reach of high capitalism. Decisively influencing the design of later arcades in Genoa, Naples, Rome and Munich—all sites of the intensified nationalism of the last half of the 19th century—these characteristics made the centrality of Milan's Galleria not just exceptional but absolute. For it became a secular *axis mundi* representing to Italy the Milanese pretension to be the country's moral center, and representing to the world the claims of the new Italian state on advanced bourgeois civilization.

—EDWARD W. WOLNER

SANT'AMBROGIO
Milan, Italy

Fourth century: Original church built (apses, southwest tower survive). **Ninth century:** Sanctuary built. **12th century:** Church rebuilt; atrium added. **1123:** Northwest tower begun. **Ca. 1281:** Northwest tower completed. **Ca. 1492:** Cloisters begun; **Architect:** Donato Bramante (1444-1514).

Sant'Ambrogio: Milan, Italy, 4th century

Sant'Ambrogio, western bay

Publications

BRIVIO, ERNESTO: *Guida della basilica di S. Ambrogio*. Milan, 1978.
PATETTA, LUCIANO: "Bramante e la trasformazione della basilica di Sant'Ambrogio a Milano." *Bollettino d'arte* 21 (1983): 49-74.
PORTER, ARTHUR KINGSLEY: *Lombard Architecture*. 4 vols. New Haven, Connecticut, 1915-17.
"Sant'Ambrogio." In *Le chiese di Milano*. Milan, 1985.

*

The Romanesque aesthetic is often closely related to the varied types of vaulting found in the interiors of churches. This is especially true in Lombardy, where early experiments in ribbed vaulting produced dramatic, centralized volumes. The Basilica of Sant'Ambrogio reveals the greatest advancement of the Lombard Romanesque aesthetic, and its nave is a marvel of broad, vaulted spaces.

Sant'Ambrogio is located on the site of Saint Ambrose's fourth-century church, and the present nave and side aisles rest upon those earlier foundations. The vast width of the church is, therefore, a remnant of the Early Christian design. The aisled basilica of four bays ends in a raised choir with three apses, and the entire fabric of the church incorporates fragments of various building campaigns into a harmonious whole.

The church is approached through an atrium, which, in its present form, was added in the late 12th century. The grand entrance court with vaulted walkways and plain, solid walls dominates the exterior and marks a return to the axiality of Roman and Early Christian churches. The exterior of the basilica is primarily constructed in brick, with accents of stone, and

Sant'Ambrogio, nave toward east

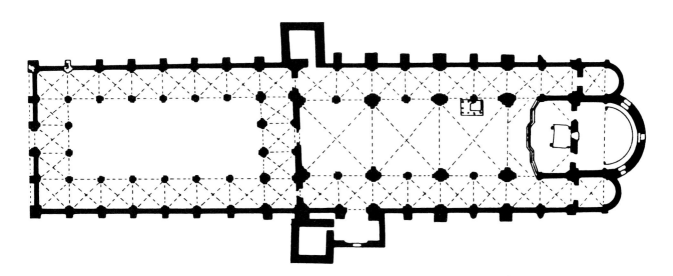

there is little detail to detract from the massiveness of the walls.

The gabled facade is rather austere in comparison with the sculpturally banded facades with lion portals usually found in Lombardy. A preference for planar, earthbound surfaces is revealed, although the five great arches of the loggia provide a dramatic counterpoint to the flatness of the facade. This alternation of solid and void creates a severe rhythm, which is repeated, in modified form, on the walls of the interior. The low, broad proportions of the exterior are relieved somewhat by the vertical articulation of the engaged colonnettes that divide the facade into five parts. Two flanking bell towers, set back from the facade, also provide massings that counteract the overall effect of horizontality.

Much of the light coming into the interior enters through the openings of the facade, as there are no clerestory windows along the central aisle. The rather wide spaces of the nave are divided into three square, double bays covered with ribbed groin vaults. The ribs of the vaults have rectangular profiles, as do the ribs of the semicircular transverse arches. The combination of square bays with these semicircular arches forms domical units that create an undulating movement of volumes. The vaults are supported by alternating, compound piers with richly sculpted capitals. This alternation of support creates a syncopation, which adds vitality to the progression of spaces toward the altar.

The two-story elevation includes a gallery with twin, round-headed arches in each bay, and the void of the arches contrasts with the subtly molded quality of the piers and wall surfaces. In addition to the play of shadow and light found in the nave, there is also a coloristic effect created by the polychromy of brick and stone.

Although the basilica has no transept, there is a clearly defined spatial separation between the nave proper and the raised sanctuary. The bay in front of the barrel-vaulted choir has an octagonal brick drum supporting a low tower. Openings in the tower create a circle of light around the ciborium, which shelters a Carolingian antependium known as the Paliotto of Sant'Ambrogio. The spotlight effect further enhances the position of the altar as the focal point of the basilica.

Beyond the altar is the raised sanctuary added to Sant'Ambrogio in the ninth century. The axial movement that began in the atrium reaches its culmination in the choir. The harmony of effect that is achieved is all the more remarkable in light of the span of time between the construction of the sanctuary and the atrium.

The lateral exteriors of the basilica experienced a striking transformation when Donato Bramante designed new cloisters for both the canons and the monks of Sant'Ambrogio. While preserving the traditional conventual arrangement, Bramante dramatically increased the scale, creating an imposing and decidedly new monumentality of form. The elevation of the monk's double cloister also experimented with the Doric and Ionic orders in an exploration of simplified elegance. The Renaissance expansion of the exterior was coordinated with a corresponding extension of the interior, where chapels were built between the buttresses along both side-aisle walls.

—KATHRYN McCLINTOCK

SAN LORENZO
Milan, Italy

Fourth century: Original church built, including chapels of San Aquilino and San Ippolito. **Sixth century:** Chapel of San Sisto built. **1071:** Church damaged in fire and remodeled; three exterior towers, groin vaults of ambulatory, octagonal piers or the exedrae built. **16th century:** Diagonal arches joining the inner piers, exterior drum, dome built. **19th century:** Facade added.

Publications

CALDERINI, ARISTIDE; CHIERICI, GINO; and CECCHELLI, CARLO: *La basilica di S. Lorenzo Maggiore in Milano.* Milan, 1951.

CHIERICI, GINO: *La basilica di S. Lorenzo in Milano.* Milan, 1938.

San Lorenzo: Milan, Italy, 4th century

San Lorenzo

MONNERET DE VILLARD, UGO: "Antichi disegni riguardanti il San Lorenzo di Milano." *Bollettino d'arte del Ministero dell'Istruzione* 5, 7 (Rome, 1911).

*

The original dedication of the Church of San Lorenzo in Milan, possibly correctly identified with the Basilica Portiana that is mentioned in early documents, is unknown, as is its original function. The traditional view that the church was a palace church was challenged recently by Richard Krautheimer, who suggested that the church, which lay outside the walls of the Roman city, was built by the late Roman Emperor Gratian as a cathedral for the Arians. Whatever the religious and sociological climate of its origin, the Church of San Lorenzo was unique in the architecture of Italy and was one of the most complex among Early Christian buildings in the West.

Although much of the present appearance was a result of later alterations, the essential elements of the original, fourth-century structure were retained. A 1071 fire necessitated extensive repairs. From that period or slightly later came three of the four exterior towers, the groin vaults of the ambulatory, and the present octagonal piers of the exedrae. To the 16th century date the diagonal arches joining the inner piers, the high exterior drum, and the octagonal dome, which replaced an original square drum and lower timber, or groin-vaulted, dome. The present facade is 19th-century.

In front of the church lay a large atrium with a monumental propylaeum at the west. The propylaeum still stands, consisting of a colonnade of reused columns with Corinthian capitals supporting an entablature. These columns, like much of the material used in the building of San Lorenzo, were *spoglia*.

Although the dome was rebuilt and raised, the original exterior impression of a tightly assembled body of spaces is still conveyed. The large geometric volumes of apses, dome and corner towers hug the central core of the church. This multitowered exterior became the norm in later medieval church architecture.

Subsidiary chapels attached to the exterior of the apses give the whole the feel of a revolving compound. Fortunately, a large, open outdoor space surrounds San Lorenzo today, allowing a rare perspective in comparison with the usual cramped location of ancient buildings in busy urban centers. There one can truly experience the massiveness and majesty of the structure in a comprehensive view. It is there, too, that the beauty of the workmanship can be appreciated, with its masonry of thick bricks and thin mortar beds of the highest quality and attractiveness.

The design of the church was not new. The centralized plan, based on the projection of four apses from the four sides of a square and an inner distribution of piers and exedrae that echoed the outer profile, produced an "aisled tetraconch" design. The same type appeared earlier in Constantine's Golden Octagon in Antioch, Syria. The plan was also common in fourth-century baths and palaces, but none survives intact like San Lorenzo.

The entrance to the church through the center of the west apse today brings one face to face with the Baroque altar. The central "nave" is spacious, tall and wide; the structure appears

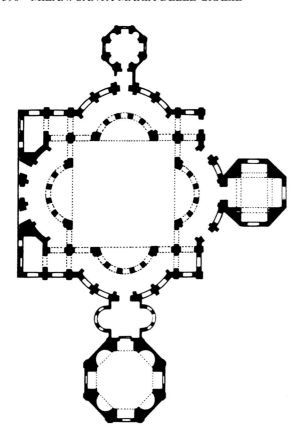

solid. The heaviness of the walls and piers, and even moldings—in part, a result of later remodelings—was typically Roman. It established a "space defined by structure," rather than an ethereal structure defined by a neverending space, so common to later Byzantine, double-shell buildings.

The stone piers also assert their structural strength and that of the interior as a whole. The walls, once sheathed in marble, now expose their nude brickwork; the original dome mosaic is also gone now. The four interior exedrae bend away from the center and open the space to diverse views into the surrounding shell, without vanishing into it. The definition of the central space is retained by the angular corner piers, once forming a square but now forming an octagon, and by the flat wall surfaces above the wide, round arches of the semidomes. Without doubt the building is complicated, but in no way is it mysterious or does it hide the components that make it stand.

The corner piers of the square were spanned by tall arches in two stories, corresponding to the two-story elevation of the surrounding shell with its ground floor ambulatory and second-story gallery. The four exedrae were also of two stories, each with a double row of arcades, originally resting on columns and having five openings each. The repetition of round arches in ascending tiers is purely Roman in inspiration, as seen, for example, in the classic designs of the Colosseum or the aqueducts. The arcades carry heavy projecting cornices (perhaps more emphatic than the original stucco moldings) that continue across the piers, creating horizontal lines to balance the verticals of the columns. The articulation of the flat pilasters is also of later date and gives a relief-like, sculptural appearance. The linear quality is echoed in the surface carving of the remodeled upper walls. The interior was well lit from windows in the ambulatory, gallery and drum.

Two of the three subsidiary chapels attached to the outer sides of the apses—the spacious Chapel of San Aquilino to the

south and the Chapel of San Ippolito to the east—belong to the same original construction as San Lorenzo. San Aquilino was probably built as the imperial mausoleum. It was treated as a separate building to which one entered from the ambulatory of San Lorenzo through an attached, double-apsed and square, barrel-vaulted atrium.

The exterior of San Aquilino is octagonal, and the domed, two-story interior has alternating semicircular and straight niches. The walls are closed and solid. The nudeness of San Lorenzo is present there, too, due to the loss of much of the original marble and mosaic decoration, with the exception of substantial remains of two famous fourth-century mosaics in the south niches. The gallery, with its large, round-arched windows, is no more than a low passage cut into the thickness of the wall. The design is consistent with, but simpler than, the design of the church.

The somewhat smaller Chapel of San Ippolito is entered directly from the east ambulatory, and it, too, is octagonal on the outside. The bare, vaulted interior has four rectangular niches in the shape of a Greek cross. The smallest chapel, San Sisto, on the north side, was added in the sixth century. It is almost identical in plan to San Aquilino and is entered through a very small, square atrium. Most interesting are the remains of the ancient floor and doors.

In some ways, San Lorenzo pointed the way to later Byzantine developments of the double-shell design, though these were created in an essentially different, Eastern aesthetic. Wall mass was denied, verticality predominated, light shaped space, and structural members were dematerialized through intricate surface carving or light-reflecting mosaics. In other ways, San Lorenzo was the forerunner of later medieval developments in the West, where the integrity of the wall was reinstated, where walls formed spatial boundaries, where the structure of a building was "read" in its essential shapes, and where towers and volumes were stacked around central cores.

—PAULA D. LEVETO-JABR

SANTA MARIA DELLE GRAZIE
Milan, Italy

1464-72: Original complex built; **Architect:** Giuniforte Solari. **1492:** New choir built, apse end extended; **Architect:** Donato Bramante (1444-1514). **1495-ca. 1497:** Fresco of the Last Supper painted in refectory of convent; **Artist:** Leonardo da Vinci (1452-1519).

Publications

PEDRETTI, CARLO: "The Original Project for the S. Maria Delle Grazie." *Journal of the Society of Architectural Historians.* 32 (1973): 30-42.

*

Santa Maria delle Grazie in Milan is a Dominican church and friary, famous now for the fresco of the *Last Supper* by Leonardo da Vinci to be found in the refectory. The complex was erected on land granted the Dominicans of Pavia by Count Gaspare Vimercato, commander of the forces of Francesco Sforza, duke of Milan. The support continued; Ludovico Sforza, wishing to

Santa Maria delle Grazie: Milan, Italy, 1464-82

Santa Maria delle Grazie

give expression to his power and authority through new buildings in Milan, chose Santa Maria delle Grazie as the court
church and the burial place for his family. This required a more
splendid structure, and in March 1492 the archbishop, Guido
d'Antonio, laid the foundations for a new choir designed by
Donato Bramante; it was to rise over what had been built there
by Giuniforte Solari 20 years earlier. The monastery itself was
decorated throughout—hence the fresco by Leonardo. The nave
and facade were to be rebuilt, and designs were submitted in
1497, but because of political events that led to the expulsion
of Ludovico in 1499, these last projects were never completed.

The church is divisible into two sections; the older parts by
Solari and the great, new tribune by Bramante. The facade of
the church is of a type—traditional in Lombardy—spare in
decoration and marked only by a small marble portal. The
church itself is similarly spare but expanded to an extraordinary
scale. In a sense it is a variation on the idea found in the Old
Sacristy of San Lorenzo, Florence, and since that was built as a
memorial chapel for the Medici, this may have been a deliberate
adaptation of the type by Bramante, done this time for the
Sforzas. The wide space of the church is flooded with light
from the great niches and the rows of windows in the huge
dome, so that the walls seem like thin shells; this thinness is
further enhanced by the delicate and economical motifs Bramante set throughout, something perhaps at odds with the vast
space. Indeed, it may be said that this was the last work, of
this intention, that could still be carried out in the technical and
formal language of the 15th century, Bramante turning afterward
to Rome and the monumental traditions of Roman architecture.
The other parts of the complex are necessarily less impressive.
Behind the tribune is the presbytery, rectangular in shape, ending

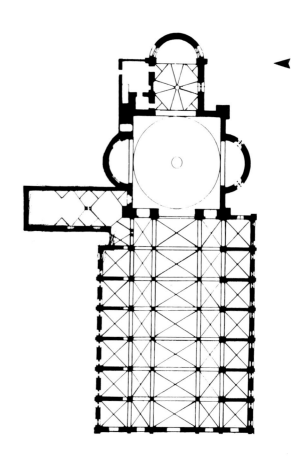

in an apse; to the left is a small cloister, perhaps by Bramante, and beyond that the Sagrestia Vecchia, also by Bramante, also rectangular in plan, with a small apse.

The refectory, or *cenacolo vinciano,* is at the other end of the complex and is a separate building, approached by a small atrium, added in the 17th century. It is a long rectangular space, built also by Solari; there, on the far wall, is the fresco of the *Last Supper,* painted there between 1495 and 1497 by Leonardo. The work began to disintegrate almost immediately: Pietro Aretino spoke of it by 1547 as virtually ruined. The whole room, together with other parts of the complex, was badly damaged in 1943. It is being carefully restored, however, in a campaign begun in the early 1980s under the supervision of Pinin Brambilla Barcilon, reinforcing work done there in 1953 by Mauro Pellicoli. During the war, the neighboring Choistro Grande o dei Morti, also by Solari, was destroyed but has been rebuilt.

Besides the *Last Supper,* the church and friary contain a number of other interesting works. Opposite the *Last Supper* is a fresco of the Crucifixion by Donato di Montorfano, done in 1495. In the chapels of the church are the 15th-century tomb of Francesco Olgiati, a general of Francesco II Sforza; the tombs of the Della Torre family (1483), by Attilio and Tomaso Cazzaniga; in the fourth chapel on the right, a group of frescoes by Gaudenzio Ferrari (ca. 1540); and in the farthest chapel to the right, an altar painting by Marco d'Oggiono. In the corner of the small cloister is a painting, in monochrome, by Bartolommeo Suardi, il Bramantino; at the other end is a bust of Ludovico il Moro, set in a black marble frame of the late 17th century. Yet it is, of course, to the fresco of the *Last Supper* that visitors have been drawn over the centuries; and any account we make of that work now, whatever evidence the last cleaning reveals to us, will depend in part on the testimonies and visual records of those visitors; most notable are a copy by the French artist Andŕe Dutertre done about 1790, just before the occupation of the buildings by Napoleon's troops, and another once-famous copy of Giuseppe Bossi done in 1810, which was destroyed in World War II and is known now only in photographs.

—DAVID CAST

CATHEDRAL OF SANTA MARIA LA NUOVA
Monreale, Sicily

1174-82: Construction of main church. **1172-89:** Cloisters built. **1770:** Portico added. **1807:** Northern tower damaged by lightning.

Publications

DEMUS, OTTO: *The Mosaics of Norman Sicily.* London, 1949.
KITZINGER, E.: *The Mosaics of Monreale.* Palermo, 1961.
KRÖNIG, W.: *The Cathedral of Monreale.* Palermo, 1965.

*

In the 12th and 13th centuries, when the Cathedral of Santa Maria la Nuova was built in Monreale, Sicily was home to a unique mixture of peoples, faiths and cultures. The island had come under Norman rule in the 11th century, which meant that Roman Catholicism was the official religion. Wisely, however,

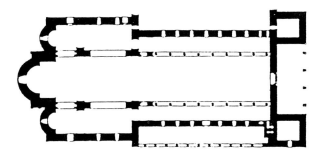

the sizable Orthodox and Muslim Greek and Moorish populations were granted religious freedom. Beyond embracing religious tolerance, the Normans were apparently well able to cooperate with other established groups, utilizing the particular expertise of each. Sicilian architecture of that period is proof of this mutual ability to cooperate. The Romanesque Monreale Cathedral, which survives today much in its original state, is the most significant product of that confluence of cultures. The architecture, though peculiar to Sicily in many respects, shows a Norman influence, following models of Early Romanesque northern churches. The mosaics, the cathedral's chief glory, are Byzantine. Many other decorative features, particularly the decoration of the exterior and of the nave ceiling, are Islamic. The sculpture, on the other hand, is by and large Catalan and Provençal in orientation, while the bronze doors in the western and northern portals must have been executed by Pisan and Apulian masters. Although it does not seem that any attempt was made to achieve a stylistic synthesis out of the diverse elements, the cathedral, particularly its breathtaking interior, shows a happy coexistence of divergent traditions. The result was an ensemble of overwhelming beauty.

Founded in 1174 by William II of Sicily and consecrated in 1267, the cathedral was originally part of the royal complex at Monreale in the Conca d'Oro, situated on a mountainous slope above Palermo. The carefully selected site affords a magnificent view of the sea, the bay and the city of Palermo itself. The complex consisted of a royal palace (now the archiepiscopal seminary), an archiepiscopal palace and a monastery besides the cathedral, which formed the center of the complex. In plan and elevation, the building closely followed nearby Cefalù Cathedral, which was under construction when work at Monreale was begun. Cefalù was built on a cruciform plan with extremely shallow transepts. The emphasis was placed on the three-apse east end, where work was first begun. The three-aisle basilican nave was built last on a reduced plan, so that the nave is lower than the transepts. The unusual distribution of height again added to the weight of the east end. Cefalù's western facade is fronted by a central portal flanked by two towers as was typical of Romanesque architecture north of the Alps.

What was the result of circumstance at Cefalù became design at Monreale. In its severe simplicity, the western facade with its central portal and scarcely articulated flanking towers stands in startling contrast to the highly elaborate east end. The only visual connection of the western facade to the elaborately decorated east end is the row of interlaced blind arches above the central portico. The exterior of the east end, on the other hand, is completely covered with a forest of such interlaced, blind pointed arches, each again inlaid with stones of different colors

Cathedral of Santa Maria la Nuova: Monreale, Sicily, Italy, 1174-82

in Islamic motifs. The soft pinks and yellows of the arches against the white wall provide an enchanting color scheme, but as a whole the decoration is overwrought and completely obscures the architecture.

The western facade is the part of the building that has undergone the most change in the course of the centuries. The central portico, which hides the original portal and seems so completely out of place, is in fact an addition of the 1770s. The asymmetry of the design of the western facade is exaggerated by the fact that the northern tower lost its spire when it was hit by lightning in 1807.

The three-aisle nave behind the facade is covered by an open wood ceiling painted with Islamic designs. The ceiling is a conservative feature, since Romanesque churches elsewhere were being vaulted by that time as a consequence of fireproofing requirements. The side aisles are separated from the central nave by Corinthian gray granite columns supporting Islamic pointed arches. A heavy arch and cornice mark the transition to the crossing, which is covered by a saddle roof. The shallow transepts, covered by groin vaults, barely project. The sanctuary

terminates in three tall apses, the straight part of which is covered by barrel vaults.

The inlaid floors, the painted ceiling and arches, and the mosaics on the upper wall surfaces of the nave, for all their polychrome richness, do not detract from the powerful focus on the sanctuary and the central apse beyond. This is due in part to the fact that the nave is the same height as the transepts, but more particularly because of the repetition of diminishing shapes, which gives the entire interior a tunnel-like quality, drawing the eye ineluctably to the east end. The arch at the end of the nave is echoed by that at the end of the crossing, by the longitudinal barrel vault in the first part of the apse, and by the arch that marks the transition to the semicircular termination of the apse with its pointed semidome. The interior architecture, then, privileges to an unusual degree the mosaics in the termination of the apse.

The semicircular wall space is divided into levels by continuous cornices as at Cefalù, but where Cefalù has three stages, Monreale has four. The lower level is taken up by the altar. The second level is pierced by the central (and only) window,

Cathedral of Santa Maria la Nuova

which is flanked by mosaics of saints on each side. The third level depicts the Madonna and Child surrounded by angels. The half figure of the Pantocrator, right hand raised and holding the Book of Life in his left, towers over the ensemble, dominating the entire cathedral. Again the example was furnished by Cefalù, which in turn was derived from the Pantocrator at the Church of the Dormition at Daphni, Greece. It is possible that Daphni exercised a direct influence on Monreale: whereas the Cefalù Pantocrator is characterized by a weary, melancholy mien, at Monreale he wears the severe, almost unforgiving, expression of the Daphni model. In his indomitable power and presence, the Monreale Pantocrator truly presides over the cathedral. Upon crossing the western threshold, one encounters the mosaic of Christ, which—with the Virgin and angels immediately below him, and the whole ringed by the saints—establishes the hierarchy of the Christian faith. Mosaics of the apostles Peter and Paul are arranged in rather similar schemes in the side apses, and the remaining wall spaces are devoted to an inventory of lesser Christian sainthood and the range of biblical history. This wealth of divine history is a forceful reminder of man's humble position in the divine scheme.

Since Monreale Cathedral's consecration in the 13th century, work there has consisted principally of repairs and restorations, following upon serious neglect in the 14th century. Several chapels were added in the course of the centuries, which neither significantly added to nor detracted from the cathedral. The unfortunate 18th-century western portico was balanced by a rather more felicitous northern portico facing the erstwhile royal palace. That later ages have largely respected this Romanesque monument to the unique cultural confluence of 12th-century Sicily may be due as much to the extraordinary power of the variegated ensemble as it is to the fact that Sicily ceased to be a major political and cultural center with the collapse of Norman rule in the late 13th century.

—MARIJKE RIJSBERMAN

CASTEL NUOVO
Naples, Italy

1279-82. Architects: Planned by Pierre d'Angicourt; built by Paumier d'Arras and Pierre de Chaulnes. **Mid 15th century:** Remodeled; **Architect:** Guglielmo Sagrera. **1495:** Reconstruction begun; **Architect:** Francesco di Giorgio Martini. **1499:** Bastions added; **Architect:** Antonio Marchesi. **18th century:** Remodeling. **1871-75:** Most bastions removed during remodeling.

Publications

WITTKOWER, RUDOLF: *Art and Architecture in Italy 1600-1750*. Harmondsworth, England, 1973.

Castel Nuovo: Naples, Italy, 1279-83

The Castel Nuovo, the "New Castle", rises above a hill in the southeastern part of Naples, looking out over what is called the Bacino Angioino. The castle takes its name from the fact that it was established after the two other such structures in Naples: the Castel de'Ovo, begun about 1130, and the Castel Capuano (or La Vicaria), which was founded in the second half of the 12th century; these earlier structures are in the northeast part of the city, near the road to Capua, the Porta Capuano.

The Castel Nuovo, known also as the Maschio Angioino ("Angevin Tower"), was established by Charles of Anjou, between 1279 and 1282 on the site of a house of the Franciscans, Santa Maria ad Palatium. The work began under the architectural direction of Pierre d'Angicourt, the court builder responsible also for the castles at Lucera (1270-84) and Canosa (1271). The whole structure was remodeled by Alfonso I of Aragon in the mid-15th century, with the Spanish architect Guglielmo Sagrera, to become both a fortress and a proper royal residence; commentators of the period suggested that the residential aspect may have been modeled on the ideas of Vitruvius. A range of bastions was added, begun in 1499 by Antonio Marchesi, and a second moat, which was remodeled extensively in the 18th

century by Ferdinand IV. The bastions were mostly removed when further work was done between 1871 and 1875.

The form of the original castle nonetheless remains: an irregular range of rooms around a central courtyard, marked by four massive towers at the corners. On the west, between the Torre di San Giorgio and the Torre del Beverello, an enormous 18th-century screen covers the older parts. To the north, a large public room, the Sala dei Baroni, added by Sagrera, now functions as the seat of the Consiglio Communale. To the east, a range of rooms is screened by a 15th-century masonry wall. The famous Arch of Alfonso is situated on the south. The arch is the most significant work of Renaissance Naples, and was built between 1454 and 1467 to record the triumph of Alfonso that had taken place in Naples some 11 years earlier.

Alfonso was but one of several famous rulers who lived in the Castel Nuovo after Charles of Anjou. Most notable among them was Charles' immediate successor, King Roberto, whose court was described by Boccaccio and who was responsible for the magnificent Capella Palatina (Church of Santa Barbara), which was once decorated with paintings by Giotto. After Alfonso and then Ferdinand I, whose court was notable for the

Castel Nuovo

many famous scholars in residence, the castle was occupied by Spanish kings: Charles V after 1535, John of Austria after 1575, and then until the end of the 18th century the Bourbon kings, most famous of them Don Carlo di Borbone, king in the mid-18th century. In most recent years, the castle has been the home of a number of cultural institutions, especially the Società Napoletana di Storia Patria, founded in 1875 under the patronage of Benedetto Croce, among others. The Castel Nuovo is also the seat of the Biblioteca Comunale Cuomo.

Apart from the great Arch of Alfonso, the castle contains a number of other important works of art. Behind the arch is another portal, the so-called Porta de Bronzo (1460s), which shows the coronation of Ferdinand I and six bas-reliefs telling the story of his various triumphs. Within the Cappella Palatina is an elegant 15th-century portal—perhaps by the artist of the Arch of Alfonso—with the most delicate reliefs, including one in the lunette of the Madonna and Child by Andrea dell'Aquila. In the sacristy is a Madonna by the 15th-century sculptor Domenico Gagini and a ciborium, with a relief of the Last Supper, by Jacopo della Pila. To the side of the chapel, leading to the Sala dei Baroni, is a magnificent winding staircase of some 147 steps. Leading from the Sala dei Baroni back to the rooms of the west range is the Portale del Trionfo, which was decorated with a relief by Francesco Laurana that was destroyed in a fire in 1919. On the outside is another relief by Gagini showing the entry of Alfonso into the Castel Nuovo.

Despite the fact that Naples has been changed and built up in the past few years, the Castel Nuovo is an imposing monument that can suggest even now the local and artistic position it must have enjoyed in the Renaissance city.

—DAVID CAST

SAN FRANCESCO DI PAOLA
Naples, Italy

1808: Colonnade of piazza built; **Architect:** Leopoldo Laperuta. **1817:** Building of church begun; **Architect:** Pietro Bianchi (1787-1849). **1831:** Building completed.

Publications

VENDITTI, A.: *Architettura neoclassica a Napoli.* Naples, 1961.

The Church of San Francesco di Paola was designed by the Swiss architect Pietro Bianchi under the orders of Ferdinand I, king of the Two Sicilies, and begun in 1817. The building was part of Napoléon's great scheme for what is now the Piazza del Plebiscito, begun by Joachim Murat, king of Naples during Napoléon's reign; a great colonnade was to be built around the piazza to regularize the space opposite the Palazzo Reale. This colonnade, designed by Leopoldo Laperuta and begun in 1808, was semi-elliptical in plan—obviously modeled on Giovanni Lorenzo Bernini's colonnade in front of St. Peter's in Rome. Bianchi's church was set into the colonnade, directly opposite the Palazzo Reale.

The whole complex in Naples was yet another instance of the form, so popular in Italian neoclassicism in those years, of a design based on either the Parthenon or the Pantheon, with attachments spreading out; similar buildings from about the same time include the Chiesa della Madre di Dio in Turin (1818-31) by Ferdinando Buonsignore and the Rotonda at Ghisalba (1834) by Luigi Cagnola. Bianchi had studied with Cagnola, and like his master, he knew his archaeology. But Bianchi was not bound by it, and his variations at San Francesco on the design of the Pantheon are subtle and effective. The portico is Ionic hexastyle, *in antis,* with pierced end walls. There is no attic, but in its place are two domed cylindrical chapels (in one plan there were to be four, one at each corner) that work visually to link the main dome with the portico and the colonnade that joins it.

The great dome inside (about 53 meters in height) rises to a far greater height proportionally than that of the Pantheon; the San Francesco dome is articulated, below a cornice line, with 34 Corinthian columns of marble from Mondragone; above are 34 equal pilasters, and between them and the lantern at the top is a pattern of "collapsing" squared coffers. Despite its regularity, all this work is rich in effect, and eight statues, placed at regular intervals around the circle, add to this richness; the sculptors included Carlo Finelli, Giuseppe de Fabris and Toto Angeli. Also decorating the church are works of art brought from other churches: an altar of lapis lazuli by Anselmo Canigiano, made in 1641, and a painting of the Circumcision by Antonio Campi, from 1586.

In the church's interior, but especially in the exterior design, Bianchi was able to blend very successfully a range of elements—some from Rome, some from Palladio, some from the Baroque—mixing parts that were to be understood separately with others that were to be seen together, creating a notable effect that may be called urban scenography. All the parts of this design may be based on earlier plans of Giovanni Antonio Selva (1751-1819), who had traveled throughout Europe and seen several other examples; certainly the idea of using a monument like the Pantheon, with a colonnade attached, can be seen in plans by Giacomo Quarenghi and in one for Washington, D.C., by Robert Mills.

San Francesco di Paola: Naples, Italy, 1808

It is perhaps too much to say that any of these imitations surpass their models, but Bianchi—using as his first step the earlier work of Laperuta—achieved nonetheless an extraordinarily successful combination of diverse elements that was of great significance in the history of architecture in Naples. The turn to neoclassicism in Naples came from a variety of sources, or as Nikolaus Pevsner noted, "with Joseph Bonaparte and Joachim Murat, the Pantheon and the Piazza of St. Peter's, or indirectly via Marie-Joseph Peyre and the style of the Parisian *Grands Prix.*"

—DAVID CAST

PIAZZA VIGLIENA (I QUATTRO CANTI)
Palermo, Sicily, Italy

1608: Building begun; **Architects:** Until 1617 Giulio Lasso; after 1617 Mariano Smiriglio (1569-1636); **Sculptors:** *Autumn* and *Winter* by Nunzio la Mattina; *Spring* and *Summer* by Gregorio Tedeschi; Spanish monarchs by Carlo d'Aprile.

Publications

BOSCARINO, S.: *Sicilia barocca: architettura e città.* Rome, 1986.
BLUNT, ANTHONY: *Barocco siciliano.* Milan, 1968.
CARONIA ROBERTI, SALVATORE: *Il barocco in Palermo.* Palermo, 1935.
GUIDONI MARINO, ANGELA: "La componente scenografica nell'urbanistica barocca in Sicilia." Pp. 123-128 in *La scenografia barocca.* Bologna, 1982.
WITTKOWER, RUDOLF: *Art and Architecture in Italy 1600-1750.* Harmondsworth, England, 1973.

*

Inspired by, but more impressive than, Pope Sixtus V's Quattro Fontane (1588) in Rome, the Quattro Canti (begun 1608) stand proudly, each screen over one hundred feet tall, at the intersection of Via Toledo and Via Maqueda in the center of the old city of Palermo. They are one of the few surviving results of Palermo's ambitious program of urbanization and rivalry with Rome. Their position, form and iconography reveal much about the intentions of urbanization projects, urban ideologies and the relationships between civil and ecclesiastical, Spanish and Sicilian powers in early-17th-century Palermo.

During the 16th century, the Spanish faced a growing fear of the disintegration of their empire throughout Europe, and particular tension with the Turks in Sicily and the Mediterranean. In Sicily, this unease seems to have prompted the systematic idealization and mythologizing of Palermo (which gradually eclipsed Messina as the seat of government), initiating the era of rule by propaganda, which reflected the growing gap between the city's real significance and the pretensions of its most powerful inhabitants. As their reputation depended on it, the Spanish viceroys undertook conspicuous urban "embellishments." Thus were opened Via Toledo (from the Royal Palace to the

Piazza Vigliena (I Quattro Cante): Palermo, Sicily, Italy, 1608

sea) in the 1560s and Via Maqueda in the 1590s. These streets cut Palermo into four sections, and it was at their intersection that Viceroy Vigliena began a fine Baroque octagon, the Quattro Canti, in 1608. If Rome provided the most obvious model for this development, the "Ochavo" in Valladolid (1561-95) may also have been influential. But the intention of the Viceroy was to celebrate the *status quo* in Sicily in general and Palermo in particular.

The Quattro Canti is composed of four screens, divided into three stories by Tuscan, Ionic and Corinthian orders. The four seasons, Spanish sovereigns and Palermitan saints are represented in statuary in the lower, middle and upper stories, respectively. Thus nature, Spanish rule and local religious beliefs are conflated into an unequivocal statement about urban power.

Begun by Giulio Lasso in 1608, only the bare architectural structure was ready by 1620; after 1617, the work was directed by the Senate's architect, Mariano Smiriglio (1569-1636). The modeling is florid, stiff and undistinguished: "Autumn" and "Winter" are by Nunzio la Mattina, "Spring" and "Summer" by the Florentine sculptor Gregorio Tedeschi; the Spanish monarchs—Philip IV, Philip III, Philip II and Charles V—are by Carlo d'Aprile.

In addition to marking spectacularly two important routes through the city, linking the Royal Palace, cathedral and other significant churches, the Senate and aristocratic palaces, the Quattro Canti successfully screened the slums behind from the view of resident aristocrats and important foreign visitors. Their principal function, however, was to provide a permanent focus, or theater, for temporary religious festivities or political gatherings—hence the piazza's popular name, "Teatro del Sole." Religious and political festivals (especially the feast of Saint

Rosalia) and their attendant hierarchical processions were an important element in governing 17th-century Palermo. Altars, arches, canopies and baldachinos, made of wood, card, papier-mâché, brightly painted and illuminated with thousands of candles and torches, were set up between and below the screens during *feste*. Themes echoed those of the permanent architecture: the protection of the city by its patron saints, the virtues of the Spanish monarchy, the natural blessings with which Palermo was bestowed and which reflected divine favor and the necessary harmony prevailing between these powers. Thus urban interventions functioned as propaganda to celebrate, articulate and strengthen the alliance between the aristocracy and the Catholic Church—in spite of the stifling effect of that alliance on independent economic, cultural or intellectual initiatives within the city.

—HELEN HILLS

CERTOSA
Pavia, Italy

1396-1402: Construction begun, foundations completed; **General Contractor:** Bernardo da Venezia. **1402-34:** Living quarters, communal buildings and service areas built, construction of church begun. **1461-97:** Monastary completed, interior decoration of church completed. **1474-55:** Facade of church built;

Certosa: Pavia, Italy, 1396-1402

Architects: Begun by Giovanni Solari, decorations by Cristoforo Mantegazza, Giovanni Amadeo. **1497:** Church consecrated. **1895:** Monastery restored

Publications

DURELLI, G., and DURELLI, F.: *La Certosa di Pavia*. 1853.

*

The Certosa of Pavia is a Carthusian monastery and church near Milan, at the edge of the private park of its founder, the duke of Milan, Gian Galeazzo Visconti. The whole complex was a home for the Carthusians, a strict, contemplative religious order. But it was also intended to be a monument to the Visconti family, for Gian Galeazzo chose the church to be his burial place; he included in his will a description of the tomb he wanted, reportedly expecting that his two wives and their deceased would also be buried there. The Carthusians, appropriately, were especially noted for their intercessory prayers on behalf of a particular dynasty or family. Construction was begun

on the site in 1396, and records from that year name Bernardo da Venezia as the general contractor. But the progress was slow, and by 1402 only the foundations had been completed. It was then that the prior of the monastery chose Antonio da Crema to be the *ingeniere* for the site, and it was he who was responsible for the subsequent building of the living quarters for the monks, the communal buildings and the service areas, including kitchens and storerooms and areas for the lay brothers.

By the time all these parts were completed (ca. 1434), the construction of the church was also under way, though little was done to it for the next decade. But between 1451 and 1454 another attempt was made to resume the building. The monastery was finally completed after 1461 when the newest duke, Francesco Sforza, assumed control and appointed his own superintendent, Bartolommeo Gadio, to set up a new building office that would be in charge of the project. The church was given its present interior decoration in the last few years of the 15th century, and was consecrated on 3 May 1497. The facade, which had been begun in 1474, was intermittently worked on until 1555, and its upper parts are still incomplete.

For all this history of starts and stops, however, the whole complex is remarkable. The church, which is dedicated to Santa Maria delle Grazie, is a notable example of quattrocento Lombard architecture. Around the church are the offices of the monks, including the so-called Great Cloister, which is surrounded by the cells of the monks and is one of the great repositories of Milanese religious sculpture. The colonnade, with some 122 divisions in all, have richly ornamented columns and wall capitals that hold up a superstructure, itself embellished with a large number of molded figures. The Small Cloister between the Great Cloister and the church is similarly embellished with sculpture, and the space is filled with a fountain that makes this area softer in effect and more intimate.

The church itself is full, inside and out, of decorations. The facade begun by Giovanni Solari and decorated by Cristoforo Mantegazza and Giovanni Amadeo, has a whole range of detail: a rich portal, perhaps designed by Gian Cristoforo Romano; medals along the basement that were done in imitation of Roman coins; and a form of polychrome decoration across the front that serves to make order out of all the varying elements set into it. The inside of the church is more harmonious, the style being between that of Italian Gothic architecture and what came soon after in the Renaissance. Among the remarkable works in the church are a painting of Saint Ambrose and Saints (1490) by Andrea Bergognone, the tomb statues of Ludovico il Moro and Beatrice d'Este (1499) by Cristoforo Solari, two bronze candelabras (1580) by Annibale Fontana, and the tomb of Gian Galeazzo Viconti (1497) by Gian Cristoforo Romano. In the chapels to the right of the nave are a number of 17th-century paintings by such artists as Camillo Procaccini, Guercino and Carlo Cornara.

The later history of the complex is mixed. The Carthusian order itself was suppressed in 1782, and after much discussion and many delays the buildings were taken over by the state. Much of the Certosa suffered during that period of neglect; however, in 1895 a general restoration of the whole monastery was begun, especially in the area of the large cloister, where the walls were reconsolidated and the roofs of the cells and corridor were replaced. All this work was done with a proper sense of history, and the result is a monument properly and gloriously preserved, and one, as the guidebooks say, that is one of the most suggestive in all Italy.

—DAVID CAST

PISA CATHEDRAL
Pisa, Italy

1063: Cathedral begun. **1104-10:** Construction nearly completed; **Architect:** Buschettus. **1117:** Church consecrated. **1153:** Baptistery foundation laid; **Architect:** Diotisalvi. **1174:** Construction of campanile begun and immediately suspended. **Ca. 1185:** Ground story of Baptistery completed. **1246:** Baptismal font installed; **Architect:** Guido da Como. **Ca. 1250:** Original facade of church demolished; basilica extended three bays to the west; new facade built. **1250-65:** Exterior of Baptistery remodeled; **Architect:** Nicola Pisano (d. 1284). **Ca. 1260-1394:** Transverse arches and diaphragm walls added to Baptistery gallery; destruction and rebuilding of exterior Baptistery gallery wall; new covering for Baptistery built and cupoletta added to cone. **1261-72:** Nave of cathedral extended; **Architect:** Rainaldus. **1275-84:** Construction of Campanile resumed and again halted. **1278-83:** Campo Santo built; **Architect:** Giovanni di Simone. **1350:** Campanile completed; belfry added; **Architect:**

Tommaso Pisano. **14th-15th century:** Interior frescoes and Gothic tracery in courtyard added to Campo Santo.

Publications

KOSEGARTEN, ANTJE: "Die Skulpturen der Pisani am Baptisterium von Pisa: Zum Werk von Nicola und Giovanni Pisano." *Jahrbuch der Berliner Museen* 10 (1968): 14-100.
SANPAOLESI, PIERO: *Il Duomo di Pisa.* Pisa, 1975.
SMITH, CHRISTINE: *The Baptistery of Pisa.* New York, 1978.
SMITH, CHRISTINE: "The Date and Authorship of the Pisa Duomo Facade." *Gesta* 19, 2 (1980): 95-108.
SMITH, CHRISTINE: "East or West in 11th-Century Pisan Culture: The Dome of the Cathedral and Its Western Counterparts." *Journal of the Society of Architectural Historians* 43 (October 1984): 195-208.

*

One of the most elegant groupings of ecclesiastical buildings of the medieval period, the complex at Pisa consists of a cathedral, baptistery, bell tower and enclosed cemetery. The complex is a monument to the city's expansion in the 11th century to become a dominant Mediterranean power, a position the city held for more than 200 years. Pisa's location on the west coast of Italy, near the "Via Francigena" (the land route of commerce and pilgrimage), encouraged trade, travel and military exploits, but not without a long period of armed conflict with both Saracen and Italian rivals. The culminating Battle of Palermo (1062) brought the Pisans final success. To celebrate their victory, they vowed to dedicate a new cathedral to the Virgin; it was at that time that the construction of the city's ecclesiastical center began.

The complex is located on the northwest edge of the medieval city, in an area archaeologists have discovered to be rich in ancient Roman and medieval ruins. This area may have served as the religious center as early as the ninth century, but certainly by the 10th, as attested in documents that refer to a baptistery there. Further evidence to support this theory came from excavations in the Campo Santo during the 1930s which uncovered the ruins of a non-Roman octagonal foundation believed to have been the original baptistery.

One of the most interesting features of the cathedral complex is its stylistic harmony, a harmony which extends beyond the marble facing and arcading common to all. Scholars have debated how this harmony was achieved, and whether it is due to an original plan for the complex as a whole. This harmony is all the more curious because the complex was built over a period of 400 years in a series of overlapping campaigns from the foundation of the cathedral in 1063 to the completion of the cemetery, or Campo Santo, in 1464. It is likely that this stylistic harmony is due to the continuous existence of a "Piazza Workshop" on this site. This workshop, established for the cathedral, defined the architectural and decorative vocabulary used throughout the complex in the following centuries.

The monuments on the piazza have often been referred to as the earliest and finest examples of the style of the Pisan Romanesque. This style is characterized there by ground-story blind arcades, multicolored revetment, the reuse of ancient *spolia*, and freestanding arcades. With subtle variations, these elements are repeated in all four buildings, regardless of the date of execution, and suggest a constant turning back by each generation of builders to the earliest designs for the complex and, hence, to the city's period of glory.

The need for a new cathedral became apparent with the city's growing importance as a center for trade and as a stop along

Pisa Cathedral: Pisa, Italy, 1063

the route for pilgrims visiting Rome or the Holy Land. Indeed, the grandeur of scale and richness of materials used at the cathedral and throughout the piazza suggest that visitors were being appealed to by the Pisans to believe that their city could compete in magnificence with any other.

Begun in 1063 by an unknown architect, the cathedral was brought to near-completion by Buschettus, an architect associated with the cathedral from 1104 to 1110. The original cathedral, three bays shorter than it is today, was consecrated by Pope Gelasius II in 1117. By about 1250 the basilica was extended three bays to the west, a complicated process that involved demolishing the completed facade, then utilizing much of that material in the new facade. The cathedral, which rests upon a white marble pavement, is an elliptically domed, five-aisle basilica with apse and double-aisle transepts. This plan has been described as an elaborated joining of three basilicas, each with its own apse. The interior and exterior are faced with colored marble bands and ancient *spolia*.

The striped revetment of the cathedral is the earliest example of this mural effect in Pisa, though a Pisan tradition of decorated facades had earlier found expression in buildings ornamented with majolica bowls or plaques placed into a brick surround. The new fashion for a multicolored mural facing was also coming into vogue in Florence around the same time. The Florentine taste was for a more geometric patterning in white and black stones, with accents of green and pink; in Pisa, however, the taste was for a more pictorial, subtle arrangement of color and pattern. The origin of this type of revetment is unknown, though it surely lies in remnants of ancient Roman decorative stonework and mosaics, much of which still survives in these cities.

The Baptistery, often compared with the Holy Sepulchre in Jerusalem, is a large rotunda located on the east-west axis of the cathedral. The interior consists of three levels: ground story, gallery and cupola; this is reflected on the exterior in a ground story, combined clerestory and gallery, and cupola. Its covering is a truncated cone enclosed within a dome. The interior is remarkable for its simplicity of plan, underscored by the clarity of space and effect of light. As with the cathedral, the baptistery may exhibit the Pisans' desire to commemorate their achievements. For example, five of the eight columns on the ground-floor interior were brought from Elba and Sardinia in 1159 and 1162. These islands had been conquered by Pisa in the early 11th century, and it has been suggested that the columns were brought to Pisa as trophies.

Knowledge of the building history of the baptistery is partially based on four inscriptions found in the interior. Two inscriptions refer to its foundation in 1153, a third to the architect Deotisalvi, of whom very little is known, and a fourth to a rebuilding campaign of 1278. It is believed that the initial building campaign extended over approximately 100 years: from the foundation of the baptistery in 1153, through the completion of the ground story by circa 1185, to the installation of the baptismal font, by Guido da Como, in 1246.

A recent structural analysis of the baptistery suggests that this early structure was unstable, perhaps due to the lateral thrust from the covering to the gallery wall, where structural and architectural inconsistencies have been found. It has been suggested that several stages of rebuilding in the gallery occurred from circa 1260 to the closing of the oculus circa 1394: these include the installation of transverse arches and diaphragm walls, and a partial destruction and rebuilding of the exterior

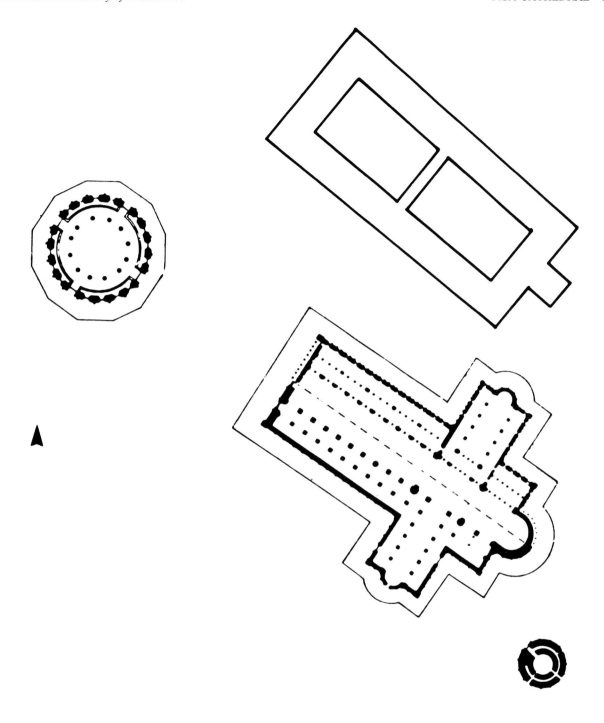

gallery wall. With the reconstruction of the gallery, a new covering was built, and a *cupoletta* added to the cone.

The circular bell tower, or campanile, is characteristically Italian in its detachment from the church. The eight stories of arcading (six of them are open, spiraling galleries) are closely reminiscent of the arcades of the cathedral's facade. Begun in 1174, construction was almost immediately suspended for approximately 100 years. The second campaign, too, was brief, from 1275 to 1284. The final campaign was concluded around 1350 with the construction of the belfry by Tommaso Pisano. These long delays were due to several factors: the desire to complete the cathedral and baptistery, unavailability of funds for yet another monument at a time of economic decline for the city, and, most perplexing to the Pisans, structural problems

that appeared from the start. When the foundations began to settle unevenly, the tower took on a marked slant. The second building campaign attempted to "correct" this problem by overloading the upward side as building continued. This resulted in a decidedly banana-shaped tilt.

The Campo Santo, literally "Holy Field," was begun to house earth brought from the Holy Land as ballast in Pisan ships. The simplest of the four buildings, its plan is that of an elongated classical atrium. The marble exterior wall repeats the motif of Pisan Romanesque blind arcading, accentuated by a Gothic tabernacle over one door. Begun in 1278 by architect Giovanni di Simone, it was largely completed by 1283. Further additions to the Campo Santo in the 14th and 15th centuries included the many interior frescoes and the sculpted Gothic

Pisa Cathedral

SANT'APOLLINARE IN CLASSE
Near Ravenna, Italy

Ca. 532: Building begun. **549:** Church completed and dedicated. **Seventh century:** Mosaics on lower apse wall and triumphal arch added. **Ninth century:** Apse floor raised; crypt added.

Publications

DEICHMANN, F. W.: *Ravenna, Haupstadt des spätantiken Abendlandes*. Wiesbaden, Germany, 1976.
MILBURN, ROBERT: *Early Christian Art and Architecture*. Berkeley and Los Angeles, 1988.
VON SIMSON, OTTO G.: *Sacred Fortress: Byzantine Art and Statecraft in Ravenna*. Chicago, 1948.

*

The beautiful Church of Sant'Apollinare in Classe, the former port city of Ravenna, is typical of Ravennate churches built during the fifth and sixth centuries in the way that it blends traditional elements of the Early Christian basilica with local characteristics and imported Byzantine characteristics. Dedicated to the titular saint and sole martyr of the city, Saint Apollinaris, the imposing structure today stands in uncommon isolation from surrounding buildings and is visible from a distance.

The handsome brickwork of the deservedly bare exterior consists of closely spaced courses of long, thin bricks imitative of Byzantine masonry. Nowhere is masonry as appealing as in the series of exquisite churches built at that time in Ravenna. The brick arcades surrounding windows of the aisle and clerestory walls, a decorative device common to north Italian architecture and found especially in Milan, adds a rhythmic articulation to the exterior. The pilasters at the corners of the exterior walls also are north Italian features.

The front facade is dominated by the tripartite arrangement of the tall, central nave and the wide, lower side aisles. The narthex with its short lateral towers, now lost, remained secondary in the overall exterior profile. The bell tower is a later medieval addition. At the east end three polygonal apses project on the exterior, the main apse appearing tall against the east nave wall and the two flanking side apses much lower in comparison and abutting the small, square sacristy chapels that project from the end of the side aisles.

The church was entered through three doors in the west wall aligning with the nave and aisles. The longitudinal, three-aisle plan is based on proportions of 1 to 1.3 overall width to length, and 1 to 3.3 nave width to height. The triple-apse plan of the east end concedes to Aegean church design and possibly to Byzantine liturgical requirements. The three apses, though polygonal on the exterior in keeping with Ravennate traditions, are semicircular on the interior. The main apse is deeper on the inside than it appears to be on the outside, where it is, in part, encased between the side chapels. In many ways the design is similar to the earlier, fourth-century church of San Giovanni Evangelista in Ravenna.

Separating the nave and aisles are wide arcades with 24 gray-veined, imported marble columns resting on carved pedestals and supporting impost blocks, all of which were made for this church. Sant'Apollinare, as other Ravennate basilicas, used 12 columns per arcade, perhaps symbolically referring to the 12 apostles. Wind-blown acanthus capitals in deeply cut Constantinopolitan style added a dramatic movement as the eye was swept toward the apse. The impost capitals were probably also

tracery added to the Romanesque-style arcades surrounding the courtyard.

These four buildings comprise the ecclesiastical center of Pisa, and served both religious and political purposes. Today, the Piazza del Duomo, also called the Piazza dei Miracoli, is surrounded by the city's walls (to the north and west, begun in the 11th century), the archbishop's palace (to the east, late 16th century) and the Hospital of Santa Chiara (to the south, founded 1258). The isolation of the four monuments within these confines, and the relative peace and quiet there, even with the ever-present tourist traffic, conflicts with the image of the piazza as it must have existed in an earlier age. Traversed by two roads, the piazza was surrounded well into the 15th century by hostels, shops, a hospital and cemetery, a well, numerous private residences and a cloister. The piazza was, itself, the focal point for Pisan citizens and their international visitors.

The piazza, and all it holds, is a monument to the power and wealth of Pisa, and its construction closely followed the city's fortunes. It seems that in Pisa, as elsewhere in Europe at that time, ecclesiastical architecture went hand in hand with secular achievements. The cathedral was founded to commemorate Pisa's ascendancy as a military and commercial power in the Mediterranean. The baptistery and campanile were constructed at the height of this power; indeed, the richness of the materials used suggests a desire to display the mangnificence of the city's wealth. The Campo Santo, founded shortly before Pisa's decline, is a repetition of designs and motifs originating with the cathedral and the period of Pisa's glory. How ironic that Pisa's decline in military strength, wealth and independence coincided with the construction of a cemetery built as a reliquary for land that Pisa once took pride in protecting.

—MARJORIE OCH

Sant'Apollinare in Classe: Near Ravenna, Italy, ca. 532

inspired by contemporary architecture in Constantinople or Salonika.

The spacious interior was flooded with light from large, round-arched windows in the nave, aisles and apses, the well-lit interior, again, reflecting Contantinopolitan trends. Only the western bay of the nave was blind.

Sant'Apollinare in Classe represents the best surviving example of the Early Christian basilica, though somewhat altered by later modifications, such as the raising of the apse floor in conjunction with the installation of a crypt in the ninth century. Though extremely well preserved, the pristine interior has lost its original floor, marble revetment and ceiling decoration, but the original apse mosaics survive. The style of the mosaic in the semidome points in a new direction, with unnatural spaces, unreal facial masks and abstract gold grounds. The mosaics on the lower apse wall and on the triumphal arch wall date somewhat later, to the seventh century. Other relics that adorn the interior are the seventh-century episcopal throne, the ninth-century marble ciborium and altar, and columns from a fragmentary ninth-century ciborium.

The building of Sant'Apollinare spreads over two important periods of Ravenna's history. Initiated under the Ostrogoths between 532 and 536 with the backing of the banker Julianus Argentarius, the basilica was completed under Byzantine rule, in 549, and dedicated by Archbishop Maximian. Both personalities were also behind the building and completion of San Vitale in Ravenna. The political and economic personalities contributing to the construction of the church complete the story of its origin.

—MARJORIE OCH

SANT'APOLLINARE NUOVO
Ravenna, Italy

Ca. 490: Church construction begun. **Ca. 550:** Lowest rows of mosaics redone; image of Theodoric removed. **Eight century:** Apse destroyed in earthquake. **10th century:** Belltower added.

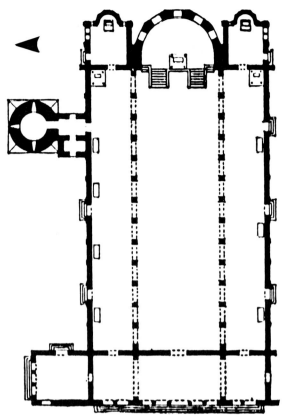

Sant'Apollinare in Classe

16th century: Portico in front of facade added; floor levels raised. **1950:** Apse rebuilt on original foundations.

Publications

DEICHMANN, F. W.: *Ravenna, Haupstadt des spätantiken Abendlandes.* Wiesbaden, Germany, 1976.

MILBURN, ROBERT: *Early Christian Art and Architecture.* Berkeley and Los Angeles, 1988.

VON SIMSON, OTTO G.: *Sacred Fortress: Byzantine Art and Statecraft in Ravenna.* Chicago, 1948.

The Church of Sant'Apollinare Nuovo in Ravenna is designed on a simple Early Christian basilical plan and elevation. The architecture can be described at brief, but the true magnificence and attraction of the church belongs to its extensive and beautiful mosaic decoration.

Except for the mosaics, the church is bare today, both inside and out. The bell tower and portico in front of the facade are both later additions, belonging to the 10th and 16th centuries,

respectively. The original apse, too, was lost in an eighth-century earthquake, and today's apse dates to 1950 when it was restored on the foundations of the original. The present floor, also, has been raised by approximately 1.20 meters above the original floor level, and the height of the arcades was equally raised in the 16th century, giving the interior its present squat appearance. Despite these later alterations, the church retains many of its original Early Christian architectural characteristics.

Specifically, local and imported elements were merged in typically Ravennate fashion. The polygonal exterior profile of the apse, for example, though semicircular on the interior, is a feature that stems ultimately from the Aegean area. The regular, fine brick masonry laid in thin mortar beds with wooden stretchers in the walls follows Milanese masonry techniques. The original semidome of the apse was built with hollow, interlocked, terra-cotta tubes, a technique that migrated to southern and central Italy from northern Africa.

Other features stem ultimately from Syria, such as the pilasters on the exterior walls that continue as brick arches around the windows. The marble columns of the interior, and possibly also their elaborate capitals, were imported from Constantinople. This combination of eastern and western, Roman and Constantinopolitan traits is typical of Ravenna, due to its strategic location between East and West.

The interior arrangement of Sant'Apollinare Nuovo is standard for the basilica plan: nave and two aisles, apse and arcade. The arcades consist of 24 columns, 12 on each side. The columns sit on low bases and are crowned with capitals supporting high impost blocks decorated with crosses. The use of impost blocks shows further Constantinopolitan influence. The proportions, though, exhibit the local preference in favor of increased overall width, tall nave and wide arcades. The spaciousness inherent in the proportions is enhanced by the numerous, and consistently large, windows in both nave and aisles, as well as in the apse. As a result, the interior is light and open. Three windows apparently pierced the apse wall, while at Sant'Apollinare in Classe, near Ravenna, the number was even greater, and five windows lit the apse.

Aesthetically, the combination of arched and linear elements in the interior architecture imparts an animated rhythm to the plain, smooth walls of the nave. The architectural rhythm of the arched colonnade is echoed in the round-arched windows of the clerestory above, and repeated in the windows of the aisles, the apse windows, and in the huge round arch of the apse itself. The arched rhythms complement the vertical and horizontal lines of columns and cornices, and these architectural lines are, in turn, echoed in the mosaic processions of vertically aligned saints, martyrs and prophets on either side of the nave above the colonnade. The human rhythms of figures in the narrative scenes at the top of the walls heighten the sense of movement countering stasis.

The smooth wall surfaces of Early Christian basilicas, almost without exception, carried decorations that transformed the plain interiors into shimmering, glorious tapestries of biblical and religious images, as in Sant'Apollinare Nuovo. Visitors were entranced by this imagery and were invited to "read" the walls in such a way that they became visual as well as structural supports. The interior of Sant'Apollinare Nuovo is exceptional in the way that the architecture and decoration interact and complement each other.

The history of the church's patronage charts the political course of late-fifth-century and early-sixth-century Ravenna. Begun around 490-500 A.D. under the Ostrogothic king Theodoric (ruled 493-526), Sant'Apollinare was built as Theodoric's palace church in the new Ostrogothic capital. The lavishness of the interior mosaic decoration, more so than any architectural

Sant'Apollinare Nuovo: Ravenna, Italy, ca. 490

richness, reflects the wealth of the founder. While Theodoric was an Arian, rejecting the belief that Christ was the son of God, nothing in the style of the building or even in the mosaics indicates a peculiarly Arian style or approach. The palace church was originally dedicated to Christ, then later, under Byzantine rule in 561, rededicated to Saint Martin and restored to orthodoxy. The present dedication to Saint Apollinare was acquired at a still later date.

Theodoric's building campaigns seem to have been extensive, and to have included three other structures in Ravenna—Santo Spirito, the Arian cathedral and baptistery, and his mausoleum—as well as buildings at Pavia and Verona. At Sant'Apollinare Nuovo, in the lower row of mosaics, on the nave wall near the entrance, the king was depicted standing in front of his palace facade with a retinue of soldier guards. His image was obliterated when, around 550 A.D., after the Byzantine conquest, the lowest rows of mosaics were redone. The broader, sociopolitical history of the church is, therefore, embedded in the history of its architectural and decorative modifications.

—MARJORIE OCH

SAN VITALE
Ravenna, Italy

Ca. 547: Church built. **16th century:** Portico built; **Architect:** Andrea da Valle.

Publications

DEICHMANN, F. W.: *Ravenna, Haupstadt des spätantiken Abendlandes.* Wiesbaden, Germany, 1976.

MACDONALD, WILLIAM: *Early Christian and Byzantine Architecture.* New York, 1985.

MILBURN, ROBERT: *Early Christian Art and Architecture.* Berkeley and Los Angeles, 1988.

VON SIMSON, OTTO G.: *Sacred Fortress: Byzantine Art and Statecraft in Ravenna.* Chicago, 1948.

San Vitale: Ravenna, Italy, ca. 547

The special kind of development that characterizes Ravenna in general and the Church of San Vitale in particular can be fully appreciated only against the turbulent series of events that accompanied the breakup of the Roman Empire. Following the death of Theodosius in 395 A.D., the empire was divided between his two sons, with Honarius ruling the west from Rome itself, and Arcadius governing the east from his capital in Byzantium. Rome was first invaded and sacked by Visigoths in 410, who then went on to occupy Provence and Spain. They were followed in turn by Vandals in 455, Heruleans in 476, and finally the Ostrogoths under Theodoric, who took what was left of the city in 495. Because of depleted resources and the need for a better location from which to establish commerce, the Ostrogothic capital was moved to Ravenna in 526.

Each of these various barbaric kingdoms, in fact if not by conquest, actually considered itself to be the partial vassal of the emperor of the east, who was then the only remaining representative of the Classical legacy of Rome. After his victory over Licinius in the hills above Chrysopolis in 324, which was just across the Bosporus from Byzantium, Constantine did all

he could to ensure that the architectural evidence of that legacy was reestablished. This brought about an important shift in the perceptions of those who inhabited what remained of the old Roman Empire, which was then largely made up of Greek-speaking Christians. A great period in the history of the eastern empire opened in 527. When Justinian the Great took the throne, he deliberately sought to recapture both the territory and the architectural grandeur of the past, and when he died in 565, Byzantium extended from the Euphrates in the east to the Pillars of Hercules in the west.

One of Justinian's first commissions in Constantinople was the Church of SS. Sergius and Bacchus, which was started in the first year of his reign, marking the beginning of an extraordinarily creative period of architectural experimentation that also produced the Hagia Sophia in that same city, and San Vitale and the Baptistry and Church of San Apollinare in Classe in Ravenna. In plan, the Church of SS. Sergius and Bacchus, which has been called the sister church to San Vitale, is an irregular octagon, inscribed within a rectangle, with a portico attached to one of the narrow ends of the rectangle, and an apse

San Vitale

located on the other. The octagon is covered with a dome, which is divided into 16 sections. These sections are further divided into eight flat areas, which alternate with eight concave surfaces above the angles of the octagon. Pairs of columns between each of the piers that hold up the dome are alternatively arched or trabeated, with verd antique marble used on one set and red synnada on the other. The visual effect is like that of a moving curtain circling around inside of the surrounding rectangular space, which seems to move further outward when the exedrae curve toward the corners of the exterior envelope.

Whereas the Church of San Vitale, built nearly 20 years after SS. Serguis and Bacchus, in 547, is also based on a centralized, octagonal plan, it does not stand within a rectilinear enclosure, and consequently seems to have a great deal more formal vibrancy. The idea for this form has been attributed to a bishop named Ecclesius, who is said to have been inspired by the new church architecture that he saw in Constantinople while visiting there with Pope John I, on a mission organized by Theodoric

to resolve the Arian controversy. An inscription by the historian Andreas Agnellus, in his *Liber Pontificalis,* records that a patron named Julianus Argentarius, who was a banker entrusted with the responsibility of the reinvestment of tax revenue in new buildings, arranged for the construction of the church. It was dedicated to Saints Vitalis, Gervase and Protase, whose relics are still kept in a marble urn to the left of the apse.

In form, the church has a high central octagon which supports a cupola and is surrounded by a lower octagon containing both the ambulatory and the *matronaeum,* or women's gallery, as well as the presbytery and the side chapels. This creates a logically graduated design in which the chancel and apse totally occupy one of the eight sides of the octagon. Light enters the church through windows in the cupola, and this light is further diffused by the triforia before it reaches the interior. Fragments of colored glass, discovered in 1930, indicate that it was once used in these windows, which would make San Vitale the oldest surviving example of the use of stained-glass windows in a

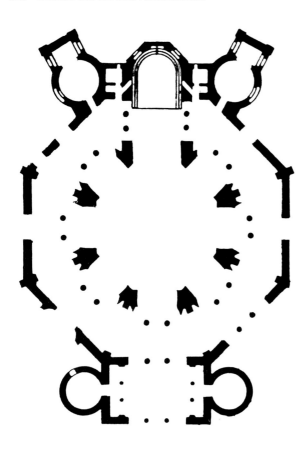

Christian church. Considering that the interior is also covered in mosaics, which make the ecclesiastical architecture that was produced in Ravenna from the time of Galla Placida onward historically unique, the overall effect of this layering of light must have been overwhelming. The style of the mosaics, which are still substantially intact within the church, was obviously influenced by the Justinian school. Here, they form an entire catechism, using the concept of salvation as the basis of the lesson, and vignettes from both the Old and New Testaments as examples.

On the exterior of the building, brickwork techniques and the use of corner buttresses clearly show a northern Adriatic, and specifically Milanese, influence, in which the rough surface of the exterior is used to heighten the contrast with a mysterious and jewel-like interior. The walls were built with brick that is only four centimeters thick, which has led to speculation that these were brought especially from Constantinople, as they were for all of the buildings patronized by Julianus Argentarius. As seen today, the elongated, tubular narthex, which is offset from the centerline of the apse, gives a totally different impression of entry than originally would have been the case. This portico, which was added by Andrea da Valle in the 16th century, has replaced an open atrium and quadriporticus that would had allowed direct access from the narthex into the ambulatory. From there, the sanctuary, which was once surrounded by open-work screens that are now in the National Museum, would have been visible in perspective through the columns of the triforia. In spite of these changes, San Vitale remains an extremely valuable document of a highly innovative period, and the completeness of both the built fabric and the mosaics make it doubly important as an example of the sacred architecture of the transitional period between the late Roman Empire and the Middle Ages.

—JAMES M. STEELE

CITTÀ UNIVERSITARIA
Rome, Italy

1932-35: Construction; **Chief architect:** Marcello Piacentini. **1934-35:** Physics Institute; **Architect:** Giuseppe Pagano. **1934-35:** Mathematics Faculty; **Architect:** Gio Ponti. **1934-35:** Mineralogy Institute; **Architect:** Giovanni Michelucci. Other architects included Pietro Aschieri, Giuseppe Capponi, Arnaldo Foschini, and Gaetano Rapisardi.

Publications

Giuseppe Pagano: Architettura tra guerre e polemiche. Florence, 1991.
LUPANO, MARIO: *Marcello Piacentini*. Rome, 1991.
PATETTA, LUCIANA: *L'architettura in Italia 1919-1943: Le polemiche*. Milan, 1972.
PONTI, LISA LICITRA (ed.): *Gio Ponti: The Complete Works, 1923-78*. Cambridge, Massachusetts, and London, 1990.

In May 1932 the University of Rome and the Kingdom of Italy announced plans for the construction of a new home for Rome's principal secular institution of higher learning. The site chosen for the university was between the remains of the Pretorian Camp and the newly built Stazioni Termini in the part of Rome that had been filled with princely villas before the ancient city had become the capital of the new kingdom in 1871. The complex was to contain 16 new buildings. The head of state, Benito Mussolini, envisioned the creation of an educational institution of international stature and treated the construction of the new campus as an undertaking of national importance. Il Duce's favorite architect, Marcello Piacentini, received the commission to direct the design and execution of the huge project. Mussolini desired that the architecture of the new Città Universitaria (University City) reflect the ideals of the ruling Fascist Party.

Early in his control of the state, Mussolini stated the need to direct the arts into certain acceptable channels. In 1928, at Perugia, addressing a convention of artists and architects, he proclaimed: "Today Italy is a great people of great possibilities. . . . Today . . . we are also morally united. Now, on a foundation so well prepared, a great art can be reborn, which can be traditional as well as modern. It is necessary to create, otherwise we will be the exploiters of an old patrimony: it is necessary to create a new art of our times, a Fascist art." His words were carefully chosen to establish certain themes. This art was to be new, but linked to the past. This art was to be modern, but related to a Roman, Mediterranean and classic Italic tradition.

Fascist architecture was charged with two conflicting and competing tasks. It must honor, preserve and recreate the monumental modes of the Roman spirit (*Romanità*) and, concurrently, adapt modern building techniques and developments to its stated ideal of a totally new and totalitarian society. Fascist architecture was expected to obey the dictums of both *Romanità* and modernism.

In December 1925 on the Campidoglio, framed by Michelangelo's Capitoline Palaces, while addressing the new governor of Rome, Mussolini outlined the Fascist program for the rebuilding of Rome, and by extension, for all of Italy. This statement was the potent pronouncement of his architectural policy. He demanded that Fascist architecture solve the vexing problem *"della necessità e della grandezza."* Fascism would attempt to recreate the Italic style on a modern and united base. Further, the

Città Universitaria: Rome, Italy, 1932-35

artist, freed from need and inspired by his "*sacro entusiasmo*," which alone is capable of stimulating the creative faculties, would respond to the call of the party and the people by integrating the past with the present. The party was disposed to use architecture for political propaganda, permitting it only a certain limited freedom, while pressing it into the service of the state.

Fascist architecture was to rest on certain specific foundations and pragmatic ideals. Despite the pragmatic nature of the regime and its ability to suit its policy to its current needs, the underlying concepts remained consistent; only the interpretation varied.

The party established several concepts to guide the architect in creating these new Fascist monuments in a land already filled with the monuments of many ages. The new architecture, like Roman architecture, would rest on the principle of responding as an adequate or fitting expression of a determined content and an established function. The new architecture would be linear, as linear styles are a moving reflection of a linear lifestyle, of rapidity which moves toward a goal. Modern man is a realist, needing movement, sport, clarity, health, education. These needs demand and produce a rationalist architecture. That rationalist architecture, however, must also express the fact that the "Fascist twentieth century is characteristically Roman." The style would be forced to follow two trends, tearing itself asunder to perform an imposed and impossible task.

G. E. Kidder-Smith has noted that modernism did not at first take too readily in Italy, where it conflicted with the longstanding post-Baroque tradition of nonlinear architecture. Once accepted, however, the style was "naturalized" to suit the need and temperament of "this highly creative country." Still, the pre-Baroque tradition in Italian architecture had stressed the linear, the horizontal and the arch, so it might be said that

modern rationalist architecture was, indeed, a continuation of an interrupted tradition stretching unbroken from Roman through Early Christian, Romanesque and even Gothic to the Renaissance and the linear architecture of Filippo Brunelleschi, Leon Battista Alberti and Andrea Palladio.

The Fascist state was aware of the need to provide the nation with all the required signs of a modern society: the Fascist revolution was to rebuild the nation according to concepts of light and cleanliness. The rebuilding of the nation was to provide jobs, to employ the veterans of the Great War, to stimulate the economy, and to heal and redeem the Italian people after centuries of oppression, disunity, regionalism and division. Fascism would have to bring into being new housing, hospitals, prisons, public services and schools. It would also have to provide new roads, bridges, and cities for a new, Fascist Italy.

In 1932 the Fascist Party celebrated its tenth year in power. Within the previous ten years, through incessant propaganda, the party had firmly established its classic antecedents, its *Romanità;* it could now begin to stress the opposite polarity of its bipartite policy, its progressive nature, its *modernità*. Now, Fascism would and could express "the simplicity that represents the hygiene of the spirit, the economy of the times, the clarity of the idea, the right line." The party was ready to accept publicly the rationale of the futurist movement and marry it to its own version and vision of *Romanità*.

In this atmosphere and under these concepts the planning for the new university began. The new institution was to house some 12,000 students in 16 new structures. Piacentini selected 11 architects to assist him, chosen from various Italian cities, reinforcing the idea that this was a national, not just a local, effort. The official dedication of the new campus took place just three years later, in October 1935, a year in which Fascist architectural theory was to change once again as Mussolini was completing his conquest of Ethiopia. He proclaimed that Fascist architecture would from then on be imperial architecture, an architecture of substance and international renown. However, this new imperial phase of Fascism was in some ways anticipated in the scale, monumentality and neoclassicism of the university campus.

Symmetry and axial organization govern the composition. Various university buildings flank a major axis that terminates at the Administration Building. The grid-like plan of the university recalls those Roman camps and towns built in many parts of the Roman Empire, with a striking resemblance to the plan of Diocletian's retirement palace at Split on the Adriatic. The plan has also been likened to traditional Italian town centers, especially the planned centers of the Renaissance, as at Pienza, and even to the interior arrangement of Christian churches. The architects responsible were given general freedom in their individual designs, but all buildings were required to follow general guidelines regarding cornice heights and exterior facing materials.

The individual buildings reflect the various strains in official Fascist architectural policy. Piacentini's Administration Building, a stripped neoclassical design sheathed in marble and travertine, stands at the focal point of the campus. An imposing flight of stairs leads to the main entrance, which is framed by narrow, unadorned piers rather than columns, stressing the straight line. The facade is rigidly symmetrical, and the fenestration is repetitive and uninspired, devoid of any framing. The Administration Building reflects the striving for a modern neoclassical style but results rather in a severe but cumbersome structure. The Physics Building, by Giuseppe Pagano, reflects a sober functional style, more in accord with the concepts of rationalist architecture. One of the few buildings that attempted to follow the guidelines and yet strives to fulfill the potential of modernism was Giuseppe Capponi's Botany Building. Because it was not visible from the formal axis of the campus and because it was required to have greenhouses, the building has extensive glazing, with one of the first glass curtain walls in Rome, expressing some of the concepts that Antonio Sant'Elia had explored in his futurist architecture.

Rome's Città Universitaria reflected the divergent trends in official Fascist architecture—Roman, neoclassical, futurist, rationalist—all held in uneasy harmony by the strict, rigid and linear plan of the campus, which reflected the Fascist Party's ability, with some success, to contain the divergent strains in national life. The party attempted to impose a uniform system on a nation rich in the diversity of its regionalism, and the plan, design, and execution of the university campus were a measure of just how well the Fascist Party had, in times of peace, been able to impose that seeming uniformity while allowing limited diversity. That the university continues to function even now is a testament of the ability of the capital of Italy, as a reflection of its people, to absorb and contain diverse and divergent architectural expressions.

—DONALD FRICELLI

IL GESÙ
Rome, Italy

1568-84: Church begun; **Architects:** Giacomo Barozzi da Vignola (1507-73, retired from project in 1571), Giovanni Tristano

(took over in 1571). **1571-75:** Facade redesigned and completed; **Architect:** Giacomo della Porta. **1672-85:** Vault decorated; **Artists:** Giovanni Battista Gaulli, known as Baciccio, and Antonio Raggi.

Publications

ACKERMAN, JAMES S.: "The Gesù in Light of Contemporary Church Design." In WITTKOWER and JAFFE: *Baroque Art: The Jesuit Contribution.* New York, 1972.

BUCHOWIECKI, W.: *Handbuch der Kirchen Roms.* Vienna, 1974.

HOWE, EUNICE D.: "The Church of Il Gesù Explicated in a Guidebook of 1588." *Extrait de la Gazette des beaux-arts* (December 1985).

SCHWAGER, K.: "La chiesa del Gesù del Vignola." *Bollettino del Centro Internazionale di Studi di Architettura "Andrea Palladio"* 19 (1977): 251-271.

*

The architectural design of Il Gesù rivals that of any other 16th-century church in respect to originality as well as influence. Vignola, in his plan for the mother church of the Jesuit order, responded to religious goals newly formulated at the Council of Trent. He designed a spacious church with a longitudinal axis, side chapels rather than aisles, a wide transept and a dome over the crossing. Giacomo della Porta's facade fused the verticality with the breadth, a fitting prelude to the interior of the church. Il Gesù immediately became the prototype for the Counter-Reformation church, and subsequently served as a model for the great baroque churches of Rome.

The architects who participated in the construction of Il Gesù were influenced by a unique combination of practical and aesthetic concerns. Della Porta's facade represents the culmination of a development initiated by Leon Battista Alberti at Santa Maria Novella more than a century earlier. Giant volutes visually connect the width of the nave with a wider base at the lower level. The classical orders articulate the surface of the aedicular facade, and a crowning pediment completes the pyramidal form. The interior of the church, best viewed from the entrance to the nave, is impressive for its scale and harmonious proportions. At the time of its construction, Il Gesù was the largest church in Rome, and it was completed in a remarkably short time (1568-84).

The first Jesuit church was Santa Maria della Strada on the Piazza degli Altieri, entrusted to the newly founded order in 1540. When Saint Ignatius of Loyola obtained permission for a new church and cloister, projects were commissioned from Giovanni di Bartolomeo Lippi (died 1568), known as Nanni di Baccio Bigio or Nanni Lippi. Nanni, who belonged to the Sangallo workshop, produced an undistinguished plan which, however, was unusual in having a wide nave with side chapels and a spacious choir, features surely desired by the order. The foundation stone was laid in 1550 but no work was done, due to a lack of funds, and the initial plans were discarded. Then the opportunity arose to reassign the project to Michelangelo, who was present at a second foundation ceremony in 1554. Only a sketch from another architect's hand annotated by Michelangelo (Uffizi Arch. 1819) suggests his intentions.

In 1568 yet another foundation ceremony took place, as Cardinal Alessandro Farnese had taken over funding of the project. He commissioned a plan from his architect, Giacomo Barozzi (1507-73), known as Vignola, for a church on an enlarged site. The spacious nave and connecting chapels allowed ample room for the swelling congregation. Unlike earlier plans,

Il Gesù: Rome, Italy, 1568-84

Il Gesù

the three chapels on each side of the nave are linked by passage-ways, and by domed precincts toward the transept. The acoustics of the barrel vault impacted on preaching in the nave, a point of deliberation between the Jesuits and Cardinal Farnese, whose will prevailed. A choir, reserved for the priests, was distinct from the nave, but the longitudinal plan drew attention to the high altar.

The interior of Il Gesù bears Vignola's imprint in its harmoni-ous proportions and classical details. He oversaw the construc-tion of the nave, articulated by paired, Corinthian pilasters and a projecting cornice, as far as the crossing, and his plan antici-pated a dome spanning the width of the nave. Although com-pleted later, the cylindrical vault above the architrave belonged to the original design. There, in the upper reaches of the nave, windows were inserted into the spandrels of the vault, allowing light to flood the interior. Illumination from the windows in the vault and the drum of the cupola resembled divine light, which attracted the congregation to the high altar. Originally, whitewashed walls lent the interior an imposing austerity, lost when the vault was decorated by Giovanni Battista Gaulli, known as Baciccio, and Antonio Raggi (1672-85).

Vignola left the project in 1571. Nominally, his replacement was the Jesuit architect Giovanni Tristano, but in fact Giacomo della Porta, who took over as architect of the facade, was his real successor. Vignola's preliminary idea for the facade appeared on a foundation medal in 1568. He proposed a colossal order at ground level, and an equally broad attic story punctuated by a Serlian window. Alternative designs by Vignola emphasized the verticality of the two-story facade, but his final project attempted to synthesize competing elements. An engraving by Mario Cartaro of 1573, which incidentally assured the unexe-cuted facade its own legacy, indicates the methodical application of a measured classicism to the final project.

Della Porta forged a bolder solution, which depended on massing at the center to suggest elevation, and thus height. Engaged Corinthian columns flank the main portal, and free-standing columns frame the window above, while paired pilas-ters form a screen across the facade. The facade has a plastic quality, although conventional sculptural decoration is limited. There are full-size figures in niches at the lower level, while two massive coats-of-arms are suspended along the central axis. (The lower shield with the Jesuit emblem was designed by Bartolomeo Ammannati). Volutes frame the second story, like gigantic bookends with sculpted heads tucked into the upper

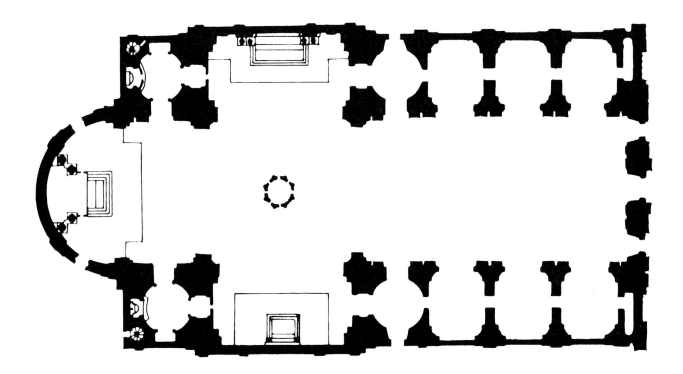

Il Gesù

corners; these scrolls relieve the angular surfaces of the facade and reflect the curvature of the pediment in the central bay. The commemorative inscription in the entablature dates the completion of the facade to 1575, which also marked the beginning of its widespread influence.

—EUNICE D. HOWE

PALAZZO BARBERINI
Rome, Italy

1628-33: Construction (rebuilding of existing structure); **Architects:** Carlo Maderno (1556-1629); completed by Giovanni Lorenzo Bernini (1598-1680), assisted by Francesco Borromini (1599-1667). **1633:** Staircase built; **Architect:** Pietro da Cortona (1596-1669). **1633-39:** Ceiling painted in Gran Salone; **Artist:** Pietro da Cortona.

Publications

BLUNT, ANTHONY: "The Palazzo Barberini: the Contributions of Maderno, Bernini and Pietro da Cortona." *Journal of the Warburg and Courtauld Institutes* 21 (1958): 256-287.
POSSE, HANS: "Das Deckenfresko des Pietro da Cortona im Palazzo Barberini und die Deckenmalerie in Rom." *Jahrbuch der Preussischen Kunstsammlungen* 40 (1919): 93-118, 126-173.
WADDY, PATRICIA: "The Design and Designers of Palazzo Barberini." *Journal of the Society of Architectural Historians* 35, 3 (1976): 151-185.

*

The Barberini played a major role in the political and artistic life of 17th-century Rome, and the great palace that was built on the western slope of the Quirinal Hill was intended to provide a fitting locale for and advertisement of the family's eminence. The site, of irregular shape, was bounded on the east by Strada Felice (now Via XX Settembre), on the south by Strada Pia (now Via delle Quattro Fontane). Strada Felice intersected with Strada Pia at Quattro Fontane, one of the principal points on the pilgrimage route confirmed under Sixtus V in 1590. In addition, the location was on the edge of and well above the city proper in the 17th century, which would have made any building there visible in silhouette against the open country behind. To the northwest lay SS. Trinità dei Monti, with beyond it the great bulk of Villa Medici; to the southwest was the papal palace on the spur of the Quirinal, while almost due west on the other side of the river lay St. Peter's. The site was thus well chosen to bring the name and presence of the Barberini to the attention of every visitor to the city. This was of no small importance, as Maffeo Barberini had been elected to the throne of Peter as Pope Urban VIII in 1623. It was he who gave the land for the palace to his nephew Taddeo in 1626.

As the principal Roman architect of the day, the elderly Carlo Maderno was the obvious choice as supervisor of the project.

Palazzo Barberini: Rome, Italy, 1628-33

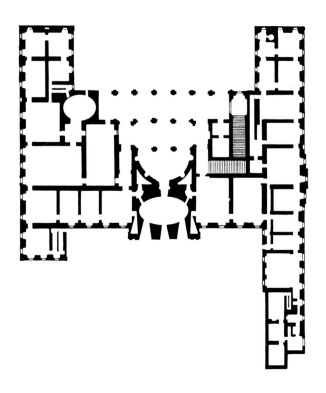

Maderno was appointed architect in 1627, and among those gathered around him was his nephew Francesco Castelli (later Borromini); it is to Borromini's hand that the surviving drawings of the lower floor plan and principal elevation have been attributed. Those drawings were completed before Maderno's death in early 1629, and demonstrate that the final design was approved in its essential features under Maderno.

As the building was to be a city residence but was to stand on an elevated position on the edge of the city proper, in the manner of a suburban villa, its design presented novel problems. The solution was to use the plan and massing of a villa combined with the scale and articulation of a city palace. The plan as drawn was U-shaped when seen from the west, the principal view, in the manner of Villa Farnesina, while at the center of the west facade was a three-story arcade suggesting the formal dignity of a town palace, reminiscent of the Cortile di San Damaso in the Vatican. The building was entered through the lowest level of the arcade, which was developed in depth and terminated in a grotto-like recess. Above, on the principal floor, the center of the plan was marked by a huge salon to the west, toward the city, and an elliptical room to the east, toward the garden. Between the first and second floors a stair rose in straight flights around a square well, an innovation in stair design. All of those features were to appear in the finished building. After Maderno's death he was replaced as supervisor by Giovanni Lorenzo Bernini, who had worked earlier under Barberini patronage, making his appointment a logical one. What his influence was on the final result is not so easy to show.

To begin with, the drawings prove that the design was complete before Bernini's appointment as chief of the work. Second,

Palazzo Barberini, rear facade

Bernini was not an architect, so it should not follow that he would have set out to change significantly what had already been approved simply because he was made supervisor of the project. Third, the building as built reveals no more than a small number of changes from the drawings. For example, the arcaded centerpiece of the principal facade was drawn with Tuscan pilasters at the third level, surmounted only by a cornice; as built, the pilasters are composite and multiplied, with an architrave and frieze added above. Again, the flanking wings projecting to each side of the center were drawn with windows against plain wall surfaces; as built, the wall surfaces were articulated by pilaster strips. The windows of the flanking wings as drawn were framed more simply at the first and second levels, more elaborately at the third level; as built, the third-level windows were framed simply as those on the second level. Apart from these few details the main facade was built as drawn.

The garden facade presents more problems of understanding, mostly because it appears to have been left permanently incomplete. The massing is awkward and asymmetrical, and the central element in the form of a triumphal arch is not integrated with the rest of the composition. The triumphal arch surely belongs to Maderno; the lower facade elements to either side each carry four windows that can only be by Borromini.

In the interior there are two spaces, the vestibule at the top of the main stair, and the great salon beyond, notable for strikingly original details. In each space the details can only be from the hand of Borromini once more, characterized as they are by those revolutionary juxtapositions found in all of Borromini's work. It is difficult to avoid the conclusion that Bernini's influence on the final shape of the palace was slight.

Although there is no evidence for a complete program of decoration for the main rooms of the palace, the decorations that were executed were of considerable size and complexity. Above all, the ceiling of the huge salon at the center of the plan, directly behind the principal facade, was not merely the outstanding feature of the palace but a masterwork of the entire 17th century. It was executed between 1633 and 1639 to the designs of Pietro da Cortona, and depicted the Triumph of Divine Providence, and of the Barberini, and was second in size only to Michelangelo's ceiling for the Sistine Chapel. It was constructed as a spectacular combination of quadratura and atmospheric perspective, unmatched before or after for illusionistic complexity.

Although unfinished both inside and out, Palazzo Barberini nonetheless occupied a critical position in the history of the Renaissance palace. It was the first town palace to adopt the massing of the villa, the first to build movement in perspective into its spatial sequences, the first to place a vast salon with a dynastic allegory painted on its vaulted ceiling at the center of its plan—all of which features were to appear together in numerous subsequent examples.

While the only project on which the three greatest figures of the Roman Baroque—Giovanni Lorenzo Bernini, Francesco Borromini, Pietro da Cortona—all employed their talents, Palazzo Barberini can in no sense be seen as an artistic whole. Yet it was one of the first great dynastic monuments clearly intended to be carried out as a complete work of art, designed and decorated as a whole by contemporary artists. To the extent that it did not achieve the intended artistic unity, it was a failure; to the extent that its example influenced all later palace building in the 17th and 18th centuries it was an extraordinary success.

—BERNARD M. BOYLE

International Dictionary of Architecture

PALAZZO DELLA CANCELLERIA
Rome, Italy

1484: Building begun; **Architect:** Designs attributed to Donato Bramante (1444-1514), Andrea Bregno, or Antonio da Sangallo. **1495:** Facade completed. **1503:** Construction resumed. **1511:** Construction completed. **Early 16th century:** Salone di Studio and Capella del Pallio decorated; **Artists:** Perino del Vaga and Francesco Salviati respectively. **1546:** Sala dei Cento Giorni decorated; **Artist:** Giorgio Vasari. **1719:** Sala Riaria decorated; **Artist:** Antonio Valeri. **1939:** Building restored.

Publications

LAVAGNINO, EMILIO: *Il Palazzo della Cancelleria e la chiesa di San Lorenzo in Damaso*. Rome, 1924.

SCHIAVO, ARMANDO: *Il Palazzo della Cancelleria*. Rome, 1964.

*

The Palazzo della Cancelleria, the Palace of the Chancellery, is one of the most important monuments of the Early Renaissance in Rome. It was a model for many of the later palaces in the city, such as the Palazzetto Turchi and the Palazzo Santori, and then, even centuries later, for the first design of the Villard Houses in New York City by Joseph Morrill Wells, which were incorporated in 1882-85 into the final scheme for this complex by McKim, Mead and White.

The design of the Palazzo della Cancelleria has been attributed often to Donato Bramante, but he was not in Rome until the construction, which seems to have begun a little before 1485, was well under way. It is now usual to attribute the plan to Andrea Bregno, an architect in Rome, or to Antonio da Sangallo the Elder from Florence. But to some scholars, the parallels there with details in part of the hospital at Urbino suggest someone like Francesco di Giorgio Martini or Baccio Pontelli, who was working in Rome in those years but had been trained earlier in Urbino. The participation of Bramante at some point, however, especially in the courtyard, is still possible.

Activity on the site began about 1483, the year that Cardinal Raffaello Riario was appointed titular bishop of San Lorenzo in Damaso, a church established there in A.D. 380; he had both the old palace, built by his predecessor in the mid-century, and the church completely demolished. Work was proceeding by 1485; by 1495, as we know from the inscription that runs the full length of the church, the facade was completed, and in that year the chapter took possession of the new church. A second stage of building began about 1503, but by 1511, to judge from a detail of the title given Cardinal Riario in the inscriptions on some of the windows, construction was complete. The building itself was confiscated from the Riario family after their participation in a plot against Pope Leo X, and it became for many years the seat of the ecclesiastical magistrates; in 1798 it was the home of the Tribunale della Repubblica, in 1810 that of the Imperial Court, in 1848 that of the Roman Parliament, and in 1849 the Roman Republic was proclaimed there. But after 1870 it became the seat of the Chancellery Cardinals of the Roman Catholic Church, a right confirmed in the Lateran pact of 1929.

Palazzo della Cancelleria: Rome, Italy, 1485

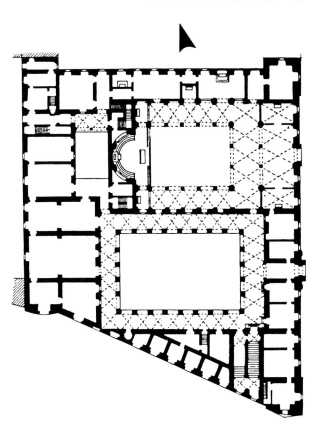

Palazzo della Cancelleria Court

It is now also the home of the Pontificia Accademia Romana di Archaeologia.

The design of the whole complex was marked by a range of new ideas. Embedded within the carefully regularized plan, which accommodated itself very carefully to the irregular site that faces both the Via del Corso and the Via Pellegrini, is an internal courtyard and the new Church of San Lorenzo in Damaso, set parallel to one another, the service rooms at the ground level and above running around and to the back of the courtyard. There is a long, regular wall surface on the front on the Via Pellegrini; at either end are slightly projecting corner bays, and in between, at ground level, is a series of shops and *botteghe,* a detail of obvious economic significance and one—whether or not this was consciously modeled on the similar idea found in the old Roman *insulae*—that was to be much imitated in other palaces in the city. On the facade on the Corso around the corner was a grander scheme of articulation, a simple, rusticated facade at the ground floor with two richly marked entrance doors, the larger leading into the courtyard of the complex, the smaller into the Church of San Lorenzo in Damaso, and above this two more floors, rusticated again, but with a series of windows surrounded by carefully cut, paired pilasters.

Such a facade was new to Rome; the idea of paired pilasters had been seen only in Florence at the Palazzo Rucellai or in Bernardo Rossellino's work at Pienza, and it is these elements, the windows and the frieze with its inscription running the full length of the facade, that seem to come directly from Leon Battista Alberti and the new Palazzo Ducale at Urbino. The same newness can be seen in the great courtyard, which is like that of Urbino, the only other courtyard built in the Early Renaissance on a similar scale, for the courtyards of the new palaces in Florence were smaller and defined by the cornices that project at their heights as enclosed spaces. The one earlier

model in Rome, the courtyard of the Palazzetto di San Marco, was a garden court, rather than, as here, a wide, open space. The highest level of columns is closed and forms part of the service rooms. The motifs in this courtyard, rosettes and capitals of a great delicacy and corner pilasters with ringed shafts are also new. It was these refinements that led scholars to propose the name of Bramante; yet this may be a strain of architecture from Urbino, given new and particular form in a Roman setting, and could well have been created by someone like Francesco di Giorgio or Baccio Pontelli.

Several of the interior rooms at the Cancelleria are richly decorated, most famously, or infamously, the so-called Sala dei Cento Giorni, or Room of a Hundred Days, decorated in unseemly haste by Giorgio Vasari in 1546 with scenes from the life of Pope Paul III; the Salone di Studio and the Capella del Pallio, done in the early 16th century by, respectively, Perino del Vaga and Francesco Salviati; and the Sala Riaria, or Aula Magna, commissioned from the otherwise unknown artist Antonio Valeri by Lodovico Segardi in 1719 under Pope Clement XI, restored most recently in 1939.

—DAVID CAST

PALAZZO CHIGI
Rome, Italy

1664: Construction begun (rebuilding of existing structure); **Architect:** Giovanni Lorenzo Bernini (1598-1680). **1745:** Addition built; **Architect:** Nicola Salvi (1697-1751), assisted by Luigi Vanvitelli (1700-73).

Palazzo Chigi: Rome, Italy, 1664

Publications

GOLZIO, VINCENZO: *Documenti artistici sul Seicento nell' Ar-chivio Chigi*. Rome, 1939.
LEFEVRE, RENATO: ''Della Porta e Maderno a Palazzo Chigi.'' *Palladio* 21 (1971): 151-158.

*

In 1657 Cardinal Fabio Chigi rented a 16th-century palace on the Piazza dei SS. Apostoli. Four years later, he bought it from the Colonna family and, in 1664, the cardinal engaged Giovanni Lorenzo Bernini to undertake major renovations. The old building with its courtyard by Carlo Maderno (1556-1629) was to be masked with a modern facade. Bernini flanked a central section of seven bays with recessed wings of three bays each, terminating their corners with quoins. He relied on the lateral bays with their horizontal rustication to frame and compress the central bays, and to draw the spectator's peripheral vision back to the palace's elegant center.

Bernini's use of pilasters to articulate exterior walls of both religious and secular structures was a characteristic approach that reflected his conservatism in architecture. In his reliance on pilasters for the front of the Palazzo Chigi, he departed from such prominent Renaissance models as Baldassare Peruzzi's Villa Farnesina or the Palazzo Farnese, the facades of which were articulated by a repetition of pedimented windows. Another Roman model only partially noted by Bernini was the late-15th-century Cancelleria, a magnificent structure as the official center of Church government, with its facade of paired pilasters confined to single stories. Bernini also did not follow Raphael's Palazzo Vidoni-Caffarelli, which used double half columns to demarcate bays of the *piano nobile*. Michelangelo's architecture on the Capitoline Hill, however, provided a grand prototype for Bernini's use of the colossal order, but he restrained Michelangelo's muscularity with his choice of pilasters instead of half columns for the Palazzo Chigi. From the plainer ground level serving as a base, Bernini extended the pilasters as independent units on the *piano nobile*. He added a powerful cornice to the structure. The intended appearance of the palace with its balustrade and statues is recorded in engravings, but the open balustrade above with its planned statuary was never carried out.

Bernini distinguished the entrance at the center of the facade with freestanding Tuscan columns, and a balcony and window above. He expanded the Roman context for his palace by matching Michelangelo's Palazzo Farnese in the number of bays and stories, in the use of quoins, and in the emphatic vertical emphasis of the central portal with its columns, balcony and cartouche. The resulting structure assumed an aristocratic air.

Bernini had already used the motif of stepped-back wings in his Palazzo Ludovisi (di Montecitorio) of 1650. That, too, was a broad facade, but of 25 bays with wings advancing toward the center in rhythms of 3-6-7-6-3.

He provided the ground-level windows of the Palazzo Chigi with flat pediments. He placed alternating triangular and segmented pediments on the fenestration of the *piano nobile,* then reversed the sequence in the lateral bays to further distinguish them from the central projection. He gave the facade additional focus by topping his central portico with a balustrade, above which he placed a window tabernacle defined by paired half columns. Bernini continued the emphatic stress on the vertical in the window's broken pediment, on which he superimposed a cartouche with the Chigi arms.

In 1665, for Louis XIV's new wing of the Louvre, Bernini sent two facade designs to Paris which proved to be too extravagant even for the French king. Bernini's third design, which he presented in Paris in person, shared many elements with the Palazzo Chigi then undergoing construction in Rome, but the king rejected it as well.

Bernini's classical balance in the Palazzo Chigi was disrupted after 1745 when the palace was bought by the prominent Odescalchi family, who asked Nicola Salvi to expand the building. Assisted by Luigi Vanvitelli, Salvi doubled the facade's eight pilasters of the composite order to 16, and added paired entrances to replace Bernini's central one. The palace evolved into one with a broad facade with stepped-back wings, the grand sweep of which replaced Bernini's refined sense of proportion. His clean reiteration of Renaissance ideals gave way to a dissipation of energy through Salvi's repetitive bays. Bernini had conceived of the center as a visual fulcrum to link the facade bays in a measured processional. This interpretation vanished in the sweep of Salvi's new facade, which also destroyed Bernini's sense of hierarchy and proportion. Salvi's renovations for the Odescalchi involved the practical expansion of public and private quarters, but he broadened the scope of the palace visually with new intentions. Salvi created a scenographic vista, but in the process the regal character of Bernini's Palazzo Chigi, as his exemplary statement in palace architecture, was lost to future generations.

—EDWARD J. OLSZEWSKI

PALAZZO FARNESE
Rome, Italy

1515: Building begun; **Architect:** Antonio da Sangallo the Younger (1483-1546). **1534:** Designs revised, palace enlarged.

Palazzo Farnese: Rome, Italy, 1515

Palazzo Farnese, piazza: Before 1515

In 1495 Cardinal Alessandro began buying land in the area near the Campo dei Fiori for the construction of his palace and the large piazza before it. In the early 16th century, that area was one of two in Rome favored by the wealthiest cardinals for their private residences (the other was the area around the Piazza Navona). Cardinals required large palaces for their households (up to several hundred persons), as well as for hosting state and church functions. Indeed, the size of palace and household was an indication of wealth, power and prestige.

In 1515 the Palazzo Farnese was designed for the sizable household of Cardinal Alessandro, approximately 300 persons. Upon his accession to the papal throne, however, Alessandro desired to build an even larger, more magnificent structure. Although construction had progressed beyond the *piano nobile* by 1534, significant alterations were deemed necessary. One of the major changes to the palace was its extension into the piazza by 14 to 16 feet.

At the time Sangallo began the Palazzo Farnese, he was involved in the design and construction of the Palazzo Baldassini in Rome (1514-23). Similarities between the two facades have been noted; both have in common an emphasis on the horizontality of the three stories, with the verticals merely suggested by the alignment of the windows. Most interesting, however, is the manner in which the two palaces are distinguished from one another and reflect the private and public concerns of the patrons. Both Farnese and Baldassini were collectors of antiquities; their palaces show a refined use of classical elements to achieve a Vitruvian decorum appropriate to each patron—the one a man of the highest political, social and religious standing in Rome, the other a jurist.

The extent of the Palazzo Farnese's completion by the time of Sangallo's death in 1546 is difficult to ascertain; while construction is documented through letters, drawings and contracts,

1546: Building halted. **1547:** Cornice built, designs revised; **Architect:** Michelangelo (1475-64). **After 1565:** Rear wing begun; **Architect:** Giacomo Barozzi da Vignola (1507-73). **1586-92:** Building completed. **1589:** Facade completed; **Architect:** Guglielmo della Porta (1532-1602). **1597-1604:** Interior frescoes, gallery, painted; **Artist:** Annibale Carracci (1560-1609).

Publications

BOURDON, PIERRE: "Un plafond du Palais Farnèse." *École française de Rome: Mélanges d'archéologie et d'histoire* 27 (1907): 3-22.
BOURDON, PIERRE, and LAURENT-VIBERT, ROBERT: "Le palais Farnèse d'après l'inventaire de 1653." *École française de Rome: Mélanges d'archéologie et d'histoire* 29 (1909): 145-198.

*

The Palazzo Farnese is, perhaps, the most magnificent Renaissance palace in Rome. It was begun in 1515 by Antonio da Sangallo the Younger for Cardinal Alessandro Farnese, the future Pope Paul III (1534-49), and his family. The palace was left unfinished at the time of Sangallo's death in 1546; adding to the complexity of its building history, the palace was completed by several architects in the following decades. Recent research suggests that Sangallo's original design was respected by those architects, among them Michelangelo, Giacomo da Vignola and Guglielmo della Porta.

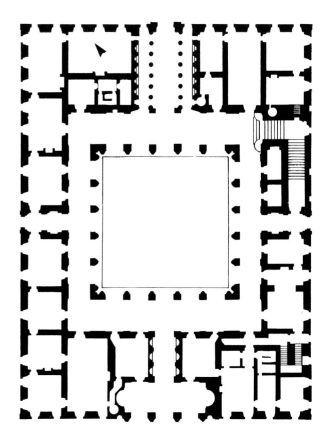

the interpretation of this material varies among scholars. It is generally believed that Sangallo completed the upper story of the front wing, the right wing to the *piano nobile,* and the rear wing to the ground level. However, recent research suggests that the right wing may have been completed beyond the *piano nobile.*

Michelangelo was given the responsibility of the palazzo upon Sangallo's death. It may have been Michelangelo's winning design for the cornice which earned him that position, although his reputation was without question. According to Giorgio Vasari, the competition was held just before Sangallo's death; designs were submitted by Vasari, Michelangelo, Sebastiano del Piombo, Perino del Vaga and Sangallo. Sometime early in 1547 a full-size wooden model of Michelangelo's cornice was set up on the palace for the pope's inspection; by July 1547 the cornice was partially completed.

Michelangelo's cornice was the first significant break from Sangallo's palace design. Sangallo's exterior facade cornice was closer in conception to a Vitruvian model in that it had been proportioned to the top floor only. Michelangelo's cornice, though similar in decorative detail to Sangallo's, was designed in proportion to the entire facade. This contrast spurred a heated debate between disciples of Michelangelo and those who remained faithful to the deceased Sangallo. Sangallo's supporters accused Michelangelo of intending to ruin the palace both visually and structurally. As constructed, however, Michelangelo's cornice type set a new standard of monumentality for later palaces.

Sangallo's design for the entrance to the palace had been simple: spanning the bay above the entrance were arches which rested on freestanding and applied columns; a small papal coat of arms was placed within the tympanum. Michelangelo altered that design and added a sculpted coat of arms, thus relieving the horizontaly of Sangallo's original design at the focal point of the facade by overlapping the verticals with the horizontals.

It is likely that Michelangelo planned some geometric design for the pavement of the piazza. Had such a design been executed, it would have served as a much-needed transitional field between the urban setting and the palace. As it exists today, the palace looms over the great expanse of the piazza, emphasizing its isolation rather than establishing itself as an integral element within the urban fabric.

Michelangelo's contributions to the Palazzo Farnese are characteristic of his approach to Sangallo's design; significant additions were made with the aim of achieving monumentality and an architectural tension unlike the stability typical of Sangallo's work. Nevertheless, Sangallo's fundamental design was maintained.

The palace remained unfinished at the time of Michelangelo's death in 1564, although the Farnese family had taken up residence there many years earlier. The rear wing was finally begun by Vignola at the time of Cardinal Alessandro II Farnese's residence (after 1565). The architecture of the palace was completed under the patronage of Duke Alessandro Farnese of Parma, who lived in the palace from 1586 to 1592, with additional decorative programs by his successor, Cardinal Odoado Farnese.

In architectural terms, the Palazzo Farnese shares much with its Renaissance predecessors in Rome. At the same time, however, the aims of the Farnese to create a grand urban focus for their power, and the accomplishments of the architects to monumentalize that vision, surpassed those earlier examples as a model for later palaces that crossed the boundary between public and private.

—MARJORIE OCH

PALAZZO MASSIMO ALLE COLONNE
Rome, Italy

1532-36. Architect: Baldassare Peruzzi (1481-1536).

Publications

WURM, H.: *Der Palazzo Massimo alle Colonne.* Berlin, 1965.

*

The Palazzo Massimo alle Colonne by Baldassare Peruzzi exemplifies the Mannerist architectural tendencies that developed in Italy early in the 16th century. Rome had been a thriving artistic center during the Renaissance, but the dissolution of Raphael's shop at his death in 1520, as well as the Sack of Rome in 1527, aided in part in bringing about the Mannerist style.

The Palazzo Massimo was built for the brothers Pietro and Angelo Massimo, from a prominent Roman family, to replace a palace owned by the Massimo family on the same site that had been destroyed by fire during the Sack of Rome. The palace received the additional name *"alle colonne"* due to the unusual colonnade along the facade. A document of 28 February 1532 reveals Pietro Massimo's desire to rebuild the palace by regularizing what remained of the structure and building a new facade. The actual site consisted of two separate palaces on adjoining lots, one for each brother, which were systematized by Peruzzi. The irregularity of the site as well as a bend in the street in front of the palace led to the use of a curved facade, which sought to acknowledge rather than disguise this irregularity, thus creating a unique feature that has made the building famous.

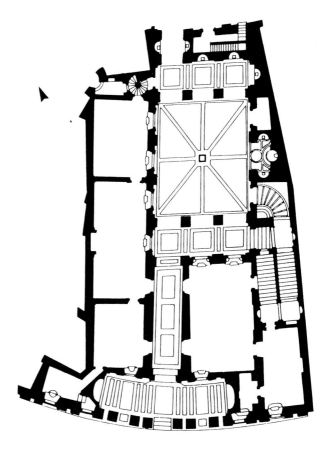

Palazzo Massimo alle Colonne: Rome, Italy, 1532-36

Peruzzi had returned to Siena following the Sack of Rome, but he was seen working at the Church of St. Peter's again in 1531, and returned definitively to Rome in 1534 to become the *capomaestro* at St. Peter's. Therefore, Peruzzi's work on the Palazzo Massimo dates from about 1534 until his death early in 1536, which did not allow him to see his work completed at the palazzo.

Three plans of the palace by Peruzzi exist today in the Uffizi in Florence. The most important drawing, number A368, shows the original rectangular ground plan of the first palazzo, seen with a straight loggia in front, a central corridor through the width of the building, and a large, trapezoidal *cortile* in the back right of the building. Therefore, the use of a loggia, a rare feature often attributed completely to Peruzzi, appeared in the first building, and Peruzzi's contribution extended only to the convex shape introduced in the second palace loggia. Although the use of the loggia on the first story seems unprecedented, it may have been requested by the patron in order to recall a loggia located on the earlier palace that had been destroyed. The source for this type of portico comes from Early Christian churches located in Rome, or suburban villas seen outside of Rome. A loggia located on a private, urban palace remained a rare feature.

The Palazzo Massimo as rebuilt by Peruzzi is characterized by a convex open loggia in the middle of the first story, supported by paired columns. The loggia is classical in nature, but the pairing of columns with pilasters at the edges is a typical Mannerist variation. The facade is accentuated on each side of the loggia by paired pilasters that squeeze windows tightly between each bay, creating a tension in spacing. The second story has windows topped by Mannerist sculptural molding rather than by simpler classical pediments. The third story and

attic level both have small mezzanine windows surrounded by flat framing that have no classical source and that break purposefully from the size ratios of the lower windows, making a visual transition upward that seems illogical. The courtyard also shows Mannerist elements, such as the strange attic windows above the first-story loggia, which serve to mask the great discrepancy between the heights of the two stories, but break the visual unity between the two stories.

Peruzzi was trained in the Renaissance tradition in the shop of Raphael in Rome, and was certainly familiar with Bramante's extremely classical Palazzo Carini in Rome (ca. 1510), as well as Raphael's Roman Palazzo Branconio dall'Aquila (ca. 1515), which already showed some freedom in decorative detail that diverged from the High Renaissance ideal. Peruzzi's first Roman palace commission was the Farnesina (1511), which shows a more strict adherence to the classical ideals found in the architectural treatise of the ancient Roman scholar Vitruvius, a text that was revived by Renaissance architects.

Peruzzi's work of the 1520s shows a definitive turn toward Mannerism, however, and this could be seen for the first time on the facade of his Palazzo Fusconi-Pighini in Rome (1521), where he inverted the Doric and Ionic orders, breaking with classical precedent. In defense of his less restrained use of classical elements, Peruzzi argued that Vitruvius did not discuss all the possibilities of ancient classical architectural vocabulary, but gave only a restricted and incomplete study. Thus, Peruzzi thought of his Mannerist vocabulary not as a rejection of the classicism of the High Renaissance, but as an expansion on classical architectural vocabulary in order to create a greater variety in building articulation. The Palazzo Massimo alle Colonne, in the unprecedented use of a slight curve in the facade as well as the innovative use of an open loggia on the first floor, clearly exemplifies these Mannerist ideals.

—ALLISON PALMER

PIAZZA DEL CAMPIDOGLIO
Rome, Italy

Ca. 1546: Reconstruction of existing piazza planned; **Architect:** Michelangelo (1475-1564). **Ca. 1550-55:** Loggias built; **Architect:** Giacomo Barozzi da Vignola (1507-73). **1564-68:** Palazzo dei Conservatori built; **Architect:** Michelangelo. **1579:** Campanile built. **From 1592:** Palazzo del Senatore built; **Architect:** Michelangelo; completed by Girolamo Rainaldi (1570-1655). **1644-55:** Capitoline Museum built; **Architect:** Michelangelo; executed by Girolamo Rainaldi.

Publications

ASHBY, T.: "The Capitol in Rome: Its History and Development." *Town Planning Review* 12: 159-173.

D'OSSAT, G. DE ANGELIS, et al.: *Il Campidoglio di Michelangelo.* Milan, 1965.

PECCHIAI, P.: *Il Campidoglio nel cinquecento sulla scorta dei documenti.* Rome, 1950.

SPEZZAFERRO, LUIGI, and TITTONI, MARIA ELISA (eds.): *Il Campidoglio e Sisto V.* Rome, 1991.

VENTURI, ROBERT: "The Campidoglio: A Case Study." *Architectural Review* (May 1953).

*

On 10 December 1537, on the ancient Capitoline Hill, Michelangelo Buonarroti was made a citizen of Rome. The Capitoline Hill, which in antiquity had borne witness to Roman triumphs from throughout the Mediterranean world, retained both a political and symbolic significance to the Roman people. The site itself, however, was devoid of its former radiant grandeur. By

Piazza del Campidoglio: Rome, Italy, ca. 1546

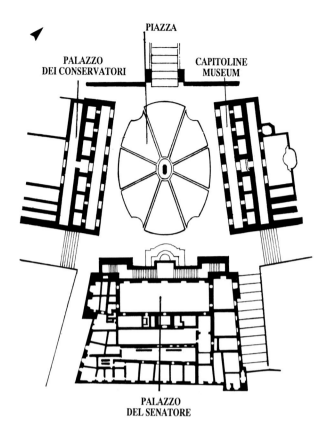

PIAZZA

PALAZZO
DEI CONSERVATORI

CAPITOLINE
MUSEUM

PALAZZO
DEL SENATORE

statue, on a base designed by Michelangelo, was set in place in front of the Palazzo del Senatore. With that beginning, Michelangelo made plans to design the piazza, redesign the facades of the two existing structures, and construct a third palace, the Palazzo Nuovo, on the northern side of the hill, opposite the Palazzo dei Conservatori. Construction of the Piazza del Campidoglio was not completed until the mid-17th century. Fortunately, Michelangelo's intentions were preserved in three engravings dating from 1567 (plan), 1568 and 1569 (views). These engravings guided the completion of the project, and retain for us Michelangelo's conception, from which we can compare later alterations.

Michelangelo's solution to the irregularity of the existing buildings and piazza was both inventive and practical. The new facade designs for the Palazzo del Senatore and the Palazzo dei Conservatori would utilize existing structures. The campanile of the Palazzo del Senatore, however, needed to be moved. Atop the center of the palazzo, the campanile would define the axis not only of the buildings, but also of the piazza as a whole. To complete the symmetry of the piazza, the Palazzo Nuovo would flank the northern side of the Palazzo del Senatore, directly opposite the Palazzo dei Conservatori. That 80-degree angle between the existing Palazzo dei Conservatori and Palazzo del Senatore was repeated in the orientation of the Palazzo Nuovo, creating a trapezoidal shape for the piazza. At the center of the trapezoid, in line with the senate-house campanile, stood the bronze statue of Marcus Aurelius. The base which Michelangelo designed for the ancient equestrian statue was primarily oval, and from that base an oval pavement pattern was expanded within the trapezoidal shape of the piazza. Twelve complex, geometric interlocking grids, emanating from a twelve-pointed star pattern at the base of the statue, were designed in the pavement within the oval.

The symbolism of the oval-and-star pattern has engendered various interpretations. Charles de Tolnay views the oval as suggesting a terrestrial globe, implying a *caput mundi* significance. James Ackerman discusses a cosmological meaning to be found in the pavement pattern, while David Summers establishes a correspondence between the oval and the form of the human head, asserting the anatomical basis of the microcosmic tradition which was the context of Michelangelo's creativity. Formally, the oval plan within the trapezoidal shape creates both a central and axial focus, simultaneously responding to and defining the space of the piazza.

Michelangelo designed five entrances to the Campidoglio, including an axial *cordonata* as the main access from the city. Ascending the *cordonata*, one is greeted by what Ackerman rightly has described as a "crescendo of forms." As more and more of the piazza is revealed, from the campanile of the Palazzo del Senatore to the intricate pavement design, the diversity of parts is inexorably bound to a unity of design and purpose. On either side, in the Palazzo dei Conservatori and the Palazzo Nuovo, a monumental rhythm, established by the use of the giant Corinthian pilasters, carries one's attention to the climax of the imposing senate house. Unlike the vestibule of the Laurentian Library, where Michelangelo challenged expectations of support and ornament, in the Palazzo dei Conservatori the structural support is disclosed in the giant pilasters, which primarily bear the load of the cornice. The pilasters, along with the columns which support the entablature of the portico, are the measured, skeletal components of the design, components whose form directly communicates their function. The central entrance to the palace is noted only by the more ornate pedimental window above; the monumental longitudinal rhythm of the piazza proceeds nearly undisturbed to the Palazzo del Senatore.

the early 16th century, the architecture was eclectic and the setting was mundane. Michelangelo's design would transform the Capitoline Hill, which the Romans termed Campidoglio, into a unified complex of space and buildings, the plan of which evolved from the architect's profound concern with the human figure in art. For Michelangelo and later architects, the Piazza del Campidoglio truly gave new meaning to the concept of monumentality in architectural design.

On that December day in 1537, only two buildings occupied the Campidoglio. The Palazzo del Senatore sat at the eastern end, with its back to the ancient Roman forum just below the hill. Initially constructed in the 12th century, the Palazzo del Senatore, with its towering campanile, was typical of governmental palaces in northern Italy. To the south of the senate house, and set at an 80-degree angle to it, was the Palazzo dei Conservatori. Built in the 15th century, the conservator's palace housed offices and an art museum enhanced later in the century by Pope Sixtus IV. In keeping with the historical importance of the Campidoglio, the museum housed many of Rome's ancient treasures, including the Etruscan bronze *She Wolf*, a symbol of the city. The varying architectural styles and barren piazza contributed to a setting which hardly confirmed the dignity of its significance. In addition, no major access road led to the hill from the city itself.

Rome's lack of a civic center had become especially apparent during the visit of Emperor Charles V in 1536. Pope Paul III (Alessandro Farnese) lamented that there was no ceremonial site in which visiting dignitaries could be received publicly. A year later, Paul III, over Michelangelo's objections, planned to move the ancient bronze equestrian statue of Marcus Aurelius from the basilica precinct of San Giovanni in Laterano to the Campidoglio. The piazza was leveled, and in January 1538 the

The giant pilasters of the senate house, now ornamental, contribute to the insistent unity established by their use in the flanking palaces. But here is another of Michelangelo's inventive yet practical solutions to the necessities demanded by architecture. A triangular stairway occupies the lower register of the facade. It allows immediate access to the main floor, while extending only minimally into the space of the piazza. Atop the stairway, on the axis established by the *cordonata,* the *Marcus Aurelius* statue and the campanile above, a baldachin provides a sheltered focus for ceremonial events.

The stairway serves additional purposes; its triangular design leads from the flanking palaces to the climax of the visual "crescendo," while it also acts as the backdrop for two ancient colossal sculptures of reclining river gods, one of which was altered to represent Rome's Tiber River. Respecting the ancient tradition of sculpture on the Capitoline Hill, as well as the Renaissance exhibition of sculpture in the Palazzo dei Conservatori, Michelangelo integrated sculpture throughout his design. Like the *Marcus Aurelius,* the statues and their judicious placement offered a tangible link to the splendor of Rome's past.

As Bramante had done in the Cortile del Belvedere, which most probably influenced aspects of the Campidoglio design, Michelangelo created an architectural and environmental space. It is, in one sense, a monumental and solemn stage where the public functions of Rome would be enacted with nobility and *virtù.* Yet however grand the environment of the Campidoglio, it responds to us in a more immediate way.

Within the microcosmic/macrocosmic tradition, Michelangelo understood architecture as analogous to the human figure. As the body is symmetrical, with features which are both independent and interdependent, so too the architectural "features" of the Campidoglio, ordered about a longitudinal axis, are resolved with an individual, yet coherent relationship. Michelangelo's design allows us to participate in the Piazza del Campidoglio not only as witnesses to an event, but also with an empathetic understanding of our environment.

—BERNARD SCHULTZ

PIAZZA NAVONA
Rome, Italy

1475: Foundations of ancient stadium leveled, ground paved.
1574: Two fountains built (subsequently altered); **Architect:** Giacomo della Porta (1532-1602). **1645:** Palazzo Pamphili built; **Architect:** Girolamo Rainaldi. **1645:** Initial plans for Church of Sant'Agnese created; **Architect:** Carlo Rainaldi (1611-91). **1648:** Church of Sant'Agnese commisioned. **1650:** Fountain of the Four Rivers built; **Architect:** Giovanni Lorenzo Bernini (1598-1680). **1652:** Church of Sant'Agnese built; **Architects:** Carlo Rainaldi (head architect until 1653 and after 1657), Francesco Borromini (1599-1667, head architect 1653-57), Bernini (1598-1680), Girolamo Rainaldi.

Publications

EIMER, GERHARD: *La fabbrica di S. Agnese in Navona.* 2 vols., Stockholm, 1970-71.
MONTANELLI, I., et al.: *Piazza Navona, Isola dei Pamphili.* Rome, 1978.

*

The Piazza Navona, a large, rectangular square located in the center of Rome, was originally built as a raceway during the Roman Imperial Age. This track, called the Circus Flaminius, was inaugurated by Domitian in 86 A.D. to celebrate the Capitoline Contest, an event derived from the athletic games of Olympia. Domitian built an odeum and a stadium next to each other on the southern side of the square near the modern Corso Vittorio Emmanuele, while the amphitheater stretched around the northern side of the square. The stadium was used for many years after the rule of Domitian for gladiator games, until the amphitheater was destroyed by fire in 217 A.D. The square today maintains this rather unusual long, rectangular shape enclosing the oval area that was used for the race track.

After the establishment of Christianity in Rome, this square became famous as the site of the martyrdom of Saint Agnes. The square was then called the Stadio Agonale, or Campo di Agone, through the Middle Ages, in reference to a small church built there to commemorate the death of the saint. In 1123 Pope Callisto II rebuilt the church and officially named it Sant'-Agnese. The remains of the stadium had filled in with dirt and grass by that time, and the foundations were being used for market stalls and shops.

It was not until the 15th century that the square began to be regularized with important architectural commissions, including the Church of San Giacomo degli Spagnoli, built on the south end by Bernardo Rossellino. In 1450 Giovanni Rucellai was still able to see the foundations of the ancient stadium, but these were finally destroyed in 1475 when Pope Sixtus IV leveled and paved the ground, and imposed the first zoning laws in that area. The square was then enlivened with a larger population brought by the market that was moved to the Piazza Navona in 1477 from the Capitoline Hill. In the 16th century Pope Gregory XIII commissioned Giacomo della Porta to build two fountains, one at each end of the piazza. These fountains, completed in 1574, show a Mannerist arrangement of four tritons blowing water through conch shells, surrounded by a balustrade.

In the middle of the 17th century, this piazza became the site selected by Pope Innocent X Pamphili as his papal enclave. It was Innocent's grandiose plan that transformed the square into the area that exists today. Beginning in 1645 he commissioned a family palace to be built by Girolamo Rainaldi near where the medieval Church of Sant'Agnese had recently been demolished. The Palazzo Pamphili was built quickly, because Rainaldi used the original boundaries of older buildings, such as the Palazzo Mellini, attached to the Palazzo Pamphili, and the area adjacent to the Palazzo Braschi, owned by Dona Olimpia Pamphili, to build his structure. The first ground plan, signed by Rainaldi, was dated June 1645, and construction was begun shortly thereafter. The facade appears as a simple Late Renaissance design with subtle Mannerist articulation of the decorative window moldings.

In 1648 Innocent X commissioned the building of the monumental Baroque Church of Sant'Agnese. Documents suggest that the church was planned in 1645, however, which would

Piazza Navona: Rome, Italy, 1475

show that the idea of creating a complete papal enclave did not develop with the project, but was the initial impetus for the work. This church, begun in 1652 across from the Palazzo Pamphili, was built through the next decade by Girolamo and his son Carlo Rainaldi, as well as by Francesco Borromini and Giovanni Lorenzo Bernini. It is characterized by a centralized plan covered by a monumental facade with a very dynamic, concave form topped by a tall dome that was meant to rival the Church of St. Peter's.

Although the separate contributions of each architect remain unclear, the majority of the work falls into the oeuvre of the

Rainaldi. Carlo Rainaldi designed the Greek-cross plan with an octagonal interior formed from beveled columns detached from the four edges of the crossing. Disengaged columns first appeared in Rainaldi's plans for the ciborium of Santa Maria della Scala (1646). Borromini took over in 1653, completed the interior above the niches, and rebuilt the exterior to his design. The dynamic undulations of the facade, so characteristic of Borromini, can also be seen in the facade of his Church of San Carlo alle Quattro Fontane in Rome (1665). At some point Bernini or Carlo Fontana may have contributed the more classical triangular pediment and high, flat attic to the facade. Carlo

Piazza Navona, Church of Sant'Agnese, building detail: 1652

Rainaldi then replaced Borromini in 1657, and finished the work on the exterior above the entablature.

In 1650 Innocent X commissioned Bernini to build a grandiose fountain topped by an obelisk, which was to symbolize the triumph of Christianity through the four parts of the world. This fountain, called the Fountain of the Four Rivers, is located in the middle of the square, between the two Renaissance fountains by Della Porta. Bernini's fountain consists of allegorical sculptures of the four major rivers of the world: the Danube of Europe, seen with a horse and the coat-of-arms of Pope Innocent X; the Nile of Africa, seen veiled to demonstrate the unknown source of the river, and with a lion; the Rio de la Plata of America, seen with an armadillo and coins showing the great wealth of the newly discovered continent; and the Ganges of Asia, seen with a palm tree, serpent, and a long oar representing the long, navigable waters of the river. These figures are situated in a travertine grotto that holds a granite obelisk above.

This theatrical work not only displayed the triumph of Christianity in all four corners of the world with Rome as the center of Catholicism, but also emphasized Innocent X's participation in these gains. Thus, the square, begun as an ancient Roman stadium, had grown to become one of the most important squares of the Baroque age.

—ALLISON PALMER

Piazza Navona, fountain: 1650

PIAZZA DEL POPOLO
Rome, Italy

1472-77: Santa Maria del Popolo built; **Architect:** Attributed to Andrea Bregno. **1572-78:** Fountain built; **Architect:** Giacomo della Porta (1532-1602). **1655:** Porta Flaminia decorated; **Architect:** Giovanni Lorenzo Bernini (1598-1680). **1662:** Piazza designed; **Architect:** Carlo Rainaldi (1611-91). **1662:** Santa Maria di Monte Santo begun; **Architect:** Carlo Rainaldi. **1673-75:** Construction on Santa Maria di Monte Santo halted, designs revised, and work completed; **Architects:** Bernini (1598-1680) and Carlo Fontana (1634-1741). **1675-79:** Santa Maria de'Miracoli built; **Architect:** Carlo Rainaldi and assistant Carlo Fontana. **1810-16:** Piazza redesigned and rebuilt; **Architect:** Giuseppe Valadier.

Publications

CIUCCI, G.: *La Piazza del Popolo*. Rome, 1974.

The grand scale of Piazza del Popolo is an anomaly among the more intimate spaces of Rome, Italy. The Piazza was first laid out along a north-south axis during the Renaissance and Baroque periods. In the 19th century, during the French occupation, the Piazza underwent a monumental expansion in the neoclassical style, which added an east-west axis to the plan and showed a strong French influence.

Theatricality was an important theme of the Piazza del Popolo, which was situated along the processional route through the heavenly city. The processional route was used for the grand entries organized to welcome visiting religious and secular dignitaries. The layout of the processional route evinced a clear sense of a sequentially ordered ceremony, a journey through a series of spiritual gates to the inner sanctum of the holy city. The Piazza del Popolo was one of these spiritual gates. The Renaissance and Baroque design made a kind of stage of the piazza, with the buildings functioning as a backdrop. The piazza was truncated in plan. Initially two streets branched off from it, the Corso and the Via di Ripetta, funneling movement toward the medieval Churches of Santa Maria di Montesanto and Santa Maria dei Miracoli.

Piazza del Popolo: Rome, Italy, 1472-77

Early in the 16th century, this fork was changed to a trident by the addition of a third street, the Via del Babuino, planned by Pope Leo X and carried out by Antonio da Sangallo. The trident was the first of its kind, and served to define the two churches. The design creates a scenic arrangement that follows the normative descriptions of theatrical design by such architectural theorists as Leon Battista Alberti, Andrea Palladio and Sebastiano Serlio, with their emphasis on the proscenium arch. In the layout of the Piazza del Popolo, the churches function as a proscenium arch, while the three avenues serve as painted backdrops.

The formation of the trident enhances the drama of the Piazza del Popolo. Each of the avenues may be associated with one of three recognized dramatic types, comedy, tragedy and satire. Comedy was conventionally represented by ordinary buildings on theatrical backdrops, the equivalent of which are the homes along the Via del Babuino. Tragedy was associated with royal surroundings, which are found on the Corso, the central arm of the trident. Lined with the grand palazzos of the Roman nobility and Rome's temporal and spiritual institutions, the Corso extends directly into the heart of the city, ending at the summit of the ancient capital, the Campidoglio. Satire was symbolized in the theater by natural landscape. The Via di Ripetta represents satire by connecting the Piazza del Popolo directly to the Tiber River.

The neoclassical expansion of the piazza, while respectful of history, made some important new changes. The north-south orientation of the old plan was crossed by an east-west axis. The design of the expanded piazza was based on the classical Roman axial urban plans shaped by the *cardo* (north-south axis) and *decumanus* (east-west axis). The neoclassical expansion employed monumental planning to express a secular rationalism of a decidedly French bent. It suggests a liberal interpretation of the divine circle, and its iconographic program is cosmological in nature. Setting the parameters of the cosmological scheme are statues of four lions, representing the four seasons and eternal time, and statues of four sphinxes, representing divine knowledge.

The east-west orientation is defined by an allegorical theme, opposing nature and culture. Nature is represented by Neptune, placed on the Tiber River side of the piazza, across from Romulus and Remus, the mythical founders of civilization. On the Monte Pincio terraces are the Prisoner statues and the rostral columns, recalling victorious battle and the Arch of Constantine from classical antiquity. A bas-relief represents a rationalist Fame, which is synonymous with virtue and culture, crowning the genius of the arts and sciences. Although the 19th-century Piazza del Popolo incorporates the mythos of antiquity, the impetus to do so derives from a sense of historical duty rather than a revival of belief in the world views the supernatural beings represent. Thus the café at the summit of the Monte Pincio suggests voyeuristic rather than spiritual tendencies.

The neoclassical design also refers to theatrical architecture, but uses classical Greek rather than Roman models, dispensing with the proscenium, for instance. The view from the Monte Pincio hill, overlooking the oval stage of the Piazza del Popolo, the Tiber River, the Castle Sant'Angelo and St. Peter's, uses the cityscape as the stage scenery. The neoclassical theater design faces west, with the Roman proscenium to its left, giving a panoramic view of the stage of the city, observing St. Peter's historically, rather than as a living sacred space of spiritual enlightenment.

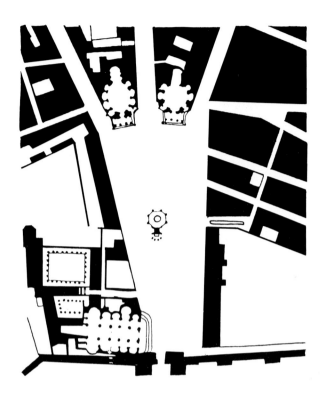

The point of integration of the north-south and east-west axes represents the intended merging of the less-than-harmonious cultural intentions of Rome and France. In actuality, the political and theological views of the Romans, pursuing the interests of the pontifical states, and the French, seeking to realize the ideals of the *nouveau regime,* remained fixed in opposite directions. Ironically, while the Piazza del Popolo was a culmination of the evolution of many centuries of public ritual and ceremony, it was realized at a time when the city as the stage for public ritual was becoming more and more irrelevant.

—LORNA ANNE McNEUR

SANT' ANDREA AL QUIRINALE
Rome, Italy

1658: Construction begun; **Architect:** Giovanni Lorenzo Bernini (1598-1680). **1660:** Main lantern added. **Ca. 1662:** Sculptural decor and rose and white marble revetment added. **1668:** Main altar chapel designed. **Ca. 1670:** Porch and entry facade constructed. **1676:** Entry wing-walls added.

Publications

BAUER, G.: "Gian Lorenzo Bernini: The Development of an Architectural Iconography" (Ph.D. dissertation). Princeton, New Jersey, 1974.

BORSI, F.: *La chiesa di S. Andrea al Quirinale.* Rome, 1967.

BRAUER, H., and WITTKOWER, RUDOLF: *Die Zeichnungen des Gianlorenzo Bernini.* Berlin, 1931.

CONNORS, J.: "Bernini's S. Andrea al Quirinale: Payments and Planning." *Journal of the Society of Architectural Historians* 41 (March 1982): 15-37.

FROMMEL, C. L.: "S. Andrea al Quirinale: genesi e Bstruttura." In GIANFRANCO SPAGNESI and MARCELLO FAGIOLO (eds.): *Gianlorenzo Bernini architetto e l'architettura europea del sei-settecento.* Rome, 1983.

MARDER, TOD A.: "The Evolution of Bernini's Designs for the Facade of Sant'Andrea al Quirinale: 1658-76." *Architectura* 21, No. 2 (1990): 108-132.

SMYTH-PINNEY, JULIA M.: "The Geometrics of S. Andrea al Quirinale." *Journal of the Society of Architectural Historians* 48 (March 1989): 53-65.

VARRIANO, J.: *Italian Baroque and Rococo Architecture.* New York, 1986.

WITTKOWER, RUDOLF: *Art and Architecture in Italy 1600-1750.* 3rd ed., Harmondsworth, England, 1973.

*

Sant' Andrea al Quirinale, designed by Giovanni Lorenzo Bernini at the height of his architectural career, provided him with an important first opportunity to create a complete ecclesiastical structure. The church's oval plan with drumless oval dome appears to confirm Bernini's belief in using forms sanctioned by classical and Renaissance traditions, particularly as established by Serlio and Vignola, as the foundation for his design. Further evidence of Bernini's apparent traditionalism is furnished by the basically conservative forms used in his other two contemporaneous small central-plan churches: the Greek-cross plan of San Tomaso di Villanova (1658-61), and the Pantheon-like round church of Santa Maria dell'Assunzione (1662-64).

Scholars differ regarding the relative importance of Bernini's church architecture, and particularly Sant' Andrea, which is universally accepted as the most original, complex and successful of the three churches. When Bernini's traditionalism is stressed, Sant' Andrea is judged to be a building of only localized interest that is heavily overshadowed in originality by Francesco Borromini's efforts at San Carlo alle Quattro Fontane and Sant' Ivo alla Sapienza. However, when the innovative characteristics of the church of Sant' Andrea, some of which are outlined below, are examined, a more positive evaluation emerges both of Sant' Andrea's quality and of Bernini's considerable architectural talents.

Plans for the rebuilding of the Jesuits' conventual church on the Via Pia opposite the long arm of the Quirinal Palace had been delayed for years. When the financial support of Cardinal Camillo Pamphili and the approval of Pope Alexander VII (Chigi) were given in the summer of 1658, it took Bernini a scant month to establish a first oval plan that by October 1658 was being used to begin the foundations of the new church adjacent to the existing convent. Subsequent changes in design over the following 18 years are recorded in a series of drawings from Bernini's workshop and attest to his continual involvement with the building as it changed markedly in response to programmatic and budgetary revisions. Recent scholarship has revealed that many of the features earlier accepted as integral aspects of a cohesive initial design effort were in fact modified piecemeal over more than a decade: the main lantern (added 1660), the sculptural decor and the rose and white marble revetment on the interior (after 1662), the main altar chapel with its lantern (designed in 1668), the porch and entry facade (after 1670), and the entry wing-walls (1676) were all modifications of the original design. The conceptual, iconographical and spatial clarity of the building, whose parts are drawn into a powerful

Sant'Andrea al Quirinale: Rome, Italy, 1658

experiential unity, is an especially amazing feat given the temporal discontinuity in its design and construction.

Preexisting site constraints and a program calling for five
altars initially led Bernini to propose a pentagonal plan for the
church, which was quickly set aside. The approved oval plan,
pushed back from the street and initially set in a courtyard to
avoid competition with the pope's residence, had to be positioned with its minor axis leading from entrance to main altar.
This highly unusual orientation of the oval, whose long axis
would ordinarily coincide with the path from entry to altar,
allows the energetic thrust of the axis of entry to be balanced
by the transverse pull of the oval. This balance is reinforced
by the incorporation of vestibule and altar spaces to extend the

oval's short axis, and by Bernini's innovation of using pilasters
rather than chapel openings to terminate the oval's long axis.
The total length of the open space from entry door to altar
painting thereby exactly equals the length of the opposing cross
axis. In effect as well as in measure, a true central plan was
created.

The spatial interactions of the interior are even more richly
complex, however, as an examination of the architectural promenade reveals, because experiences initiated by architectural
elements are enhanced by the coordinated impact of sculpture
and light. The visitor to the church enters the vestibule carved
from the *poche* of the chapel ring, pauses at the edge of the
main oval space, and faces the triptych of the main altar aedicule

Sant'Andrea al Quirinale

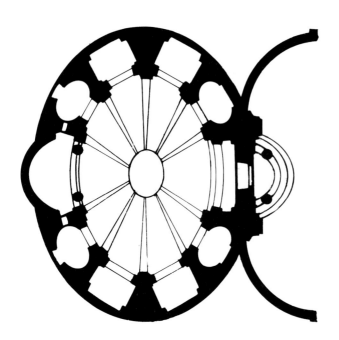

with its flanking chapels. The figure of Saint Andrew, perched above the altar pediment, gestures to the lantern opening in the main dome from whence light floods downward, thus creating diagonal relationships between the visitor at the entry, the figure of the saint, and the dome. The skeletal elements of the pavement, pilasters and dome ribs further reinforce the visitor's upward view to the main lantern.

In counterpoint, the curvilinear surfaces of the walls and coffered dome and the powerful sweep of the main entablature insist upon an essential rotundity that is emphasized and yet softened by the gentle wave of fishermen, putti and garlands draped above and between the windows that are cut into the lowest zone of the dome. The visitor then proceeds to the altar aedicule, where light again streams down from a lantern; putti and angels ascend on gilded rays, transporting the painted image of a crucified Saint Andrew up to the second altar dome. This establishes another complementary diagonal relationship between the visitor, the saint, and a dome. Thus, Bernini successfully coordinated multiple interactions among the horizontal axes of path and oval, the vertical axes of central and altar domes, the diagonal relationships of lines of sight, light and sculptural gesture, and the rotundity and centripetal forces of ovals and domes.

The design of the grand marble facade and the low, concave quadrant walls that form the entry piazza also attests to Bernini's genius. Although they were late additions, these new elements seem inevitable, so coherently are they wedded to the form and concept of the main body of the church. The semicircular porch bursts outward through the tall, flat, pedimented gateway, and yet is tied horizontally to the low chapel ring behind by the taut band of cornice. The still lower quadrant walls enclose the negative piazza space in counterpoint to the positive volume of the church. The standard view of the building on the diagonal allows all of these curvilinear elements to be seen in concert, and in opposition to the orthogonality of the giant temple front that firmly continues the major cornice-line of the tall, oval cylinder encasing the main dome. Perhaps most important, the interactions of these exterior elements become dynamic spatial and psychological prefigurations of the primary elements of the interior. Thus Sant' Andrea exists as a superb example of the unity not only of exterior with interior, but also of the arts of painting, sculpture and architecture in a paradigmatic yet unique whole.

—JULIA M. SMYTH-PINNEY

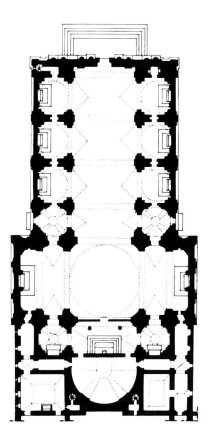

SANT' ANDREA DELLA VALLE
Rome, Italy

1591: Construction on foundations of nave and first four chapels begun; **Architect:** Francesco da Volterra (died 1594). **1603:** Building halted; agreement for decoration of side chapels arranged; **Architect:** Matteo Castello. **1608:** New designs introduced, building resumed; **Architect:** Carlo Maderno (1556-1629); **Assistant architect:** Francesco Borromini (1599-1667). **1614:** Tombs of Piccolomini popes transferred to church from St. Peter's; **Architect:** Paolo Taccone. **1614-15:** Sculptures added; **Sculptor:** Pietro Bernini (1598-1680). **1615:** Altar fresco painted; **Artist:** Giovanni Lanfranco (1582-1647). **1621-25:** Frescoes in cupola painted; **Artist:** Giovanni Lanfranco; frescoes in presbytery painted; **Artist:** Domenichino (1581-1641). **1622:** Frescoes on choir and pendentives painted; **Artist:** Domenichino. **1623:** Construction halted. **1650s-66:** Construction of facade resumed and completed; **Architects:** Carlo Rainaldi (1611-91) and Carlo Fontana (1634-1714). **1671:** Cappella Ginetti built; **Architect:** Carlo Fontana. **1671-75:** Relief and statues added to Cappella Ginetti; **Architect:** Antonio Raggi (1624-96). **18th, 19th, 20th centuries:** Extensive restorations and remodeling.

Publications

HIBBARD, HOWARD: "The Early History of Sant' Andrea della Valle." *Art Bulletin* 43 (1961): 289-318.

*

The Church of Sant' Andrea della Valle, standing on what is now the Corso Vittorio Emanuele, is one of the great churches of the Counter-Reformation; it was built for the Theatine Order, which had been confirmed in 1540 by Pope Paul III Farnese. In 1584 the Theatines decided to found a church and a *casa* in the center of Rome, and four years later Cardinal Alfonso Gesualdo agreed to underwrite the cost of a new church. Several architects were involved in its construction. Plans were drawn up by Giacomo della Porta, in association with a Theatine architect, Padre Francesco Grimaldi. The new church was begun in 1591, and the construction of the foundations of the nave and the first four chapels proceeded under the supervision of Francesco da Volterra, with ground level being reached in 1594, the year he died. Building continued until 1603, when Cardinal Gesualdo

died and funding ceased; the next few years were marked by litigation between Gesualdo's heirs and the Theatines. But matters were eventually settled, and in 1606 more property was acquired for the expansion and completion of the church.

In 1608 Carlo Maderno was selected by Alessandro Peretti, Cardinal Montalto, to produce a set of new plans for the church. The form was essentially that of the Church of Il Gesù, which had been designed by Vignola in 1568, the church with which Sant' Andrea has always been compared. However, Sant' Andrea has a deeper tribune and more strongly projecting transepts, with the nave articulated by a series of high chapel arches; these arches are separated by clustered Corinthian pilasters that are linked across the vault by raised bands. The chapels are wider than they are long, and are separated and illuminated by large windows that fit the arches leading from the nave into the chapels. The ceiling of the nave is high, higher than that of Il Gesù, resulting in a reduction of the wall surface to a far more sculptured mass than in any of the immediately preceding churches, and invoking the highly active relationship of space and solid that was to be a constant effect of Baroque architecture.

The same might be said for the form of the dome. Like that of Il Gesù, it is completely independent of the rest of the church, and is not visible from the front; however, Sant' Andrea's dome is modeled less on the dome of Il Gesù than on that at St. Peter's, where Maderno's addition of a nave to Michelangelo's centrally planned church also resulted in separating the dome visually from the rest of the building. Yet the dome of Sant' Andrea is smaller than that of St. Peter's, with fewer buttresses and ribs; in its proportion, too, Sant' Andrea's dome is higher and slimmer, with the lines of force running visibly up to the lantern at the top, which was designed by Maderno's young assistant, Francesco Borromini. With its richer and deeper elaboration of the forms to be seen below, the lantern offered a hint of the spatial richness that Baroque architecture was to feature.

Sant'Andrea della Valle: Rome, Italy, 1591

Sant'Andrea della Valle

In the 1620s Maderno prepared a number of designs for the facade, but construction was stopped soon after it began when, in 1623, Cardinal Montalto died. Nothing more was done until the 1650s, when Cardinal Francesco Peretti Montalto died and left income in his will for the construction of the facade. The work was resumed by Carlo Rainaldi and Carlo Fontana, with the church finally being completed in 1666. The facade was built on the ground plan laid out by Maderno, but where Maderno had turned back to his own design at Santa Susanna, with its stepped central section and two clearly marked levels, Rainaldi, expanding the size of the whole facade to cover the area of the church, increased the sense of verticality: he produced a design where the play of the elements in the two-story aedicular facade seems to take place like a performance, as Howard Hibbard put it, "entirely above our heads." This is antique architecture perhaps, but antiquity on the scale of Nero or Trajan.

The church inside is full of works by distinguished artists. Under an agreement of 1603, the Theatines persuaded four noble patrons—Cardinal Maffeo Berberini, Orazio Rucellai, Pietro Paolo Crescenzi and Leone Strozzi—to decorate the side chapels at their own expense. These chapels are full of the richest sculptured decoration, mostly by Matteo Castello. In addition, the tombs of the Piccolomini popes, by the 15th-century sculptor Paolo Taccone, were transferred to Sant' Andrea from St. Peter's in 1614. In the cupola are frescoes by Giovanni Lanfranco showing the *Glory of Paradise* (ca. 1621-25); in the presbytery are others by Domenichino of about the same date, and in the left transept, an altar painting (ca. 1615) by Giovanni Lanfranco. Other paintings in the church are by Mattia Preti, Carlo Cicagnani and Domenico Passignano; there are also sculpted pieces by Francesco Mocchi and Domenico Guidi. Various changes were made in the 18th and 19th centuries, and early in this century the whole church was extensively restored and redecorated. Most notably, the white, unfluted columns in the nave were fluted and gilded in imitation of those in the chancel; the bands of the nave vaults were decorated, and paintings between them were executed by Silvio Galimberti, Virgino Monti and other artists. The church was newly inaugurated on 31 March 1907.

—DAVID CAST

SAN CARLO ALLE QUATTRO FONTANE
Rome, Italy

1634: Church designs commissioned; dormitory, cloisters and refectory begun; **Architect:** Francesco Borromini (1599-1667). **1638-41:** Church built. **1646:** Church consecrated. **1665-67:** Facade built; **Architects:** Borromini (lower story), completed by Bernardo. **1682:** Sculptural decoration on facade completed; **Sculptors:** Borromini and Antonio Raggi (1624-86).

Publications

ARGAN, GIULIO CARLO: *Borromini*. Verona, 1952.
BLUNT, ANTHONY: *Borromini*. Harmondsworth, England, 1979.
HEMPEL, EBERHARD: *Francesco Borromini*. Vienna, 1924.
PORTOGHESI, PAOLO: *The Rome of Borromini*. New York, 1968.
SEDLMAYR, HANS: *Die Architektur Borrominis*. Munich, 1930.
STEINBERG, LEO: *Borromini's San Carlo alle Quattro Fontane: A Study in Multiple Form and Architectural Symbolism*. New York, 1977.
WITTKOWER, RUDOLF: *Art and Architecture in Italy, 1600-1750*. Harmondsworth, England, 1982.

Francesco Borromini's great opportunity to establish himself as an architect came in 1634, with the commission to design the monastery of San Carlo alle Quattro Fontane for the order of the Spanish Discalced Trinitarians in Rome. This church, along with Pietro da Cortona's contemporary church of SS. Luca e Martina, inaugurated the Roman High Baroque period and is truly one of its masterpieces. It achieves Baroque richness and complexity using exclusively architectural means; the limited resources of the Trinitarians did not allow for use of the rich materials that characterize Giovanni Lorenzo Bernini's church of Sant'Andrea al Quirinale just down the block.

The site for the monastery is both small and irregular. The bounding street frontages are less than 80 and 150 feet long and are at an obtuse angle to each other, with the corner chamfered off to contain one of the four fountains that give the church its name. On this small parcel, Borromini was challenged to place a church, a refectory, a dormitory, a library, a cloister and a garden. Borromini met the challenge brilliantly. He placed the church on the corner with its facade on the shorter street frontage. Next to it he placed the cloister. Behind church and cloister runs a three-story monastery block containing the refectory at the first level, the dormitory at the second and the library at the third. The large space behind the monastery is devoted to the garden.

Both cloister and church illustrate Borromini's fascination

San Carlo alle Quattro Fontane, dome interior: Rome, Italy, 1634

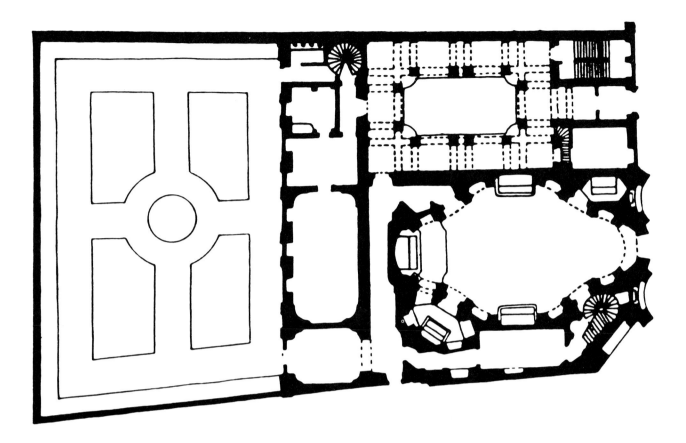

San Carlo alle Quattro Fontane

with geometrical manipulation. The cloister begins as a simple rectangular space. In it is inserted a two-story octagon defined by columns of alternating wide and narrow spacing; at the lower level the wide bays carry arches, while the narrow bays have straight entablatures. At the corners, the entablatures, and the wall segments above them, bulge inward as if the mass of the building were pressing into the open space.

The church retains the cloister's central octagonal spatial unit defined by pairs of columns, but with a difference; the diagonal wall segments they define are straight rather than curved. What is straight and planar in the cloisters is concave in the church, and what is convex in the cloisters is straight in the church. In the church the walls of the larger bays on the longitudinal and cross axes bow out to form narthex, sanctuary and side chapels. The straight walls are fixed and solid, the curved walls plastic and membranous; equilibrium is created between dynamic space and solid structure. The space has a dynamic pulsating character at ground level that is in contrast to the simple elliptical dome that constitutes the upper zone of the church.

Borromini was the first Baroque master to create plan forms by overlapping geometrical units. His extant drawing of the plan clearly reveals that all critical features of the plan evolve from a lozenge formed by two equilateral triangles circumscribed about tangent circles. The apexes of the lozenge mark the extremities of the concave forms at ends and sides; they are also the centers of the arcs that describe the long sides of the ellipse of the nave vault. Although the lozenge disappears as a visible form in the resultant space, vestiges of it remain in the straight segments of wall that support the dome's pendentives. All of the geometric figures employed to create the plan merge to form the single pulsating space that is the church. The unitary character of the space is emphasized by the entablature of the

Corinthian columns that decorate all surfaces. The round columns hide the intersections of straight and curved wall segments (the arrises show only in the entablature), adding to the church's pulsating, visually nondeterminate geometry. The columns are double-functioning elements, belonging equally to, and defining the ends of, both the straight and curved wall segments.

Although the elliptical plan form has a dynamic directional character, it is not the longitudinal axis but rather the vertical axis that is dominant in San Carlo. The church is almost twice as tall as it is long, and the height is emphasized by the treatment of the dome coffering; the coffers diminish in size as they move up in space, adding to the illusion of great depth. The emphasis on height makes the greater longitudinal dimension of the elliptical plan incidental.

While the facade of San Carlo was not built until the 1660s, Borromini's plan drawings of the 1630s indicate that a curved facade was planned from the start. If it had been built then, it would have vied with Cortona's church of SS. Luca e Martina for the distinction of being the first of the Roman High Baroque curved church facades. What is uncertain, since it was done by Bernardo after Borromini's death, is how much of the upper story is Borromini's design. Certainly the painted oval medallion supported by sculpted angelic figures is not Borromini's; this piece seems to have been borrowed from the design for the high altar at Bernini's church at Castel Gandolfo. Considering the intense dislike Borromini felt for Bernini, it is inconceivable that he would have used one of Bernini's designs. In addition, the tall false wall of the upper story, which obscures all view of the dome, is also inconsistent with Borromini's work; it too is probably Bernardo's invention.

The lower story and the lower portion of the upper story were constructed before Borromini's death under his supervision, however. The powerful double S-curve of the lower facade is an outstanding example of the Baroque fascination with movement. The interior space presses the wall out at its center, whereas the exterior space exerts greater pressure at each side of the oval interior plan form, causing the facade to indent. Interior space and exterior space are in equilibrium; the facade is the membrane in between.

—C. MURRAY SMART, JR.

SANTA COSTANZA
Rome, Italy

Ca. 330: Construction of mausoleum or baptistery for Emperor Constantine's daughter Constantina. **1256:** Building converted to a church.

Publications

STETTLER, M.: ''Zur Rekonstruktion von S. Costanza.'' *Römische Mitteilungen* 58 (1943): 76-86.

*

To the southwest of the seventh-century Basilica of Sant'Agnese on the Via Nomentana in Rome stands the older, round building of Santa Costanza. Though seen together, the two structures

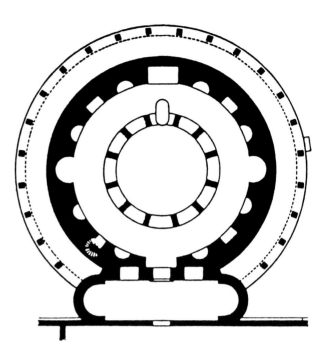

belong to separate historical developments.

The history of the construction of Santa Costanza is controversial. Only fragments of walls survive of the large, fourth-century cemeterial basilica to which Santa Costanza was once attached, either as an integral part or as a later addition. Since Constantina, Constantine's daughter, built the cemeterial basilica, some scholars have attributed the round building to her as well. The association was made early, for her memory survives in the Christianized dedication of the building to a fictitious ''Santa Costanza,'' first recorded in 865. The building may have served as Constantina's mausoleum, or as the baptistery, the latter mentioned in fourth-century documents but not identified elsewhere at the site.

This uncertainty concerning the origin of the building, either as a mausoleum or as a baptistery, is compounded by the fact that Early Christian baptisteries were modeled on Late Roman mausolea. Iconographic boundaries between secular and religious art and architecture were not drawn clearly in the fourth century, as evidenced in the mosaic decoration of this same interior and elsewhere, on Early Christian sarcophagi, for example. Perhaps careful reexamination of early excavation reports combined with future excavation and a comparative study of masonry techniques will help to clarify the origin of the building.

The architectural style of Santa Costanza belongs to the Roman architectural tradition. Consisting of three concentric rings, the plan is circular with a diameter of 22.5 meters. The plan includes an exterior peripteral portico, now lost, but once covered by a barrel vault supported on columns. The second ring forms an interior barrel-vaulted ambulatory. And the third ring, the central core, is covered by a tall drum supporting a dome and resting on an arcade of 24 paired, monolithic columns aligned radially, each pair joined by a single impost block and entablature.

Santa Costanza: Rome, Italy

The interior was originally relented from the northeast side of the basilica leading into a wide, but shallow, atrium ending in double lateral apses. The same arrangement of double-apsed atrium and round mausoleum reappeared later in the fourth century against the south transept of the basilica of Old St. Peter's in Rome. The double-apse atrium provided the transition from the straight walls and rectangular spaces of the basilica to the curved walls and circular spaces of the mausoleum. Externally, the curved, double apses of the atrium softened the abrupt juncture between rectangular and round volumes. The atrium also acted as a transitional hall between two monumental interiors with differing functions.

On the exterior, roof levels rose at three different heights over the portico, the ambulatory and over the tall dome of the central core, producing a tiered effect. Roofs over the side apses of the atrium were the shortest in height. Opposite the atrium on the rear side of the exterior, a square roof rose from the ambulatory roof over the small domed bay of the niche opposite the entrance. This terracing of the exterior masses produced a geometric clarity consistent with the individual interior spatial units.

Inside, the ambulatory wall was punctuated with 11 shallow, round-arched niches—in addition to the entrance "niche"—that are alternately rectangular and semicircular in plan, reminiscent, in their design, of the plan of the Pantheon. Three elements in the elevation suggest an inscribed Greek cross: the dimensions of the four niches on opposite and transverse axes from the entrance are larger than the other niches along the diagonal axes, the four axial niches open at floor level in the wall while the niches along the diagonal axes open at a height approximately 90 centimeters above the floor, and the arcade arches along the axes are wider and higher than the other arches of the arcade.

The building was designed as if the side aisle and nave of a basilica had been wrapped in a circle. Seventeen small windows pierced the ambulatory wall, but the space remains dark, while the 12 large, round-arched windows that pierced the drum of the dome flooded the inner core with light. The dark aisle, the tall arcade, the entablatures, the monolithic columns, the flat wall beneath the lighted clerestory, the tiered roofs—all were elements stemming from the longitudinal basilica.

The structure is open and spacious, but not billowing; the supports are visible, not concealed; the design is simple, not

Santa Costanza

complex. All features comes from the Roman past. But the building exhibits a lightness and verticality that seem new. It is this lightness and verticality, perhaps, that inspired the builders of the later Lateran baptistery.

The architectural simplicity of the building contributes to its classicity, for as a design, it is complete and whole. The surviving mosaic compartments in the ambulatory vault, with their evenly spaced objects against the unifying white ground, complement the clean, simple lines of the architecture. Originally, the walls of the domed core, now bare, were covered with marble panels and stucco pilasters, and the dome was decorated with mosaics including biblical scenes and resembling a celestial canopy. The richness of the mural decoration was echoed in the ornate composite capitals of the columns and in the complex, tall imposts and entablatures. Architectural simplicity and decorative lavishness became the hallmark of Early Christian building.

—PAULA D. LEVETO-JABR

SAN GIOVANNI IN LATERANO
Rome, Italy

312-13: Church founded. **440:** Baptistery altered. **5th, 8th, 9th, 10th, 12th, 13th, 15th and 16th century:** Church repeatedly renovated and redecorated. **9th century:** Nave damaged in earthquake. **Late 9th and early 10th century:** Nave rebuilt. **12th century:** Cloister built. **14th century:** Nave damaged in

fire and reconstructed. **15th century:** Nave rebuilt again, nave piers strengthened. **1562:** Wooden ceiling constructed; **Architect:** Daniele da Volterra. **1646-49:** Nave reconstructed; **Architect:** Francesco Borromini (1599-1667). **1730-35:** Capella Corsini built and decorated; **Architect:** Alessandro Galilei; **Sculptors:** Filippo della Valle, Giovanni Battista Maini (1690-1752), among others. **1732:** New facade added; **architect:** Alessandro Galilei. **1876-86:** Apse destroyed, new apse and long chancel built; **Architects:** Virgilio and Francesco Vespignani (based on simplied version of plans by Busiri-Vici).

Publications

ECHOLS, ROBERT: ''A Classical Barrel Vault for San Giovanni in Laterano in a Borromini Drawing.'' *Journal of the Society of Architectural Historians* 51 (June 1992): 146-160.
FISCHER, M. F.: ''Die Umbaupläne des Giovanni Battista Piranesi für den Chor von S. Giovanni in Laterano.'' *Münchner Jahrbuch der bildenden Kunst* 19 (1968).
SPADA, VIRGILIO: ''Relatione della fabrica di San Giovanni in Laterano.'' In KLAUS GÜTHLEIN: ''Quellen aus dem Familienarchiv Spada zum römischen Barock.'' *Römisches Jahrbuch für Kunstgeschichte* 18 (1979).

*

San Giovanni in Laterano, the Cathedral of Rome and first of the basilican churches built following Constantine's defeat of Maxentius, is now a Baroque transformation of the fourth-century structure.

Founded in about 312-313 by Constantine on private property

San Giovanni in Laterano: Rome, Italy, 312-13

in the suburban greenbelt outside the civic center of Rome, the church stands on the site of the imperial army barracks that earlier had displaced parts of a large private house that possibly was the Laterani family residence confiscated by Nero in 65 A.D. The plan of San Giovanni was typical of the Early Christian basilicas based on Roman civic basilicas and, as the first of those constructed by Constantine, was a prototype for later Christian churches. It consisted of a nave ending in a semicircular apse and double outer aisles. The nave was set off from the inner aisles by trabeated red granite columns, while smaller green marble columns divided the inner and outer aisles. Attached to each side of the aisles near the apse were sacristies. The question of whether a transept was part of the original plan has not been settled, but the evidence seems to indicate that it was not, but was added later to correspond to the plan of the more popular St. Peter's Basilica. Internal decoration of the fourth-century building included marble revetment of the aisle arcades and part of the aisle walls, in contrast to the open timber ceiling.

Throughout the long history of San Giovanni in Laterano, repairs to damaged portions and additions to the fabric of the church changed it and expanded it, although it seems that the Early Christian character of the building was retained carefully and deliberately at every stage. Renovation, redecoration and additions occurred in the fifth, eighth, ninth, 10th, 12th, 13th, 15th and 16th centuries before the church was drastically altered in a complex reconstruction of the nave from 1646 to 1649 by Francesco Borromini; he redefined the internal order of the cathedral while retaining some elements of the venerable fabric of the original basilica. The other significant alteration was the addition of a new facade by Alessandro Galilei in 1732. In further internal reorganization, in 1764, Pope Clement XIII commissioned Giovanni Battista Piranesi to build a new apse, but the project was cancelled. Finally, in 1876-86, Virgilio and Francesco Vespignani destroyed the old apse and built a new apse and long chancel based on a simplified version of plans by Busiri-Vici of 1880.

The original nave suffered damage during a ninth-century earthquake and was repaired shortly afterward in the late ninth and early 10th centuries. Then, in the 14th century, a fire further damaged the nave, which was repaired shortly afterward and again in the mid-15th century, when the nave piers were strengthened. Those repairs were obviously piecemeal and makeshift, for, in the middle of the 17th century, the nave had deteriorated to the extent that the north wall was leaning dangerously inward, and the nave columns were encased in brick to enable them to support the entablature.

In response to the condition of San Giovanni, in 1646 Pope Innocent X charged Borromini with the repair and restoration of the nave for the celebration of the upcoming Holy Year in 1650. To repair the nave, Borromini reinforced the old walls by connecting them to new walls that forced them nearly into plumb, and by cutting away part of the north nave wall that still extended inward. To support these new doubled nave walls, Borromini removed the nave columns and replaced them with massive piers, which took the place of pairs of the original red granite columns. Borromini decorated these piers with pairs of giant Corinthian pilasters, which framed small aedicular niches designed to hold statues. These massive piers perform a dual function. The first of these is symbolic, for the presence of the

San Giovanni in Laterano

doubled pilasters is reminiscent of the spacing of the original columns of the old basilican nave; the second is the practical one of hiding much of the reconstruction of the old walls. Five large arches open from the nave into the inner aisles, while an 11th arch flanked by chamfered bays frames the inner wall of the main entrance. Borromini demolished the dark, low aisles and replaced them with alternating wide and narrow bays following the new configuration of the nave. In the inner aisles, he contrasted the wide, well-lit bays vaulted by pendentives with narrow, dark bays crowned by shallow sail domes. For the outer lower aisles, he employed flat vaulting.

Borromini did not complete his comprehensive plan for the interior of the church. He had planned a new vault for the nave and had anticipated the planning of a buttress system in the nave walls, although the details of that system have not survived. A stone vault would have led to the demolition of the gilded, coffered, wooden ceiling constructed in 1562 by Daniele da Volterra, a follower of Michelangelo. The ceiling was left intact, possibly in the mistaken belief that it was by Michelangelo himself, but more probably because of lack of funds.

Borromini decorated the nave walls and the aisle vaults with his characteristically symbolic sculptural forms. Carved angel heads form the keystones of the aisle vaults and are used as consoles in the outer aisles. He designed the 12 niches in the nave for statues of the apostles, which were produced in a major sculptural project of the 18th century in Rome. He framed the niches with pairs of the old green marble columns from the aisles. Over the niches, he superimposed rectangular panels; above these he placed oval openings, which he possibly intended to leave as openings in the nave wall to reveal what remained

of the old and putative original Constantinian walls behind them. The niches were filled in later, however, and the intended effect of displaying original wall fragments as relics in what amounted to giant wall reliquaries was lost. Borromini was more successful in the enclosure of the old tombs of popes and cardinals in the piers and walls of the outer aisles. Though these tombs and all other ornamentation and reconstruction by Borromini were dramatic, the new interior reveals a certain amount of restraint of his typically flamboyant and undulating Baroque style.

Borromini's restrained Baroque interior was followed in the early 18th century by the construction of a new classical Baroque facade by Alessandro Galilei, a Florentine architect who won the competition held by Pope Clement XII, the Corsini pope who favored his Florentine countrymen for the many Roman projects he initiated.

Galilei's classical front halted a growing tendency in late Roman Baroque architecture toward an Italian version of the Rococo style. Among his sources were St. Peter's Basilica in Rome and St. Paul's Cathedral in London, with which Galilei became acquainted during a trip to England from 1714 to 1718. Like the facade of St. Paul's and other classical church fronts with central pedimented porticoes, Galilei's facade is a stylistic correction of Carlo Maderno's flawed, problematical front of St. Peter's. At San Giovanni, Galilei used a similar forward projection of pilasters from the sides to the center, where engaged columns and a triangular pediment form an aedicular frame for the entrance. He also employed the giant Corinthian order for his pilasters and engaged columns. Galilei employed a wide entablature like that of St. Peter's, but he did not have to contend with the excessive width of the attic story imposed upon Maderno by Michelangelo's apse elevation. Galilei thus created a streamlined version of Maderno's facade. For the Cathedral of Rome and the first of the patriarchial basilicas, Galilei created a facade of classical restraint worthy of the simplicity of the early basilica.

—JOYCE M. DAVIS

SANT'IVO DELLA SAPIENZA
Rome, Italy

1643-ca.1650: Church built; **Architect:** Franceso Borromini (1599-1667). **1660:** Decoration completed.

Publications

BORROMINI, FRANCESCO: *Opera . . . Cavata da suoi originali: Cioè, la chiesa e fabrica della Sapienza di Roma, con le vedute in prospettiva e con lo studio delle proporzioni geometriche, piante, alzate, profili e spaccati*. Rome, 1720.
HERZ, ALEXANDRA: "Borromini, S. Ivo, and Prudentius." *Journal of the Society of Architectural Historians* 48 (June 1989): 150-157.
OST, HANS: "Borrominis römische Universitätskirche S. Ivo alla Sapienza." *Zeitschrift für Kunstgeschichte* 30 (1967): 101-142.
SCOTT, JOHN BELDON: "S. Ivo alla Sapienza and Borromini's Symbolic Language." *Journal of the Society of Architectural Historians* 41 (December 1982): 294-317.
SEDLMAYR, HANS: *Die Architektur Borrominis*. Munich, 1930.

*

Early in his career, Francesco Borromini received the commission that was to produce his masterpiece—the design of the church for the Roman university, Sant'Ivo della Sapienza. The church was to be placed at the end of the long two-story, arcaded court designed by Giacomo della Porta for the Archiginnasio. Construction began in 1643 and was substantially complete a decade later, although the decoration continued through 1660.

In Sant'Ivo, Borromini produced an exceptionally successful example of a complex, centralized church plan created by overlapping geometric figures. The plan diagram can be described as follows: Two large equilateral triangles are superimposed to produce a six-pointed star with a regular hexagon at its center. The points of intersection of the two triangles are connected with the center of the hexagon to create six lozenges, each composed of two small equilateral triangles. Circles are circumscribed about the cross-diameters of three alternating lozenges. Circles of the same diameter are drawn with their centers at the outer apexes of the other three alternating lozenges. Segments of the resulting diagram yield all elements of the plan, which

Sant'Ivo della Sapienza: Rome, Italy, 1642-ca. 1650

Sant'Ivo della Sapienza

consists of a convex curve where one of the outer circles intersects a triangle, which yields to a straight wall segment, which intersects with a concave curve from one of the inner circles, which leads to another straight wall segment, and so on around the interior perimeter of the space.

The space that results from this play of geometry epitomizes the Baroque fascination with movement. Semicircular bays alternate with sharply angular ones which focus upon convex wall segments; interior space exerting outward pressure seems to be restrained by exterior space pushing in. Clusters of three giant-order Corinthian pilasters—a two-sided one on the arris between pairs of adjacent bays plus an additional flanking one on each wall—form piers that hold the opposing spatial forces in equilibrium and support an entablature that runs unbroken around the space. The mass of the enclosing wall is emphasized by the niches that are carved into it.

Above the entablature the bays and the pilasters of the ground plan continue up directly, with no intervening stage, to form the dome where the complex geometry of the ground plan resolves into a hemispherical space by means of doubly curved surfaces, aedicular window frames and camouflaging sculptural ornament. The pilasters are transformed into ribs which are gathered up into a simple pattern radiating from the circular aperture of the lantern that marks the center of the church. Complex forms have evolved into a single simple one. The result is magical. The apparent geometry of the space seems to change with the movement of the vantage point.

As at San Carlo alle Quattro Fontane, space and motion are everything. The color palette is limited to white and gold, although recent discoveries indicate that Borromini also used shades of pale gray as well; the material is plaster, and all decoration is derived from architectural means and simple geometric figures.

The six-pointed star is a symbol of wisdom—an appropriate icon for a university church. Borromini also intended the six bays of the church to represent the head, body and four wings of the bee, the emblem of the Barberini family of Borromini's first papal client, Pope Urban VIII. The Chigi and Pamphili family arms are also present in the decoration.

The two Baroque concerns that energize the interior space—movement and opposing forces in equilibrium—also characterize the exterior of Sant'Ivo. The facade is organized in four

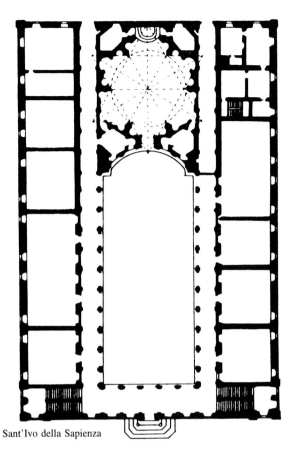

Sant'Ivo della Sapienza

vertical stages. The first is a concave two-story exedra that continues the arcades of della Porta's *cortile* as blind arches. At its center, on the longitudinal axis of the court, the concave facade is tangent to the convex projection of one of the sides of the tall hexagonal drum that rises above it. The concave lower facade is shaped by the arcade of the *cortile* that sweeps around the end of the court and pushes into the mass of the church. In contrast, the drum reveals the pressure of the interior space, which seems to be pushing out through the piers at the angles of the central organizing hexagon. These convex drum segments prepare the visitor for the star-shaped space found inside. The piers continue as volutes up through the undulating pyramid that covers the drum to the hexagonal lantern, where they are transformed into paired-column piers. The lantern is a reversal of the drum below; its sides are open and concave rather than closed and convex. It resembles the famous little Roman temple at Baalbek. It is crowned with a spiral that seems to gather up the forces expressed by the piers and volutes into a single moving line that dissipates through the open iron finial into the atmosphere.

Of the Roman Baroque architects, only Borromini chose to use the northern Italian form for the dome, a form which obscures the interior space from exterior view behind a vertical mass that counters the dome's outward thrust and diverts it to the vertical mass of the building. A strong vertical line formed by the door and the window above it in the lower facade carries through the window of the drum and a corresponding window of the lantern to the final resolution in the spiral that supports the crowning orb. This vertical line not only expresses vertical movement, but also serves to unite the four disparate vertical stages into a single composition.

—C. MURRAY SMART, JR.

SANTA MARIA DEGLI ANGELI
Rome, Italy

1563: Tepidarium of the Baths of Diocletian (A.D. 298-306) transformed into a church. **Architect:** Michelangelo (1475-1564). **1749:** Church remodeled. **Architect:** Luigi Vanvitelli (1700-73).

Publications

WADDY, PATRICIA: "Brunelleschi's Design for S. Maria degli Angeli in Florence." *Marsyas* 15 (1970-72): 36-45.

*

In 1561 Michelangelo was commissioned by Pope Pius IV to construct the Church of Santa Maria degli Angeli in the great central hall of the ancient Roman Baths of Diocletian. Michelangelo died in 1564, and the pope in 1565, thus, neither architect nor patron lived long enough to see the church completed as planned. In fact, little of Michelangelo's design can be detected under the Baroque decorations added by successive architects. Nevertheless, Santa Maria degli Angeli is symbolically and architecturally representative of the Catholic Reform Church in the mid-16th century.

Interest in this building project prior to Michelangelo's tenure as chief architect is known through early-16th-century drawings by Giuliano da Sangallo and Baldassare Peruzzi, both of whom may have been asked by the papacy to submit designs for a church. No buildings resulted from those plans. Interest in the project did not return until 1541, when a pious Sicilian priest, Antonio del Duca, was inspired by visions to petition Pope Paul III to take up the transformation of the baths into a Christian monument dedicated to the cult of the angels. It took nine years for the papacy to respond to del Duca; in the Holy Year of 1550 the grounds were consecrated by Julius III, who also had temporary altars installed in the hall of the baths. The papacy was not committed to a complete renovation until Pius IV (1559-65) initiated his program for urban renewal. The Baths of Diocletian, located along the new Via Pia begun by Pius, complemented the pope's urban planning in that area. The commission was handed over to Michelangelo, along with the Porta Pia in the same area.

In the design of the new church, Michelangelo was faced with the problem of how to make use of surviving ancient walls. The issue was architectural as well as liturgical, and its solution would determine the orientation, function and character of the interior space. If the great hall were used as transept, the church would be left without a nave; if the hall were used as nave, the area to the northeast (formerly the *frigidarium*) would need major construction to balance it with the southwest projection (the surviving walls of the *tepidarium* and *caldarium*). Michelangelo's decision to use the great hall as transept suggests that architect and patron desired to maintain the integrity of the surviving walls and, perhaps, to keep construction costs to a minimum.

Evidence from drawings and engravings prior to Baroque embellishments suggests that Michelangelo altered the existing walls very little apart from allowing for chapels. In his design, Michelangelo utilized much that survived from antiquity: an exedra from the *caldarium* became the entrance to the church, the *tepidarium* served as a vestibule, and the huge hall, surviving largely intact, became the transept. The hall or transept was covered with cross vaults, thus emphasizing the expansiveness

Santa Maria degli Angeli: Rome, Italy, 1563

Santa Maria degli Angeli

of the space below; these cross vaults are the only surviving elements from Michelangelo's design.

Such a plan, based on the Greek cross, was liturgically significant for the resident Carthusians. The Carthusian Order required privacy from the visiting lay congregation, and this need was easily accommodated by the construction of the chancel beyond the altar, isolated in part by ancient columns supporting an entablature and blind arch. The large transept was thus given over entirely to public worship. The chancel designed by Michelangelo was rebuilt and enlarged several times before reaching its final, and current, form in the late 18th century.

After Michelangelo's death, a number of architects and designers added to the interior and exterior of the church. Initially, interior window frames were added and the facade was decorated. In the 18th century, however, the interior was dramatically remodeled by a series of architects. Luigi Vanvitelli, appointed architect to the Carthusians in 1749, was given the task of harmonizing the contributions made by the numerous architects who followed Michelangelo. According to the taste of the time, Vanvitelli embellished the interior, except the vaults, with stucco and veneer. These alterations intended, no doubt, to enrich the simple but grand spaces of the interior, but had the effect of disrupting the unity of design planned by Michelangelo for the walls and vaults.

According to Giorgio Vasari, Michelangelo himself had gone to Pius IV with a plan to renovate the ancient baths into a Christian temple. Vasari's account, though inaccurate, is significant for its recognition of Michelangelo's religiosity in his final years. At mid-century, Michelangelo was preoccupied with exploring in sculpture and poetry the theme of salvation. His obsession with the power and dignity of the human body through the study of classical form became subservient to meditations on Christian themes of death and resurrection. It is not surprising that Vasari would have inferred from the master's other work that the impetus for constructing a Christian church from the ruins of antiquity originated with Michelangelo.

—MARJORIE OCH

SANTA MARIA MAGGIORE
Rome, Italy

5th century: Basilica built to replace previous 4th-century church; nave, triumphal arch wall and corresponding mosaics still remain. **12th century:** Cosmatesque floor added. **13th century:** Transept and apse rebuilt. **Ca. 1296:** Apsidal mosaics of the coronation of the Virgin installed; **Artist:** Jacopo Torriti. **14th century:** Belltower built. **Early 16th century:** Ceiling decorated; **Artist:** Designs attributed to Giuliano da Sangallo (1443-1516). **1564-73:** Sforza Chapel added; **Architect:** Giacomo della Porta (1532-1602), original designs by Michelangelo (1475-1564). **1585:** Sistine chapel built; **Architect:** Domenico Fontana (1543-1607). **1611:** Pauline chapel built; **Architect:** Flaminio Ponzio. **1673:** Exterior of apse designed; **Architect:** Carlo Rainaldi. **18th century:** Baldachin added. **1743:** Facade built; **Architect:** Ferdinando Fuga (1699-1781).

Publications

CECHELLI, C.: *I mosaici della basilica di S. Maria Maggiore.* Rome, 1967.

JOHNS, CHRISTOPHER M. S.: "Clement XI and Santa Maria Maggiore in the Early 18th Century." *Journal of the Society of Architectural Historians* 45 (September 1986): 286-293.

MILBURN, ROBERT: *Early Christian Art and Architecture.* Berkeley and Los Angeles, 1988.

SCHWAGER, KLAUS: "Zur Bautätigkeit Sixtus V und S. Maria Maggiore in Rome." In *Miscellanea Bibliothecae Hertzianae.* Munich, 1961.

*

The approach to Santa Maria Maggiore today, sitting as it does on a summit of the Esquiline, is indeed majestic. The east end or back, with its curved, double-leveled staircase and domes flanking the apse, presents as monumental and inviting a facade as the front, which looks more like a parliamentary building. In fact, the church is usually entered from the back, which is the more frequented access from the Piazza dell'Esquilino. Both entrances are odd in that they encompass the whole of the building in both width and height, so the familiar profile of a church with a higher nave and lower side aisles, or aisles from which subsidiary chapels project, is not seen here.

The earliest, fourth-century basilica is now entirely lost, and much of the present appearance stems from later, 12th- to 18th-century additions or alterations to the fifth-century Early Christian basilica. An 18th-century facade, for example, is juxtaposed against a Romanesque bell tower. The historical and stylistic incongruity of this superposition of style upon style through centuries of use and patronage is a hallmark of church architecture and decoration in Italy. The specialized historian usually visits to study one period or another, trying to divest the church of its multilayered past.

Whereas the exterior is completely remodeled, the most visible remains of the three-aisle Early Christian basilica lie in the interior proportions of the church, with its spacious nave. The triumphal arch wall that originally connected directly to the apse now separates the nave from the present, 13th-century transept and apse. The transept and apse design came about as a concession to minimal "modernization" according to contemporary Gothic standards. Today the fifth-century triumphal arch and 13th-century apse are obscured by the huge 18th-century baldachin that surmounts the altar in front of the arch.

The original interior decoration represented the so-called "Sistine Renaissance." This was a renaissance, or revival, of classical Roman architectural types and motifs in the buildings of Pope Sixtus III, to whom the pilgrimage church of Santa Maria Maggiore is attributable on the basis of a dedicatory mosaic inscription on the triumphal arch. A Christian classicism—an assimilation of pagan tastes by high-ranking Christian officials—of a kind seen in Santa Maria Maggiore and in other buildings erected or remodeled by Sixtus III (such as the Lateran Baptistery and Santo Stefano Rotondo), emerged only after the final defeat of paganism in 395 A.D. In 410, after the sack of Rome, the last vestige of Roman rule disappeared and the pope assumed a role equal to that of former emperors. We could say that Sixtus III was the first "classical" pope, in the same sense that Constantine was the first "Christian" emperor: each, from a different perspective, translated pagan classicism into a Christian idiom.

The nave of Santa Maria Maggiore is flanked by tall colonnades with columns surmounted by Ionic capitals resembling the original capitals. These support a classical entablature. Naves with colonnades and entablatures appeared before, in

Santa Maria Maggiore

Constantinian basilicas. The patterns of the 12th-century Cosmatesque floor and of the beautiful early-16th-century gilded, coffered ceiling echo the strong horizontals produced by the entablatures and emphasize the longitudinal axis of the church, carrying the eye straight to the altar. On the upper wall tall, flat, fluted pilasters rose to the top of the clerestory and roof, a clear indication that the wall above the entablature was treated as a single story, near equal in height to the colonnade. The double order of columns finds prototypes in Roman architecture of the imperial period. Above the tall pilasters ran a classical scroll-leaf, stucco border.

Today the interior is dominated to such an extent by the central nave that the side aisles, baptistery and many chapels, added later, fade from view. The fact that the nave appears to be isolated is due to the unusually dark interior, a result of the reduction in the number of nave windows to half their original number. With more light and without the later side chapels, the aisles would have been illuminated, too.

The true wealth of the church is seen in the original nave and arch mosaics. Forty-two Old Testament scenes illustrating stories from the lives of Moses, Joshua, Abraham and Jacob, lined the nave walls between the columns and the windows. These culminated in a New Testament cycle of events from the life of Christ depicted in four registers on the arch wall. As one walked from the entrance to the arch, the "stories" unfolded. The mosaic panels in the nave were originally framed by separate aediculae with colonnettes carrying small pediments. These are now lost, as is the rest of the three-dimensional sculpturing of the upper wall, with the exception of the tall, fluted pilasters mentioned above. Another double order of columns rose inside the pilasters, flanking the mosaic panels, below, and the windows, above.

Santa Maria Maggiore: Rome, Italy, 5th century

The historical context of the church is revealed by the decorative mosaic program, although its meaning is still debated. The theme of the mosaics had been related to the decision of the Church Council of Ephesus, in 431, to recognize the dual natures of Christ, both human and divine, and the divine motherhood of Mary. The mosaic program and architectural style have also been interpreted as an embodiment of the political aspirations of the pope.

The mosaics are considered masterpieces of Early Christian art, a revival of the pagan classicism found in late-fourth-century illustrated epic manuscripts, completely consistent with the revival of the classical style in the architectural. But they are as problematic as they are revelatory, for despite the exceedingly high quality and costliness of their execution, they are done in too small and miniaturistic a scale to be seen at such great height. This problem, too, was a classically Roman one, for the artist who designed Trajan's Column in Rome made the same—dare it be said—mistake. Perhaps in an effort to correct this effect, in several of the mosaic panels nearest the arch the artist enlarged the figure scale and reduced the number of figures, thus simplifying the iconography of the scenes. Much later, Michelangelo would make a similar in-progress correction to the iconography of the Old Testament scenes on the vault of the Sistine Chapel.

Possibly with more light to reflect off of the gold glass mosaic *tesserae* and if the mosaics were cleaner and better preserved, the interior walls would glisten as they must have when the church was first built. The richness of the architectural decoration—columns, capitals, marbles and mosaics—reflected the prestige of its patron and a high point in Early Christian Rome.

—PAULA D. LEVETO-JABR

SAN PAOLO FUORI LE MURA
Rome, Italy

Ca. 380: Original construction. **13th century:** Cloister added. **Architects:** Vassalletto family. **1823:** Church destroyed by fire, but 5th- and 13th-century mosaics survived.

Publications

"Borromini per San Paolo fuori le mura: Il classico, l'allegoria, la città." *Ricerche di storia dell'arte* 4 (1977): 57-77.

*

To form a general idea of the character of the church of San Paulo Fuori-le-Mura it is necessary to keep in mind the importance and scope of the reconstruction that followed the fire of 1823. Even if the plan of the original building had been respected, the use of new materials, particularly for new supports, has fundamentally altered the impression the viewer receives.

Nothing remains but the wall of the great apse, which is probably for the most part that of the original apse. Originally, it was certainly not pierced with windows.

The great church constructed toward the end of the fourth century and surviving until 1823 had nothing in common with a still earlier building, attributed to the middle of the fourth century, except the connection with the monument built over the tomb of Saint Paul. After the construction of the late fourth century, however, the plan remained basically the same, in spite of all the alterations the church underwent. The plan was that of a basilica preceded by an atrium with four porticoes. (The paleochristian versions of those porticoes were destroyed in the 16th century.) It has a central nave with two lateral naves on each side, the inner lateral nave being higher than the exterior one. Light comes from the clerestory windows, since the two lateral naves are covered by a single roof on each side. East of the nave, a large transept forms the transition to the great apse. (Between 1130 and 1145 the transept was divided in two by an arcaded wall, constructed to support the roof, which seemed unstable after the fire of 1115.) The most striking feature of this ensemble is its size: the building was approximately 128 meters long and 65 meters wide, 25 meters of which were taken up by the central nave alone. The height of the central nave, which was lined with columns, was about 30 meters. On the whole, one receives the impression that the builders wished to construct a church that could equal St. Peter's. It is, in fact, quite similar in certain respects, significantly different in others—probably quite deliberately so.

Two types of columns, differing in the kinds of marble used, are cited in numerous sources. If the designs, of uniformity or variety in decoration, are considered common for the period,

San Paulo fuori le Mura: Rome, Italy, ca. 380

San Paulo fuori le Mura

the irregular distribution of the two types brings to mind the partial rebuilding under Leo the Great (Pope 440-461). It was shown recently that the church was originally built with a single type of column made out of Carrara marble. The desire for uniformity is also evident in the fact that the width of the transept, and both the height and the width of the lateral naves, are all identical. All these elements demonstrate the care with which the builders strove for unity, which makes for a significant difference from the Constantinian aesthetics of St. Peter's.

While keeping the simplicity of the design in mind, some decorative elements must also be mentioned, since their presence and distribution were essential to the architect's desired effects. The description of the Roman poet Prudentius, a contemporary of its construction, is very useful here. It is important to recall, in attempts to understand the decorative wealth, that the basilica was also an imperial foundation. The most important decorative elements are first and foremost the ceilings of gilded coffers, which in themselves inspired contemporaries with awe, and which covered the transept, the principal nave and undoubtedly the lower, lateral naves. Then there are the mosaics, primarily those of the apse and of the triumphal arch. Gold and light were symbols of God, and enhanced the sense of a divine presence in the sanctuary. It remains unknown whether the naves were in fact decorated with mosaics, or whether these mosaics existed only in plan. Some of the ornamentation was redone during the restoration undertaken under Leo. Stucco and frescoes were also added at that time, on the walls above the colonnades of the central nave and below the clerestory in particular.

The renovations of the sanctuary and of the monument to

Saint Paul initiated by Gregory the Great (Pope 590-604) also deserve mention, even though they did not significantly alter the architecture of the church. In fact, these renovations, comparable to near contemporary ones at St. Peter's, highlight with particular clarity the relationship between the sainted body and the altar. The paving stones of the transept are elevated above the pavement of the naves by 90 cm. As a consequence, the apostle's sanctuary, behind which a crypt was dug, was almost completely buried. (There is no certainty as to the form of this first crypt, but it is likely that the ring-shaped crypt under the apse does not date back further than the ninth century, at which time this type was widely adopted.) The altar is therefore placed right above the tomb of the saint, so that Mass is celebrated over the body of the apostle.

Subsequently, during the Middle Ages and in modern times, the architecture proper was not altered—except for repairs such as the construction of the wall in the transept mentioned above—but the ornamentation was modernized, so to speak. The mosaic in the apse dates to the early 13th century, and the frescoes in the nave were repainted late in the same century. The construction of a large canopy over the altar, also in the late 13th century, and the transformation of the facade with a new window design and a beautiful mosaic are more important, as they distanced the church in a more decisive manner from its paleochristian origins. It seems unnecessary to record the details of the renovations up to 1823, which did not significantly alter the basic structure of the building, but only modified its appearance.

—J. -M. SPIESER
Translated from the French by Alla Melamed

ST. PETER'S
Rome, Italy

1506-13: Building begun on the site of Basilica of Constantine, four central piers nearly complete, nave of Basilica of Constantine removed; **Architect:** Donato Bramante (1444-1514). **1514:** Bramante died, new architects took over, plans revised; **Architect:** Raphael (1483-1520); **Assistant architects:** Giuliano da Sangallo (1443-1516), Fra Giocondo (died in 1515). **1520-46:** Plans revised, construction continued; **Architects:** Antonio da Sangallo the Younger (1483-1546), Baldassare Peruzzi (1481-1536). **1546-64:** After Sangallo's death, plans revised, construction continued, south arm of crossing, drum of dome, transept completed; **Architect:** Michelangelo (1475-1564). **1588:** Height of dome extended; **Architect:** Giacomo della Porta (1532-1602). **1603-06:** Inner mosaic decoration of dome added. **1607-12:** Facade built; **Architect:** Carlo Maderno (1556-1629). **1612-24:** Interior decoration begun, barrel vaulting of front arm prolonged, communicating chapels at sides added; **Architect:** Carlo Maderno (1556-1629). **1624:** Church consecrated. **1624-30:** Baldachin built to mark altar; **Architect:** Giovanni Lorenzo Bernini (1598-1680). **1629:** Maderno died, Bernini named chief architect. **1642:** Two campenili at the ends of the facade built; **Architect:** Bernini. **1658:** Piazza of St. Peter's begun; **Architect:** Bernini.

Publications

ACKERMAN, JAMES S.: *The Architecture of Michelangelo*. Rev. ed., Harmondsworth and Baltimore, 1970.

BARDESCHI-CIULICH, LUCILLA: "Documenti inediti su Michelangelo e l'incarico di San Pietro." *Rinascimento* 17 (1977): 235-275.

BRINCKMANN, ALBERT E.: "Das Kuppelmodell für San Pietro in Rom." *Repertorium für Kunstwissenschaft* 43 (1921): 92-97.

COOLIDGE, JOHN: "Vignola, and the Little Domes of St. Peter's." *Marsyas* 2 (1942): 63-123.

St. Peter's: Rome, Italy, 1506-13

St. Peter's, toward Basilica

DI STEFANO: *La cupola di San Pietro: storia della costruzione e dei restauri*. Naples, 1963.

FRANCIA, ENNIO: *1506-1606: Storia della costruzione di San Pietro*. Rome, 1977.

FREY, DAGOBERT: *Bramantes St. Peter-Entwurf und seine Apokryphen*. Vienna, 1915.

HOFMANN, THEOBALD: *Entstehungsgeschichte des St. Peter in Rom*. Zittau, 1928.

KELLER, FRITZ-EUGEN: "Zur Planung am Bau der römischen Peterskirche im Jahre 1564-1565." *Jahrbuch der berliner Museen* 18 (1976): 24-50.

KITAO, T. K.: *Circle and Oval in the Square of St. Peter's; Bernini's Art of Planning*. New York, 1974.

KÖRTE, WERNER: "Zur Peterskuppel des Michelangelo." *Jahrbuch der königlichen preussischen Kunstsammlungen* 53 (1932): 90-112.

LAVIN, I.: *Bernini and the Crossing of St. Peter's*. New York, 1968.

LEES-MILNE, JAMES: *Saint Peter's*. London, 1967.

LICHT, MEG: "*I Ragionamenti*—Visualizing St. Peter's." *Journal of the Society of Architectural Historians* 44 (May 1985): 111-128.

MARCHINI, GIUSEPPE: "Quattro piante per il San Pietro di Roma." *Bollettino d'arte* 41 (1956): 313-317.

MARIANI, VALERIO: *Michelangelo e la facciata di San Pietro*. Rome, 1943.

METTERNICH, FRANZ GRAF WOLFF: *Die Erbauung der Peterskirche in Rom im 16. Jahrhundert*. Vienna, 1972.

MILLON, HENRY, and SMYTH, CRAIG H.: "Michelangelo and St. Peter's: Observations on the Interior of the Apses, a Model of the Apse Vault, and Related Drawings." *Römisches Jahrbuch für Kunstgeschichte* 16 (1976): 137ff.

ORBAAN, J. A. F.: "Zur Baugeschichte des Peterskuppel." *Jahrbuch der königlich-preussischen Kunstsammlungen* 38, supplement (1917): 189-207.

POLLAK, OSKAR: "Ausgewählte Akten zur Geschichte der römischen Peterskirche (1535-1621)." *Jahrbuch der königlich-preussischen Kunstsammlungen* 36, supplement (1915): 21-117.

SCHIAVO, ARMANDO: "La cupola di S. Pietro." *Bollettino del Centro di Studi di Storia dell'Architettura* 6 (1952): 14-26.

SCHIAVO, ARMANDO: *San Pietro in Vaticano, forme e strutture*. Rome, 1960.

THELEN, HEINRICH: *Zur Entstehungsgeschichte der Hochalter-Architektur von St. Peter in Rom*. Berlin, 1967.

THOENES, C.: "Studien zur Geschichte des Petersplatzes." *Zeitschrift für Kunstgeschichte* 26 (1963): 97-145.

VON GEYMÜLLER, HEINRICH: *Die ursprünglichen Entwicklungen für S. Peter in Rom*. 2 vols., Vienna and Paris, 1875-80.

VOSS, H.: "Bernini als Architekt an der Scala Regia und an den Kolonnaden von St. Peter." *Jahrbuch der preussischen Kunstsammlungen* (1922).

WITTKOWER, RUDOLF: "Zur Peterskuppel Michelangelos." *Zeitschrift für Kunstgeschichte* N.F. 2 (1933): 348-370.

"Zur Baugeschichte des St. Peter." *Jahrbuch der königlich-preussischen Kunstsammlungen* 31, supplement (1911): 1-95.

"Zur Baugeschichte des St. Peter." *Jahrbuch der königlich-
preussischen Kunstsammlungen* 33, supplement (1913): 1-
153.
"Zur Baugeschichte des St. Peter." *Jahrbuch der königlich-
preussischen Kunstsammlungen* 37, supplement (1916): 22-
135.

*

The story behind the evolution of St. Peter's as it appears today
entails far more than a chronological listing of each of the
successive architects who were involved with it over several
centuries. Instead, it represents nothing less than a particularly
venal struggle between some of the most brilliant talents of the
quattrocento, who all seem to have been determined to leave
their own, individual stamp upon what each of them must have
realized was to become the architectural symbol of Christendom.

Julius II, who was elevated to the papacy in 1503, was arguably the most important of all of these protagonists because of the
critical part that he played in deciding to replace the dilapidated
Basilica of Constantine in the first place. Showing a determination that was entirely consistent with his name, which he felt
made him the natural sucessor to the Caesars, Julius did not
hesitate to order the demolition of the old basilica, which had
been sanctified by tradition as having been built over the tomb
of St. Peter. His motive in doing so was not only to enlarge
the church, which by then had become much too small in
comparison to its increasing stature, but also to make it the
most beautiful building in Rome, which he was determined to
make the *caput mundi* once again. This intention, which is

clearly documented in a letter that Pope Julius sent to Henry
VIII of England in January 1506, was quickly followed by the
laying of a foundation stone for the new church in April of that
same year.

A medal that the pope had struck to commemorate the occasion remains as one of the most reliable representations of the
Greek-cross plan proposed by Donato Bramante, whom the
Pope had named as the first *architetto della fabbrica.* That
architect's unwillingness or failure to produce more complete
documentation of his concept was an important factor in the
confusion that followed. The Greek-cross plan that was proposed by Bramante was considered to be revolutionary at the
time, especially since it was proposed as a replacement for
one following the basilica typology, which had such deeply
established historical roots in Rome itself. Having originally
been used to accommodate a magistrates court, the basilica was
adapted as a church by the early Christians because it conformed
so easily to emerging liturgical needs, with a nave and side
aisles that provided the necessary separation between the procession and observation that were becoming integral to each service. By changing to a centralized rather than a longitudinal
form, and therefore stressing purely commemorative aspects,
Bramante was taking a fundamentally different position on the
character that St. Peter's was to have in the future.

This concept not only was based on the desire to achieve a
strong and memorable form that a central dome would provide,
but was also meant to recall intentionally an entirely separate
tradition of ancient mausolea and Christian martyria that had
already begun to be creatively explored in the Byzantine east
during the reign of Justinian. The Hagia Sophia in Constantinople, for example, which was dedicated in 537, is the most

St. Peter's, nave view east

St. Peter's, dome exterior: 1546-64

impressive evidence of this inventiveness. With four massive piers forming a square base for a large central dome, this church represents one of the most obvious prototypes for the type of space that Bramante had in mind.

Far from coming to Justinian in a dream, as the emperor wanted his subjects to believe, the Hagia Sophia has been shown to represent the complete synthesis of the axial, basilican plan, using forecourt, nave, side aisles and apse, with a politically motivated need to express the equality of church and state. By providing a central dome, which scholars such as Andre Graber have linked to the early Christian cult of martyrs, Justinian also made it possible for both emperor and patriarch to meet underneath it at the conclusion of a religious service, symbolizing the unity of church and state. The dome was undeniably celestial, not only meant to be a metaphor for the sky vault, but also, as in this case, meant to signify the heavenly witness of the union of the earthly church with its heavenly master. Side galleries, rather than acting as the aisles in a basilica, were seen as the place from which the public could visually ratify the union of political and religious authority, and this ratification became almost as important as the celebration of the service itself. While the centralized martyria form, which can be traced back to such circular Late Roman structures as the Temple of Minerva Medici (260 A.D.), soon became the norm in Byzantium, and the central dome of the Hagia Sophia established a line of architectural evolution that continued on in the East for nearly a thousand years, the basilica form continued on in the west through the Romanesque and Gothic periods, until the pattern was broken by Bramante in his plan for St. Peter's.

While historians still debate the origin of the dome itself, Bramante certainly had several Latin prototypes to refer to, and he has been universally praised for the way in which he intuitively assimilated the spirit of each of these into his design.

These prototypes, which ranged in age from the Roman Pantheon to the numerous studies of centrally planned churches by Leonardo da Vinci, all seemed to him to provide the most promising architectural form with which to commemorate the burial place of the one apostle from whom all successive popes would trace their authority. Bramante's genius, in this case, lay not only in his ability to achieve a perfect blending of Late Classical and Early Christian forms, but also in his visceral understanding of classical proportions, as transmuted into Hellenistic and Roman construction techniques.

By the time of Pope Julius II's death in 1513, and Bramante's death one year later, the nave of the Basilica of Constantine had been almost completely removed, and the four central piers of the new church were nearly in place. Their spacing, which was carefully derived from the span of the combined width of both the middle and outer aisles of old St. Peter's, and their crossing, which arched over the place where its nave once stood, not only served to commemorate the dimensions of the previous church, but also set irrevocably those of the monumental structure that was to follow.

Using earlier Roman models as examples, along with other domes that had already been built in the early Renaissance, Bramante had been determined to cover his central piers with a single shell, in order that it, along with its colonnaded drum, would produce the simple, powerful silhouette that he desired. He had already achieved such a model in his Tempietto of San Pietro in Montorio, but on a far smaller scale; also, there were persistent doubts that such a dome could be built to the span required. In the year before his death, alarming cracks began to develop in the central piers even before the weight of a dome was superimposed on them, and Leo X, who became pope in 1513, felt it necessary to call in Giuliano da Sangallo, as well as Fra Giocondo, to collaborate with Bramante on structural matters.

Three months after his master's death, the painter Raphael, whom Bramante had specifically appointed as his successor, was named chief architect of St. Peter's, and Antonio da Sangallo the Younger was designated as his assistant. By that time, the entire foundation of the church had begun to shift, and the cracks in the massive central piers had widened to the extent that the public was becoming alarmed. Because of these concerns, and in order to clear up the confusion surrounding Bramante's intentions, Raphael ordered the first wooden model of his predecessor's design to be built. This model initially was successful in defusing the debate about whether the church should have a Greek- or Latin-cross plan, which had continued in the absence of any physical representation of Bramante's idea.

While little tangible progress on the building itself was achieved under Raphael's supervision, which was partially due to the fact that Leo X, as a Medici, was more interested in embellishing his home city of Florence than he was in Rome, a new method of supervision was established during Raphael's tenure. Rather than continuing to have the responsibility for both planning and supervision combined in one person, as had been the case throughout the Middle Ages, Raphael created the office of "coadjutor" during his term in office. That position might be best compared to that of project manager today. The result of this division was to relieve the architect of the supervisory and construction-related tasks that had previously been considered part of that position.

In addition, Raphael also realized that the traditional use of both a model and plans were not comprehensive enough to convey all of the detail of a building as monumental and complex as St. Peter's to its craftsmen. Detailed elevations were also

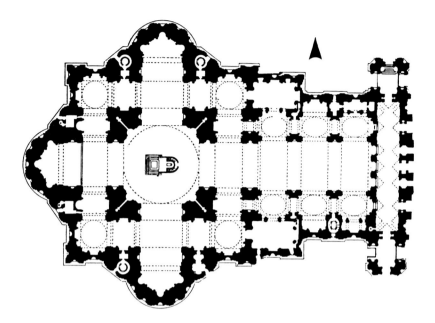

introduced that refined the Renaissance reliance upon single-point perspective renderings and verbal instructions from the architect to the master masons. Raphael's basilican plan, as well as the elevations and sections that accompany it, is the first fully documented scheme of St. Peter's. Copies of these drawings, which are now in the Paul Mellon Collection in Washington, D.C., show a repetition of the core of the Bramante plan, as indicated on the Julian commemorative medal, with a longitudinal extension of the nave. In this nave, the piers forming the aisles repeat the outline of Bramante's four central supports. Raphael also designed ambulatories around the transepts that Bramante intended, underscoring the doubts at that time about the ability of the interior walls to support the thrust of a high, single-shell dome.

Raphael, however, finally fell victim to the criticisms and intrigues of Antonio da Sangallo the Younger, who took over the post of chief architect in 1520, along with Baldassare Peruzzi, beginning another complex chapter in the construction of the church. Like Raphael, Sangallo also proposed a basilican plan, adding high corner towers to the facade that greatly reduced the visual impact of the central dome. During his supervision, much progress was made in the vaulting of the area over the crossing, as well as on the floor, which was raised 3.2 meters, or 12 feet 6 inches above that of the original Constantine Basilica, to counteract settlement. The niches in Bramante's four central piers were also filled in to solve the problem of structural cracks, giving them the relatively smooth surface that they have today. Following Raphael's lead, Sangallo also had a costly wooden model made of his scheme in 1539, which still survives, showing a highly ornate wedding cake of a building that is far removed from the classical simplicity of the original concept. Contemporary etchings by Marten Van Heemskerck that were done in 1534 show the confused state of affairs that still existed at that time, with parts of the old church mixed in with the new construction of the central area.

This confusion was dramatically clarified when Michelangelo took over as chief architect following Sangallo's death in 1546. Massive contributions from Spain between 1540 and 1546, which were made possible by the large amounts of gold coming from Mexico and South America at that time, had done much to set the stage for a final, determined campaign to complete the church, and Michelangelo certainly had the strength of will to do so. In a gesture of great piety, he agreed to carry on with no pay, continuing the work for the next 18 years until his death in 1564; his refusal to accept payment not only placed him above the manipulations of the Fabbrica, which advised the pope on matters regarding construction, but also gave all his arguments added moral force. Considering the great cost and time involved in the building of the wooden model of the Sangallo scheme, Michelangelo's submission of an entirely new one, to Pope Paul III, representing an entirely new scheme in model form, was a very courageous act. While his model has not survived, engravings executed by Etienne Dupérac in 1569 clearly show his intention to return to the simplicity and clarity of Bramante's original scheme.

After quickly beginning a program to clear the site of any remaining parts of the old basilica, Michelangelo wisely decided to return Sangallo's complex but structurally stable combination of secondary vaults around the completed core, but otherwise proposed an entirely different direction than had been taken by his immediate predecessors. Instead of the double set of exterior walls and the longitudinal plan that had been proposed by Raphael and further complicated by both Peruzzi and Sangallo, Michelangelo resolved the structural problems that had been largely responsible for their complications. By thickening and strengthening the external envelope in order to make it possible for it to absorb the thrust of the dome, he was able to eliminate the ambulations and chapels that had begun to obliterate the clarity of the core. Michelangelo claimed to have restored Bramante's plan, but his own, bolder version surpassed the original in directness and strength.

The dome and system of minor domes shown in the Dupérac engravings are reminiscent of ancient Roman thermae, and can also be traced back to Bramante. Determined to retain a hemispherical form, but aware of the structural difficulties posed by a single shell, Michelangelo is known to have sent to Florence for a survey of Filippo Brunelleschi's dome. This was built using a double shell and a crude but effective device of a large chain wrapped around the base of the drum to restrain thrust. However, in striving to retain a lower, hemispherical outline, which would provide a more compact composition and have classical as well as global connotations, Michelangelo was reintroducing the problems of thrust that Brunelleschi had partially offset by building his dome with a far higher vertical profile. In spite of Michelangelo's repetition of both the double shell and chain technique, as well as his strengthening of the outer perimeter, these questions of the optimum height to span were to remain one of the main elements of contention after the architect's death. As the Dupérac engravings prove, the perfect hemisphere shown there was later changed to a higher profile by Giacomo della Porta in 1588. In spite of this single variation, the central core of the church, including the idea of a commanding central dome that was initiated by Bramante, is of Michelangelo's design, and conveys a unified sense of power and integrity that would not have existed had he not become involved in the project.

Instead of relying upon a single, frontal elevation at the beginning of a longitudinal nave to create a processional impression, as had been the case in the past, Michelangelo approached the exterior skin of his centrifugal core as an entity in itself, just as he approached a block of rough marble when beginning to sculpt it. As Le Corbusier so forcefully pointed out in his *Vers une Architecture,* where he used Michelangelo's treatment of the exterior of this church as the paramount example of exterior form becoming the plastic expression of interior space, the inert stone of the outer walls of St. Peter's came alive in the hands of this brilliant artist. Repetitive vertical pilasters, which are similar to those used by Michelangelo on the flanking wings of the Piazza di Campidoglio, offset the circular horizontal movement of the main form of the church and create repetitive patterns of light and shade that were obviously meant to be seen in the round. As at the Campidoglio, Michelangelo took great care to balance the vertical of the massive Corinthian order that he used at St. Peter's with vertical elements in order to allow the columns to continue to suggest upward movement, but not to dominate the composition. A top story, one third as high as the external walls, caps this facade, in order to provide a similar kind of balance.

At the time of Michelangelo's death, the south arm of the crossing had been finished, as was the drum of the dome and what now amounts to the transept of the present church. Considerable progress was made on this plan by the energetic Pope Sixtus V, but following his death in 1590, Clement VIII was not quite as enthusiastic about architectural matters.

Early in the 17th century, however, the old debate about the advantages of a Latin-cross plan began once again, with those opposing a centralized scheme using the issue of anticipated attendance at the most important shrine of Christendom as their sharpest argument. In a final vote by the College of Cardinals, which missed being unanimous by only a single ballot, the decision was made to adopt the Latin-cross plan, and to extend Michelangelo's extremely narrow portico by three bays. In 1607

a competition was held for the design of the facade of this extended nave, which was won by Carlo Maderno. His portico, which greatly resembles the proportions of the facade of the Constantine Basilica, completely obliterated any visual appreciation of Michelangelo's scheme from the square in front of the church, but its completion finally cleared the way for the consecration of the building in 1624.

While Le Corbusier, among others, virulently criticized the Maderno design, such a screen wall is a traditional element in many Italian Renaissance churches, and the addition of a facade of similar size was a foregone conclusion once the decision to extend Michelangelo's short nave was made. Giovanni Lorenzo Bernini's universally admired and extremely elegant colonnade, which was added in the early part of the 18th century, inadvertently continued this containment, blocking from public view what is perhaps the greatest synthesis of art and architecture ever known.

—JAMES M. STEELE

ST. PETER'S SQUARE
Rome, Italy

1629-69. Architect: Giovanni Lorenzo Bernini (1598-1680).
1656-67: Colonnades constructed.

Publications

KITAO, TIMOTHY K.: *Circle and Oval in the Square of St. Peter's: Bernini's Art of Planning.* New York, 1974.

*

Pope Urban VIII, when he was Cardinal Maffeo Barberini, singlehandedly opposed the lengthening of the nave of St. Peter's as designed by Michelangelo, because he knew that the facade proposed by Carlo Maderno would effectively block out the previous architect's sculptural treatment of the exterior walls of the church. The facade was built nonetheless, but only a few years after his ascension, the new pope was able to offset that artistic loss by appointing Giovanni Lorenzo Bernini in 1629 to succeed Maderno as architect of St. Peter's. For the next 40 years, Bernini, often considered to be the most brilliant interpreter of the High Baroque, worked wonders at the Vatican, with his realization of his plan for the square in front of the cathedral unanimously regarded as the most wondrous of all.

Urban VIII (pope 1623-44) and Bernini were well matched in intelligence and temperament, and had an artist-to-patron relationship that was remarkably similar to that between Michelangelo and Julius II. The trust that was placed in Bernini was first put to the test after the commissioning of an enormous baldachin, which was constructed between 1626 and 1633, and required substantial foundations that had to penetrate down to the pavement level of the original Constantinian basilica and the sacred Christian mausoleums beneath it. The resolute confidence that Bernini displayed in dealing with the controversy that surrounded those foundations was later shaken by his attempt to correct the ungainly width of Maderno's facade by adding bell towers at each end. Structural miscalculations, which led to cracks in the facade and the removal of the towers, were a major setback for the artist, resulting in a period of relative inactivity during the tenure of Pope Innocent (1644-55). However, with

St. Peter's

the next pope, Alexander VII (1655-67), all was forgotten, and on the first day after his election he asked Bernini to consider ways in which a sense of order could be achieved in front of the basilica.

The colonnades which the architect proposed were quickly seen to be an inspired solution to a seemingly intractable problem, and construction, which took 11 years to complete, was begun in 1656. When the work was begun, St. Peter's Square might more accurately have been described as a disorderly trapezoid struggling to accommodate a small piazzetta directly in front of Maderno's facade, as well as public viewing of the papal balcony, an Egyptian obelisk placed in front of the basilica amidst great fanfare by Pope Sixtus V (1685-90), and the Santo Spirito quarter, which formed a residential wall to the south. Using the obelisk as a center, the architect created an ellipse, which required the removal of some of Santo Spirito, but generally resolved all of those diverse conditions, and finally allowed the basilica to become the visual terminus of the urban axis set up by the Via Alessandrina, as it should be.

Bernini strengthened this axis in several ingenious, barely perceptible ways, such as by connecting the colonnades with the facade of the church in arms that are splayed outward to create an optical illusion of nearness, just as Michelangelo did in his redesign of the Campidoglio. Bernini also carried out a gradual lowering of the street itself, in order to ensure that the bronze doors of the basilica would still be visible from the end of the axis at the bridge crossing over the Tiber to the Castel Sant'Angelo, nearly 850 meters away. Recent research by Leonardo Benevolo has revealed the infinite care that Bernini took in making slight alterations to the elevating of both the Via Alessandrina and the Via della Conciliazione, which he saw as

a logical extension of his design. This care also included his establishment of a uniform slope toward the obelisk of Sixtus V—which had to remain stationary because of the great difficulty in moving it—and the inversion of this grade by a small but visually significant percentage toward the east in order to tilt the whole piazza toward the Castel Sant'Angelo.

The construction of the two ranks of double porticoes that Bernini created, in what he saw as a "maternal gesture" to accept the faithful, was further complicated by the downhill slope, which made a difficult alignment even more precarious. While the changes that Bernini made to the streets outside the square were removed in 1936, destroying the delicate balance that he set up on this axis, his porticoes provide a constantly shifting perspective as one sees the church facade through them, and are the perfect answer to a problem that once seemed impossible to solve.

—JAMES M. STEELE

SANTO STEFANO ROTONDO
Rome, Italy

Ca. 468-83: Construction. **Sixth century:** East arm converted into chapel. **Seventh century:** Small aspe built. **Eighth century:** Renovations made. **12th century:** Church damaged and subsequently renovated. **1450-54:** Structure rehabilitated; **Architect:** Bernardo Rossellino (1409-1464).

Santo Stefano Rotondo: Rome, Italy, 468-83

Publications

BANFI, FLAVIO: "La Chiesa di Santo Stefano sul monte Celio in Roma." *Annuario dell'Istituto Ungherese di Storia dell'Arte di Firenze* 1 (1947): 3-21.

BANFI, FLAVIO: "La Chiesa di Santo Stefano sul monte Celio e il monastero dei frati Paolini al Monte Celio in Roma." *Capitolium* 28 (1953): 289-300.

BANFI, FLAVIO: "Santo Stefano Rotondo." *L'urbe* 15, No. 1 (1952): 3-9.

BENEDETTI, LUIGI: *Santo Stefano Rotondo*. Rome, 1962.

CORBETT, SPENSER: "Santo Stefano Rotondo." *Rivista di archeologia cristiana* 36 (1960): 249-261.

GENTILE ORTONA, ERMINIA: "Santo Stefano Rotondo e il restauro del Rossellino." *Bollettino d'arte* 67 (1982): 99-106.

GERO, LADISLAO: *Santo Stefano Rotondo, la chiesa nazionale degli ungheresi di Roma*. Budapest, 1944.

KRAUTHEIMER, RICHARD: "Santo Stefano Rotondo a Roma e la chiese del Santo Sepolcro a Gerusalemme." *Rivista di archeologia cristiana* 12, Nos. 1-2 (1935): 52-102.

LIPINSKY, ANGELO: "Santo Stefano Rotondo sul Monte Celio a Roma." *Arte cristiana* 53 (1965).

MACK, CHARLES R.: "Nicholas V and the Rebuilding of Rome: Reality and Legacy." In HELLMUT HAGER and SUSAN MUNSHOWER (eds.): *Light on the Eternal City: Observations*

Santo Stefano Rotondo

and Discoveries in the Art and Architecture of Rome. University Park, Pennsylvania, 1987.

ROSSI, G. B.: "La basilica di Sto. Stefano ed il monastero di S. Erasmo." *Studi di diritto e storia* (1886).

ROSSI, SARA: "Santo Stefano Rotondo a Roma." *Architettura* 4 (1959): 774-779.

SANDOR, RITZ: "La nuova Gerusalemme dell'apocalisse e Santo Stefano Rotondo." *L'urbe* 30, Nos. 4-5 (1976): 12-26.

THIERRY, ANTONIO: "Il restauro di Santo Stefano Rotondo." *Italia nostra* 49 (1966): 15-21.

                                  *

The Church of Santo Stefano, on the Caelian Hill in Rome, is one of the city's most important examples of ecclesiastical architecture. Although the church was believed to have once formed a part of the Markets of Nero, recent investigations have demonstrated that the building was erected as a church during the reign of Pope Simplicius (468-83). Its plan was in keeping with the architectural symbolism of the period and in emulation of the supposed centrality of the Church of the Holy Sepulcher in Jerusalem. Santo Stefano Rotondo, as built, consisted of a series of three concentric circles, the largest 213 feet in diameter, upon which were inscribed the four equal arms of a Greek cross. A high tambour surrounded the central altar. The brick walls of the tambour rose from an architrave carried on 22 granite columns with Ionic capitals. The clerestory of the circular tambour wall was pierced by 22 round-headed windows, flooding the area below in light. Encircling this focal area was an annular nave bordered by an arcade of 36 Corinthian columns. The four arms of the Greek cross radiated from this second circle. Four separate atriums occupied the spaces between the protruding arms of the cross. The third circle was a solid wall that both formed the outer ends of the arms of the cross and enclosed the atrium areas between them.

In the centuries subsequent to its completion, several restorations were carried out which significantly altered the character of the early Christian structure. A century after the church was erected, the eastern arm of the cross was converted into a chapel dedicated to the martyr saints Primus and Felician. There, Pope Theodore I (642-49) built a small apse decorated with mosaics.

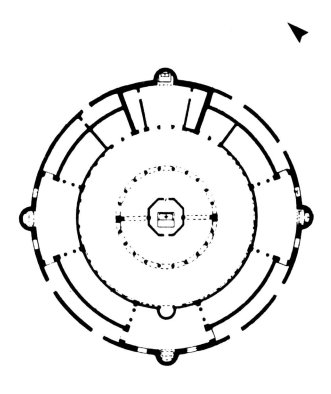

By the eighth century, the fabric of the tambour was in danger of collapse, and was buttressed by Pope Hadrian I (772-95) with a transverse wall across the altar area. The depredations wrought by the followers of the antipope Anacletes II (1130-38) so ruined the church that Pope Innocent II (1130-43) was forced to undertake a drastic program of renovation. That project reduced the church to its present circumference of 131 feet. The net effect of the work done under Pope Innocent was that the outer circle of walls was eliminated. The exterior wall (already partially destroyed) was detached from the building and converted into a precinct wall about the remaining building core. This meant the elimination of all but the eastern arm (the Chapel of Sts. Primus and Felician) of the cross. The middle colonnade thus became the new external wall and the arcades, accordingly, were bricked up. A section of the old outer annular wall was retained next to the martyrs' chapel and an entrance portico attached to it. This portico consisted of five arches resting upon columns with simple beveled capitals. One of the eight original gates led from the portico through part of the old northeastern atrium into the body of the restored church.

The 12th-century alteration in the design and size of Santo Stefano often has been attributed to the important Renaissance restorations carried out as part of the overall efforts to renew Rome by Pope Nicholas V (1447-55). The artist Francesco di Giorgio is partially responsible for this notion, making the claim in his treatise on the history of architecture; he was echoed by Andrea Fulvio, who stated that it was under Nicholas V that the church was reduced in size. The error of these opinions, repeated by some modern authorities, is demonstrated by an examination of the fabric of the church and by the description of the church in the memoirs of Giovanni Rucellai, which indicated that only the innermost circle of columns was visible on his visit in 1450 (before the intervention of Pope Nicholas).

In 1446 Santo Stefano was described by Flavio Biondo as being in a roofless state with ruined mosaics and cracked marble panels. Four years later, Pope Nicholas set aside funds to begin a thorough structural rehabilitation of the old structure as part of his program of refurnishing the 40 station churches in Rome. The extant payment records pertaining to the project all date to the years 1453-54. From the nature of the work carried out at that time, it is evident that the bulk of the substantial restoration must have been undertaken during the three previous years. The fabric was repaired, a new wooden roof installed, an area adjoining the martyrs' chapel set apart for a sacristy, and the anteroom between the porch and the church proper vaulted.

The bulk of the work must have been carried out under the direction of the Florentine sculptor and architect Bernardo Rossellino, whose name figures prominently in the surviving payment records. To redirect the illumination of the interior, 36 round windows were inserted in the arcades walled up in the 12th century. In the clerestory of the tambour, eight twin-lighted window frames of the Florentine variety were installed within the old fifth-century openings, while the remainder of the original windows were bricked up. This more even distribution of light reflects the precepts of Leon Battista Alberti, with whom Rossellino was collaborating in Rome. Much of Pope Nicholas' repairs to Santo Stefano should be termed a beautification project. Apparently, few structural changes were made and, once the essential stabilization had been effected, attention was turned to embellishments. Remaining from that Renaissance intervention, in addition to the windows, are the still largely intact wooden ceiling with carved consoles, the soberly impressive entrance portal, triangular stone corbels in the anteroom, a double door frame through which the annular nave is entered from the anteroom, the sacristy door frame, and a handsome *lavacro* in the sacristy. A painted *stemma* of Pope Nicholas and several carved inscriptions attest to the renovation.

The complex of buildings for the little convent which abuts the northern side of Santo Stefano apparently is of later date. This is demonstrated by the fact that two of Rossellino's round windows were walled up when a wing of this establishment was attached to the exterior of the annular wall of the church, by the character of the corbels in the cloister of the convent, and by the decoration of the walls around the cloister yard. A well in the yard bears the *stemma* of Pope Leo X (1513-21), and the convent would appear to date from his papacy.

—CHARLES R. MACK

SPANISH STEPS AND SANTA TRINITÀ DEI MONTI
Rome, Italy

1502: Church begun; **Architect:** Giacomo della Porta (1532-1602). **1570:** West facade of church completed. **1587:** Twin towers of church finished. **1627-29:** Barcaccia fountain built; **Architect:** Giovanni Lorenzo Bernini (1598-1680). **1723-26:** Steps built; **Architect:** Francesco de Sanctis (1693-1731). **1786:** Obelisk in road set up. **Early 19th century:** Church restored.

Publications

BANDINI, C.: "La scalinata e Piazza di Spagna." *Capitolium* 7 (1931): 327-340.

FORTINI, E.: *Descrizione della venerabile chiesa dedicata alla Ssma. Trinità.* Rome, 1853.

HEMPEL, EBERHARD: "Die spanische Treppe." In *Festschrift Heinrich Wölfflin.* Munich, 1924.

Spanish Steps and SS. Trinità dei Monti: Rome, Italy, 1502

LORET, MATTIA: "La scalinata della Trinità dei Monti vista dal suo autore." *Atti V Congresso Nazionale di Studi Romani* 3 (1942): 456-462.

LOTZ, WOLFGANG: "Bernini e la scalinata di Piazza di Spagna." *Colloqui del Sodalizio* Series 2, 1 (1969): 100-110.

LOTZ, WOLFGANG: "Die Spanische Treppe: Architektur als Mittel der Diplomatie." *Römisches Jahrbuch für Kunstgeschichte* 12 (1969): 39-94.

PECCHIAI, P.: *La scalinata di Piazza di Spagna.* Rome, 1941.

*

In a city of perspectives, vistas and focal points, the Spanish Steps and the Church of Santa Trinità dei Monti are surely the most celebrated, a happy combination of designs spanning more than two centuries. Piazza, steps and church together form the culmination of a narrow kilometer-long axis leading from Alessandro Secchi's former landing place beside the Tiber (Porto di Ripetta) and crossing on its way the busy thoroughfare of Il Corso. Since the history of all three was bound up almost wholly with the French, it is gently ironic that the description "Spanish" became popularly attached to both piazza and steps, merely through the proximity of the Spanish Embassy. The little square was long called Piazza della Trinità, but that name has transferred itself to the space at the top.

Charles VIII of France bought a villa on the Pincio hill in 1494 and there set up a monastery of Minims, an order founded in France by St. Francesco di Paola. The church, on the brink of a steep wooded bank, was begun in 1502. Mostly, however, it is attributed to Giacomo della Porta (architect of Il Gesù and of substantial works in other churches of Rome, including St. Peter's); the west-facing facade is dated 1570, and the twin towers were finished in 1587, together with the twin flights of steps to the entrance.

The idea of formal steps to replace the earlier rough tracks up the hillside was first mooted in 1577. Eventually, in 1660, following an offer of funds by the chargé d'affaires at the French Embassy, there was a limited competition for designs. Some of these survive in drawings, and they reflect a determination to assert French power in papal territory—notably with an equestrian statue of Louis XIV that would have looked down on the Spanish Embassy and rivaled that of Marcus Aurelius on the Capitoline hill. The pope, however, sided with the Spaniards and vetoed the proposal, and it was not resurrected until half a century later by his successor, Clement XI. After further wrangling, the monks insisted on the appointment of their own architect, Francesco de Sanctis. Perhaps as a compromise, the French king's statue was omitted.

Inevitably de Sanctis' Baroque design, carried out in 1723-26, bore close resemblances to the unrealized ones. He catalogued the requirements he was fulfilling, namely, that it should be an effective setting for festivities, that it should form an attractive rendezvous and promenade for the citizens, that it should be pleasing as a whole when seen from a distance, and that the drainage should be good. The last is important in a city subject to sudden violent rainstorms. He pointed out also the allusion to the church's dedication to the Trinity with three flights of steps and three terraces. That, however, is a misleading simplification of the wonderfully varied grouping and branching, merging and separating that carry the eye up and up, following the lines of the balustered parapets, to the topmost terrace, always overtopped by the church above. For the pedestrian, faced with 138 steps in actually 11 separate flights, the main pause for breath is at the broad terrace that occurs after the sixth flight. The initial three flights, usually brightly

thronged with flower sellers, and converging like an inverted wineglass as they rise, are really each three separate stairs running parallel and punctuated by brief landings. Then a single very broad concave flight rises to the first terrace, which is a kind of recessed stage backed by a wall and balustrade—its theatrical character being emphasized by the ordinary buildings flanking it like parts of a set. The fifth and sixth flights rise on either side to the main promenade, a considerable flat area quite hidden from below. Two more, convex this time, then go up to a broad landing backed by another high wall that comes forward in a semicircle from the roadway at the top. To reach that, the steps divide into alternative branches, of three flights each, clasping the semicircle.

Even then, 34 steps must be scaled to reach the church doorway. The obelisk in the road was set up in 1786. It detracts somewhat from the value of the church as a focal point and draws attention to the fact that the church's axis is different from that of the main vista. From there another, much longer axis (the Via Sistina) goes off toward the Basilica of Santa Maria Maggiore.

The Trinità Church, used nowadays by the Sisters of the Sacred Heart, is pre-Baroque, though that does not make it any less accomplished a participant in the grand Baroque townscape of the Spanish Steps. In plan and classical design it is unremarkable; like so many others it was evidently adapted from a Gothic building and probably has medieval walling embedded in it. Only the ribbed vault of the crossing is exposed now, incongruously. The pilasters alternating with coffered arches and supporting a simple clerestory are all very standard for their date. In spite of damage by soldiery in 1799, much of the decorative work in the side chapels is from the 16th century. It includes some important pictures by Daniele da Volterra.

Also part of the whole composition, intermediate in date (1627-29) between the church and the steps, is the Barcaccia (barque) fountain in the floor of the Piazza di Spagna. That is an appropriate description of its position; the water pressure there was too low to permit another of the stately gushing entertainments in stone and water that occur so often in Rome. It is generally agreed to be a work of the young Giovanni Lorenzo Bernini, who 30 years later was to be one of those invited to produce a design for the steps. Those who look for symbolic meanings have many from which to select: the "ship of the Church," as in Giotto's poem "Navicella," or the ship of the Barberini family firing water cannon to calm the world, as in a poem of Pope Urban VIII, or an allusion to the pretended sea fights formerly staged in the piazza. The ancient Romans made similar fountains, and the curious general form of an elegant high-ended boat flooding with water and aground in little more than an elliptical puddle was certainly suggested by them. Bernini embellished it with bees and suns, Barberini emblems, which lend credence to an association with Pope Urban (himself a Barberini).

—ANTHONY NEW

TEMPIETTO IN SAN PIETRO IN MONTORIO
Rome, Italy

1502: Constructed; **Architect:** Donato Bramante (1444-1514). **Early 17th century:** Crypt renovated; altar, porch, dome, and lantern altered.

Tempietto in San Pietro in Montorio: Rome, Italy, 1502

Publications

WAETZOLDT, S.: "Bemerkungen zu Bramantes Tempietto." *Sitzungsberichte der Kunstgeschichtlichen Gesellschaft zu Berlin* New series 11 (1962-63).

The Tempietto, or "little Temple," designed by Donato Bramante and built in 1502 at the Church of San Pietro in Montorio in Rome, is taken to be one of the most exemplary buildings of the High Renaissance. The site was that of the martyrdom of Saint Peter, and the Tempietto, which was a foundation of the king of Spain, is in the most basic sense a monument: while the interior is articulated with all the refinements of Renaissance architecture, it is too small to be used; the building is essentially designed to be looked at, or as Sebastiano Serlio, a contemporary, put it, "erected solely in memory of Saint Peter the Apostle." The interior is only about 14 feet in diameter, and about half of the pavement is taken up by the altar and the altar steps, so there is no room for any sizable congregation.

The idea of such a round building was not new; there had been others in the quattrocento, and if we think of an Early Christian church in Rome, like Santo Stefano Rotondo, we see an even older tradition for circular monuments to celebrate the martyrs of the church. Yet what is new about the Tempietto within the tradition of Renaissance architecture is that the cella, as in the manner of classical, or rather classical Greek design, is surrounded by a colonnade and an architrave, above which then runs a balustrade, a new element in Renaissance decoration. The intervals between the columns are equal all the way around, and there is no indication of where the altar is set within the building. Beyond this, the Tempietto has vaulting done in an ancient manner, and the dome, which is hemispherical in section, is made of cemented masonry. Yet Bramante, against the usual manner in antiquity, made the dome spring, not from the order articulated in the lower sections, but from an intermediate story, the height of which is almost equal to the radius of the diameter. The model there was the Pantheon and, like the Pantheon, a relationship is suggested between the circular form of the ground plan, the height of the cylinder of the dome and the hemisphere of the dome.

According to Sebastiano Serlio, the plan of the Tempietto was not carried out in full, for the Tempietto, which now stands in a square court, was originally to have been surrounded by a cloister of columns, one-and-a-half times the width and height of those of the colonnade. This probably would have made the Tempietto itself seem both higher and wider, for the columns in the Tempietto colonnade would have been taken, by analogy, to be the same height as those that surrounded them.

It is interesting to see the other accommodations for the spectator. The dome is not interrupted by the line of the entablature, and when the door is open, any spectator standing in front of the building would see the altar with the Crucifixion of St. Peter on it, framed by the entrance to the cella, giving the whole a clear iconographic meaning and suggesting in one view both the event of the martyrdom and, from the surrounding architecture, a celebration of that martyrdom.

All this allowed Bramante to construct a piece of religious architecture, true to its purpose, yet with a language of classical design much richer than anything done in the previous century. The architectural vocabulary for this came to Bramante from his early training in Urbino and his knowledge of the theory of Leon Battista Alberti; this may be especially true for the idea of the visual pyramid and the one spectator, occupying the correct view point for the whole. To this Bramante added a

vocabulary that was more purely classical than anything he had designed in the more vernacular style of his early years in Milan. His next move after the Tempietto was to the great exedra of the Cortile of the Belvedere in the Vatican.

It should be noted that the figure of the apostle in the altar niche at the Tempietto is modern, but the relief there is original. The crypt under the Tempietto was renovated early in the 17th century and alterations were made at the same time to the altar, the porch, the dome and the lantern.

—DAVID CAST

TREVI FOUNTAIN
Rome, Italy

1732: Work begun on fountain; **Architect:** Nicola Salvi (1697-1751). **1735:** Facade of connecting palazzo completed. **1736:** Lateral wings of connecting palazzo completed. **1736-62:** Sculptural work on fountain done; **Principle Sculptors:** Salvi, Gian Battista Maini (d. 1752); Central figures, Ocean, his coach, seahorses, and Tritons made; **Designer:** Maini, **Carver:** Pietro Bracci; relief of Agrippa's Meeting with the Architect of the Aquiduct done; **Sculptor:** Andrea Borgondi; figure of Fame made; **Sculptor:** Bengalia; statues of Health and Fertility done; **Designs:** Gian Battista Maini, **Carver:** Filippo Della Valla.

Publications

PINTO, JOHN: *The Trevi Fountain.* New Haven, Connecticut, and London, 1986.
SCHIAVO, A.: *La Fontana di Trevi e le altre opere di Nicola Salvi.* Rome, 1956.

The Trevi Fountain, a theatrical aquatic tableau set in front of a private palace, is one of the most important projects of city planning launched in Rome in the early 18th century. This assemblage of classical sculptural and architectural forms combined with the dramatic display of water effects and simulated elements of nature link the Baroque monument to Rome's ancient past and to the modern picturesque movement of the 18th century.

The fountain, which forms an outdoor stage setting of various materials for the enactment of its water exhibit, echoes similar ensembles of mixed media introduced in Rome by Giovanni Lorenzo Bernini in the 17th century, while the juxtaposition of water, sculpture and architecture evokes the older traditions of waterworks and artificial grottoes popular in ancient Roman and Italian Renaissance gardens. Further, many of the details, such as the sculptural plants and trees creating the illusion of a natural setting and the artificially crumbling pilaster at the farthest eastern corner of the palace facade resembling the deteriorating form of an ancient ruin, reveal Nicola Salvi's interest in nature and the increasingly popular picturesque movement.

The fountain was constructed on the site of one of the supply points of the Aqua Virgo (Acqua Vergine), the aqueduct constructed by Agrippa in 19 B.C. to bring water from a spring east of Rome to the Baths of Agrippa behind the Pantheon. After Gothic invaders damaged the aqueduct in the sixth century and suspended the flow of water, Pope Adrian I repaired it in the late eighth century and redirected its final point of delivery to

Trevi Fountain: Rome, Italy, 1732

a new small fountain at the foot of the Quirinal Hill, near the site of the present fountain. The convergence of three streets (*tre vie*) at this point is a possible source of the name for the site.

Modern antecedents of Salvi's fountain include simple structures by Leon Battista Alberti in 1450 and Guglielmo della Porta in 1564. A third early version was begun by Bernini in the middle of the 17th century in another part of the square, but his project was not completed. In 1629 Pope Urban VIII appointed Bernini architect of the Acqua Vergine and directed him to build a new fountain. The fountain, as envisioned by Bernini, included an expanded piazza to provide more space for a large and imposing fountain. By 1643, he had moved the

outlets of the fountain from the eastern part of the square to the north and demolished many houses in the area to provide a clear view of the piazza from the summer residence of the popes in the Quirinal Palace; but his only construction was a new fountain base, which was demolished for the construction of Salvi's design. The relocation, however, of the fountain so that it was no longer on axis with any of the entrances to the piazza was significant, because it established the Baroque element of surprise for the later fountain that would not be completely visible outside the piazza. The death of his patron Urban VIII in 1645, however, and the shortage of funds brought Bernini's active involvement in the fountain project to an end. And papal politics later directed Bernini's efforts as well as the

Trevi Fountain

flow of water from the Acqua Vergine, as Urban VIII's successor, Innocent X, commissioned from Bernini the Four Rivers Fountain, which drew large volumes of water away from the Trevi Fountain and into the Piazza Navona.

The Trevi Fountain became a point of interest again when an earthquake damaged the aqueduct in 1703. Pope Clement XI announced a design competition for a fountain in 1703 but rejected all entries in favor of a Bernini-inspired composition of his own that would have enlarged the piazza around a reassembled Antonine column set up in front of a palace facade. Nothing came of it, however, because of the shortage of funds,

and Clement XI thus made only structural repairs. The fountain project was introduced again by Benedict XIII, who approved a design by Paolo Benaglia; but the pope died in 1730, before Benaglia's project could be completed. Benedict's successor, Clement XII, after first canceling Benaglia's enterprise, held a competition about which little is known except that apparently only four architects were invited to participate. Then, in 1732, he held a second contest, open to all sculptors and architects working in Rome. One primary requirement for the design was the inclusion, in the plan, of the new facade of the palace of the Poli ducal family, who, in 1722-23, had purchased the entire site facing the piazza for additions to their palace, including the desired fountain to be attached to their new facade. After first choosing and then rejecting, in succession, designs by Lambert Sigisbert Adam and Luigi Vanvitelli, the pope and his committee chose a project by Nicola Salvi.

Work began on the fountain in 1732, and the first stage of completion was a model of the palace facade presented in 1733. The facade of the palace itself was completed in 1735, and the lateral wings were complete by 1736. The sculptural forms proceeded very slowly, however, because many sculptors and stonecutters were involved. And there were some design changes as the sculptural work moved forward. Benedict XIV, who succeeded Innocent XIII in 1740, was not happy to inherit the unfinished project and attempted to complete it quickly; but progress was slowed by the deaths of some of the principals: Salvi in 1751, after catching cold working in the waters; sculptor Giovanni Battista Maini in 1752; and Benedict XIV himself in 1758. The fountain was completed finally in 1762 under Clement XIII.

Salvi's Baroque stage consists of a complex scene of tritons and sea horses in a rocky plateau inundated by a triple cascade of falling water. Towering above them is the giant figure of Oceanus, the active and powerful ruler of all waters, standing on a large shell chariot. Salvi consulted ancient and contemporary literary sources for his imagery and created a universe in miniature, in which the powerful ruler of the waters of the earth rides through the waters in his shell chariot driven by two sea horses, one of whom is active, the other passive. The inundation of water in the cascade duplicates the symbolical circular flow of water from earth to heaven and back as described by Aristotle, and hints also of the modern scientific inquiry into the circulation of water, with which Salvi was familiar. Additional symbols brought into play were large sculptural snakes representing the healthful effects of water. These snakes, whose heads were broken in the 19th century, also added another component to this seminal architectural venture of the 18th century. Like the crumbling corner pilaster, they also suggested the typical growth and decay visible in Roman ruins throughout the city in the 18th century as witnessed by Salvi's contemporary Giovanni Battista Piranesi, a Venetian architect who, in numerous etchings, depicted the decay of ancient Roman ruins overgrown with vines and weeds.

Although Salvi's architectural design was chosen the winner, the final version of the fountain also exhibited the styles of other artists working on the project. Maini was commissioned to design the central group of Oceanus and a shell chariot pulled by tritons and sea horses. His first group of models, carved in stucco and set in place in 1738, caused a disagreement with Salvi; a compromise between them led to a second version of the group put in place in 1741-42. In 1759-61 marble copies of these models were produced by Pietro Bracci and set in place on the fountain.

The total concept of the fountain, however, belonged to Salvi, whose early studies of mathematics and philosophy prepared him for the comprehensive stylistic and iconographical program he developed for the integrated ensemble of sculpture and architecture. His scientific concerns were addressed in the design and construction of the water cascade, which so clearly demonstrates the philosophical theme of the circular flow of water. And his interest in nature and all its elements placed him ahead of his 18th-century contemporaries. His interest in nature and science was balanced, though, by his reverence for classical antiquity, which is well represented in the Trevi Fountain. Oceanus stands in front of a semicircular niche, which is coffered like that of Hadrian's Pantheon. And the backdrop of Oceanus' water display, which seems at first to be the *scena*

frons of an ancient Roman theater, is, in reality, the facade of the Palazzo Poli. At the center of the facade is a giant triumphal arch close in size, scale and decoration to the grandiose Arch of Constantine. A high, rusticated base further links the palace facade to ancient Roman sources, while the giant Corinthian pilasters in the lateral bays and engaged columns in the central arch vividly recall the giant order introduced by Michelangelo in the Capitoline Palace facade and the apse elevation of St. Peter's Basilica. Salvi apparently also knew the designs for a 17th-century project by Pietro da Cortona to move the Trevi Fountain to the Piazza Colonna, because, in those drawings, Cortona had anticipated Salvi's design of a palace facade combined with a monumental fountain.

The secondary sculpture of the fountain includes the plants and other natural forms in the rockwork of the fountain and the figural sculptures devoted to the legendary history of the fountain, its allegorical symbolism, and the dedicatory inscriptions honoring its benefactors. Statues representing Health and Fertility, which were produced as full-scale models by Maini, were carved in stone by Filippo Della Valla and set in the lateral niches in 1760. Above the niches, a pair of relief scenes represent the beginning of the aqueduct. On the left is Andrea Borgondi's depiction of Agrippa's meeting with the architect of the aqueduct; the relief on the right by Giovanni Battista Grossi shows the possible source of the aqueduct's name as a young virgin shows the site of the spring to Agrippa's troops. And on the attic, statues resting on the tops of the cornice blocks of the central columns, carved by four different sculptors, represent the gifts of vegetation presented throughout the four seasons of the year. On the roofline of the balustrade, two figures of Fame by Benaglia support the coat of arms, by stonecutters Francesco Pincelotti and Giuseppi Poddi, of Innocent XII, who commissioned the square and whose feat is described in the attic inscription below, like similar heraldic tributes to triumphant Roman emperors. The friezes below bear the names of the popes who followed Clement XII and brought the fountain to a conclusion.

The Trevi Fountain, which was funded by a public lottery and consequently has been subject to the opinion of the people of Rome and the world, has been a favored monument of the public throughout its history, although it has not always been well received by art critics. Democratic tastes have prevailed, however: the fountain has increased in popularity and today remains one of Rome's favorite tourist spots.

—JOYCE M. DAVIS

THE VATICAN
Vatican City, Rome, Italy

847-55: First version of the Vatican Borgo constructed. **1447-55:** Vatican Borgo designs revised, bastion still stands; **Architect:** Leon Battista Alberti (1404-72). **1198-1216:** Papal Palace built. **1277-80:** Additions to Papal Palace built. **1377:** Papal Palace rebuilt. **Early 15th century:** Residential north wing added to Papal Palace; **Designer:** Pope Nicholas V (under guidance of Alberti's original designs for the Vatican Borgo). **Late 15th century:** Tower added to residential wing; **Architect:** Antonio da Sangallo the Elder (1443-1516). **1473-78:** Sistine Chapel constructed. **1481:** Sistine Chapel fresco decorations begun. **1485-87:** Villa Belvedere built. **1503-21:** Papal Palace's eastern front built; **Architects:** Donato Bramante (1444-1514), Raphael (1483-1520). **1505:** Belvedere Court designed; **Architect:** Bramante. **1508-13:** Stanze della Segnatura, Stanze di

Vatican, Cortile di Belvedere and Giardino della Pigna: Rome, Italy, 1505

Eliodoro painted, Papal Palace, frescoes painted; **Artist:** Raphael. **1508-12:** Sistine Chapel ceiling painted, roof restored; **Artist:** Michelangelo (1475-1564); **Architect:** Bramante; **1534-41:** *The Last Judgement* Sistine Chapel altar wall painted, two end windows eliminated; **Artist:** Michelangelo. **1540:** Sala Regia designed; **Architect:** Antonio da Sangallo the Younger (1483-1546); **Stuccoists:** Perino del Vaga (1501-1547; also known as Pietro Bonaccorsi), Daniele da Volterra. **1540s:** Pauline Chapel built and decorated; **Architect:** Antonio da Sangallo the Younger. **1559-65:** Villa Pia built; **Architect:** Pirro Ligorio (ca. 1500-1583). **Late 16th century:** Vatican Library constructed. **18th century:** Braccio Nuova added. **1971:** Papal Audience Hall built; **Architect:** Pier Luigi Nervi (1891-1979).

Publications

ACKERMAN, JAMES S.: *The Cortile del Belvedere.* Vatican City, 1954.

ANCEL, RENÉ: "Le Vatican sous Paul IV: Contribution à l'histoire de palais pontifical." *Revue Bénédictine* 24 (1908): 48-71.

DEHIO, GEORG: "Die Bauprojekte Nicolaus V." *Repertorium fuer Kunstwissenschaft* 3 (1880): 241-257.

DE TOLNAY, C.: *Michelangelo: The Sistine Ceiling.* Princeton, New Jersey, 1969.

FROMMEL, CHRISTOPHER L.: "Antonio da Sangallos Cappella Paolina." *Zeitschrift für Kunstgeschichte* 27: 1-42.

MAGNUSON, TORGIL: "The Project of Nicholas V for Rebuilding the Borgo Leonino in Rome." *Art Bulletin* 36 (June 1954): 89-115.

REDIG DE CAMPOS, DEOCLECIO: "I Palazzi Vaticani." *Roma cristiana* 18 (1967).

SMITH, GRAHAM: *The Casino of Pius IV.* Princeton, New Jersey, 1977.

The Vatican and the Basilica of St. Peter's in Rome. 2 vols. Paris, 1882.

VOSS, H.: "Bernini als Architekt an der Scala Regia und an den Kolonnaden von St. Peter." *Jahrbuch der preussischen Kunstsammlungen* (1922).

WASSERMAN, JACK: "The Palazzo Sisto V in the Vatican." *Journal of the Society of Architectural Historians* 21 (1962): 26-35.

WITCOMBE, CHRISTOPHER L. C. EWART: "Sixtus V and the Scala Santa." *Journal of the Society of Architectural Historians* 44 (December 1985): 368-379.

*

The Vatican, as we know it today, serves its original function as the seat of the papacy. It still consists of an impressive array of structures with diverse functions, buildings which include the primary residence of the pope, ceremonial chapels, halls of state, a library, private gardens and an extensive series of rooms housing the papal art collections—the Museo del Vaticano. In addition, the Vatican has operated as an independent city-state since the Lateran Treaty of 1929, with the result that government services reside within historic structures as well as utilitarian buildings. The most notable modern building constructed to fit the needs of the 20th-century papacy was designed by Pier Luigi Nervi in 1971. Rising to the south of St. Peter's, the papal audience hall with its shell-shaped vault reminds the present-day visitor of the Vatican's central role as the focus of pilgrimage.

Public access to Vatican buildings is limited to the museums and galleries, whereas special privileges are required for entrance to other historic sites. The Church of St. Peter's adjoins the Vatican Palace for the convenience of the pope and resident

Vatican, great niche detail: 847-55

ecclesiastics. Fortified walls encircle the whole precinct, marking the original boundaries of the Vatican City, with the old entrance gate of Porta Angelica connecting the Piazza of St. Peter's with the city to the north. The 20th-century Via della Conciliazione runs along a straight axis from the Tiber to the piazza, and the perimeter of the present Vatican city. Not only has the modern city of Rome grown up around the enclosed entity of the Vatican, but the relationship of the Vatican to its physical environment has changed dramatically since its genesis in the early Middle Ages.

Pope Leo IV (847–55), who had the first walls raised in order to protect the tomb of Saint Peter, created a distinct precinct which became known as the Leonine City, or the Vatican Borgo. The walls ran from the foot of the Janiculum at the Tiber River toward the hills and around St. Peter's, turning back in the direction of Castel Sant'Angelo to the north. This early attempt to carve out an urban district which was both habitable and defensible resulted in an autonomous identity for the Vatican. Subsequent popes, aware of the need for better fortification, directed their architects to strengthen the walls. A passageway for the popes, the so-called "Corridor" along the northern walls of the Leonine City, joined the papal palace to the Castel Sant'Angelo, which served as a fortress during times of strife. Nicholas V (1447–55), probably on the advice of Leon Battista Alberti, conceived of an ideal urban plan for the Vatican Borgo. The bastion which stands at the junction of the walls and the Vatican Palace formed part of his visionary building project. As architects expanded the Vatican, particularly to unpopulated areas to the north and west, the defensive walls grew in size and stature. The present-day visitor circumnavigates these tall, brick fortifications in order to gain entrance to the Vatican museums.

Such defensive measures went hand in hand with the decision of the papacy to transfer the papal residence from San Giovanni

Vatican, garden: 847-55

in Laterano to St. Peter's. Evidently, a palace existed at the Vatican from the sixth to 10th centuries, but the nucleus of the present structure dates from the papacy of Innocent III (1198–1216). Nicholas III (1277–80) ordered significant additions, and Gregory XI (1370–78) rebuilt the palace after his return from Avignon in 1377. The popes of the Early Renaissance continued to divide their time between palaces at the Lateran and Vatican, although isolated building projects testify to the increasing stature of the palace.

The plans made by Nicholas V, with the guidance of Alberti, proved to be pivotal for the Vatican Palace. The pope had a new wing of the palace built to the north in a style which launched a Renaissance building vocabulary for domestic architecture of mid-15th-century Rome. The brick structure has a three-story facade punctuated by marble detailing, cross-bar windows along the *piano nobile,* horizontal ledges and a crenellated roof line reminiscent of medieval fortification. The papal apartments in the interior are commodious and well illuminated. A small chapel, decorated with frescoes by Fra Angelico, was built for the private services of the pope. Although he also desired a new ceremonial chapel, Nicholas V continued to use the *capella magna* founded by Gregory XI. For each of these endeavors, the names of builders, rather than an identifiable architect, appear in the documents. Yet, there is little doubt about the participation of Alberti, who served as adviser to the pope and composed his *Ten Books on Architecture* during residency at the papal court. Just as Alberti's ideas surely guided the work of Bernardo Rossellino, who was in charge of building the new choir for the Church of St. Peter's, he must have been the source of building projects in the Vatican. Only one addition to Nicholas' residential wing took place during the later 15th century, the massive tower built by Antonio da Sangallo the Elder for Alexander VI (1492–1503).

The next phase of palace construction, an eastern front, was begun under Julius II (1503–12) and continued under Leo X (1513–21). Bramante, who was succeeded by Raphael, introduced the massive scale and harmonious proportions of High Renaissance architecture to the principal facade of the papal palace, just as he also planned for other portions of the Vatican complex. The eastern facade was composed of four stories, with the upper three consisting of classical arcades rising above the Vatican walls. Bramante applied a system of piers, pilasters and engaged columns, patterned after the Colosseum. Raphael

oversaw the installation of stucco and fresco decoration in the antique manner. The Bramante-Raphael facade eventually formed one side of the Courtyard of San Damaso, and this wing of the palace dominated views of the Vatican during the 16th century. Sixtus V (1585–90) directed the completion of an adjacent palace on a slightly lower level which superseded the earlier papal residence. Domenico Fontana designed the large, square palace which now rises over the north side of the Piazza of St. Peter's. Here the pope delivers the papal benediction in full view of the pilgrims below.

An equally potent symbol of the Vatican is the Sistine Chapel, now open to visitors as part of the Vatican museums but still considered the ceremonial chapel of the popes. In particular, the conclaves for papal elections are held in the chapel, circumstances requiring security and privacy. Such prerequisites influenced the architectural design of the original building. The exterior of the chapel is notable for its austerity; the brick walls are relieved only by high windows placed over a simple cornice. An oblong structure situated at the southwest corner of the papal palace, the Sistine Chapel approximated a fortified bastion overlooking the hills to the north and west.

The chapel takes its name from the founder, Sixtus IV (1471–84), who oversaw its construction from about 1473 to 1478. In respect to church architecture, the dimensions of the building are unusual, for it is three times as long as it is wide, and twice as high. Some scholars have suggested that the pope, the former Francesco della Rovere, sought a model in the Temple of Jerusalem, as described in the Book of Kings. More certainly, the Franciscan scholar was attached to the model of the late-13th-century basilica of St. Francis at Assisi, where the scheme of decoration in the interior followed a similar pattern. It is likely that the shallow barrel vault of the Sistine originally was painted with a starry, blue sky. A clerestory of simple proportions illuminates the interior, while the lower half of the wall elevation is marked by a cornice below the entablature. Frescoes cover the entire surface of the walls, in three distinct bands of decoration. Although it was moved closer to the entrance during the 16th century, a marble screen or *cancellata* has always divided the presbytery from the space occupied by the laity. Only the pavement, a type of "neo-Cosmatesque" work, recalls the early chapel on that site, the *cappella magna.*

The architecture of the Sistine Chapel clearly was designed for the decoration of the interior walls and, as such, was driven by the programmatic intentions of the pope and his humanist advisers. However, the scale of the project (it was the largest building in the Vatican complex, excepting Old St. Peter's) and its innovative design are the products of a rare combination of technical expertise and aesthetic judgment. Scholarly opinion is divided about the architect or architects responsible. The names of Giuliano da Sangallo, Andrea Bregno and Leon Battista Alberti can be dismissed on circumstantial grounds, while Baccio Pontelli and Giovannino dei Dolci each deserve consideration. Pontelli, a Florentine, is mentioned by Giorgio Vasari as the architect of Sixtus IV and, although undocumented in Rome during the period when the Sistine Chapel was under construction, he may well have supervised the project from afar. Giovannino, another Florentine woodworker, was employed at the palace in the capacity of a builder, and may have directed work at the site. The project was conceived and executed efficiently, with a hiatus in the work occurring before the fresco decoration was undertaken in 1481. Except for a sacristy added under Innocent VIII (1484–92), subsequent alterations to the chapel were limited to shoring up the structure. When Michelangelo was engaged to paint the ceiling in 1508–12, Bramante restored the roof; and when Michelangelo repainted the altar wall in 1534–41, two windows at the end were eliminated.

A series of rooms at ground level adjoined the Sistine Chapel, linking the Church of St. Peter's with the Vatican Palace. The great reception hall, named the Sala Regia, was designed by Antonio da Sangallo the Younger in 1540. The massive barrel vault is covered with stuccowork executed by Perino del Vaga and Daniele da Volterra, and illuminated by a Serlian window at one end. The Pauline Chapel, named after its founder, Paul II (1534–50), is located on the opposite end of the Sala Regia. Sangallo was the architect of the tall, narrow chapel which was designed to hold the two frescoes by Michelangelo.

The nucleus of the Vatican museums dates back to the papal collection assembled by Pope Julius II. He installed antiquities, including the renowned Laocoon, in a square courtyard adjoining the Belvedere villa. The villa proper had been built, by an unknown architect, for Innocent VIII in 1485-87 on a hill to the north of the papal palace. Julius II commissioned Bramante to design a court linking the villa of Innocent VIII to the papal palace. Bramante's ambitious plan for the Vatican rivaled antiquity in its dimensions, form and symbolism. The architecture of the Belvedere Court recreated the ambience of imperial Rome, a vast pleasure palace for a patron who claimed the secular authority of the ancient Roman empire. Bramante turned to the examples of the Temple of Fortune at Praeneste as well as the classical villa. In a like manner, the new Church of St. Peter's, rising at the other side of the Vatican Palace, represented the pope's spiritual claims to the Chair of the Apostle.

The Belvedere Court, begun in 1505, was notable from the beginning for its grandiose scale, about 950 by 225 feet. Bramante began by designing arcades to serve as the long arms of the courtyard to frame and connect the three levels. The lower end of the enclosed space, near the Vatican Palace, served as a theater for outdoor spectacles. At the center of the upper end, Bramante inserted a large hemicycle in the wall and preceded it with semicircular steps, creating a giant exedra. There he installed the bronze pinecone which had formerly graced the forecourt of Old St. Peter's. Gardens, elaborate ramps and connecting steps traversed the intermediate, terraced landscape. The total effect was created for a strategic point from the papal apartments, where the pope could command a perspective view of architecture, sculpture and theater. Construction of the court continued into the later 16th century and, despite alterations to Bramante's plan, the elevation of the side walls adheres to his rhythmic grouping of arches and narrow bays.

A critical blow was dealt to Bramante's project in the late 16th century with the construction of the new Vatican Library under Sixtus V. The first papal library had occupied the lower story of the Vatican Palace. Founded by Nicholas V, the library had been expanded to include a Biblioteca Latina and a Biblioteca Greca by Sixtus IV. Yet, the necessity of larger quarters resulted in the construction of a new wing by Domenico Fontana. The new library spanned the width of the Belvedere Court and thereby fractured Bramante's plan. The 18th-century Braccio Nuovo, a section of the papal museum, was added parallel to the library, completing the dissection of the Belvedere Court.

Pirro Ligorio designed the Villa Pia or Casino for Pope Pius IV (1559-65), who desired a pleasure retreat in the Vatican gardens. The architecture of the *villa suburbana,* conceived for overnight stays, derived from the humanist revival of the antique type, as described by Leon Battista Alberti, and elaborated by Sebastiano Serlio. Ligorio devised an elegant, diminutive version of the villa type, a casino with a forward pavilion, an oval court in the middle and the main building to the rear. The disposition of the rooms conformed to the landscape, with terraces at three levels, and open loggias above fountains. The symmetrical plan was an intrinsic feature of villa design; only the tower at one side produces a picturesque effect reminiscent of a rustic environment. Statuary, inscriptions and stuccowork cover the surface of the walls, signaling a program of decoration steeped in humanist complexity.

—EUNICE D. HOWE

VILLA FARNESINA
Rome, Italy

1505-1511. **Architect:** Baldassare Peruzzi (1481-1536). **1515-17:** Hall of Perspectives painted; **Artist:** Peruzzi. **1517:** *Marriage of Alexander and Roxanne* painted; **Artist:** Sodoma. **1518-19:** Loggia of Psyche painted; **Artist:** Raphael, with help from Giulio Romano and Giovanni da Udine. **16th century:** Hall of Galatea painted; **Artists:** Peruzzi and Sebastiano del Piombo.

Publications

FROMMEL, C. L.: *Die Farnesina und Peruzzis architektonisches Frühwerk.* Berlin, 1961.
GERLINI, E.: *La Villa Farnesina in Roma.* Rome, 1949.
GERLINI, E.: *Villa Farnesina alla Lungara Roma.* Rome, 1988.

*

The Villa Farnesina took its name from the Farnese family, who acquired it in 1579 as a pendant to their Palazzo Farnese on the opposite bank of the Tiber. It was the original commission of Agostino Chigi (1466-1520), banker to a succession of popes including Alexander VI Borgia, Julius II della Rovere and Leo X de' Medici. Intended as a residence for Chigi's mistress, Imperia, it was completed only after her death. Chigi then took a youthful Venetian courtesan, Andreosia, by whom he had four children before they were married by Leo X in 1519.

Agostino is the Sienese patron who had commissioned chapels from Raphael in Santa Maria del Popolo and Santa Maria della Pace. He had lent money to the Venetians, rented tolfa

Villa Farnesina: Rome, Italy, 1505-1511

mines and, ever the entrepreneur, even set up a printing press in the villa's basement in 1515, its first and only volume a Greek Pindar.

The villa was the masterpiece of Chigi's fellow countryman, the painter and architect Baldassare Peruzzi. Peruzzi began the Farnesina the same decade as Donato Bramante began the Tempietto and Basilica of St. Peter. Peruzzi gave the Farnesina a less insistent grouping of orders than is found in the earlier Roman Palazzo di Cancelleria (1486-96) or in the urban facade of Leon Battista Alberti's Palazzo Rucellai in Florence (1446-51).

Within the villa's two-story elevation small openings hint at a basement level, a mezzanine above the ground floor and an attic above the second level. Peruzzi gave the villa a symmetrical plan in the shape of a square horseshoe, but with an irregular arrangement of interior space. Yet the leisurely plan, with its wide, comfortable staircases and pleasant arrangement of rooms, attests to Peruzzi's strengths as an architect.

Tuscan order pilasters define the window bays of both of the villa's stories, and with the rectangular window aediculae and stucco facing emphasize the essential flatness of the walls, the pilasters serving as suitable frames for the illusionistic fresco paintings that have long since disappeared. Stronger accents are reserved for mezzanine windows that hang from the architrave of the first story, and the relief stucco *putti* that enframe attic windows in the entablature. Peruzzi reserved his boldness for the villa's interior.

The garden loggia, framed within extended lateral wings and now enclosed to protect the Raphael-school fresco decorations, was the original entrance, rather than the staid doorway on the opposite side that is entered from the street today. The Loggia

of Psyche (1518-19), painted by Raphael with considerable shop assistance from Giulio Romano and Giovanni da Udine, contains figures of grand volumes in illusionistic scenes. Lunettes harbor deities silhouetted against a blue sky within the confines of a simulated bower. On the ceiling are two scenes of *Psyche Received on Mt. Olympus* and the *Wedding of Cupid and Psyche* as simulated tapestries. The loggia, with its fictive tapestries and simulated trellis, has the aspect of an open pergola appropriately melding house and garden. It is a superb example of the illusionistic interests of artists in the early decades of the 16th century, making Peruzzi one of the important Renaissance innovators in this genre.

The Hall of Galatea contains Peruzzi's painted program honoring the villa's patron. He placed Chigi arms within the ceiling's central octagon flanked by two elongated, eight-sided panels containing the patron's pictorial horoscope with allegorical personifications showing the alignment of planets and constellations for 1 December 1466, accepted as Chigi's birthday. This ceiling arrangement is surrounded by 10 hexagons and 14 vaults containing mythological scenes. Peruzzi's paintings are characterized by figures of vigorous interior modeling and varied outline placed in the frontal plane against neutral backdrops, yet somewhat stiff and dry in pose. There is throughout, however, a clear articulation of architectural detail. Some of the paintings in the lunettes by Sebastiano del Piombo, such as his *Fall of Icarus,* use a blue sky as background, with figures of softer modeling although somewhat awkward anatomies.

The wall bays contain a fresco by Sebastiano of the one-eyed giant Polyphemus, adjacent to Raphael's painting of the sea nymph Galatea. It is with good reason that the room takes its name from Raphael's splendid wall fresco. The landscapes

Villa Farnesina

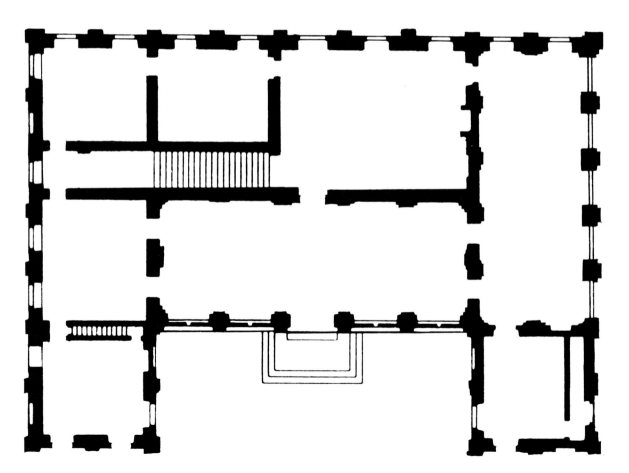

on the remaining bays of the wall were later additions associated with Gaspard Dughet. The decoration of the Sala, which was originally an open loggia that was enclosed, was never completed with other narrative scenes, probably due to the flooding of the Tiber in 1514, which damaged Raphael's and Sebastiano's frescoes.

On the second level, the grandest room in size and conception is the Hall of Perspective (1515-17), painted by Peruzzi. Portions of the walls are painted surfaces made to appear as columned porches opening on to views of the surrounding hills. They remind the viewer of the illusionistic perspective of Bramante's choir for Santa Maria presso San Satiro in Milan, except that here Peruzzi has advanced Bramante's study of space by opening the walls to the landscape vista beyond.

The room had previously conveyed a regal quality due to 19th-century porphyry overpaint. This had thickened the columns and cropped the illusionistic vistas beyond, but the recently cleaned frescoes of the Hall of Perspective now display slender columns of green variegated marble lending an appropriately open, airy freshness to the interior.

Adjacent is Chigi's bedroom, with the splendid fresco of the *Marriage of Alexander and Roxanne* by Sodoma (ca. 1517). The subject is appropriate to the room and allegorizes the love affair of its patron.

The Villa Farnesina continues to impress by its charm and comfort. Jacopo Sansovino paid it the ultimate compliment by repeating its plan in 1540 in his Villa Garzone in Pontecasale.
—EDWARD J. OLSZEWSKI

VILLA GIULIA
Rome, Italy

1551-55: Construction; **Architects:** Giacomo Barozzi da Vignola (1507-73), Giorgio Vasari (1511-74), Bartolomeo Ammannati (1511-92). **1560s:** Additions made. **20th century:** Etruscan Museum added.

Publications

COOLIDGE, JOHN: "The Villa Giulia: A Study of Central Italian Architecture in the Mid-Sixteenth Century." *Art Bulletin* 25 (September 1943): 177-225.

FOSSI, MAZZINO: *Bartolomeo Ammannati: Architetto.* Florence, 1967.

GIORGANI, P.: "Ricerche intorno a Villa Giulia." *Arte* 10 (1907).

STEFANI, E.: "Villa Giulia: la primitiva sistemazione architettonica della facciata retrostante al ninfeo." *Bollettino d'arte* 30 (1936).

Villa Giulia, the suburban Roman retreat of Pope Julius III, Giovanni Maria Ciocchi del Monte, was the architectural proving ground for at least two Mannerist architects, Giacomo Barozzi da Vignola (1507-73) and Bartolomeo Ammannati (1511-92). Each had major responsibilities for the design of the handsome villa where the pope wished to retire from Vatican intrigues and entertain his friends. Initially, however, the pope called a countryman, the ubiquitous Giorgio Vasari from Arezzo (1511-74), to help him formulate a comprehensive plan to remodel existing structures on the large estate he had inherited, Vigna Giulia. He also desired a new architectural focal point that reflected his own aesthetics. This structure became known as Villa Giulia. According to Vasari's plausible account, he alone worked out the master plan according to a program advanced by the pope. Before Vasari returned to his Medici projects for Duke Cosimo I in Florence, he recommended Barozzi (called "Vignola" after his birthplace) to Julius. As papal architect, Vignola immediately began work on the villa proper, or casino, in 1551.

After a lengthy approach from the Tiber River, past a fountain and earlier buildings on the property, Vignola's distinctive new facade soon presented itself to view. The architect designed a taut-surfaced, symmetrical composition alive with heavy rustication on the portal and flanking windows. Corner quoins of the same texture wrap the exterior edges of the elevation, unifying the facade's composition. The rough stone-like ornamentation recalls that favored by Sebastiano Serlio (1475-1554), whose books on architecture had begun to appear as early as 1537. The Roman architecture of an earlier papal artist, Raphael

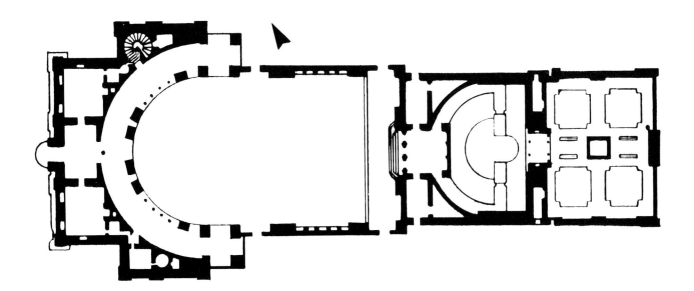

Villa Giulia, courtyard facade: Rome, Italy, 1551-55

(1483-1520), and that of his associate, Giulio Romano (1499-1566), also influenced the design. The Villa Giulia was Vignola's first major commission in Rome, and he naturally drew upon available contemporary as well as antique models. As nothing about the design resembles known architecture by Vasari, it can be safely assumed that the synthesis of styles on the villa was Vignola's.

As the major surface decoration of the facade, he designed a tripartite Roman triumphal arch to frame the entrance. He then repeated that device, with minor variations, directly above on the second level. These arches announced the motif that would recur throughout the villa and garden architecture, suggesting associations between its ambitious owner and the glories of ancient Rome; no matter that Julius was a provincial from Monte Sansovino near Arezzo.

Immediately beyond the villa's entrance portal awaits a rectangular foyer flanked on either side by large rooms used for dining by the pope and his frequent guests. All private apartments are above. The mass of the building, less than one third as deep as it is wide, is only one room in depth. Through another triumphal arch on the opposite side of the foyer, a visible garden space filled with additional architectural forms beckons. It is at this point that Vignola presented his architectural surprise, and one of the villa's great pleasures.

Just a step outside of the far door curves a high, vaulted, loggia that reaches out gracefully to embrace the carefully designed scenic vista beyond. Nothing about the villa architecture quite prepares one for the generous loggia. The ends of this handsome arc lead to nothing in particular, but that in no way diminishes the delight of the loggia itself. There the delicate

fresco imagery of Taddeo Zuccari (1529-66) and Prospero Fontana (1512-97) mirrors the influence of the newly excavated Roman palace of the emperor Titus. Cupids peer from painted arbors above, graceful female figures stroll along the walls, and an array of intertwining floral and leaf forms frames Greco-Roman-style look-alikes. It has been advanced that Julius wanted the loggia to function as an area for temporary stepped seating so that his guests could enjoy his lavish theatrical and musical spectacles in the garden space beyond. From the triumphal arches of the entrance to the Roman-inspired loggia and garden architecture, Julius III continued to suggest parallels, if not a continuum, between himself and the grandeur of antiquity.

Beyond the center of the curved loggia, the garden architecture attributed to Ammannati stretches. This second artist, also engaged on the advice of Vasari, began work on a dramatic nymphaeum in 1552, but Vignola, as papal architect, appears to have had some influence on the design, at least in the beginning. On the villa proper, according to an extant commemorative medal struck in 1553, Vignola planned two facade towers with domes to be echoed in the garden by two domed kiosk shapes above the sides of the grotto. The kiosks were completed, but not the towers, and a later nymphaeum wall, possibly Ammannati's, enveloped and obscured Vignola's kiosks. Although the pope called Michelangelo and other architects to consult on the project, the garden architecture remains predominantly Ammannati's creation.

Faithful to the original concept, all garden forms follow the central axis proceeding from the entrance portal and progressing through two garden spaces to arrive at a tripartite niche in the back wall. Forms are symmetrical, but a second incidence of the unexpected occurs in Ammannati's sunken grotto and nymphaeum. This type of construction was known from Roman villas of antiquity, but its three-story depth, preceded by a loggia of triumphal arches and hidden from casual view, quite stuns the viewer with its sudden magnificence. A curving staircase descends each side of the nymphaeum, which Ammannati designed with one rectilinear side and a sweeping, connecting curve. The use of the curve immediately recalls that of Vignola's arc on the casino loggia, while Ammannati's repetition and reversal of that curve introduce an element of playfulness quite appropriate for the nymphaeum-grotto form.

Vasari appears to have consulted with Ammannati on the nymphaeum, taking credit for the fountain on the lowest level, where Vignola had earlier worked with the hydraulics. Ammannati continued to construct the arched loggia above at the second level between 1553 and 1555, when construction ceased due to Julius' death. The second-level loggia blends well with the side walls that attempt to enclose the entire garden area and connect it to the villa. On stylistic grounds, the walls can be attributed to Ammannati.

Loggia three, repeating the familiar tripartite triumphal-arch motif, and the remainder of the top floor of the nymphaeum were executed in the 1560s and are virtually the only additions made to Villa Giulia until the wing for the Etruscan Museum was added in the 20th century.

A true exemplar of Mannerism, Villa Giulia embraces nearly all of Mannerism's architectural vagaries. The distinctive manner of each participating architect is clearly visible; each utilized classical elements in unpredictable and novel ways. The unexpected reigns side by side with classical regularity, rough texture plays against smooth, curves counter rectilinearity, and restless forms contrast with tranquil ones. Nearly every part of the villa and grounds denies the viewer closure in some way, and questions arise where one might logically expect answers. How many of these anticlassical characteristics are due to the capricious personality of the pope, to the designs of multiple architects, or to the intellectual, social and artistic climate of the time in which the villa was designed can never be fully ascertained, but the Pope Julius-Vasari-Vignola-Ammannati creation is, without doubt, one of the major Mannerist structures of the 16th century.

—PHILANCY N. HOLDER

VILLA MADAMA
Rome, Italy

1516: Villa designed; **Architect:** Raphael (1483-1520). **1523-24:** Work continued after Raphael's death (1520), some interior decorations, gardens and fountains completed; **Architects:** Antonio da Sangallo the Younger (1483-1546), Giulio Romano (1499-1546), Giovanni da Udine. **1527:** Villa extensively damaged in fire.

Publications

COFFIN, D. R.: "The Plans of the Villa Madama." *Art Bulletin* (1967): 111ff.
FROMMEL, L.: "La Villa Madama e la tipologia della villa romana ne Rinascimento." *Bollettino del Centro Internazionale di Studi di Architettura "Andrea Palladio"* (1969): 47-64.

*

The Villa Madama in Rome was designed by Raphael as a suburban retreat on Monte Mario, north of the Vatican Borgo, for Cardinal Giulio de' Medici, later Pope Clement VII. History, as David Coffin notes, has been harsh with this villa, which is now only a fragment of the great scheme Raphael planned; contributing to the problems was Raphael's death in 1520, just a few years into the project, although the work was continued by his assistants, Antonio da Sangallo, Giulio Romano and Giovanni da Udine. Delays followed; but in 1523, with the election of Clement VII, work was resumed and by the end of the next year, some of the interior decorations were finished, and many of the gardens and fountains were in place.

In 1527, however, during the Sack of Rome, the villa was burned; what is there now is essentially the villa as it was in 1524, changed over the years to make it more habitable. The only surviving parts of the original building are the stumps of the rotunda, five rooms and a loggia, and parts of the garden. In 1536 the villa passed to Madama Margherita di Parma, daughter of Charles V—hence its name—and then later to the Bourbons of Naples; it is now owned by the state.

Villa Madama: Rome, Italy, 1516

Villa Madama

What Raphael had planned we know of from a letter—perhaps by Raphael himself—of about 1516, addressed to his friend Baldassare Castiglione. The villa was to have two entrances, one at the southeast end where a road came up from the Vatican, and the whole building was planned to lie along an axis, from southeast to northwest, that could serve to keep it as cool as possible in the hot Roman summers. A huge entrance court was to open out behind the southeast entrance, leading through a vestibule and an atrium, and at the east end of the complex, the upper part of a round tower was to serve as a winter garden house; toward the north corner, the coolest part, were to be the cardinal's apartments. Near this, and at the northwest end of the axis of the villa, a huge garden loggia was planned, with an exedra to the southwest and a fountain in the center, the whole serving as a kind of garden room. Cut into the hillside beside the villa, to the southwest, there was to be a semicircular theater; in the basement, at the level of the stable court, terraced in front of the building, there was to be also a vestibule that Raphael compared to an ancient *cryptoporticus,* and beyond it, rooms modeled on those of the ancient Roman baths.

All this, as Raphael showed in his letter, was based on what he took to be the model of classical antiquity, details picking up the account of Pliny's Villa at Laurentium; this would have been a perfect reference, since Pope Leo X, who was very interested in his cousin's plans, owned a copy of the letter of Pliny that describes his famous villa. Everything was classical. And if this was true of the form of the plan—it was believed that Pliny's villa had been set in the shape of the letter O—all the details of the splendid and rich decorations were intended to express the same. These were supervised by Giovanni da Udine and Giulio Romano, with perhaps Baldassare Peruzzi helping in part, Giovanni concentrating on the stucco work, Giulio doing the paintings, many of which showed scenes from Ovid.

As a whole, this was the new form of decoration described as *alla grottesca,* that is, based on what was found in newly discovered Roman buildings, all of which looked like grottoes. Niches and monochrome stuccowork in the lower parts were set in this villa below highly decorated ceilings, filled with scenes of the Four Seasons in the guise of Proserpina, Ceres,

Villa Madama, ceiling fresco

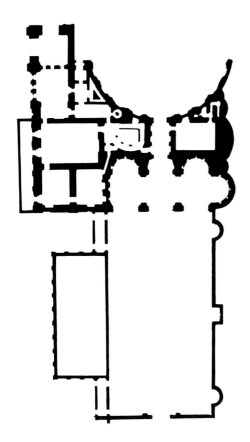

Bacchus and Vulcan alternating with the Four Elements, these being the deities Jupiter, Juno, Neptune and Pluto with Proserpina; these images became standard in the villa decorations of the 16th century. Other parts included scenes from the Greek writer Philostratus, plus a whole range of more general designs of *putti* playing with swans or throwing balls or apples—references to the *palle,* or balls, on the Medici coat of arms.

Outside in the gardens were remarkable elements such as the famous grotto designed by Giovanni da Udine that had an elephant's head in the center of a wall set into the hillside; a fountain in the woods with a lion's head, surrounded by water plants; and a nymphaeum and a grotto. All around were Roman antiquities, some of which were recorded by Marten van Heemskerck in his sketchbook of 1532-35. The most famous of these perhaps was a set of eight seated Muses, now in the Prado, Madrid, that had been found a few years earlier at Hadrian's Villa at Tivoli and were then set, appropriately enough, in this modern version of that famous older building.

The whole Villa Madama, as we would expect only from Raphael, was an extraordinary idea; no one simple system is to be found in the plan (this was what he had already experimented with at the Palazzo Branconio dell'Aquila), and much was done throughout (as in his plans for the Chigi Chapel at Santa Maria dell Popolo) to emphasize the possibility of particular internal views and vistas. And the whole building was decorated—in a way no earlier architect had been able to accomplish so well—to suggest in its plan, in the account of life it suggested and the details of its ornaments, the atmosphere of an ancient Roman villa. This was a new stage in the history of the antique revival in the Renaissance; like all the earlier attempts, it was based both on the material remains of antiquity that the artists and patrons of the Renaissance knew and how they chose to interpret them as guides for the way they wanted to live.

—DAVID CAST

SIENA CATHEDRAL
Siena, Italy

1226-47: Construction. **1265-68:** Pulpit; **Designer/Sculptor:** Nicola Pisano. **1285-87:** Western facade; **Architect:** Giovanni Pisano. **1316:** Baptistery added at east end, choir extension. **Ca. 1340:** Reconstruction on cathedral begun, foundations and piers of new nave built, construction abandonded. **Ca. 1370:** Centerpiece of western facade.

Publications

CARLI, E.: *Il Duomo di Siena*. Genoa, 1979.

Siena Cathedral bears witness both to the innovative vigor and exquisite sensibility of the Gothic age and to its vaulting ambitions, sometimes unaccompanied by the knowledge and means to avert disaster in their realization. The surviving structure essentially dates from the second quarter of the 13th century, though it is chiefly notable for later additions. The building

Siena Cathedral

is neighbored by the ruins of a fortunately abortive attempt, undertaken in the mid-14th century, to more than quadruple the cathedral in size.

More than once Sienese authorities took their chances on the structural stability of the cathedral and its planned expansions. In 1316 work on a baptistery was begun at the east end, which was also to provide the substructure for an extension of the choir by two bays. In 1622 a team of experts headed by Lorenzo Maitani—who had just finished a reconstruction at Orvieto Cathedral to prevent its threatened collapse—came to the conclusion that the expansion, by then well under way, endangered the existing building and had to be abandoned immediately. In spite of the extremely strongly worded recommendations of their own experts, the Sienese decided to finish the work come what might. Their recklessness paid off: the expanded choir has now survived for more than six centuries and shows no sign of structural weakness.

In the 1340s, well before the Baptistery expansion was completed, a new and much more grandiose plan was hatched, which would have made the existing building into the transept of a much larger, much higher cathedral. A series of designs was submitted attempting to deal with the transformation of the old nave and choir into transepts and with the thorny problem of the crossing, which would be pulled off-center in the projected 95-degree shift in orientation. Such was the urgency of the Sienese dream that work was actually begun, even though no satisfactory or even adequate designs had been submitted. The foundations and piers of the new nave were built, and the old nave was heightened. Fortunately, a lack of funds forced the abandonment of the project before too much damage had been done. Only the piers and foundations of the new nave, which clearly would have been inadequate for the grand superstructure they were intended to carry, survive. At about the same time,

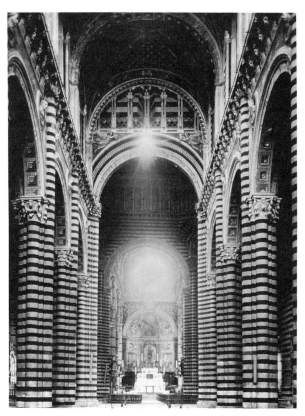

Siena Cathedral, view toward altar

Siena Cathedral, west front: Siena, Italy, 1226-47

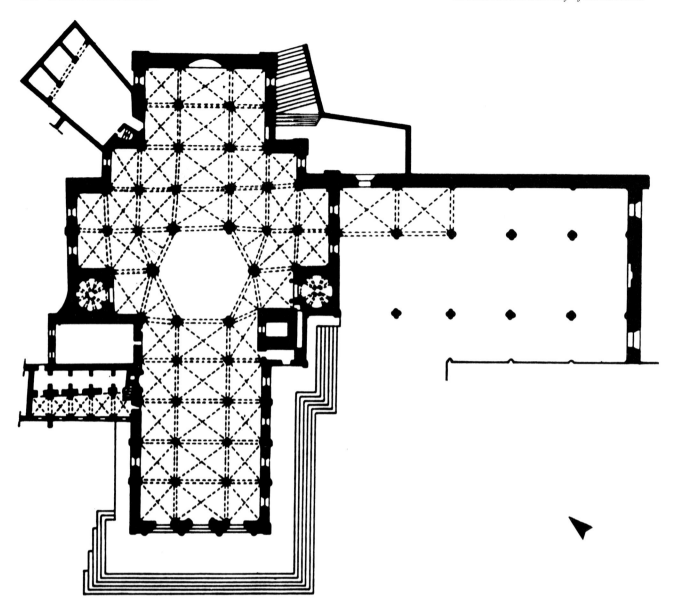

the still unfinished Baptistery facade had to be abandoned and completed in the most stopgap manner, spoiling the entire design. The Sienese twice courted disaster, then, and were twice lucky. Spurred by phenomenal economic growth and competition with other cities, they undertook schemes of potentially calamitous consequences, and still managed to leave behind a beautiful example of early Tuscan Gothic largely unaffected by the later misadventures.

Work on the cathedral was begun in about 1226, and that first campaign was mostly completed by 1247. The result was a cathedral on a cruciform plan with a three-aisle nave and straight-ended choir. The side aisles were as wide and almost as high as the central nave, which was originally covered by a barrel vault. (When the nave was heightened in the 14th century, a groin vault was put in its place.) The transepts were just one bay deep, while the hexagonal domed crossing was almost as wide as the aisles. By means of squinches the hexagon was transformed into a dodecagon and then into the circle of the cupola, which carries a lantern. John White has described the style of the earliest building as an ''adventurous and influential extension of the Romanesque vocabulary of form,'' with some Gothic detailing, principally in the windows and the drum. The

Romanesque Cathedral of Pisa may have provided the general plan of the building, while the nave has much in common with the Church of Notre-Dame la Grande in Poitiers, France. The heavy cornice just below the springing of the original nave vault, on the other hand, is similar to those in the southern Italian cathedrals of Bari, Barletta and Ruovo. Both the interior and the exterior were decorated with the banded marbling typical of the Tuscan Romanesque. Particularly in the interior, the striping of the columns and walls has a tendency to dissolve architectural form into surface ornamentation, and stands in the way of a clear apprehension of space.

Later additions were more clearly in a Gothic idiom, particularly the sculptural western facade, which is the most impressive architectural feature of the surviving building. The lower part of the facade was designed and built by Giovanni Pisano in 1285-87, and exercised as much influence on subsequent developments in sculpture as in architecture. Three portals of identical size (in accordance with the identical widths of the nave and aisles behind them) dominate the first story of the facade. As is typical of the Italian Gothic but in sharp contrast to the French tradition, the jambs between the portals are bare of sculpture. In general, this first story is of great simplicity. Above the portals, however, the facade becomes very elaborate, with an abundance of sculpted figures and deep, rich ornamental carving. The emphasis shifts from the center to the highly sculptured corner turrets. The turrets themselves, with their off-center niches, are also characterized by a heavy emphasis on the outer edges. The addition in the 1370s of the centerpiece, which is a little wider than the jambs of the central portal, repeats this pattern of outward expansion in the upper levels. The horizontal thrust completely breaks the vertical impetus so closely associated with Gothic architecture. Indeed, the outward displacement and vertical discontinuities are unique in Gothic building. The design for the Baptistery facade, by an unknown author, emulated Pisano's western facade, but in its half-finished state the relationship is not easy to discern.

Pisano's sculptured figures (some of which have been removed to the Museo dell'Opera del Duomo) inhabit this facade as if carrying on their lives in their natural environment. Breaking free of the architectural setting, they walk, talk, stride out of doorways and even interact with each other, as if unaware of the fact that they have become ornaments in a stone landscape. They are modeled with an emphasis on realistic detail rather than symbolic content—a sculptural development of overwhelming importance, which had been prefigured principally in the work of Giovanni's father, Nicola Pisano.

Nicola's work is also represented at Siena Cathedral, in the monumental pulpit dating from 1265-68. An octagon with high-relief panels is raised on columns over a cruciform platform. Four of the columns are carried on the backs of animals, while the Virtues form the transition from the columns to the upper octagon. A central column rests on a group made up of Philosophy and the seven Liberal Arts. The elaborate iconographic program of the upper panels includes five scenes from the life of Christ, and a Last Judgment. The Siena pulpit was itself an important milestone in Nicola's development: for the first time, the sculpture was completely integrated with the architecture of the piece, notably in the upper cornice, which blends fully with the relief panels. Moreover, the figures were characterized by a much greater liveliness of realistic detail, which de-emphasized their symbolic impact. The realism of the Siena pulpit, radiating a warmly human spirituality, was a development away from the allegorical stasis of his earlier work as in the Pisa pulpit, and also a movement toward Giovanni Pisano's treatment of the Siena facade figures. Nicola's workshop for the Siena pulpit, it may be noted in passing, included not only such sculptors as Arnolfo di Cambio, but also the teenaged Giovanni himself.

Siena Cathedral also boasts a gorgeous stained-glass oculus of uncertain attribution. In all likelihood, it was designed by a fresco painter, possibly Cimabue. The window is also characterized by an unusual degree of realism, due in part to the fact that the leading, almost without exception, was made to coincide with the contours of the figures. Another contributing factor is the casualness with which the individual scenes spill over into the framing borders. The window is divided into nine panels, the central three of which depict the Burial, Assumption and Coronation of the Virgin. The corner panels are taken up by the four Evangelists, and the middle side panels hold the figures of the patron saints of Siena. Duccio di Buoninsegna was responsible for the enormously influential Siena altarpiece known as the *Maestà,* which unfortunately has been dismembered. Although for the most part it is preserved in the Opera del Duomo, the remainder has been scattered across Italy.

Although the original architecture was by no means clearly a product of the Gothic style, later alterations make Siena Cathedral an important example of the Tuscan Gothic tradition. Its wealth of innovative and influential sculpture, glass and painting

also reserves an important place in the history of Gothic art for Siena Cathedral. At the same time, the forest of crumbling piers which adjoins the south transept is a poignant reminder of the unbridled desire for height and magnitude that sometimes blinded late medieval men to reality's practical requirements.

—MARIJKE RIJSBERMAN

PALAZZO PUBBLICO
Siena, Italy

1298-1348: Palazzo constructed; **Architects:**Agostino di Giovanni and Agnolo di Vebntura; **Painters:** Simone Martini, Ambrogio Lorenzetti, Spinello Aretino, Taddaeo di Bartolo among others. **1304:** Upper loggia at back begun. **1307-10:** Wings added. **1327:** Hall of the Grand Council built. **1338-48:** Torre della Mangia and Piazza del Campo built. **1341:** Crown of Torre del Mangia designed; **Architect:** Lippo Memmi. **1560:** Hall of the Grand Council converted into chief theater of Siena; **Architect:** Riccio. **1680-81:** Wings extended upwards. **1753:** Theater rebuilt; **Architect:** Galla di Bibiena.

Publications

CAIROLA, ALDO: *Il Palazzo Pubblico di Siena.* Rome, 1963.
DIDRON, A.: "Sienne: chapelle du palais municipale." *Annales archéologiques* 16 (1856): 5-25, 282-291.
JENKINS, MARIANA: "The Iconography of the Hall of the Consistory in the Palazzo Pubblico, Siena." *Art Bulletin* 54 (December 1972): 430-451.
SANTI, LIONETTO: *Il Palazzo Comunale e il Campo di Siena.* Siena, 1950.

*

Siena's Palazzo Pubblico, constructed between 1298 and 1348, a product of the short-lived Gothic period in Italy, is joined by the Torre della Mangia, the tallest and most graceful of the Italian municipal towers. The Piazza del Campo, built between 1338 and 1348, is a carefully delineated semicircular open civic plaza, curved opposite and visually framing the city hall. Both the palazzo and the piazza date from medieval times, not a period of major plaza planning and development. The city even from its early days has had an appreciation for the open plaza for traditional public events. Twice a year, July 2 and August 16, since 1656 the plaza has hosted horse races and related festivities known as the Palio Festival or as the Palio delle Contrade.

The Gothic style, coming late in Italy, was considered a product of the barbarous north, and was never prominently used in the same way that it was in northern Europe. Educated Italians were aware, after all, that Classical antiquity was Italian antiquity. In addition, the Gothic was in competition with the flourishing Romanesque, which was associated with the image of Italy's Early Christian heritage. But the Gothic was accepted between 1200 and 1400 because it was the architecture with the general approval of the Church.

Tuscany's city-states, as a matter of public pride, competed at that time to develop their social, political, economic and physical prowess, and today their grand civic buildings remain functional in their original uses. Churches and cathedrals too

Palazzo Pubblico: Siena, Italy, 1298-1348

Palazzo Pubblico

were planned to be larger or grander than those of the neighboring city-states. Siena and Florence were strong rivals attempting to surpass each other in architectural excellence. The city halls of each, the Palazzo Vecchio presiding over the Piazza della Signora in Florence and the Palazzo Pubblico as the backdrop for the Piazza del Campo in Siena, were monuments of pride and distinction to these two city-states.

Siena, whether planned or whether evolved by intuition, is carefully sited on three hills. The Piazza del Campo is near the gravity center of the city in a low point between the hills on the site of a former Roman forum. The Piazza del Campo is a masterpiece as a medieval plaza. As early as 1262, municipal regulatory ordinances determined the height, size and character of the houses facing the piazza. A street, separated from the piazza floor by a stone curb and randomly spaced columns, follows the exterior edges of the plaza and is used for parade and ceremonial functions. The brick and stone pavers set in the radiating configuration follow the shape of the peripheral edges, and the downward-sloping half-bowl surface is integral with the lineal fan-pattern mosaic stones focusing on the Palazzo Pubblico. The radiating brick bonds articulate the stone inlay lines breaking the piazza surface into pie-shaped sectors, emphasizing the visual focus leading the eye to the front of the Palazzo Pubblico. As a product of the planning of the city, the municipal ordinances, the spatial design and the lineal articulation of the open space, the Palazzo Pubblico becomes the dominant feature within the complex.

The piazza may be entered from any of 11 dark, narrow streets—the axis of each trained on the Palazzo Pubblico—and offers a sudden visual sensation of light and change of scale. Enhancing this effect are the lines on the piazza floor and the

tall, vertical accent of the Mangia tower joining the Palazzo Pubblico. At the center of the piazza is the Fonte Gaia by Jacopo della Quercia. Following the peripheral edges of the space is a series of cafes open to the public.

Contributing to the design of the Palazzo Pubblico in the 14th century were Agostino di Giovanni and Agnolo di Ventura. Because of fires and additions to the structure, it is unknown when periods of construction took place, suggesting that it was a collective effort and possibly the reason why the building is not homogeneous. The fenestration of the brick facade facing the piazza does have a sophisticated order and visual rhythm composed of three stories with carefully spaced triforium, and lancet arched windows at the second and third levels, significant of the Italian Gothic period. This facade is capped by a crenellated merlon parapet and a partial fourth story also capped by a parapet with battlements. The ceiling lines are articulated at the second floor with a discontinuous band of blind arches, and the fourth floor with a continuous one.

The interior spaces of the Palazzo Pubblico comprise an atrium and a number of halls richly decorated with frescoes and paintings. The atrium walls are supported by a series of round arches and groined vaults resting on octagonal columns with Corinthian capitals. The two ground-floor halls contain a *Coronation of the Virgin* by Sano di Pietro and a *Resurrection* by Sodoma. In the Sala del Nove or della Pace above are frescoes by Ambrogio Lorenzetti representing the effects of just and unjust government; the Sala del Mappamondo was painted by Simone Martini, and the Ciappella della Signoria by Taddeo di Bartolo; the Sala di Balia has frescoes by Spinello Aretino with scenes from the life of Pope Alexander III, and another room painted by local artists displays periods of contemporary

Italian history. The former hall of the grand council, built in 1327, was converted into the chief theater of Siena by Riccio in 1560, and, after being twice destroyed by fire, was rebuilt in 1753 from Bibbiena's designs.

The light, elegant and soaring Torre della Mangia, built in 1338-48 at the northeast corner of the Palazzo Pubblico, is 334 feet high, the chapel was erected at the tower's foot as a public offering of thanks after the Plague of 1348. The brick tower was erected as a watch station with a clock-bell function. The top, constructed of stone, is the most visually embellished element, with a lower balcony extended beyond the exterior walls, supported by buttresses, a Gothic defensive detail or machicolation, extending out and up from the walls to support the overhanging floor. The top level is smaller than the tower walls but is attractively animated with round-arched openings. Both levels are protected by a crenellated merlon parapet.

—GORDON ECHOLS

PALAZZO CARIGNANO
Turin, Italy

1679: Construction begun; **Architect:** Guarino Guarini (1624-83).

Publications

CHEVALLEY, GIOVANNI: "Il Palazzo Carignano a Torino." *Bollettino della Società piemontese di archeologia e belle arti* 5 (January-June 1921): 4-14.

CRAVERO, DAVIDE GIOVANNI: "Il Palazzo Carignano." *Atti e rassegna tecnica del Società degli ingegneri e degli architetti in Torino* 5 (1951): 55-63.

MILLON, HENRY A.: "Guarino Guarini and the Palazzo Carignano in Turin." Ph.D. Dissertation. Harvard University, Cambridge, Massachusetts, 1964.

*

The Palazzo Carignano in Turin is a secular design which makes full use of the dynamic forms and dramatic lighting of Baroque churches. Designed by the Theatine monk Guarino Guarini, it was built for Emanuele Filiberto di Carignano, the oldest male of a cadet branch of the House of Savoy, who, through a succession of deaths and marriages, had recently become a potential heir to the Duchy of Savoy. His new position in the hierarchy of the duchy required a palace equal to his noble status, and Guarini, who was invited to Turin in order to aggrandize the ecclesiastical buildings in the Savoyan capital, was entrusted with raising the status of the princes of Carignano.

The design for the Palazzo Carignano owes a great debt to Giovanni Lorenzo Bernini's designs for the Louvre Palace, which Guarini would have seen during his residence in Paris. Bernini's first two designs, both of which were rejected, featured projecting curvilinear facades similar to church designs such as his Sant' Andrea al Quirinale in Rome. The concave-convex-concave plan of Guarini's facade, however, is closer in form to Francesco Borromini's work, especially the facade of San Carlo alle Quattro Fontane in Rome. The undulating facade of the Palazzo Carignano responds to the form of the grand salon and stairs, which are the focal point of the design. Guarini worked through several variants of the design before arriving

at the final disposition of stairs and central hall. Originally the oval salon was placed on the facade with the stairs following the curve of the oval on the garden elevation. Then, in a series of variants, Guarini reversed the position of the stairs and freed the stairs from the oval curve of the salon.

The sequence of spaces leading up to the grand salon on the *piano nobile* is carefully orchestrated through curving paths and controlled illumination. After passing through a hexagonal guard chamber, one enters an oval room on the ground level, with double columns supporting the floor of the grand salon above and arches open to the garden. The path leading to the grand salon then turns either right or left to a rectangular chamber, from which a curved set of stairs ascends to the room above. The gentle curve of the stairs is sufficient to hide the top from view but leave a landing visible at the midpoint. This landing has the only window along the flight of stairs so that it becomes an intermediate point of destination. The stair risers bow outward in a manner reminiscent of Michelangelo's vestibule at the Laurentian Library, then reverse their curvature at the landing to pull one up to the well-lit antechamber at the top of the stairs.

The grand salon is much changed from Guarini's time, and physical evidence suggests that his untimely death contributed to a change in its final form. The engraved elevation in Guarini's treatise shows a lower central pavilion than actually built, and currently there are large masses of masonry above the current vault that appear as if they were the springing and surcharge for a higher vault, perhaps employing interlacing ribs. Since Guarini died about two years before completion of the forward section of the palace, it may be that Guarini altered the original design, but did not leave sufficient instructions to complete it after his death. Alternatively, if Guarini did intend to build one of his unusual domes of interlacing ribs, it could be that no one had sufficient expertise (or confidence) to complete the design. When Savoy annexed the Italian peninsula to form the modern Italian state, the first subalpine parliamentary sessions were held in the grand salon of the Palazzo Carignano, with desks and seating on risers occupying the volume of the room. The ceiling, too, has been altered so that a determination of the original form is difficult. Surviving designs intended for the central vaulted hall of the Castello di Racconigi (formerly in the Quirinale, "Sav. Car.," Cat. 95, now Archivio dello Stato di Torino) give tantalizing evidence of perforated vaults with interlacing ribs which Guarini was capable of designing for secular palaces, but a lack of further evidence leaves only imaginative speculation as to his final intentions.

The exterior elevation of the Palazzo Carignano also contains echoes of Borromini's work in Rome. The use of brick without a stucco or stone veneer is a technique that Borromini used in Rome, although Guarini's brick surface is less uniform and not as crisply defined. Guarini also followed Borromini's practice of dividing the elevation with flat pilaster strips. This technique, used by Guarini on his earlier Theatine College in Messina and at Racconigi, was embellished with molded brick star patterns, which enliven the facade. The windows on the *piano nobile* have an anthropomorphically inspired aedicule that looks like a native American with a feathered headdress, a reference to the prince of Carignano's titular command of a French regiment that served in the New World. The anthropomorphic nature of this form, too, recalls Borromini's window aedicule on the side elevation of San Carlo alle Quattro Fontane showing a Trinitarian with a three-cornered hat.

Since the location for the Palazzo Carignano was a new quarter of the city extending toward the Po River, the original design was for a block palace with gardens toward the Po. Later drawings focus only on the front half of the palace, suggesting that a phased construction was intended in the final plans.

Palazzo Carignano: Turin, Italy, 1679

Guarini also developed a number of variants for the arrangement of rooms in the residential wings, among them a double loaded corridor, somewhat of a rarity in the days before reliable artificial lighting. The remaining half of the palace block was completed in the 19th century, copying the star-encrusted elevation of the original. However, the new addition used pressed instead of hand-molded brick, the contrast aptly illustrating the qualities of the different materials. To the 19th century also belongs the pediment over the entrance announcing the birth of Vittorio Emanuele II, who served as the first king of a united Italy nearly 200 years after construction of the palace.

The dramatic use of light with gradually unfolding vistas in the spatial sequence leading up to the grand salon anticipated the 18th-century German palaces by architects such as Johann Lukas von Hildebrandt and Balthasar Neumann. Guarini's genius was his ability to take the dramatic impact of his church interiors and, through controlled lighting and dynamic forms, organize a sequence of spaces with an equally dramatic impact.

—ELWIN C. ROBISON

PALAZZO MADAMA
Turin, Italy

1718-21. Architect: Filippo Juvarra (1678-1736).

Publications

BERNARDI, MARZIANO: *Palazzo Madama*. Turin, 1954.
MALLÉ, LUIGI: *Palazzo Madama in Torino*. Turin, 1970.

*

Filippo Juvarra is known as an architect who borrowed widely from existing architectural work, choosing his sources carefully, and always reinterpreting his prototypes. There is no question that the design of the facade of the Palazzo Madama was influenced directly by the garden front of the palace of Versailles. However, Juvarra transformed and improved the French prototype. At Versailles, Louis Le Vau and, later, Jules Hardouin-Mansart, used a design that articulates three almost-equal stories. The palace is so attenuated that none of its architectural features are capable of relieving its overwhelmingly horizontal character. Moreover, the ground floor and attic story are only slightly less tall than the *piano nobile,* and the three floors are clearly separated from each other by the continuous horizontal lines created by the balustrade and cornice. Juvarra shortened, strengthened and simplified his base story by eliminating Versailles' round window heads and by expressing the bay divisions by means of prominent rusticated piers. These piers carry the colossal order of Corinthian pilasters and columns that organize the second and third stories into a single *piano nobile;* the windows of what appears to be the third level are incorporated into the bays created by these powerful vertical elements. Juvarra retained Versailles' round-headed windows at the *piano nobel* level, but they have been used at the Palazzo Madama as special design features to add interest to this most important

Palazzo Madama, stair hall: Turin, Italy, 1718-21

floor. At Versailles, Le Vau used four freestanding columns carrying projecting entablatures to mark the centers of his two projecting wings: Hardouin-Mansart expanded this feature into a six-column set to mark the center of the entire composition. These projecting-column features seem restless at Versailles; the length of the facade is so great that something much more monumental is required to impart the necessary *gravitas* to the design. In contrast, the compact form of the Palazzo Madama, its division into three three-bay sections, and the added height and emphasis given to the *piano nobile* give Juvarra's design the weight and monumentality that Versailles is lacking.

The project as originally envisioned constituted a major re-modeling and extension of the medieval castle, enveloping it and creating a new town palace for the queen mother. The irregular quadrilateral block of the 14th-century castle would have been surrounded by new construction and would have been visible only in its round towers, reconstructed with conical roof turrets and allowed to project above the mass sufficiently to complement the central emphasis of the facade. Of this grand scheme, only the central pavilion facing the piazza was executed. This pavilion was intended to project from the center of a 19-bay facade, which was to be terminated by taller pavilions at the ends. The terminal pavilions would have been decorated with four freestanding columns in an a:b:a arrangement borrowed literally from Le Vau's Versailles design. If executed in its entirety, it would have been a great Italian Baroque palace similar to and on the scale of Giovanni Lorenzo Bernini's third design for the Louvre.

Unlike Guarini's Palazzo Carignano in the same city, or the early designs of Bernini and Pietro da Cortona for the Louvre, the Palazzo Madama is designed almost entirely in planes and straight lines. Only the round-headed windows of the *piano nobile* depart from the strict orthogonal grid. No sculpted, pulsating, organic mass exists here. Juvarra's design eschews the sculptural qualities of Guarino Guarini's work in favor of a classical Baroque style influenced by Michelangelo, Palladio, and Bernini, as well as Le Vau and Hardouin-Mansart.

The great space behind the new facade is devoted entirely to a foyer-staircase hall. Each end of the barrel-vaulted space is filled with a stair which doubles back on itself to reach a central bridge that leads to the state apartments of the palace. The sides of the bridge are concave, and it is supported by a domical vault carried on freestanding columns; the bridge is one of the few plastic elements in the design. The entire foyer space is flooded with light from the great round-headed windows and the mezzanine windows above them (which turn out not to be in a mezzanine at all). From the inside the impression is that the entire front wall is a curtain of glass. No stair nearly so grand as this had ever been built in Italy, and very few of comparable magnificence had been built elsewhere. It competes favorably with the Escalier des Ambassadeurs at Versailles and the fanciful central European Baroque stairs of J. B. Fischer von Erlach, Johann Lukas von Hildebrandt and Balthasar Neumann. The idea is French; Le Vau had designed a similar stair for an unexecuted project for the Louvre that had been published and disseminated widely. Its decoration is Italian, however, and recalls the decorative details of Pietro da Cortona and Francesco Borromini. Exuberant, naturalistic motifs appear next to flat, almost neoclassical features.

Anthony Blunt, in *Baroque and Rococo: Architecture and Decoration* (1978), said about the Palazzo Madama: "The Palazzo Madama is a typical example of the workings of the

Palazzo Madama

Late International Baroque: a French plan, known in Rome and Vienna, is treated in a manner which derives from Roman Baroque; and on the exterior French elements in the windows and the reliefs are worked into a whole which is directly inspired by Bernini.''

—C. MURRAY SMART, JR.

PALAZZINA STUPINIGI
Turin, Italy

1719-33. Architect: Filippo Juvarra (1678-1736).

Publications

BERNARDI, MARZIANO: *La palazzina di caccia di Stupinigi.* Turin, 1958.
MALLÉ, LUIGI: *Stupinigi un capolavoro del settecento europeo tra barocchetto e classicismo: architettura, pittura, scultura, arredamento.* Turin, 1972.
PASSANTI, M.: "La palazzina di caccia di Stupinigi." *Architettura* (August 1957).

*

The Palazzina Stupinigi is a hunting lodge on a grand scale done by Filippo Juvarra for King Vittorio Amedeo II. Its formal organization is based upon the Italian star-shaped plan in which corresponding units are grouped around a central core—a plan

form that had been used with particular success by J. B. Fischer von Erlach in his palace for Count Althan and by Germain Boffrand in the Château de Malgrange. However, the scale of Stupinigi is so vast that the result is completely different from its smaller villa prototypes. In its general appearance and its decorative exterior detail, Stupinigi presents the simplest classical design of any of Juvarra's works; however, its main salon is among the finest examples of Italian Rococo interior design.

Stupinigi's central pavilion and the diagonal arms that it generates are the focus of a vast landscape layout that skillfully manipulates form, rhythm, and enclosure to masterful effect. The spatial sequence begins with a long, straight road lined with trees; as it approaches the palace, the avenue of trees is bordered by stables and service buildings that close off the view of the fields and begin the buildup of architectural forms. Arrival at the palace proper is announced by the opening up of the allée into a semicircular entrance court formed by the continuation of the service buildings. A circular court-within-a-court, half projecting into the entry court and half penetrating the palace complex, is the first of three contrasting exterior geometric forms; the circle leads first to a square, which is followed by an octagon that is the actual entry court of the palace. All three spaces are formed by extensions of the low, story-and-a-half palace wings that build in height only as they approach their intersection with the central oval pavilion form. This pavilion is the central generating point for the park design beyond the palace; a large formal circular park, with axial and concentric paths, connected to the palace by a rectangular garden link. All spaces interpenetrate in a manner similar to Guarino Guarini's interior spaces, creating a pulsating, dynamic exterior spatial sequence.

The building itself seems to be an infinitely extended, open organism which interacts with the system of exterior spaces it

Palazzo Stupinigi, interior hall

Palazzo Stupinigi: Turin, Italy, 1719-33

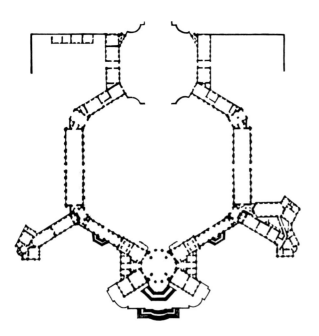

The *salone delle feste* at Stupinigi is truly festive indeed. The space is more like a church than a ballroom, and, in fact, has many similarities to the unexecuted design of the new cathedral for Turin that occupied much of Juvarra's time during that period. Its exterior wall is oval in shape. In this oval space sits a cage structure made up of four piers carrying a saucer dome. The inner structure is connected to the outer one by undulating mezzanine balconies and, at the ceiling level, by two large and two small apses. The space is much taller than it is wide. The color scheme—white and bright pastel hues—and the *trompe l'oeil* niches, trophies and heavenly scene painted on the ceiling dematerialize the mass and make the structure seem weightless. Although the frescoes and the spaces were conceived in Baroque terms, they achieve a Rococo lightness of feeling.

In *Late Baroque and Rococo Architecture* (New York, 1974), Christian Norberg-Schulz writes: "The *Zweischaligkeit* and the vertical continuity of the space have a strong affinity with contemporary churches in Central Europe, to which the *salone* in Stupinigi forms the most splendid secular counterpoint. Although Stupinigi does not show the sophisticated articulation of the Belvedere in Vienna or the equilibrated monumentality of the Residenz in Würzburg, it may be considered the most ingenious of all eighteenth-century palaces. It offers a new and valid interpretation of the Baroque concepts of centralization and extension, and, in spite of its scale, expresses the intimate and sensuous approach of that epoch."

—C. MURRAY SMART, JR.

creates. It is designed with a simplicity that is Rococo in feeling. The effect is of an intimacy and simplicity at odds with the palace's vast size. The traditional Italian palace base story has been eliminated entirely, and the *piano nobile* has been brought to the ground. The central salon gives access directly to the entrance court in front and to the gardens behind. Its facades are divided into panels by pilasters that have lost all reference to the orders except on the central mass itself. Similarly, windows have lost their classical aedicular frames. Decoration is lavished in the interior, however, particularly in the stunning *trompe l'oeil* central salon.

SAN LORENZO
Turin, Italy

1670-79. Architect: Guarino Guarini (1624-83).

Publications

CREPALDI, GIUSEPPE MICHELE: *La real chiesa di San Lorenzo in Torino*. Turin, 1953.
DENINA, LUIGI, and PROTO, ALESSANDRO: "La real chiesa

San Lorenzo: Turin, Italy, 1670-79

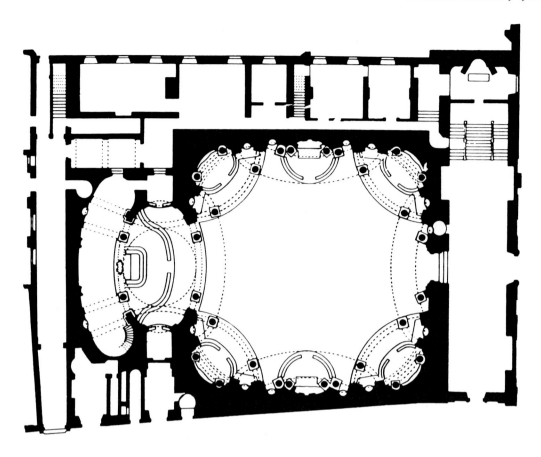

di San Lorenzo in Torino." *Architettura italiana* 15 (1920): 34-38.

ROBISON, ELWIN C.: "Guarino Guarini's Church of San Lorenzo in Turin." Ph.D. Dissertation. Cornell University, Ithaca, New York, 1985.

TORRETTA, GIOVANNI: *Un analisi della capella di S. Lorenzo di Guarino Guarini.* Turin, 1966.

VANDERPERREN, JOS, and KENNES, JOSE: "Die sistematische ruimtelijke wereld van Guarino Guarini." Fifth-year architectural thesis. Brussels, 1974.

The ducal Church of San Lorenzo in Turin is one of Guarino Guarini's most important extant works. It includes all of the design concepts and motifs that characterize his oeuvre: domes of interlacing ribs, interpenetrating spaces, vaults based on conic sections, and forced perspective. Guarini's church replaced an earlier longitudinal church formerly dedicated to Santa Maria del Presepe. It was inadequate for the needs of the Savoyan Duchy, and in 1634 responsibility for the church was given to the Theatine Order. That same year the cornerstone was laid for the new church, but Savoy soon became mired in political difficulties resulting in occupation by French troops from 1640 until 1657. Little if any construction seems to have been accomplished on this plan.

With the departure of occupying troops, work began once again on the church. Documents from 1661 list payments for some construction work on the site, perhaps referring to the oratory and Chapel of the Santa Sepolcro located under the porticoes (now the oratory of the Beata Vergine Addolorata). In 1664 contracts were let for construction of a design by Amedeo di Castellamonte, but no record of the design remains.

However, a different pattern of marble veneering near the entrance of the church and the shading outline in the *poché* of Guarini's engraved ground plan for the church may be surviving elements of the Castellamonte plan.

Having previously resided in Rome and Paris, Guarini must have been viewed as an up-to-date designer capable of building structures appropriate for a major European capital, which was what the Duchy of Savoy hoped to make of Turin. Not long after Guarini's arrival in Turin in late 1666, he was redesigning the Chapel of the SS. Sindone. The court must have been pleased with his efforts, for Guarini was next asked to redesign Castellamonte's plan for San Lorenzo in 1668 or 1669, construction beginning in January of 1670. Guarini likely reused the foundations of the Castellamonte design, for the account book lists few deliveries of stone and no payments to excavators. Other restrictions were present in his design due to the oratory and chapel that existed toward the Piazza Castello, which precluded a longitudinal plan.

The interior of San Lorenzo is dominated by a 15-meter-diameter dome over the congregational space. The dome, composed of an octagonal arrangement of structural ribs, has an elliptical profile, chosen by Guarini both because of its great strength and because it avoids what he felt was the flat, depressed appearance of hemispherical domes. The eight interlacing ribs of the dome form a large oculus, which opens into a brightly lit lantern above with its own set of interlacing ribs; the contrast in light between the main dome and upper lantern makes the lantern seem much higher than its actual elevation, creating a forced vertical perspective. The main dome is visually supported by four hollow, pendentive-like forms, which are perforated and terminated in a torsional arch with two small columns. They are obviously too weak to support the large expanse of masonry, and the observer is left wondering how

San Lorenzo, dome interior

post-World War II restorations, leaving the plain monochromatic surfaces seen today.

The dome of interlacing ribs was repeated by Guarini in a project for the Church of the Padri Somaschi in Messina. Later Bernardo Vittone used interlacing ribs in a nonstructural way in several of his small chapels, notably the Sanctuary at Vallinotto (1738-39) and Santa Chiara in Bra (1742). Central European architects were more interested in Guarini's interpenetrating spaces, although Johann Lukas von Hildebrandt did design a similarly planned church dedicated to Saint Lawrence in Gabel (1699-1711).

There is a strong resemblance between the geometry of the dome of San Lorenzo and a small dome near the *mihrab* of the Great Mosque in Cordoba, the Octagon at Ely, kitchen vaults at Durham, and early Romanian churches. Before proposing direct influence of such examples in Guarini, however, it should be noted that Leonardo shows a dome with the same geometric plan in his sketchbooks. This is not to suggest that Guarini might have somehow found access to Leonardo's work, but rather that an architect working on dome geometries might independently arrive at such a plan. While Guarini might have been influenced by any (or all) of the above examples, we should first look at Guarini's own skills and knowledge before searching far afield for sources for his designs. Certainly San Lorenzo displays ample evidence of Guarini's creativity and skill in manipulating complex volumes and geometries.

—ELWIN C. ROBISON

the dome stands up. In fact, Guarini hid massive brick arches behind the interior surface which support the dome and its large lantern. To the east of the congregational space is a smaller domed presbytery housing the altar. Its dome, a conventional hemisphere, has a hexagonal arrangement of ribs, providing a theme and variation to the main dome. This presbytery space pushes into, or interpenetrates, the main domed space so that although a large Serlian arch divides the two spaces, there is a strong dynamic connection between them. The six chapels ringing the main space likewise interpenetrate the congregational area, creating an undulating movement that activates the wall surface.

The striking geometry of the dome should not lull us into thinking that its design was solely a geometric exercise. Guarini's skill as a geometrician enabled him to achieve aesthetic and optical aims within the confines of a tightly organized geometry. The major and minor axes of the ellipse of the dome control the placement of the side chapels, internal wall structure, and serve as the center of a star-shaped pattern in the floor which represents the governing geometric diagram for the design.

Work on the main walls proceeded through 1675, when work began on the small vault over the altar. The upper walls were completed by 1677, when Guarini chose to halt building for a year, presumably to let the mortar completely cure before subjecting it to the stresses of the main vault loads. The main dome was vaulted in 1678, with the upper lantern finished the following year, the planting of the cross being celebrated with fireworks on 27 October 1679. Guarini also designed the main altar, finished the year following his death, and may have been the original designer of the side chapels, all six having been reworked in subsequent years. The main dome had canvas paintings fastened between the ribs in 1689 which were replaced with Pietro Fea's frescos of 1822; these were removed in the

SUPERGA
Turin, Italy

1717-31. Architect: Filippo Juvarra (1678-1736).

Publications

CARBONERI, NINO: *La reale chiesa di Superga di Filippo Juvarra*. Turin, 1979.
PAROLETTI, M.: *Description historique de la basilique de Superga*. Turin, 1808.
TELLUCCHINI, A.: *L'arte dell'architetto Filippo Juvarra in Piemonte*. Turin, 1926.

＊

Baroque architects favored grand, theatrical building situations; numerous monasteries were built on mountain sites during that period, both in Italy and in the other Catholic countries of Europe. The Superga is certainly one of the most impressive of these. It is an immense monastery dominated by a votive church and located on a mountain overlooking the plain of Turin and the Alps beyond. It was built to celebrate the 1706 military victory over the French.

From the first days of the Renaissance onward, Italian architects were fascinated with the problems posed by the centrally planned domed church. Juvarra was no exception to this rule. His masterpiece, the Superga, is the most important of his experiments with this form. It benefited from the experience he had gained from his earlier centrally planned church designs, particularly the design for the Church of the Venaria Reale.

Basilica di Superga: Turin, Italy, 1717-31

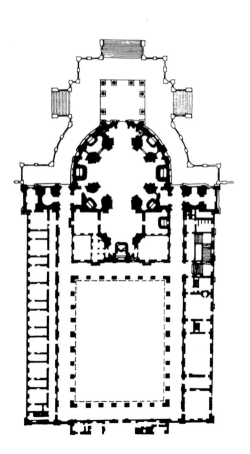

The Superga's importance is not that it demonstrated new design approaches or was forward-looking in its design; rather, it is interesting because it is a brilliant explication of current design ideas composed in an imaginative and skillful way.

The church is cylindrical in form with the vertical zones of nave, drum and dome equal in height, making the central space three times as tall as it is wide. It engages (and, for all practical purposes, obscures) the monastery by means of a great screen wall, which projects to either side of the church from the rear portion of the nave. This screen wall supports towers capped with Germanic onion-shaped cupolas, which flank and frame the dome. From the exterior these wings suggest transepts; however, they do not contain spaces that open into the body of the church at all.

Entry to the church is by means of a large, square, pedimented porch with four Corinthian columns on each side. On the side of the porch that engages the drum that is the body of the church, the columns become pilasters in the center and engaged columns at the corners. The width of the porch is the same as the width of the screen-wall projection on each side of the church. The major axis proceeds through alternating large and small spaces to the high altar: porch, narthex, circular nave, a connecting link comparable to the narthex, octagonal choir and oval sanctuary. The octagonal choir is actually the center of a Greek cross; its chamfered piers support pendentives that carry a circular entablature which supports a dome that is not visible from the exterior.

In the main body of the church, eight columns carry a circular entablature which supports the drum. The spacing of the columns is alternately wide, narrow, wide, etc., with the wide spaces opening to spaces on the longitudinal and cross axes and the narrow spaces opening to chapels on the diagonals. The column spacing, and the fact that the walls behind the columns on the major axes are flat and the walls behind the columns on the diagonal axes are curved, in plan suggests a Greek-cross layout comparable to that of the choir; in reality, however, the space does not take the form of a Greek cross. There is no pendentive zone, and the columns carry a continuous circular entablature. Juvarra combined in the Superga two different forms of the centralized church: a Greek-cross choir and sanctuary and a Pantheon-type nave. (In the latter the dome rises from a cylindrical space.) There is nothing of Guarino Guarini's pioneering interpenetration of dynamic spatial units in this building; Juvarra returned to the carefully proportioned, individually articulated spaces of northern Italian Renaissance tradition.

The decorative details inside were borrowed from both Francesco Borromini (the plastic three-dimensional window frames) and Giovanni Lopenzo Bernini (the coffers and ribs of the dome), but the color scheme of pale blue, yellow and gray is uniquely 18th century in character. The exterior effect is a variant of Borromini's Sant'Agnese in Agone in Rome, combined with Michelangelo's dome, drum and portico for St. Peter's. (The silhouette of the Superga's campaniles is actually closer in character to Borromini's original design for Sant'-Agnese than the towers as ultimately built.) The extreme verticality of the design, both in space and form, makes the design Juvarra's own. There is no question that Juvarra intended a shrine that is a vertical focus in relationship to the landscape; consequently, it is quite different from the urban prototypes from which he borrowed so successfully.

—C. MURRAY SMART, JR.

DUCAL PALACE
Urbino, Italy

Ca. 1455-ca. 1465: Construction begun. **Ca. 1465-ca. 1774:** Construction continued; **Architect:** Luciano Laurana (ca. 1420/25-80). **Ca. 1474-82:** Construction completed; **Architect:** Francesco di Giorgio.

Publications

MARCHINI, GIUSEPPE: "Aggiunte al palazzo ducale di Urbino." *Bollettino d'arte* 45 (1960): 73-80.

ROTONDI, PASQUALE: *The Ducal Palace of Urbino.* New York, 1969.

ROTONDI, PASQUALE: *Francesco di Giorgio nel palazzo ducale di Urbino.* Milan, 1970.

SALMI, M.: *Piero della Francesca e il palazzo ducale di Urbino.* Florence, 1945.

*

"A city in the form of a palace," as Baldassare Castiglione described it in the *Cortegiano,* the Ducal Palace at Urbino is the symbol and perfect synthesis of Renaissance culture.

The palace was built according to the wishes of Federigo da Montefeltro, one of the brightest and most ingenious politicians and military men of the 15th century. He developed a form of cultural patronage that was among the most advanced of his time, by investing the abundant profits of his military campaigns in prestigious art, both secular and religious. Seeking to make

Urbino a center not only of political power but of cultural innovation and experimentation, Federigo also invited the most influential and eminent figures of 15th-century Italy to the court of Montefeltro. Among the architects, sculptors, painters, literary men and intellectuals who visited the court, Leon Battista Alberti, Piero della Francesca, Luciano Laurana, Francesco di Giorgio Martini, Giusto di Gand, Domenico Rosselli and Ambrogio Barocci are the most well known.

The Ducal Palace is the most important monument of the city of Urbino. It is situated on the western slope of the Poggio hill, presenting its clearly articulated and complex facade dominated by turrets to the surrounding countryside. From the valley, the extraordinary nature of the building is visible in all its airy grace. It seems lifted from a fairy tale, in spite of the audacity of its engineering. On the side of the city, the structure seems relatively more compact, with its long facade on the Piazza Rinascimento, and the "winged" small facade on the Piazza Federigo.

The structure is designed as a series of clearly articulated and complex spaces and volumes, developed planimetrically at different levels, and with a variety of projecting and retracting elements (courtyards, gardens, loggias, passages, ramps, monumental and winding staircases). The complex is not, however, the work of a single designer, but resulted rather from the work and ideas of a group of architects and artists, contributing to the project in the course of the 15th and 16th centuries. Out of that concatenation of artistic experience, a formally harmonious architectural synthesis emerged, a synthesis unanimously held to be among the most surprising achievements in western architectural history.

The project was first initiated in the middle of the 15th century, when Federigo da Montefeltro purchased and consolidated some medieval houses on the Piazza Rinascimento, close to what had been the traditional residence of the Montefeltro family (now the site of the university). On the whole, those initial alterations were carried out in a linear and fairly traditional manner. The first real innovation occurred with the arrival at the court of Luciano Laurana, a Dalmatian architect who was responsive to new architectural trends. He developed a design for a number of new buildings. These have the calm and composed monumentality and the new handling of geometry and space which Piero della Francesca and Leon Battista Alberti (one-time guests at the court of Urbino) had also adopted in their work. Laurana's contributions to the complex take up most of the area between the old Montefeltro property and the Castellare, close to the Duomo, around the large *cortile d'onore* (courtyard of honor).

However, it was with the work of Francesco di Giorgio Martini, the Sienese architect who arrived at Urbino in the 1470s after Laurana's departure, that the palace acquired the appearance it has today. The articulation of volumes and spaces, first designed by Laurana and further developed by Francesco di Giorgio, are part of the ambitious project of creating an open and welcoming residence, to be substantially different from the old, medieval, fortified castles. The architecture was to display the aspirations of a prince in touch with the latest developments in humanist thought.

Although Laurana gave the first impetus to that project, it was Francesco di Giorgio who left a new and unmistakable imprint on it, with his designs of the so-called "winged" northern facade, the hanging gardens toward the valley, and the winding stairs to the Data (the ducal stables situated down hill from the palace) and to the Mercatale (market square). The architecture is dominated by spatial design and a formal order principally based on a search for movement and a negation of symmetry. The final result has a machine-like articulation.

Ducal Palace: Urbino, Italy, ca. 1455-ca. 1465

Francesco di Giorgio, who was also a hydraulics engineer, supervised most of the construction and technical organization of the basements. He designed the water-supply system, with its complex and effective hydraulic mechanisms, which served stables and kitchens, washhouses and bathrooms, and used both water and snow reserves. The Sienese artist and architect was also responsible for many of the decorative designs in the interior. He designed corbels, bas-reliefs, friezes, heraldic crests, fireplaces, doorways and inlaid doors. He was also responsible for the pavilion ceilings, the free arrangement of doors and windows, and the rich base of the "winged" facade, featuring the long stone bench with the *macchine di guerra e di pace* (instruments of war and peace) design in the tiling. All the designs were carried out by the Lombard and Tuscan master craftsmen employed in the palace workshop, and by such accomplished artists as Cosimo Rosselli, Giacomo Cozzarelli and Federico Barocci.

In spite of the lengthy collaboration of so many different artists on the interior ornamentation, the final result also has an extraordinarily spatial quality and a homogeneous refinement. Everywhere a synthesis of opposites is pursued and successfully achieved, from the *Sala del Trono,* an enormous space with a light and spacious monumentality, to the *Studiolo,* a small meditation cell with extraordinary carved wall paneling. The *Studiolo* is a unique ideological synthesis and artistic creation, which combines the ideal spirit of the palace with an air of privacy and secrecy. Other examples are the *Cappella del perdono* and the *Tempietto delle muse,* both diminutive spaces blending the sacred and profane, and the *Cortile d'onore,* defined and arranged with extraordinary grace and a perfect geometry of proportions. In addition, there are the numerous other spaces, which held the most important works of art collected by the families of Montefeltro and della Rovere: paintings, arras and sculptures by such masters as Piero della Francesca, Paolo Uccello, Giusto di Gand, Luca Signorelli, Pedro Berruguete, Giovanni Santi, Federico Barocci, Timoteo Viti, besides Raphael and Titian. Today, the Ducal Palace houses the Galleria Nazionale della Marche, the most complete and prestigious art collection in the region, thus juxtaposing the art and architecture of the Renaissance in an immediate and appropriate manner.

The importance of the palace at Urbino must be measured not only by its own intrinsic value, but also by the upheaval it

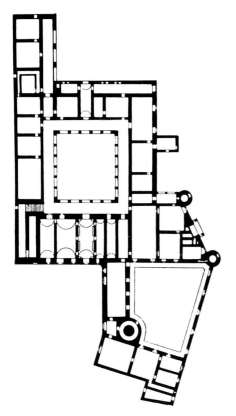

Ducal Palace

decadence, removing it far from the splendors of its earlier days. First losing its functions as a political and cultural center, the palace was subsequently denuded of both its furniture and art treasures, which were either taken to Rome and Florence or put up for auction. (Federigo's library, today at the Vatican, is one example among many.) The building has been reclaimed as a national monument only in this century, undergoing a series of restorations of a very high quality, and becoming again a much-researched object of study.

—GIANNI VOLPE
Translated from the Italian by Luisa Guglielmotti

CA' D'ORO
Venice, Italy

1421-ca. 1431: Palace built on foundations of an earlier house; **Architect:** Marin Contarini. **1427-28:** Wellhead in courtyard built; **Sculptor:** Bartolomeo Bon. **Ca. 1438:** Balconies completed; **Masons:** Nicolo Romanello and Gasparin Rosso.

Publications

CECCHETTI, B.: "La facciata della Ca' d'Oro dello scalpello di Giovanni e Bartolomeo Buono." *Archivio Veneto* 31 (1886): 201ff.

brought about in the city. Laid out in the direction of the western countryside and the Apennine mountains, toward the road to Urbania and Arezzo, the palace and its complex system of annexes, including the Mercatale, substantially modified the structure and image of the city. Until the palace was constructed, the city had its center in the area of Porta Lavagine on the eastern slope turned toward the Adriatic, and had been viewed and painted mostly from that side. The completion of the Ducal Palace, so majestic and so representative of the age, shifted the center to the area of Porta Valbona in the western part of the city. Since then, Urbino has been associated most strongly with the palace, and has been painted only from the western side.

Although Urbino remained a walled city, it was no longer closed and unattractive as it had been in the Middle Ages. The presence of the palace opened up the city, placing it in a continuous relationship with the surrounding countryside. This openness was achieved by the architectural plan of Federigo's palace, incorporating courtyards, hanging gardens, loggias, terraces and wide windows. The resulting cityscape was entirely new, not least because of the vertical impetus of the turrets, whether viewed from the valley or from the other side. From the square between the two wings, the palace appears open and welcoming, suggestive of the sweeping internal spaces.

The work of Luciano Laurana and Francesco di Giorgio Martini, even though it is quantitatively prominent and formally distinctive, does not make up the sum of the creative achievements associated with the palace. Possibly Donato Bramante, and certainly Girolama Genga and Brandani contributed to the complex during the period when it was in the possession of the della Rovere family.

When the Duchy of Urbino was transfered to the Holy See (1631), the palace and the duchy itself entered a period of

Ca' d'Oro: Venice, Italy, 1421-ca. 1431

The Cà d'Oro (House of Gold) is the most famous and richly decorated of the many surviving Venetian medieval palaces. It was built in the years after 1421 by a nobleman, Marin Contarini, whose father Antonio was a senior statesman and a candidate for the ducal throne in the years immediately prior to the palace's construction.

In some respects the house is traditional. Like most such palaces it combined two functions under one roof: the residential accommodation of a merchant nobleman together with the storage and ancillary rooms necessary for him to trade in spices, fabrics and other luxury goods. These latter functions occupied the ground and mezzanine floors, above which there are two spacious apartments.

The plan, like the facade is, asymmetrical, the result of Contarini's decision to re-use the foundations of an earlier house on the site, which he had first bought and then demolished. In its asymmetry the house is rather atypical, since most new palaces of that period were formal and symmetrical in both plan and principal facade.

Nevertheless, the house contains many other traditional features, among them the private inner courtyard, with an open stair rising to the principal *piano nobile.* The courtyard itself is also approached by a typical stone gateway, and in the center is the well, with a notable contemporary wellhead, carved for Contarini by Bartolomeo Bon in 1427-28.

On the upper floors, the chief feature is the great hall or *pòrtego,* 30 meters in length, and terminating at its southern end, on both *piani nobili,* with fine traceried *logge,* each with memorable views over the Grand Canal. The other living accommodations are all reached from the great hall.

The palace's most notable feature is the Grand Canal facade, the element on which Contarini spent more time and expense than any other. He engaged two master masons, the local man Giovanni Bon (and his son Bartolomeo) and a Milanese, Matteo Raverti. To Raverti and his large team of assistants were assigned the main staircase, the entrance gateway and the two *logge* onto the Grand Canal. The Bon workshop was responsible for most of the remaining stonework, including the ground-floor arcade, the pendant-traceried windows and the crenellation.

Contarini himself took an extremely close interest in the entire construction process, constantly refining his requirements and adding new features. Although the basic structure was complete by about 1431, masons such as Nicolo Romanello and Gasparin Rosso were still on site carving additional balconies as late as 1438.

The whole appearance of the rich facade is highly fragmented for the same reason; in particular, Raverti's two *logge* were designed in almost complete isolation from the other elements of the facade, and the detailed design of features such as the crenellation was not finalized until much of the facade was complete.

The house acquired its soubriquet through Contarini's decision to decorate many parts of the facade with gold leaf, as well as with pigments such as lapis lazuli, red, white and black. The extensive use of gold leaf was probably unique for a house in this period, an ostentatious display of the great wealth and power of the numerous Contarini clan.

The richly carved stonework represents the later Venetian Gothic style at its most characteristic and refined. The Cà d'Oro was to be succeeded by many other Gothic palaces in the period up to about 1460, but none were as elaborately decorated, and none were sheathed entirely with marble. In this and many other respects the house has close links with the Palazzo Ducale, particularly with the Porta della Carta, where several of Contarini's own masons, including the Bons, later worked. Raverti's

first-floor loggia at the Cà d'Oro is also modeled on the tracery at the Palazzo Ducale, although it is considerably more refined in detail.

—RICHARD J. GOY

DOGE'S PALACE
Venice, Italy

Ninth century: Palace founded. **1170:** Palace rebuilt. **1340-65:** Molo wing rebuilt. **1400:** Central window added to Molo wing; **Architect:** Pier Paolo Masegne. **1424:** Ziani's Palace of Justice demolished. **1424-ca. 1438:** Piazzetta wing built; **Architect:** Attributed to Filippo Calendario. **1438-ca. 1444:** Porta della Carta built; **Architects:** Bartolomeo Bon and Giovanni Bon. **1444-60s:** Porta extended. **1462-71:** Foscari arch built. **1483:** Original Ziani wing destroyed by fire; reconstruction begun; **Architect:** Antonio Rizzo. **Late 1560s:** Statues of Mars and Neptune added to Scala dei Giganti; **Sculptor:** Jacopo Sansovino (1486-1570). **1574:** Interior Senate and Collegio damaged in fire; remodeling begun. **1577:** Molo wing damaged by fire; rebuilding begun; **Architect:** Antonio da Ponte. **Ca. 1600:** Prisons added; **Architect:** Antonio da Ponte. **Ca. 1600:** Bridge of Sighs built; **Architect:** Contini.

Publications

ARSLAN, EDOARDO: "Qualche appunto sul Palazzo Ducale di Venezia." *Bollettino d'arte* 50 (1965): 58ff.
BASSI, ELENA: "Appunti per la storia del Palazzo Ducale di Venezia, 1 e 2." *Critica d'arte* 9, Nos. 51 and 52 (1962): 25-38; 41-53.
BASSI, ELENA: "Il Palazzo Ducale nel '400." *Bollettino del Centro Internazionale di Studi di Architettura "Andrea Palladio"* 6/2 (1964): 181-187.
CADORIN, GIUSEPPE: *Pareri di XV architetti, e notizie storiche intorno al Palazzo Ducale di Venezia.* Venice, 1838.
DA MOSTO, ANDREA: *Il dogi di Venezia nella vita pubblica e privata.* 2nd ed. Milan, 1960.
Il palazzo ducale di Venezia. Turin, 1971.
LAURITZEN, PETER, and ZIELCHE, ALEXANDER: *The Palaces of Venice.* New York, 1978.
LORENZI, GIAMBATTISTA (ed.): *Monumenti per servire alla storia del Palazzo Ducale di Venezia.* Venice, 1868.
McANDREW, JOHN: *Venetian Architecture of the Early Renaissance.* Cambridge, Massachusetts, and London, 1980.
ZANOTTO, FRANCESCO: *Il Palazzo Ducale di Venezia.* 4 vols. Venice, 1842-61.

*

As the seat of government of the Venetian Republic from the ninth century until its fall to Napoleon in 1797, the Doge's Palace is imbued with great symbolic as well as architectural importance. Although its built history is as long and complex as that of the Republic itself, the present structure epitomizes in many ways the peaks of creativity and individuality of Venetian architecture.

Little is known of the earliest structures on the site, which was chosen originally for its commanding strategic location and control over the great basin of San Marco. The first definitive rebuilding was begun in the 1170s under the doge Sebastiano

Doge's Palace: Venice, Italy, 9th century

Ziani; by then, the earliest structures had outgrown their defensive requirements, and so Ziani's buildings were constructed with many open arcades and *logge,* in a broadly Byzantine style, but establishing a precedent for the later reconstructions.

Ziani's palace had three wings, around a central courtyard, each wing housing one element of the government of the republic (the fourth side was formed by the flank wall of San Marco), and this function-zoning was largely retained in subsequent reconstructions. The three basic functions were the residence of the doge, the elected head of state; the great hall for the assemblies of the Maggior Consiglio, the chief governing council of the republic; and third, the palace of justice.

Doge Ziani's reconstruction located the ducal apartments on the east side of the site, along a narrow canal, the Rio di Palazzo. The most prominent wing, though, was that along the quay or Molo, and this was where the Maggior Consiglio was located. The third wing occupied the western side, forming one flank of the Piazzetta of San Marco.

This palace survived until 1340, when the Signoria, the inner cabinet of government, decreed that the Molo wing should be rebuilt chiefly to house satisfactorily the Maggior Consiglio, which had increased notably in numbers and far outgrown the Ziani wing. It was also intended to form the centerpiece of the government of what was by that time a very wealthy mercantile empire. The exterior of the 1340 Molo wing survives largely unchanged today, and it incorporated the remains of some of Ziani's earlier structure at the east end. The Molo wing was structurally complete by about 1365, although the great central window was not added until 1400, the work of Pier Paolo delle Masegne.

The decision to locate the vast hall of the Maggior Consiglio

on the second floor (partly for reasons of security) meant that it was supported by two lower stories of ancillary accommodation, the appearance of which was rendered lighter by continuous colonnades. These are characteristic examples of Late Venetian Gothic tracery, surmounted by the great, largely solid mass of the hall, the internal dimensions of which are 54 by 25 meters, and 15 meters in height. Visually, the mass of the hall is broken by a row of large windows, formerly with elaborate tracery; by the delicate diaper pattern of pink and white stone that covers the wall surface; and by the elegant stone crenellation. The last owes much to Middle Eastern precedents, the result of Venice's close trade links with Cairo and Damascus. Although the Molo wing dominates the whole waterfront by its bulk, in detail it exhibits the most characteristic traits of Late Venetian Gothic: lightness of detailing, strong chiaroscuro, and in the capitals and the central window a close integration of architecture and sculpture.

The completion of the Molo wing was almost immediately followed by the demolition of Ziani's Palace of Justice, which began in 1424. As with the Molo wing, the master builder for the new Piazzetta wing is not known, but is believed to be Filippo Calendario. The design principles already established were continued along the Piazzetta frontage for a further 12 bays, stopping a little short of the corner of San Marco. All three external corners of the palace are enlivened with fine Gothic sculptures (*Adam and Eve*; *The Drunkenness of Noah*; *The Judgment of Solomon*), the authorship of which, however, is still the subject of much debate.

The Piazzetta wing was structurally complete by about 1438, and incorporated a great central window similar to that on the Molo facade. In the same year, Giovanni and Bartolomeo Bon were commissioned to design and carve the Porta della Carta, the new chief ceremonial entrance to the palace, which fills the space between the Piazzetta wing and San Marco.

The Porta della Carta (probably completed ca. 1444) represents the apogee of Late Venetian Gothic, with architecture and sculpture fully integrated. It incorporates many iconographic sculptures, including the four Virtues (Prudence, Charity, Temperance, Fortitude), and a figure of the incumbent doge, Francesco Foscari, kneeling in front of the winged lion, symbol of the republic. At the apex is the figure of Justice, by Bartolomeo Bon.

The slow, piecemeal reconstruction of the Doge's Palace continued with the extension of the *porta* into the central courtyard in the form of the Foscari Loggia and Foscari Arch. These are the work of many different artists and sculptors, including Bon, Antonio Bregno and, later, Antonio Rizzo. The arch is transitional, part Gothic and part Early Renaissance; unlike the *porta,* though, it suffers from an ill-defined overall form and an excess of arbitrary decoration. The arch was not finally completed until the 1460s.

At that time, the original Ziani wing still survived on the east side of the courtyard, but it was destroyed by fire in 1483, thus necessitating the final stage of reconstruction. This was begun by Antonio Rizzo, who built the Scala dei Giganti to terminate the new axis formed by the Porta della Carta and Foscari Loggia; the election of a new doge was announced to the people from the top of these stairs.

Rizzo also designed the lower two orders of the long east wing facing the courtyard. They are a curious and at least partially successful exercise in a transitional style, the ground-floor Early Renaissance forms rather less convincing than the more purely Gothic arcading above them. Rizzo also completed the lower facade onto the Rio di Palazzo, again in a hybrid but rather more disciplined manner. Work on the east wing was continued under Pietro Solari (il Lombardo), who added the two uppermost orders of the facade. Typical of his work, these facades are clad with elaborate but insubstantial decorative stonework, excessively fussy compared with the lower orders. Lombardo was succeeded in turn as *proto* (chief surveyor) by Spavento and the Scarpagnino.

When finally completed, this wing was the largest and most complex of the three, containing, as well as the ducal apartments, the two large halls of the Senate and Collegio, and the accommodation for the Council of Ten, the body responsible for state security. When Jacopo Sansovino became *proto,* he added the two giants (Mars and Neptune) at the top of the Scala dei Giganti, and the Scala d'Oro, a masterpiece of High Renaissance stucco work.

Two disastrous fires in 1574 and 1577 necessitated further considerable reconstruction, all of which survives today. The first fire gutted the newly completed Senate and Collegio, while the second destroyed the interior of the Molo wing, including the hall of the Maggior Consiglio. All of the internal decoration was lost, although the basic structure survived. Although it was originally intended to hold a competition for a completely new structure, more conservative views in the government prevailed, and the Gothic shell of the Molo wing was retained.

The new interiors contain many fine "program" works, dedicated to the glory and myth of the republic. The decorations vary considerably in their detailed style and in their success; the Maggior Consiglio remains a magnificent hall, incorporating some important pictures in the heavy, gilded, coffered ceiling typical of the late 16th century. But Tintoretto's *Paradiso* on the east wall (said to be the largest oil-on-canvas painting in the world) is far from being his most successful work, being excessively repetitious and unclearly structured.

The other fine interiors rebuilt after the fires are all in the Rio di Palazzo wing. One of the most ornate is the Hall of the Senate, designed by Antonio da Ponte; again, there is an elaborate coffered ceiling, of more note than the individual paintings, although the central panel is by Tintoretto.

The other large hall is the Collegio, perhaps the finest of all. The ceiling contains a magnificent group of works by Paolo Veronese, while the wall paintings include three from Tintoretto's workshop. Other than the ducal apartments, the two other significant rooms in this wing are the Hall of the Four Doors (with an overpowering stucco ceiling) and the Hall of the Council of Ten, a much more austere room, with two surviving works by Veronese.

The Doge's Palace was extended further soon after these reconstructions were complete, by the building of the new prisons, across the Rio di Palazzo. The architect was again Antonio da Ponte, and the facade is a severe classical composition, all of white Istrian stone. The prisons are joined to the palace by the little Bridge of Sighs (Ponte dei Sospiri) in a rather frivolous (and perhaps inappropriate) Baroque style (ca. 1600) by Contini.

—RICHARD J. GOY

LIBRARY OF ST. MARK'S
Venice, Italy

1536-53. Architect: Jacopo Sansovino.

Publications

LORENZETTI, GIULIO: "La libreria sansoviniana di Venezia." *Accademie e biblioteche d'Italia* 2 (1928-29).
LOTZ, WOLFGANG: "Sansovinos Bibliothek von S. Marco und die Stadtbaukunst der Renaissance." In *Kunst des Mittelalters in Sachsen. Festschrift für Wolf Schubert.* Weimar, 1967.
LUXORO, MARIA: "La biblioteca di S. Marco nella sua storia." *Collana di monografie delle biblioteche d'Italia* 1 (1954).

*

Considered the first building in Venice to be truly classical in its vocabulary, Jacopo Sansovino's Library of St. Mark's along the Piazzetta in that city has been admired for centuries for its sculptural virtuosity and impressive handling of ancient forms, in which he combined the language of classicism and the language of the High Renaissance. The building illustrates Sansovino's debt to Donato Bramante, and its fundamental syntax, using superimposed orders, derives from the Theater of Marcellus in Rome (11 B.C.) Andrea Palladio called the Library of St. Mark's the "richest and most ornate building since antiquity," and it clearly influenced his remodeling of the Palazzo della Ragione (Basilica) in Vicenza, where work began in 1549. Both buildings employ arcades on two stories to create a screen with the strong textural effect of light and shade. The travel writer Karl Baedeker called the library "perhaps the most magnificent secular edifice in Italy."

When Sansovino arrived in Venice from Rome, he found inns, butcher shops and wooden public lavatories in the Piazzetta. His commission resulted from the creation of the library as a repository for Greek and Latin manuscripts that had been held in the Doge's Palace. After about 10 years of work, part of the

Library of St. Mark's: Venice, Italy, 1536-53

inner vault collapsed, attributable possibly to moisture penetration and an especially frigid winter, and Sansovino spent a short time in prison because of the structural failure. Twenty-one bays, of which only 16 were finished before Sansovino's death, run parallel to the Piazzetta, and three follow the canal. From 1583 to 1588 Vincenzo Scamozzi oversaw the completion of the building according to Sansovino's plan.

The library presents a two-story, white Istrian stone facade with a distinctly horizontal emphasis. The ground story is mostly an open arcade, and the upper story contains a reading room and stacks. The design becomes more sculptural with height, and the interiors of the library were enriched by Venetian painters: Tiziano Vecelli (ca. 1490-1576, known as Titian), Jacopo Robusti (1518-94, known as Tintoretto) and Paolo Cagliari (1528-88, known as Veronese). In the spandrels of the Doric lower story recline river gods, and winged female figures rest in the spandrels of the upper Ionic story. The result is a wall barely visible.

Contrasting in era and architectural language to the Doge's Palace across from it on the Piazzetta, the library nevertheless relates to the palace in scale, texture and civic importance. Having created sorely needed unity for the Piazzetta, the library is significant for its place in the conceptual development of urban design history. It employs a formula related to that of the Doge's Palace, namely, a balcony or loggia over an open arcade. It illustrates also the structural and aesthetic challenge of placing small openings over large ones, without risking too much mass in the upper story. By introducing the three-part Venetian window—developed presumably first by Bramante in his Sala Regia in the Vatican, but identified usually as a Serlian or Palladian motif—to the upper story, Sansovino lightened and dematerialized its mass.

At the ground-level arcade, piers with engaged Doric columns support a Doric frieze of triglyphs and metopes. The entrance is at the center and leads to a barrel-vaulted stair. At the upper level the rhythmic pattern continues, but the order is Ionic and the Venetian window pattern and balustrade create a greater mass for the structural support of the coffered vault of the reading room inside. Next to the reading room lies a vestibule, used for a classroom. Above the architrave runs a tall and deeply sculpted frieze, influenced most likely by that of the Villa Farnesina in Rome (1509-11), designed by Baldassare Peruzzi. Sansovino's frieze, however, represents a uniquely firm integration of sculpture and architecture, with festoons hung from *putti* positioned above structural points. Additional sculpture occurs in the forms of human and lion heads at the uppermost point of each arch and above the swoop of each festoon. Lozenge openings punctuate the frieze at the center of each bay.

Atop the upper balustrade sculptures of human figures, placed above each set of columns, pose against the sky. This treatment of the balustrade deeply impressed Andrea Palladio, who adorned balustrades in a similar fashion. Finally, obelisks pierce the sky above pilastered corners.

The Library of St. Mark's impressed not only Palladio, but also several New World architects. Notable tributes to the library include the north and south arcades of Shepley, Rutan and Coolidge's design of the Art Institute of Chicago (1892) as well as their design of the Chicago Public Library (1897).

—PAUL GLASSMAN

Library of St. Mark's

PALAZZO CORNER DELLA CA' GRANDE
Venice, Italy

1545-56. Architect: Jacopo Sansovino (1486-1570).

Publications

LAURITZEN, PETER, and ZIELCHE, ALEXANDER: *The Palaces of Venice*. New York, 1978.

*

With the Palazzo Corner della Ca' Grande, Jacopo Sansovino brought the High Renaissance system of palace design to Venice: the building employs the Venetian mode of planning, with a central entrance vestibule, the *gran salone,* leading to a spacious courtyard toward the rear of the building. The primary innovation in the design of the facade consists of uniting the balconies of the three central windows into one, achieving a particular emphasis on and tight rhythm in the entrance bays.

On the site of a Gothic residence purchased by Zorzi Corner before his death in 1527, the building was destroyed by fire in 1532, and Sansovino was asked to rebuild it. Work began in about 1545, and several antecedents elucidate the cumulative achievement of Sansovino's palazzo.

A vigorously rusticated ground floor and upper stories articulated by paired columns derive from Donato Bramante's interpretation of classicism for the Palazzo Caprini in Rome (ca. 1510), later known as the House of Raphael, because the painter bought it in 1517. No longer standing, it is known from an engraving: it consisted of only two stories, instead of the more typical three popularized in Florence, with the first story featuring carefully dressed stonework of uniform texture on the ground level and the second introducing paired engaged columns. Raphael employed a similar system in the Palazzo Vidoni Caffarelli in Rome (ca. 1515-20). The triple-arched entrance loggia leading to a courtyard relates to Giuliano Romano's garden facade for the Palazzo del Tè at Mantua (1527-34).

The strongest and most durable relationship, however, exists between the Palazzo Corner and perhaps its most direct antecedent, the Palazzo Canossa in Verona (begun ca. 1530) by Michele Sanmicheli. He, too, employed Bramante's Roman prototype, with its system of a rusticated ground floor and engaged paired order on the *piano nobile.* Sanmicheli flattened almost all of the textural effects, however; it remained, therefore, for Sansovino to express fully the *chiaroscuro* effect of three-dimensionality achieved by deep rustication and engaged columns.

In all respects, therefore, the Palazzo Corner is more Mannerist and perhaps more adventurous in its design than Sansovino's earlier Palazzo Dolfin, begun in 1538. The Palazzo Dolfin features a calmer, even number of bays—the entrance was not through the main waterfront facade—while the Palazzo Corner, with its odd number of bays, is more animated. Both employ superimposed orders; Doric for the ground story, Ionic for the middle, and Corinthian for the top. Ground-story rustication and lozenge openings in the uppermost frieze of the Palazzo Corner, however, differentiate it from its predecessor. Furthermore, the segmental ground-floor window arches in the Mannerist work appear squeezed between the podia of the overscaled brackets of its mezzanine windows; as in the Palazzo Vidoni-Caffarelli, recesses separate the bases of the columns and the

Palazzo Corner della Ca' Grande: Venice, Italy, 1545-56

balustrades, lending to the facade the dramatic effects of shade and shadow. Both exhibit three stories: the Palazzo Dolfin presents central bays in the upper stories divided in half, while the Palazzo Corner has bays consistent in width, with broader central window openings at the loggias.

In plan the main stair runs unobtrusively at a right angle off the long, vaulted *gran salone*. The generous use of rusticated pilasters in the courtyard is probably again a result of Sansovino's experience of the Palazzo del Tè, and the skillful attention to sculptural detail there is most evident in the circular metopes that, at the corners, are superseded by ovals.

The Palazzo Corner's influence permeated the design of palazzos in Venice until nearly 1750. Notable examples inspired by the Palazzo Corner are the Palazzo Pesaro by Baldassare Longhena (begun in 1652 and completed by Antonio Gaspari), the ca' Ressonico (formerly Bon) by Baldassare Longhena (begun in 1667), the Palazzo Corner della Regina by Domenico Rossi (begun in 1724), and the Palazzo Grassi by Giorgio Massari (begun in 1748).

—PAUL GLASSMAN

PIAZZA SAN MARCO
Venice, Italy

8th century: Doge's Place. **1063-71:** Basilica of St. Mark—transformation of the original church (ca. 830). **13th century:** Basilica of St. Mark—domes added. **15th century:** Basilica of

St. Mark—additions made to facade. **1536:** Library of St. Mark—construction begun. **1536:** Mint—construction begun.

Publications

BETTRINI, S.: *L'architettura di San Marco (origini e significato)*. Padua, 1946.

DEMUS, OTTO: *The Church of San Marco in Venice: History, Architecture, Sculpture*. Washington, D.C., 1960.

FORLATI, FERDINANDO: "Storia e restauri del San Marco di Venezia." *Palladio* 15 (1965): 71-85.

FRADELETTO, A. (ed.): *Il campanile di S. Marco riedificato: studi, ricerche, relazioni*. Venice, 1912.

LOTZ, WOLFGANG: "La Trasformazione sansoviniana di Piazza S. Marco e l'urbanistica del cinquecento." *Bollettino del Centro Internazionale di Studi di Architettura "Andrea Palladio"* 8 (1966): 114-122.

PASINI: *Il tesoro di San Marco*. Venice, 1885-87.

ROBERTSON, HOWARD: *Architecture Arising*. London, 1944.

SAMONÀ, GIUSEPPE, et al.: *Piazza San Marco: l'architettura, la storia, le funzioni*. Venice, 1976.

UNRAU, JOHN: *Ruskin and St. Mark's*. 1984.

The open space Piazza San Marco, delineated by the Basilica of St. Mark, the Doge's Palace, the Procuratie Vecchie, the Fabbrica Nuova and the Library of St. Mark's is perhaps the world's most perfectly designed and constructed civic plaza, and surely one of its greatest outdoor spaces. The piazza is the most significant space and building complex of the city of Venice. Other elements that compose the space and the closure are the bell tower or the Campanile; the two granite columns from Constantinople that are surmounted by the lion of Saint Mark, patron saint of the city, and the statue of Saint Theodore, patron saint before the body of Saint Mark was brought to the city; and Leopoldi's three flagpoles in front of the church.

Venice was the primary gateway to the Orient from Europe as well as a port of entry to the European continent for the Asian trade routes. Many wealthy merchants, their families and political overseers under the leadership of the Doge built and enjoyed the economic and cultural fruits of this early commercial city. The origins of the city date back to the ninth century from the discovery of the small, scattered islands at a strategic location on the Adriatic Sea. The Italian builders sunk piles into the marshy land, stabilizing the foundations for building construction.

The first building of importance was the Doge's Palace, constructed as a fortress outside the city walls, during the latter part of the eighth century. The first Chapel of St. Mark, a small wooden structure that was originally the private chapel for the first Doge's Palace, was begun in 827 as a sepulcher to contain the body and relics, brought from Alexandria in Egypt, of Saint Mark; he subsequently became the patron saint of Venice in place of Saint Theodore. In 976 the church and palace were burned in a rebellion against Doge Candiano IV.

The church was rebuilt by Pietro Orseolo, and was enlarged and remodeled in about 1063 under the orders of Doge Contarini. This design and construction incorporated the Byzantine Greek-cross plan of equal arms derived from the emperor Justinian's Church of the Holy Apostles at Constantinople (536-546) after the remodeling of 1063. The west nave is surrounded on three sides by a narthex, the roof and a triforium supported by an elaborate series of columns and round arches. Above the narthex is a wide gallery spatially interacting with the triforium. Four large bronze horses, which were removed from a Greco-Roman

Piazza San Marco: Venice, Italy

triumphal quadriga, brought to Venice by Doge Enrico Dandolo in 1204, are placed in the center of the gallery. (In more recent times these horses have been replaced by accurate reproductions because of environmental deterioration of the originals. The originals have been placed in a small chamber on the second floor.)

A large central dome was erected at the transept and nave crossing, with two smaller, symmetrically located domes over the north and south transepts and similar domes over the west nave and the chancel to the east. Each of the five domes is framed with a series of wood members to support the outer shell, and is sprung from the supporting walls and quadripartite piers with pendentives. Each is topped with a Byzantine lantern. Clerestory windows and elaborate mosaics occur at the inner shell of each dome.

The church was completed in 1071 and consecrated between 1084 and 1096. In 1106 it was again damaged by fire but was repaired; it thereafter served as the doge's chapel, with many late additions and embellishments.

European church architecture from the Gothic school, influenced by St. Front at Périgueux in France, superseded the Byzantine style near the end of the 14th century, when the upper

archivolts, pinnacles and window traceries were added to the exterior. Finally, the Renaissance school in the 17th century usurped the Gothic, giving the edifice the influences of three architectural periods and elaborate polychrome interior Greek mosaic compositions.

The architectural details of the church are subordinated by the elaborate mosaics, the primary decoration of the interior. The walls and arches are encased by marble, porphyries and alabaster taken from previous ancient structures, sawn into slabs and placed to create bands of color. During that period of the evolution of the church, the doges in some modest way continued to embellish the church, so it is difficult to assign specific times to the details. Marble columns, brought from Alexandria and other eastern cities, enriched the five-bay facade facing the piazza with the arch traceries decorated with mosaics. The corners are rounded, and the mosaics follow the curve; therefore, visually no break appears in the wall sections, allowing for a continuance of the mosaic iconography. The purpose of the mosaics is to reflect light in the dome interior, symbolically declaring the radiance of heaven and God's word.

Because of the unstable earth and changing water table of the city, the crypts below the nave, the chancel and the three

St. Mark's Basilica, Piazza San Marco

apses at the ends of each wing, and the floors of the sublevels have sunk and are frequently below water. Due to this instability, the floors of the church have raised or settled, producing an uneven surface.

In addition to the central plaza in front of the cathedral, there are four additional secondary plazas delineated by specific buildings, creating a composition of voids and solids. The so called "Piazzetta," the smaller arm of the L-shaped space, is the primary entrance to the Piazza, located between the Doge's Palace and the Library. The third and smaller piazza is on the north side of the church; the fourth, the Molo, is between the Doge's Palace and the lagoon; and the fifth is the Giardino Reale between the Procuratie Nuove and the lagoon. This complex of plazas and buildings defines the composition that is considered one of the most important open spaces in the world.

The plaza was much smaller during its initial period and through the early 15th century. The buildings of the plaza facade were devoted to residential purposes and were constructed of rough brick masonry. The north walls were removed and replaced with the Procuratie Vecchie, a long row of administrative offices for use by the Venetian officials referred to as Procurators, in 1480-1517. The clock tower, the Torre dell'Orologio, was built at the east end of the south wall, facing the Piazzetta, with an arched port leading from the plaza to the primary land-based street, the Merceria, in 1499.

Jacopo Tatti, surnamed Il Sansovino, a Florentine architect and a refugee from the sacking of Rome in 1527, gave the Piazza its final form. In 1529 Sansovino was appointed *Proto dei Procuratori di Supra,* the most eminent position the republic could assign to an architect, and he became responsible for the continuous development of St. Mark's, the Piazza, the Procuratie Vecchie and the procurators' offices. On the western side of the Piazzetta, presently facing the Doge's Palace, the Library (or *Libreria*) and the Mint (or *Zecca*) were begun in 1536 by Sansovino. The library was first housed in the church, later in the Doge's Palace, and in 1537 the procurators made the decision to house the manuscripts in a new and larger building to face the Doge's Palace on the Piazzetta. This edifice was a Renaissance masterpiece for the purpose of housing the volumes given to the city by the Greek scholar Cardinal Bessarione, and to provide reading rooms. Andrea Palladio referred to the building as "probably the richest and most ornate edifice since ancient times." The rather simple ground-floor arcade is composed of columns with Doric capitals supporting the arches above, which in turn carry the more decorative columns with Ionic capitals and a continuous balustrade and balcony across the entire face. This long, 21-bay arcade at the ground floor on the east facade was designed to be used as a shelter from the morning sun and the frequently inclement weather, for recreation and for open commercial activities. At the ceiling level of the second floor, across the entire east and south faces, the architect placed an elaborate entablature, dentiles and a balustrade parapet above the roof level, interrupted by equally spaced pedestals bearing statues and life-size figures. Sansovino placed the reading room and the stacks on the second floor to protect the invaluable manuscripts from the frequent flooding.

Two primary concerns faced Sansovino—the siting and the outline of the building, which were both solved with the same design. The bell tower, or the Campanile, had been erected in timber in about 888, as an attachment to the original north

St. Mark's Basilica, Piazza San Marco

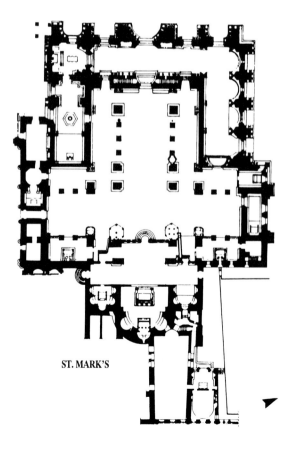

ST. MARK'S

facade of the Piazza. By moving this facade back, thus creating a greater east opening, the Piazza better frames the church. The new library and the *Procuratie* were removed from the Campanile, leaving it as a freestanding tower. This allowed the new library a parallel face to the Doge's Palace, providing a building with an arcaded facade, and giving an animated west wall to the Piazzetta.

An important feature of the Library of St. Mark's (Libreria Sansoviniana) is the visual relation of scale and harmony it echoes with the lower two floors of the facade of the Doge's Palace. The interaction of the composition of these two structures, facing each other across the Piazzetta, offers the pedestrian a sense of belonging. It appears that Sansovino's goal was to interpret the Gothic architecture of the Doge's Palace in the Renaissance spirit of the time.

The Mint, begun in 1536, with a forbidding three-story facade, faces the Canale di San Marco. The ground-level face is of heavy cut stone clearly exposing the joints, the spring stones, and the voussoirs in each of the arches of a colonnade. The upper two levels are of similar stonework, with large rectangular windows, pediments above each of the third-story openings, and with heavy stone outlookers at the ceiling levels. The visual effect is rustic and stern, with an air of strength and impregnability.

Sansovino's death in 1570 required that the building be completed by Vincenzo Scamozzi in 1584. In that year Scamozzi began the removal and new construction of the Procuratie Nuove, the administrative offices on the south face of the Piazza.

The later refinements of the elements of the Piazza included the south side of the Procuratie Nuove, which was undertaken by Scamozzi in 1584 and completed in 1640 by Baldassare Longhena. The floor of the piazza, one of the basic unifying elements of the complex, was accomplished between 1722 and 1735. The square was completed in 1810, with the closing of the west end with the Fabricca Nuova. The present Campanile was rebuilt after its collapse in 1902.

—GORDON ECHOLS

IL REDENTORE
Venice, Italy

1577-92. Architect: Andrea Palladio (1508-80).

Publications

MURRAY, PETER: "Palladio's Churches." *Arte in Europa: Scritti di storia dell'arte in onore di E. Arslan* (1966): 597-608.

PUPPI, LIONELLO: *Andrea Palladio: The Complete Works.* New York, 1986.

SINDING LARSEN, S.: "Palladio's Redentore: A Compromise in Composition." *Art Bulletin* (1965): 419-437.

SORAVIA, GIOVANNI BATTISTA: *Le chiese di Venezia descritte ed illustrate.* 3 vols. Venice, 1822-24.

TIMOFIEWITSCH, VLADIMIR: *The Chiesa del Redentore.* University Park, Pennsylvania, and London, 1971.

TIMOFIEWITSCH, VLADIMIR: *Die sakrale Architektur Palladios.* Munich, 1968.

WITTKOWER, RUDOLF: *Palladio and English Palladianism.* London, 1974.

ZORZI, GIAN GIORGIO: *Le chiese e i ponti di Andrea Palladio.* Venice, 1966.

*

Andrea Palladio had not just one but three opportunities to shape Venice's outer bank of islands, and thereby to shape the look of harborside Venice itself. On the Guidecca not far from San Giorgio Maggiore, Palladio designed, around 1577, the small, centralized Church of Santa Maria della Presentazione, or La Zitelle, part of a religious institution that aided poor girls. Further along the Guidecca is Il Redentore, or the Church of the Redeemer, undertaken by the Venetian Senate in thanksgiving for the city's deliverance from the ravaging plague of 1575-76. The swelling masses of all these churches punctuate and further unify the slowly curving wall of three-story buildings on the islands of San Giorgio and the Guidecca. Magnificently scaled in relation to the Guidecca proper, the broad waterway in front, and Venice itself, their domed silhouettes, paired towers and stately white stone facades embrace, herald and step up to the city, forming an urban gateway that fashions from the elements of a classical serenity one of the world's most picturesque skylines.

On a smaller site than San Giorgio's, Il Redentore is that much more compact. The elevation adumbrates the church's compressed plan through changes in plane and coded pediments. In contrast to San Giorgio, the full pediment on a giant order demarcating the nave this time appears against a rectangular attic, a motif sanctioned for Palladio by the Roman Pantheon, whose rectangular attic rises over that temple's barrel-vaulted

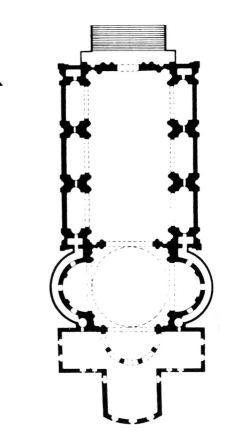

vestibule, as Palladio's does over Il Redentore's shallow entrance bay and tunnel-vaulted nave. Second pediments occupy a recessed plane and indicate chapel width. Just behind and below the attic, a tertiary set of half pediments calls off the position of the exterior buttresses for the nave vault.

Although the facade does not lack sculptural power, it does not have San Giorgio's impact or vertical momentum. Gone are the massive plinths used in San Giorgio's giant order, replaced by the stairs and the podium to which they lead. Palladio substituted pilasters for engaged columns in the two flanking members of the giant order, their flat surfaces further reducing the sculptural heft of the facade. He compressed the impressive vertical reach of San Giorgio's principal order by framing the pediment within the rectangular attic and hipping the attic roof. These two features visually step up to the monumental dome, whose more forward position gives it a dominance over the facade not true of the San Giorgio elevation. Palladio also introduced a new intermediate scale: the door surround's own order and pediment further tame the gigantism of San Giorgio by mediating between the human proportions of the two lateral wall niches and the giant order of the principal temple front.

The tight proximity of niche and door pediments to the colossal members of that frame compresses the facade's organization horizontally as well. So does substituting chapels for aisles, withdrawing the transepts into the body of the church, and placing the bell towers at a rearward visual tangent to the dome, giving them the character of minarets and evoking Venice's historic ties to the Byzantine and Islamic worlds.

Despite its vertical and horizontal compression, however, the facade's proportional ratios created a stateliness appropriate to the Feast of the Redeemer, held annually on the third Sunday of July. In a pilgrimage as unique to Venice as the penitential

Il Redentore: Venice, Italy, 1577-92

Il Redentore

church's principal dome. The two truncated transepts and the monk's-choir columnar screen make up three exedral volumes that shape space, buttress the crossing dome, contrast their quarter spheres with its semisphere, and provide a more centralized reading for the church's eastern end than any previous Italian Renaissance attempt to join longitudinal with Greek-cross plans. The tighter site, more compact plan and greater interior sculptural power and consistency of Il Redentore give it a spatial unity that the amplitude of San Giorgio obviates.

—EDWARD W. WOLNER

SAN GIORGIO MAGGIORE
Venice, Italy

1559-1610: Refectory (1559-63); cloister (1579-1614); church (1566-1610). **Architect:** Andrea Palladio (1508-80). **1602-10:** Facade completed. **Architect:** Vincenzo Scamozzi (1548-1616). **1641-53:** Library and grand staircase added. **Architect:** Baldassare Longhena (1598-1682).

Publications

DAMERINI, G.: *L'isola e il cenobio di S. Giorgio Maggiore.* Venice, 1956.
FORLATI, FERDINANDO: *S. Giorgio Maggiore: Il complesso monumentale e i suoi restauri (1951-1956). In memoriam.* Padua, Italy, 1977.
LUND, H.: "The Facade of San Giorgio Maggiore." *Architectural Review* (1963).
MURRAY, PETER: "Palladio's Churches." In *Arte in Europa: Scritti di storia dell'arte in onore di E. Arslan.* Milan, 1966: 597-608.
PUPPI, LIONELLO: *Andrea Palladio: The Complete Works.* New York, 1986.
SORAVIA, GIOVANNI BATTISTA: *Le chiese di Venezia descritte ed illustrate.* 3 vols. Venice, 1822-24.
TIMOFIEWITSCH, VLADIMIR: "Ein neuer Bietrag zu der Baugeschichte von S. Giorgio Maggiore." *Bollettino del Centro Internazionale di Studi "Andrea Palladio"* 5 (1963): 330-339.
TIMOFIEWITSCH, VLADIMIR: *Die sakrale Architektur Palladios.* Munich, 1968.
WITTKOWER, RUDOLF: *Palladio and English Palladianism.* London, 1974.
ZORZI, GIAN GIORGIO: *Le chiese e i ponti di Andrea Palladio.* Venice, 1966.

ascent of the Spanish Steps on knees alone was to Rome, Venetians walked across the water on an axis with the church by means of a flotilla of barges and boats temporarily laced together. The procession and the ritual held on Il Redentore's steps and podium was political pageantry as well. Palladio's church was its center stage, its authoritative frontality augmenting and reflecting back onto the doge, the councilors and other dignitaries the piety and legitimacy of a merchant oligarchy.

On a nave and chapel plan like that of Leon Battista Alberti's Sant'Andrea in Mantua, the interior of Il Redentore is to San Giorgio as Filippo Brunelleschi's San Spirito is to his earlier San Lorenzo—a leap forward in the sculptural modeling of walls. Hollowed out of each nave pier between two giant engaged columns are semidomical niches on upper and lower levels. The lateral ends of each chapel are also semidomical cavities, ones scooped out of the transverse tongue walls that help brace the piers against the barrel vault. The continuous three-dimensional curves that outline the nave vault over each thermal window reveal the vault's thickness more fulsomely than the pointed terminations for the clerestory cuts in San Giorgio's tunnel vault. On a much larger scale, the columnar screen between altar and monk's choir also defines a semicylindrical, semidomical volume, thus eliminating the inconsistency in San Giorgio between the curved membering of nave piers and transept walls on the one hand, and the occupation of a mere single plane by the *altar's* columnar screen on the other.

Indeed, Il Redentore possesses a greater spatial unity as well as a heightened sculptural power and consistency. A single uninterrupted entablature completely outlines the church's interior and marks the spring line of chapel, nave, transept, altar and crossing vaults. Instead of competing with one another, chancel and crossing spaces have been pulled in under the

Few Western buildings have so decisively shaped the image of an entire city as Andrea Palladio's San Giorgio Maggiore. In its smallest field of urban relations it brilliantly refigures key aspects of the architecture of the Piazzetta-Piazza San Marco. Both locations exploit an island flatness that seems on approach, to suspend their buildings between sea and sky. Each exhibits a picturesque skyline in whose distant views an assertively vertical, freestanding campanile dominates the semispherical envelopes of church domes, and in whose closer views crucifixes, saints and secular figures animate lanterns, roof balustrades and pediment angles. The Basilica of St. Mark's and the Benedictine Abbey Church of San Giorgio possess facades that

San Giorgio Maggiore: Venice, Italy, 1559-1610

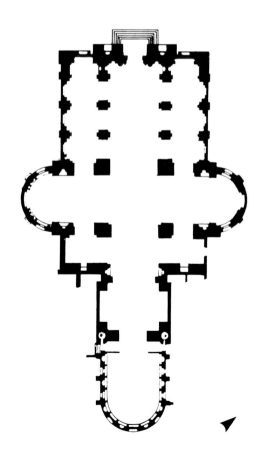

even in the Italian tradition of demonstrative western fronts possess exceptional scenographic and urbanistic power. At once soft and vivid, the color and material contrasts at San Giorgio and the Piazzetta are essentially the same: turquoise water and moisture-laden azure skies set off the whiteness of marble or Istrian stone, heighten the dusky rose, salmon or sienna hues of brick, painted stucco or marble inlay.

Yet San Giorgio engages a larger field of urban relations than these. Where St. Mark's newly cleaned polychrome lusters arch across one end of the city's most celebrated and ceremonial public square, San Giorgio sits astride Venice's most singular junction of major waterways, island groupings and uninterrupted sightlines. Whether seen along the Riva, through the heraldic columns of the Piazzetta, from the head of the Grand Canal and the Dogana, or out on the far end of the curving island chain of the Giudecca, San Giorgio commands Venice's most sweeping cityscapes. It does so by mediating between human and heroic scales, between urban foregrounds and the distant sea, between a chaste, self-contained classical purity and a declarative sculptural power, between a luminous and a spectral whiteness determined by clear or overcast skies, between scenography and a revelation of the church's spacial organization through superimposed nave and aisle pediments.

On the island itself, however, San Giorgio is a world apart from the city. Where many of Venice's most notable buildings show dramatically uneven settlement, San Giorgio shows none, its vertically emphatic facade the very embodiment of a building's first physical and metaphysical imperative: to stand upright and immovable, to work with and transcend gravity. The church's western front distances itself from Palladio's earlier Venetian facade for San Francesco della Vigna and from Palladio's later imitators at several other Venetian churches by means

San Giorgio Maggiore

of its larger scale, more balanced proportions, bolder sculptural power, subtler integration of rectilinear and curving forms, and its more careful adjustment of aisle to nave pediments.

Neither Jacopo Sansovino's sculpturally dense State Library nor heftier Baroque facades for several Venetian churches and fraternal organizations possess San Giorgio's heroic dimensions, its counterpoint of high relief against extensive areas of flat or unornamented surface, or the subtlety evident in such features as the convex curvature in the giant-order frieze, a curvature which appears to cushion the heaviness of the nave pediment and its formidable modillions. No Italian Renaissance architect had employed weightier garlands than Palladio here. Few had given attached columns a three-quarter girth before engaging them into the wall. None had used them in a colossal order. Only Michelangelo's gigantism at St. Peter's surpassed the titanic power of San Giorgio, but the earlier master's marshaled intensities were not balanced by Palladio's proportional equilibrium. For these reasons, no other Renaissance or Baroque church facade in Italy tells as strikingly from a distance.

Inside, the sculptural potency is less assertive, controlled by the necessary repetition of motifs along the length of nave and aisle bays, by the light-reflecting smoothness of all vaulted surfaces and by an unexampled clarity of organization that precisely codifies the church's different functions and spaces. Thus, barrel vault, unfluted Corinthian columns, schematically articulated capitals, and thermal clerestory windows of just one open central light together distinguish the nave. As it frames the most spiritually charged area of the church, the altar's architecture is correspondingly intensified through shifts to a groin vault, fluted columns and pilasters, intricately articulated capitals, larger thermal windows with three open lights, and a change in level. Other variations in vaulting, fenestration, column treatment or level set off the work's choir, transepts, aisles and

crossing.

In its swelling transepts and apse, in the width of its nave and aisles, San Giorgio possesses an amplitude and proportional equilibrium that contrasts with most Venetian Renaissance churches, whose restricted sites often result in unduly vertical proportions. On clear days a soft pale pink light of a sereneness that complements the architecture washes the vaults. While the church's sculptural potency is less assertive inside, arresting sculptural episodes do occur: set into apsidal walls, the tabernacle frames for the transept altar are one of the first major instances of broken pediments curving through three dimensions.

Yet the design is not without its puzzling features. The emphatically two-story columnar screen separating the monk's choir from the chancel ruptures the vertical consistency of the giant order used throughout the nave, crossing and chancel. Compared with its first level, the screen's serliana appears top-heavy, an interloper used nowhere else in the church. It does not sculpt or frame space as fulsomely as the church's curving arches, vaults and transepts, a weakness of the western nave wall as well. The nave entablature powerfully breaks forward over every column but carries nothing, for the spring line of the barrel vault rests on the pier behind the attached columns. The sculptural richness of the pilasters, columns and entablature is belied by the smooth surface of the uncoffered barrel vault. Its creamy color adds to its floating character, weightlessly detached from the substantial piers and arches. Rising off pendentives and a drum, the crossing dome competes for attention with the chancel.

Adjacent to the church is a square cloister whose arcades Palladio carried on coupled columns. His treatment of the corner piers is perhaps the most elegant of all Renaissance attempts to solve the problems posed by joining two arcades to one another at right angles. Without the blatant weakness of Michelozzo's corner columns at the Palazzo Medici in Florence or the paired pilasters squeezed into the angles of the L-plan piers at Luciano Laurana's Urbino palace, Palladio's corner piers and attached columns are at once heftier than Donato Bramante's at the cloister of Santa Maria della Pace, Rome, and more graceful than Antonio da Sangallo's at the Palazzo Farnese, Rome.

—EDWARD W. WOLNER

SANTA MARIA DELLA SALUTE
Venice, Italy

1631-81. Architect: Baldassare Longhena (1598-1682).

Publications

SEMENZATO, CAMILLO: *L'architettura di Baldassare Longhena*. Padua, 1954.
SORAVIA, GIOVANNI BATTISTA: *Le chiese di Venezia descritte ed illustrate*. 3 vols. Venice, 1822-24.
WITTKOWER, RUDOLF: *Santa Maria della Salute*. New York, 1958.
WITTKOWER, RUDOLF: "Santa Maria della Salute." *Saggi e memorie di storia dell'arte* 3 (1963): 33-54.

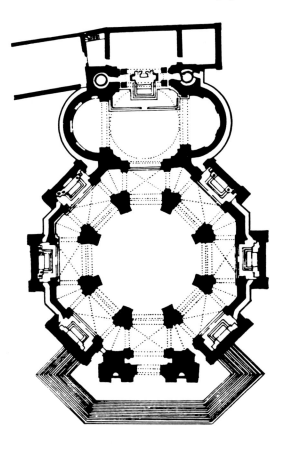

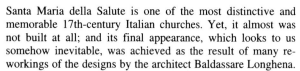
Santa Maria della Salute: Venice, Italy, 1631-81

Santa Maria della Salute is one of the most distinctive and memorable 17th-century Italian churches. Yet, it almost was not built at all; and its final appearance, which looks to us somehow inevitable, was achieved as the result of many reworkings of the designs by the architect Baldassare Longhena.

During the terrible plague of 1630, the doge and senate of the Republic of Venice decided to erect a church *ex voto.* Santa Maria della Salute, therefore, is primarily a votive temple, imbued with religious and civic symbolism. This duality is encapsulated in its name, meaning both Health and Salvation. Its conspicuous site, chosen by a commission of senators, where the Giudecca Canal and Grand Canal join the Bacino di San Marco, both parallels the hilltop sites of votive temples and marks the spot where the Dogana (customs house) joins the city. A symbol of health, well-being and the Virgin's protection of Venice, the church was thus also intended to function visually as an anchor for trade—that activity which was so risky, yet so essential, to the city. The prominent site and the expense were justified by the important political message the church was intended to convey.

When the competition was opened in 1631, 11 projects were submitted, but only two received serious consideration. These were Longhena's centrally planned church and a longitudinal design submitted by Fracao and Rubertini, praised for good distribution, good lighting and spaciousness. Stipulations included that the building should harmonize with the site and make a grand impression while leaving sufficient space for the building of a monastery—for the PP. Somaschi, the only religious order to have been founded in Venice. There were also three precise requirements: first, that from the entrance the whole church space should be visible unobstructed; second, that light should be evenly distributed throughout; third, and most interesting, that the high altar should dominate the view from

the main entrance, while the other altars should come into view as one proceeded toward the east end. To meet this last requirement, Longhena took over a dramatic device used in the Redentore Church by Andrea Palladio where the entrance to the chancel framed the high altar from the entrance most effectively. But whereas Palladio's church unfolds down a single axis, Longhena made new vistas open up around the spectator in all directions. From the entrance, only the high altar can be seen; from the center of the octagon, each altar is revealed.

Longhena chose a centralized plan for traditional, iconographic and aesthetic reasons. Not only was the urban setting best served by a centralized solution, but sanctuaries and churches dedicated to the Virgin were traditionally centrally planned. Moreover, for Longhena that form symbolized a divine mystery: "The mystery contained in the dedication of this church to the Blessed Virgin made me think, with what little talent God has bestowed on me, of building the church in *forma rotonda,* i.e., in the shape of a crown," Longhena himself wrote in his first report.

His plan is dominated by an octagon surrounded by an ambulatory, a late antique form, commonly used during the medieval period, but eschewed by Renaissance and post-Renaissance architects because the ambulatory makes it impossible to create a design with completely regular sub-units. By making the sides of consecutive pillars in the octagon parallel to each other (as at San Vitale, Ravenna), Longhena provided the visually important units of the ambulatory as well as the chapels with regular geometrical shapes.

Within the octagon, the visitor's lines of vision are carefully controlled as required by the commission. The octagon's centralization could not have been carried further: the sanctuary, up three steps, appears only loosely connected to it, following the north Italian Renaissance tradition of disjunction between

Santa Maria della Salute, high altar

most Venetian architecture, which depends on Venetian traditions. In particular, his debt to Palladio is great. Had the Venetian Republic not needed the support of the Catholic world in its struggle against the Turks, Santa Maria della Salute would have been even more starkly Venetian. As it was, four Venetian saints were replaced by angels so that on the dome the image of the Virgin, the symbol of Counter-Reformation ideology, was no longer rivaled by Venetian patriotism.

—HELEN HILLS

PALAZZO CHIERICATI
Vicenza, Italy

1550: Palazzo designed; **Architect:** Andrea Palladio (1508-80). **1554:** Construction halted; three left bays and first central bay completed. **Before 1557:** Frescoes and stuccowork begun; **Artists:** Bartolomeo Ridolfi and Eliodoro Forbicini. **17th century:** Construction completed according to Palladio's designs. **Late 17th century:** Roofline sculptures added. **1855:** Palazzo converted into municipal museum of Vicenza.

Publications

ACKERMAN, JAMES S.: *Palladio*. Harmondsworth, England, 1977.
GODFREY, F. M.: *Italian Architecture up to 1750*. New York, 1971.

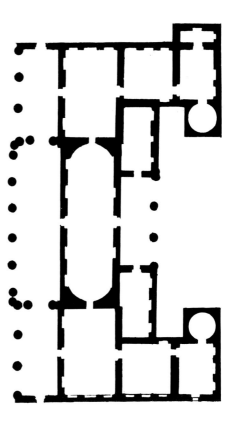

main room and sanctuary in centralized plans. Here, a secondary dome crowns an apsed space, where shape and details depend on IL Redentore: giant pilasters replace columns, and normal windows in two tiers replace the segmental mullioned windows of the octagon.

The exterior is dramatic and forcefully connected with the interior, in a manner very unlike that of the Roman architects of the time. The main facade, based on a triumphal arch motif, corresponds exactly to the interior arches of the octagon. Indeed, its conception as a *scena frons* is clear when the central door is open to reveal the series of consecutive arches inside. This drama was enacted annually on the Festa della Salute, held on the Feast of the Presentation of the Virgin, when the doge himself made a processional visit to the church. The 15 steps in front of the church refer to the Temple of Solomon in Jerusalem (where the Presentation itself was supposed to have occurred). Santa Maria della Salute should, then, be understood in terms of civic drama, rather like contemporary ephemeral architecture created for the celebration of significant politico-religious events.

The exterior of the chapels flanking the main entrance are treated like little facades and are, in fact, adaptations of Le Zitelle (ca. 1570) across the Giudecca.

The thrust of the large dome is carried through the vast picturesque scrolls resting on the arches of the ambulatory, so that the side walls of the chapels are abutments to the dome. The subsidiary dome, over the sanctuary, differs boldly from the main dome. Stilted in the Byzantine-Venetian tradition, it stands on a simple circular brick drum and is framed by two campanili.

Longhena stressed the originality of his design in two memoranda to the committee, but there is much in his church, as in

MAGRINI, A.: *Il palazzo del Museo Civico in Vicenza*. Vicenza, 1855.

PÉE, H.: *Die Palastbauten des Andrea Palladio*. Würzburg, 1939.

PUPPI, LIONELLO: *Andrea Palladio: The Complete Works*. New York, 1986.

WITTKOWER, RUDOLF: *Architectural Principles in the Age of Humanism*. New York, 1962.

WITTKOWER, RUDOLF: *Palladio and Palladianism*. New York, 1974.

WUNDRAM, M., and PAPE, T.: *Andrea Palladio 1508-1580: Architect Between the Renaissance and the Baroque*. Cologne, 1989.

ZORZI, GIAN GIORGIO: *Le opere pubbliche e i piazzi privati di Andrea Palladio*. Vicenza, 1965.

The urban residence planned by Andrea Palladio (1508-80) and his client, Giralomo Chiericati, in Vicenza remains one of the most singular domestic structures of the mid-16th century. The generally accepted image of "palazzo" is that of the earlier, austere Florentine tradition, to which the Palazzo Chiericati bears no relationship. Where familiar Tuscan Renaissance structures presented closed facades and turned inward toward their courtyards, Palladio's Palazzo Chiericati, although also arranged around a courtyard, flung open its facade on two levels and provided a new, alternative solution. To find any earlier residence with similar characteristics, one must turn to Roman frescoes at Stabia, where an artist of the first century B.C. painted a two-story, colonnaded villa open to the sea, but when Palladio

studied and observed in Rome, those frescoes remained buried under ash and lava. It should be remembered, however, that by the time of the Palazzo Chiericati in 1550, Palladio was thoroughly cognizant of the writings of the Roman architect-author Vitruvius, who provided him a direct line to antiquity and in whose writing he found descriptions of domestic architecture as well as advice about city planning. Palladio's own first-hand observations of extant ancient monuments provided him another ready architectural lexicon.

Vicenza's once-forlorn Piazza d'Isola, now Piazza Matteotti, supplied the site for the stucco-over-brick Palazzo Chiericati and encouraged Palladio to think in terms of redesigning the entire area. He intended the palazzo to be but one link in an encompassing chain of open loggias and adjacent structures surrounding the piazza, a vision unfortunately unfulfilled. Versions of the connecting-loggia device, recalling the Greek stoa, appeared in his later villa designs.

The Palazzo Chiericati as it exists today is remarkably faithful to Palladio's original drawings. Only his own changes to the second-level facade and the overwhelming roof-line sculptures added in the 17th century were absent in the initial design. The drawings demonstrate that ratio and proportion were to Palladio what they were to Donato Bramante, Leon Battista Alberti and other Renaissance architects, as well as to Vitruvius before them. For all, mathematics was the propelling force toward a harmonious solution, but Palladio's interpretations of harmony were not always those of his illustrious predecessors.

On the Palazzo Chiericati facade, the height of a column encounters expected repetition in the depth of the loggia and the decorative Ionic capitals find traditional placement on the second-level loggia above the more severe Doric capitals on

Palazzo Chiericati: Vicenza, Italy, 1550

the ground floor, but Palladio's design of the two superimposed colonnades contains some unexpected twists. The columns of the upper level do not dutifully diminish in height, as was customary in earlier Renaissance and classical design. Both colonnades are of the same height, an example of Palladio's personal decision-making. It is this pushing and pulling of accepted classical practice that led to the highly original solutions of the structure and the application of the term "Mannerism" to Palladio's architecture.

To Albertian and Vitruvian practices, Palladio contributed his Mannerist ingenuity and refinements, breaking away from more severe classicism. With the opened Chiericati facade, he leapt beyond classical preference by his design of a three-part vertical division of the facade. The center third of the palazzo facade advances slightly in front of the sections on either side of it and is marked by unexpected clusters of columns on the outer edges of the forward section. This innovation may have occurred for structural reasons, the needs of the client, artistic device, or all three reasons, but it demonstrates Palladio's pragmatic approach to the canons of antiquity. When his client reacted negatively to the small size of his grand salon, which resulted from the rhythmic repetition of the second loggia above the first, Palladio responded with a resourceful solution. He extended the salon space forward through the center section of the top exterior loggia and supported it below with the clusters of four columns. As a result, Chiericati had a salon of impressive dimensions in which to entertain his friends and Palladio had an unprecedented exterior solution with a three-part vertical facade composition.

A second incidence of Palladio's pragmatism is the use of the low podium, or crepidoma, on which he elevated the palazzo. Rather than completely resulting from a classical reference, however, the location of the site at the bottom of a rising street influenced the decision. Rain easily converted the Piazza d'Isola to marsh. By raising the mass of the building, Palladio avoided moisture problems and also provided space for storage of wine in cellars beneath the palazzo.

In the Chiericati, Palladio's use of mathematics to determine all its architectural relationships is clear; refinements, such as his use of multiples of six, became a signature. The foyer, in its length and width, echoes the proportions of the palazzo's rectangular plan on a smaller scale. Interior rooms, all with similar longitudinal axes, decrease progressively in floor area as they flow behind the facade, each room retaining one dimension of the room preceding it.

In addition to Palladio's adaptations of, and changes to, classical canons, and his years of study of the architecture of antiquity, it is well to remember that while he lived in Rome, he also eagerly absorbed the styles of Bramante, Raphael and Michelangelo, the titans of his own century. The Palazzo Chiericati strongly reflects Bramante's Tempietto of 1503. This involves more than the use of similar balusters between the bays on the *piano nobile* or the preference for the post-and-lintel bay system. Were the Chiericati's symmetrical facade molded into a circular form, it would immediately evoke the image of Bramante's influential Tempietto. And what evolving architectural talent living in Rome could avoid being dazzled by Michelangelo's powerful designs under way on the Campidoglio Hill and the rising dome of St. Peter's, also under construction?

These are the contemporary influences that the architect brought back to Vicenza and which found their way to the Palazzo Chiericati. In addition to Palladio's use of the alternating semicircular and triangular pediments Michelangelo favored above window entablatures, he elected to dress the pediments of the five centered windows of the grand salon with pairs of sculpted, reclining figures reminiscent of those found in

Michelangelo's Medici Chapel in Florence's San Lorenzo Church, a direct acknowledgement of the genius of the older master.

Palladio, like that other great synthesizer of the Renaissance, Raphael, drew on both past and contemporary styles to produce architecture that paid homage to all, but which became uniquely his own. Through his four books of architecture first published in 1570, Palladio, in turn, influenced centuries of later architectural design. His Palazzo Chiericati, which is in excellent condition, has functioned as Vicenza's municipal museum since 1855.

—PHILANCY N. HOLDER

LA ROTONDA (Villa Almerico)
Vicenza, Italy

Ca. 1567-68. Architect: Andrea Palladio (1508-80).

Publications

BURGER, FRITZ: *Die Villen des Andrea Palladio*. Leipzig, 1909.
GOEDICKE, CHRISTIAN; SLUSALLEK, KLAUS; and KUBELIK, MARTIN: "Thermoluminescence Dating in Architectural History: the Chronology of Palladio's Villa Rotonda." *Journal of the Society of Architectural Historians* 45 (December 1986): 396-407.
HEINEMANN, W.: *Die Villenbauten des Andrea Palladio*. Berlin, 1909.
ISERMEYER, C. A.: "Die Villa Rotonda von Palladio." *Zeitschrift für Kunstgeschichte* (1967): 207-221.

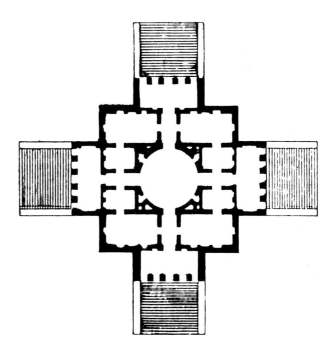

LOTZ, WOLFGANG: "The Rotonda: A Secular Building with a Dome." In *Studies in Italian Renaissance Architecture.* Cambridge, Massachusetts, 1977.

MANTESE, G.: "La Rotonda." *Vita Vicentina* 1 (1967): 23-24.

PUPPI, LIONELLO: *Andrea Palladio: The Complete Works.* New York, 1986.

SEMENZATO, C.: "La Rotonda di Andrea Palladio." *Bollettino del Centro Internazionale di Studi di Architettura "Andrea Palladio"* (1968).

ZORZI, GIAN GIORGIO: *Palladian Villas.* Venice, 1958.

ZORZI, GIAN GIORGIO: *La Rotonda di Andrea Palladio.* Vicenza, 1910.

*

Built in 1567-68 by Andrea Palladio, the Rotonda is properly known as the Villa Almerico, since it was designed for the wealthy Vicentine cleric Paolo Almerico following his departure from the papal court and his retirement to his home city.

Its design represents the culmination of Palladio's approach to the rural villa as a distinct cinquecento typology, a development that can be traced from his Villa Gazzotti at Bertesina (early 1540s) through the Villa Badoer at Fratta Polèsine (after 1556). The Rotonda was previously believed to date from about 1550, but recent research has confirmed that the building dates from the later 1560s, and it is thus correctly seen as a mature work of Palladio.

Most of Palladio's villas served two distinct practical functions as well as their aesthetic and symbolic ones. They were country retreats for a nobleman and his family to take their *villeggiatura,* their extended escape from the pressures of public life and the heat of the city summer; they were also working farmhouses, bases from which extensive estates were administered.

In most cases, therefore, the villa formed the nucleus for a group of ancillary, more utilitarian structures. During two decades, Palladio refined the basic form of his villas such that the house often had a symmetrical plan about one axis, with a principal facade to the approach road and *cortile,* while the

La Rotonda, Villa Capra: Vicenza, Italy, ca. 1567-68

other enjoyed views over the estate. The facades were simple, but classically derived, often incorporating a pediment and central portico. The shorter elevations had no prospect, but were extended by means of two long wings (*barchesse*) containing such ancillary functions of the "farmhouse villa" as barns, stables and storage for farm equipment. These wings, themselves sometimes terminating in smaller pavilions (such as those at Villa Barbaro, Maser) gave grandeur and scale to the overall symmetrical composition, with the villa prominent in the center.

The Villa Almerico departs from this highly developed arrangement in only one vital respect, which allowed Palladio to perfect the villa form there in a unique manner. The house stands on the brow of a low hill, close to the center of Vicenza; Palladio himself described the site as "suburban," and it was not therefore surrounded by extensive rural estates. Since the villa was to be so close to the city and was not to be a working farmhouse, it was not necessary for Palladio to provide the villa with *barchesse* or outbuildings; Almerico used the house chiefly to entertain friends from Vicenza who came to dine and admire the prospects. It is thus strictly hardly a villa at all, but rather a *belvedere,* a freestanding structure set in a landscape.

The specific site features further influenced Palladio's design. The eminence had attractive views in three directions, with the road approach from the fourth. This topography (and the lack of the need for *barchesse*) meant that he could design a fully centralized villa, with no defined front or back, but composed fully "in the round." The villa was thus intended to be seen from an infinite number of locations in the surrounding landscape, and from it, too, many different prospects could be seen.

The plan is therefore square, centralized on both axes. A series of rooms is ranged around the perimeter of the square, with four larger *saloni* in the corners. A smaller hallway is aligned on the center of each facade, and these four halls extend back into the body of the house, where they all converge on a central space, the famous rotunda from which the villa's popular name derives.

All of the chief spaces are designed according to a series of harmonic proportions, while the rotunda (loosely derived from the Roman Pantheon) unifies the whole spatial composition, receiving its light from a central lantern. The plan of the villa is extended outward on all four faces by prominent hexastyle Ionic porticoes, from which imposing steps lead down to the garden.

There is one principal story of accommodation, above a basement of ancillary rooms such as kitchens, and there is a low attic. The raising of the *piano nobile* not only conveniently locates these ancillary rooms, but gives the *piano nobile* more extensive views over the countryside.

All four facades are treated in the same manner. Palladio's use of the classical temple pronaos as a device for giving emphasis and *gravitas* to a villa entrance had by then been developed in his own work over twenty years. Although Palladio's pronaos was derived from classical sources, in antiquity the pronaos had been used only for temples; except for Giuliano da Sangallo's rather tentative version at the Villa Medici at Poggio, the device had never been used for a private house before Palladio. His own development of the motif had reached early maturity at the Villa Foscari ("La Malcontenta") in about 1560; there, too, a hexastyle portico projects well forward from the solid cube of the villa itself, and the *piano nobile* is again raised above a basement, with external steps down to the garden. At the Rotonda, though, the composition is balanced on all four sides, and given further centralization by the low dome, which unifies the rectangular and triangular forms below it.

What Palladio achieved at the Rotonda, therefore (but nowhere else), was a form that was pure and symmetrical from all vantage points, the porticoes and their steps reaching outward and downward into the landscape, while the landscape itself is partially enclosed within the intercolumniation of the spacious porticoes.

Palladio intended to develop this form even further at the Villa Trissino at Meledo, which was never built. This house, closely modeled on the Rotonda, was to form the centerpiece of a grandiose composition, again on the crest of a hill, but with *barchesse* and colonnades in terraces down the hillside from the summit of the villa itself. As a composition, this form (shown in the *Quattro Libri*) was to be extremely influential on later country houses and public buildings.

Indeed, the mature Palladian villa, exemplified by La Malcontenta and the Villa Almerico, was to have extensive influence, largely as a result of the publication of the *Quattro Libri* in 1570, and the many later translations. Lord Burlington's grand tour in 1715 and the English translations of the *Quattro Libri,* beginning in the same year, marked a turning point in Palladio's influence. Burlington and William Kent's Chiswick House and Colen Campbell's Mereworth are both direct *hommages* to the Rotonda; later, in the United States, Thomas Jefferson was strongly influenced by the villa, notably at Monticello (ca. 1770) and the State Capitol at Richmond, Virginia. The more general classical revival in Europe in the later 18th century led to a further "discovery" of the purity of Palladio's forms; in particular, the application of a temple portico to a wide variety of buildings of many different functions makes this element of the Palladian villa perhaps the most universally imitated of all architectural elements since the Renaissance.

—RICHARD J. GOY

NETHERLANDS

EIGEN HAARD HOUSING ESTATE
Amsterdam, Netherlands

1913-21. Architect: Michel de Klerk (1884-1924).

Publications

DE WIT, WIM (ed.): *The Amsterdam School, Dutch Expressionist Architecture, 1915-1930.* Cambridge, Massachusetts, 1983.

FRAMPTON, KENNETH, and FUTAGAWA, YUKIO: *Modern Architecture: 1851-1919.* New York, 1983.

FRANK, SUZANNE: *Michel De Klerk 1884-1923, Architect of the Amsterdam School.* New York, 1984.

KRAMER, PIET: "De Bouwwerken van Michel de Klerk." *Wendingen* 9-10 (1924).

SEARING, HELEN: "Eigen Haard: Workers' Housing and the Amsterdam School." *Architectura* 2 (1971): 148-175.

SHARP, DENNIS: "Michel de Klerk and the Eigen Haard Development." *GA Houses* 3 (1979): 8-23.

*

The decorative form of expression which became known as the Amsterdam school gained recognition through the work of Michel de Klerk. Probably the most significant example of the Amsterdam school's earlier years is de Klerk's work for the Eigen Haard Housing Society at the Spaarndammerplantsoen in Amsterdam. There are in fact three blocks of housing designed by de Klerk at this site in which it is possible to trace the origins of the style. The first block was designed for the Hille Company and the other two for Eigen Haard, whose name means "Own Hearth."

De Klerk's success at the Eigen Haard scheme was to provide the formal attributes of urban architecture while at the same time developing the style of expressionism of the Amsterdam school. The first block, designed for Hille, indicates possible formal precedents for the style. De Klerk provided parabolic gable devices on the elevation, which are reminiscent of the work of the Viennese architect of the Secession, Joseph Maria Olbrich. In previous work for Hille, de Klerk had used wavelike patterns in timber and wrought-iron detailing.

De Klerk drew upon several sources for his inspiration, but he worked best when designing in traditional materials. His skill in detailing of tilework, brick and timber can be seen in the first of the Eigen Haard schemes. Tilework and polychromatic brickwork are used to provide a lively elevational expression of curvilinear treatment. Also of note on this block are the formal motifs of cylindrical forms used to express communal entrances and give emphasis to the corners. This motif would be incorporated into the work of other designers of the Amsterdam school.

When the Eigen Haard scheme is discussed, the work usually referred to is that of de Klerk's second block for the society. The scheme was developed on a triangular plot of land with a sharp apex, and the block varied in height from one to five stories; also, a school not designed by de Klerk had to be incorporated into the design. Due to the form and detailing, the scheme is known as "The Ship." Indeed, during the renovation of the scheme one source of inspiration for de Klerk was clearly apparent, for the timber-roof superstructure at the apex of the block revealed construction reminiscent of the hull of a boat.

The anomaly found at Eigen Haard, and in other work by the Amsterdam school, is that the rich formal expression given to the housing schemes contrasted with rather basic plan types for the dwellings. This was a result of the way planning was organized in Amsterdam, for while the plan types were to a large extent determined by the builder, the appearance had to be acceptable to "commissions of beauty." Thus, while the basis of Eigen Haard was that of the provision of social housing for workers, de Klerk was required to provide a satisfactory aesthetic solution. However, this form of design has been criticized as merely facade architecture.

De Klerk's architectural language at Eigen Haard incorporates ideas and detailing from Indonesian design; there are also features associated with northern European villages and examples of decorative motifs, symbolic elements and formal expression. Yet, the design of Eigen Haard does not appear eclectic, for de Klerk had drawn these disparate features into a unified urban composition.

Two of the most delightful features of the scheme, which illustrate the refinement of de Klerk's architecture, occur at the opposite end of the block from the highly expressionist form of the post office at the apex. One of these features is an oriel-bay bulbous form that is expressed in brick detailing and extends over three stories at a corner of the block. The form tapers with increase in height, but despite the complexity of the device, de Klerk accomplished the design with consummate ease. The other feature of note is a spire that is a part of a reentrant feature of the perimeter block. The spire is essentially a formal device; it is part of de Klerk's concept of an urban village and possibly relates to sketches he made on a study visit to Scandinavia prior to work on this scheme.

Although de Klerk did not visit the Dutch East Indies, there was keen interest in the forms of Indonesia in Holland and de Klerk was in close contact with the people who had visited Indonesia, such as the first influence on his work, Ed Cuypers, who introduced de Klerk to the formal aspects of architecture. This influence can be found in a small hut for the Eigen Haard Housing Society in the central court of the scheme, which is almost a literal interpretation of an Indonesian village hut. Also, the detailing of doorways, sometimes with prow-like forms, is evocative of an eastern influence.

In terms of the historical development of the period, de Klerk's work for Eigen Haard should not be underestimated. Other than the use of parabolic and curvilinear devices, a connection with art nouveau is difficult to define. De Klerk's work is basically artistic and decorative. The inventiveness of the expressionist forms was more complex and developed earlier than north German expressionism. De Klerk and the Amsterdam school, particularly at Eigen Haard, sought to reconcile a complexity of formal devices with urban expression.

—E. S. BRIERLEY

Zaanstraat Flats, Eigen Haard Housing: Amsterdam, Netherlands, 1913-21

HERENGRACHT
Amsterdam, Netherlands

16th century: Development of "Three Canal Plan"; **Architect:** Franz Hendrickszoon Oetgens. **1612ff:** Construction of "Three Canal Plan."

Publications

VERMEULEN, FRANS A. J.: *Handboek tot de Geschiedenis der Nederlandsche Bouwkunst.* 3 vols. The Hague, 1928-41.

Amsterdam is one of the few great cities of Europe which have preserved the appearance of a single short time period in the city center. In the case of Amsterdam, that period was the 17th century. The development of the cityscape, according to a plan determined by unified aesthetic principles, is particularly clearly visible today on the Herengracht. The development of the Herengracht both reflects urbanistic and architectural developments and gives insight into the social relationships of this city of merchants at the highest moment of its development.

To gain a proper understanding of the architecture of the Herengracht, an overview of the history of the city is indispensable. It was not until 1275 that Amsterdam obtained city privileges. What was then a fishing village could consequently be

Herengracht: Amsterdam, Netherlands, 17th century

expanded on both sides of the Amstel River into an extensive settlement. The damming up of the Amstel and the diversion of the river to the left and right of the old riverbed created the basic urban structure. The city's first layout was completed with fortifications, and ditches and canals, which reshaped the mouth of the Amstel into a delta. The "Three Canal Plan" was a significant further expansion of the existing structure. It was developed at the end of the 16th century by Frans Hendrickszoon Oetgens, who was later to become burgomaster, and the city carpenter Hendrick Jacobszoon Straets, with the participation of the surveyor Lucas Dackerts. The plan called for a tripling of the developed area to 800 hectares, and drew on the building code of 1565. That code, which remained in force until the 19th century, regulated the installation and inspection of foundation piles, the sanitary arrangements of the buildings, and the construction and financing of streets and walks. The plan for the expansion of Amsterdam, which was passed by the citizenry after intense debate, had become necessary as a consequence of enormous population increases in the wake of the blockade of Antwerp and the Scheldt River by the Spanish in 1585. The blockade had spurred a massive flow of refugees to Amsterdam, so that the population jumped from 32,000 in 1567 to 105,000 in 1622. The influx of merchants from the southern Low Countries, with their farflung mercantile connections, reaching from the Levant to Russia, caused an enormous economic upsurge. By 1609, Amsterdam maintained shipping connections with nearly 700 ports. A further consequence was the foundation of the Commodities and Stock Exchange on the Dam in 1612. The construction of canals according to the "Three Canal Plan," begun in 1612 by the surveyor and architect Daniel Stolpaert,

allowed merchant ships to sail into the center of the city.

The construction of the Herengracht had a determining influence on future developments. With its width of 22 meters, it functioned as a thoroughfare, the Keizersgracht and Prinsengracht being subsidiary arteries. All three canals ended at the present Leidsegracht. Smaller canals and cross streets connected the main canals, creating segments further subdivided with gardens and courtyards. A defensive wall some 8 kilometers long, fitted out with 26 bastions, surrounded the newly developed area. The work of laying the foundations of the quays, banking up the building sites and erecting the walls and buildings themselves was accomplished with the simplest tools. The community supplied cheap labor by sentencing convicts to forced labor on the construction of canals.

The "Three Canal Plan" not only subdivided the newly developed city area, but assigned different sections to different social strata. The three grand canals were reserved for the leading merchants with their monumental town houses. The petty bourgeois, artisans, immigrants and Jews lived in the area to the west, the "Jordaan" (from the French "*Jardin*"). As a whole, the "Three Canal Plan" reflected Baroque planning principles, which also shaped the 17th-century fortifications. At the same time, the plan pursued the Renaissance ideal of the star-shaped city. The mighty self-representation of a citizenry dominated by prosperous merchants was expressed in the planning and development of the Herengracht. More than a question of aesthetics, urban planning and architecture became a medium of propaganda.

Engravings of the 18th century in particular evoke an accurate image of the architecture of the Herengracht with its connected facades, an architecture which in many instances has been preserved. The bridge over the Leidsegracht offers the best view of the unified design of the ensemble, for which master Justus Vingboons (1620/21-98) and his brother Philips (1614-78) were responsible. Two types of houses are to be found in the ranges along the canal. One type has a high, generally four-story facade, with three windows on each floor, and is crowned by a tall, narrow gable with curved sides. The facade is invariably set over a basement also pierced by windows. Stoops consisting of two flights of stairs laid parallel to the wall complete the designs. While this building type was a variant of the typical town house of the Low Countries, the other type used villa and palace architecture in a Palladian style. The facades are wider and afford space for five windows on each of the three or four stories. The center sometimes projects in the manner of a bay. Most are crowned with a gable done in an antique manner. Classical elements, however, are also present in the first type, mostly in the form of pediments over the windows, doors and gables, or as garlands under the windows. By and large, however, the facades remained unornamented. The large windows, admitting as much light as possible to the interiors, dominate the designs. The reduction of decorative elements, a consciousness of hygiene and the cementing of social barriers by means of architecture may all be seen as reflexes of a Calvinist ethic, which was the spiritual foundation of the Dutch economy.

—KUNIBERT BERING
Translated from the German by Marijke Rijsberman

SCHEEPVAARTHUIS
Amsterdam, Netherlands

1912-15. Architects: J. M. van der Mey (1868-1949), Michel de Klerk (1884-1924) and Pieter L. Kramer. **1925:** Enlargement.

Publications

DE WIT, WIM (ed.): *The Amsterdam School, Dutch Expressionist Architecture, 1915-1930.* 1984.
FANELLI, GIOVANNI: *Architettura moderna in Olanda: 1900-1940.* Florence, 1968.
Nederland Bouwt in Baksteen: 1800-1940. Rotterdam, 1941.
Nederlandse Architectuur, 1910-1930: Amsterdamse School. Amsterdam, 1975.
OUD, J. J. P.: *Holländische Architektur.* Munich, 1926.
VAN ZUYDEWIJN, H. J. F. DE ROY: *Amsterdamse Bouwkunst, 1815-1940.* Amsterdam, 1969.

The Scheepvaarthuis in Amsterdam was the first significant monument of the Amsterdam school of Dutch expressionism. Its triumvirate of designers, J. M. van der Mey, Michel de Klerk and Pieter L. Kramer, had all worked for various periods in the office of Eduard Cuypers. Cuypers in turn was the nephew of P. J. H. Cuypers, the designer of the Rijksmuseum (1885) and the Amsterdam Central Station (1890) and the most important 19th-century Dutch eclectic architect. Between the elder Cuypers and the young trio of Scheepvaarthuis designers stands the magisterial example of Hendrik Petrus Berlage.

Berlage's Amsterdam Exchange (1897-1903) stands as perhaps the most significant building in the history of Dutch architecture. In it Berlage purged the Dutch brick-building tradition of its eclectic ornamentation and subordinated it to the integrity of the flat wall plane, relieved by architectonic sculpture. Berlage thus returned to primitive forms and to the facts of construction as an antidote to an exhausted eclectic tradition. This severe style of Berlage, subsequently employed on other commissions, exerted an immense influence on Dutch designers in the first decade of the century, but became ultimately a stale orthodoxy against which the best and brightest of the rising generation rebelled. This certainly describes Michel de Klerk, who became the seminal genius of the Amsterdam school.

De Klerk availed himself of the liberal working conditions in Eduard Cuypers' atelier to undertake a number of unexecuted projects in which the style of the Scheepvaarthuis was progressively developed. Despite the fact that van der Mey was the first to leave Cuypers' employ and organized the new studio, de Klerk must be regarded as its primary designer. Pieter Kramer would subsequently follow de Klerk's lead in developing Dutch expressionism, achieving particular prominence after de Klerk's premature death in 1924. Van der Mey remained at best a minor figure in the Amsterdam school.

The Scheepvaarthuis necessarily invites comparison to Berlage's Exchange, both for its similarities and for its striking antitheses. Like the Exchange, it uses the traditional Dutch building material—brick—complemented by architectonic sculpture and the other decorative arts. The Scheepvaarthuis designers extracted these elements from the severe Berlagian style, however, and developed them to "Baroque excess," as Berlage later described de Klerk's work. The disciplined wall surfaces of the elder master dissolve in the Scheepvaarthuis into a veritable orgy of inventive detail. Novel effects of brick coursing, carved stone sculpture, ornamental woodcarving and wrought iron are orchestrated into a restless pattern of surface effects in which angular forms replace the mural integrity of Berlage's style. Sculpture by H. A. van den Eynde and Hildo Krop, wrought iron by Theodore Nieuwenhuis, and art glass by Willem Bogtman complement the architectural detail. Thus the Scheepvaarthuis, and by extension the Amsterdam school which it initiated, continued the tradition of the ensemble as a total work of art (*Gesamtkunstwerk*) which the art nouveau embodied at the turn of the century, imparting a special preciocity to the heritage of the Arts and Crafts movement.

By 1914 the *Gesamtkunstwerk* had been preempted in much of Europe by the concepts of serial production and industrial design associated with the Deutscher Werkbund. From this perspective then, the Scheepvaarthuis appears conservative if not retardataire. This is even more apparent if one considers the reinforced-concrete structure of the Scheepvaarthuis, designed by Adolf van Gendt. Unlike Berlage's Exchange, where bearing walls and structure are frankly expressed, the concrete frame of the Scheepvaarthuis is masked by an intricate applied facade. So although the inventive virtuosity of de Klerk and his colleagues temporarily breathed new life into the Dutch brick-building tradition, the mannered conservatism of the Scheepvaarthuis prefigured the ultimate failure of Dutch expressionism.

The plan of the Scheepvaarthuis was at first appearance dictated by its site—an irregular angle between the Prins Hendrikkade and the Waalseilandsgracht. Originally the building presented an asymmetrical facade to the Prins Hendrikkade; its enlargement in 1925 repositioned the original end pavilion as a central bay. The site was a basic flatiron configuration, with the main entrance porch at the salient angle leading to the lobby and central, top-lighted stairhall. If this configuration was hardly

Scheepvaarthuis: Amsterdam, Netherlands, 1912-15

original, it did invite a strategy of planning by triangulation, reinforcing the angular morphology of the ornamental detail. This appears in the details of the internal stairhall as well, the only point where the concrete structure is at all visible to inspection. The flatiron site also suggested the profile of a ship, thus giving rise to a symbolic connection between the building's form and its function as a shipping office. Such gestalt identification may seem tenuous to functionalist critics, but it became part of the Scheepvaarthuis' mystique and presumably influenced Fritz Höger's Chilehaus in Hamburg (1923-24).

The Scheepvaarthuis, the seminal monument of Dutch expressionism, was in place in the neutral Netherlands by 1916, when Germany was still embroiled in the war. The spiritual angst and catharsis often used to explain German expressionism played no role in the Netherlands, where the Amsterdam school, ultimately related by both similarity and antithesis to the earlier work of H. P. Berlage, very nearly became the national style in the late teens and early twenties, despite the competing claims of De Stijl. Nearly but not quite, for it must be admitted that the Amsterdam school contained the seeds of its own demise—seeds already apparent in the Scheepvaarthuis. It turned back to the spirit of eclectic and picturesque detail of P. J. H. Cuypers and ignored the reductive, even primitive, conservatism of H. P. Berlage. By the early 1930s Dutch architects had abandoned the Amsterdam school, either for a return to the explicit eclecticism of the Delft Reaction, or to the functional and structural rationalism of the International Style. The Scheepvaarthuis is thus a monument to a fascinating but ultimately transitory episode of modern architecture.

—JAY C. HENRY

STOCK EXCHANGE
Amsterdam, Netherlands

1898-1903. Architect: Hendrik Petrus Berlage (1856-1934).

Publications

BANHAM, REYNER: *Theory and Design in the First Machine Age.* New York, 1960.

BERLAGE, HENDRIK PETRUS: *Amerikaansche Reisherinneringen.* Rotterdam, Netherlands, 1913.

BERLAGE, HENDRIK PETRUS: *Concerning Style in Architecture and the Art of Furniture-Making.* 1904.

BERLAGE, HENDRIK PETRUS: *Gedanken über Stil in der Baukunst.* Leipzig, 1905.

BERLAGE, HENDRIK PETRUS: *Grundlagen und Entwicklung der Architektur.* Berlin, 1908.

BERLAGE, HENDRIK PETRUS: ''The Relationship between Architecture and Society.'' *De Beweging* 1 (January 1916): 5.

E. R.: Article on Amsterdam Stock Exchange. *De Eendracht* (14 November 1903).

EISLER, M.: *Der Baumeister Berlage.* 1921.

FANELLI, GIOVANNI: *Architettura moderna in Olanda 1900-1940.* Florence, 1968.

FRAMPTON, KENNETH, and FUTAGAWA, YUKIO: *Modern Architecture: 1851-1919.* New York, 1983.

GRATEMA, H. P.: *Berlage Bouwmeester.* 1925.

GRINBERG, DONALD: *Housing in the Netherlands 1900-1940.* Netherlands, 1977.

Stock Exchange: Amsterdam, Netherlands, 1898-1903

POLANO, S.: *Hendrik Petrus Berlage: Complete Works*. New York, 1988.

REININK, ADRIAAN WESSEL: *Amsterdam en de Beurs van Berlage: Reacties van tijdgenoten*. The Hague, 1975.

SEARING, HELEN: "Berlage and Housing, 'the most significant modern building type.'' *Nederlands Kunsthistorisch Jaarboek* 25 (1974): 133-179.

SINGELENBERG, PIETER, and BOCK, MANFRED: *H. P. Berlage, Bouwmeester, 1856-1934*. The Hague, 1975.

SINGELENBERG, PIETER: *H. P. Berlage: Idea and Style—The Quest for Modern Architecture*. Utrecht, 1972.

"Un architetto e una città: Berlage ad Amsterdam." *Casabella* 249 (March, 1961): 36-53.

*

For three decades Hendrik Petrus Berlage was preeminent in the architectural profession in the Netherlands. The new Amsterdam Stock Exchange was the cornerstone of his national and international reputation.

Between 1898 and 1903 Berlage gradually refined both his formal language and theory of architecture in the crucible of the controversy surrounding the design and building of a new Stock Exchange for Amsterdam. He had made significant advances in the immediately preceding years in his designs for "De Algemeene" (Amsterdam, 1892-94), and "De Nederlanden van 1845" (The Hague, 1894-95; Amsterdam, 1895-96), but the full development and integration of these ideas were achieved in the Stock Exchange.

The Exchange was to be an important focus for the aspirations of the city fathers and, in many ways, of the nation as a whole; so it is small wonder that its design was fraught with controversy. The symbolic potential and scope for political chicanery had produced a plethora of designs from all manner of architects as early as the 1870s, and a series of competitions followed in the 1880s, all without a definite result. The scandal continued until 1896 when the new chairman of the Exchange committee, M. W. F. Treub, suggested the appointment of Berlage as "artistic adviser." In the event, he did not just advise; behind closed doors he prepared completely new designs of his own.

During the full period of his involvement in the design of the Exchange (which he began as early as 1884), the plan changed remarkably little because the brief had been clearly and fully worked out at an early stage. It was the stylistic development that was so radical.

In the competition design of 1885 the Exchange was a palatial Dutch Renaissance building with a close relationship to the Oude Kerk, and the new Central Station then still under construction by the great P. J. H. Cuypers. Both were only a short walk away. Berlage had clearly mastered this historicist idiom, and there was plenty of scope for contributions by craftsmen and artists.

From 1896, when Berlage was appointed "aesthetic adviser" to the project, the design began its radical transformation. The national rationalism of Cuypers gave place to a direct influence by Eugène-Emmanuel Viollet-le-Duc, evident in the projecting main entrance, which is related to a drawing by Viollet-le-Duc for Pierrefonds.

Increasing sobriety of detail can be seen in the treatment of the tower in drawings of 1897, but more important is Berlage's growing concern with the handling of planes and volumes, and the new role of mathematics in the coordination of the elements of architecture. The "definitive" design (a term used advisedly because the building continued to evolve on site) of 1898 shows how tightly mathematics controlled the architectural composition. The diagonal grid is based on the "Egyptian triangle," described by Viollet-le-Duc in his *Entretiens*.

As Berlage maintained in his first book, *Concerning Style in Architecture and the Art of Furniture-Making* (1904), what is true in principle of the building on a large scale is true of furniture and design on a small scale. Strict geometrical control was exercised in the design of all the fittings, furniture and objects of use as well as elements of architecture.

Architecture was by no means a neutral matrix for the development of an iconographic scheme, as appears to have been more the case in the 1885 competition design. Its rational, ordering principles of mathematics and structure, and indeed the very materials themselves, all became the bearers of meaning in later designs. In 1911 Berlage wrote in "Concerning Brick": "Doesn't a building in brick embody the democratic idea in a way?" considering its unity in plurality.

In Berlage's work, each material is recognized as having its own character and proper function arising out of that character and its capabilities. Brick produced the beautifully modulated wall plane; hewn stone, transitional elements; and iron, miraculous spans. Each has its own function, and its characteristic color allows that function to be clearly read within a restrained structural polychromy.

Unity of purpose, diversity of function—"unity in diversity"—was both an architectural and a social principle for Berlage. The unity in diversity of the society, he believed, can be read in the contemporary style of architecture. Berlage maintained in his article "The Relationship between Architecture and Society" that "The architectural style puts its stamp on the whole period and is the yardstick for the whole culture. A stylistic relationship arises amongst all the different arts." (*De Beweging*, I, January 1916, p.5). The role of the architect in this process is obviously central. It is the architect who is the leader, the coordinator whose function it is to establish "unity in diversity" and eventually "unity between opposites," which was the program of the Exchange.

Berlage chose collaborators whose linear, tectonic stylistic development was closely related to his own. True to his rationalistic training, the technical means were crucial. The machine and industrial processes were a hallmark of the age, and mechanized stylistic forms were already emerging in the arts. Forms were to be "naturally geometric" or crystalline.

A. J. Derkinderen, Jan Toorop and R. N. Roland-Holst were the painters in Berlage's team. On the same principle he added Lambertus Zijl (for stonework) and J. Mendes da Costa (for woodwork). There was a most fascinating addition to this inner circle, the poet Albert Verwey, who together with Berlage worked out the iconographic scheme. Their theme was a utopian Amsterdam; architect and artists were to be instruments of social change.

The painting, woodwork and sculpture were all vigorous, but none was allowed to dominate or disturb the unity of the building. Characteristically even the angular sculptures of Zijl were all carved back into the wall, remaining subordinate to the architecture and allowing the wall plane to continue unbroken. The iconographic program is about trade and its function in society, but it was not calculated to flatter the brokers; and the paintings by Roland-Holst represent trade and industry, and as one might expect from the husband of Henriette Roland-Holst, an early feminist/socialist writer, the sympathy is for labor.

This polemic was not lost on contemporaries. Soon after the Exchange was opened an article signed only with the initials E. R. appeared in the magazine of the Christian Workers' Union

in Eindhoven. E. R. wrote: "Let the conscious worker consider this building thoughtfully. . . . It is not the spare simplicity of the Exchange which gives it its beauty, but that it is the manifestation of the great movement of its age, the people's movement." (*De Eendracht*, November 14, 1903).

The Netherlands at that time was a divided society. Berlage would not have considered the Exchange to be a perfected *Gesamtkunstwerk*, because this division was reflected in its architecture. The actual client for the building was the people of Amsterdam, not specifically the brokers; and he built very much on behalf of his client. Nevertheless, the institution Berlage was housing was antipathetic to many of his own stated ideals. An architecture of paradox can never be completely resolved, but as an embodiment of an ideal it can be, as in the Exchange, breathtaking in its clarity and precision.

—ALLAN DOIG

WESTERKERK
Amsterdam, Netherlands

1613-31. Architect: Hendrik de Keyser (1565-1621). **1638:** Tower completed. **1685:** Eastern gallery added.

Publications

HITCHCOCK, HENRY-RUSSELL: *Netherlandish Scrolled Gables of the Sixteenth and Early Seventeenth Centuries*. New York, 1978.

KEYSER, HENDRIK DE: *Architectura moderna*. Amsterdam, 1631. Facsimile edition: Soest, Netherlands, 1971.

NEURDENBURG, ELISABETH: *Hendrick de Keyser: Beeldhouwer en Bouwmeester van Amsterdam*. Amsterdam, 1929.

OZINGA, M. D.: *De Protestantsche Kerkenbouw in Nederland van Hervorming tot franschen Tijd*. Amsterdam, 1929.

ROSENBERG, JAKOB; SLIVE, SEYMOUR; and TER KUILE, E. H.: *Dutch Art and Architecture: 1600-1800*. 3rd ed. Harmondsworth, England, 1977.

VERMEULEN, FRANS A. J.: *Handboek tot de Geschiedenis der Nederlandsche Bouwkunst*. 3 vols. The Hague, 1928-41.

*

In 1613, in the heyday of the city's prosperity following the Spanish capture of Antwerp a generation before, a start was made on the third and most important enlargement of Amsterdam, including the concentric Herengracht, Keizersgracht and Prinsengracht, and the Jordaan.

To the city's formerly Catholic churches (of which only two out of the six, the Oude Kerk and the Nieuwe Kerk, survive in their original form) were added three others, the Zuiderkerk (South Church, 1611), the Noorderkerk (North Church, 1623) and the Westerkerk (West Church). For the last and finest the city council commissioned Hendrick de Keyser, who had already designed the other two, and chose a splendid site between the Keizersgracht and the Prinsengracht—actually at a bend in the latter allowing an unimpeded view of the tower from two sides (the wide Raadhuisstraat which opens up the south side still further was not formed until 1895-96). The Zuiderkerk was the only church of the three which de Keyser was to see completed.

Primarily a sculptor, his most famous work being the tomb

Westerkerk: Amsterdam, Netherlands, 1610-30

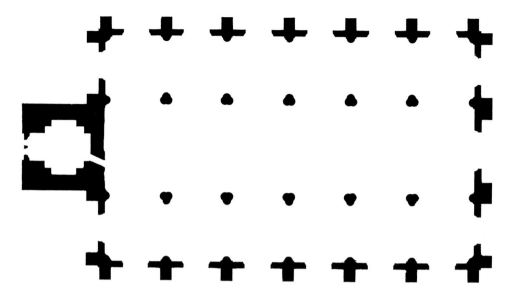

effigy of Prince William the Silent in the New Church at Delft, de Keyser was only secondarily an architect, engineer and inventor. Yet his impress was evident on many of the important buildings of that first quarter of the so-called Golden Century, including also the Montelbaanse and Mint towers, the Haarlemmerpoort, the East India House and the Old Exchange on the Rokin. He worked in other Dutch towns and even as far afield as Denmark.

Church building had virtually stood still for two centuries, except that the old Catholic churches had had to be reordered by the Reformers in order to give priority to preaching instead of emphasizing the high altar. The proclamation of the Word of God centered on the pulpit, and the pulpit could not go where the altar had been because the Word spoken from that distance in a large building became unintelligible. So the pulpit was placed in the middle of the nave.

The oldest specifically Protestant church in Holland, that at Willemstad (begun 1594), eight-sided with no columns to block the view of the preacher, is a type that was often followed subsequently, an equal-armed Greek cross in its internal layout. The Westerkerk, however, reverted in a sense to the traditional plan, a Latin cross within a rectangle, but here with two bold transepts instead of only one. Of the six bays the second and the fifth open into cross arms with ridges almost as high as the nave—much more emphatically than at the Zuiderkerk. So the Westerkerk can actually be considered as two Greek crosses side by side with the pulpit at the point of junction. Externally this duality stands out strongly in the pairs of steep gable ends to the transepts—variants of the traditional Dutch "bell" gables, topped by miniature pediments—and further emphasis and strength are provided by pairs of entablatured columns in two stories, forming buttresses at every outer corner of the transepts and of the body of the church. The disposition of spaces and volumes is still medieval, but the effect has ceased to be Gothic. Leaving aside the classical details, this is just as much due to the cool, clear, generous light of plain windows—15 at the lower level and 21 at the upper. Because the church stands relatively free of other buildings (which in Holland is unusual in the center of a great town), the lightness is a powerful factor. Outside is warm brown brick with mathematically precise white stone dressings. Inside is the reverse; white walls contrast with the gray sandstone (now painted) of columns, arches and vault ribs. The windows too are medieval in general shape but are subdivided throughout in an insistent rhythm of nine small panes, three by three, and with tracery reinterpreted in a classical manner.

Ingeniously, each internal pier is a cluster of three Doric columns, two of them supporting the semicircular arches and the upper walls of the nave, and one the transverse ribs of the aisle vaults. Above the arches an entablature disembodied from the columns forms a base for a row of flat pilasters, which punctuate the tall clerestory and support a wooden barrel vault that broadens at each junction with the transepts into octopartite squares. An eastern gallery, a separate wooden superstructure on stone Doric columns, was added in 1685 for orphan children and was the scene of a tragic collapse of the roof in 1704.

As well as the hexagonal pulpit with its curving stair and great canopy, other rich woodwork (altered and simplified over the years) contrasts with the cool clarity of the interior. Enclosed pews surround many of the column bases, and stalls are ranged in two banks against the outer walls. The organ, originally by the celebrated builder Roelof Duijschot, was installed in 1683-86 and is largely housed in the tower. Its case, standing on four marble Ionic columns and six pilasters, is embellished beneath with luxuriant acanthus leaves, an angel and a pair of cherubs holding garlands, and above with other rich carvings and paintings. At the east end of the church are two ornate oak entrance lobbies with Corinthian columns at their corners, the northeast one being crowned with an open arched and domed *templum*. Outside, the rather ponderous stone door surrounds shelter-carved emblems of mortality, typical of the 17th century, under segmental pediments.

The tower, known as Lange Jan ("Long John"), appears in countless views of the city. When the church was opened in 1631, ten years after de Keyser's death, only the massive brick lower part up to the balustrade had been completed. This, rising to just above the nave ridge, is of three stories, with pairs of louvered belfry windows in the top stage. Its giant scale becomes evident at close quarters when one sees the generously sized *koster*'s house, nestling against the south face, with its own three stories rising no higher than the tower's bottom stage. The thickening of the angles into broad piers gives a tremendous sense of strength and power, and leaves no doubt about the safety of the steeple above.

De Keyser had intended the steeple to be similar to that of the Zuiderkerk, the lowest of the three stages being square with engaged Doric pillars (as in fact they exist, though at the Zuiderkerk they are freestanding, and there the tower is at a

Westerkerk

corner of the church). Above would have been an octagonal and a hexagonal stage, of wood clothed with lead and very open in design so as to let the bell sounds out (in the Low Countries the smaller carillon bells are hung high on open steeples). Here there are 42 bells altogether. Drawings exist showing in precise detail what de Keyser intended. Whether the steeple as built was redesigned by his son Peter or by the father's assistant Cornelis Danckerts (a bricklayer by trade) or by another designer, Jacob van Campen, has long been a matter of controversy. As completed in 1638, the steeple virtually repeats in its two top stages the design of the lowest, with corner columns at each level and diminishing in size as it rises. On top, as de Keyser always intended, is a large imperial crown, Amsterdam's privileged civic symbol awarded in 1486 by Maximilian, emperor of Austria. In addition, on the four sides of the bottom stage of the steeple (here also timber-framed but faced with stone) are shields of the city arms in high relief—further proof, if any were needed, of Amsterdammers' pride in one of their most distinguished buildings, where Rembrandt lies buried and where their queen was married.

—ANTHONY NEW

SCHRÖDER HOUSE
Utrecht, Netherlands

1923-24. Architect: Gerrit Rietveld (1888-1964), with Truus Schröder.

Publications

BROWN, THEODORE M.: *The Work of Gerrit Rietveld, Architect.* Cambridge, Massachusetts, 1970.
FRAMPTON, KENNETH, and FUTAGAWA, YUKIO: *Modern Architecture: 1920-1945.* New York, 1983.
HOFMANN, WERNER, and KULTERMANN, UDO: *Modern Architecture in Color.* New York, 1970.
NAGAO, S., and TOMINAGA, Y.: "The Schröder House (1924)." *Space Design* (March 1976).
"Niet een landhuis maar een gewoon huis." *Bouwkundig Weekblad* 44 (The Hague, 1926).
OVERY, PAUL: *The Rietveld Schröder House.* Cambridge, Massachusetts, 1988.
RIETVELD, GERRIT: *Schröder Huis.* Amsterdam, 1963.
Rietveld Schröderhuis 1925-1975. Exhibition catalog. Utrecht, 1975.
SALOMON, ITZAK: "Mrs. Schroder and Her House." *Forum* (May 1980).

*

The Schröder House in Utrecht, designed by Gerrit Rietveld in collaboration with his client Truus Schröder, has arguably been more influential than any other domestic building of its time, with its flexible, partionable, open first-floor space and built-in equipment and furniture. Together with his Red Blue Chair, the prototype of which was designed in about 1918, the house was to become one of the icons of De Stijl and of the Modern Movement, with which Rietveld was associated from 1919. The house, in which Schröder lived for 60 years until her death in 1985, has been painstakingly restored, and is open to the public.

The interior owed much to Schröder, particularly the sliding and folding partitions that divide the first-floor space in seven different ways. (She also worked with Rietveld on a number of other designs from the 1920s until the 1950s, specializing in the organization of the interiors and the use of color.) When its plan was first published, the house was credited to Rietveld and Schröder, but after World War II, with the institutionalization of modernism and its largely male pioneers, Schröder's name was omitted from the credits.

In 1921 Rietveld had redesigned a room for Schröder in the large, rambling, 19th-century apartment in central Utrecht where she lived with her family. After her husband died in 1923 she asked him to work on a new house where she and her three children could live more intimately. Rietveld wanted a completely open-plan first floor, but she insisted on partitions that could be closed, open, or placed in a variety of half-open, half-closed combinations to create different spaces for living, sleeping, entertaining and working. This area included bedrooms for Schröder's son and two daughters, and a dining/sitting area. Only the lavatory and bathroom and her own tiny bedroom, in which there was room for little more than the bed, were separated. Downstairs the house was organized more conventionally, with a kitchen, a study and a room originally intended as a garage. (This became a studio that Rietveld used as an atelier for his architectural practice until 1932.) These rooms were linked by strips of glass above the communal walls, which let in extra light and created a sense of sociality in these otherwise private areas.

Schröder and her children moved in at the end of 1924, and the interior was finished by the autumn of 1925. The house cost much less than other comparable Modern Movement houses—about the same as a lower-middle-class terrace house in the Netherlands at the time. Although Schröder was a relatively

Schröder House: Utrecht, Netherlands, 1923-24

wealthy woman, the austerity and simplicity of the design were intended to inscribe a new view of life in which luxury was replaced by inexpensive materials and simple fitments enhanced with primary color and an imaginative formal invention.

Rietveld was familiar with the "ideal" projects by Theo van Doesburg and Cornelis van Eesteren designed for the De Stijl architectural exhibition at the Léonce Rosenberg exhibition in Paris in 1923. He had made the model for the Hôtel Particulière, but he did not visit the exhibition, although he had no doubt seen photographs of the drawings and models for the other two major designs, the Maison Particulière and the Maison d'Artiste, with their free use of space and "deconstructive" experiments with abstract planes and primary colors. These designs and some models for kiosks and street furniture by the Utrecht artist Willem van Leusden, also shown in the De Stijl exhibition, may have influenced the fluid and apparently disconnected planes of the the Schröder House facades, although these are close to the visually separate wooden elements used in Rietveld's early furniture, and also suggest the sliding partitions of the first-floor interior.

In 1924 van Doesburg published the manifesto, "Towards a Plastic Architecture," in the *De Stijl* magazine. This reads like a description of the Schröder House, although the house was already designed when the manifesto was published; van Does-

burg, who was living in Paris, had not yet seen any drawings or photographs of the house, however, nor apparently had Rietveld and Schröder read the manifesto before it was published. This called for the interrelation of the exterior and the interior; a balanced asymmetry without a dominant facade consisting of "space-cells" created by overlapping planes and balconies, producing a "hovering" effect and the illusion of defying gravity; a "mobile" interior with movable walls or screens; and an "organic" use of color to create an equilibrium between the different architectural elements.

Rietveld and Schröder seem to have simultaneously realized the architectural ideas which van Doesburg was in the process of theorizing. The play between the apparently formal qualities of the exterior and the ingeniousness of the interior, with its specially designed fittings and equipment, creates a dynamic tension which gives the Schröder House its extraordinary presence, even today when restored and unlived in. This was the result of the close dialogue which took place between the architect and his client/codesigner, and her determination that the house should continue to be a physical embodiment of a way of life even after her death (it was made over to a trust which would restore and maintain it for the public to visit).

—PAUL OVERY

POLAND

CHURCH OF ST. MARY
Gdansk, Poland

1343-1502: Construction. **1447:** Eastern part of basilica completed. **1484-98:** Side naves widened, and new external walls built. **Builders (from late 14th century on):** Henryk Ungeradin, Claus Sweder, Master Steffen, Master Michal, Jan Brandt and Henryk Hetzel. **1945:** Heavily damaged during World War II. **1946-83:** Reconstruction works conducted.

Publications

DOMANSKA, H.: *Sladami gdanskich zabytkow*. Gdansk, 1987.
KLOEPPEL, O.: *Die Marienkirche in Danzig und das Huttengeheimnis vom Gerechten Steinmessengrund*. Danzig, 1935.
KRZYZANOWSKI, L.: *Gdansk*. Warsaw, 1987.
MILOBEDZKI, A.: *Zarys dziejow architektury w Polsce*. Warsaw, 1988.

*

The construction of the Church of St. Mary started in 1343 and was interrupted and resumed a number of times until its completion in 1502. The scale of the church and resultant structural problems with its enormous height and spans exceeded the financial and technological resources of one generation. Through time the design concept continuously evolved and adjusted to current architectural trends.

The eastern part of the basilica was completed in 1447. It had a rather centralized character due to the width of the presbytery, which was almost equal to the width of the intersecting transept. The names of the first builders remain unknown. In 1484-98, the side naves were widened and new external walls were erected. Starting from the last quarter of the 14th century, construction works were conducted by Henryk Ungeradin, Claus Sweder, Master Steffen, Master Michal, Jan Brandt, and Henryk Hetzel (who built the vaults).

The Church of St. Mary is the biggest Gothic church in Poland, with three naves 105 meters (345 feet) long and a three-nave transept 66 meters (217 feet) wide. The basilica can house 25,000 people. The greatness and importance of the church lie not only in its scale, however. The spatial composition and architectural details of St. Mary's exemplify trends in the late medieval construction of sacral buildings in Gdansk. One has to realize that there were not too many places in the country where architecture was so strongly connected with the local urban population and its culture.

The cultural development of Gdansk achieved its apogee in the 15th and 16th centuries, and that period resulted in many magnificent buildings. When, in 1454, the region returned to Poland, Gdansk became independent from the feudal Teutonic Order administration. Gdansk inherited the tradition of masonry building developed by the Teutonic knights, and enriched that tradition with influences of art from the Netherlands and Flanders. From the middle of the 15th century, a specific Gdansk style developed; its roots were in architecture of castles and churches erected by the grand masters and palaces of the Prussian bishops, combined with Flemish influences both in architectural concepts and ornamentation. This architectural Gdansk

school spread to all of Pomerania, the provinces in the east and the south up to the Vistula River.

As mentioned, the main body of St. Mary's Church consists of three naves and a three-nave transept. Each nave is covered with an independent steep, Gothic, pitched roof, hidden behind the gable walls.

A system of buttresses was designed inside the church. Flying buttresses were seldom constructed in Poland, mostly because of climate considerations. In Polish masonry and stone Gothic buildings the external heavy buttresses prevailed. The Late Gothic churches in Eastern Pomerania often had buttresses hidden inside, as in the earlier St. Mary's in Torun (ca. 1370).

Hidden buttresses in St. Mary's, Gdansk, resulted in plain external wall surfaces through which a few large windows were pierced. These plain, stern walls contrast sharply with richly decorated gable walls equipped with as many as 10 slender spires. The gable walls were grouped three together, wherever three roof fronts occurred.

St. Mary's late Gothic hall-building, with its hidden buttresses, approaches perfection in its spatial and light interior. It is more reminiscent of a representative hall of secular palaces than of a medieval church. The conformity of space is assured with the high concentration and density of ribs dividing vaults. The ribs "span" the supports rather than transform loads to single columns. These columns look as if they bear the umbrella of the roof, as opposed to the traditional arrangements of columns defining the outlines of particular naves.

The chain of chapels, placed in spaces between buttresses, suggest a width that is larger than the actuality, and also decrease the image of directional, structural arrangements in the longitudinal direction.

The vaults closing the interior at the height of 27 meters (89 feet) are not fan or lierne vaults, but rather form sophisticated arrangements of surfaces placed on a complicated, dense web of ribs giving the impression of shells as opposed to traditional vaults. The side naves are covered with rib and panel vaults that produce an intricate play of shadows as a result of the frustums of numerous pyramids cut into the vaults. The richness of the ceilings contrasts strongly with the simplicity of white, plain walls and columns.

A single, massively powerful tower with a tent roof was erected on the axis of symmetry of the church. The tower, equipped with external buttresses, has a clear horizontal division at five levels. It reaches 80 meters (260 feet) and shows strong influence of Flanders' architecture. The tower provides one of the dominant accents in the Gdansk cityscape.

In 1945, during the final battles of World War II, the church suffered heavy damage. The Gothic timber trusses of the roof were burned down and nearly 40 percent of the vaults collapsed. Many invaluable furnishings were destroyed or looted.

Reconstruction, begun in 1946, continued through 1983. The restoring of vaults required the most highly qualified masons. One of the columns in the presbytery, weakened by artillery shells and weather conditions, would not bear the weight of the new vaults and had to be protected with reinforced concrete rings. At the same time, the three remaining presbytery columns were strengthened, and now they look more massive than the original Gothic ones.

Because of the many elements missing, the interior looks emptier than in the past. The main 16th-century altar by Master Michal of Augsburg has been reinstalled, along with the

Church of St. Mary: Gdansk, Poland, 1343-1502

15th-century sculptures of the Madonna and Pietà. Side altars of Saints Barbara, James, Martin, Simon and Jude, and the famous 17th-century canvas *The Deeds of Mercy* by Anthony Moller again enrich the church, but many elements of the interior have not been returned to Poland and remain in neighboring countries. Other artifacts are in museum collections, including the National Museum in Warsaw.

—JERZY ANDRZEJ STARCZEWSKI

Publications

FISCHINGER, A.: *Kaplica Zygmuntowska*. Warsaw, 1981.
FRANASZEK, A.: *Wawel*. Warsaw, 1988.
LAUTERBACH, A.: *Die Renaissance in Krakau*. Munich, 1911.
PRZYBYSZEWSKI, B.: *Muratorzy i kamieniarze zajeci przy budowie zamku królewskiego na Wawelu 1502-1536*. Warsaw, 1955.
SZABLOWSKI, J. (ed.): *Wawel*. Kraków, 1965.

*

SIGISMUND CHAPEL, WAWEL CATHEDRAL
Kraków, Poland

1518-33. Architect: Bartolomeo Berrecci (Florentine, worked in Kraków from 1516 until his death in 1537). **Late 16th century:** Tombs added for the Jagiellonian rulers. **1591-92:** Dome covered with gold-plated tiles.

The Sigismund Chapel is one of the most interesting architectural monuments in the Wawel Castle complex in Kraków, Poland. Wawel Castle has the same significance for the Poles as the Escorial for the Spanish or Buckingham Palace and Westminster Abbey for the British.

Sigismund Chapel: Kraków, Poland, 1516-33

The preserved relics of stone building on the Wawel Hill date from about the second half of the 10th century, the time of the Christianization of Poland (A.D. 966). Wawel gradually grew in importance to become the center of political power and eventually became the capital of the Polish kingdom, until 1596 when the capital was moved to Warsaw. First the ducal and later a royal residence, Wawel Castle was expanded from a Romanesque building to become a magnificent Gothic castle during the reign of King Casimir the Great (ruled 1333-70). The creation of the office of bishop in Kraków at the beginning of the 11th century was followed by the erection of the first cathedral. It was twice destroyed by fire and replaced by the Gothic structure that has remained until today. Ladislaus the Short was the first ruler to make the cathedral the place for coronation and burial of the Polish kings.

The 16th century was the golden age in Polish history. Politically and economically, Poland became one of the most powerful countries in Europe. The last two kings of the Jagiellonian dynasty, Sigismund I the Old (ruled 1506-48) and Sigismund August (ruled 1548-72), modernized Wawel Castle, turning it into a magnificent Renaissance residence. Sigismund I married the Italian princess Buona Sforza, who brought with her from Italy many outstanding artists and architects.

The Sigismund Chapel was built as an addition to Wawel Cathedral. It is considered one of the most outstanding examples of the Italian art in central Europe. It is often called "The Pearl of Renaissance architecture in Poland." Founded by Sigismund I, the chapel had a religious purpose and at the same time was to become the royal burial mausoleum. The architect was Bartolomeo Berrecci, Florentine architect and sculptor who went to Kraków in 1516 and remained there until his death in 1537. With a number of Italian and Polish stonecutters, Anthony of Fiesole, Bernard Zanobii, John Cini of Siena, Nicolaus Castiglione, John Maria Padovano, Stanisław Brzezina and others, Berrecci worked 15 years on the chapel that became the work of his lifetime and the leading symbol of the Polish architectural golden age.

The project was completed probably as soon as 1516, and in 1517 was presented to the king, who accepted it, introducing only few changes. Construction began the next year and was completed in 1533. In the succeeding years some furnishings were added, and in 1538 the sterling silver altar was installed. In the second half of the 16th century, Princess Ann the Jagiellon, daughter of Sigismund I, ordered some changes, since the chapel had become the mortuary mausoleum of the last Jagiellonian kings. The sculpture of Sigismund August was added and placed over the sculpture of his father to create a double-level tomb.

On the other wall the tomb of Ann the Jagiellon was added in front of the royal stalls. This tomb and subsequent changes were completed from 1574 to 1575 by Santi Gucci, an outstanding Florentine architect and sculptor. In 1591-92, the dome was covered with gold-plated tiles. The chapel was restored several times during the following centuries, but no changes or remodeling have been introduced. To the present the chapel has retained its original shape and decoration.

The Sigismund Chapel is a square structure erected in natural stone, covered with a hemispherical dome and equipped with a central lantern. The geometry and plan of the chapel were derived from the circle, which in the time of the Renaissance was considered an ideal form. The pilasters are connected with the base and headers and create interesting wall divisions. The square body is transformed into an octagonal drum with circular windows. From outside, the gray limestone walls produce a striking contrast against the golden dome and the lantern decorated with the royal crown and golden cross.

The inside looks even more impressive. The pilasters, the base and the arcades of each wall create the solution that reminds one of the four triumphal Roman arches placed on the four sides of the square. One of them serves as an entrance, two others house royal tombs; the altar is located in the fourth one.

In parts of the walls adjacent to the dome there are interesting floral decorations with animals and humans. The dome itself is decorated with five rows of rosettes, 80 in all, each of them of different original design. In niches near the corners Berrecci placed statues of six saints, Solomon and David. The statues were carved in red marble from Hungary, the same material that was used for the royal tombs and fresco decorations. At the top of the lantern, Berrecci placed the inscription "Bartholo Fiorentino Opifice" (Work of Bartholo of Florence). The lantern and eight circular windows provide intensive natural lighting characteristic of the Renaissance interior, and contrasting with the relatively dark Gothic naves of Wawel Cathedral.

The bronze entrance gate and bronze candleholders were crafted by Hans Vischer in Nuremberg between 1530 and 1534. The sterling-silver altar was made by a group of Nuremberg artists according to the design of Hans Dürer.

The Sigismund Chapel, an outstanding example of the architecture and sculpture of the period, exemplifies the ideals of humanism and the contemporary artistic theories. Berrecci, on a very large scale, was applying ancient motifs. Ancient principles inspired him in planning divisions of walls, shaping semicircular arches and dome, as well as selecting mural and stone decoration. Even the sculptures of kings, carved in the tombs, link them to the Renaissance visions of Mars, the god of war. The realistic, precise sculptures, representing all the details, show the royal figures asleep, waking in the time of the final judgment.

The chapel became a model for the future work as well as for research on Renaissance architecture in Poland.

—JERZY ANDRZEJ STARCZEWSKI

CASTLE OF THE TEUTONIC KNIGHTS
Malbork, Poland

Ca. 1275-ca. 1400: Chapels, High Castle, Middle Castle and Lower Castle constructed. **16th-17th centuries:** Redecorations, renovations and new buildings executed. **Early 19th-early 20th century:** Reconstruction and restoration conducted. **1945:** Severely damaged during World War II. **1959:** Reconstruction begun.

Publications

ADAMY, RUDOLF: *Architektonik des gothischen Stils*, Hannover.

CHODYN AASKI, A. R.: *Zamek Malborski w obrazach i kartografii*. Warsaw, 1988.

CLASEN, K. H.: *Marienburg und Marienwerder*. Berlin, 1931.

GOAARSKI, K.: *Dzieje Malborka*. Gdansk, 1973.

GUERQUIN, B.: *Zamek w Malborku*. Warsaw, 1971.

QUAST, F. VON: "Schloss Marienburg." *Neues Preussische Provinzial Blatt* 11 (1851).

STEINBRECHT, C.: *Schloss Marienburg in Preussen. Führer durch seine Geschichte und Bauwerke*. Berlin, 1917.

ZBIERSKA, E.: *Zamek w Malborku*. Warsaw, 1982.

Castle of the Teutonic Knights: Malbork, Poland, ca. 1275-ca. 1400

The Castle of Malbork occupies a special place in the history of architecture and politics in Poland. The castle was built by the Teutonic Knights, who were called in by Polish princes early in the 13th century to protect their territories against the aggression of pagan Prussian tribes. In 1226 the Order of Teutonic Knights, having just concluded its crusades and resided for nearly 10 years in Hungary, was given the Chelmno region of Poland. Later, by conquest, the Teutonic Knights spread along the Vistula River to northern Pomerania.

The history of Malbork Castle is not well documented, and the dates of construction and later remodeling remain hypothetical. The available sources quote the year 1275, in which construction of "Marienburg" Castle and the adjacent town (both later renamed Malbork by the Poles) was begun. Five years later the convent was opened. Malbork was a novel type of conventual building, combining strategic with religious functions. Unlike military structures in Poland, which were built mostly of timber and dirt, and unlike ecclesiastical buildings erected mostly in wood and natural stone, Malbork Castle was built mostly of brick.

For a long time, architectural historians associated the castle with western European architectural traditions. Recent Polish studies explain the specific character and form of Malbork Castle as a quite unique and original concept, developing out of the newly established conventual canons following Dominican law (1244). Dominican monks observed strict architectural regulations regarding geometric layouts, in which the integrated inner yards were completely surrounded with the church and monastery buildings.

The building site was first enclosed with ramparts. The construction of the High Castle continued through the mid-14th century. According to research by Szczesny Skibinski (published 1982), the earliest structure was a chapel dedicated to Saint Anne, erected in two stages at the end of the 13th century and beginning of the 14th. In the second stage, during the second quarter of the 14th century, the builders completed the structure, and modified the eastern part of the vaults to a tripartite system, also to be found at the Teutonic Castle at Lochstadt. Skibinski suggests that the original solution derived from St. Mary's Chapel at Auxerre. St. Anne's Chapel at Malbork is a two-level structure, adapted from the architectural concept of the Sainte-Chappelle in Paris. The rectangular courtyard of the High Castle was surrounded by high buildings with Gothic arcades and high steep roofs in the 14th century.

Archaeological and architectural studies, conducted between 1978 and 1982 by Antoni Pawlowski, confirmed earlier suggestions by Busching and Clasen that the construction of buildings of the Middle Castle was also begun before 1280. Construction continued after 1310, and the most significant part of the early Middle Castle was the west wing, with the Great Refectory. The latter, constructed 1318-24, was a splendid interior space measuring 49 by 98 feet. Its fan vaults, supported on three slim black granite columns, demonstrate not only the designers' imagination and sense of beauty, but also the builders' engineering skill.

In 1309 the grand master moved from Venice to Malbork, and the castle became the official headquarters of the Teutonic Order, which became more and more powerful with the conquest of new territories. As to wealth and architectural splendor, the residence of the grand master is comparable to royal residences in Europe. The most impressive interiors of the residence were the Winter Refectory, with vaults 39 by 39 by 25.6 feet, supported with a single stone column; and the Summer Refectory, 46 by 46 by 31.8 feet, constructed in the rectangular tower between 1382 and 1390. At the end of the 14th century arcades were added, mostly for the purpose of connecting the different buildings. The whole was surrounded by a system of double defensive walls. The moat was filled with water, except for the moat dividing the High Castle and Middle Castle, which remained empty.

Completed in about 1400, the Middle Castle abounds in architectural and structural solutions exhibiting the highest level of workmanship and engineering skill. The masons and stonecutters created vaults optimally shaped to accommodate gravity. Decorations, however, were subjugated to defensive considerations. The origins of particular solutions are controversial, but Clasen sees connections to English architecture (York), and to the Château de Poitiers and the Papal Palace in Avignon, both in France. Mural decorations, however, exhibit a strong resemblance to those found in the religious architecture of Krolewiec and Kwidzyn.

The Lower Castle, situated to the north of the High Castle, was completed in the 14th century, with its own infrastructure: a defensive system with ramparts, walls and towers, as well as storage areas, grain elevators and stables.

The town, granted a charter in 1276, developed on the southern side, along the Nogat River. An elongated marketplace was set parallel to the river. The town was enclosed with brick walls in 1352-83.

In 1410, after the defeat of the Teutonic Knights at the battle of Grunwald, Malbork managed to resist a Polish siege. After the siege new fortifications were erected, but in 1457 Malbork was incorporated into the Commonwealth of Poland and Lithuania, as a result of the Thirteen Years' War. Until 1772 the castle served as one of the residences of the Polish kings, and was administered by a Polish constable. In the 16th century it was redecorated in the Renaissance style. In the 17th century new buildings were added, and the main courtyard of the High Castle was reconstructed in the Baroque style.

In 1772 Malbork was taken by Frederick the Great of Prussia, and turned into warehouses and barracks. By the beginning of the 19th century, the devastation was so advanced that total demolition was considered. Only a campaign launched by lovers of old architecture saved the complex from destruction. Subsequent reconstruction was undertaken by the architects Karl Friedrich Schinkel, Friedrich August Stüler and Gersdorff. From 1850 to 1887 the restoration of the castle was the responsibility of Ferdinand von Quast. Unfortunately, his activity was not based on scientific methods, but rather on a personal, romantic vision of the past. In 1887 Conrad Steinberg was named chief coordinator of the reconstruction. His main purpose was to restore the original Gothic character of the buildings, by removing all the additions in the Renaissance and Baroque styles executed by the Polish builders. Where no original Gothic fragments could be discovered, Steinberg introduced new pseudo-Gothic decorative elements of his own. The works were continued until the outbreak of World War I.

Malbork suffered severe damage in 1945, as a result of the German invasion, especially in the eastern part, of which nearly 80 percent was laid waste. The reconstruction of the castle began in 1959, under the auspices of the Polish Ministry of Culture, and was only recently completed. The conservation works were conducted with an historical-analytical approach, and new technology was used, such as X-ray screening, laser analysis, thermophotography and ultrasonic tests. Today the castle serves as a museum.

—JERZY ANDRZEJ STARCZEWSKI

TOWN HALL
Poznan, Poland

1550: Construction begun on new town hall; **Architect:** Jan Baptista di Quadro. **1782-84:** Neoclassical decorations and tower top added. **1910-13:** Major alterations executed under Prussian occupation. **1945:** Severely damaged during World War II. **1945-54:** Restored to pre-1910 appearance.

Publications

JAKIMOWICZ, T.: *Ratusz Poznański*. Warsaw, 1979.
KONDZIELA, H.: *Stare Miasto w Poznaniu*. Poznan, 1975.
MIŁOBĘDZKI, A.: *Zarys dziejów architektury w Polsce*. Warsaw, 1988.

*

The city of Poznan contains one of the most interesting town halls surviving from the Renaissance. Poznan, the seat of the bishop and the ducal residence, received its urban status in 1253. Soon after, a Gothic town hall was erected. The tower, the symbol of power and the city's prosperity, was added probably at the beginning of the 16th century.

Not much information is available about this early hall except that it was two stories high. In 1536 the Town Hall was destroyed by a fire that consumed the city. Eight years later a carpenter named Hanusz reconstructed the wooden structure of the spire, but the problem of the weakened walls remained.

In 1550 the city council brought Jan Baptista di Quadro, an Italian mason, from Lugano. Born in the region of Lake Como, di Quadro understood the local style there. His design did not follow the canons of the prevailing great Western Renaissance. To the contrary, it was quite remote from Renaissance monumentality and was characteristic for its decorative approach.

Di Quadro, instructed to enlarge the Town Hall in the western direction and to add one story, fully satisfied the expectations of the city council. In 1552, in appreciation for his efforts, he was appointed the city mason for a period of 10 years.

Di Quadro's free, almost fantastic, concept of the reconstruction of the Town Hall and his nonclassical approach in comparison to orthodox Renaissance design made the solution one of the most interesting in central Europe. Di Quadro transformed the Gothic provincial structure into an ''original'' modern Renaissance building. At the front, he built a three-story loggia decorated with arcades. The symmetrical solution of the loggia corresponded with the axis of symmetry of the top wall surrounding the roof. The wall, called *corona muralis,* was a flat vertical structure with three miniature towers representing the coats of arms of many Polish towns, including Poznan. It symbolized the jurisdictional law and order of the Renaissance town.

Di Quadro's concept of the symmetrical elevation resulted in the layout of interiors with two grandiose symmetrical staircases and magnificent halls. The most interesting interior of the first floor, the Chamber (called in Polish *sien*), is covered with a barrel vault with lanterns through which the natural light penetrates. On the second floor, the Renaissance Hall, also called ''the Great Chamber,'' fills the whole width of the Town Hall. Covered with coffer vaults supported by two columns located on the axis of symmetry of the building, it served as a seat of the court. In the adjacent Royal Chamber the sessions of the city council took place.

The di Quadro design exemplified the city council's tendency for modernization of the town. The upper, well-educated class of Poznan had high aspirations that were reflected in the utilitarian,

Town Hall: Poznan, Poland, 1550

pragmatic yet artistic program of the newly reconstructed Town Hall.

Throughout the ages the Town Hall has been renovated several times. New polychrome decorations and a new neoclassical helmet for the tower were completed in 1782-84. Changes in 1910-13, during the Prussian occupation, spoiled the Renaissance character of the building. The additional floor was added and windows were pierced out at the top of the facade. In the Royal Chamber the historical vaults were altered. The Polish crown decorated with an eagle sitting on the top of the tower was replaced with a Prussian crown.

In 1945, during the final battles of World War II, the Town Hall suffered severe damage. Another fire destroyed the tower and partially gutted the top floor. One of the small spires in the corner of the facade and the upper part of the facade itself were partly ruined. The fresco and stucco decorations in the most beautiful interiors were stained with smoke.

The conservation work undertaken in 1945 continued until 1954. Long and ardent studies were required to recover the historic shape of the building. This work was conducted by the architect Slawski.

Preliminary repairs included the removal of water from flooded basements, strengthening of the walls and providing a temporary roof. In 1947 an engineering proposal for the tower was submitted by Lucjan Ballenstaedt. The spire was completed within a year.

From 1949 to 1950 the most important work included the removal of the flat roof and demolition of the top floor added during 1910-13. The window openings in the facade were filled with bricks, and a new roof sloped inward, identical to that designed by di Quadro.

The change in function from the administrative center to a museum, decided in the 1950s, required changes in organization of circulation and fire exits. A new reinforced-concrete staircase connecting all the floors was added in the northern part of the building.

The restoration of the elevations and the interiors was the responsibility of the Bureau for Historical Conservation, Poznan Chapter, and was guided by Aleksander Holas. The historical studies for conservation of the interior frescoes and decoration were completed by Anna Gogalanka. These studies required the thorough analysis of old written and iconographical sources up to the year 1910.

The projects of painted decorations and frescoes of the facades were prepared by Jan Piasecki. According to that proposal the royal portraits gallery was placed back on the front facade. Since the iconographical documentation proved to be fragmentary and not quite certain, the artist introduced his own concept of Renaissance facade painting. The fresco technology, however, was done in the most traditional way, and the particular mixtures were derived from the time of the Italian Renaissance.

Since the conservation the front elevation of the Town Hall is most impressive. The building, open to the marketplace, is a three-story arcaded loggia. The number of arcades of the third floor doubles. The arcades are supported on columns from which half-columns arise, bearing beams that divide the particular stories. The frescoes and stuccos play with the intricate shadows of the rich architectural elevation and strongly contrast with the flat, stern facade from which three handsome towers, covered with helmets, shoot into the sky.

—JERZY ANDRZEJ STARCZEWSKI

TORUŃ TOWN HALL
Toruń, Poland

Ca. 1393-ca. 1399: Construction begun on new town hall; **Architect:** Probably Master Andrzej. **1602-05:** Reconstruction executed; **Architect:** Probably Anthony van Opbergen. **1619:** Spires and window frames added. **1703:** Structure gutted by fire during Swedish siege. **1728-38:** Building reconstructed. **1957-64:** Restoration conducted.

Publications

GASIOROWSKI, E.: *Ratusz w Toruniu*. Warsaw, 1970.
GRUBER, K.: "Das Rathaus in Thorn." *Deutsche Kunst und Denkmalpflege* (1940-41): 50ff.
HEUER, R.: *Thorn*. Berlin, 1931.
SOKOLSTOWSKA, K.: *Ratusz Staromiejski w Toruniu*. Torun, 1952.

*

The Toruń Town Hall is one of the most interesting buildings of the medieval Old Town and one of the most magnificent of Europe. Researchers, historians, architects and writers agree on the highest qualities of its appearance, proportions and sophisticated details expressed by the 17th-century Latin description: *"elegantissimum,. . .quale nullibi videbis,. . .ut nihil ad perfectionem architecturae requiratur."*

When compared with other medieval town halls of Europe, Toruń's is not only larger but shows originality and specific architectural solutions that developed during its 700-year history. This history coincides with the past of Toruń, a city famous for its trade and enterprise.

The town of Toruń was formally established in 1233 by the Teutonic Order. Situated on the Vistula River, at the ford on the east-west route, it became an important inland harbor that connected lower and upper regions of the estuary. The town also participated in the trade of agricultural products produced in eastern and southern Poland to western Europe, mostly through the Dutch and Flemish harbors.

In 1454, Toruń, retaining its status as **Respublicae Thorunensis**, became part of Poland, and King Casimir Jagiellon received a tribute from the city and the knights of the region. From then through 1793, when Toruń was annexed to Prussia, it served as a royal residence, and the kings visited the city practically every year. In 1520, 1576 and 1626, Parliament's sessions took place in the town hall.

The history of the building began in 1259, when the two-story markethouse was erected on the site of the later western wing of the town hall. The privilege of 1274 granted a permit for construction of the second building, which was built on the site of the eastern wing and housed stalls of the merchants. At the same time, the lower part of the tower was built. Thus, in 1280, two parallel buildings were standing with an axis of symmetry in the north-south direction. In 1343, Toruń gained permission for closing the complex into the form of a rectangular building with an inner court.

The cloth hall and the stalls of the merchants looked like typical trade buildings in northwest Europe at that time. The strong resemblance of the Toruń tower to the tower of Bruges proves strong links with that region besides trade. On the other hand, the exterior screening wall brings associations with the town hall of Lübeck, but the combination of the tower with screen wall created a unique solution that has not been applied in any other city.

At the end of the 14th century the buildings were in poor repair, and there was even danger of collapse. The privilege of 1393 gave permission for demolition of the old buildings and the construction of a new town hall that in plan could be eight feet bigger than the old buildings. The document of 1393 was of great importance because it provided precedence of a building construction permit according to the submitted architectural project. The construction must have been completed before 1399, when city documents mentioned taxes paid by the users of the new building.

The new town hall was a masonry building, two stories high. The four wings covered a rectangle 43.7 by 52.4 meters and surrounded the interior yard. The cellars occupied the entire area, including the yard. The three-track vaults of the cellars were supported by external walls and intermediate granite columns.

The entrances at both ends of the east and the west wings provided perfect circulation. In the building the municipal institutions and market facilities were located under one roof and coexisted in a perfect way. The cellars were designed for storing wine, and the market stalls occupied the main floor. On this floor an architect designed also the scales and the city court.

The longer wings were covered with brick Gothic vaults. The vaults over the scales and the court had special decorative character. The interiors received their natural lighting through

Town Hall: Toruń, Poland, ca. 1393-ca. 1399

high Gothic windows located over the stalls of "poorer" hawkers who could not afford to pay rent for internal stalls and had them placed outside the building.

The large scale of the building, its proportions, the tower and the strong vertical divisions with pilasters closed by pointed arches at the top prove that the architect had in mind not only a functional solution but also an expression of the splendor and importance of the town hall.

The architect was probably Master Andrzej, a Pole. The project proves the maturity of the designer, who was able to implement new technical solutions while achieving outstanding artistic effects. The town hall's formal resemblance to a number of important buildings of Flanders and Pomerania (Malbork Castle) show that the architect was acquainted with monumental architecure of the 14th century.

In the 16th century the technical state of the town hall deteriorated so much that complete restoration was imminent. The reconstruction was probably done to the plans of Anthony van Opbergen, the Gdansk architect who built the royal castle at Kronberg. In the years 1602-05 all the works were completed. The current requirements of the Renaissance style brought changes in the characteristic Gothic shape of the building. But at the same time, the architect showed understanding and a good taste. By adding the additional story and using light brick gables in the style of the Dutch Renaissance, he smoothed the shape of the building. Other additions comprising small spires in four corners of the roof and stone window framings were completed in 1619. The latter were not only beautifully decorated, but proved also the engineering prowess of the builders, who applied among other novelties sophisticated iron reinforcements. The tower received slim spires. Later the interiors were redecorated.

The most important interiors on the second floor (the Hall of the Council and the Royal Chamber) received Late Baroque marble and alabaster portals of priceless artistic value. Several doors were replaced with richly ornamented doors of silver inlay with lavish intarsia. However, the cellars and the main floor retained their original Gothic appearance.

During the Swedish siege in 1703, the town hall was completely burned down and remained in ruins for more than 20 years. In 1728 the building was covered with a roof and thus protected against further deterioration. The reconstruction of the interiors was completed by 1738. Despite the Baroque additions (new modest gables and a pilaster to support the leaning western wall), the building still retained its stern Gothic appearance. The tower received the temporary roof structure that has survived to the present.

The fall of the Respublicae Thorunensis resulted in slow deterioration of the town hall. The commercial spaces were replaced with offices of the growing bureaucracy. The large halls and other interiors were divided with partition walls. According to the designs of F. Quast, the Baroque pilaster on the western wall was reconstructed in pseudo-Gothic style. During World War II, the Nazis planned major alterations of the building, but fortunately implemented only a few changes in the cellars of the eastern wing.

After the war the town hall was turned into a museum. The technical state of the building required vast conservation works, which were completed in 1957-64. The work included removal of all the 19th-century additions and details. The wooden roof structure has been replaced with a steel one, and all timber floors and stairs were replaced by reinforced-concrete equivalent structures. Research on the interiors and architectural details has resulted in interesting discoveries. Among others, in the southern wall of the tower, Gothic frescoes dating from circa 1330 have been found.

—JERZY ANDRZEJ STARCZEWSKI

OLD TOWN RECONSTRUCTION
Warsaw, Poland

1939-44: Warsaw extensively destroyed during World War II. **1945:** Reconstruction of the city begun; **Chief architect:** Mieczyslaw Kuzma. **1953:** Reconstruction of the Old Town completed.

Publications

CHRÓŚCICKI, J. A., and ROTTERMUND, A.: *Atlas of Warsaw's Architecture*. Warsaw, 1978.
CIBOROWSKI, A.: *Warszawa, O zniszczeniu i odbudowie miasta*. Warsaw, 1964.
LORENZ, S.; ZACHWATOWICZ, J.; BIEGAŃSKI, P.; and GIEYSZTOR, A.: *The Old Town and the Royal Castle in Warsaw*. Warsaw, 1988.
ZACHWATOWICZ, J. (ed.): *Budownictwo i Architektura w Polsce 1945-1966*. Warsaw, 1968.

*

A map drawn by Ptolomeo shows a ford through the Vistula River in the middle of its length, more or less in the place where the present Old Town of Warsaw lies. But even if archaeological discoveries demonstrate that there were some early settlements on the Warsaw territory, the first official mention goes back to 1262, when the small fortress Jazdów, located on the high western bank of the river, was burned down by invaders. At the end of the 13th century, Warsaw received an urban legislature, and in 1339 it was chosen as the site for the international tribunal settling a dispute between the Polish king Casimir the Great and the Teutonic Order of Knights.

In the 13th century, Warsaw had defensive walls along the steep slope of the river embankments. The system was closed with horseshoe-shaped double walls, beginning and ending at the river, in the 14th century. The medieval Old Town, with a total area of about 22 acres, had about 150 building sites, each 30 feet wide and 115 to 130 feet long. There was a rectangular marketplace 240 by 310 feet in the center, and the adjacent castle of the Mazovian Dukes, the rulers of the province of Mazovia, was located on the southern side. In the 14th century, two Gothic churches were erected, the Parish Church of St. John and the Augustinian Church of St. Martin, with an adjacent monastery.

As the trade and administrative center of the Mazovia province, Warsaw developed rapidly. The town within the defensive walls, located at the intersection of the Vistula and the east-west trade route, soon proved to be too small. A second town, referred to as the New Town, was founded in 1408, north of the walls. Fifteen years later, Warsaw was named the official capital of Mazovia. After a tragic fire in 1431, which consumed most of the city, the city council issued new regulations prohibiting timber construction. The new Gothic masonry city evolved in the wake of those regulations.

The year 1526 brought the death of the last prince of Mazovia, and the province was incorporated into the Kingdom of Poland. After the fire of the Royal Castle in Kraków, in 1596, King Sigismund III Vasa moved the capital from Kraków to Warsaw. The decision was politically motivated: at that time, royal elections took place at Warsaw, and the central geographical location was suitable for the seat of government of the commonwealth of the Kingdom of Poland and the Grand Duchy of Lithuania.

When the capital was moved to Warsaw, the Gothic castle

Old Town reconstruction: Warsaw, Poland, 1945-53

of the Mazovian princes was promoted to royal status, and underwent extensive architectural changes. It was first enlarged and decorated in the Renaissance style. In the 18th century, the Saxon kings remodeled the castle in the Baroque style.

The development of the city reflects the historical destiny of the nation. It grew in times of peace, active trading and prosperity, but stagnated when Poland was partitioned, and also during the Russian occupation. The city grew again from 1918, when Poland regained its independence, to 1939, when it was invaded by Germany. At the outbreak of World War II, the population had reached 1.3 million. Ten percent of residents lived in the Old and New Towns.

During World War II, Warsaw was destroyed in three stages. The 1939 siege of the city involved the destruction of about 12 percent of the buildings. In 1943, during and after the uprising of the Jews in the Ghetto, the central district of the city was completely leveled. Finally, during and after the uprising of 1944, Warsaw suffered almost total destruction. Survivors were forced to leave the city, and the special German demolition brigades dynamited the remnants of any buildings that had architectural or cultural value. The Russian army waited for several months for orders to cross the river, allowing the Nazis to complete their task. When, eventually, the Red army ''liberated'' Warsaw, on 17 January 1945, there were no inhabitants among the deserted ruins. The destruction was assessed at 85 percent. Out of 957 registered historical buildings, 782 were completely razed and 141 were badly damaged. None of the surviving 34 were in the Old Town. The city was covered with 20 million cubic meters of debris and ruins.

The Old and New Towns of Warsaw and the Royal Castle all shared in the city's destiny. The castle was partly destroyed in 1939, but many pieces of architectural decoration and artistic furniture were saved from the burning palace by members of the Polish Resistance and employees of the National Museum. After the Germans entered Warsaw, a campaign to destroy the castle was begun: 10,000 holes were drilled in the foundation walls in preparation for its demolition. The task was carried to completion after the uprising of 1944.

Despite this unprecedented destruction, it was clear that Warsaw had to be rebuilt. The reconstruction of the country was impossible without the reconstruction of its capital, especially the Old Town, which was the nucleus of Warsaw's urban development and the cultural center of Poland. The decision to reconstruct Warsaw and its historic districts was made almost immediately after the liberation of the city. Although superstructures had been razed, most of the foundations and basements survived. The restoration project first concentrated on protecting the fissured and dangerously leaning outer walls, and collecting the thousands of fragments and architectural details found in the ruins. At the same time, the architects collected architectural and iconographic documentation of the city from all over Poland. The miraculously saved collection of nearly 60 canvases, representing 18th-century views of Warsaw by the royal painter Bernardo Bellotto, proved of great value in historical studies. (Bellotto, nephew of the great Canaletto, spent most of his life in Warsaw. He was a master of precise, almost photographic representation of cityscapes, showing both layout and architectural detail.)

From the point of view of urban planning, it was agreed that the reconstruction was to respect the layout of the Old and New Towns. At the same time, the rebuilt Old Town had to meet the spatial requirements and technical facilities appropriate to the expectations of 20th-century inhabitants. The early master plan for Warsaw designated the Old and New Towns as primarily residential and tourist areas. Mieczysław Kuźma, who had been appointed chief architect of reconstruction of the Old Town, was responsible for the design concept.

The question arose in what style the Old Town should be rebuilt. It was agreed that the image of the Old Town should not be limited to a single historical period. According to Piotr Bieganski, a leading expert and consultant, it was necessary to reconstruct all the important stages, as evidence of the practical and creative town-planning trends throughout the city's history. The specific character of the task confronting the conservators, architects and town planners required the reconstruction not only of the earliest and most attractive historical buildings, but also of those which, as a result of political, economic and artistic vicissitudes, represented opposing trends.

The difficulties of the undertaking, seeming insuperable at first, arose from a lack of practical experience in resolving so vast and unique a problem as the reconstruction of an entire city. Neither theoretic knowledge nor the mass of archival material provided sufficient direction in the decision-making process. Only a minute examination of extant buildings and fragments, together with the experts' architectural intuition, made it possible to resolve some fundamental doubts, and to develop a reconstruction strategy. Not only matters of conservation were involved, but also engineering problems, and above all problems arising out of decisions concerning the spatial administration of the Old and New Towns. Of the utmost importance was the choice of criteria as to what was to be preserved, particularly in instances where extant parts of buildings exhibited traces of different historical stages, each possessing an artistic value worth preserving.

The destruction had uncovered interesting Gothic walls and arches under Baroque facades, Renaissance decorations under 19th-century stucco. From beneath the ruined houses, the outline of the medieval defense system appeared. The defensive walls turned out to have been integrated into buildings constructed on the site of the former moat. The reconstruction experts also found the foundations of the former barbican, and the remnants of a bridge over the moat.

The general principle of reconstruction preserved the medieval town plan and Gothic buildings with some additions dating to the Renaissance and Baroque. By ignoring 19th-century additions, extensive courtyards were created, recalling the earliest form of the Old Town area, and providing the necessary space for contemporary residents. This decision also made room for miniature greenbelts behind the serried ranks of houses lining the medieval streets.

The Old Town owed its development not only to its location on the banks of the Vistula, but also to the ford and the later bridge across the river. Before World War II, the two important thoroughfares, running north-south and east-west, intersected at Castle Square. The reconstruction of the Old Town as a residential district necessitated a reorganization of traffic circulation. Two important decisions were made: the east-west highway was directed through a tunnel built under Castle Square, and north-south traffic was directed through Miodowa Street, outside the walls of the Old Town. Through-traffic was thus eliminated, and local traffic was restricted to a minimum.

The reconstruction of the Old Town was completed by 1953. Two years later the New Town was officially opened to the public. The reconstruction of the Royal Castle did not run so smoothly, despite the Polish parliament's decision of 1949 to rebuild. Economic and political reasons prevented the realization of reconstruction plans. Bolesław Bierut, the first secretary of the Communist Party, found the plans for the reconstruction

of the castle unsatisfactory. In his opinion, the palace was too small, and since he planned to make it his own residence, he felt that an additional story was desirable. That, in turn, met with strong opposition from the leading experts in the restoration of historic buildings. After the death of Bierut, the reconstruction of the Royal Castle again became a political issue. The Communist Party blocked all initiatives, and discussion of the possibility of reconstruction was forbidden. The issue seemed nonexistent if one listened to official propaganda in the state-censored mass media. After 15 years, the party yielded to public demands, and agreed to initiate reconstruction. The castle has been rebuilt with the financial aid of Polish emigrants, particularly Polish Americans.

Jan Bogusławski was appointed chief architect in charge of reconstruction. Technical documentation of the castle, compiled before World War II, and more than 3,000 photographs were used to determine the nature of the restorations. Several thousand sculptural and architectural elements, 16 fireplaces, and hundred of pieces of original furniture and furnishings, saved in 1939, were used in the reconstruction process. The interiors have been furnished with more than 300 canvases by famous painters, including the Bellotto collection. Consequently, the castle not only has been reconstructed, but has retained a considerable degree of authenticity.

—JERZY ANDRZEJ STARCZEWSKI

WILANÓW PALACE
Warsaw, Poland

Ca. 1680-82: Residence built for King John III Sobieski; **Architect:** Augustyn Locci, Jr. **1683-96:** Palace enlarged, including addition of second story, Baroque interiors and gardens. **Artists:** Andreas Schlüter, Stefan Szwaner, Jerzy E. Szymonowicz-Siemiginowski, Jan Reisner, Claude Callot, Michelangelo Palloni. **1723-31:** Symmetrical wings added to sides of palace; **Architects:** Giovanni Spazio and Jan Zygmunt Deybel; **Artists:** Jozef Rossi, Louis de Silvestre, Francesco Fumo, Pietro Innocente Comparetti, Jan Jerzy Plersch. **1781-94:** Remodeling executed; **Architect:** Szymon Bogumil Zug. **1945:** Severely damaged during World War II. **1955-65:** Reconstruction and technical improvements conducted; **Chief architects:** Stefan Deubel and Jacek Cydzik.

Publications

CYDZIK, J., and FIJALKOWSKI, W.: *Wilanow, Dzieje—Architektura—Konserwacja.* Warsaw, 1989.
MIŁOBEDZKI, A.: *Zarys Dziejów Architektury w Polsce.* Warsaw, 1988.

*

The estate of Wilanów, situated 7 miles south of downtown Warsaw, was bought by King John III Sobieski in 1677. The site, a flat terrace 13 feet above a small estuary of the Vistula River, was ideal for a country summer residence. Such a location suited fashionable theories of planning by Vitruvius and Andrea Palladio, who advised taking advantage of the richness of the natural environment. The place was renamed *Villanova,* but was almost immediately polonized into Wilanów.

In about 1680 the royal secretary, Augustyn Locci Jr., an

Wilanów Palace: Warsaw, Poland, ca. 1680-82

amateur architect of Italian heritage, designed a modest single-story manor, in the typical style of the nobility, on the foundation of an old demolished building. It was located exactly in the center of the future palace. In 1681-82 Locci enlarged the residence by a half story, adding symmetrically arranged galleries with monumental towers.

The richly decorated front elevation was representative of the reigning Baroque style. The sculptural mural decorations created an intricate play of light and shadow, combining architectural and artistic effects. The garden facade created just the opposite effects. It combined a Sarmatian fantasy and richness with the sophistication of Roman villas. The sculptural treatment of column capitals and pilasters followed the architectural detailing of Michelangelo's Capitol. But Locci did not strictly copy the architecture of Rome, capital of the Baroque—he applied it to suit ''the Polish sky and customs.'' The role of the king himself in the design process cannot be overappreciated, since his concepts and Sarmatian taste guided not only Locci but also the other artists participating in the construction. The mural decorations were done by the local masters Jan and Antoni, the Italian stonecutters Francesco Cerisola and Santino Madernati, and the painter Jan Apelles.

After 1683, when the king returned triumphant from the Battle of Vienna, in which Polish and Austrian forces led by the king defeated the Turks, and until his death in 1696, the palace continued to be altered and enlarged. Between 1692 and 1696, the second story was added to the main wing, and the towers were covered with sophisticated copper helmets, each decorated with a statue of Atlas carrying the globe. The king supervised the artists, a team made up of the sculptors Andreas Schlüter

and Stefan Szwaner, and the painters Jerzy E. Szymonowicz-Siemiginowski, Jan Reisner, Claude Callot and Michelangelo Palloni. As a result of their abilities, the Wilanów palace received the silhouette of a Late Baroque Italian villa. Fijałkowski, a leading Polish expert on architectural conservation, finds a close resemblance between Wilanów and Rome's Villa Doria Pamphili, built by Giovanni Francesco Grimaldi and decorated by Alessandro Algardi.

The interiors were decorated with painted ceilings, frescoes, tapestries and wall hangings made of luxurious fabrics. The gardens were laid out in the Italian-French style. The large representative courtyard with its beautiful stone gate and another adjacent entrance yard dominated the front view. Two-level gardens spread alongside the palace and behind it. Designed with fountains, gilt sculptures, and a stone parapet with Baroque decorations and grottoes, it demonstrated the taste of Queen Marysieńka, who tried to enrich the palace and its surroundings with elements from her native France.

After the death of John Sobieski, his son Prince Alexander continued the enlargement of Wilanów, constructing two symmetrical wings, which formed a U-shape together with the main building. The building was further altered and added to between 1723 and 1731 by subsequent owners: Elżbieta Sieniawska, her daughter Maria Zofia Denhoffowa-Czartoryska, and August II the Strong. Architects Giovanni Spazio and Jan Zygmunt Deybel designed the buildings; the ornamentation was the work of the painters Jozef Rossi and Louis de Silvestre, and the sculptors Francesco Fumo, Pietro Innocente Comparetti and Jan Jerzy Plersch. Between 1781 and 1794 Izabela Lubomirska, wife of Prince Marshal and then owner of the palace, hired the well-known Varsovian architect Szymon Bogumił Zug for a general reconstruction and remodeling of the interiors. Zug also designed the bathhouse, the kitchen in the courtyard and the guardhouse. The gardens were rearranged in the Late Baroque style, and the former King John's grange was turned into a romantic English-Chinese park.

In the 19th century Wilanów belonged to the magnate family of the Potockis. Christian Piotr Aigner erected several romantic buildings in the gardens. The Gothic gallery was replaced with the neo-Renaissance north wing by Franciszek Maria Lanci. Henry Marconi designed the Potockis' mausoleum. In 1892 Wilanów was inherited by the Branicki family and remained their property until 1945, when it was nationalized by the government of the Polish People's Republic. The palace and the park were heavily damaged during World War II, and the government initiated a full restoration program to preserve the palace as a national monument.

The reconstruction of 1955-65 included a technical modernization of the building. Wet and dry rot was eliminated. Waterproof insulation, steel roofs, fireproof floors and staircases, and air-conditioning were installed. In addition, facades and interiors were restored, following an intensive research program. In three rooms, the original Late Baroque ceiling paintings were discovered, as well as wall and ceiling paintings from the time of Sieniawska. After the removal of layers of plaster and paint, a number of polychrome wooden ceilings were also uncovered. The scope of the conservation work included the reconstruction of stucco, wood paneling, painted ceilings and wall fabrics. Great care was given to restoring original shapes, textures and colors.

The palace now serves as a chapter of the National Museum. Part of the ground floor in the main wing is used as a reception and residence for heads of state visiting Poland.

—JERZY ANDRZEJ STARCZEWSKI

CHURCH OF THE MOST BLESSED VIRGIN MARY
Sand Island, Wrocław, Poland

1334-75: Gothic church built to replace 12th-century church. **Builder:** Probably Pieszko. **1390:** Holy Family Chapel added (remodeled in 1694). **1430:** Gothic spire added to tower (removed in 1730); **Architect:** Father Jodok of Głucholazy. **1439:** Chapel of St. John Nepomuk added. **1466-69:** Chapel of St. Anthony added; **Architect:** Jodok Tauchen. **1945:** Heavily damaged during World War II. **1946-48:** Vaults and roof reconstructed; **Architect:** W. Rawski. **1961-63:** Gothic interior restored; **Architect:** E. Malachowicz.

Publications

CZERNER, O.: "Chór kapłański i lektorium kościoła NMP we Wrocławiu w XIV w," *Kwartalnik Architektury i Urbanistyki* 3-4 (1965).

CZERNER, O., and ARCZYŃSKI, S.: *Wrocław, Krajobraz i architektura.* Warsaw, 1976.

MAŁACHOWICZ, E.: *Ostrów Tumski i Wyspy we Wrocławiu.* Warsaw, 1988.

In the 10th century, Wrocław and the whole province of Silesia, previously part of Moravia, was incorporated into the Kingdom of Poland. In the year 1000, King Boleslaus the Brave founded Wrocław Cathedral, which raised the importance of the city, putting it on a par with Gniezno and Poznań. The transfer of the Polish capital to Cracow, which took place under the reign of Casimir the Restorer, increased traffic along the east-west trade routes, and determined the development of Wrocław.

The historic center of Wrocław, which has retained its specific, unique architectural and urban character, is situated on a group of islands in the Oder. The eastern islands in the group include Cathedral Island, Mill Island and Sand Island. Cathedral Island, or Ostrów Tumski, which provided some natural defenses, became a stronghold, with fortifications built from the ninth through the 11th century. The castle on Cathedral Island fell under the jurisdiction of the church upon the extinction of the Piast dynasty in 1335, even though formally it became the property of King Władysław IV. The other islands formally belonged to the town, but enjoyed considerable freedom and privileges.

On Sand Island, timber building predominated until 1149, when the Augustinian Church of the Most Blessed Virgin Mary was built from stone. (Augustinian monks, traveling to Poland from northern France, first settled at Ślęża Mountain, but were moved by Piotr Włast and resettled in Wrocław.) According to research done by Olgierd Czerner, who investigated the remnants of the old foundations during reconstructions after World War II, the first church was a stone, single-nave, two-tower Romanesque basilica. It had a transept and a rectangular chancel with side chapels and a crypt. In the 13th century, the monks erected the masonry building of the monastery.

Even though only a few elements of the foundations of the Romanesque church survived, Czerner was able to determine the approximate shape of the structure. Among the granite foundation blocks, the sandstone tympanum placed there by the founder was discovered. The bas-relief shows Maria, widow of Piotr Włast, and her son Świętosław, offering a model of the church to the Virgin Mary. The inscription reads, "*Has matri veniae/Tibi do Maria Mariae/Has offert aedes/Swentoslaus mea proles.*" ("Oh Mary, Mother of God's Mercy, let me, Maria, and my son, Świętosław, dedicate this holy building to you as our gift.") The discovered remnants of the Romanesque church demonstrate a wealth of architectural detail and highly accomplished craftsmanship. Czerner found two granite column bases of beautiful proportions, and some stone blocks from the old church, stuccoed and covered with preserved Romanesque frescoes. The latter were used as foundations for the later Gothic church.

The development of the monastery and an increase in the number of monks first resulted in the enlargement of the church itself. In the middle of the 13th century, a brick chancel was added to the stone body of the church. Elongated in shape, with a simple flat front wall, the outline of the chancel was unearthed from the dirt during the reconstructions after World War II, and is now open to the public.

The enlargement of the church did not satisfy the ambitions of the monks, and in 1334 a new Gothic structure was begun. Even though Bishop Przecław of Pogorzela consecrated the new church in 1369, construction continued until 1375, and the decoration of the interior was not completed before 1390. The builder of the 14th-century construction was probably Pieszko ("*magister Pesco Murator apud beatam Virginem*"), who also built the Church of Mary Magdalene and the Chapel of St. Mary at the cathedral, both in Wrocław. The body of the church consists of three brick naves, all of the same height. The naves were strengthened with rather heavy buttresses, whose depth

Church of the Most Blessed Virgin Mary: Sand Island, Wrocław, Poland, 1334-75

decreased at four different levels, giving them a stair-like appearance. The thickness of the buttresses remained constant. The interiors were covered with threefold vaults, each supported at three points, and reinforced with stone and brick ribs. Other architectural details include carved stone supports of the ribs, window frames, and decorated keystones on the arches. Some of these are characteristic of the Silesian Gothic of the second half of the 14th century. The stucco walls were covered with frescoes. The northern nave has three subsidiary chapels, fitted between the buttresses: the Holy Family Chapel (1390), the Chapel of St. John Nepomuk (1439) and the Chapel of St. Anthony, erected by Jodok Tauchen in the years 1466-69. In 1694 the Holy Family Chapel was remodeled in the Baroque style.

In the 15th century the interior was enriched with a stone lectorium, which divided the chancel from the principal nave. A number of frescoes were completed between 1465 and 1477, which have been preserved in fragments. The church originally had stained-glass windows, mentioned in a chronicle of 1666, but they were replaced in that year with clear glass.

Of the two towers, only the southern one was completed and, in 1430, covered with a Gothic spire by Father Superior Jodok of Głuchołazy. It caught fire several times. After 1730 the spire was replaced with a simple tent roof. The interior, also heavily damaged by fire, was redone in the Silesian Baroque. According to information by Stenus, writing in 1512, the church had three independent steep pitched roofs over the three naves. Stone gutters ran along the walls between the naves. The roof structure burned a number of times. In the 18th century, the three roofs were replaced with one steep pitched roof, which survived until World War II.

The war damage and fire of 1945 not only destroyed the roof, but also all Baroque furnishings and decorations. Most of the vaults collapsed, and the eastern wall of the chancel was ruined. The reconstruction of the church was conducted in two stages. W. Rawski rebuilt the vaults and the roof (1946-48). E. Małachowicz restored the Gothic appearance of the interior (1961-63). Since all the Baroque furnishings were destroyed, the interior has been equipped with Gothic altars, a baptistery in the 15th-century style, and new stained-glass windows.

Adjacent to the church stands the monastery complex. The main Baroque building was erected after 1709, according to a design by Johann Georg Kalkbrenner. Destroyed in 1945, it was rebuilt in the years 1956-59. The old medieval wing of the monastery was not rebuilt. Gothic bricks from that building were used for the reconstruction of the church.

—JERZY ANDRZEJ STARCZEWSKI

PORTUGAL

ABBEY CHURCH
Alcobaça, Portugal

1153: Foundation. **1178ff:** Construction. **1252:** Dedication. **14th century:** Cloister and annexes added. **16th-18th centuries:** Expansions to the south and east. **1725:** Baroque facade; **Architect:** Giovanni Turriano. **1930:** Restoration.

Publications

CHICÓ, MÁRIO TAVARES: *A arquitectura gótica em Portugal.* Lisbon, 1954.

COCHERIL, MAUR: *Notes sur l'architecture et le décor dans les abbayes cisterciennes du Portugal.* Paris, 1972: 49-102, 138-143.

COCHERIL, MAUR: *Routier des abbayes cisterciennes du Portugal.* Paris, 1978: 221-304.

COCHERIL, MAUR: *Alcobaça, abadia cisterciense de Portugal.* Lisbon, 1989.

DIAS, PEDRO (ed.): *História da arte em Portugal. O Gótico.* Vol. 4. Barcelona, 1986: 14-22.

DIMIER, ANSELME: *Recueil de plans d'eglise cisterciennes.* Supplement. Paris, 1967: 56.

GUSMÃO, ARTUR DE: *A real abadia de Alcobaça.* Lisbon, 1948.

PARREAUX, A.: *Excursion à Alcobaça et Batalha.* Paris, 1956.

SEQUEIRA, GUSTAVO DE MATOS: *Inventário artistico do Distrito de Leiria.* Lisbon, 1955: 5-15.

*

The Cistercian Abbey of Santa Maria at Alcobaça, located some 100 kilometers north of Lisbon, was founded in 1153 as a direct filiation of Saint Bernard's headquarters at Clairvaux. It was the second settlement of the Cistercian order in Portugal. The abbey was founded by the Portuguese king Dom Afonso Henriques, and its fate was intimately connected with that of his kingdom, which had just achieved independence from Spain. Afonso and his successors granted the abbey numerous privileges, with the result that it became one of the wealthiest and most powerful, and became the religious and intellectual center of the country. Only the French invasion of 1810 and the subsequent dissolution of the Cistercian order in Portugal in 1834 put an end to the abbey's prosperity.

The complex, which was restored in 1930 and today serves as a museum, grew to its present size during the course of eight centuries. The original complex was essentially laid out according to the Cistercian ideal plan, with the not-quite-unique exception that the monastic buildings were separately situated, to the north of the church. The location of the monastic buildings may be explained by the course of the river, which was indispensable to monastic housekeeping. The cloister and its annexes were erected in the early 14th century, and they constitute, in spite of later alterations in the western wing, an impressive example of medieval Cistercian architecture. From the 16th century to the 18th century, the abbey was expanded to the south and to the east. Members of the royal family were buried in the abbey, and their tombs are outstanding examples of Portuguese Gothic sculpture.

The abbey church is of exceptional significance, not only for the architectural history of Portugal but for all of Europe. According to an inscription on the passage to the cloister, the present building was begun in 1178, and was a replacement of a modest earlier structure. That original church had been executed according to the so-called Bernardine Formula, and had a square apse. The surviving church was dedicated in 1252, but was certainly not complete at that time. The cruciform structure has a nave of three aisles and 13 bays, and a transept with two aisles which ends in a square chapel on the eastern side. The central nave ends in a choir with ambulatory, which has a polygonal 9/16 end with radial chapels. The radial chapels in turn have trapezoidal ends. The sacristy is a narrower continuation of the northern arm of the transept.

The principal spaces are almost identical in height (central nave and transept 20.1 meters high, lateral aisles and presbytery 19.4 meters high), and are all covered with groin vaults. The structure is illuminated by windows in the lateral naves, by roses in the facade and by the two rows of windows in the clerestory of the presbytery. The exterior has a squarish, closed appearance, with buttresses on the southern and eastern sides. On the northern side the church adjoins the cloister. The choir has open buttresses. The Baroque facade, which incorporates parts of the Early Gothic portal, was erected in 1725 by the Italian Frei Giovanni Turriano.

The interior is imposing both for its dimensions and the quality of the stonework. It is articulated by compound piers, both in the nave and transept. The cruciform center is marked by powerful engaged columns, though more slender versions of these are set in the corners of some of the bays. The fairly shallow vault is supported by strongly projecting wall arches and profiled ribs, which rise across varied capitals decorated with a flowerbud motif. The rib intersections have no keystones. In the central nave the engaged columns are coffered in three different ways, to mark the three different sections of the space: the first four bays (counting from the crossing) contain the monks' choir, the next two the choir for the sick, and the next four the choir for converts. The unusually narrow and steep lateral naves, which are barely more than 2 meters wide, served as passages. The presbytery has a two-level elevation. Powerful columns are set on a continuous base at the level of the arcades. Small windows alternating above these pierce the wall. The clerestory is very long. Windows, set over the engaged columns of the lower third, pierce the base of the vault.

The Abbey Church of Alcobaça is extremely similar in plan to Clairvaux III, and may well be the most precise and best preserved image of the destroyed model, both with regard to structure and to proportion. With its 106 meters, Alcobaça is exactly of the same length, and is after Vaucelles (destroyed) and Pontigny the third-largest church of the Cistercian order.

An individual trait of the church at Alcobaça is the similarity in height of the different principal spaces, which rarely occurs in Cistercian architecture, and then mostly in connection with local traditions (as at Haina, Germany). Such local traditions do not seem to have existed in Portugal, which may point to peculiarities in the support system as an immediate cause for this design. An influence from southern France is another possibility. The elevation of the choir uses elements of Pontigny, which like Alcobaça was built after the model of Clairvaux. The robust exterior, however, connects the Portuguese structure with other Cistercian abbeys of the Iberian peninsula, for instance with Santes Creus in Catalonia.

Abbey Church: Alcobaça, Portugal, 1178ff

There is hardly any doubt that the Church of Alcobaça was built by French workmen or under the direction of French masters, and that this was the way in which the constructive systems of Burgundian Gothic architecture were brought into Portugal. Admittedly, attempts had been made before to construct groin vaults for single building elements, but Alcobaça was the first Portuguese building completely in the Gothic style. The new building realized at Alcobaça did not immediately find imitators. As becomes clear in a comparison with Évora Cathedral, built at the same time, Romanesque elements continued to be used well into the 13th century. It was the architecture of the mendicant orders—which, however, picked up other aspects of the Gothic style than did the Cistercian order—that later helped to establish the Gothic style in Portugal.

It is not to be ruled out, however, that the spatial design of Alcobaça had an influence on the composition of the Convent Church of Batalha, which was founded in 1388 by João I, in gratitude for the victory over the Castilians. During the Manueline era many churches were built on the same principles of relative aisles of equal height as Alcobaça, but whether this was due to Alcobaça's example is unclear.

The Church of the Cistercian Abbey of Alcobaça appears not to have been created out of indigenous architectural traditions, nor to have had an immediate influence on them. For research into medieval architecture and its dissemination by the Cistercian order, however, the church is of great importance. Although the matter of height was developed independently of the Burgundian example, and thus demonstrates the multiplicity of possibilities afforded by the Cistercian models, the church is a faithful copy of the model with regard to plan. For the reconstruction of the lost building of Clairvaux III, the Abbey Church of Alcobaça may be the most important point of departure.

—BARBARA BORNGÄSSER KLEIN
Translated from the German by Marijke Rijsberman

MONASTERY OF SANTA MARIA DA VITÓRIA
Batalha, Portugal

1388-1402: Transeptal chapels, walls of central axial chapel, walls and piers of nave and aisles, aisle vaults, south transept portal, lower portions of cloister galleries, chapter house, vaults of east and south cloister galleries constructed; **Architect:** Afonso Domingues (died in 1402). **1402-25:** Vaults over central axial chapel, transept, nave, aisles, vaulting of west and north cloister galleries, great stellar vault of chapterhouse, east window constructed; **Architect:** Huguet (or Ouguete) (died in 1440). **1426-34:** Founder's Chapel constructed; **Architect:** Huguet. **1434-38:** Lower half of central octagon and its radiating chapels constructed; **Architect:** Huguet. **1503-09:** Vestibule linking church and Capelas Imperfeitas, great portal of Capelas Imperfeitas constructed; **Architect:** Mateus Fernandes (died 1515). **1509-15:** Pier and buttress extensions of central octagon constructed; **Architects:** Mateus Fernandes and/or Diogo Boytac. **1500-19:** Tracery panels inserted into gallery arcades; **Architect:** Diogo Boytac or Mateus Fernandes. **1755:** Flêches over Founders Chapel and over north transept damaged. **1840-1936:** Restoration.

Publications

CHICÓ, M. T.: *A arquitectura gótica em Portugal*. Lisbon, 1981.
DA SILVA BARROS, C. V.: *Le monastère de Batalha*. Lisbon, 1969.
DE ALBUQUERQUE, L.: *Memória inédita acerca do edifício monumental da Batalha*. Lisbon, 1854.
DE AZEVEDO, C.: *Churches of Portugal*. New York, 1985.
História da arte em Portugal. Oporto, 1948. Vol. 2: 20-56.
LAMBERT, E.: "L'église du monastère dominicain de Batalha et l'architecture cistercienne." *Mélanges d'études portugaises, offerts à G. Le Gentil*. Lisbon, 1949: 243-256.
LAMBERT, E.: *Etudes médiévales*. Toulose, 1956. Vol. 3: 277-81, 292.
MURPHY, J. K.: *History and Description of the Royal Convent of Batalha*. London, 1792.
Plans, Elevations, Sections and Views of the Church of Batalha. London, 1795.
SMITH, R. C.: *The Art of Portugal: 1500-1800* New York, 1968: 52-54.
WATSON, W. C.: *Portuguese Architecture*. London, 1908: Chapters 4, 12.

*

The Dominican Monastery of Santa Maria da Vitória, at Batalha (Portuguese for battle), was founded by Dom João I to commemorate his decisive victory over the Spanish in the battle of Aljubarrota. Fought on 14 August 1385 some ten miles south of the monastery's actual location, this battle assured Portuguese independence from Spain for the next two centuries. That Batalha remains even today a potent symbol of national pride and unity is evident by the fact that Portugal's Unknown Soldier of World War I is entombed with full military honors in the monastery's great chapterhouse.

Architecturally, Batalha is significant for possessing not only one of Portugal's largest Gothic buildings, but also one of Europe's most extensive and best-preserved monastic ensembles from the later Middle Ages. In this essay, only the most original and influential structures of this vast complex will be critically analyzed.

However magnificent and impressive Batalha's later additions may be, none are more important and significant for Gothic architecture in Portugal than the monastery's majestic yet soberly conceived church. Begun in 1388 by Afonso Domingues, a native architect presumably responsible for the mid-14th-century chevet of Lisbon's cathedral, the Dominican church at Batalha demonstrates continuity with the past while also revealing some new, precedent-setting features. Like earlier mendicant churches in Portugal, Batalha also employs a Cistercian-type ground plan, recognizable as such by the treatment of the east end as a series of contiguous chapels opening directly off the transept arms. But unlike its mendicant predecessors, Batalha's chevet is more impressive and more regularly organized, since all four of its transeptal chapels are of equal depth, width and height and, like the wider and taller chancel they flank, each is terminated by a polygonal apse. But what renders Batalha's east end so arresting and original is the loftiness of the chancel, which is nearly as high as the nave itself (26.50 meters), and the two-story scheme of its apsidal fenestration. (All measurements are approximate.) This elegant handling of the east end

Monastery of S. Maria: Batalha, Portugal, 1388-1402

later provided the inspiration for the chevets of such major churches as that of the Carmelites in Lisbon and the cathedral at Guarda.

The western half of Batalha also displays a combination of old and new ideas. The employment in the nave of a two-part elevation consisting of a tall arcade and a short clerestory adheres to well-established local traditions. But quite unlike the two-story mendicant and nonmendicant churches of earlier generations, Batalha is rib-vaulted (rather than timber-roofed), the nave piers thick (2.65 meters) and closely spaced, and the outer walls massive. All this, in combination with the narrowness of the nave (8.20 meters) and the extreme steepness of its proportions (1:3.2), endows Batalha with a distinctly nonmendicant air. Grandeur, strength and soaring verticality characterize the nave as well as the aisles. The spaciousness and openness that one generally associates with mendicant architecture both in Portugal and elsewhere in Europe are conspicuously, and perhaps purposely, absent at Batalha.

Surviving medieval documents suggest that in this monastery the principal task of the Dominican friars was not preaching, but rather praying for the deceased members of the royal house of Aviz, most of whom were buried at Batalha, including Prince Henry the Navigator. Such royal patronage may account for one of the church's most striking features: its great size and length relative to others in Portugal. For even if Batalha had a large community of friars, the nave, where the choir stalls were normally located (in the easternmost bays), seems, nevertheless, inordinately long, an impression that is further strengthened when the town of Batalha's tiny lay population is also taken into consideration. It is not inconceivable to think that a certain

degree of architectural display, particularly in length and height, was deliberately designed into this church as a means of emphasizing the emerging power and prestige of the Portuguese monarchy. And it is no less conceivable that its considerable length (80 meters), although not necessarily its grandeur and monumentality, was expressly desired by the Dominicans for purely functional reasons. The two aisles, each eight bays long, would have provided places for the erection of the many altars the friars needed for their private masses. The establishment of altars in the aisles is well documented for similarly planned mendicant churches in Italy, where, as in Batalha, their east ends are sparsely furnished with chapels.

When Afonso Domingues died in 1402, Huguet was chosen to complete the church. He was clearly conversant with the formal vocabulary of northern Late Gothic, but his allegedly foreign—and particularly English—origin has never been confirmed. To Huguet must be attributed the vast majority of the rib vaults. Although his use of longitudinal ridge-ribs finds ample precedent in earlier Portuguese architecture, he went a step further by also employing transverse ridge-ribs in both the nave and transept vaults.

More interesting and significant for later Gothic architecture in Portugal are Huguet's vaults in the chancel; they indicate familiarity with, if not direct knowledge of, English and French vaulting practices. The straight portion of the chancel is crowned by a ribbed, pointed barrel vault with short side penetrations and diagonal ribs traversing two successive bays. Structurally and aesthetically, this vault may be regarded as a simpler and smoother version of the vaults erected in the early 13th century at the church of Airvault, in Anjou, France. The vaulting system of the Batalha chancel quickly found fertile soil in Portugal, as numerous 15th- and 16th-century churches testify. In certain of these, the vaults show remarkable similarities in design and structure with Late Gothic vault construction in central and eastern Europe.

Huguet also executed the west front of the church. Particularly interesting and controversial there is the blind vertical paneling that ripples across the walls above the portal and central window, and along the outer face of the inner buttresses. Whether English Perpendicular is the source for Huguet's graphic fantasies is another issue surrounding this architect which remains unresolved.

At the request of João I, Huguet in 1426 initiated construction of the Founder's Chapel along the church's south flank. A mausoleum for the king and members of the Aviz dynasty, the chapel is a centrally planned structure composed of an elegant octagonal core rising from within and above a square ambulatory. The stellar-vaulted lantern, the central core's upper section, is carried aloft by highly stilted arches springing from the eight compound piers that define the chapel's octagonal inner base. The cusping on these stilted arches is so prominent and visually stimulating that it immediately captures the viewer's attention and even holds it at the expense of other interesting features. The Founder's Chapel thus recalls, but more boldly, Huguet's earlier use of cusping in the triumphal arch of the church's chancel and in the intrados of the nave's westernmost flying buttresses. Perhaps the later Portuguese penchant for cusping architecturally prominent arches has its roots in Huguet's oeuvre at Batalha.

In addition to the church, Huguet also completed the monastery's Royal Cloister and chapterhouse, both begun by Afonso Domingues and only half-finished at the time of his death. Particularly dramatic was the effect this midstream change of architects had on the chapterhouse's final appearance. Huguet rejected the conventional nine-bay, three-aisle plan of his predecessor for a unified spatial scheme. Over a vast and totally unencumbered area 19.30 by 19.30 meters square, he erected a breathtaking eight-pointed stellar vault which for sheer audacity alone merits admiration.

Directly east of the church, Huguet initiated construction of an octagonal funerary rotunda with radiating chapels. Commissioned around 1434 by Dom Duarte I, this grand project was never fully realized, hence its name, the Capelas Imperfeitas, or Unfinished Chapels. During Portugal's exuberant Manueline Period (late 15th and early 16th centuries) an unsuccessful attempt was made to finish this royal pantheon.

The first phase, completed by Mateus Fernandes in 1509, involved the construction of a vaulted vestibule in order to link the rotunda to the church's east end. Communication between vestibule and octagon was facilitated by the erection of a lavishly and intricately carved doorway of truly monumental proportions (5.5 meters deep, 8 meters wide and 13.70 meters high). Viewed from the vestibule, this double-splayed and many-layered portal is composed of an inner series of trilobed arches framed externally by two orders of multiple concave arches swinging in a curve and countercurve movement. The uncanny resemblance between Batalha's doorway and the main north-porch portal of Bristol's St. Mary Redcliffe has long been recognized.

On the rotunda side, the great doorway is dominated instead by a huge arch, itself the aggregate of a series of cusped, interlaced round- and ogee-shaped arches, with the peaks of the latter terminating in bushy crockets. This side, however, resembles not the aforementioned portal of St. Mary Redcliffe, but rather the stellate tomb-recesses along the church's south aisle. If there is indeed a relationship between Batalha and Bristol as these correspondences suggest, chronological reasons

alone would argue in favor of an English origin for the Batalha design, since the Bristol monuments antedate the portal of the Capelas Imperfeitas by nearly two centuries. Given the dynastic links between England and the Portuguese royal house, and more important, the vigorous trade conducted by Bristol merchants with Portugal in the 15th and 16th centuries, English influence at Batalha cannot be discounted even if it cannot be documented.

On the rotunda itself, work resumed around 1510, only to be definitively abandoned a generation later. During that period little else was accomplished beyond raising the piers and buttresses to their present 25-meter height. Although Mateus Fernandes may have had a hand in this new Manueline construction, the ornamental detailing, which is fleshy and undulating, points to Diogo Boytac. He is known to have worked at Batalha until at least 1519, and it is almost certain that he was responsible for the stone tracery panels now filling the arcades of the Royal Cloister. These screen inserts, carved in Boytac's lush, organic style, contrast sharply, but not unpleasantly, with the harder and more refined forms of the cloister's original, late 14th- and early 15th-century fabric.

—RICHARD A. SUNDT

JERONYMITE MONASTERY
Belém, Portugal

1501: Construction begins; **Architects:** Diogo Boytac (*fl.* 1490-1525), João de Castilho (*fl.* 1515-52). **1540-51:** Apse rebuilding begins; **Architect:** Diogo de Torralva (1540-51). **1571:** Apse completed; **Architect:** Jerónimo de Ruão.

Publications

"As relações artísticas entre Portugal e Espanha na época dos descobrimentos." *Actas do II simpósio luso-espanhol de história da arte 28. 6. bis 2. 7. 1983 a Coimbra*. Coimbra, Portugal, 1987.
ATANÁZIO, M. C. MENDES: *A arte do Manuelino*. Lisbon, 1984.
HAUPT, ALBRECHT: *Die Baukunst der Renaissance in Portugal*. 2 vols. Frankfurt, 1890-95.
MOREIRA, RAFAEL: *Jeronimos*. Lisbon, 1987.
SMITH, R. C.: *The Art of Portugal, 1500-1800*. London, 1968.

*

The Jeronymite Monastery of Belém (Bethlehem) just outside the gates of Lisbon, not far from the mouth of the Tagus River, is the chief work of the era of Manuel I, both in terms of its architecture and of its ideological expressiveness. It was an age on the threshold between the Middle Ages and modernity, and the time when Portugal became a world power as a consequence of its maritime explorations. Mostly built in the first quarter of the 16th century, the complex combines Late Gothic structural principles with Plateresque decorative forms and dynastic symbolism, which give the monument an unmistakably Portuguese character.

The monastery was a royal foundation, dating from 1496, and was planned as a burial site for the Aviz dynasty. At the same time, it served as the site of devotion for departing and returning sailors. The present building is a replacement of a hermitage founded by Prince Henry the Navigator and subject

Jeronymite Monastery: Belém, Portugal, 1502

to the Order of Christ. The earlier structure was no longer sufficient for the practical and ideological requirements of the new age. The new monastery, entrusted to the Jeronymites, was financed by profits reaped in the colonies. Its ornamentation was to be worthy of the ascending colonial empire. Together with the neighboring Tower of Belém, the Jeronymite Monastery formed the outpost of the capital of the former colonial power of Portugal.

On Epiphany Day, 1501, the foundation stone for the epochal monument was laid. The first master of the works was Diogo Boytac or Boutaca (ca. 1460-1528), an artist possibly of French origin, who had already been involved with the construction of the Mosteiro de Jesus at Setúbal. A now-lost document indicated that he planned a complex with four cloisters, much larger than the previous building. Not all of Boytac's designs were actually executed, however. Only the church, which lies parallel to the river on an east-west axis, the cloister immediately to the north of the church, and an arcaded west wing with dormitories in the upper floor (altered in the 19th century) were built. The southern facade, which faces the river, must have impressed all travelers with its length of more than 300 meters.

The plan of this church—with its three naves of equal height, and its transept which barely juts out—was conceived under Boytac's supervision. The system of supports and the peculiar vault, which pulls together the entire interior space, were completed after 1517 by João de Castilho (1475-1552), an architect and sculptor of Spanish origin, who was involved in all of King Manuel's important commissions. The complex net vault of the nave is supported by six octagonal pillars, which are 25 meters high and completely covered with ornamentation in the Renaissance style. The transept vault is cantilevered. The building is

a technical as well as an artistic masterpiece, and withstood the earthquake of 1755 completely undamaged. The exterior is defined by the richly decorated frames of the portals, on which a complex figurative iconography unfolds itself. The decoration of the western portal portrays the presentation of the royal founder and his wife to St. Jerome—a theme derived from the Carthusian Monastery of Champmol. The southern portal contains a long cycle representing Henry the Navigator in the center of a missionary iconography. Foreign masters were employed for the sculptural decoration also, principally the Frenchman Nicolas Chanterenne and Diogo de Castilho, who was João's brother.

João de Castilho was active at Belém until about 1530, and the Sacristy and parts of the Cloister may be ascribed to him. The *capela-mor* (literally, "main chapel"), intended as a pantheon for Manuel and his successors, on the other hand, was demolished in 1563 and reconstructed by Diogo de Torralva in a Mannerist style, close to that of the Escorial in Spain. Torralva was responsible for the design, but Jean de Rouen completed the construction. The unornamented cube-like exterior expresses the clear articulation of the interior with Ionic and Corinthian columns, which are continued in the ribs of the coffered vault. The structure of this tunnel-like space exercised a great influence on numerous 17th-century buildings. The design of the choir stands in conscious contrast to the Late Gothic forms of the earlier buildings.

The cloister, planned by Boytac but executed mainly by João de Castilho, is the most magnificent example of Manueline architecture, poised to embrace the Renaissance. The square, two-level structure has six bays to each wing, covered with net vaults. Four of the six bays are opened up by a wide and deep

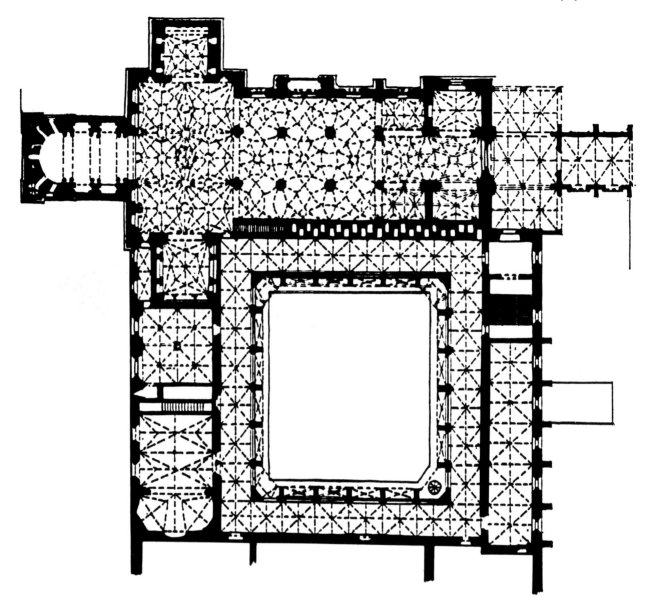

arcade, set between powerful buttresses. While Late Gothic forms dominate in the interior, the facades turned to the court-yard prominently display Plateresque decorative elements, which may have to be credited to João de Castilho. The orna-mentation of flat surfaces and the placement of the traceried columns within the arcades dissolve the massiveness of the structure into a delicate filigree. The entire building, with the gradually diminishing round arches and the emphasis on hori-zontals, already points in the direction of the Renaissance. The proximity to Spanish monuments is unmistakable. Torralva's stone parapet, which is decorated with medallions, was already entirely in the new taste. The sacristy and the chapter house, both covered with Late Gothic vaults, are located on the eastern side, while the refectory is to be found on the western side.

The cloister was probably intended not only for the monks' devotions, but to have a representative function. As in the church, Late Gothic structures are ornamented in a Renaissance style, combining figurative representations with emblematic motifs, such as the Cross of the Order of Christ, the armillary sphere and coats of arms. The single elements come together in an impressive decor, whose iconographic program has not nearly been exhaustively interpreted.

The expansion of the Jeronymite Monastery at Belém was motivated not only by the requirements of pastoral care, but, more important, carried the ideological burden of a rising colo-nial power in the process of creating its own image. Moreover, thoughts of a rapprochement or reunification of Spain and Portu-gal had revived. Manuel had plans to marry his son João with Leonora of Austria, who was the sister of the later emperor Charles V. In 1517 the decision was made to move the burial sites of the Aviz dynasty from the Convent of Santa Maria da Vitória in Batalha to Belém. Manuel himself wished to be buried "in the choir chapel, before the altar, under the steps," without the benefit of a raised tomb, "so that the people could walk over it." His plan came to nothing in the face of opposition from the monks, however. Manuel and his family found their last resting place in the choir and the transept only in the second half of the 16th century.

In the 19th century the Jeronymite Monastery became the focus of Portuguese nationalism. As the point of departure of the great maritime explorations, shrouded in legend, the building retained its ideological value also after (or, perhaps, *especially* after) the collapse of the colonial empire. The building took on a rich life in Portuguese literature, for example. In 1894 the cenotaphs of Vasco da Gama and Luis de Camões were placed in the first bays of the nave. Many more graves of Portuguese poets and politicians in the cloister buildings followed.

Given this historical background, the past and present significance of the Jeronymite Monastery, like its artistic importance, becomes clear. As a royal foundation and burial site, and as the point of departure and return of the heroic maritime voyages, the building had to manifest visibly the claims and powers of a great nation. For the quality of its architecture and the complexity of its decorative programs, the Jeronymite Monastery at Belém must be considered one of the peak achievements not only of Portuguese architecture but of all European architecture.
—BARBARA BORNGÄSSER KLEIN
Translated from the German by Marijke Rijsberman

ROYAL PALACE
Queluz, Portugal

1747-58: Main block construction; **Architect:** Mateus Vicente de Oliveira (1706-86). **1758-86:** Formal gardens laid out, 'Don Quixote' wing designed, interiors decorated; **Architect:** Jean-Baptiste Robillion (d.1782). **1792:** Construction completed.

Publications

KUBLER, GEORGE, and SORIA, MARTIN: *Art and Architecture in Spain and Portugal and their American Dominions, 1500-1800.* Harmondsworth, 1959.
WATSON, W. C.: *Portugese Architecture.* London, 1908.

*

The Palace of Queluz, near Lisbon, is the premier Portuguese example of the courtly, French-inspired Rococo style of the mid-18th century. Its design reflects the shift away from the Italian models of the Portuguese Baroque or "Joanine" style cultivated by J. F. Ludovice at Mafra, and the ascendance around mid-century of a Portuguese taste for French fashions in architecture, planning and interior decoration.

Adjoining the original nucleus of the Castelo Rodrigo hunting pavilion of the late 16th century, the main block, or *corps-de-logis,* was designed in the manner of a French *château de plaisance* for the brother of King José I (ruled 1750-77), L'Infant D. Pedro III and his wife (later Queen Maria I). It was begun in 1747 by the Portuguese military engineer Mateus Vicente de Oliveira (1706-86), Ludovice's most important pupil. In 1758 Mateus Vicente was called away to assist in the reconstruction of earthquake-torn Lisbon, and the French goldsmith Jean-Baptiste Robillion (died 1782) assumed the works. Between 1758 and Dom Pedro's death in 1786, he laid out the formal gardens, designed the "Dom Quixote" wing in the Louis XIV mode, and decorated the interiors in a rich French Rococo style.

Although the palace complex was not finished until 1792, it corresponded in spirit and style to the aristocratic values of the

Royal Palace: Queluz, Portugal, 1747-58

royal court of the Bragança family, whose power and artistic values were challenged by the reforming priorities of the marquis of Pombal, the Portuguese prime minister during the reign of King José I. The severe style of functional architecture and the Vaubanesque *urbanisme militaire* adapted by Pombal in his reconstruction of Lisbon after the earthquake of 1755 has been seen as the stylistic and spiritual antithesis of the decoratively elegant Queluz. However, both ''Pombaline'' Lisbon and courtly Queluz illustrate, albeit in very different ways, the wider preference in late-18th-century Portugal for French models—classicizing, Rococo or military—over the heavier Italianate forms of the old Joanine.

The Château of Queluz has often been compared to the Sans-Souci Palace in Potsdam (1745-47), built for Frederick the Great by Georg Wenzeslaus von Knobelsdorff, and to the Amalienburg pavilion in the Nymphenburg Park in Munich (1734-39), by François Cuvilliés the Elder. A formal analysis of the facade of the main building at Queluz, however, suggests closer parallels with the late-17th-century French architecture favored by Louis XIV. Laid out in a formal, symmetrically planned ''U'' with a main *corps-de-logis,* flanking pavilions and a *cour d'honneur* leading to the gardens, Queluz illustrates the Portuguese military engineer's integration of French formal planning and stylish Rococo ornament with the same Joanine concern for a quality decorative finish that characterized Ludovice's work at Mafra.

The Rococo style of Queluz was essentially a Portuguese decorative overlay on a château in the Louis XIV mode of Jules Hardouin-Mansart's Pavilion at Marly (1679). Stripped of its ornament, the main garden facade by Mateus Vicente would closely resemble that of Mansart's château. Both facades are two-story compositions with giant pilasters and a three-bay frontispiece crowned by a triangular pediment. The pilasters support straight, unadorned entablatures. In Queluz, however, the composition has been condensed into seven bays, which are more widely spaced than the nine bays of Marly, and which follow a 2-3-2 grouping created by the four pairs of overlapping pilasters that define the frontispiece and the ends of the pavilion. The triangular pediment is carved with the Portuguese royal escutcheon and garlands on each side. A typically Portuguese tile roof is visible behind the balustrade that runs on either side of the pediment. The fenestration is also a key element in the decorative system of the facade. Sculptural ornamentation in the form of floral motifs and cartouches framing *putti* is limited to the tops of the segmental frames around the French doors. On the upper story, these doors open onto grilled balconies with bases defined by a stringcourse which, supported by pairs of consoles, extend the length of the facade. The central door of the main story is framed by paired columns and a curvilinear frame, which is echoed in the frame and rippled pediment (of Joanine derivation) in the French door above. The ochre and pink plaster finishes on the wall surfaces, otherwise unadorned, give dainty Rococo coloring to the whole.

Mateus Vicente's work at Queluz demonstrates that the Portuguese military engineer trained in the Academia Militar in Lisbon and at Ludovice's school at Mafra could work comfortably in a complex French international idiom that fused rococo decoration and *style Louis XIV* architecture. It also reflected the desire of the Portuguese aristocracy on the eve of the Lisbon earthquake to speak that idiom through architecture, to emulate the artistic achievements of the French *roi soleil* by using French models and, when necessary, French artists to create a courtly pleasure palace that was to be, as one writer put it, the Versailles that Portugal never had. Robillion's ''Dom Quixote'' wing (1774-86), with its paired Doric columns supporting straight entablatures surmounted by military trophies like those found

at Versailles, is the most characteristically Louis XIV aspect of the palace. But the Versailles comparison should not be pushed too far. In its much more intimate scale and in its original function as a retreat house, an escape from the pompous routine of the court, Queluz is more akin to the tradition of Ange-Jacques Gabriel's Petit Trianon in the park at Versailles than to Louis XIV's grandiose palace.

—DAVID K. UNDERWOOD

CHRISTO CHURCH
Tomar, Portugal

1160ff: Construction; **Architect:** Gualdim Pais. **Early 16th century:** Nave, chapter room constructed; **Architect:** Diogo de Arruda (*fl.* 1508-1531). **1557-62:** Main cloister constructed; **Architects:** Diogo de Torralva (1500-66), F. Terzia.

Publications

DIAS, PEDRO (ed.): *História da arte em Portugal. O manuelino.* Lisbon, 1986.
HAUPT, ALBRECHT: *Die Baukunst der Renaissance in Portugal.* 2 vols. Frankfurt, 1890-95.
MENDES ATANÁZIO, M. C.: *A arte do manuelino.* Lisbon, 1984.
SEQUEIRA, GUSTAVO DE MATOS: *Inventário artístico de Portugal. Distrito de Santarém.* Lisbon, 1949.
SMITH, R. C.: *The Art of Portugal, 1500-1800.* London, 1968.

*

Two significant complexes dating from different eras are combined in the Church of the Order of Christ at Tomar. The fort-like central church, built by the Knights Templar, was built in the second half of the 12th century. The annex of the Order of Christ, serving as choir and chapterhouse, by João de Castilho and Diogo de Arruda, was built in the early 16th century. This annex is a key work of Manueline architecture, and is the best preserved example of the style.

The Order of the Knights Templar, founded in 1119 to protect pilgrims traveling to the Holy Land, had been active in the reconquest of Portugal. As a reward they were granted land by Afonso Henriques, the first Portuguese king. The Templars' Castle at Tomar, some 100 kilometers north of Lisbon, was built, on a site chosen for defensive reasons, in 1160 by Gualdim Pais. Besides parts of the outer walls, the church has been preserved. It is a 16-cornered structure with flying buttresses. In the interior a two-level domed octagon separates the sanctuary from the ambulatory. The doubling of the side walls of the central space and disjunctions in the execution lead to the suspicion that the circular aisle and the outer walls were added later. A comparison of the plan with other centralized buildings of the order in Segovia, Paris and Laon or with that of the Church of Eunate must therefore remain inconclusive. In spite of such imponderables, the building is an outstanding example of Late Romanesque architecture. The pictorial and sculptural decoration, both of high quality, dates from the 16th century.

In 1312 the Order of the Templars was dissolved, but the Portuguese king Dini immediately created the Order of Christ in its stead. The Order of Christ took over all the properties of the Templars. The new order was intimately connected with Portugal's ascendancy as a colonial power, and the spiritual

Christo Church: Tomar, Portugal, 1510-14

care of the conquered territories was entrusted to it. The transformation of the Templars' Castle into the Monastery of the Order of Christ was thus motivated both by pragmatic reasons and by the need to represent the might of the colonial empire in a suitable architectural style. In an initial campaign two cloisters were erected in the southeast corner of the compound. Under Manuel I, who was both king of Portugal and grand master of the order, the expansion of the church was undertaken. The earlier structure had for long been inadequate for the growing community of monks, and there was no chapter house. Two of the northern sides of the outer walls were torn down to make room for the new Church of the Order of Christ.

Diogo de Arruda erected a rectangular two-story space, whose six bays were covered with net vaults. João de Castilho, court architect of Manuel I, and hailing from the Biscaye area, took over after Arruda left the project. He created the wide pointed arches at the new and old structures. Medallions of the Evangelists and the cross of the order were painted on the arch. The famous choir stall by Olivier of Ghent (1509) was destroyed during the French invasion of 1810.

The Church of the Knights of Christ is a key work of the Manueline style, whose essential achievement lies in the decoration of upper surfaces and the subtle expression of ideological content. The exuberant decoration of the exterior, also the work of João de Castilho, stands in stark contrast to the sparing but impressive ornamentation of the interior. The portal, the window surrounds, the massive, stepped buttresses and the continuous frieze display the entire Manueline repertoire of decorative motifs. These decorations also constitute a political program: royal coats of arms and emblems, nautical instruments, ropes and cables, marine flora and fauna are part of the pictorial world, and are interwoven with the religious images placed under the cross of the order. As on the southern portal of the Jeronymite Monastery at Belém, the central portal is surrounded by a Late Gothic traceried arch, which rises the entire height of the facade. Under this arch a complex iconographic program unfolds itself. Traditional Christian elements representing prophets, saints and a central Mary figure are combined with an armillary sphere above the archivolt. As a symbol of nautical science, the presence of the sphere demonstrates the importance of maritime concerns in the Manueline era. The great maritime explorations of the time were understood as Christian missions, and thoughts of a New Crusade to liberate the holy sites revived.

At Tomar, as also in other churches if the early 16th century, secular elements came to take up a foreground position in decorative programs. The most prominent example of the rich imagination and creative power of the Manueline era are the outer surrounds of the windows of the chapter house, attributable either to Diogo de Arruda or to João de Castilho. Algae, coral, mussels and ships' cables are twined across the walls like vines. The entire composition is supported by a kneeling figure (the artist?), who is crowned and flanked by the emblems of the Portuguese royal dynasty, the cross of the order, and another armillary sphere.

The imaginative naturalistic and emblematic decorative motifs to be found at the Church of the Order of Christ at Tomar typify the art of an era on the threshold between the Middle Ages and modernity, which translates the experience of the age of world exploration into images. In such artistic expression it becomes clear that the reign of Manuel I must be seen as a transitional epoch, both artistically and societally. Formally, the traditions of the Late Gothic are still dominant, but the glorification of the Aviz dynasty and its achievements has clearly modern features.

—BARBARA BORNGÄSSER KLEIN
Translated from the German by Marijke Rijsberman

RUSSIA

ANDRONIKOV MONASTERY
Moscow, Russia

1420s: Construction; **Architect:** Andrey Rublyov. **1504:** Refectory completed. **1812:** Damaged in the great Moscow fire, later restored.

Publications

RIASANOVSKY, N.: *A History of Russia*. New York: Oxford University Press. 1977.
VOYCE, R.: *Russian Architecture*. New York, 1948.

*

Like so many old Russian monasteries, the Andronikov rises picturesquely like a small fortress on a high bluff overlooking a river. It is historically remarkable as one of the first monasteries established by followers of Saint Sergius (1321-91), whose monastic foundations during the next century would reach, in a great and somewhat mysterious wave of colonization, to the furthest corners of the Russian North. It was the first of the "outer ring" of monasteries defending Moscow to the west, south and east: some 3 kilometers from the Kremlin, it stands now in an obscure suburb, dominating not the Moskva River, but its little tributary the Yauza (once navigable and important), where the "Golden Horn" rivulet flows into it.

An impressive gateway gives access to the grassy courtyard, in the middle of which rises the Cathedral of the Savior Not-Made-By-Hands (a dedication to an ancient and revered iconographic type). This remarkable structure, dated to the 1420s (replacing an original wooden church), is by half a century the oldest standing building in Moscow, and the only fully preserved specimen in the capital of the Early Muscovite style of architecture: two other such churches survive at Zvenigorod, one at the Trinity Monastery (Zagorsk), and a very modest specimen at the village of Kamenka. Exiguous as the cathedral's remains are, the style is important, since it represents the revival in Central Russia of stone architecture after a century and a half of Tatar domination that had cut short the fine building tradition of Vladimir-Suzdal, the latter's revival or continuation in certain respects, and the appearance of features that were to have a greater development subsequently in Muscovy.

The Andronikov cathedral, like the others, is of quite modest dimensions (about 19 meters by 12 meters externally), but is strikingly monumental with its pyramidal outline rising in four tiers of *kokoshniki* (decorative gables, thought to resemble a woman's headdress, *kokoshinik*) to a drum whose walls are perceptibly canted inward to give an illusory perspective effect

Andronikov Monastery: Moscow, Russia, 1420s

of greater height. This overall tendency toward pyramidality, already visible in pre-Tatar Kievan architecture, is here pursued more consistently. The characteristic Old Russian tripartite division of the main walls through pilasters or engaged shafts is retained, but here the central wall division is wider and roofed at nearly twice the height of the outer gables. The pilasters no longer correspond exactly to the interior structure. There is no midwall frieze (as at Zvenigorod and the Trinity monastery) to interrupt the vertical thrust of the forms. The east wall is a triple apse: the north, west and south walls each have a rather grand recessed portal, approached by flights of steps, culminating in a pointed ogee. The ogee form is echoed in the *kokoshniki;* though pointed arches are occasionally found in late pre-Tatar buildings, it was with the Early Muscovite style that ogees became a characteristic feature of Russian medieval architecture. The church has been much restored, partly as a result of damage in the great Moscow fire of 1812 (some of the blocks of local limestone from which it was built still show traces of scorching), partly because the original roofline—as in most early Russian buildings—had been obliterated by the latter imposition of a simple pitched roof.

The ground plan of the Andronikov cathedral is the standard Orthodox "cross-in-square," of three bays, without a narthex. However, the interior space is no longer roughly cubical, as in Vladimir or Novgorod churches, but because of the rising arches supporting the external tiers of *kokoshniki* it shares the exterior's dynamic pyramidality. Of the original wall paintings only some foliar motifs on window splays survive. Yet these fragments are unusually precious in that they represent the work of a team led by Andrey Rublyov, greatest of Old Russian artists: it is also possible (from the wording of a mid-15th-century source) that Rublyov planned the building itself. In any case Rublyvov spent his last years in the monastery, and his death (29th January 1420) was noted on a now-lost tombstone. The monastic buildings house the Andrey Rublyov Museum (and restoration-workshop) of Old Russian art, and it is under this name that the monastery is most generally known nowadays.

Not only does the Andronikov contain Moscow's earliest church: it boasts one of its earliest domestic buildings, the Refectory (1504). It is a simple structure, built into the monastery wall, with small paired windows in a facade articulated by a central pilaster strip, under a "hood" (*kolpak*) pitched roof: inside, its low vaults are supported on a central pier, like the 15th-century Faceted Palace in the Kremlin. A second church, that of St. Michael, in Moscow Baroque style (1694 onward) adjoins the Refectory.

—R. R. MILNER-GULLAND

G.U.M. DEPARTMENT STORE
Moscow, Russia

1889-93: Design and construction; **Architect:** Aleksandr Nikanorovich Pomerantsev (1848-98). **1953:** Restoration.

Publications

IKONNIKOV, A.: *Russian Architecture of the Soviet Period.* trans. Lev Lyapin. Moscow: Raduga Publishers 1988.
RANDALL, F.B.: *Stalin's Russia.* New York: The Free Press, 1965.
RIASANOVSKY, N.: *A History of Russia.* New York: Oxford University Press. 1977.
VOYCE, R.: *Russian Architecture.* New York, 1948.

*

The famous Red (derived from the Russian word *krasny,* meaning "beautiful") Square is bordered by several culturally and politically monumental edifices. On the south end of the square is St. Basil's Cathedral (1555-61), a symbol of the Russian Orthodox Church. At the opposite, north end is the Historical Museum (1874-83), displaying exhibits of the rich heritage of the peoples of the country. Forming the west border of the Red Square are the Kremlin, an area inhabited since the 11th century and traditionally the seat of state power, and the Lenin Mausoleum (1930)—both housing the leaders, dead or alive. Finally, opposite the Kremlin, on the east side, is located a symbol of Russian commerce and trade: the G.U.M. (Generalny Universalny Magazin, or General Universal Store) Department Store designed and built by the architect Aleksandr Nikanorovich Pomerantsev in 1889-93.

The Red Square has been the familiar site of mass military and civilian parades, and the long front of the G.U.M. Department Store has served as the parades' stage backdrop. Invariably, during the holidays the facade was adorned with immense boards of portraits and slogans, as if to cover the "undignified, utilitarian" purpose of the building. Indeed, the presence of a department store on the Red Square had been questioned during the Soviet reign since the Red stars first shone on the Kremlin towers. The G.U.M. was to be razed for ideological reasons to make room for structures and open spaces to mark the victory of the Communist political and social order in the Soviet Union. For that reason, the Cathedral of Christ the Savior (1812, architect Konstantin Ton), located across from the west wall of the Kremlin, was demolished in 1931, to clear the site for the Palace of the Soviets—which was envisioned as the model of socialist realism in architecture.

The G.U.M. was to be replaced by a "politically correct" structure for the National Commissariat of Heavy Industry. A competition held in 1934-36 showed entries of gigantic dimensions to house the industry bureaucrats. Fortunately, the "Stalin Plan" (1935) for the reconstruction of the city of Moscow was not fully implemented for the city core. Neither the Palace of the Soviets nor the National Commissariat for Heavy Industry was built. So, the G.U.M. has remained among those humans and buildings alike which survived the purges of Stalinism.

The design and construction of the Upper Trading Rows (Verkhniye Torgoviye Ryadi), as the G.U.M. Department Store was known before the 1917 Revolution, were part of the Russian nationalist movement. Like architects in other European countries at the end of the 19th century and at the turn of the 20th century, Russian architects also searched for their national expression in the Russian architecture of the past. Four buildings were designed with emphasis on the national spirit in the arts and built on the Red Square and in its proximity. Two of these buildings exploring the "Russian Style"—the Historical Museum (1874-83) by the Anglo-Russian architect Vladimir Sherwood, and the neighboring building facing the Revolution Square (formerly Voskresenskaya Square), the Lenin Museum (formerly the City Hall) by architect Dmitriy Chichagov, completed in 1892—are dark red brick, overdecorated structures. These museums feature many traditional medieval and Byzantine Russian architectural motifs. There are tent roofs, octagonal

G.U.M. Department Store: Moscow, Russia, 1889-93

G.U.M. Department Store

towers and pinnacles, *kokoshniki* (a form based on women's headdresses of the old Russia), wall paneling and ornate window surrounds. Similarly eclectic, also executed in the Russian Style, are the two other structures on the Red Square: the G.U.M. by Pomerantsev and the Middle Trading Rows (Sredniye Torgoviye Ryadi, 1894) by R. I. Klein.

The G.U.M. Department Store is grandiose not just in its size but in its concept, too. Derived from the building type referred to in Europe as the "passage," it is like the Galleria Vittorio Emanuele in Milan (1865-87) by architect Giuseppe Mengoni—a covered shopping mall. Though the 250-meter front facing the Red Square is characteristic of the Russian Style, the interior is ingenious, with the use of daylighted indoor pedestrian streets, executed in iron, glass and concrete. In the layout, there are three longitudinal vaulted skylight galleries and three transversal passages connecting the building to the Red Square. Each arcade contains three levels, with rows of shops on the first and second levels, and offices on the third level. Continuous balconies access the second-floor shops, and arched bridges span the galleries on the second and third levels. At the time of the building's construction, nothing equaled the size of the complex, with its space for some 1,200 shops.

There are two underground levels serving the complex: the first basement for service, deliveries and storage, and the second basement for a heating plant and electrical generators. Engineering design of the building was done by Vladimir Shchukov, who was known for his innovative designs of large metal-frame structures. In the architect-engineer collaboration, the use of reinforced concrete, iron and glass provided space for circulation and light, and eliminated the need for thick masonry bearing walls. The outcome of the building was an attempt to fuse the national with the rational—at that time a trend among European architects of progressive persuasion. The G.U.M. was restored in 1953. Official statistics claim that it handles some 350,000 customers a day.

—PETER LIZON

KAZAN RAILWAY STATION
Moscow, Russia

1913-26: Construction; **Architect:** Aleksei V. Shchusev (1873-1949).

Publications

AFANAS'EV, K.: "Zodchiy A.V. Shchusev." *Arkhitektura SSSR* 8:29-35 (1967).

DRUZHINA-GEORGIEVSKAIA, E. V., and KORNFELD, I. A.: *Zodchii A. V. Shchusev*. Moscow, 1955.

KOPP, ANATOLE: *L'architecture de la période Stalinienne*. Grenoble, France, 1978.

NOVIKOV, I.: "Traditsii natsional'nogo zodehestva v tvorchesve A.V. Shcuseva." *Arkhitektura SSSR* 5:15-21 (1953).

SOKOLOV, N. B.: *A.V. Shchusev*. Moscow, 1952.

After the demise of the Jugendstil, Russian architecture principally turned to neoclassicism. A revival of Old Russian architecture, in the so-called "Russian style," took place at the same time. The roots of this architectural movement are actually to be found in the historical eclecticism of the second half of the 19th century, when several architects found a new source of inspiration in the Russian-Byzantine architectural tradition. The Russian style of the beginning of this century, however, was more lively and more sculptural than its 19th-century predecessor.

Aleksei Shchusev, Kazan Station's principal architect, had received a classical training, but, after he finished his education, he displayed an interest in the Russian architectural tradition and in the restoration of monuments. It is hardly surprising, then, that he started out in the Russian style as an independent architect. His most important work from that period is undoubtedly the Kazan Station (Kazanski Vokzal) in Moscow. Shchusev won a competition organized in 1910, which had made the so-called Russian style a requirement. The task of the architect was the design of the station building and its interior, while traffic arrangements and construction problems were the responsibility of the railway administration's engineers.

Shchusev prepared a number of variant designs starting in 1911. The first version of the facade was subdued in comparison with later designs. In 1913 construction could finally be undertaken. Since the project was relatively extensive, Shchusev had a number of assistants, among whom was the later constructivist Ivan Golosov. Among the artists involved with the project, the painter A. N. Benois (Benua) of the "Mir Isskustva" (World of

Kazan Railway Station: Moscow, Russia, 1913-26

Art) group was the most prominent. The start of World War I slowed down construction, which did not begin in earnest until 1916.

The station was Shchusev's most important commission before the Revolution. It is a terminal with a facade 205 meters long. Besides the arrivals and departures hall, the building contained waiting rooms for the different social classes, a mail and telegraph office, a boiler room, storage areas and housing for railway employees. Behind the facade, three iron-and-glass halls covered the tracks. Shchusev had little to do with that part of the station, since the halls were designed by the engineers Shukhov and Loleyt. The facade is asymmetrical, and each function has been articulated separately, so that the design suggests a row of buildings rather than a single common facade. Such a solution would have been impossible within the dominant classical style. The design of the facade was determined not only by the nascent Russian style, but also by the location of the station on Kalanchevskoy Square. Shchusev attempted to give a lively appearance to the long facade, which has a 90-degree angle in the middle. Architectonically the complex is dominated by a tower, whose form is derived from the towers of the Kazan and Moscow kremlins. The sculptural decoration of the bell tower and several other parts is in turn inspired by the Moscow Baroque. Shchusev prepared himself thoroughly for the design of the details. He made several trips to Astrakhan, to Niznyi Novgorod and to Kazan, where he studied local monuments to enrich his repertoire of old architectural forms. The public sections of the interior of the station were richly furnished with frescoes and stucco reliefs.

After the Revolution, construction was resumed in about 1923. Shchusev designed an expansion for the station, the "Club of the October Revolution." Shchusev used concrete and metal for the facade of the club, instead of the brick and stone of the station proper, possibly in response to the ideas of the avant-garde. Work on details and small changes in the station project led to its completion only in 1940. After 1928, Shchusev was not heavily involved with the project, so that Kazan Station is properly considered part of Shchusev's pre-Revolutionary oeuvre.

—OTAKAR MÁČEL
Translated from the German by Marijke Rijsberman

KREMLIN
Moscow, Russia

1326-27: Cathedral of the Dormition constructed. **1330:** Church of the Redeemer in the Wood (Spas na Boru) constructed. **1358:** Monastery of the Miracles constructed. **Late 14th century:** Church of the Virgin's Nativity constructed. **1471-79:** New Cathedral of the Dormition; **Architects:** Begun by Miskin and Krivtsov; completed by Aristotele Fioravanti (ca. 1415-ca. 1486). **1482-89:** Cathedral of the Annunciation built; **Architects:** Masters from Pskov. **1484-86:** Church of the Deposition of the Robe; **Architects:** Masters from Pskov and Moscow. **1485:** Taynitskaya Tower; **Architect:** Antonio Fryazin. Senate Tower and Alarm Tower constructed. **1487:** Beklemishevskaya Tower; **Architect:** Marco Ruffo. **1487-91:** Granovitaya (Faceted) Palace (burned and rebuilt after fires in 1547 and 1571); **Architects:** Marco Ruffo and Pietro Solario. **1488-90:** Peter, 2nd Nameless and 1st Nameless Towers, Annunciation Tower constructed. **1489:** Vodovzvodnaya Tower; **Architect:** Antonio

Fryazin. **1490:** Konstantin-Yelena Tower constructed. **1490:** Borovitskaya Tower; **Architect:** Pietro Solario. **1491:** Nikolskaya Tower (rebuilt in 1817-18); **Architect:** Pietro Solario. **1491:** Savior Tower (superstructure added in 1625); **Architect:** Pietro Solario. **1492:** Corner Arsenal Tower; **Architect:** Pietro Solario. **1495:** Middle Arsenal Tower; **Architect:** Alevisio Novi. **1495:** Commandant Tower constructed. **1495:** Armory Tower constructed. **1495-99:** Trinity Tower constructed. **1505-08:** Cathedral of the Archangel Michael; **Architect:** Alevisio Novi. **1505-08:** Ivan the Great Bell Tower (heightened in 1600); **Architect:** Marco Bono (Fryazin). **1532-43:** Belfry added to Ivan the Great Bell Tower; **Architect:** Petrok Maliy. **1624:** Filaret Annex (rebuilt in 19th century) added to Ivan the Great Bell Tower; **Architect:** Bazhen Ogurtsev. Gate of the Redeemer and Church of St. Sergius constructed. **1635-36:** Terem Palace constructed. **1645-55:** Cathedral of the Twelve Apostles and Patriarch's Palace (since altered); **Architect:** D. L. Okhlebinin. Palace of the Tsar constructed. **Mid-17th century:** Poteshnyy Palace constructed. **1672-88:** Superstructure for Trinity Tower constructed. **1680:** Little Tsar Tower constructed. **1680s:** Tent roofs added to towers. **1736:** Arsenal completed. **1776-90:** Senate; **Architect:** Matvey Kazakov (1738-1812). **1809-17:** Church of St. Catherine; **Architect:** Karl I. Rossi (1775-1849). **1815:** Restorations begun. **1838-49:** Great Kremlin Palace; **Architect:** Konstantin A. Thon. **1844-51:** Armory (Oruzheinaya Palace); **Architect:** Konstantin A. Thon. **1932-34:** Military School (later the Presidium of the Supreme Soviet); **Architect:** Ivan I. Rerberg (1869-1932). **1959-61:** Palace of Congresses; **Chief architect:** M. V. Posokhin.

Publications

BERTON, KATHLEEN: *Moscow: An Architectural History.* New York, 1991.
IKONNIKOV, A.: *Russian Architecture of the Soviet Period.* trans. Lev Lyapin. Moscow, 1988.
RANDALL, F.B.: *Stalin's Russia.* New York, 1965.
RIASANOVSKY, N.: *A History of Russia.* New York, 1977.
SCHMIDT, ALBERT J.: *The Architecture and Planning of Classical Moscow.* 1988.
VOYCE, R.: *Russian Architecture.* New York, 1948.

*

The Moscow Kremlin (*kreml'*, a word probably related to *kremen'*, flint) is not unique, but is one of several similarly named citadels in medieval towns of central Russia. It outstrips all others, of course, in the magnificence of its walls and towers, the fine buildings within them, and the treasures of art they contain: it is justly one of the most famous architectural ensembles of the world. This concise account begins with an outline of the Kremlin's overall history, including mention of the early structures, nearly all now vanished; continues with a description of the series of magnificent buildings that transformed its appearance in a generation or so from 1475 onward, and still lend it its special distinction; and concludes with mention of some of its many miscellaneous treasures.

The Kremlin was in the Middle Ages often called *detinets*, the "place of the retainers" or princely bodyguard, characteristic of pre-Tatar Russian cities. It was always more than merely a palace compound, however: its transformation from living heart of the capital of Muscovy into a ceremonial and administrative center was gradual, and completed only in modern times. The establishment of a fortress on the Moskva River between its little tributaries, Neglinka and Yauza, is dated in the chronicles

Kremlin: Moscow, Russia, 14th century

to 1156, nine years after the first mention of Moscow (though it is clear the site was inhabited earlier); it was then an outpost of the Vladimir principality, whose heritage it was later to assume. Like most Russian fortresses, the Kremlin occupies a bluff rising well over 100 feet above the river: the old place name Borovitsky Hill indicates there was a pine wood there. The first Kremlin, occupying perhaps a third of its modern territory, was defended by a wooden stockade and ditch; part of the latter, five meters deep, has been excavated. Masonry churches, then walls (1367), appeared only from the early 14th century, when Moscow had established its own princely dynasty and, under the Tatars, had set in train the political processes that would lead in the next century to its hegemony over the Russian lands. The material used was "white stone," a good local limestone; brick began to be used only after the mid-15th century. Those structures have all vanished, but considerable parts of the undercrofts of the Church of St. Lazarus (concealed within the Great Palace) and of the Annunciation Cathedral, both dating from the 1390s, survive.

Tatar raids and a long civil war (mid-15th century) interrupted the building and maintenance of the Kremlin. Ivan III ("the Great," 1462-1505), the ruler most responsible for establishing Muscovy's power and prosperity, initiated a huge program of restoration and rebuilding. Vasily Yermolin not only carried out building work but in 1464 set up carved and painted figures of Saint George and Saint Demetrius over the main gate—the earliest known freestanding Russian sculpture. In the 1470s Moscow masons began the rebuilding of the great Cathedral of the Dormition, but after two years the walls collapsed, perhaps as the result of an earth tremor, but also—in the judgment of

a team of builders from Pskov, summoned by Ivan as troubleshooters—because of poorly mixed mortar. Ivan (whose second wife, a Byzantine princess, had been brought up, after the Fall of Constantinople, in Italy) empowered his ambassador in Venice to hire an expert engineer, the Bolognese Aristotele Fioravanti, to recommence the work. He was first in a series of northern Italians—Marco Ruffo, Antonio Fryazin ("the Frank"), Pietro Antonio Solario, Alevisio Fryazin, Alevisio Novy ("the New"), Marco Bono—who in the space of four decades were responsible for the Dormition Cathedral, the Kremlin walls, the Faceted Palace, the Archangel Michael Cathedral and the base of the great belfry. Meanwhile, the Pskov builders, having refused to undertake the Dormition, nevertheless busied themselves in Muscovy both in the Trinity Monastery and the Kremlin, where they constructed two small but exquisite churches on the Cathedral Square. About all these late-15th-to-early-16th-century buildings, more below.

Ivan III's son, Vasily III, continued and completed his father's works in the Kremlin, but during the long reign of his successor, Ivan IV, there was less building activity within its walls. Much remarkable building took place outside it, of course, and in particular the unique church now known as St. Basil's (the Intercession on the Moat, 1555) is as organically linked with the Kremlin, close to which it stands, as with the city beyond: it was the object of the czar's annual "Entry into Jerusalem" procession that left the main Kremlin Gate and wound through Red Square before ascending its steps. Various ecclesiastical and palace buildings of the period have not survived. Boris Godunov (1598-1605), however, had grandiose plans for the Kremlin. He planned to build a "Holy of Holies," derived from

Kremlin, Archangel Cathedral

the Holy Sepulchre in Jerusalem, and thus probably intended to take over for the Kremlin the status of "symbolic Jerusalem" from St. Basil's outside it. From Boris Godunov's plans one great achievement was realized: the completion of the belfry Ivan Velikiy (i.e., "Big John"—dedicated to Saint John Climacus and not, as is usually thought, referring to Ivan III). An inscription below its dome implies that it was intended to celebrate the new dynasty Czar Boris hoped to found.

In the first half of the 17th century, after the "Time of Troubles" and establishment of the Romanov dynasty (1613), much new building took place. The main entrance, renamed the Savior Gate, was adorned with a grand spire and a clock by an English (maybe Scots or Irish) expert, Christopher Galloway or Halloway, working with the Russian Bazhen Ogurtsov. The latter also organized the reconstruction of the main domestic quarters, the Terem Palace (which still stands). Other towers also acquired superstructures. Later in the century several most picturesque small churches were added to the palace complex.

In mid-century the ambitious Patriarch Nikon closed off the north side of Cathedral Square with a long range of buildings serving the patriarchate, and terminating in the church first dedicated to Saint Philip, later rededicated to the Twelve Apostles. From the second half of the 17th century there also survives the smaller Poteshny ("Entertainment") Palace, location of the first court theater, with its surprising jettied upper story.

At the beginning of the 18th century, with the foundation of St. Petersburg, it might have been expected that no more funds would be expended on the Kremlin and that it would sink into obscurity. But this was far from the case: the 18th century was a crucial period for the Kremlin's appearance and development. Moscow continued to be regarded as the country's second capital and the Kremlin as its ceremonial heart. Peter the Great, despite disliking and fearing the Kremlin as a residence, strengthened its military significance with massive outer earthworks and founded in 1702 the vast "Petrine Baroque" building of the Arsenal, which occupies much of its northwest side. The

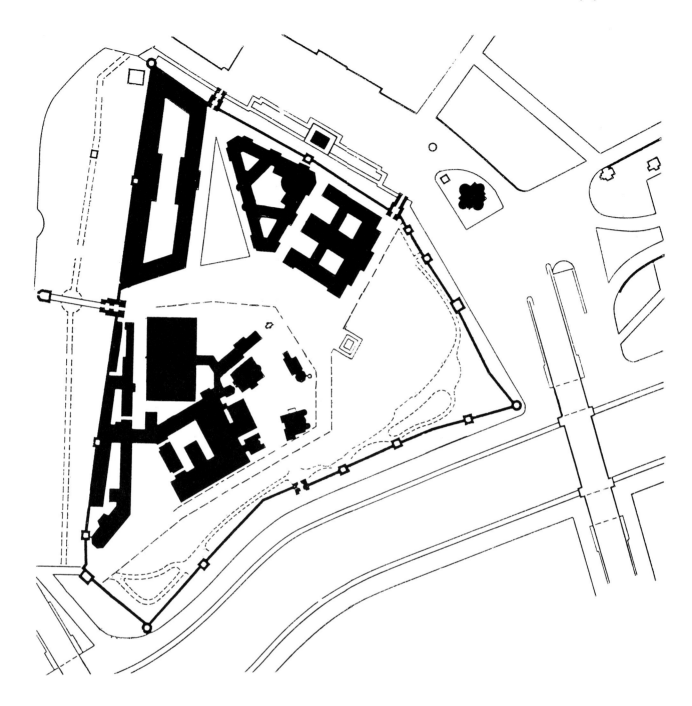

Arsenal was dogged by problems and delays, and was still under construction well into the second half of the century, yet the resulting building is rather impressive.

The Arsenal was a formative influence on Vasiliy Bazhenov, the *Wunderkind* of Russian 18th-century architecture, who, at the age of 30 in 1767 received the grand commission from Catherine II to rebuild the entire palace area (while preserving the ancient cathedrals). His breathtaking scheme can be judged from his surviving scale model: it involved a colonnaded south-facing facade 630 meters long, which might well have been one of the finest expressions of European neoclassicism—however one might assess its impact on the medieval atmosphere

of the Kremlin as a whole. For several years much preliminary work was done, including the demolition of part of the south perimeter wall. But the state's resources were overstretched by the Russo-Turkish War, and the project was never realized; nor was a later plan for a regularized neoclassical Kremlin by Bazhenov's near-contemporary and rival, M. F. Kazakov. However, Kazakov did manage to give the Kremlin the unobtrusive, yet magnificent, domed Senate building (1776)—across a small garden from the Arsenal, and deliberately a foil to it. Kazakov ingeniously utilized an awkwardly shaped site through a pentagonal courtyard framing the great domed entrance rotunda close to the northeast walls.

The 19th and 20th centuries did more harm than good to the Kremlin's appearance—though few would object to the attractive gardens laid out in its south and east parts. At the beginning of the 19th century a good many ancient buildings (including Czar Boris' Palace) were demolished, but the greatest threat to the Kremlin came in 1812, when a vengeful Napoléon attempted to blow up the Kremlin structures on his departure from Moscow in 1812. Much damage was in fact done, particularly to the main belfry complex, while the Nikolsky Tower (at the north apex) had to be rebuilt, with rather odd mock-Gothic features. Many visitors might well conclude, however, that the biggest single piece of 19th-century vandalism was the construction (from 1838 on) of the present Great Kremlin Palace, designed by K. Ton: despite a certain cheerfulness, it is a building quite out of scale with its surroundings, lumpish yet somehow tentative in applied quasi-Old-Russian detailing and graceless dome. By contrast, the rectilinear glass-and-concrete Palace of Congresses (1959-61), housing an auditorium for 6,000, is less obtrusive than might be expected (and draws in concertgoers to experience the unrivaled vision of the Kremlin by night). Its construction did not involve wanton demolition—such as took place from the late 1920s, with the loss of several churches, including that of the Miracle (Chudov) Monastery, which, though largely a 16th-century rebuilding, stood on a very early substructure. The large, vapid, neoclassical pastiche of the Supreme Soviet building (1932) now occupies its site. Under Stalin the Kremlin was for the first time in its history closed to general public access, and its reopening after his death had symbolic importance, though it should be noted that by no means all of its territory or significant buildings can be visited without special permission.

As mentioned, the Kremlin's unique ensemble of buildings dating from the four decades from 1475 deserves further examination. All, save the walls, are located on the splendid stone-paved Cathedral Square.

The first and largest cathedral, dedicated to the Dormition (Assumption) of the Virgin, was begun by Aristotele Fioravanti (after the series of events outlined above) in 1475 and dedicated in 1479: it was painted by the leading artist Dionisy and his team in 1481, and a little of that early fresco-work survives. Fioravanti's plan for the Dormition is entirely Russo-Byzantine, and were it not for the chronicle record we should scarcely detect any "Italianisms" in the church's architecture; it is constructed of small limestone blocks with brick vaulting. The rather plain north and south facades are articulated by pilasters into four great bays; the five apses to the east scarcely project, and the whole has a "box-like," monolithic feel. The five rather crowded domes are supported on piers of round section: the interior is airy and majestic. As the chief cathedral church of Muscovy, it was a repository for notable icons of all periods back to pre-Tatar times; the south doorway has splendid damascene work panels of the 12th and 13th centuries brought from Suzdal in 1410. Fioravanti traveled to Vladimir and the Russian North. The Vladimir Dormition (12th century) was partly his model—though it is a more complex and aesthetically engaging building—and the Moscow Dormition has, in its uncompromising simplicity, an archaic feel in terms of the architectural development of early Muscovite Russia. It nevertheless served as an example for much subsequent "official" church architecture.

The Faceted Palace (*Granovitaya Palata*), an unexpected Florentine palazzo of 1487-91, projects into Cathedral Square from the amorphous east flank of the palace complex. Its externally rusticated upper story contains the great audience chamber of the czars, its vaults springing from a massive central pier. The fenestration was remodeled in the 1680s.

The Cathedral of the Annunciation (1482) and Church of the Deposition of the Robe (Rizpolozheniye, 1484), standing respectively to north and south of the Faceted Palace and likewise attached to the palace complex, can conveniently be treated together: both were the work of the Pskov builders summoned by Ivan III, and their small scale, picturesque and dynamic forms contrast interestingly with the Dormition Cathedral. Both stand on high foundation stories, make much use of ogees, have complex rooflines and employ terra-cotta frieze ornamentation. The originally three-domed Annunciation, palace chapel to the czars, has had a complicated building history that still gives rise to questions. The broad galleries were covered over and integrated into the church probably soon after the latter's construction. Further changes were made in the reign of Ivan IV, including the construction of domed corner chapels, the installation of a beautiful jasper floor, of damascene paneled doors, and probably of the elaborate low-relief door surrounds; recent scholars believe the iconostasis—one of the finest in the world—was assembled (using earlier works) then. Much original wall painting (done by Dionisiy's son Feodosiy in 1508) survives; later scenes in the galleries include worthies of antiquity, including Aristotle, Homer and Virgil. This is doubtless the most interesting church interior in the Kremlin. The tiny, beautiful Deposition Church gives an idea of how the Annunciation must have looked when new, though its good frescoes are, in fact, later (1644).

The Cathedral of the Archangel Michael, prominently located, was commissioned by Ivan III in his last year of life (1505). It was the royal burial church of Muscovy, and today much of the interior is taken up by rows of carved and painted stone tombs under recent glass and bronze canopies. The well-preserved frescoes are from the mid-17th century. The Italian architect Alevisio "the New" (Novy) adhered to the standard Orthodox cross-in-square plan, but gave the exterior a wealth of already High Renaissance detailing: the heavy cornices and scallops at the head of each bay were much imitated in Muscovite architecture. The portals have delicate, luxuriant low-relief ornamentation carved on soft stone.

The history of the great bell tower, symbol of the Kremlin (1505, 1600) has been mentioned already. It rises in diminishing octagonal stories, their walls becoming successively thinner, to a gilded dome and cross at a height of 81 meters. To hang more bells, a further elaborate structure was built on the north side of the bell tower in 1532 (by Petrok Maliy, probably another Italian) and added to by Patriarch Filaret in 1624. It was severely damaged by Napoléon in 1812, and in its rebuilt form shows neoclassical detailing.

Finally, there are the great brick walls of the Kremlin, which form an irregular triangle $2\frac{1}{4}$ kilometers long and enclose an area of 28 hectares (69 acres). They vary in height from 5 to 19 meters, in thickness from $3\frac{1}{2}$ to $6\frac{1}{2}$ meters; their elegant swallowtail battlements (projecting more than 2 meters) testify to their North Italian inspiration. Work was begun in 1485, on the section fronting the Moskva River, under Antonio Fryazin (the "Frank," i.e., Westerner), and continued under various Italian specialists until 1516, when the defenses were completed by channeling the little Neglinka River into a moat (now it flows through a pipe). There are 18 towers, plus a bridgehead tower to the west and the picturesque Tsar's Turret to the east; five of the towers originally had gateways. The present superstructures were added in the 17th century, the illuminated ruby stars in the 1930s. Most of the southern wall was demolished in the 1770s, and what we see now is an adroit late-18th-century rebuilding; the southwest and north apical towers were largely destroyed by Napoléon and subsequently reconstructed.

No account of the architecture of the Kremlin can limit itself entirely to the fabric of its buildings. Wall paintings, icons, carvings and church furniture are an integral part of them.

Most movable treasures of the czars (including such paraphernalia as coaches, thrones and crowns) have been installed in the museum of the Armory, an undistinguished building by K. Ton near the southwest corner. The great icons, however, mostly remain in the cathedrals, each of which has examples antedating the present fabric. The earliest are in the Dormition (where there are also iconic frescoes on a stone screen); there is a fine Saint Michael of ca. 1400 in the Archangel Cathedral, while the greatest ensemble is constituted by the two middle tiers of the iconostasis in the Annunciation. On stylistic grounds it is clear that these must originate nearer the beginning than the end of the 15th century. A chronicle records that the earlier church on the site was painted in 1405 by Theophanes the Greek, Audrey Rublyov and Prokhor of Gorodets—the greatest painters of the age—and most 20th-century art historians have assumed that these artists' panels somehow escaped destruction by fire and were reinstalled. Recent scholarship casts doubt on this; but the icons are undoubtedly early, whatever their history, and this icon screen is probably the finest in the world.

An object of exceptional artistic and historic worth in the Dormition is the carved wooden throne canopy of Ivan IV, carrying scenes affirming the supposed Byzantine heritage of the czars (through Vladimir Monomakh). Many objects of ecclesiastical importance are kept and shown in the patriarchal range of buildings. Within the palace complex the wall paintings are generally recent, but the magnificent "Golden Grille"—of gilded wrought-iron work—dating from 1670, still stands at the entrance to the Church of the Savior Behind the Golden Grille; the church is swallowed up in the palace, but its astonishing

collection of small domes, glimpsed behind the Church of the Deposition of the Robe, glitter with the applied ceramic that is an important element of Muscovite architecture.

More than 20 great bells were rung from the belfry: the largest in the world, though, the "Tsar Bell" cast in 1733, was never hung or rung. A fire in 1737 caused an 11-ton slice of it to crack off; the remainder served for a time as a chapel. More remarkable still is "Tsar Cannon," now standing nearby but formerly part of the large collection of old weaponry in the Arsenal. The largest cannon ever made, it was cast as early as 1586 by Andrey Chokhov, and never fired.

—R. R. MILNER-GULLAND

LENIN STATE LIBRARY
Moscow, Russia

1928-1941. Architects: Vladimir A. Shchuko (1878-1939) and Vladimir G. Gelfreikh (1885-1967).

Publications

L-OV: "Novoe zdanie Leninskoi biblioteki, kak monumentalnyi pamiatnik epokhi." *Stroitelstvo Moskvy* 7 (1929): 18-21.
MESTNOV, A.: "Konkurs na sostavlenie proekta novogo zdaniia biblioteki im. Lenina." *Stroitelstvo Moskvy* 6 (1928): 3-8.

Lenin State Library: Moscow, Russia, 1928-1941

"Moskovskie arkhitekturnye organizatsii po povodu konkursa na zdanie Leninskoi biblioteki." *Stroitelstvo Moskvy* 7 (1929): 22.

"Protest." *S. A.* 3 (1929): 88.

*

Often cited as one of the world's largest libraries, the Lenin State Library of the Union of Soviet Socialist Republics was designed and built during the transitional period in Soviet history marked by the onset of the cult of personality centered on Joseph Stalin (1879-1953). The history of the construction of the library spans the years 1928 to 1941, and reflects the changes that took place in Soviet government and culture during that time. The design of the building is marked by certain contradictions that can be explained by its transitional status.

The library as a new building type was considered extremely important in the new Soviet society, along with workers' clubs and schools. Library design was continuously researched throughout the 1920s, eventually expanding into an elaborate complex serving multiple cultural, educational and scientific functions. In 1928 an open competition was announced for the design of the Lenin Library in Moscow. The journal *Stroitelstvo Moskvy* (*Construction of Moscow*) called this competition the most significant event in the architectural life of Moscow in recent years, and underscored the potential importance of the structure as one of the principal edifices of the capital and a memorial to the founder of the Soviet state. The academicians Vladimir Alekseevich Shchuko and Aleksei Viktorovich Shchusev and the constructivist Vesnin brothers were formally invited to submit designs to the competition. The first prize of five prizes in the first phase of the competition went to the entry by Markov, Fridman and Fridman, who submitted a design in the tradition of *architecture parlante,* symbolically shaped in the form of an open book. The jury was unable to choose a design deemed worthy of construction, so the first-prize winner and the three invited competitors were asked to further develop their designs and submit them in a second round of the competition, which took place in 1929.

The selection of Shchuko's design for the second round generated a negative reaction from the modernist architects, who considered his project reactionary in its use of classical motifs. Both Shchuko and his collaborator, Vladimir Georgeivich Gelfreikh, had continued to design in the neoclassical style throughout the 1920s. An example of their collaboration in this style is the Propylaea of the Smolny Institute in Leningrad (1922-25). A joint proclamation of protest against the results of the Lenin Library competition was issued, and statements by the architectural associations OSA (Society of Contemporary Architects), ARU (Society of Architects-Urbanists), ASNOVA (Association of New Architects) and the architectural circle of VKHUTEIN (Higher State Artistic-Technical Institute) were published in the journals *Stroitelstvo Moskvy* and *Sovremennaya Arkhitektura* (*Contemporary Architecture*). The association ARU attributed the perceived failure of the competition to the composition of the jury, which was restricted to members of the notoriously conservative Moscow Architectural Society, which organized the competition. This protest campaign eventually forced the jury to reconsider its decisions and caused Shchuko and Shchusev to revise their projects. Shchusev's new design was in the constructivist style, bearing no resemblance to his earlier scheme. Shchuko responded by retaining the same basic plan, but created a more streamlined, modern facade, eliminating all classical references with the exception of an abstract allusion to a classical entrance portico.

The controversy over the Lenin Library competition illustrates the continuous confrontation throughout the 1920s between the modernists, who were determined to break completely with the past, and the traditional, "Old School" architects, who remained loyal to the classical canons of the prerevolutionary Academy. This temporary victory of modern architecture is often considered the apex of its influence in the Soviet Union, but an influence that did not persist into the next decade. The design by Shchuko and Gelfreikh was ultimately chosen, and construction began in 1932, but not according to the revised version submitted in the second round of the competition. In fact, the final design reflects a return to their controversial initial project. The original entry made an overt classical reference in the form of a ceremonial, classicizing entrance portico, which, in fact, appeared discontinuous with the rest of the facade. It was that feature that caused the most controversy after the first round of the competition and which was eliminated in the revised design. It was also the most prominent feature reinstated when official taste reverted to a more classical style. The final version of the Lenin Library reflects the official rejection of modern architecture in the early 1930s in favor of a more traditional style that came to be known as socialist realism. Socialist realism in architecture is marked by a tendency toward monumentality and an adherence to motifs based on classical forms, but not copying them. This is the style that was accepted as the most suitable architectural expression of Soviet ideology in the 1930s.

The monumental dimensions and the extensive use of columns and ornamental sculpture place the Lenin Library in the category of socialist realism, but the nonacademic planning and asymmetrical cubic massing of the building complex reflect its debt to the functional modern design developed in the 1920s by such architects as the Vesnin brothers. The nonacademic plan features a complex of six buildings arranged asymmetrically around two courtyards. This plan was introduced in the initial design of 1928 and was retained in subsequent revisions, with only minor alterations. Each building in the library complex serves a different function. The vast reading hall is turned perpendicular to the main building of the complex on Marx Prospekt and is linked to the nine-story book repository along Marx and Engels Street. On the Kalinin Prospekt side are additional reading rooms, reference rooms and administrative offices. All the buildings are linked at their southeastern corner by a wide terrace, which serves to emphasize the importance of the corner site. The complex is located near the Kremlin, at the intersection of two major thoroughfares of Moscow. From the terrace, access to the complex is gained through the main entrance, into the main building of the library, or through the colonnade, into one of the two courtyards. The terrace level is connected to the street level by a series of flights of steps, while the transition from terrace to building complex is defined by a marble colonnade which is continuous with the black granite-faced columns of the portico of the main entrance. The square, matchstick-like granite and marble columns have schematic capitals and bases of no distinguishable order.

In the sense that the Lenin Library displays characteristics of modern design while adhering to the new aesthetic requirements dictated by the state in the 1930s, it is very much a transitional structure. The style of the complex straddles the style of overt modern design and the reappearance of heavily decorated classical architecture. The exteriors of the buildings that face the street underwent the most alteration throughout the 1930s as changes occurred in official artistic and architectural thought.

The architects continuously amended their design by adding additional decorative sculpture. Allegorical statues depicting different trades and professions adorn the roofs along Marx and Kalinin Prospekts. These sculptures represent figures that were considered representative of the new Soviet society, such as the figures of a worker, a *kolkhozhnik* and a scholar. Relief panels set into the main facade form two horizontal bands of sculpture that intersect the dominant vertical elements, reflecting the framework of the structure. Symbolically appropriate for a library, famous scientists and writers are represented in these panels. In addition, the attic over the entrance portico bears an overt classical reference in the form of a two-tiered heroic frieze, which is partially obscured by a large panel bearing the name of the library. All of this sculpture has contributed to the library's reputation as one of the most decorated buildings of postrevolutionary Moscow.

The initial program of the Lenin Library competition required that the design take into account surrounding historical monuments and buildings and avoid entering into visual competition with them. Shchuko's inclusion of classical motifs in his first design of the library can be seen as an attempt to suggest visual continuity with surrounding buildings such as the Pashkov House, an example of 18th-century Russian classicism. The Pashkov House had housed the Lenin Library prior to the construction of the new complex and now serves as an annex, housing general and children's reading rooms. The competition requirement of visual conformity reflects the belief of the city planners of Moscow in preserving continuity between the old and the new in the development of the historically evolved urban environment. After 1931, architectural uniformity was codified with the acceptance of socialist realism as the official style in the arts. By the end of 1933, all architectural projects were being strictly monitored in order to enforce the new aesthetic canon of the state. The shift in official taste toward socialist realism in architecture is believed to have been initiated by the choice of the winning project in the competition for the Palace of the Soviets in Moscow. Shchuko and Gelfreikh collaborated with B. M. Iofan on the design of the palace from 1931 to 1939, the year of Shchuko's death. The Palace of the Soviets was to be the focal point of a projected ensemble of structures flanking a newly widened avenue bordering the Kremlin. The Lenin Library was to be one of these subsidiary structures and therefore was expected to harmonize with the scale and classicizing style of the future dominant structure. The addition of a colonnade to the design served both purposes. Some aspects of the design of the Lenin Library are reflected in models of the palace, suggesting an active interrelationship between the two designs. For example, the conspicuous two-tiered heroic frieze in the attic above the entrance portico of the Lenin Library appears in some versions of the design of the Palace of the Soviets by Iofan, Shchuko and Gelfreikh, as does the stripped classical style based on the square column.

The facades of the Lenin Library were continuously redesigned as tastes changed, even while the building was already under construction. Like many architects of the "Old School," Shchuko and Gelfreikh were skillful at responding to the stylistic trends of the day, whether it be constructivism or socialist realism. This is a skill that can be seen as an extension of their prerevolutionary practice of making the most fashionable choice among the currently approved historical styles. This flexibility resulted in the construction of a building complex that combined a modern plan with traditional facades. The history of the design and construction of the structure runs parallel to a period of intensive reorientation of architectural thought in the Soviet Union. For the modernist architects who prevailed in the 1920s, the primary concern of architecture was social transformation, while for the social realists of the 1930s, architecture became an ideological tool. Influences from both trends are evident in the final, built version of the Lenin Library.

—OLYA SHEVCHENKO

LOMONOSOV UNIVERSITY
Moscow, Russia

1949-53. Architects: Lev V. Rudnev, Sergei Y. Chernyshev, Pavel V. Abromisov, and Alexander H. Khryakov, with engineer Vsevolod Nasonov.

Publications

KONNIKOV, A.: *Russian Architecture of the Soviet Period.* trans. Lev Lyapin. Moscow, 1988.
KOPP, ANATOLE: *L'Architecture de la perióde Stalinienne.* Grenoble, France, 1978.
KREIS, BARBARA: "Moskauer Monumentalarchitektur." *Bauwelt* 25 (1978): 986-90.
RANDALL, F.B.: *Stalin's Russia.* New York, 1965.
RIASANOVSKY, N.: *A History of Russia.* New York, 1977.
VORIGA, J. P.: "L'Architecture et le Réalisme Socialiste." *L'Architecture d'Aujourd'hui* 158 (1971): 48-53.

*

The grandiose main building of Lomonosov State University, on the Lenin Hills overlooking Moscow, was built between 1949 and 1953 by the architects Lev Rudnev, Sergei Chernyshev, Pavel Abromisov and Alexander Khryakov, and the engineer Vsevolod Nasonov. Once the tallest building in the city of Moscow, its height is now exceeded only by that of the Ostankino Television Tower. The main tower contains the university's teaching and research departments, while the flanking wings house dormitory rooms for 6,000 students, a restaurant, a swimming pool, a cinema, a library and bookshops. The central block is 240 meters (790 feet) high and contains 36 stories; the wings have 17 stories.

The university was founded in 1755 by Michael Lomonosov (1711-65), a "Renaissance man" whom the poet Aleksandr Pushkin called "the first Russian University." Born to a peasant family, Lomonosov was educated in Russia and Germany. He became known as a grammarian, poet, scientist, economist, historian, craftsman and inventor. Lomonosov University, the first institution of higher learning in Russia, is the largest university in the Soviet Union today.

While its dramatic design, prominent size and location 73 meters (240 feet) above the Moskva River make it an important landmark for the southwest part of the city, the university structure is not unique. It is the largest of a group of seven skyscrapers of very similar design that were erected in a ring encircling central Moscow following a central urban plan established in 1947. Each of the skyscrapers has the same prominent central block with a tall spire, flanking wings and similar decorative motifs; from many viewpoints in the city two or more of these structures are visible. The other six buildings are a high-rise housing unit on the Kotelnicheskaya Embankment, the Ukraina and Leningradskaya Hotels, and administrative buildings in Smolenskaya, Lermontovskaya and Vosstaniya Squares. Historical records indicate that, despite the obvious similarity of their

Lomonosov University: Moscow, Russia, 1949-53

designs, each of these seven buildings was designed by a different architect or group of architects; such conformity is a witness to the centralized state control and the suppression of individual personality and creativity within the Soviet state. An eighth structure, intended for the area of Zaryadye, near the Kremlin, was never built. Because of their size and importance in the Soviet capital, these skyscrapers served as models for many of the new official buildings built throughout the U.S.S.R. in the postwar period.

The ring of skyscrapers was built under the rule of Joseph Stalin; this assertive group of buildings was certainly intended to reflect the triumph and grandeur of the Soviet state and the power of the current ruler. While other structures erected under Stalin are crumbling due to hurried construction, lack of funds and poor materials, the ring of skyscrapers was built during a relatively prosperous period of Stalin's rule, and the buildings, constructed with fine materials, are still in good condition.

The design of the university building and its peers reveals the inherent conservatism in Soviet architecture during the Stalin period: their only modern features are the high-rise design and the steel-frame construction. In the university building, the architectural motifs that define the design, and especially the combination of architecture with allegorical and didactic sculpture, were all drawn from traditional 19th-century styles, while the monumental scale and extravagant decoration reveal the inspiration of Roman imperial architecture during that period. The huge scale, strict symmetry and the hierarchical design of the stepped forms that crescendo up to the central spire were surely meant to express the power and control of the Soviet state and the hierarchical nature of Communist society. This conservative architecture was a reaction to the abstract modernism promulgated by earlier Soviet architects: Vladimir Tatlin, El Lissitsky, Kasimir Malevich and Konstantin Melnikov.

An ornamental garden at the front of the building extends from a terrace above the riverbank to granite steps and a colossal classical entrance portico lined with heavy columns; flanking the path and the entrance are sculptures and rostral columns. At the roofline are classical urns, obelisks and allegorical sculptures that draw attention up to the gigantic star that surmounts the spire. Like the stars on the other skyscrapers, this reference to the Soviet state was certainly intended to match the famous ruby stars that replaced the Romanoff eagles on the historic spires of the Kremlin wall in 1937; Stalin's ring of Soviet buildings thus continued the form and ideology of the Soviet Kremlin to more distant parts of the city. The star atop the university building is in perfect alignment with the center of Lenin Stadium and the Bell Tower of Ivan the Great in the Kremlin.

The same sense of magnificence can also be found in some of the Moscow metro stations built during the same time period. The stations of the Circle Line, built between 1944 and 1954, combine austerity of basic design with an elaborate overlay of fine materials, ornate decoration and, in a few cases, allegorical and inspirational subject matter exalting the Soviet worker and the state. These stations reflect the same interests as the grandiosity and the ornateness evidenced in the Lomonosov University building.

—DAVID G. WILKINS

MELNIKOV HOUSE
Moscow, Russia

1927-29. Architect: Konstantin Melnikov (1890-1974).

Publications

L-NOV: "Neudachnye konstruktsii." *Stroitelstvo Moskvy* 10 (1929): 19-20.
LUKHMANOV, NIKOLAI: "Tsilindricheskii dom." *Stroitelstvo Moskvy* 4 (1929): 16-22.
ZHEITS, V.: "O tsilindricheskom dome arkhitektora Melnikova." *Stroitelstvo Moskvy* 10 (1929): 18-19.

*

The master builders of 20th-century architecture asserted their design philosophies of what a modern residence should be through their trend-setting houses. What Le Corbusier established with Villa Savoye (1928-30), Ludwig Mies van der Rohe with Villa Tugendhat (1928-30) and Frank Lloyd Wright with Fallingwater (1936-39), Konstantin Melnikov achieved with his own house built in 1927-29. With their respective houses, all of the architects succeeded in breaking away from tradition, from the eclecticism of the 19th-century bourgeois house, to designs for a new family: liberal and intellectual, whose new life-style required not only different spatial arrangements of house functions but also an architectural image reflecting social and political changes and the 20th-century advancement of technology. These new houses were devoid of any decoration, embellishment or ornament. The aesthetic strength was in the direct and truthful expression of structure, functions and building materials, of how the sun entered the residential spaces, and how solid and void and light and shadow played on the architectural form.

The young artists in the Soviet Union who became the heralds of the revolutionary society were searching for a new language in architecture to express the ideals of the new social and political order established in the country. Architectural constructivism, as the movement of the Russian avant-garde came to be known in the West, was established through a dynamic, articulated, machinistic vocabulary of forms full of high contrasts.

Konstantin Melnikov was one of the acknowledged and influential leaders of the Soviet architectural avant-garde of the 1920s. A prolific designer, for a decade he entered all important architectural competitions and carried out numerous commissions. He won the competition for the Soviet Pavilion at the 1925 International Exhibition of Decorative Arts in Paris. The pavilion established Melnikov as an architectural innovator and presented to the world the exuberant designs of the Soviet avant-garde. In appreciation for the successful show in Paris, the Soviet government gave Melnikov a parcel of land on which to build his house. The fashionable area of Arbat in Moscow was chosen for the lot. At the turn of the century, it was an area of art nouveau apartment buildings that housed artists, writers, musicians and well-to-do merchants.

Throughout his career in architectural design, Melnikov was preoccupied with curves, and especially with the circle. His 1923 entry to the Palace of Labor competition was an asymmetrical composition organized from a circular colonnaded plaza. Both the large and small auditoriums have images of large, sloped, megaphone-like forms. A rotating series of curved sections stacked in a vertical cylinder, which was to constantly change the building silhouette, was used in the entry for the Leningrad Pravda competition in 1924. Melnikov evolved a method of combining a set of intersecting cylinders. This strategy was used in a number of designs for housing and public buildings and in the house he designed for himself. A direct connection to the geometry of the house is evident in his 1927 competition design for the Zuyev Factory Workers' Club. It is a linear composition of two pairs of intersecting cylinders. Also, the design for the Burevestnik Workers' Club, built in 1929, features a four-story cylinder defining the plaza of the main entry to the building. The five floor-to-ceiling glass bays opened the cylinder to the natural light and to the views from the street as well. In the invited competition for the Frunze Military Academy in 1930, Melnikov's design consisted of 12 cylinders organized in three rows, like soldiers in a military parade.

His house is composed of two cylinders, each 10 meters in diameter; they are joined at one third of their volume, which forms a footprint of the numeral 8. The front cylinder is 8 meters high, and the back one is 11 meters high. The exterior perimeter wall is 50 centimeters thick. The brick of this double cylindrical wall is built in a diagonal system of a diamond-shaped pattern which forms a series of some 124 diamond "openings." Half of these diamond "openings" make room for the hexagonal windows and the other half of the "openings" are "covered" to create air-cushion thermal-insulation pockets in the wall. The floors of the house are designed as a system of two-way wood joists coffered in the 50-by-50-centimeter pattern. The dimensions of each joist are 2.5 by 22 centimeters. The underlayment flooring and the ceiling are made out of 2.9-by-9-centimeter tongue-and-groove boards placed diagonally over the coffered joists. Such a sturdy two-way structural system of floors was used because of the 9-meter clear span from the perimeter bearing walls of the two cylinders. Melnikov used masonry construction for the cylindrical walls to utilize the traditional skills of Russian masons who had built numerous churches throughout the country. Concrete and steel were scarce in the Soviet Union at the time, and the architect knew that Russian construction workers were experienced in building with bricks and wood.

The house featured a number of amenities, including a central, hot-air, gravity-operated heating system, internal telephone, gas water heater and gas kitchen stove with a ventilator hood. (At my last visit in the house, the heating was working very efficiently. While the temperature outside was minus 30 degrees Fahrenheit, there was shirt-sleeve comfort inside the house.) A waste-disposal system was originally piped from the kitchen to the coal-burning furnace to burn refuse. Today, however, the

Melnikov House: Moscow, Russia, 1927-29

heating is supplied from a district heating plant (every building in central Moscow is hooked to it), so waste cannot be burned in the house anymore.

The house has three floors and a roof terrace. The centrally placed entry door leads to an air lock. The foyer opens to a hall from where stairs lead up to the second floor. The dining room and the kitchen, which open doorless to the hall, are all in the front cylinder of the house. The hall turns then into a corridor (placed on the longitudinal axis of the numeral 8) that leads to the back cylinder of the first floor. On the left, next to the kitchen, are the bathroom and lavatory, and further down

are two workrooms for children. On the right, at the end of the corridor, is the family dressing room. A large mirror in the dressing room was placed at the termination of the longitudinal axis of the house. Next to the dressing room is a workroom for sewing, ironing and related tasks. The volume of the first floor is divided into 11 spaces, so the curvature of the external wall is hardly felt. But on the second floor, the space explodes when the living room, 4.7 meters high and occupying the entire front cylinder, is flooded by a floor-to-ceiling glass wall of daylight. In the living room, one becomes aware of the interplay of penetration of the volume of one cylinder into the other when a chunk of the back cylinder hangs into the volume of the living room. The bedroom is placed in the back of the second floor. Lit by 12 hexagonal windows, the bedroom was common to all four members of the family. A double bed for the parents in the center is visually separated by two partial partitions, behind which are single beds for the children. All three beds were built in to the floor. A spiral stair from the living room leads to the third-floor studio. Illuminated by 38 hexagonal windows in three horizontal bands, the studio is 4.7 meters high and occupies the entire third-floor volume of the back cylinder. The juxtaposition of the front cylinder with the back-cylinder volume of the studio is implemented by a cantilevered balcony extending from the roof terrace of the house. The balcony was, according to the Melnikov's son, Viktor, the architect's favorite place to sketch the first ideas of his designs. From that vantage point, the numerous views, framed by the hexagonal windows, reveal multiple images of inspiration from the outside world projected on the curved wall of the room.

The curvelinear plan and the different way of articulating the various elements of the house generated a set of complex interior effects. Two rooms, identical in their shape and dimensions (the living room and the studio), produce completely different stimuli. The difference is in the two-story glass wall in one and the 38 hexagonal windows combined in a complex pattern in the other, and in the intricate play of projections through division and interpenetration of the two cylinders.

The aesthetic message and the sensory impact of the spatial events are awesome, and a visit to the house remains an unforgettable experience. The result of Melnikov's innovative approach in architectural design employed in this house is on par with the breakthrough houses designed by his contemporaries Le Corbusier, Frank Lloyd Wright and Ludwig Mies van der Rohe.

—PETER LIZON

METRO STATIONS
Moscow, Russia

Begun in 1932. Chief engineer: L. M. Kaganovich. **1935:** First stage of Kirovsko-Frunzenskaia Line completed. **1938:** Gorkovsko-Zamoskvoretskaia Line completed (extended in 1943); first stage of Arbatsko-Pokrovskaia Line completed. **1938-39:** Maiakovskaia Station completed; **Architect:** A. N. Dushkin. **1952:** Komsomolskaia Station (now Koltsevaia Station) completed; **Architects:** Aleksei V. Shchusev and A. Zabolotnaya. **1954:** Koltsevaia (Circle) Line completed; **Late 1950s-1960s:** Kaluzhsko-Rizhskaia, Filevskaia and Tagansko-Krasnopresnenskaia Lines completed.

Publications

DRUZHINA-GEORGIEVSKAIA, E. V., and KORNFELD, I. A.: *Zodchii A. V. Shchusev*. Moscow, 1955.
GRABAR, IGOR E.; AFANASEV, K. N.; and BACHINSKY, N. M.: *Proizvedeniia akademika A. V. Shchuseva udostoennye Stalinskoi premii*. Moscow, 1954.
VLASOV, ALEKSANDR V.: ''Nash put. Vsesoiuznoe soveshchanie sovetskikh arkhitektorov.'' *Arkhitektura SSSR* 6 (1937): 23-25.

In 1902 the city council of czarist Moscow rejected an offer by the American banking firm of Werner and Company to construct an underground railway. The plans drawn by American engineers were discovered 30 years later by the commissar of transportation, L. M. Kaganovich, who presented them to the Central Committee of the Communist Party. It was decided in June 1931 that a subway would be built.

The Soviet government set up the Metrostroi Building Trust, which provided with the most advanced Soviet-made equipment. Construction of the first line began in 1932 under the personal leadership of Joseph Stalin. Kaganovich was appointed chief engineer, and Nikita Khrushchev was named foreman of the actual construction. After a year of investigation and experimentation, the real construction began, and by 1934 more than 60,000 workers from all over the Soviet Union were engaged in the enormous task of building the first line of the Moscow Metropolitan, or Metro. Built primarily by unskilled labor, the first 16 kilometers were completed and opened for service in May 1935.

The subway was immediately incorporated into Stalin's ''Great Plan.'' Approved in 1935, that plan was to put an end to the rapid deterioration of the capital city, thus marking the fall of the old Moscow and the beginning of a new socialist center. Stalin had decided that the modernization of Moscow would serve as a model for the Soviet Union and for the world. The subway was perhaps the greatest success, exhibiting efficiency, new techniques in construction and engineering, and, most of all, the lavish and ornate Stalinesque architecture. Stalin's efforts to create an image of greatness and power took precedence over more practical social reforms. He saw that not only was the Metro crucial to the development of his new capital, but it was an excellent source of propaganda, too.

The stations were built during a period of historical eclecticism in Soviet architecture. Extremely decorative in design, the early structures built during the late 1930s through the early 1950s were often referred to as ''underground palaces.'' The best architects, sculptors, painters, stone carvers and molders worked on combining monumental design with examples of traditional Soviet architecture. Red granite, golden smalto, jasper, marble, mosaics and sculptured reliefs are only a sample of the materials and techniques used by these artists to enhance the themes of heroism of the Russian people.

Developments in Soviet architecture are reflected in the designs of the prewar stations through the early 1950s. Facades of the stations, for example, were embellished with Corinthian columns and pillars, classical emblems, and Renaissance-style loggias with classical cornices and pediments. Similar styles are reflected in many of the administrative buildings, residences and theaters built during that period.

An innovative development that greatly affected the interior designs of several stations was the distinction made between pier and column-type construction. Maiakovskaia Station has one of the most successful column-type designs. Named for the Russian poet Vladimir Maiakovsky, Maiakovskaia Station was built in 1938-39 by architect A. N. Dushkin and engineer R. A. Sheinfain. The station is best known for its open-air design facilitated by a unique column-type construction. The standard type of construction for most of the early stations comprises three separate vaulted halls with massive walls flanked by gateways through which passengers can move from one side of the track to the other. At the Maiakovskaia Station the heavy walls are replaced by stainless-steel columns and arches. By eliminating the heavy structure, the space becomes one immense hall, very similar to the arcade-like interior of the G.U.M., the state department store built in the late 19th century. The spacious interior design allows for more efficient handling of large flows

Metro Stations: Moscow, Russia, 1932

Metro Stations

of passengers as well as a unique and complex ceiling structure. Built into the vaulted ceiling of the central hall are 36 oval cupolas with mosaics in multicolored smalto.

Of the stations noted for their combined architectural styles, innovative interiors and thematic artistry, Komsomolskaia Station (recently changed to Koltsevaia) is most outstanding. Located on Komsomolskaia Square, the station was built in 1952 on the Kirovsko-Frunzenskaia Line, the first completed subway line. The station was designed by Aleksei V. Shchusev and A. Zabolotnaya and others. Classical in style, the facade displays a row of Corinthian columns marking the entrance to a three-railway terminal. The entrances are decorated with mosaics, paintings, sculptures and applied art by noted artists such as A. A. Deineka, P. Korin and M. G. Manizer. Each work pays tribute to Russia's military history, glorifying the past and the heroic deeds of the Soviet people. Conceived as a monument to victory and triumph, the entrance to the trains is semi-apsidal with arched ceilings covered in highly decorative Rococo and Baroque plaster reliefs. The overall effect is further dramatized by a row of ballroom-size crystal chandeliers.

The ostentatious, monumental and often overdecorated interiors and pseudoclassical exteriors of the pre-1950s stations were not found in the designs of stations after Stalin's death. Since the late 1950s construction has been standardized, making it possible to accelerate the rate while decreasing the costs. Unlike the early stations, many are now duplicated and differentiated only by colors or materials.

From the time of its inception to the present, construction on the subway has not ceased. Today the subway is about 200 kilometers long, housing 132 stations, and carries 7 million passengers daily. Only the cost has remained constant, a single five-kopeck copper coin will take you anywhere you wish to go in Moscow.

—LESLIE A. BROTHERS

PALACE OF THE SOVIETS (COMPETITIONS)
Moscow, Russia

1923: First competition for the Palace of Labor. **1931:** International Competition for the Palace of the Soviets. **1932:** Invited Competition for Twelve Soviet Teams. **1932-33:** Competition for Five Collectives. **1957-59:** Final competitions for the Palace of the Soviets.

Publications

BADOVICI, JEAN: "Le Moment héroique de l'architecture moderne en URSS." *L'Architecture vivante* (Spring-Summer 1933): 5-6.

BARDI, P. M.: "La Soi-disant Architecture russe." *Architecture d'aujourd'hui* 2, 8 (1932): 73-74.

COOKE, CATHERINE, and KAZUS, IGOR: *Sowjetische Architekturwettbewerbe 1924-1936.* Laren, Netherlands, 1991.

DE FEO, V.: *URSS: Architettura 1917-1936.* Rome, 1963.

Palace of the Soviets, Boris Iofan's entry: Moscow, Russia, 1923

Palace of the Soviets, Le Corbusier's entry

HAMLIN, TALBOT: "Style Developments in Soviet Russia." *American Quarterly on the Soviet Union* 1 (April 1938): 15-20.

ILIN, MIKHAIL A.: "The Building Season of 1931 in Moscow." *VOKS Bulletin* 10-12 (1931): 83-87.

SCHMIDT, HANS: "The Soviet Union and Modern Architecture." In ELEAZAR LISSITZKY: *Russia: An Architecture for World Revolution*. Cambridge, Massachusetts, 1970: 218-222.

ROCCO, GIOVANNI: "Architettura dell'URSS." *Rassegna di architettura* (September 1935): 313-325.

VLASOV, ALEKSANDR V.: "Nash put. Vsesoiuznoe soveshchanie sovetskikh arkhitektorov." *Arkhitektura SSSR* 6 (1937): 23-25.

WOZNICKI, S. T.: "USSR—On the Problems of Architecture." *T-Square* 2 (November 1932): 80-83.

ZAPLETIN, N. P.: "Magnitostroi arkhitektury." *Stroitelstvo Moskvy* 5-6 (1933): 10-32.

*

The evolution of Soviet architecture from its beginnings in 1917 to the present may be traced in the epic struggle to design the Palace of the Soviets, a building to house meetings and congresses of the legislative branch of the government and the Soviet Communist Party—an equivalent of the United States Capitol or the British Houses of Parliament.

Successive design competitions for the Palace of the Soviets, held at crucial moments in the social, political and cultural life of the Soviet Union, heralded substantial changes in architectural design philosophy and in architecture as an art form. Designs for the Palace of the Soviets which received official recognition serve as a paradigm of architectural form in the periods that followed. The evolution of Soviet architecture can be described in three phases centered around three separate series of architectural competitions. The design competitions were held in 1922-23, 1931-33, and 1957-59. Designs submitted in these three series of competitions can be seen as trendsetters in the evolution of Soviet architecture.

Revolutionary architecture, from the so-called "Heroic Period" that began with the revolutionary year 1917 and lasted until 1932-33, resulted from the search for new expression for the newly born society. As the Soviet Union approached normalization upon fulfilling the task of its first five-year plan, it was decided to construct—for all the world to see—a brick-and-mortar monument to house massive All-Union congresses and demonstrations. Though the resources at hand really did not permit such a building to be realized, a great competition was presented in 1923 for a combined government center and central house of culture, the Palace of Labor (later renamed the Palace of the Soviets). This complex was to contain two auditoriums, offices, an observatory, a radio broadcasting center, several museums, a library and a 6,000-seat restaurant. While the results of this competition were to mark the beginning of modern Soviet architecture, the program also was typical of a certain gigantism, which was to reappear throughout the period of socialist realism; it was a gigantism that expressed the desire to outdo the capitalist world, even in the scale of its buildings.

During that first phase there arose a new architectural school—constructivism—which embodied some of the most progressive elements of 20th-century architecture. The form vocabulary of architectural constructivism was defined in the 1923 competition design of Viktor, Leonid and Aleksandr Vesnin, which, both in functional conception and in architectural forms, opened the way for modern architecture in the Soviet Union. The Vesnin brothers' design broke with both classical composition and symbolic and romantic trends, though such approaches were represented elsewhere in the competition.

In spite of the obvious superiority of the Vesnins' entry, which placed only third, the first prize went to Nikolai Trotsky, who later was to make a name for himself in Leningrad with eclectic, supermonumental compositions. Anatole Kopp, a French scholar of Soviet architecture, characterized Trotsky's scheme for the Palace of Labor as an overblown cross of Ledoux and Palladio. Pantelemon Golosov, who joined the constructivists in 1924, obtained fifth prize for a symbolist gesture toward machine aesthetics—an enormous mass surmounted by the inevitable spiral inscribed in a gigantic, geared wheel.

If the competition marked the beginning of architectural constructivism, it also revealed the influence that the old school still retained—and was to cling to—through the years. The composition of the jury explains why the first prize went to a neoclassical design. Apart from representatives of the Party, the government and the Moscow Soviet, the jury included Aleksei Shchusev, Ivan Zholtovsky and others who had received their training well before the Revolution, and in the purest academic tradition.

The project of the Palace of Labor, like many competition subjects of the time, was never built. Sufficient resources were unavailable, and eventually the requirements changed.

A few years later, the first stage of the Palace of the Soviets competition aimed to establish the program for an international competition, to choose the site for the palace, and to examine possible solutions for the future building. The results of the 16 projects submitted by invitation showed a wide spectrum of styles, and established the program for the All-Union Open Competition—known as the International Competition—of 1931. A new site was chosen, too: a decision was made to tear down the Cathedral of Christ the Savior, southwest of the Kremlin walls, to create a large space open to the Moskva River. By then, the total proposed area for the palace had grown to a grandiose 39,000 square meters, including a large auditorium for 15,000 spectators and a small auditorium with 5,900 seats, a library and exhibition halls.

The competition drew 160 entries and 112 project proposals, including 24 entries from abroad. The three grand prizes were awarded to Ivan Zholtovsky and Boris M. Iofan, both from the Soviet Union, and to the American Hector Hamilton. Those three awards represented a similar selection to those of the awards from the competitions for the Chicago Tribune tower and the League of Nations building in Geneva. Equally, the jury gave preference to the designs composed in traditional canons using historicizing forms: the classical manner was common for all the top awards.

The project of academician Zholtovsky of Moscow was traditional in form: the composition was surrounded by Italian colonnades decorated with numerous figurative sculptures. However, the very strict classicism Zholtovsky had applied to match the Kremlin's architecture was not considered to be expressive of the new society.

Iofan, a 28-year-old Muscovite, presented a sober, symmetrical plan of a circular auditorium separated by a central plaza from a smaller, semicircular auditorium, the whole accentuated by a tower surmounted by a statue; it was the tower—without function, and reminiscent, too, of American skyscrapers— to which the jury objected.

The design by Hamilton, submitted with the motto "Simplicity," consisted of two symmetrical wings joined by an accentuated mass in the middle. The building exploited almost the whole site, but with little relationship to the surroundings. The strict symmetry and uniformity of the facade did not express the nature of the palace; the image was that of a large, bureaucratic building, massive and without character.

Designs that reflected the new in architecture ended in defeat. Le Corbusier, Walter Gropius, Erich Mendelsohn, Moisei Ginsburg, the Vesnins and Nikolai Ladovsky were apparently much ahead of their time. Even so, a handful of progressive intellectuals around the world expected modern architecture to break through the conservatism, prudence and conventional criteria of one of the important juries. It did not happen.

The competition jury comprised 70 professionals from various field: architects and engineers, and representatives of theater, literature, painting and sculpture, among others. The jury issued a resolution that attested to wide participation by the proletarian Soviet public; projects, project proposals, sketches and details done by Soviet citizens showed the exceptional

social and political importance of the event. In addition, the jury reviewed 12 invited projects, three from the Soviet Union and nine from Germany, the United States, France and Italy. These schemes were of great value, the jury report stated, especially because they exhibited detailed solutions of structure, acoustics, visibility, circulation and transportation. According to the jury, this collective contribution was to be used in the future development of the project.

While all awards and prizes were indeed distributed, none of the competition entries was recommended for construction. Notably absent from the roster of prize winners were the names of constructivist participants. Their reputation, however, must have been sufficiently strong and lasting in architectural circles. The ideological constructivist leaders, such as the Vesnin brothers, Ginsburg and the rationalist Ladovsky, were later invited to take part in the Invited Competition for Twelve Soviet Teams.

Ginsburg collaborated with Gustav Hassenpflug, a member of Ernst May's team of German architects, on a resolutely functional proposal, despite the fact that in some respects the competition tended to encourage gigantism and impracticality. Internal functions of the project were clearly expressed on the exterior. Circulation and natural illumination defined structural elements of the large auditorium. It was a confession of purity of forms.

Ladovsky, leader of the rationalist movement, entered a design of organic, curved forms. The main auditorium, a hemisphere with the expressed, sloped lines of inner movement, was balanced by the volume of the small auditorium ensemble, which was dominated by a cylindrical glass tower. The separation of the two auditoriums was further enhanced by the main auditorium's ramp-like, externally expressed balcony levels.

Ilya Golosov's design showed his renunciation of the constructivist movement. His project was already expressing a new line in Soviet architecture—a precursor to socialist realism— that was historicist and overwhelmed by decorative elements.

The ideological pressure on constructivists during that period had been strenuous, and not all of them were strong enough to carry on with their architectural ideals. Also, the political atmosphere insisted on the method of socialist realism, later so clearly defined in the construction of many neoclassical buildings. Therefore, some of the modernist architects reexamined their beliefs.

The psychological effect of this change in architecture was a degradation of intellect; basically, architects were advised to reassess the old aesthetic values of architecture. The reappraisal of the classical inheritance disturbed many contemporary architects, such as Grigori Barkhin, who designed no buildings after 1933. He concentrated instead on large-scale planning and urbanism, ventures in which he did not have to encourage architectural design that sanctioned the eclectic socialist realism. The Vesnin brothers, Ginsburg, Melnikov, El Lissitzky, Ladovsky and Ivan Leonidov did not want to give up their beliefs, and were gradually pushed out of the mainstream of events in Soviet architecture.

Among the projects submitted to the International Competition from abroad were entries of the leading personalities of modern European architecture. Walter Gropius' central, compact composition was a presentation of the functionalist discipline in the careful combination of the required areas. The rational expression, achieved by organizing the spaces in a circular configuration, was repetitive and yet dynamic. The two great halls were connected through a central, cylindrical body. Excellent circulation inside the building still left the ground floor open between the two sections of the total composition, allowing demonstrators to march along the stages of both auditoriums. Nonetheless, the jury criticized the fact that the marching masses would have to walk up and down the stairs to cross the core plateau of the building.

Le Corbusier's project received the most attention. In fact, though it officially received no award at all, that design seemed to be destined for construction. The design, however, lost only in the competition. In the history of modern architecture, Le Corbusier's proposal is recognized as one of the most influential designs, whose significance lay in the truthful expression of the internal functions and the courageous, exposed structural system. The inventive proposition for the structure of the halls, to be carried by the suspension of the ceilings to the external load-bearing elements, became a landmark in the development of modern world architecture. Even so, the jury viewed the project as too utilitarian, and not expressive of the great idea of the palace—the monument to socialism.

In the early 1930s a tendency toward new realist architecture, expressed officially as an application of the best traditions of classical architecture in the forms of national architecture, was becoming increasingly apparent. Though Soviet constructivism still persisted—and indeed posed a hope for progressive architects from Germany, where modern architecture was condemned by the National Socialists as Bolshevist art—Party hardliners and antimodernists, together with defenders of classical expression in architecture, easily found grounds to criticize the cosmopolitan and formalist movements that had penetrated the Soviet Union. They attacked Le Corbusier, Hannes Meyer, Ernst May, Mart Stam, Andre Lurçat, Walter Gropius, Erich Mendelsohn, Bruno Taut, Theo van Doesburg and other visitors from the West. To strengthen its position, the Party consolidated all groups of artists—architectural, artistic, literary, musical and theatrical—on the basis of the creative method of socialist realism.

The next step was a limited competition in 1932—the Invited Competition for Twelve Soviet Teams—that excluded foreigners, but did not include leading constructivists; it was to be constructivism's last fight against the burgeoning realism. Officials were by then stressing the absolute necessity of monumentalism, simplicity, unity and elegance of architectural expression, and the need to employ both techniques along with the best methods of classical architecture. That competition, once more, did not yield a winner, but Boris Iofan's neoclassical scheme received the highest rating. Not only did his entry predict the final design, but it also embodied the aspirations of the ruling Stalinism and its dictatorial architectural expression.

The long struggle to find a final winning project ready for construction continued with the limited Competition for Five Collectives (1932-33), in which the only constructivists represented were the Vesnins. The winning design by Iofan was basically the same scheme submitted in the second Invited Competition for Twelve Soviet Teams. A monumental entrance was added, however, consisting of long, lateral colonnades arranged all around the main floor. It was decided to top Iofan's scheme with a powerful sculpture of Lenin, rising 50 to 75 meters, thereby introducing the idea of the Palace of the Soviet as pedestal for the figure of Lenin. Iofan was instructed to develop the project using the best elements of other entries, and to consider the possible collaboration of other architects in the project's execution. In effect, the destiny of the Palace of the Soviets had fallen into the hands of politicians, and particularly Stalin. Architect Iofan was reduced to the role of draftsman for a dictator's caprice.

The verdict of the jury had gone precisely along the lines of Frank Lloyd Wright's bitter characterization of jury work in general. As had happened at other competitions, the jury grouped the designs into three categories: progressive idea (the Vesnins), cast out; historical attitude (academic architects), rejected; and mediocre solution (Iofan), accepted. This mediocre plan would later become the basis for a bombastic design for a monument which would have the effect of ridiculing the majestic ideals of socialism and communism and their leader, Lenin—an outcome that was difficult even to imagine in its full dimensions.

It took about three years from approval of the preliminary design in 1934 to completion of working drawings in 1937, and the building itself was scheduled to be completed in the following years. The foundations of the large auditorium, which were to support the enormous pedestal with the Lenin statue, included two circular walls of almost 30 meters in depth, each one 3.5 meters thick. Radially, the foundation walls were connected by 32 joint beams. The construction of this remarkably elaborate project was interrupted by World War II, however, and the building was never continued. The huge foundations, which had been completely laid, were later used for an underground water-heating and filtration plant serving a year-round, open-air, circular swimming pool. This unique recreational facility has served the Moscow public usefully and enjoyably—some would say more usefully and enjoyably than had the original scheme been carried out.

After World War II, the Soviet Union set about repairing the devastation, and whole cities were rebuilt from the ground up. In Moscow, the official style, sometimes referred to as Stalin Gothic, took the form of inflated spire buildings in an unconsidered, neoclassical mode, often with eccentric, even humorous, variations—bundled-wheat Corinthian capitals and a baroque heraldry of hammers, sickles, shields and stars. The spire buildings—symbols of the oppressive weight of the dogma of Stalin's rule on the very spirit of the nation—now serve only as painful reminders of the waste and excesses of those years.

With the de-Stalinization instigated by Nikita Khrushchev in 1956, the stirrings of a trend toward ideological coexistence prompted Russian architects, especially those of the younger generation, to reach back into their own heritage and to knit together the break in their great architectural tradition. One glimmer of hope was the Kremlin Palace of Congresses (1959-60) by M. Posokhin and others, an adequate, if somewhat ostentatious, step (particularly in the interior) into the idiom of the International Style, and out of the chaotic eclecticism of the years before 1953.

But the actual beginning of the third phase of Soviet architecture, a rebirth of modern architecture, was marked by the new competition for the Palace of the Soviets. The All-Union Conference on Construction and Architecture (1954) condemned embellishment and asked for recognition of contemporary technology, economy and standardization of the construction industry.

As in the 1930s, this competition (1957-59) of both open and invited rounds did not yield a winner, and it was necessary to repeat the contest. However, the results were quite the opposite of those in the 1930s: while at that time the constructivists were pushed out by neoclassical designs, this time the schemes of V. G. Gelfreikh and Boris Iofan, representing the long-established style of socialist realism, were rejected by the jury and did not even get the chance to compete in the second, closed contest.

Ivan Zholtovsky and Ivan Fomin, submitting in the first competition stage heavily academic designs, but again sensing the political trends of the times, quickly rediscovered and dusted off modernist forms that they had never liked or understood. The traditionalists, however, did not suffer such a drastic fall as had the constructivists in the 1930s. The old school was still important and perhaps even admired, but it was significant that those architects could no longer design as they had in the years of so-called socialist realism.

—PETER LIZON

RUSAKOV WORKERS' CLUB
Moscow, Russia

1927: Construction; **Architect:** Konstantin Melnikov (1890-1974).

Publications

FRAMPTON, KENNETH, and FUTAGAWA, YUKIO: *Modern Architecture: 1920-1945*. New York, 1983.
HOFMANN, WERNER, and KULTERMANN, UDO: *Modern Architecture in Color*. New York, 1970.
KHAN-MAGOMEDOV, S. O.: "Kluby segodnia i vchera." *Dekorativnoe iskusstvo SSSR* 9 (1966): 2-6.
LUKHMANOV, N.: *Arkhitektura kluba*. Moscow, 1930.

*

When the Exhibition of Decorative Arts was envisaged in Paris in 1925, the Union of Soviet Socialist Republics had not been recognized by the United States and had just barely been recognized by France. Russia, never having exhibited in an international exhibition, now decided to show its architectural aspect. At the same time, the exhibit would portray the effects of Soviet life upon the new forms, in distinction from European architecture, as the committee put it. In opposition to the wealth and luxury of other countries, the Soviets presented the freshness and the artistic originality of the revolutionary epoch.

And this was exactly what the architect Konstantin Melnikov succeeded in doing with his great glass expanses, his interrelation of exterior and interior spaces by the oblique passage of the stairway across the pavilion, and his audacious utilization of wood, affirming structures instead of camouflaging them. The diagonal direction of the passageway, again, was a symbolic gesture of the dynamic advancement in the new social order. The exhibits in the pavilion were dominated by the work of constructivists and were far more radical than those of other countries, including Germany.

Perhaps the only rival to Melnikov's Soviet Pavilion at the 1925 Paris Exhibition of Decorative Arts was Le Corbusier's Pavilion de L'Esprit Nouveau. While the latter was distin-

Rusakov Workers' Club: Moscow, Russia, 1927

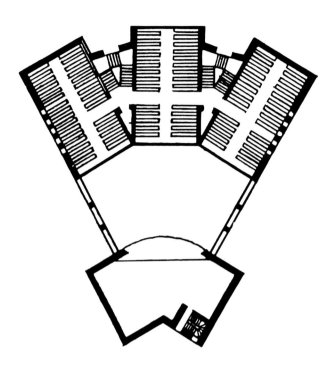

guished by a certain logical clarity, Melnikov's pavilion aspired to have the impact of a poster, with its vigorous colors, decorative lettering and emblems, and expansive composition. Its daring dynamics, the frank simplicity of its materials and the lightness of the pavilion, as well as its rapid erection, stood in contrast to the theatrical monumentality of neighboring pavilions.

Melnikov, one of the most imaginative architects of the 20th century, provided a range of new formal solutions beginning with the Soviet Pavilion in Paris, and continuing with his famous clubs for workers. However, his design solutions were provocative, and polemics were stimulated further. Discussion was fierce, experiments daring and innovation intrepid. Many new ideas were to emerge. But the path of development was by no means uniform. Melnikov invariably devised new solutions in plan and volume, and gave them direct and dramatic expression in the massing of his forms.

In the latter half of the 1920s, the workers' club became a new architectural theme in Melnikov's work. He designed seven clubs between 1927 and 1929, six of which were built. It was a search for a new kind of public building, and together with that a new form of public life; it was a search without tradition and without a clear program. The "club" was a major theme of the period, second in priority, perhaps, only to housing. Much was written about clubs at that time, and especially about those designed by Melnikov. They were disturbing, paradoxical and extraordinary, neither familiar nor even alike. Practically beginning afresh each time, Melnikov sought different solutions and never remained content with past achievements.

This is not to say that he was not guided by principles. Generally, in both the external appearance and the functional construction of the interiors of Melnikov's clubs, there is a system of complex and evolving spatial volumes, by means of which he endeavored to compose a flexible and multipurpose

environment with minimal expenditure. The auditorium, which in fact occupies a great part of a club's volume, was always planned with due consideration of its possible use in parts, its segmentalization by means of special movable screens into several smaller auditoriums. However, technical problems prevented the realization of most of this. The most experimental aspects of the clubs were those that suffered most radically. They were criticized at the time without allowance for the fact that they were substantially incomplete. Melnikov's principle of fluid space—space that is not related solely to a proposed function but undergoes transformations and develops somewhat freely—was in itself progressive. There Melnikov can be seen to have adopted a functional attitude ahead of that of the constructivists, whose "functional method" led rapidly toward a fragmentation of the building by a clear emphasis upon the individual function of each element.

Melnikov's subsequent structural innovations led to extremely varied exterior forms, which resulted in each case in an unprecedented spatial solution to the building. Putting aside the traditional means of articulating the exterior to indicate the social character of the club, such as pediments and porticoes, Melnikov developed new means of articulation. Spacious terraces and external staircases were moved out to cross diagonally in front of facades. He achieved dynamic organization of the masses of a building, and emphasized the entrances and main facade.

This expression of mass attained its most acute formulation in the Rusakov Club (built in 1927 for workers of the Moscow Tramway Factory), where parts of the auditorium project over the facade. At the time, this building was one of the most famed examples of modern Soviet architecture. The theater could be divided into three parts along radial lines converging on the stage, thus forming three volumes whose ends are expressed as cantilevered masses projecting beyond the facade. However, these powerful, reinforced-concrete cantilevered projections drew criticism from the press. They were seen to represent a naive naturalistic symbolism—in no way a part of Melnikov's architectural ideas—and also, simply, a "tendency toward formalism." These reproaches were repeated later when Melnikov's principle of suspending part of the auditorium above the facade had gained wide acceptance in the designs of other contemporary buildings that required auditoriums or other spaces for spectators. Perhaps one reason for these attacks was the unexpected and extraordinary nature of the expressive means developed by Melnikov and the paradoxical nature of his architectural concepts.

Paradox was a characteristic feature of his talent. Both the cantilevers of the Rusakov Club and the staircase of the Paris pavilion were paradoxical in their splitting up of rectangular volume. What was seen as "formalism" and lack of logic was in fact only Melnikov's extraordinary use of his own strict logic—not only in functional and constructive respects but also in the organization of architectural forms. The pie-shaped footprint of the building corresponds to the fan-like seating organization of the auditorium, with the spectators' point of entry and the foyer in the wide end of the pie, and the stage with the back service in the narrow end of the pie. The jutting masses of the three auditorium balconies dominating the front facade seem to be supported by the vertical glazed shafts of stairs. Large graphic signs are incorporated into the three projecting masses. The side elevations express the served and serving parts of the composition. The inclined floor of the auditorium, the rhythm and sizes of fenestration are directly related to the diagonal geometry of the pie-shaped floor plan. While the served part of the composition is finished in stucco, the rear elevation—the stage house—is finished in utilitarian red brick. Clearly, the architect succeeded in his effort to create a legible expression for the new building type. The architectural image of the Rusakov Workers' Club communicates its purpose to the observer.

The chilly appearance of a factory, of smooth surfaces in brick and concrete, of large flat areas of glass in characteristically small frames, were typical of the time and were not confined to Melnikov's work, for in the late 1920s and early 1930s a general tendency developed among leading architects toward the noneclectic and the undecorated. It was a kind of romance of industrialism set up against established ideas. All of this helped to unite the principal groups of leftist architecture—OSA (the Organization of Contemporary Architects) and ASNOVA (Association of New Architects)—separated by the cold functionalism of one and the romantic verve of the other. The indefatigable fantasist Melnikov belonged, in effect, to the latter. Besides, there was a certain amount of urban romanticism in the projects of the most austere constructivists, though they would perhaps have been unwilling to recognize this. The strictly functional bases of their most daring aspirations had become law for them. On the other hand, an acknowledged aim of maximum attention to aesthetics did not prevent their enemies from ensuring the functional modernity of their own buildings, their economic viability or their role in the social organization of public life.

—PETER LIZON

ST. BASIL'S
Moscow, Russia

Early 17th century: Construction; **Architects:** Posnik and Barma. **1626, 1668, and 1737:** Restored after damage from fires.

Publications

BERTON, KATHLEEN: *Moscow: An Architectural History*. New York, 1991.
SCHMIDT, ALBERT J.: *The Architecture and Planning of Classical Moscow*. 1988.
VOYCE, R.: *Russian Architecture*. New York, 1948.

*

The Church of Basil the Blessed was commissioned by Czar Ivan IV (the Terrible) as a national votive church to commemorate his capture of the Tartar stronghold of Kazan on the day of the Feast of the Intercession, 1 October 1552; Ivan's later conquest of Astrakhan is also honored there. The original dedication was to the "Protection and Intercession of the Virgin Mary," but for centuries the church had been known as St. Basil's after Vasily Blazheny, a holy man who died in 1552 and was buried there. The architects are traditionally identified as the Russians Posnik and Barma. The church played an important role in Moscow's Palm Sunday procession. After St. Basil's was damaged by fires in 1626, 1668 and 1737, it was restored to replicate its appearance in the early 17th century.

St. Basil's bizarre multicolored domes have become a popular international symbol for Russia and the Union of Soviet Socialist Republics; located in Moscow's main square next to the Kremlin, the traditional center of Russian and Soviet power, the church's fantastic shape and unexpected decoration make it

immediately recognizable. Théophile Gautier described St. Basil's as "without doubt the most original monument in the world: it recalls nothing that one has ever seen, and belongs to no known style." Uniquely Russian, St. Basil's is the most dramatic development of Russian church architecture as it evolved over a number of centuries from Byzantine prototypes.

The church was intended from the beginning to be a monument to imperial power and military might. Its design refers directly to Ivan's conquest over the infidel, for eight wooden churches commemorating the eight sieges of Kazan originally surrounded a central cathedral dedicated to the Intercession of the Virgin. Eventually they were joined and executed in masonry.

St. Basil's central element, a bold octagonal tower with a tent roof, is surrounded by four dramatically elevated domes on octagonal bases that alternate with four lower domes on polygonal bases; the building's unity stems from the repeated rhythm of high and low domes around a central tower. Undulating walls carry the forceful rhythm of the upper part of the church to ground level to create a complex polygonal ground plan. In the 17th century the internal logic of the plan was destroyed when a chapel, a bell tower and a raised covered gallery with tent-roofed porches were added. The profusion of forms on the exterior is related to the interior, which is honeycombed with individual chapels. The frescoes of the interior date from the 18th and 19th centuries.

The architectural iconography of St. Basil's emphasized Ivan's patronage and the church's function as a votive monument. The source for the central tower with its tent roof has been identified as the Church of the Ascension at Kolomenskoe (1530s), which was built by Ivan's father, Vasily III, probably in thanksgiving for Ivan's birth. The tent roof was particularly identified with votive structures; Kolomenskoe's tent roof had been inspired by votive churches erected by noble families in the first part of the 16th century. St. Basil's large scale, eccentric plan, unusual combination of tent roof with domes, and the alternation and irregular height of the subsidiary domes combine to create a unique structure. Ivan's motivation may have been to create a new and distinct identity for his rule and for his capital in Moscow, in sharp contrast with the more conservative structures characteristic of the earlier centers of power at Novgorod and Kiev. St. Basil's was especially identified with the government because the Czar's Great Treasury was stored there during the later 16th century.

The architects are traditionally identified as Posnik and Barma, but another theory holds that Barma ("Mumbler") was Posnik's nickname; no other work by an architect named Posnik or Barma is known. Popular sources report that Ivan blinded the architects so that they could never build another church as

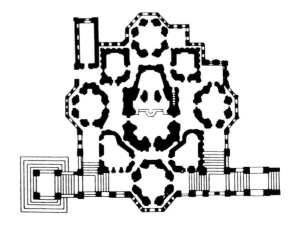

St. Basil's: Moscow, Russia, early 17th century

beautiful as St. Basil's, but no early documents support this tale. It probably developed as an explanation for the building's unparalleled design and as yet another example of the cruelty traditionally attributed to Ivan. Ivan IV's choice of Russian architects is in contrast to the Italian architects imported by Ivan III and is another indication of the particular Russian emphasis in Ivan IV's political program. Makari, the metropolitan (bishop) of Moscow, is also thought to have played a role in the design of the church.

The ultimate source for Byzantine and Russian multidomed structures such as St. Basil's was the five-domed, centrally planned Church of the Holy Apostles built for the Byzantine emperor Justinian I in Constantinople in the sixth century. It had a central dome and four lower domes at the corners, and inspired many replicas. Many Byzantine and Byzantine-inspired churches have the raised exterior domes which are the ultimate source for the extravagant elevated domes of Russian religious structures, but the origins of the distinctive onion-shaped domes of Russian church architecture are still controversial.

St. Basil's uniqueness is heightened by the multicolored, patterned decoration of the lower walls and, especially, of the tent vault and domes, but this was not a part of the original design. Originally the eight subsidiary domes had a lower, rounded profile and were probably gilded; the onion-shaped domes were added in the late 16th or early 17th century. Their raised decoration and extravagant polychromy were completed in the 17th century, and during the same period the floral decoration of the lower walls was added. These colorful designs suggest the influence of Russian folk art—embroideries, traditional wooden architecture, metalwork, enamels and other traditional decorative arts. These peculiarly Russian motifs are another aspect of the patriotic and national quality that characterizes St. Basil's.

—DAVID G. WILKINS

ADMIRALTY
St. Petersburg, Russia

1704: Construction. **1710-30:** Reconstruction. **1732-38:** Reconstruction of tower; **Architect:** I. K. Korobov. **1806-23:** Reconstruction; **Architect:** Adrian Dmitrievich Zakharov (1761-1811).

Publications

EGOROV, IURII ALEKSEEVICH: *The Architectural Planning of St. Petersburg.* Athens, Ohio, 1969.

HAMILTON, G.H.: *The Art and Architecture of Russia.* Harmondsworth, 1954.

HAUTECOEUR, L.: *L'architecture classique à St. Pétersbourg à la fin du XVIIIe siècle.* 1912.

LANCERAY, N.: "Adrien Zakharov et l'Amirauté à St. Pétersbourg." *Starye Gooy* 12 (1911):3-64.

MILNER-GUILLAND, ROBIN: "Art and Architecture in the Petersburg Age; 1700-1860." in AUTY, ROBERT and OBLENSKY, DIMITRI (eds.): *An Introduction to Russian Art and Architecture.* 1980.

One of the oldest and largest structures in St. Petersburg, the Admiralty was the main center of urban growth in the mainland part of the city along the left bank of the Neva River. The building is the nucleus of a grand ensemble of central plazas: Palace Square, Senate Square and St. Isaac's Square. It also constitutes a point of focus for the entire arc-and-radial layout of the city center. The Admiralty tower, crowned by a gilt spire, is a dominant architectural landmark. Nevsky Prospekt, Gorokhovaia Street and Vosnesensky Prospekt form a symmetrical "trident" which is oriented toward the Admiralty, as are Galernaia and Millionnaia streets along the Neva. In the area of the Neva watershed, the silhouette of the Admiralty tower provides a counterpoint to the bell tower of Peter and Paul Cathedral (1712-33, by Domenico Trezini), which rises over the walls of the St. Petersburg, or Peter and Paul, Fortress.

The Admiralty is recognized as the pinnacle of high classicism—also called the Empire style—in Russia. It is unsurpassed in its expressiveness and rich artistic content, in the delicacy of its composition, and in its combination of architectural form and monumental sculpture. It acquired these qualities during a thorough reconstruction carried out in the early 19th century under the direction of Adrian D. Zakharov. But the building's history predates that event by a century.

The Admiralty shipyard, the birthplace of the Russian navy, was laid out in 1704, only a year and a half after the founding of St. Petersburg. The design was drafted by Peter the Great who knew both architecture and the craft of shipbuilding. The shipyard was situated on the southern shore of the Great Neva River arm, downstream from St. Petersburg Fortress. The structure combined the functions of a shipyard, a fortress and an administrative center.

The architecture of the original Admiralty resembled that of similar structures in the Netherlands. An elongated main building and two symmetrical wings at right angles formed three sides of a rectangular yard, open on its long side to the Neva. The yard enclosed a production zone. The building was unpretentious and sincerely utilitarian, constructed of mud over a wooden framework. In the tradition of vertical architecture, which became popular in St. Petersburg during the first half of the 18th century, a small spired tower provided the central axis of the main building with its only accent. A moat and an earthen rampart with five bulwarks encircled the original Admiralty.

The reconstruction of 1710-30 transformed the Admiralty into a more imposing structure and strengthened its central place in the urban plan of the city. The first addition was a new stone tower with a high spire crowned by a sculpture of a small ship. H. van Boleos, a Dutch engineer, constructed the wooden spire. Subsequently, the earthen buildings were replaced, in stages, with brick ones. These projects were completed under the direction of I. K. Korobov, architect of the Admiralty board, who had studied construction work in the Netherlands. He doubled the building plan, placing production and storage facilities inside the main buildings but retaining the original layout with an open-sided square. A canal, which flowed at both ends into the Neva, was dug between the exterior and interior wings.

Korobov's plans called for the central tower to be rebuilt (1732-38) from the bottom up, to a total height of 72 meters. That gave the Admiralty a more imposing and expressive stature, in sharp contrast to the horizontality of its extended wings. The graduated composition of the tower did not have the plasticity of detail peculiar to the Baroque style. Rather, the smooth planes of the facades and their polished pilasters were closer to the classical style. The wooden structure of the spire, consisting of four-sided and eight-sided prismatic parts with an eight-sided pyramidal top, has been preserved and is a unique example of the engineering arts of the time.

Admiralty: St. Petersburg, Russia, 1704

The Admiralty in many ways predetermined the character of the development of the left-bank section of the city, which later became the city center. Simultaneously with the erection of Korobov's tower, three central rays (the "trident" streets) were laid out, completing the skeleton of the mainland layout. During the course of the 18th century, the esplanade encircling the shipyard-fortress was replaced by a system of monumental squares, completed in the first half of the 19th century.

The movement toward a unified cityscape was fundamental to the architecture of Russian high classicism. The prosaic and utilitarian appearance of the Admiralty's wings ceased to meet the requirements of its location at the structural nucleus of the St. Petersburg city center. Attempts to lend the entire building a classical character and monumental appearance can be observed in the unrealized plans of Charles Cameron and Giacomo Quarenghi from the early 1800s.

The task was finally completed by Zakharov, who was appointed chief architect of the Admiralty board in 1805. His creation synthesized the devices of Russian classicism of the turn of the 18th century and the artistic innovations of the new French architectural school led by Claude-Nicolas Ledoux. From this combination arose the phenomenon of the Russian

Empire style, of which Zakharov was a main proponent.

Reconstruction of the Admiralty began in 1806 and was completed in 1823, 12 years after its architect's death. Zakharov roughly duplicated the configuration of the old building. Proceeding from considerations of rational economy, he used the old walls and even preserved in part the axes of the embrasures. But that prevented neither the realization of a fundamentally new stylistic conception nor the creation of an exceptionally integrated and polished composition. Glancing at the building, it is difficult to believe that it was not rebuilt from the ground up. In truth, the complex as a whole had two faces. Its exterior wings, the main entrance of which faces the area's central squares, accommodated the Ministry of the Navy, an educational institution, and a museum among others. The courtyard continued to be the site of a shipyard, and the interior wings had a more modest and ordinary appearance.

The exterior facades are striking in their ceremonial grandeur and stern monumentalism. The architect brilliantly solved the complex problem of rhythmic organization in the horizontally extending wings (the main one is 407 meters in length, and the lateral wings are 163 meters each). Expressiveness is achieved through a precisely balanced distribution of mass, and the regular alternation of neutral surfaces with powerful accents.

Zakharov reworked the walls of Korobov's tower, treating its base like a huge, massive cube cut across by an arc. Rounded sculpture and reliefs effectively set off the smooth lapidary surface of the wall. The geometric abstraction of mass and contour and the stark tectonics of simple forms characterize this expressive cube. It summons associations with the work of Ledoux and the graphic compositions of Etienne-Louis Boullée and Moitte. The second tier of the tower is surrounded by a grand, airy Ionic colonnade which provides a counterpoint to the powerful, static foundation. The old gilt spire with its little ship weathervane was completely preserved as an original attribute of the cityscape and symbol of the Admiralty's history. However, this very element is the only one that remains somewhat alien in the overall design of the building.

The flanks of the main facade are organized around three axes, a form much loved in Russian classicism. The symmetrical six-column portico-loggias on the sides are overshadowed by the central 12-column one. The same combination of three porticoes, but with large spaces between them, is repeated on the lateral facades. The six-column portico-loggias are repeated on all the exterior corners of the building (12 times altogether), thereby connecting its facades. The tower foundation's cubic motif is carried on, in different proportions, in the pavilions terminating the wings, which are visible from the Neva side.

Thus, in its overall structure, the Admiralty variously combines several uniform elements. This approach lends the enormous structure not only a compositional unity, but also richness and diversity. The leitmotif of Roman Doric porticoes is like a fugue of many voices. Zakharov succeeded in endowing the very surface of the walls with a rare expressivity and a strikingly severe power and cool clarity that testify to the influence of French architecture. Unlike Karl Rossi, whose major works exhibit a preoccupation with exterior effect, Zakharov achieved a remarkable dimensional expressiveness.

The most interesting feature of the Admiralty's interior is the main vestibule and front stairway. Its two-tiered spatial composition with heavy arcade below and airy colonnade above spans the entire height of the building.

Zakharov achieved a synthesis of the architectural arts with unprecedented artistic strength and depth of vision. The monumental sculpture tends toward fundamental dimensional accents and concentrates around the central tower. The massive sculptural groups of sea nymphs by F. F. Shchedrin balance the

heavy base of the tower. Allegorical statues on the tower's colonnade extend the light vertical lines of the columns. The principal thematic bas-relief, *The Establishment of the Navy in Russia* (by I. I. Terebenev), adorns the attic of the cube. The sculptural ensemble of the Admiralty confirms its multiple function as the home of the Russian navy, a symbol of the port city, and a monument to the military victories of Russia. Its heroic spirit and solemnity were especially in keeping with the mood of Russian society after the victory over Napoleon in the War of 1812.

Zakharov's Admiralty became an indisputable compositional dominant in the Russian capital. It had a determining influence on the last stages of Russian classicism, particularly the work of Karl Rossi and V. P. Stasov. When the fortifications that had surrounded it were removed (1816-18), the Admiralty assumed an organizing role among the central squares of St. Petersburg.

In the 1870s a landscaped garden was planted on the embankment along the Neva, in front of the Admiralty's main facade, and the interior courtyard was built up with multistory buildings. This noticeably reduced the building's resonance in the larger scheme of the city and detracted from the clarity of the Admiralty's design. But the character of the building itself has undergone negligible changes on the whole and has survived to our time in its entirety.

—BORIS M. KIRIKOV
Translated from the Russian by Gwenan Wilbur

EXCHANGE (BOURSE)
St. Petersburg, Russia

1804-10: Construction of Bourse, embankment and Rostral Columns; **Architect:** Thomas de Thomon (1754-1813). **1826-32:** Northern and southern warehouses constructed. **1913-14:** Restoration and reconstruction of Bourse; **Architects:** F. I. Lidval and M. M. Peretiatkovich. **1927:** Public garden laid out; **Architect:** L. A. Ilyin.

Publications

BERCKENHAGEN, EKHART: *St. Petersburg um 1800: Architekturzeichnungen Thomas de Thomon.* Exhibition catalog. Berlin, 1975.
EGOROV, IURII ALEKSEEVICH: *The Architectural Planning of St. Petersburg.* Athens, Ohio, 1969.
HAMILTON, G. H.: *The Art and Architecture of Russia.* Harmondsworth, 1954.
LOUKOMSKI, GEORGES: "Thomas de Thomon." *Apollo* 42 (1945): 297-304.
OSHCHEPKOV, C. D.: *Arkhitektor Thomon.* Moscow, 1950.
THOMON, THOMAS DE: *Recueil de plans et facades des principaux monuments contruits a Saint-Petersbourg et dans les differentes provinces de l'Empire de Russie.* St. Petersburg, 1809.

*

The architectural complex of the St. Petersburg Bourse is one of the greatest achievements of mature Russian classicism. This lovely ensemble in the central part of St. Petersburg is insepara-

Exchange: St. Petersburg, Russia, 1804-10

bly linked with the panorama of the Neva River embankments and has become one of the symbols of the city.

The Bourse is located on one of the most prominent sites in the city center—the eastern promontory (''the arrow'') of Vasilievsky Island, where the Neva divides into the Great and the Little Neva. The essence of Thomas de Thomon's grand architectural scheme is a precise spatial composition organized around the Bourse building, with other structures laid out symmetrically along the northern and southern banks of the island.

Beginning in the early 18th century, the ''arrow'' of Vasilievsky Island was a port of trade and the business center of St. Petersburg. Peter the Great chose it for the location of his stock exchange, which went for a long time without its own building. In the 1780s, the architect Giacomo Quarenghi roughed out a separate Bourse building on the promontory of Vasilievsky Island, but neither its placement nor its architectural character conformed to new requirements. In connection with the rapid growth of trade, the new Bourse building had to be much larger.

In 1801 Thomas de Thomon completed his first plan for the Bourse. The 40-year-old architect, a graduate of the Académie in Paris, had arrived in St. Petersburg only a year earlier. He was a fine draftsman, but not a very experienced architect. Prior to his arrival in Russia, he had had no construction experience. Thomon had studied ancient architecture in Italy for a few years, and he later became the forefather of Hellenism in St. Petersburg architecture of the classical period.

While working out his first design for the Bourse, Thomon relied upon the tradition of the French academic school and developed approaches that can be traced in the works of his classmates in the Paris Académie, foremost among them Pierre

Bernard and Jean Jacques Tardieu. Like many of his contemporaries, Thomon relied on the designs of the *''Grand Prix d'architecture,''* having inherited from French architecture a passion for gigantic scale. Although such projects were purely rhetorical for his French colleagues, Thomon made a concrete attempt to link the Bourse with a specific location and the surrounding buildings. The influence of the St. Petersburg architectural school on his design is unmistakable. Thomon worked tirelessly for four years, with the constant creative support and advice of the St. Petersburg Academy of Arts, to put together a final version of his design for the Bourse. The recommendations of A. D. Zakharov, well-known architect and professor at the academy, were especially helpful.

Thomon instantly found the fundamental elements of his composition: the central location of the Bourse building, its flanking rostral columns and the precisely delineated embankment of the ''arrow'' with its gently sloping ramps. The principal shortcomings of the first design versions derived from the requirement of incorporating Quarenghi's old Bourse into the new construction. Later, that requirement was dropped, and the unfinished building was dismantled.

In the process of working on his design, Thomon vastly improved the proportions of the Bourse. He made the building more compact, replaced porticoes on the facades with an unbroken exterior colonnade, improved the floor plan, increased the size and plasticity of the planned rostral columns and set them farther off from the Bourse. Early in 1804, the emperor Alexander I approved the sixth and final design.

Work began with shoring up of the ''arrow'' promontory of Vasilievsky Island, which jutted more than 100 meters into the channel of the Neva. This made room for a spacious plaza, not only in front of the Bourse building, but also behind it. An active and decisive reorganization of the site allowed Thomon to transform the appearance of the entire riverfront ensemble of St. Petersburg with only one building and the transfigured embankment.

The simple and clear-cut proportions of the Bourse are reminiscent of a Greek peripteral temple. The building is rectangular, with a peaked roof, and is surrounded by a powerful colonnade of 44 smooth Doric columns on a massive granite stylobate with a wide staircase and lateral ramps. In contrast with ancient temples, the slopes of the roof are not supported by columns, but cover only the main body of the building. The colonnade thus appears to stand away from the walls, forming a wide gallery on all sides. This lends the building an air of breadth and spaciousness in harmony with the Neva panorama.

The attic story accommodates two monumental sculptural groups, *Neptune with Two Rivers* and *Navigation and Mercury with Rivers*. The main entrance leads into the building's vestibule, through which one can enter the central hall. The enormous space of the hall is covered by a cylindrical segmented arch supported by perfectly smooth walls, crowned by a Doric entablature. The severe and majestic building is striking in its grand scale and stately spirit.

A spacious semicircular plaza is laid out in front of the Bourse, pointing upstream along the Neva. The plaza is ringed by a granite embankment with ramps extraordinary in their composition. They slope gently toward the Neva, with parapets topped by massive granite globes on pedestals. Along the sides of the plaza two monumental Doric columns rise to a height of 32 meters; these columns are decorated with images of rostra—the prows of ships—whence the term rostral columns. Colossal figures carved out of white Pudostsky stone, symbolizing the great Russian rivers Volga, Dniepr, Neva and Volkhov, sit on the pedestals of the columns.

The Bourse ensemble is designed to be viewed from great distances: both from the St. Petersburg embankments and from ships sailing by on the Neva. Its color scheme is felicitous, being based on an effective contrast between the dark granite of the embankment, the reddish rostral columns and the light silhouette of the Bourse. The Bourse ensemble became a fundamental compositional focus in the cityscape, uniting other earlier architectural components on the banks of the Neva, such as the Peter and Paul Fortress and the Winter Palace. Firmly planted against the currents of the Neva, as if dividing it into two branches, the monumental ensemble of the Bourse was designed to symbolize the naval power of the Russian government.

Most of the structural work on the Bourse ensemble was completed in 1810. However, the war with Napoleon delayed the opening of the Bourse for six years. Thomas de Thomon died in 1813, at the peak of his creative powers, and did not witness this event. The "arrow" ensemble was completed after the major flood of 1824, when the warehouses designed by Thomon and Zakharov in 1804 were erected along the northern and southern sides of the Bourse. Since then, the Bourse has remained essentially unchanged. The most extensive restoration was carried out in 1914, when the architects F. I. Lidval and M. M. Peretiatkovich replaced the wooden structure of the grand hall's arch with reinforced concrete.

After the Revolution of 1917, the Bourse was closed. Since then, the building has housed the Central Naval Museum. Recently the question of restoring the building to its original function has been discussed.

—ALEKSANDR V. KOBAK
Translated from the Russian by Gwenan Wilbur

KAZAN CATHEDRAL
St. Petersburg, Russia

1801-11: Construction; **Architect:** Andrei Nikiforovich Voronikhin (1760-1814). **1834:** Installation of new silver iconostasis; **Architect:** K. A. Ton. **1910-11:** Restoration of cathedral; **Architect:** A. P. Aplaksin. **1932:** Cathedral closed and converted into the Museum of the History of Religion and Atheism. **1950-60:** Restoration of the facade.

Publications

APLAKSIN, A. P.: *Kazanskij sobor: Istoricheskoe issledovanie o sobore i ego opisanie*. St. Petersburg, 1911.
GRIMM, G. G.: *Atkhitektor Voronikhin*. Moscow, 1963.
HAMILTON, G. H.: *The Art and Architecture of Russia*. Harmondsworth, 1954.
HAUTECOEUR, L.: *L'architecture classique a St. Petersbourg a la fin du XVIIIe siecle*. 1912.
LISOVSKIJ, V. G.: *Andrej Voronikhin*. Leningrad, 1971.
PANOV, V. A.: *Arkhitektor Voronikhin*. Moscow, 1937.
SHURYGIN, Y. I.: *Kazanskij sobor*. Leningrad, 1987.

Kazan Cathedral is an integral element in the architectural appearance of Nevsky Prospekt, the central boulevard of St. Petersburg. The cathedral is among the first and best works of early-19th-century Russian high classicism.

The history of the site on which Kazan Cathedral now stands dates back to the first half of the 18th century, when a Baroque church with a stately, spired bell tower was erected there by the architect M. G. Zemtsov. The church housed an important Russian holy relic, an icon of Our Lady of Kazan, which had been brought to St. Petersburg during the reign of Peter the Great. However, the original church soon appeared too modest, not only for the significance accorded it among St. Petersburg places of worship, but also for its location on the main thoroughfare of the rapidly growing Russian capital. At the end of the 18th century, two well-known architects, Giacomo Quarenghi and N. A. Lvov, worked out designs for a new church, which, however, remained on paper.

In 1799 Emperor Paul I held a competition for the design of the new Kazan Cathedral. However, as none of the participating architects—Pietro Gonzaga, Charles Cameron and Thomas de Thomon—came up with a convincing alternative, A. N. Voronikhin was commissioned a year later to build the cathedral according to his own designs. The 40-year-old Voronikhin was descended from the serfs of Count A. S. Stroganov, a well-known patron of the arts and president of the Academy of Arts. Through his own extraordinary talent, and with Stroganov's support, Voronikhin became the leading architect of his time.

Paul I required that the new Kazan Cathedral should recall St. Peter's Basilica in Rome, with its famous colonnade by Giovanni Lorenzo Bernini. That condition complicated the project immensely. As is generally known, Bernini had built his colonnade as an addition to the main facade of the Roman cathedral 100 years after its completion. Bernini's colonnade is lower than the cathedral itself and encloses the self-contained area of the cathedral's facing square. The topography of Kazan Cathedral's site ruled out such an approach. Since the altar in an Orthodox church must face east, and Nevsky Prospekt itself runs east-west, the cathedral would inevitably have to "turn" its lateral north facade toward the street. To carry out the emperor's order, it followed that the main entrance with the colonnade

Kazan Cathedral: St. Petersburg, Russia, 1801-11

would open onto narrow Meshchansky Street, which leads off Nevsky Prospekt.

Voronikhin succeeded in finding a solution to that problem. First of all, he placed the exterior colonnade on the side of the main boulevard rather than at the main entrance. This violated canons of church construction, but fully addressed the larger task of city planning. Second, rather than close off the square facing Nevsky Prospekt with columns, he opened it up to meet the city's main thoroughfare. Finally, he connected the colonnade organically with the building itself by using harmonious proportions and rhythm. From the vantage point of Nevsky Prospekt, the bulk of Kazan Cathedral is completely disguised by the colonnade, which is of the exact same height. This made

it possible to "hide" the asymmetry of the structure on the Nevsky Prospekt side. In fulfilling the emperor's requirement of an exterior colonnade, Voronikhin simultaneously happened upon a completely original architectural solution.

As depicted in Voronikhin's plan, the cathedral building forms a Latin cross, set far back from Nevsky Prospekt. The northern facade is bordered by a grand colonnade consisting of 96 fluted Corinthian columns, arranged in four rows and crowned with a high entablature with a light balustrade. The flowing curve of the colonnade frames an open semicircular square in front of the building. At the center of the entire composition is a stately six-column portico ending in a triangular fountain. A light cupola on a high drum pierced by rectangular windows rises over the portico. The wings of the colonnade end in monumental portals, which function as passageways.

Voronikhin's colonnade, connecting the cathedral with its surroundings, was the first in the history of Russian architecture to play a role in the formation of the cityscape. Kazan Cathedral opens up to meet the city: a sense of spaciousness permeates its colonnade and portico, as if the street and the embankment are drawn in by its gigantic lateral portals. The complexity of the cathedral's design foreshortens the perspective in countless ways.

Kazan Cathedral's architecture is not only monumental and triumphant, but is also harmonious and refined in its decorative details. This building heralded a new stage of Russian architecture—the high classicism in the Empire style of the first third of the 19th century. If the stately refinement and grace of Voronikhin's architecture had its precursor in late-18th-century French and Russian classicism, the principles of monumentality, of unified building complexes, and of active interplay with the surroundings belong entirely to the Empire period.

Voronikhin's design was approved in the fall of 1800, and construction of the cathedral went on for 10 years. The exterior facing of the walls, colonnade and reliefs was executed in light-colored Pudostsky limestone, quarried in the vicinity of St. Petersburg. The cathedral cupola is an important engineering innovation devised by Voronikhin: it spans 17 meters and is executed in wrought-iron latticework. The cupola's interior composition resembles that of Jacques Germain Soufflot's Panthéon in Paris.

The sculptural decoration of Kazan Cathedral is unique. Its designer achieved a synthesis of architecture and sculpture hitherto unknown in the architecture of Russian classicism. Leading masters of the Academy of Arts worked on the sculptural decoration of the cathedral. The bronze sculptures of saints in the northern portico were done by S. S. Pimenov, I. P. Martos and V. I. Demuth-Malinovsky. The large bas-relief friezes above the lateral passageways and above the altar, the square panels and ornamental reliefs between the wall pilasters are the works of I. P. Martos, I. P. Prokofiev, F. G. Gordeev and G. Rachett. The north doors of the cathedral are copies of Lorenzo Ghiberti's famous "Doors of Paradise" in the Florentine Baptistery.

The interior of Kazan Cathedral creates a feeling of grandeur and spaciousness. The exterior colonnade is answered in the interior by rows of monolithic columns in red Finnish granite with gilded Corinthian capitals. In arranging the interior and exterior columns, the architect preserved a unified rhythm. The lines of exterior columns carry on a spontaneous dialogue with those of the interior. Among contributors to the creation of the cathedral's interior were such distinguished Russian painters as V. L. Borovikovsky, V. K. Shebuev, O. A. Kiprensky and A. E. Yegorov.

Not long before construction was completed, Voronikhin decided to develop his original intention and proposed to complete and balance the cathedral's composition by erecting a second exterior colonnade on the southern facade. However, that grandiose project was never realized. Instead, a cast-iron fence was built to encircle the square in front of the western facade of the cathedral. This was one of the last and most wonderful works of the architect. Comparable to the fence around St. Petersburg's Summer Garden, Voronikhin's iron-work fence is among the best in the city.

Completed not long before the start of the war with Napoleon, Kazan Cathedral became a distinctive war memorial, housing numerous captured banners, standards, keys to seized fortresses and other war trophies. The memorial significance of the cathedral greatly increased after Mikhail I. Kutuzov, hero of the War of 1812, was interred in the northern chapel, and monuments

to field marshals Kutuzov and Mikhail Barclay de Tolly were erected on the square.

After construction was completed, the cathedral underwent a few modifications. In the 1830s a new silver iconostasis was added, designed by architect Konstantin A. Ton. The most extensive restoration, under the direction of architect A. P. Aplaksin, was timed to coincide with the cathedral's 100th anniversary.

In 1932 Kazan Cathedral was closed to worship and turned into a museum of the history of religion and atheism. During the postrevolutionary struggle against religion, the interior and artistic decoration of the building suffered significant damage. From 1950 to 1960 it underwent another thorough restoration after having sustained more damage during the siege of Leningrad during World War II.

—ALEKSANDR V. KOBAK
Translated from the Russian by Gwenan Wilbur

PETERHOF PALACE
Petrodvorets, near St. Petersburg, Russia

1714: Construction begins; **Architect:** Andreas Schlüter. **1715-24:** Construction of Grand Cascade; **Architects:** J.-B. LeBlond, J. F. Braunstein and N. Michetti. **1717-20:** Interior decoration. **1721:** Damaged in fire. **1722-24:** Restoration of damaged sections and addition of galleries and side blocks. **1747-51:** Restoration of palace; **Architect:** B. F. Rastrelli. **1763-75:** Refurnishing of palace interiors; **Architects:** J.-B. Vallin de la Mothe and Y. M. Velten. **1779-85:** Construction of Korpus za Gerbom Building; **Architects:** Y. M. Velten and I. E. Iakovlev. **1845-50:** Remodeling of interiors in eastern block; **Architect:** A. I. Shtakenshneider. **1941-44:** Palace destroyed during World War II. **1945-80s:** Restoration work; **Architects:** V. M. Savkov and E. V. Kazanskaia.

Publications

ARKHIPOV, N. I. and RASKIN, A. G.: *Petrodvorets.* Leningrad/Moscow, 1961.
GIRIEVICH, I. M., ZNAMENOV, V. V. and MIASOEDOVA, E. G.: *Bolshoi Petergoffskij Dvorets.* Leningrad, 1979.
RASKIN, A.: *Petrodvorets; dvosrtsovo-parkovy ansambl' 18 veka.* Leningrad, 1975.
USPENSKIJ, A. I.: *Imperatorskie dvortsy.* Moscow, 1913.
VOJNOV, V.: "Andres Shluter: arkhitektor Petra 1: k voprosy o formirovanii stilia 'petrovskoe barokko'." *Sovetskoe isskusstvoznanie.* 1 (1976).

*

Peterhof Palace was the center of the emperor's summer residence park and palace complex in Peterhof. Renamed Petrodvorets in 1944, Peterhof was a small town near St. Petersburg. According to Peter I's plan, the Bay of Finland coastal area was to become a gigantic ensemble, consisting of the high nobility's summer residences. Building of the summer palace began in 1714; the palace was named Peterhof, after the emperor.

The noted German architect Andreas Schlüter composed the project, following Peter I's drawings. The French architect Jean-Baptiste LeBlond directed the construction of the palace; he slightly modified the original composition and completed the

Peterhof Palace: near St. Petersburg, Russia, 1714

first version of the palace. The building was located on the shore terrace edge, and consisted of a central block with a triangular gable and two smaller side blocks. Using LeBlond's designs, Johann Friedrich Braunstein fashioned the palace interiors, of which only Peter I's Cabinet has been preserved. Ornamental floral patterns, combined with symbols of power, the sciences and the arts, were carved on the oak panels which decorated the Cabinet walls. Exquisite carving was carried out according to Nicolas Pineau's drawings.

In 1720 the Italian architect Nicolo Michetti added two symmetrical wings, connected by arcade galleries to the main building. The new wings repeated the design of the palace's side blocks, unifying the extended construction, composed of similar segments of different height.

Four architects of different aesthetic schools, then, created the first version of Peterhof Palace. The palace design combined Baroque with classical traits. This stylistic duality was characteristic of early-17th-century St. Petersburg architecture. It fused austere, flat structures with a picturesque intricacy of gables, roofs and balustrades adorned with sculpture.

In the mid-17th century, the building underwent a comprehensive reconstruction. Bartolomeo Francesco Rastrelli, the major architect of the Russian Baroque period, created new designs for the palace at the request of Empress Elizabeth, Peter's daughter.

Elizabeth approved Rastrelli's project in 1747. Originally commissioned by Peter, the palace had a memorial significance, so Rastrelli preserved its former tripartite composition and main stylistic features. He included the original building in his new three-story construction. It consisted of a central block and two side blocks. Rastrelli also built two wings and connected them by galleries to the side blocks of the main building. He achieved spatial expressiveness by varying the rhythmic organization of the facades. Patterns of pilasters and gables accentuated the interplay of the facade's structural parts.

Rastrelli employed Peter I's period techniques without attempting to achieve the plasticity and dynamism characteristic of his other works. The Peterhof Palace facade was modest and flat. The high, figured roof, characteristic of early-17th-century architecture, played an important part in the palace's appearance. Rastrelli raised high, gilded cupolas adorned with domes and relief patterns over the side blocks. Above the east block, he built a five-dome structure resembling those of Moscow

churches in the late 17th century. The two-headed eagle, emblem of the Russian empire, crowned the west block. The sophisticated forms of the roof and domed cupolas endowed the building with a fanciful Baroque silhouette, clearly visible from the Bay of Finland side. Thus, Rastrelli both maintained the memorial significance of Peter's ensemble and created a palace in the Russian High Baroque style.

By 1775 building and furnishing of the palace were complete. Rastrelli created an enfilade of six ceremonial halls and many reception rooms, to suit Empress Elizabeth's court reception ritual. The enfilade opened onto the upper landing of the Ceremonial Staircase, located in the palace's west block. The enfilade's numerous mirrors reflected its splendid decorations and created the impression of an infinitely multiplying space. The walls seemed unable to contain the decorative exuberance of the interiors. The Ceremonial Staircase, the Ballroom, the Audience Hall and the Chapel retained their Baroque appearance until 1941. Gilded wood carving covered the wall surfaces, corresponding to the parquet floor patterns. The carving set off the mirrors, doors and windows and served as a background for frescoes and decorated ceilings.

Already during the 1760s and 1770s, the architects Jean-Baptiste Vallin de la Mothe and Y. M. Velten refurnished a series of Rastrelli's interiors in the early neoclassical style. Vallin de la Mothe decorated two galleries, employing authentic Chinese lacquered screens and Chinese-style gold fretwork as the main elements of adornment. The Chinese galleries contained the empress' collection of Chinese and Japanese decorative art. At the same time, Vallin de la Mothe refurnished the Great Petrovsky Hall, which originally had been created by Le Blond and was later included in the ceremonial enfilade by Rastrelli. The hall was renamed the Gallery of Graces. Instead of gilded wood carving, the hall was decorated with tapestries and portraits of women by Pietro Rotari. Concurrently, Velten created the Dining, Throne and Chesmensky Halls in the classical style. He blended them into the former Rastrelli enfilade. Sculpture was the main element of the Dining Hall and the Throne Hall decorations. Twelve paintings by J. F. Gakkert, depicting Chesmensky Battle scenes, decorated Chesmensky Hall. Velten also refurnished the Lounge, Partridge Room, Bedroom and Throne Room. However, during these reconstructions, the interior planning and the facade's Baroque appearance remained intact.

Peterhof Palace, pavillion

Later remodeling did not alter the palace's character. In the 1840s A. I. Shtakenshneider partially reorganized some of the rooms in the building's eastern part, which were intended for Princess Olga Nikolaevna.

The center of the imperial residence ensemble, Peterhof Palace was erected on the border between the Upper and Lower Parks. The Upper Park was oriented toward the palace, while the Lower Park opened onto the Bay of Finland. Facing the Lower Park and Bay of Finland, the palace crowned the perspective of Morskoi Canal in the Lower Park. The Grand Cascade, begun in 1715, was set into the slope of the terrace in front of the palace and forms a unified whole with it. With 64 fountains,

the Grand Cascade was one of the largest fountain complexes in the world, a grandiose triumphal construction, glorifying Russia's victory during the Northern War (1700-21). With its 22-meter-high jet, *Samson Lacerating the Lion's Jaws* was the largest fountain in the cascade. This fountain was an allegorical memorial to the Battle of Poltava, which brought a decisive victory to the Russian army.

Until 1917 the 18th-century palace and park complex at Peterhof remained the Russian emperor's official summer residence. After the Revolution it became a museum. During the World War II, military actions were undertaken in the Peterhof area, and the palace was largely destroyed. Restoration began in 1945, and currently, Peterhof Palace functions as a museum of 18th-century Russian culture.

—IRENA A. KOSTAREVA
Translated from the Russian by Konstantine Klioutchkine

PUSHKINO PALACE (GREAT PALACE)
Tsarkoe Selo, near St. Petersburg, Russia

1710-24: Construction begins; **Architect:** J. F. Braunstein. **1741-51:** Reconstruction of palace; **Architects:** M. G. Zemtsov, A. V. Kvasov and S. I. Chevakinsky. **1748-52:** Reconstruction; **Architects:** S. I. Chevakinsky and Bartolomeo Francesco Rastrelli (1700-1771). **1748-53:** Hermitage Pavilion built; **Architects:** M. G. Zemtsov and Bartolomeo Francesco Rastrelli. **1748-54:** MonBijou Pavilion built; **Architect:** Bartolomeo Francesco Rastrelli. **1749-63:** Grotto Pavilion; **architect:** Bartolomeo Francesco Rastrelli. **1752-56:** Reconstruction of the palace; **Architect:** Bartolomeo Francesco Rastrelli. **1754-57:** Katalnaia Gorka Pavilion built; **Architect:** Bartolomeo Francesco Rastrelli. **1778-84:** Zubovsky Wing built; **Architect:** Y. M. Velten. Chapel Wing built; **Architect:** I. V. Neelov. **1779-84:** Interior decoration of the palace; **Architect:** Charles Cameron (ca. 1740-1812). **1780-83:** Cold Bath and Cameron Gallery built; **Architect:** Charles Cameron. **1941-43:** Palace destroyed by occupying Nazi forces. **1957:** Restoration begun; **Architect:** A. A. Kedrinsky.

Publications

ARKIN, D. E.: *Rastrelli.* Moscow, 1954.

BENUA, A.: *Tsarskoye Selo v tsarstvovanie imperatritsy Elizavety Petrovny.* St. Petersburg, 1910.

BRONSHTEJN, S. S.: *Arkhitektura goroda Pushkina.* Moscow, 1940.

DENISOV, Y. and PETROV, A.: *Zodchij Rastrelli. Materialy k izucheniu tvorchestva.* Leningrad, 1963.

KOZ'MIAN, G. K.: *Rastrelli.* Leningrad, 1976.

MATVEEV, A. A.: *Rastrelli.* Leningrad, 1938.

OVSIANNIKOV, Y.: *Franchesko Bartolomeo Rastrelli.* Leningrad, 1982.

PETROV, A. N.: *Dvortsy i parki.* Leningrad, 1969.

VIL'CHKOVSKIJ, S. N.: *Tsarkoye Selo.* St. Petersburg, 1910.

*

The park and palace ensemble of Tsarskoe Selo (nowadays called Pushkin) is the most luxurious of the suburban residences in the environs of St. Petersburg. It was developed during the 18th century. In 1710 a small suburban country estate was founded at Tsarskoe Selo—a village which Peter the Great had presented to his wife, Catherine I, in 1708. After the death of Peter and Catherine, the estate was inherited by Peter's daughter, Elizabeth. When she ascended the throne, Elizabeth decided to turn Tsarskoe Selo into a grand official residence—a ''Russian Versailles.'' Construction was begun in the 1740s on Elizabeth's initiative, and resulted in the creation of a magnificent park and palace complex, the architectural symbol of Elizabeth's epoch and of the High Baroque style.

The first wooden palace of Catherine I at Tsarskoe Selo was replaced with stone buildings designed by the architect Johann Friedrich Braunstein. Construction was completed in 1724, and their outside appearance was modest.

Architect M. G. Zemtsov first attempted to realize Elizabeth's idea of expanding the palace. A. V. Kvasov, who began reconstruction in 1743, and then S. I. Chevakinsky both elaborated on Zemtsov's ideas. The main compositional traits of this palace complex corresponded to the traditional country-estate scheme of early-18th-century suburban residences, such as the palaces at Peterhof and Oranienbaum. The Great Palace at Tsarskoe Selo was divided into independent components: a tall central wing, and side wings containing a chapel and a greenhouse. The side wings were connected with the central wing by one-story galleries which formed a gigantic, semicircular courtyard in front of the main west facade.

The palace retained that appearance until Bartolomeo Francesco Rastrelli started working in Tsarskoe Selo, first as a decorator, designing the iconostasis for the palace church (1748). He began reconstructing the palace four years later, following the composition outlined by his predecessors to create a new palace, the main element of a park and palace ensemble for Elizabeth.

Rastrelli accentuated the most peculiar feature of the palace—its gigantic length of more than 300 meters. He rejected the previous three-part composition and consolidated the earlier components into one huge mass. Rastrelli converted the one-story galleries into high-ceilinged chambers. In order to install a grand staircase in the side wing of the palace, the greenhouses were moved into a new wing, which was crowned with one dome. A decorative five-domed church corresponds to it on the other side of the palace. The building was finished with a sculptured balustrade.

The great length of the palace's facade determined its architectural character, marked by clear vertical detailing and measured accents which intensify toward the center of the building. The central wing, distinguished by its high roof, has three axes with porticoes and pediments. The porticoes of the two side axes, also crowned by high roofs, echo the central portico.

An entablature divides the facade into two tiers. The second and third floor are united by mighty three-quarter columns. Their rhythm clearly reproduces the main architectonic peculiarities of the facades. Piers between the windows of the first floor are ornamented with figures of Atlas, which seem to carry the entire weight of the walls and colonnades of the upper floors. These white and gilt atlantes and the columns and column pedestals are delineated against a background of azure walls, forming a row of verticals dividing the facade.

Rastrelli's facades are extraordinary in their profusion of Baroque detailing of columns, pilasters and masonry. The window embrasures create an impression of visual activity. The whimsical contours of the window casings, interlaced into garlands, nearly obscure the narrow piers and crosspieces between the tiers of windows and break up the clear tectonics of the wall. The walls practically disappear behind decorations which visually divide, shorten and enrich the length of the facade. The sculptural formulation of the Great Palace's facades is a splendid achievement in the history of Russian decorative art. These extensive works were completed from 1753 to 1755 according to models done by sculptor Johann Dunker.

The Great Palace became the compositional center of the park ensemble. The main western facade faces the courtyard, which is encircled by wings of identical semicircular galleries housing courtiers' apartments. The New Garden adjoins the courtyard, while the opposite, eastern facade faces the Old Garden.

Pavilions—characteristic of 18th-century parks—were added to the regular park created by Rastrelli. The main walk of the Old Garden ends at the Hermitage pavilion. This pavilion was

Pushkino Palace, Atlantes detail: St. Petersburg, Russia, 1710-24

conceived by Zemtsov, and the architectural formulation of its facades was carried out by Rastrelli. A grotto—another favorite attribute of Baroque parks—is located on the bank of the Great Pond. Together with the MonBijou (Monbezh) and Katalnaia Gorka pavilions, which have not been preserved, these elements played an important role in shaping the Tsarskoe Selo park ensemble.

The interior plan of the Great Palace is in close keeping with its general composition. The main entrance to the building is located on the southern facade, in the side wing of the palace. Rastrelli used a similar architectural solution in the Winter Palace in St. Petersburg. A suite of rooms begins at the grand staircase, creating an effect of endlessly extending space. The

scale of the interiors echoes that of the facades, intensifying toward the largest halls—the Great Hall and the Picture Gallery. Five grand halls lead into these largest halls, splendidly displaying Rastrelli's talent as a decorator. The key decorative elements are columns and carved, gilt panels. These decoratively rich and colorful "antechambers" end at the main ceremonial space—the White Hall. This hall manifests Rastrelli's favorite device of elusive spatial expansion. The hall has two tiers of windows and occupies the entire floor. The windows on both sides alternate with mirrored piers, creating an impression of endless, light and airy space. The White Hall's main ornamentation is gilt paneling, whose design, along with that of the parquet, demonstrates Rastrelli's inexhaustible creativity. A great num-

Pushkino Palace

ber of notable artists worked under Rastrelli's supervision to complete his interiors for the Great Palace.

After Rastrelli's design was completed in 1756, the palace remained unchanged for about 15 years. When Elizabeth died, the palace was inherited by Catherine II, who was satisfied neither with its size nor with its Baroque interiors. The erection of two three-story wings on the sides of the main courtyard was the first change to Rastrelli's composition. I. V. Neelov designed the Chapel Wing, and Y. M. Velten designed the "Zubovsky" wing by the grand staircase. As a result of the remodeling, Rastrelli's grand staircase was destroyed and a new one erected in the center of the palace. The transfer of the main entrance to the middle of the facade broke up the suite stretching along the whole building, thus violating Rastrelli's fundamental principle of interior spatial organization.

In 1779 Charles Cameron, newly arrived in Russia from Scotland, was immediately involved in the project at Tsarskoe Selo. He designed a number of classical interiors for the Great Palace. Cameron, an expert on antique art and the work of Andrea Palladio, introduced a new aesthetic to Rastrelli's grand halls and extensive wings. Cameron created two groups of rooms in the Great Palace: private chambers for Catherine II in the new wing—the Bedroom, Snuff-box Room, Domed Room, the Silver Study—and apartments for Paul, heir to the throne, and his wife in the northern part of the palace. Cameron replaced two of Rastrelli's halls in the southern half of the palace with the enormous Lionsky and Arabesque Halls—two of his most perfect interiors. An orderly decorative principle governs the Arabesque Hall. A gilt frieze, twin fluted composite pilasters and vertical rectangular panels typical of classicism adorn the hall. The interior includes a decorative ceiling, which is one of Cameron's best and was created under the influence of Titian's murals and Raphael's loggias in the Vatican Palace. The interior of Lionsky Hall is characteristic of Cameron's elegant treatment of various precious materials: its walls are trimmed in gold silk intricately stitched with garlands, vases and arabesques.

The interior of the palace was hardly modified during the 19th century. The work that V. P. Stasov and Ippolito Monighetti did on the grand staircase during that time was comparable neither in scale nor in quality to the interiors of Rastrelli and Cameron.

The numerous additions to the Great Palace during the second half of the 18th century transformed it into an extraordinarily large complex of not entirely homogeneous buildings. From 1780 to 1783, Cameron added an independent classical ensemble onto the palace on the Old Garden side. In this ensemble, buildings of different functions—the Cameron Gallery, Cold Baths with "Agate Rooms," Hanging and Colored Gardens and the Ramp—cohere under a general artistic unity of ancient Roman motifs. But the nature of Cameron's distinctive architectural creations, created at the dawn of the cult of antiquity in Russia, was not in harmony with the Great Palace.

The Great Palace of Tsarskoe Selo was owned by the Russian imperial family until 1917. In 1918 it was turned into a museum. During World War II, it suffered barbarous destruction, and all of its interiors were lost. Restoration and recreation of the interiors began in 1957.

—MARIA L. MAKOGONOVA
Translated from the Russian by Gwenan Wilbur

ST. ISAAC'S CATHEDRAL
St. Petersburg, Russia

1818-58: Construction; **Architect:** Auguste Richard de Montferrand (1786-1858).

Publications

EGOROV, IURII ALEKSEEVICH: *The Architectural Planning of St. Petersburg*. Athens, Ohio, 1969.

St. Isaac's Cathedral is one of the largest domed structures in Europe. This cathedral for the Russian capital completed the layout of central squares in St. Petersburg. Its 102-meter-high golden cupola dominates the panorama of the Neva River and the entire city center. The construction of this gigantic building involved 14,000 people and spanned 40 years (1818-58). Designed in the early years of Russian high classicism, the cathedral was completed during the ascendency of eclecticism. Its technical peculiarities represented an enormous step in the development of building techniques in Russia. St. Isaac's Cathedral is one of the most complex and fascinating buildings in St. Petersburg.

The existing St. Isaac's has a long prehistory, dating back to the beginning of the 18th century. A first wooden church was erected in 1710 near the Admiralty shipyard in honor of Saint Isaac of Dalmatia, whose saint's day also marks the birthday of Peter the Great. Seven years later, G. I. Mattarnovi designed a stone cathedral with a tall bell tower and spire to replace that homely structure. The new church stood too near the bank of the Neva, and settling caused the building's walls to crack. In 1761 S. I. Chevakinsky, distinguished architect of the Russian Baroque, drew up an unrealized plan for a new cathedral and city square—St. Isaac's Square.

In 1768 Antonio Rinaldi designed a third St. Isaac's Cathedral in the spirit of early classicism. Paul I ordered Vincenzo Brenna to complete the construction. Brenna simplified the plan and replaced marble with brick. This hastily completed and undistinguished cathedral was not in keeping with its central location in the cityscape.

In 1809 a competition was held for the design of a fourth St. Isaac's Cathedral. Despite the participation of leading architects, the competition did not result in an approved design. After Napoleon's defeat, work resumed on the design of a central cathedral for St. Petersburg, and in 1818 Alexander I unexpectedly approved a design submitted by a young and still unknown French architect, Auguste de Montferrand.

Montferrand, a 30-year-old graduate of the École Royale d'Architecture in Paris, had recently arrived in St. Petersburg. He was a skillful graphic artist, but an inexperienced architect, unacquainted with the Russian architectural tradition. His task was complicated by the emperor's requirement that he preserve Rinaldi's cathedral to a large extent. St. Petersburg specialists took quick note of Montferrand's lack of specialized architectural and technical knowledge, which was especially apparent in the exterior effect of his design. He clearly relied on his teachers Percier and Fontaine, as well as on the work of the late-18th-century Paris Académie.

St. Isaac's Cathedral: St. Petersburg, Russia, 1818-58

Concurrent with the approval of Montferrand's design, a "Commission for the Reconstruction of St. Isaac's Cathedral" was established. Work on the foundations was begun, and monolithic granite columns for the porticoes were prepared in Finland. However, shortly thereafter the architect A. Modui wrote a note demonstrating the shortcomings of the design and proving Montferrand's deficiency as a builder. As a result, work was suspended in 1822, and the Academy of Arts created a special commission to rework the design of St. Isaac's Cathedral. Members of the commission included such prominent Russian architects as V. P. Stasov, A. I. Melnikov, the Mikhailov brothers and V. I. Beretti, each of whom proposed his own variant of the design.

Montferrand followed the commission's recommendations and made good use of them in a new design, which was approved in 1825 and had little in common with his original plan. A central cupola with a drum surrounded by columns was the new design's dominant feature. He set four significantly smaller cupolas, or belfries, away from the main cupola, giving the building a solid pyramidal silhouette. Montferrand clearly borrowed his main motifs from well-known French architectural monuments—in particular the cupola and circular colonnade of the Paris Panthéon, and the portico of the Church of the Madeleine, in whose construction Montferrand had participated before leaving for Russia. At the same time, Montferrand succeeded in bringing together all the best suggestions of the Russian architects who made up the commission. The cathedral's proportions improved significantly, its scale became more imposing, and its facades acquired a finished appearance.

The rectangular building is compact, crowned by a columned dome with a golden cupola. Large windows break up the smooth planes of the walls, which are ornamented with corner pilasters. The Corinthian colonnades of the porticoes on all four facades of the cathedral provide an expressive contrast to the powerful smoothness of the walls. A striking color scheme of gray marble walls, red granite portico columns and gilt cupolas emphasizes the building's splendor. The wider facades face two city squares: St. Isaac's Square to the south, and Decembrists Square and the Neva embankment to the north.

According to Montferrand's original idea, the portico columns were erected before the wall masonry. The necessary hoisting gear and scaffolding for this project were devised by the distinguished engineer A. A. Betankur. The walls and pylons of St. Isaac's Cathedral were made of brick with layers of stone. Subsequently, 24 columns, weighing 64 tons each, were lifted 40 meters to encircle the drum under the cupola. After completing the walls, Montferrand modified the design, substituting square side belfries with monolithic columns for the round belfries shown in the plans.

A particularly innovative feature is the cathedral's cupola, which rises 21.8 meters above the roof and consists of three shells. An interior spherical cupola is encased in a second, conical cupola supporting a heavy lantern and the metal structure of the third, exterior cupola of gilt copper. The first and second shells were the first in the history of construction technique to be completely executed in prefabricated cast-iron and iron elements. Montferrand's construction was a variant of the cupola of St. Paul's Cathedral in London, whose architect, Christopher Wren, was the first to replace the middle spherical shell with a conical one.

Other technical innovations characterized the construction of the cathedral: an air-heating system; bas-reliefs and sculptures created by means of galvanoplasty; and a special process of gilding the cathedral's cupolas, which to this day retain their original brilliance.

The cathedral's facades are faced with massive slabs of gray marble. The monolithic portico columns and the cupola's colonnade are of dark rose-colored granite, quarried in Finland. Sculptural compositions of the masters I. P. Vitali, S. S. Pimenov, A. V. Loganovsky and P. K. Klodtom, among others, play a significant role in the composition of the facades. The arrangement of decorative sculpture reinforces the architectural role of fundamental structural elements, particularly the portico fountains and the angular aspects of the attic and the central dome.

Construction on St. Isaac's Cathedral drew to a close in 1841. There were two plans for the interior of the cathedral, one of which was by the well-known Bavarian architect Leo von Klenze. However, Montferrand also won that competition. The interior was designed during the period of transition from classicism to romanticism and historicism—hence the luxuriant, richly decorated and stylistically diverse interior, which contained architectural forms of the Italian Renaissance and 17th-century Baroque.

The interior of St. Isaac's Cathedral is stunning in its magnificence and diversity. It is a monumentally decorative ensemble, uniting the expressive means of architecture, sculpture and monumental painting. Its design makes wide use of colored marble. The walls are faced in light Italian marble, the columns and pilasters are done in rose-colored Tiudian marble, the panels and medallions in yellow Siena and green Genoa marble, the floor in gray Finnish marble.

Especially striking three-tiered iconostases in the form of enormous triumphal arches were manufactured in the St. Petersburg lapidary works. They are done in white marble, with columns and inlays of malachite and lapis lazuli. The large stained-glass panel behind the altar was made in Munich by M. E. Einmiller.

There are approximately 150 ceiling frescoes and oil paintings inside the cathedral. Prominent masters of the Russian academic school contributed to these paintings. At Montferrand's suggestion, the icons in the iconostases and the paintings on the interior of the cupola were replaced with mosaics. These were executed after the architect's death by a specially founded mosaic department at the Academy of Arts, marking the beginning of a renaissance in mosaic art in Russia.

Many of the cathedral's treasures were lost to the Bolsheviks after the Revolution, and the church was closed in 1928. During the rule of Joseph Stalin the cathedral housed an antireligious museum. During World War II the building suffered significant damage. After a restoration unique in its scale and diversity, St. Isaac's Cathedral was reopened as a museum and architectural monument.

—ALEKSANDR V. KOBAK
Translated from the Russian by Gwenan Wilbur

SMOLNY MONASTERY
St. Petersburg, Russia

1748-57: Construction of convent; Smolny Cathedral begun; **Architect:** Bartolomeo Francesco Rastrelli (1700-71). **1746-08:** Home for Widowed Noblewomen built (now the Smolny Institute); **Architect:** Giacomo Quarenghi (1744-1817). **1769:** Smolny Cathedral completed. **1833-35:** Interior of cathedral completed; **Architect:** Vasili P. Stasov (1769-1848). **1860s:** Reconstruction of facades on western wings; **Architect:** P. I. Tamansky. **1875-82:** Installation of new iconostases; **Architect:** M. Y. Mesmakher. **1923:** Cathedral closed and turned into an administrative building. **1943:** Monastery damaged in World War II. **1946:** Restoration work begun on cathedral. **1953:** Restoration of southwestern wing of monastery. **1974:** Smolny Monastery becomes a museum.

Publications

ARKIN, D. Y.: *Rastrelli*. Moscow, 1954.
DENISOV, Y. and PETROV, A.: *Zodchij Rastrelli. Materialy k izucheniu tvorchestva*. Leningrad, 1963.
FEDOTOVA, T. P.: "K probleme piatiglavia v arkhitekture barokko pervoj poloviny XVII veka." *Russkoe iskusstvo barokko* Moscow, 1977.
KOZ'MIAN, G. K.: *B. F. Rastrelli*. Leningrad, 1976.
MIKHAILOV, A.: *Rastrelli i traditsii russkoj arkhitektury*. Moscow, 1951.
PILIAVSKIJ, V.I.: *Stasov-arkhitekor*. Leningrad, 1963.
PILIAVSKIJ, V.I.: *Smol'nyj*. Leningrad, 1970.
ROZADEEV, B. A.: *Smol'nyj*. Leningrad, 1958.
VIPPER, B. R.: *Arkhitektura russkogo barokko*. Moscow, 1978.

The Smolny Monastery complex occupies a significant and unique place in mid-18th-century Russian architecture. It is the only integral Baroque ensemble in St. Petersburg, in which the creative will of its architect, Bartolomeo Francesco Rastrelli, thoroughly and freely expressed the originality of High Baroque Russian architecture of the 1740s and 1750s.

Empress Elizabeth I desired that the monastery be built on the bank of the Neva River, on the former site of Smoliany Dvor, where resin had been stored for use at the Admiralty shipyard. Peter I's Smoliany House had been the first building erected near Smoliany Dvor, followed by a small recreational palace for Elizabeth. Although Smoliany Dvor was torn down in the first half of the 18th century, the name "Smolny" became attached to the location and was passed on to the monastery. In 1748, when the monastery foundation was laid, the area was still secluded and unpopulated.

Peter I had regarded the Neva as the main thoroughfare of the city. Elizabeth, continuing Peter's tradition of city planning, chose to locate the Smolny Monastery for women downstream from, and on the same bank as, the Aleksandr Nevsky Monastery for men. In the panorama of the Neva, approaching the center of the capital, these picturesque architectural ensembles emerge like symbols of the two reigns under which they were built.

Rastrelli began to work out a design for Smolny Monastery in 1747. Its prominent place in the larger plan of the city had a determining influence on the monastery's architecture, which is characterized by large proportions, extensive detailing and a picturesque cathedral. The idea of an ensemble is fundamental to the design. The complex is compositionally closed: the central cathedral is surrounded by cloisters in the form of a cross, each with its own small corner chapel. A high outer wall conforms to the contours of the wings.

The cathedral in Rastrelli's original plan had one cupola and the wavy vertical contouring typical of the Roman Baroque style. The architect began reworking that plan in 1749, when

Smolny Monastery: St. Petersburg, Russia, 1748-57

the empress ordered him to imitate two exemplary works of ancient Russian architecture: Uspensky Cathedral and the Bell Tower of Ivan the Great in the Moscow Kremlin. He modified the spatial composition of the cathedral and added a grand bell tower to the ensemble. Among the traditional architectural forms Rastrelli adopted in his new design for the cathedral were the five-domed structure and a floor plan centered around a Greek cross. The five-domed approach enjoyed a comeback from 1740 to 1750, after a 50-year period dominated by Baroque stylistics.

Slightly earlier, Rastrelli had begun the Andreevsky Church in Kiev. This church and the numerous variants of the design for Smolny Cathedral represent interpretations of a single architectural intention. The main mass is crowned by the tall, faceted dome of the central cupola and four delicate belfries with cupolas. In the Kiev church and in the models of Smolny Monastery, completed under Rastrelli's supervision in the early 1750s, the smaller cupolas are spaced widely around the central dome.

Both the overall composition and the dome with its paired columns were inspired by the Church of Sant'Agnese in Agone, Rome, by Rainaldi and Francesco Borromini, and the Superga basilica in Turin by Francesco Juvarra. Smolny's close relationship to the Italian Baroque is emphasized in the tense dynamism of its masses. The four delicate, extended belfries in Rastrelli's final design are tightly gathered around the drum of the central cupola, obscuring its massiveness and simultaneously serving as buttresses. As a result, the church's form acquires a unity and characteristic dynamic upward thrust. The entablature, which is broken up in many places, encircles the cathedral and divides its mass into two parts. The orderly vertical divisions of the facades emphasize the visual easing upward of the building's mass through the headlong thrust of the imposing clusters of columns on the emphatically tiered exterior corners, modulating into the lighter, paired pilasters of the second tier. The plasticity of the cathedral's facades is enriched by generous decorative modeling of the capitals and ornamental window frames with heads of cherubim.

Unfortunately, the 140-meter bell tower projected in the plans for the western part of the monastery was never built. Rastrelli created a few different versions of it before he arrived at the composition shown in the project models. In the final project he rejected a literal reproduction of the Moscow paradigms, creating a free, Baroque interpretation of ancient Russian pillared bell towers. The mighty upward flight of the bell tower intensifies the mass of the cathedral while displacing the principal compositional center of the entire complex.

The domes of the smaller churches situated at the corners of the cloister quadrangle add an accent to the spatial resolution of the monastery's composition. These domes describe a second five-domed pattern, echoing the five domes of Smolny Cathedral. This composition, unique in Russian architecture, strikingly characterizes Rastrelli's spatial approach and his mastery of perspective.

The predominance of vertical lines on the facades of the smaller churches and the similarity of their domes to those of the cathedral's central cupola serve as an additional link, unifying the entire ensemble. The monastery cloisters, including the refectory and other rooms, are also architecturally related to the cathedral. The main facades of the cloisters form a two-tiered arcade. The peculiarities of a northern climate did not allow for the open first-floor galleries proposed in the plans, which would have enlivened the ensemble and enhanced the delicacy of the facades. However, double semicolumns and sculptural and wrought-iron decoration create a rich play of light and shadow and greatly influence the formulation of the facades.

Smolny Monastery remained under construction for many years, with a number of interruptions. The cathedral, finally completed in 1769 after Rastrelli had already left St. Petersburg, never received its Baroque interior trim. Only one of the smaller monastery churches was decorated according to Rastrelli's plan. This interior is especially interesting, since the original interior decoration of most Baroque buildings in St. Petersburg has been lost.

Although the architectural complex retains the name Smolny Monastery, it never actually housed a monastery. After construction was complete, Empress Catherine II designated the building as a school for women, and later as a charitable institution. From 1833 to 1835, during the period of late classicism when Baroque architecture was considered "in bad taste," the architect V. P. Stasov created a strictly ordered interior for the Cathedral of the Resurrection. Only a frieze sculptured with crosses and heads of cherubim above the massive cornice echoes the rich decorative detailing of the cathedral's facades.

During the same period, Stasov also modified the plan of Smolny Monastery. He built an open entrance in the western facade, flanking it with the classical porticoes of two new wings. This opened up the composition toward the city, an essential departure from the planning conceptions of Elizabeth's era. A wide, semicircular plaza erected by Stasov on the western side of the monastery also connects the ensemble with the urban environment.

Smolny Monastery, witness to several architectural epochs, visually reflects the stylistic evolution of Russian architecture of the 18th and 19th centuries. In the early 1860s, when interest in the architecture of the past took the form of stylization and Stasov's classicism seemed to detract from the Baroque masterpiece, the symmetrical western wings were rebuilt in the neo-Baroque style by architect P. I. Tamansky.

The various architectural modifications of Smolny Cathedral never went as far as full-scale reconstruction. Both the Baroque facades and the classical interior retain their stylistic purity to this day.

—MARIA L. MAKOGONOVA
Translated from the Russian by Gwenan Wilbur

WINTER PALACE
St. Petersburg, Russia

1732-35: Construction of Third Winter Palace; **Architect:** B. F. Rastrelli (1700-1771). **1752-53:** Reconstruction of the Third Winter Palace; **Architect:** B. F. Rastrelli. **1754-62:** Construction of the Fourth Winter Palace; **Architect:** B. F. Rastrelli. **1762-70:** Palace interiors completed; **Architects:** Y. M. Velten, J.-B. Vallin de la Mothe and A. Rinaldi. **1764-75:** Construction of the Maly Hermitage building; **Architect:** J. B. Vallin de la Mothe. **1795:** Georgian Hall added to eastern facade; **Architect:** G. Quarenghi. **1837:** Fire destroys palace interior. **1838-39:** Interior restoration; **Architects:** V. P. Stasov and A. P. Briullov. **1896-1901:** Laying out of a square by western facade; **Architect:** N. I. Kramskoi. **1922:** Palace becomes the State Hermitage.

Publications

ARKIN, D. Y.: *Rastrelli*. Moscow, 1954.

BORISOVA, E. A.: *Russkaia arkhitektura vtoroj poloviny XIX veka*. Moscow, 1979.

DENISOV, Y. and PETROV, A.: *Zodchij Rastrelli. Materialy k izucheniu tvorchestva*. Leningrad, 1963.

Winter Palace: St. Petersburg, Russia, 1754-62

EGOROV, IURII ALEKSEEVICH: *The Architectural Planning of St. Petersburg*. Athens, Ohio, 1969.

Ermitazh: Istoriia stroitel'stva i arkhitektura zdanij. Leningrad, 1989.

KOZ'MIAN, G. K.: *F.-B. Rastrelli*. Leningrad, 1976.

OL, G. A.: *Arkhitektor Briullov*. Leningrad/Moscow, 1955.

OVSIANNIKOV, Y.: *Franchesko Bartolomeo Rastrelli*. Leningrad, 1982.

PILIAVSKIJ, V. I.: *Zimnij dvorets*. Leningrad, 1960.

PILIAVSKIJ, V. I.: *Stasov-arkhitektor*. Leningrad, 1963.

VIPPER, B. P.: *Arkhitektura russkogo barokko*. Moscow, 1978.

*

The Winter Palace that exists today is the fourth imperial Winter Palace to be built on the bank of the Neva River in St. Petersburg. The first two were built at the beginning of the 18th century for Emperor Peter I (the Great), and were small in scale. From 1732 to 1735 the young Bartolomeo Francesco Rastrelli built a more extensive palace—the third Winter Palace—for Empress Anna. Twenty years later, at the zenith of his powers, the architect first set about rebuilding his earlier palace and then designed and erected a new, grand palace for Empress Elizabeth. This fourth palace was a masterpiece of the Russian Baroque style and marked the apex of Rastrelli's creative activity.

Its status as the main civic building of the capital and its important position in the panorama of the "main street" of St. Petersburg—the Neva—demanded that the Winter Palace should architecturally dominate the St. Petersburg city center. Rastrelli addressed this requirement with brilliant originality.

The Winter Palace is very grand, with a massive rectangular frame enclosing a spacious enclosed courtyard. Having rejected the country-estate design scheme of his earlier palaces, Rastrelli created the Winter Palace in the spirit of one of his earlier works, the Stroganov Palace, as an urban block of houses, calculated to be viewed from all sides.

The elongated, sculpturally detailed facades of the Winter Palace serve an organizing principle. A continuous entablature divides the facades into two tiers. The lower tier forms a monumental foundation for the second tier, whose imposing Corinthian and composite columns unify the composition of the ground floor with that of the second and third stories.

The facades of the Winter Palace face the Neva, Admiralty Prospekt and Palace Square, on which Rastrelli planned to erect a statue of Peter I designed by his father, the artist Carlo Bartolomeo Rastrelli. The northern facade, which faces the Neva, is the widest and grandest of the facades. Its rhythmic, orderly groupings of architectural detail around two prominent axes create a ceremonial, balanced composition—an unbroken, two-tiered colonnade. This part of the palace was designed to be viewed against a vast, open expanse of water.

The southern facade, which faces Palace Square and is as extensive as its northern counterpart, was executed differently. The northern and southern facades are in fact opposites in their composition, rhythm and plasticity. A three-tiered main entrance cuts across the central axis of the southern facade, which is considerably more pronounced than the two side axes. The architectural masses increase in plasticity toward the center, creating an impression of an almost sculptural dynamic, which is especially strong when viewing the walls in foreshortened perspective, from the vantage point of Khalturin Street, which ends at the corner of the palace. The plasticity of the facade is enhanced by clusters of architectural details. The columns come together in imposing groupings at the corners, and the porticoes mark the center of the axes. The compositional development culminates in the central axis and imposing double columns of the central portico, which echoes the three-part organization of the entire facade.

Both the eastern and western facades feature deep *cours d'honneur* and two side axes. They differ only in their details. Although the eastern facade at one time opened onto the Winter Canal, it is now closed off by the Maly Hermitage building, which was built in the late 18th century.

Rastrelli's imaginative treatment of each of the four facades created a unique building with an inimitable and distinctive appearance. The palace gives an overall impression of integrated plasticity and diverse perspective: it is a polished composition of freely interpreted, individual architectural forms.

The spontaneous interaction of architecture and decorative detailing plays a major role in the organization of the Winter Palace's facades and accentuates all aspects of the composition. Sculptural decoration not only distinguishes the facades, but also develops and enhances the plastic character of the entire volume of the building. Plasticity and architecture act in unison.

The many decorative elements obey a system of architectural divisions, enhancing it with sculptural detail. Rastrelli placed the most striking accents in the pediments and column caps. The window frames add to an impression of inexhaustible diversity. The architect employed 22 different types of window frames combined with 12 different types of window embrasures.

An original approach to color scheme adds an additional accent to the building's decoration. The Winter Palace's present color does not correspond to the artist's intention. According to Rastrelli's plan, the white and azure detail and white stone sculpture should be viewed against a background of sand-colored walls.

The decorative plasticity of the Winter Palace is based on an interpretation of the triumphal theme. This theme emerges in the many emblems and allegories, military attributes, banners, heads of warriors, armed Cupid figures and military accessories. The decorative sculptural relief builds in intensity from the first to the third floor, culminating in the rounded sculpture of the pediments and the vases and figures of the balustrade. Such a sculptural ensemble served to strengthen the Winter Palace's formative role in the larger plan of the city. Its azure detailing lent it a characteristic silhouette, opening up the self-enclosed mass of the palace through the airy horizontal sculptured balustrade.

The original stone sculpture of the balustrade was replaced at the end of the 19th century. The statues which exist today were worked out of a different material: copper leaf. Although they retained their original configuration, the new sculptures were marked by poor optic adjustment, rigid contours and static modeling. These undistinguished figures failed to present a formal continuation of the columns, as the original sculpture had done. Thus, Rastrelli's delicate and organic synthesis of architecture and sculpture was violated.

The Winter Palace's layout is systematically functional, and can be observed in the placement, in each of the building's corners, of four indispensable elements of mid-18th-century palace construction: a main staircase, a throne room, a chapel and a theater. These elements are connected by suites of rooms designed by Rastrelli. The five large halls of the Nevsky Suite ran from the main Jordan Staircase to the enormous throne room; the Western Suite from the throne room to the theater; the Southern Suite from the theater to the chapel; the Bolshoi Suite from the Jordan Staircase to the chapel. The creation of such a precise and systematic interior plan in the Winter Palace evolved from many previous interior designs, including the experience of working through analogous problems in Peterhof and Tsarskoe Selo.

Rastrelli did not complete his work on the interior of the Winter Palace. Catherine II's ascension to the throne and the appearance in the early 1760s of a new architectural style in Russia—classicism—precipitated his resignation.

After 1762 the interior accommodations of the Winter Palace were completed for the new empress by Y. M. Velten, Jean-Baptiste Vallin de la Mothe and Antonio Rinaldi, who introduced changes to the Baroque trim of the halls and living quarters until those rooms gradually acquired a peculiarly classical appearance. From the late 18th through the first third of the 19th century nearly all the grand halls and the emperor's family apartments were completely redesigned by distinguished classicist architects. Only the main staircase, the large and small chapels, the chapel antechamber and the first-floor galleries retained Rastrelli's detailing.

From 1780 to 1790, Giacomo Quarenghi and I. N. Starov worked on the Winter Palace. During that time the throne room and theater were demolished, and a new Nevsky Suite was built. In 1795, Quarenghi added a new, enormous throne room to the eastern facade. This so-called Georgian Throne Room, bicolored with a severe Corinthian colonnade and multicolored marble decoration is very effective. In 1820 K. I. Rossi created perhaps the most famous room of the Winter Palace in the eastern wing—the Military Gallery of 1812. In 1830 Auguste de Montferrand took part in the interior decoration. He redesigned the rooms by the main staircase, and added more new halls: the Fieldmarshals Hall and the Petrovsky Hall.

The palace halls, drawing rooms and private chambers composed a series of ensembles known today only through sketches. A catastrophic fire destroyed most of the building in 1837.

The restoration of the Winter Palace was carried out very quickly—in two years—and was a tremendous feat, heralding a turning point in the history of 19th-century Russian architecture. The architecture of the completely reworked, revitalized palace interiors was an early example of the new artistic language which replaced classicism: eclecticism.

Meanwhile, the earlier detailing of a significant number of halls was restored. The architect V. P. Stasov directed this work, following the classical tradition. Paradoxically, he revealed his fidelity to classicism in resurrecting the few Rastrelli interiors which had been preserved before the fire—the main staircase, the chapel and its antechamber. While recreating the general Baroque flavor of the earlier composition, Stasov endowed it with the symmetry and decorative elements of classicism, adding a classical severity and monumentality to Baroque forms.

The designs and sketches that have been preserved allow for comparison between the earlier classical decor of the Nevsky and Bolshoi Suites, the Georgian Hall and the Military Gallery of 1812 and Stasov's elaborations. To a great degree, Stasov's Georgian Hall corresponds to the original, almost entirely reproducing the compositional scheme by Giacomo Quarenghi, with its paired columns supporting a second-floor gallery. Stasov retained the general compositional approach of his predecessors in other halls as well. But by introducing his own more decorative approach to order and detailing, he created qualitatively new interiors, more monumental and ceremonial.

Stasov's work on the Winter Palace, ultimately loyal to the canons of classicism, belongs to the final stage of the style's development, while the creative activities of A. P. Briullov, who also participated in the palace's restoration, belong to the new architectural epoch which replaced classicism. Briullov's work manifests many of the characteristics of eclecticism: the free reign of imagination, a diversity of artistic impressions and decorative forms, and references to historical prototypes. These features are evident not only in the architecture of several of Briullov's grand halls—the Aleksandrovsky Hall, the White Hall, the Grand Dining Hall—but also in his detailing of the inner chambers of Emperor Nicholas I and members of his family—the Pompeian Dining Hall, the Gothic Drawing Room, the Crimson Drawing Room and the Moorish Bath.

The structural renovation of the halls, a brilliant experiment of the Russian engineering school, deserves special attention among the various restorative works at the Winter Palace. The installation of a fireproof metal internal structure in ceilings of considerable span required new construction techniques. Leading St. Petersburg architects and engineers of the 1830s successfully dealt with these problems. Three types of metallic constructions were prepared in the St. Petersburg Aleksandrovsky Iron Works: riveted thin-walled girders for smaller spans, triangular roof trusses, and trussed girders for the ceilings of the great palace halls (the Heraldic, the Georgian, and the Concert Halls and the Maly and Bolshoi front halls). These unique strutted systems, monuments of European construction technique, were devised by the engineer M. E. Clark and have survived the test of time.

The post-fire renovation of the Winter Palace has survived practically unmodified. The second half of the 19th and the early 20th centuries saw a few isolated changes. The interior decor of the living chambers was redone during that period by A. I. Shtakenshneider, Ernst Gotthilf Bosse, V. A. Shreiber, Ippolito Monighetti, L. L. Bonshtedt and V. A. Shreter.

Among the changes to the exterior appearance of the Winter Palace were the addition of a new entrance on the Neva side, which somewhat broke up the perspective of the facade, and also the laying-out of a garden with a fountain in front of the western facade.

Until 1917 the Winter Palace remained the main residence of the Russian imperial family, the Romanovs. Since 1922 the building has housed the State Hermitage, one of the most splendid museums in the world.

—MARIA L. MAKOGONOVA
Translated from the Russian by Gwenan Wilbur

SPAIN

CASA MILÁ
Barcelona, Spain

1905-10. Architect: Antoni Gaudí (1852-1926).

Publications

BASSEGODA NONELL, JUAN: *El Gran Gaudí*. Barcelona, 1989.
BORRAS, MARIA LLUISA: "Casa Batllo, Casa Mila." *Global Architecture* 17 (1972).
COLLINS, GEORGE R.: *Antonio Gaudí*. New York, 1960.
FRAMPTON, KENNETH, and FUTAGAWA, YUKIO: *Modern Architecture: 1851-1919*. New York, 1983.

HOFMANN, WERNER, and KULTERMANN, UDO: *Modern Architecture in Color*. New York, 1970.
MARTINELL, CÉSAR: *Gaudí: His Life, His Theories, His Work*. Cambridge, Massachusetts, 1975.
RUSSELL, FRANK (ed.): *Art Nouveau Architecture*. London, 1979.
SWEENEY, JAMES JOHNSON, and SERT, JOSÉ LUIS: *Antonio Gaudí*. London and New York, 1961.

*

The Casa Milá in Barcelona is one of Antoni Gaudí's pivotal works. Its cut stone facade is a traditional load-bearing structure, but radical conceptions abound, such as the formal indetermi-

Casa Milá: Barcelona, Spain, 1905-10

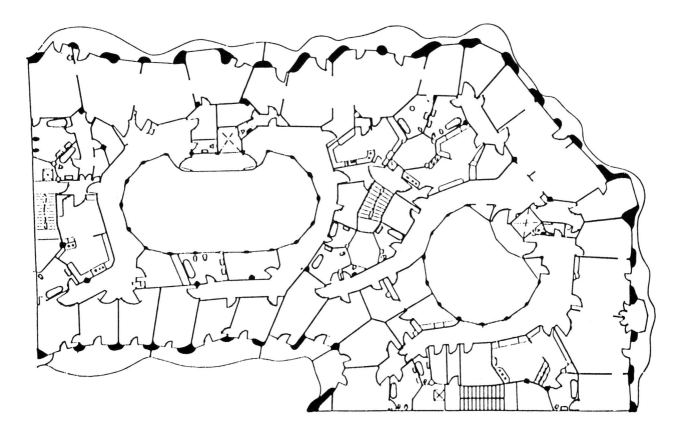

nacy of the facade, the independent interior structural frame, the free plan and the novel adaptations of the layout for elevators and automobiles. Its popular name, "La Pedrera" (the quarry), alludes to a resemblance to natural rock formations. The suggestive, abstract, ahistoric forms encourage such interpretations, which, as symbolist art, can support many readings without favoring any one.

Casa Milá was built for the businessman Pere Milá i Camps, who was enthusiastic about Gaudinian aesthetics, and his wife, Roser Segìmon i Artells, who was not. The mixed-use building had a commercial floor elevated above street level, a very large owner's apartment with more than 20 rooms in the *piano nobile,* and apartments in the upper five stories. The builder, Josep Bayó, had constructed Gaudí's Casa Batlló, and understood the difficulties of working with the architect.

The plan of Casa Milá is unusual and innovative. Since elevators were provided, in order to save space Gaudí eliminated the grand staircase to the upper floors, and included only two service stairs. There is a grand stair in the main court that leads only to the *piano nobile,* a source of confusion for many visitors to the building. Gaudí consolidated the multiple airshafts and small courts typical in a building of this scale into two large roughly oval courts, connected to each other by a driveway. Between the two courts a spiral ramp descends to the basement, originally intended as carriage house and stables, but adapted to accommodate automobiles during construction. The structural system consists of interior point supports. Brick or stone piers hold iron girders with regularly spaced iron beams between them. Catalan brick vaults span between the beams. Curved peripheral iron beams isolate and connect the facade to the floors. Since the structural system is independent of partitions, no two floors have the same plan.

Casa Milá is at the corner of the elegant Passeig de Gracia and Carrer de Provença in the Eixample, the 1859 northwestern urban expansion of Barcelona designed by Ildefonso Cerdà. City blocks in the Eixample have broad 20-meter chamfered corners; thus, every intersection becomes a small piazza with four diagonally oriented facades. Buildings at corner sites must address these piazzas.

Continuous undulating floors, like sea waves or sand dunes, define the facade of Casa Milá. The sea connection is strengthened by the mazes of Josep Maria Jujol's wrought-iron balconies, resembling seaweeds deposited on a beach, and by the grotto-like entrances. Gaudí envisioned an automatic sprinkling system to encourage climbing vines to cover balconies and stone surfaces. The facade appears to wrap continuously around its three sides, but closer examination reveals a three part division, with different compositional strategies in each.

The short Passeig de Gracia elevation has a formal, nearly symmetrical organization. Three piers hold an axial projecting bay. The central pier thrusts illegally onto the sidewalk, supporting a great three-dimensional arch that projects like an eyebrow over a major window of the *piano nobile.* The central pier stops above the *piano nobile,* and the two lateral ones gradually step closer together on the upper five stories. The central bay becomes narrower and less prominent as it rises, and is expressed as only a small double scroll at the cornice.

A similarly organized elevation faces the corner, with a central art nouveau doorway of flowing glass and iron by Jujol leading into the principal court. Some lower balconies have plate-glass floors held by metal beams to allow more light to apartments below. An unexecuted monumental bronze group of the Virgin and Child with the archangels Michael and Gabriel by the sculptor Carlos Mani was to top this corner.

The organization of the long facade on Carrer de Provença is much freer, with an almost random pattern of openings. Major supports at ground level become minor secondary supports or even voids above, and vice-versa. No architectural precedents exist for such a remarkably indeterminate composition: its roots are in natural forms.

An attic level caps the building, exceeding the legal height limit by up to 10 meters. Thin parabolic arches span across the depth of the building, which varies because of the irregular plan and the two curved courts. As a result, the height and inclination of the arches also vary, creating an undulating mansard. The upper roof is an eerie spectacle of sculptural chimneys and stairway towers on stepped platforms that rise and fall with the crowns of the parabolic arches below. Modern apartments built in the attic in 1954 have been removed recently to recover this unusual interior space.

—SERGIO L. SANABRIA

GERMAN PAVILION
Barcelona, Spain

1929. Architect: Ludwig Mies van der Rohe (1886-1969).
1986: Reconstructed.

Publications

BIER, JUSTUS: "Mies van der Rohe's Reichspavillon in Barcelona." *Form* 4 (15 August 1929): 423-430.
BONTA, JUAN PABLO: *Mies van der Rohe: Barcelona 1929—An Anatomy of Architectural Interpretation*. Barcelona, 1975.
FRAMPTON, KENNETH, and FUTAGAWA, YUKIO: *Modern Architecture: 1920-1945*. New York, 1983.
GENZMER, WALTHER: "Der Deutsche Reichspavillon auf der internationalen Ausstellung Barcelona." *Baugilde* 11 (1929): 1654-1657.
RUBIO TUDURI, N. M.: "Le Pavillon de l'Allemagne à l'exposition de Barcelone par Mies van der Rohe." *Cahiers d'art* 4 (1929): 408-412.
SCHULZE, FRANZ: *Mies van der Rohe: A Critical Biography*. Chicago and London, 1985.
SPAETH, DAVID: *Mies van der Rohe*. New York and London, 1985.

*

Among the icons of modern architecture, Ludwig Mies van der Rohe's Barcelona Pavilion had an exceedingly short life, lasting barely eight months, but it went on to become the most celebrated no-longer-existing building of the 20th century. Nearly 60 years later, the pavilion was reconstructed on the very same spot where it stood during the World's Exposition in the summer of 1929. Inaugurated in June 1986, after years of trans-Atlantic correspondence and research and 16 months of construction, the replica pavilion was completed at the cost of $1 million.

German Pavilion, International Exposition: Barcelona, Spain, 1929

German Pavilion, International Exposition

Mies was originally commissioned in 1928 by the Weimar Republic to design two buildings for the exposition that would represent the new Germany. One was an exhibition space to display industrial products, designed in collaboration with Lily Reich, an interior designer; the other was an architectural space to be expressive of the industrial potential of the country. The distinction is worth noting. The latter—Barcelona Pavilion—in fact had no functional program and nothing to show but itself. It also demonstrated Mies' immense talent. Although few architects or critics saw the actual building that year, the pavilion was critically acclaimed. Neither Philip Johnson nor Henry-Russell Hitchcock ever saw it, yet they included it in their "International Style" show at the Museum of Modern Art in 1932. The Barcelona Pavilion became an instant celebrity. As Arthur Drexler wrote in 1960, even if Mies had not built anything else, the German Pavilion would have assured him lasting fame.

During the exposition, the pavilion itself was neither the most popular nor the most visited exhibition building. That honor fell to the Pueblo Español a small collage city representing each region of Spain. While the Pueblo Español remained in place and has been in continuous use to this day, the pavilion suffered a different fate. It was dismantled; the marble was returned to Germany, and the steel sold for scrap on the spot.

The recent history of the pavilion's reconstruction can be traced back to 1957, when Oriol Bohigas, then secretary of the Grupo R (a group of rationalist Catalan architects), wrote to Mies in Chicago, proposing reconstruction. Mies replied, saying he would supervise the project at cost, but feared materials would be extremely expensive. Nothing came of that first attempt. In the late 1970s, two other Catalan architects, Emili Donato and Ignasi de Solá-Morales, separately pursued the

issue again. Both felt the pavilion should be rebuilt in time to commemorate the 50th anniversary of its construction. Again the idea died. But in 1981, when Bohigas was appointed director of Barcelona's Department of Urbanism, he immediately initiated the Barcelona Pavilion project, and helped create the Mies van der Rohe/German Pavilion Foundation to supervise construction and maintenance through public and private financing. Three local architects were named to oversee the reconstruction: Cristian Cirici, of Studio Per (which includes Oscar Tusquets, Lluis Clotet and Pep Bonet), Fernando Ramos, director of Barcelona's School of Architecture, and Ignasi de Solá-Morales, historian and critic.

Reconstructing the pavilion proved to be a tremendous, almost scientific undertaking. Original photographs, sketches and drawings, some of which provided contradictory information, were consulted. The original set of working drawings had been lost for years. The largest part of the extant material was found in New York, at the Museum of Modern Art's Mies van der Rohe Archive, and part was extracted from local newspapers of the time. Several functional, material and detailing decisions were made at the outset. First, the pavilion had to be as faithful as possible to the original conception. Second, the new building, unlike the original, had to be permanent without altering visible detailing. Finally, the building had to retain its obvious open qualities while serving as a formal reception and exhibition space.

To accommodate the first priority, the architects felt it necessary to create a hollow podium, so that drainage inclines could be avoided. Even a slight inclination of one percent would not permit every wall to meet the base at 90 degrees, as in the original. In the replica, rain and possibly snow will drain in

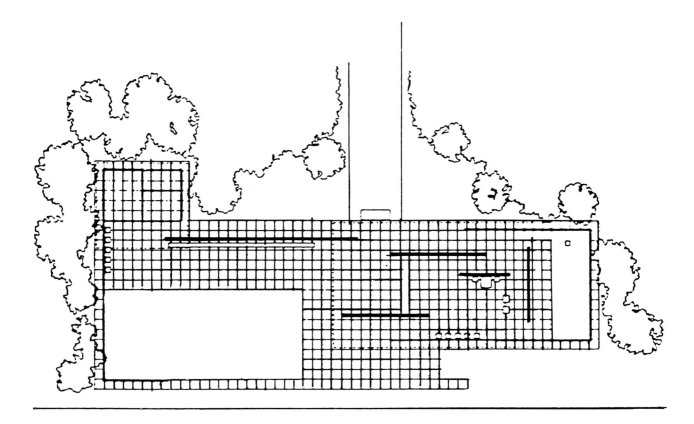

between travertine marble slabs supported underneath by steel posts, like a computer-room floor. (Standing water would seep into the stone by capillary action and darken it over time.) Drainage from the roof slab is concealed inside the marble walls. The green marble slabs, 1 meter by 2 meters in size, for the exterior walls are also mounted on steel supports to allow for servicing or replacement at a future date.

In order to maintain the Barcelona Pavilion without its disputed glass doors (Mies originally designed it without them, but two pairs were installed later), the architects installed an invisible light-beam alarm system. This system, coupled with round-the-clock security guards, protects the building and grounds from intruders. The roof slab incorporates heating coils embedded in the concrete, which will radiate heat during evening or winter functions, thus avoiding visible grilles and radiators altogether. Only the small annex, which is used as office space for the German Pavilion Foundation, is air-conditioned by concealed units.

The original chromium-plated mullions and cross-shaped columns proved vulnerable over time. During experiments *in situ,* the chromium plating oxidized, requiring constant maintenance and polishing. In its place, the architects specified polished stainless steel, which is virtually maintenance-free without losing the sparkling qualities intended by Mies.

Interior day and evening lighting was accomplished by means of a glass light chimney duplicating that designed by Mies. During the daytime, the chimney will glow with natural sunlight from a skylight above, and at night it will be artificially illuminated from within. It is interesting to note that the technology used in 1929 to sandblast glass of such large proportions (3 meters by 3 meters) is no longer in use today, prompting the architects to settle for standard white opaque glass. Additional artificial lighting will be provided as required by movable floor-light cans.

Replicating the original green-tinted glass remained a problem: how to determine from black-and-white photographs its reflective qualities, tint, shade and degree of transparency. The architects tried several samples, photographing them against natural light and comparing them with period photographs. They finally selected the one they thought came closest, but this substitution will always remain the subject of debate.

On first observation, the reconstructed German Pavilion is spatially magnificent and materially sublime. Most striking, however, in the translation from photographs to reality, is its monumental character, never before captured through camera lenses. Georg Kolbe's statue *Evening* has always provided the wrong visual scale. In published photographs, which never included a human figure, the statue appeared life-size; in fact it is taller. In proportion, the walls, which never seemed tall, are in fact rather monumental. The statue, coupled by Mies' idea that there be no scale-providing elements—say, moldings—on the walls, left no real clues as to actual scale.

Another aspect now perceptible is the complete casualness of the spaces within, in contrast to the geometrical or structural rigor most people associate with Mies van der Rohe. Although the plan is a suprematist composition, the pavilion spatially is a more picturesque composition of naturally flowing open spaces. The pavilion is both opaque and transparent, from side to side and front to back. As Kenneth Frampton has pointed out, both the marble walls and the glass partitions are reflective: The glass, which reflects marble patterns, seems solid, while the marble, reflecting glass mullions and interiors, seems transparent.

Any faithful reproduction remains just that: a copy, a facsimile. Without the original *Zeitgeist* of the age that inspired it or the original mind that conceived it, the new Barcelona pavilion may become just a souvenir of the modern past that was, but no longer is. Everything that has been said and written about the building will probably now have to be said and written again, but this time with the protagonist close at hand. Mies' critics may still wonder: Why go through all that trouble? Why bother to revive the pavilion? Why rebuild it at all? Philip Johnson just may have the right answer: "... and why not?"

—WARREN A. JAMES

Sagrada Familia: Barcelona, Spain, 1883-1926

SAGRADA FAMILIA
Barcelona, Spain

1883-1926. Architect: Antoni Gaudí (1852-1926). Note: Building remains incomplete.

Publications

COLLINS, GEORGE R.: *Antonio Gaudí.* New York, 1960.

COLLINS, GEORGE R., and BASSEGODA, JUAN: *The Designs and Drawings of Antonio Gaudí.* Princeton, New Jersey, 1983.

FRAMPTON, KENNETH, and FUTAGAWA, YUKIO: *Modern Architecture: 1851-1919.* New York, 1983.

HITCHCOCK, HENRY-RUSSELL: "The work of Antonio Gaudí i Cornet." *Architectural Association Journal* (November 1958): 86-98.

JOEDICKE, JÜRGEN: "Willkür und Bindung im Werk von Antonio Gaudí." *Bauen und Wohnen* 5 (1960): 181-187.

MARTINELL, CÉSAR: *Gaudí: su vida, su teoria, su obra.* Barcelona, 1967. English translation, 1975.

PUIG BOADA, ISIDRO: *El templo de la Sagrada Familia.* Barcelona, 1929.

ZERBST, RAINER: *Antoni Gaudí i Cornet—A Life Devoted to Architecture.* Cologne, 1988.

*

So many books have been written about Antoni Gaudí and his best-known structure that it is difficult to disentangle the myths from the facts. He had always been to the public of Barcelona a highly controversial architect, but this did not mean that for most of his life he was a lone figure, an outsider, a single genius. He started to retreat from life only toward the end of his days, when he was concentrating on his building.

From the 1920s through to the 1940s there was little foreign interest in Gaudí's work. In Nikolaus Pevsner's first edition of *Pioneers in Modern Design,* neither Gaudí nor this temple appear; in the second edition (1949) there is a footnote. Serious comment began in the late 1950s, when curtain walling and the International Style started to pall, and the parabolic hyperboloid became a favorite construction figure. Gaudí must, however, be seen in the context of cultural aspirations of late-19th-century Barcelona, where he pursued the same ideals as Lluís Domènech and Josep Puig i Cadafalch, revising traditional methods, and exploiting new materials and technologies.

Gaudí was engaged in the construction of the temple for the greater part of his life, from 1883 to his death in 1926. The concept for the church was proposed by a Catalan publisher of means, Josep Maria Bocabella, who was concerned about the spread of anarchism as a political doctrine. He set up a society dedicated to St. Joseph, his patron saint and also the patron saint of the family and the worker; its aim was to build a church to expiate the sins of the city, and to welcome everyone from worker to factory owner. The funds were to come from public subscription.

Before Gaudí was appointed, the original architect, Francesc del P. del Villar, had constructed the crypt in neo-Gothic fashion. In Gaudí's lifetime that style was maintained in the eastern facade and the apse wall, but he had a deep desire to improve on Gothic. "Gothic," he was supposed to have said, "is an art of formula—my idea is to better that style, to give Gothic a life it could not reach through mere geometry: but to try and conquer three centuries of architecture is a titanic enterprise for one man." He proposed to set aside the method of arch and flying buttress, and by the use of inclined columns and parabolic forms to bring down the pressure of the upper elements straight to the ground instead of directing it to the edges and the buttresses. In this way he intended to achieve an exaggerated upward thrust. The basic plan was to be basilical, with five naves and a crossing with three naves. The basic measurements, according to Isiduro Puig Boada, were: nave with apse, 95 meters; crossing, 60 meters; central nave width, 15 meters; lateral naves, 7.5 meters, making a total width of 45 meters; and width of transept, 30 meters.

In the planning of the upward thrust, Gaudí worked in strong, continuous lines which emphasized the plastic flow of stone rather than the angular cut, and he overlaid the surfaces with liturgical symbolism, thus creating a spiritual counterpart, as it were, of Domènech's Palau de la Música, but on an infinitely greater scale. Many of the exterior shapes can be associated with simplified natural forms, on to which are grafted realistic sculptures and polychrome ceramic tiles.

Only one facade and one tower out of four, corresponding to the eastern front, were put up in his lifetime; this facade represents the birth and infancy of Jesus. This is now composed of four bottle-shaped towers, each constructed in the form of a helix, topped by finials covered in mosaics set into complicated three-dimensional patterns. The towers are slotted and contain staircases spiraling around an open void, which was to hold suspended long, tubular, tuned bells. The towers arise over three portals over which is draped flowing stone, like snow, out of which rises a green Christmas tree, ending in the star of Bethlehem at mid-level of the towers. The whole carries an unmistakable explosion of joy at the divine birth.

The opposite facade, facing west, is a post-World War II construction, following certain designs of Gaudí. It consists of skeletal forms, depressed arches, denuded of color, into which have been set recently a Crucifixion on the upper story, and on the lower, at the entrance level, a flagellation of Christ, thus expressing the Passion. This facade is also flanked by four towers that were begun in the 1970s.

The major facade, facing south, at the end of the main nave, was to be the "Facade of Glory," whose elements were never clearly delineated, also with four towers. Over the center of the crossing was to be placed an enormous dome, 170 meters high, surrounded by towers representing the four evangelists. The central nave would rise to 45 meters, and the side aisles to 30 meters. A great illuminated cross was to crown the dome, designed to be seen from Majorca. The whole was set squarely in one of the blocks of Ildefonso Cerdà's grid, according to the original architect's plan. Gaudí would have preferred to twist the axis of the temple around 90 degrees to afford richer perspectives from the four streets that mark off the curtilage, and develop a star-shaped surround, but it proved too expensive.

In this basilica Gothic angularity has been subordinated to a complicated treatment of curve and twisted three-dimensional forms, the spiral and the parabola, all of which were present in other works of Gaudí, especially the crypt of the unfinished church of the workers' settlement outside Barcelona, called the Colònia Güell. Henry-Russell Hitchcock has called the temple the greatest ecclesiastical monument *in posse* of the turn of the century.

However, Gaudí's disciples have continued to follow from where Gaudí left off. There has been continuous pressure on them to stop; as early as 1960 Walter Gropius, Le Corbusier and others signed a letter calling on the authorities to make them desist. Further, the present-day architects associated with the 1992 Olympic Games claim that what is being added is mediocre and superficial, that reinforced concrete has replaced stone. But work goes on, and a great deal of money has come in, especially from Japan. It is not likely that plans for the completion of the nave in the 1990s will be easily set aside. Gaudí could not say in his lifetime when the temple would be finished. He said his client had all the time in the world and more.

—ROBERT BRIAN TATE

BURGOS CATHEDRAL
Burgos, Spain

1221-60: Construction. **1260-80:** Reconstruction and expansion; **Architect:** Master Enricus. **1519-23:** Escalera Dorada constructed; **Architect:** Diego de Siloe (ca. 1495-1563). **1523-26:** Chapel of the Constable constructed; **Architects:** Diego de Siloe, Felipe Vigarny (ca. 1470-1573).

Publications

BRANNER, ROBERT: *La cathédrale de Bourges et sa place dans l'architecture gothique.* Bourges and Paris, 1962: 172-176.

FLÓREZ, FR. HENRIQUE: *España sagrada.* Vol. 26. Madrid, 1771.

GARRIDO GARRIDO, MANUEL: *Documentación de la catedral de Burgos, 804-1183/1184-1222.* 2 vols. Burgos, 1983.

JUSTI, CARL: *Miscellaneen aus drei Jahrhunderten spanischen Kunstlebens.* Berlin, 1908: 1-40.

KARGE, HENRIK: "Gotische Architektur in Kastilien und León, 12.-14. Jahrhundert." In SYLVAINE HÄNSEL and HENRIK KARGE (eds.): *Spanische Kunstgeschichte. Eine Einführung.* Vol. 1. Berlin, 1991: 113-131.

KARGE, HENRIK: "La cathédrale de Burgos. Organisation et technique de la construction." In ROLAND RECHT (ed.): *Les bâtisseurs des cathédrales gothiques.* Exhibition catalog. Strasbourg, 1989: 139-163.

KARGE, HENRIK: *Die Kathedrale von Burgos und die spanische Architektur des 13. Jahrhunderts. Französische Hochgotik in Kastilien und León.* Berlin, 1989.

LAMBERT, ELIE: *L'art gothique en Espagne aux XIIe et XIIIe siècles.* Paris, 1931: 218-238.

LÓPEZ MATA, TEÓFILO: *La Catedral de Burgos.* Burgos, 1950.

MANSILLA Y REOYO, DEMETRIO: *Catálogo documental del Archivo Catedral de Burgos, 804-1416.* Madrid and Barcelona, 1971.

MARTÍNEZ Y SANZ, MANUEL: *Historia del Templo Catedral de Burgos, escrita con arreglo a documentos de su archivo.* Burgos, 1866. Reprint, Burgos, 1983.

PEREDA LLARENA, F. JAVIER: *Documentación de la catedral de Burgos, 1254-1293/1294-1316.* 2 vols. Burgos, 1984.

PONZ, ANTONIO: *Viage de España.* Vol. 12. 2nd ed. Madrid, 1788: 19-50.

SERRANO, DOM LUCIANO: *D. Mauricio, obispo de Burgos y fundador de su catedral.* Madrid, 1922.

STREET, GEORGE EDMUND: *Some Accounts of Gothic Architecture in Spain* Vol. 1. 2nd ed. New York, 1914: 13-38.

TORRES BALBÁS, LEOPOLDO: *Arquitectura gótica.* Vol. 7 in *Ars Hispaniae.* Madrid, 1952: 69-77.

WELANDER, CHRISTOPHER: "The Architecture of the Cloister of Burgos Cathedral." In ERIC FERNIE and PAUL CROSSLEY (eds.): *Medieval Architecture and its Intellectual Context: Studies in Honour of Peter Kidson.* London, 1990: 159-168.

*

Burgos is Castile *in nuce.* This is true not only for the entire historical situation, but also for the Gothic architecture of the area. Together with the royal Cistercian convent, Las Huelgas, at the edge of the city, Burgos Cathedral uniquely embodies 13th-century architectural developments in Castile. A close relationship to French models, which is characteristic of 13th-century Castilian cathedrals, is combined with structural elements of local heritage, deriving from Spanish-Islamic examples.

Burgos Cathedral: Burgos, Spain, 1221-60

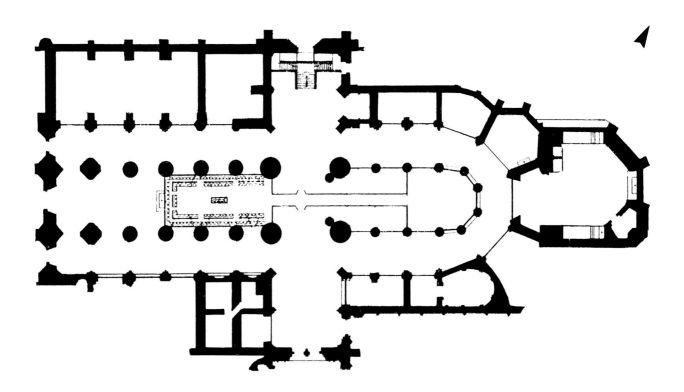

Burgos Cathedral's significance for European architectural history rests not only on the high quality of its forms: no church building outside medieval France possesses a greater wealth of first-rate Gothic architectural sculpture. Only the cathedrals of Strasbourg and León are comparable in this respect.

The Gothic cathedral, situated on the incline of the hill with the city fortifications, stands on the site of an earlier building constructed late in the 11th century, about which virtually nothing is known. Numerous annexes and expansions undertaken in later centuries have definitively shaped the appearance of the Gothic church, which is richly varied if perhaps somewhat difficult to assimilate at first sight. Its incomparable artistic wealth of works, dating from the 13th century through the 18th century, is primarily due to the fact that no extensive restorations were undertaken in the 19th or 20th centuries. A nearly untouched image of Old Spanish church decoration has thus been preserved.

In 1221—two years after the wedding of King Ferdinand III the Holy of Castile (ruled 1217-53) and Beatrix von Hohenstaufen took place in the old Romanesque cathedral—the foundation stone for the new Gothic structure was laid. Bishop Mauricio, who had accompanied the bride from Germany at the order of the king, initiated the construction. Chapter statutes—the so-called "Concordia Mauriciana"—bear witness to the fact that the chapter began using the new choir in 1230, indicating that the structure was roofed over only nine years after the start of construction. The surviving choir, with side aisles and ambulatory, goes back to that earliest section of the Gothic cathedral. Two spacious radial chapels on the northern side of the choir, however, belong to a fragmentarily preserved ring of radial chapels built between 1270 and 1280. The choir originally had radial chapels, but those were much smaller. The reconstruction

of the earliest chapels hinges on a series of stumps of vault ribs in the ambulatory, broken off some time after construction. These truncated stumps show that the ambulatory bays were originally covered with sexpartite rib vaults, rather than the present five-part vaults. If one continues the stumps of the broken ribs, one finds that each leads to two spots on the originally semicircular outer wall, marking the entrance pillars of small chapels. Those chapels, which were not interconnected, had an unambiguous relationship to the example of Bourges Cathedral in France, which in general served as a model for Burgos Cathedral.

Together with the main choir area, the beginnings of two rectangular chapels were erected on the eastern side of the transept. The northern one of them, which has been preserved, was under construction in 1230. Its two eastern windows originally had an unobstructed view. Already in mid-century, however, additional chapels were built along the northern choir side aisle. The lower arcades of the southern transept portals were finished before 1230. The upper arcades of the portal and the side walls were built according to a modified design in about 1235. Both arms of the transept stood around 1250 (northern portal around 1245), and so did the side walls of the nave and the eastern bays of the central nave. The design of the transepts and nave is clearly different from that of the choir, whose architectonic system was nevertheless preserved. A further stylistic change was implemented in about 1250. Until the consecration of the cathedral in 1260, the western bays of the central nave and the first two levels of the western facade were executed in a more advanced style. A document written by King Alfonso X the Wise in 1257 indicates that the western main portal was used by the king. It is likely that the entire cathedral was roofed over by 1260.

During the reign of Alfonso X (1252-84), the essentially completed cathedral was subjected to an extensive expansion program in the current Rayonnant Gothic style. The tracery galleries at the ends of the transept were built (ca. 1260), the third story of the western facade (ca. 1265), the two-story cloister (ca. 1265-70) and the new ring of radial chapels around the ambulatory (1270-80). That last change had already been prepared before 1260, by means of the construction of choir chapels and new chapel entrance pillars in the ambulatory (next to the original small chapels). As a result of most recent measurements it has been possible to determine that the cloister and chapel ring were built according to a unified geometric plan, which indicates that the expansion of the cathedral was conceived as a single artistic project. This also becomes clear if one takes into account the close connection of architecture and monumental sculpture in the facades and in the cloister. The design of the expansions was apparently the work of Master Enricus, the first known master of the cathedral works, who was active in Burgos at least between 1261 and his death in 1277. At his death, he was also master of the works of León Cathedral.

Unfortunately, the surviving written sources give no precise information about the organization or financing of the cathedral workshop. The bishops and the cathedral chapter appear together as sponsors of the construction. The initiative for the construction of the new cathedral appears to have been Bishop Mauricio's, of whom the Cartularium of the cathedral archives expressly say *"incepit dominus Mauricius episcopus burgensis fabricam ecclesiae burgensis."* On 22 June 1221 King Ferdinand III granted Bishop Mauricio some settlements in gratitude for the fact that the bishop accompanied Beatrix von Hohenstaufen from Germany to Spain. The bishop thus acquired a new source of funds immediately before the laying of the foundation stone on 20 July 1221, which he could use to finance the new construction. However, the new revenues from the large Benedictine abbeys in the diocese may have been much more important: since the early years of the 13th century the abbeys owed the bishop tithes over their entire income. This tax right had been enforced against the powerful Oña Abbey only in 1218. Burgos Cathedral's construction, therefore, also documents the establishment of centralized episcopal power over the Benedictine abbeys, which had for long been autonomous, and which in the 12th century still had a much stronger economic position than the bishop and his chapter. Mauricio's connection with the king is also to be seen as an important precondition making construction of the cathedral possible.

The architectonic system of the nucleus of the building finished in 1260 was modeled on the choir of Bourges Cathedral (ca. 1195-1215), down to the design of details. This is true for the striking motif of the richly articulated triforium, which was set in multifoil arcades, one to each bay; for the three types of pillars used (the pillars have star-shaped or rectangular or round stepped centers, with eight engaged columns); for the ambulatory chapels; and for the openings in the vaults at the end of the choir. However, the five-nave design of Bourges was reduced to a much smaller three-nave layout. The inner side aisles of the French cathedral's choir served as models for the central nave at Burgos, so that a far-reaching similarity of proportions in the elevation of these building sections was preserved. Bourges' structure was simplified and simultaneously made more systematic, which is particularly obvious in the clearer disposition of the different types of pillars. Bourges itself was modeled on the Cathedral of Notre-Dame in Paris, which originally seems to have had small radial chapels similar to the ones at Bourges. Churches in the vicinity of Paris and Bourges, such as Moret-sur-Loing (with respect to the choir) and St.-Leu-d'Esserent (with respect to the nave), are strikingly similar to Burgos in

the structure of the walls. A clear kinship exists between the sculpture of the southern transept portals of Burgos and the cathedrals of Paris, Amiens and Bourges.

A particular Parisian connection became apparent in the most recent measurements taken of Burgos Cathedral: while the building sections constructed after 1230 did not consistently use any particular foot measurement, the choir as the oldest building part most definitely did. The first architect of Burgos determined all the essential dimensions of the choir on the basis of multiples of a 32.62-centimeter foot, which is the medieval Parisian royal foot (about 32.5 to 32.7 centimeters). This foot was used in the layout of the choir with astounding exactitude, to the point where even the longest stretches, both in plan and elevation, deviate from the ideal measurement by less than 5 centimeters, and often less than 1 centimeter. The clear height of the choir is 80 feet (measured: 26.07-26.1 meters), the total width including the flying buttresses is 96 feet (measured: 31.29-31.32 meters), the depth of the bays 18 feet (measured: 5.83-5.92 meters), the height of the choir side aisles 30 feet (measured: 9.77 meters) and the center of the choir 72 feet (measured: 23.49 meters). These results prove that the design of the choir was based on a simple numerical relationship of round numbers: the height of the central aisle of the choir is thus four times the depth of the bays and three fourths of the total width of the choir.

Tours and the Loire region take up a key position in the mediation of northern French architecture to Spain. The choir at St.-Martin in Tours (begun before 1220, finished ca. 1250), started immediately before Burgos, was a close copy of the choir at Bourges, and is identifiable as the middle step between Bourges and Burgos through some details. The identification is confirmed by the design of the clerestory windows at Burgos, which correspond almost exactly to the choir chapel windows at Tours Cathedral (before 1230). These artistic connections become understandable only when we recall the historic significance of the northern leg (Via Turonensis) of the Jacob's Road, which led through Burgos. Along this road the exchange of products and ideas between northern France and Castile took place. Moreover, the Jacob's Road had an immediate influence on the layout of Burgos Cathedral: the inviting transept (which is the part most clearly differentiated from Bourges, and rather similar to the transept at Santiago de Compostela) is explained by the presence of the pilgrim's road leading along the northern side.

The architectonic structure of Burgos Cathedral is purely French, but the architectural ornamentation gives the building an unmistakably Spanish character. Clear examples are to be found in the Spanish Romanesque. The tendency toward untectonic surface decoration, particularly in the Burgos triforium, goes back to Islamic art, which remained influential even after the Reconquista, because Muslim construction workers continued to be employed in Christian Spain. The integration of an Islamic decorative style with the French Gothic architecture was paralleled by Toledo Cathedral, built at the same time as Burgos (after ca. 1222). The kinship of Burgos and Toledo cathedrals, which both stand in the stylistic tradition of Paris, Bourges and Tours, is apparently related to their special connection with the Castilian royal court: Burgos was Castile's most important seat of government until the conquest of Seville in 1248, and Toledo Cathedral, the seat of the Spanish primate, was singled out by a long tradition of royal burials.

The architectural idiom of the expansions done after 1260—which probably mark the horizons of Master Enricus' knowledge—was determined to a high degree by the Paris Rayonnant Gothic architecture, particularly of the 1240s and 1250s. The southern rose window of St. Denis served as the model for the southern rose window at Burgos, for example. The crocket ornamentation of the windows of the western tower at Burgos goes back to the western tower of Notre-Dame Cathedral. The windows of the Burgos cloister are similar to those of the Ste. Chapelle. The unusual layout of the later ring of radial chapels at Burgos was modeled on that of the demolished Franciscan Church in Paris. It was principally buildings of the French royal house, with which Castile maintained a close connection, which were used as examples. The artistic orientation toward Parisian models thus had the same royal connection that the expansion of Burgos Cathedral had.

The expansion proclaims the connection with the Castilian royal house mostly in the monumental sculpture. The representation on the northern wall of the cloister of Ferdinand the Holy presenting the wedding ring to Beatrix von Hohenstaufen is almost programmatic. Together with the representation of the wedding, it is to be seen as one of the best and most poignant founder's portraits of the 13th century. Alfonso the Wise based his royal ambitions on his maternal Hohenstaufen connection. In 1257 Alfonso was indeed elected Roman-German king in Frankfurt-am-Main, although he failed to establish himself in Germany. Through the emphasis on the Castilian king's imperial claim, which derived from the royal wedding at Burgos, the bishop and chapter of Burgos simultaneously laid claim to a privileged position in the kingdom.

—HENRIK KARGE
Translated from the German by Marijke Rijsberman

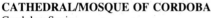

CATHEDRAL/MOSQUE OF CORDOBA
Cordoba, Spain

785-87: Mosque construction; **Architect:** Abd ar-Rahman I ibn Mu'awiyah. **832-48:** Prayer hall extended; **Architect:** Abd er-Rahman II. **951:** Courtyard extended; **Architect:** Abd er-Rahman III. **962-68:** Extended, remodeled; **Architect:** Hakam II. **987:** Width extended; **Architect:** Al-Mansur. **1523-1607:** Gothic chapel constructed.

Publications

BORRAS GUALIS, GONZALO M.: *El islam de Cordoba al mudejar.* Madrid, 1990.
SORDO, E.: *Moorish Spain: Cordoba, Seville, Granada.* New York, 1963.

*

The Cathedral of Cordoba evolved through a series of architectural and cultural changes. The Arabs who conquered Spain in 711 transformed the site of an ancient Visigothic church into a great congregational mosque, which in turn was converted into a Christian cathedral after the Spanish armies reconquered the Iberian Peninsula. During the centuries of Muslim dominance, Cordoba became the center of Islamic culture and influence in the West, and this great mosque grew to become the third largest in the Islamic world. It represents a high point in early Islamic architecture and decoration, and influenced architecture throughout Spain and North Africa for centuries.

The mosque was begun in 785 by Abd ar-Rahman I, the last of the once-powerful Umayyad princes, overthrown by the

Cathedral/Mosque of Cordoba, doorway in enlargement of Al Hakim II: 962-68

Cathedral/Mosque of Cordoba, dome in maqsurah of Al Hakim II: 962-68

Cathedral/Mosque of Cordoba: Cordoba, Spain, 785-87

Abbasids in 750 and forced to flee to the outskirts of the vast Islamic empire he once helped rule. Cordoba became a new dynastic capital from which Abd ar-Rahman I ruled Spain as an independent kingdom. The Cordoba mosque was built to symbolize this new Islamic state and to compete with the grand monuments of Europe and the Middle East. Its design was extraordinary, using longitudinal aisles with double tiers of horseshoe arches banded with alternating red brick and white stone voussoirs. The upper arches are supported on narrow piers which rest on slender, marble columns borrowed from ancient Visigothic and Roman buildings. Although some of these features can be found in earlier mosques in Syria and Palestine, its design recalls Roman engineering works and native Visigothic architectural traditions. Nevertheless, the system of vaulting developed in the Cordoba mosque is unique and may have resulted from the structural necessity of raising the height of the prayer hall in order to accommodate the use of short, locally available columns. The effect is a forest of seemingly insubstantial columns and ethereal arches that defies structure and dematerializes space, initiating a trend that became elaborated and refined in later centuries of Islamic architecture in North Africa and Spain.

As Cordoba grew, the mosque was enlarged four times, retaining an exceptional harmony of style throughout each addition. Between 832 and 848 Abd er-Rahman II extended the length of the prayer hall eight bays in the *qibla* direction, the direction of the holy city of Mecca, which is always faced during prayer. In 951 Abd er-Rahman III extended the courtyard, surrounded it with an arcade and built the present *minaret,* used to call the faithful to prayer. Between 962 and 968 Hakam II carried out the most significant and magnificent alterations when

he extended the mosque 12 bays further, remodeled the *mihrab,* the symbolic niche that indicates the *qibla* direction, and added the *maqsura,* an enclosed area designated exclusively for the ruler. A final addition was made in 987 when al-Mansur extended the width of the mosque by adding eight new aisles and enlarged the courtyard accordingly, continuing in the style initiated by Abd ar-Rahman I more than two centuries earlier.

The innovative additions of Caliph Hakam II represent a culmination in the development of early Islamic architecture in Spain. His *mihrab* design utilizes a wide horseshoe arch in a rectangular frame and is unusual in that it encloses an octagonal chamber, which became the standard form for *mihrabs* in most later Spanish and North African mosques. The importance and beauty of the *mihrab* is accentuated by the *maqsura,* defined by a series of elaborate polylobed and interlacing arches supported on slender marble columns. Four domes were constructed to emphasize the *mihrab* area, each supported by an intricate system of decorative, interlaced ribs. The central dome in front of the *mihrab* uses eight arched and interlocking ribs, rising from an octagonal base and supporting a great gouged dome. The structure breaks the architectural form into multiple surfaces, which are enlivened by rich mosaics of gold and floral designs executed by Byzantine craftsmen brought from Constantinople. This accentuates the dramatic and decorative effect of the structure, and influenced domes and decorative use of these structural elements throughout Spain and North Africa.

In 1236 Cordoba was captured by Christian armies, and by the end of the 15th century a Gothic chapel had been built in the northern part of al-Hakam II's extension. In 1523 the clergy received permission from King Charles V to build a Gothic cathedral in the middle of the prayer hall of the mosque, and

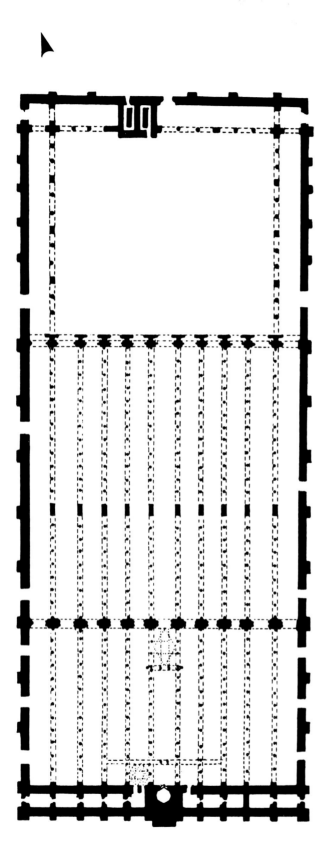

construction continued until 1607. The cathedral addition is unremarkable and even destructive, as expressed by King Charles himself in his comments upon visiting Cordoba in 1526: ''If I had known what you wished to do, you would not have done it, because what you are carrying out there is to be found elsewhere, and what you had formerly does not exist anywhere else in the world.'' Certainly his words ring true to this day, where the Great Mosque at Cordoba represents an unsurpassed integration of architecture and decoration and one of the most unique and influential monuments in the architecture of the Islamic world.

—THOMAS GENSHEIMER

ALHAMBRA
Granada, Spain

1238: Construction begun. **14th century:** Construction of Court of the Lions and Court of the Myrtles.

Publications

GRABAR, OLEG: *The Alhambra*. Cambridge, Massachusetts, 1978.
JONES, OWEN and GOURY, JULES: *Plans, Elevations, Sections and Details of the Alhambras*. 2 vols. London, 1936-1845.

*

The Alhambra is one of the finest examples of western Islamic, or ''Moorish,'' architecture to be found in North Africa or Islamic Spain. Begun in 1238 by the first Nasrid ruler, Mohammed ibn Yusuf ibn Nasr (also known as Ibn al-Ahmar), it was built during a time of waning Islamic power in Spain. At the time of the Alhambra's initial construction, Toledo had long fallen into Christian hands (as early as 1085), the ancient capital of the Islamic empire at Cordoba followed in 1236, and within a decade Seville would also succumb to advancing Castilian armies. The palace complexes and gardens of the Alhambra are rare treasures which survive as a reminder of the once great Islamic civilization that flourished for centuries in Spain following its introduction by Arab armies in the early eighth century. The surrender of the Alhambra's keys by Boabdil, the last ruler of the great Nasrid Dynasty, to the Christian monarchs Ferdinand and Isabella in 1492, without firing a shot, was a fitting symbol of the Reconquista and the steady decline of Muslim influence throughout the western reaches of the Islamic world.

The Alhambra derives its name from al-Qal'at al-Hamra, meaning ''the red fort,'' which refers to the red bricks used in the construction of earlier fortifications built on the site in the ninth and 11th centuries. Impressively located on a defensible spur, with its back against the towering range of the Sierra Nevada mountains, the Alhambra commands a magnificent view of the city of Granada below. Incorporating the earlier compact citadel of the Alcazaba and most of the 11th-century fortification walls of a palace from the Berber Zirid Dynasty, the Alhambra complex presents a stern front to the outsider, emphasizing the defensive network of 22 towers, crenelated walls and massive gates. Granada was never the capital of a powerful empire, but rather a weak kingdom which preferred to use diplomacy rather than warfare in its dealings with the

Alhambra: Granada, Spain, 14th century

Alhambra, Court of the Myrtles

Christians. The walls of the Alhambra, as formidable as they appear from below, were meant less for defensive purposes than to provide a setting that was fitting and symbolically appropriate for the princely image and courtly life of an Islamic ruler. The Alhambra was not solely a palace structure, but a royal city with a range of social and economic activities. To the west of the palace, the Alcazaba once served as military headquarters, barracks and jail, while to the south and east, within the Alhambra walls there were shops, workshops, dwellings, baths, an Islamic school and a great mosque, all of which served to separate the ruler and his court from the life of the larger city, a tradition at the roots of Islamic concepts of urban planning. The extensive fortifications and the palace structures are all that survive of this princely city of the last Islamic rulers in Spain.

The symbolic significance of the design of the Alhambra pervades the architecture and decoration. Bastions and fortifications express the preeminent power of the ruler, great domed audience halls mirror great heavenly spheres, and gardens depict serene images of paradise as represented in the Koran. Even as one enters the main arched gateway of the Bab al-Shari'ah (Gate of Law), the visitor is greeted by an image of an open hand sculpted on the keystone, whose extended fingers serve to remind the follower of the five obligations of the Muslim faith: belief in one God and Mohammed as his prophet, prayer five times daily, giving alms, fasting during the holy month of Ramadan and, if possible, making a pilgrimage to Mecca.

The palace complex represents an accumulation of halls, courtyards, gardens and private rooms, many of whose specific uses are not clearly known. Typical of Islamic architecture, the elements in the Alhambra focus inward, presenting a plain exterior facade that hides the beauty and decorative elaboration

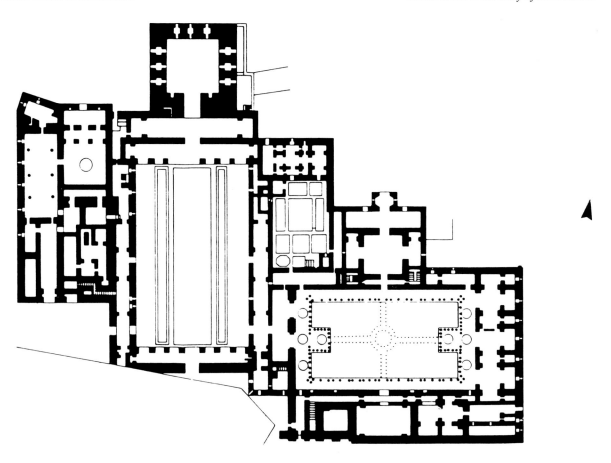

of the interior, emphasizing privacy and seclusion, which are qualities important to Islamic culture. The most significant complexes are the Court of the Lions and the Court of the Myrtles, both built in the 14th century and attributed, respectively, to Yusuf I (ruled 1333-54) and Mohammad V (ruled 1354-59 and 1362-91). The design of these complexes may have been influenced by the gardens and pavilions of the Generalife, a summer retreat built to the north of the Alhambra complex and attributed to Isma'il Ibn-Faraj (ruled 1314-25), but initial construction may have begun much earlier. Although much of the gardens surrounding this complex were remodeled at a later date, the essence of the design of the Generalife focuses around a rectangular courtyard enclosing a lavish garden and narrow pool of water running its entire length, with low fountains accentuating the middle and both ends. Building complexes and porticoes frame the narrow ends, including a mirador as part of the northern complex, a room for enjoying the view of the Alhambra and the valley below.

A similar arrangement can be seen in the Court of the Myrtles, except the gardens are pushed to the sides as the pool is enlarged, emphasizing the static beauty of the water as it reflects the undulating roofline and the dominating mass of the Comares Tower. Delicately arched porticoes line the narrow ends of the court, providing a place for viewing the garden, and leading out on the northern end to a great, square hall, the Hall of the Ambassadors. This hall occupies the main tower of the Alhambra, and its nine large windows provide views of the valley below. It contains a 60-foot-high domed room, with walls elaborately decorated with colored glazed tiles, intricately carved and painted stucco, and a ceiling made up of 8,017 pieces of inlaid colored woods. This elaborate setting is believed to have been the throne room and audience hall, intentionally

recreating the cosmic imagery of the Koranic seven heavens as a means of reinforcing the power of the ruler. This imagery is augmented by elaborate calligraphic inscriptions of poetry and Koranic verses that ring the upper walls and inner arches, proclaiming the glory of heaven and the power of the ruler.

To the east of Court of Myrtles are the Royal Baths and the Gardens of Daraxa, whose surrounding apartments most likely served as living quarters and as the location of the harem, but what survives today is entirely the result of restorations in the 16th century. Linking the Daraxa to the Court of the Lions is the Hall of Two Sisters, a rectangular room crowned by a pair of great domes composed of thousands of stalactite *muqarnas* squinches, an ornamental method of vaulting frequently found in Islamic architecture where the spanning corner arches are divided into a seemingly infinite number of small units, masking the transition from the walls to the dome. The image created is of a shimmering dome of heaven, hovering suspended and appearing to rotate as light from the upper windows illuminates the shadows and the multitude of curved surfaces. It is an architecture of illusion, which attains a dream-like quality through the mesmerizing use of ornament, concealing the mass and structure behind a veil of insubstantiality.

The Court of the Lions has a similar courtyard garden plan, but with a very different treatment of water. There the use of water is dynamic as it flows in thin channels that link the pavilions on all sides of the courtyard to a central fountain, dividing the garden into quadrants. It is a scheme familiar to Persian garden design yet on a more intimate, typically Andalusian scale. The central fountain is a grand composition of a large alabaster basin resting on the backs of 12 stone lions spraying water from their maws, and is believed to be a remnant of the 11th-century palace formerly on this site. Such figural

Alhambra, Court of Lions

representation is rare in Islamic arts, yet occasionally this Koranic prohibition is neglected. In the Hall of the Kings on the east side of the court, there are even more unusual ceiling paintings depicting the 10 rulers of the Nasrid Dynasty in a style reminiscent of European medieval painting. To the south of the court is the Hall of Two Sisters with another great *muqarnas* dome, this time rising from an eight-pointed star.

The greatest beauty of the Alhambra is less in the great vaulted spaces and elaborate decoration than in the way the buildings unite interior and exterior spaces and the artful integration of water, vegetation and architecture. In one sense the Alhambra lacks the sense of monumentality and grandeur associated with Western tastes, and even in terms of artistic innovation, the Alhambra also fails to stand out. But these were not the aims of the architecture of the Alhambra, whose goal was to create a luxurious and symbolic environment, one of intense pleasure to the senses. In this sense the Alhambra not only succeeds, but represents the ultimate refinement of a style which creates an enduring image of incredible beauty unparalleled in the Western and Islamic worlds.

—THOMAS GENSHEIMER

PALACE OF EMPEROR CHARLES V IN THE ALHAMBRA
Granada, Spain

1527: Palace designed; **Architect:** Pedro Machuca (*fl*.1517-50). **1551-63:** West portal complete; **Architects:** Pedro Machuca, Luis Machuca (d.1570). **1612:** Annular vault completed. **1633:** Work stopped.

Publications

GÓMEZ-MORENO Y MARTÍNEZ, MANUEL: ''Palacio de Carlos V.'' *Revista de España* 18 (1885): 191-225.
GÓMEZ-MORENO Y MARTÍNEZ, MANUEL: *Las águilas del renacimiento español*. Madrid, 1941.
JUSTI, CARL: ''Anfänge der Renaissance in Granada.'' *Jahrbuch der königlich-preussischen Kunstsammlungen* 12 (1891): 186-187.

Palace of Emperor Charles V in the Alhambra: Granada, Spain, 1527

LOUKOMSKI, GEORGE: "The Palace of Charles V at Granada."
  Burlington Magazine 84 (1944): 119-124.
ROSENTHAL, EARL E.: *The Palace of Charles V in Granada.*
  Princeton, New Jersey, 1985.

*

The Palace of Emperor Charles V in the Alhambra of Granada was the first High Renaissance building outside Italy. Its design was begun in 1527 by Pedro Machuca, a painter trained in Rome, probably in Raphael's studio. His only other known architectural work was a catafalque of 1549 for Maria de Portugal, first wife of Philip II. Construction on the palace started in May 1533 and continued desultorily into the 17th century. In 1551 Pedro was succeeded as architect by his son Luis, who died in 1570.

Although never finished and largely uninfluential in Spain, the palace must be counted among the finest architectonic creations of the *Italian* Renaissance, reflecting up-to-date Roman ideas without taint from the exuberance associated with Spanish Plateresque architecture. Its plan is highly regular, square on the exterior, with major two-story facades on the south and west sides, and a large, severe interior circular courtyard with superimposed Doric and Ionic orders. The only important departure from radial symmetry is a large octagonal chapel on the northeast corner. The external facades follow the two-story High Renaissance palace type established by Donato Bramante at the House of Raphael in Rome, with a rusticated ground floor and a *piano nobile* articulated by orders and tabernacle windows.

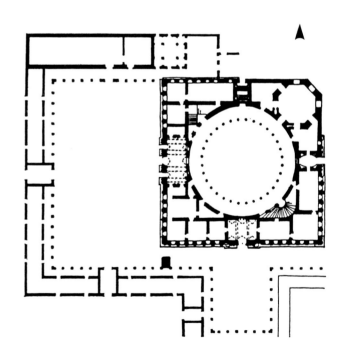

Palace of Emperor Charles V in the Alhambra

The exterior facades are unusually rich. The ground floor has an expressively plastic bolstered rustication articulated by Tuscan pilasters, a disciplined version of a motif seen in the first century A.D. at the Porta Maggiore in Rome. This design anticipated the use of rusticated orders by Michele Sanmicheli in the Palazzo Bevilacqua in Verona in the 1530s, and by Giacomo Vignola in Rome, in the portal of the Villa Giulia of 1550. The Ionic *piano nobile* has a rich wall layering surpassing in complexity the late work of Raphael at the Palazzo Vidoni Caffarelli in Rome. Alternating pediments and lintels above windows are tightly framed in their bays, generating a tense density. Pilasters are arranged in compound rhythmic patterns at corners and portals, recalling similar framing and centralizing intensifications used by Giulio Romano at the Palazzo del Te in Mantua.

Richly sculptured central portals in each facade reinforce this centralizing character. The south portal has a pedimented Ionic doorway surmounted by a Corinthian imperial window, or Serliana. This upper window was completed and probably designed under Luis' directorship. The west portal, more imposing, has three bays with pedimented doorways, and paired Doric orders below surmounted by Ionic above. Only the lower level of the west portal was completed before Luis' death. The sculptural program of the portals, established early, includes war-trophy reliefs, battle scenes, winged Victories, personifications of Fame and History, plus curious representations of the globe flanked by columns and Victories. According to Earl Rosenthal it expresses an imperial promise to defend Granada from a feared Turkish invasion, and to extend the Christian domain beyond the Pillars of Hercules, fulfilling a vow of the Knights of the Burgundian Order of the Golden Fleece, to which Charles V belonged.

Rosenthal has argued against classifying Pedro Machuca as a Mannerist, pointing out that nearly every motif in his vocabulary can be found in High Renaissance buildings in Rome, and that Machuca returned to Spain in 1520, before the full establishment of Mannerism in Rome. This is certainly true of the exquisitely simple and powerful Bramantesque design of the circular inner court, where no extraneous element diverts attention from the steady rhythm of the two-story colonnade. It is also true that the original design of the exterior facades was closer to a high-minded Roman classicism than was the finished structure. Based on evidence provided by a 16th-century elevation of the west facade formerly in Lord Burlington's collection, now at the Metropolitan Museum in New York, Rosenthal notes that a celebrated, perversely Mannered feature of the palace, the asymmetric arrangement of alternating pediments and lintels on the windows of the *piano nobile* of the west facade, resulted from a construction error during the directorship of Luis Machuca. Indeed, the palace has a classical restraint and purity which would not be seen again in Spain until the second half of the 16th century, in the work of Juan de Herrera. This is due to the simple underlying geometric forms, and a strict canonical use of orders as proportional regulating devices, with none of the enrichments and distortions usual in the contemporary Spanish work of Alonso de Covarrubias or Diego de Siloe. Its complexity is not playful, as in the more willful compositions of Giulio Romano or Baldassare Peruzzi.

Nonetheless, there are features in Pedro Machuca's original facade designs which show a stylistic development based on the tense juxtapositions characterizing the late work of Raphael, comparable to that of many contemporary Roman architects. Since Machuca's architectural training appears to have been the result of free observation of contemporary practice in Rome, architecturally its Spanish location is accidental. Thus his work should be seen as a natural development of the currents of artistic thinking prevalent in Rome at the time of Machuca's departure, and by 1527 those developments had led its most prominent practitioners, not unlike Pedro Machuca, to an increasingly affected, i.e., Mannerist, style.

—SERGIO L. SANABRIA

LEÓN CATHEDRAL
León, Spain

Early 9th century: Original cathedral constructed. **Late 10th century:** Original cathedral destroyed in military campaign of Al-Mansur of Cordoba. **1065-73:** New cathedral built. **Ca. 1255-1303:** Construction of new cathedral. **17th and 18th centuries:** Vaults collapsed and were rebuilt. **1869:** Reconstruction begun; **Architects:** Juan de Madrazo and Demetrio de los Rios.

Publications

CÓMEZ RAMOS, RAFAEL: *Las empresas artísticas de Alfonso X el Sabio.* Seville, 1979.
ESBERT, R. M.; ORDAZ, J.; et al.: "Petrographic and Physical Study of the Building Stones from León Cathedral (Spain)." *Rapporti della Soprintendenza per i Beni artistici storici per le provincie di Bologna, Ferrara, Forlì e Ravenna* 31 (1981).

León Cathedral: León, Spain, early 9th century

FRANCO MATA, ANGELA: *Escultura gótica en León*. León, 1976.

FRANCO MATA, ANGELA: "Alfonso X el Sabio y las catedrales de Burgos y León." *Norba-Arte* (Universidad de Extremadura), 7 (1987): 71-81.

KARGE, HENRIK: *Die Kathedrale von Burgos und die spanische Architektur des 13. Jahrhunderts. Französische Hochgotik in Kastilien und León*. Berlin, 1989.

KARGE, HENRIK: "Gotische Architektur in Kastilien und León, 12.-14. Jahrhundert." SYLVAINE HÄNSEL and HENRIK KARGE (eds.): *Spanische Kunstgeschichte. Eine Einführung*. Vol. 1. Berlin, 1991.

LINEHAN, PETER: "La Iglesia de León a mediados del siglo XIII." *León y su historia* Vol. 3 (1975).

NIETO SORIA, JOSÉ MANUEL: *Iglesia y poder real en Castilla. El episcopado, 1250-1350*. Madrid, 1988.

RIVERA BLANCO, JAVIER: *La Catedral de León y su museo*. León, 1979.

*

No other building outside of France, except for Cologne Cathedral, is as indebted to the northern French High Gothic style as is León Cathedral in northern Spain. In its architectonic elegance and its great expanses of glass, the church is an integral expression of the Rayonnant Gothic, which was developed during the reign of Louis IX, and most impressively realized in the additions at St. Denis dating to 1231, in Amiens Cathedral and in the Ste. Chapelle in Paris. In the Spanish architectural landscape, however, the High Gothic is a foreign element, and León Cathedral never had any significant influence on its immediate environment. The importance of the cathedral derives not only from the subtlety of its architecture, but also from the abundance of the partially projecting sculpture on its six portals, on the walls of the cloister and on a series of important tombs. The cathedral is also famous for its medieval glass, whose total area is surpassed only by that of Chartres Cathedral.

During restorations of the cathedral in the late 19th century, the foundations of the Romanesque predecessor to the present cathedral were discovered. The earlier building was constructed at the initiative of Bishop Pelayo, between 1065 and 1073, and was itself a replacement of an early-ninth-century cathedral. That earliest structure had been laid waste in one of the military campaigns of Al-Mansur of Cordoba in the late 10th century. Pelayo's cathedral, which had three naves and three apses, was a massive brick construction. The contrast with the slender, dressed-stone Gothic cathedral that replaced it could not have been greater.

The chronicler Lucas de Túy recorded that Bishop Manrique, who died in 1205, had initiated a new construction, but no traces of the work can be found anywhere in the surviving structure. The present Gothic building was more likely begun completely anew in about 1255. In 1254 Martín Fernández—who was chancellor to Alfonso X the Wise of Castile and León—was made bishop of León. In the following year Alfonso granted the León church financial privileges and some lands yielding timber for construction. In 1258 the king ceded the royal tithes for the entire diocese to the cathedral, so that debts could be paid off. In the same year, the Council of Madrid granted indulgences to all who contributed to the construction of the new building. The chapels radiating from the choir ambulatory were among the structures built first. The Santiago Chapel and the San Clemente Chapel were reputedly founded in 1258.

While the early history of León Cathedral is clear, later developments have gone largely uninvestigated. The available documents indicate only in general terms that construction of the eastern parts was undertaken first, and was substantially completed in the second half of the 13th century. In 1303 the work was called complete. The style of the cathedral is so unified throughout as to yield little information concerning the chronology of construction. Extensive later restorations also obscure the precise building history. Vaults collapsed and were restored in the 17th and 18th centuries. By the mid-19th century damage was so extensive that far-reaching reconstructions became inevitable. After attempts to restore the building, undertaken without plans and without success under the cathedral architects Matías Laviña and Andrés Hernández Callejo, reconstruction was finally begun in a professional manner by Juan de Madrazo in 1869. After his death in 1880, the work was carried on by Demetrio de los Ríos. Both architects pursued a purifying reconstruction of the original design, and to that purpose they erected a multitude of pillars, flying buttresses and vaults, and completely reconstructed the tracery of the windows, the south transept facade with the two portals, the upper parts of the western facade and of the end of the choir, and large parts of the side walls. Photographs of the building taken before the restoration indicate, however, that only the articulation of the south and west facade was altered.

The distinctly French character of León Cathedral is already

León Cathedral, west facade

evident in the plan, which—as has long been recognized—was derived from that of Reims Cathedral. Both nave and transept have three aisles in both cathedrals, and the transept arms consist of two bays. The León nave of six bays, however, is significantly shorter than the Reims nave of 10 bays. It may be noted, though, that the Reims nave was originally shorter in plan: the present facade reflects the addition of four nave bays on the western end during an expansion that was begun in about 1260. León Cathedral, in consequence, faithfully reflects the original plan of Reims Cathedral. At Reims as at León, the choir of five bays is connected by the shallower eastern bay to the chevet. The ambulatory consists of five bays and has five radial chapels in both buildings. The chapels of León are distinct from those at Reims in their polygonal plan and in the fact that the chapel at the end of the central axis does not project. The western towers of León, unlike those of Reims, are placed at the sides of the western facade of three bays. In spite of these differences, the similarities in plan to the much earlier Reims Cathedral are astonishing, and can only be understood as a conscious architectural quotation.

The architectural system at León, however, is not backward-looking, but used the contemporary forms of the Rayonnant Gothic of the mid-13th century. In this vein, the two-level elevation of the walls of the lateral naves at Reims was adopted, but translated into Rayonnant forms, as in the nave of St. Denis. (There is no continuous band connecting the column capitals.) The freestanding piers on the sides of the central nave at León are cantoned pillars, around which are set three engaged columns breaking through the level of the capitals. The triforia are pierced with windows, and the clerestory is made completely of glass. The unusual articulation of the two levels gives the triforia and the clerestory the appearance of a single unit. They both have two double arches, each of which is topped with an oculus. The

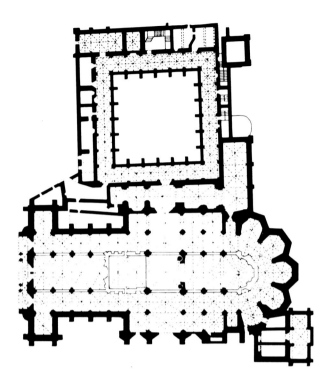

oculi are framed with narrow lancet windows. This design also evinces a Reims influence, but in this instance it concerns the Parish Church of St. Jacques. The western bay at St. Remi (renovated in the late 12th century) may also have been a model. There is also evidence of a relationship between León Cathedral and Chalons-sur-Marne, particularly in the development of the triforia and the windows. These observations point to a concrete connection between León Cathedral and the architecture of the Champagne region.

Questions concerning the identity of the architect responsible for the design of the cathedral arise here. In February 1261 a certain Simon, "*operis eiusdem [Legionensis] ecclesie magister*" (master of the works), was noted as a witness on a document. The name has not been traced further, so it is not possible to connect it with any known historical personage. The case is quite different with Enricus, who, at his death on 10 July 1277, was described as head of the cathedral works at León and Burgos. The Obituarium of León and the Calendarium (Vol. 73) of Burgos give the same date, so that the identity of this master of the works is not in doubt. Burgos was most probably Master Enricus' base of operations, since he was indirectly mentioned there already in 1261 (when Master Simon was still active at León), by his son, Juan Anrric. The deaths of his daughter Helisabeth in 1277 and of his wife Mathia in 1308 are recorded only in the Burgos Calendarium, further supporting the supposition that Burgos was Enricus' home.

In fact, certain elements at León Cathedral point unmistakably to Burgos Cathedral, particularly the three sculpture portals: the tympanum of the middle south transept portal at León follows the composition of the tympanum on the southern portal at Burgos (ca. 1235-40). The northern transept portal leading to the cloister copies the cloister portal at Burgos (1265-70), both in the architectural and in the sculptural design. Although

the porches of the western portals at León derive from the transept facades at Chartres, the cube-like shape of the portal facade again points to the example of Burgos. The design of the León portals is strikingly independent from the architectonic structure of the church itself. Particularly the northern portal appears like an unconnected quotation of Burgos Cathedral. The suspicion arises then that Master Enricus, to whom the Burgos cloister with its rich sculpture can be ascribed with certainty, was responsible only for the portals at León.

The architecture proper of León Cathedral, however, has no connection whatever with Burgos or any other Spanish buildings. This state of affairs can only be explained by the supposition that a French architect (Simon?), most likely from the Champagne area, was commissioned to design the cathedral and came to Spain accompanied by his own assistants and craftsmen, so that a more or less closed French workshop was active at León. It is admittedly unclear who could have paid for such a workshop, because the cathedral chapter was torn by internal controversy, and had very few funds. A key figure in the construction of the cathedral seems to have been Martín Fernández, who in 1254 accepted the position, vacant for two years then, of bishop of León. As chancellor to Alfonso the Wise, he belonged to the court of Castile—in one document Alfonso called him his "servant." He also had good connections with the papal Curia. It is not insignificant that Alfonso the Wise and the bishop of León are represented together in one of the cathedral windows. It cannot be an accident that immediately after Martín Fernández became bishop the construction of the cathedral was begun, with impressive royal backing, and after the most "modern" French designs. It is certainly reasonable to connect the modernity of this royal cathedral with the innovations pursued by Alfonso the Wise, particularly in his far-sighted legislation.

—HENRIK KARGE
Translated from the German by Marijke Rijsberman

EL ESCORIAL
Madrid, Spain

1562: Designed; **Architect:** Juan Bautista de Toledo (d.1567). **1567:** South façade, Court of the Evangelists constructed; **Architect:** Juan Bautista de Toledo. **1572-84:** Spires, gables, infirmary constructed; **Architect:** Juan de Herrera (ca. 1530-97). **1645-54:** Burial-vault constructed; **Architect:** Alonso Carbonell (*fl.* 1620-1660). **1785:** Ministers' houses constructed; **Architect:** Juan de Villanueva (1739-1811). **1793:** North staircase in court palace constructed; **Architect:** Juan de Villanueva.

Publications

CERVERA VERA, LUIS: *Las Estampas y el Sumario de El Escorial por Juan de Herreray*. Madrid, 1945.
CHUECA GOITIA, F.: Arquitectura del siglo XVI (Ars Hispaniae, vol XI). Madrid, 1953.
CHUECA GOITIA, FERNANDO: *Arquitectura del Siglo XVI*. In *Hispaniae XI*. Madrid, 1953.
El Escorial 1563-1963. 2 vols. Madrid, 1963.
HERRERA, JUAN DE: *Sumario y Breve Declaracion de los Diseños y estampas de la fabrica de San Lorençio el Real del Escurial, Madrid, 1589*. Madrid, 1954.

El Escorial, main facade: Madrid, Spain, 1567

IÑIGUEZ ALMECH, FRANCISCO: *Las Trazas del Monasterio de S. Lorenzo de El Escorial.* Madrid, 1965.

KUBLER, G.: *Building the Escorial.* Princeton, New Jersey, 1981.

KUBLER, G. and SORIA, M.: *Art and Architecture in Spain and Portugal and their American Dominions, 1500-1870.* Pelican History of Art, Harmondsworth, 1959.

KUBLER, GEORGE and SORIA, MARTIN: *Art and Architecture in Spain and Portugal and Their American Dominions, 1500-1800.* Baltimore, 1959.

KUBLER, GEORGE: "Galeazzo Alessi e l'Escuriale." pp. 599-603 in *Galeazzo Alessi e l'Architettura del Cinquecento.* Genoa, Italy, 1975.

LOPEZ SERRANO, MATILDE: *Trazas de Juan de Herrera y sus seguidores para el Monasterio del Escorial.* Madrid, 1944.

TAYLOR, RENE: "Architecture and Magic: Considerations on the Idea of the Escorial." pp. 81-109 in Howard Hibbard (ed.), *Essays in the History of Architecture Presented to Rudolf Wittkower.* London, 1967.

WILKINSON, CATHERINE: "Planning a Style for the Escorial: An Architectural Treatise for Philip of Spain." *Journal of the Society of Architectural Historians* 44 (March 1985): 37-47.

*

The monastery of San Lorenzo El Real del Escorial, situated on a sheltered southern slope in the Guadarrama mountain range, was built during the turbulent years of the Counter-Reformation, in which Spain played a major role. A compact rectangular structure, of local pale gray granite, the Escorial rises majestically above its surroundings. Its formidable exterior, fortress-like in appearance, with severely plain walls punctuated by rows of tiny windows, and towers at its four corners, shuns the outer world, reflecting the introspective, isolationist and austere personality of Philip II, who shaped its design from the start. The Escorial was designed by Philip as a royal retreat and mausoleum (à la Diocletian's Palace at Split, Yugoslavia, which it resembles in part), and as such it stands at the end of a long line of European palace monasteries.

Oriented east-west in traditional Christian fashion, the monastery is organized symmetrically around a strong central axis, a principle of design favored by both ancient Roman and contemporary Italian Renaissance architects. In the central section, at the heart of the monastery, towering above all else, and facing a large interior courtyard, the Patio de los Reyes (Courtyard of the Kings), the Church of San Lorenzo dominates the design. The apse of the church with its attendant additions (the rooms of Philip II, which open onto the high altar, the picture galleries and the throne room) projects out from the eastern face of the monastery, breaking the basic rectangle of the plan. In the eastern half of the monastery two large courtyards flank the church, and in the west to either side of the Patio de los Reyes four small courtyards are arranged in a cruciform pattern, a design derived from Filarete's Ospedale Maggiore in Milan, which was often copied in Renaissance Spain. The resulting overall plan of the monastery resembles the grid-iron upon which Saint Lawrence was martyred.

On the western facade three strong vertical accents—the tall central block and corner towers—offset the dominant horizontal lines of the exterior walls. Engaged Palladian-style pavilions

El Escorial, church facade

are separated from the central pedimented section by low, narrow, recessed areas with pitched roofs, which blend with the corridors surrounding the Patio de los Reyes. The overall effect of tall corner towers separated slightly from, and looming above, the central section, recalls Santa Maria del Carignano in Genoa by Galeazzo Alessi. Seen from above, the Church of San Lorenzo forms a Latin cross; a hemispherical dome designates the crossing. Raised on a tall cylindrical drum, and surmounted by a tall lantern with a slender spire, the dome provides the dominant vertical accent of the monastery, playing off against the slightly shorter, rectangular towers of the church facade, a contrast of forms also present on Alessi's church.

The plan of San Lorenzo reflects the contemporary state of Renaissance church design. Enjoined from building centralized churches by the Council of Trent in 1563, Renaissance architects turned their genius to creating centralized designs with longitudinal formats. In San Lorenzo the central focus was cleverly achieved on the interior by dividing the rectangular plan of the church into a large square—which represents the main body of the church—and a complex vestibule, with choir tribune above. The latter is "a normal feature of Spanish church design." The plan of the square is Italianate, recalling to some extent Michelangelo's St. Peter's, but even more strongly Santa Maria del Carignano. The dome, resting on pendentives, is supported by four massive crossing piers. It dominates the space, the large arched windows of its drum admitting plentiful light to the crossing below. Extending outward from the pendentives, barrel-vaulted nave and transept arms form a Greek cross within the square, leaving four subsidiary areas in the corners. The outlines of the church are rectilinear in keeping with the lines of the monastery. The nave walls, with their ponderous arcades and giant fluted pilasters, also betray Italian influence, as do

mark the three main entrances to the monastery, relieving the monotony of the smooth ashlar courses. The central pavilion consists of a splendid two-story engaged pedimented portico, wider at the bottom than at the top, recalling the western facades of certain contemporary Italian churches (such as Santa Caterina dei Funari in Rome). The two flanking entrances, decorated with identical pavilions in very low relief, are clearly subordinate. They are differentiated from the rest of the facade by flat pilasters marking their edges, and by a decorative pedimented section, rising above the strongly dentilated cornice of the monastery, which, like the roof combs of Mayan architecture, serve as false fronts. Large arched windows complete the vertical accent of the subsidiary pavilions, and hint at the Roman arcades found within the side sections of the monastery. The facade is completed by the corner towers, which, by virtue of their slender Flemish spires, soar higher than the central portion of the facade, balancing its impressive bulk.

Thus directed by the architectural design to the main entrance, and prepared by the church-like pavilion of the central facade, the visitor proceeds through the vestibule, and out into the Patio de los Reyes, finally to face the western aspect of the Church of San Lorenzo. The axial progression that leads there, to a holy structure at the back of an enclosed courtyard open to the sky, recalls the typical arrangement of the ancient Roman temple precinct.

The Church of San Lorenzo, designed in part by the Italian architect Paciotto, is so well integrated into the surrounding monastery that the corridors which flank the Patio de los Reyes run up against its two western towers. Its charming facade, with a two-story central section and tall corner towers, resembles somewhat Giacomo della Porta's western elevation for Sant'Atanasio dei Greci in Rome. At the Escorial, however, the towers

El Escorial, library

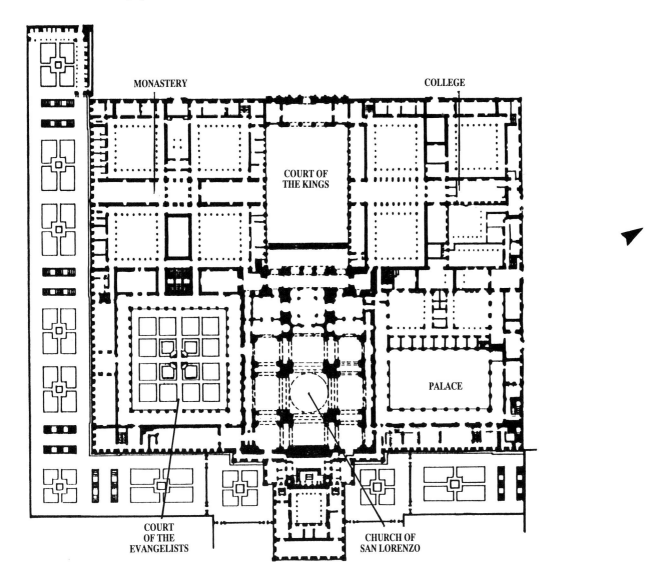

MONASTERY

COLLEGE

COURT OF
THE KINGS

PALACE

COURT
OF THE
EVANGELISTS

CHURCH OF
SAN LORENZO

the Palladian windows, which serve as part of the clerestory. The somber gray granite and the squat proportions—by Italian standards—of the walls give the interior of San Lorenzo a solemn, dignified atmosphere, which is modified somewhat by touches of painting in the vaulting, and by the ornate *retablo*, which, in true Spanish fashion, covers the entire altar wall.

Turning to the northern and southern sections of the Escorial—which house the Royal Palace and College, and the Cloister and Chapter Halls of the monastery, respectively—one finds that the cold, forbidding aspect of the exterior walls gives way to a series of charming, intimate courtyards. Roman arcades on piers, stacked one above the other, surround all of the smaller western courtyards (save one), admitting plentiful light to the rooms beyond. Arcaded courtyards are common in Spain, "a country whose buildings were always arranged to face inwards," but until then they were usually in the form of an arcade on columns, not piers. Of the two large eastern courtyards which flank the Church of San Lorenzo, the Claustro de Los Evangelistas in the southeast corner is particularly inviting. Two superimposed arcades on piers, decorated with engaged columns—the lower order Doric, the upper order Ionic—surround this delightful courtyard. This design, which was popular

with ancient Roman and Italian Renaissance architects alike, may have been inspired by the recently built courtyard of the Palazzo Farnese in Rome. The garden is arranged in squares with two central paths crossing at right angles in the center, and subsidiary paths to either side in each direction, a layout borrowed from Roman planned cities and put to new use. A domed shrine with four arched entrance ways, dedicated to the four Evangelists, occupies the center of the garden, the small dome and its lantern echoing that of the nearby church. Square pools issue forth from the corners of the shrine, each overlooked by a statue of one of the Evangelists. Inside the western section of this cloister the visitor encounters the celebrated, spacious imperial staircase, the first of its kind.

The monumental grandeur of the Escorial, which above all reflects the taste of Philip II, was admired by many a contemporary visitor. In its plain severity of line, corner towers, restrained touches of classicism, and Flemish roofs, it was a direct successor to a number of 16th-century Spanish buildings, among them a series of palaces built by Luis de Vega. Philip preferred this plain style to the prevailing fussy and unfocused Spanish Plateresque, which was heavily influenced by Moorish design precepts. The Escorial set the tone for Spanish architecture of the second half of the century. Its lasting influence is evident in subsequent centuries, for although Spanish architecture became more ornate once again, the ornament was applied in a more focused, classical manner to be part of the structure, rather than applied to it willy-nilly in a two-dimensional design. Spurred on by the building of the Escorial, Spanish architecture shook off the last vestiges of Moorish influence, and entered the European mainstream.

—PATRICIA MARX

MUSEO DEL PRADO
Madrid, Spain

1785-1819: Construction; **Architect:** Juan de Villanueva (1739-1811). **1914-20:** Expansion on eastern end of building. **1928-30:** Monumental entrance on northern side constructed.

Publications

CHUECA GOITIA, F.: *La vida y las obras del arquitecto Juan de Villanueva*. Madrid, 1949.
GAVILANES, PEDRO MOLEÓN: *La Arquitectura de Juan de Villanueva. El Proceso del Proyecto*. Madrid, 1988.
KUBLER, G. and SORIA, M.: *Art and Architecture in Spain and Portugal and Their American Dominions, 1500-1800*. Harmondsworth, 1959.
SAMBRICIO, CARLOS: *La Arquitectura española de la Ilustración*. Madrid, 1986.
VEGA, RAMÓN GUERRA DE LA: *Juan de Villanueva. II. Museo del Prado y Jardín Botánico*. Madrid, 1987.

*

The Museo del Prado lies on the Salón del Prado in Madrid, a promenade laid out in the vicinity of the Palace of Buen Retiro in the middle of the 18th century. The museum was not originally planned as a picture gallery. At the recommendation of his minister Floridablanca, Charles III decided to erect a building for the Natural Science Museum, which had long been insufficiently accommodated, and for the Academy of Sciences. The new complex, with a botanical garden and an astronomical observatory, was to be a park for the education and recreation of the citizens of Madrid. The museum was to be the temple in this realm of science. After proposals by Ventura Rodríguez for a peristyle had been rejected, Juan de Villanueva prepared the first designs for the future museum in 1785. One of the early sketches called for a central rotunda, connected by means of porticoes and *paseos* to two exedrae. A spacious auditorium was to lie on a second axis, parallel to the first, communicating with the rotunda by means of a narthex. Sequences of rooms were to lead out from the auditorium to corner pavilions. The division into different building blocks was based on the function of the building as a museum, academy and gathering place. Besides this early sketch, a wooden model has survived, showing some changes that accord with the later realization of the building.

Work probably began as early as 1785, and had progressed

Museo del Prado: Madrid, Spain, 1785-87

significantly by 1808, when French troops marched into Madrid and used the structure as a horse stable. The building was definitively completed in 1819, and made into a royal museum. It has served as a national museum since 1868. Between 1914 and 1920, the complex was expanded on the eastern side, while a monumental entrance to the upper story on the northern side was created between 1928 and 1930.

The actual building fundamentally retained the layout foreseen in the first design, but was limited to only one cross axis. The *paseos* were transformed into Ionic colonnades at the level of the upper story, while the ground floor is articulated with arcades and square niches. An attic story and a wreath frieze with a marked profile provide closure at the top, hiding the height of the roofs. The facades of the corner pavilions are opened to the park with a loggia and a portico at different levels. The pavilions themselves were enlarged with respect to the original design, and the northern one was furnished on the inside with a rotunda inspired by the Pantheon. At the center of the complex lies the projecting Tuscan portico, which provides entrance to the Aula Magna, or Great Hall, a semicircular space oriented at right angles to the facade. The exhibition spaces have coffered half-barrel vaults and domes in the style of classical Roman architecture.

In the addition of different building blocks, Villanueva referred to his own earlier buildings, such as the Casita del Principe in El Escorial. In the Museo del Prado, Villanueva's structural principles reflect functional concerns, as these had been determined by the original purpose of the building as museum, academy and meeting place.

Villanueva's designs for the Prado take their place in the long succession of theoretical and practical formulations of the relatively young building type of museum. At the Paris and Rome Academies, this theme was often set as an examination assignment for students. Moreover, there was hardly a seat of government that did not furnish itself with a building to present artistic and scientific collections in the late 18th century. Immediate examples for the Madrid museum are to be found in the Vatican museums, particularly in the Museo Pio-Clementino, knowledge of which may have been brought to Spain by Count Floridablanca, who was the delegate to the Holy See. As to the design and the layout of the interior, there is an academy project by the Frenchman Louis François Trouard, which won a prize in 1753. The designs for the Prix de Rome of 1778/79 also elaborate on the museum theme with elements such as barrel-vaulted galleries, rotundas and colonnades. In the clear disposition of the building masses, the learned but lively use of ancient motifs, Villanueva rose above the academic projects to create a key building of Spanish neoclassical architecture.

—BARBARA BORNGÄSSER KLEIN
Translated from the German by Marijke Rijsberman

CATHEDRAL OF SANTIAGO DE COMPOSTELA
Santiago de Compostela, Spain

Ca. 1070-ca. 1100: Original church enlarged. **1658-67:** Canopy projected. **1680:** Reloj tower constructed. **1738-49:** Central panel constructed; **Architect:** Fernando de Casas y Novoa (1711-1794).

Publications

ALCOLEA, S.: *La catedral de Santiago de Compostela*. Madrid, 1948.
CHAMOSO LAMAS, M.: "La capilla del Pilar en la catedral de Santiago." *Archivo español de arte* 14 (1940/41).
CONANT, KENNETH J.: *The Early Architectural History of the Cathedral of Santiago de Compostela*. Cambridge, Massachusetts, 1926.
JACOBS, MICHAEL: *Northern Spain: The Road to Santiago de Compostela*. San Francisco, 1991.
LOUIS, R.: "Les fouilles dans la cathédrale Saint-Jacques de Compostelle." *Bulletin de la société nationale des antiquaires de France* (1954/55): 152.
MULLINS, E.: *The Pilgrimage to Santiago*. New York, 1974.

Santiago de Compostela was one of the most important pilgrimage centers of the Middle Ages, rivaled only by Rome and Jerusalem. The cult of Saint James Major, whose body was believed to have been discovered at Compostela in the ninth century, gained momentum in the 10th century and burgeoned to such an extent that by the late 11th century a new and larger church was needed to accommodate the throngs of pilgrims. The roads which brought pilgrims from north of the Pyrenees across the kingdoms of Navarre, Leon and Castile to Santiago also served as conduits for cultural exchange, creating a connection between the Christian territories of the Iberian peninsula and the European north. This connection, which manifested itself culturally, artistically and liturgically, increased under Alfonso VI, king of Leon and Castile. In his efforts to wrest territory from Moorish domination, he received assistance from French knights and Cluniac clerics. Saint James, who was said miraculously to have joined Christian soldiers in a victorious battle against the infidel, became Saint James *matamoros*—the Moor-slayer—patron saint of the *Reconquista*. When the Peace of God was proclaimed in Catalonia in 1027 and extended in the late 1060s, pilgrimages to his shrine became popular. And in the following decade, with the help of funds supplied by Alfonso VI, planning for the large-scale reconstruction of the Cathedral of Santiago de Compostela was begun.

The flow of ideas across national and regional boundaries, fostered by the Pilgrimage Road and Alfonso's ties with France, had an impact on the development of Santiago in the late 11th century. The cathedral is similar in design to four Romanesque churches, all with important relics, located on the pilgrimage roads north of the Pyrenees. These churches, which have come to be known as the "pilgrimage group," include St.-Martin at Tours, Ste.-Foy at Conques, St.-Sernin at Toulouse and St.-Martial at Limoges, as well as Santiago de Compostela. Tours and Limoges are no longer extant, but the others are strikingly similar to one another. All have, or had, an aisled nave (long, except at Conques); a wide, aisled transept; a capacious sanctuary; and an apse with an ambulatory and radiating chapels. There has been considerable debate about which of these churches came first and how they are related to one another. For many years St.-Martin at Tours was believed to have been the progenitor of the group, but it now appears that all five may have been under construction at roughly the same time, and the question of which was begun before the others has not yet been adequately resolved. Santiago bears the closest resemblance to Toulouse, except that it is a little shorter and has two, rather than four, side aisles flanking the nave. The two churches were rivals; Toulouse also claimed to have the relics of Saint James, but the pilgrims continued to go to Santiago to venerate the saint.

Cathedral of Santiago de Compostela: Santiago de Compostela, Spain, 1738-49

Today Santiago's exterior is dominated by Baroque work constructed between 1650 and 1750. In the 17th century, Santiago's preeminence as a pilgrimage center began to falter. To boost its stature and reaffirm Saint James as Spain's sole patron saint, the cathedral's exterior was given a facelift. Its Churrigueresque facade is wide and imposing with its elaborate twin towers, one for bells, the other for the *carrac*, the Easter rattle. The Reloj tower, constructed in 1680, was nearly as influential in Galicia as the Cathedral of Seville's Giralda tower was in Andalusia. The medieval exterior of brown granite, turned gray over time, was less elaborate than the Baroque additions, but its height and the nine towers, which were planned and executed over several centuries, made the cathedral visible to the pilgrim approaching from a distance. Like Toulouse, Santiago was heavily fortified. Though the process of fortification may initially have been undertaken in response to a local uprising in the early 12th century, Santiago's development into an ecclesiastical citadel gave it a militant presence befitting a shrine to the patron saint of the *Reconquista*. Aymery of Picaud, whose "Pilgrim's Guide" of about 1130 (part of the Codex of Calixtus II) provides some insight into how at least one pilgrim experienced the church, described Santiago as "gorgeous with towers." But the focus of his narrative is the building's portals and interior. Three elaborately carved portals, one at the end of each transept arm and one in the west facade, open into a cathedral whose interior remains largely Romanesque.

The ultimate goal of the medieval pilgrimage to Santiago was the shrine of Saint James housed in the cathedral's apse. Several features establish the east end as the building's focal point. The sanctuary, which has received Baroque embellishments, is elevated over the foundations of the early church, in which the relics of the saint were originally believed to have been interred in the ninth century. These form the core of the

present church, maintaining a tangible link with the past through the saint's tomb, from which, it was believed, his remains could never be removed—a good defense against Toulouse's claims. While the nave, which has no clerestory windows, is relatively dim, light floods the crossing through windows in the tower, and windows also illuminate the radiating chapels. Aymery commented on the sanctuary's luminosity. He counted five windows "from which the altar of the Apostle receives a good light." He noted that the high altar is "embellished by the splendor of celestial lights" in tones that recall the light metaphysics Abbot Suger of St.-Denis derived from Pseudo-Dionysius the Areopagite.

The pilgrim's path continued once he or she entered the church. Like the other churches in the pilgrimage group, Santiago de Compostela was designed to facilitate the movement of large numbers of people toward the shrine. Pilgrims passed through the church on two well-defined axes converging at the crossing. They could move west to east when they entered through the western Portico de la Gloria, or along a lateral north-south axis if they entered through the transept. The principal entrance, for medieval French pilgrims at least, was the north portal, the Puerta Francigena, which Aymery used as a point of departure for his description of the interior. Aymery saw the nave and the two arms of the transept as three naves, distinct compartments meeting, to use his words, "at the four middle piers which dominate the church." In both the nave and the transept there is a strong momentum toward the crossing established by the long tunnel vault and the narrow, undifferentiated bays, which create a rapid, unbroken rhythm. The horizontal impetus is countered by a strong vertical axis created by the narrow nave, the high 68-foot vault and the shafts, which rise up to the capitals that cushion the transverse arches.

From the west, the view of the sanctuary was once blocked

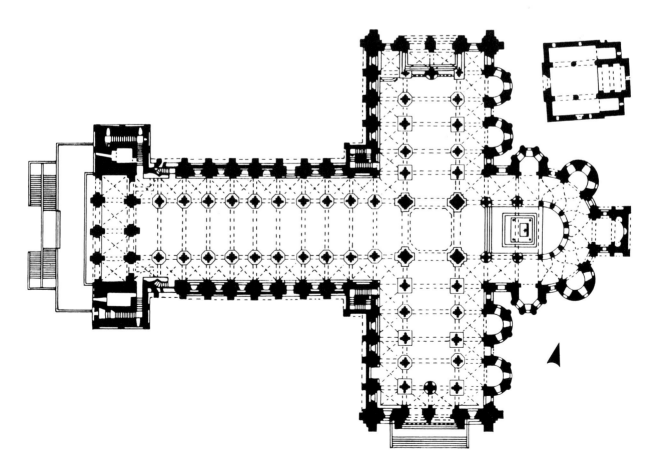

Cathedral of Santiago de Compostela, nave showing Romanesque vaulting

by an enclosed choir placed just in front of the crossing. Like the other churches in the pilgrimage group, Santiago was designed to serve the dual function of shrine for the relics of a widely-venerated saint and place of worship for the clerics whose role it was to protect the relics. From the early 12th century, the choir provided a private space for the devotions of the cathedral's canons, which Bishop Diego Gelmirez (who presided over the early construction of the Romanesque church) placed under the rule of Saint Augustine. As a result, the church functioned as a semimonastic foundation comparable to the other four pilgrimage churches, which were all monastic. The nave aisles bypass the choir, allowing devotions to continue uninterrupted by visitors. The side aisles and the galleries above them continue around the church, providing corridors for the pilgrimage traffic. The relatively narrow bays and heavy piers of the nave arcade screen the side aisles, covered with groin vaults, so that they become well-defined passageways. The galleries above provide yet another level for movement through the church. Aymery recommended that visitors go up to the triforium level (which he saw as another set of aisles), "for he who visits the triforium, if sad when he ascends, once he has seen the preeminent beauty of this temple, is rejoiced and filled with gladness." Although the nave is dim for lack of a clerestory, the pilgrim's journey through the aisles and galleries was well lit (before some of the windows were blocked up) by one window per bay on each level.

The crossing, set apart from the nave and transepts by its illumination and verticality, forms a pivotal, transitional space beyond which the pilgrims could move into the apse. The aisles leading into the ambulatory allowed people to circulate around the shrine of Saint James and exit on the opposite side, without the sort of jam-up that had occasionally been a problem in

churches not designed to accommodate the smooth flow of visitors. The nine apsidal chapels, five in the apse and four more in the transept, provided additional altars for worship. Designed for dynamic movement through three naves, along two axes, and on two levels, Santiago de Compostela was planned to facilitate the progress of the faithful toward the final goal of the pilgrimage, the shrine of Saint James, symbol of Christianity's triumph over the infidel. The common characteristics it shares with important pilgrimage churches north of the Pyrenees attests to broader cultural connections between northern Spain and France forged by political alliances and communication along the Pilgrimage Road.

—KATHERINE SOLOMONSON

CATHEDRAL OF SEVILLE
Seville, Spain

1401: Construction begins. **1439-49:** Construction; **Mason:** Maestro Carlin. **1454:** Two portals sculpted; **Sculptor:** Lorenzo Mercadante. **1479-1482:** Choir stalls constructed; **Sculptor:** Pieter Dancart. **1495-1506:** Crossing tower constructed; **Architects:** Simón de Colonia and Alonso Rodríguez. **1511:** Tower collapsed. **1514-17:** Nave vault, transepts, crossing vaults constructed; **Architects:** Juan de Badajoz, Juan de Álava (1505-37), Juan Gil de Hontañón, Enrique Egas (d.1534). **1888:** Crossing tower collapsed.

Cathedral of Seville, vault detail: 1514-17

Cathedral of Seville: Seville, Spain, 1401

Publications

CHUECA GOITIA, FERNANDO: *Arquitectura del Siglo XVI.* Madrid, 1953.

CHUECA GOITIA, FERNANDO: *Historia de la Arquitectura Española, Edad Antigua y Edad Media.* Madrid, 1965.

GÓMEZ-MORENO, M.: ''La catedral de Sevilla.'' *Boletin de la Real Academia de la Historia* 92 (1928).

KUBLER, G. and SORIA, M.: *Art and Architecture in Spain and Portugal and their American Dominions, 1500-1870.* Pelican History of Art, Harmondsworth, 1959.

LAMPEREZ Y ROMEA, V.: *Juan de Colonia.* Valladolid, Spain, 1904.

TORRES BALBAS, LEOPOLDO: *Arte y Arquitectura Gotica.* Madrid, 1952.

*

The Cathedral of Seville is an exceptional Late Gothic church, unusual not only for its enormous scale, but also for its spatial character, which was to be widely influential in Spain and Latin America. It has a five-aisle Latin-cross plan with lateral chapels between buttresses and a flat chevet. The central nave is approximately 36 meters high, comparable to Chartres Cathedral, but the four 25-meter-tall side aisles give it a broad horizontal expanse, 60 meters wide, reminiscent of a hall church. The interior elevation of the central nave has two stories, a nave arcade and a clerestory with a narrow passage at its base. Possi-

ble precedents for Seville are the Toledo Cathedral, also of five aisles and with a two-story nave elevation, and Cologne Cathedral, of similar section, if taller and narrower.

Work began in 1401, when the chapter approved the demolition of the western bays of the 12th-century Almohad Friday Mosque. The mosque had served as cathedral since its rededication after Ferdinand III's conquest of Seville in 1248. The *sahn,* or courtyard, of the mosque would become the cloister of the new cathedral, and the splendid minaret its bell tower, the *Giralda.* The canons intended the new church to be the largest in Christendom, retracing in plan the outline of the vast prayer hall of the mosque. The statutes of 1401 record this intention: ''Let a church be built such and so fine that there be no other unlike [sic] it.'' A fire at the Alcázar of Madrid in 1734 destroyed the large parchment plan of the cathedral produced at that time. Falcón Márquez tentatively attributes the first plan to Alonso Martínez, master mason of the cathedral from 1386 to 1396. It seems unlikely that a local mason in a city where previous Gothic work was of a distinctly Mudéjar style, and of brick, would have designed a stone structure of this magnitude and quality. The master was more likely a foreigner, familiar with Rhenish and Burgundian architecture.

Construction proceeded slowly due to straitened economic conditions in Seville, but foreign masons and artists appear in the account books. In 1434 a master Isambret served as consultant for a few days. He was probably a Flemish architect responsible for work in Daroca, Zaragoza and Palencia. Maestro Carlin was master mason from 1439 to at least 1449. He may be the French architect who in 1408 designed an unexecuted facade for

Cathedral of Seville, crossing tower, vaults and flyers from Giraldo: 1514-17

Barcelona Cathedral. The Breton sculptor Lorenzo Mercadante arrived in Seville in 1454, and was responsible for the terracotta sculptures of two portals, begun in 1464. In 1479 the Flemish sculptor Pieter Dancart took over work on the choir stalls, and three years later began the monumental retable filling the entire height of the sanctuary behind the altar, completed by Jorge Fernández Alemán after 1505.

In 1495 Simón de Colonia, architect of Burgos Cathedral, was released by his archbishop to work in Seville, where vaults of the nave were still under construction and those of the crossing and sanctuary were not yet begun. Although appointed master mason, Simón was mainly a consultant for the design of the crossing tower, modeled after that of the cathedral in Burgos, began by his father Juan de Colonia. In 1506 master Alonso Rodríguez completed the tower, which collapsed in 1511 due to weakness in two crossing piers.

Juan Gil de Hontañón was appointed master mason in 1513, concurrently with Alonso Rodríguez, who apparently died that same year. Earlier Juan de Badajoz and Juan de Álava had presented reports and plans for the reconstruction of the crossing and adjacent vaults. On 20 March 1514, Juan Gil presented to the chapter his final plans, including a low, conservative vaulted crossing tower, and three extraordinarily elaborate rib vaults for the adjacent bays of transepts and nave, each of a different design. Juan de Álava and Enrique Egas, master mason of Toledo Cathedral, acted as consultants for this proposal. Although the chapter preferred a sumptuous wooden roof for the crossing, fearing the weakness of the crossing piers, the consultants reinstated Juan Gil's project in 1515. The nave vault was completed that year, and the transepts and crossing vaults in 1517. Small, slightly pointed triple windows illuminate the

interior lantern enough to exalt it above the magnificent gloom of the great hall. The fears of the chapter were, belatedly, well founded, as the crossing tower collapsed again, in 1888.

Continuous additions were made to the cathedral in the 16th century, when the wealth and prestige of Seville were at its peak. The final additions, including the transept portals, the main portal of the west facade, and the cathedral archive and offices were not completed until the 20th century.

—SERGIO L. SANABRIA

TRANSPARENTE, CATHEDRAL OF TOLEDO
Toledo, Spain

1721-32: Construction; **Architect:** Narciso Tomé (*fl.* 1715-42).

Publications

"El Transparente de la catedral de Toledo (1721-1732)." *Archivo Español de Arte*, July-Sept. 1969 (issued Jan. 1971), pp. 255-288.

GUDIOL Y RICHART, J.: *La catedral de Toledo*. Madrid, 1948.

KUBLER, G.: Arquitectura espanola, 1600-1800 (Ars Hispaniae, vol. XIV). Madrid, 1957.

KUBLER, G. and SORIA, M.: *Art and Architecture in Spain and Portugal and their American Dominions, 1500-1800*. Pelican History of Art. Harmondsworth, 1959.

"Narciso Tomé's Transparente in the Cathedral of Toledo (1721-1732)." *Journal of the Society of Architectural Historians*, May 1970, pp. 9-23.

*

Narciso Tomé's Transparente in Toledo Cathedral is one of the most important examples of 18th-century art in Spain, yet it stands apart from the rest of the architecture and sculpture produced in that period. The term "Churrigueresque," which has been attached frequently to the Transparente in the past, is an inadequate label for a structure that differs in almost every respect from contemporary works by Alberto Churriguera or Pedro de Ribera. It serves to point up, however, that Tomé's altarpiece fits into a current of Baroque architecture of extraordinary richness that was the prevalent mode of expression in Spain during a considerable portion of the 18th century.

The construction of the Transparente was undertaken to provide a showcase in which the exposed Sacrament could be venerated from both the choir and the ambulatory of the church. The need for this double exposure resulted from the organization of the typically Spanish eastern end of the Gothic Cathedral of Toledo. The choir is separated from the side aisles and ambulatory by a high stone screen, and the monumental retable behind the high altar goes up to the vault in the center bay. The *manifestador*, a receptacle set into the retable for the exposition of the Blessed Sacrament, was only visible from the choir; the wall behind it gave no indication to those walking in the ambulatory of the presence of the Sacrament when it was exposed in the high altar. The opening of a window into the small chamber behind the altar which housed the monstrance was the obvious solution to this problem, and the intention of creating a *transparente* in its present location went back to 1579. A subsequent effort to erect such a structure dates to the first decade of the 18th century (ca. 1706-09), but the commission for the present

Transparente, Cathedral of Toledo: Toledo, Spain, 1721-32

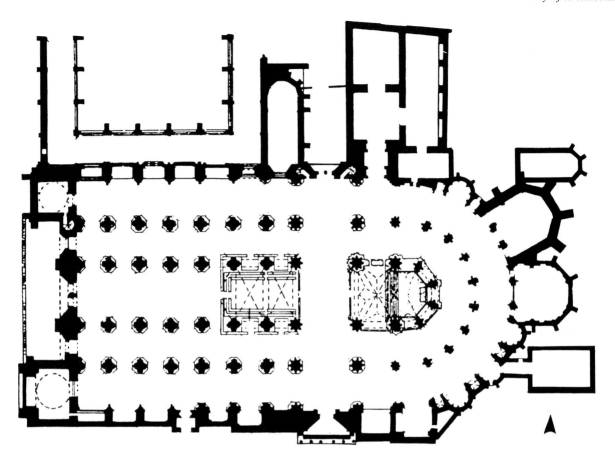

Transparente dates to the last few months of 1720. This final initiative came from Cardinal Astorga (1656-1734) soon after attaining the see of Toledo, in August of 1720.

The selection of the architect who was to be in charge of this commission was somewhat fortuitous. Teodoro Ardemans (1664-1726), the *maestro mayor* (chief architect) of the cathedral, was also royal architect, and at that time was actively engaged in the design of the palace of La Granja. Antonio Tomé and his son Narciso, whose center of operations was the small town of Toro in the province of Valladolid, were probably chosen by D. Fernando Merino y Franco, the *canónigo obrero* in charge of the cathedral works, because he also came from Toro and was already acquainted with them.

Antonio Tomé's role in this undertaking must have been minor, for his name disappeared from the books of the cathedral after his initial trip to Toledo, accompanied by Narciso, in the last months of 1720. On 10 June 1721, Narciso Tomé and the *canónigo obrero* signed the designs for the Transparente, much as it would be executed. By the end of 1722, a stucco model of Narciso's design had been finished by Diego Tomé, his sculptor brother, and a drawing signed on 10 April 1724 provided the design for the painting of the new vault over the outer ambulatory. The execution of the project took eight more years, and on 29 May 1732, Archbishop Astorga passed a decree of final payment to be made to Narciso Tomé. In June, the altar was consecrated with splendid attendant celebrations.

The symbolic program of the Transparente is primarily a compilation of representations alluding to the mystery of the Sacrament. In order to make their content more evident, pertinent quotations from Scripture are used throughout in connection with the images. The idea of the whole was to express the power of the Eucharist both by a single statement and by cumulative reassertions of the theme in various forms. The author of the program is not disclosed by any source, but given its complexity one can assume that it was the result of deliberations between the archbishop and the chapter, Tomé only giving it concrete form.

The structure that serves as a frame for the tabernacle chamber is divided into two tiers, defined by superimposed orders. The lower tier has as its center the figures of the Virgin and Child enthroned in a niche. The Christ Child points at an orb of the world decorated with a relief of the Fall of Man; the sacrifice of Christ for the redemption of man's sins embodied by the eucharist is tied to its first cause by the infant's gesture. To left and right of the niche, two gilded bronze reliefs depict formal parallels to the mystery of the Sacrament: David receiving from Ahimelech the hallowed bread, and David being offered bread and wine by Abigail.

In the center of the altar structure, contained within the lines of the lower entablature, is a "glory" of golden rays and angels, its core the sheet of glass that marks the location of the exposed Sacrament, and in its center a golden sun. The four archangels are placed among the golden rays at the cardinal points.

In the upper tier, a small three-wall "room" encloses a Last Supper, the institution of the Eucharist, and above it stands a statue of Faith. To her right and left, standing on the entablature over the order, are Hope and Charity. The Theological Virtues appear frequently in connection with the Sacrament; in fact, the image of Faith was often used as the support for monstrances in the 17th and 18th centuries.

The remainder of the sculpture in this portion of the Transparente is dedicated to honor local saints and the men more directly responsible for its execution. To right and left of the main orders at both levels are the patron saints of Toledo and its cathedral, Saints Leocadia and Casilda, and Saints Eugene and Ildefonsus. Above the Last Supper, in the broken pediment, two angels support the bronze coat of arms of the cathedral, a relief of Saint Ildefonsus receiving a chasuble from the Virgin. The coats of arms of the *canónigo obrero*, of Archbishop Astorga and of Pope Benedict XIII are also included in this upper tier.

Part of the project for the new Transparente was to provide additional light for the altar and the chamber for the monstrance, the *camarin*, and in order to achieve this, Tomé dismantled a portion of the 13th-century vault facing the new altar. The masonry between the ribs of one half of the vault was removed and, covering the opening, a kind of dormer almost as high as the nave was erected, resting partially on the ambulatory piers and partly on the vaults of the inner and outer ambulatories.

In the area of the opening of the vault, four sculpted prophets holding large tablets with their prophecies regarding the Sacrament stand above the arch of the ambulatory, silhouetted against the light from the new window. In the half dome and walls of the new structure that replaced the Gothic vault is painted a scene from Judges: the armies of Midian routed by Gideon; and in the spandrel over the ambulatory arch is depicted the story of Joseph and the cup hidden in Benjamin's sack of grain, from Genesis. In the part of the vault that remained standing over the inner ambulatory, a fresco depicts Saint John's Apocalyptic Vision.

The Transparente is an unparalleled example in Spain of the concept of the unity of the visual arts, which Giovanni Lorenzo Bernini had first brought into existence in the 17th century (in the Cornaro Chapel Santa Maria della Vittoria, Rome), and which also informs the Cathedra Petri in St. Peter's in Rome. Like Bernini, Tomé combined sculpture, painting, architecture and natural light to create an illusionistic experience in which the boundaries between reality and artifice dissolve before the beholder, to inflame his soul with religious fervor. In the complex design of the Transparente there is hardly any ornament introduced for its own sake. The jagged, frothy forms than envelop the columns, for instance, support the conceit that the structure is emerging from a disintegrating cloud where the heads of cherubs still float; these forms serve an illusionistic conception that expresses the mysterious power of the Eucharist, source of the extraordinary vision that confronts the visitor.

—NINA A. MALLORY

SWEDEN

KALMAR CATHEDRAL
Kalmar, Sweden

1660-78: Foundations laid and early construction. **Architect:** Nicodemus Tessin the Elder. **1682:** Consecration of building as Karlskyrka. **1703:** Building completed.

Publications

ALMQVIST, OSVALD: "Taflan angaende ny folkskola i *Kalmar." Arkitektur 29* 1913.
ROSELL, INGRID, and BENNETT, ROBERT: *Kalmar Domkyrka. Sveriges Kyrkor. Småland.* Vol. 3, 4. Stockholm, 1989.

*

The conflict between Lutheranism and the Italian Baroque was resolved in Kalmar Cathedral (1660-1703), one of the most architecturally significant churches in Sweden and northern Europe. It is one of a relatively small number of completely Baroque churches in Sweden and was, from its beginning, designed as part of a comprehensive city plan for Kalmar. The Kalmar Cathedral, which compares favorably to European churches of the time, is also one of the nation's most well-preserved cathedrals. Not only was it designed by Sweden's leading architect of the period, Nicodemus Tessin the Elder, but it was the only major ecclesiastical project by Tessin to be realized. Beyond that, as a building designed by the royal architect, begun and supported by the crown, paid for with national and local funds, and built in the strategically located town of Kalmar, this edifice—along with the town plan and other proposed and built structures for it—was also used as a political statement to assert the strength of absolute monarchs and their northern empire.

The city of Kalmar, situated on the Baltic coast of the province of Småland in southern Sweden, was an important defense point in Sweden. Its castle, a 16th-century fortification with towers and moat, had figured prominently in Swedish military history since the early Vasa kings. Kalmar continued to serve as a strategic point in the 17th century, when the aggressive political posturing of powerful Swedish sovereigns aimed at complete control of the Baltic. Historians call the years 1653-60 the planning stage of the cathedral, when the relocation and reorganization of the city of Kalmar on the island of Kvarnholmen for military reasons necessitated new town plans and a new cathedral. Already during the 1630s, it was deemed unwise to have the main elements of the city so near the fortication of Kalmar Castle. Many plans for a new town plan and cathedral were drawn up during the following decades. By 1658 the population of the city had been relocated, serious planning of the

Kalmar Cathedral: Kalmar, Sweden, 1660-1708

Kalmar Cathedral

cathedral had commenced, and the king encouraged nationwide support of the project.

Nicodemus Tessin the Elder began planning the cathedral during the reign of King Karl X. When he started to make new designs for the church, he had already been to Italy, where he had become enamored of Baroque classicism. His was a vision of a modern Italian Baroque, a new and revolutionary style in Sweden at that time. The only major precedent for its use in church architecture in Sweden was the Katarina Church in Stockholm designed by Jean de la Vallée (begun in 1656, and destroyed by fire in 1990).

Three main factors set parameters for the cathedral's design: limits on height based on defense considerations; the location of the church on Stortorget (the main square) as dictated by the town plan; and a need for reconciliation between the doctrines and worship service of Lutheranism and the style and symbolic associations of the Italian Baroque, a style linked to Roman Catholicism. Indeed, it was far more radical in Sweden at that time to use this style for a church than for a palace. The site on the square required some elongation of the ground plan and also some external compatibility with the proposed Court House, also designated for Stortorget. In order to respect Lutheran doctrine and worship, much consideration had to be given to the form of the interior. A rather uninterrupted volume of space was preferred, because it could symbolize the oneness of God and the unity of the community of believers. The Lutheran form of worship had a dual focus, the service and many rituals being initiated from the altar, and a sermon being delivered from the pulpit, which had to be accommodated on the design. In addition, the importance of congregational participation in worship, particularly in the singing of hymns, as well as the presence of a large and powerful organ were important considerations. Long naves and cruciform plans were traditional. Thus, the form of

worship helped to shape the form of the body of the church.

Since the 17th century, historians have speculated about the possible influence of Italian churches on Tessin's design for this church. The Roman character of his work may have been inspired by direct knowledge of the architecture of Girolamo and Carlo Rainaldi, as well as careful study of the buildings in Rome. Historians have made comparisons between Tessin's resolution and possible Italian sources, including the Rainaldis' plans for Sant'Agnese, Girolamo Rainaldi's design for Santa Lucia in Bologna, Il Gesù in Rome and even a drawing by Sebastiano Serlio.

Tessin's early plans reveal an interest in central planning in octagonal form, Baroque corner pavilions and the Greek-cross plan. However, in trying to create a design that worked well with Lutheranism and the location, the perfect Greek cross was transformed into a cross with a somewhat elongated nave. Tessin's design evolved into one that possessed both the compact character of a central plan and the feeling of length of a Latin cross. In 1660 the foundations of the church were laid, beginning the first of what historians have divided into three major building campaigns: 1660-78, a slow period of construction troubled by financial problems; 1678-82, a time in which building was completed enough to celebrate the building's consecration as Karlskyrka (Karl's Church) in 1682; and 1692-1703, the period in which the cathedral's completion was given priority. Tessin, who was directly involved with the project during its first two campaigns, saw the cathedral in a partial state of completion when he died in 1681. Undoubtedly, his death was one factor explaining the difficulties the edifice faced over the next decade. The church was completed by Tessin's stepson, Abraham Svanskold, and the German Rudolf Bientz under the supervision of Hans Wachtmeister, Admiral of the Fleet.

The Kalmar Cathedral is a large, dignified edifice with a powerful and stable presence created by perfect symmetry on all four sides and a compact centralized massing grounded by four towers and four raised fronts. It has an animated skyline and carefully worked-out details, but it is a planar and "calm" edifice relative to Italian sources. One of the most-written-about issues of this building is the fact that it is without a dome or cupola. The idea of this kind of Baroque crowning member was considered for the proposed Court House of the square. The domelessness of the cathedral, which has been a controversial issue for some historians, meant that elevated pediments on all four sides of the edifice were emphasized to fashion a unique visual appearance for the Swedish Baroque church.

In the end, Tessin's design is quintessentially Baroque, reflective of a keen knowledge of sophisticated Italian classicism, but, nevertheless, distinctly Swedish, particularly "Tessinesque." In achieving a reconciliation between the Italian Baroque and Swedish Lutheranism, and between military, civic and ecclesiastical considerations, Kalmar Cathedral is a strikingly independent resolution and one of Tessin's greatest architectural triumphs.

—KARIN M. E. ALEXIS

CITY HALL
Stockholm, Sweden

1907-23: Construction; **Architect:** Ragnar Östberg (1866-1945).

Publications

DAHL, DAVID: "Stockholms Stadshus." *Arkitekten* 26 (1924): 179-192.

EASTON, J. MURRAY: "The Stadshus at Stockholm." *Architectural Review* 55, 326 (January 1924): 1-6.

FRAMPTON, KENNETH, and FUTAGAWA, YUKIO: *Modern Architecture: 1851-1919*. New York, 1983.

ÖSTBERG, RAGNAR: *The Stockholm Town Hall*. Stockholm, 1929.

STRÖMBON, SVEN: "The New Townhall of Stockholm." *Burlington Magazine* 43 (1923): 208-214.

*

The Stockholm City Hall by Ragnar Östberg draws its surrounding world together in two ways. First, the location of the city hall on a prominent point on the eastern tip of Kungsholmen Island, along Lake Mälaren's edge, provides the building with a landmark status and allows it to establish a dominant presence over the surrounding environment of lake and land. The tower is a point of reference bringing the seemingly disparate pieces of the Stockholm urban fabric together. Second, Östberg assembled the best artists and artisans in Sweden to execute the paintings, frescoes, mosaics, sculptures and interior surface treatments. As a result, the Stockholm City Hall is Sweden's most famous National Romantic building, and is among the world's finest civic structures.

Though Östberg received the commission of the city hall in 1907, he had developed proposals for a new law courts complex on the site beginning in 1901. The city hall plan developed from the original law courts design studies, which included a symmetrical plan with an exterior reminiscent of the medievalizing qualities seen in Martin Nyrop's Copenhagen City Hall. In Östberg's first proposals for the Stockholm City Hall (from 1908), the plan began to exhibit the significant asymmetries that are seen in the final design of 1913. Despite the continued refinement of the project over the course of its production, and until its completion in 1923, Östberg never fully departed from the original conception of a building formed around two courtyards, one interior and one exterior.

Urban in strategy, the site organization includes a waterside terrace mediating between Lake Mälaren and the south facade of the building, an exterior civic court and the interior "Blue Hall" formed by the building proper, a public square to the north of the city hall that is configured by a proposed Committee House, and a small park to the north of the Committee House. The terrace and city hall have been completed, but the rest of the original plan remains on paper. The building volumetrics reinforce the planning strategy: the tower roots the complex to the prominent point on the site, while the south facade has Venetian windows and a colonnade, responses to the terrace access from the lake. The western and northern facades are more restrained in quality, while the east facade is scaled to its lakeside location.

The exterior civic court is a small piazza formed by red brick walls, with a large entry stair that leads to a vestibule and then the Blue Hall. The Blue Hall, which receives its name from the original intention of finishing it in blue tile, is an interior, skylighted piazza of red brick and accented with a marble loggia and staircase that is Venetian in expression. This hall is the interior embodiment of the exterior civic court, and its elements are of a scale that recalls a small, intimate, exterior urban space.

City Hall: Stockholm, Sweden, 1907-23

Many of the major ceremonial spaces surround the Blue Hall, including the famous Golden Hall. The Stockholm City Hall not only carries on the Scandinavian tradition of being ordered around a courtyard, but elaborates the concept of an interior court seen in Nyrop's Copenhagen City Hall and numerous 19th-century Nordic civic buildings. Östberg's use of courtyards as both organizing spaces and spaces of civic action influenced architects Erik Gunnar Asplund and Alvar Aalto, among others.

In addition to the Blue Hall, other significant rooms include the Golden Hall, the Prince's Gallery, the Council Chamber and the Three Crowns Chamber. These interiors, plus the many others that exist in this extensive building, showcase the excellent work of numerous Swedish artists and artisans. The Golden Hall, where the ball honoring Nobel prizewinners is traditionally held, is a blaze of glittering golden mosaics by the painter Einar Forseth. The dominant element is a representation of the mythical Queen of Lake Mälaren. Decorated by elegant, delicate frescoes representing the motif "Stockholm's Shores," the Prince's Gallery is so named for the artist, the Swedish royal prince, Eugene. The Council Chamber, executed in its primitive Swedish red and wooden paneling, and the Three Crowns Chamber with its silk brocade wall hangings, are representative of the variety of themes and motifs that decorate the state and council suites. The overall ensemble of building, decoration and art continued the late-19th-century concept, represented by the English Arts and Crafts movement, of a totally integrated work of art. Architect, artist and craftspeople have come together there in a close working relationship to forge a memorable experience.

The Stockholm City Hall is a truly romantic and eclectic assembly of elements. The exterior is of red brick with a copper roof, and combines a picturesque volumetric composition with Italianate detail qualities. In this building the Nordic National Romantic style, with its vernacular and medieval associations, is modified by Venetian elements: the southern colonnade, a tripartite window, balconies and sculpture. Other exotic elements act as counterpoints to the somber, Nordic fortress quality of the volume: onion domes, spires and bell towers all meet the sky in a fantasy of forms. In the end, it is the great red brick walls which bind the many forms and elements together, for they create a datum that allows for the muliplicity of pieces to be reconciled into a completed unity.

The Stockholm City Hall is not only a fitting setting for conducting the business of this great city, but is an appropriate environment for ceremonies surrounding the Nobel prize. It is there that Marconi, Einstein, Fermi, Kipling, Mann, Hesse, Camus and Hemingway, among the many greats, have dined and danced in celebration of receiving the Nobel.

　　　　　　　　　　　　　　　　—WILLIAM C. MILLER

DROTTNINGHOLM
Stockholm, Sweden

1662: Construction begun; **Architects:** Nicodemus Tessin the Elder (1615-81) and Nicodemus Tessin the Younger (1654-1728). **1740s-1750s:** Additions; **Architect:** Carl Hårleman. **1753:** Chinese pavilion built (later destroyed by fire). **1762-69:** Theater and New Chinese Pavilion built; **Architect:** Carl Fredrik Adelcrantz (1716-96).

Publications

BEIJER, AGNE: *Court Theatres of Drottningholm and Gripsholm.* New York, 1972.
DONNELLY, MARIAN C.: "Theaters in the Courts of Denmark and Sweden from Frederik II to Gustav III." *Journal of the Society of Architectural Historians* 43, 4 (December 1984): 328-340.
MALMBORG, BOO VON: *Drottningholm.* Stockholm, 1966.
SETTERWALL, ÅKE C. E.; FOGELMARCK, STIG; and GYLLEN-SVÄRD, BO: *The Chinese Pavilion at Drottningholm.* Malmö, Sweden, 1974.
SILFVERSTOLPE, G., and STAVENOW, ÅKE: "Drottningholm." In ALBIN ROOSVAL (ed.): *Svenska slott* New Series 1:401-480.
WRANGEL, FREDRIK ULRIK: *Tessinska palatset: ett bidrag till öfverståthållarehusets i Stockholm historia.* Stockholm, 1912.

*

The palace and grounds of Drottningholm (begun 1662), a royal estate outside of Stockholm, were a dramatic departure from Swedish architecture of the mid-17th century. One of northern Europe's most important Baroque buildings and gardens, often called the "Versailles of Sweden," it set the architectural standard in Sweden during the late 17th century and continued to hold a place of great influence during the 18th century. Designed by Nicodemus Tessin the Elder and completed by Nicodemus Tessin the Younger, it was instrumental in directing Swedish architecture toward Baroque classicism.

The history of Drottningholm began before the erection of the present palace and garden. Located on Lake Mälar outside of Stockholm, it has been the site of two royal palaces. The first palace was built in 1579 by Queen Katarina Jagellonica, the wife of King Johan III, Gustavus Vasa's second-oldest son. It received its name from Drottning Katarina (*drottning* means queen in Swedish). The palace and grounds later became one of the estates of the De la Gardie family. Little is known about the appearance of the original palace, which was destroyed by fire in 1661. That year the property was purchased from Magnus Gabriel de la Gardie by Queen Hedvig Eleonora, who envisioned a new and modern palace, which would serve the dual purpose of a country retreat and a monument to her husband, King Karl X, who had died just one year earlier in 1660. The new palace was not an "official" royal project in that it was commissioned by the queen for her use. Ironically, Drottningholm, a grand monument to the Carolinian monarchs, a symbol of their absolute power, was not completed until after the fall of the Swedish Baltic empire.

Becoming the architect of Drottningholm was pivotal in the career of Nicodemus Tessin the Elder. When he received this commission, it meant that he had won the day in architecture in Sweden after years of competition with Jean de la Vallée. As the royal architect of Hedvig Eleonora and in charge of Drottningholm, he was the undisputed leader of Swedish architecture. Tessin would devote most of the remainder of his life to this ambitious project.

Tessin's vision for the new palace at Drottningholm was the most modern conception of architecture in Sweden at the time. Even his early designs for the palace, dating from the 1660s, represent a distinct break with Swedish architecture of the immediate past, the Swedish Renaissance, which often retained medieval and picturesque elements. By the time Tessin began drawing up plans for the palace, he had visited the Continent and absorbed the modern Baroque, which he used for his design of

Drottningholm Palace: near Stockholm, Sweden, 1662ff

Kalmar Cathedral (begun in 1660). The designs and, finally, the building and grounds of Drottningholm evolved toward an uncompromising classicism with no discernible link to earlier Swedish architecture. Four factors determined the character and development of Drottningholm: the impact of Baroque classicism, particularly French influences; French Baroque landscape architecture; the purpose of the palace as a country retreat and not a military defense point; and the location on Lake Mälar.

Early plans indicate that Tessin considered the inclusion of a center tower flanked by domes, a hieratic program that may have given this domestic commission the authority of civic or even ecclesiastical architecture. Tessin's choice of a French Baroque palace style for Drottningholm contrasts with his use of an Italian Baroque ecclesiastical style for Kalmar Cathedral. The French influence is clearly seen in the character and disposition, particularly the pavilion system and mansard roofs, as well as the grand staircase of the palace. Although it was conceived before Louis XIV's palace and grounds of Versailles, early drawings for Drottningholm reveal knowledge of André Le Nôtre and the Château of Vaux-le-Vicomte in France.

Drottningholm, not in any sense a copy, represents an inventive, adaptive and distinctly Tessinesque Baroque style. This work was conceived and executed as a grand palace oriented toward the lakefront as the beginning point of a formal procession with terraces and steps leading to the palace and into its grand hall and staircase. As in Tessin's designs for Kalmar Cathedral and related to the European Baroque, Drottningholm was given a formal classical treatment ruled by an exacting symmetry extending from the palace into the garden. From its beginning, a program comprised of a dominant center building flanked by two low-riding, laterally extending arms culminating in framing pavilions crowned by domes endowed this brick-and-sandstone edifice with the hierarchy, formality and dignity offered by French Baroque classicism.

The rich Baroque classicism continued on the interior as the look of rich Italian marble and stone, classical details and refinements replaced the darker appearance of wood found in earlier 17th-century palaces. Designed by Nicodemus Tessin the Elder and Nicodemus Tessin the Younger, the interior was adorned by highly skilled stucco artists Giovanni and Carlo

Carove, an Italian father-and-son team; sculptors Nicolas Cordier, Evrard Chaveau and Nicolas Millich, who was responsible for much of the marble statuary, including the figures of Minerva, Apollo and the Muses; and painters David Klocker Ehrenstrahl, Cornelius van der Meulen, Johan Sylvius and Johan Philip Lemke. Ceiling paintings and other artworks seized by Swedish military forces during successful campaigns abroad also embellished Drottningholm.

Together these architects and artists brought to Drottningholm a Baroque unity of the arts and a Baroque theatrical character before unknown to Sweden. The grand hall and staircase, one of the most outstanding features of the palace, exemplifies their success in transposing to a Swedish setting a Baroque vision of architecture as the mother of the arts working in perfect harmony with sculpture and painting. Designed by the elder Tessin and completed by his son as the centerpiece of the design, the lavish, ornate and processional grand stairhall has some of the best works of sculpture and painting in the palace, including striking *trompe l'oeil* painting of the 1680s. It exemplifies how very specific elements from French and Italian Baroque buildings were successfully paraphrased, thereby demonstrating how well versed its architects and foreign-born artists were with current European art. The arrangement of classical statues, along with figures in court dress looking down the staircase as if to greet those who ascend, was inspired by the Ambassador's Room at the Quirinal Palace in Rome and by the Ambassador's Stairway and Guardroom at Louis XIV's Versailles. The use of this motif became a symbolic gesture expressing the importance and sophistication of the Swedish monarchs by linking their new palace with powerful and cultured European leaders. The program at Drottningholm enjoyed its own fame through well-publicized engravings.

The State Bedroom, begun by Tessin the Elder in 1668 and based on engravings by Jean Le Pautre, a Parisian artist, clearly shows a debt to the ceremonial French Baroque. Originally, this room was painted in gold and black as a symbol of royalty and mourning in memory of the dead king, and decorated with paintings by Ehrenstrahl about the history of the royal family. It was one of the most lavish Baroque bedrooms in Sweden and northern Europe.

The French influence was reasserted by Nicodemus Tessin the Younger, who made some important changes to the exterior, such as the elimination of the proposed tower in his father's plan, but is most evident in the design of the interior and the vast formal gardens. His plan for the Gallery Karl XI, which dates from the 1690s (1689-90), includes ceiling paintings by Sylvius dealing with the theme of Virtue and Vice, and wall paintings by Lemke depicting military victories, particularly the Scanian Wars. The well-known Hall of State is adorned with murals by Sylvius dating from the 1690s, depicting the four continents and the olympian gods. The walls of the room were redesigned by F. W. Scholander to complement the ceiling paintings. Tessin the Younger was also largely responsible for the chapel, dating from the 1680s and 1690s, a central room with dome containing a painting of the Last Supper by G. E. Schroder.

The beginnings of the garden date back to Tessin the Elder and the 1660s (before Versailles), but it was Tessin the Younger who created a design of such excellence that it gave Drottningholm the nickname the "Versailles of Sweden." Early on, formality ruled the scheme, making itself felt in all elements, including the axial plan, uncompromising symmetry, tree-lined avenues, formal box-hedge patterns in star shapes and geometric labyrinth forms, pools and fountains, and statuary. Sculpture by the Flemish master Andriaen de Vries, taken during war, became an important part of the design. The influence of French

Baroque planning and the work of Le Nôtre can be seen in the system of parterres that were laid in the 1680s.

During the 18th century, Carl Gustav Tessin was responsible for the completion of Drottningholm; Carl Hårleman, a student of Tessin the Younger, was the architect in charge of additions made during the 1740s and 1750s. The development of the palace was greatly influenced by Crown Princess Lovisa Ulrika, to whom Drottningholm was given as a wedding present from her husband King Frederik I in 1744. Due to Hårleman's addition of a second story over the arms of the palace, the sense of the French pavilion system was almost completely lost. An interest in the French Rococo and chinoiserie during that period is reflected in room redecorations. Hårleman's Green Antechamber dates from the 1740s; Jean Eric Rehn's famous library dates from the 1760s.

The 18th century brought new buildings to the estate that also reflect contemporary continental taste. The Chinese Pavilion, presented to Lovisa Ulrika on her 34th birthday in 1753 by her husband, also testifies to the impact of the Rococo on art in Sweden. The direct source of this garden pavilion pleasure palace was the so-called "Lust Palace" (1747) at Rheinsberg Palace belonging to the crown princess' brother, Frederik II of Prussia. The pavilion was destroyed by fire, and a new Chinese Pavilion (1763-69) was designed by Carl Fredrik Adelcrantz with the assistance of Jean Eric Rehn and with paintings by Johan Pasch, the leading exponent of Rococo painting in Sweden. Its Red and Yellow Rooms reveal a debt to interiors found in William Chambers' *Designs of Chinese Buildings, Furniture, Dresses, Machines and Utensils* (1757). Today it is almost completely intact. The Theater (1762-66) also for Lovisa Ulrika, was designed by Adelcrantz with advanced stage machinery, still in use, by the Italian engineer Donato Stopani in 1766. Renovated in 1921, it is one of the most important 18th-century theaters. During the 18th century, other important changes were the addition of a formal garden by Adelcrantz and the building of a Glade Theater with stage.

—KARIN M. E. ALEXIS

PUBLIC LIBRARY
Stockholm, Sweden

Ca. 1922-28; Architect: Erik Gunnar Asplund (1885-1940).

Publications

FRAMPTON, KENNETH, and FUTAGAWA, YUKIO: *Modern Architecture: 1920-1945.* New York, 1983.

FUTAGAWA, YUKIO (ed.): *GA 62: Woodland Crematorium, Stockholm, 1935-40, Woodland Chapel (1918)-20, Stockholm Public Library (1920):-28.* Tokyo, 1982.

HOLMDAHL, GUSTAV; LIND, SVEN IVAR; and ÖDEEN, KJELL (eds.): *Gunnar Asplund Architect, 1885-1940.* Stockholm, 1950.

"Stockholm Public Library." *Global Architecture* 62 (1982).

TYNELL, KNUT: "Stockholms stadsbibliotek." *Arkitektur* (1922): 146-154.

WREDE, STUART: *The Architecture of Erik Gunnar Asplund.* Cambridge, Massachusetts, 1980.

Public Library: Stockholm, Sweden, 1920-28

In 1918 Erik Gunnar Asplund was retained to assist in determining the requirements for a public library in Stockholm. As the library was to be the first public library in Sweden, Asplund traveled to the United States in 1920 to study what was then the most developed system of public libraries in the world. Though it was originally intended that Asplund prepare a competition brief for the library, in 1921 he presented schematics in which many of the essential elements of the final design were present. At that time the building committee decided Asplund was the most suitable designer for the job. Yet, when completed in 1928, Asplund's Stockholm Public Library was already considered stylistically outdated by Swedish avant-garde architects. Critics of the period felt the building stood on the border between two fundamentally different sensibilities, representing a dated classicism in a period of emerging modernist rationality. But Asplund's classicism incorporated a series of architectural meanings that modernism seldom had the capacity to realize.

A large cylindrical drum appears to root the Stockholm Public Library to its site on Observatory Hill, while the cubic mass of the complex is rotated slightly off the orthogonal grid of central Stockholm. The rotation intensifies the sense of monumentality, and accords the building landmark status within the extant context. The notion of the building being a compact, taut-skinned mass that would not be overpowered by the steeply sloping site was an early design decision. Though the plan order of the composition remained essentially the same throughout the design process, both the site planning and the volumetric development underwent two fundamentally different explorations for expression.

The original design of 1921 was positioned on Svaevägen,

and formed an edge to the plaza located to the north at the corner with Odengatan. The plan consisted of a square suite of spaces ordered around a circular central space housing the lending collection. A large dome, with skylight coffers, surmounted the round hall containing three stepping tiers of bookshelves. A processional staircase led from the entry, up several flights, to the lending hall. The exterior had the appearance of a normative 19th-century bourgeois apartment complex, the gargantuan-scaled entry portico notwithstanding. The dome crowned the entire composition, and, with the interior staircase, formed the central conception of the building: the staircase, the ascent to the world of books, represented the pathway to knowledge, while the dome, as metaphor for the mind, and its spherical rotunda housed the brain.

Though maintaining the same compositional *parti* and system of meanings, the final design was abstracted into two simple volumetric elements: cube and cylinder. The cube is formed by reading rooms that make a square in plan, and access the cylindrical lending hall at four tangential points. A more compact, but no less ceremonial, staircase still leads from entry to rotunda. The central space is taller and narrower, though keeping the stepping tiers of shelving, but has a flat ceiling and high clerestory windows. On the exterior, the lightly rendered rusticated base and simple stringcourses reinforce the geometric purity of the volumes. Well-proportioned, punched window openings, without overt classical decoration, are carefully arranged on the taut stucco facade. In powerful juxtaposition to the simple, delicate rendering of the exterior mass are the three overscaled, Egyptianesque entry portals. The light touch of the exterior detail qualities is also evident in the interior spaces of the library. The entry foyer, with its black polished stucco and delicate surface sculpture, also provides a fitting beginning for the staircase to the lending hall. The staircase receives further emphasis through the use of an Egyptian portal frame. As an entity, the building represents a consistent synthesis from conception through detail. But the library is not without humor, as is seen in the painter Nils Dardel's dream fantasy mural for the children's story room, or the naked figures of Adam and Eve used as door handles at the main entry.

The austerity of Asplund's library design often invites comparison with the work of the French Enlightenment architects Claude-Nicolas Ledoux and Etienne-Louis Boullée. Ledoux's Rotunde de la Villette is often cited as a potential source, but Boullée's work was published only after Asplund's death. More often overlooked is the influence of Scandinavian neoclassicists such as C. F. Hansen, M. G. Bindesbøll, N. Tessin and C. L. Engel. Eighteenth-century neoclassicism paralleled the strong political, intellectual and economic development occurring in Scandinavia at the time. The work produced in that "golden age" informed the so-called Nordic classicism of the 1920s, and continues as a source for precedent today.

Asplund also designed the terrace upon which the library sits and the park along Sveavägen. The terrace, built in 1930 and functionalist in expression, marks Asplund's shift to modernism. It is in keeping with his contemporaneous design for the 1930 Stockholm Exhibition. Though this might have created an aesthetic conflict, the light and transparent terrace acts as a kind of underscoring to the solid monumentality of the library volume. Designed shortly after the library was completed, the park has a large reflecting pool that corresponds to the orthogonal geometry of the context. Framed within the formal order of surrounding trees, we see reflected in the pool the powerful rotated presence of the library. In counterpoint, Asplund designed the landscape of Observatory Hill to appear as an untouched, naturalistic setting. Approached from the south or north, the austere, cubic volume of the library sits in contrast to the natural, even romanticized, appearance of the site. Both the larger urban context and the immediate landscape setting have been acknowledged in the design.

—WILLIAM C. MILLER

ROYAL PALACE
Stockholm, Sweden

1692-1754; Architect: Nicodemus Tessin the Younger (1654-1728).

Publications

KOMMER, BJÖRN R.: *Nicodemus Tessin der Jüngere und das Stockholmer Schloss*. Heidelberg, 1974.

OLSSON, MARTIN (ed.): *Stockholms slotts historia*. 3 vols. Stockholm, 1940-41.

SETTERWALL, ÅKE C. E.: *The Royal Palace, Stockholm*. Stockholm, 1948.

WRANGEL, FREDRIK ULRIK: *Tessinska palatset: ett bidrag till öfverståthållarehusets i Stockholm historia*. Stockholm, 1912.

A new aesthetic in Swedish architecture is represented by the Royal Palace in Stockholm (1692-1754). The palace, located in the oldest part of the city, on an island in the heart of Stockholm, brought to Sweden a robust Baroque classicism that stood in marked contrast to the castles of the Vasa Era, the 16th-century Swedish Renaissance, and to 17th-century palaces, including Drottningholm. It also signaled a new direction in the career of its architect, Nicodemus Tessin the Younger, by demonstrating how he had departed from the course set by his father, Nicodemus Tessin the Elder. The new Baroque style and rhythmic classical organization of the palace presented a vision of modernism in turn-of-the-century Sweden. During the 18th century, the palace was the center of Swedish cultural life, with all eyes on the achievements of Tessin and his successors. The palace's interiors, dating from the 1730s and 1740s, were the most modern in Sweden. Their early use of the current French Rococo style anticipated the popularity of the style during and after the 1760s. As the palace has been the residence of the royal family since 1754, it has experienced change and modernization; however, its exterior is a well-preserved Tessin design, and its interior has retained Baroque features dating back to the 1692-through-1710 period, and still houses some of Sweden's and northern Europe's most outstanding mid-18th-century Rococo rooms.

The realization of a palace of this scale and style in Sweden was made possible by a close and dynamic relationship between the architect Nicodemus Tessin the Younger and Queen Hedvig Eleonora. Tessin had been interested in the idea of a new royal palace in Stockholm since his return from Paris. Early on, the queen was concerned with making the Tre Kronor, the medieval royal castle, into a modern edifice befitting the authority of the Vasa dynasty. This set the stage for Tessin to convince King Karl XI to rebuild the royal castle.

A fire in 1686 led to discussion of a bridge linking the north end of the castle to northern Stockholm, and to the rebuilding of the northern castle itself. In 1692 construction of a new northern wing based on Tessin's design was begun; foreign artists, particularly French designers, were engaged to work on the project. Modifications and additions, including new state and royal residences, and a royal chapel were near completion in 1697, the year the king died and the year the great fire of May 7 destroyed the old castle. The north wing and much of Tessin's new building survived. However, the chapel, transformed by Tessin from a Gothic to a Baroque form, was gutted. This sumptuous, highly ornate Baroque sanctuary swelled into one great volumetric space to create a feeling of largeness and vastness reminiscent of Nicodemus Tessin the Elder's design for Kalmar Cathedral.

The fire made the creation of a new royal palace a necessity. A comprehensive master plan was drawn up by Tessin and approved by the Council of the Realm by June 1697. Thus, the erection of a new royal palace commenced during a period in which Sweden was still a great northern power. The undertaking of a building of such a large scale and high quality made Hedvig Eleonora one of the greatest patrons of art of the day, and it called international attention to Sweden, Hedvig Eleonora and Tessin. As the commission attracted a body of talented foreign artists, designers and craftsmen to Stockholm, the character of Swedish cultural life was dramatically improved.

Factors that influenced the development of the design were the direct impact of Tessin's "grand tour," which facilitated an intimate understanding of the implications of a full-bodied Baroque derived from Italian and French classicism, and the restrictions of the site. Some speculate that the design of the oldest part of the palace, the northern wing dating from the 1690s, may have been somewhat indebted to mid-century ideas

Royal Palace: Stockholm, Sweden, 1692-1754

of the architect Jean de la Vallée, and to Tessin's own design for a palace in Swedish Pomerania, dating from 1680, but never built. The most important influence on the northern wing was Giovanni Lorenzo Bernini's projects for the Louvre, which Tessin had seen during his most recent trip to Paris. His designs for the palace have also been compared with Vignolas' Villa Farnese at Caprarola, and with Versailles itself. The influence of the Roman Baroque can be seen in the use of the triumphant-arch motif as a main entry, that of the palace at Caprarola is brought to mind by the double ramps of Lejonbacken, and that of Versailles is recalled by the royal apartments connected by a grand ceremonial hall. The plan, elevation and character of the palace are based on the Italian palace type of the Renaissance and Baroque periods.

The limitations of the somewhat awkward site of the old palace set natural parameters. The design of the palace had to consider the existing foundation of the Tre Kronor. The size and form of the palace were also restricted by the waterfront location and close proximity to the existing Storkyrkan, the Cathedral of Stockholm. Tessin's design resolved this problem by creating two curved (instead of squared) wings, which took Storkyrkan into consideration and maximized available space to allow for a huge and formal palace, expressive of the great power of the Swedish Empire (although it was faltering at that time). The restrictive site also caused some imbalance on the south facade, which Tessin visually lessened by concentrating ornamentation near entrances. The grand triumphant arch used as the entry on this front was also a monument to King Karl XII after his victory at the Battle of Narva.

Tessin's master plan included the Hall of State, a Baroque interior known for its classical statuary and decorations by French artists; a large Royal Chapel; the Gallery of Karl XI, also a Baroque room completed before 1710; a long third-floor gallery with paintings by the French artist Jacques Foucquet and sculpture by his countryman René Chaveau; and a Royal Opera, which was never realized. The period of political and economic decline that followed the defeat of King Karl XII adversely affected construction of the palace. When Tessin died in 1728, he was succeeded by competent architects and designers; his own son, Carl Gustav, became the surveyor of public works and buildings, whose principal responsibility was the completion of the palace. Carl Hårleman, who was the architect in charge, respected Tessin's plans, but made his own contributions to the interior; Cronstedt and Carl Fredrik Adelcrantz also worked on the project. The interior included what was the latest in French fashion of the mid-18th century in rooms, such as the Pillared Hall (with Rococo work by Johan Pasch), as well as outstanding examples of the Gustavian Style, a late-18th-century Swedish neoclassicism.

From its inception, Tessin's plan stood apart from anything in Sweden. The palace itself is a bold and severe edifice with the visual force and drama of Baroque monumentalism and Baroque stage effects. It is an Italian Renaissance-Baroque palace type with a square plan arranged around a central open court for which an equestrian statue of Karl XI (based on an equestrian of Louis XIV) was intended. This Roman Baroque palace possessed an uncompromising hierarchy achieved by a grandiose classicism, an absolute symmetry and an imposing location. Its theatrical disposition can be seen well from near and far on the north side, with the ceremonial entry ramps that zigzag across the lateral projection of the wall, on the east, where rectangular wings extend beyond the body of the palace, and on the west, where circular arms create a natural defense point. In contrast to the broken skyline of the Tre Kronor, the horizontality and regularity of the palace's roofline create a sense of continuity and unity of design whose beauty is dependent upon classical laws of proportion, weight and priority. Without much ornamentation and high relief, the tight, compact, self-contained wall surface gives the palace a feeling of sobriety—which bespeaks a nordic solemnity and strangely foreshadows Nordic classicism of the 20th century—and a feeling of austerity, which somehow seems appropriate for a monument completed after the decline of a great empire.

—KARIN M. E. ALEXIS

SWITZERLAND

GOETHEANUM
Dornach, Switzerland

1913-20: Construction; **Architect:** Rudolf Steiner (1863-1925). **1922:** Destruction by fire. **1924-28:** Second Goetheanum constructed; **Architects:** Rudolf Steiner and Ernst Aisenpreis.

Publications

FRAMPTON, KENNETH, and FUTAGAWA, YUKIO: *Modern Architecture: 1851-1919*. New York, 1983.
KEMPER, C.: *Der Bau: Studien zur Architektur und Plastik des ersten Goetheanum*. Stuttgart, 1966.
PEHNT, WOLFGANG: *Rudolf Steiner: Goetheanum, Dornach*. Berlin, 1991.
RUMÉ, G.: "Rudolf Steiner." *Architecture Mouvement Continuité* 39 (June 1976): 23-29.
STEINER, RUDOLF: *Wege zu einem neuen Baustil*. 1926. English edition: *Ways to a New Style in Architecture*. London, 1927.
STEINER, RUDOLF: *Der Baugedanke des Goetheanum*. Stuttgart, 1958.
ZIMMER, ERICH: *Rudolf Steiner als Architekt*. Stuttgart, 1971.

*

Fourteen of the 17 buildings designed between 1913 and 1925 by the Austrian-born anthroposophist Rudolf Steiner (1863-1925) were associated with his Goetheanum project sited on a hilltop at the edge of Dornach, just southeast of Basel. However, the complete "colony" of stylistically related buildings he envisioned did not completely come to pass. Though some details of Steiner's early designs (including the first Goetheanum) showed similarities to Jugendstil, and though his design production in general has often been classified as expressionist, Steiner stated that he intended his buildings to be primitive, beginning illustrations of an entirely new style of architecture.

Steiner was an early advocate of a broad, holistic understanding of functionalism, and his design approach can be termed organic functionalism. He saw his buildings as integrated design "organisms," wherein each visible form imaged its function(s) in relation to the building and to its human users. In addition, Steiner's forms were organic not because, as in most Jugendstil design, they stylized existing forms in nature, but because they were designed after the same *principles* observed in the organic world.

Functionally, the Goetheanum presented a complex design problem. Among other purposes, Steiner intended the Goetheanum to be an example of a *Gesamtkunstwerk;* to serve as an artistic, experiential introduction to the elaborate metaphysical teachings of his anthroposophy; to pay homage to the scientific and philosophical views of the German poet-scientist Goethe, whose complete scientific writings Steiner had edited; to be an appropriately designed theater and world headquarters for the Anthroposophical Society founded by Steiner in 1913; and to be an indication for a new, modern style of architecture, applicable to any type of building or design project.

The Goetheanum was first planned as a large theater-temple for lectures and theatrical performances in Munich. After Mu-

nich authorities rejected a 1911 building application, Steiner, who had no formal architectural training, began working with Stuttgart architect Carl Schmid-Curtius and later other collaborators to design his Goetheanum for a newly donated site at Dornach. Construction began in 1913 and by 1920 the structure was far enough completed to be used for several events.

Raised on a concrete pedestal above the surrounding subalpine landscape, the dual-domed Goetheanum was approximately 272 feet long by 243 feet wide. The interior diameter of the large dome reached 110 feet. The rounded shapes of the concrete base were designed to be, Steiner said, "an extension of the rocky subsoil" so that "nature's shapes pass over effortlessly into the forms of the building." On this substratum arose an enormous sculpture-building, carved out of laminated American oak and roofed with grayish-blue slate from Norway.

A five-lobed, carved motif based on the pentagram was repeated in seven variations throughout the building and represented only one example of Steiner's application of the Goethean principle of organic metamorphosis. Steiner stated his intention to move from a static architectural conception of support and load to an active, organic principle of growth, wherein one form "grew" or "metamorphosed" out of another one. Another prominent example of designed metamorphosis was the progression of carved wood forms on the column bases and capitals and on the architraves of the interior auditorium.

Steiner considered the interior of the Goetheanum to be more important architecturally than the exterior. The west entrance of this axial building led into a dramatically zoomorphic, concrete entry hall of columned arches and continued up a curving staircase, fashioned in freely modeled shapes meant to express the stairway's structural dynamics. Above this was the rear entrance to the auditorium, which seated more than 900 people. The interior was elaborately decorated with carved wood ornament and sculpture, soaring columns, engraved colored-glass windows, and watercolor murals on the two dome ceilings.

The most prominent architectural feature of the Goetheanum was the two huge, interlocking domes of unequal size, unique in architectural history. Braced timber construction was used for the separate but joined interior and exterior dome shells, and the domes were encircled with an oval ring anchor. Two perpendicular wings on the exterior north and south were added as buttresses at the juncture of the two domes. Steiner chose the unusual design of two interpenetrating domes to express "the duality of that which is revealed and of that which comes to meet it." The larger dome, the auditorium, represented the physical, temporal world of human life, while the smaller dome, the stage, conveyed the spiritual, eternal world. The interpenetration of the world of spirit and idea with the sensory world was a key concept of Steiner's anthroposophy, as well as a hoped-for result of the lectures and performances offered in the Goetheanum. This qualitative distinction between the two different interior spaces was reinforced throughout in intricate detail of colors, forms and ground plan.

When the first Goetheanum was destroyed by arson on New Year's Eve 1921-22, Steiner designed in a rather different style a larger replacement building of reinforced concrete. Functionally and formally, his new design attempted to express the qualities of concrete, the expansion and changed character of his anthroposophical movement since the time of the first building, the use of insurance money, and the quality of a protective, fortress-like enclosure for the spiritual-cultural activities to occur within.

Goetheanum: Dornach, Switzerland, 1913-20

Under the general direction of architect Ernst Aisenpreis, the more angular and monumental second Goetheanum was constructed between 1924 and 1928 and represented a pioneering achievement in large-scale, free-form, unfinished reinforced-concrete construction using irregularly shaped wooden form-work. The east-west, axially oriented building is approximately 308 feet long at ground level. Raised on a new concrete base, the sculptural exterior of the second Goetheanum (the only part completely designed by Steiner before his death) reveals an expressive polarity between the simply articulated stage block in the east and the plastically animated and projecting forms of the west facade. While the basically cruciform plan of the first Goetheanum has been retained, in this second structure expanded side wings reinforced by a multifaceted slate roof, rising to about 122 feet and spanning the boundary between the cubic eastern block and the trapezoidal western block, create a clear third element between the other two. This tripartite articulation expresses Steiner's later conceptions of a fundamental threefold constitution observable in both society and human nature, and it helps present a more monumental and forceful exterior expression than in the first Goetheanum. The interior was completed later by others, partially following a few general indications by Steiner.

—DAVID ADAMS

TURKEY

CHURCH OF CHRIST IN CHORA
Istanbul [Constantinople], Turkey

Ca. 1050: Reconstruction of earlier church. **1303-21:** Additions, restorations and decorations.

Publications

ALPATOV, M.: "Die Fresken der Kachrije-Djami in Konstantinopel." *Münchner Jahrbuch der bildenden Kunst* 6 (1929).

MATHEWS, THOMAS F.: *Early Churches of Constantinople, Architecture and Liturgy.* University Park, Pennsylvania, 1971.

MÜLLER-WIENER, W.: *Bildlexikon zur Topographie Istambuls.* Tübingen, Germany, 1979.

VAN MILLINGEN, E.: *Byzantine Churches in Constantinople.* London, 1912.

*

The church of the Monastery of Chora, now known as Kariye Camii is, in its present form, a reconstruction of earlier buildings initiated by the statesman Theodore Metochites at the beginning of the 14th century. However, to understand the building's originality and place in the history of church architecture, it is necessary to recognize what belongs to earlier building phases. It seems that the church initially—that is, when it was rebuilt in about 1080 on the site of a ruined older building—had an inscribed Greek-cross plan, which was typical for its date.

The sebastocrator Isaac Comnenus seems to have been responsible for a reconstruction, which for historical reasons must be dated to about 1120, and undoubtedly followed an earthquake. That reconstruction, which replaced the Greek-cross plan, introduced a characteristic new element—a larger dome, whose support system used pendentives as a transition to the weight-bearing piers. The piers formed the corners of the naos and were connected to each other with barrel vaults. A number of monuments in Constantinople's architecture testify to the popularity of this plan, whether it was reduced to a central nucleus formed by the dome and its support system—as seems to have been the case at Chora—or was integrated into monumental extensions. It is possible that Chora was the first example of the reintroduction of that kind of plan in 12th-century Byzantine architecture. Its principal characteristic is to allow increases in available space without compromising stability. It has been suggested, interestingly, that revived interest in this type of architecture was linked to attempts to promote plans considered ancient and traditional (which were used effectively between the sixth and ninth centuries).

In this case, the use of the plan seems both to have imparted

Church of Christ in Chora

Church of Christ in Chora, inner narthex to south: Istanbul, Turkey, ca. 1050

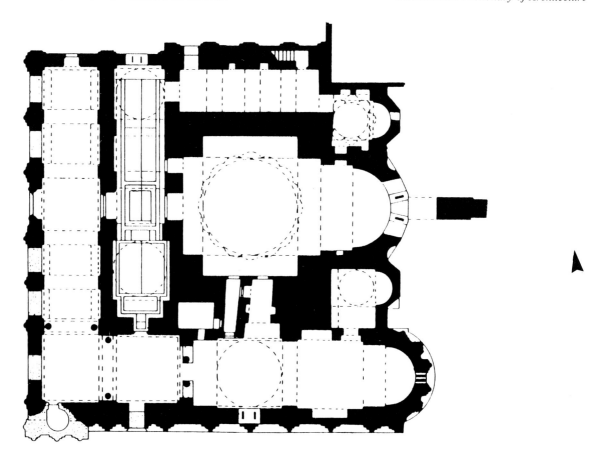

greater stability to a church constructed on difficult terrain, and to have enhanced the monumentality of the interior. Survivals from that phase of the church's history make it possible to say, with greater certainty than was feasible for the preceding phase, that the church was constructed with great care, according to a system of geometrical relations, both in plan and elevation. This system may be compared to that used in the Church of the Virgin Kosmosoteira at Pherae in northern Greece, also founded by Isaac Comnenus, in 1152.

Little is known about the church at Chora between the 12th century and the beginning of the 14th century, at which time it was again reconstructed, at the instigation of Theodore Metochites. Theodore was one of the most important men of the age, a great figure both intellectually and politically. (However, he was exiled when Andronicus II, to whom he was close, abdicated and Andronicus III came to power.) The major reconstruction and redecoration of the church, which Theodore directed, may be regarded as an expression of the ideas and tastes of a person who belonged to the highest and most developed circles of Byzantine society. This fact is reflected primarily in the appearance of the church, particularly the decorative structure of its facades, where the traditional Byzantine technique of alternating layers of rubble with layers of brick is combined with a discreet but lively animation of the walls utilizing an elegant architectural vocabulary. Interior architectural ornamentation is of an equally restrained elegance, which highlights the wealth and quality of the marble revetments, mosaics and frescoes, which are essential to the impact of the interior.

It seems that only the naos proper was not reconstructed during that campaign, with the exception of the dome, which

must have collapsed or was otherwise sufficiently damaged to require reconstruction. Perhaps the most salient feature of the new complex is the relationship between the church with its double narthex, the funeral chapel on the south side, and the annex to the north.

Noteworthy among the additions typical of the Palaeologan period are the mostly open exterior narthex and the presence of a bell tower on its southern side (where a minaret is now to be found). Bell towers were virtually unknown in Byzantine architecture before the Latin invasion, the faithful traditionally being summoned to worship by a simander. As in other churches of the same period, the impression is of a somewhat irregular disposition, as if overcoming the constraints inherent in each separate space weighed more heavily than considerations of harmony in overall composition. This state of affairs resulted most often from later additions of annexes to an existing structure, but at Kariye Camii the whole was built in a single campaign. A notable asymmetry results from the prominence of the southern bay of the interior narthex, which is also marked off from the rest of the structure by its iconographic program. A large mosaic represents the sebastocrator Isaac, praying to the Virgin and Christ. It is thinkable that Theodore Metochites wished to honor his imperial predecessor by designing a section of the narthex as a separate chapel, preserving a design characteristic of earlier church architecture, prior to the full development of the narthex. These disjunctions notwithstanding, the ornamentation of the facades attempts to evoke a unified impression.

The funeral chapel, intended for the founder, is one of a well-known series of funeral churches and church annexes built by

Byzantine aristocrats, and inspired by imperial monuments. The originality of the Chora annex, decorated with frescoes of exceptional quality, resides in its unusual length and the unity of the interior. The northern annex, which has a second story, is an altogether exceptional structure. Recently it has been suggested, with great plausibility, that the two-story building housed the monastery library, of which Metochites was particularly proud.

The church of the Chora Monastery is therefore an altogether exceptional monument, showing the possibilities of Constantinople's architecture of the first quarter of the 14th century, but which may yet be compared with monuments built elsewhere, particularly in Thessalonica. However, less and less favorable political and economic conditions prevented the full realization of the promises contained in this building.

—J.-M. SPIESER
Translated from the French by Alla Melamed

HAGIA SOPHIA
Istanbul [Constantinople], Turkey

---

360 A.D.: First basilica completed. **404 A.D.:** Destroyed by fire. **532 A.D.:** Second basilica damaged by fire. **6th Century:** Rebuilt by Justinian. **Architects:** Anthemius of Tralles and Isidorus of Miletus.

Publications

Aya Sofia Constantinople, As Recently Restored by Order of H. M. the Sultan Abdul Medjid. London, 1852.

DOWNEY, GLANVILLE: "Byzantine Architects, Their Training and Methods." *Byzantion*, 18 (1946)-48: 99-118.

HUXLEY, G. L.: *Anthemius of Tralles: A Study in Later Greek Geometry.* Cambridge, Massachusetts, 1959.

KAEHLER, H.: *Hagia Sophia.* Berlin and New York, 1967.

MACDONALD, WILLIAM L.: "Design and Technology in Hagia Sophia." *Perspecta* 4 (1957): 20-27.

MANGO, CYRIL A.: *The Art of the Byzantine Empire, 312-1453.* Englewood Cliffs, New Jersey, 1972.

MATTHEWS, THOMAS F.: *The Byzantine Churches of Istanbul: A Photographic Survey.* University Park, Pennsylvania, 1976.

MATTHEWS, THOMAS F.: *The Early Churches of Constantinople.* London, 1971.

MILBURN, ROBERT: *Early Christian Art and Architecture.* Berkeley and Los Angeles, 1988.

MÜLLER-WIENER, W.: *Bildlexikon zur Topographie Istambuls.* Tübingen, Germany, 1979.

SCHNEIDER, A. M.: *Die Sophienkirche in Konstantinopel.* Berlin, 1939.

SWIFT, E. W.: *Hagia Sophia.* New York, 1940.

UNDERWOOD, P. A.: "A Preliminary Report on Some Unpublished Mosaics in Hagia Sophia." *American Journal of Archaeology* Vol. 55, 4 (1951).

VAN MILLINGEN, E.: *Byzantine Churches in Constantinople.* London, 1912.

Hagia Sophia

Hagia Sophia: Istanbul, Turkey, 360 A.D.

VAN NICE, ROBERT L.: *St. Sophia in Istanbul: An Architectural Survey*. Locust Valley, New York, 1965.

WHITTEMORE, T.: *The Mosaics of St. Sophia at Istanbul*. Reports 1-4. Oxford, 1952.

*

The overpowering spatial drama, gigantic scale, and architectural and structural innovations of Hagia Sophia place it among the most memorable examples of world architecture. Built in

a prominent position above the Sea of Marmara, it dominated Constantinople's skyline for many centuries. A number of early writers describe the building, including Procopius in *On the Buildings (of Justinian)*, Agathias in his *Histories*, and Paulus Silentarius, who especially comments on the liturgical furnishings.

The first Hagia Sophia, a basilica begun by Constantine, was brought to completion and dedicated by Constantius in 360; it seems to have replaced the nearby church of Hagia Irene (Divine Peace) as the cathedral of Constantinople. Hagia Sophia (Divine Wisdom) was dedicated to Jesus Christ as the embodiment of Divine Wisdom and as the Word Incarnate; the church's patronal

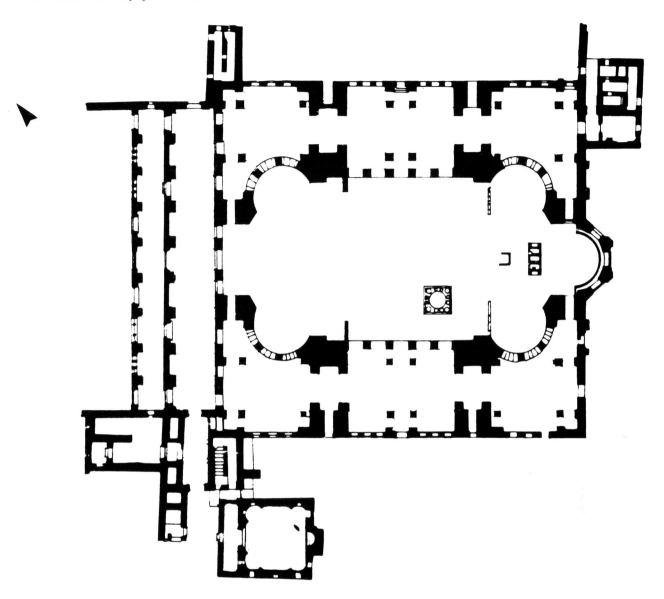

festival was Christmas. The popular designation as "Santa Sophia" or "Saint Sophie," which suggests that the structure is dedicated to a particular saint, is misleading.

The first Hagia Sophia was destroyed by fire during a riot in 404. The second, built by Theodosius II, was damaged by fire in the Nika revolt of 532. Although most of the brick and stone basilica was probably left standing, the victorious Justinian decided to demolish the remains in order to create a new cathedral that could be specifically identified with his patronage and power. The idea of an enormous domed structure was probably Justinian's, and Hagia Sophia's capitals are decorated with his monogram and that of his Empress Theodora. When the new Hagia Sophia was completed, Justinian is reported to have announced: "Glory to God who has thought me worthy to finish this work. Solomon, I have outdone you!" He thus declared himself to be the creator of a Christian building that was greater than the most important Old Testament structure, Solomon's Temple in Jerusalem.

The two documented architects, Anthemius of Tralles and Isidorus of Miletus, were engineers and mathematicians; they were almost certainly approached by Justinian because of his desire to construct a domed structure of enormous scale. Working together with the emperor, Anthemius and Isidorus conceived a building that went beyond the limitations of the master builders of the age. Anthemius, probably the older of the two, should be considered the major figure; in contemporary documents his name is given first, and Procopius emphasizes Anthemius' role in his account of the building. No other work by either Anthemius or Isidorus is documented, but a 10th-century source credits them with the design of two innovative churches built for Justinian in Constantinople, the Church of the Holy Apostles and SS. Sergius and Bacchus. Anthemius, who was trained in geometry, is documented as a designer of elaborate mechanical devices, while Isidorus, a student of the work of Archimedes and a master of advanced geometry, wrote a commentary on a treatise about vaulting. The structural evidence at Hagia Sophia suggests that their original conception was so daring and ethereal that the structure had to be progressively strengthened during construction to guarantee its stability.

Hagia Sophia's effect of spatial unity and spiritual transcendence is best captured in the description written by Procopius, a historian at Justinian's court: "The sun's light and its shining rays fill the temple. One would say that the space is not lit by the sun without, but that the source of light is to be found within, such is the abundance of light. . . . So light is the construction, the dome seems not to rest on a solid structure, but to cover the space with a sphere of gold suspended in the sky. . . . The scintillations of the light forbid the spectator's gaze to linger on the details; each one attracts the eye and leads it on to the next. The circular motion of one's gaze reproduces itself to infinity. . . . The spirit rises toward God and floats in the air, certain that He is not far away, but loves to stay close to those whom He has chosen.''

The sense of a suspended dome must have been even more impressive originally, when the sweep of a lower dome would have been virtually continuous with the rising curves of the giant pendentives. The windows that ring the base of the dome were originally larger and would have provided a ring of light below the dome that, in combination with the gold glass mosaics of the dome itself, would have dematerialized the structure at this point. The effect of suspension is emphasized by the groupings of half domes to the east and west.

The half domes and the walls that surround a spectator standing in the nave are regularly pierced with windows or with colonnades leading into the galleries and aisles, and the space of these secondary areas is likewise bounded only by walls pierced with windows. As a result, the interior seems continuous and limitless, and the bulk of the piers is hidden.

As the site for coronations and other imperial functions, Hagia Sophia had important political connotations. The huge nave, centered under the dome of heaven, was reserved for the court liturgy enacted by the clergy, the patriarch, the emperor and many attendants. The people gathered in the aisles and galleries, where they would have had only a partial view of the nave and dome; women may have been restricted to the galleries. A portion of the galleries was set aside for the royal family; it was there that the throne of the empress was located.

Hagia Sophia is crowned and centralized by its great dome, but the plan also encompasses the longitudinal emphasis of the early Christian basilica. Attention is directed toward the altar by the grouping of half domes that abut the main dome to the east; the impact of a centralized space created by the dome is so great, however, that it is not immediately apparent that the space of the central area is actually more than twice as long as it is wide.

The ethereal and dematerialized effect established by the hovering dome was originally enhanced by a rich and sumptuous treatment of all the interior surfaces, from the shimmering marble revetment of the pavement and the lower walls to the intricate lacy treatment of capitals and arcades and the mosaics of the upper walls, vaults and domes. To stress Constantinople's role as the imperial capital, Justinian had rare marbles and monolithic stone columns quarried in many areas of the empire. Procopius wrote: ''The whole ceiling is overlaid with pure gold which is beautiful as well as ostentatious. Yet the reflections from the marbles prevail, vying with the gold.'' The Justinianic mosaics, most of which seem to have been of glass, consisted of vast expanses of gold with crosses and geometric or floral borders. Originally the windows were filled with colored glass. After iconoclasm, figural mosaics were added, including seraphim in the pendentives, a Madonna and Child and flanking angels in the main apse, a series of standing bishops, a Deesis and other dedicatory mosaics offered by rulers.

The original entrance led through a large atrium, an exonarthex and a narthex. The original Justinianic bronze doors, decorated with simple crosses, survive. Unfortunately, virtually all the other Christian furnishings, including gold lamps, a silver chancel screen, a monumental pulpit with marble columns supporting a golden dome adorned with semiprecious stones, and other elements have been lost. The Muslim additions of *mihrab* and *minbar* are still in place.

The walls are constructed of thin brick, with stone used only for the main and secondary piers. The vaults, which are constructed of brick, are remarkably light and thin. Iron clamps and tie bars, as well as timber tie bars, apparently strengthened the structure from the beginning. Hagia Sophia's construction in less than five years was extremely rapid, especially given its scale.

The exterior of the building is dominated by the great central dome, the half domes that cluster below it, and the massive buttresses. The exterior is now painted an intense rosy red based on the color used in Justinian's day.

Justinian's church proved to be such an impressive religious structure that Sinan, the greatest Turkish architect, and his patron Suleiman the Magnificent used it as a model and an inspiration for many later mosques, including the Suleimaniyeh in Istanbul and the Selimiyeh at Edirne. As a result, Justinian's great church influenced the design of Ottoman mosques throughout the Middle East.

—DAVID G. WILKINS

ST. IRENE
Istanbul [Constantinople], Turkey

740: Major structural changes to earlier church (original structure built in 532, and partially rebuilt in 564).

St. Irene: Istanbul, Turkey.

Publications

MATTHEWS, THOMAS F.: *The Early Churches of Constantinople*. London, 1971.

MÜLLER-WIENER, W.: *Bildlexikon zur Topographie Istambuls*. Tübingen, Germany, 1979.

VAN MILLINGEN, E.: *Byzantine Churches in Constantinople*. London, 1912.

*

It is now known that the church of St. Irene at Constantinople, as it stands today, does not contain a single element built prior to the reign of Justinian (ruled 527-565). The architectural complex was erected after the destruction by fire of an earlier church, during the rebellion of 532. The construction of the new church was undertaken on an open and level site, no longer presenting any constraints that had to be taken into account. Besides the church proper, which is itself preceded by an atrium following the Paleochristian model, there are a number of secondary buildings and a passage, on the southern side, connecting St. Irene to its great neighbor, St. Sophia. The function of the secondary buildings is hard to determine, particularly where it concerns the buildings to the south, but also those to the north, of the church.

St. Irene is an original and important example of Byzantine architecture, but for a long time it failed to gain the recognition it deserves. The primary reason for the neglect is the difficulty in dating some of its characteristic features, arising from the fact that the church was subject to extensive reconstructions at least twice. Possibly it was also neglected, by the general public if not the researchers, because of the building's austere character in its present state of preservation. In fact, one most remembers it for the surviving mosaic cross in the vault of the apse—a rare vestige of the iconoclastic era—and for the monumental semicircular *synthronon* that follows the outline of the apse. The *synthronon* is perhaps the most striking surviving example of this type of ornamentation common in Paleochristian basilicas. It dates from 740, and probably replaced an earlier identical *synthronon*. However, apart from these two features, practically nothing survives of the original ornamentation, not even the marble facing which must have clad its walls, as it did in other churches of equal importance. It is impossible to determine whether this is due to maltreatment during the Byzantine era, or to the fact that, after the Ottoman conquest, St. Irene was not converted to a mosque, as many other churches were, but to an arsenal where arms and military trophies were kept.

It is now known that the church of Justinian's times was a true domed basilica. The dome covered the central section of the naos, and was supported by four barrel vaults. However, the western side was lengthened by an extra barrel-vaulted bay. There were galleries along three sides, which opened onto the central space through a triple arcade. This reconstruction of the earlier design was made possible by a clarification of the uncertainties introduced by a historical source, which mentioned a fire in 564. U. Peschlow's analyses have shown that there are no traces of significant reconstruction in the church itself before 740. The fire of 564 must have concerned the annexes to the south, between St. Irene and St. Sophia. Peschlow's conclusions are significant for the history of Byzantine architecture, because they prove that a domed basilica supported by barrel vaults was

St. Irene: Istanbul, Turkey, 740

constructed some time after St. Sophia but well before the end of the sixth century—undoubtedly in mid-century or a little later. The difficult issue of dating domed basilicas, which constitute a limited number of important buildings, is thus at least partially resolved. A starting date for the construction of such buildings can now be given—a date much earlier than was previously supposed. Such an early date is also supported by the recently proposed new dating of St. Sophia of Thessalonica.

The domed basilica of Justinian's times was badly damaged in an earthquake in 740, and the church resulting from the reconstruction was conceived in an entirely new and original manner. In effect, the entire upper section of the church above the galleries was reconstructed then. The most spectacular change was the introduction of an elliptical, domical vault over the western part of the naos, which must have presented considerable construction problems, given the rectangular plan of that section. The exterior of the church received its characteristic look on the western side of the central dome as a result of this modification. The dome itself was apparently reconstructed with the insertion of a drum, not present previously, which allowed for a greater elevation. At the same time, the barrel vaults were

enlarged to cover the entire width of the galleries, giving greater amplitude to the interior volume.

—J.-M. SPIESER
Translated from the French by Alla Melamed

SS. SERGIUS and BACCHUS
Istanbul [Constantinople], Turkey

525-30: Original construction.

Publications

MACDONALD, WILLIAM: *Early Christian and Byzantine Architecture*. New York, 1985.

SS. Sergius and Bacchus: Istanbul, Turkey, 525-30

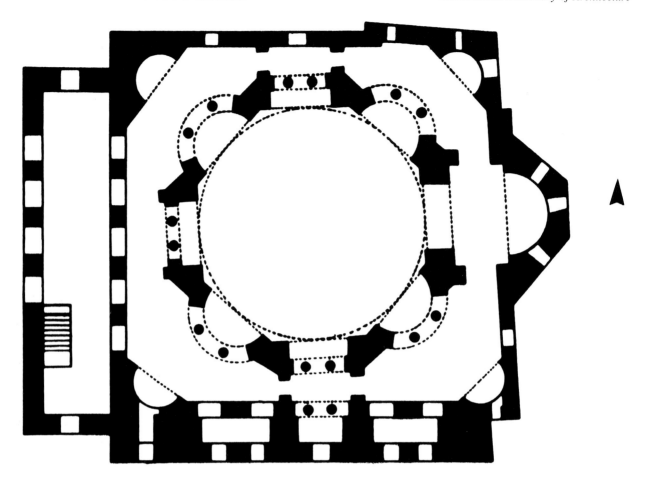

MATTHEWS, THOMAS F.: *Early Churches of Constantinople, Architecture and Liturgy*. University Park, Pennsylvania, 1971.

MÜLLER-WIENER, W.: *Bildlexikon zur Topographie Istambuls*. Tübingen, Germany, 1979.

VAN MILLINGEN, E.: *Byzantine Churches in Constantinople*. London, 1912.

*

The church consecrated to Saints Sergius and Bacchus in Constantinople is one of the most paradoxical monuments of Byzantine architecture. It is virtually unknown in spite of its significance, and it combines innovations with traditional elements, an original design with clumsy execution. In a manner of speaking, its plan anticipates to an equal degree those of San Vitale in Ravenna and of the Hagia Sophia. Such a statement is easily understood, and presents itself forcefully in a comparison of the plans of these three monuments, but it is not necessarily historically significant. It is mentioned here not to point out a historical relationship, but to further an appreciation of the monument, which, in the chronology of Constantinople churches, stands between the Church of St. Polyectus—famous

for its extraordinarily rich architectural ornamentation, though not for elevation or details of design—and the new St. Sophia.

Apart from the obviously projecting apse and the narthex, the church has a nearly square exterior plan. It appears massive because of a dome that barely disengages itself from its drum, and in spite of the articulation of buttresses that correspond, on the outside, to the concave parts of the dome. Some marked irregularities appear in this exterior envelope, and they remain as difficult to explain as are the interior irregularities. They do not, in any case, appear to be due to the presence of older walls, which might have hampered construction. The exterior square surprisingly encloses an octagonal interior plan. Irregularities are apparent there as well, particularly in the way the octagon is fit into the square. These irregularities cannot be explained except by ineptitude in execution, an ineptitude that appears astonishing in light of the quality of the design. A difference in ability between the architect and the team of engineers comes to mind, but our almost complete ignorance of the ways in which construction work was organized in the Byzantine world makes a more definite interpretation impossible.

The interior space is dominated by the dome. The supporting piers are placed so close to the outside walls as to leave only a narrow passage. In spite of being relatively small (about 15 meters in diameter), the cupola dominates the visitor's spatial impressions. Those impressions are reinforced by several factors. One of these, purely accidental, is the disappearance—during the course of the centuries and probably particularly after the building's conversion to a mosque—of the ornamentation, which was most likely polychrome. It must also be kept in

SS. Sergius and Bacchus

both predates and evidently influenced them, the capitals of SS. Sergius and Bacchus are the oldest of the type dated with certainty. Without a doubt they are the most remarkable.

—J.-M. SPIESER
Translated from the French by Alla Melamed

YEREBATAN CISTERN
Istanbul [Constantinople], Turkey

Fifth Century: Constructed.

Publications

STRZYGOWSKI and FORCHEMIR: *Die Byzantinischen Wasserbehälter von Konstantinopel.* Vienna, 1893.

*

Yerebatan Cistern, with its 12 rows of 28 columns, is the largest and most impressive of the closed cisterns in Istanbul. Although such utilitarian structures were never meant to be visited, Yerebatan Cistern, lit dramatically with artificial lighting, is now open to the public; as the visitor enters the empty interior from above ground, the effect is one of descending into a grandiose underground hypostyle hall. Known during the Byzantine period as Basilica Cistern because it was located below the public square known as the Stoa Basilica, Yerebatan Cistern is popularly known today as the "Underground Palace."

Since the advent of civilization at Istanbul's site on the Bosporus, there has been a limited supply of fresh water; there are no rivers in the urban area and local springs cannot supply ample water for a large settlement. The Romans built aqueducts to bring water to fountains, open reservoirs and closed cisterns near and in the city. The reservoirs and cisterns stored water for the growing population and were also intended to provide water in case of a prolonged siege of this strategic port city. Byzantine Constantinople had as many as six open reservoirs and more than 50 closed cisterns, but many of them were small cisterns attached to specific buildings (there were no fewer than three cisterns for the Hagia Sophia, for instance). Even one of the smallest of the open reservoirs, built in 421 by Aetius, prefect of Constantinople, was so large that it is in use today as a stadium. The Hagios Makoie Reservoir, built under the emperor Anastasius (491-518) and the largest open reservoir surviving in Istanbul, could hold 375,000 cubic meters (99 million gallons) of water.

Yerebatan Cistern, which dates from the fifth century, may be an enlargement of a cistern built by Constantine the Great (ruled 306-377). Its grandiose scale reflects its imperial purpose as the reservoir for the Great Palace of the Byzantine Emperors; after the Turkish conquest, Yerebatan Cistern served the Topkapi Sarayi Palace. Originally 140 meters (460 feet) by 70 meters (230 feet) with a floor area of 9,800 square meters (106,000 square feet), the cistern had a capacity of approximately 50 million gallons.

Binbirdirek Cistern, the second-largest of Istanbul's closed

mind, however, that the system of supports does not have much vertical impetus, in spite of the presence of galleries along three sides. The supports at the ground floor are capped with an architrave above the columns, continuing like a ribbon along the piers, which breaks the vertical movement. (The ends of the straight sides and exedras are marked by the piers bearing most of the dome's weight. Between piers there are always two columns slightly set back.) The absence of arcuation at the lower level results in the lack of one of the principal factors in the dynamism of San Vitale's interior space. The use of arcuation in the galleries does not compensate for the lack of it in the supports. The colonnades of the galleries, undoubtedly because of their great size, also have a certain heaviness, and seem to squash the interior space.

These considerations should not make one forget the strengths of the interior space, deriving from the disposition of the octagon. The octagon consists of alternating straight sides along the north-south and east-west axes, and exedras in the corners. This aspect of the design made it possible to connect the piers on the straight sides with great semicircular arches (or, if one prefers, by small barrel vaults), and to cover the exedras by small half domes, the connection being made by small pendentives. This plan also permitted an original treatment in the dome, which consists of 16 alternating straight and concave segments over the arches and pendentives, respectively.

To conclude, it must be pointed out that one of the principal originalities of the church is its sculptural ornamentation. The capitals, architraves and corbels are graced with fine, very shallow sculpture, not really in relief but very elaborate, which has been compared to lace worked in stone. Even if one knows now that the even more innovative sculpture of St. Polyectus

Yerebatan Cistern: Istanbul, Turkey, 5th century

cisterns, with a capacity of almost 19 million gallons, was built a century after Yerebatan; it is known romantically (and incorrectly) as "the Cistern of a Thousand and One Columns." At Binbirdirek, the vaults are supported by 224 double columns joined by stone tie-rods. Binbirdirek's columns, plain and uniform, are undecorated except for the occasional monogram of a stonemason on am impost capital. Binbirdirek Cistern has had a number of other uses; in the 19th century it became a workshop for the production of thread; more recently it has been used as a storehouse.

Yerebatan Cistern was apparently built with haste and economy, for the builders incorporated ancient Roman and Early Christian columns and capitals of different sizes and designs, as well as Byzantine Corinthian columns and capitals. Spolia columns that did not reach the necessary uniform height were raised on blocks. Two massive spolia blocks have huge Medusa heads carved in relief; one of these pagan images was set into place upside down, while the second is sideways. While the builders may have assumed these would never be seen, to a modern visitor their effect is distinctly surrealistic. Yerebatan is vaulted with low pendentive domes of brick embedded in thick mortar, demonstrating how Byzantine construction techniques were gradually shifting from the earlier solid stonework or concrete toward the thin brick vaulting so characteristic of the later Byzantine tradition.

—DAVID G. WILKINS AND REBECCA L. WILKINS.

YUGOSLAVIA

MONASTERY CHURCH (CHURCH OF THE ASSUMPTION)
Gračanica, Yugoslavia

1311: Commissioned by King Milutin. **1321:** Construction begun. **Ca. 1570:** Exonarthex constructed.

Publications

MILLET, G.: *L'ancien art serbe: Les Églises*. Paris, 1919.
PETKOVIC: *La Peinture serbe du moyen âge*. Belgrade, 1930.
VERCORS: *L'art médiéval Yougoslave*. Paris, 1950.

*

The Church of the Assumption of the Mother of God, also commonly referred to as "Gračanica," is the only extant structure of the monastery complex at Gračanica, located in the autonomous region of Kosovo, in the Yugoslav republic of Serbia. Originally planned as a mausoleum, the church was commissioned by the Serbian king Milutin in 1311. Like numerous other churches of the same period, the Church of the Assumption was constructed on the site of two earlier structures. The earliest church on this site was a three-aisle basilica with three apses located at its eastern end. By the 13th century, this structure was replaced by a smaller, single-aisle structure without apses.

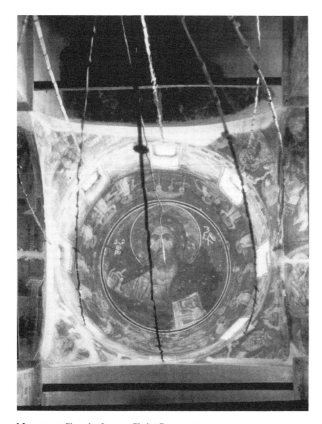

Monastery Church, fresco, Christ Pantocrator

The Church of the Assumption stylistically is best described as a Late Byzantine structure. As such, its architectural significance for that period has varied from scholar to scholar. It has been described as a significant example of Late Byzantine design in local, regional and international terms. The church is constructed of masonry bearing walls of brick, sandstone and limestone. The material is assembled in a cloissoné manner with alternating coursing, which rests upon a drywall foundation. A great discrepancy exists between the quality of the craftsmanship between the interior and the exterior masonry. The exterior stonework by far exceeds the workmanship of the interior. It may be surmised that the original intent was for the exterior surface to remain exposed, while the interior was to be left for embellishment with fresco.

In plan, the Church of the Assumption at Gračanica is a flawed rectangle. Its original design consisted of centralized naos, esonarthex, sanctuary, ambulatory wings and lateral chapels, with a gallery located above. Subsequently, an exonarthex was added west of the original structure in about 1570. As previously described, the naos occupies the central location in the building. Its plan is square, and thus is defined by four square piers. A dome, resting on an octagonal drum, rises above, while the ceiling is barrel-vaulted to the east.

Divided by a tribelon to the east of the naos is the sanctuary. Above is a blind dome. On the east wall of this space is a prothesis niche.

To the opposite side of the naos and connected to it by a low-rising, arched opening is the esonarthex. Oval in form, it is covered by a barrel-vaulted ceiling and a central groin vault. Two domes, again resting on octagonal drums, are located in the corners.

Extending from the esonarthex and located to the north and south of the naos are two ambulatory wings, both of which are barrel-vaulted. A staircase is located in the north wall of the southern wing.

Lateral chapels flank the church to the east of the ambulatory wings, and further connect to both the naos and sanctuary. Each chapel terminates to its east in an apse, enclosing an altar. A dome, resting upon an octagonal drum, functions as the ceiling of each chapel.

Above the esonarthex, and reached by the stairs in the ambulatory wing, is the barrel-vaulted gallery chamber. Double windows provide natural lighting from the exterior wall, while repeating the same into the naos below.

The exterior reads clearly as a carefully constructed Byzantine church. The two-story masonry facades are complemented by a lead-tile-clad roof. Three facades are similar in design, while the east is altered by the existence of its apses. Each of the primary facades is divided by pilasters into three bays, with the third being the highest. Each bay is further defined by a window, consisting of small circular glass quarrels embedded in a mortar base. Each window is adorned with arched surrounds.

The interior, although lacking in fine craftsmanship, is constructed primarily of sandstone. Frescoes cover most surfaces, often depicting textures such as fabric and marble *trompe l'oeil*.

Although scholars may argue about Gračanica's place in the global sphere, one cannot deny the quality of the composition of its parts, the careful placement of materials and the skillfulness of its engineering. As such, it stands as one of the best ecclesiastical examples of its era in the Byzantine sphere of influence and in the Kosovo region.

—ANDREA URBAS

Monastery Church, west facade: Gračanica, Yugoslavia, 1321

RELATED, NON-EUROPEAN AREAS

Australia

SYDNEY OPERA HOUSE
Sydney, Australia

1960-1973: Construction; **Architect:** Jørn Utzon (1918-).

Publications

ARUP, OVE, and KUNZ, C. J.: "Sydney Opera House." *Civil Engineering* 41 (1971).

BRADLEY, ANTHONY, and SMITH, TERRY (eds.): *Australian Art and Architecture*. Melbourne, 1980.

KEYS, PETER, and BREWER, COLIN: "The Sydney Opera House." *Architecture in Australia* (December 1965).

"The Sydney Opera House." *Architecture in Australia* (September 1960).

"The Sydney Opera House: What Happened and Why." *Architectural Record* 141, 5 (1967): 189-192.

UTZON, JØRN: *Sydney Opera House*. Sydney, 1962.

The Sydney Opera House was created by an act of political will and, in large measure, the problems which dogged its development had a political origin. Jørn Utzon, its architect, was not a political person.

It goes without saying that nothing, much less one of the greatest buildings of the 20th century, is created without some pain—it would be surprising if it were otherwise. The opera house gave Sydney a focus and an identity, which, up until then, it had lacked. The building expressed, in a fresh manner, the essence of its maritime location, surrounded as it is on three sides by the waters of Sydney Harbor, at the same time flanking the open front door of the city.

It is a porch and a veranda all in one—a sensuous welcome to anyone entering the city by sea—whether seen from beneath the great steel arch of the harbor bridge, from the surrounding foreshore of the harbor, or from the office towers and hotels overlooking Circular Quay. Since its completion in 1973, the Sydney Opera House has become the special symbol of the city. Quite what it says is not easy to express: there is the generous freedom of the forms, of spherical surfaces that glide over one another and climb to an elevated climax. Its open

Opera House: Sydney, Australia, 1960-73

shells shelter one another. They have a certain anonymous additive quality normally associated with the vernacular. It is a building like a ship, with its sail-like shell roofs over the two main halls—really two vessels berthed side by side.

In 1956 there was considerable interest in shell concrete and the structures of Felix Candela. However, it was Eero Saarinen who, perhaps more than any other American architect, transformed shell concrete into an expressive medium. His TWA Terminal, designed in the same year as Utzon's Opera House, is similar in its arrangement—flower petals balanced against one another in pairs to Utzon's shell unit. Whereas Saarinen's TWA Terminal shells lean outward, the Utzon shells, as realized, lean inward against one another for stability. They too, leaned outward originally, as can be seen in the competition sketches.

Both Saarinen and Utzon had adopted a "free" structural form, neither of which was crippled by a harsh geometry. There was not a circle, right angle or parabola to be seen. The TWA Terminal building retained its free form, but Utzon's design was subsequently criticized on account of this. The consulting engineers Ove Arup and Partners, called in to make adjustments to Utzon's designs, proved unequal to the challenge and insisted that the shells be controlled by geometry. This is one of the pervasive myths of the Sydney Opera House—that Utzon's concept for the shells was unbuildable. The TWA Terminal, completed in 1964, shows this to be untrue; there was also the criticism that the original shells, as sketched by Utzon, were too flat and horizontal. Once again the rebuttal is to be found in TWA.

Like Saarinen's TWA Terminal, the Sydney Opera House freed architects from what was a restricted ideology. By giving each auditorium its own separate envelope defined in accordance with volumetric and acoustic requirements—that is, the internal functions of the opera house—while adopting a sculptural solution for the roof shells in response to the requirement to be seen from all sides and above, Utzon challenged the modernist dictum that the outside should reflect what occurs on the inside; that the outside forms should directly mirror the interior functions. The design was widely viewed as undermining this leading tenet of functionalist dogma.

Sydney Harbour was formed by the flooding of two valleys. It is shaped like a large hand, with many inlets and points adding greatly to its interest. Bennelong Point, on which the opera house is sited, is one of two points on either side of Circular Quay, the main ferry passenger terminus for the city. It had previously been occupied by Fort Macquarie and, later, by an electric tram shed.

The essence of Utzon's design lies in his imaginative response to the harbor itself. A number of the competition entries were better planned and more efficient, but, by and large, they ignored their setting.

Many of the subsequent complications and later difficulties stemmed from this subordination of the functional relationships. Utzon alone appreciated the importance of place and subordinated all other considerations so that his exterior forms deal with the issue of where the building is in the landscape. The "free" shaping of the shells was the result. He did this with enormous sensitivity and poetic flair so that his building suggests both the sensual richness of opera as a musical form at the same time that it subtly encapsulates its maritime surroundings.

Another problem was the building's relationship to the city—how best to arrive and enter the opera and symphony concert halls. Utzon pushed the building out into the harbor on a seawall-enclosed base, with a platform from which he sculpted the stepped seating ramps so they resemble a pair of Greek theaters. The hall foyers are located on the north facing the water, with

the stages opposite the city. The operagoer approaches the halls from below, climbs a monumental flight of stairs, then moves around the stage backs and sides to be seated. These side spaces, pressed between the exposed V-shaped concrete ribs composing the underside of the roof shells and the timber hall casings, are among the most dramatic spaces in the opera house, their excitement being enhanced by glimpses through to the water. Each stage is serviced from below by lifts.

The white tiled shell roofs were mounted on the expansive, brown, precast, concrete-clad platform. The main hall is straddled by three asymmetrical shells, the minor hall by two, with a restaurant in a sixth shell on its own on the southwestern corner of the platform. A stunning, narrow canyon-like space is formed between the cleavage of the two principal halls. The open ends of the shells were to have been enclosed by a suspended saddle-shaped membrane of glass, resembling a Frei Otto-like cable saddle network, but this was subsequently rationalized to a stiff hood that spills out brusquely over the foyer edges.

Jørn Utzon's involvement ended on 28 February 1966, when his tendered resignation was accepted by the New South Wales minister for public works, Davis Hughes. The project was completed by Hanson, Todd and Partners; and Rudder, Littlemore, and Rudder, with Peter Hall as designer.

The competition had called for a building that contained two halls, one large and one small. The large hall was to seat 3,500 people for symphony concerts, large-scale opera, ballet and dance, choral works, pageants and mass meetings. The small hall was to seat 1,200 people for drama, intimate opera, chamber music, concerts, recitals and lectures. There was to be a 250-seat restaurant, light refreshment rooms, two meeting rooms seating 100 and 200 people, lounges, cloakrooms and bars "easily accessible to the exterior for day-to-day use." Following Utzon's departure, opera was relegated to the small hall, and the large hall was devoted to symphony concert performances.

The interiors as completed fall far short, in regard to both quality and concept, of those proposed by Utzon. The design of the halls is disappointing, the small opera hall being the best of the two in terms of scale and in the unity of its forms. In place of Utzon's grand synthesis—each detail and part being related to the geometry and thought animating the whole—the work has been determined pragmatically almost on an ad hoc basis, with the result that the quality varies considerably.

It was Utzon, and not Ove Arup and Partners, who ultimately supplied the geometrical model of the shells by obtaining them from the surfaces of two spheres, and who sought to harmonize the auditorium vaults by generating them from revolving drums in a series of radial slices converging on the stage areas. It was Utzon who insisted on prefabrication, but at the same time humanized the results by combining similar units to create variety and to adapt each solution to its unique context. These principles, such as the "kit of parts" and "additive form," he was to pursue and refine in his subsequent projects.

The Sydney Opera House is important because it challenged the rationalism of modern architecture with a romantic Scandinavian expressionism whose form appeals to an emotional sensibility. The freshness of the architecture, which has not aged in the least or become any less enjoyable with time, points to something that was lacking—the proper recognition of place as supplying much more than an objective scientific rationale for building decisions. Instead, buildings may find their inspiration in the uniqueness of their site and, in turn, illuminate and translate in human terms what those surroundings mean culturally. By binding a building to its site, as happened with the Sydney Opera House, Utzon showed how place could give meaning and an identity to an entire city.

—PHILIP DREW

Hong Kong

HONG KONG BANK
Hong Kong

1979-85. Architect: Foster Associates (Norman Foster, born 1935).

Publications

DAVIES, COLIN: *High Tech Architecture.* New York, 1988.

DODWELL, C. R. (ed.): *Norman Foster, Architect: Selected Works 1962-84.* Exhibition catalog. Manchester, 1984.

"Foster Associates: Hongkong and Shanghai Banking Corporation Headquarters." *Architectural Design* (March/April 1981).

"Foster Associates: The Architecture of the Near Future." *Space Design* (special issue, March 1982).

"Hongkong and Shanghai Bank." *Architectural Review* (special issue, April 1986).

"Hongkong and Shanghai Banking Corporation." *GA Document* 16.

KING, FRANK (ed.): *Eastern Banking: Essays in the History of the Hongkong and Shanghai Banking Corporation.* London, 1983.

LAMBOT, IAN: *The New Headquarters for the Hongkong and Shanghai Banking Corporation.* Hong Kong, 1986.

WILLIAMS, STEPHANIE: *Hongkong Bank: The Building of Norman Foster's Masterpiece.* London and Boston, 1989.

*

Completed in 1985 to the designs of Foster Associates, the 47-story headquarters building for the Hong Kong Bank represents the most imaginative office building of the decade.

Hong Kong is the world's third-largest financial center, and the Hong Kong and Shanghai Bank was a major force in the colony, with a picture of its building on Hong Kong's $500 notes. Since 1864 the bank had occupied its site at 1 Queens Road Central, facing Statue Square and the harbor. The bank built its first headquarters building on the site in 1886, and that ornate classical building was replaced in 1935 by Palmer and Turner's stone tower, at 220 feet and the tallest building in Asia. By the 1970s the Palmer and Turner building was dwarfed by its neighbors, and was clearly due for replacement.

In 1979 the Hong Kong and Shanghai Bank, later known simply as the Hong Kong Bank, invited seven of the leading architectural practices of the world to submit designs for a new building with the brief that it was to be "the best in the world." The inclusion of Foster Associates was a brave gesture, for they had never built a high-rise or a major urban structure. It may well have been their lack of experience at building conventional office towers that led Foster Associates to come up with an original solution and to win the competition.

The Foster office has always enjoyed the demand for change inherent in most organizations, and to enable the bank building to change, it has been given big open floor areas, with services, stairs, structure and other vertical elements pulled to four great towers placed on each of the two side streets. Recalling the servicing towers at Louis Kahn's Richards Medical Research Building in Philadelphia, the eight great towers at Hong Kong

are a dominant feature of the architecture; they give the building a richness of expression lacking in most modern office towers, with their central cores and identical skin all around. The design that won the competition had all eight towers the same height, with great trusses spanning between them, but as the design developed, the towers were made to vary in height to respond to the daylight requirements of the Hong Kong building code, which forced the height down to 35 stories on Des Voeux Road and 28 stories on Queens Road. This variation in height, contained within the firm geometry of the building, gives interest and richness to the design.

Standing next to each of the eight service towers is a structural element consisting of four round steel columns. In the competition-winning scheme, Warren trusses spanned between the towers three times in the height of the building, and intermediate floors were hung from these. The structure between these towers went through many stages of development before the final "coat hanger" scheme was adopted. In this design the four tubes forming each column are linked together at each story level, and these cross-links have splayed haunches, an example of the muscular revealing of structure that is consistent throughout the design. Five times in the height of the building are the "coat hanger" cantilevers, forming and marking the double-height floors. From the outer points of these cantilevers, hangers drop to support the intermediate floors, and all this structure is clearly revealed on the outside to give the building its characteristic image.

The 33-meter space between the column clusters provides the open office floors supported at mid-span by hangers extending down from the ends of the coathangers. The other ends of the coat hangers, extending outward from the column clusters, also have hangers. These hangers support staircases, lifts and service modules. Some of the service modules contain mechanical and air-handling plant, and others contain the lavatories; these elements of the building were prefabricated, with all their fittings and finishes, in Japan and delivered to the site at night for hoisting into place. But it was not only the service modules that were completely made in another country: because Hong Kong has a limited manufacturing base, the architects toured the world for the best products and the best prices. The steel frame was made in England, the gray aluminum cladding was made in the United States and, in contrast to all this sophisticated Western technology, the Chinese *Fung-Shui* experts had to be satisfied that the designs would bring good luck to the bank.

In the past, service runs in office buildings have been within the suspended ceiling. The Foster office had experience with under-floor servicing from the Willis, Faber and Dumas building in Ipswich, and developed the idea further at Hong Kong. 1200 sq floor panels cover a 600 void containing air conditioning and other services, with air introduced into the offices by circular grilles in the floor.

Most office buildings of this size are served impersonally by lifts. In this building the lifts stop at the five double-height floors, which occur at the same level as the coat hangers of the structure. So these double-height spaces become meeting places, and break the building down into units of comprehensible size. From the double-height floors, access to the office floors is by escalator.

The completed building can be seen as a complete rethinking of the office tower as a building type. It can also be seen as achieving the architects' ambition of bringing the craft of building nearer to the level of production in the aerospace industry, and of giving it an image to suit.

—JOHN WINTER

Hong Kong Bank Headquarters: Hong Kong, China, 1979-85

Syria

KRAK DES CHEVALIERS
Syria

Ca. 1142-92: Knights Hospitallers remodeled 11th-century Moslem fortress. Three towers added later. Restored. **Late 12th-early 13th century:** Inner defenses built. **Latin occupation:** Inner gatehouse, inner northwest postern tower and chapel added before it became a hospital. **Gothic period:** Vaulted loggia in upper court built.

Publications

BOASE, T. S. R.: *Castles and Churches of the Crusading Kingdom.* London, 1967.

DESCHAMPS, PAUL: *Les châteaux des croises en Terre-Sainte: Le Crac des Chevaliers.* Paris, 1934.

KING, D. J. C.: "The Taking of Le Krak des Chevaliers in 1271." *Antiquity* 23 (1949): 83-92.

LAWRENCE, T. E.: *Crusader Castles.* Oxford, 1988.

*

Medieval military science finds its most complete and dramatic expression in the castle of Krak des Chevaliers. Sitting atop a mountain ridge more than 2,000 feet above the valley floor, the bold silhouette of Krak seems to grow out of the terrain. It is a manmade addition to the precipitous defenses of nature, improving and expanding upon the lack of accessibility provided

Krak des Chevaliers: Syria, ca. 1142-92

by the site. The approaches to the fortress are controlled through careful design, and the massive defenses of ashlar masonry reduce the need for a large garrison of men.

Removed from the main lines of attack, Krak's position overlooking the valley gave it an extended view of the approaches to Tripoli, an invaluable position in the frontier defenses of the Crusaders. As long as Krak remained in the hands of the Hospitallers, the Moslem reconquest of the Levant could not be completely successful. It is a testament to the castle's imposing presence that Saladin decided against attacking it in 1187, and Krak did not fall into Arab hands until 1271. It is noteworthy that when the garrison did surrender, it was as the result of treachery rather than because the inner defenses had been compromised.

The core of the fortress consists of an irregular polygon conforming to the outlines of the escarpment. A circuit wall forms the boundary of the polygon and is strengthened by semicircular towers. This inner wall overlooks an outer wall, the latter added after Saladin's campaign. The presence of this double line of defense created a concentric plan, which was not employed in Europe until the end of the 13th century. The multiplication of fortified walls at Krak made the catapults of attackers less effective, and also gave the Hospitallers a platform for counteraction in the event that the first line was breached.

The south flank of the castle was the side most vulnerable to attack and was also the area of greatest fortification. Between the inner and outer circuit walls was a ditch carved out of the rock, serving both as an obstacle and a reservoir. Behind the ditch rises a great sloped wall of stone flanked by two semicircular towers. This massive batter is sloped to discourage escalation as well as sapping, while the towers allowed the defenders to fire upon attackers approaching the base of the wall.

The inner wall and towers are also provided with passageways that have arrow slits for archers, and the batter is crowned by a series of machicolations, permitting the dropping of missiles upon the enemy below. The main defensive front was further strengthened by the addition of three inner towers, buttressing the batter. This defensive system of fortification was the most advanced found in the medieval world during the 12th and 13th centuries, reflecting the constant adaptation of the builders at Krak to new developments in siegecraft.

The inner and outer circuit walls are connected by a long, bent ramp on the east face. This ramp leads from an outer gatehouse into the courtyard where conventual buildings abut the inner wall. These buildings are often multistory and are vaulted throughout in stone. The three massive towers on the south side provided housing for the knights, while great vaulted chambers along the north and west faces held the kitchen, latrines and staff living quarters, as well as a covered well. The chapel, with a pointed barrel vault in the northeast corner, faces a chapter house and loggia, exquisitely covered with ribbed vaults and ornamented with delicate Gothic tracery.

The monastic character of the Hospitallers is as fully expressed in the inward-turning buildings of the courtyard as their military character is revealed in the massive fortifications of the ashlar walls. The chapel and chapter house reflect contemporary developments in French ecclesiastical architecture, particularly those of Provence and Burgundy. The defenses of Krak, however, were superior to any European developments in 13th-century military architecture. Even the design of Château Gaillard, said to reflect the influence of Crusader technology, was not as advanced as the concentric plan of Krak des Chevaliers, built almost a century earlier.

—KATHRYN McCLINTOCK

THE
AMERICAS

BRAZIL

FEDERAL CAPITAL COMPLEX
Brasília, Brazil

1956-61. Architect: Oscar Niemeyer (born 1907).

Publications

"Brasília." *Acropole* (São Paulo; special issue, July/August 1970).

COSTA, LUCÍO: "L'Urbaniste défend sa capitale." *Architecture: Formes et fonctions* (Lausanne). 14 (1968).

"Cultural Scientific Institute, Brasília." *AC: International Asbestos Cement Review* (April 1980).

EVENSON, NORMA: *Two Brazilian Capitals: Architecture and Urbanism in Rio de Janeiro and Brasília.* New Haven, Connecticut, 1973.

HOLSTON, JAMES: *The Modernist City: An Anthropological Critique of Brasília.* Chicago, 1989.

MAGALHAES, A., and FELDMAN, E.: *Doorway to Brasília.* Philadelphia, 1959.

NIEMEYER, OSCAR: *Minha experiência em Brasília.* Rio de Janeiro, 1961.

NIEMEYER, OSCAR: *Textes et dessins pour Brasília.* Paris, 1965.

STAUBLI, WILLY: *Brasília.* Stuttgart, 1965.

*

The new capital of Brazil, replacing Rio de Janeiro in that capacity in 1960, Brasília is a monument to the determination and political ambition of President Juscelino Kubitschek, of modern Brazil's major planner and architect, Lúcio Costa and Oscar Niemeyer, respectively, and of the masses of Brazilian laborers who erected the frontier "city of the future" practically overnight. More than any other modern planning achievement, the creation of the Brazilian capital was the opportunity to realize the modernist dream of a futuristic city that would be both a work of art that symbolized national modernization as well as a motor for that development. An architect's rather than a planner's image of the modernist utopia, Brasília represents the realization of a primarily Corbusian ideal of the mechanized motor city created by a single architect striving for a unity of formal conception with an emphasis on technical and rational considerations in urban design. A large-scale laboratory for the evolution of International Style forms, the city reflects Niemeyer's unique capacity for pushing modern architecture to its formal and technical limits. Building upon Costa's plan, he created within its vast spaces a unified ensemble of distinct architectural monuments noteworthy for their classic volumetric purity, dynamic plastic richness and provocative visual power.

A project of unprecedented scope and colossal scale, Brasília was intended both to initiate and to represent Kubitschek's campaign for Brazilian development, advertised in the slogan "Fifty years of progress in five." Aware of the political vicissitudes of Brazilian political administrations and determined not to let his own project founder in the regime of a less-inspired successor, Kubitschek focused on building a city quickly rather than taking the time to plan it thoroughly beforehand. Inseparable from the city's development was the president's support of Brazil's fledgling automobile and aviation industries. While Brasília's great distance from Brazil's major cities on the Atlantic coast meant that the new capital would be accessible primarily by airplane, its regional and interior circulation system of multilane superhighways demanded the automobile. Perhaps the most stunning aspect of Brasília's achievement is that the city and the technical infrastructure required to make it function were for the most part completed during Kubitschek's relatively short administration (1956-60).

Although the dream of a new capital in the Brazilian hinterland dates back to late colonial times and the movement for an independent Brazil, it was not until 1891 that the legislative groundwork for the new city was laid. A constitutional article called for the setting aside of 14,400 square kilometers on the central plateau, and a bill was passed authorizing the exploration and demarcation of the site. After a number of field studies and postponements of the decision, a site was finally chosen in 1953, during the Vargas administration. Three criteria were essential for the selection of the site. First, it had to be centrally located with respect to the population of the nation. Second, it needed to be centrally located to stimulate interregional transport and communications linkages. It had long been observed that too much of Brazil's population and economic activity had been concentrated in the Atlantic coastal cities. Third, proximity to interstate borders was sought because it would foster political and administrative unification of the nation. A fourth, unstated criterion concerned Brasília's projected role in the politics of Brazilian "developmentalism": the capital was to be a new "center" from which capitalist wealth, modern technology and "democratic" ideology would "trickle down" to the masses and the underdeveloped regions of the vast nation.

By April 1955 an expanded site (58,014 square kilometers) of gentle, shrubby savanna terrain bordering the states of Minas Gerais and Goiás had been surveyed during a 10-month period using aerial photography, a technique introduced into Brazil in 1927 by the French planner Alfred Agache in his master plan for Rio de Janeiro. Agache had tried in vain to enact a plan that would reform the old capital and its inefficient government bureaucracy. But Rio, with its long colonial history, its seductive beaches and culture, and its touristy atmosphere of leisurely self-indulgence, was widely considered unfit for the responsibilities of a serious administrative center of the future.

Elected to the presidency without a majority mandate, Kubitschek saw in the creation of a new capital not only a chance to reform the old Brazil, but also a means to insure the popular legitimation he so urgently needed. Perceiving and adroitly manipulating the widespread popular interest in the idea of a new capital, he moved quickly to secure congressional authorization for the establishment of a government corporation (NOVACAP) to oversee the city's construction. Niemeyer was appointed its director and headed the jury convened to judge the competition entries submitted for the design of the new capital. A number of projects were put forth, all characterized by their appropriation of garden-city planning elements: functional zoning, traffic separation systems, the use of a greenbelt as an urban divider, and residential areas ordered according to superblocks and neighborhood units. In the vast spatial context of the Brazilian central plateau, however, most of the proposals suffered from a fragmentation of space and forms, and from an excessive concern with a rational geometric ordering that was generally insensitive to the topography of the site. They

Federal Capital Complex, Congress: Brasília, Brazil, 1956-61

were generalized solutions which, in their oversimplification and schematization of functions and spaces, reflected a European textbook solution. But the successful design would have to be above all *Brazilian,* flexible to the needs of the future (as yet not very clearly defined by the architects), and responsive to the inspired spirit of willful improvisation that had been the very soul of Kubitschek's effort from the start.

The winning project by Lúcio Costa was at once the least detailed and the most brilliant of the entries. Costa presented his plan as a sudden inspiration, the product of a moment's creative extemporization based on his own intuitive understanding of the problem. For Costa, the plan of Brasília had to be above all a national symbol and a monumental work of art that

would clearly and appealingly express the goal and function of a monumental capital. In a few freehand sketches and a brief statement, Costa presented the idea of the capital in terms of a great crossing of monumental axes that was, on one level, an emblem of the primal act of bringing civilization to a virgin territory, and on another level, a visual expression of the marriage of the government functions of one axis and the domestic functions of the other. For Costa, it was the pleasing aesthetic idea and the creative artist that ruled supreme. The creation of an attractive image that could be appreciated in the same immediate way that a man appreciates a beautiful woman—this was the essence of his plan and the key to his civilizing act of consummation. As he put it: "When we see a beautiful

Federal Capital Complex, Ministry of Defense

woman we don't need much time to know we are pleased.''
What was important was the dramatic overture and conquest
of the ''virgin'' land. The details of this difficult ''marriage''
between inspired art and a reformed society, between ruling
well and living right, could be worked out in good time. Sooner
or later, it was assumed, the benefits of the actions of the genius,
taken on behalf of the people, would ''trickle down.''

The Brasília plan stressed a unity of artistic conception that
was perhaps most evident to those arriving in the city by plane
and glimpsing it for the first time from above. Falling in love
with such an image after a superficial aerial glance, of course,
presumes the same infatuation for modern transportation forms
that we find in Le Corbusier. But whereas Le Corbusier had
preferred the ocean liner, Costa's Brasília plan, appropriately,
describes the body of a huge aircraft: the long and straight
government axis is the fuselage—its cockpit is the brain center
in the governmental complex of the Praça dos Tres Poderes
(Plaza of the Three Powers). The great arcing axis that intersects
the fuselage describes the wings. It is on this curving ''domestic'' axis that we find the residential districts of the bureaucrats
whose idealistically projected rational behaviors were to determine the future direction of this new urban machine. Their
efficient performance was essential to the capital's flight plan:
Brasília could never have taken off without them. Adding to
the aviation theme is the fact that the multilane superhighways,
traffic interchanges and interurban transport terminals that define the center of the city were conceived in the high-speed
spirit of an airport: avenues became runways for cars which,
once cleared for departure on the speedway, could find little
chance of turning back. The death of the traditional urban street

system and the rise of the one-way access ramp celebrate unidi-
rectional velocity and the city's uncompromising commitment
to forward progress.

If Brasília was a city that left many of the details to the
imagination, it fell to the sculptural imagination of Niemeyer
to fill in at least the main architectural details. In designing the
major structures of the new city, he focused his efforts on the
governmental structures along the monumental axis. Within the
spatial, formal and political hierarchy of the modernist utopia,
the ''control center'' in and around the Plaza of the Three
Powers received the most lavish attention. Against the bleak
rectangular backdrop of the twin slabs of the Secretariat, Niemeyer cast the two curving compositions (one concave, the other
convex) of the Congress and Chamber of Deputies. Enamored of
the free-form curve, Niemeyer there achieved a sculptural power
that depended not on its sympathetic reflection of the curving
forms of the natural landscape, as the forms designed in his
native Rio often did, but on the stark juxtaposition and visual
contrast of the rectilinear and the curvilinear. What unites the
forms and unifies the composition is the purity of interior volume they define and the complexity of the vast urban spaces with
which they interact. As works of urban sculpture, Niemeyer's
buildings in Brasília are incomparable; as functioning works
of architecture, they have often been intensely criticized for
sacrificing social depth to the aesthetic effect of the impressive
facade.

Niemeyer's Alvorada and Planalto Palaces exemplify his interest in creating visually rich urban facades behind which lie
the simplest International Style rectangular boxes of glass and
concrete. By encasing these boxes in systems of concrete arches,

columns and piers, an appearance of incredible structural lightness and a weightless, ephemeral quality is achieved: there is nothing here of the brutalistic treatment that characterized Le Corbusier's capital in the Punjab, Chandigarh. Instead, Niemeyer's extroverted buildings achieve an almost classic refinement and a timeless, floating monumentality; they are above all products of and interactive participants in the vast space and unique urban drama that are Brasília.

Innovative structural expression and the interpenetration of exterior space and interior volume are themes forcefully explored in the Brasília Cathedral. The powerful sculptural presence created by its curving structural members, with its glazed interstices and crown-like superstructure, is again accentuated by its placement against the backdrop of the uninspired rectangular slabs of the ministry buildings beyond. In Niemeyer's Brasília, the masterpieces shine forth all the more because so much of the city's architecture celebrates the monotonously standardized and prefabricated, the simplified and regularized, the disciplined and the redundant. In a city in which the strictest governmental control was to regulate what was built and how, it was Niemeyer's good fortune to have a fairly exclusive carte blanche on artistic freedom.

In addition to the major buildings along the monumental axis, including a supreme court, the foreign ministry, the theater and the commercial sector with hotels, banks and shopping facilities, Niemeyer also standardized Brasília's housing into four basic types: six-story apartment blocks (accounting for 90 percent of the total housing in the city); lower-cost, three-story units; single-family units (one- or two-story); and row houses. Following Le Corbusier, he saw the multifamily apartment building as the best solution to the problem of modern housing.

Although Brasília's impressive utopian urbanism and bold monuments have taken their deserved places in the critical histories of modern architecture, many of the important details that were not addressed by the original "planning" remain to be worked out. Most pressing of all are the social details: Brasília's working people. The question of where these "details" are to be housed has not been resolved. Or perhaps it has. The vast labor force required to construct the city could not be accommodated in the original housing proposals. What has emerged as a result is a peripheral ring of "temporary" workers' camps that have become permanent shantytowns for the lower classes of Brasília. For all its impressive beauty, the modernist "utopia" has failed to transform fundamentally the Brazilian society it supposedly sought to reform.

—DAVID UNDERWOOD

MINISTRY OF EDUCATION AND HEALTH
Rio De Janeiro, Brazil

1936-43: Construction; **Architects:** Oscar Niemeyer (1907-) and Lúcio Costa (1902-).

Publications

BRUAND, Y.: *Arquitectura Contemporânea no Brasil.* São Paulo, 1981.
EVENSON, NORMA: *Two Brazilian Capitals: Architecture and Urbanism in Rio de Janeiro and Brasília.* New Haven, Connecticut, 1973.
FRAMPTON, KENNETH, and FUTAGAWA, YUKIO: *Modern Architecture: 1920-1945.* New York, 1983.

*

The Ministry of Education and Health Building in Rio de Janeiro (1936-43) was the first monumental public structure in the style of Corbusian modernism to be officially sanctioned and erected in Brazil. Commissioned by the reform-minded minister of education, Gustavo Capanema, the building was the complex product of a fruitful artistic and technical collaboration between Le Corbusier and a talented team of young Brazilian architects and artists headed by Lúcio Costa and Oscar Niemeyer.

Dissatisfied with the academic- and historicist-style entries selected in a design competition sponsored in 1935, Capanema, who presided over the jury, paid the winners their cash prizes and called on Costa (who had submitted a disqualified project) to come up with a new, more modernist solution that would move Brazil forward into the mainstream of modern European architecture. Capanema's arbitrary action, though initially creating an outrage, was gradually accepted in part because of the increasing public recognition that Costa, who had initiated the curricular reform of Rio's Escola de Belas Artes in 1930-31, was the undisputed leader of the new generation of Brazilian architects. In an apparent effort to minimize the perception of the arbitrariness of his decisions and to "democratize" the design process, Capanema called on three other architects who had submitted disqualified modernist projects—Carlos Leão, Affonso Reidy and Jorge Moreira—to participate with Costa in elaborating a new design. A team composed of the best young Brazilian architects, it was felt, would result in a better, more broadly based Brazilian work. To this group of four would be added two others: Ernani Vasconcellos, whose inclusion was insisted upon by his usual collaborator Moreira, and the energetic and ambitious Oscar Niemeyer, who, determined not to be left out, imposed his own participation on his colleagues by calling attention to his work as Costa's chief draftsman. This definitive design team, formed in early 1936, was a highly homogeneous group: all were students of the reformed fine arts academy, and all were committed to the functionalist principles of Le Corbusier.

The team's commitment to Corbusian doctrine was reinforced by the intimate personal contact with the European master that occurred during his six-week stay in Rio beginning in July 1936. Invited to consult on the Ministry project and a plan for a *cidade universitária,* Le Corbusier delivered a series of conferences and soon assumed leadership over the initial planning for the Ministry. The evolution of the design and the form of the building as it was executed, however, illustrate that the Brazilian team went well beyond Le Corbusier's tutelage to create their own richer, more characteristically Brazilian masterpiece, one that would advertise the progress of Brazilian modernism internationally.

Le Corbusier's contribution, most strongly felt in the early stages of the design, consisted in moving the Brazilians away from certain academic tendencies that characterized early Brazilian functionalism. Rejecting their preference for symmetrical dispositions and absolute regularity of masses, he proposed a more plastic solution that called for a sweeping, horizontal mono-block instead of the beaux-arts U-form composition they preferred. Building upon Le Corbusier's innovation but rejecting his suggestion of a waterfront site for the building, the Brazilian team elaborated their design from his second project,

Ministry of Education and Health: Rio de Janeiro, Brazil, 1936-43

one with an asymmetrical disposition of masses that was nonetheless sensitive to the surrounding street pattern of the chosen center-city lot. From that, the team worked out a number of important adaptations that resulted most importantly in an emphasis on the vertical character of the building and its adaptability to the local climate. The Brazilian variant of Le Corbusier's ''fixed'' *brise-soleil* (sunbreaker), a concrete grid proposed for the facades of a 1933 Algiers project, was the horizontal *quebra-sol,* a system of movable louvers that could be adjusted for increased luminosity in accordance with the changing angle of the sun. The application of the *quebra-sol* system across the

entire facade resulted in greater balance between horizontal elements and the verticality of the block and, more important, in an increased plastic effect, and greater unity, proportion and formal purity.

Le Corbusier's original proposal for a composition of three distinct volumes—the principal office block, the exposition salon (perpendicular to the main block) and the conference salon (across from the exposition salon)—was carefully modified by the Brazilian design team into two continuous perpendicular volumes. This new arrangement, achieved by placing the exposition and conference salons on the same axis, resulted in a more unified composition. The main block and exposition wing thus intersect at the conference salon, which was not constructed on pilotis but directly on the ground floor. The height of the conference chamber demanded that the pilotis of the main block be increased in height from the original four meters to 10 if the intersection of the two wings was to be visually and volumetrically congruous. The team's handling of the height and structural details of their own, more slender pilotis led to an effect very different from that intended by Le Corbusier. In the exposition wing, the pilotis were moved outward from the body of the structure and conceived as columns that supported their superstructure with small consoles or brackets of reinforced concrete. The result was the new sense of daring structural lightness that is often associated with the work of Oscar Niemeyer, who was probably also behind the suggestion that the pilotis of the main block be heightened. In 1940, Costa left the direction of the team to Niemeyer, whose impact on the plastic

conception of the ensemble was by that time the preponderant force in the evolution of the design.

The overall impact of the Brazilian modifications to Le Corbusier's ideas was the creation of a work that was at once more monumental and more dynamic. To this must be added the typically Brazilian interest in formal lyricism and decorative exuberance manifest in the colorful *azulejo* (ceramic tile) wall panels of Cândido Portinari. The inclusion of the *azulejos* by Portinari, the works of the sculptors Bruno Giorgi, Antônio Celso and Jacques Lipchitz, and the landscape gardening of Roberto Burle Marx marks the Ministry building as a milestone in Brazilian artistic collaboration and the first major example of Brazilian modernism's valorization of architecture as a *tour-de-force* showcase of a multimedia ensemble of great plastic richness and formal unity.

—DAVID K. UNDERWOOD

CANADA

MISSISSAUGA CITY HALL
Mississauga, Toronto, Canada

Ca. 1982: Construction; **Architects:** Kirkland and Jones.

Publications

ARNELL, P. and BICKFORD, T., ed.: *Mississauga City Hall, A Canadian Competition*. 1984.

JONES, E. and KIRKLAND, M.: "The Design of the City Hall." *Mississauga City Hall: A Canadian Competition*. New York, 1985.

MURRAY DE FORT-MENARES, A.: "Issues of Hierarchy and Social Ritual: Mississauga City Hall." *SSAC Bulletin* 4 (1985).

*

If Kirkland and Jones' Mississauga City Hall emerges as one of Canada's premier monuments of postmodernism, it is a distinction derived from broadly cast contemporary discourse involving not only the polemics of architectural style, but also the critical problematics of sense and meaning of place in the last, mass-mediated and technocratic, decades of the 20th century. Aesthetically, the building is a pastiche of distinctive formal elements borrowed flagrantly from the seemingly contradictory vocabularies of Italian Renaissance classicism and rural Ontario vernacular, thus objectifying the double coding that postmodernism often involves and inviting the wide and abstract interpretation that metaphor in architecture always engenders. Culturally, the building presents parallel conflations of sense and meaning of place concerning the connotations and denotations of a civic structure. Traditionally, the city hall is an urban typology, but in Mississauga, a suburb situated approximately 16 kilometers due west of Toronto, there is no city per se; the traditionally monumental, place-making urban form must derive its context from the suburban strip development that surrounds it. Indeed, if the blurring of traditionally clear-cut domains of ideology and place, and the celebration of difference are the hallmarks of postmodernism, then Mississauga City Hall, which blurs the urban with the suburban, the suburban with the rural, the historicized with the vernacular, and the public accountability of civic architecture with the esoteric gamesmanship of interpreting and burlesquing precedent, is most assuredly a building of its era.

A 1982 competition determined the design of Mississauga City Hall. Of 246 submissions, the Kirkland and Jones scheme was the unanimous selection of a jury which included such luminary tastemakers as architect James Stirling and Phyllis Lambert, founder of the Canadian Center of Architecture. The overarching appeal of the scheme may well have derived from the broadly based cultural cohesions the architects sought to embody in their design. Kirkland and Jones drew their conceptual references from two Ontario traditions: climatically influenced site situation and regional vernacular precedent. In keeping with the milieu of the province's acclaimed civic structures—the Dominion Parliament Buildings in Ottawa, Toronto's Old and New City Halls, and the Ontario Provincial Legislative Buildings, also in Toronto—the Mississauga building faces south. Yet in contrast to those urban precedents, the architects asserted a rural paradigm, the farmsteads which once dominated Mississauga, suggesting that the building becomes indigenous to Ontario through its aggregation of clustered building parts, designed to recall the formal play among farmhouses, silos and barns. However, it is demanding to find the metaphor of the silo in the great drum that houses Mississauga's Council Chamber or to identify the windmill that is purportedly the source of the city hall's clock tower, a highly referential element that also evokes urban town squares.

Ultimately, the building attains its formal cohesion through intentionally hierarchic and monumental devices, subsumed in the language of Italian Renaissance classicism although the city hall recalls the villa as readily as it does the *palazzo communale*. No doubt, this merger of memories of accessible and referential traditions appealed to the jury. Mississauga City Hall's pluralistic and essentially narrative content emerged on the highest waves of early postmodern monuments such as Philip Johnson's AT&T Building (New York, 1978-84), Michael Graves' Portland (Oregon) Municipal Services Building (1980) and Charles Moore's Piazza d'Italia (New Orleans, 1975-80). The 1982 date of the Mississauga competition was still early in the postmodern era, and its concern for bringing high cultural concerns more closely in step with daily life and shared cultural experiences common to both the producers and consumers of the built environment as a cultural text were undoubtedly at the forefront of the architect's, and the jurors', minds.

For Mississauga, however, the environmental constructs of daily life, are, in reality, the contemporary architectural lowest common denominator of the suburban commercial strip and its equally anonymous housing stock. In the absence of satisfactory local references, on a site a stone's throw from a regional shopping center and ringed by 12-story towers, it is not surprising that Kirkland and Jones were compelled to draw from known traditions to create a recognizably public building. Like an ancient temple and, in spite of the sea of parking that surrounds it, to attain monumentality, the building is lifted on a base five feet above ground level. A broad entry piazza, with elegant reflecting pool conceived to function as a skating rink in winter months, and flanking arcades terminating in pyramid-roofed pavilions establish a formal and ritualistic procession toward the principal (south) elevation. Its inherent classicism, subsuming the essence of a temple front in its elevational treatment, is a foil to the careful articulation of its parts—including the aforementioned council chamber, administrative areas, theater, gallery, conservatory and the imagistically forceful clock tower—that is clearly discerned from the north elevation. As a multipurpose facility housing both government and community uses, the city hall becomes a city in miniature, an urban village concisely packaged for its suburban site. The city hall's architectonic content becomes its own context, making its own memories of urban experience.

Inside, a skylighted "great hall" unifies the functionally disparate building. Here again, classical proportions prevail in geometrically disposed interior elevations and ornamentation, but the material richness of their treatment, replete with verde alpe Carerra marble banded with black granite rising above a pink marble floor, underscores the traditional political and

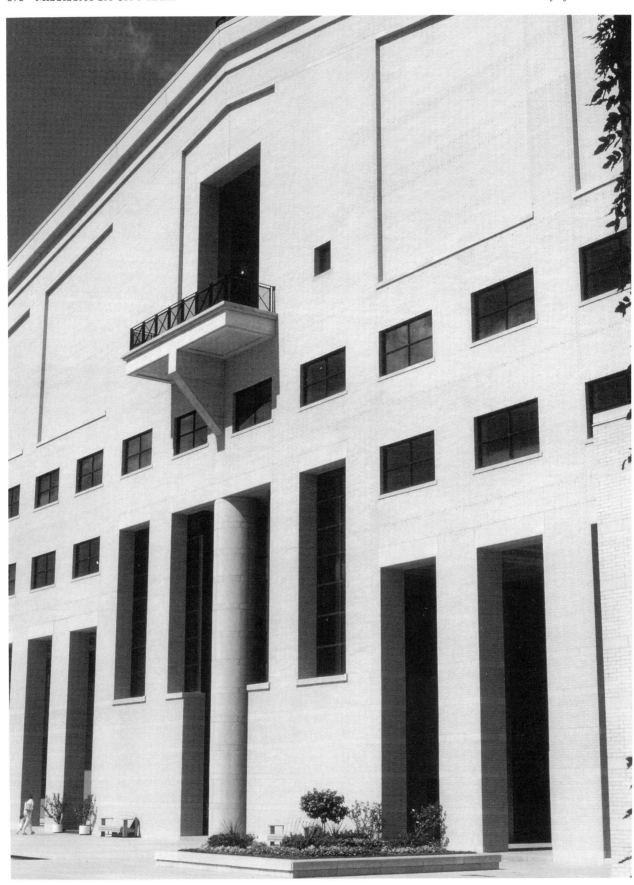

Mississauga City Hall: Mississauga, Toronto, Canada, ca. 1982

economic connotations of a palace of government, rather than those of a culturally accessible palace of the people. It thus objectifies Michel Foucault's interpretation of power as a construct of cultural hierarchy. The esoteric gamesmanship of postmodernism is also well at work in the design of the monumental stair that leads from the great hall to the administrative tower. The stair, a burlesque of Michelangelo's Laurentian Library stair, intellectually undercuts the architects' expressed intentions, their purported high regard for the regional vernacular. Equally problematic is the collision of classical paradigm, contemporary abstraction and materials, and native folk tradition in the handling of the council chamber, a cylindrical space defined by paired Tuscan columns and capped with a domed ceiling. Painted to evoke the color of the evening sky, the dome features a portrayal of the native American legend of the Great Bear and the Seven Hunters, which is uncomfortably juxtaposed against the council room frieze, emblazoned with the names of the 12 municipalities and communities that comprise Mississauga. Again, the postmodern blunting of traditions, even within the regional context, is jarring at best.

Historian Fredric Jameson has labeled postmodernism the culture of late capitalism. Certainly, the sumptuous interiors of Mississauga City Hall speak to the conspicuous consumption that characterized the 1980s in North America. Unfortunately, that may be the level on which Mississauga City Hall is most accessible to its larger public who may easily be alien to the building's profuse historical allusions and associations. Though Kirkland and Jones strived to cultivate a necessarily fragmented urban environment in an expression that subsumes distant histories and is sensitive to vernacular tradition and local history, there is little intimacy or particularized sense of place here. It is hard to create historical continuity when a community's collective memory may well be a short one. With little variation, Kirkland and Jones' great hall could serve equally well in a hotel or upscale shopping mall. Ultimately, the building becomes very much part of the late-modern milieu its architects seemed to strive so determinedly to counter.

It is worth noting that Kirkland and Jones failed to win a single institutional commission since Mississauga City Hall, quite possibly a result of the controversial content, imagery and sense of place of the building—all problems of appropriateness of expression. The architects' partnership was dissolved in 1988, with Jones returning to his native England one year later. Among projects that would follow Mississauga City Hall, 163 Queens Street, a mixed-use structure in downtown Toronto, evokes the character of the 19th-century warehouses indigenous to its neighborhood, sharing Mississauga City Hall's contextual and material concerns, while the firm's S. A. Armstrong Limited Headquarters at Scarborough involves self-reflexive treatment of a stark modernist aesthetic that recalls Walter Gropius' Bauhaus building. Only their entry for the Waterloo Clay and Glass Gallery Competition attained the formal and conceptual complexity of Mississauga City Hall in a scheme that evoked metaphors of craft process through a juxtapositioning of postmodern classicism and late-modern minimalism.

Kirkland and Jones' Mississauga City Hall reflects the concerns and questions of its period. The building engenders syntactical and grammatical liberties that are, at best, difficult to interpret in the context of a public building. Mississauga City Hall suggests that postmodernism can engage recognizable imagery in abstract ways, but it also—and more critically for the community it was built to serve—raises critical questions as to whether architecture can use history without invoking the ideology that underlies that history.

—ETHEL S. GOODSTEIN

HABITAT (EXPO '67)
Montreal, Quebec, Canada

1962-67: Planning and construction; **Architect:** Moshe Safdie.

Publications

BRUMFIELD, WILLIAM CRAFT: *Gold in Azure: One Thousand Years of Russian Architecture*. Boston, Massachusetts, 1983.
"Habitat '67." *Beyond Left and Right*. Edited by Richard Kostelanetz. New York, 1968.
"Habitat '67." *Building Management* (Toronto) (October 1965).
"Habitat '67." *Engineering News Record* (April 1965).
Habitat '67. Ottawa, 1967.
"Habitat '67." *Progressive Architecture* (October 1966).
HOFMANN, WERNER, and KULTERMANN, UDO: *Modern Architecture in Color*. New York, 1970.
JACOBS, DAVID: "Habitat '67." *Horizon* (Winter 1967).
KOMENDANT, A. E.: "Post Mortem on Habitat '67." *Progressive Architecture* (March 1968).
"On From Habitat." *Design* (October 1967).
"Post Mortem on Habitat: Anatomy of a System." *Royal Institute of British Architects Journal* (London) (November 1967).
PYKE, ALEXANDER: "Habitat '67." *Architectural Design* (March 1967).
SAFDIE, MOSHE: *Beyond Habitat*. Cambridge, Massachusetts, 1970.

*

Habitat—or more accurately, Habitat '67, to distinguish it from Moshe Safdie's related projects elsewhere—is arguably Canada's most internationally famous residential structure. Because of that, Safdie's local reputation once had a rather superhuman character. Certainly his achievement—an approach to high-density lodgings avoiding uniformity and monotony in spite of a strictly reduced vocabulary of modular components—was a major innovation even though it had affinities with other, more utopian projects like Le Corbusier's Unité d'Habitation. Habitat is all the more notable since it was the result of a thesis prepared while Safdie was still a student at McGill University. But several of the things the building is most well known for in public eyes were not, in fact, successful. Moreover, it should be pointed out that part of the building's notoriety is due to the typically "'60s" media blitz that surrounded its construction.

First things first: Habitat probably would never have seen the light of day were it not for the fact that Montreal "accidentally" received permission to present the World Exposition of 1967. A couple of Quebec senators had presented to the Bureau International des Expositions a proposal for a fair to accompany Canada's centennial celebrations, but the proposal was refused, and permission was given instead to the U.S.S.R. By 1962, however, the U.S.S.R. had decided to forgo the project. Montreal mayor Jean Drapeau hurriedly resubmitted the proposal and managed to win the competition. The country started to gear up for a major round of nationalism, the effects of which are still being felt in some cultural sectors.

The exhibition had to have a theme, of course, and the intelligentsia assembled for the purpose decided "Man and His World" was appropriate, for it satisfied the conditions of the "first category" established by the Bureau—that is, that the expo cover the full range of human activity. The Expo '67 administrators did not want to put up any money for a residential

Habitat, Expo '67: Montreal, Canada, 1967

showpiece, but given the exhibition's theme, they were more than happy to lend a helping hand in most other respects.

Although the Expo '67 engineers and technicians were occasionally unsympathetic to Safdie and his team, Habitat was constructed entirely in the same atmosphere of international expectations. Given that Habitat represented an unorthodox solution to certain architectural problems on both the theoretical and practical planes, it exploited a full and very contemporary expression of modernity. Popular feeling, of course, was that Canada strongly wanted to represent itself to the rest of the world as quintessentially modern in its celebratory hundredth year, so Safdie was encouraged to push hard for Habitat. In addition, his proposal also spoke of historic human roots, for the result strangely resembled the clustered traditional architecture of the ancient Middle East and the geometrically scattered hill towns of medieval Europe. Taken together, these two sets of associations led to the reception of Safdie's project as a fusion of the traditional vernacular with a highly sophisticated modernist modular system.

The transcendental '60s mentality that led to Marshall McLuhan's postulate of the global village virtually determined that Safdie's modernist village would thus be read as a universal prototype. Even the choice of name made this clear: "Habitat" was expressly chosen because it meant the same in both English and French, and of course it connoted generic buildings for domestic uses around the world. (The name, incidentally, was not Safdie's. It was suggested by Jean-Louis Lalonde, a Montreal architect with connections to cement manufacturers who put up the money for the feasibility studies.) In any case, part of the fame of the building is due to the way in which it has

been received and worn, as it were, like a badge of Canadian international identity.

Safdie's thesis tried to present an economical solution to an international problem: how to provide inexpensive and adequate housing in the face of rapid population growth and escalating land costs. His project was not so much an innovation as a reworking of some of the standard modernist solutions, particularly those that looked forward to prefabrication and high-density residential complexes incorporating office and retail components. The latter were desirable since the site was to be the Mackay Pier directly alongside the St. Lawrence River, rather removed from the downtown area. Ironically, these were the first areas of the proposal to be phased out in the interest of economy. The prefabrication was retained, though not in the impractical form originally envisaged.

A principal factory was established directly on the site to mass-produce the basic components of the building, which were obsessively related in the popular press to children's building blocks. This is not surprising, given that the full selection of 15 dwelling types was achieved simply by arranging combinations of one, two and three reinforced-concrete modules. (Some sort of plastic would have been a preferred material, but the need for great resistance to compression and speed of construction forced a more obvious choice.) The factory produced residential units to be grouped into dwellings of one to four bedrooms, one and two stories, and about 600 to 1,700 square feet. Some of the features within these repeated units were also prefabricated, particularly the bathrooms. By happy coincidence, a plastics firm was already working on a prototype for a fiberglass bathroom, and Safdie managed to pique the firm's interest. However, despite these unequivocal assembly-line elements, the overall result cannot properly be described as fully prefabricated; all sorts of additional components were required for decorative, functional and structural reasons when the units were hoisted into place.

Each of the boxes was to be lifted into a position in an ostensibly organic, three-dimensional grid structure. Apart from the open interior of the whole, which reduced the visual mass and wind resistance, the overall configuration was reminiscent of a ziggurat. The units ranged in weight from 70 to 90 tons, so the technical team had to devise a special crane mounted on rails. Of course, that was the least of the problems. The units were to be staggered so that virtually every one had some sort of overhang. The motivations for this were aesthetic and humanistic—privacy, acoustics, visual variety, individual views—but they introduced fresh technical problems, like individually designed reinforcements in addition to the planned post-tensioned links between pairs of units. In various ways, the overhangs and projections were provided with ingenious self-watering roof gardens built on top of the projecting unit below, in turn necessitating Swiss-designed plumbing traps to replace the traditional vent stacks that would otherwise spoil each garden. Most of the balconies were unique enough to make prefabrication financially imprudent, so individual finishing was necessary there as well.

Safdie's original thesis was to provide very low-budget housing, so he first imagined a Habitat nearly five times the size of the finished version. Technical innovations drove the unit cost up into the "luxury" zone, so some of the dwellings, as well as a planned interior school, shops and offices were arbitrarily removed, leaving about 160 self-contained homes constructed of some 350 units. This of course led to a vicious circle, since the fewer the dwellings, the more each had to contribute to costs such as for specialized retooling and innovative machinery. By 1965, when tendering was still under way, it had already become apparent that costs were expected to be around $10 million, or about $60,000 per unit. This was an astronomical sum for mid-1960s Canada, especially given that the Canadian dollar was then much stronger in international markets than it is today. (The whole package would then have seemed all the more frightening to prospective buyers, since condominiums were not as common as they are now.)

The dwellings are arranged in three groups separated by gardens at the entrances and by vertical components covering stair towers and elevator shafts. The alternating axes of the boxes replace a monolithic visual mass with a planar, dynamic shuttling to and fro. This openness, of course, quite completely defeats the original purpose of reinventing high-density housing, although it generates considerable visual interest. The light along the St. Lawrence can be quite intense here, especially when winter snows bounce it off the vertical surfaces, none of which seem to lie in quite the same plane as the others, thus emphasizing variety. The majority of the houses are placed so that three of the walls have windows or other openings, creating a psychological impression of privacy. All of them are tied to two wide interior streets wrapped in curved Plexiglass tubes at the fifth and tenth levels. Here and there within these streets are public areas for meetings and play, but despite the decoration and greenery intended to alleviate the concrete, they are as underused as most such interiors in apartment complexes.

The streets also serve a structural purpose, for they add further resistance to wind, a common problem along the river's edge. Directly beneath the pavements within these streets are service ducts that lead directly to the mechanical systems housed in the vertical cores paralleling the stair towers. Only pedestrian traffic is permitted immediately around the base of the structure;

vehicles circulate one level below grade. A regular bus route connects the somewhat remote complex with the business district.

Habitat was imagined as a housing alternative in the utopian strain, but its loose connections with Expo '67 ensured that it would be isolated, much like a showpiece, rather than immersed in the urban clutter for which it was a solution. If nothing else, however, it does offer hope that harmonious variety can replace the visual monotony of typical mass housing, and that humanitarian concerns for individuality are viable in an increasingly restricted and restricting economy.

—ROBERT J. BELTON

DOMINION PARLIAMENT BUILDINGS
Ottawa, Ontario, Canada

1861-67. Architects: Thomas Fuller (1822-98) and Herbert Chilion Jones (1836-1923), with subsidiary buildings by F. W. Stent and Augustus Laver (1839-98). **1916:** Destroyed by fire, and rebuilt by J. A. Pearson (1867-1940) and J. O. Marchand (1873-1936).

Publications

ARMSTRONG, ALAN H.: "Profile of Parliament Hill." *Journal of the Royal Architectural Institute of Canada* 34, 9 (1957): 327-331.

*

The 19th century was a great period of nationalistic patrimony of the arts. Although by the second half of the 1800s, the rhetorical power of architecture to convey sociopolitical and cultural agendas was evident in the great urban schemes of Napoleon III's Paris or Franz Josef's Vienna, in North America, where both Canada and the United States aggressively sought cultural parity with western Europe, the capacity of architecture to signify ideology and values was of unique importance. For Canada, whose heritage was colored by the concomitant influences of British and French domination, identifying a national expression in the arts and architecture free from colonial limitations and introspection was widely desired, but rarely achieved. Alan Gowans, the foremost historian of Canadian architecture, has suggested in his book *Building Canada* that in the design of the Dominion Parliament Buildings such a national style, "Picturesque Eclecticism," distinct from yet related to European precedents was achieved. However, in spite of their nationalistic conceptual underpinnings, the Parliament buildings are more correctly considered in a larger architectural historical context. When in 1859 the decision to establish the capital at Ottawa was reached, two aesthetics dominated the western tradition, the English High Victorian Gothic and the French academic classical; it is difficult to envision a public building in bicultural Canada failing to adopt one of these vocabularies. With close economic and then-predominant cultural ties to Great Britain, it is no surprise that Canada's Houses of Parliament emulated the British models.

London's Houses of Parliament (A.W.N. Pugin and Charles Barry, completed 1836) were symbolically rich and eminently identifiable. Although Pugin and Barry's archaeologically correct interpretation of the English Gothic vocabulary had already

Dominion Parliament Buildings: Ottawa, Ontario, Canada, 1861-67

influenced Canadian architecture, with particular force in ecclesiastical design, including Ottawa's Notre-Dame Basilica (1844-78), by 1859 the style was outmoded. It was a freer interpretation of historical precedent, clearly influenced by the contemporary taste for the picturesque, that the Parliament buildings demanded.

Picturesquely situated on a cliff above the Ottawa River and the Rideau Canal, the Dominion Parliament buildings comprise three structures, regularly organized in a U-shaped site plan. Thomas Fuller, architect with partner H. Chilion Jones of the central block, was keenly familiar with the burgeoning High Victorian Gothic mode that responded to the dictates of John Ruskin, expressed in his *Seven Lamps of Architecture* (1849) and

Stones of Venice (1853), for richly textured and polychromed surfaces and powerfully expressive forms drawn broadly from medieval vocabularies. Arriving from his native England in Toronto in 1856, Fuller was undoubtedly familiar with Deane and Woodward's strongly Ruskinian Oxford Science Museum, begun in 1855, and Gilbert Scott's 1857 project for the Foreign Service Office in London. So too would he have known one of Canada's first significant High Victorian Gothic buildings, University College in Toronto, begun in 1856 by Toronto architects Cumberland and Storm. Fuller's Parliament Building is informed by each of these paradigms.

Self-consciously eclectic, the Center Block of Parliament is asymmetrically massed with various heights attained through divergently shaped towers and roofs. Fenestration includes crisp, pointed window details and Norman-influenced carvings decorate the main portal. Decorative detail and formal articulation are uniformly rich. The great central tower, influenced by the 15th-century Gothic architecture of Flanders, creates the perpendicular character that has led to the building's incorrect official description as "Early English." The river elevation of Parliament is dominated by its library, which is interiorly ornate, and in elevation recalls Late English Gothic chapter houses, such as that at Westminster Abbey. The library was the only element of the Center Block to survive a 1916 fire. Reconstruction of the Center Block by John A. Pearson and J. Omer Marchand followed closely Fuller's 1859 design, but with greater stylistic consistency and archaeological correctness. So too, the reconstructed edifice has lost the textural richness of Fuller's subtle but purposeful polychromy.

The flanking Eastern and Western Blocks of the Parliament group, executed by Frederick Warburton Stent and Augustus Laver, were built at the same time as Fuller's Center Block, and echo its elemental eclecticism and High Victorian Gothic character. There too, an active massing and roofscape of pinnacles and towers, with irregular stonework, contribute to the visual richness of this free interpretation of the language of the Middle Ages that Ruskin, the predominant voice of contemporary British theory, prescribed. The Eastern Block remains in its original appearance, while the West Block has undergone a number of additions.

In the inherent eclecticism of the High Victorian Gothic expression, critics of Canadian culture have seen an appropriate merger of French and British tradition through the common ancestry of the Gothic. So too have the Parliament buildings served not only as a symbol of Canadian government, but also, as R. H. Hubbard noted in the *Architectural Review,* as "a perpetual reminder of the traditionalism which seems so paradoxical in a young country." In light of these interpretations, the significance of the Parliament buildings is vested in the use of architectural rhetoric to signify commonly held national aspirations. They are not strictly imitative of any specific medieval models or styles, but strive—as Ruskin advised—to evolve a new aesthetic predicated on an understanding of the transcendent principles and associations of the Gothic style. For the remainder of the 19th century, the Parliament buildings would exemplify a Canadian response to the High Victorian Gothic taste that, for all intents and purposes, constituted a national symbol of the new Dominion of Canada, and that would persist in such important Canadian buildings of the late 19th century as Edward Lennox's Toronto City Hall (1890); Bruce Price's Chateau Frontenac, Quebec (1890); and William G. Storm's Victoria College, Toronto (1892).

—ETHEL S. GOODSTEIN

UNIVERSITY COLLEGE
Toronto, Ontario, Canada

1856-58. Architects: Frederic Cumberland (1821-81) and William Storm.

Publications

ARTHUR, ERIC: *Toronto, No Mean City.* 3rd ed. Toronto, Buffalo and London, 1986.
GOWANS, ALAN: *Building Canada.* 2nd ed. Toronto, 1968.

HUBBARD, R.: "Canadian Gothic." *Architectural Review* (August 1954).
LANGTON, W. A. (ed.): *Early Days in Upper Canada: Letters of John Langton.* Toronto, 1926.
TROLLOPE, ANTHONY: *North America.* New York, 1862.

*

Constructed during the decade preceding the confederation of Canada, University College is both an inheritor of the architectural heritage of colonial Upper Canada and a harbinger of a modern architectural expression for the new nation. In their design for this building, Cumberland and Storm—one of 19th-century Toronto's most influential architectural offices—responded to a demand for the abandonment of colonial imitation, rigid historicism and introspection in Canadian architecture by adopting the freer interpretation of models of the past preferred by the burgeoning High Victorian Gothic movement. The significance of University College, the first structure built for the University of Toronto, must be understood in this larger context of Canadian architectural history.

Established in the early 1790s as the capital of Upper Canada, Toronto (then the town of York) developed in a period when classicism was synonymous with British colonial institutions and power; it is telling that Edward Walsh's proposal for a House of Assembly at York (1804), like much of the town's early architecture, exemplified the Georgian style. The employ of the classical language matured with the city. In Thomas Young's King's College (1842-45, demolished 1886), it was a sophisticated and archaeologically correct, Greek Revival classicism that signified the institution's domination by Anglicans who controlled the province's political and social life. As the population of Toronto increased and diversified, the domination of a public institution by one denomination was questioned; in 1849 King's College became the University of Toronto, a secular school. Nevertheless, identifying an appropriate language for University College would not be as simple as refuting the stately Doric of King's College and propounding the emergent Gothic Revival, the style of the British Houses of Parliament and of the ecclesiological movement. It too was symbolic of Anglican domination.

The design of University College was marked by a battle of the styles fought by architect Frederic Cumberland and his ally, university Vice-Chancellor John Langton, and Governor General Sir Edmund Head. Like many 19th-century architects Cumberland, who had worked as a civil engineer in England before immigrating to Canada in 1847, was a master of many styles; his St. James' Cathedral (1850-52), a monument of ecclesiological correctness in the manner of A. W. N. Pugin, and his addition to Osgoode Hall (1857), an exercise in Renaissance Revival, demonstrate the architect's virtuosity. In 1856 Cumberland traveled to England, where Deane and Woodward's Oxford Science Museum, which embodied the aesthetic, ethical and theoretical underpinnings of John Ruskin's *Stones of Venice,* was secularizing and popularizing the Gothic. According to Eric Arthur, Cumberland knew Ruskin, and his first scheme for University College reflects the profound effect of what he saw at Oxford. That Gothic scheme was rejected by the governor general, who believed Siena's Palazzo Pubblico provided a more suitable model. Ultimately, Cumberland's sensibilities prevailed; his final solution was no mean aesthetic compromise but a thoughtful assimilation of the principles of Ruskin that combined the essence of tradition with the symbols of discrete historic styles.

Like the Oxford Science Museum, University College is a

University College: Toronto, Ontario, Canada, 1856-58

picturesque block, influenced by the medievally derived quadrangle plans of Oxford and Cambridge, anchored by a central tower and punctuated with end pavilions. However, its asymmetrical massing and widely varied roofscape are more aggressive, and its overall appearance and detailing less homogeneous than that of Deane and Woodward's building. Moreover, unlike the pointed and perpendicular Venetian Gothic that Ruskin preferred and Deane and Woodward employed at Oxford, Cumberland and Storm's University College is distinctly Romanesque. Its bulky, square-headed and heavily buttressed south tower recalls towers of Norman parish churches and castle keeps. A single round-arched opening comprises the tower's entrance, an exquisitely crafted portal ornamented with moldings of alternating foliated, geometric and chevron motifs and carried on jamb columns with foliated capitals and richly carved shafts, and recalls such English Romanesque models as the portal of Lincoln cathedral. So too the round arch predominates fenestration articulation, exemplified by the first-floor windows of the south elevation, where paired round-arched openings in a larger round-arched revetment reflect the main portal in their richly carved moldings, tympana and shafts. Treatment of the University College quadrangle cloisters, derived from both Ruskin and early English sources, also reflects Cumberland and Storm's understanding of precedent.

The interior of University College, programmed to accommodate a wide range of academic, administrative and residential functions, also followed English precedents. Detail drawings for stone carvers of capitals are evidence of the faithful interpretation of Romanesque sculpted foliage and beasts that Ruskin propounded. An 1850 perspective drawing of the Convocation

Hall reveals exposed trusses springing from corbel shafts, chevron moldings and round-arched clerestory. Although University College's public spaces retain their original Ruskinian character in rich, naturalistically conceived capitals, they are wholly the result of an 1890 restoration undertaken by David B. Dick following a fire that destroyed the entire east wing.

Although Vice-Chancellor Langton deemed Cumberland and Storm's design a "hybrid" absent of any distinctive style, University College initially proved a critical success. According to British novelist Anthony Trollope, it was "the glory of Toronto ... a Gothic building [that] will take rank not after, but next to, the [Parliament] buildings at Ottawa." Contemporary critics have emphasized the eclecticism of the building and the richness of its decorative detail, generally agreeing that in form and spirit, University College embodies the High Victorian Gothic movement. Even in the secular context of the reestablished university, the implicit morality and monastic allusions of the design are clearly in the spirit of Ruskin. The building is the product of a period during which polemics and associational emotions engendered in style were the overarching determinants of good architecture.

While it is the fine balance of picturesque massing and careful attention to historically derived detail that distinguishes Cumberland and Storm's solution, the building is absent of the formal assimilation that characterized the Richardsonian Romanesque Revival style that would become predominant in the city by the end of the century. University College is more correctly compared to the romantic eclecticism of earlier North American Romanesque Revival architecture, including James Renwick's Smithsonian Institution in Washington, D.C. (1847).

Although the last of Cumberland and Storm's Toronto buildings, the Chapel of St. James the Less (1860), adhered strictly to Gothic Revival style, William Storm later produced fine Romanesque Revival buildings, Victoria College (1889) and St. Andrew's Church (1874-75), that reflect the aggressive, yet picturesque, forms of University College. By establishing a great precedent for Toronto's Romanesque Revival works of the 1880s and 1890s, including R. A. Waite's Provincial Legislative Buildings (1886-93), E. J. Lennox's Old City Hall (1889-99) and David Dick's University of Toronto Library (1891), University College provided a keystone in the transition from colonial imitation to a freer understanding of precedent that fostered a much-desired North American character in Canadian architecture.

—ETHEL S. GOODSTEIN

MEXICO

MEXICO CITY CATHEDRAL
Mexico City, Mexico

1563: Construction begins; **Architect:** Juan Gómez de Mora. **1580s:** Conversion to double basilican form; **Architect:** Claudio Arciniega. **1612:** Exterior walls partially completed, vaulting of four chapels completed. **1623:** Two vaults completed; **Architect:** Claudio Arciniega. **1786:** Facade constructed; **Architect:** José Damián Ortiz de Castro. **1813:** Construction completed.

Publications

FERNANDEZ, JUSTINO: *Outline of Mexican Art.*
KUBLER, GEORGE, and SORIA, MARTIN: *Art and Architecture in Spain and Portugal and their American Dominions, 1500-1800.* Harmondsworth, England, 1959.
TOUSSAINT, MANUEL: *La catedral de México y el Sagrario Metropolitano.*

*

The Cathedral of Mexico City is strikingly unified despite the two and a half centuries taken for its construction. It reflects its conception in the severe Renaissance mode of the Escorial of Philip II and Juan de Herrera and its completion by neoclassicists. Gothic and Baroque elements also contribute to its structure and ornamentation. In elevation the cathedral was conceived as a level-roofed hall church and was converted to its double basilican form by Claudio de Arciniega in the 1580s. The largest ecclesiastical building in the Americas, the cathedral is based upon a rectangular plan consisting of two adjoining squares and measuring 110 meters in length.

The exterior is massive. Though the exterior is broken by powerful towers and a steep-lanterned dome, the dominant impression is of horizontality, marked in diagonal and side views by the extended tiers of balustrades over the chapels, the aisles and the nave. Though softened by the warmth of the buff stone, the whole is severe, shaped by a Herrerean sensibility. The portals on the sides demonstrate the thawing of that sensibility as they rise from a sober Tuscan lower story, through a more ornamented middle stage, to an upper story suggestive of the Baroque with twisting columns and fragmentary double pediment.

The principal south facade balances the verticality of its buttresses and towers with strong horizontal emphasis. The broad bases of the towers are united with the intervening sections by relating the pilasters at their corners to the sturdy rectangular buttresses that flank the central portal. All these elements are

Mexico City Cathedral: Mexico City, Mexico, 1563

welded to the plane of the main wall behind them by pairs of giant inverted consoles. Above the consoles strong horizontal accents run across the top of the entire facade.

The three portals have simple semicircular arched doorways flanked by pairs of restrained Tuscan columns and which at the wider central portal enclose niches containing statues. Above the doorways are religious scenes carved in low relief in contrasting whitish stone, also flanked by pairs of columns. Those of the side portals are Corinthian, dramatically twisted and ornamented, expressing the Baroque zest for animation that swept Mexico just before the opening of the 18th century.

The lower of the two belfry stages of the towers is restrained but marked by a complex pattern of arched openings for bells. The towers remained unfinished for more than a century after the completion of the vaulting of the interior. The settling of the structure in the soft former lake bed and the threat of recurring earthquakes caused grave concern for the effect of the weight of the additional belfry and terminal stages. In designing these elements, the short-lived neoclassical architect José Damián Ortiz de Castro achieved the appearance of ponderous solidity without excessive weight by constructing for the upper belfry stage a relatively light, hollow inner octagon faced with thin piers at the four corners, and by constructing a bell-shaped top of thin and light *tezontle* stone braced with beams of cedar and faced with a thinner veneer of cut stone, which was held in place by iron hoops.

After the completion of the towers, the Spanish-born sculptor Manuel Tolsá finished the cathedral with a hard-edged arch and a square clock stage softened with statuary at the top of the facade, a palisade of pilasters and segmentally arched pedimented windows to face the octagonal drum of the dome, and a very tall lantern to raise the height of the dome closer to that of the towers.

In the interior of the cathedral, Claudio Arciniega's design called for raising the vault of the nave above those of the flanking aisles and for raising the aisle vaults above the level of those covering the tiers of chapels at the sides. Arciniega was probably responsible for changing the decoration of the aisle vaults from ribbed Gothic designs used in the northern peripheral chapels to saucer domes with spoke-like ribs, more in keeping with Renaissance taste. Two ribbed Gothic vaults were constructed as late as 1623 to cover the sacristy. Arciniega cut lunettes containing triple windows in the wall rising above the entrances to the chapels. These windows provide ample light for the aisles. The nave, towering above the aisles to a height of 29 meters, is covered by a barrel vault, intersected in each bay by transverse vaulting in order to provide light through similar triple windows. The principal architectural features of the interior—the barrel-vaulted nave—the saucer-domed aisles, and the tall piers decorated by fluted Tuscan half columns that continue up across the barrel vault as transverse arches—are drawn from the Renaissance vocabulary of classical forms, but the whole has the tall, airy lightness of a Gothic cathedral.

The retables of the chapels constitute an anthology of Mexican styles, early and late Baroque and neoclassical. Two features of the interior are outstanding: the choir placed in the nave near the entrance with a screen constructed to Mexican specifications at Macao in the Far East, and handsomely carved Baroque stalls and a *retablo* facing the entrance, the two latter elements primarily replicas because of a fire in 1967. The great Retable of the Kings at the far end of the nave with its four giant *estipité* columns was designed by the Spaniard Jerónimo de Balbás in 1718. It educated a remarkable generation of Mexican retable makers.

Adjoining the cathedral is the Sagrario Metropolitano, which was designed by another Spaniard, Lorenzo Rodríguez, in 1749.

Its interior is laid out as a cross in a square, tall and light-filled, but conservative in ornamentation in accord with the cathedral. The superb screen facades, which cascade down to the corners of the structure and set powerful compressed *estipité*-decorated portals of light *chiluca* stone against descending panels of soft, dark rose *tezontle,* applied the lesson of Balbás to church exteriors. These facades set off the final inspired phase of the Mexican Baroque.

—JAMES EARLY

UNIVERSITY CITY
Mexico

1950: Construction of first buildings begun; **Architects:** Enrique del Moral and Mario Pani.

Publications

"Mexico City University: Its New Campus and Buildings."
    Northwest Architect (September-October 1952).
MYERS, I. E.: *Mexico's Modern Architecture.* New York, 1952.
WHITE, NORVAL: *The Architecture Book.* New York, 1976.

*

The largest single building project in modern Mexican history, the University City of Mexico (the main campus of the institution officially named the Universidad Nacional Autonoma de Mexico, hereafter referred to as the UC) was acclaimed internationally as an architectural coming of age for that country, a reconciliation of past and present, cosmopolitan and indigenous, which culminated in functional contemporary forms of distinctive local character. It has now been 40 years since groundbreaking on the project began, and the UC's student population has grown by about 1,000% in that time. As an exercise in architectural semiotics and modern contextualism, the questions the project raised, perhaps more than the answers it provided, continue to be of vital interest.

From its inception, the UC's planners had aimed at forms somehow expressive of the region. Dissatisfaction with the perceived sterility and materialism of modern functionalist architecture began mounting in Mexico in the mid 1930s, less than a decade after its introduction into the country. Among its many functions, the UC was to be a grand symbol of both Mexico's rich national history and myth, and its potential for progress. Carlos Lazo, director-general of the UC project, discussed the planner's role in effecting an appropriately broad-based, humanistic habitat for this ideal when in about 1950 he wrote: "The world has felt a terrific technico-social impact, caused by the slowness of the evolution . . . of human consciousness . . . in comparison to the tremendous recent surge of technological development. But the modern world is clearly showing its need and hope for equilibrium. . . . Planning . . . attempts to take its place as a synthesizing, coordinating agent for the problems of the immediate future. As far as possible, within the limitations of space and time, we are applying this concept of planning to the University City. Thus, we hope to do our part toward blending humanistic thought with the vital, basic necessities of Mexico, both now and in the years to come."

Founded in 1551, the University of Mexico is the oldest such institution in the Americas. After 400 years its facilities had

University City, library: Mexico City, Mexico, 1950

spread across the city of Mexico and its outlying regions, variously housed in outmoded structures no longer able to satisfy modern operational requirements. To remedy this situation, the Mexican government in 1946 acquired 1,730 acres in the 5,000-year-old lava fields at the city's southern outskirts—an area known as El Pedregal: "the Rocky Place." Some 200 million pesos, at the time equal in buying power to about $90 million (U.S.), were allocated for construction. Enrique del Moral and José Villagran Garcia, of the National School of Architecture, were asked to make a preliminary study. Del Moral, Mario Pani and Mauricio Campos were then commissioned in 1947 to prepare projects, establish a competition for the award of the 52 individual building commissions, and develop an overall plan. The primary aim of this plan, according to Pani and del Moral (Campos having died shortly after the project's initiation), was "to create unity, physical and pedagogical, which would make for an ease of communication between the different schools, for the convenience of students, professors and researchers." By 1950 Lazo had been appointed director-general and ground was broken for the first buildings. Just two years later, when Mexican President Miguel Aleman officially dedicated the site, 150 architects, artists and engineers and 6,000 workmen had completed 80 percent of a campus whose sometimes overwhelmingly vast spaces were designed to accommodate 30,000 students and 15,000 faculty and staff.

The logistical considerations of so great and expedient an undertaking were formidable. Not the least of Lazo's concerns was to coordinate the high volume of necessary manpower and material resources in such a way that construction throughout the rest of the nation would not be paralyzed. His budget, though large, was not unlimited. One key solution was found in the

extensive use of a locally available material: the rough lava stone of the Pedregal, which accounted for about 90 percent of the material originally used at the UC. Traditional masonry techniques employed in the generally low-lying campus buildings (few structures are more than three stories tall; consequently, only a few required expenditure for elevators) and the use of local stone minimized the level of difficulty confronted by a mostly untrained local labor force. Site-drawn materials reduced transportation costs and promoted aesthetic integration between buildings and landscape. These economically grounded motives provided for especially successful results in the 110,000-seat Olympic Stadium, whose stands were formed by piling up earth excavated in making the stadium's bowl, and then facing the exterior dirt walls with lava. Very little concrete was used. Lazo related the building process there to the earth's natural formation of volcanoes: "We have built a volcano," he said, and in fact, the finished stadium does bear strong resemblance to the mountains visible from campus. In a related vein were Alberto Arai's fronton courts, also built of lava and modeled on the truncated pyramids of nearby Teotihuacan. It is of interest that the two most overtly regionalizing structural forms at the UC should be sports facilities. As one faculty member explained, "The stadium and frontones tell us, 'Remember your ancestry—but remember it in play only. The past may beckon us but it can never be a reality.' "

While Pani and del Moral's plan did establish certain criteria aimed at promoting unity between the various campus structures, individual architects, and teams, were given great latitude in their designs, and were encouraged to consult directly with the faculties whom their designs would eventually serve. Most of the architects involved had come to maturity in the doctrinaire

University City, School of Medicine

functionalist climate present in Mexico since the late 1920s, and many of the buildings have a rational underpinning and cubic severity that springs directly from the International Style. Even so, the autonomy accorded the architects provided for a far greater formal range—and qualitative inconsistency—than can be seen, for example, at Ludwig Mies van der Rohe's IIT campus in Chicago (1939-52).

Much of this diversity is due to the applied ornament which clothes many of the structures, the most prominent case being Juan O'Gorman's mosaic-clad library tower. According to O'Gorman and other artists and architects involved at the UC, the murals, mosaics and sculptures that appear throughout the campus attempted an integration of all the plastic arts, including architecture—an art, in O'Gorman's words, "of our time, in our tradition, and expressing the aspirations of our people." The country's best-known artists, among them the politically radical muralists Diego Rivera and David Alfaro Siqueros, carried out designs at the UC. In the social realist manner of these artists, most of the artwork at the UC is representational and didactic in character, putting forth imagery from Mexican history and legend, and glorifying the country's native Indian culture and the humble nobility of the peasant class. Not everyone shared O'Gorman's enthusiasm for the result. Alonso Mariscal, head of the National School of Architecture in the early 1950s, found the campus buildings' exterior ornamentation the "principal mistake" of the overall design, "anachronistic and as unnecessary as tatooing," while Sibyl Moholy-Nagy criticized the library tower for its "continuous mural that leaves not a square inch of the building material free to breath." O'Gorman cited the example of medieval cathedrals as precedential for the UC's attempted unification of the visual arts;

but unlike Gothic cathedrals, almost none of the UC's ornament is related to structure. Many of the larger murals (e.g., Siqueros' sculpted mural on the south wall of the Central Administration Building) have a billboard-like scale and bluntness which, regardless of independent aesthetic merit, would not adversely affect the visual or functional quality of structure by being removed.

Unlike public universities in the United States, the UC was established to serve a national, rather than state or local, constituency. How effectively it does this is debatable. There seems never to have been any doubt about its placement in Mexico City. The city, like its Aztec counterpart, Tenochtitlan, has always been the uncontested cultural, financial and administrative center of the country. The UC's central position within the nation is proclaimed by the presence of landscaping plants and colored mosaic stones brought as "tribute" from all the states of the republic. The country feeds the capital, and the presence there of the nation's preeminent educational institution is yet another contributing factor to its magnetic appeal. Mexico's extremely centralized bureaucracy ensures that most UC graduates who are able to find employment within their respective fields will do so in the capital.

Like other "academical villages" the UC has received criticism for its isolation from the community beyond its walls. As critic Roberto Segre noted, "It is an intellectual elite which receives the message of nativist recovery attempted in Mexico City." This claim may seem particularly pointed in a developing country with marked social divisions, but the most obvious goal of all educational institutions is the promotion of learning, and by this, upward mobility for the societies and individuals they serve. This is, naturally, a gradual and ongoing process. With the UC's population now hovering at around 300,000 students plus faculty and staff, it would appear to be working at or near peak capacity toward providing such opportunities to the public at large.

The choice of the Pedregal site itself raises questions of social and physical exclusion/inclusion. By the early 1940s, when its population had grown to more than two million, Mexico City's outlying areas could be seen dividing into two distinct suburban sectors. The north and east were populated almost exclusively by the poor and working classes; equal upper class exclusivity applied to the southern and western sectors. Clearly, the projected scale of the UC project demanded an amount of land unavailable, barring extensive demolition, anywhere near the city's core. A site at the urban periphery was thus necessary. The chosen Pedregal site lies directly south of the elegant old San Angel district. Even today, with an extensive subway system in place, most traffic must pass through the city's center, and students from the working-class neighborhoods to the city's north and east often spend several hours of each day in transit. Those from the wealthier areas have far more direct access.

Still regarded as a wasteland by most Mexicans, the Pedregal attracted the UC's planners because it was inexpensive to acquire and available for exploitation. Since the early 1940s, however, the Pedregal had come to be valued by some as a distinctively "regional" landscape. The Pedregal harbored relics directly linking present to past: recently dug from its lava was a circular stone temple, called Cuicuilec, then the oldest known structure in the Americas: of even greater vintage were the remains found there of ancient American ancestors. There too were dramatic views of distant volcanoes, types of vegetation found in few other places in the world, and the ruggedness of a virgin landscape untouched by colonial impact. Luis Barragán, beginning in 1945 with his exclusive residential development, Los Jardines del Pedregal, was the first builder to recognize the area's economic and aesthetic potential. He himself was following the lead of the painters Diego Rivera and Dr. Atl, who had long praised the Pedregal as a native beauty. But Barragán's achievement was seen at the time to be mainly in the realm of landscaping, and the expensive homes built by his clients could not bear the same broad nationalistic messages as put forth in a public institution like the UC.

As has been noted, it was to the builders' advantage to use the good local stone of the Pedregal. Lazo and others alluded to a nationalist/humanist impulse which supported the regionalized forms they employed, and as we have seen, there were significant economic arguments for these as well. But the site forced, as well as facilitated, this incipient regionalism. As architect and critic Max Cetto wrote, "Irregular topography . . . forced the architects to avoid a rigid spatial organization." A flexible, inclusive design approach, seen in the overall plan and in many of the individual structures, was demanded by an ancient, unyielding landscape.

—KEITH EGGENER

UNITED STATES

HYATT REGENCY HOTEL (PEACHTREE CENTER)
Atlanta, Georgia, U.S.A.

From 1960. Architect: John Portman (born 1924). **1960-61:** Merchandise Mart; **1963-67:** Hyatt Hotel; **1971:** 200-room addition to Hyatt Hotel; **1975:** Shopping gallery; **1979:** Apparel Mart; **1976:** Westin Peachtree Plaza Hotel; **1982:** 350-room addition to Hyatt Hotel. **1985:** Atlanta Mariott Marquis Hotel. **1989:** Inforum and Peachtree Center Athletic Club.

Publications

"Atlanta." *Architectural Forum* (April 1969).
"Architect/Developer John Portman." *Journal of the Royal Institute of British Architects* (December 1977).
GOLDBERGER, PAUL: "John Portman and Associates." *Global Architecture* 57 (1981).
GOLDBERGER, PAUL: "John Portman—Hyatt Regency Hotels." *Global Architecture* 28 (1974).
"Hotels" and "In Progress: Portman Projects." *Progressive Architecture* (February 1978).
"John Portman: Atlanta's One-Man Urban Renewal Program." *Architectural Record* (January 1966).
PORTMAN, JOHN, and BARRETT, JONATHAN: *The Architect as Developer.* New York, 1976.
RIANI, PAOLO: *John Portman.* Washington, D.C., 1990.

*

The Hyatt Regency Hotel is significant as the archetype for the late-20th-century downtown atrium hotel. Following its construction in 1967, it influenced countless atrium buildings designed for institutional, commercial (wholesale and retail), office and hotel use.

While Portman had experimented with the concept of a multistory lobby with overlooking balconies at his Antoine Graves Houses (1965), a housing project for the elderly commissioned by the Atlanta Housing Authority, the Hyatt Regency Atlanta was the architect's first masterful design in the idiom. It introduced typical Portman features: visible movement (elevators, escalators and people), nature (trees in planters, vines overhanging balconies, water and natural light), patterned paving, prominent large-scale sculpture, color and spatial excitement.

Within three months of its opening, the 800-room Hyatt Regency was 94.6 percent occupied, and immediately became an Atlanta tourist attraction, fulfilling the architect's goal to create a place downtown which people would enjoy visiting and using. A 200-room addition in 1971 introduced Portman's first glass-encased cylinder of hotel rooms, which he repeated in Peachtree Center at the 73-story landmark hotel, the Westin Peachtree Plaza (1976). Portman had built other glass cylinders, in the meantime, at the four corners of Chicago's Hyatt Regency O'Hare Hotel (1971), at the 1500-room Bonaventure Hotel in Los Angeles (composed of five cylinders in 1977), and at the cylindrical glass towers of Detroit's Renaissance Center (1976). Thus, Atlanta's Hyatt Regency addition of 1971 repeated the archetypal role of the original hotel, but in different form. This

was not the last phase of the Hyatt Regency's history: 350 more rooms were added to the hotel in 1982.

The Hyatt Regency Hotel remains a key element in the design of John Portman's Peachtree Center, a mixed-use urban center for the heart of downtown Atlanta. Portman began Peachtree Center with the construction of the Merchandise Mart (1960-61), his first completed project both designed and developed by the "entrepreneur-architect." Its success immediately stimulated further development, and Peachtree Center today is still evolving to create what Portman calls a "coordinate unit," an urban model in which all the necessities of life are available within walking distance. (This has not been realized in 30 years, however, including built housing, although the master plan calls for it eventually.) The development thus far has achieved a multiuse complex of coordinated office towers (1965, 1968, 1970, 1974, 1976, 1985 and 1988) and commercial and recreational buildings; the latter include a shopping gallery (1975) and Apparel Mart (1979), a high-tech/computer commercial mart called Inforum (1989), the recent Peachtree Center Athletic Club (1989), and two noteworthy hotels, the Westin Peachtree Plaza Hotel (mentioned above and the world's tallest, 1976) and the Atlanta Marriott Marquis (1985).

Portman's latest Peachtree Center hotel, the Marriott Marquis, is spatially overpowering—the atrium concept has been extended to a cavernous 50 stories—and the lobby is unquestionably dramatic; it, too, has become a tourist attraction. Similarly, the recently redesigned five-level skylit atrium lobby of the Peachtree Plaza Hotel has been made more stylishly chic and offers "stage-prop" pavilions of neoclassical style and intentional theatrics. With its original atrium design and fittings intact, the Hyatt Regency remains architecturally the most successful of the architect's three Atlanta hotels. All three share Portman's revolutionary design concept of "turning the downtown hotel inside out" in order to transform a dismal city-center hotel into a festive place for people.

The architect's emphasis on the reaction of people to his buildings, and his concern as a designer for the "psychology of space" (space as people experience it), motivated his effort to redesign the urban hotel. He has sought to transform the typical dark and uninviting downtown hotel lobby and inhospitable bedrooms overlooking alleys and blank brick walls (the empty environments occupied by solitary and lonely individuals as captured in paintings by the American artist Edward Hopper) to an architecture which celebrates life, an architecture of diversion, entertainment and fantasy.

Portman cites such places of amusement as Tivoli Gardens in Copenhagen and the imaginative streets and plazas of Walt Disney (Disneyland, Disney World's Magic Kingdom) as models for his vision. But such models contribute both to what is successful and to what is not in his spaces. If his Peachtree Center hotels sought to offer stages on which people would enact daily-life dramas, the recently revamped Peachtree Plaza Hotel lobby may be too theatrical and the Marriott Marquis' space too melodramatic. The five levels of the Peachtree Plaza lobby overlook a crowded bazaar of elongated, pedimented pavilions sparkling with theater lights, postmodern cosmetics and Palladian burlesque. The exaggerated supervolume and plasticity of the Marriott lobby, at twice the height of the Hyatt Regency lobby, approach architectural slapstick; the hotel is loved by many conventioneers whose initial impression, upon entering this megaspace, is as immediate as a loud smack, but

Hyatt Regency Hotel: Atlanta, Georgia, 1963-67

who find, in the afterglow, a stinging feeling that the space dehumanizes.

It is by means of such contrasts with the immediately adjacent Portman hotels in Atlanta's Peachtree Center that the original Hyatt Regency Hotel retains its crown. More effectively, the Hyatt Regency lobby offers a space which involves people—an environment for social interaction. Trees, plants and water bring life inside. The movement of people and objects (elevator cabs, for example) further energizes the space. Indeed, Portman's signature elevators at the Hyatt Regency, with their futuristic, carnival-like space-cab design, cling to open interior walls and propel their occupants in semiprivate rockets to rotating restaurants in the sky, and they have become as popular as amusement rides at Disney World.

The Hyatt Regency, Atlanta, introduced both the design tricks and the architectural language of John Portman's contemporary atrium hotel. It established a significant late-20th-century building type, and it offered the architect his first renowned exercise, and one of his best, in architecture conceived as a social art.

—ROBERT M. CRAIG

CATHOLIC CATHEDRAL
Baltimore, Maryland, U.S.A.

1808-21. Architect: Benjamin Henry Latrobe (1764-1820).
1863: Portico added (according to original plans).

Publications

KIMBALL, FISKE: "Latrobe's Designs for the Cathedral of Baltimore." *Architectural Record* 42, 6 (December 1917).

*

The Catholic Cathedral of Baltimore, America's first such structure, was an unusual and unprecedented exercise in Roman-inspired design by Benjamin Latrobe. Impressed by the opportunity to do something of importance, and pleased by having been asked by Bishop Carroll to comment on the sketches for a proposed cathedral, Latrobe ended up offering his design free of charge. Beginning with his designs of late 1804, the project occupied part of his attention through his final design of 1808. Subsequent construction was halted during the War of 1812 and by the economic depression that followed it until 1817, and the building was not dedicated until two years after Latrobe's death, in 1821. The unusual and discordant, vaguely Eastern, onion domes were not of Latrobe's design, and replaced the rounded tops that echoed the shape of the central dome.

Latrobe had originally submitted two designs: an earlier version of the structure as built, and a design in the prevailing ecclesiastical Gothic style, which the English-born architect knew from his substantial European travels preceding his immigration to the United States. And although Greek and Roman Revival buildings were gaining popularity both in England and

St. Mary's Catholic Cathedral: Baltimore, Maryland, 1805-21

St. Mary's Catholic Cathedral

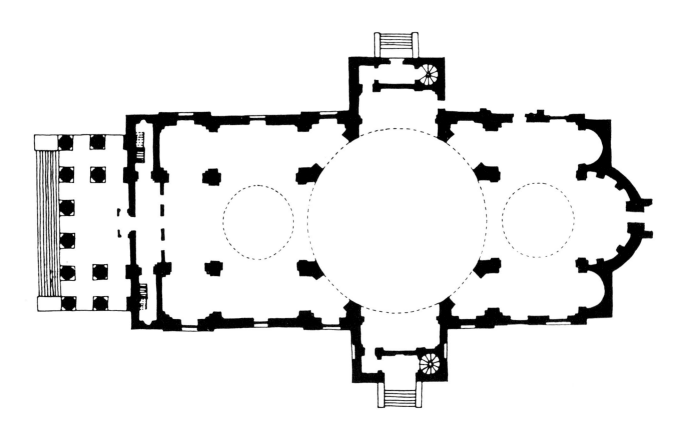

Europe, he had no clear precedent for a large church. When the bishop and his advisers decided on the more classical design, the architect faced a fairly unusual problem for one designing a major ecclesiastic building: the downtown location and preexisting structures provided for a lot that was both narrower and shorter than was desirable.

In his seventh and final design of 1808, and in response to continued interference by powerful members of the Catholic community, Latrobe was forced to simplify his original design; one change was the removal of the inner piers at the crossing, and that necessity, providentially, helped create his masterpiece. Instead of having four shallow saucer-shaped domes surrounding the central one, he unified and simplified the entire design by having the dome span the entire 65 feet of the nave. The modified Greek cross, with its integrated main and side aisles, is both simple and dignified. By taking the unusual steps of eliminating the pendentives ordinarily associated with such a dome and using masonry vaulting—the latter a technology found only in Southwestern mission churches—Latrobe created a light and unified interior space that excites our admiration today as much as it did for those who first beheld it at the dedication. The cathedral interior is consistent with the architect's predilection for simplicity and comprehensibility of design, and the direct and powerful effect of the relationship of the dome to the nave is his magnificent solution to clarifying, rather than segmenting, the space.

The interior decoration is also noteworthy, for, as Latrobe was still at work on the United States Capitol, he convinced Bishop Carroll to allow him to employ the highly experienced Italian sculptor Andrei for the Ionic capitals and other detail work. Thus, a higher quality of carving than was ordinarily available made its mark on this building.

Understandably, the dome is the most significant feature on the exterior of the cathedral, and the shortness of the modified Greek cross enhances the visibility and effect of the comparatively shallow dome more than would a conventional longitudinal format. The exterior panels, of cut stone, reveal the interior plan and, just as the interior spaces both admit the outside light and define their relationship to each other, so do the exterior forms reveal the interior design. The curved spaces in which the windows are set replay the shapes of the vaulting as well as prefigure the quality of light to be found inside. Finally, the column capitals exhibit the first American use of curved-corner ears to create the illusion of a basic Ionic form when seen from either the facade or the sides.

The portico was finally completed to the architect's design by his son, John, in 1863 and is faithful to the original plan. The choir was lengthened with equal fidelity to the spirit of the original design and detailing, an appropriate addition that fulfilled Latrobe's original desire for additional length to the building. The stained-glass windows are a mid-20th-century addition, and certainly change the color and quality of light entering the building, though not the general effect of the design.

The Catholic Cathedral of Baltimore is more than an ecclesiastical building of historic importance. By its grace and simplicity, through Latrobe's articulation of interior and exterior spaces, and through the balance of classical design and technical and structural innovation, the architect made an enduring and aesthetically satisfying contribution to American architecture. The cathedral is unconventional in its combination of dedication to the spirit of Vitruvius, its simple floating dome, and in the simplicity and logic of its plan; it stands as a testament to Latrobe's creativity and awareness of the relationship between structure and design.

—DAVID M. SOKOL

FALLINGWATER (Kaufmann House)
Bear Run, Pennsylvania, U.S.A.

1936-39. Architect: Frank Lloyd Wright (1867-1959).

Publications

FRAMPTON, KENNETH, and FUTAGAWA, YUKIO: *Modern Architecture: 1920-1945*. New York, 1983.
"Frank Lloyd Wright." *Architectural Forum* (special issue, January 1938).
GILL, BRENDAN: *Many Masks: A Life of Frank Lloyd Wright*. New York, 1987.
HITCHCOCK, HENRY-RUSSELL: *In the Nature of Materials: The Buildings of Frank Lloyd Wright, 1887-1941*. New York, 1942.
HOFFMANN, DONALD: *Frank Lloyd Wright's Fallingwater: The House and Its History*. New York, 1978.
HOFMANN, WERNER, and KULTERMANN, UDO: *Modern Architecture in Color*. New York, 1970.
KAUFMANN, EDGAR, JR.: "Twenty-Five Years of the House on the Waterfall." *Architettura* 82/8, 4 (August 1962): 222-258.
KAUFMANN, EDGAR, JR.: *Fallingwater, A Frank Lloyd Wright Country House*. 1986.
RUDOLPH, PAUL: "Frank Lloyd Wright—Fallingwater." *Global Architecture* 2 (1970).
TWOMBLY, ROBERT C.: *Frank Lloyd Wright: His Life and His Architecture*. New York, 1979.
ZEVI, BRUNO: "Alois Riegl's Prophecy and Frank Lloyd Wright's Falling Water." *Architettura* 82/8, 4 (August 1962).

*

Nestled by a stream amidst a dense cover of woods in rural southwestern Pennsylvania stands one of the most remarkable designs of the 20th century. The structure, built between 1936 and 1939, was intended as a summer home and weekend retreat for Pittsburgh department store magnate Edgar J. Kaufmann and his wife, Lillian.

The building is known as Fallingwater and was designed by Frank Lloyd Wright, America's preeminent architect of the 20th century. It is not surprising that Wright designed such a stunning country house, for he had already drafted many astounding buildings dating back to the 1890s.

Yet, it is rather amazing that Fallingwater's design appeared when the architect was nearly 70 years old, when his career was in a tailspin and his financial resources were next to nothing. Furthermore, there might not have been a Fallingwater had Wright not turned his Wisconsin-based home-studio/office Taliesen (meaning "shining brow") into a teaching facility. Born of extreme economic necessity, Wright's school attracted aspiring architectural interns on fellowships, among them Edgar Kaufmann, Jr. He enthusiastically introduced his father and mother to architect Wright. In addition to a lifelong friendship, their meeting produced Fallingwater, its eventual guest house, and a handsome commission. Wright's career soared thereafter, never to be diminished again.

Fallingwater is a multilevel country house situated on a natural rock footing just above a falls on a creek called Bear Run. Its various floors and balconies involve extensive use of cantilevered, reinforced concrete. The home was ingeniously constructed around and above stubwalls plus a central core of stone walls containing a kitchen, stacked bedrooms and utilities

Fallingwater (Kaufmann House): Bear Run, Pennsylvania, 1936-39

Fallingwater (Kaufmann House)

Fallingwater (Kaufmann House)

paraphernalia. All of this functions as a vertically massing weight or anchor flush to a rocky hillside slope. Such alignment of space and weight effectively counterbalances horizontal slab floor/balconies, which are probably the most prominent feature in the overall design with their sleek, daring and weightless appearance.

Weightlessness is an aesthetic key (however deceptive) to Fallingwater. Horizontal slabs appear to float above and below long frieze-ribbons of glass, and collectively levitate above a stream just as it spills over the ledge of a falls. The setting of this home is not just picturesque, it is dramatic.

Fallingwater is also deceptively serene because a complex structure operates behind its facade. Part of the structural complexity is due to design alterations, following initial construction, to accommodate the client's wishes. However, such alterations are small compared to Wright's compositional essay of masses and voids, insistent horizontality opposing energetic verticality, rough textured courses of limestone versus smooth concrete deck walls, anchoring forms opposing cantilevering forms, the fluid space within the home and the flowing water underneath it. Fallingwater is, then, an arrangement of balanced opposites not unlike those in a Japanese print or a Piet Mondrian painting. It is natural and familiar, incorporating native stone, as well as wood and glass, which reflect its surroundings and permit nature to come into the house, at least indirectly.

This country house for the Kaufmanns is not simple regarding other connections with nature either. The hillside, the falls and the highly convex-concave dwelling collectively suggested for Wright a cave image in the sense of shelter, security and privacy. Perhaps it is the sense of insulation from the industrialized and urbanized world that Fallingwater and its protective Bear Run

Nature Conservancy provide that ultimately pleased Wright.

It seems that Wright idolized Thomas Jefferson and his auto-biographical home, Monticello. Jefferson, an amateur architect and dutiful statesman, wrote more than once that he was happiest when at Monticello and especially when he was redesigning his home, the English landscape grounds that surround it, or had his hands in the soil of his beloved kitchen garden. More than refreshing experiences, they constituted his world by choice, a microcosm of nature from which he obtained moral sustenance.

By the 1920s Wright had come to feel seriously alienated by the industrial world and disgusted with shoddy industrialized production, not to mention a vicious press that castigated him for marital entanglements. It is quite possible that through the rebuilding of his home-studio Taliesen during that decade he was identifying with Jefferson and even rivaling Monticello. For Wright—who had grown up on this land, its rolling hills, tilled fields, woods and nearby Wisconsin River—all this likely became a retreat, perhaps even an escape.

Whatever his deep-seated or subconscious motivations, throughout a career covering nearly six decades, Wright advocated a natural architecture and its thorough integration into nature. Thus, Fallingwater, like Taliesen before it, became directly part of its site and did so through integration of local materials, horizontal orientation and sensitivity to client needs. Fallingwater is almost camouflaged like a living, growing organism. In a romantic sense, this identification with unity of place for Wright may furthermore be seen as attempting to relive an early American pioneer experience.

On the other hand, it is also true that site-specific, nearly unique homes can be prohibitively expensive for most people.

In addition, Fallingwater, the Dana-Thomas House (Springfield, Illinois, 1904) and several other Wright homes routinely exceeded their originally projected high costs. There were also delays due to new or untried construction procedures. In that light, Fallingwater and its cousins may ultimately reflect quite another sort of union, one between a moneyed, tolerant client and an ambitious architect. Thus, despite Wright's often-published and -quoted advocacy for a moral architecture, built naturally, or for Usonian houses, there are contradictions. Despite rampant worship of this architect in the late 20th century, Wright loved best a totally free rein to design everything connected with a project—the building, its interior, the detailing, furniture, lighting fixtures—everything!

Generally one associates an efficient and economic platform with Wright. One came to expect a brilliant imagination disciplined by Midwestern practicality in Wright. In Fallingwater those qualities are present even with a carte blanche budget. The architectural community is fortunate that Frank Lloyd Wright was not interested in revival styles and other eclecticism.

—TOM DEWEY II

BOSTON PUBLIC LIBRARY
Boston, Massachusetts, U.S.A.

1887-95. Architect: McKim, Mead and White [Charles Follen McKim (1847-1909), William R. Mead (1846-1928), Stanford White (1853-1906)]. **1969-73:** Addition built; **Architect:** Philip Johnson (born 1906).

Publications

JORDY, WILLIAM H.: ''The Beaux-Arts Renaissance: Charles McKim's Boston Public Library.'' In *American Buildings and Their Architects: Progressive and Academic Ideals at the Turn of the Twentieth Century*. Garden City, New York, 1972.

''Prize Designs for the Public Library Building, Boston, Massachusetts.'' *American Architect and Building News* 17 (14 February 1885).

Boston Public Library: Boston, Massachusetts, 1887-95

Boston Public Library, annex by Philip Johnson: 1969-73

ROTH, LELAND M. (ed.): *A Monograph of the Work of McKim, Mead and White 1879-1915*. New York, 1974.

ROTH, LELAND M.: *McKim, Mead and White, Architects*. New York, 1983.

*

Ralph Adams Cram, whose good taste for the refined and the correct has never been doubted, characterized the Boston Public Library as having "a serene Classicism, reserved, scholarly, delicately conceived in all its parts, beautiful in that sense in which things have always been beautiful in periods of high human culture "(*My Life in Architecture,* 1936).

Unlike bold, domineering, symbol-sending Trinity Church facing it across Copley Square, the Public Library stands a solid, silent barrier containing not the high-pitched voice of a sermonizing rector, but thousands of captured writings resting in linear regularity, and expressed on the exterior by fenestration as repetitious as the arches of the Roman Colosseum.

It is said that the architect, Charles Follen McKim, had assisted in 1872 with the designing of Trinity, but his heart must not have been in the work, as Stanford White soon became the lead draftsman for the project. McKim had spent three years at the École des Beaux-Arts in Paris. He apparently liked the clarity, directness and standardization of classic design as taught there to the combination of medieval forms preferred by H. H. Richardson. Furthermore, Trinity was built in the 1870s, while the library (1887-95) was the product of a new generation that was clearly in favor of classical architecture reinterpreted.

For some years it had become evident that the old library building was no longer serving the avid reading habits of Boston's citizens. Thus the legislature helped the city by appropriating funds. After some bitterness over control, the trustees of the library were requested to select an architect and to manage the contract procedures. S. A. B. Abbott, former mayor and a trustee, became the strong, moving force. He knew McKim and had approved highly of the architect's design for the Villard Houses in New York. Abbott's selection of McKim was mainly on the basis of his ability to create a monumental building, one about which Oliver Wendell Holmes later said, "This palace is the people's own!"

Without question the exterior design of the library is formally related to Henri Labrouste's Bibliothèque Ste.-Geneviève (1845), which McKim had surely seen while in Paris. Labrouste showed considerable originality in symbolizing on the exterior the library's interior purpose, in veering away from classical reinterpretation yet harboring classical illusions, and in daring to use exposed iron posts and arches to vault the enormous reading room. By contrast, McKim gave his library a sheltered elegance, a strong sense of classical proportions, and a distinctively studied and finished quality. Labrouste's is archaic and exciting, a process not fully realized; while McKim's is of the Golden Age, a fabric brilliantly conceived and elaborately decorated, yet lacking sensuality in its severity and coldness. But the library is also related to the arched flank of San Francesco at Rimini where L. B. Alberti displayed the full power of classicism to moderate favorably between grand architectural form and delicate decoration.

The conservative exterior hides the splendor within where sculpture, painting and rich materials abound. It was McKim and Abbott who led the campaign to decorate the interior. They insisted that the whole project was an enhancement of culture for the entire country and therefore ought to have artistic representation worthy of the enterprise. Beyond McKim's architectural partners, Stanford White and William Mead, it was Augustus Saint-Gaudens who first became aware of the great artistic opportunity available at the library. Saint-Gaudens recalled much later his first introduction to McKim when "a devouring love for ice cream brought us together." Ice cream has little to do with architectural decoration, but friendship and admiration of talent do.

Over a period of several years (1887 to 1897) about ten notable artists were persuaded to contribute their special artistry. Augustus Saint-Gaudens was privileged to create two groups to stand at the entrance, but these were never completed; however, the panels over the doorway and four bronze memorials in the court are his. The bronze entrance doors are by Daniel Chester French. The grand stair hall has formidable, though kind, lions that Louis Saint-Gaudens would not show in public until his brother had approved and done some finishing touches. The expansive walls of the stairs have murals by Puvis de Chavannes—a major success by the popular French artist. James McNeill Whistler and John La Farge had projects that failed to materialize. John Singer Sargent shyly chose an upper hallway for his murals on the evolution of religion, which he completed over a period of 26 years. Young Edwin Austin Abbey, working at his studio in Fairford, Gloucestershire, England, chose for his murals in the book-delivery room the legend of the Holy Grail, a story Abbey thought appropriate because it was known everywhere, thus paralleling the contents of the library's books, which concerned all countries. The medallions in the spandrels of the facade arches depicting marks and trade devices of printers are the work of Domingo Mora, who had earlier worked on the sculpture at Trinity Church.

The inner courtyard, whose obvious function is to provide light to rooms facing it, was done in very handsome brickwork with stone-arched arcades like those of the Palazzo Cancelleria in Rome. It is a pity that the tranquility and seclusion of the space are not more frequently sought by visitors.

The new addition, almost doubling the old building in volume, is from a 1964 design by Philip Johnson. The two parts join physically and jar visually. Each has it own scale, each its own interior spatial mood, each its own entrance, as though to admit a difference of opinion. The old looks back to even older ages for its inspiration; the new addition rejoices in its freedom from the past. The main purposes served are to cope with a large borrowing public, and to make more space for special department libraries.

While the original library was being built, many complaints were leveled at it that may be grouped under the headings of architects, costs, use and aesthetics. Major buildings—all buildings—are inevitably victims of criticism on these same issues. Newspapers said that a local architect should have been chosen; the public agreed that the cost was too great, but liked the result; librarians preferred a different stack system; other architects and connoisseurs found fault with the rigid classicism; and there were all those undigested, ill-formed opinions that were proffered for a number of biased reasons. Yet the building continued to be built from the original plans with very little, if any, regard for public or private opinion. The clamor and criticism subsided when the doors opened and Boston discovered what a beautiful pearl had emerged from the wetlands of the Back Bay.

—PAUL F. NORTON

CITY HALL
Boston, Massachusetts, U.S.A.

1962-69. Architects: Kallmann, McKinnell and Knowles [Gerhard Kallmann (born 1915), Noel McKinnell (born 1935), Edward Knowles (born 1929)].

Publications

"Boston City Hall." *Arkitekten* 26 (1963).

"Boston City Hall." *Casabella* (January 1963).

"Boston's Emerging Architectural Monument." *Architectural Forum* (November 1966).

A Competition to Select an Architect for the New City Hall in the Government Center of the City of Boston. Boston, 1961.

"Facade: Boston City Hall." *Architects' Journal* (January 1969).

FITCH, JAMES MARSTON: "City Hall, Boston." *Architectural Review* 147, 880: 398-411.

"A Great Plaza for Boston's Government Center." *Architectural Record* (March 1964).

HOFMANN, WERNER, and KULTERMANN, UDO: *Modern Architecture in Color.* New York, 1970.

"La Tourette Comes to Boston: Boston City Hall." *Architects' Journal* (July 1962).

McQUADE, WALTER: "Toughness Before Gentility Wins in Boston." *Architectural Forum* (August 1962).

MERTZ, J. G.: "Ein Projekt für die Boston City Hall." *Werk* (Zurich, February 1963).

MOHOLY-NAGY, SIBYL: "Boston's City Hall: It Binds the Past to Its Future." *Architectural Forum* (January/February 1969).

"Projet pour l'Hôtel de Ville de Boston, Etats Unis." *Architecture d'aujourd'hui* (February 1963).

SCHMERTZ, MILDRED F.: "The New Boston City Hall." *Architectural Record* 145, 2: 133-144.

SPREIREGEN, PAUL: "The Boston Government Center: A Study in Urban Design." *Arts and Architecture* (October 1965).

City Hall: Boston, Massachusetts, 1962-69

The Boston City Hall is a bold concrete-and-brick structure related more to the British architectural movement of the New Brutality, in which structure and services are dominantly expressed, than to any American idiom of the 1960s. Although the New Brutality had several roots, it was strongly influenced by Le Corbusier, especially his Maisons Jaoul in Paris (1955), which were constructed of cheap load-bearing stock bricks and *béton brut* in which the formwork of the beams and slabs are crudely emphasized. Even so, the overall form of the City Hall more clearly parallels Corbusier's design for the Monastery of Sainte-Marie de la Tourette (1956-60). The reason that this British movement became the expression for the City Hall is that two of the three architects—Gerhard Kallman, a German by birth, and Noel McKinnell—were trained in Britain. Together with Edward Knowles, an American-trained architect, they taught at Columbia University when they entered, and won, the two-stage competition, the first stage attracting 256 entrants from which eight finalists were chosen. William Wurster, Walter Netsch, Ralph Rapson and Pietro Belluschi acted as the four major jurors, and they were unanimous in their decision.

Siting the City Hall within a large plaza had been decided in 1960 when Edward Logue of the Boston Redevelopment Authority, together with the architect I. M. Pei, located the center for federal, state and local government in the Scollay Square area, as part of the master plan of Boston. Fitzgerald Expressway (Interstate 93) had cut off the North End from the remainder of Boston, and to its west lay the decayed and dilapidated warehouse district of Scollay Square, where cheap

stores, seedy bars and other low-class entertainments proliferated. The area was ripe for removal and gentrification. Government Center was the result, conceived as a square surrounded by federal and state buildings with the City Hall located at its center. Pedestrian walkways were to be through the City Hall with peripheral activities around the square, half-a-million square feet in extent. In some ways City Hall Square reflects the piazza at medieval Siena, with the town hall having a central court as does the Boston City Hall. City Hall Square is, of course, too large, bleak, impersonal and dominated by all types of adverse microclimatic conditions to be successful. Only on rare occasions, such as when the city's athletic teams became champions, has the square been fully utilized.

Since there is a major level change between City Hall Square and the Faneuil Hall/Quincy Market redevelopment across Congress Street, traffic is introduced into the building at the lowest level of the brick base. This three-story 57-foot-high base without windows is meant to be contextual. Beacon Hill to the east, Sears Crescent, the only building on the square to be retained, and Faneuil Hall are all of brick. To have located windows in the brick base would either have mimicked or clashed with these historic structures. Material context did not mean stylistic copying. The concrete was meant to simulate Boston's stone structures, and although the building reads as a unified whole, each elevation is different. On various sides, for example, canopies overhang the library and mayor's office to express major elements within the design.

In the base, parking, the heating plant and computer center

are located. A main east entrance leading to the second and third levels introduces 5,000 Bostonians daily into the building to pay taxes and conduct other local business. Rooflights from the brick plaza provide natural daylighting to the Treasurer's Department below. The council chamber, library, mayor's and council members' offices are at the fifth level, accessed from the grand, almost Piranesian, main south lobby. The brick base and concrete middle ceremonial level are then capped by three administrative floors, stepped out with *brise soleil* and supported on huge Corbusian "pilotis," or rather fins, supporting Vierendeel trusses. Internal materials consist of concrete and brick, complemented on ceremonial floors by metallic surfaces, exotic woods, fabrics and neutral color schemes.

Architecturally the designers wanted the building to be "a celebration of government" and "an architecture for the people." The building was presented with an American Institute of Architects' Honors Award in 1969, one of only 16 throughout the United States in that year.

—LAWRENCE WODEHOUSE

MASSACHUSETTS STATE HOUSE
Boston, Massachusetts

1795-97. Architect: Charles Bulfinch (1763-1844). **1802:** Wood dome changed to copper by silversmith Paul Revere. **1831:** Rear addition; **Architect:** Isaiah Rogers. **1853-55:** Further expansion to rear; **Architect:** Gridley F. Bryant. **1874:** Dome covered in gold leaf. **1886-87:** Large rear addition; **Architects:** John Hubbard Sturgis (1834-88) and Charles Brigham. **1896:** Rehabilitation of Bulfinch Front; **Architects:** Cummings, Andrews and Everett. **1913-19:** Side wings added.

Publications

BULFINCH, ELLEN SUSAN: *The Life and Times of Charles Bulfinch, Architect.* Boston and New York, 1896.
"Charles Bulfinch, the First American Architect." *Architecture* 52 (December 1925): 431-436.
FORBES, JOHN D.: "Shepley, Bulfinch, Richardson and Abbott, Architects: An Introduction." *Journal of the Society of Architectural Historians* 17 (1958): 19-31.
HITCHCOCK, HENRY-RUSSELL, and SEALE, WILLIAM: *Temples of Democracy: The State Capitols of the USA.* New York, 1976.
HOWELLS, JOHN MEAD: "Charles Bulfinch, Architect." *American Architect* 93 (June 1908): 195-200.
KIRKER, HAROLD, and KIRKER, JAMES: *Bulfinch's Boston, 1787-1817.* New York, 1964.
KIRKER, HAROLD: *The Architecture of Charles Bulfinch.* Cambridge, Massachusetts, 1978.
PICKENS, BUFORD: "Wyatt's Pantheon, the State House in Boston and a New View of Bulfinch." *Journal of the Society of Architectural Historians* 29 (May 1970): 124-131.
PIERSON, WILLIAM H., JR.: "American Neoclassicism—The Traditional Phase: Charles Bulfinch." In *American Buildings and Their Architects: The Colonial and Neo-Classical Styles.* Garden City, New York, 1970.
PLACE, CHARLES A.: *Charles Bulfinch, Architect and Citizen.* Boston and New York, 1925.
QUINCY, JOSIAH: *A Municipal History of the Town and City of Boston during Two Centuries.* Boston, 1852.
SHANNON, M. A. S.: "Architecture of Charles Bulfinch." *American Magazine of Art* 17 (August 1925): 431-437.

*

Designed by Charles Bulfinch in 1785, the Massachusetts State House was (with Thomas Jefferson's Virginia Capitol) among the first of an entirely new building type, the public assembly hall for the conduct of state government. Its domed form was to set the standard profile for virtually every American state capitol designed in the next two centuries, and also for the United States Capitol building in Washington D.C., whose original wooden copper-clad dome was completed by Bulfinch in 1819-25.

Son of a prosperous Boston merchant and professional family, Bulfinch became interested in architecture as a youth. After graduating from Harvard College he was sent on the grand tour in 1785-87, spending some time in London, where he studied the most recent work by William Chambers, John Soane and James Wyatt. About 10 months after his return to Massachusetts, Bulfinch boldly presented to the committee considering the construction of a new legislative house a plan of his own that was based, as he said, on modern European sources, but that had been adapted "to the convenience and necessities of the country" and also incorporated "an air of magnificence, without departing from economy."

Although construction was delayed for several years, and the final plan was modified slightly, the State House as built in 1795-97 apparently reflected the essence of Bulfinch's original scheme. Moreover, Bulfinch was appointed to the committee of three that undertook and supervised construction of the new statehouse. Bulfinch's specific inspiration was the domed central section of Chambers' new Somerset House in London, begun in 1776. Although Massachusetts had vigorously pursued freedom from English government control, Bulfinch successfully convinced officials that his building scheme, although based on English sources, was modern in concept and would suitably house the new legislative requirements. Built of brick (unlike Chambers' stone prototype), the Massachusetts State House was a rectangular mass, with a square central legislative chamber covered by a low dome. Externally this was announced by a high wooden false dome with lantern, echoing the lower, more Roman dome atop Somerset House. To the right, in the north wing, was a smaller chamber for the senate, and mirroring this in the wing to the south were offices for the governor, his council and other auxiliary facilities. The central legislative chamber, with its clipped corners, broad segmental arches and low domed ceiling, seems to have been patterned after James Wyatt's very popular Pantheon in London (1770-72).

For the front elevation Bulfinch adapted the central motif of Somerset House—a rusticated base with round-headed windows, and an upper section with an engaged Corinthian order—by making it three-dimensional. Below is a broad arcaded entrance portico of seven bays, supporting an open Corinthian colonnade above that provides a broad porch overlooking the Boston Common. The greater breadth of Bulfinch's portico also resembles a similar wide portico built at Heveningham Hall, Suffolk, by Robert Taylor in 1778-80.

Massachusetts State House: Boston, Massachusetts, 1795-98

Although white marble was used for lintels and keystones, most of the decorative trim was of wood, expertly carved by shipwright/carpenters, and painted white. The tall dome was also of wood, sheathed in canvas, originally whitewashed and later painted to resemble lead. In 1802 it was covered in copper by silversmith Paul Revere. Today the dome is an even more distinctive and brilliant landmark in Boston, since in 1874 it was covered in gold leaf and has remained gilded since.

Bulfinch's Massachusetts State House served as a model for several later state capitols, either in plan arrangement or domed profile. The New Hampshire Capitol (1816-19) emulated its plan; the Vermont Capitol (1832) had a similar profile translated into heavier Greek and Roman components. When Maine was split off from Massachusetts and became a separate state, Bulfinch was engaged in 1828 to design its new capitol in Augusta. At the insistence of the Maine legislators, Bulfinch prepared a modification of the capitol in Boston, incorporating a lower dome on a square base, and a broad octastyle portico using heavier Roman Doric columns.

In 1831, due to an expanding legislature in Massachusetts, an addition was built onto the rear by Isaiah Rogers, creating a T-shaped layout; this was expanded again by Gridley F. Bryant in 1853-55. A highly elaborate proposal, made by Bryant in 1866, for further remodeling Bulfinch's statehouse was rejected. Fortunately subsequent political differences prevented both abandonment of the Massachusetts State House for a new location further west in the state, as well as significant renovation; Bryant's expansion proposal of 1866 would have nearly obliterated Bulfinch's original design.

By 1886, when the need for more space was urgent, artistic taste had shifted so that Bulfinch's building, which was associated with the nation's beginnings, was viewed more positively. A large addition (1886-87) was designed by Sturgis and Brigham for the rear of Bulfinch's building, bridging over Mount Vernon Street, and built of yellow brick to match the exterior of the Bulfinch building, which was painted yellow at the time. No taller than Bulfinch's building, the addition continued the same cornice line, but since the ground fell away behind the old statehouse, the farthest part of the new addition was nearly five stories tall. Brigham's recessed windows and classical details closely emulated Bulfinch's work, although the details throughout were cut in stone. Although large, the addition worked well visually with the original building and was judged a great success. Side wings, set back from the Bulfinch front, were added in 1913-19.

The original Bulfinch front section was, by 1892, suffering badly from neglect, but when a suggestion was broached that it be torn down and a new front built, citizens from across the state protested. After deliberation, it was decided in 1896 to execute a thorough rehabilitation in what was then called the Bulfinch Front. Carried out by Cummings, Andrews and Everett, the work entailed insertion of steel beams, replacement of rotten wood, restoration of original decorations and addition of new embellishments (such work would not be called restoration by today's standards).

The Massachusetts State House has proven to be a venerable model, and an important vestige of those critical years when the new nation was defining itself and shaping new buildings to house representative government.

—LELAND ROTH

TRINITY CHURCH
Boston, Massachusetts, U.S.A.

1873-77: Construction. **Architect:** Henry Hobson Richardson (1838-1886).

Publications

ADAMS, A. J.: "Birth of a Style: Henry Hobson Richardson and the Competition Drawings for Trinity Church, Boston." *Art Bulletin* 62 (1980): 409-433.

Monographs of American Architecture Vol. 1: *Austin Hall, Harvard Law School, Cambridge, Mass.*, Vol. 3: *Ames Memorial Building*, Vol. 5: *Trinity Church, Boston, Mass.*, Boston, 1886-1888.

RICHARDSON, H. H.: *A Description of Trinity Church.* Boston.

"Strength in conception; clearness in expression; breadth in treatment; imagination; and a love for repose and massive dignity of aspect, and often for an effect which in the widest meaning of the word we may call 'romantic.' "

These are the words Mrs. Van Rensselaer used in 1888 to describe the whole of Henry Hobson Richardson's architectural work, yet she could have been characterizing only the qualities of Trinity Church. What Van Rensselaer said one hundred years ago is still true today. In spite of all the large new buildings rising around it, Trinity retains a dignity and correctness of place and scale with regard to the plaza before it. Trinity reminds

one of the ancient formative years of Christianity in the Western World, while standing today as a bulwark of the faith against the rank commercialism intruding on its presence.

Born as the result of a disaster and the existence of a great, foresighted rector, Trinity, like the great medieval cathedrals of Europe, has not outgrown its purpose and its usefulness to mankind. The reason for this lies in part with the site chosen for the new church after the previous building on Summer Street had burned—all but the stone walls. The site was selected in the new Back Bay area, which was becoming the choice for dwellings of the professional class. As streets nearby are still inhabited by a large population, Trinity continues to serve the community, as well as provide for residents of the inner suburbs.

Perhaps the greater reason for the success of Trinity is its architectural design. As the first nationally important work by Richardson, one that was immediately conceded a masterpiece, the architect was able to build his whole career upon this renowned achievement. For the last decade of his life Richardson had more clients than he could satisfy; his office was filled with young, aspiring architects, several of whom were later to become well known in their own right. But the large congregation of Trinity always said it was Phillips Brooks' church, seeming to believe that the good qualities of the building were owing to the rector's planning that was merely carried out by its architect. The truth probably lies somewhere in between. Brooks and Richardson became very good friends and listened well to each other. They respected each other's strengths and weaknesses. Brooks knew the Bible and how he wished to preach his evangelical sermons. Richardson had little interest in organized religion; he was an organizer of space and materials. When Richardson became fully aware of what Brooks wanted,

Trinity Church: Boston, Massachusetts, 1873-77

Trinity Church, interior stained glass

and the rector in turn became convinced that he had found an architect who could almost miraculously turn his wants into physical reality, then the church could be built.

The architect created a wide, short plan, almost a Greek-cross plan, but modified to have a broad, semicircular apse at the east end of the chancel, and a nave slightly longer than the transepts. By placing the pulpit at the point joining the chancel and the north transept. Brooks could preach familiarly to his congregation while easily being seen and heard. The close proximity of the rector and his congregation was imperative, for it was Brooks' sermons that thrilled not only the members of his parish, but also those persons of many other denominations than the Episcopal that flocked to the church.

The design with which Richardson won the competition, over the formidable opposition of several better-known rivals, such as Peabody and Stearns and Richard Morris Hunt, had a very tall, progressively tapering tower over the crossing. Its base was narrower than the width of the nave that formed a Latin cross with a characteristic nave longer than the transepts. When the church bought an additional piece of property to the north, Richardson was able to expand the width of the nave and transepts, creating a space more pleasing to Brooks. Both men were familiar with the Romanesque style, Richardson having seen it during his student days in the 1860s in Paris, and Brooks at his Philadelphia church before he was lured to Boston and by travel to France. Richardson probably enjoyed the robustness and massive stonework of the Romanesque, while Brooks was attracted by the interior spatial features, perhaps even imagining the pleasure of preaching in the Auvergnate types that he had visited, with their central towers and Greek-cross plans. Brooks was convinced that the early church of the Romanesque age

was superior to the church as it developed in the age of the Gothic cathedrals. He saw the early church as more directly concerned with the words of the Bible, as he was himself, than the Roman Catholic Church, which had adopted doctrine that Brooks believed suppressed certain human freedoms.

As the plan of the church was revised to meet Brooks' demands, so was the tower over the greatly expanded interior body. The tower by then reached such proportions as to dominate the whole exterior of the building and the square in front. The bold simplicity of it gave ample opportunity for decoration. On close inspection it may be seen that there is scarcely a square foot of exterior surface that is not in some way a part of the decorative scheme. Enrichment is everywhere. The same is clearly true of the interior, where all surfaces are painted, often with superb frescoes by John La Farge, and every window is filled with gorgeous color from the use of stained-glass windows whose presence not only adds to the ever-changing brilliance of exterior light brought within, but gives room for the visual expression of biblical themes—themes that Phillips Brooks most wanted displayed.

There is no other church in America that better demonstrates the unity of faith, architecture and decoration than Trinity. Very likely this is owing to the continuous cooperation of Brooks and Richardson, but also to their assistants at the church such as the Building Committee and the Window Committee, the enormous energy and talent of John La Farge, and the draftsmen at Richardson's office. When all these parties generously combined their efforts, the result was a monument of near perfection.

As proof of the building's integrity, that is, its suitability for its purpose, its inventive use of old, symbolic form, and its open declaration of the texture and solidity of the building materials, one can perceive historically that its influence was immense upon the designing of buildings in America for the rest of the century. And although the formal aspects of Trinity are not in detail or decoration those of today, there are still many lessons to be learned there by contemporary architects.

—PAUL F. NORTON

LARKIN BUILDING
Buffalo, New York, U.S.A.

1904. Architect: Frank Lloyd Wright (1867-1959).

Publications

FRAMPTON, KENNETH, and FUTAGAWA, YUKIO: *Modern Architecture: 1851-1919*. New York, 1983.

HITCHCOCK, HENRY-RUSSELL: *In the Nature of Materials: The Buildings of Frank Lloyd Wright, 1887-1941*. New York, 1942.

QUINLAN, JACK: *Frank Lloyd Wright's Larkin Building*. Cambridge, Massachusetts, 1990.

WRIGHT, FRANK LLOYD: "The New Larkin Administration Building." *Larkin Idea* (November 1906). Reprint: *Prairie School Review* 7 (First Quarter, 1970): 15-19.

*

The ways of client-architect relationships have been such that an architect has often been given the commission for a new residence by a satisfied client, but the commission for the Larkin Building is a classic example of a reversal of that process. It also amply illustrates the power of Frank Lloyd Wright to impress the clients for whom his houses were built. In this case, W. E. Martin, of Oak Park, fell under the spell of Wright and the early prairie houses in his neighborhood. Before long, the architect was building at roughly the same time Martin's new home in Oak Park, a home for Martin's brother Darwin in

Larkin Building: Buffalo, New York, 1904

Buffalo, five other homes for family and friends of the brothers in Buffalo, and two commercial structures. The E-Z Polish Company of Chicago was owned by the brothers and run by W. E., and the Larkin Company in Buffalo was served by Darwin Martin as chief financial officer. It was Darwin who, having caught the Wright fever from his brother, proposed the Oak Park architect for the new administrative headquarters being planned next to the factory. Thus, in 1902-05, Wright was responsible for two commercial buildings spawned by his residential clients, with the Larkin to become one of the most important structures of his career.

Though demolished in 1949-50 when the firm no longer had any use for it (the site is still vacant 40 years later), the Larkin Building long had the distinction of being one of the most successfully designed commercial buildings of its era. It was pioneering in several important ways. Building on a site in close proximity to factories and railroad sidings, Wright (in a format he was to follow even more fully in Unity Temple, two years later) minimized contact with the outer world with a combination of a building essentially sealed off from its surroundings. A massive, fortress-like brick building, with the first commercial use of double-glazed windows, the Larkin Building included a pioneering form of mechanical air-conditioning that was based on cold running water and the use of fans to distribute the freshened air. Wright also included the Foster & Glidden-designed vacuum cleaning system marketed by that Oak Park firm in recognition of the need for maintaining an office setting free of the pollutants found in and created by the factory. He even thought to use an unusually hard light-colored brick for the interior, as it was easy to keep clean and increased the brightness in the office spaces.

It is especially interesting that Wright, the experienced architect of domestic structures who could drive Darwin Martin's wife to distraction by the way he sacrificed her domestic needs to his aesthetic sense, worked long and hard to make every part of the Larkin Building functional. In addition to dealing with the issue of cleanliness, he successfully sought to eliminate clutter through a greater use of metal and other nonconventional materials for all the surfaces. He designed metal desks with seats that were attached to and swung out from the desks, thus giving unlimited access to the floor surface. Further, he used metal in creating built-in storage and file cabinets, again making it unnecessary to move things for cleaning and, at the same time, permitting more open space with less clutter; even the wires for desk lamps and telephones were run through underground conduits into each work station. Even at the most mundane level, in the bathrooms, Wright utilized toilets that cantilevered from the wall. The bathrooms themselves were quartered in a separate wing of the building, along with the cafeteria and other amenities.

The heavy exterior of the building, twice as long as it was wide, was set on its side with the short facade facing the street and the length stretching back toward the factories: it thus served as an entrance into the entire Larkin complex. Imposing and sealed as the environment was, the exterior was true to the design of the interior, revealing the number of floors and its basic organization through the arrangement of the windows and brick courses dividing the floors.

In spite of the massive, even forbidding, dark-brick exterior of the building, Wright used his double-glazed windows and the overhead skylight to flood the five-story interior with daylight, though the employees, seated in the center of the atrium, had no direct access to any of the windows. He also permitted more than the usual amount of light to enter by moving all the stairs to the corners of the building, creating a more open space. Finally, out of concern for the workers' comfort and utmost in

protection from fire in such a space, Wright experimented with Magnesite, a recently patented man-made fireproofing material, using it for the floors and most of the work surfaces.

Few buildings, either near the turn of the century or long thereafter, exhibited as much sensitivity to both efficiency and human safety as did the Larkin Building, and the description and photographs that are its only ongoing record give ample substantiation for the architect's often-noted pride in producing such an innovative landmark of commercial design.

—DAVID M. SOKOL

DULLES INTERNATIONAL AIRPORT
Chantilly, Virginia, U.S.A.

1958-62. Architect: Eero Saarinen (1910-61).

Publications

"Eero Saarinen." *Architecture & Urbanism* (April 1984).

HOFMANN, WERNER, and KULTERMANN, UDO: *Modern Architecture in Color*. New York, 1970.

MCQUADE, W.: "Eero Saarinen, A Complete Architect." *Architectural Forum* (April 1962): 102-119.

PAPADEMETRIOU, P.C.: "Coming of Age: Eero Saarinen and Modern American Architecture." *Perspecta* 21 (1985): 116-141.

"Recent Work of Eero Saarinen." *Zodiac* 4 (1959): 30-67.

SAARINEN, A.: *Eero Saarinen on His Work*. New Haven, 1962.

SAARINEN, EERO: "Our Epoch of Architecture." *Journal of the American Institute of Architects* 18 (1952): 243-247.

SPADE, R. and FUTAGAWA, Y.: *Eero Saarinen (Masters of Modern Architecture series)*. New York, 1968.

SPADE, RUPERT: *Eero Saarinen*. 1971.

TEMKO, A.: *Eero Saarinen (Makers of Contemporary Architecture series)*. New York, 1962.

*

From the outset, the "Washington International Airport," as the project was known in the office of Eero Saarinen and Associates, was conceived as a gateway to the capital city, although its form owed as much to its location in Virginia's Piedmont Valley. Eero Saarinen, who died in September 1961 only 10 months before its completion, stated that he initially wanted to "place a strong form between earth and sky that seems both to rise from the plain and hover over it."

The airport's image is its suspended roof form, a compact structure 170 feet wide and 600 feet long. The design *parti*, aesthetically potent as it is, was arrived at only after a rigorous analysis of all aspects of the problem. Originating as a commission to Ammann and Whitney Engineers, the project was a collaboration between consultants; yet in many ways, Dulles Airport (named in the waning days of the Eisenhower Administration) is best representative of the Saarinen method. At the time of its inception, the project was to rewrite standards as the nation's first all-jet airport planned from the outset for expansion. Its 9,600-acre site could fit over Washington's northwest area, and all of National Airport could fit into the space reserved for the terminal area. Central to the solution was Saarinen's wish to facilitate an indeterminate expansion with a concept that would limit disruption to operations, and to mitigate

Dulles International Airport: Chantilly, Virginia, 1958-62

distances for passenger travel. From this emerged the decision to dispense with the standard American "finger" terminal arrangement for a centralized, linear shed for passengers, separate and remote servicing for planes, and a link between both functions.

Saarinen was unique among his contemporaries in recognizing, as critic Cranston Jones observed, that "the valid approaches to modern architectural problems are vastly more varied than any single-minded approach would indicate," a search for form rooted in functionalism, but also concerned with expanding a formal language into "... an updated *architecture parlante*, not a style but ... a literary architecture that would arouse emotions and affect sentiments," as noted by John Jacobus. On one level, the concept of the Mobile Lounge, a vehicle to connect passenger from terminal to plane, not as a bus but as a direct extension of the departure lounge itself, was the conceptually correct innovation, one which brought the passenger to the plane rather than the plane to the passenger. To achieve Dulles Airport, the Lounge had to be invented. It was Saarinen's success as a practitioner that the concept was developed and adopted. However, his idea was not to celebrate technology, but rather to put it in service of a higher conception of the issues within the problem. The architectural container ultimately became the connection between all elements of the airport, and the symbol of its synthesis of functions.

At Dulles Airport, Saarinen sought to retain the unchanging scale of pedestrian circulation in the face of an enormous shift in technological and environmental scale. The concern for the passenger begins a scenographic experience which orchestrates movement from its start on a 17-mile access road, linked to

Washington's Beltway system, such that most of the 27-mile trip is on high-speed, no-intersection parkways. As Edgar Kaufmann, Jr., described the approach, "as the perspective shifts, the road relaxes, and there, on its two extended, concave podia, rises a temple to the friendly power of flight." The passenger engages the terminal directly, since grade-separated vehicular arrival points locate all entries at ticket counters; the interior "great hall" concept is created by an unobstructed space in which support functions appear as furniture, and the distance from arrival to Mobile Lounge is only a few hundred feet.

The terminal's form, described by Saarinen, "resembles a huge, continuous hammock suspended between concrete trees." The hovering image is achieved by the projecting thrust of the main support piers, 65 feet high on the field side, and 43 feet on the approach side. Structurally, the 16 pairs of supports are cantilever beams, braced against the thrust of the hanging suspension roof by large footings and a main floor acting like a strut between opposing supports. Technologically, the free-span interior was achieved by prefabricated planks spanning 10 feet between steel cables slung across the span in a catenary curve, an innovative erection method that did not necessitate interior scaffolding. The monolithic integrity of the roof was achieved by poured concrete "ribs" between adjacent rows of planks. The autonomy of the roof structure is maintained by the design of the infill glass, which furthers and counterpoints its curved geometry, and while resistant to wind loading, remains a gossamer transparent membrane.

The dynamic geometry of Dulles Airport draws upon multiple allusions; its curvilinear forms recall the 1920s drawings of

Dulles International Airport

Erich Mendelsohn, thereby reinstating expressionist architecture as a source, as well as the great arrival train sheds of the 19th century, or in its whiteness, a Federal architecture. As critic Peter Carter summarized, "Saarinen was aware of today's technology in its widest sense . . . as a means of achieving a many-faceted architectural expression within the tradition of the modern masters. To advance the symbolic and environmental content of that tradition he explored special architectural vernaculars for each project . . . it precluded the possibility of a personal style, a fact which set him apart from any of his contemporaries."

—PETER PAPADEMETRIOU

DRAYTON HALL PLANTATION
Charleston, South Carolina, U.S.A.

1738-42: House constructed. **Architect:** Believed to be Peter Harrison (1716-1775).

Publications

RAVENEL, BEATRICE ST. JULIEN: *Architects of Charleston.* Charleston, S.C, 1945.

Drayton Hall was the first major neo-Palladian structure in America (two earlier neo-Palladian designs, both presumably by the painter John Smibert, were Whitehall in Middletown, Rhode Island (1729), for the philosopher George Berkeley, and St. Pauls' College in Bermuda, the latter never executed).

The house was built in 1738-42 for the Honourable John Drayton, member of the King's (i.e., Governor's) Council, who is recorded to have been indifferent in his education, so he could not have been the architect of his own house. In spite of years of diligent searching, no mention of any architect has been found. Peter Harrison, within whose style the house falls, is known to have visited Charleston several times as a mate on his brother's merchant ship in the period 1738-42. Moreover, many aspects of the design of Drayton reappear in other American buildings with strong Harrison connections, so unless and until documentation of a different architect appears, Harrison would be the most likely choice.

Drayton's most prominent feature is a double-decked (Ionic over Doric) tetrastyle portico with recessed porches on the land, or west, front, based on Andrea Palladio's design at the Villa Pisani in Italy; this was the first such portico in America. Other such porticoes appeared at the Statehouse II, Williamsburg, Virginia (possibly by Peter Harrison, 1749, demolished); Battersea, Petersburg, Virginia (possibly by Harrison, ca. 1765, altered); Stuyvesant House, New York (also perhaps by Harrison, ca. 1756, demolished); Hibbert House, Kingston, Jamaica (ca. 1765, hexastyle, altered); Brewton House, Charleston, South Carolina (by Ezra Waite, 1768); Shirley, Charles City, Virginia (added ca. 1769); Monticello I, near Charlottesville, Virginia (Thomas Jefferson, ca. 1772, demolished); W. Washington

Drayton Hall: Charleston, South Carolina, 1738-42

House, Charleston, South Carolina (William Miller, ca. 1772); Lansdowne, Philadelphia (possibly by Robert Smith, ca. 1773, hexastyle, demolished); Kershaw House, Camden, South Carolina (Miller, 1775, reconstructed); Annfield, Berryville, Virginia (possibly by John Ariss, ca. 1790); Dr. Wicks House, Falmouth, Massachusetts (1790); and Essex County Courthouse, Salem, Massachusetts (ca. 1790, demolished).

Drayton is built of brick laid in Flemish bond with incomplete belt courses. It is seven bays wide by six bays deep, and stands two stories tall over a high basement. The mansard roof, which is surmounted by two chimneys, stands over a modillioned cornice atop a full, if simple, entablature. On the river front, a handsome divided stone staircase leads to a rich Doric pedimented doorcase, and the central three windows on the floor above are framed in pedimented Ionic aedicules. A large, unsupported pediment on the roof is almost certainly a 19th-century alteration.

Inside the river front is a two-story hall with divided stairs of mahogany with rich carving and baroque balusters. The center of the house is occupied by one large, fully paneled room on each floor—the Doric "great hall" downstairs and the ballroom above. However, after construction had begun, the owner decided to enlarge these rooms at the expense of the stairhall, which caused the communicating wall to be placed some distance away from the foundation wall intended to support it, and this part of the house has always had structural problems as a result (evidence that the architect was not present after construction was begun). These structural problems are finally being addressed with modern technology by the present owners.

The two great rooms and the eight lesser rooms were all richly decorated with raised paneling, carved woodwork, pilasters,

entablatures and molded ceilings, but the greatest glory lay in the William Kent-style mantels and overmantels. Some of the original ceilings and mantels have disappeared, but the house is nonetheless surprisingly intact. In fact, Drayton Hall has never had wiring, plumbing or central heating installed, and the present owners are obligated to maintain that condition. Moreover, the house is displayed almost entirely unfurnished, which permits the magnificent woodwork to be seen to best advantage with no distractions. One unfortunate alteration is that the original 12-over-12 sash windows were replaced in the 19th century by 6-over-6 windows.

A crude, period manuscript sketch (probably not by the architect) shows the intention of building a pair of large formal dependencies, each with a cupola, to form a forecourt on the land side. The dependencies, one of which was likely a stable/carriage house and the other plantation offices, were to have been connected to the house by colonnaded quadrants, but the whole scheme was never executed. Later in the 18th century, a pair of small, simple pedimented dependencies were built to form a forecourt. Whereas the basement of the main house rests essentially on top of the sandy soil, the later dependencies had their basements well below grade. Late in the 19th century, a tremendous earthquake rocked the area, destroying many of the finest buildings. Drayton Hall survived almost intact, skating over the surface, but one of the dependencies was destroyed and the other damaged, only to fall victim to a hurricane not long afterward.

During the Civil War, the owner saved the house from destruction at the hands of a Union army by reporting that the house was being used as a smallpox hospital. Since 1974 the house and surrounding 632 acres have been owned by the National Trust for Historic Preservation in partnership with the Historic Charleston Foundation, and it is open to the public. Previously, it had been owned by seven generations of the Drayton family.

One official of the National Trust has described Drayton Hall as "the most beautiful house in America"; if Peter Harrison was indeed the architect, such an achievement is all the more extraordinary for what was probably his earliest executed design.

—JOHN F. MILLAR

UNIVERSITY OF VIRGINIA
Charlottesville, Virginia, U.S.A.

1817-26: Construction; **Architect:** Thomas Jefferson (1743-1826).

Publications

BINNEY, I. M.: 'University of Virginia." *Country Life* 163 (12 January 1978): 74-77.

BINNEY, I. M.: 'University of Virginia, II." *Country Life* 163 (19 January 1978): 142-145.

BROWN, GLENN: "Letters from Thomas Jefferson and William Thornton, Architect, Relating to the University of Virginia." *American Institute of Architects Journal* 1 (1913): 21-27.

BRUCE, PHILIP A.: *History of the University of Virginia*. 5 vols. New York, 1920-22.

GOLDBERGER, PAUL: 'Ten Buildings with a Style of Their Own." *Portfolio* 1/2 (June-July 1979): 32-39.

LE COAT, G.: 'Thomas Jefferson et l'architecture metaphorique: le village academique a l'Université de Virginie." *RASCAR* 3, Part 2 (1976): 8-34.

'Mr. Jefferson's Rotunda." *HUD Challenge* 3 (December 1972): 7-9.

O'NEAL, W.B.: *Jefferson's Fine Arts Library: His Selections for the University of Virginia Together with His Own Architectural Books*. Charlottesville, Virginia, 1976.

WOODS, MARY N.: "Thomas Jefferson and the University of Virginia: Planning the Academic Village." *Journal of the Society of Architectural Historians* 44 (October 1985): 266-283.

YETTER, G. H.: 'Stanford White at the University of Virginia: Some New Light on the Old Question." *Journal of the Society of Architectural Historians* 40 (December 1981): 320-325.

*

Thomas Jefferson concluded his career in architecture with the building of the University of Virginia. Considered by Jefferson's contemporaries in architecture as a significant building project in the young history of American architecture, its stature has only increased over the years. As a gentleman architect, Jefferson experimented with many architectural ideas throughout his life. The University of Virginia represents the culmination of many of these ideas, combined with his ideas on educational reform.

Jefferson's academical village consists of 17 main buildings in four parallel rows running in a north-south direction. The two exterior rows consist of three two-story hotels, dining halls with living quarters for the proprietor above, connected by one-story student dormitories, each row facing outward through an arcade. The two interior rows consist of five two-story pavilions, classrooms with living quarters for the professor above, again connected by one-story student dormitories, facing each other through colonnades across a lawn open to the south but closed off on the north by the three-story Rotunda.

Designed not only as a village for learning, but also as a dictionary of classical architecture, the buildings around the central lawn show four of the five classical orders. Jefferson wanted the buildings to serve as examples for the architectural lecturer, so he designed four Doric pavilions, four Ionic pavilions and two Corinthian pavilions, and connected them all with a Tuscan colonnade. Not only does the decoration of each pavilion serve as an example of the classical orders, the pavilions also serve as examples of cubic architecture, a form Jefferson had worked with throughout his career.

As early as 1779 Jefferson experimented with the idea of using the cubic temple form, in his remodeling of the Governor's Palace at Williamsburg. Then in his design for the Virginia State Capitol in Richmond, Jefferson successfully fit a modern government building into the ancient religious form, using the Maison Carrée in Nîmes, France, as his model. At his university, Jefferson used the cubic temple form in his pavilions, placing more historical examples at the northern end of the lawn, and using more modern ideas as the pavilions progress southward, with the final pavilions being examples more of the neoclassical rather than the classical. Jefferson did ask for help from his friends William Thornton and Benjamin Henry Latrobe in designing the facades of the pavilions, and two of the original drawings for the pavilions have the word "Latrobe" written in the upper corner by Jefferson.

Latrobe can also be credited with giving Jefferson the idea for using a domed structure as the central building on the lawn. In early plans Jefferson did not distinguish the form of the central building from that of the pavilions. After receiving a letter in which Latrobe drew the central building as a domed structure, Jefferson designed his central building after the perfect model of spherical architecture, the Pantheon in Rome. Here again, the Rotunda represents the culmination of Jefferson's experimentation with spherical architecture. In 1770 Jefferson designed a domed, octagonal chapel, which contained a sphere within its walls and between the floor and ceiling. Although he designed numerous domes after that, Jefferson never built his pure example of spherical architecture until he built the Rotunda at the university.

All of these make the University of Virginia aesthetically important in the history of architecture, but Jefferson's design is even more important, in the field of education as well as the field of architecture, in its conceptual idea. Prior to that time most universities based their education around theology. In making his main central building a library, Jefferson moved the emphasis of his university to knowledge of the sciences rather than theology. Also, Jefferson introduced the concept of the elective system, whereby a student could choose a field of study and take classes in that field, rather than all students taking the same set of courses. This system worked well in Jefferson's village design, with each professor teaching only one subject in his pavilion.

Architecturally, Jefferson also broke from the traditional university building type. Prior to this, most colleges consisted of one large building with classrooms and dormitories under one roof. In fact, Jefferson's addition to the main building at the

Rotunda, University of Virginia: Charlottesville, Virginia, 1817-26

College of William and Mary simply completed the quadrangle of the original building, much like the English colleges it was patterned after. By spreading his classrooms out, and placing the student rooms between them, Jefferson hoped to avoid the pitfalls of these large buildings. He felt these buildings were dark and unhealthy, allowing disease to pass easily around the educational community. By having the student rooms open onto an exterior colonnade rather than an interior corridor, Jefferson hoped to provide a healthier environment for the students. He also hoped that the professors would police the students near their pavilions and cut down on rowdiness, an idea that did not always work. Additionally, by designing his university as a series of smaller buildings, he argued, it could be built over a period of several years, as the money became available, rather than all at once as a single building would have to be.

As his last architectural effort, the University of Virginia represents the culmination of Jefferson's architectural and educational ideas. There he brought together his best examples of cubic and spherical architecture, two forms that pervade his career. His new ideas about education needed a new form in which to be housed, and that he provided in a unified series of pavilions and student rooms which departed from the standard building type of the day. Even though Jefferson's building type did not catch on in the academic world, it is still viewed as one of the most significant developments in American architecture.

—RICHARD L. HAWKINS

AUDITORIUM BUILDING
Chicago, Illinois, U.S.A.

1887-89. Architects: Dankmar Adler (1844-1900) and Louis H. Sullivan (1856-1924).

Publications

ANDREW, DAVID S.: *Louis Sullivan and the Polemics of Modern Architecture: The Present against the Past.* Urbana, Illinois, and Chicago, 1985.
HASBROUCK, W. R.: 'Chicago's Auditorium Theater.'' *Prairie School Review* (Third Quarter, 1967).
O'GORMAN, JAMES F.: *Three American Architects: Richardson, Sullivan, and Wright, 1865-1915.* Chicago and London, 1991.
PERLMAN, DANIEL H.: *The Auditorium Building: Its History and Significance.* Chicago, 1976.
SCOTT, JIM, and SAMUELSON, TIM: "Auditorium Album." *Inland Architect* 33, 5 (September/October 1989): 64-71.

Even one hundred years after its completion, and with most of the interior space drastically modified and given over to different uses than were originally planned, the Auditorium Building is still one of the most imposing and dramatic buildings of its type, and the masterpiece of the firm of Dankmar Adler and Louis Sullivan.

Chicagoans have long enjoyed a reputation for both civic boosterism and large-scale construction, with ''the largest'' and ''the tallest'' being favorite descriptive terms. Ferdinand Peck, who had been the leading spirit behind the great Opera Festival of 1885, was such a Chicago booster, albeit one with a particular commitment to music and the visual arts. He, more than anyone else, flushed with the success of the festival, pushed for and made possible the creation of a new permanent facility for opera and other major musical events; he had also been pleased with the quality and the speed with which Adler and Sullivan had renovated the Interstate Exposition Building to make the Opera Festival possible. With a string of successful theaters and music palaces to their credit and with the support of Peck and other powerful Chicagoans who were established clients, Adler and Sullivan were chosen to create what was, for its time, not only the tallest and largest building in the city, but—at over 100,000 tons—the most massive in the world.

The challenges that the partners so masterfully faced were both varied and complex: they had the unusual task of developing a building of varied uses, including a hotel, concert hall and commercial space; without the benefit of the usual bisymmetrical design, they had to design and harmonize three facades of different lengths; and the combination of the vast auditorium area and the off-center tower created the necessity for previously untested structural solutions to the problem of uneven settlement. Not least among the challenges to Adler and Sullivan was the chore of pleasing the various illustrious and powerful members of the board, many of whom had commissioned major structures themselves, and all certain that they knew what was needed in a building that would serve as such a conspicuous place in their city.

Looking at the completed building (which eventually cost over $3 million, over 50 percent more than originally planned), after its several major design modifications, it is easy to see the strong influence of H. H. Richardson. While the rusticated masonry and the massive arches directly show the influence of

the recently deceased older man's newly completed Wholesale Store for Marshall Field, Sullivan, the principal author of the Auditorium's design, had admired the work of Richardson since the former had observed his buildings as a teenager in Boston. Perhaps more than any one American architect, Richardson's historical references were to provide the only examples acceptable to Sullivan, as he worked his way toward a total repudiation of the past, with the Auditorium, and in his designs for the Standard Club in Chicago (1887), the Opera House in Pueblo, Colorado (1889), and the Dooly Block in Salt Lake City (1890-91). While a commission and a building of the first significance, the Auditorium Building is still Sullivan's great creation in a retrogressive mode.

The massive and noble facades, particularly the great loggia along the south end of the building, fail to reveal the uses of the interior space, subordinating those expressions of function to a larger rhythmic order. Further, considering the major Chicago buildings that already revealed something more about their metal construction, Sullivan could have followed their example on both the facades and the great interior space. Keenly aware of such buildings as the recently completed Home Insurance Building (1884-85) and the contemporary Rookery (1885-86), Sullivan chose to subordinate his knowledge of the structural potential of the building to create a satisfying aesthetic effect through its massing. The solidity of the structure, combined with masonry in the service of verticality, makes one of the strongest statements about a public building in traditional, though not classical, terms.

The interior of the Auditorium, while divided among many uses, and especially in the great concert hall itself, is still a great monument to the skills of both Adler and Sullivan, an acoustical gem second in size only to La Scala, and the summation of all of Sullivan's early conceptions about design and decoration. Almost 6,000 electric lights serve as a key element in the immense room, playing off the brilliant predominant gold of the arches and the large skylight of colored glass. Geometric and foliated areas each have their part in developing the richness of pattern, play off against each other, yet contribute to a satisfying whole.

The other great spaces of the building are no longer visible, but their impact was so strong that critics from around the country noted that Sullivan's accomplishments in designing both interior and exterior had made his reputation as a preeminent designer secure, putting to rest the accusation that he was only a decorator. And though it is still difficult to separate out completely the contributions of each partner, the Auditorium Building is a true collaboration of two people with separate yet overlapping strengths. Without Adler's profound knowledge of engineering and the latest in acoustical theory, and without Sullivan's feel for formal order and the balance of structure and ornament, the Auditorium Building would never have become the monument that it immediately became and still remains.

—DAVID M. SOKOL

HOME INSURANCE BUILDING
Chicago, Illinois, U.S.A.

1884-85: Constructed; **Architect:** William LeBaron Jenney (1832-1907).

Auditorium Building: Chicago, Illinois, 1887-89

Home Insurance Building: Chicago, Illinois, 1884-85

Publications

BAUMANN, FREDERICK: "Improved Construction of High Buildings." *Sanitary News* 3 (15 March 1884): 123.

LARSON, GERALD R., and GERANIOTIS, ROULA MOUROU-DELLIS: "Toward a Better Understanding of the Evolution of the Iron Skeleton Frame in Chicago." *Journal of the Society of Architectural Historians* 46 (March 1987): 39-48.

TURAK, THEODORE: "Remembrances of the Home Insurance Building." *Journal of the Society of Architectural Historians* 44 (March 1985): 60-65.

*

William Le Baron Jenney's Home Insurance Building marks a discrete but important step in the development of the curtain-walled skyscraper that has dominated American construction in the 20th century. It has often been referred to as the first skyscraper, but such a claim obscures its actual contribution to the development of tall office buildings. It was not the tallest building in its day, nor did it have an independent metal frame. Even its architectural form did not differ significantly from contemporary tall buildings. However, Jenney's inclusion of iron columns within the supporting masonry piers was a critical step toward the development of independently framed structures, which have significantly impacted American architecture.

Jenney was not a prolific builder of tall buildings, but he is remembered as a pioneer of skyscraper construction because of the creative solution he devised for limiting the bulk of the supporting piers for the Home Insurance Building. One of the difficulties in building tall masonry buildings without an iron frame is that the masonry walls must be thickened in order to carry safely the weight of each successive floor. However, such thick walls would reduce available floor area for rental and the natural light and air that could be brought into interior spaces. Jenney reduced the size required for the masonry piers by inserting cast-iron columns into the piers. He did not take full advantage of this technique, however, as the first and second stories (ground and first stories by European nomenclature) had piers of solid granite 4 feet thick at ground level tapering to 2 feet 10 inches at the third story. Columns were inserted into the piers from the third to the ninth stories, but the detailing of the masonry piers clearly indicates that the iron columns were not intended to support the masonry piers, but only partially to relieve them of their load. For example, transfer girders were built into the exterior walls only at the fourth, sixth, and ninth stories, and these girders were intended only to support mullion loads, not to support directly the masonry of the piers. In other words, Jenney's use of iron columns was not intended to supplant the supporting function of the wall, but only to supplement it.

Another innovation employed in the Home Insurance Building that has been used to justify its being called the "first" skyscraper was the first inclusion of rolled-steel structural members in a building. During construction Jenney was persuaded by the Carnegie Corporation to substitute Bessemer process steel girders for the wrought-iron girders specified (and used up to the sixth floor). However, Bessemer process steel is not really steel in the modern sense because alloys can be controlled only through careful selection of ores. The process of bubbling oxygen through the molten metal to burn off the carbon produced a metal that was about 15% stronger than wrought iron but was not a steel as is used today, with carefully controlled carbon and alloy contents. This inclusion of Bessemer process steel in the upper floors tells us more about the developing steel industry than it does about building technology.

One of the reasons that Jenney's Home Insurance Building has held such a prominent position in the history of the skyscraper is the patent battle initiated by Leroy S. Buffington. Buffington was granted a patent on independent framed construction in May of 1888, nearly three years after Jenney's Home Insurance Building was completed. However, Buffington claimed that the principles contained in the patent were developed in unbuilt skyscraper projects done in 1881-82, several years before design of the Home Insurance Building began. During the ensuing court battles that resulted as Buffington attempted to enforce his patent, Chicago architects closed ranks behind their colleague and pronounced Jenney as the originator of the skyscraper. It seems likely that their testimony in the proceedings was influenced by the fact that Buffington could have exacted a royalty on every building constructed using independent-frame construction if his patent were upheld. In fact, another Chicago architect, Frederick Baumann, published an article on iron-frame construction in March of 1884, one month before Jenney's notes show calculations for the iron columns in the piers. Clearly, Jenney was not the only architect working on the problem of iron-frame construction, and should be remembered not as the inventor of the iron-frame office building, but rather as the individual who took the critical first step in implementing some of the elements necessary for iron-frame construction.

Architecturally, the 10-story Home Insurance Building (later extended two additional stories) was similar to other Chicago commercial structures with a defined base and large windows set into a regular grid of vertical piers and horizontal spandrels. This similarity is not surprising, because the overall structural system was similar to earlier tall buildings. In these buildings the internal grid of iron columns and beams was stabilized by exterior and interior masonry walls. These buildings, like the Home Insurance Building, did not have an independent metal frame. To provide independent support a metal skeleton must have either diagonal bracing or rigid joints to prevent racking or sidesway. Just like its contemporaries, the Home Insurance Building depended upon its exterior load-bearing masonry party walls and interior walls to provide lateral stability, since its iron skeleton did not have rigid connections to prevent horizontal movement. The cast-iron columns, rectangular in section and filled with concrete, had brackets cast into the section to support the wrought-iron and steel girders. The girders sat on these shelves without any direct bolted or riveted connection holding them together. The only positive tie between girders and columns was a one-inch-diameter iron rod, which was bent into a notch cut into the top flange of the girders. However, such a tie could not transfer internal bending forces between column and girder, for the hook in the rod would simply bend under forces due to wind loading. In fact, the use of cast-iron columns, whose brittle properties preclude the development of high tensile stresses typical in rigid connections, probably would have caused a structural failure in the absence of the masonry walls, which stiffened the structure and aided in resisting lateral wind forces and sidesway. It was not until the mid-1890s that skyscrapers were built with beam and column connections that had sufficient rigidity and strength to support a tall building without the contribution of interior and exterior walls.

Although Jenney did not develop a fully independent iron frame in his design of the Home Insurance Building, he did take the first crucial step of inserting metal columns into exterior walls. Although both Buffington and Baumann may have better understood independent framing principles, Jenney was the first actually to integrate iron columns with a masonry wall system. While Jenney's technical contribution is limited by the fact that the columns in the exterior walls were not integrated into an independent supporting system, nevertheless the Home Insurance Building remains an important step in the development of the American skyscraper.

—ELWIN C. ROBISON

ILLINOIS INSTITUTE OF TECHNOLOGY
Chicago, Illinois

1942-58. Architect: Ludwig Mies van der Rohe (1886-1969). **1942-43:** Minerals and Metals Research Building; **1944-46:** Engineering Research Building; **1945-46:** Alumni Memorial Hall; **1945-46:** Perlstein Hall; **1945-46:** Wishnick Hall; **1945-50:** Laboratory for Institute of Gas Technology; **1948-50:** Administration Building for American Institute of Railroads; **1949-52:** St. Savior Chapel; **1950-52:** Mechanical Engineering Building; **1951-53:** Carmen Hall; **1952-53:** Commons Building; **1952-55:** Bailey Hall; **1952-55:** Cunningham Hall; **1950-56:** S. R. Crown Hall; **1955-57:** Siegel Hall and Physics-Electronics Research Building; **1955-58:** Metals Research Building.

Publications

"Building Groups: IIT Campus." *Arts and Architecture* 66 (Summer 1949).

CADBURY-BROWN, H. T. (ed.): "Ludwig Mies van der Rohe." *Architectural Association Journal* (special issue, July/August 1959).

CARTER, PETER (ed.): "Mies van der Rohe." *Architectural Design* (special issue, March 1961).

"Crown Hall, Illinois Institute of Technology." *Architectural Record* 120 (August 1956): 134-139.

"Drawings for the Library and Administration Building, Illinois Institute." *Architects' Journal* (January 1946).

HOFMANN, WERNER, and KULTERMANN, UDO: *Modern Architecture in Color.* New York, 1970.

"Metals and Minerals Research Building, Illinois Institute of Technology." *Architectural Forum* 79 (November 1943).

SCHULZE, FRANZ: *Mies van der Rohe: A Critical Biography.* Chicago and London, 1985.

SPAETH, DAVID: *Mies van der Rohe.* New York and London, 1985.

SWENSON, A., and CHENG, P.: *Architectural Education at IIT, 1938-1978.* Chicago, 1980.

WINTER, JOHN: "Crown Hall." In *Modern Buildings.* London, 1969.

*

Ludwig Mies van der Rohe immigrated to the United States in 1938 to be director of architecture at the Armour (later Illinois) Institute of Technology in Chicago. In addition to developing a new curriculum for architectural education, loosely based on his experience as director of the Bauhaus (Dessau and Berlin, 1930-33), Mies was given the opportunity to plan and design a new campus for IIT.

By the 1930s, the once-fashionable neighborhood in which the Armour Institute was located had become a slum. However, rather than moving Armour to a new location, Henry Heald, the institution's first president after the merger between Armour and Lewis Institute, saw the new campus as acting as a catalyst

for revitalizing Chicago's South Side. In cooperation with various other institutions in the vicinity, including Michael Reese Hospital, the newly formed Illinois Institute of Technology began to acquire and clear land between 31st and 35th streets to the north and south, respectively, Michigan Avenue to the east, and the New York Central Railroad's tracks to the west. Since more than 3,000 separate parcels of land had to be assembled, Mies soon came to understand that he would have to think in terms of decades rather than years for the realization of his plan. An overall structure was necessary, but that structure had to be flexible enough to allow for possible change as the institution grew and/or changed its mission.

Not since Thomas Jefferson designed the University of Virginia had an architect been permitted to design an entire campus. Unlike the virgin Charlottesville site, the IIT campus had to be painstakingly inserted into an existing neighborhood. Mies was well aware of both the possibilities and the difficulties presented by such a commission. Above all, he felt the campus should be unified. Mies' analysis of the problem suggested the use of a module or ordering device, large enough and flexible enough to accommodate classrooms, laboratories and offices. Further, such a module should be repetitive so as to be economic and efficient in terms of construction. On the grounds of economy and flexibility, Mies explored the possibilities skeleton construction offered. Such a system appealed to his sense of order, for, as he believed, "only a clear expression of the structure would give us an architectural solution which would last." After a number of preliminary studies, some of which replaced the existing pattern of Chicago's streets with a different structure, Mies was brought to accept the existing gridiron. On this grid of streets intersecting at right angles, he superimposed a three-dimensional module 24 feet by 24 feet by 12 feet. Initially, all building dimensions were to have been whole-number multiples of 24 feet in plan and 12 feet in height. With few exceptions, Mies adhered to this module. The exceptions: his proposed Library (1944) and Administration Building and the completed S. R. Crown Hall (1950-56).

It is characteristic of many of Mies' preliminary designs for the campus, as well as the final version, that the principal buildings are arranged symmetrically about an axis perpendicular to the short dimension of the site (east/west). However, the device of allowing individual buildings to relate asymmetrically to each other was to afford elision or overlap between one building and the next. This strategy allowed Mies to create a series of open landscaped spaces of various sizes that define but do not enclose space. By virtue of those "shifts," he was able to combine the new buildings and the existing pattern of streets into a coherent and unified whole. At IIT there is never that sense of enclosure or containment characteristic of the medieval quadrangle. Rather, there is always the sense of the existence of a continuum, the idea that space is everywhere, articulated and made visible by architecture and landscape architecture. Alfred Caldwell's (born 1903) landscaping, reminiscent of the Illinois prairie, complements the architecture, reinforcing Mies' understanding of space and the existence of the "greater whole," as he termed it.

In the Minerals and Metals Research Building (1942-43), the first of the structures built on the new campus, affords a sense of the power and appropriateness of Mies' vision. His mastery of architecture, his understanding of the structure and order are evident down to the smallest details. As one contemporary critic described it, "Like his earlier buildings in Europe, the laboratory is distinguished by the utmost simplicity in the handling of structure and materials." In developing the structural system

Chapel, Illinois Institute of Technology: Chicago, Illinois, 1942-58

for the campus buildings, Mies had already accepted the discipline of skeletal steel construction. However, within this discipline, he had refined a new vocabulary, one whose elements consisted of rolled steel stations: angles, channels, I-beams and H-columns. In so doing, he made a new language for architecture from the means technology and society had placed at his disposal. The result, according to Mies: "Real forms of a real world." As Philip Johnson wrote about Mies' project for the Library and Administration Building, "Steel is joined to steel or steel to glass with all the taste and skill that formerly went into the chiseling of a stone capital or the painting of a fresco." What Johnson described was Mies' careful attention to detail, a quality found even in the most utilitarian and economical of

his buildings as well as in the most expensive of them.

Commencing with the end of World War II and continuing to his retirement from the faculty in 1958, Mies' work on the campus proceeded slowly but without serious interruption. While the majority of the buildings were constructed in steel, a few, for reasons of economy or war-related material shortages, were reinforced-concrete structures. Of these, the apartment buildings, Carmen Hall (1951-53), Bailey Hall (1952-55) and Cunningham Hall (1952-55), with their exposed, stepped-back skeletal structured infilled with brick spandrels and operating windows, derive from Mies' earlier work on the Promontory Apartments, Chicago (1946-49). As budgets and building programs allowed, for some of the other buildings on the campus

Mies continued to investigate the architectural possibilities of exposed-steel construction, using the vocabulary he developed during the war. Of these, St. Savior Chapel (1949-52), the Commons (1952-53) and Crown Hall were not required by the building code to have fireproofed structures. Together they represent a clear, concise history of steel construction unencumbered by the requirement of applied fire protection.

Crown Hall is perhaps the most worthy of attention because it is the clearest expression of Mies' ideas about the relationship between structure and space on the IIT campus. Housing the College of Architecture, Planning and Design, in Crown Hall Mies challenged the limits of structure and technology and realized the first of his large-scale "universal" spaces. The roof, measuring 120 feet by 220 feet, is suspended from four plate girders 6 feet 3 inches deep, 60 feet on center. At each end of the column-free space, the roof cantilevers an additional 20 feet. The resultant space, only partially subdivided by free-standing partitions 8 feet tall and two service cores extending from floor to ceiling, is, as Mies observed, "the clearest structure we have done, best to express our philosophy." At Crown Hall's dedication, Eero Saarinen observed that the building made an important statement regarding individuality and universality. "Great architecture," according to Saarinen, "is both universal and individual. . . . The universality comes because there is an architecture expressive of its time. But the individuality comes as an expression of one man's unique combination of faith and honesty and devotion and beliefs in architecture—in short, his moral integrity."

Mies' moral integrity did not necessarily mean that he was an easy person to get along with. When, after 20 years as director of the department of architecture, in declining health, and with his practice demanding more of his time, Mies resigned, IIT's administration took the opportunity to replace Mies as campus architect. Despite letters and telegrams protesting the decision, including one from Le Corbusier (1887-1965), the board of trustees appointed Skidmore, Owings and Merrill to replace Mies. As Mies recalled shortly after his resignation, "They [the board of trustees] decided that it was better to work with other people and have some local man in the field. They then felt they had made a mistake by doing that and they asked me to make one of the other buildings. I said: 'No. The campus was planned as a unit and, if it cannot be a unit, I have to be satisfied with a torso.'" The torso includes the following classroom and laboratory facilities: Alumni Memorial Hall (1945-46), Perlstein Hall (1945-46), Wishnick Hall (1945-46), Siegel Hall (1955-57); for the IIT Research Institute, the Engineering Research Building (1944-46), the Mechanical Engineering Building (1950-52), the Physics-Electronics Research Building (1955-57), the Metals Research Building (1955-58); for the Institute of Gas Technology, a laboratory facility (1945-50); and for the American Association of Railroads, an Administration Building (1948-50), a Mechanical Engineering Building (1948-53), a laboratory building (1955-57). In addition, Mies designed the boiler plant (1945-50) for the campus.

In retrospect, it seems obvious that Mies should come to Chicago and that the largest body of his completed works be located in the city whose architectural legacy includes William Le Baron Jenney (1832-1907), Louis Sullivan (1856-1924) and Frank Lloyd Wright (1867-1959). Chicago provided Mies with the environment and the means, the technology, with which he might accomplish his work. IIT provided Mies with the nearly unprecedented opportunity to see that vision of architecture realized. The campus is a tribute to his overwhelming talent and his profound insight into the problem of architecture in a technological age.

—DAVID SPAETH

JOHN HANCOCK CENTER
Chicago, Illinois, U.S.A.

1965-70: Construction; **Architects:** Louis Skidmore (1897-1962), Nathaniel Owings (b. 1903), John O. Merrill (1896-1975).

Publications

"Analysis and Design of the 100-Story John Hancock Center in Chicago." with S. H. Iyengar and J. P. Colaco, in *Acier Stahl Steel* (Brussels) (June 1968).

Architecture of Skidmore, Owings and Merrill 1963-1973. Introduced by Arthur Drexler, Stuttgart, 1974.

"Computer Design of the 100-Story John Hancock Center." With S. H. Iyengar and J. P. Colaco, in *Journal of the American Society of Civil Engineers* (December 1966).

"The John Hancock Center." *Civil Engineering* (October 1967).

KHAN, FAZLUR: "The John Hancock Center." *Civil Engineering* 37 (October 1967).

KHAN, FAZLUR: "100-Story John Hancock Center in Chicago—A Case Study of the Design Process." *IABSE Journal* J-16/82 (August 1982).

BILLINGTON, DAVID P.: *The Tower and the Bridge: The New Art of Structural Engineering.* Princeton, New Jersey, 1983.

*

Designed by the Chicago office of Skidmore, Owings and Merrill, the 100-story John Hancock Center is one of the world's tallest buildings. Set a couple of blocks back from the lakefront, it towers above Chicago's North Michigan Avenue. The building's image is strong and in accordance with the Chicago tradition of bold structures; the tower is a simple rectangle on plan, tapers in as it rises, and has clearly expressed wind bracing on all facades—never has the engineering of a very tall building been expressed so clearly.

The brief was for a mixture of functions—a department store, small shops, offices, housing and parking—corresponding to the surrounding area, which consists of high-quality apartments, professional offices and shops. An early design of the architects proposed a 70-story apartment tower and a 45-story office tower, but that arrangement led to cramped planning, particularly at ground level; one solution was to place one tower on top of the other, a concept that received much support from research into the structures of very tall buildings being carried out at that time by SOM's brilliant structural engineer, Fazlur Khan.

The final building has shopping in the basement extending up to the fourth floor, parking from the sixth to the 12th floor, offices from the 13th to the 41st floors, apartments from the 46th to the 92nd floors, and then restaurants, viewing areas, television studios and mechanical plant. "Sky lobbies" at various places in the tower provide elevator lift interchanges and communal spaces.

Architecturally, the different functions are played down. The structure is so powerful that one has to look for the differences: parking floors may be neutral, office floors may have higher headroom, apartments may have opening windows and recessed balconies, but the mullion spacing is maintained throughout, and the varying functions in no way affect the calm of the facade.

In terms of planning, the taper helps, as apartments need less depth than the offices, which are placed in the lower levels where the tower is fatter.

John Hancock Center: Chicago, Illinois, 1965-70

The building will be remembered for its clearly expressed diagonals. We are accustomed to seeing diagonal bracing on tall engineering structures—electricity pylons, suspension-bridge towers, radio masts. In architecture, the strength of the classical tradition is such that diagonal members required to resist horizontal forces were usually suppressed in conventional high-rise buildings, and could be concealed in the walls surrounding the elevators. Gothic architecture was more structurally based and had no inhibitions about enjoying to the full any structural requirement for a diagonal member—witness the loving celebration of the flying buttress. In the 18th century that tradition died out, but with the advent of iron construction and the understanding of the static forces within a structure, the diagonal returned with London's Crystal Palace (1850-51), a famous early example.

Interest in diagonals continued in metal structures, such as the Eames House in 1949, but the real revival came soon after World War II with the studies of Myron Goldsmith and Jim Ferris at the Illinois Institute of Technology. These architects later moved to the San Francisco office of Skidmore, Owings and Merrill, and produced a design for the Norton Building in Seattle, a metal cage with clear diagonals on all four sides. The Norton building was only 17 stories high, and opinion was that the scale was too small to give such prominence to the bracing; however, the idea was pursued by the same office in its 27-story Alcoa Tower in San Francisco's Golden Gate Center.

The John Hancock tower consists of a core in the center and a trussed tube in the external wall plane, with no interior columns between core and perimeter. The stiffness in the tube is provided by the diagonals and by those floors which align with the point where the diagonals meet the corner columns. By taking horizontal forces in this way, dramatic savings in structure were made: the weight of structural steel in the Hancock tower is 29.7 pounds per square foot compared with 45 pounds per square foot for average medium-height buildings in the Chicago area. With the realization that the world's resources are not infinite, there is a moral as well as a financial imperative to use material efficiently even if the result is forms which are unfamiliar, and the Hancock tower is a step along the way.

In addition to its structural inventiveness, the Hancock tower is also a pioneer "24-hour building"—with its many different uses, it can contribute to the life of the community in a way that a single-function building can never do. Here again is a pointer to future developments.

At many architectural levels, this building is little better than average. The entrance, the treatment at ground level, the parking ramp are all unworthy of the tower. But the sheer bravado of the form and the obvious brilliance and clarity of its structure make a memorable addition to the Chicago skyline and to the continuing development of metal towers.

—JOHN WINTER

860-880 LAKE SHORE DRIVE APARTMENTS
Chicago, Illinois

1949-51. Architect: Ludwig Mies van der Rohe (1886-1969).

Publications

HILBERSEIMER, LUDWIG: *Ludwig Mies van der Rohe*. Chicago, 1956.

HOFMANN, WERNER, and KULTERMANN, UDO: *Modern Architecture in Color*. New York, 1970.

JORDY, WILLIAM H.: "The Laconic Splendor of the Metal Frame: Ludwig Mies van der Rohe's 860 Lake Shore Apartments and His Seagram Building." *American Buildings and Their Architects: The Impact of European Modernism in the Mid-Twentieth Century*. Garden City, New York, 1972.

"Ludwig Mies van der Rohe." *Inland Architect* (special issue, March 1986).

SCHULZE, FRANZ: *Mies van der Rohe: A Critical Biography*. Chicago and London, 1985.

SPAETH, DAVID: *Mies van der Rohe*. New York and London, 1985.

*

The 860-880 Lake Shore Drive Apartments in Chicago, built between 1949 and 1951, were the first realization of Ludwig Mies van der Rohe's long-cherished dream of the glass-tower skyscraper. Exemplifying the ideas and goals of the International Style, the 26-story twin towers of glass and steel evoked the image of a new city. Unprecedented in the lightness, clarity and airiness of the skeleton frame design, the apartment buildings became a symbol of modern architecture and tolled the death knell for the brick-and-terra-cotta Chicago skyscraper of the 1930s and 1940s.

The two rectangular towers, whose exteriors are identical, are set on an irregular plot directly facing Lake Michigan. They are positioned at right angles to each other, to maximize the lake view from the apartments. The steel canopy connecting the two buildings echoes the forms of the canopies over the entrance doorways. Both towers are raised on pilotis in a design that reputedly goes back to Le Corbusier. The Lake Shore Drive Apartments, however, have a completely glassed-in ground floor, where Le Corbusier left the pilotis uncovered.

The pilotis are continued in steel columns that rise the height of the buildings, in a three-by-five-bay plan. Steel spandrels at each floor span the columns. Both columns and spandrels consist of a steel core surrounded with two inches of concrete, to conform to the Chicago Building Code's fireproofing requirements, and are covered with black steel plate on the exterior. Mies resolved the problem of wind load by stiffening the structure with the introduction of a sheer wall in the inner service core.

The structural elements of the full-length columns and spandrels demarcating floors are also the main elements of articulation. The spaces in the resulting grid are entirely filled with floor-to-ceiling glass panels set in aluminum frames. The basic grid of columns and spandrels is underscored by the mullions subdividing the windows. I-beams welded onto the exterior of the columns and mullions relieve the flatness of the design. Mies compared the I-beam in 20th-century architecture to the classical orders, as symbols of antiquity, in ancient Greek and Roman building. At the Lake Shore Drive Apartments the I-beam functions as an icon of modernity. The strong vertical impetus of the towers is enhanced by the emphasis on the vertical elements of articulation of the I-beams. Much of the liveliness of the design derives from the reflections of sky and clouds in the glass, and from the lives within the apartments, signs of which are always visible from the outside.

The apartments themselves are laid out on an open plan, leaving the residents considerable freedom in arranging the interior space. Dividing walls separate the bedrooms from the

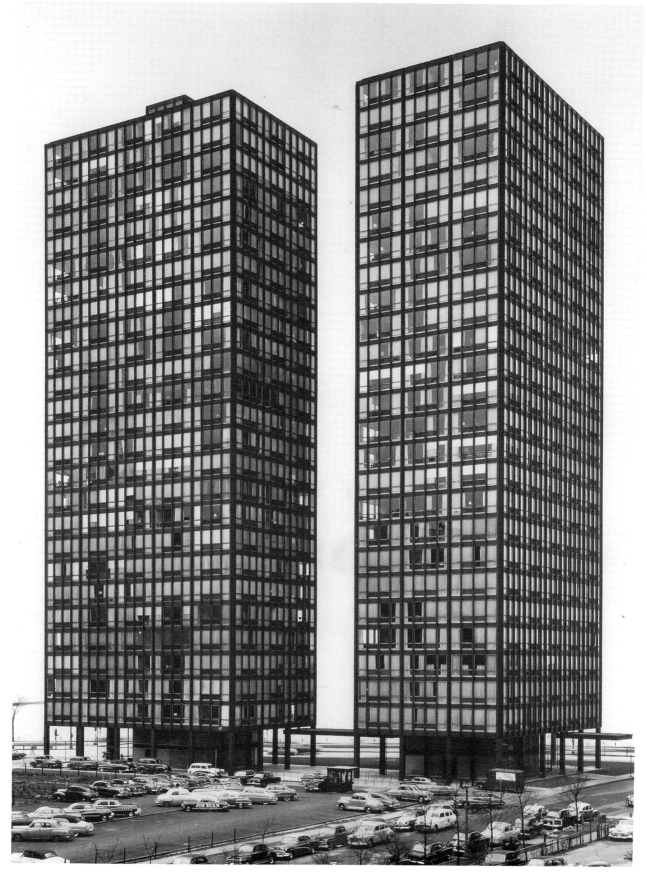

860-880 Lake Shore Drive Apartments: Chicago, Illinois, 1949-51

rest of the space. All the apartments were fitted out with light-gray draperies, to cushion the impact of the sun and possibly to prevent a too-riotous appearance on the exterior. The draperies were insufficient in a climatological regard, however, and the apartments are uncomfortable during Chicago's hot summers. The glass-and-steel construction has something of a hot-house effect, while the building lacks the vents for central air-conditioning. The windows do not open to allow for the installation of window units either.

As the first of Ludwig Mies van der Rohe's glass-tower skyscrapers to be built, the Lake Shore Drive Apartments became paradigmatic of skyscraper design for the next quarter of a century. Now somewhat dwarfed and crowded by the highrises that have sprung up all around it, the Lake Shore Drive Apartments still provide a vibrant accent along the Chicago lakeshore.

—LISA PINCUS

MARQUETTE BUILDING
Chicago, Illinois, U.S.A.

1893-94: Constructed; **Architects:** William Holabird (1854-1923) and Martin Roche (1853-1927). **1905:** Addition. **1980:** Restored.

Publications

BRUEGMANN, R.: *Holabird & Roche and Holabird & Root: An Illustrated Catalog from the Collection in the Art Institute of Chicago.* New York, 1990.
CONDIT, C. W.: *American Building Art: The Nineteenth Century.* New York, 1960.
CONDIT, CARL: *Chicago School of Architecture. History of Commercial & Public Building in the Chicago Area 1875-1925.* Chicago, 1964.
"Holabird, William." Vol. 9, pages 127-128 in *Dictionary of American Biography.* New York, 1943.
WINKLER, FRANZ: "Some Chicago Buildings Represented by the Work of Holabird and Roche." *Architectural Record* 31:313-387, 1912.

*

The Marquette Building, known for its unabashed expression of structure and function, is considered a key example of what came, by the 1940s, to be called the Chicago school. Peter Brooks, acting through his agent Owen Aldis, began planning the building in 1893. Their correspondence reveals Aldis' formula for the well-planned office building, a formula that he developed through his involvement with other major commissions, including the Montauk Building, the Monadnock Building and the Rookery. All office space was to be first-class, he said. There should be plenty of light and air; the design should lend itself to easy and inexpensive maintenance; provisions should be made for changes in the locations of partitions and utilities; and the public parts of the building, such as the lobby and corridors, should make a good impression. Though the Marquette Building was not the first to be designed with these factors in mind, it is a particularly good example of their effective coalescence.

To provide light and air to all of the offices, Holabird and Roche gave the building, which appears monolithic from its street facades, an E-shaped plan. The central, shorter wing houses the elevators, while the two end wings contain offices, the inner ones overlooking a large light court lined with a newly developed white enameled brick (the same type used in Louis Sullivan's Guaranty Building in Buffalo) that reflected light and was easy to clean. Even after the introduction of the electric light, daylight continued to be an important source of illumination. Wide horizontal windows, their panes separated by unusually slender mullions, fill each bay, allowing light to flood the building's interior.

It is possible, to a certain extent, to read the building's function from the design of its street facades; the disposition of the windows reflects the function of the interior spaces. The windows in the building's shaft consist of a bisected fixed pane flanked by narrower movable sashes. The central mullion allows each bay to be partitioned into more than one office if need be, providing the flexibility of use Aldis specified. Chicago windows, with one large fixed pane flanked by narrower movable windows, fill the second story of the base. These uninterrupted central panes were particularly appropriate for larger offices occupying at least an entire bay and businesses requiring a good deal of open floor space, such as the Banker's National Company, which had quarters on the second floor when the building first opened. The Marquette Building thus lent itself well to a varied and shifting tenancy. The fact that it received an addition in 1905 and was restored for future use in 1980 testifies to the long-term viability of its planning.

The Marquette Building's design indicates its structure as well as its function. The projecting piers and recessed spandrels embracing wide panes of glass mirror the steel frame that supports the building. Because the structural bays are not bisected by heavy piers or mullions, the steel frame is expressed more forcefully than in some of the building's notable contemporaries, such as Sullivan's Guaranty Building or Holabird and Roche's own Pontiac and Old Colony buildings. The Marquette Building's design has been criticized, however, for certain "architectonic defects" that show a "misguided traditionalism," including its heavy piers—especially the rusticated corner piers. These features, together with the rusticated base, may, in fact, have made the building more appealing to potential tenants by conveying a sense of solidity that some people—even vociferous advocates of structural expression—found reassuring.

The Marquette Building's monumentality and richness of finish—far from being extraneous, as some later critics have contended—also contributed to its desirability. In their 1948 book *The Story of Chicago,* Joseph and Caroline Kirkland said of the Marquette Building: "The design of the whole is after the style of the Italian Renaissance architecture which combines size and solidity with beauty and dignity." Although it is almost invisible in most published photographs of the building, classical ornament abounds on its exterior, covering the base, the rusticated piers and the bracketed cornice. It was no secret that there were tenants who wanted beauty as well as light, air and well-planned offices, as Aldis knew when he requested that the public areas of the building be given special care. In its article on the Marquette Building, *Inland Architect* gave as much space to the mosaics, Italian marble and mahogany woodwork in the lobby and corridors as to the perfect light, freedom from noise, and up-to-date temperature control.

Located at a prominent corner in the Loop, the Marquette Building is a monument to the early Illinois explorer Jacques Marquette, whose deeds are commemorated in bronze panels over the entrance and in a series of mosaics in the marble lobby. To be sure, the building *was* designed to be functional, but the concept of function held by its early patrons, users and viewers was more broadly defined than by later critics. As such, it stands

Marquette Building: Chicago, Illinois, 1893-94

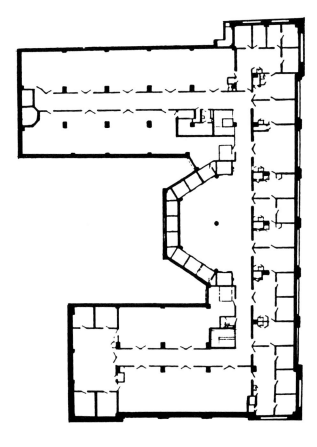

as an important example of skyscraper planning as it developed in late-19th-century Chicago, and it established the pattern that Holabird and Roche would maintain—with greater or lesser degrees of elaboration, depending on the client—for the next 20 years.

—KATHERINE SOLOMONSON

MARSHALL FIELD WHOLESALE STORE
Chicago, Illinois, U.S.A.

1885-87: Constructed; **Architect:** Henry Hobson Richardson (1838-1886). **1930:** Demolished.

Publications

HITCHCOCK, H.-R.: *The Architecture of H. H. Richardson and His Times.* New York, 1936.
O'GORMAN, J.: "The Marshall Field Warehouse: Materials Toward a Monograph." *Journal of the Society of Architectural Historians* (October 1978).
O'GORMAN, J. F.: *H. H. Richardson: Architectural Forms for an American Society.* Chicago, 1987.
OCHSNER, JEFFREY KARL: *H. H. Richardson Complete Architectural Works.* 1982.
VAN RENSSELAER, M.G.: *Henry Hobson Richardson and His Works.* New York, 1969.

Henry Hobson Richardson's Marshall Field Wholesale Store, built at West Adams and South Franklin Streets in Chicago, represented the epitome of his mature neo-Romanesque style. This urban U-shaped building, with its seven stories and nearly 500,000 square feet of interior space, reflected the architect's goals of a massive yet quiet and simple structure. Richardson believed it was one of his most important designs, well suited for its American urban setting.

With its direct geometric Romanesque design of large arched windows, solid red granite and red sandstone walls, and skillful arrangement of exterior tiers, the Field Store echoed the images of a dynamic, industrializing America. Its unified, solid and secure appearance represented the consolidation, concentration and power of large-scale capitalism in an age of enterprise. Shed of ornamentation, elemental in design and stately in appearance, the Field Store was the prototype for urban architecture; its presence and dignity made it appropriate for cities seeking an architecture both quiet and secure. The building was an early and very successful example of organic architecture, growing out of its environment and its era, reflecting its purpose as a center for trade with a masculine clientele. This structure, devoid of frills and fancy, utilitarian and matter-of-fact, said it was a place of trade and commerce; customers and passers-by alike knew the purpose of the building. This functional design made it an early example of design elements embraced by later architects such as Louis Sullivan and Frank Lloyd Wright.

The Marshall Field Wholesale Store was both progressive and retrospective in its influence. Its massive stone walls were interrupted by simple semicircular arched window openings, creating an open-cage building of simple and direct lines. Twentieth-century architects of the modern and International Style embraced these principles of highlighting a structure's skeleton in its design and of producing buildings of sheer simplicity. In this aspect of his exterior designs, especially in his later years, Richardson produced an exemplary American urban style. At a time when American Gothic and Second Empire styles dominated much post-Civil War architecture, he emphasized the vernacular style of the unpretentious and unadorned. By demonstrating that the simple, unified and massive could be both artistic and stately, Richardson returned American architecture to its democratic and rational roots. That legacy of direct architectural statements appeared in buildings such as Adler and Sullivan's Chicago Auditorium Building and McKim, Mead and White's Public Library for Boston, whose design was influenced by two of Richardson's former assistants, Charles F. McKim and Stanford White. As one of America's most successful architects in the 1880s, Richardson had demonstrated the value of organic and functional architecture to an increasingly technological and urban America.

Yet Richardson's innovations or reforms were expressed in the language of a much earlier time and place. Rounded arches, heavy stone exteriors, massive walls and traditional structural techniques made Richardson as much traditionalist as reformer. Although the Field Store's exterior had elements of a modern style to emerge in the next century, it also spoke in traditional terms. The heavy masonry exterior, with its allusions to an earlier New England textile-mill style, covered a rather conventionally designed interior. The lower half of the Field building had a regular grid of terra-cotta-covered iron columns supporting each floor; heavy timbers were the structural material for the upper stories. These hardly were great innovations in building technology and served to reinforce traditional ideas about architectural style and structural design.

From this perspective, Richardson is properly considered, as the architectural historian H.-R. Hitchcock said, the last great traditional architect, not the first modern one. His buildings such

Marshall Field Wholesale Store: Chicago, Illinois, 1885-87

as the Field Store exemplified the culmination of an architectural tradition which endorsed the use of historical forms and styles identified with late-19th-century urban America. These massive and solid buildings dominated urban architecture well into the 20th century and became hallmarks of the crowded, polluted, concrete and stone landscape of the industrial city. When Americans embraced the openness and space of the clean and green suburbs in the car culture of this century, these symbols of an earlier urban America seemed anachronistic, and many, like the Field Store in 1930, suffered the undeserved fate of the wrecker's ball.

Had Richardson's Marshall Field Wholesale Store survived in downtown Chicago, as did Sullivan's Auditorium Building, it would serve today as a monument to an astute architect who incorporated an historical style into a structure appropriate to its time, purpose and place. As modern architects grope for architectural statements relevant to their time, Richardson's achievement with the Field Store in the late 19th century reminds us that most successful architecture is rooted in functionalism

and elegance. The Field Store reflected both, and served its role well for almost half a century. Although it stimulated modern movements of organic and utilitarian or vernacular designs, it also reinforced the techniques used in traditional structures and celebrated an earlier historical style.

As in almost any artistic endeavor, a field must have a master consolidator of a style before developments move in a new direction. H. H. Richardson served that role to the fullest. By creating masterpieces such as the Marshall Field Wholesale Store, he demonstrated the value of the traditional and, at the same time, the potential of the modern. In doing so, Richardson influenced many architects who embraced the limits of traditionalism. With these buildings he also demonstrated to others the challenge and capacity for innovation and invention by rejecting prevailing styles and developing designs true to their own time and purpose. For many historians of American architecture the Field Store symbolized the best of late-19th-century urban design.

—H. J. EISENMAN

MONADNOCK BUILDING
Chicago, Illinois, U.S.A.

1889-91: Constructed; **Architects:** Daniel H. Burnham (1846-1912) and John Wellborn Root (1850-1891). **1892:** Building extended; **Architects:** William Holabird (1854-1923) and Martin Roche (1853-1927).

Publications

FRAMPTON, KENNETH, and FUTAGAWA, YUKIO: *Modern Architecture: 1851-1919.* New York, 1983.
HOFFMANN, DONALD: *The Architecture of John Wellborn Root.* Baltimore, 1973.
HOFFMANN, DONALD: "John Root's Monadnock Building." *Journal of the Society of Architectural Historians* 26 (1967): 269-277.
HOFMANN, WERNER, and KULTERMANN, UDO: *Modern Architecture in Color.* New York, 1970.
OVERBY, OSMUND R.: "Monadnock Block." Unpublished report, Washington, 1963.
REBORI, A. N.: "The Work of Burnham & Root, D.H. Burnham & Co. and Graham, Burnham & Co." *Architectural Record* 38, 1 (July, 1915): 32-168.

*

The Monadnock Building in Chicago is a study in contradiction: aesthetically it looks forward to the Modern Movement of the 20th century, yet structurally it is a dinosaur, using the older load-bearing-wall technology of previous centuries. It was one of many speculative office buildings built for investors attempting to cash in on the spectacular economic development taking place in Chicago in the final decades of the 19th century. Understanding the speculative basis of the Monadnock Building aids in interpreting its contradictory nature.

While many eastern cities experienced a relatively flat period of economic growth in the 1880s and 1890s, Chicago boomed due to its function as a transportation hub for the developing American West. Investors Peter and Shepard Brooks recognized the greater opportunities present in Chicago than in their native Boston and purchased land in the Loop, the Chicago business district. Such speculation on land had driven prices to astronomical levels. High land costs demanded full exploitation of the site in order to recoup investment, one of many factors that led to the large number of tall office buildings constructed in Chicago during those decades.

The original design for the Monadnock Building by the firm of Burnham and Root was much modified by the cautious Boston investors. John Wellborn Root proposed an ornamented neo-Egyptian building complete with gradated colors of brick that was different in style and color but similar in use of applied ornament to commissions like the Rookery in Chicago, the *San Francisco Tribune* Building and the Society for Savings Building in Cleveland. In addition, he proposed a structure of steel columns similar to those being built in these and other contemporary tall office buildings. However, this plan was rejected by the Brookses: on the one hand they distrusted the steel structure because of the potential for corrosion, and on the other

the ornamented elevations were considered too expensive for a speculative building.

Root's response to these requests by the client was to eliminate the steel columns in the outer walls, employing the traditional load-bearing walls that had characterized American masonry construction practice until only a few years previous. What was nontraditional, however, was the tremendous thickness of the walls required to carry the weight of 16 stories. Without the introduction of steel columns, the building loads required a wall thickness of over 6 feet 4 inches at the base. This extreme thickness has many economic consequences; not only do construction costs escalate because of the sheer volume of masonry required, but the thickness of the walls significantly reduces the square footage of rental area available on the lower floors; in addition, the weight of these walls has caused large settlement of the foundations. The building does have an interior row of steel columns (well protected from rain penetration that can occur in exterior walls), which eliminates further loss of floor area and additional settlement that would occur if an interior masonry wall were used. Nevertheless, the Monadnock Building represents the practical limit of load-bearing-wall construction using conventional-strength bricks and mortar.

The other requirement of the Brookses, that of eliminating unnecessary ornament, was brilliantly handled by Root. He removed the polychromatic treatment of the brick and the neo-Egyptian ornament while still retaining a chiseled outward flair of the cornice. The planar wall surfaces are interrupted by faceted strips of bay windows, which increase light and air in the offices. The chamfered corner, which widens as it approaches the top, is countered by a graceful outward curve that thickens the wall at its base. More than a vestige of the neo-Egyptian project, this curve physically broadens the base of the building, increasing its resistance to wind loads.

At the time of its construction, the Monadnock Building towered above neighboring structures, exposing it to large wind pressures. Both designers and investors were concerned about its performance in wind, as was later evidenced when, during a violent storm, deflection measurements were taken with a plumb bob down an elevator shaft and telegraphed to the anxious Boston investors. The thick, tapering walls were aided in their lateral resistance to wind by massive masonry cross walls, which stiffen the long side walls. Relatively lightweight portal braces were also included to develop lateral resistance to wind pressures, but since these braces are directly attached to the masonry wall it is unlikely that the masonry-brace connection can develop enough strength to significantly resist wind loads.

Contemporary criticism was not entirely favorable, and Montgomery Schuyler was one of the few critics who appreciated the raw power of the building's form. Certainly the clients were unimpressed, as in 1892 they commissioned Holabird and Roche to complete the extension of the building along Dearborn Street, originally called the Katahdin, but now referred to as Monadnock II. Built with an early steel frame and more conventional ornament, it is technically superior to Burnham and Root's load-bearing structure, but the architectural form lacks the boldness and power of Monadnock I.

Although dwarfed today by taller buildings that surround it, the Monadnock Building arrests the attention of the observer with its massive brick walls. Sharing the simple massing of later curtain-wall skyscrapers, it is distinguished from them by the bold flair and deeply set windows of the supporting walls. Its paradoxical nature—aesthetically advanced while structurally backward—is the product of investment pressures, mistrust of new technology, and Root's sensitive handling of this large commercial office building.

—ELWIN C. ROBISON

Monadnock Building: Chicago, Illinois, 1889-91

RELIANCE BUILDING
Chicago, Illinois, U.S.A.

1890-95: Construction; **Architects:** John Wellborn Root and Charles B. Atwood (1849-1895) of D.H. Burnham and Co. firm.

Publications

CONDIT, CARL W.: *The Chicago School of Architecture*. Chicago, 1964.

FRAMPTON, KENNETH, and FUTAGAWA, YUKIO: *Modern Architecture: 1851-1919*. New York, 1983.

FREITAG, JOSEPH KENDALL: *Architectural Engineering*. New York, 1895.

JENKINS, CHARLES E.: "A White Enameled Building." *Architectural Record* 4 (January-March 1895): 299-306.

*

The Reliance Building in Chicago remains as one of the clearest statements of the potential of curtain-wall construction in tall buildings. The rapid erection of the steel work, the use of a visibly nonstructural cladding and the large window area of the cantilevered bays demonstrated the economic and aesthetic

Reliance Building: Chicago, Illinois, 1890-95

advantages of what was then called "veneer construction," or as it is now known, curtain-wall construction.

Plans for the Reliance Building and construction on the ground level were begun in 1890, while John Wellborn Root was chief designer for what was then called the firm of Burnham and Root. However, after Root's untimely death in January 1891, Charles B. Atwood took over as chief designer. Atwood radically changed the concept of the design, eliminating the heavy exterior walls of the earlier plan and replacing them with lightweight glazed terra-cotta. Traditionally used as nonstructural fireproofing material, terra-cotta used on the exterior clearly demonstrated the independence of the steel frame from the exterior cladding. Although the terra-cotta sections were cast into patterns with Gothicizing motifs, the overall impression of the building is one where the taut skin follows the outlines of the steel frame and cantilevered bays holding large windows.

Architecturally the Reliance Building broke away from the heavy masonry forms and eclectic ornament favored by Root. However, Atwood did not import a new architectural style upon his arrival from the East Coast. Instead, he absorbed the straightforward approach to tall commercial buildings that distinguished Chicago architecture. Formally, the Reliance Building owes a great debt to the work of Holabird and Roche completed just before Atwood's involvement in the Reliance commission, especially the Tacoma Building (1887-89), which shared projecting bays of windows and horizontal articulation of the spandrels with the Reliance Building. However, the larger window area, bolder and simpler projecting bays, and slab roof anticipated 20th-century skyscraper forms in a way the Tacoma Building did not.

Not only did the Reliance Building develop new forms in terms of architectural aesthetics, but it was innovative in its use of building technology as well. The previous building on the site had leases with a later expiration time on the upper floors than on the lower floors. Rather than let the lower levels remain empty (and economically unproductive) the upper floors were underpinned, and construction on the foundations and lower steelwork proceeded while the upper floors were still occupied. This work, directed by Root, is distinguished by its granite cladding and comprises the ground-level storefronts. When the lease on the upper floors expired on 1 May 1894, demolition and construction proceeded at breakneck speed; by 8 November 1894 all 16 stories were closed in, with only interior work remaining.

The structural frame of the Reliance Building, designed by Edward Shankland, looks similar to modern frames, but it differed significantly in terms of calculation method and conceptualization. Modern frames are considered as rigid or fixed frames, with beams and columns connected so that hinging or rotation at the joint is prevented. The advantage of a rigidly connected frame is that diagonal braces which might impinge on windows or restrict interior spaces are not necessary. However, calculating the stresses in the beams and columns of a rigid frame was practically impossible in the 1890s. Such frames generate high internal bending forces called moments. Calculating the accumulation of multiple stories of these internal bending forces was too complex. Instead, engineers assumed the presence of hinges where one story joined the lower story. Rigidity was provided by either massive portal arches, knee braces or, in the case of the Reliance Building, by 24-inch-deep plate girders riveted to the columns. Engineers realized their assumption of a hinge in the frame was incorrect, but they also realized that it was conservative, i.e., the frame was actually stronger than its calculated strength with the hinges assumed. Thus, safety was ensured while opening up the interior spaces without the inconvenience of diagonal bracing.

The structural frame of the Reliance Building used the Gray column, a patent system using riveted plates and T-sections. Breaking with accepted practice, columns were not interrupted by horizontal base plates, but instead were riveted together with splice plates at alternating stories. Such splices are more rigid than base plates, which interrupt the continuity of the column, and enabled designers to route piping inside the hollow form of the columns.

Atwood's contribution to skyscraper design was followed in 1895-96 with the more vertically oriented Fisher Building in Chicago. It, too, used lightweight terra-cotta cladding combined with large windows set in a more Gothicizing form. Unfortunately, Atwood's personal difficulties interfered with his professional career, leading to his dismissal and subsequent death in late 1895. Despite the brevity of Atwood's employment in Chicago, the Reliance Building remains as one of the most important achievements of the Chicago school. More than any other single building of its time, the Reliance Building prophetically anticipated both the architectural form and structural technology that would revolutionize architecture in the 20th century.

—ELWIN C. ROBISON

SCHLESINGER AND MAYER STORE [CARSON PIRIE SCOTT STORE]
Chicago, Illinois, U.S.A.

1899-1904. Architect: Louis H. Sullivan (1856-1924). **1906:** Addition of five bays on the south; **Architect:** D. H. Burnham and Company. **1960-61:** Addition of three bays to the south; **Architect:** Holabird and Root.

Publications

BENSON, SUSAN PORTER: "Palace of Consumption and Machine for Selling: The American Department Store, 1880-1940." *Radical History Review* 21 (Fall 1979): 199-221.

COMMISSION ON CHICAGO HISTORICAL AND ARCHITECTURAL LANDMARKS: *Carson Pirie Scott & Company Building*. Chicago, 1979.

CONDIT, CARL W.: *The Chicago School of Architecture: A History of Commercial and Public Building in the Chicago Area, 1875-1925*. Chicago, 1964.

DESMOND, HENRY W.: "{The Schlesinger and Mayer Building} Another View—What Mr. Louis Sullivan Stands For." *Architectural Record* 16 (July 1904): 61-67.

FRAMPTON, KENNETH, and FUTAGAWA, YUKIO: *Modern Architecture: 1851-1919*. New York, 1983.

"The New Schlesinger and Mayer Building, Chicago." *Brickbuilder* 12 (May 1903): 101-104.

SIRY, JOSEPH: *Carson Pirie Scott: Louis Sullivan and the Chicago Department Store*. Chicago and London, 1988.

SMITH, LYNDON: "The Schlesinger and Mayer Building: An Attempt to Give Functional Expression to the Architecture of a Department Store." *Architectural Record* 16 (July 1904): 53-60.

Schlesinger and Mayer Store: Chicago, Illinois, 1899-1904

SULLIVAN, LOUIS: "Sub-Structure at the New Schlesinger and
    Mayer Store Building." *Engineering Record* 47 (21 Febru-
    ary 1903): 194-196.
VAN ORMER, GERALDINE: "Louis Sullivan's Ornamentation
    as Exemplified in the Carson, Pirie, Scott Building." Mas-
    ter's thesis. Pennsylvania State University, University Park,
    Pennsylvania, 1960.

*

Schlesinger and Mayer (Carson Pirie Scott and Company since
1904) was probably Louis Sullivan's most important contribution to modern architecture after the dissolution of his partnership with Dankmar Adler in 1895. The client, the architect, the
critical community and the general public all understood the
significance of whatever appeared on the site at the junction of

Madison and State streets, which was at the time and for many
years afterward the major intersection in the commercial district
of Chicago.

Adler and Sullivan had worked with the clients a decade
earlier, designing a residence for the highly successful dry-
goods merchant Leopold Schlesinger in 1884. Then the firm he
headed began to occupy large segments of the square block at
the intersection of the city's north/south and east/west axis.
Because of Adler and Sullivan's reputation for getting major
remodeling projects completed in months rather than years, and
Adler's connections with the owners, the architectural partners
were granted several commissions for interior and exterior remodeling, for additions, and for designs meant to harmonize
the diverse facades of the newly joined structures.

Even before they finally decided to erect an entirely new
department store on the site, the clients hired Sullivan rather
than his ex-partner for another round of facade work on one of
the properties facing the Wabash Avenue side of the block; this
was a strong indication of the high esteem in which the designer

was held and, perhaps, the result of the visibility of his 1886 article in *Lippincott's,* "The Tall Office Building Artistically Considered."

While Sullivan's design responses to the constantly shifting plans of the clients are interesting in themselves, the real importance of the completed design is rooted in his understanding of the client's long-range plans almost as much as in the harmony and balance he achieved. That is because a large part of his exterior design conception had already been developed in preparation for uniting the diverse properties with a unified horizontal format. Thus, by the spring of 1898, when Schlesinger and Mayer proposed a major new department store instead of the continued piecemeal approach, Sullivan was able to work even more quickly than usual and incorporated at least some of his prior exterior plans into his overall conception for what he knew would make or break his reputation in his solo practice.

Sullivan's success in creating tall buildings of impressive proportions and breathtaking verticality was attested to at a national level, and critics had joined the community of business boosters in glorying in the height of such recent commercial structures as the Wainwright Building in St. Louis, Missouri (1890) and the Guaranty Building in Buffalo, New York (1894-95). However, not willing to rely on the same approach to verticality in a building that was to be not only tall, but long, Sullivan invented an entire new image for the American department store at the same time as his design acknowledged the tension between the vertical and the horizontal.

The architect made later additions to the store, through the year 1903, but the external appearance of the building remained based on his brilliant synthesis between the vertical and the horizontal: by having the marble blocks that comprised the horizontal and the vertical skin of the building at the same depth, neither direction was stressed. Further, as the bays are wider than they are tall, and as the building is a lot longer than it is high, the corner tower provides the vertical thrust that was needed to balance the inexorable pull on the eye down the block. That vertical thrust is created by the rounded corner, leading the eye upward as it reaches the richly ornamented entrance with its more vertical windows, at the intersection of State and Madison.

Instead of the verticality that led the viewer's attention skyward in Sullivan's previous designs, the majestic horizontal rhythm of the Schlesinger and Mayer facades was also of symbolic importance. Given the unusually large showcase windows, with their ornate, luxurious and arresting design, the viewer—a potential customer—is encouraged to stop in front of each display space. Walking along either facade of the building, the even more magnificent decoration surrounding the rounded main entrance is there to lead one into the place where all the splendidly displayed wares can actually be purchased. And while it is impossible to know just how conscious the architect was of the commercial value of his design, it was successful enough to set a standard for an entire genre of urban department stores.

The use of ornamental iron as a major design tool reached a new level of maturity in this building, and Sullivan was to utilize his understanding of its potential in both the interiors and the exteriors of the commissions that came to him in the last years of his practice. His jewel-like banks for small towns throughout the midwest have little else in common with the Schlesinger and Mayer Department Store, but the major role of iron ornament was possible only because of the architect's explorations on his greatest solo project.

Each of the three major elements of the design contributes to making Schlesinger and Mayer the impressive structure it remains today: the balance of vertical and horizontal elements,

the development of a new typology for the urban department store, and the careful and strategic use of a rich but nonderivative and imaginative ornamentation that contrasts so well with the restraint of the exterior facades.

—DAVID M. SOKOL

SEARS TOWER
Chicago, Illinois, U.S.A.

1974-76: Constructed; **Architects:** Louis Skidmore (1897-1962), Nathaniel A. Owings (b.1903), and John O. Merrill (1896-1975).

Publications

BLAKE, PETER: "SOM Puts the Bones Outside the Skin." *Architectural Forum* 120 (1959): 92-95.
BOYLE, MICHAEL: "Architectural Practice in America 1865-1965: Ideal and Reality." pp. 309-344 in KOSTOF, SPIRO (ed.): *The Architect: Chapters in the History of the Profession.* New York, 1977.
DANZ, E.: *Architecture of Skidmore, Owings & Merrill, 1950-1962.* New York, 1962.
DREXEL, ARTHUR and MENGES, AXEL: *The Architecture of Skidmore, Owings & Merrill: 1963-1973.* New York, 1974.
DREXLER, A.: *Architecture of Skidmore, Owings and Merrill.* London, 1974.
FISCHER, ROBERT: "Optimizing the Structure of the Skyscraper." *Architectural Record* 152 (1972): 97-104.
GIEDION, SIGFRIED: "The Experiment of SOM." *Bauen und Wohnen* 12 (1957): 113-117.
HITCHCOCK, H.-R. (ed.): *Architecture of Skidmore, Owings and Merrill 1950-1962.* London, 1963.
HITCHCOCK, H.R. and E. DAUZ: *Skidmore, Owings and Merrill.* London, 1963.
WOODWARD, CHRISTOPHER: *Skidmore, Owings & Merrill.* New York, 1970.

*

Designed by Skidmore, Owings and Merrill and built at the western edge of the Chicago Loop in 1974, the Sears Tower is big in all senses of the word: at 1,470 feet it is the world's tallest inhabited building, and its 4.4 million square feet of floor space make it second only to the Pentagon in building size.

The John Hancock Center (1970) had been created in Skidmore, Owings and Merrill's Chicago office, with Bruce Graham as partner in charge and Fazlur Khan as engineer. "Technology is our art form," said Khan, so when the same designers tackled the design of the even bigger Sears Tower, one might have expected a continuation of the fascination with height and the straightforward expression of a clear, inventive, economical structure. Chicago was the city that gave us the skyscraper and the clearly expressed metal frame in the 1870s, but these aspects of the city's inventiveness reached their furthest development with Graham and Khan in the 1970s.

Sears Tower: Chicago, Illinois, 1974-76

The site is a whole city block, and the client, the Sears, Roebuck department-store and mail-order company, wanted to gather under one roof its various offices, which were scattered in different parts of Chicago. To develop the site economically and to provide space for expansion, the architects designed a building much larger than that needed by Sears, which planned to occupy some 40 percent of the space, with 7,000 of its own employees in a building that provides work space for 16,500. The upper part of the tower was, therefore, leased to other tenants.

For its own employees' work areas, Sears wanted very large floor plates. The company was advised, however, that such large areas would not rent well, so the rental areas needed to be smaller. The designers' response was to make a building that would be reduced in size as it ascended, giving large floor areas for Sears at lower levels and shallower floor depths for rental at higher levels. As at the John Hancock tower, the designers turned this functional need to slim the upper floors into an aesthetic and technical advantage.

The plan form and the structure of the Sears Tower consist of nine tubes. Each tube is a 75-foot square with columns placed 15 feet on center around the periphery, with no columns within the squares. The columns and the beams around the floors form a cellular tube frame, with rigid connections to take wind loads. This use of rigid connections was, in some respects, a backward step from the diagonal bracing at the John Hancock tower, but the designers achieved a relatively efficient structure by tying the tubes together and by using a very deep plan form at low level, where horizontal forces are greatest. The use of diagonals would not have been practical, because where the tubes touch, there is a need to pass freely between the columns in an open office layout.

The nine tubes at low level reduce to two at the top; this reduction had its origins in the need for shallower offices in the rental areas and in structural requirements, but it was exploited to give the building its form and its distinctive silhouette. New York skyscrapers of the 1930s had setbacks for stylistic and for daylighting reasons, but usually the structural framing was contorted to achieve the desired massing. At Sears the appearance can be regarded as the effortless result of function and structure. The lowest 49 stories, originally occupied by Sears, consist of the full complement of nine squares; two opposite corner tubes stop at the 50th floor, and the other two stop at the 91st floor, leaving two to extend to the full 109 stories.

The service cores are located in the unlit spaces in the center of the building, and great skill was exercised in reducing the core appropriately as the plan area reduces. Twice in the height of the building, sky lobbies provide interchange points from the high-speed elevators to the local elevators serving the intermediate floors. Five times in the height of the building are mechanical floors, which are faced with louvers; some diagonal bracing is placed in these floors so that not all wind forces have to be taken on rigid connections.

The frame is steel, and the cladding is gray aluminum and gray glass. The cladding is impeccably detailed but decidedly neutral, even a bit dull. It is as if the architects, having dazzled us with structure and silhouette, had no energy left to make a similar contribution at the detail level.

Sears Tower took office buildings to new heights. After Sears came a pause. The Empire State Building was the climax of one stage of skyscraper building: its record as world's highest stood for a quarter of a century, and it was only overtaken when fresh structural ideas made even greater heights economical. Sears had a similar role. It awaits the challenge of new designers with new ideas and values. Until then, it remains the highest.

—JOHN WINTER

STATE OF ILLINOIS CENTER
Chicago, Illinois, U.S.A.

1985: Constructed; **Architect:** Helmut Jahn (b.1940).

Publications

MILLER, N.: *Helmut Jahn.* New York, 1986.
YALE SCHOOL OF ARCHITECTURE: *Helmut Jahn.* 1982. Exhibition Catalog.

Arguably the most audacious building completed in Chicago in the 1980s, the State of Illinois Center was commissioned from Helmut Jahn of Murphy/Jahn in cooperation with Lester B. Knight and Associates. To many it marks Jahn's arrival as a force in the history of modern (or late-modern) architecture and in the enlargement of its influence. It has been met with vehement criticism, having been called an exile from an alien land and accused of rejecting all historical references for this mixed-use, governmental office building. Described as a crystal palace for the 20th century, it was intended to be a metaphor for the open nature of democratic government. Jahn sought a design that would reinforce the existing urban patterns of Chicago's street grid and accommodate the pedestrian patterns that deviate from it.

The priorities for the design of the building were the expression of its governmental status; its relation to the 10-story City and County Building to the south, designed by Holabird and Roche and completed in 1906; its links to the subway and elevated rapid transit lines; and the reestablishment of the social role of architecture.

Occupying an entire block within the Chicago Loop (the area of downtown Chicago circumscribed by the elevated rapid-transit line tracks), the 17-story building is distinguished by its 160-foot-diameter atrium. Its southeast section is sliced away to form a sloped setback in curved segments, gesturing to the Daley Center, a 31-story governmental office building designed by C. F. Murphy Associates (Murphy/Jahn's predecessor firm), and creating a new plaza at the corner. A granite screen-wall dematerializes and diminishes toward the entry at the southeast corner, leading to an interior rotunda that serves as an alternative to the exterior open spaces along the urban corridors of Dearborn and Clark streets. The crystalline, translucent whole reveals a central space that can be perceived from the outside, penetrating the entire height of the building and terminating in a lantern in the form of a sloped, truncated cylinder.

On the north, east and west sides of the building, Jahn adhered fully to the prescription of the street grid. A 2-foot 6-inch vertical division governs alternating strips of reflective-glass vision panels and opaque colored-glass panels; a 30-by-30-foot structural module governs the bay system. On the east and west sides, the curtain wall steps back gradually, while along the north side, against the elevated rapid transit line tracks on Lake Street, the curtain wall rises straight up.

At the entry, a slice of clear silicone glazing at the center of the dome-like, sweeping curved wall, which is stretched tautly to midway along the east side, reveals the interior, and a keystone pattern in the glazing reinforces this entry point. A covered walkway envelopes the curved section with a detail employed

State of Illinois Building: Chicago, Illinois, 1985

previously by Jahn in the 701 Fourth Avenue South building in Minneapolis: round piers stand behind flat pilasters that diminish in width from top to bottom.

Inside, the space glitters and presents an unexpected baroque nobility; it is grand in its complexity, assured in its hyperactivity. A glass-walled antechamber leads inward, where layers of activity celebrate movement, with open office floors, expressed emphatically by reflective baby-blue spandrel panels, shimmering above a ground level of retail shops. Freestanding banks of elevators with exposed mechanics reveal bolts, ducts and cables. The tracery of the curtain wall adds to the dizzying effect of the pattern of the subterranean food court, open to the atrium above, which recalls the pattern Michelangelo gave the plaza of the Campidoglio in Rome.

Having revitalized Chicago's waning architectural dialectic, the State of Illinois Center is already set firmly within the city's architectural history. Its disturbing complexity, brazen nonconformity, tense relationship with its more venerable neighbors, and ungracefully aging materials make it either a landmark experiment in form-giving or a misdirected urbanistic exercise.

—PAUL GLASSMAN

TRIBUNE TOWER COMPETITION
Chicago, Illinois, U.S.A.

1922: Competition announced. **1923:** Competition documented. **1922-25:** Tower constructed; **Architects:** John Mead Howells (1868-1959) and Raymond Hood (1881-1934).

Publications

Chicago Tribune. *The International Competition for a New Administration Building for the Chicago Tribune MCMXXII.* Chicago, 1923.

SOLOMONSON, KATHERINE: "Chicago's Cathedral of Commerce." *Chicago History* Spring (1989).

TIGERMAN, STANLEY, and COHEN, STUART E.: *Chicago Tribune Tower Competition and Late Entries.* New York, 1980.

WANSCHER, VILHELM: "The Chicago Tribune Building." *Arkitekten* 25 (1923): 22-28.

*

On 10 June 1922, the *Chicago Tribune* challenged architects from all over the world to design a skyscraper which was to be no less than the most beautiful building in the modern world. The competition developed into one of the largest and certainly one of the best-publicized competitions ever held. Timed for the celebration of the newspaper's 75th anniversary, the Chicago Tribune Competition was planned as a massive publicity stunt. Even while the *Tribune*'s editors exploited the competition for its advertising value, they also wanted it to be educational. Through newspaper articles, a traveling exhibition of selected drawings, and a book that reproduced all but three of the submitted entries, the *Tribune* hoped to have a positive impact on the beautification of the American city (especially Chicago) by providing new and better models for skyscraper design. In so doing, the *Tribune* asserted its self-appointed role as arbiter of design standards, a role architects and arts organizations claimed as their own. Although the *Tribune* was ultimately unable to influence the course of future architecture to the extent that it had hoped, the competition and the traveling exhibition that followed it stirred up considerable interest among architects as well as the general public.

The *Tribune* ultimately received 263 entries, 204 of them by the final deadline. Nearly all of the original entries have been lost, but most of the perspective drawings were reproduced in the *Tribune*'s 1923 book documenting the competition. This book, which shows designs ranging from Bauhaus to Byzantine Revival submitted by some of the most prominent architects of the day as well as some who had probably never before designed anything bigger than a cottage, has been regarded as an encyclopedic overview of the state of skyscraper design in 1922. The fact that the entries represent a variety of responses to a single commission makes it particularly interesting to compare them. At the same time, the very requirements to which they responded were, in some ways, idiosyncratic enough that many of the entries are unlike anything that had ever been constructed—or ever would be.

One of the competition program's unusual features was that the *Tribune* presented no budget, and it vowed to construct the winning design regardless of cost. Another was that the Chicago building code allowed buildings to rise to a height of 400 feet, but the top 140 feet could not be occupied. Because, unlike most real estate speculators, the *Tribune* was willing to pay for unused space as well as any special effects the architect wished

to devise, many of the designs are more structurally or ornamentally complex than usual, with elaborate crowns devoted purely to the beauty—and the advertising value—the *Tribune* desired. Because the *Tribune*'s editors wanted their building to capture the spirit of the newspaper and ennoble the city of Chicago, they received a number of designs crowned with newspaper symbols ranging from globes to radio towers. The *Tribune*'s site also presented the architect with an unusual set of conditions. Located in a newly developing part of town, the site was exceptionally constricted for a Chicago lot, though unobstructed on three sides. This encouraged a three-dimensional approach to design, an approach becoming increasingly common following the institution of New York's 1916 zoning law that required setbacks. And it also offered architects the rare opportunity to design a towering skyscraper that would become a monumental vista point in a new urban scheme.

The *Tribune*'s two editors, Robert R. McCormick and Joseph Patterson, set up the competition so that they could maintain maximum control over its conduct and outcome. Although the competition was held under the supervision of the American Institute of Architects; the jury had a ratio of four *Tribune* employees (the two editors and two subordinates who were unlikely to argue with them) to one architect, who apparently differed with the majority opinion but who was sorely outnumbered. It is also evident that there were some irregularities in the competition's conduct and that anonymity might not have been strictly guarded. After weeks of deliberation, the three top prizes went to New Yorkers John Mead Howells and Raymond Hood, the Finnish architect Eliel Saarinen, and the Chicago firm of Holabird and Roche.

Although the *Tribune* received entries from architects working in 23 nations, the Chicago Tribune Competition was only nominally international. While other notable international competitions had jurors from several countries and programs in several languages, the *Tribune*'s jury was made up exclusively of Chicagoans and the program was issued in English only. Foreign architects were given a later deadline, but judging started weeks before, when only a few foreign entries had actually arrived. Moreover, foreign architects were at a considerable disadvantage because they would have known little or nothing about the competition's sponsors, nor would they have been privy to the active debate about skyscraper design in the American architectural press. When the *Tribune* announced the competition's outcome, it smugly stated that the competition proved the superiority of American design. The competition was set up to bear this out in accordance with the ardent patriotism of its sponsors.

The competition's results stimulated considerable discussion in the architectural press. Most of it centered on the relative merits of the two top prize winners and their truthful expression of structure. Howells and Hood's Gothic design was widely praised, but its detractors were disturbed by the breakdown of structural logic at the crown. Some felt that the use of flying buttresses (which Louis Sullivan described as "the monster on top") to crown a steel-framed building was illogical, especially because these simulacra of masonry supports supported nothing, but even some of the most negative critics admitted that the building as a whole had its good features. Those who preferred Saarinen's design praised it for its expression of the steel frame clear to the building's summit, its vertical impetus, and its graceful and well-integrated solution to the problem of designing a skyscraper with setbacks. The American architectural press was utterly mute when it came to the more avant-garde designs submitted by architects such as Walter Gropius and Adolph Meyer, and Bruno Taut. Because nearly all of these designs arrived after the competition's deadline, it is possible

Tribune Tower: Chicago, Illinois, 1922-25

that no one saw them until the *Tribune* published its book on the competition in the fall of 1923.

Despite a few detractors, the Gothic Tribune Tower was actually quite popular during the 1920s. Thousands of people took the trip to the top to gaze over Chicago through a screen of flying buttresses. The building was admirably designed to suit the *Tribune*'s advertising purposes. It answered the *Tribune*'s desire for a distinctive silhouette which could be read on the skyline from all directions and which would lend itself well to photographs. The building's crown, which provided a sort of elevated public space, was also designed for night illumination. And its Gothic style, according to *Tribune* articles, symbolized the newspaper's high, quasi-spiritual aspirations transcending the merely commercial.

The competition's later historiography reads like a barometer of changing attitudes in architectural criticism. By the late 1920s, Saarinen's design was hailed as the ''beacon of the future'' and heir to Sullivan's work, while Howells and Hood's design was relegated to being the representative of a period of murky darkness which was believed to have started with the World's Columbian Exposition in 1893. By the 1940s Saarinen had been displaced by Gropius and Meyer, ignored in the 1920s, as heirs to what had become known as the Chicago school. Lönberg Holm's entry, which was never submitted, was also elevated to a position of prominence. This perspective reigned for more than 30 years until studies in the 1980s started to reassess Howells and Hood's entry and historicism in general.

The Chicago Tribune Competition has been hailed as a watershed in skyscraper design. To be sure, it is significant for having drawn together such a range of entries, from the European avant-garde, which eventually assumed preeminence in the United States, to the more traditional historicizing designs that had predominated for the past several decades. Yet, although Howells and Hood's entry was not as influential as the *Tribune* hoped it would be, it did not mark the end of the skyscraper's ''enslavement'' to the past. Gothic, classical, Mayan and Egyptian skyscrapers would continue to be built throughout the 1920s. At the same time, the European avant-garde entries went wholly unnoticed in the United States. Some have said that Eliel Saarinen's design represented a turning point in the approach to the setback skyscraper. It was certainly hailed as important in the early 1920s, but in retrospect it appears that part of his success was due to the design's effective amalgamation of trends that were already under way. Unlike the Tribune Tower, however, Saarinen's entry did influence the design of a number of later skyscrapers, the best known of which is Hood's American Radiator Building in New York City (1924). The competition's greatest legacy may not be so much in what was actually constructed in its wake but in the discussion it fostered, both in its own time and in the succeeding decades as it assumed its place in the changing discourse on modern architecture.

—KATHERINE SOLOMONSON

WORLD'S COLUMBIAN EXPOSITION, 1893
Chicago, Illinois, U.S.A.

Architects: Frederick Law Olmsted (1822-1903), Daniel H. Burnham (1846-1912), John Wellborn Root (1850-91). **Participating architects:** Administration Building: Richard Morris Hunt (1827-95); Machinery Hall: Robert S. Peabody (1845-1917) and John G. Stearns (1843-1917); Agriculture Building: Charles F. McKim (1847-1909), William R. Mead (1846-1928),

and Stanford White (1853-1906); Manufacturers and Liberal Arts Building: George Post (1837-1913); Electricity Building: Henry Van Brunt (1832-1903) and Frank Howe; Mines and Mining Building: S. S. Beman; Transportation Building: Dankmar Adler (1844-1900) and Louis H. Sullivan (1856-1924); Horticulture Building: William Le Baron Jenney (1832-1907); Fisheries Building: Henry Ives Cobb (1859-1931); Women's Building: Sophia Hayden; Art Pavilion: Charles B. Atwood (1849-95).

Publications

ADAMS, J. C.: ''What a Great City Might Be: A Lesson from the White City.'' *New England Magazine* 14 (March 1896): 3-13.

American Architect and Building News Various articles in Vols. 28-46 (1890-94).

APPELBAUM, STANLEY: *The Chicago World's Fair of 1893: A Photographic Record*. New York, 1980.

APPELBAUM, STANLEY: *The Chicago World's Fair of 1893*. 1980.

BADGER, R.: *The Great American Fair: The World's Columbian Exposition and American Culture*. Chicago, 1979.

BUNNER, H.: ''Making of the White City.'' *Scribner's Magazine* 12 (October 1892): 398-418.

BURG, DAVID F.: *Chicago's White City of 1893*. Lexington, Kentucky, 1976.

BURNHAM, DANIEL H.: *The World's Columbian Exposition: The Final Official Report of the Director of Works*. Chicago, 1898.

CRAVATH, J. R.: ''Electricity at the World's Columbian Exposition.'' *Review of Reviews* 8 (July 1893): 35-39.

''Detail of the Peristyle, World's Fair Grounds, Chicago, Illinois.'' *American Architect and Building News* 42 (4 November 1993): 63, illustration.

FERREE, BARR, and SCHUYLER, MONTGOMERY: ''Architecture at the World's Fair.'' *Review of Reviews* 8 (September 1893): 318-319.

''The Fine Arts Building, from the North, World's Columbian Exposition, Chicago, Illinois.'' *American Architect and Building News* 42 (23 December 1993): 152, illustration, plans.

''The Fine Arts Gallery, World's Columbian Exposition, Chicago, Illinois.'' *American Architect and Building News* 38 (22 October 1992): 61, illustration.

GILBERT, JAMES: *Perfect Cities: Chicago's Utopias of 1893*. Chicago, 1991.

GRILLE, C. J. A., and FALCONNET, H.: *Revue technique de l'Exposition universelle de Chicago en 1893*. Paris, 1894.

HINES, THOMAS: *Burnham of Chicago*. New York, 1974.

HIRSCHL, J. H.: ''The Great White City.'' *American Heritage* 11 (October 1960): 8-21, 75.

HOFFMANN, DONALD: *The Architecture of John Wellborn Root*. Baltimore, 1973.

Inland Architect and News Record Various articles in Vols. 17-22 (1891-93).

''Interior Decoration of Dome, Fine Arts Building, World's Columbian Exposition, Chicago, Illinois.'' *Inland Architect and News Record* 22, 5 (December, 1893):48-49.

JOHNSON, R. (ed.): *A History of the World's Columbian Exposition Held in Chicago in 1893*. 4 vols. New York, 1897.

KARLOWICZ, TITUS M.: ''D. H. Burnham's Role in the Selection of Architects for the World's Columbian Exposition.'' *Journal of the Society of Architectural Historians* 29 (October 1970): 247-254.

World's Columbian Exposition: Chicago, Illinois, 1893

KARLOWICZ, TITUS M.: "Notes on Columbian Exposition's Manufactures and Liberal Arts Building." *Journal of the Society of Architectural Historians* 33 (October 1974): 214-218.

"Lessons of the Chicago World's Fair: An Interview with the Late Daniel H. Burnham." *Architectural Record* 33/1 (1913): 34-44.

MILLET, F. D.: "Decoration of the Exposition." *Scribner's Magazine* 12 (December 1892): 692-709.

MILLET, F. D.: "Designers of the Fair." *Harper's Magazine* 85 (November 1892): 872-883.

MOORE, CHARLES: *Daniel H. Burnham, Architect, Planner of Cities.* 2 vols. Boston, 1921.

MOORE, CHARLES: "Lessons of the Chicago World's Fair: An Interview with the Late Daniel H. Burnham." *Architectural Record* 33 1 (1913):34-44.

PALMER, A. F.: "Some Lasting Results of the World's Fair." *Forum* 16 (December 1893): 517-523.

ROTH, LELAND M.: *McKim, Mead and White, Architects.* New York, 1983.

SCHUYLER, MONTGOMERY: "Last Words about the World's Fair." *Architectural Record* 3 (January-March 1894): 291-301.

SULLIVAN, LOUIS H.: *The Autobiography of an Idea.* New York, 1924.

TSELOS, DIMITRI: "The Chicago Fair and the Myth of the 'Lost Cause'." *Journal of the Society of Architectural Historians* 26, (December 1967): 259-268.

TUNNARD, C.: "A City Called Beautiful." *Journal of the Society of Architectural Historians* 9 (March-May 1950): 31-35.

VAN BRUNT, HENRY: "Architecture at the World's Exposition." *Century* 22 (May, July, August, September and October 1892).

WALTON, W.: *World's Columbian Exposition, 1893; Official Illustrated Publication; Art and Architecture.* 11 vols. Philadelphia, 1893.

WILSON, WILLIAM H.: *The City Beautiful Movement.* Baltimore, 1989.

WOOD, R. W.: *Architectural Details from the Buildings at the World's Columbian Exposition.* Boston, 1893.

In 1893 the city of Chicago was host to a major international industrial exposition which marked an important turning point in the American embrace of emblematic classicism for public buildings and in the rise of the planning profession in the United States.

The World's Columbian Exposition was planned to occur in 1892 to celebrate the discovery of the new world by Columbus. Although the first proposal for such a fair was made in 1882, protracted wrangling over the site of the host city and in obtaining the necessary authorization from the United States Congress resulted in delays that meant the fair did not actually open to the public until the spring of 1893. Several Eastern Seaboard cities, particularly New York, felt certain that one of their number would be selected; the campaign mounted by the city of Chicago was countered with derisive remarks suggesting that a fair there would be little better than a bumpkin's cattle show.

Once Chicago was officially designated host city in the spring of 1890, a local committee was formed. At the same time, the eminent landscape architect Frederick Law Olmsted was engaged by the committee to plan the grounds, and the prominent local architectural firm of Burnham and Root was appointed as consulting architects. Olmsted at first hoped for a fair site in Lincoln Park on Chicago's north side, but he eventually agreed to a larger site in undeveloped and marshy Jackson park, on the city's south side.

Meanwhile, John Wellborn Root (Daniel Burnham's partner) began sketching out possible fair buildings in a delicately ornamented Romanesque style, but the late beginning date meant that no single individual or architectural firm could design all the required buildings. Accordingly, Burnham's appointment was changed to chief of construction, and in December 1890 he requested permission to select 10 major architects to design the principal buildings of the fair, with all the remaining minor buildings to be designed by Burnham and Root. Burnham's authorization to select architects also made it possible for him to tap esteemed architects from eastern cities and the Midwest, thereby squelching fears of a tasteless display. The eastern architects, who had been waging a battle to establish professional standards—particularly the right to supervise construction to ensure that building followed construction drawings—were reluctant to design the fair's buildings due to the distance of their offices from the fair site, but Burnham assured them that they would have full control of their creative work. They then all agreed on a planning meeting in Chicago in January 1891.

When the selected architects assembled in Chicago in January, they immediately decided that the buildings of the fair be unified in style and character, and from that followed their subsequent selection of a classical style for the main buildings around the Court of Honor lagoon; classicism was the one style they all knew in common, and, moreover, the details of the various buildings could be worked out by crews of draftsmen working for Burnham in Chicago. Root, meanwhile, had caught a cold at the first gathering of the architects and died of pneumonia within four days, while Burnham and the assembled architects concluded their planning session.

By mutual consent, the main buildings were portioned out. Richard Morris Hunt of New York took the centrally located Administration Building. Peabody and Stearns of Boston selected the Machinery Hall. McKim, Mead and White of New York chose the Agriculture Building. George B. Post of New York elected to design the huge Manufactures and Liberal Arts Building. Van Brunt and Howe of Kansas City, Missouri, chose the Electricity Building. Flanking it was the Mines and Mining Building selected by S. S. Beman of Chicago. North of this axially aligned and compact group of buildings was a second group of buildings more loosely arranged around an irregular lagoon. This group included the Transportation Building chosen by Chicago architects Adler and Sullivan. Next to it was the Horticulture Building by Chicago architect William Le Baron Jenney. Nearby was the Fisheries Building designed by Henry Ives Cobb of Chicago. At the northern edge of this group was the Women's Building accommodating special activities for women; it was designed by one of the nation's first women architects, Sophia Hayden. At the northern end of the lagoon was the imposing classical Art Pavilion designed by Charles B. Atwood, who had become Root's replacement.

The Chicago fair was significant for a number of reasons. One was the importance of the interrelationship of buildings and the spaces between them, the result of the early work of Olmsted in planning the grounds. Related to this, too, was the deliberate placement of buildings according to functional activity, so that the principal exhibition buildings were at the southern end of the fair site, with the smaller and stylistically diverse state and national pavilions at the northern end of the grounds behind the Art Pavilion. Extending in an L to the west of the northern end of Jackson Park was a third area devoted to amusements and entertainments, the most striking of which was the huge revolving wheel, rising to 265 feet, designed by George W. G. Ferris (smaller Ferris wheels immediately became a staple American carnival ride). The organization of the grounds implemented a system of zoning by use, the first large-scale application of this principle in American planning.

Also among the important contributions was the widespread application of technology, particularly the various ways electricity was employed. Imbedded in the outer plaster shells of all the buildings were tens of thousands of incandescent electric bulbs, powered by huge generators in the Electricity Building. This was the first commercial installation of the newly developed alternating-current system of electrical transmission, thereby allowing the fair to operate on a 24-hour basis; once the exhibits were closed to visitors, grounds crews began overnight cleaning and repairs so that the fair opened new each morning. Electric motors were also used to power an electric sidewalk that extended out into Lake Michigan, and electric storage batteries were used to power launches that plied the lagoons and canals. Particularly important, too, was the use of alternating-current electricity to power mass-transit trains that ran around the periphery of the grounds on an elevated track.

Other technical matters had important ramifications. One, noticed by fairgoers, was the absence of utility lines overhead. The careful planning of the grounds beforehand meant that large utility tunnels were provided, through which ran the electrical power lines, telephone lines and telegraph lines, and the wiring for the fair's fire alarm system; in real cities of the period it was not uncommon for a dense tangle of overhead lines to blot out the sun in some narrow streets. Another development was the large-scale commercial use of spray-painting of all the buildings, although this materially changed the final appearance of the fair. As originally planned, the fair buildings were all to have been painted in a rainbow of colors; Louis Sullivan, in fact, was relying on this to create the bold patterns on his Transportation Building. When time ran out for the intricate polychrome painting, spray-painting in off-white was selected as a last-ditch effort to get the fair opened in time. Sullivan, however, insisted that his building be painted, since his alone did not incorporate large masses of three-dimensional sculpture to relieve otherwise flat surfaces.

A year after the Columbian Exposition closed, in 1894, the esteemed architecture critic Montgomery Schuyler published his reflections on the artistic success of the fair. He identified three elements contributing to the enormous popular success of the fair. One was the careful attention of the planners, architects and artists in creating a unity of ensemble in the buildings. This was effected by the buildings' three-dimensional arrangement, their variation within the common architectural language of classicism, and the sensitive integration of mural painting and decorative sculpture, as well as sculpture placed throughout the grounds. Another component was the sheer magnitude of the enterprise, which made the sense of unity all the more appreciated as one moved from area to area. The World's Columbian Exposition was planned and designed at a scale that approached that of a small city. The third component was the thoroughness of the illusion that pervaded the fair; it was like a dreamland that never relaxed in strengthening that illusion (and it is this same delight in an all-pervading illusion that draws millions of visitors to the various Disney theme parks and others like it today). The possible negative effect that concerned Schuyler, however, was that most visitors would associate the classicism of the fair with its success, and would take the desire to build classical buildings back to their hometowns, as in fact actually happened. Planning, ensemble and unity did not necessarily reside particularly in classical buildings, as Schuyler tried to convince his readers. Insofar as the fair did persuade hundreds of American city leaders to build classical town halls, courthouses, libraries and art galleries, Sullivan's famous prophetic diatribe that "the damage of the fair will last half a century" was accurate. But what Sullivan missed was the enormous positive effect the fair had in encouraging the planning of cities, for 1893 marks the beginning of the planning profession in the United States. If the hundreds of landscaped boulevards and the axially arranged complexes of white civic buildings built in the half century after 1893 were classically articulated, nevertheless their gracious provisions of open public space and harmonious proportions have become appreciated civic ornaments.

—LELAND M. ROTH

Wexner Center for the Visual Arts

WEXNER CENTER FOR THE VISUAL ARTS
Columbus, Ohio

1983-89. Architects: Peter Eisenman (b. 1932), Richard Trott and Laurie Olin.

Publications

"AD Profile 82: Wexner Center for the Visual Arts." *Architectural Design* (November/December 1989).
ARNELL, PETER, and BICKFORD, TED (eds.): *A Center for the Visual Arts: The Ohio State University Competition.* New York, 1984.
"Eisenmanamnesie." *Architecture † Urbanism* (special issue, August 1988).
MONEO, RAFAEL, and VIDLER, ANTHONY: *Wexner Center for the Visual Arts, Ohio State University.* New York, 1989.
SOMOL, ROBERT E.: "Wexner Center for the Visual Arts." *Domus* (January 1990).

*

The Wexner Center at the Ohio State University in Columbus is one of the art world's more controversial buildings. Sponsored by the university and the clothing tycoon Leslie Wexner, its principal architects were Peter Eisenman and Richard Trott.

Critics have complained that the structure's intricacies are inappropriate backdrops for contemporary art works. Its exhibition spaces, nestled below the complex angles of the ceilings, are intended to resemble lofts. However, museum installations allow the Wexner Center to be arranged for various kinds of art, such as the exhibit "Passage de l'Image."

The convertible spatial ordering of the Center suits its purposes, but the design is mainly symbolic. The building stands for a confrontation between past and future, and for an intimate relationship to its site. Two of its principal features indicate the structure's temporal dimensions. At the southern end, where the major entrance and lobby are situated, fragmented brick masses are reminiscent of the Armory towers that stood nearby until their destruction in 1958. Marking the Center's north-south spine, a white gridded steel framework visually collides with the brick masses. The framework suggests a scaffold, a temporary structure erected to prepare for what lies ahead, in this case the art of the 21st century. The collision of spaces represents the collision of past and future.

The contextual solutions are more inherently architectural. Peter Eisenman used the asymptote between the northeast edge of the University's Oval and the linear east-west axis of the grid of Columbus as the base of the design. From this base, the Center was connected to two existing auditoriums, Mershon and Weigel. These auditorium spaces complement the Wexner Center, not only because they are used for events sponsored by the Center, but because their volumetric massing is echoed by other bays, some of which are earth mounds. The earth mounds cover such partial basement spaces as libraries and storage. Their formation is breathtaking: long-bladed grasses indigenous to the region are set off by beds of German red sandstone.

Wexner Center for the Visual Arts, from the south: Columbus, Ohio, 1983-89

Moreover, the fragmented views resulting from this maze of angular masses are vaguely reminiscent of imagery in pre-industrial European towns.

If there is any formal precedent for this design it is the Museum of Decorative Arts in Frankfurt by Richard Meier, where there are two overlaid, rotational grids, one following the line of the Main River shore, the other a street line of Frankfurt. The Wexner Center joins the grid of Columbus with the University's Oval. Eisenman referred to this as the meeting of "town and gown," for both the city and the university attend Center events.

Authorship of the Wexner Center's design is attributed to Peter Eisenman, although Richard Trott and others really did make contributions. Trott was partly responsible for the towers; he was an alumnus of Ohio State University and had fond memories of the previous Armory that had once housed campus activities such as dances. Trott and his firm also designed the interior divisions of the administrative towers, a rather difficult problem well executed. The construction of the complex was overseen by Trott's Columbus-based office. The structure was mostly a post-and-lintel design with curtain walls. James Rudy from Trott's office was involved with overseeing the structure, and he also was in charge of making the connection between the Center and Mershon Hall. Laurie Olin of Hanna Olin Landscape Architects was also involved in the design. Olin and Eisenman had both taught at Harvard, where they discussed aspects of the plan. Apparently it was Olin who indicated that the asymptote to the Oval could form the germinating point for the Wexner Center's development, and he was consulted for the beautiful landscaping. The landscaping was a response to pressing environmental concerns.

The culmination of these architects' efforts are intricate patterns that harken to the past, accommodate the present, and at the same time invite the future. The architects' vision was remarkably elaborate. In fact, critic Michael Sorkin reported that after he accompanied Eisenman on a tour through the Center, Eisenman himself was actually lost in the labyrinth of complex spaces.

—SUZANNE S. FRANK

HAYSTACK MOUNTAIN SCHOOL OF ARTS AND CRAFTS
Deer Isle, Maine

1961: Buildings constructed; **Architect:** Edward Larrabee Barnes.

Publications

"The Architecture of Edward Larabee Barnes." *Journal* (June 1979) : 9-29.

*

The counterpoint composition of Edward Larrabee Barnes' Haystack Mountain School of Arts and Crafts, which tumbles down a precipitous slope on Maine's Deer Isle, stands as a highpoint of his career. The shingled shed-roofed volumes of Haystack signaled a point of transition in modern architecture in which concern for context determined materials and forms. The pitched roofs of the individual buildings departed from the orthodox geometry of modernism, and their reductive forms contributed to Barnes' exploration of a purely volumetric architecture. Haystack was acclaimed for its subtle expression of context, which reflected its siting conditions, local history and materials.

Haystack marked a significant step in the evolution of Barnes' design philosophy, initially formed during his training at Harvard. While Barnes was steeped in the formal discipline of the Harvard Graduate School of Design as taught by Walter Gropius and Marcel Breuer, his introduction during the late 1950s to the village architecture of the Greek island of Mykonos was a turning point in his pursuit of a more personal approach, which was first expressed in his woodland camps such as Haystack and Camp Hidden Valley (1961), and his dormitories for St. Paul's School (1961).

In his adaptation of vernacular architecture, Barnes chose to focus attention on a single form, used as a physically independent motif, but linked to similar forms through spatial relationships and a circulation "spine" inspired by the narrow village streets of Mykonos. Utilizing the concept of village architecture as a departure point, the undisciplined, random forms of village architecture were transformed in Barnes' interpretation by rigorous geometry and an underlying framework.

At Haystack, the simple volumes of the various classrooms appear to cascade freely down the sloping, heavily wooded site. In fact, the units are highly organized through the employment of the connective vertical "spine" staircase which runs downhill through the composition, and stem-like "street" platform walkways which branch out horizontally from the central staircase. The longer building units are clustered near the central vertical stair; these break up into smaller units as they are dispersed on the stems farther away from the center. The interior spaces of the individual structures are clearly revealed by the exterior forms. Their expression as pure volume is accentuated through the use of a single material and minimal detailing, and the shingled exteriors further serve to evoke the vernacular of Maine fishing villages. The structures, elevated on piles, gracefully ride down the hillside without disturbing the site or vegetation.

All of these features reflect Barnes' philosophy of "continu-

ity," which he explained in his 1965 article "Remarks on Continuity and Change" published in *Perspecta:* "In architectural terms continuity means the use of fewer materials, an emphasis on what is alike, not on what is different; the elimination of unnecessary articulation; the use of land without the wholesale use of the bulldozer. It means designing with respect for adjoining buildings ... finally, it means thinking of each building as part of a process, not as a world unto itself ... I am arguing for architecture which is in harmony with its environment ... And I am arguing for the unified statement."

Compositionally, the bold triangular roof forms impart a feeling of movement and tension to the design. At Haystack, a distinctive push-pull effect is created by the pitched roof lines alternatively echoing and counterpointing the fall of the slope to the sea. In *Perspecta,* Barnes simply stated: "The design grows out of this slope. That is its strength."

The pitched roof forms and diagonal lines of Haystack reflect the emerging desire of architects in the 1960s to break away from the cubical massing of the International Style. The prototype for Haystack actually dates from the 1950s with Barnes' unbuilt Osborn Studio project (1951). The simple form of the Osborn Studio was created by the removal of a triangular wedge from a larger conceptual rectangular block, and all elevations of the studio are related proportionally. Shed-roofed forms characterized much of Barnes' subsequent built work, and the late architectural historian C. Ray Smith observed in his book *Supermannerism* that Barnes was one of the leading architects to popularize the diagonal form during the 1960s with his shed-roofed buildings. Besides Haystack, these included the Cowles House (1963), Studios for Two Composers (1963), Adirondack Vacation House (1964), Righter Beach House (1964), Hilltop House (1965), W. D. Richards School (1964), Bennington College dormitories (1966) and the Hecksher House (1974). Barnes' employment of a spine as an organizing device for Haystack would resurface in his later work such as the Wye Institute (1968), the Fuqua School of Business (1978) and the Dallas Museum of Art (1984).

Haystack has proven to be one of Barnes' most influential projects, and it won a 1965 citation in landscape architecture from the Architectural League of New York. Vincent Scully noted not only the striking pitched roofs of the Haystack School, but also its vernacular shingled siding in his discussion of the modern revival of the Shingle and Stick styles in *The Shingle Style Today.* Scully cited Barnes' Haystack School as an influence in Charles Moore's Sea Ranch in California (1965-66), and he further pointed to Barnes' influence on the architects who worked in his office at that time, such as Giovanni Pasanella and Jaquelin Robertson. Cervin Robinson has also taken note of the attention which Haystack brought to Barnes in the 1960s, and other talented young architects who worked in his firm during that period, such as Charles Gwathmey. Gwathmey's house and studios for Robert Gwathmey (1966-67) clearly evoke the familiar wood-sided Barnesian prime forms.

In its synthesis of vernacular references with a formal modern vocabulary, Haystack was a significant and influential departure for its time. Today, the concept of contextualism is frequently distorted by a trendy superficiality, a too-literal reading, or by gross exaggeration. In light of these excesses, Barnes' subtle evocation of context at Haystack has continuing meaning, and demonstrates that sensitive design rooted in a modern idiom can exist in perfect harmony with its natural setting.

—BARBARA KOERBLE

Haystack Mountain School of Arts and Crafts: Deer Isle, Maine, 1961

KIMBELL ART MUSEUM
Fort Worth, Texas, U.S.A.

1966-72. Architect: Louis I. Kahn (1901-74).

Publications

JOHNSON, NELL E. (compiler): *Light is the Theme: Louis I. Kahn and the Kimbell Art Museum*. Fort Worth, Texas, 1975.

JORDY, WILLIAM H.: "Kimbell Art Museum, Fort Worth, Texas; Library, Philips Exeter Academy, Andover, New Hampshire." *Architectural Review* (June 1974): 318-342.

LOBELL, JOHN: *Between Silence and Light: Architecture of Louis Kahn*. 1979.

Louis I. Kahn: Sketches for the Kimbell Art Museum. Fort Worth, Texas, 1978.

"Louis I. Kahn—Yale University Art Gallery; Kimbell Art Museum, Fort Worth." *Global Architecture* 38 (1976).

RONNER, HEINZ; JHAVERI, SHARAD; VESELLA, ALESSANDRO: *Louis I. Kahn: The Complete Works 1935-1974*. Boulder, Colorado, 1977.

*

The Kimbell Art Museum is one of the recognized masterpieces of modern architecture. Many architects and critics regard it as the most perfect postwar American building. As a building of such distinction it can serve as an assay of the strengths and weaknesses of modern architecture in general and postwar American architecture in particular.

Using a visible interlay of the most modern materials—concrete, glass, and steel—with the most ancient—marble and wood—Louis Kahn created an interlacing of dreams and aspirations, of the base with the noble, of the profane with the sacred. The interlay achieves greatness by expressing and yet transcending the circumstances of time and place. One could state that the limitations of this architecture are precisely that of the reconciliation between the desire for transcendence with the act of acceptance.

In its overall form, parallel to the street, the Kimbell is reminiscent of a large concrete high-security building, a telephone switching center, a biochemical research laboratory, an aircraft assembly plant. As one looks at the side, one becomes aware that this seeming industrial building is broken into five transverse vaulted sections—and a sixth at the back, which with no external wall appears as an incomplete "back porch." Grand expectations are aroused, fulfilled and broken.

These transverse vaults look like columbaria, like a safe-deposit center, like a spirits warehouse; they conjure images of Roman or Etruscan tombs. As Kahn observed, "My mind is full of Roman greatness and the vault so etched itself in my mind that, though I cannot employ it, it's there always ready. . . . The vault, rising not high, not in an august manner, but somehow appropriate to the size of the individual. And its feeling of being home and safe come to mind."

The greatness of the Roman Empire at the time of the Vietnam agony of the American is successfully reconciled with the human scale of American republicanism—home and empire, Fort Worth and Rome, Louis Kahn and Thomas Jefferson. The character of museum as tomb or repository is reconciled to that of workshop, laboratory, plant. The massive, low, expansive

Kimbell Art Museum: Fort Worth, Texas, 1966-72

marble-clad facade stands in juxtaposition with the concrete base, with the concrete outline, and the travertine fill of the transverse vaults. In its synthesis of these contradictories the building vaults over the horns of the dilemmas they pose and transcends them. Yet, the very statement of the contradictions is their acceptance; the acceptance is the confession of the need for transcendence.

Internally it is rightly said that "light is the theme." It is telling that the premiere laudatory work on the building which has *Light is the Theme* as its title is illustrated with black-and-white photos only: an essay not in color but in black and white, an austere and old-fashioned purist monochrome.

As one opens this book, one is confronted by a right-profile portrait of Kahn as an old man; on the reverse side of the page the rear portico of the Kimbell as entrance—in three-quarter profile. Behold the man. *Si monumentum requiris, circumspice.* Enter, and you have penetrated into the self-portrait, the tomb, the treasure repository not only of the donor, as if the Kimbells were some Texan Medici, but also of Kahn. Only shades dwell there; the colors are perhaps that of the "illustrations," the artwork; but the building, like some archaic sculpture, has been bleached and washed clean of the appliqué pigments one imagines to have been there. It is as if externally and internally these works of art had been wrapped into a building of clean linen cloth; the texture and the color of a black-and-white simulacrum of travertine and polished concrete.

Laid in its own new tomb, what a magnificent interment for this body of classic art, for the patron, for the architect. What a magnificent foretaste, what portentous foreshadowing of interment and preservation for the visitor—you never looked as good in life! In the diffused light of the inside it is as if any longing for someone to come from heaven and roll aside the stone were an impiety. No angel will come, there is no promise of a face like lightning nor of a raiment as white as snow. There is something, someone interred here without hope of resurrection of the dead. Transcend and accept light and shadow as if in a cave. The longing for color is fulfilled only within the imaginary "other side" of the sacred works of art.

Inside and out, finally a necropolis: a magnificent entombment of the needs, wants, longings, neuroses, passions, motives, addictions, protrusions, dreams, images and illusions which fed and were fed by the Modern Movement, by modern American architecture. In transcending the spheres of architecture as technical exercise and self-expression, there is the acceptance of the mortality of the idea itself.

—JOSEPH B. JUHASZ

INDETERMINATE FACADE SHOWROOM [Best Products Showroom]
Houston, Texas, U.S.A.

1974-75. Architects: SITE [Alison Sky, Michelle Stone and James Wines].

Publications

"Best Fassade." *Deutsche Bauzeitung* (September 1975).

Buildings for Best Products, U.S.A. Exhibition catalog. New York, 1979.

BZDAK, M. J.: "Indeterminate Facade, Best Products Showroom." In TOD A. MARDER (ed.): *The Critical Edge;*

Controversy in Recent American Architecture. Cambridge, Massachusetts, and London, 1985: 137-148.

DIAMONSTEIN, BARBARALEE: *American Architecture Now II.* New York, 1985.

"La Façade Indeterminate, Magasin Best." *Architecture d'aujourd'hui* (February 1981).

"La Façade Indeterminée." *Architecture Concept* (September 1975).

MARSH, PETER: "Crumbling Facades." *Building Design* (6 August 1976).

NAKAMURA, TOSHIO: "Indeterminate Facade." *Architecture and Urbanism* (July 1975).

PONTI, LISA: "Pre-disastro nel Texas." *Domus* (October 1975).

RAGGI, FRANCO: "SITE. Indeterminate Facade." *Casabella* (March 1976).

"SITE: Architecture and Environmental Architecture." *Space Design* (special issue, August 1981).

"SITE—Best Showrooms." *Nikkei Architecture* (July 1977).

SITE: *SITE Projects and Theories.* Bari, Italy, 1978.

WINES, JAMES: *De-Architecture.* New York, 1988.

The Indeterminate Facade Showroom for the Best Products Company was designed in 1974-75 by the architectural design group known as SITE. Located in the Almeda-Genoa Shopping Center in Houston, the critically controversial showroom features a tall facade of white brick punctured and "eroded" at the edges, with a distressing expanse of apparently loose brick spilling onto the traditional pedestrian canopy. Termed "de-architecture" by SITE's spokesperson, James Wines, the unusual design was an attempt to create an artistic statement within the ordinarily unimaginative setting of the commercial strip mall.

SITE, an acronym for Sculpture in the Environment, was formed in 1970 by Alison Sky, Michelle Stone and James Wines. The members of SITE, while allied in their architectural vision, approach the design process through varied disciplines: Sky through training in art and literature, Stone via photography and sociology, and Wines as a sculptor. As a group, they seek to create structures that function not only as architecture but also as art, to assert a subtle interplay of the building and its immediate environment, and to infuse their work with humorous twists that cause the viewer to question the traditional boundaries between architecture and its surroundings. SITE's catalog-showroom designs for the Best Products Company based in Richmond, Virginia, are the firm's most publicized work to date.

SITE began its association with Best with a work titled "Peeling Project" (1971-72), which involved renovation of the facade of an existing building in Richmond, Virginia. The facade, when completed, featured a brick wall which appeared to peel away from the underlying cement, and thus, like many of SITE's subsequent projects, confronted the viewer directly with its potential instability. Other projects for Best included the Notch Showroom, Sacramento, California (1976-77), in which the building entrance was incorporated into a jagged cavity created through the removal and separation of a chunk of the corner of the building; the Tilt Showroom, Towson, Maryland (1976-78), characterized by a facade that appeared as though it had been lifted and then set down again to balance precariously on one pointed end; and the Forest Building, Richmond, Virginia (1978-80), which involved the incorporation of adjacent trees directly into the building, making it appear as though the facade and the body of the building had been pushed apart through the sheer force of nature. Similarly, the Indeterminate Facade

Indeterminate Facade Showroom (BEST Products Showroom): Houston, Texas, 1974-75

Showroom, through its inclusion of seemingly random passages of deterioration, comments on the corrosive effect of nature over time.

While many architects of the postmodern era seek to reach the public and draw them in through the overt use of historical symbols, SITE's formula for engaging the viewer has always related directly to the reexamination of common expectations. However, the ideas that support the work of SITE, and in particular their Indeterminate Facade Showroom, are not entirely without art-historical precedent, despite the buildings' apparent lack of formal historical references. Much has been made of the underlying commonality of approach between SITE and the Italian Mannerist work of Giulio Romano, architect of the Palazzo del Tè, Mantua, Italy (1525-35). Both the Indeterminate Facade and the Palazzo del Té exploit the viewer's traditional perception of a building as a place of stability, shelter and enclosure. Where the Palazzo del Té accomplishes this by presenting traditional structural elements (keystones, triglyphs) stripped of their structural function and used instead in a decorative manner, the Indeterminate Facade modernizes the concept through the avoidance of direct historical reference, and focuses instead on the potential for instability in the familiar construction materials of brick and mortar.

Other observers make reference to the connection between the Best Products showrooms and English follies of the 18th and 19th centuries, such as those found in Hagley Park in Worcestershire. More akin to garden sculpture, the follies were, like the showrooms, constructed in a false state of ruin in order to create a picturesque and romantic playground.

SITE's approach can also be linked to that of the Dada artists working in the early 20th century, whose work forced the public to constantly reevaluate ordinary objects by placing them in new contexts or by juxtaposing them with incongruous partners. For instance, Man Ray's *Gift* of 1913, which combines an ordinary household iron with spikes, thus suggesting the destruction of garments coming within its contact, can be compared to the Indeterminate Facade. Both create an air of unease, forcing us to ponder new meanings, to rethink an object, or a building, in a new way. At the same time, both utilize irony in an attempt to reach the viewer's most basic emotions.

Following its construction, the Indeterminate Facade for Best Products created a certain amount of controversy due to its unconventionality, and generated an abundance of scholarly debate within the architectural press. Despite mixed reactions, ranging from fear for physical safety to delight in the building's novelty, the sales recorded at the Houston shop exceeded the Best Products Company's estimated goals by 40 percent.

—MEREDITH ARMS

WALTER GROPIUS HOUSE
Lincoln, Massachusetts, U.S.A.

1937. Architect: Walter Gropius (1883-1969), with Marcel Breuer (1902-81).

Publications

CANTACUZINO, SHERBAN: *Modern Houses of the World.* London, 1964.
CORMIER, LESLIE HUMM: *Walter Gropius, Emigré Architect—Works and Refuge—England and America in the '30s.* Ph.D. dissertation. Brown University, Providence, Rhode Island.
FORD, JAMES, and MORROW, KATHERINE: *The Modern House in America.* New York, 1940.
SUMMERS, NEIL: "Analyzing the Gropius House as Energy-Conscious Design." *American Institute of Architects Journal* (February 1977).
WINKLER, ROBERT: *Das Haus des Architekten.* Zurich, 1954.

The Walter Gropius House sits stark white and emphatic in a New England apple orchard. This landmark modern house speaks to us of clarity and purity of form in an era of architectural ambiguity; its dual message is of modernism and the vernacular.

The house is a classic of the International Style. Built in 1937, it is a white, asymmetrical, volumetric box. The ornament is inherent in the design as punched voids of shadow and functionally elegant architectural elements: glass brick, steel supports and industrial staircase. Though the cube is reminiscent of the man-made aesthetic of the 1920s and 1930s, the house also embraces its local landscape. The "stretched skin" facade is articulated with natural textures of fieldstone and clapboards, juxtaposed with the industrial appendages.

Gropius' design concept was twofold: to use the modern vocabulary to express the character of the New England Colonial house. Commenting on "the old Colonial houses painted white," he wrote, "This white colour is the best invention of New England architecture, fitting so lovely into the green surround." And, "a very strong bond proved to be the beautiful architecture I have found in New England . . . the style which has so much in common with the principles of modern architecture."

The white architecture which Gropius favored is the architecture of the Greek Revival and the Federal periods whose forms are well-proportioned rectangles, triangles and cylinders. There is a monumental dignity about the white, wooden buildings, sited in open fields, proclaiming themselves as counterpoint to nature, just as Gropius was to site his white, wooden house.

The specific Colonial antecedent of the Gropius House is the Stearns-Cole-Smith House (1782), in which Gropius was living while designing his modern house just down Sandy Pond Road. As an emigré architect, Gropius must have derived the texture, the humanity of the American house from this experience. Gropius the artist can be appreciated by examining the very different architectural sources from which he adapted his house, for he was able to synthesize here an American vernacular with its apparent opposition, European modernism, creating from the reconciliation a wholly new form.

Specific modern precedents for the Gropius House can be traced to Marcel Breuer's Bristol Pavilion (1936) for the west elevation, to Le Corbusier's Villa Stein (1927) for the front elevation, and especially to Gropius' own Director's House at the Dessau Bauhaus (1925).

The west facade, like Breuer's work, is a very abstract composition of verticals, horizontals and slabs of constructivist influence, with elements simultaneously pulling apart and joining together, creating a tension which merges with a nature-oriented romanticism of pergola and trellis. Gropius, however, improved on Breuer's pavilion by circumscribing it with the streamlined box and tight machine-like character of the house.

The front elevation shows the influence of one of the most renowned residences of the 1920s, Le Corbusier's Villa Stein, which impressed Gropius greatly. These modernist works are white, smooth cubes with industrial banded windows and punched voids that both enframe and contrast with nature. Though the proportions of the Villa Stein are more regularly balanced between horizontal and vertical planes, and the Gropius House is a predominant horizontal, the relationship of the houses can be clearly observed by mentally canceling the upper story of the Le Corbusier building, and then comparing the works. From the Villa Stein, Gropius also borrowed the metaphor of the airplane wing over the doorway, to create movement, thrust and depth on a flat facade. When Gropius assimilated an architectural element, however, he always inverted it in some original way, here rotating and extending the wing to a sideways position, just as he had rotated the traditional placement of the New England clapboard 90 degrees to a vertical placement. What particularly differentiates Gropius' work from Le Corbusier's is scale and emotional content, for as Le Corbusier's aim at the Villa Stein was toward cool monumentality, Gropius

Gropius House: Lincoln, Massachusetts, 1937

followed the backroads of simplicity and human scale in America.

Though Gropius was a master synthesizer, his most significant point of reference for the house in Lincoln was within his own oeuvre: the Director's House at the Dessau Bauhaus, which he had designed for himself a dozen years before. The front elevation of the work is a cubist composition made architecture, a completely flat white plane, punctuated with consciously placed rectangles of solid and void. As in his earlier Fagus Factory (1911), the corner window hangs apparently unsupported, a contradictory element in the architecture, which adds to the dynamic tension of the facade. It is a daring composition, one Gropius could have created only in the heyday of avant-garde European modernism. It is a geometric foil to nature; it relates instead to architecture. Its aesthetic appeal is to intellect unencumbered by emotion or tradition.

The stylistic shift from the Dessau house to the Lincoln house reflects a change in Gropius the man as well as the architect. With his emigration to America, he moved from European abstraction to contextualism, empiricism, and to what William H. Jordy has called American regionalism. The stark geometry and abstract symbolism of Dessau were mediated by the time of the Lincoln house design. The absolute planarity of the Dessau facade at Lincoln is interrupted by the projecting canopy and spiral staircase. The surface is textured and windows no longer float unsupported. The tension of the composition is much more restrained. Whereas the Dessau facade dares to be physically ambiguous, the Lincoln house creates a sense of totality and closure. Dessau is pure artistic abstraction. Lincoln is, simply put, more house-like. Contemplating the concept of house, Gropius once wrote that the modern house "is imbued with the 'tension,' a spiritual life of its own, as it were, beyond the value of the house."

For his own American house, refugee architect Walter Gropius looked to sources as wide-ranging as the New England vernacular farmhouse, to European constructivism, to Le Corbusier's French villa style, and he played all these themes against his German Bauhaus compositions. Thus, the Gropius House in Lincoln may truly be the epitome of an International Style.

—LESLIE HUMM CORMIER

LOVELL HEALTH HOUSE
Los Angeles, California, U.S.A.

1927. Architect: Richard Neutra (1892-1970).

Publications

BOESIGER, WILLY (ed.): *Richard Neutra, Buildings and Projects, 1923-1966*. 3 vols. New York, 1951-66.
DREXLER, ARTHUR, and HINES, THOMAS S.: *The Architecture of Richard Neutra: From International Style to California Modern*. Exhibition catalog. New York, 1982.
FRAMPTON, KENNETH, and FUTAGAWA, YUKIO: *Modern Architecture: 1920-1945*. New York, 1983.
HINES, THOMAS S.: *Richard Neutra and the Search for Modern Architecture*. New York and Oxford, 1982.
HOFMANN, WERNER, and KULTERMANN, UDO: *Modern Architecture in Color*. New York, 1970.
McCOY, ESTHER: *Richard Neutra*. New York, 1960.
NEUTRA, DIONE (ed): *Richard Neutra, Promise and Fulfillment, 1919-1932*. 1986.

*

Set at the edge of one of the long, narrow canyons composing the Hollywood Hills of Los Angeles, the Lovell Health House is perhaps the most dramatically sited of all the buildings defining the 1920s International Style. Its sobriquet "Health" relates to Dr. Philip Lovell, a naturopath who believed in drugless healing with reliance on a vegetarian diet, exercise, open-air sleeping and nude sunbathing. Lovell and his wife Leah—sister of Harriet Freeman, for whom Frank Lloyd Wright had designed a house in Los Angeles—traveled in a small Southern California avant-garde circle which included architect R. M. Schindler. Schindler had already designed a beach house near Los Angeles for the Lovells, a house later recognized as a modernist masterpiece in its own right, but perhaps because Schindler was not known for the structural soundness of his buildings, the Lovells turned to Richard Neutra in 1927 to design their city house on this precarious site.

Given full freedom in the design, other than responding to the client's request for open sleeping porches, private areas for sunbathing, and a specially designed kitchen, Neutra indulged the Lovells' progressive vision by erecting America's first steel-framed house, its complex facade composed of white concrete and steel casement windows fully expressing the spaces within. The upper floor of the house, devoted to sleeping rooms and the entrance foyer, is sited at the canyon rim, with a level sidewalk extending out to the cul-de-sac street that leads up from the valley below. From the street the house appears largely enclosed. The sidewalk terminates at a blank front door, the garage nestles along the narrow street somewhat downhill from the house entrance, and the house itself faces away from the street, overlooking the canyon and opening itself to the vast Los Angeles Basin extending to the Pacific Ocean 20 kilometers to the west.

From the canyon below, however, the view of the house is spectacular, and it must have been even more so when the starkly white, angular house stood out from the nearly barren hillside of desert scrub. The composition projects out and cascades down the hill, where a series of low concrete walls below the house suggest a terraced buttress to keep the building in place. The main house itself is highly transparent, with a glass-walled stairwell leading to the principal rooms on the lower floor, and beneath them a secluded outdoor swimming pool for Philip Lovell's nude sunbathing. Neutra indulged in only one act of dry architectural humor, by embedding Model-T Ford headlights in the stair walls leading down through the core of the house. The building complex sprawls along the top edge of the site in the form of an L, one leg devoted to the house and the other a long arm leading to the garage and to Leah Lovell's kindergarten rooms, where she conducted innovative programs for young children.

Early photographs, as well as Neutra's preliminary designs, show how this site challenged the architect's ability to embrace modernist principles of pure volumes and clarity of massing. Neutra's first sketches show a series of cubic forms marching up the hill, hugging it with an architectural timidity not yet realizing the tradition-shattering possibilities of the modernist medium in the late 1920s. In his final design, however, Neutra leapt to a radical conclusion that seems obvious only in retrospect. He tore the building away from the hill, jutting it out in defiance to the slope, extenuating its seemingly cantilevered cubes ever farther from the hill as they rose. The planar cap of

Lovell Health House: Los Angeles, California, 1927

the flat roof, set over the entire building, was finished on the far outer end by a decorative parapet. This parapet served the modernist house much as a cornice served a Beaux-Arts building, but Neutra's flourish was vertical rather than horizontal, declaring the building's defiance toward its moorings rather than tying it to them.

Constructed less than two years after Le Corbusier's Villa Stein, the Lovell House already shunted the International Style toward a picturesqueness that violated the minimalist purity of its European provenance. It eschewed the expansive stucco planes articulated by slices of ribbon windows that characterized much of the 1920s International Style, in favor of cantilevered and corbeled volumes with expanses of glass associated primarily with industrial buildings. That the house's volumetric complexity affronted contemporary modernist apologists was already apparent by Henry-Russell Hitchcock and Philip Johnson's commentary in their 1932 book for *The International Style* exhibition. Though they included the Lovell House, they noted how its design was "complicated by the various projections and the confusing use of metal and stucco spandrels." Yet a glance at their own published photograph of the house demonstrates how different it had to be from other International Style buildings of the period. There were other hillside houses, to be sure, but none that had to accommodate itself to the apex of a steep, V-shaped canyon in a semi-arid Mediterranean climate.

Even beyond the requirements of its setting, the Lovell House's composition was certainly informal compared to the mainstream of 1920s modernist work. This informality may have been jarring in Europe, but it responded well to Los Angeles' quirky reputation as an easy, sun-baked environment where ordinary people lived differently. Neutra himself admired southern California for its "mentally footloose" attitude, as he stated in his 1962 autobiography, *Life and Shape*, where "one can do most anything that comes to mind and is good fun." He was pleased to work in an artistic climate where he could try "something independent of hidebound habituation."

Neutra's design proved to be a radical departure not only from the early principles of European modernism, but from his own more traditional modernist Jardinette Apartments of 1927 in Los Angeles, if one could speak by then of a modernist tradition at all. Its combination of tension and harmony with the site demonstrated the ability of the International Style to enhance rugged, nonurban settings and served as a prototype for two generations of modernist houses sited daringly in the Los Angeles hills.

—PAUL H. GLEYE

MUSEUM OF CONTEMPORARY ART
Los Angeles, California, U.S.A.

1981-83: Renovation of Temporary Contemporary; **Architect:** Frank Gehry. **1981-86:** Construction; **Architect:** Arata Isozaki (b. 1931).

Publications

FLACKE, C.: "Isozaki's MOCA." *The New Criterion* (April 1987).

FRAMPTON, K.: "Arata Isozaki's MOCA." *Domus* (November 1986).

GOLDBERGER, P.: "Arata Isozaki." *Architectural Digest* (March 1989).

JENCKS, C.: *Post-Modernism: The New Classicism in Art and Architecture.* New York, 1987.

KOSHALEK, R., STEWART, D. B. and YATSUKA, H.: *Avata Isozaki: Architecture 1960-1990.* Catalogue. New York, 1991.

"Project by Arata Isozaki for the Museum of Contemporary Art" in *Casabella* (May 1983).

RASTOFER, D.: "Isozaki: The Art of Construction." *Architectural Record* (January 1988).

SEARING, HELEN: *New American Art Museums.* 1983.

VILADAS, P.: "On MOCA." *Progressive Architecture* (November 1986).

*

The Los Angeles Museum of Contemporary Art is composed of two complementary structures. The Temporary Contemporary (TC), located in Little Tokyo, opened in the fall of 1983 as an interim exhibition space. Originally a hardware store, a warehouse, and finally a car garage, it was re-leased in 1986 to the Los Angeles Museum of Contemporary Art until the year 2038. Its renovation by California architect Frank Gehry now complete, the TC has been assessed as "a prince among spaces." The second structure, the Museum of Contemporary Art (MOCA), opened in California Plaza in December 1986. It was Arata Isozaki's first major commission outside Japan, a commission that has received international acclaim.

MOCA is a singularly successful synthesis of the eclectic interests that have marked Isozaki's architecture since the 1960s: his particular postmodern commitment to the use of classical form, motifs from architectural history, and advanced technology, plus a firm belief in the metaphorical power of building forms and materials to make architectural statements of expressive complexity. Isozaki's work holds in tension a dialectic between tectonic form and sensual color and surface, between art and architecure, between East and West. His sense of the diversity of life determines his belief that creativity should come from multiple sources. Kenneth Frampton has observed that it is because of the numerous dualities inherent in Isozaki's architecture that he may qualify as a universal figure of our time.

California Plaza is a mixed-use development in the Bunker Hill section of downtown Los Angeles. MOCA is presently bounded by an office tower on the south, residential condominiums on the east and Grand Avenue on the west. A hotel is planned on the north. The museum contains 24,500 square feet of exhibition space, an auditorium, a library, café, bookstore, offices and extensive service areas. The museum complex is housed in two major structures, each comprising a series of rectangular, interrelated cubes of various sizes, ranging from two to seven stories in height. They are two to three stories within, and two to four stories above a preexisting five-story parking facility, which continues in service. As has been noted, the only way that Isozaki could compete with the neighborhood was to fragment the museum into a village in a valley of skyscrapers.

Museum of Contemporary Art: Los Angeles, California, 1981-86

The two sections of the museum symbolize the East versus the West, or, as Isozaki says, ''Yin/Yang versus the Golden Section.'' The larger section on the north side of the complex is dominated by a monumental barrel vault, a building shape much favored by Isozaki (possibly derived from Louis Kahn's Kimbell Museum in Fort Worth, Texas, 1972). The vault, 53 feet in height, projects on tall stilts over the plaza/atrium, uniting the museum's two sections. It terminates in a Palladian motif (the ''West'') which directly confronts three glass pyramids (the ''East'') on top of the long, low cubic mass that makes up the museum's south section.

The vault merges with two major cubic masses containing offices, auditorium, bookstore and storage, behind which stretches a much lower rectangle of gallery space, topped by eight pyramids. Like the three pyramids on the south structure, these too are glass-topped, providing skylighting for the museum's galleries, all of which are underground. Floors are granite throughout, and interior walls are a unique mixture of white crystallized glass and sandstone. The galleries are extraordinarily flexible, of different heights, widths and lengths, capable of many kinds of subdivision.

The monumental Palladian vault contains the library, overlooked by the boardroom one level above. The boardroom has a small balcony on the west and a roof terrace on the east. The library vault, as it bridges over the pedestrian path of the two-level plaza/atrium, functions as a metaphorical entrance gate to the museum: directly beneath on the plaza level is a green aluminum-clad cube containing the ticket booth. The vault, like most of the museum's major masses, is faced in burnt-red Indian sandstone from India, with a base of red granite. The vault's

barrel is sheathed in green copper, as are all of the pyramids. The cubic mass to which the vault is directly connected is recessed, its lower two-thirds a wall of glass brick, its top third clad in dark green aluminum panels set in a playful rotated grid with pink channels. The honed and rough cleft facings of red sandstone and granite alternate in a subtle pattern of horizontal striations, particularly vivid in southern California's brilliant light. This facing is applied in a strop-and-anchor system, tied to the reinforced-concrete walls beneath. The green metallic skins and the red cubic masses provide dramatic contrasts similar to that of the Palladian vault with the pyramids.

The vault's 20-foot-high window is translucent white onyx (not unlike that in Skidmore, Owings and Merrills' Beinecke Rare Book Room at Yale University, 1964), providing filtered light to the library. The plaza directly below functions as a sculpture court. The atrium below the plaza is reached by a grand stairway, giving access to a large entry gallery, skylit by the largest pyramid. The plaza/atrium is dominated by another playful note—a long, brilliant, curvilinear wall that connects and articulates the two levels. This is Isozaki's famous ''Marilyn Monroe curve'' (also used in his ''Monroe chair''). Like all gallery walls, it is made of white crystallized glass, and, continuing into the main entry, it is Isozaki's witty metaphor for the local, welcoming goddess of Hollywood.

Contrary to the criticism that his visual metaphors are not articulated overtly enough at MOCA, Isozaki's metaphorical subtlety is in fact appropriately subordinated to his bold, eclectic composition. Structural form, sensuous color, texture and shape are juxtaposed in an animated collage of vibrant harmony.

—ANN CROWE

Johnson Glass House: New Canaan, Connecticut, 1945-49

JOHNSON GLASS HOUSE
New Canaan, Connecticut, U.S.A.

1945-49: Construction; **Architect:** Philip Johnson (b.1906).

Publications

FUTAGAWA, YUKIO (ed.): *Johnson House, New Canaan, Connecticut.* Tokyo, 1972.
"House at New Canaan, Connecticut." *Architectural Review* (September 1950): 152-159.
JOHNSON, PHILIP: *Philip Johnson: Architecture 1949-65.* New York, 1966.
STERN, ROBERT A. M.: "The Evolution of Philip Johnson's Glass House 1947-48." *Oppositions* (Fall 1977).
WHITE, NORVAL: *The Architecture Book.* New York, 1976.

*

Since its completion in 1949, Philip Johnson's Glass House has become an icon of modern American architecture. Designed by the architect as his own country retreat, this house summarized, in built form, some of the innovative ideas of the new architecture of the 20th century associated most closely with the work of Ludwig Mies van der Rohe. These revolutionary principles included the continuity of space between inside and outside via a thin, transparent membrane; the incorporation of new building techniques for residential uses, such as steel construction and large expanses of glass; and the open floor plan where interior rooms were dispensed with, and replaced by partitions of luxurious materials.

There is, however, a significant difference between the Glass House by Johnson and, say, the Farnsworth House by Mies van der Rohe, which was designed simultaneously but completed two years later. Besides the obvious difference in commissioning client—in one case the architect was his own client and the other involved a private client—there was a profound difference in basic conception. One house was designed by an American for a specific American landscape, the other was designed by a European for a generic landscape. This distinction is worth noting, because Mies often thought in universal terms, not tied to specific sites, program or the needs of others, while Johnson was interpreting and filtering those very same ideas for a specific site and client (himself), also bringing along his own set of cultural (and, as will be seen, curatorial) predispositions.

A European concept of nature and landscape is intrinsically different from an American concept of nature and landscape—especially after dramatic political and social changes, such as those which occurred just prior to Mies' arrival in America in the wake of two world wars. No such cataclysmic, and thus catalytic, changes had taken place on American soil or in American society. For Mies, architecture carried heavy social and political weight, for Johnson it did not. He was simply building a country house for himself in a lot in Connecticut.

The early acclaim of the Glass House had to do, obviously, with its well-known architect; he had already been the first architecture curator at the Museum of Modern Art, curating, among other exhibitions, the acclaimed "International Style" in 1932. The critical and sustained success of the house as a seminal work of architecture to this day has to do with something else, however, and that is its ability to generate and elicit, like any good work of art, numerous and multiple responses. The house, built entirely of large panes of glass supported by a black steel frame, reflects its immediate surroundings, disappearing at times into the seasons, like a chameleon changing with the

landscape, or a house made out of mirrors, with multiple reflections. That Mies always called glass a reflective material, not just a transparent material, coincides with this interpretation. But it is not just a highly reflective house, it is also a place for reflection. For Johnson, the house serves as a place to reflect on architecture, art and nature. He himself has called it "a clearing house for ideas," a place for sorting them out. A monk has his enclosed cell for reflection; for Johnson the house is his cell, albeit an open one.

Kenneth Frampton has written that the house is also a series of metaphorical houses, one within the other, like a Russian doll. There is a progression from inside to outside: a beige wool rug inside holds together a suite of classic furniture by Mies, over a "woven carpet" of terra-cotta bricks laid in herringbone pattern, which forms the base of the house itself, over a larger green lawn as a *tapis vert* defined by trees, on which the actual house sits. Frampton also describes the house as analogous to an open loggia, where a series of vertical columns defines a linear space. The house is rectangular in plan, and its floating roof is held by eight steel columns, four on each long side of the rectangle.

Another possible interpretation is that the house is like a museum display case. Not only does it hold precious objects, like a jewel box, it also sits in the landscape the way an exhibition piece is shown in a museum. So the house is both a museum in miniature inside, and outside a large display case sitting in the larger museum of its natural setting (the Albertian notion of a small city being like a large house, and conversely a large house being like a small city comes to mind). In the first, the objects exhibited are modern pieces of furniture, pure objects floating in space. Two rectangles made out of wood and one cylinder made of brick define virtual exhibition spaces. Viewed from the outside, the house is sited in the landscape in such a way as to resemble a display case, in relationship to other objects (pavilions) in the exhibit (estate). The estate becomes, in a sense, an exhibition of architectural pieces.

Over the years Johnson has built several additional pavilions, among them a folly on the lake, a sculpture gallery, a painting gallery, a guest house and a library studio. The entire compound is thus a permanent exhibition designed and curated by Johnson set in a classic American landscape. Each object, the Glass House being the most important one of them all, sits in the landscape in relationship to the others. All the pavilions, in concert, resemble a small village of houses, or an academic campus.

Johnson, in fact, uses the Acropolis as a precedent that influenced him when designing the site plan. In that context, the Glass House is the Parthenon, a temple on the hill. Much is made of the angles of vision, as one walks about the site. The house is never approached frontally but obliquely, in Greek fashion, so that a short side and a long side of the rectangular box are framed and visible in perspective. Johnson controlled the available angles of vision by the footpaths demarcated on the lawn, recalling also, as Frampton has pointed out, the Harvard Yard Johnson was familiar with as a graduate student.

Another aspect, rarely discussed but described by Paul Rudolph, is the lighting scheme of the house. Johnson designed a series of special effects with night lighting. He could light up the house's interior and its immediate exterior edge, to make it float in total darkness; light up the trees to highlight their shapes, and dim the house itself, so that the house was an actor on a stage; or he could flood the property with light and turn off the lights of the house completely so it would disappear. That Johnson was able to experiment and bring out each of these qualities of the house makes it a memorable architectural experience, day or night.

Finally, the site on which the house is situated, and the surrounding land which Johnson has acquired and manipulated over the years, is as important as the house itself. One plays off the other, making the house extremely site-specific, while the site is house-specific. It is a rare occurrence indeed, but in great works of architecture where this symbiosis is generated, it becomes a common theme. Whether one thinks of Fallingwater by Frank Lloyd Wright, the Barcelona Pavilion by Mies van der Rohe, or even Villa Savoye by Le Corbusier, it is this intimate relationship between architecture and nature that sets them apart. The Glass House exemplifies not only some of the greatest achievements of the Modern Movement in the 20th century, it is also located in one of the greatest of natural sites for such great work.

—WARREN A. JAMES

AT&T BUILDING
New York City, New York, U.S.A.

1979-84. Architects: Philip Johnson (born 1906), with John Burgee (born 1933).

Publications

FRAMPTON, KENNETH: *Philip Johnson—Processes: The Glass House, 1949, and AT&T Corporate Headquarters, 1978.* Cambridge, Massachusetts, 1978.
GOLDBERGER, PAUL: "The Man Who Designed a Chippendale Skyscraper." *Observer Magazine* (London, 17 December 1978).
"Johnson/Burgee." *Progressive Architecture* (Special issue, February 1984).
JOHNSON, PHILIP: *Writings.* New York, 1979.
JOHNSON, PHILIP, and BURGEE, JOHN: *Philip Johnson/John Burgee, Architecture 1979-1985.* New York, 1986.
MILLER, NORY: *Johnson/Burgee Architects.* New York, 1979.

*

Ever since it appeared on the cover of the *New York Times* in the fall of 1977, for its shockingly new traditionalism, this skyscraper, built for what was then the world's largest corporation, became an instant symbol of the postmodern movement. No other large-scale building, except for the earlier but smaller Portland Municipal Building by Michael Graves, summarizes and represents all the main points of that movement. It incorporates issues of contextualism, historical continuity, classical vocabulary, traditional building methods and traditional city-making urbanism.

It is noteworthy that the AT&T Building's architect, Philip Johnson, was an early patron and advocate of the International Style—bringing the movement in full force to the United States with the "International Style" exhibition and a book of the same title in 1932. However, widely discredited and disparaged, the movement and the style by the late-1970s had lost their conviction and pervasiveness. A new debate ensued (modern versus traditional) in architecture, paving the way for historical, eclectic and mixed styles. The AT&T Building was built proof of the viability and validity (vitality being something else) of this mode of design.

The building itself, located on narrow Madison Avenue, presents its entire frontal elevation to the avenue, extending 200 feet from 55th to 56th streets. It rises, without property or building setbacks, straight up from the sidewalk to its pediment for a total of 648 feet (with only 37 usable floors, instead of the possible 48), above a large, open loggia at street level. It is a standard steel-frame building clad in pink granite of great thickness with traditional detailing. Stone had not been used for skyscrapers for decades, and when it was, it was a thin veneer. Ultra-thin and light glass curtain walls were the norm. Ironically, the building's typical floor plan, a simple rectangle, does not deviate much from the Seagram Building, by Ludwig Mies van der Rohe (in which Johnson designed the Four Seasons restaurant) of 20 years earlier, which is often seen as the apotheosis of modernism. The differences between modernism and classicism are thus, seemingly, only skin-deep. The AT&T proved that classicism was possible with modern means.

However, the breakthrough of the AT&T was its soaring, classically inspired vertical composition. Like a Greek or Roman column, with base, shaft and capital, this building incorporates the tripartite compositional device at a megastructure scale. Like the earlier skyscrapers of the 1920s and 1930s in New York and Chicago, the AT&T recalled the romanticism of an earlier epoch, but at the *end* of the century. Ostensibly a corporate world headquarters (AT&T was later divested and now occupies but a fraction of the space), this building was in fact a marketing success for the company; as John D. Butts, chairman of the board at AT&T, once said: "We would like the building to say, loud and clear, 'We love New York.'" To a city on the edge of bankruptcy, this building met its aspirations as well as those of the architect. Philip Johnson even appeared holding a model on the cover of *Time* magazine, such was the shock of the new-old.

Costing more than $200 million, it became the most expensive skyscraper ever built in America, a Roman enterprise to match the image of its corporate patron. But perhaps the most controversial features of the building are located at the bottom and at the top. With a three-story-high arch marking the entrance, together with oculi and a glass-roofed arcade on the back, the base was pure gigantic and triumphant classicism not seen since McKim, Mead and White's Municipal Building of 1914. The street-level main lobby (there is another "sky" lobby for elevator transfers) was designed to hold a newly gilded statue, *Golden Boy,* from the top of the previous company headquarters downtown. At the top of the building, a broken pediment, which was to spew steam and have dramatic lighting at night, was likened to a Chippendale highboy cabinet (although the latter was derived from classical buildings in the first place, not the other way around). If historical references were going to be used, as Johnson had done, most critics feared an architectural free-for-all. All periods of history, they said, could be used, plagiarized, appropriated and cannibalized by less adept hands.

But it was precisely that liberation for which architects were looking. Modernism had, in a sense, enslaved them earlier, and Johnson had liberated them now. No longer was modernism dogma, the only set of rules; now architects could invent, "be free as the devil," as Raymond Hood, the first architect of Rockefeller Center—significantly enough, the large-scale project of its day—had said a generation earlier. Interestingly enough, either by accident or by design, next to the new-old AT&T Building is the new-new IBM Building, designed by Edward Larrabee Barnes and built almost simultaneously. The contrast is startling: symmetry versus asymmetry, tripartite composition versus an extruded prism, articulated facades versus smooth facades, recessed glass versus flush glass, traditional ornament versus absence of ornament, and so on. These are the

AT&T Building: New York City, 1979-84

only two built versions of the polarized postmodern debate standing side by side.

On close pedestrian observation the loggia, with its elaborate paving pattern, is populated on hot summer days (it is in the shade most of the daytime), but the dust and din of the avenue and the wind and shadows during the winter months make it a difficult space to enjoy for long, unlike the IBM Building's glass-enclosed winter garden next door. However, for all the AT&T's luxurious materials, including gold leaf, the main lobby with its heroic gilded statue seems humanly scaled—tall, narrow and intimate at the same time: in essence, a civic, honorable and monumental gesture to the city.

The stone detailing throughout, "the thicker, the better," as Johnson wanted, is very convincing—except, as Paul Goldberger of the *New York Times* pointed out, for the middle "shaft" portion of the building. It could have been deeper if the glass had been recessed further. For all its efforts and effects, he said, it is a shallow facade, deeper than wallpaper but not deep enough to carry, at least visually, structural weight. The figural quality of the broken pediment, an attempt to cut a recognizable presence in the skyline, is at times visible for miles despite midtown's tall-building clutter. A boring flat roof it is not, and even without the steam and lights at night, it has become part of the mythic Manhattan skyline, along with the Empire State and Chrysler buildings.

In the final analysis, this is a seminal and opportune building. Five hundred years from now the AT&T will be remembered, both as a turning point in the history of architecture during the late 20th century, and as a symbol of the persistence of classicism through the ages. It opened many corporate doors for an entire generation of architects to practice this mode of design, allowing party-hat tops on skyscrapers, thick-stone tall buildings, insouciant but sensitive uses of history, and civic monumentality. At the same time it recalled old humanist values by the use of a language present in the history of architecture for two thousand years, and that was no small feat. New skyscraper forms simply followed.

—WARREN A. JAMES

BATTERY PARK CITY
New York City, New York, U.S.A.

1979. Architects: Alexander Cooper and Stanton Eckstut.

Publications

GANDELSONAS, MARIO, and PASTIER, JOHN (eds.): *Cesar Pelli: Buildings and Projects 1965-1990.* New York, 1990.
GOLDBERGER, PAUL: *The City Observed—New York: A Guide to the Architecture of Manhattan.* New York, 1979.
"Pelli Unveils Battery Park City Plan." *Building Design* (5 June 1981).
WOLFE, GERARD R.: *New York: Twenty Walking Tours of Architecture and History.* 1988.
"World Financial Center." *Architecture and Urbanism* No. 233 (February 1990): 66-89.

*

Collaboration and cooperation are key terms in describing the success of the new development of Battery Park City. The

project involves a combination of public and private money, the incorporation of residential, commercial and public space, a governmental organizing body, private developers, and a number of architects and artists. Located across from the financial district in Lower Manhattan, the landfill site was ready for development in the early 1970s. The financial crisis in the 1970s in New York City, however, prevented the further development of the area. In 1979 Battery Park City Authority, the public body in charge of the land, hired the urban development firm of Cooper, Eckstut Associates to revise the original plan.

The 1979 master plan by Alexander Cooper and Stanton Eckstut changed the conception of Battery Park City, from a separate unit attached to New York to a natural extension of Lower Manhattan. This new design, reflecting a shift in urban development, was far more realistic and sensitive to the needs of the city. The mixed land use includes 42 percent residential, 9 percent commercial, 30 percent open spaces for public use, and 19 percent streets and avenues. While the architecture was designed as a cohesive unit, there were also restrictions in the plan to maintain diversity and to connect the buildings and spaces to the rest of the city. Parcels of land were given to different developers, who, in turn, hired architects to design the buildings.

The most dramatic complex of buildings is the World Financial Center, designed by Cesar Pelli and Associates. The six million square feet of office space is divided into four towers, accompanied by smaller "gate houses." The four towers vary in height from 34 to 51 stories, adding complexity to the skyline. Pelli's towers also provide the 110-story World Trade Center towers with a sense of perspective and scale. The setbacks of Battery Park City's granite-and-glass skins recall skyscrapers of the 1920s, further connecting the complex to the city.

The World Financial Center is accompanied by two central

Battery Park City, winter garden

Battery Park City: New York City, 1979

public areas: the Winter Garden and the World Financial Center Plaza. The Winter Garden, also designed by Pelli, provides a visual and functional junction for the Financial Center and a backdrop for the Plaza. The glass with steel ribbing encloses a lofty 120 feet. It has been likened to 19th-century European train stations and called a modern Crystal Palace. Clear glass allows the Winter Garden to change with the moods of the day, while a double row of palm trees creates a constant, peaceful environment.

The World Financial Center Plaza also embraces a restful atmosphere. The 3.5-acre waterfront plaza is a collaborative design by Cesar Pelli, artists Scott Burton and Siah Armajani, and landscape architect M. Paul Friedberg. Both Burton and Armajani create art which, rather than being removed and esoteric, is incorporated into public spaces with a subtle ease. Burton's granite benches and tables in the plaza provide both comfortable seating and sculptural articulation. Armajani's railings with the words of Walt Whitman and Frank O'Hara are not outspoken artistic statements, but an integration of art with functional elements.

The plaza is connected to other public gardens and spaces by the 1.2-mile Esplanade, running the length of Battery Park City. Taking precedent in public spaces such as the Brooklyn Heights Promenade, this walkway along the Hudson River unites the entire project. In particular, it joins the art projects that are an important aspect of Battery Park City. "South Cove," located at the southern end of Battery Park City, was designed by artist Mary Miss, in collaboration with landscape architect Susan Child and architect Stanton Eckstut. The area combines sculptural forms in its circular jetty and walkways with a natural, romantic atmosphere in the disorder of boulders and shrubbery.

Ned Smyth's "Upper Room" is a more deliberately sculptural artscape. The colonnaded courtyard located at the intersection of Albany Street and the Esplanade creates a mysterious but inviting environment of both residents and visitors. Other art projects include Richard Artschwager's "Sitting/Stance," and "Rector Gate" by R. M. Fisher. Also in planning is a formal garden by Alexander Cooper and Jennifer Bartlett.

The public art collection, parks and walkways at Battery Park City enhance the commercial appeal and attract tourism; they also create a more comfortable residential environment. Residential plans are a major portion of Battery Park City. The housing complexes take up 42 percent of the area and will eventually provide up to 14,000 apartments. The residential developments were designed under the strict regulations of Cooper and Eckstut's plan, enforced by the Battery Park City Authority. The requirements insured that the buildings would be diverse, appearing to have cropped up in increments, rather than appearing to be a homogenous megastructure. They are unified by the stone bases, masonry walls and punched windows—features that invoke the residential buildings of New York's Upper East and West sides.

Although the original plans for Battery Park City had incorporated lower-, middle- and high-income housing, the 1979 plan eliminated all the subsidized housing. To compensate for the lost lower-income housing, the Battery Park City Authority, under Meyer Frucher, devised a plan to channel a portion of Battery Park City's revenue into subsidized housing throughout New York City. The financial success of Battery Park City, even before its completion, seems to insure that the revenues will be significant.

The World Financial Center, residential development and

public spaces have received significant praise from New York critics. While it is too soon to know all of the implications of the planning and implementation, Battery Park City appears to be a success. Its immediate impact and importance lie in its successful incorporation of historical references to early-20th-century architecture in New York; its effective implementation of a master plan, which maintains diversity and unity; and the emphasis on public spaces that incorporate art into life. The overall concern seems to be the creation of a city environment that is friendly to its inhabitants. This postmodern idea has been adopted for Battery Park City, however: the theory is tempered by practicality and regulation. One of the greatest criticisms of postmodernism is that architecture becomes a series of eclectic and artistic statements, lacking practicality and relevance. The urban, artistic and architectural design of Battery Park City combines modernism with new understanding of what makes a city work, and creates a mixed-use space on a human scale.

—MELISSA CARD

BROOKLYN BRIDGE
New York City, New York, U.S.A.

1869-83. Architects: John Roebling (1806-69) and Washington Roebling (1837-1926).

Publications

BILLINGTON, DAVID P.: *The Tower and the Bridge: The New Art of Structural Engineering*. Princeton, New Jersey, 1983.
FRAMPTON, KENNETH, and FUTAGAWA, YUKIO: *Modern Architecture: 1851-1919*. New York, 1983.
McCULLOUGH, DAVID: *The Great Bridge*. New York, 1972.
TRACHTENBERG, ALAN: *Brooklyn Bridge: Fact and Symbol*. New York, 1965.

*

The Brooklyn Bridge is one of the technological and aesthetic triumphs of the 19th century. Linking the formerly separate cities of Brooklyn and New York, the bridge was a daring feat of suspension technology for its time. Perhaps even more impressive is the bridge's aesthetic impact, from the graceful arc of its roadbed as it springs effortlessly over the East River to the spidery web of its cables draped from the hulking towers. The bridge has become part of the iconography of the city, while the heroism of the men who built the bridge has become part of its folklore.

By the 1840s there was an obvious need to link the burgeoning cities of Brooklyn and New York by a bridge to replace the overtaxed ferry services, but the great width of the river proved to be daunting. The engineer John Roebling, already a noted bridge designer, first proposed a suspension bridge across the river in 1857, but it was not until 1865 that he prepared plans for such a structure. Roebling's prior accomplishments included the building of suspension bridges over the Niagara River in upstate New York (1851-55) and the Allegheny River in Pittsburgh (1857-60). Before construction of the Brooklyn Bridge could begin, however, he died in 1869 from complications resulting from a work-related accident.

Roebling's son and assistant, Washington, assumed the position of chief engineer on the Brooklyn Bridge project, and

Brooklyn Bridge: New York City, 1869-83

carried it to its completion in 1883. The rigors of the job also took their toll on the younger man. In 1872 he fell victim, like many of his laborers, to the so-called caisson disease—a paralysis that results from changes in air pressure—while working on the bridge's foundations. The younger Roebling remained partially paralyzed and in poor health for the rest of his life. Using field glasses and with the assistance of his wife, he supervised the remainder of the bridge's construction from his house in Brooklyn. There were intermittent charges of fraud and corruption, and there was a failed attempt to remove Roebling as chief engineer. After 13 years of construction, and at a cost of more than $13 million and 20 lives, the bridge was dedicated on May 24, 1883. Roebling, too weak to leave his house, watched the ceremony from his window.

Although the bridge has long been surpassed in length, its physical dimensions are still impressive. The roadbed is 85 feet wide and 5,989 feet long, of which the central span is 1,595½ feet. Draped from the 276-foot-high masonry towers are steel cables 16 inches in diameter. Thousands of vertical steel suspenders and diagonal stays create the distinctive diamond pattern between the main cables and the roadbed. The bridge has been designed to carry a load three times greater than its normal capacity.

Immediately upon its completion, the bridge was declared to be an aesthetic triumph. Only in the choice of pointed arches and a projecting cornice on each of the towers has the design of the bridge been criticized as needlessly historicist; however, these features give the structure a romantic silhouette, in keeping with its heroic provenance, as well as the visual solidity required to convince early doubters of its strength. Equally romantic and enduring in their appearance are the battered walls of the anchorages. The approaches are carried on Florentine arcades that allow for the passage of streets on either shore. Despite the removal of transit lines and the reconfiguration of the approaches and the main deck, the bridge remains essentially intact. Its centennial was marked in 1983 with a fireworks spectacle that rivaled the festivities on opening day.

Like a revered icon, the bridge has become more than just a transportation link between Manhattan and Brooklyn. It is the frame through which the skyscrapers of Manhattan are viewed and the lofty path from the mundane world of the outer borough's neighborhoods to the sophistication of the big city. Numerous writers, from Walt Whitman to Hart Crane, have extolled its virtues in print, and legions of painters and photographers, including Joseph Stella and Edward Steichen, have attempted to capture its visual beauty. A monument to 19th-century American ingenuity, the Brooklyn Bridge continues to inspire a society that has largely lost faith in technological progress.

—ROBERT WOJTOWICZ

CENTRAL PARK
New York City, New York, U.S.A.

1858: Construction begun; **Architect:** Frederick Law Olmsted (1822-1903).

Publications

BARLOW, ELIZABETH: *Frederick Law Olmsted's New York.* New York, 1972.

FEIN, H.: *Landscape into Cityscape: Frederick Law Olmsted. Plans for a Greater New York.* Ithaca, New York, 1967.

LANCASTER, CLAY: "Central Park, 1851-1951." *Magazine of Art* 44 (April 1951): 123-128.

OLMSTED, FREDERICK LAW, JR., and KIMBALL, THEODORA (eds.): *Frederick Law Olmsted 1822-1903.* 2 vols. Cambridge, Massachusetts, 1937.

REED, HENRY HOPE, et al.: *Bridges of Central Park.* New York, 1990.

REED, HENRY HOPE, and DUCKWORTH, SOPHIA: *Central Park, a History and a Guide.* New York, 1967.

SCHUYLER, DAVID, and CENSER, JANE TURNER (eds.): *The Years of Olmsted, Vaux and Company.* Baltimore, 1992.

Designed by Frederick Law Olmsted, Central Park in New York City is not only embedded in an urban landscape, but itself seems to contain the ruins of a lost city. The architectural structures scattered across the park, particularly when viewed in aerial photographs, take on the features of urban remains. In fact, Central Park is one of the last masterpieces of the tradition in park architecture that intentionally created cityscapes within park settings. Other notable examples of this tradition can be found in French and Italian gardens of the Renaissance and Baroque periods.

Olmsted's choice of a basically urban frame of reference

Central Park: New York City, 1858

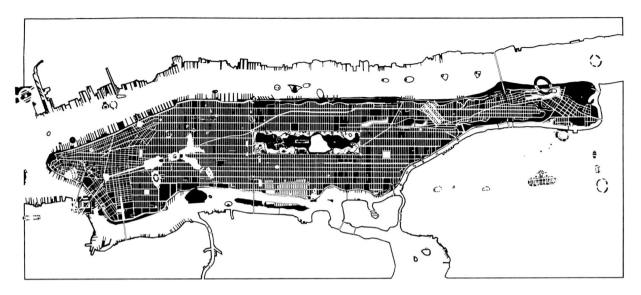

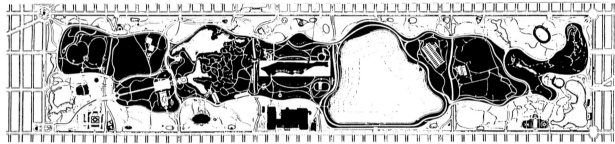

Central Park: Plan of Manhattan (top); plan of Central Park (bottom)

may appear even more surprising in a park created to grant relief to city dwellers from the unnatural conditions of urban life. In an account of his work on the project, Olmsted explained his choices by the unusual nature of the task entrusted to him: "The form and position of Central Park are peculiar . . . and such that precedent with dealing with it is rather to be sought in the long and narrow boulevards of some of the old continental European cities, than in the broad parks with which from its area in acres, we are most naturally led to compare it."

The "city" within Central Park is in some ways a mirror image of the city that surrounds it. Centrally located on the long, thin island of Manhattan, and defined by the existing street grid, the park's rectangular shape was inevitable. However, when one superimposes the plan of Manhattan on the plan of Central Park some distinct similarities in layout emerge.

Olmsted began the design of the park by setting down the major road systems, organizing them in a similar configuration to that of the existing major road structure of New York. The Main Drive in Central Park is a continuous loop, which describes a shape curiously similar to the outline of Manhattan. The transverse roads cut through the park in the same way that the major crosstown streets of Manhattan cut across the island, and they serve the same purpose of directly connecting the east and west sides. Broadway and the Grand Promenade parallel one another in their diagonal orientation to the Manhattan grid. In plan, the crosstown streets of New York are diagonally intersected by Broadway in the way that the transverse roads of Central Park are intersected by the Grand Promenade. Considering actual intersections of the Grand Promenade with the transverses undesirable, however, Olmsted dropped the transverse roads to a depth of about twelve feet below the surface of

the park, to avoid congestion at intersections and any traffic disturbances in the landscape. He thus created the illusion of a continuous landscape, while simultaneously segmenting it into smaller sections, employing a device reminiscent of the English "ha ha," or sunken fence.

Both Broadway and the Grand Promenade are determined by pre-existing conditions, a little arbitrarily in the case of the Grand Promenade. Broadway follows an old Indian trail cutting across Manhattan, and the Grand Promenade follows the line of sight between an intersection (in the south-east corner of the park) of the Main Drive with one of the transverses and Vista Rock. Olmsted himself described the process by which the direction of the Grand Promenade was determined: "Vista Rock, the most prominent point in the landscape of the Lower Park, here first comes distinctly into view, and fortunately in a direction diagonal to the boundary lines."

In the overall plan of the park Vista Point, together with Belvedere Castle nearby, corresponds to Columbus Circle in the layout of the city. The location of the former rectangular reservoir within Central Park is analogous to the placement of the park itself within Manhattan. Columbus Circle sits at the southwest corner of the park just as Belvedere Castle sits at the southwest corner of what used to be the reservoir. And Belvedere Castle concludes the axis of the Grand Promenade just as Columbus Circle creates a significant pause in Broadway at Central Park. A similar correspondence exists between Union Square and that section of the Grand Promenade called the Mall.

Olmsted divided the park into the "Lower Formal" and the "Upper Natural" sections, corresponding to the two original reservoirs. The lower reservoir, later transformed to public playing fields, was rectangular and the upper "naturally" shaped.

Both the opposition between the reservoirs and that between the Lower and Upper Park parallel the historical development of Manhattan, which was developed first on the southern end, while the northern end was left as wilderness. The road structure further divides the park into sections, each designed as a different type of landscape. There are pastoral and formal settings, areas designed for strolling and promenading, and spaces for playing and exercise. The smaller segments of the park can be seen as neighborhoods within the park, analogous to the distinctly different neighborhoods of the city defined by the major crosstown streets and avenues. Considering its complexity, the park takes on the nature of a city clothed in foliage. In spite of its enormous size, Central Park looks small when one considers the numerous varieties of landscape that it contains.

Along the diagonal axis in the park Olmsted placed the elements of an English mansion. "In giving [the Grand Promenade] this prominent position," Olmsted wrote, "we look at it in the light of an artificial structure on a scale of magnitude commensurate with the size of the park, and intend in our design that it should occupy the same position of relative importance in the general arrangement of the plan that a mansion should occupy in a park prepared for private occupation." The "mansion" was designed to give individual users a sense of personal ownership in the park. As the equivalent of a private mansion set in a private park and reserved for the use and enjoyment of a single family, Olmsted wished to create a mansion in a park for the use of the "family" of New Yorkers. An additional motive for this arrangement, which encouraged the visitor to consider the park with the eye of a landowner surveying his estate, was to ensure a respectful use of the public space.

The Grand Promenade functions as the grand entrance to the mansion. The 72nd Street entrance is the equivalent of the carriage entrance, including the terrace where Sunday strollers paraded their finery. The terrace overlooks Bethesda Fountain and the romantic landscape of the lake and the rambles beyond. The axis of the Grand Promenade continues visually through the landscape to Belvedere Castle at Vista Point, built at a tiny scale in order to heighten the illusion of distance. To the east of the Mall is the arbor, and further along a flower garden that later served as a miniature sailboat pond. Olmsted provided numerous places along the formal axis of the park for the then fashionable custom of public promenading.

Although New York City has grown dramatically since Olmsted designed his monument to urban living, Central Park continues to be a vital part of the life and image of the city.

—LORNA ANNE McNEUR

CHRYSLER BUILDING
New York City, New York, U.S.A.

1928-30. Architect: William Van Alen (1883-1954).

Publications

BLETTER, R. H., and ROBINSON, C.: *Skyscraper Style—Art Deco New York*. New York, 1975.
CLUTE, E.: "The Chrysler Building, New York." *Architectural Forum* 53 (October 1930).
FRAMPTON, KENNETH, and FUTAGAWA, YUKIO: *Modern Architecture: 1920-1945*. New York, 1983.
ISOZAKI, ARATA: *The Chrysler Building*. Tokyo, 1984.
STERN, R. A. M., GILMARTIN, G. and MELLINS, T.: *New York 1930: Architecture and Urbanism between the Two World Wars*. New York, 1987.

The formal and symbolic flamboyance of Walter P. Chrysler's and William Van Alen's Chrysler Building was occasionally witty, often elegant and resolutely unorthodox. The building's origins in a real estate scheme by speculator William H. Reynolds to erect the tallest structure in the world, its novel forms of corporate advertising, its several phases of design under the successive ownerships of Reynolds and Chrysler, and its provision of the *mise-en-scène* for the most dramatic episode in the race for height that characterized skyscraper development in the late 1920s and early 1930s have exercised an irresistible appeal for the many historians who have recounted these episodes, in no single source with richer detail and more nostalgic panache than in the Stern, Gilmartin and Mellins text *New York 1930*.

Yet what the Chrysler Building's architecture revealed about the larger culture continually goes unexamined. Most significant in this regard was Chrysler's pursuit of a distinct corporate identity and a suitable monument to his own career as a self-made man. Like the Fisher Brothers of Detroit or Irwin S. Chanin in New York City, Chrysler merged traditional frontier values of self-reliance with modern ones associated with the technological and organizational agglomerations unique to the 1920s. Chrysler might be termed an artisan-entrepreneur because of his experience as a designer of automobile parts and engineering tools. His largely self-taught mastery of aspects of industrial design tied him to the 19th-century tradition of the amateur and the apprentice, while his design activity itself and his development of 20th-century economies of scale within the automobile industry gave him the status of a modern organizational pioneer. Whether as the manager between 1908 and 1920 of the Buick division of General Motors or of his own automobile companies in the 1920s, Chrysler, a railroad master machinist from the frontier town of Eillis, Kansas, was an innovator in the design of engines, transmissions and mechanical components, as well as in assembly-line and front-office divisions of labor. Many of his contemporaries credited him with revolutionizing the aesthetics of moderately priced cars.

Chrysler vividly embedded these experiences in a skyscraper iconography that expressed the distinct 1920s version of the traditional American myth of the self-made man. On the Chrysler Building's expressionist-inspired observation deck, Chrysler installed a glass case displaying the first set of machine tools he had fashioned as a boy of 18. One level above and framing three sides of Chrysler's private dining room was a glass mural whose life-size automotive workers and their tools were raised in polished black-glass relief against a frosted blue ground. In the main lobby Edward Turnball's 97-foot-by-110-foot ceiling mural *Energy, Result, Workmanship, and Transportation* culminated in a huge painted image of the Chrysler Building itself. These three exhibits more pointedly expressed the highlights in Walter Chrysler's self-begotten career than the better-known hubcap frieze or the eagle-head and radiator-cap gargoyles high on the building exterior. Examples of Van Alen's architectural wit, these latter two icons also exemplified business boosterism in the 1920s, virtually identifying America's well-being with that of big business, and expressing a patriotism that the historian William Preston Slossen in 1930 characterized as nearly "religious in its intensity."

Chrysler's creative propensities were also evident in his sensitivity to unusual materials and elaborate ornamental detailing, with which he had had considerable experience in the design

Chrysler Building: New York City, 1928-30

of cars. His skyscraper, along with those of the Fisher Brothers and Chanin, established a standard of rich interior fittings that exceeded the comparatively chaste material sheen of the Woolworth Building lobby, or that of the Nebraska State Capitol, the most sumptuous of earlier skyscraper interiors. That the lobbies of many office buildings became more opulent during the boom period of 1925 to 1929, or that skyscraper patrons were certainly aware of the publicity value inherent in the use of exotic materials does not gainsay the fact that Chrysler, Chanin and the Fisher Brothers were the first and only skyscraper patrons of the 1920s to authorize their architects to employ such expensive materials so lavishly, nor the notion that given the developer's own design experience a significant element of aesthetic choice entered into their authorization.

Thus, just after Chrysler had purchased the lease and the Van Alen plans for the building, he, in his own words, "made the final choice for the marbles in the corridors." In the spatially dynamic triangular lobby, yellow Sienna appeared on the floor, red Moroccan on the walls, and amber onyx and blue marble were used as trim. In addition, Chrysler selected the Oriental, English, Cuban and American hardwoods used to create the inlaid sumptuousness of the elevator doors and cabs, none of whose interiors repeated the others, and all of which Chrysler pictured as "the work of some extraordinarily gifted cabinetmaker."

However assertively modern the appointments for most portions of the building, Chrysler also mandated traditional decors in two key locations. Placed within the space framed by the building's metal crown of superimposed arches, the Cloud Club—an association for executives in the automobile, airplane, steel and oil industries—reassuringly offered its aesthetically conservative clientele a Georgian lobby, a Tudor lounge and coffee areas, and a Breton taproom. Designed by French and Company, Chrysler's office itself exuded a medieval ambience by virtue of heavy plasterwork, leaded windows and elaborate wooden doors.

In sum, the Chrysler Building was a grandiloquent representation of Chrysler's epiphanies as a self-made man. It reflected those moments when he realized the full scope of his possibilities in the expansively optimistic world of the 1920s, an historical period that mixed with astonishing providence the rewards of 19th-century values with those of modern systems, those of artistic endeavor with those of industry, those of naive enterprising wonder with those of self-promotion or self-aggrandizement. His building didactically made available to everyone the entrepreneur's experience of success, an experience summarized in painted images and material metaphors, all of which referred back to the creative will of the developer.

—EDWARD W. WOLNER

EMPIRE STATE BUILDING
New York City, New York, U.S.A.

1929-31: Construction; **Architects:** Richmond Shreve (1877-1946), William Lamb (1883-1952), and Arthur Harmon (1878-1958).

Publications

GIES, JOSEPH: "The Tallest Building: The Empire State." pp. 59-81 in *Wonders of the Modern World*. New York, 1966.
HELLER, STEVEN et. al.: *Empire State Building Book*. New York, 1980.
ROBINSON, C. and BLETTER, R. H.: *Skyscraper Style: Art Deco New York*. New York, 1975.
WHITE, NORVAL: *The Architecture Book*. New York, 1976.

*

The architectural, commercial and popular success of the Empire State Building depended on a highly rationalized design process, and equally efficient advertising and construction campaigns. Skillful designers of Manhattan office buildings, architects Shreve, Lamb and Harmon were familiar with the imperatives of design and construction efficiency that maximized investors' returns by filling the building with tenants as soon as possible. The investors for the project included the popular former New York State governor Alfred Smith; together with the building's name, Smith's association was meant to give a purely commercial operation the intimation of something more public, to increase its marketability beyond that secured by erecting the world's tallest building, which it became less than a year after the completion of the Chrysler Building, then the highest structure in the world.

Moreover, as the Depression set in and overbuilt Manhattan office space increasingly stood empty, the investors countered with novel publicity operations such as crowning the building with a multistory mooring mast for dirigibles (never fully successful), and exhibiting Lewis Hine's eloquent photographs of the vertiginous work of steel frame assembly, a portfolio commissioned by the investors to advertise the building's available office space.

That 3,500 laborers were able to erect an average five and a half stories of the building a week, and that no more than a year elapsed between ground-breaking ceremonies and the arrival of the first tenants depended on technical and organizational advances. The increasing height and size of skyscrapers since the turn of the century had resulted in improvements to such equipment as steam shovels, jacks and derricks. In the 1920s engineers gave elevators the increased speeds, more comfortable deceleration and more accurate landing alignments that taller buildings required.

Contractors William and Paul Starrett subsumed such improvements and the design process itself within a Taylorized construction schedule that William Starrett had been elaborating and refining since his leadership during World War I in the rapid construction of domestic military training facilities. The Starretts maximized the number of building operations carried out simultaneously or in overlapping sequences. In carefully coordinated operations, members of the steel frame arrived by train from Pittsburgh only hours after fabrication, were shipped from the train station to the building site, and were used immediately to eliminate losses of time and money due to storage. Powerful derricks on cantilevered platforms were especially designed for this job. To an extent not true of previous skyscraper building operations, elevators, including some salvaged from the demolished 19th-century Waldorf-Astoria Hotel, carried construction crews and some lightweight building materials in the interests of saving time. For the same reason, portable kitchens served lunch at a floor level appropriate for the building height achieved that week, preventing the inefficiency attendant on bringing hundreds of workers to the ground to eat.

Empire State Building: New York City, 1929-31

The financial imperatives behind such innovations also favored two formal developments in the skyscraper, both epitomized in the design of the Empire State Building: maximum density of development on central lucrative sites, and the extrusion of a tower to exploit the advertising value of visibility on the skyline. In its requirements for natural lighting on streets and building interiors, the New York City zoning ordinance reinforced both tendencies, the former by pulling the building into a series of setbacks, and the latter by allowing a tower to rise to an unlimited height within a floor area no larger than about 25 percent of the lot size.

The Empire State Building, like most art deco skyscrapers, was modernistic, not modernist. It was deliberately less pure, more flamboyant and populist than European theory allowed. It appeared to be a sculpted or modeled masonry mass, giving to business imagery a substantial character that executives would not have found in the European emphasis on the expression of interior volumes and apparently weightless buildings. The Empire State's uninterrupted metal mullions gleaming in the sunlight further emphasized the building's radical height rather than the horizontality and structural articulation sought after in Europe. Its commanding silhouette carried a figural crown that gracefully met the sky, rather than a flat termination that effaced a portion of it.

The building's first five stories were pulled out in front of the rest of the building, effectively putting the great height and bulk of the skyscraper at a comfortable remove from passersby. Inside, the lobby was stylistically transitional. It possessed the material richness of the late 1920s in its modernistic chevron flooring and stripings, but it was also Moderne or streamlined, its mezzanine bridge, metal handrails and round corners inspired by transport design. It was one of the last three buildings of the era (the others being the Chrysler and Daily News buildings) to express a skyscraper narcissism. A large wall-mosaic of marble and aluminum inlay figured forth a map of metropolitan New York dominated by a huge elevation of the Empire State Building itself, the sun's rays radiating out from its mooring mast in celebration of the building's completely rationalized and improbable elegance.

—EDWARD W. WOLNER

GRAND CENTRAL TERMINAL
New York City, New York, U.S.A.

1907-13: Construction; **Architects:** Charles A. Reed (1857-1911) and Allen H. Stem (1856-1931), Whitney Warren (1864-1943) and Charles D. Wetmore (1866-1941).

Publications

FITCH, JAMES MARSTON, and WAITE, DIANA S.: *Grand Central Terminal and Rockefeller Center: A Historic-Critical Estimate of Their Significance*. Albany, New York, 1974.
MIDDLETON, W. D.: *Grand Central . . . The World's Greatest Railway Terminal*. San Marino, California, 1977.

Grand Central Terminal: New York City, 1907-13

As with the rest of the burgeoning city, the terminus for the railway that ran along Fourth (later Park) Avenue in Manhattan moved progressively uptown until it reached 42nd Street in 1871. By that time, the three railroads which entered from the north were under the control of Cornelius Vanderbilt. Marking the new facilities was a three-story red brick building trimmed with cast iron painted white, and crowned by rounded mansard roofs over pavilions in the Second Empire manner. Forty years later, this building (subsequently enlarged and remodeled) was to be replaced by Grand Central Terminal.

The immediate cause was an accident that killed 15 persons in 1902 when two trains collided in the tunnel beyond the marshaling yards, which was filled as usual with smoke and steam. This prompted the electrification of the system and the total rebuilding of the railroad's facilities to a comprehensive plan drawn up by the railroad's chief engineer (and later, vice-president), William J. Wilgus.

Included in his proposals were the construction of two levels of tracks (express and suburban), the lowest roughly 50 feet below Park Avenue to allow for its continuation to the north (connecting with the crosstown streets bridged over them), and the lease of the air rights above the open spaces between for hotels, apartment buildings and office towers to finance the operation.

Four firms were invited to submit plans for a new terminal. Two were well known: McKim, Mead and White (then engaged in the design of Pennsylvania Station), and D. H. Burnham and Company. Two were less familiar: Samuel Huckel of Philadelphia (who had worked for Wilgus previously), and Reed and Stem of St. Paul, Minnesota. The three extant designs (that of Burnham was lost) depict very large buildings with no special

character particular to their use. However, the entry by Reed and Stem, selected in 1903, incorporated an elevated roadway around the terminal to connect the two lengths of Park Avenue, a magnificent neoclassical ''court of honor'' over the air rights behind the station (this might have been added later), and a system of ramps instead of staircases within it, to facilitate access to the tracks.

As it turned out, Reed and Stem's success was to be short-lived. Charles Reed was Wilgus' brother-in-law, but Whitney Warren was a cousin and friend of William K. Vanderbilt, who was chairman of the railroad's board. Submitting its own design after the competition had been judged, the firm of Warren and Wetmore was authorized to share the commission and ultimately took over the project.

Warren had studied at the École des Beaux-Arts, and lived in Paris until he was 30. His firm's initial design featured a top-heavy tripartite facade where a six-story rectilinear window wall sat on an arched base under a multistoried attic. Between this first scheme and the final elevation of 1910, the definitive metaphor and associated form for the railroad station type was evolved.

A congruence of ideas seems to have led to this conclusion. Previous stations had used arched openings to give expression to the station shed. The ''city beautiful'' movement, stemming from the rebuilding of Paris, indicated that a station could be its ''gateway'' or ''portal.'' The neoclassical ideal suggested the triumphal arch as an appropriate precedent.

Grand Central Terminal was well placed to be conceptualized as the gateway to New York City. At that time, little building of quality had been erected north of the station, which stood astride a major line of access through Manhattan and to the nation beyond.

However, the design for the facade of Grand Central Terminal is more symbolic than literal. Its three great arched windows that order the broad rhythm of its parts are raised above the roadway, which tops the entrance level, thereby compromising their functional use as portals. (Inside, they are shared between the smaller waiting room and space above, and do not even open up to the main concourse beyond.) The everyday world exists below. The ideal form sits aloof as a separate treatment of its civic purpose.

The scale is so monumental that the entrance wall at the base of the facade reads in the drawings as the building's plinth. The main feature itself is marked by the clarity, simplicity and elegance of its composition. Embellishing the skyline at the entablature in front of the hipped roof, the statue of Mercury represents the glory of commerce supported by moral and mental energy in the guise of Hercules and Minerva.

Missing from the project is the imposing public square that would have provided a suitable setting and allowed the facade to be viewed as a whole, instead of being contorted by the relative narrowness of 42nd Street and the road that bridges over it (opened in 1919). It might also have permitted vehicular movement along the sides of the building. For in resolving the issue of through-traffic by means of a viaduct along the building's central axis, the architectural response to the notion of the "gateway to the city" had been compromised.

In a way, this was made more apparent when the New York Central Building (also by Warren and Wetmore) was erected immediately behind the terminal in 1929. There, the traffic was allowed to travel alongside the newly constructed residential blocks and through the arched base of the office structure, while its tower dramatically closed the vista from the north (at least, until the effect was almost ruined by the addition of the Pan-Am Building).

Yet if the form of Grand Central Terminal fails to make complete sense within its immediate context, its space provides the essential mediation between the metropolis and the outside world. The main concourse, ramped below street level, is a block wide and 125 feet high, its vaulted ceiling adorned with selected constellations. A noble staircase leads to a gallery and the adjacent side street. The whole is sheathed in marble and simulated Caen stone. Light floods through its huge end windows and the lunettes above, revealing its gracious proportions. Even with the recent fashion for glass-roofed atria (and the decline of rail travel), Grand Central Terminal remains one of the great urban places in the public life of New York City.

—ANTHONY JACKSON

GUGGENHEIM MUSEUM
New York City, New York, U.S.A.

1956-59. Architect: Frank Lloyd Wright (1867-1959). **1985-92:** Addition; **Architect:** Gwathmey/Siegel Associates.

Publications

"Guggenheim Museum." *Global Architecture* 36.
HOFMANN, WERNER, and KULTERMANN, UDO: *Modern Architecture in Color*. New York, 1970.
JORDY, WILLIAM H.: "The Encompassing Environment of Free-Form Architecture: Frank Lloyd Wright's Guggenheim Museum." *American Buildings and Their Architects: The Impact of European Modernism in the Mid-Twentieth Century*. Garden City, New York, 1972.
"The New Guggenheim '92." *Art in America* 80 (September 1992): 106-119.
PFEIFFER, BRUCE BROOKS: *The Guggenheim Correspondence*. 1986.
WRIGHT, FRANK LLOYD: *The Solomon R. Guggenheim Museum*. New York, 1960.
WRIGHT, FRANK LLOYD: "The Modern Gallery: For the Solomon R. Guggenheim Foundation, New York City." *Magazine of Art* 39 (January 1946).

*

The Guggenheim Museum had one of the longest gestation and planning periods of any structure by Frank Lloyd Wright: it began with talks between the architect and the curator of the Guggenheim collection in 1943, but it was not dedicated until shortly after the architect's death in 1959. Though the preliminary drawings were approved by Solomon Guggenheim in 1944 and the working drawings were completed in mid-1946, the project was delayed over and over, first by World War II, then by the cost of building. Later, there were questions about the site (the last parcel was acquired in 1951), about the use of glass and the choice of interior materials, about the best way to angle the walls; all of these issues took time and pushed the project ever further into the future. The director of the museum could not be bullied as easily as many of Wright's clients had been, and the elderly architect lost several major battles.

Wright had originally contemplated a horizontal building when first approached about a museum to house the potential client's collection of nonobjective art, but even as rich a man as Solomon Guggenheim could not afford a sufficiently large piece of prime New York real estate to accomplish such an aim. Consequently, the architect developed his startling design based on the concept of the spiral as a solution to a vertical museum. He had utilized such a form several times before, in projects dating back to the mid-1920s, and while working on the Guggenheim Museum itself, he was to use the spiral for projects as diverse as the Morris Store in San Francisco, in several houses of the early 1950s, and for a variety of projects that never came to fruition.

Wright consciously drew forth associations with the ancient Near Eastern form of the ziggurat, and proposed that it could be utilized with the wider part on either the top or the bottom. Although there was a functional reason for working one's way down the spiral while viewing the paintings, there seems little doubt that the architect was delighted with the possibility of seeming to defy gravity by having the entire edifice poised on the tip of the spiral. Given Wright's known disinterest in the nonobjective art collected by the Guggenheim family, it is unlikely that he made any formal comparison between the building and the work of the Russian constructivists, who used such forms as the spiral as part of their geometric conceptions and as a way of playing with the third dimension without having to take refuge in traditional representational art. Nonetheless, there are certainly parallels between the museum's design and the intellectual interests of artists such as Wassily Kandinsky, Kasimir Malevich and El Lissitsky, on the one hand, and Hilla Rebay, the first curator of the collection (and the person who

Guggenheim Museum: New York City, 1956-59

had first contacted Wright about designing a museum for the Guggenheims). Indeed, it is probable that Wright, never as unaware of the work of other architects as he pretended to be, was actually aware of an unbuilt design for a spiral/vertical museum earlier planned but never executed by Le Corbusier, himself a nonobjective artist of no small accomplishment.

With all of the inevitable arguments and changes of plan behind, the final steps in constructing the tightly coiled building proceeded through the late 1950s to completion. And though the spiral is often too tight—the walls too sharply curved—to handle either the larger paintings or the viewer's ability to step back a sufficient distance for their viewing, the plan of having the visitor ride to the top of the building and walk down the spiral and out of the exhibition was and remains a satisfying experience in most situations. Even some thirty years later, the conception captures the imagination of the museum visitor.

To the extent that the design is less than perfect for its intended use, it is only fair to note that the architect was forced by economics to work on such a small lot. If he had been granted more space and thus the room for a larger and more gradual spiral, the "walls" would have sloped more gradually and permitted the hanging of larger works. Also, if he had not had to make room for the theater, dining area and other amenities, an even more majestic presence might have been established.

As a museum design, per se, Wright's spiral solution was brilliant, laying the groundwork for others who might wish to learn from his mistakes and the needs of a changing collection. Knowing that one is to walk through the exhibition and never be more than half a turn from an elevator should one want to make a quick exit without either retracing one's steps or walking

to the end of a horizontal space is satisfying to the viewer and, psychologically, lessens museum fatigue. Again, at the end of a career of 70 years, and almost half a century after his first innovative commercial design for the Larkin Building, the greatest American architect of the 20th century brilliantly solved problems for a type of building he had never before designed.

—DAVID M. SOKOL

HAUGHWOUT BUILDING
New York City, New York, U.S.A.

1857: Construction; **Architect:** John P. Gaynor (ca. 1826-1889).

Publications

KOEPER, F.H.: *The Gothic Skyscraper: A History of the Woolworth Building and Its Antecedents.* Ph.D. diss., Department of Architecture, Harvard University, 1969.

*

At the time of its construction in 1857 at the northeast corner of Broadway and Broome Street in Manhattan, the Haughwout Building was a combination of progressive and retrogressive elements. Although the architect, John P. Gaynor, chose to

Haughwout Building: New York City, 1857

erect a prefabricated cast-iron building, he disguised the modern building method behind a fashionable Venetian Renaissance facade. This use of European architectural styles and historic detailing was a logical way to validate the new building material and technique: it affirmed the building's respectability while confirming the reliability of the new building method. It was also a disappointment to many architects and critics of the period, who had hoped that through the use of iron, a fresh architectural language independent of past styles would be developed there.

Gaynor designed the Haughwout Building to accommodate the successful housewares business. He took advantage of the corner location by carrying the facade across both street fronts and using as much glass as possible at the ground, or showroom, level. On the first floor, each of the window bays consists of a sheet of glass in an iron frame and set between Corinthian columns. The centered triple doorway which faces Broadway is also made of iron and glass. This arrangement opens the entire showroom to the outdoors, which must have been quite a startling sight in the late 1850s. The only visible means of support for the upper stories are two rows of thin, elegant iron columns.

The remaining four stories of the building are much more conservative and identical to each other. Gaynor used a version of the Palladian window motif: an arched window on a small order of Corinthian columns placed between piers with engaged Corinthian columns. Each story is separated by a strong entablature and pedestal bands, a clear demarcation that gives the building a horizontal emphasis. A prominent entablature with a slight outward curve designates the line of the flat roof. Placed on the second floor above the center door is a large circular clock with the twelve o'clock position corresponding to the

keystone of the window arch. Unfortunately, this clock is no longer working and has been painted black to blend in with the rest of the building.

Gaynor relied upon Daniel Badger's Architectural Iron Works to fabricate and construct the Haughwout Building. Badger's establishment was one of the two dominant cast-iron businesses in New York during the 1850s. The other major firm was that of James Bogardus, who is credited with devising and popularizing the system of prefabricating cast-iron factory buildings. In his book of 1856, *Cast-Iron Buildings—Their Construction and Advantages,* Bogardus claimed: "The first complete cast-iron edifice ever erected in America, or in the world, was that of inventor, James Bogardus—being his manufactory on the corner of Centre and Duane Streets in New York." As a rejoinder, Badger declared in the catalog of the Architectural Iron Works published in 1865: "The first person who practically used Iron as a building material for the exterior was Daniel D. Badger, the President of the Architectural Iron Works. In the year 1842, Mr. Badger erected, in the city of Boston, the first structure of Iron ever seen in America." Badger gave his firm the advantage by hiring architects, molders and modelers to design both stock items and custom orders. One of the architects employed by Badger was George H. Johnson, an English builder who became known for his participation in the development of terra-cotta fireproofing for iron buildings.

It is not known whether Gaynor designed the facade of the Haughwout Building or chose stock items from Badger's catalog. Some of the motifs from the Haughwout Building are found on other cast-iron buildings in New York. It is possible that Gaynor designed the motifs and either used them on a few of his buildings or permitted the Architectural Iron Works to reuse his compositions.

The use of prefabricated cast iron had certain advantages over traditional masonry. A cast-iron building was more quickly and economically constructed than a comparable masonry structure. Iron could replicate the most intricate and detailed stone carving repeatedly and consistently through mass production. Cast iron is also much stronger and lighter than masonry. Iron forms can be reduced with no fear of compromising structural strength and without forfeiting beauty. Cast iron permitted, for the first time in architectural history, the size of the window openings to determine the width of the exterior bays, which previously had been restricted by the strength of the building material.

The Haughwout Building contained the first Otis passenger elevator equipped with automatic safety devices, which prevented the elevator from falling. The elevator had become a safe and practical means of transportation between the different floors of a building. No longer did the height of a building have to be restricted by the number of flights of stairs that a client was willing to walk.

The Haughwout Building is an important reminder that cast-iron construction was a precursor to 20th-century building techniques. Both prefabrication and modular design are used in cast-iron and 20th-century buildings. The vertical supports and horizontal beams that made up the structural support of cast-iron buildings are prototypes of the steel-cage construction of skyscrapers. Iron-and-glass facades evolved into curtain walls. Although the Haughwout Building shares these elements with the other cast-iron buildings of the 19th century, its most pragmatic contribution to 20th-century architecture was the first commercial passenger elevator. Skyscrapers would not exist without the technology to construct them, but their upper stories would not be occupied without an effortless means of transportation to reach them.

—LORETTA LORANCE

LEVER HOUSE
New York City, New York, U.S.A.

1952: Construction; **Architects:** Louis Skidmore (1897-1962), Nathaniel Owings (b.1903), John O. Merrill (1896-1975).

Publications

Architecture of Skidmore, Owings and Merrill 1950-62. Introduction by Henry-Russell Hitchcock. Stuttgart, 1962.

HOFMANN, WERNER, and KULTERMANN, UDO: *Modern Architecture in Color.* New York, 1970.

"Lever House Complete." *Architectural Forum* 96 (1952): 69, 110-111.

"Lever House Gets Landmark Status." *Building Design* (8 April 1983).

"Lever House, New York: Glass and Steel Walls." *Architectural Record* 111 (1952): 130-135.

"Lever's Landmark Status Upheld." *American Institute of Architects Journal* (April 1983).

"New York's Lever House Landmark Is Sold and Saved." *Building Design* (21 October 1983).

"25-year Award Goes to Lever House." *American Institute of Architects Journal* (March 1980).

*

The appearance of Lever House was widely praised on its completion (and also widely copied). Even Lewis Mumford, no mindless eulogist of the modern style, thought it was "a building of outstanding qualities . . . comfortable, gracious and handsome." Just 10 years later, Reyner Banham was belittling it by association with the advertising values of nearby Madison Avenue. It was this caricature of Lever House that was taken into the 1970s by the new generation of critics who were intent on demolishing the values of their predecessors and replacing them with their own ambitions.

The initial impact of Lever House stemmed from its solution to a basic concern of architects of the Modern Movement: the integration of technology and style within a pure geometric form. One interpretation of this formula was to be derived from the life's work of Ludwig Mies van der Rohe (whom Gordon Bunshaft met in 1940). In the 1920s, Mies had argued that the underlying principles of metal-frame structures could be best understood when they were faced with glass. His later designs for high-rise buildings attempted to realize this aim. But in the aesthetics of the era, glass was more than just a translucent wall panel.

By that time, the mystical qualities of glass that had been advocated by the expressionists, some of whom also doubled as functionalists (or vice versa), had been assimilated into the architectural mainstream. Interestingly, Sigfried Giedion hardly mentioned Mies in *Space, Time and Architecture,* but equated the glass curtain wall with his notion of space-time, and compared the glazed corner of the Bauhaus building with a Picasso cubist head. In this image, glass was no longer conceived as window but as transparent volume.

In practical terms, however, this was still quite difficult to achieve. Probably, the motivation to resolve the issue had also been lacking. European architects of the modern style had been more interested in following Le Corbusier's example of exploring form in light (leading Henry-Russell Hitchcock and Philip Johnson to warn that glass walls were perhaps "too fragile" for permanent buildings—an echo of John Ruskin's denunciation of the Crystal Palace). In the United States, architects were too interested in the rich effects to be achieved by mixing traditional and new materials in what became known as the art deco style.

World War II and the rise of Mies van der Rohe as the guru of the moment changed the direction of the profession. Required to construct enormous factories for the production of armaments, the construction industry developed new techniques and standards. Such buildings might cover acres of land, be artificially lit and air-conditioned, and have prefabricated, lightweight walls which could be assembled rapidly. With the end of the war, the companies making these materials and products looked for, and actively promoted, other uses in more conventional building types.

At the same time, architects once more began to be interested in the glass aesthetic. Pietro Belluschi designed the Equitable Building in Portland, Oregon (1945-48), with an aluminum and glass facade that was almost flush. The United Nations Secretariat Building in New York City (1947-50) had glass walls measuring over 150,000 square feet. Yet neither of these buildings quite captured the essence of the quest. The first was another essay in frame and infill. The second was still conceived as a solid form. The problem was not as simple as it seemed.

The achievement of Lever House was to make it look simple and inevitable. Decades of trying to conceive how a glass-faced building might be constructed was resolved with a wraparound grid of steel mullions and horizontal strips, holding heat-resistant glass, and sheathed in extruded stainless steel.

To some extent, the solution was made possible by a change in the New York City building code, which, after almost 50 years of specifying curtain walls as a masonry thickness, had just redefined them in terms of their fire rating. This allowed the glass spandrel panels to be set in front of four-inch cinder-block walls, plastered outside and insulated inside. On the other hand, the hybrid system also permitted the humidity within the airspace to corrode the subframe, and the movement of the metal to break the glass panes (resulting in the current random pattern of slightly different blue-green colors).

Creating a glazed volume was one step in the design. The next was to expose and celebrate it as an ideal form.

Within itself, this was achieved by a number of devices. The *parti* featured the vertical block as a separate unit over a raised hollow horizontal base. Opened up to the street, the site itself became a public (if somewhat forbidding) space. Floating above this podium, the 21-story slab was turned at right angles to Park Avenue, its solid back hidden at the rear, its form articulated by the recess at the third story where the building's outer columns were exposed. Completing the illusion, its front face was cantilevered almost 10 feet to hover over the hedge that lined the podium roof (which also served as the employees' dining room terrace).

Outside itself, the elegantly proportioned glass box stood in pristine contrast to its backdrop of masonry-walled neighbors. Reputed to house more millionaires than anywhere else in the world, Park Avenue between the world wars had been lined with solid apartment houses. Two events changed this situation. The major landowners in the area got it rezoned for business use, and the Depression and subsequent rent controls made luxury apartments unprofitable. Lever House was to be the first new building on the block when, as Nathaniel Owings was later to say, it "added its own slender beauty to the lovely old-world charm of that part of Park Avenue."

Unfortunately, the juxtaposition between old and new forms was soon to be eliminated. Within a decade most of the apartment buildings close to Lever House had been replaced by ordinary curtain-walled office buildings (although McKim, Mead and White's Racquet and Tennis Club still remains across the street). Lost in acres of reflective glass, Lever House was

Lever House: New York City, 1952

to be condemned for the excesses of its imitators. But in its own day, it stood for the culmination of a professional dream that saw modern architecture as the symbol (and savior) of contemporary life. And even if that vision has now faded, Lever House continues to be an outstanding example of its type.

—ANTHONY JACKSON

LINCOLN CENTER
New York City, New York, USA

1955-70: Construction; **Architects:** Breuer, Saarinen, Johnson, Harrison and Abramovitz. **1959-62:** Philharmonic Hall constructed; **Architect:** Max Abramovitz. **1961-64:** New York State Theater constructed; **Architect:** Philip Johnson. **1961-65:** Vivian Beaumont Theater constructed; **Architect:** Eero Saarinen. **1962-66:** Metropolitan Opera constructed; **Architect:** Wallace Harrison. **1965-69:** Juilliard School constructed; **Architect:** Pietro Belluschi.

Publications

"Philip Johnson and John Burgee: Avery Fisher Hall." *Interiors* (February 1977).
SPADE, R. and FUTAGAWA, Y.: *Eero Saarinen.* New York, 1968.
YOUNG, EDGAR B.: *Lincoln Center: The Building of an Institution.* New York, 1980.

Created during 1955-70 as part of an urban-renewal project, the Lincoln Center for the Performing Arts has established itself as a major regional and national location for the study, performance and broadcast of dance, operatic, chamber and symphonic works. Its story, however, also involves power politics, acoustical disaster and corrective reconstruction.

Late in 1954, Robert Moses, chairman of the Committee on Slum Clearance in New York City, together with Mayor Robert Wagner, designated a broad swath of the residential area west of Central Park as a Title I urban-renewal zone. Because it included the area west of the intersection of Columbus Avenue and Broadway, the designated zone took on the name of that intersection and became known as the Lincoln Square Urban Renewal Project. Altogether it comprised 17 blocks between 62nd and 70th streets. Moses, who had strong negative prejudices against the ethnic groups living in that area, was ready to use whatever powers of eminent domain were necessary to clear the area and prepare it for redevelopment. Altogether more than 7,000 families were evicted, and although 4,400 new apartment units were scheduled for construction, 4,000 of these were to be luxury units. Early in 1955 Moses contacted architect Wallace K. Harrison, asking what he thought of the idea of a new opera house as part of the renewal project.

At the same time, wealthy benefactors and officers of the major performing-arts institutions began exploratory meetings to discuss the construction of a new opera house, and Moses offered a portion of the Lincoln Square redevelopment area for its site. The discussions gradually broadened to include an adjoining facility for the New York Philharmonic Orchestra and other arts organizations. In June 1956, Lincoln Center for the Performing Arts was incorporated to carry out the design,

Lincoln Center: New York City, 1955-70

Lincoln Center, Philharmonic Hall, 1959-62

construction and operation of the individual arts buildings. The details of financing and organization of the opera and symphonic hall were placed in the hands of John D. Rockefeller III. The arts center grew in scope as other agencies joined, including the Juilliard School of Music in 1957, the Repertory Theater Association in 1960, and the New York Public Library in 1961.

The site for the arts center was expanded from an original four acres to 14 acres, to become a super block extending from 62nd to 65th streets, between Columbus Avenue and Amsterdam Avenue. The basic site plan developed by Harrison provided for a square central plaza fronting on Columbus Avenue, a fountain in its center, and defined by the large masses of the New York State Theater on the south, the Metropolitan Opera to the west and Philharmonic Hall on the north. Behind these, and on the adjoining block north of 65th Street, were to be additional structures housing a library and museum of the performing arts, the Vivian Beaumont Theater, the Juilliard School and a high school for the performing arts.

Ground was broken in May 1959. Each of the major buildings was designed by a separate architect. First to be constructed was Philharmonic Hall, begun in 1959 and opened in 1962; it was designed by Max Abramovitz and cost $17 million. Philharmonic Hall suffered from such severe acoustic problems that major artists and orchestras soon refused to perform there. The interior was gutted and a completely new auditorium built in 1976; designed by Philip Johnson in consultation with acoustical adviser Cyril Harris, the new Avery Fisher Hall interior cost $4.5 million. The Metropolitan Opera was designed by Wallace Harrison, with a seating capacity of 3,800 and a large entrance lobby housing a sinuous, baroque grand staircase. Construction of the opera began in 1962; when it opened in 1966, its cost

had grown to $46.9 million. The New York State Theater, designed by Philip Johnson, was begun in 1961 and opened in 1964; its cost was $20.4 million, met largely by state appropriations. The Vivian Beaumont Theater, designed by Eero Saarinen and built from 1961 to 1965, cost $9 million. To its rear and connected to the opera was the library and museum section designed by Gordon Bunshaft of Skidmore, Owings and Merrill.

North of 65th Street and connected to the remainder of Lincoln Center by an elevated pedestrian bridge is the Juilliard School, designed by Pietro Belluschi with Catalano and Westermann. The most complex of the buildings because of internal engineering requirements (rooms are wrapped around two auditoriums), and because of its physical connection to the adjoining LaGuardia High School of Performing Arts (also designed by Belluschi), the Juilliard School was the last to be built, in 1965-69; its cost rose to $24.3 million. Included in the Juilliard School complex is a separate auditorium for chamber music, Alice Tully Hall, designed by Belluschi and opened to acclaim in 1969.

The exteriors of the major buildings—Philharmonic Hall, the Metropolitan Opera and the New York State Theater—have been criticized as being overscaled, featureless and unconvincing evocations of classical architecture by architects who were champions of the Modern Movement. The buildings' external sheathing of travertine provides some warmth of color and texture. The rhythm established by the paired columns in Johnson's New York State Theater is considered more successful in comparison with the other two buildings. The red and gold interior of the Metropolitan Opera has been described as shrill, but the remodeled interior of Avery Fisher Hall has served well both visually and acoustically. Critics have generally agreed that the three rather vacuous main buildings benefit greatly from the works of modern sculpture and painting incorporated in them, including works by Yaacov Agam, Lee Bentocou, Alexander Calder, Marc Chagall, Richard Lippold, Jacques Lipschitz, Seymour Lipton, Henry Moore and Elie Nadelman, among others. Only Saarinen's theater and Belluschi's Juilliard School have been warmly received by critics for their unique architectural characters.

In a financial assessment prepared in 1969, covering the years since 1956, the total cost of land, construction and operations came to about $185 million; of this, some $148 million (80%) had been donated by individuals, foundations and corporations, and $37 million (20%) had come from city, state and federal sources.

Although the dramatic arts of television were initially studied for inclusion in Lincoln Center, television officials decided full incorporation of studios was unnecessary. Robert Sarnoff of RCA and William S. Paley of CBS, however, strongly advised from inception that all facilities should be designed to facilitate broadcasts. As a result, "Live from Lincoln Center" has become a standard offering on television stations across the United States, with regular broadcasts of opera, orchestra, and chamber performances.

Although the development was criticized at the outset as a patrician imposition in a residential neighborhood, efforts were taken from the start to make Lincoln Center accessible physically and economically to the citizens of the city, and it has indeed become a vital center for the arts both regionally and for the nation.

—LELAND M. ROTH

METROPOLITAN MUSEUM OF ART
New York City, New York, U.S.A.

1874-80: First wing constructed; **Architect:** Calvert Vaux (1824-1895). **1888:** Second wing constructed; **Architect:** Theodore Weston. **1895:** Entrance wing constructed; **Architects:** Richard Morris Hunt (1827-1895), Richard Howland Hunt, George B. Post (1837-1913). **1904-26:** North and south wings constructed; **Architects:** Charles McKim (1847-1909), William Mead (1846-1928), Stanford White (1853-1906). **1967:** New additions designed; **Architect:** Kevin Roche (b.1922).

Publications

"Calvert Vaux." *Harper's Weekly* 39 (1895): 1130.
FRANCIS, DENNIS STEADMAN: *Architects in Practice, New York City 1840-1900.* New York, 1980.
HOWE, WINIFRED E.: *A History of the Metropolitan Museum of Art.* New York, 1913.
ROTH, LELAND M.: *McKim, Mead and White, Architects.* New York, 1983.
SIGLE, JOHN DAVID: "Bibliography of the Life and Works of Calvert Vaux." *American Association of Archeological Bibliographers: Papers* 5 (1968): 69-106.

*

The architectural history of the Metropolitan Museum of Art reflects the changing character of how art museums generally have been understood in the United States since the 19th century.

Founded in 1870 for the primary purpose of encouraging popular instruction in the arts, the Metropolitan has undergone a transformation from being primarily an educational institution to one that exists mainly to conserve and collect original works of art. This programmatic evolution has played an important role in shaping the physical plant of the Metropolitan.

The museum's construction history spans virtually every decade of its 111-year existence, and among American museums, the Met's piecemeal evolution—its multiple "wings" divided into areas according to the established canons of modern art history—perhaps best illustrates the struggle of translating into a successful design an ambiguous institutional program. In addition to practical concerns—the need for adequate light and secure space, for example—the art museum in America carries with it associations of complex, often contradictory values, including education, history, scholarship, money, social class, as well as aesthetics. The buildings that make up the Metropolitan Museum stand therefore as a compendium of stylistic interpretations reflecting these issues, from the eclectic 19th-century revivalism of Calvert Vaux's original design, to the turn-of-the-century Beaux-Arts classicism of Richard Morris Hunt and McKim, Mead and White, to Kevin Roche's steel, stone and glass modernism of the last 25 years.

Modeled after the South Kensington Museum (now the Victoria and Albert), the Metropolitan was founded with the conviction that the instruction of art and an awareness of aesthetic issues, including "proper" taste, would enlighten the character and spirit of society, and perhaps even elevate its moral station as well. According to the original charter, the Met would establish "... a library of art, encourage and develop the study of the fine arts, and the application of arts to manufacture and practical life. ..." The museum would institutionalize the exaltation of aesthetic ideals.

In the new Metropolitan building, the form of that expression would be understood in both stylistic and practical terms. The aesthetic ideas of theorists like John Ruskin, William Morris and Augustus Pugin had not only helped to inspire the instructional imperative of museums, they also encouraged notions of a "correct" architecture, one not of classical rationality but of emotional resonance. Art and its pursuit clearly fell within the domain of the latter; thus, by the mid-19th century, Gothic forms were thought to be most appropriate for museums.

On the other hand, a contemporary building, the technologically advanced "greenhouse" structure of Joseph Paxton's Crystal Palace (1851), appealed to utilitarian considerations which style alone could not address. The sensational London building—after which a smaller copy was erected in New York City—met basic practical needs of light and flexible space for the display not only of art, but of industrial and trade commodities as well. A proper site for the new museum, where the uplifting and enlightening experiences of a visit would be enhanced, was also considered. Again like the South Kensington Museum in London, the new Metropolitan would be located within another important 19th-century manifestation of civic betterment, the urban park.

For their new building, therefore, the founders of the museum—progressive-thinking artists, writers and philanthropists such as William Cullen Bryant, John Jay and Frederic E. Church—turned, not surprisingly to an architect who was well versed in the Gothic idiom and who had helped establish the urban park movement in the United States. They chose Calvert Vaux, an English-trained designer active in local civic and philanthropic organizations, who had collaborated with Frederick Law Olmsted in the development of New York's "greensward" plan for a central park in Manhattan.

In the new Met building, Vaux incorporated a steel and

Metropolitan Museum of Art: New York City, 1874-80

glass roof, following the same utilitarian principles as Paxton's "greenhouse" scheme. The style and plan of Vaux's modest red-brick structure had been scaled down from a more ornate and ambitious multiwing scheme, surrounding a series of enclosed interior courts, to a single Ruskinian Gothic structure. Originally, he had envisioned a sequence of pavilions organized around a hierarchy of courts and corridors similar to the organizational layouts of 19th-century German museums. The simpler scheme meant that the more complex issue of plan and design as interpretative means for the understanding of art also remained basic. When it opened in 1880, the new museum would display a modest collection of plaster casts, architectural models, paintings and decorative arts arranged somewhat haphazardly in the large glass-covered central space. Thus the architecture acted more as a container for objects rather than as an organizational determinant for the historical, stylistic or other critical interpretation of art.

Soon after, in 1888, the completion of the museum's second wing, a red-brick Renaissance scheme of broad arches and stylized columns designed by Theodore Weston—an undistinguished architect for the New York City Parks Department—signaled the gradual move toward the kind of monumentality that is associated with the face of the Metropolitan Museum today, but it contributed little to a coherent presentation of the collections.

As entrepreneurs amassed private collections toward the end of the century, American museums expanded, becoming both repositories for these holdings and civic monuments memorializing the individual collectors. The instruction of art as a priority waned; its accumulation and the social nourishment of its sources increased. At about the same time, the Metropolitan

hired Richard Morris Hunt to prepare designs for the museum's expansion into its designated five-block park site. Since the Met's founding, Hunt had lobbied the city park commissioners and the museum board (of which he was an original member) to be the Metropolitan's sole architect, but because of political and professional rivalries, he had been denied. When the opportunity finally came in 1893, Hunt was considered the dean of American architects, an experienced practitioner whose private houses for New York's society elite, including the Vanderbilts, the Lenoxes and the Marquands (Henry Marquand was president of the Met at the time) won him recognition comparable to that of his civic and commercial projects. Indeed, his social standing as well as his professional stature contributed to the museum board's selection of Hunt as its new architect.

Hunt had worked with Olmsted and Daniel Burnham in designing the Main Administration Building and grounds for the 1893 World's Columbian Exposition in Chicago. Highly acclaimed, it inspired Hunt's new five-block undertaking for the redesign of the Met's master plan. Continuing Vaux's earlier court-surrounding schemes, Hunt produced a layout even more grandiose than at the Columbian exposition, enveloping the elaborate new museum with a neoclassical Beaux-Arts shell. But the plans were short-lived. Funds were available only for an entrance wing, and after completing just a handful of presentation drawings for this abbreviated exterior, Hunt died in 1895. His son, Richard Howland Hunt, together with George B. Post, an established Beaux-Arts architect (and one of the senior Hunt's prize pupils) completed the job. The resulting new Fifth Avenue entrance facade contrasted dramatically with the earlier Weston and Vaux wings and seemed deliberately to obliterate them from the street. The imposing Beaux-Arts scheme mimicked a Roman triumphal arch, and the palatial staircase inside the domed ''great hall'' ceremoniously heralded in giant letters the epiphany of PAINTINGS awaiting the visitor at the top. The museum now seemed to glorify the possessor of art, in much the same way palaces might announce the wealth of a monarch.

Ultimately, however, it would be McKim, Mead and White's somewhat more restrained classicism that characterized the flanking wings to the north and south of Hunt's entry pavilion and that at last completed the museum's face to the city. Built between 1904 and 1926, the wings provided the Met with the appearance—along Fifth Avenue at least—of architectural continuity. Inside, however, the galleries were a hodgepodge of contextual installations (a Roman atrium for antiquities), amassed individual collections (the Morgan bequest) and ''old-fashioned'' case displays of object types (such as porcelain and minor antiquities).

In the 1950s and 1960s, the Metropolitan built several ''service'' buildings, including a new library and an auditorium. But the selection in 1967 of Kevin Roche, John Dinkeloo and Associates as architects for the museum marked a concerted attempt by the trustees to again fulfill the larger architectural potential of the original five-block Central Park site. The new master plan set forth a program not only of architectural additions, but of collections refinement, ''logical traffic patterns'' and ''decentralization,'' the latter concept being an especially important guide in determining the new administrative and programmatic agenda. In fact, decentralization meant that the Metropolitan would become not an institution united by ''encouraging and developing the study of fine arts . . . and of advancing the general knowledge of kindred subjects,'' as its original

charter intended, but rather, it would further evolve into a series of different museums, each governed by curators at the mercy of a well-endowed board.

Given such a program of ''disunity,'' Roche's accomplishment in designing all seven of the museum's new wings during the past 24 years may be better appreciated. He has endowed them with an exterior coherence which, if nothing else, alerts the passerby in Central Park that within the building there exists a singularity of purpose, although what it might be, the stark glass, steel and stone modernism of its forms does not reveal. With the ''greenhouse'' construction of the new wings, Roche basically followed Paxton's Crystal Palace model from the previous century, hoping that the new ''gently sloping walls of glass set in a tubular steel skeleton would serve as a stylistic and spiritual bond with the Park.'' Although Roche has to a large extent accomplished this goal, the architecture could not—nor should it—overcome a more basic institutional disjunction. The concept of decentralization has left the museum without an interpretative framework. Today it remains a series of individual museums through which visitors must ''island hop'' (as a recent museum publication stated) from one culture to the next. Almost in spite of its architecture, these ''museums'' lack a coherent institutional vision for how to understand art or to relate it to contemporary culture.

Ironically, in the last major addition to the Metropolitan, the expanded European Sculpture and Decorative Arts galleries and garden court, Roche abandoned the modern geometric formalism of his earlier wings and instead reverted to a 19th-century type of historicism—an incongruous amalgam of styles perhaps fitting to an institution that boasts of its encyclopedic collections. Roche has designed a pyramidal steel and glass roof enclosing a narrow French garden court. The atrium is bounded on the south side by a new limestone facade resembling the Petit Trianon at Versailles; on the north side it incorporates the now-fossilized Renaissance Revival Weston facade. But without the accompanying moral resonance that distinguished the thinking of the Met founders and theoreticians like Pugin, Ruskin and their protégés, Roche's solution seems more an attempt to placate the contextual demands of an individual department's curatorial staff rather than a concerted effort at continuing the architectural vision of his earlier wings.

—PETER L. DONHAUSER

Metropolitan Museum of Art

PENNSYLVANIA STATION
New York City, New York, U.S.A.

1902-10: Constructed; **Architects:** Charles McKim (1847-1909), William Mead (1846-1928), Stanford White (1853-1906). **1964:** Demolished.

Publications

BURGESS, GEORGE H., and KENNEDY, MILES C.: *Centennial History of the Pennsylvania Railroad Company.* Philadelphia, 1949.

CONDIT, CARL W.: *The Port of New York: A History of the Rail and Terminal System from the Beginnings to Pennsylvania Station.* Chicago, 1980.

COUPER, WILLIAM: *A History of the Engineering, Construction, and Equipment of the Pennsylvania Railroad Company's New York Terminal and Approaches.* New York, 1912.

Pennsylvania Station: New York City, 1902-10

DIEHL, LORRAINE: *The Late, Great Pennsylvania Station.* New York, 1985.

FRAMPTON, KENNETH, and FUTAGAWA, YUKIO: *Modern Architecture: 1851-1919.* New York, 1983.

MUMFORD, LEWIS: "The Disappearance of Pennsylvania Station." *New Yorker* 34 (7 June 1958): 106-113.

RICHARDSON, WILLIAM S.: "The Architectural Motif of the Pennsylvania Station." *A History of the Engineering, Construction, and Equipment . . . .* New York, 1912: 77-78.

RICHARDSON, WILLIAM S.: "The Terminal—The Gate of the City." *Scribner's* 52 (October 1912): 401-416.

ROTH, LELAND M.: *McKim, Mead and White, Architects.* New York, 1983.

SCHOTTER, H. W.: *The Growth and Development of the Pennsylvania Railroad Company.* Philadelphia, 1927.

*

Pennsylvania Station, built in New York City in 1902-10, was the last, most complex and grandest building created by architects McKim, Mead and White. It was described by historian Carl Condit as the "greatest of all creations of the American building art." This spacious classical building was the epitome of railroad-station design, offering luxurious spatial release to the long-distance passenger arriving in New York. It was designed as an impressive portal to the city, but later was abused and demolished after little more than a half century of service. Its demolition prompted the rise of a vigorous historical preservation movement, in New York City and across the United States.

By the late 19th century, the Pennsylvania Railroad was the major competitor with the New York Central Railroad for the business of long-distance travel from the Northeast to Chicago and points west. Unfortunately for the Pennsylvania Railroad, the New York Central had easy access to Manhattan Island, since its rail lines were built on the east side of the Hudson and from the north crossed onto Manhattan Island via a short bridge over the East River. The Pennsylvania tracks, in contrast, approached New York City from the west, across New Jersey, and ended in Jersey City, where passengers were obliged to transfer to ferries over the Hudson to reach Manhattan. Prior to 1900 there was no practicable way to put rails over or under the broad expanse of the Hudson River.

The developments that made possible constructing a Pennsylvania Station on Manhattan Island occurred during the decade before the turn of the century. First came the perfection of horizontal-tunneling technology in 1890, permitting construction of a long tunnel through the rocky soil under the Hudson River, and second was the development of heavy electric traction engines in France during 1897-1900. These could provide smokeless power through the long underwater tunnel, pulling the long transcontinental trains into New York City.

The vast project was put under the direction of Samuel Rea, assistant to the president of the Pennsylvania Railroad. It was further subdivided into four components, three largely engineering and one combining engineering and architecture: the North River Division for the tunnel under the Hudson (under the direction of engineer Charles M. Jacobs), the East River Division for tunneling under the East River to Brooklyn (under the direction of engineer Alfred Noble), the Meadows Division for trackage and facilities in New Jersey (under the direction of engineer William H. Brown), and the Terminal Division for construction of the station itself (under the direction of engineer George W. Gibbs, who worked directly with the architects).

The elaborate scheme provided for two tracks, crossing the Hackensack Meadows from Jersey City; these would descend into a tunnel under the Hudson, expand to a fan of tracks under midtown Manhattan, continue as four tracks in tubes under the East River, and eventually ascend and connect with the Long Island Railroad at Long Island City. The rail lines below ground were to run in an unprecedented tunnel of more than 5.1 miles, of which 1.5 miles were under water.

In April 1902, Alexander J. Cassatt, president of the Pennsylvania Railroad, gave the commission for the new Pennsylvania Station to McKim, Mead and White, with Charles Follen McKim in charge. Cassatt had become acquainted with McKim during 1901-02, when the latter served on the Senate Park Commission charged with replanning Washington, D.C. McKim and his fellow committee member, Daniel H. Burnham, had successfully persuaded Cassatt to remove a late-19th-century railroad station that had been built across the Mall originally planned in 1791 by Pierre L'Enfant. As a result of the relocation, Burnham was asked by Cassatt to design a new Union Station north of the United States Capitol in Washington. Now McKim was given the task of planning an even far more complicated station in New York.

Not only were there major engineering difficulties involved with the New York station, but the entire track system and the trains on it were to be 45 feet below street level. Only the architectural character of the station building itself would announce the presence of the railroad, and thus it had to serve as a visual advertisement of the power and importance of the Pennsylvania Railroad.

The solution for the station, planned by McKim and his assistant, William S. Richardson (1873-1931), was brilliant though flawed in two respects, one of which ultimately doomed the building to destruction. The station filled two entire New York city blocks and measured 430 and 780 feet. Externally it was wrapped by a continuous classical peristyle of massive Tuscan Doric columns, rising nearly 44 feet with entablature. At the entrances and along the Seventh Avenue colonnade, the columns stood free, but for the long sections of wall, these changed to pilasters. The thick columns were powerful elements amid the surrounding four-story residence and business buildings. Just west of the center of the building rose the vaults of a huge waiting room shaped like a three-bay Roman bath and based, in fact, on the tepidarium of the Baths of Caracalla in Rome, but increased in size about 20 percent in all directions to measure 102 by 278 feet. The broad lunette windows and gables rose above the cornice of the station and could be seen from the street. Corridors, passageways and bridges over vehicular roadways led from all sides toward this central waiting room where stairs descended to the main pedestrian floor located 14 feet below the street.

The exterior of the station and the huge waiting room were classical in form and detail, making reference to the public architecture of the surrounding city. But immediately west of the waiting room was the concourse, an enclosed volume even broader, 208 by 315 feet, vaulted entirely in glass carried by open-web steel arches and columns. From this light-flooded room, stairs descended to the 20 tracks below. The concourse was designed, William Richardson wrote, as a transitional zone between the unadorned utilitarian modern machinery of the trains below and the formal architecture of the station above. The massive stone architecture of the station was, in fact, cladding on a steel frame whose slender columns penetrated through the maze of tracks below ground.

Coincidentally, in 1902-03, the New York Central Railroad

system embarked on building a new station to rival Pennsylvania Station, setting up a competition among four architectural firms. The general plan developed by the winning firm of Reed and Stem of St. Paul, Minnesota, improved on that of Pennsylvania Station by using ramps throughout for pedestrian circulation, but what eventually caused the demise of Penn Station was McKim's original insistence that it be a horizontal building. East of the waiting room were two great open air wells providing ventilation for the track area so far below the streets. Early in the design process, Pennsylvania railroad officials had suggested building a vertical office tower over this available space, but McKim refused, fearing this would compromise the design of the station.

Although architectural critic Lewis Mumford (once the antagonist of the Classical Revival) wrote glowingly in 1958 of McKim's planning clarity and spatial flow in Pennsylvania Station, railroad officials and the general public had been persuaded that such architectural excess was completely outmoded and without value. By 1962 a scheme was devised by the railroad to demolish the station, to retain about 15 feet above the concourse level for a more "efficient" station, and build over the two-block area a tall speculative office slab and a broad cylinder, housing a new Madison Square Garden. Had McKim been persuaded to add an office tower in 1910, perhaps the pressure for economic development of the site in the 1960s would have been diminished (as the Pan Am Building addition erected in 1963 atop Grand Central Station enabled it to survive).

Despite vigorous protests against demolition from many citizens, art critics and architects—in New York and across the country—Pennsylvania Station came down and was replaced by two buildings of no cultural or artistic merit whatever, however economically productive they were purported to be in the short term. The seemingly unthinkable loss of Pennsylvania Station galvanized New York citizens in support of legislation that made it possible for designated historic and architectural landmarks to be saved thereafter. The great loss of Pennsylvania Station has meant, at least, the ongoing preservation and restoration of Grand Central Station and the retention of numerous other buildings of merit in New York City and beyond.

—LELAND M. ROTH

ROCKEFELLER CENTER
New York City, New York, U.S.A.

1929-39: Construction; **Architects:** L. Andrew Reinhard (1891-1964), Henry Hofmeister (1891-1962), Harvey Wiley Corbett (1873-1954), Wallace K. Harrison (b. 1895), Raymond Hood (1881-1934), Jacques André Foulihoux (1879-1945). **1947:** Office building added. **1950:** Office building added. **1960:** Time Life Building erected. **1960s:** More office buildings included. **1973:** Three office buildings constructed.

Publications

BALFOUR, ALAN: *Rockefeller Center: Architecture as Theater.* New York, 1978.
FITCH, JAMES MARSTON, and WAITE, DIANA S.: *Grand Central Terminal and Rockefeller Center: A Historic-Critical Estimate of Their Significance.* Albany, New York, 1974.
FRAMPTON, KENNETH, and FUTAGAWA, YUKIO: *Modern Architecture: 1920-1945.* New York, 1983.

Rockefeller Center: New York City, 1929-39

HASKELL, DOUGLAS: "The Super Block as a Core: Unity and Harmony at Rockefeller Center." *Architectural Forum* (January-February 1966).

HOOD, RAYMOND M.: "The Design of the Rockefeller Center." *Architectural Forum* (January-June 1932).

JORDY, WILLIAM H.: "Rockefeller Center and Corporate Urbanism." In *American Buildings and Their Architects: The Impact of European Modernism in the Mid-Twentieth Century*. Garden City, New York, 1972.

KRINSKY, CAROL HERSELLE: *Rockefeller Center*. London and New York, 1978.

*

Rockefeller Center is a complex of office buildings and theaters, also containing shops, restaurants, and public spaces, located in central Manhattan between Fifth and Seventh avenues. It is so renowned as an essential element in New York's cityscape that some Americans were dismayed when in 1989, Japanese gained a majority financial interest in it.

It was erected in several stages, the first and most famous being that of 1929-39 between Fifth and Sixth avenues, 48th and 51st streets. In 1947 another office building was added at the north; in 1950 an office building at Fifth Avenue and 48th Street replaced a church formerly on the site and was incorporated into the center; in 1960 the center expanded across Sixth Avenue when the Time and Life Building was erected; in the early 1960s more new office buildings and a hotel on Sixth

Avenue were included in the center; and in 1973 three office buildings were completed on the three blocks south of the Time and Life Building, with which their plans were coordinated.

The initial group of office buildings, theaters and a central open space is the most significant part of Rockefeller Center, an opinion shared by the general public, architects and urban planners. Earlier office buildings had usually been built individually, unrelated to their neighbors, or if conceived as a group (e.g., those north of Grand Central Terminal), they were built on every inch of space that could be used within the city's zoning regulations (in force since 1916). Rockefeller Center's owner, John D. Rockefeller, Jr., its planners, the firm of Todd, Robertson and Todd, and its architects judiciously sacrificed some square footage in order to produce a building group of such high quality that its beauty and utility would commend it to renters even during the Depression, when it was built, and for a long time thereafter. They did so by staggering the building heights, paring down the building bulk or disguising it, leaving unprecedented open space in commercial premises, and adding such amenities as a connection to the subway system, an underground truck delivery area to reduce congestion on the streets, and plantings as well as works of art. The buildings are arranged with a balanced asymmetry that retains the formal appeal and dignity of classicism while allowing for visual variety, the introduction of small plazas, the presence of some sunlight, the relief offered by trees and flowers, and visual incidents to reduce monotonous long stretches of wall.

The center began before the stock market crash of 1929 as a project with high office buildings around a plaza that fronted upon a new Metropolitan Opera House. Rockefeller leased the nearly three-block site from Columbia University and engaged the Todd firm to manage the operation, its principal, John R. Todd, having successfully developed many office buildings in Manhattan. When, after the crash, certain owners of the Metropolitan Opera could no longer help to finance a new Opera House, the project became purely commercial. Radio interests, then expanding, were invited to replace the opera as major tenants and became the focus of the plan; for that reason, the RCA Building, the tallest of the center's structures, replaced the Opera House on the center block. In order to simplify access to it, and also to increase street frontage for profitable shops, a private street was added to the east of the RCA Building and its two neighboring blocks. Having already promised the city an open plaza, the owner and his associates understood the adverse criticism that would follow its elimination, so they allowed a smaller plaza to remain. This plaza, at the heart of the center and east of the RCA Building, was designed with statuary, a fountain and plantings to increase its conspicuousness, and it was later improved with the famous ice-skating rink (the inspiration for numerous others) and the colorful flags of the United Nations. The plaza is sunk one story below grade so as to provide a perimeter for shops (originally) and restaurants (since the mid-1930s), which zoning restrictions prohibited at grade level.

Buildings lower than the RCA surround the plaza on its other sides. They are office towers of several different heights on the north and south, and six-story twin buildings to the east along Fifth Avenue. (Two more such buildings were later erected on the north block, providing welcome human scale amidst Manhattan's high-rises.) The twins, separated by a promenade with fountain pools and planter beds, were kept low to allow visual access along the promenade to the plaza and the RCA Building, revealing the latter as the climax of architectural steps upward. This was important to the center's financial prospects, because while Fifth Avenue was highly prestigious, the area toward Sixth Avenue to the west was then blighted; therefore, everything had to be done to link the western part of the property to Fifth Avenue. The promenade slopes downward to entice people westward, and it is lined with shops to engage their attention as well as to make profitable use of the building frontage. Even the planters and fountains, placed in the center of the promenade, force visitors to move close to the shops. Only later were benches added to the planter beds; the original aim was to keep people moving westward into or around the plaza and beyond it. For this reason, among others, pedestrian circulation both above and below grade was comprehensively planned and is excellent.

Flanking the RCA Building were two theaters, one now replaced by an office building. Because fire code restrictions kept them at low height, they deferred to and enhanced the RCA Building. Theaters, being air-conditioned and artificially lit, do not need more street frontage than is required for attractive signs and entrances. Minimal space was allocated on Sixth Avenue for entrances and marquees, which were visible from the theater district farther west. The theater auditoriums could be tucked into much of the side-street space between the private street and Sixth Avenue. The surviving theater, Radio City Music Hall, is one of the world's largest, with a seating capacity of over 6,000 and excellent sight lines. A vast shell with a ceiling suggesting successive bursts of sun rays, the auditorium was designed with thoroughly contemporary machinery and the world's largest theater organ. The grand foyer with a sweeping staircase and balconies overlooking it has custom-designed cubist-inspired carpeting, sculptured reliefs and an enormous mural, while lounges on four levels incorporate specially designed wallpapers, rugs, statues and reliefs, paintings and furniture,

some created by prominent artists of the day, such as Stuart Davis, Isamu Noguchi and Donald Deskey, the interior designer who created much of the furniture and coordinated much of the Music Hall's visual art. (Some of it has been removed for its protection.)

Works of art, some of them coordinated thematically, were commissioned for every building at Rockefeller Center. Lee Lawrie, a modernistic academic sculptor, executed many reliefs and the statue of Atlas on the center's north block; Paul Manship designed the gilded "Prometheus" in the central plaza. The owners destroyed an unfinished fresco by Diego Rivera when they could not persuade him to remove Lenin's portrait and other provocative images. In the postwar phases of the center, Josef Albers and Haum Gabo were among the artists employed. This shift in taste from modified academicism to abstraction parallels the change in architectural style. From a conservative modernism with traditional elements in the planning (balanced forms, focus on a climactic monument at the center, traditional window designs, decoration at doors and cornices), the architects moved to the simplified prismatic shapes and technological explicitness of the postwar era.

Within the three associated firms of architects, those closest to the project were L. Andrew Reinhard, Henry Hofmeister, Harvey Wiley Corbett early and Wallace K. Harrison later, and Raymond Hood, assisted at times by Carl Landefeld, George Pauley and, for the Music Hall, Edward Durell Stone. Reinhard and Hofmeister were concerned primarily with planning for maximum economic return; they had previously worked with the Todd development firm. Corbett was a kind of overseer whose staff also was concerned with design, while Hood and his associates were called in for their ability to introduce more contemporaneity in style. The architects worked as a team, and no single firm is responsible for the design; overall planning and determination of space needs and profitability were done by the Todd firm. After Hood's death in 1934, the young Wallace Harrison assumed more responsibility. He, with his later partner Max Abramovitz, was responsible for the postwar buildings which were done without the Todds and Robertson.

The postwar buildings deserve less attention than their predecessors. One office tower terminates the private street at the north, providing a satisfying urban design element. The Time and Life Building was significant for 1960 in expressing the interior arrangement of columns and ducts on the exterior, and in allowing space for a small plaza and fountain that improved Sixth Avenue. The three buildings south of it have monotonously similar vertical stripes, but they include formal plazas along Sixth Avenue, the central two set back to add some variety to the streetscape; zoning requirements also mandated small plazas at their western ends, which are attractively furnished. All the buildings, of all phases, are admirably maintained.

Much of the 1930s part of Rockefeller Center has been designated as a New York City landmark, along with much of the Music Hall's interior and the RCA Building's lobby. Alterations to areas not designated do not vitiate the whole. The center merits designation for the low-rise and open-space relief that it offers in a crowded city, its well-ordered plan and formality countering the urban clamor, and its importance as a model for enlightened commercial developments. The RCA Building (now renamed GE) continues to thrust gracefully into the sky; its 65th-story Rainbow Room, little changed from 1934, is among the world's most glamorous restaurants, and its underground shopping streets, leading to the subway, inspired others elsewhere. While not formally avant-garde, Rockefeller Center nonetheless illustrates the eternal Vitruvian principles of utility, soundness and delight.

—CAROL HERSELLE KRINSKY

ST. JOHN THE DIVINE
New York City, New York, U.S.A.

1892-1911: Construction of the choir and four arches; **Architects:** George L. Heins (1860-1907) and Christopher Grant LaFarge (1862-1938), with Gustavino the Younger. **1919-41:** Construction continued; **Architect:** Ralph Adams Cram (1863-1942). **1979:** Construction of transepts, west facade towers, and choir roof begun.

Publications

CRAM, RALPH ADAMS: *Church Building*. 3rd ed. Boston, 1924.
HALL, EDWARD H. (ed.): *A Guide to the Cathedral of St. John the Divine in the City of New York*. New York, 1965.
HAMLIN, A. D. F.: *A Study of the Designs for the Cathedral of St. John the Divine*. New York, 1924.
LA FARGE, CHRISTOPHER GRANT: "The Cathedral of Saint John the Divine." *Scribner's Magazine* 41 (1907): 385-401.
MUCHIGROSSO, ROBERT: *American Gothic: The Mind and Art of Ralph Adams Cram*. Washington, D.C., 1980.
NORTH, ARTHUR TAPPAN: *Ralph Adams Cram*. 1931.
TUCCI, DOUGLASS SHAND: *Ralph Adams Cram, American Medievalist*. Boston, 1975.
TUCCI, DOUGLASS SHAND: *Treasures: A Guide to Stained Glass and Architectural Sculpture at the Cathedral Church of St. John the Divine in New York*. New York, 1976.
WICKERSHAM, GEORGE W., II: *The Cathedral Church of St. John the Divine*. New York, 1977.

The idea of building an Episcopal cathedral in New York City was first raised in 1828, but it was not until 1873 that a charter granting its erection was obtained. A tree-lined site of about 13 acres on the height above Morningside Avenue at 111th Street was selected in 1887. The following year a competition was held for the design of the cathedral to be consecrated to Saint John the Divine. George L. Heins and C. Grant LaFarge won the commission with a design combining Richardsonian Romanesque with Byzantine motifs. The design was based on a Latin-cross basilican plan 520 feet long, and called for a conical spire at the crossing of the apse and aisled nave.

The cornerstone was laid on Saint John's Day (December 27) of 1892, and construction began immediately afterward. The seven chapels radiating from the eastern end of the planned apse were built first. The chapels were designed specifically to accommodate the different ethnic groups of the city's immigrant population, and were appropriately called "The Chapels of Tongues." In 1897 the first on-site services were held in the crypt basement. By 1911, the choir and the four gigantic arches supporting the dome over the crossing were completed. The choir had eight polished granite gray columns, 55 feet in height, with white marble capitals. Polished red jasper covered the base of the ambulatory wall. The choir was furnished with a white marble throne, and white stone reredos. The stained-glass windows, designed by James Powell and Sons of London, depicted narrative scenes from the Revelation of Saint John the Divine. The inner shell of the crossing dome, which was 162 feet high at the apex, was unique for being clad with laminated tile made to cantilever. The dome's red tile and its mosaic work depicting Christ, all designed by Gustavino the Younger, further intensified the polychrome effect of the interior.

Following disagreements between LaFarge and the bishop,

the architect Ralph Adams Cram was selected to continue construction in 1916. Cram had extensive experience with church architecture, having done such important buildings as the Church of St. Thomas in New York City, the Chapel at West Point, the Princeton Chapel in New Jersey, and the Fourth Presbyterian Church in Chicago. Cram's most important contribution was to change St. John's style from Romanesque to Gothic, to give it greater elegance, grace and verticality. The Gothic also provided more space for glass, another important factor to Cram.

Construction was resumed in 1919 with the widening of the nave, from three to five aisles. Two years later, work on the northern transept was begun. Cram also lengthened the long arm of the Latin cross from 520 to 601 feet, heightened the piers and installed a sexpartite vault system. The semidome was removed, as well as the vaulting in the apse and choir. These were replaced by an eight-ribbed, seven-portion Gothic vault over the apse, and three quadripartite vaults over the choir. The clerestory windows of the choir are lit by artificial lighting. Cram planned a change in the line of the roof over the choir, to give it a loftier effect. However, World War II interrupted construction, and the roofline is still low, as LaFarge designed it.

The most vexing construction problem involved in the change from LaFarge's Romanesque to Cram's Gothic concerned the creation of a tower or "lantern" over the crossing. After many preliminary designs, the interior crossing square was altered to accommodate a lofty lantern tower, rising to a height of 400 feet, and recessed or tapered back from its base.

In 1931 an ornate altar with a wooden canopy was installed in the apse, and organs were placed on each side of the sanctuary. By the end of 1941 Cram's reconstructions were concluded with the demolition of the old temporary wall separating the nave from the crossing. Architects have humorously referred to that momentous event as "the most constructive destruction in the history of New York."

A third building campaign was initiated in 1972. Actual construction, resumed in 1979, was preceded by the consecration of a roofed-over stoneyard on the northwest side of the building, which functions as a workshop where local stoneworkers receive instruction in the craft of stone-building and sculpture from English master masons. These artisans are now working on the incomplete transepts, the west facade towers, the crossing and the choir roof besides the sculptural ornamentation.

Ultimately, the plan is to complete St. John's by the year 2050. Until then, as one art critic wrote, "It is a mess, but a tremendously powerful one!" St. John's is rightly known as the last cathedral of the Western world.

—GEORGE M. COHEN

SEAGRAM BUILDING
New York City, New York, U.S.A.

1954-58. Architects: Ludwig Mies van der Rohe (1886-1969) and Philip Johnson (born 1906).

Publications

DREXLER, ARTHUR: "Seagram Building." *Architectural Record* 124 (July 1958): 139-147.
JORDY, WILLIAM H.: "The Laconic Splendor of the Metal

Nave, St. John the Divine: New York City, 1892-

Seagram Building: New York City, 1954-58

Frame: Ludwig Mies van der Rohe's 860 Lake Shore Apartments and His Seagram Building." *American Buildings and Their Architects: The Impact of European Modernism in the Mid-Twentieth Century*. Garden City, New York, 1972.

JORDY, WILLIAM H.: "Seagram Assessed." *Architectural Review* (December 1958).

SCHULZE, FRANZ: *Mies van der Rohe: A Critical Biography*. Chicago and London, 1985.

SPAETH, DAVID: *Mies van der Rohe*. New York and London, 1985.

WINTER, JOHN: *Modern Buildings*. London, 1969.

*

Ludwig Mies van der Rohe's 38-story office tower, built to accommodate the administrative headquarters for the House of Seagram and prestige tenant space, possesses the dignity and majesty associated with traditional architectural symbols of princely power. It shares a Renaissance regard for scale and proportion. Set as a piece of sculpture on a podium, it draws upon classical awareness of placement. This steel-framed tower, clad in a meticulously detailed somber skin of tinted glass and bronze, was hailed as the epitome of Mies' credo of "less is more." It convinced a jaundiced public that "modern" did not have to mean flashy glitter and neon lights, and impacted upon the existing conceptions of what constituted a building and urban space. For decades it stood as the standard by which other corporate images were judged.

The Seagram Building's regal yet delicate image of discreet metal and glass broke with the traditional masonry-and-window facades of pre-World War II steel-framed high-rise structures. Along with the Lever Brothers tower located diagonally up the street, it became the form setter for office towers throughout the world. The amorphous metal and glass skin shouted modernity to its viewers. Gone were the heavy opaque stone overcoats of the prewar structures. The Seagram Building appeared to wear a transparent raincoat to shield it from the weather.

The sophisticated and carefully proportioned rectangular tower is set back 90 feet from the street line, endowing it with stature and dignity. The impact was particularly striking in relation to its building-line-hugging neighbors, which relentlessly followed a rigid metropolitan grid in order to maximize their volume and thus their rental income. Set on a private podium, its opulent materials created a restrained display of monetary power. This corporate image impressed a public accustomed to heavy-handed buildings slavishly following zoning setback rules, crowding out light and air at the sidewalk level. The Seagram Building rose majestically from a sunlit plaza textured with reflecting pools, fountains and an exotic imported variety of bronze-toned weeping beech trees.

Frustratingly, a closer examination of the building reveals flaws that come from subverting the honesty of individual parts of the structure in an attempt to create an illusion of consistency where none can or even should exist. One can sense how compromises and even outright fakery were resorted to in order to maintain the image of the basic intellectual concept. Given a richer, more ornate, palette, these "flaws" could have been accepted as necessary variations, lost in a texture of multiple variations. In Mies' pedantic striving for "purity," integrity was subverted and consistency forced.

Mies broke construction as well as aesthetic traditions with his detailing of the curtain wall. He brought the glass to within inches of the floor. The ensuing impact on someone in an exterior room can be as intimidating as standing at the edge of a cliff. The only exterior barrier, other than the floor-to-ceiling glass, is the thin vertical lines of the mullions, which are spaced almost five feet apart. Building Department officials threw their hands up in frustration; their codes demanded masonry separation between windows, from the top of one window to the bottom of the one above. Now there was no separation, no place to put the masonry, thus the letter of the law was unviolated. Today, more sophisticated codes require a horizontal projection to prevent flames from leaping out of a window into one above.

The need to provide a wind-bracing system for the tower presented the designers with a difficult dilemma. The tower plan, a pristine rectangle when seen from Park Avenue, also encompasses a stubby T at the rear. This was necessitated by the offset location of the building core, which contains the stairs, elevators, washrooms and mechanical shafts. The 87-foot, 7-inch depth of the main rectangular tower made it necessary to offset the location of the core to provide a meaningful amount of space between it and exterior windows along Park Avenue. The final size and location of the core severely limited the availability of space within it for placement of wind bracing. The solution was to extend the wind bracing, located within two of the core walls, beyond the core and into the exterior walls of the rear stub.

Placing walls of solid concrete wind bracing against the exterior raised the issue of how to express it. Windows cannot rationally be placed in front of an opaque wall. Rather than interrupt the relentless pattern of the glass and bronze curtain walls with a different texture, the architects carefully substituted a green marble slab for the tinted glass of the office areas. Located within the shadow-clothed building recesses along the side streets, this camouflaging is undetectable from Park Avenue, and thus the subterfuge remains unnoticed by most.

The location and expression of louvers required by the building's supply and exhaust air needs presented another problem that led to an inventive and curious solution. The building is too tall to have only one vertical zone for supply and exhaust ducts, and contains two zones. The louvers for the mechanical system serving the upper floors surround the building's top, and are clearly articulated. Louvers for the lower zone presented a far more difficult problem. Ultimately devised were two exterior boxes, one placed on each side of the building's core at the main lobby level. Located outside the enclosed lobby, they are still underneath the overhang of the building tower; their tops, which do not extend to the underside of the building soffit above, house the necessary louvers totally out of sight. These boxes act as air-intake shafts, conducting fresh air to the air-handling and treatment spaces in the cellar below. This is a clever solution that completely disguises the nature and location of the air-handling system, and is totally at odds with Mies' statements about purity and honesty. Exhaust air is spilled out at the rear of the building through louvers concealed in a deep recess along the property line.

The designer's desire for total control over the final image extended to every possible detail and concern. Venetian blinds, their blades fixed rigidly at a 45-degree angle, are provided at each window, and can be set only at fully raised, fully lowered, or mid-height positions. The pattern of the perimeter ceiling light fixtures is identical at every ceiling level. The building must appear organized and tidy to all who pass by, day and night. The leases prevent any tenant from modifying these items. No variation or individuality is tolerated.

By classically dividing the front elevation of the building into five framing bays, and then subdividing each framing bay into six mullion bays, the architects produced a 4-foot $7\frac{1}{2}$-inch module which in turn controlled the location of all partitions intersecting an outer wall. Most building materials, such as ceiling tile, are manufactured on one-foot multiples. Rather than adjust the Seagram Building's carefully determined overall dimensions, special fractional-size tiles were manufactured to conform to the unique module and thus not tarnish a forced image of relentless precision.

The much-acclaimed sunlit plaza, while providing a dramatic forecourt for the tower, fails to provide human spaces. In order to reach the plaza side walls, the only surface appropriable for sitting, people must tightrope-walk along a nine-inch-wide strip of pavement that separates the walls from the reflecting pools and planting areas. And, sadly, the handsome beech trees could not tolerate the contaminated air of the city, and died.

After the building was completed, the city fathers dealt a death blow to hopes of emulations of the gracious plaza size by ruling that the owners would be taxed on the basis of the full building bulk that could have been built under the zoning code, rather than on the actual structure which had so magnanimously allowed for the creation of a public oasis of light and air.

The Seagram Building's initial acclaim was due to the clean, unadorned lines of its massing and curtain-wall system, honesty of detail and gift of open space to the public, issues that closer scrutiny and the unfolding of events ultimately revealed were not all successfully resolved.

Perhaps the main reason the Seagram Building met with such instant initial acclaim was that it broke with stereotypes, and did so with dignity. The final judgment, given the test of time, is that while the building contains flaws and fakes, it is still beautiful and uplifting. The whole is indeed greater than the parts.

—DAVID GUISE

UNITED NATIONS HEADQUARTERS
New York City, New York, U.S.A.

1947-52. Design committee: Le Corbusier, Oscar Niemeyer, Howard Robertson. **Architects:** Wallace K. Harrison and Max Abramovitz.

Publications

LE CORBUSIER: *UN Headquarters*. New York, 1947.
OUD, J. J. P.: "United Nations Headquarters." *Royal Institute of British Architects Journal* (October 1948).
WHITE, NORVAL: *The Architecture Book*. New York, 1976.

*

The Permanent Headquarters of the United Nations comprises two adjacent buildings overlooking Manhattan's East River. The two buildings are the Secretariat, completed in 1950, and the General Assembly, finished two years later. The political importance of the buildings is obvious; architecturally, their interest lies in the first use of curtain walling on a grand scale and in a design process involving an international committee.

After the end of World War II, there was much debate over the location of the permanent headquarters of the United Nations. For a while, Flushing Meadow in Queens was favored, and buildings were designed for that site; however, by 1947 the East River site had been selected and an international team of architects assembled. The architects were Soilleux of Australia, Gaston Brunfaut of Belgium, Oscar Niemeyer of Brazil, Ernest Cormier of Canada, Liang Ssu-ch'eng of China, Le Corbusier

of France, Sven Markelius of Sweden, Wallace Harrison of the United States, Bassov of the Soviet Union, Robertson of the United Kingdom and Julio Vilamajó of Uruguay. Later they were joined by others. Le Corbusier, Niemeyer and Harrison were the key players in this oddly assorted team.

Harrison was a leading American commercial architect, the guiding light behind the Rockefeller Center development of the 1930s. Immensely competent and on the spot, he was the natural person to see the project through; but it was just as natural that he should quarrel with Le Corbusier, a mercurial genius who was everything that Harrison was not. Le Corbusier undoubtedly behaved badly, but equally undoubtedly, the concept of the building was his.

Le Corbusier had been denied a place in the 1927 competition for the League of Nations headquarters in Geneva, allegedly for using the wrong ink on the competition drawings. He was determined not to miss out this time. He did not wish to work with a group of architects for whom he had little respect, so he set up a design studio before the international team had been assembled. Le Corbusier produced his famous model 23A and pushed other designs aside. Model 23A had a tall Secretariat tower parallel to the river, and a low Assembly Building, but the junction of the two was awkward. Niemeyer, who a few years previously had helped to realize Le Corbusier's Ministry of Education Building in Rio de Janeiro, stepped in to improve his old mentor's design by pulling the Assembly Block away from the tower as a separate building. The resulting model, numbered 32, was the basis of the final scheme.

Le Corbusier respected Harrison's ability to get things done, and in fact it may have been his confidence in Harrison's patience and competence that gave him the freedom to behave in such an arrogant way. But Le Corbusier was not the sort of architect to fly back to Paris and leave Harrison to sort out the details. Le Corbusier fought hard for *brise-soleils* of the type he had designed in the 1930s for an unbuilt apartment tower in Algiers. But facts, and perhaps American building traditions, were too strong for him: snow and ice would have accumulated and dropped off projections to the danger of passersby, so the flush skin prevailed.

The ever-patient Harrison, concealing whatever rage he may have felt at Le Corbusier claiming all the credit, proceeded to build the building after the international team had departed. Problems abounded. The shape of the low block was a dumbbell derived from two auditoriums placed back to back; the brief was changed to just one great assembly room, but Harrison kept the exterior shape to avoid the trauma of bringing the international team back to New York. But the integrity of the building was hurt, and it was hurt again when a dome was added as a concession to conservative American opinion.

When the building was completed in 1952, there was much acrimony in architectural circles. Supporters of Le Corbusier argued that their hero had designed a great building, the culmination of all his thoughts on tall buildings, only to have it debased by lesser men. Supporters of Harrison were annoyed that Le Corbusier should claim so much of the credit when all he had done was a few sketches and a model, leaving Harrison to see the project through and to deal with all the problems. Other architects on the international team felt that they had been sidelined.

But while architects bickered, the world had acquired a new image. The 40-floor Secretariat was a great square box, with its main facades fully glazed. Suddenly every tall building in the world looked overcomplicated and old-fashioned. The setbacks and fancy tops of earlier skyscrapers were seen as redundant styling. The glazed facades were a triumph, as nothing of this scale had been attempted before; the glazing is held well

United Nations Headquarters: New York City, 1947-52

forward of the structure, and the black masonry behind the wire-glass spandrel panels gives the facades a reflectivity on a scale that was completely new. The internal core left the skin unencumbered, and the two short ends were faced in smooth marble. The service floors, as indicated on Le Corbusier's model 23A, give a welcome horizontal proportion to the tower.

The idealism of the United Nations shone as a hopeful beacon to humanity in the postwar world. The United Nations building, at the moment of its completion, gave architectural form to those ideals. But architecture moved on, as architecture will, and the completion of Skidmore, Owings and Merrill's Lever House on Park Avenue, with the glass skin apparently taken around all sides, suddenly made the United Nations slab look tentative and a bit hesitant. The United Nations had effectively ended the fantasy of the art deco skyscrapers, but it took Lever House to give a new kind of fantasy to the office tower.

—JOHN WINTER

WOOLWORTH BUILDING
New York City, New York, U.S.A.

1911-13: Construction; **Architect:** Cass Gilbert (1859-1934).
1980-81: Renovation.

Publications

AUS, G.: "Engineering Design of the Woolworth Building." *American Architect* 103:(26 March 1913): 157-70.

"Construction of the Woolworth Building." *Engineering Record* 66:4 (27 July 1912): 97-100.

"Elevator Safety in World's Highest Building." *Engineering Record* 70:10 (5 September 1914): 231-33.

"The Highest Office Building." *American Architect* 105:1986 (14 January 1914): 19-20.

HOLZMAN, S. F.: "Design of the Woolworth Building." *Engineering Record* 68:1 (5 July 1913): 22-24.

JONES, R.A.: "Mr. Woolworth's Tower: The Skyscraper as Popular Icon." *Journal of Popular Culture* 7:3 (Fall 1973): 408-24.

KIRKHAM, GUY: "Cass Gilbert, Master of Style." *Pencil Points* 15 (1934): 541-556.

KOEPER, F.H.: *The Gothic Skyscraper: A History of the Woolworth Building and Its Antecedents.* Ph.D. diss., Department of Architecture, Harvard University, 1969.

"The Method of Excavating the Cellar of the Woolworth Building in New York." *Engineering Record* 65:17 (27 April 1912): 472-73.

SCHUYLER, MONTGOMERY: "The Towers of Manhattan and Notes on the Woolworth Building." *Architectural Record* 33:2 (February 1913): 98-122.

SCHUYLER, MONTGOMERY: *The Woolworth Building.* New York, 1913.

"Six Hundred-Foot Drop Tests Woolworth Building Elevators." *Engineering Record* 70:10 (5 September 1914): 266-67.

"Steel Erection for the Woolworth Building." *Engineering Record* 65:26 (29 June 1912): 714-15.

"The Steel Substructure of the Woolworth Building in New York City." *Engineering Record* 65:7 (17 February 1912): 177-78.

"The Tallest Office Building. Erection of the Woolworth Building, New York." *Scientific American* 108:10 (8 March 1913): 224-25, 233.

"Water Supply System in the Fifty-Five Story Woolworth Building, New York." *Engineering Record* 68:2 (12 July 1913): 44-45.

"Wind Bracing in the Woolworth Building." *Engineering Record* 65:8 (24 February 1912): 220-221.

"The Woolworth Building Foundations." *Engineering Record* 64:9 (26 August 1911): 256-57.

"The Woolworth Building, New York City." *The Builder* 100:5 (May 1911): 644-46.

"The Woolworth Tower: A Technology Revisited, a Material Understood, a Landmark Restored." *Architectural Record* 169:11 (Mid-August 1981): 90-95.

The Woolworth Building, a justly celebrated skyscraper, was commissioned by the F. W. Woolworth Company in 1910 and erected at 230 Broadway, New York City, in 1911-13. The company was founded by Frank Winfield Woolworth in 1879 and flourished to an unparalleled degree, its annual sales passing $100 million by the time of World War I. By 1910 Woolworth was able to afford the best in office skyscrapers, and that is exactly what he got. He awarded the commission for architectural design to Cass Gilbert in 1910 on the basis of his admiration for the architect's West Street Building in New York, erected in 1905-07. The choice guaranteed that the program of design would include the talented structural engineer Gunvald Aus, who had been associated with Gilbert since 1900. A series of revisions were made in the preliminary plans during the fall of 1910, and the acquisition of a lot adjacent to the original property (233 Broadway) made possible the final and much-expanded plan of January 1911. The result comprised a main block facing Broadway with a height of 30 stories, a central tower 85 feet square rising an additional 25 stories for an overall height of 760 feet, and two wings at 30 stories extending to the west of the main volume. The distinct parts of the entire structure are clearly revealed in overall view of its external appearance.

The enclosing envelope of the building, a light largely transparent curtain wall of glass and terra-cotta, was given a strong vertical emphasis by continuous pilasters and recessed spandrels interrupted only by horizontal courses at the third and 25th stories and at the top of the main shaft that give the building a clear but restrained tripartite division. The elegant formal character of the elevations intensified the difficult technical problems posed by structural necessities and the process of construction. The average depth of bedrock at the site is 115 feet below grade level, and the water-saturated burden, combined with the extreme irregularity of the rock surface, dictated the use of pneumatic caissons to protect the workers during the tedious and dangerous process of excavation, leveling the rock, and emplacing the concrete footings and steel base plates of the columns.

The elaborate steel frame, rising 840 feet from the column base to the top of the tower, required special wind bracing to maintain rigidity for this lightly clad skyscraper, which was the highest building in the world at the time. The entire structure was treated as a vertical cantilever bending before the horizontal force of the wind, and the massive but precisely detailed steel frame carrying the glass and terra-cotta envelope with its attenuated verticality required continuous portal-arch bracing from grade level to the 28th floor. This engineering masterpiece represented the most extensive use of the technique in building construction. The vertical depth of the arch bracing and the

Woolworth Building: New York City, 1911-13

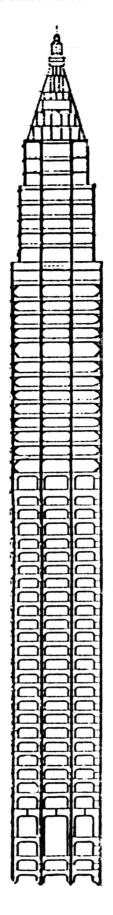

width of the massive steel columns fixed the width of the pilasters in the Broadway elevation of the Woolworth. A modification of the portal arches in the facade of the building was used in the column-and-girder frames that extended through the depth of the main block and the west wings, where technical solutions also controlled the dimensions of the terra-cotta pilasters and the associated window and spandrel proportions.

The formal treatment of the Woolworth elevations is marked predominantly by the vertical continuity of the pilasters running upward through the base block, the main shaft of the tower, and the diminished shaft above it, to the attenuated pyramidal roof that caps the whole complex. This verticality is intensified by the thin mullions rising between the pilasters. The horizontal emphasis provided by the demarcation of the base from the main block and the two setbacks (the form anticipating the New York Zoning Ordinance of 1916) complete the formal expression of the distribution of loads and what Gunvald Aus called the "lines of strength" in the steel frame. The dominant lines are those of the columns, the primary members of the frame, which gather within themselves all the wind and gravity loads and transmit them to the concrete footings that support the vertical elements.

The beauty of this highly kinetic pattern is enhanced by the Gothic ornamental detail that is an integral part of the terra-cotta envelope and helps to give the building its aerial delicacy. Perhaps the most impressive characteristic of the ornament is that the architect found it unnecessary to expand the scale of details at great height above the street, with the paradoxical consequence that the ornamental richness at high elevations carries the same aesthetic force when seen from the street as it does at the setback level. The architect's control of this visual complexity gives the building the powerful unity that strengthens all the formal details.

Montgomery Schuyler said that the tower is the "noblest offspring" of skeleton construction, and it clearly embodies the aesthetic and functional validity of Louis Sullivan's theory of the tall building's tripartite division. One may well argue that the union of technical, functional and formal design of the Woolworth has seldom been surpassed among office buildings. There was every reason to welcome the renovation of the building that was undertaken in 1980-81.

—CARL W. CONDIT

UNITY TEMPLE
Oak Park, Illinois, U.S.A.

1905-08: Constructed; **Architect:** Frank Lloyd Wright (1867-1959).

Publications

FRAMPTON, KENNETH, and FUTAGAWA, YUKIO: *Modern Architecture: 1851-1919.* New York, 1983.
HOFMANN, WERNER, and KULTERMANN, UDO: *Modern Architecture in Color.* New York, 1970.

*

Unity Temple was Frank Lloyd Wright's first major work. The project was commissioned in 1904 by the Building Committee of the Unity Church in Oak Park, Illinois, led by the Universalist

Unity Temple: Oak Park, Illinois, 1905-08

pastor Dr. Johonot. Wright rejected the architectural precedent of many New England churches and obtained approval for his concept of a temple to follow the motto "The Worship of God and the Service of Man." Wright conceived of the temple as a single room for worship, balanced by another room for secular activities. The idea of a cubical noble room coincided with Wright's concern with "the destruction of the box." It is likely that Wright set himself the problem of the "perfect box" and then proceeded to demolish it to demonstrate his thesis of organic architecture, which called for the natural flow of spaces to achieve continuity both inside and outside the building.

The design process of the building began with the consideration of the use of materials. The budget, $45,000 for a room to seat 400 worshippers, made it necessary for Wright to experiment with reinforced concrete, a relatively new material at the time. As concrete could be easily molded, it suited the idea of the cube as formwork would be identical to all sides. It followed that the roof would also be a slab, to be supported by four large pillars along the diagonals of the square plan instead of by the corners of the cube, thus reducing the span of the slab. The space between the pillars and the walls would be filled with tiered seating, which would bring the congregation closer to the lectern situated to one side of the cube.

The next consideration was the environment. Noise from Lake Street was to be excluded by the elimination of windows at low levels. Natural lighting was provided at the roof by a double glaze system, supported by cross beams giving the interior the necessary diffused daylight. Worshippers entered the church by means of an internal court not open to the street. To minimise disturbance, late arrivals were led through a depressed foyer and entered the church discreetly, almost imperceptibly,

around the sides of the lectern. Similarly, worshippers could ascend to the galleries behind the pillars, again out of sight of the main body of the congregation. To ensure comfort in the large space, heated air circulated through the hollowed out pillars.

The interior of the Unity Temple consists of painted exposed concrete with timber molds to provide continuity around the internal walls. The external walls are exposed aggregate. Wright also designed the light fittings, which could be lowered for repair.

To enhance the theme of unity, Wright's design encouraged the congregation to leave the church by moving towards the pastor at the lectern instead of by way of the more conventional rear door. This innovative plan for congregation circulation was, however, disregarded.

The secular section, known as Unity House, shares the common court. Again the "box" was expanded to be less "boxy," as the center portion housing the main activities was joined by two other cubes forming the Sunday School, and balconies were provided around these extensions to repeat the theme of the tiered seating of the Temple. The auxiliary rooms, a kitchen and a sewing room, were connected to one side. The elevations of Unity House are similar to those of Unity Temple, with four closets at the four corners to repeat the "cube" theme of the Unity Temple.

Wright's account of the design of Unity House indicated that it was a difficult problem; thirty-four studies were made before the final solution was adopted. The harmony between the two structures was achieved through similar materials and proportions. Nevertheless, the larger mass of Unity Temple gave it dominance over the smaller, more delicate Unity House.

Unity Temple

Characteristic of Wright's work, Unity Temple was conceived through a clear and logical design process. Beginning with the notion of integrity to embrace the requirements of good design, Wright abandoned the conventional style and look of the cube at its simplest form, modifying and reshaping that cube until it suited his purposes. Unity Temple demonstrated Wright's ethos of organic architecture through an uninhibited flow of spaces and a natural expression of materials. He succeeded in bringing the harmony of the whole through the complementary massing and external treatment of the Unity Temple and Unity House, and the consequential balance of the two internal spaces.

The Unity Temple introduced a bold new architectural style that considered basic geometry, available building technology, and environmental considerations. Wright developed this style further at the Larkin Building in Buffalo, New York, and demonstrated the potential of reinforced concrete as an integrated building material at the Kaufmann House ("Fallingwater"), Bear Run, Pennsylvania (1936), the Johnson & Sons Inc. Building, Racine, Wisconsin (1950), and the H. C. Price Tower, Bartlesville, Oklahoma (1953).

The Unity Temple and Unity House stand today as testimony to Wright's extraordinary ability to compose three-dimensional solids in a strong rectilinear form. Wright's experiment with the cube at Unity Temple pioneered architectural cubism much as Pablo Picasso pioneered the style in painting and sculpture.

—B. P. LIM

Unity Temple

MUMMERS THEATER
Oklahoma City, Oklahoma, U.S.A.

1966-71. Architect: John M. Johansen (b. 1916).

Publications

BLAKE, PETER: "The Mummers Theater." *Architectural Forum* 134 (March 1971): 30-37.
JOHANSEN, JOHN M.: "John M. Johansen Declares Himself." *Architectural Forum* 124 (January-February 1966): 64-67.
JOHANSEN, JOHN M.: "The Mummers Theater: A Fragment Not a Building." *Architectural Forum* 129 (May 1968).
JOHANSEN, JOHN M.: "New Town." *Architectural Forum* 127 (September 1967): 44-53.
KOERBLE, BARBARA: "A Mummer's Tale." *Cite: The Architecture and Design Review of Houston* 25 (Fall 1990): 14-17.
PASTIER, J.: "Something Else Altogether in Oklahoma City." *American Institute of Architects* 70 (August 1981): 40-46.
SUCKLE, ABBY (ed.): *By Their Own Design.* New York, 1980.

*

For many architects, John M. Johansen's Mummers Theater in Oklahoma City has been a compelling and influential source occupying a special niche in the history of 1960s design.

Mummers Theater: Oklahoma City, Oklahoma, 1966-71

Johansen's design, at once emblematic of the sixties and of his own willful personality, challenged accepted modernist practices with its confrontational assemblage of industrial components. It was a building that shocked the public and delighted many architects who applauded Johansen's foray into the exploitation of new materials and compositional methods. The Mummers Theater is an achievement all the more striking when contrasted with the classical modernity espoused during that period by Philip Johnson, Edward Durrell Stone, Minoru Yamasaki, and Skidmore, Owings and Merrill.

The genesis of this remarkably novel design resulted from the pairing of the talents of progressive Oklahoma City theater director Mack Scism with the support of a Ford Foundation challenge grant. Scism recruited stage designer David Hays, and the two men selected Johansen, who had previously designed Clowes Memorial Hall in Indianapolis (1963) and the Mechanic Theater in Baltimore (1966), as the architect of the Mummers. The Ford Foundation grant did much to permit the full flowering of this design, as Ford officials fully backed Johansen by threatening to withdraw financial support if the architectural integrity of the design was compromised by a skeptical board in Oklahoma City.

With the Mummers design Johansen broke with his previous neo-Brutalist work, such as the Mechanic Theater, and developed a more expressive approach in which light spanning elements and heavy structural parts were delineated through the use of contrasting materials and eye-popping primary colors. Johansen's local sources were grain elevators, quarrying lifts and brightly painted junked automobiles. As Johansen explained to Robert Hughes in an interview for *Time,* he was looking for "a kind of slang . . . I want my things to look brash and incisive and immediate. They should respond to what people actually need, the way slang and jargon respond to quick needs in communication."

Formally derived from the organization of electronic circuitry, the Mummers represented the culmination of his exploration of the prototype in the Goddard Library at Clark University in Worchester, Massachusetts (1968), and was the capstone of his career. The basic program components included a 600-seat thrust theater, a children's school and a 240-seat arena theater, which surrounded a central court and cooling tower. The original design concept was tailored to the experimental theater productions favored by Scism, and the thrust stage was planned by Hays as an island floating in space surrounded by an open moat.

Johansen's explanation of the seemingly eccentric assembly of the building's components appeared in his 1968 article "The Mummers Theater: a Fragment Not a Building," published in *Architectural Forum.* He wrote: "The design process, if the term can be used at all, is not one of composing but of rigging or assemblage. Each element, whether enclosed functional space, conveyor tube, or structural member, goes about its work directly and independently; sometimes with utter disregard for the other elements, or for occupants it is not required to accommodate at that place or moment. The way of dealing with functional elements then might be to 'position' them, i.e., to satisfy functional relationships; to 'prop' them, i.e., to support with structure; to 'connect' them, i.e., to provide circulation and distribution."

The stylistic evolution that led Johansen to this ground-breaking design is an interesting saga; Johansen's explorations in the 1960s certainly paralleled those of the metabolists, and he admired the work of Archigram. Johansen also drew from the writing of Marshall McLuhan, who, in *Understanding Media,* wrote of an analogy between electronic communication and the human central nervous system, an analogy that compelled Johansen to compare the people tubes of the Mummers to arteries in a body.

Johansen's trip to the Gulf of Mexico in the 1960s to study the prefabricated Grand Isle island mine might have further inspired him to exploit industrialized building techniques. Johansen's subsequent 1966 "Leapfrog City" proposal for interconnecting towers and bridges that appeared in his article "New Town" (*Architectural Forum,* September 1967) relates directly to the Mummers' ramped conveyor tubes for people.

The design quickly brought Johansen acclaim in the architectural press, and he subsequently received a 1972 AIA Honor Award for the Mummers. Yet Johansen's critical success was tempered by a lack of local acceptance, and the building was viewed as an affront to community sensibilities, even though it played a pivotal role in urban renewal plans for downtown Oklahoma City. The fate of the Mummers Theater provides a case study of what happens when a progressive design is interjected into a community that is completely unprepared and uncomprehending of the architect's intent. Local antagonism has dogged the theater since its opening, leading to calls for its demolition, and attempts to obscure the structure with vines and trees. As a performing facility, the Mummers has experienced a checkered history, following the political ouster of its

founding director within two years of its opening. Subsequently, closures of one resident theatrical company after another occurred; all were unable to support the overhead of operating the facility with the modest local appetite for theater. The innovative thrust stage was soon replaced by more conventional proscenium staging favored for amateur productions.

Concern about the building's current dilapidated condition has recently arisen, and nearly $2 million has been raised from state and local sources to refit and remodel the Mummers Theater. These plans do not include a resident theatrical company, but instead the building will become a multiuse facility, used primarily for performing arts but also for meetings and lectures. The renovation plans by Elliot and Associates, an Oklahoma City firm, will include functional improvements, but also propose a transformation of interior spaces to make the building more palatable to the general public. The question remains whether this radical and confrontational building can be made more mannerly, and whether a polite Mummers will still evoke the vanguard design of the experimental 1960s.

—BARBARA KOERBLE

NATIONAL FARMERS BANK
Owatonna, Minnesota, U.S.A.

1906-08. Architect: Louis H. Sullivan (1856-1924).

Publications

BENNETT, CARL K.: "A Bank Built for Farmers." *Craftsman* 15 (November 1908): 176-185.

DE WIT, WIM: "The Banks and the Image of Progressive Banking." In *Louis Sullivan: The Function of Ornament.* Chicago, St. Louis and New York, 1986.

FRAMPTON, KENNETH, and FUTAGAWA, YUKIO: *Modern Architecture: 1851-1919.* New York, 1983.

GEBHARD, DAVID: "Letter to the Editor." *Prairie School Review* 4 (Third Quarter 1967): 33-36.

MILLET, LOUIS J.: "The National Farmers' Bank of Owatonna, Minn." *Architectural Record* 24 (October 1908): 249-258.

MILLETT, LARRY: *The Curve of the Arch: The Story of Louis Sullivan's Owatonna Bank.* St. Paul, Minnesota, 1985.

SPRAGUE, PAUL E.: "The National Farmers' Bank, Owatonna, Minnesota." *Prairie School Review* 4 (Second Quarter 1967): 5-21.

WARN, ROBERT R.: "Part I: Bennett and Sullivan, Client and Creator." *Prairie School Review* 10 (Third Quarter 1973): 5-15.

WEINGARDEN, LAUREN S.: *Louis H. Sullivan: The Banks.* Cambridge, Massachusetts, 1987.

ZABEL, CRAIG: "The Prairie School Banks of Frank Lloyd Wright, Louis H. Sullivan, and Purcell and Elmslie." Ph. D. dissertation. University of Illinois, Urbana-Champaign, Illinois, 1984.

---

*

The National Farmers Bank at Owatonna, Minnesota, was the first of a series of small-town banks that Louis Sullivan sporadically built across the Midwest during the final, difficult years

National Farmers Bank: Owatonna, Minnesota, 1906-08

of his life. This one-time builder of skyscrapers during the heyday of the Chicago school concentrated his vision of a modern American architecture into these diminutive Prairie school monuments on ''Main Street'' during the first two decades of the 20th century. In some respects, this building type closely matched his interests. Such agricultural towns as Owatonna were closer to a life in tune with nature that he romantically idealized than was an urban giant such as Sullivan's own Chicago. Moreover, a small-town bank as a community financial center seemed to provide more of an opportunity for developing Sullivan's ideal of a democratic architecture than did speculative office skyscrapers.

Carl K. Bennett, vice-president of the National Farmers Bank and son of the bank's president, wanted something other than a routine classical temple for the bank building. He was drawn to Sullivan through his writings. The design that Sullivan and his chief draftsman, George G. Elmslie (who made major contributions to the design), developed combined a ''strongbox'' image of a monumental brick block, evocative of security, and an

inviting appearance denoting a community-minded, progressive financial institution. In his *Kindergarten Chats*, Sullivan had condemned the use of classical temple-like buildings for modern banks. His alterative at Owatonna was an astylar cubical block, with a single Richardsonian arch on each facade. Such a design combined the strength of his earlier burial vaults, such as the Getty Tomb in Chicago (1890), with the welcoming nature of his enormous entrance arches, as on the Transportation Building for the World's Columbian Exposition in Chicago (1893).

Sullivan was always sensitive to the scale of these prairie towns. Although his Owatonna bank monumentally claims its prominent corner site (across from the town's Central Park) with a single-story structure rising to the height of a three-story building, it stands above its neighbors in a subtle manner and nearly equals in height the corner building across the street (which then housed a rival bank). Adjoining the banking room is a Sullivan-and-Elmslie-designed annex; this two-story structure originally contained rental offices, a store and a print shop (as well as a printing plant and warehouse at the back). It maintains the scale of the prototypical two-story Italianate storefronts found along such Midwestern "Main Street" settings as Owatonna.

The basic composition of an arcuated "strongbox" does not depart sharply from some contemporary Beaux-Arts classical banks. However, Sullivan's bank exterior is radical in its unconventional proportions, exceptional sensitivity to materials and unique ornament. His block emphasizes the horizontal and seems to hug the ground on which it stands. In contrast to the cold stone facades of the typical Beaux-Arts bank, Sullivan and Elmslie crafted a rich tapestry of warm, natural colors on the facades with their use of a reddish-brown stone base supporting walls of rough and varicolored "Oriental" bricks embroidered with bands of colorful terra-cotta ornament and glass mosaic. It is a virtuoso display of Sullivan's distinctive organic ornament (almost all of the bank's ornament was designed by Elmslie under Sullivan's supervision). Botanical forms controlled by geometric patterns romantically embellish and balance the rational geometry of the overall building and its openings. Sullivan would later describe one of his banks as a "jewel box."

The general floor plan of the bank is the building's most conventional feature (and is where the client had the greatest influence). The axial arrangement of an entrance vestibule leading into a central public lobby and terminating with a tellers' screen and vault could be found in numerous banks across the country in the early 20th century. This ceremonial procession leading symbolically to the vault topped with that icon of banking, the clock, suggests a quasireligious aura for such "temples" to money as the Owatonna bank. The efficient arrangement of the bank's departments around the lobby emphasized public service. The president's office was prominently located at the front corner of the bank. Such amenities as a Farmers' Exchange and a special lounge for women were included, truly making this bank a community center.

While the lower section of this banking room emphasized business, with its sensible craftsman furniture and Roman brick partitions, the upper reaches of the banking room are decorated with a lyrical vision of nature brought indoors. A visual poem of colorful organic ornament dominates in one of the most extraordinary interior decorative displays in the United States. Glazed terra-cotta, polychromatic stencils, decorative plaster work, exuberant cast iron and opalescent glass windows combine into what Sullivan called a "color tone poem" and a "color symphony." It is evocative of springtime, of nature's renewal, complementing Sullivan's own mission to foster a new American architecture. Sullivan brought the sophisticated decorative program down to the realm of this bank's clientele by including large murals (by Oskar Gross) on the inner walls of grazing cows and hardworking farmers, the ultimate sources of this dairy community's wealth, whose financial well-being this bank protected and promoted.

By 1908, when this building was completed, Sullivan's personal and professional life was clearly in decline. Foreseeing only a dim future, Elmslie chose to leave Sullivan in 1909 (and in association with William G. Purcell began to build his own impressive series of banks, including several in southern Minnesota). Nonetheless, the Owatonna bank stood as an optimistic revelation of Sullivan's ideas about architecture and received extensive attention in periodicals, including a glowing critique by the client, Carl K. Bennett, in *The Craftsman*. This one-of-a-kind prairie bank drew many visitors, particularly other bankers interested in a new building that would be distinctive yet functional. Sullivan proceeded to build an extraordinary, but limited, series of small-town banks during the ensuing decade, although none of them is as harmonious as his first, the National Farmers Bank at Owatonna.

—CRAIG ZABEL

EASTERN PENITENTIARY
Philadelphia, Pennsylvania, U.S.A.

1823-29. **Architect:** John Haviland (1792-1852).

Publications

JOHNSTON, N. B.: "John Haviland, Jailor to the World." *Journal of the Society of Architectural Historians* 23 (May 1964).

*

Although well regarded among his contemporaries as an architect whose practice was devoted to the Greek Revival, John Haviland's reputation among historians has long rested on his achievement in the design of the Eastern Penitentiary. Before the commission for its design, his reputation had already been established by the publication of *The Builder's Assistant* and the design of the Cridland Villa (1818), the First Presbyterian Church (1820) and St. Andrew's Episcopal Church (1822). His interest in the commission extended beyond that of an architect eager to further his practice, however, for he was genuinely concerned about the reform of prisons. While the extent of his involvement in local efforts to improve the conditions in prisons has not been determined, in 1818 the legislature of the Commonwealth of Pennsylvania authorized the construction of a penitentiary in Pittsburgh. Haviland's scheme was rejected, but in 1821 the construction of the Eastern Penitentiary in Philadelphia was authorized and his design selected.

Attempts at the reform of prisons by the Quakers had yielded a system based upon the solitary confinement of a prisoner in a cell for the term of the sentence. To accommodate this system, Haviland devised a scheme based on a radial plan: from a rotunda radiated single-story cell blocks, each cell having its own yard for exercise. Because of its central position, the rotunda permitted easy observation of all corridors. Although credit for the scheme has usually been awarded to Haviland, less grand versions apparently had been adopted for prisons and asylums in Britain at least as early as the years of his apprenticeship in London. As remarkable as the plan was, even more notable was the manner in which this design differed from others by Haviland during that period.

His previous designs had been renditions of models from antiquity, some of which were faithfully archaeological in their imitation. Clearly the facade of the penitentiary was inspired by those of prisons in his native Britain and by the Gothic Revival. Stripped of nearly all ornament, it boasted turrets, crenellation, a distinct silhouette and even a portcullis. Windows in the formidable walls were narrow slits, reminiscent of arrow loops found in castles. Despite its lack of references to classicism in its details, the scheme was symmetrical. Innovative in plan and receptive to the influences of style in elevation, the design addressed the issues raised by reforms in penology.

Yet the Pennsylvania System was never popular in the United States, so Haviland's scheme was not widely adopted there. Soon after construction was under way, however, representatives of several states and foreign governments arrived to inspect the prison. Not only was the design preferred over the plan of the panopticon, but its popularity was soon widespread, due in part to its inclusion in two reports on prisons in the United States—that by William Crawford, published in 1834 in London, and that by F.-A. Demetz and A.-G. Blouet, published in 1837 in Paris. Charles Barry's plan for Pentonville Prison in London and E.-J. Gilbert's adoption of a radial scheme for the Prison de la Nouvelle Force demonstrated "the significant influence

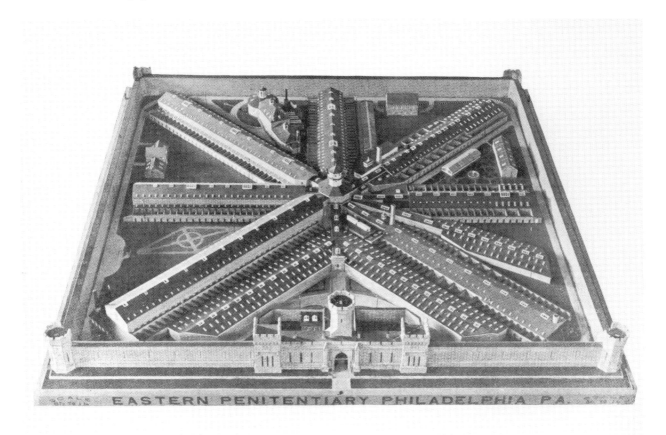

Eastern Penitentiary, bird's eye view: Philadelphia, Pennsylvania, 1823-29

abroad of the Eastern Penitentiary," as Henry-Russell Hitchcock noted. The radial plan inspired designs for prisons elsewhere on the Continent, including Spain, Belgium and Prussia. Among the most notable influences were those on prisons in Japan in the latter half of the 19th century, some of which adopted not only the plan but the style of the Gothic Revival as well.

The acclaim with which the scheme was greeted bore testimony to how successfully Haviland had provided ease of surveillance, some degree of comfort in the cells with a recognition of the importance of sanitation, illumination and ventilation, and, moreover, a style that was appropriate for penology in those decades.

—JED PORTER

MERCHANTS' EXCHANGE
Philadelphia, Pennsylvania, U.S.A.

1832-34: Construction; **Architect:** William Strickland (1788-1854).

Publications

GILCHRIST, AGNES ADDISON: *William Strickland, Architect and Engineer, 1788-1854*. Philadelphia, 1950.

GILLIAMS, E. L.: "A Pioneer American Architect—William Strickland." *Architectural Record* 23 (February 1908): 133.
HAMLIN, TALBOT: *Greek Revival Architecture in America*. New York, 1944.

*

William Strickland's Merchants' Exchange in Philadelphia is one of the most original and impressive Greek Revival buildings in the United States. The exchange was commissioned by the city's merchants, who had outgrown the relative informality of meeting at local coffeehouses by the second quarter of the 19th century. While the site chosen for the building was strategically located in the heart of the city's old financial center, its triangular shape posed special problems for the architect. The program of the building was also relatively complex. Strickland, an ardent practitioner of the Greek Revival style, was well aware of the style's limitations in the design of modern building types, but with his characteristic versatility, he produced an elegant marble design in which classical details were freely adapted to the building's unusual form and purpose.

The plot at Third and Walnut streets is slightly elevated and is diagonally sliced by Dock Street, one of very few streets to disrupt William Penn's 17th-century gridiron plan. Realizing that this would ensure a generous, angled view of his building, Strickland turned what seemed to be a disadvantage into an asset. He set the main rectangular block of the exchange to the

Merchants' Exchange: Philadelphia, Pennsylvania, 1832-34

rear of the site, and, at the center of the main facade, he placed a semicircular central bay that nearly fills the acute angle at the eastern corner.

Strickland surrounded the curved main facade with a two-story Corinthian colonnade that recalls the portico of the former Bank of the United States (Samuel Blodget, Jr., 1795-97) on Third Street. The main floor of the exchange was raised on a high basement, reached by curving flights of stairs (now restored) that flank the main portico. Strickland terminated the design with a cylindrical lantern, modeled after the Choragic Monument of Lysicrates in Athens, which echoes at reduced scale the portico beneath it. Strickland would have known this and other ancient Greek monuments through James Stuart and Nicholas Revett's *Antiquities of Athens,* his favorite sourcebook. Although less prominently situated, the rear facade, facing Third Street, is articulated by a pedimented Corinthian portico set *in antis,* which again subtly recalls the main facade of Blodget's bank across the street. Massive Tuscan columns frame the rear entrance at the basement level. The sides of the building are distinguished by tripartite windows on the upper levels, and

directly below by doors flanked by thin columns with lotus-leaf capitals. This last motif was copied after capitals on the Tower of the Winds in Athens.

Strickland's interiors were as elaborate as the exterior, although the original configuration of the rooms has been lost through renovations over the years. Originally, there was a post office on the ground level and rooms for the exchange on the upper levels. A library was located behind the curving portico, its ceiling rising to the great height of 35 feet. The exchange room on the Third Street side of the building at one time had mosaic floors and frescoed ceilings. Marble was used extensively in the building's interior decoration. Strickland engaged the finest artisans and craftsmen in Philadelphia to carry out his design.

At the time of the exchange's completion, Philadelphia was already in decline as a financial center, having been eclipsed gradually by New York City after the opening of the Erie Canal in 1825. The merchants' exchange was dissolved after the Civil War, and the building underwent a series of renovations and adaptations. The building subsequently housed the city's corn

Merchants' Exchange, dome detail

exchange (1866) and the stock exchange (1875), and for the second quarter of the 20th century, it was used as the city's produce exchange. In 1952 the National Park Service restored the exterior of the building, which was to be used as its offices.

The building is best viewed from Walnut Street, where the full scenographic sweep of the curving main facade can be appreciated, and the portico of Blodget's bank can be glimpsed at the head of Dock Street to the right. A monument to Philadelphia's financial and cultural aspirations, the refined Greek classicism of the Merchants' Exchange helped secure the city's reputation as the "Athens of America."

—ROBERT WOJTOWICZ

PHILADELPHIA SAVING FUND SOCIETY BUILDING
Philadelphia, Pennsylvania, U.S.A.

1929-32. **Architects:** George Howe (1886-1955) and William Lescaze (1896-1969).

Publications

"Another Look at PSFS." *Architectural Forum* (June 1964).
BROOKS, H. ALLEN: "PSFS: A Source for Its Design." *Journal of the Society of Architectural Historians* 27 (December 1968).

FRAMPTON, KENNETH, and FUTAGAWA, YUKIO: *Modern Architecture: 1920-1945*. New York, 1983.
HITCHCOCK, HENRY-RUSSELL: "Howe and Lescaze." In *Modern Architecture International*. Exhibition catalog. New York, 1932.
"Howe and Lescaze." *Architecture d'aujourd'hui* 4 (special issue, November/December 1933).
JORDY, WILLIAM H.: "Philadelphia Saving Fund Society Building: Its Development and Its Significance in Modern Architecture." *Journal of the Society of Architectural Historians* 21 (May 1962): 47-83.
JORDY, WILLIAM H.: "The American Acceptance of the International Style: George Howe and William Lescaze's Philadelphia Saving Fund Society Building." In *American Buildings and Their Architects: The Impact of European Modernism in the Mid-Twentieth Century*. Garden City, New York, 1972.
STERN, ROBERT A. M.: "Philadelphia Saving Fund Society Building: Beaux-Arts Theory and Rational Expressionism." *Journal of the Society of Architectural Historians* 21 (May 1962): 84-102.
WRIGHT, HENRY: "Philadelphia Saving Fund Society Building." *Architectural Forum* (May 1964).

*

The Philadelphia Saving Fund Society Building is not merely the best example of a high-rise building of the International Style in the United States, it is one of the best skyscraper designs of any period. There has always been a controversy between historians concerning the designer of PSFS. Was it George Howe, who made early drawings that William Lescaze claimed never to have seen, or was it designed from conception to completion by Lescaze in the New York office of the partnership?

Howe was originally approached by the bank for a design at Market and Twelfth streets in Philadelphia in 1926. He produced a design in the Beaux-Arts idiom based upon entries in the *Chicago Tribune* Tower competition of 1922. Howe had trained at the École des Beaux-Arts in Paris, but by 1929 he was convinced that modern architecture was the direction in which he wished to continue architectural practice, and thus he needed a partner conversant in the modern idiom. He met Lescaze as early as June 1928, proposed a partnership during January 1929, and signed articles of agreement on 1 May 1929. Howe was to be responsible for administrative duties, while Lescaze was to be the architectural designer within the partnership.

During March of 1929, Howe had produced four schemes for the new bank building, including one dated March 20 which was regulated by existing streets, adjacent structures and building lines. This drawing was not so different from the massing of the 32-story structure as finally built. James Willcox, the bank president, had a strong impact upon the design through his meetings over a three-and-one-half-year period with Howe. Willcox wanted assurances that the bank would not look like a warehouse structure and asked Howe to give his word as a gentleman that the final result would be a respectable building, and not an advertising novelty for the glorification of its architects.

Most historians who have written about the model of the building agree that it had the appearance of a layered cake with its horizontal emphasis of windows and spandrels between. Robert Stern, the biographer of Howe, stated that it "would have been the biggest marshmallow sandwich of all time." After

Philadelphia Saving Fund Society Building: Philadelphia, Pennsylvania, 1929-32

inspecting the model, Willcox demanded a vertical emphasis to the structure on the exterior of the office tower, thus making a major design decision. PSFS would have been more mainstream International Style had the original horizontal layering been retained and the structure minimized as a design element, thereby bringing the design into closer conformity with attributes of the International Style as defined by Henry-Russell Hitchcock and Philip Johnson in their 1932 Museum of Modern Art exhibition and publication, *The International Style.*

Sources for the design have been attributed to a large number of buildings. Knud Lönberg-Holm's design (not entered, but widely published) for the Chicago Tribune Tower competition has certain similarities. Lescaze wrote to the Bauhaus in Germany for publications by J. J. P. Oud and Walter Gropius which illustrated Lönberg-Holm's design. Lescaze also made annual trips to Europe, during which time he visited the latest buildings by advanced designers in Holland, Germany and France. E. Otto Osswald's Stuttgart Tageblatt-Turm Building, illustrated in the *Architectural Record* during February 1929, has cantilevering similar to the PSFS tower, and designs of office towers by Richard Neutra for his proposed Rush City Reformed of 1926 resemble the PSFS design.

It was Lescaze's idea, however, to incorporate stores at ground level in a building located in the shopping and transportation hub of Market and Twelfth. On the second level, accessed by elevators and stairs, is the dominant banking hall expressed on the exterior by a huge aluminum window curving around the corner and set in a wall plane of polished charcoal-colored granite. Internally, tellers' counters were of Belgian black polished marble, piers were alternately dark gray and white marble, floors were gray rubber, and furniture was chrome, upholstered in dark blue leather. Eighteen-foot-deep steel trusses spanned 63 feet across the banking floor to support the tower above, and in turn are supported on steel columns going down to caisson foundations below basement level. Immediately above the banking hall were three floors for bank offices, above which was rentable space slightly cantilevered out over Market Street. There the external material was buff-colored limestone, the same material used for the columns. Brick was used below sill level for the spandrels on all floors of the tower.

The name of the building spelled out would have been impossible to read at any distance. Lescaze therefore made a mock-up of the initials PSFS, 26 feet high, and positioned them on top of the building. The letters could be seen by the bank directors more than a mile away. A penthouse suite for bank executives, plus an observatory (now a television station), topped the building, and letters of white porcelain enamel and red neon strips identified it as the PSFS building.

On plan the office tower is the downstroke of the T, and the service core at the rear of the site is in the cross bar. This core contains the entrance and elevators to the tower, the fire stairs, toilets and duct work. Heat and humidity during the summer of 1931 convinced the building committee to incorporate air-conditioning into the whole building. This was an innovative feature, first used in a high-rise building in San Antonio in 1928. The whole of the 20th floor was used to house the air-conditioning machinery, with other spaces on the roof and in the trusses over the banking floor commandeered for additional equipment.

Lescaze with his able assistants, including Walter Baermann and Alfred Clauss, detailed the whole building. This included partitions, doors, lighting fixtures, desks, hardware, radiators, grills, baffles, safety deposit boxes and rooms, tubular furniture, clocks, and even the salt and pepper shakers for the executive dining room.

—LAWRENCE WODEHOUSE

RICHARDS MEDICAL RESEARCH BUILDING
Philadelphia, Pennsylvania, U.S.A.

1957-64. Architect: Louis I. Kahn (1901-74).

Publications

HOFMANN, WERNER, and KULTERMANN, UDO: *Modern Architecture in Color.* New York, 1970.

JORDY, WILLIAM H.: "Medical Research Building for Pennsylvania University." *Architectural Review* (February 1961): 99-106.

JORDY, WILLIAM H.: "What the Building 'Wants to Be': Louis I. Kahn's Richards Medical Research Building at the University of Pennsylvania." In *American Buildings and Their Architects: The Impact of European Modernism in the Mid-Twentieth Century.* Garden City, New York, 1972.

MAKI, FUMIHIKO: "Louis I. Kahn—Richards Medical Research Building, Pennsylvania." *Global Architecture* 5 (1971).

RONNER, HEINZ; JHAVERI, SHARAD; and VASELLA, ALESSANDRO: *Louis I. Kahn: The Complete Works, 1935-1974.* Boulder, Colorado, 1977.

*

The Richards Medical Research Building is one of the rare projects by any architect that can truly be regarded as a turning point in the history and practice of architecture. As a turning point it has one foot planted in the contemporary standards by which buildings of its own time were designed and evaluated. Yet, in many ways from its very inception it had another foot in the air, ready to be planted, a foot that could be perceived then and can still be perceived today as the next step, a change in direction, a step forward.

Aesthetically, it confirmed the contemporary belief that beauty came from self-expression on the part of the architect and from the artful translation of function to form: program to design. The self-expressive aspects are immediately perceivable in the massing. Functionally, the complex reinvents a form language for a laboratory as a place of intellectual work as well as a research factory.

Yet, as Vincent Scully immediately perceived, it goes well beyond these two criteria for beauty. Its innermost beauty is purely formal without any reference to the specifics of Louis Kahn or of the brief, the program—it is *spirituelle,* it is transcendent, it is subtle and esoteric, it is neither about the imagination of the architect nor the needs of science, research or the user, but it is about form, it is about architecture.

Functionally, the turning point can be identified as the reaction to users' complaints about the open floor plan, and the resultant additional heating and air-circulation problems encountered when partitions were put in at the insistence of users. Is the building faulty because users modified or rather unilaterally abrogated the open floor plan? The dilemma for the critic can be summed up in the eloquent words of a user in a letter written to the sociologist-architectural critic Robert Gutman in 1971: "I suspect that nowhere in the history of 20th century architecture could one find an edifice which, over the same interval of time, has: i) Enhanced the stature of its creator in the

Richards Medical Research Building: Philadelphia, Pennsylvania, 1957-64

eyes of his profession (students of architecture swarm around this building like Beatle Fans at a rock festival) and ii) Seriously impeded the progress of medical science, because of its gross inadequacies from the viewpoint of those who have to use it.''

While Kahn himself regarded the complaints about the malfunctioning of Richards with pain and seriousness, at least partially accepting the contemporary judgment that users' needs are definers of the success of a building, the architectural profession and architectural critics embrace it as a success, one suspects, in part as a response to what they perceive to be the ill-informed tyranny of the user. This is especially so because the ''failure'' does not come either from Kahn's ''egotistic self-expression'' or from ''hyperfunctionalism'' but rather from what he perceived to be, and what other architects continue to perceive to be formally *good* architecture, or formal expressions of the users' desires rather than their needs.

Architects were already used to complaints about buildings that were impractical because of being beautiful at the expense of ''function'' or because of following a social program at the expense of contemporary taste. One suspects that architects rallied around Richards because the building accepts and shows familiarity with these criteria, but it also goes a step beyond them: ''The building *wants* to have an open plan; you should appreciate the conceptual and formal brilliance of an open plan.'' After Richards modern architecture could no longer address needs alone.

Psychologically, the building goes beyond either mechanical or traditionally ''humanistic'' conceptions of the welfare of the users, or indeed of the ''nature'' of the users themselves. Kahn's distinction between needs and desires recognizes the imperative to be mechanically efficient as well as to provide latitude for the comfort and the self-expressive acts of users: but in talking of and designing around ''desire'' he goes beyond these criteria.

Desires, after all, refer to pure ''oughts,'' not to ''is''-es or to the egotistic wish to be special and different. Kahn dared to utter a verbal and an architectural ''ought'' when that word was thought to have been superseded by the ''is'' or by the idiosyncratic. He attempted a monument to the universality neither of need nor of idiosyncrasy but of desire—at a time when such ideas were thought to be totally out of fashion, but, paradoxically, architects were at least ready to see and hear such anathema.

A first step in a new direction is also a last step in the old direction—and it is fair to ask what the change in direction in architecture that Richards signaled left behind. Many still mourn the more socially conscious and technically driven or the more humanistic architecture that preceded the postmodern era. These people fairly ask whether the change in direction signaled by Richards was not in fact a forward, but rather a ''to the rear, march!''

—JOSEPH B. JUHASZ

UNIVERSITY OF PENNSYLVANIA LIBRARY
Philadelphia, Pennsylvania, U.S.A.

1887-91: Construction; **Architects:** Frank Furness (1839-1912), Allen Evans. **1986-91:** Alterations; **Architects:** Robert Venturi (b. 1925), John Rauch (b. 1930), and Denise Scott Brown (b. 1931).

Publications

O'GORMAN, JAMES F.; THOMAS, GEORGE E.; and MYERS, HYMAN: *The Architecture of Frank Furness*. Philadelphia, 1973.

THOMAS, GEORGE E.: ''Furness Building Restoration.'' In ANN STRONG and GEORGE E. THOMAS: *The Book of the School, 100 Years*. University of Pennsylvania Graduate School of Fine Arts, Philadelphia, 1990.

WILLIAMS, TALCOTT: ''Plans for the Library of the University of Pennsylvania.'' *Library Journal* 13 (August 1888): 237-243.

*

Viewed from the perspective of formalist architectural history, the complex massing and red tonality of Frank Furness' design for the Library of the University of Pennsylvania was aesthetically obsolete even before it was completed in 1891. Henry Hobson Richardson's Marshall Field Wholesale Store in Chicago and McKim, Mead and White's Boston Public Library had signaled a change in the aesthetic direction of American architecture toward the simple volumes and classical proportions that would characterize the next generation. But viewed from the modern perspective, it is quite as possible to see Frank Furness' library as a step away from the dependence on the forms of the past toward a modern ahistorical approach. This method started from a rational plan established by a team of consultants, and then developed its forms without preconceptions, resulting in one of the most original buildings of its era.

In 1886 the University of Pennsylvania charged a building committee headed by a Shakespearean scholar and professor, Horace Howard Furness, with developing plans for the best collegiate library in the world. In this they were competing with Harvard University, whose president in the previous decade had understood the growing importance of the university library as the center of ''any system of comprehensive training'' (Moses King, *Harvard and its Surroundings,* Cambridge, 1882, p. 25). Dr. Furness assembled a team of experts including Justin Winsor, the librarian of Harvard University, which had just completed a book-storage building addition to its facility, and Melvil Dewey, the inventor of the modern book-cataloging system and director of Columbia University's Library Reference Bureau. The university suggested as designer Frank Furness, Horace's brother, and also at that time the campus architect.

In the summer of 1887, plans were developed for a triangular plot on the west side of the campus; the apex would contain the reading room entered through a projecting portico into a stair tower which advanced from the main volume paralleling the diagonal of the site. With card catalog and call desk flanking the room and a quiet reading room surrounded by seminar alcoves for special collections beyond, the logic of the building would be immediately apparent to the user. Attached on the east end would be a self-sustaining, fireproof, glass-floored and steel-framed bookstack wing encased in a masonry shell, recalling the similar structure at Harvard, but here integrated into the composition. Most remarkable was its removable end wall, which would permit the construction of additional stack arcades as the book collection grew. Though a change in the

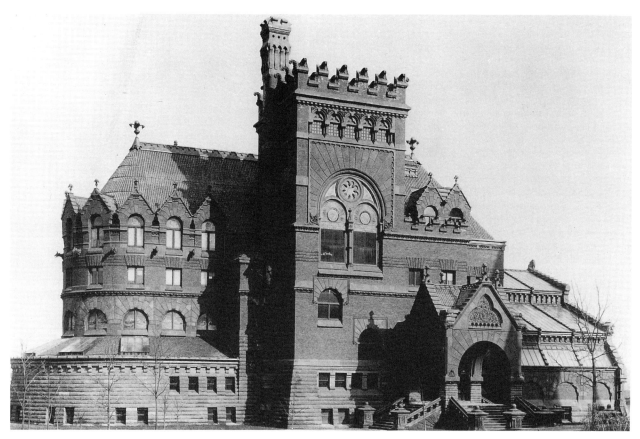

Library of the University of Pennsylvania: Philadelphia, Pennsylvania, 1887-91

site caused the architects to invert the plan, the basic scheme remained unchanged. It certainly pleased Dewey, who wrote: "The plans I sketched with Mr. Furness late that evening, seem to me better than any college library has yet adopted. I should like to see your building by all odds the best model for similar institutions to follow and it will be a great pleasure if I can be of any service in that direction" (Dewey to Provost William Pepper, 20 April 1888, University of Pennsylvania Archives). It was a scheme strikingly similar to that advocated by the *Encyclopedia Britannica* in its 1888 edition (H.R. Tedder and E. C. Thomas, "Libraries," v.XIV, KAO-LON, London, 1888, p. 536).

The functional plan devised by the library consultants was resolved by Furness in a design that combined the spare volume of a railroad trainshed for the bookstack building abutted against a complex cathedral-like volume housing the reading room and other public spaces. Public spaces were differentiated from service uses; circulation was denoted by a great tower whose largest window at the top indicated the presence of an auditorium above the reading room.

Furness' detailing was similarly direct in its use of materials; stone and brick were reserved for the structural piers; terracotta, with a picked surface, spans openings and caps dormers and parapets in violently overscaled forms far removed from their ostensible medieval sources. Within, iron, cast for newels and columns, rolled for stringers and wrought for the balustrade, celebrates its multiple states in the great cataract of the main stair that begins at the top of the tower and tumbles to its overscaled conclusion at the entrance. Unadorned rolled-steel girders, carrying the auditorium, form the ceiling of the inner

reading room. But most astonishing was the glittering light-filled iron-and-steel bookstack that anticipated the Miesian glass and steel paradigm within a greenhouse roof hidden behind rustic masonry arcades.

Though such a scheme was within the range of Victorian expressionism of the previous decade, it was remarkable in the late 1880s. More astonishing was the force with which Furness' convictions of expression of purpose and differentiation of function were held long after they had been supplanted by Beaux-Arts formalism or masked by historical revivals. How Furness' clients continued to encourage and support what the rest of the nation viewed as outlandish design tells much about Philadelphia's isolation from the national mainstream after the Centennial in 1876. Philadelphians were sustained in their contrary behavior by regional myths centered in the 18th-century red city of the American Revolution which resulted in an additional generation of brick architecture.

For a generation, Furness' firm made the major alterations to the building, extending the bookstack in the same direction, though in a different form from the original plan, and subdividing the four-story-high reading room with an inserted floor. In the 1930s plans were made to clad the entire structure in academic Gothic; by the 1940s demolition was proposed. In the 1950s, Frank Lloyd Wright visited the library and proclaimed, "It is the work of an artist." With Wright's advocacy, the building was preserved; beginning in 1986 it has been restored as the Fine Arts Library of the University of Pennsylvania under the direction of Venturi, Rauch and Scott-Brown.

—GEORGE THOMAS

PORTLAND BUILDING
Portland, Oregon, U.S.A.

1980-82: Construction; **Architect:** Michael Graves (b. 1934).

Publications

ARNELL, PETER; BICKFORD, TED; and WHEELER, KAREN V. (eds.): *Michael Graves: Buildings and Projects, 1966-1981*. New York, 1982.

BUREAU OF GENERAL SERVICES, PORTLAND: *The Portland Building*. Portland, Oregon, 1986.

GILBERT, DAVID L.: "The Portland Building." In TOD A. MARDER: *The Critical Edge: Controversy in Recent American Architecture*. Cambridge, Massachusetts, 1985, 162-174.

MACRAE-GIBSON, GAVIN: *The Secret Life of Buildings: An American Mythology for Modern Architecture*. Cambridge, Massachusetts, 1985.

"Portland Civic Center." *Architecture interieure créé*. (August/September 1983).

*

The Portland Building (officially the Portland Public Services Building), built in 1980-82, generated significant local, national and international critical comment, both positive and negative, because it was the first publicly funded large office building to be built in the style termed "postmodern." Prior to 1979 only a few private residences and corporate headquarters had demonstrated this alternative to the tediously restrained glass box long promoted by International Style modernism. The Portland Building gave postmodernism the sanction it had lacked, generated public acceptance and significantly helped to end the 40-year dominance of International Style modernism.

By February 1979 the city of Portland was leasing office space in different downtown buildings. It was decided then that the critical need for additional office space for the city's various public services could best be met by sponsoring a competition for a new building. Requirements were determined, including square footage, and a budget was fixed, calling for a building of 356,000 square feet (406,705 gross square feet), to cost no more than $22.4 million, or $55.13 per square foot. To make certain that the cost limit would not be exceeded, it was also decided that the construction of the building would be done using the "design-build" concept, with the winning architect, his engineering consultants and the builder all entering into contracts stipulating the total cost and the date of completion; cost overruns would be the responsibility of this team, and severe penalties were to be charged to the team for every day that construction passed the deadline. This was a new procedure at that time.

In June 1979 a search was begun for design-build teams willing to participate in the competition under these conditions; eventually 11 teams were identified, and of these, three were selected to prepare finished entries. The three teams were led by Arthur Erickson of Vancouver, British Columbia, Michael Graves of Princeton, New Jersey, and Mitchell-Giurgola of Philadelphia, Pennsylvania. In February 1980 three designs were presented to the jury made up of six Portland political and business leaders, with the architect Philip Johnson engaged as professional adviser. The jury recommended to the city council the striking postmodern design by Michael Graves (his team included the Pavarini Construction Company of Greenwich, Connecticut, and the Hoffman Construction Company of Portland, Oregon, with Emery Roth Architects of New York City). Of the three proposals, Graves' was the only one that provided all of the space needed at the specified cost limit, in a highly energy-efficient building that was strikingly original.

Surprised by Graves' unusual design, and pressured by local architects and citizens who considered Graves' arresting proposal an affront, the city council requested that the Graves and Erickson teams make slight modifications to their designs for reconsideration (in particular, Graves was to remove architectural ornament). In April the two modified proposals were resubmitted, with the Graves design again being chosen. Construction began in July 1980, and the building was completed for dedication on 2 October 1982. With change orders for an additional $2.2 million, the final cost was $24.6 million, or not quite $60.54 per square foot overall, with the office section costing $56 per square foot.)

When the Graves design was first made public during the restudy of the initial proposals, comment in local papers, national news media and professional journals was highly mixed. Many criticized the choice of Graves, who had yet to build a large structure and who was then known as a theoretical designer and artist but not yet as an established architect. Portlanders, unaccustomed to Graves' bold decorative forms and bright colors, thought themselves the butt of a monumental joke. Letters to the editor of the Portland *Oregonian* described the Graves design as "the funniest thing I have seen," and called it a "jukebox," a misplaced "Christmas package" and a "turkey." Other writers, however, both in Portland and across the country, believed the building a "landmark," poetically alluding to classical Greek, Roman and Renaissance buildings, with art deco boldness, forming a refreshing break with the familiar and dull architectural formulas of the 1950s, 1960s and 1970s.

As the building went up, professional and public attacks diminished and gradually changed to acceptance; indeed, Portlanders were happy to be at center stage in the architectural world, even if they did not quite understand the symbolism incorporated in Graves' design.

Graves had given study to the setting of the building, making abstracted references to the nearby classical Federal Courthouse (1930-31), and especially to the two flanking government buildings—the mannerist City Hall (1895) and the massive Roman classical Multnomah County Courthouse (1909-13), both by early Portland architects Whidden and Lewis. Graves' design, divided into stepped base, midsection and penthouse, was also an allusion to classical design principles. On the east and west sides, the stepped base was punctuated by large block-like central pavilions marking the major entrance on the west and a garage entrance on the east. The bold colors—turquoise in the base, terra-cotta and cream in the midsection and light blue for the penthouse—were selected by Graves to refer to trees, earth and sky.

The most visible and dramatic of the embellishments Graves had specified were fluttering sculptural garland banners attached to tondi on the north and south walls, and a large allegorical sculptural figure of *Portlandia*, inspired by the female figure on the city seal. Funded with a "1 percent for art" city appropriation, and with additional funds donated by local businesses and individuals, sculptor Raymond J. Kaskey was commissioned to create the kneeling figure. It was Kaskey's decision to create

Portland Building, Civic Center: Portland, Oregon, 1980-82

a hollow *repoussé* figure in hammered copper, supported by an internal steel armature, recreating the technique used by Frédéric-Auguste Bartholdi in making the Statue of Liberty. Work on *Portlandia* commenced in 1982, and the 6.5-ton figure was installed in October 1985 on top of the entrance-pavilion base block on the east side of the building. The female figure, who would be 50 feet tall if standing, kneels on one knee and extends a hand downward, in greeting to passersby below.

Although Graves alluded to the classical public buildings of the turn of the century, his singular color scheme and greatly overscaled embellishments were not easily understood by the general public; the human figure of *Portlandia,* however, was loved by the city's citizens, who readily underwrote the growing

cost of its fabrication. The criticisms leveled against the building regarding its ephemeral color scheme, which relies on painted concrete, and the easily damaged soft interior surfaces in the public areas do not take full cognizance of the extremely limited budget.

Following the Portland Building competition, Graves received a series of important commissions for other public and corporate buildings, including the Public Library in San Juan Capistrano, California (1980-82), the Humana Building in Louisville, Kentucky (1982), Riverbend Music Center in Cincinnati, Ohio (1983), and the Swan and Dolphin Hotels at Disney World, Lake Buena Vista, Florida (1986-90). Hence, the Portland Building marks a decisive turn in the advancement of Graves' career, as well as a turning point in the public acceptance of postmodernism in public and corporate architecture. The Portland Building may possibly be seen as a major turning point in the architecture of the late 20th century.

—LELAND M. ROTH

VIRGINIA STATE CAPITOL
Richmond, Virginia, U.S.A.

1785-99: Construction; **Architect:** Thomas Jefferson (1743-1826). **1904-05:** Refurbishment.

Publications

HITCHCOCK, HENRY-RUSSELL, and SEALE, WILLIAM: *Temples of Democracy: The State Capitols of the U.S.A.* New York, 1976.

KIMBALL, FISKE: "Jefferson and the Public Buildings of Virginia." *Huntingdon Library Quarterly* 12 (1949): 2-3.

KIMBALL, FISKE: "Thomas Jefferson and the First Monument of the Classical Revival in America." *Journal of the American Institute of Architects* 3 (1915): 371-380, 421-434, 473-491.

Thomas Jefferson, third president of the United States, was a writer, scholar and gifted amateur architect as well as a politician. Before becoming president, Jefferson had been a member of the Colonial House of Burgesses, the Virginia House of Delegates, and was elected governor of the Commonwealth of Virginia in 1779. These experiences provided him with insight for the creation of a public architecture for the new republic composed of individual states. As a product of his architectural ability, the Virginia Capitol became a monument of national and international prominence.

Jefferson's proposal to establish Richmond as the capital city of Virginia was approved by the House of Delegates in 1780. Immediately, he submitted a bill to the assembly to support the erection of buildings to serve as the seats of and to provide an image for the new state governmental functions. Separate edifices were to be built "with walls of brick or stone, and Porticos where the same may be convenient or ornamental, and with pillars or pavements of stone." In addition to a "house for the use of the General Assembly to be called the Capitol," there were to be structures to accommodate the legislative judicial and executive divisions of the government and a public market. A later bill was approved to include these governmental functions within a single structure. Shortly before Jefferson's appointment in 1785 as the United States' minister to France, he was named to a plural directorate to find a site for the new capitol structure for Virginia.

Because of his knowledge of architecture, Jefferson was officially requested by the Directors of the Public Buildings in Virginia to consult with an architect on plans for the capitol. Jefferson was interested in classical styles; he was a scholar of Palladian detail, and had studied plates and developed designs

Virginia State Capitol: Richmond, Virginia, 1785-99

in that particular vernacular before his sojourn in France. That gave him a greater understanding of classical architecture during his on-site visits to Roman monuments. His travels took him to a Roman temple, the Maison Carrée at Nîmes, which had been restored by Louis XV, with the reputation as the finest existing example of ancient architecture. It was Jefferson's primary source for his design for the Virginia Capitol, although his design featured Ionic rather than Corinthian capitals, because of the latter's difficulty.

Charles-Louis Clérisseau, a French neoclassical architect, assisted Jefferson in preparing plans and a plaster model of the capitol for submission to the Commonwealth. The design included offices, halls and a central foyer, illuminated by windows, with the symmetrical portico of hexastyle Ionic columns supporting the traditional entablature and pediment, contained within the envelope of the classic temple form.

From 1904 to 1905, during refurbishment of the building, the symmetrical wings projecting from each side of the original structure to house the Senate and House chambers of the General Assembly were added; the portico stairs designed by Jefferson were constructed, in addition to radical alterations to the interior of the capitol.

With the Virginia Capitol, Jefferson introduced Classical Revival architecture to the United States. The building also preceded anything similar abroad. The Classical Revival movement already had begun in Europe, but the style had been used primarily in garden temples and commemorative monuments, not on such a large scale as in the capitol or in a public building. In England, the leader in the Classical Revival, the temple form was not used for any monumental building until 1830. The Virginia Capitol also predated the Madeleine in Paris, the first great European temple reproduction, by more than 20 years. "In the classical movement America was thus not merely a follower—rather, a leader in pressing it to its extreme consequences," wrote Jefferson scholar Fiske Kimball.

Still, while the Virginia Capitol was a pioneering use of the Classical Revival style, this architectural form's popularity in the United States also was influenced by the degree to which it caught on in Europe, particularly in England. British architecture retained great influence on that of its former colony during the early 19th century. In turn, the Virginia Capitol had great influence on other government and commercial buildings in the United States, with many of them adopting Greek and Roman temple forms.

—GORDON ECHOLS

WAINWRIGHT BUILDING
St. Louis, Missouri, U.S.A.

1890-91: Constructed; **Architects:** Dankmar Adler (1844-1900) and Louis H. Sullivan (1856-1924). **1981:** Renovations.

Publications

ANDREW, DAVID S.: *Louis Sullivan and the Polemics of Modern Architecture: The Present against the Past.* Urbana, Illinois, and Chicago, 1985.

FRAMPTON, KENNETH, and FUTAGAWA, YUKIO: *Modern Architecture: 1851-1919.* New York, 1983.

HITCHCOCK, HENRY-RUSSELL: "Sullivan and the Skyscraper." *Royal Institute of British Architects Journal* (July 1953): 353-361.

JORDY, WILLIAM H.: "Functionalism as Fact and Symbol: Louis Sullivan's Commercial Buildings, Tombs, and Banks." *American Buildings and Their Architects: Progressive and Academic Ideals at the Turn of the Twentieth Century.* Garden City, New York, 1972.

O'GORMAN, JAMES F.: *Three American Architects: Richardson, Sullivan, and Wright, 1865-1915.* Chicago and London, 1991.

RANDALL, JOHN D.: *The Art of Office Building: Sullivan's Wainwright and the St. Louis Real Estate Boom.* Springfield, Illinois, 1972.

SPRAGUE, PAUL E.: 'The Wainwright—Landmark Built and Saved." *Historic Preservation* (October-December 1974): 5-11.

SULLIVAN, LOUIS: "The Tall Office Building Artistically Considered." *Lippincott's Magazine* 57 (1896): 403-409.

TWOMBLY, ROBERT: *Louis Sullivan: His Life and Work.* New York, 1986.

*

In 1890 the St. Louis financier Ellis Wainwright commissioned the Chicago architectural firm of Adler and Sullivan to create in downtown St. Louis an office building rising to the then-amazing height of 10 stories. Wainwright had met the architects a few years before at a St. Louis meeting of the Association of Western Architects. Apparently, Sullivan at first had some difficulty conceiving a design for this structure. According to his young draftsman, Frank Lloyd Wright, Sullivan was walking the streets of Chicago one night in frustration and the solution came to him in a flash. Sullivan later would write, "It was a very sudden and volcanic design (made literally in three minutes) and marks the beginning of a logical and poetic expression of the metallic frame construction."

This new style of building used the current construction developments of reinforced concrete in its foundation, with steel columns and girders braced and riveted and encased in fireproof tiles. The exterior walls were carried on steel spandrel shelves at every story. Nonbearing interior partitions could be easily rearranged according to tenant needs. The building's height was made practical by the inclusion of passenger elevators. While these technological developments were not new, the expression of the building's height as the essential feature of its design was truly innovative. Until the Wainwright Building, no architect had used the height of these new, taller buildings as the guiding principle of their decoration.

The dominant visual feature of the Wainwright Building, the accented vertical pier, does not span the full height of the building's facade. The lowest section of the facade was originally an arrangement of nine separate shops, each with its own free access. The original door and display-window arrangement was modified in a 1981 renovation into large glass windows topped by a horizontal string of transom-like panes. The horizontality of the base was further emphasized by a second story of small offices, which read on the facade as unadorned rectangular windows punched through the surface of the wall. Between the third and ninth stories, the window mullions are designed to appear as a continuous pier. They are even decorated at the bottom and again at the top as though these vertical piers should be read as a classical-style column with a capital and a base.

The sill ledge of the third-floor windows and a molded stringcourse above the ninth help to visually contain this area of the facade. Between the windows of these floors there are decorated spandrel panels made of cast terra-cotta. Each floor is unified with its own distinctively designed spandrel panels, whose images are based upon foliate motifs. This large middle

Wainwright Building: St. Louis, Missouri, 1890-91

section of the building's facade (this includes the second floor as well), was conceived of by Sullivan in order to serve like the cells of a honeycomb or rabbit warren, where the workers produced their daily tasks. The larger offices were arranged along the outside walls, with the smaller offices placed along the inside of the U-shaped building.

The 10th floor reads very differently from all the others on the facade. Comprised of rather small porthole windows surrounded by elaborate terra-cotta swirls of leaves, it serves visually as a decorative cornice for the facade. This top floor served as catch-all for the building, with lavatories for the offices, a barbershop, as well as areas for the mechanical systems and the large steam mains for the building. Originally there were no restrooms on the working floors, and additional lavatories were located in the basement along with storage areas, the electrical plant, pumps, engines, and a boiler under the light court.

The Wainwright Building was designed in a U-shaped arrangement in order to create a central light well. Brochures advertising later Sullivan buildings for potential customers made much of the natural light provided by this type of design. "The plan of the building . . . is of the form of the letter U, with a

wide and light court . . . the building is so well lighted that every office or room in the building will have direct outside light and air." The Wainwright light court was constructed of white mortar and white enamel-faced brick, which helped reflect light back into the building.

The street-side facades of the Wainwright Building are constructed of red Missouri granite, reddish-brown ashlar sandstone, red brick, red mortar and cast decorative terra-cotta panels. The whole creates a unified image coloristically, especially since only the east and south facades and a little bit of the north are decoratively arranged, as mentioned above. The west facade and most of the north facade were constructed plainly of brick and mortar.

All over, the building interior areas and fittings were decoratively arrayed, especially the vestibules, elevator waiting areas and lavatories. In the lobby above the first-floor elevator-bank area was a stained-glass skylight in a pattern reminiscent of Adler and Sullivan's elaborately decorative stencil patterns. The polished brass door pulls were embossed with the initials W.B.

In an early and successful example of historic preservation and adaptive reuse, the state of Missouri purchased the decaying Wainwright Building in 1974 for use as offices. The state held a competition to provide designs for the building's remodeling, as well as the construction of additional adjacent buildings to complement and enhance the historic skyscraper. In 1981 the Wainwright Building renovation was completed, and the building now houses offices for the state of Missouri. The additional building abutting the original Wainwright was designed to "flow" into the older historic space. The original light court was converted to an atrium lobby, with a walkway bridging the open end of the "U" on each floor. The new exterior is constructed of a similar terra-cotta toned brick and mortar. The windows in the new portion of the building are even constructed of solid teak, as were the original Wainwright windows.

—JOYCE K. SCHILLER

CITY PLANS FOR WASHINGTON, D.C.
Washington, D.C., U.S.A.

1791: Commission for building capital awarded; **Architect:** Pierre Charles L'Enfant (1754-1825). **1902:** McMillan Commission report; **Architects:** Daniel Burnham (1846-1912), Charles McKim (1847-1909), Frederick L. Olmsted (1822-1903), Augustus St. Gaudens.

Publications

BUTLER, J. F.: "Competition 1792: Designing a Nation's Capitol." *Capitol Studies* 4 (1976).

CAEMMERER, HANS PAUL: *The Life of Pierre Charles L'Enfant.* Washington, D.C., 1950.

FLEXNER, J. T.: "Great Columbian Federal City." *American Art Journal* 2 (Spring 1970).

HINES, THOMAS S.: *Burnham of Chicago: Architect and Planner.* New York, 1974.

JENNINGS, J. L. S.: "Artistry as Design: L'Enfant's Extraordinary City." *Quarterly Journal of the Library of Congress* (Summer 1979).

KITE, E. S.: *L'Enfant and Washington 1791-1792.* Baltimore, 1929.

LOWRY, BATES (ed.): *The Architecture of Washington, D.C.* 2 vols. Princeton, New Jersey, 1982.

MOORE, CHARLES: *Daniel H. Burnham, Architect, Planner of Cities.* 2 vols. Boston, 1920.

NATIONAL CAPITAL PLANNING COMMISSION: *Comprehensive Plan for the National Capital.* Washington, D.C., 1974.

PEETS, ELBERT: "Washington as L'Enfant Intended It." In *On the Art of Designing Cities: Selected Essays of Elbert Peets.* Cambridge, Massachusetts, 1968.

REPS, JOHN W.: *Monumental Washington: The Planning and Development of the Capital Center.* Princeton, New Jersey, 1967.

VERHEYEN, E.: "James Hoban's Design for the White House in the Context of the Planning of the Federal City." *Architecture* 11 (1981): 66-81.

*

Strolling down the Mall in Washington, D.C., with the profile of the United States Capitol dominating the eastern horizon, the commanding presence of the Washington Monument at the

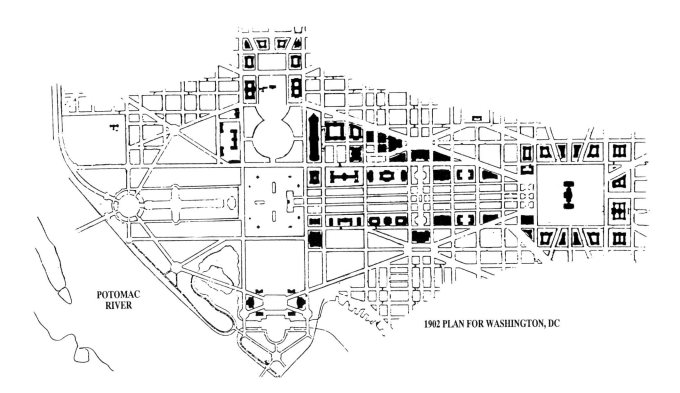

POTOMAC RIVER

1902 PLAN FOR WASHINGTON, DC

intersection of the axis to the White House, the Lincoln Memorial at the edge of the Potomac and the graceful rotunda of the Jefferson Memorial to the south, it is easy to imagine that the city has always been this way. There is a sense of order and balance, the architecture is harmonious, and the symbolism inherent in this vista appears to capture the critical themes in United States history. The tranquility, however, is deceiving. What seems so natural and complete actually has a more tumultuous and more interesting background. Like most large cities, the contemporary scene in Washington is composed of layers. In this case, decisions juxtapose grandiose classical plans with eras of random laissez-faire building and a process of expansion and refinement that continues today.

The earliest phase in this development began in spring 1791 when Major Pierre Charles L'Enfant, an expatriate French engineer and loyal soldier during the American Revolution, was hired on the recommendation of George Washington to design the permanent capital of the United States. The site was a 10-mile-square parcel of land at the junction of the Potomac and Anacostia rivers. As the location was largely uninhabited, L'Enfant considered it to have great potential; during the next several months he carefully surveyed the territory and devised a scheme that ingeniously blended function, topography and symbolism.

His scheme was inspired by, and was perhaps even intended to rival, European capitals (several plans of which L'Enfant had borrowed from Thomas Jefferson). The framework for the city was a grid of north-south, east-west streets covering approximately eight square miles. Then superimposed on these utilitarian roads was a series of squares, circles and radial avenues that would give Washington a truly monumental scale. The boulevards were to measure 160 feet wide and, as a sign of optimism, the total area described in the proposal was as large as the already thriving Philadelphia.

Within this layout, each branch of government—legislative, executive and judicial—had its own location on a high point in the landscape commanding impressive views. In particular, "Congress House" would dominate Jenkins Hill, a knoll L'Enfant regarded as "a pedestal waiting for a monument." At the intersection of the axes from the White House and the Capitol, there was to be an equestrian statue of George Washington. And the avenue going east from the Capitol to the Anacostia River was designed as bustling shopping arcade and ceremonial gateway. There were instructions concerning the Supreme Court, a naval monument, markets and even a national church. Finally, the "Grand Avenue" (today's Mall) would stretch from the west facade of the Capitol to the Potomac River, and was to be used for gardens and embassy residences.

As a concept, L'Enfant's ambitious plan was meant to instill confidence in a fledgling nation and enhance its credibility at a time when, both within the United States and abroad, grave doubts existed about its future. Unfortunately, while his proposal was impressive initially, the reality was that it went well beyond the needs and resources of the country. Streets were surveyed and a few monumental buildings completed, but in general, during the first half of the 19th century, growth was slow and erratic. When Charles Dickens visited in 1842, he referred to the town as that "City of Magnificent Intentions" with "spacious avenues that begin in nothing and lead nowhere; [and] streets, mile-long, that only want houses, roads and inhabitants." In 1851 the Mall was landscaped as a romantic English garden and reflected the capital's relaxed and spontaneous—rather than planned—character.

After the Civil War, the pace of development improved significantly, but by that time the 18th-century proposal was a vague memory. Ignoring the intended use of the Mall as a public

garden, a railroad was constructed below the Capitol; downtown, the area south of Pennsylvania Avenue was referred to as "Murder Bay," and an arbitrary variety of eclectic styles, rather than a chaste classicism, became the norm in architecture. Thus, as the District of Columbia was about to celebrate its centennial, there was little to recall L'Enfant's vision except pattern and the occasional glimpse of several grand buildings in a new "wilderness" of haphazard expansion.

By the beginning of the 20th century, the solution to these confused circumstances was another plan—the 1902 McMillan Commission report that set forth recommendations guiding the rebirth of Washington as an elegant, monumental city. The document was prepared by a distinguished team: architects Daniel Burnham and Charles McKim, landscape designer Frederick Law Olmsted, Jr., and sculptor Augustus St. Gaudens. Motivation for their effort came from several sources. There was the popular success of the 1893 World's Columbian Exposition in Chicago with its lavish Beaux-Arts pavilions and parks. There was a spurt of major building-related technical advances—for example, steel-frame construction, electric lighting, telephones and elevators—that reaffirmed the confidence of designers to control and shape the environment. And politically, there was the easily won victory in the 1898 Spanish-American War that almost transformed the United States overnight into an international imperial power.

Responding to these precedents, the commission prepared a scheme that at once reflected and surpassed L'Enfant's ideas. The group renewed the emphasis on axial composition and classical architecture. In the central city, they relocated the railroad and opened up and extended the Mall to a proposed Lincoln Memorial. On the sides of this broad park, they planted trees and created a promenade of monuments and sculptures framed by great museums. Along Pennsylvania Avenue, they laid out a new civic center with a hospital, market, armory and city hall. Around the White House and Capitol Hill, they suggested the construction of numerous office buildings as the home for various executive and legislative agencies. Clearly, many of these concepts can be seen in Washington as it presently exists.

The McMillan Commission also looked to the future in another important way. It envisioned not only a city but a metropolis, an urban area that would go far beyond the boundaries of L'Enfant's design and even the original 100-square-mile tract that George Washington had endorsed. That aspect of the 1902 plan advocated the development of parkways from Mount Vernon, Virginia, to Great Falls, Maryland. It incorporated an extensive park system that stretched from downtown into the surrounding suburbs. It advised using portions of the waterfront as a major shipping and commercial center. And it prescribed a list of neighborhood amenities, including schools, playgrounds and local pools, that it felt were essential components of every residential community.

Since the commission's report presented a persuasive remedy to decades of neglect and piecemeal planning, reaction was overwhelmingly positive and, under the watchful eyes of the Commission of Fine Arts, many of its features were carried out. By the late 1930s, however, certain of its planning objectives seemed dated as forces unforeseen by Burnham and his colleagues began shaping the region. The ever-increasing size of the Depression- and war-era federal government, complex automobile transportation problems, the emergence of a new, modern style of architecture and the necessity to coordinate resources and decision making among local, state and federal jurisdictions demanded new approaches.

That was the beginning of a third layer in Washington's planning history. Conceptually, it is a design whose hallmark is a monumental core surrounded by neighborhoods and satellite towns, each with its own architectural and political identity. In this situation, agencies rather than individuals establish the guidelines for growth. Some—the Council of Governments, for instance—deal with metropolitan concerns such as pollution, health care and employment. Others—including the District Planning Commission and the National Capital Planning Commission—address citywide, county or intercounty issues: land use, schools and parks. In this category, one of the more important themes has been the "wedges and corridor" strategy that seeks to channel development along specific transportation routes (the corridors) while encouraging green space and low-density uses in between (the wedges). Still a third group—including the Pennsylvania Avenue Development Corporation, which has fostered the rebuilding of the north side of Pennsylvania Avenue into a boulevard of monumental offices, hotels, public squares and an embassy, and the Architect of the Capitol—which has refined the image of Capitol Hill as a modern Acropolis—executes detailed architectural proposals for specific areas within the city.

In this system, planning responsibilities have been divided and the focus has shifted from grand architectural schemes to a combination of an abstract allocation of urban resources complemented with various three-dimensional design projects. Now, because ideas come from many directions, success emerges not from inspiration but from cooperation and consensus building. In the final analysis, the method is appropriately democratic and represents an extension of the classical belief that if two heads are better than one, many heads are better than two. In Washington, D.C., then, L'Enfant's first city has become a tale of multiple cities, and the genius of one has been enriched by the genius of many.

—THOMAS WALTON

LINCOLN MEMORIAL
Washington, D.C., U.S.A.

1911: Lincoln Memorial Commission awarded; **Architect:** Henry Bacon (1866-1924). **1922:** Constructed.

Publications

FLETCHER, BANISTER: *A History of Architecture*. 4th. ed. New York, 1977.
HITCHCOCK, HENRY-RUSSELL: *Architecture: Nineteenth and Twentieth Centuries*. Baltimore, 1977.
KIDNEY, WALTER C.: *The Architecture of Choice: Eclecticism in America, 1880-1930*. New York, 1974.
SCULLY, VINCENT: *American Architecture and Urbansim*. New York, 1969.
TALLMADGE, THOMAS E.: *The Story of Architecture in America*. 3rd ed. New York, 1936.

*

In the Lincoln Memorial, architecture, sculpture, painting, setting and the legacy of Abraham Lincoln have combined to create an image that has taken on powerful symbolic aspects. In the years since its completion in 1922, the memorial has been perceived as an emblem of freedom, racial equality and democratic virtues, and has provided the setting for dramatic events that have reverberated in the minds of Americans. Marian Anderson's 1939 open-air recital on the steps of the memorial, sponsored by Secretary of the Interior Harold Ickes and First Lady Eleanor Roosevelt, was a New Deal response to the racial prejudice of the Daughters of the American Revolution. The 1963 March on Washington in support of civil rights culminated in Martin Luther King's "I Have a Dream" address, delivered in front of the memorial. In the realm of cinematic myth, a midnight visit to the Lincoln Memorial by James Stewart as Senator Jefferson Smith steeled him to oppose his corrupt colleagues in *Mr. Smith Goes to Washington*, Frank Capra's 1939 romantic fable on democracy. The Lincoln Memorial has achieved a symbolic resonance that transcends both its architecture and the historical accomplishments of Abraham Lincoln.

The Lincoln Memorial was one of the final American products of the Beaux-Arts tradition of urban design. Pierre L'Enfant's 1791 plan for the city of Washington, inspired by the Baroque gardens of Europe, was an earlier expression of that tradition, but it had been only partially implemented by the turn of the 20th century. In 1902 the Senate Park Commission, consisting of Daniel Burnham, Charles McKim, Frederick Law Omsted, Jr., and Augustus Saint-Gaudens, unveiled a plan for Washington that essentially revived and expanded L'Enfant's original scheme. The members of the commission were thoroughly imbued with Beaux-Arts principles and consciously relied on European precedents in their planning.

A key recommendation of the commission was to realize long-standing proposals to erect a suitable monument to Abraham Lincoln in Washington. The commission's comprehensive plan called for a memorial to Lincoln to be sited on reclaimed marsh land at the western end of the Mall. Renderings of the proposed memorial, a mammoth portico in the Greek Doric order apparently designed by McKim, were produced to illustrate the 1902 plan. Not until 1911 did Congress establish a Lincoln Memorial Commission, which accepted the recommendation of the newly formed Fine Arts Commission, chaired by Burnham, to award the design of the Lincoln Memorial to Henry Bacon.

Bacon had received much of his training in the offices of McKim, Mead and White, and his design for the Lincoln Memorial was firmly within the Beaux-Arts tradition, both in its siting and its architecture. The memorial, set within a *rond-point* and raised on a terrace at the end of a tree-lined reflecting pool, effectively terminates the two-mile-long vista that originates with the Capitol building, sympathetically extending L'Enfant's original plan for the Mall. The horizontal mass of the memorial balances the verticality of both the Capitol and the Washington Monument, the dominant feature on the Mall itself.

In his design for the Lincoln Memorial, Bacon simplified and made more abstract McKim's proposed portico of 1902. Bacon's memorial, a modified Greek Doric peripteral temple, is an example of a classicism willing to innovate in form, and seeking to display the most exquisite taste in details. Bacon departed from antique authority in using an attic instead of a saddle roof and by placing the entrance on the long side of his temple, facing the Mall. From a distance, the bold, crisp, basic geometric forms of the colonnade and attic convey an elemental power, augmented by the play of light and shadow along the colonnade. Close up, the delicately carved details, including Greek antefixae and an attic frieze of American eagles linked by garlands, seem somewhat overrefined and inert. The overall impression of the white marble temple is one of repose and stasis.

In keeping with the Beaux-Arts conception of the role of monumental architecture, the Lincoln Memorial incorporates an iconographic program centering on the concept of national unity. The 36 peripheral columns represent the 36 states in

Lincoln Memorial: Washington, D.C., 1922

existence at the outbreak of the Civil War. Their names and dates of admission to the Union are inscribed in the entablature. The frieze on the attic walls contains the names of the 48 states that formed the nation in 1922. A bridge across the Potomac from the grounds of the Lincoln Memorial to the military cemetery at Arlington, Virginia, completed in 1932, reinforces the memorial's symbolic message of national reunification through the sacrifice of war.

Within the top-lit interior of the memorial, Daniel Chester French's monumental seated Lincoln seems to gaze down upon the visitor with wisdom and weary determination. The architectural setting and imposing sculptural form unite to invoke feelings of awe and reverence. In two chambers flanking the central statue and separated from it by screens of Ionic columns are tablets containing Lincoln's Gettysburg Address and Second Inaugural Address. Above these texts are allegorical mural paintings by Jules Guerin intended to represent abstract principles (such as "Freedom and Liberty," "Unity" and "Charity") exemplified in the life of Lincoln.

In the Lincoln Memorial, the Beaux-Arts approach to design, by 1911 thoroughly assimilated by leading American architects, is made to serve American commemorative purposes. True to the best academic traditions, painting and sculpture collaborate with architecture, the mother art, to deliver symbolic messages. The Beaux-Arts classicism of the Lincoln Memorial successfully conveys qualities like power, authority, dignity, nobility and purity. Expunged from this multimedia representation of Lincoln are the earthiness, homespun humor, political shrewdness and deep personal ambition that were part of the man's makeup.

The memorial transforms Abraham Lincoln from a democratically elected president to a figure of myth. Yet, we often prefer the Lincoln of myth to the complex figure of Lincoln the man, and perhaps need to call upon that myth when we want to resuscitate the possibilities for equality and freedom in American life. Its expressive range may be limited and tenuously related to democratic ideals, but the collaborative achievement of Bacon, French and Guerin in the Lincoln Memorial embodies the Lincoln myth and makes it available for periodic attempts at national regeneration.

—ROBERT W. BLYTHE

NATIONAL GALLERY OF ART
Washington, D.C., U.S.A.

1936-37: Original Gallery (now West Building) designed; **Architect:** John Russell Pope (1874-1937). **1941:** West Building constructed; **Architects:** Otto Eggers (1882-1964) and Daniel Higgins (1886-1953). **1971-78:** East Building constructed; **Architect:** I. M. Pei (b. 1917).

Publications

Drawings for the East Building, National Gallery of Art, Exhibition catalog. Washington, D.C. 1978.

National Gallery of Art, from mall: Washington, D.C., 1941

HUDNUT, JOSEPH: "The Last of the Romans: Comment on the Building of the National Gallery of Art." *Magazine of Art* 34 (1941): 169-173.

MCLANATHAN, RICHARD (compiler): *East Building, National Gallery of Art: A Profile*. Wahington, D.C. 1978.

"John Russell Pope." *Journal of the Royal Institute of British Architects* 45 (1937): 102.

STANTON, PHOEBE: "A Note on John Russell Pope, Architect, 1874-1937." Part 2, in The Baltimore Museum of Art *Annual IV: Studies in Honor of Gertrude Rosenthal*. Baltimore, 1972: 60-69.

SWALES, FRANCIS S.: "Master Draftsman, VIII: John Russell Pope." *Pencil Points* 5 (1924): 64-80, 90.

*

The National Gallery of Art in Washington, D.C., comprises two buildings of significance. The original gallery building, now referred to as the West Building, was designed between 1936 and 1937 by John Russell Pope and completed after the death of the architect by his successors Eggers and Higgins. The more recent East Building was designed in 1978 by I. M. Pei and Partners. As early as 1924 plans for a National Gallery of Art had been entertained. Charles Platt, architect of the Freer Gallery in Washington, had prepared a scheme for a building to be located on the Mall adjacent to the Museum of Natural History. The project was stalled due to concerns about the site selection as well as the lack of sufficient funding for construction.

The present building and its "seed" collections were a gift to the American people from Andrew W. Mellon, secretary of the treasury under Presidents Harding, Coolidge and Hoover. Mellon, an avid collector of fine art, assembled an unparalleled group of old-master paintings and sculpture, which he intended to serve as the basis for a national museum. With the later additions of the Kress and Widener collections, the National Gallery rapidly attained a world-class status. Mellon foresaw that the building should inevitably aspire to the standards of the world's great national museums. He selected the celebrated architect John Russell Pope to produce a design that would harmonize with his collection as well as those of future donors.

Knowing that he was in ill health, Pope wasted little time on the design of the gallery building. In the spring of 1937, the architect's physician proposed an operation. Pope declined surgery with the knowledge that his chances for survival were slim. The design of the new building quickly took shape, and by the time of the architect's death in August 1937 the form of the building had largely been settled upon. Pope and Mellon had decided on a neoclassical scheme to be located on the northern edge of the Mall near the eastern tip of the Federal Triangle.

Pope oriented the major front of the building to respond to the 1903 McMillan Commission's projected vision of the Mall. The exterior of the building is rendered in rose-colored Tennessee marble. It was desired not to interrupt the wall space of the building with windows in order to provide for the maximum flexibility of gallery spaces, and since an elaborate system of skylighting had been designed by the architect. Consequently, the modulation of the exterior surfaces of the building tested the architect's abilities to manipulate the proportion and character without the luxury of fenestration. Pope rose to the occasion by employing taut, elegantly proportioned surfaces, blind windows

National Gallery of Art

and a minor order of Ionic pilasters. The composition is punctuated at its center by an Ionic portico that is presented in unison with a Pantheon-like dome. The ensemble is anchored at its perimeter by a series of low walls that extend the configuration of the building onto the surrounding site, cleverly masking the building's service courts.

On the interior, the Pope building is organized around a central space that recalls the rotunda of Karl Friedrich Schinkel's Altes Museum in Berlin. The rotunda and entry portico establish the major axis of the building, while a series of sculpture galleries and garden courts develop along the line of the rotunda's cross-axis. Adjacent to these grand spaces are located suites of top-lit gallery rooms. The configuration of these rooms can be changed at will because the structure of the building has been relegated to the perimeter of the gallery areas. Pope employed state-of-the-art climate control, lighting and security systems, making the National Gallery of Art the premier museum building of its day.

Both Mellon and Pope foresaw the possibility of expansion of the museum on to an adjacent site, but it was not until the late 1960s that serious thought was given to a new building project. I. M. Pei was selected as architect for the new building, which again was to be funded with Mellon money. Pei, in formulating his scheme for an addition, did not attempt to follow the neoclassical paradigm that had inspired his predecessor. The architect of the museum expansion selected a minimalist version of the modern style. Although Pei chose to distance himself from the language of classicism, he selected materials to match the initial gallery, necessitating the reopening of quarries in Tennessee. Faced with a difficult trapezoidal site, Pei decided upon a triangular geometry to organize the space and

structure of the building. The site for the new building was considerably smaller than the site for the original gallery. Pei distributed the program for the building over five levels, in contrast to the original building, which is organized around a main floor and basement level. Consequently, in Pei's building many of the exhibition spaces are illuminated solely by means of artificial lighting, whereas the Pope building provides daylighting in nearly all of the important gallery rooms.

The Pei building also is organized around a large central space conceived of as a place for the exhibition of sculpture and other large-scale works of art. The space is covered by a smartly detailed space frame and system of skylights that evenly illuminate the interior. Alexander Calder was commissioned to produce the monumentally scaled mobile that intensifies the already dynamic character of the court.

Both buildings share a common bond in that they seem to have signified the end of their respective movements. Pope, often deemed "the last of the Romans," produced a monument to classicism that has been unequaled since its construction. Likewise, Pei's building can be said effectively to signal the close of his particularly formal brand of modernism, a style that eschewed the conceptual and social ideals of the heroic period of the movement. Since the completion of the ensemble, both strategies for making architecture have been called into question. Pope's building can now be said to appear more modern than his contemporaries gave him credit for. His handling of functional and technical problems was paramount in the production of a comfortable and flexible building. Pei's building, though superficially and stylistically steeped in modernism, retains many of the functional problems (particularly because of its relentless formalism) that proponents of the movement sought to eliminate.

—BRIAN KELLY

UNITED STATES CAPITOL
Washington, D.C., U.S.A.

1793: Commission awarded; **Architect:** William Thornton (1759-1828). **1803-12:** North and south wings constructed; **Architect:** Benjamin Henry Latrobe (1764-1820). **1814:** Burned by British during War of 1812. **1815-17:** North and south wings rebuilt; **Architect:** Latrobe. **1819-27:** Rotunda and first dome constructed; **Architect:** Charles Bulfinch (1763-1844). **1851-65:** Wings and new dome added; **Architect:** Thomas U. Walter (1804-87).

Publications

BANISTER, TURPIN C.: "The Genealogy of the Dome of the United States Capitol." *Journal of the Society of Architectural Historians* 7, Nos. 1-2 (1948): 1-31.

BENNETT, WELLS: "Stephen Hallet and His Designs for the National Capitol, 1791-94." *Journal of the American Institute of Architects* 4 (1916): 290-295, 324-330, 376-383, 411-418.

BROWN, GLENN: *History of the United States Capitol.* Washington, D.C., 1900-03.

BUTLER, JEANNE FOLLEY: "Competition 1792: Designing a Nation's Capitol." *Capitol Studies* 4 (1976): 63-70.

CAMPIOLI, MARIO E.: "Building the Capitol." In CHARLES E. PATTERSON (ed.): *Building Early America.* Radnor, Pennsylvania, 1976: 202-231.

"The First Architect in America, Benjamin Henry Latrobe; Notes and Letters on the Erection of the Capitol at Washington." *Appleton's Booklovers Magazine* 6, 3 (September 1905).

HAZELTON, GEORGE C., JR.: *The National Capitol: Its Architecture, Art and History.* New York, 1914.

KIMBALL, FISKE, and BENNETT, WELLS: "William Thornton and the Design of the United States Capitol." *Art Studies, Medieval and Modern* 1 (1923): 76-92.

MADDEX, DIANE: *Historic Buildings of Washington, D.C.* Pittsburgh, 1973.

NORTON, PAUL F.: *Latrobe, Jefferson and the National Capitol.* New York and London, 1977.

UNITED STATES GOVERNMENT PRINTING OFFICE: *Documentary History of the Construction and Development of the United States Capitol Building and Grounds.* Washington, D.C., 1904.

*

The United States Capitol is a complex interweave of several classically derived architectural styles. The winning design (1793) by William Thornton was Federal in style; Benjamin Henry Latrobe constructed the interiors of the north and south wings (1803-12; 1815-18) in a predominantly Greek-inspired rational neoclassicism; Charles Bulfinch returned to Roman

United States Capitol: Washington, D.C., 1803-12

models in the rotunda and dome (1819-29) of the first building; and Thomas U. Walter added wings and a new dome (1851-65) in a Victorian version of Renaissance architecture. On the exterior, this melange has some believable coherence, but on the interiors the full range of eclecticism is evident, as one can clearly discern the hand of each of the four major architects who most contributed to the Capitol's present form.

Thomas Jefferson had suggested to Pierre Charles L'Enfant, the planner of Washington, that the Capitol's design he based on "some one of the models of antiquity which have the approbation of thousands of years." No elevation of L'Enfant's Capitol is known, but the outstanding feature of its plan, known from his 1791-92 maps of Washington, was a vast circular space overlooking the Mall. It seems to have influenced the most unusual aspect of Thornton's design: two domed rotundas, one near the center of the building and a second, projecting one facing the Mall. The dome on the west was eliminated due to program changes and financial constraints, and a low, Pantheon-type dome with porticoes on the east and west was centered between the two legislative wings. What remains of Thornton's Federal-style design are the four exterior wall segments flanking the present east and west porticoes and some interior plan features, principally oval and semicircular rooms. His exterior-wall articulation is a graceful, elegant and compact interpretation of a palazzo type with a smooth, rusticated basement story, segmentally pedimented windows supported by brackets on the *piano nobile*, and square attic windows. On each wall segment he gave prominence to the central of the five bays by creating blind, round-arched frames with circular-headed windows for the main story, and bull's-eye windows in the attic. The order was Corinthian, as the Capitol was viewed as the most important public structure to be erected in the new federal city.

Latrobe's major contribution to the Capitol's exterior is his design for the much-admired east portico, whose present marble facade is a 1958-62 reproduction of the original sandstone. A pedimented, octastyle temple form supported by a deep and wide staircase projects in front of a colonnade that physically and visually links the original House and Senate wings, giving dominance to the center section of the Capitol, which was to contain the "Hall of the People." Latrobe's interiors are the major architectural glory of the Capitol. The three chambers, the Supreme Court on the ground story of the north wing, the Senate directly above it, and the Hall of Representatives (now Statuary Hall) on the main story of the south wing exist today as museum rooms. They all follow the same basic pattern: extended semicircles with a screen of columns across their radii divide the body of each room from semiprivate retiring areas that faced exterior walls, thus lighting the interiors through a system of filtered, rather than direct, sunlight.

The Supreme Court is the most powerful of Latrobe's spaces. It combines heavy Greek Doric columns, Roman butterfly vaults and medieval ribs in a formally and spatially exciting room for which there is no true precedent in architectural history. Latrobe fused architectural principles derived from each of these historical eras to create a unique solution to the difficult problem of designing a majestic room on the ground floor which, in turn, must support the weight of another large room above it. Throughout his Capitol interiors Latrobe employed the same spatial principle to make relatively small spaces appear monumental. Layering of space within, for instance, the Supreme Court—a vaulted ring outside the piers that support the half dome, the corridor behind the screen of Doric columns, and the faceted surface of the dome—creates the illusion of expanding rather than confining space.

The old Senate and House chambers are rebuildings of earlier rooms that had been destroyed by British forces during the War of 1812. In the Senate, the original natural light from east-facing windows and the cupola have been shut off, thus deadening its multifaceted forms and surfaces. A screen of gray Potomac marble columns (with Ionic capitals of white Carrara marble) supports a visitors' gallery parallel to the east front; Bulfinch's balcony carried on slender cast-iron colonnettes was added along the room's semicircular perimeter. Statuary Hall is the second of Latrobe's rooms for the House of Representatives. Its subtle color harmonies of matte brown sandstone, polished and variegated gray marble columns, and elaborately carved white Corinthian capitals (derived from the Choragic Monument to Lysicrates in Athens and carved in Carrara, Italy) are presently masked by an inappropriate paint scheme and heavy curtains hanging between the columns. Each of Latrobe's major chambers has a series of vestibules—the most famous of which have columns whose capitals are derived from corncobs and tobacco leaves—located outside the Supreme Court chamber. While these lobbies all display Latrobe's genius for manipulating small spaces, the vestibules with his American orders represent a fundamental contribution to Latrobe's iconographic program for the Capitol, which depended on invented and borrowed American symbols.

The west-central projecting wing was built by Bulfinch in the 1820s, and partially followed Latrobe's design. Its unpedimented portico has an unusual arrangement of two sets of double columns framing one set of single columns, a motif Bulfinch had used on his Massachusetts State House (1797). His articulation of the north and south sides of the wing, where double pilasters were used on the inside angles (but not on the outside edge), was presumably done to strengthen these corners, but the effect is nonetheless disjointed. Bulfinch's most lasting contribution to the Capitol is the rotunda. His interest in permanently recording pre- and post-Revolutionary events is evidenced by sculptural panels placed above the rotunda's four doors. The subjects range from Columbus' discovery of America to Daniel Boone fighting the Indians. Bulfinch's basic definition of architecture as elegantly decorated surfaces is seen in the decorative sculpted panels set between the historical panels. In conjunction with John Quincy Adams, Bulfinch initiated the tradition of pedimented sculpture on the Capitol's east front with Enrico Causici's *Genius of America* (1826).

The contrast between the measured rhythm of Thornton's Federal-style facades and the staccato and sculpturally more robust wall treatment of Walter's Renaissance Revival-style extensions (1851-60) is an instructive comparison between two sensibilities within the broad spectrum of the classical architectural tradition. Although Walter continued the horizontal regulating line of the original building, the scale of his two wings set at right angles to the earlier Capitol (increasing its length from 352 to 731 feet) and the plasticity of his wall surfaces transformed the Capitol from a neoclassical to a Victorian building. His extensions were executed in a warm-toned marble, and light reflections of Walter's walls and columns contrast sharply with the absorption of light by the painted sandstone of the original building.

The Capitol's cast-iron dome, designed by Walter with the assistance of army engineer Montgomery C. Meigs, is still considered an outstanding engineering feat. Iron was selected to be fireproof, lightweight, inexpensive and quick to assemble. The outer dome rises from a ring cantilevered 14 feet from Bulfinch's octagonal masonry drum; it is separated from the inner dome by 36 continuous trusses. This skeletal structure allows for large areas of glass on four levels of windows, giving it an open, airy appearance from both the interior and exterior despite its weight of nine million pounds. The dome's bold, three-dimensional character directly relates it to Walter's wings;

together they overwhelm the delicacy of the original building but give the Capitol its vivid, highly articulated silhouette.

The Capitol's extensions have some of the finest extant mid-Victorian interiors in America, which were overseen by Meigs. The ground floor of the Senate (north) wing was decorated by the Italian-born fresco painter Constantino Brumidi in arabesques and *groteschi* derived from Roman interiors as interpreted by High Renaissance architects. Brumidi incorporated numerous species of American birds, animals and plants into the overall decorative scheme while inserting into it illusionistically painted frames for portraits and history paintings. The *piano nobile* continues the historical themes but is more elaborately decorated with gilded, three-dimensional plaster used for frames, decorative panels and the rosettes of shallow domes and vaults. Rich, somber tones of browns and purples are set off by the light-reflecting gold and elaborate bronze staircases reserved for the use of members of Congress. Opulent entrance vestibules and the imperial public staircases are constructed in white and veined brown marbles, and include Walter's American variant on the Corinthian order. The splendor of the Capitol's extensions was meant to express the wealth and artistic maturity of the nation by the mid-19th century.

—PAMELA SCOTT

UNITED STATES TREASURY
Washington, D.C., U.S.A.

1836: Commission awarded; **Architect:** Robert Mills (1781-1855). **1836-42:** Construction; **Architect:** Robert Mills. **1855-69:** Exterior and interior reconstructed; **Architects:** Thomas U. Walter (1804-1887), Amni B. Young (1800-1874), Isaiah Rogers (1800-1869), and Alfred B. Mullett (1834-1890).

Publications

BRYAN, JOHN MORRILL: *Robert Mills, Architect 1781-1855.* Columbia, S.C, 1976.

CLARK, A. C.: "Robert Mills, Architect and Engineer." Columbia Historical Society *Records* 40-41 (1940): 1-32.

GALL, M.: "Mills, the Master Builder." *South Carolina Magazine* (January 1950): 12-13, 60-61.

GALLAGHER, H. M. P.: "Robert Mills, America's Finest Native Architect." *Architectural Record* 65 (April-May, 1929): 387-93, 478-84; 66 (July 1929): 67-72.

GALLAGHER, HELEN MAR PIERCE: *Robert Mills.* New York, 1935.

HALL, L.: "Mills, Strickland, and Walter: Their Adventure in a World of Science." *Magazine of Art* 40 (November 1947): 266-71.

"Robert Mills, Architect and Engineer." *Architectural Record* 40 (December 1916): 584-86.

Robert Mills, Architect of the Washington Monument, 1781-1855. New York, 1935.

NEWCOMB, R.: "Robert Mills, American Greek Revivalist." *Architect* (9 March 1928): 697-99.

WILSON, C. C.: "Robert Mills, Architect." University of South Carolina *Bulletin* 77 (February 1919).

The United States Treasury Building is the product of five major American architects, although it is generally thought to be solely the work of Robert Mills. In 1836 President Andrew Jackson chose Mills' design for a fireproof building to replace the first Treasury Building (1798-1800), which had been destroyed by fire three years earlier; the original structure had been designed by George Hadfield and rebuilt by James Hoban after the British burned it in 1814. Mills' design was monumental in comparison. Even today the Treasury Building does not have the diminutive look of most early-19th-century buildings in the United States. Its plan—central barrel-vaulted corridors flanked by groin-vaulted offices—deviated from earlier American public buildings in its regularity and organization of space according to a module, rather than in suites of interconnected rooms. This plan has proved to be adaptable to changing office conditions, having been in continuous office use since its erection, like Mills' two other contemporaneous Washington office buildings, the Patent Office (1836-40) and the General Post Office (1839-41). In scale and vaulted construction throughout, Mills was truly building for permanence.

Mills' Treasury Building design was shaped like the letter E, with the three porticoed wings facing the White House and the spine along 15th Street articulated by a giant Ionic colonnade 460 feet in length. Mills himself likened it to both the Greek Temple of Diana at Ephesus (significantly, one of the Seven Wonders of the Ancient World) and to Alexandre Brongniart's Paris Bourse (1808), an instant modern classic. The Ionic order he selected is that of the Erechtheion on the Athenian Acropolis, the Ionic capital most commonly reinterpreted by American Greek Revival architects. The building was originally constructed of sandstone from Acquia, Virginia, which proved to be too soft for external use. Mills' colonnade was replaced by a granite copy in 1908, but the coffered ceiling behind it remains. Due to repeated street gradings, the Treasury Building base is now higher than intended, and a beautiful and intricate cast-iron fence Mills designed to mask its blank walls was destroyed and has not been replicated.

Mills oversaw construction of the spine and the central wing. In 1855 Thomas U. Walter proposed a design to complete the building in the form of the figure 8. The north, south and west facades were to have giant octastyle porticoes, while each corner was to be terminated with a square pavilion. Mills is often accused of shutting off the reciprocal vista along Pennsylvania Avenue between the White House and the Capitol, but it was actually the plan by Walter that was responsible for this effect. Over the next 14 years Walter's exterior envelope was erected wing-by-wing in granite by three architects, Ammi B. Young (in conjunction with the engineer Alexander T. Bowman), Isaiah Rogers and Alfred B. Mullett. Although they adhered to the basic exterior pattern established by Walter with only minor modifications, each left his personal stamp on the interiors.

With the exception of his magnificent double geometrical staircase, Mills' interiors are not spatially or decoratively interesting, as he was pressed by Congress to maximize office space at the expense of architectural grandeur. His flying stairs and their surrounding corridors supported by plain Doric columns, derived from those of the Temple of Apollo at Delos, are spatially exciting and beautifully integrated into his plan. The double curve of every rise of stairs is complemented by the scalloped profile of the treads, which are cantilevered from the walls and corbeled against one another.

The New England architect Ammi B. Young introduced iron as a structural and decorative material in his Treasury Building wing constructed between 1855 and 1862. With this material came a new system of construction and his own American order, a variant of the Corinthian in which he introduced eagles beneath

United States Treasury: Washington, D.C., 1836-42

the volutes and a key grasped by a fist (a Treasury Department emblem) between them. The iron balustrades of his staircases also incorporate emblems adopted as American symbols, including fasces and oak leaves. These were designed by J. Goldsborough Bruff, who also devised several bronze gas chandeliers that included American Indians, buffalos, cougars and rattlesnakes, a vestige of his own participation in the California Gold Rush. Unfortunately they have been lost. In corridors and rooms cast-iron columns and pilasters carry cast-iron beams with shallow brick vaults between them. The result is an entirely different spatial experience, one that is basically trabeated rather than arcuated. This system of construction was repeated in the remaining two wings. On the exterior Young introduced monolithic granite columns cut from the quarry on the diagonal for added strength, a remnant of his New England building heritage.

Isaiah Rogers was appointed supervising architect of the Treasury Department in 1862. He oversaw construction of the west wing that faces the White House, introducing only minor changes to Walter's master plan. That wing's octastyle portico projects in front of a wide colonnade to help visually bridge the building's 466-foot length, a feature Walter adopted from Benjamin Henry Latrobe's design for the east portico of the Capitol.

Alfred B. Mullett's major contribution to the Treasury is his Cash Room, a double-story rectangle circumscribed by a balcony whose bronze railing was designed by Goldsborough Bruff. It contains numerous natural elements intertwined in its running acanthus-leaf motif, including grapes, corn, cotton, wheat, shells and starfish, all of which refer to various aspects of the United States' economy overseen by agencies of the Treasury Department. Seven varieties of variegated Italian and

American marbles in subtle shades of gray, pink, yellow, white and red cover the walls, which are articulated by double pilasters, Corinthian below the balcony and composite above. The gilded plaster bracketed and shell cornice provides the transition to a flat iron-beamed ceiling. White and yellow marble floors in a simple geometric pattern are countered by reproductions of elaborately sculptural bronze chandeliers.

—PAMELA SCOTT

WASHINGTON NATIONAL MONUMENT
Washington, D.C., U.S.A.

1845: Commission awarded; **Architect:** Robert Mills (1781-1855). **1848-54:** Initial construction; **Architect:** Robert Mills. **1876-84:** Completed.

Publications

BRYAN, JOHN MORRILL: *Robert Mills, Architect 1781-1855.* Columbia, S.C, 1976.
GALLAGHER, HELEN PIERCE: *Robert Mills, Architect of the Washington Monument, 1781-1855.* New York, 1935.
GALLAGHER, H. M. P.: "Robert Mills, America's Finest Native Architect." *Architectural Record* 65 (April-May, 1929): 387-93, 478-84; 66 (July 1929): 67-72.

Washington National Monument: Washington, D.C., 1848-54

HOYT, WILLIAM D.: "Robert Mills and the Washington Monument in Baltimore." *Maryland Historical Magazine* 34 (1939): 144-160; 35 (1940): 178-189.

LANDY, JACOB: "The Washington Monument Project in New York." *Journal of the Society of Architectural Historians* 28 (1969): 291-297.

MILLER, J. JEFFERSON: "The Designs for the Washington Monument in Baltimore." *Journal of the Society of Architectural Historians* 23 (1964): 19-28.

"Robert Mills, Architect and Engineer." *Architectural Record* 40 (December 1916): 584-86.

ZUKOWSKY, JOHN: "Monumental American Obelisks: Centennial Vistas." *Art Bulletin* 58, 4 (1976): 574-581.

*

The Washington National Monument is one of more than a dozen monuments designed by Robert Mills during his long and fruitful career (1800-55), which spanned the half century during which architects struggled to gain a precarious professional footing in the United States. Of these, five specifically honored George Washington, but the only other one to be completed is the Baltimore Washington Monument, begun in 1813. It was the earliest architectural monument to eulogize Washington, and, at 170 feet, was the tallest triumphal column in the world. As with many of his contemporaries, Mills saw size as a measure of quality and directly equated it with American greatness. In retrospect it appears that this attitude toward architecture probably reflects the influence of the sheer physical size of the country. Also, the majority of American buildings during Mills' lifetime were set on the ground rather than in a landscape. This seems to be particularly true of the Washington National Monument, but the view of it today is quite different from what Mills intended.

Nothing is known of the design he entered in the 1836 competition sponsored by the Washington National Monument Society, a group of the national capital's military and civic leaders. It, and the other competing designs, were not judged sufficiently grand by the society, or "coextensive with the nation," according to their minutes. The only other design by an architect of note was a posthumous one by George Hadfield (ca. 1767-1826), which was entered by one of his former students. Gideon Shryock (1802-80) corresponded with the society, but his design, if he sent one, has not been found.

By 1845, when the American public, which had been making contributions to the national monument for a dozen years, began to be skeptical about the structure's eventual erection, a design by Mills was solicited. No further competition was held. His thinking about a suitable monument to Washington was wide-ranging. Numerous sketches by Mills exist for obelisks with and without bases, for triumphal arches surmounted by a colossal statue of Washington, and even for a giant, medieval-revival reliquary sheltering a statue. A lengthy, undated document in Mills' hand describes a rusticated stepped pyramid 1,000 feet square and 680 feet high. Seven vaulted levels were to contain statues of the "worthies of the Revolution," and a massive, 100-foot-high statue of Washington for the summit was so large that Mills said it would be built as a work of architecture rather than sculpture. (Enrico Causici's 14-foot-tall statue atop the Baltimore Washington Monument was carved in four pieces and erected under Mills' superintendence.)

The society's intention, expressed from the outset, was to build the largest monument in the world, for which the group at first expected to pay $1 million. However, they proceeded to finance their initial pledge to erect a monument by small private contributions alone. The design the society selected seems to have been favored because it was capable of being built at costs ranging from $100,000 to $1 million, depending on the size of each of its elements. It consisted of two parts: a 600-foot obelisk, which would rise from the center of a circular colonnaded base 250 feet in diameter. Portrait and emblematic sculpture were an integral part of this design, as they had been for the Baltimore Washington Monument. Numerous 20th-century interpretations of Mills as an architect of stark, geometric forms do not consider the relationship between his own initial preferences and what his clients wanted or could afford. The obelisk alone was dedicated to the first president, while the four relief sculptures at its base were to depict his major Revolutionary War victories at Yorktown, Trenton, Monmouth and Brandywine. The single star at its summit was to signify his immortality. The roof of the pantheon base was meant to be a belvedere where visitors could view not only that sculpture and an additional group consisting of a quadriga driven by Washington, but also the surrounding city and, through cupolas lighting the gallery below, the sculpture located there. The base was to commemorate Washington's contemporaries, the civil and military heroes of the Revolution. Thirty Doric columns, 45 feet high and 12 feet in diameter, were to represent the states in the Union in 1845 and the signers of the Declaration of Independence, statues of whom were to be placed in niches cut in the rotunda wall behind the colonnade. Further statues on the interior of the fathers of the Revolution were to be supplemented by a cycle of history paintings recounting the major events of the era.

The cornerstone was laid on 4 July 1848, and drew the largest crowd yet seen in the capital. Before the monument was actually begun, the society recognized the near-impossibility of raising the necessary funds solely through private contributions, and settled on an intermediate stage of construction whereby the obelisk would be completed and its stepped-pyramid foundations inscribed with the names of the heroes until such time as the pantheon could be reasonably undertaken. Construction was halted in March 1854 due to disruptions by the Know-Nothing political party, whose anti-Catholic platform was spurred on by the inclusion of a memorial stone sent by the Vatican, the "Pope's Stone," actually a piece of the Temple of Concordia from the Roman Forum. Another factor not generally recognized is that the hundreds of stonemasons were predominantly Irish Catholic laborers.

Construction did not resume until 1876 when centennial fever and federal sponsorship joined to complete the monument. Tastes had changed, and numerous mid-Victorian solutions of how to cover the 170-foot stump were suggested. However, under the direction of Thomas Lincoln Casey of the Army Corps of Engineers, construction of the obelisk went forward with some minor changes. The height was set at 555 feet, because measurements of Egyptian obelisks in Rome showed their heights to be 10 times the width of their bases. Casey redesigned the pyramidion at the top to be 50 feet high, and removed Mills' two Egyptian Revival doorways with cavetto cornices and winged orbs that were on the north and south faces. Built of Symington's pure white crystalline marble on the exterior with a Potomac gneiss core, the Washington Monument was the tallest building in the world when it was completed in 1884, to be surpassed by the Eiffel Tower only five years later. Its actual height is indeed 555 feet, $5\frac{1}{8}$ inches, and it weighs 80,378 tons.

—PAMELA SCOTT

Architect Index

119
Fischer von Erlach, Joseph Emanuel, 107
Flasar, Frantisek, 151
Fontana, Carlo, 630, 635
Fontana, Domenico, 649
Forbat, Fred, 311
Forbes, William, 515
Foschini, Arnaldo, 610
Foster, Norman, 865
Foulihoux, Jacques André, 977
Fowke, Captain Francis, 433
Francesco di Giorgio, 571, 697
Freiburg, Johann von, 580
Frisoni, Donato Guiseppe, 364
Fryazin, Antonio, 761
Fuchs, Kamil, 146
Fuga, Ferdinando, 649
Fuller, Thomas, 881
Furness, Frank, 1001

G

Gabriel, Ange-Jacques, 254, 286, 293
Gaddi, Taddeo, 555
Galilei, Alessandro, 642
Galla di Bibiena, 685
Gandon, James, 533
Garnier, Charles, 248
Gaudí, Antoni, 802, 807
Gaynor, John P., 967
Gehry, Frank, 950
Gelfreikh, Vladimir G., 766
Gervin I, Abbot, 197
Gervin II, Abbot, 197
Gibberd, Frederick, 402
Gibbs, James, 380, 449, 496
Gilbert, Cass, 986
Gil de Hontañón, Juan, 830
Giocondo, Fra, 654
Giotto, 540
Glucholazy, Father Jodok of, 744
Godwin the Mason I, 371
Gómez de Mora, Juan, 886
Gowan, James, 396
Graham, James Gillespie, 519
Graves, Michael, 1003
Gropius, Walter, 311, 321, 323, 947
Guarini, Guarino, 688, 692
Guimard, Hector, 244
Gustavino the Younger, 980
Gwathmey/Siegel Associates, 966

H

Hakam II, 812
Halliday, J. Theo, 408
Hansen, C. F., 165
Hardouin-Mansart, Jules, 234, 256, 286
Häring, Hugo, 311

Hårleman, Carl, 839
Harmon, Arthur, 963
Harrison, Peter, 909
Harrison, Wallace, 971
Harrison, Wallace K., 977, 984
Harsdorff, C. F., 162
Hase, C. W., 328
Haviland, John, 994
Hawksmoor, Nicholas, 380, 413, 444, 452, 470, 493, 498, 512
Hayden, Sophia, 938
Heins, George L., 980
Heintz, Josef, the Elder, 304
Héré de Corny, Emmanuel, 218
Herkommer, J. J., 364
Herland, Hugh, 425
Hermogenes, 61
Herrera, Juan de, 822
Higgins, Daniel, 1012
Hilbert, Kamil, 154
Hild, Józef, 529
Hildebrandt, Johann Lukas von, 103, 105, 113, 366
Hoffmann, Josef, 132
Hofmeister, Henry, 977
Höger, Fritz, 326
Hohenberg, F. H. von, 119
Holabird, William, 923, 927, 930
Holl, Elias, 304
Holland, Henry, 377
Hood, Raymond, 936, 977
Horta, Victor, 130
Howe, Frank, 938
Howe, George, 997
Howells, John Mead, 936
Huguet, 748
Hültz, Johann, 280
Hunt, Richard Howland, 973
Hunt, Richard Morris, 938, 973

I-J

Iakovlev, I. E., 789
Iktinos, 6
Il Cronaca, 551
Ilyin, L. A., 785
Inwood, Henry William, 454
Inwood, William, 454
Isidorus of Miletos, 851
Isozaki, Arata, 950
Jackson, T. G., 143
Jahn, Helmut, 934
Jamaer, P. V., 127
James of St. George, 524
Janák, Pavel, 149
Janececk, 146
Janyns, Henry, 371
Jefferson, Thomas, 911, 1005
Jenney, William Le Baron, 913, 938
Joedicke, Jürgen, 342
Johansen, John M., 990

Mique, Richard, 293
Miskin, 761
Mnesikles, 6
Mocker, Josef, 154
Montferrand, Auguste Ricard de, 795
Montreuil, Eudes de, 261
Montreuil, Pierre de, 261
Moosbrugger, Caspar, 364
Moral, Enrique del, 887
Mullett, Alfred B., 1017
Mylne, John, Jr., 518
Mylne, Robert, 518

N-O

Nash, John, 377, 439
Neelov, I. V., 792
Nervi, Pier Luigi, 672
Nesfield, W. A., 482
Neumann, Johann Balthasar, 362, 366
Neutra, Richard, 949
Niemeyer, Oscar, 871, 874
Nouvel, Jean, 233
Novi, Alevisio, 761
Odo of Metz, 302
Oetgens, Franz Hendrickszoon, 721
Ogurtsev, Bazhen, 761
Okhlebinin, D. L., 761
Olbrich, Joseph Maria, 122
Olin, Laurie, 941
Oliveira, Mateus Vicente de, 753
Olmsted, Frederick Law, 938, 959, 1009
Opbergen, Anthony van, 738
Oppenord, Gilles-Marie, 264
Orsenigo, Simone da, 580
Ortiz de Castro, José Damianode, 886
Östberg, Ragnar, 837
Otto, Frei, 342
Owings, Nathaniel A., 919, 932, 969

P

Paatelainen, Raili, 182
Paesschen, Hans Hendrik van, 125
Pagano, Giuseppe, 610
Paine, James, 386
Pais, Gualdim, 754
Palladio, Andrea, 578, 709, 711, 715, 717
Pani, Mario, 887
Parigi, A., 547
Parigi, G., 547
Parker, Barry, 417
Parler, Peter, 148, 154
Paxton, Joseph, 415
Peabody, Robert S., 938
Pearson, J. A., 881
Pei, I. M., 241, 1012
Peretiatkovich, M. M., 785
Perret, Auguste, 212

Persius, Ludwig, 350, 352
Peruzzi, Baldassare, 623, 654, 674
Piacentini, Marcello, 610
Piano, Renzo, 224
Pietilä, Reima, 182
Pisano, Andrea, 540
Pisano, Giovanni, 682
Pisano, Nicola, 601
Pisano, Tommaso, 601
Playfair, William H., 519
Pollaiuolo, Tommaso del, 551
Post, George B., 973
Polykleitos the Younger, 29
Pomerantsev, Aleksandr Nikanorovich, 758
Ponte, Antonio da, 700
Ponti, Gio, 610
Ponzio, Flaminio, 649
Pope, John Russell, 1012
Porta, Giacomo della, 612, 627, 630, 649, 654, 663
Porta, Guglielmo della, 622
Portman, John, 891
Posnik, 781
Posokhin, M. V., 761
Post, George, 938
Poynter, Ambrose, 439
Prager, Karel, 151
Primaticcio, Francesco, 205
Pritchard, Thomas Farnolls, 505

Q-R

Quadro, Jan Baptista di, 736
Quarenghi, Giacomo, 796, 798
Quintillus, P., 26
Raffield, John, 439
Raggi, Antonio, 635
Rainaldi, Carlo, 627, 630, 635, 649
Rainaldi, Girolamo, 625, 627
Rainaldus, 601
Raphael, 654, 670, 679
Rapisardi, Gaetano, 610
Rastrelli, Bartolomeo Francesco, 789, 792, 796, 798
Rauch, John, 1001
Rawski, W., 744
Redman, Henry, 374
Reed, Charles A., 964
Reginald of Ely, 380
Reinhard, L. Andrew, 977
Rejsek, Matej, 148
Rejt, Benedikt, 154, 158
Rerberg, Ivan I., 761
Riccio, 685
Richardson, Henry Hobson, 904, 925
Rietveld, Gerrit, 729
Rinaldi, A., 798
Rios, Demetrio de los, 819
Ristoro, Fra, 566
Rizzo, Antonio, 700
Robillion, Jean-Baptiste, 753
Robinson, Thomas, 512

NOTES ON CONTRIBUTORS

ADAM, Bernd. Academic adviser, Institute for Architecture and Art History, University of Hannover, Germany. Leader of a project for the investigation of the history of the old town halls in Hannover. **Essay:** Hannover: Altes Rathaus.

ADAMS, David. Director, Center for Architectural and Design Research, Grass Valley, California. Author of essays and booklets on art and architecture, with special emphasis on American stained glass and German expressionist architecture. Contributor to *Journal of the Society of Architectural Historians.* **Essay:** Dornach: Goetheanum.

ALEXANDER, Robert L. Emeritus professor of art history, University of Iowa, Iowa City. Senior editor, *The Papers of Robert Mills.* Author of *The Architecture of Maximilian Godefroy,* 1974; *The Architecture of Russell Warren,* 1979; *The Sculpture and Sculptors of Yazilikaya,* 1986; numerous articles and lectures on architectural history. **Essay:** Maximilian Godefroy.

ALEXIS, Karin M. E. Art and architectural historian, Center for Advanced Study in the Visual Arts, National Gallery of Art, Washington, D.C. Coordinator of the Smithsonian Institution's Art History Series Certificate Program. Author of numerous articles on art and architecture. **Essays:** Russell Sturgis; Tessin Family; Kalmar Cathedral; Stockholm: Drottningholm; Stockholm: Royal Palace.

ANDREOTTI, Libero. Assistant professor of architecture, Georgia Institute of Technology. Assistant editor, *Journal of Architectural Education.* Author of a book on Italian art and architecture during fascism (in progress); numerous lectures and articles on Italian Rationalism and architectural theory and criticism. **Essay:** Como: Casa del Fascio.

ARMS, Meredith. Doctoral candidate in American art and architectural history, Rutgers University. Historic preservation consultant, Sullebarger Associates, Oldwick, New Jersey. **Essays:** Pietro Belluschi; John Hejduk; James Gallier, Sr.; Houston, Texas: Indeterminate Facade Showroom.

BADENOCH-WATTS, Teresa S. Assistant professor of art history, Potsdam College, State University of New York. Author of *The Works of Johann Heinrich Müntz (1727-1798)* (catalogue exhibition), 1992. Contributor to journals. **Essays:** Charles De Wailly; Simon Du Ry; Richard Boyle, Third Earl of Burlington; Kassel: Löwenburg; London: Chiswick House.

BAHR, Carolin. Formerly affiliated with Institute for Art History, Justus-Liebeg-Universität, Giessen. Author of articles in *GieBener Kunstweg* and *Wege zur Kunst.* **Essays:** Heinrich von Ferstel; Theophilus Hansen.

BALAKIER, Ann Stewart. Associate professor of art history, University of South Dakota, Vermillion. Author of *The Newton Connection* (in preparation). **Essays:** Lieven De Key; Louis Le Vau; Pieter Post; Michele Sanmicheli; Jacob Van Campen; Berkshire: St. George's Chapel, Windsor.

BARNES, Carl F., Jr. Professor of art history and archaeology, Oakland University, Rochester, Michigan. Author of *Villard de Honnecourt, the Artist and His Drawing: A Critical Biography,* 1982. Former president of International Center of Medieval Art and Association Villard de Honnecourt for the Interdisciplinary Study of Science, Technology and Art. **Essays:** Villard de Honnecourt; William of Sens.

BELTON, Robert J. Faculty member, McMaster University, Hamilton, Ontario, Canada. **Essays:** Ernest Cormier; Moshe Safdie; Montreal: Habitat (Expo '67).

BERING, Kunibert. Instructor, Ruhr-Universität Bochum, Germany. Author of *Fra Angelico,* 1984; *Baupropagand der Frührenaissance in Florez-Rom-Pienza,* 1984; *Kunst und Staatsmetaphysik des Hochmittelalters in Italien,* 1986; numerous articles about art and architecture in the Middle Ages and the 20th century. **Essays:** Camillo Sitte; Amsterdam: Herengracht.

BINDING, Gunther. Professor of art history, University of Cologne, Germany. Author of numerous books and articles about architecture, including *Ordensbaukunst in Deutschland,* 1985; *Architektonische Formenlehre,* 1987; *Masswerk,* 1989; *Deutscher Fachwerkbau,* 1989; *Das Dachwerk,* 1991; *Baubetrieb im Mittelalter,* 1993. **Essays:**

Parler Family; Würzburg: Residenz.

BLYTHE, Robert W. Historian, National Park Service, Atlanta, Georgia. Past treasurer of Chicago chapter, Society of Architectural Historians. **Essays:** Charles Bowler Atwood; Minard Lafever; Washington, D.C.: Lincoln Memorial.

BOGNAR, Botond. Professor of architecture, University of Illinois at Urbana-Champaign. Architectural essayist, critic and photographer. Correspondent for *Architecture and Urbanism,* Tokyo, Japan. Author of *Contemporary Japanese Architecture: Its Development and Challenge,* 1985; *The New Japanese Architecture,* 1990. **Essays:** Tadao Ando; Fumihiko Maki; Kazuo Shinohara.

BOHAN, Peter. Professor and chair of Department of Art History, State University of New York, College at New Paltz. Formerly gallery director, College at New Paltz, and assistant curator, Yale University art gallery. Author of *Early American Gold,* 1963; articles on James Burton. **Essays:** Decimus Burton; James Burton.

BOKER, Hans J. Contributor. **Essay:** Cologne Cathedral.

BORNGÄSSER-KLEIN, Barbara. Specialist in Iberian architecture, Ibero-Amerikanisches Institut Preussischer Kulturbesitz, Berlin, Germany. **Essays:** Juan Gomez de Mora; Francisco Hurtado; Ventura Rodríguez; Diogo de Torralva; Juan de Villanueva; Alcobaça: Abbey Church; Belém: Jeronymite Monastery; Madrid: Museo del Prado; Tomar: Christo Church.

BOYLE, Bernard M. Professor of architecture, Arizona State University, Tempe. Editor, *Materials in the Architecture of Arizona, 1870-1920,* 1976; *Blain Drake: Forty Years of Architecture in Arizona,* 1992. Author of articles on Roman and modern architecture; numerous lectures on architecture and historic preservation. **Essays:** Pietro da Cortona; Herculanuem; Nîmes: Maison Carrée; Nîmes: Pont du Gard; Rome: Forum Romanum; Rome: Palazzo Barberini; Rome: Theater of Marcellus.

BRIERLEY, E. S. Senior lecturer in architecture, De Montfort University, Leicester. Author of *De Stijl and the Amsterdam School,* 1979; *J. L. M. Lauwerik's Proportional Systems and Geometrical Structure Drawings,* 1980; *J. B. Bakema, An Architect's Social Attitude to Design,* 1985; numerous lectures and articles on 20th-century European architecture and urbanism. **Essays:** Michel De Klerk; Van den Broek and Bakema; Van der Vlugt and Brinkman; Amsterdam: Eigen Haard Housing.

BROTHERS, Leslie A. Scholar of art history and museum studies. Formerly assistant to curator of photography, Virginia Museum of Fine Arts. Contributor of reviews to *New Art Examiner.* **Essay:** Moscow: Metro Stations.

BROWN-MANRIQUE, Gerado. Professor of architecture, Miami University, Oxford, Ohio. Formerly visiting critic at University of Oregon. Author of *The Ticino Guide,* 1989; *Words and Works: Writings and Projects,* 1989; numerous essays and research presentations on design and parallel issues, and the work of contemporary architects, including O. M. Ungers and the Tendenza architects. **Essays:** Leon Krier; Rob Krier; Aldo Rossi; Oswald Mathias Ungers; Karlsruhe: Marktplatz; Berlin: Altes Museum; Berlin: Gross-Siedlung Siemensstadt; Berlin: IBA.

BUGSLAG, Jim. Visiting assistant professor, University of Victoria, British Columbia. Author of several lectures and articles about medieval stained glass and design. **Essays:** Henry of Reyns; Gloucester Cathedral; Bourges: House of Jacques Coeur; Carcassonne: City Walls and Fortifications; Centula: St. Riquier; Caernarvonshire: Caernarvon Castle; Oxford: Christ Church College; Oxford: Queen's College; Paris: Hôtel de Cluny; Périgueux: St. Front; York: Minster; Vézelay: La Madeleine.

ČAČKOVIĆ, Dražen. Architect, Arex Corporation, Pleasantville, New York. Assistant professor of art and architecture, Lehigh University, Bethlehem, Pennsylvania, and Kansas State University. Formerly coeditor, *Architecture Update.* Author of *Il Gruppo 7: A Bibliography of Periodical Literature,* 1987; *Luciano Boldessari: A Bibliography of Books and Periodical Literature,* 1989; articles and lectures on contemporary architecture. **Essay:** Banfir, Belgiojoso, Peresutti and Rogers (BBPR).

CAMERON, K. C. Reader in French and Renaissance studies, University of Exeter. Editor, *Montaigne and His Age,* 1981; *From Valois to Bourbon,* 1989. Author of *Henri III, a Maligned or Malignant King: Satirical Iconography of Henri de Valois,* 1978; numerous articles on late 16th-century satirical iconography. **Essays:** London: Mansion House; Paris: Madeleine; Paris: Sacré Coeur; Paris: Val de Grâce; Reims Cathedral; Vaux-le-Vicomte: Château.

CARD, Melissa. Graduate student in art history, Rutgers University. **Essays:** Holabird and Roche; Cesar Pelli; New York City: Battery Park City.

CAST, David. Professor of the history of art, Bryn Mawr College, Bryn Mawr, Pennsylvania. Former president of Philadelphia chapter of Society of Architectural Historians. Author of *The Calumny of Apelles,* 1981. **Essays:** Franco Albini; Galeazzo Alessi; Jacques-Denis Antoine; François-Joseph Bélanger; Jacques-François Blondel; Alexandre-Théodore Brongniart; Bernardo Buontalenti; Charles Cameron; Carlo Castellamonte; Mauro Coducci; P. J. H. Cuypers; Robert de Cotte; Hendrik De Keyser; Peter Ellis; Il Filarete; Jacques Gondouin; Harrison and Abramovits;

Nicholas Hawksmoor; Johann Lukas von Hildebrandt; Guiseppe Japelli; Pietro Lombardo; Carlo Maderno; François Mansart; Hugh May; Eugenio Montuori; John Nash; Giovanni Battista Nolli; Gilles-Marie Oppenord; Roger Pratt; Raphael; Giuliano da Sangallo; Vincenzo Scamozzi; Giles Gilbert Scott; James Smith; Robert Smythson; Robert A. M. Stern; William Talman; Giuseppe Valadier; John Vanbrugh; Henry Yevele; London: British Museum; London: Christ Church, Spitalfields; London: Westminster Hall, Houses of Parliament; London: St. Stephen's Chapel, Houses of Parliament; London: Paddington Station; London: Regent's Park; Milan Cathedral; Milan: Santa Maria Delle Grazie; Naples: Castle Nuovo; Naples: San Francesco di Paola; Pavia: Certosa; Rome: Palazzo Della Cancelleria; Rome: Sant' Andrea Della Valle; Rome: Tempietto; Rome: Villa Madama; Yorkshire: Castle Howard.

CHELAZZI, Giuliano. Architect in private practice, Florence, Italy. Contributor to *Pan Arte, Deutsche Bauzeitung* and *L'Architettura.* **Essays:** Arnolfo di Cambio; Filippo Brunelleschi; Michelozzo; Florence: Cathedral; Florence: Ospedale Degli Innocenti; Florence: Palazzo Pitti.

CHRISTENSEN, Ellen A. Doctoral candidate in art history, Northwestern University, Evanston, Illinois. Author of *Government Architecture and British Imperialism: Patronage and Imperial Policy in London, Pretoria and New Delhi (1800-1931)* (thesis: Northwestern University), in preparation; lectures and articles on Edwin Lutyens and Frank Lloyd Wright. **Essays:** Herbert Baker; Owen Jones; Gottfried Semper: Aston Webb.

CLARKE, Timothy. Writer in London, England. Author of numerous articles on architecture and design. **Essays:** London: Battersea Power Station; Paris: La Défense.

COHEN, George M. Professor of art history, Hofstra University, Hempstead, New York. Contributor to *American Artist, Art Voices, Arts Magazine, Art International, College Arts Journal* and other periodicals. Author of *A History of American Art,* 1971. **Essays:** James Bogardus; Charles Bulfinch; Georges-Eugène Haussmann; Raymond M. Hood; William Le Baron Jenney; Pierre Lescot; James Renwick; John A. and Washington Roebling; John Hubbard Sturgis; Richard Upjohn; New York City: St. John the Divine.

COHEN, Pamela A. Graduate student in art history, Rutgers University. **Essay:** Clorindo Testa.

CONDIT, Carl W. Emeritus professor of history and art history, Northwestern University, Evanston, Illinois. Author of books and articles on the history of architecture, building technology and urban technology, published from 1948 to 1982. **Essay:** New York City: Woolworth Building.

COOK, Jeffrey. Regents' professor of architecture, Arizona State University, Tempe. Founding editor, *Passive Solar Journal.* Author of *The Architecture of Bruce Goff,* 1978; *Award Winning Passive Solar Buildings,* 1984; *Passive Cooling,* 1989; *Anasazi Places,* 1992. **Essays:** Sebastiano Serlio; Paolo Soleri.

COOLEDGE, Harold N., Jr. Emeritus professor of art and architectural history, Clemson University, Clemson, South Carolina. Author of *Lusitania,* 1978; *Samuel Sloan, Architect of Philadelphia, 1815-1884;* articles on mid-19th-century architecture and the work of Samuel Sloan. **Essay:** Samuel Sloan.

CORMIER, Leslie Humm. Faculty of Fine Arts, Harvard University Extension, Boston, Massachusetts. Author of articles and lectures on European emigre modernism and its synthesis with American idiom. **Essays:** Walter Gropius; E. Maxwell Fry; The Architects Collaborative (TAC); Lincoln, Massachusetts: Gropius House.

CRAIG, Robert M. Associate professor of architectural history, Georgia Tech, Atlanta. Author of *Guide to Atlanta Architecture,* in preparation. Contributor to *Southern Home.* **Essays:** Charles Sumner and Henry Mather Greene; Edwin Landseer Lutyens; Bernard Maybeck; Julia Morgan; A. W. N. Pugin; Henry Hobson Richardson; Charles Francis Annesley Voysey; Atlanta, Georgia: Hyatt Regency Hotel; Surrey: Tigbourne Court, Hambledon.

CROWE, Ann Glen. Assistant professor of art history, Virginia Commonwealth University, Richmond. Contributor of reviews for *Artpapers.* Author of *The Art of Goya and the Duchess of Alba (1792-1802),* (dissertation: Stanford University). Past president, Ibero-American Society for Eighteenth-Century Studies. **Essays:** Frank Gehry; Arata Isozaki; Los Angeles, California: Museum of Contemporary Art.

CURL, James Stevens. Professor of architectural history, De Montfort University, Leicester, England. Formerly architectural editor, *The Survey of London.* Formerly architect to the Scottish Committee for European Architectural Heritage Year. Author of *A Celebration of Death,* 1980; *The Egyptian Revival,* 1982; *The Life and Work of Henry Roberts (1803-76), Architect,* 1983; *The Londonderry Plantation, 1609-1914,* 1986; *Victorian Architecture,* 1990; *The Art and Architecture of Freemasonry,* 1991; *Classical Architecture,* 1992; *Encyclopaedia of Architectural Terms,* 1992; *Gregorian Architecture,* 1993; numerous articles on architecture, planning, music and the environment. **Essays:** Osvald Almqvist; Asam Brothers; Georg Bähr; George Basevi; John Francis Bentley; Colen Campbell; William Chambers; François Cuvilliés; George the Elder Dance; Dientzenhofer Brothers; Kilian Ignaz Dientzhofer; Friedrich Wilhelm von Erdmannsdorff; Josef Anton Feuchtmayer; Johann Michael Fischer; Johann Bernhard Fischer von Erlach; James

Gandon; Friedrich von Gärtner; Friedrich Gilly; Henry Holland; Leo von Klenze; Georg Wenzeslaus von Knobelsdorff; Carl Gotthard Langhans; Caspar Moosbrugger; Roger Mulholland; Edward Lovett Pearce; Matthaeus D. Pöppelmann; Jacob Prandtauer; John Rennie; Humphry Repton; Henry Roberts; Karl Friedrich Schinkel; Andreas Schlüter; James Stuart; Robert Taylor; Michael and Peter Thumb; Friedrich Winbrenner; Dominikus and Johann Baptist Zimmerman; Berlin: Brandenburg Gate; Berlin: Neue Wache; Dublin: Custom House; Lübeck: Marktplatz; Munich: Amalienburg; Munich: Königsbau; Munich: Propyläen; Munich: St. John Nepomuk; Munich: Michaelskirche; Potsdam: Nikolaikirche; Potsdam: Palace of Sans Souci; Salzburg: Schloss Mirabell; Steinhausen: Pilgrimage Church; Vienna: Hofburg; Vienna: Karlskirche; Vienna: Piaristenkirch; Vienna: Schloss Schönbrunn; Vienna: Belvedere; Vierzehnheiligen: Pilgrimage Church; Weingarten: Abbey Church.

DALE, Antony. Author of *James Wyatt, Architect,* 1956. **Essay:** Frank Lloyd Wright.

DAVIS, Joyce M. Associate professor of art, Valdosta State College, Georgia. Formerly associate professor of architecture and art, Southern University, Baton Rouge, Louisiana. Author of *Lakeland's Unique Architectural Heritage,* 1987; articles on Lakeland, Florida, women artists, African-American women artists. **Essays:** Lancelot "Capability" Brown; Jules Hardouin-Mansart; André Le Nôtre; London: Banqueting House, Whitehouse; Middlesex: Syon House, Isleworth; Nottinghamshire: Wollaton Hall; Oxfordshire: Blenheim Palace; Paris: Panthéon (Ste. Geneviève); Paris: Place des Vosges; Paris: Place Vendôme: Paris: St. Sulpice; Rome: San Giovanni in Laterano; Rome: Trevi Fountain; Versailles: Park.

DELGADO, Annabel. Architect and president, Architectural Design Consultants, Miami, Florida. Coeditor of *New City Journal.* Formerly visiting lecturer in design, University of Miami, Coral Gales, Florida. Cofounder of Miami Design Alliance. Contributor of book reviews to periodicals. **Essays:** Henri Labrouste; Auguste Perret; Le Raincy: Church of Notre Dame; Paris: Bibliothèque Nationale.

DEWEY, Tom II. Associate professor, University of Mississippi. Author of numerous exhibition catalogues. **Essays:** Henry Van de Velde; Bear Run, Pennsylvania: Fallingwater; Brussels: Palais Stoclet.

DIXON, Susan M. Scholar of the history of art. Formerly teaching assistant, Cornell University. **Essays:** Ferdinando Fuga; Alessandro Galilei; Carlo Lodoli; Carlo Marchionni; Giovanni Batitista Piranesi; Luigi Vanvitelli; Bernardo Antonio Vittone.

DOIG, Allan. Assistant curate, St. Helen's Church, Abingdon, England. Formerly lecturer in history and theory of Art, University of Kent. Author of *The Architectural Drawings Collection of King's College, Cambridge,* 1979; *Theo van Doesburg: Painting into Architecture, Theory into Practice,* 1986. **Essays:** Theo Van Doesburg; Amsterdam: Stock Exchange.

DONHAUSER, Peter L. Doctoral candidate in fine arts, New York University. Assistant museum educator, Metropolitan Museum of Art. Author of articles, lectures and reviews on architecture. **Essay:** New York City: Metropolitan Museum of Art.

DONNELLY, Marian C. Emeritus professor of art history, University of Oregon, Eugene. Fellow of Royal Society of Arts, London. Past president of Society of Architectural Historians. Author of *New England Meeting Houses of the Seventeenth Century,* 1968; *A Short History of Observatories,* 1973; *Architecture in the Scandinavian Countries,* 1992. **Essays:** Carl Fredrik Adelkrantz; Carl Ludwig Engel; Christian Heinrich Grosch; Copenhagen: Amalienborg; Copenhagen: Bourse; Copenhagen: Rosenborg Palace; Helsinki: Senate Square.

DREW, Philip. Architectural historian and critic, Sydney, Australia. Australian correspondent, *Architecture and Urbanism.* Author of *Third Generation: The Changing Meaning of Architecture,* 1973; *Frei Otto: Form and Structure,* 1976; *Tensile Architecture,* 1979; *Two Towers,* 1980; *The Architecture of Arata Isozaki,* 1982; *Leave of Iron: Glenn Murcutt, Pioneer of an Australian Architectural Form,* 1985; *Harry Seidler: Four Decades of Architecture,* 1992; *Veranda: Embracing Place,* 1992; *Real Space: Martorell, Bohigas, Mackay, Puigdomenech,* 1993; numerous articles and lectures on tensile, contemporary and Australian architecture and criticism. **Essays:** Walter Burley Griffin; Frei Otto; Jørn Utzon; Sydney: Opera House.

DROST, Uwe. Assistant professor of architecture, University of Maryland, College Park. Director, International Forum of Young Architects; president of Office of Independent Architecture; president of INTERFACE Consulting. Numerous lectures on contemporary urban design and contemporary German architecture. **Essays:** Günther Behnisch; Egon Eiermann; Hugo Häring; Hans Scharoun; Bruno Taut; Cologne: Werkbund Exposition, 1914; Munich: Olympic Games Complex.

DUNLOP, Ian G. D. Vicar and canon, Salisbury Cathedral. Author of *Versailles,* 1956, 1970; *Châteaux of the Loire,* 1969; *Palaces and Progresses of Elizabeth I,* 1982; *Royal Palaces of France,* 1985; *Burgundy,* 1990. **Essays:** Sébastian le Prestre de Vauban; Beauvais Cathedral; Blois: Château; Chambord: Château; Chartres Cathedral; Dumfriesshire: Drumlanrig Castle; Paris: Louvre; Paris: Notre-Dame Cathedral; Salisbury Cathedral; Versailles: Palace; Versailles: Petite Trianon;

Versailles: Grand Trianon.

EARLY, James. Professor of English, Southern Methodist University, Dallas, Texas. Author of *Romanticism and American Architecture,* 1965; *Colonial Mexico: Architecture in the Society of Vice Regal New Spain* (in preparation). **Essay:** Mexico City: Cathedral.

ECHOLS, Gordon. Professor of landscape architecture, Urban Planning and Architecture, Texas A&M University, College Station, Texas. Author of *The Early Indigenous Architecture of Texas,* 1993; numerous articles on Spanish colonial planning and architecture. **Essays:** Churriguera Family; Thomas Jefferson; Josep Lluís Sert; Thomas U. Walter; Paris: Eiffel Tower; Paris: Unesco Headquarters; Richmond, Virginia: Virginia State Capital; Siena: Palazzo Pubblico; Venice: Piazza San Marco.

EGGENER, Keith. Doctoral candidate in history of art, Stanford University, Stanford, California. Author of lectures and articles on Mexican modernist architecture. **Essays:** Luis Barragán; Felix Candela; Juan O'Gorman; José Villagran Garcia; Gregori Warchavchik; Mexico: University City.

EISENMAN, H. J. Professor of history, University of Missouri—Rolla. Author of article on Frank Lloyd Wright in *Great Lives from History: American Series,* 1987. **Essay:** Chicago, Illinois: Marshall Field Wholesale Store.

ELMAS, Cynthia. Graduate student in art history, Rutgers University. **Essays:** Jacques Ignace Hittorff; Percier and Fontaine.

ERDMANN, Biruta. Associate professor of art history, East Carolina University, Greenville, North Carolina. Author of introduction to *The Architectural Heritage of Greenville, North Carolina,* 1988. **Essay:** Leopold Eidlitz.

FAWCETT, Peter. Architect. Professor of architecture and head of Department of Architecture and Planning, University of Nottingham, England. Contributor to *Ulster Architect;* numerous lectures and articles on interwar and postwar British architecture. Exhibitor of architectural drawings at national exhibitions. **Essays:** Mario Botta; Johannes Duiker; Frederick Gibberd; Herman Hertzberger; Denys Lasdun; Le Corbusier; Berthold Lubetkin; Robert Hogg Matthew; Basil Spence; Aldo Van Eyck; Liverpool: Metropolitan Cathedral; Marseilles: Unité d'Habitation; London: London Zoo (Penguin Pool/Gorilla House); London: National Gallery Competition; Poissy: Villa Savoye.

FAZIO, Michael W. Professor of architecture, Mississippi State University. Coeditor of *Arris,* the journal of the Southeast Society of Architectural Historians. **Essay:** Benjamin H. Latrobe (with Patrick Snadon).

FERKIN, Robert. Registered interior designer. Author of paper "Harwell Hamilton Harris: His Legacy in American Architecture." Member of Society of Architectural Historians. **Essay:** Hans Hollein.

FRANK, Suzanne S. Associate adjunct professor of architectural history, New York Institute of Technology. Member of Society of Architectural Historians. Author of *Michel DeKlerk (1884-1923): An Architect of the Amsterdam School,* 1984; *House 6—Peter Eisenman's Dream House Revisited* (forthcoming). **Essays:** Peter Eisenman; Columbus, Ohio: Wexner Center for the Visual Arts.

FRICELLI, Donald. Assistant professor of art history, Fordham University, New York City. Formerly assistant professor, Adelphi College, Garden City, New York. Lecturer in Italian art and architecture. Author of *The Architecture of Giorgio Vasari's Uffizi.* **Essays:** Bartolomeo Ammannati; Leonardo da Vinci; Giorgio Vasari; Florence: Uffizi; Rome: Città Universitaria.

GARMAZ, Magdalena. Assistant professor of architecture, Auburn University, Alabama. Formerly architect in Yugoslavia. Author of articles and lectures on Jože Plečnik. **Essay:** Jože Plečnik.

GENSHIEMER, Thomas. Doctoral candidate in architectural history, University of California, Berkeley (dissertation on medieval Islamic cities of East Africa). **Essays:** Cordoba: Cathedral/Mosque of Cordoba; Granada: Alhambra.

GLASSMAN, Paul. Director, Morris-Jumel Mansion, New York City. Contributor to *Inland Architect.* Formerly assistant director, The Frank Lloyd Wright Home and Studio Foundation and visiting lecturer in architectural history, school of Art Institute of Chicago. Past vice president, Chicago Society of Architectural Historians. **Essays:** Daniel Hudson Burnham; Helmut Jahn; Jacopo Sansovino; Chicago: State of Illinois Center; Venice: Library of St. Mark's; Venice: Palazzo Corner.

GLEYE, Paul H. Head of experimental workshop, Bauhaus, Dessau, Germany, and member of Architecture faculty, Montana State University. Author of *The Architecture of Los Angeles,* 1981. **Essay:** Los Angeles: Lovell Health House.

GOODSTEIN, Ethel S. Associate professor of architecture, University of Arkansas, Fayetteville. Formerly associate professor of architecture, University of Southwestern Louisiana. Author of articles in *International Journal of Canadian Studies, American Review of Canadian Studies* and *Critical Studies in Mass Communication;* numerous papers on 19th- and 20th-century North American and British architecture. Member of southeast chapter of Society of Architectural Historians. **Essays:**

Arthur Erickson; Mississauga City Hall; Ottawa: Dominion Parliament Buildings; Toronto: University College.

GOY, Richard J. Author of *Chioggia and the Villages of the Venetian Lagoon,* 1985; *Venetian Vernacular Architecture,* 1988; *The House of Gold: Building a Palace in Medieval Venice,* 1993; numerous articles on the history and architecture of Venice. **Essays:** Venice: Ca' D'Oro; Venice: Doge's Palace; Vicenze: La Rotonda.

GREENE, Francis J. Professor in Department of Languages and Fine Arts, St. Francis College, Brooklyn Heights, New York. Author of articles on French culture and literature. Member of Society of Architectural Historians; member of board of directors, The United Nations Association. **Essays:** Cuthbert Brodrick; Otto Wagner; Liverpool: St. George's Hall; Vienna: Majolica House; Vienna: Postal Savings Bank.

GUILES-CURRAN, Susan. Doctoral candidate in art history, Rutgers University, New Brunswick, New Jersey. **Essays:** Irving Gill; Hector Guimard.

GUISE, David E. Emeritus professor of architecture, City College of New York. Former visiting adjunct professor at University of Pennsylvania and Columbia University. Author of articles on progressive architecture, published in *New York Times* and *Encyclopaedia Britannica Yearbook.* **Essay:** New York City: Seagram Building.

GÜVEN, Suna. Associate professor of architectural history and chair of Department of Architecture, Middle East Technical University, Ankara, Turkey. Member of editorial board of *Journal of the Faculty of Architecture.* Author of articles on Roman architecture. **Essays:** Hermogenes; Vitruvius; Aspendos; Miletos.

HABEL, Dorothy Metzger. Associate professor of art history, University of Tennessee, Knoxville. Author of numerous articles on 17th- and early 18th-century architecture and planning in Rome. **Essays:** Giovanni Antonio De Rossi; Filippo Raguzzini; Carlo Rainaldi.

HAWKINS, Richard L. Security supervisor, Monticello, the home of Thomas Jefferson, Charlottesville, Virginia. **Essay:** Charlottesville: University of Virginia.

HENRY, Jay C. Professor of architecture, University of Texas at Arlington. Author of *Architecture in Texas, 1895-1945,* 1993; numerous papers on Texas and American architecture and European modernism. **Essays:** Fritz Höger; Amsterdam: Scheepvaarthuis; Hamburg: Chilehaus.

HERBERT, Gilbert. Mary Hill Swope Professor of Architecture and Town Planning, Technion: Israel Institute of Technology, Haifa. Formerly teacher at University of Witwatersrand, Johannesburg, and University of Adelaide, South Australia. Author of *The Synthetic Vision of Walter*

Gropius, 1959; *Martienssen and the International Style: The Development of Modern Architecture in South Africa,* 1975; *Pioneers of Prefabrication: The British Contribution in the Nineteenth Century,* 1978; *The Dream of the Factory-Made House: Walter Gropius and Konrad Wachsmann,* 1984. **Essays:** Erich Mendelsohn; London: St. Pancras Station and Hotel; Stuttgart: Schocken Department Store.

HESSE, Michael. Professor of history of art, Universität Heidelberg, Germany. Author of *Von der Nachgotik zur Neugotik,* 1984; *Studien zu Renaissance und Barock,* 1986; numerous articles and lectures on modern and contemporary architecture and the fine arts. **Essays:** Dominikus Böhm, Josef-Paul Kleihues; Charles Le Brun; Johann Santini-Aichel.

HILES, Timothy W. Assistant professor of art history, University of Tennessee, Knoxville. Author of articles on Morris Louis; lectures and papers on fin de siècle painting and sculpture. **Essay:** Paris: Métro Stations.

HILLS, Helen. Lecturer in art history, Keele University. Author of *Marmi Mischi in Seventeenth-Century Palermo* (in press). **Essays:** Baldassare Longhena; Andrea Pozzo; Palermo: Piazza Vigliena; Venice: Santa Maria Della Salute.

HOLDER, Philancy N. Emeritus professor of art history, Austin Peay State University, Clarksville, Tennessee. Author of *Cortona in Context, the History and Architecture of an Italian Hill Town,* 1992; numerous articles and lectures. **Essays:** Rome: Villa Giulia; Vicenza: Palazzo Chiericati.

HOLLIDAY, Peter J. Assistant professor of art history, California State University, San Bernardino. Editor of *Narrative and Event in Ancient Art,* 1993. Author of numerous articles on classical art and architecture. **Essays:** Rome: Arch of Constantine; Rome: Arch of Titus; Rome: Temple of Fortuna Virilis.

HORNIK, Heidi J. Assistant professor of art, Baylor University, Waco, Texas. Author of exhibition catalogues; papers on Michele di Ridolfo del Ghirlandaio. **Essay:** Florence: Santa Maria Novella.

HOWE, Eunice D. Associate professor of art history, University of Southern California, Los Angeles. Author of *The Hospital of Santo Spirito and Pope Sixtus IV,* 1978; *Andrea Palladio, the Churches of Rome,* 1991; numerous lectures and articles on Roman urbanism, Italian painting, papal patronage and guidebooks to Rome. **Essays:** Donato Bramante; Giacomo Del Duca; Luciano Laurana; Giacomo della Porta; Antonio da Sangallo the Younger; Giacomo Barozzi da Vignola; Rome: Il Gesù; Rome: Vatican.

HURLEY, Kent C. Associate professor of architecture and

assistant dean, Technical University of Nova Scotia. Former editor for Tech Press. Lecturer in architectural conservation and the English country house. **Essay:** Norfolk: Holkham Hall.

HÜTTEL, Richard. Author of *Kustos Graphische Sammlung; Spiegelungen einer Ruine-Leonardos Abendmahl im 19. und 20. Jahrhundert,* 1993; numerous articles about Leonardo's *Last Supper,* capital town and symbolism of a ground plan. **Essays:** Gottfried Böhm; Nancy: Place Royale (Place Stanislas).

ISTVANFI, Gyula. Professor of history of architecture, Technical University of Budapest, Hungary. **Essays:** Budapest: East Railway Station; Budapest: St. Stephen's Basilica; Budapest: University Church.

JACKSON, Anthony. Formerly professor of architecture, Technical University of Nova Scotia, Halifax, Canada. Author of *The Politics of Architecture,* 1970; *A Place Called Home,* 1976; numerous articles on theoretical aspects of architecture. **Essays:** William Morris; New York City: Grand Central Terminal; New York City: Lever House.

JACKSON, Neil. Architect and architectural historian. Lecturer in architecture, University of Nottingham. Author of *F. W. Troop, Architect,* 1985; *Nineteenth Century Bath Architects and Architecture,* 1991; numerous articles on 19th- and 20th-century architecture. **Essays:** William Adam; William Bruce; William Henry Playfair; Aberdeenshire: Craigievar Castle; Edinburgh: Holyroodhouse.

JAMES, Warren A. Architect. Principal, James & Associates, New York City. Formerly designer at Robert A. M. Stern Architects, New York, and Ricardo Bofill/Taller de Arquitectura, Barcelona and Paris. Author of *Ricardo Bofill/ Taller de Arquitectura: Buildings and Projects, 1960-1988,* 1988; *Kohn Pederssen Fox: Architecture and Urbanism, 1986-1992,* 1993; numerous articles on contemporary architects and architecture. Member of American Institute of Architects, National Institute for Architectural Education and Architectural League. **Essays:** Ricardo Bofill; New Canaan Connecticut: Johnson Glass House; New York City: AT&T Building; Barcelona: German Pavilion.

JUHASZ, Joseph B. Associate professor of architecture and planning, University of Colorado, Boulder. Author of *Environments: Notes and Selections on Objects, Spaces and Behavior* (with Steven Friedman), 1974. **Essays:** Michael Graves; Victor Horta; Louis Kahn; Charles W. Moore; Brussels: Hôtel Tassel; Fort Worth: Kimbell Art Museum; Philadelphia: Richards Medical Research Building.

KARGE, Henrik. Assistant professor of art history, University of Kiel, Germany. Author of *Die Kathedrale von Burgos und die Spanische Architektur des 13. Jhs.,* 1989; *Spanische Kunstgeschichte. Eine Einführung,* 2 vols., 1992; numerous lectures and articles about Spanish art and architecture, German gothic architecture, 19th-century historiography of art and architecture. **Essays:** Burgos Cathedral; León Cathedral.

KAROL, Eitan. Partner of Louis Karol Architects International. Formerly curator of Charles Holden exhibition. **Essay:** Charles Holden.

KELLY, Brian. Principal, Brian Kelly-Matt Bell, Architecture-Urban Design. Assistant professor of architecture, University of Maryland. **Essays:** Bertram Grosvenor Goodhue; John Russell Pope; James Stirling; Stuttgart: Neue Staatsgalerie; Washington, D.C.: National Gallery of Art.

KILINSKI, Karl II. Professor of art history, Southern Methodist University, Dallas, Texas. Author of *Classical Myth in Western Art,* 1985; *Boeotian Black Figure Vase Painting of the Archaic Period,* 1990; numerous articles in *American Journal of Archaeology, Antike Kunst, Arts Magazine, Hesperia* and *Greek, Roman and Byzantine Studies.* President and national trustee, Texas chapter of Society for the Preservation of the Greek Heritage. **Essays:** Delphi; Mycenae.

KIRIKOV, Boris M. Art critic. Vice-director, State Museum of History, St. Petersburg. Lecturer in history of art, St. Petersburg University. Author of several books, pamphlets and articles on 19th- and 20th-century architecture of St. Petersburg, history of church architecture, charity and necropolis of St. Petersburg. **Essays:** Giacomo Quarenghi; Karl Ivanovich Rossi; Thomas de Thomon; Konstantin A. Ton; Adrian D. Zakharov; St. Petersburg: Admiralty.

KOBAK, Aleksandr. Historian and chief expert, St. Petersburg Cultural Foundation; author of several books and numerous articles on 19th- and 20th-century architecture of St. Petersburg, history of church architecture, charity and necropolis of St. Petersburg. **Essays:** St. Petersburg: Exchange; St. Petersburg: St. Isaac's Cathedral.; St. Petersburg: Kazan Cathedral.

KOERBLE, Barbara. Free-lance writer, Fort Worth, Texas. Author of numerous articles on architecture. **Essays:** Edward Larrabee Barnes; Deer Isle, Maine: Haystack School; Oklahoma City: Mummers Theater.

KOSTAREVA, Irena. Historian and senior researcher, State Museum of the History of St. Petersburg. **Essays:** St. Petersburg: Peterhof Palace.

KRINSKY, Carol Herselle. Professor of fine arts, New York University, New York City. Past president, Society of Architectural Historians. Author of *Vitruvius de* *architectura, 1521—,* 1969; *Synagogues of Europe: Architecture, History, Meaning,* 1985; *Gordon Bunshaft of Skidmore, Owings and Merrill,* 1988; numerous articles and lectures on American and European architecture and urbanism. **Essay:** New York City: Rockefeller Center.

LEACH, Neil. Lecturer in architecture, University of Nottingham, England. Translator of Leon Battista's *On the Art of Building in Ten Books* (with others), 1988. **Essays:** Florence: San Lorenzo—New Sacristy; Florence: San Lorenzo—Old Sacristy.

LEACH, Peter. Author of *James Paine,* 1988; articles on aspects of 17th- and 18th-century English architecture. **Essays:** John Carr; James Paine; Derbyshire: Kedleston Hall.

Le ROY, Christian. Professor of ancient history, University of Paris I. Editor-in-chief, *Revue Archéologique.* Author of *Fouilles de delphes; Les Terres cuites architecturales;* numerous articles on archaeology, epigraphy and ancient history. **Essay:** Pergamon.

LESER, Petra. Assistant professor of art history, University of Cologne, Germany. Author of *Der Architekt Clemens Klotz (1886-1969),* 1991. **Essays:** Elias Holl; Johann Balthasar Neumann; Augsburg: Zeughaus; Ottobeuren: Abbey Church.

LEVETO-JABR, Paula D. Formerly instructor at Georgia State University and Indiana University, Bloomington. Member of archaeological excavations. Author of articles on Byzantine art. **Essays:** Aachen: Royal Chapel; Milan: San Lorenzo; Rome: Colosseum; Rome: Pantheon; Rome: Santa Costanza; Rome: Santa Maria Maggiore.

LEWIS, Michael J. Historiographer, Canadian Centre for Architecture, Montreal, Quebec. Author of *The Collected Works of Frank Furness* (with others), 1991; *The Politics of the German Gothic Revival: August Reichensperger,* 1993; various articles on American and German architecture. **Essays:** Georg Ludwig Friedrich Laves; Detlef Lienau; Bruce Price.

LIM, B. P. Professor and head of School of Architecture and Industrial Design, Queensland Institute of Technology, Brisbane, Australia. Editor of *The Indoor Environment of Buildings,* 1989. Author of *Architectural Detailing for the Tropics* (with E. Lip), 1988. **Essays:** John Andrews; Harry Seidler; Oak Park, Illinois: Unity Temple.

LITTLE, Bryan. Author of *The Building of Bath,* 1948; *The Life and Works of James Gibbs,* 1955; *Bath Portrait,* 1961; *English Historic Architecture,* 1964; *Catholic Churches since 1623,* 1966; *English Cathedrals,* 1972; *Sir Christopher Wren: A Historical Biography,* 1975; *Bristol: An Architectural History* (with Andor Gomme and Michael Jenner), 1979. **Essays:** James Gibbs; Wood Family; Bath:

Circus/Crescent/Square; Bristol: St. Mary Redcliffe; Cambridge: King's College; Canterbury Cathedral; London: St. Martin-in-the-Fields; Oxford: Radcliffe Library.

LIZON, Peter. Professor of architecture, University of Tennessee. Coauthor of *Handbook of Architectural Design Competitions,* 1981; and *American Institute of Architects Guidelines for the Management of Quasi-Competitions,* 1982. Author of *Smyrna Airport Design Competition,* 1992; *The Palace of the Soviets: The Paradigm of Architecture in the U.S.S.R.,* 1993; numerous articles on practice, theory and criticism of architecture and planning. **Essays:** Moisei Ginsburg; Josef Havlíček; Vladimír Karfík; Jan Kotěra; Ödön Lechner; Konstantin Melnikov; Vesnin Brothers; Brno: Villa Tugendhat; Moscow: Rusakov Workers' Club; Moscow: G.U.M. Department Store; Moscow: Melnikov House; Moscow: Palace of the Soviets (Competitions); Prague: National Theater.

LONG, Christopher. Researcher, Texas State Historical Association. Formerly teaching assistant, University of Texas at Austin. Contributor to *Austin American-Statesman.* **Essays:** Josef Hoffmann; Adolf Loos; Joseph Maria Olbrich; Vienna: Secession Building.

LORANCE, Loretta. Doctoral candidate in art history, City University of New York. Formerly affiliated with The Metropolitan Museum of Art, New York City. **Essays:** R(ichard) Buckminster Fuller; Paul Marvin Rudolph; Antonio Sant'Elia; New York City: Haughwout Building.

LOWERSON, J. R. Reader in history, University of Sussex. Former editor of *Southern History.* Author of *A Short History of Sussex; Sport and the English Middle Classes, 1870-1916;* numerous historical papers. **Essays:** Amiens Cathedral; Bradford-on-Avon: St. Lawrence; Brighton: Royal Pavilion; Paris: La Sainte-Chapelle.

LUKER, Maurice S. III. Architectural historian in Campus Planning Office, Cornell University. Member of College Art Association. **Essays:** Philibert De L'Orme; Anet: Château.

MACDONALD, A. J. Senior lecturer in architecture, University of Edinburgh, Scotland. Author of *Wind Loading on Buildings,* 1975. Founding member, Edinburgh Center of Architectural History. **Essays:** William Burn; Thomas Hamilton; Edinburgh New Town.

MÁCEL, Otakar. Associate professor of history of architecture, University of Technology, Delft, Holland. Author of *Stühle aus Stahl,* 1980; *The Museum of the Continuous Line* (with J. Van Geest), 1986; *Eiu Stuhl macht Geschichte* (with W. Möller), 1992; articles on modern architecture and design. **Essays:** Peter Behrens; Bohuslav Fuchs; Josef Gočár; J. J. P. Oud; Aleksei V. Shchusev; Fedor Shekhtel; Berlin: AEG Turbine Factory;

Moscow: Kazan Railway Station.

MACK, Charles R. Professor of art history and William J. Todd Professor of the Italian Renaissance, University of South Carolina, Columbia. Author of *Pienza: The Creation of a Renaissance City,* 1987; *Paper Pleasures,* 1992; numerous lectures and articles on Renaissance art and architecture. Past president and board member of southeast chapter of Society of Architectural Historians and Southeastern College Art Conference. **Essays:** Leon Battista Alberti; Lorenzo Ghiberti; Giuliano da Maiano; Bernardo Rossellino; Paestum; Florence: Palazzo Rucellai; Florence: Palazzo Strozzi; Florence: Santa Croce/Pazzi Chapel; Mantua: Sant' Andrea; Rome: Santo Stefano Rotondo.

MADIGAN, Brian. Assistant professor of art history, Wayne State University, Detroit, Michigan. Author of articles on Greek, Roman and late-Antiquity art and archaeology. **Essay:** Thomas Archer.

MAKOGONOVA, Maria. Art critic. Curator of architecture section, State Museum of the History of St. Petersburg. Lecturer in the history of architecture, St. Petersburg Institute of Culture. **Essays:** Bartolomeo Francesco Rastrelli; St. Petersburg: Smolny Monastery; Tsarkoe Selo: Pushkino Palace; St. Petersburg: Winter Palace.

MALLORY, Nina A. Professor of art, State University of New York at Stony Brook. Author of *Bartolomé Esteben Murillo,* 1983; *El Greco to Murillo: Spanish Painting in the Golden Age, 1556-1700,* 1990; numerous articles on Spanish architecture and painting. **Essays:** Narciso Tomé; Toledo: Transparente, Cathedral of Toledo.

MANNELL, Joanne. Assistant professor of art history, Montana State University. Bozeman, Montana. Author of articles on Roman architecture and architectural ornament. **Essays:** Split: Imperial Palace of Diocletian; Tivoli: Hadrian's Villa.

MARX, Patricia A. Adjunct professor of art history, American University. Member of Archaeological Institute of America. **Essays:** Iktinos; Kallikrates; Mnesikles; Athens: Acropolis; Madrid: El Escorial; Nîmes: Amphitheater.

McCLINTOCK, Kathryn Marie. Part-time instructor in art history, The Pennsylvania State University, University Park. Author of *The Sculpture of San Nicola at Bari* (dissertation). **Essays:** Bari: San Nicola; Milan: Sant' Ambrogio; Syria: Krak des Chevaliers.

McKEAN, John. Designer and critic. Head of Interior Architecture, University of Brighton, England. Formerly head of History Unit, University of North London School of Architecture and Interior Design. Author of *Learning*

from Segal, 1988; *The Royal Festival Hall,* 1992; *The Crystal Palace,* 1993. **Essays:** Joseph Paxton; Alison and Peter Smithson; Alexander Thomson; Leicester: Engineering Faculty Building; London: Crystal Palace; London: Royal Festival Hall.

McKINNEY, David D. Program development associate, John F. Kennedy Center for the Performing Arts, Washington, D.C. Author of numerous articles and lectures on Horace Walpole and 18th-century English architecture. **Essays:** Charles Harrison Townsend; Middlesex: Strawberry Hill, Twickenham.

McNEUR, Lorna Anne. Lecturer in architecture, Cambridge University. Formerly design teacher at Carleton and Waterloo universities, Canada. Contributor to journals. **Essays:** New York City: Central Park; Rome: Piazza del Popolo.

MICHELSON, Elizabeth Munch. Free-lance writer on decorative arts and architecture. Curator, New Milford Historical Society, Connecticut. M.A., Cooper Hewitt Museum Master's Program, Parson School of Design. **Essay:** William Kent.

MILLAR, John F. Architectural historian and former museum director. Author of *The Architects of the American Colonies,* 1968; *Classical Architecture in Renaissance Europe, 1419-1585,* 1987; *A Handbook on the Founding of Australia 1788,* 1988; *The Harrison Guide* (in preparation). **Essays:** Peter Harrison; Hans Hendrik van Paesschen; Charleston: Drayton Hall.

MILLER, William C. Professor of architecture and dean, University of Utah. Author of *Alvar Aalto: An Annotated Bibliography,* 1984; numerous articles on Aalto and Finnish architecture. **Essays:** Alvar Aalto; Erik Gunnar Asplund; Kay Fisker; Arne Jacobsen; Sven Markelius; Ragnar Östberg; Ivar Tengbom; Paimio: Tuberculoisis Sanatorium; Stockholm: City Hall; Stockholm: Public Library; Seinäjoki: Civic Center.

MILNER-GULLAND, R. R. Reader in Russian studies, University of Sussex, England. Author of *Introduction to Russian Art and Architecture* (with J. E. Bowlt), 1980; articles on Russian, Byzantine and medieval English art and architecture. **Essays:** Vasili Ivanovich Bazhenov; Moscow: Andronikov Monastery; Moscow: Kremlin.

MOFFETT, Marian Scott. Professor of architectural history, University of Tennessee, Knoxville. Coeditor, *Arris.* Author of *A History of Western Architecture* (with Lawrence Wodehouse), 1989; *East Tennessee Cantilever Barns* (with Wodehouse), 1993; articles and lectures on vernacular architecture. **Essays:** Roland Anthony Wank; Conques: Church of Ste. Foy; Shropshire: Iron Bridge.

MOORE, R. J. Senior lecturer in architectural history, University of Newcastle, New South Wales, Australia. Numerous articles and lectures on Ruskin and Victorian architecture. Member of Society of Architectural Historians of Australia and New Zealand. **Essays:** William Butterfield; John Ruskin; George Gilbert Scott; George Edmund Street.

MORGAN, William. Professor of fine arts, University of Louisville, Kentucky. Formerly architecture critic, *Courier-Journal.* Author of *The Almighty Wall,* 1983; *Collegiate Gothic,* 1989; numerous articles on architecture. **Essay:** Reima and Raili Pietilä.

MORGENTHALER, Hans R. Assistant professor of architecture, University of Colorado at Denver. Author of *The Early Sketches of German Architect Erich Mendelsohn (1887-1953): No Compromise with Reality,* 1992; articles and lectures on Erich Mendelsohn and contemporary architecture. **Essays:** August Endell; Ely Jacques Kahn; Karl Moser; Rudolf M. Schindler; Bernard Tschumi.

MUNK-JØRGENSEN, Wivan. Contributor. **Essays:** Michael Gottlieb Bindesbøll; C. F. Hansen; Peder Vilhelm Jensen-Klint; Copenhagen Cathedral.

MURTA, K. H. Professor of architecture, University of Sheffield. Member of Ecclesiastical Architects and Surveyors; chairman of Board of Architectural Education. Contributor to *Architectural Review; Architects Journal; RIBA Journal.* **Essays:** John Ninian Comper; Inigo Jones; Edward S. Prior; Northumberland: Seaton Delaval.

NEW, Anthony. Architect in private practice, London. Consultant architect to Derby Cathedral and numerous churches. Fellow of Society of Antiquaries and Royal Institute of British Architects. Author of *Observer's Guide to Cathedral,* 1972; *Cathedrals of Britain,* 1980; *The Abbeys of England and Wales,* 1985; *The Abbeys of Scotland,* 1988. **Essays:** Amsterdam: Westerkerk; Durham Cathedral; Exeter Cathedral; Laon Cathedral; Lincoln Cathedral; London: St. James the Less, Westminster; London: St. Mary Woolnoth; London: Tower of London; London: Westminster Abbey; Middlesex: Hampton Court Palace; Rome: Spanish Steps.

NICOLETTA, Julie. Doctoral candidate in history of Art, Yale University. Author of *Structures for Communal Life: Shaker Dwelling Houses at Mount Lebanon, New York* (thesis; in progress). Member of Society of Architectural Historians and Vernacular Architecture Forum. **Essays:** Henry Austin; Charles Bridgeman; William Strickland; William Thornton; Ithiel Town.

NOFFSINGER, James P. Emeritus professor of architecture, University of Kentucky. Taught at Kansas University, University of Minnesota and Insitut Teknologie Bandung (Indonesia). Architect for U.S. Commission of Fine Arts and Historic American Building Survey of U.S. Department of the Interior. Past national director of Society of Architectural Historians. Author of numerous bibliographies on Japanese architects. **Essays:** Kunio Maekawa; Antonin Raymond; Kenzo Tange.

NORTON, Bettina A. Writer and historian, Cambridge, Massachusetts. Formerly director of Cambridge History Society and registrar of print collection, Essex Institute. Author of *History of the Boston Naval Shipyard, 1800-1974,* 1974; *Edwin Whitefield: Nineteenth-Century North American Scenery,* 1977; *Trinity Church: The Story of an Episcopal Parish in the City of Boston,* 1977; *To Create and Foster Architecture: The Contributions of the Boston Architecture Center,* 1989. **Essays:** Asher Benjamin; Henry Van Brunt.

NORTON, Paul F. Emeritus professor of art history Program, University of Massachusetts, Amherst; past chair, for thirteen years, of Department of Art. Formerly editor of *Journal of the Society of Architectural Historians.* Author of *Amerhert, A Guide to its Architecture,* 1977, and *Latrobe, Jefferson and the National Capitol,* 1977; numerous articles on architects and architecture. **Essays:** Samuel Pepys Cockerell; Samuel McIntire; Boston Public Library; Boston: Trinity Church.

OCH, Marjorie. Independent scholar. Author of essays on Italian medieval and Renaissance art, architecture and 19th-century American painting and illustration. **Essays:** Francesco Primaticcio; Florence: Palazzo Vecchio; Florence: San Miniato al Monte; Pisa Cathedral; Ravenna: Sant' Apollinare in Classe; Ravenna: Sant' Apollinare Nuovo; Rome: Palazzo Farnese; Rome: Santa Maria Degli Angeli.

O'CONNELL, Lauren M. Assistant professor of art history, Ithaca College. Author of numerous lectures on French revolutionary architecture, Viollet-le-Duc and 19th-century nationalism. **Essays:** Jean-Baptiste Rondelet; Eugène Emmanuel Viollet-le-Duc.

OLSZEWSKI, Edward J. Professor of art history, Case Western Reserve University, Cleveland, Ohio. Formerly president of Midwest Art History Society. Author of *Giovanni Battista Armenini, on the True Principles of the Art of Painting,* 1977; *The Draftsman's Eyes,* 1981. **Essays:** Giovanni Lorenzo Bernini; Carlo Fontana; Giulio Romano; Pirro Ligorio; Baldassare Peruzzi; Matti Rossi; Mantua: Palazzo del Tè; Rome: Palazzo Chigi; Rome: Villa Farnesina.

O'ROURKE, Desmond. Consulting architect in Washington, D.C., and Helsinki, Finland. Author of articles and lectures on Finnish architecture. Member of Finnish Association of Architects. **Essays:** Erik Bryggman; Aarne Ervi; Aarno Ruusuvuori; Tampere: Kaleva Church.

OVERY, Paul. Lecturer in history of art and design, Goldsmiths College, University of London. Art critic, *Times,* London. Author of *De Stijl,* 1969; *The Rietvel Schröder House* (coauthor), 1988; *Kadinsky: The Language of the Eye,* 1991; numerous lectures and articles on early 20th-century art, architecture and design. **Essays:** Gerrit Thomas Rietveld; Utrecht: Schröder House.

PALEY, Richard. Graduate student in art history, Rutgers University. **Essay:** Carlo Scarpa.

PALMER, Allison. Doctoral candidate in art history, Rutgers University, New Jersey. **Essays:** Cosimo Fanzago; Francesco Ricchino; Rome: Palazzo Massimo; Rome: Piazza Navona.

PAPADEMETRIOU, Peter. Professor, New Jersey Institute of Technology. Author of articles on Eero Saarinen. **Essays:** Eero Saarinen; Chantilly: Dulles International Airport.

PAWELEC, Katharina. Assistant professor of art history, Justus-Liebig-Universität, Giessen, Germany. Author of *Medieval Art,* 1990; *Die Aachener Bronzegitter; Studien zur Karolingischen Ornamntik Um 800.;* several lectures and articles about Karolingian architecture and minor arts. **Essays:** Juan de Herrera; Juan Bautista de Toledo.

PERDUE, Susan Holbrook. Scholar of architectural history, with an emphasis on early 20th-century American architecture and landscape design. **Essay:** Parker and Unwin.

PINCUS, Lisa L. Received master's degree from New York University. **Essay:** Chicago: 860-880 Lake Shore Drive Apartments.

PITLUGA, Kurt. Doctoral candidate, Pennsylvania State University. Formerly teaching assistant in art history. Author of *The Collegiate Architecture of Charles Z. Klauder* (dissertation). **Essay:** George Browne Post.

PLATT, Frederick. Writer on American life between the Civil War and World War I. Author of *The Architecture of Horace Trumbauer* (in preparation). **Essays:** Horace Trumbauer.

PLUMMER, David. Masters candidate in architecture, University of Texas at Austin. **Essay:** Pier Luigi Nervi.

POLETTI-ANDERSON, Anita. Doctoral candidate, University of Virginia, Charlottesville. Formerly writer and researcher at Université Catholique de Louvain's centre d'Histoire de L'Architecture et de Bâtiment. **Essays:** Etiènne-Louis Boullée; Claude-Nicolas Ledoux.

PORT, M. H. Emeritus professor of modern history, Queen Mary and Westfield College, University of London.

Formerly editor of *The London Journal;* editor of *The Commissions for Building Fifty New Churches,* 1986. Author of *Six Hundred New Churches,* 1961; *History of the King's Works, vol. VI, 1782-1851* (with others), 1973; *The Houses of Parliament* (with others), 1976; numerous articles on 19th-century British architecture. **Essays:** Charles Barry; Robert Smirke; William Wilkins; James Wyatt; Jeffry Wyatville; Berkshire: Windsor Castle; London: Houses of Parliament; London: Law Courts; London: Reform Club; London: St. John, Bethnal Green; London: St. Pancras Church; London: Somerset House.

PORTER, Jed. Assistant professor of architecture, University of Kentucky. Member, Society for Industrial Archeology. **Essays:** John Haviland; Philadelphia: Eastern Penitentiary.

PRICE, Patricia Lynn. Doctoral candidate in architectural history, University of Virginia, Charlottesville. Dissertation topic concerns Renaissance architectural theory in Italy and France. **Essays:** Germain Boffrand; Du Cerceau Family; Jacques Lemercier.

PTACEK, Robin. Assistant professor in visual arts department, University of Maryland, Baltimore. **Essays:** Kutna Hora: Cathedral of St. Barbara; Prague: St. Vitus' Cathedral; Prague: Černín Palace; Prague: St. Nicholas; Prague: Vladislav Hall; Tabor: Zizka Square.

RATTNER, Donald M. Director, Institute for the Study of Classical Architecture, New York Academy of Art, New York City. Author of numerous articles and lectures on classical architecture. **Essays:** Athens: Choragic Monument of Lysicrates; Athens: Tower of the Winds.

RIJSBERMAN, Marijke. Multilingual free-lance writer and editor, Chicago. **Essays:** Salomon De Brosse; Caprarola: Palazzo Farnese; Fontainebleau Palace; Monreale: Cathedral of Santa Maria La Nuova; Siena Cathedral; Vienna: St. Stephen's Cathedral.

RING, Trudy. Free-lance writer and editor, Chicago. **Essays:** Victor Louis; Bordeaux: Grande Théâtre.

ROBERTS, Ann. Associate professor of history of art, University of Iowa, Iowa City. Contributor of articles on Netherland's art of the late middle ages to *Art Belletin, Oud Holland* and *Burlington Magazine.* **Essay:** Bruges: Town Hall (Stadhuis).

ROBISON, Elwin C. Associate professor of architecture and environmental design, Kent State University. Book review editor, *Architronic: The Electronic Journal of Architecture.* Author of *Architectural Technology before the Scientific Revolution* (with others), 1993; numerous lectures and articles on Guarini, Palladio and early skyscrapers. **Essays:** Guarino Guarini; Andrea Palladio; Chicago: Home Insurance Building; Chicago: Monadnock Building;

Chicago: Reliance Building; Maser: Villa Barbaro; Turin: Palazzo Carignano; Turin: San Lorenzo.

ROSENBLUM, Charles L. Free-lance writer. Doctoral candidate in history of architecture, University of Pittsburgh, Pennsylvania. Formerly public relations coordinator in New Haven, Connecticut. **Essays:** Gustave Eiffel; Romaldo Giurgola; Charles Gwathmey; Kevin Roche; Heinrich Schickhardt; Stanley Tigerman.

ROTH, Leland M. Marion Dean Ross Professor of Architectural History, University of Oregon, Eugene. Former member of board of directors, Society of Architectural Historians. Author of *A Concise History of American Architecture,* 1979; *McKim, Mead and White, Architects,* 1983; *Understanding Architecture,* 1992; several articles and book chapters on planning and industrial workers' housing and vernacular house design from 1860-1920. **Essays:** Carrère and Hastings; Ralph Adams Cram; Ernest Flagg; Cass Gilbert; John Mead Howells; Richard Morris Hunt; McKim, Mead and White; Peabody and Stearns; John Wellborn Root; John Mills Van Osdel; Boston: Massachusetts State House; Chicago: World's Columbian Exposition, 1893; New York City: Lincoln Center; New York City: Pennsylvania Station; Portland: Portland Building.

RUDOLF, Moira. Art historian, special trustees for St. Thomas's Hospital, London. Author of articles for *St. Thomas's Hospital Gazette* and various journals. Member of Society of Architectural Historians of Great Britain. **Essays:** Joseph Bonomi; Thomas Harrison; Thomas Leverton; John Soane; Liverpool: Anglican Cathedral.

SAINT, Andrew. Architectural historian, London. Two-time winner of Alice Davis Hitchcock Medallion of Great Britain Society of Architectural Historians. Author of *Richard Norman Shaw,* 1976; *The Image of the Architect,* 1983; *Towards a Social Architecture,* 1987. **Essays:** London: Sir John Soane's Museum; Strasbourg Cathedral.

SANABRIA, Sergio L. Associate professor of architecture, Miami University, Oxford Ohio. Numerous lectures and articles on 16th-century Spanish architect Rodrigo Gil de Hontañón. **Essays:** Antonio Gaudí; Rodrigo Gil de Hontañón; Juan Guas; Diego de Siloe; Simón de Colonia; Lorenzo Vazquez; Barcelona: Casa Milá; Granada: Palace of Emperor Charles V in the Alhambra; Metz Cathedral; Seville: Cathedral.

SAUNDERS, Ann Loreille. Historian. Fellow of University College, London and Society of Antiquaries of London. Honorary editor to London Topographical Society and Costume Society. Author of *John Bacon R. A.,* 1961; *Regent's Park,* 1969, 1981; *Art and Architecture of London,* 1984, 1988, 1992. **Essay:** London: Hampstead Garden Suburb.

SCHILLER, Joyce K. Lecturer, St. Louis Art Museum, St. Louis, Missouri. Author of numerous lecture and articles on 19th- and 20th-century art and architecture. **Essays:** Albert Kahn; St. Louis: Wainwright Building.

SCHULTZ, Bernard. Professor of art history and chair of division of art, West Virginia University. Author of *Art and Anatomy in Renaissance Italy,* 1985; *Art Past/Art Present* (with David G. Wilkens), 1990; lectures and articles on interdisciplinary relationships between art and medical history. **Essays:** Michelangelo; Florence: San Lorenzo—Laurentian Library; Rome: Piazza del Campidoglio.

SCHULZE, Franz. Professor of art, Lake Forest College. Contributing editor, *Art News* and *Inland Architect;* corresponding editor, *Art in America.* Author of *Fantastic Images: Chicago Art Since 1945,* 1972; *One Hundred Years of Architecture in Chicago,* 1976; *Ames van der Rohe: A Critical Biography,* 1985. **Essays:** Philip Johnson; Ludwig Mies van der Rohe.

SCHUMACHER, Thomas L. Professor of architecture, University of Maryland, College Park. Author of *The Danteum,* 1985; *Surface and Symbol: Giusseppe Terragni and the Architecture of Italian Nationalism,* 1991; numerous articles on modern architecture and urbanism. **Essays:** Marcello Piacentini; Giuseppe Terragni.

SCOTT, Pamela. Visiting lecturer, Cornell University, Washington, D.C. Editor of *The Papers of Robert Mills, 1781-1855* (microfilm edition), 1990. Author of *Buildings of the District of Columbia* (with others), 1993; numerous lectures and articles on Washington, D.C., architecture and early American iconography. **Essays:** George Hadfield; Robert Mills; Alexander Parris; Isaiah Rogers; Washington, D.C.: United States Capital; Washington, D.C.: United States Treasury; Washington, D.C.: Washington National Monument.

SEBESTA, Judith Lynn. Professor of classics, University of South Dakota. **Essay:** Ostia Antica.

SENARCLENS DE GRANCY, Antje. Contributor. **Essay:** Paris: Institut de Monde Arabe.

SHAPIRO, Ellen R. Assistant professor of art history, Massachusetts College of Art, Boston. Former associate editor, *Assemblage.* Author of numerous articles on Italian architecture of the 1920s and 1930s. **Essays:** Ernesto Basile; Gruppo 7; Gio Ponti; Giuseppe Sommaruga.

SHEVCHENKO, Olya. Doctoral candidate, City University of New York. **Essay:** Moscow: Lenin State Library.

SILBERBERG-PEIRCE, Susan. Assistant professor of art history, Colorado State University, Fort Collins, Colorado.

Consultant and photo archival specialist, documentation of Roman wall painting, The Getty Center; photographer of ancient Roman architecture. Author of numerous lectures on Greek and Roman art and architecture. **Essays:** Segesta; Rome: Baths of Diocletian.

SMART, C. Murray, Jr. Professor of architecture, University of Arkansas, Fayetteville. Member of editorial board, *Victorians Institute Journal.* Author of *Muscular Churches,* 1989; numerous articles on 19th-century British architecture. Past president, Southeast Society of Architectural Historians. **Essays:** George Frederick Bodley; Francesco Borromini; William Burges; C. R. Cockerell; Deane and Woodward; Filippo Juvarra; W. Eden Nesfield; John Loughborough Pearson; Anthony Salvin; Richard Norman Shaw; Alfred Waterhouse; London: Natural History Museum; London: New Scotland Yard; Oxford: Keble College; Rome: San Carlo Alle Quattro Fontane; Rome: Sant'Ivo Della Sapienze; Turin: Superga; Turin: Palazzo Madama; Turin: Plazzina Stupinigi.

SMITHSON, Peter D. Architect in private practice. **Essay:** Oxfordshire: Rousham Park.

SMYTH-PINNEY, Julia M. Registered architect. Associate professor of architecture, University of Kentucky. Numerous lectures on the Italian Renaissance and baroque architecture. **Essay:** Rome: Sant' Andrea al Quirinale.

SNADON, Patrick. Associate professor of architecture, Mississippi State University. Author of articles on A. J. Davis, B. H. Latrobe and 19th-century American architecture and interiors. **Essays:** Alexander Jackson Davis; Benjamin H. Latrobe (with Michael W. Fazio).

SOKOL, David M. Professor of history of architecture, University of Illinois at Chicago. Former chair of Oak Park Historic Preservation Commission; former vice president of Unity Temple Restoration Foundation. Editor, Cambridge Monographs on American Artists. Author of *American Architecture and Art,* 1976; *American Decorative Arts and Old World Influences,* 1980; *Life in Nineteenth-Century American,* 1981; *Otto Neumann,* 1988; numerous articles on Frank Lloyd Wright, American landscapes and Chicago architecture. **Essays:** George Grant Elmslie; Louis Sullivan; Baltimore: Catholic Cathedral; Buffalo: Larkin Building; Chicago: Auditorium Building; Chicago: Schlesinger and Mayer Store; New York City: Guggenheim Museum.

SOLOMONSON, Katherine M. Assistant professor, College of Architecture and Landscape Architecture, University of Minnesota. Formerly architectural historian, San Mateo County Historic Resources Inventory. Author of book in progress on Chicago Tribune Tower Competition; articles and book reviews on medieval and modern topics. **Essays:** Chicago: Marquette Building; Chicago: Tribune

Tower Competition; Santiago de Compostela: Cathedral.

SOO, Lydia M. Assistant professor of architecture, Ohio State University, Columbus. **Essays:** Claude Perrault; Christopher Wren; London: Royal Hospital, Greenwich; London: St. Mary-le-Bow; London: St. Paul's Cathedral; London: St. Stephen Walbrook.

SPAETH, David Anthony. Professor of architecture, University of Kentucky, Lexington. Author of *Ludwig Mies van der Rohe: An Annotated Bibliography and Chronology,* 1979; *Ludwig K. Hilberseimer: An Annotated Bibliography,* 1981; *Mies van der Rohe,* 1985; numerous articles and lectures. **Essays:** Charles O. Eames; Tony Garnier; Ludwig Karl Hilberseimer; Chicago: Illinois Institute of Technology; Dessau: Bauhaus; Stuttgart: Weissenhofsiedlung.

SPENCE, Rory. Lecturer in architecture, University of Tasmania, Launceston, Australia. Formerly architect and writer in London, England, and Sydney, Australia. Author of *Catalogue of the Drawings Collection of the Royal Institute of British Architecture, T-2,* 1984; articles on contemporary Australian architecture. **Essays:** Lars Eliel Sonck; Philip Speakman Webb; Helsinki: Telephone Company Building; Tampere Cathedral.

SPIESER, Jean-Michel. Professor of history of art, Université des Sciences Humaines de Strasbourg, Strasbourg Cedex, France. Author of *Thessalonique et ses monuments du IVeau VIe s.,* 1984; *Caričin Grad II; Le quartier sud-ouest de la ville haute* (with others), 1990; articles on early Christian and Byzantine art and archaeology. **Essays:** Instanbul: St. Irene; Instanbul: Church of Christ in Chora; Instanbul: SS. Sergius and Bacchus; Rome: San Paolo Fuori Le Mura; Thessalonica: St. Demetrios.

STARCZEWSKI, Jerzy Andrzej. Assistant professor of architecture, Drury College, Springfield, Missouri. Formerly senior faculty, Warsaw Technological University, Warsaw, Poland. Formerly participated in reconstruction of historic buildings in Poland. Author of *Budownictwo Ogólen* (with others), 1965-75; numerous papers on architecture and building. **Essays:** Matthew Nowicki; Gdansk: Church of St. Mary; Kraków: Sigismund Chapel, Wawel Cathedral; Malbork: Castle of the Teutonic Knights; Poznan: Town Hall; Torun: Town Hall; Warsaw: Old Town Reconstruction; Warsaw: Wilanow Palace; Wroclaw: Church of the Most Blessed Virgin Mary.

STEELE, James M. Associate professor of architecture, Texas Tech University, Lubbock. Formerly architect in private practice, Doylestown, Pennsylvania. **Essays:** Raimondo D'aronco; Bruce Goff; Marc-Antoine Laugier; Jean Prouvé; Robert Venturi; Athens: Agora; Ephesos; Prienne; Ravenna: San Vitale; Rome: St. Peter's Rome: St. Peter's Square.

STEVENSON, Christine. Lecturer in the history of art, Reading University, Reading, England. Editor of *Architectural History*. Author of articles about C. F. Hansen, John Wood the Elder, Danish painting and industrial design around 1800 and the design of 18th-century hospitals and lunatic asylums. **Essays:** Robert Adam; George the Younger Dance; [Hans] Christian Hansen; Martin Nyrop; Carl Petersen.

SULLEBARGER, Beth. Principal, Sullegargers Associates (consulting firm in historic preservation). Editor, *Historic Preservation: Forging a Discipline*. President Emerita, Preservation Alumni, Inc. **Essays:** Othmar Ammann; James H. Dakin.

SUNDT, Richard A. Associate professor of art history, University of Oregon, Eugene. Author of articles on Mendicant architecture. Treasurer, Association Villard de Honnecourt for the Interdisciplinary Study of Science, Technology and Art. **Essay:** Batalha: Monastery of Santa Maria da Vitória.

TATE, Robert B. Corresponding fellow of Institut d'Estudis Catalans, Barcelona and Real Academia de la Historia, Madrid. Fellow of British Academy and Royal Historial Society, London. **Essays:** Lluís Domenèch; Barcelona: Sagrada Familia.

THAYER, Preston. Doctoral candidate, University of Pennsylvania. Project coordinator of *Buildings of the United States* series, Society of Architectural Historians. **Essays:** Isambard K. Brunel; Thomas Telford.

THOMAS, Christopher. Staff member at University of Western Ontario. **Essay:** Henry Bacon.

THOMAS, George. Professor, University of Pennsylvania, Philadelphia. Author of *The Architecture of Frank Furness* (with James O'Gorman and Hyman Myers), 1973; *Frank Furness: The Complete Works* (with Jeffrey Cohen and Michael Lewis), 1991. **Essays:** Frank Furness; Philadelphia: Library of the University of Pennsylvania.

TOMLINSON, R. A. Professor of ancient history and archaeology and head of department, University of Birmingham, England. Chairman of managing committee, British School at Athens. Author of *Argos and the Argolid*, 1972; *Greek Sanctuaries*, 1976; *Greek Architecture*, 1989; *The Athens of Alma Tadema*, 1991; *From Mycenae to Constantinople*, 1992. **Essays:** Hippodamos; Akragas; Syracuse; Tiryns.

TURAK, Theodore. Emeritus professor of art history, American University, Washington, D.C. Author of *William Le Baron Jenney: A Pioneer of Modern Architecture*, 1986; numerous articles on the Chicago School of Architecture and French influences on American architecture. **Essays:** J. N. L. Durand; Paris: Les Halles Centrales.

UNDERWOOD, David K. Assistant professor of art history, Rutgers University, New Brunswick, New Jersey. Author of articles on Brazilian architecture. **Essays:** Aleijadinho; Roberto Burle Marx; Lucio Costa; João Federico Ludovice; Oscar Niemeyer; Matteus Vicente de Oliveira; Affonso Eduardo Reidy; Carlos Raúl Villanueva; Brasília: Federal Capital Complex; Queluz: Royal Palace; Rio de Janeiro: Ministry of Education and Health.

URBAS, Andréa. Assistant professor of architecture, Ball State University. Formerly historical architect, State Historic Preservation Office, Arizona and Illinois. **Essays:** A. J. Downing; Porec: Euphrasius Basilica; Pula: Amphitheater; Gračanica: Monastery Church; Trogir: Trogir Cathedral; Zadar Cathedral; Zadar: Church of St. Donato.

VAN BERGEIJK, Herman. Free-lance architectural historian. Visiting professor at various European and American universities. Author of *M. P. Berlage: Architettura, estetica, urbanistica*, 1985; *W. M. Dudok: Architect and Urbanist*, 1994; numerous lectures and articles on Italian, German and Dutch architecture. **Essays:** Hendrik Petrus Berlage; Willem Marinus Dudok; Philips Vingboons.

VAN SCHOUTE, Roger. Director of Archaeology and History of Art, Catholic University of Louvain, Belgium. **Essays:** Louvain: Town Hall (with Monique Van Schoute); Tournai Cathedral (with Monique Van Schoute).

VIGNUOLO, Lisa. Graduate student in art history, Rutgers University. **Essays:** I. M. Pei; Paris: Louvre, Pyramide.

VINCENT, Marc. Doctoral candidate in history of art, University of Pennsylvania. Author of lectures and articles on Louis Kahn and Paul Cret. **Essays:** Jean-François-Thérèse Chalgrin; Paul Philippe Cret; Ange-Jacques Gabriel; Charles Garnier; Jacques-Germain Soufflot; Paris: Arc de Triomphe; Paris: Les Invalides; Paris: Opéra; Paris: Place de la Concorde.

VOLKMAN, Nancy J. Associate professor of landscape architecture, Texas A&M University, College Station, Texas. Specialist in landscape history and historic landscape preservation. Coauthor of *Landscapes in History: Design and Planning in the Western Tradition*, 1993; numerous articles on 19th-century landscape architect H. W. S. Cleveland. Member of State Board of Review for National Register of Historic Places. **Essays:** John Notman; Frederick Law Olmstead; Charles Adams Platt; Calvert Vaux.

VOLPE, Gianni. Architect. Author of numerous essays on architecture of the Italian Renaissance. Member of Accademia Rafaello di Urbino. **Essays:** Francesco di Giorgio; Urbino: Ducale Palace.

WALDEN, Russell. Reader in history of contemporary architecture, Victoria University, Wellington, New Zealand. Formerly senior lecturer, Birmingham School of Architecture, England. Author of *Voices of Silence: The Chapel of Futuna,* 1986. **Essay:** Ronchamp: Notre-Dame-du-Haut.

WALKER, Frank Arneil. Professor of architecture, University of Strathclyde, Glasgow, Scotland. Author of architectural guides, including *South Clyde Estuary,* 1986; *Central Glasgow,* 1989; *Glasgow,* 1992; *North Clyde Estuary,* 1992; numerous articles on architecture and urban form. **Essays:** William Richard Lethaby; Charles Rennie Mackintosh; Glasgow School of Art.

WALTON, Thomas. Associate professor of architecture and planning, Catholic University of America, Washington, D.C. Editor, *Design Management Journal.* Author of articles on design. **Essays:** Pierre Charles L'Enfant; Washington, D.C.: City Plans.

WARDEN, P. Gregory. Associate professor of art history, Southern Methodist University, Dallas, Texas. Consulting scholar, The University Museum, Philadelphia. Formerly editor of *Perspective.* Author of *The Extramural Sanctuary of Demeter and Persephone at Cyrene, Libya. Final Reports IV,* 1990; numerous lectures and articles on Etruscan and Roman art and archaeology. President, Dallas chapter of Archaeological Institute of America. **Essays:** Apollodorus of Damascus; Rabirius; Pompeii.

WEIDENHOFFER, Hansjörg. Free-lance art historian in Graz, Austria. Author of *Der Salzburger Hofbaumeister Giovanni Gaspare Zuccalli,* 1987; *Sakramentschäuschen in Österreich,* 1991. **Essay:** Enrico Zuccalli.

WHITE, Charles W. Associate professor of architecture, Texas A&M University, College Station. Formerly staff member of Aphrodisias archaeological expedition in Turkey. Author of papers and articles on Hellenistic architecture in the Near East. **Essays:** Baalbek; Palmyra.

WILKINS, Ann Thomas. Lecturer in classics, University of Pittsburgh and Duquesne University, Pittsburgh, Pennsylvania. Formerly faculty member at Vassar College and the University of Michigan. Author of *Hero or Villain: Sallust's Portrayl of Catiline,* 1993; numerous lectures on ancient art, architecture and literature. **Essays:** Epidauros; Olympia.

WILKINS, David G. Professor of the history of art and architecture, University of Pittsburgh. Author of *Donatello* (with Bonnie A. Bennett); *History of the Duquesne Club* (with Mark Brown and Lu Donnely); *Art Past/Art Present* (with Bernard Schultz and Katheryn Linduff). Founding member of Preservation Pittsburgh. **Essays:** Sinan; Florence: Ponte Vecchio (with Rebecca L. Wilkins); Instanbul: Yerebatan Cistern (with Rebecca L. Wilkins);

Instanbul: Hagia Sophia; Moscow: Lomonosov University; Moscow: St. Basil's.

WILLIS, Alfred. Architecture librarian, Kent State University. Author of numerous lectures and articles on Belgian architecture, architectural drawings and architectural literature. **Essays:** François Hennebique; Lucien Kroll; André Lurçat; Edward Durrell Stone; Antwerp: Grote Markt; Antwerp: Town Hall; Brussels: Grand' Place.

WINTER, John. Architect in private practice, London. Council member of London Architectural Association. Formerly visiting professor at Cambridge University, Yale University, Syracuse University and Toronto University. Author of *Modern Architecture,* 1969; *Industrial Architecture,* 1970. **Essays:** Ove Arup; Marcel Breuer; Serge Ivan Chermayeff; Wells Coates; Ralph Erskine; Norman Foster; Richard Meier; Richard Neutra; Richard Rogers; Owings and Merrill Skidmore (SOM); Owen Williams; Minoru Yamasaki; F. R. S. Yorke; Nottinghamshire: Boots Factory, Beeston; Chicago: John Hancock Center; Chicago: Sears Tower; Hong Kong Bank; London: Lloyd's of London; New York City: United Nations Headquarters; Paris: Centre Georges Pompidou.

WITTKOPP, Gregory M. Curator of Collections, Cranbrook Academy of Art Museum, Bloomfield Hills, Michigan. Director of restoration of Saarinen House (Eliel Saarinen's home and studio) at Cranbrook Academy of Art. Formerly curator of exhibitions, Saginaw Art Museum, Saginaw, Michigan. **Essays:** Eliel Saarinen; Helsinki: Railway Station and Administration Building.

WODEHOUSE, Lawrence. Professor of architectural history, University of Tennessee, Knoxville. Coeditor, *Arris.* Author of *Ada Louise Huxtable: A Bibliography,* 1981; *White of McKim, Mead and White,* 1988; *The Roots of International Style Architecture,* 1989; *A History of Western Architecture* (with Marian Scott Moffett), 1989; *East Tennessee Cantilever Barns* (with Moffett), 1993; numerous articles on 19th- and 20th-century American architecture. **Essays:** C. R. Ashbee; Joseph Emberton; George Howe; William Lescaze; Alfred B. Mullett; Edward Tuckerman Potter; William Appleton Potter; M. H. Baillie Scott; Stanford White; Ammi B. Young; Boston: City Hall; Philadelphia: Philadelphia Saving Fund Society Building.

WOJTOWICZ, Robert. Assistant professor of art history, Old Dominion University, Norfolk, Virginia. Author of several articles on Lewis Mumford. **Essays:** New York City: Brooklyn Bridge; Philadelphia: Merchants' Exchange.

WOLNER, Edward W. Assistant professor of architectural history, Ball State University, Muncie, Indiana. Author of *Walter W. Ahlschlager: American Architecture and Urban Society in the 1920s,* (in progress);

numerous conference papers and articles on the relationship between Chicago architecture and Chicago's development between 1835 and 1910 and on 1920s skyscrapers in midwest American cities. **Essays:** Milan: Galleria Vittorio Emanuele II; Milan: Central Railway Station; New York City: Chrysler Building; New York City: Empire State Building; Venice: Il Redentore; Venice: San Giorgio Maggiore.

YARWOOD, Doreen. European consultant. Writer and artist. Author of *Robert Adam,* 1970; *Architecture of*

Europe, 1974, 1983; *English Interiors,* 1984; *Chronology of Western Architecture,* 1987.

ZABEL, Craig. Associate professor of art history, Pennsylvania State University. Previously taught at Dickinson College, University of Virginia and University of Illinois at Urbana-Champaign. Coeditor, *American Public Architecture: European Roots and Native Expressions.* Author of articles on George Grant Almslies, Prairie School bank buildings, public architecture, recent American architects, Eadweard Muybridge and Anselm Kiefer. **Essay:** Owatonna: National Farmers Bank.

PHOTO CREDITS